M.R.G.

To my children: Josh, Erin, Bryn, Lynsey, and Jake

R.G.S.

To Karyn, a joy in my life

PREFACE

The appearance of yet one more casebook in the area of substantive criminal law, which already has well over 15 such materials, seems to demand some explanation. It is not, after all, initially apparent why the currently available materials cannot satisfy the need for an introduction to criminal law.

The explanation we offer is simple. First, many of the presently available materials do not appear to have a viewpoint, a firm position on the role of the criminal law. This book takes such a viewpoint. It is that the purpose of the criminal law is to reflect the moral standards of our society and to punish those who, with culpability and awareness, violate those moral norms. The roots of this concern with moral blameworthiness—*mens rea*—trace back at least 3,000 years. Even in primitive societies, distinctions were made between those who acted coldly, with intention to harm, and those who did not.

In the past century, that crucial ingredient of the criminal law has often been lost. Yet perhaps the most striking aspect of criminal law in the past 150 years has been the abandonment of the retributivist viewpoint in favor of a positivist, utilitarian approach to criminal liability. The evidence is everywhere: in the development of strict liability, the enhancement of negligence as a proper basis of criminal vulnerability, and the lagging of the distinction between justified and excused acts, and numerous other changes in the law. It seems clear that the tendency is to reject *mens rea* and replace that doctrine by an emphasis upon harmful consequences. Yet by failing to chronicle these changes and relate them to the underlying changes in criminal theory, many case-books tend to divide the criminal law into digestible chunks, rather than stress the interrelations of the various parts of the whole. Moreover, it is only with such a historical perspective that current doctrines are explicable. As Sir Leslie Stephens declared,

> At every point the system is determined by the circumstances of its growth, and you can no more account for its oddity or its merits, without considering its history, than you can explain the structure of a bat or a seal, without going back to previous forms of life. The growth of the criminal law . . . is closely connected with the development of the moral sentiments of the community: with all the great political and social revolutions and with the changes of the ecclesiastical constitution and the religious beliefs of the nation.

L. Stephen, *The Life of Sir James Fitzjames Stephen* 414 (1895).

This quotation suggests a second difference between this casebook and others: the stress on the historical developments of criminal law theory and doctrine. Throughout these materials, the historical roots of the criminal law are emphasized, and the various trends and changes in that movement are highlighted.

Particularly clear is the trend, in the last 20 years, to return to the earlier notions of subjective culpability as the basis of criminal liability. Like the earlier movement toward objectification, the return to retributivist-based notions of moral culpability is everywhere evident: in many aspects of the Model Penal Code, in the growing rejection of "presumptions," in the increasing willingness to view so-called affirmative defenses as requiring only that the defendant meet the burden of production rather than the burden of proof, and in the more careful analysis by the judiciary of the place of liability-escaping (or -reducing) techniques. In a sense, the present movement toward "sentencing reform," which stresses both equality and desert, reinforces the change in criminal theory taking place. Surely the two are related. This book stresses that relationship.

These approaches minimize the notion that criminal law is today primarily a process of reading and interpreting statutes. They ask instead whether the statutes—even when properly interpreted—are consistent with the theoretical underpinnings of the criminal law. In an era when the practice of criminal law rarely focuses in fact on culpability, but is an administrative mechanism for dealing with scores of criminal charges mitigated by processes of plea bargaining, emphasis on statutory language seems unduly nice. A concern with first principles seems more consistent and more fruitful an approach.

After a brief discussion of some elementary procedural matters, the materials explore the basic foundations of the criminal law: the criminal sanction, with increased attention in this third edition to conceptual questions regarding punishment, and the *actus reus* and *mens rea* principles. While not aimed at the study of particular crimes per se, the materials consider several crimes whose characteristics illuminate the basic foundations and principles.

The law of homicide is examined to exemplify the problem of grading offenses for purposes of imposing punishment, sometimes the ultimate penalty of death for certain homicides. The crime of rape is investigated for essentially two reasons: 1) to illustrate the role historical social stereotypes (in this case sexual ones) play in the law and to examine the problems created in redefining legal doctrine when those stereotypes are seriously challenged; and 2) as a vehicle for examining special *actus reus* and *mens rea* issues arising through the presence of the factor of consent in the law of rape. Finally, the materials present several inchoate crimes in order to explore the role of harm within the criminal law and to provide a vehicle for studying differentiated *mens rea* elements for various *actus reus* elements of a given offense.

The book concludes with a look at accomplice liability and an examination of theories of defense. The defense doctrines present a final opportunity to consider the *actus reus* and *mens rea* principles as they relate to the issue of appropriate employment of the punitive sanction.

Throughout these materials, certain reference sources constantly appear. Rather than cite them fully on each occasion, they are abbreviated as follows:

Blackstone	W. Blackstone, *Commentaries on the Law of England* (1969) (cites will be to volume 4, unless otherwise indicated)
Dressler	J. Dressler, *Understanding Criminal Law* (2d ed. 1955)
Fletcher	G. Fletcher, *Rethinking Criminal Law* (1978)
Hale	M. Hale, *Pleas of the Crown* (1678)
Hall	J. Hall, *General Principles of Criminal Law* (1961)
Hart	H. L. A. Hart, *Punishment and Responsibility* (1968)
Holmes	O. W. Holmes, Jr., *The Common Law* (1881)
LaFave and Scott	W. LaFave and A. Scott, *Criminal Law* (2d ed. 1986)
Model Penal Code (MPC)	American Law Institute, Model Penal Code, Proposed Official Draft (1962)
Packer	H. Packer, *The Limits of the Criminal Sanction* (1967)
Plucknett	T. F. Plucknett, *A Concise History of the Common Law* (5th ed. 1956)
Pollock and Maitland	F. Pollock and W. Maitland, *History of English Law* (2d ed. 1898)
Stephen	J. Stephen, *History of the Criminal Law of England* (1883)
Williams	G. Williams, *Criminal Law: The General Part* (2d ed. 1961)

Martin R. Gardner
Richard G. Singer
April, 2001

Acknowledgments

Richard Singer is grateful for the research assistance as well as the guide to the unchartered country of computerland that Pat Cronin and Leslie Wade provided. Secretarial assignments were so split amongst many persons for so long, over so many drafts, at so many schools that it is not feasible to mention all who gave of their skill, time, and sanity. Therefore, here is a general thank you to all those who helped at Rutgers-Newark, Cardozo, and Rutgers-Camden Law Schools. A special thanks, however, to Mary Ann Purvenas for her help on the second edition.

Martin R. Gardner expresses appreciation for the support provided by the Ross McCollum Research Fund at the University of Nebraska, College of Law; for the research assistance of Joseph Kehon; and for the secretarial support of Vida Eden.

PERMISSIONS

(The following authors and publishers have kindly granted permission to include excerpts from their works in this casebook. Instead of acknowledging their permissions on the pages where they appear, we have chosen to list their permissions below. Some materials are excerpted in more than one section of the book, but acknowledgment is indicated below in the chapter of first appearance. Within chapters, permissions are listed alphabetically by author, not by order of appearance.—Eds.)

West Publishing Company and West Services, Inc., St. Paul, MN, for permission to use *Westmate Software* and materials obtained via *Westlaw* employed in preparing this casebook.

CHAPTER 1

K. C. Davis, *American Comments on American and German Prosecutors*, from Discretionary Justice in Europe and America 70–72 (K.C. Davis, ed. 1976), copyright 1976 by the University of Illinois Press, Champaign, IL. Reprinted by permission.

P. Devlin, *Trial by Jury* 7–12 (1966), copyright 1966 by Stevens & Sons Ltd., London, U.K. Reprinted by permission of Associated Book Publishers (U.K.), London, U.K.

J. Herman, *The German Prosecutor*, from Discretionary Justice in Europe and America 16, 58–59 (K. C. Davis ed. 1976), copyright 1976 by the University of Illinois Press, Champaign, IL. Reprinted by permission.

J. Van Dyke, *Jury Selection Procedures* ix, 57, 150–51 (1979), copyright 1979 by John Van Dyke, Honolulu, HI. Reprinted by permission.

G. Williams, *The Proof of Guilt* 271–72 (3d ed. 1963), copyright 1963 by Sweet & Maxwell Limited, London, U.K. Reprinted by permission.

CHAPTER 2

F. A. Allen, *The Erosion of Legality in American Criminal Justice: Some Latter-Day Adventures of the Noella Poena Principle*, 29 Ariz. L. Rev. 385, 389–90 (1987), copyright 1987 by the Arizona Board of Regents, Tucson, AZ. Reprinted by permission.

Alschuler, *Sentencing Reform and Prosecutorial Power: A Critique of Recent Proposals for "Fixed" and "Presumptive" Sentencing*, 126 U. Pa. L. Rev. 550, 563–69, 577 (1978), copyright 1978 by the University of Pennsylvania Law Review, Philadelphia, PA. Reprinted by permission.

American Law Institute (ALI), Model Penal Code, Proposed Official Draft (1962), copyright 1962 by the American Law Institute, Philadelphia, PA. Reprinted with the permission of The American Law Institute.

J. Andenaes, *The General Preventive Effects of Punishment*, 114 U. Pa L. Rev. 949, 955–57, 961–62, 970, 982–83 (1966), copyright 1966 by the University of Pennsylvania Law Review, Philadelphia, PA. Reprinted by permission.

Antunes and Hunt, *The Deterrent Impact of Criminal Sanctions: Some Implications for Criminal Justice Policy*, 51 U. Det. J. Urb. L. 145, 158–59 (1973), copyright 1973 by the University of Detroit Journal of Urban Law, Detroit MI. Reprinted by permission.

Armstrong, *The Retributivist Hits Back*, from The Philosophy of Punishment 138, 155 (H. Acton ed. 1969), copyright 1969 by St. Martin's Press, Incorporated, New York, NY. Reprinted by permission.

Ashworth, *Punishment and Compensation: Victim Offenders and the State*, Oxford J.L. Stud. 86,98 (1986), copyright Oxford University Press, Oxford, UK. Reprinted by permission of Oxford University Press.

Bedau, *Concession to Retribution in Punishment*, from Justice and Punishment 51, 64 (J. Cederblom and W. Blizek eds. 1977), copyright 1977 by J. Cederblom and W. Blizek. Published by Ballinger Publishing Co., Cambridge, MA. Reprinted by permission.

Cohen, *Moral Aspects of the Criminal Law*, 49 Yale L. J. 987, 1013 (1940), copyright 1940 by the Yale Law Journal Co., New Haven, CT. Reprinted by permission.

P. Devlin, *The Enforcement of Morals* 7–10, 12–22 (1968), copyright 1968 by Oxford University Press, Oxford, UK. Reprinted by permission of Oxford University Press.

E. Durkheim, *The Division of Labor in Society* 108–9 (W. D. Halls trans. 1984). Reprinted with the permission of The Free Press, a division of Macmillan, Inc. Translation copyright 1984 by Higher and Further Education Division, Macmillan Publishers Ltd. Copyright 1984 by the Free Press, New York, NY.

Epstein, *Crime and Tort: Old Wine in Old Bottles*, from Assessing the Criminal 231, 243 (R. Barnett and J. Hogel eds. 1977), copyright 1977 by R. Barnett and J. Hogel. Published by Ballinger Publishing Co., Cambridge, MA. Reprinted by permission.

J. Feinberg, *Doing and Deserving* 95–100, 105, 110–11, 114 (1970), copyright 1970 by Princeton University Press, Princeton, NJ. Reprinted by permission.

G. Fletcher, *Rethinking Criminal Law* 408–9, 836 (1978), copyright 1978 by Little, Brown and Company, Boston, MA. Reprinted by permission.

Gardiner, *The Purpose of Criminal Punishment*, 21 Mod L. Rev. 117, 122–23 (1958), copyright 1958 by the Modern Law Review Limited, Stevens and Sons Ltd., London, UK. Reprinted by permission.

H. L. A. Hart, *Punishment and Responsibility* 3–6, 9, 11–12, 25–27, 39–40, 45–48 (1968), copyright 1968 by Oxford University Press, Inc., New York. Reprinted by permission.

Jeffries, *Legality, Vagueness, and the Construction of Penal Statutes*, 71 Va L. Rev. 189, 196–97, 206–8 (1985), copyright 1985 by the Virginia Law Review, Charlottesville, VA. Reprinted by permission.

Kahan, *What Do Alternatives Sanctions Mean?*, 63 U. Chi. L. Rev. 591-601 (1996), copyright 1996 by the Chicago Law Review, Chicago, Ill. Reprinted by permission.

Kant, *The Metaphysical Elements of Justice* 100–1 (J. Ladd trans. 1985), copyright 1985 by Macmillan Publishing Company, New York, NY. Reprinted by permission.

Mann, *Punitive Civil Sanctions: The Middleground between Criminal and Civil Law*, 101 Yale L. J. 1795, 1844–47, 1861–63 (1993). Reprinted by permission.

Martinson, *New Findings, New Views: A Note of Caution Regarding Sentencing Reform*, 7 Hofstra L. Rev. 243, 252–55 (1979), copyright 1979 by the Hofstra Law Review Association, Hempstead, NY. Reprinted by permission.

M. Moore, *Responsibility, Character, and Emotions* from The Moral Worth of Retribution 179, 181–87, by F. Schoeman, copyright 1987 by Cambridge University Press. Reprinted with the permission of Cambridge University Press.

Morris, *Persons and Punishment*, 52 The Monist 475–76, 483, 485–87, 489–90 (Oct. 1968), copyright 1968, *The Monist*, La Salle, IL 61301. Reprinted by permission.

N. Morris, *The Future of Imprisonment* 14–17 (1974), copyright 1974 by The University of Chicago Press, Chicago, IL. Reprinted by permission.

J. Murphy, *Three Mistakes about Retributivism*, 31 Analysis 166–69 (1971), copyright 1971 by Jeffrie Murphy, Tempe, AZ. Reprinted by permission.

H. Packer, *The Limits of the Criminal Sanction* 18, 24–25, 49–51, 53–55, 57–58, 65–69, 249–50, 264–67, 296, 301–5, 312 (1968). Excerpted with the permission of the publisher, Stanford University Press, Stanford, CA. Copyright 1968 by Herbert L. Packer.

L. Radzinowicz, I *A History of English Criminal Law* 411 fn. 40 (1957), copyright 1957 by Stevens and Sons Limited, London, UK. Reprinted by permission.

Smith, *The Element of Chance in Criminal Liability*, 1971 Crim. L. Rev. 63, 73, copyright 1971 by Sweet & Maxwell Limited, London, UK. Reprinted by permission.

A. von Hirsch, *Doing Justice: The Choice of Punishment* 26 (1976), copyright 1976 by Andrew von Hirsch. Reprinted by permission of Hill and Wang, a division of Farrar, Straus and Giroux, Inc., New York, NY.

A. von Hirsch and Anders Ashworth eds., *Principled Sentencing* 101–8, copyright 1992 by Andrew von Hirsch and Andrew Ashworth. Reprinted with the permission of Northeastern University Press, Boston, MA.

A. von Hirsch, *The Sentencing Commission Functions* 3–15, 177–82, from The Sentencing Commission and Its Guidelines by Andrew von Hirsch, Kay A. Knapp, and Michael Tonry, copyright 1987 by Andrew von Hirsch, Kay A. Knapp, and Michael Tonry. Reprinted with the permission of Northeastern University Press, Boston, MA.

Nigel Walker, *Punishment, Danger and Stigma: The Morality of Criminal Justice* 24–25, 28–30, 37–42 (1980), copyright 1980 by Basil Blackwell, Ltd., New York, NY. Reprinted by permission.

R. Wasserstrom, *Some Problems with Theories of Punishment*, from Justice and Punishment 173, 178–79 (J. Cederblom and W. Blizek eds. 1977), copyright 1977 by J. Cederblom and W. Blizek. Published by Ballinger Publishing Co., Cambridge, MA. Reprinted by permission.

James Q. Wilson, *Thinking about Crime* 121 (rev. ed. 1983), copyright 1975 by Basic Books, Inc. Second revised edition copyright 1983 by Basic Books, Inc., New York, NY. Reprinted by permission of Basic Books, Inc., Publishers.

F. Zimring, *Making Punishment Fit the Crime: A Consumer's Guide to Sentencing Reform*, from *The Pursuit of Criminal Justice—Essays from the Chicago Center* 271–72 (1977), copyright 1977 by the University of Chicago Law School, Chicago, IL. Reprinted by permission.

CHAPTER 3

Norval Morris, *Somnambulistic Homicide: Ghosts, Spiders and North Koreans*, 5 Res Judicatae 29, 29–33 (1955), copyright 1955 by Melbourne University Law Review (formerly Res Judicatae), Victoria, Australia. Reprinted by permission.

New York Times, Ault, February 7, 1968, copyright 1968 by The New York Times Company and the Associated Press, New York, NY. Reprinted by permission.

R. Perkins and R. Boyce, *Criminal Law* 795–97 (3d ed. 1982), copyright 1982 by Foundation Press, Inc., Westbury, NY. Reprinted by permission.

CHAPTER 4

Brown, *Self-Defense in Homicide from Strict Liability to Complete Exculpation*, 1958 Crim. L. Rev. 583, 583, copyright 1958 by the Criminal Law Review, London, UK. Reprinted by permission.

Fletcher, *The Individualization of Excusing Condition*, 47 S. Cal. L. Rev. 1269, 1292–93, 1299–301 (1974), copyright 1974 by the Southern California Law Review, University of Southern California, Los Angeles, CA. Reprinted by permission.

Fletcher, *The Theory of Criminal Negligence: A Comparative Analysis*, 119 U. Pa. L. Rev. 401, 421–22 (1971), copyright 1971 by the University of Pennsylvania Law Review. Reprinted by permission.

Jerome Hall, *General Principles of Criminal Law* 126, 213–15, 217, 219–22, 382, 387 (1961), copyright 1961 by The Mickie Co., Charlottesville, VA. Reprinted by permission.

Jerome Hall, *Interrelations of Criminal Law and Torts: I*, 43 Colum. L. Rev. 753, 767–68 (1943), copyright 1943 by the Directors of the Columbia Law Review Association, Inc., New York, NY. All rights reserved. Reprinted by permission.

Hart, *Book Review*, 74 Yale L.J. 1325 (1965), copyright 1965 by the Yale Law Journal Co., New Haven, CT. Reprinted by permission.

Levitt, *Extent and Function of the Doctrine of Mens Rea*, 17 Ill. L. Rev. 578, 578, 580–81 (1923). Reprinted by special permission of Northwestern University School of Law, Chicago, IL.

Remington and Helstad, *The Mental Element in Crime—A Legislative Problem*, 1952 Wis. L. Rev. 645, 666–67, copyright 1952 by the University of Wisconsin, Madison, WI. Reprinted by permission.

Robinson and Grall, *Element Analysis in Defining Criminal Liability: The Model Penal Code and Beyond*, 35 Stan. L. Rev. 681, 695–96 (1983), copyright 1983 by Paul H. Robinson, Camden, NJ. Reprinted by permission of Paul H. Robinson and the Board of Trustees of the Leland Stanford Junior University.

J. W. C. Turner, *The Mental Element in Crimes at Common Law*, 6 Cambridge L.J. 31, 36 (1934), copyright 1934 by Cambridge University Press, New York, NY. Reprinted by permission.

Wasserstrom, *Strict Liability in the Criminal Law*, 12 Stan. L. Rev. 731, 736–41 (1960), copyright 1960 by the Board of Trustees of the Leland Stanford Junior University, Stanford, CA. Reprinted by permission.

Glanville Williams, *Criminal Law: The General Part* 90, 241 (2d ed. 1961), copyright 1961 by Sweet & Maxwell Limited. Reprinted by permission of Associated Book Publishers (U.K.) Ltd., London, U.K.

Barbara Wootton, *Crime and the Criminal Law* 52–53, 66, 75–79 (1963), copyright 1963 by Sweet & Maxwell Limited. Reprinted by permission of Associated Book Publishers (U.K.) Ltd., London, UK.

CHAPTER 5

Walter Berns, *For Capital Punishment* 172–73 (1979), copyright 1979 by Basic Books, Inc., New York, NY. Reprinted by permission.

B. N. Cardozo, *Law and Literature*, from Selected Writings of Benjamin Nathan Cardozo 338, 383–84 (M. Hall ed. 1975), copyright 1975 by Matthew Bender and Company, Inc., New York, NY. Reprinted by permission.

Crump and Crump, *In Defense of Felony Murder*, 8 Harv. J.L. & Pub. Pol'y 359, 363–64, 367–71 (1985), copyright 1985 by Harvard Society for Law & Public Policy, Inc., Cambridge, MA. Reprinted by permission.

G. Fletcher, *Reflections on Felony-Murder*, 12 Sw. U.L. Rev. 413, 426–28 (1981), copyright 1981 by the Southwestern University Law Review, Los Angeles, CA. Reprinted by permission.

Gegan, *A Case of Depraved Heart Murder*, 49 St. John's L. Rev. 417, 457 (1975), copyright 1975 by the St. John's Law Review, Jamaica, NY. Reprinted by permission.

Wayne R. LaFave and Austin W. Scott, Jr., *Criminal Law, Second Edition* 85–86, 389, 624 (1986), copyright 1986 by West Publishing Co., St. Paul, MN. Reprinted by permission.

Lempert, *Desert and Deterrence: An Assessment of the Moral Bases of the Case for Capital Punishment*, 79 Mich. L. Rev. 1177, 1177–80, 1182–86, 1207–8 (1981), copyright 1981 by Michigan Law Review Association, Ann Arbor, MI. Reprinted by permission.

T. F. Plucknett, *A Concise History of the Common Law* 445–46 (5th ed. 1956), copyright 1956 by Little, Brown and Company, Boston, MA. Reprinted by permission.

Sayre, *Mens Rea*, 45 Harv. L. Rev. 974, 997–98 (1932), copyright 1932 by the Harvard Law Review Association, Cambridge, MA. Reprinted by permission.

E. van den Haag, *The Death Penalty: A Debate* 69 (1983) by Plenum Publishing Corporation, New York, NY. Reprinted by permission.

Weschler and Michael, *A Rationale of the Law of Homicide I and II*, 37 Colum. L. Rev. 701, 707–9, 721–22, 744–46, 1280–83 (1937), copyright 1937 by the Directors of the Columbia Law Review Association, Inc., New York, NY. All rights reserved. Reprinted by permission.

W. White, *The Death Penalty in the Eighties* 135–36 (1987), copyright 1987 by The University of Michigan Press, Ann Arbor, MI. Reprinted by permission.

F. Zimring and G. Hawkins, *Capital Punishment and the American Agenda* 162–63, 180–82 (1986), copyright 1986 by Cambridge University Press, New York, NY. Reprinted by permission.

CHAPTER 6

Estrich, *Rape*, 95 Yale L.J. 1087, 1090–95 (1986). Reprinted by permission of The Yale Law Journal and Fred B. Rothman & Company from The Yale Law Journal, vol. 95, pages 1090–95.

Henderson, *Rape and Responsibility*, 11 Law & Phil. 127, 130–31 (1992). Reprinted by permission of Kluwer Academic Publishers.

Husak and Thomas, *Date Rape, Social Convention, and Reasonable Mistake*, 11 Law & Phil. 95, 116, 122–26 (1992). Reprinted by permission of Kluwer Academic Publishers.

Schulhofer, *Taking Sexual Automony Seriously: Rape Law and Beyond*, 11 Law & Phil. 35, 40–41 (1992). Reprinted by permission of Kluwer Academic Publishers.

Stefan, *The Protection Racket: Rape Trauma Syndrome, Psychiatric Labeling, and Law*, 88 Nw. U.L. Rev. 1271, 1273 (1994). Reprinted by permission of the Northwestern University Law Review.

CHAPTER 7

Ashworth, *Belief, Intent, and Criminal Liability*. Oxford Essays in Jurisprudence, 3d Series 7, 29–31, J. Eckelaar and I. Bell eds. (1989). Reprinted by permission.

G. R. Blakey and B. Gettings, *Racketeer Influenced and Corrupt Organizations (RICO): Basic Concepts—Criminal and Civil Remedies*, 53 Temple L. Q. 1009, 1011–14, 1021–25, 1029–31, 1033–35 (1980). Reprinted by permission from the Temple Law Review, formerly Temple Law Quarterly, vol. 53 (1980). Copyright 1980 Temple University of the Commonwealth System of Higher Education, Philadelphia, PA.

Burke and Kadish, *Conspiracy*, from Encyclopedia of Crime and Justice 235 (Sanford H. Kadish editor-in-chief 1983), copyright 1983 by The Free Press, a division of Macmillan, Inc., New York, NY. Reprinted with permission of The Free Press, an imprint of Macmillan Publishing Company.

Duff, *Criminal Attempts*, from Intention, Agency and Criminal Liability 184, 186–92 (1990). Reprinted by permission of Blackwell Publishers, Oxford, UK.

Note, *Chance, Freedom and Criminal Liability*, 87 Colum. L. Rev. 125, 137–40 (1987). Reprinted by permission of the Columbia Law Review.

Note, *Conspiracy: Statutory Reform since the Model Penal Code*, 75 Colum. L. Rev. 1122, 1183–87 (1975), copyright 1975 by the Directors of the Columbia Law Review Association, Inc., New York, NY. All rights reserved. Reprinted by permission.

Note, *Developments in the Criminal Law—Criminal Conspiracy*, 71 Harv. L. Rev. 920, 933, 996 (1959), copyright 1959 by the Harvard Law Review Association, Cambridge, MA. Reprinted by permission.

Schulhofer, *Harm and Punishment: A Critique of Emphasis on the Result of Conduct in the Criminal Law*, 122 U. Pa. L. Rev. 1497, 1514–17 (1974). Reprinted by permission of the University of Pennsylvania Law Review.

CHAPTER 8

American Bar Association (ABA), *Commentary*, from 3 American Bar Association Standards for Criminal Justice, Sentencing Alternatives and Procedures 18.164–69 (2d ed. 1980), copyright 1980 by Little, Brown and Company, Boston, MA. Reprinted by permission.

K. Brickey, 1 *Corporate Criminal Liability*, 20-22, 41, 46-47, 49-51 (1984), copyright 1984 by West Group. Reprinted with permission.

K. Brickey, 1 *Corporate Criminal Responsibility*, from Encyclopedia of Crime and Justice 253, 256–61 (Sanford H. Kadish editor-in-chief 1983), copyright 1983 by The Free Press, a division of Macmillan, Inc., New York, NY. Reprinted with permission of The Free Press, an imprint of Macmillan Publishing Company.

Note, *Developments in the Law—Corporate Crime*, 92 Harv. L. Rev. 1270–71 (1979), copyright 1979 by the Harvard Law Review Association, Cambridge, MA. Reprinted by permission.

Sayre, *Criminal Responsibility for the Acts of Another* 43 Harv. L. Rev. 689, 702–6, 722 (1930), copyright 1930 by the Harvard Law Review Association, Cambridge, MA. Reprinted by permission.

CHAPTER 9

Alldridge, *Duress and the Reasonable Person*, 34 No. Ire. L. Q. 125, 138 (1983), copyright 1983 by the Northern Ireland Law Quarterly, Queen's University, Belfast, No. Ireland. Reprinted by permission.

Alldridge, *The Coherence of Defences*, 1983 Crim. L. Rev. 665, 665-66 (1983), copyright (1983) by Criminal Law Review. Reprinted by permission.

F. Allen, *The Crimes of Politics* 29, 57 (1974), copyright 1974 by The President and Fellows of Harvard College. Reprinted by permission of Harvard University Press, Cambridge, MA.

American Bar Association (ABA), *ABA on Criminal Justice Mental Health Standards* 316–17, 323 (1984), copyright 1984 by Little, Brown and Company, Boston, MA. Reprinted by permission.

American Bar Association, *Report of the Standing Committee on Association Standards for Criminal Justice and Commission on the Mentally Disabled*, 108 Rep. of the ABA 715, 717 (1983) (recommendation approved by the House of Delegates, February 9, 1983, 108 Rep. of the ABA at 380 (1983), copyright 1983 by the American Bar Association, Chicago, IL. Reprinted by permission.

American Psychiatric Association, *Diagnostic and Statistical Manual of Mental Disorders, Third Edition, Revised* 324 (1987), copyright 1987 by the American Psychiatric Association, Washington, DC. Reprinted by permission.

American Psychiatric Association, *Statement on the Insanity Defense* (December 1982), copyright 1982 by the American Psychiatric Association, Washington, DC. Reprinted by permission.

J. Andenaes, *The General Part of the Criminal Law of Norway* 156, 170 (1965), copyright 1965 by New York University School of Law, New York, NY. Reprinted by permission.

N. Angier, *Elementary, Dr. Watson. The Neurotransmitters Did It*, New York Times, January 21, 1994. Reprinted by permission of the New York Times.

Ashworth, *Self-Defense and the Right to Life*, 34 Cambridge L.J. 282, 289–90 (1975), copyright 1975 by Cambridge University Press, New York, NY. Reprinted by permission.

Bonnie, *The Moral Basis of the Insanity Defense*, 69 A.B.A. J. 194–96 (1983), copyright 1983 by the American Bar Association. Reprinted with permission from the February 1983 ABA Journal, The Lawyer's Magazine, published by the American Bar Association, Chicago, IL.

Brandt, *A Utilitarian Theory of Excuses*, 78 Phil. Rev. 337 (1969), copyright 1969 by The Philosophical Review, Cornell University, Ithaca, NY. Reprinted by permission.

Delgado, *Ascription of Criminal States of Mind: Toward a Defense Theory for the Coercively Persuaded ("Brainwashed") Defendant*, 63 Minn. L. Rev. 1, 8–11, 19 (1978), copyright 1978 by the Minnesota Law Review, Minneapolis, MN. Reprinted by permission.

Delgado, *"Rotten Social Backgrounds": Should the Criminal Law Recognize a Defense of Severe Environmental Deprivation?*, 3 Law & Inequality 9, 54–56, 75–77 (1985), copyright 1985 by Law & Inequality, Minneapolis, MN. Reprinted by permission.

J. Dressler, *New Thoughts about the Concepts of Justification in the Criminal Law: A Critique of Fletcher's Thinking and Rethinking*, 32 UCLA L. Rev. 61, 84–85 (1984), copyright 1984, The Regents of the University of California. All rights reserved. Reprinted by permission of the UCLA Law Review, Los Angeles, CA.

J. Dressler, *Professor Delgado's "Brainwashing" Defense: Courting a Determinist Legal System*, 63 Minn. L. Rev. 335, 342–43, 346–49, 354, 359–60 (1979), copyright 1979 by the Minnesota Law Review, Minneapolis, MN. Reprinted by permission.

Eisenberg and Micklow, *The Assaultive Wife: "Catch 22 Revised,"* 3 Women's Rights Law Rep. 138, 159 (1977). Reprinted by permission.

Eser, *Justification and Excuse*, 24 Am. J. Comp. L. 621, 635–36 (1976), copyright 1976 by the American Journal of Comparative Law, University of California, Berkeley, CA. Reprinted by permission.

J. German and A. Singer, *Punishing the Not Guilty: Hospitalization of Persons Acquitted by Reason of Insanity*, 29 Rutgers L. Rev. 1011, 1037–38, 1053–54, 1064–66 (1976), copyright 1976 by the Rutgers Law Review, Newark, NJ. Reprinted by permission.

A. Goldstein, *The Insanity Defense* 50–51 (1967), copyright 1967 by Yale University Press, New Haven, CT. Reprinted by permission.

Goldstein and Katz, *Abolish the "Insanity Defense"—Why Not?*, 72 Yale L.J. 853–54, 864–66, 868 (1963), copyright 1963 by Yale Law Journal Co., New Haven, CT. Reprinted by permission of the Yale Law Journal Company and Fred B. Rothman & Company.

R. Kent Greenawalt, *The Perplexing Borders of Justification and Excuse*, 84 Colum. L. Rev. 1897, 1900–5, 1910, 1927 (1984), copyright 1984 by the Directors of the Columbia Law Review Association, Inc., New York, NY. All rights reserved. Reprinted by permission.

Gross, *Some Unacceptable Excuses*, 19 Wayne L. Rev. 997, 1001–2 (1973), copyright 1973 by the Wayne Law Review, Detroit, MI. Reprinted by permission.

Hall, *Comments on Justification and Excuse*, 24 Am. J. Comp. L. 638–40 (1976), copyright 1976 by the American Journal of Comparative Law, University of California, Berkeley, CA. Reprinted by permission.

Hitchler, Motive as an Essential Element of Crime, 35 Dick. L. Rev. 105. 105. 110–11 (1931), copyright 1931 by the Dickinson Law Review, Carlisle, PA. Reprinted by permission.

D. Husak, *Motive and Criminal Liability* (as appeared in Criminal Justice Ethics, vol. 9, no. 1 [Winter/Spring 1989] pp. 3–14). Reprinted by permission of The Institute for Criminal Justice Ethics, 899 Tenth Avenue, New York, NY 10019.

S. Kadish, *Excusing Crime*, 75 Calif. L. Rev. 257, 278–81, 284–85 (1987), copyright 1987 by the California Law Review, Berkeley, CA. Reprinted by permission.

Kadish, *The Decline of Innocence*, 26 Cambridge L.J. 273–75 (1968), copyright 1968 by Cambridge University Press, New York, NY. Reprinted by permission.

A. Matthews, *Mental Disability and the Criminal Law* 90–92 (1970), copyright 1970 by the American Bar Foundation, Chicago, IL. Reprinted by permission.

G. Melton, J. Petrila, N. Poythress, and C. Slobogin, *Psychological Evaluations for the Courts* 114–15, 118–19 (1987), copyright 1987 by The Guilford Press, New York, NY. Reprinted by permission.

Ira Michenburg, *A Pleasant Surprise: The Guilty but Mentally Ill Verdict Has Both Succeeded in Its Own Right and Successfully Preserved the Traditional Role of the Insanity Defense*, 55 U. Cin. L. Rev. 943, 987–91 (1987), copyright 1987 by the University of Cincinnati College of Law, Cincinnati, OH. Reprinted by permission.

M. Moore, *Causation and the Excuses*, 73 Calif. L. Rev. 1091, 1137–39 (1985), copyright 1985 by the California Law Review, Berkeley, CA. Reprinted by permission.

Norval Morris, *Madness and the Criminal Law*, 53–74 (1982), copyright 1982 by The University of Chicago, IL. Reprinted by permission.

Morse, *Culpability and Control*, 142 U. Pa. L. Rev. 1587, 1637–40 (1994). Reprinted by permission of the University of Pennsylvania Law Review.

Morse, *Excusing the Crazy: The Insanity Defense Reconsidered*, 58 S. Cal. L. Rev. 777, 782–83, 788 (1986), copyright 1986 by the Southern California Law Review, University of Southern California, Los Angeles, CA. Reprinted by permission.

Morse, *Undiminished Confusion in Diminished Capacity*, 75 J. Crim. L. & Criminology 1, 5–9, 40–42 (1984), copyright 1984 by Stephen J. Morse, Philadelphia, PA. Reprinted by special permission of Stephen J. Morse and Northwestern University School of Law, Chicago, IL.

Newman and Weitzer, *Duress, Free Will and the Criminal Law*, 30 S. Cal. L. Rev. 313–16 (1957), copyright 1957 by the Southern California Law Review, University of Southern California, Los Angeles, CA. Reprinted by permission.

Note, *The Genetic Defense: Excuse or Explanation?*, 35 Wm. and Mary L. Rev. 353, 390, 393–96 (1994). Reprinted by permission of the William and Mary Law Review.

Note, *Justification: The Impact of the Model Penal Code on Statutory Reform*, 75 Colum. L. Rev. 914, 922–23 (1975), copyright 1975 by the Directors of the Columbia Law Review Association, Inc., New York, NY. All rights reserved. Reprinted by permission.

P. Robinson, *Criminal Law Defenses: A Systematic Analysis*, 82 Colum. L. Rev. 119, 203–4, 234 (1982), copyright 1982 by Paul H. Robinson, Camden, NJ. Reprinted by permission of Paul H. Robinson and the Directors of the Columbia Law Review Association, Inc.

Rosen, *On Self Defense, Imminence, And Women Who Kill Their Batterers* 71 N. Car. L. Rev. 371, 380-81 (1993). Reprinted by permission.

Rosenthal, *Duress In The Criminal Law*, 32 Crim. L. Q. 199, 203-4 (1989-90). Reprinted from (1989-90) 32 Criminal Law Quarterly 199 with the permission of Peter Rosenthal and Canada Law Book Inc., 240 Edward Street, Aurora, Ontario, L4G 3S9 Canada.

Schmolesky, *County Court of Ulster County v. Allen and Sandstrom v. Montana: The Supreme Court Lends an Ear but Turns Its Face*, 33 Rutgers L. Rev. 261, 266, 295 (1981), copyright 1981 by the Rutgers Law Review, Newark, NJ. Reprinted by permission.

Sendor, *Mistake of Fact: A Study in the Structure of Criminal Conduct*, 25 Wake For. L. Rev. 707, 776 (1990). Reprinted by permission of the Wake Forest University Law Review.

Slobogin, *A Rationale Approach to Responsibility*, 83 Mich. L. Rev. 820, 832–33 (1985). Reprinted by permission of the Michigan Law Review.

Smith, *Comment: R. v. Howe*, 1987 Crim. L. Rev. 480–82, copyright 1987 by Sweet & Maxwell Limited, London, UK. Reprinted by permission.

A. Stone, *The Insanity Defense on Trial*, 33 Harv. L. Sch. Bull. 15, 21 (Fall 1982), copyright 1982 by the Harvard Law School Bulletin, Cambridge, MA. Reprinted by permission.

H. Wales, *An Analysis of the Proposal to "Abolish" the Insanity Defense in S.I.: Squeezing a Lemon*, 124 U. Pa. L. Rev. 687, 710 (1976), copyright 1976 by the University of Pennsylvania Law Review, Philadelphia, PA. Reprinted by permission.

A. Wertheimer, *Coercion*, 148–49 (1987). Reprinted by permission of Princeton University Press.

Whitaker, *Daughter Freed after Mercy Killing of Father*, May 24, 1979, p. 1, Washington Post, copyright 1979 by the Washington Post, Washington, D.C. Reprinted by permission

Glanville Williams, *Offences and Defences*, 2 Legal Stud. 233, 233–36 (1982), copyright 1982 by Legal Studies, University College of Wales, Aberystwyth, UK. Reprinted by permission.

Williams, *The Theory of Excuses*, 1982 Crim. L. Rev. 732, 741–42, copyright 1982 by Sweets & Maxwell Limited, London, UK. Reprinted by permission.

TABLE OF CONTENTS

	Page
PREFACE	V
ACKNOWLEDGMENTS	VII
PERMISSIONS	VIII

CHAPTER 1 A SHORT SKETCH OF THE CRIMINAL JUSTICE SYSTEM 1

§ 1.01 An Overview, ... 1
    President's Commission on Law Enforcement and Administration of Justice, *The Challenge of Crime in a Free Society* (1968), ... 1

§ 1.02 The Uniqueness of the Criminal Process—The Players on the Scene, ... 4
    [A] The Burden of Proof, ... 5
        In re Winship 1970, ... 5
        Notes and Questions, ... 8
    [B] The Public Prosecutor, ... 11
        Commonwealth v. Malloy (1982), ... 12
        Notes and Questions, ... 14
        Enker, Perspectives on Plea Bargaining, The President's Commission on Law Enforcement and Administration of Justice,
        Task Force Report: The Courts (1967), ... 16
        Notes on the German Prosecutor and the Issue of Plea Negotiation, ... 17
        Note, ... 19
    [C] Defense Counsel, ... 20
    [D] The Jury, ... 21
        United States Constitution, Sixth Amendment, ... 21
        [1] Historical Sketch, ... 22
            Devlin, *Trial by Jury* (1966), ... 22
            Note, ... 24
        [2] Jury Selection, ... 24
            Taylor v. Louisiana (1975), ... 24
            Notes and Questions, ... 28
            Note on Jury Size and Unanimity, ... 32
            Note on Jury Nullification 33

	Page
CHAPTER 2 PUNISHMENT, ...	37
§ 2.01 Introduction, ...	37
§ 2.02 The Concept of Punishment, ...	39
Notes and Questions, ...	39
Fletcher	39
Packer	40
[A] The Definition of Punishment, ...	40
Hart, *Punishment and Responsibility* (1968)	40
Notes and Questions	41
Fleming v. Nestor (1960)	42
Notes and Questions	47
Feinbert, *The Expressive Function of Punishment* (1970)	48
Notes and Questions	51
[B] Punishment and Nonpunitive Sanctions	51
[1] Punishment versus Preventive Detention	51
United States v. Salerno (1987)	52
Notes and Questions	57
Kansas v. Hendricks (1997)	58
Notes and Questions	68
[2] Punishment versus Coercive Therapy	68
In re De La O (1963)	68
Wasserstrom, *Some Problems with Theories of Punishment* (1977)	73
In re Felder (1978)	74
Notes and Questions	77
[3] Punishment versus Regulatory Penalties	78
Brown v. Multnomah County District Court (1977)	78
Notes and Questions	82
Roe v. Farwell (1998)	83
Notes and Questions	94
[4] Punishment versus Compensation	96
People v. Pettit (1979)	97
Notes and Questions	99
Hudson v. United States (1997)	100
Notes and Questions	108
[5] Punishment versus Tax	109
Department of Revenue of Montana v. Kurth Ranch (1994)	109
Notes and Questions	115
[6] Forfeiture: Punishment versus Actions in Rem, ...	116

Page

   Austin v. United States (1993) 116
   Notes and Questions 123
   Bennis v. Michigan (1996) 125
   Notes and Questions 137
   United States v. Ursery (1996), ... 139
   Notes and Questions 152
  [C] Punitive Civil Sanctions: The Shrinking of Criminal
   Law? 153
   Mann, *Punitive Civil Sanctions: The
   Middleground between Criminal and
   Civil Law* (1992) 153

§ 2.03 The Justification of Punishment 156
  [A] Introduction 156
   Model Penal Code § § 1.02, 7.01 156
   Comprehensive Crime Control Act of 1984 (1988) . . . 157
   California Penal Code § 1170 (1976) 158
  [B] Utilitarianism 159
   [1] Deterrence 159
    Plato, *Protagoras* (1952) 159
    Radzinowicz, *A History of English
    Criminal Law* (1957) 160
    Bentham, *The Rationale of Punishment* (1830) . . 160
    Bentham, *An Introduction to the Principles
    of Morals and Legislation* (1789) 160
    Notes 162
   [2] Incapacitation 168
    Von Hirsch, *Incapacitation* (1992) 169
    Notes and Questions 172
   [3] Rehabilitation 173
    Packer 173
    Hart, *Punishment and Responsibility* (1968) 175
    Cohen, *Moral Aspects of the
    Criminal Law* (1940) 176
    Morris, *The Future of Imprisonment* (1974) 177
    Note 178
   [4] Denunciation 179
    Stephen 179
    Durkheim, *The Division of Labor
    in Society* (1933) 180
    Walker, *Punishment, Danger and Stigma:
    The Morality of Criminal Justice* (1980) 181
    Kahan, *What Do Alternatives Sanctions Mean?*
    (1996) 182
    Note 188
  [C] Retributivism 188

	Page
[1] Just Deserts and the Obligation to Punish	188
Kant, *The Metaphysical Elements of Justice* (1965)	188
Murphy, *Three Mistakes about Retributivism* (1971)	189
Moore, *The Moral Worth of Retribution* (1987)	191
Walker, *Punishment, Danger and Stigma: The Morality of Criminal Justice* (1980)	195
Notes and Questions	197
[2] Just Deserts as a Limiting Principle	198
Armstrong, *The Retributivist Hits Back* (1969)	198
Hart, *Punishment and Responsibility* (1968)	199
Packer	199
Notes and Questions	201
[3] Just Deserts and the Right to Be Punished	202
Morris, *Persons and Punishment* (1968)	202
Notes and Questions	204
[D] Putting Theory into Practice	204
United States v. Bergman (1976)	205
[E] Capital Punishment	211
§ 2.04 Sentencing and Proportionality	211
[A] Indeterminate or Determinate Sentences?	211
Von Hirsch *The Sentencing Commission's Functions* (1987)	212
Notes and Questions	223
Alschuler *Sentencing Reform and Prosecutorial Power: A Critique of Recent*	225
Note on Federal Sentencing Guidelines	227
[B] Proportionality of Punishment	230
Harmelin v. Michigan (1991)	230
Notes and Questions	240
Bedau, *Concessions to Retribution in Punishment* (1977)	242
United States v. Bajakajian (1998)	242
Notes and Questions	252
§ 2.05 *Nulla Poena Sine Lege:* The Legality Principle	252
[A] Judicial Creation of Crimes	252
Shaw v. Director of Public Prosecutions (1962)	252
Notes and Questions	256
[B] Vagueness and Overbreadth	257
Jeffries, *Legality, Vagueness, and the Construction of Penal Statutes* (1985)	258
Notes and Questions	260

	Page
[C] Statutory Interpretation	262
Allen, *The Erosion of Legality in American Criminal Justice: Some Later-Day Adventures of the* Nulla Poena *Principle* (1987)	262
Keller v. Superior Court 1970	263
Notes and Questions	272
Johnson v. State of Florida 1992	274
Notes and Questions	278

§ 2.06 What Conduct Should Be Punished? 280

    [A] Constitutionally Protected Conduct 281
        Griswold v. Connecticut (1965) 281
        Notes and Questions 283

    [B] Policy Issues 286
        [1] The Role of Harm 286
            Hall 287
            Notes and Questions 289

        [2] Immorality as Sufficient Ground for Criminal Liability 290
            Devlin, *The Enforcement of Morals* (1968) 290
            Notes and Questions 294
            Packer 295
            Notes and Questions 300

CHAPTER 3 THE REQUIREMENTS OF AN ACT 303

§ 3.01 Acts" 303
    Martin v. State (1944) 304
    People v. Wu (1991) 305
    Morris, *Somnambulistic Homicide: Ghosts, Spiders, and North Koreans* (1955) 313
    Notes and Questions 315
    People v. Decina (1956) 317
    Notes and Questions 320
    Robinson v. California (1962) 320
    Model Penal Code § 2.01 323
    Notes and Questions 323

§ 3.02 Knowing Failure to Act 325
    [A] Generally 325
        People v. Shaughnessy (1971) 325
        Notes and Questions 326

    [B] Possession 327
        People v. Ackerman (1971) 327
        Notes and Questions 329

	Page
§ 3.03 Omissions	329
Jones v. United States (1962)	329
Notes and Questions	332
§ 3.04 Causation	335
[A] Eggshell Victims	336
[B] Acts of Victims	337
Stephenson v. State (1932)	337
Notes and Questions	339
[C] Acts of Third Parties	341
[1] Criminal Acts	341
[2] Negligent Acts	341
Regina v. Benge and Another (1865)	341
[D] Nonhuman Forces	343
Model Penal Code § 2.03	344
Notes and Questions	345

CHAPTER 4 THE IMPORTANCE OF *MENS REA* 347

§ 4.01 Introduction	347
§ 4.02 The Development of the Common Law Requirement of *Mens Rea*	349
Further Readings on the History of *Mens Rea*	352
§ 4.03 The Notion(s) of *Mens Rea*	352
[A] Intent and Recklessness	352
[i] Oblique Intent	352
[ii] "Specific" and "General" Intents	353
Regina v. Pembliton (1874)	354
Regina v. Faulkner (1877)	356
Notes and Questions	358
Regina v. Cunningham (1957)	359
Notes and Questions	360
Commonwealth v. Pierce (1884)	363
Questions	365
[B] Negligence as a Criminal Predicate	365
Holmes	365
Hall, *Interrelations of Criminal Law and Torts: I* (1943)	367
Notes and Questions	368
Santillanes v. State (1993)	370
United States v. Garrett (1993)	374
Notes and Questions	378
§ 4.04 The Interpretation of *Mens Rea* Words in Criminal Statutes	378

	Page

[A] Generally 378
Remington and Helstad, *The Mental Element in Crime: A Legislative Problem* (1952) 379
Note 379

[B] Applying *Mens Rea* to Elements of the Offense 379
Cotterill v. Penn (1936) 380
Notes and Questions 381
United States v. X-Citement Video, Inc., et al. (1994) 382
Problems 388

§ 4.05 The Impact of the Model Penal Code 390

[A] The Model Penal Code 390
Notes 391

[B] Analysis of "Material Elements" 392

[C] Recklessness as the "Default" *Mens Rea* Requirement 393

[D] Conflicts between Subsections (3) and (4) of MPC § 2.02 394

[E] Mixed Elements 395

[F] Interpretation Problems 395

§ 4.06 The Impact of Mistake 396

[A] Mistake of Fact 396
Turner, *The Mental Element in Crimes at Common Law* (1934) 396
State v. McDonald (1879) 397
Stern v. The State (1874) 398
Notes, Questions, and Recommended Reading 399
Notes on Honest versus Reasonable Mistakes of Fact 400
People v. Ryan (1993) 402
Notes and Questions 406
Note on "Willful Blindness" 408

[B] Ignorance and Mistake of Law 408

    [1] Ignorance of Law 408
        United States v. Moncini (1989) 408
        Notes and Questions 411

    [2] Mistake of Law 416

        [a] Reliance on a Court 417
            State v. Striggles (1926) 417
            Notes and Questions 419

        [b] Reliance on Counsel 420
            Staley v. State (1911) 420
            Notes and Questions 421

	Page
[c] Reliance on an Official	423
State v. Huff (1897)	423
Notes and Questions	423
[d] Relaxing the Common Law	425
Notes and Questions	427
Cheek v. United States (1991)	427
Notes and Questions	434

§ 4.07 "Strict" Criminal Liability 437

    [A] Generally 437
        Commonwealth v. Mixer (1910) 438
        State v. Williams (1952) 442
        Notes and Questions 445
        Morissette v. United States (1952) 446
        Notes and Questions 449
        Regina v. Prince (1875) 450
        Notes and Questions 454
        Sayre, *The Present Significance of* Mens
        Rea *in Criminal Law* (1934) 456
        Notes and Questions 456
        Wasserstrom, *Strict Liability in the
        Criminal Law* (1960) 457
        Notes and Questions 459

    [B] The Federal View 460
        United States v. Park (1975) 461
        Notes and Questions 467
        Staples v. United States (1994) 468
        Notes and Questions 480

§ 4.08 The Future of *Mens Rea* 481
    Levitt, *Extent and Function of the Doctrine
    of* Mens Rea (1923) 481
    Wooton, *Crime and the Criminal Law* (1963) 482
    Note 483
    Hart, *Book Review* (1965) 483
    Note 484

CHAPTER 5 HOMICIDE **485**

§ 5.01 Introduction 485
    Plucknett 485

§ 5.02 The *Actus Reus:* Causing the Death of a Person 486

    [A] The Timing of Causation 486
        State v. Minster (1985) 486
        Notes and Questions 489

    [B] What is Death? 490
        State v. Fierro (1979) 490
        Notes and Questions 492

	Page
[C] Who Is a Person?	493
Keeler v. Superior Court (1970)	493
Notes and Questions	493
[D] The Implications of Causing One's Own Death	495
In Re Joseph G. (1983)	495
Notes and Questions	499
Washington v. Glucksberg (1997)	500
Notes and Questions	507

§ 5.03 The *Mens Rea* 509
  Sayre, *Mens Rea* (1932) 509

  [A] Murder 510
    Blackstone 510
    Stephen, *A Digest of the Criminal Law* (1878) ... 510
    Note on Degrees of Murder 511

    [1] Intent-to-Kill Murder 514
      People v. Haack (1976) 514
      Notes and Questions 516
      State v. Bingham (1985) 517
      Notes and Questions 521
      People v. Waters (1982) 523
      Notes and Questions 526
      People v. Lucero (1988) 529
      Notes and Questions 532

    [2] Depraved Heart Murder 534
      Banks v. State (1919) 534
      Notes and Questions 535
      Pears v. State (1983) 537
      Notes and Questions 540
      Commonwealth v. Malone (1946) 542
      Questions 543
      Northington v. State (1981) 543
      Notes and Questions 545

    [3] Intent-to-Cause-Serious-Bodily-Injury Murder ... 546
      Commonwealth v. Dorazio (1950) 546
      Director of Public Prosecutions v. Smith (1961) 548
      Notes and Questions 550

    [4] Felony Murder 551
      [a] In General 551
        State v. McKeiver (1965) 551
        Notes and Questions 552
        People v. Aaron (1980) 553
        Notes and Questions 560

      [b] "Dangerous" Felonies? 561
        People v. Patterson (1989) 562
        Notes and Questions 571

				Page
		[c] Duration of the Felony		573
		[d] The Merger Doctrine		574
			People v. Sears (1970)	574
			Notes and Questions	579
		[e] Causation Limitations		581
			State v. Canola (1977)	581
			Notes and Questions	586
			People v. Antick (1975)	588
			Notes	591
		[f] Abolish Felony Murder?		591
	[B] Manslaughter			595
		[1] Voluntary Manslaughter: The Provocation Formula		595
		Stephen, *A Digest of the Criminal Law* (1877)		595
		Tripp v. State (1977)		596
		Note		601
		People v. Berry (1976)		603
		Notes and Questions		606
		Director of Public Prosecutions v. Camplin (1978)		610
		Notes and Questions		615
		[2] Involuntary Manslaughter		617
			[a] Criminal Negligence Manslaughter	617
			Fitzgerald v. State (1896)	617
			State v. Barnett (1951)	620
			Notes and Questions	622
			State v. Williams (1971)	625
			Notes and Questions	628
			People v. Strong (1975)	629
			Questions	631
			[b] Unlawful Act Manslaughter	632
			United States v. Walker (1977)	632
			Notes and Questions	634
§ 5.04 The Death Penalty				635
	[A] Moral and Policy Issues			635
		[1] Retribution		635
		Lempert, *Desert and Deterrence: An Assessment of the Moral Bases of the Case for Capital Punishment* (1981)		635
		Notes and Questions		639
		[2] Deterrence		640
	[B] Legal Issues			644
		Tison v. Arizona (1987)		644
		Notes and Questions		657

	Page
A Brief Consideration of Supreme Court Cases	658
Bibliographic Note	661

CHAPTER 6 RAPE 663

§ 6.01 Introduction 663
    Blackstone 663
    Estrich, *Rape* (1986) 665
    Henderson, *Rape and Responsibility* (1992) 667
    Schulhofer, *Taking Sexual Autonomy Seriously:*
    Rape Law and Beyond (1992) 668

§ 6.02 *The Actus Reus* 669

    [A] Force, Threats, and Nonconsent 671
        Commonwealth v. Berkowitz (1994) 671
        Notes and Questions 673
        People v. Iniguez (1994) 675
        Notes and Questions 681

    [B] Deception 684
        Boro v. Superior Court (1985) 684
        Notes and Questions 687

    [C] The Marital Exemption 689
        Warren v. State (1985) 689
        Notes and Questions 692

§ 6.03 The *Mens Rea* 693

    [A] Subjective Fault 693
        Director of Public Prosecutions v. Morgan (1975) ... 693
        Notes and Questions 699
        Reynolds v. State (1983) 700
        Notes and Questions 704

    [B] Objective Liability 705
        State v. Smith (1989) 705
        Notes and Questions 709
        Fletcher 710
        Notes and Questions 712

    [C] Strict Liability 714
        People v. Williams (1993) 714
        Notes and Questions 717

§ 6.04 Evidentiary Considerations 718
    Dressler 718
    Notes and Questions 721

§ 6.05 Grading 722
    Notes and Questions 724

Chapter 7 Inchoate Crimes 725

§ 7.01 Introduction 725
§ 7.02 Attempt 726
    [A] Background 726
    [B] The *Actus Reus* 727
        Regina v. Eagleton (1855) 727
        Notes and Questions 728
        United States v. Jackson (1977) 728
        Notes and Questions 735
        McQuirter v. State (1953) 737
        Notes and Questions 738
        State v. Otto (1981) 739
        Notes and Questions 744
    [C] The *Mens Rea* 746
        Thacker v. Commonwealth (1922) 746
        Notes and Questions 748
        People v. Krovarz (1985) 748
        Notes and Questions 753
    [D] Renunciation 756
        People v. Staples (1970) 756
        Notes and Questions 757
    [E] Attempting Inchoate Crimes 758
    [F] Impossibility 759
        People v. Jaffe (1906) 759
        People v. Dlugash (1977) 762
        Notes and Questions 766
        United States v. Oviedo (1976) 767
        Notes and Questions 769
    [G] Grading 769
    [H] The Relevance of Resulting Harm 770
        Ashworth, *Belief, Intent, and Criminal Liability* (1989) 770
        Duff, *Criminal Attempts* (1990) 772
        Schulhofer, *Harm and Punishment: A Critique of Emphasis on the Results of Conduct in the Criminal Law* (1974) 775
        Notes and Questions 777
        Note, *Chance, Freedom and Criminal Liability* (1987) 778
§ 7.03 Conspiracy 780
    [A] Background 780
        [1] Rationale of Conspiracy Law 780

		Page
	[2] Procedural Aspects	783
[B]	Conspiratorial Objectives	786
[C]	The *Actus Reus*	787
	[1] The Agreement	787
	Weniger v. United States (1931)	787
	Notes and Questions	790
	[2] Parties to the Agreement	792
	State v. St. Christopher (1975)	792
	Notes and Questions	795
	Gebardi v. United States (1932)	797
	Iannelli v. United States (1975)	799
	Notes and Questions	802
[D]	The *Mens Rea*	803
	People v. Lauria (1967)	803
	Notes and Questions	809
	United States v. Blankenship (1992)	810
	Notes and Questions	814
	Note on the Corrupt Motive Doctrine	814
	United States v. Feola (1974)	815
	Notes and Questions	824
[E]	Single or Multiple Conspiracies	825
	Kotteakos v. United States (1946)	826
	Notes and Questions	829
[F]	Renunciation and Withdrawal	833
[G]	Grading of Punishment	834
	Note, *Conspiracy: Statutory Reform since the Model Penal Code* (1975)	834
[H]	RICO,	836
	Blakey and Gettings, *Racketeer Influenced and Corrupt Organizations (RICO): Basic Concepts— Criminal and Civil Remedies* (1980)	836
	United States v. Sutherland (1981)	838
	United States v. Licavoli (1984)	845
	Notes and Questions	849

CHAPTER 8 COMPLICITY 851

§ 8.01 Accomplice Liability 851
    Blackstone 851
    Notes 852

    [A] *Actus Reus* 853
        The Queen v. Coney (1882) 853
        Notes and Questions 856
        Wilcox v. Jeffery (1951) 857

	Page
Questions	858
State ex rel. Attorney General v. Tally (1894)	859
Notes and Questions	861

    [B] *Mens Rea* 862
        State v. Gladstone (1970) 862
        State v. Ellrich (1952) 864
        Notes and Questions 865
        United States v. Giovanetti (1990) 866
        Notes and Questions 869
        State v. Etzweiler (1984) 870
        Notes and Questions 875

    [C] Primary and Secondary Liability 879
        State v. Hayes (1891) 879
        Regina v. Cogan and Leak (1975) 881
        Notes and Questions 883

§ 8.02 The Conspiracy—Complicity Doctrine 884
    Pinkerton v. United States (1946) 884
    Notes and Questions 887

§ 8.03 Vicarious Liability 890

    [A] Liability of Natural Persons 890
        Allen v. Whitehead (1929) 890
        Notes and Questions 892
        Commonwealth v. Koczwara (1959) 895
        Notes and Questions 898

    [B] Corporate Criminality 899
        K. Brickey, *Corporate Criminal Liability* (1984) 899
        State v. Christy Pontiac-GMC, Inc. (1984) 901
        Notes and Questions 905
        United States v. Hilton Hotels Corporation (1972) 906
        Notes and Questions 908
        Coffee, *Corporate Criminal Responsibility* (1983) 910
        Note 918

CHAPTER 9 DEFENSES 919

§ 9.01 The Postulate of Free Will 919
    Lynch v. Director of Public Prosecutions (1975) 919
    State v. Sikora (1965) 919
    Notes 926

§ 9.02 Classifying Defenses 926
    Blackstone 926
    Hart 927
    Robinson, *Criminal Law Defenses:*
    A Systematic Analysis (1982) 928

	Page
Note	932
Williams, *Offences and Defences* (1982)	932

§ 9.03 Justification versus Excuse 935

[A] The Distinction 935
Hall, *Comments on Justification and Excuse* (1976) 935
Eser, *Justification and Excuse* (1976) 935
Note 936

[B] The Distinction Challenged 937
Dressler, *New Thoughts about the Concept of Justification in the Criminal Law: A Critique of Fletcher's Thinking and Rethinking* (1984) 937
Greenawalt, *The Perplexing Borders of Justification and Excuse* (1984) 937
Notes 938

§ 9.04 The Procedural Implications of Classifying Defenses 939

[A] Elements Generally 942
State v. Segovia (1969), ... 942
Notes and Questions 944

[B] Elements and Affirmative Defenses 946
Mullaney v. Wilbur (1975) 946
Notes and Questions 953
Patterson v. New York (1977) 954
Notes and Questions 964
McMillan v. Pennsylvania (1986) 965

[C] Elements and Presumptions 973
Ulster County Court v. Allen (1979) 973
Notes and Questions 981
Sandstrom v. Montana (1979) 983
Notes and Questions 988

§ 9.05 Specific Defenses 991

[A] Acts "in Extremis" 991

[1] Duress 991

[a] Generally 991
Blackstone 991
Stephen 991
Wertheimer, *Coercion* (1987) 992
Newman and Weitzer, *Duress, Free Will, and the Criminal Law* (1957) 992
Regina v. Hudson and Taylor (1971) 994
Model Penal Code § 2.09 997

[b] Rationale of Duress 997

[C] Definitional Controversies 999

		Page
	[d] Homicide and Duress	1000
	[e] Other Considerations	1001
[2]	Superior Orders	1002
[3]	Necessity	1003
	Blackstone	1003
	Regina v. Dudley and Stephens (1884)	1004
	Perka v. The Queen (1984)	1008
	Notes and Questions	1017
	[a] Codifying Necessity	1020
	Model Penal Code § 3.02	1021
	New York Penal Law § 35.05	1021
	German Penal Code 1969 (1975) § § 34 and 35	1022
	Swedish Penal Code (1963) Ch. 24 § § 4 and 5	1022
	Notes and Questions	1023
[4]	Self-Defense	1024
	Blackstone	1025
	Model Penal Code § § 3.04 and 3.09	1026
	[a] The Rationale of Self-Defense and Doctrinal Confusion	1027
	[b] Mistake and "Imperfect Self Defense"	1029
	[c] The "Retreat" Rule	1030
	[d] The "Rules" of Self-Defense	1033
	State v. Wanrow (1977)	1035
	Notes and Questions	1038
	State v. Norman (1989)	1043
	Notes and Questions	1057
[5]	Defense of Property/Habitation	1060
	Law v. Maryland (1974)	1060
	Notes and Questions	1064
[6]	Law Enforcement Defenses	1067
	Tennessee v. Garner (1985)	1067
	Notes and Questions	1076
[B] Mental Abnormality		1078
[1]	Incompetency to Stand Trial	1078
[2]	Insanity and Execution	1080
	Notes and Questions	1082
[3]	The Defense of Insanity	1083
	[a] Development of Tests for Insanity ABA Standing Committee On Association Standards for Criminal Justice, *Proposed Criminal*	1083

        Justice Mental Health Standards
        (1984) 1083
        Daniel M'Naghten's Case (1843) 1084
        Notes and Questions 1085
        Commonwealth v. Tempest (1981) 1090
        Note on Volitional Impairment 1092
        United States v. Pollard (1959) 1093
        Note 1095
        Morse, *Culpability and Control* (1994) .. 1096
        Note on the Model Penal Code
        Approach 1097
        State v. Johnson (1979) 1098
        Notes and Questions 1103

    [b] Disposition of Offenders Not Guilty by
        Reason of Insanity 1105
        Jones v. United States (1968) 1105
        Notes and Questions 1108
        Foucha v. Louisiana (1992) 1110
        Notes and Questions 1115

    [c] The Rationale of the Defense of
        Insanity 1118
        Bentham, *Theory of Legislation* (1914) .. 1118
        Brandt, *A Utilitarian Theory of*
        Excuses (1969) 1118
        Goldstein and Katz, *Abolish the "Insanity*
        Defense"—Why Not? (1963) 1119
        Kadish, *The Decline of Innocence*
        (1968) 1121
        Morse, *Excusing the Crazy: The Insanity*
        Defense Reconsidered (1985) 1122
        Kadish, *Excusing Crime* (1987) 1123
        Moore, *Causation and the*
        Excuses (1985) 1124
        Notes and Questions 1126

    [d] Insanity and Automatism 1128
        Fulcher v. State (1981) 1128
        Notes and Questions 1131

    [e] Burden of Proof and the Insanity
        Defense 1132

[4] Diminished Capacity 1133
    United States v. Brawner (1972) 1133
    Notes 1135
    Morse, *Undiminished Confusion*
    in Diminished Capacity (1984) 1135
    Notes and Questions 1137
    Johnson v. State (1982) 1139

	Page
Notes and Questions	1144
People v. Wetmore (1978)	1145
Notes and Questions	1149

    [5] New Alternatives 1150

        [a] The Guilty but Mentally Ill Verdict 1150
            Mickenberg, *A Pleasant Surprise: The Guilty but Mentally Ill Verdict Has Both Succeeded in Its Own Right and Successfully Preserved the Traditional Role of the Insanity Defense* (1987) 1150
            Note 1153

        [b] Abolition of the Defense of Insanity 1153
            Morris, *Madness and the Criminal Law* (1982) 1154
            Note 1159
            Wales, *An Analysis of the Proposal to "Abolish" the Insanity Defense in S.I.: Squeezing a Lemon* (1976) 1159
            Stone, *The Insanity Defense on Trial* (1982) 1160
            Bonnie, *The Moral Basis of the Insanity Defense* (1983) 1160

[C] Intoxication 1162
    People v. Low (1987) 1164
    Model Penal Code § 2.08 1169
    People v. Kelly (1970) 1169
    Notes 1174
    Montana v. Egelhoff (1996) 1178
    Notes and Questions 1196
    Note on Alcohol and Drug Addiction 1197

[D] Entrapment 1198
    Sherman v. United States (1958) 1198
    Notes and Questions 1204

[E] Expanding Excuses 1205

    [1] In General 1205
        Williams, *The Theory of Excuses* (1982) 1205
        Aristotle, *Nicomachean Ethics* 1205
        United States v. Bailey (1978) 1206
        Notes and Questions 1210

    [2] General Issues of Free Will and Science 1210
        Gross, *Some Unacceptable Excuses* (1973) 1212

        [a] Physiologically Based Excuses for
            Criminality 1212
            XYY 1212
            Genetic Causation 1213

		Page
	Note, *The Genetic Defense: Excuse or Explanation?* (1993)	1213
	Angier, *Elementary, Dr. Watson.*	
	The Neurotransmitters Did It	1216
	Complicating Factors	1217
	Premenstrual Syndrome (PMS)	1218
	Hypoglycemia	1220
	Senility and Alzheimer's Disease	1220
	Sleep Disorders	1221
	Brain Scan Evidence	1221
	Suggested Reading	1221
[b]	Psychologically Based Excuses for Criminality	1221
	Brainwashing	1221
	Pathological Behavior	1224
	Other Concerns	1224
[c]	Sociologically Based Excuses for Criminality	1224
	"Rotten Social Background" (RSB): "I'm Depraved on Accounta I'm Deprived"	1224
	Kadish, *Excusing Crime* (1987)	1226
	Notes	1226

[3] The Role of Motive 1228

    [a] The General Doctrine 1228
        Regina v. Hicklin (1868) 1228
        Notes and Questions 1229

    [b] Specific Cases 1233
        Euthanasia 1233
        State v. Forrest (1987) 1233
        Whitaker, *Daughter Freed after Mercy Killing of Father* (1979) 1238
        Notes and Questions 1240
        Political Offenders: Civil Disobedients and Terrorists 1243
        United States v. Merkt (1986) 1243
        Notes 1246
        Allen, *The Crimes of Politics* (1974) 1247
        Note 1248

APPENDIX—MODEL PENAL CODE, ... APP-1

TABLE OF CASES, ... TC-1

TABLE OF STATUTES, ... TS-1

TABLE OF MODEL PENAL CODE, ... MPC-1

INDEX, ... I-1

Chapter 1
A Short Sketch of the Criminal Justice System

§ 1.01 An Overview

President's Commission on Law Enforcement and Administration of Justice,

The Challenge of Crime in a Free Society 70–78 (1968)

America's System of Criminal Justice

* * *

The criminal justice system has three separately organized parts—the police, the courts, and corrections—and each has distinct tasks. What each one does and how it does it has a direct effect on the work of the others. The courts must deal, and can only deal, with those whom the police arrest; the business of corrections is with those delivered to it by the courts. How successfully corrections reforms convicts determines whether they will once again become police business and influences the sentences the judges pass; police activities are subject to court scrutiny and are often determined by court decisions. . . .

The popular, or even the lawbook, theory of everyday criminal process oversimplifies in some respects and overcomplicates in others what usually happens. That theory is that when an infraction of the law occurs, a policeman finds, if he can, the probable offender, arrests him and brings him promptly before a magistrate. If the offense is minor, the magistrate disposes of it forthwith; if it is serious, he holds the defendant for further action and admits him to bail. The case then is turned over to a prosecuting attorney, who charges the defendant with a specific statutory crime. This charge is subject to review by a judge at a preliminary hearing of the evidence and in many places, if the offense charged is a felony, by a grand jury that can dismiss the charge, or affirm it by delivering it to a judge in the form of an indictment.*

The chart on the following page* . . . sets forth in simplified form the process of criminal administration and shows the many decision points along its course. Since felonies, misdemeanors, petty offenses, and juvenile cases generally follow quite different paths, they are shown separately.

If the defendant pleads "not guilty" to the charge he comes to trial; the facts of his case are marshaled by prosecuting and defense attorneys and presented, under the supervision of a judge, through witnesses, to a jury. If the jury finds

---

* [In most states a felony may be charged either by grand jury indictment or by "information," i.e., a formal charge prepared by the prosecuting attorney without the advice of the grand jury. In federal cases, felonies are chargeable only by grand jury indictment pursuant to the Fifth Amendment of the United States Constitution unless waived.—Eds.]

* [The chart has been omitted from this book.—Eds.]

the defendant guilty, he is sentenced by the judge to a term in prison, where a systematic attempt to convert him into a law-abiding citizen is made, or to a term of probation, under which he is permitted to live in the community as long as he behaves himself.**

Some cases do proceed much like that, especially those involving offenses that are generally considered "major:" serious acts of violence or thefts of large amounts of property. However, not all major cases follow this course and, in any event, the bulk of the daily business of the criminal justice system consists of offenses that are not major—breaches of the peace, crimes of vice, petty thefts, assaults arising from domestic or street-corner or barroom disputes. These and most other cases are disposed of in much less formal and much less deliberate ways.***

* * *

[T]he transformation of America from a relatively relaxed rural society into a tumultuous urban one has presented the criminal justice system in the cities with a volume of cases too large to handle by traditional methods. One result of heavy caseloads is highly visible in city courts, which process many cases with excessive haste and many others with excessive slowness. In the interest both of effectiveness and of fairness to individuals, justice should be swift and certain; too often in city courts today it is, instead, hasty or faltering. Invisibly, the pressure of numbers has effected a series of adventitious changes in the criminal process. Informal shortcuts have been used. The decision making process has often become routinized. Throughout the system the importance of individual judgment and discretion, as distinguished from stated rules and procedures, has increased. In effect, much decision making is being done on an administrative rather than on a judicial basis. Thus, an examination of how the criminal justice system works and a consideration of the changes needed to make it more effective and fair must focus on the extent to which invisible, administrative procedures depart from visible, traditional ones, and on the desirability of that departure.

The Police

At the very beginning of the process—or, more properly, before the process begins at all—something happens that is scarcely discussed in law books and is seldom recognized by the public: law enforcement policy is made by the policeman. For policemen cannot and do not arrest all the offenders they encounter. It is doubtful that they arrest most of them. A criminal code, in practice, is not a set of specific instructions to policemen but a more or less rough map of the territory in which policemen work. How an individual

---

** [Note that a "not guilty" verdict is not a declaration that the defendant did not commit the crime. Instead, it simply means that the government was unable to prove the prima facie case "beyond a reasonable doubt" or the defendant successfully bore the burden of a "defense" to the particular crime. These principles are discussed *infra* Chapter 9.—Eds.]

*** [One approach to such disputes is the use of mediation. This approach is especially favored in intrafamily and neighbor disputes because of its conciliatory approach to dispute resolution. For a rather complete discussion, see N. Rogers and R Salem, A Student's Guide to Mediation and the Law (1987).—Eds.]

policeman moves around the territory depends largely on his personal discretion.

That a policeman's duties compel him to exercise personal discretion many times every day is evident. Crime does not look the same on the street as it does in a legislative chamber. How much noise or profanity makes conduct "disorderly" within the meaning of the law? When must a quarrel be treated as a criminal assault: at the first threat, or at the first shove, or at the first blow, or after blood is drawn, or when a serious injury is inflicted? How suspicious must conduct be before there is "probable cause," the constitutional basis for an arrest? Every policeman, however complete or sketchy his education, is an interpreter of the law.

* * *

Finally, the manner in which a policeman works is influenced by practical matters: the legal strength of the available evidence, the willingness of victims to press charges and of witnesses to testify, the temper of the community, the time and information at the policeman's disposal. Much is at stake in how the policeman exercises this discretion. If he judges conduct not suspicious enough to justify intervention, the chance to prevent a robbery, rape, or murder may be lost. If he overestimates the seriousness of a situation or his actions are controlled by panic or prejudice, he may hurt or kill someone unnecessarily. His actions may even touch off a riot.

The Magistrate

In direct contrast to the policeman, the magistrate before whom a suspect is first brought usually exercises less discretion than the law allows him. He is entitled to inquire into the facts of the case, into whether there are grounds for holding the accused. He seldom does. He seldom can. The more promptly an arrested suspect is brought into magistrate's court, the less likelihood there is that much information about the arrest, other than the arresting officer's statement, will be available to the magistrate. Moreover many magistrates, especially in big cities, have such congested calendars that it is almost impossible for them to subject any case but an extraordinary one to prolonged scrutiny.

In practice the most important things, by far, that a magistrate does are to set the amount of a defendant's bail and in some jurisdictions to appoint counsel. Too seldom does either action get the careful attention it deserves. In many cases the magistrate accepts a waiver of counsel without ensuring that the suspect knows the significance of legal representation.

* * *

The persistence of money bail can best be explained not by its stated purpose but by the belief of police, prosecutors, and courts that the best way to keep a defendant from committing more crimes before trial is to set bail so high that he cannot obtain his release.

The Prosecutor

The key administrative officer in the processing of cases is the prosecutor. Theoretically the examination of the evidence against a defendant by a judge at a preliminary hearing, and its reexamination by a grand jury, are important parts of the process. Practically they seldom are because a prosecutor seldom has any difficulty in making a *prima facie* case against a defendant. In fact most defendants waive their rights to preliminary hearings and much more often than not grand juries indict precisely as prosecutors ask them to. The prosecutor wields almost undisputed sway over the pretrial progress of most cases. He decides whether to press a case or drop it. He determines the specific charge against a defendant. When the charge is reduced, as it is in as many as two-thirds of all cases in some cities, the prosecutor is usually the official who reduces it.

* * *

The Plea and the Sentence

When a prosecutor reduces a charge it is ordinarily because there has been "plea bargaining" between him and a defense attorney. The issue at stake is how much the prosecutor will reduce his original charge or how lenient a sentence he will recommend in return for a plea of guilty. There is no way of judging how many bargains reflect the prosecutor's belief that a lesser charge or sentence is justified and how many result from the fact that there may be in the system at any one time ten times as many cases as there are prosecutors or judges or courtrooms to handle them, should every one come to trial. In form, a plea bargain can be anything from a series of careful conferences to a hurried consultation in a courthouse corridor. In content it can be anything from a conscientious exploration of the facts and dispositional alternatives available and appropriate to a defendant, to a perfunctory deal. If the interests of a defendant are to be properly protected while his fate is being thus invisibly determined, he obviously needs just as good legal representation as the kind he needs at a public trial. Whether or not plea bargaining is a fair and effective method of disposing of criminal cases depends heavily on whether or not defendants are provided early with competent and conscientious counsel.

* * *

In perhaps nine-tenths of all cases there is no trial; the defendants are self-confessedly guilty.

§ 1.02 THE UNIQUENESS OF THE CRIMINAL PROCESS—THE PLAYERS ON THE SCENE

In a significant number of ways, the law has recognized that the criminal process and the substance of criminal law are unique. This section explores some of those ways.

[A] The Burden of Proof

IN RE WINSHIP

Supreme Court of the United States

397 U.S. 358 (1970)

Mr. JUSTICE BRENNAN *delivered the opinion of the Court.*

This case presents the single, narrow question whether proof beyond a reasonable doubt is among the "essentials of due process and fair treatment" required during the adjudicatory stage when a juvenile is charged with an act which would constitute a crime if committed by an adult. . . .

* * *

I

. . . The requirement that guilt of a criminal charge be established by proof beyond a reasonable doubt dates at least from our early years as a Nation. The "demand for a higher degree of persuasion in criminal cases was recurrently expressed from ancient times, [though] its crystallization into the formula beyond a reasonable doubt' seems to have occurred as late as 1798. It is now accepted in common law jurisdictions as the measure of persuasion by which the prosecution must convince the trier of all the essential elements of guilt." . . . Although virtually unanimous adherence to the reasonable-doubt standard in common-law jurisdictions may not conclusively establish it as a requirement of due process, such adherence does "reflect a profound judgment about the way in which law should be enforced and justice administered." *Duncan v. Louisiana,* 391 U.S. 145, 155 (1968).

Expressions in many opinions of this Court indicate that it has long been assumed that proof of a criminal charge beyond a reasonable doubt is constitutionally required. . . . [T]he Court said in *Brinegar v. United States,* [338 U.S. 160, 174 (1949)], that "[g]uilt in a criminal case must be proved beyond a reasonable doubt and by evidence confined to that which long experience in the common-law tradition, to some extent embodied in the Constitution, has crystallized into rules of evidence consistent with that standard. These rules are historically grounded rights of our system, developed to safeguard men from dubious and unjust convictions, with resulting forfeitures of life, liberty and property." *Davis v. United States,* [160 U.S. 469, 488 (1895)], stated that the requirement is implicit in "constitutions . . . [which] recognize the fundamental principles that are deemed essential for the protection of life and liberty." In *Davis* a murder conviction was reversed because the trial judge instructed the jury that it was their duty to convict when the evidence was equally balanced regarding the sanity of the accused. This Court said: "On the contrary, he is entitled to an acquittal of the specific crime charged, if upon all the evidence, there is reasonable doubt whether he was capable in law of committing crime. . . . No man should be deprived of his life under the forms of law unless the jurors who try him are able, upon their consciences, to say that the evidence before them . . . is sufficient to show beyond a reasonable doubt the existence of every fact necessary to constitute the crime charged."

The reasonable-doubt standard plays a vital role in the American scheme of criminal procedure. It is a prime instrument for reducing the risk of convictions resting on factual error. The standard provides concrete substance for the presumption of innocence—that bedrock "axiomatic and elementary" principle whose "enforcement lies at the foundation of the administration of our criminal law." *Coffin v. United States,* [156 U.S. 432, 453 (1895)]. As the dissenters in the New York Court of Appeals observed, and we agree, "a person accused of crime . . . would be at a severe disadvantage, a disadvantage amounting to a lack of fundamental fairness, if he could be adjudged guilty and imprisoned for years on the strength of [the preponderance of evidence standard], the same evidence as would suffice in a civil case." 24 N.Y.2d, at 205, 247 N.E.2d, at 259.

The requirement of proof beyond a reasonable doubt has this vital role in our criminal procedure for cogent reasons. The accused during a criminal prosecution has at stake an interest of immense importance, both because of the possibility that he may lose his liberty upon conviction and because of the certainty that he would be stigmatized by the conviction. Accordingly, a society that values the good name and freedom of every individual should not condemn a man for commission of a crime when there is reasonable doubt about his guilt. . . .

Moreover, use of the reasonable-doubt standard is indispensable to command the respect and confidence of the community in applications of the criminal law. It is critical that the moral force of the criminal law not be diluted by a standard of proof which leaves people in doubt whether innocent men are being condemned. It is also important in our free society that every individual going about his ordinary affairs have confidence that his government cannot adjudge him guilty of a criminal offense without convincing a proper factfinder of his guilt with utmost certainty.

Lest there remain any doubt about the constitutional stature of the reasonable-doubt standard, we explicitly hold that the Due Process Clause protects the accused against conviction except upon proof beyond a reasonable doubt of every fact necessary to constitute the crime with which he is charged.

* * *

II

* * *

Finally, we reject the . . . suggestion that there is, in any event, only a "tenuous difference" between the reasonable-doubt and preponderance standards. The suggestion is singularly unpersuasive. . . . [C]ommentators [accurately observe] that "the preponderance test is susceptible to the misinterpretation that it calls on the trier of fact merely to perform an abstract weighing of the evidence in order to determine which side has produced the greater quantum, without regard to its effect in convincing his mind of the truth of the proposition asserted." . . .

[The Court went on to hold that the "beyond a reasonable doubt standard" was constitutionally required in delinquency adjudications as well as criminal trials.]

Reversed.

Mr. JUSTICE HARLAN, *concurring.*

* * *

[T]he choice of the standard for a particular variety of adjudication does, I think, reflect a very fundamental assessment of the comparative social costs of erroneous factual determinations.

To explain why I think this so, I begin by stating two propositions, neither of which I believe can be fairly disputed. First, in a judicial proceeding in which there is a dispute about the facts of some earlier event, the factfinder cannot acquire unassailably accurate knowledge of what happened. Instead, all the factfinder can acquire is a belief of what probably happened. The intensity of this belief—the degree to which a factfinder is convinced that a given act actually occurred—can, of course, vary. In this regard, a standard of proof represents an attempt to instruct the factfinder concerning the degree of confidence our society thinks he should have in the correctness of factual conclusions for a particular type of adjudication. Although the phrases "preponderance of the evidence" and "proof beyond a reasonable doubt" are quantitatively imprecise, they do communicate to the finder of fact different notions concerning the degree of confidence he is expected to have in the correctness of his factual conclusions.

A second proposition, which is really nothing more than a corollary of the first, is that the trier of fact will sometimes, despite his best efforts, be wrong in his factual conclusions. . . .

The standard of proof influences the relative frequency of erroneous outcomes. If, for example, the standard of proof for a criminal trial were a preponderance of the evidence rather than proof beyond a reasonable doubt, there would be a smaller risk of factual errors that result in freeing guilty persons, but a far greater risk of factual errors that result in convicting the innocent. Because the standard of proof affects the comparative frequency of these two types of erroneous outcomes, the choice of the standard to be applied in a particular kind of litigation should, in a rational world, reflect an assessment of the comparative social disutility of each.

When one makes such an assessment, the reason for different standards of proof in civil as opposed to criminal litigation becomes apparent. In a civil suit between two private parties for money damages, for example, we view it as no more serious in general for there to be an erroneous verdict in the defendant's favor than for there to be an erroneous verdict in the plaintiff's favor. . . .

In a criminal case, on the other hand, we do not view the social disutility of convicting an innocent man as equivalent to the disutility of acquitting someone who is guilty. As MR. JUSTICE BRENNAN wrote for the Court in *Speiser v. Randall,* 357, U.S. 513, 525–26 (1958):

There is always in litigation a margin of error, representing error in factfinding, which both parties must take into account. Where one party has at stake an interest of transcending value—as a criminal defendant his liberty—this margin of error is reduced as to him by the process of placing on the other party the burden . . . of persuading the factfinder at the conclusion of the trial of his guilt beyond a reasonable doubt.

In this context, I view the requirement of proof beyond a reasonable doubt in a criminal case as bottomed on a fundamental value determination of our society that it is far worse to convict an innocent man than to let a guilty man go free. It is only because of the nearly complete and long-standing acceptance of the reasonable-doubt standard by the States in criminal trials that the Court has not before today had to hold explicitly that due process, as an expression of fundamental procedural fairness, requires a more stringent standard for criminal trials than for ordinary civil litigation.

NOTES AND QUESTIONS

1. What is a "reasonable doubt"? What does it mean to be convinced *beyond* such a doubt? In a series of cases decided after *Winship,* the Court appeared to hold that any attempts to "redefine" the term *reasonable doubt* would result in reversal because the force of the term would be diluted—for example, *Cage v. Louisiana,* 498 U.S. 39 (1990); *Boyce v. California,* 494 U.S. 370 (1990). In two decisions in 1994, however, the Court upheld instructions that defined reasonable doubt, respectively, as "not a mere possible doubt, because everything relating to human affairs and depending on moral evidence, is open to some possible or imaginary doubt" or as requiring a "moral certainty" and an "actual and substantial doubt." *Sandoval v. California,* 114 S.Ct. 1239 (1994); *Victor v. Nebraska,* 114 S.Ct. 1239 (1994). The California Supreme Court, however, removed "moral certainty" and "moral evidence," finding "warning signals" in *Sandoval* that these words might be too vague. *People v. Freeman,* 882 P.2d 249 (Cal., 1994).

2. How *much* proof is "beyond a reasonable doubt"? Can the concept be quantified? Should it be? See Tribe, *A Further Critique of Mathematical Proof,* 84 Harv. L. Rev. 1810, 1817 (1971). Is there any difference between this standard operationally and "preponderance of the evidence"? For some intriguing studies demonstrating that, while judges and juries sometimes disagree on how much proof is necessary, they do agree that "beyond a reasonable doubt" is different from "preponderance," see Simon, *Judges' Translations of Burdens of Proof into Statements of Probability* (1969); Trial Law Guide 103; Simon and Mahan, *Quantifying Burdens of Proof,* 5 Law and Soc'y Rev. 319 (1971); Simon, *"Beyond a Reasonable Doubt"—An Experimental Attempt at Quantification,* 6 J. Applied Behavioral Sci. 203 (1970). *See also* L.S.E. Jury Project, *Juries and the Rules of Evidence,* 1973 Crim. L. Rev. 208. *See also United States v. Fatico,* 458 F. Supp. 388 (S.D.N.Y. 1978), where Judge Weinstein published a poll of his fellow jurists as to how much proof was required for proof beyond a reasonable doubt. The results were intriguing. All judges agreed that proof by a preponderance required over 50 percent. Most found the "clear and convincing" standard to required 60 to 75 percent, but

some also found that this same "quantity" was required by the "clear, unequivocal and convincing" standard. Finally, four judges thought that proof beyond a reasonable doubt was met by an 85 percent standard, two a 90 percent standard, one a 95 percent standard, one an 80 percent standard, and one a 76 percent standard. On the other hand, the court in *McCullough v. State,* 99 Nev. 72, 657 P.2d 1157 (1983), held that a trial judge erred when he suggested to the jury that beyond a reasonable doubt was "about" 75 percent. Said the court, "The concept of reasonable doubt is inherently qualitative. Any attempt to quantify it may impermissibly lower the prosecution's burden of proof, as it is likely to confuse rather than clarify."

3. The *substance of Winship* may well have been diluted in the past 20 years by a series of techniques that redefine what facts are "necessary to constitute the crime." Some of these developments are discussed in section 9.04, *infra.* For a general discussion, see Note, *Winship on Rough Waters: The Erosion of the Reasonable Doubt Standard,* 106 Harv. L. Rev. 1093 (1993).

4. In the history of Anglo-American law, two primary methods have been used to ascertain the truth of a plaintiff's (or prosecution's) allegations. The first is the ordeal; the second the jury. Virtually every society has placed reliance upon the intervention by God, both to decide individual cases of supposed liability and to indicate the future (soothsayers, etc.). In *Superstition and Force* (1870), H. Lea meticulously traces the history of resort to God in various civilizations. Not surprisingly, there is great similarity among them in the techniques used.

Some of these techniques relied almost solely on natural forces, controlled by God without any direct participation by man. Thus, for example, the Hebrews often relied upon lot. African tribes required suspects to drink poison, swallow emetics, or obtain an item guarded by a snake. Indians, Slavs, and the English threw suspects into water, but with different rules. For the first two, drowning (sinking) proved guilt, while for the English the notion was that the water, blessed by the priest, would reject anything evil, while accepting innocence. Thus, sinking was a sign of innocence while floating to the top was a sign of guilt. Russians, like the Puritans in Salem, used the water ordeal to detect witches. V. Chaldize, Criminal Russia 15 (1977).

By far the most popular ordeals in all these societies appear to have involved fire or burning. The Slavs and English used the hot iron ordeal—the accused was required to hold a piece of hot iron for a specific length of time. If, after three days, the wounds healed, the accused was declared acquitted; if not, a finding of guilt, usually followed by hanging, ensued. A variation of this was the Indian technique in which an accused had to walk in circles with the iron— the more serious the crime, the wider the circles. Other societies such as Spain and Sweden varied the weight of the iron. Lea, *supra* at 236–237, describes the widespread use of these techniques:

> From Spain to Constantinople, and from Scandinavia to naples, it was appealed to with confidence as an unfailing mode of ascertaining the will of heaven. . . . The ordeal even became partially naturalized among the Greeks. . . . In the middle of the thirteenth century, the Emperor Theodore Lacaris demanded that Michael Paleologus, who afterwards wore the imperial crown, should clear himself of an accusation in this manner.

English process varied somewhat. The accused could accept, as an alternative to the ordeal, either trial by battle or trial by "wager of law." The first would appear to be self-explanatory; in fact, however, there was a professional band of champions who undertook business throughout the realm to fight on behalf of defendants (or plaintiff-prosecutors). Courts would arrange the dates of battle to accommodate the schedule of these champions. Some great landowners were engaged in so much litigation that they maintained their own full-time champions. *Plucknett* 117. Trial by battle was not available, however, if the accused had been indicted by the king.

Wager of law required the defendant to find a fixed number of persons (usually 12) to take a solemn oath that he was innocent. These "compurgators" were not asked to swear to the facts of the case, but merely that the accused was an honest, credible person; it was essentially a test of character and reputation.

The ordeals were generally preferred by the Church. Individual priests, who determined whether the accused had been "cured" after the ordeal, were able both to consolidate their power and, on occasion, to accept bribes. Moreover, they could manipulate the results in various ways, such as the intensity of the heat with which the iron was heated before the accused took hold of it. *Plucknett* at 114, cites Peter the Chanter, who indicated that he believed he had a duty to make the result come out "right."

The ordeals ceased in 1215, however, when the Lateran Council forbade priests from participating in them. Without the blessing of the Church, there could be no assurance that the results were ordained by God, and the ordeals became virtually a dead letter. Thereupon, the common law turned toward another system of determining guilt—the jury. The history of that institution is traced, §1.02 [D] *infra*.

The "standard of proof" in the ordeals was, of course, absolute: God would determine, without doubt, the liability of the defendant. But with the abolition of the ordeals and the consequent growth of the jury system, some articulated standard for determining criminal liability became necessary. For several centuries the standard varied, but for the main juries were told that they should convict the accused only if there was *no doubt* about his guilt. This, in turn, led some countries (not, however, England, at least in the main) to turn to torture, not as a means of punishment, but as a pretrial means of obtaining the confession of the accused, which was then accepted at trial. See J. Langbein, Torture and the Law of Proof (1976).

With the growth during the 1600s and 1700s of the rules of evidence, much evidence that earlier would have been admitted in the jury trial came to be excluded. Morano opines that it was this movement that ultimately resulted in the striking of the "no doubt" standard, and its replacement, in the late 1700s, by the "beyond a reasonable doubt" standard which is generally used today. Morano, *A Reexamination of the Development of the Reasonable Doubt Rule,* 55 B.U. L. Rev. 507 (1975).

5. In *Addington v. Texas,* 449 U.S. 418 (1979), the Court held that proof beyond a reasonable doubt was not required before civilly committing a person alleged to be mentally ill. What factors arepresent in a criminal adjudication that are not present in such a commitment? *See* Chapter 2 *infra*.

[B] The Public Prosecutor

Public prosecutors are relatively new to the Anglo-Saxon world. When crime and tort were the same proceedings and two possible remedies could result from one trial, it made sense that the plaintiff was also the prosecutor. Therefore, private prosecution was the norm of the day. This was also particularly relevant when trial was either by battle or by ordeal since in trial by battle, one might well expect that the plaintiff would be willing to take on the defendant on the field of battle and, in trial by ordeal, the officiating judge sometimes ordered the plaintiff to disprove the response of the defendant by going through the ordeal himself. For these and other reasons, in both situations private prosecution made a great deal of sense.

But even when crime and tort became distinct procedures, the concept of private prosecution in criminal trials persisted. Indeed, there was no public police or public prosecutor to speak of in England until roughly the mid-19th century.

The genesis of public prosecution in the United States is still somewhat of a historical mystery. Roscoe Pound, Criminal Justice in America 150–51 (1930), has described the process:

> We departed radically from the English system by setting up public prosecutors. In the very spirit of our formative era we provided an independent public prosecutor for each local circuit or district, or sometimes for each county . . . suggested partly by the French *procurer du roi* of the old regime, but also made to the pattern of the English attorney general. His powers were those of the attorney general, and usually he had complete independence as the local organ of the state in criminal matters. The public prosecutor was conspicuously adapted to the country of independent neighborhoods, with local institutions, local offenders, and problems of local order and security which obtained in the fore part of the nineteenth century.

In most states, the district attorney, county attorney, or the prosecuting attorney is an elected official. It has been suggested that election to the office came in the wave of American Jacksonian populism, but in many states it appears to have become elective, rather than appointive, much later.[*]

These elected prosecutors are not responsible to any higher authority; they do not fall within the office of the state attorney general. That office has particular jurisdiction, often described by statute, which usually does not conflict with the jurisdiction of the local prosecutor. In most states, the state attorney general is appointed rather than elected, and is thus subject indirectly to the electorate.

The federal system is different. Although the attorney general of the United States and a few very close subordinates are appointed by the President (with the advice and consent of the Senate), the day-to-day prosecutions are conducted by United States Attorneys, one for each federal judicial district in the country. These officers also are appointed by the President with Senate concurrence. Subordinates to these prosecutors (called Assistant United States Attorneys) are not subject to political decisions and are not expected

---

[*] See Yobel and Naughton, Law Enforcement in Colonial New York 328–330 (1994).

to resign if a new administration is elected. Although these posts are essentially civil service posts and could be held for life, most assistant U.S. attorneys leave after three or four years to enter private practice. This system generally establishes a "professional" prosecutor who is not dependent on political forces, except in the broadest sense of that term.

Moreover, since the prosecutor is often affiliated with a political party, he often has to seek the support of that party's leaders and therefore is put in the dangerous position of excessive sensitivity to these leaders in criminal matters. For this reason among others, federal law now requires the appointment of a "special prosecutor" to investigate charges against any administrative official. 8 U.S.C. § 591 (1973). In theory the special prosecutor is independent of political pressures because his job terminates after the single investigation is complete.

As with any government position, the election of district attorneys is beset with the familiar issues of popularity versus qualifications, party affiliation, and so on. However, these familiar issues become aggravated by the very nature of the office: to prosecute crime. An incumbent prosecutor is forced to run on his record and thus may prosecute harshly those people and those crimes that the electorate may dislike and similarly fail to prosecute those people whom the electorate admires.

COMMONWEALTH V. MALLOY

Superior Court of Pennsylvania

304 Pa. Super. 297, 450 A.2d 689 (1982)

CIRILLO, Judge

This case raises the novel issue of whether the victim of an alleged crime has standing to appeal, without the consent of the district attorney, a judicial determination dismissing a complaint for the prosecution's failure to establish a *prima facie* case. For the reasons which follow, we conclude that a victim/complainant lacks the authority and power to appeal and, therefore, this appeal must be quashed.

On February 20, 1980, private criminal complaints were executed by David Rosen of the appellant corporation, Paula-Arlen Vending Machine Co. (hereinafter "appellant"), against James P. Michener and Heidi Malloy (hereinafter "defendants"). Each of the defendants was charged with theft by unlawful taking or disposition, theft by deception and criminal conspiracy. The complaints alleged that the defendants, former employees of appellant, drew and endorsed numerous checks on appellant's account without authority, in an attempt to deprive the company of monies. On March 10, 1980, the District Attorney of Lehigh County approved the complaints.

The District Attorney allowed the appellant's private counsel to represent the Commonwealth at the preliminary hearing held on April 17, 1980. After that hearing, District Justice Ralph Beck determined that a *prima facie* case had been established on all charges against both defendants. On June 4, 1980, informations were filed against the defendants on the charges alleged in the complaints.

Petitions for writs of *habeas corpus* were filed on behalf of both defendants, on June 5, 1980, in the Lehigh County Court of Common Pleas. The writs alleged a failure by the Commonwealth to establish a *prima facie* case at the preliminary hearing. Writs of *habeas corpus ad subjiciendum* were issued and a hearing was scheduled for June 30, 1980. The hearing was conducted by the Honorable Maxwell E. Davison, who reviewed the preliminary hearing transcript and the memorandum of law submitted by counsel. On July 28, 1980, the complaints against both defendants were dismissed because of the prosecution's failure to prove a *prima facie* case.

On August 20, 1980, appellant privately filed notices of appeal from the order dismissing the complaints, because the district attorney refused to appeal or authorize appellant to do so on behalf of the Commonwealth. On October 29, 1980, the district attorney filed a motion to quash the appeals, challenging appellant's standing to appeal. The motion was denied by our Court on February 10, 1981, ". . . without prejudice to the parties to address the standing issue in their briefs."

Inquiry into the power of a private citizen to appeal in a criminal prosecution without the authorization or approval of the district attorney involves a consideration of the significance of the distinction between public and private wrongs and the role of the district attorney in conducting criminal prosecutions.

It is a well-settled principle of law that a crime is an offense against the sovereignty, a wrong which the government deems injurious not only to the victim but to the public at large, and which it punishes through a judicial proceeding in the Commonwealth's name. Though the same wrongful act may constitute both a crime and a tort, the tort is a private injury which is to be pursued by the injured party. Criminal prosecutions are not to settle private grievances but are to rectify the injury done to the Commonwealth. The individual who is the victim of a crime only has recourse in a civil action for damages.[1]

This special position which criminal prosecutions hold in our system has long been recognized by our courts, as evidenced in *Hutchinson v. Bank of Wheeling,* 41 Pa. 42, 45 (1861):

> The private wrong was not merged in the public one, nor is the public prosecution intended to supersede the private action. Their purposes are entirely different. The person wronged is not chargeable with the conduct of the prosecution, and therefore not affected by an acquittal. Even a conviction and sentence do not discharge his right of action. . . .

and more recently in *Commonwealth v. Walker,* 468 Pa. 323, 331, 362 A.2d 227, 231 (1976):

> One of the purposes of the criminal law is to punish offenses against the Commonwealth, as defined by the Legislature, and it follows, that "[t]he

---

[1] We note that numerous civil suits are pending between the various parties based on the same circumstances.

criminal prosecution is for the injury done to the Commonwealth, and not for the injury done to the individual who may, if entitled, obtain redress through a civil action. . . . "

* * *

[State statute] provides that the district attorney is the one ". . . who shall sign all bills of indictment and conduct in court all criminal and other prosecutions, in the name of the Commonwealth. . . ." In the performance of his duties, the district attorney is a quasi-judicial officer with the duty to seek justice, not just convictions. He is obligated to perform this task intelligently and impartially. The prosecutor is under no compulsion to prosecute every alleged offender, and the decision to prosecute or not to prosecute is a matter within his discretion. . . .

* * *

Thus, the district attorney is permitted to exercise sound discretion to refrain from proceeding in a criminal case whenever he, in good faith, thinks that the prosecution would not serve the best interests of the state. This decision not to prosecute may be implemented by the district attorney's refusal to approve the private criminal complaint at the outset, or, once the proceedings have commenced[,] by withdrawing his approval and discontinuing the prosecution of the complaint.

* * *

[The Court reviewed cases denying standing to crime victims to challenge judicial determinations foreclosing further prosecution of the alleged crime.]

* * *

The above discussion clearly illustrates that the state, represented by the District Attorney, is the party plaintiff in a criminal prosecution; the victim/complainant is not considered a party to the proceeding. The victim acts only as a prosecuting witness.[2] . . . Since appellant, as victim or witness, lacks "party" status in this criminal prosecution, he has no standing to appeal and therefore, this appeal must be quashed.

Appeal quashed

NOTES AND QUESTIONS

1. The traditional reluctance of courts to require a prosecutor to take action against every person about whom a complaint is made by any citizen may be understandable. See, for example, *Pagach v. Klein,* 193 F.Supp. 630 (S.D.N.Y. 1961). But suppose the grand jury, after being convened by the

---

[2] A prosecuting witness has been defined as: The private person upon whose complaint or information a criminal prosecution is founded and whose testimony is mainly relied on to secure a conviction at the trial. . . .

prosecutor, seeks to indict someone the prosecutor does not? Is there any justification, at that point, for the courts' refusing to step in? *See United States v. Cox,* 542 F.2d 167 (5th Cir. 1967). During the Watergate investigation, the special prosecutor strenuously and successfully urged the grand jury not to seek to indict President Nixon, but to name him as an unindicted co-conspirator, fearing, apparently, that the issue of whether a sitting president could be indicted might itself delay further proceedings. Suppose the grand jury had ignored this advice and named the president in the indictment, but the special prosecutor had refused to sign it? Rule 7(c) of the Federal Rules of Criminal Procedure requires the signature of the prosecutor before a "true bill" may be returned.

2. The prosecutor's decision to prosecute is not quite as absolute as her decision not to prosecute. Although many cases hold that "selective enforcement" is not unconstitutional per se, this may not be so where the selection itself is based upon a discriminatory purpose. Thus, in *United States v. Falk,* 479 F.2d 616 (7th Cir. 1973), the court ordered a hearing where the defendant made out a prima facie case that the prosecution was brought primarily to stifle his dissent from the Vietnam War. See also *United States v. Berrois,* 501 F.2d 1207 (2d Cir. 1974). However, in *United States v. Swanson,* 509 F.2d 1205 (8th Cir. 1975), the court held that a decision by the IRS to give special priority to tax evasions by attorneys and certified public accountants was based on a rational classification and was not discriminatory.

3. In *Imbler v. Pachtman,* 424 U.S. 409 (1976), the United States Supreme Court confronted for the first time the question of the tort liability of a prosecutor under the Federal Civil Rights Act (42 U.S.C. §1983). The Court continued the common law tradition (see *Yaselli v. Goff,* 275 U.S. 503 (1927)) that prosecutors are absolutely immune from malicious prosecution suits. The court, however, noted that the immunity was dependent on the functions that the prosecution was performing. It specifically limited its holding to the "initiating [of] a prosecution and in presenting the State's case," thus leaving unconsidered the areas of administration and investigation.

4. Does a private attorney acting as a criminal prosecutor enjoy the same immunity as a district attorney? In *Voytko v. Ramada Inn of Atlantic City,* 445 F. Supp. 315 (D.N.J. 1975), the Ramada Inn filed criminal complaints against Voytko for nonpayment of a hotel bill. The grand jury refused to indict Voytko, but the law firm retained by the Ramada Inn filed new charges under the New Jersey Disorderly Persons Act. The district attorney did not appear in court to prosecute the charges. Therefore, under N.J. Rules of Practice 7:4–4(b), an associate of the law firm retained by the Ramada Inn actually prosecuted the case. The charges were dismissed at the end of the prosecution's case for failure of proof. Voytko thereupon brought a damage suit against the associate. The District Court found that a private prosecutor who was granted leave to bring a criminal prosecution was absolutely immune from liability.

5. Neb. Rev. Stat. sec. 29–1606 (1995):

It shall be the duty of the county attorney of the proper county to inquire into and make full examination of all the facts and circumstances connected with any case on preliminary examination, as provided by law, touching the commission of any offense wherein the offender shall be committed to jail, or become recognized or held to bail. If the prosecuting attorney shall determine in any such case that an information ought not to be filed, he shall make, subscribe, and file with the clerk of the court a statement in writing, containing his reasons, in fact and in law, for not filing an information in such case. . . .

6. In *State v. Winne,* 12 N.J. 152, 96 A.2d 63 (1953), the court held that the state could indict a county prosecutor for failing to investigate complaints relating to gambling violations even though the indictment did not charge that the failure was willful or corrupt. *Winne* seems to be an isolated case, both nationally and in New Jersey.

ENKER, PERSPECTIVES ON PLEA BARGAINING

The President's Commission on Law Enforcement and Administration of Justice,
Task Force Report:

The Courts 108–11 (1967)

I. DESCRIPTION OF PLEA BARGAINING

[A] Pleading Guilty to a Reduced Charge

1. "Plea bargaining," or its popular euphemism "the negotiated plea," actually takes on a variety of forms and occurs in varied legal and factual contexts. In what is probably its best known form, the "plea bargain" consists of an arrangement between the prosecutor and the defendant or his lawyer, whereby in return for a plea of guilty by the defendant, the prosecutor agrees to press a charge less serious than that warranted by the facts which he could prove at trial. "Less serious" in this context usually means an offense which carries a lower potential maximum sentence. In such instances the defendant's motivation for pleading guilty is to limit the judge's sentencing discretion to the lesser maximum. Similar results are obtained when the defendant agrees to plead guilty to a given charge in return for a prosecutor's promise not to charge him with being a multiple offender or to drop added counts in a multicount indictment.

2. It is equally common in plea bargaining for reduced charges to be motivated by the opposite goal, namely, to maximize the judge's sentencing discretion. In this type of agreement the defendant pleads guilty to a lesser charge than is warranted by the facts, not to reduce the potential maximum sentence, but to avoid a legislatively mandated minimum sentence or a legislative direction precluding the availability of probation. . . .

[B] "On the Nose" Guilty Pleas

1. Plea bargaining need not necessarily take the form of a reduction of the charges. A defendant may plead guilty to a charge that accurately describes his conduct in return for a general promise of leniency at sentencing or a more

specific promise of probation or of a sentence that does not exceed a specific term of years. . . .

2. One further type of plea bargain merits attention. This may be called the "tacit bargain." In this instance, there are no formal or explicit negotiations between the defense and the prosecution. Defendant, aware of an established practice in the court to show leniency to defendants who plead guilty, pleads guilty to the charges in the expectation that he will be so treated. This expectation is almost invariably satisfied without the need to enter into any negotiations or make any explicit promises. . . .

NOTES ON THE GERMAN PROSECUTOR AND THE ISSUE OF PLEA NEGOTIATION

1. Joachim Hermann, *The German Prosecutor,* in Discretionary Justice in Europe and America 16, 58–59 (K.C. Davis, ed., 1976):

Americans may have considerable difficulty imagining a criminal justice system based on the concept that the prosecuting authority should have limited, rather than pervasive and uncontrolled, discretionary powers. A system of this kind does, however, exist. Prosecuting attorneys in West Germany are required, except in certain situations specified in the codes and statutes, to prosecute all charges for which there is sufficient evidence to justify a conviction.[1] The German prosecutor is not without discretion; the scope of his discretion has increased steadily and is still growing. Unlike the American situation, however, the discretion of the prosecutor in this system is strictly limited by the Code of Criminal Procedure; it is guided by statutory standards and, to a certain extent, is controlled by the courts.

The striking difference between the two systems reasonably causes Americans to wonder how the German prosecutor manages to do his job, despite this restricted discretion, in a way that seems to be accepted by the public. . . .

* * *

When a prosecuting attorney decides not to prosecute, he must obtain approval of his superior and officially close the case. A file is opened for each case and recorded in a central register in the local office. Superiors are thus able to follow the activities of individual prosecutors in each case.

When a prosecutor closes a case, he gives written reasons for his action. In the more difficult cases he communicates the reasons for the decision orally to his superiors. These reasons, whether oral or written, provide an effective means for supervisors to standardize and structure the exercise of discretion. At the same time, the requirement of providing reasons restricts the prosecutor's decision to close a case. . . .

---

[1] The duty is stated in §152(2) of the West German Code of Criminal Procedure: "Except as otherwise provided by law, it [i.e., the prosecution] is obligated to take action in case of all acts which are punishable by a court and capable of prosecution, so far as there is a sufficient factual basis." An English translation of the Code is published in 10 *American Series of Foreign Penal codes: The German Code of Criminal Procedure* (H. Niebler trans. 1965).

To complete the picture of the German prosecutor's activities, one more factor should be mentioned. The prosecutor in a sense is isolated from the facts. He must investigate all offenses brought to his attention, but the initial investigation is typically performed by the police authorities. The police are legally obligated to investigate all cases other than petty misdemeanors and petty infractions, but in fact this duty is not discharged. Police officers exercise broad and unknown discretionary powers. As long as no file is opened and no superior is present, the police officer's discretion cannot be controlled. A study of police activities found that the police often did not investigate cases in which a misdemeanor or when a felony was committed. Police officers freely exercise their power to label acts as criminal or not criminal, and they often downgrade traffic violations. Thus, most cases are screened and sifted before they reach the prosecutor.

* * *

The German system of criminal procedure, unlike the American system, tries to control prosecutorial activities with the rule of compulsory prosecution and the concept of restrained discretion.

* * *

2. Davis, *American Comments on American and German Prosecutors,* in Discretionary Justice in Europe and America 70–72 (K.C. Davis, ed., 1976):

The German system seems carefully planned in each facet. The American system seems obviously unplanned. . . . The American system is the product of an accretion over nearly two centuries of small decisions which prosecutors have made largely in their own interest.

The system of judicial unreviewability for abuse of prosecutorial discretion is likewise unplanned, although it stems from judges rather than from prosecutors. It grew up during the nineteenth century, when the dominant attitude was that "interference of the Courts" with executive departments "would be productive of nothing but mischief." Even as late as 1900 the Supreme Court summarized the law: "It has been repeatedly adjudged that the courts have no general supervising power over the proceedings and action of the various administrative departments of government." But during the twentieth century, judicial reviewability of administrative discretion has become the norm, because of the discovery that courts can provide a meaningful check without substituting judgment. The unreviewability of prosecutors' discretion for abuse is a clear departure from the prevailing assumption that courts should protect against abuse of administration discretion. The main reason for the departure, I think, is that the present generation of judges recoils from reviewing prosecutors' discretion because the volume of new judicial business would be so enormous. The judges' own interests largely determine their decisions on a major question of judicial policy. I do not speak critically; on the contrary, the very best judges take the most pride in the quality of their work, and they are the ones who properly have the strongest interests in protecting that quality against the threat of a huge volume of new business. The conflict of interest is not the fault of the judges, for it is built into the system. . . .

The lack of legal control of American prosecutors' discretion is aggravated by the unplanned failure to insulate their discretionary choices from political or other ulterior influence. We insulate our judges; one with an interest at stake may not ethically try to influence a judicial decision outside the courtroom, and by and large the ethical principle is obeyed. But we have no such tradition against influencing prosecutors' decisions. Senators and Congressmen often help constituents to escape prosecution; their intervention is called "casework" and is not generally deemed unethical. And a U.S. attorney or other prosecutor is peculiarly vulnerable to political influence, because most American prosecutors use their offices as stepping stones to higher political positions. They often welcome requests for favors from those who wield political power, because they may ask favors in return. When the politician says to the prosecutor, "Please do me a favor; X is an old friend of mine and a good fellow," the prosecutor may initially decide to deal with the X case on its merits. But he may then postpone action, with the idea that when he gets to it he will decide it on the merits; then after a while he finds that the X case is too stale to pick up. He has done the favor without ever making a decision to do it. Or perhaps he has even done the favor after making a decision not to do it.

Americans can learn from Germans how to formulate a plan to insulate prosecutors from political influence. The main idea is to make the prosecutor's office nonpolitical—to make it not a stepping stone to elective office. Anyone who becomes an assistant prosecutor in Germany is on a career ladder; he has reached that position on his merits, and if he goes on up the ladder, perhaps to the bench, the promotions will be on the merits. He can gain nothing by doing a politician a favor; he is more likely to lose by doing such a favor. The tradition is strongly established that each political party avoids any advantage for its own members (as against members of the opposition party) in promoting prosecutors or judges. The result is that favors are neither asked nor expected.

* * *

Note

The Davis book generated a substantial debate concerning the degree and types of discretion in the office of continental prosecutors, in particular the German office. See Goldstein and Marcus, *The Myth of Judicial Supervision in Three "Inquisitorial" Systems: France, Italy and Germany,* 87 YaleL.J. 240 (1977). Professors Langbein (University of Chicago) and Wienreb (Harvard) responded to Goldstein and Marcus in 87 Yale L.J. 1549 (1978), which was followed by a surrebuttal, 87 YaleL.J. 1570 (1978). See also Langbein, *Land Without Plea Bargaining: How the Germans Do It,* 78 Mich.L. Rev. 204 (1980); and J. Langbein, Comparative Criminal Procedure: Germany (1977).

Most heatedly discussed in these and other volumes is the power of the prosecutor to "plea bargain" (to agree to drop some counts of an indictment, urge a lighter sentence, or prosecute on a lesser included offense), in exchange for the defendant's plea of guilty. This appears to be a relatively new phenomenon historically, but has already been widely accepted by the courts.

Yet, the discretion in plea bargaining is not absolute. The U.S. Supreme Court in *Santobello v. New York,* 404 U.S. 257 (1971), required a prosecutor to keep any plea bargaining promise made to a defendant. Thus, a prosecutor cannot promise to seek a reduced sentence and then say nothing at sentencing. Indeed, the bargain made by one prosecutor must be kept by a prosecutor who replaces him on the case.

However, a prosecutor's failure to bargain with one co-defendant while bargaining with the other does not violate the first's equal protection or due process rights. *Newman v. United States,* 382 F.2d 479 (D.C. Cir. 1967) and *Dear Wing Jung v. United States,* 312 F.2d 73 (9th Cir. 1963). Moreover, a prosecutor can refuse to recommend acceptance of lesser pleas in a homicide case for some defendants unless all the defendants plead guilty to lesser charges. *People v. Henzey,* 24 A.2d 764, 263 N.Y.S.2d 678 (1965).

In *Bordenkircher v. Hayes,* 434 U.S. 357 (1978), the Court found, 5–4, that the decision of the prosecutor to bring an habitual criminal charge against a defendant after his refusal to plead guilty to the originally charged offense did not violate the due process rights of the defendant. Hayes refused to plead guilty to a charge of entering a forged investment in the amount of $88.30 in return for the promise of the prosecutor to recommend a five-year sentence. The prosecutor further stated that if Hayes did not accept the bargain, the prosecutor would seek an indictment under the Kentucky Habitual Criminal Act which mandates a life sentence. Hayes refused to bargain, was convicted of both offenses, and was sentenced to a life term. The Court stated that, "[i]t follows, that, by tolerating and encouraging the negotiation of pleas, this Court has necessarily accepted as constitutionally legitimate the simple reality that the prosecutor's interest at the bargaining table is to persuade the defendant to forego his right to plead not guilty."

The practice of plea bargaining has come under increasing scrutiny. Although it is often declared that the pressures of the system would always make plea bargaining necessary, historical surveys indicate that plea bargaining began as late as the 1910s. See Alschuler, *Plea Bargaining and Its History,* 79 Colum. L. Rev. (1979). The National Advisory Commission on Criminal Justice Standards and Goals (1973) recommended the abolition of plea bargaining by 1978; that goal has not been achieved.

[C] Defense Counsel

When juries were fact-givers rather than fact-finders (see §1.02 [D] *infra.*) there was little need for lawyers. But even as the role of the jury changed, the common law clung to the notion that lawyers were unnecessary for fair adjudication of any dispute, including a criminal matter. In England from 1550 to 1800, prisoners indicted for felony were, by law, denied the assistance of counsel in presenting their case. The judge bore the responsibility for seeing that the proceedings were sufficient in law. The rule might have disappeared sooner if the possibility of lengthening the trials had not been administratively unthinkable. In many cases, there was no prosecutor, either private or public, and one should remember that even in those cases where there was some sort of prosecutor, it was generally a private, rather than a state-employed, prosecutor.

But with the establishment of rules of evidence and trial procedure, the rule was relaxed somewhat and, by a statute of 1695, prisoners indicted of treason were given a right to counsel. Thereafter, the exclusion of lawyers in felony cases was scarcely supportable. During the 18th century, it became normal for counsel to be permitted to conduct a case or at least to prompt the accused.

On the other hand, until the abolition—in the late 19th century—of the rule that the defendant was not a competent* witness, the judge would so inform the jury of the defendant's lack of competency as a witness. It would seem that the defendant could have benefitted from that as much as he theoretically benefitted from having counsel present.**

Only in 1963 did the Supreme Court of the United States decide that every charged felon was entitled to counsel, and that if the accused could not afford to pay for a lawyer, the state was obligated to provide one free of charge. *Gideon v. Wainwright,* 372 U.S. 335 (1963). Later this principle was extended to reach all those imprisoned for offenses, whether felonies or misdemeanors. *Argersinger v. Hamlin,* 407 U.S. 25 (1972); *Scott v. Illinois,* 440 U.S. 367 (1979). There was, however, early evidence that these decisions were often ignored. See S. Krantz, *Right to Counsel in Criminal Cases* (1976).

Some states have a statewide office of "public defender" which represents indigents; in some states, these offices are established on a county basis. But in the majority of states, counsel are selected from among members of the bar at large to represent indigent defendants. The results are sometimes not in accord with a hoped-for standard of justice. The "draft" system requires attorneys unfamiliar with criminal law or procedure to master those areas within a relatively short time; that some fail should not be surprising. What is more surprising is the alleged weakness of some public defenders who, after all, soon become skilled experts in those processes as well as in plea bargaining. But when the heavy caseloads that these attorneys are compelled to carry are considered, the attacks on the general level of competence are brought more clearly into focus.

[D] The Jury

UNITED STATES CONSTITUTION
SIXTH AMENDMENT

In all criminal prosecutions, the accused shall enjoy the right to a speedy and public trial, by an impartial jury of the state and district wherein the crime shall have been committed. . . .

---

* *Competent* in this context would mean that the court would allow the defendant to testify, not that he was physically or mentally unable to testify.

** For a discussion of trials during this period, see generally Langbein, *The Criminal Trial before the Lawyers,* 45 U. Chi. L. Rev. 263 (1978).

[1] Historical Sketch

Although the jury is often said to be one of the major innovations in justice (civil as well as criminal) that the common law has established, this is not totally accurate. Juries are found in other civilizations, although it is true that this history was unknown at the time the jury was created in England, as described in the excerpt from Devlin, *infra*.

In ancient Greece, for example, the change from the ordeal to jury trial in criminal cases can be traced through the drama. In *Antigone,* by Sophocles (circa 496–406 BC), the guards appointed to prevent the burial of Polynices offer to go through the ordeal of hot iron or fire to demonstrate their innocence; in the same play, Cleon, without a jury, decrees Antigone's death. In *Orestia* by Aeschylus (circa 525–456 BC), however, Orestes, pursued by the Furies, is tried by a jury of Athenians summoned by Athena. This body—called the Areopagus because they convened on the Hill of Ares—was the most important jury in Greece, and heard homicide cases for several centuries. In other trials, however, dicasts—citizens of Athens who volunteered to sit on a jury, and who were then selected by lot—decided the fate of the offender. These bodies were often very large; Socrates (470?–399 BC) was condemned by a jury of 500, deciding by majority vote.*

Roman procedure developed a jury system as well. Initially, a defendant appeared before a magistrate for conviction and sentence, but if the sentence was severe, he could appeal to the *judicium populi*—in which the entire community would be asked to vote. In later times, this developed into the *judicia publica,* a representative group of citizens who voted on matters of criminal liability.**

Jury trials, however varied, apparently disappeared early in the Middle Ages; the institution reappeared again only in England after the Norman Conquest of 1066, as Lord Devlin demonstrates:

P. Devlin, Trial by Jury 7–12 (1966)

It was King Henry II [1133–1189; reigned 1154–1189] who was directly responsible for turning the jury into an instrument for doing justice and Pope Innocent III [1161–1216; Pope 1198–1216] who was indirectly responsible for its development as a peculiarly English institution. Henry II understood well the importance of extending the royal jurisdiction as a means of enlarging the royal power; and also the royal purse, for the conduct of litigation was in those days a profitable business. A jury which gave the King information for administrative purposes could also be used to give him information which would enable him to decide a dispute. The primitive nature of the older methods was in the second half of the twelfth century beginning to be recognized; the use of the jury was not only a superior procedure but was also one which could be used only in the King's courts, since he alone could compel

---

* For further elaboration, see R. Bonner, Lawyers and Litigants in Ancient Athens (1972); D. Macdowell, Athenian Homicide Law in the Age of the Orators (1963).

** J. Jones, The Criminal Courts of the Roman Republica and Principate (1972).

the taking of an oath. By the Grand Assize and other petty assizes Henry ordained that in a dispute about the title to land a litigant might obtain a royal writ to have a jury summoned to decide the matter. The character of the jurors was not thereby altered. They were men drawn from the neighborhood who were taken to have knowledge of all the relevant facts (anyone who was ignorant was rejected) and were bound to answer upon their oath and according to their knowledge which of the two disputants was entitled to the land. When a party got twelve oaths in his favor, he won. This is the origin of the trial jury, though there was as yet no sort of trial in the modern sense. . . .

* * *

In November 1215 Pope Innocent III prohibited trial by ordeal. That at least was the immediate effect of the decree of the Fourth Lateran Council, though in form it merely forbade ecclesiastics from taking part in it. On the Continent, where the science of law and legal procedure was much further advanced than in England, the judges were quick to devise new and more rational forms of proving guilt. In England—the Crown was then in the infancy of Henry III [1207–1272; reigned 1216–1272]—the judges who went out on circuit were left to improvise. The goals had to be delivered. For fifty years crimes had been tried by ordeal and the older modes had become things of the past. Something had to be devised and it was natural that the judges should use the jury. Was the prisoner willing to be judged by the neighborhood? Would he "put himself upon his country"? If so, let him plead Not Guilty and take their verdict. The old phrase is today still occasionally used when the prisoner is given in charge to the jury: "and by his plea he hath put himself upon God and the country which country ye are." If he would not put himself on his country, he got no trial at all and in the early days was probably condemned simply on the presentment of the grand jury or at best was kept in prison until he did plead. . . .

At first no sharp distinction was drawn between the jurors who presented and those who tried. It was not until 1352 that it was enacted by a statute of Edward III [1312–1377; reigned 1337–1377] that no indictor should be put on the inquest. By that time the petty jury, formed on the model of the jury of the Grand Assize, was an established part of the process. The process was still, and for many years remained, an inquest—an inquiry of those who were supposed to know. . . .

* * *

At first the information was supplementary and given haphazardly—perhaps privately to one or two of the jurors by the plaintiff or defendant (much as a party interested in the decision of a committee might nowadays buttonhole one of the members and put his point of view) or perhaps publicly in response to a general invitation. The idea of the reception of evidence matured slowly. It began by the parties putting their case, but not really distinguishing between pleadings, evidence and argument. It ended with the jury as it is today—a body whose strict duty is to "hearken to the evidence" and return a verdict accordingly, excluding from their minds all that they have not heard in open court. If any one of them has any knowledge of the facts, he must state it publicly, and the result of that today would probably be that he would be asked not to serve. Jurors are still drawn from the neighborhood, but only because it would be inconvenient for them to be brought from afar.

NOTE

Not all believe that the jury is a sound invention. Dean Griswold, of Harvard Law School, called the jury "at best . . . the apotheosis of the amateur. Why should anyone think that 12 persons brought in from the street, selected in various ways, for their lack of general ability, should have any special capacity for deciding controversies between persons?"Griswold, *Harvard Law School Dean's Report* 5–6 (1962–63).

Glanville Williams' disdain for the jury is scarcely less evident:

If one proceeds by the light of reason, there seems to be a formidable weight of argument against the jury system. To begin with, the twelve men and women are chosen haphazardly. There is a slight property qualification—too slight to be used as an index of ability, if indeed the mere possession of property can ever be so used; on the other hand, exemption is given to some professional people who would seem to be among the best qualified to serve—clergymen, ministers of religion, lawyers, doctors, dentists, chemists, justices of the peace (as well as all ranks of the armed forces). The subtraction of relatively intelligent classes means that it is an understatement to describe a jury, with Herbert Spencer, as a group of twelve people of average ignorance. There is no guarantee that members of a particular jury may not be quite unusually ignorant, credulous, slow-witted, narrow-minded, biased or temperamental. The danger of this happening is not one that can be removed by some minor procedural adjustment; it is inherent in the English notion of a jury as a body chosen from the general population at random.

G. Williams, The Proof of Guilt 271–72 (3d ed., 1963)

[2] Jury Selection

TAYLOR v. LOUISIANA

Supreme Court of the United States

419 U.S. 522 (1975)

Mr. JUSTICE WHITE *delivered the opinion of the Court.*

When this case was tried, Art. VII, §411 of the Louisiana Constitution, and Art. 402 of the Louisiana Code of Criminal Procedure provided that a woman should not be selected for jury service unless she had previously filed a written declaration of her desire to be subject to jury service. . . .

Appellant, Billy J. Taylor, was indicted by the grand jury of St. Tammany Parish, in the Twenty-second Judicial District of Louisiana, for aggravated kidnaping. On April 12, 1972, appellant moved the trial court to quash the petit jury venire drawn for the special criminal term beginning with his trial the following day. Appellant alleged that women were systematically excluded from the venire and that he would therefore be deprived of what he claimed to be his federal constitutional right to "a fair trial by jury of a representative segment of the community". . . .

The Twenty-second Judicial District comprises the parishes of St. Tammany and Washington. The appellee has stipulated that 53% of the persons eligible for jury service in these parishes were female, and that no more than 10% of the persons on the jury wheel in St. Tammany parish were women. During the period from December 8, 1971 to November 3, 1972, 12 females were among the 1,800 persons drawn to fill petit jury venires in St. Tammany Parish. It was also stipulated that the discrepancy between females eligible for jury service and those actually included in the venire was the result of the operation of La. Const., Art. VII, §41, and La. Code Crim. Proc., Art. 402. In the present case, a venire totaling 175 persons was drawn for jury service beginning April 13, 1972. There were no females on the venire.

* * *

II

The Louisiana jury-selection system does not disqualify women from jury service, but in operation its conceded systematic impact is that only a very few women, grossly disproportionate to the number of eligible women in the community, are called for jury service. In this case, no women were on the venire from which the petit jury was drawn. The issue we have, therefore, is whether a jury-selection system which operates to exclude from service an identifiable class of citizens constituting 53% of eligible jurors in the community comports with the Sixth and Fourteenth Amendments.

* * *

III

Our inquiry is whether the presence of a fair cross section of the community on venires, panels, or lists from which petit juries are drawn is essential to the fulfillment of the Sixth Amendment's guarantee of an impartial jury trial in criminal prosecutions.

* * *

[I]n *Carter v. Jury Commission,* 369 U.S. 320, 330 (1970), the Court observed that the exclusion of Negroes from jury service because of their race "contravenes the very idea of a jury—'a body truly representative of the community'. . . . "At about the same time it was contended that the use of six-man juries in noncapital criminal cases violated the Sixth Amendment for failure to provide juries drawn from a cross section of the community, *Williams v. Florida,* 399 U.S. 78 (1970). In the course of rejecting that challenge, we said that the number of persons on the jury should "be large enough to promote group deliberation, free from outside attempts at intimidation, and to provide a fair possibility for obtaining a representative cross section of the community. . . ."

* * *

We accept the fair-cross-section requirement as fundamental to the jury trial guaranteed by the Sixth Amendment and are convinced that the requirement has solid foundation. The purpose of a jury is to guard against the exercise of arbitrary power—to make available the common sense judgment of the community as a hedge against the overzealous or mistaken prosecutor and in preference to the professional or perhaps over conditioned or biased response of a judge. *Duncan v. Louisiana,* 391 U.S. at 155–156. This prophylactic vehicle is not provided if the jury pool is made up of only special segments of the populace or if large, distinctive groups are excluded from the pool. Community participation in the administration of the criminal law, moreover, is not only consistent with our democratic heritage but is also critical to public confidence in the fairness of the criminal justice system. Restricting jury service to only special groups or excluding identifiable segments playing major roles in the community cannot be squared with the constitutional concept of jury trial. . . .

IV

We are also persuaded that the fair-cross-section requirement is violated by the systematic exclusion of women, who in the judicial district involved here amounted to 53% of the citizens eligible for jury service. This conclusion necessarily entails the judgment that women are sufficiently numerous and distinct from men and that if they are systematically eliminated from jury panels, the Sixth Amendment's fair-cross-section requirement cannot be satisfied. This very matter was debated in *Ballard v. United States,* [329 U.S. 187 (1946)]. Positing the fair-cross-section rule, there said to be a statutory one, the Court concluded that the systematic exclusion of women was unacceptable. The dissenting view that an all-male panel drawn from various groups in the community would be as truly representative as if women were included, was firmly rejected:

> The thought is that the factors which tend to influence the action of women are the same as those which influence the action of men—personality, background, economic status—and not sex. Yet it is not enough to say that women when sitting as jurors neither act nor tend to act as a class. Men likewise do not act as a class. But, if the shoe were on the other foot, who would claim that a jury was truly representative of the community if all men were intentionally and systematically excluded from the panel? The truth is that the two sexes are not fungible; a community made up exclusively of one is different from a community composed of both; the subtle interplay of influence one on the other is among the imponderables. To insulate the courtroom from either may not in a given case make an iota of difference. Yet a flavor, a distinct quality is lost if either sex is excluded. The exclusion of one may indeed make the jury less representative of the community than would be true if an economic or racial group were excluded.

329 U.S., at 193–194.[12]

V

There remains the argument that women as a class serve a distinctive role in society and that jury service would so substantially interfere with that function that the State has ample justification for excluding women from service unless they volunteer, even though the result is that almost all jurors are men. It is true that *Hoyt v. Florida,* 368 U.S. 57 (1961), held that such a system did not deny due process of law or equal protection of the laws because there was a sufficiently rational basis for such an exemption. But *Hoyt* did not involve a defendant's Sixth Amendment right to a jury drawn from a fair cross section of the community and the prospect of depriving him of that right if women as a class are systematically excluded. The right to a proper jury cannot be overcome on merely rational grounds. There must be weightier reasons if a distinctive class representing 53% of the eligible jurors is for all practical purposes to be excluded from jury service. No such basis has been tendered here.

The States are free to grant exemptions from jury service to individuals in case of special hardship or incapacity and to those engaged in particular occupations the uninterrupted performance of which is critical to the community's welfare. . . . It would not appear that such exemptions would pose substantial threats that the remaining pool of jurors would not be representative of the community. A system excluding all women, however, is a wholly different matter. It is untenable to suggest these days that it would be a special hardship for each and every woman to perform jury service or that society cannot spare any women from their present duties. This may be the case with many, and it may be burdensome to sort out those who should be exempted from those who should serve. But that task is performed in the case of men, and the administrative convenience in dealing with women as a class is insufficient justification for diluting the quality of community judgment represented by the jury in criminal trials.

* * *

VII

* * *

It should also be emphasized that in holding that petit juries must be drawn from a source fairly representative of the community we impose no requirement that petit juries actually chosen must mirror the community and reflect the various distinctive groups in the population. Defendants are not entitled to a jury of any particular composition. *Fay v. New York,* 332 U.S. 261, 284 (1947); *Apodaca v. Oregon,* 406 U.S., at 413 (plurality opinion); but the jury

---

[12] Controlled studies of the performance of women as jurors conducted subsequent to the Court's decision in Ballard have concluded that women bring to juries their own perspectives and values that influence both jury deliberation and result. See generally Rudolph, *Women on Juries—Voluntary or Compulsory?,* 44 J. Am. Jud. Soc. 206 (1961); 55 J. Sociology & Social Research 442 (1971); 3 J. Applied Social Psychology 267 (1973); 19 Sociometry 3 (1956).

wheels, pools of names, panels, or venires from which juries are drawn must not systematically exclude distinctive groups in the community and thereby fail to be reasonably representative thereof.

The judgement of the Louisiana Supreme Court is reversed and the case remanded to that court for further proceedings not inconsistent with this opinion.

So ordered.

Mr. JUSTICE REHNQUIST, *dissenting.*

* * *

I cannot conceive that today's decision is necessary to guard against oppressive or arbitrary law enforcement, or to prevent miscarriages of justice and to assure fair trials. Especially is this so when the criminal defendant involved makes no claims of prejudice or bias. The Court does accord some slight attention to justifying its ruling in terms of the basis on which the right to jury trial was read into the Fourteenth Amendment. It concludes that the jury is not effective, as a prophylaxis against arbitrary prosecutorial and judicial power, if the "jury pool is made up of only special segments of the populace or if large, distinctive groups are excluded from the pool.". . . It fails, however, to provide any satisfactory explanation of the mechanism by which the Louisiana system undermines the prophylactic role of the jury, either in general or in this case. The best it can do is to posit "—a flavor, a distinct quality,' "which allegedly is lost if either sex is excluded. . . . However, this "flavor" is not of such importance that the Constitution is offended if any given petit jury is not so enriched. . . . This smacks more of mysticism than of law. The Court does not even purport to practice its mysticism in a consistent fashion—presumably doctors, lawyers, and other groups, whose frequent exemption from jury service is endorsed by the majority, also offer qualities as distinct and important at those at issue here.

* * *

Absent any suggestion that appellant's trial was unfairly conducted, or that its result was unreliable, I would not require Louisiana to retry him (assuming the State can once again produce its evidence and witnesses) in order to impose on him the sanctions which its laws provide.

NOTES AND QUESTIONS

1. *Sixth versus Fourteenth Amendment:* Are the Sixth Amendment and Fourteenth Amendment challenges compatible? Under the latter, the argument is made that a specific group, (e.g., women) are denied equal protection by a process that excludes them from jury service because they *are not* a distinct group whose exclusion is consistent with equal protection; yet under the Sixth Amendment argument raised in *Taylor,* the very reason that they cannot be excluded is that they *are* a distinct group with distinct "perceptions and values." Is there a way to reconcile these contentions?

2. *Equal Protection Issues:* What are the "differences" between, for example, men and women, and black and white, that demand that they be given equal access to the jury box, while at the same time arguments are made and accepted, in the pursuit of other goals, that they must be treated equally? In *Johnson v. Louisiana,* 406 U.S. 356 (1972), Mr. Justice Marshall, dissenting from the holding that unanimity was not required by the Constitution (see Note below), declared,

> I respectfully reject the suggestion of my brother POWELL that the doubts of minority jurors may be attributable to "irrationality" against which some protection is needed. For if the jury has been selected properly, and every juror is a competent and rational person, then the "irrationality" that enters into the deliberation process is precisely the essence of the right to a jury trial. Each time this Court has approved a change in the familiar characteristics of the jury, we have reaffirmed the principle that its fundamental characteristic is its capacity to render a common sense, layman's judgment, as a representative body drawn from the community. To fence out a dissenting juror fences out a voice from the community, and undermines the principle on which our whole notion of the jury now rests. . . . The juror whose dissenting voice is unheard may be a spokesman, not for any minority viewpoint, but simply for himself—and that, in my view, is enough.

Is the Sixth Amendment categorization of groups as "cognizable" limited to "suspect" classifications? If so, how can we explain *Taylor,* since women are not (yet) a "suspect" classification? If not, what other groups fall within the *Taylor* rationale? Distinguishable ethnic groups appear to fall within the "cognizable" label—for example, *State v. Plenty Horse,* 85 S.D. 401, 184 N.W.2d 654 (1971) (Native Americans); *State v. Guirlando,* 152 La. 570, 93 So. 796 (1922) (Italians): *International Longshoremen Warehouseman's Union v. Ackerman,* 82 F.Supp. 65 (D. Haw. 1943) (Filipinos). In 1946, the Court ruled that "daily wage earners" were a cognizable class, *Thiel v. Southern Pacific Co.,* 328 U.S. 217 (1946), and in 1974 assumed, for purposes of argument, that "the young" were such a group, *Hamling v. United States,* 418 U.S. 87 (1974). But see *Chase v. United States,* 468 F.2d 141 (8th Cir. 1972). Lower courts have classified the less educated, *United States v. Cohen,* 275 F.Supp. 724 (D. Md. 1974), and Roman Catholics, *Juarez v. State,* 102 Tex. Crim. 297, 277 S.W. 1091 (1925), as such groups. Are there any Fourteenth Amendment problems raised by these cases?

In addition to the Sixth Amendment challenge presented in *Taylor,* the courts have countenanced challenges based upon the equal protection clause, where members of a given group have been excluded from grand jury venires. (*E.g., Strauder v. West Virginia,* 100 U.S. 303 (1880), and its progeny [cases collected in *Castaneda v. Partida,* 430 U.S. 482, n.12 (1977)]; *Carter v. Jury Commission of Greene County,* 396 U.S. 320 (1970). These challenges are now allowed even where the defendant is not a member of the group excluded; see, for example, *Peters v. Kiff* 407 U.S. 493 (1971), perhaps on an analogy to *Barrows v. Jackson,* 346 U.S. 249 (1953). Compare the relief granted in *Taylor* with that granted in *Carter, supra.* Cf. Note, *Twelve Good Persons and True: Healy v. Edwards and Taylor v. Louisiana,* 9 Harv. C.R. L. Rev. 561 (1974).

In effect, the argument is that all persons should have an equal opportunity to serve upon a jury, and the exclusion of a particular group violates that group's equal protection.

3. *The Reach of Taylor:* In *Taylor,* the statute excluded women unless they "opted in" to the jury system. In *Duren v. Missouri,* 439 U.S. 357 (1979), the statute allowed women to "opt out"—to seek exemption—without further explanation. The Court condemned such a procedure because it *assumed* that women might be "otherwise engaged" (e.g., in caring for children) without requiring a showing of such activity. Some groups (such as doctors, firemen, policemen, and lawyers), however, are still allowed to opt out and in some states are actually precluded from serving. What justifies these exemptions? Are they susceptible to the same challenge as in *Duren?* Are they subject to a challenge that they preclude a representative jury? See *Rawlins v. Georgia,* 201 U.S. 638 (1906).

4. *The Jury Selection Process:* (a) *The "Pool" and the "Venire":* The process of jury selection begins by attempting to determine who all the eligible people are who could serve on a jury. How can a state do that? Until the 1970s, little attention was paid to this issue and systems varied widely. Some states and the federal system relied upon the "key man" system, in which clerks, judges, jury commissioners, or others would ask friends, acquaintances, and so on for the names of persons who would be "worthy" of sitting on a jury. This method has now been abandoned almost everywhere. See *New Hampshire v. Elbert,* 121 N.H. 43, 424 A.2d 1147 (1981). The federal system and many others now use voting lists, sometimes supplemented by driver's license (or additional, supplemental) lists. What problems are there with either of these methods? Are there other ways to ensure a broader jury "pool"? See Note, 55 N.Y.U. L. Rev. 1266 (1980). This "pool," after those with exemptions and hardships are removed (see n.3, *supra*), constitutes "the venire"—the group of eligible jurors from which a specific jury will be chosen.

(b) *Challenges to Individual Jurors:* Once the jury venire is selected, counsel (or the judge in some states and in the federal system) makes inquiries ("voir dire") of the jurors. When a juror shows obvious bias or is believed to be potentially biased (e.g., is a relative of the victim or the accused), he may be challenged by counsel "for cause." The number of such challenges is, of course, unlimited, since the presence of even one such biased member on the jury would presumably skew the impartiality of the jury. Although there is sometimes a dispute over what constitutes "cause," this area of the law has remained somewhat uncharted because of the availability of "peremptory" challenges to jurors for which counsel need give no reason. It is believed that this allows each side to remove from the venire persons whom counsel guesses might unduly influence the rest of the jurors against his position, but cannot challenge for cause.

In *Batson v. Kentucky,* 476 U.S. 79 (1986), the Court held that if a defendant makes a "*prima facie* case" of discrimination by showing that the prosecutor, using "peremptory" challenges, has disproportionately struck blacks from the venire, the equal protection clause requires the prosecutor to demonstrate that she had nondiscriminatory reasons for her action. Although *Batson* was premised on the equal protection rights of the *defendant,* since that time the

Court, focusing on the equal protection rights of potential jurors, has applied *Batson* to civil litigation, *Edmondson v. Leesville Concrete Co.,* 500 U.S. 614 (1990), and to challenges made by criminal defendants, *Georgia v. McCollum,* 505 U.S. (1992). In *J.E.B. v. Alabama Ex rel T.B.,* 114 S. Ct. 1419 (1994), the Court extended the rationale to challenges based on gender. However the Court has emphasized that its holdings are not based on the Sixth Amendment, but on the equal protection clause. See *Holland v. Illinois,* 493 U.S. 474 (1990). What problems does such a holding present? What is the purpose of such a holding? See Singer, *Peremptory Holds: A Suggestion (Only Half Specious) of a Solution to the Discriminatory Use of Peremptory Challenges,* 62 U. Det. L. J. 275 (1985). See also Alschuler, *The Supreme Court and the Jury: Voir Dire, Peremptory Challenges and the Review of Jury Verdicts,* 50 U. Chi. L. Rev. 153 (1989); Broderick, *Why the Peremptory Challenge Should Be Abolished,* 65 Temple L. Rev. 369 (1992); Note, 17 Nova L. Rev. 1367 (1993).

5. Van Dyke, Jury Selection Procedures ix (1977):

The North Carolina jury took only 75 minutes to find Joan Little not guilty of killing her jailer, who (she stated) had tried to assault her sexually. The defense team had spent 10 days in July 1975 to question 150 prospective jurors in an effort to find a panel it considered sympathetic to the young black woman's plea of self-defense. The 10-day examination—similar to others involving significant political and social issues—was the culmination of the nine-month—long Joan Little Fair Trial Jury Project, an undertaking that cost nearly $40,000, most of it spent on a seven-member team of professional sociologists, psychologists, and pollsters. The project involved over 1,000 telephone interviews, the use of a computer to correlate attitudes and demographic data, and detailed questioning of prospective jurors—with a psychic and body-language expert on hand to be sure that nonverbal clues would not be missed—in order to decide which jurors to remove from the panel through challenges. The $40,000 was only part of the total defense cost of $325,000, most of it raised from citizens around the country in a sophisticated direct-mail campaign.

Is this what it takes to assemble an impartial jury. . . ?

Was the defense team seeking an "impartial" or a "partial" jury?

6. When is a jury required? As will be more carefully explored in Chapter 2, *infra,* the line between tort and crime, and between regulation and crime, is often tenuous. The Sixth Amendment seems to require a jury whenever the defendant is accused of a "crime." But in *Baldwin v. New York,* 399 U.S. 66 (1970), the Court declared that a jury trial was not required under that amendment unless the possible jail sentence was more than six months, even though the offense was a "crime." Similarly, jury trials have not been held to be required for "noncrimes," even though confinement is possible, for example, juvenile proceedings, *McKeiver v. Pennsylvania,* 403 U.S. 528 (1971), or commitment proceedings, *Comm. v. Barboza* 387 Mass. 105, 438 N.E.2d 1064 (1982). In *Blanton v. Nevada,* 489 U.S. 538 (1989), the Court held that a jury is not required in driving-while-intoxicated cases, even though the collateral or direct consequences, such as loss of a driver's license, may be severe.

7. For further reading, see National Jury Project, Jury Work: Systematic Techniques (1987). See also Bennett, *Psychological Methods of Jury Selection*

in the Typical Criminal Case, Criminal Defense, March-April 1977, vol. 4, no. 2 (National College of Public Defenders and Criminal Defense Lawyers): Broeder, *Voir Dire Examination: An Empirical Study,* 38 S.C. L. Rev. 503 (1965); Note, 27 Stan. L. Rev. 1493 (1975); Dogin and Tevelin, *Jury Systems of the Eighties: Toward a Fairer Cross-Section and Increased Efficiency,* 11 U. Toledo L. Rev. 939 (1980).

NOTE ON JURY SIZE AND UNANIMITY

In *Johnson v. Louisiana,* 406 U.S. 356 (1972), the Court held that jury unanimity was not required by the Constitution, although defendant argued that a nonunanimous verdict was conclusive evidence that the prosecutor had not proved the case beyond a reasonable doubt as required by Winship. This holding is particularly troublesome in light of *Williams v. Florida,* 399 U.S. (1971), which held that the states could have juries of fewer than 12 members.

The *Johnson and Williams* decisions on unanimity and size of juries spurred a wave of continuing empirical research. The results are mixed, though some findings constantly appear—some that support the majority decisions, others that refute them: (1)Six-person juries are more likely to have predeliberation majorities and do not, in fact, discuss minority views as thoroughly. (2)However, there seems to be no significant difference in the final verdicts determined by 6-or 12-person juries, unanimous or not. See Padawer-Singer et al., *An Experimental Study of Twelve vs. Six Member Juries under Unanimous vs. Nonunanimous Decisions,* in B. Sales, *Psychology in the Legal Process* 77 (1977); Lempert, *Uncovering Non-discernible Differences: Empirical Research and the Jury Size Cases,* 73 Mich. L. Rev. 643 (1975); M.J. Saks, *Jury Verdicts: The Role of Group Size and Social Decision* (1977). In *Ballew v. Georgia,* 435 U.S. 320 (1978), confronted with this information challenging the notion that there was no difference in jury operation dependent on size, the Court held that a five-person jury was too small. Finally, *Birch v. Louisiana,* 441 U.S. 130 (1979), held that six-person juries had to be unanimous in a criminal case.

Jury unanimity was not required in Greece and Rome. There, majority vote was sufficient, whether the jury was small or in the hundreds. Moreover, even in early times in England, there was no actual requirement of unanimity, although there was the appearance of it. With the jury of compurgators, the defendant was apparently entitled to ask as many persons as he wished to swear to his version of the facts; it was only if he could not find 12 so willing that he was found guilty, even if the 12 were a small minority of all those he sought to ask.

When the jury became a fact-finding body, with the abolition of the ordeals, however, the standard became quite strict (*see* §1.02[A], *supra*) and unanimity appeared to become the rule. Although it has theoretically remained the rule ever since, some states, as the *Johnson* case shows, did not abide by it (although Louisiana may itself be slightly different because of its civil law background).

England abolished the requirement of jury unanimity by statute in 1967. No continental system requires unanimity of jurors. Indeed, many allow conviction on the basis of a simple majority vote. See Damaska, *Evidentiary Barriers to Conviction and Two Models of Criminal Procedure,* 121 U. Pa. L. Rev. 506 (1973).

In Greece, where juries appear to have originated, the size of the jury was quite variable. There are references to juries of 1,500 and even 6,000, although those seem to be jury lists, not actual juries. The Areopagus varied in size each year. The same variation in size occurred in early Rome.

With the introduction of the jury into England by King Henry II (1133–89; reigned 1154–89), the initial size seems to have been 12. There is some indication, however, that the size of the jury varied for a substantially long period of time in Medieval England. See W. Forsyth, History of Trial by Jury 109 (1875), suggesting that fewer than 12 would suffice. *Plucknett* at 121–23 cites a case that shows juries of eight being summoned from each of four neighboring villages. It should be noted, perhaps, that in a grand jury, where only a majority is required to bring in an indictment, the number in the grand jury is 23—of which a majority is 12. Many Biblical explanations of this number have been offered; the 12 tribes of Israel, the 12 patriarchs, the 12 offices of Solomon, the 12 Apostles—but the number 12 seems to have been magical in other cultures—the jury convened by Athena to try Orestes in the *Oresteia* by Aeschylus (525–456 BC) consisted of 12 persons. Forsyth suggests that the number stems from Scandinavian sources.

NOTE ON JURY NULLIFICATION

One of the important reasons for requiring a "representative" jury in criminal cases, even more than in civil cases, is the ability of the jury to "nullify" the law simply by finding the defendant not guilty, regardless of the legal standards that are explicated to them in the judge's instructions. This is not possible in civil cases since either side may appeal, but in criminal cases, the nullification power is given procedural weight by precluding the prosecution from appealing a verdict of not guilty. Although this is explained under the theory that the defendant who is acquitted cannot (by virtue of our constitution) be placed in "jeopardy" twice, the same rule applies in England, which does not have the constitutional language upon which American courts rely.

Nullification has, of course, always been a power of the triers, or givers, of fact. But when "juries" were givers of fact, it was not unknown for judges to fine, and even imprison jurors whose "testimony" the judge found perjured. See generally H. Lea, The Duel and the Oath (U. Pa. Reprint Series, 1973). This process was known as "attainting" the jury.

Although it was in decline from the middle of the 15th century on, the threat of "attaint" sometimes persuaded juries to follow the "law," even when they disagreed with it. In a landmark case, however, the power of judges to punish jurors who "falsely" returned a verdict of not guilty was conclusively denied. *Bushell's Case,* Vaughn 135, 6 Howell's State Trial 999 (1670). William Penn was tried on a charge of giving a treasonous speech; while there was no doubt that Penn had given the speech and that it was, within the meaning of the law, "treasonous," the jury acquitted. The trial judge thereupon fined each member of the jury. Four, including Bushell, refused to pay the fine and were imprisoned. Bushell then sought a writ of habeas corpus, contending that the fine was illegal. In a monumental decision, the court agreed.

This story could be carried out at length in the English history alone. But one thing should be noted: In many of the leading English cases, including *Bushell's,* the charge against the defendant was "seditious" libel—a "political" crime, in which the jury would have to determine, at least, publication, while the judge might otherwise decide the legal question of whether the words were, in fact, libelous. Yet the jury's ability and right to so "decide" the law expanded far beyond the scope of libel and other political affairs. By the time the United States was established, most American writers, including John Adams, Thomas Jefferson, and Alexander Hamilton, agreed that the jury should be the "determiner" of law. Hamilton, in fact, gave it one of the most impassioned defenses:

> That in the general distribution of powers in our system of jurisprudence, the cognizance of the law belongs to the court, of fact to the jury; that as often as they are not blended, the power of the court is absolute and exclusive. That in civil cases it is always so, and may rightfully be so exerted. That in criminal cases, the law and fact being always blended, the jury, for reasons of a political and peculiar nature, for the security of life and liberty, is entrusted with the power of deciding both law and fact.
>
> . . .
>
> That inal cases, nevertheless, the courts are the constitutional advisers of the jury in matter of law; who may compromise their conscience by lightly or rashly disregarding it, but may still more compromise their consciences by following it, if exercising their judgements with discretion and honesty have a clear conviction that the charge of the court is wrong.

Sparf v. United States, 156 U.S. 51 (1895) (quoting 7 *Hamilton's Works* 335, 336 (ed. 1886)).

This "right" was so strongly protected that one of the counts of impeachment against Supreme Court Justice Samuel Chase in 1805 was that he, while sitting as a trial judge, had failed to instruct the jury of its power to decide the law. Scheflin, *Jury Nullification: The Right to Say No,* 45 So. Cal. L. Rev. 168, 176 (1972).

Of course, to propose that the jury has the right to determine the law may itself beg the question. On questions of so-called "mixed fact and law," a fact finder necessarily "determines" the law when finding the "fact," such as negligence or perhaps self-defense. But it seems reasonably clear that his is not what the 18th century proponents of nullification had in mind. As Dean Roscoe Pound put it, the

> doctrine that jurors were judges of the law belongs with (an) ultra individualistic political and legal philosophy. The citizen is invited to judge for himself . . . whether and how far to obey or to enforce the law as it stands in the book . . . to judge of its conformity to his personal ideals and to ascertain its validity.

R. Pound, Criminal Justice in America 130 (1930).

In short the "right" of nullification was "part and parcel" of an egalitarian society in which every actor was the equivalent of the government.

For the first half of the 19th century, American courts accepted virtually without question not only the power of the jury to disregard the "law," but also the need of the judge to so instruct them. One theoretical support of this view was that the judge (often, in those days, someone not formally educated in the law) was "only a witness" when he gave instructions and that, like any other witness, he would be disbelieved by the jury. As the organized bar became stronger and as legal education became a prerequisite for judgeships, the notion that the jury should be informed of its power to disregard the judge's instructions came under sustained attack. The watershed decision was *Sparf and Hansen v. United States,* 156 U.S. 51 (1895), in which the Court held, 5–4, that, in federal trials, the jury need not be informed of its nullification power. The majority and dissenting opinions, totaling over 100 pages, carefully and exhaustively review the history, case law, and policy issues involved.

After *Sparf,* the current ran swiftly against open recognition of jury nullification power. Only two states, both in their constitutions, now adhere to the proposition that the jury has the right, of which it should be informed, to determine the law. *Wyley v. Warden,* 372 F.2d 742 (4th Cir. 1967); Note, 3 Det. C. L. Rev. 873 (1981). Oregon voters in 1990 rejected, by referendum, an initiative enshrining nullification into the state's constitution. A large number of states, however, still have nullification clauses, often in their constitution, for cases of "criminal" or "seditious" libel.

The argument today is over whether the jury should be *informed* of its actual power. (The Oregon initiative described above would have required such an instruction.) There is no suggestion that the prosecution should be able to appeal a "wrong" verdict. Indeed, most observers of the criminal justice system have ardently supported nullification; Roscoe Pound, for example, declared that "jury lawlessness is the great corrective" of the law. Pound, *Law in Books and Law in Action,* 44 Am. L. Rev. 12, 18–19 (1910). But obviously, if the corrective is to work properly, the jury must be fully representative in order to adequately reflect the community's view as to the harshness of the law.

The subject stirs substantial debate during times of political tribulation, such as that engendered by the antiwar movement in the late 1960s and early 1970s. For representative writings concerning the issue, see Kunstler, *Jury Nullification in Conscience Cases,* 10 Va. J. Int'l Law 71 (1969); Richardson, *Jury Nullification: Justice or Anarchy?,* Case and Comment 30 (Mar.—Apr. 1975); Scheflin, *Jury Nullification: The Right to Say No,* 45 S.C. L. Rev. 168 (1972); Simson, *Jury Nullification in the American System: A Skeptical View,* 54 Tex L. Rev. 488 (1976); Note, 12 Suffolk U. L. Rev. 968 (1978); Note, 74 Yale L.J. 170 (1964). See also M. Kadish and S. Kadish, Discretion to Disobey 45–66 (1973); *United States v. Moylan,* 417 F.2d 1002 (4th Cir.), *cert. denied* 397 U.S. 910 (1969); *United States v. Dougherty,* 473 F.2d 1113 (D.C. Cir. 1973); *United States v. Kryske,* 836 F.2d 1013 (6th Cir. 1988).

Nullification, of course, need not be total. In many instances, the jury may indicate its displeasure with the law by convicting of a lesser offense on the supposition that this will result in a lesser penalty. This was widespread in

England and America in the 18th century, when literally scores of felonies were punishable by death. In larceny cases, juries committed what Blackstone called "pious perjury," *Blackstone,* at 239, by "downgrading" the value of goods stolen so that capital punishment could not be imposed. See, for example, Beattie, *Crime and the Courts in Surrey:* 1736–1753, in Crime in England: 1660–1800 155 (J. C. ed. 1977); Langbein, *Shaping the Eighteenth-Century Criminal Trial: A View from the Ryder Sources,* 50 U. Chi. L. Rev. 1 (1983). This practice, as well as jury acquittals, was one of the main forces that ultimately resulted in therepeal of many of the capital statutes in the early 19th century.

Chapter 2
Punishment

§ 2.01 INTRODUCTION

American criminal law traces its ancestry to the primitive Anglo-Saxon legal tradition which drew few distinctions between crime and tort. The primary concern of the early law was to discourage blood feuds (precipitated by acts of private vengeance against those engaging in injurious conduct) by providing "sanctions," essentially compensatory in nature, for acts resulting in injury. Whether or not the injuring party had intended harm or even been negligent, the victim and his family were entitled to compensation (called *bot* if he survived; *wer* if he died) based, not on the amount of injury, but upon his social class. From the 13th century on, however, the criminal law began to be distinguished from tort by, among other things, the requirement of *mens rea* which is central to criminal theory. (See *infra*, Chapter 4.)

By Blackstone's time, the differences between crime and tort were thought to be obvious:

> The distinction of public wrongs from private, of crimes and misdemeanours from civil injuries, seems principally to consist in this: that private wrongs, or civil injuries, are an infringement or privation of the civil rights which belong to individuals, considered merely as individuals; public wrongs, or crimes and misdemeanours, are a breach and violation of the public rights and duties, due to the whole community, considered as a community, in its social aggregate capacity. As if I detain a field from another man, to which the law has given him a right, this is a civil injury, and not a crime; for here only the right of an individual is concerned, and it is immaterial to the public which of us is in possession of the land: but treason, murder and robbery are properly ranked among crimes; since, besides the injury done to individuals, they strike at the very being of society, which cannot possibly subsist where actions of this sort are suffered to escape with impunity.
>
> In all cases the crime includes an injury: every public offense is also a private wrong, and somewhat more; it affects the individual, and it likewise affects the community. Thus, treason in imagining the king's death involves in it conspiracy against an individual, which is also a civil injury; but as this species of treason in its consequences principally tends to the dissolution of government, and the destruction thereby of the order and peace of society, this denominates it a crime of the highest magnitude. Murder is an injury to the life of an individual; but the law of society considers principally the loss which the state sustains by being deprived of a member, and the pernicious example thereby set for others to do the like. Robbery may be considered in the same view; it is an injury to *private* property; but, were that all, a civil satisfaction in damages might atone for it: the *public*

mischief is the thing, for the prevention of which our laws have made it a capital offense.

In these gross and atrocious injuries the private wrong is swallowed up in the public: we seldom hear any mention made of satisfaction to the individual; the satisfaction to the community being so very great. And, indeed, as the public crime is not otherwise avenged than by forfeiture of life and property, it is impossible afterwards to make any reparation for the private wrong, which can only be had from the body or goods of the aggressor.

Blackstone 5–6

Blackstone's easy distinctions appear a bit too easy, however. His identification of "public wrongs" as the distinguishing characteristic of the criminal law is contested by some who argue that criminal and tort law vindicate exactly the same private interests in personal integrity, property possessed or owned, and maintenance of certain relationships. Epstein, *Crime and Tort: Old Wine in Old Bottles* in Assessing the Criminal 231, 238–40 (R. Barnett and J. Hagel eds., 1977). On the other hand, while the situation was doubtless different in Blackstone's day, today a variety of public wrongs routinely trigger governmentally initiated noncriminal actions (e.g., administrative fines, tax actions) brought in the public interest. Indeed, perceived difficulty in discerning the distinctive features of the criminal law has led some to conclude, "There are no certain and universal qualities which at once stamp an act with the character of a crime." J. Austin, *Jurisprudence, Lecture* XXVII (1875). *See also* Holmes at 44 (the law of crime and tort supposedly unified through principles of objective liability).

While Blackstone's account may prove inadequate, a host of theorists nevertheless maintain that the distinction between criminal law and civil law is not merely a matter of arbitrary label. See generally, e.g., Fletcher; Hall. State and federal constitutions as well as courts and legislatures presume the uniqueness of the criminal law by mandating in its context a variety of protections not necessarily required in civil actions. Compare, e.g., *In re Winship,* 397 U.S. 358 (1970) (due process requires the state to prove guilt of the accused in criminal cases "beyond a reasonable doubt"), with *Addington v. Texas,* 441 U.S. 418 (1979) ("proof beyond a reasonable doubt" of statutory grounds for hospitalization is not constitutionally required in civil commitment proceedings). The authors of this casebook share the belief that the criminal law is theoretically unique. The materials in this chapter begin the search for the distinctive features of the criminal law by attending to the criminal sanction. We take seriously the observation of a leading commentator: "If we wish to understand the criminal law, we must first understand its most prominent feature: the infliction of punishment." Fletcher, at 409.

Understanding punishment in turn raises two kinds of problems considered in the present chapter: (1) conceptual issues about the meaning of punishment and how it differs from civil sanctions and (2) moral issues relating to the justification of punishment. The latter problem, a theme recurring throughout this book, is introduced in the present chapter by a consideration of various theories offered as justifications for punishment in both general and particular cases. Problems of fairly allocating punishment are next considered in materials dealing with sentencing and proportionality. The chapter concludes with an examination of the problem of determining what conduct is appropriately punished and how, when, and by whom such conduct is to be defined. As you proceed, consider whether the imposition of punishment (as opposed to, say, the criminal actor's moral culpability, see, e.g., Hall, 242–43) is indeed the defining characteristic of the criminal law.

§ 2.02 The Concept of Punishment

Note

Professor George Fletcher has observed that in order to understand the "deep structure" of the criminal law, one must understand "how we mark the boundaries of *criminal punishment* as opposed to other coercive sanctions. . . that are burdensome but non-criminal." G. Fletcher, *Basic Concepts of Criminal Law* 4, 5 (1998). Indeed, "[w]ithout punishment and the institutions designed to measure and carry out punishment, there is no criminal law [because] the institution of punishment provides the distinguishing features of criminal law." *Id.* at 25.

This section examines the question: What is punishment? As evidenced by the recent spate of Supreme Court cases included herein, the question has proven to be perplexing. The cases illustrate Fletcher's observation that "[f]athoming the contours of punishment depends not on the positive law of particular [jurisdictions] but on the results of philosophical and conceptual inquiry." *Id.* at 25-26. As, you consider the following materials consider, on the other hand, whether Professor Douglas Husak is correct in his view that philosophical inquiry itself may be of limited value given the "vagueness in the term 'punishment.'" D. Husak, *Review Essay: Philosophical Analysis and the Limits of the Substantive Criminal Law*, 18 Crim. J. Ethics 58, 60 (1999).

Fletcher

408–09

The best candidate for a conceptual proposition about the criminal law is that the infliction of "punishment" is sufficient to render a legal process criminal in nature. In the United States, the labelling of a process as "criminal" triggers certain basic constitutional guarantees, such as the right to counsel and the right to a jury trial. As a test for when processes are criminal, the Supreme Court unhesitatingly invokes the concept of "punishment" as the relevant criterion. That a sanction is inflicted in the criminal courts for a violation of the criminal code is sufficient to classify the sanction as "punitive," but there are recurrent problems in assessing the punitive nature of other sanctions, such as administrative commitment, expatriation, deportation, fines for custom violations and the deprivation of Social Security benefits. That the legislature has identified these sanctions as civil in nature does not control the constitutional issue, for if the sanction is punitive, if it constitutes "punishment," then regardless of the legislative label, the process is criminal and the constitutional guarantees apply.

Packer

18

What we mean by a "crime" or an "offense" is simply conduct that is forbidden by law and to which certain consequences, called punishment, will apply on the occurrence of stated conditions and following a stated process. A crime is not merely any conduct forbidden by law; it is forbidden conduct for which punishment is prescribed and which is formally described as a crime by an agency of government having the power to do so. The standard case presents no problem under this definition. Bank robbery is a crime; breach of contract is not. Marginal questions may and do frequently arise about whether certain kinds of forbidden conduct for which unpleasant consequences may be imposed shall be treated as a "crime" for various purposes . . . even though they have not previously been formally described as a crime. But the definition of crime is inescapably tautological. Crime is whatever is formally and authoritatively described as criminal. It is not surprising that this definition tells us nothing about what the content of a law of crimes is or ought to be. In order to give a material, as opposed to a formal, definition of crime, one would first have to solve the puzzles about punishment . . .

[A] The Definition of Punishment

Hart, *Punishment and Responsibility*

4–6

Here I shall simply draw upon the recent admirable work scattered through English philosophical journals and add to it only an admonition of my own against the abuse of definition in the philosophical discussion of punishment. So . . . I shall define the standard or central case of "punishment" in terms of five elements:

(i) It must involve pain or other consequences normally considered unpleasant.

(ii) It must be for an offense against legal rules.

(iii) It must be of an actual or supposed offender for his offense.

(iv) It must be intentionally administered by human beings other than the offender.

(v) It must be imposed and administered by an authority constituted by a legal system against which the offense is committed.

In calling this the standard or central case of punishment I shall relegate to the position of sub-standard or secondary cases the following among many other possibilities:

(a) Punishments for breaches of legal rules imposed or administered otherwise than by officials (decentralized sanctions).

(b) Punishments for breaches of non-legal rules or orders (punishments in a family or school).

(c) Vicarious or collective punishment of some member of a social group for actions done by others without the former's authorization, encouragement, control or permission.

(d) Punishment of persons [other than under (c)] who neither are in fact nor supposed to be offenders.

The chief importance of listing these sub-standard cases is to prevent the use of what I shall call the "definitional stop" in discussions of punishment. This is an abuse of definition especially tempting when use is made of conditions (ii) and (iii) of the standard case in arguing against the utilitarian claim that the practice of punishment is justified by the beneficial consequences resulting from the observance of the laws which it secures. Here the stock "retributive" argument is: If this is the justification of punishment, why not apply it, when it pays to do so, to those innocent of any crime, chosen at random, or to the wife and children of the offender? And here the wrong reply is: That, by definition, would not be "punishment" and it is the justification of punishment which is in issue. Not only will this definitional stop fail to satisfy the advocate of "Retribution", it would prevent us from investigating the very thing which modern skepticism most calls in question: namely the rational and moral status of our preference for a system of punishment under which measures painful to individuals are to be taken against them only when they have committed an offense. Why do we prefer this to other forms of social hygiene which we might employ to prevent anti-social behaviour and which we do employ in special circumstances, sometimes with reluctance? No account of punishment can afford to dismiss this question with a definition.

NOTES AND QUESTIONS.

1. Is Hart's definition adequate to distinguish "criminal" from "civil" law? What does he mean by "an offense against legal rules"? If *offense* is synonymous with *crime,* is not the definition of punishment circular and thus inadequate to distinguish the criminal law from its civil counterparts? On the other hand, if *offense* means every violation of a legal rule, would it not follow that an "unpleasant" sanction such as an injunction issued by the National Labor Relations Board constitutes punishment under Hart's definition? What about tort damages, certainly "unpleasant" to the defendant, assessed for negligence *per se* based on violations of statutory norms? If these sanctions constitute punishment, are the labor and tort proceedings in fact "criminal" despite their seemingly "civil" natures? See Fletcher, 411; Wasserstrom, *Some Problems with Theories of Punishment,* in Justice and Punishment 173, 177–87 (J. Cederblom and W. Blizek, eds. 1977).

2. Can the difficulties discussed in the previous note be solved by unpacking Hart's notion that punishment "involve[s] unpleasant consequences for an offense"? Does Hart really mean, "Punishment must be imposed *for the sake* of inflicting pain or other consequences normally considered unpleasant"? If so, are the labor injunction and tort judgment punishments? Moreover, in what sense are those sanctions imposed "for an offense"? See Fletcher, 410–11.

3. On the other hand, if punishment is defined in terms of acting "for the sake of inflicting pain," has a traditional *justification* of punishment (e.g., the

retributive interest in giving offenders their just deserts) been incorporated into the *definition* of punishment? See, e.g., Baier, *Is Punishment Retributive?*, in Philosophical Perspectives on Punishment 16, 18 (G. Ezorsky, ed. 1972): "[P]unishment is the name of a method, or system, of inflicting hardship, the aim of which is to hurt all and only those who are guilty of an offense." (Emphasis in original.)

Should the definitional and justificatory questions of punishment be kept analytically distinct? Are difficulties created, for example, by Thomas Hobbes' definition?:

> A punishment, is an Evill inflicted by publique Authority, on him that hath done, or omitted that which is Judged by the same Authority to be a Transgression of the Law; to the end that the will of men may thereby the better be disposed to obedience. . . . [A]ll evill which is inflicted without intention, or possibility of disposing the Delinquent, or (by his example) other men, to obey the Lawes, is not Punishment; but an act of hostility; because without such an end, no hurt done is contained under that name.

T. Hobbes, *Leviathan* 353, 355 (Pelican Classics, C. B. MacPherson ed. 1971). For the virtues of keeping distinct the conceptual and justificatory issues of punishment, see J. Kieinig, *Punishment and Desert* 10–13 (1973).

4. Consider Hart's definition in both its original and "unpacked" versions as a vehicle for deciding *Flemming v.Nestor* which follows.

FLEMMING V. NESTOR

Supreme Court of the United States

363 U.S. 603 (1960)

Mr. JUSTICE HARLAN *delivered the opinion of the Court.*

[Appellee, Nestor, immigrated to the United States in 1913 and lived continuously in this country until 1956. He was then deported pursuant to the immigration laws for having been a member of the Communist Party from 1933 to 1939. During the time of Nestor's association with the Party, membership therein was not illegal and did not constitute statutory grounds for deportation until Congress so stipulated in 1940, one year after Nestor quit the Party.

In 1954, Congress enacted § 202(n) of the Social Security Act which provided for cutting off Social Security benefits for persons who had been deported because of: unlawful entry to the United States, "subversive" activities including membership in the Communist Party, convictions for designated crimes, or being a narcotics addict or prostitute. Nestor had made regular contributions to the Social Security fund from 1936 to 1955. Subsequent to his deportation, the Government invoked § 202(n) and terminated Nestor's Social Security payments, which he had begun to receive in 1955. Nestor, whose wife remained in the United States, successfully contested the termination in federal district court arguing, among other things, that the termination constituted punishment unconstitutionally imposed without a judicial trial and contrary to the prohibitions against bills of attainder and *ex post facto* laws. The Government brought a direct appeal to the Supreme Court.]

* * *

[Appellee's] most insistently pressed constitutional objections rest upon Art. I, § 9, cl. 3, and Art. III, § 2, cl. 3, of the Constitution, and the Sixth Amendment.[6] It is said that the termination of appellee's benefits amounts to punishing him without a judicial trial . . . and that the punishment exacted is imposed for past conduct not unlawful when engaged in, thereby violating the constitutional prohibition on *ex post facto* laws. Essential to the success of each of these contentions is the validity of characterizing as "punishment" in the constitutional sense the termination of benefits under § 202(n).

In determining whether legislation which bases a disqualification on the happening of a certain past event imposes a punishment, the Court has sought to discern the objects on which the enactment in question was focused. Where the source of legislative concern can be thought to be the activity or status from which the individual is barred, the disqualification is not punishment even though it may bear harshly upon one affected. The contrary is the case where the statute in question is evidently aimed at the person or class of persons disqualified.

. . . Only the other day the governing inquiry was stated, in an opinion joined by four members of the Court, in these terms:

> The question in each case where unpleasant consequences are brought to bear upon an individual for prior conduct, is whether the legislative aim was to punish that individual for past activity, or whether the restriction of the individual comes about as a relevant incident to a regulation of a present situation, such as the proper qualifications for a profession.

De Veau v. Braisted, 363 U.S. 144, 160, 80 S. Ct. 1146, 1155 (plurality opinion). . . .

[T]hough the governing criterion may be readily stated, each case has turned on its own highly particularized context. Where no persuasive showing of a purpose "to reach the person, not the calling," . . . has been made, the Court has not hampered legislative regulation of activities within its sphere

---

[6] Art. I, § 9, cl. 3:

No Bill of Attainder or *ex post facto* Law shall be passed.

Art. III, § 2, cl. 3:

The Trial of all Crimes, except in Cases of Impeachment, shall be by Jury; and such Trial shall be held in the State where the said Crimes shall have been committed. . .

Amend. VI:

In all criminal prosecutions, the accused shall enjoy the right to a speedy and public trial, by an impartial jury of the State and district wherein the crime shall have been committed, which district shall have been previously ascertained by law, and to be informed of the nature and cause of the accusation; to be confronted with the witnesses against him; to have compulsory process for obtaining witnesses in his favor, and to have the assistance of counsel for his defence.

of concern, despite the often severe effects such regulation has had on the persons subject to it. Thus, deportation has been held to be not punishment, but an exercise of the plenary power of Congress to fix the conditions under which aliens are to be permitted to enter and remain in this country. . . . Similarly, the setting by a State of qualifications for the practice of medicine, and their modification from time to time, is an incident of the State's power to protect the health and safety of its citizens, and its decision to bar from practice persons who commit or have committed a felony is taken as evidencing an intent to exercise that regulatory power, and not a purpose to add to the punishment of ex-felons. . . .

Turning, then, to the particular statutory provision before us, appellee cannot successfully contend that the language and structure of § 202(n), or the nature of the deprivation, requires us to recognize a punitive design. . . . Here the sanction is the mere denial of a noncontractual governmental benefit. No affirmative disability or restraint is imposed, and certainly nothing approaching the "infamous punishment" of imprisonment. . .

[The Court reviewed the legislative history of § 202(n) and found that its purpose was nonpunitive. Earlier in its opinion, the Court had posited that § 202(n) could be understood as a means, under the spending power of Congress, to limit Social Security payments to United States residents, thereby promoting economic conditions within the United States. This was so even though certain classes of deportees and some nonresidents were recipients of benefits under the statute. Applying a presumption of constitutionality, the Court found that § 202(n) was rationally related to a nonpunitive purpose.]

Appellee argues that this history demonstrates that Congress was not concerned with the fact of a beneficiary's deportation—which it is claimed alone would justify this legislation as being pursuant to a policy relevant to regulation of the Social Security system—but that it sought to reach certain grounds for deportation, thus evidencing a punitive intent. It is impossible to find in this meager history the unmistakable evidence of punitive intent which, under principles already discussed, is required before a Congressional enactment of this kind may be struck down. Even were that history to be taken as evidencing Congress' concern with the grounds, rather than the fact, of deportation, we do not think that this, standing alone, would suffice to establish a punitive purpose. . . . The legislative record, however, falls short of any persuasive showing that Congress was in fact concerned alone with the grounds of deportation. To be sure Congress did not apply the termination provision to all deportees. However, it is evident that neither did it rest the operation of the statute on the occurrence of the underlying act. The fact of deportation itself remained an essential condition for loss of benefits, and even if a beneficiary were saved from deportation only through discretionary suspension by the Attorney General . . . § 202(n) would not reach him.

Moreover, the grounds for deportation [illegal entry, conviction of a crime, engaging in subversive activity] referred to in the Committee Report [as triggering application of § 202(n)], embrace the great majority of those deported, as is evident from an examination of the four omitted grounds [for deportation which do not trigger § 202(n)], summarized in the margin.[13] Inferences drawn from the omission of those grounds cannot establish, to the degree of certainty required, that Congressional concern was wholly with the acts leading to deportation, and not with the fact of deportation. To hold otherwise would be to rest on "slight implication and vague conjecture" against which Chief Justice Marshall warned. . . .

The same answer must be made to arguments drawn from the failure of Congress to apply § 202(n) to beneficiaries voluntarily residing abroad. . . . Congress may have failed to consider such persons; or it may have thought their number too slight, or the permanence of their voluntary residence abroad too uncertain, to warrant application of the statute to them, with its attendant administrative problems of supervision and enforcement. Again, we cannot with confidence reject all those alternatives which imaginativeness can bring to mind, save that one which might require the invalidation of the statute.

Reversed.

[The dissenting opinions of Mr. Justice Black and of Mr. Justice Douglas are omitted.]

Mr. JUSTICE BRENNAN, with whom The CHIEF JUSTICE and Mr. JUSTICE DOUGLAS join, *dissenting.*

When Nestor quit the Communist Party in 1939 his past membership was not a ground for his deportation. . . . It was not until a year later that past membership was made a specific ground for deportation. This past membership has cost Nestor dearly. It brought him expulsion from the country after 43 years' residence—most of his life. Now more is exacted from him, for after he had begun to receive benefits in 1955—having worked in covered employment the required time and reached age 65—and might anticipate receiving them the rest of his life, the benefits were stopped pursuant to § 202(n) of the Amended Social Security Act. His predicament is very real—an aging man deprived of the means with which to live after being separated from his family and exiled to live among strangers in a land he quit 47 years ago. The common sense of it is that he has been punished severely for his past conduct.

* * *

The Court's test of the constitutionality of § 202(n) is whether the legislative concern underlying the statute was to regulate "the activity or status from which the individual is barred" or whether the statute "is evidently aimed at the person or class of persons disqualified." It rejects the inference that the statute is "aimed at the person or class of persons disqualified" by relying upon the presumption of constitutionality. This presumption might be a basis for

---

[13] They are: (1)persons institutionalized at public expense within five years after entry because of "mental disease, defect, or deficiency" not shown to have arisen subsequent to admission . . . ; (2)persons becoming a public charge within five years after entry from causes not shown to have arisen subsequent to admission . . . ; (3)persons admitted as nonimmigrants . . . who fail to maintain, or comply with the conditions of, suchstatus . . . ; (4)persons knowingly and for gain inducing or aiding, prior to or within five years after entry, any other alien to enter or attempt to enter unlawfully. . .

sustaining the statute if in fact there were two opposing inferences which could reasonably be drawn from the legislation, one that it imposes punishment and the other that it is purposed to further the administration of the Social Security program. The Court, however, does not limit the presumption to that use. Rather the presumption becomes a complete substitute for any supportable finding of a rational connection of § 202(n) with the Social Security program. For me it is not enough to state the test and hold that the presumption alone satisfies it. I find it necessary to examine the Act and its consequences to ascertain whether there is ground for the inference of a congressional concern with the administration of the Social Security program. Only after this inquiry would I consider the application of the presumption.

The Court seems to acknowledge that the statute bears harshly upon the individual disqualified, but states that this is permissible when a statute is enacted as a regulation of the activity. But surely the harshness of the consequences is itself a relevant consideration to the inquiry into the congressional purpose. . . .

It seems to me that the statute itself shows that the sole legislative concern was with "the person or class of persons disqualified." Congress did not disqualify for benefits all beneficiaries residing abroad or even all dependents residing abroad who are aliens. If that had been the case I might agree that Congress' concern would have been with "the activity or status" and not with the "person or class of persons disqualified." The scales would then be tipped toward the conclusion that Congress desired to limit benefit payments to beneficiaries residing in the United States so that the American economy would be aided by expenditure of benefits here. Indeed a proposal along those lines was submitted to Congress in 1954, at the same time § 202(n) was proposed, and it was rejected.

Perhaps, the Court's conclusion that regulation of "the activity or status" was the congressional concern would be a fair appraisal of the statute if Congress had terminated the benefits of all alien beneficiaries who are deported. But that is not what Congress did. Section 202(n) applies only to aliens deported on one or more of 14 of the 18 grounds for which aliens may be deported.

H.R. Rep. No. 1698, 83d Cong., 2d Sess. 25, 77, cited by the Court, describes § 202(n) as including persons who were deported "because of unlawful entry, conviction of a crime, or subversive activity." The section, in addition, covers those deported for such socially condemned acts as narcotic addiction or prostitution. The common element of the 14 grounds is that the alien has been guilty of some blameworthy conduct. In other words Congress worked its will only on aliens deported for conduct displeasing to the lawmakers.

This is plainly demonstrated by the remaining four grounds of deportation, those which do not result in the cancellation of benefits. Two of those four grounds cover persons who become public charges within five years after entry for reasons which predated the entry. A third ground covers the alien who fails to maintain his nonimmigrant status. The fourth ground reaches the alien who, prior to or within five years after entry, aids other aliens to enter the country illegally.

* * *

[Justice Brennan then argued that exempting the four classes of deportees from termination under § 202(n) was explainable only in terms of a view by Congress that persons in those classes were less blameworthy than those in the classes covered by the statute.]

This appraisal of the distinctions drawn by Congress between various kinds of conduct impels the conclusion, beyond per adventure that the distinctions can be understood only if the purpose of Congress was to strike at "the person or class of persons disqualified." The Court inveighs against invalidating a statute on "implication and vague conjecture." Rather I think the Court has strained to sustain the statute on "implication and vague conjecture," in holding that the congressional concern was "the activity or status from which the individual is barred." Today's decision sanctions the use of the spending power not to further the legitimate objectives of the Social Security program but to inflict hurt upon those who by their conduct have incurred the displeasure of Congress. The Framers ordained that even the worst of men should not be punished for their past acts or for any conduct without adherence to the procedural safeguards written into the Constitution. . . .

Section 202(n) imposes punishment in violation of the prohibition against ex post facto laws and without a judicial trial. I therefore dissent.]

NOTES AND QUESTIONS

1. Three years after *Nestor,* the Court in *Kennedy v. Mendoza-Martinez,* 372 U.S. 144 (1963), considered, among other things, whether involuntary expatriation imposed upon those leaving the country to evade the draft in time of war constituted "punishment" so as to trigger the Sixth Amendment right to jury trial. In finding the sanction punitive, the Court offered the following "test":

> The punitive nature of the sanction here is evident under the tests traditionally applied to determine whether an Act of Congress is penal or regulatory in character, even though in other cases this problem has been extremely difficult and elusive of solution. Whether the sanction involves an affirmative disability or restraint, whether it has historically been regarded as a punishment, whether it comes into play only on a finding of *scienter,* whether its operation will promote the traditional aims of punishment—retribution and deterrence, whether the behavior to which it applies is already a crime, whether an alternative purpose to which it may rationally be connected is assignable for it, and whether it appears excessive in relation to the alternative purpose assigned are all relevant to the inquiry, and may often point in differing directions. Absent conclusive evidence of congressional intent as to the penal nature of a statute, these factors must be considered in relation to the statute on its face. . . .

372 U.S. at 168–69.

While the *Mendoza-Martinez* majority saw the expatriation statute as punitive in purpose, Justices Stewart and White argued in dissent that the statute was a nonpunitive attempt by Congress to preserve troop morale and was thus not a measure retributively directed toward draft evaders themselves. For a discussion of *Mendoza-Martinez,* see Comment, *The Concept of Punitive Legislation and the Sixth Amendment: A New Look at Kennedy v. Mendoza-Martinez,* 32 U. Chi. L Rev. 290 (1965).

Does the Court's decision in *Mendoza-Martinez* call into question its earlier opinion in *Perez v. Brownell,* 356 U.S. 44 (1958), in which the Court held that a statutory provision imposing involuntary expatriation upon American citizens voting in foreign elections constituted a nonpunitive regulation of foreign affairs? *Perez* was eventually overruled on the grounds that Congress lacks power to involuntarily strip persons of their citizenship. *Afroyim v. Rusk,* 387 U.S. 253 (1967). See also *Trop v. Dulles,* 356 U.S. 86 (1958) (expatriation following court-martial conviction for wartime desertion constitutes "punishment" for purposes of Eighth Amendment ban against cruel and unusual punishments) (plurality opinion).

2. Are the decisions in *Nestor* and *Mendoza-Martinez* compatible? Apart from considerations of the possibly differing purposes of the sanctions in the two cases, can the cases be reconciled in terms of formal and symbolic distinctions between the sanctions themselves? Does expatriation carry punitive connotations not shared by withholding Social Security benefits? Consider the following excerpt:

FEINBERG, *THE EXPRESSIVE FUNCTION OF PUNISHMENT*

Doing and Deserving, 95–100, 105, 110–11, 114 (1970)

Recent influential articles [treating the problem of punishment] have quite sensibly distinguished between questions of definition and justification, between justifying general rules and particular decisions, between moral and legal guilt. So much is all to the good. When these articles go on to *define* "punishment," however, it seems to many that they leave out of their ken altogether the very element that makes punishment theoretically puzzling and morally disquieting. Punishment is defined in effect as the infliction of hard treatment by an authority on a person for his prior failing in some respect (usually an infraction of a rule or command). There may be a very general sense of the word "punishment" which is well expressed by this definition; but even if that is so, we can distinguish a narrower, more emphatic sense that slips through its meshes. Imprisonment at hard labor for committing a felony is a clear case of punishment in the emphatic sense. But I think we would be less willing to apply that term to parking tickets, offside penalties, sackings, flunkings, and disqualifications. Examples of the latter sort I propose to call *penalties* (merely). . . .

Rather than look for a characteristic common and peculiar to the penalties on which to ground the distinction between penalties and punishments, we would be better advised, I think, to turn our attention to the examples of punishments. Both penalties and punishments are authoritative deprivations for failures; but, apart from these common features, penalties have a miscellaneous character, whereas punishments have an important additional characteristic in common. That characteristic, or specific difference, I shall argue, is a certain expressive function: punishment is a conventional device for the expression of attitudes of resentment and indignation, and of judgments of disapproval and reprobation, on the part either of the punishing authority himself or of those "in whose name" the punishment is inflicted. Punishment, in short, has a *symbolic significance* largely missing from other kinds of penalties.

The reprobative symbolism of punishment and its character as "hard treatment," though never separate in reality, must be carefully distinguished for purposes of analysis. Reprobation is itself painful, whether or not it is accompanied by further "hard treatment," and hard treatment, such as fine or imprisonment, because of its conventional symbolism, can itself be reprobatory. Still, we can conceive of ritualistic condemnation unaccompanied by any further hard treatment, and of inflictions and deprivations which, because of different symbolic conventions, have no reprobative force. . . . [B]oth the "hard treatment" aspect of punishment and its reprobative function must be part of the *definition* of legal punishment.

That the expression of the community's condemnation is an essential ingredient in legal punishment is widely acknowledged by legal writers. Henry M. Hart, for example, gives eloquent emphasis to the point:

What distinguishes a criminal from a civil sanction and all that distinguishes it, it is ventured, is the judgment of community condemnation which accompanies . . . its imposition. . . . [6] Professor Hart's compendious definition needs qualification in one respect. The moral condemnation and the "unpleasant consequences" that he rightly identifies as essential elements of punishment are not as distinct and separate as he suggests. It does not always happen that the convicted prisoner is first solemnly condemned and then subjected to unpleasant physical treatment. It would be more accurate in many cases to say that the unpleasant treatment itself expresses the condemnation, and that this expressive aspect of his incarceration is precisely the element by reason of which it is properly characterized as punishment and not mere penalty . . . the very walls of his cell condemn him, and his record becomes a stigma.

To say that the very physical treatment itself expresses condemnation is to say simply that certain forms of hard treatment have become the conventional symbols of public reprobation. This is neither more nor less paradoxical than to say that certain words have become conventional vehicles in our language for the expression of certain attitudes, or that champagne is the alcoholic beverage traditionally used in celebration of great events, or that black is the color of mourning. Moreover, particular kinds of punishment are often used to express quite specific attitudes (loosely speaking, this is part of their "meaning"); note the differences, for example, between beheading a nobleman and hanging a yeoman, burning a heretic and hanging a traitor, hanging an enemy soldier and executing him by firing squad.

---

[6] Henry M. Hart, *The Aims of the Criminal Law,* Law and Contemporary Problems 23 (1958), II, A, 4.

* * *

A philosophical theory of punishment that, through inadequate definition, leaves out the condemnatory function not only will disappoint the moralist and the traditional moral philosopher; it will seem offensively irrelevant as well to the constitutional lawyer, whose vital concern with punishment is both conceptual, and therefore genuinely philosophical, as well as practically urgent. . . .

* * *

The distinction between punishments and mere penalties, and the essentially reprobative function of the former, can also help clarify the controversy among writers on the criminal law about the propriety of so-called strict liability offenses—offenses for the conviction of which there need be no proof of "fault" or "culpability" on the part of the accused. If it can be shown that he committed an act proscribed by statute, then he is guilty irrespective of whether he had any justification or excuse for what he did. . . .

* * *

The rationale of strict liability in public welfare statutes is that violation of the public interest is more likely to be prevented by unconditional liability than by liability that can be defeated by some kind of excuse; that, even though liability without "fault" is severe, it is one of the known risks incurred by businessmen; and that, besides, the sanctions are *only fines,* hence not really "punitive" in character. On the other hand, strict liability to *imprisonment* (or "punishment proper") "has been held by many to be incompatible with the basic requirements of our Anglo-American, and indeed, any civilized jurisprudence."[22] What accounts for this difference in attitude? In both kinds of case, defendants may have sanctions inflicted upon them even though they are acknowledged to be without fault; and the difference cannot be merely that imprisonment is always and necessarily a greater harm than a fine, for this is not always so. Rather, the reason why strict liability to imprisonment (punishment) is so much more repugnant to our sense of justice than is strict liability to fine (penalty) is simply that imprisonment in modern times has taken on the symbolism of public reprobation.

* * *

Public condemnation, whether avowed through the stigmatizing symbolism of punishment or unavowed but clearly discernible (mere "punitive intent"), can greatly magnify the suffering caused by its attendant mode of hard treatment. Samuel Butler keenly appreciated the difference between reprobative hard treatment (punishment) and the same treatment without reprobation:

> . . . we should hate a single flogging given in the way of mere punishment more than the amputation of a limb, if it were kindly and courteously performed from a wish to help us out of our difficulty, and with the full

---

[22] Richard A. Wasserstrom, *Strict Liability in the Criminal Law,* Stanford L. R. 12 (1960), 730.

consciousness on the part of the doctor that it was only by an accident of constitution that he was not in the like plight himself. So the Erewhonians take a flogging once a week, and a diet of bread and water for two or three months together, whenever their straightener recommends it.[27]

Even floggings and imposed fastings do not constitute punishments, then, where social conventions are such that, they do not express public censure. . . .

NOTES AND QUESTIONS

1. Under Feinberg's definition, is the termination of Social Security benefits in *Nestor* punishment? What about the sanction of expatriation in *Mendoza-Martinez*?

2. If Feinberg's theory is correct, did the Supreme Court act inconsistently in finding expatriation to be punishment in *Mendoza-Martinez* but not in *Perez v. Brownell, supra,* p. 48?

[B] Punishment and Nonpunitive Sanctions

The previous section introduced the problem of defining punishment. As evidenced by the Supreme Court's attempts in *Nestor* and *Mendoza-Martinez* to differentiate punishment from nonpenal regulation, an understanding of punishment entails the ability to distinguish it from other sanctions. The present section continues the definitional exploration by contrasting punishment with several analogous nonpunitive sanctions.

The Court's examination of the "punishment" sanction has proven to be a difficult and perplexing process. As the following cases illustrate, the Court has generated a body of law difficult to comprehend. One commentator characterized the Court's performance as "an incoherent muddle,". . . "so inconsistent that it borders on the unintelligible." Logan, *The Ex Post Facto Clause and the Jurisprudence of Punishment*, 35 Am. Crim. L. Rev. 1261, 1268, 1280 (1998). As you read the following cases defining and identifying punitive sanctions, consider whether the Court's definition of punishment is driven by the particular constitutional challenge before the Court.

[1] Punishment versus Preventive Detention

In *Bell v. Wolfish*, 441 U.S. 520 (1979), the United States Supreme Court assessed the Constitutional character of the confinement imposed upon jailed detainees awaiting trial. The Court first recognized that detainees may not be "punished," since punishment of the unconvicted would violate due process. The Court found, however, that jailing pretrial detainees was nonpunitive even in overcrowded facilities where inmates possessed limited access to outside reading material and were subjected to body cavity searches after contact visits. The Court found pretrial jailing permissible so long as the detention reasonably related to the nonpunitive purpose of ensuring presence

---

[27] Erewon, new and rev. edn. (London: Grant Richards, 1901), Ch. 10.

at trial, notwithstanding the fact that jail facilities routinely house both pretrial detainees and convicted offenders.

The Court expounded on the meaning of punishment by referring to the tests articulated in *Mendoza-Martinez:*

> The factors identified in *Mendoza-Martinez* provide useful guideposts in determining whether particular restrictions and conditions accompanying pretrial detention amount to punishment in the constitutional sense of that word. A court must decide whether the disability is imposed for the purpose of punishment or whether it is but an incident of some other legitimate governmental purpose. . . . Absent a showing of an expressed intent to punish on the part of detention facility officials, that determination generally will turn on "whether an alternative purpose to which [the restriction] may rationally be connected is assignable for it, and whether it appears excessive in relation to the alternative purpose assigned [to it]." . . . Thus, if a particular condition or restriction of pretrial detention is reasonably related to a legitimate governmental objective, it does not, without more, amount to "punishment."[20] Conversely, if a restriction or condition is not reasonably related to a legitimate goal—if it is arbitrary or purposeless—a court permissibly may infer that the purpose of the governmental action is punishment that may not constitutionally be inflicted upon detainees *qua* detainees. Courts must be mindful that these inquiries spring from constitutional requirements and that judicial answers to them must reflect that fact rather than a court's idea of how best to operate a detention facility.

UNITED STATES V. SALERNO

Supreme Court of the United States

481 U.S. 739 (1987)

Chief Justice REHNQUIST *delivered the opinion of the Court.*

The Bail Reform Act of 1984 (Act) allows a federal court to detain an arrestee pending trial if the Government demonstrates by clear and convincing evidence after an adversary hearing that no release conditions "will reasonably assure . . . the safety of any other person and the community." The United States Court of Appeals for the Second Circuit struck down this provision of the Act as facially unconstitutional, because, in that court's words, this type of pretrial detention violates "substantive due process." We granted *certiorari* because of a conflict among the Courts of Appeals regarding the

---

[20] This is not to say that the officials of a detention facility can justify punishment. They cannot. It is simply to say that in the absence of a showing of intent to punish, a court must look to see if a particular restriction or condition, which may on its face appear to be punishment, is instead but an incident of a legitimate nonpunitive governmental objective. . . . Retribution and deterrence are not legitimate nonpunitive governmental objectives. . . . Conversely, loading a detainee with chains and shackles and throwing him in a dungeon may ensure his presence at trial and preserve the security of the institution. But it would be difficult to conceive of a situation where conditions so harsh, employed to achieve objectives that could be accomplished in so many alternative and less harsh methods, would not support a conclusion that the purpose for which they were imposed was to punish.

validity of the Act. We hold that, as against the facial attack mounted by these respondents, the Act fully comports with constitutional requirements. We therefore reverse.

Responding to "the alarming problem of crimes committed by persons on release," Congress formulated the Bail Reform Act of 1984, 18 U.S.C. § 3141 et seq. (1982 ed., Supp. III)

* * *

To this end, the Act requires a judicial officer to determine whether an arrestee shall be detained. Section 3142(e) provides that "[i]f, after a hearing pursuant to the provisions of subsection (f), the judicial officer finds that no condition or combination of conditions will reasonably assure the appearance of the person as required and the safety of any other person and the community, he shall order the detention of the person prior to trial.". . .

The judicial officer is not given unbridled discretion in making the detention determination. Congress has specified the considerations relevant to that decision. These factors include the nature and seriousness of the charges, the substantiality of the Government's evidence against the arrestee, the arrestee's background and characteristics, and the nature and seriousness of the danger posed by the suspect's release. . . .

Respondents Anthony Salerno and Vincent Cafaro were arrested. . . after being charged in a 29-count indictment alleging various Racketeer Influenced and Corrupt Organizations Act (RICO) violations, mail and wire fraud offenses, extortion, and various criminal gambling violations. The RICO counts alleged 35 acts of racketeering activity, including fraud, extortion, gambling, and conspiracy to commit murder. At respondents' arraignment, the Government moved to have Salerno and Cafaro detained pursuant to § 3142(e), on the ground that no condition of release would assure the safety of the community or any person. The District Court held a hearing at which the Government made a detailed proffer of evidence. The Government's case showed that Salerno was the "boss" of the Genovese crime family of La Cosa Nostra and that Cafaro was a "captain" in the Genovese family. According to the Government's proffer . . . the two respondents had participated in wide-ranging conspiracies to aid their illegitimate enterprises through violent means. The Government also offered [evidence] . . . that Salerno personally participated in two murder conspiracies. . . .

The District Court granted the Government's detention motion, concluding that the Government had established by clear and convincing evidence that no condition or combination of conditions of release would ensure the safety of the community or any person:

> The activities of a criminal organization such as the Genovese Family do not cease with the arrest of its principals and their release on even the most stringent of bail conditions. The illegal businesses, in place for many years, require constant attention and protection, or they will fail. Under these circumstances, this court recognizes a strong incentive on the part of its leadership to continue business as usual. When business as usual involves threats, beatings, and murder, the present danger such people pose in the community is self-evident.

Respondents appealed, contending that to the extent that the Bail Reform Act permits pretrial detention on the ground that the arrestee is likely to commit future crimes, it is unconstitutional on its face. Over a dissent, the United States Court of Appeals for the Second Circuit agreed. . . . The Court of Appeals also found our decision in *Schall v. Martin,* 467 U.S. 253 (1984), upholding postarrest, pretrial detention of juveniles, inapposite because juveniles have a lesser interest in liberty than do adults.

II

Respondents . . . rely upon the Court of Appeals' conclusion that the Act exceeds the limitations placed upon the Federal Government by the Due Process Clause of the Fifth Amendment. . . .

A

* * *

Respondents . . . argue that the Act violates substantive due process because the pretrial detention it authorizes constitutes impermissible punishment before trial . . . The Government, however, has never argued that pretrial detention could be upheld if it were "punishment." The Court of Appeals assumed that pretrial detention under the Bail Reform Act is regulatory, not penal, and we agree that it is.

As an initial matter, the mere fact that a person is detained does not inexorably lead to the conclusion that the government has imposed punishment. . . . To determine whether a restriction on liberty constitutes impermissible punishment or permissible regulation, we first look to legislative intent. Unless Congress expressly intended to impose punitive restrictions, the punitive/regulatory distinction turns on " 'whether an alternative purpose to which [the restriction] may rationally be connected is assignable for it, and whether it appears excessive in relation to the alternative purpose assigned [to it].'," quoting *Kennedy v. Mendoza-Martinez.* . . .

We conclude that the detention imposed by the Act falls on the regulatory side of the dichotomy. The legislative history of the Bail Reform Act clearly indicates that Congress did not formulate the pretrial detention provisions as punishment for dangerous individuals. Congress instead perceived pretrial detention as a potential solution to a pressing societal problem. There is no doubt that preventing danger to the community is a legitimate regulatory goal.

Nor are the incidents of pretrial detention excessive in relation to the regulatory goal Congress sought to achieve. The Bail Reform Act carefully limits the circumstances under which detention may be sought to the most serious of crimes. See 18 U.S.C. § 3142(f) (detention hearings available if case involves crimes of violence, offenses for which the sentence is life imprisonment or death, serious drug offenses, or certain repeat offenders). The arrestee is entitled to a prompt detention hearing, ibid., and the maximum length of pretrial detention is limited by the stringent time limitations of the Speedy Trial Act.[4] Moreover, as in *Schall v. Martin,* the conditions of confinement

---

[4] We intimate no view as to the point at which detention in a particular case might become excessively prolonged, and therefore punitive, in relation to Congress' regulatory goal.

envisioned by the Act "appear to reflect the regulatory purposes relied upon by the" Government. As in *Schall,* the statute at issue here requires that detainees be housed in a "facility separate, to the extent practicable, from persons awaiting or serving sentences or being held in custody pending appeal." We conclude, therefore, that the pretrial detention contemplated by the Bail Reform Act is regulatory in nature, and does not constitute punishment before trial in violation of the Due Process Clause.

* * *

. . . We have repeatedly held that the Government's regulatory interest in community safety can, in appropriate circumstances, outweigh an individual's liberty interest. For example, in times of war or insurrection, when society's interest is at its peak, the Government may detain individuals whom the government believes to be dangerous. . . . Even outside the exigencies of war, we have found that sufficiently compelling governmental interests can justify detention of dangerous persons. Thus, we have found no absolute constitutional barrier to detention of potentially dangerous resident aliens pending deportation proceedings. . . . We have also held that the government may detain mentally unstable individuals who present a danger to the public . . . and dangerous defendants who become incompetent to stand trial. . . . We have approved of postarrest regulatory detention of juveniles when they present a continuing danger to the community. *Schall v. Martin, supra.* Even competent adults may face substantial liberty restrictions as a result of the operation of our criminal justice system. If the police suspect an individual of a crime, they may arrest and hold him until a neutral magistrate determines whether probable cause exists. . . . Finally, respondents concede and the Court of Appeals noted that an arrestee may be incarcerated until trial if he presents a risk of flight, or a danger to witnesses.

* * *

The government's interest in preventing crime by arrestees is both legitimate and compelling. . . . The Bail Reform Act, . . . narrowly focuses on a particularly acute problem in which the Government interests are overwhelming. The Act operates only on individuals who have been arrested for a specific category of extremely serious offenses. Congress specifically found that these individuals are far more likely to be responsible for dangerous acts in the community after arrest. Nor is the Act by any means a scattershot attempt to incapacitate those who are merely suspected of these serious crimes. The Government must first of all demonstrate probable cause to believe that the charged crime has been committed by the arrestee, but that is not enough. In a full-blown adversary hearing, the Government must convince a neutral decision maker by clear and convincing evidence that no conditions of release can reasonably assure the safety of the community or any person. While the Government's general interest in preventing crime is compelling, even this interest is heightened when the Government musters convincing proof that the arrestee, already indicted or held to answer for a serious crime, presents a demonstrable danger to the community. Under these narrow circumstances, society's interest in crime prevention is at its greatest.

* * *

... Given the legitimate and compelling regulatory purpose of the Act and the procedural protections it offers, we conclude that the Act is not facially invalid under the Due Process Clause of the Fifth Amendment.

The judgment of the Court of Appeals is therefore, Reversed.

Justice MARSHALL, with whom Justice BRENNAN joins, *dissenting.*

* * *

... The majority concludes that the Act is a regulatory rather than a punitive measure. The ease with which the conclusion is reached suggests the worthlessness of the achievement. The major premise is that "[u]nless Congress expressly intended to impose punitive restrictions, the punitive/regulatory distinction turns on " 'whether an alternative purpose to which [the restriction] may rationally be connected is assignable for it, and whether it appears excessive in relation to the alternative purpose assigned [to it].' " "The majority finds that "Congress did not formulate the pretrial detention provisions as punishment for dangerous individuals," but instead was pursuing the "legitimate regulatory goal" of "preventing danger to the community." Concluding that pretrial detention is not an excessive solution to the problem of preventing danger to the community, the majority thus finds that no substantive element of the guarantee of due process invalidates the statute.

This argument does not demonstrate the conclusion it purports to justify. Let us apply the majority's reasoning to a similar, hypothetical case. After investigation, Congress determines (not unrealistically) that a large proportion of violent crime is perpetrated by persons who are unemployed. It also determines, equally reasonably, that much violent crime is committed at night. From amongst the panoply of "potential solutions," Congress chooses a statute which permits, after judicial proceedings, the imposition of a dusk-to-dawn curfew on anyone who is unemployed. Since this is not a measure enacted for the purpose of punishing the unemployed, and since the majority finds that preventing danger to the community is a legitimate regulatory goal, the curfew statute would, according to the majority's analysis, be a mere "regulatory" detention statute, entirely compatible with the substantive components of the Due Process Clause.

The absurdity of this conclusion arises, of course, from the majority's cramped concept of substantive due process. The majority proceeds as though the only substantive right protected by the Due Process Clause is a right to be free from punishment before conviction. The majority's technique for infringing this right is simple: merely redefine any measure which is claimed to be punishment as "regulation," and, magically, the Constitution no longer prohibits its impo-sition. . . . [T]he majority's argument is merely an exercise in obfuscation.

Throughout the world today there are men, women, and children interned indefinitely, awaiting trials which may never come or which may be a mockery of the word, because their governments believe them to be "dangerous." Our

Constitution, whose construction began two centuries ago, can shelter us forever from the evils of such unchecked power. Over 200 years it has slowly, through our efforts, grown more durable, more expansive, and more just. But it cannot protect us if we lack the courage, and the self-restraint, to protect ourselves. Today a majority of the Court applies itself to an ominous exercise in demolition. Theirs is truly a decision which will go forth without authority, and come back without respect.

I dissent.

[The dissenting opinion of Justice Stevens is omitted.]

NOTES AND QUESTIONS

1. If pretrial detention is not punishment, why do courts often require that convicted offenders be given credit against their prison sentences for jail time spent pretrial? See, e.g., *In re Trambitas,* 96 Wash. 2d 329, 635 P.2d 122 (1981).

2. Does pretrial detention become "punishment" for purposes of the Eighth Amendment prohibition against cruel and unusual punishments if a jailor physically abuses a detainee? See *Johnson v. Glick,* 481 F.2d 1028, 1032 (2d Cir. 1973).

3. To what extent is Salerno detained because of *who he is* (a mob "boss" perceived to be dangerous) rather than for *what he has done?* If he is detained as a response to his present status rather than because of his past offenses, is he being "punished" under Hart's definition? See § 2.02 [A]. On the other hand, but for Salerno's alleged offenses, he would not be subject to detention under the Federal Bail Reform Act. Does that not suggest that his detention is, in a sense at least, *for an offense?* If so, is his detention punishment after all?

For other examples of detentions for "status," see *Predators and Politics: A Symposium on Washington's Sexually Violent Predators Statute,* 18 U. Puget Sound L. Rev. 505 (1992); Robinson, *Foreword, The Criminal—Civil Distinction and Dangerous Blameless Offenders,* 83 J. Crim. L. & Criminology 693 (1993); *In re Blodgett,* 510 N.W. 2d 910 (Minn. 1994) (upholding "psychopathic personality" statute against due process and equal protection attacks).

4. Salerno was incarcerated to prevent him from acting in undesirable ways. Sometimes courts incarcerate people to induce them to act in certain ways, specifically to adhere to particular orders (for example, to pay child support) of the court. In such cases of "civil contempt," incarceration is viewed as remedial and nonpunitive. On the other hand, where the court incarcerates an individual for an insult to the court, the context is "criminal contempt" and the incarceration is punitive. The distinction has traditionally been understood as follows:

> At common law, contempts were divided into criminal contempts, in which a litigant was punished for an affront to the court by a fixed fine or period of incarceration; and civil contempts, in which an uncooperative litigant was

incarcerated (and in later cases fined) until he complied with a specific order of the court.

International Union, United Mine Workers of America v. Bagwell, 512 U.S. 821, 840 (1994) (Scalia, J. concurring).

The *United Mine Workers* case held that contempt fines in the amount of $52 million issued against the union for violations of a labor injunction constituted a "serious criminal sanction" and thus could be imposed only through a jury trial. The Court found that the fines were not compensatory but rather were levied for widespread, ongoing, out-of-court violations of an entire code of conduct imposed by the lower court. Under these circumstances, the Court found the fines to be punitive.

KANSAS V. HENDRICKS

Supreme Court of the United States

521 U.S. 346 (1997)

Justice THOMAS *delivered the opinion of the Court.*

In 1994, Kansas enacted the Sexually Violent Predator Act, which establishes procedures for the civil commitment of persons who, due to a "mental abnormality" or a "personality disorder," are likely to engage in "predatory acts of sexual violence." The State invoked the Act for the first time to commit Leroy Hendricks, an inmate who had a long history of sexually molesting children, and who was scheduled for release from prison shortly after the Act became law. Hendricks challenged his commitment on, inter alia, "substantive" due process, double jeopardy, and ex post facto grounds. The Kansas Supreme Court invalidated the Act, holding that its pre-commitment condition of a "mental abnormality" did not satisfy what the court perceived to be the "substantive" due process requirement that involuntary civil commitment must be predicated on a finding of "mental illness." The State of Kansas petitioned for certiorari. Hendricks subsequently filed a cross-petition in which he reasserted his federal double jeopardy and ex post facto claims. We granted certiorari on both the petition and the cross-petition, and now reverse the judgment below.

I

A

The Kansas Legislature enacted the Sexually Violent Predator Act (Act) in 1994 to grapple with the problem of managing repeat sexual offenders. Although Kansas already had a statute addressing the involuntary commitment of those defined as "mentally ill," the legislature determined that existing civil commitment procedures were inadequate to confront the risks presented by "sexually violent predators." In the Act's preamble, the legislature explained:

> [A] small but extremely dangerous group of sexually violent predators exist who do not have a mental disease or defect that renders them

appropriate for involuntary treatment pursuant to the [general involuntary civil commitment statute]. . . . In contrast to persons appropriate for civil commitment under the [general involuntary civil commitment statute], sexually violent predators generally have anti-social personality features which are unamenable to existing mental illness treatment modalities and those features render them likely to engage in sexually violent behavior. The legislature further finds that sexually violent predators' likelihood of engaging in repeat acts of predatory sexual violence is high. The existing involuntary commitment procedure . . . is inadequate to address the risk these sexually violent predators pose to society. The legislature further finds that the prognosis for rehabilitating sexually violent predators in a prison setting is poor, the treatment needs of this population are very long term and the treatment modalities for this population are very different than the traditional treatment modalities for people appropriate for commitment under the [general involuntary civil commitment statute].

As a result, the Legislature found it necessary to establish "a civil commitment procedure for the long-term care and treatment of the sexually violent predator." The Act defined a "sexually violent predator" as:

any person who has been convicted of or charged with a sexually violent offense and who suffers from a mental abnormality or personality disorder which makes the person likely to engage in the predatory acts of sexual violence.

A "mental abnormality" was defined, in turn, as a "congenital or acquired condition affecting the emotional or volitional capacity which predisposes the person to commit sexually violent offenses in a degree constituting such person a menace to the health and safety of others."

As originally structured, the Act's civil commitment procedures pertained to: (1) a presently confined person who, like Hendricks, "has been convicted of a sexually violent offense" and is scheduled for release; (2) a person who has been "charged with a sexually violent offense" but has been found incompetent to stand trial; (3) a person who has been found "not guilty by reason of insanity of a sexually violent offense"; and (4) a person found "not guilty" of a sexually violent offense because of a mental disease or defect.

The initial version of the Act, as applied to a currently confined person such as Hendricks, was designed to initiate a specific series of procedures. The custodial agency was required to notify the local prosecutor 60 days before the anticipated release of a person who might have met the Act's criteria. The prosecutor was then obligated, within 45 days, to decide whether to file a petition in state court seeking the person's involuntary commitment. If such a petition were filed, the court was to determine whether "probable cause" existed to support a finding that the person was a "sexually violent predator" and thus eligible for civil commitment. Upon such a determination, transfer of the individual to a secure facility for professional evaluation would occur. After that evaluation, a trial would be held to determine beyond a reasonable doubt whether the individual was a sexually violent predator. If that determination were made, the person would then be transferred to the custody of the Secretary of Social and Rehabilitation Services (Secretary) for "control, care and treatment until such time as the person's mental abnormality or personality disorder has so changed that the person is safe to be at large."

In addition to placing the burden of proof upon the State, the Act afforded the individual a number of other procedural safeguards. In the case of an indigent person, the State was required to provide, at public expense, the assistance of counsel and an examination by mental health care professionals. The individual also received the right to present and cross-examine witnesses, and the opportunity to review documentary evidence presented by the State.

Once an individual was confined, the Act required that "[t]he involuntary detention or commitment . . . shall conform to constitutional requirements for care and treatment." Confined persons were afforded three different avenues of review: First, the committing court was obligated to conduct an annual review to determine whether continued detention was warranted. Second, the Secretary was permitted, at any time, to decide that the confined individual's condition had so changed that release was appropriate, and could then authorize the person to petition for release. Finally, even without the Secretary's permission, the confined person could at any time file a release petition. If the court found that the State could no longer satisfy its burden under the initial commitment standard, the individual would be freed from confinement.

B

In 1984, Hendricks was convicted of taking "indecent liberties" with two 13-year-old boys. After serving nearly 10 years of his sentence, he was slated for release to a halfway house. Shortly before his scheduled release, however, the State filed a petition in state court seeking Hendricks' civil confinement as a sexually violent predator. On August 19, 1994, Hendricks appeared before the court with counsel and moved to dismiss the petition on the grounds that the Act violated various federal constitutional provisions. Although the court reserved ruling on the Act's constitutionality, it concluded that there was probable cause to support a finding that Hendricks was a sexually violent predator, and therefore ordered that he be evaluated at the Larned State Security Hospital.

Hendricks subsequently requested a jury trial to determine whether he qualified as a sexually violent predator. During that trial, Hendricks' own testimony revealed a chilling history of repeated child sexual molestation and abuse, beginning in 1955 when he exposed his genitals to two young girls. At that time, he pleaded guilty to indecent exposure. Then, in 1957, he was convicted of lewdness involving a young girl and received a brief jail sentence. In 1960, he molested two young boys while he worked for a carnival. After serving two years in prison for that offense, he was paroled, only to be rearrested for molesting a 7-year-old girl. Attempts were made to treat him for his sexual deviance, and in 1965 he was considered "safe to be at large," and was discharged from a state psychiatric hospital.

Shortly thereafter, however, Hendricks sexually assaulted another young boy and girl he performed oral sex on the 8-year-old girl and fondled the 11-year-old boy. He was again imprisoned in 1967, but refused to participate in a sex offender treatment program, and thus remained incarcerated until his parole in 1972. Diagnosed as a pedophile, Hendricks entered into, but then abandoned, a treatment program. He testified that despite having received professional help for his pedophilia, he continued to harbor sexual desires for children. Indeed, soon after his 1972 parole, Hendricks began to abuse his own stepdaughter and stepson. He forced the children to engage in sexual activity with him over a period of approximately four years. Then, as noted above, Hendricks was convicted of "taking indecent liberties" with two adolescent boys after he attempted to fondle them. As a result of that conviction, he was once again imprisoned, and was serving that sentence when he reached his conditional release date in September 1994.

Hendricks admitted that he had repeatedly abused children whenever he was not confined. He explained that when he "get[s] stressed out," he "can't control the urge" to molest children. Although Hendricks recognized that his behavior harms children, and he hoped he would not sexually molest children again, he stated that the only sure way he could keep from sexually abusing children in the future was "to die." Hendricks readily agreed with the state physician's diagnosis that he suffers from pedophilia and that he is not cured of the condition; indeed, he told the physician that "treatment is bull----."

The jury unanimously found beyond a reasonable doubt that Hendricks was a sexually violent predator. The trial court subsequently determined, as a matter of state law, that pedophilia qualifies as a "mental abnormality" as defined by the Act, and thus ordered Hendricks committed to the Secretary's custody.

Hendricks appealed, claiming, among other things, that application of the Act to him violated the Federal Constitution's Due Process, Double Jeopardy, and Ex Post Facto Clauses. The Kansas Supreme Court accepted Hendricks' due process claim. The court declared that in order to commit a person involuntarily in a civil proceeding, a State is required by "substantive" due process to prove by clear and convincing evidence that the person is both (1) mentally ill, and (2) a danger to himself or to others. The court then determined that the Act's definition of "mental abnormality" did not satisfy what it perceived to be this Court's "mental illness" requirement in the civil commitment context. As a result, the court held that "the Act violates Hendricks' substantive due process rights."

The majority did not address Hendricks' ex post facto or double jeopardy claims. The dissent, however, considered each of Hendricks' constitutional arguments and rejected them.

II

[The Court agreed with the argument by the State of Kansas that the Act's definition of "mental abnormality" satisfied substantive due process requirements.]

B

We granted Hendricks' cross-petition to determine whether the Act violates the Constitution's double jeopardy prohibition or its ban on ex post facto lawmaking. The thrust of Hendricks' argument is that the Act establishes criminal proceedings; hence confinement under it necessarily constitutes punishment. He contends that where, as here, newly enacted "punishment" is predicated upon past conduct for which he has already been convicted and forced to serve a prison sentence, the Constitution's Double Jeopardy and Ex Post Facto Clauses are violated. We are unpersuaded by Hendricks' argument that Kansas has established criminal proceedings.

The categorization of a particular proceeding as civil or criminal "is first of all a question of statutory construction." We must initially ascertain whether the legislature meant the statute to establish "civil" proceedings. If so, we ordinarily defer to the legislature's stated intent. Here, Kansas' objective to create a civil proceeding is evidenced by its placement of the Sexually Violent Predator Act within the Kansas probate code, instead of the criminal code, as well as its description of the Act as creating a "civil commitment procedure." Nothing on the face of the statute suggests that the legislature sought to create anything other than a civil commitment scheme designed to protect the public from harm.

Although we recognize that a "civil label is not always dispositive," we will reject the legislature's manifest intent only where a party challenging the statute provides "the clearest proof" that "the statutory scheme [is] so punitive either in purpose or effect as to negate [the State's] intention" to deem it "civil." In those limited circumstances, we will consider the statute to have established criminal proceedings for constitutional purposes. Hendricks, however, has failed to satisfy this heavy burden.

As a threshold matter, commitment under the Act does not implicate either of the two primary objectives of criminal punishment: retribution or deterrence. The Act's purpose is not retributive because it does not affix culpability for prior criminal conduct. Instead, such conduct is used solely for evidentiary purposes, either to demonstrate that a "mental abnormality" exists or to support a finding of future dangerousness. . . . In addition, the Kansas Act does not make a criminal conviction a prerequisite for commitment persons absolved of criminal responsibility may nonetheless be subject to confinement under the Act. An absence of the necessary criminal responsibility suggests that the State is not seeking retribution for a past misdeed. Thus, the fact that the Act may be "tied to criminal activity" is "insufficient to render the statut[e] punitive."

Moreover, unlike a criminal statute, no finding of scienter is required to commit an individual who is found to be a sexually violent predator; instead, the commitment determination is made based on a "mental abnormality" or "personality disorder" rather than on one's criminal intent. The existence of a scienter requirement is customarily an important element in distinguishing criminal from civil statutes. The absence of such a requirement here is evidence that confinement under the statute is not intended to be retributive.

Nor can it be said that the legislature intended the Act to function as a deterrent. Those persons committed under the Act are, by definition, suffering from a "mental abnormality" or a "personality disorder" that prevents them from exercising adequate control over their behavior. Such persons are therefore unlikely to be deterred by the threat of confinement. And the conditions surrounding that confinement do not suggest a punitive purpose on the State's part. The State has represented that an individual confined under the Act is not subject to the more restrictive conditions placed on state prisoners, but instead experiences essentially the same conditions as any involuntarily committed patient in the state mental institution. Because none of the parties argues that people institutionalized under the Kansas general civil commitment statute are subject to punitive conditions, even though they may be involuntarily confined, it is difficult to conclude that persons confined under this Act are being "punished."

Hendricks focuses on his confinement's potentially indefinite duration as evidence of the State's punitive intent. That focus, however, is misplaced. Far from any punitive objective, the confinement's duration is instead linked to the stated purposes of the commitment, namely, to hold the person until his mental abnormality no longer causes him to be a threat to others. If, at any time, the confined person is adjudged "safe to be at large," he is statutorily entitled to immediate release.

Hendricks next contends that the State's use of procedural safeguards traditionally found in criminal trials makes the proceedings here criminal rather than civil. . . . The numerous procedural and evidentiary protections afforded here demonstrate that the Kansas Legislature has taken great care to confine only a narrow class of particularly dangerous individuals, and then only after meeting the strictest procedural standards. That Kansas chose to afford such procedural protections does not transform a civil commitment proceeding into a criminal prosecution.

Finally, Hendricks argues that the Act is necessarily punitive because it fails to offer any legitimate "treatment." Without such treatment, Hendricks asserts, confinement under the Act amounts to little more than disguised punishment. Hendricks' argument assumes that treatment for his condition is available, but that the State has failed (or refused) to provide it. The Kansas Supreme Court, however, apparently rejected this assumption, explaining:

> It is clear that the overriding concern of the legislature is to continue the segregation of sexually violent offenders from the public. Treatment with the goal of reintegrating them into society is incidental, at best. The record reflects that treatment for sexually violent predators is all but nonexistent. The legislature concedes that sexually violent predators are not amenable to treatment under [the existing Kansas involuntary commitment statute]. If there is nothing to treat under [that statute], then there is no mental illness. In that light, the provisions of the Act for treatment appear somewhat disingenuous.

It is possible to read this passage as a determination that Hendricks' condition was untreatable under the existing Kansas civil commitment statute, and thus the Act's sole purpose was incapacitation. Absent a treatable mental illness, the Kansas court concluded, Hendricks could not be detained against his will.

Accepting the Kansas court's apparent determination that treatment is not possible for this category of individuals does not obligate us to adopt its legal conclusions. We have already observed that, under the appropriate circumstances and when accompanied by proper procedures, incapacitation may be a legitimate end of the civil law. Accordingly, the Kansas court's determination that the Act's "overriding concern" was the continued "segregation of sexually violent offenders" is consistent with our conclusion that the Act establishes civil proceedings, especially when that concern is coupled with the State's ancillary goal of providing treatment to those offenders, if such is possible. While we have upheld state civil commitment statutes that aim both to incapacitate and to treat, we have never held that the Constitution prevents a State from civilly detaining those for whom no treatment is available, but who nevertheless pose a danger to others. A State could hardly be seen as furthering a "punitive" purpose by involuntarily confining persons afflicted with an untreatable, highly contagious disease. Similarly, it would be of little value to require treatment as a precondition for civil confinement of the dangerously insane when no acceptable treatment existed. To conclude otherwise would obligate a State to release certain confined individuals who were both mentally ill and dangerous simply because they could not be successfully treated for their afflictions.

Although the treatment program initially offered Hendricks may have seemed somewhat meager, it must be remembered that he was the first person committed under the Act. That the State did not have all of its treatment procedures in place is thus not surprising. What is significant, however, is that Hendricks was placed under the supervision of the Kansas Department of Health and Social and Rehabilitative Services, housed in a unit segregated from the general prison population and operated not by employees of the Department of Corrections, but by other trained individuals. And, before this Court, Kansas declared "[a]bsolutely" that persons committed under the Act are now receiving in the neighborhood of "31.5 hours of treatment per week."

Where the State has "disavowed any punitive intent"; limited confinement to a small segment of particularly dangerous individuals; provided strict procedural safeguards; directed that confined persons be segregated from the general prison population and afforded the same status as others who have been civilly committed; recommended treatment if such is possible; and permitted immediate release upon a showing that the individual is no longer dangerous or mentally impaired, we cannot say that it acted with punitive intent. We therefore hold that the Act does not establish criminal proceedings and that involuntary confinement pursuant to the Act is not punitive. Our conclusion that the Act is nonpunitive thus removes an essential prerequisite for both Hendricks' double jeopardy and ex post facto claims.

III

We hold that the Kansas Sexually Violent Predator Act comports with due process requirements and neither runs afoul of double jeopardy principles nor constitutes an exercise in impermissible ex post facto lawmaking. Accordingly, the judgment of the Kansas Supreme Court is reversed.

Justice KENNEDY, *concurring.*

I join the opinion of the Court in full and add these additional comments.

Though other issues were argued to us, as the case has matured it turns on whether the Kansas statute is an ex post facto law. A law enacted after commission of the offense and which punishes the offense by extending the term of confinement is a textbook example of an ex post facto law. If the object or purpose of the Kansas law had been to provide treatment but the treatment provisions were adopted as a sham or mere pretext, there would have been an indication of the forbidden purpose to punish. The Court's opinion gives a full and complete explanation why an ex post facto challenge based on this contention cannot succeed in the case before us. All this, however, concerns Hendricks alone. My brief, further comment is to caution against dangers inherent when a civil confinement law is used in conjunction with the criminal process, whether or not the law is given retroactive application.

It seems the dissent, too, would validate the Kansas statute as to persons who committed the crime after its enactment, and it might even validate the statute as to Hendricks, assuming a reasonable level of treatment. As all Members of the Court seem to agree, then, the power of the state to confine persons who, by reason of a mental disease or mental abnormality, constitute a real, continuing, and serious danger to society is well established. Confinement of such individuals is permitted even if it is pursuant to a statute enacted after the crime has been committed and the offender has begun serving, or has all but completed serving, a penal sentence, provided there is no object or purpose to punish. The Kansas law, with its attendant protections, including yearly review and review at any time at the instance of the person confined, is within this pattern and tradition of civil confinement. In this case, the mental abnormality, pedophilia, is at least described in the DSM-IV.

Notwithstanding its civil attributes, the practical effect of the Kansas law may be to impose confinement for life. At this stage of medical knowledge, although future treatments cannot be predicted, psychiatrists or other professionals engaged in treating pedophilia may be reluctant to find measurable success in treatment even after a long period and may be unable to predict that no serious danger will come from release of the detainee.

A common response to this may be, "A life term is exactly what the sentence should have been anyway," or, in the words of a Kansas task force member, "So be it." The point, however, is not how long Hendricks and others like him should serve a criminal sentence. With his criminal record, after all, a life term may well have been the only sentence appropriate to protect society and vindicate the wrong. The concern instead is whether it is the criminal system or the civil system which should make the decision in the first place. If the civil system is used simply to impose punishment after the State makes an improvident plea bargain on the criminal side, then it is not performing its proper function. These concerns persist whether the civil confinement statute is put on the books before or after the offense. We should bear in mind that while incapacitation is a goal common to both the criminal and civil systems of confinement, retribution and general deterrence are reserved for the criminal system alone.

On the record before us, the Kansas civil statute conforms to our precedents. If, however, civil confinement were to become a mechanism for retribution or general deterrence, or if it were shown that mental abnormality is too imprecise a category to offer a solid basis for concluding that civil detention is justified, our precedents would not suffice to validate it.

Justice BREYER, with whom Justices STEVENS and SOUTER *join*, **and with whom Justice GINSBURG joins as to Parts II and III**, *dissenting.*

Kansas, concedes that Hendricks' condition is treatable; yet the Act did not provide Hendricks (or others like him) with any treatment until after his release date from prison and only inadequate treatment thereafter. These, and certain other, special features of the Act convince me that it was not simply an effort to commit Hendricks civilly, but rather an effort to inflict further punishment upon him. The Ex Post Facto Clause therefore prohibits the Act's application to Hendricks, who committed his crimes prior to its enactment.

* * *

II

Kansas' 1994 Act violates the Federal Constitution's prohibition of "any. . . ex post facto Law" if it "inflicts" upon Hendricks "a greater punishment" than did the law "annexed to" his "crime[s]" when he "committed" those crimes in 1984. The majority agrees that the Clause " 'forbids the application of any new punitive measure to a crime already consummated.' " But it finds the Act is not "punitive." With respect to that basic question, I disagree with the maj

In this circumstance, with important features of the Act pointing in opposite directions, I would place particular importance upon those features that would likely distinguish between a basically punitive and a basically nonpunitive purpose. And I note that the Court, in an earlier civil commitment case, looked primarily to the law's concern for treatment as an important distinguishing feature. I do not believe that a particular law's lack of concern for treatment, by itself, is enough to make an incapacitative law punitive. But, when a State believes that treatment does exist, and then couples that admission with a legislatively required delay of such treatment until a person is at the end of his jail term (so that further incapacitation is therefore necessary), such a legislative scheme begins to look punitive.

The focus upon treatment, as a kind of touchstone helping to distinguish civil from punitive purposes, is not surprising, for one would expect a nonpunitive statutory scheme to confine, not simply in order to protect, but also in order to cure. That is to say, one would expect a nonpunitively motivated legislature that confines because of a dangerous mental abnormality to seek to help the individual himself overcome that abnormality (at least insofar as professional treatment for the abnormality exists and is potentially helpful, as Kansas, supported by some groups of mental health professionals, argues is the case here). Conversely, a statutory scheme that provides confinement that does not reasonably fit a practically available, medically oriented treatment objective, more likely reflects a primarily punitive legislative purpose.

. . . [T]he Kansas statute insofar as it applies to previously convicted offenders, such as Hendricks, commits, confines, and treats those offenders after they have served virtually their entire criminal sentence. That time-related circumstance seems deliberate. The Act explicitly defers diagnosis, evaluation, and commitment proceedings until a few weeks prior to the "anticipated release" of a previously convicted offender from prison. But why, one might ask, does the Act not commit and require treatment of sex offenders sooner, say soon after they begin to serve their sentences?

An Act that simply seeks confinement, of course, would not need to begin civil commitment proceedings sooner. Such an Act would have to begin proceedings only when an offender's prison term ends, threatening his release from the confinement that imprisonment assures. But it is difficult to see why rational legislators who seek treatment would write the Act in this way providing treatment years after the criminal act that indicated its necessity. And it is particularly difficult to see why legislators who specifically wrote into the statute a finding that "prognosis for rehabilitating. . . in a prison setting is poor" would leave an offender in that setting for months or years before beginning treatment. This is to say, the timing provisions of the statute confirm the Kansas Supreme Court's view that treatment was not a particularly important legislative objective.

[A] state is free to commit those who are dangerous and mentally ill in order to treat them. Nor does my decision preclude a State from deciding that a certain subset of people are mentally ill, dangerous, and untreatable, and that confinement of this subset is therefore necessary. . . . But when a State decides offenders can be treated and confines an offender to provide that treatment, but then refuses to provide it, the refusal to treat while a person is fully incapacitated begins to look punitive.

* * *

In *Kennedy v. Mendoza-Martinez*, this Court listed seven factors that helped it determine whether a particular statute was primarily punitive for purposes of applying the Fifth and Sixth Amendments. Those factors include whether a sanction involves an affirmative restraint, how history has regarded it, whether it applies to behavior already a crime, the need for a finding of scienter, its relationship to a traditional aim of punishment, the presence of a nonpunitive alternative purpose, and whether it is excessive in relation to that purpose. This Court has said that these seven factors are "neither exhaustive nor dispositive," but nonetheless "helpful." Paraphrasing them here, I believe the Act before us involves an affirmative restraint historically regarded as punishment; imposed upon behavior already a crime after a finding of scienter; which restraint, namely confinement, serves a traditional aim of punishment, does not primarily serve an alternative purpose (such as treatment) and is excessive in relation to any alternative purpose assigned.

This is to say that each of the factors the Court mentioned in *Mendoza-Martinez* on balance argues here in favor of a constitutional characterization as "punishment." It is not to say that I have found "a single 'formula' for identifying those legislative changes that have a sufficient effect on substantive crimes or punishments to fall within the constitutional prohibition." We have not previously done so, and I do not do so here.

III

To find that the confinement the Act imposes upon Hendricks is "punishment" is to find a violation of the Ex Post Facto Clause.

The statutory provisions before us amount to punishment primarily because, as I have said, the legislature did not tailor the statute to fit the nonpunitive civil aim of treatment, which it concedes exists in Hendricks' case.

I therefore would affirm the judgment below.

NOTES AND QUESTIONS.

1. Does *Hendricks* hold that the Constitution permits civil commitment of dangerous but non-treatable persons? After *Salerno*, page 52 of the casebook, is there reason to doubt the constitutionality of preventative detention for persons such as Hendricks? Does the length of detention (limited period pending trial in *Salerno,* indefinite period of time in *Hendricks*) make a difference as a constitutional matter?

2. Was the commitment of Hendricks "punishment" under Hart's definition, page 40 of the casebook?

3. As a policy matter, is the civil commitment mechanism reflected in the *Hendricks* case a good idea? Would it be a better idea to simply increase the term of imprisonment for "sexually violent predators"?

4. In *Allen v. Illinois*, 478 U.S. 364 (1986), the Supreme Court held that commitment of "sexually dangerous" person for purposes of "care and treatment" constituted a "non-punitive" disposition and thus not within the purview of the Fifth Amendment privilege against self-incrimination. While the commitment statute at issue in *Allen* was not triggered unless the state proved at least one act of sexual assault, the Court saw such proof and antecedent conduct as evidence not of an attempt to punish past misdeeds but to show the accused's mental condition and to predict future behavior.

5. For critical commentary on *Hendricks* and "sexual violent predator" legislation, See, e.g., Logan, *The Ex Post Facto Clause and the Jurisprudence of Punishment*, 35 Am. Crim. L. Rev. 1261 (1998); La Fond, *Washington's Sexually Violent Predator Law: A Deliberate Misuse of the Therapeutic State for Social Control*, 15 Puget Sound L. Rev. 655 (1992).

[2] Punishment versus Coercive Therapy

IN RE DE LA O

Supreme Court of California

59 Cal.2d 128, 28 Cal. Rptr. 489, 378 P.2d 793 (1963)

SCHAUER, Justice

This matter is before us on an order to show cause issued upon an application for writ of *habeas corpus* filed on behalf of David De La O, who is confined in the California Rehabilitation Center.

Petitioner was charged by criminal complaint in the municipal court with a violation of Health and Safety Code section 11721, a misdemeanor, in that on a particular date "in the City of Pasadena, County of Los Angeles, State of California" he "did wilfully and unlawfully use and be addicted to the unlawful use of narcotics. . . . " Petitioner waived jury trial; he was found guilty as charged, and a motion for new trial was denied. Thereafter that court on its own motion suspended proceedings in the criminal action over which it had jurisdiction, and certified petitioner to the superior court for proceedings therein pursuant to Penal Code section 6450.[1] No judgment imposing imprisonment, fine, or other penal sanction has been entered in the criminal case.

The superior court conducted a hearing and examination in accordance with the terms of Penal Code section 6450. Petitioner was represented by counsel and evidence was received. . . . At the conclusion of the hearing the superior court made appropriate findings and entered an order adjudging petitioner to be "a narcotic drug addict within the meaning of Section 6450 of the Penal Code" and committing him to the custody of the Director of Corrections "for placement as provided for by law, for a period of five years, except as earlier discharge is provided for by law." Petitioner's demand for a jury trial in the superior court on the issue of addiction was denied.

Petitioner contends that the subject statute (Pen. Code, § 6450, and related sections) is unconstitutional because it provides criminal penalties for an illness—narcotics addiction—thus imposing cruel and unusual punishment within the meaning of *Robinson v. California* (1962), 370 U.S. 660 [*infra* this book at page 320]. . . .

In *Robinson* . . . the United States Supreme Court held unconstitutional as there applied the provision of Health and Safety Code section 11721 making it a criminal offense to "be addicted to the use of narcotics." The precise language of the subject holding is . . . "We hold that a state law which *imprisons* a person thus afflicted *as a criminal,* even though he has never touched any narcotic drug *within the State* or been guilty of any irregular behavior *there,* inflicts a cruel and unusual punishment in violation of the Fourteenth Amendment." (Italics added.) Yet in that decision . . . the high court recognized "The broad power of a State to regulate the narcotic drugs traffic *within its borders*" (italics added), and observed that "Such regulation, it can be assumed, could take a variety of valid forms. A State might impose

---

[1] Penal Code section 6450 provides in pertinent part: "Upon conviction of a defendant of any crime in a municipal or justice court, if it appears to the judge that the defendant may be addicted or by reason of repeated use of narcotics may be in imminent danger of becoming addicted to narcotics, such judge shall adjourn the proceedings or suspend the imposition of the sentence and certify the defendant to the superior court.

"The superior court shall direct the sheriff to file a petition to ascertain if such defendant is addicted to narcotics or is in imminent danger of becoming addicted thereto. Proceedings shall be conducted in substantial compliance with Sections 5353, 5053, 5054, and 5055 of the Welfare and Institutions Code.

"If, after a hearing and examination, the judge shall find that the defendant charged is a narcotic drug addict, or by reason of repeated use of narcotics is in imminent danger of becoming addicted thereto, and is not ineligible for the program under the application of Section 6452 hereof, he shall make an order committing such defendant to the custody of the Director of Corrections for a period of five years, except as this chapter permits earlier discharge. If, upon the hearing, the judge shall find that the defendant is not a narcotic drug addict and is not in imminent danger of becoming addicted to narcotics, he shall so certify and return the defendant to the municipal or justice court which certified such defendant to the superior court for such further proceedings as the judge of such municipal or justice court deems warranted."

criminal sanctions, for example, against the unauthorized manufacture, prescription, sale, purchase, or possession of narcotics within its borders. In the interest of discouraging the violation of such laws, or in the interest of the general health or welfare of its inhabitants, a State might establish a *program of compulsory treatment* for those addicted to narcotics. Such a program of treatment might require *periods of involuntary confinement*. And *penal sanctions* might be imposed for failure to comply with established *compulsory treatment* procedures." (Italics added.)

We recognize at once that an essential part of the procedural foundation for petitioner's current restraint is his conviction of violating Health and Safety Code section 11721. We note also that petitioner's "status" or "chronic condition" of being (in California) unlawfully "addicted to the use of narcotics" . . . is considered to constitute a sufficient ground for conviction of violating section 11721 and therefore to *prima facie* establish the status of eligibility for initiation of the procedures contemplated by Penal Code section 6450. The case at bench, however, differs from *Robinson* in these, among other, vital respects: (1) no judgment of conviction of violating Health and Safety Code section 11721 has here been entered; (2) petitioner is not being held under any penal sanction—rather, the criminal action is suspended; and (3) he is being held under involuntary restraint for compulsory treatment and rehabilitation procedures as provided by Penal Code section 6450.

The issue is whether the statutory scheme here challenged (a) "imprisons" petitioner "as a criminal," or (b) constitutes "compulsory treatment" of petitioner as a sick person requiring "periods of involuntary confinement." If the former, it would be unconstitutional under Robinson as cruel and unusual punishment . . . if the latter, it would be valid under the same decision as a constitutionally permissible exercise of the state's power to regulate the narcotic drug traffic.

The criteria by which this issue is to be determined, however, are not so easily defined. In *Robinson* little difficulty was experienced by the majority in holding on the issues then before them that Health and Safety Code section 11721 imposed criminal penalties, in view of that statute's provision that any person "convicted" of a violation thereof "is guilty of a misdemeanor" and shall be "sentenced to serve" a term of "not less than 90 days nor more than one year in the county jail." No such provision appears in the measure (Pen. Code § 6450) under which petitioner is currently restrained. Rather, analysis of the present statute—its origin, purpose, terms, operation, and effect—discloses not just one but a number of factors to be considered in this connection, of varying relevance and weight.

The court rejected petitioner's arguments that Section 6450 imposed criminal sanctions because (1) the statute appears in that part of the state Code entitled "Of Imprisonment and the Death Penalty" and (2) custody rests under the jurisdiction of the Department of Corrections.]

Petitioner stresses the fact that his commitment is for a minimum of six months and a maximum of five years. . . . It is argued that neither the minimum nor the maximum is in any way related to the treatment or rehabilitation of the addict as a sick person, and hence that these requirements show a legislative intent to imprison the addict as a criminal. While superficially appealing, the argument does not withstand analysis in the light of the facts of narcotics addiction and rehabilitation.

First, there is medical evidence that the addict will benefit from a minimum period of confinement and control during which he is deprived of narcotics, thus permitting the withdrawal symptoms to run their course and alleviate at least his physiological dependence on drugs. In recognition of this fact, the Legislature has long provided for just such a minimum term of confinement under the Narcotic Drug Addicts Law of the Welfare and Institutions Code—the provisions of which were characterized as "civil procedures" by the Court in *Robinson*. . . . Once it is conceded that *some* minimum period of confinement of the narcotics addict is constitutionally permissible, the precise length of that period is largely a matter for the reasonable judgment of the Legislature. Here that period is fixed at six months. It is true that the above cited provisions of the Welfare and Institutions Code fix the period at three months, but the Legislature is allowed some leeway in translating into exact figures such medically imprecise concepts as the minimum beneficial term of confinement. Indeed, these same Welfare and Institutions Code provisions originally fixed the minimum at eight months . . . and at the federal narcotics hospitals at Lexington and Fort Worth the recommended minimum period of confinement believed necessary for rehabilitation is four to six months. . . . In the circumstances, the Legislature's choice of the figure of six months does not appear to be unreasonable.

Second, the fact that a maximum of five years is placed on the term of confinement does not make it any the less a confinement that is essentially for an indeterminate period. Each of the relevant sections of the subject statute provides that the addict shall be committed for the fixed period "except as this chapter permits earlier discharge." The proviso refers, of course, to the procedures set up for parole and subsequent discharge from the program. Similarly indeterminate commitments are authorized for narcotic drug addicts confined under Welfare and Institutions Code section 5355 ("for an indeterminate period of not less than three months nor more than two years"); and indeterminate commitments without fixed maximum terms are provided for mentally ill persons, . . . sexual psychopaths . . . and defective or psychopathic delinquents. Thus the use of the device of indeterminate commitment in the subject statute appears neither novel nor invalid per se.

* * *

When the indeterminate commitment aspect of the subject statute is thus viewed in its proper light, there is obviously no merit in petitioner's further contention that he has been "sentenced to serve five years" for a misdemeanor in violation of Penal Code section 19a (one-year maximum for misdemeanors).

It will be observed, however, that whereas the maximum period of confinement of a person committed under Penal Code section 6450 (such as petitioner here) is five years, that maximum is fixed at ten years in the case of one committed under section 6451 (applicable to a defendant convicted of "any crime in any superior court"). It is contended that this longer maximum term for felons can be justified only as a penal sanction. But "It is generally accepted that addiction is largely the result of personal inadequacy, emotional instability, and social maladjustment" [Eldridge, *Narcotics and The Law* (1962), p.123.] As the author points out (*ibid.,* fn. 3), "Such causal factors actually play a large part in most criminal activity." If a principal cause of narcotics addiction is the psycho-social maladjustment of the user, and if a person convicted of a felony tends to suffer from greater psycho-social maladjustment than one convicted of a misdemeanor, then it would not seem unreasonable to expect that a longer period of readjustment and rehabilitation may be necessary for the felon-addict than for the misdemeanant-addict.

[The court discussed and rejected petitioner's arguments that section 6450 imposed criminal sanctions because (1)the penal code provides that a person committed under 6450 shall be deemed a prisoner committed to state prison for purposes of laws prohibiting escape; (2)the same agency that determines parole for convicts in state prison passes on his parole; and (3)he was processed through the same reception center as convicts going to prison, his moustache shaved, his fingerprints taken, his mail censored, and his visitation privileges limited.

Among the court's reasons for rejecting such claims were (1)the stated purpose of the facility housing petitioner includes "segregation, confinement, employment, education, treatment and rehabilitation of addicts and those in imminent danger of becoming addicts"; (2)the commitment procedures do not involve trial by jury as in criminal cases but rather incorporate the special civil procedures of the Welfare and Institutions Code; and (3)similar commitment steps apply to those not charged with crime, including persons voluntarily committing themselves.]

[Petitioner alleges that he] "is being incarcerated and treated in the same manner as if he were a felon." It appears, however, that the branch of the California Rehabilitation Center where petitioner is confined is physically and administratively distinct from the other facilities at Chino and consists of 16 buildings including dormitories, gymnasium, mess hall, academic and vocational buildings, and others; that the California Rehabilitation Center employs a full-time psychiatrist and professionally trained counselors and therapists; and that petitioner is given daily group therapy and twice weekly intensive therapy in small units of not more than 15 men, all under the direction of trained counselors. In addition, the California Rehabilitation Center provides a specially selected vocational and academic program.

. . . From the declarations of purpose and other provisions discussed hereinabove it appears that in enacting the subject statute the Legislature intended to create a new program for the confinement (which in truth is a quarantine rather than penal sanction), treatment, and rehabilitation of narcotics addicts. . . .

[W]e are of the opinion that the demonstrably civil purpose, mechanism, and operation of the program outweigh its external "criminal" indicia, and hence that petitioner's commitment and confinement thereunder do not constitute cruel and unusual punishment within the meaning of *Robinson v. California*. . . .

. . . The order to show cause is discharged and the petition for habeas corpus *is denied.*

WASSERSTROM, *SOME PROBLEMS WITH THEORIES OF PUNISHMENT*

Justice and Punishment 173, 178–79 (1977)

(J. Cederblom and W. Blizek, eds.)

What I propose is that for the purpose of distinguishing between some of the clearest cases of punishment and some of the clearest cases of, what might be termed, unpleasant coerced treatments (and one must do this if we are to assess the view that wrongdoers ought always to be treated rather than punished), the following constitutes a relatively helpful elucidation of many of the key features.

I think that we would be punishing someone if:

1. We believed that he or she had done some action; and
2. We believed that he or she was responsible at the time he or she acted; and
3. We believed that his or her action was blameworthy; and
4. We publicly inflicted some unpleasantness upon him or her; and
5. We publicly inflicted that unpleasantness upon him or her in virtue of the fact that he or she did the action in question, that he or she was responsible when he or she acted, and that he or she was blameworthy for having so acted; and furthermore
6. We determined—within at least some limits—at the time of our decision to punish what the nature and magnitude of the unpleasantness would be; and, finally,
7. In making the determination we would regard any of the following factors as relevant—although none need be decisive:
   a. The immorality of the actor and his or her action,
   b. The way in which others similarly situated were dealt with,
   c. The probable effect of the punishment upon the actor's future conduct,
   d. The probable effect upon others of punishing the actor.

As for treatment, we would be treating someone if:

1. We believed that he or she was in a certain state or condition, and
2. We acted in a certain way toward or upon him or her, and
3. We acted in this way in virtue of the fact that acting in this way would alter his or her condition in a manner beneficial to him or her, and

4. The decision as to what constituted appropriate treatment was always subject to revision upon a showing either:

   a. That an alternative response would be more beneficial to him or her, or

   b. That his or her condition has altered so as no longer to require that, or any other, further response.

IN RE FELDER

Family Court, Onondoga County

93 Misc. 2d 369, 402 N.Y.S.2d 528 (1978)

EDWARD J. MCLAUGHLIN, Judge.

This juvenile delinquency proceeding involves a designated felony pursuant to the *Juvenile Justice Reform Act of* 1976 (L. 1976, ch. 878), N.Y. Family Court Act §§ 711–767, 29A *McKinney's Consolidated Laws* 1977. It presents a case of first impression for this court. Respondent, a boy of fifteen, allegedly committed a robbery in the first degree, Penal Law § 160.15, a designated felony. FCA § 712(h). When the case came before the Court, the Respondent moved for a jury trial, asserting that under *Baldwin v. New York,* 399 U.S. 66 (1970), an individual charged with a crime where the penalty could exceed six months imprisonment is entitled to a jury trial. The respondent alleged that since he can be confined in a secure facility for a period of time up to twelve months, pursuant to section 753-69 a(4)(a)(ii) of the Family Court Act, the *Baldwin* doctrine applied, and he is entitled to a trial by jury.

On the other hand, the petitioner alleged that the United States Supreme Court decision in *McKeiver v. Pennsylvania,* 403 U.S. 528 (1971), is controlling. *McKeiver* holds that a juvenile charged with a delinquency, which precludes, by definition, criminal consequences and tried in a civil court, does not have a due process right to a jury trial. Petitioner further alleged that while New York is not constitutionally precluded from granting a jury trial under *McKeiver,* it has determined not to do so. . . .

The issue before the court, then, is whether the instant proceeding is controlled by *McKeiver* or by *Baldwin.* Specifically, the question turns on whether this is a juvenile proceeding within the meaning of *McKeiver,* or, whether so many of the attributes of a juvenile proceeding have been discarded that the proceeding is in effect "criminal" in nature and thus within the ambit of *Baldwin.*

A. IS A DESIGNATED FELONY PROCEEDING A JUVENILE PROCEEDING?

The concept of designated felony was created as a part of the *Juvenile Justice Reform* Act of 1976.

The Legislature has chosen to label this new "designated felony concept" as a "juvenile" proceeding. It is axiomatic that this court is not bound by that designation if, in fact, the new proceeding is indeed a criminal proceeding. The Supreme Court recognized this principle in *Trop v. Dulles,* 356 U.S. 86, at 94 (1958), when the Court taught us:

But the Government contends that this statute does not impose a penalty. . . . We are told this is so because a committee . . . said it "technically is not a penal law." How simple would be the tasks of constitutional adjudication and of law generally if specific problems could be solved by inspection of labels pasted on them. . . .

B. BACKGROUND OF THE JUVENILE JUSTICE SYSTEM

The fundamental substantive distinction between a juvenile proceeding and a criminal proceeding is that a juvenile disposition is limited to treatment, while a criminal proceeding may impose punishment regardless of whether the punishment results in retribution and/or, deterrence. [The Court reviewed the history of the juvenile court movement as a rehabilitative alternative to the criminal law.]

* * *

It is against this background that *McKeiver v. Pennsylvania, supra,* must be viewed. It is true that *McKeiver* stated that in a juvenile proceeding trial by jury is not a constitutional requirement. The Court specifically refused to abandon the salutary goals of the juvenile system and rejected the jury trial because it could "tend once again to place the juvenile squarely in the routine of the criminal process." . . . Indeed, the Court acknowledged that when a child is adjudicated as a juvenile, but treated as a criminal, an inconsistency results, for the Court stated: "Of course there have been abuses. . . . We refrain from saying at this point that these abuses are of a constitutional dimension." . . . In effect, the Court deferred until a more appropriate occasion the determination of when a juvenile disposition fails to meet the rehabilitative premise of the juvenile system. The determination in *McKeiver* that in a juvenile proceeding a jury trial is not required, is, therefore, necessarily limited to those proceedings that are juvenile in nature. Thus, there is no requirement of a jury trial in family court where the disposition is rehabilitative and non-penal. When, however, the protections provided to the juvenile criminal offender have been so eroded away that what is actually a punishment is characterized as a treatment, an abuse of constitutional dimension has occurred, and a jury trial is required before punishment, although appropriate, may be inflicted.

C. BACKGROUND OF THE 1976 ACT

In response to the reported increase in the frequency and severity of crimes committed by juveniles, the Legislature in the 1976 session enacted the *Juvenile Justice Reform Act* (L. 1976, ch. 878). This bill significantly amended Article 7 of the Family Court Act. The express purpose of Article 7 was redefined to include, for the first time, consideration of the needs of the community: "In any juvenile procedure under this article, the court shall consider the needs and best interests of the respondent as well as the need for protection of the community." FCA § 711. To this end, the Legislature created restrictive placement. Rejecting proposals to transfer seriously violent juveniles to the adult criminal system, the Legislature adopted restrictive placement as a method of dealing with the juveniles within the juvenile system.

D. AN ANALYSIS OF THE 1976 ACT

A significant change made by the *Juvenile Justice Reform Act* is the requirement that restrictive placement may be ordered for a juvenile found to have committed a designated felony, when the court determines that a juvenile requires such restrictive placement. FCA § 753-a. Once restrictive placement is ordered by the court, the delinquent must remain in the placement for twelve months, if the placement results from an adjudication on a Class A designated felony, or for six months, if the placement results from the adjudication of any designated felony. FCA § 753-a(3)(a)(ii); (4)(a)(ii). Further, during the period of restrictive placement, the right to petition the court to stay the execution, to set aside, modify, or vacate the disposition is suspended. It is this suspension of the provisions of part six, Article 7, of the Family Court Act which distinguishes a restrictive placement disposition from all other dispositions under Article 7. Thus, the Legislature has created a definite sentence of placement nearly indistinguishable from definite sentences imposed upon adults under section 70.20(2) of the Penal Law.

Further, in mandating the minimum period of restrictive placement, when restrictive placement has been found to be needed at all, the Legislature has introduced two other concepts of the criminal justice process previously unknown in the juvenile system. First, the length of the commitment is determined by the act committed rather than by the needs of the child, and second, the sentence is mandatory. In effect, the Legislature has determined that a child who at the time of his dispositional hearing requires restrictive placement will continue to require restrictive placement for the entire period of the minimum sentence. Prior to the enactment of this statute, the court was only required to determine that at the time of the dispositional hearing the needs of the child were for placement in an institution and that at any time during that initial period, if the child was successfully rehabilitated, he was entitled to release. Consistent with this philosophy of treatment was the provision that if at the end of the initial placement the child was not successfully rehabilitated, then, the period of placement could be extended. In effect, once the court makes a finding that restrictive placement is needed at the time of the disposition, the act then mandates a minimum sentence, a result which is more harsh on the juvenile than is the criminal procedure for the adult who is entitled to an indeterminate sentence in nearly all cases. . . .

The distinction between indeterminate and determinate sentencing is not semantic, but indicates fundamentally different public policies. Indeterminate sentencing is based upon notions of rehabilitation, while determinate sentencing is based upon a desire for retribution or punishment.

In his vigorous dissent in *In re Gault,* 387 U.S. 1 (1967), Mr. Justice Stewart succinctly distinguished the purpose and mission of the juvenile system of justice from the purpose and mission of the criminal system. "The object of the one [juvenile] is correcting a condition. The object of the other [criminal] is conviction and punishment for a criminal act." . . . By mandating restrictive placement in a secure facility for a minimum of six months, the Legislature has created a disposition that more nearly resembles a punishment than a treatment and, thereby, has blurred the clearly distinct objectives of the juvenile justice system with those of the criminal justice system.

* * *

E. TREATMENT

The Juvenile Justice Reform Act requires that treatment be available at restrictive placement facilities. The availability and quality of treatment available to the respondent is not at issue here. What is at issue is the mandatory time period required for treatment. . . .

* * *

Juveniles . . . have a right to treatment. . . . Moreover, one court has found that " 'the right to treatment' includes the right to *individualized* care and treatment." *Nelson v. Heyne*, 491 F.2d 352, at 360 (7th Cir.), *cert. denied*, 417 U.S. 976, . . . (1974) (emphasis in the original). The reasoning of the court in *Nelson* is helpful in analyzing time limited restrictive placement:

> Because children differ in their need for rehabilitation, individual need for treatment will differ . . . Without a program of individual treatment the result may be that the juveniles will not be rehabilitated, but warehoused, and that at the termination of detention they will likely be incapable of taking their proper places in free society; their interests and those of the state thereby being defeated.

Id.

Clearly, treatment may result in a cure in six days, or in six weeks, or in six months, or in one year, or never! By setting a mandatory minimum time period for restrictive placement, treatment becomes indistinguishable from punishment.

* * *

[While it found the sanction to be punitive and not therapeutic, the court refrained from ordering a jury trial which was clearly precluded without statutory authorization. Instead, the court forbade restrictive placements in designated felony proceedings tried without juries.]

NOTES AND QUESTIONS

1. Other New York courts disagree with *Felder* and hold that juveniles do not enjoy a right to jury trial when subjected to the sanctions imposed in designated felony proceedings. *People v. Young*, 99 Misc. 2d 328, 416 N.Y.S.2d. 171 (Fam. Ct., Monroe County 1979); *In re William M.*, 90 Misc. 2d 173, 393 N.Y.S.2d 535 (Fam. Ct., Kings County 1977).

2. If the *Felder* court is correct in concluding that therapeutic sanctions are inherently "indeterminate" and punitive ones "determinate," is the sanction in *De La O* (commitment for six months to five years) therefore "punishment?"

3. For a discussion of the concept of punishment and its relation to the juvenile justice system, see Gardner, *Punishment and Juvenile Justice: A Conceptual Framework for Assessing Constitutional Rights of Youthful Offenders,* 35 Vand. L. Rev. 791 (1982).

[3] Punishment versus Regulatory Penalties

BROWN V. MULTNOMAH COUNTY DISTRICT COURT

Supreme Court of Oregon

280 Or 95, 570 P.2d 52 (1977)

Linde, J.

In the course of revising the Oregon Vehicle Code in 1975 (Or. L. 1975, ch. 451) the legislative assembly placed the first offense of driving a motor vehicle under the influence of intoxicants (DUII) into a statutory category of "traffic infractions" as distinguished from "traffic crimes." ORS 484.365. The question before us is whether, in the light of the entire statutory scheme, this offense may be tried without the . . . safeguards guaranteed defendants in criminal prosecutions [under the Oregon Constitution].

Charged in district court with a first offense DUII, petitioner moved for an order appointing counsel for him as an indigent, granting him trial by jury, and requiring the state to prove its case beyond a reasonable doubt. These rights are expressly excluded in the trial of traffic infractions under the code, ORS 484.390(1), ORS 484.375(1), (2), and the district court denied all three demands. . . .

II

* * *

It is beyond dispute that the legislature may define and enforce obligatory conduct by means other than the criminal law, as it does in taxation, or injunctive orders, or in creating private remedies, which may extend beyond compensatory damages. It may employ licenses—in effect, exemptions from a prohibition—conditioned upon prescribed qualifications and upon adherence to prescribed standards of conduct. It may take custody of persons in involuntary commitment or juvenile proceedings. . . . [I]t may decide to repeal criminal prohibitions, to define civil obligations enforceable by the state and its agencies, and to replace one with the other, so long as constitutional limits are observed.

The Oregon Vehicle Code represents a systematic effort to match legal sanctions and procedures with the types of conduct to be regulated. In some respects it is a hybrid of elements drawn from civil, criminal, and administrative law models. It treats fines, forfeitures, and loss of licenses as "civil penalties," to be imposed for "traffic infractions" either by administrative acceptance of voluntary payment, . . . or by a court upon a trial without a jury and upon proof "by a preponderance of the evidence," the standard used in civil cases. . . . It authorizes the judge to suspend a driver's license for nonpayment of a fine. . . . It allows appeals by the prosecution as well as the defendant. . . . It treats as crimes, triable by criminal procedure, all "major," . . . or "serious," . . . traffic offenses other than DUII. . . . But it extends many of the typically criminal procedures of arrest, detention, release on bail or recognizance, and plea to traffic infractions as well as to traffic crimes. . . . On the other hand, it excludes infractions as a basis of legal disabilities or disadvantages attached to convictions of crime, . . . including impeachment as a witness. . . . As we have said, the use of these diverse elements in devising a system of traffic laws is within the state's discretion unless it departs from a constitutional standard. . . .

III

There is no easy test for when the imposition of a sanction is a "criminal prosecution" within the meaning of the constitutional guarantees. The starting point, of course, is the law under which the sanction is imposed. When the legislature has defined conduct as a criminal offense, it is a criminal offense for constitutional purposes even if the same consequences could have been attached to the same conduct by civil or administrative proceedings. But it does not follow that a law can avoid this result simply by avoiding the term "criminal" in defining the conduct to be penalized. Constitutional guarantees have more substance than that.

A number of indicia have been used to determine whether an ostensibly civil penalty proceeding remains a "criminal prosecution" for constitutional purposes. . . . All are relevant, but none is conclusive on what we believe is the ultimate determination.

A. Type of Offense

On the whole, it is not very helpful to refer to the "gravity" or the "nature" of the offense as a criterion, since this is the legislative judgment which the state claims to have made in "decriminalizing" it. The offense may have been a crime at common law, or at the time the constitution was adopted, or for a long time thereafter. Similarly, it may involve traditional elements of *mens rea* or a lower degree of culpability. These characteristics can bear on whether the downgrading marks a genuine change in the public assessment of the conduct or merely seeks procedural short-cuts, but they do not mean that what was once a crime can never be regulated by other means.

Traffic offenses as we know them are largely a 20th-century phenomenon. They may well have been assigned to the courts in criminal form as much because the form was familiar and the courts available as by any deliberate choice among alternatives. This does not prevent a later decision not to treat traffic offenses as crimes.

B. Penalty

The prescribed penalty is generally regarded as the single most important criterion, at least when it involves imprisonment. Indeed, "decriminalization" of one-time criminal offenses ordinarily assumes that the sanction of imprisonment must be abandoned, and the state's main argument is that the line between traffic infractions and traffic crimes can be defended by this criterion alone. We agree that "imprisonment" cannot be used as "punishment" for a civil offense; but here, too, as much depends on the significance of those words as on the confinement itself. The law employs compulsory confinement in looking after persons suffering from mental incapacity or infectious disease, or children in need of supervision or protection, in securing material witnesses or aliens awaiting deportation, without turning these into criminal cases, so long as the detention is for a non-punitive purpose and ends with that purpose. It is the punitive use of detention, not the detention as such, that defines the criminal offense.

By the same token, the absence of potential imprisonment does not conclusively prove a punishment non-criminal. . . . [A] large fine may be as severe, in practical terms, as a short imprisonment, and so strikingly severe as to carry the same punitive significance.

The Oregon Vehicle Code presently sets the maximum fines for traffic infractions at $50 for a Class D infraction, $100 for Class C, $250 for Class B, and $1,000 for a Class A infraction. . . . Class A includes only two named offenses: Driving while under the influence of intoxicants and failure to perform the duties of a driver involved in an accident resulting only in property damage, . . . although others may fall into that class. . . .

Courts are understandably reluctant to pick a particular sum of money as the rigid measure of a defendant's constitutional rights, for this measure has less history and much less stability than the six months of jail chosen as the measure of a federal petty offense . . . Two federal courts of appeals have recently drawn the line at $500 . . . If a line must be drawn, this is plausible, even if it cannot be conclusive nor permanent. It proves little about a $1,000 fine for driving under the influence of intoxicants that much larger civil penalties are levied against business enterprises for violations of various regulations in the course of business. We deal here with fines payable by ordinary individuals for misconduct unrelated to the pursuit of a profitable activity, not by regulated truckers or cabdrivers, and indeed with the rights of a petitioner who claims the right to counsel as an indigent. In this context a $1,000 fine, if not in itself a criminal rather than civil penalty, must be at the margin of legislative discretion. At the least it is strong evidence of the punitive significance that the legislature meant to give this fine.

C. Collateral Consequences

No similar significance attaches to the direct or collateral suspension or revocation of a driver's license for a traffic offense. The offense does not become "criminal" rather than "civil" merely because the loss of a license is a great inconvenience, so long as the suspension or revocation reflects a legislative, judicial, or administrative judgment that a traffic offender should not continue to drive. Again the question is whether the deprivation is regulatory or another form of punishment, as for instance its imposition for nonpayment of a fine. . . .

D. Punitive Significance

Evidence of punitive intent has led the United States Supreme Court to hold ostensibly nonpenal sanctions to the constitutional standards for crimes. . . . Th[e][*Mendoza-Martinez*] test [*supra,* p.52] requires courts to face the issue of the criteria of "punishment," one of the oldest and most difficult issues in law. It is not made easier when phrased in terms of the purpose of the law. The purposes of criminal law (apart from incapacitating dangerous offenders by confinement) are customarily stated to be "retribution and deterrence" meaning deterrence both of the individual defendant and of persons in his situation generally. But deterrence is equally a purpose of other sanctions, so that "punishment" cannot be deduced from it, and retribution is purposive only in the sense of a legislative aim to reflect the outrage of the public or the victims of the condemned acts. And this aim, in turn, is confined by the constitutional prohibition against vindic-tive justice. "What distinguishes a criminal from a civil sanction and all that distinguishes it," a leading scholar concluded, "is the judgment of community condemnation which accompanies and justifies its imposition."[14] The stigma of that condemnation can accompany the imposition of a sanction whether it is imprisonment, a fine, or something else; and its presence in a judgment of conviction, as much as the potential sanction itself, makes the right to a jury peculiarly appropriate to a criminal prosecution.

This test, whether a judgment carries stigmatizing or condemnatory significance, has been criticized for its difficulty. . . . True, we have no litmus paper for punitive significance, and that used by the United States Supreme Court shows red and blue in inconsistent patterns. In part this difficulty is unavoidable, since the significance of a law may differ in the eyes of legislators, of defendants, and of the general public. Moreover, their views can change with time, and a legislative decision to decriminalize an offense may lead the public's perception as well as follow it. The very language of the law contributes to the problem when civil penalties are imposed in the familiar terms of criminal law, no doubt because they are familiar. "Penalty" is cognate to penal and punishment, and the code itself states that infractions are "punishable." . . . A defendant who is asked to declare whether he is "guilty," . . . or who is "convicted" as such, . . . may reasonably conclude that the judgment carries the stigma of condemnation. Again, these terms of the code are only relevant to the issue, not conclusive.

[The court discussed legislative history of the DUII provision which indicated that driving while intoxicated was perceived to be as serious as other traffic offenses tried as crimes. The court concluded that the legislature intended to "decriminalize" the procedure [for dealing with first-offense DUII] rather than the "offense" itself. The court found further evidence of the "seriousness" of DUII by noting that that offense is treated in much the same manner under the law of arrest (booking, fingerprinting, detention in jail, etc.) as felonies and misdemeanors.]

V

On reviewing these elements we conclude that, on balance, the code's offense of driving under the influence of intoxicants, and its enforcement and punishment, retains too many penal characteristics not to be a "criminal prosecution" under . . . the constitution. . . .

---

[14] Hart, *The Arms of the Criminal Law,* 23 Law and Contemp. Prob. 401, 404 (1958)

* * *

The code represents a good faith effort to deal with traffic offenses in the regular courts in forms other than criminal law. Nothing prevents such a decriminalization of traffic offenses, if it is fully carried out. Nor need it exclude the offense of driving under the influence of intoxicants. We hold only that, considering the magnitude of the potential fine, the secondary sanctions in case of nonpayment, the relationship of DUII to the other major traffic offenses, the evident legislative desire to emphasize the seriousness of this offense while facilitating its punishment, and the retention of criminal law enforcement procedures, the 1975 code did not free this offense from the punitive traits that characterize a criminal prosecution. Accordingly, petitioner is entitled to the constitutional and statutory protections afforded in the prosecutions of the other major traffic offenses that remained traffic crimes under the code. The decision of the Court of Appeals is reversed with instructions to remand the case to the circuit court in accordance with this opinion.

Reversed.

NOTES AND QUESTIONS

1. In the preceding case, the Oregon court encountered the same problem that troubled the Supreme Court in *Nestor* and *Mendoza-Martinez:* how to distinguish the criminal sanction from noncriminal regulatory penalties. The problem has also perplexed the commentators. See, e.g., Mann, *Punitive Civil Sanctions: The Middle ground between Criminal and Civil Law,* 101 Yale L.J. 1795 (1992); Chen, *Constitutional Limits on Using Civil Remedies to Achieve Criminal Law Objectives: Understanding and Transcending the Criminal— Civil Law Distinction,* 42 Hastings L.J. 1325 (1991); Clark, *Civil and Criminal Penalties and Forfeitures: A Framework for Constitutional Analysis,* 60 Minn. L. Rev. 379 (1976); Charney, *The Need for Constitutional Protections in Civil Penalty Cases,* 59 Cornell L. Rev. 478 (1974).

2. Professor Herbert Packer identified regulation along with punishment, treatment, and compensation, as the four categories of sanctions. He defined regulation and distinguished it from compensation as follows:

> Regulation may be defined as the control of future conduct for general purposes excluding the interests of identifiable beneficiaries. It is public rather than private. It differs from Compensation also in that it is typically administered by agencies of government. In prototype, Regulation resembles one branch of Compensation, the injunction or other special order directing an individual to do or not to do certain things in the future. The difference is that in the case of Regulation there is no identifiable beneficiary. Regulation may be legislative in form, *e.g.,* a general directive that motorists obtain driver's licenses; or it may be adjudicative, *e.g.,* an order by the Federal Trade Commission directing Company X to stop advertising that its cigarettes are good for you. Typically, Regulation can be reinforced by other forms of sanction. A good example is found in the antitrust laws. The

government may bring a suit for an injunction against anticompetitive practices. That is a case of Regulation. The same anticompetitive practices may have injured or threatened to injure some other person, who may bring an action for injunctive relief and for damages. The sanctioning method here is Compensation. Finally, the same anti-competitive practices may provide the basis for the government to bring a criminal prosecution in which the responsible persons may be fined and put in jail. This is a case of Punishment.

Packer, 24–25.

Why does Packer characterize as "punishment" the use of fines or jail terms in response to anticompetitive practices? Why are such sanctions, especially fines, not (also?) "regulation"? Is the punishment/regulation distinction clarified by his view that punishment characteristically is "imposed for the dominant purpose of preventing offenses against legal rules or of exacting retribution from offenders, or both"? *Id.* at 31.

3. The drafters of the Model Penal Code attempted to distinguish crimes and punishments on the one hand from regulatory offenses and sanctions on the other, as follows:

Classes of Crimes; Violations.

(1) An offense defined by this code or by any other statute of this State, for which a sentence of [death or of] imprisonment is authorized, constitutes a crime. Crimes are classified as felonies, misdemeanors, or petty misdemeanors.

[(2), (3), and (4) define felonies, misdemeanors, and petty misdemeanors.]

(5) An offense defined by this Code or by any other statute of this State constitutes a violation if it is so designated in this Code or in the law defining the offense or if no other sentence than a fine, or fine and forfeiture or other civil penalty is authorized upon conviction or if it is defined by a statute other than this Code which now provides that the offense shall not constitute a crime. A violation does not constitute a crime and conviction of a violation shall not give rise to any disability or legal disadvantage based on conviction of a criminal offense.

Model Penal Code § 1.04

ROE v. FARWELL

United States District Court, D. Massachusetts.

999 F. Supp. 174 (1998)

YOUNG, District Judge.

I. INTRODUCTION

This case presents to this Court questions faced in many jurisdictions across this country regarding the constitutionality of sex offender registration and notification statutes commonly referred to as "Megan's Laws" after seven year old Megan Kanka of New Jersey who was abducted, raped, and murdered on July 29, 1994 by a neighbor who lived across the street and was a released sex offender previously convicted of sex offenses against young girls. Neither Megan's parents, neighbors, nor the local police department knew about this sex offender's presence in their community. In response to this tragedy, the New Jersey legislature passed the Sex Offender Registration and Community Notification Acts on October 31, 1994. Spurred, in part, by the tragedy of Megan Kanka and other children at the hands of known sex offenders, the remaining states, including Massachusetts, soon enacted their own version of Megan's Law.

The case presently before this Court seeks a declaratory judgment that the Massachusetts Megan's Law, Mass. Gen. Laws ch. 6 §§ 178C-178P, is unconstitutional on its face and as applied to the plaintiff John Roe ("Roe") in that it violates the terms of his plea agreement, as well as the Ex Post Facto, Double Jeopardy, Cruel and Unusual Punishment, Bill of Attainder, Equal Protection, and Due Process Clauses of the United States Constitution. Roe sought a preliminary injunction and this Court combined the hearing thereon with trial on the merits. Trial on a statement of agreed facts was held on July 2, 1997.

II. Statutory Scheme

The Massachusetts legislature enacted the Massachusetts Sex Offender Registration and Community Notification Act ("the Act") on July 31, 1996. It became effective on October 1, 1996. The Act amended Mass. Gen. Laws ch. 6 by adding sections 178C to 178O. These new sections impose registration and notification requirements on "sex offenders." Under the statute, a sex offender is "a person convicted of a sex offense. . . on or after August first, nineteen hundred and eighty-one." The Act defines eleven crimes as sex offenses, along with attempt to commit any of the listed sex offenses and violation of similar crimes in other states.

The Act requires that all sex offenders residing in Massachusetts register in person with their local police department. The police department submits the registration data to the Criminal History Systems Board who sends such data to the police departments where the sex offender intends to live and work, to the police department where the offense was committed, and to the Federal Bureau of Investigation. A sex offender must notify the police department where he or she is registered of any change in his or her residential or work address five days prior to establishing a new residence. Failure to register is a misdemeanor punishable by two and one-half years in a house of correction or by a fine of not more than one thousand dollars or both.

The Act establishes an annual procedure for the verification of the registration data that includes an in-person appearance by the sex offender at his or her local police department. The annual registration requirement terminates "twenty years after the sex offender has been convicted or adjudicated or has been released from all custody or supervision, whichever last occurs, unless the sex offender was convicted of two or more sex offenses committed on different occasions, in which case the duty to register shall last for the offender's life." A sex offender may apply to have the registration obligation terminated upon a showing, by clear and convincing evidence, "that [he] has not committed a sex offense within fifteen years following conviction, adjudication, or release from all custody or supervision, whichever is later, and is not likely to pose a threat to the safety of others."

Under the Act, the Criminal History Systems Board is responsible for establishing and maintaining a computerized sex offender registry. This registry is expected to contain a file on each sex offender including specified registration data.

The Act establishes a Sex Offender Registry Board, a subdivision of the Criminal History Systems Board, responsible for 1) establishing guidelines for assessing the recidivism risk of sex offenders; 2) applying the guidelines to determining the risk level of a particular sex offender; 3) creating guidelines for police departments in distributing sex offender registry information; and 4) making recommendations to the Superior Court on a sex offender's recidivism level and community notification plan when an offender, who has a right to judicial review, has requested a hearing. Pursuant to its regulatory authority under the Act, the Sex Offender Registry Board has promulgated guidelines both for assessing a sex offender's risk of recidivism, and for a police department's dissemination of sex offender registry information.

The Act establishes a three-tiered notification system based on a sex-offender's risk of recidivism. The greater the risk of recidivism, the greater the level of notification. Broader community notification is required where the risk of recidivism is moderate (level two) or high (level three). Where the risk is moderate, community notification of organizations "likely to encounter" the sex offender (e.g., schools, day care centers, religious and youth organizations, and sports leagues) is required. Where the risk is high, community notification of organizations "likely to encounter" the sex offender and individuals "likely to encounter" the sex offender is required.

Under the level-two community notification requirement, the local police department, where the sex offender resides or works, is required to provide the relevant community organizations with the sex offender's 1) name; 2) home and work address; 3) information about the sexual offense or offenses committed and the date of the conviction or convictions; 4) his or her age, sex, race, height, weight, eye and hair color; and 5) a photograph (hereinafter "sex offender registry information"). Under the level-three community notification requirement, extensive community notification is required. In addition to notifying organizations in the community which are "likely to encounter" the sex offender, the local police department is required to notify individual members of the public who are "likely to encounter" the sex offender. Such notification is to occur by using local cable television stations, local newspapers, or the public posting of information. All notices to the community under the level-two or the level-three notification procedures are required to contain a criminal penalties warning against the use of sex offender registry information to commit a crime or to discriminate or harass a sex offender.

Another element of the public disclosure system established under the Act is public initiated access to sex offender registry information. Two provisions of the Act permit a person to request and obtain sex offender information. Under Section 178I, any person who is eighteen years of age or older may request verification of whether a person is a sex offender, his or her sex offenses, and the date of his or her convictions from the Criminal History Systems Board.

Under section 178J, any person may inquire at a local police department about whether a sex offender resides or works in a particular geographic area or whether a specific person is a sex offender. Such inquiry must be for the purposes of protecting the inquirer or a minor child or other person in the inquirer's care, custody, or control. If a sex offender is identified, the police department will provide the inquirer with the sex offender registry information for the sex offender, including the sex offender's home address or work address, if such address is within a one mile radius of a specified geographic area or on a specified street. Like the community notification notices, any report issued contains a criminal penalties warning for the illegal use of sex offender registry information.

III. Facts

Roe is a resident of Lynn, Massachusetts. He owns a company which manufactures porcelain dental fittings. One of his employees was a thirty-three year old female. From the beginning of her employment with Roe, she was subjected to Roe's inappropriate touching, hugging, and attempts to kiss her. When she informed Roe that she intended to leave her position because of his conduct, he threatened to kill her. On February 11, 1990, when this employee was working late, Roe approached her and stated, "I feel whorish, and I'm going to make love to you." When the employee rejected this unwanted advance, Roe grabbed her around the shoulders, tried to kiss her, and then forced her to a stairwell where he forcibly removed her pants, underpants, and shoes. When the employee struggled in her attempts to protect herself, Roe put both hands around her neck and attempted to choke her, saying, "If you don't open your legs I'll kill you!" He subjected her to vaginal penetration with his fingers and penis and performed cunnilingus on her. Roe forced her to masturbate his penis. Then, he led her to a room with a cot and continued to rape her and to sodomize her. This brutalization continued for one-and-a half to two hours. At the end of this brutal attack, Roe threatened to kill her if she did not return to work the next day.

A criminal complaint charging Roe with one count of assault and battery, three counts of rape, two counts of indecent assault, and one count of threats was filed against Roe. Roe was tried and convicted on both the rape and indecent assault and battery charges. He was sentenced to eight to fifteen years at MCI Cedar Junction. Following his conviction, the victim filed a civil suit against him.

In December 1991, after serving nine months of his sentence, Roe won a motion for a new trial. Prior to this trial, he entered into a conditional plea bargain agreeing to plead guilty to all of the criminal charges against him in exchange for a recommended sentence of time served, no probation, and a stipulation that Roe was not subject to the sanctions imposed by Massachusetts Sexually Dangerous Persons Act. Additionally, an agreement to dismiss the civil suit, based on Roe's guilty plea, was executed on November 6, 1992. The Superior Court accepted Roe's plea bargain and on November 1992, he pled guilty to two counts of rape and three counts of indecent assault and battery. Based on the evidence in the record, Roe has no other criminal history.

Roe is a sex offender, as he was convicted of crimes constituting sex offenses under the Act. Therefore, he is subject to its registration and public disclosure requirements. To date, Roe has registered with his local police department, but he has not been given a risk-designation under the Act.

* * *

VII. Ex Post Facto And Double Jeopardy Issues

A. LEGAL STANDARD

The Ex Post Facto Clause of the United States Constitution prohibits the legislative enactment of a law which: "1) makes a prior action, which legal when done, criminal, and punishes such action; 2) aggravates a crime, or makes it greater than it was, when committed; 3) changes the punishment, and inflicts a greater punishment, than the law annexed to the crime, when committed; 4) alters the legal rules of evidence, and requires less, or different testimony than the law required at the time of the commission of the offense in order to convict the offender." Roe claims a violation of the Ex Post Facto Clause asserting that the Act "changes the punishment and inflicts a greater punishment, than the law annexed to the crime, when committed." The Ex Post Facto Clause applies only to criminal statutes. See, e.g., *Kansas v. Hendricks,* [§ 2.02[B][1] *supra*]. The Double Jeopardy Clause prohibits multiple punishments for the same offense. *United States v. Ursery*, [§ 2.02[B][6] *infra*]. For a violation of either the Ex Post Facto Clause or the Double Jeopardy Clause to exist, the registration or community notification requirements of the Act must be deemed "punishment."

The Supreme Court doctrine on whether a civil sanction constitutes punishment has developed most substantively in the area of double jeopardy. See, e.g., *Hendricks* [and] *Usery*. This punishment analysis also has been applied to assessing Ex Post Facto challenges. The analytical matrix culled from these opinions does not produce a single standard, and the applicability of any such framework to sex offender registry provisions is blurry. Circuit Courts attempting to glean an applicable standard of analysis in the specific context of sex offender registry provisions have relied on the intent-effects test articulated by the Supreme Court in *Ursery* and *Hendricks* to devise an analytical protocol for assessing whether the registration or notification provisions constitute "punishment."

Ursery delineates a two-part test for assessing whether a civil sanction constitutes "punishment" under the Double Jeopardy Clause. The first part of this inquiry is a determination of legislative intent. Indication of express remedial or nonpunitive intent will result in a conclusion that such a statute does not constitute punishment, unless the party challenging the statute can demonstrate by "the clearest of proof" that the purpose or effect of the statute is so great as to negate the remedial intent.

In *Hendricks,* the Supreme Court held that a Kansas statute authorizing the civil commitment of violent sexual predators was constitutional as such commitment did not constitute punishment and, therefore, did not violate either the Ex Post Facto or the Double Jeopardy Clauses though enacted after the plaintiff committed his crimes and applied to plaintiff upon his release from prison. [The court outlined the holding in *Hendricks*.]

* * *

The sanction at issue in *Hendricks* civil commitment of a sexually dangerous person following release from prison is closely analogous to the Massachusetts requirement that a sex offender register with law enforcement and conform to community notification requirements. Both sanctions attempt "to grapple with the problem of managing repeat sexual offenders" or the problem of recidivism. Therefore, in evaluating whether the registration and notification requirements constitute punishment, this Court employs the *Ursery-Hendricks* framework.

B. REGISTRATION PROVISIONS

1. Legislative Intent

The determination of "whether a particular statutorily defined penalty is civil or criminal is a matter of statutory construction." On its face, the intent of the Massachusetts legislature in requiring sex offenders to register is to provide the appropriate officials with the necessary information to aide law enforcement in the prevention of sexual offenses and in the investigation of particular sexual offenses when they occur. The legislative history confirms this construction. In the initial bills proposed by both the State Senate and House of Representatives, which are the basis for the Act, the legislature stated that:

> The legislature further finds that law enforcement agencies' efforts to protect their communities, conduct investigations and quickly apprehend sex offenders are impaired by the lack of information about sex offenders who live within their jurisdiction. . . . Registration will provide law enforcement with additional information critical to preventing sexual victimization and to resolving incidents involving sexual abuse and exploitation promptly.

2. Effects Do Not Negate the Remedial Intent

Despite the clear indication of remedial intent on the part of the legislature in its enactment of this Act, "where a party challenging the statute provides 'the clearest proof' that the statutory scheme is so punitive either in purpose or effect as to negate the State's intention to deem it 'civil,' ". . . the statutory scheme will be deemed to constitute punishment. In assessing whether the statutory scheme is sufficiently punitive in its purpose or effect, the Supreme Court has continued to acknowledge the utility of the seven factors delineated in *Kennedy v. Mendoza-Martinez*, but also has continued to hold that these factors are neither exhaustive nor dispositive on the punishment inquiry. Federal and state courts have split on the applicability or continued viability of these factors to the Megan's Law context. This Court disagrees with those courts who have concluded that the *Mendoza-Martinez* factors are inapposite to the punishment inquiry concerning Megan's Laws. This Court concludes that the *Mendoza-Martinez* factors provide a useful analytical framework to the punishment analysis and, although not dispositive, are applicable to assess whether a statute is punitive or regulatory. This Court recognizes that because the Supreme Court has not assigned a weight or priority to any of these factors there is the potential for "unmanageable indefiniteness." Nonetheless, taking its cue from the Supreme Court, this Court rules that certain of the factors provide a most helpful analytical approach. . . .

3. Application of the *Mendoza-Martinez* Factors

In an attempt to meet his heavy burden under the effects test, Roe evaluates the registration provisions using the *Mendoza-Martinez* factors. Although this Court disagrees with Roe's implied argument that these factors are dispositive or that all factors are relevant, it considers some of these arguments to show that Roe has failed to demonstrate by the "clearest proof" that the purpose or effect of the statute is so great as to negate the remedial intent.

a. Affirmative Disability or Restraint

Roe avers that the registration requirements of the Act are an affirmative disability or restraint because they impose an annual verification procedure and potentially subject sex offenders to police interrogations or line-ups. This Court disagrees. The physical act of registering is not an affirmative disability or restraint. The registration requirements do not affirmatively disable or restrain a sex offender's choice of residence, movement within the state or out of the state, or activities. The registration requirements do not prevent a sex offender from holding or pursuing a particular profession.

b. Historically Regarded as a Punishment

Despite Roe's arguments to the contrary, "registration is typically and historically a regulatory measure." The registration of sex offenders assists law enforcement in its criminal investigation of such offenses. In this respect, felon registration provisions are a common nonpunitive device to assist law enforcement.

c. Promotes Retribution and Deterrence

Registration is not retributive but it does have a deterrent purpose. By requiring a sex offender to register, the legislature attempts to discourage recidivism by alerting the sex offender to the fact that he can easily be apprehended by law enforcement officials and is under the watchful eye of law enforcement. The fact that the Act serves a deterrent purpose does not affirmatively establish that it is punitive. As the Supreme Court has recognized, deterrence "may serve civil as well as criminal goals."

d. Legitimate Purpose

Registration ensures that law enforcement has sufficient information on sex offenders to assist them in criminal investigations, apprehensions, and prosecutions. Presently, most of the information is available in the criminal history records maintained by the Criminal History Systems Board. The registration requirements make such information more readily available to law enforcement not for the purposes of harassment, as Roe contends, but to promote public safety and efficacious law enforcement. There is no evidence that the registration provisions will result in any other outcome.

e. Excessiveness Beyond Legitimate Purpose

Although a sex offender is unable to terminate his or her duty to register until at least fifteen years after his or her conviction or release from prison, this effect alone does not amount to the "clearest proof" required to cause a statute with a clear remedial purpose to be deemed punitive. By compelling the registration of sex offenders, the legislature is reasonably advancing its law enforcement and public safety objectives.

In support of his position that the registration provisions of the Act are punitive, Roe relies on the California Supreme Court's decision *In re Reed*. In that case, the court held that a mandatory sex offender registration statute inflicts punishment and violates the California constitution's prohibition against cruel and unusual punishment where the sex offender has committed a misdemeanor as such registration constitutes punishment. The court applied the *Mendoza-Martinez* factors and determined the registration provision to be punitive. A central part of the court's reasoning was its proportionality analysis where it determined that the punishment of registration far exceeded the actual offense and was treated more severely than more serious sex-related crimes or other serious crimes. The plaintiff's offense was a misdemeanor involving the solicitation of a police officer by the plaintiff in a public restroom which the court characterized as a "relatively simple sexual indiscretion." In the court's opinion, the plaintiff did not represent the type of person who the legislature intended to be subjected to the registration requirements in order to assist law enforcement efforts. In addition, the court found that several more serious sex-related misdemeanors were not subject to registration, including prostitution. Thus, the Court concluded that the punishment was not in proportion to the crime and constituted cruel and unusual punishment under state law.

This case is readily distinguishable from *In re Reed*. First, the specific crimes listed as sex offenses under Mass. Gen. Laws ch. 6, § 178C are felonies. More importantly, the crimes for which Roe was convicted are felonies. Secondly, the constitutional issue in *In re Reed* was whether the sex offender registry provision violated the cruel or unusual punishment provisions of the California constitution. The *Reed* court focused not on the punishment aspect of the provision but on the proportionality inquiry in determining that the statute constituted cruel or unusual punishment as applied to the plaintiff, a misdemeanor sex-offender. The reasoning of the *Reed* court is not apposite to the facts of this case.

* * *

The registration provisions of the Act do not constitute punishment in violation of either the Ex Post Facto or Double Jeopardy Clauses. This conclusion is tempered by the recognition that, unlike some Megan's Laws, this Act does not permit a sex offender to challenge his duty to register. Indeed, at least three justices of the Supreme Judicial Court view registration as "a continuing, intrusive, humiliating regulation of the person himself." Even so, this is not enough to render the registration provisions punishment under the Constitution of the United States.

C. Public Disclosure Provisions

Roe avers that the community notification and public access provisions of the Act, i.e. §§ 178I, 178J and 178K, are punitive because such public disclosure 1) is historically punishment; 2) serves the traditional goals of punishment; 3) is an affirmative disability and restraint due to the effect of public stigma towards him as a sex offender on his personal life and professional life; 4) is an affirmative disability and restraint due to the greater disclosure of information on Roe than is available through judicial proceedings or criminal records; 5) is conducted under a punitive scheme; 6) results in excessively harsh effects on sex offender, i.e., threats and harassment; and 7) is too broad permitting disclosure to persons who are not vulnerable to or threatened by Roe's presence in their community.

1. Legislative Intent

In reviewing the legislative history of the Act, it is apparent that the legislature believed that public disclosure or notification was a central element in advancing the public safety objectives of the Act. In the initial bills, the legislature stated that:

> In balancing offenders' rights with the interest of public security, the legislature finds that releasing information about sex offenders to law enforcement agencies and, under certain circumstances, to the public will further the primary governmental interest of protecting children and other vulnerable populations from potential harm.

* * *

a. Historically Punishment

Roe argues that public disclosure of his sex offenses is punitive, as such disclosure is analogous to the wearing of a "Scarlet Letter." Contrary to Roe's contention, federal courts addressing this issue, have rejected the historical punishment analogies. ("Public shaming, humiliation, and banishment all involve more than the dissemination of information."); ("Stigmatization penalties of an earlier era primarily served distinctively punitive goals and operated through significantly different mechanisms than community notification [provisions]"); ("wanted" posters [are] at least as apt an analogy as historical shaming punishments). The dissemination of information regarding criminal conduct, without more, is not punishment when done to advance a legitimate government purpose or objective. The more apt analogy to the public disclosure of sex offender registry information is "the required dissemination of information generated by our criminal justice system and the subsequent dissemination of 'rap sheet' information to regulatory agencies, bar associations, prospective employers and interested members of the public." This Court agrees that historical shaming punishments are not identical to notification or public disclosure, in large part because historical shaming punishments entailed more than the dissemination of information. First, the intent of such punishment was punitive. Whipping, branding, stockading, banishment were the punishment for the offender's particular transgression. Notification, on the other hand, occurs after the sex offender has been punished. It is not a substitute for punishment. Second, such punishment "required the physical participation of the offender and typically required direct confrontation between the offender and members of the public." The purpose, method, and process of such punishment are completely different from public notification. . . .

* * *

c. Traditional Goals of Punishment: Deterrence and Retribution

Roe avers that the dissemination of his address and identity will result in public ostracism. He asserts that such a consequence is an objective of the Act in order to deter future criminal conduct. As the deterrence of future criminal conduct is an objective of the Act, he argues that the Act is punitive. The Supreme Court has explicitly stated that deterrence "may serve civil as well as criminal goals." *Ursery*. The legislative history here demonstrates that the objective behind public disclosure of sex offender registry information was to "further the primary governmental interest of protecting children and other vulnerable populations from potential harm." The goal of public notification is to reduce the likelihood of re-offense by a sexual offender by giving law enforcement necessary information to be aware of potential dangers, the public necessary information in order to take appropriate steps to minimize a harmful encounter with a sex offender, and to deter the sex offender from reoffending because of the increased likelihood of apprehension. This deterrence objective is insufficient to render the notification provisions punitive, as there are underlying legitimate governmental public security purposes.

Nothing in the legislative history of this Act indicates a retributive intent on the part of the legislature. The fact that as a result of the public disclosure provisions, Roe may be subject to physical threats, harassment, and may find his employment situation impaired does not constitute retribution on the part of the government. The Act specifically warns of criminal penalties for the misuse of sex offender registry information. Any person who uses sex offender registry information to commit a crime against a sex offender or to illegally discriminate or to harass a sex offender is guilty of a misdemeanor and is subject to a fine and imprisonment.

d. Affirmative Disability or Restraint

1) Effects on Personal and Professional Lives

Roe asserts that the compelled disclosure of private information, its compilation, and its subsequent disclosure to law enforcement and the public is punitive. First, he argues that this public disclosure "has a potentially devastating effect on Roe's personal and professional lives." The Commonwealth counters that such claims are speculative, as there have been no reported incidents of harassment, violence, or discrimination related to the release of sex offender registry information in Massachusetts or in Roe's hometown of Lynn. Circuit courts that have addressed this issue have not been persuaded by arguments concerning the risk of physical violence, stigma, or impairment of employment opportunities such as Roe advances here. ("Although we do not doubt that the Act has had unfortunate consequences for many subject to its operation, we do not agree that these detrimental consequences suffice to transform the regulatory measure of community notification into punishment."). . . . Second, the effects of a statute having a remedial purpose must be extremely burdensome to constitute punishment. Third, it is the direct effects, not the indirect effects of a statute, that must be assessed. Public stigma or ostracism, vigilantism, loss of employment are indirect effects of public disclosure provisions which are neither encouraged, condoned, nor tolerated under the Act. Guided by the reasoning of these decisions, this Court concludes that the potential effect on Roe's personal and professional life is not punitive.

2) Greater Disclosure of Information

For the public disclosure provisions to pass constitutional muster, they must be "reasonably related" to the legislative purpose: a perfect fit is not required. The central inquiry is whether the public disclosure provisions of this Act are carefully tailored to meet the objectives of the legislature, i.e., providing law enforcement and, under certain circumstances, the public with information about potential recidivists in order to prevent re-offense and to assist in the investigation, apprehension, and prosecution of a re-offense.

a) Community Notification Provisions

Since the breadth of the community notification provisions varies with an offender's classification, and since Roe has not yet been classified, this Court declines to press this aspect of the analysis further at this time and expresses no opinion thereon.

b) Public Access Provisions

The public access provisions, of course, do not depend on Roe's classification level so the issues presented by this aspect of the case are ripe for decision.

Pursuant to the Guidelines for Dissemination of Sex Offender Information, under either section 178I or 178J, any person who makes a request for information based on his or her need for protection or for the protection of a minor child or another person in his or her custody is entitled to obtain sex offender registry information on any sex offender who is either specifically identified or who resides within a one mile radius of a particular address or resides on a specified street regardless of whether the sex offender, based on his or her prior sex offenses, can be deemed to create a public safety risk to the inquirer.

The Supreme Judicial Court appears to have rejected precisely this interpretation. ("If the Legislature intended that requirements of § 178J are to apply to an inquiry under § 178I, it is unclear why some but not all the requirements of § 178J are included in § 178I in substantially identical language."). Instead that court treats the sections as separate and discrete provisions for the purpose of assessing their remedial or punitive character (concluding that section 178I lacks an explicit remedial or regulatory purpose). The Commonwealth, nonetheless, asks this Court to reject the Supreme Judicial Court's construction of section 178I as lacking a remedial purpose (reading the provisions in tandem and applying the prudential requirements of section 178J to inquiries under section 178I). What the Commonwealth asks is beyond the power of this Court to grant. The interpretation of state law by the highest court of the state is conclusive on this Court. That interpretation becomes a part of the state law itself. Because the Supreme Judicial Court has ruled that section 178I lacks a remedial purpose, the provisions of that section cannot be applied to Roe as violative of the Ex Post Facto and Double Jeopardy Clauses. [The court found that although § 178I constituted "punishment," it was not cruel and unusual punishment.]

* * *

XIII. Conclusion And Order

[A] Since the Supreme Judicial Court has declared that section 178I has no remedial purpose, this Court declares that its provisions cannot be enforced in any respect against John Roe.

[B] Save as to paragraph A above . . . this Court declares the Act, in all other respects, constitutional when tested against the provisions of the Constitution of the United States.

* * *

It is SO ORDERED.

NOTES AND QUESTIONS.

1. In *In re Reed*, 191 Cal. Rptr. 658 (1983), a case noted and distinguished in *Roe*, the California Supreme Court found a sex offender registration requirement to be punitive in part because it found a "deterrent" purpose in the registration requirement: "the legislative intent was surely to deter recidivism by facilitating the apprehension of past offenders". Is "facilitating the apprehension of past offenders" the kind of "traditional aim of punishment" that the *Mendoza-Martinez* Court had in mind when it listed "deterrence" among its list of defining characteristics of punishment?

Does Justice Richardson in his dissent in *Reed* more accurately capture the possible purposes of the registration requirement as "deterr[ing] those already once convicted from repeating the offense and assist[ing] in the apprehension of those recidivist offenders who had not been so deterred"? Does such a view suggest a "non-punitive" purpose?

2. Does the *Roe* court adequately distinguish *Reed*? Does the *Roe* court offer any basis for distinguishing *Reed* on the issue of whether registration requirements constitute "punishment" as opposed to the issue of whether registration requirements, once found to be punitive, are disproportionate punishment in *Reed* and *Roe* respectively?

3. The California courts have limited the *Reed* case to its facts. In *People v. Fioretti*, 54 Cal. App. 4th 1209, 63 Cal. Rptr.2d 367 (1997), the Court of Appeals held that the sex offender registration requirements did not constitute "punishment" for purposes of ex post facto clause application.

The court distinguished *Reed* as a case concerning a misdemeanor defendant (unlike Fioretti, who had been convicted of a felony sex offense) raising a claim of cruel or unusual punishment rather than an ex post facto claim. The court explained:

Appellant argues that *Reed* represents the law in California, standing for the proposition that sex offender registration requirements are to be considered a form of punishment for all purposes. We believe the holding in *Reed* is more properly limited to its particular circumstances and to the legal issue addressed by the court in that case. The court in *Reed* emphasized the fact that defendant was an otherwise exemplary citizen who was involved in a "relatively simple sexual indiscretion" with no victim. . . . Appellant, on the other hand, was convicted of a felony sex offense, namely lewd and lascivious conduct upon a child. . . . Furthermore, at the time *Reed* was decided, only three other states besides California had sex offender registration laws, all of which were less stringent than California's. . . .Now sex offender registration laws are a widely accepted means of aiding law enforcement authorities in preventing and investigating sex crimes, and have been found by courts addressing the issue to have a legitimate regulatory purpose. In *Reed*, the court held simply that insofar as section 290 requires registration of all persons convicted [of specified sex offenses] it violates [the Cruel or Unusual Punishments Clause]. We do not believe that holding is susceptible of the broad application appellant would give it to ex post facto claims. . . . 54 Cal. App. At 1216-17, 63 Cal. Rptr. At 372.

Are the *Fioretti* court's attempts to distinguish *Reed* convincing? A few courts in other jurisdictions have found sex offender registration statutes to be punitive and thus inapplicable retroactively under ex post facto clause provisions. See, e.g., *State v. Calhoun*, 669 So. 2d 1359, 1363 (La. App. 1996).

4. Are the notification provisions of recent "Megan's Laws" more "punitive" in nature than mere registration provisions such as those at issue in *Reed* ? Some courts, contrary to *Roe*, have found statutes embracing registration and notification provisions to be "punitive" and thus unconstitutional ex post facto laws. See, e.g., *Rowe v. Burton*, 884 F. Supp. 1372, 1385 (D. Alaska 1994). Other courts have found that registration provisions are non-punitive while notification provisions constitute ex post facto punishment. See, e.g., *State v. Myers,* 260 Kan. 669, 923 P.2d 1024 (1996).

A majority of courts have found that neither registration nor notification provisions constitute punishment for purposes of ex post facto clause application. Note, *Scarlet Letter Sex Offender Databases and Community Notification: Sacrificing Personal Privacy for a Symbol's Sake*, 35 Am. Crim. L. Rev. 333, 358 n.40 (1998).

5. Is there a "shaming" aspect to the sex offender notification provisions? If so, how does such an aspect relate to the question of whether the provision is "punitive" or not? For a discussion of recent use of shaming sanctions as alternatives to traditional forms of punishment, see Garvey, *Can Shaming Punishments Educate?*, 65 U. Chi. L. Rev. 733 (1998); Kahan, *What Do Alternative Sanctions Mean?*, 63 U. Chi. L. Rev. 591, 630-52 (1996); Massaro, *Shame, Culture, and American Criminal Law,* 89 Mich. L. Rev. 1880 (1991); Whitman, *What is Wrong With Shame Sanctions?*, 107 Yale L.J. 1055 (1998).

Are any of the following penalties, noted in the above articles, "punishment"?

a) An offender convicted of DWI is ordered to paste a bumper sticker on his car that reads "CONVICTED DWI";

b) An offender convicted of DWI has his face and name broadcast on community access TV;

c) An offender convicted of theft is ordered to wear a t-shirt stating: "I am on felony probation for theft";

d) An offender convicted of sexual assault is ordered to post a sign in his yard that reads: "DANGEROUS SEX OFFENDER";

e) A landlord whose building is condemned as a slum is placed under house arrest in one of his rat-infested tenements;

f) A man convicted of stealing steaks is ordered to give a "shaming speech," approved of in advance by the court, on the steps of the local courthouse.

[4] Punishment versus Compensation

The above cases and materials have illustrated, in a variety of contexts, the significance of the punitive sanction in setting apart the criminal law. Nowhere is the analytical power of the concept of punishment more prominent, however, than in accounting for the differences between criminal and tort law, a distinction generally understood to rest entirely on "the interests affected and the remedy afforded by the law." W. Prosser and P. Keeton, *Law of Torts* 7 (5th ed. 1984). Crimes are offenses against the public at large and are punished by the state, while torts are wrongs against individual persons who seek compensation for their injuries by privately bringing legal actions against their wrongdoers. See Fletcher, *Compensation and Punishment*, 14 Creighton L. Rev. 691 (1981).

Historically, as mentioned in this chapter's Introduction, § 2.01, supra, tort and crime shared a common ancestry in an essentially compensatory medieval legal system. With the emergence of centralized authority, the criminal law began to assume a distinct identity. Where offenders were once required to pay *bot* to their victims, they eventually were also ordered to make money payments to the king *(wite)*. The distinction between compensation and punishment had thus begun. For a time, tort claims for compensatory damages could be joined with criminal actions imposing punishment. Plucknett, 457. As punitive sanctions were increasingly employed, however, victim reparation became less a concern to the criminal law, until by the end of the 14th century the common law precluded joint imposition of criminal and tort sanctions. *Id.* at 458–59; Hitchler, *Crimes and Civil Injuries*, 39 Dick. L. Rev. 23, 33 (1934).

Today tort damages are collaterally available to the victims of many crimes. Of course, as a practical matter, many criminal defendants lack sufficient resources to compensate their victims.

However theoretically distinct, crime and tort continue to share many similarities. Both are directed, in part at least, toward the control of antisocial behavior by relying on deterrence theory. Holmes, *Lecture IL*. Moreover, the sanctions employed by the two systems sometimes appear similar. The imposition of punitive damages in tort cases casts an apparently criminal shadow over a system that denies the procedural protections of the criminal process. See generally, Note, *The Imposition of Punishment by Civil Courts: A Reappraisal of Punitive Damages,* 41 N.Y.U. L. Rev. 1158 (1966); Note, *Criminal Safeguards and the Punitive Damages Defendant,* 34 U. Chi. L. Rev. 408 (1967).

The distinction between tort and crime is further blurred by resurgence of interest in governmentally initiated actions to require criminal defendants to pay compensation. The following cases illustrate this trend. The *Pettit* case reflects the movement toward victim reparation, imposed in most jurisdictions as a condition of probation established at the discretion of sentencing judges rather than as an explicit sanction set by the legislature. The *Hudson* case examines whether statutory requirements that defendants compensate the state for its law enforcement expenses are themselves punitive.

PEOPLE V. PETTIT

Court of Appeals of Michigan

88 Mich. App. 203, 276 N.W.2d 878 (1979)

WALSH, Presiding Judge

Defendant was charged with negligent homicide. . . . A second count was added to the information: driving while impaired . . . Pursuant to negotiations between the prosecutor and defense counsel, defendant pleaded guilty to count II and the prosecutor moved to dismiss count I. The circuit court judge accepted defendant's guilty plea and count I was dismissed. On April 20, 1978, defendant was placed on probation for two years. On appeal defendant challenges the propriety of one of the conditions of his probation: that he pay restitution in the amount of $1,295 to cover the funeral expenses for the child who died in the automobile accident which gave rise to the charge in count I ($795), and the expenses incurred in the repair of the automobile in which the child had been riding ($500).

The circuit judge was within his statutory sentencing authority in imposing restitution as a condition of probation. . . .

Restitution may be imposed as to the "whole loss caused by a course of criminal conduct upon conviction of a crime arising out of that conduct." . . .

The issue in the instant case is whether the losses for which restitution was ordered were caused by the impaired driving for which the defendant stood convicted. Defendant argues that this can be established only by civil judgment or, at the least, by a hearing approximating a civil trial at which defendant would have the benefit of procedural safeguards available in a civil proceeding.

Similar argument was raised and rejected in *People v. Good,* 287 Mich. 110, 115–116, 282 N.W. 920, 923 (1938):

> Appellant claims that this provision violates the due process clause of both Federal and State Constitutions, U.S.C.A. Const. Amend. 14; Const. Mich.

art. 2, § 16, in that it does not provide for a hearing on the question of damages to be assessed, nor does it give a defendant an opportunity to interpose the defenses, such as the contributory negligence of a decedent, which are available to him in civil proceedings; also that the notice of a criminal prosecution is "not appropriate to a proceeding in which civil damages may be assessed."

The arguments of appellant are based upon the erroneous assumption that damages are "assessed" by the court when restitution is made a condition of probation. Such is not the case. No judgment is rendered for, nor could a writ of execution issue to enforce the collection of, the sum specified. A defendant in such instance is merely given the alternative of abiding by the conditions imposed or else suffering the imposition and execution of a sentence which ordinarily follows a verdict of guilty. This defendant was not deprived of any of his rights without due process; rather he was given the additional privilege of avoiding the usual penalty of his crime by the payment of a sum of money and the observance of the other conditions attached to his probation. Consequently it was not a deprivation of due process of law to deny defendant a hearing on the question of the amount of "damages" to be imposed as a condition of probation and the statute, . . . is ample notice of the possibility that such a condition might be imposed.

Due process does not require the same type of proof which would be required in a civil proceeding. Nevertheless, the proper exercise of judicial discretion would require, and we hold that, in cases where restitution is ordered as a condition of probation, there must be persuasive support in the record for the sentencing judge's conclusion that the losses for which restitution is ordered were caused by the criminal conduct of the defendant.[2]

We find such support in the instant record. Defendant was convicted of driving while impaired. The sentencing judge reviewed the presentence report prepared by the probation department. The presentence report contained the statement of the investigating officer that defendant was at fault in the fatal collision. In open court both defendant and his attorney expressed their agreement with the contents of the pre-sentence report. From this the sentencing judge reasonably concluded that the child's losses were caused by defendant's criminal conduct (i.e., by his driving while impaired). After sentencing, defendant's attorney moved for review of the conditions of probation. The sentencing judge deleted a requirement that defendant pay $208 for the headstone of the child's grave, since that amount had not been set forth in the presentence report. Defendant did not contend that the funeral and car repair expenses were inaccurate or unreasonable, nor did he move to withdraw his guilty plea.

---

[2] Of course, restitution must not be used as a substitute for determination in the proper forum of a defendant's civil liability: Criminal and civil liability are not synonymous. A criminal conviction does not necessarily establish the existence of civil liability. Civil liability need not be established as a prerequisite to the requirement of restitution as a probation condition; such restitution for personal injury, therefore, generally should be more limited in scope than civil damages. In the instant case we believe that restitution should encompass only those losses which are easily ascertained and measured, and which are a direct result of the defendant's criminal acts. *People v. Heil,* 79 Mich. App. 739, 748–749, 262 N.W.2d 895, 900 (1977).

The record clearly indicates the purpose of the restitution payments. The condition of restitution was reasonable and just. It was not designed as a substitute for determination of defendant's civil liability.

* * *

Affirmed.

Notes and Questions

1. As noted by the *Pettit* court, sentencing judges do not engage in assessments of comparative fault of the victim and the offender in ordering restitution. See also *State v. Morse,* 45 Wash. App. 197, 723 P.2d 1209, 1210 (1986). Some commentators see the refusal to take contributory fault of the victim into account as a defining characteristic of the criminal law that distinguishes it from tort.

> [I]n the tort law alone the fundamental question is always, which of the two parties to the lawsuit should bear the loss, where a decision in favor of the one necessarily precludes a decision in favor of the other? The equities between parties must, therefore, be resolved on a comparative basis. . . . The criminal law stands in sharp opposition, for it does not labor under such a comparative constraint. If two parties are involved in a dispute, each will escape punishment only if the state's prosecution is frustrated, and *vice versa.* But the state can choose to dispose of the case of each individual party to a private dispute in a manner that does not prejudice . . . the other. In criminal cases, therefore, it is possible to measure the conduct of each individual against an ideal standard of judgment, rather than by constant comparison to the conduct of another party.

Epstein, *Crime and Tort: Old Wine in Old Bottles* in Assessing the Criminal 231, 243 (R. Barnett and J. Hogel eds. 1977).

2. What is the purpose of restitution in criminal sentencing? Consider: "Restitution as a sentencing device can be viewed in two conceptually different ways. It can be viewed (1) as a method for summarily awarding a victim civil damages resulting from criminal conduct, or (2) as a sanction imposed *to punish* criminal conduct." (Emphasis in original.) *State v. Dillon,* 51 Or. App. 729, 732, 626 P.2d 959, 961 (1981). Most courts, *Dillon* included, seem to favor the punitive interpretation. See, e.g., *State v. Wright,* 156 N.J. Super. 559, 562, 384 A.2d 199, 201 (1978):

> While restitution of monies unlawfully obtained is specifically authorized as a condition of probation under N.J.S.A. 2A:168–2, we know of no comparable authority whereby this requirement may be imposed as part of a custodial sentence. The design of penalties for crime is a legislative and not a judicial function and authority to impose punishment must be found in statutory law.

Along the same lines, courts have held that defendants committing their offenses prior to the passage of a statute authorizing expanded use of restitution cannot be subject to that sanction even though their sentencing occurs after the restitution statute is in force. "It is well settled that where a criminal statute increases the punishment for previously committed crimes, the statute may not be applied retroactively." *People v. Winston,* 92 A.D.2d 740, 741, 461 N.Y.S.2d 89, 89–90 (1983). Is this conclusion consistent with the Supreme Court's failure to see a violation of the ex post facto clause in *Flemming v. Nestor, supra*? Is restitution "punishment" under the definition(s) of that concept provided by these materials?

3. Restitution is not always employed as a condition of probation. Some statutes permit its use in conjunction with other punitive sanctions, including imprisonment. See, e.g., the discussion of the New York scheme of restitution in *People v. Bertucci,* 132 Misc. 2d 1051, 506 N.Y.S.2d 399 (1986). For a British perspective on the victim reparation issue, see Ashworth, *Punishment and Compensation: Victims, Offenders and the State,* 6 Oxford J.L. Stud. 86 (1986).

4. Some statutes authorize courts to impose fines and to direct all or a portion thereof as restitution to the victim. See, e.g., Ariz. Rev. Stats. § 13-804(A) (Cum. Supp. 1986). Are such sanctions any more or less punitive than the award of restitution in *Pettit?*

Sometimes the characterization of a sanction as a "fine" as opposed to an order for "restitution" can be crucial. See, e.g., *State in Interest of D.G.W.,* 70 N.J. 488, 361 A.2d 513 (1976), holding that a juvenile court could order a youthful offender, as a condition of probation, to provide restitution for property he had damaged. The court saw the restitution order as consistent with the rehabilitative goals of the juvenile system, but noted that fines, on the other hand, are inherently punitive and thus could not be imposed by juvenile courts. The D. G. W. court ordered the minor to pay $156.50 as restitution. Under what circumstances would a similar money payment be a fine?

HUDSON v. UNITED STATES

Supreme Court of the United States

522 U.S. 93 (1997)

Chief Justice REHNQUIST *delivered the opinion of the Court.*

The Government administratively imposed monetary penalties and occupational debarment on petitioners for violation of federal banking statutes, and later criminally indicted them for essentially the same conduct. We hold that the Double Jeopardy Clause of the Fifth Amendment is not a bar to the later criminal prosecution because the administrative proceedings were civil, not criminal. Our reasons for so holding in large part disavow the method of analysis used in *United States v. Halper,* 490 U.S. 435, 448 (1989), and reaffirm the previously established rule exemplified in *United States v. Ward,* 448 U.S. 242, 248-249 (1980).

During the early and mid-1980's, petitioner John Hudson was the chairman and controlling shareholder of the First National Bank of Tipton (Tipton) and the First National Bank of Hammon (Hammon). During the same period, petitioner Jack Rackley was president of Tipton and a member of the board of directors of Hammon, and petitioner Larry Baresel was a member of the board of directors of both Tipton and Hammon.

An examination of Tipton and Hammon led the Office of the Comptroller of the Currency (OCC) to conclude that petitioners had used their bank positions to arrange a series of loans to third parties, in violation of various federal banking statutes and regulations. According to the OCC, those loans, while nominally made to third parties, were in reality made to Hudson in order to enable him to redeem bank stock that he had pledged as collateral on defaulted loans.

On February 13, 1989, OCC issued a "Notice of Assessment of Civil Money Penalty." The notice alleged that petitioners had violated 12 U.S.C. 84(a)(1) and 375b (1982) and 12 CFR 31.2(b) and 215.4(b) (1986) by causing the banks with which they were associated to make loans to nominee borrowers in a manner that unlawfully allowed Hudson to receive the benefit of the loans. The notice also alleged that the illegal loans resulted in losses to Tipton and Hammon of almost $900,000 and contributed to the failure of those banks. However, the notice contained no allegation of any harm to the Government as a result of petitioners' conduct. "After taking into account the size of the financial resources and the good faith of [petitioners], the gravity of the violations, the history of previous violations and other matters as justice may require, as required by 12 U.S.C. 93(b)(2) and 504(b)," OCC assessed penalties of $100,000 against Hudson and $50,000 each against both Rackley and Baresel. On August 31, 1989, OCC also issued a "Notice of Intention to Prohibit Further Participation" against each petitioner. These notices, which were premised on the identical allegations that formed the basis for the previous notices, informed petitioners that OCC intended to bar them from further participation in the conduct of "any insured depository institution."

In October 1989, petitioners resolved the OCC proceedings against them by each entering into a "Stipulation and Consent Order." These consent orders provided that Hudson, Baresel, and Rackley would pay assessments of $16,500, $15,000, and $12,500 respectively. In addition, each petitioner agreed not to "participate in any manner" in the affairs of any banking institution without the written authorization of the OCC and all other relevant regulatory agencies.

In August 1992, petitioners were indicted in the Western District of Oklahoma in a 22-count indictment on charges of conspiracy, misapplication of bank funds, §§ 656 and 2, and making false bank entries, § 1005. The violations charged in the indictment rested on the same lending transactions that formed the basis for the prior administrative actions brought by OCC. Petitioners moved to dismiss the indictment on double jeopardy grounds, but the District Court denied the motions. The Court of Appeals affirmed the District Court's holding on the nonparticipation sanction issue, but vacated and remanded to the District Court on the money sanction issue. The District Court on remand granted petitioners' motion to dismiss the indictments. This time the Government appealed, and the Court of Appeals reversed. That court held, following *Halper,* that the actual fines imposed by the Government were not so grossly disproportional to the proven damages to the Government as to render the sanctions "punishment" for double jeopardy purposes. We granted certiorari because of concerns about the wide variety of novel double jeopardy claims spawned in the wake of *Halper*. We now affirm, but for different reasons.

The Double Jeopardy Clause provides that no "person [shall] be subject for the same offence to be twice put in jeopardy of life or limb." We have long recognized that the Double Jeopardy Clause does not prohibit the imposition of any additional sanction that could, "'in common parlance,'" be described as punishment. The Clause protects only against the imposition of multiple criminal punishments for the same of

Whether a particular punishment is criminal or civil is, at least initially, a matter of statutory construction. A court must first ask whether the legislature, "in establishing the penalizing mechanism, indicated either expressly or impliedly a preference for one label or the other." Even in those cases where the legislature "has indicated an intention to establish a civil penalty, we have inquired further whether the statutory scheme was so punitive either in purpose or effect," as to "transfor[m] what was clearly intended as a civil remedy into a criminal penalty."

In making this latter determination, the factors listed in *Kennedy v. Mendoza-Martinez*, 372 U.S. 144, provide useful guideposts, including: (1) "[w]hether the sanction involves an affirmative disability or restraint"; (2) "whether it has historically been regarded as a punishment"; (3) "whether it comes into play only on a finding of scienter "; (4) "whether its operation will promote the traditional aims of punishment-retribution and deterrence"; (5) "whether the behavior to which it applies is already a crime"; (6) "whether an alternative purpose to which it may rationally be connected is assignable for it"; and (7) "whether it appears excessive in relation to the alternative purpose assigned." It is important to note, however, that "these factors must be considered in relation to the statute on its face," and "only the clearest proof" will suffice to override legislative intent and transform what has been denominated a civil remedy into a criminal penalty.

Our opinion in *United States v. Halper*, marked the first time we applied the Double Jeopardy Clause to a sanction without first determining that it was criminal in nature. In that case, Irwin Halper was convicted of, violating the criminal false claims statute, based on his submission of 65 inflated Medicare claims each of which overcharged the Government by $9. He was sentenced to two years' imprisonment and fined $5,000. The Government then brought an action against Halper under the civil False Claims Act. The remedial provisions of the False Claims Act provided that a violation of the Act rendered one "liable to the United States Government for a civil penalty of $2,000, an amount equal to 2 times the amount of damages the Government sustains because of the act of that person, and costs of the civil action." Given Halper's 65 separate violations of the Act, he appeared to be liable for a penalty of $130,000, despite the fact he actually defrauded the Government of less than $600. However, the District Court concluded that a penalty of this magnitude would violate the Double Jeopardy Clause in light of Halper's previous criminal conviction. While explicitly recognizing that the statutory damages provision of the Act "was not itself a criminal punishment," the

District Court nonetheless concluded that application of the full penalty to Halper would constitute a second "punishment" in violation of the Double Jeopardy Clause.

As [this Court saw it in] *Halper*, the imposition of "punishment" of any kind was subject to double jeopardy constraints, and whether a sanction constituted "punishment" depended primarily on whether it served the traditional "goals of punishment," namely "retribution and deterrence." Any sanction that was so "overwhelmingly disproportionate" to the injury caused that it could not "fairly be said solely to serve [the] remedial purpose" of compensating the government for its loss, was thought to be explainable only as "serving either retributive or deterrent purposes."

The analysis applied by the *Halper* Court deviated from our traditional double jeopardy doctrine in two key respects. First, the *Halper* Court bypassed the threshold question: whether the successive punishment at issue is a "criminal" punishment. Instead, it focused on whether the sanction, regardless of whether it was civil or criminal, was so grossly disproportionate to the harm caused as to constitute "punishment." In so doing, the Court elevated a single *Kennedy* factor whether the sanction appeared excessive in relation to its nonpunitive purposes to dispositive status. But as we emphasized in *Kennedy* itself, no one factor should be considered controlling as they "may often point in differing directions." The second significant departure in *Halper* was the Court's decision to "asses[s] the character of the actual sanctions imposed," rather than, as *Kennedy* demanded, evaluating the "statute on its face" to determine whether it provided for what amounted to a criminal sanction.

We believe that *Halper*'s deviation from longstanding double jeopardy principles was ill considered. As subsequent cases have demonstrated, *Halper*'s test for determining whether a particular sanction is "punitive," and thus subject to the strictures of the Double Jeopardy Clause, has proved unworkable. We have since recognized that all civil penalties have some deterrent effect. If a sanction must be "solely" remedial (i.e., entirely nondeterrent) to avoid implicating the Double Jeopardy Clause, then no civil penalties are beyond the scope of the Clause. Under *Halper*'s method of analysis, a court must also look at the "sanction actually imposed" to determine whether the Double Jeopardy Clause is implicated. Thus, it will not be possible to determine whether the Double Jeopardy Clause is violated until a defendant has proceeded through a trial to judgment. But in those cases where the civil proceeding follows the criminal proceeding, this approach flies in the face of the notion that the Double Jeopardy Clause forbids the government from even "attempting a second time to punish criminally."

Finally, it should be noted that some of the ills at which *Halper* was directed are addressed by other constitutional provisions. The Due Process and Equal Protection Clauses already protect individuals from sanctions which are downright irrational. The Eighth Amendment protects against excessive civil fines, including forfeitures. The additional protection afforded by extending double jeopardy protections to proceedings heretofore thought to be civil is more than offset by the confusion created by attempting to distinguish between "punitive" and "nonpunitive" penalties.

Applying traditional double jeopardy principles to the facts of this case, it is clear that the criminal prosecution of these petitioners would not violate the Double Jeopardy Clause. It is evident that Congress intended the OCC money penalties and debarment sanctions imposed for violations of 12 U.S.C. §§ 84 and 375b to be civil in nature. As for the money penalties, both 12 U.S.C. §§ 93(b)(1) and 504(a), which authorize the imposition of monetary penalties for violations of §§ 84 and 375b respectively, expressly provide that such penalties are "civil." While the provision authorizing debarment contains no language explicitly denominating the sanction as civil, we think it significant that the authority to issue debarment orders is conferred upon the "appropriate Federal banking agenc[ies]." That such authority was conferred upon administrative agencies is prima facie evidence that Congress intended to provide for a civil sanction.

Turning to the second stage of the *Ward* test, we find that there is little evidence, much less the clearest proof that we require, suggesting that either OCC money penalties or debarment sanctions are "so punitive in form and effect as to render them criminal despite Congress' intent to the contrary." First, neither money penalties nor debarment have historically been viewed as punishment. We have long recognized that "revocation of a privilege voluntarily granted," such as a debarment, "is characteristically free of the punitive criminal element." . . .

Second, the sanctions imposed do not involve an "affirmative disability or restraint," as that term is normally understood. While petitioners have been prohibited from further participating in the banking industry, this is "certainly nothing approaching the 'infamous punishment' of imprisonment." Third, neither sanction comes into play "only" on a finding of scienter. The provisions under which the money penalties were imposed, allow for the assessment of a penalty against any person "who violates" any of the underlying banking statutes, without regard to the violator's state of mind. "Good faith" is considered by OCC in determining the amount of the penalty to be imposed, but a penalty can be imposed even in the absence of bad faith. The fact that petitioners' "good faith" was considered in determining the amount of the penalty to be imposed in this case is irrelevant, as we look only to "the statute on its face" to determine whether a penalty is criminal in nature. Similarly, while debarment may be imposed for a "willful" disregard "for the safety or soundness of [an] insured depository institution," willfulness is not a prerequisite to debarment; it is sufficient that the disregard for the safety and soundness of the institution was "continuing."

Fourth, the conduct for which OCC sanctions are imposed may also be criminal (and in this case formed the basis for petitioners' indictments). This fact is insufficient to render the money penalties and debarment sanctions criminally punitive, particularly in the double jeopardy context. . . .

Finally, we recognize that the imposition of both money penalties and debarment sanctions will deter others from emulating petitioners' conduct, a traditional goal of criminal punishment. But the mere presence of this purpose is insufficient to render a sanction criminal, as deterrence "may serve civil as well as criminal goals." For example, the sanctions at issue here, while intended to deter future wrongdoing, also serve to promote the stability of the banking industry. To hold that the mere presence of a deterrent purpose renders such sanctions "criminal" for double jeopardy purposes would severely undermine the Government's ability to engage in effective regulation of institutions such as banks.

In sum, there simply is very little showing, to say nothing of the "clearest proof" required by *Ward*, that OCC money penalties and debarment sanctions are criminal. The Double Jeopardy Clause is therefore no obstacle to their trial on the pending indictments, and it may proceed.

The judgment of the Court of Appeals for the Tenth Circuit is accordingly *Affirmed*.

* * *

Justice STEVENS, *concurring in the judgment.*

. . .

III

Despite my disagreement with the Court's decision to use this case as a rather lame excuse for writing a gratuitous essay about punishment, I do agree with its reaffirmation of the central holding of *Halper* and *Department of Revenue of Mont. v. Kurth Ranch*. Both of those cases held that sanctions imposed in civil proceedings constituted "punishment" barred by the Double Jeopardy Clause. Those holdings reconfirmed the settled proposition that the Government cannot use the "civil" label to escape entirely the Double Jeopardy Clause's command, as we have recognized for at least six decades. That proposition is extremely important because the States and the Federal Government have an enormous array of civil administrative sanctions at their disposal that are capable of being used to punish persons repeatedly for the same offense, violating the bedrock double jeopardy principle of finality. "The underlying idea, one that is deeply ingrained in at least the Anglo-American system of jurisprudence, is that the State with all its resources and power should not be allowed to make repeated attempts to convict an individual for an alleged offense, thereby subjecting him to embarrassment, expense and ordeal and compelling him to live in a continuing state of anxiety and insecurity. . . ." However the Court chooses to recalibrate the meaning of punishment for double jeopardy purposes, our doctrine still limits multiple sanctions of the rare sort contemplated by *Halper*.

IV

Today, as it did in *Halper* itself, the Court relies on the sort of multi-factor approach to the definition of punishment that we used in *Kennedy v. Mendoza-Martinez* to identify situations in which a civil sanction is punitive. Whether the Court's reformulation of *Halper*'s test will actually affect the outcome of any cases remains to be seen. Perhaps it will not, since the Court recommends consideration of whether a sanction's " 'operation will promote the traditional aims of punishment retribution and deterrence,' " and " 'whether it appears excessive in relation to the alternative [non-punitive] purpose assigned.' " Those factors look awfully similar to the reasoning in *Halper*, and while we are told that they are never by themselves dispositive, they should be capable of tipping the balance in extreme cases. The danger in changing approaches midstream, rather than refining our established approach on an incremental basis, is that the Government and lower courts may be unduly influenced by the Court's new attitude, rather than its specific pr

It is, of course, entirely appropriate for the Court to perform a lawmaking function as a necessary incident to its Article III responsibility for the decision of "Cases" and "Controversies." In my judgment, however, a desire to reshape the law does not provide a legitimate basis for issuing what amounts to little more than an advisory opinion that, at best, will have the precedential value of pure dictum and may in time unduly restrict the protections of the Double Jeopardy Clause. "It is not the habit of the Court to decide questions of a constitutional nature unless absolutely necessary to a decision of the case." Accordingly, while I concur in the judgment of affirmance, I do not join the Court's opinion.

Justice SOUTER, *concurring in the judgment.*

I concur in the Court's judgment and with much of its opinion. As the Court notes, we have already recognized that *Halper's* statements of standards for identifying what is criminally punitive under the Fifth Amendment needed revision, *United States v. Ursery*, [*infra*, page 139], and there is obvious sense in employing common criteria to point up the criminal nature of a statute for purposes of both the Fifth and Sixth Amendments.

* * *

My acceptance of the *Kennedy-Ward* analytical scheme is subject to caveats, however. As the Court points out, under *Ward*, once it is understood that a legislature intended a penalty to be treated as civil in character, that penalty may be held criminal for Fifth Amendment purposes (and, for like reasons, under the Sixth Amendment) only on the "clearest proof" of its essentially criminal proportions. While there are good and historically grounded reasons for using that phrase to impose a substantial burden on anyone claiming that an apparently civil penalty is in truth criminal, what may be clear enough to be "clearest" is necessarily dependent on context, as indicated by the cases relied on as authority for adopting the standard in *Ward*. . . . I read the requisite "clearest proof" of criminal character, then, to be a function of the strength of the countervailing indications of civil nature (including the presumption of constitutionality enjoyed by an ostensibly civil statute making no provision for the safeguards guaranteed to criminal defendants).

I add the further caution, to be wary of reading the "clearest proof" requirement as a guarantee that such a demonstration is likely to be as rare in the future as it has been in the past. We have noted elsewhere the expanding use of ostensibly civil forfeitures and penalties under the exigencies of the current drug problems, a development doubtless spurred by the increasingly inviting prospect of its profit to the Government. Hence, on the infrequency of "clearest proof," history may not be repetitive.

Justice BREYER, with whom Justice GINSBURG joins, *concurring in the judgment.*

I agree with the majority and with JUSTICE SOUTER that *United States v. Halper* does not provide proper guidance for distinguishing between criminal and non-criminal sanctions and proceedings. I also agree that *United States v. Ward* and *Kennedy v. Mendoza-Martinez* set forth the proper approach.

I do not join the Court's opinion, however, because I disagree with its reasoning in two respects. First, unlike the Court I would not say that " 'only the clearest proof' " will "transform" into a criminal punishment what a legislature calls a "civil remedy." I understand that the Court has taken this language from earlier cases. See *Ward*. But the limitation that the language suggests is not consistent with what the Court has actually done. Rather, in fact if not in theory, the Court has simply applied factors of the *Kennedy* variety to the matter at hand. In *Department of Revenue of Mont. v. Kurth Ranch*, [*infra*, page 109], for example, the Court held that the collection of a state tax imposed on the possession and storage of drugs was "the functional equivalent of a successive criminal prosecution" because, among other things, the tax was "remarkably high"; it had "an obvious deterrent purpose"; it was "conditioned on the commission of a crime"; it was "exacted only after the taxpayer ha[d] been arrested for the precise conduct that gives rise to the tax obligation"; its alternative function of raising revenue could be equally well served by increasing the fine imposed on the activity; and it departed radically from "normal revenue laws" by taxing contraband goods perhaps destroyed before the tax was imposed. This reasoning tracks the non-exclusive list of factors set forth in *Kennedy,* and it is, I believe, the proper approach. The "clearest proof" language is consequently misleading, and I would consign it to the same legal limbo where *Halper* now

Second, I would not decide now that a court should evaluate a statute only " 'on its face,' " rather than "assessing the character of the actual sanctions imposed." *Halper* involved an ordinary civil-fine statute that as normally applied would not have created any "double jeopardy" problem. It was not the statute itself, but rather the disproportionate relation between fine and conduct as the statute was applied in the individual case that led this Court, unanimously, to find that the "civil penalty" was, in those circumstances, a second "punishment" that constituted double jeopardy. Of course, the Court in *Halper* might have reached the same result through application of the constitutional prohibition of "excessive fines." But that is not what the Court there said. And nothing in the majority's opinion today explains why we should abandon this aspect of *Halper*'s holding. Indeed, in context, the language of *Kennedy* that suggests that the Court should consider the statute on its face does not suggest that there may not be further analysis of a penalty as it is applied in a particular case. Most of the lower court confusion and criticism of *Halper* appears to have focused on the problem of characterizing—by examining the face of the statute—the purposes of a civil penalty as punishment, not on the application of double jeopardy analysis to the penalties that are imposed in particular cases. It seems to me quite possible that a statute that provides for a punishment that normally is civil in nature could nonetheless amount to a criminal punishment as applied in special circumstances. And I would not now hold to the con

That said, an analysis of the *Kennedy* factors still leads me to the conclusion that the statutory penalty in this case is not on its face a criminal penalty. Nor, in my view, does the application of the statute to the petitioners in this case amount to criminal punishment. I therefore concur in the result.

NOTES AND QUESTIONS

1. How significant is the *Hudson* Court's conclusion that questions of criminal punishment will be analyzed "on the face" of statutes rather than "assessing the character of actual sanctions imposed"? Under this approach, how would the *Halper* case be decided?

2. If the monetary penalties in *Hudson* are not "criminal punishment" for purposes of the double jeopardy clause might they nevertheless be "fines" for purposes of the excessive fines clause of the Eighth Amendment? See the *Bajakajian* case, *infra*, page 243.

3. As noted in *Hudson*, the *Halper* Court found that the $130,000 civil penalty constituted punishment for purposes of the double jeopardy clause. Yet the *Halper* Court suggests in dicta that "nothing in today's ruling precludes the Government from seeking the full civil penalty against a defendant who has not been punished for the same conduct, *even if the civil sanction imposed is punitive.*" Does this mean that in "civil" proceedings seeking the "punitive civil sanction" the defendant is not entitled to the array of protections provided within the "criminal" process? If so, does *Halper* call into question *Mendoza-Martinez's* holding, *supra* at p. 52, that because expatriation constituted punishment, the defendant was entitled to the protections of the "criminal" process where the government argued the proceedings should be treated as noncriminal and regulatory in nature? This problem is discussed by Justice Scalia in his dissenting opinion in the *Kurth Ranch* case, other opinions *infra* at p. 109. Justice Scalia argues that *Halper* applies a different test for determining "punishment" for purposes of double jeopardy analysis than the test (significantly more deferential to the government) applied in *Mendoza-Martinez* to determine whether the expatriation proceeding constituted a "criminal prosecution" for purposes of the sixth amendment (rights to counsel, trial by jury, etc.) See 511 U.S. 798, 805-808 (Scalia J. dissenting).

4. After *Halper,* should the *Brown* case, *supra* § 2.02 [B][3], be rethought? If punishment can be administered in civil proceedings, what distinguishes criminal from civil law? Is the following useful?

> The very machinery of the criminal law may be seen as providing an official and authentic form of condemnation of particular behavior: conviction in a court of law, the imposition of sentence and the execution of that sentence. . . . In practical terms it is simply the legislative choice of this procedure or process which marks out crimes from civil wrongs: otherwise, it is not possible to account for the large number of strict liability offenses which now form part of the criminal law.
>
> If however, we search for the "essence" of criminal liability rather than for the identifying mark of all crimes, it is perhaps to be found in a

combination of (a) the relative gravity of the harm, loss, or damage concerned and (b) the fact that the offender may be said to have *chosen* to inflict it, in the sense that he knew what he was doing and had some control over his conduct.

Ashworth, *Punishment and Compensation: Victims Offenders and the State,* 6 Oxford J. L. Stud. 86, 98 (1986). Does the "essence" of criminal liability (and criminal law itself) rest in the fact that criminal offenders "choose to inflict their harms" (*i.e.,* they possess *"mens rea"*)? See Chapter 4. Or is *mens rea* required in the criminal law because punishment cannot be justified without personal culpability? See Gardner, *The Mens Rea Enigma: Observations on the Role of Motive in the Criminal Law Past and Present,* 1993 Utah L. Rev. 635, 641–64.3.

5. Some commentators heralded *Halper* as legitimizing "hybrid punitive sanctions" (more-than-compensatory-mo ney sanctions) in civil proceedings. See e.g. Mann, *Punitive Civil Sanctions: The Middle ground between Criminal and Civil Law,* 101 Yale L. J. 1795, 1840–43 (1992). Professor Mann saw *Halper* as an important break from the Court's earlier jurisprudence that employed an array of fictions to avoid findings of "punishment" in hybrid punitive sanction cases in order to escape burdening civil actions with the procedural requirements of the criminal process. Such fictions included simply adhering to legislative labels (if a hybrid sanction is labeled "civil," it is therefore nonpunitive), seeing hybrid sanctions as "rough compensation" rather than punishment, and seeing hybrid actions as regulation aimed at deterring but not punishing undesirable conduct.

6. For an argument in favor of adhering to legislative labels as the basis for distinguishing criminal and civil proceedings, see Cheh, *Constitutional Limits on Using Civil Remedies to Achieve Criminal Law Objectives: Understanding and Transcending the Criminal—Civil Law Distinction,* 42 Hastings L. J. 1325, 1348–64 (1991).

[5] Punishment versus Taxation

DEPARTMENT OF REVENUE OF MONTANA v. KURTH RANCH

Supreme Court of the United States

511 U.S. 767 (1994)

Justice STEVENS *delivered the opinion of the Court.*

This case presents the question whether a tax on the possession of illegal drugs assessed after the State has imposed a criminal penalty for the same conduct may violate the constitutional prohibition against successive punishments for the same offense.[1]

---

[1] The Fifth Amendment provides that "No person shall . . . be subject for the same offence to be twice put in jeopardy of life or limb. . . . " U.S. Const., Amdt. 5. The Double Jeopardy Clause protects against a second prosecution for the same offense after acquittal, a second prosecution for the same offense after conviction, and multiple punishments for the same offense. . . .

I

Montana's Dangerous Drug Tax Act took effect on October 1, 1987. The Act imposes a tax "on the possession and storage of dangerous drugs," and expressly provides that the tax is to be "collected only after any state or federal fines or forfeitures have been satisfied." The tax is either 10 percent of the assessed market value of the drugs as determined by the Montana Department of Revenue (DOR) or a specified amount depending on the drug ($100 per ounce for marijuana, for example, and $250 per ounce for hashish), whichever is greater. The Act directs the state treasurer to allocate the tax proceeds to special funds to support "youth evaluation" and "chemical abuse" programs and "to enforce the drug laws."

In addition to imposing reporting responsibilities on law enforcement agencies,[5] the Act also authorizes the DOR to adopt rules to administer and enforce the tax. Under those rules, taxpayers must file a return within 72 hours of their arrest. The Rule also provides that "[a]t the time of arrest law enforcement personnel shall complete the dangerous drug information report as required by the department and afford the taxpayer an opportunity to sign it." If the taxpayer refuses to do so, the law enforcement officer is required to file the form within 72 hours of the arrest. The "associated criminal nature of assessments under this act" justifies the expedited collection procedures. The taxpayer has no obligation to file a return or to pay any tax unless and until he is arrested.

II

The six respondents, all members of the extended Kurth family, have for years operated a mixed grain and livestock farm in central Montana. In 1986 they began to cultivate and sell marijuana. About two weeks after the new Drug Tax Act went into effect, Montana law enforcement officers raided the farm, arrested the Kurths, and confiscated all the marijuana plants, materials, and paraphernalia they found. . . . The raid put an end to the marijuana business and gave rise to four separate legal proceedings.

In one of those proceedings, the State filed criminal charges against all six respondents in the Montana District Court, charging each with conspiracy to possess drugs with the intent to sell, or, in the alternative, possession of drugs with the intent to sell. Each respondent initially pleaded not guilty, but subsequently entered into a plea agreement. On July 18, 1988, the court sentenced Richard Kurth and Judith Kurth to prison and imposed suspended or deferred sentences on the other four family members.

The county attorney also filed a civil forfeiture action seeking recovery of cash and equipment used in the marijuana operation. The confiscated drugs were not involved in that action, presumably because law enforcement agents had destroyed them after an inventory. The respondents settled the forfeiture action with an agreement to forfeit $18,016.83 in cash and various items of equipment.

---

[5] Section 5(1) of the Act provides that "[a]ll law enforcement personnel and peace officers shall promptly report each person subject to the tax to the department, together with such other information which the department may require, in a manner and on a form prescribed by the department." Mont. Code Ann. § 15.-25-113(1) (1987).

The third proceeding involved the assessment of the new tax on dangerous drugs. Despite difficulties the DOR had in applying the Act for the first time, it ultimately attempted to collect almost $900,000 in taxes on marijuana plants, harvested marijuana, hash tar and hash oil, interest, and penalties. The Kurths . . . initiated the fourth legal proceeding triggered by the raid on their farm: a petition for bankruptcy under Chapter 11 of the Bankruptcy Code.

In the bankruptcy proceedings, the Kurths objected to the DOR's proof of claim for unpaid drug taxes and challenged the constitutionality of the Montana tax. After a trial, the Bankruptcy Court held most of the assessment invalid as a matter of state law, but concluded that an assessment of $181,000 on 1,811 ounces of harvested marijuana was authorized by the Act. It held that assessment invalid under the Federal Constitution.

. . . [T]he Bankruptcy Court decided that the assessment constituted a form of double jeopardy. . . .

The District Court affirmed. . . .

The Court of Appeals for the Ninth Circuit also affirmed. . . .

While this case was pending on appeal, the Montana Supreme Court two lower state court decisions that had held that the Dangerous Drug Tax was a form of double jeopardy. . . . Over the dissent of two Justices, the State Supreme Court found that the legislature had intended to establish a civil, not a criminal, penalty and that the tax had a remedial purpose other than promoting retribution and deterrence. . . .

The Montana Supreme Court's decision is directly at odds with the conclusion reached in the federal proceedings involving the Kurths. We therefore granted certiorari to review the decision of the Court of Appeals. We now affirm its judgment.

[The court discussed *United States v. Halper.*]

* * *

IV

Criminal fines, civil penalties, civil forfeitures, and taxes all share certain features: They generate government revenues, impose fiscal burdens on individuals, and deter certain behavior. All of these sanctions are subject to constitutional constraints. . . . A defendant convicted and punished for an offense may not have a nonremedial civil penalty imposed against him for the same offense in a separate proceeding. . . .

As a general matter, the unlawfulness of an activity does not prevent its taxation. . . . Montana no doubt could collect its tax on the possession of marijuana, for example, if it had not previously punished the taxpayer for the same offense, or, indeed, if it had assessed the tax in the same proceeding that resulted in his conviction. Here, we ask only whether the tax has punitive characteristics that subject it to the constraints of the Double Jeopardy Clause.

Although we have never held that a tax violated the Double Jeopardy Clause, we have assumed that one might. In the context of other constitutional requirements, we have repeatedly examined taxes for constitutional validity. We have cautioned against invalidating a tax simply because its enforcement might be oppressive or because the legislature's motive was somehow suspect. . . . Yet we have also recognized that "there comes a time in the extension of the penalizing features of the so-called tax when it loses its character as such and becomes a mere penalty with the characteristics of regulation and punishment." *A. Magnano Co. v. Hamilton,* 292 U.S. 40, 44 (1934) [citing *Child Labor Tax Case,* 259 U.S. 20, 38 (1922)]. That comment . . . indicates that a tax is not immune from double jeopardy scrutiny simply because it is a tax..

. . . Whereas fines, penalties, and forfeitures are readily characterized as sanctions, taxes are typically different because they are usually motivated by revenue-raising rather than punitive purposes. Yet at some point, an exaction labeled as a tax approaches punishment, and our task is to determine whether Montana's drug tax crosses that line.

We begin by noting that neither a high rate of taxation nor an obvious deterrent purpose automatically marks this tax a form of punishment. In this case, although those factors are not dispositive, they are at least consistent with a punitive character. A significant part of the assessment was more than eight times the drug's market value—a remarkably high tax. That the Montana legislature intended the tax to deter people from possessing marijuana is beyond question.[18] The DOR reminds us, however, that many taxes that are presumed valid, such as taxes on cigarettes and alcohol, are also both high and motivated to some extent by an interest in deterrence. Indeed, although no double jeopardy challenge was at issue, this Court sustained the steep $100-per-ounce federal tax on marijuana in *United States v. Sanchez,* 340 U.S. 42 (1950). Thus, while a high tax rate and deterrent purpose lend support to the characterization of the drug tax as punishment, these features, in and of themselves, do not necessarily render the tax punitive. . . .

Other unusual features, however, set the Montana statute apart from most taxes. First, this so-called tax is conditioned on the commission of a crime. That condition is "significant of penal and prohibitory intent rather than the gathering of revenue." Moreover, the Court has relied on the absence of such a condition to support its conclusion that a particular federal tax was a civil rather than a criminal sanction. In this case, the tax assessment not only hinges on the commission of a crime, it also is exacted only after the taxpayer has been arrested for the precise conduct that gives rise to the tax obligation in the first place. Persons who have been arrested for possessing marijuana constitute the entire class of taxpayers subject to the Montana tax.

Taxes imposed upon illegal activities are fundamentally different from taxes with a purerevenue-raising purpose that are imposed despite their adverse effect on the taxed activity. But they differ as well from mixed-motive taxes that governments impose both to deter a disfavored activity and to raise

---

[18] For example, although the Act's preamble evinces a clear motivation to raise revenue, it also indicates that the tax will provide for anticrime initiatives by "burdening" violators of the law instead of "law abiding taxpayers"; that use of dangerous drugs is not acceptable; and that the Act is not intended to "give credence" to any notion that manufacturing, selling, or using drugs is legal or proper. 1987 Mont. Laws, ch. 563, p.1416.

money. By imposing cigarette taxes, for example, a government wants to discourage smoking. But because the product's benefits—such as creating employment, satisfying consumer demand, and providing tax revenues—are regarded as outweighing the harm, that government will allow the manufacture, sale, and use of cigarettes as long as the manufacturers, sellers, and smokers pay high taxes that reduce consumption and increase government revenue. These justifications vanish when the taxed activity is completely forbidden, for the legitimate revenue-raising purpose that might support such a tax could be equally well served by increasing the fine imposed upon conviction.

The Montana tax is exceptional for an additional reason. Although it purports to be a species of property tax—that is, a "tax on the possession and storage of dangerous drugs," it is levied on goods that the taxpayer neither owns nor possesses when the tax is imposed. Indeed, the State presumably destroyed the contraband goods in this case before the tax on them was assessed. If a statute that amounts to a confiscation of property is unconstitutional . . . a tax on previously confiscated goods is at least questionable. A tax on "possession" of goods that no longer exist and that the taxpayer never lawfully possessed has an unmistakable punitive character. This tax, imposed on criminals and no others, departs so far from normal revenue laws as to become a form of punishment.

Taken as a whole, this drug tax is a concoction of anomalies, too far-removed in crucial respects from a standard tax assessment to escape characterization as punishment for the purpose of Double Jeopardy analysis.

V

* * *

This drug tax is not the kind of remedial sanction that may follow the first punishment of a criminal offense. Instead, it is a second punishment within the contemplation of a constitutional protection that has "deep roots in our history and jurisprudence," . . . and therefore must be imposed during the first prosecution or not at all. The proceeding Montana initiated to collect a tax on the possession of drugs was the functional equivalent of a successive criminal prosecution that placed the Kurths in jeopardy a second time "for the same offence."

The judgment of the Court of Appeals is affirmed.
It is so ordered.

Chief Justice REHNQUIST, *dissenting.*

* * *

The proper question to be asked is whether the Montana Drug tax constitutes a second punishment under the Double Jeopardy Clause for conduct already punished criminally. The Court asks the right question, but reaches the wrong conclusion.

Taxes are customarily enacted to raise revenue to support the costs of government. ("[T]axes are typically different [than fines, penalties, and forfeitures] because they are usually motivated by revenue-raising purposes"). It is also firmly established that taxes may be enacted to deter or even suppress the taxed activity. Constitutional attacks on such laws have been regularly turned aside in our previous decisions. . . .

The Court's opinion today . . . proceeds to hold that a high tax rate and a deterrent purpose "lend support to the characterization of the drug tax as punishment." The Court then discusses "[o]ther unusual features" of the Montana tax which, it concludes, brands this tax as a criminal penalty.

The Court first points to its conclusion that the so-called tax is conditioned on the commission of a crime, a conclusion which the State disputes, and for good reason. The relevant provision of the rule . . . which provides that the tax return "shall be filed within 72 hours of arrest," merely acknowledges the practical realities involved in taxing an illegal activity.[2] Then . . . the Court states that the justifications for mixed motive taxes—imposed both to deter and to raise revenue—vanish "when the taxed activity is completely forbidden."

A second "unusual feature" identified by the Court is that the tax is levied on drugs that the taxpayer neither owns or possesses at the time of taxation. But here, the Court exalts form over substance. Surely the Court is not suggesting that the State must permit the Kurths to keep the contraband in order to tax its possession. . . . ("It would be strange if one carrying on a business the subject of an excise should be able to excuse himself from payment by the plea that in carrying on the business he was violating the law"). And although Montana's "Dangerous Drug Tax" is described as a tax on storage and possession, it is clear from the structure and purpose of the Act that it was passed for the legitimate purpose of raising revenue from the profitable underground drug business.

* * *

. . . I do not find the conditioning of the tax on criminal conduct and arrest to be fatal to this tax's validity; this characteristic simply reflects the reality of taxing an illegal enterprise. . . .

After averaging the effective tax rates on the two marijuana products, the Court concludes that Montana's tax rate of four times the market value appears to be "unrivaled." That may be so. But the proper inquiry is not whether the tax rate is "unrivaled," but whether it is so high that it can only be explained as serving a punitive purpose. When compared to similar types of "sin" taxes on items such as alcohol and cigarettes, these figures are not so high as to be deemed arbitrary or shocking. This is especially so given both

---

[2] Other potential schemes for taxing illegal drug possession will face similar pitfalls. Because the activity sought to be taxed is illegal, individuals cannot be expected to voluntarily identify themselves as subject to the tax. The Minnesota scheme cited by respondents provides for the anonymous purchase of tax stamps prior to, and independent of, any criminal prosecution. Minn. Stat. §§ 297D.01 *et seq.* (1992). Not surprisingly, when asked at oral argument "Does Minnesota collect any money off that scheme. . . Not too many stamps being sold?", counsel for respondents admitted, amidst laughter, that he did not know the answer. Tr. of Oral Arg. 41.

the traditional deference accorded to state authorities regarding matters of taxation, and the fact that a substantial amount of the illegal drug business will escape taxation altogether.[5]

In short, I think the Court's conclusion that the tax here is a punishment is very much at odds with the purpose and effect of the Montana statute. . . . After reviewing the structure and language of the tax provision and comparing the rate of taxation with similar types of sin taxes imposed on lawful products, I would reach the contrary conclusion—that the Montana tax has a nonpenal purpose of raising revenue, as well as the legitimate purpose of deterring conduct, such that it should be regarded as a genuine tax for double jeopardy purposes.

[The dissenting opinion of Justice O'Connor is omitted.]

[The dissenting opinion of Justice Scalia, with whom Justice Thomas joins, is omitted.]

NOTES AND QUESTIONS

1. Does the *Kurth* Court essentially embrace the following observation of professor Leo Katz: Taxes aimed at discouraging conduct and incidentally at raising revenue are nonpunitive "penalties" where the conduct, say smoking cigarettes, is not itself prohibited, but become "punishments" where the conduct taxed is prohibited? See L. Katz, *Bad Acts and Guilty Minds,* 27 (1987). Is such a view consistent with the definitions of punishment outlined earlier in this chapter? See § 2.02[A], *supra.*

2. In *Helverling v. Michell,* 303 U.S. 391 (1938), the Court rejected a taxpayer's claim that a tax proceeding following a criminal prosecution constituted double jeopardy. After Michell was acquitted on a criminal charge of tax evasion, the government brought an action to recover 50 percent of his tax deficiency over and above the amount of the deficiency itself. The Court, rejecting Michell's claim that the second proceeding constituted an attempt to punish him for tax evasion, noted that

> [T]he remedial character of sanctions imposing additions to a tax has been made clear by this court. . . . They are provided primarily as a safeguard for the protection of revenue and to reimburse the Government for the heavy expense of investigation and the loss resulting from the taxpayer's fraud.

Id. at 401.

Can this characterization of the sanction in *Helvering* survive after *Kurth Ranch?*

---

[5] The federal tax on cigarettes is currently at 1.2 cents per cigarette, or 24 cents per package. 26 U.S.C. § 5701(b). While this does not exceed the cost of a pack of cigarettes, the current proposal to boost the cigarette tax to 99 cents per pack could lead to a total tax on cigarettes in some jurisdictions at a rate higher than the 80% rate utilized in this case for the marijuana bud. . . .

[6] Forfeiture: Punishment versus Actions in Rem

AUSTIN V. UNITED STATES

Supreme Court of the United States

509 U.S. 602 (1993)

Justice BLACKMUN *delivered the opinion of the Court.*

In this case, we are asked to decide whether the Excessive Fines Clause of the Eighth Amendment applies to forfeitures of property under 21 U.S.C. §§ 881(a)(4) and (a)(7). We hold that it does and therefore remand the case for consideration of the question whether the forfeiture at issue here was excessive.

I

On August 2, 1990, petitioner Richard Lyle Austin was indicted on four counts of violating South Dakota's drug laws. Austin ultimately pleaded guilty to one count of possessing cocaine with intent to distribute and was sentenced by the state court to seven years' imprisonment. On September 7, the United States filed an *in rem* action in the United States District Court for the District of South Dakota seeking forfeiture of Austin's mobile home and auto body shop under 21 U.S.C. §§ 881(a)(4) and (a)(7).[1] Austin filed a claim and an answer to the complaint.

On February 4, 1991, the United States made a motion, supported by an affidavit from Sioux Falls Police Officer Donald Satterlee, for summary judgment. According to Satterlee's affidavit, Austin met Keith Engebretson at Austin's body shop on June 13, 1990, and agreed to sell cocaine to Engebretson. Austin left the shop, went to his mobile home, and returned to the shop with two grams of cocaine which he sold to Engebretson. State authorities executed a search warrant on the body shop and mobile home the following day. They discovered small amounts of marijuana and cocaine, a .22 caliber revolver, drug paraphernalia, and approximately $4,700 in cash. In opposing summary judgment, Austin argued that forfeiture of the properties would violate the Eighth Amendment.[2] The District Court rejected this argument and entered summary judgment for the United States.

---

[1] These statutes provide for the forfeiture of:

"(4) All conveyances, including aircraft, vehicles, or vessels which are used, or are intended for use, to transport, or in any manner to facilitate the transportation, sale, receipt, possession, or concealment of [controlled substances, their raw materials, and equipment used in their manufacture and distribution.]

* * * * *

"(7) All real property, including any right, title, and interest (including any leasehold interest) in the whole of any lot or tract of land and any appurtenances or improvements, which is used, or intended to be used, in any manner or part, to commit or facilitate the commission of a violation of this subchapter punishable by more than one year's imprisonment. . . . "
Each provision has an "innocent owner" exception. See §§ 881(a)(4)(c) and (a)(7).

[2] "Excessive bail shall not be required, nor excessive fines imposed, nor cruel and unusual punishments inflicted." U.S. Const., Amdt. 8.

The United States Court of Appeals for the Eighth Circuit "reluctantly agree[d] with the government" and affirmed. . . .

We granted certiorari . . . to resolve an apparent conflict with the Court of Appeals for the Second Circuit over the applicability of the Eighth Amendment to *in rem* civil for feitures.

II

Austin contends that the Eighth Amendment's Excessive Fines Clause applies to *in rem* civil forfeiture proceedings. We have had occasion to consider this Clause only once before. In *Browning-Ferris Industries v. Kelco Disposal, Inc.,* 492 U.S. 257 (1989), we held that the Excessive Fines Clause does not limit the award of punitive damages to a private party in a civil suit when the government neither has prosecuted the action nor has any right to receive a share of the damages.

[The Court considered and rejected the argument that the Excessive Fines Clause applies only to "criminal" cases.]

* * *

The purpose of the Eighth Amendment, putting the Bail Clause to one side, was to limit the government's power to punish. The Cruel and Unusual Punishments Clause is self-evidently concerned with punishment. The Excessive Fines Clause limits the Government's power to extract payments, whether in cash or in kind, "as *punishment* for some offense." "The notion of punishment, as we commonly understand it, cuts across the division between the civil and the criminal law." "It is commonly understood that civil proceedings may advance punitive and remedial goals, and, conversely, that both punitive and remedial goals may be served by criminal penalties." Thus, the question is not, as the United States would have it, whether forfeiture under §§ 881(a)(4) and (a)(7) is civil or criminal, but rather whether it is punishment.[6]

In considering this question, we are mindful of the fact that sanctions frequently serve more than one purpose. We need not exclude the possibility that a forfeiture serves remedial purposes to conclude that it is subject to the limitations of the Excessive Fines Clause. We, however, must determine that it can only be explained as serving in part to punish. We said in *Halper* that "a civil sanction that cannot fairly be said solely to serve a remedial purpose, but rather can only be explained as also serving either retributive or deterrent purposes, is punishment, as we have come to understand the term." We turn, then, to consider whether, at the time the Eighth Amendment was ratified, forfeiture was understood at least in part as punishment and whether forfeiture under §§ 881(a)(4) and (a)(7) should be so understood today.

---

[6] For this reason, the United States' reliance on *Kennedy v. Mendoza-Martinez* is misplaced. The question in [that case] was whether a nominally civil penalty should be reclassified as criminal and the safeguards that attend a criminal prosecution should be required. See *Mendoza-Martinez,* 372 U.S., at 167, 184. In addressing the separate question whether punishment is being imposed, the Court has not employed the tests articulated in *Mendoza-Martinez.* See, e.g., *United States v. Halper,* 490 U.S. 435, 447 (1989). [But see *Hudson v. United States,* § 2.02[B][5] *supra,* ed.]

III

A

Three kinds of forfeiture were established in England at the time the Eighth Amendment was ratified in the United States: deodand, forfeiture upon conviction for a felony or treason, and statutory forfeiture. Each was understood, at least in part, as imposing punishment.

At common law the value of an inanimate object directly or indirectly causing the accidental death of a King's subject was forfeited to the Crown as a deodand. The origins of the deodand are traceable to Biblical and pre-Judeo—Christian practices, which reflected the view that the instrument of death was accused and that religious expiation was required. See O. Holmes, *The Common Law,* c. 1 (1881). The value of the instrument was forfeited to the King, in the belief that the King would provide the money for Masses to be said for the good of the dead man's soul, or insure that the deodand was put to charitable uses. 1 W. Blackstone, *Commentaries.* When application of the deodand to religious or eleemosynary purposes ceased, and the deodand became a source of Crown revenue, the institution was justified as a penalty for carelessness.

As Blackstone put it, "such misfortunes are in part owing to the negligence of the owner, and therefore he is properly punished by such forfeiture."

The second kind of common-law forfeiture fell only upon those convicted of a felony or of treason. "The convicted felon forfeited his chattels to the Crown and his lands escheated to his lord; the convicted traitor forfeited all of his property, real and personal, to the Crown." Such forfeitures were known as forfeitures of estate. These forfeitures obviously served to punish felons and traitors . . . and were justified on the ground that property was a right derived from society which one lost by violating society's laws.

Third, "English Law provided for statutory forfeitures of offending objects used in violation of the customs and revenue laws." The most notable of these were the Navigation Acts of 1660 that required the shipping of most commodities in English vessels. Violations of the Acts resulted in the forfeiture of the illegally carried goods as well as the ship that transported them. The statute was construed so that the act of an individual seaman, undertaken without the knowledge of the master or owner, could result in forfeiture of the entire ship. Yet Blackstone considered such forfeiture statutes "penal."

. . . [W]e [have] observed that statutory forfeitures were "likely a product of the confluence and merger of the deodand tradition and the belief that the right to own property could be denied the wrongdoer." Since each of these traditions had a punitive aspect, it is not surprising that forfeiture under the Navigation Acts was justified as a penalty for negligence. . . .

B

Of England's three kinds of forfeiture, only the third took hold in the United States. "Deodands did not become part of the common-law tradition of this country." The Constitution forbids forfeiture of estate as a punishment for treason "except during the Life of the Person attainted," U.S. Const., Art. III,

§ 3, cl. 2, and the First Congress also abolished forfeiture of estate as a punishment for felons. "But–[l]ong before the adoption of the Constitution the common law courts in the Colonies—and later in the states during the period of Confederation—were exercising jurisdiction *in rem* in the enforcement of [English and local] forfeiture statutes.'"

* * *

C

Our cases also have recognized that statutory *in rem* forfeiture imposes punishment. . . .

The same understanding of forfeiture as punishment runs through our cases rejecting the "innocence" of the owner as a common-law defense to forfeiture. In these cases, forfeiture has been justified on two theories—that the property itself is "guilty" of the offense, and that the owner may be held accountable for the wrongs of others to whom he entrusts his property. Both theories rest, at bottom, on the notion that the owner has been negligent in allowing his property to be misused and that he is properly punished for that negligence.

The fiction "that the thing is primarily considered the offender," has a venerable history in our case law. See [e.g.,] *Dobbins's Distillery* [*v. United States,* 96 U.S. 395, 401 (1878)] ("[T]he offence is attached primarily to the distillery, and the real and personal property used in connection with the same, without any regard whatsoever to the personal misconduct or responsibility of the owner"). Yet the Court has understood this fiction to rest on the notion that the owner who allows his property to become involved in an offense has been negligent. Thus . . . the Court said that "ascribing to the property a certain personality, a power of complicity and guilt in the wrong," had "some analogy to the law of *deodand*." It then quoted Blackstone's explanation of the reason for deodand: "'that such misfortunes are in part owing to the negligence of the owner, and therefore he is properly punished by the forfeiture.'"

In none of these cases did the Court apply the guilty-property fiction to justify forfeiture when the owner had done all that reasonably could be expected to prevent the unlawful use of his property. . . . The more recent cases have expressly reserved the question whether the fiction could be employed to forfeit the property of a truly innocent owner. If forfeiture had been understood not to punish the owner, there would have been no reason to reserve the case of a truly innocent owner. Indeed, it is only on the assumption that forfeiture serves in part to punish that the Court's past reservation of that question makes sense.

* * *

We conclude, therefore, that forfeiture generally and statutory *in rem* forfeiture in particular historically have been understood, at least in part, as punishment.

IV

We turn next to consider whether forfeitures under 21 U.S.C. §§ 881(a)(4) and (a)(7) are properly considered punishment today. We find nothing in these provisions or their legislative history to contradict the historical understanding of forfeiture as punishment. Unlike traditional forfeiture statutes, §§ 881(a)(4) and (a)(7) expressly provide an "innocent owner" defense. See § 881(a)(4)(C) ("no conveyance shall be forfeited under this paragraph to the extent of an interest of an owner, by reason of any act or omission established by that owner to have been committed or omitted without the knowledge, consent, or willful blindness of the owner"); § 881(a)(7) ("no property shall be forfeited under this paragraph, to the extent of an interest of an owner, by reason of any act or omission established by that owner to have been committed or omitted without the knowledge or consent of that owner"). . . . These exemptions serve to focus the provisions on the culpability of the owner in a way that makes them look more like punishment, not less. . . . The inclusion of innocent-owner defenses in §§ 881(a)(4) and (a)(7) reveals a . . . congressional intent to punish only those involved in drug trafficking.

Furthermore, Congress has chosen to tie forfeiture directly to the commission of drug offenses. Thus, under § 881(a)(4), a conveyance is forfeitable if it is used or intended for use to facilitate the transportation of controlled substances, their raw materials, or the equipment used to manufacture or distribute them. Under § 881(a)(7), real property is forfeitable if it is used or intended for use to facilitate the commission of a drug-related crime punishable by more than one year's imprisonment.

The legislative history of § 881 confirms the punitive nature of these provisions. When it added subsection (a)(7) to § 881 in 1984, Congress recognized "that the traditional criminal sanctions of fine and imprisonment are inadequate to deter or punish the enormously profitable trade in dangerous drugs." It characterized the forfeiture of real property as "a powerful deterrent."

The Government argues that §§ 881(a)(4) and (a)(7) are not punitive but, rather, should be considered remedial in two respects. First, they remove the "instruments" of the drug trade "thereby protecting the community from the threat of continued drug dealing." Second, the forfeited assets serve to compensate the Government for the expense of law enforcement activity and for its expenditure on societal problems such as urban blight, drug addiction, and other health concerns resulting from the drug trade.

In our view, neither argument withstands scrutiny. Concededly, we have recognized that the forfeiture of contraband itself may be characterized as remedial because it removes dangerous or illegal items from society. The Court, however, previously has rejected government's attempt to extend that reasoning to conveyances used to transport illegal liquor. . . . In that case it noted: "There is nothing even remotely criminal in possessing an automobile." The same, without question, is true of the properties involved here, and the Government's attempt to characterize these properties as "instruments" of the drug trade must . . . [fail].

The Government's second argument about the remedial nature of this forfeiture is no more persuasive. We previously have upheld the forfeiture of goods involved in customs violations as "a reasonable form of liquidated damages." But the dramatic variations in the value of conveyances and real property forfeitable under §§ 881(a)(4) and (a)(7) undercut any similar argument with respect to those provisions. The . . . "forfeiture of property [is] a penalty that ha[s] absolutely no correlation to any damages sustained by society or to the cost of enforcing the law."

Fundamentally, even assuming that §§ 881(a)(4) and (a)(7) serve some remedial purpose, the Government's argument must fail. "[A] civil sanction that cannot fairly be said solely to serve a remedial purpose, but rather can only be explained as also serving either retributive or deterrent purposes, is punishment, as we have come to understand the term." *Halper.* In light of the historical understanding of forfeiture as punishment, the clear focus of §§ 881(a)(4) and (a)(7) on the culpability of the owner, and the evidence that Congress understood those provisions as serving to deter and to punish, we cannot conclude that forfeiture under §§ 881(a)(4) and (a)(7) serves solely a remedial purpose.[14] We therefore conclude that forfeiture under these provisions constitutes "payment to a sovereign as punishment for some offense," . . . and, as such, is subject to the limitations of the Eighth Amendment's Excessive Fines Clause.

V

The judgment of the Court of Appeals is *reversed* and the case is remanded to that court for further proceedings consistent with this opinion.

It is so ordered.

Justice SCALIA, *concurring in part and concurring in the judgment.*

We recently stated that, at the time the Eighth Amendment was drafted, the term "fine" was "understood to mean a payment to a sovereign as punishment for some offense." . . . I write separately to explain why I consider this forfeiture a fine, and to point out that the excessiveness inquiry for statutory *in rem* forfeitures is different from the usual excessiveness inquiry.

I

* * *

In order to constitute a fine under the Eighth Amendment the forfeiture must constitute "punishment," and it is a much closer question whether statutory *in rem* forfeitures, as opposed to *in personam* forfeitures, meet this

---

[14] In *Halper,* we focused on whether "the sanction as applied in the individual case serves the goals of punishment." . . . In this case, however, it makes sense to focus on §§ 881(a)(4) and (a)(7) as a whole. *Halper* involved a small, fixed-penalty provision, which "in the ordinary case . . . can be said to do no more than make the Government whole. The value of the conveyances and real property forfeitable under §§ 881(a)(4) and (a)(7), on the other hand, can vary so dramatically that any relationship between the Government's actual costs and the amount of the sanction is merely coincidental. . . . Furthermore, as we have seen, forfeiture statutes historically have been understood as serving not simply remedial goals but also those of punishment and deterrence. Finally, it appears to make little practical difference whether the Excessive Fines Clause applies to all forfeitures under §§ 881(a)(4) and (a)(7) or only to those that cannot be characterized as purely remedial. The Clause prohibits only the imposition of "excessive" fines, and a fine that serves purely remedial purposes cannot be considered "excessive" in any event.

requirement. The latter are assessments, whether monetary or in-kind, to punish the property owner's criminal conduct, while the former are confiscations of property rights based on improper use of the property, regardless of whether the owner has violated the law. Statutory *in rem* forfeitures have a long history. The property to which they apply is not contraband . . . nor is it necessarily property that can only be used for illegal purposes. The theory of *in rem* forfeiture is said to be that the lawful property has committed an offense.

However the theory may be expressed, it seems to me that this taking of lawful property must be considered, in whole or in part . . . punitive. Its purpose is not compensatory, to make someone whole for injury caused by unlawful use of the property. Punishment is being imposed, whether one quaintly considers its object to be the property itself, or more realistically regards its object to be the property's owner. . . .

The Court apparently believes, however, that only actual culpability of the affected property owner can establish that a forfeiture provision is punitive, and sets out to establish (in Part III) that such culpability exists in the case of *in rem* forfeitures. In my view, however, the caselaw is far more ambiguous than the Court acknowledges. We have never held that the Constitution requires negligence, or any other degree of culpability, to support such forfeitures. A prominent 19th-century treatise explains statutory *in rem* forfeitures solely by reference to the fiction that the property is guilty, strictly separating them from forfeitures that require a personal offense of the owner. See 1 J. Bishop, *Commentaries on Criminal Law* §§ 816, 824, 825, 833 (7th ed. 1882). If the Court is correct that culpability of the owner is essential, then there is no difference (except perhaps the burden of proof) between the traditional *in rem* forfeiture and the traditional *in personam* forfeiture. Well-established common-law distinctions should not be swept away by reliance on bits of dicta.

. . . *Even if* punishment of personal culpability is necessary for a forfeiture to be a fine; and *even* if *in rem* forfeitures in general do not punish personal culpability; the *in rem* forfeiture in this case is a fine. As the Court discusses in Part IV, this statute, in contrast to the traditional *in rem* forfeiture, requires that the owner not be innocent—that he have some degree of culpability for the "guilty" property. Here, the property must "offend" and the owner must not be completely without fault. Nor is there any consideration of compensating for loss, since the value of the property is irrelevant to whether it is forfeited. That . . . make[s] the entire discussion in Part III dictum. Statutory forfeitures under § 881(a) are certainly payment (in kind), *to a sovereign as punishment* for an *offense.*

II

That this forfeiture works as a fine raises the excessiveness issue, on which the Court remands. I agree that a remand is in order, but think it worth pointing out that on remand the excessiveness analysis must be different from that applicable to monetary fines and, perhaps, to *in personam* forfeitures. . . .

. . . Unlike monetary fines, statutory *in rem* forfeitures have traditionally been fixed, not by determining the appropriate value of the penalty in relation to the committed offense, but by determining what property has been "tainted" by unlawful use, to which issue the value of the property is irrelevant. Scales used to measure out unlawful drug sales, for example, are confiscable whether made of the purest gold or the basest metal. But an *in rem* forfeiture goes beyond the traditional limits that the Eighth Amendment permits if it applies to property that cannot properly be regarded as an instrumentality of the offense—the building, for example, in which an isolated drug sale happens to occur. Such a confiscation would be an excessive fine. The question is not *how much* the confiscated property is worth, but *whether* the confiscated property has a close enough relationship to the offense.

. . . The relevant inquiry for an excessive forfeiture under § 881 is the relationship of the property to the offense: Was it close enough to render the property, under traditional standards, "guilty" and hence forfeitable?

I join the Court's opinion in part, and concur in the judgment.

[The opinion of Justice Kennedy, with whom the Chief Justice and Justice Thomas join, concurring in part and concurring in the judgment is omitted.]

NOTES AND QUESTIONS

1. A commentator has described forfeiture as "the most popular 'new' [sanction] for law enforcement officials." Cheh, *Constitutional Limits on Using Civil Remedies to Achieve Criminal Law Objectives: Understanding and Transcending the Criminal—Civil Law Distinction,* 42 Hastings L. J. 1325 (1991). Forfeiture manifests both *in personem* and *in rem* dimensions. The former are aspects of the criminal case against the defendant with the forfeiture affecting only the interests of the defendant in the property. *Id.* at 1340. *In rem* actions, on the other hand, are civil actions brought against the property in order to seize it. The rationales for seizure include removing contraband (the "guilty property" theory); confiscating property used to produce, store, or transport contraband (the "instrumentalities" theory as represented by *Austin*); and denying possessors the use of "proceeds and profits" derived from illegal activity. *Id.* at 1341. All of these categories are broadly defined. "Contraband" includes virtually anything so designated by the legislature, including such things as adulterated products and cars with falsified identification numbers. *Id.* "Instrumentalities" include "any property having even the most tangential connection to criminal activity such as real property where a crime was planned." *Id.* "Profits and proceeds" include the profits from a business fraudulently obtained, as well as any enterprise or goods in which money from criminal activities has been invested with the possibility existing that an entire business enterprise can be forfeited if the defendant has committed crimes in her management or conduct of it. *Id.* at 1341–42.

Not surprisingly, the explosive growth of both state and federal forfeiture schemes to combat criminal activity has triggered a spate of scholarly comment. See, e.g., Fried, *Rationalizing Criminal Forfeiture,* 79 J. Crim. L. & Criminology 328 (1988); Note, *Constitutional Rights and Civil Forfeiture Actions,* 88 Colum. L. Rev. 390 (1988); Comment, *The Scope of Real Property*

Forfeiture for Drug-Related Crimes Under the Comprehensive Forfeiture Act, 137 U. Pa. L. Rev. 303 (1988).

2. In reaching the conclusion that the forfeiture involved in the *Austin* case constituted a form of punishment, the Court relied extensively on the analysis of *United States v. Halper,* largely repudiated in the *Hudson* case, *supra* § 2.02[B][5]. Does the Court's repudiation of *Halper* in *Hudson* call into question the continued viability of *Austin* ?

3. The *Austin* Court reserved the question of whether forfeiture of the goods of "a truly innocent person" is constitutionally permissible. Would forfeitures in such situations be "punishment" so as to be governed by the Eighth Amendment or by the due process doctrine precluding punishment without a conviction of guilt? Does forfeiture of an innocent person's property involve imposing "unpleasant consequences for an offense" under Hart's definition, *infra,* p. 483, or express the community condemnation essential for punishment according to Feinberg, *supra,* p.48? See *Bennis v. Michigan, infra* this section.

See *United States v. A Parcel of Land,* 113 S.Ct. 1126 (1993), where the Court held that protection afforded "innocent owners" under the forfeiture provision of the Comprehensive Drug Abuse Prevention and Control Act of 1970 is not limited to bona fide purchasers who acquire their property interests before the acts giving rise to the forfeiture took place.

4. *Austin* recognizes the possibility that a given punitive forfeiture may constitute an "excessive fine" under the Eighth Amendment. See also *Alexander v. United States,* 509 U.S. 544 (1993). Does Justice Scalia identify in his *Austin* opinion the proper standard: If the property was "close enough" to the offense under "traditional standards" to be forfeitable, it is not an excessive fine? Would this mean, for example, that a defendant making a single minor drug deal from the telephone of his million-dollar home could forfeit his home on the instrumentality theory even if he had not used illegally detained assets in purchasing the home? If this result appears unlikely, consider the *Harmelin* case, *infra* p. 231 § [B], where the Court declined to find a mandatory life sentence without possibility of parole for possession of a quantity of cocaine to be excessive punishment under the cruel and unusual punishments clause of the Eighth Amendment. Is there reason to believe the Court will more rigorously scrutinize forfeitures under the excessive fines clause than it has imprisonment under the cruel and unusual punishments clause? Would the "tax" in *Kurth Ranch* survive "excessiveness" scrutiny? See *United States v. Bajakajian,* § 2.04[B], *infra.*

For an evaluation and criticism of Scalia's position *in Austin,* see Note, *Proportionality in Civil Forfeiture,* 62 Geo. Wash. L. Rev. 456, 475–77 (1994).

5. Note that even though the forfeiture provisions constituted punishment in *Austin,* the double jeopardy clause would not preclude punishing Austin twice: once in the South Dakota action and again in the federal forfeiture proceeding. Under the "dual sovereign" doctrine, the same offense may be tried and punished separately by state and federal sovereignties as well as by separate states having jurisdiction over the matter. W. LaFave and J. Israel, *Criminal Procedure* 1083–85 (2d ed., 1992).

Bennis v. Michigan

Supreme Court of the United States

516 U.S. 442 (1996)

Chief Justice REHNQUIST *delivered the opinion of the Court.*

Petitioner was a joint owner, with her husband, of an automobile in which her husband engaged in sexual activity with a prostitute. A Michigan court ordered the automobile forfeited as a public nuisance, with no offset for her interest, notwithstanding her lack of knowledge of her husband's activity. We hold that the Michigan court order did not offend the Due Process Clause of the Fourteenth Amendment or the Takings Clause of the Fifth Amendment.

Detroit police arrested John Bennis after observing him engaged in a sexual act with a prostitute in the automobile while it was parked on a Detroit city street. Bennis was convicted of gross indecency. The State then sued both Bennis and his wife, petitioner Tina B. Bennis, to have the car declared a public nuisance and abated as such under §§ 600.3801 and 600.3825 of Michigan's Compiled Laws.

Petitioner defended against the abatement of her interest in the car on the ground that, when she entrusted her husband to use the car, she did not know that he would use it to violate Michigan's indecency law. The Wayne County Circuit Court rejected this argument, declared the car a public nuisance, and ordered the car's abatement. In reaching this disposition, the trial court judge recognized the remedial discretion he had under Michigan's case law. He took into account the couple's ownership of "another automobile," so they would not be left "without transportation." He also mentioned his authority to order the payment of one-half of the sale proceeds, after the deduction of costs, to "the innocent co-title holder." He declined to order such a division of sale proceeds in this case because of the age and value of the car (an 11-year-old Pontiac sedan recently purchased by John and Tina Bennis for $600); he commented in this regard: "[T]here's practically nothing left minus costs in a situation such as this."

The Michigan Court of Appeals reversed, holding that regardless of the language of Michigan Compiled Law § 600.3815(2), Michigan Supreme Court precedent interpreting this section prevented the State from abating petitioner's interest absent proof that she knew to what end the car would be used. Alternatively, the intermediate appellate court ruled that the conduct in question did not qualify as a public nuisance because only one occurrence was shown and there was no evidence of payment for the sexual act.

The Michigan Supreme Court reversed the Court of Appeals and reinstated the abatement in its entirety. It concluded as a matter of state law that the episode in the Bennis vehicle was an abatable nuisance. Rejecting the Court of Appeals' interpretation of § 600.3815(2), the court then announced that, in order to abate an owner's interest in a vehicle, Michigan does not need to prove that the owner knew or agreed that her vehicle would be used in a manner proscribed by § 600.3801 when she entrusted it to another user. The court next addressed petitioner's federal constitutional challenges to the State's abatement scheme: The court assumed that petitioner did not know of or consent to the misuse of the Bennis car, and concluded in light of our decisions in *Van Oster v. Kansas*, 272 U.S. 465 (1926), and *Calero-Toledo v. Pearson Yacht Leasing Co.*, 416 U.S. 663 (1974), that Michigan's failure to provide an innocent-owner defense was "without constitutional consequence." The Michigan Supreme Court specifically noted that, in its view, an owner's interest may not be abated when "a vehicle is used without the owner's consent." Furthermore, the court confirmed the trial court's description of the nuisance abatement proceeding as an "equitable action," and considered it "critical" that the trial judge so comprehended the statute.

We granted certiorari in order to determine whether Michigan's abatement scheme has deprived petitioner of her interest in the forfeited car without due process, in violation of the Fourteenth Amendment, or has taken her interest for public use without compensation, in violation of the Fifth Amendment as incorporated by the Fourteenth Amendment. We affirm.

The gravamen of petitioner's due process claim is not that she was denied notice or an opportunity to contest the abatement of her car; she was accorded both. Rather, she claims she was entitled to contest the abatement by showing she did not know her husband would use it to violate Michigan's indecency law. But a long and unbroken line of cases holds that an owner's interest in property may be forfeited by reason of the use to which the property is put even though the owner did not know that it was to be put to such use.

Our earliest opinion to this effect is Justice Story's opinion for the Court in *The Palmyra,* 12 Wheat. 1, 6 L.Ed. 531 (1827). *The Palmyra*, which had been commissioned as a privateer by the King of Spain and had attacked a United States vessel, was captured by a United States war ship and brought into Charleston, South Carolina, for adjudication. On the Government's appeal from the Circuit Court's acquittal of the vessel, it was contended by the owner that the vessel could not be forfeited until he was convicted for the privateering. The Court rejected this contention, explaining: "The thing is here primarily considered as the offender, or rather the offence is attached primarily to the thing." In another admiralty forfeiture decision 17 years later, Justice Story wrote for the Court that in *in rem* admiralty proceedings "the acts of the master and crew. . . bind the interest of the owner of the ship, whether he be innocent or guilty; and he impliedly submits to whatever the law denounces as a forfeiture attached to the ship by reason of their unlawful or wanton wrongs." *Harmony v. United States*, 2 How. 210, 234 (1844).

In *Dobbins's Distillery v. United States*, 96 U.S. 395 (1878), this Court upheld the forfeiture of property used by a lessee in fraudulently avoiding federal alcohol taxes, observing: "Cases often arise where the property of the owner is forfeited on account of the fraud, neglect, or misconduct of those intrusted with its possession, care, and custody, even when the owner is otherwise without fault . . . and it has always been held . . . that the acts of [the possessors] bind the interest of the owner . . . whether he be innocent or guilty."

In *Van Oster v. Kansas*, 272 U.S. 465 (1926), this Court upheld the forfeiture of a purchaser's interest in a car misused by the seller. Van Oster purchased an automobile from a dealer but agreed that the dealer might retain possession for use in its business. The dealer allowed an associate to use the automobile, and the associate used it for the illegal transportation of intoxicating liquor. The State brought a forfeiture action pursuant to a Kansas statute, and Van Oster defended on the ground that the transportation of the liquor in the car was without her knowledge or authority. This Court rejected Van Oster's claim:

> It is not unknown or indeed uncommon for the law to visit upon the owner of property the unpleasant consequences of the unauthorized action of one to whom he has entrusted it. Much of the jurisdiction in admiralty, so much of the statute and common law of liens as enables a mere bailee to subject the bailed property to a lien, the power of a vendor of chattels in possession to sell and convey good title to a stranger, are familiar examples. . . . They suggest that certain uses of property may be regarded as so undesirable that the owner surrenders his control at his peril. . . .
>
> It has long been settled that statutory forfeitures of property entrusted by the innocent owner or lienor to another who uses it in violation of the revenue laws of the United States is not a violation of the due process clause of the Fifth Amendment.

The *Van Oster* Court relied on *J.W. Goldsmith, Jr.-Grant Co. v. United States*, 254 U.S. 505 (1921), in which the Court upheld the forfeiture of a seller's interest in a car misused by the purchaser. The automobile was forfeited after the purchaser transported bootleg distilled spirits in it, and the selling dealership lost the title retained as security for unpaid purchase money. The Court discussed the arguments for and against allowing the forfeiture of the interest of an owner who was "without guilt," and concluded that "whether the reason for [the challenged forfeiture scheme] be artificial or real, it is too firmly fixed in the punitive and remedial jurisprudence of the country to be now displaced."

In *Calero-Toledo v. Pearson Yacht Leasing Co.*, 416 U.S. 663 (1974), the most recent decision on point, the Court reviewed the same cases discussed above, and concluded that "the innocence of the owner of property subject to forfeiture has almost uniformly been rejected as a defense." Petitioner is in the same position as the various owners involved in the forfeiture cases beginning with *The Palmyra* in 1827. She did not know that her car would be used in an illegal activity that would subject it to forfeiture. But under these cases the Due Process Clause of the Fourteenth Amendment does not protect her interest against forfeiture by the government.

Petitioner relies on a passage from *Calero-Toledo*, that "it would be difficult to reject the constitutional claim of . . . an owner who proved not only that he was uninvolved in and unaware of the wrongful activity, but also that he had done all that reasonably could be expected to prevent the proscribed use of his property." But she concedes that this comment was obiter dictum, and "[i]t is to the holdings of our cases, rather than their dicta, that we must attend." And the holding of *Calero-Toledo* on this point was that the interest of a yacht rental company in one of its leased yachts could be forfeited because of its use for transportation of controlled substances, even though the company was "'in no way . . . involved in the criminal enterprise carried on by [the] lessee' and'had no knowledge that its property was being used in connection with or in violation of [Puerto Rican Law].'" Petitioner has made no showing beyond that

The dissent argues that our cases treat contraband differently from instrumentalities used to convey contraband, like cars: Objects in the former class are forfeitable "however blameless or unknowing their owners may be," but with respect to an instrumentality in the latter class, an owner's innocence is no defense only to the "principal use being made of that property." However, this Court's precedent has never made the due process inquiry depend on whether the use for which the instrumentality was forfeited was the principal use. If it had, perhaps cases like *Calero-Toledo*, in which Justice Douglas noted in dissent that there was no showing that the "yacht had been notoriously used in smuggling drugs . . . and so far as we know only one marihuana cigarette was found on the yacht," might have been decided differently.

The dissent also suggests that *The Palmyra* line of cases "would justify the confiscation of an ocean liner just because one of its passengers sinned while on board." None of our cases have held that an ocean liner may be confiscated because of the activities of one passenger. We said in *Goldsmith-Grant*, and we repeat here, that "[w]hen suchapplication shall be made it will be time enough to pronounce upon it."

Notwithstanding this well-established authority rejecting the innocent-owner defense, petitioner argues that we should in effect overrule it by importing a culpability requirement from cases having at best a tangential relation to the "innocent owner" doctrine in forfeiture cases. She cites *Foucha v. Louisiana*, 504 U.S. 71 (1992), for the proposition that a criminal defendant may not be punished for a crime if he is found to be not guilty. She also argues that our holding in *Austin v. United States*, that the Excessive Fines Clause limits the scope of civil forfeiture judgments, "would be difficult to reconcile with any rule allowing truly innocent persons to be punished by civil forfeiture."

In *Foucha* the Court held that a defendant found not guilty by reason of insanity in a criminal trial could not be thereafter confined indefinitely by the State without a showing that he was either dangerous or mentally ill. Petitioner argues that our statement that in those circumstances a State has no "punitive interest" which would justify continued detention requires that Michigan demonstrate a punitive interest in depriving her of her interest in the forfeited car. But, putting aside the extent to which a forfeiture proceeding is "punishment" in the first place, *Foucha* did not purport to discuss, let alone overrule, *The Palmyra* line of cases.

In *Austin*, the Court held that because "forfeiture serves, at least in part, to punish the owner," forfeiture proceedings are subject to the limitations of the Eighth Amendment's prohibition against excessive fines. There was no occasion in that case to deal with the validity of the "innocent-owner defense," other than to point out that if a forfeiture statute allows such a defense, the defense is additional evidence that the statute itself is "punitive" in motive. In this case, however, Michigan's Supreme Court emphasized with respect to the forfeiture proceeding at issue: "It is not contested that this is an equitable action," in which the trial judge has discretion to consider "alternatives [to] abating the entire interest in the vehicle."

In any event, for the reasons pointed out in *Calero-Toledo* and *Van Oster*, forfeiture also serves a deterrent purpose distinct from any punitive purpose. Forfeiture of property prevents illegal uses "both by preventing further illicit use of the [property] and by imposing an economic penalty, thereby rendering illegal behavior unprofitable." This deterrent mechanism is hardly unique to forfeiture. For instance, because Michigan also deters dangerous driving by making a motor vehicle owner liable for the negligent operation of the vehicle by a driver who had the owner's consent to use it, petitioner was also potentially liable for her husband's use of the car in violation of Michigan negligence law. "The law thus builds a secondary defense against a forbidden use and precludes evasions by dispensing with the necessity of judicial inquiry as to collusion between the wrongdoer and the alleged innocent owner."

* * *

At bottom, petitioner's claims depend on an argument that the Michigan forfeiture statute is unfair because it relieves prosecutors from the burden of separating co-owners who are complicit in the wrongful use of property from innocent co-owners. This argument, in the abstract, has considerable appeal. . . . Its force is reduced in the instant case, however, by the Michigan Supreme Court's confirmation of the trial court's remedial discretion, and petitioner's recognition that Michigan may forfeit her and her husband's car whether or not she is entitled to an offset for her interest in it.

We conclude today, as we concluded 75 years ago, that the cases authorizing actions of the kind at issue are "too firmly fixed in the punitive and remedial jurisprudence of the country to be now displaced." The State here sought to deter illegal activity that contributes to neighborhood deterioration and unsafe streets. The Bennis automobile, it is conceded, facilitated and was used in criminal activity. Both the trial court and the Michigan Supreme Court followed our longstanding practice, and the judgment of the Supreme Court of Michigan is therefore *Affirmed*.

Justice THOMAS, *concurring*.

I join the opinion of the Court.

Mrs. Bennis points out that her property was forfeited even though the State did not prove her guilty of any wrongdoing. The State responds that forfeiture of property simply because it was used in crime has been permitted time out of mind. It also says that it wants to punish, for deterrence and perhaps also for retributive purposes, persons who may have colluded or acquiesced in criminal use of their property, or who may at least have negligently entrusted their property to someone likely to use it for misfeasance. But, the State continues, it does not want to have to prove (or to refute proof regarding) collusion, acquiescence, or negligence.

As the Court notes, evasion of the normal requirement of proof before punishment might well seem "unfair." One unaware of the history of forfeiture laws and 200 years of this Court's precedent regarding such laws might well assume that such a scheme is lawless a violation of due process. As the Court remarked 75 years ago in ruling upon a constitutional challenge to forfeiture of the property of an innocent owner:

> If the case were the first of its kind, it and its apparent paradoxes might compel a lengthy discussion to harmonize the [statute at issue] with the accepted tests of human conduct. . . . There is strength . . . in the contention that . . . [the statute at issue] seems to violate that justice which should be the foundation of the due process of law required by the Constitution.

But the Court went on to uphold the statute, based upon the historical prevalence and acceptance of similar laws.

This case is ultimately a reminder that the Federal Constitution does not prohibit everything that is intensely undesirable. As detailed in the Court's opinion and the cases cited therein, forfeiture of property without proof of the owner's wrongdoing, merely because it was "used" in or was an "instrumentality" of crime has been permitted in England and this country, both before and after the adoption of the Fifth and Fourteenth Amendments. . . .

The limits on what property can be forfeited as a result of what wrongdoing for example, what it means to "use" property in crime for purposes of forfeiture law are not clear to me. Those limits, whatever they may be, become especially significant when they are the sole restrictions on the state's ability to take property from those it merely suspects, or does not even suspect, of colluding in crime. It thus seems appropriate, where a constitutional challenge by an innocent owner is concerned, to apply those limits rather strictly, adhering to historical standards for determining whether specific property is an "instrumentality" of crime. The facts here, however, do not seem to me to be obviously distinguishable from those involved in *Van Oster* and in any event, Mrs. Bennis has not asserted that the car was not an instrumentality of her husband's crime.

If anything, the forfeiture in *Van Oster* was harder to justify than is the forfeiture here, albeit in a different respect. In this case, the trial judge apparently found that the sales price of the car would not exceed by much the "costs" to be deducted from the sale; and he took that fact into account in determining how to dispose of the proceeds of the sale of the car. The state statute has labeled the car a "nuisance" and authorized a procedure for preventing the risk of continued criminal use of it by Mr. Bennis (forfeiture and sale); under a different statutory regime, the State might have authorized the destruction of the car instead, and the State would have had a plausible argument that the order for destruction was "remedial" and thus noncompensable. That it chose to order the car sold, with virtually nothing left over for the State after "costs," may not change the "remedial" character of the State's action substantially. And if the forfeiture of the car here (and the State's refusal to remit any share of the proceeds from its sale to Mrs. Bennis) can appropriately be characterized as "remedial" action, then the more severe problems involved in punishing someone not found to have engaged in wrongdoing of any kind do not arise.

Improperly used, forfeiture could become more like a roulette wheel employed to raise revenue from innocent but hapless owners whose property is unforeseeably misused, or a tool wielded to punish those who associate with criminals, than a component of a system of justice. When the property sought to be forfeited has been entrusted by its owner to one who uses it for crime, however, the Constitution apparently assigns to the States and to the political branches of the Federal Government the primary responsibility for avoiding that result.

Justice GINSBURG, *concurring*.

I join the opinion of the Court and highlight features of the case key to my judgment.

The dissenting opinions target a law scarcely resembling Michigan's "red light abatement" prescription, as interpreted by the State's courts. First, it bears emphasis that the car in question belonged to John Bennis as much as it did to Tina Bennis. At all times he had her consent to use the car, just as she had his. And it is uncontested that Michigan may forfeit the vehicle itself. The sole question, then, is whether Tina Bennis is entitled not to the car, but to a portion of the proceeds (if any there be after deduction of police, prosecutorial, and court costs) as a matter of constitutional right.

Second, it was "critical" to the judgment of the Michigan Supreme Court that the nuisance abatement proceeding is an "equitable action." That means the State's Supreme Court stands ready to police exorbitant applications of the statute. It shows no respect for Michigan's high court to attribute to its members tolerance of, or insensitivity to, inequitable administration of an "equitable action."

Nor is it fair to charge the trial court with "blatant unfairness" in the case at hand. That court declined to order a division of sale proceeds, as the trial judge took pains to explain, for two practical reasons: the Bennises have "another automobile," and the age and value of the forfeited car (an 11-year-old Pontiac purchased by John and Tina Bennis for $600) left "practically nothing" to divide after subtraction of costs.

Michigan, in short, has not embarked on an experiment to punish innocent third parties. Nor do we condone any such experiment. Michigan has decided to deter Johns from using cars they own (or co-own) to contribute to neighborhood blight, and that abatement endeavor hardly warrants this Court's disapprobation.

Justice STEVENS, with whom Justice SOUTER and Justice BREYER join, *dissenting*.

For centuries prostitutes have been plying their trade on other people's property. Assignations have occurred in palaces, luxury hotels, cruise ships, college dormitories, truck stops, back alleys and back seats. A profession of this vintage has provided governments with countless opportunities to use novel weapons to curtail its abuses. As far as I am aware, however, it was not until 1988 that any State decided to experiment with the punishment of innocent third parties by confiscating property in which, or on which, a single transaction with a prostitute has been consummated.

The logic of the Court's analysis would permit the States to exercise virtually unbridled power to confiscate vast amounts of property where professional criminals have engaged in illegal acts. Some airline passengers have marijuana cigarettes in their luggage; some hotel guests are thieves; some spectators at professional sports events carry concealed weapons; and some hitchhikers are prostitutes. The State surely may impose strict obligations on the owners of airlines, hotels, stadiums, and vehicles to exercise a high degree of care to prevent others from making illegal use of their property, but neither logic nor history supports the Court's apparent assumption that their complete innocence imposes no constitutional impediment to the seizure of their property simply because it provided the locus for a criminal transaction.

In order to emphasize the novelty of the Court's holding, I shall first comment on the tenuous connection between the property forfeited here and the illegal act that was intended to be punished, which differentiates this case from the precedent on which the Court relies. I shall then comment on the significance of the complete lack of culpability ascribable to petitioner in this case. Finally, I shall explain why I believe our recent decision in *Austin v. United States* compels reversal.

I

For purposes of analysis it is useful to identify three different categories of property that are subject to seizure: pure contraband; proceeds of criminal activity; and tools of the criminal's trade.

The first category—pure contraband—encompasses items such as adulterated food, sawed-off shotguns, narcotics, and smuggled goods. With respect to such "objects the possession of which, without more, constitutes a crime," the government has an obvious remedial interest in removing the items from private circulation, however blameless or unknowing their owners may be. The States' broad and well-established power to seize pure contraband is not implicated by this case, for automobiles are not contraband.

The second category—proceeds—traditionally covered only stolen property, whose return to its original owner has a powerful restitutionary justification. Recent federal statutory enactments have dramatically enlarged this category to include the earnings from various illegal transactions. Because those federal statutes include protections for innocent owners, cases arising out of the seizure of proceeds do not address the question whether the Constitution would provide a defense to an innocent owner in certain circumstances if the statute had not done so. The prevalence of protection for innocent owners in such legislation does, however, lend support to the conclusion that elementary notions of fairness require some attention to the impact of a seizure on the rights of innocent parties.

The third category includes tools or instrumentalities that a wrongdoer has used in the commission of a crime, also known as "derivative contraband." Forfeiture is more problematic for this category of property than for the first two, both because of its potentially far broader sweep, and because the government's remedial interest in confiscation is less apparent. Many of our earliest cases arising out of these kinds of seizures involved ships that engaged in piracy on the high seas, in the slavetrade, or in the smuggling of cargoes of goods into the United States. These seizures by the sovereign were approved despite the faultlessness of the ship's owner. Because the entire mission of the ship was unlawful, admiralty law treated the vessel itself as if it were the offender. Moreover, under "the maritime law of the Middle Ages the ship was not only the source, but the limit, of liability."

The early admiralty cases demonstrate that the law may reasonably presume that the owner of valuable property is aware of the principal use being made of that property. That presumption provides an adequate justification for the deprivation of one's title to real estate because of another's adverse possession for a period of years or for a seizure of such property because its principal use is unlawful. Thus, in *Dobbins's Distillery v. United States*, we upheld the seizure of premises on which the lessee operated an unlawful distillery when the owner "knowingly suffer[ed] and permitt[ed] his land to be used as a site" for that distillery. And despite the faultlessness of their owners, we have upheld seizures of vehicles being used to transport bootleg liquor, or to smuggle goods into the United States in violation of our customs laws.

While our historical cases establish the propriety of seizing a freighter when its entire cargo consists of smuggled goods, none of them would justify the confiscation of an ocean liner just because one of its passengers sinned while on board. The principal use of the car in this case was not to provide a site for petitioner's husband to carry out forbidden trysts. Indeed, there is no evidence in the record that the car had ever previously been used for a similar purpose. An isolated misuse of a stationary vehicle should not justify the forfeiture of an innocent owner's property on the theory that it constituted an instrumentality of the crime.

This case differs from our historical precedents in a second, crucial way. In those cases, the vehicles or the property actually facilitated the offenses themselves. Our leading decisions on forfeited conveyances, for example, involved offenses of which transportation was an element. In *Van Oster v. Kansas*, for example, the applicable statute prohibited transportation of intoxicating liquor. In *Calero-Toledo v. Pearson Yacht Leasing Co.*, similarly, a yacht was seized because it had been used "to transport, or to facilitate the transportation of" a controlled substance. Here, on the other hand, the forfeited property bore no necessary connection to the offense committed by petitioner's husband. It is true that the act occurred in the car, but it might just as well have occurred in a multitude of other locations. The mobile character of the car played a part only in the negotiation, but not in the consummation of the offense.

In recent years, a majority of the members of this Court has agreed that the concept of an instrumentality subject to forfeiture also expressed as the idea of "tainted" items must have an outer limit. In *Austin*, the Court rejected the argument that a mobile home and auto body shop where an illegal drug transaction occurred were forfeitable as "instruments" of the drug trade. . . . The car in this case, however, was used as little more than an enclosure for a one-time event, effectively no different from a piece of real property. By the rule laid down in our recent cases, that nexus is insufficient to support the forfeiture here.

The State attempts to characterize this forfeiture as serving exclusively remedial, as opposed to punitive ends, because its goal was to abate what the State termed a "nuisance." Even if the State were correct, that argument would not rebut the excessiveness of the forfeiture, which I have discussed above. But in any event, there is no serious claim that the confiscation in this case was not punitive. The majority itself concedes that " 'forfeiture serves, at least in part, to punish the owner.' " At an earlier stage of this litigation, the State unequivocally argued that confiscation of automobiles in the circumstances of this case "is swift and certain 'punishment' of the voluntary vice consumer." Therefore, the idea that this forfeiture did not punish petitioner's husband and, a fortiori, petitioner herself–is simply not sustai

Even judged in isolation, the remedial interest in this forfeiture falls far short of that which we have found present in other cases. Forfeiture may serve remedial ends when removal of certain items (such as a burglar's tools) will prevent repeated violations of the law (such as housebreaking). But confiscating petitioner's car does not disable her husband from using other venues for similar illegal rendezvous, since all that is needed to commit this offense is a place. In fact, according to testimony at trial, petitioner's husband had been sighted twice during the previous summer, without the car, soliciting prostitutes in the same neighborhood. The remedial rationale is even less convincing according to the State's "nuisance" theory, for that theory treats the car as a nuisance only so long as the illegal event is occurring and only so long as the car is located in the relevant neighborhood. The need to "abate" the car thus disappears the moment it leaves the area. In short, therefore, a remedial justification simply does not apply to a confiscation of this type.

II

Apart from the lack of a sufficient nexus between petitioner's car and the offense her husband committed, I would reverse because petitioner is entirely without responsibility for that act. Fundamental fairness prohibits the punishment of innocent people.

The majority insists that it is a settled rule that the owner of property is strictly liable for wrongful uses to which that property is put. Only three Terms ago, however, the Court surveyed the same historical antecedents and held that all of its forfeiture decisions rested "at bottom, on the notion that the owner has been negligent in allowing his property to be misused and that he is properly punished for that negligence." *Austin v. United States.* According to *Austin,* even the hoary fiction that property was forfeitable because of its own guilt was based on the idea that " 'such misfortunes are in part owing to the negligence of the owner, and therefore he is properly punished by the forfeiture.' " It is conceded that petitioner was in no way negligent in her use or entrustment of the family car. Thus, no forfeiture should have been permitted. The majority, however, simply ignores *Austin*'s detailed analysis of our case law without explanation or co

Even assuming that strict liability applies to "innocent" owners, we have consistently recognized an exception for truly blameless individuals. The Court's opinion in *Calero-Toledo v. Pearson Yacht Leasing Co.* established the proposition that the Constitution bars the punitive forfeiture of property when its owner alleges and proves that he took all reasonable steps to prevent its illegal use. The majority dismisses this statement as "obiter dictum," but we have assumed that such a principle existed, or expressly reserved the question, in a line of cases dating back nearly 200 years. In one of its earliest decisions, the Court, speaking through Chief Justice Marshall, recognized as "unquestionably a correct legal principle" that "a forfeiture can only be applied to those cases in which the means that are prescribed for the prevention of a forfeiture may be employed." *Peisch v. Ware*, 4 Cranch 347, 363 (1808). In other contexts, we have regarded as axiomatic that persons cannot be punished when they have done no wrong. I would hold now what we have always assumed: that the principle is required by due process.

The unique facts of this case demonstrate that petitioner is entitled to the protection of that rule. The subject of this forfeiture was certainly not contraband. It was not acquired with the proceeds of criminal activity and its principal use was entirely legitimate. It was an ordinary car that petitioner's husband used to commute to the steel mill where he worked. Petitioner testified that they had been married for nine years; that she had acquired her ownership interest in the vehicle by the expenditure of money that she had earned herself; that she had no knowledge of her husband's plans to do anything with the car except "come directly home from work," as he had always done before; and that she even called "Missing Persons" when he failed to return on the night in question. Her testimony is not contradicted and certainly is credible. Without knowledge that he would commit such an act in the family car, or that he had ever done so previously, surely petitioner cannot be accused of failing to take "reasonable steps" to prevent the illicit behavior. She is just as blameless as if a thief, rather than her husband, had used the car in a criminal episode.

While the majority admits that this forfeiture is at least partly punitive in nature, it asserts that Michigan's law also serves a "deterrent purpose distinct from any punitive purpose." But that is no distinction at all; deterrence is itself one of the aims of punishment.

Even on a deterrence rationale, moreover, that goal is not fairly served in the case of a person who has taken all reasonable steps to prevent an illegal act.

Forfeiture of an innocent owner's property that plays a central role in a criminal enterprise may be justified on reasoning comparable to the basis for imposing liability on a principal for an agent's torts. Just as the risk of respondeat superior liability encourages employers to supervise more closely their employees' conduct, so the risk of forfeiture encourages owners to exercise care in entrusting their property to others. But the law of agency recognizes limits on the imposition of vicarious liability in situations where no deterrent function is likely to be served; for example, it exonerates the employer when the agent strays from his intended mission and embarks on a "frolic of his own." In this case, petitioner did not "entrust" the car to her husband on the night in question; he was entitled to use it by virtue of their joint ownership. There is no reason to think that the threat of forfeiture will deter an individual from buying a car with her husband or from marrying him in the first place if she neither knows nor has reason to know that he plans to use it wrongfully.

The same is true of the second asserted justification for strict liability, that it relieves the State of the difficulty of proving collusion, or disproving the lack thereof, by the alleged innocent owner and the wrongdoer. Whatever validity that interest might have in another kind of case, it has none here. It is patently clear that petitioner did not collude with her husband to carry out this offense.

The absence of any deterrent value reinforces the punitive nature of this forfeiture law. But petitioner has done nothing that warrants punishment. She cannot be accused of negligence or of any other dereliction in allowing her husband to use the car for the wholly legitimate purpose of transporting himself to and from his job. She affirmatively alleged and proved that she is not in any way responsible for the conduct that gave rise to the seizure. If anything, she was a victim of that conduct. In my opinion, these facts establish that the seizure constituted an arbitrary deprivation of property without due process of law.

III

The Court's holding today is dramatically at odds with our holding in *Austin v. United States*. We there established that when a forfeiture constitutes "payment to a sovereign as punishment for some offense" as it undeniably does in this case it is subject to the limitations of the Eighth Amendment's Excessive Fines Clause. For both of the reasons I have already discussed, the forfeiture of petitioner's half-interest in her car is surely a form of "excessive" punishment. For an individual who merely let her husband use her car to commute to work, even a modest penalty is out of all proportion to her blameworthiness; and when the assessment is confiscation of the entire car, simply because an illicit act took place once in the driver's seat, the punishment is plainly excessive. This penalty violates the Eighth Amendment for yet another reason. Under the Court's reasoning, the value of the car is irrelevant. A brand-new luxury sedan or a ten-year-old used car would be equally forfeitable. We have held that "dramatic variations" in the value of conveyances subject to forfeiture actions undercut any argument that the latter are reasonably tied to remedial ends.

I believe the Court errs today by assuming that the power to seize property is virtually unlimited and by implying that our opinions in *Calero-Toledo* and *Austin* were misguided. Some 75 years ago, when presented with the argument that the forfeiture scheme we approved had no limit, we insisted that expansive application of the law had not yet come to pass. "When such application shall be made," we said, "it will be time enough to pronounce upon it." That time has arrived when the State forfeits a woman's car because her husband has secretly committed a misdemeanor inside it. While I am not prepared to draw a bright line that will separate the permissible and impermissible forfeitures of the property of innocent owners, I am convinced that the blatant unfairness of this seizure places it on the unconstitutional side of that line.

I therefore respectfully dissent.

Justice KENNEDY, *dissenting.*

The forfeiture of vessels pursuant to the admiralty and maritime law has a long, well-recognized tradition, evolving as it did from the necessity of finding some source of compensation for injuries done by a vessel whose responsible owners were often half a world away and beyond the practical reach of the law and its processes. The prospect of deriving prompt compensation from *in rem* forfeiture, and the impracticality of adjudicating the innocence of the owners or their good-faith efforts in finding a diligent and trustworthy master, combined to eliminate the owner's lack of culpability as a defense. Those realities provided a better justification for forfeiture than earlier, more mechanistic rationales. The trade-off, of course, was that the owner's absolute liability was limited to the amount of the vessel and (or) its cargo. For that reason, it seems to me inaccurate, or at least not well supported, to say that the owner's personal culpability was part of the forfeiture rationale. . . . [E]ven the well-recognized tradition of forfeiture in admiralty has not been sufficient for an unequivocal confirmation from this Court that a vessel in all instances is seizable when it is used for criminal activity without the knowledge or consent of the owner.

We can assume the continued validity of our admiralty forfeiture cases without in every analogous instance extending them to the automobile, which is a practical necessity in modern life for so many people. At least to this point, it has not been shown that a strong presumption of negligent entrustment or criminal complicity would be insufficient to protect the government's interest where the automobile is involved in a criminal act in the tangential way that it was here. Furthermore. . . the automobile in this case was not used to transport contraband, and so the seizure here goes beyond the line of cases which sustain the government's use of forfeiture to suppress traffic of that sort.

This forfeiture cannot meet the requirements of due process. Nothing in the rationale of the Michigan Supreme Court indicates that the forfeiture turned on the negligence or complicity of petitioner, or a presumption thereof, and nothing supports the suggestion that the value of her co-ownership is so insignificant as to be beneath the law's protection. For these reasons, and with all respect, I dissent.

NOTES AND QUESTIONS

1. Is the Court's finding that the forfeiture of the Bennis' car is remedial rather than punitive at odds with *Austin*'s finding that the forfeiture of a mobile home and car repair shop constitutes a punitive forfeiture? Is it consistent with the test forwarded in *Hudson*, § 2.02[4] *supra*, to determine what constitutes punishment?

2. Was Mrs. Bennis, by entrusting her husband with the use of the car she co-owned with him, negligent? Does the majority rule stand for the proposition that co-owners of property are strictly liable for the criminal activities of the other? If so, is that theoretically sound?

If Mr. and Mrs. Bennis co-owned the car, presumably, Mrs. Bennis may not have been able to prevent Mr. Bennis from using the car. Even if Mrs. Bennis knew or had reason to know Mr. Bennis was going to take the car and use if for solicitation and fornication with a prostitute, could she have stopped him from using the car for criminal purposes?

3. If forfeiture of the Bennis's car is justifiable, is the answer the same if the state attempts to seize their house, business or yacht if Mr. Bennis had taken the prostitute "home," to his place of business, or to a yacht? See, *Colero-Toledo v. Pearson Yacht Leasing Co.*, 416 U.S. 663 (1974).

4. The Court noted that there was an increase in prostitution in the area in which Mr. Bennis was discovered with the prostitute. If the same conduct occurred in another area of town where prostitution was not a common problem, would the State have had a basis for declaring the car a nuisance and therefore be justified in its forfeiture proceeding?

5. Was Mrs. Bennis "punished" for the illegal conduct of her husband? Is so, would Mrs. Bennis have a different (a better?) argument than the "takings" argument?

6. The Court in *Austin* seemed to retreat from the common law idea that forfeiture of property following criminal behavior is levied against the thing and instead agreed that it is imposed against the criminal actor. Is *Bennis* a return to the former conceptualization used at common law?

7. When a fine is imposed as punishment for criminal behavior, presumably the spouse of the offender also suffers because the cost of paying the fine depletes the total family resources. Is the situation in *Bennis* any different where the state seizes a car from a married couple? Is it any different when a spouse is sentenced to a lengthy prison term or to the electric chair? Is any of this suffering "punishment"?

8. If the government had seized the Bennis's late model Lexis might the outcome of the case have been different? Consider the language used by the trial court that even after the sale of the car minus costs, there would have been no money left to give to Mrs. Bennis. Should the value of the item determine whether seizure constitutes a legal or illegal forfeiture?

9. If the forfeiture of the mobile home and car repair shop in *Austin* is subject to the Excessive Fines Clause in the Eighth Amendment, might the *Bennis* facts also be subjected to such scrutiny? If so, why did Mrs. Bennis fail to challenge the forfeiture of the car as an excessive fine under the Eighth Amendment? See *Austin*, p. 116, *supra*. See also, *Bajakajian*, 2.04[B] *infra*. Had this issue been so raised, would forfeiture of the car have constituted an excessive fine? Against Mr. Bennis? Against Mrs. Bennis?

UNITED STATES v. URSERY

Supreme Court of the United States

518 U.S. 267 (1996)

Chief Justice REHNQUIST delivered the opinion of the Court.

In separate cases, the United States Court of Appeals for the Sixth Circuit and the United States Court of Appeals for the Ninth Circuit held that the Double Jeopardy Clause prohibits the Government from both punishing a defendant for a criminal offense and forfeiting his property for that same offense in a separate civil proceeding. We consolidated those cases for our review, and now reverse. These civil forfeitures (and civil forfeitures generally), we hold, do not constitute "punishment" for purposes of the Double Jeopardy Clause.

I

Michigan Police found marijuana growing adjacent to respondent Guy Ursery's house, and discovered marijuana seeds, stems, stalks, and a growlight within the house. The United States instituted civil forfeiture proceedings against the house, alleging that the property was subject to forfeiture under 84 Stat. 1276, as amended, 21 U.S.C. § 881(a)(7) because it had been used for several years to facilitate the unlawful processing and distribution of a controlled substance. Ursery ultimately paid the United States $13,250 to settle the forfeiture claim in full. Shortly before the settlement was consummated, Ursery was indicted for manufacturing marijuana, in violation of § 841(a)(1). A jury found him guilty, and he was sentenced to 63 months in prison.

The Court of Appeals for the Sixth Circuit by a divided vote reversed Ursery's criminal conviction, holding that the conviction violated the Double Jeopardy Clause of the Fifth Amendment of the United States Constitution. The court based its conclusion in part upon its belief that our decisions in *United States v. Halper* and *Austin v. United States*, [casebook, p. 116] meant that any civil forfeiture under § 881(a)(7) constitutes punishment for purposes of the Double Jeopardy Clause. Ursery, in the court's view, had therefore been "punished" in the forfeiture proceeding against his property, and could not be subsequently criminally tried for violation of 21 U.S.C. § 841(a)(1).

[The Court reviewed a companion case arising from the Ninth Circuit Court of Appeals in which property was seized under 18 U.S.C. § 981 (a)(1)(A)].

We granted the Government's petition for certiorari in each of the two cases, and we now reverse.

II

The Double Jeopardy Clause provides: "[N]or shall any person be subject for the same offence to be twice put in jeopardy of life or limb." U.S. Const., Amdt. 5. The Clause serves the function of preventing both "successive punishments and . . . successive prosecutions." The protection against multiple punishments prohibits the Government from " 'punishing twice, or attempting a second time to punish criminally for the same offense.'

In the decisions that we review, the Courts of Appeals held that the civil forfeitures constituted "punishment," making them subject to the prohibitions of the Double Jeopardy Clause. The Government challenges that characterization of the forfeitures, arguing that the courts were wrong to conclude that civil forfeitures are punitive for double jeopardy purposes.

A

[The Court reviewed prior cases dealing with questions of multiple punishment under the double jeopardy clause.]

* * *

B

Our cases reviewing civil forfeitures under the Double Jeopardy Clause adhere to a remarkably consistent theme . . . [concluding that] *in rem* civil forfeiture is a remedial civil sanction, distinct from potentially punitive *in personam* civil penalties such as fines, and does not constitute a punishment under the Double Jeopardy Clause.

In the case that we currently review, the Court of Appeals recognized as much, concluding that "the law was clear that civil forfeitures did not constitute 'punishment' for double jeopardy purposes." Nevertheless, that court read three of our decisions to have "abandoned" [that] oft-affirmed rule. According to the Court of Appeals, through our decisions in *Halper*, *Austin*, and *Department of Revenue of Mont. v. Kurth Ranch*, [casebook, p.109] we "changed [our] collective mind," and "adopted a new test for determining whether a nominally civil sanction constitutes 'punishment' for double jeopardy purposes.". . . We turn now to consider whether *Halper*, *Austin*, and *Kurth Ranch* accomplished the radical jurisprudential shift perceived by the Courts of Appeals.

[The court reviewed the facts of *Halper*].

* * *

. . . We determined [in *Halper*] that our precedent had established no absolute and irrebuttable rule that a civil fine cannot be 'punishment' under the Double Jeopardy Clause. Though it was well established that "a civil remedy does not rise to the level of 'punishment' merely because Congress provided for civil recovery in excess of the Government's actual damages," we found that our case law did "not foreclose the possibility that in a particular case a civil penalty . . . may be so extreme and so divorced from the Government's damages and expenses as to constitute punishment." Emphasizing the case-specific nature of our inquiry, we compared the size of the fine imposed on Halper, $130,000, to the damages actually suffered by the Government as a result of Halper's actions, estimated by the District Court at $585. Noting that the fine was more than 220 times greater than the

Government's damages, we agreed with the District Court that "Halper's $130,000 liability is sufficiently disproportionate that the sanction constitutes a second punishment in violation of double jeopardy." We remanded to the District Court so that it could hear evidence regarding the Government's actual damages, and could then reduce Halper's liability to a nonpunitive level.

In *Austin,* we considered whether a civil forfeiture could violate the Excessive Fines Clause of the Eighth Amendment to the Constitution, which provides that "[e]xcessive bail shall not be required, nor excessive fines imposed. . . ." [T]he Government . . . initiated a civil forfeiture proceeding against Austin's mobile home and auto shop, contending that they had been "used" or were "intended for use" in the commission of a drug offense. Austin contested the forfeiture on the ground of the Excessive Fines Clause, but the District Court and the Court of Appeals held the forfeiture constitutional.

We limited our review to the question "whether the Excessive Fines Clause of the Eighth Amendment applies to forfeitures of property under 21 U.S.C. §§ 881(a)(4) and (a)(7)." We began our analysis by rejecting the argument that the Excessive Fines Clause was limited solely to criminal proceedings: The relevant question was not whether a particular proceeding was criminal or civil, we determined, but rather was whether forfeiture under §§ 881(a)(4) and (a)(7) constituted "punishment" for the purposes of the Eighth Amendment. In an effort to answer that question, we. . . [took] a categorical approach that contrasted sharply with *Halper*'s case-specific approach to determining whether a civil penalty constitutes punishment. Ultimately, we concluded that "forfeiture under [§§ 881 (a)(4) and (a)(7)] constitutes 'payment to a sovereign as punishment for some offense,' and, as such, is subject to the limitations of the Eighth Amendment's Excessive Fines Clause."

In *Kurth Ranch*, we considered whether a state tax imposed on marijuana was invalid under the Double Jeopardy Clause when the taxpayer had already been criminally convicted of owning the marijuana which was taxed. . . . [W]e determined that the tax was motivated by a " 'penal and prohibitory intent rather than the gathering of revenue.' " Concluding that the Montana tax proceeding "was the functional equivalent of a successive criminal prosecution," we affirmed the Court of Appeals' judgment barring th

We think that the Court of Appeals for the Sixth Circuit and the Court of Appeals for the Ninth Circuit misread *Halper, Austin*, and *Kurth Ranch*. None of those decisions purported to overrule the well-established teaching [that civil forfeitures are not punishment under the Double Jeopardy Clause]. *Halper* involved not a civil forfeiture, but a civil penalty. That its rule was limited to the latter context is clear from the decision itself, from the historical distinction that we have drawn between civil forfeiture and civil penalties, and from the practical difficulty of applying *Halper* to a civil forfeiture.

In *Halper*, we emphasized that our decision was limited to the context of civil penalties: "What we announce now is a rule for the rare case, the case such as the one before us, where a fixed-penalty provision subjects a prolific but small-gauge offender to a sanction overwhelmingly disproportionate to the damages he has caused. The rule is one of reason: Where a defendant previously has sustained a criminal penalty and the civil penalty sought in the subsequent proceeding bears no rational relation to the goal of compensating the Government for its loss, but rather appears to qualify as 'punishment' in the plain meaning of the word, then the defendant is entitled to an accounting of the Government's damages and costs to determine if the penalty sought in fact constitutes a second punishment." The narrow focus of *Halper* followed from the distinction that we have drawn historically between civil forfeiture and civil penalties. [W]e have distinguished civil penalties such as fines from civil forfeiture proceedings that are *in rem*. While a "civil action to recover . . . penalties, is punitive in character," and much like a criminal prosecution in that "it is the wrongdoer in person who is proceeded against . . . and punished," in an *in rem* forfeiture proceeding, "it is the property which is proceeded against, and by resort to a legal fiction, held guilty and condemned." Thus, though for Double Jeopardy purposes we have never balanced the value of property forfeited in a particular case against the harm suffered by the Government in that case, we have balanced the size of a particular civil penalty against the Government's harm.

It is difficult to see how the rule of *Halper* could be applied to a civil forfeiture. Civil penalties are designed as a rough form of "liquidated damages" for the harms suffered by the Government as a result of a defendant's conduct. The civil penalty involved in *Halper*, for example, provided for a fixed monetary penalty for each false claim count on which the defendant was convicted in the criminal proceeding. Whether a "fixed-penalty provision" that seeks to compensate the Government for harm it has suffered is "so extreme" and "so divorced" from the penalty's nonpunitive purpose of compensating the Government as to be a punishment may be determined by balancing the Government's harm against the size of the penalty. Civil forfeitures, in contrast to civil penalties, are designed to do more than simply compensate the Government. Forfeitures serve a variety of purposes, but are designed primarily to confiscate property used in violation of the law, and to require disgorgement of the fruits of illegal conduct. Though it may be possible to quantify the value of the property forfeited, it is virtually impossible to quantify, even approximately, the nonpunitive purposes served by a particular civil forfeiture. Hence, it is practically difficult to determine whether a particular forfeiture bears no rational relationship to the nonpunitive purposes of that forfeiture. Quite simply, the case-by-case balancing test set forth in *Halper*, in which a court must compare the harm suffered by the Government against the size of the penalty imposed, is inapplicable to civil forfeiture.

We recognized as much in *Kurth Ranch*. In that case, the Court expressly disclaimed reliance upon *Halper*, finding that its case-specific approach was impossible to apply outside the context of a fixed civil-penalty provision. Reviewing the Montana marijuana tax, we held that because "tax statutes serve a purpose quite different from civil penalties, . . . *Halper*'s method of determining whether the exaction was remedial or punitive simply does not work in the case of a tax statute." This is not to say that there is no occasion for analysis of the Government's harm. . . . The point is simply that *Halper*'s case-specific approach is inapplicable to civil forfeitures.

In the cases that we review, the Courts of Appeals did not find *Halper* difficult to apply to civil forfeiture because they concluded that its case-by-case balancing approach had been supplanted in *Austin* by a categorical approach that found a civil sanction to be punitive if it could not "fairly be said solely to serve a remedial purpose." But *Austin*, it must be remembered, did not involve the Double Jeopardy Clause at all. *Austin* was decided solely under the Excessive Fines Clause of the Eighth Amendment, a constitutional provision which we never have understood as parallel to, or even related to, the Double Jeopardy Clause of the Fifth Amendment. The only discussion of the Double Jeopardy Clause contained in *Austin* appears in a footnote that acknowledges our decisions holding that "[t]he Double Jeopardy Clause has been held not to apply in civil forfeiture proceedings . . . where the forfeiture could properly be characterized as remedial. . . ."

We acknowledged in *Austin* that our categorical approach under the Excessive Fines Clause was wholly distinct from the case-by-case approach of *Halper*, and we explained that the difference in approach was based in a significant difference between the purposes of our analysis under each constitutional provision. It is unnecessary in a case under the Excessive Fines Clause to inquire at a preliminary stage whether the civil sanction imposed in that particular case is totally inconsistent with any remedial goal. Because the second stage of inquiry under the Excessive Fines Clause asks whether the particular sanction in question is so large as to be "excessive," a preliminary-stage inquiry that focused on the disproportionality of a particular sanction would be duplicative of the excessiveness analysis that would follow. Forfeitures effected under 21 U.S.C. §§ 881(a)(4) and (a)(7) are subject to review for excessiveness under the Eighth Amendment after *Austin*; this does not mean, however, that those forfeitures are so punitive as to constitute punishment for the purposes of double jeopardy. The holding of *Austin* was limited to the Excessive Fines Clause of the Eighth Amendment, and we decline to import the analysis of *Austin* into our double jeopardy jurisprudence.

In sum, nothing in *Halper*, *Kurth Ranch*, or *Austin*, purported to replace our traditional understanding that civil forfeiture does not constitute punishment for the purpose of the Double Jeopardy Clause. Congress long has authorized the Government to bring parallel criminal proceedings and civil forfeiture proceedings, and this Court consistently has found civil forfeitures not to constitute punishment under the Double Jeopardy Clause. It would have been quite remarkable for this Court both to have held unconstitutional a well-established practice, and to have overruled a long line of precedent, without having even suggested that it was doing so. *Halper* dealt with *in personam* civil penalties under the Double Jeopardy Clause; *Kurth Ranch* with a tax proceeding under the Double Jeopardy Clause; and *Austin* with civil forfeitures under the Excessive Fines Clause. None of those cases dealt with the subject of this case: *in rem* civil forfeitures for purposes of the Double Jeopardy Clause.

We turn now to consider the forfeitures in these cases. . . . Because it provides a useful analytical tool, we conduct our inquiry within the framework of the two-part test used in [earlier cases]. First, we ask whether Congress intended proceedings under 21 U.S.C. § 881, and 18 U.S.C. § 981, to be criminal or civil. Second, we turn to consider whether the proceedings are so punitive in fact as to "persuade us that the forfeiture proceeding[s] may not legitimately be viewed as civil in nature," despite Congress' intent.

There is little doubt that Congress intended these forfeitures to be civil proceedings. . . . "Congress' intent in this regard is most clearly demonstrated by the procedural mechanisms it established for enforcing forfeitures under the statute[s]." Both 21 U.S.C. § 881 and 18 U.S.C. § 981, which is entitled "Civil forfeiture," provide that the laws "relating to the seizure, summary and judicial forfeiture, and condemnation of property for violation of the customs laws . . . shall apply to seizures and forfeitures incurred" under § 881 and § 981. Because forfeiture proceedings under the customs laws are *in rem*, see 19 U.S.C. § 1602 *et seq.*, it is clear that Congress intended that a forfeiture under § 881 or § 981, . . . would be a proceeding *in rem*. Congress specifically structured these forfeitures to be impersonal by targeting the property itself. "In contrast to the *in personam* nature of criminal actions, actions *in rem* have traditionally been viewed as civil proceedings, with jurisdiction dependent upon seizure of a physical object."

Other procedural mechanisms governing forfeitures under § 981 and § 881 also indicate that Congress intended such proceedings to be civil. Forfeitures under either statute are governed by 19 U.S.C. § 1607, which provides that actual notice of the impending forfeiture is unnecessary when the Government cannot identify any party with an interest in the seized article, and by § 1609, which provides that seized property is subject to forfeiture through a summary administrative procedure if no party files a claim to the property. And 19 U.S.C. § 1615, which governs the burden of proof in forfeiture proceedings under § 881 and § 981, provides that once the Government has shown probable cause that the property is subject to forfeiture, then "the burden of proof shall lie upon [the] claimant." In sum, "[b]y creating such distinctly civil procedures for forfeitures under [§ 881 and § 981], Congress has 'indicate[d] clearly that it intended a civil, not a criminal sanction.'"

Moving to the second stage of our analysis, we find that there is little evidence, much less the "'clearest proof'" that we require . . . [that the forfeiture proceedings in the instant case] are so punitive in form and effect as to render them criminal despite Congress' intent to the contrary. The statutes involved in this case are, in most significant respects, indistinguishable from those reviewed, and held not to be punitive, in [earlier cases].

Most significant is that § 981(a)(1)(A), and §§ 881(a)(6) and (a)(7), while perhaps having certain punitive aspects, serve important nonpunitive goals. Title 21 U.S.C. § 881(a)(7), under which Ursery's property was forfeited, provides for the forfeiture of "all real property . . . which is used or intended to be used, in any manner or part, to commit, or to facilitate the commission of" a federal drug felony. Requiring the forfeiture of property used to commit federal narcotics violations encourages property owners to take care in managing their property and ensures that they will not permit that property to be used for illegal purposes. . . . In many circumstances, the forfeiture may abate a nuisance. . . .

Other considerations that we have found relevant to the question whether a proceeding is criminal also tend to support a conclusion that § 981 (a)(1)(A) and §§ 881(a)(6) and (a)(7) are civil proceedings. First, in light of . . . the long tradition of federal statutes providing for a forfeiture proceeding following a criminal prosecution, it is absolutely clear that *in rem* civil forfeiture has not historically been regarded as punishment, as we have understood that term under the Double Jeopardy Clause. Second, there is no requirement in the statutes that we currently review that the Government demonstrate scienter in order to establish that the property is subject to forfeiture; indeed, the property may be subject to forfeiture even if no party files a claim to it and the Government never shows any connection between the property and a particular person. Though both § 881 (a) and § 981 (a) contain an "innocent owner" exception, we do not think that such a provision, without more indication of an intent to punish, is relevant to the question whether a statute is punitive under the Double Jeopardy Clause. Third, though both statutes may fairly be said to serve the purpose of deterrence, we long have held that this purpose may serve civil as well as criminal goals. We recently reaffirmed this conclusion in *Bennis v. Michigan,* where we held that "forfeiture . . . serves a deterrent purpose distinct from any punitive purpose." Finally, though both statutes are tied to criminal activity, . . . this fact is insufficient to render the statutes punitive. It is well settled that "Congress may impose both a criminal and a civil sanction in respect to the same act or omission." By itself, the fact that a forfeiture statute has some connection to a criminal violation is far from the "clearest proof" necessary to show that a proceeding is criminal.

We hold that these *in rem* civil forfeitures are neither "punishment" nor criminal for purposes of the Double Jeopardy Clause. The judgments of the Court of Appeals for the Sixth Circuit and of the Court of Appeals for the Ninth Circuit are accordingly reversed.

It is so ordered.

Justice KENNEDY, *concurring.*

I join the Court's opinion and add these further observations.

In *Austin v. United States*, we described the civil *in rem* forfeiture provision of 21 U.S.C. § 881 (a)(7) at issue here as punitive. In *Libretti v. United States*, we reviewed 21 U.S.C. § 853, which in almost identical terms provides for criminal forfeiture of property involved in or derived from drug crimes. We held that the "fundamental nature of criminal forfeiture" is punishment. Today the Court holds that the civil *in rem* forfeitures here are not punishment implicating the protections of the Double Jeopardy Clause. I write to explain why, in my view, our holding is consistent with both *Austin* and *Libretti*.

The Fifth Amendment provides that no person shall "be subject for the same offence to be twice put in jeopardy of life or limb." We have interpreted the Double Jeopardy Clause to "protec[t] against a second prosecution for the same offense after acquittal, against a second prosecution for the same offense after conviction, and against multiple punishments for the same offense."

Although there is language in our cases to the contrary, civil *in rem* forfeiture is not punishment of the wrongdoer for his criminal offense. We made this clear in [an earlier case where we said:] "[This] forfeiture proceeding . . . is *in rem*. It is the property which is proceeded against, and, by resort to a legal fiction, held guilty and condemned as though it were conscious instead of inanimate and insentient. In a criminal prosecution it is the wrongdoer in person who is proceeded against, convicted and punished. The forfeiture is no part of the punishment for the criminal offense. The provision of the Fifth Amendment to the Constitution in respect of double jeopardy does not apply."

Embracing the rule . . . that the Double Jeopardy Clause applies only to *in personam* punishments of the wrongdoer and not *in rem* forfeitures, does not imply that forfeiture inflicts no punishment. Though I have expressed my doubts about the view expressed in *Austin*, that throughout history forfeitures have been intended to punish blameworthy owners, I did not there question the punitive nature of § 881 (a)(7), nor do I now. Under this statute, providing for the forfeiture of real property used to facilitate a drug offense, only the culpable stand to lose their property; no interest of any owner is forfeited if he can show he did not know of or consent to the crime.

The key distinction is that the instrumentality-forfeiture statutes are not directed at those who carry out the crimes, but at owners who are culpable for the criminal misuse of the property. The theory is that the property, whether or not illegal or dangerous in nature, is hazardous in the hands of this owner because either he uses it to commit crimes, or allows others do so. The owner can be held accountable for the misuse of the property. The same rationale is at work in the statutory provisions enabling forfeiture of currency "used or intended to be used" to facilitate a criminal offense, § 881 (a)(6). Since the punishment befalls any property holder who cannot claim statutory innocence, whether or not he committed any criminal acts, it is not a punishment for a person's criminal wrongdoing.

Forfeiture, then, punishes an owner by taking property involved in a crime, and it may happen that the owner is also the wrongdoer charged with a criminal offense. But the forfeiture is not a second *in personam* punishment for the offense, which is all the Double Jeopardy Clause prohibits.

Civil *in rem* forfeiture has long been understood as independent of criminal punishments. . . .

Distinguishing between *in rem* and *in personam* punishments does not depend upon, or revive, the fiction . . . that the property is punished as if it were a sentient being capable of moral choice. It is the owner who feels the pain and receives the stigma of the forfeiture, not the property. The distinction simply recognizes that Congress, in order to quiet title to forfeitable property in one proceeding, has structured the forfeiture action as a proceeding against the property, not against a particular defendant. Indeed, the Government will often file a forfeiture complaint without any knowledge of who the owner is. True, the forfeiture statutes require proof of a violation of a drug trafficking or other offense, but the purpose of this predicate showing is just to establish that the property was used in a crime. In contrast to criminal forfeiture civil *in rem* forfeiture actions do not require a showing that the owner who stands to lose his property interest has committed a criminal offense. The offenses committed by Ursery, . . . [were] proffered as evidence that the property was used in a crime, but this does not make forfeiture a punishment for those offenses.

* * *

[I]n the context of this case and the precedents bearing upon it, I am not sure the test [applied by the Court] adds much to the clear rule . . . that civil *in rem* forfeiture of property involved in a crime is not punishment subject to the Double Jeopardy Clause. As to the first prong of the test, any *in rem* proceeding is civil. As to the second prong, so long as forfeiture hinges on the property's use in a crime, there will always be the remedial purpose the Court identifies of preventing property owners from allowing their goods to be used for illegal purposes. . . .

[The concurring opinion of Justice Scalia, with whom Justice Thomas joins, is omitted.]

Justice STEVENS, *concurring in the judgment in part and dissenting in part.*

The question the Court poses is whether civil forfeitures constitute "punishment" for purposes of the Double Jeopardy Clause. Because the numerous federal statutes authorizing forfeitures cover such a wide variety of situations, it is quite wrong to assume that there is only one answer to that question. For purposes of analysis it is useful to identify three different categories of property that are subject to seizure: proceeds, contraband, and property that has played a part in the commission of a crime. . . .

[Proceeds of unlawful activity] are not property that respondents have any right to retain. The forfeiture of such proceeds, like the confiscation of money stolen from a bank, does not punish respondents because it exacts no price in liberty or lawfully derived property from them. . . .

None of the property seized in *Ursery* constituted proceeds of illegal activity. Indeed, the facts of that case reveal a dramatically different situation. Respondent Ursery cultivated marijuana in a heavily wooded area not far from his home in Shiawassee County, Michigan. The illegal substance was consumed by members of his family, but there is no evidence, and no contention by the Government, that he sold any of it to third parties. Acting on the basis of the incorrect assumption that the marijuana plants were on respondent's property, Michigan police officers executed a warrant to search the premises. In his house they found marijuana seeds, stems, stalks, and a growlight. I presume those items were seized, and I have no difficulty concluding that such a seizure does not constitute punishment because respondent had no right to possess contraband. Accordingly, I agree with the Court's opinion insofar as it explains why the forfeiture of contraband does not constitute punishment for double jeopardy purposes.

The critical question presented in [*Ursery*] arose, not out of the seizure of contraband by the Michigan police, but rather out of the decision by the United States Attorney to take respondent's home. There is no evidence that the house had been purchased with the proceeds of unlawful activity and the house itself was surely not contraband. Nonetheless, 21 U.S.C. § 881 (a)(7) authorized the Government to seek forfeiture of respondent's residence because it had been used to facilitate the manufacture and distribution of marijuana. Respondent was then himself prosecuted for and convicted of manufacturing marijuana. In my opinion none of the reasons supporting the forfeiture of proceeds or contraband provides a sufficient basis for concluding that the confiscation of respondent's home was not punitive. . . .

I

In recent years, both Congress and the state legislatures have armed their law enforcement authorities with new powers to forfeit property that vastly exceed their traditional tools. In response, this Court has reaffirmed the fundamental proposition that all forfeitures must be accomplished within the constraints set by the Constitution. This Term the Court has begun dismantling the protections it so recently erected. In *Bennis v. Michigan*, the Court held that officials may confiscate an innocent person's automobile. And today, for the first time it upholds the forfeiture of a person's home. On the way to its surprising conclusion that the owner is not punished by the loss of his residence, the Court repeatedly professes its adherence to tradition and time-honored practice. As I discuss below, however, the decision shows a stunning disregard not only for modern precedents but for our older ones as well.

* * *

[T]he modern understanding of how the Double Jeopardy Clause applies in nominally civil proceedings . . . has been developed in a trio of recent decisions: *Halper*, *Austin*, and *Kurth Ranch*. The court of appeals found that the combined effect of two of those decisions *Halper* and *Austin* established the proposition that forfeitures under 21 U.S.C. § 881 (a)(7) implicated double jeopardy. This Court rejects that conclusion. . . .

It is the majority, however, that has "misread" *Halper, Austin*, and *Kurth Ranch* by artificially cabining each to a separate sphere and treating the three as if they concerned unrelated subjects. In fact, all three were devoted to the common enterprise of giving meaning to the idea of "punishment," a concept that plays a central role in the jurisprudence of both the Excessive Fines Clause and the Double Jeopardy Clause. *Halper* laid down a general rule for applying the Double Jeopardy Clause to civil proceedings: "[A] civil sanction that cannot fairly be said solely to serve a remedial purpose, but rather can only be explained as also serving either retributive or deterrent purposes, is punishment, as we have come to understand the term. . . . We therefore hold that under the Double Jeopardy Clause a defendant who already has been punished in a criminal prosecution may not be subjected to an additional civil sanction to the extent that the second sanction may not fairly be characterized as remedial, but only as a deterrent or retribution." In the past seven years, we have applied that same rule to three types of sanctions: civil penalties, civil forfeitures, and taxes.

The first was the subject of *Halper* itself. The defendant had been convicted for submitting 65 false claims for reimbursement (seeking $12 for each, when the actual services rendered entitled him to only $3) to a Medicare provider, and sentenced to imprisonment for 2 years and a $5,000 fine. The Government then brought a civil action against him for the same offenses. The penalty for violating the civil false-claims statute consisted of double the Government's damages plus court costs and a fixed fine of $2,000 per false claim. Accordingly, the Government sought a penalty of $130,000, although the defendant's fraud had caused an actual loss of only $585. Applying the definition of "punishment" given above, the Court first held that the fixed $2,000 fine served a remedial purpose because it was designed to compensate the Government "roughly" for the costs of law enforcement and investigation. Despite finding that the fine was not by nature punitive, the Court went on to consider whether the sanction "as applied in the individual case" amounted to punishment. It answered that question in the affirmative, for the applied sanction created a "tremendous disparity" with the amount of harm the defendant actually caused. The Court explained that, as a rule, a fixed penalty that would otherwise serve remedial ends could still punish the defendant if the imposed amount was out of all proportion to the damage done.

The second category of sanctions civil forfeitures was the subject of *Austin*. In that case, the Government sought to forfeit the petitioner's mobile home and auto body shop as instrumentalities of the drug trade . . . because he had sold cocaine there. Applying *Halper*'s definition of punishment, we held that [the forfeitures] must be considered to qualify as such, partly because forfeitures have historically been understood as punishment and more importantly because no remedial purpose underlay the sanction the statute created. Merely compensating the Government for its costs, as in *Halper*, could not justify the forfeiture scheme because "[t]he value of the conveyances and real property forfeitable . . . can vary so dramatically that any relationship between the Government's actual costs and the amount of the sanction is merely coincidental." Accordingly, we held that any forfeiture was subject to the constraints of the Excessive Fines Clause of the Eighth Amendment.

The Court expends a great deal of effort attempting to distinguish *Austin* away as purely an excessive fines case. The Court states, for example, that it is "difficult to see" how one would apply the "rule of *Halper* "to a civil forfeiture such as was present in *Austin*. But the Court conflates the two different rules that *Halper* announced. As discussed above, *Austin* expressly quoted *Halper* and followed its general rule that a sanction should be characterized as "punishment" if it serves any punitive end. It relegated to a footnote *Halper'* s narrower rule the one for the "rare case," which requires an accounting of the Government's damages and costs because it had already decided that the statute was of a punitive character. That approach was perfectly appropriate. There is no need to determine whether a statute that is punitive by design has a punitive effect when applied in the individual case. *Halper* is entirely consistent with *Austin*, because it determined first that the sanction there generally did not have a punitive character before it considered whether some applications might be punitive nonetheless.

The majority implies that *Austin*'s "categorical approach" is somehow suspect as an application of double jeopardy jurisprudence but *Kurth Ranch* definitively refutes that suggestion. The sanction there was a tax imposed on marijuana and applied to a taxpayer who had already been prosecuted for ownership of the drugs sought to be taxed. Again applying *Halper*'s definition of punishment, we considered the nature of the tax, focusing on several unusual features that distinguished it from ordinary revenue-raising provisions, and concluded that it was motivated by a "penal and prohibitory intent." On that basis, we held that imposition of the tax after criminal prosecution of the taxpayer violated double jeopardy. The approach taken was thus identical to that followed in *Austin*. By considering and rejecting each of the asserted "remedial" interests served by the sanction, we reasoned that the tax had an "unmistakable punitive character" that rendered it punishment in all of its applications.

The claim that *Halper*'s "case-by-case" method is "impossible to apply" to forfeitures or taxes, thus misses the point. It is true that since fixed penalties can serve only one remedial end (compensation), it is easy to determine whether a particular fine is punitive in application. Forfeitures and taxes, generally speaking, may have a number of remedial rationales. But to decide if a sanction is punitive, one need only examine each claimed remedial interest and determine whether the sanction actually promotes it. Many of our cases have followed just such an approach, regardless of whether any nonpunitive purpose can be "quantif[ied]," The majority itself embarks on such an inquiry. . . . Furthermore, even in the context of forfeitures and taxes, nothing prevents a court from deciding that although a sanction is designed to be remedial, its application in a particular case is so extreme as to constitute punishment.

In reaching the conclusion that the civil forfeiture at issue yielded punishment, the *Austin* Court surveyed the history of civil forfeitures at some length. That history is replete with expressions of the idea that forfeitures constitute punishment. . . .

Remarkably, the Court today stands *Austin* on its head a decision rendered only three years ago, with unanimity on the pertinent points and concludes that § 881 (a)(7) is remedial rather than punitive in character. Every reason *Austin* gave for treating § 881 (a)(7) as punitive the Court rejects or ignores. Every reason the Court provides for treating § 881 (a)(7) as remedial *Austin* rebuffed. The Court claims that its conclusion is consistent with decisions reviewing statutes "indistinguishable" "in most significant respects" from § 881 (a)(7), but ignores the fact that *Austin* reached the opposite conclusion as to the identical statute under review here.

First, the Court supposes that forfeiture of respondent's house is remedial in nature because it was an instrumentality of a drug crime. It is perfectly conceivable that certain kinds of instruments used in the commission of crimes could be forfeited for remedial purposes. Items whose principal use is illegal for example, [a] distillery . . . might be thus forfeitable. But it is difficult to understand how a house in which marijuana was found helped to substantially "facilitate" a narcotics offense, or how forfeiture of that house will meaningfully thwart the drug trade. In *Austin*, we rejected the argument that a mobile home and body shop were "instruments" of drug trafficking simply because marijuana was sold out of them. I see no basis for a distinction here.

Second, the Court claims that the statute serves the purpose of deterrence, which helps to show that it is remedial rather than punitive in character. That statement cannot be squared with our precedents. *Halper* expressly held, and *Austin* and *Kurth Ranch* reaffirmed, that "a civil sanction that cannot fairly be said solely to serve a remedial purpose, but rather can only be explained as also serving either retributive or deterrent purposes, is punishment" for purposes of the Double Jeopardy Clause. " 'Retribution and deterrence are not legitimate nonpunitive governmental objectives.'" To say otherwise is to renounce *Halper*'s central holding. If deterrence is a legitimate remedial rationale "distinct from" any punitive purpose, then the $130,000 fine in *Halper* could not be condemned as excessive because it plainly served a powerful deterrent function. It was a premise of the Court's analysis in that case that deterrence could not justify a penal sanction. As in *Bennis v. Michigan*, where the Court first announced this new view of deterrence, it simply ignores *Halper* without explanation or co

For good measure, the Court also rejects two considerations that persuaded the majority in *Austin* to find 21 U.S.C. § 881 (a)(7) a punitive statute. The Court first asserts that the statute contains no scienter requirement and property may be forfeited summarily if no one files claim to it. Property that is not claimed, however, is considered abandoned; it proves nothing that the Government is able to forfeit property that no one owns. Any time the Government seeks to forfeit claimed property, it must prove that the claimant is culpable, for the statute contains an express "innocent owner" exception. Today the Court finds the structure of the statute irrelevant, but *Austin* said that the exemption for innocent owners "makes [the statute] look more like punishment."

Finally, the Court announces that the fact that the statute is "tied to criminal activity" is insufficient to render it punitive. *Austin* expressly relied on Congress' decision to "tie forfeiture directly to the commission of drug offenses" as evidence that it was intended to be punitive.

The recurrent theme of the Court's opinion is that there is some mystical difference between *in rem* and *in personam* proceedings, such that only the latter can give rise to double jeopardy concerns. The Court claims that [for some time] we have drawn this distinction for purposes of applying relevant constitutional provisions. That statement, however, is incorrect. We have repeatedly rejected the idea that the nature of the court's jurisdiction has any bearing on the constitutional protections that apply at a proceeding before it. "From the relevant constitutional standpoint, there is no difference between a man who 'forfeits' $8,674 because he has used the money in illegal gambling activities and a man who pays a 'criminal fine' of $8,674 as a result of the same course of conduct." Most recently, in our application of *Halper*'s definition of punishment, we stated that "[w]e do not understand the Government to rely separately on the technical distinction between proceedings in rem and proceedings *in personam*, but we note that any such reliance would be misplaced."

The notion that the label attached to the proceeding is dispositive runs contrary to the trend of our recent cases. In *Halper* we stated that "the labels 'criminal' and 'civil' are not of paramount importance" in determining whether a proceeding punishes an individual. In *Kurth Ranch* we held that the Double Jeopardy Clause applies to punitive proceedings even if they are labeled a tax. . . . It is thus far too late in the day to contend that the label placed on a punitive proceeding determines whether it is covered by the Double Jeopardy Clause.

The pedantic distinction between *in rem* and *in personam* actions is ultimately only a cover for the real basis for the Court's decision: the idea that the property, not the owner, is being "punished" for offenses of which it is "guilty." Although the Court prefers not to rely on this notorious fiction too blatantly, its repeated citations to [earlier precedent] make clear that the Court believes respondent's home was "guilty" of the drug offenses with which he was charged. On that rationale, of course, the case is easy. The owner of the property is not being punished when the Government confiscates it, just the property. The same sleight-of-hand would have worked in *Austin*, too: The owner of the property is not being excessively fined, just the property itself. Despite the Government's heavy reliance on that fiction in *Austin*, we did not allow it to stand in the way of our holding that the seizure of property may punish the owner.

Even if the point had not been settled by prior decisions, common sense would dictate the result in this case. There is simply no rational basis for characterizing the seizure of this respondent's home as anything other than punishment for his crime. The house was neither proceeds nor contraband and its value had no relation to the Government's authority to seize it. Under the controlling statute an essential predicate for the forfeiture was proof that respondent had used the property in connection with the commission of a crime. The forfeiture of this property was unquestionably "a penalty that had absolutely no correlation to any damages sustained by society or to the cost of enforcing the law." As we unanimously recognized in *Halper*, formalistic distinctions that obscure the obvious practical consequences of governmental action disserve the "'humane interests'" protected by the Double Jeopardy Clause. Fidelity to both reason and precedent dictates the conclusion that this forfeiture was "punishment" for purposes of the Double Jeopardy Cl

* * *

Accordingly, I respectfully dissent from the judgment in *United States v. Ursery*.

NOTES AND QUESTIONS

1. Both *Austin* and *Ursery* involved forfeiture actions under the same statute, 21 U.S.C. § 881. How can forfeitures under the same statute, applied to very similar facts, constitute punishment in *Austin* for the purposes of Eighth Amendment and yet not in *Ursery* for the purpose of the Fifth Amendment?

2. If the forfeiture described in Ursery is not meant to punish, what is its purpose? Is it meant to deter? If so, how is it different from a fine, a form of punishment?

Are forfeitures effective deterrents? If a criminal risks conviction and perhaps a fine, prison sentence or death, is it realistic to assume that the additional risk of forfeiting property will effectively deter the criminal behavior?

[C] Punitive Civil Sanctions: The Shrinking of the Criminal Law?

Many of the selections in § 2.02[B] illustrate what Professor Kenneth Mann, in the article excerpted immediately below, has described as "a dramatic shift in the jurisprudence of sanctions" toward the use of punishment in civil proceedings. As more and more jurisdictions employ in "civil actions" punitive mechanisms such as multiple damages, monetary penalties, forfeitures, and taxes on illegal activity, questions are raised about the extent to which the criminal law retains *sui generis* identity as a legal category. See Coffee, *Does "Unlawful" Mean "Criminal"?: Reflections on the Disappearing Tort/Crime Distinction in American Law*, 71 B.U. L. Rev. 193 (1991). If "punishment" is no longer the defining characteristic of the criminal law, what is? Is the uniqueness of the criminal law best understood by its imposition of certain forms of punishment, imprisonment, and the death penalty, for example? If so, what are the implications of the movement toward such sanctions as house arrest and community service as alternatives to imprisonment? See A. Von Hirsch, *Censure and Sanctions* 2 (1993).

In any event, do these trends suggest that in the future the criminal law will play a less dominant role in responding to certain types of socially undesirable activity as civil law mechanisms become more prominent? The following excerpt, from an article critically assessed in Coffee, *Paradigms Lost: The Blurring of the Criminal and Civil Law Models—And What Can Be Done*, 101 Yale L.J. 1875 (1992), addresses the question by offering an explanation for the emergence of punitive civil sanctions and an assessment of their future implications for the criminal law.

MANN, *PUNITIVE CIVIL SANCTIONS: THE MIDDLEGROUND BETWEEN CRIMINAL AND CIVIL LAW*

101 Yale L.J. 1795, 1844–47, 1861–63 (1992)

Legislative adoption of punitive civil sanctions—multiple damages, forfeitures, and penalties—grew rapidly during the middle of the century and has continued to expand in recent years. In 1979, Colin Diver found that twenty-seven federal departments and independent agencies enforced 348 civil statutory penalties. Since that time, Congress has added new punitive civil sanctions, increased their size, and made their imposition procedurally easier. Not only are there many new statutes on the books, but administrative agencies also tend to impose sanctions rather than refer cases for criminal prosecution. Several factors have contributed to the rapid development of punitive civil sanctions. These include a changed philosophy of sanctioning, the general expansion of sanctioning, the growth of the administrative state, and reforms in procedural rules.

A. THE CHANGING PHILOSOPHY OF SANCTIONING

At the outset of this Article, I argued that in their paradigmatic forms, criminal and civil law serve different purposes: the former punishment, the latter compensation. Changing perceptions of the nature of law, starting with

Beccaria on the Continent and Bentham in England, began to force a revision in the conventional bifurcation between punishment and compensation.

Among Bentham's contributions, which would profoundly affect the law of sanctions, was the introduction of utilitarian theory into jurisprudence, moving law away from Kantian ideas of metaphysical imperatives. This gradual shift replaced notions of right and desert with concepts rooted in behavioral science. Utilitarianism became the basis of a legal theory in which the object of the law was to manipulate pain and pleasure to achieve the greatest good. It was this understanding of law as manipulating behavior that bridged the gap between criminal and civil law.

Utilitarian philosophy contributed greatly to deterrence theory, which encouraged the use of middleground punitive sanctions. The two axioms of deterrence ideology held that the more severe the sanction, the greater its deterrent effect, and that deterrent effect varied directly with the probability of a sanction's actual application. This perspective viewed the obligation to pay an injured party as a disincentive to causing injury, rather than as a form of compensatory justice. Where damages failed to promote better behavior, the solution arguably was to augment the size of the civil money payment.

With the development of deterrence ideology, the difference between the purposes of criminal and civil law decreased. While prominent differences remained with respect to other aspects of the paradigms, such as the elements of the criminal offense or the cause of action, with respect to sanctions the results for criminal and civil defendants became increasingly similar. Differences in severity, found within criminal and civil law as well as between the two, came to be understood as a matter of quantity rather than quality. This idea contradicted basic normative differences in the conventional paradigms, in which punishment had been distinctive to the criminal process.

Utilitarianism thus brought jurists and scholars to a new awareness of the middleground; the theory highlighted the possibility of controlling parties by placing costs on them in the civil law. The awareness of this possibility coincided with the development of tort law as a form of legitimate coercion rather than as a legal tool for righting a wrong through compensation. With further integration of utilitarianism into legal analysis, economic theories of law came close to eliminating all differences between civil and criminal law. Within that analytic framework, both civil and criminal law create negative sanctions for wrongful behavior. Posner put it this way:

> In cases where tort remedies are an adequate deterrent, because optimal tort damages, including any punitive damages, are within the ability to pay of the potential defendant, there is no need to invoke criminal penalties. The criminal (= tortious) conduct probably will be deterred. [C]riminal sanctions generally are reserved, as theory predicts, for cases where the tort remedy bumps up against a solvency limitation.

As the purposes of civil and criminal sanctions came to be understood as similar, so did the purposes of civil and criminal law generally. Civil law could more often achieve what, under the conventional paradigms, would have been conceived as a task for the criminal law. Deterrence ideology, with its philosophical background of law and economics, became a significant causal factor in the growth of punitive civil sanctions.

* * *

The vast growth in punitive civil sanctions has broad implications for future legal sanctioning. A society in which many offenders can be made to pay severe civil penalties has compelling reasons to shrink the criminal law. A newly conceptualized three-paradigm jurisprudence of sanctioning—composed of criminal, punitive, and remedial sanctions—would reserve criminal law for a much smaller proportion of all sanctionable offenses. As the most extreme form of the state's punitive power, the criminal law would be invoked only when necessary to maintain a public threat of severe punishment for those who cause the most harm in the most blameworthy circumstances.

Under the new tripartite structure, the growth of punitive civil sanctions would result in more sanctioning, and consequently more social control, than would occur under a legal regime in which the government could only choose between criminal and compensatory civil sanctions. Under the traditional paradigmatic structure, a broad range of offenses goes entirely unsanctioned. Potential targets of enforcement probably perceive this result as an expression of society's jealousy of freedom of action. In the tripartite structure, therefore, the rise of punitive civil sanctions may bring with it the specter of increasing governmental intrusion into private and corporate life for the purpose of greater social control; while the change in sanctioning capacity has an Orwellian hue, the actual consequences of these developments will depend on how the implementation of these sanctions is checked and controlled.

. . . A new paradigm can be established in the middleground between civil and criminal law. This new approach would levy punitive monetary sanctions (but not as punitive as criminal sanctions) in response to behavior that is culpable (but not egregious enough to require criminal sanctions). Severely punitive monetary sanctions would require especially stringent procedures (but not as stringent as criminal procedures).

These changes would reflect the appropriate position of the criminal law in an era in which specialized agencies wield growing prosecutorial responsibilities. As punitive civil sanctions are used with greater frequency to punish and deter wrongdoers, criminal law should become more of a residual sanction. It should continue to reinforce social solidarity around basic values, but routine sanctioning should be achieved through state-invoked punitive civil sanctions, which are capable of a broader reach because of their less serious implications and their less burdensome procedural setting.

* * *

Criminal law has a distinctive normative role, and it should be reserved for the most damaging wrongs and the most culpable defendants. Middle ground jurisprudence presents a special opportunity for reform, permitting the criminal law to be scaled back where it has been overextended—with respect to petty and middle-range crimes, regulatory and administrative offenses, and some of the so-called victimless crimes where the use of criminal sanctions has long been controversial. Punitive civil penalties can both increase sanctioning power and reduce reliance on criminal law for a range of intermediate offenses, particularly those committed by the middle class in the course of their occupations. [Footnotes omitted.]

§ 2.03 THE JUSTIFICATION OF PUNISHMENT

[A] Introduction

Because it entails the purposeful infliction of suffering, the imposition of punishment raises serious ethical problems. To be morally tolerable, punishment must be administered only for good reason.

Theorists classically have offered two kinds of general justifications for the criminal sanction. One is utilitarian—punishment is imposed to achieve desirable consequences, specifically to minimize criminal conduct. The other is retributive—punishment is imposed to do justice, whether or not beneficial consequences are obtained.

While various theorists have defended relatively "pure" utilitarian or retributive theories, respectively, most actual systems of punishment are grounded in both types of justifications, often resulting in an uneasy compromise between competing considerations. Utilitarian interests in deterrence or rehabilitation may pull toward one or several punitive dispositions, while the retributive demands of justice may pull toward still others. Consider, for example, the following statutory statements of punitive purpose:

MODEL PENAL CODE

§ 1.02

Purposes; Principles of Construction.

(1) The general purposes of the provisions governing the definition of offenses are:

    (a) to forbid and prevent conduct that unjustifiably and inexcusably inflicts or threatens substantial harm to individual or public interests;

    (b) to subject to public control persons whose conduct indicates that they are disposed to commit crimes; . . .

* * *

    (e) to differentiate on reasonable grounds between serious and minor offenses. . . .

(2) The general purposes of the provisions governing the sentencing and treatment of offenders are:

    (a) to prevent the commission of offenses;

    (b) to promote the correction and rehabilitation of offenders;

    (c) to safeguard offenders against excessive, disproportionate or arbitrary punishment; . . .

* * *

(e) to differentiate among offenders with a view to a just individualization in their treatment;

* * *

§ 7.01

Criteria for Withholding Sentence of Imprisonment and for Placing Defendant on Probation.

(1) The Court shall deal with a person who has been convicted of a crime without imposing sentence of imprisonment unless, having regard to the nature and circumstances of the crime and the history, character and condition of the defendant, it is of the opinion that his imprisonment is necessary for protection of the public because:

(a) there is undue risk that during the period of a suspended sentence or probation the defendant will commit another crime; or

(b) the defendant is in need of correctional treatment that can be provided most effectively by his commitment to an institution; or

(c) a lesser sentence will depreciate the seriousness of the defendant's crime. . . .

* * *

COMPREHENSIVE CRIME CONTROL ACT OF 1984

18 U.S.C. § 3553 (1988 Supp.)

(a) Factors To Be Considered In Imposing A Sentence. The court shall impose a sentence sufficient, but not greater than necessary, to comply with the purposes set forth in paragraph (2) of this subsection. The court, in determining the particular sentence to be imposed, shall consider

(1) the nature and circumstances of the offense and the history and characteristics of the defendant;

(2) the need for the sentence imposed

(A) to reflect the seriousness of the offense, to promote respect for the law, and to provide just punishment for the offense;

(B) to afford adequate deterrence to criminal conduct;

(C) to protect the public from further crimes of the defendant; and

(D) to provide the defendant with needed educational or vocational training, medical care, or other correctional treatment in the most effective manner;. . . .

* * *

CALIFORNIA PENAL CODE

§ 1170 (1977 amend.)

(a)(1) The Legislature finds and declares that the purpose of imprisonment for crime is punishment. This purpose is best served by terms proportionate to the seriousness of the offense with provision for uniformity in the sentences of offenders committing the same offense under similar circumstances. The Legislature further finds and declares that the elimination of disparity and the provision of uniformity of sentences can best be achieved by determinate sentences fixed by statute in proportion to the seriousness of the offense as determined by the Legislature to be imposed by the court with specified discretion.

These materials do not attempt to resolve the debate between utilitarians and retributivists, but will merely illustrate the strengths and weaknesses of the respective positions. As the various theories are considered, it will be helpful to consider the following insights from H.L.A. Hart, *Punishment and Responsibility* 3, 9, 11 (1968):

[W]hat is most needed is not the simple admission that instead of a single value or aim (Deterrence, Retribution, Reform or any other) a plurality of different values and aims should be given as a conjunctive answer to some single question concerning the justification of punishment. What is needed is the realization that different principles (each of which may in a sense be called a "justification") are relevant at different points in any morally acceptable account of punishment. What we should look for are answers to a number of different questions such as:

What justifies the general practice of punishment? To whom may punishment be applied? How severely may we punish? In dealing with these and other questions concerning punishment we should bear in mind that in this, as in most other social institutions, the pursuit of one aim may be qualified by or provide an opportunity, not to be missed, for the pursuit of others. Till we have developed this sense of the complexity of punishment . . . we shall be in no fit state to assess the extent to which the whole institution has been eroded by, or needs to be adapted to, new beliefs about the human mind. . . .

* * *

. . . I shall assume that Retribution, defined simply as the application of the pains of punishment to an offender who is morally guilty, may figure among the conceivable justifying aims of a system of punishment. Here I shall merely insist that it is one thing to use the word Retribution *at this point* in an account of the principle of punishment in order to designate the General Justifying Aim of the system, and quite another to use it to secure that to the question "To whom may punishment be applied?" (the question of Distribution), the answer given is "Only to an offender for an offence". Failure to distinguish Retribution as a General Justifying Aim from retribution as the simple insistence that only those who have broken the law—and voluntarily broken it—may be punished, may be traced in many writers. . . . We shall distinguish the latter from Retribution in General Aim as "retribution in Distribution". Much confusing shadow-fighting between utilitarians and their opponents may be avoided if it is recognized that it is perfectly consistent to assert *both* that the General Justifying Aim of the practice of punishment is its beneficial consequences and that the pursuit of this General Aim should be qualified or restricted out of deference to principles of Distribution which require that punishment should be only of an offender for an offence. Conversely it does not in the least follow from the admission of the latter principle of retribution in Distribution that the General Justifying Aim of punishment is Retribution though of course Retribution in General Aim entails retribution in Distribution. . . .

* * *

. . . [T]hough we may be clear as to what value the practice of punishment is to promote, we have still to answer as a question of Distribution "Who may be punished?". . . . [I]f in answer to this question we say "only an offender for an offence" this admission of retribution in Distribution is not a principle from which anything follows as to the severity or amount of punishment; in particular it neither licenses nor requires, as Retribution in General Aim does, more severe punishments than deterrence or other utilitarian criteria would require.

[B] Utilitarianism

[1] Deterrence

Deterrence theory provides a widely embraced rationale for imposing the punitive sanction. Under this theory, punishment is imposed to deter the commission of crime. Deterrent effects are purportedly achieved in two ways: by dissuading would-be criminals through the threat of punishment for criminal acts (general deterrence) and by discouraging individual convicted criminals from committing subsequent offenses by inflicting them with punishment (special defence). The following selections reflect both varieties of deterrence theory and suggest some objections to their validity.

PLATO, *PROTAGORAS*

139 (trans. W.R.M. Lamb [1952])

. . . No one punishes the evil doer under the notion . . . that he has done wrong, only the unreasonable fury of a beast acts in that way. But he who undertakes to punish with reason does not avenge himself for past offense, since he cannot make what was done as though it had not come to pass; he looks rather to the future, and aims at preventing that particular person and others who see him punished from doing wrong again.

RADZINOWICZ, *A HISTORY OF ENGLISH CRIMINAL LAW*

411, fn. 40 (1957) (quoted therein)

For it is very hard, my lord, said a convicted felon at the bar to the late excellent Judge Burnet, to hang a poor man for stealing a horse. You are not to be hanged, sir, answered my ever honoured and beloved friend, for stealing a horse, but you are to be hanged that horses may not be stolen.

BENTHAM, *THE RATIONALE OF PUNISHMENT*

19, 41 (1830)

Pain and pleasure are the great springs of human action. When a man perceives or supposes pain to be the consequence of an act, he is acted upon in such a manner as tends, with a certain force, to withdraw him, as it were, from the commission of that act. If the apparent magnitude, or rather value of that pain be greater than the apparent magnitude or value of the pleasure or good he expects to be the consequence of the act, he will be absolutely prevented from performing it. The mischief which would have ensued from the act, if performed, will also by that means be prevented.

* * *

The observation of rules of proportion between crimes and punishments has been objected to as useless, because they seem to suppose, that a spirit of calculation has place among the passions of men, who, it is said, never calculate. But dogmatic as this proposition is, it is altogether false. In matters of importance, every one calculates. Each individual calculates with more or less correctness, according to the degrees of his information, and the power of the motives which actuate him, but all calculate. It would be hard to say that a madman does not calculate. Happily, the passion of cupidity, which on account of its power, its constancy, and its extent, is most formidable to society; is the passion which is most given to calculation. This, therefore, will be more successfully combated, the more carefully the law turns the balance of profit against it.

BENTHAM, *AN INTRODUCTION TO THE PRINCIPLES OF MORALS AND LEGISLATION*

170–88 (1789)

§ I. *General View of Cases Unmet for Punishment*

I. The general object which all laws have, or ought to have, in common, is to augment the total happiness of the community; and therefore, in the first place, to exclude, as far as may be, everything that tends to subtract from that happiness: in other words, to exclude mischief.

II. But all punishment is mischief: all punishment in itself is evil. Upon the principle of utility, if it ought at all to be admitted, it ought only to be admitted in as far as it promises to exclude some greater evil.

III. It is plain, therefore, that in the following cases punishment ought not to be inflicted.

1. Where it is *groundless:* where there is no mischief for it to prevent; the act not being mischievous upon the whole.
2. Where it must be *inefficacious:* where it cannot act so as to prevent the mischief.
3. Where it is *unprofitable,* or too expensive: where the mischief it would produce would be greater than what it prevented.
4. Where it is *needless:* where the mischief may be prevented, or cease of itself, without it: that is, at cheaper a rate.

* * *

OF THE PROPORTION BETWEEN PUNISHMENTS AND OFFENSES

* * *

Rule 1. . . . The first object . . . is to prevent, in as far as it is worthwhile, all sorts of offences; therefore, *[t]he value of the punishment must not be less in any case than what is sufficient to outweigh that of the profit of the offence.*

* * *

Rule 2. But whether a given offence shall be prevented in a given degree by a given quantity of punishment, is never any thing better than a chance; for the purchasing of which, whatever punishment is employed, is so much expended in advance. . . .

The greater the mischief of the offence, the greater is the expense, which it maybe worth while to be at, in the way of punishment.

Rule 3. The next object is, to induce a man to choose always the least mischievous of two offences; therefore

Where two offences come in competition, the punishment for the greater offence must be sufficient to induce a man to prefer the less.

Rule 4. When a man has resolved upon a particular offence, the next object is, to induce him to do no more mischief than what is necessary for his purpose: therefore

The punishment should be adjusted in such manner to each particular offence, that for every part of the mischief there may be a motive to restrain the offender from giving birth to it.

Rule 5. The last object is, whatever mischief is guarded against, to guard against it at as cheap a rate as possible: therefore

The punishment ought in no case to be more than what is necessary to bring it into conformity with the rules here given.

Rule 6. It is further to be observed, that owing to the different manners and degrees in which persons under different circumstances are affected by the same exciting cause, a punishment which is the same in name will not always either really produce, or even so much as appear to others to produce, in two different persons the same degree of pain: therefore

That the quantity actually inflicted on each individual offender may correspond to the quantity intended for similar offenders in general, the several circumstances influencing sensibility ought always to be taken into account.

* * *

Rule 7. Want of certainty must be made up in magnitude. These things being considered, the three following rules may be laid down by way of supplement and explanation to Rule 1.

To enable the value of the punishment to outweigh that of the profit of the offence, it must be increased, in point of magnitude, in proportion as it falls short in point of certainty.

Rule 8. *Punishment must be further increased in point of magnitude, in proportion as it falls short in point of proximity.*

Rule 9. *Where the act is conclusively indicative of a habit, such an increase must be given to the punishment as may enable it to outweigh the profit not only of the individual offence, but of such other like offences as are likely to have been committed with impunity by the same offender.*

Notes

1. Bentham's views provide the foundation for the classical theory of deterrence. Many of his assumptions have come under attack. Particularly controversial is his view that human behavior is premised on a rational calculus of costs and benefits. Consider Gardiner, *The Purpose of Criminal Punishment,* 21 Modern L. Rev. 117, 122–23 (1958):

> [T]he belief in the value of deterrence rests on the assumption that we are rational beings who always think before we act, and then base our actions on a careful calculation of the gains and losses involved. These assumptions, dear to many lawyers, have long since been abandoned in the social sciences. No economist would seriously maintain them today, and even to the uninformed the movements of shares on the stock exchange—where one might expect to see Bentham's principle of "enlightened self-interest" vindicated most clearly—demonstrate that men's actions are governed quite as much by fear or greed as by reason; and that the ability to ignore hard facts, and to see only what you want to see, is shared by a surprisingly large and influential section of the community.

Amongst criminals, foresight and prudent calculation is even more conspicuous by its absence. . . .

Even though there is no consensus amongst doctors about the exact description of the so-called "psychopaths," experienced Prison Medical Officers, and for that matter, Prison Governors, are agreed that there is a type of prisoner who is quite incapable of foresight, who cannot learn even from the experience of punishment, much less from the threat of it. Yet other offenders, notably some sex offenders (but also others subject to compulsive behaviour) are sometimes at the mercy of their impulses, and unable, without proper help and treatment, to control themselves adequately. Such persons are frequently in conflict, not only with society, but also with themselves.

Gardiner probably overstates the case against the Benthamite position. Some economists do suggest that "criminals respond to changes in opportunity costs, in the probability of apprehension, in the severity of punishment, and in other relevant variables, as if they were indeed the rational calculators of the economic model." R. Posner, *Economic Analysis of Law* 164–65 (2d ed. 1977).

Regarding the role deterrence plays in the lives of criminals, both present and would-be, consider J. Wilson, *Thinking about Crime* 121 (rev. ed. 1983):

People are governed in their daily lives by rewards and penalties of every sort. We shop for bargain prices, praise our children for good behavior and scold them for bad, expect lower interest rates to stimulate home building and fear that higher ones will depress it, and conduct ourselves in public in ways that lead our friends and neighbors to form good opinions of us. To assert that "deterrence doesn't work" is tantamount to either denying the plainest facts of everyday life or claiming that would-be criminals are utterly different from the rest of us. They may well be different to some degree—they most likely have a weaker conscience, worry less about their reputation in polite society, and find it harder to postpone gratifying their urges—but these differences of degree do not make them indifferent to the risks and gains of crime. If they were truly indifferent, they would scarcely be able to function at all, for their willingness to take risks would be offset by their indifference to loot. Their lives would consist of little more than the erratic display of animal instincts and fleeting impulses.

2. Other common objections to the classical deterrence theory are noted, and responded to, by Johannes Andenaes, a modern proponent of general deterrence. In his article, *The General Preventive Effects of Punishment,* 114 U. Pa. L. Rev. 949, 955–57 (1966), Andenaes addressed "certain untenable contentions . . . frequently introduced . . . into discussions of general prevention:"

"*Our knowledge of criminals shows us that the criminal law has no deterrent effects.*"

The fallacy of this argument is obvious. If a man commits a crime, we can only conclude that general prevention has not worked in his case. If I interview 1000 prisoners, I collect information about 1000 men in whose cases general prevention has failed. But I cannot infer from this data that general prevention is ineffective in the cases of all those who have not committed crimes. General prevention is more concerned with the psychology of those obedient to the law than with the psychology of criminals.

"The belief in general prevention rests on an untenable rationalistic theory of behavior."

It is true that the extreme theories of general prevention worked out by people like Bentham . . . were based on a shallow psychological model in which the actions of men were regarded as the outcome of a rational choice whereby gains and losses were weighed against each other. Similar simplified theories are sometimes expressed by police officials and by authors of letters to newspaper editors asking for heavier penalties. But if we discard such theories, it does not follow that we have to discard the idea of general prevention. Just as fear enters the picture when people take a calculated risk in committing an offense, fear may also be an element in behavior which is not rationally motivated. . . . [M]odern theories of general prevention take into account both deterrence and moral influence, and they concede that the effects involved may be "unconscious and emotional, drawing upon deep rooted fears and aspirations."

* * *

"Because people generally refrain from crimes on moral grounds, threats of penalty have little influence."

The premise contains a large measure of truth, but it does not justify the conclusion. Three comments are necessary. (a)Even if people on the whole do not require the criminal law to keep them from committing more serious offenses, this is not true for offenses which are subject to little or no moral reprobation. (b)Even though moral inhibitions today are adequate enough to prevent the bulk of the population from committing serious crimes, it is a debatable question whether this would continue for long if the hazards of punishment were removed or drastically minimized. It is conceivable that only a small number of people would fall victim to temptation when the penalties were first abolished or greatly reduced, but that with the passage of time, crime would attract the weaker souls who had become demoralized by seeing offenses committed with impunity. The effects might gradually spread through the population in a chain reaction. (c) Even though it be conceded that law-abiding conduct in certain areas predominantly depends upon non-legal conditions, this does not mean that the effects of the legal machinery are not extremely valuable from a community point of view. Let us imagine a fictitious city which has 1,000,000 adult male inhabitants who commit 100 rapes annually. Suppose, then, that abolishing the crime of rape led to an increase in the number of rape cases to 1,000. From a social-psychological point of view one might conclude that the legal measures were quite insignificant: 999,000 males do not commit rape even when the threat of penalty is absent. If observed from the view point of the legal machinery, however, the conclusion is entirely different. A catastrophic increase of serious cases of violence has occurred. In other words, the increase in rape has demonstrated the tremendous social importance of general prevention.

3. Providing empirical documentation of the deterrent effects of punishment has proven a difficult task. Some anecdotal evidence exists as illustrated by the following from Andenaes, id. at 961–62:

Reports on conditions of disorganization following wars, revolutions or mutinies provide ample documentation as to how lawlessness may flourish when the probability of detection, apprehension and conviction is low. In these situations, however, many factors work together. The most clear cut examples of the importance of the risk of detection itself are provided by cases in which society functions normally but all policing activity is paralyzed by a police strike or a similar condition. For example, the following official report was made on lawlessness during a 1919 police strike, starting at midnight on July 31st, during which nearly half of the Liverpool policemen were out of service:

In this district the strike was accompanied by threats, violence and intimidation on the part of lawless persons. Many assaults on the constables who remained on duty were committed. Owing to the sudden nature of the strike the authorities were afforded no opportunity to make adequate provision to cope with the position. Looting of shops commenced about 10 p.m. on August 1st, and continued for some days. In all about 400 shops were looted. Military were requisitioned, special constables sworn in, and police brought from other centers.

* * *

Unfortunately none of these reports tells us whether the rise in criminality was due to increased activity among established criminals or whether noncriminals participated as well.

4. Because deterrence theory makes empirical claims—that a relation exists between penalties, certainty of capture, and crime rates—the theory is subject to empirical evaluation. In 1978, the National Research Council of the National Academy of Sciences published a report assessing all empirical studies of deterrence, *NRC, Deterrence and Incapacitation: Estimating the Effects of Criminal Sanctions on Crime Rates* (1978). The council found that reported evidence consistently shows a negative association between crime rates and the risks of apprehension, conviction, or imprisonment. However, the Council cautioned that such data did not necessarily establish the deterrent effect of punishment. Inaccurate measuring of the rate of crime is always a possibility that precludes firm conclusions about deterrent effect. Moreover, incapacitating offenders may reduce crime. Thus the negative association between imprisonment and crime rates may be a consequence of an incapacitative, or a combined incapacitative and deterrent, effect. Finally, the negative association between crime and sanctions could be interpreted as an "inverse causal effect" "whereby jurisdictions impose lower sanctions because they have higher crime rates which cannot be met by an overburdened criminal justice system. Such concerns led the Council to urge "scientific caution," and to conclude that "we cannot yet assert that the evidence warrants an affirmative conclusion regarding deterrence" (*id.* at 4–7).

Commentators continue to urge caution. "Surveys of the available research have shown that there are relatively few studies which have genuinely identified the existence and extent of general deterrent effects flowing from the legal penalty, and that it would be unsafe to generalize from these specific studies to broad policy prescriptions." *Principled Sentencing* 57 (A. von Hirsch and A. Ashworth eds. 1992)

For a retort to the NRC's work, see Ehrlich and Mark, *Fear of Deterrence,* 6 J. Leg. Stud. 293 (1977).

5. The above excerpt from Andenaes describing the effects of the Liverpool police strike suggests a relationship between effective law enforcement and deterrence: Where risk of apprehension and conviction is low, crime appears to increase. As Bentham appreciated, deterrence is a function of both the certainty and the severity of punishment. Consider the assessment of the certainty—severity relationship in Antunes and Hunt, *The Deterrent Impact of Criminal Sanctions: Some Implications for Criminal Justice Policy,* 51 J. Urban L. 145, 158–59 (1973):

> [C]ertainty, considered by itself, has a moderate deterrent effect for all crimes, while severity acting alone is not associated with lower rates of crime. When certainty and severity are combined, . . . then the impact of severity is filtered through the certainty value. This means that increasing severity in a condition of low certainty will have little effect on crime rates.

* * *

> It seems clear from a scientific point of view that the key to resolving the conflicting goals of our criminal justice system lies in increasing the certainty of detection, prosecution, and punishment. Severity has only slight effects in generally deterring crime, and could safely be left at its current level or even reduced without exerting much impact on reducing crime rates. Furthermore, high severity has adverse consequences on the probability of post-prison crime. Thus, the goal of special deterrence may be facilitated not by increasing (or even by decreasing) the severity of punishment. On the other hand, we believe that increasing the certainty of detection, prosecution, and punishment will have important beneficial consequences for both general and specific deterrence. The evidence indicates that increased certainty will act as a general deterrent to reduce levels of crime. Further, increased certainty should facilitate special deterrence by eliminating the feeling of those who are incarcerated that they have been unfairly singled out for punishment while most of those guilty of the same crime remain unpunished.

On the other hand, consider Andenaes, *supra,* p. 163 n.2, at 970:

> It seems reasonable to conclude that as a general rule, though not without exceptions, the general preventive effect of the criminal law increases with the growing severity of penalties. Contemporary dictatorships display with almost frightening clarity the conformity that can be produced by a ruthlessly severe justice.

> However, it is necessary to make two important reservations. In the first place, . . . what is decisive is not the actual practice but how this practice is conceived by the public. Although little research has been done to find out how much the general public knows about the penal system, presumably most people have only vague and unspecified notions. Therefore, only quite

substantial changes will be noticed. Only rarely does a single sentence bring about significant preventive effects.

In the second place, the prerequisite of general prevention is that the law be enforced. Experience seems to show that excessively severe penalties may actually reduce the risk of conviction, thereby leading to results contrary to their purpose. . . .

See also Nagel, *Trade-off in Crime Reduction among Certainty, Severity, and Crime Benefits,* 35 Rutgers L. Rev. 100 (1982) (concluding that certainty is more significant than severity only in some contexts).

6. Empirical considerations aside, deterrence theory raises moral issues. A traditional objection to deterrence as the justification for punishment rests in the theory's apparent insensitivity to the demands of justice. Suppose a serious crime were commonly being committed and no offenders were being apprehended. Would not deterrence theory permit, indeed perhaps require, the state to frame an innocent person and publicize his conviction and punishment if he were universally thought guilty and if substantial deterrence could likely be achieved thereby? For consideration of this problem, see Rawls, *Two Concepts of Rules,* in Philosophy of Law 556 (J. Feinberg and H. Gross eds. 1975).

Professor Andenaes notes a similar, but less dramatic, moral objection to grounding punishment on deterrence theory. Andenaes, *supra, p.* 90 n.2, at 982–83:

. . . [I]t has often been said that punishment, in this context, is used not to prevent future violations on the part of the criminal, but in order to instill lawful behavior in others. The individual criminal is merely an instrument, he is sacrificed in a manner which is contrary to our ethical principles. This objection carries least weight in relation to general preventive notions connected with legislation. The law provides, for example, that whoever is found guilty of murder is liable to life imprisonment or that whoever drives a car when he is intoxicated is to be given a prison sentence of thirty days. Such penal provisions have been laid down with an aim to preventing anyone from performing the prohibited acts. If we accept the provisions as ethically defensible, we also have to accept the punishment prescribed in each individual case. . . .

* * *

The question, however, comes to a head when the individual penalty is decided by general prevention considerations, in other words, exemplary penalties.

* * *

. . . There is an element of *ex post facto* law involved in such sentences. Although the judge operates within the framework of the law, such sentences are not, in fact, applications of previously established norms. The judge establishes a norm to suit the situation. Nor does the result square with the ideal of equality before the law. The procedure calls to mind a practice which—at least according to historical novels—was commonly used in former times when a number of soldiers committed mutiny or similar grave violations: the commanding officer would have a suitable number of soldiers shot in order to instill fear and give warning, and the remaining soldiers were readmitted to service without penalty.

Such ethical doubts become even stronger if the individual sentence depends upon the kind of publicity—and hence the kind of preventive effect—which is expected. Suppose a judge is faced with two similar cases within a short interval. In the first case, the courtroom is filled with journalists, and the outcome of the trial is likely to become known to millions of readers. In the second case, the listener's benches are empty and, in all probability, the verdict will not spread far beyond the circles of those who are present in the courtroom. Is it defensible for the judge to pass heavy judgment in the first instance because the sentence is likely to gain much publicity and consequently bring about strong general preventive effects, while the defendant in the second case is merely given a warning because punishment in his case would only mean personal suffering, and would not yield results from a social point of view? Such speculation upon the general preventive effects of the individual sentence easily become tinged with cynicism and for ethical reasons this approach is only acceptable within very narrow limits.

[2] Incapacitation

Certain sanctions such as imprisonment, the death penalty, and banishment have the effect of preventing or seriously limiting the ability of the offenders upon whom they are visited to commit further offenses against citizens in ordinary society. Therefore, by "incapacitating" crime-prone offenders the amount of crime is arguably reduced.

Advocates of incapacitation argue that it offers a crime control strategy free of the kinds of questionable assumptions about human nature considered in the materials on deterrence. See J. Wilson, Thinking About Crime 145 (rev. ed. 1983). Unlike deterrence and rehabilitation (which is considered in the next section of these materials), incapacitation is said to work by "definition" so long as three factual conditions exist: Some offenders must repeatedly commit crime; offenders taken out of society must not be "immediately and completely" replaced by different offenders; and the form and conditions of incapacitation itself must not increase the criminal activity of those incapacitated sufficiently to offset the crimes prevented by the incapacitation. *Id.* at 145–46.

Consider the extent to which the above three factual conditions actually obtain and might vary depending upon the crime and the nature of the incapacitative disposition. Even assuming that the three conditions are met, incapacitation nevertheless is, as the following materials illustrate, a controversial basis for restricting liberty.

Von Hirsch, *Incapacitation*

Principled Sentencing 101-8

(A. von Hirsch and A. Ashworth eds. 1992)

Incapacitation is the idea of simple restraint: rendering the convicted offender incapable, for a period of time, of offending again. Whereas rehabilitation involves changing the person's habits or attitudes so he or she becomes less criminally inclined, incapacitation presupposes no such change. Instead, obstacles are interposed to impede the person's carrying out whatever criminal inclinations he or she may have. Usually, the obstacle is the walls of a prison, but other incapacitative techniques are possible—such as exile or house arrest.

Incapacitation has, usually, been sought through predicting the offender's likelihood of reoffending. Those deemed more likely to reoffend are to be restrained, for example, by imposition of a term of imprisonment—or of a prison term of longer duration than they otherwise would receive. . . .

Who, then, is likely to reoffend? Prediction research in criminology has had a more than sixty-year history. . . . The basic research technique has been straightforward enough. Various facts about convicted criminals are recorded: previous arrests and convictions, social and employment history, prior drug use, and so forth; and those factors that are, statistically, more strongly associated with recidivism are identified. The prediction instrument, based on these factors, is then constructed and tested. The studies suggest that a limited capacity to predict does exist. Certain facts about offenders—principally, their previous criminal records, drug habits, and histories of unemployment—are (albeit only to a modest extent) indicative of increased likelihood of recidivism.

Incapacitation was an important (although often less visible) element in the traditional rehabilitative penal ethic. Sentencing judges and correctional officials were supposed to gauge not only offenders' treatment needs but their likelihood of recidivism. "Curable" offenders were to be treated (in the community, if possible), but those judged bad risks were to be restrained. The traditional view had its appeal precisely because it thus offered both therapy and restraint. One did not have to assume that all criminals really were treatable, but merely that some might be. Therapy could be tried on the potentially responsive, but always with a fail-safe: the offender who seemed unsuitable for treatment could be separated from the community.

* * *

In the early 1970s, some penologists began raising doubts about predictive restraint in sentencing. . . . [Critics noted] that prediction in sentencing does not have to be left to a judge's personal judgment. Before a defendant is incarcerated on incapacitative grounds, the degree of harmfulness of the predicted conduct, and its required degree of likelihood, could be specified in advance. The predictions could also rely, not on someone's intuitive sense of who is a bad risk, but on statistically tested forecasting methods. The question asked is whether—once these threshold requirements are met—it is fair to rely on forecasts of dangerousness in deciding the sentence.

In this connection, [commentators pointed] to the tendency of forecasts of criminality to overpredict. Although statistical forecasting methods can identify groups of offenders having higher than average probabilities of recidivism, these methods show a disturbing incidence of "false positives." Many of those classified as potential recidivists will, in fact, not be found to offend again. The rate of false positive is particularly high when forecasting serious criminality—for example, violence. The majority of those designated as dangerous turn out—when the predictions are followed up—to be persons who are not found to commit the predicted acts of violence when allowed to remain at large.

* * *

False positives put the justice of predictive sentencing into question. Ostensibly, the offender classified as dangerous is confined to prevent him or her from infringing the rights of others. But to the extent the classification is mistaken, the offender would not have committed the infringement. The person's liberty is lost merely because people *like* him or her will offend again, and we cannot specify which of them will actually do so.

* * *

. . . [Some defenders of predictive sentencing concede the false positive problem and admit that in predicting dangerousness] at least half of those classified as risks will mistakenly be so classified. With such a high incidence of error, how then can sentencing on the basis of dangerousness be justified? It can only be [justified, these defenders suggest,] by the idea of shifting the burden of risk. An unconvicted dangerous person is entitled to remain at large, and any risk to potential victims must be borne by them. Once the person acts on the dangerous inclinations and is convicted for seriously harming others, however, we become entitled to shift the risk of victimization (in this case, of mistaken confinement) to the offender. Error is unavoidable, and the question is, who should bear its costs?. . . .

. . . [Such views raise a number of questions.] [E]ven if restraining the dangerous were justifiable on . . . such . . . "shifting of risk" [grounds,] one still has not explained why an offender's *punishment* should be extended on that ground. Punishment, [for many commentators,] involves not only deprivation but blame—so that increasing punishment implies the offender to be more blameworthy. . . . There is nothing about a convicted offender's dangerousness—that is, the mere likelihood of offending again as contrasted with the degree of culpability for crimes already committed—which renders him or her more to blame. Thus if confining offenders beyond their deserved term of punishment were justifiable at all, that confinement would be civil, not criminal.

* * *

In the early 1980s, a number of studies, based mainly on interviews with incarcerated offenders, suggested that offense patterns are highly skewed, even among those individuals who recidivate after being convicted. While some recidivists reoffended only occasionally, others appeared to revert to serious criminality frequently. If incapacitative techniques could be targeted to the latter group—to the frequent, serious violators—might these techniques not offer hope, after all, for reducing crime?

It was during this period that Peter Greenwood, a Rand Corporation researcher, published a report on a prediction technique which he termed "selective incapacitation." The technique, derived from interviews with confined offenders, made use of a few simple indicia of dangerousness, concerned mainly with the offender's criminal, unemployment, and drug-use histories. It was designed to identify "high-rate" predators—those who would commit violent offenses (such as robbery) frequently. Because so many robberies were being committed by a small group of active predators, he argued, identifying and isolating these persons could considerably reduce the incidence of such crimes. Greenwood devised a method of projecting the resulting crime reduction effect. He estimated that imposing longer prison terms for the high-rate offenders could reduce the robbery rate by as much as 15 to 20 percent, without even any significant increase in prison populations.

Greenwood's suggestions generated considerable interest among criminologists and policymakers [who argued, among other things, that selective incapacitation is] not unfair or undeserved . . . because desert sets merely the broadest outer limits on permissible punishments. Reliance on status factors such as employment is no serious problem, because such factors are used by the criminal justice system in other contexts. The possible inaccuracies of the prediction technique should be no bar to use, because the technique is superior to the informal predictive judgments that judges and prosecutors make today. . . .

The optimism . . . about selective incapacitation was soon challenged, however. Objections were raised both about the empirical soundness of the technique and about its ethics. . . .

The empirical objections [questioned] whether Greenwood's factors can identify high-rate offenders, once official data that courts must rely upon are utilized, instead of offenders' self-reports of their own criminal activities. The projections of large crime-reduction effects are also suspect. Those projections rely on questionable extrapolations, from the criminal activity of *incarcerated* offenders to the activity of offenders generally. The projections also appear to make unrealistic estimates of such important factors as the anticipated length of offenders' criminal careers. In 1986, a research panel of the National Academy of Sciences examined these issues, and concluded that selective incapacitation, at least today, has a much more modest crime-reduction potential than Greenwood. . . . claim[s].

The ethical objection to selective incapacitation . . . consists chiefly in the strategy's conflict with the requirements of proportionality. Selective incapacitation relies upon factors (e.g., early criminal history, drug use, and so forth) that have little bearing on the blameworthiness of the criminal conduct for which the offender stands convicted. The strategy can have significant crime prevention effects by its own proponents' reckoning, moreover, only if disparities among those convicted of comparable offenses are very large: the prison sentences visited on "high-risk" felons must be *much* longer than those visited on lower-risk felons convicted of the same offense. To sustain such large disparities, proportionality must either be disregarded entirely or be treated as only marginal constraint.

Notes and Questions

1. The problem of reliably identifying those offenders posing the greatest danger of subsequent recidivism has always plagued proponents of the incapacitation theory. As von Hirsch points out, the tendency has been to "overpredict" dangerousness through both clinical and statistical forecasts of violent conduct at a "false positive" rate of over 60 percent. J. Monahan, *Predicting Violent Behavior: An Assessment of Clinical Techniques* 73–80, 101–04 (1981). The problem is so substantial that a task force of the American Psychological Association concluded, 33 Am. Psychologist 1099, 1110 (1978):

> It does appear from reading the research that the validity of psychological predictions of violent behavior, at least in the sentencing and release situations we are considering, is extremely poor, so poor that one could oppose their use on the strictly empirical grounds that psychologists are not professionally competent to make such judgments.

2. Predicting future behavior in terms of facts about the person raises ethical problems. If, for example, race is an obviously inappropriate factor, why not past juvenile or adult "records," alcohol or drug use, and employment history? If chronic unemployment counts heavily in favor of increasing incapacitative sentences, is the offender in a sense being punished "for" being unemployed? See J. Wilson, *Thinking About Crime* 158 (rev. ed. 1983). Consider A. von Hirsch, *Doing Justice: The Choice of Punishments* 26 (1976): "[P]redictive restraint poses special ethical problems. The fact that the person's liberty is at stake reduces the moral acceptability of mistakes of over-prediction. Moreover, one may question whether it is ever just to punish someone more severely for what he is expected to do, even if the prediction was accurate."

Commentators raise other moral objections to incapacitation. Consider Packer, 49–51:

> Incapacitation, then, is a mode of punishment that uses the fact that a person has committed a crime of a particular sort as the basis for assessing his personality and then predicting that he will commit further crimes of that sort. It is an empirical question in every case whether the prediction is a valid one. To the extent that the prediction is valid, utilitarian ethics can approve the use of punishment for incapacitative purposes, on the view that the pain inflicted on persons who are punished is less than the pain that would be inflicted on their putative victims and on society at large if those same persons were left free to commit further offenses.

* * *

There are kinds of conduct that are typically repetitive. Persons who commit theft because they suffer from kleptomania are apt to go right on doing so. Narcotics offenders, if they happen to be addicts, are by definition likely to repeat their offenses. We have learned that there is a typical syndrome involved in the writing of bad checks. It is an activity of such a compulsive sort that repeat performances are highly probable. In cases of this sort, the empirical basis for making the kind of prediction upon which the incapacitative rationale necessarily rests is quite strong. But note the paradox that this involves. The case for incapacitation is strongest in precisely those areas where the offender is least capable of controlling himself; where his conduct bears the least resemblance to the kind of purposeful, voluntary conduct to which we are likely to attach moral condemnation. Baldly put, the incapacitative theory is at its strongest for those who, in retributive terms, are the least deserving of punishment. That is not, of course, enough to disqualify it as a basis for punishment. It does, however, suggest a certain tension between the concept of blameworthiness as a prerequisite of punishment and the dictates of the incapacitative claim. Perhaps the way to dissolve that tension is to abandon blameworthiness as a condition for the imposition of punishment. That is the thrust of the behavioral theory that presents one horn of the criminal law's contemporary dilemma. Incapacitation as a basis for punishment seems particularly attuned to the demands of the behavioral position.

. . . The logic of the incapacitative position drives us to say that until the offender stops being a danger we will continue to restrain him. What this means, pushed to its logical conclusion, is that offenses that are universally regarded as relatively trivial may be punished by imprisonment for life. It means that, at least, unless we have some basis for asserting that lengthy imprisonment is a greater evil than the prospect of repeated criminality.

3. To the extent that offenders are incapacitated for their perceived dangerous present status rather than for their past criminal actions, are they being "punished"? Reconsider the material at the beginning of this chapter on the meaning of punishment, especially *United States v. Salerno, supra* at p.52. To what extent is incapacitation a justification of "punishment" rather than a basis for coercive state intervention of another sort?

[3] Rehabilitation

PACKER

53–55, 57–58

The most immediately appealing justification for punishment is the claim that it may be used to prevent crime by so changing the personality of the offender that he will conform to the dictates of law; in a word, by reforming him. In that ideal many have seen the means for resolving the moral paradox of the utilitarian position: that punishment is an instrumental use of one man for the benefit of other men. Perhaps "resolving" is too strong a word. After all, the goal sought by the rehabilitative ideal is not reform for its own sake or even for the sake of enabling its object to live a better and a happier life. We hope that he will do so, but the justification is a social one: we want to reform him so that he will cease to offend. He is still being made use of. . . .

* * *

What are the significant characteristics of a system of punishment based on the goal of rehabilitation? Principally, such a system is—like incapacitation—offender-or iented rather than offense-oriented. If rehabilitation is the goal, the nature of the offense is relevant only for what it tells us about what is needed to rehabilitate the offender. To be sure, that relevance is greater than is commonly supposed. In the present state of our knowledge about the human personality and the springs of human action we cannot afford to ignore what a man has done as an index of the kind of man he is and, consequently, of what measures are required to make him better. Still, what he has done is only one measure, and a rough one at that, of what he is. The rehabilitative ideal teaches us that we must treat each offender as an individual whose special needs and problems must be known as fully as possible in order to enable us to deal effectively with him. Punishment, in this view, must be forward-looking. The gravity of the offense, however measured, may give us a clue to the intensity and duration of the measures needed to rehabilitate; but it is only a clue, not a prescription. There is, then, no generally postulated equivalence between the offense and the punishment, as there would be in the case of the retributive or even the deterrent theory of punishment.

It follows from this offender-oriented aspect of the rehabilitative ideal that the intensity and duration of punishment are to be measured by what is thought to be required in order to change the offender's personality. Unlike the related goal of incapacitation, the inquiry is not into how dangerous the offender is but rather into how amenable to treatment he is. If a writer of bad checks can be cured of his underlying disorder only by five years of intensive psychotherapy, then that is what he is to receive. And, of course, no one knows at the outset how much of what kind of therapy will be needed in his or anyone else's case, so it cannot be said in advance what the duration of his punishment will be. It ends whenever those in authority decide that he has been rehabilitated. Of course, if he does not yield to treatment and is thought to present a danger, he will not be released. . . .

There are two major objections to making rehabilitation the primary justification for punishment. The first probably comes very close to settling the matter for present purposes. It is, very simply, that we do not know how to rehabilitate offenders, at least within the limit of the resources that are now or might reasonably be expected to be devoted to the task. The more we learn about the roots of crime, the clearer it is that they are nonspecific, that the social and psychic springs lie deep within the human condition. To create on a large scale the essentials of a society that produced no crime would be to remake society itself. To say this is not to suggest that the goal of so improving society is not worthwhile, or that there is any superior social goal. It is merely to suggest that this is a task to be undertaken in the name of objectives and using techniques that far transcend the prevention of undesirable behavior. One trouble with the rehabilitative ideal is that it makes the criminal law the vehicle for tasks that are far beyond its competence. Surely the point does not require laboring that a general amelioration of the conditions of social living is not a task that can be very well advanced in the context of the institutions and processes that we devote to apprehending, trying, and dealing with persons who commit offenses.

Let us suppose, though, that the side effects of some yet-to-be-discovered means of changing the human personality are not such as we would consider objectionable. To put it another way, suppose that the existing empirical objection to the rehabilitative ideal is removed. Should that ideal be permitted to dominate our punishment system? It is with this question that the second major objection to rehabilitation as the primary goal of punishment emerges. If people can be changed for the better without suffering effects that would generally be considered unfortunate, is there any moral case against compelling them to undergo measures designed to produce such change, given the predicate that they have by their past behavior demonstrated a readiness to commit offenses of a sort whose future occurrence will now be reduced? It may be enough to measure our present fumbling efforts against that millennial prospect and assert that until it arrives the question is academic. It may also be that when the day of the good-behavior pill comes, we will be on the one hand so insensitive to such interferences with the personality and on the other hand so eager to enjoy the increased security that its wholesale administration to offenders promises that questions of this order will seem as academic then as they do now. But if weconsider the moral dimensions of the question, the answer is by no means clear. Is it quixotic to assert that man has a right to be bad? Perhaps that right will appear to have little substance when the means of change is more readily at hand than it is today. Yet I have serious doubts on this point, and I am impelled to ask whether a theory of punishment that requires acquiescence in compelled personality change can ever be squared with long-cherished ideals of human autonomy.

Hart, *Punishment and Responsibility*

25–27 (1968)

It is . . . important to see precisely what the relation of Reform to punishment is because its advocates too often misstate it. "Reform" as an objective is no doubt very vague; it now embraces any strengthening of the offender's disposition and capacity to keep within the law, which is intentionally brought about by human effort otherwise than through fear of punishment. Reforming methods include the inducement of states of repentance, or recognition of moral guilt, or greater awareness of the character and demands of society, the provision of education in a broad sense, vocational training and psychological treatment. Many seeing the futility and indeed harmful character of much traditional punishment speak as if Reform could and should be the General Aim of the whole practice of punishment or the dominant objective of the criminal law. . . .

Of course this is a possible ideal but is not an ideal for punishment. Reform can only have a place within a system of punishment as an exploitation of the opportunities presented by the conviction or compulsory detention of offenders. It is not an alternative General Justifying Aim of the practice of punishment but something the pursuit of which within a system of punishment qualifies or displaces altogether recourse to principles of justice or proportion in determining the amount of punishment. This is where both Reform and individualized punishment have run counter to the customary morality of punishment.

There is indeed a paradox in asserting that Reform should "predominate" in a system of Criminal Law, as if the main purpose of providing punishment for murder was to reform the murderer, not to prevent murder; and the paradox is greater where the legal offence is not a serious moral one: e.g., infringing a state monopoly of transport. The objection to assigning to Reform this place in punishment is not merely that punishment entails suffering and Reform does not; but that Reform is essentially a remedial step for which *ex hypothesi* there is an opportunity only at the point where the criminal law has failed in its primary task of securing society from the evil which breach of the law involves. Society is divisible at any moment into two classes: (i)those who have actually broken a given law and (ii)those who have not yet broken it but may. To take Reform as the dominant objective would be to forego the hope of influencing the second and—in relation to the more Serious offenses— numerically much greater class. We should thus subordinate the prevention of first offenses to the prevention of recidivism.

COHEN, *MORAL ASPECTS OF THE CRIMINAL LAW*

49 Yale L.J. 987, 1013 (1940)

Let us abandon the light-hearted pretension that any of us know all cases of criminality can be readily cured, and ask the more modest and serious question: To what extent can criminals be reeducated or reconditioned so that they can live useful lives? It would indeed be illiberal dogmatism to deny all possibility and desirability of effort along this line. Yet we must keep in mind our human limitations.

If the causes of crime are determined by the life of certain groups, it is foolish to deal with the individual as if he were a self-sufficient and self-determining system. We must deal with the whole group to which he naturally belongs or gravitates and which determines his morals. Otherwise we have to adapt him completely to some other group or social condition, which is indeed a very difficult problem in social engineering.

And here we must not neglect the question of cost. When we refer to any measure as impracticable, we generally mean that the cost is too great. There is doubtless a tremendous expense in maintaining our present system of punishment. But this expense is not unlimited. Suppose that fiendish perpetrators of horrible crimes on children could be reformed by being sent first for several years to a special hospital. Will people vote large funds for such purposes when honest law-abiding citizens so often cannot get adequate hospital facilities? Suppose that we find that a certain social environment or that an elaborate college course will reform a burglar or gunman, would our community stand for the expense when so many worthy young people cannot afford to go to college because they have to go to work? We certainly should not give even the appearance of reward for criminality. Let us not forget that there is always a natural resentment in any society against those who have attacked it. Will people be satisfied to see one who is guilty of horrible crimes simply reformed, and not give vent to the social horror and resentment against the miscreant?

Morris, *The Future of Imprisonment*

14–17 (1974)

"Rehabilitation," whatever it means and whatever the programs that allegedly give it meaning, must cease to be a purpose of the prison sanction. This does not mean that the various developed treatment programs within prisons need to be abandoned; quite the contrary, they need expansion. But it does mean that they must not be seen as purposive in the sense that criminals are to be sent to prison for treatment. There is a sharp distinction between the purposes of incarceration and the opportunities for the training and assistance of prisoners that may be pursued within those purposes. The system is corrupted when we fail to preserve this distinction and this failure pervades the world's prison programs.

* * *

[I]t seems to me clear that the treatment model suffers from two fallacies, one empirical, the other psychological.

First, the empirical defect. Can we predict the likelihood of criminal behavior in the community by observing the prisoner's response to prison training programs? For present purposes it is necessary to telescope shelves of statistical analysis of parole prediction tables and base expectancy rates for different categories of offenders into overly dogmatic propositions. . . What it all comes to is this: Prison behavior is not a predictor of community behavior.

* * *

Second, there is the psychological fallacy that corrupts the individual treatment model. The model of medical treatment that underlies the present advocacy of prison training programs is itself flawed. It suffers fundamentally from a belief that psychological change can be coerced. In psychological treatment of abnormal behavior it is widely agreed that conventional psychotherapy, particularly if it is of the psychoanalytic variety, must be voluntarily entered into by the patient if it is to be effective. By contrast, in physical medicine the cooperation of the patient, although desirable, is not always necessary—an antibiotic works on a patient held down for the injection—and "cure" is a substantially different concept. Yet, in penology the analogy with physical medicine has been accepted since the Quakers first prescribed compulsory segregated religious observance and enforced penitence as their principal specifics.

NOTE

In the 1970s, several empirical studies concluded that rehabilitation programs had no appreciable effect on recidivism rates of those exposed to the programs. See, e.g., Robinson and Smith, *The Effectiveness of Correctional Programs,* 17 Crime & Delinq. 67 (1971). A study published in 1976 analyzed all written reports of the effects of correctional rehabilitation programs between 1945 and 1967 and concluded, essentially, that "nothing works." D. Lipton, R. Martinson, and J. Wilks, *The Effectiveness of Correctional Treatment [ECT]* (1976). More recently, however, a somewhat less pessimistic picture was painted by Martinson, one of the authors of the *ECT* study. In Martinson, *New Findings, New Views: A Note of Caution Regarding Sentencing Reform,* 7 Hofstra L. Rev. 243, 252–55 (1979), he stated:

> Any conclusion in scientific inquiry is held provisionally, subject to further evidence. . . . [N]ew evidence from our current study leads me to reject my original conclusion and suggest an alternative more adequate to the facts at hand. . . .
>
> Different procedures were used in the two surveys. *ECT* is based primarily on the findings of evaluation research—a special kind of research which was applied to criminal justice on a wide scale for the first time in California during the period immediately following World War II. This research is experimental—that is, offenders are often randomly allocated to treatment and nontreatment groups so that comparison can be made of outcome. Our current study, however, compares the reprocessing rates of groups receiving treatment with roughly comparable groups who receive the "standard processing" given to most offenders across the United States.

* * *

> In brief, *ECT* focused on summarizing evaluation research which purported to uncover *causality;* in our current study we reject this perspective as premature and focus on uncovering *patterns* which can be of use to Policymakers in choosing among available treatment programs. . . .

* * *

> . . . More precisely, treatments will be found to be "impotent" under certain conditions, beneficial under others, and detrimental under still others. The current study, by enabling us to uncover a major category of *harmful treatment,* is an advance on ECT. It enables us to indicate, at least roughly, the conditions under which a treatment program will fall into one of three categories: (1) beneficial (the program *reduces* reprocessing rates); (2) neutral (*no impact,* positive or negative, can be determined); and (3) detrimental (the program *increases* reprocessing rates).
>
> The most interesting general conclusion is that no treatment program now used in criminal justice is inherently either substantially helpful or harmful. The critical fact seems to be the *conditions* under which the program is delivered. For example, our results indicate that a widely used program,

such as formal education, is detrimental when given to juvenile sentenced offenders in a group home, but is beneficial (decreases reprocessing rates) when given to juveniles in juvenile prisons. Such startling results are found again and again in our study, for treatment programs as diverse as individual psychotherapy, group counseling, intensive supervision, and what we have called "individual/help" (aid, advice, counseling).

[4] Denunciation

STEPHEN

81–82

. . . [T]he sentence of the law is to the moral sentiment of the public in relation to any offense what a seal is to hot wax. It converts into a permanent final judgment what might otherwise be a transient sentiment. The mere general suspicion or knowledge that a man has done something dishonest may never be brought to a point, and the disapprobation excited by it may in time pass away, but the fact that he has been convicted and punished as a thief stamps a mark upon him for life. In short, the infliction of punishment by law gives definite expression and a solemn ratification and justification to the hatred which is excited by the commission of the offense, and which constitutes the moral or popular as distinguished from the conscientious sanction of that part of morality which is also sanctioned by the criminal law. The criminal law thus proceeds upon the principle that it is morally right to hate criminals, and it confirms and justifies that sentiment by inflicting upon criminals punishments which express it.

* * *

. . . I am also of opinion that this close alliance between criminal law and moral sentiment is in all ways healthy and advantageous to the community. I think it highly desirable that criminals should be hated, that the punishments inflicted upon them should be so contrived as to give expression to that hatred, and to justify it so far as the public provision of means for expressing and gratifying a healthy natural sentiment can justify and encourage it.

* * *

. . . No doubt they are peculiarly liable to abuse, and in some states of society are commonly in excess of what is desirable, and so require restraint rather than excitement, but unqualified denunciations of them are as ill-judged as unqualified denunciations of sexual passion. The forms in which deliberate anger and righteous disapprobation are expressed, and the execution of criminal justice is the most emphatic of such forms, stand to the one set of passions in the same relation in which marriage stands to the other.

* * *

DURKHEIM, *THE DIVISIONS OF LABOR IN SOCIETY*

108–9 (Simpson trans. 1933)

Although [punishment] proceeds from a quite mechanical reaction, from movements which are passionate and in great part non-reflective, it does play a useful role. Only this role is not where we ordinarily look for it. It does not serve, or else only serves quite secondarily, in correcting the culpable or in intimidating possible followers. From this point of view, its efficacy is justly doubtful and, in any case, mediocre. Its true function is to maintain social cohesion intact, while maintaining all its vitality in the common conscience. Denied so categorically, it would necessarily lose its energy if an emotional reaction of the community did not come to compensate its loss, and it would result in a breakdown of social solidarity. It is necessary, then, that it be affirmed forcibly at the very moment when it is contradicted, and the only means of affirming it is toexpress the unanimous aversion which the crime continues to inspire, by an authentic act which can consist only in suffering inflicted upon the agent. Thus, while being the necessary product of the causes which engender it, this suffering is not a gratuitous cruelty. It is the sign which witnesses that collective sentiments are always collective, that the communion of spirits in the same faith rests on a solid foundation, and accordingly, that it is repairing the evil which the crime inflicted upon society. That is why we are right in saying that the criminal must suffer in proportion to his crime, why theories which refuse to punishment any expiatory character appear as so many spirits subversive of the social order. It is because these doctrines could be practiced only in a society where the whole common conscience would be nearly gone. Without this necessary satisfaction, what we call the moral conscience could not be conserved. We can thus say without paradox that punishment is above all designed to act upon upright people, for, since it serves to heal the wounds made upon collective sentiments, it can fill this role only where these sentiments exist, and commensurately with their vivacity. Of course, by warning already disturbed spirits of a new enfeeblement of the collective soul, it can even stop attacks from multiplying, but this result, however useful, is only a particular counter blow. In short, in order to form an exact idea of punishment, we must reconcile the two contradictory theories which deal with it: that which sees it as expiation, and that which makes it a weapon for social defense. It is certain that it functions for the protection of society, but that is because it is expiatory. Moreover, if it must be expiatory, that does not mean that by some mystical virtue pain compensates for the error, but rather that it can produce a socially useful effect only under this condition.

WALKER, *PUNISHMENT, DANGER AND STIGMA: THE MORALITY OF CRIMINAL JUSTICE*

28–30 (1980)

[The expressive (denunciatory) view] holds that the justification for penalising an offender is that doing so expresses an important statement about the offense. A penalty declares, in effect, that in the society the offense in question is not tolerated. On the expressive view this is not sufficiently declared by laws which merely prohibit certain conduct: penalties must be provided and people must be sentenced.

It is important to be clear whether a "denouncer" (as I shall call someone who holds this view) is really a "reducer," [one who believes that punishment reduces the frequency of crime] or something else. If he believes that the point of declaring society's non-toleration of this or that sort of law-breaking is to strengthen people's disapproval of it, and so reduce its frequency, he is simply a reducer who believes in a particular technique. . . .

If, on the other hand, the denouncer denies that he is a mere reducer, he must tell us what it is that makes the expression of non-toleration a good thing. Sociologically-minded denouncers usually give Durkheim's answer to this question: that denunciation promotes social cohesion. If this is offered as a justification (and not as a mere description) it is implied that social cohesion is a good thing, and the answer is again a utilitarian one, although rather vaguer and harder to test than the reductive version.

It is possible, however, to be a less utilitarian denouncer, who justifies penalties by talking not of any future benefit but simply of the immediate satisfaction which they give to people who know and disapprove of the offense, in much the same way as funerals and other ceremonials give satisfaction to most if not all participants. This is probably the version of the expressive justification which comes nearest to being both non-utilitarian and non-retributive: I call it "ceremonial denunciation."

It should be easy to distinguish any version of the denunciatory justification from retributivism, although it is possible to confuse the two:

> . . . I will start with retribution. The Old Testament concept of an eye for an eye and a tooth for a tooth no longer plays any part in our criminal law. There is, however, another aspect of retribution . . . it is that society, through the courts, must show its abhorrence of particular types of crime. . . . The courts do not have to reflect public opinion. On the other hand the courts must not disregard it. Perhaps the main duty of the court is to *lead* public opinion. [*Regina v. Sargeant,* 60 CR App. R. 74 (1974).]

But that is by the way. In either form the expressive view is clearly distinguishable from the retributive. For if denunciation is to be achieved the penalty must be publicly announced, whereas retribution can be achieved by secret punishment.

Paradoxically, however, denouncers could not exist without retributivists. For the penalty could not have any of the effects in which denouncers believe (whether the giving of immediate satisfaction or the promotion of disapproval or social cohesion) unless the people upon whom it is meant to have this effect regarded it as just in the retributive sense. This paradox, however, does not imply that the expressive view is really retributivism after all; for the latter demands that the penalty be genuinely appropriate to the offender's culpability, or actually inflicted on a culpable offender, whereas all the denouncer can demand is that those at whom he aims his effect should *believe* it to be retributively appropriate. Moreover, he cannot logically demand that the penalty should actually be inflicted: merely that it should (i)be publicly ordered and (ii)be thought to have been inflicted.

A few denouncers, however, have a more limited aim than influencing public opinion or giving satisfaction to those who are outraged by an individual offense. They see the penalty as a symbolic way of telling the offender something. That something may be either society's disapproval or the inherent wickedness of his act. This view does not require that the penalty be publicized; but it seems to require that the offender himself believe that it is going to be inflicted, in order to make him take its symbolism seriously.

Kahan, *What Do Alternatives Sanctions Mean?*

63 U Chi. L. Rev. 591-604 (1996)

Imprisonment is the punishment of choice in American jurisdictions. In everyday life, the modes of human suffering are numerous and diverse: when we lose our property, we experience need; when we are denounced by those whose opinions we respect, we feel shame; when our bodies are tormented, we suffer physical pain. But for those who commit serious criminal offenses, the law strongly prefers one form of suffering—the deprivation of liberty—to the near exclusion of all others. Some alternatives to imprisonment, such as corporal punishment, are barely conceivable. Others, including fines and community service, do exist but are used sparingly and with great reluctance.

The singularity of American criminal punishments has been widely lamented. Imprisonment is harsh and degrading for offenders and extraordinarily expensive for society. Nor is there any evidence that imprisonment is more effective than its rivals in deterring various crimes. For these reasons, theorists of widely divergent orientations from—economics-minded conservatives to reform-minded civil libertarians—are united in their support for alternative sanctions.

The problem is that there is no political constituency for such reform. If anything, the public's commitment to imprisonment has intensified in step with the theorists' disaffection with it. In the last decade, prison sentences have been both dramatically lengthened for many offenses and extended to others that have traditionally been punished only with fines and probation.

What accounts for the resistance to alternative sanctions? The conventional answer is a failure of democratic politics. Members of the public are ignorant of the availability and feasibility of alternative sanctions; as a result, they are easy prey for self-interested politicians, who exploit their fear of crime by advocating more severe prison sentences. The only possible solution, on this analysis, is a relentless effort to educate the public on the virtues of the prison's rivals.

I want to advance a different explanation. The political unacceptability of alternative sanctions, I will argue, reflects their inadequacy along the expressive dimension of punishment. The public rejects the alternatives not because they perceive that these punishments won't work or aren't severe enough, but because they fail to express condemnation as dramatically and unequivocally as imprisonment.

This claim challenges the central theoretical premise of the case for alternative sanctions: that all forms of punishment are interchangeable along the dimension of severity or "bite." The purpose of imprisonment, on this account, is to make offenders suffer. The threat of such discomfort is intended to deter criminality, and the imposition of it to afford a criminal his just deserts. But liberty deprivation, the critics point out, is not the only way to make criminals uncomfortable. On this account, it should be possible to translate any particular term of imprisonment into an alternative sanction that imposes an equal amount of suffering. The alternatives, moreover, should be preferred whenever they can feasibly be imposed and whenever they cost less than the equivalent term of imprisonment.

This account is defective because it ignores what different forms of affliction mean. Punishment is *not* just a way to make offenders suffer; it is a special social convention that signifies moral condemnation. Not all modes of imposing suffering express condemnation or express it in the same way. The message of condemnation is very clear when society deprives an offender of his liberty. But when it merely fines him for the same act, the message is likely to be different: you may do what you have done, but you must pay for the privilege. Because community service penalties involve activities that conventionally entitle people to respect and admiration, they also fail to express condemnation in an unambiguous way. This mismatch between the suffering that a sanction imposes and the meaning that it has for society is what makes alternative sanctions politically unacceptable.

The importance of the expressive dimension of punishment should be evident. It reveals, for one thing, that punishment reformers face certain objective constraints. The social norms that determine what different forms of suffering mean cannot be simply dismissed as the product of ignorance or bias; rather, they reflect deeply rooted public understandings that mere exhortation is unlikely to change. But there are also more hopeful implications. If we can understand the expressive dimension of punishment, we should be able to perceive not only what kinds of punishment reforms won't work but also which ones will. Careful attention to social norms might allow us to translate alternative sanctions into a punitive vocabulary that makes them a meaningful substitute for imprisonment.

* * *

I. The Expressive Dimension of Punishment

Does it make sense to conceive of punishment as a language? Many observers in many different places and at many different times have concluded that it does. Durkheim seems to have had this idea in mind, for example, when he characterized punishment as a "sign indicating [] the sentiments of the collectivity," as did Hegel, when he described it as the "annul[ment of a] crime, which otherwise would have been held valid." James Fitzjames Stephen, the nineteenth-century English political theorist and judge, understood punishment to be the means by which "law gives definite expression and a solemn ratification . . . to the hatred which is excited by the commission of an offence. . . ." Various contemporary philosophers, including Jean Hampton, Joel Feinberg, and Robert Nozick, have also emphasized the expressive dimension of punishment.

But theirs is not the orthodox view. "Deterrence" and "retributivism" dominate mainstream theorizing. The proponents of these accounts frequently deride the expressive theory or, even more contemptuously, ignore it altogether.

Disrespect for the expressive theory can be attributed to two causes. The first is its obscurity. The writings of Hegel and Durkheim are filled with dense abstractions, like "annulment," "negation," and "collective conscience." Contemporary philosophers, while more precise in their terminology, still fail to connect their accounts to actual institutions and practices.

Focusing on the abstract quality of such theorizing, critics assail the expressive position as either incoherent or derivative. Crimes, as historical events, are not genuinely "annulled" or "negated" by punishment, they point out. And if expression of condemnation were the salient ingredient of punishment, why wouldn't society be content simply to criticize the criminal verbally? Maybe annulment can be understood less literally as a "righting of the moral balance" upset by the criminal's acts; and maybe expression of disapproval through hard treatment can be defended as discouraging criminality. But if this is how we must reformulate the expressive theorists' arguments, then their account dissolves into conventional retributive and deterrence theories and thus need not be independently taken into account. Or so it is claimed.

The second difficulty for the expressive theory is that it appears strikingly illiberal. Deterrence justifies punishment to prevent harm to others; retributivism confines it to those who voluntarily choose to inflict such harm. The expressive theory, by contrast, appears to emphasize neither consequences nor choices, but rather the enforcement of society's moral values. In his famous rejoinder to Lord Devlin, who had used the expressive theory to criticize proposals to decriminalize homosexuality, H.L.A. Hart assailed this justification for punishment as "belong[ing] to the prehistory of morality." "The idea that we may punish offenders against a moral code, not to prevent harm or suffering or even the repetition of the offence but simply as a means of venting or emphatically expressing moral condemnation, is uncomfortably close to human sacrifice as an expression of religious worship."

I believe that the conventional disregard for the expressive view is ill-considered. The expressive theory, properly understood, is less imperial than the conventional deterrence and retributive theories; it doesn't purport to explain everything of significance in criminal law and may, in fact, be constrained by other important considerations. Nonetheless, theorizing that excludes the expressive dimension of punishment generates incomplete explanations of what the criminal law is and unreliable prescriptions of what it should be.

* * *

A. What Punishment Says and How

Actions have *meanings* as well as consequences. Part of being rational consists in selecting actions that, against the back ground of social norms, express meanings appropriate to our purposes and goals. Along some dimension, for example, five thousand dollars might be equivalent in value to everything I would do with and for a friend during a certain period of time. But if my goal is to be her *friend*, then giving her the money and sharing my time with her are not interchangeable; giving money in lieu of time fails to convey the respect and affection that being a good friend requires.

This is a general account of expressive rationality; the expressive theory of punishment can be viewed as a special instance of this account. Under this view, we can give a satisfactory account of crime and punishment only if we pay close attention to their social meaning.

* * *

Under the expressive view, the signification of punishment is moral condemnation. By imposing the proper form and degree of affliction on the wrongdoer, society says, in effect, that the offender's assessment of whose interests count is wrong. It follows, moreover, that when society deliberately forgoes answering the wrongdoer through punishment, it risks being perceived as endorsing his valuations; hence the complaint that unduly lenient punishment reveals that the victim is worthless in the eyes of the law.

The contention that the expressive theory supports illiberal results is based on a specious form of generalization. Expressive arguments can be used to justify the criminalization of homosexuality, but the expressive theory entails neither this nor any other form of intolerance. Indeed, the expressive theory illuminates a critical part of what is wrong with such laws. The injustice of a prohibition on same-sex sodomy, for example, consists at least as much in the disrespect it expresses toward gays as it does in the impingement of anyone's liberty to engage in particular sexual acts. From an expressive point of view, hate crime legislation can be used to criticize the devaluation of gays just as effectively as sodomy laws can be used to entrench it.

The expressive theory also underscores the importance of form and convention in punishment. Military service might in some sense be equivalent to imprisonment if we consider their effects on a person's liberty. But the reason that only imprisonment and not conscription is regarded as punishment is that against the background of social norms only imprisonment expresses society's authoritative moral condemnation.

The formal and conventional underpinnings of what different forms of affliction signify constrain society's options for expressing condemnation. Just as it would be irrational for a person who wishes to express respect and affection for a friend to offer her money rather than shared experiences, so would it be irrational for society to attempt to condemn a wrongdoer by imposing an affliction that does not signify condemnation within that society. Punishment, as a language, has a vocabulary uniquely suited for getting its meaning across.

* * *

. . . In some societies, and even in ours at an earlier time, public denunciation by itself might have been sufficient to convey condemnation of a wrongdoer, but such is clearly not true today. Imagine that a judge proposed only to denounce a brutal rapist rather than to sentence him to prison. Such a sentence would no doubt be regarded as inadequate for purposes of deterrence and retribution. But even beyond that, mere verbal denunciation would be understood to trivialize the offense: the way for society to show that it takes rape seriously, and to show that it genuinely condemns a particular rapist, is to make him suffer in an appropriate way. For inflicting–punishment as for many other–purposes actions speak louder than words.

B. Expressive Condemnation vs. Retributivism and Deterrence

According to its critics, the expressive theory can be saved from incoherence only at the expense of its analytical independence. Clarifying the theory inevitably merges the expressive account into deterrence or retributivism, making independent study of the expressive view unnecessary.

A defender of the expressive theory might respond in one of two ways. First, she could attempt to develop an abstract conception of the expressive position that is in fact analytically independent of either deterrence or retributivism. She could then show that this account either is or should be the basis of criminal law. This strategy attacks the claim of derivativeness head-on.

A second strategy is less ambitious. It essentially demurs to the claim of analytical interdependence. It might be the case that any plausible conception of the expressive view can be fit into the framework of deterrence or retributivism, but it would be fallacious to conclude that the expressive theory can therefore be ignored; that conclusion would follow only if it were possible to develop plausible conceptions of deterrence and retributivism that make no reference to the expressive function of criminal law. And that, the defender of the expressive view would try to show, cannot be done.

I want to pursue this second strategy in the next part of this essay. To set it up, I will consider how retributivism and deterrence theories can be analytically related to and distinguished from the expressive theory.

Start with very basic conceptions of retributivism and deterrence. "Retributivism is the view that punishment is justified by the moral culpability of those who receive it. A retributivist punishes because, and only because, the offender deserves it." Deterrence, in contrast, asserts that punishment is justified because it averts future harm. Society should punish, on this view, only if the expected benefits of a particular penalty exceed the expected costs of imposing it.

The core idea of retributivism that an individual should be punished "because, and only because, [he] deserves it"–is vague. It is possible to give content to this notion without reference to expressive condemnation; one might say, for example, that an individual deserves punishment when "he renounces a burden which others have voluntarily assumed and thus gains an advantage which others . . . do not possess," or when human beings naturally intuit that the individual has engaged in "a wrong action [that] . . . calls for the infliction of suffering or deprivation on the agent." But it is also possible to use the expressive view to inform desert. On this account, an individual deserves punishment when he engages in behavior that conveys disrespect for important values. The proper retributive punishment is the one that appropriately expresses condemnation and reaffirms the values that the wrongdoer denies.

The expressive theory can also be used to inform deterrence. One way in which it might do so is by supplying a consequentialist theory of value. Without a theory for identifying which outcomes are socially disvalued and how much, it is impossible to know what to deter or how to allocate limited punishment resources among different forms of wrongdoing. Again, one could attempt to specify a consequentialist theory of value perhaps wealth-maximization that is indifferent to expressive sensibilities. Or one could overtly draw on these sensibilities to identify preferred outcomes. . . . [O]ne might conclude that a white man who kills an African-American out of racial hatred should be punished more severely than a woman who kills the abuser of her child in anger, even if equal punishment would maximize social wealth; when expressive considerations are taken into account, racist killings are deemed to harm society more than are impassioned killings of child molesters.

Another way that the expressive theory might reinforce deterrence is through preference formation. The law can discourage criminality not just by "raising the cost" of such behavior through punishments, but also through instilling aversions to the kinds of behavior that the law prohibits. The latter is often referred to as the "moralizing" or "moral educative" effect of punishment.

The moralizing effect of criminal law depends on a variety of mechanisms, all of which are reinforced by the expressive character of the law. The first is preference adaptation. To avoid cognitive dissonance, citizens form aversions to the kinds of behavior—whether rape, theft, or insider trading—that the law tells them are unworthy of being valued. This sort of preference adaptation is most likely to take place when citizens perceive the law as expressing society's moral condemnation of such conduct.

The law also moralizes by shaping relevant "belief-dependent" preferences. Empirical studies show that the willingness of persons to obey various laws is endogenous to their beliefs about whether others view the law as worthy of obedience: if compliance is perceived to be widespread, persons generally desire to obey; but if they believe that disobedience is rampant, their commitment to following the law diminishes. Even a strong propensity to obey the law, in other words, can be undercut by a person's "desire not to be suckered." When the law effectively expresses condemnation of wrongdoers, however, it reassures citizens that society does indeed stand behind the values that the law embodies.

Finally, the law moralizes through goodwill. Individuals are more disposed to obey particular laws, whether or not those laws accord with their moral beliefs, when they perceive the criminal law as a whole to be basically just. They are more likely to have this perception when criminal punishment confirms, rather than disappoints, shared expectations about what behavior is worthy of moral condemnation.

Theorists who dismiss the expressive theory can't draw on it to support retributivism or deterrence reasoning in any of these ways. Thus, the question should not be whether expressive condemnation can be successfully disconnected from deterrence and retribution, but whether it's possible to develop sensible conceptions of the latter theories without reference to the expressive view. I believe that it isn't; punishment theorizing that disregards the expressive view is necessarily incomplete. . . .

NOTE

As the above excerpts suggest, denunciatory justifications of punishment are not always utilitarian in nature. For a largely nonutilitarian discussion of denunciation, see generally J. Feinberg, *The Expressive Theory of Punishment* in Doing and Deserving 98–118 (1970). Consider the relationship of denunciation to retributive theory as it is discussed in the immediately following materials.

[C] Retributivism

[1] Just Deserts and the Obligation to Punish

KANT, *THE METAPHYSICAL ELEMENTS OF JUSTICE*

100–01 (Ladd trans. 1965)

The law concerning punishment is a categorical imperative, and woe to him who rummages around in the winding paths of a theory of happiness looking for some advantage to be gained by releasing the criminal from punishment or by reducing the amount of it. . . . If legal justice perishes, then it is no longer worthwhile for men to remain alive on this earth. . . .

* * *

Only the Law of retribution (*jus talionis*) can determine exactly the kind and degree of punishment; it must be well understood, however, that this determination [must be made] in the chambers of a court of justice (and not in your private judgment). All other standards fluctuate back and forth and, because extraneous considerations are mixed with them, they cannot be compatible with the principle of pure and strict legal justice.

Murphy, *Three Mistakes About Retributivism*

31 Analysis 166–69 (1971)

Retributive theories of punishment maintain that criminal guilt merits or deserves punishment, regardless of considerations of social utility. Such theories may be put forth for either of two reasons: (1) It could be argued (e.g., by a Moral Sense theorist) that the claim is a primitive and unanalysed proposition which is morally ultimate. Every ethical theory necessarily involves at least one such primitive (e.g., "happiness is good", "freedom is to be respected", etc.) and the retributivist may be offering this as his candidate. We can, he may argue, just *intuit* the "fittingness" of guilt and punishment. (2) It might be maintained (as it was, I believe, by both Kant and Hegel) that the retributivist claim is demanded by a general theory of political obligation which is more plausible than any alternative theory. Such a theory will typically provide a technical *analysis* of such notions as crime and punishment and will thus not regard the retributivist claim as an indisputable primitive. It will be argued for as a kind of theorem within the system.

The objection to the first sort of theory is obvious: the retributivist may be able to *intuit* the fittingness of guilt and punishment, but most of us cannot—not, at any rate, in a sense strong enough to make us want to appeal to the notion in justifying punishment. Thus the first theory is subject to all the classical objections to intuitionism, and these do not have to be repeated here. Let us, then, try to make sense of a theory of the second sort. What sort of theory of political obligation would render it plausible?

Consider a quasi-contractual model . . . that seeks to analyze political obligation in terms of *reciprocity*. Such a model will proceed as follows: In order to enjoy the benefits that a legal system makes possible, each man must be prepared to make an important sacrifice—namely, the sacrifice of obeying the law even when he does not desire to do so. Each man calls on others to do this, and it is only just or fair that he bear a comparable burden when his turn comes. Now if the system is to remain just, it is important to guarantee that those who disobey will not thereby gain an unfair advantage over those who obey voluntarily. Criminal punishment thus attempts to maintain the proper balance between benefit and obedience by insuring that there is no profit in criminal wrongdoing. . . .

* * *

Rule utilitarians often maintain that retributivism, to be coherent, must involve a tacit appeal to utility—i.e., must tacitly presuppose that the principle "Do not allow men to profit from their criminal wrongdoing" has more desirable social consequences than any alternative principle. But I should argue that Kant's theory, for example, is (i) perfectly coherent and (ii) quite independent of utilitarian considerations. His principle is that no man should profit from his own wrongdoing, and retribution attempts to keep this from happening. If a man does profit from his own wrongdoing, from his disobedience, this is *unfair* or *unjust,* not merely to his victim, but to all those who have been obedient. Now it may be, as the utilitarian might argue, that such unfairness—if widespread—would have socially undesirable consequences. But this is not Kant's argument. His argument is that the *injustice* or *unfairness itself,* regardless of consequences, demands retribution. . . .

But if this line is taken, the utilitarian may argue, retributivism becomes obviously unreasonable—a bit of primitive, unenlightened and barbaric emotionalism. But why is retributivism so condemned? Typically the charge is that infliction of punishment, with no attention to utility, is pointless vengeance. But what is meant by the claim that the activity in question is pointless? If "pointless" is to be analyzed as "disutilitarian", then the whole question is being begged. One cannot refute a retributive theory merely by noting that it is a retributive theory and not a utilitarian theory. This is to confuse refutation with redescription. That the maximization of social utility is important is no more *obviously* true than that a man should not unfairly profit from his own criminal wrongdoing; and, if the utilitarian proposes simply to dig in his heels on the former, it is important to note that the charge of emotionalism cuts both ways.

* * *

Another common criticism against the Kantian theory may be regarded as Marxist in character. Kant's theory, it may be argued, involves an ideal utopian model of society which is in fact so utterly different from the actual character of society as to render it useless in understanding or evaluating any existing practice of criminal punishment. Indeed, the theory is dangerous. For it allows us to hide from ourselves the vicious character of actual social arrangements and thereby perpetuate gross injustice.

Let me elaborate: Punishment as retribution (paying a kind of "debt" to one's fellow-citizens) makes good sense with respect to a community of responsible individuals, of approximate equality, bound together by freely adopted and commonly accepted rules which benefit everyone. This is an ideal community, approximating what Kant would call a kingdom of ends. In such a community, punishment would be justly retributive in that it would flow as an accepted consequence of accepted rules which benefited everyone (including, as citizen, the criminal). But surely existing human societies are not *in fact* like this at all. Many people neither benefit nor participate but rather operate at a built-in economic or racial disadvantage which is in fact, if not in theory, permanent. The majority of criminals who are in fact punished are drawn from these classes, and they utterly fail to correspond to the model which underlies the retributive theory. Surely we delude ourselves in appealing to the retributive theory to justify their punishment.

The moral doubts raised here are extremely important. However, they may be doubts which testify to *strengths* rather than weaknesses in a retributive theory of the Kantian variety. Decent men surely want to object to the wanton handing out of punishments to those who, in a socially uneven community, always get the short end of the stick. But does not Kant's theory explain (or at least give one good reason) *why* we do want to object? Just punishment rests upon reciprocity; and is not one of the most serious moral problems confronting most existing communities the absence of such reciprocity, the absence of a balance between benefit and burden? Punishment is unjust in such a setting because it involves pretending (contrary to fact) that the conditions of justified punishment are met. Thus could not Kant, given his theory, easily share the Marxist skepticism about punishing in certain actual states? I believe that he could.

Moore, *The Moral Worth Of Retribution*

Responsibility, Character, and the Emotions 179, 181–87

(F. Schoeman ed. 1987)

Retributivism is the view that punishment is justified by the moral culpability of those who receive it. A retributivist punishes because, and only because, the offender deserves it. Retributivism thus stands in sharp contrast to the utilitarian views that justify punishment of past offenses by the greater good of preventing future offenses. It also contrasts sharply with rehabilitative views, according to which punishment is justified by the reforming good it does the criminal.

* * *

Retributivism is a very straightforward theory of punishment: we are justified in punishing because and only because offenders deserve it. Moral culpability (desert) is in such a view both a sufficient as well as a necessary condition of liability to punitive sanctions. Such justification gives society more than merely a right to punish culpable offenders. It does this, making it not unfair to punish them, but retributivism justifies more than this. For a retributivist, the moral culpability of an offender also gives society the *duty* to punish. Retributivism, in other words, is truly a theory of justice such that, if it is true, we have an obligation to set up institutions so that retribution is achieved.

Retributivism, so construed, joins corrective justice theories of torts, natural right theories of property, and promissory theories of contract as deontological alternatives to utilitarian justifications; in each case, the institutions of punishment, tort compensation, property, and contract are justified by the rightness or fairness of the institution in question, not by the good consequences such institution may generate. . . . Once the deontological nature of retributivism is fully appreciated, it is often concluded that such a view cannot be justified. You either believe punishment to be inherently right, or you do not, and that is all there is to be said about it. . . .

. . . Retributivism is no worse off in the modes of its possible justification than any other deontological theory. In the first place, one might become a kind of "reluctant retributivist." A reluctant retributivist is someone who is somewhat repelled by retributivism but who nonetheless believes: (1) that there should be punishment; (2) that the only theories of punishment possible are utilitarian, rehabilitative, retributive, or some mixture of these; and (3) that there are decisive objections to utilitarian and rehabilitative theories of punishment, as well as to any mixed theory that uses either of these views in any combination. Such a person becomes, however reluctantly, a retributivist by default.

In the second place, positive arguments can be given for retributivism that do not appeal to some good consequences of punishing . . . Coherence theories of justification in ethics allow two nonconsequentialist possibilities here:

1. We might justify a principle such as retributivism by showing how it follows from some yet more general principle of justice that we think to be true.

2. Alternatively, we can justify a moral principle by showing that it best accounts for those of our more particular judgments that we also believe to be true.

In a perfectly coherent moral system, the retributive principle would be justified in both these ways, by being part of the best theory of our moral sentiments, considered as a whole.

The first of these deontological argument strategies is made familiar to us by arguments such as that of Herbert Morris, [see p. 116 *infra*] who urges that retributivism follows from some general ideas about reciprocal advantage in social relations. Without assessing the merits of these proposals one way or another, I wish to pursue the other strategy. I examine the more particular judgments that seem to be best accounted for in terms of a principle of punishment for just deserts.

These more particular judgments are quite familiar. I suspect that almost everyone at least has a tendency—one that he may correct as soon as he detects it himself, but at least a tendency—to judge culpable wrongdoers as deserving of punishment. Consider some examples Mike Royko has used to get the blood to the eyes of readers of his newspaper column:

> The small crowd that gathered outside the prison to protest the execution of Steven Judy softly sang "We Shall Overcome". . . . But it didn't seem quite the same hearing it sung out of concern for someone who, on finding a woman with a flat tire, raped and murdered her and drowned her three small children, then said that he hadn't been "losing any sleep" over his crimes.
>
> I remember the grocer's wife. She was a plump, happy woman who enjoyed the long workday she shared with her husband in their ma-and-pa store. One evening, two young men came in and showed guns, and the grocer gave them everything in the cash register. For no reason, almost as an afterthought, one of the men shot the grocer in the face. The woman stood only a few feet from her husband when he was turned into a dead, bloody mess. She was about 50 when it happened. In a few years her mind was almost gone, and she looked 80. They might as well have killed her too.

* * *

[Reprinted by permission: Tribune Media Services]

Most people react to such atrocities with an intuitive judgment that punishment (at least of some kind and to some degree) is warranted. Many will quickly add, however, that what accounts for their intuitive judgment is the need for deterrence, or the need to incapacitate such a dangerous person, or the need to reform the person. My own view is that these addenda are just "bad reasons for what we believe on instinct anyway," to paraphrase Bradley's general view of justification in ethics.

To see whether this is so, construct a thought experiment of the kind Kant originated. Imagine that these same crimes are being done, but that there is no utilitarian or rehabilitative reason to punish. The murderer has truly found Christ, for example, so that he or she does not need to be reformed; he or she is not dangerous for the same reason; and the crime can go undetected so that general deterrence does not demand punishment (alternatively, we can pretend to punish and pay the person the money the punishment would have cost us to keep his or her mouth shut, which will also serve the ends of general deterrence). In such a situation, should the criminal still be punished? My hypothesis is that most of us still feel some inclination, no matter how tentative, to punish. That is the particular judgment I wish to examine. . . .

The Case against Retributive Judgments

The puzzle I put about particular retributive judgments is this: Why are these particular judgments so suspect—"primitive," "barbarous," "a throwback"—when other judgments in terms of moral desert are accorded places of honor in widely accepted moral arguments? Very generally, there seem to me to be several explanations (and supposed justifications) for this discriminatory treatment of retributive judgments about deserved punishment.

(1) First and foremost there is the popularly accepted belief that punishment for its own sake does no good. "By punishing the offender you cannot undo the crime," might be the slogan for this point of view. I mention this view only to put it aside, for it is but a reiteration of the consequentialist idea that only further good consequences achieved by punishment could possibly justify the practice. Unnoticed by those who hold this position is that they abandon such consequentialism when it comes to other areas of morals. It is a sufficient justification not to scapegoat innocent individuals, that they do not deserve to be punished; the injustice of punishing those who do not deserve it seems to stand perfectly well by itself as a justification of our practices, without the need for further good consequences we might achieve. Why do we not similarly say that the injustice of the guilty going unpunished can equally stand by itself as a justification for punishment, without need of a showing of further good consequences? It simply is not the case that justification always requires the showing of further good consequences.

Those who oppose retributivism often protest at this point that punishment is a clear harm to the one punished, and the intentional causing of this harm requires some good thereby achieved to justify it; whereas *not* punishing the innocent is not a harm and thus does not stand in need of justification by good consequences. Yet this response simply begs the question against retributivism. Retributivism purports to be a theory of justice, and as such claims that punishing the guilty achieves something good—namely, justice—and that therefore reference to any other good consequences is simply beside the point.

One cannot defeat the central retributivist claim—that justice is achieved by punishing the guilty—simply by assuming that it is false.

The question-begging character of this response can be seen by imagining a like response in areas of tort, property, or contract laws. Forcing another to pay tort or contract damages, or to forgo use and possession of something, is a clear harm that corrective justice theories of tort, promissory theories of contract, or natural right theories of property are willing to impose on defendants. Suppose no one gains anything of economic significance by certain classes of such impositions—as, for example, in cases where the plaintiff has died without heirs after his cause of action accrued. "It does no good to force the defendant to pay," interposed as an objection to corrective justice theories of tort, promissory theories of contract, or natural right theories of property simply denies what these theories assert: that something good is achieved by imposing liability in such cases—namely, that justice is done.

This "harm requires justification" objection thus leaves untouched the question of whether the rendering of justice cannot in all such cases be the good that justifies the harm all such theories impose on defendants. I accordingly put aside this initial objection to retributivism, relying as it does either on an unjustifiable discrimination between retributivism and other deontological theories, or upon a blunderbuss assault on deontological theories as such.

(2) A second and very popular suspicion about retributive judgments is that they presuppose an indefensible objectivism about morals. Sometimes this objection is put metaphysically: There is no such thing as desert or culpability. More often the point is put as a more cautious epistemological modesty: "Even if there is such a thing as desert, we can never know who is deserving." For religious people, this last variation usually contrasts us to God, who alone can know what people truly deserve. . . . We might call this the "don't play God" objection.

One way to deal with this objection is to show that moral judgments generally (and judgments about culpability particularly) are both objectively true and knowable by persons. . . . A striking feature of the "don't play God" objection is how inconsistently it is applied. Let us revert to our use of desert as a limiting condition on punishment: We certainly seem confident both that it is true and that we can know that it is true, that we should not punish the morally innocent because they do not deserve it. Neither metaphysical skepticism nor epistemological modesty gets in our way when we use lack of moral desert as a reason not to punish. Why should it be different when we use presence of desert as a reason to punish? If we can know when someone does *not* deserve punishment, mustn't we know when someone *does* deserve punishment? . . .

Analogously, consider our reliance on moral desert when we allocate initial property entitlements. We think that the person who works hard to produce a novel deserves the right to determine when and under what conditions the novel will be copied for others to read. The novelist's labor gives him or her the moral right. How can we know this—how can it be true—if desert can be judged only by those with godlike omniscience, or worse, does not even exist? Such skepticism about just deserts would throw out a great deal that we will not throw out. To me, this shows that no one really believes that moral desert does not exist or that we could not know it if it did. Something else makes us suspect our retributive judgments than supposed moral skepticism or epistemological modesty.

WALKER, *PUNISHMENT, DANGER AND STIGMA: THE MORALITY OF CRIMINAL JUSTICE*

24–25, 37–42 (1980)

[The revival of interest in the retributive . . . justification] for punishment is a reaction against the utilitarian approach, which is becoming unpopular partly because of the excessive prison terms imposed in the United States in the name of rehabilitation or public protection, and partly because of discouraging evidence about the efficacy of sentences designed to reform or deter. . . .

[The retributivist] holds that the justification for inflicting a penalty is that the offender deserves it because of his offense. The pure retributivist also believes that the severity of the penalty should match the offender's culpability. Culpability varies according to the gravity of the harm done, intended or consciously risked, the offender's motives and any circumstances relevant enough to mitigate or aggravate it. . . .

* * *

A . . . serious criticism [of these views] is the difficulty which retributive sentencers feel, or ought to feel, in deciding what kind and amount of punishment corresponds to the culpability of this or that offender. The decision involves two difficult feats of estimation: the assessment of his culpability and the prediction of the amount of suffering which different punishments will impose on him. It is much easier to say whether a man is or is not culpable than to say exactly how culpable: even his intimates can only guess at the strengths of the impulses, temptations or pressures to which he was subject. As for how much he will suffer from six months' or 12 months' imprisonment, or from a £100 fine, this is equally incalculable. It is not surprising that some modern retributivists have given up the hope of matching the quantum of punishment to the culpability of the offender, and argue that their objective is not commensurability but mere proportionality . . . together with the avoidance of obvious inconsistencies (such as imprisoning one accomplice and fining the other).

The most difficult question for the retributivist, however, is "Why *should* breaches of laws (or rules) be penalised?" Many moral philosophers have wrestled with this question, and offered a variety of answers. Most of the answers fall into one of three groups:

a. that punishment *purges* the offender's guilt by making him suffer. Undoubtedly this is sometimes true as a psychological statement. Some people feel guilty about some of the things they do; and some of those who feel guilty feel less guilty if they undergo suffering (voluntarily, accidentally or compulsorily) which they can in some way link to the offense. Moreover, there are also people who feel less censorious towards an offender who has been made to suffer for an offense. These, however, are mere psychological truths, and are not even true about all offenders or all their condemners. They do not alter the fact that an offender has acted culpably, and they do not therefore satisfy those who want a nonpsychological reason for retributive punishment, as distinct from a mere explanation.

* * *

c. that punishment is an effort to cancel the offense: to bring about a state of affairs in which it is as if it had not been committed. This is sometimes possible. A thief who has stolen money can sometimes be made to return it; and unless the owner was beggared by the theft he is no worse off. A vandal can be made to pay for the restoration of what he has damaged; and if it is not an irreparable work of art nobody else suffers. Such situations, however, are rare. Even if the loss or damage is of a kind which is capable of being put right, the offender usually lacks the means to do so. (State compensation is a more effective way of restoring the *status quo ante* where this is at all possible: but that is not punishing the offender.) In fact, we tend to *distinguish* between penalty and restitution. This being so, in what sense does a fine or a prison sentence cancel the offense? Only in some non-literal sense. For example, a society might regard the doing of wrong to a wrongdoer as a *symbol* of the cancellation which they would have liked to achieve in reality. If this is what is being argued, it belongs to the expressive justification rather than the retributive; for the symbolic function would be adequately performed if people believed that the offender had been punished, whether he had in fact been or not.

d. that punishment is deserved by the offender. Philosophers, however, do not find it easy to explain what is meant by "deserving." It has even been suggested that a desert is "a right;" but a right is something that one claims or not, as one wishes, and it is only in special circumstances that offenders claim the right to be punished. More plausible is the suggestion that offenders have forfeited a right, variously defined as the right not to be deliberately made to suffer, or the right to one's liberty and property. It does not much matter how the right is defined; for the notion of a *forfeited* right cannot provide the positive justification for punishing which the retributivist needs. The notion of desert seems to involve the belief that a person who has acted culpably should suffer for his action, and that unpunished wrong-doing is somehow a greater evil than punished wrong-doing.

A satisfactory retributive answer to the question, "Why should offenses be punished?" has to meet a number of requirements:

(i) it must make retribution clearly distinguishable from mere vengeance or denunciation;

(ii) it must allow penalties to be proportional to rather than commensurate with culpability;

(iii) it must account psychologically for the retributivist's feeling that unpunished wrongdoing is a greater evil than punished wrongdoing (without implying that it is sufficient to explain it psychologically);

(iv) it must make punishment not permissible but obligatory (in the absence of excuses). If it made it merely permissible, some other positive justification for it would have to be found; and if the retributive answer did not supply this, it would follow that the answer must be nonretributive.

Some people would also argue that:

(v) the answer must also make it clear why the natural or accidental consequences of wrongdoing are not punishment. If, for example, a burglar is injured by barbed wire or by an outraged householder, is his injury distinguishable from punishment? If so, is this reconcilable with the fact that even a retributively minded sentencer might well lighten his sentence because of the injury he had suffered? Some people feel that guilt is partially—or even wholly—purged by suffering which is the natural or accidentalresult of the wrongdoing.

Only one answer seems to meet all these points: that *retributive punishment is a penalty imposed in fulfilment of a requirement in a rule that it should be imposed on those who have infringed a rule.* As has already been said, this is what distinguishes it from mere vengeance, which is inflicted for emotional reasons. It also distinguishes it from denunciation, which requires only the belief that the offender will suffer the penalty. It allows the penalty to be proportional rather than commensurate to culpability; for the rule need not insist on commensurability. It provides a psychological explanation of the feeling that an unpunished infringement is worse than a punished one. Man is a rule-making, rule-following animal, and most of his activities—linguistic, social, recreational and sexual—are governed by rules or conventions. There is nothing like conforming with a rule for inducing a feeling of propriety or even righteousness. An unpunished infraction means two infractions.

Notes and Questions

1. For further elaboration of the "benefit/burden" theory as a basis for justifying punishment, see H. Morris, *On Guilt and Innocence* 33–34 (1976). For an additional critique of the theory, see Murphy, *Marxism and Retribution,* 2 Phil. & Pub. Aff. 217 (1973).

2. As theories of justice, most forms of retributivism tend to focus on the crime, and not the individual traits of the criminal, in urging that the severity of punishment be equivalent to the gravity of the offense. Moreover, each offender committing that offense is generally thought equally deserving of the same punishment. But does justice not demand attention to the situation of each particular offender? Suppose the "same" punishment of one-month imprisonment is imposed on (a) a "hardened" criminal and (b) a "middle-class" offender. Is the one-month sentence "the same" for each? What of an offender who has claustrophobia but is sentenced to a prison with especially small cells? What of an offender who is likely to be the subject of a prison rape? Finally,

what of the offender whose sentence is one year, but who, from all medical evidence, has only six months to live? Is his sentence one for "life"? If so, should it be shortened? Which, if any, of these factors are relevant in considering whether punishments are equal even if they are of equal length?

For a detailed discussion of the problem of fitting severity of punishment to gravity of offense, see Bedau, *Concessions to Retribution in Punishment,* in Justice and Punishment 51 (J. Cederblom and W. Blizek eds. 1977), and Pincoffs, *Are Questions of Desert Decidable?, id.* at 75, 85–86.

3. Another aspect of some varieties of retributivist theory is that the criminal has demonstrated disrespect for the rights of his victims as well as for the general rights of society, and so must be similarly disrespected. Sir James Fitzjames Stephens expressed this as saying that there was a "right to hate" the criminal. For recent discussions of this corner of retributivism, see J. Murphy and M. Hampton, *Forgiveness and Mercy* (1988), and the review of that book, Dressler, *Hating Criminals: How Can Something That Feels So Good Be So Wrong?,* 88 Mich L. Rev. 1448 (1990). See also Pillsbury, *Emotional Justice: Moralizing the Passions of Criminal Punishment,* 74 Cornell L. Rev. 655 (1989); Pillsbury, *Evil and the Law of Murder,* 24 U.C. Davis L. Rev. 437 (1990).

[2] Just Deserts as a Limiting Principle

Armstrong, *The Retributivist Hits Back*

The Philosophy of Punishment 138, 155 (H. Acton ed. 1969)

[A] retributive theory is essential, because it is the only theory which connects punishment with desert, and so with justice, for only as a punishment is deserved or undeserved can it be just or unjust. What would a just *deterrent* be? The only sense we could give to it would be a punishment which was just from the retributive point of view and which also, as a matter of fact, deterred other people. "But", it may be objected, "you are only talking about *retributive* justice." To this I can only reply: What other sort of justice is there?

A vital point here is that justice gives the appropriate authority the *right* to punish offenders up to some limit, but one is not necessarily and invariably *obliged* to punish to the limit of justice. Similarly, if I lend a man money I have a right, in justice, to have it returned; but if I choose not to take it back I have not done anything unjust. I cannot claim more than is owed to me but I am free to claim less, or even to claim nothing. For a variety of reasons (amongst them the hope of reforming the criminal) the appropriate authority may choose to punish a man less than it is entitled to, but it is never just to punish a man more than he deserves. It is a mistake to argue . . . that, on the retributive theory, to punish a man less than the exact amount due is an injustice similar to punishing an innocent man. The retributive theory is not, therefore, incompatible with mercy. Quite the reverse is the case—it is only the retributive idea that makes mercy possible, because to be merciful is to let someone off all or part of a penalty which he is recognised as having deserved.

HART, *PUNISHMENT AND RESPONSIBILITY*

11–12 (1968)

The standard example used by philosophers to bring out the importance of retribution in Distribution is that of a wholly innocent person who has not even unintentionally done anything which the law punishes if done intentionally. It is supposed that in order to avert some social catastrophe, officials of the system fabricate evidence on which he is charged, tried, and convicted and sent to prison or death. Or. it is supposed that without resort to any fraud more persons may be deterred from crime if wives and children of offenders were punished vicariously for their crimes. In some forms this kind of thing may be ruled out by a consistent, sufficiently comprehensive utilitarianism. Certainly expedients involving fraud or faked charges might be very difficult to justify on utilitarian grounds. . . . Certainly vicarious punishment of an offender's family might [avert some evils,] and legal systems have occasionally though exceptionally resorted to this. An example . . . is the Roman *Lex Quisquis,* providing for the punishment of the children of those guilty of majestas. In extreme cases many might still think it right to resort to these expedients but we should do so with the sense of sacrificing an important principle. We should be conscious of choosing the lesser of two evils, and this would be inexplicable if the principle sacrificed to utility were itself only a requirement of utility

. . . [The] moral importance of the restriction of punishment to the offender cannot be explained as merely a consequence of the principle that the General Justifying Aim is Retribution for immorality involved in breaking the law. Retribution in the Distribution of punishment has a value quite independent of Retribution as Justifying Aim. This is shown by the fact that we attach importance to the restrictive principle that only offenders may be punished, even where breach of this law might not be thought immoral. Indeed even where the laws themselves are hideously immoral as in Nazi Germany, e.g., forbidding activities (helping the sick or destitute of some racial group) which might be thought morally obligatory, the absence of the principle restricting punishment to the offender would be a further *special* iniquity; whereas admission of this principle would represent some residual respect for justice shown in the administration of morally bad laws.

PACKER

65–69

Law, including the criminal law, must in a free society be judged ultimately on the basis of its success in promoting human autonomy and the capacity for individual human growth and development. The prevention of crime is an essential aspect of the environmental protection required if autonomy is to flourish. It is, however, a negative aspect and one which, pursued with single-minded zeal, may end up creating an environment in which all are safe but none is free. The limitations included in the concept of culpability are justified not by an appeal to the Kantian dogma of "just deserts" but by their usefulness in keeping the state's powers of protection at a decent remove from the lives of its citizens

. . . I see an important limiting principle in the criminal law's traditional emphasis on blameworthiness as a prerequisite to the imposition of punishment. But it is a *limiting* principle, not a justification for action. It is wrong to say that we should punish persons simply because they commit offenses under circumstances that we can call blameworthy. It is right to say that we should not punish those who commit offenses unless we can say that their conduct is blameworthy. . . .

* * *

It seems desirable to make clear also the extent of the difference between the views I have been setting forth and what I conceive to be the essence of the retributive position. That position views the imputation of blame or culpability to the offender as in itself a sufficient justification for the imposition of criminal punishment. This view is sometimes expressed forthrightly; at other times it is masked by assertions that punishment on the basis of moral fault strengthens the moral fiber of the individual being punished, or constitutes education for good citizenship, or something of that sort. That kind of assertion has a pharisaical ring to it made less attractive, if anything, by its Pollyannaish overtones. Punishment is not a virtue, only a necessity.

The view I take of the role of culpability in the justification for punishment is an instrumental one. I see this limitation on the utilitarian position as desirable—not for any inherent quality that it possesses but because it serves ends that I think require attention in a criminal system. It does so in several different ways. First, it establishes a firm basis for resisting the attenuation of the offense as a component in the definition of punishment. Without an offense—a more or less specifically defined species of conduct—there can be no basis for imputing blame. A man may be a danger to others, or in need of help, or any other equivalent in the current cant that denotes an inconvenient human being whom we would like to get out of the way; but unless he has committed an offense, unless he has done something rather than merely been something, we cannot say that he has been culpable. And, it follows from the view taken of culpability as a necessary condition, that he cannot be found guilty through the criminal process and subjected to criminal punishment. . . .

Another aspect of this instrumental case for culpability is that there is a rough correspondence between the dictates of the culpability limitation and aspects of the desirable operation of the criminal sanction. People ought in general to be able to plan their conduct with some assurance that they can avoid entanglement with the criminal law; by the same token the enforcers and appliers of the law should not waste their time lurking in the bushes ready to trap the offender who is unaware that he is offending. It is precisely the fact that in its normal and characteristic operation the criminal law provides this opportunity and this protection to people in their everyday lives that makes it a tolerable institution in a free society. Take this away, and the criminal law ceases to be a guide to the well-intentioned and a restriction on the restraining power of the state. Take it away is precisely what you do, however, when you abandon culpability as the basis for imposing punishment. While it may often serve the state's purposes not to interfere with its citizens unless they have acted with foresight, on many occasions their foresight or lack of it may seem immaterial. If we leave to a purely utilitarian calculus the decision whether a man's innocence or ignorance shall count for him, the answer on any given occasion will be uncertain. Only by providing the shield of a culpability requirement can this desirable aspect of the criminal law be preserved.

Finally, the singular power of the criminal law resides . . . not in its coercive effect on those caught in its toils but rather in its effect on the rest of us. That effect, . . . is a highly complex one. It includes elements of coercion and of terror: if I do as he did, I too shall suffer for it. But it also includes conscious and unconscious moralizing and habit-forming effects that go far beyond the crassness of a narrowly conceived deterrence. If it is not thought enough of a justification that the law be fair, the argument may seem appealing that a criminal law system cannot attract and retain the respect of its most important constituents—the habitually law-abiding—unless it *is seen to be fair*. And whatever fairness may be thought to mean on the procedural side, its simplest (if most neglected) meaning is that no one should be subjected to punishment without having an opportunity to litigate the issue of his culpability. Even imagining a system in which, once forbidden physical conduct has taken place, no excuses are listened to is enough to show the importance of making culpability a necessary condition of liability to punishment.

NOTES AND QUESTIONS

1. Retributive theory operates as a limiting principle in at least two ways: by requiring blameworthiness as a precondition of punishment and by requiring that punishment be proportionate to blame. Whatever its merits as a theory requiring "an eye for an eye," the *lex talionis* principle also demands *"no more than* an eye for an eye." Would similar requirements of personal blameworthiness and proportionality be entailed in a purely utilitarian model of punishment?

2. For an account similar to Packer's of the role of retribution in punishment theory, see H.L.A. Hart, *Punishment and Responsibility* 180–83 (1968). For a discussion of the resurgence of retributive theory in the 1970s, see Gardner, The *Renaissance of Retribution—An Examination of Doing Justice,* 1976 Wis. L. Rev. 781. For a critical view of this resurgence, see Dolinko, *Three Mistakes of Retributivism,* 39 UCLA L. Rev. 1623 (1992).

[3] Just Deserts and the Right to Be Punished

MORRIS, *PERSONS AND PUNISHMENT*

52 The Monist 475, 476, 483, 485–87, 489–90 (1968)

My aim is to argue for four propositions concerning rights that will certainly strike some as not only false but preposterous: first, that we have a right to punishment; second, that this right derives from a fundamental human right to be treated as a person; third, that this fundamental right is a natural, inalienable, and absolute right; and, fourth, that the denial of this right implies the denial of all moral rights and duties. . . .

* * *

. . . [W]ith punishment there is an attempt at some equivalence between the advantage gained by the wrongdoer—partly based upon the seriousness of the interest invaded, partly on the state of mind with which the wrongful act was performed—and the punishment meted out. Thus, we can understand a prohibition on "cruel and unusual punishments" so that disproportionate pain and suffering are avoided. With therapy attempts at proportionality make no sense. It is perfectly plausible giving someone who kills a pill and treating for a lifetime within an institution one who has broken a dish and manifested accident proneness. We have the concept of "painful treatment." We do not have the concept of "cruel treatment." Because treatment is regarded as a benefit, though it may involve pain, it is natural that less restraint is exercised in bestowing it, than in inflicting punishment. Further, protests with respect to treatment are likely to be assimilated to the complaints of one whose leg must be amputated in order for him to live, and, thus, largely disregarded. To be sure, there is operative in the therapy world some conception of the "cure being worse than the disease," but if the disease is manifested in conduct harmful to others, and if being a normal operating human being is valued highly, there will naturally be considerable pressure to find the cure acceptable.

* * *

Now, it is clear I think, that were we confronted . . . between a system of just punishment and a thoroughgoing system of treatment, a system, that is, that did not reintroduce concepts appropriate to punishment, we could see the point in claiming that a person has a right to be punished, meaning by this that a person had a right to all those institutions and practices linked to punishment. For these would provide him with, among other things, a far greater ability to predict what would happen to him on the occurrence of certain events than the therapy system. There is the inestimable value to each of us of having the responses of others to us determined over a wide range of our lives by what we choose rather than what they choose. A person has a right to institutions that respect his choices. Our punishment system does; our therapy system does not.

Apart from those aspects of our therapy model which would relate to serious limitations on personal liberty, there are clearly objections of a more profound kind to the mode of thinking I have associated with the therapy model.

First, human beings pride themselves in having capacities that animals do not. . . .

Second, if all human conduct is viewed as something men undergo, thrown into question would be the appropriateness of that extensive range of peculiarly human satisfactions that derive from a sense of achievement. For these satisfactions we shall have to substitute those mild satisfactions attendant upon a healthy well-functioning body. Contentment is our lot if we are fortunate; intense satisfaction at achievement is entirely inappropriate.

Third, in the therapy world nothing is earned and what we receive comes to us through compassion, or through a desire to control us. Resentment is out of place. We can take credit for nothing but must always regard ourselves—if there are selves left to regard once actions disappear—as fortunate recipients of benefits or unfortunate carriers of disease who must be controlled. . . .

Fourth, attention should also be drawn to a peculiar evil that may be attendant upon regarding a man's actions as symptoms of disease. The logic of cure will push us toward forms of therapy that inevitably involve changes in the person made against his will. The evil in this would be most apparent in those cases where the agent, whose action is determined to be a manifestation of some disease, does not regard his action in this way. He believes that what he has done is, in fact, "right" but his conception of "normality" is not the therapeutically accepted one. When we treat an illness we normally treat a condition that the person is not responsible for. He is "suffering" from some disease and we treat the condition, relieving the person of something preventing his normal functioning. When we begin treating persons for actions that have been chosen, we do not lift from the person something that is interfering with his normal functioning but we change the person so that he functions in a way regarded as normal by the current therapeutic community. We have to change him and his judgments of value. In doing this we display a lack of respect for the moral status of individuals, that is, a lack of respect for the reasoning and choices of individuals. They are but animals who must be conditioned. I think we can understand and, indeed, sympathize with a man's preferring death to being forcibly turned into what he is not.

Finally, perhaps most frightening of all would be the derogation in status of all protests to treatment. If someone believes that he has done something right, and if he protests being treated and changed, the protest will itself be regarded as a sign of some pathological condition, for who would not wish to be cured of an affliction? . . .

* * *

. . . [I]f we look at the responses I suggested would give rise to feelings of shame, we may rightly be troubled with the appropriateness of this response in any community in which each person assumes burdens so that each may derive benefits. In such situations might it not be that individuals have a right to a system of punishment so that each person could be assured that inequities in the distribution of benefits and burdens are unlikely to occur and if they do, procedures exist for correcting them? Further, it may well be that, everything considered, we should prefer the pain and suffering of a system of punishment to a world in which we only experience shame on the doing of wrong acts, for with guilt there are relatively simple ways of ridding ourselves of the feeling we have, that is, gaining forgiveness or taking the punishment, but with shame we have to bear it until we no longer are the person who has behaved in the shameful way. Thus, I suggest that we have, wherever there is a distribution of benefits and burdens of the kind I have described, a right to a system of punishment.

. . . [A] man has the right to be punished rather than treated if he is guilty of some offense. And, indeed, one can imagine a case in which, even in the face of an offer of a pardon, a man claims and ought to have acknowledged his right to be punished.

* * *

When we talk of not treating a human being as a person or "showing no respect for one as a person" what we imply by our words is a contrast between the manner in which one acceptably responds to human beings and the manner in which one acceptably responds to animals and inanimate objects. When we treat a human being merely as an animal or some inanimate object, our responses to the human being are determined, not by his choices, but ours in disregard of or with indifference to his. And when we "look upon" a person as less than a person or not a person, we consider the person as incapable of rational choice. In cases of not treating a human being as a person, we interfere with a person in such a way that what is done, even if the person is involved in the doing, is done not by the person but by the user of the person.

Notes and Questions

1. Is Morris's argument limited to the notion that the offender has a right to punishment where coercive therapy is the only alternative, or does his position also embrace a right to be punished regardless of the alternatives?

2. Suppose a given offender prefers a "therapeutic" disposition to a punitive one. Is he entitled as a rational "person" to waive his "right to punishment" in favor of a regimen of therapy? Suppose he desires a therapeutic alternative but none exists in his jurisdiction?

For examples of how Morris's theory might relate to some "real world" issues, see Gardner, *The Right to Be Punished–A Suggested Constitutional Theory,* 33 Rutgers L. Rev. 838 (1981); Gardner, *The Right of Juvenile Offenders to Be Punished: Some Implications of Treating Kids as Persons,* 68 Neb. L. Rev. 182 (1989). For a theory similar to Morris's, see Lewis, *Humanitarian Theory of Punishment,* 6 Res Jud. 224 (1953).

[D] Putting Theory into Practice

The problem of justifying punishment is a matter of deep concern to theorists and legal policy makers, but it is also of great practical importance in the day-to-day workings of the criminal justice system. Indeed, in "indeterminate" sentencing systems common in many jurisdictions, the problem of dispensing appropriate punishment is perhaps the most important issue confronted by lawyers and judges within the criminal system, given the fact that most defendants waive their trial rights by pleading guilty. In light of the theories of punishment examined above, consider the following case. What punishment, if any, should be imposed?

UNITED STATES v. BERGMAN

United States District Court

Southern District New York

416 F. Supp 496 (1976)

SENTENCING MEMORANDUM

FRANKEL, District Judge.

Defendant is being sentenced upon his plea of guilty to two counts of an 11-count indictment. The sentencing proceeding is unusual in some respects. It has been the subject of more extensive submissions, written and oral, than this court has ever received upon such an occasion. The court has studied some hundreds of pages of memoranda and exhibits, plus scores of volunteered letters. A broad array of issues has been addressed. Imaginative suggestions of law and penology have been tendered. A preliminary conversation with counsel, on the record, preceded the usual sentencing hearing. Having heard counsel again and the defendant speaking for himself, the court postponed the pronouncement of sentence for further reconsideration of thoughts generated during the days of studying the briefs and oral pleas. It seems fitting now to report in writing the reasons upon which the court concludes that defendant must be sentenced to a term of four months in prison.[1]

I. DEFENDANT AND HIS CRIMES

Defendant appeared until the last couple of years to be a man of unimpeachably high character, attainments, and distinction. A doctor of divinity and an ordained rabbi, he has been acclaimed by people around the world for his works of public philanthropy, private charity, and leadership in educational enterprises. Scores of letters have come to the court from across this and other countries reporting debts of personal gratitude to him for numerous acts of extraordinary generosity. (The court has also received a kind of petition, with fifty-odd signatures, in which the signers, based upon learning acquired as newspaper readers, denounce the defendant and urge a severe sentence. Unlike the pleas for mercy, which appear to reflect unquestioned facts inviting compassion, this document should and will be disregarded.) In addition to his good works, defendant has managed to amass considerable wealth in the

---

[1] The court considered, and finally rejected, imposing a fine in addition to the prison term. Defendant seems destined to pay hundreds of thousands of dollars in restitution. The amount is being worked out in connection with a state criminal indictment. Apart from defendant's further liabilities for federal taxes, any additional money exaction is appropriately left for the state court.

ownership and operation of nursing homes, in real estate ventures, and in a course of substantial investments.

Beginning about two years ago, investigations of nursing homes in this area, including questions of fraudulent claims for Medicaid funds, drew to a focus upon this defendant among several others. The results that concern us were the present indictment and two state indictments. After extensive pretrial proceedings, defendant embarked upon elaborate plea negotiations with both state and federal prosecutors. A state guilty plea and the instant plea were entered in March of this year. (Another state indictment is expected to be dismissed after defendant is sentenced on those to which he has pled guilty.) As part of the detailed plea arrangements, it is expected that the prison sentence imposed by this court will comprise the total covering of the state as well as the federal convictions.

For purposes of the sentence now imposed, the precise details of the charges, and of defendant's carefully phrased admissions of guilt, are not matters of prime importance. Suffice it to say that the plea on Count One (carrying a maximum of five years in prison and a $10,000 fine) confesses defendant's knowing and wilful participation in a scheme to defraud the United States in various ways, including the presentation of wrongfully padded claims for payments under the Medicaid program to defendant's nursing homes. Count Three, for which the guilty plea carries a theoretical maximum of three more years in prison and another $5,000 fine, is a somewhat more "technical" charge. Here, defendant admits to having participated in the filing of a partnership return which was false and fraudulent in failing to list people who had bought partnership interests from him in one of his nursing homes, had paid for such interests, and had made certain capital withdrawals.

The conspiracy to defraud, as defendant has admitted it, is by no means the worst of its kind; it is by no means as flagrant or extensive as has been portrayed in the press; it is evidently less grave than other nursing-home wrongs for which others have been convicted or publicized. At the same time, the sentence, as defendant has acknowledged, is imposed for two federal felonies including, as the more important, a knowing and purposeful conspiracy to mislead and defraud the Federal Government.

II. THE GUIDING PRINCIPLES OF SENTENCING

Proceeding through the short list of the supposed justifications for criminal sanctions, defense counsel urge that no licit purpose could be served by defendant's incarceration. Some of these arguments are plainly sound; others are not.

The court agrees that this defendant should not be sent to prison for "rehabilitation." Apart from the patent inappositeness of the concept to this individual, this court shares the growing understanding that no one should ever be sent to prison *for rehabilitation*. That is to say, nobody who would not otherwise be locked up should suffer that fate on the incongruous premise that it will be good for him or her. Imprisonment is punishment. Facing the simple reality should help us to be civilized. It is less agreeable to confine someone when we deem it an affliction rather than a benefaction. If someone must be imprisoned—for other, valid reasons—we should seek to make rehabilitative resources available to him or her. But the goal of rehabilitation cannot fairly serve in itself as grounds for the sentence to confinement.[3]

Equally clearly, this defendant should not be confined to incapacitate him. He is not dangerous. It is most improbable that he will commit similar, or any, offenses in the future. There is no need for "specific deterrence."

Contrary to counsel's submissions, however, two sentencing considerations demand a prison sentence in this case:

First, the aim of general deterrence, the effort to discourage similar wrongdoing by others through a reminder that the law's warnings are real and that the grim consequence of imprisonment is likely to follow from crimes of deception for gain like those defendant has admitted.

Second, the related, but not identical, concern that any lesser penalty would, in the words of the Model Penal Code, § 7.01(1)(c), "depreciate the seriousness of the defendant's crime."

Resisting the first of these propositions, defense counsel invoke Immanuel Kant's axiom that "one man ought never to be dealt with merely as a means subservient to the purposes of another."[4] In a more novel, but equally futile, effort, counsel urge that a sentence for general deterrence "would violate the Eighth Amendment proscription against cruel and unusual punishment." Treating the latter point first, because it is a short subject, it may be observed simply that if general deterrence as a sentencing purpose were now to be outlawed, as against a near unanimity of views among state and federal jurists, the bolt would have to come from a place higher than this.[5]

As for Dr. Kant, it may well be that defense counsel mistake his meaning in the present context.[6] Whether or not that is so, and without pretending to authority on that score, we take the widely accepted stance that a criminal punished in the interest of general deterrence is not being employed "merely as a means Reading Kant to mean that every man must be deemed more than the instrument of others, and must "always be treated as an end in himself,"[7] the humane principle is not offended here. Each of us is served by the enforcement of the law—not least a person like the defendant in this case, whose wealth and privileges, so long enjoyed, are so much founded upon law. More broadly, we are driven regularly in our ultimate interests as members of the community to use ourselves and each other, in war and in peace, for social ends. One who has transgressed against the criminal laws is certainly among the more fitting candidates for a role of this nature. This is no arbitrary selection. Warned in advance of the prospect, the transgressor has chosen,

---

[3] This important point, correcting misconceptions still widely prevalent, is developed more fully by Dean Norval Morris in *The Future of Imprisonment* (1974).

[4] Quoting from I. Kant, *Philosophy of Law* 1886 (Hastie trans. 1887).

[5] To a large extent the defendant's Eighth Amendment argument is that imprisoning him because he has been "newsworthy" would be cruelly wrong. This thought is accepted by the court without approaching the Constitution. (See below.) The reference at this point is meant to acknowledge, if only to reject, a seemingly broader submission.

[6] See H.L.A. Hart, *Punishment and Responsibility* 243–44 (1968).

[7] Andenaes, *The Morality of Deterrence,* 37 U. Chi. L. Rev. 649 (1970). See also O. Holmes, Common Law 43–44, 46–47 (1881).

in the law's premises, "between keeping the law required for society's protection or paying the penalty."[8]

But the whole business, defendant argues further, is guesswork; we are by no means certain that deterrence "works." The position is somewhat overstated; there is, in fact, some reasonably "scientific" evidence for the efficacy of criminal sanctions as deterrents, at least as against some kinds of crimes.[9] Moreover, the time is not yet here when all we can "know" must be quantifiable and digestible by computers. The shared wisdom of generations teaches meaningfully, if somewhat amorphously, that the utilitarians have a point; we do, indeed, lapse often into rationality and act to seek pleasure and avoid pain. It would be better, to be sure, if we had more certainty and precision. Lacking these comforts, we continue to include among our working hypotheses a belief (with some concrete evidence in its support) that crimes like those in this case—deliberate, purposeful, continuing, non-impulsive, and committed for profit—are among those most likely to be generally deterrable by sanctions most shunned by those exposed to temptation.[11]

The idea of avoiding depreciation of the seriousness of the offense implicates two or three thoughts, not always perfectly clear or universally agreed upon, beyond the idea of deterrence. It should be proclaimed by the court's judgment that the offenses are grave, not minor or purely technical. Some attention must be paid to the demand for equal justice; it will not do to leave the penalty of imprisonment a dead letter as against "privileged" violators while it is employed regularly, and with vigor, against others. There probably is in these conceptions an element of retributiveness, as counsel urge. And retribution, so denominated, is in some disfavor as a reason for punishment. It remains a factor, however, as Holmes perceived,[12] and as is known to anyone who talks to judges, lawyers, defendants, or people generally. It may become more palatable, and probably more humanely understood, under the rubric of "deserts" or "just deserts."[13] However the concept is formulated, we have not yet reached a state, supposing we ever should, in which the infliction of punishments for crime may be divorced generally from ideas of blameworthiness, recompense, and proportionality.

III. An Alternative, "Behavioral Sanction"

Resisting prison above all else, defense counsel included in their thorough memorandum on sentencing two proposals for what they call a "constructive," and therefore a "preferable" form of "behavioral sanction." One is a plan for Dr. Bergman to create and run a program of Jewish vocational and religious high school training. The other is for him to take charge of a "Committee on Holocaust Studies," again concerned with education at the secondary school level.

---

[8] H.L.A. Hart, *supra* n.6, at 23.

[9] See, e.g., F. Zimrig and G. Hawkins, *Deterrence* 168–71, 282 (1973).

[11] For some supporting evidence that "white-collar" offenses are somewhat specially deterrable, see Chambliss, *Types of Deviance and the Effectiveness of Legal Sanctions,* 1967 Wis. L. Rev. 703, 708–10.

[12] See O. Holmes, *Common Law* 41–42, 45 (1881).

[13] See A. von Hirsch, *Doing Justice* 45–55 (1976); see also N. Morris, *The Future of Imprisonment* 73–77 (1974).

A third suggestion was made orally at yesterday's sentencing hearing. It was proposed that Dr. Bergman might be ordered to work as a volunteer in some established agency as a visitor and aide to the sick and the otherwise incapacitated. The proposal was that he could read, provide various forms of physical assistance, and otherwise give comfort to afflicted people.

No one can doubt either the worthiness of these proposals or Dr. Bergman's ability to make successes of them. But both of the carefully formulated "sanctions" in the memorandum involve work of an honorific nature, not unlike that done in other projects to which the defendant has devoted himself in the past. It is difficult to conceive of them as "punishments" at all. The more recent proposal is somewhat more suitable in character, but it is still an insufficient penalty. The seriousness of the crimes to which Dr. Bergman has pled guilty demands something more than requiring him to lend his talents and efforts to further philanthropic enterprises. It remains open to him, of course, to pursue the interesting suggestions later on as a matter of unforced personal choice.

IV. "Measuring" the Sentence

In cases like this one, the decision of greatest moment is whether to imprison or not. As reflected in the eloquent submissions for defendant, the prospect of the closing prison doors is the most appalling concern; the feeling is that the length of the sojourn is a lesser question once that threshold is passed. Nevertheless, the setting of a term remains to be accomplished. And in some respects it is a subject even more perplexing, unregulated, and unprincipled.

Days and months and years are countable with a sound of exactitude. But there can be no exactitude in the deliberations from which a number emerges. Without pretending to a nonexistent precision, the court notes at least the major factors.

The criminal behavior, as has been noted, is blatant in character and unmitigated by any suggestion of necessitous circumstance or other pressures difficult to resist. However metaphysicians may conjure with issues about free will, it is a fundamental premise of our efforts to do criminal justice that competent people, possessed of their faculties, make choices and are accountable for them. In this sometimes harsh light, the case of the present defendant is among the clearest and least relieved. Viewed against the maxima Congress ordained, and against the run of sentences in other federal criminal cases, it calls for more than a token sentence.[14]

On the other side are factors that take longer to enumerate. Defendant's illustrious public life and works are in his favor, though diminished, of course, by what this case discloses. This is a first, probably a last, conviction. Defendant is 64 years old and in imperfect health, though by no means so ill, from what the court is told, that he could be expected to suffer inordinately more than many others of advanced years who go to prison.

---

[14] Despite Biblical teachings concerning what is expected from those to whom much is given, the court has not, as his counsel feared might happen, held Dr. Bergman to a higher standard of responsibility because of his position in the community. But he has not been judged under a lower standard either.

* * *

How, then, is the particular sentence adjudged in this case? As has been mentioned, the case calls for a sentence that is more than nominal. Given the other circumstances, however—including that this is a first offense, by a man no longer young and not perfectly well, where danger of recidivism is not a concern—it verges on cruelty to think of confinement for a term of years. We sit, to be sure, in a nation where prison sentences of extravagant length are more common than they are almost anywhere else. By that light, the term imposed today is not notably long. For this sentencing court, however, for a nonviolent first offense involving no direct assaults or invasions of others' security (as in bank robbery, narcotics, etc.), it is a stern sentence. For people like Dr. Bergman, who might be disposed to engage in similar wrongdoing, it should be sufficiently frightening to serve the major end of general deterrence. For all but the profoundly vengeful, it should not depreciate the seriousness of his offenses.

V. Punishment in or for the Media

Much of defendant's sentencing memorandum is devoted to the extensive barrage of hostile publicity to which he has been subjected during the years before and since his indictment. He argues, and it appears to be undisputed, that the media (and people desiring to be featured in the media) have vilified him for many kinds of evil doing of which he has in fact been innocent. Two main points are made on this score with respect to the problem of sentencing.

First, as has been mentioned, counsel express the concern that the court may be pressured toward severity by the force of the seeming public outcry. That the court should not allow itself to be affected in this way is clear beyond discussion. Nevertheless, it is not merely permissible, but entirely wholesome and responsible, for counsel to bring the expressed concern out in the open. Whatever our ideals and mixed images about judges, it would be naive to doubt that judges have sometimes been swept by a sense of popular demand toward draconian sentencing decisions. It cannot hurt for the sentencing judge to be reminded of this and cautioned about it. There can be no guarantees. The sentencer must confront and regulate himself. But it bears reaffirmance that the court must seek to discount utterly the fact of notoriety in passing its judgment upon the defendant. Defense counsel cite reported opinions of this court reflecting what happens in a large number of unreported cases, by the present sentencer and many others, in which "unknown" defendants have received prison sentences, longer or shorter than today's, for white-collar or comparably nonviolent crimes. The overall run of cases, with all their individual variations, will reflect, it is hoped, earnest efforts to hew to the principle of equal treatment, with or without publicity.

Defendant's second point about his public humiliation is the frequently heard contention that he should not be incarcerated because he "has been punished enough." The thought is not without some initial appeal. If punishment were wholly or mainly retributive, it might be a weighty factor. In the end, however, it must be a matter of little or no force. Defendant's notoriety should not in the last analysis serve to lighten, any more than it may be permitted to aggravate, his sentence. The fact that he has been pilloried by journalists is essentially a consequence of the prestige and privileges he enjoyed before he was exposed as a wrongdoer. The long fall from grace was possible only because of the height he had reached. The suffering from loss of public esteem reflects a body of opinion that the esteem had been, in at least some measure, wrongly bestowed and enjoyed. It is not possible to justify the notion that this mode of nonjudicial punishment should be an occasion for leniency not given to a defendant who never basked in such an admiring light at all. The quest for both the appearance and the substance of equal justice prompts the court to discount the thought that the public humiliation serves the function of imprisonment.

Writing, as judges rarely do, about a particular sentence concentrates the mind with possibly special force upon the experience of the sentencer as well as the person sentenced. Consigning someone to prison, this defendant or any other, "is a sad necessity." There are impulses of avoidance from time to time— toward a personally gratifying leniency or toward an opposite extreme. But there is, obviously, no place for private impulse in the judgment of the court. The course of justice must be sought with such objective rationality as we can muster, tempered with mercy, but obedient to the law, which, we do well to remember, is all that empowers a judge to make other people suffer.

* * *

. . . Defendant will surrender to begin service of his sentence at 10:30 a.m. on July 7, 1976.

It is so ordered.

[E] Capital Punishment

[The special problem of justifying the death penalty is considered in the materials on the law of homicide, *infra* at § 5.04.]

§ 2.04 SENTENCING AND PROPORTIONALITY

[A] Indeterminate or Determinate Sentences?

As illustrated by the *Bergman* case, wide judicial discretion in imposing sanctions is often a characteristic of sentencing policy. Not only are courts vested with broad authority to administer punishment within a wide range of possible sanctions, but judicially imposed sentences are themselves subject to subsequent adjustment by parole boards and other administrative functionaries. Such sentencing is thus "indeterminate" in the sense that the actual penalty to be served is unknown prior to the time of sentencing and even thereafter. Under "determinate" sentencing, on the other hand, sentences for given offenses are known prior to the time of, or at least at, the time of sentencing.

As a manifestation of the rehabilitative ideal, indeterminate sentencing became popular in the 20th century. Its aim is to individualize sanctions in terms of the offender's need for rehabilitation and propensity for future dangerousness.

Recently, discretionary sentencing has come under attack. A variety of "determinate sentencing" alternatives have been proposed and sometimes adopted. This section considers some of the more significant aspects of the current determinate sentencing movement.

VON HIRSCH, *THE SENTENCING COMMISSION'S FUNCTIONS*

von Hirsch, Knapp, and Tonry,

The Sentencing Commission and Its Guidelines 3–15, 177–82 (1987)

Sweeping discretion in the determination of sentence prevailed during the first six decades of this century. . . . Typically, American statutes set only the maximum penalties for different crimes, and the judge had the choice of any sentence within that limit: a fine, probation, a jail sentence, or a shorter or longer term in state prison. When the offender was sentenced to prison, the parole board could release him at any time after a specified fraction (in most states, one-third) of his sentence had elapsed. Within these wide limits, no standards governed the decisions of sentencing judges or parole boards, and those decisions ordinarily could not be appealed.

This wide discretion was ostensibly justified for rehabilitative ends: to enable judges and parole officers familiar with the case to choose a disposition tailored to the offender's need for treatment. Actually, the discretion may not have helped the cause of penal rehabilitationism much, because it was a blank check which judges and parole officials could use as they wished. . . .

Beginning in the 1970s, disenchantment with discretionary sentencing began to develop. It stemmed, in part, from growing skepticism about the therapeutic model of punishment. . . . Penal treatments did not seem to be working well: once tested carefully, few such programs had a measurable influence on recidivism. Aside from such program failures came a broader loss of faith in human malleability. Not only in sentencing but in other state interventions into the lives of persons whose conduct was deemed deviant, the difficulties of compelling or inducing changed behavior were becoming apparent. Finally, the fairness of the rehabilitative sentence came into question: was it really fair to make the severity of the offender's penalty depend, not on the degree of reprehensibleness of his own criminal choices, but on someone else's estimate of his supposed "needs" for treatment?

As rehabilitationism lost its dominance, other penal philosophies came to the fore. One influential school of thought emphasizes the offender's deserts and would make the sentence comport with the gravity of his criminal conduct. Another school emphasizes incapacitation: imprisoning offenders whose early criminal records and social histories suggest they are likely to return to crime. There have been sharp disagreements between these schools of thought. . . . But both philosophies are suited to embodiment in explicit standards for sentencing. If penalties are to be based on the seriousness offenders' criminal conduct, then guidelines can help judges gauge the conduct's gravity and the appropriate, deserved penalty. If penalties are to be based, instead, on the statistical probability of offending again, such probabilities, and the appropriate incapacitative measures, can also be set forth in explicit standards.

As these shifts in penal philosophy were occurring, broad sentencing discretion itself came under fire. Unguided authority to sentence, it began to be recognized, allows discrepant decisions. When judges and parole boards are free to determine the quantum of punishment without standards or guidelines, they are apt to decide similar cases differently. While some courts seem to have developed "going rates" of sentence for various typical situations, these are little more than statistical norms—from which individual judges are free to deviate whenever and for whatever reason they choose.

More fundamentally, critics asserted, discretionary sentencing meant sentencing uncontrolled by considered policy. Dispositional patterns in a particular state emerged largely by happenstance, the product of the attitudes and practices of those occupying the bench at the moment. There was no coherent pattern of sentences sought, and hence no opportunity to consider the wisdom or practicability of seeking such outcomes. The time seemed ripe for bringing purpose and order to sentencing.

THE UNSUITABILITY OF LEGISLATIVE STANDARDS

As interests in regulating sentencing grew, the method of regulation initially most used was legislative: the state legislature would prescribe a detailed schedule of prescribed or recommended sanctions for various crimes. . . .

. . . When called upon to write specific punishments for crimes, a legislative body has two vulnerabilities. First, it has little time available: given the press of other legislative business, it cannot devote much effort and thought to developing a coherent rationale; comparing proposed penalties with one another; projecting the standards' impact on sentencing practice and on the limited resources of the correctional system; and, once the penalties have gone into effect, reviewing the manner in which they have actually been administered. Second, legislatures face particularly troublesome pressures in the sentencing field. Many voters fear crime and criminals, and few convicted offenders do (or even may) vote. Once a legislative body begins debating specific penalties, legislators have considerable incentives to adopt posturing stances of "toughness" and few incentives for giving thought to the *justice* of proposed penalties—for considering seriously whether the proposed sanctions would treat convicted criminals (that unpopular minority) fairly and deservedly. With such difficulties apparent, observers began to ask whether the legislature might better delegate the task of setting sentencing standards to a specialized body—one more insulated from political pressures and with more time and expertise to devote.

* * *

. . . Explicit standards for *judges'* sentencing decisions . . . are a necessity. To write such standards, a standard-setting body is needed: not the legislature, but a specialized rule maker.

The Sentencing Commission

The idea for such a rule-making body can be credited to a former law professor and federal judge, Marvin E. Frankel. In a 1972 book, he proposed creation of a sentencing commission. The commission would be authorized by statute to write detailed guidelines for sentencing. Its members would be appointed by the jurisdiction's chief executive, with senatorial advice and consent; they would consist of judges, prosecutors, defense attorneys, scholars, and citizens, backed by a full-time professional staff. Judges would be required to follow the guidelines in their sentencing decisions, except where they could give satisfactory reasons for deviation. Under the enabling statute, the guidelines would become law either automatically after the commission approved them (in the absence of a legislative resolution of disapproval), or else upon submission to and approval by the legislature. In either case, the commission would be responsible for writing the guidelines, and was supposed to have enough leisure, expertise, and insulation from outside pressures to draft them with care. After the guidelines went into effect, the commission would collect information on their implementation and amend and refine them accordingly.

The sentencing commission's mission was to be prescriptive: to decide the future direction of sentencing policy. The study of past sentencing practice would be a useful first step, indicating what factors had been given primary emphasis in judges' everyday sentencing decisions. The next and critical step, however, would be a normative evaluation of that past practice. Is it rational? Is it fair? Ought the practice continue to be followed? If not, how should it be changed? . . .

The commission's guidelines were supposed to structure the judge's discretion, not eliminate it. Judges would still interpret and apply the guidelines and could deviate from them in special circumstances. They would be called upon to do what their legal background has trained them to do: to apply generalized norms to particular cases, with whatever complexities of interpretation that involves, and to decide when there are sufficient grounds for departing from those norms in unusual situations. They would no longer be called upon to act in a legal void—to make decisions about people's liberty without explicit standards to guide their actions.

Frankel's proposal generated a great deal of interest, and by the end of the 1970s, several states began taking action. . . . For federal crimes, the U.S. Sentencing Commission has been established. . . . Of these various efforts, the first—and in many respects the most sophisticated to date—has been Minnesota's guidelines.

The Format of the Guidelines

Let me begin a sketch of sentencing commission guidelines with a description of their usual format. The guidelines are numerical and definite. Usually, their principal feature is a sentencing grid: a two dimensional table of prescribed sanctions. The vertical axis of the grid, or offense score, grades the seriousness of various species of criminal conduct. The horizontal axis, or offender score, rates characteristics of the offender—such as the extent of his prior criminal record. Across the grid is drawn a so-called dispositional (or in—out) line. Above the line are prescribed prison sanctions of varying duration, and below it are lesser sanctions. In each grid cell above the line, a numerical range of imprisonment is prescribed: the grid cell applicable to convicted armed robbers having two prior felony convictions might contain a range of, say, thirty-eight to forty-four months in prison.

* * *

In a grid, the range in any particular cell prescribes only the *normally* appropriate sentences. A sentencing court is authorized to deviate from the cell range on account of aggravating and mitigating circumstances. Such deviations are to be invoked, however, only in unusual situations—and the guidelines themselves may contain a suggested list of factors that qualify as mitigating or aggravating.

Once established, the guidelines system is policed through appellate review. The higher courts are authorized to hear sentence appeals and to determine compliance with the guidelines. In so doing, those courts are supposed to develop a supplementary jurisprudence—on, for example, how to interpret the commission's list of aggravating and mitigating factors.

* * *

The Guidelines and "Disparity"

One of the major charges against discretionary sentencing was, as I noted, its apparent tendency to produce disparate outcomes. It has thus been tempting to define the sentencing commission's mission purely as that of promoting consistency or reducing disparity. Such a formulation of the guidelines' aim, however, is insufficient.

Disparity cannot be determined in a vacuum. It consists of differences in sentence that cannot be accounted for on the basis of the purpose or purposes sought to be achieved. Does it constitute disparity when unemployed offenders receive more severe sentences than employed ones? That depends on the rationale. If the aim is to punish offenders as they deserve, it is disparity—because an offender's employment status ordinarily is not germane to the reprehensibleness of his criminal conduct. If, on the other hand, the aim is to sentence offenders according to their risk of recidivism, it is not necessarily disparity, because available studies suggest a link between joblessness and recidivism. In order to combat or even to identify disparity, the first step needed is the specification of a rationale. Yet that is precisely what is missing in a discretionary sentencing system.

Consistency is, also, no guarantee of the rationality or fairness of a system. Sentencing offenders invariably according to their height or weight would be consistent but nevertheless irrational. What is needed is a considered judgment of what the basis of the sentence should be. Only then has a standard been created against which "disparity" can be measured and judged.

What, then, is the mission of a sentencing commission? It is threefold: selecting a rationale, considering prison population constraints, and developing a tariff. . . .

Choosing the Rationale

The sentencing commission, in fashioning its guidelines, must choose a rationale. Should the system emphasize punishing offenders proportionately to the gravity of their crimes? Or should it rely, instead, more heavily on the degree of risk offenders pose? Or should there be some other purpose? The choice of rationale is critical because it will determine what features of the offense or of the offender should be relied upon in determining the punishment. On a rationale emphasizing proportionality and desert, the factor primarily to be relied upon is the seriousness of the current crime. On a predictive rationale, however, the primacy would shift to factors that are indicative of risk—chiefly, . . . the offender's previous criminal record and his social and employment history. The commission does not have to choose one rationale to the exclusion of all others, but, where a hybrid rationale is used, it is still necessary to decide which aim should have preeminence.

A sentencing commission is well suited to this task: it can consider the rationale for the system as a whole and make its choice in an informed fashion. When considering treatment or deterrence, the commission can inform itself of the extent and limits of present knowledge of treatment and deterrent effects. When considering incapacitation, it can examine prediction research to see how well we can forecast recidivism, and where the empirical and ethical problems lie. When considering desert, it can—by examining the literature on that subject—acquaint itself with the criteria for proportionality.

With the rationale formulated, the commission is in a position to identify the factors chiefly to be relied upon and the comparative weight they should be given. Choosing between desert and incapacitation, for example, enables the commission to decide the weight to be given the current offense relative to the prior record and other information about the offender.

A striking illustration of this policy-making process has been provided by Minnesota's sentencing commission. The Minnesota commission studied judges' decisions about whether or not to impose a prison sentence. It found that, under previous judicial practice, the main determinant of an offender's going to prison was the length of his criminal record. An offender with a string of lesser felonies would be imprisoned; a first offender with a considerably more serious conviction would not. In other words, the dispositional line on the grid—the line separating prison from nonprison dispositions—would be steep (emphasizing the criminal record) were past practice made the basis of the guidelines. The commission then proceeded to consider whether this practice was desirable and should be continued.

To make that decision the commission developed models comparing the slope of the dispositional line on two rationales: a desert rationale, and an incapacitative one relying on prediction of risk. After consulting the literature on desert and prediction, the commission determined that a desert rationale would have a relatively flat line, giving primary weight to the seriousness of the current offense—whereas a predictive rationale would (because of the link between previous record and recidivism) have a much steeper line, emphasizing the prior record, as the state's previous practice did. With this in mind the commission was able to debate the rationale, and eventually it decided that a more desert-oriented rationale was preferable. The commission thereupon chose as its dispositional line one which, it asserted, reflected a "modified" desert conception; the line was flat for most cases, albeit steep for offenders with lengthy criminal histories. The result of this decision was a substantial change from prior policy. The seriousness of the offense is given considerably more importance in the guidelines than it had under the state's past practice, and the extent of the criminal history is given much less.

* * *

Controlling the Growth of Prison Populations

Many jurisdictions, both in the United States and elsewhere, have been experiencing sharp rises in prison populations. The result has been prison overcrowding, with its attendant evils of deteriorating living conditions. If crowding is endemic and serious, the conventional palliatives offer little hope. Emergency release, accelerated parole, and similar stopgap measures are only short-term solutions—and soon generate opposition, as involving the "premature" release of undeserving or dangerous felons. New prison construction is costly, time-consuming, and (if prison commitments continue unabated) creates space that itself soon will be filled. Crowding can be effectively prevented only by controlling the inflow into the prisons and the length of stay there.

Inflow and length of stay can be influenced through sentencing guidelines. Minnesota, again, provides the model. The Minnesota sentencing commission devised its guidelines so that, given anticipated conviction rates, the aggregate prison population would not exceed the capacity of the state's prisons. The commission accomplished this by projecting the impact of its tentatively proposed guidelines on prison populations, comparing those projections with the rated capacity of the state's prison system, and then making the appropriate adjustments to yield the final guidelines.

* * *

Why should a sentencing commission adopt such population targets? The plainest reason is ethical. Overcrowding makes the daily discomforts of prison life much worse, and it exacerbates frictions that can lead to violence. A civilized society should not commit offenders to institutions that lack room for them.

A population constraint has another use: it forces those who write sentencing guidelines to treat them as a choice of priorities. When a population constraint is imposed and population projections are systematically used in writing the guidelines, the commissioners are made aware that they are dealing with a system of scarce resources—which cannot possibly imprison all those whom various constituencies might prefer to see confined. With explicit population targets it becomes clear that a choice must be made of whom it is most important to imprison: those whose crimes are serious or those who have substantial criminal records can be chosen, but not all of both groups. The need to make such a choice can promote consensus within the commission and can also help the commission explain its work by pointing out the tradeoffs: how getting tougher with one group of offenders would necessitate more leniency with another group. . . .

* * *

Beyond such philosophical arguments stands another, simpler reason for considering prison space: namely, to ensure that the guidelines are implemented as written. To the extent that their full application would overtax available penal resources, the guidelines will have to be disregarded in everyday sentencing decisions. . . .

Developing the Tariff

The third task for the commission is to develop a tariff: to provide specific guidance on the amount of punishment ordinarily called for by various types of cases. Such a baseline for everyday sentencing decisions is what has been lacking from discretionary systems.

If the guidelines use a grid format, the commission develops the tariff by filling in the cells in the grid. By supplying ranges in the grid's cells, the commission indicates when imprisonment is called for, and what periods of imprisonment ordinarily are appropriate. The judges' role then becomes that of applying and interpreting the tariff in their everyday sentencing decisions and deciding when to deviate from the tariff in suitable special circumstances.

This tariff-construction work is the commission's most laborious task. Different species of criminal conduct must be graded in seriousness—which involves assessing the harm and culpability of a wide variety of criminal acts. Offenders' criminal histories, and any other appropriate offender factors, need also to be graded. . . . Finally, the ranges of normally prescribed punishments need to be decided upon—work involving complex comparative judgments, in which the commission needs to bear in mind its chosen rationale and its prison-population targets. The guidelines are only as good as the tariff. Little is accomplished if the chosen rationale is ignored when the numbers are written in the grid cells, or if the prescribed punishment ranges are too broad to provide significant guidance to judges.

Once the tariff is thus developed, the question of departures needs also to be addressed. What burden of persuasion must be met before departures from the grid's ranges are permitted? What are the permitted grounds for departure? If departures are too readily permitted, the guidelines become merely precatory; if they are stringently restricted, then the guidelines become too rigid.

The Minnesota guidelines . . . most significant features are (1)the scoring system for crime seriousness, (2)the criminal history scoring system, (3)the sentencing grid, and (4)the rules governing departures.

* * *

Crime Seriousness

The offender's current offense is graded according to the offense of conviction. The guidelines assign scores from 1 (lowest) to 10 (highest) to the various statutory offense categories or subcategories. Examples of the crimes assigned to the various grades are as follows:

Offense Score	Crime Category
10	Murder—intentional but not premeditated
9	Felony murder
8	Assault—great bodily harm
7	Armed robbery Burglary—with weapon or assault
6	Burglary of occupied dwelling
5	Burglary of unoccupied dwelling
4	Nonresidential burglary Theft over $2500
3	Theft ($250–$2500) Possession of heroin
2	Various lesser theft-related felonies
1	Unauthorized use of vehicle Marijuana possession

Criminal History

The criminal history score is based upon the offender's prior *convictions.* Prior arrests not leading to conviction are not counted. Each prior felony conviction counts one point. Each prior gross misdemeanor conviction counts *one-half point,* and each prior misdemeanor conviction counts *one-quarter* point. There are special rules for: (1) crimes committed while on probation or parole, and (2) prior crimes as a juvenile.

The Sentencing Grid

The sentencing grid . . . sets forth (1) when imprisonment presumptively is appropriate, and (2) the presumptive duration of prison sentences. Unless the offender loses "good time" for infractions committed in prison, he will serve two-thirds of any prison sentence in confinement and the remaining one-third under supervision in the community.

On [Table A–1's] grid . . . cells with recommended prison terms are below the heavy black line (known as the dispositional line). In each such cell, the single number is the recommended

TABLE A-1 Minnesota Sentencing Grid

Criminal History Score

Seriousness Levels of Conviction Offense		0	1	2	3	4	5	6 or more
1	Unauthorized use of motor vehicle Possession of marijuana	N	N	N	N	N	N	19 18–20
2	Theft-related crimes Aggravated forgery	N	N	N	N	N	N	21 20–22
3	Theft crimes	N	N	N	N	19 18–20	22 21–23	25 24–26
4	Nonresidential burglary Theft crimes (over $2500)	N	N	N	N	25 24–26	32 30–34	41 37–45
5	Residential burglary Simple robbery	N	N	N	30 29–31	38 36–40	46 43–49	54 50–58
6	Criminal sexual conduct, 2nd degree	N	N	N	34 33–35	44 42–46	54 50–58	65 60–70
7	Aggravated robbery	24 23–25	32 30–34	41 38–44	49 45–53	65 60–70	81 75–87	97 90–104
8	Criminal sexual conduct, 1st degree Assault, 1st degree	43 41–45	54 50–58	65 60–70	76 71–81	95 89–101	113 106–120	132 124–140
9	Murder, 3rd degree Murder, 2nd degree (felony murder)	105 102–108	119 116–122	127 124–130	149 143–155	176 168–184	205 195–215	230 218–242
10	Murder, 2nd degree (with intent)	120 116–124	140 133–147	162 153–171	203 192–214	243 231–255	284 270–298	324 309–339

Notes: "N" denotes a presumption of a nonimprisonment sentence.

duration of sentence. The range below that number is the range within which the judge may sentence without supplying reasons. Any sentence outside that range constitutes a departure from the guidelines.

Above the dispositional line, the cells prescribe a presumption of a sentence other than imprisonment, designated as "N." This nonimprisonment sentence may, within the judge's discretion and statutory limits, include a jail term of up to one year, or else probation, fine, or other community disposition. The guidelines, in other words, limit the use and duration of imprisonment—but leave discretion in the choice among nonprison sanctions. (The actual guidelines provide, in each cell above the line, a number representing the duration of reconfinement upon revocation of probation or other stayed prison sentence—but these numbers are not reproduced here.)

Departures

The guidelines provide that the court may depart from the grid's presumptive sentences, only in "substantial and compelling circumstances."

Certain circumstances may not be considered as grounds of departure. These are:

- Race
- Sex
- Employment factors, including:
  1. occupation or impact of sentence on profession or occupation
  2. employment history
  3. employment at time of offense
  4. employment at time of sentencing
- Social factors, including:
  1. educational attainment
  2. living arrangements at time of offense or sentencing
  3. length of residence
  4. marital status
- The exercise of constitutional rights by the defendant during the adjudication process.

A *nonexclusive* list of mitigating factors is provided. The court may impose a sentence less severe than the indicated range if the court makes the appropriate substantial—and—compelling finding. The list consists of the following four items:

1. The victim was an aggressor in the incident.
2. The offender played a minor or passive role in the crime or participated under circumstances of coercion or duress.
3. The offender, because of physical or mental impairment, lacked substantial capacity for judgment when the offense was committed. The voluntary use of intoxicants (drugs or alcohol) is not included.

4. Other substantial grounds exist which tend to excuse or mitigate the offender's culpability, although not amounting to a defense.

A *nonexclusive* list of aggravating factors is likewise provided, consisting of the following seven items:

1. The victim was particularly vulnerable owing to age, infirmity, or reduced physical or mental capacity, which was known or should have been known to the offender.

2. The victim was treated with particular cruelty for which the individual offender should be held responsible.

3. The current conviction is for an offense in which the victim was injured and there is a prior felony conviction for an offense in which the victim was injured.

4. The offense was a major economic offense, identified as an illegal act or series of illegal acts committed by other than physical means and by concealment or guile to obtain money or property, to avoid payment or loss of money or property, or to obtain business or professional advantage. Two or more of the circumstances listed below combine to form an aggravating factor with respect to the offense:

    a. the offense involved multiple victims or multiple incidents per victim;

    b. the offense involved an attempted or actual monetary loss substantially greater than the usual offense or substantially greater than the minimum loss specified in the statutes;

    c. the offense involved a high degree of sophistication or planning or occurred over a lengthy period of time;

    d. the defendant used his or her position or status to facilitate the commission of the offense, including a position of trust, confidence, or fiduciary relationship;

    e. the defendant has been involved in other conduct similar to the current offense as evidenced by the findings of civil or administrative law proceedings or the imposition of professional sanctions.

5. The offense was a major controlled-substance offense, identified as an offense or series of offenses related to trafficking in controlled substances under circumstances more onerous than the usual offense. (Specific factors that are aggravating with respect to such major drug offenses are then listed.)

6. The offender committed, for hire, a crime against the person.

7. The offender committed a crime against the person in furtherance of criminal activity by an organized gang. An "organized gang" is defined as an association of five or more persons, with an established hierarchy, formed to encourage gang members to perpetrate crimes or to provide support to gang members who do commit crimes.

NOTES AND QUESTIONS

1. Under the Minnesota Sentencing Guidelines, a person convicted of six or more charges of "unauthorized use of a motor vehicle" suffers a "presumptive" sentence of 19 months imprisonment. Is this sentence consistent with the "modified desert" rationale of the system? Is a repeat offender more "deserving" of imprisonment than a first offender? See R. Singer, Just Deserts 67–74 (1979). Should the Minnesota system distinguish between offenders convicted of six counts of that offense and those convicted of that offense in six separate prosecutions?

Traditionally an offender's criminal history has played an informal but substantial role in the sentencing judge's decision. Today, many states and the federal government have legislatively mandated that sentences be dramatically enhanced in cases where the offender has a certain number of prior convictions. These statutes often require long prison sentences, often life without possibility of parole, for repeat offenders. The statutes vary in both the number and the type of criminal offenses required to trigger the sentence enhancement. A common type of enhancement statute is triggered by conviction of a specified number of felonies of any kind. Laws that tie enhancement to conviction of any felony, can, in certain circumstances, mandate excessive punishment. See *Solem v. Helm,* 463 U.S. 277 (1994), discussed in the *Harmelin* case, *infra* at p. 231 (sentence of life in prison without possibility of parole for uttering a bad $100.00 check, based on the prior commission of seven minor nonviolent felonies, violates the Eighth Amendment).

In 1994, Congress enacted a so-called "three strikes and you're out" statute providing mandatory life imprisonment for defendants convicted of three predicate felonies. Violent Crime Control and Law Enforcement Act of 1994, Pub. L. No. 103–322, § 70001, 108 Stat. 1796 (1994). In light of the materials considered earlier in this chapter, is such a statute sound on utilitarian or retributive grounds?

2. Does the choice of 10 categories of crime seriousness in the Minnesota model accurately capture the problem of grading crimes? Consider the following from F. Zimring, Making Punishment Fit the Crime: A Consumers' Guide to Sentencing Reform 10–11 (1977), in assessing the presumptive sentencing model proposed by the Twentieth Century Fund's Fair and Certain Punishment:

> The *incoherence of the criminal law.* Any system of punishment that attaches a single sanction to a particular offense must define offenses with a morally persuasive precision that present laws do not possess. In my home state of Illinois, burglary is defined so that an armed housebreaker is guilty of the same offense as an 18-year-old who opens the locked glove compartment of my unlocked station wagon. Obviously, no single punishment can be assigned to crime defined in such sweeping terms. But can we be precise?
>
> The problem is not simply that any such penal code will make our present statutes look like Reader's Digest Condensed Books; we lack the capacity to define into formal law the nuances of situation, intent and social harm

that condition the seriousness of particular criminal acts. For example, the sample code provides six years in prison for "premeditated assault" in which serious harm was intended and two years for assaults where serious harm was not intended. While there may be some conceptual distinction between these two mental states, one cannot confidently divide hundreds of thousands of gun and knife attacks into these categories to determine whether a "Fair and Certain Punishment" is six years or two.

Rape, an offense that encompasses a huge variety of behaviors, is graded into three punishments: six years (when accompanied by an assault that causes bodily injury); three years (when there is no additional bodily harm); and six months (when committed on a previous sex partner, with no additional bodily harm). Two further aggravating conditions are also specified. Put aside for a moment the fact that prior consensual sex reduces the punishment by a factor of six and the problem that rape with bodily harm has a "presumptive sentence" one year longer than intentional killing. Have we really defined the offense into its phenologically significant categories? Can we rigorously patrol the border between forcible rape without additional bodily harm and that with further harm—when that distinction can mean the difference between six months and six years in the penitentiary?

I am not suggesting that these are problems of sloppy drafting. Rather, we may simply lack the ability to comprehensively define in advance those elements of an offense that should be considered in fixing a criminal sentence.

3. As von Hirsch points out, the Minnesota system is based on a defined sentencing rationale—in that case one emphasizing just deserts conceptions. Sometimes policy makers articulate a theoretical rationale as the basis for sentencing reform but implement a system at odds with the rationale. For example, in the late 1960s a New York commission charged with revising sentencing policy determined that penal sanctions were to be imposed to deter crime and rehabilitate and incapacitate offenders. See Allen, *Retribution in a Modern Penal Law: The Principle of Aggravated Harm*, 25 Buff. L. Rev. 1, 2–3, 6–11, 16, 19–20 (1975). The commission expressly rejected retribution as a sentencing consideration. *Id.* Yet, when the commission implemented its system, it based its sentences largely on the basis of the amount of harm caused by the offender's act, even if the harm (or its absence) was a largely fortuitous consequence of the act. For example, if a person acts recklessly and creates a grave risk of death, he will be punished much more severely if his act causes death than if his very same act results in no harm. *Id.* Sentencing premised on such a principle of "aggravated harm" is arguably at odds with the articulated grounds for sentencing (deterrence, rehabilitation, and incapacitation) while it is arguably more at home with the rejected ground of retribution. *Id.*

4. Do the Minnesota guidelines adequately meet the goal of limiting sentencing discretion? Should, for example, the list of mitigating and aggravating factors be exclusively, rather than nonexclusively, defined?

5. Even if the rehabilitative ideal is abandoned, should parole boards be retained to "check" the severity of the penalty structure? Some suggest that

parole boards possess lower political visibility than legislatures and judges and thus can transform "lengthy judicial sentences into more realistic terms of actual confinement." Commentary, *American Bar Association Standards for Criminal Justice, Sentencing Alternatives and Procedures* 18.241–42 (2d ed. 1980). On this view, parole boards can mitigate sentencing severity with minimal political objection because the public accepts the idea that individuals change, or at least mature, over time and thus offers less resistance to an early release system than to short sentences in the first instance. Moreover, a parole agency is arguably able to detect the disparities that result because of plea bargaining and is not compelled to accept them because it is not intimately involved in the day-to-day pressures of caseload management. *Id.* at 18.245. Finally, parole boards can accommodate changing social attitudes over time toward different crimes and adjust sentences accordingly.

In addition to the issues addressed by the Minnesota guidelines, should reform movements confront other problem areas of discretion? See R. Singer, Just Deserts 123–35 (1979). Consider the following:

ALSCHULER, *SENTENCING REFORM AND PROSECUTORIAL POWER: A CRITIQUE OF RECENT PROPOSALS FOR "FIXED" AND PRESUMPTIVE* SENTENCING

126 U. Pa.L.Rev. 550, 563–69, 577 (1978)

Any reform of sentencing practices, whether great or small and whether taking the form of fixed sentences, presumptive sentences or sentencing guidelines, can be undercut by the practice of plea bargaining. The advocates of dramatic change in our system of criminal punishment have dutifully noted that prosecutors do, in effect, make sentencing decisions in formulating charges and in negotiating pleas of guilty. They have even proclaimed that "there can be no practical understanding of any sentencing system without an appreciation of the role played by plea bargaining." Sometimes after these brief glances in the direction of reality, however, and sometimes without them, the reformers have for the most part ignored the dominant reality of prosecutorial sentencing power. They have usually sought to leave this power as they found it without pausing to consider the effects of a still-unchecked power to bargain on the achievement of their objectives.

It seems unlikely that today's reformers are truly content with the regime of prosecutorial power as it is. There is hardly any objection to judicial sentencing discretion that does not apply in full measure to prosecutorial sentencing discretion—a discretion which has been, in practice, every bit as broad and broader. As much as judicial discretion, the discretion of American prosecutors lends itself to inequalities and disparities of treatment because of disagreements concerning issues of sentencing policy. Like judicial discretion, prosecutorial discretion permits at least the occasional dominance of illegitimate considerations such as race and personal or political influence in sentencing decisions. It may also lead to a general perception of unfairness, arbitrariness and uncertainty and may even undercut the deterrent force of the criminal law.

There are additional objections to prosecutorial sentencing discretion that do not apply with nearly so much force to judicial discretion. The exercise of prosecutorial discretion is more frequently made contingent upon a waiver of constitutional rights. It is generally exercised less openly. It is more likely to be influenced by considerations of friendship and by reciprocal favors of a dubious character. It is commonly exercised for the purpose of obtaining convictions in cases in which guilt could not be proven at trial. It is usually exercised by people of less experience and less objectivity than judges. It is commonly exercised on the basis of less information than judges possess. Indeed, its exercise may depend less upon considerations of desert, deterrence and reformation than upon a desire to avoid the hard work of preparing and trying cases. In short, prosecutorial discretion has the same faults as judicial discretion and more.

The *laissez-faire* attitude of sentencing reformers toward this concentration of governmental power in prosecutors' offices is probably not the product of blindness or indifference. It is probably best explained by a pervasive sense that, for one reason or another, the institution of plea bargaining is impregnable. Perhaps the reformers have accepted the claim that trial courts would be swamped if the power of prosecutors to bargain for guilty pleas were substantially restricted, or they may have agreed that efforts to restrict the bargaining process would merely drive it underground. Furthermore, the reformers probably have little desire to engage in what they see as a fruitless political battle. They may sense that sentencing reform will have a rough enough time in the political arena without a hopeless charge at the prosecutor's well-entrenched—and very comfortable—way of doing business.

. . . [F]rom my perspective, the worthwhile goal of sentencing reform might almost as well be forgotten if plea bargaining cannot be restricted.

* * *

The defenders of plea bargaining sometimes debate whether the bargaining process should focus on the number and severity of the charges against a defendant or instead on specific sentence recommendations. Plea bargaining in a world of fixed sentencing, however, would combine the worst features of both forms of negotiation. Under the current system of criminal justice, the principal advantage of charge bargaining is that it involves a measure of shared discretion and tends to intrude less dramatically upon the judicial sentencing function. Even after a charge-reduction bargain has been fully effected, a trial judge is likely to retain a significant choice in the sentence to be imposed, and he may exercise this discretion without undercutting the credibility of the prosecutor who struck the bargain. When plea negotiations focus on prosecutorial sentence recommendations, by contrast, judges usually follow the course of least resistance and simply ratify the prosecutors' sentencing decisions. The advantage that charge bargaining exhibits in our current system of criminal justice would plainly disappear in a system of fixed sentences. Under a fixed-sentencing regime, bargaining about the charge would be bargaining about the sentence. A nonjudicial officer would determine the exact outcome of every guilty plea case, and every defendant who secured an offer from a prosecutor in the plea bargaining process would be informed of the precise sentence that would result from his conviction at trial and also of the precise lesser sentence that would result from his conviction by plea.

Although plea negotiation in a system of fixed sentencing would not have the same ad-vantages as charge bargaining today, it would retain the same defects. The principal virtue of sentence-recommendation bargaining in our current system of justice is that it permits a reasonably precise adjustment of the concessions that a defendant will receive by pleading guilty. Charge bargaining is not as capable of making fine-adjustments but must proceed by leaps from one charge to another. . . .

* * *

[M]any of today's reformers couple their proposals for increased certainty in sentencing with proposals for a substantial reduction in the severity of criminal punishments. To the extent that the reformers accomplish this second objective, the plea bargaining leverage of prosecutors is likely to be reduced. A prosecutor who can threaten only a penalty of three years following a defendant's conviction at trial plainly has less bargaining power than a prosecutor who can threaten a sentence of twenty-five years. Nevertheless, a caveat of Professor Franklin Zimring is worth repeating: "Once a determinate sentencing bill is before a legislative body, it takes only an eraser and pencil to make a one-year 'presumptive sentence' into a six-year sentence for the same offense." Political forces may push sentencing reform away from the humanitarian objectives of its authors and toward a sterner model. Even if liberal reformers were to succeed initially in securing a reduction in penalties, instances in which a legislatively specified penalty appeared too lenient would probably attract more public attention than cases in which the penalty appeared too severe. Politicians pressed to find issues upon which to campaign can always propose an increase in the penalty for whatever crime has caught the public's eye.

* * *

. . . Eliminating or restricting the discretionary powers of parole boards and trial judges is likely to increase the powers of prosecutors, and these powers are likely to be exercised without effective limits through the practice of plea bargaining. The substitution of fixed or presumptive sentences for the discretion of judges and parole boards tends to concentrate sentencing power in the hands of officials who are likely to allow their decisions to be governed by factors irrelevant to the proper goals of sentencing—officials moreover, who typically lack the information, objectivity, and experience of trial judges.

Note on Federal Sentencing Guidelines

Throughout much of the 20th century, rehabilitation was a primary consideration in federal sentencing. After a decade of study, Congress determined that the sentences given under the indeterminate sentencing model then in place lacked the uniformity necessary to fair application of the law and the certainty required to inspire public confidence and deter crime. Those conclusions led Congress to pass the Federal Sentencing Reform Act of 1984, which drastically changed the federal sentencing process.

The Federal Sentencing Reform Act of 1984 (SRA) created the United States Sentencing Commission (Commission), an independent commission in the judicial branch, and directed the Commission to promulgate guidelines to be used by federal courts when sentencing criminal offenders. Additionally, the SRA specified that the guidelines embrace a presumptive sentencing model with maximum sentences for prison offenses not exceeding minimums by more than 25 percent or six months, whichever is greater, except that cases with a minimum term of 30 years or more may carry a maximum of life imprisonment. Under the guidelines that eventually emerged, sentencing judges are required to impose sentences within the guidelines "unless the court finds that an aggravating or mitigating circumstance exists that was not adequately taken into account by the Sentencing Commission in formulating the guidelines and should result in a sentence different from that described." If a sentence is outside the guidelines, "the court is to state the specific reason for deviating from the guidelines." Either side may appeal a sentence and obtain appellate review of—among other issues—a judge's decision to impose a sentence deviating from the guidelines.

The Commission's initial set of Sentencing Guidelines (Guidelines) went into effect on November 1, 1987. The Guidelines are aimed at furthering the basic purposes of punishment in the federal system: "deterring crime, incapacitating the offender, providing just punishment, and rehabilitating the offender." United States Sentencing Commission, *Sentencing Guidelines and Policy Statements* 1 (1987). In attempting to accommodate those diverse interests, the Guidelines specifically reject adopting "a single philosophical theory" of sentencing. Moreover, the Guidelines attempt no assessment of the primacy of one sentencing purpose if (when?) it conflicts with others.

In determining the appropriate sentencing ranges for each offense, the Commission empirically established the average sentences actually being served within each offense category under the former system. In many instances, the Guidelines mirror pre-Guideline practice. The result is thus essentially a descriptive attempt to make sentences more uniform as opposed to extensive normative reshaping of the sentencing process. In defining the sentences, the Commission established a 43-level sentencing table with sentencing levels in rows that overlap with the levels in the preceding and succeeding rows. Such overlap "preserves the maximum degree of allowable discretion for the judge within each level." *Sentencing Guidelines and Policy Statements* at 11. In determining the sentence, the judge first categorizes the offense according to the Guidelines, then takes account of the specific enhancements provided in the Guidelines (e.g., possession of a weapon) and certain mitigating factors, and then calculates a criminal history score. This will lead the judge to the applicable range of sentences. See Ashworth, *Principled Sentencing* 260 (A. von Hirsch and A. Ashworth eds. 1992).

Although shortly after its inception some appellate courts struck down the SRA and the Guidelines it spawned as unconstitutional on separation of powers grounds—see, e.g., *United States v. Seluk*, 691 F.Supp 525 (D. Mass.

1988)—the Supreme Court eventually upheld the constitutionality of the statutory scheme, *United States v. Mistretta,* 488 U.S. 361 (1989). Constitutional objections to specific parts of the Sentencing Guidelines still persist, however. See, e.g., *United States v. Jackson,* 506 U.S. 1023 (2nd Cir. 1992), *cert. den.,* 113 S.Ct. 664 (1992) (vacating district court's decision that the enhanced penalty provisions for cocaine base offenses are unconstitutionally vague), *on resent.,* 856 F.Supp. 176, (S.D.N.Y.) 1994 (holding that the enhanced penalty provisions do not violate equal protection or cruel and unusual punishment); but see, *United States v. Clary,* 846 F.Supp. 768 (E.D. Mo. 1994) (enhanced penalty provisions for crack cocaine offenses violate equal protection clause because Congress was influenced and motivated by unconscious racism when enacting the provision). Additionally, objections that sentencing courts incorrectly applied the Guidelines generate numerous appeals. See, e.g., *United States v. Jackson,* 30 F.3d, (1st Cir. 1994) (vacating and remanding for resentencing as the sentencing court's downward departure from Guidelines was not supported by legally sufficient reasons). Some have concluded that there has been "a seemingly endless line of criminal appeals marching stolidly to the beat of the Federal Sentencing Guidelines." *United States v. Ocasio-Rivera,* 991 F.2d 1, 2 (1st Cir. 1993).

The commentators have also roundly criticized the Guidelines. Some object to the inflexibility of the system, Alschuler, *The Failure of the Sentencing Guidelines: A Plea for Less Aggregation,* 58 U. Chi. L. Rev. 901, 925–28 (1991), as well as to its failure to choose between possible rationales for punishment, see, e.g., Alschuler, *Departures and Plea Agreements under the Sentencing Guidelines,* 117 F.R.D. 459, 461–63 (1988). Others lament the perceived increase in judicial time and effort required to reach sentencing decisions due to the bulk and complexity of the Guidelines. Cabranes, *Sentencing Guidelines: A Failed Utopian Experiment,* Nat'l L.J., July 27, 1992, at 18.

Other critics fault Congress for continuing to involve itself in the details of sentencing policy despite its creation of a specialized agency possessed of expertise in the field. Throughout the time the Commission has been in existence, Congress has continued to legislate mandatory minimum sentences for certain offenses. In all, there are roughly 60 mandatory minimum penalty statutes in federal law today, although only four (covering drug and firearm violations) are used frequently. See, *United States Sentencing Commission, Special Report to Congress: Mandatory Minimum Penalties in the Federal Criminal Justice System* (Aug. 1991) 10 and Appendix A (which contains a full list of federal mandatory minimum sentences).

Both commentators and judges have frequently noted that mandatory sentences and the Guidelines often combine to mandate unfairly harsh sentences. See, e.g., Carmody, *Revolt to Sentencing Is Gaining Momentum,* Nat'l L.J., May 17, 1993, at 10 (reporting that two emeriti judges refuse to take drug cases because they believe the statute's mandatory sentencing provisions are too harsh). Moreover, the Guidelines contain a number of offense characteristic provisions, most notably in the area of drug offenses, that are questionable. See, e.g., *United States v. Marshall,* 908 F.2d 1312, 1332–33 (7th Cir. 1990) (Posner J. dissenting) (calling calculation of sentence based on the weight of a carrier substance, where the drug amount is often minuscule in comparison to the substance on which it is transported, in an LSD case "crazy" and "looney"). [Note that currently the carrier medium for LSD is taken into account to determine statutory mandatory minimum sentences, *Chapman v. United States,* 500 U.S. 453 (1991) but not in determining the "base offense level" under the Guidelines, U.S. Sentencing Comm'n, Federal Sentencing Guidelines Manual, 117–18 (1993)].

For additional assessments of the Federal Guidelines movement, see generally Robinson, *Dissent from the United States Sentencing Commission's Proposed Guidelines,* 77 J. Crim. L. & Criminol ogy, 1112 (1986); Silets and Brenner, *Commentary on the Preliminary Draft of the Sentencing Guidelines Issued by the United States Sentencing Commission in September 1986, id.* at 1069. See also Robinson, *A Sentencing System for the 21st Century?,* 66 Tex. L. Rev. 1 (1987); *Sentencing Symposium,* 27 Am. Crim L. Rev. 231 (1989); *Federal Sentencing Guidelines Symposium,* 29 Am. Crim L. Rev. 899 (1992); *Symposium, A Decade of Sentencing Guidelines: Revisiting the Role of the Legislature,* 28 Wake Forest L. Rev. 185 (1993).

[B] Proportionality of Punishment

HARMELIN V. MICHIGAN

Supreme Court of the United States

501 U.S. 957 (1991)

Justice Scalia announced the judgment of the Court and delivered the opinion of the Court with respect to Part V, and an opinion with respect to Parts I, II, III, and IV, in which THE CHIEF Justice joins.

Petitioner was convicted of possessing 672 grams of cocaine and sentenced to a mandatory term of life in prison without possibility of parole [under a statute requiring a life sentence for possession of "more than 650 grams" of cocaine]. The Michigan Court of Appeals initially reversed his conviction because evidence supporting it had been obtained in violation of the Michigan Constitution. . . . On petition for rehearing, the Court of Appeals vacated its prior decision and affirmed petitioner's sentence, rejecting his argument that the sentence was "cruel and unusual" within the meaning of the Eighth Amendment. . . . The Michigan Supreme Court denied leave to appeal, and we granted certiorari. . . .

Petitioner claims that his sentence is unconstitutionally "cruel and unusual" for two reasons. First, because it is "significantly disproportionate" to the crime he committed. Second, because the sentencing judge was statutorily required to impose it, without taking into account the particularized circumstances of the crime and of the criminal.

I

The Eighth Amendment, which applies to the states by virtue of the Fourteenth Amendment, . . . provides: "Excessive bail shall not be imposed, nor cruel and unusual punishment inflicted." In *Rummel v. Estelle,* 445 U.S. 263 (1980), we held that it did not constitute "cruel and unusual punishment" to impose a life sentence, under a recidivist statute, upon a defendant who had been convicted, successively, of fraudulent use of a credit card to obtain $80 worth of goods or services, passing a forged check in the amount of $28.36, and obtaining $120.75 by false pretenses. We said that "one could argue without fear of contradiction by any decision of this Court that for crime concededly classified and classifiable as felonies, that is as punishable by significant terms of imprisonment in a state penitentiary, the length of the sentence actually imposed is purely a matter of legislative prerogative." We specifically rejected the proposition asserted by the dissent, that unconstitutional proportionality could be established by weighing three factors: (1)the gravity of the offense, (2)penalties imposed within the same jurisdiction for similar crimes, and (3)penalties imposed in other jurisdictions for the same offense. A footnote in the opinion, however, said: "This is not to say that a proportionality principal would not come into play in the extreme example mentioned by the dissent, . . . if a legislature made overtime parking a felony punishable by life imprisonment."

* * *

. . . [W]e uttered what has been our last word on the subject to date [in] *Solem v. Helm,* 463 U.S. 277 (1983), [which] set aside under the Eighth Amendment, because it was disproportionate, a sentence of life imprisonment without possibility of parole, imposed under the South Dakota recidivist statute for successive offenses that included three convictions of third-degree burglary, one of obtaining money by false pretenses, one of grand larceny, one of third-offense driving while intoxicated, and one of writing a "no account" check with intent to defraud. . . .

It should be apparent that our 5–4 decision eight years ago in *Solem* was scarcely the expression of clear and accepted constitutional law. . . . Accordingly, we have addressed anew, and in greater detail, the question of whether the Eighth Amendment contains a proportionality guarantee . . . We conclude from this examination that *Solem* was simply wrong; the Eighth Amendment contains no proportionality guarantee.

[In omitted portions of Parts I, II, III, and IV, Justice Scalia traces the historical development of the Eighth Amendment and its interpretation by the Court. This discussion leads him to the conclusion that *Solem v. Helm* should be overruled because the Constitution does not embrace a general principal of proportionality. In the retained portion of Part III, he specifically addresses and criticizes the proportionality doctrine as formerly applied under the three-part test required by *Solem.*]

III

. . . While there are relatively clear historical guidelines and accepted practices that enable judges to determine which modes of punishment are "cruel and unusual," proportionality does not lend itself to such analysis. Neither Congress or any state legislature has ever set out with the objective of crafting a penalty that is "disproportionate," yet . . . many enacted dispositions seem to be so—because they were made for other times or other places, with different social attitudes, different criminal epidemics, different public fears, and different prevailing theories of penology. This is not to say that there are no absolutes; one can imagine extreme examples that no rational person, in no time or place, could accept. But for the same reason these examples are easy to decide, they are certain never to occur. The real function of a constitutional proportionality principal, if it exists, is to enable judges to evaluate a penalty that some assemblage of men and women has considered proportionate—and to say that it is not. For that real-world enterprise, the standards seem so inadequate that the proportionality principle becomes an invitation to imposition of subjective values.

This becomes clear, we think, from a consideration of the three factors that *Solem* found relevant to the proportionality determination: (1) the inherent gravity of the offense, (2) the sentences imposed for similarly grave offenses in the same jurisdiction, and (3) sentences imposed for the same crime in other jurisdictions. . . . As to the first factor: Of course some offenses, involving violent harm to human beings, will always and everywhere be regarded as serious, but that is only half the equation. The issue is what else should be regarded to be as serious as these offenses, or even to be more serious than some of them. On that point, judging by the statutes that Americans have enacted, there is enormous variation—even within a given age, not to mention across the many generations ruled by the Bill of Rights. The State of Massachusetts punishes sodomy more severely than assault and battery . . . whereas in several States, sodomy is not unlawful at all. In Louisiana, one who assaults another with a dangerous weapon faces the same maximum prison term as one who removes a shopping basket "from the parking area or grounds of any store without authorization[;]" . . . and [a] battery that results in "protracted and obvious disfigurement" merits imprisonment "for not more than five years," one half the maximum penalty for theft of livestock or an oilfield seismograph. We may think that the First Congress punished with clear disproportionality when it provided up to seven years in prison and up to $1,000 in fine for "cut[ting] off the ear or ears, cut[ting] out or disabl[ing] the tongue, put[ting] out an eye, cut[ting] off any limb or member of any person with intention to maim or disfigure," but provided the death penalty for "run[ning] away with [a] ship or vessel, or any goods or merchandise to the value of fifty dollars." . . . But then perhaps the citizens of 1791 would think that today's Congress punishes with clear disproportionality when it sanctions "assault by wounding" with up to six months in prison, unauthorized reproduction of the "Smokey Bear" character or name with the same penalty, offering to barter a migratory bird with up to two years in prison, and purloining a "key suited to any lock adopted by the Post Office Department" with a prison term of up to 10 years. Perhaps both we and they would be right, but the point is that there are no textual or historical standards for saying so.

The difficulty of assessing gravity is demonstrated in the very context of the present case: Petitioner acknowledges that a mandatory life sentence might not be "grossly excessive" for possession of cocaine with intent to distribute. . . . But surely whether it is a "grave" offense merely to possess a significant quantity of drugs—thereby facilitating distribution, subjecting the holder to the temptation of distribution, and raising the possibility of theft by others who might distribute—depends entirely upon how odious and socially threatening one believes drug use to be. Would it be "grossly excessive" to provide life imprisonment for "mere possession" of a certain quantity of heavy weaponry? If not, then the only issue is whether the possible dissemination of drugs can be as "grave" as the possible dissemination of heavy weapons. Who are we to say no? The Members of the Michigan Legislature, and not we, know the situation on the streets of Detroit.

The second factor suggested in *Solem* fails for the same reason. One cannot compare the sentences imposed by the jurisdiction for "similarly grave" offenses if there is no objective standard of gravity. Judges will be comparing what they consider comparable. Or, to put the same point differently: when it happens that two offenses judicially determined to be "similarly grave" receive significantly dissimilar penalties, what follows is not that the harsher penalty is unconstitutional, but merely that the legislature does not share the judges' view that the offenses are similarly grave. Moreover, even if "similarly grave" crimes could be identified, the penalties for them would not necessarily be comparable, since there are many other justifications for a difference. For example, since deterrent effect depends not only upon the amount of the penalty but upon its certainty, crimes that are less grave but significantly more difficult to detect may warrant substantially higher penalties. Grave crimes of the sort that will not be deterred by penalty may warrant substantially lower penalties, as may grave crimes of the sort that are normally committed once-in-a-lifetime by otherwise law-abiding citizens who will not profit from rehabilitation. Whether these differences will occur, and to what extent, depends, of course, upon the weight the society accords to deterrence and rehabilitation, rather than retribution, as the objective of criminal punishment (which is an eminently legislative judgment). In fact, it becomes difficult even to speak intelligently of "proportionality," once deterrence and rehabilitation are given significant weight. Proportionality is inherently a retributive concept, and perfect proportionality is the *talionic* law. . . .

As for the third factor mentioned by *Solem*—the character of the sentences imposed by other States for the same crime—it must be acknowledged that that can be applied with clarity and ease. The only difficulty is that it has no conceivable relevance to the Eighth Amendment. That a State is entitled to treat with stern disapproval an act that other States punish with the mildest of sanctions follows *a fortiori* from the undoubted fact that a State may criminalize an act that other States do not criminalize at all. Indeed, a State may criminalize an act that other States choose to reward—punishing, for example, the killing of endangered wild animals for which other States are offering a bounty. What greater disproportion could there be than that? "Absent a constitutionally imposed uniformity inimical to traditional notions of federalism, some State will always bear the distinction of treating particular offenders more severely than any other State." . . . Divers ty not only in policy, but in the means of implementing policy, is the very *raison d'être* of our federal system. Though the different needs and concerns of other States may induce them to treat simple possession of 672 grams of cocaine as a relatively minor offense . . . nothing in the Constitution requires Michigan to follow suit. The Eighth Amendment is not a ratchet, whereby atemporary consensus on leniency for a particular crime fixes a permanent constitutional maximum, disabling the States from giving effect to altered beliefs and responding to changed social conditions.

V

Petitioner claims that his sentence violates the Eighth Amendment for a reason in addition to its alleged disproportionality. He argues that it is "cruel and unusual" to impose a mandatory sentence of such severity, without any consideration of so-called mitigating factors such as, in his case, the fact that he had no prior felony convictions. He apparently contends that the Eighth Amendment requires Michigan to create a sentencing scheme whereby life in prison without possibility of parole is simply the most severe of a range of available penalties that the sentencer may impose after hearing evidence in mitigation and aggravation.

As our earlier discussion should make clear, this claim has no support in the text and history of the Eighth Amendment. Severe, mandatory penalties may be cruel, but they are not unusual in the constitutional sense, having been employed in various forms throughout our Nation's history. As noted earlier, mandatory death sentences abounded in our first Penal Code. They were also common in the several States—both at the time of the founding and throughout the 19th century. . . .

Petitioner's "required mitigation" claim, like his proportionality claim, does find support in our death-penalty jurisprudence. We have held that a capital sentence is cruel and unusual under the Eighth Amendment if it is imposed without an individualized determination that punishment is "appropriate"—whether or not the sentence is "grossly disproportionate." . . . Petitioner asks us to extend this so-called "individualized capital-sentencing doctrine," . . . to an "individualized mandatory life in prison without parole sentencing doctrine." We refuse to do so.

Our cases creating and clarifying the "individualized capital sentencing doctrine" have repeatedly suggested that there is no comparable requirement outside the capital context, because of the qualitative difference between death and all other penalties. . . .

It is true that petitioner's sentence is unique in that it is the second most severe known to the law; but life imprisonment with possibility of parole is also unique in that it is the third most severe. And if petitioner's sentence forecloses some "flexible techniques" for later reducing his sentence . . . it does not foreclose all of them, since there remain the possibilities of retroactive legislative reduction and executive clemency. In some cases, moreover, there will be negligible difference between life without parole and other sentences of imprisonment—for example, a life sentence with eligibility for parole after 20 years, or even a lengthy term sentence without eligibility for parole, given to a 65-year-old man. But even where the difference is the greatest, it cannot be compared with death. We have drawn the line of required individualized sentencing at capital cases, and see no basis for extending it further.

The judgment of the Michigan Court of Appeals is, Affirmed.

Justice KENNEDY, with whom Justice O'CONNOR and Justice SOUTER join, *concurring in part and concurring in the judgment.*

I concur in Part V of the Court's opinion and in the judgment. I write this separate opinion because my approach to the Eighth Amendment proportionality analysis differs from Justice Scalia's. . . . *[S]tare decisis* counsels our adherence to the narrow proportionality principle that has existed in our Eighth Amendment jurisprudence for 80 years. Although our proportionality decisions have not been clear or consistent in all respects, they can be reconciled, and they require us to uphold petitioner's sentence. . . .

[In Part I of his concurring opinion, Justice Kennedy reviews the Court's decisions, concluding that they establish a limited proportionality requirement that does not require "strict proportionality between crime and sentence," but that does forbid "extreme sentences grossly disproportionate to the crime."]

II

With these considerations stated, it is necessary to examine the challenged aspects of petitioner's sentence: its severe length and its mandatory operation.

Petitioner's life sentence without parole is the second most severe penalty permitted by law. It is the same sentence received by the petitioner in *Solem*. Petitioner's crime, however, was far more grave than the crime at issue in *Solem*.

The crime of uttering a no account check at issue in Solem was "'one of the most passive felonies a person could commit.'" . . . It "involved neither violence nor threat of violence to any person," and was "viewed by society as among the less serious offenses." The felonies underlying the defendant's recidivism conviction, moreover, were "all relatively minor." . . . The *Solem* Court contrasted these "minor" offenses with "very serious offenses" such as "a third offense of heroin dealing," and stated that "[n]o one suggests that [a statute providing for life imprisonment without parole] may not be applied constitutionally to fourth-time heroin dealers or other violent criminals."

Petitioner was convicted of possession of more than 650 grams (over 1.5 pounds) of cocaine. This amount of pure cocaine has a potential yield of between 32,500 and 65,000 doses. From any standpoint, this crime falls in a different category from the relatively minor, nonviolent crime at issue in *Solem*. Possession, use, and distribution of illegal drugs represents "one of the greatest problems affecting the health and welfare of our population." . . . Petitioner's suggestion that his crime was nonviolent and victimless . . . is false to the point of absurdity. To the contrary, petitioner's crime threatened to cause grave harm to society.

Quite apart from the pernicious effects on the individual who consumes illegal drugs, such drugs relate to crime in at least three ways: (1) A drug user may commit crime because of drug-induced changes in physiological functions, cognitive ability, and mood; (2) A drug user may commit crime in order to obtain money to buy drugs; and (3) A violent crime may occur as part of the drug business or culture. . . . Studies bear out these possibilities, and demonstrate a direct nexus between illegal drugs and crimes of violence. To mention but a few examples, 57 percent of a national sample of males arrested in 1989 for homicide tested positive for illegal drugs . . . The comparable statistics for assault, robbery, and weapons arrests were 55, 73 and 63 percent, respectively. In Detroit, Michigan in 1988, 68 percent of a sample of male arrestees and 81 percent of a sample of female arrestees tested positive for illegal drugs. . . . Fifty-one percent of males and seventy-one percent of females tested positive for cocaine. And last year an estimated 60 percent of the homicides in Detroit were drug-related, primarily cocaine-related.

These and other facts and reports detailing the pernicious effects of the drug epidemic in this country do not establish that Michigan's penalty scheme is correct or the most just in any abstract sense. But they do demonstrate that the Michigan Legislature could with reason conclude that the threat posed to the individual and society by possession of this large an amount of cocaine—in terms of violence, crime, and social displacement—is momentous enough to warrant the deterrence and retribution of a life sentence without parole. . . .

* * *

Petitioner and *amici* contend that our proportionality decisions require a comparative analysis between petitioner's sentence and sentences imposed for other crimes in Michigan and sentences imposed for the same crime in other jurisdictions. Given the serious nature of petitioner's crime, no such comparative analysis is necessary. Although *Solem* considered these comparative factors after analyzing "the gravity of the offense and the harshness of the penalty," it did not announce a rigid three-part test.

. . . *Solem* is best understood as holding that comparative analysis within and between jurisdictions is not always relevant to proportionality review. The Court stated that "it may be helpful to compare sentences imposed on other criminals in the same jurisdiction," and that "courts may find it useful to compare the sentences imposed for commission of the same crime in other jurisdictions." . . .

A better reading of our cases leads to the conclusion that intra-and inter-jurisdictional analyses are appropriate only in the rare case in which a threshold comparison of the crime committed and the sentence imposed leads to an inference of gross disproportionality. In *Solem and Weems v. United States* 217 U.S. 349 (196)], decisions in which the Court invalidated sentences as disproportionate, we performed a comparative analysis of sentences after determining that the sentence imposed was grossly excessive punishment for the crime committed. . . .

The proper role for comparative analysis of sentences, then, is to validate an initial judgment that a sentence is grossly disproportionate to a crime. This conclusion neither "eviscerate[s]" *Solem,* nor "abandon[s]" its second and third factors, as the dissent charges. . . . In light of the gravity of petitioner's offense, a comparison of his crime with his sentence does not give rise to an inference of gross disproportionality, and comparative analysis of his sentence with others in Michigan and across the Nation need not be performed.

Petitioner also attacks his sentence because of its mandatory nature. Petitioner would have us hold that any severe penalty scheme requires individualized sentencing so that a judicial official may consider mitigating circumstances. Our precedents do not support this proposition, and petitioner presents no convincing reason to fashion an exception or adopt a new rule in the case before us. The Court demonstrates that our Eighth Amendment capital decisions reject any requirement of individualized sentencing in noncapital cases.

Justice WHITE, with whom Justice BLACKMUN and Justice STEVENS join, *dissenting*.

The Eighth Amendment provides that "[e]xcessive bail shall not be required, nor excessive fines imposed, nor cruel and unusual punishments inflicted." Justice Scalia concludes that "the Eighth Amendment contains no proportionality guarantee." Accordingly, he says *Solem v. Helm,* "was simply wrong" in holding otherwise, as would be the Court's other cases interpreting the Amendment to contain a proportionality principle. Justice Kennedy, on the other hand, asserts that the Eighth Amendment's proportionality principle is so "narrow," that *Solem's* analysis should be reduced from three factors to one. With all due respect, I dissent.

[The dissenters argue that the Court's cases embody a proportionality component as recognized in *Solem v. Helm.*]

While Justice Scalia seeks to deliver a swift death sentence to *Solem,* Justice Kennedy prefers to eviscerate it, leaving only an empty shell. The analysis Justice Kennedy proffers is contradicted by the language of *Solem* itself and by our other cases interpreting the Eighth Amendment.

In *Solem,* the Court identified three major factors to consider in assessing whether a punishment violates the Eighth Amendment: "the gravity of the offense and the harshness of the penalty,"; "the sentences imposed on other criminals in the same jurisdiction,"; and "the sentences imposed for commission of the same crime in other jurisdictions." Justice Kennedy, however, maintains that "one factor may be sufficient to determine the constitutionality of a particular sentence," and that there is no need to consider the second and third factors unless "a threshold comparison of the crime committed and the sentence imposed leads to an inference of gross disproportionality." *Solem* is directly to the contrary, for there the Court made clear that "no one factor will be dispositive in a given case," and "no single criterion can identify when a sentence is so grossly disproportionate that it violates the Eighth Amendment," "[b]ut a combination of objective factors can make such analysis possible."

Justice Kennedy's abandonment of the second and third factors set forth in *Solem* makes any attempt at an objective proportionality analysis futile. The first prong of *Solem* requires a court to consider two discrete factors—the gravity of the offense and the severity of the punishment. A court is not expected to consider the interaction of these two elements and determine whether "the sentence imposed was grossly excessive punishment for the crime committed." Were a court to attempt such an assessment, it would have no basis for its determination that a sentence was—or was not—disproportionate, other than the "subjective views of individual [judges]," . . . which is the very sort of analysis our Eighth Amendment jurisprudence has shunned. . . .Justice Kennedy asserts that "our decisions recognize that we lack clear objective standards to distinguish between sentences for different terms of years," citing *Rummel* and *Solem* as support. But *Solem* recognized that "[f]or sentences of imprisonment, the problem is not so much one of ordering, but one of line-drawing. It is clear that a 25-year sentence generally is more severe than a 15-year sentence, but in most cases it would be difficult to decide that the former violates the Eighth Amendment while the latter does not. Decisions of this kind, although troubling, are not unique to this area. The courts are constantly called upon to draw similar lines in a variety of contexts." . . . The Court compared line-drawing in the Eighth Amendment context to that regarding the Sixth Amendment right to a speedy trial and right to a jury before concluding that "courts properly may look to the practices in other jurisdictions in deciding where lines between sentences should be drawn." Indeed, only when a comparison is made with penalties for other crimes and in other jurisdictions can a court begin to make an objective assessment about a given sentence's constitutional proportionality, giving due deference to "public attitudes concerning a particular sentence."

Because there is no justification for overruling or limiting *Solem,* it remains to apply that case's proportionality analysis to the sentence imposed on petitioner. Application of the *Solem* factors to the statutorily mandated punishment at issue here reveals that the punishment fails muster under *Solem* and, consequently, under the Eighth Amendment to the Constitution.

Petitioner, a first-time offender, was convicted of possession of 672 grams of cocaine. The statute under which he was convicted . . . provides that a person who knowingly or intentionally possesses any of various narcotics, including cocaine, "[w]hich is in an amount of 650 grams or more of any mixture containing that substance is guilty of a felony and shall be imprisoned for life." No particular degree of drug purity is required for a conviction. Other statutes make clear that an individual convicted of possessing this quantity of drugs is not eligible for parole. A related statute . . . which was enacted at the same time as the statute under which petitioner was convicted, mandates the same penalty of life imprisonment without possibility of parole for someone who "manufacture[s], deliver[s], or possess[es] with intent to manufacture or deliver," 650 grams or more of a narcotic mixture. There is no room for judicial discretion in the imposition of the life sentence upon conviction. The asserted purpose of the legislative enactment of these statutes was to " 'stem drug traffic' " and reach " 'drug deale rs.' "

The first *Solem* factor requires a reviewing court to assess the gravity of the offense and the harshness of the penalty. . . . The mandatory sentence of life imprisonment without possibility of parole "is the most severe punishment that the State could have imposed on any criminal for any crime," for Michigan has no death penalty.

Although these factors are "by no means exhaustive," . . . in evaluating the gravity of the offense, it is appropriate to consider "the harm caused or threatened to the victim or society," based on such things as the degree of violence involved in the crime and "[t]he absolute magnitude of the crime," and "the culpability of the offender," including the degree of requisite intent and the offender's motive in committing the crime.

Drugs are without doubt a serious societal problem. To justify such a harsh mandatory penalty as that imposed here, however, the offense should be one which will always warrant that punishment. Mere possession of drugs—even in such a large quantity—is not so serious an offense that it will always warrant, much less mandate, life imprisonment without possibility of parole. Unlike crimes directed against the persons and property of others, possession of drugs affects the criminal who uses the drugs most directly. The ripple effect on society caused by possession of drugs, through related crimes, lost productivity, health problems, and the like, is often not the direct consequence of possession, but of the resulting addiction, something which this Court held in *Robinson v. California* [376 U.S. 660 (1962)], cannot be made a crime.

To be constitutionally proportionate, punishment must be tailored to a defendant's personal responsibility and moral guilt. . . . Justice Kennedy attempts to justify the harsh mandatory sentence imposed on petitioner by focusing on the subsidiary effects of drug use, and thereby ignores this aspect of our Eighth Amendment jurisprudence. While the collateral consequences of drugs such as cocaine are indisputably severe, they are not unlike those which flow from the misuse of other, legal, substances. For example, in considering the effects of alcohol on society, the Court has stressed that "[n]o one can seriously dispute the magnitude of the drunken driving problem or the States' interest in eradicating it," . . . but at the same time has recognized that the severity of the problem "cannot excuse the need for scrupulous adherence to our constitutional principles," . . . Thus, the Court has held that a drunken driver who has been prosecuted for traffic offenses arising from an accident cannot, consistent with the Double Jeopardy Clause, subsequently be prosecuted for the death of the accident victim. Likewise, the Court scrutinized closely a state program of vehicle checkpoints designed to detect drunken drivers before holding that the brief intrusion upon motorists is consistent with the Fourth Amendment. It is one thing to uphold a checkpoint designed to detect drivers then under the influence of a drug that creates a present risk that they will harm others. It is quite something else to uphold petitioner's sentence because of the collateral consequences which might issue, however indirectly, from the drugs he possessed. Indeed, it is inconceivable that a State could rationally choose to penalize one who possesses large quantities of alcohol in a manner similar to that in which Michigan has chosen to punish petitioner for cocaine possession, because of the tangential effects which might ultimately be traced to the alcohol at issue. . . .

The "absolute magnitude" of petitioner's crime is not exceptionally serious. Because possession is necessarily a lesser included offense of possession with intent to distribute, it is odd to punish the former as severely as the latter. . . . Nor is the requisite intent for the crime sufficient to render it particularly grave. To convict someone under the possession statute, it is only necessary to prove that the defendant knowingly possessed a mixture containing narcotics which weighs at least 650 grams. There is no *mens rea* requirement of intent to distribute the drugs, as there is in the parallel statute. Indeed, the presence of a separate statute which reaches manufacture, delivery, or possession with intent to do either, undermines the State's position that the purpose of the possession statute was to reach drug dealers. . . .

There is an additional concern present here. The State has conceded that it chose not to prosecute Harmelin under the statute prohibiting possession with intent to deliver, because it was "not necessary and not prudent to make it more difficult for us to win a prosecution." The State thus aimed to avoid having to establish Harmelin's intent to distribute by prosecuting him instead under the possession statute. Because the statutory punishment for the two crimes is the same, the State succeeded in punishing Harmelin as if he had been convicted of the more serious crime without being put to the test of proving his guilt on those charges.

The second prong of the *Solem* analysis is an examination of "the sentences imposed on other criminals in the same jurisdiction." As noted above, there is no death penalty in Michigan; consequently, life without parole, the punishment mandated here, is the harshest penalty available. It is reserved for three crimes: first-degree murder; manufacture, distribution, or possession with intent to manufacture or distribute 650 grams or more of narcotics; and possession of 650 grams or more of narcotics. Crimes directed against the persons and property of others—such as second-degree murder; rape; and armed robbery—do not carry such a harsh mandatory sentence, although they do provide for the possibility of a life sentence in the exercise of judicial discretion. It is clear that petitioner "has been treated in the same manner as, or more severely than, criminals who have committed far more serious crimes."

The third factor set forth in *Solem* examines "the sentences imposed for commission of the same crime in other jurisdictions." No other jurisdiction imposes a punishment nearly as severe as Michigan's for possession of the amount of drugs at issue here. Of the remaining 49 States, only Alabama provides for a mandatory sentence of life imprisonment without possibility of parole for a first-time drug offender, and then only when a defendant possesses ten kilograms or more of cocaine. Possession of the amount of cocaine at issue here would subject an Alabama defendant to a mandatory minimum sentence of only five years in prison. Even under the Federal Sentencing Guidelines, with all relevant enhancements, petitioner's sentence would barely exceed ten years. Thus, "[i]t appears that [petitioner] was treated more severely than he would have been in any other State." Indeed, the fact that no other jurisdiction provides such a severe, mandatory penalty for possession of this quantity of drugs is enough to establish "the degree of national consensus this Court has previously thought sufficient to label a particular punishment cruel and unusual." . . .

Application of *Solem's* proportionality analysis leaves no doubt that the Michigan statute at issue fails constitutional muster. The statutorily mandated penalty of life without possibility of parole for possession of narcotics is unconstitutionally disproportionate in that it violates the Eighth Amendment's prohibition against cruel and unusual punishment. Consequently, I would reverse the decision of the Michigan Court of Appeals.

[The dissenting opinions of Justices Marshall and Justice Stevens, with whom Justice Blackmun joins, are omitted.]

NOTES AND QUESTIONS

1. Is the proportionality principle essentially abandoned if knowing possession of large amounts of cocaine is punished exactly the same as murder by

torture? Suppose the defendant in *Harmelin* had been asked by a friend to simply hold the drugs for him as a favor for a short period of time. Could the defendant receive a life sentence under the Michigan statute if he is apprehended and convicted for possession under these circumstances even though he neither uses, deals in, nor profits from illegal drugs? Would such a defendant essentially be at the mercy of the prosecutor? Given the view of the evils of cocaine expressed by some members of the *Harmelin* Court, might some prosecutors seek life sentences against *mere* possessors on deterrence theory grounds?

Suppose the Michigan statute required a life sentence for possession of specified quantities of cocaine whether or not the possessor knows the possessed substance is cocaine. After *Harmelin,* does any constitutional principle preclude a sentence of life imprisonment? See the materials *infra* on the "act" of possession, § 3.02[B], on "mistake of fact," § 4.06[A], and on "strict liability," § 4.07.

Subsequent to the United States Supreme Court's opinion in *Harmelin,* the Michigan Supreme Court held unconstitutional, under that state's prohibition against cruel or unusual punishment, the statutory provision upheld under the Eighth Amendment by the *Harmelin* Court. *People v. Bullock,* 440 Mich. 15, 485 N.W.2d 866 (1992). Does it make sense to claim that the criminal law embraces a "proportionality principle" if the same punishment is constitutionally disproportionate under state but not under federal law?

2. Compare Justice Scalia's views on proportionality in his *Harmelin* opinion with those expressed in his concurring opinion in the *Austin* case, *supra* p. 79, relating to when fines might be "excessive" under the Eighth Amendment. Does it make sense to maintain a constitutionally mandated proportionality principal for "excessive fines" but not for excessive imprisonment?

3. As should be clear from *Harmelin,* judicial findings of unconstitutional disproportionality in sentences of imprisonment have been a rare phenomenon. A few lower courts have invalidated prison sentences under proportionality analysis similar to that rejected by Justice Scalia in *Harmelin.* See, e.g., *Downey v. Perini,* 518 F.2d 1288 (6th Cir. 1975) (60 years prison for possession and sale of "very small" amounts of marijuana violates the Eighth Amendment); *In re Lynch,* 503 P.2d 921 (1972) (life sentence for second indecent exposure offense violates cruel or unusual punishments proscription of the California Constitution).

On the other hand, most courts routinely reject claims of unconstitutionally excessive imprisonment. See, e.g., *McDougle v. Maxwell,* 203 N.E.2d 334 (1964) (20-year sentence for operating a motor vehicle without the owner's consent not unconstitutional).

4. How substantial is the claim that assessing the relative seriousness of crime is essentially a "subjective" enterprise? Assuming that at least a rough ranking of crime according to relative seriousness can be achieved, what is the proper "proportionate" punishment for each? For an illustration of the divergence of scholarly opinion about which penalties are proportionate to given crimes, compare the kinds and degrees of penalties recommended in A. von Hirsch, Doing Justice 106–17, with those spelled out in D. Fogel, We Are the Living Proof: The Justice Model for Corrections 254–55 (1975).

Is the problem of proportioning punishment even less "objective" when individual culpability considerations are factored in? Consider the following:

BEDAU, *CONCESSIONS TO RETRIBUTION IN PUNISHMENT*

Justice and Punishment 51, 64

(J. Cederblom and W. Blizek eds. 1977)

. . . Even if we can agree that a malicious killer is morally and legally more culpable than an accidental killer, how are we to answer the question, "How much more culpable is he—twice as culpable? ten times? seven and one half times?" Second, the principle needs a mode of measurement for degrees of harm inflicted by different offenses. Granted that murder is more harmful than rape, how much worse is it in terms of harm to the victim (or to society)? Twice as harmful? Ten times as harmful? The concepts of culpability and harmfulness are not like the concepts of temperature or ductility because we lack standard units in terms of which to measure them, something we do not lack for the latter. Third, we need a way of combining the two concepts—culpability and harmfulness—into one common concept of gravity of offense. Without a common measure for these concepts, there is no way of telling, e.g., whether an offense that falls on the midpoint of the culpability scale and the bottom of the harmfulness scale is exactly as grave or half as grave, or twice as grave, as an offense that falls on the mid-point of the harmfulness scale but at the bottom of the culpability scale. Culpability and harmfulness seem to be not even as like each other as the proverbial apples and oranges; the latter are, after all members of a common genus, whereas no genus subsumes both degrees of fault and degrees of harm.

UNITED STATES V. BAJAKAJIAN

Supreme Court of the United States

524 U.S. 321 (1998)

Justice THOMAS delivered the opinion of the Court

Respondent Hosep Bajakajian attempted to leave the United States without reporting, as required by federal law, that he was transporting more than $10,000 in currency. Federal law also provides that a person convicted of willfully violating this reporting requirement shall forfeit to the government "any property. . . involved in such offense." The question in this case is whether forfeiture of the entire $357,144 that respondent failed to declare would violate the Excessive Fines Clause of the Eighth Amendment. We hold that it would, because full forfeiture of respondent's currency would be grossly disproportional to the gravity of his offense.

I

On June 9, 1994, respondent, his wife, and his two daughters were waiting at Los Angeles International Airport to board a flight to Italy; their final destination was Cyprus. Using dogs trained to detect currency by its smell, customs inspectors discovered some $230,000 in case in the Bajakajians' checked baggage. A customs inspector approached respondent and his wife and told them that they were required to report all money in excess of $10,000 in their possession or in their baggage. Respondent said that he had $8,000 and that his wife had another $7,000, but that the family had no additional currency to declare. A search of their carry-on bags, purse, and wallet revealed more cash; in all, customs inspectors found $357,144. The currency was seized and respondent was taken into custody. A federal grand jury indicated respondent on three counts. Count One charged him with failing to report, as required by 31 U.S.C. § 5316(a)(1)(A), that he was transporting more than $10,000 outside the United States, and with doing so "willfully," in violation of § 5322(a). Count Two charged him with making a false material statement to the United States Customs Service, in violation of 18 U.S.C. § 1001. Count Three sought forfeiture of the $357,144 pursuant to 18 U.S.C. § 982(a)(1), which provides:

> The court, in imposing sentence on a person convicted of an offense in violation of section . . . 5316, . . . shall order that the person forfeit to the United States any property, real or personal, involved in such offense, or any property traceable to such property. 18 U.S.C. § 982(a)(1).

Respondent pleaded guilty to the failure to report in Count One; the Government agreed to dismiss the false statement charge in Count Two; and respondent elected to have a bench trial on the forfeiture in Count Three. After the bench trial, the District Court found that the entire $357,144 was subject to forfeiture because it was "involved in" the offense. The court also found that the funds were not connected to any other crime and that respondent was transporting the money to repay a lawful debt. The District Court further found that respondent had failed to report that he was taking the currency out of the United States because of fear stemming from "cultural differences": Respondent, who had grown up as a member of the Armenian minority in Syria had a "distrust for the Government."

Although § 982(a)(1) directs sentencing courts to impose full forfeiture, the District Court concluded that such forfeiture would be "extraordinarily harsh" and "grossly disproportionate to the offense in question," and that it would therefore violate the Excessive Fines Clause. The court instead ordered forfeiture of $15,000, in addition to a sentence of three years of probation and a fine of $5,000 the maximum fine under the Sentencing Guidelines because the court believed that the maximum Guidelines fine was "too little" and that a $15,000 forfeiture would "make up for what I think a reasonable fine should be."

The United States appealed, seeking full forfeiture of respondent's currency as provided in § 982(a)(1). The Court of Appeals for the Ninth Circuit affirmed. Applying Circuit precedent, the Court held that, to satisfy the Excessive Fines Clause, a forfeiture must fulfill two conditions: The property forfeited must be an "instrumentality" of the crime committed, and the value of the property must be proportional to the culpability of the owner. A majority of the panel determined that the currency was not an "instrumentality" of the crime of failure to report because " '[t]he crime [in a currency reporting offense] is the withholding of information,. . . not the possession or the transportation of the money.'" The majority therefore held that § 982(a)(1) could never satisfy the Excessive Fines Clause in cases involving forfeitures of currency and that it was unnecessary to apply the "proportionality" prong of the test. Although the panel majority concluded that the Excessive Fines Clause did not permit forfeiture of any of the unreported currency, it held that it lacked jurisdiction to set the $15,000 forfeiture aside because respondent had not cross-appealed to challenge that forfe

Judge Wallace concurred in the result. He viewed respondent's currency as an instrumentality of the crime because "without the currency, there can be no offense," and he criticized the majority for "strik[ing] down a portion of the statue. He nonetheless agreed that full forfeiture would violate the Excessive Fines Clause in respondent's case, based upon the "proportionality" prong of the Ninth Circuit test. Finding no clear error in the District Court's factual findings, he concluded that the reduced forfeiture of $15,000 was proportional to respondent's culpability.

Because the Court of Appeals' holding that the forfeiture ordered by § 982(a)(1) was per se unconstitutional in cases of currency forfeiture invalidated a portion of an act of Congress, we granted certiorari.

II

The Eighth Amendment provides: "Excessive bail shall not be required, nor excessive fines imposed, nor cruel and unusual punishments inflicted." This Court has had little occasion to interpret, and has never actually applied, the Excessive Fines Clause. We have, however, explained that at the time the Constitution was adopted, "the word 'fine' was understood to mean a payment to a sovereign as punishment for some offense." The Excessive Fines Clause thus "limits the government's power to extract payments, whether in cash or in kind,'as punishment for some offense.'" Forfeiture payments in kind are thus "fines" if they continue punishment for an offense.

[The Court found that the forfeiture involved in the case constituted a punitive fine. The Court also suggested that had the action been a "civil, *in rem* forfeiture" rather than an *in personam* action brought against respondent, no "fine" would have been imposed.]

III

Because the forfeiture of respondent's currency constitutes punishment and is thus a "fine" within the meaning of the Excessive Fines Clause, we now turn to the question of whether it is "excessive."

A

The touchstone of the constitutional inquiry under the Excessive Fines Clause is the principle of proportionality: The amount of the forfeiture must bear some relationship to the gravity of the offense that it is designed to punish. Until today, however, we have not articulated a standard for determining whether a punitive forfeiture is constitutionally excessive. We now hold that a punitive forfeiture violates the Excessive Fines Clause if it is grossly disproportional to the gravity of a defendant's offense.

The text and history of the Excessive Fines Clause demonstrate the centrality of proportionality to the excessiveness inquiry; nonetheless, they provide little guidance as to how disproportional a punitive forfeiture must be to the gravity of an offense in order to be "excessive." Excessive means surpassing the usual, the proper, or a normal measure of proportion. The constitutional question that we address, however, is just how proportional to a criminal offense a fine must be, and the text of the Excessive Fines Clause does not answer it.

Nor does its history. The Clause was little discussed in the First Congress and the debates over the ratification of the Bill of Rights. As we have previously noted, the Clause was taken verbatim from the English Bill of Rights of 1689. That document's prohibition against excessive fines was a reaction to the abuses of the King's judges during the reigns of the Stuarts, but the fines that those judges imposed were described contemporaneously only in the most general terms. Similarly, Magna Charta which the Stuart judges were accused of subverting required only that amercements (the medieval predecessors of fines) should be proportioned to the offense and that they should not deprive a wrongdoer of his livelihood:

> A Free-man shall not be amerced for a small fault, but after the manner of the fault; and for a great fault after the greatness thereof, saving to him his contenement; (2) and a Merchant likewise, saving to him his merchandise; (3) and any other's villain than ours shall be likewise amerced, saving his wainage. Magna Charta, 9 Hen. III, ch. 14 (1225), 1 Stat. at Large 6-7 (1762 ed.).

None of these sources suggests how disproportional to the gravity of an offense a fine must be in order to be deemed constitutionally excessive.

We must therefore rely on other considerations in deriving a constitutional excessiveness standard, and there are two that we find particularly relevant. The first, which we have emphasized in our cases interpreting the Cruel and Unusual Punishments Clause, is that judgments about the appropriate punishment for an offense belong in the first instance to the legislature. The second is that any judicial determination regarding the gravity of a particular criminal offense will be inherently imprecise. Both of these principles counsel against requiring strict proportionality between the amount of a punitive forfeiture and the gravity of a criminal offense, and we therefore adopt the standard of gross disproportionality articulated in our Cruel and Unusual Punishments Clause precedents.

In applying this standard, the district courts in the first instance, and the courts of appeals, reviewing the proportionality determination de novo, must compare the amount of the forfeiture to the gravity of the defendants' offense. If the amount of the forfeiture is grossly disproportional to the gravity of the defendant's offense, it is unconstitutional.

B

Under this standard, the forfeiture of respondent's entire $357,144 would violate the Excessive Fines Clause. Respondent's crime was solely a reporting offense. It was permissible to transport the currency out of the country so long as he reported it. Section 982(a)(1) orders currency to be forfeited for a "willful" violation of the reporting requirement. Thus, the essence of respondent's crime is a willful failure to report the removal of currency from the United States. Furthermore, as the District Court found, respondent's violation was unrelated to any other illegal activities. The money was the proceeds of legal activity and was to be used to repay a lawful debt. Whatever his other vices, respondent does not fit into the class of persons for whom the statute was principally designed: He is not a money launderer, a drug trafficker, or a tax evader. And under the Sentencing Guidelines, the maximum sentence that could have been imposed on respondent was six months, while the maximum fine was $5,000. Such penalties confirm a minimal level of culpability.

The harm that respondent caused was also minimal. Failure to report his currency affected only one party, the Government, and in a relatively minor way. There was no fraud on the United States, and respondent caused no loss to the public fisc. Had his crime gone undetected, the Government would have been deprived only of the information that $357,144 had left the country. The Government and the dissent contend that there is a correlation between the amount forfeited and the harm that the Government would have suffered had the crime gone undetected. We disagree. There is no inherent proportionality in such a forfeiture. It is impossible to conclude, for example, that the harm respondent caused is anywhere near 30 times greater than that caused by a hypothetical drug dealer who willfully fails to report taking $12,000 out of the country in order to purchase drugs.

Comparing the gravity of respondent's crime with the $357,144 forfeiture the Government seeks, we conclude that such a forfeiture would be grossly disproportional to the gravity of his offense. It is larger than the $5,000 fine imposed by the District Court by many orders of magnitude, and it bears no articulable correlation to any injury suffered by the Government.

C

Finally, we must reject the contention that the proportionality of full forfeiture is demonstrated by the fact that the First Congress enacted statutes requiring full forfeiture of goods involved in customs offenses or the payment of monetary penalties proportioned to the goods' value. It is argued that the enactment of these statutes at roughly the same time that the Eighth Amendment was ratified suggests that full forfeiture, in the customs context at least, is a proportional punishment. The early customs statutes, however, do not support such a conclusion because, unlike § 982(a)(1), the type of forfeiture that they imposed was not considered punishment for a criminal offense.

Certain of the early customs statutes required the forfeiture of goods imported in violation of the customs laws, and, in some instances, the vessels carrying them as well. These forfeitures, however, were civil *in rem* forfeitures, in which the Government proceeded against the property itself on the theory that it was guilty, not against a criminal defendant. Such forfeitures sought to vindicate the Government's underlying property right in customs duties, and like other traditional *in rem* forfeitures, they were not considered at the

Founding to be punishment for an offense. They therefore indicate nothing about the proportionality of the punitive forfeiture at issue here.

Other statutes, however, imposed monetary "forfeitures" proportioned to the value of the goods involved. These "forfeitures" were similarly not considered punishments for criminal offenses. . . .

The early monetary forfeitures . . . were considered not as punishment for an offense, but rather as serving the remedial purpose of reimbursing the Government for the losses accruing from the evasion of customs duties. They were thus no different in purpose and effect than the *in rem* forfeitures of the goods to whose value they were proportioned. By contrast, the full forfeiture mandated by § 982(a)(1) in this case serves no remedial purpose; it is clearly punishment. The customs statutes enacted by the First Congress, therefore, in no way suggest that § 982(a)(1)'s currency forfeiture is constitutionally proportional.

* * *

For the foregoing reasons, the full forfeiture of respondent's currency would violate the Excessive Fines Clause. The judgment of the Court of Appeals is Affirmed.

Justice KENNEDY, with whom THE CHIEF JUSTICE, Justice O'CONNOR, and Justice SCALIA join, *dissenting.*

For the first time in its history, the Court strikes down a fine as excessive under the Eighth Amendment. The decision is disturbing both for its specific holding and for the broader upheaval it foreshadows. At issue is a fine Congress fixed in the amount of the currency respondent sought to smuggle or to transport without reporting. If a fine calibrated with this accuracy fails the Court's test, its decision portends serious disruption of a vast range of statutory fines. The Court all but says the offense is not serious anyway. This disdain for the statute is wrong as an empirical matter and disrespectful of the separation of powers. The irony of the case is that, in the end, it may stand for narrowing constitutional protection rather than enhancing it. To make its rationale work, the Court appears to remove important classes of fines from any excessiveness inquiry at all. This, too, is unsound; and with all respect, I dissent.

II

Turning to the question of excessiveness, the majority states the test: A defendant must prove a gross disproportion before a court will strike down a fine as excessive. This test would be a proper way to apply the Clause, if only the majority were faithful in applying it. The Court does not, however, explain why in this case forfeiture of all of the cash would have suffered from a gross disproportion. The offense is a serious one, and respondent's smuggling and failing to report were willful. The cash was lawful to own, but this fact shows only that the forfeiture was a fine; it cannot also prove that the fine was excessive.

The majority illuminates its test with a principle of deference. Courts "'should grant substantial deference to the broad authority that legislatures necessarily possess'" in setting punishments. Again, the principle is should but the implementation is not. The majority's assessment of the crime accords no deference, let alone substantial deference, to the judgment of Congress. Congress deems the crime serious, but the Court does not. Under the congressional statute, the crime is punishable by a prison sentence, a heavy fine, and the forfeiture here at issue. As the statute makes clear, the Government needs the information to investigate other serious crimes, and it needs the penalties to ensure compliance.

A

By affirming, the majority in effect approves a meager $15,000 forfeiture. The majority's holding purports to be narrower, saying only that forfeiture of the entire $357,144 would be excessive. This narrow holding is artificial in constricting the question presented for this Court's review. The statute mandates forfeiture of the entire $357,144. The only ground for reducing the forfeiture, then, is that any higher amount would be unconstitutional. The majority affirms the reduced $15,000 forfeiture on de novo review, which it can do only if a forfeiture of even $15,001 would have suffered from a gross disproportion. Indeed, the majority leaves open whether the $15,000 forfeiture itself was too great. Money launderers, among the principal targets of this statute, may get an even greater return from their crime.

The majority does not explain why respondent's knowing, willful, serious crime deserves no higher penalty than $15,000. It gives only a cursory explanation of why forfeiture of all of the money would have suffered from a gross disproportion. The majority justifies its evisceration of the fine because the money was legal to have and came from a legal source. This fact, however, shows only that the forfeiture was a fine, not that it was excessive. As the majority puts it, respondent's money was lawful to possess, was acquired in a lawful manner, and was lawful to export. It was not, however, lawful to possess the money while concealing and smuggling it. Even if one overlooks this problem, the apparent lawfulness of the money adds nothing to the argument. If the items possessed had been dangerous or unlawful to own, for instance narcotics, the forfeiture would have been remedial and would not have been a fine at all. If respondent had acquired the money in an unlawful manner, it would have been forfeitable as proceeds of the crime. As a rule, forfeitures of criminal proceeds serve the nonpunitive ends of making restitution to the rightful owners and of compelling the surrender of property held without right or ownership. Most forfeitures of proceeds, as a consequence, are not fines at all, let alone excessive fines. Hence, the lawfulness of the money shows at most that the forfeiture was a fine; it cannot at the same time prove that the fine was excessive.

B

1

In assessing whether there is a gross disproportion, the majority concedes, we must grant "'substantial deference'" to Congress' choice of penalties. Yet, ignoring its own command, the Court sweeps aside Congress' reasoned judgment and substitutes arguments that are little more than specul

Congress considered currency smuggling and non-reporting a serious crime and imposed commensurate penalties. It authorized punishments of five years' imprisonment, a $250,000 fine, plus forfeiture of all the undeclared cash. Congress found the offense standing alone is a serious crime, for the same statute doubles the fines and imprisonment for failures to report cash "while violating another law of the United States." 31 U.S.C. § 5322(b). Congress experimented with lower penalties on the order of one year in prison plus a $1,000 fine, but it found the punishments inadequate to deter lucrative money laundering. The Court today rejects this judgment.

The Court rejects the congressional judgment because, it says, the Sentencing Guidelines cap the appropriate fine at $5,000. The purpose of the Guidelines, however, is to select punishments with precise proportion, not to opine on what is a gross disproportion. In addition, there is no authority for elevating the Commission's judgment of what is prudent over the congressional judgment of what is constitutional. The majority, then, departs from its promise of deference in the very case announcing the standard.

The Court's argument is flawed, moreover, by a serious misinterpretation of the Guidelines on their face. The Guidelines do not stop at the $5,000 fine the majority cites. They augment it with this vital point: "Forfeiture is to be imposed upon a convicted defendant as provided by statute." The fine thus supplements the forfeiture; it does not replace it. Far from contradicting congressional judgment on the offense, the Guidelines implement and mandate it.

2

The crime of smuggling or failing to report cash is more serious than the Court is willing to acknowledge. The drug trade, money laundering, and tax evasion all depend in part on smuggled and unreported cash. Congress enacted the reporting requirement because secret exports of money were being used in organized crime, drug trafficking, money laundering, and other crimes. Likewise, tax evaders were using cash exports to dodge hundreds of millions of dollars in taxes owed to the Government.

The Court does not deny the importance of these interests but claims they are not implicated here because respondent managed to disprove any link to other crimes. Here, to be sure, the Government had no affirmative proof that the money was from an illegal source or for an illegal purpose. This will often be the case, however. By its very nature, money laundering is difficult to prove; for if the money launderers have done their job, the money appears to be clean. The point of the statute, which provides for even heavier penalties if a second crime can be proved, is to mandate forfeiture regardless. It is common practice, of course, for a cash courier not to confess a tainted source but to stick to a well-rehearsed story. The kingpin, the real owner, need not come forward to make a legal claim to the funds. He has his own effective enforcement measures to ensure delivery at destination or return at origin if the scheme is thwarted. He is, of course, not above punishing the courier who deviates from the story and informs. The majority is wrong, then, to assume *in personam* forfeitures cannot affect kingpins, as their couriers will claim to own the money and pay the penalty out of their master's funds. Even if the courier confessed, the kingpin could face an *in personam* forfeiture for his agent's authorized acts, for the kingpin would be a co-principal in the commission of the crime.

In my view, forfeiture of all the unreported currency is sustainable whenever a willful violation is proven. The facts of this case exemplify how hard it can be to prove ownership and other crimes, and they also show respondent is far from an innocent victim. For one thing, he was guilty of repeated lies to Government agents and suborning lies by others. Customs inspectors told respondent of his duty to report cash. He and his wife claimed they had only $15,000 with them, not the $357,144 they in fact had concealed. He then told customs inspectors a friend named Abe Ajemian had lent him about $200,000. Ajemian denied this. A month later, respondent said Saeed Faroutan had lent him $170,000. Faroutan, however, said he had not made the loan and respondent had asked him to lie. Six months later, respondent resurrected the fable of the alleged loan from Ajemian, though Ajemian had already contradicted the story. As the District Court found, respondent "has lied, and has had his friends lie." He had proffered a "suspicious and confused story, documented in the poorest way, and replete with past misrepresentation."

Respondent told these lies, moreover, in most suspicious circumstances. His luggage was stuffed with more than a third of a million dollars. All of it was in cash, and much of it was hidden in a case with a false bottom.

The majority ratifies the District Court's see-no-evil approach. The District Court ignored respondent's lies in assessing a sentence. It gave him a two-level downward adjustment for acceptance of responsibility, instead of an increase for obstruction of justice. It dismissed the lies as stemming from "distrust for the Government" arising out of "cultural differences." While the majority is sincere in not endorsing this excuse, it nonetheless affirms the fine tainted by it. This patronizing excuse demeans millions of law-abiding American immigrants by suggesting they cannot be expected to be as truthful as every other citizen. Each American, regardless of culture or ethnicity, is equal before the law. Each has the same obligation to refrain from perjury and false statements to the Government.

In short, respondent was unable to give a single truthful explanation of the source of the cash. The multitude of lies and suspicious circumstances points to some form of crime. Yet, though the Government rebutted each and every fable respondent proffered, it was unable to adduce affirmative proof of another crime in this particular case.

Because of the problems of individual proof, Congress found it necessary to enact a blanket punishment. One of the few reliable warning signs of some serious crimes is the use of large sums of cash. So Congress punished all cash smuggling or non-reporting, authorizing single penalties for the offense alone and double penalties for the offense coupled with proof of other crimes. The requirement of willfulness, it judged, would be enough to protect the innocent. The majority second-guesses this judgment without explaining why Congress' blanket approach was unreasonable.

Money launderers will rejoice to know they face forfeitures of less than 5% of the money transported, provided they hire accomplished liars to carry their money for them. Five percent, of course, is not much of a deterrent or punishment; it is comparable to the fee one might pay for a mortgage lender or broker. It is far less than the 20-26% commissions some drug dealers pay money launderers. Since many couriers evade detection, moreover, the average forfeiture per dollar smuggled could amount, courtesy of today's decision, to far less than 5%. In any event, the fine permitted by the majority would be a modest cost of doing business in the world of drugs and crime.

Given the severity of respondent's crime, the Constitution does not forbid forfeiture of all of the smuggled or unreported cash. Congress made a considered judgment in setting the penalty, and the Court is in serious error to set it aside.

III

The Court's holding may in the long run undermine the purpose of the Excessive Fines Clause. One of the main purposes of the ban on excessive fines was to prevent the King from assessing unpayable fines to keep his enemies in debtor's prison. Concern with imprisonment may explain why the Excessive Fines Clause is coupled with, and follows right after, the Excessive Bail Clause. While the concern is not implicated here for of necessity the money is there to satisfy the forfeiture the Court's restrictive approach could subvert this purpose. Under the Court's holding, legislators may rely on mandatory prison sentences in lieu of fines. Drug lords will be heartened by this, knowing the prison terms will fall upon their couriers while leaving their own wallets untouched.

At the very least, today's decision will encourage legislatures to take advantage of another avenue the majority leaves open. The majority subjects this forfeiture to scrutiny because it is *in personam*, but it then suggests most *in rem* forfeitures (and perhaps most civil forfeitures) may not be fines al all. The suggestion, one might note, is inconsistent or at least in tension with *Austin v. United States*. In any event, these remarks may encourage a legislative shift from *in personam* to *in rem* forfeitures, avoiding *mens rea* as a predicate and giving owners fewer procedural protections. By invoking the Excessive Fines Clause with excessive zeal, the majority may in the long run encourage Congress to circumvent it.

IV

The majority's holding may not only jeopardize a vast range of fines but also leave countless others unchecked by the Constitution. Non-remedial fines may be subject to deference in theory but overbearing scrutiny in fact. So-called remedial penalties, most *in rem* forfeitures, and perhaps civil fines may not be subject to scrutiny at all. I would not create these exemptions from the Excessive Fines Clause. I would also accord genuine deference to Congress' judgments about the gravity of the offenses it creates. I would further follow the long tradition of fines calibrated to the value of the goods smuggled. In these circumstances, the Constitution does not forbid forfeiture of all of the $357,144 transported by respondent. I dissent.

NOTES AND QUESTIONS

1. Both the *Bajakajian* majority and the dissent agree that the test for excessiveness is whether the fine is "grossly disproportionate to the gravity of the defendant's offense." Given the sharp difference of opinion between the majority and the dissent, however, as to whether the statutory forfeiture in *Bajakajian* was excessive under this test, is there reason to doubt the usefulness of the test? Will its application inevitably be reduced to an exercise of subjective judgment by judges? Could the Court have ameliorated the subjectiveness of the test by augmenting it with more "objective" components such as the intra-jurisdictional and inter-jurisdictional comparisons sometimes invoked in assessments of cruel and unusual punishments under the Eighth Amendment? See *Harmelin v. Michigan* page 231 of the casebook, and *Solem v. Helm*, 463 U.S. 277 (1983).

2. Does the *Bajakajian* Court's suggestion that "*in rem* forfeitures" are not "fines" call the *Austin* Case § 2.02[B][6] into question?

§ 2.05 *NULLA POENA SINE LEGE*: THE LEGALITY PRINCIPLE

In addition to the justificatory issues already considered, the "principle of legality," summarized in the ancient maxim, *nulla poena sine lege* ("no punishment without law") provides a distinct set of normative constraints upon the imposition of punishment. One aspect of the legality ideal, the interest in avoiding retroactively punishing conduct not criminally proscribed prior to its inception, was alluded to earlier in this chapter in *Flemming v. Nestor* (p. 35, *supra*) and its consideration of the constitutional prohibition against *ex post facto* legislation. The retroactivity problem is again considered here as well as the related issues of institutional competency to define crime (the problem of judicial creation of crime) and adequate specificity in criminal rules (the vagueness and overbreadth problems).

[A] Judicial Creation of Crimes

SHAW V. DIRECTOR OF PUBLIC PROSECUTIONS

House of Lords [1962] App. Cas. 220

[Shaw, was convicted, *inter alia,* of conspiracy to corrupt public morals. The Crown based its charge on the fact that Shaw had joined with others in publishing a magazine that advertised the services of prostitutes by providing their names, addresses, phone numbers, sexual proclivities, and nude photographs. The indictment charged:

> Conspiracy to corrupt public morals. Particulars of offense. [Shaw] conspired with certain persons who inserted advertisements in issues of a magazine entitled "Ladies Directory" numbered 7, 7 revised, 8, 9, 10 and a supplement thereto, and with certain other persons whose names are

unknown, by means of the said magazine and the said advertisements to induce readers thereof to resort to the said advertisers for the purposes of fornication and of taking part in or witnessing other disgusting and immoral acts and exhibitions, with intent thereby to debauch and corrupt the morals as well of youth as of divers other liege subjects of Our Lady The Queen and to raise and create in their minds inordinate and lustful desires.

Shaw was sentenced to nine months' imprisonment.

The Lords dismissed Shaw's appeal, holding (Lord Reid dissenting) that conspiracy to corrupt public morals constituted a common law misdemeanor and that sufficient evidence existed to support Shaw's conviction.]

VISCOUNT SIMONDS. . . .

. . . I am concerned only to assert what was vigorously denied by counsel for the appellant, that such an offense [conspiracy to corrupt public morals] is known to the common law and that it was open to the jury to find on the facts of this case that the appellant was guilty of such an offense. I must say categorically that, if it were not so, Her Majesty's courts would strangely have failed in their duty as servants and guardians of the common law. Need I say, my Lords, that I am no advocate of the right of the judges to create new criminal offenses? . . . But I am at a loss to understand how it can be said either that the law does not recognize a conspiracy to corrupt public morals or that, though there may not be an exact precedent for such a conspiracy as this case reveals, it does not fall fairly within the general words by which it is described. . . . In the sphere of criminal law I entertain no doubt that there remains in the courts of law a residual power to enforce the supreme and fundamental purpose of the law, to conserve not only the safety and order but also the moral welfare of the State, and that it is their duty to guard it against attacks which may be the more insidious because they are novel and unprepared for. That is the broad head (call it public policy if you wish) within which the present indictment falls. . . . The same act will not in all ages be regarded in the same way. The law must be related to the changing standards of life, not yielding to every shifting impulse of the popular will but having regard to fundamental assessments of human values and the purposes of society. . . . I now assert, that there is in that court a residual power, where no statute has yet intervened to supersede the common law, to superintend those offenses which are prejudicial to the public welfare. Such occasions will be rare, for Parliament has not been slow to legislate when attention has been sufficiently aroused. But gaps remain and will always remain since no one can foresee every way in which the wickedness of man may disrupt the order of society. . . .

* * *

The appeal . . . should . . . be dismissed

LORD TUCKER. . . .

Counsel for the appellant put in the forefront of his address the submission that there is no such offense known to the law as a conspiracy to corrupt public morals. . . . I would invite your Lordships to pause to consider for a moment how far-reaching are the consequences of such a proposition if it be correct.

It has for long been accepted that there are some conspiracies which are criminal although the acts agreed to be done are not *per se* criminal or tortious if done by individuals. Such conspiracies form a third class in addition to the well-known and more clearly defined conspiracies to do acts which are unlawful, in the sense of criminal or tortious, or to do lawful acts by unlawful means. Assuming that the corruption of public morals by the acts of an individual may not be criminal or tortious, does it follow that a conspiracy by two or more persons to this end is not indictable? . . .

* * *

[T]he decision of this case does not depend upon a detailed examination of the old authorities in order to ascertain whether in every case the act or acts in question, whether performed or proposed, constituted common law misdemeanours in themselves at the date of the decisions. If they did, then the conspiracy alleged was admittedly criminal, but if they did not, it would, in my view, be equally criminal if the acts were of a nature to satisfy a jury that they were wrongful in the sense of being calculated to corrupt and deprave public morals. . . .

* * *

[T]he appeal . . . fails.

LORD MORRIS OF BORTH-Y-GEST. . . .

It is said that there is a measure of vagueness in a charge of conspiracy to corrupt public morals, and also that there might be peril of the launching of prosecutions in order to suppress unpopular or unorthodox views. My Lords, I entertain no anxiety on these lines. Even if accepted public standards may to some extent vary from generation to generation, current standards are in the keeping of juries, who can be trusted to maintain the corporate good sense of the community and to discern attacks upon values that must be preserved. If there were prosecutions which were not genuinely and fairly warranted juries would be quick to perceive this. There could be no conviction unless 12 jurors were unanimous in thinking that the accused person or persons had combined to do acts which were calculated to corrupt public morals. My Lords, as time proceeds our criminal law is more and more being codified. Though it may be that the occasions for presenting a charge such as that [involved here] will be infrequent, I concur in the view that such a charge is contained within the armoury of the law, and that the jury were in the present case fully entitled to decide the case as they did.

I would dismiss the appeal

LORD HODSON. . . .

That prostitution is not a punishable offense does not involve that it is regarded as a lawful activity. . . . I do not see any reason why a conspiracy to encourage fornication and adultery should be regarded as outside the ambit of a conspiracy to corrupt public morals. . . .

Since a criminal indictment is followed by the verdict of a jury it is true that the function of *custos morum* is in criminal cases ultimately performed by the jury, by whom, on a proper direction, each case will be decided. This I think is consonant with the course of the development of our law. One may take, as an example, the case of negligence where the standard of care of the reasonable man is regarded as fit to be determined by the jury. In the field of public morals it will thus be the morality of the man in the jury-box that will determine the fate of the accused, but this should hardly disturb the equanimity of anyone brought up in the traditions of our common law.

I would dismiss the appeal.

Appeal dismissed.

LORD REID

In my opinion there is no such general offense known to the law as conspiracy to corrupt public morals. Undoubtedly there is an offense of criminal conspiracy and undoubtedly it is of fairly wide scope. In my view its scope cannot be determined without having regard first to the history of the matter and then to the broad general principles which have generally been thought to underlie our system of law and government and in particular our system of criminal law.

I agree with R.S. Wright J. when he says . . . "There appear to be great theoretical objections to any general rule that agreement may make punishable that which ought not to be punished in the absence of agreement." And I think, or at least I hope, that it is now established that the courts cannot create new offenses by individuals. . . . [If they could] it would leave it to the judges to declare new crimes and enable them to hold anything which they considered prejudicial to the community to be a misdemeanour. However beneficial that might have been in days when Parliament met seldom or at least only at long intervals it surely is now the province of the legislature and not of the judiciary to create new criminal offenses. Every argument against creating new offenses by an individual appears to me to be equally valid against creating new offenses by a combination of individuals.

* * *

Even if there is still a vestigial power of this kind it ought not, in my view, to be used unless there appears to be general agreement that the offense to which it is applied ought to be criminal if committed by an individual. Notoriously, there are wide differences of opinion today as to how far the law ought to punish immoral acts which are not done in the face of the public. . . . Parliament is the proper place, and I am firmly of opinion the only proper place, to settle that. . . .

* * *

It may, perhaps, be said that there is no question here of creating a new offense because there is only one offense of conspiracy—agreeing or acting in concert to do an unlawful act. In a technical sense that is true. But in order to extend this offense to a new field the court would have to create a new unlawful act: it would have to hold that conduct of a kind which has not hitherto been unlawful in this sense must now be held to be unlawful. It appears to me that the objections to that are just as powerful as the objections to creating a new offense. The difference is a matter of words; the essence of the matter is that a type of conduct for the punishment of which there is no previous authority now for the first time becomes punishable solely by a decision of a court.

* * *

Finally I must advert to the consequences of holding that this very general offense exists. It has always been thought to be of primary importance that our law, and particularly our criminal law, should be certain: that a man should be able to know what conduct is and what is not criminal, particularly when heavy penalties are involved. Some suggestion was made that it does not matter if this offense is very wide: no one would ever prosecute and if they did no jury would ever convict if the breach was venial. Indeed, the suggestion goes even further: that the meaning and application of the words "deprave" and "corrupt" . . . or the words "debauch" and "corrupt" in this indictment ought to be entirely for the jury, so that any conduct of this kind is criminal if in the end a jury think it so. In other words, you cannot tell what is criminal except by guessing what view a jury will take, and juries' views may vary and may change with the passing of time. . . .

NOTES AND QUESTIONS

1. Historically, most of the ancient English offenses were created by courts without the aid of statute. However, even before the rise of Parliament, the courts had become less active in creating and defining crime as a body of precedent evolved that, through the doctrine of *stare decisis,* constrained judicial innovation.

At first, Parliament merely filled gaps in the common law, leaving the judge-made law intact. In time, the legislative process assumed the expanded tasks of crime creation through codifying the common law and supplementing and correcting it with new legislation. *Shaw* raises the question of the extent to which courts retain residual authority to create criminal liability.

2. What problems are created by Viscount Simond's view that the courts retain "residual power to enforce the supreme and fundamental purpose of the law, to conserve . . . the moral welfare of the state . . . and to guard it against attacks which may be the more insidious because they are novel and unprepared for"?

3. As between courts and legislatures, is one of the bodies more appropriate as the institutional source of the criminal law than the other? Is the problem of "common law crimes" merely the retroactivity problem, the problem of punishing offenders for conduct which was not (clearly?) criminal at the time of its commission? Suppose in cases involving possible first-time extensions of criminal liability, courts issued "prospective" rulings. Would the problem of "common law crimes" thereby be solved? Suppose, for example, the Lords had held in *Shaw* that the facts established the crime of conspiracy to corrupt public morals but that only future offenders in Shaw's position could be

punished. Do arguments still support the view that legislatures rather than courts are the appropriate source of the criminal law? See Jeffries, *Legality, Vagueness, and the Construction of Penal Statutes,* 71 Va. L. Rev. 189, 201–05 (1985).

4. Suppose that prior to Shaw's production of *The Ladies' Directory* a statute made criminal "conspiracy to corrupt public morals." Would Lord Reid find Shaw's conviction under the statute more acceptable than under a judge-made law? Would Lord Reid be impressed by Lord Morris's confidence in the good sense of the jury in upholding public morality? Are there problems with entrusting such discretion to the jury? Is Lord Hodson's analogy to jury discretion in tort cases convincing in the context of *Shaw?*

5. Does Lord Tucker adequately address the problem(s) posed by Shaw's conviction by citing the proposition that historically conspiracy could be committed even though the act(s) agreed to be done are not themselves criminal or even tortious? Consider the material on conspiracy, *infra* at § 7.03 of this book.

6. For critical reaction to the *Shaw* case, see H.L.A. Hart, Law, Liberty and Morality 7–12 (1963); Comment, 75 Harv. L. Rev. 1652 (1962).

7. While a fair number of American jurisdictions permit judicial innovation in the area of criminal defenses, the creation of new offenses by courts is extremely rare. In fact, it is safe to say that the doctrine of common law crimes has been virtually abolished in this country. Only a few exceptions exist. See, e.g., *Commonwealth v. Keller,* 35 D. & C. 2d 615 (Pa. Court of Common Pleas, 1964) (conviction upheld for "indecent disposition of a dead body" even though no statute nor prior case proscribed such conduct—court invoked its authority to find criminal "acts which injuriously affect public morality"); *Willard v. State,* 174 Tenn. 642, 130 S.W.2d 99 (1939) ("public drunkenness" held by court to be criminal in absence of statute or case precedent).

Do judicially created defenses (e.g., a court recognizing the defense of necessity in a situation not covered by statute or prior case law) raise any of the same problems created by judicially created offenses? See Gardner, *The Mens Rea Enigma: Observations on the Role of Motive in the Criminal Law Past and Present,* 1993 Utah L. Rev. 635, 743–47.

[B] Vagueness and Overbreadth

Under the Due Process Clauses of the Fifth and Fourteenth Amendments, criminal statutes or other authoritative sources of criminal liability must be defined in sufficiently certain terms so that "[n]o one may be required at peril of life, liberty or property to speculate as to the meaning of the [law]. All are entitled to be informed as to what the State commands or forbids." *Lanzetta v. New Jersey,* 306 U.S. 451, 453 (1939). This due process rule, known as the "void-for-vagueness" doctrine, embraces, among other things, the concern for "fair warning" (also promoted by the proscription against *ex post facto* legislation) and the opposition to judicially created crimes.

While certainty in statutory language is a virtue, the Supreme Court nevertheless has recognized the inherent limitations in the use of language as well as the impossibility of defining *a priori* all the factual variations that manifest the general evil sought to be avoided by legislative drafters. The Court has thus sometimes permitted legislators to employ imprecise terminology to provide a net large enough to catch all those falling within the purpose of a given statute even though it is unclear whether certain marginal offenses fall within the statutory language. Moreover, the Court has often upheld statutes embracing value-laden terminology. Thus, in *United States v. Ragen,* 314 U.S. 513, 523 (1941), the Court upheld the conviction of a defendant for wilfully taking an "unreasonable" tax deduction, saying, "The mere fact that a penal statute is so framed as to require a jury upon occasion to determine a question of reasonableness is not sufficient to make it too vague to afford a practical guide to permissible conduct."

The Supreme Court case law suggests no litmus-paper test for determining whether a criminal statute is void for vagueness. Yet, a degree of consistency in the Court's performance may be appreciated if it is understood that the vagueness doctrine is not exclusively grounded in the fair notice value.

JEFFRIES, *LEGALITY, VAGUENESS, AND THE CONSTRUCTION OF PENAL STATUTES*

71 Va. L. Rev. 189, 196–97, 206–08 (1985)

[The constitutional doctrine of void-for-vagueness] is the operational arm of legality. It requires that advance, ordinarily legislative crime definition be meaningfully precise—or at least that it not be meaninglessly indefinite. As the Supreme Court stated in an early and oft-quoted formulation, "a statute which either forbids or requires the doing of an act in terms so vague that men of common intelligence must necessarily guess at its meaning and differ as to its application, violates the first essential of due process of law."[17] The connection to legality is obvious: a law whose meaning can only be guessed at remits the actual task of defining criminal misconduct to retroactive judicial decisionmaking.

The difficulty is that there is no yardstick of impermissible indeterminacy. As Justice Frankfurter said, unconstitutional indefiniteness "is itself an indefinite concept."[18] The inquiry is evaluative rather than mechanistic; it calls for judgment concerning not merely the degree of indeterminacy, but also the acceptability of indeterminacy in particular contexts. As Professor Amsterdam has taught us, a paramount concern is whether the law's uncertain reach implicates protected freedoms.[19] Other factors considered in the vagueness inquiry include the nature of the governmental interest, the feasibility of being more precise, and whether the uncertainty affects the fact or merely the grade of criminal liability.

---

[17] *Connally v. General Constr. Co.,* 269 U.S. 385, 391 (1926).

[18] *Winters v. New York,* 333 U.S. 507, 524 (1948) (Frankfurter, J., dissenting).

[19] See Note, *The Void-for-Vagueness Doctrine in the Supreme Court,* 109 U. Pa. L. Rev. 67 (1969). This note has inevitably become dated (especially with reference to the growing use of the vagueness doctrine by state courts), but it remains the classic treatment.

Additionally, the courts may legitimately be concerned about the degree to which prosecutorial authority is centralized or dispersed. Prosecutors in this country have enormous discretion, and their decisions are largely unconstrained by law. Our chief (and admittedly inadequate) response to the potential for abuse is to tighten the procedural criteria for a criminal conviction, so that prosecutors, though largely uncontrolled in deciding not to proceed, at least are subject to a careful post-audit of their decisions to begin prosecution. The vagueness doctrine provides a secondary constraint by eliminating laws that invite manipulation—specifically, those for which the individualized adjudication of guilt is an unusually inadequate check on police and prosecutorial action.

In assessing the potential for official manipulation, judges often seem to entertain differing assumptions about federal law enforcement as compared to state, and especially local, law enforcement. The distinction is especially vivid with respect to the "worst case" of racial discrimination. Many vagueness cases are irresistibly suggestive of racial bias,[21] and the invalidation of the laws involved often may plausibly be viewed as a prophylactic against such abuse. A review of modern vagueness decisions by the Supreme Court supports the hypothesis that the Court sees this danger chiefly at the local level and is (probably correctly) relatively unconcerned about the potential for racially discriminatory enforcement of federal law. Indeed, it may well be that federal statutes benefit from a more general (and sometimes misplaced) assumption of federal prosecutorial restraint.

These and perhaps other factors combine to render modern vagueness review contextual and impressionistic. . . . While the inquiry cannot be quantified, the vagueness doctrine does bar wholesale legislative abdication of lawmaking authority and thus works, albeit irregularly, as a goad toward effective advance specification of criminal misconduct.

* * *

Consider the vagueness doctrine. The invalidation of indefinite laws is routinely justified on grounds of notice. Other reasons are also given, but the requirement of fair warning is always included and usually given pride of place. Yet the actual administration of the vagueness doctrine belies this rationale. For one thing, the kind of notice required is entirely formal. Publication of a statute's text always suffices; the government need make no further effort to appraise the people of the content of the law. . . . It may be objected that no more effective means is possible where the intended recipient of the information is the entire populace or some broad segment thereof, rather than an identifiable individual or entity. But this argument at most explains why publication should sometimes suffice; it does not explain why no further obligation is ever considered. Nor does it explain why publication in some official document, no matter how inaccessible, is all that is required. In short, the fair warning requirement of the vagueness doctrine is not structured to achieve actual notice of the content of the penal law.

---

[21] See, e.g., *Papachristou v. City of Jacksonville,* 405 U.S. 156 (1972) (vagrancy prosecution of two white women and two black men riding together down the town's main thoroughfare).

A more telling point concerns the permissible sources of specificity in the penal law. Among many disputed aspects of the vagueness doctrine, one settled rule is that the precision required of a criminal statute need not appear on its face. Facial uncertainty may be cured by judicial construction. Indeed, judicial specification will be accepted as sufficient even where it amounts to a wholesale rewriting of the statutory text. Thus, the "fair warning" that the law regards as the "first essential of due process" may be discoverable only by a search of the precedents. As every first-year law student knows (and has not had time to forget), this process of research and interpretation is anything but easy. For the trained professional, the task is time-consuming and tricky; for the average citizen, it is next to impossible. Where there is a lawyer at hand, this kind of notice may be meaningful. But in the ordinary case, the notice given must be recovered from sources so various and inaccessible as to render the concept distinctly unrealistic.

And what if notice fails? What if an individual acts in honest ignorance of the law's commands or in the mistaken belief that his conduct is lawful? The answer, of course, is that we punish him anyway. *Ignorantia juris neminem excusat* states the entrenched policy of the penal law. In some jurisdictions, a defense of estoppel bars prosecution where the government has affirmatively misled the individual, but where the government is not responsible for the error, ignorance of the law is no excuse.

NOTES AND QUESTIONS

1. In addition to the interest in assuring fair notice, Professor Jeffries suggests two additional bases underlying the void-for-vagueness doctrine: avoiding governmental intrusions into areas of protected rights and controlling abuse of governmental discretion. Consider, for example, the Jacksonville City Ordinance invalidated under the vagueness doctrine in *Papachristou v. City of Jacksonville,* 405 U.S. 156 at fn.I (1972):

> Jacksonville Ordinance Code § 26-57. Rogues and vagabonds, or dissolute persons who go about begging, common gamblers, persons who use juggling or unlawful games or plays, common drunkards, common night walkers, thieves, pilferers or pickpockets, traders in stolen property, lewd, wanton and lascivious persons, keepers of gambling places, common railers and brawlers, persons wandering or strolling around from place to place without any lawful purpose or object, habitual loafers, disorderly persons, persons neglecting all lawful business and habitually spending their time by frequenting houses of ill fame, gaming houses, or places where alcoholic beverages are sold or served, persons able to work but habitually living upon the earnings of their wives or minor children shall be deemed vagrants and, upon conviction in the Municipal Court shall be punished as provided for Class D offenses.

Fair notice problems are created by much of the language of the ordinance—what does it mean to be a "lewd, wanton, and lascivious" person? Who are "habitual loafers"?

The *Papachristou* Court was not merely concerned with the notice problem, however. As Professor Jeffries suggests, the vagueness issue was exacerbated by the potential for police manipulation to invade areas of protected rights. The uncertainty and breadth of the language permitted virtually unchecked discretion to arrest as a "vagrant" whomever the officer desired. As Jeffries notes in the above excerpt, arresting and prosecuting racially mixed couples bore the earmarks of governmental interference with the "vagrant's" rights to be free from racial discrimination. Moreover, the ordinance posed a potential chilling effect on the exercise of other constitutional rights. Surely taking a walk is permissible, perhaps constitutionally protected, activity. Yet, if "strolling around from place to place" . . . is a crime (or can be one if a police officer decides to see it as such) "innocent" strollers may be dissuaded from engaging in cherished pedestrian activity. The ordinance thus provided insufficient "breathing space" for protected activity.

Furthermore, the Jacksonville provision invited abuse of discretion even where protected rights were not at stake. One of the defendants in *Papachristou* was arrested when he and his companion drove up to his girlfriend's residence. Some police officers were already present and in the process of arresting another man. When defendant and his companion began backing out of the driveway, the officers signaled them to stop and asked them to get out of the car, which they did. The police then searched the car but found nothing illegal therein. Defendant was, nevertheless, arrested for "loitering" because he was standing on the driveway, an act which the officers admitted was done only at their command.

2. Vagrancy statutes have been characterized as "punishing by analogy." Foote, *Vagrancy Type Law and Its Administration,* 104 U. Pa. L. Rev. 603, 609 (1956). Police allegedly have utilized vagrancy provisions as a means of arresting "suspicious" persons whom they lack probable cause to arrest for the "suspected" offense. Sometimes searches incident to the vagrancy arrest would turn up contraband and evidence of other criminality that could then be used against the defendant for those other crimes.

3. *Papachristou* has called all vagrancy statutes into constitutional question. Is the following Model Penal Code provision constitutional after *Papachristou*?

A person commits a violation if he loiters or prowls in a place, at a time, or in a manner not usual for law-abiding individuals under circumstances that warrant alarm for the safety of persons or property in the vicinity. Among the circumstances which may be considered in determining whether such alarm is warranted is the fact that the actor takes flight upon appearance of a peace officer, refuses to identify himself, or manifestly endeavors to conceal himself or any object. Unless flight by the actor or other circumstances makes it impracticable, a peace officer shall prior to any arrest for an offense under this section afford the actor an opportunity to dispel any alarm which would otherwise be warranted, by requesting him to identify himself and explain his presence and conduct. No person shall be convicted of an offense under this Section if the peace officer did not comply with the preceding sentence, or if it appears at trial that the explanation given by the actor was true and, if believed by the peace officer at the time, would have dispelled the alarm.

MPC § 250.6

4. Is the MPC loitering provision constitutional in light of *Koilender v. Lawson,* 461 U.S. 352 (1983), which held void for vagueness a California statute that declared guilty of disorderly conduct every person

> who loiters or wanders upon the streets or from place to place without apparent reason or business and who refuses to identify himself and to account for his presence when requested by any peace officer so to do, if the surrounding circumstances are such as to indicate to a reasonable man that the public safety demands such identification.

The Court held the statute invalid on its face, noting that a judicial gloss requiring "credible and reliable" identification, if anything, made matters constitutionally worse by injecting additional statutory uncertainty. (Did the gloss have this effect?) The Court saw the statute as vesting "virtually complete discretion in the hands of the police to determine whether the suspect has satisfied the statute and must be permitted to go on his way." *Id.* at 358. The statute thus became "a convenient tool" for discriminatory and abusive enforcement. Possible racial discrimination was again a factor in *Lawson,* given the fact that the defendant was a black man of unusual appearance who routinely walked late at night in wealthy and predominantly white residential neighborhoods.

Suppose the defendant in *Lawson* had refused to provide any identification when requested by the officer. Would the statute still be unconstitutional? If so, to what extent is "fair notice" a concern? Can *Lawson* be understood essentially in terms of the statute's susceptibility to arbitrary and discriminatory enforcement?

5. In *City of Chicago v. Morales,* 527 U.S. 41 (1999), the Supreme Court struck down a city ordinance prohibiting "street gang members" from "loitering" (defined by the ordinance as "remaining in any one place with no apparent purpose") with one another or with other persons in any public place. In finding that the ordinance "affords too much discretion to the police and too little notice to citizens who wish to use the public streets," the Court opined that an ordinance directly prohibiting gang members from intimidating citizens would be constitutional. However, because the Chicago ordinance "broadly cover[ed] a significant amount of additional activity" the Court found it unconstitutionally vague.

6. For an argument that much of the recently enacted "antistalking" legislation suffers from unconstitutional vagueness and overbreadth, as well as a number of other constitutional infirmities, See Faulkner and Hsiao, *And Where You Go I'll Follow: The Constitutionality of Anti stalking Laws and Proposed Model Legislation,* 31 Harv. J. Legis. 1 (1994).

[C] Statutory Interpretation

ALLEN, THE EROSION OF LEGALITY IN AMERICAN CRIMINAL JUSTICE:
SOME LATER-DAY ADVENTURES OF THE NULLA POENA PRINCIPLE

29 Ariz. L. Rev. 385, 389–90 (1987)

The language of statutes defining criminality and specifying penalties produces conflicting readings, and authoritative resolution of the conflicts is required. In the ordinary course of events, the judicial interpretation will be made after, not before, the behavior alleged to be criminal is committed; and if the dispute concerning statutory meaning was a substantial one, the rendering of the subsequent authoritative interpretation may impinge substantially on the principle of prior notice to prospective offenders embraced in the *nulla poena* maxim. Nor does the matter end here. The judicial interpretation itself is a product of language, and may display the characteristic fallibilities of statutory language plus some of its own. Thus, interpretation breeds new interpretation, and the result can often be to enlarge rather than reduce the departure from the *nulla poena* ideal. There comes a point, of course, in which the deficiencies of statutory language cannot be ignored, and courts may disregard statutes on grounds of *casus omissus* or invalidate them by invoking the constitutional doctrine of void for vagueness. These doctrines are employed sparingly by the courts, however; one may feel all too sparingly. Yet even a more liberal application of the vagueness doctrine would leave untouched the overwhelming majority of statutes presenting problems of ambiguity, omission, and inexactitude. The requirements of an operating system of criminal justice demand considerable judicial accommodation to the defects of statutory language. Counsels of perfection do not flourish in the context of day-to-day operations.

Even if one could conceive of a legal prescription stated with perfect clarity and admitting of no readings other than that intended by the writer, a need for interpretation might ultimately arise because the context in which the statute operates has changed. For centuries we have been told that murder is the killing of another human being with malice aforethought. But has an accused "killed" when by reason of his act the victim has suffered "brain death" but whose heart beat and respiration are being maintained by artificial means? The question could not have arisen when the murder formula was first articulated, for the circumstances supposed could occur only when medical technology entered into its present stage of development. Having arisen, the question must be answered by interpretation, unless it has been anticipated and resolved in advance of adjudication by a statutory modification of the murder definition.

KEELER V. SUPERIOR COURT

Supreme Court of California

2 Cal.3d 619, 470 P.2d 617 (1970)

MOSK, Justice.

In this proceeding for writ of prohibition we are called upon to decide whether an unborn but viable fetus is a "human being" within the meaning of the California statute defining murder (Pen. Code § 187). We conclude that the Legislature did not intend such a meaning, and that for us to construe the statute to the contrary and apply it to this petitioner would exceed our judicial power and deny petitioner due process of law.

[After 16 years of marriage, petitioner, Keeler, and his wife received an interlocutory decree of divorce. On February 23, 1969, five months after obtaining the decree, Keeler stopped his wife's car as she was driving on a mountain road. She was well into the third trimester of a pregnancy by another man. Keeler said to her, "I hear you're pregnant," assisted her from her car, examined her abdomen and remarked, "You sure are. I'm going to stomp it out of you." He then shoved his knee into her abdomen and struck her several times in the face. The fetus, which according to the wife and her obstetrician had manifested movements *in utero* prior to the attack by Keeler, was delivered stillborn with a fractured skull.]

An information was filed charging petitioner, in Count I, with committing the crime of murder (Pen. Code § 187) in that he did "unlawfully kill a human being, to wit Baby Girl Vogt, with malice aforethought." In Count II petitioner was charged with wilful infliction of traumatic injury upon his wife . . . , and in Count III, with assault on Mrs. Keeler by means of force likely to produce great bodily injury. . . . His motion to set aside the information for lack of probable cause . . . was denied, and he now seeks a writ of prohibition. . . .

I

Penal Code section 187 provides: "Murder is the unlawful killing of a human being, with malice aforethought." The dispositive question is whether the fetus which petitioner is accused of killing was, on February 23, 1969, a "human being" within the meaning of this statute. If it was not, petitioner cannot be charged with its "murder" and prohibition will lie.

Section 187 was enacted as part of the Penal Code of 1872. Inasmuch as the provision has not been amended since that date, we must determine the intent of the Legislature at the time of its enactment. But section 187 was, in turn, taken verbatim from the first California statute defining murder, part of the Crimes and Punishments Act of 1850. . . . Penal Code section 5 (also enacted in 1872) declares: "The provisions of this Code, so far as they are substantially the same as existing statutes, must be construed as continuations thereof, and not as new enactments." We begin, accordingly, by inquiring into the intent of the Legislature in 1850 when it first defined murder as the unlawful and malicious killing of a "human being."

It will be presumed, of course, that in enacting a statute the Legislature was familiar with the relevant rules of the common law, and, when it couches its enactment in common law language, that its intent was to continue those rules in statutory form. . . .

* * *

. . . [I]t appears that by the year 1850–the date with which we are concerned—an infant could not be the subject of homicide at common law *unless it had been born alive.* Perhaps the most influential statement of the "born alive" rule is that of Coke, in mid-17th century: "If a woman be quick with childe, and by a potion or otherwise killeth it in her wombe, or if a man beat her, whereby the childe dyeth in her body, and she is delivered of a dead childe, this is a great misprision [i.e., misdemeanor], and no murder; but if the childe be born alive and dyeth of the potion, battery, or other cause, this is murder.". . . In the 18th century, . . . Coke's requirement that an infant be born alive in order to be the subject of homicide was reiterated and expanded by both Blackstone and Hale.

Against this background, a series of infanticide prosecutions were brought in the English courts in mid-19th century. In each, a woman or her accomplice was charged with murdering a newborn child, and it was uniformly declared to be the law that a verdict of murder could not be returned unless it was proved the infant had been born alive.

* * *

By the year 1850 this rule of the common law had long been accepted in the United States.

While it was thus "well settled" in American case law that the killing of an unborn child was not homicide, a number of state legislatures in the first half of the 19th century undertook to modify the common law in this respect. The movement began when New York abandoned the common law of abortion in 1830. The revisers' notes on that legislation recognized the existing rule, but nevertheless proposed a special feticide statute which, as enacted, provided that "The wilful killing of an unborn quick child, by any injury to the mother of such child, which would be murder if it resulted in the death of such mother, shall be deemed manslaughter in the first degree." . . . At the same time the New York Legislature enacted a companion section . . . which, although punishing a violation thereof as second degree manslaughter, was in essence an "abortion law" similar to those in force in most states today.

In the years between 1830 and 1850 at least five other states followed New York and enacted, as companion provisions, (1) a statute declaring feticide to be a crime, punishable as manslaughter, and (2) a statute prohibiting abortion. In California, however, the pattern was not repeated. Much of the Crimes and Punishments Act of 1850 was based on existing New York statute law; but although a section proscribing abortion was included in the new Act the Legislature declined to adopt any provision defining and punishing a special crime of feticide.

We conclude that in declaring murder to be the unlawful and malicious killing of a "human being" the Legislature of 1850 intended that term to have the settled common law meaning of a person who had been born alive, and did not intend the act of feticide—as distinguished from abortion—to be an offense under the laws of California.

Nothing occurred between the years 1850 and 1872 to suggest that in adopting the new Penal Code on the latter date the Legislature entertained any different intent. The case law of our sister states, for example, remained consonant with the common law. . . .

Any lingering doubt on this subject must be laid to rest by a consideration of the legislative history of the Penal Code of 1872. The Act establishing the California Code Commission . . . required the commissioners to revise all statutes then in force, correct errors and omissions, and "recommend all such enactments as shall, in the judgment of the Commission, be necessary to supply the defects of and give completeness to the existing legislation of the State." . . . In discharging this duty the statutory schemes of our sister states were carefully examined, and we must assume the commissioners had knowledge of the feticide laws noted hereinabove. Yet the commissioners proposed no such law for California, and none has been adopted to this day.

That such an omission was not an oversight clearly appears, moreover, from the commissioners' explanatory notes to Penal Code section 187. After quoting the definitions of murder given by Coke, Blackstone, and Hawkins, the commissioners conclude: "A child within its mother's womb is not a 'human being' within the meaning of that term as used in defining murder.["] . . .

* * *

It is the policy of this state to construe a penal statute as favorably to the defendant as its language and the circumstances of its application may reasonably permit; just as in the case of a question of fact, the defendant is entitled to the benefit of every reasonable doubt as to the true interpretation of words or the construction of language used in a statute. . . . We hold that in adopting the definition of murder in Penal Code section 187 the Legislature intended to exclude from its reach the act of killing an unborn fetus.

II

The People urge, however, that the sciences of obstetrics and pediatrics have greatly progressed since 1872, to the point where with proper medical care a normally developed fetus prematurely born at 28 weeks or more has an excellent chance of survival; i.e., is "viable;" that the common law requirement of live birth to prove the fetus had become a "human being" who may be the victim of murder is no longer in accord with scientific fact, since an unborn but viable fetus is now fully capable of independent life; and that one who unlawfully and maliciously terminates such a life should therefore be liable to prosecution for murder under section 187. We may grant the premises of this argument; indeed, we neither deny nor denigrate the vast progress of medicine in the century since the enactment of the Penal Code. But we cannot join in the conclusion sought to be deduced: we cannot hold this petitioner to answer for murder by reason of his alleged act of killing an unborn—even though viable—fetus. To such a charge there are two insuperable obstacles, one 'Jurisdictional' and the other constitutional.

Penal Code section 6 declares in relevant part that "No act or omission" accomplished after the code has taken effect "is criminal or punishable, except as prescribed or authorized by this Code, or by some of the statutes which it specifies as continuing in force and as not affected by its provisions, or by some ordinance, municipal, county, or township regulation.". . . Stated differently, there are no common law crimes in California.

Settled rules of construction implement this principle. Although the Penal Code commands us to construe its provisions "according to the fair import of their terms, with a view to effect its objects and to promote justice" (Pen. Code § 4), it is clear the courts cannot go so far as to create an offense by enlarging a statute, by inserting or deleting words, or by giving the terms used false or unusual meanings . . . Penal statutes will not be made to reach beyond their plain intent; they include only those offenses coming clearly within the import of their language. . . .

Applying these rules to the case at bar, we would undoubtedly act in excess of the judicial power if we were to adopt the People's proposed construction of section 187. As we have shown, the Legislature has defined the crime of murder in California to apply only to the unlawful and malicious killing of one who has been born alive. We recognize that the killing of an unborn but viable fetus may be deemed by some to be an offense of similar nature and gravity; but as Chief Justice Marshall warned long ago, "It would be dangerous, indeed, to carry the principle, that a case which is within the reason or mischief of a statute, is within its provisions, so far as to punish a crime not enumerated in the statute, because it is of equal atrocity, or of kindred character, with those which are enumerated." [*United States v. Wiltberger* (1820), 18 U.S. (5 Wheat) 76, 96.] Whether to thus extend liability for murder in California is a determination solely within the province of the Legislature. For a court to simply declare, by judicial fiat, that the time has now come to prosecute under section 187 one who kills an unborn but viable fetus would indeed be to rewrite the statute under the guise of construing it. Nor does a need to fill an asserted "gap" in the law between abortion and homicide—as will appear, no such gap in fact exists—justify judicial legislation of this nature: to make it "a judicial function 'to explore such new fields of crime as they may appear from time to time' is wholly foreign to the American concept of criminal justice" and "raises very serious questions concerning the principle of separation of powers." (*In re Davis* (1966), 242 Cal. App. 2d 645, 655–656 and fn. 12, 51 Cal. Rptr. 702.)

The second obstacle to the proposed judicial enlargement of section 187 is the guarantee of due process of law. Assuming *arguendo* that we have the power to adopt the new construction of this statute as the law of California, such a ruling, by constitutional command, could operate only prospectively, and thus could not in any event reach the conduct of petitioner on February 23, 1969.

The first essential of due process is fair warning of the act which is made punishable as a crime. "That the terms of a penal statute creating a new offense must be sufficiently explicit to inform those who are subject to it what conduct on their part will render them liable to its penalties, is a well-recognized requirement, consonant alike with ordinary notions of fair play and the settled rules of law." [*Connally v. General Constr. Co.* (1926), 269 U.S. 385, 391. . . .]

This requirement of fair warning is reflected in the constitutional prohibition against the enactment of *ex post facto* laws. . . . When a new penal statute is applied retrospectively to make punishable an act which was not criminal at the time it was performed, the defendant has been given no advance notice consistent with due process. And precisely the same effect occurs when such an act is made punishable under a preexisting statute but by means of an unforeseeable *judicial* enlargement thereof. [*Bouie v. City of Columbia* (1964), 378 U.S. 347. . . .]

In *Bouie* two Negroes took seats in the restaurant section of a South Carolina drugstore; no notices were posted restricting the area to whites only. When the defendants refused to leave upon demand, they were arrested and convicted of violating a criminal trespass statute which prohibited entry on the property of another "after notice" forbidding such conduct. Prior South Carolina decisions had emphasized the necessity of proving such notice to support a conviction under the statute. The South Carolina Supreme Court nevertheless affirmed the convictions, construing the statute to prohibit not only the act of entering after notice not to do so but also the wholly different act of remaining on the property after receiving notice to leave.

The United States Supreme Court reversed the convictions, holding that the South Carolina court's ruling was "unforeseeable" and when an "unforeseeable state court construction of a criminal statute is applied retroactively to subject a person to criminal liability for past conduct, the effect is to deprive him of due process of law in the sense of fair warning that his contemplated conduct constitutes a crime." Analogizing to the prohibition against retrospective penal legislation, the high court reasoned

> Indeed, an unforeseeable judicial enlargement of a criminal statute, applied retroactively, operates precisely like an ex post facto law. . . . An *ex post facto* law has been defined by this Court as one "that makes an action done before the passing of the law, and which was innocent when done, criminal; and punishes such action," or "that *aggravates a crime,* or makes it *greater* than it was, when committed." *Calder v. Bull,* 3 Dall. 386, 390. If a state legislature is barred by the *Ex Post Facto* Clause from passing such a law, it must follow that a State Supreme Court is barred by the Due Process Clause from achieving precisely the same result by judicial construction. . . . The fundamental principle that "the required criminal law must have existed when the conduct in issue occurred," Hall, *General Principles of Criminal Law* (2d ed. 1960), at 58–59, must apply to bar retroactive criminal prohibitions emanating from courts as well as from legislatures. If a judicial construction of a criminal statute is "unexpected and indefensible by reference to the law which had been expressed prior to the conduct in issue," it must not be given retroactive effect.
>
> *Id.,* at 61. . . .

The court remarked in conclusion that "Application of this rule is particularly compelling where, as here, the petitioners' conduct cannot be deemed improper or immoral." . . . In the case at bar the conduct with which petitioner is charged is certainly "improper" and "immoral," and it is not contended he was exercising a constitutionally favored right. But the matter is simply one of degree, and it cannot be denied that the guarantee of due process extends to violent as well as peaceful men. The issue remains, would the judicial enlargement of section 187 now proposed have been foreseeable to this petitioner?

* * *

Turning to the case law, we find no reported decision of the California courts which should have given petitioner notice that the killing of an unborn but viable fetus was prohibited by section 187. . . .

Properly understood, the often cited case of *People v. Chavez* (1947), 77 Cal. App. 2d 621, 176 P.2d 92, does not derogate from this rule. There the defendant was charged with the murder of her newborn child, and convicted of manslaughter. She testified that the baby dropped from her womb into the toilet bowl; that she picked it up two or three minutes later, and cut but did not tie the umbilical cord; that the baby was limp and made no cry; and that after 15 minutes she wrapped it in a newspaper and concealed it, where it was found dead the next day. The autopsy surgeon testified that the baby was a full-term, nine-month child, weighing six and one-half pounds and appearing normal in every respect; that the body had very little blood in it, indicating the child had bled to death through the untied umbilical cord; that such a process would have taken about an hour.

* * *

Chavez . . . stands for the proposition—to which we adhere—that a viable fetus "in the process of being born" is a human being within the meaning of the homicide statutes. But it stands for no more; in particular it does not hold that a fetus, however viable, which is not "in the process of being born" is nevertheless a "human being" in the law of homicide. On the contrary, the opinion is replete with references to the common law requirement that the child be "born alive," however that term is defined, and must accordingly be deemed to reaffirm that requirement as part of the law of California.

* * *

We conclude that the judicial enlargement of section 187 now urged upon us by the People would not have been foreseeable to this petitioner, and hence that its adoption at this time would deny him due process of law.

Let a peremptory writ of prohibition issue restraining respondent court from taking any further proceedings on Count I of the information, charging petitioner with the crime of murder.

BURKE, Acting Chief Justice *(dissenting).*

The majority hold that "Baby Girl" Vogt, who, according to medical testimony, had reached the 35th week of development, had a 96 percent chance of survival, and was "definitely" alive and viable at the time of her death, nevertheless was not a "human being" under California's homicide statutes. In my view, in so holding, the majority ignore significant common law precedents, frustrate the express intent of the Legislature, and defy reason, logic and common sense.

The majority cast a passing glance at the common law concept of quickening, but fail to explain the significance of that concept: At common law, the quickened fetus was considered to be a human being, a second life separate and apart from its mother. As stated by Blackstone, in the passage immediately preceding that portion quoted in the majority opinion "Life is the immediate gift of God, a right inherent by nature in every individual; *and it begins in contemplation of law as soon as an infant is able to stir in the mother's womb."* . . .

Modern scholars have confirmed this aspect of common law jurisprudence. As Means observes, "The common law itself prohibited abortion after quickening and hanging a pregnant felon after quickening, *because the life of a second human being would thereby be taken,* although it did not call the offense murder or manslaughter."

* * *

This reasoning explains why the killing of a quickened child was considered "a great misprision," although the killing of an unquickened child was no crime at all at common law. . . . Moreover, although the common law did not apply the labels of "murder" or "manslaughter" to the killing of a quickened fetus, it appears that at common law this "great misprision" was severely punished. As late as 1837, the wilful aborting of a woman quick with child was punishable by death in England. . . .

Thus, at common law, the killing of a quickened child was severely punished, since that child was considered to be a human being. The majority would have us assume that the Legislature in 1850 and 1872 simply overlooked this "great misprision," codifying and classifying criminal offenses in California, or reduced that offense to the lesser offense of illegal abortion with its relatively lenient penalties.

In my view, we cannot assume that the Legislature intended a person such as defendant, charged with the malicious slaying of a fully viable child, to suffer only the mild penalties imposed upon common abortionists who, ordinarily, procure only the miscarriage of a nonviable fetus or embryo. . . . To do so would completely ignore the important common law distinction between the quickened and unquickened child.

Of course, I do not suggest that we should interpret the term "human being" in our homicide statutes in terms of the common law concept of quickening. At one time, that concept had a value in differentiating, as accurately as was then scientifically possible, between life and nonlife. The analogous concept of viability is clearly more satisfactory, for it has a well defined and medically determinable meaning denoting the ability of the fetus to live or survive apart from its mother.

The majority opinion suggests that we are confined to common law concepts, and to the common law definition of murder or manslaughter. However, the Legislature, in Penal Code sections 187 and 192, has defined those offenses for us: homicide is the unlawful killing of a "human being." Those words need not be frozen in place as of any particular time, but must be fairly and reasonably interpreted by this court to promote justice and to carry out the evident purposes of the Legislature in adopting a homicide statute. Thus, Penal Code section 4, which was enacted in 1872 along with sections 187 and 192, provides: "The rule of the common law, that penal statutes are to be strictly construed, has no application to this Code. All its provisions are to be construed according to the fair import of their terms, with a view to effect its objects and to promote justice." . . .

* * *

We commonly conceive of human existence as a spectrum stretching from birth to death. However, if this court properly might expand the definition of "human being" at one end of that spectrum, we may do so at the other end. Consider the following example: All would agree that "Shooting or otherwise damaging a corpse is not homicide." In other words, a corpse is not considered to be a "human being" and thus cannot be the subject of a "killing" as those terms are used in homicide statutes. However, it is readily apparent that our concepts of what constitutes a "corpse" have been and are being continually modified by advances in the field of medicine, including new techniques for life revival, restoration and resuscitation such as artificial respiration, open heart massage, transfusions, transplants and a variety of life-restoring stimulants, drugs and new surgical methods. Would this court ignore these developments and exonerate the killer of an apparently "drowned" child merely because that child would have been pronounced dead in 1648 or 1850? Obviously not. Whether a homicide occurred in that case would be determined by medical testimony regarding the capability of the child to have survived prior to the defendant's act. And that is precisely the test which this court should adopt in the instant case.

The common law reluctance to characterize the killing of a quickened fetus as a homicide was based solely upon a presumption that the fetus would have been born dead. . . . Based upon the state of the medical art in the 17th, 18th and 19th centuries, that presumption may have been well-founded. However, as we approach the 21st century, it has become apparent that "This presumption is not only contrary to common experience and the ordinary course of nature, but it is contrary to the usual rule with respect to presumptions followed in this state." (*People v. Chavez* . . .)

* * *

The majority suggest that to [include a viable fetus as a "human being"] would improperly create some new offense. However, the offense of murder is no new offense. Contrary to the majority opinion, the Legislature has not "defined the crime of murder in California to apply only to the unlawful and malicious killing of one who has been born alive." Instead, the Legislature simply used the broad term "human being" and directed the courts to construe that term according to its "fair import" with a view to effect the objects of the homicide statutes and promote justice. (Pen. Code § 4.) What justice will be promoted, what objects effectuated, by construing "human being" as excluding Baby Girl Vogt and her unfortunate successors? Was defendant's brutal act of stomping her to death any less an act of homicide than the murder of a newly born baby? No one doubts that the term "human being" would include the elderly or dying persons whose potential for life has nearly lapsed; their proximity to death is deemed immaterial. There is no sound reason for denying the viable fetus, with its unbounded potential for life, the same status.

The majority also suggest that such an interpretation of our homicide statutes would deny defendant "fair warning" that his act was punishable as a crime. . . . Aside from the absurdity of the underlying premise that defendant consulted Coke, Blackstone or Hale before kicking Baby Girl Vogt to death, it is clear that defendant had adequate notice that his act could constitute homicide. Due process only precludes prosecution under a new statute insufficiently explicit regarding the specific conduct proscribed, or under a preexisting statute "by means of an unforeseeable judicial enlargement thereof."

Our homicide statutes have been in effect in this state since 1850. The fact that the California courts have not been called upon to determine the precise question before us does not render "unforeseeable" a decision which determines that a viable fetus is a "human being" under those statutes. Can defendant really claim surprise that a 5-pound, 18-inch, 34-week-old, living, viable child is considered to be a human being?

The fact is that the foregoing construction of our homicide statutes easily could have been anticipated from strong *dicta in People v. Chavez*. . . . he court in *Chavez* held that a viable child killed during, but prior to completion of the birth process, was a human being under the homicide statutes. However, the court did not hold that partial birth was a prerequisite, for the court expressly set forth its holding "Without drawing a line of distinction applicable to all cases." In *dicta,* the court discussed the question when an unborn infant becomes a human being under the homicide statutes, as follows: "There is not much change in the child itself between a moment before and a moment after its expulsion from the body of its mother, and normally, while still dependent upon its mother, the child for some time before it is born, has not only the possibility but a strong probability of an ability to live an independent life."
. . . "[I]t would be a mere fiction to hold that a child is not a human being because the process of birth has not been fully completed, when it has reached that state of viability when the destruction of the life of its mother would not end its existence and when, if separated from the mother naturally or by artificial means, it will live and grow in the normal manner.". . .

* * *

The trial court's denial of defendant's motion to set aside the information was proper, and the peremptory writ of prohibition should be denied.

NOTES AND QUESTIONS

1. Would there have been an unconstitutional failure to provide "fair notice" if the *Keeler* court had permitted the murder statute to be applied in that case? Suppose Baby Vogt had been "born alive" but died 10 minutes after birth of prenatal injuries inflicted by Keeler. Could Keeler then be charged with murder? If so, does he receive "fairer notice" than he possessed in the actual case? Do undesirable policy implications result if liability for murder hinges on the distinction between causing the death of a stillborn fetus on the one hand and committing prenatal injuries that cause the death of an infant after it is born on the other?

Suppose, prior to his actions, Keeler had sought a legal opinion on the issue of murder liability in California for killing a viable fetus. Would the opinion have provided any "notice" to Keeler that his proposed actions might constitute murder?

Are the "notice" problems in Keeler distinguishable from those in the *Bouie* case described in the *Keeler* opinion? Would the concerns that motivated the Supreme Court to invalidate the statutes in *Papachristou and Lawson*, noted above at pages 155–57, similarly move the Court to invalidate a reading of the California murder statute to cover the facts of *Keeler?*

While *Keeler* represents the majority rule, some courts have rejected the *Keeler* reasoning and found in prospective rulings that a viable fetus is a human life for purposes of homicide statutes even though the legislature has not so provided. See *Commonwealth v. Cass*, 392 Mass. 799, 467 N.E.2d 1324 (1984); *State v. Home*, 282 S.C. 444, 319 S.E.2d 703 (1984).

2. Apart from constitutional considerations, does the *Keeler* court correctly interpret the murder statute? Shortly after the *Keeler* decision, the California legislature broadened the murder statute to include the "killing of a human being or a fetus" except where fetal death occurs in the course of a legal abortion or where "consented to by the mother." 1970 Cal. Laws ch. 1311 § 1. Does the statutory revision influence your assessment of the *Keeler* court's performance? Does the revision suggest that the court "misread" the legislative intent or does it simply make the court's point that defining criminal liability is a legislative matter?

3. Does the principle of legality require that courts follow the oft-stated rule that criminal statutes be "strictly construed" in favor of defendants? What results if strict construction is applied in *Keeler*? While thoroughgoing application of strict construction promotes the principle of legality, might it sacrifice other values?

4. Suppose that a doctor surgically separates conjoined—also called Siamese—twins who share a single heart, realizing that the twin left without the heart will die soon after surgery. Without the surgery both twins would likely suffer early deaths; but with the surgery, the twin left with the heart may live a normal life. Could the doctor be convicted of homicide for killing a "human being" when the twin left without a heart dies? Could the doctor argue that the Siamese twins constituted only one life and not two because a heart is essential to human life and only one heart existed? If such an argument made sense historically, would its force be diminished by the fact that it is now possible to transplant hearts and to insert artificial hearts? For a situation that raises some of these questions, see David Brown, *Twin "Stable and Awake," Surgeon Says Surviving Girl Listed in Critical Condition*, Washington Post, August 22, 1993, A at 3. Would your answer be different if the twins shared a brain? See L. Katz, Bad Acts and Guilty Minds 104–113 (1987).

JOHNSON V. STATE OF FLORIDA

Supreme Court of Florida

602 So. 2d 1288 (1992)

HARDING, J.

The issue before the court is whether section 893.13(1)(c)(1), Florida Statutes (1989), permits the criminal prosecution of a mother, who ingested a controlled substance prior to giving birth, for delivery of a controlled substance to the infant during the thirty to ninety seconds following the infant's birth, but before the umbilical cord is severed. Johnson presents four arguments attacking the applicability of section 893.13(1)(c)(1) to her conviction: (1) the district court's interpretation of the statute violates the legislature's intent; (2) the plain language of the statute prevents her conviction; (3) the conviction violates her constitutional rights of due process and privacy; and (4) the State presented insufficient evidence to show that she intentionally delivered cocaine to a minor. . . . The State contends that the district court correctly found that the statute's plain language prohibits the delivery of the controlled substance to a minor, and that the conviction does not violate Johnson's constitutional rights.

We adopt Judge Sharp's analysis [in the lower court opinion] concerning the insufficiency of the evidence to support Johnson's conviction and her analysis concerning the legislature's intent in section 893.13(1)(c)(1). . . . The text of Judge Sharp's dissent is as follows:

Johnson appeals from two convictions for delivering a controlled substance to her two minor children in violation of section 893.13(1)(c)(1), Florida Statutes (1989).[1] The state's theory of the case was that Johnson "delivered" cocaine or a derivative of the drug to her two children via blood flowing through the children's umbilical cords in the sixty-to-ninety-second period after they were expelled from her birth canal but before their cords were severed. The application of this statute to this concept of "delivery" presents a case of first impression in this state. Because I conclude that section 893.13(1)(c)(1) was not intended to apply to these facts, I would vacate the convictions and remand for the entry of a judgment of acquittal.

The record in this case establishes the following facts. On October 3, 1987, Johnson delivered a son. The birth was normal with no complications. There was no evidence of fetal distress either within the womb or during the delivery. About one and one-half minutes elapsed from the time the son's head emerged from his mother's birth canal to the time he was placed on her stomach and the cord was clamped.

---

[1] Section 893.13(1)(c)(1), Florida Statutes (1989), provides as follows:

893.13 Prohibited acts; penalties.—(c) Except as authorized by this chapter, it is unlawful for any person 18 years of age or older to deliver any controlled substance to a person under the age of 18 years, or to use or hire a person under the age of 18 years as an agent or employee in the sale or delivery of such a substance, or to use such person to assist in avoiding detection or apprehension for a violation of this chapter. Any person who violates this provision with respect to: 1. A controlled substance . . . is guilty of a felony of the first degree. . . .

The obstetrician who delivered Johnson's son testified he presumed that the umbilical cord was functioning normally and that it was delivering blood to the baby after he emerged from the birth canal and before the cord was clamped. Johnson admitted to the baby's pediatrician that she used cocaine the night before she delivered. A basic toxicology test performed on Johnson and her son was positive for benzoylecgonine, a metabolite or "breakdown" product of cocaine.

In December 1988, Johnson, while pregnant with a daughter, suffered a crack overdose. Johnson told paramedics that she had taken $200 [worth] of crack cocaine earlier that evening and that she was concerned about the effects of the drug on her unborn child. Johnson was then taken to the hospital for observation.

Johnson was hospitalized again on January 23, 1989, when she was in labor. Johnson told Dr. Tompkins, an obstetrician, that she had used rock cocaine that morning while she was in labor. With the exception of finding meconium stain fluid in the amniotic sack, there were no other complications with the birth of Johnson's baby daughter. Approximately sixty-to-ninety seconds elapsed from the time the child's head emerged from her mother's birth canal until her umbilical cord was clamped.

The following day, the Department of Health and Rehabilitative Services investigated an abuse report of a cocaine baby concerning Johnson's daughter. Johnson told the investigator that she had smoked pot and crack cocaine three to four times every-other-day throughout the duration of her pregnancy with her daughter. Johnson's mother acknowledged that Johnson had been using cocaine for at least three years during the time her daughter and son were born.

At Johnson's trial, Dr. Tompkins testified that a mother's blood passes nutrients, oxygen and chemicals to an unborn child by a diffusion exchange at the capillary level from the womb to the placenta. The umbilical cord then circulates the baby's blood (including the exchange from its mother) between the placenta and the child. Metabolized cocaine derivatives in the mother's blood thus diffuse from the womb to the placenta, and then reach the baby through its umbilical cord. Although the blood flow is somewhat restricted during the birthing process, a measurable amount of blood is transferred from the placenta to the baby through the umbilical cord during delivery and after birth.

Dr. Shashi Gore, a pathologist and toxicologist, testified that cocaine has a half life of about one hour. This means that half of the amount of the drug remains in a person's blood stream for about one hour. The remainder gradually decreases over a period of forty-eight to seventy-two hours. The liver metabolizes the cocaine into benzoylecgonine which travels through the kidneys and into the urine until it is voided.

When Dr. Gore was asked whether a woman who had smoked cocaine at 10:00 p.m. and again between 6:00 and 7:00 a.m. the following morning and delivered a child at 1:00 p.m. that afternoon would still have cocaine or benzoylecgonine present in her blood stream at the time of delivery, the response was yes. When asked whether a woman who had smoked cocaine sometime the night before delivering a child at 8:00 in the morning would still have cocaine or benzoylecgonine in her system at the time of the child's birth, the response again was yes.

Dr. Stephen Kandall, a neonatologist, testified for the defense that it was impossible to tell whether the cocaine derivatives which appeared in these children's urine shortly after birth were the result of the exchange from the mother to her children before or after they were born because most of it took place from womb to the placenta before the birth process was complete.

He also testified that blood flow to the infant from the placenta through the umbilical cord to the child is restricted during contractions. Cocaine also constricts the passage of blood dramatically but benzoylecgonine does not. Dr. Kandall admitted that it is theoretically possible that cocaine or other substances can pass between a mother and her baby during the thirty-to-sixty-second period after the child is born and before the umbilical cord is cut, but that the amount would be tiny.

I submit there was no medical testimony adequate to support the trial court's finding that a "delivery" occurred here during the birthing process, even if the criminal statute is applicable. The expert witnesses all testified about blood flow from the umbilical cord to child. But that blood flow is the child's and the placenta through which it flows, is not part of the mother's body. No witness testified in this case that any cocaine derivatives passed from the mother's womb to the placenta during the sixty-to-ninety seconds after the child was expelled from the birth canal. That is when any "delivery" would have to have taken place under this statute, from one "person" to another "person."

Further, there was no evidence that Johnson timed her dosage of cocaine so as to be able to transmit some small amount after her child's birth. Predicting the day or hour of a child's birth is difficult to impossible even for experts. Had Johnson given birth one or two days later, the cocaine would have been completely eliminated, and no "crime" would have occurred. But since she went into labor which progressed to birth after taking cocaine when she did, the only way Johnson could have prevented the "delivery" would have been to have severed the cord before the child was born which, of course, would probably have killed both herself and her child. This illustrates the absurdity of applying the delivery-of-a-drug statute to this scenario.

However, in my view, the primary question in this case is whether section 893.13(1)(c)(1) was intended by the Legislature to apply to the birthing process. Before Johnson can be prosecuted under this statute, it must be clear that the Legislature intended for it to apply to the delivery of cocaine derivatives to a newborn during a sixty-to-ninety second interval, before severance of the umbilical cord. I can find no case where "delivery" of a drug was based on an involuntary act such as diffusion and blood flow. Criminal statutes must be strictly—not loosely—construed. § 775.021(1). . . .

Further, in construing a statute, we must consider its history, the evil to be corrected, the intention of the Legislature, the subject to be regulated and the objects to be attained. Legislative intent is the polestar by which the courts must be guided. Legislative intent may be express or it may be gathered from the purpose of the act, the administrative construction of it, other legislative acts bearing upon the subject, and all the circumstances surrounding and attendant upon it.

[Judge Sharp then reviewed the legislative history.]

From this legislative history, it is clear that the Legislature considered and rejected a specific statutory provision authorizing criminal penalties against mothers for delivering drug-affected children who received transfer of an illegal drug derivative metabolized by the mother's body, *in utero*. In light of this express legislative statement, I conclude that the Legislature never intended for the general drug delivery statute to authorize prosecutions of those mothers who take illegal drugs close enough in time to childbirth that a doctor could testify that a tiny amount passed from mother to child in the few seconds before the umbilical cord was cut. Criminal prosecution of mothers like Johnson will undermine Florida's express policy of "keeping families intact" and could destroy the family by incarcerating the child's mother when alternative measures could protect the child and stabilize the family.

* * *

Neither judges nor prosecutors can make criminal laws. This is the purview of the Legislature. If the Legislature wanted to punish the uterine transfer of cocaine from a mother to her fetus, it would be up to the Legislature to consider the attending public policy and constitutional arguments and then pass its legislation. The Legislature has not done so and the court has no power to make such a law.

[Judge Sharp then discussed cases from other jurisdictions rejecting arguments that mothers will be deterred from using drugs and induced to seek treatment if they risk criminal liability in cases similar to *Johnson*. Those cases suggest a likely opposite effect of potential criminal liability: the woman will likely either abort the child or avoid treatment out of a fear of prosecution.]

There can be no doubt that drug abuse is one of the most serious problems confronting our society today. Of particular concern is the alarming rise in the number of babies born with cocaine in their systems as a result of cocaine use by pregnant women. Some experts estimate that as many as eleven percent of pregnant women have used an illegal drug during pregnancy, and of those women, seventy-five percent have used cocaine. Others estimate that 375,000 newborns per year are born to women who are users of illicit drugs.

It is well-established that the effects of cocaine use by a pregnant woman on her fetus and later on her newborn can be severe. On average, cocaine-exposed babies have lower birth weights, shorter body lengths at birth, and smaller head circumferences than normal infants. Cocaine use may also result in sudden infant death syndrome, neural-behavioral deficiencies as well as other medical problems and long-term developmental abnormalities. The basic problem of damaging the fetus by drug use during pregnancy should not be addressed piecemeal, however, by prosecuting users who deliver their babies close in time to use of drugs and ignoring those who simply use drugs during their pregnancy.

* * *

However, prosecuting women for using drugs and "delivering" them to their newborns appears to be the least effective response to this crisis.[5] Rather than face the possibility of prosecution, pregnant women who are substance abusers may simply avoid prenatal or medical care for fear of being detected. Yet the newborns of these women are, as a group, the most fragile and sick, and most in need of hospital neonatal care. A decision to deliver these babies "at home" will have tragic and serious consequences. . . .

In summary, I would hold that section 893.13(1)(c)(1) does not encompass "delivery" of an illegal drug derivative from womb to placenta to umbilical cord to newborn after a child's birth. If that is the intent of the Legislature, then this statute should be redrafted to clearly address the basic problem of passing illegal substances from mother to child *in utero,* not just in the birthing process.

* * *

[Judge Sharp's opinion concludes.]

At oral argument the State acknowledged that no other jurisdiction has upheld a conviction of a mother for delivery of a controlled substance to an infant through either the umbilical cord or an *in utero* transmission; nor has the State submitted any subsequent authority to reflect that this fact has changed. The Court declines the State's invitation to walk down a path that the law, public policy, reason and common sense forbid it to tread. Therefore, we quash the decision below, answer the certified question in the negative, and remand with directions that Johnson's two convictions be reversed.

It is so ordered.

NOTES AND QUESTIONS

1. What would result in *Johnson* if the case arose in a jurisdiction with no specific statutes requiring "strict construction" in interpreting penal statutes?

---

[5] As the AMA Board of Trustees Report notes, possession of illicit drugs already results in criminal penalties and pregnant women who use illegal substances obviously are not deterred by existing sanctions. Thus the goal of deterrence is not served. To punish a person for substance abuse ignores the impaired capacity of these individuals to make rational decisions concerning their drug use. "In all but a few cases, taking a harmful substance such as cocaine is not meant to harm the fetus but to satisfy an acute psychological and physical need for that particular substance. If a pregnant woman suffers from a substance dependency, it is the physical impossibility of avoiding an impact on fetal health that causes severe damage to the fetus, not an intentional or malicious wish to cause harm." Punishment is simply not an effective way of curing a dependency or preventing future substance abuse. Stated another way: However the initial use of a drug might be characterized, its continued use by addicts is rarely, if ever, truly voluntarily. Drug addiction tends to obliterate rational, autonomous decision making about drug use. Drugs become a necessity for dependent users, even when they would much prefer to escape their addiction. In virtually all instances, a user specifically does not want to harm her fetus, yet she cannot resist the drive to use the drug. Thus it is not plausible to attribute to drug-using women a motive of causing harm to the fetus.

Would it be unconstitutional to extend a "delivery statute" such as Florida's to a woman in Ms. Johnson's situation? Would she lack required notice? Would such application of the statute illegally discriminate against her on the basis of gender?

2. If a jurisdiction chose to deal with the evils of drug abuse by imposing criminal penalties against pregnant women who "deliver" drugs to their children, must such statutes be limited only to those "deliveries" occurring following birth and before the umbilical cord is severed? Must the child be "born" to be a "person" to whom another delivers illegal drugs? Suppose a statute prohibited "delivering drugs to a fetus"? How might the woman's right to choose an abortion relate to these questions?

In some states it is arguably possible to find a mother guilty of a felony if she transmits the HIV virus through the umbilical cord even if the mother does not know that she is HIV-positive at the time she conceives the child. See Closen and Isaacman, *Are AIDS-Transmission Laws Encouraging Abortion?* A.B.A.J., December 1990, at 77.

3. As a policy matter, is criminal punishment of Ms. Johnson a good idea? Are any of the theories or goals of punishment promoted thereby? Consider the materials *infra* at § 2.06.

4. At least one court has found a state child abuse statute applicable to a situation where a pregnant mother ingested crack cocaine during the third trimester of her pregnancy causing her baby to be born with cocaine metabolites in its system. See *Whitner v. State*, 328 S. C. 1, 492 S.E.2d 777 (1996). In noting that South Carolina had long held that viable fetuses were "persons" holding certain rights and privileges, the court stated that "the prevention of children's problems" was "the most important strategy" as a matter of state legislative policy. The court added:

> The abuse or neglect of a child at any time during childhood can exact a profound toll on the child herself as well as on society as a whole. However, the consequences of abuse or neglect which takes [sic] place after birth often pale in comparison to those resulting from abuse suffered by the viable fetus before birth. This policy of prevention supports a reading of the word "person" [under the child abuse statute] to include viable fetuses. Furthermore, the scope of the Children's Code is quite broad. It applies "to all children who have need of services." When coupled with the comprehensive remedial purposes of the Code, this language supports the inference that the legislature intended to include viable fetuses within the scope of the Code's protection.

Dissenters in *Whitner* argued that the statute should be strictly construed in favor of the defendant. For the dissenters, the majority's finding that viable fetuses were "persons" was based on decisions in areas of civil wrongful death and common law feticide and were thus inapplicable to the context of statutory child abuse. The dissenters further objected as follows:

> In construing this statue to include conduct not contemplated by the legislature, the majority has rendered the statute vague and set for itself the task of determining what conduct is unlawful. Is a pregnant woman's failure to obtain prenatal care unlawful? Failure to take vitamins and eat

properly? Failure to quit smoking or drinking? Although the majority dismisses this issue as not before it, the impact of today's decision is to render a pregnant woman potentially criminally liable for myriad acts which the legislature has not seen fit to criminalize. To ignore this "down-the-road" consequence in a case of this import is unrealistic.

The majority attempts to support an overinclusive construction of the child abuse and neglect statute by citing other legal protections extended equally to a viable fetus and a child in being. The only law, however, that specifically regulates the conduct of a mother toward her unborn child is our abortion statute under which a viable fetus is in fact treated differently from a child in being.

The majority argues for equal treatment of viable fetuses and children, yet its construction of the statute results in even greater inequities. If the statute applies only when a fetus is "viable," a pregnant woman can use cocaine for the first twenty-four weeks of her pregnancy, the most crucial period for the fetus, and be immune from prosecution under the statute so long as she quits drug use before the fetus becomes viable. Further, a pregnant woman, under the majority opinion, now faces up to ten years in prison for ingesting drugs during pregnancy but can have an illegal abortion and receive only a two-year sentence for killing her viable fetus.

As a policy matter, is criminal punishment of the mother in *Whitner* justified? Are any of the theories of punishment discussed earlier in this Chapter promoted by her conviction?

For critical commentary of *Whitner* see, e.g., Comment, *Fatal Abuse Prosecutions: The Triumph of Reaction Over Reason*, 47 DePaul L. Rev. 989 (1998); Comment, *Looking for a Solution: Determining Fetal Status for Prenatal Drug Abuse Prosecutions*, 38 Santa Clara L. Rev. 1255 (1998).

§ 2.06 WHAT CONDUCT SHOULD BE PUNISHED?

With its recognition of the crime of "conspiracy to corrupt public morals," the Shaw case raises the issue of the appropriateness of employing the criminal law to regulate immoral conduct that may manifest little immediate "harm." This section considers this issue as well as the general policy problem of determining when conduct is appropriately subjected to the criminal sanction. The materials begin, however, by attending to examples of constitutional protection of certain conduct thus restricting its criminalization. While a variety of constitutional provisions insulate conduct in certain circumstances from criminal regulation, see e.g., *Wisconsin v. Yoder,* 406 U.S. 205 (1972) (free exercise clause protects Amish parents against punishment under compulsory education law for failing to send their teenage children to school); *Texas v. Johnson,* 491 U.S. 397 (1989) (free speech clause protects against punishment under flag desecration statute where political protester burns the American flag), these materials focus on constitutional issues relating to the protection of consensual sexual activity in private. This context provides an opportunity to raise questions about the appropriate reach of the criminal law in an area of expanding constitutional protection that may pose challenges to traditional mores.

[A] Constitutionally Protected Conduct

GRISWOLD v. CONNECTICUT

Supreme Court of the United States

381 U.S. 479 (1965)

Mr. Justice DOUGLAS *delivered the opinion of the Court.*

Appellant Griswold is Executive Director of the Planned Parenthood League of Connecticut. Appellant Buxton is a licensed physician and a professor at the Yale Medical School who served as Medical Director for the League at its Center in New Haven—a center open and operating from November 1 to November 10, 1961, when appellants were arrested.

They gave information, instruction, and medical advice to *married persons* as to the means of preventing conception. They examined the wife and prescribed the best contraceptive device or material for her use. Fees were usually charged, although some couples were serviced free.

The statutes whose constitutionality is involved in this appeal are §§ 53–32 and 54–196 of the General Statutes of Connecticut (1958 rev.). The former provides: "Any person who uses any drug, medicinal article or instrument for the purpose of preventing conception shall be fined not less than fifty dollars or imprisoned not less than sixty days nor more than one year or be both fined and imprisoned." Section 54–196 provides: "Any person who assists, abets, counsels, causes, hires or commands another to commit any offense may be prosecuted and punished as if he were the principal offender."

The appellants were found guilty as accessories and fined $100 each, against the claim that the accessory statute as so applied violated the Fourteenth Amendment. The Appellate Division of the Circuit Court affirmed. The Supreme Court of Errors affirmed that judgment. We noted probable jurisdiction.

* * *

Coming to the merits, we are met with a wide range of questions that implicate the Due Process Clause of the Fourteenth Amendment. . . . We do not sit as a super-legislature to determine the wisdom, need, and propriety of laws that touch economic problems, business affairs, or social conditions. This law, however, operates directly on an intimate relation of husband and wife and their physician's role in one aspect of that relation.

The association of people is not mentioned in the Constitution nor in the Bill of Rights. The right to educate a child in a school of the parents' choice—whether public or private or parochial—is also not mentioned. Nor is the right to study any particular subject or any foreign language. Yet the First Amendment has been construed to include certain of those rights.

[The Court discusses previous cases where Bill of Rights protections were extended to embrace rights not expressly specified in the text of the Constitution.]

The foregoing cases suggest that specific guarantees in the Bill of Rights have penumbras, formed by emanations from those guarantees that help give them life and substance. . . . Various guarantees create zones of privacy. The right of association contained in the penumbra of the First Amendment is one, as we have seen. The Third Amendment in its prohibition against the quartering of soldiers "in any house" in time of peace without the consent of the owner is another facet of that privacy. The Fourth Amendment explicitly affirms the "right of the people to be secure in their persons, houses, papers, and effects, against unreasonable searches and seizures." The Fifth Amendment in its Self-Incrimination Clause enables the citizen to create a zone of privacy which government may not force him to surrender to his detriment. The Ninth Amendment provides: "The enumeration in the Constitution, of certain rights, shall not be construed to deny or disparage others retained by the people."

We have had many controversies over these penumbral rights of "privacy and repose." . . . These cases bear witness that the right of privacy which presses for recognition here is a legitimate one.

The present case, then, concerns a relationship lying within the zone of privacy created by several fundamental constitutional guarantees. And it concerns a law which, in forbidding the use of contraceptives rather than regulating their manufacture or sale, seeks to achieve its goals by means having a maximum destructive impact upon that relationship. Such a law cannot stand in light of the familiar principle, so often applied by this Court, that a "governmental purpose to control or prevent activities constitutionally subject to state regulation may not be achieved by means which sweep unnecessarily broadly and thereby invade the area of protected freedoms." . . . Would we allow the police to search the sacred precincts of marital bedrooms for telltale signs of the use of contraceptives? The very idea is repulsive to the notions of privacy surrounding the marriage relationship.

We deal with a right of privacy older than the Bill of Rights—older than our political parties, older than our school system. Marriage is a coming together for better or for worse, hopefully enduring, and intimate to the degree of being sacred. It is an association that promotes a way of life, not causes; a harmony in living, not political faiths; a bilateral loyalty, not commercial or social projects. Yet it is an association for as noble a purpose as any involved in our prior decisions.

Reversed.

Mr. Justice GOLDBERG, whom THE CHIEF JUSTICE and Mr. Justice BRENNAN join, *concurring.*

I agree with the Court that Connecticut's birth-control law unconstitutionally intrudes upon the right of marital privacy, and I join in its opinion and judgment.. . . .

* * *

. . . [I]t should be said of the Court's holding today that it in no way interferes with a State's proper regulation of sexual promiscuity or misconduct. As my Brother Harlan so well stated . . . [:]

Adultery, homosexuality and the like are sexual intimacies which the State forbids but the intimacy of husband and wife is necessarily an essential and accepted feature of the institution of marriage, an institution which the State not only must allow, but which always and in every age it has fostered and protected. It is one thing when the State exerts its power either to forbid extra-marital sexuality or to say who may marry, but it is quite another when, having acknowledged a marriage and the intimacies inherent in it, it undertakes to regulate by means of the criminal law the details of that intimacy.

In sum, I believe that the right of privacy in the marital relation is fundamental and basic. . . . Connecticut cannot constitutionally abridge this fundamental right, which is protected by the Fourteenth Amendment from infringement by the States. I agree with the Court that petitioners' convictions must therefore be reversed.

[The concurring opinions of Justices Harlan and White, and the dissenting opinions of Justices Black and Stewart are omitted.]

Notes and Questions

1. The *Griswold* case is frequently viewed as a case protecting "procreative choice." Subsequent cases tend to emphasize the rationale of protecting procreative choice, and do not limit constitutional protections to persons who are married. For instance, in *Eisenstadt v. Baird,* 405 U.S. 438, 453 (1972), the Court held unconstitutional a state statute that criminalized the distribution of contraceptives to unmarried persons but not to married couples. The Court stated that "if the right of privacy means anything, it is the right of the *individual,* married or single, to be free from unwanted governmental intrusions into matters so fundamentally affecting a person as the decision whether to bear or beget a child." Moreover, in *Carey v. Population Services International,* 431 U.S. 678 (1977), the Court struck down a state ban on distribution of contraceptives to minors.

Others see *Griswold* as a case protecting a more general right to "privacy." Support for that view is often drawn from the words of Justice Douglas in his Griswold opinion: "Would we allow the police to search . . . marital bedrooms for. . . the use of contraceptives?" To what extent does the privacy rationale extend beyond protection of activities occurring in the *marital* bedroom?

2. In *Roe v. Wade,* 410 U.S. 113 (1973), the Court seemingly drew from both the procreative choice and privacy rationales in invalidating statutes prohibiting abortions, at least those performed in the first trimester of pregnancy. The Court's recognition of constitutional protection of a woman's right to make abortion decisions has been followed by a steady stream of cases aimed at

defining the extent of the right as it collides with state attempts to regulate abortion, often through the criminal law. See *Planned Parenthood v. Casey,* 505 U.S. 833 (1992), and cases cited therein.

3. Some view *Griswold* and its progeny as embracing broad protection for a right to engage in sexual intimacy in private with other consenting adults. The Court, in a 5–4 decision, rejected such a right, at least in the context of homosexual activity, in *Bowers v. Hardwick,* 478 U.S. 186 (1986). In upholding a Georgia statute criminalizing sodomy, the Court noted:

> This case does not require a judgment on whether laws against sodomy between consenting adults in general, or between homosexuals in particular, are wise or desirable. . . . The issue presented is whether the Federal Constitution confers a fundamental right upon homosexuals to engage in sodomy and thus invalidates the laws of many States that still make such conduct illegal and have done so for a very long time. . . .
>
> [The Court then held that the *Griswold* line of cases did not go so far as to extend the right of privacy to cover private consensual homosexual sodomy or any other private consensual sexual activity that is not connected with family, procreation, or marriage.]
>
> Even if the conduct at issue here is not a fundamental right, respondent asserts that there must be a rational basis for the law and that there is none in this case other than the presumed belief of a majority of the electorate in Georgia that homosexual sodomy is immoral and unacceptable. This is said to be an inadequate rationale to support the law. The law, however, is constantly based on notions of morality, and if all laws representing essentially moral choices are to be invalidated under the Due Process Clause, the courts will be very busy indeed. Even respondent makes no such claim, but insists that majority sentiments about the morality of homosexuality should be declared inadequate. We disagree, and are unpersuaded that the sodomy laws of some 25 states should be invalidated on this basis.

478 U.S. at 190, 196.

Justice Blackmun, joined by Justices Brennan, Marshall, and Stevens, dissented, arguing that the state could not constitutionally punish private acts of sodomy between consenting adults.

> The statute at issue . . . [d]enies individuals the right to decide for themselves whether to engage in particular forms of private, consensual sexual activity. The Court concludes that [the statute] is valid essentially because "the laws of . . . many States . . . still make such conduct illegal and have done so for a very long time." . . . But the fact that moral judgments expressed by statutes . . . may be "natural and familiar" . . . ought not to conclude our judgment upon the question whether statutes embodying them conflict with the Constitution of the United States. . . . I believe that "[i]t is revolting to have no better reason for a rule of law than that so it was laid down in the time of Henry IV." It is still more revolting if the grounds on which it was laid down have vanished long since and the rule simply persists from blind imitation of the past. I believe we must analyze respondent's claim in the light of the values that underlie the constitutional right to privacy. If that right means anything, it means that before

Georgia can prosecute its citizens for making choices about the most intimate aspects of their lives it must do more than assert that the choice they have made is an "abominable crime not fit to be named among Christians." . . .

478 U.S. at 199, 200. (Blackmun, J., dissenting.)

4. The statute at issue in *Hardwick* also applies to heterosexual sodomy between both married and unmarried couples. After *Hardwick,* what results if a married couple is prosecuted for sodomy under a statute similar to Georgia's? For a pre-*Hardwick*, but post-*Eisenstadt* no. 1, p. 172, decision, see *State v. Bateman,* 547 P.2d 6 (Az. 1976) (*en banc*) (holding state statutes prohibiting sodomy and "lewd and lascivious" acts constitutional despite application to married couples based on state interest in protecting the "moral welfare" of its people). What if an unmarried heterosexual couple is charged with sodomy? See *Schochet v. Maryland,* 320 Md. 714, 580 A.2d 176 (Md. Ct. Spec. App. 1990) (statute criminalizing "unnatural and perverted sexual practices" interpreted as not prohibiting consensual, noncommercial, heterosexual activity between adults in the privacy of the home so as to avoid serious constitutional question); *Post v. State,* 715 P.2d 1105 (Okla. Crim. App. 1986), *reh. den.* 717 P.2d 1151 (1986), *cert. den.* 479 U.S. 890 (1986) (overturning heterosexual sodomy conviction on grounds that federal constitutional right to privacy extends to matters of sexual gratification at least with respect to heterosexuals).

5. The *Hardwick* majority stated that it "would be difficult, except by fiat, to limit the claimed right to homosexual conduct while leaving exposed to prosecution, adultery, incest, and other sexual crimes . . . committed in the home." Can you think of any principled distinction that would allow criminal prosecution of such acts as adultery, incest, statutory rape, and bestiality while still recognizing a right for adults to engage in private, consensual, noncommercial, homosexual activity? If such a distinction can be drawn, could a state still punish fornication? See *State v. Saunders,* 381 A.2d 333 (N.J. 1977) (invalidating New Jersey's fornication statute on grounds that such sexual activities between adults are protected by right to privacy under state and federal constitutions). See generally Note, *Fornication, Cohabitation, and the Constitution,* 77 Mich. L. Rev. 252 (1978); Note, *Constitutional Barriers to Civil and Criminal Restrictions on Pre-and Extra-Marital Sex,* 104 Harv. L. Rev. 1660 (1991); Siegel, *For Better or Worse: Adultery, Crime & the Constitution,* 30 J. Fam. L. 45 (1991).

6. In *Hardwick,* the Court stated that the decision "raises no question about . . . state court decisions invalidating [homosexual sodomy] laws on state constitutional grounds." Moreover, outside of the context of sodomy, some state courts have recognized fairly broad protection of privacy rights under state constitutional provisions. See, e.g., *Ravin v. State,* 537 P.2d 494 (Alaska 1975) (state constitutional provision embracing the right to privacy violated by state law criminalizing possession of marijuana in the home by adults for personal use). Such arguments have not fared as well on federal constitutional grounds. See *People v. Shepard,* 409 N.E.2d 840 (N.Y. 1980) (possession of marijuana in the home by adults not protected under federal right to privacy); *State v. Erickson,* 574 P.2d 1 (Alaska 1978) (federal right to privacy does not preclude criminalization of cocaine possession in the home by adults).

7. In some states it is arguably possible to find a mother guilty of a felony if she transmits the HIV virus to her child through the umbilical cord even if the mother does not know that she is HIV-positive at the time the child is conceived. See Closen and Isaacman, *Are Aids-Transmission Laws Encouraging Abortion?*, A.B.A.J., December 1990, at 77. Would the right to privacy, specifically the "procreative choice" aspect, contained in *Griswold* and its progeny prohibit enforcement of such a law against mothers contracting AIDS through sexual activity? Would it make a difference if the woman is not married or if the child is not fathered by her husband if she is married?

[B] Policy Issues

Assuming that no constitutional barriers preclude punishing conduct deemed undesirable, when is it advisable as a policy matter to make such conduct criminal? What considerations should policy makers take into account in deciding when to impose the criminal sanction? These materials address such questions by examining the relationship between harmful conduct and criminal liability. The following excerpts and notes raise three issues: (1) whether all conduct harmful to identifiable victims should be criminalized; (2) whether conduct that merely risks harm to identifiable victims should be criminalized; and (3) whether conduct deemed immoral that neither harms nor raises a risk of harm to identifiable victims should be criminalized. After discussing the first two issues in the context of a general discussion of the role harm plays in criminal theory, this chapter concludes by highlighting the debate surrounding whether the criminal law should be utilized simply to enforce moral principle.

[1] The Role of Harm

The criminal law is generally perceived as the paradigmatic instance of the law's prohibition of "harm." Murder, rape, assault, and even gambling in some way suggest harm to others. But as the rules surrounding attempt, conspiracy, and solicitation (discussed in detail in Chapter 7 *infra*) graphically demonstrate, "harm," in its usual sense, is not always a prerequisite to criminal liability. The criminal law will often intervene before "harm" has occurred if there exists a substantial risk of criminal consequences. There are, of course, numerous other instances in which this is true. Reckless (or drunken) driving, possession of burglary tools, perjury (where harm might not occur because the fact finder might find the truth in any event), and possession of drugs are examples where the criminal law intervenes even though there is no necessity that "harm" occur. One commentator has gone so far as to say, "Though 'harm' is still the official theoretical basis for labeling anything 'crime,' it seems clear that our current system depends far more heavily on 'danger' and 'dangerousness.' Indeed the main historical trend seems to have been from 'harm' to 'danger' to 'dangerousness.'" Seney, *A Pond as Deep as Hell—Harm, Danger and Dangerousness in Our Criminal Law,* 18 Wayne L. Rev. 569, 632 (1972).

Clearly, however, current law has not abandoned the concept of harm. Much dangerous activity not resulting in harm is left unpunished, although for reasons not always easy to articulate. Consider, for example, a variation on a famous theme noted in 3 *Stephen* 311. Suppose two trains are being driven by Engineers A and B, respectively. Both A and B fall asleep for five minutes while operating their trains. When A awakes he discovers that his train is moving inexorably toward an obstruction on the tracks that will cause the train to derail. Had he not fallen asleep, A would have had notice of the obstruction in ample time to have stopped the train. A's train hits the obstruction and derails; several passengers are killed. When B awakes, however, absolutely nothing untoward occurs. While A and B are both equally negligent and "dangerous," only A will be subject to criminal liability because criminal negligence traditionally requires harmful consequences.

Along these lines, consider the following:

> . . . Suppose that a driver, X, overtakes on the brow of a hill when he cannot see whether anything is coming in the opposite direction. If anything were coming, there would certainly be a crash and, obviously, someone might be killed. But nothing is coming and no harm is done. Certainly X ought to be convicted of dangerous driving; but to convict him of attempted murder would be rather startling. Yet there is evidence that he was reckless whether he caused death and if recklessness is indistinguishable in law from intention, there is equally evidence that he was guilty of attempted murder. . .

Smith, *The Element of Chance in Criminal Liability,* 1971 Crim. L. Rev. 63, 73.

The emphasis on harmful consequences is further puzzling in the context of the traditional approach, which punishes attempts less severely than "completed" crimes. Suppose that X intends to kill Y, aims a loaded gun at Y's heart, and pulls the trigger but does not kill Y because the bullet hits a metal badge which Y, unbeknownst to X, happened to be wearing over his heart. X will be guilty of attempted murder and punished less severely than he would have been had Y died, even though X has manifested all the characteristics of a murderer. Why should the fortuitous presence of a metal badge affect X's liability?

Conversely if X intends only minor harm, what is the purpose of punishing X more severely, as the law sometimes does, if she causes more harm than was intended (or risked, where X is reckless)? The following materials address these and other issues. See also § 7.02[H], *infra.*

HALL

213–15, 217, 219–22

It should, indeed, evoke little wonder that "harm" is a central notion of penal theory. "The problem of evil" is deeply imbedded in the human drama, and the proscribed harms have played the major role in it. It was passionate reaction against grievous wrongs which long ago set into motion the course of legal history that culminated in modern penal law; and any thorough discussion of that law can hardly exaggerate the significance of those stimuli.

It is said or implied . . . that many crimes are not harmful, indeed, that some of them, e.g., criminal attempts, the possession of burglar's tools or counterfeit money, have no effect whatever; and, also, that legislatures forbid all sorts of consequences, some of which may be ethically neutral or even good. The corollaries are that harm is not essential in penal law and that "harm" can mean no more than the effect of any proscribed behavior or conduct. . . . [O]n that premise, there is no possibility of acquiring any knowledge of penal effects. In that formal perspective, the effect of any criminal conduct is only an "X." In practice, however, it is impossible to restrict the meaning of "effect" in that way, as any lawyer who has participated in a criminal trial will aver.

Certainly, there is nothing formal about being robbed or killed, and in early societies criminal law was for the most part limited to the proscription of such observable injuries. But in a more advanced view, a harm is a negation, a disvalue, the lack of a natural condition, and the like. Thus, harm implies the existence of values, interests or natural conditions. . . .

* * *

It should be recognized, . . . that penal harms, while they refer to, are far from being restricted to, physical injuries. In libel, kidnaping, perjury, political crimes, many sexual offenses and others, there is no physical injury; and in still others . . . the physical injury may be insignificant. Since it is generally agreed that there are actual harms in these crimes, the notion of "criminal harm" must be stated in terms of intangibles such as harm to institutions, public safety, the autonomy of women, reputation and so on. In short, harm signifies the loss of a value. Regardless of the materiality of any object, its value always involves personal appraisal of, and attitudes towards, that object, i.e., people value things; hence the locus of a value or a disvalue is not simply in the thing itself. In addition, penal harm must be defined in relation to conduct expressing mentes reae. Penal harm, accordingly, has certain normative-empirical references. It is a complex of fact, valuation and interpersonal relations—not an observable thing or effect, as is sometimes assumed. Only if the incorporeality of penal harm is borne in mind, can the more difficult questions regarding the so-called "inchoate" or "formal" crimes be elucidated.

. . . Any conduct has at least two references or dimensions: It originates in an actor and, to some extent, by the mere fact of its presence, it alters pre-existing conditions, i.e., it has some effect. For example, the taking possession of burglar's tools or narcotics by persons who intend to use them illegally alters the previous condition of affairs. The quality of daily life is impaired by such conduct; and one need only ask whether he would want to live in a community where attempts to kill and to commit robberies and arsons were frequent, to indicate that there are harmful effects of such conduct not only in the apprehension aroused but also in the increased danger of becoming the victim of a more serious crime.

This is the externality of the penal harm by reference to which its correlate, criminal conduct, is distinguished from merely unethical intentions and unethical actions which are not criminal. "Penal harm" also serves to limit the legal effect of an offender's moral culpability and thus to distinguish the ethics of legal punishment from the purely ethical evaluation of immoral conduct. In sum, criminal conduct is legally significant in relation to a penal harm; and any conduct which actualizes a *mens rea* alters the external world, it has effect. If, nevertheless, certain preparations are not penalized in the common law and other legal systems, the reason is a practical one of policy; in logic and theory a harm has been committed.

* * *

. . . [T]he principle of harm serves the following purposes:

1. It is essential in distinguishing the ethics of criminal law ("penal policy") from pure ethics.

2. Craftsmanship depends on the availability of precise tools; and the need to resolve the ambiguity of "act" also supports the distinction of harm and conduct. In addition to the analytical gain, there are practical needs that are served, e.g., in solving various jurisdictional questions and problems involving double jeopardy.

3. It provides a rational basis for punishment as well as for the differentiation of punishments, i.e., in proportion to the gravity of the harm. It is also important in corrective treatment since an offender's harm-doing must be considered in determining his dangerousness.

4. As the summation of all the specific proscribed harms, the principle of harm functions as an essential organizational construct. Other principles of criminal law, especially those concerning conduct and causation, presuppose that of harm. If harm is excluded, conduct and causation become irrelevant, and the combined result is a great loss in the systematization of the criminal law.

Notes and Questions

1. Is Hall correct in his view that the principle of harm "is essential in distinguishing the ethics of criminal law from pure ethics"? For example, does the principle of harm explain why telling lies is generally left to the arena of "pure ethics" rather than being subjected to regulation under the criminal law?

2. Is Hall correct in his view that the principle of harm provides a "rational basis for the differentiation of punishments, i.e., in proportion to the gravity of the harm"? Why is it "rational" to punish attempts less severely than completed crimes? How would Hall account for the fact that a growing minority of states now hold that attempts should be punished as severely as completed crimes? See Model Penal Code § 5.05.

[2] Immorality as Sufficient Ground for Criminal Liability

DEVLIN, *THE ENFORCEMNET OF MORALS*

7–10, 12–22 (1968)

I think it is clear that the criminal law as we know it is based upon moral principle. In a number of crimes its function is simply to enforce a moral principle and nothing else. The law, both criminal and civil, claims to be able to speak about morality and immorality generally. Where does it get its authority to do this and how does it settle the moral principles which it enforces? Undoubtedly, as a matter of history, it derived both from Christian teaching. But I think that the strict logician is right when he says that the law can no longer rely on doctrines in which citizens are entitled to disbelieve. It is necessary therefore to look for some other source.

In jurisprudence, as I have said, everything is thrown open to discussion and, in the belief that they cover the whole field, I have framed three interrogatories addressed to myself to answer:

1. Has society the right to pass judgment at all on matters of morals? Ought there, in other words, to be a public morality, or are morals always a matter for private judgment?

2. If society has the right to pass judgment, has it also the right to use the weapon of the law to enforce it?

3. If so, ought it to use that weapon in all cases or only in some; and if only in some, on what principles should it distinguish?

I shall begin with the first interrogatory and consider what is meant by the right of society to pass a moral judgment, that is, a judgment about what is good and what is evil. The fact that a majority of people may disapprove of a practice does not of itself make it a matter for society as a whole. Nine men out of ten may disapprove of what the tenth man is doing and still say that it is not their business. There is a case for a collective judgment (as distinct from a large number of individual opinions which sensible people may even refrain from pronouncing at all if it is upon somebody else's private affairs) only if society is affected. Without a collective judgment there can be no case at all for intervention. . . .

* * *

This view—that there is such a thing as public morality—can be justified by *a priori* argument. What makes a society of any sort is community of ideas, not only political ideas but also ideas about the way its members should behave and govern their lives; these latter ideas are its morals. Every society has a moral structure as well as a political one: or rather, since that might suggest two independent systems, I should say that the structure of every society is made up both of politics and morals. . .

* * *

. . . [S]ociety means a community of ideas; without shared ideas on politics, morals, and ethics no society can exist. Each one of us has ideas about what is good and what is evil; they cannot be kept private from the society in which we live. If men and women try to create a society in which there is no fundamental agreement about good and evil they will fail; if, having based it on common agreement, the agreement goes, the society will disintegrate. For society is not something that is kept together physically; it is held by the invisible bonds of common thought. If the bonds were too far relaxed the members would drift apart. A common morality is part of the bondage. The bondage is part of the price of society; and mankind, which needs society, must pay its price.

* * *

I think, therefore, that it is not possible to set theoretical limits to the power of the State to legislate against immorality. It is not possible to settle in advance exceptions to the general rule or to define inflexibly areas of morality into which the law is in no circumstances to be allowed to enter. Society is entitled by means of its laws to protect itself from dangers, whether from within or without. Here again I think that the political parallel is legitimate. The law of treason is directed against aiding the king's enemies and against sedition from within. The justification for this is that established government is necessary for the existence of society and therefore its safety against violent overthrow must be secured. But an established morality is as necessary as good government to the welfare of society. Societies disintegrate from within more frequently than they are broken up by external pressures. There is disintegration when no common morality is observed and history shows that the loosening of moral bonds is often the first stage of disintegration, so that society is justified in taking the same steps to preserve its moral code as it does to preserve its government and other essential institutions. The suppression of vice is as much the law's business as the suppression of subversive activities; it is no more possible to define a sphere of private morality than it is to define one of private subversive activity. . . . You may argue that if a man's sins affect only himself it cannot be the concern of society. If he chooses to get drunk every night in the privacy of his own home, is any one except himself the worse for it? But suppose a quarter or a half of the population got drunk every night, what sort of society would it be? You cannot set a theoretical limit to the number of people who can get drunk before society is entitled to legislate against drunkenness. The same may be said of gambling. The Royal Commission on Betting, Lotteries, and Gaming took as their test the character of the citizens as a member of society. They said: "Our concern with the ethical significance of gambling is confined to the effect which it may have on the character of the gambler as a member of society. If we were convinced that whatever the degree of gambling this effect must be harmful we should be inclined to think that it was the duty of the state to restrict gambling to the greatest extent practicable."

. . . How is the law-maker to ascertain the moral judgments of society? It is surely not enough that they should be reached by the opinion of the majority; it would be too much to require the individual assent of every citizen. English law has evolved and regularly uses a standard which does not depend on the counting of heads. It is that of the reasonable man. He is not to be confused with the rational man. He is not expected to reason about anything and his judgment may be largely a matter of feeling. It is the viewpoint of the man in the street—or to use an archaism familiar to all lawyers—the man in the Clapham omnibus. He might also be called the right-minded man. For my purpose I should like to call him the man in the jury box, for the moral judgment of society must be something about which any twelve men or women drawn at random might after discussion be expected to be unanimous. . . .

Immorality then, for the purpose of the law, is what every right-minded person is presumed to consider to be immoral. Any immorality is capable of affecting society injuriously and in effect to a greater or lesser extent it usually does; this is what gives the law its *locus standi*. It cannot be shut out. But . . . the individual has a *locus standi* too; he cannot be expected to surrender to the judgment of society the whole conduct of his life. It is the old and familiar question of striking a balance between the rights and interests of society and those of the individual. . . .

* * *

[I]t is possible to make general statements of principle which it may be thought the legislature should bear in mind when it is considering the enactment of laws enforcing morals.

I believe that most people would agree upon the chief of these elastic principles. There must be toleration of the maximum individual freedom that is consistent with the integrity of society. It cannot be said that this is a principle that runs all through the criminal law. Much of the criminal law that is regulatory in character—the part of it that deals with *malum prohibitum* rather than *malum in se*—is based upon the opposite principle, that is, that the choice of the individual must give way to the convenience of the man. But in all matters of conscience the principle I have stated is generally held to prevail. It is not confined to thought and speech; it extends to action, as is shown by the recognition of the right to conscientious objection in wartime; this example shows also the conscience will be respected even in times of national danger. The principle appears to me to be peculiarly appropriate to all questions of morals. Nothing should be punished by the law that does not live beyond the limits of tolerance. It is not nearly enough to say that a majority dislike a practice; there must be a real feeling of reprobation. . . . I do not think one can ignore disgust if it is deeply felt and not manufactured. Its presence is a good indication that the bounds of toleration are being reached. Not everything is to be tolerated. No society can do without intolerance, indignation, and disgust; they are the forces behind the moral law, and indeed it can be argued that if they or something like them are not present, the feelings of society cannot be weighty enough to deprive the individual of freedom of choice. . . . But matters of this sort are not determined by rational argument. Every moral judgment, unless it claims a divine source, is simply a feeling that no right-minded man could behave in any other way without admitting that he was doing wrong. It is the power of common sense and not the power of reason that is behind the judgments of society. But before a society can put a practice beyond the limits of tolerance there must be a deliberate judgment that the practice is injurious to society. There is, for example, a general abhorrence of homosexuality. We should ask ourselves in the first instance whether, looking at it calmly and dispassionately, we regard it as a vice so abominable that its mere presence is any offense. If that is the genuine feeling of the society in which we live, I do not see how society can be denied the right to eradicate it.

. . . I return therefore to the simple and observable fact that in matters of morals the limits of tolerance shift. Laws, especially those which are based on morals, are less easily moved. It follows as another good working principle that in any new matter of morals the law should be slow to act. By the next generation the swell of indignation may have abated and the law be left without the strong backing which it needs. But it is then difficult to alter the law without giving the impression that moral judgment is being weakened. This is now one of the factors that is strongly militating against any alteration to the law on homosexuality.

A third elastic principle must be advanced more tentatively. It is that as far as possible privacy should be respected. This is not an idea that has ever been made explicit in the criminal law. Acts or words done or said in public or in private are all brought within its scope without distinction in principle. But there goes with this a strong reluctance on the part of judges and legislators to sanction invasions of privacy in the detection of crime. The police have no more right to trespass than the ordinary citizen has; there is no general right of search; to this extent an Englishman's home is still his castle. . . .

This indicates a general sentiment that the right to privacy is something to be put in the balance against the enforcement of the law. Ought the same sort of consideration to play any part in the formation of the law? Clearly only in a very limited number of cases. When the help of the law is invoked by an injured citizen, privacy must be irrelevant; the individual cannot ask that his right to privacy should be measured against injury criminally done to another. But when all who are involved in the deed are consenting parties and the injury is done to morals, the public interest in the moral order can be balanced against the claims of privacy. . . .

The last and the biggest thing to be remembered is that the law is concerned with the minimum and not with the maximum; there is much in the Sermon on the Mount that would be out of place in the Ten Commandments. We all recognize the gap between the moral law and the law of the land. No man is worth much who regulates his conduct with the sole object of escaping punishment, and every worthy society sets for its members standards which are above those of the law. We recognize the existence of such higher standards when we use expressions such as "moral obligation" and "morally bound." The distinction was well put in the judgment of African elders in a family dispute: "We have power to make you divide the crops, for this is our law, and we will see this is done. But we have not power to make you behave like an upright man."

It can only be because this point is so obvious that it is so frequently ignored. Discussion among lawmakers, both professional and amateur, is too often limited to what is right or wrong and good or bad for society. There is failure to keep separate the two questions I have earlier posed—the question of society's right to pass a moral judgment and the question of whether the arm of the law should be used to enforce the judgment. The criminal law is not a statement of how people ought to behave; it is a statement of what will happen to them if they do not behave; good citizens are not expected to come within reach of it or to set their sights by it, and every enactment should be framed accordingly.

The arm of the law is an instrument to be used by society, and the decision about what particular cases it should be used in is essentially a practical one. Since it is an instrument, it is wise before deciding to use it to have regard to the tools with which it can be fitted and to the machinery which operates it. . . .

* * *

. . . The line that divides the criminal law from the moral is not determinable by the application of any clear-cut principle. . . . The boundary between the criminal law and the moral law is fixed by balancing in the case of each particular crime the pros and cons of legal enforcement in accordance with the sort of considerations I have been outlining. . . . But the true principle is that the law exists for the protection of society. It does not discharge its functions by protecting the individual from injury, annoyance, corruption, and exploitation; the law must protect also the institutions and the community of ideas, political and moral, without which people cannot live together. Society cannot ignore the morality of the individual any more than it can his loyalty; it flourishes on both and without either it dies.

NOTES AND QUESTIONS

1. For a view similar to Devlin's, see E. Durkeim, The Division of Labor in Society 93–107 (Simpson trans., 1933). For a critique of Devlin's views, see H.L.A. Hart, *Law, Liberty, and Morality* (1963); Dworkin, *Lord Devlin and the Enforcement of Morals,* 75 Yale L.J. 662 (1962). For support of Devlin's view that "there is no principled line following the contours of the distinction between immoral and harmful conduct such that only grounds referring to the latter may be invoked to justify criminalization," see G. Dworkin, *Devlin Was Right: Law and the Enforcement of Morality,* 40 Wm. & Mary L. Rev. 927 (1999). See also the responses to Dworkin from Murphy, *Moral Reasons and the Limitations of Liberty,* 40 Wm. & Mary L. Rev. 947 (1999) and Becks, *Crimes Against Autonomy: Gerald Dworkin on the Enforcement of Morality,* 40 Wm. & Mary 959 (1999).

2. Is Devlin mistaken in his conclusion that it is impossible to set theoretical limits on the state's power to legislate against immorality? If he is mistaken, what are the theoretical limits?

3. Assuming that society is bound together by a "common morality," is its enforcement by the criminal law necessarily appropriate? Does Devlin provide an adequate standard for determining the content of the "common morality"?

Packer

249–50, 264–67, 296,301–5, 312

. . . In our present state of comparative ignorance about the sources and control of human conduct there is no escape from the use of punishment (whether criminal or not) as a device for reducing the incidence of behavior that we consider antisocial. There is also no escape from the conclusion that punishment is morally ambiguous: we cannot be sure that it does more good than it does harm. This tension between inevitability and ambiguity necessitates adherence to a set of doctrinal complexities that place certain limits on the means by which the system of criminal punishment may seek to prevent crime.

* * *

. . . [T]he criminal sanction, inflicting as it does a unique combination of stigma and loss of liberty, should be resorted to only sparingly in a society that regards itself as free and open. But what are the criteria that ought to guide the exercise of legislative judgment regarding the appropriate occasions for invoking the criminal sanction? How are we to decide what kinds of conducts should be made criminal?

* * *

In a sense, all limiting criteria reduce themselves to a simple prescription: first things first. The criminal sanction is the law's ultimate threat. Being punished for a crime is different from being regulated in the public interest, or being forced to compensate another who has been injured by one's conduct, or being treated for a disease. The sanction is at once uniquely coercive and, in the broadest sense, uniquely expensive. It should be reserved for what really matters.

Considerations of several kinds enter into a determination of what "things" should be considered "first." On the credit side of the ledger are the social gains that will accrue from the successful prevention or reduction of the conduct in question, discounted by the prospects of achieving success (however defined). On the debit side are the moral and practical costs, reckoned in terms of values other than the prevention of antisocial conduct. Finally, there is the question of alternatives: what other means of social control are available to achieve the same ends? The question of alternatives is particularly crucial. If there are readily available alternatives that avoid or minimize the formidable battery of objections and obstacles . . . , they must be carefully weighed. If there are not, we must face, rather than reject out of hand, the alternative of doing nothing.

* * *

IMMORALITY: AN INSUFFICIENT CONDITION

If the immorality of conduct is a generally necessary condition for invocation of the criminal sanction, is it a generally sufficient one? That is the gist of the "law and morals" debate. Conventional morality, it is asserted, is what holds society together. It must be not only taught but enforced. The enforcement of morals needs no other justification. The usual lines of attack upon this argument are, first, that there is no easy way to determine what should count as immoral and, second, that other considerations (primarily of enforceability) should also be taken into account in determining whether immoral conduct should be made criminal. To these may be added a third: it simply is not true that we use the criminal law to deal with all conduct that we consider immoral; even the most extreme of legal moralists have never pressed for that. Therefore, unless the choice of proscribed conduct is to be purely whimsical, we must take other factors into consideration.

It is generally considered immoral to break a promise simply because it has become inconvenient to keep it. Not only is it regarded as immoral, but the conduct of the ordinary business of life would be greatly changed if the tendency to break promises frivolously became widespread. Yet we do not put promise-breakers in jail. What they do may be viewed as both immoral and harmful; but it does not result in the invocation of the criminal sanction. Examples could be multiplied, but the point is surely obvious. For whatever reasons—the availability of other sanctions (legal and extra-legal), the difficulty of agreeing about categories of excuse, the varying social importance attributed to different kinds of promises—we withhold the sanction of legal condemnation.

The extent of disagreement about moral judgments is an obvious reason for hesitancy about an automatic enforcement of morals. There have been monolithic societies in which a static and homogeneous ethnic, religious, and class structure conducts to widely shared acceptance of a value system. But that is hardly a description of the reality of twentieth-century American society, or of its pluralistic and liberal aspirations. In a society that neither has nor wants a unitary set of moral norms, the enforcement of morals carries a heavy cost in repression. We don't begin to agree about the "morality" of smoking, drinking, gambling, fornicating, or drug-taking, for example, quite apart from the gap between what we say and what we do. The more heterogeneous the society, the more repressive the enforcement of morals must be.

. . . [T]he enforcement of morals is a costly indulgence. Immorality clearly should not be viewed as a sufficient or even a principal reason for proscribing conduct as criminal. Morals belong to the home, the school, and the church; and we have many homes, many schools, many churches. Our moral universe is polycentric. The state, especially when the most coercive of sanctions is at issue, should not seek to impose a spurious unity upon it.

. . . If a legislator can think of no better reason to proscribe conduct than that he (or his constituency) abhors it, he had better think twice about doing it.

"HARM TO OTHERS"

For the past hundred years, since the appearance of Mill's great essay On Liberty, the terms of the debate on law and morals have been set, almost immovably, by his declaration that "the only purpose for which power can be rightfully exercised over any member of a civilized community, against his will, is to prevent harm to others."

* * *

. . . [I]t has to be conceded that Mill's formula solves very little. Later in his essay Mill extends his concept of "harm to others" to include "risk of damage" to the interests of others, and it is usually possible to make a more or less plausible argument that any given form of conduct involves that risk in some way. The question is not one of whether or not there will be harm done; it is one of the remoteness and probability of the harm. Some things are more harmful than others. Homicide is more harmful than muttering voodoo incantations; rape is more harmful than reading dirty books. And in a world of limited resources, we need to draw discriminations about the gravity and remoteness of harms. Seen in this light, "harm to others" is a prudential criterion rather than a hard and fast distinction of principle.

"Harm to others" does not, of course, mean identifiable others. It has become fashionable to talk about "victimless crimes," meaning those in which there is no immediately identifiable victim to lodge a complaint. The absence of an identifiable victim can make enforcement difficult, and can encourage undesirable enforcement practices. But the prospect of these difficulties should not end the inquiry into the wisdom of any given use of the criminal sanction. Many offenses against the administration of government are "victimless crimes" in the sense that there is nobody to complain. Consensual transactions like bribery and espionage are admittedly difficult to detect because of the absence of an identifiable victim; yet they do not necessarily cause so little "harm to others" that we can forget about subjecting them to the criminal sanction.

The "harm to others" formula seems to me to have two uses that justify its inclusion in a list of limiting criteria for invocation of the criminal sanction. First, it is a way to make sure that a given form of conduct is not being subjected to the criminal sanction purely or even primarily because it is thought to be immoral. It forces an inquiry into precisely what bad effects are feared if the conduct in question is not suppressed by the criminal law. Second, it immediately brings into play a host of secular inquiries about the effects of subjecting the conduct in question to the criminal sanction. One cannot meaningfully deal with the question of "harm to others" without weighing benefits against detriments. In that sense, it is a kind of threshold question, important not so much in itself as in focusing attention on further considerations relevant to the ultimate decision. It is for these two instrumental reasons rather than for either its intrinsic rightness or its ease of application that it deserves inclusion.

* * *

. . . [I]t may be useful to try to establish some kind of bench mark for the optimal use of the criminal sanction. The criteria for choice seem so clear that it may be trite to rehearse them. They include the following:

(1) The conduct is prominent in most people's view of socially threatening behavior, and is not condoned by any significant segment of society.

(2) Subjecting it to the criminal sanction is not inconsistent with the goals of punishment.

(3) Suppressing it will not inhibit socially desirable conduct.

(4) It may be dealt with through even-handed and nondiscriminatory enforcement.

(5) Controlling it through the criminal process will not expose that process to severe qualitative strains.

(6) There are no reasonable alternatives to the criminal sanction for dealing with it.

* * *

SEX OFFENSES

The debate over criminal laws forbidding certain varieties of sexual conduct has become the *locus classicus* of modern interest in the limits of criminal law. . . . What the consenting adult does in private has become everybody's business to the precise extent that debate waxes hot over whether it is nobody's business.

* * *

One point that may well be unique to the problem of deviate consensual sexual relations is that by far the most powerful sanction is that of social stigma. There is little or no evidence to suggest that the criminal law exerts a deterrent influence that would not be present even if there would be a substantial increase in the number of people who smoke marijuana or gamble or get abortions if those criminal prohibitions were relaxed; it seems implausible to suppose that a similar effect would occur if the laws against sexual deviations were changed. The reason is twofold: first, the strong pressures that impel people with homosexual tendencies to engage in deviate relations probably ensure that most who would do so are doing so already; second, the stigma that attaches even in so permissive a society as ours would militate against the advent of many new recruits. This is not to say that casual and situational experimentation might not increase if existing proscriptions were relaxed, but rather to suggest that it is unlikely that many people would change their predominant sexual patterns simply because of a change in the law. . . .

* * *

. . . For the criminal law to threaten the private sexual behavior of consenting adults, it must run afoul of many limiting criteria. . . . Some of the reasons listed below for not invoking the sanction where such behavior is concerned are self-explanatory; others will require some comment.

(1) Rarity of enforcement creates a problem of arbitrary police and prosecutorial discretion.

(2) The extreme difficulty of detecting such conduct leads to undesirable police practices.

(3) The existence of the proscription tends to create a deviant subculture.

(4) Widespread knowledge that the law is violated with impunity by thousands every day creates disrespect for law generally.

(5) No secular harm can be shown to result from such conduct.

(6) The theoretical availability of criminal sanctions creates a situation in which extortion and, on occasion, police corruption may take place.

(7) There is substantial evidence that the moral sense of the community no longer exerts strong pressure for the use of criminal sanctions.

(8) No utilitarian goal of criminal punishment is substantially advanced by proscribing private adult consensual sexual conduct.

The only countervailing argument is that relaxation of the criminal proscription will be taken to express social approval of the conduct at issue. There is little enough . . . to that general proposition. It becomes peculiarly vacuous when addressed to this issue, where the social taboo is so much stronger than the legal prohibition. It does not pay a statute much of a compliment, a justice of the Supreme Court once remarked, to say that it is not unconstitutional. It may also be said that it does not express much approval of a behavior pattern to say that it is not criminal.

The enforcement ratio of private consensual sex offenses must show incredibly heavy odds against arrest—perhaps one in ten million? There is an inherent unfairness in that situation regardless of how equitably discretion is exercised, which is to say, even if it is perfectly random. But it is not. The scanty available evidence suggests that enforcement takes place mainly in a context in which other mores, not reinforced by law, are being flouted, as for example, where the partners are of different races. While this is outrageous, it is also understandable. If no systematic efforts are made to enforce these criminal proscriptions, their detection and prosecution must be triggered by something extrinsic to the conduct itself. With no guidance as to the social interests that ought to be protected (and there can be none), those enforcing the law must fall back on their own individual scheme of values.

Knowledge that the law is unenforced has a bad effect both on those who violate it and on the public at large. The violators are contemptuous of a law that they perceive to be both unjust and ineffectual. They react against it by strengthening their own identification as an outlaw group. As social stigma apart from the criminal law begins somewhat to relax, this isolating effect of the criminal proscription becomes even more objectionable than formerly. Otherwise law-abiding citizens see themselves as rebels against society, not because of society's deeds or even society's thoughts, but simply because of some words in a book. Imaginary offenses turn out to have effects that are far from imaginary.

* * *

... The problem [of private consensual sexual conduct among adults] does not bulk large quantitatively in the misallocation of resources to the criminal sanction with which we are presently afflicted. It would bulk much larger if law enforcement were ever to undertake a really massive assault on illegal sexual conduct. The prevalence of the conduct bespeaks the futility of attempts to suppress it. . . .

NOTES AND QUESTIONS

1. Applying criteria similar to Packer's, Norval Morris and Gorden Hawkins argue for the "decriminalization" of the following conduct:

   a) Public drunkenness;

   b) Acquisition, purchase, possession, or use of controlled substances;

   c) Gambling (certain fraudulent and cheating gambling practices will remain criminal);

   d) Disorderly conduct and vagrancy (laws should be enacted which precisely stipulate the conduct proscribed and define the circumstances in which the police should intervene);

   e) Abortion performed by a qualified medical practitioner in a registered hospital;

   f) Sexual behavior between consenting adults in private including: adultery, fornication, illicit cohabitation, statutory rape and carnal knowledge, bigamy, incest, sodomy, bestiality (cruelty to animals may be criminalized);

   g) Attempted suicide;

   h) Checks drawn on insufficient funds (intent to defraud may be criminalized);

   i) Non-support of family.

N. Morris and Q. Hawkins, The Honest Politician's Guide to Crime Control, 2–28 (1969).

Do you agree with these authors' conclusions? Does the list of offenses to be decriminalized go too far? Not far enough?

2. Consider the *Johnson* case, *supra* at p. 275. Is criminalization the best way to deal with the problem of "crack mothers" and "crack babies"? The law reviews have been sated with discussions. See, e.g., Moss, *Substance Abuse during Pregnancy,* 13 Harv. Women's L.J. 278 (1990); Roberts, *Punishing Drug Addicts Who Have Babies: Women of Color, Equality and the Right of Privacy,* 104 Harv. L. Rev. 1419 (1991); Note, 23 J. Marshall. L. Rev. 393 (1990); *Note,* 65 Wash. L. Rev. 377 (1990). Note the comment of one trial court quashing an indictment in such a case: "There is no familial bond more intimate and more fundamental than that between the mother and the fetus she carries in her womb. This court will not permit the destruction of this relationship by the prosecution." N.Y. Times, October 18, 1990.

3. Do this Chapter's earlier materials dealing with the conceptual and justificatory problems of punishment aid in deciding whether given conduct should be within the reach of the criminal law?

Chapter 3
The Requirement of an Act

§ 3.01 "Acts"

For well over 500 years, one maxim has guided criminal law: *Actus non facit reum, nisi ens sit rea*(there is no criminal act unless there is a criminal mind). Thus both an act and a guilty mind are requisites for liability (with some exceptions that we will explore later). Here we are concerned only with the first part of the first requirement: that there be an *act* that is attributable to the defendant.

The criminality of the act is not here in question. Thus if A, an army private, intends to murder B, his captain, and shoots with all malice in his heart, but it turns out that the person shot is really an enemy soldier, A is not guilty of the enemy's death because he did not commit a *criminal* act—it is not a crime to kill an enemy in time of war. Though A did not commit an *actus reus*, he did act. His "defense" should not be confused with the question of whether he acted at all. Similarly, if A threatens B with death unless B drives at 80 miles per hour and B violates the speeding laws by doing so, it is inaccurate to say that B did not "act." His defense, if there is one, is in terms of voluntariness of his act, rather than of whether he acted per se.

Providing a definition for acts and distinguishing them from mere bodily movements is a difficult matter. There are two principal ways to define an act: as a muscular contraction of some sort or as a muscular contraction combined with circumstances. This definitional problem is compounded by the imprecision of language, a difficulty that, as we will see later, can cause major problems in interpreting statutes. Thus we commonly say that someone "drove" a car or "shot" someone. Yet the "act," particularly if defined as a "muscular contraction," consists only of pressing one's foot on the accelerator or pulling one's finger on a trigger. The rest is circumstance. Consider, for example, cases where the car has no gas or the gun is unloaded. The same physical acts of the defendant are present, yet the results are different, because the circumstances (gas, bullet) are different. Thus, if one asks whether the defendant *acted,* there will be different responses depending on whether one focuses solely on the physical muscular act or on the totality of circumstances.

The requirement that there be an act is not a requirement that there be harm, in any tangible sense. Inchoate crimes, such as attempt, involve no actual harm to an object or person; yet there has been an act, and that act, if combined with the proper mental state, may be defined by the legislature as a crime. Thus in the military example above, A may be guilty of *attempted* murder of the captain if his intent can be proved, but not of the captain's—or anyone else's—actual murder. A *killed* the enemy, but did not *murder* him.

Why require an act? The reason usually given is the impossibility of proving a mere mental state. The classic statement is that of Chief Justice O'Brian:

"The thought of man is not triable, for the devil himself knoweth not the thought of man." But that statement seems clearly overbroad, since we do strive to know the thoughts of people—indeed, it is on the basis of (perceived) differing mental states that the criminal law apportions guilt. For example, an intentional killing is punished more severely than a negligent killing. Perhaps the real reason is that we want to be sure that the defendant's *mind* was aware of his act. As Holmes 54–55, put it:

> The reason for requiring an act is that an act implies a choice, and that it is felt to be impolitic and unjust to make a man answerable for harm, unless he might have chosen otherwise. But the choice must be made with a chance of contemplating the consequence complained of, or else it has no bearing on responsibility for that consequence. If this were not true, a man might be held answerable for everything which would not have happened but for his choice at some past time.

MARTIN V. STATE

Criminal Appeals Court of Alabama

31 Ala. App. 334, 17 So. 2d 427 (1944)

SIMPSON, J.:

Appellant was convicted of being drunk on a public highway, and appeals. Officers of the law arrested him at his home and took him onto the highway, where he allegedly committed the proscribed acts, viz., manifested a drunken condition by using loud and profane language.

The pertinent provisions of our statute are: "Any person who, while intoxicated or drunk, appears in any public place where one or more persons are present . . . and manifests a drunken condition by boisterous or indecent conduct, or loud and profane discourse, shall . . . be fined."

Under the plain terms of this statute, a voluntary appearance is presupposed. The rule has been declared . . . that an accusation of drunkenness . . . cannot be established by proof that the accused, while in an intoxicated condition, was involuntarily and forcibly carried to that place by the arresting officer. . . .

Reversed and Remanded

People v. Wu

California Court of Appeals, Fourth District, Division 2

286 Cal. Rptr. 868 (1991)

OPINION BY: TIMLIN

I

Introduction

Helen Wu, also known as Helen Hamg Ieng Chau (defendant), was convicted of the second degree murder of her son, Sidney Wu (Sidney), following trial by jury. Her motion for a new trial was denied and she was sentenced to a prison term of 15 years to life. She contends that the court committed reversible error by (1) refusing to instruct the jury on the defense of unconsciousness, and (2) refusing to instruct the jury on her theory of the case.

* * *

The prosecution's theory seems to have been that defendant killed Sidney because of anger at Sidney's father, and to get revenge. The defense's theory was that defendant believed that Sidney, who lived with his father in the United States, was looked down upon and was ill-treated by everyone except his paternal grandmother because he had been borne out of wedlock, and that when she learned that the grandmother was dying of cancer, she felt trapped and, in an intense emotional upheaval, strangled Sidney and then attempted to kill herself so that she could take care of Sidney in the afterlife.

* * *

II

Facts

Defendant was born in 1943 in Saigon, China. At the age of 19, in about 1962 or 1963, she moved to Macau. She married and had a daughter, who was 25 years old at the time of the trial of this matter in February 1990. In 1963, she met Gary Wu (Wu), the son of one of her friends. That same year Wu went to the United States, and married Susanna Ku. He opened several restaurants in the Palm Springs area.

After eight years of marriage, defendant was divorced, and became employed, writing statistics for greyhound races.

In 1978 or 1979, defendant was contacted by Wu, who had heard that she was divorced and had a daughter. Wu told her his marriage was unsatisfactory because his wife could not have children. According to defendant, Wu told her he planned to divorce his wife. They discussed the possibility that defendant could come to the United States and conceive a child for Wu. Defendant believed Wu would marry her after he divorced his wife. Defendant was in love with Wu and Wu gave defendant money to deposit in a joint bank account and sent her $20,000 so she could apply for a visa to the United States.

In November 1979, defendant came to the United States. When defendant arrived, he hugged and kissed her, told her his divorce proceedings would be completed soon and he definitely would marry her. Defendant lived with Wu's mother. Wu's wife believed she was a family friend. At Wu's request defendant had brought $15,000 of the money he had sent her and they opened a joint account together.

In December 1979 or January 1980, Wu and his wife Susanna were divorced; however, Wu did not tell defendant that he had obtained a divorce. Defendant conceived a child by Wu in the early part of 1980, and then moved into an apartment, where she was visited by Wu. After the child, Sidney, was born in November 1980, Wu apparently made no overtures regarding marriage. Depressed, defendant, who could not speak English, could not drive, and who had no support system in the United States, told Wu she intended to return to Macau, apparently expecting that this information would cause him to try to persuade her to stay.

Wu did not try to persuade defendant to stay, so in February 1981, she returned home but left Sidney with Wu. She could not take the baby because no one knew she had a baby and she and Sidney would have been humiliated in China. She told only her closest friend, Chung, who had already learned of defendant's pregnancy from Chung's daughters who were going to college in the United States, that she had borne a child out of wedlock; such a thing was apparently considered to be particularly shameful among people of defendant's culture.

From 1981 to 1988 defendant regularly asked Wu to bring Sidney to visit her, but to no avail. In 1981, Wu said he could only come for the summer and defendant told him she wanted Sidney to stay and if he could not, then she did not want to see him because it would be harder after he left. In 1984, Wu asked defendant to visit him but she did not want to come until she was married, then she and her son would have dignity and status.

In September 1987, Wu told defendant he needed money for his restaurant business. She finally told him that if he would bring Sidney to visit her, she would loan him money for his restaurants.

In January 1988, Wu brought Sidney, who was then seven years old, to visit defendant in Hong Kong. Defendant showed him $100,000 cash and a receipt for a certificate of deposit of a million Hong Kong dollars. Both the cash and the deposited funds had been loaned to defendant by Chung [a friend], after defendant admitted to Chung that she had lured Wu into bringing Sidney to see her with the promise of a loan. On that visit, Wu proposed marriage, but defendant declined, depressed over the fact that the marriage proposal seemed to be because of "her" money, and because she did not know if Wu were still married or not. Defendant was so discouraged by these beliefs that she attempted to throw herself out of the window of Chung's apartment, but was restrained by Chung, Chung's daughter, and a servant.

. . . .

During the next year defendant worked and traveled with Chung. She wanted to see Sidney but she did not know if Wu was still married and did not want to upset her son's life. In August 1989, defendant, who was on a vacation trip to Las Vegas and San Francisco with Chung, as Chung's guest, apparently heard that Wu's mother, Sidney's paternal grandmother, was terminally ill, so she came to Palm Springs to visit. While there, she was told by the grandmother that when the grandmother died, she, defendant, should take Sidney because Wu would not take good care of him. She was given similar advice by Sandy, Wu's cousin.

Toward the end of August, Wu told defendant that they were going to Las Vegas. Defendant stated she did not want to go. Wu told her it was important that she go, as "she was the main character" because they were going to be married. Defendant and Wu were married on September 1. On September 5, they went to Los Angeles to consult an attorney about immigration law. Defendant, following the marriage and consultation, was still of the opinion that Wu had married her because of his belief that she had a lot of money. During the drive home from Los Angeles, this belief was reinforced by Wu's comments. When she asked if he had married her for her money, he responded that until she produced the money, she had no right to speak. Defendant asked Wu whether the marriage was not worthwhile simply for the purpose of legitimizing Sidney, and Wu replied that many people could give him children. Defendant told Wu he would be sorry. She later explained that remark meant that she was thinking about returning to Macau and killing herself. . . .

On September 9, the evening of the killing, defendant was playing with Sidney. Earlier that day defendant had interceded on Sidney's behalf when Wu hit Sidney when Sidney would not get out of the family car. Wu had gone to the restaurant to put on two birthday parties, apparently for his friend Rosemary. Defendant and Sidney played and talked, and defendant told Sidney that she knew what he liked because of the mother—child bond between them.

Sidney told defendant that Wu said she was "psychotic" and "very troublesome." He then told defendant that Rosemary was Wu's girlfriend, and that the house they lived in belonged to Rosemary. He also told her that Wu made him get up early so Wu could take Rosemary's daughters to school in the morning and if he did not get up, Wu would scold and beat him. He said Wu loved Rosemary more than him. Defendant began to think about what she had been told by Sidney's grandmother and Sandy concerning her taking care of Sidney. She began to experience heart palpitations and to have trouble breathing. She told Sidney she wanted to die, and asked him if he would go too. He clung to her neck and cried. She then left the bedroom, and obtained a rope by cutting the cord off a window blind. She returned to the bedroom and strangled Sidney. According to defendant, she did not remember the strangling itself. She stopped breathing, and when she started breathing again, she was surprised at how quickly Sidney had died. She then wrote a note to Wu to the effect that he had bullied her too much and "now this air is vented. I can die with no regret," but did not mention Sidney's killing in the note. She then attempted to strangle herself, failed, went to the kitchen and slashed her left wrist with a knife, and then returned to the bedroom and lay down next to Sidney on the bed, having first placed a waste-paper basket under her bleeding wrist to catch the blood so that the floor would not be dirtied.

Wu returned home several hours later, and discovered defendant and Sidney. He called the police, and the paramedics were also summoned. The police determined that Sidney was dead. The paramedics tested defendant's vital signs, and determined that although her pulse and blood pressure were normal, she exhibited a decreased level of consciousness. . . .

Dr. Saul Faerstein, a physician specializing in psychiatry, testified, after reviewing pictures of the wounds on defendant's wrists, that they did not appear to have been inflicted by a "malingerer," that they were the type of wound which a layperson, particularly one who was agitated, severely depressed, or confused, might make in a serious attempt to commit suicide. He also testified, as to the decreased state of consciousness in which defendant was found, that defendant might have fainted and then remained in a reduced level of consciousness, but that "we're talking about something more than fainting here," and "there are many, people may disassociate, people may have emotional reactions which are acute and severe, where suddenly they become confused, as a result of shock, as a result of some acute shock. Clearly the circumstances of what was going on with her son were overwhelming kinds of trauma that she was experiencing, and I believe that the shock she was experiencing were [sic] traumatic but psychological in origin."

Chung testified that two days after Sidney's death, she received a telephone call from Wu, who was fishing for information about how defendant had accumulated the money he believed she possessed. Chung evaded his questions, and then Wu told her that defendant had strangled Sidney and "committed" suicide, but that defendant had been saved. Chung then hired an attorney in Hong Kong to help defendant. . . .

III

A. The Trial Court Committed Reversible Error by Refusing to Instruct the Jury on the Defense of Unconsciousness

Defendant contends that the trial court committed reversible error by refusing to give the following instruction on unconsciousness:

A person who commits what would otherwise be a criminal act, while unconscious, is not guilty of a crime.

This rule of law applies to persons who are not conscious of acting but who perform acts while asleep or while suffering from a delirium of fever, or because of an attack of [psychomotor] epilepsy, a blow on the head, the involuntary taking of drugs or the involuntary consumption of intoxicating liquor, or any similar cause.

Unconsciousness does not require that a person be incapable of movement.

Evidence has been received which may tend to show that the defendant was unconscious at the time and place of the commission of the alleged crime for which [he][she] is here on trial. If, after a consideration of all the evidence, you have a reasonable doubt that the defendant was conscious at the time the alleged crime was committed, [he][she] must be found not guilty. (CALJIC No. 4.30.)

Defendant contends that the evidence that due to her extreme emotional and psychological distress she was not conscious of her act of strangling her child was sufficient evidence to justify giving this instruction. The People contend that there was no evidence of unconsciousness "deserving of the jury's consideration" to justify giving the instruction, given that defendant's own testimony, and that of the defense experts, was that she consciously strangled the child so that they could be united in death and a post-death afterlife, and also because she testified that she strangled her son, and told other witnesses "how quickly her son died along with details surrounding the strangulation."

* * *

After reviewing all the evidence related to defendant's awareness of her act of strangling Sidney at the moment of the act, we agree with defendant that there was sufficient evidence to require the giving of an instruction on unconsciousness.

According to Dr. Ching-Piao Chien, M.D., one of defendant's expert witnesses and a board certified psychiatrist:

Q: Did Helen tell you what were the details of the strangulation of Sidney?

A: No. She did not remember the act afterward.

Q: Did you find that to be unusual?

A: Not unusual. When somebody has such a heat of passion or emotional status, under such a strong stress, it is not uncommon to have that kind of memory loss. But sometimes we call that a fugue state or dissociation or dissociated disorder.

* * *

A: Fugue state is kind of a mental status that when somebody cannot understand the reality that they are facing, there's a kind of automatic mechanism that change the mentality into different state. Like dreaming state or different state that usually don't retain the memory.

"To give you some example, if a child is killed in front of the mother by a truck, brain's splattered—I have seen a patient, I mean the mother, who was supposed to have been in deep shock or grief, suddenly start laughing like as if nothing happened. And laughing is a kind of counter mechanism of her grief shock or sadness that she cannot accept.

Q: Well, based upon what you heard from Helen and reviewed from the materials, was Helen in a fugue state when she strangled Sidney?

A: Obviously.

Q: Why is it obvious?

A: Because that kind of emotion, mixed emotional of the despair, anger, disappointment, depression, sadness, hopelessness, everything all sudden come up to her mind that she thought the only way out is to go to the heaven together with the son. And that is not kind of comfortable thing for people to think long time ahead or to plan.

So obviously, she was under a kind of heat of emotion or I call it heat of passion that went out like a dreamy state.

* * *

Dr. Chien also testified, during cross-examination:

Q: She perceived that she was going to kill her son first, clearly because that's what happened before she wrote the note?

A: Right.

Q: So she made a decision; right? She had to decide.

* * *

That is, is she going to shoot the boy, is she going to strangle him, is she going to poison him, or is she going to run over him with a truck or whatever.

Q: Doctor, she told you she picked up the scissors?

A: Yes.

Q: So she had to think about it before she did it. At least she had to say, "Ah, there is a pair of scissors. Let me pick them up." Right? Or—

A: Sometime there's a behavior in the human being that they did something without really knowing what is going on.

Q: Doctor, nonetheless, she still, in order to kill the boy, she first of all had to decide to kill him. Then she had to decide how to do it. Right?

A: Actionwise, yes. That's a fact.

Q: All right.

A: However, I'm not sure about the mentality process, mental process you are talking about.

According to Dr. Terry Gock, a clinical psychologist:

* * *

Helen was relating [in her sessions with him] that, that, that the sequence of what happened that night, in regard to the death of Sidney, was not very clear. However, she felt she—what she remembered was that she cut some rope from the window blinds and strangled Sidney. And she sort of recalled that she was sort of puzzled or she thought that it was so easy to, to kill Sidney.

Defendant herself testified as follows:

Q: What did you do after you got the piece of rope?

A: I only recall that I strangled myself and I also strangled my son.

Q: Which did you do first?

A: I don't recall.

Q: Do you remember where Sidney was when you strangled him?

A: I don't even know where he was.

Q: Did you strangle him with the piece of rope from the blinds?

A: Yes.

Q: Do you remember talking to some doctors about this?

A: I don't recall.

Q: Okay. What did Sidney do when you were strangling him?

A: I don't know what happened. I don't even know.

Q: Do you remember telling Dr. Chien that, how quickly and easily Sidney died?

A: I don't recall.

Q: Do you remember telling Dr. Gock that you strangled Sidney but you do not recall him as struggling against you? Do you remember that?

A: Actually, I don't even know what happened myself.

Q: Well, didn't you tell Dr. Chien that you had trouble breathing at that time?

A: Yes.

Q: Did you have trouble breathing at the time you were strangling Sidney?

A: At night already I could not breathe. Also I had headaches, severe headaches.

Q: What happened after you strangled Sidney?

A: I don't recall. I got knife and rope—I strangled myself and I strangled my son. But how, I really don't know.

* * *

Q: But you don't remember the actual strangulation of Sidney. Is that what you're saying?

A: That's correct.

Q: But Mrs. Wu, can you explain to us why you remember talking with Sidney, remember going and cutting the rope, you remember writing a note, and in fact have identified the note, you remember going to the sink and cutting your wrist, you remember going back to the sink and cutting your wrist, you remember going back into the bedroom and worrying about getting blood on the floor, you remember laying down with Sidney? Why don't you remember the actual strangulation of Sidney if you remember everything else?

A: I don't know.

John Bernard Melia, a firefighter/paramedic who responded to Wu's call to 911, testified that [after he administered several tests aimed at determining levels of consciousness] defendant appeared to have "a decreased level of consciousness," that this level of consciousness did not change during the trip to the hospital, and that he could not tell why defendant's level of consciousness was decreased, but that it did not appear to be from loss of blood. He also stated that oxygen was administered to defendant in the hope and expectation that it would improve her level of consciousness, but that it did not appear to cause any significant increase in defendant's level of consciousness.

The above evidence was sufficient to have supported a finding by the jury, if they had been instructed on unconsciousness, that although defendant might have consciously contemplated killing Sidney before she actually strangled him, the actual act of strangulation was committed while she was in a fugue state, i.e., in a state in which she acted without conscious thought and was unconscious of her act of strangulation at the time she committed it. A reasonable jury could have further concluded that the reason defendant "knew" she had strangled Sidney was not because she actually *remembered* the strangulation based on a conscious awareness of her acts as she strangled the child, but because she inferred, given the circumstances, that she had strangled him.

Obviously, the prosecuting attorney and the trial court were very influenced by the fact that defendant "knew" she had strangled Sidney, as well as by the fact that she remembered information related to her behavior and thoughts immediately preceding and following the strangulation of her child. However, if, indeed, defendant was unconscious while strangling Sidney, the fact that she had planned Sidney's death, and had even obtained the rope immediately before using it to strangle the child, would not be a sufficient basis upon which to deny giving the requested instruction on unconsciousness, given that to support a conviction for a criminal act there must be a "joint operation of act and intent."

* * *

[A] defendant is entitled to an instruction on any defense which is supported by substantial evidence [;] in determining whether such evidence exists, the trial court must not weigh the credibility of witnesses, nor focus on the fact there is conflict in the evidence, but must resolve any doubts as to the credibility and sufficiency of the evidence in favor of the defendant.

Here, an instruction on unconsciousness was clearly warranted. The evidence that defendant was not conscious of strangling Sidney, and that she acted in a "fugue" state during the actual strangulation, was substantial and of such nature that a jury could reasonably conclude therefrom she was not conscious when she killed Sidney.

* * *

In conclusion, because the jury was not instructed on unconsciousness, despite the existence of evidence to support the giving of such an instruction, and because the issue of unconsciousness was not resolved adversely to defendant under the other instructions given, we must reverse her conviction.

Editor's note: The opinion above was "withdrawn from publication" by order of the California Supreme Court. It thus has no precedential value even in that state. Nevertheless, the issues that it raises are sometimes presented in actual trials, and it is therefore helpful to use the case, if only as a hypothetical.

Morris, Somnambulistic Homicide: Ghosts, Spiders, and North Koreans

5 Res Judicata 29 (1955)

The unreported case of *The King v. Cogdon,* heard in the Supreme Court of Victoria before Mr. Justice Smith in December, 1950, though clear as to its facts and unchallengeable in law, compels consideration of some of our basic premises of responsibility for criminal actions.

Mrs. Cogdon was charged with the murder of her only child, a daughter called Pat, aged nineteen. Pat had for some time been receiving psychiatric treatment for a relatively minor neurotic condition of which, in her psychiatrist's opinion, she was now cured. Despite this, Mrs. Cogdon continued to worry unduly about her. Describing the relationship between Pat and her mother, Mr. Cogdon testified: "I don't think a mother could have thought any more of her daughter. I think she absolutely adored her." On the conscious level, at least, there was no reason to doubt Mrs. Cogdon's deep attachment to her daughter.

To the charge of murdering Pat, Mrs. Cogdon pleaded not guilty. Her story, though somewhat bizarre, was not seriously challenged by the Crown, and led to her acquittal. She told how, on the night before her daughter's death, she had dreamt that their house was full of spiders and that these spiders were crawling all over Pat. In her sleep, Mrs. Cogdon left the bed she shared with her husband, went into Pat's room and awakened to find herself violently brushing at Pat's face, presumably to remove the spiders. This woke Pat. Mrs. Cogdon told her she was just tucking her in. At the trial, she testified that she still believed, as she had been told, that the occupants of a nearby house bred spiders as a hobby, preparing nests for them behind the pictures on their walls. It was these spiders which in her dreams had invaded their home and attacked Pat. There had also been a previous dream in which ghosts had sat at the end of Mrs. Cogdon's bed and she had said to them, "Well, you have come to take Pattie." It does not seem fanciful to accept the psychological explanation of these spiders and ghosts as the projections of Mrs. Cogdon's subconscious hostility towards her daughter; a hostility which was itself rooted in Mrs. Cogdon's own early life and marital relationship.

The morning after the spider dream she told her doctor of it. He gave her a sedative and, because of the dream and certain previous difficulties she had reported, discussed the possibility of psychiatric treatment. That evening Mrs. Cogdon suggested to her husband that he attend his lodge meeting, and asked Pat to come with her to the cinema. After he had gone Pat looked through the paper, not unusually found no tolerable program, and said that as she was going out the next evening she thought she would rather go to bed early. Later, while Pat was having a bath preparatory to retiring, Mrs. Cogdon went into her room, put a hot water bottle in the bed, turned back the bed-clothes, and placed a glass of hot milk beside the bed ready for Pat. She then went to bed herself. There was some desultory conversation between them about the war in Korea, and just before she put out her light Pat called out to her mother, "Mum, don't be so silly worrying there about the war, it's not on our front door step yet."

Mrs. Cogdon went to sleep. She dreamt that "the war was all around the house," that soldiers were in Pat's room, and that one soldier was on the bed attacking Pat. This was all of the dream she could later recapture. Her first "waking" memory was of running from Pat's room, out of the house to the home of her sister who lived next door. When her sister opened the front door Mrs. Cogdon fell into her arms, crying, "I think I've hurt Pattie."

In fact Mrs. Cogdon had, in her somnambulistic state, left her bed, fetched an axe from the woodheap, entered Pat's room, and struck her two accurate forceful blows on the head with the blade of the axe, thus killing her.

Mrs. Cogdon's story was supported by the evidence of her physician, a psychiatrist and a psychologist. The burden of the evidence of all three, which was not contested by the prosecution, was that Mrs. Cogdon was suffering from a form of hysteria with an overlay of depression, and that she was of a personality in which such dissociated states as fugues, amnesias, and somnambulistic acts are to be expected. They agreed that she was not psychotic, and that if she had been awake at the time of the killing no defence could have been spelt out under the *McNaughten Rules.* * They hazarded no statement as to her motives, the idea of defence of the daughter being transparently insufficient. However, the psychologist and the psychiatrist concurred in hinting that the emotional motivation lay in an acute conflict situation in her relations with her own parent; that during marital life she suffered very great sexual frustration; and that she over-compensated for her own frustration by over-protection of her daughter. Her exaggerated solicitude for her daughter was a conscious expression of her subconscious emotional hostility to her, and the dream ghosts, spiders, and Korean soldiers were projections of that aggression. How manifold can be the possible motives for a "motiveless" killing!

At all events the jury believed Mrs. Cogdon's story, and regarded the presumption that the natural consequences of her acts were intended as being completely rebutted by her account of her mental state at the time of the killing, and by the unanimous support given to it by the medical and psychological evidence. She was acquitted. It must be stressed that insanity was not pleaded as a defence—she was acquitted because the act of killing itself was not, in law, regarded as her act at all.

---

* [The *McNaughten Rules,* relating to insanity, are discussed infra, §9.05 [G] [3].—Eds.]

This case illustrates the impossibility of applying the maxim *actus non facit reum nisi mens sit rea* as if it covered the field of criminal liability, as if it were possible satisfactorily to sever "act" from "intention." Here the mental element in the *actus reus,* its voluntary quality, was lacking; or, put alternatively, the physical element in the *mens rea,* the consciousness of action, was likewise lacking. This lack can be stated either way, and both are confusing.

The better course is taken by J.W.C. Turner, who in his article on the *Mental Element in Crimes at Common Law* adds to his statements of the requirements of *actus reus* and *mens rea* a third and independent requirement, namely, that "it must be proved that the conduct was voluntary," and when discussing this voluntary conduct as a prerequisite to criminal liability includes a somnambulistic action as involuntary and therefore exculpatory.

Thus, Mrs. Cogdon's action not being "voluntary," no question of criminal liability arose. But . . . this concept of a "voluntary action" itself conceals many philosophical and psychological difficulties. Mrs. Cogdon escapes basically because of the state of her consciousness; not because she had no conscious intention or rational motive to kill, a state she shares with many convicted murderers. She was "asleep: "had she been "awake" her only defence would have been one of insanity. This defence might have succeeded, not because she fitted the *McNaughten Rules,* in fact she did not, but because when a mother kills a daughter to whom she is apparently and consciously deeply attached, the Bench and the jury will strive to squeeze her case into the psychologically rigid and narrow confines of the *McNaughten Rules.*

But the difference between being "asleep" and "awake" is not absolute. Consciousness is not like a light, either off or on; it is a finely graded scale ranging from death to the extreme awareness of the artist. Indeed, with the electroencephalograph we can even chart certain variations of consciousness between people, and in one person at different times. Had Mrs. Cogdon been "awake," that is, just a little more conscious, a little more aware of her actions, then her act may have had to be regarded as "voluntary." The line is an extremely fine one, as is shown by the fact that in and during her dream Mrs. Cogdon was "aware" of the axe, her daughter and the soldiers. . . . Nor would Mrs. Cogdon's position have been legally different even if she could have then recalled all the dream, including the killing. Her exculpation lay not in the state of her memory but in her inability to bring into consciousness her emotional motivations, and consequently her diminished awareness of the deed.

Notes and Questions

1. What does the *Martin* court mean when it says that the police "took" Martin onto the highway? Suppose that they had simply ordered him to walk out of his house onto the road; is the same issue presented as in the situation where they carry him to the road? Why would Martin not be "acting" when the police carry him unto the road? Is there a difference in Martin's "non-action" in that situation and that of Cogdon and arguably of Wu? Exactly what is the difference?

2. Are you satisfied that there was sufficient evidence for the jury to perhaps find that Ms. Wu was not "acting" relative to her son's death. Did she have a motive, perhaps subconscious, for desiring his death? Does her "state of mind" have anything to do with whether or not she "acts"?

3. Was Ms. Cogdon "acting" at the time the injury occurred to her daughter? Does it matter that what Ms. Cogdon "thought" she was doing was a "good thing"? Thirty years after reporting on *Cogdon,* Professor Morris raised a variation: A defendant, while sleepwalking, kills his lover because, in his "dream," he believes that she is having intercourse with another man, and the defendant wishes to kill the other man. N. Morris, *Madness and the Criminal Law* 92 (1982). Is that a different case? Why?

4. Defendant, having fallen asleep on the sofa of a public hotel, is shaken by the porter, who tells him that he must leave. Defendant shoots the porter, killing him; his defense is that he committed no actus reus because he was "asleep" and therefore unconscious of the shooting. Should he be convicted of murder? *Fain v. Commonwealth,* 78 Ky. 183 (1879). Suppose the evidence showed that defendant knew that, upon waking, he sometimes became violent? The *Fain* court declared:

> If the prisoner is and has been afflicted in the manner claimed, and knew, as he no doubt did, his propensity to do acts of violence when aroused from sleep, he was guilty of a grave breach of social duty in going to sleep in the public room of a hotel with a deadly weapon on his person, and merits, for that reckless disregard of the safety of others, some degree of punishment, but we know of no law under which he can be punished. Our law only punishes for overt acts done by responsible moral agents. If the prisoner was unconscious when he killed the deceased, he cannot be punished for that act, and as the mere fact that he had the weapon on his person and went to sleep with it there did no injury to anyone, he cannot be punished for that.

5. For a case strikingly similar to *Cogdon,* see HM *Advocate v. Fraser,* 4 Couper. 70 (Scot. 1878). See also *Bradley v. State,* 277 S.W. 147 (Tex. Cr. App. 1925); *Lewis v. State,* 196 Ga. 755, 27 S.E.2d 659 (1943). For an account of several verified homicides that have occurred during sleepwalking, see Podolsky, *Somnambulistic Homicide,* 1 Medicine, Science and the Law 260 (1961).

6. The point that Professor Morris makes about the difficulty of defining a "voluntary" act without reference to the defendant's mental state (*mens rea*) is one of many leading one writer to urge the abolition of the term *actus reus* entirely. See Robinson, *Should the Criminal Law Abandon the Actus Reus— Mens Rea Distinction?* in Action and Value in Criminal Law 187 (S. Shute, J. Gardner, and J. Horder eds. 1993).

7. See generally, Note, *Automatism: The Unconsciousness Defense to a Criminal Action,* 15 San Diego L. Rev. 839 (1978); Beck, *Voluntary Conduct, Automatism, Insanity and Drunkenness,* 9 Crim. L.Q. 315 (1966); Saunders, *Voluntary Acts and the Criminal Law: Justifying Culpability Based on the Existence of Volition,* 49 U. Pitt. L. Rev. 443 (1988); Silber, *Being and Doing,* 35 U. Chi. L. Rev. 47 (1967). For a tour de force of the metaphysical issues involved, see M. Moore, *Act and Crime* (1993).

PEOPLE v. DECINA

Court of Appeals of New York

2 N.Y.2d 133, 157 NYS 2d 558, 138 N.E.2d 799 (1956)

FROESSEL, Judge.

At about 3:30 P.M. on March 14, 1955, a bright, sunny day, defendant was driving, alone in his car, in a northerly direction on Delaware Avenue in the city of Buffalo. The portion of Delaware Avenue here involved is 60 feet wide. At a point south of an overhead viaduct of the Erie Railroad, defendant's car swerved to the left, across the center line in the street, so that it was completely in the south lane, traveling 35 to 40 miles per hour.

It then veered sharply to the right, crossing Delaware Avenue and mounting the easterly curb at a point beneath the viaduct and continued thereafter at a speed estimated to have been about 50 or 60 miles per hour or more. During this latter swerve, a pedestrian testified that he saw defendant's hand above his head; another witness said he saw defendant's left arm bent over the wheel, and his right hand extended towards the right door.

A group of six schoolgirls were walking north on the easterly sidewalk of Delaware Avenue, two in front and four slightly in the rear, when defendant's car struck them from behind. One of the girls escaped injury by jumping against the wall of the viaduct. The bodies of the children struck were propelled northward onto the street and the lawn in front of a coal company, located to the north of the Erie viaduct on Delaware Avenue. Three of the children, 6 to 12 years old, were found dead on arrival by the medical examiner, and a fourth child, 7 years old, died in a hospital two days later as a result of injuries sustained in the accident.

After striking the children, defendant's car continued on the easterly sidewalk, and then swerved back onto Delaware Avenue once more. It continued in a northerly direction, passing under a second viaduct before it again veered to the right and remounted the easterly curb, striking and breaking a metal lamppost. With its horn blowing steadily—apparently because defendant was "stooped over" the steering wheel—the car proceeded on the sidewalk until it finally crashed through a 7 1/4-inch brick wall of a grocery store, injuring at least one customer and causing considerable property damage.

* * *

Defendant was pulled out of the car by a number of bystanders and laid down on the sidewalk. To a policeman who came on the scene shortly he appeared "injured, dazed;" another witness said that "he looked as though he was knocked out, and his arm seemed to be bleeding." An injured customer in the store after receiving first aid, pressed defendant for an explanation of the accident and he told her: "I blacked out from the bridge."

When the police arrived, defendant attempted to rise, staggered and appeared dazed and unsteady. When informed that he was under arrest, and would have to accompany the police to the station house, he resisted and, when he tried to get away, was handcuffed. The foregoing evidence was adduced by the People, and is virtually undisputed—defendant did not take the stand nor did he produce any witnesses.

Defendant was indicted and charged with violating §1053-a of the Penal Law, Consol. Laws, c. 40.

We turn first to the subject of defendant's cross appeal, namely, that his demurrer should have been sustained, since the *indictment* here does not charge a crime. The indictment states essentially that defendant, *knowing* "that he was subject to epileptic attacks or other disorder rendering him likely to lose consciousness for a considerable period of time", was culpably negligent "in that he *consciously* undertook to and *did operate* his Buick sedan on a public highway" (emphasis supplied) and "while so doing" suffered such an attack which caused said automobile "to travel at a fast and reckless rate of speed, jumping the curb and driving over the sidewalk" causing the death of 4 persons. In our opinion, this clearly states a violation of §1053-a of the Penal Law. The statute does not require that a defendant must deliberately intend to kill a human being, for that would be murder. Nor does the statute require that he knowingly and consciously follow the precise path that leads to death and destruction. It is sufficient, we have said, when his conduct manifests a "disregard of the consequences which may ensue from the act, and indifference to the rights of others. No clearer definition, applicable to the hundreds of varying circumstances that may arise, can be given. Under a given state of facts, whether negligence is culpable is a question of judgment." *People v. Angelo,* 246 N.Y. 451, 457, 159 N.E. 394, 396.

Assuming the truth of the indictment, as we must on a demurrer, this defendant knew he was subject to epileptic attacks and seizures that might strike at any time. He also knew that a moving motor vehicle uncontrolled on a public highway is a highly dangerous instrumentality capable of unrestrained destruction. With this knowledge, and without anyone accompanying him, he deliberately took a chance by making a conscious choice of a course of action, in disregard of the consequences which he knew might follow from his conscious act, and which in this case did ensue. How can we say as a matter of law that this did not amount to culpable negligence within the meaning of §1053-a?

To hold otherwise would be to say that a man may freely indulge himself in liquor in the same hope that it will not affect his driving, and if it later develops that ensuing intoxication causes dangerous and reckless driving resulting in death, his unconsciousness or involuntariness at that time would relieve him from prosecution under the statute. His awareness of a condition which he knows may produce such consequences as here, and his disregard of the consequences, renders him liable for culpable negligence, as the courts below have properly held. . . . *State v. Gooze,* 14 N.J. Super. 277, 81 A.2d 811. To have a sudden sleeping spell, an unexpected heart or other disabling attack, without any prior knowledge or warning thereof, is an altogether different situation, see *Jenson v. Fletcher,* 277 A.D. 454, 101 N.Y.S.2d 75, affirmed, 303 N.Y. 639, 101 N.E.2d 759, and there is simply no basis for comparing such cases with the flagrant disregard manifested here.

Accordingly, the order of the Appellate Division should be affirmed.

DESMOND, Judge *(concurring in part and dissenting in part).*

The indictment charges that defendant knowing that "he was subject to epileptic attacks or other disorder rendering him likely to lose consciousness" suffered "an attack and loss of consciousness which caused the said automobile operated by the said defendant to travel at a fast and reckless rate of speed" and to jump a curb and run onto the sidewalk "thereby striking and causing the death" of 4 children. Horrible as this occurrence was and whatever necessity it may show for new licensing and driving laws, nevertheless this indictment charges no crime known to the New York statutes. Our duty is to dismiss it.

§1053-a of the Penal Law describes the crime of "criminal negligence in the operation of a vehicle resulting in death." Declared to be guilty of that crime is "[a] person who operates or drives any vehicle of any kind in a reckless or culpably negligent manner, whereby a human being is killed." The essentials of the crime are, therefore, first, vehicle operation in a culpably negligent manner, and, second, the resulting death of a person. This indictment asserts that defendant violated §1053-a, but it then proceeds to describe the way in which defendant is supposed to have offended against that statute. That descriptive matter . . . shows that defendant did not violate §1053-a. No operation of an automobile in a reckless manner is charged against defendant. The excessive speed of the car and its jumping the curb were "caused," says the indictment itself, by defendant's prior "attack and loss of consciousness." Therefore, what defendant is accused of is not reckless or culpably negligent driving, which necessarily connotes and involves consciousness and volition. The fatal assault by this car was after and because of defendant's failure of consciousness. To say that one drove a car in a reckless manner in that his unconscious condition caused the car to travel recklessly is to make two mutually contradictory assertions. One cannot be "reckless" while unconscious. One cannot while unconscious "operate" a car in a culpably negligent manner or in any other "manner." The statute makes criminal a particular kind of known, voluntary, immediate operation. It does not touch at all the involuntary presence of an unconscious person at the wheel of an uncontrolled vehicle. . . .

Now let us test by its consequences this new construction of §1053-a. Numerous are the diseases and other conditions of a human being which make it possible or even likely that the afflicted person will lose control of his automobile. Epilepsy, coronary involvements, circulatory diseases, nephritis, uremic poisoning, diabetes, Meniere's syndrome, a tendency to fits of sneezing, locking of the knee, muscular contractions—any of these common conditions may cause loss of control of a vehicle for a period long enough to cause a fatal accident. An automobile traveling at only 30 miles an hour goes 44 feet in a second. Just what is the court holding here? No less than this: that a driver whose brief blackout lets his car run amuck and kill another has killed that other by reckless driving. But any such "recklessness" consists necessarily not of the erratic behavior of the automobile while its driver is unconscious, but of his driving at all when he knew he was subject to such attacks. Thus, it must be that such a blackout-prone driver is guilty of reckless driving, Vehicle and Traffic Law, Consol. Laws, c.71, §58, whenever and as soon as he steps into the driver's seat of a vehicle. Every time he drives, accident or no accident, he is subject to criminal prosecution for reckless driving or to revocation of his operator's license, Vehicle and Traffic Law, §71, subd. 3. And how many of this State's 5,000,000 licensed operators are subject to such penalties for merely driving the cars they are licensed to drive? No one knows how many citizens or how many or what kind of physical conditions will be gathered in under this practically limitless coverage of §1053-a of the Penal Law and §58 and subdivision 3 of §71 of the Vehicle and Traffic Law. It is no answer that prosecutors and juries will be reasonable or compassionate. A criminal statute whose reach is so unpredictable violates constitutional rights. . . .

NOTES AND QUESTIONS

1. Assuming that Ms. Wu, Ms. Cogdon, and Mr. Decina were all "unconscious" at the time the injuries occurred in their respective cases, does it make sense to draw any distinctions between the three cases? If Mr. Decina was acting, how can it be said that Ms. Cogdon was not? If the court in *Decina* can focus on Decina's entering the car and beginning to drive, why can the jury in *Cogdon* decline to consider that she had sleepwalked before? Is *Decina* distinguishable on the ground that when he entered the car, and prior to the time of his seizure, he was "operating" the car whereas neither Wu nor Codgon could be said to have been "conscious" when the alleged homicidal act was committed?

2. Is *Decina* explicable only (or principally) on statutory interpretation grounds? Suppose that during his seizure, defendant's car had gone through a red light and he had been charged with "failing to stop at a red light." Could he be convicted, under that wording? Suppose the statutory charge were "operating a vehicle so as to cause it to run a red light"?

ROBINSON v. CALIFORNIA

Supreme Court of the United States

370 U.S. 660 (1962)

MR. JUSTICE STEWART *delivered the opinion of the Court.*

A California statute makes it a criminal offense for a person to "be addicted to the use of narcotics."[1] This appeal draws into question the constitutionality

---

[1] The statute is §11721 of the California Health and Safety Code. It provides:

No person shall use, or be under the influence of, or be addicted to the use of narcotics. Any person convicted of violating any provision of this section is guilty of a misdemeanor and shall be sentenced to serve a term of not less than 90 days nor more than one year in the county jail. The court may place a person convicted hereunder on probation for a period not to exceed five years and shall in all cases in which probation is granted require as a condition thereof

of that provision of the state law, as construed by the California courts in the present case.

The appellant was convicted after a jury trial in the Municipal Court of Los Angeles. [One police officer testified that when he arrested Robinson (there was no indication of the crime for which Robinson was arrested), he examined defendant's arm and found scar tissue consistent with the use of needles, and that defendant admitted having used narcotics occasionally. A second police officer, who examined defendant at the police station essentially corroborated this testimony, adding that there was no evidence that defendant was under the influence of drugs at the time of the examination. [Defendant denied the use of narcotics, and his alleged admissions, explaining the scar marks as resulting from an allergic condition contracted during military service.]

The trial judge instructed the jury that the statute made it a misdemeanor for a person either to use narcotics, or to be addicted to the use of narcotics. . . . That portion of the statute referring to the "use" of narcotics is based upon a condition or status. They are not identical. . . . To be addicted to the use of narcotics is said to be a status or condition and not an act. It is a continuing offense and differs from most other offenses in the fact that [it] is chronic rather than acute; that it continues after it is complete and subjects the offender to arrest at any time before he reforms. The existence of such a chronic condition may be ascertained from a single examination, if the characteristic reactions of that condition be found present.

The judge further instructed the jury that the appellant could be convicted under a general verdict if the jury agreed either that he was of the "status" or had committed the "act" denounced by the statute. "All that the People must show is either that the defendant did use a narcotic in Los Angeles County, or that while in the City of Los Angeles he was addicted to the use of narcotics."

Under these instructions the jury returned a verdict finding the appellant "guilty of the offense charged."

The broad power of a State to regulate the narcotic drugs traffic within its borders is not here in issue.

Such regulation, it can be assumed, could take a variety of valid forms. A State might impose criminal sanctions, for example, against the unauthorized manufacture, prescription, sale, purchase, or possession of narcotics within its borders. In the interest of discouraging the violation of such laws, or in the interest of the general health or welfare of its inhabitants, a State might establish a program of compulsory treatment for those addicted to narcotics. Such a program of treatment might require periods of involuntary confinement. And penal sanctions might be imposed for failure to comply with established compulsory treatment procedures. *Cf. Jacobson v. Massachusetts,* 197 U.S. 11 (1905). . . .

It would be possible to construe the statute under which the appellant was convicted as one which is operative only upon proof of the actual use of

---

that such person be confined in the county jail for at least 90 days. In no event does the court have the power to absolve a person who violates this section from the obligation of spending at least 90 days in confinement in the county jail.

narcotics within the State's jurisdiction. But the California courts have not so construed this law. Although there was evidence in the present case that the appellant had used narcotics in Los Angeles, the jury were instructed that they could convict him even if they disbelieved that evidence. The appellant could be convicted, they were told, if they found simply that the appellant's "status" or "chronic condition" was that of being "addicted to the use of narcotics." And it is impossible to know from the jury's verdict that the defendant was not convicted upon precisely such a finding.

* * *

This statute, therefore, is not one which punishes a person for the use of narcotics, for their purchase, sale or possession, or for antisocial or disorderly behavior resulting from their administration. It is not a law which even purports to provide or require medical treatment. Rather, we deal with a statute which makes the "status" of narcotic addiction a criminal offense, for which the offender may be prosecuted "at any time before he reforms." California has said that a person can be continuously guilty of this offense, whether or not he has even used or possessed any narcotics within the State, and whether or not he has been guilty of any antisocial behavior there.

It is unlikely that any State at this moment in history would attempt to make it a criminal offense for a person to be mentally ill, or a leper, or to be afflicted with a venereal disease. A State might determine that the general health and welfare require that the victims of these and other human afflictions be dealt with by compulsory treatment, involving quarantine, confinement, or sequestration. But, in light of contemporary human knowledge, a law which made a criminal offense of such a disease would doubtless be universally thought to be an infliction of cruel and unusual punishment in violation of the Eighth and Fourteenth Amendments. . . .

We cannot but consider the statute before us as of the same category. In this Court counsel for the State recognized that narcotic addiction is an illness. Indeed, it is apparently an illness which may be contracted innocently or involuntarily.[9] We hold that a state law which imprisons a person thus afflicted as a criminal, even though he has never touched any narcotic drug within the State or been guilty of any irregular behavior there, inflicts a cruel and unusual punishment in violation of the Fourteenth Amendment. To be sure, imprisonment for ninety days is not, in the abstract, a punishment which is either cruel or unusual. But the question cannot be considered in the abstract. Even one day in prison would be a cruel and unusual punishment for the "crime" of having a common cold.

---

[9] Not only may addiction innocently result from the use of medically prescribed narcotics, but a person may even be a narcotics addict from the moment of his birth.

Reversed.

MODEL PENAL CODE §2.01[*]

(1) A person is not guilty of an offense unless his liability is based on conduct which includes a voluntary act or the omission to perform an act of which he is physically capable.

(2) The following are not voluntary acts within the meaning of this section:

  (a) a reflex or convulsion;

  (b) a bodily movement during unconsciousness or sleep;

  (c) conduct during hypnosis or resulting from hypnotic suggestion;

  (d) a bodily movement that otherwise is not a product of the effort or determination of the actor, either conscious or habitual.

(3) Liability for the commission of an offense may not be based on an omission unaccompanied by action unless:

  (a) the omission is expressly made sufficient by the law defining the offense; or

  (b) a duty to perform the omitted act is otherwise imposed by law.

NOTES AND QUESTIONS

1. Were Martin, Wu, Cogdon, Decina, or Robinson acting within the meaning of the MPC?

2. Why does *Robinson* find it objectionable to punish a person for his status? Does it matter whether the status is (or is not) one that is usually voluntarily acquired? Does it matter whether the status is (or is not) one that is almost always acquired through the commission of a criminal act?

---

[*] The Model Penal Code [MPC] is the culmination of a thirty-year effort by The American Law Institute, an association of judges, practicing attorneys, and academics. It is the most recent in a series of attempts, here and in England, to codify the criminal law. Almost all of the predecessor efforts in both countries, over the past two centuries, have failed. In England, periodic attempts at codification in 1845, 1848, 1852, 1861, and 1976 all failed miserably. This was also the fate of the famous draft criminal code proposed by the most famous criminal jurist of the last century, Sir James Fitzjames Stephen; other commonwealth countries, however, did adopt the Stephen Code in large part. See *Symposium,* 19 Rutgers L. J. 530 (1988). Yet the Model Penal Code has been accepted, in large part, by a large number, probably a majority, of states. Although the "common law" of crimes no longer truly exists in either country, and all criminal laws have been put in statutory form (*nullum crimen sine lege*—without a law there is no crime), the statutes of every state have been a patchwork of heterogenous and often conflicting legislation, enacted sporadically and often without much thought. Ironically, with the adoption of the MPC by so many states in this country, revivified codification movements in England and in Canada arose. The Canada Law Revision Commission has recommended a full revision of that country's code. In England, the Criminal Revision Committee, an official government body, published many working papers on the criminal law, but these have been unfruitful. In sharp contrast are the continental countries, which for nearly two centuries have had an integrated and relatively consistent set of criminal statutes, which are periodically updated as a group.

3. Could the California legislature make it a crime for a person, while addicted to narcotics, (a)to enter the state; (b)to rent a hotel room; (c)to buy a magazine; or (d)to appear in public? What about "being a narcotics addict and failing to be cured of such addiction"?

4. If having a common cold may not be punished, what of going into public with a common cold? See S. Butler, *Erewhon; R. v. Vatandillo,* 4 M. & S. 72 (1815) (it is a common law offense to carry a child infected with smallpox into public). Many persons initially interpreted *Robinson* as saying that narcotics addiction was a disease and that it was unconstitutional to punish (but not compulsorily treat or confine) someone for having a disease even if the diseased person "acted" in some way. This was then extended to argue that "inherent aspects" of the disease could also not be prosecuted. Thus possession and use of narcotics by an addict could not, according to this interpretation, be punished either. The first interpretation was rejected in *Powell v. Texas,* 392 U.S. 514 (1968), where a majority upheld the conviction of an alcoholic who violated a statute prohibiting being "found in a state of intoxication in public." The *Powell* Court found that the crime charged entailed an "act" sufficient to distinguish the situation from the "mere status" involved in *Robinson.* The Court did not clearly reject the "inherent aspects" extension of *Robinson,* however. Four dissenting Justices argued that any act that was "part of the pattern" of alcoholism could not constitutionally be punished under *Robinson.* A fifth Justice—White—agreed with this conclusion, but held that public drunkenness was not "part of the pattern" of chronic alcoholism. Although these five would seem to have given sustenance to the "inherent aspects" approach, *Powell* has generally been read as rejecting that view, and there is little movement toward resurrecting the question. See *infra,* 9.05C. Thus, while it would be unconstitutional, under *Robinson,* to punish a person for *having* tuberculosis, it would be constitutional to punish such a person for "acting" within the state (e.g., coming into public places).

5. *Robinson* and Powell raise a problem with which we will be constantly concerned: civil alternatives to criminal confinement. If narcotics addicts, alcoholics, or the mentally ill may be hospitalized in the absence of an act, as the dicta in *Robinson* states, what is the difference to the "patients" or to the rest of us how the process by which they are committed is labeled? Are these systems and others alternatives to criminal law? Are there distinctions—and, if so, what are they? Reconsider the material on punishment-therapy, *supra,* pp.68—78, especially in *Re De La O, supra,* p.68.

§ 3.02 KNOWING FAILURE TO ACT

[A] Generally

PEOPLE v. SHAUGHNESSY

District Court of Nassau County

66 Misc. 2d 19, 319 N.Y.S.2d 626 (1971)

JOHN S. LOCKMAN, Judge.

On October 9th, 1970, shortly before 10:05 P.M., the Defendant in the company of her boyfriend and two other youngsters proceeded by automobile to the vicinity of the St. Ignatius Retreat Home, Searingtown Road, Incorporated Village of North Hills, Nassau County, New York. The Defendant was a passenger and understood that she was headed for the Christopher Morley Park which is located across the street from the St. Ignatius Retreat Home and has a large illuminated sign, with letters approximately 8 inches high, which identifies the park. As indicated, on the other side of the street the St. Ignatius Retreat Home has two pillars at its entrance with a bronze sign on each pillar with 4 to 5 inch letters. The sign is not illuminated. The vehicle in which the Defendant was riding proceeded into the grounds of the Retreat House and was stopped by a watchman and the occupants including the Defendant waited approximately 20 minutes for a Policeman to arrive. The Defendant never left the automobile.

The Defendant is charged with violating §1 of the Ordinance prohibiting entry upon private property of the Incorporated Village of North Hills, which provides: "No person shall enter upon any privately owned piece, parcel or lot of real property in the Village of North Hills without the permission of the owner, lessee or occupant thereof."

* * *

The problem presented by the facts in this case brings up for review the primary elements that are required for criminal accountability and responsibility. It is only from an accused's voluntary overt acts that criminal responsibility can attach. An overt act or a specific omission to act must occur in order for the establishment of a criminal offense.

* * *

The principle which requires a voluntary act or omission to act had been codified in the Revised Penal Law, §15.10 and reads as follows in part: "The minimal requirement for criminal liability is the performance by a person of conduct which includes a voluntary act or the omission to perform an act which he is physically capable of performing. . . ."

* * *

In the case at bar, the People have failed to establish any act on the part of the Defendant. She merely was a passenger in a vehicle. Any action taken by the vehicle was caused and guided by the driver thereof and not by the Defendant. If the Defendant were to be held guilty under these circumstances, it would dictate that she would be guilty if she had been unconscious or asleep at the time or even if she had been [a] prisoner in the automobile. There are many situations which can be envisioned and in which the trespass statute in question would be improperly applied to an involuntary act. One might conceive of a driver losing control of a vehicle through mechanical failure and the vehicle proceeding onto private property which is the subject of a trespass.

In the case of the Defendant now before the Court, the very first and essential element in criminal responsibility is missing, an overt voluntary act or omission to act and, accordingly, the Defendant is found not guilty.

NOTES AND QUESTIONS

1. In both *Decina* and *Shaughnessy* it is certainly beyond dispute that, at the actual moment of injury, the defendant was not, in any morally relevant sense, "acting." Yet in *Decina,* the court moved back the focus of time to a moment at which the defendant clearly did "act." If the law could be so elastic, what is the point of the requirement of an "act," since, at some pre-injury moment of time, there will always be an act? See Ashworth, *Reason, Logic and Criminal Liability,* 91 Law Q. Rev. 102 (1975).

2. Assuming that Decina's (earlier) act was voluntary, and that there was some mens rea at that point, should the crime not be defined, e.g., as "entering a car with the knowledge of the (high) possibility of death if a seizure occurs," rather than charging the defendant as though he had been acting at the time the injury occurred and punishing him for manslaughter? Does that not penalize this defendant equally with the defendant who in fact was "acting" recklessly at the time of the injury? Are they equally culpable? Compare the issue of intoxication, §9.05C, *infra*.

3. Defendant is found asleep in his car on the side of the road. He is clearly intoxicated though there is no bottle of liquor in the car. Can he be convicted of being in "actual physical control of a car while under the influence of intoxicating liquor?" See *State v. Webb,* 78 Ariz. 8, 274 P.2d 338 (1954). Suppose a clearly intoxicated defendant has entered his car and put his key in the ignition? See *State v. Daly,* 64 N.J. 122, 313 A.2d 194 (1974); *Sweeny v. State,* 40 N.J. 359, 192 A.2d 573 (1963).

Defendant is charged with violation of a statute providing that "Any person who when driving or attempting to drive, or when in charge of, a motor-vehicle on a road. . . is under the influence of drink . . . to such an extent as to be incapable of having proper control of the vehicle" is guilty of an offense. Defendant, clearly under the influence, suddenly awoke to find that the car in which he had been sleeping was moving. He steered it to a median strip, some 300 yards down the road. He states that he feared to stop it sooner, because the road was oily and he thought the car might skid. What is the result? *In re Kitson,* 39 Crim. App. 66 (1955).

4. What of the person who accidentally starts a fire and then fails to put it out, *Commonwealth v. Cali,* 247 Mass. 20, 141 N.E. 510 (1923), or who, having accidentally driven his car on a constable's toe, fails to remove it when requested to do so? *Fagan v. Metropolitan Police Commissioner,* 3 All E.R. 442 (1968). Or what of the "innocently-born heroin addict" (mentioned in footnote 9 of *Robinson*) who, becoming aware at age 18 that he is addicted, refuses to undergo treatment? Are these cases different from the cases of "omissions" considered in §3.03 infra?

5. The Academic Group of the Criminal Law Committee proposes the following:

(1) Where it is an offense to be at fault in causing a result, a person who causes the result by an act done without the fault required commits the offense if, after doing the act and with the fault required, he fails to take reasonable steps which might have prevented the result occurring or continuing.

[B] Possession

PEOPLE V. ACKERMAN

Criminal Appeals Court of Illinois

2 Ill. App. 3d 903, 274 N.E.2d 125 (1971)

Mr. Justice STOUDER *delivered the opinion of the court:*

This is an appeal by Jeffrey Ackerman, Defendant, from his conviction and sentence for the offense of possession of 140 tablets more or less of LSD.

On the morning of April 9, 1970, the postmaster of the Macomb, Illinois post office noticed that a package wrapped as a book rattled when shaken. He called the sheriff and in the presence of the sheriff and a deputy sheriff the package was opened. Inside the package was a book with its pages glued together and inside the pages was a cut-out section containing about 140 pills identified by a test conducted on the spot as LSD. The package was rewrapped for delivery in due course. The package was addressed to Gary Lang, c/o Jeffrey Ackerman, 916 Henninger, Macomb, Illinois. Neither the name nor the address of the sender appeared on the package. Henninger Hall is a dormitory of Western Illinois University at Macomb and the defendant, a Western Illinois student, resides at Room 916 in such Hall. No student named Gary Lang is registered at Western Illinois University.

After ascertaining that the package would be delivered at about noon, the sheriff, deputy sheriff, postal inspector and agent of the Illinois Bureau of Investigation set up a surveillance of the first floor of Henninger Hall. At about 2 P.M. the defendant came into Henninger Hall, went to his mail box and withdrew therefrom a notice that there was a package for him. He went to the counter where packages were ordinarily delivered, presented his notice, received the package, signed a receipt therefore, put the package under his arm and headed for the elevator. While so proceeding he was stopped and arrested. The package, previously opened and examined in the post office, was taken from him.

Defendant testified that he returned to Henninger Hall to get a notebook for his next class and that he had received the package as described and that he had the package under his arm when arrested. However he denied that he knew what was in the package, that he had ordered any such package, that he knew where the package had come from and that he did not know any Gary Lang.

It is well settled that knowledge is an essential element in the chain of proof of the crime of possession of narcotics. . . . Ill. Rev. Stat. 1969, par. 4–2, ch. 38, defines voluntary possession in the following language, "Possession is a voluntary act if the offender knowingly procured or received the thing possessed, or was aware of his control thereof for a sufficient time to have been able to terminate his possession." Possession as so described is an essential element of the offense of possession of a narcotic or dangerous drug. . . .

[T]he element of knowledge is seldom susceptible of direct proof. In a narcotic case knowledge sufficient to convict a person ". . . may be proved by evidence of acts, declarations or conduct of the accused from which the inference may be fairly drawn that he knew of the existence of the narcotics at the place where they were found." See *People v. Mack,* 12 Ill. 2d 151, 145 N.E.2d 609.

The State insists there is sufficient evidence from which knowledge may be inferred.

* * *

In *People v. Mosley* ([131] Ill. App. 2d [722]), 265 N.E.2d 889, a recent case dealing with this problem, the court held that presence of marijuana in the trunk of a car without other evidence relating such presence to some conduct of the defendant other than his occupancy of the car as a passenger was insufficient to give rise to any fair or reasonable inference of knowledge or possession.

[I]t is our opinion that the evidence fails to show acts, declarations or conduct which fairly support any inference of knowledge by defendant that the package contained LSD. In this respect the State itself refers to defendant's conduct as suspicious or not normal, characterizations which are difficult to justify from the evidence at best and insufficient to support the burden imposed upon the State. All the evidence shows is that defendant received a package in the course of normal mail delivery and placed the package under his arm for about five seconds. Such evidence is of little more probative value than the evidence of the discovery of the LSD in the package in the post office.

[T]he evidence is insufficient to support the conviction. . . .

* * *

Judgement reversed.

NOTES AND QUESTIONS

1. Originally courts held that a person could not be criminally punished for mere "possession," since this was not an act. See, e.g., *Rex v. Heath,* Russ & Ry. 184, 168 Eng. Rep. 750 (1810). Most state statutes today, however, follow the wording of the statute involved in *Ackerman* [which was taken verbatim from §2.01(4) of the Model Penal Code].

2. Distinguish: (a)Unknown to and unsolicited by D, X puts a package of cocaine into D's coat pocket while the coat is hanging in a closet; (b)D knows that X has put the package in the coat but (1)has no idea what the package contains; (2)believes the package contains golf balls; (3)knows the package contains a white powder, but believes that the white powder is sugar. In which instances, if any, does D "possess" the cocaine?

§ 3.03 OMISSIONS

JONES V. UNITED STATES*

United States Court of Appeals

District of Columbia Circuit

308 F.2d 307 (1962)

WRIGHT, Circuit Judge.

Appellant, together with one Shirley Green, was tried on a three-count indictment charging them jointly with (1)abusing and maltreating Robert Lee Green, (2)abusing and maltreating Anthony Lee Green, and (3)involuntary manslaughter through failure to perform their legal duty of care for Anthony Lee Green, which failure resulted in his death. At the close of evidence, after trial to a jury, the first two counts were dismissed as to both defendants. On the third count, appellant was convicted of involuntary manslaughter. Shirley Green was found not guilty.

* * *

A summary of the evidence, which is in conflict upon almost every significant issue, is necessary for the disposition of both arguments. In late 1957, Shirley Green became pregnant, out of wedlock, with a child, Robert Lee, subsequently born August 17, 1958. Apparently to avoid the embarrassment of the presence of the child in the Green home, it was arranged that appellant,

---

* [Footnotes are renumbered.—Eds.]

a family friend, would take the child to her home after birth. Appellant did so, and the child remained there continuously until removed by the police on August 5, 1960. Initially appellant made some motions toward the adoption of Robert Lee, but these came to naught, and shortly thereafter it was agreed that Shirley Green was to pay appellant $72 a month for his care. According to appellant, these payments were made for only five months. According to Shirley Green, they were made up to July 1960.

Early in 1959 Shirley Green again became pregnant, this time with the child Anthony Lee, whose death is the basis of appellant's conviction. This child was born October 21, 1959. Soon after birth, Anthony Lee developed a mild jaundice condition, attributed to a blood incompatibility with his mother. The jaundice resulted in his retention in the hospital for three days beyond the usual time, or until October 26, 1959, when, on authorization signed by Shirley Green, Anthony Lee was released by the hospital to appellant's custody. Shirley Green, after a two or three day stay in the hospital, also lived with appellant for three weeks, after which she returned to her parents' home, leaving the children with appellant. She testified she did not see them again, except for one visit in March, until August 5, 1960. Consequently, though there does not seem to have been any specific monetary agreement with Shirley Green covering Anthony Lee's support,[1] appellant had complete custody of both children until they were rescued by the police.

With regard to medical care, the evidence is undisputed. In March, 1960, appellant called a Dr. Turner to her home to treat Anthony Lee for a bronchial condition. Appellant also telephoned the doctor at various times to consult him concerning Anthony Lee's diet and health. In early July, 1960, appellant took Anthony Lee to Dr. Turner's office where he was treated for "simple diarrhea." At this time the doctor noted the "wizened" appearance of the child and told appellant to tell the mother of the child that he should be taken to a hospital. This was not done.

On August 2, 1960, two collectors for the local gas company had occasion to go to the basement of appellant's home, and there saw the two children. Robert Lee and Anthony Lee at this time were age two years and ten months respectively. Robert Lee was in a "crib" consisting of a framework of wood, covered with a fine wire screening, including the top which was hinged. The "crib" was lined with newspaper, which was stained, apparently with feces, and crawling with roaches. Anthony Lee was lying in a bassinet. One collector testified to seeing roaches on Anthony Lee.

On August 5, 1960, the collectors returned to appellant's home in the company of several police officers and personnel of the Women's Bureau. At this time, Anthony Lee was upstairs in the dining room in the bassinet, but Robert Lee was still downstairs in his "crib." The officers removed the children to the D.C. General Hospital where Anthony Lee was diagnosed as suffering from severe malnutrition and lesions over large portions of his body, apparently caused by severe diaper rash. Following admission, he was fed repeatedly, apparently with no difficulty, and was described as being very hungry. His death, 34 hours after admission, was attributed without dispute to

---

[1] It was uncontested that during the entire period the children were in appellant's home, appellant had ample means to provide food and medical care.

malnutrition. At birth, Anthony Lee weighed six pounds, fifteen ounces—at death at age ten months, he weighed seven pounds, thirteen ounces. Normal weight at this age would have been approximately 14 pounds.

Appellant argues that nothing in the evidence establishes that she failed to provide food to Anthony Lee. She cites her own testimony and the testimony of a lodger, Mr. Wills, that she did in fact feed the baby regularly. At trial, the defense made repeated attempts to extract from the medical witnesses opinions that the jaundice, or the condition which caused it, might have prevented the baby from assimilating food. The doctors conceded this was possible but not probable since the autopsy revealed no condition which would support the defense theory. It was also shown by the disinterested medical witnesses that the child had no difficulty in ingesting food immediately after birth, and that Anthony Lee, in the last hours before his death, was able to take several bottles, apparently without difficulty, and seemed very hungry. This evidence, combined with the absence of any physical cause for nonassimilation, taken in the context of the condition in which these children were kept, presents a jury question on the feeding issue.

Moreover, there is substantial evidence from which the jury could have found that appellant failed to obtain proper medical care for the child. Appellant relies upon the evidence showing that on one occasion she summoned a doctor for the child, on another took the child to the doctor's office, and that she telephoned the doctor on several occasions about the baby's formula. However, the last time a doctor saw the child was a month before his death, and appellant admitted that on that occasion the doctor recommended hospitalization. Appellant did not hospitalize the child, nor did she take any other steps to obtain medical care in the last crucial month. Thus there was sufficient evidence to go to the jury on the issue of medical care, as well as failure to feed.

Appellant takes exception to the failure of the trial court to charge that the jury must find beyond a reasonable doubt, as an element of the crime, that appellant was under a legal duty to supply food and necessities to Anthony Lee.

The problem of establishing the duty to take action which would preserve the life of another has not often arisen in the case law of this country.[2] The most commonly cited statement of the rule is found in *People v. Beardsley*, 150 Mich. 206, 113 N.W. 1128, 1129, 13 L.R.A.—N.S. 1020:

> The law recognizes that under some circumstances the omission of a duty owed by one individual to another, where such omission results in the death of the one to whom the duty is owing, will make the other chargeable with manslaughter. . . . This rule of law is always based upon the proposition that the duty neglected must be a legal duty, and not a mere moral obligation. It must be a duty imposed by law or by contract, and the omission to perform the duty must be the immediate and direct cause of death.

There are at least four situations in which the failure to act may constitute breach of a legal duty. One can be held criminally liable: first, where a statute

---

[2] The problem has evoked considerable study. See, e.g, Holmes, The Common Law, p. 278 (1881); Moreland, A Rationale of Criminal Negligence, ch. 10 (1944); Hughes, *Criminal Omissions*, 67 Yale L.J. 590, 620—26 (1958); Annot., 10 A.L.R. 1137 (1921).

imposes a duty to care for another;[3] second, where one stands in a certain status relationship to another;[4] third, where one has assumed a contractual duty to care for another; and fourth, where one has voluntarily assumed the care of another and so secluded the helpless person as to prevent others from rendering aid.

It is the contention of the Government that either the third or the fourth ground is applicable here. However, it is obvious that in any of the four situations, there are critical issues of fact which must be passed on by the jury—specifically in this case, whether appellant had entered into a contract with the mother for the care of Anthony Lee or, alternatively, whether she assumed the care of the child and secluded him from the care of his mother, his natural protector. On both of these issues, the evidence is in direct conflict, appellant insisting that the mother was actually living with appellant and Anthony Lee, and hence should have been taking care of the child herself, while Shirley Green testified she was living with her parents and was paying appellant to care for both children.

In spite of this conflict, the instructions given in the case failed even to suggest the necessity for finding a legal duty of care. The only reference to duty in the instructions was the reading of the indictment which charged, inter alia, that the defendants "failed to perform their legal duty." A finding of legal duty is the critical element of the crime charged and failure to instruct the jury concerning it was plain error.

* * *

Reversed and remanded.

NOTES AND QUESTIONS

1. The common law of tort rarely imposed liability for failure to prevent injury. Administrative reasons might explain some of this reluctance: (a) Who, of a large number of people knowing of the danger, has the duty to act? (b) What level of danger activates the duty? (c) What if the rescuer is injured? (d) What if the person rescued is injured by the rescuer? (e) What if the rescuer misperceives the presence of danger or its extent?

Are these reasons sufficient in the tort context? Are they sufficient in the criminal context? Are there other reasons, in the criminal context, for not imposing a duty even if it were to be imposed in the tort law?

One such explanation is the protection of the autonomy of those who would be placed under a duty. Another is that to "legalize" a moral duty degrades that duty. Some feminists suggest that the explanation is gender:

> The moral imperative that emerges repeatedly in interviews with women is an injunction to care, a responsibility to discern and alleviate the "real

---

[3] See, e.g., D.C. Code §22-902; *Craig v. State,* 220 Md. 590, 155 A.2d 684.

[4] *Regina v. Smith,* 8 Carr. & P. 153 (Eng. 1837) (master to apprentice); *United States v. Knowles,* 26 Fed. Cas. 800 (No. 15,540) (ship's naster to crew and passengers); cf, *State v. Reitze,* 86 N.J.L. 407, 92 A. 576 (innkeeper to inebriated customers).

and recognizable trouble" of this world. For men, the moral imperative appears rather as an injunction to re spect the rights of others and thus to protect from interference the rights to life and self-fulfillment.

C. Gilligan, In a Different Voice 100 (1982).

2. The *Jones* court suggests that one basis upon which a defendant may incur liability is the presence of a contractual undertaking. Must there be a "contract"? Or is a voluntary "undertaking" sufficient? Suppose that Jones was not being paid to care for the child. Should that make a difference? What is the basis of the "undertaking"? In *Regina v. Stone,* [1977] Q.B. 354, one of the defendants was a mistress of the owner of the house. The owner's sister was incapable of taking care of herself, and the defendant sometimes helped wash and feed her. A neighbor also assisted. Several neighbors, concerned about the sister's deteriorating health, either urged the defendant to contact a doctor or made efforts themselves. The sister died from toxemia, spreading from infected bed sores. Only the defendant (and her lover, the victim's brother) were charged. Why not the neighbors? Had they not "undertaken" the same duty? Are these questions the same as, or only similar to, those asked in the tort context? Compare *Erie R.R. v. Stewart,* 40 F.2d 855 (6th Cir. 1930) (train company held liable in tort where watchman it employed to warn car drivers of oncoming trains was absent, on the theory that public had come to rely upon warnings by watchman), with *R. v. Smith,* 11 Cox C.C. 210 (1869) (guard on railroad tramway was not guilty of manslaughter when he was absent from work). On the other hand, why should a breach of contract ever be grounds for establishing criminal liability? Why is the civil remedy for such a breach not sufficient in itself?

3. Why should it be necessary to prove a contract, or even an "undertaking," in order to establish a duty to act? Why is it not sufficient that the defendant is aware of the danger to the victim, and can avoid that danger by minimum action? For example, in *Jones,* were the gas collectors under a duty to notify authorities? Was the doctor? If not, why not? Is the possible reason that it seems harsh to hold them for homicide? Might they be held liable for a different offense? Some states now require by statute that doctors or other designated persons notify state authorities if they see a neglected or battered child, and they penalize failure to so report as a misdemeanor, punishable by fine and imprisonment. See U. DeFrancis and C. Lucht, Child Abuse Legislation in the 1970's (1974). Should the duty extend to teachers? To others who may see such children? Some states severely restrict those who are under a duty to take action or report. Others, such as Nebraska, impose a broad duty:

28-711, Neb. Rev. Stat.

When any physician, medical institution, nurse, school employee, social worker, or other person has reasonable cause to believe that a child has been subjected to abuse or neglect or observes such child being subjected to conditions or circumstances which reasonably would result in abuse or neglect, he or she shall report such incident or cause a report to be made to the proper law enforcement agency.

Many foreign codes have imposed a duty to rescue, or to take action to obtain help, at least where the defendant can do so without apparent danger to himself. These codes provide small penalties for the failure to act, whether or not the victim is harmed. See generally Larquier, *French Penal Law and Duty to Aid,* 38 Tul. L. Rev. 81 (1963); Feldbragge, *Good and Bad Samaritans,* 14 Amer. J. Comp. L. 630 (1966). See, e.g., Vt. Stat. Ann. tit. 12, 519 (1973):

>519. Emergency medical care

(a) A person who knows that another is exposed to grave physical harm shall, to the extent that the same can be rendered without danger or peril to himself or without interference with important duties owed to others, give reasonable assistance to the exposed person unless that assistance or care is being provided by others. . . .

* * *

. . .

(c) A person who willfully violates subsection (a) of this section shall be fined not more than $100.00.

See Franklin, *Vermont Requires Rescue,* 25 Stan. L. Rev. 51 (1972). Why is the sanction so small? Should a "nonrescuer" be liable for the death of the victim? See also Minn. Stat. Ann. §604.05(I) (1988).

4. *Jones* recognizes a duty established by "status." Generally, a parent who negligently withholds necessities from his child when he has the means to supply them is held liable if the child starves to death. The crime is generally manslaughter, rather than murder, although murder is sometimes charged as it was in *State v. Stehr,* 92 Neb.75, 139 N.W. 676 (1913).See also *Queen v. Senior,* [1899] 1 Q.B. 283; *Regina v. Wagstaffe,* 10 Cox C.C.530 (1868). Cf. Knox v. Comm., 735 S.W.2d 711 (Ky. 1987) (mother has no duty to prevent rape of her daughter).

The leading case on liability of a husband for failure to care for his wife is *Territory of Montana v. Manton,* 8 Mont. 95, 19 P. 387 (1888). The defendant and his wife had been out carousing. On their way home the wife fell into the snow within calling distance of the house. Her husband, who left her outside all night, and brought her into the house the next morning, was found guilty of manslaughter after she died of exposure to the cold. In *State v. Smith,* 65 Me. 257 (1876), defendant left his insane wife in a cold upper room with no fire with only a piece of canvas for a covering; he was held guilty of manslaughter when she froze to death. For a recent case, see *Commonwealth v. Konz,* 498 Pa. 639, 450 A.2d 638 (1982), holding that there is no duty to provide or obtain medical aid if the deceased spouse has chosen, while competent, not to seek such aid himself.

With other relationships the law is even more loathe to impose a duty to act. A famous case is *People v. Beardsley,* cited in *Jones.* Defendant's mistress attempted suicide after he told her he would not leave his wife. He took no action to obtain a doctor. The court found no liability. If the lover had provided the mistress with food and so forth and if the facts had been reversed (*i.e.,* he had attempted suicide), would there be a contractual obligation on the part of the mistress to take care of the lover?

5. Does imposition of a duty to act in the absence of a statute violate the maxim that there can not be criminal liability without fair warning? Do you think Ms. Jones would have understood that, by contracting with Ms. Green to care for her children, she was undertaking a duty imposed by the *criminal law*? See Fletcher, *Criminal Omissions: Some Perspectives,* 24 Amer. J. Comp. L. 703 (1976).

6. These situations must be contrasted with those where the legislature has imposed a statutory duty to act. (*e.g.,* to file income tax returns or register for the draft) and punishes with criminal sanctions failure to act. There, the only question is whether the state has the (constitutional) authority to impose such a duty. For example, in *Pollock v. Farmers' Loan & T. Co.,* 157 U.S. 429 (1895), the Supreme Court of the United States held that Congress could not, consistent with the Constitution, impose an income tax, a decision that was reversed only with the adoption of the Sixteenth Amendment to the Constitution.

7. If a bartender has a common law or statutorily established duty to prevent persons from leaving a bar while inebriated, is he criminally liable if such a person injures another? See *Judgment of the (German) Supreme Court,* 13 November 1963, 19 BGHST. What if the state has adopted "social host liability" in the tort context, e.g., *Kelly v. Gwinnell,* 96 N.J. 538, 476 A.2d 1219 (1984)?

8. A common hypothetical raised in early criminal law treatises considered whether a doctor who refused to provide treatment to a terminally ill person could be said to have acted. A corollary of this hypothetical, which is now not hypothetical, is the doctor's liability if, after providing "extraordinary" life support, he simply failed to provide it further or, alternatively, turns off a life support machine. In which instances has the doctor acted? See *Barber v. Superior Court,* 147 Cal. App. 3d 1006, 105 Cal. Rptr. 484 (1983). Is this kind of case best handled by such analysis, or should questions of euthanasia and so on be dealt with head on? See §9.05[E][3][b][i], *infra*.

9. Additional recommended readings include: Fox, *Physical Disorder, Consciousness and Criminal Liability,* 63 Colum. L. Rev. 645 (1963); Frankel, *Criminal Omissions: A Legal Microcosm,* 11 Wayne L. Rev. 367 (1965); Greenawalt, *"Uncontrollable" Actions and the 8th Amendment,* 69 Colum. L. Rev. 927 (1969).

§ 3.04 Causation

As any student who has grappled with tort law knows that questions of "cause" and "proximate cause" raise delicate and perplexing enigmas. This is true as well in the criminal law, for in those crimes requiring a result before liability is attached, the undoubted rule is that the defendant must have "caused" that result. "But for" causation is assumed; the more difficult question, in criminal law as in tort law, is "proximate causation."

As you go through the cases below, consider how a court would analyze the same problem if the victim (or survivors) were suing in tort.

[A] Eggshell Victims

It is, of course, standard lore that in torts one takes the victim as one finds him. The typical case suggested is the one of the minor battery, in which the plaintiff's head is exceptionally fragile (an eggshell), thereby causing the victim great injury, far beyond that which is foreseeable. In tort, the law requires that the defendant pay. Should the same rule be applicable in criminal law? Why? What purposes of punishment are served thereby? Is the tort analogy a good one in any event? See, e.g., *Johnson's Case,* 1 Lewin 164, 168 Eng. Rep. 999 (1827) (proving causation when there is a predisposition of the victim is too difficult); *State v. Frazier,* 339 Mo. 966, 98 S.W.2d 707 (1936) (manslaughter where defendant hit victim, who turned out to be a hemophiliac, and who died from wound).

In tort, at least until the advent of comparative negligence, the general rule was that the injurer paid for all injuries or none; damages were not (formally) reduced on grounds of "medium foreseeability" although a jury might reach such a result by compromising the amount of damages. Does the criminal law face the same restrictions? In the *Frazier* case, above, the trial court convicted the defendant of manslaughter, but sentenced him to a fine of $400 and six months in jail—the maximum punishment for a simple assault. Was the trial court eating its cake and having it too? Williams, *What Should the Code Do About Omissions?,* 7 Legal Stud. 92 (1987), argues that penalizing as manslaughter an omission resulting in death is on "an altogether inappropriate scale." He proposes a crime of "willful neglect."

Consider the following cases:

1. *Couch v. State,* 32 Ky. L. Rep. 638 (1908): Defendant recklessly fired a gun, not aiming at or hitting anyone. A pregnant woman, terrified, miscarried; she died shortly thereafter. A demurrer to an indictment for manslaughter was upheld on the basis of no causation.

2. *In re Heigho,* 18 Idaho 566, 110 P. 1029 (1910): Defendant went to Barton's house, armed with a gun. Barton's mother-in-law answered the door, and was present while defendant threatened Barton and then hit him with his fist. The mother-in-law collapsed and later died. Doctors testified that she had an aneurism of the ascending aorta that had ruptured; the excitement was said to be one of the three principal causes of her death. The court denied an application for discharge from the indictment, prior to trial.

> [I]t would be unsafe, unreasonable and often unjust for a court to hold as a matter of law that under no state of facts should a prosecution for manslaughter be sustained where death was caused by fright, fear, or terror alone, even though no hostile demonstration or overt act was directed at the person of the deceased.

[B] Acts of Victims

STEPHENSON V. STATE

Supreme Court of Indiana

205 Ind. 141, 179 N.E. 633 (1932)

[Defendant, in love with Madge Oberholtzer, kidnapped her, intending to take her to Chicago, where he intended to marry her. In the train en route to Chicago, he struck, beat, bit and wounded her. They then went to a hotel room, where the acts continued. Decedent accompanied one of defendant's accomplices ("Shorty") on a "shopping trip", during which she purchased a hat and six tablets of bichloride of mercury. After returning to the hotel room, she took the mercury, and became violently ill. Defendant had her drink a bottle of milk and suggested that he take her to a hospital, which she refused to do, apparently because he suggested that she say she was his wife. Defendant then became scared, and decided to take her home. On the way, she requested that they stop at any hospital, but he refused to do so. Arriving at his house, he put her in his garage attic. Ultimately, a friend of Stephenson's took the victim back to her own house, where she was taken to the hospital. After ten days of medical treatment, during which all her wounds but one healed, she died. The medical cause of death was apparently a combination of trauma, loss of food and rest, lack of early treatment, and the effects of the poison and infection. The indictment charged that she had taken the poison because she was "distracted with the pain and shame inflicted upon her," and that she suffered a "great distress of mind." The defendant was convicted of second degree murder.]

Per Curiam

Appellant very earnestly argues that the evidence does not show appellant guilty of murder. He points out that, at the time she took the poison she (the victim) was in an adjoining room to him, and that she swallowed the poison without his knowledge, and at a time when he was not present. From these facts he contends that she took her own life by committing suicide; that her own act in taking the poison was an intervening responsible agent which broke the causal connection between his acts and the death; that his acts were not the proximate cause of her death, but the taking of the poison was the proximate cause of death. In support of his contention, he cites *State v. Preslar* (1856), . . . ,48 N.C. 421; *State v. Shelledy* (1859), 8 Iowa 477; . . . and other cases from other jurisdictions. In the case of *State v. Preslar, supra,* the defendant in the nighttime fought with his wife, and she left to go to the home of her father. When she reached a point about two hundred yards from her father's home, she, for some reason, did not want to go in the house till morning, laid down on a bed cover, which she had wrapped around her, till daylight. The weather was cold and the next morning she could not walk, but made herself known. She afterwards died. The court held that the wife without necessity exposed herself, and the defendant was not guilty. . . . In the case of *State v. Shelledy, supra,* the defendant with others went to the home of one W. armed with revolvers, and forcibly took possession of W. and bound his arms so as to render him helpless, and in the presence of W. avowed their purpose to kill W. and placed him in a hack and started to the timber with him, and when on the banks of the Iowa river he leaped from the wagon into the water, and they permitted him to drown, while standing by, and made no effort to rescue the said W., where by reasonable effort they might have done so. The court held that defendant would be guilty of murder under these circumstances. . . . Bishop, in his work on *Criminal Law,* vol. 2, (9th Ed.) page 484, says: "When suicide follows a wound inflicted by the defendant his act is homicidal, if deceased was rendered irresponsible by the wound and as a natural result of it. . . ." We do not understand that by the rule laid down by Bishop, *supra,* that the wound which renders the deceased mentally irresponsible is necessarily limited to a physical wound. We should think the same rule would apply if a defendant engaged in the commission of a felony such as rape or attempted rape, and inflicts upon his victim both physical and mental injuries, the natural and probable result of which would render the deceased mentally irresponsible and suicide followed, we think he would be guilty of murder. . . . The evidence . . . shows that the deceased asked for money with which to purchase a hat, and it was supplied her by "Shorty," at the direction of appellant, and that she did leave the room and was taken by Shorty to a shop and purchased a hat and then, at her request, to a drug store where she purchased the bichloride of mercury tablets, and then she was taken back to the room in the hotel, where about 10 o'clock A.M. she swallowed the poison. Appellant argues that the deceased was a free agent on this trip to purchase a hat, etc., and that she voluntarily returned to the room in the hotel. This was a question for the jury, and the evidence would justify them in reaching a contrary conclusion. Appellant's chauffeur accompanied her on this trip, and the deceased had, before she left appellant's home in Indianapolis, attempted to get away, and also made two unsuccessful attempts to use the telephone to call help. She was justified in concluding that any attempt she might make, while purchasing a hat or while in the drug store to escape or secure assistance, would be no more successful in Hammond than it was in Indianapolis. We think the evidence shows that the deceased was at all times from the time she was entrapped by the appellant at his home on the evening of March 15th till she returned to her home two days later, in the custody and absolute control of appellant. Neither do we think the fact that the deceased took the poison some hours later after they left the drawing-room on the train or after the crime of attempted rape had been committed necessarily prevents it from being a part of the attempted rape. Suppose they had not left the drawing-room on the train, and, instead of the deceased taking poison, she had secured possession of appellant's revolver and shot herself or thrown herself out of the window of the car and died from the fall. We can see no vital difference. At the very moment Madge Oberholtzer swallowed the poison she was subject to the passion, desire, and will of appellant. She knew not at what moment she would be subjected to the same demands that she was while in the drawing-room on the train. What would have prevented appellant from compelling her to submit to him at any moment? The same forces, the same impulses, that would impel her to shoot herself during the actual attack or throw herself out of the car window after the attack had ceased, were pressing and overwhelming her at the time she swallowed the poison. The evidence shows that she was so weak that she staggered as she left the elevator to go to the room in the hotel, and was assisted by appellant and Gentry. That she was very ill, so much that she could not eat, all of which was the direct and proximate result of the treatment accorded to her by appellant. . . . To say that there is no causal connection between the acts of appellant and the death of Madge Oberholtzer, and that the treatment accorded her by appellant had no causal connection with the death of Madge Oberholtzer would be a travesty of justice. The whole criminal program was so closely connected that we think it should be treated as one transaction. . . . [T]he evidence was sufficient and justified the jury in finding that appellant by his acts and conduct rendered the deceased distracted and mentally irresponsible, and that such was the natural and probable consequence of such unlawful and criminal treatment, and that the appellant was guilty of murder in the second degree.

* * *

Instruction No. 43, given by the court of his own motion, told the jury that one who inflicts an injury on another is deemed by the law to be guilty of homicide, if the injury contributes mediately or immediately to the death of such other. The fact that other causes contribute to the death does not relieve the actor from responsibility. While it is true that a person cannot be killed twice, yet it is equally true that two persons can contribute to cause the death of another, in which case each will be responsible for such death.

Judgement affirmed.

NOTES AND QUESTIONS

1. What test, or tests, does *Stephenson* embrace for determining causation? Are they different from the tort tests? Should they be? The *Stephenson* case was the subject of much discussion. See, e.g., Note, 81 U. Pa. L. Rev. 189 (1933); Note, 31 Mich. L. Rev. 659 (1933); Note, 23 J. Crim. L., Criminology & Pol. Sci. 649 (1933). See generally Elliot, *Frightening a Person into Injuring Himself,* 1974 Crim. L. Rev. 15.

[P]erhaps the most typical instance of intervening cause in the form of an act, which is dependent upon a prior act, is the impulsive movement made in the effort to avoid sudden peril created by the prior act. . . . If, in the effort to save himself from apparent death or great bodily injury, one grabs a firearm which has suddenly been pointed at him, and the force thus exerted by him causes a fatal discharge not intended by the pointer, the act of pointing the weapon has caused the death. . . . [I]f a person who is suddenly attacked should, from a reasonable apprehension of immediate violence, throw himself into a river in the effort to escape, and be drowned, the assailant would be the cause of the death within the legal view. . . . While an impulsive act which is merely the normal response to fear or other emotional disturbance . . . will be imputed to him who has caused this emotional disturbance or loss of mind, the scope of proximate cause goes far beyond this. Even the deliberate act of the one threatened or endangered or that of another in his behalf, in the effort to avoid injury . . . will not be a superseding cause if it is merely the normal response of a human being to the stimulus of the situation created by the wrongdoer. . . . [I]f the act of avoidance is deliberate rather than impulsive the chain of proximate causation will be broken if the fear of danger was not well founded and the effort to avoid was made in an obviously imprudent manner.

R. Perkins and R.Boyce, *Criminal Law* 795?97 (3d ed. 1982)

Is this analysis helpful in *Stephenson* or the cases discussed there? Why should it make a difference if the action of the victim was reasonable?

2. Phoenix, Ariz., Feb. 6 (AP)—Linda Marie Ault killed herself, policemen said today, rather than make her dog Beauty pay for her night with a married man.

"I killed her. I killed her. It's just like I killed her myself," a detective quoted her grief-stricken father as saying.

"I handed her the gun. I didn't think she would do anything like that."

The 21 year-old Arizona State University coed died in a hospital yesterday of a gunshot wound in the head.

The police quoted her parents, Mr. and Mrs. Joseph Ault, as giving this account:

Linda failed to return home from a dance in Tempe Friday night. On Saturday she admitted she had spent the night with an Air Force lieutenant.

The Aults decided on a punishment that would "wake Linda up." They ordered her to shoot the dog she had owned about two years.

On Sunday, the Aults and Linda took the dog into the desert near their home. They had the girl dig a shallow grave. Then Mrs. Ault grasped the dog between her hands, and Mr. Ault gave his daughter a 22-caliber pistol and told her to shoot the dog.

Instead, the girl put the pistol to her right temple and shot herself.

The police said there were no charges that could be filed against the parents except possibly cruelty to animals.[1]

New York Times, February 7, 1968.

In terms of the analysis of Perkins and Boyce, was Linda Ault's suicide deliberate or impulsive? Should her parents be guilty of homicide?

3. Suppose that the victim's injuries are aggravated because of the victim's refusal to seek help (for example, on religious grounds)? Does it matter whether the defendant, before injuring the victim, knows of the victim's religious objections to medical aid?

4. Defendant sells Sterno, which he knows contains a small amount of lethal liquid and which he believes to a certainty the victim will drink, although (1) warning signs on the label clearly indicate the nature of the item and (2) it

---

[1] [Credit for immortalizing this event must be given to S. Kadish and M. Paulsen, *Criminal Law and Its Processes* 311 (4th ed. 1969). In a recent Florida case, a mother who forced her 17-year-old to dance in nude bars was charged with homicide when her humiliated daughter committed suicide. Is this the same as *Ault*?—Eds.]

is unquestionably not meant to be drunk. Is defendant a cause of the death when the purchaser (predictably) drinks the Sterno? *Commonwealth v. Feinberg,* 433 Pa. 558, 253 A.2d 636 (1969) (defendant held guilty of involuntary manslaughter). Is this an "impulsive" or a "deliberate" act under the Perkins-Boyce analysis?

[C] Acts of Third Parties

[1] Criminal Acts

It is black letter tort law that the intervening criminal act of a third party is a "superseding" cause, relieving the original defendant of further liability, unless the criminal act is, at the very least, foreseeable. (Usually much more is required than that.) In the absence of a finding of complicity between the two actors, discussed *infra,* Chapter 8, criminal law essentially replicates tort rules in this regard, although requiring more than mere proximate cause. See, e.g., *People v. Scott,* 29 Mich. App. 549, 185 N.W. 2d 576 (1971).

What is the result in the following: In a bar, A and B get into a verbal argument followed by a few blows. A knocks B to the floor. At this point, C, a total stranger to A, kicks B in the head. (1)A walks away; (2)A continues to kick and hit B. Later evidence shows that the kick by C was the deadly blow. Is A liable for the death? Compare *People v. Elder,* 100 Mich. 515, 59 N.W. 237 (1894), with *People v. Carter,* 96 Mich. 583, 56 N.W. 79 (1893).

[2] Negligent Acts

REGINA V. BENGE AND ANOTHER

Maidstone Crown Court

4 F. & F. 504, 176 Eng. Rep. 665 (1865)

The prisoners, Benge and Gallimore, were indicted for that on the 9th of June last they did feloniously kill and slay one Hannah Condliff. There were many other counts, each charging the manslaughter of another person on the same day.

The prosecution arose out of a fatal railway accident, which occurred on the South Eastern Railway at a place called Staplehurst, where there was a bridge, about two miles in the direction towards London from a station called Headcorn. The tidal trains of that day would be due at Staplehurst at 3:15 P.M., on Friday, the 9th of June. The prisoner Benge was foreman of a gang of plate-layers, who had been employed to repair the rails within a certain distance, including the portion of the line at Staplehurst, and for that purpose it would be necessary to take up and replace the rails. There were eight or nine men employed under the prisoner to do this work, and the other prisoner, Gallimore, was inspector of the line for the distance of 36 miles, comprising the Staplehurst part of the line. The time at which the work was done at any part of the line was left to the direction of the prisoner Benge, as the foreman of the gang. And he was furnished with a time book, in which the precise time of the arrival of the various trains on each day was marked; for each week in columns headed by the name of the day of the week. This book was clear in its arrangement, and printed in good, large, legible type, so that with the least care in its perusal, no mistake would be possible. The hour of arrival of the tidal train varied of course with the tide, and was different on each day. And on the day in question the prisoner Benge had looked at the column for Saturday—the next day—instead of Friday, the 9th. The time of arrival on the Saturday would be 5:20 P.M.; whereas the time for Friday, the day in question, would be 3:15. Thinking that the time would be 5:20, the prisoner Benge, when the last of the trains before the tidal train had passed, which was at 2:50 P.M., directed his gang to take up the rails at Staplehurst bridge, and they were accordingly taken up. There was, it will be seen, barely half an hour between the time at which the 2:50 train passed, and the time—3:15—at which the tidal train would arrive; and half an hour as it turned out, and as indeed was well known would be far too short a time to allow of the rails taken up being replaced. If the prisoner had read the time of arrival of the tidal train rightly, he would not have thought of taking up the rails, but be did not expect it until 5:20, which would have allowed nearly three hours, and the job would be completed in about an hour. He had no particular directions from the other prisoner, Gallimore, the inspector of the line; nor any particular instructions from any one. Nor was any notice sent on to the next station, Headcorn, from which the tidal trains would arrive. Neither did it appear that it was usual to send such notice, or to give notice to the driver of the trains which were to pass. It was usual, however, to send on one of the gang as a signal man with a flag in his hand, who was to go on at least 1000 yards in the direction in which the expected train was to come, and when he had got that distance he was to stand and raise a flag when it appeared, which would be seen at a distance of above 500 yards, and thus would give a distance of 1500 yards, or nearly a mile, between the train and the spot at which the rails were up, so as to allow of ample time to stop the train. Books of printed rules were in the hands of the foreman of plate-layers, and among others, of the prisoner; and these rules expressly provided that rails should not be taken up without these precautions. On the occasion in question one of the men of prisoner's gang, named Wills, was sent forward as signal man, but without (as it appeared) any particular directions from the prisoner Benge, and instead of going 1000 yards he went, as he said, only 540 yards; and there he stood till he saw the advancing train, and moved his flag. He was observed, but not until the train was too near to be stopped. The engine-driver was not paying a very sharp look-out, and though the steam was shut off, and the breaks [sic] put on, it was too late to stop the train, which was going at the rate of 50 miles an hour, and it came on to the bridge, and then running off the line at the spot where the rails were up, it dashed on to the bridge, and the catastrophe ensued in which many lives were lost.

There was evidence that at the distance of 1000 yards, the train could easily have been stopped, at any rate of speed.

* * *

Ribton, for the prisoner, submitted that there was no evidence of any criminal act or default on his part which had caused the death. It appeared that the accident could not have happened, notwithstanding the mistake which the prisoner had undoubtedly committed, if other servants of the company had done their duty; if, for instance, the flagman had gone far enough with the signal or if the engine-driver had kept a sufficient look-out, and had seen the signal, as then he must have seen it earlier than he did, and in time enough to stop the train.

* * *

Pigott, B., said, that assuming culpable negligence on the part of the prisoner which materially contributed to the accident, it would not be material that others also by their negligence contributed to cause it. Therefore he must leave it to the jury whether there was negligence of the prisoner which had been the substantial cause of the accident. In summing up the case to the jury, he said, their verdict must depend upon whether the death was mainly caused by the culpable negligence of the prisoner. Was the accident mainly caused by the taking up of the rails at a time when an express train was about to arrive, was that the act of the prisoner, and was it owing to culpable negligence on his part? His counsel had urged that it was not so, because the flagman and engine-driver had been guilty of negligence, which had contributed to cause the catastrophe; but they, in their turn, might make the same excuse, and so, if it was valid, no one could be criminally responsible at all. This would be an absurd and unreasonable conclusion, and showed that the contention of the prisoner's counsel could not be sound. Such was not the right view of the law—that of [sic] the negligence of several persons at different times and places contributed to cause an accident, any one of them could set up that his was not the sole cause of it. It was enough against any one of them that his negligence was the substantial cause of it. Now, here the primary cause was certainly the taking up of the rails at a time when the train was about to arrive, and when it would be impossible to replace them in time to avoid the accident. And this the prisoner admitted was owing to his own mistake. Was that mistake culpable negligence, and did it mainly or substantially cause the accident? The book was clearly and plainly printed, and must have been read carelessly to admit of such a mistake. Was it not the duty of the prisoner who knew the fearful consequences of a mistake to take reasonable care to be correct? And had he taken such care? Then as to its being the main cause of the accident, it was true that the company had provided other precautions to avoid any impending catastrophe, and that these were not observed upon this occasion; but was it not owing to the prisoner's culpable negligence that the accident was impending, and, if so, did his negligence the less cause it, because if other persons had not been negligent it might possibly have been avoided?

Verdict—Guilty

[D] Nonhuman Forces

Under traditional common law doctrine, an accused is not the legal cause of a result if unforeseeable natural forces intervene and cause the result. Thus if A shoots B but only wounds him, leaving him unconscious in a parking lot, where lightning strikes and kills him, A is not the legal cause of B's death. LaFave and Scott at 292. (A might be guilty of attempted murder, see §7.02, *infra*.) However, if B is rendered unconscious by A's shot in a remote parking lot on a bitter cold winter night and subsequently freezes to death, A is legally responsible for B's death assuming the actual result was foreseeable.

Model Penal Code §2.03.

Causal Relationship between Conduct and Result; Divergence between Result Designed or Contemplated and Actual Result or between Probable and Actual Result.

(1) Conduct is the cause of a result when:

(a) it is an antecedent but for which the result in question would not have occurred; and

(b) the relationship between the conduct and result satisfies any additional causal requirements imposed by the Code or by the law defining the offense.

(2) When purposely or knowingly causing a particular result is an element of an offense, the element is not established if the actual result is not within the purpose or the contemplation of the actor unless:

(a) the actual result differs from that designed or contemplated, as the case may be, only in the respect that a different person or different property is injured or affected or that the injury or harm designed or contemplated would have been more serious or more extensive than that caused; or

(b) the actual result involves the same kind of injury or harm as that designed or contemplated and is not too remote or accidental in its occurrence to have a [just] bearing on the actor's liability or on the gravity of his offense.

(3) When recklessly or negligently causing a particular result is an element of an offense, the element is not established if the actual result is not within the risk of which the actor is aware, or in the case of negligence, of which he should be aware unless:

(a) the actual result differs from the probable result only in the respect that a different person or different property is injured or affected or that the probable injury or harm would have been more serious or more extensive than that caused; or,

(b) the actual result involves the same kind of injury or harm as the probable result and is not too remote or accidental in its occurrence to have a [just] bearing on the actor's liability or on the gravity of his offense.

(4) When causing a particular result is a material element of an offense for which absolute liability is imposed by law, the element

is not established unless the actual result is a probable consequence of the actor's conduct.

NOTES AND QUESTIONS

1. Does the Code's position "solve" the dilemmas of causation by leaving the entire question to the jury? Consider L. Green, Judge and Jury 222 (1930):

> The only antidote lies in a revolt from the supremacy of rules. . . . Causal relation can be reduced to no lower terms. . . . In determining the extremes of legal protection—the problem which is hidden under the causation terminology—the sweep of judgment quickly passes beyond the reach of any rules that can be framed. And what is more, the judicial process in these cases ought to be left free of hampering restraints in fixing the limits of protection in the particular case.
>
> There is no possibility of its successfully meeting the exactions of hard cases until it is recognized that the judge, in finding a basis for judgment, must go beyond and above any range for which rules have yet been fashioned.

2. Is the Code's standard unconstitutionality vague? See *State v. Maldonado*, 137 N.J. 536, 685 A.2d 1165 (1994). See also Note, *Causation in the Model Penal Code,* 78 Colum. L. Rev. 1249 (1978).

3. In tort, joint tortfeasors are (or at least used to be) held jointly and severally liable so as to ensure compensation to the victim. Thus the rule that more than one person can be "the" proximate cause of an accident assists the purpose of compensation. Could criminal law follow such an approach by, *e.g.,* dividing a six-year prison sentence among three defendants by having each of them serve two years?

4. D beats V to the point where D erroneously believes V is dead. Testimony indicates that V would have survived without difficulty. However, D decides to get rid of the "dead" body. V dies due to this action. Of what crime is D guilty? *Thabo Meli v. Regina,* 1 All E.R. 373 (P.C. 1954); *R. v. Church,* 49 Crim. App. 206 (1965).

5. The problem of "joint causation" or "intervening cause" is often thought to arise in felony-murder cases, where, for example, the defendant robs a store and the store owner (or a police officer) shoots and kills (1)one of the robbers, (2)an innocent bystander. Most courts have now rejected a pure "proximate cause" approach to that issue. See *State v. Canola,* 73 N.J. 206, 374 A.2d 20 (1977) (reviewing cases). See Crum, *Causal Relations and Felony Murder Rule,* 1952 Wash. U.L.Q. 191; Hitchler, *The Killer and His Victims in Felony-Murder Cases,* 13 Dick. L. Rev. 3 (1948); Morris, *The Felon's Responsibility for the Legal Acts of Others,* 105 U. Pa. L. Rev. 50 (1956). See §5.03[4][e], *infra.*

However, when a defendant-robber takes a "hostage" or "shield" who is killed by the police or store owner, the courts treat the case differently, finding causal relationship. *E.g., Jackson v. State,* 286 Md. 430, 408 A.2d 711 (1979); *Pizano v. Superior Court,* 21 Cal. 3d 128, 577 P.2d 659 (1978); *State v. Kress,* 105 N.J. Super. 514, 253 A.2d 481 (1969); Note, 9 Balt. L. Rev. 508 (1980).

Arkansas has enacted an interesting "compromise." Ark. Stat. Ann. §41—1504 (91)(d) provides that it is manslaughter if, during a felony, the actor (or an accomplice) negligently kills another or a person resisting the felony kills anyone. This means if the actor (or accomplice) intentionally kills, it is still felony murder.

6. The leading and classic work on causation in the law, including the criminal law, is H.L.A. Hart and A. Honore, Causation in the Law (1959). For other discussions, see Mansfield, *A Comment on Hart and Honore,* 17 Vand. L. Rev. 487 (1964); Norrie, *A Critique of Criminal Causation,* 54 Modern L. Rev. 685 (1991); Williams, *Causation in Homicide,* Crim. L. Rev. 429 (1957); Note, *The Use of the Tort Liability Concept of Proximate Cause in Cases of Criminal Homicide,* 56 Nw. U.L. Rev. 791 (1962).

Chapter 4
The Importance of *Mens Rea*

§ 4.01 INTRODUCTION

The contention that an injury can amount to a crime only when inflicted by intention is no provincial or transient notion. It is as universal and persistent in mature systems of law as belief in freedom of the human will and a consequent ability and duty of the normal individual to choose between good and evil. A relation between some mental element and punishment for a harmful act is almost as instinctive as the child's familiar exculpatory "But I didn't mean to" and has afforded the rational basis for a tardy and unfinished substitution of deterrence and reformation in place of retaliation and vengeance as the motivation for public prosecution. Unqualified acceptance of this doctrine by English common law . . . was indicated by Blackstone's sweeping statement that to constitute any crime there must first be a "vicious will."

This statement by Mr. Justice Jackson for the Supreme Court in *Morissette v. United States,* 342 U.S. 246, 250–51 (1952), capsulized the history of the relationship between "mental state" and "act" in criminal law for literally several millennia, long before the "common law" was established in England. In the earliest Hebrew Code, a distinction is made between a person who kills intentionally and one who "lie(s) not in wait but God deliver(s) him into his hand . . . " Exodus 21:12–14. See also Kent, Israel's Laws and Legal Precedents 91, 92 (1907).

Similar distinctions appear in the Twelve Tables of Roman times established circa 450 BC:

2. Breaking a limb, unless settled for, to be punished by retaliation.
10. Whoever burns a house or a stack of corn near a house knowingly and maliciously shall be bound, beaten, and burnt. If by accident, he must pay damages.
24. Whoever knowingly and maliciously kills a free man must be put to death.
25. If a man kills his parent, veil his head, sew him up in a sack, and throw him into the river.
26. No one is to make disturbances at night in the city under pain of death.

Early English views were similar. Thus, Laws of Alfred (c. 897 AD), reprinted 1 Thorpe, Ancient Laws and Institutes of England 85 (1840) provided: "If a man have a spear over his shoulder, and any man stake himself upon it, he (should) pay the'wer' without the'wite.' If he be accused of wilfulness in the deed, let him clear himself according to wite; and with that let the wite abate." Again: "Let the man who slayeth another wilfully perish by death. Let him who slayeth another of necessity or unwillingly, as God may have sent him into his hand, and for whom he has not lain in wait, be worthy of his life and of lawful'bot' if he seek asylum." In the laws of Henry I, circa 1118 AD, we find "If someone in the sport of archery or other form of exercise kill another with a missile or by some such accident, let him repay; for the law is that he who commits evil unknowingly must pay for it knowingly," as quoted in Sayre, *Mens Rea,* 45 Harv. L. Rev. 974, 978 (1932).

The difference between "intentional" and "accidental" harms seems intuitive. There is almost universal agreement among all civilizations and societies that intentional harm doing should be punished criminally, at least if the harm (personal or social) is severe enough. And, although the issue is not fully settled, see § 4.03 [B], *infra,* the general consensus in common law and civil law countries alike is that "mere tort" negligence should not be the predicate for criminal liability. But there are intermediate stages of mental awareness of harm or the possibility of harm of which the criminal law could take cognizance. As the materials in this chapter demonstrate, the common law has long wrestled with the question of whether such intermediate mental states should be the basis of criminal liability. The distinctions between recklessness and intention, and between recklessness and negligence—both in an absolute sense and in the sense of providing different degrees of mental and moral culpability, and hence potentially different degrees of criminal liability—have evoked strong, continuing dispute in the law. As the materials in § 4.03 [A], *infra,* show, the view of the English courts changed, only to be reassessed by Parliament. That debate is not unique to England; it is the paradigmatic question on levels of liability in the criminal law.

To these questions the Model Penal Code (discussed in detail in § 4.05, *infra*) has given firm and possibly definitive answers. The Code also seeks to provide concrete guidance to the interpretation of criminal statutes, both as to the meaning of those words defining the requisite mental states and as to the application of those words to "elements" of the offense; as § 4.04, *infra,* shows, these questions need resolution in light of the chaos engendered by the common law courts giving diffuse and diverse interpretations.

Finally, § 4.07, *infra,* investigates the issue of whether *any* mental state should be required before criminal punishment is imposed. Notwithstanding Mr. Justice Jackson's declaration in *Morissette,* the past century has seen the blossoming of many so-called strict liability offenses in which the traditional requirement of *mens rea* has been or appears to have been abandoned. Indeed, immediately following his statement in *Morissette,* Justice Jackson rehearsed the development of these "offenses" before holding, in that case, that the federal statute there in question should be interpreted as requiring *mens rea* and not, as the trial court judge had done, as applying strict liability to at least some parts of the statute.

The questions raised in this chapter are the core questions of criminal liability: whether the mere doing of harm is sufficient to warrant punishment or whether there must be some awareness by the harm doer that (a)she is doing or at least risking harm (b)she is doing wrong. To these questions the retributivist and the utilitarian give different answers. Throughout these materials, echoes of the struggle between Kant and Bentham reverberate.

§ 4.02 THE DEVELOPMENT OF THE COMMON LAW REQUIREMENT OF *MENS REA*

Whether the common law,* at least since the days of the Norman Conquest, has required a *mens rea*—an intent to commit a crime—is hotly debated nearly 1000 years after the fact.* Isaacs, for example, argues vehemently that there was no such requirement; that crime and tort, being basically the same doctrine, did not require intent or any other *mens rea*.** Holmes, on the other hand, vigorously disputes that notion, arguing that (1) at best, any strict liability in the criminal law was cyclical and (2) only in the days of true "abyss" was there no such requirement.***

Much of the confusion, or uncertainty, would appear to stem from a failure to distinguish "tort" suits with materials and statutes providing for the punishment of offenders such as evidenced in the Leges Henrici Primi. Long before the Norman Conquest, the Anglo-Saxon kings had established a system of compensation in the event of injury or death. If a victim was "merely" injured, the injurer paid to the injured party what was called *bot,* based on the status of the injured party. An injury to a lord was worth more than the same injury to a serf.

If the injured party was killed, however, *wer* (also referred to as *wergild,*) was paid. This too was to buy off the blood feud that would otherwise almost surely ensue. *Wergild* continued to be an important part of the criminal law for at least 50 years after the Conquest. Then, in the latter part of the 12th century, Henry II abolished *wergild* for certain offenses to encourage persons to remove causes of action from the local "county" courts and put them in his (the king's) court, thereby consolidating his position as ruler of the entire land. As with many other reformers, however, Henry failed to accomplish fully his

---

* The term *common law* is always ambiguous. Usually, it suggests "nonstatuatory" law, but that is a misleading notion since many so-called common law rules are really interpretations Of statutes. In the criminal law, this is particularly true since (as the materials just above show) virtually every government precluded by statute (rule) certain kinds of criminal acts and made them punishable by the kind as well as by the injured party. There is no easy way, then, to distinguish between common law crimes and statutory crimes. Sir Matthew Hale suggests that the common law "began" July 6, 1189, the date of the beginning of the reign of Richard I. See M. Hale, The History of the common Law of England 4 (1713; C. Gray ed. 1971). Whether one accepts that or not, it is generally accepted that there were seven "common law" felonies. Their definitions are important, since they explain the requirements of *mens rea* as seen by the "early common law." Indeed, the contrast with later crimes, particularly those *mala prohibitum* crimes, is well worth nothing. Of one of these crimes—homicide—a sufficient amount will be said later as to allow us to delay discussion now. But the other major felonies were (1) rape, defined as unlawful sexual intercourse with a female person without her consent, (2) mayhem, defined as "maliciously depriving another of the use of such of his members as may render him less able, in fighting, either to defend himself or defeat his adversary," (3) burglary, "the breaking and entering of the dwelling of another in the nighttime with intent to commit a felony," (4) arson, "the malicious burning of the dwelling of another" (5) larceny, "the trespassory asportation and taking away of the personal property of another with intent to deprive him of it," and (6) robbery, "larceny from the person by violence or intimidation." In addition, of course, treason was a capital offense. Could any of these be done accidently? In the absence of an intent to achieve the harm?

* For a fascinating tour through Hebrew, Salic, Greek, Roman, and church contributions to the doctrine, see Levitt, *The Origins of the Doctrine of Mens Rea,* 17 Ill. Rev. 117 (1923).

** Isaacs, *Fault and Liability,* 31 Harv. L. Rev. 954 (1918).

*** O.W. Holmes, The Common Law (1881).

goal. The victim's kin could still "appeal" (bring criminal proceedings against) the defendant in local courts, thereby avoiding the king's court. Since the defendant, if found guilty, could be executed, he was usually willing to settle, or "compromise," the criminal charge. Thus, indirectly, kin still got their *wer.*

Another very important part of the early criminal law was the payment of *wite. Wite* was essentially a fine to the king—a payment by the defendant to the king in order to atone for having broken the king's peace. *Wite* was an effective method by which the king initially asserted his control over the countryside.

These three methods of compensation—not the possible criminal punishment of the offender—are referred to in our first few excerpts. But the relationship, if any, between tort (compensation) law and criminal law is unclear. Many of the statutes are, or could be seen as, ambiguous. The notion that the law in those days penalized, and even executed, persons who killed unintentionally and accidentally, is widespread, probably because of this ambiguity. The key here appears to be Henry II's desire to outlaw *wer* and replace intertribal compensation with control by the king. But King Henry was concerned that triers of fact (they were not really juries as we now know them) would find that truly culpable actors had, in fact, acted "justifiably"— that the deaths were either in self-defense, by accident, or justifiable under other rules. Such a finding would allow *wer.* Therefore King Henry provided that in cases of self-defense (or other pleas of exculpation) there would be no *wer,* and indeed, the slayer (subject only to the king's pardon) would be punished by death.[****] In effect, lack of evil intent became technically irrelevant.

From these data, scholars argued that this era was a time in which even the "morally blameless" were sent to their deaths, since self-defense (and other defenses) would not serve as an escape. Thus, they conclude, the law did not distinguish between "evil" killings and "non-evil" killings: There was no requirement of *mens rea.*

One such author, Brown, explained this perceived state of affairs in this way:

> The first business of a ruler is the elimination of all forms of self-help; this is responsible for the strict liability of earliest law. As the power of the ruler becomes more firmly established, the need for these strict rules diminishes, and in rare cases a man's efforts on his own behalf are regarded as being justified. Any such exceptions to the general principle that self-help is illegal are, however, severely restricted by the pre-requisites of necessity and public policy. They emerge only as the products of a firmly entrenched system of law which has attained a high standard of efficiency and functional precision.

Brown, *Self Defense in Homicide from Strict Liability to Complete Exculpation,* 1958 Crim. L. Rev. 583.

Hurnard (see footnote[****], *supra,* p.225) however found otherwise. According to her, almost as soon as it was enacted, the strict liability law of Henry

---

[****] N. Hurnard, The King's Pardon for Homicide Before a.d. 1307 (1969).

[****] *ID.* at 204.

II was administered with great leniency either because death was not the only punishment imposed or because the king gave pardons with great felicity, once the defendant had been convicted. This latter point meant that the king, as Brown suggested, had control—without his pardon, there would be death or exile. But since he gave his pardon widely, it may be that he recognized that failure to pardon truly "accidental" or "self-defense" killings would not increase his popularity or his power. Moreover, even if the defendant were pardoned, he still forfeited all his worldly goods to the king. Therefore, even a finding of "self-defense" did not mean that the defendant suffered no loss.

By the middle of the 13th century there was a movement to require some sort of homicidal or criminal *intent* before allowing a conviction. Bracton (a law clerk to an outstanding judge, Raleigh, during the 1230s) was the main influence here. His De Legbus Anglicae, written circa 1260, appeared under his name, covering the entire law of England.* Bracton's work was the most influential of all writings for the next half-millennium. In dealing with the law of crimes, Bracton reached back to St. Augustine,** from whom he obtained the phrase *mens rea*. Bracton's declaration that the law requires some kind of mental element in crime (but not necessarily in other actions) before it will punish the actor set the tone for criminal law for at least 500 to 550 years.

After Bracton, the law moved precipitously. Pardons became granted as a matter of course (*de coursu*) when the jury found a homicide in self-defense or accident. By Edward I's reign (circa 1276), infancy and insanity were added to the list of conditions for which a pardon should be granted. At the end of the century, the Mirror of Justice, a book whose origins are obscure and suspect, listed madmen, idiots, infants under seven, and self-defenders as having an excuse and not subject to punishment. *Mens rea* had clearly taken hold:*** "[I]n trespass the intent cannot be construed, but in felony it shall be. As when a man is shooting at the butts, and kills a man, it is not felony; and this will be so, as he had no intent to kill him."****

By the 1600s the principle was so widely accepted that Shakespeare put the concept in a play knowing that his audience would understand the essential requirement of *mens rea*:

W. Shakespeare, Hamlet Act v, sc. 2, 251–254

Hamlet, before the duel with Laertes:

Sir, in this audience

Let my disclaiming from a purposed evil

Free me so far in your most generous thoughts

---

* Frederick Weiner has suggested that it was actually Raleigh, not his clerk, who was primarily responsible for this crucial work. Weiner, *Did Bracton Write Bracton?*, 64 A.B.A.J. 71 (1978).

** Bracton was influenced by two forces: the reawareness of Roman notions of *culpa* (fault) and the church's emphasis on individual moral guilt. See, *e.g.*, Seney, *The Sybyl at Cumae: Our Criminal Law's Moral Obsolescence,* 17 Wayne L. Rev. 777, 811 (1971); Jeffrey, *The Development of Crimes in Early English History,* 47 J. Crim. L., Criminology & Police Sci. 647, 664–66 (1957).

*** *The Thorns Case,* Y.B. Mich. 6 Ed. 4, f.7, pl. 18 (1466).

That I have shot mine arrow o'er the house

And hurt my brother.

In legal terms, this basic requirement of evil was captured in Blackstone's "vicious will" referred to in *Morissette*.

FURTHER READINGS ON THE HISTORY OF *MENS REA*

Attenborough, The Laws of the Earliest English Kings (1922).

Binavince, *The Ethical Foundations of Criminal Liability*, 33 Fordham L. Rev. 1 (1964).

Brown, *The Emergence of the Psychical Test of Guilt in Homicide*, 1 Tasm. U. L. Rev. 231 (1954).

Cross, *The Mental Element in Crime*, 83 L.Q. Rev. 215 (1967).

Frankowski, Mens Rea *and Punishment in England: In Search of Interdependence of the Two Basic Components of Criminal Liability (A Historical Perspective)*, 63 U. Det. L. Rev. 393 (1986).

Gardner, *The* Mens Rea *Enigma: Observations on the Role of Motive in the Criminal Law Past and Present*, 1993 Utah L. Rev. 635.

Mueller, *On Common Law mens rea*, 42 Minn. L. Rev. 1043 (1958).

Nord, *The Mental Element in Crime*, 37 U. Det. L. J. 671 (1960).

Parker, *The Evolution of Criminal Responsibility*, 9 Alberta L. Rev. 47 (1970).

Rightmire, The Law of England at the Norman Conquest (1932).

Robertson, The Laws of the Kings of England from Edmund to Henry I (1925).

Robinson, *A Brief History of Distinctions in Criminal Culpability*, 31 Hastings L.J. 815 (1980).

Smith, *The Guilty Mind in the Criminal Law*, 76 L. Q. Rev. 78 (1960).

§ 4.03 THE NOTION(S) OF *MENS REA*

[A] Intent and Recklessness

As the materials above illustrate, the common law early condemned "intentional" criminal acts. Very few decided cases, however, define or attempt to define *intent* with regard to harm or criminal liability, perhaps because the definition is so intuitive. But two issues with regard to "intent" must be at least mentioned.

[1] Oblique Intent

The first regards so-called *oblique intention*—where the defendant does not actually desire a specific result, but understands and knows that it is "practically certain" to occur if he acts. In philosophical contexts, this is sometimes explained in terms of the "doctrine of double effect." Thus, for example, D intentionally opens the window, *knowing* that there is a gale outside and that the wind is almost certain to blow in, thereby extinguishing a candle. Can it be said that D has "intentionally" extinguished the candle, even though he did not care at all whether the candle was extinguished? In a criminal context, the example often used is that of the defendant who plants explosives near a prison wall, intending to help his friend escape, but knowing that the explosion is almost certain to kill the guard in the tower under which the explosives are placed. Has he "intentionally" killed the guard? Although the common law often finessed this question by punishing equally those who "intended" and those who acted "knowingly," the issue continues to perplex the writers if not the courts. See, *e.g.,* Boyle, *Toward Understanding the Principle of Double Effect,* 90 Ethics 527 (1980); Davis, *The Doctrine of Double Effect: Problems of Interpretation,* 65 Pac. Phil. Q. 1097 (1984); S. Uriacke, Permissible Killing 92–155 (1994); Smith, *Intention in Criminal Law,* Curr. L. Probs. 93 (1974); Williams, *Oblique Intention,* 46 Camb. L. J. 417 (1987); Williams, *Intents in the Alternative,* 50 Camb. L. J. 120 (1991).

[2] "Specific" and "General" Intents

A second common law problem with intent has been self-inflicted by the criminal law courts—the alleged distinction between a *specific* and a *general intent.* In some instances, the distinction *seems* clear: There are times when a defendant intends not merely to commit one act or crime, but to commit a subsequent crime made possible by the first. Thus a defendant who intends merely to "assault" is different from one who intends to "assault with intent to kill" and a defendant who intends to "break and enter" a building is different from one who "breaks and enters with intent to commit a felony therein." These "second" intended offenses are called *crimes of specific intent.*

Beyond this, however, nothing is clear. Some crimes, although not defined with a "with intent to" clause, are still said to be specific intent crimes. Moreover, specific intent crimes are contrasted with general intent crimes. The Comments to Model Penal Code § 2.08 offer an explication of the specific—general intent distinction:

> To the extent . . . that the actual decisions have given a concrete content to these vague conceptions, the net effect of this rule seems to have come to this: when purpose or knowledge, as those culpability factors are defined in § 2.02 of the Model Code, must be proved as an element of the offense, intoxication may generally be adduced in disproof if it is logically relevant. When, on the other hand, recklessness or negligence, as those culpability factors are defined in § 2.02, suffices to establish the offense, an exculpation based on intoxication is precluded by the law. Moreover, since recklessness is sufficient to establish *mens rea* for most offenses, intoxication is ordinarily not permitted to establish a defense, whatever its effect on the awareness or knowledge of the actor.

MPC § 2.08, Comment at 354

As the MPC commentary suggests, a major impact of the alleged distinction is in the field of intoxication, where drunkenness is said to negate a specific intent, but *never* to negate a general intent. Hall contends that this legal fiction was originally designed to allow drunken offenders to avoid liability for capital homicide (see *infra,* § 9.05[C]), Hall, *Intoxication and Criminal Responsibility,* 57 Harv. L. Rev. 1045 (1944). A straightforward acknowledgment of the untenability of the distinction occurred in *People v. Hood,* 1 Cal. 3d 444, 462 P.2d 370 (1969). There the California Supreme Court abandoned the distinction between specific and general intent, finding it opaque and confusing. But see *People v. Rocha,* 3 Cal. 3d 893, 479 P.2d 372 (1971), which appears to reintroduce the specific-general intent distinction to California law by holding that assault with a deadly weapon is a general intent crime for which the defense of intoxication is irrelevant.

The most important point for present purposes, however, is to remember that an intent to do an act is not necessarily an intent to achieve the results of that act, and that the common law has always required (or at least has always said it has required) some mental state with regard to the result. Although the opinions in *Pembliton, Faulkner,* and *Cunningham, infra,* are technically limited to interpreting the meaning of "malice" or "maliciously" within the meaning of one statute, the opinions—especially that of Judge Fitzgerald in *Faulkner*—set out the possible states of mind that the common law did, or could, regard as *mens rea. Cunningham, infra,* p.232, reflects the status of those criteria more than a half century later.

REGINA V. PEMBLITON

Court of Criminal Appeal

12 Cox C.C. 607 (1874)

At the Quarter Sessions of the Peace held at Wolver Hampton on the 8th day of January instant Henry Pembliton was indicted for that he "unlawfully and maliciously did commit damage injury, and spoil upon a window in the house of Henry Kirkhan" contrary to the provision of the stat. 24 & 25 Vict. c. 97, s. 51. This section of the statute enacts:

> Whosoever shall unlawfully and maliciously commit any damage, injury, or spoil to or upon any real or personal property whatsoever . . . shall be guilty of a misdemeanor, and being convicted thereof shall be liable . . . to be imprisoned for any term not exceeding two years with or without hard labour. . . .

LORD COLERIDGE, C.J.—I am of opinion that this conviction must be quashed. The facts of the case are these. The prisoner and some other persons who had been drinking in a public house were turned out of it at about 11 PM for being disorderly, and they then began to fight in the street near the prosecutor's window. The prisoner separated himself from the others, and went to the other side of the street, and picked up a stone, and threw it at the persons he had been fighting with. The stone passed over their heads, and broke a large plate glass window in the prosecutor's house. . . . The jury found that the prisoner threw the stone at the people he had been fighting with, intending to strike one or more of them with it, but not intending to break the window. The question is whether under an indictment for unlawfully and maliciously committing an injury to the window in the house of the prosecutor the proof of these facts alone, coupled with the finding of the jury, will do? Now I think that is not enough. . . . The Act is an Act relating to malicious injuries to property. . . .There is also the 58th section which deserves attention. "Every punishment and forfeiture by this Act imposed on any person maliciously committing any offense, whether the same be punishable upon indictment or upon summary conviction, shall equally apply and be enforced, whether the offense shall be committed from malice conceived against the owner of the property in respect of which it shall be committed, or otherwise." It seems to me on both these sections that what was intended to be provided against by the Act is the wilfully doing an unlawful Act, and that the Act must be wilfully and intentionally done on the part of the person doing it, to render him liable to be convicted. Without saying that, upon these facts, if the jury had found that the prisoner had been guilty of throwing the stone recklessly, knowing that there was a window near which it might probably hit, I should have been disposed to interfere with the conviction, yet as they have found that he threw the stone at the people he had been fighting with intending to strike them and not intending to break the window, I think the conviction must be quashed.

BLACKBURN, J. . . . A person may be said to act maliciously when he wilfully does an unlawful act without lawful excuse. The question here is can the prisoner be said, when he not only threw the stone unlawfully, but broke the window unintentionally, to have unlawfully and maliciously broken the window. I think that there was evidence on which the jury might have found that he unlawfully and maliciously broke the window, if they had found that the prisoner was aware that the natural and probable consequence of his throwing the stone was that it might break the glass window, on the principle that a man must be taken to intend what is the natural and probable consequence of his acts. But the jury have not found that the prisoner threw the stone, knowing that, on the other side of the men he was throwing at, there was a glass window and that he was reckless as to whether he did or did not break the window. On the contrary, they have found that he did not intend to break the window. I think therefore that the conviction must be quashed.

PIGOTT, B.—I am of the same opinion.

LUSH, J.—I also think that on this finding of the jury we have no alternative but to hold that the conviction must be quashed. The word "maliciously" means an act done either actually or constructively with a malicious intention. The jury might have found that he did intend actually to break the window or constructively to do so, as that he knew that the stone might probably break it when he threw it. But they have not found.

CLEASBY, B. concurred.

Conviction quashed.

REGINA v. FAULKNER

Court of Crown Cases Reserved Ireland

13 Cox C.C. 550 (1877)

The indictment was as follows: "That Robert Faulkner, on the 26th day of June, 1876, on board a certain ship called the *Zemindar*, . . . feloniously, unlawfully, and maliciously, did set fire to the said ship. . . . " It was proved that the *Zemindar* was on her voyage home with a cargo of rum, sugar, and cotton, worth 50,000 [pounds]. That the prisoner was a seaman on board, that he went into the forecastle hold, opened the sliding door in the bulk head, and so got into the hold where the rum was stored; he had no business there, and no authority to go there, and went for the purpose of stealing some rum, that he bored a hole in the cask with a gimlet, that the rum ran out, that when trying to put a spiel in the hole out of which the rum was running, he had a lighted match in his hand; that the rum caught fire; that the prisoner himself was burned on the arms and neck; and that the ship caught fire and was completely destroyed. At the close of the case for the Crown, counsel for the prisoner asked for a direction of an acquittal on the ground that on the facts provided the indictment was not sustained, nor the allegation that the prisoner had unlawfully and maliciously set fire to the ship proved. The Crown contended that inasmuch as the prisoner was at the time engaged in the commission of a felony, the indictment was sustained, and the allegation of the intent was immaterial.

At the second hearing of the case before the Court for Crown Cases Reserved, the learned judge made the addition of the following paragraph to the case stated by him for the court:

It was conceded that the prisoner had no actual intention of burning the vessel, and I was not asked to leave any question to the jury as to the prisoner's knowing the probable consequences of his act, or as to his reckless conduct.

The learned judge told the jury that although the prisoner had no actual intention of burning the vessel, still if they found he was engaged in stealing the rum, and that the fire took place in the manner above stated, they ought to find him guilty. The jury found the prisoner guilty on both counts, and he was sentenced to seven years penal servitude. . . .

* * *

Dowse, B., gave judgment to the effect that the conviction should be quashed.

BARRY, J.—A very broad proposition has been contended for by the Crown, namely, that if, while a person is engaged in committing a felony, or, having committed it, is endeavouring to conceal his act, or prevent or spoil waste consequent on that act, he accidently does some collateral act, which if done wilfully would be another felony either at common law or by statute, he is guilty of the latter felony. I am by no means anxious to throw any doubt upon, or limit in any way, the legal responsibility of those who engage in the commission of felony, or acts *mala in se;* but I am not prepared without more consideration to give my assent to so wide a proposition.

FITZGERALD, J.—[I]n order to establish the charge . . . the intention of the accused forms an element in the crime to the extent that it should appear that the defendant intended to do the very act with which he is charged, or that it was the necessary consequence of some other felonious or criminal act in which he was engaged, or that having a probable result which the defendant foresaw, or ought to have foreseen, he nevertheless persevered in such other felonious or criminal act. The prisoner did not intend to set fire to the ship—the fire was not the necessary result of the felony he was attempting; and if it was a probable result, which he ought to have foreseen, of the felonious transaction in which he was engaged, and from which a malicious design to commit the injurious act with which he is charged might have been fairly imputed to him, that view of the case was not submitted to the jury. On the contrary, it was excluded from their consideration on the requisition of the counsel for the prosecution. Counsel for the prosecution in effect insisted that the defendant, being engaged in the commission of, or in an attempt to commit a felony, was criminally responsible for every result that was occasioned thereby, even though it was not a probable consequence of his act or such as he could have reasonably foreseen or intended. No authority has been cited for a proposition so extensive and I am of opinion that it is not warranted by law. . . .

* * *

O'BRIEN, J.—[A]t the trial, the Crown's counsel conceded that the prisoner had no intention of burning the vessel, or of igniting the rum; and raised no questions as to prisoner's imagining or having any ground for supposing that the fire would be the result or consequence of his act in stealing the rum. With respect to *Reg. v. Pembliton* (12 Cox C.C. 607), it appears to me there were much stronger grounds in that case for upholding the conviction than exist in the case before us. In that case the breaking of the window was the act of the prisoner. He threw the stone that broke it; he threw it with the unlawful intent of striking some one of the crowd about, and the breaking of the window was the direct and immediate result of his act. And yet the Court unanimously quashed the conviction upon the ground that, although the prisoner threw the stone intending to strike some one or more persons, he did not intend to break the window. The courts above have intimated their opinion that if the jury (upon a question to that effect being left to them) had found that the prisoner, knowing the window was there, might have reasonably expected that the result of his act would be the breaking of the window, that then the conviction should be upheld. During the argument of this case the Crown counsel required us to assume that the jury found their verdict upon the ground that in their opinion the prisoner may have expected that the fire would be the consequence of his act in stealing the rum, but nevertheless did the act recklessly, not caring whether the fire took place or not. But at the trial there was not even a suggestion of any such ground, and we cannot assume that the jury formed an opinion which there was no evidence to sustain, and which would be altogether inconsistent with the circumstances under which the fire took place. The reasonable inference from the evidence is that the prisoner lighted the match for the purpose of putting the spiel in the hole to stop the further running of the rum, and that while he was attempting to do so the rum came in contact with the lighted match and took fire. . . .

KEOGH, J.—I am. . . of opinion, that the conviction should stand, as I consider all questions of intention and malice are closed by the finding of the jury, that the prisoner committed the act with which he was charged whilst engaged in the commission of a substantive felony. On this broad ground, irrespective of all refinements as to "recklessness" and "wilfulness," I think the conviction is sustained. . . .

* * *

NOTES AND QUESTIONS

1. The defendant in *Pembliton* threw a stone at another person presumably intending to cause serious injury to that person. Why shouldn't this "vicious will" or "evil motive" be sufficient to render the defendant guilty of "maliciously" damaging the window? Originally, *mens rea* was understood normatively as a general wicked state of mind or evil motive whose possessor was guilty of any criminal act committed while in this state of mind. See generally Gardner, *The* Mens Rea *Enigma: Observations on the Role of Motive in the Criminal Law Past and Present*, 1993 Utah L. Rev. 635; Robinson & Grall, *Element Analysis in Defining Criminal Liability: The Model Penal Code and Beyond*, 35 Stan. L. Rev. 681 (1983). On this early view, Pembliton might indeed be guilty of the crime charged even though he was unaware of the existence of the window he broke.

Pembliton thus appears to represent a different conception of *mens rea* from the original "evil motive" concept. What is that view? Does the *Pembliton* view of *mens rea* illustrate the insight that "[t]he old conception of *mens rea* must be discarded and in its place must be substituted the new conception of *mentes reae*"? Sayre, *The Present Signification of* Mens Rea *in the Criminal Law*, Harvard Legal Essays 399, 404 (1934).

2. List the various definitions of *maliciously* that each judge in *Faulkner* would accept. What is the difference among these views? Do these differences reflect different levels of moral culpability?

3. How would tort law deal with the defendant in *Pembliton* if the owner of the glass window sued him? How would tort law deal with the defendant in *Faulkner* if the owner of the ship sued him? Can the criminal law deal more accurately with the liability of the defendant for the harm inflicted upon each of the victims, actual and possible, in a way in which the tort law cannot?

REGINA v. CUNNINGHAM

Court of Criminal Appeal

41 Crim. App. 155 (1957)

* * *

Byrne, J.: The appellant was convicted at Leeds Assizes upon an indictment framed under § 28 of the Offenses against the Person Act . . . which charged that he unlawfully and maliciously caused to be taken by Sarah Wade a certain noxious thing, namely, coal gas, so as thereby to endanger the life of the said Sarah Wade.

The facts were that the appellant was engaged to be married and his prospective mother-in-law was the tenant of a house . . . which was unoccupied but which was to be occupied by the appellant after his marriage. Mrs. Wade and her husband . . . lived in the house next door. At one time the two houses had been one, but when the building was converted into two houses a wall had been erected to divide the cellars of the two houses, and that wall was composed of rubble loosely cemented. . . . [T]he appellant went to the cellar . . . wrenched the gas meter from the gas pipes, and stole it, together with its contents. . . . [I]n a statement to the police officer the appellant said: "All right I will tell you. I was short of money, I had been off work for three days, I got eight shillings from the gas meter. I tore it off the wall and threw it away." Although there was a stop tap within two feet of the meter, the appellant did not turn off the gas, with the result that a very considerable volume of gas escaped, some of which seeped through the wall of the cellar and partially asphyxiated Mrs. Wade, who was asleep in her bedroom next door, with the result that her life was endangered.

* * *

The act of the appellant was clearly unlawful and therefore the real question for the jury was whether it was also malicious within the meaning of § 28 of the Offenses against the Person Act, 1861. . . . Mr. Brodie argued, first that *mens rea* of some kind is required. Secondly, that the nature of the *mens rea* required is that the appellant must have an intention to do the particular kind of harm that was done, or alternatively he must foresee that harm may occur, yet nevertheless continue recklessly to do the act. Thirdly, that the learned judge misdirected the jury as to the meaning of the word "maliciously."[*]

We have considered . . . the following principle which was propounded by the late Professor C. S. Kenny in the first edition of his Outlines of Criminal Law, published in 1902, and repeated in the sixteenth edition edited by Mr. J.W. Cecil Turner and published in 1952:

---

[*] [In making this argument, defense counsel cited, inter alia, both *Pembliton* and *Faulkner*. Were these cites apposite?—Eds.]

In any statutory definition of a crime, malice must be taken not in the old vague sense of wickedness in general but as requiring either (1)An actual intention to do the particular kind of harm that in fact was done; or (2)Recklessness as to whether such harm should occur or not (*i.e.,* the accused has foreseen that the particular kind of harm might be done and yet has gone on to take the risk of it). It is neither limited to nor does it indeed require any ill will towards the person injured.

In our opinion, the word "maliciously" in a State crime postulates foresight of consequences.

In his summing-up the learned judge directed the jury as follows:

You will observe that there is nothing there about "with intention that that person should take it." He has not got to intend that it should be taken; it is sufficient that by his unlawful and malicious act he causes it to be taken. What you have to decide here, then, is whether, when he loosed that frightful cloud of coal gas into the house which he shared with the old lady, he caused her to take it by his unlawful and malicious action. "Malicious" for this purpose means wicked—something which he has no business to do and perfectly well knows it. "Wicked" is as good a definition as any other which you would get. The facts which face you . . . are these. Living in the house, which was now two houses but which had once been one and had been rather roughly divided, the prisoner quite deliberately, intending to steal the money that was in the meter . . . broke the gas meter away from the supply pipes and thus released the main supply of gas at large into the house. When he did that he knew that this old lady and her husband were living next door to him. . . . The wall which divided his cellar from the cellar next door was a kind of honeycomb wall through which gas could very well go, so that when he loosed that cloud of gas in that place he must have known perfectly well that gas would percolate all over the house. . . . As I have already told you, it is not necessary to prove that he intended to do it; it is quite enough that what he did was done unlawfully and maliciously.

With the utmost respect to the learned judge, we think it is incorrect to say that the word "malicious" in a statutory offense merely means wicked. We think the learned judge was in effect telling the jury that if they were satisfied that the appellant acted wickedly—and he had clearly acted wickedly in stealing the gas meter and its contents—they ought to find that he had acted maliciously in causing the gas to be taken by Mrs. Wade so as thereby to endanger her life.

In our view, it should have been left to the jury to decide whether, even if the appellant did not intend the injury to Mrs. Wade, he foresaw that the removal of the gas meter might cause injury to someone but nevertheless removed it.

Conviction quashed.

NOTES AND QUESTIONS

1. Each of the above three cases clearly holds that a "bad mind" ("vicious will" in Blackstone's terms) is not *sufficient* to sustain a conviction. Do they

hold that a vicious will is irrelevant? Suppose a defendant intends a criminally proscribed result, but with no viciousness, perhaps even with a good motive. Is his act done (1)with a vicious will in the sense that Blackstone used the term or (2)with malice as these cases define the term? The modern phrasing of this issue is whether *mens rea* is now limited to specific statutory words referring descriptively to mental state or whether, behind these words, there is also a requirement—articulated or not—that the defendant evince a "criminal" state of mind. See, *e.g.,* Pillsbury, *Evil and the Law of Murder,* 24 U. Cal. Davis L. Rev. 437 (1990), arguing that modern courts have all too easily focused on specific statutory *mens rea* words without considering the malignity at which the criminal law is aimed. See also, in a different context, Phillimore, L.J., in *Broome v. Cassell* [1971] 2 Q.B. 354, 400: "If a court is to do justice it must look at the whole case in the round. . . . Life and the things we do or say do not fall neatly into little slots. So soon as a court starts laying down rules numbered (a), (b), and (c), or (1), (2), (3), and (4), so soon is it certain to do injustice." This issue also appears in the "defenses" where a defendant who in some sense "intends" a result or acts recklessly with regard to its occurrence still seems not to have a "vicious" will (*e.g.,* the insane actor or one who acts under duress). See *infra,* Chapter 9.

2. Does *Cunningham* refine the definition(s) of *maliciously* listed in *Faulkner?* Does it restrict or broaden those definitions? Which of the judges in *Faulkner,* if any, would have found the defendant in *Cunningham* responsible? Again, contrast the result in this case with the result if Ms. Wade sued her future son-in-law in tort.

3. *Cunningham* states the usual understanding of *recklessness*—that the defendant must subjectively foresee and understand a risk that a (criminal) harm could result from his conduct. Thus a defendant who acts outrageously but does not actually foresee harm has not acted recklessly. In this sense, the term is a term of art and is to be distinguished from the common usage of the term. For example, if a person from sheer wantonness drives blindfolded down a crowded street at high speeds but does not actually foresee the possibility of harm, then she is acting outrageously (or "wantonly" or "grossly" or some other adjective) but not "recklessly" as that term is employed in *Cunningham* and most decisions. This seems to be the accepted rule in every state except Nebraska; see *State v. Kistenmacher,* 231 Neb. 318, 436 N.W. 2d 168 (1989) (interpreting statutory recklessness as an objective term).

Beyond this, however, the use of the term is quite opaque. For example, courts and commentators are divided on whether it is enough that the defendant foresee "some" risk, however remote, or whether he must understand that the risk is "substantial" or "serious." Nor is there consensus about whether the risk must in fact **be** substantial, or whether any risk is sufficient, so long as there is no "good reason" for the defendant to undertake it. Thus, for example, it is still debated (1)whether any unjustified risk, particularly of death or serious bodily harm, no matter how unlikely, is sufficient for "recklessness"; (2)whether the defendant must "know" that the risk is "substantial" or whether it is sufficient that he knows there is a risk but is wrong about the degree of risk. Nor is there consensus on whether the defendant's actual concern, should he foresee the required degree of risk, is relevant. For example, some courts say that the defendant must manifest "indifference" to the possibility of injury, raising the possibility that if the defendant foresees the risk and tries (even in a haphazard manner) to prevent its occurrence, he has not acted recklessly, even though a "reasonable person" would have still thought the risk too great. See, *e.g.,* Zimmerman, *Negligence and Moral Responsibility,* 19 Nous 199, 214–17 (1986) (differentiating between recklessness and rashness on the basis of indifference).

Assume, for example, that D is faced with 100 guns, and is told that 1 of them is loaded, but 99 are not. He picks up one of the guns, aims it at V, and shoots.

  a. Is D reckless under the facts as given?

  b. If not, suppose that, unknown to D, 99 (or 80 or 50 or 10) guns are in fact loaded. Is this recklessness?

  c. Suppose that, before shooting V, D says to V, "It's really very unlikely that I would pick the loaded gun. But just in case, here's a bullet proof vest for you." Unhappily, the vest is totally inadequate for the kind of bullets employed in the gun. Is this recklessness?

Or take a variation of the hypothetical about the driver speeding through a crowded neighborhood at noon:

  d. The defendant is an expert race car driver who has never had an accident on or off the track. He believes there is absolutely no danger to himself, his passengers, or the crowd.

  e. Defendant foresees a small possibility of injury to himself, his passengers, or the crowd, but he believes it to be very small. In fact, the chances of an accident are (according to a statistician) 30 percent. Is the answer different if the actual risk is 70 percent? Five percent?

  f. The defendant is driving five seriously injured persons to a hospital. Is the defendant acting recklessly (but arguably in a justified way) or non recklessly (assuming there is a justification)?

4. Matters are even more complicated. Whereas *Cunningham* seems to require subjectivity for "malicious" crimes, recent decisions from England have appeared to allow "objective recklessness" for statutory crimes (at least those dealing with traffic offenses). Thus Professor Smith concludes that "there are now two types of recklessness in English criminal law, commonly known as-*Cunningham*' and —*Caldwell*' recklessnesses from the leading cases in which they were recognized. . . . More unhappily still . . . it is probable that there exist more than the two principal meanings of the word." [1989] Cr. L. Rev. 377. For full discussion of these issues in English law, see Birch, *The Foresight Saga: The Biggest Mistake of All?,* [1988] Cr. L. Rev. 4; Brady, *Recklessness, Negligence, Indifference and Awareness,* 43 Mod. L. Rev. 381 (1980); *Duff, Caldwell and Lawrence: The Retreat from Subjectivism,* 3 Ox. J. Leg. Studies 77 (1983); Syrota, *A Radical Change in the Law of Recklessness?,* [1982] Cr. L. Rev. 97, Williams, *Intention and Recklessness Again,* [1982] Leg. Stud. 189.

Commonwealth v. Pierce

Supreme Judicial Court of Massachusetts

138 Mass. 165 (1884)

[The defendant, a physician, had sought to treat a patient by wrapping her wounds in kerosene-soaked rags. This ultimately resulted in her death. In the course of upholding a conviction for manslaughter, Holmes, J., defined recklessness as follows:]

Recklessness in a moral sense means a certain state of consciousness with reference to the consequences of one's acts. No matter whether defined as indifference to what those consequences may be, or as a failure to consider their nature or probability as fully as the party might and ought to have done, it is understood to depend on the actual condition of the individual's mind with regard to consequences, as distinguished from mere knowledge of present or past facts or circumstances from which some one or everybody else might be led to anticipate or apprehend them if the supposed act were done. We have to determine whether recklessness in this sense was necessary to make the defendant guilty of felonious homicide, or whether his acts are to be judged by the external standard of what would be morally reckless, under the circumstances known to him, in a man of reasonable prudence.

More specifically, the questions raised . . . are whether an actual good intent and the expectation of good results are an absolute justification of acts, however foolhardy they may be if judged by the external standard supposed, and whether the defendant's ignorance of the tendencies of kerosene administered as it was will excuse the administration of it.

So far as civil liability is concerned, at least, it is very clear that what we have called the external standard would be applied, and that, if a man's conduct is such as would be reckless in a man of ordinary prudence, it is reckless in him. Unless he can bring himself within some broadly defined exception to general rules, the law deliberately leaves his idiosyncrasies out of account, and peremptorily assumes that he has as much capacity to judge and to foresee consequences as a man of ordinary prudence would have in the same situation. [As Tindal, C.J., said:]

Instead, therefore, of saying that the liability for negligence should be coextensive with the judgment of each individual, which would be as variable as the length of the foot of each individual, we ought rather to adhere to the rule which requires in all cases a regard to caution such as a man of ordinary prudence would observe.

If this is the rule adopted in regard to the redistribution of losses, which sound policy allows to rest where they fall in the absence of a clear reason to the contrary, there would seem to be at least equal reason for adopting it in the criminal law, which has for its immediate object and task to establish a general standard, or at least general negative limits, of conduct for the community, in the interest of the safety of all.

* * *

It is clear, in the light of admitted principle and the later Massachusetts cases, that the recklessness of the criminal no less than that of the civil law must be tested by what we have called an external standard. In dealing with a man who has no special training, the question whether his act would be reckless in a man of ordinary prudence is evidently equivalent to an inquiry into the degree of danger which common experience shows to attend the act under the circumstances known to the actor. The only difference is, that the latter inquiry is still more obviously external to the estimate formed by the actor personally than the former. . . .

* * *

We have implied, however, in what we have said, and it is undoubtedly true, as a general proposition, that a man's liability for his acts is determined by their tendency under the circumstances known to him, and not by their tendency under all the circumstances actually affecting the result, whether known or unknown. And it may be asked why the dangerous character of kerosene, or "the fatal tendency of the prescription," as it was put in the fifth request, is not one of the circumstances the defendant's knowledge or ignorance of which might have a most important bearing on his guilt or innocence.

But knowledge of the dangerous character of a thing is only the equivalent of foresight of the way in which it will act. We submit that, if the thing is generally supposed to be universally harmless, and only a specialist would foresee that in a given case it would do damage, a person who did not foresee it, and who had no warning, would not be held liable for the harm. If men were held answerable for everything they did which was dangerous in fact, they would be held for all their acts from which harm in fact ensued. The use of the thing must be dangerous according to common experience, at least to the extent that there is a manifest and appreciable chance of harm from what is done, in view either of the actor's knowledge or of his conscious ignorance. And therefore, again, if the danger is due to the specific tendencies of the individual thing, and is not characteristic of the class to which it belongs, which seems to have been the view of the common law with regard to bulls, for instance, a person to be made liable must have notice of some past experience, or, as is commonly said, "of the quality of his beast." . . . But if the dangers are characteristic of the class according to common experience, then he who uses an article of the class upon another cannot escape on the ground that he had less than the common experience. Common experience is necessary to the man of ordinary prudence, and a man who assumes to act as the defendant did must have it at his peril. When the jury are asked whether a stick of a certain size was a deadly weapon, they are not asked further whether the defendant knew that it was so. It is enough that he used and saw it such as it was . . . The defendant knew that he was using kerosene. The jury have found that it was applied as the result of a foolhardy presumption or gross negligence, and that is enough. . . . Indeed, if the defendant had known the fatal tendency of the prescription, he would have been perilously near the line of murder. It will not be necessary to invoke the authority of those exceptional decisions in which it has been held, with regard to knowledge of the circumstances, as distinguished from foresight of the consequences of an act, that, when certain of the circumstances were known, the party was bound at his peril to inquire as to the others, although not of a nature to be necessarily inferred from what were known. . . .

* * *

As we have intimated above, an allegation that the defendant knew of the deadly tendency of the kerosene was not only unnecessary, but improper. . . . An allegation that the kerosene was of a dangerous tendency is superfluous, although similar allegations are often inserted in indictments, it being enough to allege the assault, and that death did in fact result from it. It would be superfluous in the case of an assault with a staff, or where the death resulted from assault combined with exposure. . . .

QUESTIONS

How does Holmes's definition of recklessness differ from Judge Fitzgerald's in *Faulkner?* From the court's in *Cunningham?* Can you distinguish between Holmes's definition and the usual definition of negligence?

[B] Negligence as a Criminal Predicate

Cunningham rejected any definition of *mens rea* that did not require some subjective awareness by the defendant of the risk of harm. But both before and since that decision, the law has debated whether any "lesser" state of mind should be endorsed as a predicate for criminal liability and, if so, how to define the parameters of that standard. Two of the great writers—Holmes and Hall—disagree vehemently on the basic issue of ever allowing negligence, however defined, to sustain criminal liability:

HOLMES

50–51, 75–76

It is not intended to deny that criminal liability, as well as civil, is founded on blameworthiness. Such a denial would shock the moral sense of any civilized community; or, to put it another way, a law which punished conduct which would not be blameworthy in the average member of the community would be too severe for that community to bear. It is only intended to point out that, when we are dealing with that part of the law which aims more directly than any other at establishing standards of conduct, we should expect there more than elsewhere to find that the tests of liability are external, and independent of the degree of evil in the particular person's motives or intentions. The conclusion follows directly from the nature of the standards to which conformity is required. These are not only external, as was shown above, but they are of general application. They do not merely require that every man should get as near as he can to the best conduct possible for him. They require him at his own peril to come up to a certain height. They take no account of incapacities unless the weakness is so marked as to fall into well-known exceptions such as infancy or madness. They assume that every man is as able as every other to behave as they command. If they fall on any one class harder than on another, it is on the weakest. For it is precisely to those who are most likely to err by temperament, ignorance, or folly, that the threats of the law are the most dangerous.

The reconciliation of the doctrine that liability is founded on blameworthiness with the existence of liability where the party is not to blame, will be worked out more fully in the next Lecture. It is found in the conception of the average man, the man of ordinary intelligence and reasonable prudence. Liability is said to arise out of such conduct as would be blameworthy in him, but he is an ideal being, represented by the jury when they are appealed to, and his conduct is an external or objective standard when applied to any given individual. That individual may be morally without stain, because he has less than ordinary intelligence or prudence. But he is required to have those qualities at his peril. If he has them, he will not, as a general rule, incur liability without blameworthiness.

* * *

It is believed that enough has now been said to explain the general theory of criminal liability, as it stands at common law. The result may be summed up as follows.

All acts are indifferent per se.

In the characteristic type of substantive crime acts are rendered criminal because they are done under circumstances in which they will probably cause some harm which the law seeks to prevent.

The test of criminality in such cases is the degree of danger shown by experience to attend that act under those circumstances.

In such cases the *mens rea,* or actual wickedness of the party, is wholly unnecessary, and all reference to the state of his consciousness is misleading if it means anything more than that the circumstances in connection with which the tendency of his act is judged are the circumstances known to him. Even the requirement of knowledge is subject to certain limitations. A man must find out at his peril things which a reasonable and prudent man would have inferred from the things actually known. In some cases, especially of statutory crimes, he must go even further, and, when he knows certain facts, must find out at his peril whether the other facts are present which would make the act criminal. . . .

In some cases it may be that the consequence of the act, under the circumstances, must be actually foreseen, if it is a consequence which a prudent man would have foreseen. The reference to the prudent man, as a standard, is the only form in which blameworthiness as such is an element of crime, and what would be blameworthy in such a man is an element; first, as a survival of true moral standards; second, because to punish what would not be blameworthy in an average member of the community would be to enforce a standard which was indefensible theoretically, and which practically was too high for that community.

In some cases, actual malice or intent, in the common meaning of those words, is an element in crime. But it will be found that, when it is so, it is because the act when done maliciously is followed by harm which would not have followed the act alone, or because the intent raises a strong probability that an act, innocent in itself, will be followed by other acts or events in connection with which it will accomplish the result sought to be prevented by the law.

HALL, *INTERRELATIONS OF CRIMINAL LAW AND TORTS: I*

43 Colum. L. Rev. 753, 767–68 (1943)

Actus non facit reum, nisi mens sit rea [No act is guilty unless there is a guilty mind.] is the most general doctrine on culpability in the criminal law. Consequently the chief application of the above analysis of Holmes' theory centers on his insistence that the rules on intentional conduct, which include the *mens rea* doctrine, are objective. . . . We can view the problem simplified thus—human conduct that is associated causally with certain harms proscribed by law, is labeled "intentional" by triers of the material facts on the basis of knowledge of certain external data. The deliberate suiting of means to ends is traditionally characterized as the operation of the "practical reason," and "intention" designates a distinctive and essential aspect of that process. Given certain facts, we must conclude that any and every rational human being in those circumstances did or did not intend the results, *i.e.*, the only sense that can be attached to certain situations is communicated by the assertion that the actor "intended" the consequences. Consequently, on the simple level of the basic mental processes embodied in the adaptation of ordinary means to attain common ends, all human beings—barring serious mental or physical defects—may properly be said to act intentionally under circumstances where any one of them could be said to have acted intentionally. Accordingly, although Holmes' theory is logically unimpeachable on his premise of great disparity between external data and internal states, nonetheless it is factually invalid. For though it is literally true that we can never say more than that, under given conditions, a rational being (and not the defendant) would or would not have "intended," yet for the reasons noted and because modern legal procedure comprises skillful methods of discovering external facts, the probabilities are high, not only that the external facts have been accurately determined, but, also, that their characterization as "intentional conduct" fits the particular defendant on trial.

In its most favorable interpretation, Holmes' theory can be rendered relevant to that view of ethics that takes motivation as its basic criterion, and to that psychology which holds motives inaccessible to outside observation. The refutation of the theory, thus interpreted, so far as externality of rules of law is concerned, takes two directions. Firstly, it challenges the tenet that motivation is unknowable to outsiders. Here the argument parallels that presented above concerning intention, and need not be elaborated further. Secondly, the doctrine that motive is irrelevant in most of the criminal law does not concede that it is unknowable. In such cases as the distraught parent who kills his child to terminate its suffering, or who steals bread to feed his starving family, the motivation is known as well as the intention. Such instances do not illustrate that the legal rules are "external" in Holmes' sense. They represent rather those marginal cases where the absolute value judgments implied in general rules give way almost entirely before ethical judgment that all but cancels out moral culpability. Normally the motives that stimulate the legally forbidden conduct are bad. The legal adaptation to the above marginal cases is more or less formal condemnation coupled with a minimum of actual penalization. The point to be stressed is that even in such marginal cases the rules do not represent the dogma Holmes asserted. The most that can be inferred is that the definitional parts of the substantive rules are restricted to certain inner states—those necessarily involved in the forbidden volitional conduct. Undoubtedly this would affect the ethical validity of the consequent legal judgments unless other avenues than those phases of the substantive rules were available to mitigate their rigor. It is true, also, that motives are much more complex than is intention and that the passing of ethical judgment requires detailed case histories. But the enormously wide range in penalties stipulated in the substantive rules themselves is concrete proof that judges must grapple with this enormously difficult problem. No other theory can account for such provisions except that which asserts that inner states are knowable and must be considered.

NOTES AND QUESTIONS

1. Is the tension between Holmes and Hall resolvable by the following observation of Holdsworth, 3 History of English Law 374 (1922)?

> We must adopt an external standard in adjudicating upon the weight of evidence adduced to prove or disprove *mens rea*. That, of course, does not mean that the law bases criminal liability upon non-compliance with an external standard. So to argue is to confuse the evidence for a proposition with the proposition proved by that evidence.

2. In addition to the arguments posed by Hall, consider the views articulated by Justice Weintraub in *State v. Weiner,* 41 N.J. 21, 194 A.2d 467 (1964), a case charging a physician with manslaughter for negligently injecting patients, who thereafter died:

> We of course must keep in mind that this is a criminal case. In a civil action for damages, the question is whether a loss shall remain where it fell or be shifted to him whose act brought it about. The test there is ordinary negligence—the failure to behave as would a reasonable man in such circumstances. The issue being only whether the victim or the actor shall bear the dollar impact, the law goes far in permitting the trier of the facts to "infer" both fault and causal connection between the fault and the loss. Indeed, if the total circumstances bespeak a likelihood of fault upon the part of a defendant, the law, for civil purposes, permits a jury to infer negligence even though the precise respect in which there was fault cannot be identified. So here, if the suit were for damages, it could be urged (we of course have no occasion here to pass upon it) that the total picture breathes the probability that defendant was careless somewhere and that his unidentifiable carelessness brought about these deaths. And in that connection, we

would not be troubled by the possibility that one of the defendant's nurses may have been the careless actor, since for the purposes of civil liability, defendant, as the employer of a nurse, must answer for her fault even though he was personally blameless.

But a criminal case is another matter. The injury to be vindicated is not the personal wrong suffered by the victim but rather an outrage to the State. And the question is not whether a defendant should absorb the dollar loss of his victim but whether his conduct justifies stamping him a criminal and sending him to State Prison. In that inquiry, the test is not ordinary negligence-behavior of which men of the highest character are capable. Rather, as phrased in 1 Warren, *Homicide* (perm. ed. 1938), § 86, p.424: "Negligence to be criminal, must be reckless and wanton and of such character as shows an utter disregard for the safety of others under circumstances likely to cause death."

And whereas a doctor is chargeable in a private suit for the negligence of his nurse-employee, he is not chargeable criminally on the basis of *respondeat superior*. . . . "For it is of the very essence of our deep-rooted notions of criminal liability that guilt be personal and individual" . . . Sayre, *Criminal Responsibility for Acts of Another,* 43 Harv. L. Rev. 689, 717 (1930). Accordingly, if defendant is to be criminally liable with respect to an act or omission of his nurse, it could not be merely because he was her employer. He could be so liable only if he directed her conduct or assented to it or failed to act with respect to it in circumstances which indicate the same wantonness or recklessness to which we have referred. And finally, whereas in civil matters the plaintiff need prove his case only by a mere preponderance of the proof, yet in a prosecution for manslaughter based upon criminal negligence the State must prove guilt beyond a reasonable doubt, a test which, despite some theoretical devaluations of it, does serve to tell the trier of the facts that a criminal trial is no guessing game.

3. There is much debate about whether, as a historical matter, the common law ever recognized negligence, as a predicate for criminal liability. In addition to the Hall excerpt, see Binavince, *The Ethical Foundations of Criminal Liability,* 33 Ford. L. Rev. 1 (1964); R. Moreland, A Rationale of Criminal Negligence (1943) (especially Chapter 1); Robinson, *A Brief History of Distinctions in Criminal Culpability,* 31 Hastings L. J. 815 (1980). To the extent that it may have, however, there seems unanimous agreement that the liability existed only in homicide cases, *see infra,* § 5.03[B][2][a], and even then the standard was "more than civil" negligence, a term never fully explicated. For example, over a century ago Judge Stephen wrote that "(t)here must be more, but no one can say how much more, carelessness than is required in order to create a civil liability" (Vol. 3, at 11). For a much fuller discussion, see Davis, *The Development of Negligence as a Basis for Liability in Criminal Homicide Cases,* 26 Ky. L. J. 209 (1938). In so-called statutory crimes that were not present in the common law, however, the courts have been much more divided about whether to allow "negligence"—and, if they do, which kind—as a basis for criminal sanctions, as the two following cases demonstrate. Some would argue that there is "less" at stake in nonhomicide cases than in homicide

prosecutions, and that even if the criminal law adheres to a rejection of negligence as a predicate in the latter situation, it might adopt such a standard (at least occasionally) in the former group. Would Hall agree? Do you?

SANTILLANES V. STATE

Supreme Court of New Mexico

115 N.M. 215, 849 P.2d 358 (1993)

FROST, J.:

We granted the defendant Vincent Santillanes' writ of certiorari to review the Court of Appeals decision affirming his conviction of child abuse under NMSA 1978, ?30-6-1(C) (Repl. Pamp. 1984). Santillanes' primary argument is that the provision in the statute under which he was convicted is unconstitutional because it improperly criminalizes ordinary civil negligence. . . .

I. FACTS

Santillanes cut his 7-year-old nephew's neck with a knife during an altercation. The jury convicted him of child abuse involving no death or great bodily injury under § 30-6-1(c) [which] reads as follows:

Abuse of a child consists of a person knowingly, intentionally or negligently, and without justifiable cause, causing or permitting a child to be:

(1) placed in a situation that may endanger the child's life or health; (2) tortured, cruelly confined or cruelly punished; or (3) exposed to the inclemency of the weather.

After the close of all evidence, defense counsel submitted a requested jury instruction to the court setting forth a criminal negligence standard rather than a civil negligence standard to define the negligence element under the statute. Defendant's Requested Instruction No. 3 stated:

An act, to be "negligence" or to be done "negligently," must be one which a reasonably prudent person would foresee as creating a substantial and unjustifiable risk of injury to Paul Santillanes. The risk created must be of such a nature and degree that the reasonably prudent person's failure to perceive it involves a gross deviation from the standard of care that a reasonably prudent person would observe in the same situation.

The requested instruction was patterned after the definition of criminal negligence in Model Penal Code § 2.02(2)(d) (1985). The trial court refused Santillanes' instruction and instead instructed the jury on a civil negligence standard. That instruction, Instruction No. 7, read:

The term "negligence" may relate either to an act or a failure to act.

An act, to be "negligence," must be one which a reasonably prudent person would foresee as involving an unreasonable risk of injury to himself or to another and which such a person, in the exercise of ordinary care, would not do.

A failure to act, to be "negligence," must be a failure to do an act which one is under a duty to do and which a reasonably prudent person, in the exercise of ordinary care, would do in order to prevent injury to himself or to another.

The trial court apparently did not instruct the jury on the definition of "intentionally."

. . . .

III. Issues

In this Court, Santillanes maintains that felony punishment should attach only to criminal behavior, in this case criminal negligence, not to ordinary civil negligence. Santillanes asserts that according felony status to acts of civil negligence violates substantive due process because the civil negligence standard is not tailored to meet the statutory goal of protecting children from abuse. Finally, Santillanes claims that as the Court of Appeals interpreted the statute, the civil negligence standard overreaches its mark and incorporates conduct that is not criminal, but rather simply negligent. Thus, he claims that the term "negligently," as interpreted, is overbroad in violation of due process of law.

The State counters that the statute, as applied, only pertains to child abuse that goes beyond merely normal action or inaction. . . . According to the State, the Court in [*State v. Coe,* 92 N.M. 320], limited the scope of the ordinary negligence standard because it interpreted the term "abuse" to require a showing of something more than just simple negligence or inadvertence even if it fell short of requiring a showing of criminal negligence. Thus, the State argues that the term "negligently," as interpreted in Coe and as applied in numerous other cases, is not constitutionally overbroad or vague. In addition, the State emphasizes that our courts have long interpreted the statute as requiring only a civil negligence standard and that there is no reason to change it now.

* * *

B. Requirement of Criminal Negligence

At common law, the conviction of a crime required satisfaction of the element of intent. . . . When a criminal statute is silent about whether a *mens rea* element is required, we do not assume that the legislature intended to enact a no-fault or strict liability crime. Instead, it is well settled that we presume criminal intent as an essential element of the crime unless it is clear from the statute that the legislature intended to omit the *mens rea* element. . . .

It is also well settled that the legislature has the authority to make negligent conduct a crime. . . . The issue in this case, then, is not whether we must read the *mens rea* element into a criminal statute because the child abuse statute contains a *mens rea* element. Rather, the question is when the legislature has included but not defined the *mens rea* element in a criminal statute, here the term "negligently," what degree of negligence is required.[2]

---

[2] It appears from our research that New Mexico's child abuse statute is unique in defining the proscribed conduct in terms of negligence rather than in terms of criminal or culpable negligence.

The State asserts that the legislature's "decision to criminalize the conduct described by [§ 30-6-1(C)] reflects a compelling public interest in protecting defenseless children" and thus was a proper exercise of the legislature's police power. . . . The State also points out that the statute has withstood many constitutional attacks. . . . While it is undisputed that the statute's purpose is both legitimate and laudable, our interpretation of this criminal statute requires that the term "negligently" be interpreted to require a showing of criminal negligence instead of ordinary civil negligence.

1. Prior Case Law. In addressing the issue of whether a civil or criminal negligence standard must be applied under the child abuse statute, the courts of this state consistently have applied a civil negligence standard. . . .

. . . .

We have stated, however, in the context of a reckless driving conviction, that mere civil negligence "not amounting to wilful or wanton disregard of consequences cannot be made the basis of a criminal action.". . . we went on to say broadly: "[m]ere negligence is not sufficient. It may be sufficient to compel the driver to respond in damages. However, when it comes to responding to an accusation of involuntary manslaughter, with the possibility of a penitentiary sentence, a different rule is called into play." . . .

Indeed, most commentators urge the application of criminal negligence for felonies instead of the civil negligence standard. Typically, the commentators explain their preference for criminal negligence over civil negligence as a standard in criminal law by relying on common-sense justifications based upon the traditional application of heightened standards of culpability to crimes punishable with jail sentences. . . .

* * *

4. Statutory Construction. It is well-settled in our state that a statute defining criminal conduct must be strictly construed. . . . Any doubts about the construction of penal statutes must be resolved in favor of lenity. . . .

We find guidance from an analogous situation in which courts have addressed whether a criminal statute that completely omits the mental state element required a showing of *mens rea* or whether it was a statute defining a strict liability crime. . . . [E]ach of the other criminal statutes in New Mexico in which "negligence" is an element also fail [sic] to define that term, but each of them is punishable as a petty misdemeanor, which is consistent with the view that only a showing of ordinary civil negligence is required. See NMSA 1978, § 30-7-4 (Repl. Pamp. 1984) (negligent use of deadly weapon); NMSA 1978, § 30-7-6 (Repl. Pamp. 1984) (negligent use of explosives); NMSA 1978, § 30-8-13 (Repl. Pamp. 1984) (negligently permitting livestock upon public highways). Conversely, when scienter is an element of the crime, the penalty generally is higher because "the infamy is that of a felony, which . . . is 'as bad a word as you can give to man or thing.'" *Morissette*, 342 U.S. at 260, see, *e.g.*, NMSA 1978, § 30-17-5(B) (Repl. Pamp. 1984) (requiring recklessness as element of negligent arson, which is a felony). In other words, when moral condemnation and social opprobrium attach to the conviction of a crime, the crime should typically reflect a mental state warranting such contempt.

We believe that there is a reasonable doubt as to the intended scope of proscribed conduct under the child abuse statute. Strictly construing the statutory language in favor of lenity, and in the absence of a clear legislative intention that ordinary civil negligence is a sufficient predicate for a felony, we conclude that the civil negligence standard, as applied to the child abuse statute, improperly goes beyond its intended scope and criminalizes conduct that is not morally contemptible. . . . We construe the intended scope of the statute as aiming to punish conduct that is morally culpable, not merely inadvertent. . . .

We also reject the State's contention that the legislature tacitly approved of the civil negligence standard as interpreted by our courts when it upgraded the violation of the child abuse statute from a fourth-degree felony to a third-degree felony in 1989. Instead, we find this concept firmly rooted in our jurisprudence: When a crime is punishable as a felony, civil negligence ordinarily is an inappropriate predicate by which to define such criminal conduct. . . .

Santillanes' defense was that his nephew injured himself when he jumped into a fishing line strung between two trees. He did not argue that he inadvertently caused the boy's throat to be cut. In addition, evidence in the record shows that his nephew's throat was cut from just below his right ear across to the left side of his neck below his jaw.

The jury found that Santillanes cut his nephew's throat with a knife during a scuffle. We believe that no rational jury could have concluded that Santillanes cut his nephew's throat, resulting in the injury described above, without satisfying the standard of criminal negligence that we have adopted today. Concluding that there could be no dispute that the element of criminal negligence was established by the evidence in the case, we hold that the error in instructing the jury on a civil negligence standard instead of a criminal negligence standard was not reversible error. . . .

D. Prospective Application

The question will arise as to whether our new interpretation of "negligently" under the child abuse statute is to be given retrospective or prospective application. . . .

It is within the inherent power of this Court to give its decision prospective or retroactive application without offending constitutional principles. . . .

Law enforcement officials in this State have relied on the civil negligence standard in the child abuse statute for at least fifteen years. Our appellate courts on several occasions have upheld such convictions and approved of the application of the tort negligence standard. "The past cannot always be erased by a new judicial declaration," and we cannot remove every trace of the convictions predicated upon the civil negligence standard from our jurisprudence. . . .

The purpose of the criminal negligence standard is to deter behavior that is culpable or, in other words, conduct that entails greater risk or fault than mere inadvertence or simple negligence. Applying this rule retroactively would not further its purpose because all such conduct was proscribed under the civil negligence standard, nor could it deter past conduct. . . .

Finally, equal administration of justice and the integrity of the judicial process requires prospective application of the criminal negligence standard in the child abuse statute. To give our holding today retroactive effect would unduly burden the criminal justice system. It could reopen old wounds and create new scars for child abuse victims and their families, wounds that they may not have forgotten, but from which they may have healed and recovered. . . . IT IS SO ORDERED.

UNITED STATES v. GARRETT

United States Court of Appeals for the Fifth Circuit

984 F.2d 1402 (1993)

GARWOOD, Circuit Judge:

Like many people trying to catch a plane around the holidays, Regina Kay Garrett was in a hurry. Unlike most, she forgot that she had a gun in her purse, or so she says. The principal question we decide today is whether the federal statute that criminalizes this conduct requires any degree of *mens rea* as an element of the offense. We hold that a "should have known" standard applies.

FACTS AND PROCEEDINGS BELOW

On December 18, 1990, Regina Kay Garrett was a ticketed passenger for and attempted to board flight 457 of L'Express Airlines, a regularly scheduled commercial commuter airline, from New Orleans to Alexandria, Louisiana. Passing through the New Orleans airport security, Garrett was stopped when the security guard monitoring the X-ray scanner noticed a dark mass in the hand bag that Garrett had placed on the conveyor belt. A consensual search of the bag was conducted and a small hand gun was discovered therein. The gun, a Browning .25 caliber semi-automatic, was loaded with six rounds in the magazine and one in the chamber. Garrett told security personnel that she had forgotten that the gun was in her purse.[1]

Garrett was charged in a one count bill of information with attempting to board an aircraft with a concealed weapon in violation of the Federal Aviation Act (the Act or the statute). See 49 U.S.C. App. § 1472(l)(1).[2] On January 23, 1992, a bench trial was held and Garrett was found guilty. Garrett was sentenced to five years' probation and a $25 special assessment. As a special condition of probation, the magistrate ordered Garrett to reside for six months in a halfway house. . . .

---

[1] Airport security officials confiscate approximately 2,500 firearms each year, or about seven a day. See McDowell, *Guns at Airports, an Everyday Event*, N.Y. Times, Dec. 29, 1992, at A9. . . . Notably, the Times reports that, "Most of those arrested. . . are like Mr. Connick: they say they simply forgot they were carrying guns to the airport." *Id.*

[2] 49 U.S.C. App. § 1472(l) provides in pertinent part: "(1) With respect to any aircraft in, or intended for operation in air transportation or intrastate air transportation, whoever—(A)while aboard, or while attempting to board such aircraft has on or about his person or his property a concealed deadly or dangerous weapon which is, or could be, accessible to such person in flight;. . . shall be fined not more than $10,000 or imprisoned not more than one year, or both."

DISCUSSION

On appeal, Garrett... argues that her conviction is invalid because the magistrate did not find that she had actual knowledge that the gun was in her purse....

* * *

II. THE STATUTE'S *MENS REA* REQUIREMENT

Garrett's... argument on appeal is that her conviction should be overturned because the government did not prove, nor even attempt to prove, that she had knowledge that the gun was in her purse when she attempted to board the L'Express flight. The government's position is that § 1472(l)(1) is a strict liability offense and contains no intent requirement whatsoever. The magistrate, eschewing both extremes, declared that "this Court is of the opinion that it would be consistent with Fifth Circuit jurisprudence and the United States Constitution to apply a 'should have known' standard to this misdemeanor offense." We agree.

A. Whether § 1472(l)(1) contains a *mens rea* requirement is a question that a number of other circuit courts seemingly addressed during the 1970's.... We believe that none of these courts were squarely presented with, or actually decided, the precise issue before us....

* * *

In determining whether § 1472(l)(1) contains a *mens rea* requirement, our overarching task is to give effect to the intent of the Congress . . . to give due respect both to the will of the Congress and the mandate of the Constitution, we construe the acts of Congress, whenever possible, so as to avoid raising serious constitutional questions....

Our effort to discern Congress' intent must begin, of course, with the statute's language. By its explicit terms . . . the statute makes no mention of *mens rea*. But before going any further, we reject a textual argument made by the government. That § 1472(l)(1) contains no *mens rea* requirement, the government maintains, must be inferred from the fact that the very next subsection does so explicitly.[16] . . . To be sure, the fact that § 1472(l)(2) speaks of willful or reckless violations of § 1472(l)(1) is convincing evidence that one need not act willfully or recklessly to violate § 1472(l)(1). One cannot infer from § 1472(l)(2), however, that § 1472(l)(1) contains no *mens rea* requirement whatsoever. There is a range of culpability between recklessness or willfulness, on the one hand, and total blamelessness, on the other, the most familiar of which is ordinary negligence. Therefore, the absence of knowledge is not the necessary converse of willfulness....

Thus, we are left with a statute which is, as we see it, silent on the question of *mens rea*. Yet, "certainly far more than the simple omission of the appropriate phrase from the statutory definition is necessary to justify dispensing with

---

[16] 49 U.S.C. App. § 1472(l)(2) provides: "Whoever willfully and without regard for the safety of human life, or with reckless disregard for the safety of human life, shall commit an act prohibited by paragraph (1)of this subsection, shall be fined not more than $25,000 or imprisoned not more than five years, or both."

an intent requirement." *United States v. United States Gypsum Co.*, 438 U.S. 422. . . . The requirement of *mens rea* as predicate to criminal liability is a fundamental precept of the Anglo-American common law. . . .

So deeply rooted is this tradition that it is presumed that the Congress intended to incorporate some requirement of *mens rea* in its definition of federal crimes, although that presumption is rebuttable. . . . A seminal case in this regard is *United States v. Delahoussaye*, 573 F.2d 910 (5th Cir. 1978), in which defendants were convicted of duck hunting in violation of federal regulations promulgated pursuant to the Migratory Bird Treaty Act, 16 U.S.C. § 703 *et seq*. These regulations prohibit the shooting of migratory game birds over a baited field. Reasoning that hunters might innocently violate these regulations by hunting over a field without knowledge that it was baited, we held that "a minimum form of scienter—the —should have known' form—is a necessary element of the offense." . . . "Any other interpretation," we said, "would simply render criminal conviction an unavoidable occasional consequence of duck hunting." . . .

Here, the text of § 1472(l)(1) provides no indication that the Congress intended to depart from the default rule of requiring some *mens rea*. Nor is there anything in the legislative history of the Federal Aviation Act that would lead us to believe that the Congress intended § 1472(l)(1) to be a wholly strict liability offense. At the same time, we think that a serious due process problem would be raised by application of this statute, which carries fairly substantial penalties, to someone who did not know and had no reason to know that he was carrying a weapon. . . . Avoiding such a construction of § 1472(l)(1), moreover, would comport with the so-called "rule of lenity"—the principle that ambiguous criminal statutes should be construed in favor of the defendant.

Therefore, in light of the principles laid down by the Supreme Court and our case law, we cannot conclude that the Congress intended § 1472(l)(1) to reach persons acting without any *mens rea* whatsoever.

. . .

C. Having declined to construe § 1472(l)(1) as a strict liability crime, it remains to be determined what level of mental culpability will support a conviction under it. We believe that the minimum level of scienter—the "should have known" standard—is appropriate and consistent with our case law.

The touchstone in our analysis is the severity of the punishment authorized by the statute. See 1 LaFave & Scott, *supra*, § 3.8, at 343 ("Other things being equal, the greater the possible punishment, the more likely some fault is required; and, conversely, the lighter the possible punishment, the more likely the legislature meant to impose liability without fault.") (footnote omitted). A violation of § 1472(l)(1) is punishable by a fine of up to $10,000 and a prison sentence of up to one year. Therefore, a violation of § 1472(l)(1), although a non-petty offense,[21] is still a misdemeanor. . . .

---

[21] Petty offenses are statutorily defined as those punishable by not more than six months in prison or a $5,000 fine. See 18 U.S.C. § 19. The petty/non-petty distinction is an important one in our law because a defendant charged with a non-petty offense has a right to a jury trial, whereas virtually no petty offenses require jury trials. . . . There is some support for the notion that those crimes for which a jury trial is required are also the ones for which some degree of *mens rea* should be required. . . .

We believe that a "should have known" standard is consistent with our prior cases in this area. . . . This case is most akin to *Delahoussaye,* in which we also applied a "should have known" standard. In *Delahoussaye,* as here, the crime at issue was a misdemeanor, although one punishable by a maximum of only six months in prison rather than one year. We decline today to go as far as *Anderson,* in which we required actual knowledge, because the crime at issue in that case was a felony that carried a possible sentence of ten years imprisonment. . . .

We conclude that one violates § 1472(l)(1) if, but only if, she either knew or should have known that the concealed weapon in question was on or about her person or property while aboard or attempting to board the aircraft.

D. There is ample evidence in the record to support the magistrate's conclusion that Garrett should have known that she was carrying the gun when she attempted to board by going through security. Garrett testified that she had traveled by air many times and that she was aware that it was illegal to try to bring a gun through airport security. And if she needed any reminder, there were two large signs in the area of the security checkpoint. The first sign, printed with large white letters upon a bright red background, stated: "CARRY NO WEAPONS OR EXPLOSIVES BEYOND THIS POINT: VIOLATORS ARE SUBJECT TO PROSECUTION UNDER FEDERAL CRIMINAL STATUTES REQUIRING PENALTIES AND/OR IMPRISONMENT." The sign also had an image of a pistol and a knife over which was superimposed a circle and a diagonal line. The other sign displayed a list of "Federal Safety and Security Inspection Rules" and informed passengers, among other things, that, "Federal regulations prohibit persons from having a FIREARM, explosive or incendiary device on or about their person or accessible property when entering or in an airport sterile area or while aboard an aircraft."

It is also relevant that the gun was in Garrett's hand bag. Garrett testified that she owns and uses seven or eight purses and that she did not remember when she put the gun in this particular bag, which was described at trial as a large leather satchel. She stated that she did not put the gun in the bag on the day of the flight, nor did she think that day to check the bag for it. On the other hand, she testified that she knew that she previously had carried the gun in that particular bag. Garrett also testified that she had put her wallet, checkbook, and makeup in the bag on the day in question. It is inferable that she would have used the bag during the day. We think it patently reasonable to require individuals in such circumstances to be aware of the presence of a firearm in their purse or equivalent bag, or, indeed, to infer that they actually have such knowledge.

In short, there is sufficient evidence in the record to support the magistrate's finding that Garrett should have known that she was carrying a firearm.[25]

---

[25] We note one additional piece of evidence. The security guard who screened Garrett's bag testified that immediately after the bag was stopped on the conveyor belt, but before the guard had said anything, Garrett threw up her hands and announced that she was a state trooper's wife. Garrett similarly testified that "I don't know if it makes any difference; I used to be married to a state policeman." The guard also testified that, unlike most passengers discovered with guns, Garrett did not appear upset or nervous. The magistrate thought that Garrett's statement "indicated at least initially some justification that she could carry the gun." It is possible to read the magistrate as suggesting that Garrett may have known what she was doing but thought it

For the reasons stated herein, Garrett's conviction and sentence are
AFFIRMED.

NOTES AND QUESTIONS

1. *Garrett* arguably adopted civil negligence as an alternative to strict liability (discussed *infra,* § 4.07). Does this mean that the court is choosing the lesser of two evils rather than the best approach?

2. The case law generally clearly indicates the resistance of the common law courts to imposing criminal liability on the basis of "mere" negligence. Yet a number of jurisdictions preclude a mistake "defense" if that mistake is "unreasonable," as opposed to its being "grossly unreasonable." See *infra*§ 4.06[A]. Are these positions reconcilable?

3. For a complete view of the Continental approach, see G. Erenius, *Criminal Negligence and Individuality* (1976). See also Alvar Nelson, *Responses to Crime: An Introduction to Swedish Criminal Law and Administration* 24–27 (1972); J. Andenaes, *The General Part of the Criminal Law of Norway* 218–22 (1965).

§ 4.04 THE INTERPRETATION OF *MENS REA* WORDS IN CRIMINAL STATUTES

[A] Generally

In addition to deciding what a specific term denoting a *mens rea* requirement (such as *reckless* or *negligent*) meant, two issues of interpretation plagued the common law courts. First, as the excerpt from Professor Remington, below, suggests, legislatures used an extraordinary number of different adverbs to describe the requisite *mens rea* for a specific crime. Although there is good reason to believe that at least in many of these cases the legislatures were either merely giving emphasis to a requirement of moral culpability or paying insufficient attention to legislative drafting, the courts were compelled, both by maxims of statutory interpretation and by the need to accord legislatures their proper role in the legal system, to assume that each different *mens rea* word in fact denoted a different mental state. Thus, *maliciously* not only had to be defined; it then had to be distinguished from *intentionally, recklessly, spitefully, wilfully, feloniously, unlawfully, wrongfully,* and the dozens of other adverbs that legislatures used to describe moral culpability.

---

was permissible. However, in the same transcribed paragraph, the magistrate also stated that "I need not decide whether [Garrett] had actual knowledge or not." In light of the latter statement, and in the absence of any express finding by the trial court on the credibility of Garrett's claim to have forgotten the gun, we view the magistrate as having found only that Garrett should have known the gun was there in her purse. . . .

REMINGTON AND HELSTAD, *THE MENTAL ELEMENT IN CRIME: A LEGISLATIVE PROBLEM*

1952 Wis. L. Rev. 645, 666–67

Suppose, for example, that a statute provides that "any person who shall wilfully. . . destroy, remove, throw down or injure any fence, hedge or wall enclosing any orchard, pasture, meadow, garden or any field whatever on land belonging to or lawfully occupied by another. . . shall be punished. . . " What does the term "wilfully" mean when used in this context? The term has at various times been given at least half a dozen different meanings. Thus, it has been held that "willfully" means intentionally as distinguished from accidentally; it has been said that it means consciously but not necessarily intentionally; it has been said that it implies a bad purpose or malice; it has been held to mean a reckless disregard for the rights of others; it has been held to mean without justifiable excuse, and various other meanings have been given the word.

Not only is little thought given by draftsmen to the structure of a statute in relation to the words signifying the requirement of a mental element, but the words themselves often are chosen merely because of habit or because they seem to sound good or because the draftsman is not certain what area of conduct he wants to cover so he inserts a "weasel word." "Maliciously," for example, hardly ever means what it seems to say, *i.e.,* spite or ill-will, yet it continues to clutter up many penal statutes, and once in a while, adding to the confusion, it is held to mean malice, spite, or ill-will toward the injured party. "Wantonly" is subject to much the same criticism as "maliciously."

NOTE

For an exhaustive recitation of case law interpretation of the various adverbs referred to in the above selection, as well as many more, see J. Edwards, *Mens Rea* in Statutory Offenses (1955).

[B] Applying *Mens Rea* to Elements of the Offense

A second issue of interpretation is illuminated by the *Cotterill* opinion, below. Assuming that a *mens rea* requirement was properly defined *per se,* and that it was satisfactorily distinguished from other "*mens rea* words," what precisely did it mean in the context of a statute? If a person who intentionally threw a stone at a person were charged (as in *Pembliton,* p. 229, *supra*) with "intentionally breaking a window," did she have to intend merely to throw the stone or also intend to break the window? This question is sometimes posed as "how far down the statute does the *mens rea* word go?" The problem was complicated by the mere rules of English syntax. *[I]ntentionally* is an adverb that modifies a verb; one cannot "intentionally" a window. Thus, a "plain meaning" approach to criminal statutes, such as that taken in *Pembliton,* would appear to make irrelevant to guilt determinations a person's mistakes (or even ignorance) of facts that, in ordinary moral discourse would be extremely relevant to a determination of moral culpability. This dilemma, moreover, was not limited to moral philosophy, since the criminal law had for centuries regarded a mistake of fact as exculpatory. Yet, arguably, the logical result of the *Cotterill* opinion, below, would be to convict. These are the issues to keep in mind while reading the next materials.

COTTERILL V. PENN

King's Bench for the County of Worcester

1 K.B. 53 (1936)

Case stated by justices for the county of Worcester.

On June 11, 1934, about 6 PM at Pedmore in the county of Worcester, Mr. Stanley Millward released a number of homing pigeons in a road near to the private garden of Mr. Joseph Samuel Penn, hereinafter called "the defendant." One of the pigeons was released some seconds before the others, and almost immediately after it had been released it was shot by the defendant, who was in his garden for the purpose of shooting wood pigeons and magpies which had materially damaged his garden. The defendant was not able to see Mr. Millward and did not know that he was in the road releasing pigeons. There was brilliant sunshine at the time, and the pigeon flew between the defendant and the sun so that he had but little opportunity of judging what kind of pigeon was there. He did not see the pigeon for more than five yards, as it came over two rows of fruit trees at least fifteen feet in height between which the defendant was standing. If he had taken time to see the bird properly and out of the glare of the sun he might have known at once that it was not a wood pigeon, but by so doing he would or might have lost his shot. The pigeon, which was the property of Mr. Arthur Millward, was different both in size and color from a wood pigeon. Owing to the defendant being partly dazzled by the sun and to the short space for which he saw the bird he could not have distinguished between a wood pigeon and a homing pigeon. The defendant picked up the bird and handed it to Mr. S. Millward very soon after and said to him that he was sorry but he had mistaken it for a wood pigeon, and he then and there offered to pay its value, but his offer was not accepted.

On the part of the informant it was contended that the honest belief that the pigeon was a wild pigeon was no defence to the information and that the defendant would only be justified in shooting the pigeon if it was actually doing damage to his crops; and that there was no obligation upon the informant to prove felonious intent in a charge of "shooting" a pigeon, but only where the charge was one of "taking." On the part of the defendant it was contended that it was necessary for the informant to prove that the pigeon was taken or killed with felonious intent; and that the defendant was entitled to kill the pigeon if he thought it was a wood pigeon which might damage his crops.

The justices were of opinion that there was no guilty mind on the part of the defendant to shoot or take the pigeon so as to deprive its owner of his property; that he shot it honestly believing it to be a wood pigeon about to alight in his garden to feed off his crops; and that, momentarily seeing one bird by itself flying low, he honestly believed that it was a wild bird, and killed it really and honestly thinking he was exercising his right of protecting his crops; and they therefore dismissed the information.

LORD HEWART C.J. The justices dismissed the information, and the question is whether in doing so they were correct in point of law.

Sect. 23 of the Larceny Act, 1861, provides that: "Whosoever shall unlawfully and wilfully kill, wound, or take any house dove or pigeon under such circumstances as shall not amount to larceny at common law, shall, on conviction," pay a penalty.

One contention on behalf of the respondent was that to sustain a charge under the section it is necessary to prove that the pigeon was killed or taken with felonious intent. In my opinion, although the section says "unlawfully and wilfully," it does not require the element of *mens rea* beyond the point that the facts must show an intention on the part of the person accused to do the act forbidden, which was here that of shooting. It seems to me to be immaterial that the bird which the respondent shot was of a different kind from that which he thought that he was shooting. If the section had used the word "maliciously," the state of mind of the person charged would have been relevant. But using the terms "unlawfully and wilfully" the section seems to me only to mean that the person accused intended to shoot and that the shooting was without a lawful excuse.

AVORY J. I am of the same opinion. I think that we should follow the case of *Horton v. Gwynne,* where Darling J. said in reference to the circumstances of that case in which there had been the shooting by the defendant of a house pigeon in the belief that it was a wild pigeon:

> In those circumstances I think that his act was both wilful and unlawful. It was not accidental. It was not as if he had shot at a crow and killed a pigeon unintentionally. The pigeon was not his property, and it was not in fact a wild one. From a very early date house pigeons were specially protected by law, as being a valuable species of property. In my opinion s. 23 was intended to protect house pigeons against being killed, not only by persons who killed them knowing them to be house pigeons, but also by persons who did not know that. A person who shoots a pigeon which turns out to be a house pigeon must take the consequences of his act.

In my view none of the other cases which have been referred to is inconsistent with *Horton v. Gwynne.*

NOTES AND QUESTIONS

1. Why is it important to Judge Avory that he distinguish the defendant in *Cotterill* from the defendant who, in the hypothetical discussed by Darling, J., in *Horton,* shoots at a crow but misses and hits a homing pigeon? Suppose that the defendant shot at the only crow in a group of 500 homing pigeons?

2. Suppose in the hypothetical suggested by Darling, J., that a homing pigeon had been painted black to look like a crow. Under the opinion in *Cotterill* would that defendant be guilty of killing a homing pigeon?

Although *Coterrill* is a quaint case, the statutory interpretation issue it poses still plagues the courts, as the following case and problems demonstrate.

UNITED STATES v. X-CITEMENT VIDEO, INC., ET AL.

Supreme Court of the United States

513 U.S. 64 (1994)

Rehnquist, C.J., *delivered the opinion of the Court:*

Rubin Gottesman owned and operated X-Citement Video, Inc. Undercover police posed as pornography retailers and targeted X-Citement Video for investigation. During the course of the sting operation, the media exposed Traci Lords for her roles in pornographic films while under the age of 18. Police Officer Steven Takeshita expressed an interest in obtaining Traci Lords tapes. Gottesman complied, selling Takeshita 49 videotapes featuring Lords before her 18th birthday. Two months later, Gottesman shipped eight tapes of the underage Traci Lords to Takeshita in Hawaii.

These two transactions formed the basis for a federal indictment under the child pornography statute [18 U.S.C. § 2252]. Evidence at trial suggested that Gottesman had full awareness of Lords' underage performances. . . . The District Court convicted respondents of all three counts. . . .

[On Appeal] Gottesman [raised] constitutional arguments. . . . [T]he Ninth Circuit reached the merits of his claims and, by a divided vote, found § 2252 facially unconstitutional. . . . The court concluded that case law from this Court required that the defendant must have knowledge at least of the nature and character of the materials. The court extended these cases to hold that the First Amendment requires that the defendant possess knowledge of the particular fact that one performer had not reached the age of majority at the time the visual depiction was produced. Because the court found the statute did not require such a showing, it reversed respondents 'convictions. . . .

Title 18 U.S.C. § 2252 (1988 ed. and Supp. V) provides, in relevant part:

"(a) Any person who—

"(1) knowingly transports or ships in interstate or foreign commerce by any means including by computer or mails, any visual depiction, if—

(A) the producing of such visual depiction involves the use of a minor engaging in sexually explicit conduct; and

(B) such visual depiction is of such conduct;

"(2) knowingly receives, or distributes, any visual depiction that has been mailed, or has been shipped or transported in interstate or foreign commerce, or which contains materials which have been mailed or so shipped or transported, by any means including by computer, or knowingly reproduces any visual depiction for distribution in interstate or foreign commerce or through the mails, if—

"(A) the producing of such visual depiction involves the use of a minor engaging in sexually explicit conduct; and

"(B) such visual depiction is of such conduct;

* * *

shall be punished as provided in subsection (b) of this section.

The critical determination which we must make is whether the term "knowingly" in subsections (1)and (2)modifies the phrase "the use of a minor" in subsections (1)(A) and (2)(A). The most natural grammatical reading, adopted by the Ninth Circuit, suggests that the term "knowingly" modifies only the surrounding verbs: transports, ships, receives, distributes, or reproduces. Under this construction, the words "knowingly" would not modify the elements of the minority of the performers, or the sexually explicit nature of the material, because they are set forth in independent clauses separated by interruptive punctuation. But we do not think this is the end of the matters, both because of anomalies which result from this construction, and because of the respective presumptions that some form of scienter is to be implied in a criminal statute even if not expressed, and that a statute is to be construed where fairly possible so as to avoid substantial constitutional questions.

. . . Some applications of [the statute] would produce results that were not merely odd, but positively absurd. If we were to conclude that "knowingly" only modifies the relevant verbs in § 2252, we would sweep within the ambit of the statute actors who had no idea that they were even dealing with sexually explicit material. For instance, a retail druggist who returns an uninspected roll of developed film to a customer "knowingly distributes" a visual depiction and would be criminally liable if it were later discovered that the visual depiction contained images of children engaged in sexually explicit conduct. Or, a new resident of an apartment might receive mail for the prior resident and store the mail unopened. If the prior tenant had requested delivery of materials covered by § 2252, his residential successor could be prosecuted for "knowing receipt" of such materials. Similarly, a Federal Express courier who delivers a box in which the shipper has declared the contents to be "film" "knowingly transports" such film. We do not assume that Congress, in passing laws, intended such results. . . .

Our reluctance to simply follow the most grammatical reading of the statute is heightened by our cases interpreting criminal statutes to include broadly applicable scienter requirements, even where the statute by its terms does not contain them. . . .

. . . *Liparota v. United States,* 471 U.S. 419 (1985), posed a challenge to a federal statute prohibiting certain actions with respect to food stamps. The statute's use of "knowingly" could be read only to modify "uses, transfers, acquires, alters, or possesses" or it could be read also to modify "in any manner not authorized by [the statute]." Noting that neither interpretation posed constitutional problems, the Court held the scienter requirement applied to both elements. . . . In addition, the Court was concerned with the broader reading which would "criminalize a broad range of apparently innocent conduct." Imposing criminal liability on an unwitting food stamp recipient who purchased groceries at a store that inflated its prices to such purchasers struck the Court as beyond the intended reach of the statute. The same analysis drove the recent conclusion in *Staples v. United States*. . . . [*infra,* see p. 322 eds]

Applying these principles, we think the Ninth Circuit's plain language reading of § 2252 is not so plain. First, § 2252 is not a public welfare offense. Persons do not harbor settled expectations that the contents of magazines and film are generally subject to stringent public regulation. In fact, First Amendment constraints presuppose the opposite view. Rather, the statute is more akin to the common law offenses against the "state, person, property, or public morals," that presume a scienter requirement in the absence of express contrary intent. Second, *Staples'* concern with harsh penalties looms equally large respecting § 2252: violations are punishable by up to 10 years in prison as well as substantial fines and forfeiture. . . . *Staples* instructs that the presumption in favor of a scienter requirement should apply to each of the statutory elements which criminalize otherwise innocent conduct. . . .

The legislative history of the statute evolved over a period of years, and perhaps for that reason speaks somewhat indistinctly to the question whether "knowingly" in the statute modifies the elements of (1)(A) and (2)(A)—that the visual depiction involves the use of a minor engaging in sexually explicit conduct—or merely the verbs "transport or ship" in (1)and "receives or distribute . . . [or] reproduce" in (2). In 1959 we held in *Smith v. California,* [361 U.S. 147 (1959)], that a California statute which dispensed with any *mens rea* requirement as to the contents of an obscene book would violate the First Amendment. When Congress began dealing with child pornography in 1977, the content of the legislative debates suggest that it was aware of this decision. See, *e.g.,* 123 Cong. Rec. 30935 (1977) ("It is intended that they have knowledge of the type of material . . . proscribed by this bill. The legislative history should be clear on that so as to remove any chance it will lead into constitutional problems"). Even if that were not the case, we do not impute to Congress an intent to pass legislation that is inconsistent with the Constitution as construed by this Court. When first passed, § 2252 punished one who "knowingly transports or ships in interstate or foreign commerce or mails, for the purpose of sale or distribution for sale, any obscene visual or print medium" if it involved the use of a minor engaged in sexually explicit conduct. Assuming awareness of *Smith,* at a minimum, "knowingly" was intended to modify "obscene" in the 1978 version.

In 1984, Congress amended the statute to its current form, broadening its application to those sexually explicit materials that, while not obscene as defined by *Miller v. California,* 413 U.S. 15 (1973), could be restricted without violating the First Amendment as explained by *New York v. Ferber,* 458 U.S. 747 (1982). When Congress eliminated the adjective "obscene," all of the elements defining the character and content of the materials at issue were relegated to subsections (1)(a) and (2)(a). In this effort to expand the child pornography statute to its full constitutional limits, Congress nowhere expressed an intent to eliminate the *mens rea* requirement that had previously attached to the character and content of the material through the word obscene.

The committee reports and legislative debate speak more opaquely as to the desire of Congress for a scienter requirement with respect to the age of minority. . . . In evaluating the proposal, the Justice Department offered its thoughts:

> The word "knowingly" in the second line of § 2251 is unnecessary and should be stricken. . . . Unless "knowingly" is deleted here, the bill might be subject to an interpretation requiring the Government to prove the defendant's knowledge of everything that follows "knowingly", including the age of the child. We assume it is not the intention of the drafters to require the Government to prove that the defendant knew the child was under age sixteen but merely to prove that the child was, in fact, less than age sixteen. . . .
>
> On the other hand, the use of the word "knowingly" in subsection 2252(a)(1) is appropriate to make it clear that the bill does not apply to common carriers or other innocent transporters who have no knowledge of the nature or character of the material they are transporting. To clarify the situation, the legislative history might reflect that the defendant's knowledge of the age of the child is not an element of the offense but that the bill is not intended to apply to innocent transportation with no knowledge of the nature or character of the material involved.

Respondents point to this language as an unambiguous revelation that Congress omitted a scienter requirement. . . . In fact, the version reported by the committee eliminated § 2252 altogether. At that juncture, Senator Roth introduced an amendment which would be another precursor of § 2252. In one paragraph, the amendment forbade any person to "knowingly transport [or] ship . . . [any] visual medium depicting a minor engaged in sexually explicit conduct." 123 Cong. Rec. 33047 (1977). In an exchange during debate, Senator Percy inquired:

> Would this not mean that the distributor or seller must have either first, actual knowledge that the materials do contain child pornographic depictions or, second, circumstances must be such that he should have had such actual knowledge, and that mere inadvertence or negligence would not alone be enough to render his actions unlawful?

Senator Roth replied:

> That is absolutely correct. This amendment, limited as it is by the phrase "knowingly," insures that only those sellers and distributors who are consciously and deliberately engaged in the marketing of child pornography . . . are subject to prosecution. . . .

The parallel House bill did not contain a comparable provision to § 2252 of the Senate bill, and limited § 2251 prosecutions to obscene materials . . . Most importantly, the new bill retained the adverb "knowingly" in § 2252 while simultaneously deleting the word "knowingly" from § 2251(a). The Conference Committee explained the deletion in § 2251(a) as reflecting an "intent that it is not a necessary element of a prosecution that the defendant knew the actual age of the child." *Id.*, at 5.[26] Respondents point to the

---

[26] The difference in congressional intent with respect to § 2251 versus § 2252 reflects the reality that producers are more conveniently able to ascertain the age of performers. It thus makes sense to impose the risk of error on producers. *United States v. United States District Court for Central District of California*, 858 F. 2d 534, 543, n. 6 (CA9 1988). Although producers may be convicted

appearance of "knowingly" in § 2251(c) and argue that § 2252 ought to be read like § 2251. But this argument depends on the conclusion that § 2251(c) does not include a knowing requirement, a premise that respondents fail to support. Respondents offer in support of their premise only the legislative history discussing an intent to exclude a scienter requirement from § 2251(a). Because § § 2251(a) and 2251(c) were passed at different times and contain different wording, the intent to exclude scienter from § 2251(a) does not imply an intent to exclude scienter from § 2251(c).[27]

The legislative history can be summarized by saying that it persuasively indicates that Congress intended that the term "knowingly" apply to the requirement that the depiction be of sexually explicit conduct; it is a good deal

---

under § 2251(a) without proof they had knowledge of age, Congress has independently required both primary and secondary producers to record the ages of performers with independent penalties for failure to comply.

[This section reads as follows (ed.): § 2251. Sexual exploitation of children: (a)Any person who employs, uses, persuades, induces, entices, or coerces any minor to engage in, or who has a minor assist any other person to engage in, or who transports any minor in interstate or foreign commerce,. . . with the intent that such minor engage in, any sexually explicit conduct for the purpose of producing any visual depiction of such conduct, shall be punished as provided under subsection (d), if such person knows or has reason to know that such visual depiction will be transported in interstate or foreign commerce or mailed, or if such visual depiction has actually been transported in interstate or foreign commerce or mailed; (b)Any parent, legal guardian, or person having custody or control of a minor who knowingly permits such minor to engage in, or to assist any other person to engage in, sexually explicit conduct for the purpose of producing any visual depiction of such conduct shall be punished as provided under subsection (d)of this section, if such parent, legal guardian, or person knows or has reason to know that such visual depiction will be transported in interstate or foreign commerce or mailed or if such visual depiction has actually been transported in interstate or foreign commerce or mailed; (c)(1) Any person who, in a circumstance described in paragraph (2), knowingly makes, prints, or publishes, or causes to be made, printed, or published, any notice or advertisement seeking or offering—(A)to receive, exchange, buy, produce, display, distribute, or reproduce, any visual depiction, if the production of such visual depiction involves the use of a minor engaging in sexually explicit conduct and such visual depiction is of such conduct; or (B)participation in any act of sexually explicit conduct by or with any minor for the purpose of producing a visual depiction of such conduct; shall be punished as provided under subsection (d). (2)The circumstance referred to in paragraph (1) is that—(A)such person knows or has reason to know that such notice or advertisement will be transported in interstate or foreign commerce by any means including by computer or mailed; or (B)such notice or advertisement is transported in interstate or foreign commerce by any means including by computer or mailed. (d)Any individual who violates this section shall be fined not more than $100,000, or imprisoned not more than 10 years, or both, but, if such individual has a prior conviction under this section, such individual shall be fined not more than $200,000, or imprisoned not less than five years nor more than 15 years, or both.]

[27] Congress amended § 2251 to insert subsection (c)in 1986. Pub. L. 99-628, 100 Stat. 3510. That provision created new offenses relating to the advertising of the availability of child pornography or soliciting children to participate in such depictions. The legislative history of § 2251(c)does address the scienter requirement: "The government must prove that the defendant knew the character of the visual depictions as depicting a minor engaging in sexually explicit conduct, but need not prove that the defendant actually knew the person depicted was in fact under 18 years of age or that the depictions violated Federal law." H. Rep. No. 99-910, p.6 (1986). It may be argued that since the House Committee Report rejects any requirement of scienter as to the age of minority for § 2251(c), the House Committee thought that there was no such requirement in § 2252. But the views of one Congress as to the meaning of an act passed by an earlier Congress are not ordinarily of great weight and the views of the committee of one House of another Congress are of even less weight.

less clear from the Committee Reports and floor debates that Congress intended that the requirement extend also to the age of the performers. But, turning once again to the statute itself, if the term "knowingly" applies to the sexually explicit conduct depicted, it is emancipated from merely modifying the verbs in subsections (1)and (2). And as a matter of grammar it is difficult to conclude that the word "knowingly" modifies one of the elements in (1)(A) and (2)(A), but not the other. . . .

For all of the foregoing reasons, we conclude that the term "knowingly" in § 2252 extends both to the sexually explicit nature of the material and to the age of the performers.

The judgment of the Court of Appeals is Reversed.

* * *

Justice SCALIA, with whom Justice THOMAS joins, *dissenting.*

Today's opinion is without antecedent. None of the decisions cited as authority support interpreting an explicit statutory scienter requirement in a manner that its language simply will not bear. . . .

There is no way in which any of these cases, or all of them in combination, can be read to stand for the sweeping proposition that "the presumption in favor of a scienter requirement should apply to each of the statutory elements which criminalize otherwise innocent conduct," even when the plain text of the statute says otherwise. All those earlier cases employ the presumption as a rule of interpretation which applies when Congress has not addressed the question of criminal intent or when the import of what it has said on that subject is ambiguous. Today's opinion converts the rule of interpretation into a rule of law, contradicting the plain import of what Congress has specifically prescribed regarding criminal intent.

In *United States v. Thomas,* 893 F. 2d 1066, 1070 (CA9), the Ninth Circuit interpreted 18 U.S.C. § 2252 to require knowledge of neither the fact that the visual depiction portrays sexually explicit conduct, nor the fact that a participant in that conduct was a minor. . . . To say, as the Court does, that this interpretation is "the most grammatical reading," or "the most natural grammatical reading," is understatement to the point of distortion—rather like saying that the ordinarily preferred total for 2 plus 2 is 4. The Ninth Circuit's interpretation is in fact and quite obviously the only grammatical reading. If one were to rack his brains for a way to express the thought that the knowledge requirement in subsection (a)(1)applied only to the transportation or shipment of visual depiction in interstate or foreign commerce, and not to the fact that that depiction was produced by use of a minor engaging in sexually explicit conduct, and was a depiction of that conduct, it would be impossible to construct a sentence structure that more clearly conveys that thought, and that thought alone. The word "knowingly" is contained, not merely in a distant phrase, but in an entirely separate clause from the one into which today's opinion inserts it. The equivalent, in expressing a simpler thought, would be the following: "Anyone who knowingly double-parks will be subject to a $200 fine if that conduct occurs during the 4:30-to-6:30 rush hour." It could not be clearer that the scienter requirement applies only to the double-parking, and not to the time of day. So also here, it could not be clearer that it applies only to the transportation or shipment of visual depiction in interstate or foreign commerce. There is no doubt. There is no ambiguity. There is no possible "less natural" but nonetheless permissible reading. . . .

The Court acknowledges that "it is a good deal less clear from the Committee Reports and floor debates that Congress intended that the requirement [of scienter] extend . . . to the age of the performers." That is surely so. In fact it seems to me that the dominant (if not entirely uncontradicted) view expressed in the legislative history is that set forth in the statement of the Carter Administration Justice Department which introduced the original bill: "The defendant's knowledge of the age of the child is not an element of the offense but . . . the bill is not intended to apply to innocent transportation with no knowledge of the nature or character of the material involved." . . .

The Court rejects this construction of the statute . . . because "as a matter of grammar it is difficult to conclude that the word knowingly' modifies one of the elements in (1)(A) and (2)(A), but not the other." But as I have described, "as a matter of grammar" it is also difficult (nay, impossible) to conclude that the word "knowingly" modifies both of those elements. It is really quite extraordinary for the Court, fresh from having, as it says, "emancipated" the adverb from the grammatical restriction that renders it inapplicable to the entire conditional clause, suddenly to insist that the demands of syntax must prevail over legislative intent—thus producing an end result that accords neither with syntax nor with supposed intent. If what the statute says must be ignored, one would think we might settle at least for what the statute was meant to say; but alas, we are told, what the statute says prevents this. . . .

I would dispose of the present case, as the Ninth Circuit did, by reading the statute as it is written: to provide criminal penalties for the knowing transportation or shipment of a visual depiction in interstate or foreign commerce, and for the knowing receipt or distribution of a visual depiction so transported or shipped, if that depiction was (whether the defendant knew it or not) a portrayal of a minor engaging in sexually explicit conduct. I would find the statute, as so interpreted, to be unconstitutional since, by imposing criminal liability upon those not knowingly dealing in pornography, it establishes a severe deterrent, not narrowly tailored to its purposes, upon fully protected First Amendment activities. . . .

Problems

1. Title 18 U.S.C. § 207(c) provides as follows:

Whoever, [being a covered government employee], within one year after such employment has ceased, knowingly acts as agent or attorney for, or otherwise represents, anyone other than the United States in any formal or informal appearance before, or, with the intent to influence, makes any oral or written communication on behalf of anyone other than the United States, to—

(1) the department or agency in which he served as an officer or employee, or any officeror employee thereof, and

(2) in connection with any . . . particular matter, and

(3) which is pending before such department or agency or in which such department or agency has a direct and substantial interest—shall be fined not more than $10,000 or imprisoned for not more than two years, or both.

Defendant discusses with employees at his old agency matters then pending before them, but seeks to introduce evidence that he did not know that the matter was then before that agency. Is such evidence relevant? See *United States v. Nofziger,* 878 F.2d 442 (D.C. Cir. 1989); Comment, 65 Notre Dame L. Rev. 803 (1990).

2. 42 U.S.C. § 6928(d) of the Resource Conservation and Recovery Act of 1976 (RCRA) provides criminal penalties for:

Any person who

(2) knowingly treats, stores or disposes of any hazardous waste . . .

(A) without having obtained a permit under § 6925 of this title . . . or

(B) in knowing violation of any material condition or requirement of such permit.

In which of the following hypotheticals is D guilty?

a. D is ordered by his employer to dump several barrels marked "golf balls" into a land fill. He believes the labels. In fact, the barrels contain a material declared a "hazardous waste" by the EPA. Must D's belief be reasonable? (*i.e.,* does it make a difference whether he hears liquid sloshing in the barrels?)

b. D knows that he is storing hazardous wastes, but believes that he has a permit to do so. In fact (1) his permit never covered such wastes, (2) his permit has expired, (3) because of technical deficiencies, his permit, which on its face allows the storage of these wastes, was never validly issued by the EPA.

c. D knows that he has a permit to store hazardous wastes, but decides to transport them to a facility that he believes has an EPA permit. The facility has no such permit. Does it matter whether D's belief is reasonable (*e.g.,* the facility has shown him a false permit)?

Compare *United States v. Johnson and Towers,* 741 F.2d 662 (3d Cir. 1984) (dictum) with *United States v. Hoflin,* 880 F.2d 1033 (9th Cir. 1989). See also *United States v. Speach,* 968 F.2d 795 (9th Cir. 1992). See Harig, *Ignorance Is Not Bliss: Responsible Corporate Officers Convicted of Environmental Crimes and the Federal Sentencing Guidelines,* 42 Duke L. J. 145 (1992); Vitiello, *Does Culpability Matter? Statutory Construction Under* 42 U.S.C.A. § 6928, 6 Tul. Envtl. L. J. 187 (1993).

3. 18 U.S.C. § 1030 (a)(5)(A) provides that anyone who "intentionally accesses a Federal interest computer without authorization, and by means of . . . such conduct alters, damages, or destroy[s] information" therein is guilty

of a felony. D, a computer hacker at Cornell University, sought to demonstrate the weakness of computer security measures at various educational, medical, and military sites. He released a "worm" program into the Internet, expecting it to migrate, undetected, without interfering with normal operations. He incorrectly calculated the number of times the worm would visit and be copied by each computer. As a result, the worm caused substantial damages, with the estimated cost of repair ranging from $2,000 to $53,000 at each location. Has D violated the statute if he honestly believed there was no danger of such damage? See *United States v. Morris,* 928 F.2d 504 (2d Cir. 1991).

§ 4.05 THE IMPACT OF THE MODEL PENAL CODE

The Model Penal Code—developed by the American Law Institute in the 1950s and adopted by that organization in 1962—sought to resolve the questions of statutory interpretation seen earlier in § 4.04. The Code also addressed the questions of minimal criminal culpability outlined in § 4.03. The Code's contribution in this regard is possibly its most important feature, although there are many other significant propositions that the Code also adopted. The Code's solution to these perplexing dilemmas has been so successful that it has been adopted, with variations, in a significant number of states; it has even influenced decisions in states not yet enacting it legislatively. In essence, the Code has given all criminal lawyers in common law jurisdictions a common language. See Singer, *Foreword,* 19 Rutgers L. J. 519 (1988). See generally, *Symposium,* 19 Rutgers L. J. 421 (1988). Reprinted below is the critical part of the Code dealing with *mens rea* issues. But before moving forward, parse this statute with extreme care and caution. As the notes following the materials indicate, there are many controversial and perplexing issues in the Code.

[A] The Model Penal Code

§ 2.02 GENERAL REQUIREMENTS OF CULPABILITY

(1) Minimum Requirements of Culpability.

Except as provided in § 2.05, a person is not guilty of an offense unless he acted purposely, knowingly, recklessly or negligently, as the law may require, with respect to each material element of the offense.

(2) Kinds of Culpability Defined.

    (a) Purposely. A person acts purposely with respect to a material element of an offense when:

        (i) if the element involves the nature of his conduct or a result thereof, it is his conscious object to engage in conduct of that nature or to cause such a result; and

        (ii) if the element involves the attendant circumstances, he is aware of the existence of such circumstances or he believes or hopes that they exist.

    (b) Knowingly. A person acts knowingly with respect to a material element of an offense when:

(i) if the element involves the nature of his conduct or the attendant circumstances, he is aware that his conduct is of that nature or that such circumstances exist; and

(ii) if the element involves a result of his conduct, he is aware that it is practically certain that his conduct will cause such a result.

(c) Recklessly. A person acts recklessly with respect to a material element of an offense when he consciously disregards a substantial and unjustifiable risk that the material element exists or will result from his conduct. The risk must be of such a nature and degree that, considering the nature and purpose of the actor's conduct and the circumstances known to him, its disregard involves a gross deviation from the standard of conduct that a law-abiding person would observe in the actor's situation.

(d) Negligently. A person acts negligently with respect to a material element of an offense when he should be aware of a substantial and unjustifiable risk that the material element exists or will result from his conduct. The risk must be of such a nature and degree that the actor's failure to perceive it, considering the nature and purpose of his conduct and the circumstances known to him, involves a gross deviation from the standard of care that a reasonable person would observe in the actor's situation.

(3) When the culpability sufficient to establish a material element of an offense is not prescribed by law, such element is established if a person acts purposely, knowingly or recklessly with respect thereto.

(4) When the law defining an offense prescribes the kind of culpability that is sufficient for the commission of an offense, without distinguishing among the material elements thereof, such provision shall apply to all the material elements of the offense, unless a contrary purpose plainly appears.

NOTES

The first thing that should be observed about the Code is that it seeks to resolve the chaos discussed by Remington and Helstad, *supra,* by limiting the kinds of culpability to four: purposely, knowingly, recklessly, and negligently. One commentator has called this the Code's "most significant and enduring achievement, a thoughtful definition of distinct levels of culpability." Robinson, *A Brief History of Distinctions in Criminal Culpability,* 31 Hastings L. J. 815 (1980). Other countries, currently in the throes of criminal codification and reform, have effectively followed the Code's lead in this regard, even though the definitions of some of the terms may vary somewhat. Thus, the Canadian Criminal Law Reform Commission has recommended that to be criminally liable for a "purposeful" crime, one must act "purposely" as to either conduct or consequences and knowingly or recklessly as to the circumstances. Recodifying Criminal Law (1987). Furthermore, the Commission would characterize as "reckless" a person who acted "purposely" as to the conduct and "recklessly" as to the consequences or circumstances. The Commission defines "recklessly" as acting "conscious that such consequences will probably result, or that such circumstances probably obtain." 2(4)(b). An alternate phrasing would require that the defendant "consciously take . . . a risk, which in the circumstances known to him is highly unreasonable to. . . . "*

The Codification of the Criminal Law: A Report to the Law Commission (1985) of the Academic Group in England has also followed the Code in limiting the levels of criminal culpability. It provides that a person acts "recklessly" with regard to a result or an attendant circumstance when "(i)he is aware of a risk that it exists or will exist or occur; and (ii)it is, in the circumstances known to him, unreasonable to take the risk." § 22(a) (1985). The Report also employs "heedlessly," defined as "(giving) no thought to whether there is a risk that it exists or will exist or occur although the risk would be obvious to any reasonable person," § 22(a). However, the proposal then goes on to say that "recklessly" is the default position of the proposed Code. *Id.,* § 24.

[B] Analysis of "Material Elements"

Model Penal Code § 2.02(1) seeks to resolve the question raised in *Cotterill, X-Citement Video,* and the problem cases by providing that a culpability element must apply to every "material element" of an offense. Thus, assuming for the moment that "house pigeon" is a "material element" of the offense in *Cotterill,* a "culpability" level must be applied to that element as well as to the verb *kills.* This approach (known as *element analysis*) is carefully analyzed in Robinson and Grall, *Element Analysis in Defining Criminal Liability: The Model Penal Code and Beyond,* 35 Stan. L. Rev. 681 (1983).

But this approach requires that we must first determine that a term in the statute in question is a "material element." This requires exploration of the definition of the term in the Code. § 1.13 of the Code provides that:

(9) "element of an offense" means (i)such conduct or (ii)such attendant circumstances or (iii)such a result of conduct as

(a) is included in the description of the forbidden conduct in the definition of the offense; or

(b) establishes the required kind of culpability; or

(c) negatives an excuse or justification for such conduct; or

(d) negatives a defense under the statute of limitations; or

(e) establishes jurisdiction or venue;

(10) "material element of an offense" means an element that does not relate exclusively to the statute of limitations, jurisdiction, venue or to any other matter similarly unconnected with

(i) the harm or evil, incident to conduct, sought to be prevented by the law defining the offense, or

(ii) the existence of a justification or excuse for such conduct.

Some words or phrases in statutes are, intuitively, elements and material elements. Thus, in *Cotterill,* it is apparent that both *kills* and *house pigeon* must be material elements—if the defendant killed a "condor" or "touched"

---

* See Model Penal Code § 2.02(2)(c), *supra.*

but did not "wound" a homing pigeon, the statute would not be violated. In the terms of the Code, these words relate to "the harm or evil. . . sought to be prevented by the law defining the offense." Thus one would characterize "house pigeon" as an attendant circumstance. But this conclusion is by negative inference—it is implausible that "house pigeon" is either a "result" or "conduct" and it therefore "must" be an "attendant circumstance." This awkwardness is made necessary by the Code's failure to define the term *attendant circumstance*—it seems closest to *facts* within the statutory framework. Whether one would characterize *kills* as conduct or result is less clear (see the discussion in § 4.05[E], *infra*), but it is obvious that it is a material element since if the defendant only touches the bird, the harm sought to be prevented (dead or wounded homing pigeons) has not occurred. Still, one must admit that at least some of this analysis is result-driven. Since an alternative reading (that "killing" or "house pigeon" is not a material element) would lead to absurd results, the conclusion is that they are material elements. In other instances, however, the point may be less evident. Take, for example, the following statute:

Any person who purposely discharges a gun in public is guilty of a misdemeanor.

Is "in public" a "material element" of the offense? Is "gun"? What is the "harm sought to be prevented" by the statute? Is it the prevention of loud noises or the possible endangerment of persons in public? The point here is not that a person who shoots a bow and arrow in public, or who causes a loud (nondangerous) explosion, should be convicted under this statute. Indeed, she cannot be convicted under the statute since she has not committed the *actus reus*. But depending on which purpose the statute is seen as serving (and therefore which facts are material elements with respect to which a defendant must act purposely), a defendant who purposely discharges an item that she does not believe is a gun, but that turns out to be a gun, or who purposely discharges what she knows to be a gun, but who believes that she is on private land, will or will not be convicted under the statute. Even the definition in MPC § 1.13(10) really leaves the question to intuition and common sense.

Again, consider a typical definition of *burglary* as "purposely breaking and entering a dwelling house in the nighttime." Is "dwelling house" a material element? Is "in the nighttime"?* Construct hypotheticals in which the defendant's guilt depends on whether these facts are or are not material elements.

[C] Recklessness as the "Default" *Mens Rea* Requirement

Suppose in the gun statute above the word *purposely* had not been included by the legislature. What is the requisite *mens rea* requirement? Leaving aside

---

* It should be noted, of course, that both "dwelling house" and "in the nighttime" have to be defined. The Code in fact does define both terms (or their analogues), but the common law grappled mightily with the latter term and somewhat tentatively with the former. Thus, for example, at what precise minute does nighttime occur? Again, is a hotel a dwelling house? What about a mobile home? Suppose there are no guests registered in the hotel when the burglary occurs, but the hotel is open to guests. Suppose the occupants of a house are gone on a four-week vacation, and the burglar knows this. These issues and many others are beyond the scope of this section and even this book. But they are not insignificant, and they become important in applying and interpreting the Code.

the possibility of strict criminal liability for the moment (see § 4.07, *infra*), it seems apparent that one of the four described *mens rea* should be necessary, but which? Here again, as *Garrett* (p. 245, *supra*) demonstrates, the courts had no fixed rule of statutory interpretation, and therefore had to struggle as to the "default" position—the floor below which criminal liability would not be imposed.

§ 2.02(3) of the Code deals with this situation by establishing as the "default" position a minimum requirement of recklessness. This rule is both procedural and substantive. Procedurally, it imposes upon the legislature the obligation to specify a *mens rea* requirement, and thus it hopes to focus the attention of the legislature on what that body really intends in a statute. Substantively, the section adopts the view in *Cunningham* that recklessness should be the minimum culpability the criminal law requires, at least unless the legislature expressly mandates that negligence [as defined by MPC § 2.02(d)] can be a predicate. This distinction between recklessness and negligence, and the unqualified preference for recklessness, embraces the view that only a defendant who subjectively is aware of his wrongdoing should, at least presumptively, be subjected to criminal liability. As Robinson and Grall, *supra* at 695–96, put it:

> A person acts "recklessly" with respect to a result if he consciously disregards a substantial risk and acts only "negligently" if he is unaware of a substantial risk he should have perceived. The narrow distinction lies in the actor's awareness of risk. The distinction, one of the most critical to criminal law, between negligence and all three higher levels of culpability, reflects that a defendant acting purposely, knowingly, or recklessly is aware of the harmful consequences that may result and is therefore both blameworthy and deterrable, but a defendant acting negligently is unaware of harmful consequences and therefore is (arguably) neither blameworthy nor deterrable. While most reject this view of negligent culpability, all nonetheless recognize that negligence represents a lower level of culpability, qualitatively different from recklessness because the negligent actor fails to recognize, rather than consciously disregards, a risk. For this reason, recklessness is considered the norm for criminal culpability, and negligence is punished only in the exceptional case.

Thus, the legislature is required to expressly state that a crime may by committed negligently.

In contrast to the Model Penal Code, the Canadian Commission, *supra,* has recommended that "purposely" be the default position of criminal culpability. Which approach is better? Is there a serious philosophical or moral issue involved in that question?

[D] Conflicts between Subsections (3) and (4) of MPC § 2.02

MPC § 2.02(4) provides a critical rule of statutory interpretation when the legislature has articulated at least once in the statutory provision at issue a culpability requirement. But however salutary this is (and it is), there are possible conflicts with MPC § 2.02(3). Consider, for example, the following statute:

Any person who, while driving a red car, negligently causes the death of another is guilty of vehicular homicide.

Assume that "red car" is a material element of the crime. If so, must the actor be reckless as to whether she is so driving, or will negligence as to this element suffice? The issue is made even more difficult because the legislature possibly could have written the statute as follows:

Any person who negligently causes the death of another while negligently driving a red car is guilty of vehicular homicide.

The question, then, is not only how one should interpret the first statute absolutely, but whether (and, if so, how) one should consider the fact that the legislature did *not* write the statute as it could have. Although MPC § 2.02(4) gives wonderful guidance to a statute that at least is fairly well drawn (and means that the legislature does not have to repeat the mental culpability required before every attendant circumstance and result element), it also potentially conflicts with MPC § 2.02(3) when the legislature has been partially, but not fully, attentive to these questions.

[E] Mixed Elements

The Code attempts to distinguish between "conduct" elements and "result" elements of a statute. But, as Robinson and Grall, *supra,* have pointed out, many verbs have both a "result" and a "conduct" aspect to them, at least unless "conduct is restricted solely to a description of muscular action." Thus, for example, *kill* (as in *Cotterill*) and *discharge* (as in the hypothetical statute above) are verbs suggesting both a conduct aspect and a result aspect. Should that be the interpretation? Or should one interpretation be preferred over the other (*i.e.,* that the legislature wished all such verbs to be viewed as describing a "result" rather than describing "conduct")? In what situations might the distinction make a difference to the liability of a defendant?

[F] Interpretation Problems

(1) You are the prosecutor when the facts of *Faulkner (supra,* p.230) come to your office. Consider §§ 220.1(1) (arson), 220.2 (causing a catastrophe), 220.3 (criminal mischief), 221.0 *et seq.* (burglary) and 221.2 (criminal trespass) of the MPC, *infra,* App. With which of these offenses, and what degree, do you think you can (successfully) charge Faulkner? What are the likely statutory interpretation issues you will face?

(2) MPC § 242.7 provides, "A person commits a misdemeanor if he [surreptitiously or contrary to law, regulation, or order of the detaining authority] introduces within a detention facility or [surreptitiously or contrary to law, regulation, or ordinance of the detaining authority] . . . provides an inmate with any weapon, tool or other thing which may be useful for escape."

(a) Which of these words are "results"? Which are "attendant circumstances"?

(b) Consider the defendant's liability in the following hypotheticals and analyze them under MPC § 242.7:

1. D gives A, whom he knows to be an inmate, a package of cigarettes. D knows there is a rule against this, but has no understanding that in prison cigarettes, as "coin of the realm," may be used to bribe other inmates for items (such as knives) or to obtain information that would be useful in attempting an escape.

2. Same hypothetical, except that A, a trustee, is acting as a secretary in the warden's office and is dressed in civilian clothes so D does not know he is an inmate.

3. I is an inmate of a halfway house. D, a plumber called to fix a leak, is not aware that the building is a halfway house, and sells I a wrench.

§ 4.06 THE IMPACT OF MISTAKE

What happens if a citizen commits a crime "by mistake"? Suppose that George sells a white powder believing it to be salt, but it turns out to be cocaine? Or suppose that he knows that it is cocaine, but believes (mistakenly) that cocaine is no longer contraband? Has George sold cocaine "purposely," "knowingly," "recklessly," or (criminally) "negligently" in violation of the criminal law? With a "vicious will"? Common law courts did not ask the question in such a way. Instead, it appears that they separated these mistakes into two separate, watertight compartments, labeled "law" and "fact," and treated them diametrically differently. As you survey these materials, consider whether the distinction drawn by the common law makes sense.

[A] Mistake or Ignorance of Fact

The case law is replete with situations where actors violate criminal statutes but claim that they were mistaken about or ignorant of a factual matter relating to the offense and thus lack criminal responsibility. Such claims, when legally recognized, are based on the theory that the actor lacked *mens rea* as a result of his mistake or ignorance in either of two ways: 1) in a general sense because the mistake or ignorance excuses the actor from moral accountability for his actions even though he engaged in the prohibited conduct with the requisite specific *mens rea*; or 2) in a specific sense because the mistake or ignorance prevents the actor from formulating the specific mental state necessary to commit the crime. While the distinction between "excuses" and "failures of proof," among others, is taken up in detail in Chapter 9, it is useful for present purposes to consider whether mistake or ignorance in the following cases operates to excuse offenders even though they possessed the specific *mens rea* required for the crime charged or renders them not guilty because their mistake or ignorance precluded formulation of the required *mens rea*.

TURNER, *THE MENTAL ELEMENT IN CRIMES AT COMMON LAW*

6 Cambridge L. J. 31, 36 (1934)

The doctrine that "mistake" may in certain cases be a valid defense has been built upon the basis of the early idea of moral guilt. It is hard to impute moral guilt to a man who had been mistaken as to facts which would have made his conduct harmless if things had been as he supposed. But in order to obtain immunity for him it was necessary to treat his mistake as rendering his conduct not really voluntary. Thus Sir Matthew Hale, writing in the Seventeenth century, said, "But in some cases *ignorantia facti* does excuse, for such an ignorance many times makes the act itself morally involuntary."

STATE V. MCDONALD

St. Louis Court of Appeals

7 Mo. App. 510 (1879)

Lewis, P. J., *delivered the opinion of the court.*

The defendant, a car-driver and conductor of the Lindell Railway, was convicted in the Court of Criminal Correction of an assault and battery committed upon the person of Oscar Wielns. The only question raised by the appeal is whether, when a passenger on a street-car has in fact paid his fare, the conductor is justified in forcibly ejecting him from the car, because he, the conductor, honestly believes that the passenger has not paid his fare, but persistently refuses so to do.

If this were a civil action for damages, there can be no question that the passenger, in the case stated, would be entitled to recover. When a passenger on a street-car has dropped his fare in the box provided and placed for that purpose, he has an absolute right to remain on the car, in an orderly manner, until it reaches his destination on the line of the railway. If the conductor, nevertheless, assuming that the fare is not paid, violates the passenger's right by putting him off the car, he manifestly does so at his peril, in so far as any question of indemnification may arise. If one wilfully destroys my property, honestly believing it to be his own, it will be no defence, against my claim for indemnity, to say that he made a mistake about the ownership. The law protects me in my property against intentional wrong-doers. If in such case either party must suffer, it should, by every rule of fairness and common sense, be he who made the mistake, rather than the other. A peaceable citizen deprived of his rights in a public conveyance, and subjected to gross indignity besides, is not to be denied redress because the servant in charge was not sufficiently observant to know the true state of the case. The learned judge who heard this cause in the court below evidently recognized these general principles, but he erred in holding them applicable to a criminal prosecution. There is here no question of indemnity to the person injured. The only question is, has the defendant committed a crime against the peace and dignity of the State?

Crime cannot exist without a criminal intent. A man at midnight discovers an intruder on his premises, under circumstances which furnish reasonable cause to apprehend that a felony is in progress or about to be perpetrated. He kills the supposed burglar, in the honest belief that nothing less will save his own life or property. It turns out that the intruder was innocent of any criminal purpose, yet his slayer has committed no crime, either in morals or in law, deserving punishment. The criminal intent was wanting. A person passes counterfeit money, being ignorant of its character and honestly believing it to be genuine; the one who receives it may recover for the wrong done him, notwithstanding the innocent mistake of the passer. And yet, an indictment against the passer of the money would fail, because he was guilty of no criminal intent. In the case before us, according to the facts stated, the defendant honestly believed that he was simply discharging his duty in putting off a passenger who refused to pay his fare, and therefore, in so doing he committed no crime. The court erred in giving instructions in support of a contrary view, and in refusing instructions prayed for by the defendant which were in harmony with the principles herein declared.

The judgment is reversed and the cause remanded.
All the judges concur.

STERN v. THE STATE

Supreme Court of Georgia

53 Ga. 229 (1874)

Myers Stern was tried at the November term, 1873, of the county court of Clarke county for the offense of allowing a minor, Frank Talmadge, to play at billiards without the consent of his parent or guardian. The evidence made out a *prima facie* case for the state, but for defense it was shown that Stern, before allowing Talmadge to play on his table had inquired as to his age and had been informed by said minor that he was an adult; that he appeared to be over twenty-one years of age, and that he was, in fact, within six months of maturity at the time that he indulged in the aforesaid game.

The county court refused to consider this testimony holding that upon proof of the playing of the game with the knowledge of the defendant, of the minority of Talmadge, and of the absence of the consent of his parent or guardian, conviction was the inevitable result.

The case was carried by certiorari to the superior court, where the judgment of the county court was affirmed, and defendant excepted.

McCay, Judge.

We agree with the counsel for the plaintiff in error that the county judge did not take a proper view of the law on the trial. To make a crime, there must be the union of act and intent, or there must be criminal negligence. It is not conclusive evidence of guilt on the part of the defendant that he permitted this young man to play at his table; that the young man was, in fact, a minor, and that the parent did not consent. These facts, it is true, make a prima facie case, and if they stood alone, the guilt of the defendant would be manifest; but evidently there was evidence of another element in the case, which, by the return of the county judge, is shown not to have been considered by him in arriving at his conclusion. There was evidence going to show that the defendant might have been honestly mistaken as to the age of the young man. It is clear to us that if the defendant, after due diligence, thought honestly that this young man was not a minor, he is not guilty. If he did so think, after proper inquiry, the element of intent does not exist; the act was done under a mistake of fact. In such a case, there is no guilt and no crime. This is the doctrine of all the books, and is, besides, common sense and common justice.

Nor is there anything in the nature of this offense which alters the rule. If one who shoots down his dearest friend by mistake, supposing him to be a dangerous wild beast or a burglar, is not guilty of any crime, surely he who permits a minor to play billiards without the consent of the parent, under the honest belief that he is not a minor but of full age, is not guilty. In both cases, however, to excuse the guilt there must be no want of proper caution on the part of the accused. He must have used due diligence, according to the circumstances and the nature of the case. But if he does this, and the evidence shows that after such caution he is still honestly mistaken, he is not guilty. We are not prepared to say that the evidence here is conclusive of an honest mistake. We do not say that the defendant was bound to have inquired of the parent. That would depend on his accessibility, and on the strength of the other circumstances indicating full age. It is impossible to lay down any general rule. Each case must depend on its own nature and circumstances. From the very nature of this offense special diligence is necessary. Everybody knows that there is uncertainty in such cases, and as the law has made the age of any billiard-player important, even in spite of this liability to mistake, every saloon keeper should act in view of the fact that he is dealing with an uncertain thing. As we have said, we do not think this evidence establishes conclusively that the defendant was honestly mistaken. We incline to the opinion of Judge Rice that there is some evidence to justify the finding, and had this conviction been by the verdict of a jury, under a legal charge as to the law, we should hesitate to disturb it. But the record shows the county judge did not consider the question of intention; he acted on the idea, that as the proof was clear of minority, the law had been violated, whatever might have been the honest opinion of the defendant. He held him to be bound to inquire of the parent—nay, on the general rule be acted on, he, perhaps, would have found him guilty if he had inquired of the parent—had the parent, either by mistake, or untruthfully, answered that the son was of age. It appears, therefore, that on the trial of this case, the judge, who acted as judge and jury, mistook the law, did not consider the evidence going to show an honest mistake, after due caution, and we send the case back to be tried again under a proper view of the law, to-wit the defendant is not guilty, if under all the circumstances, he honestly thought the young man not to be a minor, and the diligence required is that reasonable diligence which, in view of the nature of the case, a good citizen and prudent man would use.

Judgement reversed.

NOTES, QUESTIONS, AND RECOMMENDED READING

1. D, charged with sale of intoxicating liquors, sought to introduce evidence that the beverage in question—"bitters"—was not intoxicating and had been

pronounced by a United States government inspector not to require a government revenue stamp, which is required for intoxicants. The evidence was rejected by the trial court. What result on appeal? *Farrell v. State,* 32 Ohio St. 456 (1877). Was the status of the beverage a question of fact or question of law?

2. Consider the following provision of the West German Penal Code:

If a person in committing an offense did not know of the existence of factual circumstances which are part of the statutory definition of the offense, or which increase the punishment, then these circumstances may not be charged against him.

Accord: § 42, Norwegian Penal Code.

3. See generally Keedy, *Ignorance and Mistake in the Criminal Law,* 22 Harv. L. Rev. 75 (1908); Sendor, *Mistakes of Fact: A Study in the Structure of Criminal Conduct,* 25 Wake For. L. Rev. 707 (1990).

NOTES ON HONEST VERSES REASONABLE MISTAKES OF FACT

1. The court in *McDonald* acknowledges that the defendant intended to throw the passenger off, but says nevertheless that his mistake "negated" the "criminality" of this intent. What does that mean? Is it a metaphor? Is it a conclusion? In any event, the holding in *McDonald* is generally accepted as law. See *Commentary to Model Penal Code,* Tent. Draft#4, pp. 135–37 (1955). Nevertheless, a number of cases such as Stern suggest that to be a defense, the mistake made must be reasonable (made with due care). The case law is, at best, in some conflict. See, *e.g., Williams,* § 71. The first American indication that the mistake must be reasonable appears to have been dictum in an early case, *Myers v. Conn.,* 1 Conn. 502 (1816). Other early cases requiring the mistake be reasonable are self-defense cases, which may be *sui generis* [see, *e.g., Selfridge's Case,* 2 Am. St. Trials 544 (1806)], and which did not reflect the prior law. See Singer, *The Resurgence of* Mens Rea: *II—Honest but Unreasonable Mistake of Fact in Self Defense,* 28 B.C. L. Rev. 459 (1987). In later cases, primarily involving what would come to be called *public welfare offenses,* the courts imposed the requirement of reasonableness and put the burden of proof on the defendant. See, *e.g., Goetz v. State,* 41 Ind. 162 (1872). These cases, then, are the essential basis of the rule, prevalent in some states, that the mistake must be reasonable in order to excuse. Still others suggest that "a" or "the" difference as to whether a mistake must be reasonable to exonerate depends on whether the defendant is trying to justify or excuse her acts, see *infra,* § § 9.02, 9.03. This attack seems to suffer from the general problem of defining *justification*—just as McDonald might arguably be justifying his action ("it's allowed to throw off people who don't pay"), so Stern might be justifying his ("it's allowed to let people over 18 watch billiards"). For discussion of the general issue, see Hall, 343 ("The major defect in the Anglo-American criminal law on mistake of fact is the frequent requirement of —reasonableness"); Fletcher, *The Right and the Reasonable,* 98 Harv. L. Rev. 949 (1985); Howard, *The Reasonableness of Mistake in the Criminal Law,* 4

U. Queens. L. J. 45 (1961); Perkins, *Ignorance and Mistake in the Criminal Law,* 88 U. Pa. L. Rev. 35 (1939).

2. The Law Reform Commission of Canada has suggested that any mistake should be a defense to "serious" crimes, but that only a reasonable mistake should be allowed as a defense to less serious offenses. Is that position sound as a matter of policy?

3. Model Penal Code § 2.04 states

(1) Ignorance or mistake as to a matter of fact or law is a defense if: (a) the ignorance or mistake negates the purpose, knowledge, belief, recklessness or negligence required to establish a material element of the offense.

Most states have rejected this part of the MPC, preferring to require that the mistake be reasonable. Why?

4. Who decides what is a reasonable, as opposed to an honest, belief? See J. Bishop, Criminal Law 184 (8th ed. 1892):

In 1874, an Indian was tried in Washington Territory for the murder of another Indian. The defence was that he committed the homicide to save his wife from being killed through a pernicious power of the deceased. Evidence was introduced to show that, as expressed by Greene, J. in his charge to the jury, "the deceased Doctor Jackson was reputed to be a musatchee tomaawos man, a bad doctor man, a sorcerer, a man able at his will to bring unseen evil agencies to bear upon the bodies of the living; that he thus possessed the power of life and death over persons even at a distance from him, and over defendant's wife in particular; that, in defendant's presence, he threatened by use of this evil power to destroy the life of defendant's wife; that, in the presence of defendant, he professed and claimed that he by means of this power caused an actual sickness of defendant's wife, of which she lay dangerously ill at the time of his own death; that, in defendant's presence, he threatened he would cause this illness to terminate in her death; and that the only means of saving the life of defendant's wife was by killing this man, who claimed to wield over her such subtle and terrible power." It appeared in evidence that the defendant, and with him all his tribe, was born into the belief in musatchee tomaawos, and this belief controlled him in the homicide. The learned judge charged the jury that the law permitted one to kill another to save his wife's life, which the [deceased] was in the act of taking away; and though they would not themselves credit the deceased with the power attributed to him, yet if the defendant in good faith did, and this belief was a reasonable one in him, considering his education and surroundings, it would furnish him, under the circumstances proved, a good defence. And the jury acquitted him. *Territory v. Fish,* Olympia Transcript, April 11, 1874. If the learned judge committed any error in this case, it was in requiring that the mistaken belief should be a reasonable one for the defendant to entertain. I do not say that this direction was wrong, for it is supported by the language of many of the cases. Yet to my mind it would more certainly accord with just principle, and conform to other of the cases, to say that if without fault or carelessness the defendant in good faith entertained the belief, then [he should be acquitted].

See also *Williams,* 109 n. 13, relating a similar story.

The problem exists any time one culture seeks to exercise criminal jurisdiction over another culture. See generally, Mutungi, *Witchcraft and the Criminal Law in East Africa,* 5 Val. L. Rev. 524 (1971); Reedy, *A Remarkable Murder Trial; Rex. v. Sinnisiak,* 100 U. Pa. L. Rev. 48 (1951); Seidman, *Mens Rea and the Reasonable African: The Pre-Scientific World-View and Mistake of Fact,* 15 Int. and Comp. L. Q. 1135 (1966); Seidman, *Witch Murder and Mens Rea: A Problem of Society under Radical Social Change,* 28 Mod. L. Rev. 46 (1965).

PEOPLE v. RYAN

Court of Appeals of New York

82 N.Y.2d 497; 626 N.E.2d 51; 605 N.Y.S.2d 235 (1993)

KAYE, Chief Judge:

Penal Law § 220.18(5) makes it a felony to "knowingly and unlawfully possess . . . six hundred twenty-five milligrams of a hallucinogen." The question of statutory interpretation before us is whether "knowingly" applies to the weight of the controlled substance. We conclude that it does and that the trial evidence was insufficient to satisfy that mental culpability element. . . .

[T]he trial evidence revealed that on October 2, 1990 defendant asked his friend David Hopkins to order and receive a shipment of hallucinogenic mushrooms on his behalf. Hopkins agreed, and adhering to defendant's instructions placed a call to their mutual friend Scott in San Francisco and requested the "usual shipment." Tipped off to the transaction, on October 5 State Police Investigator Douglas Vredenburgh located the package at a Federal Express warehouse in Binghamton. The package was opened (pursuant to a search warrant) and resealed after its contents were verified. The investigator then borrowed a Federal Express uniform and van and delivered the package to Hopkins, the addressee, who was arrested upon signing for it.

Hopkins explained that the package was for defendant and agreed to participate in a supervised delivery to him. In a telephone call recorded by the police, Hopkins notified defendant that he got the package, reporting a "shit load of mushrooms in there." Defendant responded, "I know, don't say nothing." At another point Hopkins referred to the shipment containing two pounds. The men agreed to meet later that evening at the firehouse in West Oneonta.

At the meeting, after a brief conversation, Hopkins handed defendant a substitute package stuffed with newspaper. Moments after taking possession, defendant was arrested. He was later indicted for attempted criminal possession of a controlled substance in the second degree. . . .

[T]he police chemist testified that the total weight of the mushrooms in Hopkins' package was 932.8 grams (about two pounds), and that a 140 gram sample of the package contents contained 796 milligrams of psilocybin, a hallucinogen. He did not know, however, the process by which psilocybin appears in mushrooms, whether naturally, by injection or some other means.

Nor was there any evidence as to how much psilocybin would typically appear in two pounds of mushrooms. . . .

At the close of the People's case, defendant moved to dismiss for insufficient proof that he knew the level of psilocybin in the mushrooms, and also requested a charge-down to seventh degree attempted criminal possession, which has no weight element. Both applications were denied, defendant was convicted as charged, and he was sentenced as a second felony offender to 10 years-to-life.

The Appellate Division affirmed. The court held that a defendant must know the nature of the substance possessed, and acknowledged that the weight of the controlled substance is an element of the crime. The court declined, however, to read the statute as requiring that a defendant have actual knowledge of the weight. Instead, the court held that "the term 'knowingly' should be construed to refer only to the element of possession and not the weight requirement."

Finding ample evidence that defendant intended and attempted to possess psilocybin while knowing the nature of the substance, and that the weight of the psilocybin ultimately proved to be more than 625 milligrams, the Appellate Division sustained the conviction. Similarly, because there was no reasonable view of the evidence that the weight of the psilocybin in the mushrooms was less than 625 milligrams, the court rejected the argument that the trial court erred in refusing the charge-down. . . .

We now reverse.

Although the present case involves an attempt, analysis begins with the elements of the completed crime, second degree criminal possession of a controlled substance. Penal Law § 220.18(5) provides:

> A person is guilty of criminal possession of a controlled substance in the second degree when he knowingly and unlawfully possesses:

* * *

> 5. six hundred twenty-five milligrams of a hallucinogen.

It is undisputed that the knowledge requirement of the statute applies to the element of possession and that defendant must also have "actual knowledge of the nature of the possessed substance." . . . At issue is whether defendant must similarly know the weight of the material possessed. That is a question of statutory interpretation, as to which the Court's role is clear: our purpose is not to pass on the wisdom of the statute or any of its requirements, but rather to implement the will of the Legislature as expressed in its enactment. . . .

In effectuating legislative intent, we look first of course to the statutory language. Read in context, it seems evident that "knowingly" does apply to the weight element. Indeed, given that a defendant's awareness must extend not only to the fact of possessing something ("knowingly . . . possesses") but also to the nature of the material possessed ('knowingly . . . possesses . . . a hallucinogen"), any other reading would be strained. Inasmuch as the knowledge requirement carries through to the end of the sentence . . . eliminating it from the intervening element—weight—would rob the statute of its obvious meaning. We conclude, therefore, that there is a *mens rea* element associated with the weight of the drug.

That reading is fortified by two rules of construction ordained by the Legislature itself. First, a "statute defining a crime, unless clearly indicating a legislative intent to impose strict liability, should be construed as defining a crime of mental culpability" (Penal Law § 15.15[2]). . . . Converse ly, a crime is one of "mental culpability" only when a mental state "is required with respect to every material element of an offense" *(id.)*

By ruling that a defendant need not have knowledge of the weight, the Appellate Division in effect held, to that extent, that second degree criminal possession is a strict liability crime. That is an erroneous statutory construction unless a legislative intent to achieve that result is "clearly indicated" (Penal Law § 15.15[2]).

In a similar vein, the Legislature has provided in Penal Law § 15.15(1):

Construction of statutes with respect to culpability requirements.

1. When the commission of an offense defined in this chapter, or some element of an offense, requires a particular culpable mental state, such mental state is ordinarily designated in the statute defining the offense by use of the terms "intentionally," "knowingly," "recklessly" or "criminal negligence," or by use of terms, such as "with intent to defraud" and "knowing it to be false," describing a specific kind of intent or knowledge. When one and only one of such terms appears in a statute defining an offense, it is presumed to apply to every element of the offense unless an intent to limit its application clearly appears."

Accordingly, if a single *mens rea* is set forth, as here . . . it presumptively applies to all elements of the offense unless a contrary legislative intent is plain.

We discern no "clear" legislative intent to make the weight of a drug a strict liability element, as is required before we can construe the statute in that manner. Moreover, the overall structure of the drug possession laws supports the view that a defendant must have some knowledge of the weight.

There are six degrees of criminal possession of a controlled substance, graded in severity from a class A misdemeanor (Penal Law § 220.06 [seventh degree]) up to an A-I felony (Penal Law § 220.21 [first degree]). The definition of each begins identically: "A person is guilty of criminal possession of a controlled substance in the degree when he knowingly and unlawfully possesses * * *." The primary distinctions between one grade or another relate to the type and weight of the controlled substance, and in some instances the existence of an intent to sell (*e.g.,* Penal Law § 220.16[1]) or intent to sell combined with a prior drug conviction (*e.g.,* Penal Law § 220.09[13]).

Taking hallucinogens as an example, knowing and unlawful possession of any amount, even a trace . . . is seventh degree possession; 25 milligrams or more, fourth degree; 125 milligrams or more, third degree; and 625 milligrams, second degree. The maximum penalty for these crimes ranges from one year incarceration to a life sentence, yet the only statutory difference relates to the weight of the drugs. To ascribe to the Legislature an intent to mete out drastic differences in punishment without a basis in culpability would be inconsistent with notions of individual responsibility and proportionality prevailing in the Penal Law. . . .

In *People v. Reisman* . . . defendant—like defendant here—requested a charge-down to an offense that did not require possession of a specified amount. We rejected the claim that the trial court's failure to deliver the charge was error, first noting that the "weight of the contraband in the carton was uncontradicted." If defendant's knowledge of the weight were not anelement, and the only issue were the objective weight of the substance, that would have been sufficient to dispose of the claim, as it was for the Appellate Division here . . . But we continued:

> Moreover, the nature of the case and its circumstances depended entirely on a commercial-like shipment of the large quantity. The case could stand or fall on that proof and no other. Consequently, under no view of the facts, because there was no basis in any of the evidence, could the jury find the accused innocent of the higher crime and yet guilty of the misdemeanor which required no minimum quantity.

In the charge-down context, the Court's reference to the nature and circumstances of the case could only have been an allusion to defendant's knowledge of the weight.

In sum, the plain language of the statute, rules of construction, the format of the drug possession laws and our cases all lead to the conclusion that the Appellate Division erred in holding that there is no *mens rea* requirement associated with the weight of a controlled substance.

The People's contrary argument is based in part on a concern that it would be "prohibitively difficult," if not impossible, to secure convictions if they were required to prove that a defendant had knowledge of the weight. We disagree.

Often there will be evidence from which the requisite knowledge may be deduced, such as negotiations concerning weight, potency or price. . . . Similarly, for controlled substances measured on an "aggregate weight" basis (see, *e.g.,* Penal Law § 220.06[2]), knowledge of the weight may be inferred from defendant's handling of the material, because the weight of the entire mixture, including cutting agents, is counted. . . .

By contrast, that same inference may be unavailable for controlled substances measured by "pure" weight, like psilocybin. The effective doses of these drugs may be minuscule, and they are customarily combined with other substances to facilitate handling and use. In these circumstances it may indeed be difficult to show defendant's knowledge of the weight. Although we cannot simply read the knowledge requirement out of the statute, these "compelling practical considerations" may inform our interpretation of that element. . . .

The Legislature has decided that persons who illegally possess larger quantities of controlled substances should be punished more severely; their conduct is more repugnant and presents a greater threat to society. Because drug possession is not a strict liability crime, however, an individual is not deserving of enhanced punishment unless he or she is aware that the amount possessed is greater. A purpose of the knowledge requirement, then, is to avoid over-penalizing someone who unwittingly possesses a larger amount of a controlled substance than anticipated.

That legislative purpose can be satisfied, among other ways, with evidence that the pure weight of the controlled substance possessed by defendant is typical for the particular form in which the drug appears. This correlation between the pure weight typically found, and the pure weight actually possessed, substantially reduces the possibility that a person will unjustly be convicted for a more serious crime.

To illustrate: a person may knowingly possess 50 doses of LSD on blotter paper but, understandably, have no awareness what the pure LSD weighs; upon chemical analysis it is determined that defendant actually possessed 2.5 milligrams. If there is evidence that a typical dose of LSD weighs .05 milligrams . . . the jury could conclude, within the meaning of the statute, that defendant knowingly possessed more than 1 milligram, and convict of fourth degree possession (Penal Law § 220.09[5] [1 mg. or more]). If, however, because of some manufacturing defect unknown to defendant those 50 doses weighed 10 milligrams, defendant should not be convicted of more serious third degree possession (Penal Law § 220.16[9] [5 mg. or more]).

There may of course be other ways of proving defendant's knowledge within the meaning of the statute. Our purpose today, however, is not to survey all of the permissible methods but to clarify that the statute does in fact contain a weight-related mental culpability element.

With the foregoing principles in mind, we consider whether there was sufficient evidence to convict defendant of attempted second degree possession, an A-II felony.

[The Court concluded that the evidence was insufficient, but continued:]

That deficiency does not absolve defendant of all criminal liability. There is sufficient evidence to sustain a conviction for the lesser-included offense of attempted criminal possession of a controlled substance in the seventh degree, which does not have a weight element.

Order reversed and indictment dismissed with leave to the People to institute such proceedings as they deem appropriate. . . .

NOTES AND QUESTIONS

1. Note that *Ryan* holds that the defendant must know that the item possessed, or sold, is contraband. A contrary view existed for many years in the United States, where cases prior to 1970 usually held that defendant could be convicted even if she had no idea she was carrying drugs. This appears to have followed the 1932 Uniform Narcotic Drug Act (UNDA), which had been adopted by all 50 states. In 1970, however, the National Conference of Commissioners on Uniform State Laws rewrote the UNDA, explicitly requiring knowledge for a possession conviction. As of 1980, 42 states had legislatively adopted this approach. For English law, see *Warner v. Metropolitan*

Police Commissioner, (1969) A. C. 256. See also *Lockyer v. Gibb* (1966), 2 All E.R. 653. In *Beaver v. Queen,* (1957) S.C.R. 531 (Can.), the Supreme Court of Canada held that a defense of absense of knowledge would be valid, stressing that the statute provided a lengthy prison term for its violation.

2. *Ryan* goes further than many courts might, since it requires knowledge of factors that enhance sentencing. In a similar case, the sentencing court refused to impose a 10-year mandatory minimum sentence for possession of more than a kilogram of heroin when it found, as a matter of fact, that the defendant did not know, and could not reasonably have anticipated, that the attaché case she received contained so much heroin. On appeal, the Second Circuit reversed, holding the *finding* unsubstantiated, but apparently agreeing with the basic premise that to impose such a harsh sentence required proof of knowledge, or at least of (criminal) negligence. See *United States v. Ekwunoh,* 12 F.3d 368 (2d Cir. 1993). On remand, however, the District Court adhered to its earlier factual finding and legal conclusion. *United States v. Ekwunoh,* 888 F. supp. 369 (E.D.N.Y. 1994). The common law appears to have been much more stringent, imposing strict liability with regard to "sentencing factors." See, e.g., note 5, following *Prince, infra,* p. 312, and *McMillan, infra* p. 720.

In this regard, consider *Feola v. United States,* 420 U.S. 671 (1975), where the Supreme Court held that defendants who assaulted an undercover federal agent, not knowing of his official position, could nevertheless be convicted of assault on a federal officer. The case might, however, merely stand for the proposition that knowledge of a factor that grants jurisdiction to the federal courts is irrelevant to conviction of such a crime. See also *United States v. Brandon,* 17 F.3d 409 (1st Cir. 1994).

To test this, consider the following situation:

An English statute made assault a crime punishable by one year in prison, but an assault on a clergyman returning from divine service was deemed aggravated assault, with a two-year penalty (Section 36 of the Offenses against the Person Act [1861]). Consider the following cases and determine which crime D has committed:

   a. D intends to attack A, whom he knows is not a clergyman, but instead attacks B, mistaking him for A. B is a clergyman returning from service.

   b. D intentionally attacks B, whom he knows is a clergyman, but, unknown to him, B has just performed a divine service.

   c. D intends to attack B, a clergyman whom he knows has just performed a divine service. Instead, D mistakenly attacks V, believing V to be B.

Suppose, now, that the penalties for the crimes were the same, but were merely given different names. Would your answers change? If so, what is the holding of *Feola?*

Note On "Willful Blindness"

The requirement that the defendant "know" the facts is subject to one clearly recognized exception. Dubbed the "willful blindness" rule, it forbids the defendant to plead mistake (or ignorance) of facts where there is every reason for him to actually apprise himself of the facts, but he deliberately takes steps to avoid "knowing." There is little debate about this rule, and it appears to be well accepted. See Williams pp. 157–9; J. L. Edwards, *Mens Rea* in Statutory Offenses ch. 9 (1955); Husak and Callendar, *Wilful Ignorance, Knowledge, and the "Equal Culpability" Thesis: A Study of the Deeper Significance of the Principle of Legality,* 1994 Wisc. L. Rev. 29. Cf. Perkins, *"Knowledge" as a* Mens Rea *Requirement,* 29 Hastings L. Q. 953 (1978); Note, 102 Yale L. J. 2231 (1993). Thus in *United States v. Jewell,* 532 F.2d 697 (9th Cir. 1976), defendant agreed to drive a car from Mexico to the United States for $100. He looked over the vehicle and found nothing, concluding that customs agents would also fail to find anything *if anything was there.* Defendant was convicted of *knowingly* possessing marijuana hidden in a secret compartment in the car.

What if the "ignorance" is due, not to a conscious desire not to "know," but to a "dependent, childlike character structure by which defendant unconsciously needed" to believe that these men (her lover and other acquaintances) would never involve her in illegal activities? See *United States v. Bright,* 517 F.2d 584 (2d Cir. 1975) (evidence that the defendant did not consciously "know" that checks she possessed were stolen because she "needed" to trust her boyfriend).

[B] Ignorance and Mistake of Law

[1] Ignorance of Law

UNITED STATES v. MONCINI

United States Court of Appeals for the Ninth Circuit

882 F.2d 401 (1989)

FLETCHER, Circuit Judge:

Alessandro Moncini, a citizen and resident of Italy, appeals his conviction under 18 U.S.C. § 2252(a) for mailing child pornography from Italy to an undercover officer in the United States. . . .

FACTS

Moncini was contacted by Detective William H. Dworin of the Los Angeles Police Department after Dworin discovered Moncini's name and address in a search of an American pornography collector. Dworin sent Moncini a letter containing a photograph of a nude girl, inquiring whether Moncini would be interested in trading child pornography. Dworin led Moncini to believe the American pornography collector was a mutual acquaintance.

Moncini wrote back and asked for more pictures. Dworin complied, but Moncini did not reciprocate by sending similar pictures in return. Dworin eventually asked Moncini to send him some child pornography, offering to send Moncini more explicit material if Moncini would send him child pornography to prove his involvement "with the young ones." Moncini responded by sending some pages torn from a commercially sold pornography magazine. He subsequently mailed additional pictures and a videotape. Moncini concedes that these pictures and videotape were child pornography of the type proscribed by 18 U.S.C. § 2252.

Moncini was arrested when he arrived in New York in early 1988. He was tried in the Central District of California, which includes Valencia, the place to which the photos were sent. His motion to dismiss the indictment for lack of jurisdiction was denied on the ground that the mailings were continuing offenses which continued to take place as Moncini's letters traveled from Italy to California, giving the court territorial jurisdiction. . . .

Moncini waived jury trial. His principal defense was ignorance of the law. The district court received uncontroverted evidence in the form of an affidavit by a former member of the Italian bar that the mailing of child pornography is legal in Italy so long as it is not for commercial purposes or purposes of public display. Moncini asserts that he was unaware that his mailing of child pornography was a crime in the United States. The court convicted him and sentenced him to a year-and-a-day custodial sentence. He has completed his sentence and is now at liberty.

* * *

ANALYSIS

B. *Mens Rea*

Moncini argues that the statutory language "any person who . . . knowingly . . . mails any visual depiction," 18 U.S.C. § 2252(a) requires the government to prove that he knew his mailings were illegal under federal law. In the alternative, Moncini argues that the failure to require such proof of *mens rea* violates due process. We review these legal claims *de novo*.

1. Statutory *Mens Rea*. Section 2252(a) requires that the government prove that the defendant had knowledge of the nature of the contents of the visual depictions and that the depictions were to be transported or shipped in interstate or foreign commerce or mailed. . . . See *United States v. Brown*, 862 F.2d 1033, 1036 (3d Cir. 1988) (recipient must know that material received is child pornography but need not know precise contents of material). . . . Attempts to expand on this knowledge requirement have consistently failed. . . . We agree with the government that there is no basis for reading such a *mens rea* requirement into § 2252.

Moncini bases his statutory interpretation argument on cases construing the word *knowingly* under other statutes. However, what these statutes have in common, and what serves to distinguish them from § 2252(a), is that they all incorporate knowledge of illegality as an element of the offense. Under these statutes, the illegality is a fact of which the defendant must be aware to have the necessary *mens rea*.

For example, 31 U.S.C. § 1101 (1976), construed in *United States v. Granda,* 565 F.2d 922 (5th Cir. 1978), required any person who "knowingly" brought over $5,000 into this country to fill out a certain form; another statute, 31 U.S.C. § 1058 (1976), made it a crime "willfully" to fail to fill out this form. The court held that conviction under these statutes requires proof that the defendant knew of the reporting requirement. . . .

The decision in *Liparota v. United States,* 471 U.S. 419 (1985), is similarly distinguishable. [That case] construed 7 U.S.C. § 2024(b), which makes it a crime to "knowingly . . . acquire [food stamps] . . . in any manner not authorized by [law]." Under § 2024(b), the illegality of the acquisition is itself an element of the crime, and the word *knowingly* as used in that statute can logically be interpreted to refer to knowledge of that illegality. . . . However, as *Liparota* makes clear, § 2024(b) does not include a general "mistake of law" defense, under which a defendant could claim that he did not know it was illegal to acquire food stamps in an unauthorized manner. . . . As an additional example, *Liparota* notes that it is a defense to a charge of receiving stolen goods that one did not know the goods were stolen, even though this mistake might hinge on a mistake of law. . . by contrast, it is not a defense that one did not know that receipt of stolen goods is illegal.

The crucial difference between 7 U.S.C. § 2024(b) and 18 U.S.C. § 2252 is that the language of the former contains a genuine problem of grammatical scope: the adverb *knowingly* in § 2024(b) could conceivably modify "acquire" alone, or "acquire" in conjunction with "in any manner not authorized [by law].". . . By contrast, the word *knowingly* in § 2252(a) can at most be construed to modify "mails" in conjunction with "any visual depiction [as defined by the statute]." Thus the government must prove that the defendant had knowledge of the contents of the visual depictions and knowledge that they were to be mailed, but there is simply no reference to illegality in § 2252 which the word *knowingly* could similarly be construed to modify.

2. Constitutional Limitations. Moncini argues that without a mistake of law defense, § 2252(a) is unconstitutional as applied to him, a foreigner, for acts committed in his own country and legal there, where there is no provision in the statute to give him notice that his conduct could result in criminal sanctions in the United States. In other words, Moncini argues that the due process clause imposes limitations on the applicability of the maxim, "ignorance of the law is no excuse."

Where the defendant had whatever mental state was required for the commission of the crime and only claims that he was unaware that his conduct was proscribed by the criminal law, a mistake of law defense is seldom recognized. . . .

We do not find this to be an appropriate case in which to recognize an exception. Even assuming Moncini was ignorant of the law as he claims, he must bear the risk of the potential illegality of his conduct. . . . The child pornography laws are directly related to a commonly understood moral censure. The very nature of child pornography, which is commonly regulated throughout the world, should cause a reasonable person to investigate the laws of the United States before sending such material into this country. . . . This is not a case where due process prohibits convicting a defendant who has unwittingly broken the law through conduct which an ordinary person would not assume to be at least potentially criminal. See *Lambert v. California* [355 U.S. 255 (1957] . . . .[28]

In [*United States v. Freed,* 401 U.S. 60 (1971),] a federal statute required the registration of hand grenades. The Court upheld this law despite the fact that the statute did not require knowledge of the registration requirement, noting that "one would hardly be surprised to learn that possession of hand grenades is not an innocent act."

Moncini's conviction is. . . AFFIRMED.

NOTES AND QUESTIONS

1. *In The Matter of Etiene Barronnet and Edmond Allain,* 1 E.L. 7 B.L., 118 Eng. Rep. 337 (1852). Defendants, both Frenchmen who had fled to England for political asylum, acted as seconds in a duel in England. Their principal was killed, and they were prosecuted as aiders and abetters in his murder. (The actual shooter was apparently not located.) While pending trial, they moved for bail, which was denied. To their plea that duels were not only not illegal, but honorable acts in France, the court responded, "These two gentlemen . . . having come to this country, . . . are in precisely the same position as if they were native subjects. . . . We could not listen to a native who urged that he was ignorant of the law which he had transgressed; nor can we do so to a foreigner." Both judges strongly intimated that if the defendants were convicted, they should receive a royal pardon.

What result in *Moncini* or *Barronnet* under the Model Penal Code? See § § 2.04 and 2.02(2),(3),(4) and (9), *infra,* App.

2. *Rex v. Esop,* 7 Car. & P. 456, 173 Eng. Rep. 203 (1836), Esop was tried for an unnatural offense, committed on "board of an East India ship . . . He was native of Baghdad." His counsel argued that in his country, this was not a crime, and "a person who comes into this country and does an act, believing that it is a perfectly innocent one, cannot be convicted according to the law of England. A party must know that what he does is a crime. This is the principle upon which infants, idiots, and lunatics are held not to be answerable." The court rejected his argument, and trial proceeded; "if it is not a crime there, that does not amount to a defense here." Upon a finding that the witnesses for the prosecution acted under the influence of spite and ill will, the defendant was found not guilty.

3. The *Moncini* and *Baronnet* cases are predecessors to a current imbroglio about the so-called "cultural defense." What if the issue is confronted directly?

---

[28] In *Lambert,* a municipal ordinance made it illegal for a convicted felon to remain in Los Angeles for more than five days without registering. The Court held that this ordinance violated due process when applied to a person without actual knowledge of the registration requirement, where there was also no showing of the probability of such knowledge. 355 U.S. at 229–30. The Court emphasized that the crime of failing to register was "wholly passive," *id.* at 228, and that "circumstances which might move one to inquire as to the necessity of registration are completely lacking." *Id.* at 229.

Should a defendant have a defense if he is reared in a culture radically different from that of the jurisdiction bringing charges against him for violating one of its laws of which he is ignorant? For example: (1) a Japanese-American woman attempts to commit *oyakoshinju* (parent—child suicide) when she learns of her husband's infidelity; she lives, but her children die, and she is charged with the homicide; (2) a member of the Hmong tribe from the mountains of Laos living in the United States exercises his right under Hmong culture to execute his adulterous wife; (3) defendant, after an IRS audit, pays the agent an "honorarium" as is customary in defendant's native land. *United States v. Jung Yul Yu,* 954 F.2d 951 (3d Cir. 1991). In *People v. Wu, supra,* p. 191, the California appellate division upheld the trial court's consideration of the defendant's culture in determining her state of mind as she prepared to kill her son and then to commit suicide.

Most cases, however, involve the question of whether the defendant's cultural background is relevant at sentencing rather than in determining guilt. See *United States v. Natal Rivera,* 879 F.2d 391 (8th Cir. 1989) (assuming that sentencing guidelines preclude consideration of cultural background, no constitutional infirmity). In *United States v. Yu, supra,* the court found it unnecessary to decide whether the United States Sentencing Guidelines would allow a sentencing court to consider cultural differences, determining on the merits that the case here did not properly raise that issue. The court, citing only the *Esop* case, concluded that Congress could constitutionally prohibit such consideration.

For articles on the cultural defense, see Clinton, *Cultural Differences and Sentencing Departures,* 5 Fed. Sent. R. 348 (1993); Note, 99 Harv. L. Rev. 1293 (1986); Note, 16 Ga. J. Int'l & Comp. L. 335 (1986); Note, 27 Ind. L. Rev. 393 (1993); Comment, 9 Loy. L.A. Int'l & Comp. L. J. 751 (1987).

The concern raised by the cultural defense, of course, is that majority moral viewpoints, reflected in and reflective of, the criminal law, might become diluted by allowing subcultural viewpoints to immunize against criminal prosecution. In *Employment Division, Oregon Department of Human Resources v. Smith,* 494 U.S. 872 (1990), the Supreme Court concluded that states could constitutionally punish religiously mandated use of peyote by North American Church members, even though the use of peyote was infrequent, severely limited by church doctrine to especially important Church ceremonies, and carefully scrutinized by religious officials. Said the Court (494 U.S. at 872),

> Any society adopting [a contrary] system would be courting anarchy . . . in direct proportion to the society's diversity of religious beliefs. . . . [W]e cannot afford the luxury of deeming presumptively invalid as applied to the religious object every regulation of conduct that does not protect an interest of the highest order. It may fairly be said that leaving accommodation to the political process will place at a relative disadvantage those religious practices that are not widely engaged in; but that unavoidable consequence of democratic government must be preferred to a system in which each conscience is a law unto itself or in which judges weigh the social importance of all laws against the centrality of all religious beliefs.

Do you agree?

4. Defendants lived in Honduras, but were considering moving to South Carolina. Before they did so, they "had taken much pains to inform themselves whether there was any law of force in (the U.S.) which prohibited" the import of slaves. Finding none, they sailed for South Carolina in September. In November, South Carolina passed a law forbidding the importation of slaves. Thereafter, defendants landed in South Carolina, and the slaves were seized by the attorney general. In a suit for forfeiture, what result? Is this a question of mistake of law or ignorance of the law? See *Ham, qui tam v. McClaws,* 1 Bay's (S.C.) 93 (1789). See also *Rex v. Bailey,* Russ & Ty. 1, 168 Eng. Rep. 651 (1800); *The Cotton Planter,* 6 Fed. Cas. 620 (No. 3220) (C.C.N.Y. 1810).

5. Holmes 47–48:

Ignorance of the law is no excuse for breaking it. This substantive principle has been defended by Austin and others on the ground of difficulty of proof. If justice requires the fact to be ascertained, the difficulty of doing so is no ground for refusing to try. But every one must feel that ignorance of the law could never be admitted as an excuse, even if the fact could be proved by sight and hearing in every case. Furthermore, now that parties can testify, it may be doubted whether a man's knowledge of the law is any harder to investigate than many questions which are gone into. The difficulty, such as it is, would be met by throwing the burden of proving ignorance on the lawbreakers.

The principle cannot be explained by saying that we are not only commanded to abstain from certain acts, but also to find out that we are commanded. For if there were such a second command, it is very clear that the guilt of failing to obey it would bear no proportion to that of disobeying the principal command if known. . . .

The true explanation of the rule is the same as that which accounts for the law's indifference to a man's particular temperament, faculties, and so forth. Public policy sacrifices the individual to the general good. It is desirable that the burden of all should be equal, but it is still more desirable to put an end to robbery and murder. It is no doubt true that there are many cases in which the criminal could not have known that he was breaking the law, but to admit the excuse at all would be to encourage ignorance where the law-maker has determined to make men know and obey, and justice to the individual is rightly outweighed by the larger interests on the other side of the scales.

6. Bazelon, J., concurring in *United States v. Barker,* 514 F.2d 208, 230–232 (D.C. Cir. 1975):

The law's unwillingness to depart from the concept of absolute liability may be explained by the arguments traditionally advanced in support of the rule that ignorance or mistake of law is not a defense. . . . Those traditional arguments are three. First is that most concisely advanced by Jerome Hall:[1]

> To permit an individual to plead successfully that he had a different opinion or interpretation of the law would contradict the . . . postulates of a legal order. For there is a basic incompatibility between asserting that the law is what certain officials declare it to be . . . and asserting, also, that . . . the law is . . . what defendants or their lawyers believed it to be. A legal order implies the rejection of such contradiction.

---

[1] Hall,[General Principles of Criminal Law 361, 383 (2d ed. 1980)] . . .

On its face this argument would seem to ignore the distinction between justification for an act, which does indeed confirm its legality, and excuse for an act, which assumes illegality of the act but excuses the principal from criminal sanction because he did not freely choose to do wrong. The latter in principle implies no validation of the act. Indeed, it is in its nature an express rejection of any such view. Hall's argument also could not be that the law imposes an affirmative duty to discover what the law is since "it is very clear that the guilt of failing to obey [this duty] would bear no proportion to that of disobeying the principal command if known, yet the failure to know would receive the same punishment as the failure to obey the principal law."

Hall's argument assumes more substance when viewed in light of the second traditional argument usually attributed to Justice Holmes:[2]

> The true explanation of the rule is the same as that which accounts for the law's indifference to a man's particular temperament, faculties, and so forth. Public policy sacrifices the individual to the general good. . . . It is no doubt true that there are many cases in which the criminal could not have known that he was breaking the law, but to admit the excuse at all would be to encourage ignorance where the law-maker has determined to make men know and obey . . .

Holmes is not speaking of encouraging ignorance of the law-breaker but of encouraging ignorance of others. A failure to punish an actor might not be inconsistent with concepts of moral blameworthiness but very well might undermine the central purpose of the criminal law—"to induce external conformity to rule."

Holmes properly applies his argument in light of the purposes of the criminal law. The law in imposing absolute liability is not concerned with individual justice to the wrongdoer but with the interests of the injured party or his surviving kin and with the general reaction in society (both potential wrongdoers and those sympathetic with the injured party) to a failure to punish the act. The subtle question of the wrongdoer's intent is certainly of marginal interest to these citizens and their perception of the seriousness with which the criminal law accomplishes its purposes. Furthermore, by placing the wrongdoer in custody he may be prevented from committing more innocent, yet reprehensible acts in the future. The purpose of the criminal law is to protect society from harmful acts and if this interest were unbounded by other social interests there could be no limit to the amount or occasion of criminal punishment if it caused some marginal perception of a decrease in the incidence of harmful acts. In light of this purpose of the criminal law the existence of excusing conditions might seem anomalous indeed since it is the individuals who most likely will benefit from an excusing condition that need the greatest amount of deterrence.

The law does not fully accept this position and, to my mind, rightly so as the following countervailing arguments suggest. It does not seem realistic to assume that a purely objective criminal sanction will deter harmful acts by those who by definition did not think their actions were proscribed by law or otherwise lack the free choice not to perpetrate those harmful acts. This

---

[2] [O. Holmes, The Common Law 40, 48(1881)]. . .

is not merely an empirical statement, as the assertion that an absolute sanction will increase deterrence is not, since no evidence upon which the truth or accuracy of these propositions does exist or could exist. To determine the guilt or innocence of one person on the basis of the effect of that determination on others seems inconsistent with the concept that human beings should not be used as means to an end, but are ends in themselves. Furthermore, to determine the guilt or innocence of an individual on the basis of a prediction of future dangerousness involves the making of assumptions about individuals without a sound empirical basis, and would thus be inconsistent with modern notions of due process. To effect retribution upon an individual without consideration of his state of mind seems too barbarous for discussion and in any event the law has moved beyond retribution as a prime justification for the criminal sanction.

The question thus posed by these competing lines of argument is the extent to which the law accepts the concept of the free choice to do wrong as the basis for criminal liability. Holmes correctly recognized this fundamental question when he stated:

> If punishment stood on the moral grounds which are proposed for it, the first thing to be considered would be those limitations in the capacity for choosing rightly which arise from abnormal instincts, want of education, lack of intelligence, and all the other defects which are most marked in the criminal classes.

There is, to be sure, somewhat of a "regrettable peremptoriness of tone" to this statement inconsonant with modern sensibilities, but it phrases the question as bluntly as it should be phrased. Holmes rejects the notion that the law is enacted and administered solely on the moral grounds he has noted. However, few today would seriously dispute Judge Tuttle's observation that "the only way the law has progressed from the days of the rack, the screw and the wheel is the development of moral concepts. . . . " There is no reason to believe that this development ended in 1881. Thus, it may be seen that the tension between the two bodies of argument discussed above produces a delicate accommodation between interests of social order and individual rights, between vengeance and moral concepts of guilt. The law does not resolve these arguments. They exist in a perpetual but shifting balance producing disparate and at times illogical answers to various issues of criminal responsibility. The balance to be struck at any one point in time must not be gleaned from logical analysis of these arguments alone, but from conventional morality—the commonly held views of the people in the American community as viewed through their legal and political tradition.

7. For other true "ignorance" cases, see *Zakrasek v. State,* 197 Ind. 249, 150 N.E. 615 (1926); *Jellico Coal Min. Co. v. Comm.,* 96 Ky. 373, 29 S.W. 6 (1895); *State v. Hatch,* 64 N.J. 179, 313 A.2d 797 (1973).

8. Should there be a different approach with regard to administrative regulations, in contrast to state statutes? Consider *R. v. Ross* [1945], 3 D.L.R. 574, 1 WWR 590 (B.C. Co. Ct.). Defendant went on a hunting trip in a national park. The day after he left, an administrative declaration declaring the park off limits to hunters became effective. What result? Cf. *Johnson v. Sargant and Sons* [1918], 1 K.B. 101. In *United States v. International Minerals and*

Chemical Corp., [IMCC] 402 U.S. 558 (1971), defendant corporation moved to dismiss an indictment charging it with failure to comply with an ICC regulation requiring it to register and describe particular hazardous substances (acids) before transporting them because there was no allegation that they knew of the regulation. In reversing the trial court's granting of the dismissal, the Supreme Court, per Douglas, J., declared (402 U.S., at 565) that

> where . . . dangerous or deleterious devices or products or obnoxious waste materials are involved, the probability of regulation is so great that anyone who is aware that he is in possession of them or dealing with them must be presumed to be aware of the regulation.

Justice Stewart, joined by Harlan and Brennan, dissented (402 U.S., at 569):

> The only real impact of this decision will be upon the casual shipper who might be any man, woman or child in the nation. A person who had never heard of the regulation might make a single shipment. . . . It would be wholly natural for him to assume that he could deliver the article to the common carrier and depend upon the carrier to see that it was properly labeled and that the shipping papers were in order. Yet today's decision holds that a person who does just that is guilty of a criminal offense.

See also *United States v. Freed,* 401 U.S. 691 (1971) (also written by Justice Douglas, and holding that possessors of hand grenades cannot plead ignorance of a statutory requirement of registration upon transfer).

In *Lambert v. California,* 355 U.S. 255 (1957), however, the Court, per Mr. Justice Douglas, held that the defendant should have been allowed to introduce evidence that she was unaware of a city ordinance requiring her, as an exfelon, to register with the city police. Can the opinions of Justice Douglas in *Lambert* and *Freed—IMCC* be reconciled? Are all these cases merely regulation cases, or do they harbor a broader meaning? More recently, in *Liparota v. United States,* 471 U.S. 419 (1985), the Court, per Mr. Justice Brennan, held that under a statute penalizing anyone who "knowingly. . . possesse s [food] coupons in any manner not authorized by this chapter or the regulations issued pursuant to this chapter," the government was required to prove that the defendant knew that he was acting in violation of United States Department of Agriculture regulations. The Court expressly denied the case involved a mistake of law. *Id.,* at n. 9.

A federal statute provides that the appearance of rules and regulations in the Federal Register, which consists of roughly 75 to 80 volumes, gives legal notice of their contents. 44 U.S.C. § 307. Is this realistic? Is it even plausible? See *United States v. Freeman,* 535 F.2d 1251 (4th Cir. 1976).

These questions are explored in Note, *Ignorance of the Law as an Excuse,* 86 Colum. L. Rev. 1392 (1986), in which the author argues for a limited mistake of law defense where the defendant is engaged in "ordinary conduct" which turns out to be proscribed by statute or government regulation.

[2] Mistake of Law

Many so-called "ignorance of law" cases are really "mistake of law" cases, where the defendant knows that there is "some" law out there that might relate to her acts, but believes that the statute does not in fact reach that far. That belief can arise from a number of sources, including vague intuition. Perhaps those who rely on such intuition are suspect, or even reckless. But what about those who strive to bring themselves within the law? The common law was no more sympathetic to them, as the following materials show.

---

[a] Reliance on a Court

STATE V. STRIGGLES

Supreme Court of Iowa

202 Iowa 1318, 210 N.W. 137 (1926)

ALBERT, J.

It appears that in the early part of 1923 there was installed in several places of business in the city of Des Moines a gum or mint vending machine. The machine and its workings are fully set out in the opinion in the case of *State v. Ellis,* 200 Iowa 1228, 206 N.W. 105 [1925]. In that opinion it was judicially determined that such machine was a gambling device within the inhibition of the statute.

On August 1, 1923, in several proceedings then pending in the municipal court of the city of Des Moines, a decision was rendered holding that such machine was not a gambling device. The distributors of the machine in question thereupon secured a certified copy of said decree, and equipped themselves with a letter from the county attorney and also one from the mayor of the city, stating that such a machine was not a gambling device. Thus equipped they presented themselves to appellant, Striggles, who conducted a restaurant in the city of Des Moines, and induced him to allow them to install a machine in his place of business.

Subsequent thereto, in the early part of 1925, the Polk county grand jury returned an indictment against appellant in which it charged that he did "willfully and unlawfully keep a house, shop, and place . . . resorted to for the purpose of gambling, and he . . . did then and there willfully and unlawfully permit and suffer divers persons . . . to play a certain machine . . . being then and there a gambling device." [The appellant] offered in evidence the aforesaid certified copy of the judgment decree of the court, and the letters from the county attorney and the mayor, which were properly objected to and the objection sustained. The appellant while testifying was permitted by the court to say that the exhibits had been presented to him before he permitted the machine to be installed. He was then asked by his counsel whether he had relied on the contents of the papers when he gave his permission for installation of the machine. Objection to this line of testimony was sustained. He was also asked whether he would have permitted the machine to be installed had he believed it to be a gambling device. He was not permitted to answer this question.

It is first urged in this case that the certified copy of the judgment from the municipal court was admissible in evidence on the strength of the case of *State v. O'Neill,* 147 Iowa 513. . . . A careful reading of the case, however, shows that it has no application to the case at bar. A certain statute of this state was held to be violative of the Constitution of the United States, and therefore void, in *State v. Hanaphy,* 117 Iowa 15, . . . and *State v. Bernstein,* 129 Iowa 520. . . . The United States Supreme Court than decided *Delamater v. South Dakota,* 205 U.S. 93.*

On the strength of this opinion of the United States Court, we then overruled, the *Hanaphy* and *Bernstein* cases in *McCollum v. McConaughy,* 141 Iowa 172.

The crime with which O'Neill was charged was committed by him between the time of the filing of the opinion by this court and the filing of the opinion by the United States Supreme Court. We held in that case that the appellant could not be guilty because he was entitled to rely on the decision of this court, which held the law in question unconstitutional.

There is no case cited, nor can we find one on diligent search, holding that the decision of an inferior court can be relied upon to justify the defendant in a criminal case in the commission of the act which is alleged to be a crime. We are disposed to hold with the *O'Neill* case that, when the highest court of jurisdiction passes on any given proposition, all citizens are entitled to rely upon such decision; but we refuse to hold that the decisions of any court below, inferior to the Supreme Court, are available as a defense under similar circumstances.

The testimony offered, if available to the appellant, must be on the theory that it goes to prove his intention. It is settled law that in prohibitive statutes covering misdemeanors, where no provision is made as to intention, and the word "knowingly" or other apt words are not employed to indicate that knowledge is the essential element of the crime, intention is not an element of the crime. . . .

We are therefore of the opinion that the ruling of the district court in excluding this testimony was right.

The matters of which complaint is made should have been taken into consideration by the district court in passing sentence on a verdict of guilty, and this was apparently done in this case, as the fine assessed was the minimum.

---

* [The Iowa cases mentioned above involved the power of a state to regulate liquor in a way which, if applied to other goods, would clearly violate the dormant commerce clause. In *Hanaphy* and *Bernstein,* the Iowa Supreme Court had held that liquor was not different than other goods and that the state statutes were unconstitutional. Therefore salesmen soliciting sales of liquor by in-state purchasers from an out-of state producer were not committing crimes. In *Delamater,* the United States Supreme Court held that a similar statute in South Dakota was not unconstitutional, because Congress had, by statute, ceded some of its commerce clause authority to the states in cases of liquor regulation. The Iowa court thereupon *overruled, Hanaphy* and *Bernstein* in *McConaughy.* Are these cases apposite to a case like *Struggles?*—Eds.]

Affirmed.

NOTES AND QUESTIONS

1. In *Swincher v. Commonwealth,* 24 Ky. 1897, 72 S.W. 306 (1903), defendant was a private security guard who carried a gun pursuant to a statute allowing such persons to carry weapons, with certain minimal conditions. The court struck down the statute as unconstitutional ("the legislature could not constitutionally grant such extraordinary powers to private citizens as is here attempted") and then affirmed the defendant's conviction of carrying a concealed weapon. Is this consistent with a utilitarian viewpoint? With a retributivist viewpoint? Cf. *People v. Marrero,* 69 N.Y. 2d 382 (1987) (corrections officer who mistakenly construed statute to include him as "peace officer" who did not need permit to carry gun has no defense of mistake of law).

2. In *Brent v. State,* 43 Ala. 297 (1869), defendant was authorized, by legislative act, to raise funds for school system and was thereafter prosecuted for holding a lottery. Held: Even if the statute was illegal, "To permit the State to prosecute the said parties . . . for so doing, will be to permit the state to force advantage of its own wrong. . . . We cannot carry this rule of presumption to this extent; it must be confined to presuming that all persons know the law exists, but not that they are presumed to know how the courts will construe it. . . . To extend the rule . . . will be to implicate the legislature who passed, and the governor who approved, the act, in a charge of gross immorality and dishonesty."

3. If a defendant argues mistake of law because he did not believe his conduct came within the letter of the law, he will, as the preceding cases show, lose. But if he argues, instead, that the statute is so vague that no one could have understood the law, he may win. See, *e.g., Lanzetta v. New Jersey,* 306 U.S. 451 (1939); Note, *The Void-for-Vagueness Doctrine in the Supreme Court,* 109 U. Pa. L. Rev. 67 (1960). Is there any basis for such a distinction, or does the void for vagueness approach undermine the "mistake of law is no excuse" maxim? See Cass, *Ignorance of the Law: A Maxim Re-examined,* 17 Wm. & Mary L. Rev. 671 (1976). Compare Hall 382:

> A defensible theory of *ignorantia juris* must find its origin in the central fact noted above, namely, that the meaning of the rules of substantive penal law is unavoidably vague, the degree of vagueness increasing as one proceeds from the core of the rules to their periphery. It is therefore possible to disagree indefinitely regarding the meaning of these words. But in adjudication, such indefinite disputation is barred because that is opposed to the character and requirements of a legal order, as is implied in the principle of legality. Accordingly, a basic axiom of legal semantics is that legal rules do or do not include certain behavior; and the linguistic problem must be definitely solved, one way or the other, on that premise.

4. The court in *Striggles* cited executive or judicial leniency in sentencing as a basis for not allowing any defense of reasonable mistake of law. We will see similar reliance on prosecutorial or executive discretion in dealing with problematic "defenses"—*e.g.,* in *Dudley and Stephens, infra,* p. 751. Is this a

sensible way for the rules of the criminal law to be established? Might such officials be liable to abuse a more subjectively based rule?

[b] Reliance on Counsel

STALEY V. STATE

Supreme Court of Nebraska

89 Neb. 701, 131 N.W 1028 (1911)

ROSE, J. Alfred T. Staley, defendant, was convicted of bigamy. . . he is now seeking a reversal of the judgment against him.

A statute declares that a marriage in this state between first cousins is void. Comp. St. 1909, c. 52 § 3. Though that relationship exists between defendant and Hettie Bixler, they were married in Council Bluffs, Iowa, in 1907, when they were residents of Omaha. Under the laws of Iowa, the marriage is valid there, and consequently it is likewise valid here. . . . They lived together as husband and wife until February, 1908 when he left her in Omaha, where they were at the time residing. Without procuring a divorce, defendant was married to Pearl Stoner in Lancaster County, August 7, 1909, though his former wife is still living. These facts and conclusions are not in dispute.

Defendant argues that the conviction should not be permitted to stand for the following reasons: In entering into the second marriage, he did not intend to commit a crime. He believed in good faith that his marriage with his cousin was void, and that a divorce or an annulment of the marriage was entirely unnecessary. He was so advised by three lawyers and conscientiously relied upon their advice. A deputy county attorney of Douglas county told defendant the marriage was void and threatened him with prosecution if he did not abandon his unlawful relations with his cousin. During the trial defendant offered to prove these facts and the exclusion of proof offered for that purpose is his principal ground of complaint. Can he excuse his bigamy by showing that he was cowed by the threat of the prosecutor, and that in good faith he acted on the advice of counsel? The validity of the marriage with his cousin was a question of law and not of fact. Ignorance of facts, where there is no criminal intent, often excuses offenses; but this rule does not in general extend to ignorance of the law. That one accused of crime had endeavored to ascertain the law and had been misled by counsel or a magistrate is not generally a defense. 1 Bishop, New Criminal Law § 294. . . . This principle applies to offenses against the marriage relation. . . . The people in adopting the Constitution fully appreciated the possibility that injustice in exceptional cases would result from the enforcement of laws enacted to prevent crime and to punish criminals. To afford protection in such instances was one of the purposes in view, when the pardoning power was conferred upon the Governor.

That defendant was free from criminal intent essential to a crime is the principal feature of an able argument in his behalf. The statute denouncing bigamy does not make intent an element of the crime. It provides: "That if any married person, having a husband or wife living, shall marry any other person, every person so offending shall be imprisoned in the penitentiary not more than seven years nor less than one year." Criminal Code § 201. Malice may be implied from a willful violation of the statute and a reckless disregard of existing marital relations. Both defendant and his cousin-wife testified there never had been any domestic trouble to suggest a separation. There is proof that he knew she was pregnant when he left her. Under such circumstances, he had an accusing conscience, when he formed the purpose to abandon her, unless he was devoid of all marital sentiment and of every worthy instinct of paternity. These natural impulses of the human heart ought to have given a warning signal, even if the statutes had been silent on the subjects of bigamy and divorce. To the threatened prosecution in a court of justice his valid marriage would have been a complete defense. If, however, he was intimidated by threats of prosecution, he could have lived apart from his wife in safety during the time required for the determination of his social status in a court of justice. . . . He knew it was at least doubtful whether the marriage was void. Otherwise he would not have asked the advice of counsel. The deputy county attorney was the prosecuting officer of the state and not the attorney for defendant. Counsel may give advice, but the duty of adjudicating whether a marriage is void is a function of the courts. Lawyers and laymen alike know this. In civil controversies involving property rights only, individuals often refuse to act without an order of court; but, if the evidence on behalf of the state is believed, defendant, on the mere advice of counsel that his marriage was void, was willing to abandon his wife as an adulteress and leave her with the prospect that she would become the mother of a bastard child. The obligations of one who has voluntarily entered into the marriage relation require a greater degree of care than that exercised by defendant. He acted on the advice of counsel, at his peril, and under the law it is nodefense in this case.

[Judgment is affirmed.]

NOTES AND QUESTIONS

1. Most American jurisdictions that have considered the question hold that the fact that the defendant believed in good faith that a prior divorce was valid is no defense to a charge of bigamy if in fact the divorce is invalid. See Clark and Marshall, On Crimes, § § 5.11, 11.12 (6th ed. 1958). Most American jurisdictions also follow a similar rule where the defendant in good faith, but mistakenly, believes his or her first spouse to be dead. On the general subject see Clark and Marshall, § 5.10, dealing generally with the question of criminal intent. As to the belief that the first spouse is dead or divorced, see *Annotation,* 57 A.L.R. 792. In 1949, Delaware became the first—and apparently still the only—state to allow reliance upon counsel's advice as a defense to a charge of bigamy. *Long v. State,* 65 A.2d 489 (Del. 1949). What result in these mistake cases under § 2.04 of the MPC, *infra,*p. 289? Does it matter under the MPC whether the mistake is based on advice from a lawyer?

2. *State v. Downs,* 21 S.E. 689, 116 N.C. 1064 (1895). Defendant sold liquor within two miles of a church. He had been informed by counsel that the church

was not incorporated and therefore was not within the statute. The court observed:

> The vicarious ignorance of counsel has no greater value. . . . If ignorance of counsel would excuse violations the more ignorant counsel could manage to be, the more valuable, and sought for, in many cases, would be his advice.

Accord: *State v. Western Union Tel. Co.,* 12 N.J. 468, 97 A.2d 480 (1953).

3. *State v. Goodenow,* 645 Me. 30 (1876): Prosecution for adultery. The defendant sought to introduce evidence that his lover's former husband had deserted her and had married again and that the justice of the peace who married the two defendants charged with adultery had advised these defendants that they had the right to marry, that they believed the statement to be true, and relied upon it in good faith. The court said,

> It is undoubtedly true that the crime of adultery cannot be committed without a criminal intent, but the intent may be inferred from the criminality of the act itself. The gross ignorance of the magistrate cannot excuse them. They were guilty of negligence and fault, to take his advice. They were bound to know or ascertain the law and the facts for themselves at their peril. A sufficient criminal intent is conclusively presumed against them, in their failure to do so. The facts offered in proof may mitigate, but cannot excuse, the offense charged against them. Here it was a criminal heedlessness on the part of both the defendants to do what was done by them.

4. A county trustee's reliance on advice of counsel that a statute prohibiting him from appropriating certain funds was unconstitutional was held to be no defense to a charge of embezzlement. *Hunter v. State,* 158 Tenn. 63, 12 S.W.2d 361 (1928). Contra: *Cutter v. State,* 36 N.J.L. 135 (1873).

5. "[T]he reason for the uniform holding that the advice of counsel . . . is not a defense [is] not that the lawyer may be incompetent or corrupt, but that lawyers are not law-declaring officials; it is not their function to interpret law authoritatively." Hall 387. There appears, however, to be an exception to this view: Reliance on counsel for tax advice that turns out to be erroneous is allowed as a defense. One "explanation" for this doctrine is that the criminal provisions of the tax code require that the prosecution show that the tax evasion is "willful." Are there other explanations? See Yochum, *Ignorance of the Law Is No Excuse Except for Tax Crimes,* 27 Duq. L. Rev. 221 (1989). Holding that reasonable reliance on counsel is a defense in a charge of fraud, since the reliance negates the specific intent required, see *United States v. Walters,* 913 F.2d 388 (7th Cir. 1990). Why is it relevant only to negate "specific intent"? Is the requirement of reasonability consistent with *McDonald, supra,* p. 264? Does the principle extend to other reliances as well?

6. Even assuming that one were to adopt the Holmesian view that we wish to encourage everyone to know the criminal law, will that explain the results in some of these cases? Was Staley unaware, or mistaken, as to whether the criminal law forbade him to marry while he was still legally married? Or was his mistake, and that of Long, as to the law of domestic relations? Or was it, even more esoterically, with regard to the implications of the full faith and credit clause of the Constitution? Must every person become a constitutional lawyer to avoid the harshness of this rule?

7. Lawyers, of course, cannot ignore the ethical dilemmas of any consultation, most particularly where improper client reliance could foster criminal liability. See, *e.g.,* B. Wolfman and J. Holden, Ethical Problems in Federal Tax Practice (1981).

[c] Reliance on an Official

STATE v. HUFF

Supreme Judicial Court of Maine

89 Me. 521, 36 A. 1000 (1897)

This was a complaint for fishing for smelts with a drag seine in Damariscotta river in violation of the special laws of 1895, c. 28.

The appellant was charged with doing the acts prohibited by special statute of 1895, c. 28, enacted for the protection of smelts in the Damariscotta river. He admitted that he did the acts charged and intended to do them. He offered to show in defense, however, that he was advised by one of the fish commissioners and also by a reputable counselor-at-law that, under the circumstances, it was not unlawful to do those acts. He further offered to show that in doing those acts he acted in good faith not intending to violate any law. The court ruled out this offered defense and the appellant was convicted.

Some acts are in themselves indifferent and become criminal only when done with a particular intent. For instance, many acts become criminal only when done with an intent to defraud. In such cases the intent which makes the otherwise indifferent or innocent act criminal must be alleged and proved; and evidence tending to show the absence of the criminal intent would be admissible in defense.

Other acts, however, are sometimes made unlawful absolutely, without reference to any intent or other state of mind of the doer. In such cases no intent need be alleged or proved. The intent to do is sufficient and that can be inferred from the doing. The acts prohibited by this statute are of this latter class. They are prohibited absolutely. Having intentionally committed them, though innocent of any turpitude, the appellant has violated the statute.

Affirmed.

NOTES AND QUESTIONS

1. *State v. Foster,* 22 R.I. 163, 46 A. 833 (1900). Defendant, who owned a business in the state, wished to open a "Christmas store" elsewhere. He attempted to show that (1) he went to the state treasurer and offered to pay him the fee necessary if he was to be considered an "itinerant vender" and (2) the treasurer returned the money and told defendant he was not covered by the statute. Held: the proffer of this evidence was correctly refused.

2. A pastor in Elkton, Maryland (a town often used by eloping couples due to its being the first town in Maryland across the Delaware border), sought the advice of the county attorney as to whether he would be violating state law if he put up signs advertising his availability to perform marriages. After assurance that this was legal, he did so; his conviction for violation of the statute was upheld in *Hopkins v. State,* 193 Md. 489 (1950).

3. Defendant bought land from X; the deed was from X to defendant. Defendant then changed it to "from X to [defendant]'s wife." X agreed, and the deed was changed. Defendant was convicted of changing a public record. *People v. O'Brien,* 96 Cal. 171, 31 P. 45 (1892). The court held,

> The plea would be universally made, and would lead to interminable questions, incapable of solution. Was the defendant in fact ignorant of the law? Was his ignorance of the law excusable? The denser the ignorance the greater would be the exemption from liability. The absurdity of such a condition of the law is shown in the consummate satire of Pascal, where, speaking upon this subject, he says, in substance, that although the less a man thinks of the moral law the more culpable he is, yet under municipal law "the more he relieves himself from a knowledge of this duty the more approvedly is his duty performed."

The court does not mention that the county recorder acquiesced in this act.

4. An English statute provides that a person caring for a foster child must register. The definition of foster child is one "whose care and maintenance are undertaken for reward for a period exceeding one month." Parents of a child and a Ms. Battersby arrange for a period of at least one year that she will have primary care of their child, but that the period will never exceed 28 days in which the child is not in the care of at least one parent for at least one day. What is the result if the court interprets the statute against Ms. Battersby and charges her with criminal liability for failure to register, and she pleads ignorance of the law?

Add another fact: before entering into the agreement, Ms. Battersby asked an official of the Surrey County Council and was told that this was a legal arrangement. Held: No defense. *Surrey County Council v. Battersby* [1965], 2 W.L.R. 378.

5. D's drivers license had been revoked, but his job was at an airport, and he called the registrar of motor vehicles and was told that he could drive on the airport grounds without a license. He did so, an accident ensued, and he was prosecuted for driving without a license. Held: the lower court properly acquitted. *R. v. MacLean* [1974], 17 C.C.C.(2d) 84 (Canadian). The apparent reason was that the law of which he was ignorant (or mistaken?) was a regulation, which the registrar did not know, which made the general law applicable to airports. The court emphasized that the regulation was not really published; it did not stress his attempt to find out what the law was.

6. In *Hamilton v. People,* 57 Barb. (N.Y.) 625 (1870), defendant was convicted of voting illegally. His counsel sought to introduce evidence that both the governor and two counsels of the state Supreme Court had informed defendant that a prior conviction, imposed while he was a juvenile, would be no barrier to his voting when he achieved majority. The appellate court held that the trial court properly excluded this evidence.

7. The general "rule," even in civil cases, is that the government cannot be estopped by statements made by one of its agents. See *Merrill v. Fed. Crop. Ins. Corp.,* 332 U.S. 380 (1947); Berger, *Estoppel Against the Government,* 21 U. Chi. L. Rev. 688 (1954); Newman, *Should Official Advice Be Reliable? Proposals as to Estoppel and Related Doctrines in Administrative Law,* 53 Colum. L. Rev. 374 (1953). Nevertheless, rumblings to the contrary have surfaced in recent years. In *Haley v. Ohio,* 360 U.S. 423 (1959), the defendant, appearing before the Ohio Un-American Activities Commission, claimed the Fifth Amendment privilege against self-incrimination. The Commission not only accepted the privilege, but on several occasions informed her of that provision. Thereafter, she was prosecuted for failing to answer the Commission's questions on the grounds than an Ohio statute granted her immunity from prosecution for any answers that she might have given and therefore she had no such privilege. In reversing the conviction, the Supreme Court, per Justice Brennan, condemned the prosecution, calling it "the most indefensible sort of entrapment by the State—convicting a citizen for exercising a privilege which the State clearly had told him was available to him." 360 U.S., at 426.

Similarly, in *Cox v. Louisiana,* 379 U.S. 559 (1965), the Court invalidated a conviction for demonstrating too close to a courthouse, when the police chief had indicated the precise spot where the demonstration should occur. Still, the notion of allowing reliance on official misadvice to exculpate has not won sweeping support. See generally Note, *Applying Estoppel Principles in Criminal Cases,* 78 Yale L. J. 1046 (1969). An increasing number of cases, however, have found the government estopped. See, *e.g., People v. Markowitz,* 18 N.Y.2d 953, 223 N.E.2d 572 (1966); *United States v. Lazy FC Ranch,* 481 F.2d 985 (9th Cir. 1973); *Hansen v. Harris,* 619 F.2d. 942, 959 (2d Cir. 1980) (collecting cases), rev'd per curiam, 450 U.S. 785 (1981); *Johnson v. Williford,* 682 F.2d 868 (9th Cir. 1982). In *Johnson,* the U.S. Parole Commission, and all of its agents, over a 15-month period kept treating plaintiff/prisoner as though he were eligible for parole. After he was released and had been free for 15 months, they discovered that the statute under which he had been sentenced provided that parole was not available, and he was reincarcerated. The Ninth Circuit affirmed the district court's granting of *habeas corpus,* finding the government estopped. Among other things, the *Johnson* court said that the defendant relied, and was entitled to rely, upon the tacit interpretation of the statute which the "expert" government had given him, and he, therefore, could not be charged with "knowing" that the statute was different, although it was available for his public reading. This might have important implications for criminal law/mistake of law cases.

[d] Relaxing the Common Law

After considering the above cases, does it appear that there may be a Catch 22 in the law? After all, if a defendant does not seek assistance in interpreting a statute or the reach of the law, the court may (probably rightly) call him reckless. But if he does seek out such help, the very act may suggest that he is not sure that the course he is taking is legal, thus again subjecting him to a charge of reckless risk-taking. For example, Staley consulted three separate lawyers. Why? Could a prosecutor argue, and a fact finder conclude, that this demonstrated an obvious desire to provide protective cover in the event of a later prosecution?

There are some signs that the harsh doctrine may be ameliorating a bit. First, there is the Model Penal Code provision for reasonable reliance:

§ 2.04. Ignorance or Mistake.

(1) Ignorance or mistake as to a matter of fact or law is a defense if:

(a) the ignorance or mistake negatives the purpose, knowledge, belief, recklessness or negligence required to establish a material element of the offense; or

(b) the law provides that the state of mind established by such ignorance or mistake constitutes a defense.

(2) Although ignorance or mistake would otherwise afford a defense to the offense charged, the defense is not available if the defendant would be guilty of another offense had the situation been as he supposed. In such case, however, the ignorance or mistake of the defendant shall reduce the grade and degree of the offense of which he may be convicted to those of the offense of which he would be guilty had the situation been as he supposed.

(3) A belief that conduct does not legally constitute an offense is a defense to a prosecution for that offense based upon such conduct when:

(a) the statute or other enactment defining the offense is not known to the actor and has not been published or otherwise reasonably made available prior to the conduct alleged, or

(b) he acts in reasonable reliance upon an official statement of the law, afterward determined to be invalid or erroneous, contained in

(i) a statute or other enactment;

(ii) a judicial decision, opinion or judgment;

(iii) an administrative order or grant of permission, or

(iv) an official interpretation of the public officer or body charged by law with responsibility for the interpretation, administration or enforcement of the law defining the offense.

(4) The defendant must prove a defense arising under Subsection (3) of this Section by a preponderance of the evidence.

New Jersey has gone one step further than the MPC, granting a defense if the defendant "diligently pursues all means available to ascertain the meaning and application of the offense to his conduct and honestly and in good faith concludes his conduct is not an offense in circumstances in which a law-abiding and prudent person would also so conclude." N.J. Stat. Ann. 2C: 2-4d.

Notes and Questions

1. What, if anything, has changed to make a defense of reliance on authority now acceptable? See, for a dejected answer, Cremer, *The Ironies of Law Reform: A History of Reliance on Officials as a Defense in American Criminal Law,* 14 Cal. W.L. Rev. 48 (1978).

2. Is the part of MPC § 2.04(3) requiring an official statement of the law qualified by the "reasonable reliance" language, or must the statement only be "official"? Must the officer giving the statement actually be one empowered to give such an opinion, or is the defendant exonerated if he reasonably believed the official to have such power?

3. Defendant, hoping to be authorized to perform act X, calls the office that he (reasonably) believes to have power over the enforcement of that statute. Official Y tells him, verbally, that he may do so. Is that an "official statement"? Suppose that Y is authorized to give statements, but is wrong? Suppose he is subject to review by a higher person (*e.g.,* Y is an assistant prosecutor, but works for the prosecutor in the jurisdiction)?

4. Why does the Code not explicitly give a defendant who relies upon counsel's advice, such as Staley, a defense?

Cheek v. United States

United States Supreme Court

498 U.S. 192 (1991)

OPINION BY: White, Justice

Title 26, § 7201 of the United States Code provides that any person "who willfully attempts in any manner to evade or defeat any tax imposed by this title or the payment thereof" shall be guilty of a felony. Under 26 U.S.C. § 7203, "any person required under this title . . . or by regulations made under authority thereof to make a return . . . who willfully fails to . . . make such return" shall be guilty of a misdemeanor. This case turns on the meaning of the word "willfully" as used in § § 7201 and 7203.

I

Petitioner John L. Cheek has been a pilot for American Airlines since 1973. He filed federal income tax returns through 1979 but thereafter ceased to file returns. He also claimed an increasing number of withholding allowances—eventually claiming 60 allowances by mid-1980—and for the years 1981 to 1984 indicated on his W-4 forms that he was exempt from federal income taxes. In 1983, petitioner unsuccessfully sought a refund of all tax withheld by his employer in 1982. Petitioner's income during this period at all times far exceeded the minimum necessary to trigger the statutory filing requirement.

As a result of his activities, petitioner was indicted for ten violations of federal law. He was charged with six counts of willfully failing to file a federal income tax return for the years 1980, 1981, and 1983 through 1986, in violation of 26 U.S.C. § 7203. He was further charged with three counts of willfully attempting to evade his income taxes for the years 1980, 1981, and 1983 in violation of 26 U.S.C. § 7201. In those years, American Airlines withheld substantially less than the amount of tax petitioner owed because of the numerous allowances and exempt status he claimed on his W-4 forms. The tax offenses with which petitioner was charged are specific intent crimes that require the defendant to have acted willfully.

At trial, the evidence established that between 1982 and 1986, petitioner was involved in at least four civil cases that challenged various aspects of the federal income tax system. In all four of those cases, the plaintiffs were informed by the courts that many of their arguments, including that they were not taxpayers within the meaning of the tax laws, that wages are not income, that the Sixteenth Amendment does not authorize the imposition of an income tax on individuals, and that the Sixteenth Amendment is unenforceable, were frivolous or had been repeatedly rejected by the courts. During this time period, petitioner also attended at least two criminal trials of persons charged with tax offenses. In addition, there was evidence that in 1980 or 1981 an attorney had advised Cheek that the courts had rejected as frivolous the claim that wages are not income.

Cheek represented himself at trial and testified in his defense. He admitted that he had not filed personal income tax returns during the years in question. He testified that as early as 1978, he had begun attending seminars sponsored by, and following the advice of, a group that believes, among other things, that the federal tax system is unconstitutional. Some of the speakers at these meetings were lawyers who purported to give professional opinions about the invalidity of the federal income tax laws. Cheek produced a letter from an attorney stating that the Sixteenth Amendment did not authorize a tax on wages and salaries but only on gain or profit. Petitioner's defense was that, based on the indoctrination he received from this group and from his own study, he sincerely believed that the tax laws were being unconstitutionally enforced and that his actions during the 1980–1986 period were lawful. He therefore argued that he had acted without the willfulness required for conviction of the various offenses with which he was charged.

In the course of its instructions, the trial court advised the jury that to prove "willfulness" the Government must prove the voluntary and intentional violation of a known legal duty, a burden that could not be proved by showing mistake, ignorance, or negligence. The court further advised the jury that an objectively reasonable good-faith misunderstanding of the law would negate willfulness but mere disagreement with the law would not. The court described Cheek's beliefs about the income tax system and instructed the jury that if it found that Cheek "honestly and reasonably believed that he was not required to pay income taxes or to file tax returns," a not guilty verdict should be returned.

* * *

At the end of the first day of deliberation, the jury sent out [a] note saying that it . . . could not reach a verdict because "we are divided on the issue as to if Mr. Cheek honestly and reasonably believed that he was not required to pay income tax." When the jury resumed its deliberations, the District Judge gave the jury an additional instruction. This instruction stated in part that "an honest but unreasonable belief is not a defense and does not negate willfulness," and that "advice or research resulting in the conclusion that wages of a privately employed person are not income or that the tax laws are unconstitutional is not objectively reasonable and cannot serve as the basis for a good faith misunderstanding of the law defense." The court also instructed the jury that "persistent refusal to acknowledge the law does not constitute a good faith misunderstanding of the law." Approximately two hours later, the jury returned a verdict finding petitioner guilty on all counts.[6]

Petitioner appealed his convictions, arguing that the District Court erred by instructing the jury that only an objectively reasonable misunderstanding of the law negates the statutory willfulness requirement. The United States Court of Appeals for the Seventh Circuit rejected that contention and affirmed the convictions. . . . In its opinion in this case, the court noted that several specified beliefs, including the beliefs that the tax laws are unconstitutional and that wages are not income, would not be objectively reasonable.

II

The general rule that ignorance of the law or a mistake of law is no defense to criminal prosecution is deeply rooted in the American legal system. Based on the notion that the law is definite and knowable, the common law presumed that every person knew the law. The common-law rule has been applied by the Court in numerous cases construing criminal statutes.

The proliferation of statutes and regulations has sometimes made it difficult for the average citizen to know and comprehend the extent of the duties and obligations imposed by the tax laws. Congress has accordingly softened the impact of the common-law presumption by making specific intent to violate the law an element of certain federal criminal tax offenses. Thus, the Court almost 60 years ago interpreted the statutory term "willfully" as used in the federal criminal tax statutes as carving out an exception to the traditional rule. This special treatment of criminal tax offenses is largely due to the complexity of the tax laws. In *United States v. Murdock,* 290 U.S. 389 (1933), the Court recognized that: "Congress did not intend that a person, by reason of a bona fide misunderstanding as to his liability for the tax, as to his duty to make a return, or as to the adequacy of the records he maintained, should become a criminal by his mere failure to measure up to the prescribed standard of conduct." *Id.,* at 396.

---

[6] A note signed by all 12 jurors also informed the judge that although the jury found petitioner guilty, several jurors wanted to express their personal opinions of the case and that notes from these individual jurors to the court were "a complaint against the narrow and hard expression under the constraints of the law.". . . At least two notes from individual jurors expressed the opinion that petitioner sincerely believed in this cause even though his beliefs might have been unreasonable.

The Court held that the defendant was entitled to an instruction with respect to whether he acted in good faith based on his actual belief. In *Murdock,* the Court interpreted the term "willfully" as used in the criminal tax statutes generally to mean "an act done with a bad purpose," or with "an evil motive."

Subsequent decisions have refined this proposition. In *United States v. Bishop,* 412 U.S. 346 (1973), we described the term "willfully" as connoting "a voluntary, intentional violation of a known legal duty," and did so with specific reference to the "bad faith or evil intent" language employed in *Murdock*. Still later, *United States v. Pomponio,* 429 U.S. 10 (1976) (per curiam), addressed a situation in which several defendants had been charged with willfully filing false tax returns. The jury was given an instruction on willfulness similar to the standard set forth in *Bishop*. In addition, it was instructed that "good motive alone is never a defense where the act done or omitted is a crime." The defendants were convicted but the Court of Appeals reversed, concluding that the latter instruction was improper because the statute required a finding of bad purpose or evil motive.

We reversed the Court of Appeals, stating that "the Court of Appeals incorrectly assumed that the reference to an 'evil motive' in *Bishop,* and prior cases," . . . "requ ires proof of any motive other than an intentional violation of a known legal duty." As "the other Courts of Appeals that have considered the question have recognized, willfulness in this context simply means a voluntary, intentional violation of a known legal duty." We concluded that after instructing the jury on willfulness, "an additional instruction on good faith was unnecessary." Taken together, *Bishop* and *Pomponio* conclusively establish that the standard for the statutory willfulness requirement is the "voluntary, intentional violation of a known legal duty."

III

Cheek accepts the *Pomponio* definition of willfulness, but asserts that the District Court's instructions and the Court of Appeals' opinion departed from that definition. In particular, he challenges the ruling that a good-faith misunderstanding of the law or a good-faith belief that one is not violating the law, if it is to negate willfulness, must be objectively reasonable. We agree that the Court of Appeals and the District Court erred in this respect.

A

Willfulness, as construed by our prior decisions in criminal tax cases, requires the Government to prove that the law imposed a duty on the defendant, that the defendant knew of this duty, and that he voluntarily and intentionally violated that duty. We deal first with the case where the issue is whether the defendant knew of the duty purportedly imposed by the provision of the statute or regulation he is accused of violating, a case in which there is no claim that the provision at issue is invalid. In such a case, if the Government proves actual knowledge of the pertinent legal duty, the prosecution, without more, has satisfied the knowledge component of the willfulness requirement. But carrying this burden requires negating a defendant's claim of ignorance of the law or a claim that because of a misunderstanding of the law, he had a good-faith belief that he was not violating any of the provisions of the tax laws. This is so because one cannot be aware that the law imposes a duty upon him and yet be ignorant of it, misunderstand the law, or believe that the duty does not exist. In the end, the issue is whether, based on all the evidence, the Government has proved that the defendant was aware of the duty at issue, which cannot be true if the jury credits a good-faith misunderstanding and belief submission, whether or not the claimed belief or misunderstanding is objectively reasonable.

In this case, if Cheek asserted that he truly believed that the Internal Revenue Code did not purport to treat wages as income, and the jury believed him, the Government would not have carried its burden to prove willfulness, however unreasonable a court might deem such a belief. Of course, in deciding whether to credit Cheeks's good-faith belief claim, the jury would be free to consider any admissible evidence from any source showing that Cheek was aware of his duty to file a return and to treat wages as income, including evidence showing his awareness of the relevant provisions of the Code or regulations, of court decisions rejecting his interpretation of the tax law, of authoritative rulings of the Internal Revenue Service, or of any contents of the personal income tax return forms and accompanying instructions that made it plain that wages should be returned as income.[8]

We thus disagree with the Court of Appeals' requirement that a claimed good-faith belief must be objectively reasonable if it is to be considered as possibly negating the Government's evidence purporting to show a defendant's awareness of the legal duty at issue. Knowledge and belief are characteristically questions for the fact finder, in this case the jury. Characterizing a particular belief as not objectively reasonable transforms the inquiry into a legal one and would prevent the jury from considering it. It would of course be proper to exclude evidence having no relevance or probative value with respect to willfulness; but it is not contrary to common sense, let alone impossible, for a defendant to be ignorant of his duty based on an irrational belief that he has no duty, and forbidding the jury to consider evidence that might negate willfulness would raise a serious question under the Sixth Amendment's jury trial provision. . . . It is common ground that this court, where possible, interprets congressional enactments so as to avoid raising serious constitutional questions . . . .

It was therefore error to instruct the jury to disregard evidence of Cheek's understanding that, within the meaning of the tax laws, he was not a person required to file a return or to pay income taxes and that wages are not taxable income, as incredible as such misunderstandings of and beliefs about the law might be. Of course, the more unreasonable the asserted beliefs or misunderstandings are, the more likely the jury will consider them to be nothing more than simply disagreement with known legal duties imposed by the tax laws

---

[8] Cheek recognizes that a "defendant who knows what the law is and who disagrees with it . . . does not have a bona fide misunderstanding defense" but asserts that "a defendant who has a bona fide misunderstanding of [the law] does not 'know' his legal duty and lacks willfulness." Brief for Petitioner 29, and n. 13. The Reply Brief for Petitioner, at 13, states: "We are in no way suggesting that Cheek or anyone else is immune from criminal prosecution if he knows what the law is, but believes it should be otherwise, and therefore violates it." See also Tr. of Oral Arg. 9, 11, 12, 15, 17.

and will find that the Government has carried its burden of providing knowledge.

B

Cheek asserted in the trial court that he should be acquitted because he believed in good faith that the income tax law is unconstitutional as applied to him and thus could not legally impose any duty upon him of which he should have been aware. Such a submission is unsound, not because Cheek's constitutional arguments are not objectively reasonable or frivolous, which they surely are, but because the *Murdock—Pomponio* line of cases does not support such a position. Those cases construed the willfulness requirement in the criminal provisions of the Internal Revenue Code to require proof of knowledge of the law. This was because in "our complex tax system, uncertainty often arises even among taxpayers who earnestly wish to follow the law" and "it is not the purpose of the law to penalize frank difference of opinion or innocent errors made despite the exercise of reasonable care." . . .

Claims that some of the provisions of the tax code are unconstitutional are submissions of a different order. They do not arise from innocent mistakes caused by the complexity of the Internal Revenue Code. Rather, they reveal full knowledge of the provisions at issue and a studied conclusion, however wrong, that those provisions are invalid and unenforceable. Thus in this case, Cheek paid his taxes for years, but after attending various seminars and based on his own study, he concluded that the income tax laws could not constitutionally require him to pay a tax.

We do not believe that Congress contemplated that such a taxpayer, without risking criminal prosecution, could ignore the duties imposed upon him by the Internal Revenue Code and refuse to utilize the mechanisms provided by Congress to present his claims of invalidity to the courts and to abide by their decisions. There is no doubt that Cheek, from year to year, was free to pay the tax that the law purported to require, file for a refund and, if denied, present his claims of invalidity, constitutional or otherwise, to the courts. Also, without paying the tax, he could have challenged claims of tax deficiencies in the Tax Court, with the right to appeal to a higher court if unsuccessful. Cheek took neither course in some years, and when he did was unwilling to accept the outcome. As we see it, he is in no position to claim that his good-faith belief about the validity of the Internal Revenue Code negates willfulness or provides a defense to criminal prosecution under § § 7201 and 7203. Of course, Cheek was free in this very case to present his claims of invalidity and have them adjudicated, but like defendants in criminal cases in other contexts, who "willfully" refuse to comply with the duties placed upon them by the law, he must take the risk of being wrong.

We thus hold that in a case like this, a defendant's views about the validity of the tax statutes are irrelevant to the issue of willfulness, need not be heard by the jury, and if they are, an instruction to disregard them would be proper. For this purpose, it makes no difference whether the claims of invalidity are frivolous or have substance. It was therefore not error in this case for the District Judge to instruct the jury not to consider Cheek's claims that the tax laws were unconstitutional. However, it was error for the court to instruct the jury that petitioner's asserted beliefs that wages are not income and that he was not a taxpayer within the meaning of the Internal Revenue Code should not be considered by the jury in determining whether Cheek had acted willfully.

For the reasons set forth in the opinion above, the judgment of the Court of Appeals is vacated, and the case is remanded for further proceedings consistent with this opinion.

Justice SCALIA, *concurring in the judgment.*

I concur in the judgment of court because our cases have consistently held that the failure to pay a tax in the good-faith belief that it is not legally owing is not "willful." I do not join the Court's opinion because I do not agree with the test for willfulness that it directs the Court of Appeals to apply on remand.

As the Court acknowledges, our opinions from the 1930's to the 1970's have interpreted the word "willfully" in the criminal tax statutes as requiring the "bad purpose" or "evil motive" of "intentionally violating a known legal duty." It seems to me that today's opinion squarely reverses that long-established statutory construction when it says that a good-faith erroneous belief in the unconstitutionality of a tax law is no defense. It is quite impossible to say that a statute which one believes unconstitutional represents a "known legal duty."

Although the facts of the present case involve erroneous reliance upon the Constitution in ignoring the otherwise "known legal duty" imposed by the tax statutes, the Court's new interpretation applies also to erroneous reliance upon a tax statute in ignoring the otherwise "known legal duty" of a regulation, and to erroneous reliance upon a regulation in ignoring the otherwise "known legal duty" of a tax assessment. These situations as well meet the opinion's crucial test of "revealing full knowledge of the provisions at issue and a studied conclusion, however wrong, that those provisions are invalid and unenforceable." There is, moreover, no rational basis for saying that a "willful" violation is established by full knowledge of a statutory requirement, but is not established by full knowledge of a requirement explicitly imposed by regulation or order. Thus, today's opinion works a revolution in past practice, subjecting to criminal penalties taxpayers who do not comply with Treasury Regulations that are in their view contrary to the Internal Revenue Code, Treasury Rulings that are in their view contrary to the regulations, and even IRS auditor pronouncements that are in their view contrary to Treasury Rulings. The law already provides considerable incentive for taxpayers to be careful in ignoring any official assertion of tax liability, since it contains civil penalties that apply even in the event of a good-faith mistake, see, *e.g.,* 26 U.S.C. § § 6651, 6653. To impose in addition criminal penalties for misinterpretation of such a complex body of law is a startling innovation indeed.

I find it impossible to understand how one can derive from the lonesome word "willfully" the proposition that belief in the nonexistence of a textual prohibition excuses liability, but belief in the invalidity (*i.e.,* the legal nonexistence) of a textual prohibition does not. One may say, as the law does in many contexts, that "willfully" refers to consciousness of the act but not to consciousness that the act is unlawful. Or alternatively, one may say, as we have said until today with respect to the tax statutes, that "willfully" refers to consciousness of both the act *and* its illegality. But it seems to me impossible to say that the word refers to consciousness that some legal text exists, without consciousness that legal text is binding, *i.e.,* with good-faith belief that it is not a valid law. Perhaps such a test for criminal liability would make sense (though in a field as complicated as federal tax law, I doubt it), but some text other than the mere word "willfully" would have to be employed to describe it—and that text is not ours to write.

Because today's opinion abandons clear and long-standing precedent to impose criminal liability where taxpayers have had no reason to expect it, because the new contours of criminal liability have no basis in the statutory text, and because I strongly suspect that those new contours make no sense even as a policy matter, I concur only in the judgment of the Court.

Justice BLACKMAN, with whom Justice MARSHALL joins, *dissenting.*

It seems to me that we are concerned in this case not with "the complexity of the tax laws," but with the income tax law in its most elementary and basic aspect: Is a wage earner a taxpayer and are wages income?

The Court acknowledges that the conclusively established standard for willfulness under the applicable statutes is the "voluntary, intentional violation of a known legal duty." That being so, it is incomprehensible to me how, in this day, more than 70 years after the institution of ourpresent federal income tax system with the passage of the Revenue Act of 1913, any taxpayer of competent mentality can assert as his defense to charges of statutory willfulness the proposition that the wage he receives for his labor is not income, irrespective of a cult that says otherwise and advises the gullible to resist income tax ollections. One might note in passing that this particular taxpayer, after all, was a licensed pilot for one of our major commercial airlines; he presumably was a person of at least minimum intellectual competence.

The District Court's instruction that an objectively reasonable and good faith misunderstanding of the law negates willfulness lends further, rather than less, protection to this defendant, for it added an additional hurdle for the prosecution to overcome. Petitioner should be grateful for this further protection, rather than be opposed to it.

This Court's opinion today, I fear, will encourage taxpayers to cling to frivolous views of the law in the hope of convincing a jury of their sincerity. If that ensures, I suspect we have gone beyond the limits of common sense.

While I may not agree with every word the Court of Appeals has enunciated in its opinion, I would affirm its judgment in this case. I therefore dissent.

NOTES AND QUESTIONS

1. On remand, Cheek was again convicted, *United States v. Cheek,* 3 F.3d 1057 (7th Cir. 1993).

2. How far does *Cheek* reach? At first, courts held that it was limited to tax cases. See, *e.g., United States v. Donovan,* 984 F.2d 507 (1st Cir. 1991),

(declaring that tax law was "esoteric," but that currency reporting laws were not, therefore upholding the trial court's refusal to instruct the jury that the defendant's subjective belief that certain bank transactions need not be reported would be a complete defense). However, the Supreme Court quickly rejected this narrow view in *Ratzlaf v. United States,* 114 S. Ct. 655 (1994), applying *Cheek* to the currency reporting laws and holding that a defendant's honest mistake, even if unreasonable, would exculpate from such a charge. The *Ratzlaf* court did not suggest that *Cheek* was confined to "esoteric" or "complicated" areas of law; indeed it concluded that the bank statutes were fairly comprehensible. But even if *Cheek* were so limited, how many areas of law, particularly regulatory law, are *not* "esoteric" and "complicated"? What about copyright laws? See *United States v. Moran,* 757 F. Supp. 1046 (D. Neb. 1991). What about gun registration laws? See *United States v. Obiechie,* 30 F. 3d 309 (7th Cir. 1994). See generally Yochum, *Cheek Is Chic: Ignorance of the Law Is an Excuse for Tax Crimes—A Fashion That Does Not Wear Well,* 31 Duq. L. Rev. 249 (1993) (arguing, among other things, that tax law is not unduly complex). (Note, however, that Professor Yochum teaches tax law.)

If complexity is to be a consideration in determining whether a mistake is relevant, much less exculpating, how is that issue to be determined during a trial? Is the issue a matter of law or fact? And in either event, will there be expert witnesses, and so forth on the subject? Is such an examination too diverting from the main issue in the case?

3. Can *Cheek* be limited to statutes that use the term *wilfully* (or possibly some synonym—§ 2.02(a) of the MPC explicitly provides that *wilfully* and *knowingly* are synonymous)? Earlier decisions had suggested that *wilfully* required a specific intent that could be negated by a mistake, but that other *mens rea* words required only a general intent that was not negated by mistake. See *supra,* § 4.03[A][ii]. But if wilfulness is equated with, or is less culpable than, knowledge or purpose, then this leaves only a defendant who acts recklessly with regard to the risk of illegality without a defense of mistake of law.

4. One rather well-established exception to the *ignoratia legis* maxim is that a "claim of right," based upon a mistake of law, will excuse. See, *e.g., Brown v. State,* 28 Ark. 126 (1873); *Burns v. State,* 123 Tex. Crim. Rep. 11, 615 S.W.2d 512 (1933). Thus, a defendant who believes she has a "right" to "your" umbrella and takes it is not guilty of larceny. Why not? What *mens rea* is "negated" here that is not negated in other mistake of law claims? See MPC § 2.04. See *United States v. Walters,* 913 F2d 388 (7th Cir. 1990), holding that mistake of law (advice from counsel that deceitful actions would violate NCAA rules but would not violate law) is a defense to a charge of fraud, which, by common law definition, requires wilfulness.

5. The West German Penal Code, § 17, provides, "If in the course of the act the actor lacks the perception that he is acting wrongfully, he acts without culpability if he could not avoid making the mistake. If he could avoid making it the punishment may be mitigated in accordance with 49, subsection 1." Is this a desirable provision? Is it understandable? Which of the defendants in the cases in this section "could not have avoided" making the mistake of law in question? The Norwegian Penal Code allows (but does not require) reduction of sentence, "provided the court does not decide to acquit him for this

reason." Norwegian Penal Code § 57 (1961). Swedish courts have found three exceptions to the rule: (1) improper publication of the statute, (2) ambiguity in the statute, and (3) erroneous information regarding the meaning of a statute from an authority. Criminal Law Education and Research Center, *Responses to Crime: An Introduction to Swedish Criminal Law and Administration* 23 (1965). Asian codes also provide exculpation. See Art. 16 of the Korean Code of 1953: "Where a person commits a crime in the belief that his conduct doesn't constitute a crime under existing law, he shall not be punishable only where his mistake is based on reasonable grounds." Accord: Art. 21 II of the Japanese Criminal Code Draft (1972) and Art. 16, Chinese Criminal Code (1935), both cited in Ryu and Silving, *Comment on Error Juris,* 24 Amer. J. Comp. L. 1 689, 692 (1976).

For some readings on mistake of law, see Arzt, *Ignorance or Mistake of Law,* 24 Amer. J. Comp. L. 646 (1976); Perkins, *Ignorance and Mistake in Criminal Law,* 88 U. of Pa. L. Rev. 35 (1939); Ryu and Silving, *Error Juris: A Comparative Study,* 24 U. Chi. L. Rev. 421 (1957).

6. Why are mistakes of law and fact treated so differently? Consider the following from Fletcher, *The Theory of Criminal Negligence: A Comparative Analysis,* 119 U. Pa. L. Rev 401, 421–22 (1971):

In a transaction, such as selling a book or getting married, there is a risk that one might create a situation objectively incompatible with the law. Yet that risk is divisible into three components:

(1) a factual component: determining the content of the book or the identity of the prospective spouse.

(2) a component of legal status: determining whether the book is pornographic, or whether the prospective spouse is still married.

(3) a legal component: determining whether the selling of a pornographic book or marrying the spouse of another is prohibited by law.

There is no obvious basis for saying that the factual component of the risk of illegal conduct is different, in principle, from the two legal risks. Yet common law commentators who oppose the punishability of negligence uncritically assume there is a distinction permitting us to excuse every inadvertent factual risk and to endorse strict liability for risking a violation of the law.

In the absence of a plausible distinction between legal and factual risks, opponents of punishing negligence seem to be bound to treat every mistake of law as a complete defense to liability. Yet so far as we know, no Western legal system has ever so rigorously implemented the hypothesis that all culpability derives from known choices. One school of thought that has come close to this position is the *Vorsatztheorie* (Intent-theory) in the German and Soviet literature. It is so named because it favors treating mistakes of law as conditions, like mistakes of fact, negating the intention required for establishing an intentional offense. Yet the theory does admit of punishing conduct committed under negligent mistake of law if the offense in question may be committed negligently under the criminal code. If a theorist favored this view of mistake of law and was opposed to punishing negligence, he would be committed, in principle, to regarding every mistake of law as a complete insulation against liability for intentional and negligent crimes. This alliance of position is appealing to those seeking a consistent rejection of liability based on culpable inadvertence.

Yet this extension of skepticism about the culpability of inadvertence poses problems of its own. How would one deal under this view with the person who repeatedly violated the law out of casualness toward his legal obligations? Or how would one protect society against the morally arrogant offender who characteristically regarded his conduct as legally justified on spurious theories of justification? There is obviously a strongly felt need to justify criminal punishment in these cases. And that cannot be done unless one concedes, at least in some cases, that a man mistaken about his legal obligations might be held accountable under the criminal law.

German theorists have devised a number of rationales to justify punishment in situations in which the violator does not grasp that he is violating community norms. One approach is simply to disregard mistake of law as a defense if it is based on an "unsound conception of right and wrong." Another way is to create a separate crime of legal negligence, which would have the merit of unifying treatment of all cases of culpable inadvertence toward legal obligations. The position that has finally gained supremacy in the German courts, and which the federal legislature has adopted in its revision of the criminal code, is that negligent mistakes of law should provide no defense to liability, even as to charges of intentional criminality. With varied doctrinal techniques and with different legal implications in view, German jurists concur on the central point: actors who unknowingly but negligently violate the law are, at least sometimes, appropriately and fairly punished. A more extreme rejection of the culpability of inadvertence would offend basic sensibilities of justice in cases of insensitive and arrogant perceptions of legal duties.

§ 4.07 "Strict" Criminal Liability

[A] Generally

The objective theory of criminal law reached its apex in the acceptance by the courts of so-called strict liability criminality. The trend began in the late 19th century and increased during the 20th century, both in this country and in England. In England, strict liability was primarily restricted to instances of public, commercial activity. Many of the statutes expressly provided a defense if the defendant could show a warranty from his supplier, *e.g.,* Sale of Food & Drugs Act, 35 & 36 Vict., Ch. 63, § 25 (1875). Indeed, in what is often said to be the first strict liability English case, *R. v. Woodrow,* 15 M & W 404, 153 Eng. Rep. 907 (1846), the court said that a retailer "may take a guarantee that shall render the person with whom he is dealing responsible for all the consequences of a prosecution." Similar defenses still obtain in a number of English statutes. See L. Leigh, Strict and Vicarious Liability, ch. 4 (1982);

Wasik, *Shifting the Burden of Strict Liability,* (1982) Crim. L. Rev. 567. And many allowed any fine imposed to go to the prosecutor who, under English practice at that time, could have been the consumer who was in one way or another deceived. Thus, strict liability in crime actually filled the "privity" gap in tort-contract law that is now covered by, for example, implied warranties (U.C.C. § § 2-314–316) and products liability (Restatement of Torts [2d] § 402A). See Singer, *The Resurgence of Mens Rea: III—The Rise and Fall of Strict Liability,* 30 B. C. L. Rev. 337 (1989).

In this country, many of the early cases were concerned with morals laws, such as those prohibiting the sale of liquor, or those involved with the protection of minors from bad habits (such as purchasing liquor or being present in billiard halls or gambling houses). A complete list of cases, current as of the time, can be found in the appendix to the classic article in the field, Sayre, *Public Welfare Offenses,* 33 Colum. L. Rev. 55 (1933). Of these cases, *Mixer,* excerpted below, is typical. It demonstrates the power of legal positivism and the narrow view of constitutional restraints on state legislatures dominating American legal philosophy in the post—Civil War decades. See, *e.g.,* L. Freedman, *A History of American Law* (1973).

Most health laws were, in form, criminal statutes. That does not necessarily mean that they were the product of moral outrage, though sometimes indeed they were. But enforcement through private initiative had been largely discredited. In theory, the upsurge of concern about health did not really require fresh doctrine. The law of warranty could have been strengthened by the courts and private causes of action were available against people who sold shoddy goods; these prior rules might have been woven into an expansive law of products liability—a development now taking place in the second half of the 20th century. Yet who would or could go to court over a 10-cent can of peas? Criminalization meant that the remedy had been socialized—that the state had assumed the cost and burden of enforcement. Freedman, *supra* at 402. See also F. Allen, The Borderland of Criminal Justice, 124 (1964); Canadian Law Revision Commission, Studies of Strict Liability 173 (1974).

COMMONWEALTH V. MIXER

Supreme Judicial Court of Massachusetts

20 Mass. 141, 93 N.E. 249 (1910)

RUGG, J. This complaint. . . charges the defendant with illegally transporting intoxicating liquor into the city of Lynn, where no licenses of the first five classes for the sale of intoxicating liquor and no permits to transport such liquor into the city had been granted. The defendant, a driver in the employ of a common carrier, had upon his load for transportation in Lynn a sugar barrel, not marked by the seller or consignor as required by Rev. Laws c. 100, § 49, for packages containing intoxicating liquor. There was nothing about the appearance of the barrel to cause suspicion as to its contents, and the defendant was ignorant of the fact that it contained intoxicating liquor. The superior court refused to instruct the jury that unless the defendant knew that the barrel contained intoxicating liquor or from its appearance and all the circumstances ought reasonably to have been put on inquiry as to its contents, he should be acquitted. The question presented is whether this refusal was error. Narrowly stated the inquiry is whether a common carrier or his servant can be convicted of the crime of illegally transporting intoxicating liquor under the statute, when he does not know and has no reason to surmise that there is intoxicating liquor in a package delivered for transportation by a seller or consignor who has violated the law by failing to mark such package plainly and legibly with the kind and amount of liquor it contains.

In the prosecution of crimes under the common law apart from statute, it ordinarily is necessary to allege and prove a guilty intent, and as a general principle a crime is not committed if the mind of the person doing the act is innocent. An evil intention and an unlawful action must concur in order to constitute a crime. But there are many instances in recent times where the Legislature in the exercise of the police power has prohibited under penalty the performance of a specific act. The doing of the inhibited act constitutes the crime, and the moral turpitude or purity of the motive by which it was prompted and knowledge or ignorance of its criminal character are immaterial circumstances on the question of guilt. The only fact to be determined in these cases is whether the defendant did the act. In the interest of the public the burden is placed upon the actor of ascertaining at his peril whether his deed is within the prohibition of any criminal statute. There are many illustrations of such exercise of legislative power, as, for instance, the selling of milk below a designated standard[;] . . . the driving of an unregistered automobile[;] . . . being present where gaming implements are found[;] . . . obstructing a highway more than five minutes even though unlawful interference by trespassers[;] . . . bigamy and adultery by marriage with one honestly, upon reasonable ground, but mistakenly, supposed to be single[;] . . . killing for sale an animal under a designated age[;] . . . being present where implements for smoking opium are found[;] . . . admitting a minor to a billiard hall[;] . . . selling adulterated milk[;] . . . storing and selling naphtha [;] . . . sale of imitation butter inadvertently not wrapped as directed by the employer and required by law. . . . This principle has been very frequently applied to statutes respecting intoxicating liquor. In *Commonwealth v. Boynton,* 2 Allen, 160, it was held that one could be convicted of selling intoxicating liquor even though he had no reason to suppose that it was intoxicating. . . . The sale by a licensed liquor dealer to a minor, though made in good faith and without reason to suspect that the purchaser was below age . . . or to one honestly but erroneously supposed to be a guest on the Lord's Day[;] . . . have all been held crimes under statutes of this nature. This rule prevails generally, though not universally, throughout the United States. See cases collected in *Haynes v. State,* 118 Tenn. 709, 105 S.W. 251. . . . It was assumed in *Commonwealth v. Riley,* 196 Mass. 60, 81 N.E. 881, that the crime created by Rev. Laws, c. 100, § 50, of delivery by a regular expressman of intoxicating liquor without entering it in a book belonged to this class.

It becomes necessary to examine the terms and history of the statute upon which the present complaint is founded, and the antecedent enactments of the Legislature touching the general subject, to determine whether it falls in the same class. The local option license law now prevailing was first enacted by Stat. 1875, c. 99. It contained no provision respecting the transportation of liquors. By Stat. 1878, c. 207, the transportation of intoxicating liquors into municipalities where licenses were not granted, with intent to sell or having reasonable cause to believe that they were intended to be sold in violation of law, was forbidden, and whoever willfully violated any provision of the law was subject to punishment. . . . By the consolidation of pre-existing enactments in Pub. St[at]. 1882, c. 100, § 18, the word "willfully" was omitted, and has not since appeared in any statute touching the transportation of intoxicating liquor.

By Stat. 1906, c. 421, the Legislature made still more stringent and detailed provisions respecting the transportation of liquor into or through no-license municipalities. It was enacted by section 1 of this act, under which this complaint is framed, that "no person or corporation, except a railroad or street railway corporation, shall, for hire or reward; transport spirituous or intoxicating liquors into or in a city or town in which licenses of the first five classes for the sale of intoxicating liquors are not granted, without first being granted a permit so to do" . . . and by section 4 that "any person violating the provisions of this act shall be punished by a fine . . . or by imprisonment . . . or by both, . . . and any violation of the laws relative to the transportation of intoxicating liquors, by a person holding a permit, . . . shall render such permit void.". . . It is obvious from these successive enactments that the Legislature has been struggling to make it more and more difficult to transport liquor secretly into cities and towns where licenses are not granted. . . .

* * *

It is earnestly urged in the present case, however, that the defendant's employer, being a common carrier and as such bound to accept all packages offered to him for transportation, and as a general rule having no right to compel a shipper to disclose its contents to him when there is no reason to suspect that the package contains an illegal or dangerous object, . . . the statute ought not to be interpreted in such a way as to render him criminally liable if he was in fact innocent of any intent to transgress the law; and it is further pointed out in support of this argument that courts of other jurisdictions have held carriers liable for refusing to transport liquors contrary to an illegal local ordinance . . . and where the carrier had reason to believe that it would be illegally sold after delivery. . . .

Notwithstanding these considerations, we are not inclined to relax the rule so plainly laid down in many cases, nor to interfere with the policy of the Legislature respecting the regulation of transportation and sale of intoxicating liquors. While the rule may seem harsh at first sight in some of its applications, this raises not a question of judicial construction, but of legislative policy, with which the courts cannot interfere so long as no constitutional guaranty is infringed. Although the severity of the rule "has been criticized with inadequate understanding of the grounds for it" . . . they are pointed out with clearness by Holmes, J., in *Commonwealth v. Smith,* 166 Mass. 370, at page 375, 44 N.E. 503, at page 504, in this language:

When according to common experience a certain fact generally is accompanied by knowledge of the further elements necessary to complete what it is the final object of the law to prevent, or even short of that, when it is very desirable that people should find out whether the further elements are there, actual knowledge being a matter difficult to prove, the law may stop at the preliminary fact, and in the pursuit of its policy may make the preliminary fact enough to constitute a crime.

The Legislature may say with respect to transportation of liquors that ordinarily common carriers do not transport them without either knowing or having reasonable ground to suspect their nature, or that usually packages containing them give some evidence of their contents to those reasonably alert to detect it, or that directly or indirectly some information generally is conveyed to the carrier as to their character. . . . The language of the statute under consideration is plain and unequivocal. It contains no words, such as "willfully" or "knowingly," indicating a vicious intent as a part of the crime created. There is nothing about it to suggest an exception for the benefit of one who inadvertently violates its terms. Its phraseology discloses a legislative determination that society can best be protected against the evil aimed at by a rigorous application of an inflexible rule. There is no distinction in principle between this and the many other statutes construed in the cases we have cited. It must be assumed that the Legislature in enacting this statute in its present form had in mind the construction placed upon similar statutes. The inference is irresistible that it intended no different meaning or interpretation from that expressed in other laws of like character. Moreover railroads and street railways, common carriers which do not deliver merchandise to houses or places of business, are exempted from the operation of the statute, although they are subject to the provisions of Rev. Laws, c. 100, § 49, as are all shippers of intoxicating liquor, whether by railroad, railway or other carrier. This circumstance tends to emphasize its application to those carriers who deliver goods in such a way as to make especially difficult of detection violations of the law. Evasion of laws of this kind is well known to be more likely to be practiced when small quantities are involved. Taking into account the magnitude of the evils arising from the use of intoxicating liquors and the manifest struggle of the Legislature by successive enactments to regulate its transportation so that secrecy may be prevented, and so that those municipalities which have voted "no license" may be protected from furtive and slyly clandestine efforts to override the popular desire for freedom from its illicit traffic, an exemption ought not to be read into the statute contrary to what seems to be a deliberate legislative purpose based upon grounds of public policy. It follows from what has been said that the carrier has a right to use any reasonable efforts, by the establishment and publication of general rules, by specific inquiry, or in proper cases by the inspection of packages, or otherwise, to ascertain whether intoxicating liquors constitute any part of the goods offered for transportation, and to refuse to take any as to which this right is denied, in order to protect himself against committing the crime created by the statute. . . .

*   *   *

Exceptions overruled.

STATE v. WILLIAMS

Appeals Court of Ohio

94 Ohio App. 249, 115 N.E. 2d 36 (1952)

FESS, J. These are appeals on questions of law from judgments of the Common Pleas Court, affirming the sentences and judgments of the justice of the peace of Washington township, Sandusky county, Ohio, after an appeal therefrom to the Common Pleas Court. The three cases were tried in each court upon an agreed statement of facts.

On August 1, 1951, at about 8 PM, the defendant was driving a truck bearing Michigan license plates, en route from Venice, Ohio, to Detroit, Michigan. While stopped for a red traffic light in Fremont, Ohio, a man in a uniform wearing an Ohio game protector's badge accosted the defendant and asked him if he was carrying fish. The defendant having answered in the affirmative, upon request of the officer, the defendant drove the truck to the state highway garage where the defendant assisted the officer in inspecting the contents of the truck. The inspection revealed that the truck contained sixty-three 100-pound boxes of fish, of which 25 boxes were found to contain catfish in which more than 10 per cent by weight were found to be less than 15 inches in length.

The defendant truck driver had no knowledge of the contents of any of the boxes other than from the bill of lading, which contained the words, "2500 cat." The truck had been loaded by employees of the Cold Creek Fish Company of Venice, Ohio, and no inspection of the shipment had been made by the driver prior to or at the time of its loading. In argument it was stated that the fish in the boxes were covered with ice.

After an inspection by five game protectors the defendant was arrested on 25 charges of violating Section 1429, General Code, presumably one charge for each of the 25 boxes, and, thereafter, was released from jail upon giving bond of $2,500. . . . The defendant was found guilty and fined $25 upon each of the three charges and was assessed the costs. The remaining 22 charges are before the justice of peace, pending these appeals.

The principal error assigned in these appeals is that, in the absence of proof that the defendant had knowledge of the fact that he had possession of undersized fish, there could no conviction.

Section 1429, General Code, provides in part:

> No person shall take, catch or have in possession . . . a catfish less than fifteen inches in length. . . . All such fish caught or taken of a less length than herein prescribed shall be immediately released alive with as little injury as possible while the nets are being lifted or hauled.
>
> No person shall buy, sell, barter, give away, deliver, ship or have in possession an undersized sturgeon or any package, contained or quantity

with more than ten percent by weight of undersized fish or any other species either round or filleted mentioned in this section.

Section 1390, General Code, defines "possession" as "both actual and constructive possession and any control of things referred to."

Under the blanket penalty clause in Section 1454, General Code, a fine is imposed of not less than $15 or more than $200, in addition to costs.

It is a fundamental axiom that ignorance of the law is no defense for a violation of law. However, ignorance or mistake of fact may be proved to negative intent. But where knowledge is irrelevant, ignorance or mistake of fact is no defense, and under certain statutes defining an offense irrespective of knowledge or intent, lack of knowledge is no defense. 1 Wharton's Criminal Law, 142 to 159, § § 102 to 112.

In 1837, the abolitionist, James G. Birney, was indicted for harboring a fugitive slave. The statute did not, in terms, make scienter or intent essential to the offense. The Supreme Court held, nevertheless, that it was essential to prove that defendant knew that the mulatto girl was a fugitive slave. *Birney v. State,* 8 Ohio 230. In the opinion, Judge Wood referred to *Anderson v. State,* 7 Ohio, pt. 2,250, which held that criminality could not exist without knowledge that the instrument upon which the defendant was indicted was a forgery. In the opinion it is stated further:

> We know of no case where positive action is held criminal, unless the intention accompanies the act, either expressly or necessarily inferred from the act itself. "*Ignorantia facti* doth excuse, for such an ignorance, many times, makes the act itself morally involuntary." 1 Hales P.C., 42.

* * *

In *Crabfree v. State* (1876), 30 Ohio St. 382, the Supreme Court quoted from Bishop on Statutory Crimes, page 1021, as follows:

> And when this good faith and this due care do exist, and there is no fault or carelessness of any kind, and what is done is such as would be proper and just were the fact what it is thus honestly believed to be, there is no principle known to our criminal jurisprudence by which this morally innocent person can be condemned because of the existence of a fact which he did not know and could not ascertain. On the other hand, to condemn him would be to violate those principles which constitute the very foundation of our criminal jurisprudence. Honest error of a fact is as universal an excuse for what would be otherwise a criminal act as insanity.

In commenting on the quotation from Bishop, the court said:

> This may be a strong, but is a just statement of the excusing principle in our criminal jurisprudence. It shows the necessity of allowing a person accused of knowingly violating the law to prove on the trial the pains he took to ascertain the truth about the fact or transaction that would, if knowingly done, criminate him, as well as the further necessity of allowing him to give in evidence the nature and extent of the information thus obtained, and upon which he claimed to have acted.

* * *

In *State v. Cameron,* 91 Ohio St. 50, 109 N.E. 584, the Supreme Court again said that guilty knowledge is an essential ingredient of crime, distinguishing the adulterated food cases.

* * *

On the other hand, there is authority in Ohio for the proposition that where a statute makes an act an offense, regardless of guilty knowledge, ignorance of fact, no matter how sincere, is not a defense to a charge predicated upon such statute.

In *State v. Kelly* (1896), 54 Ohio St. 166, 43 N.E. 163, the court held that in a prosecution for the sale of adulterated molasses, it was not a defense that the accused was ignorant of the adulteration of the article sold. In its opinion, the court concluded:

> In the enactment of this statute it was the evident purpose of the General Assembly to protect the public against the harmful consequences of the sales of adulterated food and drugs, and, to the end that its purpose might not be defeated, to require the seller at his peril to know that the article which he offers for sale is not adulterated, or to demand of those from whom he purchases indemnity against the penalties that may be imposed upon him because of their concealment of the adulteration of the articles.

In *Kendall v. State,* 113 Ohio St. 111, 148 N.E. 367, the principle of the *Kelly* case was followed in a case involving the employment of a child under 14 years of age in a place of amusement. It has been held also in the following cases that lack of knowledge is no defense: *White v. State,* 44 Ohio App. 331, 185 N.E. 63 (abandoning pregnant wife); *State v. Kominis,* 73 Ohio App. 204, 55 N.E.2d 344 (sale of liquor to child under 18 inducing delinquency . . .); and *State v. Weisberg,* 74 Ohio App. 91, 55 N.E.2d 870 (selling by false or short weight).

In the interest of reconciling the conflict between the *Birney* and the *Kelly* case[s] and subsequent decisions, it is concluded that in the case of a statute defining an offense regardless of scienter where the means of knowledge are available to the accused or the act is such as to impose a duty (in the interest of the public weal) upon the offender at his peril to ascertain the fact of violation, knowledge is not an essential element to support conviction. In case an offender has the means of knowledge, scienter is inferred by reason thereof. In the cases where the offender acts at his peril, the duty is imposed upon him to ascertain the facts from which, likewise, knowledge may be inferred. For example, in the case of the sale of adulterated food or beverages, the means of knowledge are within the cognizance of the offender and not the state. *Altschul v. State,* 8 C.C. 214, 216, 4 C.D. 402. Purpose and knowledge, except where they are indicated by the character of the forbidden act, are, in most cases, insusceptible of proof. *State v. Kelly, supra,* at 178. There are also certain types of heinous crime where intent is presumed from proof of the commission of the act. From personal experience, the writer knows that a judge en route to his office and cogitating over an opinion he is about to write, who runs a red traffic light, may be wholly oblivious of the warning signal but, nevertheless, in the interest of protecting the public, he is not absolved from criminal liability on account of his lack of knowledge. . . .

* * *

On the other hand, we conclude further that upon a charge of violation of a statute not in terms including scienter, where the means of knowledge are not at hand or the circumstances are such that the accused is not bound at his peril to know the fact and obey the law, knowledge of the fact is essential to support a conviction.

The fish and game act was enacted by the General Assembly under the police power for the laudable purpose of protecting and preserving wild life for the benefit of the people of Ohio. In enacting Section 1429, General Code, the Legislature prescribed the legal weight and size of fish and prohibited the dealing and shipping of undersized fish. It provided also that no person shall have possession, actual or constructive, of any undersized fish. A perusal of the section and other provisions of the act leads to the assumption that when the General Assembly employed the term, "possession," its thoughts were directed to undersized fish in a fisherman's boat, or fish on the dock, or in the fish house, where the undersize would be obvious and apparent upon casual inspection. It cannot be assumed that the Legislature intended to denounce as criminal the possession of small fish by a person such as the defendant herein, who did not have knowledge of the undersize or the means of acquiring such knowledge.

Every reasonable presumption should be indulged in favor of the constitutionality of a statute. In a case such as this, where the validity of the act is assailed and where there may be two possible interpretations, the court must adopt the one which will bring the act into harmony with the Constitution. . . .

* * *

In the instant cases, it is stipulated that the defendant made no inspection of his cargo prior to its loading and had no knowledge that the shipment contained undersized fish. It was unreasonable and impractical to require him to inspect the shipment. As we construe Section 1429, General Code, the Legislature had no intention or purpose to make an innocent person criminally liable for the possession of undersized fish. This conclusion renders it unnecessary for us to discuss or to determine the other errors assigned.

The judgments of the Common Pleas Court and the justice court are reversed, and defendant is discharged.

Judgments reversed.

CONN and SAVORD, JJ., *concur.*

NOTES AND QUESTIONS

1. Of the explanations given in *Mixer* for supporting strict criminal liability, which are persuasive? Is the difficulty of proof, referred to in the quote from

Holmes, a sufficient justification for imposing strict liability? What of the difficulty of proving *mens rea* generally? Is the magnitude, at least in terms of harm, of such illegal transportation greater than the magnitude of harm generated by a murder? If *mens rea* is to be dispensed within crimes of this nature because of (1) the harm inflicted and (2) the possible dangerousness of a violator who is exonerated because of the failure to prove *mens rea,* why should we not abolish the requirement of proving *mens rea* in crimes such as murder, where the harm is greater?

2. Is the purpose here to make the putative defendant more wary in accepting packages? If so, who is in the best position to do that: the truck driver or the company? What could the truck driver have done to avoid liability in this case? Would a truck driver realistically have that option?

3. While there are still many statutes in this country that are construed as imposing strict liability upon defendants, the evolution from *Mixer* to *Williams* may indicate a trend against strict liability. See Singer, *The Resurgence of Mens Rea: III—The Rise and Fall of Strict Liability,* 30 B.C.L. Rev 337 (1989). What has happened in the years between these cases that could account for the difference in result? How do the respective courts view their role vis-à-vis the legislature? Are there differences in the way they view the Constitution?

4. Is the test that the *Williams* court appears to use—access to facts—sensible? Who knows better than the defendant what his *mens rea* was?

5. By now, it should not surprise you that the court relies on Justice Holmes to support an objective test. But did even Holmes go that far in the excerpts in the prior sections?

MORISSETTE V. UNITED STATES

Supreme Court of the United States

342 U.S. 246 (1952)

[One of the best known discussions of the growth of strict criminal liability is Mr. Justice Jackson's opinion in this case. The discussion was clearly dictum since the holding involved the proper construction of a federal statute that provided as follows:

> Whoever embezzles, steals, purloins, or knowingly converts to his use or the use of another, or without authority, sells, conveys or disposes of any . . . thing of value of the United States . . . [s]hall be fined not more than $10,000 or imprisoned not more than ten years or both.

The defendant, a fruit stand operator in summer and a trucker and scrap iron collector in winter, had gone hunting for deer in December 1948. While looking for a prey, he discovered some metal cylinders, about forty inches long and eight inches across, which were apparently abandoned. He decided to take three tons of them on his truck, and took them to a nearby farm where they were flattened by driving a tractor over them. The loading, crushing and transporting of these metal objects occurred in broad daylight.

The metal objects turned out to be spent bomb casings; the property on which they were found was a range owned by the Air Force. The property was posted "Danger—Keep Out—Bombing Range." Nevertheless, the range was known as good deer country and was extensively hunted. Morissette was indicted and convicted.

At the trial, he testified that he believed the casings were cast-off and abandoned. The trial court declared that if "he took it because he thought it was abandoned and he knew he was on government property. . . . That is no defense. . . . " He told the defense counsel, "I will not permit you to show this man thought it was abandoned. . . . I hold in this case that there is no question of abandoned property." [And he instructed the jury,] "[I]f this young man took this property (and he says he did), that he was on the property of the United States Government (he says it was), that it was of the value of one cent or more (and evidently it was) . . . he is guilty of the offense charged here . . . The question on intent is whether or not he intended to take the property. He says he did. Therefore, if you believe either side, he is guilty. "Defense counsel argued that the taking must have been with a felonious intent, but the trial court declared 'That is presumed by his own act.'" The Supreme Court reversed Morissette's conviction, holding that Congress did not intend to dispense with the "intent" requirement in connection with the instant statute, a variation of the traditional crime of larceny.]

Mr. Justice JACKSON *delivered the opinion of the Court.*

* * *

[Public welfare crimes] depend on no mental element but consist only of forbidden acts or omissions. This, while not expressed by the Court, is made clear from examination of a century-old but accelerating tendency, discernible both here and in England, to call into existence new duties and crimes which disregard any ingredient of intent. The industrial revolution multiplied the number of workmen exposed to injury from increasingly powerful and complex mechanisms, driven by freshly discovered sources of energy, requiring higher precautions by employers. Traffic of velocities, volumes and varieties unheard of came to subject the wayfarer to intolerable casualty risks if owners and drivers were not to observe new cares and uniformities of conduct. Congestion of cities and crowding of quarters called for health and welfare regulations undreamed of in simpler times. Wide distribution of goods became an instrument of wide distribution of harm when those who dispersed food, drink, drugs, and even securities, did not comply with reasonable standards of quality, integrity, disclosure and care. Such dangers have engendered increasingly numerous and detailed regulations which heighten the duties of those in control of particular industries, trades, properties or activities that affect public health, safety or welfare.

While many of these duties are sanctioned by a more strict civil liability, lawmakers, whether wisely or not, have sought to make such regulations more effective by invoking criminal sanctions to be applied by the familiar technique of criminal prosecutions and convictions. This has confronted the courts with a multitude of prosecutions, based on statutes or administrative regulations, for what have been aptly called "public welfare offenses." These cases do not fit neatly into any of such accepted classifications of common law offenses, such as those against the state, the person, property, or public morals. Many of these offenses are not in the nature of positive aggressions or invasions, with which the common law so often dealt, but are in the nature of neglect where the law requires care, or inaction where it imposes a duty. Many violations of such regulations result in no direct or immediate injury to person or property but merely create the danger or probability of it which the law seeks to minimize. Such offenses may be regarded as offenses against its authority, for their occurrence impairs the efficiency of controls deemed essential to the social order as presently constituted. In this respect, whatever the intent of the violator, the injury is the same, and the consequences are injurious or not according to fortuity. Hence, legislation applicable to such offenses, as a matter of policy, does not specify intent as a necessary element. The accused, if he does not will the violation, usually is in a position to prevent it with no more care than society might reasonably expect and no more exertion than it might reasonably exact from one who assumed his responsibilities. Also, penalties commonly are relatively small, and conviction does no grave damage to an offender's reputation. Under such considerations, courts have turned to construing statutes and regulations which make no mention of intent as dispensing with it and holding that the guilty act alone makes out the crime. This has not, however, been without expressions of misgiving.

* * *

After the turn of the Century, a new use for crimes without intent appeared when New York enacted numerous and novel regulations of tenement houses, sanctioned by money penalties. Landlords contended that a guilty intent was essential to establish a violation. Judge Cardozo wrote the answer:

> The defendant asks us to test the meaning of this statute by standards applicable to statutes that govern infamous crimes. The analogy, however, is deceptive. The element of conscious wrongdoing, the guilty mind accompanying the guilty act, is associated with the concept of crimes that are punished as infamous. . . . Even there it is not an invariable element. . . . [B]ut in the prosecution of minor offenses there is a wider range of practice and of power. Prosecutions for petty penalties have always constituted in our law a class by themselves. . . . That is true, though the prosecution is criminal in form.

Tenement House Department of City of New York v. McDevitt, 1915, 215 N.Y. 160, 168, 109 N.E. 88, 90.

Soon, employers advanced the same contention as to violations of regulations prescribed by a new labor law. Judge Cardozo, again for the court, pointed out, as a basis of penalizing violations whether intentional or not, that they were punishable only by fine "moderate in amount," but cautiously added that in sustaining the power so to fine unintended violations "we are not to be understood as sustaining to a like length the power to imprison. We leave that question open." *People ex rel. Price v. Sheffield Farms-Slawson-Decker Co.,* 1918, 225 N.Y. 25, 32–33, 121 N.E. 474, 477.

Thus, for diverse but reconcilable reasons, state courts converged on the same result, discontinuing inquiry into intent in a limited class of offenses against such statutory regulations.

* * *

It was not until recently that the Court took occasion more explicitly to relate abandonment of the ingredient of intent, not merely with considerations of expediency in obtaining convictions, nor with the *malum prohibitum* classification of the crime, but with the peculiar nature and quality of the offense. We referred to "a now familiar type of legislation whereby penalties serve as effective means of regulations," and continued, "such legislation dispenses with the conventional requirement for criminal conduct—awareness of some wrongdoing. In the interest of the larger good it puts the burden of acting at hazard upon a person otherwise innocent but standing in responsible relation to a public danger." But we warned: "Hardship there doubtless may be under a statute which thus penalizes the transaction though consciousness of wrongdoing be totally wanting," *United States v. Dotterweich,* 320 U.S. 277, 280–281, 284.

Neither this Court nor, so far as we are aware, any other has undertaken to delineate a precise line or set forth comprehensive criteria for distinguishing between crimes that require a mental element and crimes that do not. We attempt no closed definition, for the law on the subject is neither settled nor static. . . .

* * *

NOTES AND QUESTIONS

1. What new arguments does Jackson, or Cardozo as cited by Jackson, raise for supporting strict criminal liability? Are they persuasive?

2. One major issue in both the American and English cases was often lost in the decisions themselves: the distinction between vicarious liability and strict liability. Thus in *Barnes v. Comm.,* 19 Conn. 398 (1849), which is often said to be the first strict liability decision in this country, there was no dispute that the employee who actually sold the liquor was at least negligent in doing so and possibly was aware that the purchaser was an habitual drunkard. Thus there was *mens rea* present in the case, and the real question was whether the defendant-employer could be held responsible under criminal law theory for the acts (and *mens rea*) of his employee. These cases, therefore, are not technically speaking strict liability decisions so much as they are vicarious liability cases. See Sayre, *Criminal Responsibility for the Act of Another,* 43 Harv. L. Rev. 689 (1930); L. Leigh, *Strict and Vicarious Liability* (1982). See § 8.03, *infra.*

Although the application of vicarious liability to the criminal law was itself both novel and controversial, these cases did not raise directly the question raised in *Mixer* as to the liability of the truly unknowing actor, such as the truck driver there. Is it fair or accurate to use vicarious liability cases to support actual strict liability?

3. Strict liability was also applied in criminal cases that were sometimes summarized as "sexual activity" cases. Of these, the landmark decision was *Prince.*

REGINA v. PRINCE

Court of Criminal Appeal

L.R. 2 C.C.R. 154, (1874) 80 All Eng. L. Rept. 881, (1875) 13 Cox C.C. 138

* * *

BRAMWELL, B., *delivered the following judgment, to which the Lord Chief Baron Kelly, Cleasby, B., Grove, J., Pollock, B., and Amphlett, B., assented.*

The question in the case depends on the construction of the statute under which the prisoner is indicted. [Section 55 of the Offences against the Person Act, 1861,] enacts that "whosoever shall unlawfully take . . . any unmarried girl being under the age of sixteen years, out of the possession and against the will of her father or mother, or any other person having the lawful care of charge of her, shall be guilty of a misdemeanor." Now the word "unlawfully" means "not lawfully," "otherwise than lawfully," "without lawful cause"—such as would exist for instance on a taking by a police officer on a charge of felony or a taking by a father of his child from her school. [I]t is said . . . that that must be read as though the word "knowingly" or some equivalent word was in, and the reason given is, that as a rule *mens rea* is necessary to make any act a crime or offence, and that if the facts necessary to constitute an offence are not known to the alleged offender, there can be no *mens rea*. I have used the word "knowingly," but it will perhaps be said, that here the prisoner not only did not do the act knowingly, but knew, as he would have said or believed, that the fact was otherwise than such as would have made his act a crime; that here the prisoner did not say to himself, "I do not know how the fact is, whether she is under sixteen or not, and will take the chance," but acted on the reasonable belief that she was over sixteen: and that though, if he had done what he did, knowing or believing neither way, but hazarding it, there would be a *mens rea*, there is not one when he believes he knows that she is over sixteen. It is impossible to suppose that a person taking a girl out of her father's possession against his will is guilty of no offence within the statute unless he, the taker, knows she is under sixteen—that he would not be guilty if the jury were of opinion he knew neither one way nor the other. Let it be then that the question is whether he is guilty when he knows, as he thinks, that she is over sixteen. This introduces the necessity for reading the statute with some strange words introduced; as thus: "Whosoever shall take any unmarried girl being under the age of sixteen, and not believing her to be over the age of sixteen, out of the possession," &c. Those words are not there, and the question is whether we are bound to construe the statute as though they were, on account of the rule that *mens rea* is necessary to make an act a crime . . . [W]hat the statute contemplates, and what I say is wrong, is the taking of a female of such tender years that she is properly called a *girl,* and can be said to be in another's *possession,* and in that other's *care* or *charge.* No argument is necessary to prove this; it is enough to state the case. The Legislature has enacted that if anyone does this wrong act he does it at the risk of the girl turning out to be under sixteen. This opinion gives full scope to the doctrine of *mens rea*. If the taker believed he had the father's consent, though wrongly, he would have no *mens rea*. So if he did not know she was in anyone's possession, nor in the care or charge of anyone. In those cases he would not know he was doing the act forbidden by the statute, an act which, if he knew she was in the possession and care or charge of anyone, he would know was a crime or not according as she was under sixteen or not. He would know he was doing an act wrong itself, whatever was his intention, if done without lawful cause. In addition to these considerations one may add that the statute does use the word "unlawfully," and does not use the words "knowingly or not believing to the contrary." If the question was whether his act was unlawful there would be no difficulty as it clearly was not lawful. . . . [In *R. v. Forbes and Webb*] [a] man was held liable for assaulting a police officer in the execution of his duty, though he did not know he was a police officer [10 Cox C.C. 362]. . . . Why? Because the act was wrong in itself. So also in the case of burglary; could a person charged claim an acquittal on the ground that he believed it was past 6 AM when he entered, or in housebreaking that he did not know the place broken into was a house. . . . It seems to me impossible to say that where a person takes a girl out of her father's possession, not knowing whether she is or is not under sixteen, that he is not guilty, and equally impossible when he believes, but erroneously, that she is old enough for him to do a wrong act with safety. I think the conviction should be affirmed.

BLACKBURN, J., *delivered the following judgment to which Cockburn, CJ, Mellor, Lush, Quain, Archibald, Field and Lindley, JJ, assented.*

In this case we must take it as found by the jury that the prisoner took an unmarried girl out of the possession, and against the will of her father, and that the girl was in fact under the age of sixteen, but that the prisoner *bona fide,* and on reasonable grounds, believed that she was above sixteen, *viz.,* eighteen years old. . . . The question, therefore, is reduced to whether the words in . . . § 55, [of the Offences against the Person act, 186] . . . are to be read as if they were "being under the age of sixteen, and he knowing she was under that age." No such words are contained in the statute, nor is there the word "maliciously," "knowingly," or any other word used that can be said to involve a similar meaning. The argument in favour of the prisoner must, therefore, entirely proceed on the ground that in general a guilty mind is an essential ingredient in a crime, and that where a statute creates a crime the intention of the legislature should be presumed to be to include "knowingly" in the definition of the crime; and the statute should be read as if that word were inserted, unless the contrary intention appears. We need not inquire at present whether the canon of construction goes quite so far as above stated, for we are of opinion that the intention of the Legislature sufficiently appears to have been to punish the abductor unless the girl, in fact, was of such an age as to make her consent an excuse irrespective of whether he knew her to be too young to give an effectual consent, and to fix that age at sixteen. The section in question is one of a series of enactments beginning with sect. 50 forming a code for the protection of women and the guardians of young women. . . . Section 50 enacts that "Whosoever shall unlawfully and carnally know and abuse any girl under the age of ten years, shall be guilty of felony." Sect. 51: "Whosoever shall unlawfully and carnally know and abuse any girl being above the age of ten years and under the age of twelve years, shall be guilty of a misdemeanor." It seems impossible to suppose that the intention of the legislature in those two sections could have been to make the crime depend upon the knowledge of the prisoner of the girl's actual age. It would produce the monstrous result that a man who had carnal connection with a girl in reality not quite ten years old, but whom he, on reasonable grounds, believed to be a little more than ten, was to escape altogether. He could not, in that view of the statute, be convicted of the felony, for he did not know her to be under ten. He could not be convicted of the misdemeanor because she was, in fact, not above the age of ten. It seems to us that the intention of the legislature was to punish those who had connection with young girls, though with their consent, unless the girl was, in fact, old enough to give a valid consent. The man who has connection with a child relying on her consent does it at his peril if she is below the statutable age. The 55th section on which th epresent case arises, uses precisely the same words as those in § 50 and 51, and must be construed in the same way. . . .

* * *

BRETT, J.

[A]ccording to the statement of the case, we are to assume that it was proved on the trial that he did take an unmarried girl out of the possession and against the will of her father, and that when he did so the girl was under the age of sixteen years. But the jury found that the girl went with the prisoner willingly, that she told the prisoner that she was eighteen years of age, that he believed that she was eighteen years of age, and that he had reasonable grounds for so believing. . . . The question, therefore, is whether the findings of the jury, which are in favour of the prisoner, prevent what he is proved to have done from being unlawful within the meaning of the statute. It cannot, as it seems to me, properly be assumed that what he did was unlawful within the meaning of the statute, for that is the very question to be determined. Now on the one side it is said that the prisoner is proved to have done every particular thing which is enumerated in the Act as constituting the offence to be punished, and that there is no legal justification for what he did, and, therefore, that it must be held, as matter of law, that what he did was unlawful within the meaning of the statute, and that the statute was therefore, satisfied, and the crime completed. On the other side, it is urged, that if the facts had been as the prisoner believed them to be, and he was deceived into believing them to be, he would have been guilty of no criminal offence at all, and, therefore, that what he did was not criminally unlawful within the meaning of the criminal statute under which he was indicted. It has been said that, even if the facts had been as the prisoner believed them to be, he would still have been doing a wrongful act. The first point, therefore, to be considered would seem to be what would have been the legal position of the prisoner, if the facts had been, as he believed them to be, that is to say, What is the legal position of a man who, without force, takes a girl of more than sixteen years of age, but less than twenty-one years of age, out of the possession of her father, and against his will? . . . [I]f a man takes out of her father's possession without force, and with her consent, a daughter between sixteen and twenty-one, the father would seem to have no legal remedy for such taking. It may be that the father, if present at the taking, might resist such taking by necessary force, so that to an action for assault by the man he might plead a justification. But for a mere taking, without seduction, there is no action which the father could maintain. . . . Neither can a man who, with her consent, and without force, takes a daughter, who is more than sixteen years old, but less than twenty-one, out of her father's possession or custody, be indicted for such taking. There never has been such an indictment. . . . Upon all the cases I think it is proved that there can be no conviction for crime in England in the absence of a criminal mind or *mens rea*. Then comes the question, What is the true meaning of the phrase? I do not doubt that it exists where the prisoner knowingly does acts which would constitute a crime if the result were as he anticipated, but in which the result may not improbably end in bringing the offence within a more serious class of crime; as if a man strike with a dangerous weapon with intent to do grievous bodily harm and kills. The result makes the crime murder; the prisoner has run the risk. So, if a prisoner do the prohibited acts without car-ing to consider what the truth is as to facts, as if a prisoner were to abduct a girl under sixteen without caring to consider whether she was in truth under sixteen, he runs the risk. So, if he without abduction defiles a girl who is in fact under ten years old, with a belief that she is between ten and twelve, if the facts were as he believed he would be committing the lesser crime. Then he runs the risk of his crime resulting in the greater crime. It is clear that ignorance of the law does not excuse. It seems to me to follow that the maxim as to *mens rea* applies whenever the facts which are present to the prisoner's mind, and which he has reasonable ground to believe, and does believe to be the facts, would, if true, make his acts no criminal offence at all. It may be true to say that the meaning of the word "unlawfully" is without justification or excuse. I, of course, agree that, if there be a legal justification, there can be no crime; but, I come to the conclusion that a mistake of fact on reasonable grounds, to the extent that, if the facts were as believed, the acts of the prisoner would make him guilty of no criminal offence at all, is an excuse and that such excuse is implied in every criminal charge and every criminal enactment in England. . . .

* * *

DENMAN, J.

* * *

In the present case the jury found that the defendant believed the girl to be eighteen years of age. Even if she had been of that age she would have been in the lawful care and charge of her father as her guardian by nature. . . . Her father had a right to her personal custody up to the age of twenty-one, and to appoint a guardian by deed or will whose right to her personal custody would have extended up to the same age. The belief that she was eighteen would be no justification to the defendant for taking her out of his possession and against his will. . . . This, in my opinion, leaves him wholly without lawful excuse or justification for the act he did, even though he believed that the girl was eighteen; and, therefore, unable to allege that what he had done was not unlawfully done within the meaning of the clause. In other words, having knowingly done a wrongful act, *viz.,* in taking the girl away from the lawful possession of her father against his will and in violation of his rights as guardian by nature, he cannot be heard to say that he thought the girl was of an age beyond that limited by the statute for the offence charged against him. He had wrongfully done the very thing contemplated by the Legislature. He had wrongfully and knowingly violated the father's rights against the father's will, and he cannot set up a legal defence by merely proving that he thought he was committing a different kind of wrong from that which in fact he was committing.

Conviction affirmed.

NOTES AND QUESTIONS

1. In 1885, Parliament rewrote the statute involved in *Prince* to make reasonable mistake as to age a defense. See *Williams,* especially sec. 69, p.243. However, some 70 years later, Parliament again rewrote the statute, eliminating reasonable mistake as a defense. See G. Williams, Textbook of Criminal Law 183 (1978). See also Cross, *Centenary Reflections on Prince's Case,* 91 Law. Q. Rev. 540 (1975). Strict liability in bigamy was abandoned in *R. v. Tolson* (1889) 23 Q.B.D. 168. In a number of other instances of what might otherwise be viewed as strict liability offenses, the courts in the Commonwealth countries have allowed (reasonable) mistake of fact as an affirmative defense, on which defendant carries the burden of proof.

2. In the United States, the position, at least initially, was different. Prince was applied to bigamy cases, see n. 1 above, and to instances of statutory rape; *e.g., State v. Superior Court,* 104 Ariz. 440, 454 P.2d 982 (1969). At least 15 states, however, now allow a reasonable mistake to exculpate. The Model Penal Code § 213.6(1) provides no defense of mistake of fact as to age when a sexual offense is committed on a person under 10, and requires the defendant to prove by a preponderance of the evidence his reasonable belief as to age when the statute makes an age higher than 10 the relevant criterion. Is *Prince* properly characterized as a sexual activity case in the first place? Who was the victim under the statute? Who is the victim of § 55? Is Judge Blackburn correct that § 55 must be construed in *pari materia* with § § 50 and 51? Are the interests protected by the sections the same? Would an aunt who removed a 14-year-old niece from the control of her father who beat her every day violate § 55?

3. How can *Prince* be squared with the general doctrine that criminal statutes should be construed narrowly and that ambiguities of legislation are to be interpreted in favor of the defendant? Are the crimes punished by § § 50 and 51 of the same kind as that punished by § 55?

4. Williams at 241: "To maintain the prohibition involves punishing the unlucky ones who turn out to be wrong, while letting free those who happen to be right, and this offends the sense of justice. Perhaps Prince knew he was

committing a moral wrong. This perhaps makes us less unwilling to punish him. But put aside this possible moral wrong and suppose that, if the girl were over sixteen, Prince would be perfectly entitled to act as he did. To say that he would still act at his peril would place an undesirable restraint upon proper activities."

5. What is the wrongful or illegal act that Denman, J., asserts Prince did in fact commit? Would this extend the reach of the criminal law far beyond that contemplated by even the other judges?

Prince is usually seen as the genesis for the so-called "greater crime" doctrine—that if one knows one is committing a crime, one takes the full risk (is subject to strict liability concerning) that the crime is greater than one believes. Thus, if A steals a coin, believing it to be a normal nickel, but it turns out to be a rare coin worth thousands, A has committed not petty theft, but grand theft. As a current example, many states, following the federal model, enhance the sentence of a person selling drugs near a school yard (the drug-free school zone) or other place around which children may congregate. Virtually all courts have held that while he must know he is selling drugs, the defendant need not know that the area is within the prescribed distance from the school's boundaries. See, *e.g., United States v. Wake,* 948 F.2d 142 (5th Cir. 1991). See generally Note, 28 New Eng. L. Rev. 783 (1994). Does the same rationale apply if selling drugs near a school yard is not a sentence enhancer of a pre-existing statute, but a new statute, with a greater sentence? The same reasoning applies to statutes enhancing sentences for drug dealers who use minors in the transaction. See, *e.g., United States v. Valencia-Roldan,* 893 F.2d. 1080 (9th Cir. 1990). But see *Ryan,* supra, p. 269. And compare MPC section 2.04(2) *supra,* p. 289.

The process of increasing liability on the basis of strict liability with regard to result elements can be found in a number of other incarnations—for example, the felony murder and unlawful act manslaughter doctrines, respectively discussed *infra* at § 5.03[A][4] and [B][2][b]. Do these doctrines undercut the general premises of the criminal law?

6. After over a century of controversy, the House of Lords has recently rejected the strict liability premises of the *Prince* case. In *B. v. Director of Public Prosecutions*, H.L. [2000], 1 All E.R. 833, the court held that in order to convict a defendant for the offense of inciting a child under the age of 14 to commit an act of gross indecency, the prosecution must prove that the defendant lacked an honest belief that the child was 14 or older. The prosecution had argued that *Prince* and its progeny permitted conviction even if the defendant reasonably believed the child was over age 14. In rejecting this argument, Lord Nicholls noted, that while the child incitement statute was silent as to a mental element, the court must apply "the established common law presumption that a mental element . . . is an essential element unless Parliament has indicated a contrary intention either expressly or by necessary implication." Finding the "protection of children" as the underlying purpose of the incitement statute, Lord Nicholls saw no reason to presume that Parliament intended strict liability as to the age element. Such an interpretation in *Prince* was, for Lord Nicholls, the product of "clumsy Parliamentary drafting" and was no longer valid in light of "the nature and

weight of the common law presumption." Lord Steyn add that "*Prince* is out of line with the modern trend in criminal law which is that the defendant should be judged on the facts as he believes them to be." In this light, *Prince* is "a relic of an age dead and gone" and thus cannot be the ground for generating "a special principle of construction applicable only to age–based sexual offenses." Finally, Lord Hutton opined that "there is force in the view expressed by Blackburn J in . . . *Prince*" but "that to the extent that *Prince* can be viewed as establishing a general rule that mistake as to age does not afford a defence in age–based sexual offenses, the rule cannot prevail over the presumption [of *mens rea*]."

7. The Indiana Supreme Court, enunciating a presumption that *mens rea* is a requirement of criminal liability, has adopted a seven-prong test (borrowed from La Fave and Scott. sec. 3.8, at 342–44) to determine when a statute should be construed to require *mens rea:* (1) the legislative history, title, or contest of a criminal statute; (2) similar or related statutes; (3) the severity of punishment; (4) the danger to the public of prohibited conduct; (5) the defendant's opportunity to ascertain the operative facts and avoid the prohibited conduct; (6) the prosecutor's difficulty in proving the defendant's mental state; and (7) the number of expected prosecutions. *State v. Keihn,* 542 N.E.2d 963 (Ind. 1989). In so doing, the court held that the prosecutor must show that a defendant charged with driving with a suspended license, whichis punishable by a maximum of a year in prison and a $5,000 fine, knew that her license was suspended.

SAYRE, The Present Significance of *Mens Rea* in Criminal Law

Harvard Legal Essays 399, 408 (1934)

The line which distinguishes these "public welfare offenses" from "true crimes" is an important but not always easy one to draw. It is not dependent, as some have suggested, on whether the offense is common law or statutory. Neither is it safe to rely on the distinction between mala in se and *mala prohibita.* Nor can the criterion be rated upon the gravity or lightness of the offense. The real distinction depends upon the nature of the penalty involved and the character of the offense. If the penalty is a serious one, particularly if it involves imprisonment, ordinarily the individual interest of the defendant will loom too large to permit conviction without proof of a guilty intent. But if the maximum penalty consists of no more than a light fine, and if the character of the offense is such that infraction involves wide-spread public injury . . . the offense may fall within the category of the public welfare offense, punishable without proof of any guilty intent.

NOTES AND QUESTIONS

1. Sayre's article, *Public Welfare Offenses,* 33 Colum. L. Rev. (1933), is the classic in this area. For other discussions, most of them highly critical of strict

liability, see Davis, *Strict Liability: Deserved Punishment for Faultless Conduct,* 33 Wayne L. Rev. 1363; Kadish, *Some Observations on the Use of Criminal Sanctions in Enforcing Regulations,* 30 U. Chi. L. Rev. 423 (1963); Paulus, *Strict Liability: Its Place in Public Welfare Offences,* 20 Crim. L. Q. 445 (1978); Perkins, *The Civil Offense,* 100 U. Pa. L. Rev. 832 (1952). An outstanding student note, defending the notion of strict criminal liability, written by (now) Professor Nemerson, can be found at 75 Colum. L. Rev. 1517 (1975).

2. Some courts have allegedly equated violation of municipal ordinances with quasi-civil proceedings. For an incisive and droll analysis of the difficulties that such an approach provides, see Johns, *A Violation of a Municipal Ordinance—Is It Fish or Fowl?,* 32 Dicta 387 (1955).

3. H. Gross, A Theory of Criminal Justice 344 (1979): "Perhaps the most prominent feature of most strict liability offenses is that conviction does not affect respectability. Neither his conduct nor the punishment he receives for it stigmatizes the offender." This theme is echoed by Justice Jackson, Dean Sayre, and Judge Cardozo. Is it true? Is this an empirical question on which data would be relevant? Cf. Weiner, *The Reform of Punishment,* in Law Reform Commission of Canada, Studies on Sentencing (1974).

Wasserstrom, Strict Liability in the Criminal Law

12 Stan. L. Rev. 731, 736–41 (1960)

[T]here seem to be at least two respects in which strict liability statutes might have a greater deterrent effect than "usual" criminal statutes. In the first place, it should be noted that it might be the case that a person engaged in a certain kind of activity would be more careful precisely because he knew that this kind of activity was governed by a strict liability statute. It is at least plausible to suppose that the knowledge that certain criminal sanctions will be imposed if certain consequences ensue might induce a person to engage in that activity with much greater caution than would be the case if some lesser standard prevailed.

In the second place, it seems reasonable to believe that the presence of strict liability offenses might have the added effect of keeping a relatively large class of persons from engaging in certain kinds of activity. A person who did not regard himself as capable of conducting an enterprise in such a way so as not to produce the deleterious consequences proscribed by the statute might well refuse to engage in that activity at all. Of course, if the penalties for violation of the statute are minimal—if payment of fines is treated merely as a license to continue in operation—then unscrupulous persons will not be deterred by the imposition of this sanction. But this does not imply that unscrupulous persons would be quite so willing to engage in these activities if the penalties for violation were appreciably more severe.

[I]f we assume the strongest of all results—that a statute of this kind would lead to the disappearance of the institution involved—what conclusions are to be drawn?

The case of socially undesirable activity is easy. If the operation of the felony murder rule has the effect of inducing persons to refuse to commit felonies, there are surely few if any persons who would object to this consequence. Where socially beneficial activities, such as banking and drug distribution are concerned, the case is more troublesome. If it is further assumed that at least some of the strict liability statutes in these areas have been rigidly enforced, it is also to be noted that these institutions have not disappeared from the society. One possible conclusion to be drawn is that these strict liability offenses have been deemed to impose a not unreasonable risk. The fact that banking is still considered an extremely attractive endeavor (despite the possibility of a prison sentence for borrowing money from one's own bank) might be interpreted as evidence that people believe they can be successful bankers without violating this or a comparable strict liability statute. They believe, in other words, that they can operate with sufficient care so as not to violate the statute. Admittedly, the evidence in support of this thesis is not particularly persuasive. Perhaps most people who have gone into banking never even knew of the existence of the statute. Perhaps there is no such statute in most jurisdictions. Perhaps they knew of the statute but believed it would never attach to their conduct. And perhaps they took the statute into account incorrectly and should have been deterred by the statute. In part, the difficulty stems from the fact that there is so little empirical evidence available. It is suggested only that the above interpretation of the extent evidence is just as plausible as are the contrary inferences so often drawn.

The fact that strict liability statutes might cause the disappearance of socially desirable undertakings raises, in a specific context, one important feature of the kind of justification which might be offered for these statutes. If it is conceded that strict liability statutes have an additional deterrent effect, then a fairly plausible utilitarian argument can be made for their perpetuation.

To the extent to which the function of the criminal law is conceived to be that of regulating various kinds of conduct, it becomes relevant to ask whether this particular way of regulating conduct leads to more desirable results than possible alternative procedures. The problem is not peculiar to strict liability statutes but is endemic to the legal system as a whole.

One of the ways to prevent the occurrence of certain kinds of consequences is to enact strict liability offenses, since *ex hypothesi,* there will be an added deterrent. One of the deleterious consequences of strict liability offenses is the possibility that certain socially desirable institutions will be weakened or will disappear. The problem is twofold: first one must decide whether the additional deterrent effect of strict liability statutes will markedly reduce the occurrence of those events which the statute seeks quite properly to prevent. And second, one must decide whether this additional reduction in undesirable occurrences is more beneficial to society than the possible deleterious effects upon otherwise desirable activities such as banking or drug distribution. For even if it be conceded that strict liability offenses may have the additionally undesirable effect of holding as criminal some persons who would not on other grounds be so regarded, strict liability could be supported on the theory that the need to prevent certain kinds of occurrences is sufficiently great so as to override the undesirable effect of punishing those who might in some other sense be "innocent."

[T]he second of the two major kinds of criticism directed against strict criminal liability is that punishment of persons in accordance with the minimal requirements of strict liability—the pun ishment of persons in the absence of *mens rea*—is irreconcilable with those fundamental, long extant standards of criminal culpability which prevail in the community. The claim is made that the imposition of strict liability is inconsistent with the concept of criminal culpability—criminal culpability being defined to mean "requiring *mens rea*." But unless the argument is to be vacuous it must be demonstrated that independent reasons exist for selecting just this definition which precludes strict liability offenses from the class of actions to which the criminal sanctions are to attach.

NOTES AND QUESTIONS

1. The proffered defense of persons charged with strict liability crimes is usually mistake of fact. The courts of England, Canada, and other jurisdictions have arrived at a "halfway house" between strict liability and *mens rea* by allowing a defense of due diligence, upon which the defendant carries the burden of proof (by a preponderance). *E.g., Harding v. Price,* [1948], 1 K.B. 695, 1 All E.R. 293; *R. v. City of Sault Ste. Marie* (1978), 85 D.L.R. (3d) 161, 40 C.C.C. (2d) 353 (Sup. Ct. Can.); *Proudman v. Dayman* (1941), 67 C.L.R. 536. The Canadian Supreme Court has held that it would violate the Canadian Charter of Rights to preclude a defendant from arguing mistake of fact as a defense, at least where imprisonment is possible. *In re B.C. Motor Vehicle Act* (1985), 2 S.C.R. 486. See also Fisse, *Probability and the Proudman v. Dayman Defence of Reasonable Mistaken Belief,* 9 Melb. U.L. Rev. 477 (1974); Hutchinson, *Sault Ste. Marie, Mens Rea and the Halfway House: Public Welfare Offenses Get a Home of Their Own,* 17 Osgoode Hall L.J. 415 (1979).

Is this compromise position a "better" answer than either of the extremes? Compare Brett, *Strict Responsibility: Possible Solutions,* 37 Mod. L. Rev. 416 (1974) (no), with Levenson, *Good Faith Defenses: Reshaping Strict Liability Crimes,* 78 Corn. L. Rev. 401 (1993) (yes). Law revision commissions in both countries have gone slightly further, and urged the total abandonment of strict liability offenses, the adoption of economic regulatory provisions sanctioning negligent behavior, and placing the burden of proof of reasonableness on the defendant. See Law Reform Commission of Canada, Studies on Strict Liability (1974); English Law Reform Commission, *Working Paper* 117 Field of Inquiry (1974). This is the approach in other countries; *e.g.,* J. Andenaes, The General Part of the Criminal Law of Norway 241 (1965).

2. For a thorough study finding that there are still a number of true strict liability offenses in England, see L. Leigh, Strict and Vicarious Liability (1982). See also Peiris, *Strict Liability in Commonwealth Criminal Law,* 3 Legal Studies 117 (1983).

3. The Model Penal Code deals with strict liability offenses as follows:

§ 2.05:

(1) The requirements of culpability prescribed by Sections 2.01 and 2.02 do not apply to (a) offenses which constitute violations, [defined in § 1.04 (5)] unless the requirement involved is included in the definition of the offense or the Court determines that its application is consistent with effective enforcement of the law defining the offense. . . .

(2) . . .

(a) when absolute liability is imposed with respect to any material element of an offense . . . the offense constitutes a violation and;

(b) although absolute liability is imposed by law . . . the culpable commission of the offense may be charged and proved, in which event negligence with respect to such elements constitutes sufficient culpability.

§ 1.04 (5) An offense defined by this Code . . . constitutes a violation . . . if no other sentence than a fine, or fine and forfeiture or other civil penalty is authorized upon conviction . . . A violation does not constitute a crime and conviction of a violation shall not give rise to any disability or legal disadvantage.

[B] The Federal View

Many academicians argue that strict criminal liability violates the United States Constitution. See, *e.g.,* Hippard, *The Unconstitutionality of Criminal Liability without Fault: An Argument for a Constitutional Doctrine of Mens Rea,* 10 Hous. L. Rev. 1039 (1973); Saltzman, *Strict Criminal Liability and the United States Constitution: Substantive Criminal Law and Due Process,* 24 Wayne L. Rev. 1571 (1978). The fact, however, is that the Supreme Court has never directly addressed the question, choosing as it did in *Staples,* below, to treat the issue as one of statutory interpretation. Surely the verbiage of the Court has ebbed and flowed in its views of strict liability. Thus, in some cases, such as *United States v. Balint,* 258 U.S. 250 (1922), the Court appeared to endorse strict liability. In fact, however, the holding of the case went only to what the prosecutor had to allege in the indictment with regard to drug transactions; there was not even a conviction in the case (although it is often misread as having affirmed a conviction). Similarly strong words can be found in *Dotterweich,* cited in *Park,* below, but these words, in the context of the question certified, are clearly dictum. Contrarily, many of the Court's major opinions, such as *Morrissette,* disparage strict liability but recognize its possibility. See also *United States v. United States Gypsum Co.,* 438 U.S. 422 (1978); *Liparota v. United States,* 471 U.S. 419 (1985).

UNITED STATES v. PARK*

Supreme Court of the United States

421 U.S. 658 (1975)

Mr. Chief Justice Burger *delivered the opinion of the Court.*

We granted certiorari to consider whether jury instructions in the prosecution of a corporate officer under § 301(k) of the Federal Food, Drug, and Cosmetic Act, 21 U.S.C. § 331(k), were appropriate under *United States v. Dotterweich,* 320 U.S. 277 (1943).

Acme Markets, Inc., is a national retail food chain with approximately 36,000 employees, 874 retail outlets, 12 general warehouses, and four special warehouses. Its headquarters, including the office of the president, respondent Park, who is chief executive officer of the corporation, are located in Philadelphia, Pa. [T]he Government charged Acme and respondent with violations of the Federal Food, Drug and Cosmetic Act. Each count of the information alleged that the defendants had received food that had been shipped in interstate commerce and that, while the food was being held for sale in Acme's Baltimore warehouse following shipment in interstate commerce, they caused it to be held in a building accessible to rodents and to be exposed to contamination by rodents. These acts were alleged to have resulted in the food being adulterated within the meaning of 21 U.S.C. § § 342(a)(3) and (4)[1] in violation of 21 U.S.C. § 331(k).[2]

* * *

Acme pleaded guilty to each count of the information. Respondent pleaded not guilty. The evidence at trial demonstrated that in April 1970 the Food and Drug Administration (FDA) advised respondent by letter of insanitary conditions in Acme's Philadelphia warehouse. In 1971 FDA found that similar conditions existed in the firm's Baltimore warehouse. An FDA consumer safety officer testified concerning evidence of rodent infestation and other insanitary conditions discovered during a 12-day inspection of the Baltimore warehouse

---

* [Court footnotes are renumbered.—Eds.]

[1] Section 402 of the Act, [52 Stat. 1046,] 21 U.S.C. § 342, provides in pertinent part: A food shall be deemed to be adulterated—(a) . . . (3) if it consists in whole or in part of any filthy, putrid, or decomposed substance, or if it is otherwise unfit for food; or (4) if it has been prepared, packed, or held under insanitary conditions whereby it may have become contaminated with filth, or whereby it may have been rendered injurious to health.

[2] Section 301 of the Act, 21 U.S.C. § 331(k), provides in pertinent part:
  The following acts and the causing thereof are prohibited:

* * * * *

  (k) The alteration, mutilation, destruction, obliteration, or removal of the whole or any part of the labeling of, or the doing of any other act with respect to, a food, drug, device, or cosmetic, if such act is done while such article is held for sale (whether or not the first sale) alter shipment in interstate commerce and results in such article being adulterated or misbranded.

in November and December 1971. He also related that a second inspection of the warehouse had been conducted in March 1972. On that occasion the inspectors found that there had been improvement in the sanitary conditions, but that "there was still evidence of rodent activity in the building and in the warehouse and we found some rodent-contaminated lots of food items." . . .

The Government also presented testimony by the Chief of Compliance of FDA's Baltimore office, who informed respondent by letter of the conditions at the Baltimore warehouse after the first inspection. There was testimony by Acme's Baltimore division vice president, who had responded to the letter on behalf of Acme and respondent and who described the steps taken to remedy the insanitary conditions discovered by both inspections. The Government's final witness, Acme's vice president for legal affairs and assistant secretary, identified respondent as the president and chief executive officer of the company and read a bylaw prescribing the duties of the chief executive officer. He testified that respondent functioned by delegating "normal operating duties," including sanitation, but that he retained "certain things, which are the big, broad, principles of the operation of the company," and had "the responsibility of seeing that they all work together." . . .

At the close of the Government's case-in-chief, respondent moved for a judgment of acquittal on the ground that "the evidence-in-chief has shown that Mr. Park is not personally concerned in this Food and Drug violation." The trial judge denied the motion.

Respondent was the only defense witness. He testified that, although all of Acme's employees were in a sense under his general direction, the company has an "organizational structure for responsibilities for certain functions" according to which different phases of its operation were "assigned to individuals who, in turn, have staff and departments under them." He identified those individuals responsible for sanitation and related that upon receipt of the January 1972 FDA letter, he had conferred with the vice president for legal affairs, who informed him that the Baltimore division vice president "was investigating the situation immediately and would be taking corrective action and would be preparing a summary of the corrective action to reply to the letter." Respondent stated that he did not "believe there was anything [he] could have done more constructively than what [he] found was being done."

On cross-examination, respondent conceded that providing sanitary conditions for food offered for sale to the public was something that he was "responsible for in the entire operation of the company," and he stated that it was one of many phases of the company that he assigned to "dependable subordinates." Respondent was asked about and, over the objections of his counsel, admitted receiving, the April 1970 letter addressed to him from FDA regarding insanitary conditions at Acme's Philadelphia warehouse.[3] He

---

[3] The April 1970 letter informed respondent of the following "objectionable conditions" in Acme's Philadelphia warehouse:

1. Potential rodent entry ways were noted; ill fitting doors and door in irrepair at South west corner of warehouse: at dock at old salvage room and at receiving and shipping doors which were observed to be open most of the time.

2. Rodent nesting, rodent excreta pellets, rodent stained bale, bagging, and rodent gnawed holes were noted among bales of flour stored in warehouse.

acknowledged that, with the exception of the division vice president, the same individuals had responsibility for sanitation in both Baltimore and Philadelphia. Finally, in response to questions concerning the Philadelphia and Baltimore incidents, respondent admitted that the Baltimore problem indicated that the system for handling sanitation "wasn't working perfectly" and that as Acme's chief executive officer he was responsible for "any result which occurs in our company."

At the close of the evidence, respondent's renewed motion for a judgment of acquittal was denied. The relevant portion of the trial judge's instructions to the jury challenged by respondent is set out in the margins.[4] Respondent's counsel objected to the instructions on the ground that they failed fairly to reflect our decision in *United States v. Dotterweich*, . . . [320 U.S. 277] and to define 'responsible relationship.' The trial judge overruled, the objection. The jury found respondent guilty on all counts of the information, and he was subsequently sentenced to pay a fine of $50 on each count.[5]

The Court of Appeals reversed the conviction and remanded for a new trial. That court viewed the Government as arguing "that the conviction may be predicated solely upon a showing that . . . [respondent] was the President of the offending corporation," and it stated that as "a general proposition, some act of commission or omission is an essential element of every crime." 499 F.2d 839, 841 (CA4 1974). . . . The Court of Appeals concluded that the trial judge's instructions "might well have left the jury with the erroneous impression that Park could be found guilty in the absence of 'wrongful action on his part,' . . . and that proof of this element was required by due process." It held, with

---

3. Potential rodent harborage was noted in discarded paper, rope, sawdust and other debris piled in corner of shipping and receiving dock near bakery and warehouse doors. Rodent excreta pellets were observed among bags of sawdust (or wood shavings).

[4] In order to find the Defendant guilty on any count of the Information, you must find beyond a reasonable doubt on each count . . .

Thirdly, that John R. Park held a position of authority in the operation of the business of Acme Markets, Incorporated.

The main issue for your determination is only with the third element, whether the Defendant held a position of authority and responsibility in the business of Acme Markets. . . .

The statute makes individuals, as well as corporations, liable for violations. An individual is liable if it is clear, beyond a reasonable doubt, that the elements of the adulteration of the food as to travel in interstate commerce are present. As I have instructed you in this case, they are, and that the individual had a responsible relation to the situation, even though he may not have participated personally.

The individual is or could be liable under the statute, even if he did not consciously do wrong. However, the fact that the Defendant is pres[id]ent and is chief executive officer of the Acme Markets does not require a finding of guilt. Though he need not have personally participated in the situation, he must have had a responsible relationship to the issue. The issue is, in this case, whether the Defendant John R. Park, by virtue of his position in the company, had a position of authority and responsibility in the situation out of which these charges arose.

[5] Sections 203(a) and (b) of the Act, [52 Stat. 1043] 21 U.S.C. § § 333(a) and (b), provide:

(a) Any person who violates a provision of section 331 of this title shall be imprisoned for not more than one year or fined not more that $1,000, or both; (b) Notwithstanding the provisions of subsection (a) of this section, if any person commits such a violation after a conviction of him under this section has become final, or commits such a violation with the intent to defraud or mislead, such person shall be imprisoned for not more than three years or fined not more than $100,000, or both. . . .

one dissent, that the instructions did not "correctly state the law of the case," and directed that on retrial the jury be instructed as to 'wrongful action,' which might be "gross negligence and inattention in discharging . . . corporate duties and obligations or any of a host of other acts of commission or omission which would 'cause' the contamination of food." . . . 499 F.2d, at 842. (Footnotes omitted.)

The Court of Appeals also held that the admission in evidence of the April 1970 FDA warning to respondent was error warranting reversal, based on its conclusion that, "as this case was submitted to the jury and in light of the sole issue presented," there was no need for the evidence and thus that its prejudicial effect outweighed its relevancy. . . .

[In *Dotterweich* the Court recognized that, because the Act dispenses with the need to prove "consciousness of wrongdoing," it may result in hardship even as applied to those who share "[a] responsibility in the business process resulting in" a violation. It regarded as "too treacherous" an attempt "to define or even to indicate by way of illustration the class of employees which stands in such a responsible relation." The question of responsibility, the Court said, depends "on the evidence produced at the trial and its submission—assuming the evidence warrants it—to the jury under appropriate guidance." The Court added: "In such matters the good sense of prosecutors, the wise guidance of trial judges, and the ultimate judgment of juries must be trusted." . . .]

The rule that corporate employees who have "a responsible share in the furtherance of the transaction which the statute outlaws" are subject to the criminal provisions of the Act was not formulated in a vacuum. Cf. *Morissette v. United States,* 342 U.S. 246, 258 (1952). Cases under the Federal Food and Drugs Act of 1906 reflected the view both that knowledge or intent were not required to be proved in prosecutions under its criminal provisions, and that responsible corporate agents could be subjected to the liability thereby imposed. . . . Moreover, the principle had been recognized that a corporate agent, through whose act, default, or omission the corporation committed a crime, was himself guilty individually of that crime. The principle had been applied whether or not the crime required "consciousness of wrongdoing," and it had been applied not only to those corporate agents who themselves committed the criminal act, but also to those who by virtue of their managerial positions or other similar relation to the actor could be deemed responsible for its commission.

In the latter class of cases, the liability of managerial officers did not depend on their knowledge of, or personal participation in, the act made criminal by the statute. Rather, where the statute under which they were prosecuted dispensed with "consciousness of wrongdoing," and omission or failure to act was deemed a sufficient basis for a responsible corporate agent's liability. It was enough in such cases that, by virtue of the relationship he bore to the corporation, the agent had the power to have prevented the act complained of.

Thus, the Court has reaffirmed the proposition that "the public interest in the purity of its food is so great as to warrant the imposition of the highest standard of care on distributors." *Smith v. California,* 361 U.S. 147, 152 (1959).

In order to make "distributors of food the strictest censors of their merchandise," *id.,* the Act punished "neglect where the law requires care, or inaction where it imposes a duty." *Morissette v. United States,* 342 U.S., at 255. "The accused, if he does not will the violation, usually is in a position to prevent it with no more care than society might reasonably expect and no more exertion than it might reasonably exact from one who assumed his responsibilities." 342 U.S., at 256. Cf. Hughes, *Criminal Omissions,* 67 Yale L.J. 390 (1958). . . . The Courts of Appeals have recognized that those corporate agents vested with the responsibility, and power commensurate with that responsibility, to devise whatever measures are necessary to ensure compliances with the Act bear a "responsible relationship" to, or have a "responsible share" in, violations.

Thus *Dotterweich* and the cases which have followed reveal that in providing sanctions which reach and touch the individuals who execute the corporate mission—and this is by no means necessarily confined to a single corporate agent or employee—the Act imposed not only a positive duty to seek out and remedy violations when they occur but also, and primarily, a duty to implement measures that will ensure that violations will not occur. The requirements of foresight and vigilance imposed on responsible corporate agents are beyond question demanding, and perhaps onerous, but they are no more stringent than the public has a right to expect of those who voluntarily assume positions of authority in business enterprises whose services and products affect the health and well-being of the public that supports them. Cf. Wasserstrom, *Strict Liability in the Criminal Law,* 12 Stan. L. Rev. 731, 741–745 (1960).

The Act does not, as we observed in *Dotterweich,* make criminal liability turn on "awareness of some wrongdoing" or "conscious fraud." The duty imposed by Congress on responsible corporate agents is, we emphasize, one that requires the highest standard of foresight and vigilance, but the Act, in its criminal aspect, does not require that which is objectively impossible. The theory upon which responsible corporate agents are held criminally accountable for "causing" violations of the Act permits a claim that a defendant was "powerless" to prevent or correct the violation to "be raised defensively at a trial on the merits." *United States v. Wiesenfeld Warehouse Co.,* 376 U.S. 86, 91 (1964). If such a claim is made the defendant has the burden of coming forward with evidence, but this does not alter the Government's ultimate burden of proving beyond a reasonable doubt the defendant's guilt, including his power, in light of the duty imposed by the Act, to prevent or correct the prohibited condition. Congress has seen fit to enforce the accountability of responsible corporate agents dealing with products which may affect the health of consumers by penal sanctions cast in rigorous terms, and the obligation of the courts is to give them effect so long as they do not violate the Constitution.

We cannot agree with the Court of Appeals that it was incumbent upon the District Court to instruct the jury that the Government had the burden of establishing "wrongful action" in the sense in which the Court of Appeals used the phrase. The concept of a responsible relationship to, or a "responsible share" in, a violation of the Act indeed imports some measure of blameworthiness; but it is equally clear that the Government established a *prima facie* case when it introduced evidence sufficient to warrant a finding by the trier of the facts that the defendant had, by reason of his position in the corporation, responsibility and authority either to prevent in the first instance, or promptly to correct, the violation complained of, and that he failed to do so. The failure thus to fulfill the duty imposed by the interaction of the corporate agent's authority and the statute furnished a sufficient causal link. The considerations which prompted the imposition of this duty, and the scope of the duty, provide the measure of culpability.

Turning to the jury charge in this case, it is of course arguable that isolated parts can be read as intimating that a finding of guilt could be predicated solely on respondent's corporate position. But this is not the way we review jury instructions, because "a single instruction to a jury may not be judged in artificial isolation, but must be viewed in the context of the overall charge. . . ."

Reading the entire charge satisfies us that the jury's attention was adequately focused on the issue of respondent's authority with respect to the conditions that formed the basis of the alleged violations. Viewed as a whole, the charge did not permit the jury to find guilt solely on the basis of respondent's position in the corporation; rather, it fairly advised the jury that to find guilt it must find respondent "had a responsible relation to the situation," and "by virtue of his position . . . had authority and responsibility" to deal with the situation. The situation referred to could only be "food . . . held in unsanitary conditions in a warehouse with the result that it consisted, in part, of filth or . . . may have been contaminated with filth."

The record in this case reveals that the jury could not have failed to be aware that the main issue for determination was not respondent's position in the corporate hierarchy, but rather his accountability, because of the responsibility and authority of his position, for the conditions which gave rise to the charges against him.

Finally, we note that there was no request for an instruction that the Government was required to prove beyond a reasonable doubt that respondent was not without the power or capacity to affect the conditions which founded the charges in the information.[6]

Our conclusion that the Court of Appeals erred in its reading of the jury charge suggests as well our disagreement with that court concerning the admissibility of evidence demonstrating that respondent was advised by FDA in 1970 of insanitary conditions in Acme's Philadelphia warehouse. We are satisfied that the Act imposes the highest standard of care and permits conviction of responsible corporate officials who, in light of this standard of care, have the power to prevent or correct violations of its provisions.

Respondent testified in his defense that he had employed a system in which he relied upon his subordinates, and that he was ultimately responsible for this system.

---

[6] Counsel for respondent submitted only two requests for charge: (1) "Statutes such as the ones the Government seeks to apply here are criminal statutes and should be strictly construed," and (2) "The fact that John Park is President and Chief Executive Officer of Acme Markets, Inc. does not of itself justify a finding of guilty under Counts I through V of the Information." . . .

The testimony clearly created the "need" for rebuttal evidence. That evidence was not offered to show that respondent had a propensity to commit criminal acts, . . . or . . . that the crime charged had been committed; its purpose was to demonstrate that respondent was on notice that he could not rely on his system of delegation to subordinates to prevent or correct insanitary conditions at Acme's warehouses, and that he must have been aware of the deficiencies of this system before the Baltimore violations were discovered. The evidence was therefore relevant since it served to rebut respondent's defense that he had justifiably relied upon subordinates to handle sanitation matters.

Reversed.

NOTES AND QUESTIONS

1. Virtually every empirical study of the enforcement of regulatory crimes has concluded that criminal proceedings are brought only after the employer has been informed of some deficiency and failed to correct it. See, *e.g.,* Working Paper No. 30 of the Criminal Law Commission's Working Party (England), Strict Liability and the Enforcement of the Factories Act 1961 (1970); Law Reform Commission of Canada, Studies on Strict Liability (1974); Remington, *Liability without Fault Criminal Statutes—Their Relationship to Major Developments in Contemporary Economic and Social Policy: The Situation in Wisconsin,* 1956 Wis. L. Rev. 625; Rowan-Robinson, Watchman, and Barker, *Crime and Regulation* (1988) Crim. L. Rev. 211; Richardson, *Strict Liability for Regulatory Crime: The Empirical Research,* (1987) Crim. L. Rev. 295. In light of these data, is there need for the strict liability in criminal law? The two law reform commissions noted above concluded there was not and urged that strict liability offenses be replaced by provisions requiring negligence on the part of the defendant.

The Food and Drug Administration statute requires several steps prior to initiation of criminal proceedings, including a meeting with the defendant to determine what steps he is ready to take to alter the situation. See 21 U.S.C. § 335 (1970). See Austen, *Sanctions in Silhouette: An Inquiry into the Enforcement of the Federal Food, Drug and Cosmetic Act,* 51 Calif. L. Rev. 38 (1963); Russman, *Criminal Intent under the Federal Food, Drug and Cosmetic Act,* 7 Food Drug Comm. L.J. 336 (1942). Park refused to attend the meeting called by the FDA in this case. Does that have any bearing on the decision, since the Court did not mention it?

2. Two hours before FDA inspectors enter an otherwise spotless facility owned by the defendant, items are spoiled by the failure of a large refrigerator unit. Under *Park,* is the defendant criminally liable? If so, why? If not, why not?

Suppose that a chief executive officer's mortal enemy sneaked into a Phoenix warehouse (one supervised by the same personnel who supervised the Baltimore and Philadelphia plant) and contaminated the food. Five minutes later an FDA inspection occurred. Would *Park* hold him liable? See, *e.g., Comm v.*

N.Y. Cent. & H. Co., 202 Mass. 394, 88 N.E. 764 (1909) (malicious damage by strangers to air brakes of railroad not relevant in prosecution for failure to move train from public passage within five minutes).

3. *Park,* along with *Dotterweich,* cited in the decision, are read by some as establishing a "responsible corporate officer" doctrine, under which a person is liable essentially on the basis of his corporate title and responsibilities. Will the language of *Park* support such a reading? Will the holding? See Broudy, *RCRA and the Responsible Corporate Officer Doctrine: Getting Tough on Corporate Offenders by Sidestepping the Mens Rea Requirement,* 80 Ky. L.J. 1055 (1992); Wolf, *Finding an Environmental Felon under the Corporate Veil: The Responsible Corporate Officer Doctrine and RCRA,* 9 J. Land Use & Env. L. 1 (1993). As these titles suggest, some courts have deliberated as to whether the "RCO" doctrine applies to statutes (a) other than the FDA; and (b) that have a *mens rea* word somewhere in them. See Singer, *The Myth of the Responsible Corporate Officer Doctrine,* 6 Toxics L. Rptr. 1378 (1993).

4. In a dissenting opinion in *Park,* Mr. Justice Stewart said that the majority opinion was cast in terms of negligence. Is he correct? See Abrams, *Criminal Liability of Corporate Officers for Strict Liability Offenses—A Comment on Dotterweich and Park,* 28 UCLA L. Rev. 463 (1981). Compare Brickey, *Criminal Liability of Corporate Officers for Strict Liability Offenses,* 35 Vand. L. Rev. 1337 (1982).

5. Note that the Court put the burden of proof of "powerlessness" on the prosecution. We will consider later the issue of burden of proof generally. See § 9.04.

6. Is insanity, infancy, duress, or self-defense relevant to strict liability? See, *e.g.,* Keedy, *Insanity and Criminal Responsibility,* 30 Harv. L. Rev. 535 (1917); *R. v. Kennedy,* 7 C.C.C.2d 42, 18 C.R.N.S. 80 (1972); *R. v. Paul,* 12 C.C.C.2d 497 (1973).

STAPLES V. UNITED STATES

Supreme Court of the United States

511 U.S. 600 (1994)

Justice Thomas *delivered the opinion of the Court:*

The National Firearms Act makes it unlawful for any person to possess a machinegun that is not properly registered with the Federal Government. Petitioner contends that, to convict him under the Act, the Government should have been required to prove beyond a reasonable doubt that he knew the weapon he possessed had the characteristics that brought it within the statutory definition of a machinegun. We agree and accordingly reverse the judgment of the Court of Appeals.

I

The National Firearms Act (Act), 26 U.S.C. §§ 5801–5872, imposes strict registration requirements on statutorily defined "firearms." The Act includes within the term "firearm" a machinegun, § 5845(a)(6), and further defines a machinegun as "any weapon which shoots . . . or can be readily restored to shoot, automatically more than one shot, without manual reloading, by a single function of the trigger." § 5845(b). Thus, any fully automatic weapon is a "firearm" within the meaning of the Act.[1] Under the Act, all firearms must be registered in the National Firearms Registration and Transfer Record maintained by the Secretary of the Treasury. § 5841. § 5861(d) makes it a crime, punishable by up to 10 years in prison, see § 5871, for any person to possess a firearm that is not properly registered.

Upon executing a search warrant at petitioner's home, local police and agents of the Bureau of Alcohol, Tobacco and Firearms (BATF) recovered, among other things, an AR-15 assault rifle. The AR-15 is the civilian version of the military's M-16 rifle, and is, unless modified, a semiautomatic weapon. The M-16, in contrast, is a selective fire rifle that allows the operator, by rotating a selector switch, to choose semiautomatic or automatic fire. Many M-16 parts are interchangeable with those in the AR-15 and can be used to convert the AR-15 into an automatic weapon. No doubt to inhibit such conversions, the AR-15 is manufactured with a metal stop on its receiver that will prevent an M-16 selector switch, if installed, from rotating to the fully automatic position. The metal stop on petitioner's rifle, however, had been filed away, and the rifle had been assembled with an M-16 selector switch and several other M-16 internal parts, including a hammer, disconnector, and trigger. Suspecting that the AR-15 had been modified to be capable of fully automatic fire, BATF agents seized the weapon. Petitioner subsequently was indicted for unlawful possession of an unregistered machinegun in violation of § 5861(d).

At trial, BATF agents testified that when the AR-15 was tested, it fired more than one shot with a single pull of the trigger. It was undisputed that the weapon was not registered as required by § 5861(d). Petitioner testified that the rifle had never fired automatically when it was in his possession. He insisted that the AR-15 had operated only semiautomatically, and even then imperfectly, often requiring manual ejection of the spent casing and chambering of the next round. According to petitioner, his alleged ignorance of any automatic firing capability should have shielded him from criminal liability for his failure to register the weapon. He requested the District Court to instruct the jury that, to establish a violation of § 5861(d), the Government must prove beyond a reasonable doubt that the defendant "knew that the gun would fire fully automatically." . . .

The District Court rejected petitioner's proposed instruction and instead charged the jury as follows: "The Government need not prove the defendant knows he's dealing with a weapon possessing every last characteristic [which subjects it] to the regulation. It would be enough to prove he knows that he

---

[1] As used here, the terms "automatic" and "fully automatic" refer to a weapon that fires repeatedly with a single pull of the trigger. That is, once its trigger is depressed, the weapon will automatically continue to fire until its trigger is released or the ammunition is exhausted. Such weapons are "machineguns" within the meaning of the Act. We use the term "semiautomatic" to designate a weapon that fires only one shot with each pull of the trigger, and which requires no manual manipulation by the operator to place another round in the chamber after each round is fired.

is dealing with a dangerous device of a type as would alert one to the likelihood of regulation." Tr. 465.

Petitioner was convicted and sentenced to five years' probation and a $5,000 fine.

A

Whether or not § 5861(d) requires proof that a defendant knew of the characteristics of his weapon that made it a "firearm" under the Act is a question of statutory construction . . .

The language of the statute . . . provides little explicit guidance in this case. § 5861(d) is silent concerning the *mens rea* required for a violation. It states simply that "[i]t shall be unlawful for any person . . . to receive or possess a firearm which is not registered to him in the National Firearms Registration and Transfer Record." 26 U.S.C. § 5861(d). Nevertheless, silence on this point by itself does not necessarily suggest that Congress intended to dispense with a conventional *mens rea* element, which would require that the defendant know the facts that make his conduct illegal. . . . On the contrary, we must construe the statute in light of the background rules of the common law . . . in which the requirement of some *mens rea* for a crime is firmly embedded. . . .

[W]e have noted that the common law rule requiring *mens rea* has been "followed in regard to statutory crimes even where the statutory definition did not in terms include it. . . . Offenses that require no *mens rea* generally are disfavored," . . . and have suggested that some indication of congressional intent, express or implied, is required to dispense with *mens rea* as an element of a crime. . . .

The Government argues that Congress intended the Act to regulate and restrict the circulation of dangerous weapons. Consequently, in the Government's view, this case fits in a line of precedent concerning what we have termed "public welfare" or "regulatory" offenses, in which we have understood Congress to impose a form of strict criminal liability through statutes that do not require the defendant to know the facts that make his conduct illegal. . . .

For example, in *Balint, supra,* we concluded that the Narcotic Act of 1914, which was intended in part to minimize the spread of addictive drugs by criminalizing undocumented sales of certain narcotics, required proof only that the defendant knew that he was selling drugs, not that he knew the specific items he had sold were "narcotics" within the ambit of the statute.

Such public welfare offenses have been created by Congress, and recognized by this Court, in "limited circumstances." . . . Typically, our cases recognizing such offenses involve statutes that regulate potentially harmful or injurious items. . . . In such situations, we have reasoned that as long as a defendant knows that he is dealing with a dangerous device of a character that places him "in responsible relation to a public danger," . . . he should be alerted to the probability of strict regulation, and we have assumed that in such cases Congress intended to place the burden on the defendant to "ascertain at his peril whether [his conduct] comes within the inhibition of the statute."

. . . Thus, we essentially have relied on the nature of the statute and the particular character of the items regulated to determine whether congressional silence concerning the mental element of the offense should be interpreted as dispensing with conventional *mens rea* requirements.[3]

B

The Government argues that § 5861(d) defines precisely the sort of regulatory offense described in *Balint*. In his view, all guns, whether or not they are statutory "firearms," are dangerous devices that put gun owners on notice that they must determine at their hazard whether their weapons come within the scope of the Act. On this understanding, the District Court's instruction in this case was correct, because a conviction can rest simply on proof that a defendant knew he possessed a "firearm" in the ordinary sense of the term.

The Government seeks support for its position from our decision in *United States v. Freed,* 401 U.S. 601, (1971), which involved a prosecution for possession of unregistered grenades under § 5861(d).[4] The defendant knew that the items in his possession were grenades, and we concluded that § 5861(d) did not require Government to prove the defendant also knew that the grenades were unregistered. To be sure, in deciding that *mens rea* was not required with respect to that element of the offense, we suggested that the Act "is a regulatory measure in the interest of the public safety, which may well be premised on the theory that one would hardly be surprised to learn that possession of hand grenades is not an innocent act." Grenades, we explained, "are highly dangerous offensive weapons, no less dangerous than the narcotics involved in *Balint*." But that reasoning provides little support for dispensing with *mens rea* in this case.

As the Government concedes, *Freed* did not address the issue presented here. In *Freed,* we decided only that § 5861(d) does not require proof of knowledge that a firearm is unregistered. The question presented by a defendant who possesses a weapon that is a "firearm" for purposes of the Act, but who knows only that he has a "firearm" in the general sense of the term, was not raised or considered. And our determination that a defendant need not know that his weapon is unregistered suggests no conclusion concerning whether § 5861(d) requires the defendant to know of the features that make

---

[3] By interpreting such public welfare offenses to require at least that the defendant know that he is dealing with some dangerous or deleterious substance, we have avoided construing criminal statutes to impose a rigorous form of strict liability. See, *e.g., United States v. International Minerals & Chemical Corp.,* 402 U.S. 558, 563–564, (1971) (suggesting that if a person shipping and mistakenly thought that he was shipping distilled water, he would not violate a statute criminalizing undocumented shipping of acids). Trust strict liability might suggest that the defendant need not know even that he was dealing with a dangerous item. Nevertheless, we have referred to public welfare offenses as "dispensing with" or "eliminating" a *mens rea* requirement of "mental element," . . . and have described them as strict liability crimes. While use of the term "strict liability" is really a misnomer, we have interpreted statutes defining public welfare offenses to eliminate the requirement of *mens rea*; that is, the requirement of a "guilty mind" with respect to an element of a crime. Under such statutes we have not required that the defendant know the facts that make his conduct fit the definition of the offense. Generally speaking, such knowledge is necessary to establish *mens rea*, as is reflected in the maxim *ignorantia facti excusat* . . .

[4] A grenade is a "firearm" under the Act. 26 U.S.C. § § 5845(a)(8), 5845(f)(1)(B).

his weapon a statutory "firearm"; different elements of the same offense can require different mental states.... Moreover, our analysis in *Freed* likening the Act to the public welfare statute in *Balint* rested entirely on the assumption that the defendant knew that he was dealing with land grenades—that is, that he knew he possessed a particularly dangerous type of weapon (one within the statutory definition of a "firearm"), possession of which was not entirely "innocent" in and of itself. The predicate for that analysis is eliminated when, as in his case, the very question to be decided is whether the defendant must know of the particular characteristics that make his weapon a statutory firearm.

Notwithstanding these distinctions, the Government urges that *Freed's* logic applies because guns, no less than grenades, are highly dangerous devices that should alert their owners to the probability of regulation. But the gap between *Freed* and this case is too wide to bridge. In glossing over the distinction between grenades and guns, the Government ignores the particular care we have taken to avoid construing a statute to dispense with *mens rea* where doing so would "criminalize a broad range of apparently innocent conduct." ... In *Liparota,* we considered a statute that made unlawful the unauthorized acquisition or possession of food stamps. We determined that the statute required proof that the defendant knew his possession of food stamps was unauthorized, largely because dispensing with such a *mens rea* requirement would have resulted in reading the statute to outlaw a number of apparently innocent acts. Out conclusion that the statute should not be treated as defining a public welfare offense rested on the common sense distinction that a "food stamp can hardly be compared to a hand grenade."

Neither, in our view, can all guns be compared to hand grenades. Although the contrast is certainly not as stark as that presented in *Liparota,* the fact remains that there is a long tradition of widespread lawful gun ownership by private individuals in this country. Such a tradition did not apply to the possession of hand grenades in *Freed* or to the selling of dangerous drugs that we considered in *Balint.* ... Here, the Government essentially suggests that we should interpret the section under the altogether different assumption that "one would hardly be surprised to learn that owning a gun is not an innocent act." That proposition is simply not supported by common experience. Guns in general are not "deleterious devices or products or obnoxious waste materials," ... that put their owners on notice that they stand "in responsible relation to a public danger." ...

The Government protests that guns, unlike food stamps, but like grenades and narcotics, are potentially harmful devices.[5] Under this view, it seems that *Liparota's* concern for criminalizing ostensibly innocuous conduct is inapplicable whenever an item is sufficiently dangerous—that is, dangerousness alone should alert an individual to probable regulation and justify treating a statute that regulates the dangerous device is dispensing with *mens rea*. But that an

---

[5] The dissent relies upon the Government's repeated contention that the statute requires knowledge that "the item at issue was highly dangerous and of a type likely to be subject to regulation." But that assertion merely patterns the general language we have used to describe the *mens rea* requirement in public welfare offenses and amounts to no more than an assertion that the statute should be treated as defining a public welfare offense.

item is "dangerous," in some general sense, does not necessarily suggest, as the Government seems to assume, that it is not also entirely innocent. Even dangerous items can, in some cases, be so commonplace and generally available that we would not consider them to alert individuals to the likelihood of strict regulation. As suggested above, despite their potential for harm, guns generally can be owned in perfect innocence. Of course, we might surely classify certain categories of guns—no doubt including the machineguns, sawed-off shotguns, and artillery pieces that Congress has subjected to regulation—as items the ownership of which would have the same quasi-suspect character we attributed to owning hand grenades in *Freed*. But precisely because guns failing outside those categories traditionally have been widely accepted as lawful possessions, their destructive potential, while perhaps even greater than that of some items we would classify along with narcotics and hand grenades, cannot be said to put gun owners sufficiently on notice of the likelihood of regulation to justify interpreting § 5861(d) as not requiring proof of knowledge of a weapon's characteristics.[6]

On a slightly different tack, the Government suggests that guns are subject to an array of regulations at the federal, state, and local levels that put gun owners on notice that they must determine the characteristics of their weapons and comply with all legal requirements. But regulation in itself is not sufficient to place gun ownership in the category of the sale of narcotics in *Balint*. The food stamps at issue in *Liparota* were subject to comprehensive regulations, yet we did not understand the statute there to dispense with a *mens rea* requirement. Moreover, despite the overlay of legal restrictions on gun ownership, we question whether regulations on guns are sufficiently intrusive that they impinge upon the common experience that owning a gun is usually licit and blameless conduct. Roughly 50 per cent of American homes contain at least one firearm of some sort and in the vast majority of States, buying a shotgun or rifle is a simple transaction that would not alert a person to regulation any more than would buying a car.[9]

If we were to accept as a general rule the Government's suggestion that dangerous and regulated items place their owners under an obligation to inquire at their peril into compliance with regulations, we would undoubtedly

---

[6] [T]he dissent apparently does not conceive of the *mens rea* requirement in terms of specific categories of weapons at all, and rather views it as a more fluid concept that does not require delineation of any concrete elements of knowledge that will apply consistently from case to case. The dissent sees no need to define a class of items the knowing possession of which satisfies the *mens rea* element of the offense, for in the dissent's view the exact content of the knowledge requirement can be left to the jury in each case. As long as the jury concludes that the item in a given case is "sufficiently dangerous to alert [the defendant] to be likelihood of regulation," the knowledge requirement is satisfied. But the *mens rea* requirement under a criminal statute is a question of law, to be determined by the court. Our decisions suggesting that public welfare offenses require that the defendant know that he stands in "responsible relation to a public danger," . . . in no way suggest that what constitutes a public danger is a jury question. It is for courts, through interpretation of the statute, to define the *mens rea* required for a conviction. That task cannot be reduced to setting a general "standard," that leaves it to the jury to determine, based presumably on the jurors' personal opinions, whether the items involved in a particular prosecution are sufficiently dangerous to place a person on notice of regulation.

[9] For example, as of 1990, 39 States allowed adult residents, who are not felons or mentally infirm, to purchase a rifle or shotgun simply with proof of identification (and in some cases a simultaneous application for a permit) . . .

reach some untoward results. Automobiles, for example, might also be termed "dangerous" devices and are highly regulated at both the state and federal levels. Congress might see fit to criminalize the violation of certain regulations concerning automobiles, and thus might make it a crime to operate a vehicle without a properly functioning emission control system. But we probably would hesitate to conclude on the basis of silence that Congress intended a prison term to apply to a car owner whose vehicle's emissions levels, wholly unbeknownst to him, began to exceed legal limits between regular inspection dates.

Here, there can be little doubt that, as in *Liparota,* the Government's construction of the statute potentially would impose criminal sanctions on a class of persons whose mental state—ignorance of the characteristics of weapons in their possession—makes their actions entirely innocent.[10] The Government does not dispute the contention that virtually any semiautomatic weapon may be converted, either by internal modification or, in some cases, simply by wear and tear, into a machinegun within the meaning of the Act. . . . [I]n the Government's view, any persons who has purchased what he believes to be a semiautomatic rifle or handgun, or who simply has inherited a gun from a relative and left it untouched in an attic or basement, can be subject to imprisonment, despite absolute ignorance of the gun's firing capabilities, if the gun turns out to be an automatic.

We concur in the Fifth Circuit's conclusion on this point: "It is unthinkable to us that Congress intended to subject such law-abiding, well-intentioned citizens to a possible ten-year term of imprisonment if . . . what they genuinely and reasonably believed was a conventional semiautomatic [weapon] turns out to have worn down into or been secretly modified to be a fully automatic weapon."[11]

C

The potentially harsh penalty attached to violation of § 5861(d)—up to 10 years' imprisonment—confirms our reading of the Act. Historically, the penalty imposed under a statute has been a significant consideration in determining whether the statute should be construed as dispensing with *mens rea.* . . .

Indeed, some courts justified the absence of *mens rea* in part on the basis that the offenses did not bear, the same punishments as "infamous crimes,"

---

[10] We, of course, express no view concerning the inferences a jury may have drawn regarding petitioner's knowledge from the evidence in this case.

[11] The Government contends that Congress intended precisely such an aid to obtaining convictions, because requiring proof of knowledge would place too heavy a burden on the Government and obstruct the proper functioning of § 5861(d). Cf. *United States v. Balint,* (difficulty of proving knowledge suggests Congress did not intend to require *mens rea*) But knowledge can be inferred from circumstantial evidence, including any external indications signaling the nature of the weapon. And firing a fully automatic weapon would make the regulated characteristics of the weapon immediately apparent to its owner. In short, we are confident that when the defendant knows of the characteristics of his weapon that bring it within the scope of the Act, the Government will not face great difficulty in proving that knowledge. Of course, if Congress thinks it necessary to reduce the Government's burden at trial to ensure proper enforcement of the Act, it remains free to amend § 5861(d) by explicitly eliminating a *mens rea* requirement.

Tenement House Dept. v. McDevitt, 215 N.Y. 160, 168, 109 N.E. 88, 90 (1915) (Cardozo, J.), and questioned whether imprisonment was compatible with the reduced culpability required for such regulatory offenses. . . .

Close adherence to the early cases described above might suggest that punishing a violation as a felony is simply incompatible with the theory of the public welfare offense. In this view, absent a clear statement from Congress that *mens rea* is not required, we should not apply the public welfare offense rationale to interpret any statute defining a felony offense as dispensing with *mens rea.* But see *Balint, supra.*

We need not adopt such a definitive rule of construction to decide this case, however. Instead, we note only that where, as here, dispensing with *mens rea* would require the defendant to have knowledge only of traditionally lawful conduct, a severe penalty is a further factor tending to suggest that Congress did not intend to eliminate a *mens rea* requirement. In such a case, the usual presumption that a defendant must know the facts that make his conduct illegal should apply.

III

We emphasize that our holding is a narrow one. As in our prior cases, our reasoning depends upon a common-sense evaluation of the nature of the particular device or substance Congress has subjected to regulation and the expectations that individuals may legitimately have in dealing with the regulated items. In addition, we think that the penalty attached to § 5861(d) suggests that Congress did not intend to eliminate a *mens rea* requirement for violation of the section. As we noted in *Morissette,* "[N]either this Court nor, so far as we are aware, any other has undertaken to delineate a precise line or set forth comprehensive criteria for distinguishing between crimes that require a mental element and crimes that do not.". . . We attempt no definition here, either. We note only that our holding depends critically on our view that if Congress had intended to make outlaws of gun owners who were wholly ignorant of the offending characteristics of their weapons, and to subject them to lengthy prison terms, it would have spoken more clearly to that effect. . . . For the foregoing reasons, the judgment of the Court of Appeals is reversed and the case remanded for further proceedings consistent with this opinion.

So ordered.

Justice Ginsburg, *with whom Justice O'Connor joins, concurring in the judgment.*

Conviction under § 5861(d), the Government . . . concedes, requires proof that Staples "knowingly" possessed the machinegun . . . The question before us is not whether knowledge of possession is required, but what level of knowledge suffices: (1) knowledge simply of possession of the object; (2) knowledge, in addition, that the object is a dangerous weapon; (3) knowledge, beyond dangerousness, of the characteristics that render the object subject to regulation, for example, awareness that the weapon is a machinegun.[2]

Recognizing that the first reading effectively dispenses with *mens rea* the Government adopts the second, contending that it avoids criminalizing "apparently innocent conduct," . . . because under the second reading, "a defendant who possessed what he thought was a toy or a violin case, but which in fact was a machinegun, could not be convicted." . . . The Government, however, does not take adequate account of the "widespread lawful gun ownership" Congress and the States have allowed to persist in this country. . . . Given the notable lack of comprehensive regulation, "mere unregistered possession of certain types of [regulated weapons]—often [difficult to distinguish] from other, [non-regulated] types," has been held inadequate to establish the requisite knowledge. . . .

The Nation's legislators chose to place under a registration requirement only a very limited class of firearms, those they considered especially dangerous. The generally "dangerous" character of all guns, the Court therefore observes, did not suffice to give individuals in Staples' situation cause to inquire about the need for registration . . . Only the third reading, then, suits the purpose of the *mens rea* requirement—to shield people against punishment for apparently innocent activity.[3]

For these reasons, I conclude that conviction under § 5861(d) requires proof that the defendant knew he possessed not simply a gun, but a machinegun. The indictment in this case, but not the jury instruction, properly described this knowledge requirement. I therefore concur in the Court's judgment.

Justice Stevens, with whom Justice Blackmun joins, *dissenting.*

To avoid a slight possibility of injustice to unsophisticated owners of machineguns and sawed-off-shotguns, the Court has substituted its views of sound policy for the judgment Congress made when it enacted the National Firearms Act (or Act). Because the Court's addition to the text of 26 U.S.C. § 5861(d) is foreclosed by both the statute and our precedent, I respectfully dissent.

The Court is preoccupied with guns that "generally can be owned in perfect innocence." This case, however, involves a semiautomatic weapon that was readily convertible into a machinegun—a weapon that the jury found to be "a dangerous device of a type as would alert one to the likelihood of regulation." These are not guns "of some sort" that can be found in almost "50 percent

---

[2] Some Courts of Appeals have adopted a variant of the third reading, holding that the Government must show that the defendant knew the gun was a machinegun, but allowing inference of the requisite knowledge where a visual inspection of the gun would reveal that it has been converted into an automatic weapon.

[3] The *mens rea* presumption requires knowledge only of the facts that make the defendant's conduct illegal, lest it conflict with the related presumption, "deeply rooted in the American legal system," that, ordinarily, "ignorance of the law or a mistake of law is no defense to criminal prosecution." *Check v. United States* . . . The maxim explains why some "innocent" actors—for example, a defendant who knows he possesses a weapon with all of the characteristics that subject it to registration, but was unaware of the registration requirement, or thought the gun was registered—may be convicted under § 5861(d). Knowledge of whether the gun was registered is so closely related to knowledge of the registration requirement that requiring the Government to prove the former would in effect require it to prove knowledge of the law.

of American homes." . . . They are particularly dangerous—indeed, a substantial percentage of the unregistered machineguns now in circulation are converted semiautomatic weapons.

The question presented is whether the National Firearms Act imposed on the Government the burden of proving beyond a reasonable doubt not only that the defendant knew he possessed a dangerous device sufficient to alert him to regulation, but also that he knew it had all the characteristics of a "firearm" as defined in the statute. Three unambiguous guideposts direct us to the correct answer to that question: the text and structure of the Act, our cases construing both this Act and similar regulatory legislation, and the Act's history and interpretation.

I

Contrary to the assertion by the Court, the text of the statute does provide "explicit guidance in this case." The relevant section of the Act makes it "unlawful for any person . . . to receive or possess a firearm which is not registered to him in the National Firearms Registration and Transfer Record." 26 U.S.C. § 5861(d). Significantly, the section contains no knowledge requirement, nor does it describe a common-law crime. . . . Although the lack of an express knowledge requirement in § 5861(d) is not dispositive, . . . its absence suggests that Congress did not intend to require proof that the defendant knew all of the facts that made his conduct illegal. . . .

An examination of § 5861(d) in light of our precedent dictates that the crime of possession of an unregistered machinegun is in a category of offenses described as "public welfare" crimes.[9] Our decisions interpreting such offenses clearly require affirmance of petitioner's conviction.

II

"Public welfare" offenses share certain characteristics: (1) they regulate "dangerous or deleterious devices or products or obnoxious waste materials," . . . (2) they "heighten the duties of those in control of particular industries, trades, properties or activities that affect public health, safety or welfare," . . . and (3) they "depend on no mental element but consist only of forbidden acts or omissions," . . . Examples of such offenses include Congress' exertion of its power to keep dangerous narcotics . . . hazardous substances, . . . and impure and adulterated foods and drugs . . . out of the channels of commerce. . . .

Public welfare statutes render criminal "a type of conduct that a reasonable person should know is subject to stringent public regulation and may seriously threaten the community's health or safety." . . . Thus, under such statutes, "a defendant can be convicted even though he was unaware of the circumstances of his conduct that made it illegal." . . . Referring to the strict criminal sanctions for unintended violations of the food and drug laws, Justice

---

[9] These statutes are sometimes referred to as "strict liability" offenses. As the Court notes, because the defendant must know that he is engaged in the type of dangerous conduct that is likely to be regulated, the use of the term "strict liability" to describe these offenses is inaccurate . . . I therefore use the term "public welfare offense" to describe this type of statute.

Frank-further wrote: "The purposes of this legislation thus touch phases of the lives and health of people which, in the circumstances of modern industrialism, are largely beyond self-protection. Regard for these purposes should infuse construction of the legislation if it is to be treated as a working instrument of government and not merely as a collection of English words. . . . The prosecution . . . is based on a now familiar type of legislation whereby penalties serve as effective means of regulation. Such legislation dispenses with the conventional requirement for criminal conduct—awareness of some wrongdoing. In the interest of the larger good it puts the burden of acting at hazard upon a person otherwise innocence but standing in responsible relation to a public danger."

The National Firearms Act unquestionably is a public welfare statute. . . .

We thus have read a knowledge requirement into public welfare crimes, but not a requirement that the defendant know all the facts that make his conduct illegal. Although the Court acknowledges this standard, it nevertheless concludes that a gun is not the type of dangerous device that would alert one to the possibility of regulation.

Both the Court and Justice Ginsburg erroneously rely upon the "tradition-[al]" innocence of gun ownership to find that Congress must have intended the Government to prove knowledge of all the characteristics that make a weapon a statutory "firear[m]." We held in *Freed,* however, that a § 5861(d) offense may be committed by one with no awareness of either wrongdoing or of all the facts that constitute the offense. . . . Nevertheless, the Court, asserting that the Government "gloss[es] over the distinction between grenades and guns," determines that "the gap between *Freed*" and this case is too wide to bridge." As such, the Court instead reaches the rather surprising conclusion that guns are more analogous to food stamps than to hand grenades. Even if one accepts that dubious proposition, the Court founds it upon a faculty premise: its mischaracterization of the Government's submission as one contending that "*all guns* . . . are dangerous devices that put gun owners on notice . . . " (emphasis added). Accurately identified, the Government's position presents the question whether guns such as the one possessed by petitioner" are highly dangerous offensive weapons, no less dangerous than the narcotics" in *Balint* or the hand grenades in *Freed*. . . .

Thus, even assuming that the Court is correct that the mere possession of an ordinary rifle or pistol does not entail sufficient danger to alert one to the possibility of regulation, that conclusion does not resolve this case. Petitioner knowingly possessed a semiautomatic weapon that was readily convertible into a machinegun. The "character and nature" of such a weapon is sufficiently hazardous to place the possessor on notice of the possibility of regulation. See *Posters'N' Things, Ltd. v. United States,* U.S. —, —, (1994)(slip op., at 12).[18]

---

[18] The Court and Justice Ginsburg apparently assume that the outer limits of any such notice can be no broader than the category of dangerous objects that Congress delineated as "firearms." Our holding in *Posters'N' Things* illustrates the error in that assumption. A retailer who may not know whether certain merchandise is actually drug paraphernalia, as that term is defined in the relevant federal statute, may nevertheless violate the law if "aware that customers in general are likely to use the merchandise with drugs." The owner of a semiautomatic weapon that is readily convertible into a machinegun can certainly be aware of its dangerous nature and the consequent probability of regulation even if he does not know whether the weapon is actually

No significant difference exists between imposing upon the possessor a duty to determine whether such a weapon is registered, *Freed,* 401 U.S., at 607–610, and imposing a duty to determine whether that weapon has been converted into a machinegun.

The enforcement of public welfare offenses always entails some possibility of injustice. Congress nevertheless has repeatedly decided that an overriding public interest in health or safety may outweigh that risk when a person is dealing with products that are sufficiently dangerous or deleterious to make it reasonable to presume that he either knows, or should know, whether those products conform to special regulatory requirements. The dangerous character of the product is reasonably presumed to provide sufficient notice of the probability of regulation to justify strict enforcement against those who are merely guilty of negligent rather than willful misconduct.

The National Firearms Act is within the category of public welfare statutes enacted by Congress to regulate highly dangerous items. The Government submits that a conviction under such a statute may be supported by proof that the defendant "knew the item at issue was highly dangerous and of a type likely to be subject to regulation. . . . It is undisputed that the evidence in this case met that standard. . . . "[20]

* * *

Assuming that "innocent activity" describes conduct without any consciousness of wrongdoing, the risk of punishing such activity can be avoided only by reading into the statute the common-law concept of *mens rea:* "an evil purpose or mental culpability." . . . There are at least five such possible knowledge requirements, four of which entail the risk that a completely innocent mistake will subject a defendant to punishment. . . .

First, a defendant may know that he possesses a weapon with all of the characteristics that make it a "firearm" within the meaning of the statute and also know that it has never been registered, but be ignorant of the federal registration requirement. In such a case, we presume knowledge of the law even if we know the defendant is "innocent" in the sense that Justice Ginsburg uses the word. Second, a defendant may know that he possesses a weapon with all of the characteristics of a statutory firearm and also know that the law requires that it be registered, but mistakenly believe that it is in fact registered. *Freed* squarely holds that this defendant's "innocence" is not a defense. Third, a defendant may know only that he possesses a weapon with all of the characteristics of a statutory firearm. Neither ignorance of the registration requirement nor ignorance of the fact that the weapon is unregistered protects this "innocent" defendant. Fourth, a defendant may know that he

---

a machinegun. If ignorance of the precise characteristics that render an item forbidden should be a defense, items that are likely to be "drug paraphernalia" are no more obviously dangerous, and thus regulated, than items that are likely to be "firearms."

[20] The Court also supports its conclusion on the basis of the purported disparity between the penalty provided by this statute and those of other regulatory offenses. Although a modest penalty may indicate that a crime is a public welfare offense, such a penalty is not, as the Court recognizes, a requisite characteristic of public welfare offenses. For example, the crime involved in *Balint* involved punishment of up to five years imprisonment . . .

possess, a weapon that is sufficiently dangerous to likely be regulated, but not know that it has all the characteristics of a statutory firearm. Petitioner asserts that he is an example of this "innocent" defendant. Fifth, a defendant may know that he possesses an ordinary gun and, being aware of the widespread lawful gun ownership in the country, reasonably assume that there is no need "to inquire about the need for registration." That, of course, is not this case.[26] . . .

* * *

Accordingly, I would affirm the judgment of the Court of Appeals.

NOTES AND QUESTIONS

1. Each of the following acts has been held by at least one court to be a "public welfare offense" and hence(?) subject to characterization as a strict liability crime. How do you think each of these acts would be characterized by (a) the majority view, (b) the concurrence, (c) the dissent? Do you come away from *Staples* with a better definition of a public welfare offense than you had earlier? To what extent is the definition different from that provided by Professor Sayre in his seminal article, *supra?*

   1. Selling drugs.
   2. Driving a car over the speed limit (because the cruise control has stuck).
   3. Allowing a minor to watch billiards.
   4. Allowing a minor to drink alcohol.
   5. Killing of migratory birds.
   6. Bigamy.
   7. Selling child pornography.
   8. Having consensual sex with an underage person.
   9. Transporting subsize fish.
   10. Storing materials known to be dangerous to the environment.

2. One possible definition of a public welfare offense is that it involves danger to a large number of citizens who cannot protect themselves against that danger. Is this definition helpful? Does the *risk* engendered to the public by dumping toxic materials into the city water supply differ depending on whether the dumping is done intentionally by a group of terrorists or inadvertently by a clumsy worker in the water department? Is the question satisfactorily answered by saying that the terrorist could be convicted both of the strict liability offense and of intentionally endangering the water supply?

---

[26] Although I disagree with the assumption that "widespread lawful gun ownership" provides a sufficient reason for believing that there is no need to register guns (there is also widespread lawful automobile ownership), acceptance of that assumption neither justifies the majority's holding nor contradicts my conclusion on the facts of this case.

3. After *Staples,* how would you, as a staff member to a Congressional committee, advise the committee with regard to whether it should include a *mens rea* provision in new legislation? If you wished to impose strict liability, what *precise* language would you use in the statute?

4. For an argument that the Constitution permits strict liability regarding an element of a crime only if the legislature is constitutionally permitted to criminalize the intentional elements of the crime with the strict liability liability element removed, see Michaels, *Constitutional Innocence,* 112 Harv. L. Rev. 828 (1999). Thus for example, on this view the Court correctly intimated in *United States v. X–Citement Video, supra* p.-----, that attaching strict liability to the "depiction of a minor" element would be unconstitutional because the First Amendment would forbid punishing nonobscene, sexually explicit materials involving persons over the age of 17.

§ 4.08 THE FUTURE OF *MENS REA*

Whatever its own difficulties of interpretation, the Model Penal Code, both by § 2.02(3) and in many other ways, has sought to reassert the primacy of subjective culpability as the benchmark of the criminal law. At the same time as this development occurred, however, there were many suggesting that the requirement of *mens rea,* even in the attenuated form it had taken by the end of the 19th century, had outlived its usefulness. The next 50 years or so are likely to see a continuation and intensification of the "pro *mens rea*" and "anti *mens rea*" schools of thought concerning the role of the criminal law in society.

LEVITT, *EXTENT AND FUNCTION OF THE DOCTRINE OF* MENS REA

17 U. Ill. L. Rev. 578, 578 (1923)

The objective view . . . has gradually been gaining the ascendancy. At the present time, I think, [*mens rea*] is practically eliminated as an element of any specific crime, and maintains whatever hold it has because of the idea that a crime is an act for which the offender must be punished. This idea is tied up with the notion that punishment should not be inflicted upon one who did not act as a free moral agent and who did not possess the will to evil which is the central idea of the classical theory of punishment. Modern criminology, however, while not ignoring the will to evil, is not interested in it as a metaphysical speculation nor as a test for determining a future state of bliss or misery. It looks at the evil will as a psychological and sociological phenomenon.

I submit that if an intent cannot be discovered apart from acts and must be inferred from acts, and if the animus does not count if it does not prompt the doing of a forbidden act, it is quite obvious that the intent cannot be the essential element of a crime. The courts sententiously declare that "there can be no crime unless there is a joining of a criminal act with a criminal intent," and then they sedulously ignore the intent and examine the act. If they find the act is criminal, they assume that the intent exists and proceed to deal with the criminal. The phrase *actus non facit reum, nisi mens sit rea* means nothing to them. The judges recite it because other judges have recited it before them . . .

* * *

When the courts say . . . that a person is presumed to intend all the natural and probable consequences of his acts, they mean that if the consequences are the natural and probable results of the act which the person has performed they will infer from the existence of these consequences that the actor intended to produce these consequences. . . .

* * *

I submit, then, that in the criminal law of England and the United States there is no place now for a doctrine of intent as a necessary ingredient of a crime. In common law crimes you infer the intent from the acts or from the circumstances surrounding the acts, or from consequences growing out of the act. . . . A crime is an act. It is not an act plus an intent. *Injure actus no facit reum nisi mens sit rea* is no longer true. The modern maxim should be that most ancient one: *Actus facit reum.*

WOOTON, *CRIME AND THE CRIMINAL LAW*

52–53, 66, 75–79 (1963)

The conclusion to which this argument leads is not that the presence or absence of the guilty mind is unimportant but that *mens rea* has, so to speak—and this is the crux of the matter—got into the wrong place. Traditionally the requirement of the guilty mind is written into the actual definition of a crime. No guilty intention, no crime, is the rule. Obviously this makes sense if the law's concern is with wickedness; where there is no guilty intention there can be no wickedness. But it is equally obvious, on the other hand, that the action does not become innocuous merely because whoever performed it meant no harm. If the object of the criminal law is to prevent the occurrence of especially damaging actions, it would be absurd to turn a blind eye even to those which were due to carelessness, negligence or even accident. The question of motivation is, in the first instance irrelevant.

But only in the first instance, at a later stage, that is to say, after what is now known as a conviction, the presence or absence of guilty intention is all important for its effect on the appropriate methods to be taken to prevent a recurrence of the forbidden act. . . .

Any attempt to distinguish between wickedness and mental abnormality was doomed to failure; . . . the only solution for the future [is] to allow the concept of responsibility to "wither away" and to concentrate instead on the problem of the choice of treatment, without attempting to assess the effect of mental peculiarities or the degree or type of culpability. . . .

* * *

The proposal that we should bypass, or disregard, the concept of responsibility is only too easily misunderstood. . . . First, it is to be observed that the term "responsibility" is here used in a restricted sense, much narrower than that which it often carries in ordinary speech. The measure of a person's responsibility for his action, is perhaps best defined in terms of his capacity to act otherwise than he did. . . . [I]n the second place, to discourage the notion of responsibility does not mean that the medical condition of the offender ceases to have any importance. . . . [T]he difference is that they become relevant not to the question of determining the measure of his culpability, but to the choice of the treatment most likely to be effective in discouraging offending again. . . . [N]ext, it must be emphasized that nothing in what has been said involves acceptance of a deterministic view of human behavior. . . . [O]nce the criminal law is conceived as an instrument of crime prevention, the question whether on any occasion a man could or could not have acted otherwise than as he did can be left on one side or answered either way, as may be preferred. It is no longer relevant. . . . [T]he real difference between the psychiatric and the legal approach has nothing to do with free will or determinism, it has to do with the conception of the objective of the criminal process, with the question of whether the aim of that process is punitive or preventive, whether what matters is to punish the wrongdoer or to send him on the road to virtue, and, in order to take a stand on that issue, neither party need be a determinist.

NOTE

For other accounts of the evolution of *mens rea,* see Thornton, *Intent in Crime,* 9 Crim. L. Mag. and Rep. 139 (1887); Endlick, *The Doctrine of Mens Rea,* 13 Crim. L. Mag. and Rep. 831 (1891); Stallybrass, *The Eclipse of Mens Rea,* 52 L. Q. Rev. 60 (1936); G. Erenius, *Criminal Negligence and Individuality* (1963). See also Sayre, *Mens Rea,* 45 Harv. L. Rev. 934 (1932) ("The old conception of *mens rea*" must be discarded, and in its place must be substituted the new conception of *mentes reae.*"). Several writers have agreed with Lady Wooton that *mens rea* should be eliminated as irrelevant to the criminal law. See, *e.g.,* J. Marshall, Intention in Law and Society (1968); K. Menninger, The Crime of Punishment (1968); Gaylin, *Psychiatry and the Law, Partners in Crime,* 8 Colum. L Forum. 23 (Spring 1965).

HART, BOOK REVIEW

74 Yale L.J., 1325 (1965)

[Lady Wooton] altogether ignores an outlook on punishment which is surely common, intelligible and, except perhaps for determinists . . . perfectly defensible. According to this outlook we should restrict even punishment designed as "preventive" to those who at the time of their offence had the capacity and a fair opportunity or chance to obey the law: and we should do this out of considerations of fairness or justice to those whom we punish. This is an intelligible ideal of justice to the individual. . . . Viewed in this way as a restriction imposed on preventive punishment by considerations of fairness or justice to individuals the doctrine of *mens rea* presents an aspect of neglect which renders Lady Wooton's argument inconclusive. . . .

* * *

[T]here are equally practical objections to the wholesale elimination of *mens rea* from the criminal law. . . . The first and most important concerns individual freedom. In a system in which proof of *mens rea* was no longer a necessary condition for conviction the occasions for official interferences in our lives would be vastly increased. If the doctrine of *mens rea* were abolished, every blow, even if it was apparent that it was accidental or merely careless, and therefore not under the present law a criminal assault, would in principle be a matter for investigation under the new scheme. This is so because the possibilities of curable condition would have to be investigated. . . . No doubt under the new regime prosecuting authorities would use their common-sense; but a very great discretion would have to be entrusted to them to sift from the mass the cases worth investigation for either penal or therapeutic treatment. This expansion of police powers would bring with it great uncertainly for the individual citizen and, though official interference with his life would be more frequent, he will be less able to predict their incidence if any accidental breach of the criminal law may be an occasion for them.

A second objection is [that] . . . one of the features distinguishing punishment from treatment is that unlike a medical inspection followed by detention in a hospital, conviction by a court followed by a sentence of imprisonment is a public act expressing the odium of society for those who break the law, or at least for their conduct in doing so. As long as this odium attaches to conviction and sentence, a moral objection to their use on those who could not have helped doing as they did will always remain. On the other hand, if with the operation of the new system, conviction and imprisonment will in time be assimilated to, and no more odious than, a compulsory medical inspection . . . it seems that the law will lose an important element in its authority and deterrent force.

NOTE

For other critiques of Lady Wooton's provocative suggestion, see H. L. Hart, The Morality of the Criminal Law (1965); and Kadish, *The Decline of Innocence,* 26 Cambridge L.J. 273 (1968).

Chapter 5
Homicide

§ 5.01 INTRODUCTION

Prior to the 13th century, the law of homicide was relatively simple: anyone who caused the death of another, except in cases of killing under the king's warrant or in the pursuit of justice, was guilty and subject to punishment by death. The line between murder and manslaughter was unknown as were any legal distinctions between voluntary and involuntary homicides. The mental element was of minimal, if any, importance. Sayre, *Mens Rea,* 45 Harv. L. Rev. 974, 979–80, 994 (1932).

Beginning in the 13th century, however, a variety of forces began to converge that would eventually result in a complex and sometimes seemingly irreconcilable body of doctrine. This evolution of the law of homicide is briefly summarized by Plucknett.

PLUCKNETT

445–46

In the thirteenth century misadventure and self-defence were still recognized, not so much as defenses to a charge of homicide as circumstances entitling one to a pardon; but if these defenses were not involved, there was but one other case, and that was homicide. Whatever might be urged in mitigation of this offense could only be urged before the King as part of an appeal for pardon; it could not be considered by a court of law. It is important to remember that the prerogative of mercy was the only point at which our medieval criminal law was at all flexible; hence pardons were issued with liberality for all sorts of felonies throughout the middle ages and long afterwards, and it is in the history of pardons, therefore, that the gradual growth of a classification of homicides is to be sought. A beginning was made in 1328 when a statute called, in general terms, for restraint in issuing pardons, and in 1390 the Commons secured a statute which recognized certain pardons as issuing from the Chancery as a matter of course (no doubt cases of self-defense or misadventure); with these the statute contrasts pardons for "murders done in await, assault, or malice prepense." In such cases pardons were subjected to almost impossible conditions. The pardoning power in other cases was not touched, and so the Crown retained its normal powers and procedure for pardoning homicide, except cases of what we may call wilful murder. The distinction becomes clearer in the Tudor reigns when benefit of clergy was being redistributed among the various crimes. Thus, James Grame wilfully murdered his master, Richard Tracy, on 9th February 1497 and then pleaded his clergy. An indignant Parliament was determined that he should hang, and so attained him, and abolished clergy for his and all like cases of prepensed murder in petty treason. A number of such statutes followed in the reign of Henry VIII, and one of them uses (probably for the first time) the words "wilful murder;" from that date it is clear that the statutes have, in effect, divided the old felony of homicide into two separate crimes, "wilful murder of malice aforethought" which was not clergyable and therefore capital, and on the other hand, those homicides which were neither in self-defence, nor by misadventure. Some such division was obviously necessary, but unfortunately the boundary was generally sought in glossing the ancient formula "malice." "Manslaughter," as it came to be called, exercised the analytical skill of writers on pleas of the Crown for a century and more before very much order could be introduced, and even now serious questions as to the import of "malice" in murder have been raised.

The historical development of the law of homicide thus represents an attempt to distinguish between those killers who merit capital punishment and those who do not. To a large extent, the problem of grading homicide for purposes of punishment remains the central problem of this area of the law, especially in jurisdictions that retain the death penalty.

The grading problem focuses on issues of *mens rea*. For this reason, these materials are primarily directed to a consideration of the law's attention to the killer's state of mind at the time of the killing. The chapter begins, however, with an examination of *actus reus* matters entailed in the crime of homicide and concludes with a discussion of capital punishment, a penalty at present primarily associated with certain kinds of murder.

§ 5.02 THE *ACTUS* REUS: CAUSING THE DEATH OF A PERSON

[A] The Timing of Causation

Many of the causation issues in homicide have been addressed in the general discussion of causation, *supra* at § 3.04. The following case and its subsequent discussion, however, present a causation issue unique to homicide so it is considered here.

STATE V. MINSTER

Court of Appeals of Maryland

302 Md. 240, 486 A.2d 1197 (1985)

COUCH, Judge.

The issue here is whether we should abrogate the common law rule of "a year and a day," which bars a prosecution for murder when the victim dies more than a year and a day after being injured. Inasmuch as we believe this issue is more appropriately addressed by the legislature, we shall not abrogate the common law rule. Accordingly, we affirm the trial court's dismissal of the indictment filed against the appellee, Larry Edmund Minster.

The facts in this case are undisputed. On July 8, 1982, Minster shot the victim, Cheryl Dodgson, in the neck. As a result of the shooting, Ms. Dodgson became a quadriplegic. Minster was charged in Prince George's County Circuit Court with attempted first degree murder, assault with intent to murder, assault and battery and use of a handgun in a crime of violence. He was brought to trial in April of 1983.

Minster was convicted of attempted first degree murder and the use of a handgun in a crime of violence. He was sentenced to 20 years imprisonment for attempted murder and received a 10 year concurrent sentence for the handgun violation. . . .

* * *

On October 3, 1983, Ms. Dodgson died from injuries the State contends resulted directly from Minster's actions on July 8, 1982 one year and eighty-seven days before the victim's death. One month after Ms. Dodgson's death, Minster was indicted for first degree murder. The Circuit Court for Prince George's County dismissed the indictment because the death of Ms. Dodgson occurred more than a year and a day after the shooting. . . .

The State's issue is simply stated: should the prosecution of Minster for the murder of Cheryl Dodgson be barred by the year and a day rule. It argues that the common law rule is now archaic and, in light of medical advances in life-saving techniques, there is no sound reason for retaining the rule today. Minster argues that there are legitimate justifications for the rule's continued application; moreover, because of the number of alternatives available to replace the year and a day rule, a change in the rule should be left to the legislature.

We agree with Minster that there are a number of sound justifications for retaining this rule. As Chief Judge Orth stated . . . "[a]bolition of the rule may well result in imbalance between the adequate protection of society and justice for the individual accused, and there would remain a need for some form of limitation on causation. . . ."

* * *

Justice Musmanno, who dissented from the judicial abrogation of the rule in *Commonwealth v. Ladd,* 402 Pa. 164, 166 A.2d 501 (1960), stated this concern more fully:

> Dorothy Pierce, the alleged victim, died of pneumonia. It is possible, of course, that her weakened condition, due to the alleged hurt received thirteen months before, made her more susceptible to the attack of pneumonia. On the other hand, there is the likely possibility that the pneumonia had no possible connection with the injury allegedly inflicted by the defendant.
>
> Suppose that the pneumonia occurred two years after the physical injury, would it still be proper to charge the defendant with murder? If a murder charge can be brought two years after a blow has been struck, will there ever be a time when the Court may declare that the bridge between the blow and death has now been irreparably broken? May the Commonwealth indict a man for murder when the death occurs ten years after the blow has fallen? Twenty years? Thirty years? One may search the majority opinion through every paragraph, sentence, clause, phrase and comma, and

find no answer to this very serious question. The majority is content to open a Pandora's box of interrogation and let it remain unclosed, to the torment and possible persecution of every person who may have at one time or another injured another. I don't doubt that an "expert" of some kind can be found to testify that a slap in the face was the cause of a death fifteen years later.

If there is one thing which the criminal law must be, if it is to be recognized as just, it must be specific and definitive. . . .

* * *

In addition, a person charged with attempted first degree murder (as was the case here) can be sentenced to life imprisonment. . . . Moreover, a sentencing judge may always consider the seriousness of the injury to, or the subsequent death of, the victim. . . . The only additional conceivable punishment a first degree murder conviction entails is the death penalty. We do not believe this distinction is a sufficient reason to rescind a common law rule which has existed for over seven hundred years.[1]

Assuming, *arguendo,* that we abrogate this rule, with what do we replace it?

In *People v. Stevenson,* 416 Mich. 383, 331 N.W.2d 143 (1982), the court addressed the identical issue we address today. Five alternatives to the rule were offered to that court:

(1) The Court could retain the year and a day rule. (2) The Court could modify the rule by extending the span of time, for example, of three years and a day. California Penal Code, § 194. (3) The Court could extend the rule to any length of time it chooses, perhaps two years, five years, or ten years. (4) The Court could change the rule from an irrebuttable presumption to a rebuttable one, but with a higher burden of proof. *Cf. Serafin v. Serafin,* 401 Mich. 629, 258 N.W.2d 461 (1977), requiring clear and convincing evidence. (5) Finally, the Court could simply abolish the rule entirely, leaving the issue of causation to the jury in light of the facts and arguments in each particular case. . . .

* * *

Thus we find there is a great difference of opinion surrounding the appropriate length of the period after which prosecution is barred and some doubt whether the rule should exist at all. Consequently, we believe it is the legislature which should mandate any change in the rule, if indeed any change is appropriate in Maryland. . . .

* * *

In sum, we uphold the application of the year and a day rule in Maryland. Accordingly, we affirm the trial court's dismissal of the indictment.

---

[1] The rule has been traced back to the Statutes of Gloucester (1278) in the reign of King Edward I. *See People v. Stevenson,* 416 Mich. 383, 389, 331 N.W.2d 143, 145 (1982).

Judgment affirmed.

NOTES AND QUESTIONS

1. Are the *Minster* court's reasons for retaining the common law rule convincing? For example, are the sentencing considerations as minimal as the court makes them out to be? If a consequence of applying the year and a day rule is losing the opportunity to impose the death penalty, should the court have rejected the rule? Note that Maryland permits life imprisonment for attempted murder. Suppose the maximum penalty for attempted murder had been, say, 25 years imprisonment. Or 10 years. Would retention of the common law rule then be unjustified?

The *Minster* court also notes that sentencing judges can take the death of the victim into account when sentencing offenders convicted of attempted murder. As a sentencing consideration, what bearing should the fortuity of the victim's death have in such situations? Consider Chapter 7 on inchoate crimes, *infra,* as you think of these questions.

2. As a policy matter, of the five alternatives outlined by the *Stevenson* court referred to in Minster, which should be adopted?

3. The problem of the timing of causation in homicide cases may take on new importance in the context of the recent AIDS phenomenon. "AIDS is spread by acts, not by casual exposure. As AIDS spreads further, some are urging that those acts, including sexual acts, be treated as crimes." Field and Sullivan, *AIDS and the Criminal Law,* 15 L., Med. & Health Care 46 (1987). Assuming that it could be shown that an AIDS carrier caused the death of a victim by culpably infecting him with the presently incurable and fatal disease, the traditional law of homicide generally would not cover the case because the period of time between infection and death usually exceeds a year and a day.

Perhaps in response to a perceived deficiency in the common law rule as applied to the AIDS context, a bill proposing to make the knowing transmission of the AIDS virus second degree murder was introduced to the Criminal Justice Committee of the Louisiana House of Representatives, a jurisdiction following the year and a day rule. *AIDS Pol'y and L.,* June 17, 1987, at 7. While the Louisiana bill was defeated in committee, it is not inconceivable that such bills might eventually be enacted in light of the potential risk to life entailed in the AIDS problem. In an HIV screen of arrested Orlando-area prostitutes, 22 percent tested positive. *AIDS Pol'y and L.,* December 30, 1987, at 4. Already jurisdictions have charged some AIDS carriers with attempted manslaughter and have charged others with attempted murder for having sex with other people while infected and for selling infected blood. *Id.,* Field and Sullivan. In another case, a prison inmate carrying the AIDS virus was convicted of assault with a deadly weapon (his teeth) for biting two prison guards. *United States v. Moore,* 669 F. Supp. 289 (D. Minn. 1987).

On appeal the Eighth Circuit Court of Appeals affirmed the district court conviction in *Moore,* finding that defendant's mouth and teeth were used as deadly weapons even though insufficient evidence existed to support a finding that the bites could have transmitted the AIDS virus. *United States v. Moore,* 846 F.2d 1163 (8th Cir. 1988). But see *Brock v. State,* 555 So. 2d 285 (Ala. Crim. App. 1989), which precludes conviction for using a "dangerous instrument" causing "serious physical injury" where the state fails to show that an AIDS-infected inmate could transmit the disease by biting. On the other hand, in *State v. Haines,* 545 N.E.2d 834 (Ind. App. 1989), the court affirmed attempted murder convictions of a defendant afflicted with AIDS who intended to inflict others with the disease by spitting and throwing his blood at them and by biting and scratching them. In such circumstances the court found a genuine risk of AIDS transmission.

For additional material on AIDS and criminal law including causation issues in homicide, see Robinson, *AIDS and the Criminal Law: Traditional Approaches and a New Statutory Proposal,* 14 Hofstra L. Rev. 91 (1985); Note, *Criminal Liability for Transmission of AIDS: Some Evidentiary Problems,* 10 Crim. Just. J. 69 (1987).

4. Most jurisdictions continue to follow the year and day rule. See generally 60 A.L.R.3d 1323 (1974). Some jurisdictions have legislatively abolished the rule, *id.,* while a few courts have prospectively discarded it. *See, e.g., State v. Young,* 77 N.J. 245, 390 A.2d 556 (1978). The Model Penal Code rejects any express time limitation as a special causal requirement in homicide cases. MPC § 210.1, Comment at 9–10.

[B] What Is "Death"?

STATE V. FIERRO

Supreme Court of Arizona

124 Ariz. 182, 603 P.2d 74 (1979)

CAMERON, Chief Justice.

Defendant David Madrid Fierro was adjudged guilty of first degree murder following trial to a jury in the Maricopa County Superior Court and was sentenced to life imprisonment. We have jurisdiction of this appeal. . . .

* * *

We must answer the following question on appeal:

1. Was the evidence sufficient to support the jury's conclusion that the defendant caused the death of the victim?

* * *

The facts necessary for a resolution of this matter on appeal are as follows. Between 8 and 9 o'clock on the evening of 18 August 1977, Victor Corella was [purposely] . . . shot [by defendant] once in the chest and four times in the head. Following the shooting, Corella's body was taken to the emergency room at Maricopa County Hospital. His blood pressure was very low due to secondary bleeding from the gunshot wound to the chest area. Surgery was performed in an effort to control the bleeding. He was then taken to the surgical intensive care unit where a follow-up examination and evaluation revealed that he had suffered brain death. Corella was maintained on support systems for the next three days while follow-up studies were completed which confirmed the occurrence of brain death. The supportive measures were terminated and he was pronounced dead on 22 August 1977.

* * *

CAUSE OF DEATH

At the trial, Dr. Hugh McGill, a surgical resident at the Maricopa County Hospital, testified that:

A: After surgery he was taken to the intensive care unit. He was evaluated by a neurosurgeon who felt there was nothing we could do for his brain, he had brain death. He remained somewhat stable over the next two or three days. We had follow-up studies that confirmed our impression of brain death and because of that supportive measures were terminated and he was pronounced dead, I believe, on the 22nd.

Q: Who pronounced him dead?

A: I did.

Q: Approximately what time?

A: 3:45 pm on the 22nd of August.

Q: How many days after he was brought in did you actually pronounce him dead?

A: Would have been four days.

Dr. Hugh McGill, who performed the surgery on Corella and later pronounced him dead, and Doctor Thomas B. Jarvis, a Deputy Medical Examiner who performed an autopsy on Corella, both testified the cause of death was multiple gunshot wounds to the head.

Defendant initially argues that the termination of support systems by attendant doctors three days after Corella had suffered "brain death" was the cause of Corella's death, and that the evidence supporting the judgment of guilt to the crime of murder was therefore insufficient to convict the defendant Fierro. We do not agree.

* * *

We . . . believe that the defendant was legally dead before the life support systems were withdrawn. Although our legislature has defined dead human remains in A.R.S. § 36-301(1) and fetal death in A.R.S. § 36-301(2), it has not adopted a definition of death. A statutory definition is not necessary, however. Both the fact of death and its cause can be apparent to an ordinary layman when the condition of the body or the nature of the wound is such that no other determination is reasonable. When these obvious factors are present, it is not necessary that experts be required to testify in order to establish death and its cause. It is only where the fact of death and its cause is beyond the understanding of the average layman that expert testimony may be necessary.

The common law definition of death was as follows:

The cessation of life; the ceasing to exist; defined by physicians as a total stoppage of the circulation of the blood, and a cessation of the animal and vital functions consequent thereon, such as respiration, pulsation, etc.

Black's Law Dictionary 488 (4th ed. 1968). Thus, according to common law, as long as the person was breathing and the blood was flowing through his veins he was not dead even though his brain was no longer able to function.

Because of the increased interest in organ transplants, it was felt by some that a new definition of death was necessary. As a result, the National Conference of Commissioners on Uniform State Laws proposed the Uniform Brain Death Act that stated, "for legal and medical purposes an individual who has sustained irreversible cessation of all functioning of the brain including the brain stem, is dead." The uniform law provides that a determination of brain death must be made "in accordance with the reasonable medical standards." The *Report of the Ad Hoc Committee of the Harvard Medical School* at 205 Journal of American Medical Association 337 (1968) defined "cessation of life" as "brain death" which takes place when there is (1)unresponsiveness to normally painful stimuli; (2)absence of spontaneous movements or breathing; and (3)absence of reflexes.

In the instant case, the body of the victim was breathing—though not spontaneously, and blood was pulsating through his body before the life support mechanisms were withdrawn. Because there was an absence of cardiac and circulatory arrest, under the common law rule he would not have been legally dead. Under the Harvard Medical School test and Proposal of the National Conference of Commissioners on Uniform State Laws he was, in fact, dead before the life supports were withdrawn as he had become "brain" or "neurologically" dead prior to that time. We believe that while the common law definition of death is still sufficient to establish death, the test of the Harvard Medical School or the Commissioners on Uniform State Laws, if properly supported by expert medical testimony, is also a valid test for death in Arizona. . . . In the instant case, expert testimony was received which showed that the victim had suffered irreversible "brain death" before the life supports had been withdrawn. In effect, the doctors were just passively stepping aside to let the natural course of events lead from brain death to common law death. In either case, the victim was legally dead for the purpose of the [murder] statute. . . .

* * *

The verdict and judgment of guilt are affirmed.

Siruckmeyer, V. C. J., and Hays, Holohan and Gordon, JJ., *concur.*

NOTES AND QUESTIONS

1. Some jurisdictions have adopted brain death statutes. Absent legislative action, courts such as *Fierro* routinely uphold homicide convictions where

offenders cause brain death. For a summary of this issue in the various jurisdictions, see 42 A.L.R.4th 743 (1985).

2. Suppose that the victim in *Fierro* was not totally brain dead when brought into the hospital but was deeply comatose as a result of severe brain damage, leaving him in a vegetative state that was likely to be permanent. Although the victim manifested some minimal brain activity, family members requested medical personnel to terminate respirators and other life-sustaining equipment that had been keeping the victim's lungs and heart functioning. Does the doctor who honors such a request and terminates life-sustaining equipment commit homicide when the victim dies shortly after being taken off the equipment? See *Barber v. Superior Court,* 147 Cal. App. 3d 1006, 195 Cal. Rptr. 484 (1983). What is the result if, after the victim's death, the doctor removes some of victim's organs for subsequent use in organ transplants? See *People v. Bonilla,* 95 A.2d 396, 467 N.Y.S.2d 599 (1983) (victim was arguably brain dead when doctor terminated life support system and removed organs).

[C] Who Is a Person?

KEELER V. SUPERIOR COURT

Supreme Court of California

2 Cal. 3d 619, 470 P.2d 617 (1970)

[For the opinion in this case, see p. 264, *supra.*]

NOTES AND QUESTIONS

1. In finding that a fetus is not a person for purposes of the crime of homicide where the legislature has not specifically addressed the issue, *Keeler* represents the majority view. The factual contexts of such cases are often egregious. *See, e.g., Hollis v. Commonwealth,* 652 S.W.2d 61 (Ky. 1983), where the court found no taking of human life, and therefore no murder, where the defendant dragged his estranged wife from her parent's house into a barn and, after telling her he did not want the baby she was carrying, forced his hand up her vagina causing the death of a twenty-eight—to—thirty-week -old fetus. *See also People v. Greer,* 79 Ill. 2d 103, 402 N.E.2d at 203 (1980) (defendant improperly charged with murder after he allegedly beat his pregnant girlfriend with his fists and kicked her and struck her repeatedly with a broomstick thereby causing the death of an approximately eight-month-old fetus).

The *Keeler* approach is rejected by at least two courts, however, which have held prospectively that viable fetuses are human lives under homicide statutes even though the legislature has not explicitly so provided. *See Commonwealth v. Cass,* 392 Mass. 799, 467 N.E.2d 1324 (1984); *State v. Horne,* 282 S.C. 444, 319 S.E.2d 703 (1984).

2. Several jurisdictions have altered the common law rule by enacting feticide statutes. The California statute (defining murder in terms of "killing of a human being or a fetus") noted after the *Keeler* case in Chapter 2 at p. 274, *supra,* has been interpreted to apply to nonviable as well as viable fetal life. *See People v. Davis,* 872 P.2d 591 (Cal. 1994) (murder statute held applicable to nonviable fetuses that had passed the embryonic stage but due process prevents retroactive application). Consider the following statutory provisions:

Intentional Homicide of an Unborn Child.

(a) A person commits the offense of intentional homicide of an unborn child if, in performing acts which cause the death of an unborn child, he without lawful justification:

(1) either intended to cause the death of or do great bodily harm to the pregnant woman or her unborn child or knew that such acts would cause death or great bodily harm to the pregnant woman or her unborn child; or

(2) he knew that his acts created a strong probability of death or great bodily harm to the pregnant woman or her unborn child; and

(3) he knew that the woman was pregnant.

(b) For purposes of this Section, (1)"unborn child" shall mean any individual of the human species from fertilization until birth, and (2)"person" shall not include the pregnant woman whose unborn child is killed.

(c) This Section shall not apply to acts which cause the death of an unborn child if those acts were committed during any abortion, as defined in Section 2 of the Illinois Abortion Law of 1975, as amended, to which the pregnant woman has consented. This Section shall not apply to acts which were committed pursuant to usual and customary standards of medical practice during diagnostic testing or therapeutic treatment.

(d) Penalty. The sentence for intentional homicide of an unborn child shall be the same as for first degree murder, except that the death penalty may not be imposed.

Ill. Rev. Stat. § 9-1.2

Any person who intentionally terminates a human pregnancy after the end of the second trimester of the pregnancy where death of the fetus results commits feticide. Feticide is a class "C" felony.

This section shall not apply to the termination of a human pregnancy performed by a physician licensed in this state to practice medicine or surgery when in the best clinical judgment of the physician the termination is performed to preserve the life or health of the pregnant person or of the fetus and every reasonable medical effort not inconsistent with preserving the life of the pregnant person is made to preserve the life of a viable fetus.

Iowa Code Ann. § 707.7.

Florida law provides, "The willful killing of an unborn quick child, by any injury to the mother of such child which would be murder if it resulted in the death of such mother, shall be deemed manslaughter, a felony of the second degree. . . . " Fla. Stat. Ann. § 782.09. *See also* Minn. Stat. Ann. §§ 609.2661, 609.2662 (murder statute applies to "unborn children"). *See State v. Merrill,* 450 N.W.2d 318 (Minn. 1990) (upholding Minnesota statute as applied to nonviable fetus against equal protection and due process vagueness challenges).

3. As a policy matter, should a fetus be a person under the law of homicide? Should only viable fetuses be persons? If the taking of fetal life should be homicide, should the crime be murder, manslaughter, or the special crime of feticide?

[D] The Implications of Causing One's Own Death

In re Joseph G.

Supreme Court of California, in Banc

34 Cal. 3d 429, 194 Cal. Rptr. 163, 667 P.2d 1176 (1983)

Moss, Justice.

Joseph G., a minor, was charged in a juvenile court petition to declare him a ward of the court with murder and aiding and abetting a suicide (Pen. Code, § 401). At the contested adjudication hearing, the court sustained the petition as to the murder count but dismissed the aiding and abetting charge as inapplicable; the court further found that the murder was in the first degree.

In the case before us a genuine suicide pact was partially fulfilled by driving a car over a cliff; the primary issue is whether the survivor, who drove the vehicle, is guilty of aiding and abetting the suicide rather than the murder of his deceased partner. We conclude that, under the unusual, inexplicable and tragic circumstances of this case, the minor's actions fall more properly within the statutory definition of the former (Pen. Code, § 401).

I.

The minor and his friend, Jeff W., both 16 years old, drove to the Fillmore library one evening and joined a number of their friends who had congregated there. During the course of the two hours they spent at the library talking, mention was made of a car turnout on a curve over-looking a 300 to 350-foot precipice on a country road known as "the cliff." Both the minor and Jeff declared that they intended to "fly off the cliff" and that they meant to kill themselves. The others were skeptical but the minor affirmed their seriousness, stating "You don't believe us that we are going to do it. We are going to do it. You can read it in the paper tomorrow." The minor gave one of the girls his baseball hat, saying firmly that this was the last time he would see her. Jeff repeatedly encouraged the minor by urging, "let's go, let's go" whenever the minor spoke. One other youth attempted to get in the car with Jeff and the minor but they refused to allow him to join them "because we don't want to be responsible for you." Jeff and the minor shook hands with their friends and departed.

The pair then drove to a gas station and put air in a front tire of the car, which had been damaged earlier in the evening; the fender and passenger door were dented and the tire was very low in air pressure, nearly flat. Two of their fellow students, Keith C. and Craig B., drove up and spoke with Jeff and the minor. The minor said, "Shake my hand and stay cool." Jeff urged, "Let's go," shook their hands and said, "Remember you shook my hand." The minor then drove off in the direction of the cliff with Jeff in the passenger seat; Keith and Craig surreptitiously followed them out of curiosity. The minor and Jeff proceeded up the hill past the cliff, turned around and drove down around the curve and over the steep cliff.

Two other vehicles were parked in the turnout, from which vantage point their occupants watched the minor's car plummeting down the hill at an estimated 50 mph. The car veered off the road without swerving or changing course; the witnesses heard the car accelerate and then drive straight off the cliff. No one saw brakelights flash. The impact of the crash killed Jeff and caused severe injuries to the minor, resulting in the amputation of a foot.

Investigations following the incident revealed there were no defects in the steering or brake mechanisms. There were no skid marks at the scene, but a gouge in the pavement apparently caused by the frame of a motor vehicle coming into contact with the asphalt at high speed indicated that the car had gone straight over the cliff without swerving or skidding.

A few weeks after the crash, another friend of the minor discussed the incident with him. The minor declared he had "a quart" before driving over the cliff; the friend interpreted this to mean a quart of beer. The minor told his friend that he had "no reason" to drive off the cliff, that it was "stupid" but that he "did it on purpose." Just before the car went over the cliff, the minor told Jeff, "I guess this is it [Jeff]. Take it easy."

II.

The minor maintains that, under the peculiar circumstances presented here, he can be convicted only of aiding and abetting a suicide and not of murder. We begin by reviewing the development of the law relevant to suicide and related crimes.

At common law suicide was a felony, punished by forfeiture of property to the king and ignominious burial. . . . Essentially, suicide was considered a form of murder. . . . Under American law, suicide has never been punished and the ancient English attitude has been expressly rejected. . . .

* * *

Attempted suicide was also a crime at common law. A few American jurisdictions have adopted this view, but most, including California, attach no criminal liability to one who makes a suicide attempt. . . . It seems preposterous to argue that the visitation of criminal sanctions upon one who fails in the effort is likely to inhibit persons from undertaking a serious attempt to take their own lives. Moreover, it is clear that the intrusion of the criminal law into such tragedies is an abuse. . . .

* * *

The law has, however, retained culpability for aiding, abetting and advising suicide. At common law, an aider and abettor was guilty of murder by construction of law because he was a principal in the second degree to the self-murder of the other. Most states provide, either by statute or case law, criminal sanctions for aiding suicide, but few adopt the extreme common law position that such conduct is murder. Some jurisdictions instead classify aiding suicide as a unique type of manslaughter. But the predominant statutory scheme, and the one adopted in California, is to create a *sui generis* crime of aiding and abetting suicide. . . . The modern trend reflected by this statutory scheme is . . . to mitigate the punishment for assisting a suicide by removing it from the harsh consequences of homicide law and giving it a separate criminal classification more carefully tailored to the actual culpability of the aider and abettor.

The California aiding statute, in effect since 1873, provides simply that "Every person who deliberately aids, or advises or encourages another to commit suicide, is guilty of a felony." (Pen. Code, § 401.)

* * *

The mutual suicide pact situation, however, represents something of a hybrid between the attempted suicide and the aiding suicide scenarios. In essence, it is actually a double attempted suicide, and therefore the rationale for not punishing those who attempt suicide would seem to apply. . . .

> Suicides in pursuance of a pact are merely cases of double or multiple suicides. There can be no more justification for punishing an attempted double suicide than for punishing an attempted individual suicide. As in the case of an attempt at individual suicide, punishing the survivor of a genuine pact can serve no deterrent purpose, may hinder medical treatment, and is merely useless cruelty. It can do no more than strengthen the will to succeed in the act of self-destruction. . . .

As we have noted, attempted suicide is not a crime in California.

On the other hand, it cannot be denied that the individuals involved in the pact aid and abet each other in committing suicide: Although such individuals are thus not totally lacking in blameworthiness, their criminal responsibility would appear to fall far short of the culpability of one who actively kills another at the request of the victim. . . . We are thus faced with a dilemma: should one who attempts suicide by means of a mutual suicide pact be liable for first degree murder at one extreme, or at the other, only for aiding and abetting a suicide? The current law in California provides no options save these.

Traditionally under the common law the survivor of a suicide pact was held to be guilty of murder. . . . It has been suggested that

> the reason for imposing criminal liability upon a surviving party to a suicide pact is the "support" such a pact presents. . . . Besides the notion of "support," . . . [s]urviving a suicide pact gives rise to a presumption . . . that the participant may have entered into the pact in less than good faith. Survival, either because one party backed out at the last minute or because the poison, or other agent, did not have the desired effect, suggests that the pact may have been employed to induce the other person to take his own life.

. . . The Model Penal Code, while recognizing that "when the pact is genuine all of the arguments against treating attempted suicide as criminal apply with equal force" to the case of a suicide pact survivor, is similarly concerned with the "danger of abuse in differentiating genuine from spurious agreements" to commit suicide. Model Pen. Code, § 210.5, com. 6, at p.105.

Under the facts presented here, these concerns are not particularly appropriate. First, the trial judge was satisfied there was a genuine suicide pact between Jeff and the minor. By "genuine," we mean simply that the pact was freely entered into and was not induced by force, duress or deception. There is no evidence in the present case that Jeff's participation in the pact was anything but fully voluntary and uncoerced. Second, because of the instrumentality used there was no danger of fraud: the potential consequences for the minor of driving the car off the cliff were identical to the potential consequences for Jeff, his passenger. Finally, the suicide and the attempted suicide were committed simultaneously by the same act.

These factors clearly distinguish the present case from the murder—suicide pact situation in which one party to the agreement actively kills the other (e.g., by shooting, poison, etc.) and then is to kill himself. The active participant in that scenario has the opportunity to renege on the agreement after killing the other or to feign agreement only for the purpose of disposing of his companion and without any true intention to commit suicide himself. By contrast, in the case at hand the minor and Jeff, because of the instrumentality chosen, necessarily were to commit their suicidal acts simultaneously and were subject to identical risks of death. The potential for fraud is thus absent in a genuine suicide pact executed simultaneously by both parties by means of the same instrumentality. The traditional rationale for holding the survivor of the pact guilty of murder is thus not appropriate in this limited factual situation.

The anomaly of classifying the minor's actions herein as murder is further illustrated by consideration of Jeff's potential criminal liability had he survived. If Jeff, the passenger, had survived and the minor had been killed, Jeff would be guilty, at most, of a violation of Penal Code section 401. In order to commit suicide by this means, *i.e.,* a car, only one of the parties to the pact, the driver, can be said to "control" the instrumentality. To make the distinction between criminal liability for first degree murder and merely aiding and abetting suicide turn on the fortuitous circumstance of which of the pair was actually driving serves no rational purpose. The illogic of such a distinction has been similarly recognized in the classic example of the parties to the pact agreeing to commit suicide by gassing themselves in a closed room. If the party who turns on the gas survives, he is guilty of murder; if on the other hand, the other person survives, that person's criminal liability is only that of an aider and abettor. . . .

In light of the foregoing analysis . . . the actions of the minor constitute no more than a violation of Penal Code section 401.

The order declaring the minor a ward of the court is reversed and the cause is remanded to the trial court for further proceedings not inconsistent with this opinion.

NOTES AND QUESTIONS

1. Did the court reach the correct result in *In re Joseph G.?* Would a better result have been to hold that Jeff simply killed himself and that the defendant did no more than attempt to kill himself? Such a result would have left defendant totally free of criminal liability given the fact that California does not recognize the crime of attempted suicide. Do the policies against punishing attempted suicide outweigh those in favor of punishing aiding and abetting suicide? Could it be argued that the aiding and abetting statute was not meant to apply in genuine suicide pact situations?

2. Model Penal Code § 210.5 provides:

Section 210.5. Causing or Aiding Suicide.

 (1) Causing Suicide as Criminal Homicide. A person may be convicted of criminal homicide for causing another to commit suicide only if he purposely causes such suicide by force, duress or deception.

 (2) Aiding or Soliciting Suicide as an Independent Offense. A person who purposely aids or solicits another to commit suicide is guilty of a felony of the second degree if his conduct causes such suicide or an attempted suicide, and otherwise of a misdemeanor.

Would the defendant in *Joseph G.* "cause" or "aid" a suicide under the Code?

3. The general rule is that one who actively takes another's life at the latter's request, insistence, and so on commits murder, *People v. Matlock,* 51 Cal. 2d 682, 336 P.2d 505 (1959), while one who passively assists the deceased to take his own life commits a lesser crime (manslaughter or aiding and abetting suicide), *People v. Bouse,* 199 Or. 676, 264 P.2d 800 (1953); *In re Thomas C.,* 183 Cal. App. 3d 786, 799–800, 228 Cal. Rptr. 430, 438–39 (1986).

4. The issue of medically supervised suicide received national attention when Jack Kevorkian, a retired pathologist, began his crusade for recognition of a right for terminally ill patients to end their lives with the assistance of their physicians. Mike Williams, *Death Is Another Part of Life, Doctor Says Physician's Machine Is Latest Controversy,* Detroit Free Press, June 7, 1990, at 14A. The State of Michigan has attempted to punish Dr. Kevorkian for assisting suicides under both a theory of common law murder, *see People v. Kervorkian,* 205 Mich. App. 180, 517 N.W.2d 293 (1994), and under a 1992

statute criminalizing assisted suicide, *see Hobbins v. Attorney General,* 205 Mich. App. 192, 518 N.W.2d 487 (1994). In the latter case, the court struck down the statute under a state constitutional provision requiring that legislation have only one object. The court nevertheless offered an opinion that a ban on assisted suicide does not offend federal constitutional rights to privacy or to refuse unwanted medical treatment.

WASHINGTON V. GLUCKSBERG

Supreme Court of the United States

521 U.S. 702 (1997)

Chief Justice REHNQUIST *delivered the opinion of the Court.*

The question presented in this case is whether Washington's prohibition against "caus[ing]" or "aid[ing]" a suicide offends the Fourteenth Amendment to the United States Constitution. We hold that it does not.

It has always been a crime to assist a suicide in the State of Washington. In 1854, Washington's first Territorial Legislature outlawed "assisting another in the commission of self-murder." Today, Washington law provides: "A person is guilty of promoting a suicide attempt when he knowingly causes or aids another person to attempt suicide." Wash. Rev.Code 9A.36.060(1) (1994). "Promoting a suicide attempt" is a felony, punishable by up to five years' imprisonment and up to a $10,000 fine. At the same time, Washington's Natural Death Act, enacted in 1979, states that the "withholding or withdrawal of life-sustaining treatment" at a patient's direction "shall not, for any purpose, constitute a suicide." Wash. Rev.Code 70.122.070(1).[2]

Petitioners in this case are the State of Washington and its Attorney General. Respondents Harold Glucksberg, M. D., Abigail Halperin, M. D., Thomas A. Preston, M. D., and Peter Shalit, M. D., are physicians who practice in Washington. These doctors occasionally treat terminally ill, suffering patients, and declare that they would assist these patients in ending their lives if not for Washington's assisted-suicide ban. In January 1994, respondents, along with three gravely ill, pseudonymous plaintiffs who have since died and Compassion in Dying, a nonprofit organization that counsels people considering physician-assisted suicide, sued in the United States District Court, seeking a declaration that Wash Rev.Code 9A.36.060(1) (1994) is, on its face, unconstitutional.

[The District Court agreed with the plaintiffs and struck the statute down. A panel of the Ninth Circuit Court of Appeals reversed and the Supreme Court granted certiorari.]

---

[2] Under Washington's Natural Death Act, "adult persons have the fundamental right to control the decisions relating to the rendering of their own health care, including the decision to have life–sustaining treatment withheld or withdrawn in instances of a terminal condition or permanent unconscious condition." In Washington, "[a]ny adult person may execute a directive directing the withholding or withdrawal of life–sustaining treatment in a terminal condition or permanent unconscious condition," and a physician who, in accordance with such a directive, participates in the withholding or withdrawal of life–sustaining treatment is immune from civil, criminal, or professional liability.

We begin, as we do in all due-process cases, by examining our Nation's history, legal traditions, and practices. In almost every State indeed, in almost every western democracy it is a crime to assist a suicide. The States' assisted-suicide bans are not innovations. Rather, they are longstanding expressions of the States' commitment to the protection and preservation of all human life. Indeed, opposition to and condemnation of suicide and, therefore, of assisting suicide are consistent and enduring themes of our philosophical, legal, and cultural heritages.

More specifically, for over 700 years, the Anglo-American common-law tradition has punished or otherwise disapproved of both suicide and assisting suicide. In the 13th century, Henry de Bracton, one of the first legal-treatise writers, observed that "[j]ust as a man may commit felony by slaying another so may he do so by slaying himself." [T]hus, "[t]he principle that suicide of a sane person, for whatever reason, was a punishable felony was . . . introduced into English common law." Centuries later, Sir William Blackstone, whose Commentaries on the Laws of England not only provided a definitive summary of the common law but was also a primary legal authority for 18th and 19th century American lawyers, referred to suicide as "self-murder" and "the pretended heroism, but real cowardice, of the Stoic philosophers, who destroyed themselves to avoid those ills which they had not the fortitude to endure. . . . " Blackstone emphasized that "the law has . . . ranked [suicide] among the highest crimes."

* * *

For the most part, the early American colonies adopted the common-law approach. For example, the legislators of the Providence Plantations, which would later become Rhode Island, declared, in 1647, that "[s]elf-murder is by all agreed to be the most unnatural, and it is by this present Assembly declared, to be that, wherein he that doth it, kills himself out of a premeditated hatred against his own life or other humor: . . . his goods and chattels are the king's custom, but not his debts nor lands; but in case he be an infant, a lunatic, mad or distracted man, he forfeits nothing." Virginia also required ignominious burial for suicides, and their estates were forfeit to the crown.

Over time, however, the American colonies abolished these harsh common-law penalties. William Penn abandoned the criminal-forfeiture sanction in Pennsylvania in 1701, and the other colonies (and later, the other States) eventually followed this example. . . .

[H]owever, the movement away from the common law's harsh sanctions did not represent an acceptance of suicide; rather, as Chief Justice Swift observed, this change reflected the growing consensus that it was unfair to punish the suicide's family for his wrongdoing. Nonetheless, although States moved away from Blackstone's treatment of suicide, courts continued to condemn it as a grave public wrong.

That suicide remained a grievous, though nonfelonious, wrong is confirmed by the fact that colonial and early state legislatures and courts did not retreat from prohibiting assisting suicide. Swift, in his early 19th century treatise on the laws of Connecticut, stated that "[i]f one counsels another to commit suicide, and the other by reason of the advice kills himself, the advisor is guilty of murder as principal." His was the well established common-law view, as was the similar principle that the consent of a homicide victim is "wholly immaterial to the guilt of the person who cause[d] [his death]. " And the prohibitions against assisting suicide never contained exceptions for those who were near death. Rather, "[t]he life of those to whom life ha[d] become a burden of those who [were] hopelessly diseased or fatally wounded nay, even the lives of criminals condemned to death, [were] under the protection of law, equally as the lives of those who [were] in the full tide of life's enjoyment, and anxious to continue to live."

The earliest American statute explicitly to outlaw assisting suicide was enacted in New York in 1828, and many of the new States and Territories followed New York's example. . . . By the time the Fourteenth Amendment was ratified, it was a crime in most States to assist a suicide. . . .

Though deeply rooted, the States' assisted–suicide bans have in recent years been reexamined and, generally, reaffirmed. Because of advances in medicine and technology, Americans today are increasingly likely to die in institutions, from chronic illnesses. Public concern and democratic action are therefore sharply focused on how best to protect dignity and independence at the end of life, with the result that there have been many significant changes in state laws and in the attitudes these laws reflect. Many States, for example, now permit "living wills," surrogate health-care decision making, and the withdrawal or refusal of life–sustaining medical treatment. At the same time, however, voters and legislators continue for the most part to reaffirm their States' prohibitions on assisting suicide.

* * *

Thus, the States are currently engaged in serious, thoughtful examinations of physician–assisted suicide and other similar issues. For example, New York State's Task Force on Life and the Law an ongoing, blue–ribbon commission composed of doctors, ethicists, lawyers, religious leaders, and interested laymen was convened in 1984 and commissioned with "a broad mandate to recommend public policy on issues raised by medical advances." Over the past decade, the Task Force has recommended laws relating to end–of–life decisions, surrogate pregnancy, and organ donation. After studying physician-assisted suicide, however, the Task Force unanimously concluded that "[l]egalizing assisted suicide and euthanasia would pose profound risks to many individuals who are ill and vulnerable. . . . [T]he potential dangers of this dramatic change in public policy would outweigh any benefit that might be achieved."

Attitudes toward suicide itself have changed since Bracton, but our laws have consistently condemned, and continue to prohibit, assisting suicide. Despite changes in medical technology and notwithstanding an increased emphasis on the importance of end–of–life decision making, we have not retreated from this prohibition. Against this backdrop of history, tradition, and practice, we now turn to respondents' constitutional claim.

II

The Due Process Clause guarantees more than fair process, and the "liberty" it protects includes more than the absence of physical restraint. The Clause also provides heightened protection against government interference with certain fundamental rights and liberty interests. In a long line of cases, we have held that, in addition to the specific freedoms protected by the Bill of Rights, the "liberty" specially protected by the Due Process Clause includes the rights to marry, to have children, to direct the education and upbringing of one's children, to marital privacy, to use contraception, to bodily integrity, and to abortion. We have also assumed, and strongly suggested, that the Due Process Clause protects the traditional right to refuse unwanted lifesaving medical treatment.

But we "ha[ve] always been reluctant to expand the concept of substantive due process because guideposts for responsible decision making in this unchartered area are scarce and open-ended." By extending constitutional protection to an asserted right or liberty interest, we "to a great extent, place the matter outside the arena of public debate and legislative action. We must therefore "exercise the utmost care whenever we are asked to break new ground in this field," lest the liberty protected by the Due Process Clause be subtly transformed into the policy preferences of the members of this Court.

Our established method of substantive–due–process analysis has two primary features: First, we have regularly observed that the Due Process Clause specially protects those fundamental rights and liberties which are, objectively, "deeply rooted in this Nation's history and tradition," such that 'neither liberty nor justice would exist if they were sacrificed. Second, we have required in substantive–due–process cases a "careful description" of the asserted fundamental liberty interest. Our Nation's history, legal traditions, and practices thus provide the crucial "guideposts for responsible decision making," that direct and restrain our exposition of the Due Process Clause. As we stated recently . . . the Fourteenth Amendment "forbids the government to infringe . . . 'fundamental' liberty interests at all, no matter what process is provided, unless the infringement is narrowly tailored to serve a compelling state interest."

* * *

Turning to the claim at issue here, the Court of Appeals stated that "[p]roperly analyzed, the first issue to be resolved is whether there is a liberty interest in determining the time and manner of one's death," or, in other words, "[i]s there a right to die?" Similarly, respondents assert a "liberty to choose how to die" and a right to "control of one's final days," and describe the asserted liberty as "the right to choose a humane, dignified death," and "the liberty to shape death." As noted above, we have a tradition of carefully formulating the interest at stake in substantive-due-process cases. . . .

We now inquire whether this asserted right has any place in our Nation's traditions. Here, as discussed above, we are confronted with a consistent and almost universal tradition that has long rejected the asserted right, and continues explicitly to reject it today, even for terminally ill, mentally competent adults. To hold for respondents, we would have to reverse centuries of legal doctrine and practice, and strike down the considered policy choice of almost every State.

* * *

The history of the law's treatment of assisted suicide in this country has been and continues to be one of the rejection of nearly all efforts to permit it. That being the case, our decisions lead us to conclude that the asserted "right" to assistance in committing suicide is not a fundamental liberty interest protected by the Due Process Clause. The Constitution also requires, however, that Washington's assisted–suicide ban be rationally related to legitimate government interests. This requirement is unquestionably met here. As the court below recognized, Washington's assisted–suicide ban implicates a number of state interests.

First, Washington has an "unqualified interest in the preservation of human life." The State's prohibition on assisted suicide, like all homicide laws, both reflects and advances its commitment to this interest. This interest is symbolic and aspirational as well as practical:

> While suicide is no longer prohibited or penalized, the ban against assisted suicide and euthanasia shores up the notion of limits in human relationships. It reflects the gravity with which we view the decision to take one's own life or the life of another, and our reluctance to encourage or promote these decisions.

* * *

The State also has an interest in protecting the integrity and ethics of the medical profession. In contrast to the Court of Appeals' conclusion that "the integrity of the medical profession would [not] be threatened in any way by [physician-assisted suicide]," the American Medical Association, like many other medical and physicians' groups, has concluded that "[p]hysician-assisted suicide is fundamentally incompatible with the physician's role as healer."

Next, the State has an interest in protecting vulnerable groups including the poor, the elderly, and disabled persons from abuse, neglect, and mistakes. The Court of Appeals dismissed the State's concern that disadvantaged persons might be pressured into physician-assisted suicide as "ludicrous on its face." We have recognized, however, the real risk of subtle coercion and undue influence in end-of-life situations. Similarly, the New York Task Force warned that "[l]egalizing physician–assisted suicide would pose profound risks to many individuals who are ill and vulnerable. . . . The risk of harm is greatest for the many individuals in our society whose autonomy and well–being are already compromised by poverty, lack of access to good medical care, advanced age, or membership in a stigmatized social group." If physician-assisted suicide were permitted, many might resort to it to spare their families the substantial financial burden of end-of-life health-care costs.

The State's interest here goes beyond protecting the vulnerable from coercion; it extends to protecting disabled and terminally ill people from prejudice, negative and inaccurate stereotypes, and "societal indifference." The

State's assisted–suicide ban reflects and reinforces its policy that the lives of terminally ill, disabled, and elderly people must be no less valued than the lives of the young and healthy, and that a seriously disabled person's suicidal impulses should be interpreted and treated the same way as anyone else's.

Finally, the State may fear that permitting assisted suicide will start it down the path to voluntary and perhaps even involuntary euthanasia. The Court of Appeals struck down Washington's assisted–suicide ban only "as applied to competent, terminally ill adults who wish to hasten their deaths by obtaining medication prescribed by their doctors." Washingon insists, however, that the impact of the court's decision will not and cannot be so limited. If suicide is protected as a matter of constitutional right, it is argued, "every man and woman in the United States must enjoy it." The Court of Appeals' decision, and its expansive reasoning, provide ample support for the State's concerns. The court noted, for example, that the "decision of a duly appointed surrogate decision maker is for all legal purposes the decision of the patient himself," that "in some instances, the patient may be unable to self-administer the drugs and . . . administration by the physician . . . may be the only way the patient may be able to receive them," and that not only physicians, but also family members and loved ones, will inevitably participate in assisting suicide. Thus, it turns out that what is couched as a limited right to "physician–assisted suicide" is likely, in effect, a much broader license, which could prove extremely difficult to police and contain. Washington's ban on assisting suicide prevents such erosion.

This concern is further supported by evidence about the practice of euthanasia in the Netherlands. The Dutch government's own study revealed that in 1990, there were 2,300 cases of voluntary euthanasia (defined as "the deliberate termination of another's life at his request"), 400 cases of assisted suicide, and more than 1,000 cases of euthanasia without an explicit request. In addition to these latter 1,000 cases, the study found an additional 4,941 cases where physicians administered lethal morphine overdoses without the patients' explicit consent. This study suggests that, despite the existence of various reporting procedures, euthanasia in the Netherlands has not been limited to competent, terminally ill adults who are enduring physical suffering, and that regulation of the practice may not have prevented abuses in cases involving vulnerable persons, including severely disabled neonates and elderly persons suffering from dementia. Washington, like most other States, reasonably ensures against this risk by banning, rather than regulating, assisting suicide.

We need not weigh exactingly the relative strengths of these various interests. They are unquestionably important and legitimate, and Washington's ban on assisted suicide is at least reasonably related to their promotion and protection. We therefore hold that Wash. Rev.Code 9A.36.060(1) (1994) does not violate the Fourteenth Amendment, either on its face or "as applied to competent, terminally ill adults who wish to hasten their deaths by obtaining medication prescribed by their doctors."

* * *

Throughout the Nation, Americans are engaged in an earnest and profound debate about the morality, legality, and practicality of physician-assisted suicide. Our holding permits this debate to continue, as it should in a democratic society. The decision of the en banc Court of Appeals is reversed, and the case is remanded for further proceedings consistent with this opinion.

It is so ordered.

* * *

Justice O'CONNOR, *concurring.*

Death will be different for each of us. For many, the last days will be spent in physical pain and perhaps the despair that accompanies physical deterioration and a loss of control of basic bodily and mental functions. Some will seek medication to alleviate that pain and other symptoms.

The Court frames the issue in this case as whether the Due Process Clause of the Constitution protects a "right to commit suicide which itself includes a right to assistance in doing so," and concludes that our Nation's history, legal traditions, and practices do not support the existence of such a right. I join the Court's opinions because I agree that there is no generalized right to "commit suicide."

* * *

Every one of us at some point may be affected by our own or a family member's terminal illness. There is no reason to think the democratic process will not strike the proper balance between the interests of terminally ill, mentally competent individuals who would seek to end their suffering and the State's interests in protecting those who might seek to end life mistakenly or under pressure. As the Court recognizes, States are presently undertaking extensive and serious evaluation of physician–assisted suicide and other related issues. In such circumstances, "the . . . challenging task of crafting appropriate procedures for safeguarding . . . liberty interests is entrusted to the 'laboratory' of the States . . . in the first instance."

In sum, there is no need to address the question whether suffering patients have a constitutionally cognizable interest in obtaining relief from the suffering that they may experience in the last days of their lives. There is no dispute that dying patients in Washington and New York can obtain palliative care, even when doing so would hasten their deaths. The difficulty in defining terminal illness and the risk that a dying patient's request for assistance in ending his or her life might not be truly voluntary justifies the prohibitions on assisted suicide we uphold here.

* * *

Justice BREYER, *concurring in the judgments.*

I believe that Justice O'Connor's views, which I share, have greater legal significance than the Court's opinion suggests. I join her separate opinion, except insofar as it joins the majority. And I concur in the judgments. I shall briefly explain how I differ from the Court.

I agree . . . that the articulated state interests justify the distinction drawn between physician assisted suicide and withdrawal of life-support. I also agree with the Court that the critical question... before us is whether "te 'liberty' specially protected by the Due Process Clause includes a right" of the sort that the respondents assert. I do not agree, however, with the Court's formulation of that claimed "liberty" interest. The Court describes it as a "right to commit suicide with another's assistance." But I would not reject the respondents' claim without considering a different formulation, for which our legal tradition may provide greater support. That formulation would use words roughly like a "right to die with dignity." But irrespective of the exact words used, at its core would lie personal control over the manner of death, professional medical assistance, and the avoidance of unnecessary and severe physical suffering–combined.

* * *

I do not believe, however, that this Court need or now should decide whether or a not such a right is "fundamental." That is because, in my view, the avoidance of severe physical pain (connected with death) would have to comprise an essential part of any successful claim and because . . . the laws before us do not force a dying person to undergo that kind of pain. Rather, the laws of . . . Washington do not prohibit doctors from providing patients with drugs sufficient to control pain despite the risk that those drugs themselves will kill. And under these circumstances the laws of New York and Washington would overcome any remaining significant interests and would be justified, regardless.

Medical technology, we are repeatedly told, makes the administration of pain–relieving drugs sufficient, except for a very few individuals for whom the ineffectiveness of pain control medicines can mean, not pain, but the need for sedation which can end in a coma. We are also told that there are many instances in which patients do not receive the palliative care that, in principle, is available, but that is so for institutional reasons or inadequacies or obstacles, which would seem possible to overcome, and which do not include a prohibitive set of laws.

This legal circumstance means that the state laws before us do not infringe directly upon the (assumed) central interest (what I have called the core of the interest in dying with dignity). . . .

Were the legal circumstances different for example, were state law to prevent the provision of palliative care, including the administration of drugs as needed to avoid pain at the end of life then the law's impact upon serious and otherwise unavoidable physical pain (accompanying death) would be more directly at issue. And . . . the Court might have to revisit its conclusions in these cases.

NOTES AND QUESTIONS

1. In a companion case to *Glucksberg*, the Court held in *Vacco v. Quill,* 521 U.S. 793 (1997) that New York's prohibition on assisting suicide did not violate the Equal Protection Clause of the Fourteenth Amendment even though New

York permitted patients to refuse even lifesaving treatment. The Vacco Court observed:

> [We] think the distinction between assisting suicide and withdrawing life-sustaining treatment, a distinction widely recognized and endorsed in the medical profession and in our legal traditions, is both important and logical; it is certainly rational. . . . The distinction comports with fundamental legal principles of causation and intent. First, when a particular patient refuses life-sustaining medical treatment, he dies from an underlying fatal disease or pathology; but if a patient ingests lethal medication prescribed by a physician he is killed by that medication. The law has long used actor's intent or purpose to distinguish between two acts that may have the same result. Given these general principles, it is not surprising that many courts, including New York courts, have carefully distinguished refud sing life-sustaining treatment from suicide.

* * *

> For all these reasons, we disagree with respondents' claim that the distinction between refusing lifesaving medical treatment and assisted suicide is "arbitrary" and "irrational." Granted, in some cases, the line between the two may not be clear, but certainty is not required, even were it possible. Logic and contemporary practice support New York's judgment that the two acts are different, and New York may therefore, consistent with the Constitution, treat them differently. By permitting everyone to refuse unwanted medical treatment while prohibiting anyone from assisting a suicide, New York law follows a longstanding and rational distinction.

> New York's reasons for recognizing and acting on this distinction including prohibiting the intentional killing and preserving life; preventing suicide; maintaining physician's role as their patients healers; protecting vulnerable people from indifference, prejudice, and psychological and financial pressure to end their lives; and avoiding a possible slide towards euthanasia are discussed in greater detail in our opinion in *Glucksburg*. These valid and important public interests easily satisfy the constitutional requirement that a legislative classification bear a rational relation to some legitimate end.

521 U.S. at 800-809.

2. Is the Court correct in seeing a legal and moral distinction in effectively hastening death by refusing health care and causing death by taking positive steps to end life?

3. The critical response to *Glucksberg* has been voluminous. See, e.g., Symposium, *Physician Assisted Suicide: Facing Death After* Glucksberg *and* Quill, 83 Minn. L. Rev. 885 (1998); Harris, *Semantics and Policy in Physician–Assisted Death: Piercing the Verbal Veil*, 5 Elder L.J. 251 (1997); McConnell, *The Right to Die and the Jurisprudence of Tradition*, 1997 Utah L. Rev. 665; Shepherd, *Dignity and Autonomy After Washington v. Glucksberg: An Essay About Abortion, Death, and Crime*, 7 Cornell J.L. & Pub. Pol'y 431 (1998); Note, *Regulating Death: Oregon's Death With Dignity Act and the Legalization of Physician–Assisted Suicide*, 86 Geo. L. J. 725 (1998).

§ 5.03 THE *MENS REA*

As the earlier excerpt from Plucknett indicates, the ancient crime of homicide came to be divided into two separate crimes: murder and manslaughter, distinguishable in terms of the presence of malice aforethought in the former and its absence in the latter. The meaning and significance of the common law notion of malice aforethought are summarized by Sayre as follows:

SAYRE, *MENS REA*

45 Harv. L. Rev. 974, 997–98 (1932)

The distinction between the capital crime of murder and the less serious form of felonious homicide, which later came to be called manslaughter, depended upon the presence or absence of "malice aforethought." The subsequent history of homicide is largely the story of the shifting meanings attached to the term "malice aforethought." At the beginning, and at least until the early seventeenth century, the term designated a purely psychical element. "Malice" was construed in its popular sense as meaning general malevolence or cold-blooded desire to injure, and referred to the underlying motive rather than to the immediate intent of the actor. As shown by the Act of 2 James I, an intentional killing, whether from rage, drunkenness, or hidden displeasure, if committed "on the sudden," is considered at the opening of the seventeenth century to be without malice aforethought; and this even though there was no provocation for the killing. Lambard, who wrote in 1610, assumes that the phrase bears its natural and obvious sense of premeditation, but shows the unsatisfactory nature of this interpretation. The actual meaning of the term is gradually shifted by the use of legal fictions. Coke, whose *Third Institute* was completed in 1628, found it impossible to restrict the meaning of malice prepense to its popular, purely psychical sense. He defines murder as an unlawful killing "with malice aforethought, either expressed by the party or implied by Law." After describing express malice he sets forth three cases where malice is implied by the law: (1) a killing in the absence of provocation, or a killing by poison, (2) killing an officer or one engaged in executing a warrant in resistance to such execution, and (3) (apparently) killing while engaged in the commission of an unlawful act. Although Coke's three examples of malice implied by law smack of an actual intent to kill, if not of actual malevolence, his suggestion of implied malice was potent with wide possibilities. The floodgates were open and later courts through the fiction of implied malice found an easy way to enlarge the meaning of malice aforethought and thus to widen the actual boundaries of murder. A term used at the beginning to designate a purely psychical element was thus given a tortured and artificial meaning in order to enable courts to visit with a severe penalty killers who, in the public opinion of the day, ought not to be let off with the comparatively slight punishment attaching to clergyable offenses. So it came about that the mental requisites for murder changed according to the exigencies of the time.

[A] Murder

BLACKSTONE

199–200

[T]he killing must be committed *with malice aforethought,* to make it the crime of murder. This is the grand criterion which now distinguishes murder from other killing; and this malice prepense, . . . is not so properly spite or malevolence to the deceased in particular, as any evil design in general; the dictate of a wicked, depraved, and malignant heart; and it may be either *express or implied* in law. Express malice is when one, with a sedate deliberate mind and formed design, doth kill another: which formed design is evidenced by external circumstances discovering that inward intention; as lying in wait, antecedent menaces, former grudges, and concerted schemes to do him some bodily harm. . . . Also, if even upon a sudden provocation one beats another in a cruel and unusual manner so that he dies, though he did not intend his death, yet he is guilty of murder by express malice; that is, by an express evil design, the genuine sense of *malitia.* . . . Neither shall he be guilty of a less crime who kills another in consequence of such a wilful act as shows him to be an enemy to all mankind in general; as going deliberately, and with an intent to do mischief, upon a horse used to strike, or coolly discharging a gun among a multitude of people. So if a man resolves to kill the next man he meets, and does kill him, it is murder, although he knew him not; for this is universal malice. And if two or more come together to do an unlawful act against the king's peace, of which the probable consequence might be bloodshed, as to beat a man, to commit a riot, or to rob a park, and one of them kills a man; it is murder in them all, because of the unlawful act, the *malitia praecogitata,* or evil intended beforehand.

Also in many cases where no malice is expressed the law will imply it, as, where a man wilfully poisons another: in such a deliberate act the law presumes malice, though no particular enmity can be proved. And if a man kills another suddenly, without any or without a considerable provocation, the law implies malice; for no person, unless of an abandoned heart, would be guilty of such an act upon a slight or no apparent cause. No affront by words or gestures only is sufficient provocation so as to excuse or extenuate such acts of violence as manifestly endanger the life of another. . . . In like manner, if one kills an officer of justice, either civil or criminal, in the execution of his duty, or any of his assistants endeavoring to conserve the peace, or any private person endeavoring to suppress an affray or apprehend a felon, knowing his authority or the intention with which he interposes, the law will imply malice, and the killer shall be guilty of murder. And if one intends to do another felony, and undesignedly kills a man, this is also murder.

STEPHEN, *A DIGEST OF THE CRIMINAL LAW*

161–62 (1878)

Murder is unlawful homicide with malice aforethought.

Malice aforethought means any one or more of the following states of minds preceding or co-existing with the act or omission by which death is caused, and it may exist where that act is unpremeditated.

- (a) An intention to cause the death of, or grievous bodily harm to, any person, whether such person is the person actually killed or not;
- (b) Knowledge that the act which causes death will probably cause the death of, or grievous bodily harm to, some person, whether such person is the person actually killed or not, although such knowledge is accompanied by indifference whether death or grievous bodily harm is caused or not, or by a wish that it may not be caused;
- (c) An intent to commit any felony whatever;
- (d) An intent to oppose by force any officer of justice on his way to, in, or returning from the execution of the duty of arresting, keeping in custody, or imprisoning any person whom he is lawfully entitled to arrest, keep in custody, or imprison, or the duty of keeping the peace or dispersing an unlawful assembly, provided that the offender has notice that the person killed is such an officer so employed.

NOTE ON DEGREES OF MURDER

The types of murder described by Blackstone and Stephen have generally been incorporated into American law. However, the common law tradition is further refined in most jurisdictions in this country by a legislative division of murder into two, and sometimes three, degrees. Judge Harold Leventhal describes this development as follows:

> At common law, unlawful homicides were divided into two classes, murder and manslaughter, depending on whether the killing was with or without malice aforethought. Although the term malice aforethought was most probably intended to be applied literally when it was first introduced into the law of homicide, the courts soon converted it into a term of art. To the popular understanding of subjective malice was added an objective standard, by which negligence tantamount to recklessness might make a culpable homicide murder. The objective standard persists in the law, but what we are primarily concerned with here is not so much the extension of "malice" as the elimination of the literal significance of the word "aforethought." The courts held it sufficient to establish common law murder, subject to capital punishment, if the homicide was accompanied by the intention to cause death or grievous bodily harm, whether the slaying was calculated or only impulsive.
>
> The nineteenth century ushered in a new approach. Beginning in 1794 with Pennsylvania, state legislatures began to separate murder into two degrees, reserving the death penalty for the first degree. These statutes typically defined murder in the first degree as an intended killing, accompanied by premeditation and deliberation (as well as malice aforethought);

murder in the second degree was defined residually to include all other unlawful homicides with malice aforethought.

Austin v. United States, 382 F.2d 129, 133–34 (D.C. Cir. 1967).

The reason for dividing murder into degrees was that "the several offenses, which are included under the general denomination of murder, differ so greatly from each other in their degree of atrociousness, that it is unjust to involve them in the same punishment." Act of April 22, 1794, § 2, 15 Statutes at Large of Pennsylvania from 1682 to 1801, ch. 1777 at 174, 175 (1911). The current Pennsylvania statute provides:

Pennsylvania Consolidated Statutes Title 18

§ 2501. Criminal Homicide

(a) *Offense defined.* A person is guilty of criminal homicide if he intentionally, knowingly, recklessly or negligently causes the death of another human being.

(b) *Classification.* Criminal homicide shall be classified as murder, voluntary manslaughter, or involuntary manslaughter.

§ 2502. Murder

(a) *Murder of the first degree.* A criminal homicide constitutes murder of the first degree when it is committed by an intentional killing. [Punishable by death or life imprisonment.]

(b) *Murder of the second degree.* A criminal homicide constitutes murder of the second degree when it is committed while defendant was engaged as a principal or an accomplice in the perpetration of a felony. [Punishable by life imprisonment.]

(c) *Murder of the third degree.* All other kinds of murder shall be murder of the third degree. Murder of the third degree is a felony of the first degree. [Punishable by maximum of 20 years imprisonment.]

(d) *Definitions.* As used in this section the following words and phrases shall have the meanings given to them in this subsection. . . .

"Intentional killing." Killing by means of poison, or by lying in wait, or by any other kind of willful, deliberate and premeditated killing.

"Perpetration of a felony." The act of the defendant in engaging in or being an accomplice in the commission of or an attempt to commit, or flight after committing, or attempting to commit robbery, rape, or deviate sexual intercourse by force or threat of force, arson, burglary or kidnaping. . . .

The following are representative progeny of the original Pennsylvania formula

California Penal Code

§ 187. Murder Defined

(a) Murder is the unlawful killing of a human being, or a fetus, with malice aforethought. . . .

§ 188. Malice Defined: Express and Implied Malice

Such malice may be express or implied. It is express when there is manifested a deliberate intention unlawfully to take away the life of a fellow-creature. It is implied, when no considerable provocation appears, or when the circumstances attending the killing show an abandoned and malignant heart.

When it is shown that the killing resulted from the intentional doing of an act with express or implied malice as defined above, no other mental state need be shown to establish the mental state of malice aforethought. An awareness of the obligation to act within the general body of laws regulating society is not included within the definition of malice.

§ 189. Degrees of Murder

All murder which is perpetrated by means of a bomb, poison, or lying in wait, torture, or by any other kind of willful, deliberate, and premeditated killing, or which is committed in the perpetration or attempt to perpetrate arson, rape, robbery, burglary, mayhem, or any act punishable under Section 288 [sexual perversion], is murder of the first degree [punishable by death, imprisonment for life without possibility of parole, or imprisonment for 25 years to life]; and all other kinds of murders are of the second degree [punishable by imprisonment for 15 years to life or 25 years to life for killing a peace officer]. . . .

To prove the killing was "deliberate and premeditated," it shall not be necessary to prove the defendant maturely and meaningfully reflected upon the gravity of his or her act.

Nebraska Revised Statutes

28-302. Homicide; terms, defined. As used in sections 28-302 to 28-306 [manslaughter; motor vehicle homicide], unless the context otherwise requires:

(1) Homicide shall mean the killing of a person by another;

(2) Person, when referring to the victim of a homicide, shall mean a human being who had been born and was alive at the time of the homicide act; and

(3) Premeditation shall mean a design formed to do something before it is done.

28-303. Murder in the first degree; penalty. A person commits murder in the first degree if he kills another person (1)purposely and with deliberate and premeditated malice, or (2)in the perpetration of or attempt to perpetrate any sexual assault in the first degree, arson, robbery, kidnaping, hijacking of any public or private means of transportation, or burglary, or (3)by administering poison or causing the same to be done; or if by willful and corrupt perjury or subornation of the same he purposely procures the conviction and execution of any innocent person. The determination of whether murder in the first degree shall be punished as a Class I [Death

Penalty] or a Class IA [Life Imprisonment] felony shall be made pursuant to Sections 29-2520 to 29-2524.

28-304. Murder in the second degree; penalty. (1)A person commits murder in the second degree if he causes death of a person intentionally, but without premeditation.

(2) Murder in the second degree is a Class IB felony. [Punishable by ten years to life imprisonment.]

The Model Penal Code rejects the traditional American approach of dividing murder into degrees. Section 210.2 of the Code defines murder:

(1) Except as provided in Section 210.3(1)(b) [homicides committed under extreme emotional disturbance], criminal homicide constitutes murder when:

   (a) it is committed purposely or knowingly; or

   (b) it is committed recklessly under circumstances manifesting extreme indifference to the value of human life. Such recklessness and indifference are presumed if the actor is engaged or is an accomplice in the commission of, or an attempt to commit, or flight after committing or attempting to commit robbery, rape or deviate sexual intercourse by force or threat of force, arson, burglary, kidnaping or felonious escape.

[1] Intent-to-Kill Murder

PEOPLE v. HAACK

Supreme Court of Michigan

396 Mich. 367, 240 N.W.2d 704 (1976)

LEVIN, Justice.

The question is whether the record shows a factual basis for a plea of guilty of second-degree murder.

Arthur Haack, charged with first-degree murder, pled guilty to second-degree murder. The Court of Appeals affirmed [.]

* * *

We affirm.

During the plea-taking colloquy, Haack said that on the night of the homicide an acquaintance gave him a .45-caliber revolver to carry in his coat pocket. There were four bullets in the cylinder. Haack placed one of the empty chambers under the hammer and the other immediately to the left of it. He thought the cylinder rotated clockwise and that the hammer would strike an empty chamber if the gun was fired. He put the gun in his pocket.

At a party later that night the deceased, whom Haack had not met before, asked Haack why he had a gun. Haack responded —if you knew the people that I knew you would carry a gun too.' Haack sought to terminate the conversation. The deceased moved away. Haack overheard another person urge the deceased to leave Haack alone. Then the deceased "turned and faced me and said that if I was such a big man with the gun why didn't I shoot him."

Haack described what follows:

I figured this guy is pushing me far enough and I'm going to scare the hell out of him and let it go at that. I pulled the gun out and cocked the hammer and pulled the trigger. It fired. I found out that on a couple of makes of the older .45 revolvers that they spin counter clockwise instead of clockwise and that's what happened.

Haack contends his assertion to the judge that he believed the gun would not fire and he intended only to scare the deceased negates intent to kill, a requisite element of second-degree murder. He contends that while he intentionally pulled the trigger, the shooting was an accident. Alternatively, he contends that his belief the gun would not fire was reasonable and is a mitigating factor that reduces the offense to manslaughter. . . .

The prosecutor responds that intent to kill can be inferred from the facts recited by Haack when he offered his plea. Haack pointed a gun he knew was loaded at the deceased and intentionally pulled the trigger. . . .

* * *

Intent to kill is an element of the offense of murder. Haack's assertions to the judge that the shooting was an accident and that there were mitigating circumstances do not, however, negate a factual basis for his plea of guilty to second-degree murder . . . [I]ntent to kill may be inferred by the trier of fact[9] where the natural tendency of the defendant's behavior is to cause death. . . . [The authors have omitted references to an alternative second degree murder theory: intent-to-cause-grievous-bo dily-harm murder. This theory is discussed in the casebook at § 5.03].

"A person who kills another is guilty of the crime of murder if the homicide is committed with malice aforethought. Malice aforethought is the intention to kill, actual or implied, under circumstances which do not constitute excuse[10] or justification or mitigate the degree of the offense to manslaughter." . . .

---

[9] "The majority views—that the so-called —presumption of malice' actually authorizes merely the drawing of an inference; and that the burden of persuasion of guilt of murder (and so the negativing of facts of mitigation or justification) beyond a reasonable doubt remains always with the prosecution—are surely the correct ones if we are to abide by the guiding principle of Anglo-American criminal justice that a criminal defendant is to be considered innocent until shown by the prosecution to be guilty beyond a reasonable doubt." LaFave and Scott, Criminal Law, § 68, p.540. . . .

[10] "Homicide is —excusable' if the death is the result of an accident and the actor was not criminally negligent." . . .

Thus, as "malice aforethought" is now defined, a killing may be murder even though the actor harbored no hatred or ill will against the victim and even though he "acted on the spur of the moment." . . .

The issue here is whether a factual basis has been established for the taking of a plea.[11]

In *Guilty Plea Cases,* . . . this Court . . . 235 N.W. 132 (1975) said that on appellate review the standard to be applied in determining the adequacy of the factual basis is whether the trier of fact could properly convict on the facts as stated by the defendant. Disclaimers by the defendant during the plea taking of . . . intent to kill . . . do not preclude acceptance of a plea since on defendant's own recital a jury could properly infer the requisite participation or intent. "A factual basis for acceptance of a plea exists if an inculpatory inference can reasonably be drawn by a jury on the facts admitted by the defendant even if an exculpatory inference could also be drawn and defendant asserts the latter is the correct inference." . . .

Although Haack asserted the shooting was accidental, in deciding whether to accept his plea of guilty the judge could, on the strength of Haack's inculpatory statements, properly reject his disclaimer of intent to kill and his assertion that the shooting was accidental and accept his plea of guilty. On Haack's statement that he had pointed a revolver he knew was loaded at the deceased and intentionally pulled the trigger, a trier of fact could properly infer intent to kill.

Affirmed.

NOTES AND QUESTIONS

1. What does the *Haack* court mean when it says "intent to kill may be inferred by the trier of fact where the natural tendency of the defendant's behavior is to cause death." Does this suggest that intent is not a subjective state of mind? Or might the court be pointing out that while the issue is whether this defendant actually intended to kill, inferences about his subjective state of mind may be permissibly drawn from certain objective circumstances? Consider the court's views of how the jury should be correctly instructed as articulated in footnote 11 of the opinion. *See also* Gardner, *The Mens Rea Enigma: Observations on the Role of Motive in the Criminal Law Past and Present,* 1993 Utah L. Rev. 635, 677–78. See also § 9.04[C] of the casebook *infra* (discussing the constitutionality of inferences and presumptions in establishing guilt in criminal cases).

2. Do an assailant's verbal threats to his victim, such as "I'm going to kill you," necessarily establish his intent to kill if the assailant subsequently

---

[11] A different question would be presented if the issue were one of jury instruction, whether the judge had correctly instructed the jury on accidental death . . . or the difference between the various grades of homicide. . . . Manifestly, a properly instructed jury would be told that intent to kill is a permissible inference—not a mandatory presumption . . . that if the jury believed that the shooting was accidental the defendant should be acquitted; and that if mitigating circumstances were found, the defendant might be guilty of a lesser offense. . . .

causes the victim's death? Might the threat be seen as mere bragging rather than a manifestation of actual intent, particularly if the assailant carries out the threat through means arguably constituting nondeadly force? See *State v. Jensen,* 120 Utah 531, 336 P.2d 445 (1951) (conviction of second degree murder upheld where defendant killed victim with his fists after verbally threatening to kill victim; jury entitled to disbelieve defendant's claims that his threat was mere "big talk").

3. Should the fact that Haack used a gun (rather than, say, his fists) in killing his victim carry special evidentiary significance? "A special application of the presumption that one intends to produce the natural results of his actions is found in the deadly-weapon doctrine applicable to homicide cases: One who intentionally uses a deadly weapon on another human being and thereby kills him presumably intends to kill him." Lafave and Scott at 613.

Is the deadly-weapon doctrine justified? Does the *Haack* court correctly apply it in rejecting defendant's claim of intending only to scare but not to kill the victim?

STATE v. BINGHAM

Court of Appeals of Washington

40 Wash. App. 553, 699 P.2d 262 (1985)

WORSWICK, Chief Judge.

We are asked to decide whether the time to effect death by manual strangulation is alone sufficient to support a finding of premeditation in the absence of any other evidence supporting such a finding. We hold it is not. Accordingly, we reverse the conviction of Charles Dean Bingham for aggravated first degree murder. . . .

Leslie Cook, a retarded adult living at the Laurisden Home in Port Angeles, was raped and strangled on February 15, 1982. Bingham was the last person with whom she was seen. The two of them got off the Port Angeles—Sequim bus together at Sequim about 6 pm on February 15. They visited a grocery store and two residences. The last of these was Enid Pratt's where Bingham asked for a ride back to Port Angeles. When he was refused, he said they would hitchhike. They took the infrequently traveled Old Olympic Highway. Three days later, Cook's body was discovered in a field approximately 1/4 mile from the Pratt residence.

At trial, the State's expert testified that, in order to cause death by strangulation, Cook's assailant would have had to maintain substantial and continuous pressure on her windpipe for 3–5 minutes. The State contended that this alone was enough to raise an inference that the murder was premeditated. The trial judge agreed. . . . Therefore, it allowed the issue of premeditation to go to the jury. The jury convicted Bingham of aggravated first degree murder, rape being the aggravating circumstance. On appeal, counsel for Bingham concedes that a finding of guilty of murder was justified; he challenges only the finding of premeditation, contending that the evidence was insufficient to support it. We agree.

Premeditation is a separate and distinct element of first degree murder. It involves the mental process of thinking over beforehand, deliberation, reflection, weighing or reasoning for a period of time, however short, after which the intent to kill is formed. . . . The time required for manual strangulation is sufficient to permit deliberation. . . . However, time alone is not enough. The evidence must be sufficient to support the inference that the defendant not only had the time to deliberate, but that he actually did so. To require anything less would permit a jury to focus on the method of killing to the exclusion of the mental process involved in the separate element of premeditation.

The concept of premeditation had a slow but sure beginning in Anglo-American legal history. More than 500 years ago, English jurists arrived at the not surprising conclusion that the worst criminals—and those most deserving of the ultimate punishment—were those who planned to kill and then did so. Thus began the movement toward classification of homicides that resulted in restriction of the death penalty to those involving "malice prepensed" or "malice aforethought." When Washington's first criminal code was enacted in 1854, the Territorial Legislature abandoned this archaic language and used the phrase "deliberate and premeditated malice" in defining first degree murder. It thereby made a clear separation between a malicious intent and the process of deliberating before arriving at that intent.

Our Supreme Court recognized the need for evidence of both time for and fact of deliberation in *State v. Arata,* 56 Wash. 185, 189, 105 P. 227 (1909). Although it reversed a first degree murder conviction because a portion of an instruction was erroneous, it approved the remainder of the instruction, saying:

> In the case at bar, the court said, in substance, the law knows no specific time; if the man reflects upon the act a moment antecedent to the act, it is sufficient; the time of deliberation and premeditation need not be long; if it furnishes room for reflection *and the facts show that such reflection existed,* then it is sufficient deliberation, and closed the instruction upon this point with the statement: "There need be no appreciable space of time between the formation of the intention to kill and the killing." By these few last words the court destroyed at once all that was good in the entire statement, and gave the jury a rule which this court has frequently held was erroneous. This was reversible error. [Emphasis added.]

* * *

The subject of premeditation appears frequently in Washington cases. However, it is seldom discussed in a way that affords clear, objective guidance to trial judges in determining the sufficiency of the evidence to support it. Nevertheless, review of these cases reveals that in each one where the evidence has been found sufficient, there has been some evidence beyond time from which a jury could infer the fact of deliberation. This evidence has included, *inter alia,* motive, acquisition of a weapon, and planning directly related to the killing. . . .

Unless evidence of both time for and fact of deliberation are required, premeditation could be inferred in any case where the means of effecting death requires more than a moment in time. For all practical purposes, it would merge with intent; proof of intent would become proof of premeditation. However, the two elements are separate. Premeditation cannot be inferred from intent.

Premeditation can be proved by direct evidence, or it can be proved by circumstantial evidence where the inferences drawn by the jury are reasonable and the evidence supporting the jury's findings is substantial. . . . There was no such evidence here, either direct or circumstantial.

There was no evidence that Bingham had known Cook before February 15 or that he had a motive to kill her. By chance, they took the same bus. When Cook's companion on the bus refused to go to Sequim with her, Bingham offered to see that Cook got back to the Laurisden Home later. That was apparently still his intention when he asked for a ride at the Pratt residence. It could be inferred that between there and the field 1/4 mile away, he decided to rape her. A reasonable jury could not infer from this beyond a reasonable doubt that he also planned to kill her. There is no other evidence to support a finding of premeditation. The fact of strangulation, without more, leads us to conclude that the jury only speculated as to the mental process involved in premeditation. This is not enough. The premeditation finding cannot stand.

There remains the difficult question of how to dispose of this case. Counsel for Bingham concedes that Bingham is at least guilty of second degree murder. See RCW 9A.32.050(1)(a).[7] The jury was instructed on second degree murder as a lesser included offense and necessarily found the requisite elements in order to reach the verdict it did. . . .

Reversed. Remanded for entry of judgment and sentence for second degree murder.

PETRICH, J., *concur.*

ALEXANDER, Judge *(dissenting).*

* * *

I believe that where the evidence shows that death was caused slowly by manual strangulation in circumstances such as we have here, a rational trier of fact could be convinced beyond a reasonable doubt that the perpetrator intentionally caused death after deliberation and premeditation.

Contrary to the majority view, the law on this issue is unclear and unsettled. Washington case law and statutes do not provide a precise definition of premeditation, forcing us to examine the nature of the crime and the relationship between the concepts of intent and premeditation. "Premeditated" encompasses the mental process of thinking beforehand, deliberation, reflection, weighing or reasoning for a period of time, however short. . . . RCW 9A.32.020(1) provides:

---

[7] RCW 9A.32.050(1)(a) provides: "Murder in the second degree. (1) A person is guilty of murder in the second degree when: (a) With intent to cause the death of another person but without premeditation, he causes the death of such person or of a third person; . . ."

(1) As used in this chapter the premeditation required in order to support a conviction of the crime of murder in the first degree must involve *more than a moment in point of time.* [Emphasis added]

Premeditation may be proved by circumstantial evidence, where the inferences drawn by the jury from that evidence are reasonable. . . . A jury may infer premeditation from the facts of the crime when the defendant had an appreciable time in which to deliberate the intent to kill, though such time may be very short.

Time, then, may literally be of the essence. A number of cases have held that the element of premeditation is properly inferable from evidence of the lapse of time to death.

* * *

In *State v. Harris,* 62 Wash. 2d at 868, 385 P.2d 18, our Supreme Court found the evidence of premeditation to be sufficient in a case where the victim was struck on the head several times with a blunt instrument, struck in the face, and then strangled with a vacuum cleaner cord. The strangling was the immediate cause of death. The court held that the jury could infer premeditation from the circumstances of the killing even though the killing was unwitnessed and defendant did not testify. The "appreciable period" was the time that "elapsed between the first blow of the beating and the choking [causing death] to permit the perpetrator to form the intent to kill. . . . "

The majority seem to suggest that for a jury to find premeditation or deliberation it must have preceded the formation of intent to kill. In other words, they seem to hold, if the intent to kill is formed impulsively there can be no premeditation. Neither logic nor case law leads me to concur with that conclusion. The fact of deliberation for the requisite time is the key ingredient of premeditation. If there is opportunity for deliberation before death is caused, the jury may find that the death is not the result of an impulsive act. . . . It is not very productive, therefore, to engage in analysis or speculation over which occurred first, formation of intent to kill or reflection on that intent. Common sense suggests that premeditation exists as much if one is reflecting on an already formed intent to kill as it does when one is deliberating whether or not to kill. In either case, reflection and deliberation are present, if the deliberation is for an appreciable time. If the killing follows this process of reflection, then it is a premeditated killing.

In this case, uncontroverted evidence was presented to the jury that it takes 3 to 5 minutes to effect death by manual strangulation. The jury was, therefore, justified in concluding that an appreciable period of time elapsed from the time the defendant first placed his hand or hands on the victim's throat, regardless of what his intent might then have been, until the act of strangulation caused her death. A jury would further be justified in concluding from the circumstances of this case, as it must have done, that the defendant would necessarily have his attention riveted during this period of time on what effect the application of pressure might have on the windpipe of this "childlike" woman. It is significant that the defendant was a large man and there was little sign of struggle at the scene of the killing. These facts indicate that the death was not the result of an impulsive or spontaneous act flowing from an attempt to overcome resistance or to effect sexual contact. In short, the evidence of time-lapse and of the crime scene compels the conclusion that the defendant had ample opportunity to deliberate and premeditate on what he intended to achieve by choking his victim. The fact that he ultimately caused her death by strangulation justifies the conclusion that he intended to kill after reflecting on the deed for the requisite time.

* * *

The majority seem concerned that permitting the jury to infer premeditation in a case such as this would allow the jury to focus on the method of the killing to the exclusion of evidence concerning the mental process involved in the element of premeditation. I disagree. I do not suggest that a jury should be allowed to exclude evidence of mental process. On the other hand, they should not be precluded from considering the method of killing if its very nature provides clues to the mental process of the perpetrator.

I can only assume the Legislature must have intended by distinguishing between first and second degree murder, establishing greater penalties for first degree murder, to discourage killing when one has an opportunity to think about it. The time period during which one continuously exerts sufficient pressure on a victim's throat to block breathing which, in turn, causes unconsciousness and then death, affords a person a significant opportunity for a change of heart. If a person consciously rejects the opportunity to lessen the pressure in that period, the person may be found to have deliberated. The more time required, the greater the probability that even a slow thinker had time to reflect.

The majority correctly observes that in this case there is no evidence of prior planning. The defendant did not testify at trial and thus the jury did not know his mental state except as he revealed it to investigating officers. What a person thinks or intends is always difficult to determine in any case because we cannot pry into the mind. However, what a person does is often the best gauge of his or her thinking. The fact finder is called upon to determine whether a defendant premeditated from the facts surrounding the killing. Here, the jury concluded, as well they might, that this defendant took this mentally retarded young woman to a secluded area of Clallam County, raped her, strangled her with little difficulty for 3 to 5 minutes until she was dead, and then proceeded to bite her dead body. From this evidence a rational trier of fact could conclude beyond a reasonable doubt that the defendant was capable of reflecting and did reflect on his deed sufficiently to cause him to be guilty of premeditated murder in the first degree. The evidence supports the verdict and I would affirm.

NOTES AND QUESTIONS

1. The Court of Appeals was affirmed by the Washington Supreme Court, *State v. Bingham,* 105 Wash. 2d 820, 719 P.2d 109 (1986). In that opinion

the court stated the standard for reviewing the sufficiency of the evidence in a criminal case to be "whether, after reviewing the evidence in the light most favorable to the prosecution, *any* rational trier of fact could have found the essential elements of the crime beyond a reasonable doubt," *id.* at 111, citing *Jackson v. Virginia,* 443 U.S. 307, 319 (1979) (emphasis in original).

Under this standard of review, is the action of the Court of Appeals in *Bingham* justifiable? Does the court provide a test for determining the meaning of "premeditation?" If not, is the appellate court simply substituting its opinion for that of the jury? On the other hand, does the *Bingham* court attempt to fashion a test in terms of requiring evidence of motive to kill and "planning activity related to the killing?" If such is the test, do you agree with the court that no evidence of motive or of planning activity exists in the *Bingham* case? What about an argument that *Bingham* killed the victim to eliminate her as a witness to his crime of rape? What about the fact that the body is found in a secluded area? Does that fact evidence planning activity? Should such speculations suffice to explain the jury's finding of premeditation?

2. Is the *Bingham* court correct in its conclusion that permitting an inference of premeditation whenever "the means of death requires more than a moment in time" would merge premeditation with intent? If so, why is that consequence objectionable?

In a case similar to *Bingham,* the Tennessee Supreme Court overturned a conviction of first degree murder where the only evidence of premeditation and deliberation was that the defendant caused death by inflicting "repeated blows" upon the victim. *State v. Brown,* 836 S.W.2d 530 (Tenn. 1992). The court noted that while repeated blows might evidence premeditation and deliberation, they may also be delivered in the heat of passion with no design or reflection. Moreover, the *Brown* court emphasized the distinction between premeditation (which may be formed in an instant) and deliberation (which requires "some period of reflection"). The court cautioned against using the terms interchangeably.

3. In *Thomerson v. Lockhart,* 835 F.2d 1257 (8th Cir. 1987), the court held that sufficient evidence existed to support the jury's finding of premeditation where the petitioner killed his girlfriend after he found her in the house of an unknown man. Petitioner used his fists, hands, cord or wire, and other objects to abuse the victim's body for over an hour. The court found that although the petitioner may have begun to beat the girlfriend out of anger over her unfaithfulness, a reasonable jury could have inferred from the evidence that his actions became calculated and deliberate as he continued to assault her.

Is *Thomerson* consistent with *Bingham?*

4. Suppose that the defendant in *Bingham* had poisoned rather than strangled the victim? Many statutes include poisoning in addition to premeditation and deliberation as a basis for first degree murder. *See, e.g.,* N.C. Gen. Stat. § 14-17, which provides: "A murder which shall be perpetrated by means of poison, lying in wait . . . torture, or by any other kind of wilful deliberate, and premeditated killing . . . shall be deemed to be murder in the first degree." Why should poisoning the victim automatically constitute first degree murder while strangling her to death does not?

In interpreting such statutes, the courts are split over the question of whether murder by poison is a conclusive presumption of premeditation and deliberation, *see, e.g., Robbins v. State,* 8 Ohio St. 131 (1857), or whether killing by means of poison is a separate ground for first degree murder totally unrelated to the premeditation formula, *see, e.g., State v. Johnson,* 317 N.C. 193, 344 S.E.2d 775 (1986). Under the latter view, the prosecution need not prove any intent to kill so long as the homicide otherwise amounted to murder under theories of depraved heart, intent to cause serious bodily injury, or felony murder. See LaFave and Scott at 647. *See infra,* pp.526--93, for discussion of these theories of murder.

Could the killing in *Bingham* constitute first degree murder by "torture" under the North Carolina statute? See *People v. Steger,* 16 Cal. 3d 539, 128 Cal. Rptr. 161, 546 P.2d 665 (1976); *People v. Cardwell,* 43 Cal. 2d 864, 279 P.2d 539 (1955).

PEOPLE V. WATERS

Court of Appeals of Michigan

118 Mich. App. 176, 324 N.W.2d 564 (1982)

CYNAR, Judge.

Following a nonjury trial, defendant was convicted of first-degree murder, assault with intent to murder, and two counts of felony-firearm [possession of firearm]. . . . [D]efendant was sentenced to a term of life imprisonment for murder, life for assault with intent to murder, and two years for each felony-firearm count. He appeals as of right.

Joseph Porcelli, the victim's husband, stated that he parked their green and white 1973 Monte Carlo five or six rows behind the concession stand at the Miracle Mile Drive-In on May 2, 1980. Near the end of the first show, he noticed five young black males walk past his car toward the restrooms in the rear of the concession stand. After standing near the restrooms for some time, smoking until the movie ended, the youths walked toward the back of the drive-in. As they passed the Porcelli car, three walked on the passenger's side and two went to the driver's side. One of the individuals, standing approximately 12 to 15 feet from the driver's side, looked at Porcelli and said: "Hey, man, you got a light?" Porcelli, who smokes, was not smoking at that time. The other person on the driver's side stood approximately 20 feet away. Porcelli, who was afraid because the car was surrounded, responded politely, "Sorry, I can't help you." As the inquirer walked away, Porcelli heard another voice utter, "You can help me." The next thing he saw, heard or felt, he was struck on the side of the head, fell across his wife's lap and he heard his wife scream.

Defendant's companions on May 3, 1980, Jessie Lee King, Michael Holmes, Richard Alston and Roderick Howard, each testified at the preliminary examination. King testified that he kept a .22-caliber pistol, which he called "Marv," in his desk drawer for the pistol's owner Holmes. On May 2, 1980,

Holmes gave "Marv" to defendant to "style" for the evening. Defendant, King, Holmes, and Howard went to a Jefferson Junior High School dance, visited a McDonald's restaurant, and picked up Alston before arriving at the drive-in. There, they entered through a hole in the rear fence, proceeding to the concession stand. At the concession stand, the boys "messed around" for approximately one-half hour. While leaving the premises, they passed a green and white vehicle. Alston asked a man inside the automobile for a match. When the occupant responded that he could be of no help, the entire group walked away, except defendant, who was standing approximately eight feet from the car. Defendant said, "Can't have no match." Suddenly, King heard a shot, turned, heard another shot, and saw defendant with "Marv" drawn. According to King, defendant was eight feet from the car, holding the pistol with both hands. He stated that a "couple seconds" passed between the first and second shots. Holmes saw defendant draw the pistol and fire two shots in rapid succession into the vehicle's passenger compartment. Holmes thought that defendant held the gun with two hands. Alston also believed that defendant held the pistol with two hands. He began to run after the first shot, and heard the second shot being fired approximately four seconds later. Howard turned when he heard the shots, observing the driver's side window burst. However, he did not see the gun. The boys ran, escaped through the hole in the rear fence, and gathered at King's automobile. There, defendant stated that he did not mean to shoot; instead, he meant only to scare the couple. The following day, defendant phoned King and informed him that the lady had died. Later in the evening, King and Holmes tossed "Marv" into nearby Crystal Lake.

Defendant argues that insufficient evidence of premeditation and deliberation was introduced at trial to support his conviction. We disagree. Our review of the record shows that there was sufficient evidence introduced to justify a trier of fact in reasonably concluding that defendant is guilty beyond a reasonable doubt, and considering the entire record, it does not appear that the trial court clearly erred in finding that there was in fact premeditation and deliberation. . . .

The totality of the circumstances need to be examined in order to determine whether there is evidence to support the findings of the trier of fact; in particular, whether the findings of premeditation and deliberation are supported. . . . Premeditation and deliberation need not be established by direct evidence. The requisite state of mind may be inferred from the defendant's conduct. Such an inference, however, must have an adequate basis in the record. . . .

Testimony at trial showed that defendant acquired the pistol several hours before the killing. After leaving the gun under an armrest in King's vehicle for most of the evening, defendant carried the pistol into the drive-in. Possession of a deadly weapon in advance of a slaying is a fact from which premeditation and deliberation can be inferred. . . . However, in those cases where use of a deadly weapon has been held to evidence premeditation, there were other circumstances showing a motive or plan which would enable a trier of fact to infer that the killing was not a spur-of-the-moment decision. . . . Here, there is no direct evidence of a plan or motive existing prior to the exchange of words which preceded the shooting.

The circumstances of the killing itself, however, provide the strongest argument for a finding of premeditation and deliberation. The record shows that after Alston was denied a light, defendant stated, "Can't have no match." From this point, witness King's testimony is most illustrative, as he turned upon hearing the first shot. He saw defendant holding the pistol with two hands, the driver's side window collapsing, and the man inside the vehicle fall. After a two-to-three-second pause, another shot was fired, and King observed the woman occupant slump. It is well-settled that some time span between the initial homicidal intent and the ultimate action is necessary to establish premeditation and deliberation. . . . Here, it can be inferred that formation of a homicidal intent occurred between the time that defendant drew the weapon from his waistband and the instant he first pulled the trigger. Testimony indicates that it was the second shot that killed Deborah Porcelli. Thus, it appears that several seconds passed between the formation of a homicidal intent and the firing of the fatal gunshot. During this interval, defendant saw the window burst and the male figure fall. Before defendant squeezed the trigger again, discharging the second bullet, sufficient time passed for defendant to take a second look at the nature of his act.

In *People v. Tilley,* [405 Mich. 38, 273 N.W.2d 471 (1979)], the defendant held the murder weapon, a pistol, with two hands. Without explanation, the Supreme Court deemed this fact to be indicative of premeditation and deliberation. Presumably, the Court reasoned that the act of raising a second hand steadied the position of the weapon in the direction of the target.

Here, the trial court concluded that malice was the moving cause of the shooting, and that the shooting was not accidental or merely intended to frighten the Porcellis. The trial judge noted that at the time the defendant and his companions arrived at the drive-in, the gun was not left behind in the car as it had been on earlier occasions. The defendant carried the gun in his waistband upon entering the drive-in. Further, the court noted the remark attributed by some of the witnesses to the defendant when one of the party was refused a light was, "Oh, can't have a match, huh?" This suggested to the court an existing state of mind, a hostile feeling of the speaker, to punish or criticize in some fashion the individual who refused to give a light.

Regarding premeditation, the trial court noted that witness King, who was at the rear corner of the car, saw the man in the car drop after the first shot, then a second shot was discharged and the woman in the car fell. Defendant was closer to the car than King, and so had an even clearer view of the consequences of his actions. After the man dropped and the window fell, there could not have been a better opportunity to recognize what might happen if a second shot were fired, and the defendant chose to shoot again. The court found premeditation beyond a reasonable doubt.

We conclude that the testimony regarding the circumstances of the killing itself was sufficient to allow a trier of fact to find premeditation and deliberation proved beyond a reasonable doubt. We are convinced the trial court's determination was correct.

Affirmed.

NOTES AND QUESTIONS

1. When compared to each other, do the results in *Bingham* and *Waters* make sense? In the former, a killing by strangulation taking three to five minutes to effectuate is not premeditated, while in the latter a shooting occurring within two to three seconds of the formulation of initial homicidal intent is premeditated. Is there a principled distinction between the two cases?

2. The case law is replete in support of the notion that premeditation need not have existed for any appreciable length of time prior to the killing. So long as premeditation exists at the time of the act, "the intent (premeditation?) and the act may be as instantaneous as successive thoughts." *Murry v. State,* 713 P.2d 202, 207 (Wyo. 1986) (defendant "premeditated" when he shot and killed victim two to three minutes after obtaining a gun in response to racial slurs directed toward defendant by third parties). See also *Watson v. United States,* 501 A.2d 791 (D.C. App. 1985) (defendant committed premeditated murder when he shot and killed a police officer with the latter's service revolver seconds after wresting it away from the officer as he tried to arrest defendant).

Moreover, the notion of deliberation has received a similarly strained judicial definition. Consider, for example, *In re Thomas,* 183 Cal. App. 3d 786, 796, 228 Cal. Rptr. 430, 436 (1986), which holds that defendant killed with "deliberate intention" and thus committed second degree murder but did not "deliberate" for purposes of the first degree statute:

> [Appellant] pointing to the statutory language of "deliberate intention" for express malice, claims that the experts' evidence shows that because of his [mental] illness and his [honoring of his sister's request to kill her,] he could not and did not deliberately kill. Furthermore, he claims the judge's agreement with this is shown by his comments rejecting a finding of premeditation and deliberation for first degree murder.
>
> [Appellant's] reliance on the definition of "deliberate," in *People v. Thomas* (1945), 25 Cal. 2 880, 898–899, 156 P.2d 7, is misplaced, since the court therein was speaking of the use of the words "deliberate" and "deliberation" in the definition of first degree murder. The use of the term "deliberate intention" for malice aforethought, as required in second degree murder, is not synonymous with the term "deliberate," as used in defining first degree murder.

3. The premeditation formula has proven to be controversial with the commentators. Professors Wechsler and Michael in *A Rationale of the Law of Homicide I,* 37 Colum. L. Rev. 701, 707–9 (1937), summarize the American experience as follows:

> The most striking phase of the development of the English law was the reduction of "malice aforethought" to a term of art signifying neither "malice" nor "aforethought" in the popular sense. Strikingly analogous in the judicial development of the American law of homicide is the narrow

interpretation of "deliberation" and "premeditation" to exclude the two elements which the words normally signify: a determination to kill reached (i) calmly and (ii) some appreciable time prior to the homicide. The elimination of these elements leaves, . . . nothing precise as the critical state of mind but intention to kill. Such a result creates particular difficulty in a jurisdiction like New York where "design" to kill is, by statute, the distinguishing feature of second-degree murder. The trial judge must solemnly distinguish in his charge between the two degrees in terms which frequently render them quite indistinguishable, a procedure which obviously confers on the jury a discretion to follow one aspect of the charge or the other, if not a valid excuse for neglecting the charge entirely. The statutory scheme was apparently intended to limit administrative discretion in the selection of capital cases. As so frequently occurs, the discretion which the legislature threw out the door was let in through the window by the courts.

Benjamin Cardozo, in his lecture "Law and Literature" published in Selected Writings of Benjamin Nathan Cardozo 338, 383–84 (M. Hall ed. 1975), offers his objection to distinguishing degrees of murder in terms of premeditation:

> The difficulty arises when we try to discover what is meant by the words *deliberate* and *premeditated*. A long series of decisions, beginning many years ago, has given to these words a meaning that differs to some extent from the one revealed upon the surface. To deliberate and premeditate within the meaning of the statute, one does not have to plan the murder days or hours or even minutes in advance, as where one lies in wait for one's enemy or places poison in his food and drink. The law does not say that any particular length of time must intervene between the volition and the act. The human brain, we are reminded, acts at times with extraordinary celerity. All that the statute requires is that the act must not be the result of immediate or spontaneous impulse. "If there is hesitation or doubt to be overcome, a choice made as the result of thought, however short the struggle between the intention and the act," there is such deliberation and premeditation as will expose the offender to the punishment of death.
>
> I think the distinction is much too vague to be continued in our law. There can be no intent unless there is a choice, yet by the hypothesis, the choice without more is enough to justify the inference that the intent was deliberate and premeditated. The presence of a sudden impulse is said to mark the dividing line, but how can an impulse be anything but sudden when the time for its formation is measured by the lapse of seconds? Yet the decisions are to the effect that seconds may be enough. What is meant, as I understand it, is that the impulse must be the product of an emotion or passion so swift and overmastering as to sweep the mind from its moorings. A metaphor, however, is, to say the least, a shifting test whereby to measure degrees of guilt that mean the difference between life and death. I think the students of the mind should make it clear to the lawmakers that the statute is framed along the lines of a defective and unreal psychology. If intent is deliberate and premeditated whenever there is choice, then in truth it is always deliberate and premeditated, since choice is involved in the hypothesis of the intent. What we have is merely a privilege offered to the jury to find the lesser degree when the suddenness of the intent, the

vehemence of the passion, seems to call irresistibly for the exercise of mercy. I have no objection to giving them this dispensing power, but it should be given to them directly and not in a mystifying cloud of words. The present distinction is so obscure that no jury hearing it for the first time can fairly be expected to assimilate and understand it. I am not at all sure that I understand it myself after trying to apply it for many years and after diligent study of what has been written in the books. Upon the basis of this fine distinction with its obscure and mystifying psychology, scores of men have gone to their death.

4. Do cases like *Waters* suggest a misguided focus on premeditation as the necessary characteristic of the most heinous form of homicide? Consider the point made by 3 Stephen at 94:

As much cruelty, as much indifference to the life of others, a disposition at least as dangerous to society, probably even more dangerous, is shown by sudden as by premeditated murders. The following cases appear to me to set this in a clear light. A man passing along the road, sees a boy sitting on a bridge over a deep river and, out of mere wanton barbarity, pushes him into it and so drowns him. A man makes advances to a girl who repels him. He deliberately but instantly cuts her throat. A man civilly asked to pay a just debt pretends to get the money, loads a rifle and blows out his creditor's brains. In none of these cases is there premeditation unless the word is used in a sense as unnatural as "aforethought" in "malice aforethought," but each represents even more diabolical cruelty and ferocity than that which is involved in murders premeditated in the natural sense of the word.

5. While Stephen argues that premeditation is not a necessary condition for the most serious forms of homicide, some cases suggest that it may not be a sufficient ground for distinguishing the relative heinousness of homicide. Consider, for example, the case of *Commonwealth v. Carroll,* 412 Pa. 525, 194 A.2d 911 (1963), in which defendant and his wife experienced a long history of marital disputes. Ms. Carroll constantly objected to defendant's employment situation and defendant was concerned about his wife's sometimes sadistic discipline of their young children. The marital problems built to a head after a heated argument, lasting most of the night, over defendant's proposed change of employment which would necessitate his being away from home four nights a week for a 10-week period. After Ms. Carroll issued an ultimatum threatening to leave defendant if he took the new employment, the couple finally went to bed at about 4 AM. Approximately five minutes after their last words to each other, defendant, who had been thinking about Ms. Carroll's abuse of the children and her insulting remarks to him, remembered that he had placed a gun near the bed for her protection while he was out of town. He grabbed the gun and immediately shot and killed his sleeping wife. He then took her body to a desolate place near a trash dump.

The defendant pleaded guilty generally to an indictment charging him with murder. In a bench proceeding to determine the degree of murder, the defendant introduced psychiatric evidence to show that his act was an impulsive reaction to his feelings of being trapped in his marital situation and that had the gun been unloaded or dropped before firing, defendant would not have used the gun. The court found defendant guilty of first degree premeditated murder and sentenced him to life imprisonment.

In upholding the finding of premeditated murder, the Pennsylvania Supreme Court justified the trial court's action in terms of the following policy consideration: "society would be almost completely unprotected from criminals if the law permitted a blind or irresistible impulse or inability to control one's self, to excuse or justify a murder or to reduce it from first degree to second degree." 412 Pa. at 537, 194 A.2d at 917–18.

Do you agree with the *Carroll* court's justification for holding the defendant guilty of first degree murder? Assuming that the defendant in *Carroll* did premeditate, does he strike you as the kind of especially heinous killer meant to be identified by means of the distinction between first and second degree murder?

6. The California courts have perhaps made the most vigorous attempt to provide definitional content to the concept of premeditation. Consider the following case:

PEOPLE v. LUCERO

Supreme Court of California

44 Cal. 3d 1006, 245 Cal. Rptr. 185, 750 P.2d 1342 (1988)

BROUSSARD, Justice.

This case arises on an automatic appeal from a judgment of death imposed under the 1978 death penalty law. Defendant, Phillip Louis Lucero, was convicted of two counts of first degree murder.

Defendant presents numerous claims of error regarding . . . the guilt phase and the penalty phase of his trial. We have concluded that . . . the judgment of guilt must be affirmed.

On April 12, 1980, seven-year-old Chris Hubbard and ten-year-old Teddy Engliman were playing at the Hubbard home in the town of Yucaipa in western San Bernardino County. Chris's father, Michael Hubbard, was working in the backyard garden. Sometime between 4 PM and 4:30 PM that afternoon, he gave the girls permission to go to the nearby I Street park to play on the swings.

At 4:30 or 4:45 PM, Ruth Schultz heard defendant's goose cackling and looked out her dining room window. She saw two girls matching the description of Chris and Teddy standing at the back of defendant's lot between two fences. Defendant walked toward the girls and told them that the goose would not hurt them. The girls appeared to be coming into defendant's yard.

Shortly after 5:00, no more than 30 to 40 minutes after the girls had left for the park, Michael Hubbard became concerned by their failure to return. He and his wife made separate trips to the park but were unable to find the girls. About 5:30, Mrs. Hubbard called the San Bernardino County Sheriff's Department.

Sergeant Wallace Anton received a report of the missing girls from the sheriff's Yucaipa substation about 6 PM. In order to coordinate the search, a temporary command post was set up at the I Street park almost directly across the street from defendant's house. . . .

About 7:15, Dolores Gwaltney heard defendant's car start up and drive down the street. She lived next door to defendant and was able to recognize the car because of its defective muffler. Ten minutes later she saw the car return to defendant's driveway. Three to five minutes later she saw defendant drive away in the car. Within minutes of the car's second departure, Mrs. Gwaltney saw a fire in the rear portion of defendant's house.

Deputy Long also noticed the fire as he reported to the search command post about 7:25. He radioed the California Department of Forestry and immediately began to fight the fire with a garden hose. He was joined shortly by Deputy Vander Veen and Sergeant Anton. Long and Vander Veen crawled into the burning house searching for anyone who might be inside. No one was found.

The Department of Forestry firefighters arrived at 7:37. Sergeant Anton immediately informed Fire Captain Charles Bryant of the missing girls and asked that the captain direct his men to search the burning house. Mrs. Gwaltney telephoned defendant at his parents' house. Defendant returned to the scene with his parents in their car.

When the fire was under control, the sheriff's officers returned to the command post across the street. The firefighters then alerted sheriff's deputies to a large bloodstain on the carpet of defendant's living room. Several officers saw the bloodstain and questioned defendant. The firefighters and deputies also noticed a bloodstained bedsheet and pieces of broken glass in the living room. About the time the deputies were examining the bloodstain, the bodies of the two girls were found in a nearby dumpster wrapped in green trash bags.

Subsequent searches by homicide detectives and sheriff's criminologists verified that the stained carpet and bedsheet contained human blood. The pieces of glass came from a broken Pepsi bottle found in the living room. Additional bloodstains were discovered on the gate to defendant's front yard. Teddy Engliman's brown tennis shoes were found in the living room. A rope was lying in a doorway between the front porch and the living room. Green trash bags were discovered in the kitchen. Gasoline residue was found on the living room carpet and in the bedroom, where the fire is believed to have originated.

Searches of defendant's car revealed bloodstains on the exterior portion of the car trunk, on the driver's outside door handle, and in the interior of the car and trunk. There was a puddle of still moist blood on the bottom of the trunk compartment.

At the time of his arrest defendant's T-shirt was spotted with blood. The bottom of his left sock was saturated with blood. Dried blood was observed on one of defendant's hands.

The girls' bodies had been removed from the dumpster by 11 PM on April 12 and autopsies were performed the next day. The autopsy performed on Teddy Engliman revealed that several of the bones in her head had been fractured and that some of her teeth had been knocked out. The pathologist concluded that the injuries had been caused by a minimum of two or three blows from a blunt object. The immediate cause of death was aspiration of the blood produced by her injuries.

The autopsy of Chris Hubbard revealed an abrasion on her neck. The pathologist determined ligature strangulation to be the cause of death. He also concluded that the necklace Chris was wearing could have been used in the strangulation. Under magnification the doctor discovered "fine abrasions or little scrapes" within a discolored area on Chris' wrists. Although he thought there could be other possibilities, the pathologist testified that the marks may indicate that the victim's wrists were tied together with some kind of rough twine or rope.

The doctor found no injuries which suggested the girls had been sexually molested. Tests of vaginal and anal swabs for traces of seminal fluid also proved negative.

When Teddy's body was removed from the trash bag numerous fragments of broken glass fell out. These fragments were later identified as coming from the same broken Pepsi bottle found in defendant's living room. The blood found on defendant's living room carpet, the bedsheet, the inner tube located in the trunk of his car and defendant's sock was tested and found to be of the same type as the blood taken from Teddy Engliman during the autopsy. (It did not match that of either Chris Hubbard or the defendant.) The plastic trash bags which had contained the bodies of the victims were found to be identical in color, thickness, size, packing folds and heat seals to the trash bags found in defendant's kitchen.

The minimal cross-examination conducted by defendant during the guilt phase focused on the impression of his emotional state formed by those having contact with him during the effort to extinguish the fire and immediately thereafter. All witnesses agreed that defendant appeared surprisingly indifferent and oddly subdued given the circumstances.

The only theory of first degree murder presented to the jury was that of premeditated murder. Although the trial court properly instructed the jury in this regard, defendant contends that the evidence presented at trial is insufficient as a matter of law to support a finding of premeditation.

In *People v. Anderson* (1968), 70 Cal. 2d 15, 26–27, 73 Cal. Rptr. 550, 447 P.2d 942, we identified three categories of evidence which this court has found sufficient to sustain a finding of premeditation and deliberation: (1)facts showing planning activity; (2)facts suggesting motive; and (3)facts about the manner of killing which suggest a preconceived design. Although the evidence presented at defendant's trial was not particularly strong on any one of the *Anderson* factors, the record reveals at least some evidence in each category. When considered in combination, and viewed in a light most favorable to the prosecution . . . this evidence is sufficient to support the jury's finding of premeditated murder.

The most substantial evidence of premeditation related to planning activity, "the most important prong of the *Anderson* test. . . . " Defendant approached the children near the edge of his property and was heard to reassure them that they would not be harmed by his goose. The girls were seen entering defendant's yard and were killed inside his house. Since it is unlikely two young girls would have readily accompanied a man they did not know into a strange house, the jury could have reasonably inferred that defendant lured or compelled the victims to enter. The evidence also indicated that once inside the house defendant used a rope to bind the wrists of one girl, from which the jury could have inferred that defendant intended to immobilize one victim while he carried out his plan with respect to the other.

Defendant argues that his actions were not clearly "directed toward, and explicable as intended to result in, the killing. . . . " (*People v. Anderson, supra,* 70 Cal. 2d at p. 26, 73 Cal. Rptr. 550, 447 P.2d 942.) However, we have not always required that a murder plan be evident before characterizing conduct as planning activity. . . .

The evidence of a motive for the murders is arguably the weakest element in *Anderson'* stripartite analysis. . . .

In this case defendant intercepted the girls from their innocent journey and brought them to his house. The evidence that the younger victim's wrists had been tied suggests additional mistreatment before the murders, which may have further escalated the consequences to defendant of letting his victims go free. As far as defendant knew, no one had ever seen him with the girls. The jury may have inferred that defendant killed them in order to avoid disclosure of his conduct.[1] It should also be noted that whatever the reason for killing the first victim, once this deed was done, defendant had a strong motive to eliminate the only witness to his crime.

The evidence indicated that Chris was strangled with the necklace she was wearing. While ligature strangulation may not always evidence a premeditated murder . . . , the jury could have viewed the strangulation as a deliberate manner of killing sufficient to indicate a "preconceived design." (The manner of Teddy's killing, multiple blows to the skull from a blunt object, is much less suggestive of premeditated murder.)

The judgment as to guilt [is] affirmed.

NOTES AND QUESTIONS

1. Do the *Anderson* factors relied upon by the Lucero court provide a useful structure for appellate court review of findings of premeditation? Does the *Anderson* approach guide the *Lucero* court to the correct conclusion? How would the *Bingham* court have decided the *Lucero* case?

2. The *Anderson* case also involved the gruesome murder of a young girl. Anderson had been living with the mother of the 10-year-old victim. On the day of her death, her mother went to work, leaving her at home alone with Anderson, who had been drinking heavily for the prior two days. Later that

---

[1] This analysis does not mean that defendant's conduct prior to the killings was necessarily directed toward some lesser criminal objective and thus not "planned activity" within the meaning of *Anderson, supra,* 70 Cal. 3d at page 26, 73 Cal. Rptr. 55, 447 P.2d 942. The jury could have believed that defendant planned to kill his victims from the outset.

day, the girl's brother discovered her nude body in her bedroom with over 60 knife wounds, some severe, others superficial. Her tongue was partially amputated and a postmortem cut extended from her rectum through her vagina. Blood was splattered throughout the house. No evidence of sexual molestation prior to death was discovered. See *People v. Anderson,* 70 Cal. 2d 15, 73 Cal. Rptr. 550, 447 P.2d 942 (1968).

Anderson was convicted of first degree premeditated murder and sentenced to death. On appeal, the California Supreme Court reduced the degree of the crime to second degree murder, finding insufficient evidence of premeditation under the tripartite test (motive, planning activity, manner of killing as suggesting preconceived design). The court found no evidence of planning activity or of motive. Rather than suggesting a preconceived design, the *Anderson* court found the manner of the killing to evidence a "random, violent, indiscriminate attack rather than from deliberately placed wounds inflicted according to a preconceived design."

Did the *Anderson* court apply its test correctly? Does Anderson appear to be the kind of killer meant to be covered by the first degree murder category? Are you satisfied that as a matter of law Anderson is guilty of only second degree murder (thus avoiding a possible death penalty) while Lucero commits first degree murder (thus becoming a candidate for the death penalty)?

Keep these questions in mind as you consider the materials on capital punishment discussed in § 5.04, *infra.*

3. Following the lead of the Model Penal Code, several jurisdictions in their recent criminal law revisions have rejected use of the premeditation-deliberation formula as a basis for determining murders deserving of the greatest punishment. See, *e.g.,* New York Penal Law, § § 125.00, 125.25, 125.27. The MPC Comments to § 210.6 at 125–28 offer the following objections to this formula:

> [T]he Pennsylvania reform was undermined by the inability or unwillingness of courts to settle on any dependable content for the "deliberate and premeditated" formula. Early Pennsylvania decisions read this language to require nothing more than proof of intentional homicide. Since intent to kill is the chief meaning of the "malice aforethought" concept used to define murder generally, identifying that state of mind as sufficient for murder in the first degree blurs any distinction between the two categories of the offense. Other jurisdictions experienced similar difficulties, and modern decisions revealed continuing conflict and uncertainty about the distinguishing criteria of capital murder. At least in some jurisdictions, an intention to kill could be "deliberate" even though it was not a product of calm reflection and "premeditated" even though no appreciable time elapsed between the intention and the act.
>
> Most importantly, judicial inconsistency and obscurity are largely symptomatic of the lack of an intelligible policy underlying the Pennsylvania formulation. To the extent that the words "deliberate and premeditated" have ascertainable meaning, they suggest a plan or design conceived well in advance of the homicidal act. Under this view, a significant lapse of time between initial determination to kill and the act of killing would be the

critical evidentiary fact. When this distinction is used to define capital murder, it probably rests on the premise that there exists some dependable relation between the duration of reflection and the gravity of the offense. Crudely put, the judgment is that the person who plans ahead is worse than the person who kills on sudden impulse. This generalization does not, however, survive analysis.

Prior reflection may reveal the uncertainties of a tortured conscience rather than exceptional depravity. The very fact of a long internal struggle may be evidence that the homicidal impulse was deeply aberrational and far more the product of extraordinary circumstances than a true reflection of the actor's normal character. Thus, for example, one suspects that most mercy killings are the consequence of long and careful deliberation, but they are not especially appropriate cases for imposition of capital punishment. The same is likely to be true with respect to suicide pacts, many infanticides, and cases where a provocation gains in its explosive power as the actor broods about his injury.

It also seems clear that some purely impulsive murders will present no extenuating circumstances. The suddenness of the killing may simply reveal callousness so complete and depravity so extreme that no hesitation is required. . . . In short, the notion that prior reflection should distinguish capital from non-capital murder is fundamentally unsound.

[2] Depraved Heart Murder

BANKS v. STATE

Court of Criminal Appeals of Texas

5 Tex. Crim. 165, 211 S.W. 217 (1919)

LATTIMORE, J. . . . [Banks and a companion, Davis, were walking near a railroad track when they heard a train coming. Davis suggested shooting into the train, and handed Banks a gun for that purpose. Ballistics evidence showed that the gun Banks used was the weapon that killed the deceased, a brakeman on the train. Banks was convicted of murder, was sentenced to death, and appealed on the grounds that he had no malice aforethought, as required by common law and statute.]

No reason is assigned for such shooting, and it does not appear that appellant or any member of the party was acquainted with any of the parties on the train, and that any specific malice could be directed toward the deceased, but under our law the same is not necessary.

One who deliberately uses a deadly weapon in such reckless manner as to evince a heart regardless of social duty and fatally bent on mischief, as is shown by firing into a moving railroad train upon which human beings necessarily are, cannot shield himself from the consequences of his acts by disclaiming malice. Malice may be toward a group of persons as well as toward an individual. It may exist without former grudges or antecedent menaces. The intentional doing of any wrongful act in such manner and under such circumstances as that the death of a human being may result therefrom is malice.

That man who can coolly shoot into a moving train, or automobile, or other vehicle in which are persons guiltless of any wrongdoing toward him or provocation for such attack is, if possible, worse than the man who endures insult or broods over a wrong, real or fancied, and then waylays and kills his personal enemy. The shame of the world recently has been the unwarranted killing of persons who were noncombatants and who were doing nothing and were not capable of inflicting injury upon their slayers. Of kindred spirit is he who can shoot in the darkness into houses, crowds, or trains and recklessly send into eternity those whom he does not know and against whom he has no sort of reason for directing his malevolence. . . .

The judgment of the lower court is affirmed.

NOTES AND QUESTIONS

1. The category of murder represented in the *Banks* case is described variously as "depraved heart," "depraved mind," or "abandoned and malignant heart" murder. The different labels derive from the common law writers (see the Blackstone excerpt at the beginning of these materials on murder) and from decisions and statutes condemning as murder unintended homicide where the defendant kills under circumstances evincing extreme recklessness regarding homicidal risk. MPC, Comment to § 210.2 at 15.

While the killing in *Banks* constituted capital murder, most jurisdictions treat depraved heart killings as second degree (noncapital) murder. See, *e.g.*, N.Y. Penal Code § 125.25(2). But see Ala. Code § 13A-6-2(a)(2) and Colo. Stat. Ann. *18-3-102(1)(d) for rare statutory provisions treating depraved heart homicide as first degree murder.

Do you agree with the majority of jurisdictions, which would treat the killing by Banks as less culpable than deliberate and premeditated murder?

2. The historical origins of depraved heart murder are described in Gegan, *A Case of Depraved Heart Murder,* 49 St. John's L. Rev. 417, 457 (1975), as follows:

> The meaning of the [concept of] depraved mind murder . . . is traceable in a direct line of succession . . . back to the common law doctrine of malice aforethought and in particular, implied malice. The means used, the brutality of the act, the lack of provocation, and other circumstances were all significant to the common law in judging malice. It was a total qualitative appraisal of the actor's character in taking life, not merely of his "intent" in the modern sense of perception and conscious ratiocination.

Qualitative assessments of the actor's risk-taking conduct are matters of degree that embrace case-by-case considerations of a myriad of motives for risk creation. Therefore, statutory clarity is not the benchmark of depraved heart murder, which is commonly defined in terms of such vague standards as "depraved indifference to human life" or "the dictate of a wicked, depraved, and malignant heart." The Model Penal Code is only slightly more precise in defining unintended killing as murder when it is committed recklessly [defined in § 2.02 (2)(c)] and "under circumstances manifesting extreme indifference to the value of human life." MPC § 210.2.

3. The problem of defining unacceptable risk-taking resulting in death is elucidated in the literature. Wechsler and Michael, *A Rationale of the Law of Homicide I,* 37 Colum. L. Rev. 701, 744–46 (1937), provide the following:

[T]he matter may be summarized as follows: when death is not intended, the desirability of preventing a particular act because it may result in death, turns upon the following factors: (1) the probability that death or serious injury will result; (2) the probability that the act will also have desirable results and the degree of their desirability, in the determination of which the actor's purposes are relevant; (3) if the act serves desirable ends, its efficacy as a means, as opposed to the efficacy of other and less dangerous means.

No legislature can make these evaluations in advance for all possible acts under all possible circumstances. However, it is clear that whatever ends are thought to justify intentional homicide, when it is reasonably believed to be a necessary means to those ends, also justify acts endangering life which are not intended to kill, when they are reasonably believed to be necessary means. On the other hand, when the actor's proximate end is itself criminal or otherwise undesirable, the use of means that involve a homicidal risk obviously cannot be justified. The difficult cases are those in which the actor's ends are themselves desirable, or, at least, are not undesirable, though they would not justify intentional homicide as a means. Within this broad domain, the legislature may single out specific acts and proscribe them regardless of the actual degree of probability of good or evil results in particular cases, and may regulate others, thus providing, in effect, that any risks whatever created by the acts, in the first case, or by disregarding the regulations, in the second, shall be unjustifiable. But this can only be done to a limited extent. Beyond this, the legislature can do no more than articulate the standard to be employed by administrators in passing upon particular acts under particular circumstances. With respect to this vast residuum of behavior, the legislature can say no more, in effect, than (1) it is desirable if it is prudent and undesirable if it is not; (2) whether or not it is prudent in particular cases depends upon the desirability of the actor's ends, the efficacy and necessity of his means, and the probability that death or serious injury will result; and (3) in view of the rigor of the sanctions of the criminal law the degree of imprudence should be substantial. The difficulty of applying such a vague standard is diminished somewhat, however, by the fact that every society proceeds on some broad assumptions that provide a necessary starting point. Thus the modern world stands as firmly committed to such activities as machine production, the construction of tall buildings, the use of the automobile, the airplane and other mechanized forms of transportation, as the ancient world was committed to the use of the chariot and the wooden boat. Unless penal legislation and administration are to undertake to remake the world, in which case they had better do so explicitly, the risk of death inevitably incident to such activities must be regarded as justifiable and such death must be accepted accidental. The object of prevention can only be the creation of *unnecessary* risks by such activity. But these assumptions provide no more than a start. Once the risk is determined to be unnecessary, the difficult problem remains of determining whether or not the act creating it was nevertheless prudent.

Automobiles may be driven at many speeds and still be useful; but we frequently sanction driving at a speed that is not, in any strict sense, necessary for the use of the automobile.

Professor Fletcher has identified four important factors in assessing the acceptability and culpability of risk-taking: (1) the likelihood of causing death under the circumstances, (2) the gravity of the risk, (3) the utility of the risk, and (4) the actor's awareness of the risk being run. Fletcher at 260.

In light of these observations, compare the problem of assessing the homicide liability of the defendant in *Banks* with that facing the court in the following case.

PEARS V. STATE

Court of Appeals of Alaska

672 P.2d 903 (1983)

COATS, Judge.

While driving while intoxicated, Richard Pears caused an automobile accident in which two people died and one was injured. The state charged Pears with two counts of murder in the second degree. . . . A jury convicted Pears, . . . and Judge Jay Hodges sentenced Pears to twenty years for the murder convictions.

We affirm Pears' conviction and sentence.

Pears first argues that Judge Hodges should have dismissed the grand jury indictment for second degree murder. The second degree murder statute under which Pears was charged, AS 11.41.110(a)(2), provides:

A person commits the crime of murder in the second degree if

(2) he intentionally performs an act that results in the death of another person under circumstances manifesting an extreme indifference to the value of human life.

Pears argues that the legislature did not intend to have a motor vehicle homicide prosecuted as murder and that his offense should only have been charged as manslaughter. Manslaughter is defined in AS 11.41.120(a) and provides:

A person commits the crime of manslaughter if he

(1) intentionally, knowingly, or recklessly causes the death of another person under circumstances not amounting to murder in the first or second degree.

We find unpersuasive Pears' argument that the legislature did not intend for any motor vehicle homicide which was caused by an intoxicated driver to be charged as murder. This court discussed the relationship between second-degree murder and manslaughter in *Neitzel v. State,* 655 P.2d 325, 335–38 (Alaska Ct. App. 1982). In that case we indicated that the difference between second-degree murder and manslaughter was one of degree which was a question for the jury under proper instructions:

Under the Revised Code, negligent homicide and reckless manslaughter are satisfied by conduct creating a significant risk of death absent justification or excuse. They differ only in the actor's knowledge of the risk. In differentiating reckless murder from reckless manslaughter, the jury is asked to determine whether the recklessness manifests an extreme indifference to human life.

[T]he jury must consider the nature and gravity of the risk, including the harm to be foreseen and the likelihood that it will occur. For both murder and manslaughter, the harm to be foreseen is a death. Therefore, the significant distinction is in the likelihood that a death will result from the defendant's act. Where the defendant's act has limited social utility, a very slight though significant and avoidable risk of death may make him guilty of manslaughter if his act causes death. Driving an automobile has some social utility although substantially reduced when the driver is intoxicated. The odds that a legally intoxicated person driving home after the bars close will hit and kill or seriously injure someone may be as low as one chance in a thousand and still qualify for manslaughter. Where murder is charged, however, an act must create a much greater risk that death or serious physical injury will result.

Id., at 337.

The legislature has not indicated that no motor vehicle homicide could be charged as second degree murder. It is certainly clear that an automobile can be as dangerous a weapon as a gun or a knife and the results of its misuse just as deadly. It seems clear to us from the Revised Criminal Code that where a driver's recklessness manifests an extreme indifference to human life he can be charged with murder even though the instrument by which he causes death is an automobile. We conclude Judge Hodges did not err in refusing to dismiss the indictment charging Pears with murder in the second degree.[2]

Pears . . . contends that Judge Hodges erred in not granting his motion for judgment of acquittal for murder in the second degree. "In determining whether to grant a motion for a judgment of acquittal, the trial court must view the evidence and the inferences therefrom in the light most favorable to the state and decide whether reasonable minds could conclude that guilt had been established beyond a reasonable doubt." *Siggelkow v. State,* 648 P.2d 611, 613 (Alaska Ct. App. 1982). When we look at the evidence in the light most favorable to the state, we conclude that a jury could find that Pears committed second-degree murder. The evidence produced at trial indicated that Pears voluntarily drank in a bar to the point of intoxication. After becoming intoxicated he drove recklessly, speeding, running through stop signs and stop lights and failing to slow for yield signs. His passenger at the time, Kathy Hill, told him that his driving scared her. Pears and Kathy Hill then went to another bar and had more drinks. Pears and Hill then left the bar and while they were approaching his truck on foot, Pears was stopped by two uniformed police officers in a patrol car. One of the officers told Pears not to drive because he was too intoxicated. Pears and Hill walked back toward the

---

[2] We emphasize that a charge of second-degree murder should only rarely be appropriate in a motor vehicle homicide. The murder charge in this case is supported by the extreme facts which are set out more fully later in the opinion.

bar until the officers were out of sight. They then returned to his truck and drove away. Once again, with Hill protesting, Pears drove over the speed limit and ran red lights and stop signs. Pears then dropped Kathy Hill off and continued to drive around. Shortly before the fatal collision Pears was seen by Steve Call, who was turning his car onto the four-lane Steese Highway. According to Call, Pears' car ran a red light on the highway, going through the light at a high rate of speed and passing two cars which were stopped at the light. Call said he was going about forty-five miles per hour, the speed limit, but Pears was going faster. As they approached the next intersection Call could clearly see the red light against them and the cars stopping. Pears got around the cars which were stopping by passing them in the right turn lane, going into the intersection without braking or slowing down. Pears collided with one of the cars entering the intersection on the green light, an orange Datsun. The impact of the collision knocked the Datsun 146 feet, killing two of the three people in the car and seriously injuring the third.

We believe that a jury could have found that Pears' driving constituted circumstances manifesting an extreme indifference to human life. He was made abundantly aware of the dangerous nature of his driving by both his passenger, Kathy Hill, and the police officers who warned him not to drive. The fact that Pears drove recklessly and ran stop signs and red lights several times before the fatal collision supports the theory that he did not inadvertently run the red light when the collision occurred but that he was intentionally running the red light at high speed without regard for the fact that other cars were crossing the intersection. We believe this evidence would support a second degree murder conviction and conclude that Judge Hodges did not err in refusing to grant Pears' motion for judgment of acquittal.

The conviction [is] Affirmed.

SINGLETON, Judge, with whom BRYNER, Chief Judge, *joins concurring.*

An automobile clearly constitutes a "dangerous instrument" as that term is defined in the Revised Code. "—Dangerous instrument' means anything which, under the circumstances in which it is used, attempted to be used, or threatened to be used, is capable of causing death or serious physical injury." AS 11.81.900(b)(11). Certainly an intoxicated person in control of a dangerous instrument in a place where others are present creates a substantial and unjustifiable risk that death or serious injury will occur, see AS 11.81.900(a)(3) (defining recklessly). A person commits the crime of manslaughter if he recklessly causes the death of another person under circumstances not amounting to murder in the first or second degree. AS 11.41.120(a)(1). Consequently, a prosecutor showing that an intoxicated person drove a car and caused a death probably makes a *prima facie* case of manslaughter as defined in AS 11.41.120(a).

Before recklessness can meet the test of second-degree murder, however, it must "manifest an extreme indifference to the value of human life." As we noted in *Neitzel v. State,* 655 P.2d 325, 335–38 (Alaska Ct. App. 1982), murder, which is defined based upon the Model Penal Code, requires a finding of recklessness virtually amounting to purpose or knowledge:

In a prosecution for murder, however, the Code calls for the further judgment whether the actor's conscious disregard of the risk, under the circumstances, manifests extreme indifference to the value of human life. The significance of purpose or knowledge as a standard of culpability is that, cases of provocation or other mitigation apart, purposeful or knowing homicide demonstrates precisely such indifference to the value of human life. Whether recklessness is so extreme that it demonstrates similar indifference is not a question, it is submitted, that can be further clarified. It must be left directly to the trier of fact under instructions which make it clear that recklessness that can fairly be assimilated to purpose or knowledge should be treated as murder and that less extreme recklessness should be punished as manslaughter.

655 P.2d at 335–36, quoting A.L.I., Model Penal Code and Commentaries, Part II, § 210.2, at 21–23 (1980) (footnote omitted).

[R]eckless murder occupies the middle ground between (1)mere recklessness, creating a substantial risk of death, and (2)knowledge, creating a virtual certainty of death. Before Pears could be found guilty of murder, his recklessness must be found to approach knowledge that his acts were practically certain to cause death or serious physical injury.

Three factors, in my opinion, distinguish this case from the typical drunk driver homicide. First, Pears drove despite the fact that his companion, Kathy Hill, warned him that his driving was endangering her and other people. Second, Pears was stopped by two uniformed police officers and told not to drive and by his conduct led the police officers to believe that he would not drive. Finally, the evidence supports a finding that Pears just missed colliding with a number of other vehicles on the road prior to the eventual homicide. Given these factors, I think a *prima facie* case of murder was made. It was therefore a jury question as to whether Pears' conduct manifested extreme indifference to the value of human life.

NOTES AND QUESTIONS

1. Do you agree with the *Pears* result? How significant to the outcome is the fact that Pears had actual notice of his dangerous driving prior to the fatal collision? Should such notice always suffice to constitute the recklessness necessary for a murder conviction? See *People v. Mays,* 197 Cal. App. 3d 1229, 243 Cal. Rptr. 444 (1988), which holds that defendant's awareness that he was driving dangerously while intoxicated prior to a fatal collision did not necessarily constitute the requisite "conscious disregard for human life" necessary for a finding of malice and thus of murder. The *Mays* court opined that had the defendant possessed a history of DWI convictions or of previous enrollments in drunk driver education programs in addition to being on notice of his dangerous driving in the instant case, he may well have been guilty of murder. Why should a prior history of alcohol-related driving problems carry so much importance?

2. As *Pears* points out, unintended deaths resulting through automobile use are often treated as manslaughter rather than murder. Nevertheless, at the

urging of groups such as Mothers Against Drunk Driving, murder charges and convictions have become much more commonplace in recent years. See., *e.g.,* Christy Scatterella and Wayne Wurzer, *Mourning Families Want Stiffer Penalties for Drivers Who Drink, Kill,* Seattle Times, September 20, 1993, at A1. Are you satisfied that the distinction between murder and manslaughter is sufficiently clear? Consider the materials on involuntary manslaughter, *infra* at § 5.03[2].

Some jurisdictions have created a third level, "vehicular homicide," where the defendant's conduct does not rise to the level of culpability necessary to support a murder or manslaughter conviction. See, *e.g.,* Ark. Stat. Ann. § 27-50-307 and *Bentley v. State,* 252 Ark. 642, 480 S.W.2d 346 (1972) (driving in "reckless or wanton disregard" for safety of others may be either "negligent homicide" or manslaughter, while driving in "wilful disregard of safety of others" must be either manslaughter or murder).

Section 28-305 of the Nebraska Revised Statutes provides:

Motor vehicle homicide; penalty. (1)A person who causes the death of another unintentionally while engaged in the operation of a motor vehicle in violation of the law of the State of Nebraska or in violation of any city or village ordinance commits motor vehicle homicide. (2)Except as provided in subsection (3) of this section, motor vehicle homicide is a Class I misdemeanor. (3)If the proximate cause of the death of another is the operation of a motor vehicle in violation of section 39-669.01, 39-669.03, or 39-669.07 [reckless driving, wilful reckless driving, driving under influence of alcohol], motor vehicle homicide is a Class IV felony.

Without explaining the distinction between manslaughter (a Class III felony punishable by up to 20 years imprisonment or a $25,000 fine or both) and motor vehicle homicide (either a Class I misdemeanor punishable by one year imprisonment or a $1,000 fine or both or else a Class IV felony punishable by five years imprisonment or a $10,000 fine or both), the Nebraska Supreme Court has held that causing death with a motor vehicle may constitute either manslaughter or motor vehicle homicide. *State v. Roth,* 222 Neb. 119, 382 N.W.2d 348 (1986).

3. Given the prevalence and utility of the automobile in modern life, how should the law of vehicular homicide be defined? How should alcohol use be factored in? Should deaths caused by intoxicated drivers be *per se* treated as some level of homicide or should the state be required to prove that the intoxication was causally related to the death? For example, should an intoxicated driver be guilty of homicide if he kills someone in circumstances where a sober driver would likely not have been able to avoid killing the victim? See *People v. Chopra,* 782 P.2d 879 (Colo. App. 1989), in which the court determined that defendant's intoxication was "the proximate cause" of a vehicular homicide even though he was also fatigued at the time his car crashed, killing his passenger.

COMMONWEALTH V. MALONE

Supreme Court of Pennsylvania

354 Pa. 180, 47 A.2d 445 (1946)

MAXEY, Chief Justice

This is an appeal from the judgment and sentence under a conviction of murder in the second degree. William H. Long, age 13 years, was killed by a shot from a 32-caliber revolver held against his right side by the defendant, then aged 17 years. These youths were on friendly terms at the time of the homicide.

On the evening of February 26th, 1945, when the defendant went to a moving picture theater, he carried in the pocket of his raincoat a revolver which he had obtained at the home of his uncle on the preceding day. In the afternoon preceding the shooting, the decedent procured a cartridge from his father's room and he and the defendant placed it in the revolver.

After leaving the theater, the defendant went to a dairy store and there met the decedent. Both youths sat in the rear of the store ten minutes, during which period the defendant took the gun out of his pocket and loaded the chamber to the right of the firing pin and then closed the gun. A few minutes later, both youths sat on stools in front of the lunch counter and ate some food. The defendant suggested to the decedent that they play "Russian Poker."[3] Long replied: "I don't care; go ahead." The defendant then placed the revolver against the right side of Long and pulled the trigger three times. The third pull resulted in a fatal wound to Long. The latter jumped off the stool and cried: "Oh! Oh! Oh!" and Malone said: "Did I hit you, Billy? Gee, Kid, I'm sorry." Long died from the wounds two days later.

The defendant testified that the gun chamber he loaded was the first one to the right of the firing chamber and that when he pulled the trigger he did not "expect to have the gun go off." He declared he had no intention of harming Long, who was his friend and companion. The defendant was indicted for murder, tried and found guilty of murder in the second degree and sentenced to a term in the penitentiary for a period not less than five years and not exceeding ten years. . . .

Appellant alleges certain errors in the charge of the court and also contends that the facts did not justify a conviction for any form of homicide except involuntary manslaughter. This contention we overrule. A specific intent to take life is, under our law, an essential ingredient of murder in the first degree. At common law, the "grand criterion" which "distinguished murder from other killing" was malice on the part of the killer and this malice was not necessarily "malevolent to the deceased particularly" but "any evil design

---

[3] It has been explained that "Russian Poker" is a game in which the participants, in turn, place a single cartridge in one of the five chambers of a revolver cylinder, give the latter a quick twirl, place the muzzle of the gun against the temple and pull the trigger, leaving it to chance whether or not death results to the trigger puller.

in general; the dictate of a wicked, depraved and malignant heart;" 4 Blackstone 199.

When an individual commits an act of gross recklessness for which he must reasonably anticipate that death to another is likely to result, he exhibits that "wickedness of disposition, hardness of heart, cruelty, recklessness of consequences, and a mind regardless of social duty" which proved that there was at that time in him "the state or frame of mind termed malice. . . . "

* * *

The killing of William H. Long by this defendant resulted from an act intentionally done by the latter, in reckless and wanton disregard of the consequences which were at least sixty per cent certain from his thrice attempted discharge of a gun known to contain one bullet and aimed at a vital part of Long's body. This killing was, therefore, murder, for malice in the sense of a wicked disposition is evidenced by the intentional doing of an uncalled-for act in callous disregard of its likely harmful effects on others. The fact that there was no motive for this homicide does not exculpate the accused. In a trial for murder proof of motive is always relevant but never necessary.

All the assignments of error are overruled, and the judgment is affirmed. The record is remitted to the court below so that the sentence imposed may be carried out.

QUESTIONS

1. What is the *mens rea* for murder in *Malone?* Does the court require subjective awareness of the homicidal risk or permit a negligence standard? Should negligence be sufficient ground for murder liability?

2. Does the *Malone* court accurately assess the gravity of the risk in that case? What result if the gun had gone off the first time the defendant pulled the trigger?

NORTHINGTON v. STATE

Court of Criminal Appeals of Alabama

413 So. 2d 1169 (1981)

BOWEN, Judge.

The defendant was indicted and convicted for the murder of her five month old daughter. Sentence was life imprisonment.

> The indictment . . . charged that the defendant
> did recklessly engage in conduct which manifested extreme indifference to human life and created grave risk of death to the person of Dana Northington, and the said conduct did hereby cause the death of Dana Northington, by withholding food and medical attention from the said Dana Northington.

Under Alabama Code 1975, Section 13A-6-2(a)(2) (Amended 1977), a person commits the crime of murder if:

Under circumstances manifesting extreme indifference to human life, he recklessly engages in conduct which creates a grave risk of death to a person other than himself, and thereby causes the death of another person.

Essentially, this section is a restatement of Alabama law which defined murder in the first degree to include every homicide "perpetrated by any act greatly dangerous to the lives of others and evincing a depraved mind regardless of human life, although without any preconceived purpose to deprive any particular person of life." Alabama Code 1975, Section 13-1-70. . . .

The new statute, 13A-6-2(a)(2), removes the requirement that more than one person be endangered by the reckless conduct of the accused. Compare the phrase "any act greatly dangerous to the *lives* of others" with "conduct which creates a grave risk of death to a *person* other than himself." (Emphasis added.) However, the statute still requires conduct which manifests an extreme indifference to *human life* and not to a particular person only.

At the close of the State's evidence defense counsel requested the trial judge to exclude . . . the indictment from the consideration of the jury. The defendant argued that she could not be convicted of a count charging "universal malice" where the criminal acts of the accused were directed solely at the deceased and where the method of death alleged in the indictment (starvation) required a specific intent.

Reckless homicide manifesting extreme indifference to human life [13A-6-2(a)(2)] must be distinguished from purposeful or knowing murder [13A-6-2(a)(1)]. See American Law Institute, Model Penal Code and Commentaries, Part II, Section 210.2 (1980). Under whatever name, the doctrine of universal malice, depraved heart murder, or reckless homicide manifesting extreme indifference to human life is intended to embrace those cases where a person has no deliberate intent to kill or injure any *particular* individual.

The evidence in this case, even when viewed in the light most favorable to the prosecution, reveals that the defendant's acts and omissions were specifically directed at a particular victim and no other.

The State presented no evidence that the defendant engaged in conduct "under circumstances manifesting extreme indifference to human life" for, while the defendant's conduct did indeed evidence an extreme indifference to the life of her child, there was nothing to show that the conduct displayed an extreme indifference to human life generally. Although the defendant's conduct created a grave risk of death to another and thereby caused the death of that person, the acts of the defendant were aimed at the particular victim and no other. Not only did the defendant's conduct create a grave risk of death to only her daughter and no other, but the defendant's actions (or inactions) were directed specifically against the young infant. . . . This evidence does not support a conviction of murder as charged under Section 13A-6-2(a)(2). The function of this section is to embrace those homicides caused by such acts as driving an automobile in a grossly wanton manner, shooting a firearm into a crowd or moving train, and throwing a timber from a roof onto a crowded street. . . .

Because of the revolting and heartsickening details of this case, this Court is extremely reluctant to reverse the conviction of the defendant. Yet, because our system is one of law and not of men, we have no other choice. The judgment of the Circuit Court is reversed and the cause remanded.

Reversed and remanded.

NOTES AND QUESTIONS

1. Would the defendant in *Malone* be guilty of murder under the universal malice doctrine of *Northington?* Is the doctrine a commendable limitation on the law of unintended murder? Why should liability for murder hinge on whether a defendant's extreme indifference to human life is directed to human life generally as opposed to some particular human life? Suppose the mother in *Northington* had permitted five children to starve to death. Would that constitute universal malice? If so, is the mother indeed more culpable than the *Northington* defendant?

For a case not confronting the universal malice doctrine and upholding the second degree murder conviction of a father who knowingly permitted his infant child to die through malnutrition and dehydration, see *People v. Burden,* 72 Cal. App. 3d 603, 140 Cal. Rptr. 282 (1977).

2. Colorado statutory law explicitly embraces the concept of universal malice in distinguishing first and second degree murder. As one of a very few states treating depraved heart killings as first degree murder, Colo. Rev. Stat. § § 18-3-102(1)(d) and 18-3-103(1)(a) provide the following definitions of murder:

> A person commits the crime of murder in the first degree if . . . [u]nder circumstances evidencing an attitude of universal malice manifesting extreme indifference to the value of human life generally, he knowingly engages in conduct which creates a grave risk of death to a person, or persons, other than himself, and thereby causes the death of another.
>
> A person commits the crime of murder in the second degree if [h]e causes the death of a person knowingly, but not after deliberation. . . .

The Colorado Supreme Court commented on these provisions:

> What has consistently exercised the legislature in proscribing extreme indifference murder is aggravated recklessness, not that practical certainty of death which is at the heart of the second-degree murder statute. . . .
>
> The extreme indifference murder charge is more blameworthy than the second-degree murder charge, because the defendant's conduct demonstrates that his lack of care and concern for the value of human life generally are extreme, and that the circumstances of his actions evidence that aggravated recklessness or cold-bloodedness which has come to be known as "universal malice."

People v. Jefferson, 748 P.2d 1223, 1231–32 (Colo. 1988)

[3] Intent-to-Cause-Serious-Bodily-Injury Murder

COMMONWEALTH v. DORAZIO

Supreme Court of Pennsylvania

365 Pa. 291, 74 A.2d 125 (1950)

ALLEN M. STEARNE, Justice.

The appellant, Gustav Dorazio, appeals from the judgment and sentence entered against him on a verdict of guilty of murder in the second degree.

[Appellant, a former professional heavyweight boxer, and Blomeyer, the deceased, were both employees of a brewery and were members of rival unions, each of which sought to represent the brewery workers. At trial, the prosecution presented evidence alleging that appellant had made threats of death or serious injury to several members of rival unions if they did not cease circulating union petitions. The evidence also alleged that shortly after Blomeyer had been securing signatures to a union petition, appellant attacked him from behind, chased him into a building, and repeatedly punched Blomeyer in the head and body as he lay on the floor. After punching several other persons who had sought to prevent the further beating of Blomeyer, appellant was apprehended and taken into police custody. Blomeyer died later that day of a fractured skull, possibly caused, in the opinion of the coroner's physician, by appellant's fists.

Appellant disputed the prosecution's version of the facts, denied making threats to anyone and claimed to have fought Blomeyer in self-defense. Appellant claimed that Blomeyer's head was injured through a fall and not from the alleged beating. Appellant claimed to be helping Blomeyer to his feet at the time he was attacked by the persons alleged by the prosecution to be attempting to prevent Blomeyer's further beating.]

In reviewing a record of conviction for murder . . . , it is our duty to determine whether the degree or elements of murder in the specified degree are present; whether there is sufficient evidence from which the jury could find beyond a reasonable doubt that the degree of murder was committed by the accused.

The appellant contends that since he had no weapon of any kind in his possession the essential element of intent to kill or to do great bodily harm cannot be inferred "from the making of a mere assault, without a battery," with bare fists.

Murder in this Commonwealth, though divided by statute into degrees, is still determined by the common law. . . . The division of murder into degrees was for the purpose of fixing punishment in relation to the heinousness of the offense, not to change the common law principles. The distinguishing criterion between murder and other homicide is malice. . . .

The appellant argues that the malice necessary to support a conviction for murder cannot be imported from the use of the fists in the circumstances of this case; that such malice could only be shown by evidence that there was an intent to inflict great bodily harm.

Ordinarily where an assault is made with bare fists only, without a deadly weapon, and death results there would only be manslaughter. . . . This follows naturally from the requirement that there appear an intent to inflict great bodily harm. In *Wellar v. People,* 30 Mich. 16, this principle was well stated as follows:

It is not necessary in all cases that one held for murder must have intended to take the life of the person he slays by his wrongful act. It is not always necessary that he must have intended a personal injury to such person. But it is necessary that the intent with which he acted shall be equivalent in legal character to a criminal purpose aimed against life. . . . And if the intent be directly to produce a bodily injury, it must be such an injury as may be expected to involve serious consequences, either periling life or leading to great bodily harm. There is no rule recognized as authority which will allow a conviction of murder where a fatal result was not intended, unless the injury intended was one of a very serious character which might naturally and commonly involve loss of life or grievous mischief. Every assault involves bodily harm. But any doctrine which would hold every assailant as a murderer where death follows his act, would be barbarous and unreasonable. . . . In general, it has been held that where the assault is not committed with a deadly weapon, the intent must be clearly felonious, or the death will subject only to the charge of manslaughter. The presumption arising from the character of the instrument of violence, is not conclusive in either way, but where such weapons are used as do not usually kill, the deadly intent ought to be left in no doubt. There are cases on record where death by beating and kicking has been held to warrant a verdict of murder, the murderous intent being found. But where there was no such intent the ruling has been otherwise. . . . The willful use of a deadly weapon, without excuse or provocation, in such a manner as to imperil life, is almost universally recognized as showing a felonious intent. . . . But where the weapon or implement used is not one likely to kill or to maim, the killing is held to be manslaughter, unless there is an actual intent which shows a felonious purpose.

Whether the malice necessary to constitute murder may be implied from the use of fists alone must depend on the particular circumstances. . . . The size of the assailant, the manner in which the fists are used, the ferocity of the attack and its duration and the provocation are all relevant to the question of malice. . . . [T]he fists though not ordinarily a deadly weapon may become deadly by repeated and continued blows applied to vital and delicate parts of the body of a defenseless, unresisting victim. . . . [I]t is not necessary that the injury be intended to be permanent or dangerous to life, it is malicious to intend injury such as to seriously interfere with health and comfort. . . .

The defendant indulged himself in an unjustified, unprovoked, brutal and persistent attack upon the deceased. . . .

The judgment is affirmed and the record is remitted to the court below so that the sentence imposed may be carried out.

DIRECTOR OF PUBLIC PROSECUTIONS V. SMITH

House of Lords

[1961] A.C. 290

[Smith was driving a car knowing that stolen property was in its trunk and rear. After noticing the stolen property in the car, a police officer known to Smith directed him to stop the car. Smith slowed down as the officer walked alongside the car. Suddenly, Smith accelerated with the officer clinging to the car in hopes of preventing Smith's escape. The officer clung to the car for approximately 130 yards while Smith frantically sped down the street in an attempt to extricate the officer from the car. The officer was eventually dislodged from the car and thrown in the path of an oncoming vehicle which crushed his skull and caused other injuries from which he died. Smith drove a short distance further, removed the stolen property from the car, and returned to the site of the officer's injuries.]

VISCOUNT KILMUIR L.C.

My Lords, the respondent, Jim Smith, was convicted on April 7, 1960, of the wilful murder on March 2, 1960, of Leslie Edward Vincent Meehan, a police officer acting in the execution of his duty. Such a crime constitutes capital murder under section 5 of the Homicide Act, 1957, and, accordingly, the respondent was sentenced to death. There was never any suggestion that the respondent meant to kill the police officer, but it was contended by the prosecution that he intended to do the officer grievous bodily harm, as a result of which the officer died.

In his final direction to the jury the trial judge, Donovan J., said:

If you are satisfied that . . . he must as a reasonable man have contemplated that grievous bodily harm was likely to result to that officer . . . and that such harm did happen and the officer died in consequence, then the accused is guilty of capital murder. . . . On the other hand, if you are not satisfied that he intended to inflict grievous bodily harm upon the officer—in other words, if you think he could not as a reasonable man have contemplated that grievous bodily harm would result to the officer in consequence of his actions—well, then, the verdict would be guilty of manslaughter.

The respondent appealed to the Court of Criminal Appeal alleging misdirection by the trial judge, the main ground being that the direction cited above was wrong in that the question for the jury was what he, the respondent, in fact contemplated. The appeal was heard by the Court of Criminal Appeal on May 9 and 10, 1960, when the court allowed the appeal, substituted a verdict of guilty of manslaughter and imposed a sentence of 10 years' imprisonment. The court gave its reasons on May 18, 1960. They upheld the respondent's contention, holding that "there always remained the question whether the appellant" (the present respondent) "really did . . . realize what was the degree of likelihood of serious injury."

The matter now comes before your Lordships' House on the appeal of the Director of Public Prosecutions. . . .

My Lords, the proposition has only to be stated thus to make one realize what a departure it is from that upon which the courts have always acted. The jury must, of course, in such a case as the present make up their minds on the evidence whether the accused was unlawfully and voluntarily doing something to someone. The unlawful and voluntary act must clearly be aimed at someone in order to eliminate cases of negligence or of careless or dangerous driving. Once, however, the jury are satisfied as to that, it matters not what the accused in fact contemplated as the probable result or whether he ever contemplated at all, provided he was in law responsible and accountable for his actions, that is, was a man capable of forming an intent, not insane within the *M'Naghten* Rules and not suffering from diminished responsibility. On the assumption that he is so accountable for his actions, the sole question is whether the unlawful and voluntary act was of such a kind that grievous bodily harm was the natural and probable result. The only test available for this is what the ordinary responsible man would, in all the circumstances of the case, have contemplated as the natural and probable result. That, indeed, has always been the law. . . .

The last criticism of the summing-up which was raised before your Lordships was in regard to the meaning which the learned judge directed the jury was to be given the words "grievous bodily harm." The passages of which complaint is made are the following:

> When one speaks of an intent to inflict grievous bodily harm upon a person, the expression *grievous bodily harm* does not mean for that purpose some harm which is permanent or even dangerous. It simply means some harm which is sufficient seriously to interfere with the victim's health or comfort.
>
> In murder the killer intends to kill, or to inflict some harm which will seriously interfere for a time with health or comfort.
>
> If the accused intended to do the officer some harm which would seriously interfere at least for a time with his health and comfort, and thus perhaps enable the accused to make good his escape for the time being at least, but that unfortunately the officer died instead, that would be murder too.

My Lords, I confess that . . . I can find no warrant for giving the words "grievous bodily harm" a meaning other than that which the words convey in their ordinary and natural meaning. "Bodily harm" needs no explanation, and "grievous" means no more and no less than "really serious. . . . "

It was, however, contended before your Lordships on behalf of the respondent that the words ought to be given a more restricted meaning in considering the intent necessary to establish malice in a murder case. It was said that the intent must be to do an act "obviously dangerous to life" or "likely to kill." It is true that in many of the cases the likelihood of death resulting has been incorporated into the definition of grievous bodily harm, but this was done, no doubt, merely to emphasize that the bodily harm must be really serious, and it is unnecessary, and I would add inadvisable, to add anything to the expression "grievous bodily harm" in its ordinary and natural meaning.

. . . [O]n the facts of this case it is quite impossible to say that the harm which the respondent must be taken to have contemplated could be anything but of a very serious nature coming well within the term "grievous bodily harm."

In the result the appeal should, in my opinion, be allowed and the conviction of capital murder restored.

NOTES AND QUESTIONS

1. What is the *mens rea* for the theory of murder reflected in *Dorazio* and *Smith*? Are the two cases in agreement as to the required state of mind?

Criminal Justice Act, 1967, pt. II, ch. 80, Eliz. II overruled portions of the *Smith* case by providing,

> A court or jury, in determining whether a person has committed an offense, (a) shall not be bound in law to infer that he intended or foresaw a result of his actions by reason only of its being a natural and probable consequence of those actions; but (b) shall decide whether he did intend or foresee that result by reference to all the evidence, drawing such inferences from the evidence as appear proper in the circumstances. Is the legislative revision desirable?

2. Do the *Dorazio* and Smith cases embrace aspects of "constructive *mens rea*," elsewhere generally disdained in the criminal law? See, *e.g.*, the *Cunningham* case, supra at p.359. Do *Dorazio* and *Smith* hold that so long as the defendant intended serious bodily injury, he need not intend or even foresee the possibility of death caused through such injury?

3. As *Dorazio* and *Smith* indicate, the intent-to-inflict-serious-b odily-injury theory has been followed on both sides of the Atlantic. For a more recent American case applying the doctrine, see *Midgett v. State,* 292 Ark. 278, 729 S.W.2d 410 (1987), where the court reversed the first degree premeditated murder conviction of a father whose repeated physical abuse eventually led to the death of his eight-year-old child. The *Midgett* court sustained a second degree murder conviction, however, on the theory that the father purposely caused "serious physical injury" by delivering a fatal blow to the boy's abdomen. While the blow to the abdomen was the cause of death, the court noted that the boy was malnourished and very frail and small in stature at the time of his death. The father, on the other hand, weighed 300 pounds. An autopsy of the boy's body showed evidence of extensive and prolonged physical abuse in addition to the blow to the abdomen.

Is *Midgett* consistent with *Dorazio?* If the blow to the abdomen was the cause of death, is the evidence of the previous abuse relevant?

4. Could the defendants in *Dorazio, Smith,* and *Midgett* be found guilty of murder under the depraved heart theory?

What if the jurisdiction adheres to the universal malice doctrine?

If the depraved heart and intent-to-inflict-serious-b odily-injury doctrines overlap, why retain two doctrines? If one is to be eliminated, which should it be?

Many modern codes in American jurisdictions have abandoned the intent-to-inflict-serious-b odily-injury murder theory. See MPC, § 210.2, Comment at

29. The Model Penal Code rejects the theory on the view that "it is preferable to handle such cases under the standards of extreme recklessness contained in Sections 210.2(1)(b) and 210.3(1)(a)." *Id.*

[4] Felony-Murder

[a] In General

STATE V. MCKEIVER

Superior Court of New Jersey

89 N.J. Super. 52, 213 A.2d 320 (1965)

YANCEY, J.C.C.

Defendant was indicted by the Essex County grand jury and charged with the crime of murder.

At about 1:30 AM, October 29, 1963, defendant entered the Green Village Tavern in Newark, New Jersey. Tied around his head was a light gray handkerchief which concealed the lower part of his face. Upon entering the tavern he immediately fired a shot into the ceiling and ordered the bartender and four other persons to move to the end of the bar. Defendant then commanded these persons to place their wallets on the bar, and they complied. He then went to the back of the bar and opened the cash register and took approximately $90. After so doing, defendant picked up the wallets and ordered the victims to walk toward the front door of the tavern. As they were doing this, Mrs. Julia Yuhas toppled over and fell to the floor. Defendant, on seeing this, ran out of the front door of the tavern and disappeared.

Minutes later Mrs. Yuhas was administered first aid by the Newark Emergency Squad and was subsequently taken to Newark City Hospital. She was pronounced dead at 2:05 AM by Dr. Evke of the hospital staff. An autopsy performed by the Chief Medical Examiner, Dr. Edwin H. Albano, disclosed, in the doctor's opinion, that Mrs. Yuhas' death was "due to fright during hold-up in tavern: cardiac arrest; occlusive arteriosclerotic coronary artery disease."

Defendant was subsequently apprehended and, as stated, indicted for murder. The indictment was returned on the theory that decedent met her death as a result of defendant's actions during the course of a robbery he was committing. The State, under this indictment, contends that since death resulted during the commission of a high misdemeanor (robbery), a charge of first degree murder is appropriate under the "felony murder" theory. Defendant disagrees and has made this timely pretrial motion . . . to dismiss the indictment.

Defendant contends that his acts do not substantiate the State's charge of felony murder. He grounds this contention, and relies heavily, on the fact that there was no direct physical contact between himself and decedent, and therefore his acts were not those which would render him responsible for Mrs. Yuhas' death.

[T]he statute upon which the indictment was returned, declares: "Murder . . . which is committed in perpetrating or attempting to perpetrate arson, burglary, kidnaping, rape, robbery or sodomy, is murder in the first degree." The statute is a codification of the so-called "felony-murder rule" which was developed in England under the common law. The rule places upon a man committing a felony, or attempting to commit a felony, the hazard of being guilty of murder if he creates any substantial human risk which would actually result in the loss of life; and it does this without excluding those homicides which occur so unexpectedly that no reasonable man would have considered any risk of this nature to be involved. The English jurists reasoned that certain felonies have been attended so frequently by death or great bodily harm, even when not intended or contemplated by the particular wrongdoer, that they must be classified as dangerous. Common experience points to the presence of a substantial human risk from the perpetration of such wrongful acts as arson, burglary, rape and robbery. The intent to avoid all personal harm, formed in the mind of the transgressor at the time he embarks upon such a felony, is no reasonable safeguard that death will not result from his illegal actions.

In the instant case, the death occurred during the perpetration of an act which created substantial human risk. Defendant had in his hand a pistol, which he fired to demonstrate to the patrons of the tavern that he meant to place them in fear of losing their lives or receiving great bodily harm if they did not immediately submit to his demands. It does not matter whether he intended to do actual harm, or whether he did not contemplate decedent's death by his acts.

The death occurred during the commission of a high misdemeanor. . . . After careful consideration, I find that death occurred under circumstances which substantiate the theory of "felony-murder."

This indictment contains no clear or palpable defect. Accordingly, defendant's motion to dismiss same is hereby denied.

NOTES AND QUESTIONS

1. Suppose the defendant in *McKeiver* had committed armed robbery but had not fired a shot. Would he still be guilty of murder if a victim of the robbery died of a heart attack? See *People v. Stamp*, 2 Cal. App. 3d 203, 82 Cal. Rptr. 598 (1969), cert. denied, 400 U.S. 819 (1970). Suppose the defendant is not armed when he commits a robbery which nevertheless so frightens its victim that he dies of a heart attack?

2. The *McKeiver* court explains that the felony-murder rule is a response to the perception that "certain felonies have been attended so frequently by death or great bodily harm even when not intended or contemplated by the particular wrongdoer, that they must be classified as dangerous." Assuming the empirical accuracy of this perception, does it justify the felony-murder rule?

In fact, the empirical basis for the felony-murder rule may rest on questionable grounds. Consider the following data summarized in Model Penal Code, § 210.2 Comment at 38, n. 96:

[T]he number of all homicides which occur in the commission of such crimes as robbery, burglary, or rape is lower than might be expected. For example, comparison of the figures for solved and unsolved homicides from M. Wolfgang, Criminal Homicide (1958), with statistics on basic felonies taken from the FBI Uniform Crime Reports reveals the following for Philadelphia from 1948–1952:

Relation of Total Felonies to Homicides Occurring during the Felony

Philadelphia 1948–1952

Offense	*No. of Crimes Reported*	*No. Accompanied by Homicide*	*%*	*No. per 1000*
Robbery	6,432	38	0.59	5.9
Rape	1,133	4	0.35	35
Burglary	27,669	1	0.0036	0.36
Auto Theft	10,315	2	0.019	1.9

Similar figures are found in Cook County, Illinois, robbery statistics from 1926 to 1930. There were 71 murders committed during robberies in Cook County during 1926 and 1927. Illinois Crime Survey 610 (1929). Although robbery statistics for those years are not available, 7,196 robberies were committed in the county in 1930. Assuming this number of robberies in 1926 and 1927, it appears that only .49 percent of the robberies in those two years resulted in homicide. More recent statistics derived from N.J. State Police *Crime in New Jersey: Uniform Crime Reports* 42-45 (1975), reveal strikingly similar percentages. In 1975, 16,273 robberies were committed in New jersey, and 66 homicides resulted from these robberies, only 41 percent, a figure even lower than the earlier statistics from Cook County and Philadelphia. When other violent felonies are taken into account, this percentage drops even lower. In 1975, there were 1,382 forcible rapes and 111,264 forcible breaking and enterings in New Jersey in addition to the 16,273 robberies. These crimes resulted in 136 deaths. Thus only 10 percent of these serious felonies resulted in homicide.

PEOPLE V. AARON

Supreme Court of Michigan

409 Mich 672, 299 N.W.2d 304 (1980)

FITZGERALD, Justice.

The existence and scope of the felony-murder doctrine have perplexed generations of law students, commentators and jurists in the United States and England, and have split our own Court of Appeals. In these cases, we must decide whether Michigan has a felony-murder rule which allows the element of malice required for murder to be satisfied by the intent to commit the underlying felony or whether malice must be otherwise found by the trier of fact. We must also determine what is the *mens rea* required to support a conviction under Michigan's first-degree murder statute.

I. FACTS

In [*People v. Wright,* 80 Mich. App. 172, 262 N.W.2d (1977)], defendant was convicted by a jury of two counts of first-degree felony-murder for setting fire to a dwelling causing the death of two people. The trial court instructed the jury that proof that the killings occurred during the perpetration of arson was sufficient to establish first-degree murder. The Court of Appeals reversed the convictions, holding that it was error to remove the element of malice from the jury's consideration.

Defendant Aaron was convicted of first-degree felony-murder as a result of a homicide committed during the perpetration of an armed robbery. The jury was instructed that they could convict defendant of first-degree murder if they found that defendant killed the victim during the commission or attempted commission of an armed robbery. . . . The Court of Appeals affirmed. . . .

II. HISTORY OF THE FELONY-MURDER DOCTRINE

Felony-murder has never been a static, well-defined rule at common law, but throughout its history has been characterized by judicial reinterpretation to limit the harshness of the application of the rule. Historians and commentators have concluded that the rule is of questionable origin and that the reasons for the rule no longer exist, making it an anachronistic remnant. . . .

The first formal statement of the doctrine is often said to be *Lord Dacres' Case,* Moore 86; 72 Eng. Rep. 458 (K.B., 1535). Lord Dacres and some companions agreed to enter a park without permission to hunt, an unlawful act, *and to kill anyone who might resist them.* While Lord Dacres was a quarter of a mile away, one member of his group killed a gamekeeper who confronted him in the park. Although Lord Dacres was not present when the killing occurred, he, along with the rest of his companions, was convicted of murder and was hanged. Contrary to the construction placed on this case by those who see it as a source of the felony-murder rule, the holding was not that Lord Dacres and his companions were guilty of murder because they had joined in an unlawful hunt in the course of which a person was killed, but rather that those not present physically at the killing were held liable as principals on the theory of constructive presence. Moreover, because they had agreed previously to kill anyone who might resist them, all the members of the group shared in the *mens rea* of the crime. Thus, because *Lord Dacres' Case* involved express malice, no doctrine finding malice from the intention to commit an unlawful act was necessary or in fact utilized.

Another early case which has been cited for the origin of the felony-murder doctrine was decided after *Lord Dacres' Case.* In *Mansell & Herbert's Case,* 2 Dyer 128b; 73 Eng. Rep. 279 (K.B., 1558), Herbert and a group of more than 40 followers had gone to Sir Richard Mansfield's house "with force to seize goods under pretense of lawful authority." One of Herbert's servants threw a stone at a person in the gateway which instead hit and killed an unarmed woman coming out of Mansfield's house. The question was agreed to be whether the accused were guilty of murder or manslaughter. Since misadventure was not considered, it can be assumed that the throwing of the stone was not a careless act but that the servant who threw the stone intended at least to hit, if not kill, some person on Mansfield's side. Although the court divided, the majority held that if one deliberately performed an act of violence to third parties, and a person not intended died, it was murder regardless of any mistake or misapplication of force. The minority would have held it to be manslaughter because the violent act was not directed against the woman who died. Thus, *Herbert's* case involved a deliberate act of violence against a person, which resulted in an unintended person being the recipient of the violent act.

Some commentators suggest that an incorrect version of *Dacres' Case,* which was repeated by Crompton, formed the basis of Lord Coke's statement of the felony-murder rule:

> If the act be unlawful it is murder. As if A. meaning to steal a deer in the park of B., shooteth at the deer, and by the glance of the arrow killeth a boy that is hidden in a bush: this is murder, for that the act was unlawfull, although A. had no intent to hurt the boy, nor knew not of him. But if B. the owner of the park had shot at his own deer, and without any ill intent had killed the boy by the glance of his arrow, this had been homicide by misadventure, and no felony.
>
> So if one shoot at any wild fowl upon a tree, and the arrow killeth any reasonable creature afar off, without any evil intent in him, this is *per infortunium* (misadventure): for it was not unlawful to shoot at the wilde fowl; but if he had shot at a cock or hen, or any tame fowl of another mans, and the arrow by mischance had killed a man, this had been murder, for the act was unlawfull.

The above excerpt from Coke is, along with *Lord Dacres'* and *Herbert's* cases, most often cited as the origin of the felony-murder doctrine. Unfortunately, Coke's statement has been criticized as completely lacking in authority. . . .

At early common law, the felony-murder rule went unchallenged because at that time practically all felonies were punishable by death. It was, therefore, "of no particular moment whether the condemned was hanged for the initial felony or for the death accidentally resulting from the felony." Thus, as Stephen . . . point[s] out, no injustice was caused directly by application of the rule at that time.

Case law of Nineteenth-Century England reflects the efforts of the English courts to limit the application of the felony-murder doctrine. See, *e.g., Regina v. Greenwood,* 7 Cox, Crim. Cas. 404 (1857); *Regina v. Horsey,* 3 F & F 287, 176 Eng. Rep. 129 (1862), culminating in *Regina v. Serne,* 16 Cox, Crim. Cas. 311 (1887). In the latter case, involving a death resulting from arson, Judge Stephen instructed the jury as follows:

> [I]nstead of saying that any act done with intent to commit a felony and which causes death amounts to murder, it should be reasonable to say that any act known to be dangerous to life and likely in itself to cause death, done for the purpose of committing a felony which causes death, should be murder.

In this century, the felony-murder doctrine was comparatively rarely invoked in England and in 1957 England abolished the felony-murder rule. Section 1 of England's Homicide Act, 1957, 5 & 6 Eliz. 2, c. 11, § 1, provides that a killing occurring in a felony-murder situation will not amount to murder unless done with the same malice aforethought as is required for all other murder.

Thus, an examination of the felony-murder rule indicates that the doctrine is of doubtful origin. Derived from the misinterpretation of case law, it went unchallenged because of circumstances which no longer exist. The doctrine was continuously modified and restricted in England, the country of its birth, until its ultimate rejection by Parliament in 1957.

III. LIMITATION OF THE FELONY-MURDER DOCTRINE IN THE UNITED STATES

While only a few states have followed the lead of Great Britain in abolishing felony murder, various legislative and judicial limitations on the doctrine have effectively narrowed the scope of the rule in the United States. . . . The draftsmen of the Model Penal Code have summarized the limitations imposed by American courts as follows:

(1) "The felonious act must be dangerous to life."

(2) and (3) "The homicide must be a natural and probable consequence of the felonious act." "Death must be —proximately' caused." Courts have also required that the killing be the result of an act done in the furtherance of the felonious purpose and not merely coincidental to the perpetration of a felony. These cases often make distinctions based on the identity of the victim (*i.e.*, whether the decedent was the victim of the felony or whether he was someone else, *e.g.*, a policeman or one of the felons) and the identity of the person causing the death.

(4) "The felony must be *malum in se.*"

(5) "The act must be a common-law felony."

(6) "The period during which the felony is in the process of commission must be narrowly construed."

(7) "The underlying felony must be —independent' of the homicide."

[The court detailed the numerous judicial and legislative limitations put on the felony-murder doctrine.]

The numerous modifications and restrictions placed upon the common-law felony-murder doctrine by courts and legislatures reflect dissatisfaction with the harshness and injustice of the rule. Even though the felony-murder doctrine survives in this country, it bears increasingly less resemblance to the traditional felony-murder concept. To the extent that these modifications reduce the scope and significance of the common-law doctrine, they also call into question the continued existence of the doctrine itself.

IV. THE REQUIREMENT OF INDIVIDUAL CULPABILITY FOR CRIMINAL RESPONSIBILITY

If one had to choose the most basic principle of the criminal law in general it would be that criminal liability for causing a particular result is not justified in the absence of some culpable mental state in respect to that result. . . .

The most fundamental characteristic of the felony-murder rule violates this basic principle in that it punishes all homicides, committed in the perpetration or attempted perpetration of proscribed felonies whether intentional, unintentional or accidental, without the necessity of proving the relation between the homicide and the perpetrator's state of mind. This is most evident when a killing is done by one of a group of co-felons. The felony-murder rule completely ignores the concept of determination of guilt on the basis of individual misconduct. . . .

The felony-murder rule's most egregious violation of basic rules of culpability occurs where felony-murder is categorized as first-degree murder. All other murders carrying equal punishment require a showing of premeditation, deliberation and willfulness while felony-murder only requires a showing of intent to do the underlying felony. Although the purpose of our degree statutes is to punish more severely the more culpable forms of murder, . . . an accidental killing occurring during the perpetration of a felony would be punished more severely than a second-degree murder requiring intent to kill, intent to cause great bodily harm or wantonness and willfulness. Furthermore, a defendant charged with felony-murder is permitted to raise defenses only to the mental element of the felony, thus precluding certain defenses available to a defendant charged with premeditated murder who may raise defenses to the mental element of murder (*e.g.,* self-defense, accident). Certainly, felony-murder is no more reprehensible than premeditated murder.

The failure of the felony-murder rule to consider the defendant's moral culpability is explained by examining the state of the law at the time of the rule's inception. The concept of culpability was not an element of homicide at early common law. The early definition of malice aforethought was vague. The concept meant little more than intentional wrongdoing with no other emphasis on intention except to exclude homicides that were committed by misadventure or in some otherwise pardonable manner. Thus, under this early definition of malice aforethought, an intent to commit the felony would in itself constitute malice. Furthermore, as all felonies were punished alike, it made little difference whether the felon was hanged for the felony or for the death.

Thus, the felony-murder rule did not broaden the concept of murder at the time of its origin because proof of the intention to commit a felony met the test of culpability based on the vague definition of malice aforethought governing at that time. Today, however, malice is a term of art. It does not include the nebulous definition of intentional wrongdoing. Thus, although the felony-murder rule did not broaden the definition of murder at early common law, it does so today. We find this enlargement of the scope of murder unacceptable, because it is based on a concept of culpability which is "totally incongruous with the general principles of our jurisprudence" today.

V. The Felony-Murder Doctrine in Michigan

Michigan does not have a statutory felony-murder doctrine which designates as murder any *death* occurring in the course of a felony without regard to whether it was the result of accident, negligence, recklessness or willfulness. Rather, Michigan has a statute which makes a *murder* occurring in the course of one of the enumerated felonies a first-degree murder:

Murder which is perpetrated by means of poison, lying in wait, or other wilful, deliberate, and premeditated killing, or which is committed in the perpetration, or attempt to perpetrate arson, criminal sexual conduct in the first or third degree, robbery, breaking and entering of a dwelling, larceny of any kind, extortion, or kidnapping, is murder of the first degree, and shall be punished by imprisonment for life.

M.C.L. § 750.316; M.S.A. § 28.548.

The Michigan Legislature adopted verbatim the first-degree murder statute of Pennsylvania, the statute we have today. In creating the statutes which divided murder into degrees, it was the intention of the Pennsylvania Legislature to reform the penal laws of that state by making punishment more proportionate to the crime and, in particular, to narrow the category of capital offenses. It was not its apparent intention to adopt by statute the common-law felony-murder rule. . . .

The prosecution argues that even if Michigan does not have a statutory codification of the felony-murder rule, the common-law definition of murder included a homicide in the course of a felony. Thus, the argument continues, once a homicide in the course of a felony is proven, under the common-law felony-murder rule a murder has been established and the first-degree murder statute then becomes applicable. This Court has ruled that the term murder as used in the first-degree murder statute includes all types of murder at common law. . . .

This Court has not been faced previously with a decision as to whether it should abolish the felony-murder doctrine. Thus, the common-law doctrine remains the law in Michigan. Moreover, the assumption by appellate decisions that the doctrine exists, combined with the fact that Michigan trial courts have applied the doctrine in numerous cases resulting in convictions of first-degree felony-murder, requires us to address the common-law felony-murder issue. The cases before us today squarely present us with the opportunity to review the doctrine and to consider its continued existence in Michigan. Although there are no Michigan cases which specifically abrogate the felony-murder rule, there exists a number of decisions of this Court which have significantly restricted the doctrine in Michigan and which lead us to conclude that the rule should be abolished.

Our review of Michigan case law [previous discussion of which is here omitted] persuades us that we should abolish the rule which defines malice as the intent to commit the underlying felony. Abrogation of the felony-murder rule is not a drastic move in light of the significant restrictions this Court has already imposed. Further, it is a logical extension of our decisions as discussed above.

Accordingly, we hold today that malice is the intention to kill, the intention to do great bodily harm, or the wanton and willful disregard of the likelihood that the natural tendency of defendant's behavior is to cause death or great bodily harm. We further hold that malice is an essential element of any murder, as that term is judicially defined, whether the murder occurs in the course of a felony or otherwise. The facts and circumstances involved in the perpetration of a felony may evidence an intent to kill, an intent to cause great bodily harm, or a wanton and willful disregard of the likelihood that the natural tendency of defendant's behavior is to cause death or great bodily harm; however, the conclusion must be left to the jury to infer from all the evidence. . . .

VI. PRACTICAL EFFECT OF ABROGATION OF THE COMMON-LAW FELONY-MURDER DOCTRINE

From a practical standpoint, the abolition of the category of malice arising from the intent to commit the underlying felony should have little effect on the result of the majority of cases. In many cases where felony-murder has been applied, the use of the doctrine was unnecessary because the other types of malice could have been inferred from the evidence.

Abrogation of this rule does not make irrelevant the fact that a death occurred in the course of a felony. A jury can properly *infer* malice from evidence that a defendant intentionally set in motion a force likely to cause death or great bodily harm. . . .

The difference is that the jury may not find malice from the intent to commit the underlying felony alone. The defendant will be permitted to assert any of the applicable defenses relating to *mens rea* which he would be allowed to assert if charged with premeditated murder. The latter result is reasonable in light of the fact that felony-murder is certainly no more heinous than premeditated murder. The prosecution will still be able to prove first-degree murder without proof of premeditation when a homicide is committed with malice, as we have defined it, and the perpetration or attempted perpetration of an enumerated felony is established. Hence, our first-degree murder statute continues to elevate to first-degree murder a murder which is committed in the perpetration or attempted perpetration of one of the enumerated felonies.

* * *

In the past, the felony-murder rule has been employed where unforeseen or accidental deaths occur and where the state seeks to prove vicarious liability of co-felons. In situations involving the vicarious liability of co-felons, the individual liability of each felon must be shown. It is fundamentally unfair and in violation of basic principles of individual criminal culpability to hold one felon liable for the unforeseen and unagreed-to results of another felon. In cases where the felons are acting intentionally or recklessly in pursuit of a common plan, the felony-murder rule is unnecessary because liability may be established on agency principles.

Finally, in cases where the death was purely accidental, application of the felony-murder doctrine is unjust and should be precluded. The underlying felony, of course, will still be subject to punishment. . . .

In *Aaron,* the judgment of conviction . . . is reversed and this case is remanded to the trial court for a new trial. In Wright, the decision of the Court of Appeals [is] affirmed and [the case is] remanded to the trial court for new trial.

Notes and Questions

1. In the sections immediately following these notes and questions, the materials consider in detail many of the limitations that have been placed on the felony-murder rule as summarized by the MPC draftsmen and noted in *Aaron*. These limitations should not be understood as universally applicable in every jurisdiction recognizing felony-murder. Consider, for example, the *McKeiver* case in light of the requirement sometimes imposed that "the homicide must be a natural and probable consequence of the felonious act."

2. Aaron has not been followed by other courts even in cases where the murder statute, like the Michigan statute, is directly patterned after the Pennsylvania statute discussed *supra*, at pp.352. See, *e.g., People v. Dillon,* 34 Cal. 3d 441, 194 Cal. Rptr. 390, 668 P.2d 697 (1983), where the California Supreme Court found that "however much we may agree with the reasoning of *Aaron*," felony-murder is a creature of statute in California, thus precluding its judicial abrogation "merely because it is unwise or outdated." The court held on the basis of legislative history that the California felony-murder statute operates both as an incorporation of the common law felony-murder doctrine and as a provision establishing degrees of murder. Therefore, any killing, negligent or even accidental, occurring in the perpetration of predicate felonies is murder in California.

The *Dillon* court went on to hold, however, that certain sentences under the first degree felony-murder statute violate the state constitutional prescription of cruel and unusual punishment. The Dillon court found unconstitutional a sentence of life imprisonment imposed on a 17-year-old defendant who, while attempting to steal marijuana from a field being guarded by the deceased, panicked and shot and killed the deceased when he came after the defendant with a shotgun.

3. Are you convinced by the *Aaron* court's observation that eliminating felony-murder will have little practical effect given the fact that most felony murders involve situations where malice can be inferred on other theories? Could the defendant in *McKeiver* be convicted of murder on any theory other than felony-murder?

In *People v. Bonds,* 159 Mich. 754, 407 N.W.2d 9 (1987), the Michigan Court of Appeals denied a motion to quash an indictment charging felony-murder where defendant drove his sister to a house that he apparently intended to help burn down. The defendant carried gasoline inside the house and assisted his sister as she poured it around the premises. The pilot light from a space heater accidentally ignited the gasoline, resulting in the death of the sister. The court found that a jury could infer that defendant's actions constituted a "wilful and wanton disregard for human life" and that he set into motion a "force likely to cause death or serious bodily harm," thus satisfying the malice requirement of *Aaron*. Do you agree with the court's assessment of the evidence? Suppose defendant had taken precautions to make certain that he and his accomplice sister were alone in the house before pouring the gasoline?

For cases considering the problem of whether felony-murder applies when the deceased is a cofelon, see pp.581–91 *infra*.

4. The Model Penal Code contains no felony-murder provision. Instead, the Code finds a "rebuttable presumption" [defined in § 1.12(5)] of recklessness under the murder provision of § 210.2(1)(b) where the actor was "engaged, or is an accomplice in the commission of, or attempt to commit, or flight after committing or attempting to commit robbery, rape or deviate sexual intercourse by force or threat of force, arson, burglary, kidnaping or felonious escape." The Code Comments to § 210.2 at 38–39 explain the Code's approach:

> [T]here is no basis in experience for thinking that homicides which the evidence makes accidental occur with disproportionate frequency in connection with specified felonies. [I]t remains indefensible in principle to use the sanctions that the law employs to deal with murder unless there is at least a finding that the actor's conduct manifested an extreme indifference to the value of human life. The fact that the actor was engaged in a crime of the kind that is included in the usual first-degree felony-murder enumeration or was an accomplice in such crime, as has been observed, will frequently justify such a finding. Indeed, the probability that such a finding will be justified seems high enough to warrant the presumption of extreme indifference that Subsection (1)(b) creates. But liability depends, as plainly it should, upon the crucial finding. The result may not differ often under such a formulation from that which would be reached under some form of the felony-murder rule. But what is more important is that a conviction on this basis rests solidly upon principle.

[b] "Dangerous" Felonies?

As noted by the *Aaron* court, as early as Judge Stephen's instruction in the 1887 case of *Regina v. Serne,* courts had restricted the felony-murder rule to killings occurring in conjunction with "dangerous" felonies. Virtually all recent codifications limit felony-murder, at least in the first degree, to a list of specified felonies, each of which involves a substantial prospect of violence. MPC, § 210.2 Comment at 41.

Where no statutory list exists, the courts have struggled with defining the appropriate class of felonies to trigger the felony-murder doctrine. Even where the legislature provides listed felonies, the courts often face difficult interpretation problems because the listed felonies are often confined to first degree felony-murder leaving the courts in jurisdictions recognizing second degree felony-murder to discern for themselves those felonies which trigger second degree murder.

In such circumstances, some courts reject altogether the "inherently dangerous felony" limitation and permit any felony to support second degree murder. See, for example, *Heacock v. Commonwealth,* 228 Va. 397, 323 S.E.2d 90 (1984), where the court affirmed the conviction of a defendant who had supplied cocaine to the deceased who fatally injected the substance in the presence of the defendant.

Other courts simply assume that because death resulted due to defendant's commission of a felony, the felony was, under the circumstances, "dangerous." Thus, in *State v. Chambers,* 524 S.W.2d 826 (Mo. 1975), the court found defendant's felonious actions to be "violent" and "dangerous" when he stole a pickup truck, towed it down a major highway in darkness at a high speed, and eventually collided with an oncoming car, killing its four passengers after crossing over into its lane.

A third approach, taken by some courts, requires an assessment in the abstract of a felony's relative dangerousness in determining whether the felony may predicate felony-murder. The *Patterson* case that follows reflects this position. As you study the case and the subsequent notes and questions, consider which of the above approaches is most desirable.

PEOPLE V. PATTERSON

Supreme Court of California (in Bank)

49 Cal. 3d 615, 778 P.2d 549, 262 Cal. Rptr. 195 (1989), reh. den. Nov. 8, 1989

KENNARD, Justice.

The issue before us is whether the second degree felony-murder doctrine applies to a defendant who, in violation of Health and Safety Code section 11352, furnishes cocaine to a person who dies as a result of ingesting it. We reaffirm the rule that, in determining whether a felony is inherently dangerous to human life under the second degree felony-murder doctrine, we must consider "the elements of the felony in the abstract, not the particular —facts' of the case." . . . While Health and Safety Code section 11352 includes drug offenses other than the crime of furnishing cocaine, which formed the basis for the prosecution's theory of second degree felony-murder here, we conclude that the inquiry into inherent dangerousness must focus on the felony of furnishing cocaine, and not on section 11352 as a whole. We further hold that—consistent with the established definition of the term "inherently dangerous to life" in the context of implied malice as an element of second degree murder—a felony is inherently dangerous to life when there is a high probability that its commission will result in death.

We reverse the decision of the Court of Appeal affirming the trial court's ruling that, as a matter of law, the second degree felony-murder doctrine was inapplicable to this case. We direct the Court of Appeal to remand the matter to the trial court.

FACTUAL AND PROCEDURAL BACKGROUND

According to the testimony at the preliminary hearing, the victim Jennie Licerio and her friend Carmen Lopez had been using cocaine on a daily basis in the months preceding Licerio's death. On the night of November 25, 1985, the two women were with defendant in his motel room. There, all three drank "wine coolers," inhaled "lines" of cocaine, and smoked "cocopuffs" (hand-rolled cigarettes containing a mixture of tobacco and cocaine). Defendant furnished the cocaine. When Licerio became ill, Lopez called an ambulance. Defendant stayed with the two women until the paramedics and the police arrived. The paramedics were unable to revive Licerio, who died of acute cocaine intoxication.

The People filed an information charging defendant with one count . . . of murder. . . . Defendant was also charged with three counts of violating Health and Safety Code § 11352, in that he "did willfully, unlawfully and feloniously transport, import into the State of California, sell, furnish, administer, and give away, and attempt to import into the State of California and transport a controlled substance, to wit: cocaine."

Defendant moved . . . to set aside that portion of the information charging him with murder, contending the evidence presented at the preliminary hearing did not establish probable cause to believe he had committed murder. In opposing the motion, the People . . . relied solely on the second degree felony-murder doctrine. They argued that by furnishing cocaine defendant committed an inherently dangerous felony, thus justifying application of the rule. The trial court denied the motion. However, when the case was reassigned for trial, the court dismissed the murder charge . . . [finding] . . . that violation of . . . § 11352 . . . [is] not inherently dangerous to human life[.]

* * *

The Court of Appeal affirmed the dismissal of the murder count. Based on its review of the applicable decisions of this court, the Court of Appeal felt compelled to analyze Health and Safety Code section 11352 in its entirety (as opposed to only that portion of the statute actually violated in the present case) to determine whether defendant had committed an inherently dangerous felony. The court observed that section 11352 could be violated in various nonhazardous ways, such as transporting or offering to transport controlled substances. . . . As the court said, "The latter acts are obviously not inherently dangerous to human life." While recognizing that the murder charge against defendant rested on his furnishing cocaine to the victim, the court concluded that, viewing the statute "in the abstract," a violation of section 11352 could not be characterized as an inherently dangerous felony.

The Court of Appeal reached this conclusion reluctantly. The court noted that consideration of the entire statute, which included offenses unrelated to defendant's conduct, had brought the second degree felony-murder rule "to the brink of logical absurdity." The court suggested that "[i]f the rule is not abolished, it should be codified by the legislature with meaningful guidelines to effectuate its use."

As we shall explain, the Court of Appeal has interpreted our previous decisions in this area too broadly. In determining whether defendant had committed an inherently dangerous felony, the court should have considered only the particular crime at issue, namely, furnishing cocaine, and not the entire group of offenses included in the statute but not involved here. Thus, it is the offense of furnishing cocaine, not the statute as a whole, which must be examined "in the abstract."

DISCUSSION

1. Second Degree Felony-Murder Doctrine

There is no precise statutory definition for the second degree felony-murder rule.[5] In *People v. Ford* (1964), 60 Cal. 2d 772, 795, 36 Cal. Rptr. 620, 388 P.2d 892, we defined the doctrine as follows: "A homicide that is a direct causal result of the commission of a felony inherently dangerous to human life (other than the six felonies enumerated in Pen. Code, § 189) constitutes at least second degree murder. "In determining whether the felony is inherently dangerous, "we look to the elements of the felony in the abstract, not the particular —facts' of the case." . . .

The Court of Appeal's opinion in this case criticized the second degree felony-murder rule in its present form, suggesting the doctrine should either be completely eliminated or considerably "reformed." In response, defendant and *amici curiae* on his behalf have urged us to abolish the rule. The People and their *amici curiae,* on the other hand, have asked that we "reform" the doctrine by looking solely to the actual conduct of a defendant, thereby dispensing with the requirement that the elements of the offense be viewed in the abstract. We decline both invitations for the reasons discussed below.

The second degree felony-murder doctrine has been a part of California's criminal law for many decades. . . . In recent years, we have characterized the rule as "anachronistic" . . . and "disfavored" . . . , based on the view of many legal scholars that the doctrine incorporates an artificial concept of strict criminal liability that "erodes the relationship between criminal liability and moral culpability." . . . The Legislature, however, has taken no action to alter this judicially created rule. . . . In this case, our limited purpose in granting the People's petition for review was to determine the applicability of the second degree felony-murder doctrine to the crime of furnishing cocaine. We decline defendant's invitation that we determine the continued vitality of the rule. . . .

We also turn down the People's invitation that we expand the second degree felony-murder doctrine by eliminating the requirement . . . that the elements of the offense be viewed "in the abstract," and by adopting a new standard focusing instead on the actual conduct of a defendant in determining whether the felony is inherently dangerous.

* * *

Sound reasons support the [viewed-in-the-abstract] . . . rule. . . . "This form of analysis is compelled because there is a killing in every case where the rule might potentially be applied. If in such circumstances a court were to examine the particular facts of the case prior to establishing whether the underlying felony is inherently dangerous, the court might well be led to

---

[5] Penal Code section 189 provides in relevant part: "All murder which is perpetrated by means of a destructive device or explosive, knowing use of ammunition designed primarily to penetrate metal or armor, poison, lying in wait, torture, or by any other kind of willful, deliberate, and premeditated killing, or which is committed in the perpetration of, or attempt to perpetrate, arson, rape, robbery, burglary, mayhem, or any act punishable under Section 288, is murder of the first degree; and all other kinds of murders are of the second degree."

conclude the rule applicable despite any unfairness which might redound to so broad an application: the existence of the dead victim might appear to lead inexorably to the conclusion that the underlying felony is exceptionally hazardous."

For the reasons set forth above, we are reluctant to significantly expand the scope of the second degree felony-murder rule, as the People have urged us to do. We have repeatedly said that the felony-murder rule "deserves no extension beyond its required application." . . . Both the People's suggestion that we expand the second degree felony-murder doctrine and defendant's suggestion that we abolish it are matters appropriately left to the Legislature.

2. Determining "Inherent Dangerousness" of the Felony of Furnishing Cocaine

As discussed earlier, in determining whether defendant committed an inherently dangerous felony, we must consider the elements of the felony "in the abstract." . . . Because Health and Safety Code section 11352 also proscribes conduct other than that involved here (furnishing cocaine), the issue still to be resolved is whether we must consider only the specific offense of furnishing cocaine or the entire scope of conduct prohibited by the statute.

The Court of Appeal examined Health and Safety Code section 11352 in its entirety. It felt compelled to do so because of a series of recent cases where we held that, to determine a felony's inherent dangerousness, the statute as a whole had to be examined. . . . However, unlike the situation here, each of those cases involved a statute that proscribed an essentially single form of conduct.

* * *

In [those cases], we observed that the offense in question had a "primary element." . . . In contrast, Health and Safety Code section 11352, the statute at issue here, has no primary element. For instance, the elements of the crime of transporting a controlled substance bear no resemblance to those underlying the offense of administering such a substance; yet these two offenses are included in the same statute. . . .

The fact that the Legislature has included a variety of offenses in Health and Safety Code section 11352 does not require that we treat them as a unitary entity. Rather, we must decide whether in "[r]eading and considering the statute as a whole in order to determine the true legislative intent . . . we find [a] basis for severing" the various types of conduct it forbids. . . . There are more than 100 different controlled substances that fall within the confines of Health and Safety Code section 11352. To create statutes separately proscribing the importation, sale, furnishing, administration, etc., of each of these drugs, would require the enactment of hundreds of individual statutes. It thus appears that for the sake of convenience the Legislature has included the various offenses in one statute.

The determination whether a defendant who furnishes cocaine commits an inherently dangerous felony should not turn on the dangerousness of other drugs included in the same statute, such as heroin and peyote; nor should it turn on the danger to life, if any, inherent in the transportation or administering of cocaine. Rather, each offense set forth in the statute should be examined separately to determine its inherent dangerousness.

For the reasons discussed above, we hold the Court of Appeal and the trial court erred in concluding that Health and Safety Code section 11352 should be analyzed in its entirety to determine whether, in furnishing cocaine, defendant committed an inherently dangerous felony. Defendant, however, argues that even the more narrow offense of furnishing cocaine is not an inherently dangerous felony and therefore the trial court acted correctly in dismissing the murder charge, despite its faulty analysis. In countering that argument, the People have asked us to take judicial notice of various medical articles and reports that assertedly demonstrate that the offense of furnishing cocaine is sufficiently dangerous to life to constitute an inherently dangerous felony.

The task of evaluating the evidence on this issue is most appropriately entrusted to the trial court, subject, of course, to appellate review. We therefore direct the Court of Appeals to remand the matter to the trial court for further proceedings in light of this opinion. . . .

3. Meaning of the Term "Inherently Dangerous to Human Life"

For the guidance of the trial court on remand, we shall elaborate on the meaning of the term "inherently dangerous to life" for purposes of the second degree felony-murder doctrine.

The felony-murder rule generally acts as a substitute for the *mental state* ordinarily required for the offense of murder. . . . "Under well-settled principles of criminal liability a person who kills—whether or not he is engaged in an independent felony at the time—is guilty of murder *if he acts with malice aforethought.* The felony-murder doctrine, whose ostensible purpose is to deter those engaged in felonies from killing negligently or accidentally, operates to posit the existence of that crucial mental state—and thereby to render irrelevant evidence of actual malice or the lack thereof—when the killer is engaged in a felony whose inherent danger to human life renders logical an imputation of malice on the part of all who commit it." . . .

Implied malice, for which the second degree felony-murder doctrine acts as a substitute,[8] has both a physical and a mental component. The physical component is satisfied by the performance of "an act, the natural consequences of which are dangerous to life." . . . The mental component is the requirement that the defendant "knows that his conduct endangers the life of another and . . . acts with a conscious disregard for life." . . .

The second degree felony-murder rule eliminates the need for the prosecution to establish the *mental* component. The justification therefore is that, when society has declared certain inherently dangerous conduct to be felonious, a defendant should not be allowed to excuse himself by saying he was

---

[8] Although the second degree felony-murder doctrine operates as a substitute for implied malice, this does not mean that the doctrine results in a conclusive presumption of malice. . . . Nevertheless, in determining the proper scope of the second degree felony-murder doctrine, it is appropriate for the courts, in recognition of the Legislature's authority to define criminal offenses, to attempt to minimize the disparity between the legislatively created and the judicially recognized categories of second degree murder.

unaware of the danger to life because, by declaring the conduct to be felonious, society has warned him of the risk involved. The *physical* requirement, however, remains the same; by committing a felony inherently dangerous to life, the defendant has committed "an act, the natural consequences of which are dangerous to life" . . . , thus satisfying the physical component of implied malice.

The definition of "inherently dangerous to life" in the context of the implied malice element of second degree murder is well established. An act is inherently dangerous to human life when there is "a high probability that it will result in death.". . .

We therefore conclude . . . that, for purposes of the second degree felony-murder doctrine, an "inherently dangerous felony" is an offense carrying "a high probability" that death will result. A less stringent standard would inappropriately expand the scope of the second degree felony-murder rule reducing the seriousness of the act which a defendant must commit in order to be charged with murder.[9]

We share the concern Chief Justice Lucas has expressed in his dissent regarding the tragic effects that the abuse of illegal drugs, particularly crack cocaine, has on our society. However, it is the Legislature, rather than this court, that should determine whether expansion of the second degree felony-murder rule is an appropriate method by which to address this problem. In the absence of specific legislative action, we must determine the scope of the rule by applying the established definition of inherent dangerousness.

DISPOSITION

We reverse the decision of the Court of Appeal, and direct that court to remand the matter to the trial court for further proceedings consistent with this opinion.

LUCAS, Chief Justice, *concurring and dissenting.*

I concur in the judgment. As several prior cases have indicated, the second degree felony-murder doctrine performs a valuable function in deterring the commission of crimes which, though involving no express or implied malice, are nonetheless so inherently dangerous as to justify a murder charge when a death occurs during their commission. . . . Accordingly, the majority quite properly refuses to accept defendant's invitations (1)to abrogate the doctrine entirely, or (2)to permit consideration of other felonies not involved in the case in determining the inherent dangerousness of the defendant's own offense.

I dissent, however, to the majority's unrealistic, unwise and unprecedented definition of inherent dangerousness as involving "a high probability of death." With that one broad, gratuitous stroke, the majority has precluded application of the second degree felony-murder doctrine to most, if not all, drug furnishing offenses (as well as many nondrug offenses), . . . thereby overruling or

---

[9] We are aware that, in enacting the first degree felony-murder rule, the Legislature has determined that deaths occurring in the commission of certain felonies are punishable as first degree murder. (Pen. Code, § 189.) The fact that the Legislature has chosen to single out those offenses in this fashion, however, provides no guidance on the appropriate reach of the second degree felony-murder doctrine in general. As noted earlier, the Legislature of course has the authority to expand or to abolish the second degree felony-murder doctrine.

disapproving, *sub silentio,* several prior cases of this court and the Court of Appeal.

* * *

Because the drug furnishing statutes must be viewed *in the abstract* for purposes of applying the second degree felony-murder doctrine, as a practical matter the majority's new "high probability" requirement will be impossible to satisfy in any case arising under those statutes, for to my knowledge none of them involves drugs so dangerous that death is a *highly probable* result. At a time when our society faces a serious "crack" cocaine crisis of epidemic proportions, the majority's holding is particularly unwelcome. . . .

We recently set forth in . . . another second degree felony-murder case, the correct and proper test for determining the inherent dangerousness of an offense. There, we referred to a felony "inherently so dangerous that by its very nature, it cannot be committed without creating a *substantial risk* that someone will be killed. . . . "

* * *

Applying the foregoing test in the context of a drug furnishing offense, the relevant question would be whether furnishing a particular drug such as cocaine or heroin created a substantial risk of death. Although that test may be difficult for the prosecution to meet, the majority's alternative test will entirely foreclose the possibility of a murder charge in all of these cases.

As I have indicated, the purpose of the felony-murder rule is to *deter* the commission of inherently dangerous felonies. Certainly that purpose is furthered by deterring offenses bearing a substantial risk of death, as well as those offenses involving a greater likelihood of death. As the court in a similar case (involving heroin furnishing) explained, "knowledge that the death of a person to whom heroin is furnished may result in a conviction for murder should have some effect on the defendant's readiness to do the furnishing." . . .

The . . . "high probability of death" standard was borrowed from second degree murder cases . . . requiring proof of implied malice. Such a standard may be appropriate for measuring whether defendant's general course of conduct should warrant a murder charge based on implied malice, but it is singularly inappropriate for determining whether *felonious* conduct should lead to such a charge. Notions of implied malice have never before been imported into felony-murder, where the commission of the felony itself acts as a substitute for malice.

The anomalous and inconsistent nature of the majority's holding is confirmed by the fact that a defendant can be charged with first degree felony-murder by committing such offenses as burglary, robbery, rape or child molestation (see Pen. Code, § 189), none of which offenses, viewed in the abstract, involves a high probability of death, although each of which may present substantial risks of death. If a first degree murder charge can be based on an offense not involving a high probability of death, surely the lesser charge of second degree murder can be based on similar offenses, so long as the requisite substantial risk of death can be demonstrated.

For all the foregoing reasons, I dissent to the majority's improper new formulation of the standard for determining inherent dangerousness.

EAGLESON and KAUFMAN, JJ., *concur.*

MOSK, Justice, *dissenting.*

* * *

In my view, the correct question is whether a *violation of section 11352*—not merely "furnishing cocaine"—is a felony inherently dangerous to human life. And the trial court has already answered that question: after reviewing our decisions on the topic, the trial court ruled that "*violating section [11352] of the Health and Safety Code* [is] not so inherently dangerous that, by its very nature, it cannot be committed without creating a substantial risk that someone will be killed. And, while the felonies [charged in the case at bar] may, in many circumstances, pose a threat to human life, *the commission of the crime as defined by the statute* does not inevitably pose a danger to human life." The court therefore dismissed the murder count. . . . As will appear, our precedents amply support the court's ruling.

Shortly after this court adopted the requirement that to determine whether a felony is inherently dangerous to human life "we look to the elements of the felony in the abstract" . . . we first confronted an attempt to depart from the statutory definition of the felony. In *People v. Phillips* (1966), 64 Cal. 2d 574, 51 Cal. Rptr. 225, 414 P.2d 353, the defendant, a chiropractor, persuaded the parents of a child with eye cancer to renounce planned surgery and allow him to treat her instead by chiropractic methods, charging them for his services. When the child died the defendant was convicted of second degree felony-murder, the felony being grand theft. . . . We held that it was prejudicial error to predicate a felony-murder instruction on that offense. The Attorney General conceded that grand theft was not inherently dangerous to human life, but urged us to look at "the entire course of defendant's conduct" and to characterize the crime as "grand theft medical fraud": "this newly created —felony,' he urges, clearly involves danger to human life and supports an application of the felony-murder rule." . . .

We rejected this attempt to "abandon the statutory definition of the felony as such" . . . explaining that "To fragmentize the —course of conduct' of defendant so that the felony-murder rule applies if any segment of that conduct may be considered dangerous to life would widen the rule beyond calculation." . . . We concluded that "once the Legislature's own definition is discarded, the number or nature of the contextual elements which could be incorporated into an expanded felony terminology would be limitless. We have been, and remain, unwilling to embark on such an uncharted sea of felony-murder." . . .

The claim we rejected in *Phillips,* of course, was analytically the converse of the claim made in the case at bar: in *Phillips* the Attorney General sought to expand the statutory definition of the felony by including elements ("medical fraud") not incorporated therein by the Legislature; here the

Attorney General seeks instead to contract the statutory definition by excluding elements (the transportation, importation, sale, etc., of controlled substances) that the Legislature did incorporate therein. But the reasoning of *Phillips*—that to abandon the statutory definition of the felony would embark us on "an uncharted sea of felony-murder"—remains no less applicable to the present context.

* * *

The majority seek to distinguish the [instant statute from] authorities [requiring consideration of statutes as a whole] on the ground that in each [of the latter] the statute defines an offense having a "primary element." . . . The majority then contend there is no such "primary element" in section 11352, but their argument in support is unpersuasive. . . .

* * *

. . . [U]nder settled rules of statutory construction . . . § 11352 must be viewed in the light of both its history and its context. When so viewed, it will be seen as a deliberately crafted response by the Legislature to a single evil: trafficking in illegal narcotics.

[Justice Mosk then examines the legislative history of § 11352.]

In short, when viewed in the light of the legislative plan as a whole, section 11352 in effect prohibits different ways of engaging in the same targeted criminal conduct—trafficking in illegal narcotics. . . .

* * *

When section 11352 is thus seen in the light of its history and its place in the Legislature's elaborate plan for controlling illegal narcotics, it is clear that . . . "[t]he Legislature has not drawn any relevant distinctions" between trafficking by furnishing cocaine and trafficking by importing, transporting, or selling cocaine—or indeed any controlled substance. . . . To hold otherwise, as do the majority, is to rewrite the statute in the face of plain legislative intent to the contrary. It follows that . . . the dispositive issue here is whether a violation of section 11352 as a whole is a felony inherently dangerous to human life.

That issue is not difficult to decide. As both the trial court and the Court of Appeal correctly observed, section 11352 can be violated in various ways that do not create a substantial risk of death. For example, it is violated by one who simply carries a small amount of cocaine home in his pocket for his personal use, or by a motorist who simply offers a ride in his car to a friend who he knows is carrying a similar amount of cocaine for his own use; no other act or intent need be proved for a conviction. . . . Accordingly, as the trial court ruled, a violation of section 11352 is not "inherently so dangerous that by its very nature, it cannot be committed without creating a substantial risk that someone will be killed." . . . Because section 11352 is not a felony inherently dangerous to human life, it cannot serve as a predicate for the second degree felony-murder rule; and because the prosecutor indicated to the court that felony-murder was his sole theory on the homicide count, the court correctly dismissed that count in the interest of justice.

* * *

I would affirm the judgment of the Court of Appeal.

BROUSSARD, J., concurs.

PANELLI, Justice, dissenting.

I join fully in Justice Mosk's dissenting opinion. . . .

This case has generated both substantial disagreement and some uneasiness. The disagreement is evident in how the court has split on the issues before us. I am uneasy because we have traveled very close to the edge of our role as judges and have come perilously close to becoming legislators. We have, as the majority notes, however, tried to resolve this case simply by "applying the established definition of inherent dangerousness." . . . But we must bear in mind that both that definition and the crime, itself, are our own creations.

Although courts are often called upon to make policy choices—and this court has not shirked its responsibility to do so—our mandate to make policy in this context is not particularly strong. There are, or at least should be, no nonstatutory crimes in this state. . . . The second degree felony-murder rule, however, either creates a nonstatutory crime or increases the punishment for statutory crimes beyond that established by the Legislature. We derive such authority neither from the Constitution . . . nor from the Penal Code. . . .

My uneasiness with the second degree felony-murder rule is mirrored in the majority's adoption of the new "high probability of death" standard, which certainly will restrict the rule's future application. . . . It may also be reflected in how often the majority mentions that the Legislature has failed to act. . . . Today the majority expressly relies on that failure as a justification for continuing to "determine the scope" of this anomalous common law crime. . . . But in view of the Legislature's long-standing declaration that "[n]o act or omission . . . is criminal or punishable, except as prescribed or authorized by [the Penal Code]," I question whether subsequent legislative inaction is a sufficient justification.

In short, I am not quite convinced that the second degree felony-murder rule stands on solid constitutional ground. Since the rule permits a court to increase the punishment for certain dangerous crimes, the temptation to invoke it is great when we are facing the type of social crisis that illegal drugs have brought upon us. While I am aware of the crisis, nevertheless, I respectfully suggest that it is the Legislature that has the resources and constitutional authority to determine and define what conduct is criminal and to set the punishment for such crimes.

I would affirm the decision of the Court of Appeal.

NOTES AND QUESTIONS

1. Is the *Patterson* court's limitation of the felony-murder rule to "inherently dangerous" felonies a sound idea? Consider the following rationale for the

limitation provided in *People v. Williams,* 63 Cal. 2d 452, 458, n. 4, 47 Cal. Rptr. 7, 10, 406 P.2d 647, 650 (1965):

> The purpose of the felony-murder rule is to deter felons from killing negligently or accidentally. . . . This purpose may be well served with respect to felonies such as robbery or burglary, but it has little relevance to a felony which is not inherently dangerous. If the felony is not inherently dangerous it is highly improbable that the potential felon will be deterred; he will not anticipate that any injury or death might arise solely from the fact that he will commit the felony.

Do you agree? Can anyone be deterred from killing "accidentally"? On the other hand, wouldn't future would-be Pattersons have additional incentive to avoid transferring cocaine if the lower court eventually reimposes the felony-murder conviction?

2. Is it sound to require the court to assess a felony's relative dangerousness "in the abstract"? Consider the following observation of LaFave and Scott at 624–25:

> [I]f the purpose of the felony-murder doctrine is to hold felons accountable for unintended deaths caused by their dangerous conduct, then it would seem to make little difference whether the felony committed was dangerous by its very nature or merely dangerous as committed in the particular case. If the armed robber is to be held guilty of felony-murder because of a death occurring from the accidental firing of his gun, it seems no more harsh to apply the felony-murder doctrine to the thief whose fraudulent scheme includes inducing the victim to forego a life-prolonging operation. The requirement that the felony be "inherently dangerous" is more understandable, however, if viewed as an attempt by some courts to limit what they believe to be "a highly artificial concept that deserves no extension beyond its required application."

3. Can principled distinctions between dangerous and nondangerous felonies be drawn? Are the felonies traditionally specified for treatment as first degree murder (rape, robbery, arson, kidnaping, and burglary) themselves "inherently dangerous"? Consider, for example, *People v. Fuller,* 86 Cal. App. 3d 618, 150 Cal. Rptr. 515 (1978), in which the court held that defendants could be prosecuted for first degree felony-murder when the car in which they were driving accidentally collided with another car, killing its driver, during a high-speed automobile chase of defendant's car by the police after defendants had taken some tires from unoccupied vans during a series of daytime thefts. Because California, like several other states, had abandoned the common law's requirements of a nighttime breaking and entering of a dwelling house in order to constitute the crime of burglary, the theft of the tires from the vans technically constituted burglary under California law, thus placing defendants within the first degree felony-murder statute when they fled the scene of the burglary and killed the motorist. While burglary at common law may indeed have been an "inherently dangerous" crime, could the same be said for the California version as represented by *Fuller?*

Should the *Fuller* court have assessed the dangerousness of burglary in the context of the circumstances of that case rather than merely concluding that because the actions of the defendants met the formal definition of burglary, their conduct must also render them candidates for first degree murder? On the other hand, does the requirement that the dangerousness of a felony be assessed "in the abstract" preclude the *Fuller* court from assessing the quality of defendants' burglary within the context of their case?

4. Even when they agree to apply the "inherently dangerous" limitation, different courts sometimes reach conflicting assessments of a given felony's dangerousness. For example, while the *Phillips* case, discussed in Justice Mosk's dissent in *Patterson,* denies the inherent dangerousness of grand theft, *State v. Lashley,* 233 Kan. 620, 664 P.2d 1358 (1983), holds that the offense of theft "when viewed in the abstract" is inherently dangerous to human life and is a proper felony to support first degree felony-murder.

Similar disagreement exists over the inherent dangerousness of supplying illegal drugs to the deceased. While *Heacock v. Commonwealth,* noted *supra* in the introduction to this section, holds that any felony is sufficient to support second degree felony-murder under the Virginia statute, the court noted in dicta that the defendant "knew, or should have known" that distribution of cocaine is conduct "inherently dangerous to human life." 228 Va. at 404, 323 S.E.2d at 94. In contrast, *Sheriff, Clark County v. Morris,* 99 Nev. 109, 119, 659 P.2d 852, 859 (1983), rejects the argument that "the unlawful sale of drugs is inherently dangerous *per se,* and therefore an appropriate basis for a charge of murder when death occurs."

5. Is there an argument that Patterson did not cause the death of the deceased who willingly ingested the cocaine? Why is the death not attributed to the actions of the deceased rather than to Patterson?

6. For a general discussion of the inherently dangerous requirement in felony-murder, see Annot., 50 A.L.R.3d 397 (1973).

7. Rather than relying on the doctrine of felony-murder, some states have enacted legislation specifically punishing persons who cause deaths through drug offenses. For a case discussing such legislation and upholding its constitutionality, see *State v. Maldonado,* 137 N.J. 536, 645 A.2d 1165 (1994).

[c] Duration of the Felony

Another way in which courts and legislatures have limited the scope of the felony-murder doctrine is by imposing the requirement that the death occur "during the course, or in perpetration, of" the felony. While the cases offer little in the way of clear rules for defining the felony's duration, the courts have tended to require that the homicide and the felony be "closely connected in point of time, place, and causal relation." LaFave and Scott at 634.

The issue frequently arises in cases where the felon kills while attempting to escape apprehension for the felony. See, *e.g., Whitman v. People,* 161 Colo. 110, 420 P.2d 416 (1966), where the court found that defendants killed "in perpetration of a robbery" when they collided with another car, killing the driver as they frantically tried to avoid arrest by pursuing police officers. *People v. Gladman,* 41 N.Y.2d 123, 129, 390 N.Y.S.2d 912, 916, 359 N.E.2d 420, 424 (1976), provides the following "test" to be applied in fleeing felon cases:

The jury should be instructed to give consideration to whether the homicide and the felony occurred at the same location or, if not, to the distance separating the two locations. Weight may also be placed on whether there is an interval of time between the commission of the felony and the commission of the homicide. The jury may properly consider such additional factors as whether the culprits had possession of the fruits of criminal activity, whether the police, watchmen or concerned citizens were in close pursuit, and whether the criminals had reached a place of temporary safety. These factors are not exclusive; others may be appropriate in differing factual settings. If anything, past history demonstrates the fruitlessness of attempting to apply rigid rules to virtually limitless factual variations. No single factor is necessarily controlling; it is the combination of several factors that leads to a justifiable inference.

In addition to the issue of the dangerousness of felonious drug transactions discussed in the previous section, the courts have struggled with the problem of whether deaths caused by self-inflicted overdoses of drugs received by the deceased from the defendant are killings committed "in perpetration of" the felony of transferring controlled substances. Some courts find that the felony has terminated as soon as the drug provider and recipient part company. Thus if the fatal overdose occurs outside the presence of the defendant, felony-murder does not occur. See *State v. Mauldin,* 215 Kan. 956, 529 P.2d 124 (1974).

The question of whether the felony must precede the killing has also proven to be somewhat controversial. Suppose, for example, that Defendant accidentally kills Victim with no thoughts of robbery, but upon seeing Victim dead he decides to rob him. While an overwhelming majority of courts have concluded that a felon does not commit felony-murder where he forms felonious intent only after he commits the killing, see, *e.g., United States v. Mack,* 466 F.2d 333 (D.C. Cir. 1972); *State v. Montgomery,* 191 Neb. 470, 215 N.W.2d 881 (1974), some authority to the contrary exists. See, *e.g., Commonwealth v. Tomlinson,* 446 Pa. 241, 284 A.2d 687 (1971), but see *Commonwealth v. Spallone,* 267 Pa. Super. 486, 406 A.2d 1146 (1979).

For an extensive discussion of the duration of felonies for purposes of the felony-murder doctrine, see Annot. 58 A.L.R.3d 851 (1974).

[d] The Merger Doctrine

PEOPLE V. SEARS

Supreme Court of California

2 Cal. 3d 180, 84 Cal. Rptr. 711, 465 P.2d 847 (1970)

PETERS, Justice.

[A] jury found defendant guilty of the first degree murder of his stepdaughter Elizabeth Olives, the attempted murder of his wife Clara Sears, and the attempted murder of his mother-in-law Frances Montijo. The penalty for the murder was fixed as death. . . .

Defendant married Clara Sears in 1960. The spouses agreed that Clara and her three children by a former marriage would continue living in a cottage which she and the children had occupied before the marriage, while defendant would sleep in a nearby garage until he completed an addition to the cottage. Defendant never completed the addition, and Clara refused to let defendant sleep in the cottage even after one of her daughters married and moved out. Defendant had his meals and watched television in the cottage.

Around the end of April 1963 defendant moved to a hotel. On Sunday, May 12, defendant visited his wife. According to her testimony, defendant threatened that he would kill her and the children if she got a divorce.

On May 16, 1963, defendant completed his work for the day and went to a neighborhood tavern where he drank beer with friends until about 7:30 PM. Defendant then returned to his hotel and went to dinner with one Robert Kjaerbye. At 10 PM the two went to a tavern where defendant was a regular customer. After each man had drunk a beer, they drove approximately one block to the cottage occupied by Mrs. Sears.

Defendant and Kjaerbye entered the cottage through the unlocked front door. While Kjaerbye stayed in the living room, defendant went into the bedroom. Elizabeth was asleep and Clara was reading. Defendant told Clara that he wanted to talk with her, and she put on a robe and accompanied defendant to the kitchen. Because the floor was cold, Clara returned to the bedroom to get a pair of slippers. As she reentered the kitchen, defendant grabbed her robe and said, "If you won't want to come back to me. . . . " Then defendant unbuttoned his shirt and drew out an iron bar that he had stuck in his pants before entering the cottage. He struck Clara about the head until she lost consciousness. Elizabeth awakened and approached the kitchen. As she cried out for defendant to leave her mother alone, defendant turned on her with the iron bar. Clara regained consciousness and unsuccessfully tried to place herself between defendant and Elizabeth, but she again became unconscious.

Clara's mother, Frances Montijo, who lived next door with Clara's brother Patrick Montijo, heard the noise from her daughter's home and decided to investigate. As she approached the cottage Kjaerbye was leaving. He told her that he knew nothing of what was happening inside. Frances entered to find defendant on top of the screaming child. When defendant saw Frances, he attacked her with a knife he had taken from Clara's kitchen. After cutting her face, defendant threw Frances into a chair, rolled the iron bar against her throat and chest, and stabbed her with a barbecue fork, also taken from the kitchen.

Patrick's wife, Dolores, became concerned when Frances did not return from Clara's, and decided to investigate. As she arrived at the cottage, the injured Frances was making her escape. Dolores took Frances to a neighbor's house and went back to her own house for Patrick.

Patrick went over to the cottage. As he entered, defendant was standing over Clara with the barbecue fork in his raised hand. Patrick asked defendant what he was doing; defendant did not reply, but lunged at Patrick with the fork. A fight ensued, and defendant stabbed Patrick in the neck and chest. Defendant then ran to his car and drove away.

Elizabeth died from a knife wound that punctured her jugular vein. She also suffered numerous other cuts and bruises. Clara suffered multiple lacerations as well as a fractured jaw and a fractured arm. Frances received several wounds on her face, neck, and hands.

Defendant testified that he returned to the cottage to discuss their marital situation and effect a reconciliation; that he particularly wanted to ask her to accompany him that weekend to inspect some rental units he hoped to move to; that before entering the cottage, he saw an iron bar, picked it up and stuck it in his pants; that he intended only that his wife see the bar, hoping that she would then sit down and talk with him; and that he did not have any intent to use it on Clara or to scare her. Whether the bar was visible is disputed. Clara testified that she did not see it until defendant pulled it out from beneath his shirt.

In his argument to the jury, the prosecutor urged at some length that the first degree felony-murder doctrine was applicable, urging that defendant committed a burglary in entering the cottage. He emphasized repeatedly that burglary included an entry with an intent to commit any felony, not merely theft, and he repeatedly asserted that defendant entered with intent to assault.

The jury was instructed on first and second degree murder. In connection with the felony-murder rule, the trial judge instructed the jury:

> I will now instruct you on the law concerning first degree murder in the perpetration of burglary. The unlawful killing of a human being, whether intentional, unintentional, or accidental, which is committed in the perpetration or attempt to perpetrate burglary, the commission of which crime itself must be proved beyond a reasonable doubt, is murder of the first degree.
>
> Every person who enters any structure such as is shown by the evidence in this case, with intent to commit theft or any felony is guilty of burglary. The essence of a burglary is entering a place such as I have mentioned with such specific intent; and the crime is complete as soon as the entry is made, regardless of whether the intent thereafter is carried out.

Subsequently, the jury returned to the courtroom and asked the judge the following question. "Does assault on wife constitute a felony regardless of intent upon entering and if so, does felony-murder doctrine dictating first degree murder apply?" The court reread the felony-murder instruction, and the instruction on burglary. It did not instruct on assault with a deadly weapon or assault. The court also stated: "In answer to the specific inquiry, the court would advise that the specific intent to commit the assault must exist at the time of entry, otherwise the felony-murder rule does not apply. Does that answer your question?" Whereupon the foreman of the jury stated that he believed it did.

The jurors continued their deliberations for six hours after the above instruction before retiring for the night. The jury returned its verdict the following morning, apparently one and a half hours after resuming deliberations.

In *People v. Ireland,* 70 Cal. 2d 522, 537 et seq., 75 Cal. Rptr. 188, 450 P.2d 580, we considered the applicability of the second degree felony-murder rule to a situation where the claimed felony in the course of which the homicide occurred was an assault with a deadly weapon. We explained the felony-murder doctrine as follows:

> The felony-murder rule operates (1)to posit the existence of malice aforethought in homicides which are the direct causal result of the perpetration or attempted perpetration of all felonies inherently dangerous to human life, and (2)to posit the existence of malice aforethought and to classify the offense as murder of the first degree in homicides which are the direct causal result of those six felonies specifically enumerated in section 189 of the Penal Code. [Citations.]

We further stated [in *Ireland*]:

> We have concluded that the utilization of the felony-murder rule in circumstances such as those before us extends the operation of that rule "beyond any rational function that it is designed to serve. . . . " To allow such use of the felony-murder rule would effectively preclude the jury from considering the issue of malice—forethought in all cases wherein homicide has been committed as a result of a felonious assault—a category which includes the great majority of all homicides. This kind of bootstrapping finds support neither in logic nor in law. We therefore hold that a second degree felony-murder instruction may not properly be given when it is based upon a felony which is an integral part of the homicide and which the evidence produced by the prosecution shows to be an offense included in fact within the offense charged. . . .

We also pointed out that other jurisdictions, through a so-called "merger" doctrine, had applied similar limitations on the felony-murder doctrine and that, although it was not clear whether we would adopt the entire doctrine, "we believe that the reasoning underlying that doctrine is basically sound and should be applied to the extent that it is consistent with the laws and policies of this state. . . . "

Ireland was followed in our recent decision of *People v. Wilson,* 1 Cal. 3d 431, 82 Cal. Rptr. 494, 462 P.2d 22, where the jury was instructed on the first degree felony-murder rule on the theory that the homicide was committed in the course of a burglary because the defendant entered the premises with intent to commit a felonious assault. In *Wilson,* the defendant forcibly entered his estranged wife's apartment carrying a shotgun. He shot one man on the stairs of the apartment, shot William Washington in the living room of the apartment, broke into the bathroom, and killed Mrs. Wilson. The defendant was convicted of the second degree murder of Washington and the first degree murder of his wife. We held that there was error in instructing the jury on both the second degree and the first degree felony-murder rules.

In reversing the judgment convicting defendant of first and second degree murder, we stated with respect to the first degree felony-murder instruction:

> Here the prosecution sought to apply the felony-murder rule on the theory that the homicide occurred in the course of a burglary, but the only basis for finding a felonious entry is the intent to commit an assault with a deadly

weapon. When, as here, the entry would be nonfelonious but for the intent to commit the assault, and the assault is an integral part of the homicide and is included in fact in the offense charged, utilization of the felony-murder rule extends that doctrine "beyond any rational function that it is designed to serve." We have heretofore emphasized "that the felony-murder doctrine expresses a highly artificial concept that deserves no extension beyond its required application. . . . "

"The purpose of the felony-murder rule is to deter felons from killing negligently or accidentally by holding them strictly responsible for killings they commit. . . . " Where a person enters a building with an intent to assault his victim with a deadly weapon, he is not deterred by the felony-murder rule. That doctrine can serve its purpose only when applied to a felony independent of the homicide. In *Ireland,* we reasoned that a man assaulting another with a deadly weapon could not be deterred by the second degree felony-murder rule, since the assault was an integral part of the homicide. Here, the only distinction is that the assault and homicide occurred inside a dwelling so that the underlying felony is burglary based on an intention to assault with a deadly weapon, rather than simply assault with a deadly weapon.

We do not suggest that no relevant differences exist between crimes committed inside and outside dwellings. We have often recognized that persons within dwellings are in greater peril from intruders bent on stealing or engaging in other felonious conduct. . . . Persons within dwellings are more likely to resist and less likely to be able to avoid the consequences of crimes committed inside their homes. However, this rationale does not justify application of the felony-murder rule to the case at bar. Where the intended felony of the burglar is an assault with a deadly weapon, the likelihood of homicide from the lethal weapon is not significantly increased by the site of the assault. Furthermore, the burglary statute in this state includes within its definition numerous structures other than dwellings as to which there can be no conceivable basis for distinguishing between an assault with a deadly weapon outdoors and a burglary in which the felonious intent is solely to assault with a deadly weapon. . . .[1]

[Wilson.]

Under *Ireland* and *Wilson,* the instructions of the court on the first degree felony-murder rule and the court's answer to the question asked by the jury must be held erroneous. Those instructions and the answer could reasonably be understood to mean that if defendant entered with intent to assault his wife and stepdaughter he was guilty of burglary and that the first degree felony-murder rule was applicable. To apply the felony-murder rule to such a situation would extend the doctrine "beyond any rational function that it is designed to serve." As pointed out in Wilson, that doctrine can serve its purpose only when applied to a felony independent of the homicide, and where a person enters a building with intent to assault his victims with a deadly weapon, he is not deterred by the felony-murder rule.

---

[1] Included are any "shop, warehouse, store, mill, barn, stable, outhouse or other building, tent, vessel, railroad car, trailer coach . . . , vehicle . . . , aircraft . . . , mine or any underground portion thereof. . . . " (Pen. Code, § 459.)

The Attorney General, pointing out that there is evidence from which the jury might have concluded that defendant entered with intent to assault his wife with a deadly weapon but not his stepdaughter, urges that the felony-murder rule is applicable on the theory that the burglary based on the intent to assault the wife was independent of and collateral to the killing of the stepdaughter. It may be noted in this connection that in New York it has been held that, although the felony-murder rule does not apply where a defendant intentionally assaults each of his two victims who die as a result of the assaults, the rule is applicable if the defendant assaulted one person but killed another who came to the first's defense. (*People v. Moran,* 246 N.Y. 100, 158 N.E. 35, 36–37 (1927); *People v. Wagner,* 245 N.Y. 143, 156 N.E. 644, 646 (1927).)

However, the instructions given to the jury did not posit the applicability of the felony-murder rule upon any such theory. Moreover, we are satisfied that the distinction made by the New York cases is untenable in the light of ordinary principles of culpability. It would be anomalous to place the person who intends to attack one person and in the course of the assault kills another inadvertently or in the heat of battle in a worse position than the person who from the outset intended to attack both persons and killed one or both.

Where a defendant assaults one or more persons killing one, his criminal responsibility for the homicide should not depend upon which of the victims died but should be the greatest crime committed viewing each victim of the attack individually and without regard to which in fact died. This result is reached in application of existing principles of transferred intent, and it is unnecessary to resort to the felony murder rule. Thus if a person purposely and of his deliberate and premeditated malice attempts to kill one person but by mistake and inadvertence kills another instead, the law transfers the intent and the homicide so committed is murder of the first degree.

The error in instructing on the felony-murder rule must be held prejudicial. Although there is substantial evidence of premeditation and malice aforethought in the record, the evidence is not overwhelming, and there is conflicting evidence. The question asked of the court by the jury during its lengthy deliberations indicates that the felony-murder instruction played a decisive role in the jury's verdict.

The judgment is reversed.

NOTES AND QUESTIONS

1. Is the *Sears* court correct in its conclusion that the felony-murder doctrine "can serve its [deterrent] purpose only when applied to a felony independent of the homicide"? Does a more plausible rationale for the merger doctrine rest on the *Ireland* court's assessment of the analytical relationship between felonious assault and homicide?

2. Is it sound to draw distinctions for felony-murder purposes between felony assault burglaries and, say, felony theft burglaries? Does this distinction suggest that burglars who accidentally kill in the course of breaking and

entering intending to steal are more culpable than those who, like the defendant in *Sears,* break and enter to commit felonious assault?

Along these lines, does the *Sears* court pay sufficient attention to the point noted in the *Wilson* case that burglaries within dwellings are more dangerous than those committed in other types of buildings? These and other concerns have led some courts to reject application of the merger doctrine in situations such as *Sears.* See, *e.g., People v. Miller,* 32 N.Y.2d 157, 160–61, 344 N.Y.S.2d 342, 345–46, 297 N.E.2d 85, 87–88 (1973), where the court, after noting that burglary was one of the enumerated felonies in the New York felony murder statute, said,

> It should be apparent that the Legislature, in including burglary as one of the enumerated felonies as a basis for felony-murder, recognized that persons within domiciles are in greater peril from those entering the domicile with criminal intent, than persons on the street who are being subjected to the same criminal intent. Thus, the burglary statutes prescribe greater punishment for a criminal act committed within the domicile than for the same act committed on the street. Where, as here, the criminal act underlying the burglary is an assault with a dangerous weapon, the likelihood that the assault will culminate in a homicide is significantly increased by the situs of the assault. When the assault takes place within the domicile, the victim may be more likely to resist the assault; the victim is also less likely to be able to avoid the consequences of the assault, since his paths of retreat and escape may be barred or severely restricted by furniture, walls and other obstructions incidental to buildings. Further, it is also more likely that when the assault occurs in the victim's domicile, there will be present family or close friends who will come to the victim's aid and be killed. Since the purpose of the felony-murder statute is to reduce the disproportionate number of accidental homicides which occur during the commission of the enumerated predicate felonies by punishing the party responsible for the homicide not merely for manslaughter, but for murder, the Legislature, in enacting the burglary and felony-murder statutes, did not exclude from the definition of burglary, a burglary based upon the intent to assault, but intended that the definition be "satisfied if the intruder's intent, existing at the time of the unlawful entry or remaining, is to commit any crime."

Do you find *Sears* or *Miller* more persuasive? Apparently *Miller* is the majority view. LaFave and Scott at 638–39.

3. Outside the area of burglary, the vast majority of jurisdictions apply the merger doctrine to felonious assaults, thus precluding those crimes from generating felony-murder. A few jurisdictions, however, reject the merger rule in the felonious assault context. See, *e.g., State v. Thompson,* 88 Wash. 2d 13, 558 P.2d 202 (1977), where the court upheld the defendant's second degree murder conviction, which was premised on the theory that she committed the felony of assault in the second degree when she shot her husband and felony-murder when he died as a result of the shooting. Does *Thompson* theoretically obliterate the crime of manslaughter? Consider this question again after studying the materials on manslaughter, pp.595–635 *infra.*

The killing in *Thompson* arose during a domestic quarrel in which the deceased husband allegedly struck the defendant. Suppose the prosecution in that case had premised its felony-murder argument on the theory that the death arose in the course of defendant's commission of the felony of voluntary manslaughter and thus constituted murder.

4. Courts and legislatures have split on the application of the merger doctrine in the area of fatal child abuse. Some courts apply the doctrine, holding that felonious assaultive child abuse is an integral part of the resulting homicide, thus removing that crime as a predicate for operation of the felony murder doctrine. See, *e.g., People v. Smith,* 35 Cal. 3d 798, 201 Cal. Rptr. 311, 678 P.2d 886 (1984); *Massie v. State,* 553 P.2d 186 (Okla. Crim. 1976). Other courts reach the opposite conclusion and hold that child abuse can operate as the predicate felony for felony-murder. See, *e.g., Stokes v. McRae,* 247 Ga. 658, 278 S.E.2d 393 (1981); *State v. O'Blasney,* 297 N.W.2d 797 (S.D. 1980).

5. Which, if any, of the following crimes should be rendered unavailable as predicate felonies by the merger doctrine: Furnishing heroin, see *People v. Taylor,* 11 Cal. App. 3d 57, 89 Cal. Rptr. 697 (1970); armed robbery, see *People v. Burton,* 6 Cal. 3d 375, 99 Cal. Rptr. 1, 491 P.2d 793 (1971); kidnaping, see *People v. Kelso,* 64 Cal. App. 538, 134 Cal. Rptr. 364 (1976); child abuse by malnutrition and dehydration, see *People v. Shockley,* 79 Cal. App. 3d 669, 145 Cal. Rptr. 200 (1978); rape (sexual assault by means of a mop handle causing death by massive internal injuries), see *Commonwealth v. Cifizzari,* 397 Mass. 560, 492 N.E.2d 357 (1986); burglary (breaking and entering with intent to rape), *State v. Hinkle,* 229 N.W.2d 744 (Ia. 1975)?

6. For a general review of the merger doctrine, see Annot., 40 A.L.R.3d 1341 (1971).

[e] Causation Limitations

STATE V. CANOLA

Supreme Court of New Jersey

73 N.J. 206, 374 A.2d 20 (1977)

CONFORD, J.

Defendant, along with three confederates, was in the process of robbing a store when a victim of the robbery, attempting to resist the perpetration of the crime, fatally shot one of the co-felons. The sole issue for our resolution is whether, under N.J.S.A. 2A:113-1, defendant may be held liable for felony murder.

The facts . . . may be summarized as follows. The owner of a jewelry store and his employee, in an attempt to resist an armed robbery, engaged in a physical skirmish with one of the four robbers. A second conspirator, called upon for assistance, began shooting, and the store owner returned the gunfire. Both the owner and the felon, one Lloredo, were fatally shot in the exchange, the latter by the firearm of the owner.

Defendant and two others were indicted on two counts of murder. . . . The murder counts were based on the deaths, respectively, of the robbery victim and the co-felon. After trial on the murder counts defendant was found guilty on both and was sentenced to concurrent terms of life imprisonment. The Appellate Division unanimously affirmed the conviction for the murder of the robbery victim, and deni[ed] a motion to dismiss the count addressed to the homicide of the co-felon. [Defendant appealed the denial of the motion to dismiss this count to this court.]

Conventional formulations of the felony murder rule would not seem to encompass liability in this case. . . . [The early formulations of the felony murder rule] were concerned solely with situations where the felon or a confederate did the actual killing. . . . [T]he English courts never applied the felony murder rule to hold a felon guilty of the death of his co-felon at the hands of the intended victim. . . .

The precise issue in the present case is whether a broader concept than the foregoing—specifically, liability of a felon for the death of a co-felon effected by one resisting the felony—is required by the language of our statute applicable to the general area of felony murder. N.J.S.A. 2A:113-1. This reads:

> If any person, in committing or attempting to commit arson, burglary, kidnaping, rape, robbery, sodomy or any unlawful act against the peace of this state, of which the probable consequences may be bloodshed, kills another, *or if the death of anyone ensues from the committing or attempting to commit any such crime or act; . . . then such person so killing is guilty of murder.* (Emphasis added.)

Before attempting, through analysis of the statutory language itself, a resolution of the contrasting views of the statute entertained below, it will be helpful to survey the progress of the pertinent law in the other American jurisdictions. . . .

It is clearly the majority view throughout the country that, at least in theory, the doctrine of felony murder does not extend to a killing, although growing out of the commission of the felony, if directly attributable to the act of one other than the defendant or those associated with him in the unlawful enterprise. . . . This rule is sometimes rationalized on the "agency" theory of felony murder.[1]

A contrary view, which would attach liability under the felony murder rule for any death proximately resulting from the unlawful activity—even the death of a co-felon—notwithstanding the killing was by one resisting the crime, does not seem to have the present allegiance of any court. See *Johnson v. State,* 386 P.2d 336 (Okla. Ct. App. 1963); *Miers v. State,* 157 Tex. Cr. R. 572, 251 S.W.2d 404 (Cr. App. 1952); and *Hornbeck v. State,* 77 So. 2d 876 (Fla. Sup. Ct. 1955), in all of which either an officer or other innocent person was killed.

---

[1] The classic statement of the theory is found in an early case applying it in a context pertinent to the case at bar, *Commonwealth v. Campbell,* 89 Mass. (7 Allen) 541, 544 (Sup. Jud. Ct. 1863) as follows:

> No person can be held guilty of homicide unless the act is either actually or constructively his, and it cannot be his act in either sense unless committed by his own hand or by someone acting in concert with him or in furtherance of a common object or purpose.

At one time the proximate cause theory was espoused by the Pennsylvania Supreme Court, *Commonwealth v. Almeida,* 362 Pa. 596, 68 A.2d 595 (1949), cert. denied, 339 U.S. 924. The reasoning of the *Almeida* decision, involving the killing of a policeman shot by other police attempting to apprehend robbers, was distinctly circumvented when the question later arose whether it should be applied to an effort to inculpate a defendant for the killing of his co-felon at the hands of the victim of the crime. *Commonwealth v. Redline,* 391 Pa. 486, 137 A.2d 472 (1958). The court there held against liability. Examining the common-law authorities relied upon by the *Almeida* majority, the *Redline* court concluded:

> As already indicated, *Almeida* was, itself, an extension of the felony-murder doctrine by judicial decision and is not to be extended in its application beyond facts such as those to which it was applied.

137 A.2d at 482. The court then held that "in order to convict for felony-murder, the killing must have been done by the defendant or by an accomplice or confederate or by one acting in furtherance of the felonious undertaking." The court refused, however, actually to overrule the *Almeida* decision, thereby creating a distinction . . . between the situation in which the victim was an innocent party and the killing therefore merely "excusable" and that in which the deceased was a felon and the killing thus "justifiable."[2] Twelve years later the Pennsylvania court did overrule *Almeida* in a case involving Almeida's companion, Smith. [*Commonwealth ex rel. Smith v. Myers,* 438 Pa. 218, 261 A.2d 550 (1970).] The court noted, *inter alia,* the harsh criticism leveled against the common-law felony rule, its doubtful deterrent effect, the failure of the cases cited in *Almeida* to support the conclusions reached therein, the inappropriateness of tort proximate-cause principles to homicide prosecution, and the "will-of-the-wisp" distinction drawn by the *Almeida* court between justifiable and excusable homicides. . . .

[The court traced the influence of the Pennsylvania cases on the development of felony murder doctrine in Michigan.]

The Pennsylvania developments were also influential in Illinois. Prior to any of the Pennsylvania cases cited above, Illinois had adopted a rule of proximate causation in *People v. Payne,* 359 Ill. 246, 194 N.E. 539 (1935), where a felon's conviction of murder for the death of a bystander was affirmed despite the absence of any proof of who fired the fatal shot. The court found this fact immaterial (194 N.E. at 543):

> It reasonably might be anticipated that an attempted robbery would meet with resistance, during which the victim might be shot either by himself or someone else in attempting to prevent the robbery, and those attempting to perpetrate the robbery would be guilty of murder.

Nevertheless, following the Pennsylvania Redline decision, the Illinois courts refused to apply the proximate causation test where the decedent was an accomplice of the defendant killed by a victim of the felony. *People v. Morris,*

---

[2] Although, as will be seen, this distinction survives in a few jurisdictions, it has been criticized in principle, since, *inter alia,* the criminal immunity or liability of the third person killer is irrelevant to the criminal culpability of the accused felon. *See* Comment, 71 Harv. L. Rev. 1565, 1566 (1958).

1 Ill. App. 3d 566, 274 N.E.2d 898 (Ct. App. 1971). . . . The rationale, quite inconsistent with that applied in *Payne, supra,* was that the lethal act was not done in furtherance of the common design to commit a felony.

In the most recent Illinois case, *People v. Hickman,* 12 Ill. App. 3d 412, 297 N.E.2d 582 (Ct. App. 1973), *aff'd,* 59 Ill. 2d 89, 319 N.E.2d 511 (1974), cert. denied, 421 U.S. 913 (1975), where an officer chasing burglars mistakenly shot and killed a fellow officer, and liability was imposed pursuant to *Payne, supra,* yet another theory of differentiation of the co-felon killing cases was advanced—the dubious assumption-of-risk concept that the co-felon "assisted in setting in motion a chain of events which was the proximate cause of his death and therefore in the criminal law as in the civil law there is no redress for the victim." 297 N.E.2d at 586.

* * *

To be distinguished from the situation before us here, and from the generality of the cases discussed above, are the so-called "shield" cases. The first of these were the companion cases of *Taylor v. State,* 41 Tex. Cr. R. 564, 55 S.W. 961 (Cr. App. 1900), and *Keaton v. State,* 41 Tex. Cr. R. 621, 57 S.W. 1125 (Cr. App. 1900). In attempting to escape after robbing a train, defendants thrust the brakeman in front of them as a shield, as a result of which he was fatally shot by law officers. The court had no difficulty in finding defendants guilty of murder. The court in *Taylor* noted the correctness of the *Campbell* case doctrine that a person could not be held liable for homicide unless the act is either actually or constructively committed by him, but indicated it was inapplicable to a case where defendants forced deceased to occupy a place of danger in order that they might carry out the crime. In *Keaton,* the court said defendant would be responsible for the "reasonable, natural and probable result of his act" of placing deceased in danger of his life. The conduct of the defendants in cases such as these is said to reflect "express malice," justifying a murder conviction.

This review of the development in this country of the felony murder rule in relation to culpability for lethal acts of non-felons shows that, despite its early limitation to deadly acts of the felons themselves or their accomplices, the rule has undergone several transformations and can no longer be stated in terms of universal application. . . . But when the Pennsylvania court in *Redline, supra,* overruled, its prior holding of liability, in apparent return to the original position of the common law, a number of other jurisdictions followed suit, and the trend since has been towards nonliability; see Annot., 56 A.L.R.3d 237.

Reverting to our immediate task here, it is to determine whether our own statute necessarily mandates the proximate cause concept of felony murder, as thought by the Appellate Division majority. . . . [T]he view of the Appellate Division was that the "ensues clause" of N.J.S.A. 2A:113-1 must be deemed to have expanded the culpability of the felon to killings by others not confederated with him, if proximately related to the felonious enterprise, else the clause would be meaningless surplusage in the Act. However, other plausible motivations for the ensues clause can be postulated consistent with a legislative intent to adhere to the traditional limitations of the felony murder doctrine.

Judge Handler, dissenting below, suggested that the purpose of the clause might have been to expand the class of victims of the felon's acts to cover all killings within the *res gestae* of the felony, even if they formerly would have been considered too distant to be connected therewith, so long as in furtherance of the felony. . . . It seems to us, moreover, that the ensues clause could well have been intended to ensure effectuation of either or both of the following concomitants of the traditional felony murder rule: (a)that accidental or fortuitous homicides "ensuing" from the felony were contemplated for inclusion, the purpose of the statutory language being to repel the inference of a requisite of intent to kill, normally associated with the unqualified word "kill" as used in the initial clause of the section; and (b)that liability extend to acts of or participation by the accomplice of the killer-felon, as well as those of the killer himself. . . .

[A]ssuming the statute is facially susceptible of the interpretation here advocated by the State, it is appropriate to consider the public policy implications of the proposed doctrine as an extension of prior assumptions in this State as to the proper limitations of the felony murder rule.

Most modern progressive thought in criminal jurisprudence favors restriction rather than expansion of the felony murder rule. . . . It has frequently been observed that although the rule was logical at its inception, when all felonies were punishable by death, its survival to modern times when other felonies are not thought to be as blameworthy as premeditated killings is discordant with rational and enlightened views of criminal culpability and liability.

The final report of the New Jersey Criminal Law Revision Commission was, however, unwilling totally to reject the felony murder rule, concluding instead:

> It is true that we have no way of knowing how many of the homicides resulting in felony murder convictions were committed purposefully, knowingly or recklessly and how many were negligent or accidental. But it is our belief that this rule of law does lead some to refuse to assume a homicidal risk in committing other crimes.

The proposed New Jersey Penal Code does nevertheless offer limited defenses not hitherto available under the felony murder rule, and it confines the rule to deaths caused by the felon or his co-felons "in the course of and in furtherance of the (felony)." New Jersey Penal Code § 2C:11-3 (Final Report 1971). This is standard "agency theory" formulation and would seem intended to exclude liability for acts of persons other than felons or co-felons though generally arising out of the criminal episode.

In view of all of the foregoing, it appears to us regressive to extend the application of the felony murder rule beyond its classic common-law limitation to acts by the felon and his accomplices, to lethal acts of third persons not in furtherance of the felonies scheme. The language of the statute does not compel it, and, as indicated above, is entirely compatible with the traditional limitations of the rule. Tort concepts of foreseeability and proximate cause have shallow relevance to culpability for murder in the first degree.

Gradations of criminal liability should accord with degree of moral culpability for the actor's conduct. . . .

The judgment of the Appellate Division is modified so as to strike the conviction and sentencing of defendant for murder of the co-felon.

SULLIVAN, J. *(concurring in result only).*

The practical result of the majority holding is that even though some innocent person or a police officer be killed during the commission of an armed robbery, the felon would bear no criminal responsibility of any kind for that killing as long as it was not at the hand of the felon or a confederate. The legislative intent, as I see it, is otherwise.

The thrust of our felony murder statute, N.J.S.A. 2A:113-1, is to hold the criminal liable for any killing which ensues during the commission of a felony, even though the felon, or a confederate, did not commit the actual killing. The only exception I would recognize would be the death of a co-felon, which could be classified as a justifiable homicide and not within the purview of the statute. . . .

NOTES AND QUESTIONS

1. The *Canola* court's discussion of the case law reveals that analysis of causation issues under the felony-murder doctrine requires sensitivity as to both who the killer is and who the deceased is. In the easiest case, a felon who kills the victim of the felony will, along with his co-felons, be liable for felony-murder so long as the killing is in the course of the felony.

2. When someone other than the felon or a co-felon does the killing, the agency theory routinely precludes felony-murder liability especially where (as in *Canola*) a co-felon is the deceased. But the situation is not as clear-cut as depicted by the *Canola* court. While at the time of that case the court may have been justified in concluding that no court gave its "allegiance" to the view that felony-murder liability attaches in cases where persons resisting the crime kill co-felons, at least one court has since adopted such a view. See *State v. Baker,* 607 S.W.2d 153 (Mo. 1980) (felony-murder liability upheld against a felon whose co-felon was killed by victim of the felony on the basis that the death was the natural and proximate result of defendant felon's acts).

In *People v. Washington,* 62 Cal. 2d 777, 782–83, 44 Cal. Rptr. 442, 446, 402 P.2d 130, 134 (1965), Chief Justice Roger Traynor offered the following objection to finding felony-murder in cases like *Canola:*

> To invoke the felony-murder doctrine when the killing is not committed by the defendant or by his accomplice could lead to absurd results. Thus, two men rob a grocery store and flee in opposite directions. The owner of the store follows one of the robbers and kills him. Neither robber may have fired a shot. Neither robber may have been armed with a deadly weapon. If the felony-murder doctrine applied, however, the surviving robber could be convicted of first degree murder even though he was captured by a policeman and placed under arrest at the time his accomplice was killed.

Although the agency theory is the prevalent basis for limiting felony-murder liability in cases where co-felons are killed by nonfelons, historically a few courts denied liability on the alternative theory that where such killings constitute justifiable homicide, no unlawful killing occurs and hence no murder is committed. The court in the *Redline* case, discussed in *Canola,* expressed the point this way:

> [T]he victim of the homicide was one of the robbers who, while resisting apprehension in his effort to escape, was shot and killed by a policeman in the performance of his duty. Thus, the homicide was justifiable and, obviously, could not be availed of, on any rational legal theory, to support a charge of murder. How can anyone, no matter how much of an outlaw he may be, have a criminal charge lodged against him for the consequences of the lawful conduct of another person?

391 Pa. at 509, 137 A.2d at 483.

3. Where a nonfelon (say the victim of the felony or a police officer) while resisting the felony accidentally kills some other innocent party, the agency theory would also seemingly preclude felony-murder liability even though but for the felony the death would not have occurred. Yet some courts, as in the Illinois decision in the *Hickman* case noted in *Canola,* apply the felony-murder doctrine in these situations.

Unlike the cases where a co-felon is the deceased, the actions of the killer who resists the felony and accidentally kills an innocent bystander cannot be justified but are instead excused. Such killings are technically still unlawful. See the material dealing with the distinction between justification and excuse, *infra* at § 9.03. Does this distinction explain the different outcomes in *Canola* and *Hickman?*

However, as noted in the discussion of the case law in *Canola,* the Pennsylvania courts ultimately abandoned the justification/excuse distinction as a "will-of-the-wisp basis" for determining outcomes in felony-murder cases. A standard basis for rejecting the distinction is that it inappropriately hinges on the fortuity of the shooting ability of the nonfelon killer. (The cases almost invariably involve deaths caused by gunshots.) Thus if the shooter's aim is good and a co-felon is killed, the surviving felon(s) is (are) not guilty of felony-murder because the killing was justifiable. If, on the other hand, the killer's aim is bad and his shot misses the felons and kills an innocent bystander, felony murder is established.

Do you find the "bad aim" objection a sound basis for rejecting application of the justification/excuse distinction in felony-murder cases? Should a distinction be drawn between cases where nonfelons kill co-felons and cases where they kill innocent bystanders? If so, on what basis?

4. Suppose one felon shoots his gun at the teller of a bank, which the felon is in the process of robbing, but misses the teller and instead kills a co-felon. Would any of the theories discussed above preclude a finding of felony murder for the death of the co-felon?

Assuming that the applicable statute required the death to occur "in the commission of" or "in perpetration of" the felony, could (should) a court in such a situation conclude that the statute does not cover cases of felons killing co-felons because those killings are unrelated to the felonious purposes of the killer? Whatever the statutory language, could (should) courts in such cases simply conclude on policy grounds that the felony-murder doctrine is aimed at protecting *innocent* persons from death and is thus inapplicable when co-felons are killed? See *State v. Williams,* 254 So. 2d 548 (Fla. Dist. App. 1971) (no felony-murder liability); *Robbins v. People,* 142 Colo. 254, 350 P.2d 881 (1960) (felon commits felony murder when accidentally killing co-felon).

PEOPLE v. ANTICK

Supreme Court of California

123 Cal. Rptr. 475, 539 P.2d 43 (1975)

SULLIVAN, Justice.

Defendant Frank John Antick was charged by an amended information with burglary [and] murder. . . . A jury found defendant guilty as charged and determined that the burglary and the murder were of the first degree.

[Following a residential burglary in which a variety of household goods were stolen, the police encountered and followed a car loaded with such goods. Initially, two men were in the car but after briefly losing track of the car in traffic, the police came upon it as it was parked on the side of the road occupied by only the driver, Bose. After some suspicious actions by Bose, the police began to frisk him. Bose pulled out a gun and began to fire at the officers who returned the fire, bullets from which struck and killed Bose. Defendant, Antick, was later linked to Bose as his accomplice in the burglary and as the other person riding with him in the car when the police first encountered it.]

Defendant contends: (1) that his conviction on the murder charge was erroneous as a matter of law. . . . Count IV of the information charged defendant with murder in that on September 28, 1973, "during the perpetration of the burglary alleged in Count I of the information his copartner in the burglary, Donald Joseph Bose, initiated a gun battle which was the direct and unlawful cause of the death of the said Donald Joseph Bose." Count I charged defendant with the burglary of the Valentine residence on the same day. Thus count IV charged defendant with the murder of Bose committed during the burglary of the Valentine house.

On the murder count, the trial court instructed the jury on murder, malice, first degree felony murder and murder based on the theory of vicarious liability [based on *Taylor v. Superior Court* (1970), 3 Cal. 3d 578, 582–583, 91 Cal. Rptr. 275, 477 P.2d 131]. . . . Under these instructions, defendant's conviction of first degree murder may have been based upon either of two theories: (1) his participation in the commission of a burglary which resulted in the death of his accomplice, or (2) his vicarious liability for the crimes of his accomplice. Defendant contends that on the present record he cannot be convicted of murder under either theory.

The imputation of malice by application of the felony-murder doctrine has been limited by this court to those cases in which the actual killing is committed by the defendant or his accomplice. (*Taylor v. Superior Court*, . . . ; *People v. Gilbert* [63 Cal. 2d 690, 47 Cal. Rptr. 909, 408 P.2d 365 (1965)]; *People v. Washington* [62 Cal. 2d 777, 44 Cal. Rptr. 442, 402 P.2d 130 (1965)]). "When a killing is not committed by a robber or by his accomplice but by his victim, malice aforethought is not attributable to the robber, for the killing is not committed by him in the perpetration or attempt to perpetrate robbery. It is not enough that the killing was a risk reasonably to be foreseen and that the robbery might therefore be regarded as a proximate cause of the killing. Section 189 [defining first degree felony murder] requires that the felon or his accomplice commit the killing, for if he does not, the killing is not committed to perpetrate the felony. Indeed, in the present case the killing was committed to thwart a felony. To include such killings within section 189 would expand the meaning of the words —murder . . . which is committed in the perpetration . . . [of] robbery' . . . beyond common understanding." (*People v. Washington*, . . .)

However, we have been careful to point out that this limitation upon the felony-murder doctrine does not shield a defendant from criminal liability for murder when the elements of the crime, a homicide plus malice, can be established without resort to this doctrine. Thus, "[w]hen the defendant or his accomplice, with a conscious disregard for life, intentionally commits an act that is likely to cause death, and his victim or a police officer kills in reasonable response to such act, the defendant is guilty of murder. In such a case, the killing is attributable, not merely to the commission of a felony, but to the intentional act of the defendant or his accomplice committed with conscious disregard for life. . . . [T]he victim's self-defensive killing or the police officer's killing in the performance of his duty cannot be considered an independent intervening cause for which the defendant is not liable, for it is a reasonable response to the dilemma thrust upon the victim or the policeman by the intentional act of the defendant or his accomplice." (*People v. Gilbert*) Under these circumstances, "it is unnecessary to imply malice by invoking the felony-murder doctrine." (*People v. Washington*)

Where a murder committed in this manner is attributable not to the acts of the defendant himself, but rather to the acts of his accomplice, the defendant's vicarious liability for the killing is based upon "the rules defining principals and criminal conspiracies. . . . [For the defendant] [t]o be so guilty, however, the accomplice must cause the death *of another human being* by an act committed in furtherance of the common design." (*People v. Gilbert* italics added.)

The operation of these principles can best be illustrated by the following example. Three persons agree to commit a robbery, and during its commission one of them initiates a gun battle in which the victim or a police officer in reasonable response to such act kills another of the robbers. Since the immediate cause of death is the act of the victim or the officer, the felony-murder rule is not applicable to convert the killing into a murder. Nevertheless, the robber initiating the gun battle and the third accomplice are guilty of murder. The former commits a homicide, since his conduct is the proximate cause of the death of another human being; the intervening act of the victim or police officer is not an independent superseding cause, eliminating responsibility for the killing. Furthermore, in initiating the shootout the robber acts with malice, having intentionally and with conscious disregard for life engaged in conduct likely to kill. That this malice is directed at someone other than his crime partner who as a proximate result of the robber's acts is eventually killed "does not prevent the killing from constituting the offense of murder . . . [since] the law transfers the felonious intent from the original object of his attempt to the person killed and the homicide so committed is murder." . . . Since in the posited situation the robber initiating the gun battle is acting in furtherance of the common design of all three participants, the third robber as well may be held vicariously liable for the murder. (*People v. Gilbert.* . . .)

On the other hand, neither the felony-murder doctrine nor the theory of vicarious liability may be used to hold a defendant guilty of murder solely because of the acts of an accomplice, if the accomplice himself could not have been found guilty of the same offense for such conduct. . . .

Similar reasoning compelled our recent decision in *People v. Taylor*. . . . There Taylor was convicted of the murder of his accomplice Smith who was shot and killed by the victims during a robbery at their liquor store. Smith and one Daniels entered the store while Taylor remained in the getaway car. Taylor was found guilty on a theory of vicarious liability for the acts of his confederate Daniels who by threatening the life of one of the victims had provoked in response their return fire which killed Smith. However, Daniels had been separately tried and acquitted of the murder charge. Reversing Taylor's murder conviction but affirming his robbery conviction, we held that the doctrine of collateral estoppel precluded "the conviction of an accused based on his vicarious responsibility for the acts of a previously acquitted confederate."

Applying these principles to the case at bench, we first observe that on the uncontradicted evidence defendant himself did not participate in the immediate events which preceded his accomplice's death. Under the People's version of the facts, which we accept as accurate for purposes of this discussion, Bose initiated a gun battle with the police in order to escape apprehension for a burglary which he and defendant had recently committed. The police officer responded by killing Bose. As the immediate cause of death was the act of the officer, it is clear that the felony-murder rule does not operate to convert the killing into a murder for which defendant may be liable by virtue of his participation in the underlying burglary.

Nor may defendant be held legally accountable for Bose's death based upon his vicarious liability for the crimes of his accomplice. In order to predicate defendant's guilt upon this theory, it is necessary to prove that Bose committed a murder . . . in other words, that he caused the death of another human being [and] that he acted with malice.

It is well settled that Bose's conduct in initiating a shootout with police officers may establish the requisite malice. As we have noted on a number of occasions, a person who initiates a gun battle in the course of committing a felony intentionally and with a conscious disregard for life commits an act that is likely to cause death. . . . However, Bose's malicious conduct did not result in the unlawful killing of another human being, but rather in Bose's own death. The only homicide which occurred was the justifiable killing of Bose by the police officer. Defendant's criminal liability certainly cannot be predicated upon the actions of the officer. As Bose could not be found guilty of murder in connection with his own death, it is impossible to base defendant's liability for this offense upon his vicarious responsibility for the crime of his accomplice.

The judgment is reversed.

NOTES

1. *Antick* should be considered again after studying the material on accomplice liability in Chapter 8, *infra*. The case is useful for present purposes as a summary of the unique manner in which the California courts have interpreted the felony-murder statute. Moreover, *Antick* illustrates some of the ways in which the felony-murder rule intersects with and diverges from the doctrine of depraved heart murder.

2. Several jurisdictions have upheld convictions of felons' depraved heart killings arising during the commission of felonies. See, *e.g., People v. Braithwaite,* 63 N.Y.2d 889, 482 N.Y.S.2d 253, 472 N.E.2d 29 (1984) (felon guilty of murdering co-felon killed during shootout with robbery victim); *Blansett v. State,* 556 S.W.2d 322 (Tex. Crim. App. 1977) (felon guilty of murdering police officer accidentally killed by another police officer's gunshots in response to felon's armed attempt to release his brother from jail).

[f] Abolish Felony-Murder?

After having studied the controversial doctrine of felony-murder, brief attention should be directed to the question of whether the doctrine, even with the various attempts to limit its scope, should be retained. Many of the pros and cons of this question have been presented in the above cases and materials. The brief excerpts below are meant to supplement that discussion.

Scholarly defenses of the felony-murder doctrine are few. A rare example is reflected in the following from Crump and Crump, *In Defense of Felony Murder,* 8 Harv. J.L. Pub. Pol'y 359, 362–64, 367–71 (1985):

> Such diverse philosophers and judges as Jeremy Bentham, H.L.A. Hart, Sir James Fitzjames Stephen, Joel Feinberg, and Chief Justice Warren Burger have noted the disrespect that the law engenders when its response is disproportionate to public evaluations of the severity of an alleged violation. Many penal codes declare proportionality to be among their major objectives. The classification and grading of offenses so that the entire scheme of defined crimes squares with societal perceptions of proportionality—of "just deserts"—is a fundamental goal of the law of crimes.
>
> The felony murder doctrine serves this goal. . . . Felony murder reflects a societal judgment that an intentionally committed robbery that causes the death of a human being is qualitatively more serious than an identical robbery that does not. Perhapsthis judgment could have been embodied in a newly defined offense called "robbery-resulting-in-deat h;" but while a similar approach has been adopted in some areas of the criminal law, such a proliferation of offense definitions is undesirable. Thus the felony murder

doctrine reflects the conclusion that a robbery that causes death is more closely akin to murder than to robbery. If this conclusion accurately reflects societal attitudes, and if classification of crimes is to be influenced by such attitudes in order to avoid depreciation of the seriousness of the offense and to encourage respect for the law, then the felony murder doctrine is an appropriate classificatory device.

There is impressive empirical evidence that this classification does indeed reflect widely shared societal attitudes. . . . [C]haracterizing a robbery-homicide solely as robbery would have the undesirable effect of communicating to the citizenry that the law does not consider a crime that takes a human life to be different from one that does not—a message that would be indistinguishable, in the minds of many, from a devaluation of human life.

Another aspect of condemnation is the expression of solidarity with the victims of crime. If we as a society label a violent offense in a manner that depreciates its significance, we communicate to the victim by implication that we do not understand his suffering. He may be left with the impression that he is unprotected—or even that he is disoriented, having himself failed to understand the rules of the game. Felony murder is a useful doctrine because it reaffirms to the surviving family of a felony-homicide victim the kinship the society as a whole feels with him by denouncing in the strongest language of the law the intentional crime that produced the death.

* * *

Deterrence is often cited as one justification for the felony murder doctrine. . . . Deterrence is the policy most often recognized in the cases. Scholars, however, tend to dismiss this rationale, using such arguments as the improbability that felons will know the law, the unlikelihood that a criminal who has formed the intent to commit a felony will refrain from acts likely to cause death, or the assertedly small number of felony-homicides.

The trouble with these criticisms is that they underestimate the complexity of deterrence. There may be more than a grain of truth in the proposition that felons, if considered as a class, evaluate risks and benefits differently than members of other classes in society. The conclusion does not follow, however, that felons cannot be deterred, or that criminals are so different from other citizens that they are impervious to inducements or deterrents that would affect people in general. There is mounting evidence that serious crime is subject to deterrence if consequences are adequately communicated. The felony-murder rule is just the sort of simple, common sense, readily enforceable, and widely known principle that is likely to result in deterrence.

The argument against deterrence often proceeds on the additional assumption that felony-murder is addressed only to accidental killings and cannot result in their deterrence. By facilitating proof and simplifying the concept of liability, however, felony-murder may deter intentional killings as well. The robber who kills intentionally, but who might claim under oath to have acted accidentally, is thus told that he will be deprived of the benefit of this claim. By institutionalizing this effect and consistently condemning robbery-homicides as qualitatively more blameworthy than robberies, the law leads the robber who kills intentionally to expect this treatment for himself. Furthermore, the contrary argument proves too much even as to robbery-killings that arefactually accidental. The proposition that accidental killings cannot be deterred isinconsistent with the widespread belief that the penalizing of negligence, and even the imposition of strict liability, may have deterrent consequences.

For a thorough explanation of, if not justification for, the felony-murder rule, see Cole, *Killings During Crime: Toward a Discriminating Theory of Strict Liability,* 28 Am. Crim. L. Rev. 73 (1990).

Chief Justice Roger Traynor, in People v. Washington, 62 Cal. 2d777, 781, 44 Cal. Rptr. 442, 445, 402 P.2d 130, 133 (1965), offers the following objections to deterrence theory as a basis for justifying the felony-murder rule:

> The purpose of the felony-murder rule is to deter felons from killing negligently or accidentally by holding them strictly responsible for killings they commit. . . .
>
> It is contended, however, that another purpose of the felony-murder rule is to prevent the commission of robberies. Neither the common-law rationale of the rule nor the Penal Code supports this contention. In every robbery there is a possibility that the victim will resist and kill. The robber has little control over such a killing once the robbery is undertaken. . . . To impose an additional penalty for the killing would discriminate between robbers, not on the basis of any difference in their own conduct, but solely on the basis of the response by others that the robber's conduct happened to induce. An additional penalty for a homicide committed by the victim would deter robbery haphazardly at best. To "prevent stealing, [the law] would do better to hang one thief in every thousand by lot." (Holmes, *The Common Law,* p.58.)

Professor George Fletcher, *Reflections on Felony-Murder,* 12 Sw. U. L. Rev. 413, 426–28 (1981), offers these retributively oriented objections to the doctrine:

> There is [an] approach to the felony-murder rule, which, if valid, would justify full enforcement. In this alternative conception the principle of felony-murder reflects two unrefined ways of thinking about criminal responsibility. One mode of thought stresses the taint that inheres in causing death, whether the homicide is culpable or not. The second mode of thought takes the preliminary act of wrongdoing, the felony, as a rationale for holding the felon accountable for the deadly consequences of his actions. Both of these modes of thought require explication and criticism, for they both enjoy far more influence than they deserve.
>
> The principle of tainting dates back to the origins of prosecution for criminal homicide. In thirteenth-century England, the assumption was that if one person caused the death of another, the killing itself upset the natural order; some response was necessary to expiate the killing and thus to expunge the taint. As the Bible demands the sacrifice of a heifer in cases

of homicides by unknown persons, English law extracted two forfeitures in every case of manslaying. First, the instrument of death was forfeited to the Crown as deodand. Second, the killer forfeited his lands and his goods. These forfeitures applied in every case of unjustified killing. If, in addition, the killing occurred without excuse, that is absent the conditions of *se defendendo and per infortunium,* the slayer was subject to the death penalty for murder.

The model of taint and expiation haunts the way our courts think about criminal homicide. The felon must answer for a human death for no reason other than that he or his accomplice causes it. The felon is tainted by causing and the state responds by seeking expiation. It is important to distinguish expiating the taint of killing from justly punishing for faultfully causing death. The taint arises regardless of fault or blame; punishment is just only so far as it is proportional to fault. The notion of expiating a taint reflects a conception of the world that, if brought to consciousness, most lawyers would vehemently reject. Yet the notion of tainting might be one of the subconscious props for the contemporary persistence of the felony-murder rule.

The other unrefined mode of thought behind the rule begins not with the deadly outcome, but with the felonious background. That someone engages in a felony lowers the threshold of moral responsibility for the resulting death. If there is a principle behind this way of thinking, it is that a wrongdoer must run the risk that things will turn out worse than she expects. The same principle has motivated common law courts and legislatures to reject the claim of mistake in cases of abducting infants, statutory rape, and assaulting a police officer. If the act is wrong, even as the defendant conceives the facts to be, then she presumably has no grounds for complaining if the facts turn out to be worse than she expects. . . .

These two modes of thought—the practice of tainting and the principle that the wrongdoer runs the risk—violate a basic principle of just punishment. Punishment must be proportional to wrongdoing. When the felony-murder rule converts an accidental death into first-degree murder, then punishment is rendered disproportionate to the wrong for which the offender is personally responsible. Tainting is no substitute for criteria of moral responsibility, and the principle that the wrongdoer must run the risk explicitly obscures the question of actual responsibility for the harmful result.

The theory of just punishment is called the retributive theory. Before we criticize retribution and the *lex talionis* as outmoded, we should realize how much worse it is to make the punishment fit not the crime, but the result for which the offender is not personally to blame.

It may be that in the thinking of many people, the felony-murder rule finds its warrant in principles of deterrence as well as in the residual influence of early common law notions of taint and expiation. But of course, deterrence is not an apology for treating like cases differently; if there is no sound basis for distinguishing between thieves killing in an automobile accident and others doing so, then the remote possibility of deterring thieves from escaping the scene of the crime hardly justifies convicting [the thieves] of first degree murder.

See *People v. Fuller,* discussed in note 3, p. 572, *supra.*

Finally, for an argument that the felony-murder doctrine is unconstitutional either (1)as a presumption of malice violative of due process by shifting the burden of proof on the *mens rea* issue to the defendant or by usurping the jury function or (2)as a violation of the cruel and unusual punishments clause by imposing strict liability for a serious, nonregulatory crime, see generally Roth and Sundby, *The Felony-Murder Rule: A Doctrine at Constitutional Crossroads,* 70 Cornell L. Rev. 446 (1985).

[B] Manslaughter

[1] Voluntary Manslaughter: The Provocation Formula

STEPHEN, A DIGEST OF THE CRIMINAL LAW 164–66 (1877)

Homicide, which would otherwise be murder, is not murder, but manslaughter, if the act by which death is caused is done in the heat of passion, caused by provocation, as hereinafter defined, unless the provocation was sought or voluntarily provoked by the offender as an excuse for killing or doing bodily harm.

The following acts may . . . amount to provocation:

(a) An assault and battery of such a nature as to inflict actual bodily harm, or great insult, is a provocation to the person assaulted.

(b) If two persons quarrel and fight upon equal terms and upon the spot, whether with deadly weapons or otherwise, each gives provocation to the other, whichever is right in the quarrel, and whichever strikes the first blow.

(c) An unlawful imprisonment is a provocation to the person imprisoned, but not to the by-standers, though an unlawful imprisonment may amount to such a breach of the peace as to entitle a by-stander to prevent it by the use of force sufficient for that purpose. An arrest by officers of justice, whose character as such is known, but who are acting under a warrant so irregular as to make the arrest illegal, is provocation to the person illegally arrested, but not to by-standers.

(d) The sight of the act of adultery committed with his wife is provocation to the husband of the adulteress on the part both of the adulterer and of the adulteress.

(e) The sight of the act of sodomy committed upon a man's son is provocation to the father on the part of the person committing the offense.

(f) Neither words, nor gestures, nor injuries to property, nor breaches of contract amount to provocation within this article, except [perhaps] words expressing an intention to inflict actual bodily injury, accompanied by some act which shows that such injury is intended; but words used at the time of an assault—slight in itself—may be taken into account in estimating the degree of provocation given by a blow.

(g) The employment of lawful force against the person of another is not a provocation to the person against whom it is employed.

Provocation does not extenuate the guilt of homicide unless the person provoked is, at the time when he does the act, deprived of the power of self-control by the provocation which he has received; and, in deciding the question whether this was or was not the case, regard must be had to the nature of the act by which the offender causes death, to the time which elapsed between the provocation and the act which caused death, to the offender's conduct during that interval, and to all other circumstances tending to show the state of his mind.

TRIPP V. STATE

Court of Special Appeals of Maryland

374 A.2d 384 (1977)

MOYLAN, Judge.

Murder, which is unmitigated homicide, stands higher on the ladder of culpability than manslaughter, which is mitigated homicide. Because the negative element of non-mitigation is initially presumed, . . . and need not be proved unless and until a genuine jury question as to mitigation has been raised, the State leaps . . . to the murder plateau when it shows an intentional killing by the defendant. It . . . is not obliged to [engage in the] operation of negating mitigation unless the defendant meets his production burden. . . .

* * *

On October 12, 1974, the appellant went on a homicidal rampage . . . with a .38 caliber revolver. He shot in the chest and killed 36-year-old Hazel Wilson, with whom he had been cohabiting over a two-year period until roughly one week before the killing. [He also shot and killed Wilson's seven-year-old son, her eleven-year-old niece, and her mother, and shot and seriously wounded Wilson's eleven-year-old son.] There was no dispute as to the homicidal agency of the appellant—only as to his *mens rea* in two regards. The jury found the appellant to have been sane at the time of the attacks. The jury found the appellant guilty of four charges of murder in the first degree and of one charge of assault with intent to murder.

* * *

[A]ppellant[] conten[ds] . . . that Judge Levin committed prejudicial error by declining to instruct the jury on the subject of manslaughter. . . . The appellant is . . . correct in his preliminary assertion of law that a trial judge is obliged to instruct the jury on every essential point of law supported by the evidence when requested to do so by either side. . . .

The chink in the appellant's armor is the phrase "supported by the evidence." When instructing on the law of homicide, as when instructing on any other part of the law, it is not only required but it is, indeed, inappropriate to instruct upon a principle of law not suggested by the evidence in the case. . . .

The appellant urges that it is necessary to discuss manslaughter because it involves the same *corpus delicti* and the same homicidal agency as are involved with the murder charge but simply a lesser degree of blameworthiness—a diminished *mens rea*. This does not serve to relieve the appellant of the necessity that each principle of law to be discussed—even those involving a diminished *mens rea* for the same offense—must be supported by the evidence in the case. . . .

* * *

[I]nstructions must be restricted to those legal principles supported by the evidence and therefore material to the case at hand.

* * *

In appellate brief and argument . . . the appellant has narrowed the focus of pertinent manslaughter relief. It is not involuntary manslaughter but voluntary manslaughter being urged by him. He narrows the focus further by claiming mitigation through hot-blooded response to legally adequate provocation. The suggested form of the legally adequate provocation is strangely blurred but seems to bear an at least impressionistic resemblance to that involving the sudden discovery of a spouse in an act of adultery. We will now turn to an examination of whether the evidence supports the necessary elements for extenuation of this variety.

* * *

. . . *Whitehead v. State,* 9 Md. App. 7, 10–11, 262 A.2d 316, 319, . . . et out fully the elements of provocation:

[T]here may be a homicide which would otherwise be murder which is reduced to manslaughter by circumstances of alleviation or mitigation. Such a case is where the circumstances surrounding the homicide establish that it was provoked. For the "Rule of Provocation" to be invoked there are four requirements:

(1) There must have been adequate provocation;

(2) The killing must have been in the heat of passion;

(3) It must have been a sudden heat of passion, that is the killing must have followed the provocation before there had been a reasonable opportunity for the passionto cool;

(4) There must have been a causal connection between the provocation, the passion, and the fatal act.

Against these bench marks, we will now measure the evidence at hand.

* * *

Except for rare instances of "transferred intent," where one aims at A, misses and hits B by mistake, a defendant seeking to extenuate an intentional killing upon the theory that he killed in hot-blooded rage brought on by the provocative acts of his victim is limited to those killings where the victim is the provocateur. In the present case, Hazel Wilson was the only victim arguably in that category. In no event could the killings of [the other victims] be mitigated by even hot-blooded response to actions not of their doing. . . .

* * *

The appellant is in deep trouble when it comes to the legal sufficiency of the evidence to establish the elements of provocation. There must, of course, be established all of the elements. We conclude that the appellant failed to establish at least three of the necessary four elements. Taking the evidence in the light most favorable to the appellant, with all inferences that fairly can be drawn therefrom, he may arguably have a jury issue with respect to the fourth element:

"(4) There must have been a causal connection between the provocation, the passion, and the fatal act."

The story that emerges, from the testimony of the 11-year-old boy who lived and from the testimony of a neighboring minister who had but scant knowledge, is at best a surrealistic blur. It appeared that the appellant had been living with Hazel Wilson and her two sons for approximately two years, the last two months of which had been in the second-floor apartment at 1700 Guilford Avenue. When she would go out drinking or would make periodic visits to her former husband (or actual legal husband, for all we know), the appellant would be afflicted by fits of jealousy. He would beat Hazel Wilson. One week before the killings, the minister observed the appellant, gun in hand, dragging Hazel Wilson along. Six days before the murders, he came to the minister's church, where Hazel Wilson was then visiting, also with a gun in his hand. Events reached a critical impasse on the Tuesday, four days before the killings, when Hazel Wilson and her sons moved downstairs to the first-floor apartment and moved in with Hazel Wilson's mother. Arguments and efforts to get Hazel Wilson to return to the apartment with the appellant continued sporadically throughout the final week.

From this, it might fairly be inferred that the actions of Hazel Wilson 1) in going out and drinking, 2) in visiting periodically her husband (or ex-husband) and 3) in moving out of the second-floor apartment had provoked a passion in the appellant and that that passion was the effective cause of his decision to kill Hazel Wilson. This, however, is but one of four constituent elements, all of which must be present for legally recognizable provocation.

We turn our attention to the second necessary element:

"(2) The killing must have been in the heat of passion."

This is the subjective question of whether a particular defendant was actually in the heat of passion when he killed. (The objective, or reasonable man, question will constitute the next element to be considered.) All of the evidence in the case, clearly and decisively, indicated that the appellant was not in the heat of passion when he killed. At least a week had elapsed since the onset of domestic argument with Hazel Wilson. Four days had elapsed since she moved downstairs. Several hours before the killing, he utilized a ruse, directed toward Hazel Wilson's mother, in order to gain entrance to the downstairs apartment and particularly to the basement, where he manipulated in some fashion the lock to the basement door. After killing Hazel Wilson, he attempted to lure the other members of the family out of hiding in what inferentially appeared to be an effort to kill all witnesses to his first killing. The gun that he used was never recovered. He wore gloves at the time of the killing. He was seen by one witness in a West North Avenue grocery store less than an hour after the killing, blithely buying groceries. When he returned to the crime scene between one and one-half and two hours after the killings, he approached, with groceries in hand, feigning total ignorance of and surprise at the situation he there found.

Counterbalancing this evidence of actual, cool deliberation is not one shred of evidence indicating hot-blooded fury. . . .

* * *

The next element to be considered is the third:"

(3) It must have been a sudden heat of passion, that is the killing must have followed the provocation before there had been a reasonable opportunity for the passion to cool."

This element is the objective counterpart of the preceding one. . . . We are here concerned with the objective test of whether there had been a sufficient cooling time for the passions of an average and reasonable man to abate. Deferring for the moment consideration of the inadequacy of the cause, the cause of the appellant's distress was jealousy. Eleven-year-old Derak Wilson testified that the appellant had argued with Hazel Wilson over the fact that "she go out and get drinks" and that "she be talking to somebody else" regularly over an unspecified but significant period of time. . . . A major flare-up of . . . domestic unrest had occurred at least one week before the killings. The situation had so deteriorated that Hazel Wilson moved out at least four days before the killings. We conclude that the evidence in this regard shows clearly and decisively that there was sufficient cooling time for the average and reasonable man to have his passions abate. . . .

* * *

We were dealing with this very question when we held that a jury instruction on the subject of manslaughter was not required in *Bartram v. State* [364 A.2d 1119 (Md. App. 1976)]. There, the act of provocation was legally adequate beyond dispute: the outraged wife literally observed her husband in an act of adultery before her very eyes. There, the provoking act was rather clearly the effective cause of the killing. The fatal flaw, however, for purposes of invoking the law of provocation in that case, was the lapse of time involved between cause and effect. The law, in its wisdom, extenuates certain killings by lowering the degree of blameworthiness because it recognizes human frailty when one is in the clutches of blind and sudden fury. The long-smoldering grudge, by way of contrast, may be psychologically just as compelling a force as the sudden impulse but it, unlike the impulse, is a telltale characteristic of premeditation. The law extenuates certain killings not simply because they have been provoked but because there has also been the lack of time between the provoking cause and the impulsive response to think about the consequences or the alternatives. In the case of the spontaneous explosion, reason has no opportunity to intervene; in the case of the "slow burn," it has. We demand that it intervene whenever it can. . . .

* * *

Even in the face of blazing jealousy, what is demanded of a spouse is, *a fortiori,* demanded of one who is not a spouse.

The absolutely foreclosing aspect, as we consider the availability of the defense of provocation, is our evaluation of the first essential element of that defense:

"(1) There must have been adequate provocation."

The appellant sets himself a difficult task in arguing now that the killing was the result of hot-blooded provocation. . . .

We begin with the proposition that there must be not simply provocation in psychological fact, but one of certain fairly well-defined classes of provocation recognized as being adequate as a matter of law. . . . "Passion on the part of the slayer, no matter how violent, will not relieve him from liability for murder unless it was engendered by a *provocation which the law recognizes as being reasonable and adequate.*" (Emphasis supplied)

The most that emerges from the scant and ambiguous evidence is a state of mind in the appellant of diffuse and undifferentiated jealousy. . . . Neither "going out and getting drinks" nor "talking to somebody else" remotely constitutes an act of legally recognized provocation. To begin with, they are acts of lawful behavior which, as Perkins Criminal Law (Second Ed., 1969), points out, at 54, do not ordinarily serve as triggers for legally sufficient provocation: "[T]he provocation is itself an unlawful act of another, since a lawful act, even if it involves physical violence, is not recognized by law as a mitigating circumstance."

The same holds true with respect to Hazel Wilson's act of moving out of the upstairs apartment, where she cohabitated with the appellant, and into her mother's apartment on the first floor of the same house. . . .

Nor does the third and final possible source of the appellant's passion constitute legally recognized provocation. This source was suggested by the testimony of the neighboring minister:

"I said, —Man, you seem to be an intelligent man. What is going on? Why you all fighting and carrying on that way? Well . . . ' He said to me—tried to tell me something about her other husband, you know. Said that this Hazel was getting some money from her first husband, and what have you. She will go by there and get it every weekend. I think that was the problem that he was accusing her of her first husband."

For all which the evidence in this case reveals, Hazel Wilson's "other husband" was still her legal and, therefore, only husband.

Of the recognized varieties of action which constitute legally adequate provocation, the only one remotely suggested by the circumstances in this case is that of discovering a spouse in an act of adultery. As a necessary precondition for this type of provocation, there must be, at the very least, some significant sexual contact, if not literally intercourse itself. The law anciently required a spouse unexpectedly to discover the erring spouse *in flagrante delicto.* In its more modern and liberalized manifestations, it has been extended to situations where the spouse has suddenly been told of the other spouse's infidelity or has strong reason to believe that there has been such infidelity. Even in the liberalized forms, however, the indispensable predicate is sexual intercourse. . . . One cannot, as the appellant here apparently seeks to do, take a law which speaks exclusively of the unexpected discovery of one's legal spouse in an act of adultery and extrapolate from that a more general principle dealing with any act by any object of one's affection which gives rise to a state of jealousy.

Even more foreclosing than the innocuous nature of the acts, however, is the legally uncountenanced status of the actors. Even where the provocative act is the direct, unexpected and visual discovery of sexual intercourse in progress, the defense is still only available to the "cuckold" who is a lawful spouse. LaFave and Scott, Criminal Law, speaks to this very point, at 576: "The rule of mitigation does not, however, extend beyond the marital relationship so as to include engaged persons, divorced couples and unmarried lovers as where a man is enraged at the discovery of his mistress in the sexual embrace of another man."

* * *

Each of the four elements is a *sine qua non* for a defense of mitigation based upon hot-blooded response to legally adequate provocation. The evidence was palpably insufficient with respect to at least three of the elements, all of which would be necessary to generate a genuine jury issue. . . .

* * *

Judgments affirmed

NOTE

Although one of the authors of this casebook has shown that judges of the common law, before the middle of the 19th century, did not restrict the reach of the provocation formula, see Singer, *The Resurgence of Mens Rea: I— Provocation, Emotional Disturbance; and the Model Penal Code,* 27 B.C. L. Rev. 243 (1986), Stephen's list and the *Tripp* case reflect the widespread contrary understanding that from early on, provocation was limited to certain well-defined circumstances. Many courts that continue to apply this approach appear uneasy about operating within the rigidity of the common law structure. For example, in *Freddo v. State,* 127 Tenn. 376, 155 S.W. 170 (1913), the court upheld the second degree murder conviction of the defendant, a young railroad worker who killed a colleague after the latter had called the defendant a "son of a bitch." The court found that defendant was "a quiet, peaceable, high-minded young man," who was "morally well trained." Due to his gratitude to his foster mother who raised him after his mother died while he was an infant, defendant "respected womanhood beyond the average . . . and had a decided antipathy to language of an obscene trend or that reflected on womanhood." Deceased, a "habitually foul-mouthed, overbearing, and nagging" person, had on several occasions called defendant a "son of a bitch" knowing that he found the epithet deeply offensive. In the course of a work-related argument between the two, the deceased again hurled the epithet at defendant who became so enraged that he hit deceased with a steel bar, killing him.

The court noted that according to the writers, "no mere . . . language, however violent or offensive [is] sufficient provocation for taking life." Nevertheless the court, obviously troubled by its decision to sustain the defendant's murder conviction, urged executive clemency:

> In view of the very good character of the young plaintiff in error, as disclosed in the record, and of the peculiar motive and the circumstances under which he acted, we feel constrained to and do recommend to the Governor of the state that his sentence be commuted to such punishment as the executive may, in the light of this record and opinion, in his discretion think proper.

As early as the mid-19th century, some courts had rejected the tradition of permitting the jury to consider provocation evidence only in certain "legally sufficient" circumstances. Thus, in *Maher v. People,* 10 Mich. 212, 81 Am. Dec. 781 (1862), the court stated,

> The principle involved in the question, and which I think clearly deducible from the majority of well considered cases, would seem to suggest as the true general rule, that reason should, at the time of the act, be disturbed or obscured by passion to an extent which *might render* ordinary men, of fair average disposition, *liable* to act rashly or without due deliberation or reflection, and from passion, rather than judgment.

> In determining whether the provocation is sufficient or reasonable, *ordinary human nature,* or the average of men recognized as men of fair average mind and disposition, should be taken as the standard—unless, indeed, the person whose guilt is in question be shown to have some peculiar weakness of mind or infirmity of temper, not arising from wickedness of heart or cruelty of disposition.

> The judge, it is true, must, to some extent, assume to decide upon the sufficiency of the alleged provocation, when the question arises upon the admission of testimony, and when it is so clear as to admit of no reasonable doubt upon any theory, that the alleged provocation could not have had any tendency to produce such state of mind, in ordinary men, he may properly exclude the evidence; but, if the alleged provocation be such as to admit of any reasonable doubt, whether it might not have had such tendency, it is much safer . . . and more in accordance with the principle, to let the

evidence go to the jury under the proper instructions. [T]he question of the reasonableness or adequacy of the provocation must depend upon the facts of each particular case. That can, with no propriety, be called a rule (or a question) of law which must vary with, and depend upon the almost infinite variety of facts presented by the various cases as they arise. The law cannot with justice assume by the light of past decision, to catalogue all the various facts and combinations of facts which shall be held to constitute reasonable or adequate provocation. Scarcely two past cases can be found which are identical in all their circumstances; and there is no reason to hope for greater uniformity in the future. Provocations will be given without reference to any previous model, and the passions they excite will not consult the precedents.

In studying the following case, consider whether the courts should continue the traditional approach of limiting provocation evidence to certain circumstances or adopt the more flexible approach expressed above in the quote from *Maher*.

People v. Berry

Supreme Court of California

134 Cal. Rptr. 415, 556 P.2d 777 (1976)

SULLIVAN, Justice.

Defendant Albert Joseph Berry was charged . . . with one count of murder. A jury found defendant guilty as charged and determined that the murder was of the first degree. Defendant was sentenced to state prison for the term prescribed by law. He appeals from the judgment of conviction.

Defendant contends that there is sufficient evidence in the record to show that he committed the homicide while in a state of uncontrollable rage caused by provocation . . . and therefore that it was error for the trial court to fail to instruct the jury on voluntary manslaughter as indeed he had requested. He claims that he was entitled to an instruction on voluntary manslaughter as defined by statute since the killing was done upon a sudden quarrel or heat of passion. . . .

Defendant, a cook, 46 years old, and Rachel Passah, a 20-year-old girl from Israel, were married on May 27, 1974. Three days later Rachel went to Israel by herself, returning on July 13, 1974. On July 23, 1974, defendant choked Rachel into unconsciousness. She was treated at a hospital where she reported her strangulation by defendant to an officer of the San Francisco Police Department. On July 25, Inspector Sammon, who had been assigned to the case, met with Rachel and as a result of the interview a warrant was issued for defendant's arrest.

While Rachel was at the hospital, defendant removed his clothes from their apartment and stored them in a Greyhound Bus Depot locker. He stayed overnight at the home of a friend, Mrs. Jean Berk, admitting to her that he had choked his wife. On July 26, he telephoned Mrs. Berk and informed her that he had killed Rachel with a telephone cord on that morning at their apartment. The next day Mrs. Berk and two others telephoned the police to report a possible homicide and met Officer Kelleher at defendant's apartment. They gained entry and found Rachel on the bathroom floor. A pathologist from the coroner's office concluded that the cause of Rachel's death was strangulation. Defendant was arrested on August 1, 1974, and confessed to the killing.

At trial defendant did not deny strangling his wife, but claimed through his own testimony and the testimony of a psychiatrist, Dr. Martin Blinder, that he was provoked into killing her because of a sudden and uncontrollable rage so as to reduce the offense to one of voluntary manslaughter. He testified that upon her return from Israel, Rachel announced to him that while there she had fallen in love with another man, one Yako, and had enjoyed his sexual favors, that he was coming to this country to claim her and that she wished a divorce. Thus commenced a tormenting two weeks in which Rachel alternately taunted defendant with her involvement with Yako and at the same time sexually excited defendant, indicating her desire to remain with him. Defendant's detailed testimony, summarized below, chronicles this strange course of events.

After their marriage, Rachel lived with defendant for only three days and then left for Israel. Immediately upon her return to San Francisco she told defendant about her relationship with and love for Yako. This brought about further argument and a brawl that evening in which defendant choked Rachel and she responded by scratching him deeply many times. Nonetheless they continued to live together. Rachel kept taunting defendant with Yako and demanding a divorce. She claimed she thought she might be pregnant by Yako. She showed defendant pictures of herself with Yako. Nevertheless, during a return trip from Santa Rosa, Rachel demanded immediate sexual intercourse with defendant in the car, which was achieved; however upon reaching their apartment, she again stated that she loved Yako and that she would not have intercourse with defendant in the future.

On the evening of July 22d defendant and Rachel went to a movie where they engaged in heavy petting. When they returned home and got into bed, Rachel announced that she had intended to make love with defendant, "But I am saving myself for this man Yako, so I don't think I will." Defendant got out of bed and prepared to leave the apartment whereupon Rachel screamed and yelled at him. Defendant choked her into unconsciousness.

Two hours later defendant called a taxi for his wife to take her to the hospital. He put his clothes in the Greyhound bus station and went to the home of his friend Mrs. Berk for the night. The next day he went to Reno and returned the day after. Rachel informed him by telephone that there was a warrant for his arrest as a result of her report to the police about the choking incident. On July 25th defendant returned to the apartment to talk to Rachel, but she was out. He slept there overnight. Rachel returned around 11 am the next day. Upon seeing defendant there, she said, "I suppose you have come here to kill me." Defendant responded, "yes," changed his response to "no," and then again to "yes," and finally stated "I have really come to talk to you." Rachel began screaming. Defendant grabbed her by the shoulder and tried to stop her screaming. She continued. They struggled and finally defendant strangled her with a telephone cord.

Dr. Martin Blinder, a physician and psychiatrist, called by the defense, testified that Rachel was a depressed, suicidally inclined girl and that this suicidal impulse led her to involve herself ever more deeply in a dangerous situation with defendant. She did this by sexually arousing him and taunting him into jealous rages in an unconscious desire to provoke him into killing her and thus consummating her desire for suicide. Throughout the period commencing with her return from Israel until her death, that is from July 13 to July 26, Rachel continually provoked defendant with sexual taunts and incitements, alternating acceptance and rejection of him. This conduct was accompanied by repeated references to her involvement with another man; it led defendant to choke her on two occasions, until finally she achieved her unconscious desire and was strangled. Dr. Blinder testified that as a result of this cumulative series of provocations, defendant at the time he fatally strangled Rachel, was in a state of uncontrollable rage, completely under the sway of passion.

We first take up defendant's claim that on the basis of the foregoing evidence he was entitled to an instruction on voluntary manslaughter as defined by statute which is "the unlawful killing of a human being, without malice . . . upon a sudden quarrel or heat of passion." In *People v. Valentine* (1946), 28 Cal. 2d 121, 69 P.2d 1, this court, in an extensive review of the law of manslaughter, specifically approved the following quotation from *People v. Logan* (1917) 175 Cal. 45, 48–49, 164 P. 1121, as a correct statement of the law:

> In the present condition of our law *it is left to the jurors* to say whether or not the facts and circumstances in evidence are sufficient to lead them to believe that the defendant did, or to create a reasonable doubt in their minds as to whether or not he did, commit his offense under a heat of passion. The jury is further to be admonished and advised by the court that this heat of passion must be such a passion as would naturally be aroused in the mind of an ordinarily reasonable person under the given facts and circumstances, and that, consequently, no defendant may set up his own standard of conduct and justify or excuse himself because in fact his passions were aroused, unless further the jury believe that the facts and circumstances were sufficient to arouse the passions of the ordinarily reasonable man. . . . For the fundamental of the inquiry is whether or not the defendant's reason was, at the time of his act, so disturbed or obscured by some passion—not necessarily fear and never, of course, the passion for revenge—to such an extent as would render ordinary men of average disposition liable to act rashly or without due deliberation and reflection, and from this passion rather than from judgment.

We further held in *Valentine* that there is no specific type of provocation required . . . and that verbal provocation may be sufficient. In People v. Borches (1958), 50 Cal. 2d 321, 329, 325 P.2d 97, in the course of explaining the phrase "heat of passion" used in the statute defining manslaughter we pointed out that "passion" need not mean "rage" or "anger" but may be any "[v]iolent, intense, high-wrought or enthusiastic emotion" and concluded there "that defendant was aroused to a heat of —passion' by a series of events over a considerable period of time. Accordingly we there declared that evidence of admissions of infidelity by the defendant's paramour, taunts directed to him and other conduct, "supports a finding that defendant killed in wild desperation induced by [the woman's] long continued provocatory conduct." We find this reasoning persuasive in the case now before us. Defendant's testimony chronicles a two-week period of provocatory conduct by his wife Rachel that could arouse a passion of jealousy, pain and sexual rage in an ordinary man of average disposition such as to cause him to act rashly from his passion. It is significant that both defendant and Dr. Blinder testified that the former was in the heat of passion under an uncontrollable rage when he killed Rachel.

The Attorney General contends that the killing could not have been done in the heat of passion because there was a cooling period, defendant having waited in the apartment for 20 hours. However, the long course of provocatory conduct, which had resulted in intermittent outbreaks of rage under specific provocation in the past, reached its final culmination in the apartment when Rachel began screaming. Both defendant and Dr. Blinder testified that defendant killed in a state of uncontrollable rage, of passion, and there is ample evidence in the record to support the conclusion that this passion was the result of the long course of provocatory conduct by Rachel, just as the killing emerged from such conduct in *Borchers*.

Reversed.

NOTES AND QUESTIONS

1. Virtually every jurisdiction adopts some variation of the provocation formula as a defining characteristic of manslaughter. Some statutes mention the concept explicitly. See, *e.g.,* 18 Pa. Cons. Stat. § 2503, which provides,

> (a) *General rule.* A person who kills an individual without lawful justification commits voluntary manslaughter if at the time of the killing he is acting under a sudden and intense passion resulting from serious provocation by:
>
> (1) the individual killed; or
>
> (2) another whom the actor endeavors to kill, but he negligently or accidentally causes the death of the individual killed.

Other statutes do not specifically list provocation but implicitly incorporate its common law heritage by defining manslaughter in terms of nonmalicious killings. See, *e.g.,* Neb. Rev. Stat. § 28-305, which states, "A person commits manslaughter if he kills another without malice . . . upon a sudden quarrel." The Model Penal Code defines killings committed under the influence of "extreme emotional . . . disturbance" as manslaughter. MPC § 210.3. See the discussion of the Code standard *infra,* at pp.615–17.

2. Should the *Berry* court have concluded that whatever the past provocation, the defendant had (or should have) cooled off by the time he killed Rachel? Earlier cases, even in California, may well have ruled as a matter of law that Berry's 20-hour wait to kill his victim constituted too long a lapse of time to support a claim that the killing arose in the heat of passion. See,

for example, *People v. Ashland,* 20 Cal. App. 168, 128 P. 798 (1912), where the Court upheld the trial court's refusal to give a manslaughter instruction where defendant killed the victim, whom defendant suspected of raping his wife, after searching for him for 17 hours. The court explained,

> While the taking of life in the heat of passion will make the crime manslaughter, it will be conclusively inferred that the homicide was not committed in the heat of passion from the fact of the intervention of a long period of time between the provocation and the act of killing. In other words . . . the law will not permit the defendant to deliberate upon his wrong and, avenging it by killing the wrongdoer, set up the plea that his act was committed in the heat of passion.

See also *State v. Gounagias,* 88 Wash. 304, 153 P. 9 (1915), holding that evidence of provocation was properly excluded from defendant's murder trial. Defendant killed deceased who weeks earlier had sodomized defendant as he lay virtually unconscious in a drunken stupor. Following the assault, defendant asked deceased not to tell anyone of the experience, but deceased spread the story, resulting in numerous acquaintances directing taunts towards the defendant about the incident. Defendant suffered severe emotional trauma and frequent headaches because of the constant taunting. Defendant purchased a gun and after again being taunted and enraged by acquaintances in a coffeehouse, he went home, got his gun, went to deceased's house, and emptied the gun into the deceased's head as he slept.

The court explained its reasons for upholding defendant's conviction for murder:

> The offered evidence makes it clear that the appellant knew and appreciated for days before the killing the full meaning of the words, signs, and vulgar gestures of his [acquaintances] which, as the offer shows, he had encountered from day to day for about three weeks following the original outrage, wherever he went. The final demonstration in the coffeehouse was nothing new. It was exactly what the appellant, from his experience for the prior three weeks, must have anticipated. To say that it alone tended to create the sudden passion and heat of blood essential to mitigation is to ignore the admitted fact that the same thing had created no such condition on its repeated occurrence during the prior three weeks. To say that these repeated demonstrations, coupled with the original outrage, *culminated* in a sudden passion and heat of blood when he encountered the same character of demonstration in the coffeehouse on the night of the killing, is to say that *sudden* passion and heat of blood in the mitigative sense may be a cumulative result of repeated reminders of a single act of provocation occurring weeks before, and this, whether that provocation be regarded as the original outrage or the spreading of the story among appellant's associates, both of which he knew and fully realized for three weeks before the fatal night. This theory of the cumulative effect of reminders of former wrongs, not of new acts of provocation by the deceased, is contrary to the idea of sudden anger as understood in the doctrine of mitigation. In the nature of the thing sudden anger cannot be cumulative. A provocation which does not cause instant resentment, but which is only resented after being thought upon and brooded over, is not a provocation sufficient in law to reduce intentional killing from murder to manslaughter. . . .

The evidence offered had no tendency to prove sudden anger and resentment. On the contrary, it did tend to prove brooding thought, resulting in the design to kill. It was therefore properly excluded.

Which approach to cooling time, that of *Berry* or of *Ashland/Gounagias*, do you find preferable? Most jurisdictions hold to the view that a provoked defendant cannot have his homicide reduced to voluntary manslaughter where the time between the provocation and the death is such that a reasonable man thus provoked would have cooled. LaFave and Scott at 661.

3. The *Berry* court cites with approval the *Valentine* case for the proposition that verbal provocation may be sufficient. Some modern courts continue, however, to adhere to the position that mere words can never constitute legally adequate provocation. Thus, a wife's flaunting the fact that she committed adultery in the marital bed and disparaging her husband's sexual prowess to his face provides insufficient grounds for manslaughter when the enraged husband kills the wife. *People v. Chevalier,* 131 Ill. 2d 66, 544 N.E.2d 942 (1989).

4. Assuming that the defendant in the *Berry* case was extremely upset, frustrated, even "provoked," when he killed his wife, why should these be mitigating factors? For an argument that the traditional provocation doctrine is essentially male-biased, accommodating masculine anger that is often visited upon female victims, see Comment, *Provoked Reason in Men and Women: Heat-of-Passion Man-Slaughter and Imperfect Self-Defense,* 33 UCLA L. Rev. 1679 (1986).

Michael and Wechsler, *A Rationale of the Law of Homicide II,* 37 Colum. L. Rev. 1261, 1280–82 (1937), offers this explanation of the provocation doctrine:

> By provocation we mean the power possessed by some kinds of things and events external to human beings, of arousing in them desires by which they are moved to particular acts. We shall refer to things and events which have that potentiality as provocative circumstances; and when we wish to speak of an instance of its actualization, we shall say that the actor was provoked to a particular act. Viewing such an act as a change and the actor as the patient of the change, our present concern is with its proximate external agent, and with the probable influence of such an agent upon other men.
>
> Provocation may be greater or less, but it cannot be measured by the intensity of the passions aroused in the actor by the provocative circumstances. It must be estimated by the probability that such circumstances would affect most men in like fashion; although the passions stirred up in the actor were violent, the provocation can be said to be great only if the provocative circumstances would have aroused in most men similar desires of comparable intensity. Other things being equal, the greater the provocation, measured in that way, the more ground there is for attributing the intensity of the actor's passions and his lack of self-control on the homicidal occasion to the extraordinary character of the situation in which he was placed rather than to any extraordinary deficiency in his own character. While it is true, it is also beside the point, that most men do not kill on even the gravest provocation; the point is that the more strongly they would

be moved to kill by circumstances of the sort which provoked the actor to the homicidal act, and the more difficulty they would experience in resisting the impulse to which he yielded, the less does his succumbing serve to differentiate his character from theirs. But the slighter the provocation, the more basis there is for ascribing the actor's act to an extraordinary susceptibility to intense passion, to an unusual deficiency in those other desires which counteract in most men the desires which impel them to homicidal acts, or to an extraordinary weakness of reason and consequent inability to bring such desires into play. Moreover, since the homicidal act does not always follow closely upon the provocative circumstances and since the passions which they arouse may in the meantime gain or lose in intensity, provocation must be estimated as of the time of the homicidal act and in the light of those additional circumstances which may have intensified or diminished the actor's passions. For example, if a substantial interval of time or an apology intervened between insult and retaliation therefor, these would have to be considered in determining the extent of provocation. So, too, the immediate provocative power of a sudden and severe blow differs from that of such a blow after the actor's shock and pain have abated, and he has only his recollection of the injury to spur him on.

For an assessment of the provocation doctrine in terms of theories of both partial excuse and partial justification, see Dressler, *Rethinking Heat of Passion: A Defense in Search of a Rationale,* 73 J. Crim. L. & Criminology 421 (1982). Is it arguable that *Berry* reflects the former, and *Tripp* the latter view? See also Ashworth, *The Doctrine of Provocation,* 35 Cambridge L.J. 292 (1976).

5. Does the above excerpt from Michael and Wechsler explain why the law has traditionally embraced an "objective" standard, requiring not only that the defendant must actually be provoked but also that a reasonable person would be also? See, *e.g.,* the excerpt from *Maher v. People, supra.* See also *People v. Washington,* 58 Cal. App. 3d 620, 130 Cal. Rptr. 96 (1976), in which the defendant was convicted of murder after claiming provocation when he killed his homosexual partner during a lover's quarrel triggered by the victim's unfaithfulness and his desire to terminate his relationship with the defendant. The court rejected defendant's argument that the jury should have been instructed to measure provocation in terms of a standard applicable to "a female or to the average servient homosexual" instead of the ordinary reasonable person of "average disposition" instruction given by the trial court.

Which standard should be applied in cases such as *Washington?* Does the standard articulated by the *Berry* court ("ordinary reasonable person *under the given facts and circumstances*") suggest that the homosexuality of the defendant in *Washington* should have been taken into account in instructing the jury?

Consider the following case.

DIRECTOR OF PUBLIC PROSECUTIONS V. CAMPLIN

House of Lords

[1978] 2 All E.R. 168

LORD DIPLOCK. My Lords, for the purpose of answering the question of law on which this appeal will turn only a brief account is needed of the facts that have given rise to it. The respondent, Camplin, who was 15 years of age, killed a middle-aged Pakistani, Mohammed Lal Khan, by splitting his skull with a chapati pan, a heavy kitchen utensil like a rimless frying pan. At the time the two of them were alone together in Khan's flat. At Camplin's trial for murder before Boreham J. his only defense was that of provocation so as to reduce the offense to manslaughter. According to the story that he told in the witness box but which differed materially from that which he had told to the police, Khan had buggered him in spite of his resistance and had then laughed at him, whereupon Camplin had lost his self-control and attacked Khan fatally with the chapati pan.

In his address to the jury on the defense of provocation, counsel for Camplin had suggested to them that when they addressed their minds to the question whether the provocation relied on was enough to make a reasonable man do as Camplin had done, what they ought to consider was not the reaction of a reasonable adult but the reaction of a reasonable boy of Camplin's age. The judge thought that this was wrong in law. So in this summing-up he took pains to instruct the jury that they must consider whether—

> the provocation was sufficient to make a reasonable man in like circumstances act as the defendant did. Not a reasonable boy, as [counsel for Camplin] would have it, or a reasonable lad; it is an objective test—a reasonable man.

The jury found Camplin guilty of murder. On appeal the Court of Appeal, Criminal Division, allowed the appeal and substituted a conviction for manslaughter on the ground that the passage I have cited from the summing-up was a misdirection. The court held that the proper direction to the jury is to invite the jury to consider whether the provocation was enough to have made a reasonable person of the same age as the appellant in the same circumstances do as he did.

The point of law of general public importance involved in the case has been certified as being:

> Whether, on the prosecution for murder of a boy of 15, where the issue of provocation arises, the jury should be directed to consider the question, under § 3 of the Homicide Act 1957, whether the provocation was enough to make a reasonable man do as he did by reference to a "reasonable adult" or by reference to a "reasonable boy of 15."

My Lords, the doctrine of provocation in crimes of homicide has always represented an anomaly in English law. In crimes of violence which result in injury short of death, the fact that the act of violence was committed under provocation, which has caused the accused to lose his self-control, does not affect the nature of the offense of which he is guilty: it is merely a matter to be taken into consideration in determining the penalty which it is appropriate to impose: whereas in homicide provocation effects a change in the offense itself from murder, for which the penalty is fixed by law (formerly death and now imprisonment for life), to the lessor offense of manslaughter, for which the penalty is in the discretion of the judge.

At least from as early as 1914 the test of whether the defense of provocation is entitled to succeed has been a dual one: the conduct of the deceased to the accused must be such as (1) might cause in any reasonable or ordinary person and (2) actually causes in the accused a sudden and temporary loss of self-control as the result of which he commits the unlawful act that kills the deceased. But until the 1947 Act was passed there was a condition precedent which had to be satisfied before any question of applying this dual test could arise. The conduct of the deceased had to be of such a kind as was capable in law of constituting provocation; and whether it was or was not a question for the judge not for the jury. . . .

My Lords, this was the state of law when *Bedder [v. Director of Public Prosecutions* [1954], 2 All ER 801, [1954], 1 WLR 1119] fell to be considered by this House. The accused had killed a prostitute. He was sexually impotent. According to his evidence he had tried to have sexual intercourse with her and failed. She taunted him with his failure and tried to get away from his grasp. In the course of her attempts to do so she slapped him in the face, punched him in the stomach and kicked him in the groin, whereupon he took a knife out of his pocket and stabbed her twice and caused her death. The struggle that led to her death thus started because the deceased taunted the accused with his physical infirmity; but in the state of the law as it then was, taunts unaccompanied by any physical violence did not constitute provocation. The taunts were followed by violence on the part of the deceased in the course of her attempt to get away from the accused, and it may be that this subsequent violence would have a greater effect on the self-control of an impotent man already enraged by the taunts than it would have had on a person conscious of possessing normal physical attributes. So there might be some justification for the judge to instruct the jury to ignore the fact that the accused was impotent when they were considering whether the deceased's conduct amounted to such provocation as would cause a reasonable or ordinary person to lose his self-control. This indeed appears to have been the ground on which the Court of Criminal Appeal had approved the summing-up when they said:

> . . . no distinction is to be made in the case of a person who, though it may not be a matter of temperament is physically impotent, is conscious of that impotence, *and therefore mentally liable to be more excited unduly if* he is "twitted" or attacked on the subject of that particular infirmity.

This statement, for which I have myself supplied the emphasis, was approved by Lord Simonds L.C. speaking on behalf of all the members of this House who sat on the appeal; but he also went on to lay down the broader proposition that:

It would be plainly illogical not to recognize an unusually excitable or pugnacious temperament in the accused as a matter to be taken into account but yet to recognize for that purpose some unusual physical characteristic, be it impotence or another.

Section 3 of the 1957 Act is in the following terms:

Where on a charge of murder there is evidence on which the jury can find that the person charged was provoked (whether by things done or by things said or by both together) to lose his self-control, the question whether the provocation was enough to make a reasonable man do as he did shall be left to be determined by the jury; and in determining that question the jury shall take into account everything both done and said according to the effect which, in their opinion, it would have on a reasonable man.

My Lords, this section was intended to mitigate in some degree the harshness of the common law of provocation as it had been developed by recent decisions in this House. It recognizes and retains the dual test: the provocation must not only have caused the accused to lose his self-control but also be such as might cause a reasonable man to react to it as the accused did. Nevertheless it brings about two important changes in the law. The first is it abolishes all previous rules of law as to what can or cannot amount to provocation and in particular the rule of law that . . . words unaccompanied by violence could not do so. Secondly it makes it clear that if there was any evidence that the accused himself at the time of the act which caused the death in fact lost his self-control in consequence of some provocation however slight it might appear to the judge, he was bound to leave to the jury the question, which is one of opinion not of law, whether a reasonable man might have reacted to that provocation as the accused did.

The public policy that underlay the adoption of the "reasonable man" test in the common law doctrine of provocation was to reduce the incidence of fatal violence by preventing a person relying on his own exceptional pugnacity or excitability as an excuse for loss of self-control. The rationale of the test may not be easy to reconcile in logic with more universal propositions as to the mental element in crime. Nevertheless it has been preserved by the 1957 Act but fails to be applied now in the context of a law of provocation that is significantly different from what it was before the Act was passed.

Although it is now for the jury to apply the "reasonable man" test, it still remains for the judge to direct them what, in the new context of the section, is the meaning of this apparently inapt expression, since powers of ratiocination bear no obvious relationships to powers of self-control. Apart from this the judge is entitled, if he thinks it helpful, to suggest considerations which may influence the jury in forming their own opinions as to whether the test is satisfied; but he should make it clear that these are not instructions which they are required to follow: it is for them and no one else to decide what weight, if any, ought to be given to them.

[F]or the purpose of the law of provocation the "reasonable man" has never been confined to the adult male. It means an ordinary person of either sex, not exceptionally excitable or pugnacious, but possessed of such powers of self-control as everyone is entitled to expect that his fellow citizens will exercise in society as it is today. A crucial factor in the defense of provocation from earliest times has been the relationship between the gravity of provocation and the way in which the accused retaliated, both being judged by the social standards of the day. When Hale was writing in the 17th century pulling a man's nose was thought to justify retaliation with a sword; when Mancini [[1941] 3 All ER, [1942] AC 1] was decided by this House, a blow with a fist would not justify retaliation with a deadly weapon. But so long as words unaccompanied by violence could not in common law amount to provocation the relevant proportionality between provocation and retaliation was primarily one of degrees of violence. Words spoken to the accused before the violence started were not normally to be included in the proportion sum. But now that the law has been changed so as to permit of words being treated as provocation, even though unaccompanied by any other acts, the gravity of verbal provocation may well depend on the particular characteristics or circumstances of the person to whom a taunt or insult is addressed. To taunt a person because of his race, his physical infirmities or some shameful incident in his past may well be considered by the jury to be more offensive to the person addressed, however equable his temperament, if the facts on which the taunt is founded are true than it would be if they were not. It would stultify much of the mitigation of the previous harshness of the common law in ruling out verbal provocation as capable of reducing murder to manslaughter if the jury could not take into consideration all those factors which in their opinion would affect the gravity of taunts and insults when applied to the person to whom they are addressed. So to this extent at any rate the unqualified proposition accepted by this House in *Bedder* that for the purposes of the "reasonable man" test any unusual physical characteristics of the accused must be ignored requires revision as a result of the passing of the 1957 Act.

That he was only 15 years of age at the time of the killing is the relevant characteristic of the accused in the instant case. It is a characteristic which may have its effects on temperament as well as physique. If the jury think that the same power of self-control is not to be expected in an ordinary, average or normal boy of 15 as in an older person, are they to treat the lesser powers of self-control possessed by an ordinary, average or normal boy of 15 as the standard of self-control with which the conduct of accused is to be compared?

It may be conceded that in strict logic there is a transition between treating age as a characteristic that may be taken into account in assessing the gravity of the provocation addressed to the accused and treating it as a characteristic to be taken into account in determining what is the degree of self-control to be expected of the ordinary person with whom the accused's conduct is to be compared. But to require old heads on young shoulders is inconsistent with the law's compassion of human infirmity to which Sir Michael Foster ascribed the doctrine of provocation more than two centuries ago. The distinction as to the purpose for which it is legitimate to take the age of the accused into account involves considerations of too great nicety to warrant a place in deciding a matter of opinion, which is no longer one to be decided by a judge trained in logical reasoning but by a jury drawing on their experience of how ordinary human beings behave in real life.

In my opinion a proper direction to a jury on the question left to their exclusive determination by § 3 of the 1957 Act would be on the following lines. The judge should state what the question is, using the very terms of the section. He should then explain to them that the reasonable man referred to in the question is a person having the power of self-control to be expected of an ordinary person of the sex and age of the accused, but in other respects sharing such of the accused's characteristics as they think would affect the gravity of the provocation to him, and that the question is not merely whether such a person would in like circumstances be provoked to lose his self-control but also would react to the provocation as the accused did.

I accordingly agree with the Court of Appeal that the judge ought not to have instructed the jury to pay no account to the age of the accused even though they themselves might be of opinion that the degree of self-control to be expected in a boy of that age was less than in an adult. So to direct them was to impose a fetter on the right and duty of the jury which the 1957 Act accords to them to act on their own opinion on the matter.

I would dismiss this appeal.

LORD SIMON OF GLAISDALE . . .

The original reasons in this branch of the law were largely reasons of the heart and of common sense, not the reasons of pure juristic logic. The potentiality of provocation to reduce murder to manslaughter was . . . "in compassion to human infirmity." But justice and common sense then demanded some limitation: it would be unjust that the drunk man or one exceptionally pugnacious or bad-tempered or over-sensitive should be able to claim that these matters rendered him peculiarly susceptible to the provocation offered, where the sober and even-tempered man would hang for his homicide. Hence . . . the development of the concept of the reaction of a reasonable man to the provocation offered. . . .

The provision that words alone can constitute provocation accentuates the anomalies, inconveniences and injustices liable to follow from the *Bedder* decision. The effect of an insult will often depend entirely on a characteristic of a person to whom the insult is directed. "Dirty nigger" would probably mean little if said to a white man or even if said by one colored man to another, but is obviously more insulting when said by a white man to a colored man. Similarly, such an expression as "Your character is as crooked as your back" would have different connotation to a hunchback on the one hand and to a man with a back like a ramrod on the other. . . . In my judgment the reference to "a reasonable man" at the end of section [3 of the Homicide Act of 1957] means "a man of ordinary self-control." If this is so the meaning satisfies what I have ventured to suggest as the reasons for importing into this branch of the law the concept of the reasonable man, namely to avoid the injustice of a man being entitled to rely on his exceptional excitability (whether idiosyncratic or by cultural environment or ethnic origin) or pugnacity or ill-temper or on his drunkenness (I do not purport to be exhaustive in this enumeration).

I think that the standard of self-control which the law requires before provocation is held to reduce murder to manslaughter is still that of the reasonable person (hence his invocation in § 3 of the 1957 Act), but that, in determining whether a person of reasonable self-control would lose it in the circumstances, the entire factual situation, which includes the characteristics of the accused, must be considered. . . .

NOTES AND QUESTIONS

1. Do the opinions in *Camplin* essentially abandon an "objective" test in favor of one measuring provocation in terms of the special circumstances of each case? Suppose that in addition to being 15 years old, Camplin suffered from an emotional disturbance that caused him to become enraged whenever anyone laughed at him. Is the latter evidence admissible? If so, does not the "especially pugnacious defendant" now have an argument for mitigation? If not, would it be fair to hold Camplin for murder assuming that the reasonable 15-year-old would not have been provoked?

Camplin only applies where there is a truly young defendant. A 20-year-old defendant is to be treated as a generic reasonable man. *Regina v. Ali,* [1989] Crim. L. Rev. 736.

For the view that cultural factors unique to the defendant are relevant in determining her state of mind at the time she kills, see *People v. Wu, supra* at p. 305, in which the court, in addition to permitting an instruction on the unconsciousness defense, permitted the jury to assess defendant's emotional state by reference to her cultural background which arguably influenced her perception of the circumstances leading up to her strangulation of her son. The court specifically noted that defendant's cultural background was relevant to whether she killed "in the heat of passion."

2. Traditionally, courts denied evidence that the defendant was provoked into killing because of an emotional disturbance, a subjective consideration that by definition distinguished the defendant from the reasonable (mentally healthy) person. Thus, in *State v. McAllister,* 41 N.J. 342, 196 A.2d 786 (1964), the defendant (whose mental age was less than seven years) killed a friend during a quarrel. In appealing his conviction of murder, defendant argued that the trial court should have considered the special circumstances of his emotional and intellectual impairment, claiming that this condition rendered him more easily provoked than are ordinary adults. The court rejected defendant's contention, noting that subjective provocation generated through mental abnormality does not make a killing manslaughter since the reasonable man standard postulates a sane man. 41 N.J. at 353–4, 196 A.2d at 792.

Such an approach is arguably at odds with the position adopted by the Model Penal Code. Section 210.3 provides,

(1) Criminal homicide constitutes manslaughter when: . . .
a homicide which would otherwise be murder is committed under the influence ofextreme mental or emotional disturbance for which there is a reasonable explanation or excuse. The reasonableness of such explanation or excuse shall be determined fromthe viewpoint of a person in the actor's situation under the circumstances as he believes them to be.

The Comments to § 210.3 at 62–63 explain: . . .

> Section 210.3(1)(b) does require that the actor's emotional distress be based on "reasonable explanation or excuse." This language preserves the essentially objective character of the inquiry and erects a barrier against debilitating individualization of the legal standard.
>
> The critical element in the Model Code formulation is the clause requiring that reasonableness be assessed "from the viewpoint of a person in the actor's situation." The word "situation" is designedly ambiguous. On the one hand, it is clear that personal handicaps and some external circumstances must be taken into account. Thus, blindness, shock from traumatic injury, and extreme grief are all easily read into the term "situation." This result is sound, for it would be morally obtuse to appraise a crime for mitigation of punishment without reference to these factors. On the other hand; it is equally plain that idiosyncratic moral values are not part of the actor's situation. An assassin who kills a political leader because he believes it is right to do so cannot ask that he be judged by the standard of a reasonable extremist. Any other result would undermine the normative message of the criminal law. In between these two extremes, however, there are matters neither as clearly distinct from individual blameworthiness as blindness or handicap nor as integral a part of moral depravity as a belief in the rightness of killing. Perhaps the classic illustration is the unusual sensitivity to the epithet "bastard" of a person born illegitimate. An exceptionally punctilious sense of personal honor or an abnormally fearful temperament may also serve to differentiate an individual actor from the hypothetical reasonable man, yet none of these factors is wholly irrelevant to the ultimate issue of culpability. The proper role of such factors cannot be resolved satisfactorily by abstract definition of what may constitute adequate provocation. The Model Code endorses a formulation that affords sufficient flexibility to differentiate in particular cases between those special aspects of the actor's situation that should be deemed material for purpose of grading and those that should be ignored. There thus will be room for interpretation of the word "situation," and that is precisely the flexibility desired. There will be opportunity for argument about the reasonableness of explanation or excuse, and that too is a ground on which argument is required. In the end, the question is whether the actor's loss of self-control can be understood in terms that arouse sympathy in the ordinary citizen. Section 210.3 faces this issue squarely and leaves the ultimate judgment to the ordinary citizen in the function of a juror assigned to resolve the specific case.

In jurisdictions adopting the Code approach, the courts have divided in their interpretations of the language requiring the reasonableness of extreme mental or emotional disturbance. Some courts have permitted liberal inquiries into mental abnormalities of the defendant, see, *e.g., State v. Ott,* 297 Or. 375, 686 P.2d 1001 (1984) (error to instruct jury not to consider defendant's "personality characteristics"), while others virtually preclude such inquiries altogether, see, *e.g., State v. Russo,* 734 P.2d 156 (Haw. 1987) (no error in denying manslaughter instruction when defendant sought to introduce evidence that while mentally and emotionally disturbed, he deliberately shot victims whom he feared were about to kill him).

For a detailed discussion of the relationship of the common law and Model Penal Code approaches to voluntary manslaughter, see Singer, *The Resurgence of Mens Rea: I—Provocation, Emotional Disturbance, and the Model Penal Code,* 27 B.C. L. Rev. 243 (1986).

[2] Involuntary Manslaughter

[a] Criminal Negligence Manslaughter

FITZGERALD V. STATE

Supreme Court of Alabama

112 Ala. 34, 20 So. 966 (1896)

O. J. SEMMES, Judge.

The appellant, John Fitzgerald, was tried under an indictment charging him with murder in the first degree for killing one William Case, and was convicted of manslaughter in the second degree, and sentenced to imprisonment in the county jail for six months, and appeals. Reversed.

[T]he evidence for the state tended to show that on the night of August 19, 1893, William Case, the deceased, in company with two friends, went into a barroom wherein the defendant, John Fitzgerald, was the barkeeper, and who was, at the time, behind the bar; that, while the deceased and his friends were standing in front of the bar talking, the deceased commented on the defendant having two good-looking pistols lying on the back bar shelf; that thereupon the defendant said, "Yes; and I am a crackerjack with them," and picked up one of the pistols, and, pointing it at the deceased, fired, the ball striking the deceased in the forehead, from the effects of which wound the deceased died in December. The testimony for the defendant tended to show that he and deceased were the best of friends, and were frequently together; that at the time the deceased, with two other men, came into the barroom, and the deceased commented on the pistols lying on the back bar shelf, the defendant said, "Yes; they are crackerjacks," and picked up one of them; that he turned around, and was in the act of handing the pistol he picked up over the counter to the deceased, when the pistol fired with the above effects. The defendant, as a witness in his own behalf, testified that he did not have his hand upon the trigger, and was not pointing it at the deceased, but was passing it over the counter towards him, when it was accidentally discharged.

Murray Richardson, a witness for the state, . . . testified that two days prior to the shooting he had carried a note for the defendant to a woman. The solicitor asked said witness the following question: "When you came back, what did you tell Mr. Fitzgerald, the defendant?" The defendant objected to this question on the ground that it was irrelevant and immaterial, but the court overruled the objection, and the defendant duly excepted. The witness answered: "He asked me if I brought an answer, and I told him I did not have any answer; and he asked what she said and I told him she said she didn't want any of his notes, and nothing to do with him; and then he asked if that damned little fellow Willie Case was up there, and I told him I didn't know; that I didn't go inside." . . .

* * *

Upon the introduction of all the evidence, the court, in the general charge to the jury, instructed them, among other things, as follows: "Gentlemen of the Jury: If you should believe from the evidence, beyond a reasonable doubt, that the defendant at the bar was behind the counter, and the pistol was lying there, and that Willie Case, whom it is alleged was killed, came up to the bar, and the defendant picked up that pistol, determined beforehand to kill Willie Case, and did shoot Willie Case with that pistol, intending to kill him with the pistol, Willie Case doing nothing, and he shot him without justification, mitigation, or excuse [and] Willie Case died from the effects of the shot then [the defendant] would be guilty of murder in the first degree." To this portion of the court's general charge the defendant separately excepted, and also separately excepted to the following portion of the court's general charge: "Manslaughter in the second degree is where one person, in doing an unlawful act, which is not a felony, kills another one, not intending to kill him, or where one doing a lawful act does it in such a careless way that death is the result of the carelessness of the party, although he did not intend actually to kill the party." The court also instructed the jury, in its general charge, among other things, as follows: "It is in two categories: First, that he is doing an unlawful act, and that death is the result of the unlawful act, the defendant not intending to kill the man (that is, some other unlawful act than the killing of the man), and death results from that, that would be manslaughter in the second degree; or, second, *if the defendant is doing something he has a legal right to do, and he does that in a careless and negligent manner, and kills one by reason of his carelessness and negligence, that would be manslaughter in the second degree.*" To so much of the above quotation from the court's general charge which is emphasized the defendant duly excepted.

* * *

McCLELLAN, J. It is laid down by Bishop that "every act of gross carelessness, even in the performance of what is lawful, and, *a fortiori,* of what is not lawful, and every negligent omission of a legal duty, whereby death ensues, is indictable either as murder or manslaughter." 1 Bish. Cr. Law § 314. And that author gives the reason underlying the doctrine of criminal carelessness thus: "There is little distinction, except in degree, between a positive will to do wrong and an indifference whether wrong is done or not. Therefore, carelessness is criminal, and, within limits, supplies the place of the direct criminal intent." He says further on this subject that "there may be a degree of carelessness so inconsiderable as not to be taken into account as criminal by the law." . . . Our own adjudications are in line with these tests, and always predicate criminality, not upon mere negligence or carelessness, but upon that degree of negligence or carelessness which is denominated "gross," and which constitutes such a departure from what would be the conduct of an ordinarily careful and prudent man under the same circumstances as to furnish evidence of that indifference to consequences which in some offenses takes the place of criminal intent. . . . There can, we therefore think, be no doubt, upon authority and principle, that homicide may result from carelessness of such low degree or trivial character in the performance of a lawful act as not to involve criminality in the person so carelessly performing the act; and it follows that criminality cannot be affirmed of every lawful act carelessly performed, and resulting because of such carelessness, in the death of another. The carelessness must be aggravated, so to speak; it must be gross implying an indifference to consequences. For illustration, employing some of the circumstances involved in some of the tendencies of the evidence in the present case. The deceased, standing in front of a saloon counter, requests the defendant, who is behind the counter, to hand him a pistol lying on the shelf behind the defendant. If the latter, in complying with the request, threw the weapon down on the counter in front of deceased, and it was thereby discharged, killing deceased, this would be at least manslaughter in the second degree, though defendant did not intend to injure deceased, and did not suppose the pistol would be discharged; but if the defendant, in passing the weapon to deceased, inadvertently held the muzzle toward him, and it was accidentally discharged, with fatal results, the defendant is not criminally responsible; for, though that method of handing the weapon to the deceased involved, or may have involved, carelessness, it was of too slight a degree, tootrivial, for criminality to be affirmed of it.

The evidence before us presents three tendencies in respect of defendant's conduct on the occasion of the shooting: First. That he intentionally, and with malice, shot the deceased. This, of course, would have justified and required conviction of murder if the jury had found in line with this tendency of the evidence. Second. That the pistol was discharged without intent on the part of the defendant, but when he was in the act of pointing or aiming it at the deceased. On this phase of the evidence if believed by the jury, the defendant was guilty of manslaughter in the second degree, because of the unlawfulness of the act he was committing at the time of the shooting. . . . And, third. That the defendant did not intentionally shoot the deceased, or point or aim the pistol at him, but that, while he did not attempt to hand the weapon to the deceased in the most careful and prudent manner, or even in such a mode as would ordinarily have been adopted by careful and prudent men, was yet not guilty of that degree of carelessness which the law terms "gross," and which affords grounds for the implication of indifference to consequences on the part of the defendant. If the jury found only this character of carelessness on defendant's part, and that the homicide resulted from it, the defendant was entitled to a verdict of acquittal.

The trial court in its general charge, given *ex mero motu* to the jury, took no account of the tendency of the evidence last considered, and, in effect, instructed the jury to convict if they found that the defendant was negligent or careless in any degree in attempting to hand the pistol to deceased, and that the homicide resulted from such carelessness. This was error, on the principles we have announced, and must work a reversal of the judgment below. There was indeed no evidence in the case of gross carelessness on the part of the defendant in handling the weapon. According to the state's evidence, the defendant shot deceased either intentionally and maliciously, or while performing the unlawful act of pointing or aiming the pistol at him. The evidence on the part of the defendant was that the parties were on the friendliest of terms; that the defendant did not intend to shoot deceased; that he did not point or aim the pistol at deceased; but that, while he was handing it over the counter, in compliance with the request of deceased, he, defendant, not having his hand on the trigger, it was accidentally discharged. When reference is had to all this evidence, some of the charges requested by the defendant to the effect that if the jury should find there was not intentional shooting, and that defendant was not, at the time when the shot was fired, pointing or aiming the pistol at the deceased, but that the shot was accidental, etc., should have been given.

Reversed.

STATE v. BARNETT

Supreme Court of South Carolina

218 S.C. 415, 63 S.E.2d 57 (1951)

OXNER, Justice.

Appellant was convicted of involuntary manslaughter. It was alleged in the indictment that the homicide resulted from criminal negligence in the operation of an automobile. The exceptions on this appeal relate solely to the charge.

Error is assigned in the instructions relating to the degree of negligence necessary to sustain a conviction of involuntary manslaughter. It is said that the Court erred in charging that ordinary negligence is sufficient and that the jury should have been instructed that it was incumbent upon the State to show gross negligence or recklessness.

After defining involuntary manslaughter and distinguishing that offense from voluntary manslaughter, the Court stated that involuntary manslaughter may consist in the "killing of another without malice and unintentionally, but while one is engaged in the commission of some unlawful act not amounting to a felony and not naturally tending to cause death or great bodily harm," or in "the killing of another without malice and unintentionally but while one is negligently engaged in doing a lawful act." The jury was given the usual definition of negligence but was not instructed as to gross negligence, recklessness or wantonness. The testimony is not incorporated in the record but we assume from the charge that the State relied on the violation of certain statutes in this State regulating the operation of automobiles, and the jury was instructed that a violation of a statute of this kind constitutes negligence *per se.*

The degree of negligence necessary to establish criminal liability has perplexed the courts of England and America for centuries. The subject has at times been the source of much confusion. In the early development of the criminal law in England it was held that ordinary negligence, that is, the failure to exercise due care, was sufficient. Later it was found that this rule was too harsh. A noted English authority observed that an accident brought about by an act of ordinary negligence "may be the lot of even the wisest and best of mankind." The English courts finally concluded that more carelessness was required to create criminal liability than civil but they found it difficult to determine "how much more." They use such words as "gross," "reckless" and "culpable," and hold that it is for the jury to decide, in view of all the circumstances, whether the act was of such character as to be worthy of punishment. . . . There was a tendency in the early American decisions to follow the rule first adopted in England to the effect that ordinary negligence was sufficient. That standard was soon repudiated, however, by the great majority of the courts in this country and it is now generally held that the negligence of the accused must be "culpable," "gross," or "reckless," that is, the conduct of the accused must be such a departure from what would be the conduct of an ordinarily prudent or careful man under the same circumstances as to be incompatible with a proper regard for human life, or conduct amounting to an indifference to consequences. . . . Of course, under all the authorities the conduct of the accused must be judged in the light of the potential danger involved in the lawful act being performed. In perhaps a majority of the states, the offense of involuntary manslaughter is now defined by statute. Although variously worded, these statutes, with a few exceptions, have been construed as requiring gross negligence or recklessness. . . .

Adverting now to homicides resulting from the operation of automobiles, in almost all jurisdictions either by statute or by application of the rule governing involuntary manslaughter at common law, the rule is that the negligence necessary to convict a motorist of involuntary manslaughter must be a higher degree than is required to establish negligent default on a mere civil issue and that the proof must show recklessness or such carelessness as is incompatible with proper regard for human life. . . . Most courts have refused to consider an automobile as an inherently dangerous instrumentality so as to warrant the application of the "deadly weapon" rule. . . .

It seems to be thoroughly settled by the [South Carolina] decisions that where the instrument involved is not inherently dangerous, we follow the general rule requiring more than ordinary negligence to support a conviction for involuntary manslaughter, but hold that simple negligence causing the death of another is sufficient if the instrumentality is of such character that its negligent use under the surrounding circumstances is necessarily dangerous to human life or limb. This Court is also committed to the view that firearms and motor vehicles fall within the latter category. We shall not now undertake to develop the rationale of this distinction. It may perhaps be explained upon the theory that want of ordinary care in the handling of a dangerous instrumentality is the equivalent of culpable or gross negligence. . . .

We shall next consider the effect of the statutory offense of reckless homicide which [provides]: "When the death of any person ensues within one year as a proximate result of injury received by the driving of any vehicle in reckless disregard of the safety of others, the person so operating such vehicle shall be guilty of reckless homicide. . . . "

[T]he foregoing statute means "something more than the mere failure to exercise due care" and that "the offense denotes operation of a vehicle under such circumstances, and in such manner, as to show a wilful or reckless disregard of consequences." It will be noted that this is a greater degree of negligence than we have held necessary to support the common law offense of involuntary manslaughter where a dangerous instrumentality is involved.

[The court concluded that the legislature did not intend for the reckless homicide statute to supersede the common law offense of involuntary manslaughter in cases of death resulting from the operation of a motor vehicle.]

We have reviewed . . . the decisions in this State, as well as the authorities elsewhere, relating to involuntary manslaughter. This has been deemed necessary in deciding whether we should adhere to the rule that an automobile is an instrumentality of such character that simple negligence in its operation is sufficient to support the common law offense of involuntary manslaughter. It must be conceded that only scant support can be found for this rule in other jurisdictions. But public policy requires that due consideration should be given to the principle of *stare decisis*. . . . If a change or modification is desirable, it should come from the law-making body.

Mr. Justice Taylor and the writer desire to say that they regard the simple negligence rule in automobile homicide cases as too harsh and if the question were one of original impression, they would not be in favor of adopting it.

All exceptions are overruled and the judgment affirmed.

NOTES AND QUESTIONS

1. As noted by the *Fitzgerald* and *Barnett* courts, involuntary manslaughter traditionally consists of two types: "unlawful act" manslaughter (to be considered in the next section of this chapter) and "criminal negligence" manslaughter. As discussed in § 4.03[B], *supra,* courts and sometimes legislatures have encountered problems in defining the *mens rea* required for the latter type. The various descriptions ("criminal negligence," "gross negligence," etc.) noted in the cases suggest the difficulty in distinguishing the type of negligence necessary for involuntary manslaughter from that sufficient for tort liability. Moreover, the use of terms such as *recklessness* and *wantonness* sometimes employed to define involuntary manslaughter suggests a rejection of objective liability under a negligence standard in favor of a requirement that the defendant actually appreciate the risk of death entailed in his conduct.

This confusing situation is summarized in Wechsler and Michael, *A Rationale for the Law of Homicide I,* 37 Colum. L. Rev. 701, 721–22 (1937):

> The line dividing manslaughter from civil negligence is as shadowy as that dividing murder from manslaughter. For the most part, the negligence that is criminal is distinguished from the negligence that is not, only by the addition of an epithet such as "gross," "culpable," "wanton" or "reckless," as opposed to "ordinary" or "slight." What, if anything, these epithets mean remains for the most part undetermined. But the differences between two negligent acts that are significant for this purpose, must reside in the degree of the risk of injury they unjustifiably create, the character of the injury or the actor's awareness of the risk. There is authority for the view that the character and degree of risk distinguish criminal from non-criminal negligence, whereas awareness of the risk distinguishes murder from manslaughter. There is also authority for the view that awareness of the risk is necessary for negligence to be criminal at all, and this, indeed, is

what the epithets listed above are most likely to mean to a jury. On Holmes' view, written into the law of Massachusetts, awareness of the risk is unnecessary . . . in murder, and *a fortiori,* in manslaughter.

Even if awareness of the risk is necessary for manslaughter, as well as for murder, it is a negative and not a positive test. The jury must still determine, first, whether the danger created was unduly great, *i.e.,* whether the risk should be regarded as a normal and desirable, or as an abnormal, undesirable and, therefore, unjustifiable incident of an otherwise lawful activity; and, second, whether the unjustifiable risk was slight, great or very great. Since human beings can make only rough estimates of degrees of danger, the jury may be expected in many cases to do no more than ask itself whether the particular behavior should be punished. If awareness of the risk is necessary, cases of inadvertence are excluded, but the problem in other cases is the same. The question is left to the jury subject to a limited and uncertain censorship by the court.

Note that S.C. Code Ann. § 16-3-60 (1976) statutorily modified Barnett by establishing that the crime of criminal negligence manslaughter requires "reckless disregard of the safety of others." See *State v. McCall,* 304 S.C. 465, 469, 405 S.E.2d 414, 416 (1991).

2. Sometimes the courts during the course of a single opinion seem unable to decide whether to require a recklessness standard or to permit one grounded in negligence. Consider, for example, *Commonwealth v. Welansky,* 316 Mass. 383, 397–400, 55 N.E.2d 902, 909–11 (1944), where the court interpreted the meaning of "wanton or reckless conduct" under an indictment for involuntary manslaughter:

> To define wanton or reckless conduct so as to distinguish it clearly from negligence and gross negligence is not easy. . . . The words "wanton" and "reckless" are practically synonymous in this connection, although the word "wanton" may contain a suggestion of arrogance or insolence or heartlessness that is lacking in the word "reckless." . . .
>
> The standard of wanton or reckless conduct is at once subjective and objective. . . . Knowing facts that would cause a reasonable man to know the danger is equivalent to knowing the danger. . . . The judge charged the jury correctly when he said,
>
>> To constitute wanton or reckless conduct, as distinguished from mere negligence, grave danger to others must have been apparent, and the defendant must have chosen to run the risk rather than alter his conduct so as to avoid the act of omission which caused the harm. If the grave danger was in fact realized by the defendant, his subsequent voluntary act or omission which caused the harm amounts to wanton or reckless conduct, no matter whether the ordinary man would have realized the gravity of the danger or not. But even if a particular defendant is so stupid [or] so heedless . . . that in fact he did not realize the grave danger, he cannot escape the imputation of wanton or reckless conduct in his dangerous act or omission, if an ordinary normal man under the same circumstances would have realized the gravity of the danger. A man may be reckless within the meaning of the law although he himself thought he was careful.

The essence of wanton or reckless conduct is intentional conduct, by way either of commission or of omission where there is a duty to act, which conduct involves a high degree of likelihood that substantial harm will result to another. . . . Wanton or reckless conduct amounts to what has been variously described as indifference to or disregard of probable consequences to that other.

The words "wanton" and "reckless" are thus not merely rhetorical or vituperative expressions used instead of negligent or grossly negligent. They express a difference in the degree of risk and in the voluntary taking of risk so marked, as compared with negligence, as to amount substantially and in the eyes of the law to a difference in kind. . . . For many years this court has been careful to preserve the distinction between negligence and gross negligence, on the one hand, and wanton or reckless conduct on the other. . . .

Notwithstanding language used commonly in earlier cases, and occasionally in later ones, it is now clear in this Commonwealth that at common law conduct does not become criminal until it passes the borders of negligence and gross negligence and enters into the domain of wanton or reckless conduct. There is in Massachusetts at common law no such thing as "criminal negligence." . . .

Are you convinced that the *Welansky* opinion supports its conclusion that criminal negligence, at least as defined by MPC § 2.02(d), does not exist in Massachusetts?

3. As noted by Wechsler and Michael, some courts explicitly uphold involuntary manslaughter convictions based on grounds of negligence. For example, in *Palmer v. State,* 223 Md. 341, 164 A.2d 467 (1960), the court upheld a mother's conviction of gross or criminal negligence man-slaughter for the death of her daughter after she left her small daughter in the custody of her paramour, who frequently beat the child, finally killing her. The court found that it was not necessary for the defendant to have foreseen the death of the child so long as the death would have been foreseen by a reasonable man.

Similarly, in *People v. Bennett,* 54 Cal. 3d 1032, 2 Cal. Rptr. 8, 10–11, 819 P.2d 849, 852 (1992), the court interpreted a vehicular homicide statute's gross negligence requirement to mean "the exercise of so slight a degree of care as to raise a presumption of conscious indifference to the consequences." The court saw the test as objective: "whether a reasonable person in the defendant's position would have been aware of the risks involved."

On the other hand, other courts have unequivocally required actual awareness of risk to convict a defendant of involuntary manslaughter. See, *e.g., Bussard v. State,* 233 Wis. 11, 288 N.W. 187 (1939), where the court found that while defendant was "negligent in a high degree" in causing a death by driving his car without looking ahead, he was not guilty under Wisconsin's gross negligence manslaughter statute because he was not aware of the risk created by his conduct. Under an interpretation such as that given the Wisconsin statute by the *Bussard* court, what distinguishes involuntary manslaughter and depraved heart murder?

4. Should negligence be an adequate ground for manslaughter liability? Consider the following case.

STATE v. WILLIAMS

Washington Court of Appeals

4 Wash. App. 908, 484 P.2d 1167 (1971)

HOROWITZ, Chief Judge.

Defendants, husband and wife, were charged by information filed October 3, 1968, with the crime of manslaughter for negligently failing to supply their 17-month child with necessary medical attention, as a result of which he died on September 12, 1968. Upon entry of findings, conclusions and judgment of guilty, sentences were imposed on April 22, 1969. Defendants appeal.

The defendant husband, Walter Williams, is a 24-year-old full-blooded Sheshont Indian with a sixth-grade education. His sole occupation is that of laborer. The defendant wife, Bernice Williams, is a 20-year-old part Indian with an 11th grade education. At the time of the marriage, the wife had two children, the younger of whom was a 14-month son. Both parents worked and the children were cared for by the 85-year-old mother of the defendant husband. The defendant husband assumed parental responsibility with the defendant wife to provide clothing, care and medical attention for the child. Both defendants possessed a great deal of love and affection for the defendant wife's young son.

The court expressly found:

> That both defendants were aware that William Joseph Tabafunda was ill during the period September 1, 1968 to September 12, 1968. The defendants were ignorant. They did not realize how sick the baby was. They thought that the baby had a toothache and no layman regards a toothache as dangerous to life. They loved the baby and gave it aspirin in hopes of improving its condition. They did not take the baby to a doctor because of fear that the Welfare Department would take the baby away from them. They knew that medical help was available because of previous experience. They had no excuse that the law will recognize for not taking the baby to a doctor.
>
> The defendants Walter L. Williams and Bernice J. Williams were negligent in not seeking medical attention for William Joseph Tabafunda.
>
> That as a proximate result of this negligence, William Joseph Tabafunda died.

From these and other findings, the court concluded that the defendants were each guilty of the crime of manslaughter as charged.

Parental duty to provide medical care for a dependent minor child was recognized at common law and characterized as a natural duty. . . . In Washington, the existence of the duty is commonly assumed and is stated at times without reference to any particular statute. . . . The existence of the duty also is assumed, but not always defined, in statutes that provide special criminal and civil sanctions for the performance of that duty. . . . On the question of the quality or seriousness of breach of the duty, at common law, in the case of involuntary manslaughter, the breach had to amount to more than mere ordinary or simple negligence—gross negligence was essential. . . . In Washington, however, RCW 9.48.060[1] (since amended by Laws of 1970, ch. 49, § 2) and RCW 9.48.150[2] supersede both voluntary and involuntary manslaughter as those crimes were defined at common law. Under these statutes the crime is deemed committed even though the death of the victim is the proximate result of only simple or ordinary negligence. . . .

The concept of simple or ordinary negligence describes a failure to exercise the "ordinary caution" necessary to make out the defense of excusable homicide. RCW 9.48.150. Ordinary caution is the kind of caution that a man of reasonable prudence would exercise under the same or similar conditions. If, therefore, the conduct of a defendant, regardless of his ignorance, good intentions and good faith, fails to measure up to the conduct required of a man of reasonable prudence, he is guilty of ordinary negligence because of his failure to use "ordinary caution." If such negligence proximately causes the death of the victim, the defendant, as pointed out above, is guilty of statutory manslaughter.

The remaining issue of proximate cause requires consideration of the question of when the duty to furnish medical care became activated. If the duty to furnish such care was not activated until after it was too late to save the life of the child, failure to furnish medical care could not be said to have proximately caused the child's death. Timeliness in the furnishing of medical care also must be considered in terms of "ordinary caution." The law does not mandatorily require that a doctor be called for a child at the first sign of any indisposition or illness. The indisposition or illness may appear to be of a minor or very temporary kind, such as a toothache or cold. If one in the exercise of ordinary caution fails to recognize that his child's symptoms require medical attention, it cannot be said that the failure to obtain such medical attention is a breach of the duty owed. . . .

It remains to apply the law discussed to the facts of the instant case.

Defendants have not assigned error to the findings either on the ground that the evidence is insufficient to prove negligence or proximate cause. . . . They contended below and on appeal that they are not guilty of the crime charged. Because of the serious nature of the charge against the parent and step-parent of a well-loved child, and out of our concern for the protection of the constitutional rights of the defendants, we have made an independent examination of the evidence to determine whether it substantially supports the court's express finding on proximate cause and its implied finding that the duty to furnish medical care became activated in time to prevent death of the child. . . .

Dr. Gale Wilson, the autopsy surgeon and chief pathologist for the King County Coroner, testified that the child died because an abscessed tooth had been allowed to develop into an infection of the mouth and cheeks, eventually

---

[1] RCW 9.48.060 provided in part: "In any case other than those specified in RCW 9.48.030, 9.48.040 and 9.48.050, homicide, not being excusable or justifiable, is manslaughter."

[2] RCW 9.48.150 provides: "Homicide is excusable when committed by accident or misfortune in doing any lawful act by lawful means, with ordinary caution and without any unlawful intent."

becoming gangrenous. This condition, accompanied by the child's inability to eat, brought about malnutrition, lowering the child's resistance and eventually producing pneumonia, causing the death. Dr. Wilson testified that in his opinion the infection had lasted for approximately 2 weeks, and that the odor generally associated with gangrene would have been present for approximately 10 days before death. He also expressed the opinion that had medical care been first obtained in the last week before the baby's death, such care would have been obtained too late to have saved the baby's life. Accordingly, the baby's apparent condition between September 1 and September 5, 1968 became the critical period for the purpose of determining whether in the exercise of ordinary caution defendants should have provided medical care for the minor child.

The testimony concerning the child's apparent condition during the critical period is not crystal clear, but is sufficient to warrant the following statement of the matter. The defendant husband testified that he noticed the baby was sick about 2 weeks before the baby died. The defendant wife testified that she noticed the baby was ill about a week and a half or 2 weeks before the baby died. The evidence showed that in the critical period the baby was fussy; that he could not keep his food down; and that a cheek started swelling up. The swelling went up and down, but did not disappear. In that same period, the cheek turned "a bluish color like." The defendants, not realizing that the baby was as ill as it was or that the baby was in danger of dying, attempted to provide some relief to the baby by giving the baby aspirin during the critical period and continued to do so until the night before the baby died. The defendants thought the swelling would go down and were waiting for it to do so; and defendant husband testified, that from what he had heard, neither doctors nor dentists pull out a tooth "when it's all swollen up like that." There was an additional explanation for not calling a doctor given by each defendant. Defendant husband testified that "the way the cheek looked . . . and that stuff on his hair, they would think we were neglecting him and take him away from us and not give him back." Defendant wife testified that the defendants were "waiting for the swelling to go down," and also that they were afraid to take the child to a doctor for fear that the doctor would report them to the welfare department, who, in turn, would take the child away. "It's just that I was so scared of losing him." They testified that they had heard that the defendant husband's cousin lost a child that way. The evidence showed that the defendants did not understand the significance or seriousness of the baby's symptoms. However, there is no evidence that the defendants were physically or financially unable to obtain a doctor, or that they did not know an available doctor, or that the symptoms did not continue to be a matter of concern during the critical period. Indeed, the evidence shows that in April 1968 defendant husband had taken the child to a doctor for medical attention.

In our opinion, there is sufficient evidence from which the court could find, as it necessarily did, that applying the standard of ordinary caution, *i.e.,* the caution exercisable by a man of reasonable prudence under the same or similar conditions, defendants were sufficiently put on notice concerning the symptoms of the baby's illness and lack of improvement in the baby's apparent condition in the period from September 1 to September 5, 1968 to have required them to have obtained medical care for the child. The failure so to do in this case is ordinary or simple negligence, and such negligence is sufficient to support a conviction of statutory manslaughter.

The judgment is affirmed.

NOTES AND QUESTIONS

1. Assuming that the defendants in *Williams* indeed deeply loved and cared for their child and that they did not actually appreciate the risk to the child's health until it was too late, what is the point in prosecuting the grief-stricken parents? Are any of the purposes of punishment described in Chapter 2 promoted by convicting the parents of manslaughter or of any other crime?

2. Did the *Williams* defendants possess "normal capacities, physical and mental, for doing what the law requires"? If not, is it morally objectionable to hold them to the standard of the normal, reasonable person? See H.L.A. Hart, Punishment and Responsibility 152–58 (1968). On the other hand, is it defensible to punish the Williamses for negligence even if they do possess normal capacities for doing what the law requires?

Note that the State of Washington no longer recognizes ordinary negligence as "sufficient *mens rea*" for manslaughter. See *Wash. Rev. Code* § 9A.32.070 (1988), which now requires a criminally negligent act as required for manslaughter. See *State v. Norman,* 808 P.2d 1159, 1163–64 (Wash. Ct. App. 1991).

3. Section 210.3(a) of the Model Penal Code limits the crime of involuntary manslaughter to "homicides committed recklessly" [as defined in § 2.02(2)]. Section 210.4 of the Code provides for a separate, less serious crime when "homicide . . . is committed negligently" [defined in § 2.02(d) in terms of a "gross deviation from the standard of care that a reasonable person would observe . . . "]. The Comments to § 210.4 at 86–87 argue that punishment for negligent homicide may "stimulate care that might otherwise not be taken." At the same time, distinguishing manslaughter and negligent homicide in terms of conscious and inadvertent risk creation is important both for assessing the "dangerousness of the actor's conduct and evaluating the gravity of his moral fault." Thus, punishment for negligent homicide (imprisonment for 1 to 5 years) is less than that afforded manslaughter (imprisonment for 1 to 10 years). MPC § 6.06.

While laudable in principle, the Code's distinctions between reckless and negligent homicides are not always easy to draw in practice. Consider the following case.

People v. Strong

Court of Appeals of New York

37 N.Y.2d 568, 338 N.E.2d 602 (1975)

JASEN, Judge.

Defendant was charged, in a one-count indictment, with manslaughter in the second degree (Penal Law, § 125.15) for causing the death of Kenneth Goingsn At the trial, the defense requested that the court submit to the jury, in addition to the crime charged, the crime of criminally negligent homicide (Penal Law, § 125.10). The court refused, and the jury found defendant guilty as charged.

The sole issue upon this appeal is whether the trial court erred in refusing to submit to the jury the lesser crime of criminally negligent homicide.

"The essential distinction between the crimes of manslaughter, second degree, and criminally negligent homicide . . . is the mental state of the defendant at the time the crime was committed. In one, the actor perceives the risk, but consciously disregards it. In the other, he negligently fails to perceive the risk. The result and the underlying conduct, exclusive of the mental element, are the same." . . .

In determining whether the defendant in this case was entitled to the charge of the lesser crime, the focus must be on the evidence in the record relating to the mental state of the defendant at the time of the crime. The record discloses that the defendant, 57 years old at the time of trial, had left his native Arabia at the age of 19, emigrating first to China and then coming to the United States three years later. He had lived in Rochester only a short time before committing the acts which formed the basis for this homicide charge. He testified that he had been of the Sudan Muslim religious faith since birth, and had become one of the sect's leaders, claiming a sizable following. Defendant articulated the three central beliefs of this religion as "cosmetic consciousness, mind over matter and psysiomatic psychomatic consciousness." He stated that the second of these beliefs, "mind over matter," empowered a "master," or leader, to lie on a bed of nails without bleeding, to walk through fire or on hot coals, to perform surgical operations without anesthesia, to raise people up off the ground, and to suspend a person's heartbeat, pulse, and breathing while that person remained conscious. In one particular type of ceremony, defendant, purportedly exercising his powers of "mind over matter," claimed he could stop a follower's heartbeat and breathing and plunge knives into his chest without any injury to the person. There was testimony from at least one of defendant's followers that he had successfully performed this ceremony on previous occasions. Defendant himself claimed to have performed this ceremony countless times over the previous 40 years without once causing an injury. Unfortunately, on January 28, 1972, when defendant performed this ceremony on Kenneth Goings, a recent recruit, the wounds from the hatchet and three knives which defendant had inserted into him proved fatal.

We view the record as warranting the submission of the lesser charge of criminally negligent homicide since there is a reasonable basis upon which the jury could have found that the defendant failed to perceive the risk inherent in his actions. The defendant's conduct and claimed lack of perception, together with the belief of the victim and defendant's followers, if accepted by the jury, would justify a verdict of guilty of criminally negligent homicide. There was testimony, both from defendant and from one of his followers, that the victim himself perceived no danger, but in fact volunteered to participate. Additionally, at least one of the defendant's followers testified that the defendant had previously performed this ritual without causing injury. Assuming that a jury would not believe that the defendant was capable of performing the acts in question without harm to the victim, it still could determine that this belief held by the defendant and his followers was indeed sincere and that defendant did not in fact perceive any risk of harm to the victim.

That is not to say that the court should in every case where there is some subjective evidence of lack of perception of danger submit the lesser crime of criminally negligent homicide. Rather, the court should look to other objective indications of a defendant's state of mind to corroborate, in a sense, the defendant's own subjective articulation. . . .

Therefore, on the particular facts of this case, we conclude that there is a reasonable view of the evidence which, if believed by the jury, would support a finding that the defendant was guilty only of the crime of criminally negligent homicide, and that the trial court erred in not submitting, as requested, this lesser offense to the jury.

Accordingly, we would reverse and order a new trial.

GABRIELLI, Judge (dissenting).

[T]he evidence established defendant's awareness and conscious disregard of the risk his ceremony created and is entirely inconsistent with a negligent failure to perceive that risk. Testimony was adduced that just prior to being stabbed, Goings, a voluntary participant up to that point, objected to continuance of the ceremony saying "No, father" and that defendant, obviously evincing an awareness of the possible result of his actions, answered, "It will be all right, son." Defendant testified that after the ceremony, he noticed blood seeping from the victim's wounds and that he attempted to stop the flow by bandaging the mortally wounded Goings. Defendant further stated that when he later learned that Goings had been removed to another location and had been given something to ease the pain, he became "uptight," indicating, of course, that defendant appreciated the risks involved and the possible consequences of his acts.

Examination of the two homicide sections of the Penal Law, here involved, is important.

"A person is guilty of manslaughter in the second degree when: 1. He recklessly causes the death of another person" (Penal Law, § 125.15, subd. 1); and subdivision 3 of section 15.05 provides that a person acts "recklessly" with respect to a result when he is aware of and disregards a substantial and unjustifiable risk that such result will occur.

"A person is guilty of criminally negligent homicide when, with criminal negligence, he causes the death of another person" (Penal Law, § 125.10); and a person acts with "criminal negligence" with respect to a result when he fails to perceive a substantial and unjustifiable risk that such result will occur (Penal Law, § 15.05, subd. 4).

Simply stated, a reckless offender (manslaughter) is aware of the risk and consciously disregards it; whereas, on the other hand, the "criminally negligent" offender is not aware of the risk created and cannot thus be guilty of disregarding it.

Can it be reasonably claimed or argued that, when the defendant inflicted the several stab wounds, one of which penetrated the victim's heart and was four and three-quarter inches deep, the defendant failed to perceive the risk? The only and obvious answer is simply "no."

Moreover, the record is devoid of evidence pointing toward a *negligent* lack of perception on defendant's part. The majority concludes otherwise by apparently crediting the testimony of defendant, and one of his followers, that at the time defendant was plunging knives into the victim, the defendant thought "there was no danger to it." However, it is readily apparent that the quoted statement does not mean, as the majority assert, that defendant saw no risk of harm in the ceremony, but, rather, that he thought his powers so extraordinary that resultant injury was impossible. Thus, the testimony does not establish defendant's negligent perception for even a grossly negligent individual would perceive the patent risk of injury that would result from plunging a knife into a human being; instead, the testimony demonstrates defendant's conscious disregard of the possible consequences that would naturally flow from his acts.

This case might profitably be analogized to one where an individual believing himself to be possessed of extraordinary skill as an archer attempts to duplicate William Tell's feat and split an apple on the head of another individual from some distance. However, assume that rather than hitting the apple, the archer kills the victim. Certainly, his obtuse subjective belief in his extraordinary skill would not render his actions criminally negligent. Both, in the context of ordinary understanding and the Penal Law definition (§ 15.05, subd. 3), the archer was unquestionably reckless and would, therefore, be guilty of manslaughter in the second degree. The present case is indistinguishable. . . .

QUESTIONS

1. Assuming that the defendant in *Strong* really was unaware of the risk of death entailed in his conduct, why should that matter when he engages in conduct so obviously dangerous to human life? Do his religious motives work as a kind of defense? Should they?

2. On the other hand, if dissenting Judge Gabrielli is correct in his assessment of the facts, why is the killing not depraved heart murder rather than reckless manslaughter? How is *Strong* different from the Russian roulette situation found to be murder in *Commonwealth v. Malone supra* at 542?

[b] Unlawful Act Manslaughter

UNITED STATES V. WALKER

District of Columbia Court of Appeals

380 A.2d 1388 (1977)

KERN, Associate Judge:

Appellee was charged with two counts of involuntary manslaughter and one count of carrying a pistol without a license. The government appeals from the trial court's dismissal of the count in the indictment which charged that appellee

> feloniously, in perpetrating and attempting to perpetrate the crime of carrying a pistol without a license, involving danger of injury, did shoot Ernestine Curry with a pistol, thereby causing injuries from which the said Ernestine Curry died. . . .[3]

At the hearing on appellee's motion to dismiss this count of the indictment, the government's proffer of evidence was that appellee, while carrying a pistol without a license, dropped it in the stairwell of an apartment building, and that the gun went off, fatally wounding a bystander. Appellee's proffer was that a firearms expert had determined that when the hammer of the pistol was not cocked, it would fire on impact only if dropped at a particular angle. These proffers constitute the only explanation in the record of the incident underlying the indictment.

There is no statutory definition of manslaughter in this jurisdiction; this court had occasion in *United States v. Bradford,* D.C. App., 344 A.2d 208 (1975), however, to review at length the law of manslaughter in the District of Columbia. In respect to involuntary manslaughter, we said:

> Involuntary manslaughter is an unlawful killing which is unintentionally committed. By unintentionally it is meant that there is no intent to kill or to do bodily injury. The crime may occur as the result of an unlawful act which is a *misdemeanor involving danger of injury.* The requisite intent in involuntary manslaughter is supplied by the intent to commit the misdemeanor, or by gross or criminal negligence. . . .
>
> The state of mind in involuntary manslaughter is characterized, on the one hand, by a lack of intent to cause death or injury and, on the other, by a lack of awareness of the consequences of the act amounting to an unreasonable failure of perception [criminal negligence] . . . *or the intention to do an act which is a misdemeanor and is in some way dangerous.*

We defined the elements of involuntary manslaughter as: "(1)an unlawful killing of a human being (2)with either (a) *the intent to commit a misdemeanor dangerous in itself or* (b)an unreasonable failure to perceive the risk of harm to others." *Id.,* at 216; emphasis added.

---

[3] Another count of the indictment charged appellee with involuntary manslaughter in shooting Curry "unlawfully, feloniously, and with gross negligence" thereby fatally injuring her.

This appeal therefore presents for our determination the question whether the unlawful act of carrying a pistol without a license is also a dangerous act. The pertinent statute provides:

> No person shall within the District of Columbia carry either openly or concealed on or about his person, except in his dwelling house or place of business or on other land possessed by him, a pistol, without a license therefor issued as hereinafter provided. . . . [D.C. Code 1973, § 22-3204.]

Appellee . . . argues that the plain intent of Section 3204 is to stop the prohibited conduct before danger of injury arises, and that such danger is not a necessary concomitant of the offense. Appellee proceeds to illustrate what he deems to be the "essence" of the offense of carrying a pistol without a license by the following hypothetical:

> [T]wo persons [are] walking peaceably on a public street carrying holstered pistols. One . . . has a license to carry a pistol, but the other has *no* license. The second person is violating section 3204, and the first is not. Yet there is no difference between them in terms of the danger presented to others. [Emphasis added.]

Appellee's hypothetical and argument notwithstanding, we conclude that carrying a pistol without a license exposes the community to such inherent risk of harm that when death results, even though an unintended consequence, the defendant may be nonetheless charged with involuntary manslaughter. Appellee in the instant case was carrying a loaded handgun, which, so far as the record shows, had no purpose other than its use as a weapon. . . .

Additionally, we think it significant in assessing the dangerousness *vel non* of the unlawful act of carrying a pistol without a license that Congress has expressly required one who seeks the license to be "a suitable person to be so licensed." Issuance of these licenses is the responsibility of the Chief of the Metropolitan Police Department, and is subject to restrictive regulations which, among other things, require the applicant to be of sound mind, to be without a prior criminal record, not to be an alcoholic or user of narcotics, to "be trained and experienced in the use, functioning and safe operation of the pistol," and finally, "to be free from physical defects which would impair his safe use of the weapon."

Thus, taking up appellee's hypothetical of the two persons carrying pistols on a public street, one of whom is licensed and the other of whom is not, we conclude that Congress intended to preclude the non-licensee from being on the street with his weapon because of the danger he posed to the community as a result (1) of the inherent dangerousness of the weapon he carried, and (2) of the absence of any evidence of his capability to carry safely such a dangerous instrumentality.

. . . We now hold that a charge of violation of Section 3204 resulting in the shooting and death of another validly charges involuntary manslaughter because the misdemeanor of carrying a pistol without a license is dangerous in and of itself. Accordingly, the trial court's order must be reversed and the count at issue restored to the indictment.

So ordered

NOTES AND QUESTIONS

1. The doctrine applied by the *Walker* court is variously described as "unlawful act man—slaughter" or "misdemeanor manslaughter." It shares obvious similarities to the felony murder doctrine and has been criticized for many of the same reasons. The Model Penal Code rejects the doctrine because, like felony-murder, it "dispenses of proof of culpability and imposes liability for a serious crime without reference to the actor's state of mind." MPC, § 210.3 Comment at 77. Some jurisdictions follow the Code's lead and reject the unlawful act manslaughter rule.

The doctrine is very much alive in other jurisdictions, however. Some limit the "unlawful act" to misdemeanors but others leave open the possibility of felonies which fail to qualify as predicates for felony-murder triggering the manslaughter doctrine. See, *e.g.,* Neb. Rev. Stat. § 28-305, "a person commits manslaughter if he . . . causes the death of another unintentionally while in the commission of an unlawful act." Some jurisdictions explicitly include violations of certain city ordinances as unlawful acts. See, *e.g.,* Kan. Stat. § 21-3404 ("unlawful act[s]" include violations of "ordinances within any city within the state . . . enacted for the protection of human life or safety"). Some authority exists for treating certain noncriminal conduct as unlawful for purposes of the doctrine. See *Wallace v. State,* 232 Ind. 700, 116 N.E.2d 100 (1953) (attempted suicide though not a crime is an unlawful act).

2. The *Walker* case restricts unlawful act manslaughter to "dangerous" misdemeanors. Do you agree that carrying a pistol without a license is dangerous? Suppose the defendant in *Walker* reasonably but mistakenly believed the gun was empty. Or suppose that his accidental dropping of the gun occurred during the one and only occasion he had ever carried a gun as he acquiesced to a friend's request to take the weapon just down the hall in the same apartment building. Is a conviction for manslaughter justifiable in such circumstances?

3. In addition to the "inherently dangerous" limitation, the courts have imposed a variety of other limitations on the unlawful act manslaughter doctrine. Some have required that the unlawful act be of the *malum in se* variety. See, *e.g., Thiede v. State,* 106 Neb. 48, 182 N.W. 570 (1921) (giving the deceased homemade whiskey, though unlawful under state prohibition laws, is not *malum in se* and thus, unless accompanied by negligent conduct, not an unlawful act under manslaughter statute).

Other courts have imposed a "proximate cause" limitation. In *State v. Hupf,* 48 Del. 254, 101 A.2d 355 (1953), the court held that death resulting through defendant's violation of several motor vehicle laws constituted manslaughter so long as the death resulted "proximately" from the unlawful act. The court explained:

> Defendant argues that the common-law rule is too harsh. When applied to the operation of the motor vehicle it results, he says, in stamping as a felon any automobile operator who may, without conscious wrongdoing, have violated one of the many statutory regulations governing the use of the

automobile, if he is involved in an accident resulting in death. Thus, defendant says that the driver of an automobile taking a seriously injured person to the hospital is, under the common-law rule, equally guilty of manslaughter if he violates the speed limit and a child is killed by darting out in front of him, as is the driver who consciously attempts to pass another car upon a twisting hill and as a result is involved in a fatal collision.

The answer to this argument is that if, in such a case, the excessive speed was the proximate cause of the accident, the driver is indeed guilty, but the circumstances would go in mitigation of punishment; and that if the excessive speed was not the proximate cause of death (as might be inferred from the use of the phrase "darting out"), the driver is not guilty. The doctrine of proximate cause is an important limitation on the common-law rule that a homicide occurring in the commission of an unlawful act is manslaughter. The mere violation of the statute is not enough; the violation must be the proximate cause of the death, and that causal connection must affirmatively appear. The unlawful act must be "something more than a factor which might be denominated more properly as an attendant condition than a cause of the death."

48 Del. at 265, 101 A.2d at 360.

What result in *Walker* if the proximate cause limitation is applied?

§ 5.04 THE DEATH PENALTY

Because the death penalty was so influential in its development, the law of homicide cannot be thoroughly understood without considering the subject of capital punishment. The question of whether the State is justified in taking an offender's life has for centuries been fraught with controversy. Moreover, the law on the subject has become enormously complicated as the courts have attempted to ensure that the death penalty is fairly administered.

These materials can do no more than highlight some of the main moral and legal issues in hopes that the reader will pursue matters in more depth on her own. In considering the moral and policy dimensions of the death penalty, keep in mind Chapter 2's material on the justification of punishment in general. Justificatory issues are again taken up in this chapter because these issues are treated in the capital punishment context by a special and voluminous body of literature.

[A] Moral and Policy Issues

[1] Retribution

LEMPERT, *DESERT AND DETERRENCE: AN ASSESSMENT OF THE MORAL BASES OF THE CASE FOR CAPITAL PUNISHMENT*

79 Mich. L. Rev. 1177-86 (1981)

Those who make out a moral case for the death penalty argue in a variety of ways that those who kill others deserve to die. Indeed, to some it is our willingness to execute the murderer which affirms the high value that all participants in the debate place on human life. This is the essence of what is usually called the retributivist position. The moral argument against the death penalty starts with the principle that it is wrong intentionally to take human life. For those who regard this principle as an absolute, the fact that it is wrong to kill does not make it right to take the murderer's life. Opponents of the death penalty correctly point out that in an era when the "eye for an eye" approach to punishment has been abandoned for almost every crime, no self-evident principle demands that it be retained for homicide. They also make the more debatable argument that the state's action in taking a life degrades the values it allegedly asserts.

Both sides of the argument from morality are concerned with issues of justice. No principle of retribution allows the taking of an innocent life. Nor does the just desert theory allow personal characteristics such as sex, race, or national status to dominate indicia of moral culpability in determining punishment. Retributivists justify the death penalty despite substantial evidence that it has been inequitably applied by arguing that inequitable application is not inherent in the penalty, and that it is better that some receive their just deserts, however biased the sample executed, than that none do. For some opponents of capital punishment the inconsistency with which it is applied is enough to condemn it. These opponents need not confront the question of whether it is ultimately just to execute the murderer, for regardless of ultimate deserts, extreme penalties cannot be allowed so long as aspects of personal disadvantage play an important part in determining who from among an equally culpable lot will be subject to the extreme sanction.

There is no necessary connection between moral positions on the justice of capital punishment and empirical judgments as to whether executions deter, but, not surprisingly, moral opponents find comfort in evidence that executions do not deter while moral supporters are heartened by those studies that suggest they do. It is difficult for those whose essential case against the death penalty rests on the value of life to maintain their positions if an execution in fact trades one guilty life for several innocent ones. Even the argument from equality is clouded if the execution of each killer, however inequitably each is selected from among a larger number, prevents the death of several innocent people. Since the same features of social class which make one peculiarly eligible for capital punishment make one disproportionately likely to be a homicide victim, there may even be a kind of rough justice within classes if executions deter.

Although retributivists trace their heritage to Kant and before him to the Bible, utilitarianism is pervasive enough in modern thought that most retributivists would be troubled if a plausible case could not be made for deterrence. Death by execution is both brutal and final. It is hard to make the case for such a penalty when the only end promoted is the unprovable intuition that it is just. Nevertheless, modern retributivists have been less concerned than their opponents with the evidence bearing on deterrence. This may in part be because until recently there was virtually no empirical evidence that gave them comfort. Indeed, a desire to justify capital punishment on grounds other than deterrence has probably contributed to the revival of retributivist theories of punishment. The retributivist justification is possible—although nondeterrence be proven—because justice, however intuitive its grounding, is itself a valued end. Thus, the argument from justice does not necessarily take us beyond the questions of whether an offender deserves execution. The opposing moral claim, from the value of life, pulls us almost irresistibly to the question of whether taking an offender's life will be compensated by the preservation of lives that would otherwise be lost to murder—the empirical question addressed by the research on deterence.

Once we acknowledge that not everyone who kills another should die—and virtually all modern retributivists acknowledge this—doubts about the fairness of the process by which we select those we execute arise. I have already mentioned the difficulties some see in justifying executions when the poor or the black are over-selected for the ultimate punishment, but even less invidious inconsistencies must trouble the retributivist. For absent some self-evident principle separating murderers who deserve to die from those who do not, a *principled* basis for retributivism may only be determined inductively. If inconsistent sentencing prevents the derivation of a socially validated principle, the person who applauds the execution of the murderer is applauding what is literally unprincipled state action. While unprincipled state action may be more common than most of us would like, we usually try to avoid theories which, when applied, lead us to applaud it.

If there is solace for the retributivist, it is in his sense that the state's lack of principle leads it to spare life rather than to take it. People who deserve to die but are spared death can hardly prick one's conscience. While this view may satisfy some moralists who would otherwise have qualms about espousing an inevitably capricious system of capital punishment, it offers nothing to the skeptic. When one criminal is executed and another of apparently equal culpability spared, there is no self-evident reason why the sparing and not the execution is wrong. When a state cannot act consistently in such an important matter as determining who shall die, those who invoke moral philosophy to demand that the state be allowed to make that determination should be able to point to a consensually validated principle which assures us that the inconsistency is benign.

Retributivism is also haunted by those executions of the innocent which inevitably occur if the death penalty is allowed. It is true that documented cases in which the wrong person is executed are quite rare, and likely to remain so. But, as a purely philosophical matter, this is of little help to the retributivist. Retributivism, on its own terms, allows life to be taken only when death is deserved; it does not tolerate killing as a means to some greater social good. Retributivists are proud of their Kantian heritage, which demands that life be treated only as an end. Thus, however good a just punishment system and however much such a system demands the death penalty, the philosophy of retributivism apparently forbids the sacrifice of innocent lives as a condition for the maintenance of such a system. Ideally, of course, a system of capital punishment would not take innocent lives, but we know as a statistical matter that if a state executes often enough, some innocent lives will be lost. Although it may be a comfort not knowing what lives will be mistakenly taken, nothing about retributivism allows us to sacrifice the lives of unknown innocents in the interest of just vengeance.

As I have noted, few modern retributivists believe that all killers deserve death. They respect the law's determination that capital punishment should be reserved for the most morally culpable: those who fully intended, and perhaps rejoiced in, the suffering and death they inflicted and who, in some meaningful sense, could have done otherwise. Moral culpability, thus conceived, is a subjective state. To truly determine who are the most evil and thus the most deserving of death one would have to search people's minds. Our inability to do so means that in deciding whether to inflict the death penalty we often attend more to the circumstances of the crime than to the circumstances of the criminal. The person who slays in a peculiar or brutal way is more likely to receive the death penalty than one who dispatches his victim with a single bullet, yet the former may have been insane under all but the narrowest legal test while the latter was cool and calculating.

Indeed, the former may have been insane even under any legal test. While the mistaken conviction of those who have not killed is certainly rare, the mistaken allocation of responsibility to those who have killed may be uncomfortably common. To the retributivist one mistake is almost as bad as another, for in most retributivist schemes the unpremeditated murderer or the insane killer no more deserves to die than the innocent victim of a misidentification. In arguing from a retributivist philosophy to an actual system of state executions, retributivists are again advocating a system that will work substantial injustice as measured by the standards of the philosophical system they espouse.

The time lag between the time of the crime and the time of execution also poses problems for retributivism. Executions are justified only when the offender deserves to die. Assuming that all those sentenced to death deserved to die at the time they committed the crimes for which they were sentenced, it does not follow that they deserve death at the time it arrives. People so change with their experiences that one may sensibly conceive of individuals as different people deserving different fates at different points in time. Being on death row may be an experience that is especially likely to promote such a change in moral identity.

In short, there is a fundamental irony to the usual retributivist position. Basic principles of moral justice that are believed to justify or even demand the death of those who maliciously kill others are necessarily offended by the attempt to impose a system of state executions in an imperfect world. The emphasis that retributivists place on human beings as ends and not as means, the high value they place on innocent human life, and their insistence that retributivism (unlike revenge) respects the bounds of law combine to form a philosophy from which one cannot derive a policy that trades the wrongful execution of a few for the proper execution of many. Capital punishment implements such a policy. Conversely, any policy derived from a philosophy that is rooted in our intuitions regarding justice will be suspect if the system it prescribes distributes rewards or punishments in an invidious or inconsistent fashion. Capital punishment is such a system.

The preceding discussion focuses on the logic of deriving a system of capital punishment from the premises of retributivism. As such, it speaks to the scholarly debate but does not address the more primitive appeal of retributivism. When one person wantonly kills another we are—if our senses have not been jaded by murder after murder—outraged. Retribution in the form of killing the offender seems like an honorable thing to do.

Why do we feel there is honor in repaying death with death? I believe the reasons are largely cultural. Once we understand them we will see how it is possible—injustices aside—to be attracted by retributivism while simultaneously opposing capital punishment.

Both our history and fiction are replete with characters and communities that are thought to have acted admirably in securing the death of grievous offenders. But it is not the fact of vengeful killing that we admire. Rather, it is the process by which retribution is achieved. We honor individuals not because they redress some cosmic balance sheet, but because they risk their lives for an idea of justice. The Arthurian epic nicely highlights the way in which the degree of honor depends on the element of personal risk. The legend is also interesting for its message that the honor sought by the avenging champion is secondary to that which may be found in search of the holy.

In the case of communities the infliction of death has, historically, a different meaning. The pursuit and execution of criminals were cooperative endeavors that brought communities together to reaffirm their central values. It is not the fact that a death was repaid with a death which is salutary; rather, it is the process necessary to bring this about. Just as the linkage of a positive reinforcer with a neutral stimulus will give the stimulus a positive quality, so do the efforts associated with past accounts of retribution give retributivism its lingering good name. But once the state assumes the burden of executing, the character of the retributive process is fundamentally changed. There is no honor in watching the state execute one who in the past would have been a just target of the watcher's vengeance, nor does honor attach to the person who sets a noose or straps a convict into a chair. The meaning of executions has also changed considerably for communities. Specialized law enforcement means that citizens no longer have to come together to secure retribution, and the execution itself has become a source of passionate controversy rather than the occasion for a reassertion of communal solidarity.

Notes and Questions

1. Professor Lempert notes a variety of shortcomings in the legal system's "attempt to impose a system of state executions in an imperfect world." Would such imperfections (the inability to clearly distinguish degrees of moral culpability, for example) not likely lead some retributivists, even Kantian ones, to favor abolition of capital punishment? Would not a thoroughgoing retributivist be as likely to eschew the death penalty, given the legal system's ability to do, at best, only rough justice, as she would to favor its retention?

2. Some thoughtful commentators disagree with Professor Lempert's conclusion that there is "no honor" in state executions. Consider, for example, the following from W. Berns, *For Capital Punishment* 172–73 (1979):

> Capital punishment . . . serves to remind us of the majesty of the moral order that is embodied in our law and of the terrible consequences of its

breach. The law must not be understood to be merely statute that we enact or repeal at our will and obey or disobey at our convenience, especially not the criminal law. Wherever law is regarded as merely statutory, men will soon enough disobey it, and they will learn how to do so without any inconvenience to themselves. The criminal law must possess a dignity far beyond that possessed by mere statutory enactment or utilitarian and self-interested calculations; the most powerful means we have to give it that dignity is to authorize it to impose the ultimate penalty. The criminal law must be made awful, by which I mean awe-inspiring, or commanding "profound respect or reverential fear." It must remind us of the moral order by which alone we can live as *human* beings, and in our day the only punishment that can do this is capital punishment.

Do you agree with Lempert or Berns? Does the fact that several American states and virtually all other Western democracies in the world have abolished the death penalty bear on Berns's argument? See F. Zimring and G. Hawkins, Capital Punishment and the American Agenda 3–49 (1986). Zimring and Hawkins offer the following rebuttal to arguments like Berns's:

> Here lies the supreme irony involved in the practice of capital punishment in America today insofar as it is intended to fulfill a retributive function and satisfy vindicatory or vindictive needs. To reserve the capital sanction for one in a thousand killings, to confine its application only to those who kill during robberies, or only to those who kill police officers, or kill whites, is, in the majority of homicide cases, to increase personal and social frustration in those close to the victim by disparaging their anguish and depreciating the significance of their loss.
>
> It has been said that "capital punishment for murder exerts a moral influence by indicating that life is the most highly protected value." Viewed in this light the demand for the retention of the death penalty might be seen as representing fear that human life would be devalued by abolition. Yet abolition has precisely the reverse effect as far as the majority of homicides are concerned.
>
> The experience of abolition in other Western nations demonstrates that insofar as it is true that there is "an instinctive feeling in most ordinary men that a person who has done an injury to others should be punished for it," then that feeling is not tied inflexibly to particular penalties. The gradual erosion of support for capital punishment in the wake of abolition indicates that adjustment to a penalty scheme with one less terrible punishment can be achieved without social trauma.

Id., at 162–63.

[2] Deterrence

As suggested by the Lempert excerpt, much of the recent debate about the death penalty has centered on the question of its deterrent effect. The issue is not whether the death penalty deters, but rather whether it marginally deters more effectively than the alternative sanction of imprisonment.

The various empirical studies conducted to test the deterrent effect of the death penalty involve sophisticated issues of social science methodology largely beyond the scope of these materials. However, the following excerpts summarize some of the most important and interesting data and their interpretation by the commentators.

The Model Penal Code, § 210.6 Comments at 112–14, offers this brief sketch of the available data on deterrence:

> Chief among [the grounds for debate about the death penalty] is the efficacy of the death penalty as a deterrent. In a monograph prepared for the Institute, Professor Thorston Sellin collected data on actual imposition of the death penalty and attempted to assess the relationship, if any, between homicide rates and the authorization of death as a possible sanction for murder. Sellin selected clusters of neighboring states with similar social and economic conditions. Within each cluster he compared the experience of abolitionist and retentionist jurisdictions and found no significant or systematic difference between them: "The inevitable conclusion is that executions have no discernible effect on homicide death rates. . . . "
>
> Sellin concluded that a sentence of death is executed in a trivial fraction of the cases in which it might legally be imposed and that there is no quantitative evidence that either its availability or its imposition has noticeable influence upon the frequency of murder. The latter conclusion is not surprising when it is remembered that murders are, upon the whole, either crimes of passion, in which a calculus of consequences has small psychological reality, or crimes of such depravity that the actor reveals himself as doubtfully within the reach of influences that might be especially inhibitory in the case of an ordinary man. These factors, therefore, leave room for substantial doubt that any solid case can be maintained for the death penalty as a deterrent to murder, at least as it is employed in the United States. If this conclusion is correct, it would seem that the social need for grievous condemnation of the act can be met, as it is met in abolition states, without resorting to capital punishment.
>
> Sellin's work proved extremely influential for almost 15 years. It survived without major challenge until Professor Isaac Ehrlich's efforts to test implications of general deterrence theory in the context of capital punishment. Ehrlich looked at the relationship between the homicide rate in the nation as a whole and the "execution risk," that is, the fraction of convicted murderers who are actually put to death. He tried to hold other factors constant by the technique of multiple regression analysis. From experience in the United States from 1933 through 1967 Ehrlich drew the tentative conclusion that execution of an offender tended on the average to deter eight homicides. This finding prompted a storm of controversy that has not yet begun to abate. Sellin's work and Ehrlich's analysis have been attacked and defended on methodological grounds, and each has been tested by replication. These disputes of methodology and statistical technique are largely beyond the competence of those without special training in the field. Further research may clarify the matter, but at present the verdict must be that the existence of a significant deterrent effect from retention of the death penalty has been neither proved nor disproved.

In his dissenting opinion in *Gregg v. Georgia,* 428 U.S. 153, 234–42 (1976), Justice Marshall offered these objections to Ehrlich's pioneering work, *The*

Deterrent Effect of Capital Punishment: A Question of Life and Death, 65 Am. Econ. Rev. 397 (1975):

The Solicitor General in his *amicus* brief in these cases relies heavily on a study by Isaac Ehrlich . . . to support the contention that the death penalty does deter murder. Since the Ehrlich study . . . is the first scientific study to suggest that the death penalty may have a deterrent effect, I will briefly consider its import.

The Ehrlich study focused on the relationship in the Nation as a whole between the homicide rate and "execution risk"—the fraction of persons convicted of murder who were actually executed. Comparing the differences in homicide rate and execution risk for the years 1933 to 1969, Ehrlich found that increases in execution risk were associated with increases in the homicide rate. But when he employed the statistical technique of multiple regression analysis to control for the influence of other variables posited to have an impact on the homicide rate, Ehrlich found a negative correlation between changes in the homicide rate and changes in execution risk. His tentative conclusion was that for the period from 1933 to 1967 each additional execution in the United States might have saved eight lives.

The methods and conclusions of the Ehrlich study have been severely criticized on a number of grounds. It has been suggested, for example, that the study is defective because it compares execution and homicide rates on a nationwide, rather than a state-by-state, basis. The aggregation of data from all States—including those that have abolished the death penalty—obscures the relationship between murder and execution rates. Under Ehrlich's methodology, a decrease in the execution risk in one State combined with an increase in the murder rate in another State would, all things being equal, suggest a deterrent effect that quite obviously would not exist. Indeed, a deterrent effect would be suggested if, once again all other things being equal, one State abolished the death penalty and experienced no change in the murder rate, while another State experienced an increase in the murder rate.

The most compelling criticism of the Ehrlich study is that its conclusions are extremely sensitive to the choice of the time period included in the regression analysis. Analysis of Ehrlich's data reveals that all empirical support for the deterrent effect of capital punishment disappears when the five most recent years are removed from his time series—that is to say, whether a decrease in the execution risk corresponds to an increase or a decrease in the murder rate depends on the ending point of the sample period. This finding has cast severe doubts on the reliability of Ehrlich's tentative conclusions. Indeed, a recent regression study, based on Ehrlich's theoretical model but using cross-section state data for the years 1950 and 1960 found no support for the conclusion that executions act as a deterrent.

The Ehrlich study, in short, is of little, if any, assistance in assessing the deterrent impact of the death penalty.

The commentators tend to support Marshall's views. Lempert, for example declares: "Ehrlich's 1975 article provides no support for the proposition that the death penalty deters. . . . There is now a substantial body of research criticizing Ehrlich on technical grounds and conceptual grounds. The criticism is persuasive." Lempert, *Desert and Deterrence: Aid Assessment of the Moral Bases of the Case for Capital Punishment,* 79 Mich. L. Rev. at 1207–8. Indeed, "the body of econometric research overwhelmingly favors the conclusions that executions do not deter." *Id.*

Other commentators are more cautious. After a thorough review of the evidence, Zimring and Hawkins conclude that the various studies "do not disprove the existence of any marginal deterrent influence" of the death penalty, but the studies do establish that the influence, if any, is very slight. "There is room for debate only about whether the marginal deterrent effect is nil or very small in relation to total homicide volume." Moreover "neither Ehrlich nor anyone else has provided any evidence that capital punishment is a more effective deterrent to homicide that [sic] long prison terms. . . . We have no empirical data to tell us what the differential deterrent effects of disparate periods of incarceration are vis-a-vis the death penalty." F. Zimring and G. Hawkins, Capital Punishment and the American Agenda 180–82 (1986).

In a study only slightly less provocative than Ehrlich's, Bowers and Pierce, *Deterrence or Brutalization: What Is the Effect of Execution?,* 26 Crime & Delinquency 453 (1980), the authors explore the impact of executions on homicides in New York state between 1906 and 1963. Examining the relationship between executions and homicides in the months following executions, they find that the "brutalizing effect" of the death actually leads to two or three homicides that would otherwise not have occurred.

Finally, in what has been described by one commentator, Gorecki, *Capital Punishment: For or Against,* 83 Mich. L. Rev. 1180, 1183 (1985), as "possibly the most ingenious retentionist statement ever made," Professor Ernst van den Haag at page 69 of his book, The Death Penalty: A Debate (1983), which he co-authored with abolitionist John Conrad, offers the following defense of the death penalty:

> Suppose now one is not fully convinced of the superior deterrent effect of the death penalty. I believe I can show that even if one is genuinely uncertain as to whether the death penalty adds to deterrence, one should still favor it, from a purely deterrent viewpoint. For if we are not sure, we must choose either to (1) trade the certain death, by execution, of a convicted murderer for the probable survival of an indefinite number of murder victims whose future murder is less likely (whose survival is more likely)—if the convicted murderer's execution deters prospective murderers, as it might, or to (2) trade the certain survival of the convicted murderer for the probable loss of the lives of future murder victims more likely to be murdered because the convicted murderer's nonexecution might not deter prospective murderers, who could have been deterred by executing the convicted murderer.
>
> To restate the matter: If we were quite ignorant about the marginal deterrent effects of execution, we would have to choose—like it or not—between the certainty of the convicted murderer's death by execution and the likelihood of the survival of future victims of other murderers on the one hand, and on the other his certain survival and the likelihood of the

death of new victims. I'd rather execute a man convicted of having murdered others than to put the lives of innocents at risk. I find it hard to understand the opposite choice.

Van den Haag's argument becomes less convincing when evidence is taken into account that the death penalty might actually operate as an inducement to murder. In addition to the evidence of the "brutalizing effect" of executions noted in the Bowers and Pierce study, supra, consider the argument of Professor Welsh White that some (many?) murderers commit their crimes in hopes, conscious or subconscious, of being executed. W. White, The Death Penalty in the Eighties 152–57 (1987).

[B] Legal Issues

TISON v. ARIZONA

Supreme Court of the United States

481 U.S. 137 (1987)

Justice O'CONNOR *delivered the opinion of the Court.*

The question presented is whether the petitioners' participation in the events leading up to and following the murder of four members of a family makes the sentences of death imposed by the Arizona courts constitutionally permissible although neither petitioner specifically intended to kill the victims and neither inflicted the fatal gunshot wounds. We hold that the Arizona Supreme Court applied an erroneous standard in making the findings required by *Enmund v. Florida,* 458 U.S. 782 [1982], and, therefore, vacate the judgments below and remand the case for further proceedings not inconsistent with this opinion.

Gary Tison was sentenced to life imprisonment as the result of a prison escape during the course of which he had killed a guard. After he had been in prison a number of years, Gary Tison's wife, their three sons Donald, Ricky, and Raymond, Gary's brother Joseph, and other relatives made plans to help Gary Tison escape again. . . . The Tison family assembled a large arsenal of weapons for this purpose. Plans for escape were discussed with Gary Tison, who insisted that his cellmate, Randy Greenawalt, also a convicted murderer, be included in the prison break. . . .

On July 30, 1978, the three Tison brothers entered the Arizona State Prison at Florence carrying a large ice chest filled with guns. The Tisons armed Greenawalt and their father, and the group, brandishing their weapons, locked the prison guards and visitors present in a storage closet. The five men fled the prison grounds in the Tisons' Ford Galaxy automobile. No shots were fired at the prison.

After leaving the prison, the men abandoned the Ford automobile and proceeded on to an isolated house in a white Lincoln automobile that the brothers had parked at a hospital near the prison. At the house, the Lincoln automobile had a flat tire; the only spare tire was pressed into service. After two nights at the house, the group drove towards Flagstaff. As the group traveled on back roads and secondary highways through the desert, another tire blew out. The group decided to flag down a passing motorist and steal a car. Raymond stood out in front of the Lincoln; the other four armed themselves and laid in wait by the side of the road. One car passed by without stopping, but a second car, a Mazda occupied by John Lyons, his wife Donnelda, his 2-year-old son Christopher and his 15-year-old niece, Theresa Tyson, pulled over to render aid.

As Raymond showed John Lyons the flat tire on the Lincoln, the other Tisons and Greenawalt emerged. The Lyons family was forced into the back seat of the Lincoln. Raymond and Donald drove the Lincoln down a dirt road off the highway and then down a gas line service road farther into the desert; Gary Tison, Ricky Tison and Randy Greenawalt followed in the Lyons' Mazda. The two cars were parked trunk to trunk and the Lyons family was ordered to stand in front of the Lincoln's headlights. The Tisons transferred their belongings from the Lincoln into the Mazda. They discovered guns and money in the Mazda which they kept and they put the rest of the Lyons' possessions in the Lincoln.

Gary Tison then told Raymond to drive the Lincoln still farther into the desert. Raymond did so, and, while the others guarded the Lyons and Theresa Tyson, Gary fired his shotgun into the radiator, presumably to completely disable the vehicle. The Lyons and Theresa Tyson were then escorted to the Lincoln and again ordered to stand in its headlights. Ricky Tison reported that John Lyons begged, in comments "more or less directed at everybody," "Jesus, don't kill me." Gary Tison said he was "thinking about it." . . . John Lyons asked the Tisons and Greenawalt to "[g]ive us some water . . . just leave us out here, and you all go home." Gary Tison then told his sons to go back to the Mazda and get some water. Raymond later explained that his father "was like in conflict with himself . . . [w]hat it was, I think it was the baby being there and all this, and he wasn't sure about what to do. . . . "

The petitioners' statements diverge to some extent, but it appears that both of them went back towards the Mazda, along with Donald, while Randy Greenawalt and Gary Tison stayed at the Lincoln guarding the victims. Raymond recalled being at the Mazda filling the water jug "when we started hearing the shots. . . . Ricky said that the brothers gave the water jug to Gary Tison who then, with Randy Greenawalt went behind the Lincoln, where they spoke briefly, then raised the shotguns and started firing. . . . In any event, petitioners agree they saw Greenawalt and their father brutally murder their four captives with repeated blasts from their shotguns. Neither made an effort to help the victims, though both later stated they were surprised by the shooting. The Tisons got into the Mazda and drove away, continuing their flight. Physical evidence suggested that Theresa Tyson managed to crawl away from the bloodbath, severely injured. She died in the desert after the Tisons left.

Several days later the Tisons and Greenawalt were apprehended after a shootout at a police roadblock. Donald Tison was killed. Gary Tison escaped into the desert where he subsequently died of exposure. Raymond and Ricky Tison and Randy Greenawalt were captured and tried jointly for the crimes associated with the prison break itself and the shootout at the roadblock; each was convicted and sentenced.

The state then individually tried each of the petitioners for capital murder of the four victims as well as for the associated crimes of armed robbery, kidnaping, and car theft. The capital murder charges were based on Arizona felony-murder law providing that a killing occurring during the perpetration of robbery or kidnaping is capital murder, . . . and that each participant in the kidnaping or robbery is legally responsible for the acts of his accomplices. . . . Each of the petitioners was convicted of the four murders under these accomplice liability and felony-murder statutes.

Arizona law also provided for a capital sentencing proceeding, to be conducted without a jury, to determine whether the crime was sufficiently aggravated to warrant the death sentence. . . . The statute set out six aggravating and four mitigating factors. . . .

The judge found three statutory aggravating factors:

(1) the Tisons had created a grave risk of death to others (not the victims);

(2) the murders had been committed for pecuniary gain;

(3) the murders were especially heinous.

The judge found no statutory mitigating factor. Importantly, the judge specifically found that the crime was not mitigated by the fact that each of the petitioner's "participation was relatively minor. . . . " Rather, he found that the "participation of each [petitioner] in the crimes giving rise to the application of the felony murder rule in this case was very substantial." . . . The trial judge also specifically found, . . . that each "could reasonably have foreseen that his conduct . . . would cause or create a grave risk of . . . death. . . . "

He did find, however, three nonstatutory mitigating factors:

(1) the petitioners' youth—Ricky was 20 and Raymond was 19;

(2) neither had prior felony records;

(3) each had been convicted of the murders under the felony-murder rule. Nevertheless, the judge sentenced both petitioners to death. On direct appeal the Arizona Supreme Court affirmed. . . .

In evaluating the trial court's findings of aggravating and mitigating factors, the Arizona Supreme Court found the first aggravating factor—creation of grave risk to others—not supported by the evidence. All those killed were intended victims, and no one else was endangered. The Arizona Supreme Court, however, upheld the "pecuniary gain" and "heinousness" aggravating circumstances and the death sentences. . . . Petitioners then collaterally attacked their death sentences in state postconviction proceedings alleging that *Enmund*, . . . which had been decided in the interim, required reversal. A divided Arizona Supreme Court, interpreting *Enmund* to require a finding of "intent to kill," declared . . . the dictate of *Enmund* is satisfied [in both Raymond and Ricky Tison's cases]. . . . "

We granted certiorari in order to consider the Arizona Supreme Court's application of *Enmund*.. . .

II

In *Enmund v. Florida,* this Court reversed the death sentence of a defendant convicted under Florida's felony-murder rule. Enmund was the driver of the "getaway" car in an armed robbery of a dwelling. The occupants of the house, an elderly couple, resisted and Enmund's accomplices killed them. The Florida Supreme Court found the inference that Enmund was the person in the car by the side of the road waiting to help his accomplices escape sufficient to support his sentence of death:

> [T]he only evidence of the degree of [Enmund's] participation is the jury's likely inference that he was the person in the car by the side of the road near the scene of the crimes. The jury could have concluded that he was there, a few hundred feet away, waiting to help the robbers escape with the Kerseys' money. The evidence, therefore, was sufficient to find that the appellant was a principal of the second degree, constructively present aiding and abetting the commission of the crime of robbery. This conclusion supports the verdicts of . . . first degree . . . felony-murder. . . .

This Court, citing the weight of legislative and community opinion, found a broad societal consensus, with which it agreed, that the death penalty was disproportional to the crime of robbery—felony-murder "in these circumstances." . . . The Court noted that although 32 American jurisdictions permitted the imposition of the death penalty for felony murders under a variety of circumstances, Florida was one of only eight jurisdictions that authorized the death penalty "solely for participation in a robbery in which another robber takes life. . . . " Enmund was, therefore, sentenced under a distinct minority regime, a regime that permitted the imposition of the death penalty for felony-murder *simpliciter.* At the other end of the spectrum, eight States required a finding of intent to kill before death could be imposed in a felony-murder case and one State required actual participation in the killing. The remaining States authorizing capital punishment for felony-murders fell into two somewhat overlapping middle categories: three authorized the death penalty when the defendant acted with recklessness or extreme indifference to human life, and nine others, including Arizona, required a finding of some aggravating factor beyond the fact that the killing had occurred during the course of a felony before a capital sentence might be imposed. Arizona fell into a subcategory of six States which made "minimal participation in a capital felony committed by another person a [statutory] mitigating circumstance." . . . Two more jurisdictions required a finding that the defendant's participation in the felony was not "relatively minor" before authorizing a capital sentence. . . . Vermont fell into none of these categories.

After surveying the States' felony-murder statutes, the *Enmund* court next examined the behavior of juries in cases like *Enmund's* in its attempt to assess American attitudes towards capital punishment in felony-murder cases. Of 739 death row inmates, only 41 did not participate in the fatal assault. All but 16 of these were physically present at the scene of the murder and of these only 3, including *Enmund,* were sentenced to death in the absence of a finding that they had collaborated in a scheme designed to kill. The court found the fact that only 3 of 739 death row inmates had been sentenced to death absent an intent to kill, physical presence or direct participation in the fatal assault persuasive evidence that American juries considered the death sentence disproportional to felony-murder *simpliciter.*

Against this background, the court undertook its own proportionality analysis. Armed robbery is a serious offense, but one for which the penalty of death is plainly excessive; the imposition of the death penalty for robbery, therefore, violates the Eighth and Fourteenth Amendments' proscription "against all punishments which by their excessive length or severity are greatly disproportionate to the offenses, charged." *Weems v. United States,* 217 U.S. 349, 371 (1910); cf. *Coker v. Georgia,* 433 U.S. 584 (1977) (holding the death penalty disproportional to the crime of rape). Furthermore, the Court found that Enmund's degree of participation in the murders was so tangential that it could not be said to justify a sentence of death. It found that neither the deterrent nor the retributive purposes of the death penalty were advanced by imposing the death penalty upon Enmund. The *Enmund* Court was unconvinced "that the threat that the death penalty will be imposed for murder will measurably deter one who does not kill and has no intention or purpose that life will be taken. . . . " In reaching this conclusion, the court relied upon the fact that killing only rarely occurred during the course of robberies and such killing as did occur even more rarely resulted in death sentences if the evidence did not support an inference that the defendant intended to kill. The Court acknowledged, however, that "[i]t would be very different if the likelihood of a killing in the course of a robbery were so substantial that one should share the blame for the killing if he somehow participated in the felony. . . . "

That difference was also related to the second purpose of capital punishment, retribution. The heart of the retribution rationale is that a criminal sentence must be directly related to the personal culpability of the criminal offender. While the States generally have wide discretion in deciding how much retribution to exact in a given case, the death penalty, "unique in its severity and irrevocability, . . . " requires the State to inquire into the relevant facets of "the character and record of the individual offender. . . . " Thus, in Enmund's case, "the focus [had to] be on his culpability, not on that of those who committed the robbery and shot the victims, for we insist on "individualized consideration as a constitutional requirement in imposing the death sentence. . . . " Since Enmund's own participation in the felony murder was so attenuated and since there was no proof that Enmund had any culpable mental state, . . . the death penalty was excessive retribution for his crimes.

Enmund explicitly dealt with two distinct subsets of all felony murders in assessing whether Enmund's sentence was disproportional under the Eighth Amendment. At one pole was Enmund himself: the minor actor in an armed robbery, not on the scene, who neither intended to kill nor was found to have had any culpable mental state. Only a small minority of States even authorized the death penalty in such circumstances and even within those jurisdictions the death penalty was almost never exacted for such a crime. The Court held that capital punishment was disproportional in these cases. *Enmund* also clearly dealt with the other polar case: the felony murderer who actually killed, attempted to kill, or intended to kill. The Court clearly held that the equally small minority of jurisdictions that limited the death penalty to these circumstances could continue to exact it in accordance with local law when the circumstances warranted. The Tison brothers' cases fall into neither of these neat categories.

Petitioners argue strenuously that they did not "intend to kill" as that concept has been generally understood in the common law. We accept this as true. Traditionally, "one intends certain consequences when he desires that his acts cause those consequences or knows that those consequences are substantially certain to result from his acts. . . . " As petitioners point out, there is no evidence that either Ricky or Raymond Tison took any act which he desired to, or was substantially certain would, cause death.

The Arizona Supreme Court did not attempt to argue that the facts of this case supported an inference of "intent" in the traditional sense. Instead, the Arizona Supreme Court attempted to reformulate "intent to kill" as a species of foreseeability. The Arizona Supreme Court wrote:

"Intend [sic] to kill includes the situation in which the defendant intended, contemplated, or anticipated that lethal force would or might be used or that life would or might be taken in accomplishing the underlying felony."

. . . This definition of intent is broader than that described by the *Enmund* Court. Participants in violent felonies like armed robberies can frequently "anticipat[e] that lethal force . . . might be used . . . in accomplishing the underlying felony." Enmund himself may well have so anticipated. Indeed, the possibility of bloodshed is inherent in the commission of any violent felony and this possibility is generally foreseeable and foreseen; it is one principal reason that felons arm themselves. The Arizona Supreme Court's attempted reformulation of intent to kill amounts to little more than a restatement of the felony-murder rule itself. Petitioners do not fall within the "intent to kill" category of felony-murderers for which *Enmund* explicitly finds the death penalty permissible under the Eighth Amendment.

On the other hand, it is equally clear that petitioners also fall outside the category of felony-murderers for whom *Enmund* explicitly held the death penalty disproportional: their degree of participation in the crimes was major rather than minor, and the record would support a finding of the culpable mental state of reckless indifference to human life. We take the facts as the Arizona Supreme Court has given them to us. . . .

Raymond Tison brought an arsenal of lethal weapons into the Arizona State Prison which he then handed over to two convicted murderers, one of whom he knew had killed a prison guard in the course of a previous escape attempt. By his own admission he was prepared to kill in furtherance of the prison break. He performed the crucial role of flagging down a passing car occupied by an innocent family whose fate was then entrusted to the known killers he had previously armed. He robbed these people at their direction and then guarded the victims at gunpoint while they considered what next to do. He stood by and watched the killing, making no effort to assist the victims before, during, or after the shooting. Instead, he chose to assist the killers in their continuing criminal endeavors, ending in a gun battle with the police in the final showdown.

Ricky Tison's behavior differs in slight details only. Like Raymond, he intentionally brought the guns into the prison to arm the murderers. He could have foreseen that lethal force might be used, particularly since he knew that his father's previous escape attempt had resulted in murder. He, too, participated fully in the kidnaping and robbery and watched the killing after which he chose to aid those whom he had placed in the position to kill rather than their victims.

These facts not only indicate that the Tison brothers' participation in the crime was anything but minor, they also would clearly support a finding that they both subjectively appreciated that their acts were likely to result in the taking of innocent life. The issue raised by this case is whether the Eighth Amendment prohibits the death penalty in the intermediate case of the defendant whose participation is major and whose mental state is one of reckless indifference to the value of human life. *Enmund* does not specifically address this point. We now take up the task of determining whether the Eighth Amendment proportionality requirement bars the death penalty under these circumstances.

Like the *Enmund* court, we find the state legislatures' judgment as to proportionality in these circumstances relevant to this constitutional inquiry. The largest number of States still fall into the two intermediate categories discussed in *Enmund*. Four States authorize the death penalty in felony-murder cases upon a showing of culpable mental state such as recklessness or extreme indifference to human life. Two jurisdictions require that the defendant's participation be substantial and the statutes of at least six more, including Arizona, take minor participation in the felony expressly into account in mitigation of the murder. These requirements significantly overlap both in this case and in general, for the greater the defendant's participation in the felony-murder, the more likely that he acted with reckless indifference to human life. At a minimum, however, it can be said that all these jurisdictions, as well as six States which *Enmund* classified along with Florida as permitting capital punishment for felony-murder simpliciter, and the three States which simply require some additional aggravation before imposing the death penalty upon a felony-murderer, specifically authorize the death penalty in a felony-murder case where, though the defendant's mental state fell short of intent to kill, the defendant was a major actor in a felony in which he knew death was highly likely to occur. On the other hand, even after *Enmund,* only 11 States authorizing capital punishment forbid imposition of the death penalty even though the defendant's participation in the felony-murder is major and the likelihood of killing is so substantial as to raise an inference of extreme recklessness. This substantial and recent legislative authorization of the death penalty for the crime of felony-murder regardless of the absence of a finding of an intent to kill powerfully suggests that our society does not reject the death penalty as grossly excessive under these circumstances. . . .

Moreover, a number of state courts have interpreted Enmund to permit the imposition of the death penalty in such aggravated felony murders. We do not approve or disapprove the judgments as to proportionality reached on the particular facts of these cases, but we note the apparent consensus that substantial participation in a violent felony under circumstances likely to result in the loss of innocent human life may justify the death penalty even absent an "intent to kill." . . .

Against this backdrop, we now consider the proportionality of the death penalty in these mid range felony-murder cases for which the majority of American jurisdictions clearly authorize capital punishment and for which American courts have not been nearly so reluctant to impose death as they are in the case of felony-murder *simpliciter.*

A critical facet of the individualized determination of culpability required in capital cases is the mental state with which the defendant commits the crime. Deeply ingrained in our legal tradition is the idea that the more purposeful is the criminal conduct, the more serious is the offense, and, therefore, the more severely it ought to be punished. The ancient concept of malice aforethought was an early attempt to focus on mental state in order to distinguish those who deserved death from those who through "Benefit of . . . Clergy" would be spared. . . . Over time, malice aforethought came to be inferred from the mere act of killing in a variety of circumstances; in reaction, Pennsylvania became the first American jurisdiction to distinguish between degrees of murder, reserving capital punishment to "wilful, deliberate and premeditated" killings and felony-murders. In *Enmund,* the Court recognized . . . the importance of mental state, explicitly permitting the death penalty in at least those cases where the felony-murderer intended to kill and forbidding it in the case of a minor actor not shown to have had any culpable mental state.

A narrow focus on the question of whether or not a given defendant "intended to kill," however, is a highly unsatisfactory means of definitively distinguishing the most culpable and dangerous of murderers. Many who intend to, and do, kill are not criminally liable at all—those who act in self-defense or with other justification or excuse. Other intentional homicides, though criminal, are often felt undeserving of the death penalty—those that are the result of provocation. On the other hand, some nonintentional murderers may be among the most dangerous and inhumane of all—the person who tortures another not caring whether the victim lives or dies, or the robber who shoots someone in the course of the robbery, utterly indifferent to the fact that the desire to rob may have the unintended consequence of killing the victim as well as taking the victim's property. This reckless indifference to the value of human life may be every bit as shocking to the moral sense as an "intent to kill." . . .

Enmund held that when "intent to kill" results in its logical though not inevitable consequence—the taking of human life—the Eighth Amendment permits the State to exact the death penalty after a careful weighing of the aggravating and mitigating circumstances. Similarly, we hold that the reckless disregard for human life implicit in knowingly engaging in criminal activities known to carry a grave risk of death represents a highly culpable mental state, a mental state that may be taken into account in making a capital sentencing judgment when that conduct causes its natural, though also not inevitable, lethal result.

The petitioners' own personal involvement in the crimes was not minor, but rather, as specifically found by the trial court, "substantial." Far from merely sitting in a car away from the actual scene of the murders acting as the getaway driver to a robbery, each petitioner was actively involved in every element of the kidnaping-robbery and was physically present during the entire sequence of criminal activity culminating in the murder of the Lyons family and the subsequent flight. The Tisons' high level of participation in these crimes further implicates them in the resulting deaths. Accordingly, they fall well within the overlapping second intermediate position which focuses on the defendant's degree of participation in the felony.

Only a small minority of those jurisdictions imposing capital punishment for felony murder have rejected the possibility of a capital sentence absent an intent to kill and we do not find this minority position constitutionally required. We will not attempt to precisely delineate the particular types of conduct and states of mind warranting imposition of the death penalty here. Rather, we simply hold that major participation in the felony committed, combined with reckless indifference to human life, is sufficient to satisfy the Enmund culpability requirement. The Arizona courts have clearly found that the former exists; we now vacate the judgments below and remand for determination of the latter in further proceedings not inconsistent with this opinion. . . .

It is so ordered.

Justice BRENNAN, with whom Justice MARSHALL joins, and with whom Justice

BLACKMUN and Justice STEVENS join as to Parts I-IV-A, *dissenting.*

The murders that Gary Tison and Randy Greenawalt committed revolt and grieve all who learn of them. When the deaths of the Lyons family and Theresa Tyson were first reported, many in Arizona erupted "in a towering yell" for retribution and justice. Yet Gary Tison, the central figure in this tragedy, the man who had his family arrange his and Greenawalt's escape from prison, and the man who chose, with Greenawalt, to murder this family while his sons stood by, died of exposure in the desert before society could arrest him and bring him to trial. The question this case presents is what punishment Arizona may constitutionally exact from two of Gary Tison's sons for their role in these events. Because our precedents and our Constitution compel a different answer than the one the Court reaches today, I dissent. . . .

* * *

III

[T]he basic flaw in today's decision is the Court's failure to conduct the sort of proportionality analysis that the Constitution and past cases require. Creation of a new category of culpability is not enough to distinguish this case from *Enmund*. The Court must also establish that death is a proportionate punishment for individuals in this category. In other words, the Court must demonstrate that major participation in a felony with a state of mind of reckless indifference to human life deserves the same punishment as intending to commit a murder or actually committing a murder. The Court does not attempt to conduct a proportionality review of the kind performed in past cases raising a proportionality question, . . . but instead offers two reasons in support of its view.

A

One reason the Court offers for its conclusion that death is proportionate punishment for persons falling within its new category is that limiting the death penalty to those who intend to kill "is a highly unsatisfactory means of definitively distinguishing the most culpable and dangerous of murderers. . . . " To illustrate that intention cannot be dispositive, the Court offers as examples "the person *who tortures* another not caring whether the victim lives or dies, or the robber *who shoots* someone in the course of the robbery, utterly indifferent to the fact that the desire to rob may have the unintended consequence of killing the victim as well as taking the victim's property."

. . . Influential commentators and some States have approved the use of the death penalty for persons, like those given in the Court's examples, *who kill* others in circumstances manifesting an extreme indifference to the value of human life. Thus an exception to the requirement that only intentional murders be punished with death might be made for persons who actually commit an act of homicide; *Enmund,* by distinguishing from the accomplice case "those who kill," clearly reserved that question. But the constitutionality of the death penalty for those individuals is no more relevant to this case than it was to *Enmund,* because this case, like *Enmund,* involves accomplices *who did not kill.* Thus, although some of the "most culpable and dangerous of murderers" may be those who killed without specifically intending to kill, it is considerably more difficult to apply that rubric convincingly to those who not only did not intend to kill, but who also have not killed.

It is precisely in this context—where the defendant has not killed—that a finding that he or she nevertheless intended to kill seems indispensable to establishing capital culpability. It is important first to note that such a defendant has not committed an *act* for which he or she could be sentenced to death. The applicability of the death penalty therefore turns entirely on the defendant's mental state with regard to an act committed by another. Factors such as the defendant's major participation in the events surrounding the killing or the defendant's presence at the scene are relevant insofar as they illuminate the defendant's mental state with regard to the killings. They cannot serve, however, as independent grounds for imposing the death penalty.

Second, when evaluating such a defendant's mental state, a determination that the defendant acted with intent is qualitatively different from a determination that the defendant acted with reckless indifference to human life. The difference lies in the nature of the choice each has made. The reckless actor has not *chosen* to bring about the killing in the way the intentional actor has. The person who chooses to act recklessly and is indifferent to the possibility of fatal consequences often deserves serious punishment. But because that person has not chosen to kill, his or her moral and criminal culpability is of a different degree than that of one who killed or intended to kill.

The importance of distinguishing between these different choices is rooted in our belief in the "freedom of the human will and a consequent ability and duty of the normal individual to choose between good and evil.". . . To be faithful to this belief, which is "universal and persistent in mature systems of law," . . . the criminal law must ensure that the punishment an individual receives conforms to the choices that individual has made. Differential punishment of reckless and intentional actions is therefore essential if we are to retain "the relation between criminal liability and moral culpability" on which criminal justice depends. . . . The State's ultimate sanction—if it is ever to be used—must be reserved for those whose culpability is greatest. . . .

Distinguishing intentional from reckless action in assessing culpability is particularly important in felony-murder cases. . . .

In *Enmund,* the Court explained at length the reasons a finding of intent is a necessary prerequisite to the imposition of the death penalty. In any given case, the Court said, the death penalty must "measurably contribut[e]" to one or both of the two "social purposes"—deterrence and retribution—which this Court has accepted as justifications for the death penalty. . . . If it does not so contribute, it" —is nothing more than the purposeless and needless imposition of pain and suffering' and hence an unconstitutional punishment. . . . " Enmund's lack of intent to commit the murder—rather than the lack of evidence as to his mental state—was the decisive factor in the Court's decision that the death penalty served neither of the two purposes. With regard to deterrence, the Court was "quite unconvinced . . . that the threat that the death penalty will be imposed for murder will measurably deter one who does not kill and has no intention or purpose that life will be taken. Instead, it seems likely that —capital punishment can serve as a deterrent only when murder is the result of premeditation and deliberation.' . . . "

As for retribution, the Court again found that Enmund's lack of intent, together with the fact that he did not kill the victims, was decisive. "American criminal law has long considered a defendant's intention—and therefore his moral guilt—to be critical to the —degree of [his] criminal culpability.'"
. . . The Court concluded that "[p]utting Enmund to death to avenge two killings that he did not commit and had no intention of committing or causing does not measurably contribute to the retributive end of ensuring that the criminal gets his just deserts.". . . Thus, in *Enmund* the Court established that a finding of an intent to kill was a constitutional prerequisite for the imposition of the death penalty on an accomplice who did not kill. . . . The Court's decision today to approve the death penalty for accomplices who lack this mental state is inconsistent with *Enmund* and with the only justifications this Court has put forth for imposing the death penalty in any case.

B

The Court's second reason for abandoning the intent requirement is based on its survey of state statutes authorizing the death penalty for felony murder, and on a handful of state cases. On this basis, the court concludes that *"[o]nly a small minority of those jurisdictions imposing capital punishment for felony murder* have rejected the possibility of a capital sentence absent an intent to kill and we do not find this minority position constitutionally required."
. . . The Court would thus have us believe that "the majority of American jurisdictions clearly authorize capital punishment" in cases such as this. . . . This is not the case. First, the Court excludes from its survey those jurisdictions that have abolished the death penalty and those that have authorized it only in circumstances different from those presented here. When these

jurisdictions are included, and are considered with those jurisdictions that require a finding of intent to kill in order to impose the death sentence for felony murder, one discovers that approximately three-fifths of American jurisdictions do not authorize the death penalty for a nontriggerman absent a finding that he intended to kill. Thus, contrary to the Court's implication that its view is consonant with that of "the majority of American jurisdictions, . . . " the Court's view is itself distinctly the minority position.

Second, it is critical to examine not simply those jurisdictions that authorize the death penalty in a given circumstance, but those that actually *impose* it. Evidence that a penalty is imposed only infrequently suggests not only that jurisdictions are reluctant to apply it but also that, when it is applied, its imposition is arbitrary and therefore unconstitutional. . . . Thus, the Court in *Enmund* examined the relevant statistics on the imposition of the death penalty for accomplices in a felony murder. The Court found that of all executions between 1954 and 1982, there were "only 6 cases out of 362 where a nontriggerman felony-murderer was executed. All six executions took place in 1955." . . . This evidence obviously militates against imposing the death penalty on petitioners as powerfully as it did against imposing it on *Enmund*.

The Court in *Enmund* also looked at the imposition of the death penalty for felony murder within Florida, the State that had sentenced *Enmund*. Of the 45 murderers then on death row, 36 had been found to have "intended" to take life, and 8 of the 9 for which there was no finding of intent had been the triggerman. Thus in only one case—*Enmund*—had someone (such as the Tisons) who had neither killed nor intended to kill received the death sentence. Finally, the Court noted that in no Commonwealth or European country could Enmund have been executed, since all have either abolished or never employed a felony-murder doctrine. . . .

The Court today neither reviews nor updates this evidence. Had it done so, it would have discovered that, even including the 65 executions since *Enmund*, "[t]he fact remains that we are not aware of a single person convicted of felony-murder over the past quarter century who did not kill or attempt to kill, and did not intend the death of the victim, who has been executed." . . . Of the 64 persons on death row in Arizona, all of those who have raised and lost an *Enmund* challenge in the Arizona Supreme Court have been found either to have killed or to have specifically intended to kill. Thus, like *Enmund,* the Tisons' sentence appears to be an aberration within Arizona itself as well as nationally and internationally. The Court's objective evidence that the statutes of roughly 20 States appear to authorize the death penalty for defendants in the Court's new category is therefore an inadequate substitute for a proper proportionality analysis, and is not persuasive evidence that the punishment that was unconstitutional for *Enmund* is constitutional for the Tisons.

C

The Court's failure to examine the full range of relevant evidence is troubling not simply because of what that examination would have revealed, but because until today such an examination has been treated as constitutionally required *whenever* the Court undertakes to determine whether a given punishment is disproportionate to the severity of a given crime. . . .

* * *

The Framers provided in the Eighth Amendment the limiting principles otherwise absent in the prevailing theories of punishment. One such principle is that the States may not impose punishment that is disproportionate to the severity of the offense or to the individual's own conduct and culpability. Because the proportionality inquiry in this case overlooked evidence and considerations essential to such an inquiry, it is not surprising that the result appears incongruous. Ricky and Raymond Tison are similarly situated with Earl Enmund in every respect that mattered to the decision in *Enmund*. Like Enmund, the Tisons neither killed nor attempted or intended to kill anyone. Like Enmund, the Tisons have been sentenced to death for the intentional acts of others which the Tisons did not expect, which were not essential to the felony, and over which they had no control. Unlike Enmund, however, the Tisons will be the first individuals in over 30 years to be executed for such behavior.

I conclude that the proportionality analysis and result in this case cannot be reconciled with the analyses and results of previous cases. On this ground alone, I would dissent. But the fact that this Court's death penalty jurisprudence can validate different results in analytically indistinguishable cases suggests that something more profoundly disturbing than faithlessness to precedent is at work in capital sentencing.

IV

In 1922, "five negroes who were convicted of murder in the first degree and sentenced to death by the Court of the State of Arkansas" appealed to this Court from an order of the District Court dismissing their writ of habeas corpus. *Moore v. Dempsey,* 261 U.S. 86, 87 (1923). The crux of their appeal was that they "were hurried to conviction under the pressure of a mob without any regard for their rights and without according to them due process of law." . . . In reversing the order, Justice Holmes stated the following for the Court:

> "It certainly is true that mere mistakes of law in the course of a trial are not to be corrected [by habeas corpus]. But if the case is that the whole proceeding is a mask—that counsel, jury, and judge were swept to the fatal end by an irresistible wave of public passion, and that the State Courts failed to correct the wrong, neither perfection in the machinery for correction nor the possibility that the trial court and counsel saw no other way of avoiding an immediate outbreak of the mob can prevent this Court from securing to the petitioners their constitutional rights." *Id.,* at 91.

A

In *Furman v. Georgia,* [408 U.S. 238 (1972)], this Court concluded that the State's procedural machinery was so imperfect that imposition of the death penalty had become arbitrary and therefore unconstitutional. A scant four years later, however, the Court validated Georgia's new machinery, and in 1977 executions resumed. In this case, the State appears to have afforded petitioners all of the procedures that this Court has deemed sufficient to produce constitutional sentencing decisions. Yet in this case, as in *Moore,* "perfection in the [State's] machinery for correction" has not secured to petitioners their constitutional rights. So rarely does any State (let alone any Western country other than our own) ever execute a person who neither killed nor intended to kill that "these death sentences are cruel and unusual in the same way that being struck by lightning is cruel and unusual.". . . This case thus demonstrates, as *Furman* also did, that we have yet to achieve a system capable of "distinguishing the few cases in which the [death penalty] is imposed from the many cases in which it is not.". . .

What makes this a difficult case is the challenge of giving substantive content to the concept of criminal culpability. Our Constitution demands that the sentencing decision itself, and not merely the procedures that produce it, respond to the reasonable goals of punishment. But the decision to execute these petitioners, like the state courts' decisions in *Moore,* and like other decisions to kill, appears responsive less to reason than to other, more visceral, demands. The urge to employ the felony-murder doctrine against accomplices is undoubtedly strong when the killings stir public passion and the actual murderer is beyond human grasp. And an intuition that sons and daughters must sometimes be punished for the sins of the father may be deeply rooted in our consciousness. Yet punishment that conforms more closely to such retributive instincts than to the Eighth Amendment is tragically anachronistic in a society governed by our Constitution.

B

This case thus illustrates the enduring truth of Justice Harlan's observation that the tasks of identifying "those characteristics of criminal homicides and their perpetrators which call for the death penalty, and [of] express[ing] these characteristics in language which can be *fairly* understood and applied by the sentencing authority appear to be . . . beyond present human ability." . . . The persistence of doctrines (such as felony-murder) that allow excessive discretion in apportioning criminal culpability, and of decisions (such as today's) that do not even attempt "precisely [to] delineate the particular types of conduct and states of mind warranting imposition of the death penalty," . . . demonstrate that this Court has still not articulated rules that will ensure that capital sentencing decisions conform to the substantive principles of the Eighth Amendment. Arbitrariness continues so to infect both the procedure and substance of capital sentencing that any decision to impose the death penalty remains cruel and unusual. For this reason, as well as for the reasons expressed in *Gregg v. Georgia,* 428 U.S., at 227, I adhere to my view that the death penalty is in all circumstances cruel and unusual punishment prohibited by the Eighth and Fourteenth Amendments, and dissent.

NOTES AND QUESTIONS

1. Is the *Tison* Court on firm ground in holding that major participation in a felony with a state of mind of reckless indifference to human life deserves the same punishment as intending to aid another to commit murder or committing murder oneself? What if on remand the evidence shows that the

Tison petitioners acted with reckless indifference to the lives of the prison officials holding Gary Tison but not to the actual victims. Should the recklessness transfer to the victims. For discussion of the analogous doctrine of transferred intent, see LaFave and Scott at 283–87. Are the petitioners any less culpable if they are indifferent to the lives of guards holding their father in prison but not to the lives of the family actually victimized?

2. Is there a risk that as death penalty liability extends farther from the actual killer, negligence rather than recklessness might become the basis for imposing capital punishment? Under revolting facts such as those reflected in *Tison,* will courts and sentencers insist that the State prove the defendants *consciously* disregarded the risk of death or will temptations to exact retribution lead to imposition of the death penalty on the theory that the defendants *should have* appreciated the risk even if they actually did not? Would the *Tison* Court rule out imposition of the death penalty if imposed for gross negligence?

3. Suppose a robber accidentally kills the victim of his robbery. Under *Enmund* and *Tison,* could the State execute such a triggerman on felony-murder grounds without proving that he acted with reckless indifference to human life? If capital punishment is unjustified in these circumstances, is a noncapital sentence for felony-murder any more justified?

A Brief Consideration of Supreme Court Cases

Tison is an example of an expansive body of case law in which an often closely divided Supreme Court has struggled to set parameters for constitutionally imposing the death penalty. Complete appreciation of the intricacies and nuances of the flow of Supreme Court opinions, begun with *Furman v. Georgia,* 408 U.S. 238 (1972), cannot be achieved in the context of these materials. A few cases should be briefly highlighted, however.

Furman itself illustrates the complexity of the Court's problem and the depth of the disagreement among its members as to how to achieve its solution. The opinion consists of a short Per Curiam which, without reasoning, invalidated capital punishment as then administered in every jurisdiction. Each of the nine justices filed a separate concurring or dissenting opinion, taking over 230 pages to express their respective views.

Two of the *Furman* Justices (Brennan and Marshall) found the death penalty to be unconstitutional *per se* as cruel and unusual punishment. Justice Brennan found capital punishment, like the rack and thumbscrew, to be inherently demeaning and degrading to human life. He also objected to the arbitrary imposition of the death penalty and concluded that its infrequent employment reflected its moral unacceptability in contemporary American society. Finally, Brennan found that in the absence of evidence showing a deterrent effect superior to less severe punishments, infliction of the death penalty constituted unconstitutionally excessive punishment. Justice Marshall agreed with several of Brennan's objections and added several of his own. He maintained that the average American citizen, if fully informed on the issue, would find the death penalty "shocking to his conscience and sense of justice." Moreover, he objected to the penalty as serving no valid legislative end because it was not necessary to deter crime and could not permissibly be grounded on retributive considerations.

Three other Justices concurred in *Furman* on the narrower ground that the sentencing procedures then in use were constitutionally defective. Justice Douglas feared discrimination against racial minorities. Justice Stewart concluded that the death penalty was so "wantonly and freakishly imposed" that "death sentences are cruel and unusual in the same way that being struck with lightning is cruel and unusual." Justice White shared similar concerns by noting that "there is no meaningful basis for distinguishing the few cases in which [the death penalty] is imposed from the many cases in which it is not."

In *Furman* dissents, Chief Justice Burger and Justices Blackmun, Powell, and Rehnquist noted the long tradition of capital punishment, its acceptance by the framers of the Constitution, and its continued popular support as measured through the political process. For the dissenters, the infrequency of infliction of death suggested that the penalty was being reserved for a few extreme cases, not that it was no longer socially acceptable nor freakishly applied. Finally, the dissenters would defer to rational legislative judgments regarding the death penalty's retributive and deterrent value.

In the aftermath of *Furman,* retentionist states responded by enacting new death penalty statutes aimed at restricting sentencing discretion. In five cases decided in 1976, the Court considered a representative group of the new statutes. It struck down mandatory sentencing models in *Woodson v. North Carolina,* 428 U.S. 280 (1976) (death penalty for every person convicted of first degree murder), and *Roberts v. Louisiana,* 428 U.S. 325 (1976) (death penalty for five specified categories of murder: murder of fireman or police officer; murder in course of certain specified felonies; murder by a person previously convicted of an unrelated murder or serving a life sentence; murder by conduct intended to endanger more than one person; and murder for remuneration). The Court upheld statutes requiring consideration of special aggravating and mitigating circumstances, *Proffitt v. Florida,* 428 U.S. 242 (1976), *Gregg v. Georgia,* 428 U.S. 153 (1976), and *Jurek v. Texas,* 428 U.S. 262 (1976).

The Florida statute in *Proffitt* was modeled closely after § 210.6 of the Model Penal Code, see Appendix, *infra,* but diverged from the MPC approach by not binding the court to the judgment of the jury when it imposes a sentence of imprisonment. Also unlike the MPC, the Florida provision permitted jury decisions by majority vote.

In *Gregg,* the Court upheld a statute requiring the jury to find at least one of the 10 aggravating circumstances specified in the statute, which significantly overlaps MPC § 210.6(3). Unlike the approach of MPC § 210.6(4), however, the Georgia statute upheld in *Gregg* does not enumerate or specify mitigating factors. Instead, the Georgia scheme permits the sentencer to consider any relevant mitigating circumstance that might influence a decision not to impose the death penalty.

In *Jurek,* the Court upheld a Texas statute that defined capital murder as intentional or knowing homicide in five situations: murder of a fireman or police officer; murder committed in the course of certain specified felonies;

murder committed for remuneration; murder committed in an escape or attempted escape from prison; and murder of a prison employee by an inmate. Upon conviction of capital murder, a separate sentencing hearing is held under the Texas scheme in which the jury is informed that it can impose the death penalty only if it unanimously and affirmatively finds that the offender deliberately killed, that "there is a probability that [he] would commit criminal acts of violence that would constitute a continuing threat to society," and, if raised by the evidence, that the offender's conduct was unreasonable in response to provocation by the deceased. The Court upheld the Texas statute, seeing its five categories of capital murder as equivalents of specified circumstances of aggravation and the inquiry into the probability of future violent crimes as inviting a consideration of relevant mitigating circumstances.

A 1978 decision, *Lockett v. Ohio*, 438 U.S. 586 (1978), is noteworthy because it disapproved a statutory scheme requiring consideration of articulated aggravating and mitigating circumstances prior to imposing the death penalty. The Ohio statute in question in *Lockett* had been interpreted by the Ohio courts to require imposition of the death penalty whenever one or more of the enumerated aggravating circumstances were found against a convicted murderer and he was unable to prove one of the following three mitigating circumstances: that the victim induced the killing, that the defendant killed under "duress, coercion, or strong provocation," or that the offense was "primarily the product of psychosis or mental deficiency." The defendant in *Lockett* had sought to admit certain mitigating evidence [that she was but a secondary party to the killing, that she had no previous record of serious crime, and that her age (21) should be considered] of a nature not covered by the three specified categories. In a plurality opinion, Chief Justice Burger found that the Ohio scheme paid insufficient attention to individualizing the decision to impose the death penalty by failing to consider as mitigating factors "[every] aspect of a defendant's character or record and any of the circumstances of the offense" proffered as mitigating factors.

Moreover, in *Tuilaepa v. California*, 512 U.S. 967 (1994), the Court upheld California's approach directing sentencing jurors merely to "consider" a number of sentencing factors without telling jurors how they should weigh and evaluate any particular factor they deem relevant to the sentencing determination. The Court also rejected a vagueness argument made against three specific sentencing factors: (1) "the circumstances of the crime" committed, (2) "the presence or absence of criminal activity by the defendant which involved the use or attempted use of force or violence or the express or implied threat to use force or violence," and (3) "the age of the defendant at the time of the crime."

Question: If the concern in *Furman* centered on the problem of avoiding unguided jury discretion, does Lockett in a sense require, and Tuilaepa permit, as much?

In *McCleskey v. Kemp*, 481 U.S. 279 (1987), the Court rejected the argument that the death penalty as administered in Georgia is racially biased in violation of the equal protection and cruel and unusual punishments clauses of the Constitution. Defendant, McCleskey, a black man, was convicted of murdering a white police officer and was sentenced to death. In appealing his sentence, McCleskey introduced an elaborate statistical study demonstrating, among other things, that defendants who kill white victims in Georgia are more than four times as likely to receive the death penalty as are defendants who kill blacks. Moreover, the study showed that black defendants killing white victims have the greatest likelihood of receiving the death penalty. The case reached the Supreme Court, which accepted the reliability of the statistical study but found it insufficient to establish the unconstitutionality of McCleskey's sentence.

Question: What are the implications of a system that imposes the death penalty much more frequently on killers of white victims than on killers of black ones? Do you agree with these views of a thoughtful observer, W. White, The Death Penalty in the Eighties 135–36 (1987):

> [T]he fact that there is a substantial relationship between the race of the victim and the imposition of the death penalty shows that the death penalty continues to be arbitrarily applied. Can this arbitrariness be corrected? It seems doubtful. The courts have tried to effect reforms that reduce the extent to which race will play a part in capital sentencing. But . . . some of the forces that create racism in capital sentencing are simply too powerful to be swept away by procedural tinkering. This means that if we come to recognize the effect of race on our system of capital punishment, we will have to choose between retaining a capital punishment system that operates arbitrarily or abandoning the death penalty entirely.

In *Thompson v. Oklahoma,* 487 U.S. 815 (1988), the Court addressed the issue of imposing the death penalty for crimes committed by persons while they were minors. The *Thompson* Court decided that the State of Oklahoma could not execute a defendant who committed first-degree murder when he was only 15 years old. A four-member plurality concluded that a national consensus has arisen against executing anyone under 16 years of age at the time of his offense, therefore rendering executions of such persons cruel and unusual punishment under the Eighth Amendment. Justice O'Connor concurred in the Court's decision to preclude the execution in *Thompson* but on the narrower ground that a state may not sentence youthful offenders to death unless the legislature has spoken clearly on the matter by setting a minimum age for the death penalty. Three Justices dissented in *Thompson,* finding no national consensus against executing persons for crimes committed while they were juveniles.

Later, in *Stanford v. Kentucky,* 492 U.S. 361 (1989), the Court found no constitutional objection to sentencing 16-and 17-year-olds to death. The Court found that imposing the death penalty in such circumstances did not offend traditional or evolving societal norms.

For discussion of the issue of executing the mentally ill or retarded, see § 9.05[B][2], *infra.*

Bibliographic Note

The sources excerpted and quoted in this section (Lempert, Berns, Zimring and Hawkins, van den Haag and Conrad, and White) should be considered in their entirety by those seeking insight into the issues surrounding the death penalty. In addition, no study of the subject is complete without attention to Hugo Bedau's The Death Penalty in America (3d ed. 1982) and its extensive bibliography.

Chapter 6
Rape

§ 6.01 INTRODUCTION

The offense of rape, in one form or another, is ancient in origin, finding a place in both Mosaic and Roman law. English law punished rape with death as early as the time of King Athelstan in the tenth century. Under William the Conqueror the crime was punished by castration and loss of eyes until the common law later again treated it as a capital offense, a position adopted by a variety of American states until 1977, when the Supreme Court held the death penalty for rape to be cruel and unusual punishment. *Coker v. Georgia,* 433 U.S. 584 (1977). Today the crime is treated as a serious felony in all American jurisdictions, punishable by lengthy imprisonment, sometimes for life.

Despite its ancient pedigree and ubiquitous presence in all criminal codes, the law of rape is intensely controversial. As the concerns of women have become more engrained in social and legal consciousness, many aspects of traditional rape law and its enforcement have come under fire as embodiments of outmoded sexual stereotypes. As a result, extensive reform is under way, redefining the crime itself and revising evidentiary rules and practices affecting rape trials.

Full consideration of the range of social, cultural, and political aspects of the debate surrounding rape law is beyond the scope of these materials. Moreover, no attempt is made here to deal with the full spectrum of sexual crimes. (Some of these crimes are "lesser includeds" entailed in rape, which means that defendants acquitted of rape are nevertheless sometimes guilty of less serious offenses. See the *Berkowitz* case, *infra.*) Nor does this chapter deal specifically with the evils of homosexual rape or of female sexual assaults upon males. While these matters deserve serious attention, this chapter focuses on problems unique to the traditional crime of rape committed by male offenders upon female victims. These problems present special difficulties as reflected by the law's ongoing attempt to define and enforce this crime in a way that adequately protects the rights of victims and assures the culpability of offenders. As you study the following materials, consider whether the law of rape is or could be fashioned to accommodate the interests of both victims and those accused of the offense.

BLACKSTONE

*212

[R]ape [is] the carnal knowledge of a woman forcibly and against her will. . . .

The civil law punishes the crime of ravishment with death and confiscation of goods; under which it includes . . . the present offense of forcibly dishonoring her. . . . Also the stealing away a woman from her parents or guardians, and debauching her, is equally penal by the Emperor's edict, whether she consent or is forced. . . . And this, in order to take away from the woman every opportunity of offending in this way; whom the Roman law seems to suppose never to go astray, without the seduction and arts of the other sex; and therefore, by restraining and making so highly penal the solicitations of the men, they meant to secure effectually the honor of the woman. . . . But our English law does not entertain quite such sublime ideas of the honor of either sex, as to lay the blame of a mutual fault upon one of the transgressors only; and therefore, makes it a necessary ingredient in the crime of rape that it must be against the woman's will. . . .

. . . [B]y statute [rape] was made a felony without benefit of clergy; as was also the abominable wickedness of carnally knowing and abusing any woman child under the age of ten years; in which case the consent or non-consent is immaterial, as by reason of her tender years she is incapable of judgment and discretion. . . .

* * *

The civil law seems to suppose that a prostitute or common harlot incapable of any injuries of this kind; not allowing any punishment for violating the chastity of her, who has indeed no chastity at all, or at least has no regard to it. But the law of England does not judge so hardly of offenders, as to cut off all opportunity of retreat even from common strumpets, and to treat them as never capable of amendment. It therefore holds it to be a felony to force even a concubine or harlot; because the woman may have forsaken that unlawful course of life. . . . [The] essence of the crime is the forcible violation of the woman, it may be committed on anyone, who resists on the particular occasion, whatever may be her general conduct.

* * *

[T]he party ravished may give evidence under oath, and is in law a competent witness; but the credibility of her testimony, and how far forth she is to be believed, must be left to the jury under the circumstances of fact that concur in that testimony. For instance: if the witness be of good fame; if she presently discovered the offense, and made search for the offender; if the party accused fled for it; these and the like are concurring circumstances which give greater probability to her evidence. But, on the other side, if she be of evil fame, and stand unsupported by others; if she concealed the injury for any considerable time after she had opportunity to complain; if the place where the fact was allowed to be committed was where it was possible she might have been heard, and she made no outcry; these and the like circumstances, if unexplained, carry a strong but not conclusive, presumption that her testimony is false or feigned. The woman cannot, however, be compelled to answer whether she has not had connection with other men, or with a particular person named; but the accused may show the prosecutrix has had connection with himself or may impeach her character for chastity by general evidence.

* * *

"It is true that rape is a most detestable crime, and therefore ought to be severely and impartially to be punished with death; but it must be remembered that it is an accusation easy to be made, hard to be proved, but harder to be defended by the party accused, although innocent."[quoting Mathew Hale].

ESTRICH, *RAPE*

95 Yale L.J. 1087,1090–95 (1986)

To examine rape within the criminal law tradition is to expose fully the sexism of the law. Much that is striking about the crime of rape—and revealing of the sexism of the system—emerges only when rape is examined relative to other crimes, which the feminist literature by and large does not do. For example, rape is most assuredly not the only crime in which consent is a defense; but it is the only crime that has required the victim to resist physically in order to establish nonconsent. Nor is rape the only crime where prior relationship is taken into account by prosecutors in screening cases; yet we have not asked whether considering prior relationship in rape cases is different, and less justifiable, than considering it in cases of assault.

Sexism in the law of rape is no matter of mere historical interest; it endures, even where some of the most blatant testaments to that sexism have disappeared. Corroboration requirements unique to rape may have been repealed, but they continue to be enforced as a matter of practice in many jurisdictions. The victim of rape may not be required to resist to the utmost as a matter of statutory law in any jurisdiction, but the definitions accorded to force and consent may render "reasonable" resistance both a practical and a legal necessity. In the law of rape, supposedly dead horses continue to run.

The study of rape as an illustration of sexism in the criminal law also raises broader questions about the way conceptions of gender and the different backgrounds and perspectives of men and women should be encompassed within the criminal law. In one of his most celebrated essays, Oliver Wendell Holmes explained that the law does not exist to tell the good man what to do, but to tell the bad man what not to do. Holmes was interested in the distinction between the good and bad man; I cannot help noticing that both are men. Most of the time, a criminal law that reflects male views and male standards imposes its judgment on men who have injured other men. It is "boys' rules" applied to a boys' fight. In rape, the male standard defines a crime committed against women, and male standards are used not only to judge men, but also to judge the conduct of women victims. Moreover, because the crime involves sex itself, the law of rape inevitably treads on the explosive ground of sex roles, of male aggression and female passivity, of our understandings of sexuality—areas where differences between a male and a female perspective may be most pronounced.

* * *

. . . At one end of the spectrum is the "real" rape, what I will call the traditional rape: A stranger puts a gun to the head of his victim, threatens to kill her or beats her, and then engages in intercourse. In that case, the law—judges, statutes, prosecutors and all—generally acknowledge that a serious crime has been committed. But most cases deviate in one or many respects from this clear picture, making interpretation far more complex. Where less force is used or no other physical injury is inflicted, where threats are inarticulate, where the two know each other, where the setting is not an alley but a bedroom, where the initial contact was not a kidnaping but a date, where the woman says no but does not fight, the understanding is different. In such cases, the law, as reflected in the opinions of the courts, the interpretation, if not the words, of the statutes, and the decisions of those within the criminal justice system, often tell us that no crime has taken place and that fault, if any is to be recognized, belongs with the woman. In concluding that such acts—what I call, for lack of a better title, "non-traditional" rapes—are not criminal, and worse, that the woman must bear any guilt, the law has reflected, legitimized, and enforced a view of sex and women which celebrates male aggressiveness and punishes female passivity. And that vision, while under attack in recent years, continues to be a dominant force in our society and in the law of rape.

* * *

The traditional way of defining a crime is by describing the prohibited act (*actus reus*) committed by the defendant and the prohibited mental state (*mens rea*) with which he must have done it. We ask: What did the defendant do? What did he know or intend when he did it?

The definition of rape stands in striking contrast to this tradition, because courts, in defining the crime, have focused almost incidentally on the defendant—and almost entirely on the victim. It has often been noted that, traditionally at least, the rules associated with the proof of a rape charge—the corroboration requirement, the requirement of cautionary instructions, and the fresh complaint rule—as well as the evidentiary rules relating to prior sexual conduct by the victim, placed the victim as much on trial as the defendant. Such a reversal also occurs in the course of defining the elements of the crime. *Mens rea,* where it might matter, is all but eliminated; prohibited force tends to be defined according to the response of the victim; and nonconsent—the *sine qua non* of the offense—turns entirely on the victim's response.

But while the focus is on the female victim, the judgment of her actions is entirely male. If the issue were what the defendant knew, thought, or intended as to key elements of the offense, this perspective might be understandable; yet the issue has instead been the appropriateness of the woman's behavior, according to male standards of appropriate female behavior.

To some extent, this evaluation is but a modern response to the longstanding suspicion of rape victims. As Matthew Hale put it three centuries ago: "Rape is . . . an accusation easily to be made and hard to be proved, and harder to be defended by the party accused, tho never so innocent."

But the problem is more fundamental than that. Apart from the woman's conduct, the law provides no clear, working definition of rape. This rather conspicuous gap in the law of rape presents substantial questions of fair warning for men, which the law not so handily resolves by imposing the burden of warning them on women.

At its simplest, the dilemma lies in this: If nonconsent is essential to rape (and no amount of force or physical struggle is inherently inconsistent with lawful sex), and if no sometimes means yes, and if men are supposed to be aggressive in any event, how is a man to know when he has crossed the line? And how are we to avoid unjust convictions?

This dilemma is hardly inevitable. Partly, it is a product of the way society (or at least a powerful part of it) views sex. Partly, it is a product of the lengths to which the law has gone to enforce and legitimize those views. We could prohibit the use of force and threats and coercion in sex, regardless of "consent." We could define consent in a way that respected the autonomy of women. Having chosen neither course, however, we have created a problem of fair warning, and force and consent have been defined in an effort to resolve this problem.

HENDERSON, *RAPE AND RESPONSIBILITY*

11 Law and Philosophy 127, 130–31 (1992)

[A] primary impediment to recognition that rape is a real and frequent crime is a widely accepted cultural "story" of heterosexuality that results in an unspoken "rule" of male innocence and female guilt in law. By "male innocence and female guilt," I mean an unexamined belief that men are not responsible for their heterosexual conduct, while females are morally responsible for both their conduct and for the conduct of males. Indeed, men are entitled to act on their sexual passions, which are viewed as difficult and sometimes impossible to control; this belief also says that women should know this and avoid stimulating them if they do not wish to have sexual intercourse. Also, if men feel sexual desire, they are entitled to fulfillment of their "needs" through sexual intercourse. The flip side of the belief in men's inability to control themselves is the attribution of uncontrolled sexual passion and lust to women; it is against that lust that men must protect themselves, but if they do not, it is again not their responsibility, but the fault of the woman. On this view, woman's passion and lustfulness mean that they are already consenting to sexual activity. Women are seductive and have the power, like the Sirens, to drive men "wild," to lose control, and to therefore not be responsible. The male innocence/female guilt story is inapplicable only in the case of heterosexual relations and rape involving black men and white women, where the story is reversed: the theme in this context becomes male guilt and female innocence both in law and in culture. But otherwise, the defining story for interpreting rape in law and in fact is that of male innocence/female guilt.

SCHULHOFER, TAKING SEXUAL AUTONOMY SERIOUSLY: RAPE LAW AND BEYOND

11 Law and Philosophy 35, 40–41 (1992)

[T]he difficulty of winning convictions . . . in situations involving dates or acquaintances . . . a primary concern of both the Model Penal Code and feminist reform efforts, remains virtually unresolved.

In part, the difficulty lies imbedded in contemporary culture. Widespread attitudes about acceptable male behavior fall short of legal definitions of rape and in some respects seem impervious to change in statutory wording. Particularly striking is the finding that in some dating situations male pressure (including force) to compel intercourse is not rape or is justified in some measure by the behavior of the woman.

But legal definitions are also unsatisfactory. Beneath the seemingly universal and long-standing consensus that rape means forcible nonconsensual intercourse, there remains profound disagreement about what rape is.

What accounts for this persistent disagreement? Part of the explanation is obvious: Force and consent are not observable facts but social constructs; they mean different things to different people. Recent feminist criticism demonstrates that force and consent, as interpreted by justice system officials, reflect partial, "male" viewpoints. Standards that incorporated woman's perspectives on sexuality would accept more subtle forms of intimidation as "forcible" and would recognize that "no means no."

Yet these claims, although compelling, often prove unhelpful in understanding concrete problems. The . . . main difficulty stems not from clashing conceptions of "force" (although these are important) but more from unresolved tension (in both law and culture) between the conception of rape as a crime of violence *requiring* "force" and the conception of rape as an offense against personal autonomy, centering on "meaningful consent."

As the above materials suggest, the law of rape is controversial in its arguable embodiment of now outmoded sexual stereotypes. While it might appear a simple task to reform the law in light of the current widespread rejection of the gender roles assumed in traditional law, the crime of rape (consisting of improper male imposition and the absence of female consent) presents unique problems in defining both its *actus reus* and its *mens rea* components. Effectively defining the elements of force or threat and the offender's state of mind regarding the woman's consent is especially difficult because rape "is the only form of violent criminal assault in which the physical act accomplished by the offender . . . is an act which may, under other circumstances, be desirable to the victim." Shapo, *Recent Developments in the Definition of Forcible Rape,* 61 Va. L. Rev. 1500, 1503 (1975). "This unique feature of the offense necessitates the drawing of a line between forcible rape on the one hand and reluctant submission on the other, between true aggression and desired intimacy." MPC § 213.1 Comment at 279–80. The materials in this chapter illustrate these problems.

§ 6.02 THE *ACTUS REUS*

Rape statutes presently take a variety of forms. Here are some examples.

CODE OF VIRGINIA ANNOTATED

§ 18.2-61 Rape.—A. If any person has sexual intercourse with a complaining witness who is not his or her spouse or causes a complaining witness, whether or not his or her spouse, to engage in sexual intercourse with any other person and such act is accomplished

(i) against the complaining witness's will, by force, threat or intimidation of or against the complaining witness or another person, or

(ii) through the use of the complaining witness's mental incapacity or physical helplessness, or

(iii) with a child under age thirteen as the victim, he or she shall be guilty of rape.

MICHIGAN COMPILED LAWS ANNOTATED

750.520B. FIRST DEGREE CRIMINAL SEXUAL CONDUCT

Sec. 520b. (1) A person is guilty of criminal sexual conduct in the first degree if he or she engages in sexual penetration [defined as sexual intercourse, cunnilingus, fellatio, anal intercourse, or any other intrusion, however slight, of any part of a person's body or of any object into the genital or anal openings of another person's body, but emission of semen is not required] with another person and if any of the following circumstances exists:

* * *

(f) The actor causes personal injury [defined as bodily injury, disfigurement, mental anguish, chronic pain, pregnancy, disease, or loss or impairment of a sexual or reproductive organ] to the victim and force or coercion is used to accomplish sexual penetration. Force or coercion includes but is not limited to any of the following circumstances:

(i) When the actor overcomes the victim through the actual application of physical force or physical violence.

(ii) When the actor coerces the victim to submit by threatening to use force or violence on the victim, and the victim believes that the actor has the present ability to execute these threats.

(iii) When the actor coerces the victim to submit by threatening to retaliate in the future against the victim, or any other person, and the victim believes that the actor has the ability to execute this threat. As used in this subdivision, "to retaliate" includes threats of physical punishment, kidnapping, or extortion.

(iv) When the actor engages in the medical treatment or examination of the victim a manner or for purposes which are medically recognized as unethical or unacceptable.

(v) When the actor, through concealment or by the element of surprise, is able to overcome the victim.

Utah Code Annotated

§ 76-5-402 Rape.

(1) A person commits rape when the actor has sexual intercourse with another person without the victim's consent.

(2) This section applies whether or not the actor is married to the victim.

(3) Rape is a felony of the first degree.

Model Penal Code

§ 213.1. Rape and Related Offenses.

(1) Rape. A male who has sexual intercourse with a female not his wife is guilty of rape if:

(a) he compels her to submit by force or by threat of imminent death, serious bodily injury, extreme pain or kidnapping, to be inflicted on anyone; or

(b) he has substantially impaired her power to appraise or control her conduct by administering or employing without her knowledge drugs, intoxicants or other means for the purpose of preventing resistance; or

(c) the female is unconscious; or

(d) the female is less than 10 years old.

Rape is a felony of the second degree unless (i) in the course thereof the actor inflicts serious bodily injury upon anyone, or (ii) the victim was not a voluntary social companion of the actor upon the occasion of the crime and had not previously permitted him sexual liberties, in which cases the offense is a felony of the first degree.

* * *

Some statutes, Virginia's for example, follow Blackstone in defining rape to include both force and the absence of consent. Other jurisdictions follow Michigan in defining the offense without explicit reference to absence of consent, thus arguably requiring only force or coercion. Still other states dispense with the force requirement and, as does the Utah provision, define the offense solely in terms of absence of consent. Finally, the Model Penal Code provision, unlike the other samples, retains the common law elements of gender specificity and (along with Virginia) the marital exemption.

As you study the following cases, consider which if any of the statutory materials you find most satisfactory.

[A] Force, Threats, and Nonconsent

COMMONWEALTH v. BERKOWITZ

Supreme Court of Pennsylvania

641 A.2d 1161 (1994)

CAPPY, justice.

We granted allocatur in this case to address the question of the precise degree of force necessary to prove the "forcible compulsion" element of the crime of rape.

The Commonwealth appeals from an order of the Superior Court which overturned the conviction by a jury of Appellee, Robert A. Berkowitz. . . . The judgment of the Superior Court discharged Appellee as to the charge of rape. . . . For the reasons that follow, we affirm the Superior Court's reversal of the conviction for rape. . . .

The relevant facts of this case are as follows. The complainant, a female college student, left her class, went to her dormitory room where she drank a martini, and then went to a lounge to await her boyfriend. When her boyfriend failed to appear, she went to another dormitory to find a friend, Earl Hassel. She knocked on the door, but received no answer. She tried the doorknob and, finding it unlocked, entered the room and discovered a man sleeping on the bed. The complainant originally believed the man to be Hassel, but it turned out to be Hassel's roommate, Appellee. Appellee asked her to stay for a while and she agreed. He requested a back-rub and she declined. He suggested that she sit on the bed, but she declined and sat on the floor.

Appellee then moved to the floor beside her, lifted up her shirt and bra and massaged her breasts. He then unfastened his pants and unsuccessfully attempted to put his penis in her mouth. They both stood up, and he locked the door. He returned to push her onto the bed, and removed her undergarments from one leg. He then penetrated her vagina with his penis. After withdrawing and ejaculating on her stomach, he stated, "Wow, I guess we just got carried away," to which she responded, "No, we didn't get carried away, you got carried away."

In reviewing the sufficiency of the evidence, this Court must view the evidence in the light most favorable to the Commonwealth as verdict winner, and accept as true all evidence and reasonable inferences that may be reasonably drawn therefrom, upon which, if believed, the jury could have relied in reaching its verdict. If, upon such review, the Court concludes that the jury could not have determined from the evidence adduced that all of the necessary elements of the crime were established, then the evidence will be deemed insufficient to support the verdict. . . .

The crime of rape is defined as follows:

§ 3121. Rape A person commits a felony of the first degree when he engages in sexual intercourse with another person not one's spouse:

(1) by forcible compulsion;

(2) by threat of forcible compulsion that would prevent resistance by a person of reasonable resolution;

(3) who is unconscious; or

(4) who is so mentally deranged or deficient that such person is incapable of consent.

The victim of a rape need not resist. 18 Pa. C.S.A. § 3107. "The force necessary to support a conviction of rape . . . need only be such as to establish lack of consent and to induce the [victim] to submit without additional resistance. . . . The degree of force required to constitute rape is relative and depends on the facts and particular circumstance of the case." . . .

In regard to the critical issue of forcible compulsion, the complainant's testimony is devoid of any statement which clearly or adequately describes the use of force or the threat of force against her. In response to defense counsel's question, "Is it possible that [when Appellee lifted your bra and shirt] you took no physical action to discourage him," the complainant replied, "It's possible." When asked, "Is it possible that [Appellee] was not making any physical contact with you . . . aside from attempting to untie the knot [in the drawstrings of complainant's sweatpants]," she answered, "It's possible." She testified that "He put me down on the bed. It was kind of like—He didn't throw me on the bed. It's hard to explain. It was kind of like a push but not—I can't explain what I'm trying to say." She concluded that "it wasn't much" in reference to whether she bounced on the bed, and further detailed that their movement to the bed "wasn't slow like a romantic kind of thing, but it wasn't a fast shove either. It was kind of in the middle." She agreed that Appellee's hands were not restraining her in any manner during the actual penetration, and that the weight of his body on top of her was the only force applied. She testified that at no time did Appellee verbally threaten her. The complainant did testify that she sought to leave the room, and said "no" throughout the encounter.As to the complainant's desire to leave the room, the record clearly demonstrates that the door could be unlocked easily from the inside, that she was aware of this fact, but that she never attempted to go to the door or unlock it.

As to the complainant's testimony that she stated "no" throughout the encounter with Appellee, we point out that, while such an allegation of fact would be relevant to the issue of consent, it is not relevant to the issue of force. In *Commonwealth v. Mlinarich*, 518 Pa. 247, 541 A.2d 1335 (1988) (plurality opinion), this Court sustained the reversal of a defendant's conviction of rape where the alleged victim, a minor, repeatedly stated that she did not want to engage in sexual intercourse, but offered no physical resistance and was compelled to engage in sexual intercourse under threat of being recommitted to a juvenile detention center. The Opinion in Support of Affirmance acknowledged that physical force, a threat of force, or psychological coercion may be sufficient to support the element of "forcible compulsion," if found to be enough to "prevent resistance by a person of reasonable resolution." However, under the facts of *Mlinarich,* neither physical force, the threat of physical force, nor psychological coercion were found to have been proven, and this Court held that the conviction was properly reversed by the Superior Court. Accordingly, the ruling in *Mlinarich* implicitly dictates that where there is a lack of consent, but no showing of either physical force, a threat of physical force, or psychological coercion, the "forcible compulsion" requirement under 18 Pa. C.S. § 3121 is not met.

* * *

Reviewed in light of the above described standard, the complainant's testimony simply fails to establish that the Appellee forcibly compelled her to engage in sexual intercourse as required under 18 Pa. C.S. § 3121. Thus, even if all of the complainant's testimony was believed, the jury, as a matter of law, could not have found Appellee guilty of rape. Accordingly, we hold that the Superior Court did not err in reversing Appellee's conviction of rape.

* * *

Accordingly, the order of the Superior Court reversing the rape conviction is affirmed. [The court reinstated Appellee's conviction of indecent assault imposed by the trial court.]

NOTES AND QUESTIONS

1. The *Berkowitz* case follows the general approach in requiring evidence of physical force or threat. Was there evidence of actual force in *Berkowitz*? What about the evidence that defendant "kind of pushed" the complainant onto the bed? Apparently the jury found this to constitute "forcible compulsion." Should the court have sustained the reversal of defendant's conviction? Is there reason to believe that any of the sexual stereotypes discussed at the beginning of this chapter were at work in influencing conduct of the parties or the decision of the court or of the jury?

2. Short of unambiguous evidence of physical force or threat, does the *Berkowitz* court imply that the victim must offer some physical resistance for the force element to be established? How much resistance must she demonstrate? If the traditional requirement that the victim resist "to the utmost" has now been abandoned, see Dressler at 555, must she nevertheless put up some form of "reasonable resistance"? If the court is requiring some resistance, albeit minimal, such requirement is seemingly at odds with the Pennsylvania legislature's pronouncements: "The alleged [rape] victim need not resist the actor in Prosecutions under this chapter. Provided, however, that nothing in this section shall be construed to prohibit a defendant from introducing evidence that the alleged victim consented to the conduct in question." 18 Pa. Cons. Stat. Ann. § 3107 (1983).

Why should any resistance be required? Why doesn't "no mean no," thus ending the matter? Do victim resistance requirements place potential rape victims at risk of physical injury in addition to the harms caused by the unwanted sexual intercourse? See Ingram, *Date Rape: It's Time for "No" to Really Mean "No",* 21 Amer. J. Crim. L. 1 (1993).

On the other hand, without evidence of victim resistance, how can the force element (generally requiring something beyond the physical actions inherent in the sexual act, Perkins and Boyce at 211) be proved? Is the woman's subjective fear relevant? See the *Iniguez* case, immediately following. Would women not be likely to experience such fear in virtually any unwanted encounter with an aggressive male who is usually physically larger and stronger than themselves? See *Goldberg v. State,* 395 A.2d 1213, 1219 (Md. Spec. App. 1979); S. Estrich, *Real Rape* 67–68 (1987).

3. The *Berkowitz* court holds that the complainant's expressions of nonconsent are not relevant to the issue of force. Do you agree? Should the court have concluded that the complainant's exclamations of "no," allegedly made throughout the encounter, evidenced resistance to the defendant's advances and were thus relevant to the "forcible compulsion" element of the statute?

4. What would result if the Utah statute requiring only nonconsensual sexual intercourse (see p.670*supra*) were applied to the *Berkowitz* facts? For the view that statutory models supposedly dispensing with force requirements invariably reintroduce considerations of force (or its absence) in defining nonconsent, see Schulhofer, *Taking Sexual Autonomy Seriously: Rape Law and Beyond,* 11 Law and Phil. 35, 39 (1992). If Schulhofer is right, does it mean that rape is essentially perceived as a crime of physical violence rather than one offending female sexual autonomy? For Professor Schulhofer's proposed reforms aimed at protecting sexual autonomy, see *id.*

Not all commentators agree that rape law is essentially aimed at protecting against violence. Some see the lack of consent, protection of sexual autonomy, as the gist of the crime. See Perkins and Boyce at 211. Note that no force other than the act of sexual intercourse is required to rape an unconscious woman. Dressler at 538.

5. If absence of consent is not an element of the crime of rape under the Pennsylvania statute, what is the status of the consent issue? Would it have been a defense for the defendant in *Berkowitz* if there had been evidence of affirmative consent by the complainant? What *mens rea* implications follow from treating the consent factor as a defense rather than as an offense element? See § 6.03, *infra.* What constitutional implications follow? See § 9.04, *infra.*

6. With its reference to the *Mlinarich* case, the *Berkowitz* court suggests that "physical force, a threat of force or psychological coercion" may suffice to support the element of "forcible compulsion" if sufficient to "prevent resistance by a person of reasonable resolution." Should nonviolent threats and psychological coercion qualify? In *Commonwealth v. Rhodes,* 510 A.2d 1217, 1226 (Pa. 1986), a case predating *Mlinarich* by two years, a 20-year-old man led an 8-year-old neighbor girl to an abandoned building and, after instructing her to lay down and pull her legs up, had sexual intercourse with little resistance on her part or force on his. In upholding the man's rape conviction, the Pennsylvania Supreme Court held that "forcible compulsion" includes "not only physical force or violence but also moral, psychological or

intellectual force used to compel a person to engage in sexual intercourse against that person's will." What could the court mean by "moral" or "intellectual" force?

Should the force element in rape law be limited to physical threats and violence against the person? Should the coercion in *Mlinarich* (threat to send the young woman to a juvenile detention center) have been sufficient?

7. Consider the Michigan statute, *supra* at pp. 669–70. The statute lists examples of coercive conduct that, when used to accomplish penetration, constitutes "criminal sexual conduct." Some of the coercive conduct (threats to extort, for example) is nonviolent in nature. Moreover, the statute stipulates that "force or coercion is not limited to" any of the listed examples.

Suppose a variation on the situation presented in the movie *Forrest Gump*. A mother desperately desires to obtain an education for her son, who is said to require special educational attention. A school administrator proposes to the mother that he will admit her son to his school if she consents to have sexual relations with the administrator. If the mother consents, is the administrator guilty of criminal sexual conduct under the Michigan statute? Should he be guilty of the traditional crime of rape? If not, should new laws be enacted to prohibit such nonviolent forms of sexual exploitation? Is it useful to distinguish illegal coercion from permissible bargaining? See MPC, § 213.1, Comment at 312–14.

8. Note that while not guilty of rape, the defendant in *Berkowitz* was guilty of indecent assault, a second degree misdemeanor defined as "indecent contact with another . . . without the consent of the other person." 18 Pa. Cons. Stat. § 126 (Supp. 1994). Defendants not guilty of rape are often subject to punishment for a variety of "lesser included offenses." Compare the Model Penal Code's felony rape provisions of § 213.1 with the Code's misdemeanor sexual assault provision prohibiting "offensive . . . touching of the sexual or other intimate parts of the person of another for the purpose of arousing or gratifying sexual desire of either party." MPC § 213.4, Appendix.

PEOPLE v. INIGUEZ

Supreme Court of California (in banc)

7 Cal. 4th 847, 30 Cal. Rptr. 2d 258, 872 P.2d 1183 (1994)

ARABIAN, Justice.

Defendant Hector Guillermo Iniguez admitted that on the night before Mercy P.'s wedding, he approached her as she slept on the living room floor, removed her pants, fondled her buttocks, and had sexual intercourse with her. He further conceded that he had met Mercy for the first time that night, and that Mercy did not consent to any sexual contact or intercourse. The Court of Appeal reversed defendant's conviction for rape on the grounds that the evidence of force or fear of immediate and unlawful bodily injury was insufficient. We granted review to determine whether there was sufficient evidence to support the verdict, and to delineate the relationship between evidence of fear and the requirement under Penal Code section 261, subdivision (a)(2), that the sexual intercourse be "accomplished against a person's will," in a case where lack of consent is not disputed. We reverse the Court of Appeal.

I. Facts and Procedural Background

On June 15, 1990, the eve of her wedding, at approximately 8:30 PM, 22-year-old Mercy P. arrived at the home of Sandra S., a close family friend whom Mercy had known for at least 12 years and considered an aunt. Sandra had sewn Mercy's wedding dress, and was to stand in at the wedding the next day for Mercy's mother who was unable to attend. Mercy was planning to spend the night at her home.

Mercy met defendant, Sandra's fiancé, for the first time that evening. Defendant was scheduled to stand in for Mercy's father during the wedding.

Mercy noticed that defendant was somewhat "tipsy" when he arrived. He had consumed a couple of beers and a pint of Southern Comfort before arriving at Sandra's. Mercy, Sandra, and defendant celebrated Mercy's impending wedding by having dinner and drinking some wine. There was no flirtation or any remarks of a sexual nature between defendant and Mercy at any time during the evening.

Around 11:30 PM, Mercy went to bed in the living room. She slept on top of her sleeping bag. She was wearing pants with an attached skirt, and a shirt. She fell asleep at approximately midnight.

Mercy was awakened between 1:00 and 2:00 AM when she heard some movements behind her. She was lying on her stomach, and saw defendant, who was naked, approach her from behind. Without saying anything, defendant pulled down her pants, fondled her buttocks, and inserted his penis inside her. Mercy weighed 105 pounds. Defendant weighed approximately 205 pounds. Mercy "was afraid, so I just laid there." "You didn't try to resist or escape or anything of that nature because of your fear?" "Right." Mercy further explained that she "didn't know how it was at first, and just want[ed] to get on with my wedding plans the next day." Less than a minute later, defendant ejaculated, got off her, and walked back to the bedroom. Mercy had not consented to any sexual contact.

Officer Fragoso, who interviewed Mercy several days after the attack, testified that she told him she had not resisted defendant's sexual assault because, "She said she knew that the man had been drinking. She hadn't met him before; he was a complete stranger to her. When she realized what was going on, she said she panicked, she froze. She was afraid that if she said or did anything, his reaction could be of a violent nature. So she decided just to lay still, wait until it was over with and then get out of the house as quickly as she could and get to her fianc' and tell him what happened."

Mercy immediately telephoned her fiancé Gary and left a message for him. She then telephoned her best friend Pam, who testified that Mercy was so distraught she was barely comprehensible. Mercy asked Pam to pick her up, grabbed her purse and shoes, and ran out of the apartment. Mercy hid in the bushes outside the house for approximately half an hour while waiting for Pam because she was terrified defendant would look for her.

Pam arrived about 30 minutes later, and drove Mercy to Pam's house. Mercy sat on Pam's kitchen floor, her back to the wall, and asked Pam, "do I look like the word 'rape' [is] written on [my] face?" Mercy wanted to take a shower because she "felt dirty," but was dissuaded by Pam. Pam telephoned Gary, who called the police.

Gary and his best man then drove Mercy to the hospital, where a "rape examination" was performed. Patricia Aiko Lawson, a blood typing and serology expert, testified that there was a large amount of semen present in Mercy's vagina and on the crotch area of her underpants. A deep vaginal swab revealed that many sperm were whole, indicating intercourse had occurred within a few hours prior to the rape examination. ABO blood group, blood type B, which was consistent with defendant's, but not Gary's or Mercy's blood type, was found on the internal and external vaginal swabs and on the underpants.

The following day, Mercy and Gary married. Gary picked up the wedding dress from Sandra while Mercy waited in the car. Neither Sandra nor defendant participated in the wedding.

Defendant was arrested the same day. When asked by the arresting officer if he had had sexual intercourse with Mercy, defendant replied, "I guess I did, yes."

Dr. Charles Nelson, a psychologist, testified as an expert on "rape trauma syndrome." He stated that victims respond in a variety of ways to the trauma of being raped. Some try to flee, and others are paralyzed by fear. This latter response he termed "frozen fright."

Defendant conceded at trial that the sexual intercourse was nonconsensual. Defendant testified that he fondled Mercy without her consent, pulled down her pants, had sexual intercourse, and thereafter ejaculated. However, defense counsel argued that the element of force or fear was absent. "So if he was doing anything, it wasn't force or fear. . . . It's a situation where it looks to him like he can get away with it and a situation where his judgment is flown out the window. . . . He keeps doing it, probably without giving much thought to it, but certainly there is nothing there to indicate using fear ever entered his mind. What he was doing was taking advantage, in a drunken way, of a situation where somebody appeared to be out of it."

The jury was instructed on both rape pursuant to then Penal Code section 261, subdivision (2) and sexual battery [defined in section 243.4 as prohibiting persons from "touch[ing] an intimate part of another person . . . if the touching is against the will of the person touched and is for the purpose of sexual arousal" . . .]. Upon the jury's request for further instruction on the definition of fear of immediate and unlawful bodily injury, the court instructed in relevant part,' "fear' means, a feeling of alarm or disquiet caused by the expectation of danger, pain, disaster or the like." "Verbal threats are not critical to a finding of fear of unlawful injury, threats can be implied from the circumstances or inferred from the assailant's conduct. A victim may entertain a reasonable fear even where the assailant does not threaten by words or deed."

The jury found defendant guilty of rape. He was entenced to state prison for the midterm of six years.

The Court of Appeal reversed, concluding that there was insufficient evidence that the act of sexual intercourse was accomplished by means of force or fear of immediate and unlawful bodily injury. On the issue of fear, the court stated: "While the [defendant] was admittedly much larger than the small victim, he did nothing to suggest that he intended to injure her. No coarse or sexually suggestive conversation had taken place. Nothing of an abusive or threatening nature had occurred. The victim was sleeping in her aunt's house, in which screams presumably would have raised the aunt and interrupted the intercourse. Although the assailant was a stranger to the victim, she knew nothing about him which would suggest that he was violent. [The] event of intercourse is singularly unusual in terms of its ease of facilitation, causing no struggle, no injury, no abrasions or other marks, and lasting, as the victim testified,'maybe a minute.'"The court modified the judgment, reducing defendant's conviction of rape under section 261, former subdivision 2, to the offense of sexual battery under section 243.4, subdivision (a), and remanded for resentencing.

We granted the Attorney General's petition for review.

II. Discussion

* * *

Prior to 1980, section 261, subdivisions 2 and 3 "defined rape as an act of sexual intercourse under circumstances where the person resists, but where 'resistance is overcome by force or violence' or where 'a person is prevented from resisting by threats of great and immediate bodily harm, accompanied by apparent power of execution.' . . . " *People v. Barnes* (1986) 721 P.2d 110. . . . Under the former law, a person was required to either resist or be prevented from resisting because of threats. . . .

Section 261 was amended in 1980 to eliminate both the resistance requirement and the requirement that the threat of immediate bodily harm be accompanied by an apparent power to inflict the harm. . . . As the legislative history explains, "threat is eliminated and the victim need only fear harm. The standard for injury is reduced from great and immediate bodily harm to immediate and unlawful bodily injury." . . .

In discussing the significance of the 1980 amendments in *Barnes,* we noted that "studies have demonstrated that while some women respond to sexual assault with active resistance, others freeze,'"and "become helpless from panic and numbing fear." . . . In response to this information, "For the first time, the Legislature has assigned the decision as to whether a sexual assault should be resisted to the realm of personal choice." . . . "By removing resistance as a prerequisite to a rape conviction, the Legislature has brought the law of rape into conformity with other crimes such as robbery, kidnaping and assault, which require force, fear, and nonconsent to convict. In these crimes, the law does not expect falsity from the complainant who alleges their commission and thus demand resistance as a corroboration and predicate to conviction." . . .

At the time of the crime in this case, section 261, subdivision (2), provided, "Rape is an act of sexual intercourse accomplished with a person not the spouse of the perpetrator, under any of the following circumstances: . . . (2) Where it is accomplished against a person's will by means of force, violence, or fear of immediate and unlawful bodily injury on the person or another."[4] The deletion of the resistance language from section 261 by the 1980 amendments thus effected a change in the purpose of evidence of fear of immediate and unlawful injury. Prior to 1980, evidence of fear was directly linked to resistance; the prosecution was required to demonstrate that a person's resistance had been overcome by force, or that a person was prevented from resisting by threats of great and immediate bodily harm. . . . As a result of the amendments, evidence of fear is now directly linked to the overbearing of a victim's will; the prosecution is required to demonstrate that the act of sexual intercourse was accomplished against the person's will by means of force, violence, or fear of immediate and unlawful bodily injury.

In *Barnes,* we then addressed the question of the role of force or fear of immediate and unlawful bodily injury in the absence of a resistance requirement. We stated that [a]lthough resistance is no longer the touchstone of the element of force, the reviewing court still looks to the circumstance of the case, including the presence of verbal or nonverbal threats, or the kind of force that might reasonably induce fear in the mind of the victim, to ascertain sufficiency of the evidence of a conviction under section 261, subdivision (2). . . . Additionally, the complainant's conduct must be measured against the degree of force manifested or in light of whether her fears were genuine and reasonably grounded. "In some circumstances, even a complainant's unreasonable fear of immediate and unlawful bodily injury may suffice to sustain a conviction under section 261, subdivision (2), if the accused knowingly takes advantage of that fear in order to accomplish sexual intercourse." . . . "[T]he trier of fact —should be permitted to measure consent by weighing both the acts of the alleged attacker and the response of the alleged victim, rather than being required to focus on one or the other.' " . . . We concluded that "[i]n light of the totality of [the] circumstances" in that case, "a reasonable juror could have found that [the victim's] subsequent compliance with" defendant's insistence on sexual intercourse "was induced either by force, fear, or both, and, in any case, fell short of a consensual act"[5] . . .

Thus, the element of fear of immediate and unlawful bodily injury has two components, one subjective and one objective. The subjective component asks whether a victim genuinely entertained a fear of immediate and unlawful bodily injury sufficient to induce her to submit to sexual intercourse against her will. In order to satisfy this component, the extent or seriousness of the

---

[4] In 1990, the Legislature amended section 261, subdivision (2), to add duress and menace, and added subdivisions (b) and (c) to define these terms. In addition, the Legislature added subdivision designation (a), and redesignated former subdivisions (1)–(7) to be subdivisions (a)(1)–(a)(7). All relevant parts of section 261 remain substantively identical. Section 261, subdivision (a)(2), currently provides: "(a) Rape is an act of sexual intercourse accomplished with a person not the spouse of the perpetrator, under any of the following circumstances: . . . (2) Where it is accomplished against a person's will by means of force, violence, duress, menace, or fear of immediate and unlawful bodily injury on the person or another."

[5] "Consent" currently is, and was at the time of the crime, defined for purposes of rape prosecutions as "positive cooperation in act or attitude pursuant to an exercise of free will. The person must act freely and voluntarily and have knowledge of the nature of the act or transaction involved." § 261.6.

injury feared is immaterial. . . . "[t]he kind of physical force that may induce fear in the mind of a woman is immaterial . . . it may consist in the taking of indecent liberties or of embracing and kissing her against her will."

In addition, the prosecution must satisfy the objective component, which asks whether the victim's fear was reasonable under the circumstances, or, if unreasonable, whether the perpetrator knew of the victim's subjective fear and took advantage of it. . . . The particular means by which fear is imparted is not an element of rape. . . .

Applying these principles, we conclude that the evidence that the sexual intercourse was accomplished against Mercy's will by means of fear of immediate and unlawful bodily injury was sufficient to support the verdict in this case. First, there was substantial evidence that Mercy genuinely feared immediate and unlawful bodily injury. Mercy testified that she froze because she was afraid, and the investigating police officer testified that she told him she did not move because she feared defendant would do something violent.

The Court of Appeal stated, however, "But most importantly, the victim was unable to articulate an experience of fear of immediate and unlawful bodily injury." This statement ignores the officer's testimony as to Mercy's state of mind. Moreover, even absent the officer's testimony, the prosecution was not required to elicit from Mercy testimony regarding what precisely she feared. "Fear" may be inferred from the circumstances despite even superficially contrary testimony of the victim. . . .

In addition, immediately after the attack, Mercy was so distraught her friend Pam could barely understand her. Mercy hid in the bushes outside the house waiting for Pam to pick her up because she was terrified defendant would find her; she subsequently asked Pam if the word "rape" was written on her forehead, and had to be dissuaded from bathing prior to going to the hospital. . . .

Second, there was substantial evidence that Mercy's fear of immediate and unlawful bodily injury was reasonable. The Court of Appeal's statements that defendant "did nothing to sug-gest that he intended to injure" Mercy, and that "[a]lthough the assailant was a stranger to the victim, she knew nothing about him which would suggest that he was violent" ignores the import of the undisputed facts. Defendant, who weighed twice as much as Mercy, accosted her while she slept in the home of a close friend, thus violating the victim's enhanced level of security and privacy . . . "A person inside a private residence, whether it be their own or that of anacquaintance, feels a sense of privacy and security not felt when outside or in a semipublic structure. . . . providing the [attacker] with the advantages of shock and surprise which may incapacitate the victim(s)."

Defendant, who was naked, then removed Mercy's pants, fondled her buttocks, and inserted his penis into her vagina for approximately one minute, without warning, without her consent, and without a reasonable belief of consent. Any man or woman awakening to find himself or herself in this situation could reasonably react with fear of immediate and unlawful bodily injury. Sudden, unconsented-to groping, disrobing, and ensuing sexual intercourse while one appears to lie sleeping is an appalling and intolerable invasion of one's personal autonomy that, in and of itself, would reasonably cause one to react with fear. . . . "The essential guilt of rape consists in the outrage to the person and feelings of the victim of the rape."

The Court of Appeal's suggestion that Mercy could have stopped the sexual assault by screaming and thus eliciting Sandra S.'s help, disregards both the Legislature's 1980 elimination of the resistance requirement and our express language in *Barnes* upholding that amendment. . . . It effectively guarantees an attacker freedom to intimidate his victim and exploit any resulting reasonable fear so long as she neither struggles nor cries out. . . . "The law has outgrown the resistance concept; a person demanding sexual favors can no longer rely on a position of strength which draws no physical or verbal protest." . . . There is no requirement that the victim say, "I am afraid, please stop," when it is the defendant who has created the circumstances that have so paralyzed the victim in fear and thereby submission.[6] . . . Moreover, it is sheer speculation that Mercy's assailant would have responded to screams by desisting the attack, and not by causing her further injury or death.

The jury could reasonably have concluded that under the totality of the circumstances, this scenario, instigated and choreographed by defendant, created a situation in which Mercy genuinely and reasonably responded with fear of immediate and unlawful bodily injury, and that such fear allowed him to accomplish sexual intercourse with Mercy against her will.[7]

CONCLUSION

The judgment of the Court of Appeal is reversed, and the case is remanded to that court for further proceedings consistent with this opinion.

NOTES AND QUESTIONS

1. Would Iniguez's conduct have constituted rape under the Pennsylvania statute as interpreted in *Berkowitz?* Suppose, in light of footnote 6, Iniguez had argued that he believed Mercy had consented or at least that he didn't know that she hadn't? See the *mens rea* materials, § 6.03, *infra*.

2. Are the 1990 California legislative reforms (expanding the statute to include fear and duress as alternatives to force) desirable? Should the focus be directed to the subjective sensitivities of the victim rather than to objective manifestations of resistance or nonconsent? What kinds of duress are relevant? Are only those threatening "great and immediate bodily harm" relevant? Or might economic or psychological duress also qualify? Consider again note 7 in the Notes and Questions following *Berkowitz, supra*.

3. As the excerpt from Professor Schulhofer at the beginning of this chapter suggests, the law of rape suffers from uncertainty about the nature of the

---

[6] No defense of reasonable and good faith but mistaken belief in consent was raised by the defendant, and we therefore express no opinion on the appropriateness of such a theory under the circumstances of this case.

[7] In light of our disposition on the issue of the sufficiency of the evidence of fear of immediate and unlawful bodily injury, it is unnecessary for us to address the issue of whether the evidence of force was also sufficient to support the verdict.

crime's underlying harm. What is the essential evil of the crime of rape in the eyes of the *Iniguez* court: physical violence or affront to sexual autonomy? If the latter, are men now on notice that any act of sexual intercourse without the woman's express consent or active participation is rape?

If affront to sexual autonomy is the gist of rape, does *Iniguez* implicitly espouse the "no means no" principle? If so, does this mean that a man commits rape whenever he disregards a woman's expression of nonconsent to sexual relations, continues to sexually solicit her, and eventually has sexual relations with her without her express assent? Should the nature of his solicitations matter? Might he be guilty of rape where she, after initially refusing his advances, eventually consents in response to his continued nonviolent and nonthreatening solicitations?

4. If rape is an offense against personal autonomy, does the *Iniguez* court correctly apply its two-prong test for determining fear of immediate bodily injury? Is there sufficient evidence of subjective fear? Should fear of being "embraced and kissed against her will" be sufficient subjective fear as the court suggests? For a discussion of women's pervasive fear of rape, see West, *The Difference in Women's Hedonic Lives: A Phenomenological Critique of Feminist Legal Theory,* 3 Wis. Women's L.J. 81, 103–6 (1987).

Does the *Iniguez* court find adequate evidence that Mercy's fears were objectively reasonable? Could it be argued that virtually any woman might possess reasonable fear of potential harm at the hands of any physically stronger man (at least one whom she does not know to be gentle and nonviolent) who makes sexual advances without her express invitation? See note 2 following *Berkowitz, supra* page 673. Might that fear turn virtually any act of sexual intercourse into potential rape so long as affirmative consent is not given?

5. Aside from its expansion to include fear and duress, the California statute follows Blackstone's traditional common law formulation in requiring both force and nonconsent as *actus reus* elements. Is the force element necessary "because it should go without saying that if a woman does not want to engage in intercourse and is not consenting, the man has to force her into the act"? Henderson, *Rape and Responsibility,* 11 Law and Phil. 127, 158 (1992). Do you agree that requiring both force and nonconsent implies that women routinely consent to sex with force? "Given this sadomasochistic definition of sex at the line between intercourse and rape, it is no wonder that the legal concept of consent can coexist with a lot of force." MacKinnon, *Sex Equality,* 100 Yale L.J. 1281, 1303 (1991). Does this suggest a view of women as persons who "seek out and enjoy forced sex"? *Id.* at 1304.

6. If rape is an offense against personal autonomy rather than a crime of violence, what role, if any, should the force component play? Is it possible to account for the emphasis on force in the law of rape without assuming female sadomasochistic proclivities?

The force element is sometimes viewed as relevant as an evidentiary matter but not an essential element of the crime of rape. Rape has traditionally included not only intercourse by force or threat, but also "sexual imposition on an unconscious or otherwise incapacitated female, intimacy achieved by certain fundamental kinds of deception, and intercourse with a mentally incompetent or underage female. The unifying principle among this diversity of conduct is the idea of meaningful consent." Model Penal Code § 213.1, Comment at 301. The presence or absence of force, while not on this view an essential aspect of rape, is nevertheless relevant in indicating the evidentiary existence of nonconsent. Perkins and Boyce at 209–10. Often this evidentiary consideration becomes included as a definitional element itself. "Several states simply use language that implies the act is without the consent of the victim by describing the offense as one committed by force or against resistance." *Id.* at 210.

Ironically, after seemingly relegating the force component to mere evidentiary status in its statutory commentary, the Model Penal Code itself resurrects force as an element in defining rape in terms of "comp[ulsion] . . . by force" and "threat of imminent death" and so on. See MPC § 213.1. The Code Commentary explains this move:

> . . . [C]onsent appears to be a conceptually simple issue. Either the female assented to intercourse, or she did not. Searching for consent in a particular case, however, may reveal depths of ambiguity and contradiction that are scarcely suspected when the question is put in the abstract. Often the woman's attitude may be deeply ambivalent. She may not want intercourse, may fear it, or may desire it but feel compelled to say "no." Her confusion at the time of the act may later resolve into non-consent. Some have expressed the fear that a woman who subconsciously wanted to have sexual intercourse will later feel guilty and "cry rape." It seems plain, on the other hand, that a barrage of conflicting emotions at the time of the assault does not necessarily imply the victim's consent, although it may lead to misperception by the actor. Further ambiguity may be introduced by the fact that the woman may appear to consent because she is frozen by fear and panic, or because she quite rationally decides to "consent" rather than risk being killed or injured.

> The point, in any event, is that inquiry into the victim's subjective state of mind and the attacker's perceptions of her state of mind often will not yield a clear answer. The deceptively simple notion of consent may obscure a tangled mesh of psychological complexity, ambiguous communication, and unconscious restructuring of the event by the participants. Courts have not been oblivious to this difficulty, but in attempting to resolve it they have often placed disproportionate emphasis upon objective manifestations of non-consent by the woman. It seems plain that some courts have gone too far in this direction, although it is equally plain that one can go too far in the opposite direction.

> What is required is that a balanced inquiry be made into the factors that indicate imposition by the male as well as those that indicate non-consent by the victim. It is appropriate in this effort to focus primarily upon the conduct of the male, particularly in the more serious forms of the offense, and to seek objective verification in the actor's conduct of the overreaching and imposition that is the major characteristic of the offense in its most serious form. At the same time, however, the possibility of consent by the victim, even in the face of conduct that may give some evidence of

overreaching cannot be ignored. As intractable as the imposition-consent issue necessarily will be, it cannot be avoided.

MPC § 213.1, Comment at 302–3

For a critique of the Code's position, particularly its views regarding the "ambivalence" of women's attitudes toward male-initiated intercourse, see Estrich, *Rape,* 95 Yale L.J. 1087, 1136–41 (1986). See note 5, following the Fletcher excerpt, *infra* at pp. 513–14.

[B] Deception

BORO v. SUPERIOR COURT

California Court of Appeal, First District, Division 1

163 Cal. App. 3d 1224, 210 Cal. Rptr. 122 (1985)

NEWSOM, Associate Justice.

By timely petition filed with this court, petitioner Daniel Boro seeks a writ of prohibition to restrain further prosecution of Count II of the information on file against him . . . charging him with a violation of Penal Code section 261, subsection (4), rape: "an act of sexual intercourse accomplished with a person not the spouse of the perpetrator, under any of the following circumstances: . . . (4) Where a person is at the time unconscious of the nature of the act, and this is known to the accused."

Petitioner contends that his motion to dismiss should have been granted with regard to Count II because the evidence at the preliminary hearing proved that the prosecutrix, Ms. R., was aware of the "nature of the act" within the meaning of section 261, subdivision (4). The Attorney General contends the opposite, arguing that the victim's agreement to intercourse was predicated on a belief—fraudulently induced by petitioner—that the sex act was necessary to save her life, and that she was hence unconscious of the nature of the act within the meaning of the statute.

In relevant part the factual background may be summarized as follows. Ms. R., the rape victim, was employed as a clerk at the Holiday Inn in South San Francisco when, on March 30, 1984, at about 8:45 AM, she received a telephone call from a person who identified himself as "Dr. Stevens" and said that he worked at Peninsula Hospital.

"Dr. Stevens" told Ms. R. that he had the results of her blood test and that she had contracted a dangerous, highly infectious and perhaps fatal disease; that she could be sued as a result; that the disease came from using public toilets; and that she would have to tell him the identity of all her friends who would then have to be contacted in the interest of controlling the spread of the disease.

"Dr. Stevens" further explained that there were only two ways to treat the disease. The first was a painful surgical procedure—graphically described—costing $9,000, and requiring her uninsured hospitalization for six weeks. A second alternative, "Dr. Stevens" explained, was to have sexual intercourse with an anonymous donor who had been injected with a serum which would cure the disease. The latter, non-surgical procedure would only cost $4,500. When the victim replied that she lacked sufficient funds the "doctor" suggested that $1,000 would suffice as a down payment. The victim thereupon agreed to the non-surgical alternative and consented to intercourse with the mysterious donor, believing "it was the only choice I had."

After discussing her intentions with her work supervisor, the victim proceeded to the Hyatt Hotel in Burlingame as instructed, and contacted "Dr. Stevens" by telephone. The latter became furious when he learned Ms. R. had informed her employer of the plan, and threatened to terminate his treatment, finally instructing her to inform her employer she had decided not to go through with the treatment. Ms. R. did so, then went to her bank, withdrew $1,000 and, as instructed, checked into another hotel and called "Dr. Stevens" to give him her room number.

About a half hour later the defendant "donor" arrived at her room. When Ms. R. had undressed, the "donor," petitioner, after urging her to relax, had sexual intercourse with her.

At the time of penetration, it was Ms. R.'s belief that she would die unless she consented to sexual intercourse with the defendant: as she testified, "My life felt threatened, and for that reason and that reason alone did I do it."

Petitioner was apprehended when the police arrived at the hotel room, having been called by Ms. R.'s supervisor. Petitioner was identified as "Dr. Stevens" at a police voice lineup by another potential victim of the same scheme.

Upon the basis of the evidence just recounted, petitioner was charged with five crimes, as follows: Count I: section 261, subdivision (2)—rape: accomplished against a person's will by means of force or fear of immediate and unlawful bodily injury on the person or another. Count II: section 261, subdivision (4)—rape "[w]here a person is at the time unconscious of the nature of the act, and this is known to the accused." Count III: section 266—procuring a female to have illicit carnal connection with a man "by any false pretenses, false representation, or other fraudulent means, . . . " Count IV: section 664/487—attempted grand theft. Count V: section 459—burglary (entry into the hotel room with intent to commit theft).

A . . . motion to set aside the information was granted as to Counts I and III—the latter by concession of the district attorney. Petitioner's sole challenge is to denial of the motion to dismiss Count II.

The People's position is stated concisely: "We contend, quite simply, that at the time of the intercourse Ms. R., the victim, was 'unconscious of the nature of the act': because of [petitioner's] misrepresentation she believed it was in the nature of a medical treatment and not a simple, ordinary act of sexual intercourse." Petitioner, on the other hand, stresses that the victim was plainly aware of the nature of the act in which she voluntarily engaged, so that her motivation in doing so [since it did not fall within the proscription of section 261, subdivision (2) is irrelevant].

Our research discloses sparse California authority on the subject. A victim need not be totally and physically unconscious in order that section 261, subdivision (4) apply. In *People v. Minkowski* (1962), 204 Cal. App. 2d 832,

23 Cal. Rptr. 92, the defendant was a physician who "treated" several victims for menstrual cramps. Each victim testified that she was treated in a position with her back to the doctor, bent over a table, with feet apart, in a dressing gown. And in each case the "treatment" consisted of the defendant first inserting a metal instrument, then substituting an instrument which "felt different"—the victims not realizing that the second instrument was in fact the doctor's penis. The precise issue before us was never tendered in *People v. Minkowski* because the petitioner there conceded the sufficiency of evidence to support the element of consciousness.

The decision is useful to this analysis, however, because it exactly illustrates certain traditional rules in the area of our inquiry. Thus, as a leading authority has written, "if deception causes a misunderstanding as to the fact itself (fraud in the factum) there is no legally-recognized consent because what happened is not that for which consent was given; whereas consent induced by fraud is as effective as any other consent, so far as direct and immediate legal consequences are concerned, if the deception relates not to the thing done but merely to some collateral matter (fraud in the inducement)." Perkins and Boyce, Criminal Law (3rd. 1982) ch. 9, § 3, p.1079.

The victims in *Minkowski* consented, not to sexual intercourse, but to an act of an altogether different nature, penetration by medical instrument. The consent was to a pathological, and not a carnal act, and the mistake was, therefore, in the factum and not merely in the inducement.

Another relatively common situation in the literature on this subject is the fraudulent obtaining of intercourse by impersonating a spouse. As Professor Perkins observes, the courts are not in accord as to whether the crime of rape is thereby committed. "[T]he disagreement is not in regard to the underlying principle but only as to its application. Some courts have taken the position that such a misdeed is fraud in the inducement on the theory that the woman consents to exactly what is done (sexual intercourse) and hence there is no rape; other courts, with better reason it would seem, hold such a misdeed to be rape on the theory that it involves fraud in the factum since the woman's consent is to an innocent act of marital intercourse while what is actually perpetrated upon her is an act of adultery. Her innocence seems never to have been questioned in such acase and the reason she is not guilty of adultery is because she did not consent to adulterousintercourse. . . . "

In California, of course, we have by statute[3] adopted the majority view that such fraud is in the factum, not the inducement, and have thus held it to vitiate consent. It is otherwise, however, with respect to the conceptually much murkier statutory offense with which we here deal, and the language of which has remained essentially unchanged since its enactment [as section 261, subdivision (5), now subd. (4) in 1872].

The language itself could not be plainer. It defines rape to be "an act of sexual intercourse" with a non-spouse, accomplished where the victim is "at the time unconscious of the nature of the act . . . " § 261, subd. (4). Nor, as

---

[3] Section 261, subdivision (5) reads as follows: "Where a person submits under the belief that the person committing the act is the victim's spouse, and this belief is induced by any artifice, pretense, or concealment practiced by the accused, with intent to induce the belief."

we have just seen, can we entertain the slightest doubt that the Legislature well understood how to draft a statute to encompass fraud in the factum, § 261, subd. (5), and how to specify certain fraud in the inducement as vitiating consent. . . .

The People, however, direct our attention to Penal Code section 261.6, which in their opinion has changed the rule that fraud in the inducement does not vitiate consent. That provision reads as follows: "In prosecutions under sections 261, 286, 288a or 289, in which consent is at issue, 'consent' shall be defined to mean positive cooperation in act or attitude pursuant to an act of free will. The person must act freely and voluntarily and have knowledge of the nature of the act or transaction involved."

* * *

If the Legislature . . . had desired to correct [an] apparent oversight . . . [5] it could certainly have done so. But the Attorney General's strained reading of section 261.6 would render sections 261, subdivision (5) meaningless surplusage; and we are "exceedingly reluctant to attach an interpretation to a particular statute which renders other existing provisions unnecessary."
. . .

. . . [T]here is not a shred of evidence on the record before us to suggest that . . . Ms. R. lacked the capacity to appreciate the nature of the sex act in which she engaged. On the contrary, her testimony was clear that she precisely understood the "nature of the act," but, motivated by a fear of disease, and death, succumbed to petitioner's fraudulent blandishments.

To so conclude is not to vitiate the heartless cruelty of petitioner's scheme, but to say that it comprised crimes of a different order than a violation of section 261, subdivision (4).

Let a peremptory writ of prohibition issue restraining respondent from taking further action upon Court II, a violation of Pen. Code, § 261, subd. (4) . . .

[The dissenting opinion of Holmdahl, J. is omitted.]

Notes and Questions

1. *Boro* reflects the traditional rule that deception as to the nature of the sex act (fraud in the factum) vitiates consent and constitutes rape, while obtaining consent to sexual relations through misrepresentations (fraud in the inducement) does not constitute rape. This means that at common law a seducer is not a rapist. Dressler at 543. As a consequence, a male may use "any non-forcible —sales technique,' no matter how deceptive, to obtain the consent of a female to sexual intercourse and escape criminal punishment [for rape] thereby." *Id.* Should this be so? If, on the other hand, fraudulently induced sexual intercourse is to be punished as rape, how should the crime

---

[5] It is not difficult to conceive of reasons why the Legislature may have consciously wished to leave the matter where it lies. Thus, as a matter of degree, where consent to intercourse is obtained by promises of travel, fame, celebrity and the like—ought the liar and seducer to be chargeable as a rapist? Where is the line to be drawn?

be redefined? Is there a difference in the fraud in *Boro* and that commonly committed by males falsely expressing "love" for females simply to induce their consent to sexual relations? What about false expressions of intent or willingness to marry made to obtain sexual intercourse with the promisee?

Note that a tort action for seduction exists in some jurisdictions. W. Wadlington, Domestic Relations 129 (2d ed. 1990); Larson, *Women Understand So Little, They Call My Good Nature "Deceit": A Feminist Rethinking of Seduction,* 93 Colum. L. Rev. 374 (1993). Should seduction be actionable in tort? Should the criminal law punish it, but less severely than the crime of rape?

Should distinctions be drawn between seduction (consent obtained by "allurement, enticement, persuasion or flattery") and cases where the victim is tricked as to the identity of the person with whom she has sex? See *People v. Hough,* 159 Misc. 2d 997, 607 N.Y.S.2d 884 (1994) (defendant, twin brother of complainant's boyfriend, deceived her into act of sexual intercourse by posing as the boyfriend).

Why would the prosecutor in *Boro* concede to setting aside Count III (procuring illicit carnal connection by false pretenses) of the information?

2. If the rape statute had been held applicable in *Boro,* would the defendant have been denied adequate "notice"? See § 2.05[B] and [C], *supra.* Shortly after *Boro,* the California legislature enacted the following:

> Every person who induces any other person, except the spouse of the perpetrator, to engage in sexual intercourse, penetration of the genital or anal openings by a foreign object, substance, instrument, or device, oral copulation, or sodomy when his or her consent is procured by false or fraudulent representation or pretense that is made with the intent to create fear, and which does induce fear, and that would cause a reasonable person in like circumstances to act contrary to the person's free will, and does cause the victim to so act, is punishable by imprisonment in either the county jail for not more than one year or in the state prison for two, three, or four years.
>
> As used in this selection, "fear" means the fear of unlawful physical injury or death to the person or to any relative of the person or member of the person's family.

Cal. Penal Code § 266c (West 1988).

Why did the legislature limit the crime to situations of inducements of fear? Does the provision go far enough to address the evil of using deception to obtain sexual consent? If the statute is meant to overrule *Boro,* does it succeed?

[C] The Marital Exemption

WARREN V. STATE

Supreme Court of Georgia

255 Ga. 151, 336 S.E.2d 221 (1985)

Smith, Justice.

"When a woman says I do, does she give up her right to say I won't?" This question does not pose the real question, because rape and aggravated sodomy are not sexual acts of an ardent husband performed upon an initially apathetic wife, they are acts of violence that are accompanied with physical and mental abuse and often leave the victim with physical and psychological damage that is almost always long lasting.[4] Thus we find the more appropriate question: When a woman says "I do" in Georgia does she give up her right to State protection from the violent acts of rape and aggravated sodomy performed by her husband. The answer is no. We affirm.

The appellant, Daniel Steven Warren, was indicted by a Fulton County Grand Jury for the rape and aggravated sodomy of his wife. They were living together as husband and wife at the time. The appellant filed a pre-trial general demurrer and motion to dismiss the indictment. After a hearing, the motions were denied. The appellant sought and was issued a certificate of immediate review and filed an application for an interlocutory appeal which was granted by this court.

1. The appellant asserts that there exists within the rape statute an implicit marital exclusion that makes it legally impossible for a husband to be guilty of raping his wife.

Until the late 1970's there was no real examination of this apparently widely held belief. Within the last few years several jurisdictions have been faced with similar issues and they have decided that under certain circumstances a husband can be held criminally liable for raping his wife. . . .

What is behind the theory and belief that a husband could not be guilty of raping his wife? There are various explanations for the rule and all of them flow from the common law attitude toward women, the status of women and marriage.

Perhaps the most often used basis for the marital rape exemption is the view set out by Lord Hale in 1 Hale P.C. 629. It is known as Lord Hale's contractual theory. The statement attributed to Lord Hale used to support the theory is: "but a husband cannot be guilty of a rape committed by himself upon his lawful wife, for by their mutual matrimonial consent and contract

---

[4] "When you have been intimately violated by a person who is supposed to love and protect you, it can destroy your capacity for intimacy with anyone else. Moreover, many wife victims are trapped in a reign of terror and experience repeated sexual assaults over a period of years. When you are raped by a stranger you have to live with a frightening memory. When you are raped by your husband, you have to live with your rapist." National Center on Women and Family Law, *Clearing House Review,* November, 1984, citing Dr. David Finkelhor's testimony and statement in support of H.B. 516 to remove spousal exemption to sexual assault offenses to the Judiciary Committee, New Hampshire State Legislature (Mar. 25, 1981), p.745.

the wife hath given up herself in this kind unto her husband which she cannot retreat."

* * *

Another theory stemming from medieval times is that of a wife being the husband's chattel or property. Since a married woman was part of her husband's property, nothing more than a chattel, rape was nothing more than a man making use of his own property.

A third theory is the unity in marriage or unity of person theory that held the very being or legal existence of a woman was suspended during marriage, or at least was incorporated and consolidated into that of her husband. In view of the fact that there was only one legal being, the husband, he could not be convicted of raping himself.

These three theories have been used to support the marital rape exemption. Others have tried to fill the chasm between these three theories with justifications for continuing the exemption in the face of changes in the recognition of women, their status, and the status of marriage. Some of the justifications include: Prevention of fabricated charges; Preventing wives from using rape charges for revenge; Preventing state intervention into marriage so that possible reconciliation will not be thwarted. A closer examination of the theories and justifications indicates that they are no longer valid, if they ever had any validity.

Hale's implied consent theory was created at a time when marriages were irrevocable and when all wives promised to "love, honor, and obey" and all husbands promised to "love, cherish, and protect until death do us part." Wives were subservient to their husbands, her identity was merged into his, her property became his property, and she took his name for her own.

There have been dramatic changes in women's rights and the status of women and marriage. . . . Our State Constitution . . . provides that each spouse has a right to retain his or her own property. [The court details a variety of provisions expanding the legal rights of married women.]

Today, many couples write their own marriage vows in which they specifically decide the terms of their marriage contract. Certainly no normal woman . . . would knowingly include an irrevocable term to her revocable marriage contract that would allow her husband to rape her. Rape "is highly reprehensible, both in a moral sense and in its almost total contempt for the personal integrity and autonomy of the female victim. . . . Short of homicide, it is the —ultimate violation of self.' " . . . It is incredible to think that any state would sanction such behavior by adding an implied consent term to all marriage contracts that would leave all wives with no protection under the law from the "ultimate violation of self," . . . simply because they choose to enter into a relationship that is respected and protected by the law. The implied consent theory to spousal rape is without logical meaning, and obviously conflicts with our Constitutional and statutory laws and our regard for all citizens of this State.

One would be hard pressed to argue that a husband can rape his wife because she is his chattel. Even in the darkest days of slavery when slaves were also considered chattel, rape was defined as "the carnal knowledge of a female whether free or slave, forcibly and against her will." Georgia Code, § 4248, p.824 (1863). Both the chattel and unity of identity rationales have been cast aside. "Nowhere in the common law world—[or] in any modern society—is a woman regarded as chattel or demeaned by denial of a separate legal identity and the dignity associated with recognition as a whole human being." . . .

We find that none of the theories have any validity. The justifications likewise are without efficacy. There is no other crime we can think of in which all of the victims are denied protection simply because someone might fabricate a charge; there is no evidence that wives have flooded the district attorneys with revenge filled trumped-up charges, and once a marital relationship is at the point where a husband rapes his wife, state intervention is needed for the wife's protection.

There never has been an expressly stated marital exemption included in the Georgia rape statute. Furthermore, our statute never included the word "unlawful" which has been widely recognized as signifying the incorporation of the common law spousal exclusion. . . . A reading of the statute indicates that there is no marital exclusion. "A person commits the offense of rape when he has carnal knowledge of a female forcibly and against her will." . . . We need not decide whether or not a common law marital exemption became part of our old statutory rape law, because the rape statute that was similar to the common law definition[1] was specifically repealed in 1968, and our new broader statute, OCGA § 16-6-1, was enacted in its place which plainly on its face includes a husband.[2]

* * *

3. The appellant contends that if we find no marital exemptions under the rape . . . [statute] it would be a new interpretation of the criminal law, and to apply the statutes to him would deprive him of his due process rights.

"All the Due Process Clause requires is that the law give sufficient warning that men may conduct themselves so as to avoid that which is forbidden." [T]he rape . . . [statute is] broadly written and . . . plain on [its] face. This is a first application of [this statute] to this particular set of facts, this is not an unforeseeable judicial enlargement of criminal statutes that are narrowly drawn. . . .

---

[1] "Rape is the carnal knowledge of a female, forcibly and against her will."

[2] When our Criminal Code was revised, the drafters relied upon the Illinois Criminal Code and the Model Penal code. Both Codes included within their rape statutes an explicit marital exemption. "A male person . . . who has sexual intercourse with a female, not his wife, by force and against her will commits rape." Ill. Rev. Stat. § 11.1; "A male who has sexual intercourse with a female not his wife is guilty of rape if; . . . " Section 213.1 Model Penal Code. Our Legislature could have, but did not, include the words "not his wife." They chose instead to add the words "A person," which broadens the statute and which is in keeping with the enunciated purposes of the code. OCGA § 16-1-2.

Judgment affirmed. All the Justices concur.

NOTES AND QUESTIONS

1. As the *Warren* case notes, the Model Penal Code adopted a marital exemption for the most serious grade of rape. The Code commentary explains,

> Today, it is certainly not true that marriage results in legal abrogation of the woman's autonomy over her own person. Just as a woman may agree to date but withhold consent for intercourse, so she may marry without surrendering to sex on demand. If on occasion she refuses, the husband has no right to compel her to submit. If he does so by force or physical menace, he may be guilty of assault and subject to a range of penalties dependent on the gravity of harm threatened or caused. Liability for rape is another matter. Rape may consist of wholly non-violent conduct, but where force is used, rape carries sanctions more severe than those authorized for assault. The existence of a prior and continuing relation of intimacy, whether formalized by ceremony or achieved by long practice, is not irrelevant to the concerns of the law of rape. Explication of this conclusion requires a look at the various kinds of conduct that may be punished as rape or a related offense.
>
> First, marriage or equivalent relationship, while not amounting to a legal waiver of the woman's right to say "no," does imply a kind of generalized consent that distinguishes some versions of the crime of rape from parallel behavior by a husband. The relationship itself creates a presumption of consent, valid until revoked. At a minimum, therefore, husbands must be exempt from those categories of liability based not on force or coercion but on a presumed incapacity of the woman to consent. For example, a man who has intercourse with his unconscious wife should scarcely be condemned to felony liability on the ground that the woman in such circumstances is incapable of consenting to sex with her own husband, at least unless there are aggravating circumstances.
>
> The major context of which those who would abandon the spousal exclusion are thinking, however, is the situation of rape by force or threat. The problem with abandoning the immunity in many such situations is that the law of rape, if applied to spouses, would thrust the prospect of criminal sanctions into the ongoing process of adjustment in the marital relationship. Section 213.1, for example, defines as gross sexual imposition intercourse coerced "by any threat that would prevent resistance by a woman of ordinary resolution." It may well be that a woman of ordinary resolution would be prevented from resisting by her husband's threat to expose a secret to her mother, for example. Behavior of this sort within the marital relationship is no doubt unattractive, but it is a risky business for the law to intervene by threatening criminal sanctions. Retaining the spousal exclusion avoids this unwarranted intrusion of the penal law into the life of the family.
>
> Finally, there is the case of intercourse coerced by force or threat of physical harm. Here the law already authorizes a penalty for assault. If the actor causes serious bodily injury, the punishment is quite severe. The issue

is whether the still more drastic sanctions of rape should apply. The answer depends on whether the injury caused by forcible intercourse by a husband is equivalent to that inflicted by someone else. The gravity of the crime of forcible rape derives not merely from its violent character but also from its achievement of a particularly degrading kind of unwanted intimacy. Where the attacker stands in an ongoing relation of sexual intimacy, that evil, as distinct from the force used to compel submission, may well be thought qualitatively different. The character of the voluntary association of husband and wife, in other words, may be thought to affect the nature of the harm involved in unwanted intercourse. That, in any event, is the conclusion long endorsed by the law of rape and carried forward in the Model Code provision.

MPC § 213.1, Comment at 344–46.

Do you agree with the Code that the evil of marital rape is "qualitatively different" and less substantial than in nonmarital situations? Could it be argued that the gravity of harm is *more* substantial in marital rapes because many women report that they feel greater injury and betrayal when raped by someone they know than by someone they do not. See footnote 4 of *Warren;* see also Augustine, *Marriage: The Safe Haven for Rapists,* 29 J. Fam. L. 559, 571–72 (1991).

2. Consider the Michigan statute *supra,* pp. 669–70. Under that provision might it be rape (in the MPC Commentary example) for a husband to "extort" sex from his unwilling wife by threatening to expose a secret to her mother? If so, should a marital exemption apply under the Michigan provision? Suppose a husband "extorts" his wife's "separate property." Is there more or less reason for criminalizing his conduct than when he "extorts" sex from his wife?

3. While most states have abolished the marital exemption, many punish marital rape less severely than its nonmarital counterpart. See Comment, *Old Wine in New Bottles: The "Marital" Rape Allowance,* 72 N.C.L. Rev. 261 (1993). Should distinctions be drawn between married couples living together and those living apart? Should special rules apply to couples who live together as nonmarital cohabitants?

§ 6.03 The *Mens Rea*

[A] Subjective Fault

Director of Public Prosecutions v. Morgan

House of Lords

2 All Eng. Rep. 347 [1975]

Lord HAILSHAM:

The four appellants were all convicted at the Stafford Crown Court of various offenses connected with alleged rapes on the person of Daphne Ethel

Morgan of whom the first appellant is, or at the material time was, the husband. The second, third and fourth appellants were convicted each of a principal offence against Mrs. Morgan, and each of aiding and abetting the principal offenses alleged to have been committed by each of the other two. The appellant Morgan, who also had connection with his wife allegedly without her consent as part of the same series of events, was not charged with rape, the prosecution evidently accepting and applying the ancient common law doctrine that a husband cannot be guilty of raping his own wife. Morgan was therefore charged with and convicted of aiding and abetting the rapes alleged to have been committed by the other three.

The question certified . . . is:

Whether, in rape, the defendant can properly be convicted notwithstanding that he in fact believed that the woman consented if such belief was not based on reasonable grounds.

[Morgan, a member of the Royal Air Force, went drinking with three fellow servicemen. They talked about picking up some women for sexual activity, but Morgan suggested instead that they come to his house, declaring that his wife would be interested in having sex with all of them. He told them that his wife might struggle or feign resistance, but that this was simply her way of enjoying sexual intercourse more. They all went to the house and dragged Mrs. Morgan from her bedroom, where she was asleep. Over her vigorous protests, the three younger airmen then had sexual intercourse with her as well as committing various other sexual acts. When they were finished, Mrs. Morgan escaped to a nearby hospital and immediately declared she had been raped. The defendants testified that while the victim initially resisted, she soon actively and willingly engaged in the evening's activities, which the Court described as "a sexual orgy which might have excited unfavorable comment in the courts of Caligula or Nero."]

I mention all these details simply to show, that if, as I think plain, the jury accepted Mrs. Morgan's statement in substance, there was no possibility whatever of any of the appellants holding any belief whatever, reasonable or otherwise, in their victim's consent to what was being done.

The primary "defence" was consent. I use the word "defence" in inverted commas, because, of course, in establishing the crime of rape, the prosecution must exclude consent in order to establish the essential ingredients of the crime. There is no burden at the outset on the accused to raise the issue.

[I]t is clear that Morgan did invite his three companions home in order that they might have sexual intercourse with his wife and, no doubt, he may well have led them in one way or another to believe that she would consent to their doing so. This, however, would only be matter predisposing them to believe that Mrs. Morgan consented, and would not in any way establish that, at the time, they believed she did consent whilst they were having intercourse.

The learned judge said:

The crime of rape consists in having unlawful sexual intercourse with a woman without her consent and by force. By force. Those words mean exactly what they say. It does not mean there has to be a fight or blows have to be inflicted. It means that there has to be some violence used against the woman to overbear her will or that there has to be a threat of violence as a result of which her will is overborne. Further, the prosecution have to prove that each defendant intended to have sexual intercourse with this woman without her consent. Therefore if the defendant believed or may have believed that Mrs. Morgan consented to him having sexual intercourse with her, then there would be no such intent in his mind and he would be not guilty of the offence of rape, but such a belief must be honestly held by the defendant in the first place. He must really believe that. And, secondly, his belief must be a reasonable belief; such a belief as a reasonable man would entertain if he applied his mind and thought about the matter. It is not enough for a defendant to rely upon a belief; even though he honestly held it, if it was completely fanciful; contrary to every indication which could be given which would carry some weight with a reasonable man.

It is on the second proposition about the mental element that the appellants concentrate their criticism. An honest belief on consent, they contend, is enough. It matters not whether it be also reasonable. No doubt a defendant will wish to raise argument or lead evidence to show that this belief was reasonable, since this will support its honesty. No doubt the prosecution will seek to cross-examine or raise arguments or adduce evidence to undermine the contention that the belief is reasonable, because, in the nature of the case, the fact that a belief cannot reasonably be held is a strong ground for saying that it was not in fact held honestly at all. Nonetheless, the appellants contend, the crux of the matter is honesty and not honesty plus reasonableness. In making reasonableness as well as honesty an ingredient in this "defence" the judge, say the appellants, was guilty of a misdirection.

My first comment on this direction is that the propositions described "in the first place" and "secondly" in the above direction as to the mental ingredient in rape are wholly irreconcilable. . . . If it be true, as the learned judge says "in the first place," that the prosecution have to prove that "each defendant intended to have sexual intercourse without her consent, not merely that he intended to have intercourse with her but that he intended to have intercourse without her consent," the defendant must be entitled to an acquittal if the prosecution fail to prove just that. The necessary mental ingredient will be lacking and the only possible verdict is "not guilty." If, on the other hand, as is asserted in the passage beginning "secondly," it is necessary for any belief in the woman's consent to be "a reasonable belief" before the defendant is entitled to an acquittal, it must either be because the mental ingredient in rape is not "to have intercourse and to have it without her consent" but simply "to have intercourse" subject to a special defence of "honest and reasonable belief," or alternatively to have intercourse without a reasonable belief in her consent.

No doubt it would be possible, by statute, to devise a law by which intercourse, voluntarily entered into, was an absolute offence, subject to a "defence" of belief whether honest or honest and reasonable, of which the "evidential" burden is primarily on the defence and the "probative" burden on the prosecution. But in my opinion such is not the crime of rape as it has hitherto been understood. The prohibited act in rape is to have intercourse without the victim's consent. The minimum *mens rea* or guilty mind in most common law offenses, including rape, is the intention to do the prohibited act, and that is correctly stated in the proposition stated "in the first place" of the judge's direction.

The only qualification I would make to the direction of the learned judge's "in the first place" is the refinement that if the intention of the accused is to have intercourse *nolens volens,* that is recklessly and not caring whether the victim be a consenting party or not, that is equivalent on ordinary principles to an intent to do the prohibited act without the consent of the victim.

The alternative version of the learned judge's direction would read that the accused must do the prohibited act with the intention of doing it without an honest and reasonable belief in the victim's consent. . . . In principle, however, I find it unacceptable. I believe that *mens rea* means "guilty or criminal mind," and if it be the case, as seems to be accepted here, that mental element in rape is not knowledge but intent, to insist that a belief must be reasonable to excuse it is to insist that either the accused is to be found guilty of intending to do that which in truth he did not intend to do, or that his state of mind though innocent of evil intent, can convict him if it be honest but not rational. . . . This is to insist on an objective element in the definition of intent, and this is a course which I am extremely reluctant to adopt.

Once one has accepted, what seems to me abundantly clear, that the prohibited act in rape is non-consensual sexual intercourse, and that the guilty state of mind is an intention to commit it, it seems to me to follow as a matter of inexorable logic that there is no room either for a "defence" of honest belief or mistake, or of a defence of honest and reasonable belief and mistake. Either the prosecution proves that the accused had the requisite intent, or it does not. In the former case it succeeds, and in the latter it fails. Since honest belief clearly negatives intent, the reasonableness or otherwise of that belief can only be evidence for or against the view that the belief and therefore the intent was actually held, and it matters not whether . . . "the definition of a crime includes no specific element beyond the prohibited act." . . . Any other view, as for insertion of the word "reasonable" can only have the effect of saying that a man intends something which he does not.

[T]he appellants invited us to overrule the bigamy cases from *Regina v. Tolson* . . . onwards and perhaps also *Regina v. Prince* . . . (the abduction case) as wrongly decided at least insofar as they purport to insist that a mistaken belief must be reasonable. . . . I am content to rest my view of the instant case on the crime of rape by saying that it is my opinion that the prohibited act is and always has been intercourse without consent of the victim and the mental element is and always has been the intention to commit that act, or the equivalent intention of having intercourse willy-nilly not caring whether the victim consents or not. A failure to prove this involves an acquittal because the intent, an essential ingredient, is lacking. It matters not why it is lacking if only it is not there, and in particular it matters not that the intention is lacking only because of a belief not based on reasonable grounds.

Lord SIMON of Glaisdale:

The answer to this question, in my view, depends on the following matters: first, a distinction between crimes of basic and of ulterior intent; secondly a distinction between probative and evidential burdens of proof; thirdly, the interrelationship of these two distinctions; fourthly, ascertainment whether rape is a crime of basic or ulterior intent; and, fifthly, the general policy of the criminal law when the prosecution has provisionally discharged the burden of proving *actus reus* and *mens rea,* and the accused then alleges a belief, albeit erroneous, in a state of acts which would, if true, negative the *actus reus* and *mens rea* provisionally proved by the prosecution. After examining these five matters I shall endeavour to determine the reasons for what I believe to be the general policy of the criminal law in such circumstances.

I turn to examine, first the distinction between crimes of basic and of ulterior intent. . . . By "crimes of basic intent" I mean those crimes whose definition expresses (or, more often, implies) a *mens rea* which does not go beyond the *actus reus*. The *actus reus* generally consists of an act and some consequence. The consequence may be very closely connected with the act or more remotely connected with it; but with a crime of basic intent the *mens rea* does not extend beyond the act and its consequence, however remote, as defined in the *actus reus*.

There are crimes of ulterior intent—"ulterior" because the *mens rea* goes beyond contemplation of the *actus reus*. For example, in the crime of wounding with intent to cause grievous bodily harm, the *actus reus* is the wounding. The prosecution must prove a corresponding *mens rea* (as with unlawful wounding), but the prosecution must go further: it must show that the accused foresaw that serious physical injury would probably be a consequence of his act, or would possibly be so, that being a purpose of his act. The crime of wounding with intent to cause grievous bodily harm could be committed without any serious physical injury being caused to the victim. This is because there is no *actus reus* corresponding to the ulterior intent. One of the questions which has to be answered in this appeal is whether rape is a crime of basic or ulterior intent.

A second relevant distinction known to the modern law is that between probative and evidential burdens of proof. . . . In the criminal law the probative burden of every issue lies on the prosecution. . . . But the prosecution may adduce evidence sufficient, at a certain stage in the trial, to discharge provisionally the probative burden and thus call for some explanation on behalf of the accused (generally by evidence; though forensic analysis discounting the prosecution's case sometimes suffices): the evidential burden has shifted, though the probative burden remains on the prosecution. Again, the accused may raise a case fit for the consideration of the jury on a fresh issue. For example, although the prosecution may have provisionally discharged the onus of proving an assault, the accused may raise an issue of self-defence in a form fit for the consideration of the jury: if so, the evidential burden of disproving it will shift to the prosecution, which has, of course, also (once the defence is raised in a form fit for the consideration of the jury) the probative burden of disproving it. In this way the evidential burden of proof will often shift backwards and forwards during a trial, the probative burden remaining throughout on the prosecution.

The third matter for consideration is the interaction between these two distinctions—between crimes of basic and of ulterior intent, on the one hand,

and between probative and evidential burdens of proof on the other. Such interaction occurs because proof of the *actus reus* generally raises a presumption of a corresponding *mens rea,* an act being usually performed with foresight of its probable consequences. I emphasize the words "generally" and "usually" because the inference may not be a natural one in some circumstances. For example, a different inference as to intention may be drawn from proof that the accused drove his elbow hard into the stomach of a stranger in a crowded train from where it is proved that he did the same act when alone with the stranger in the course of an angry argument. If the crime is one of basic intent, so that the *mens rea* does not extend beyond the *actus reus,* proof of the *actus reus* is therefore, generally, sufficient *prima facie* proof of the mens rea to shift the evidential burden of proof. Thus, if the prosecution prove that the accused squeezed the trigger of a firearm and thereby wounded a victim, this will often be sufficient proof not only of the *actus reus* of unlawful wounding but also of the necessary *mens rea, i.e.,* that the accused foresaw the wounding as a likely consequence of his act or was reckless as to whether it ensued, so as to cause the evidential burden to shift and thus to call for some explanation on behalf of the accused. But if the crime is one of ulterior intent, proof of the *actus reus* tells little about *mens rea* insofar as it extends beyond the *actus reus;* so that the evidential burden does not necessarily shift on the proof of the actus reus. To prove that A wounded B, even intentionally, does not itself raise a presumption that A thereby intended to cause serious physical injury to B.

This brings me to the fourth question, namely whether rape is a crime of basic or ulterior intent. Does it involve an intent going beyond the *actus reus?* . . . The *actus reus* is sexual intercourse with a woman who is not in fact consenting to such intercourse. The *mens rea* is knowledge that the woman is not consenting or recklessness as to whether she is consenting or not. That it is nothing more can be seen by postulating an offence of rape with an ulterior intent. Rape itself involves no *mens rea* going beyond the *actus reus.*

If this is right, proof of the *actus reus* in rape—that is, proof of sexual intercourse with a woman who did not consent to it—will generally be sufficient *prima facie* proof to shift the evidential burden. If the evidential burden shifts in this way, the accused must either prove that his conduct was involuntary (which is irrelevant in the crime of rape) or he must negative the inference as to *mens rea* which might be drawn from the *actus reus.* Assuming that the prosecution have proved sexual intercourse with a woman who did not in fact consent to it, in general the only way in which the accused can shift back the evidential burden is by showing a belief in a state of affairs whereby the *actus* would not be *reus.* In the context of rape, the accused in such circumstances must, in other words, show that he believed that the woman was consenting. To say that he must show that he believed it "honestly" is tautologous but useful as emphasizing a distinction. The question is whether he must show that he believed it reasonably, and, if so, why.

It remains to consider, why the law requires, in such circumstances, that the belief in a state of affairs whereby the *actus* would not be *reus* must be held on reasonable grounds. One reason was given by Bridge, J., in the Court of Appeal:

The rationale of requiring reasonable grounds for the mistaken belief must lie in the law's consideration that a bald assertion of belief for which the accused can indicate no reasonable ground is evidence of insufficient substance to raise any issue requiring the jury's consideration.

I agree; but I think there is also another reason. The policy of the law in this regard could well derive from its concern to hold a fair balance between victim and accused. It would hardly seem just to fob off a victim of a savage assault with such comfort as he could derive from knowing that his injury was caused by a belief, however absurd, that he was about to attack the accused. A respectable woman who has been ravished would hardly feel that she was vindicated by being told that her assailant must go unpunished because he believed, quite unreasonably, that she was consenting to sexual intercourse with him. . . .

I would therefore answer the question certified for your Lordships' consideration. Yes.

Lord CROSS of Chelsea:

If the words defining an offence provide either expressly or impliedly that a man is not to be guilty of it if he believes something to be true, then he cannot be found guilty if the jury think that he may have believed it to be true, however inadequate were his reasons for doing so. But, if the definition of the offence is on the face of it "absolute" and the defendant is asking to escape his *prima facie* liability by a defence of mistaken belief, I can see no hardship to him in requiring the mistake—if it is to afford him a defence—to be based on reasonable grounds. . . . [T]here is nothing unreasonable in the law requiring a citizen to take reasonable care to ascertain the facts relevant to his avoiding doing a prohibited act. To have intercourse with a woman who is not your wife is, even today, not generally considered to be a course of conduct which the law ought positively to encourage and it can be argued with force that it is only fair to the woman and not in the least unfair to the man that he should be under a duty to take reasonable care to ascertain that she is consenting to the intercourse and be at the risk of a prosecution if he fails to take such care.

Section 1 of the 1956 Act does not say that a man who has sexual intercourse with a woman who does not consent to it commits an offence; it says that a man who rapes a woman commits an offence. . . . Rape, to my mind, imports at least indifference as to the woman's consent.

[Although a majority of the House believed that the instructions requiring "reasonable" belief of consent was erroneous, the defendants were not exculpated because a majority agreed that no jury could have found that the defendants even honestly believed that the victim was consenting.]

NOTES AND QUESTIONS

1. How does Lord Hailsham define the crime of rape? What *mens rea* is required regarding the nonconsent element? Does Lord Hailsham reach the right conclusion?

2. Does Lord Simon reach the correct conclusion (mistakes regarding consent must be reasonable)? If rape requires knowledge or recklessness regarding the nonconsent element, would not any mistake (reasonable or not) as to that element negate the required *mens rea*?

Does Lord Simon disregard the law to reach a sound result on policy grounds? Does he reach a result upholding "a fair balance between victim and accused"?

3. Do you find Lord Chelsea's "proceed at your own risk" analysis convincing? Does he assume an outmoded view of the immorality of "having intercourse with a woman who is not your wife"?

4. Not surprisingly, the *Morgan* opinion touched off great controversy. See for example, Curley, *Excusing Rape,* 5 Phil. and Pub. Aff. 325 (1976); Cowley, *The Retreat from Morgan,* [1982] Crim. L. Rev. 200; Gardner, *Reckless and Inconsiderate Rape,* [1991] Crim. L. Rev. 172. Shortly after *Morgan,* Parliament enacted the Sexual Offenses (Amendment) Act, which provides in § 1 (1),

A man commits rape if (a)he has unlawful sexual intercourse with a woman who at the time of the intercourse does not consent to it; and (b)at that time he knows that she does not consent to the intercourse or he is reckless as to whether she consents to it.

Does the statute disavow the holding in the *Morgan* case? If not, why did Parliament act?

REYNOLDS V. STATE

Court of Appeals of Alaska

664 P.2d 621 (1983)

SINGLETON, Judge.

Randall C. Reynolds was convicted of sexual assault in the first degree. . . . He received a five-year sentence. He appeals challenging his conviction and contending that . . . he should have been given more favorable jury instructions. We affirm.

Reynolds and J.D., his victim, were employees of separate businesses located in the Shoppers' Forum shopping mall in Fairbanks. On November 24, 1981, employees of the various businesses located in the mall were engaged in decorating it in anticipation of the Christmas shopping season. Reynolds and J.D. were acquainted but had never previously dated. J.D. accepted an invitation from Reynolds' father to join him, his girlfriend and Reynolds for dinner. The four went out to dinner and thereafter to a Fairbanks nightclub for drinks and dancing. J.D. allegedly asked Reynolds to take her home. Instead, he took her to his apartment. She alleges that he "forced" her to enter his apartment and used a key to close a deadbolt lock and pocketed the key, effectively preventing her from leaving. She contends that he had intercourse with her against her will and restrained her at the apartment until morning at which time he accepted her request to drive her home. She concedes that her objections were verbal, that she never forcibly resisted Reynolds and that Reynolds never threatened her or struck her. She contends that she was afraid of him particularly because she noticed a handgun on a chair in the room. She admits that Reynolds never touched or even mentioned the handgun. Reynolds testified that he had intercourse with J.D. with her consent. He contends that he did not notice anything about her behavior or demeanor which would indicate that she did not wish to have intercourse with him. Reynolds' father and his father's girlfriend testified that during the early evening J.D. seemed comfortable in Reynolds' company and satisfied to be with him.

* * *

Alaska has dispensed with any requirement that the victim resist at all. AS 11.41.470 provides in relevant part:

> Definitions. For purposes of §§ 410–470 of this chapter [sexual offenses], unless the context requires otherwise, (3) "without consent" means that a person (A) with or without resisting, is coerced by the use of force against a person or property, or by the express or implied threat of imminent death, imminent physical injury, or imminent kidnaping to be inflicted on anyone;

The code defines "force" and "physical injury" as follows:

> AS 11.81.900(b)(22) "force" means any bodily impact, restraint, or confinement or the threat of imminent bodily impact, restraint, or confinement; "force" includes deadly and nondeadly force; AS 11.81.900(b)(40) "physical injury" means physical pain or an impairment of physical condition;

Thus, the legislature has substantially enhanced the risk of conviction in ambiguous circumstances by eliminating the requirement that the state prove "resistance" and by substantially broadening the definitions of "force" and "physical injury." We are satisfied, however, that the legislature counteracted this risk through its treatment of *mens rea*. It did this by shifting the focus of the jury's attention from the victim's resistance or actions to the defendant's understanding of the totality of the circumstances. Lack of consent is a "surrounding circumstance" which, under the Revised Code, requires a complementary mental state as well as conduct to constitute a crime. . . . No specific mental state is mentioned in AS 11.41.410(a)(1) governing the surrounding circumstance of "consent." Therefore, the state must prove that the defendant acted "recklessly" regarding his putative victim's lack of consent. This requirement serves to protect the defendant against conviction for first-degree sexual assault where the circumstances regarding consent are ambiguous at the time he has intercourse with the complaining witness. While the legislature has substantially reduced the state's burden of proof regarding the *actus reus* of the offense, it has at the same time made it easier for the defendant to argue the defense of mistake of fact. The Alaska rule [distinguishes] negligence and recklessness. The senate committee suggested:

> When a statute in the code provides that a person must recklessly cause a result or disregard a circumstance, criminal liability will result if the defendant "is aware of and consciously disregards a substantial and unjustifiable risk that the result will occur or that the circumstance exists." The

test for recklessness is a subjective one—the defendant must actually be aware of the risk. On the other hand, if criminal negligence is the applicable culpable mental state, the defendant will be criminally liable if he "fails to perceive a substantial and unjustifiable risk that the result will occur or that the circumstance exists." The test for criminal negligence is an objective one—the defendant's culpability stems from his failure to perceive the risk.

In order to prove a violation of AS 11.41.410(a)(1), the state must prove that the defendant knowingly engaged in sexual intercourse and recklessly disregarded his victim's lack of consent. Construed in this way, the statute does not punish harmless conduct. . . .

Having construed the statute, we are now prepared to consider Reynolds' . . . arguments. First, he contends that there was insufficient evidence to establish that he . . . committed first-degree sexual assault against her. AS 11.41.410 provides in relevant part:

> Sexual assault in the first degree. (a) A person commits the crime of sexual assault in the first degree if, (1) being any age, he engages in sexual penetration with another person without consent of that person;

AS 11.41.470(3)(A) provides in relevant part:

> (3) "without consent" means that a person (A) with or without resistance, is coerced by the use of force against a person or property, or by the express or implied threat of imminent death, imminent physical injury, or imminent kidnaping to be inflicted on anyone . . . ;

Reynolds testified and conceded that he had sexual intercourse with J.D., *i.e.*, that he sexually penetrated her. Since "force" includes "restraint," his guilt of first-degree sexual assault turns on whether he "restrained her" with intent to have sexual intercourse and whether he recklessly disregarded her lack of consent.

In reviewing the denial of a judgment of acquittal, we apply the following test:

> [T]his court must consider the evidence and the reasonable inferences arising therefrom in the light most favorable to the state and determine if fair-minded jurors in the exercise of reasonable judgment could differ on the question of whether guilt has been established beyond a reasonable doubt. If the jurors could so differ, then the case was properly submitted to the jury.

We have carefully reviewed the record and conclude that reasonable people could differ as to the existence of the [element] of . . . "reckless disregard of lack of consent." [The court reviewed the evidence and concluded that the trial court did not err in denying Reynolds' motion for acquittal.]

* * *

Reynolds argues that the trial court incorrectly instructed the jury. He points out that the jury was not expressly told that it had to find that he "recklessly" disregarded J.D.'s lack of consent before it could convict him of first-degree sexual assault. He concedes that he did not object to the instructions on first-degree sexual assault and therefore must establish plain error to be heard on appeal. . . .

The jury was instructed as follows regarding first-degree sexual assault:

> A person commits the crime of sexual assault in the first degree if he engages in sexual penetration with another person without the consent of that person. In order to establish the crime of sexual assault in the first degree, it is necessary for the state to prove beyond a reasonable doubt the following: First, that the event in question occurred at or near Fairbanks, in the Fourth Judicial District, State of Alaska, and on or about the 25th day of November, 1981; Second, that Randall Reynolds engaged in sexual penetration with [J.D.]; and, Third, that the penetration occurred without the consent of [J.D.].

While Reynolds is correct that the foregoing instructions standing alone might be interpreted as establishing strict liability regarding J.D.'s lack of consent, any such risk disappears when we examine the other instructions. For example, the jury was told:

> In the crimes charged in the indictment there must exist a joint operation of an act or conduct and a culpable mental state. To constitute a culpable mental state is not necessary that there exist an intent to violate the law. When a person knowingly does that which the law declares to be a crime, he is acting with a culpable mental state, even though he may not know that his act or conduct is unlawful.

Significantly, the jury was given the following definition of the term "knowingly":

> A person acts "knowingly" with respect to conduct or to a circumstance described by the law when he is aware that his conduct is of that nature or that the circumstance exists. When knowledge of the existence of a particular fact must be proved by the state, that knowledge is established if a person is aware of a substantial probability of the existence of that fact, unless he actually believes that it does not exist.

In conclusion, the jury was told that, before Reynolds could be convicted of first-degree sexual assault, it had to find beyond a reasonable doubt that he knowingly did an act which the law forbids, *i.e.,* knowingly had sexual intercourse with J.D., knowing that she did not consent. Furthermore, it is clear that Reynolds and his counsel understood that this was the burden the state had to meet. In his opening statement and his final argument, defense counsel argued that Reynolds had no reason to believe that J.D. did not want to have intercourse because she never expressed her lack of consent. In rebuttal, the prosecutor conceded that J.D. needed to communicate her nonconsent in some way to Reynolds before he could be guilty of first-degree sexual assault and that it was up to the jury to decide whether J.D. had, in fact, communicated her lack of consent to Reynolds. During the trial, direct and cross-examinations of both J.D. and Reynolds focused on whether J.D. had communicated her lack of consent. On direct examination, J.D. testified that she told Reynolds several times that she wanted to go home and she did not want to kiss him or have sexual intercourse. On cross-examination, J.D. stated that she was sure that she told Reynolds she did not want to have intercourse and that he understood her. Reynolds testified that J.D. didn't say much and that she never gave him any reason to believe the incident occurred without her consent.

Under these circumstances, we are satisfied that the trial court did not commit plain error in failing to specifically instruct the jury that Reynolds had to recklessly disregard a substantial risk that J.D. did not consent to intercourse before he could be convicted of first-degree sexual assault.

* * *

The judgment is affirmed.

NOTES AND QUESTIONS

1. *Reynolds* reaches the same result as *Morgan* by applying "element analysis" as espoused by the Model Penal Code. Note, however, that nonconsent is clearly an element of rape under the Alaska statute but is not explicitly included in the definition of rape under MPC § 213.1 (rape defined in terms of sexual intercourse through "compulsion" of victim "to submit by force or threat").

2. How does the MPC treat the consent factor? What *mens rea* requirements, if any, does the Code impose regarding the woman's nonconsent? See MPC § 213.1 Comment at 304, "The definition of the offense is stated not in terms of the victim's lack of consent . . . " See the Commentary to § 213.1 at note 6 following the *Iniguez* case, *supra*. Section 2.11 of the Code provides,

Consent.

(1) In General. The consent of the victim to conduct charged to constitute an offense or to the result thereof is a defense if such consent negatives an element of the offense or precludes the infliction of the harm or evil sought to be prevented by the law defining the offense.

* * *

(3) Ineffective Consent. Unless otherwise provided by the Code or by the law defining the offense, assent does not constitute consent if:

* * *

(d) it is induced by force, duress or deception of a kind sought to be prevented by the law defining the offense. Consent would seem to negate the "comp[ulsion] . . . by force" elements. But what if the defendant mistakenly believes the woman consents? Does it matter whether this is conceptualized as a mistake about consent as opposed to a mistake about a "consent defense"? Does consent constitute an affirmative defense or a negation of an essential element of the crime? See § 9.02, infra. What consequences hinge on this distinction?

[B] Objective Liability

STATE V. SMITH

Supreme Court of Connecticut

210 Conn. 132, 554 A.2d 713 (1989)

SHEA, Associate Justice.

After a jury trial the defendant was convicted of sexual assault in the first degree in violation of General Statutes § 53a-70. In this appeal he claims error in (1) the denial of his motion for a judgment of acquittal for insufficiency of the evidence on the element of lack of consent. . . . We find no error.

Upon the evidence presented the jury could reasonably have found the following facts. On March 18, 1987, the victim, T, a twenty-six-year-old woman, and her girlfriend, A, a visitor from Idaho, went to a bar in West Haven. T was introduced by a friend to the defendant, who bought her a drink. The defendant invited her and A, together with a male acquaintance A had met at the bar, to dinner at a restaurant across the street. After dinner, the defendant having paid for T's share, the four left the restaurant. The defendant proposed that they all go to his apartment in West Haven. Because A's acquaintance had a motorcycle, the defendant gave them directions to the apartment so that they could ride there, while he and T walked.

After a twenty minute walk, the defendant and T arrived at the apartment at about 10 PM. A and her acquaintance were not there and never arrived at the apartment. When T and the defendant had entered the apartment they sat on the couch in the living room to watch television. After a while the defendant put his arm around T and told her he wanted a kiss. She gave him a kiss. She testified that "He wouldn't back off. He wouldn't let go of me. So I said "Look, I am not kidding. I really don't want to do anything. I don't know you and whatnot." The defendant still held onto T. She testified that he was "still right in my face wanting to kiss me. You know, saying so, saying that you don't think I paid for dinner for nothing, do you."

T testified that she was scared: "At first I didn't know what to do. I did spit in his face and he didn't even take it seriously. Then I tried kicking him off, which was to no avail. He was way too big for me." T described the defendant as "at least six foot two" and "at least two hundred pounds." She testified: "He told me he could make it hard on me or I could make it easy on myself, which I finally decided was probably my best bet." T understood that the defendant was determined to "have sex" with her and that either he would hurt her or she "was going to go along with it." At the point where T ceased resistance, she was "down on the couch" and the defendant was "on top of" her.

T testified that she had informed the defendant that she had to pick up her daughter, had insulted him, and had told him that he was "a big man to have to force a woman." She testified, however, that after she decided to "give in," she tried to convince the defendant that she was not going to fight and "was going to go along with him and enjoy it."

The defendant removed T's clothing as she remained on the couch and led her into the bedroom. When she declined his request for oral sex, he did not insist upon it, but proceeded to engage in vaginal intercourse with her. After completion of the act, the defendant said that he knew the victim felt that she had been raped, but that she could not prove it and had really enjoyed herself.

After they both had dressed, the defendant requested T's telephone number, but she gave him a number she concocted as a pretense. He also offered her some sherbet, which she accepted and ate while she waited for a cab that the defendant had called. T, however, placed her pink cigarette lighter underneath the couch, so that she would be able to prove she had been in the apartment. When the cab arrived, she left the apartment. She told the cab driver to take her to the police station because she had been raped. At the station she gave her account of the event to the police. The defendant was arrested. The police found T's lighter under the couch in his living room, where T had informed them it was located.

Although the defendant claims insufficiency of the evidence as the basis for his claim that he was entitled to an acquittal, he actually seeks to have this court impose a requirement of *mens rea,* or guilty intent, as an essential element of the crime of sexual assault in the firstdegree. In fact, he concedes in his reply brief that, if conviction for sexual assault in the firstdegree requires only a general intent, he cannot prevail on his claim that the evidence was insufficient to support his conviction. This court has held that our statute, § 53a-70, requires proof of only a general intent to perform the physical acts that constitute that crime. . . . "No specific intent is made an element of the crime of first degree sexual assault." . . . "It is well settled that first degree sexual assault is a general intent crime." *State v. Rothenberg,* 195 Conn. 253, 258 n.4, 487 A.2d 545 (1985). . . .

The defendant, nevertheless, urges that we adopt a construction of § 53a-70 making the mental state of the defendant the touchstone for the resolution of the issue of consent when presented in a prosecution for first degree sexual assault. He refers to this mental state as a *mens rea,* a guilty mind, and describes it as an awareness on the part of a man that he is forcing sex upon a woman against her will and that he intends to do so. In the context of the evidence in this case, the defendant claims, though he did not testify at trial, that he honestly believed that at the time the sexual act occurred that T had consented to it. He bases this claim upon her testimony that, after their preliminary encounter on the couch, and his remark that he could "make it hard" for her or she could "make it easy" on herself, she ceased resisting his advances and decided to "go along with it." T also testified that, once she decided to "give in," she acted as if she were "going to go along with him and enjoy it."

The position advocated by the defendant that the requisite *mens rea* should be an element of the crime of sexual assault in the first degree is supported by a widely publicized decision of the British House of Lords in 1975, *Director of Public Prosecutions v. Morgan.* . . . A similar position has been adopted in Alaska, where it is held that the state has the burden of proving at least "that the defendant acted 'recklessly' regarding his putative victim's lack of consent." *Reynolds v. State* . . . The Supreme Court of California has concluded that a wrongful intent is an element of a rape offense, but, contrary to *Morgan,* has held that this element would be negated if a defendant entertained a *"reasonable* and bona fide belief" that the complainant had consented. (Emphasis added.) *People v. Mayberry,* 15 Cal. 3d 143, 145, 125 Cal. Rptr. 745, 542 P.2d 1337 (1975). A recent commentary on the subject of rape also has suggested that the focus of the inquiry regarding consent in such cases should be upon the *mens rea* of the defendant rather than upon the attitude of the victim. S. Estrich, *Rape,* 95 Yale L.J. 1087, 1094–1132 (1986).

Most courts have rejected the proposition that a specific intention to have intercourse without the consent of the victim is an element of the crime of rape or sexual assault. . . . This court has implicitly discountenanced such a claim. . . . One of the complications that might arise, if such a mental element were required, involves the problem of intoxication, which is generally held to be relevant to negate a crime of specific intent but not a crime of general intent. . . . The difficulty of convicting a thoroughly intoxicated person of rape, if awareness of lack of consent were an element of the crime, would diminish the protection that our statutes presently afford to potential victims from lustful drunkards. Another related problem would be the admissibility of evidence of other similar behavior of a defendant charged with rape to prove his intent to disregard any lack of consent. Such evidence is now usually excluded as more prejudicial than probative, because only a general intent is necessary to constitute the offense. . . .

. . . A . . . provision of our own penal code, General Statutes § 53a-6(a),[1] allows the defense that a person has engaged in conduct otherwise criminal under a mistaken belief of fact where "[s]uch factual mistake negates the mental state required for the commission of an offense." This statute, however, applies only to specific intent crimes. Unless we should conclude, contrary to our precedent, that the mental state required of the actor for sexual assault in the first degree includes an awareness of lack of consent, even a reasonably founded, but nonetheless mistaken, belief as to that fact would not be available as a defense under § 53a-6(a).

Our first degree sexual assault statute, § 53a-70, applies to a person who "compels another person to engage in sexual intercourse by the use of force . . . or by the threat of use of force which . . . reasonably causes such person to fear physical injury. . . ." Although the consent of the complainant is not expressly made a defense to such a crime, it is abundantly clear that the draftsmen of our penal code endorsed the principle that "non-commercial sexual activity in private, whether heterosexual or homosexual, between consenting, competent adults, not involving corruption of the young by older persons, is no business of the criminal law." . . . A finding that a complainant had consented would implicitly negate a claim that the actor had compelled the complainant by force or threat to engage in sexual intercourse. . . .

---

[1] General Statutes § 53a-6(a) provides: "A person shall not be relieved of criminal liability for conduct because he engages in such conduct under a mistaken belief of fact, unless: (1)Such factual mistake negates the mental state required for the commission of an offense; or (2)the statute defining the offense or a statute related thereto expressly provides that such factual mistake constitutes a defense or exemption; or (3)such factual mistake is of a kind that supports a defense of justification.

While the word "consent" is commonly regarded as referring to the state of mind of the complainant in a sexual assault case, it cannot be viewed as a wholly subjective concept. Although the actual state of mind of the actor in a criminal case may in many instances be the issue upon which culpability depends, a defendant is not chargeable with knowledge of the internal workings of the minds of others except to the extent that he should reasonably have gained such knowledge from his observations of their conduct. The law of contract has come to recognize that a true "meeting of the minds" is no longer essential to the formation of a contract and that rights and obligations may arise from acts of the parties, usually their words, upon which a reasonable person would rely. . . . Similarly, whether a complainant has consented to intercourse depends upon her manifestations of such consent as reasonably construed. If the conduct of the complainant under all the circumstances should reasonably be viewed as indicating consent to the act of intercourse, a defendant should not be found guilty because of some undisclosed mental reservation on the part of the complainant. Reasonable conduct ought not to be deemed criminal.

It is likely that juries in considering the defense of consent in sexual assault cases, though visualizing the issue in terms of actual consent by the complainant, have reached their verdicts on the basis of inferences that a reasonable person would draw from the conduct of the complainant and the defendant under the surrounding circumstances. It is doubtful that jurors would ever convict a defendant who had in their view acted in reasonable reliance upon words or conduct of the complainant indicating consent, even though there had been some concealed reluctance on her part. If a defendant were concerned about such a possibility, however, he would be entitled, once the issue is raised, to request a jury instruction that the state must prove beyond a reasonable doubt that the conduct of the complainant would not have justified a reasonable belief that she had consented.

Thus we adhere to the view expressed in our earlier decisions that no specific intent, but only a general intent to perform the physical acts constituting the crime, is necessary for the crime of first degree sexual assault. We reject the position of the British courts, as well as that adopted in Alaska, that the state must prove either an actual awareness on the part of the defendant that the complainant had not consented or a reckless disregard of her nonconsenting status. We agree, however, with the California courts that a defendant is entitled to a jury instruction that a defendant may not be convicted of this crime if the words or conduct of the complainant under all the circumstances would justify a reasonable belief that she had consented. We arrive at that result, however, not on the basis of our penal code provision relating to a mistake of fact, § 53a-6(a), which is applicable only to specific intent crimes, but on the ground that whether a complainant should be found to have consented depends upon how her behavior would have been viewed by a reasonable person under the surrounding circumstances.

The defendant in this case made no request to charge upon the issue of the mental state required for the crime of sexual assault in the first degree or upon the issue of consent, nor did he except in these respects to the charge as given. On appeal his claim that a realization by a defendant of the absence of consent, or its recklessness equivalent, should be an element of the crime, as courts in Great Britain and Alaska have held, is necessarily limited to the sufficiency of the evidence to establish either an actual awareness[2] that T had not consented or a reckless disregard of her manifestations of nonconsent. Since we have rejected the subjective standard for determining the issue of consent, however, the question for us is whether the evidence is sufficient to prove that a reasonable person would not have believed that T's conduct under all the circumstances indicated her consent.

From our review of the evidence detailed previously, it is clear that the jury could properly have found beyond a reasonable doubt that T's words and actions could not reasonably be viewed to indicate her consent to intercourse with the defendant. According to her uncontradicted testimony, she expressly declined his advances, explaining that she did not know him and wanted to pick up her child. She spat in his face and "tried kicking him off." She "gave in" only after the defendant declared that "he could make it hard" for her if she continued to resist. This statement she could reasonably have regarded as a threat of physical injury. . . . Only by entertaining the fantasy that "no" meant "yes," and that a display of distaste meant affection, could the defendant have believed that T's behavior toward him indicated consent. Such a distorted view of her conduct would not have been reasonable. The evidence was more than sufficient to support the verdict.

There is no error. In this opinion the other Justices concurred.

Notes and Questions

1. In *Smith,* the court concludes that only reasonable mistakes of consent exculpate. The court reaches this conclusion in a context where victim nonconsent is not an element of the rape statute construed by the court. Would the court have reached a different conclusion if nonconsent had been an explicit element of rape? Could the court have maintained that rape is still a "general intent" crime such that unreasonable mistakes of consent are nevertheless culpable? Does a defendant act with general intent if he acts negligently? What does it mean to act with general intent regarding attendant circumstance elements of a crime? See Lord Simon's opinion in *Morgan, supra,* discussing "basic intent" crimes.

As for the *Smith* court's concerns about the role of intoxication as it relates to the nonconsent issue, see generally § 9.05[C], *infra.*

2. To what extent is the *Smith* court's holding premised on its finding that the legislature intended to leave all private consensual, noncommercial sexual activity between competent adults unregulated by the criminal law? Might the court have reached a different conclusion if fornication or adultery were crimes in Connecticut? Does the *Smith* court assume that by not criminalizing such consensual sexual activity, the legislature has found it unobjectionable

---

[2] The testimony of T that the defendant had told her, after completion of the sexual act, that "he knew that [T] felt [she] was raped but [she] couldn't prove it" is significant evidence that the defendant subjectively may have realized that T had not consented to intercourse. We hold, however, that actual awareness of lack of consent is not essential.

as a matter of public policy? Would the result in *Smith* be different if the court found nonmarital sexual activity between consenting adults to be violative of public policy?

3. In the *Mayberry* case discussed in *Smith,* the California Supreme Court reached the same conclusion reached by the Connecticut court but by arguably different means. The *Mayberry* court noted that under state statute every crime requires "a union . . . of act and intent or criminal negligence." While the rape statute did not specify nonconsent as an element of the crime, the *Mayberry* court, noting the severe penalties for the crime of rape, seemingly read the element into the offense:

> If a defendant entertains a reasonable and bona fide belief that a prosecutrix voluntarily consented to . . . engage in sexual intercourse, it is apparent he does not possess the wrongful intent that is a prerequisite . . . to a conviction of . . . rape by means of force or threat.

15 Cal. 3d at 155, 542 P.2d at 1345, 125 Cal. Rptr. at 753.

If nonconsent is an element of the crime, is the court on firm analytical ground in permitting only "reasonable" mistakes of consent to exculpate? In thinking about this question, consider the following.

FLETCHER

698–99, 701–6

The question that we shall consider is the function of consent in rape cases. Is non-consent an element of the definition? Or does consent function as a justification for fornication? In probing this specific problem we shall try to assess whether the concepts of definition and justification provide useful guidelines in prescribing when any mistake will suffice for acquittal and when the mistake must be reasonable.

The issue recently came to the fore in a cause celebre decided by the House of Lords. In a bizarre set of facts in *Regina v. Morgan,* the Lords upheld a conviction for rape but also concluded that any mistake, even an unreasonable mistake as to the victim's consent in rape cases, would preclude liability. . . .

The conclusion of the judges in *Morgan* has caused a furor in England and in Commonwealth countries. Critics have called the *Morgan* decision a "rapist's charter," for it stands for the proposition that anyone can commit rape and get away with it if he can convince a jury that he believed in good faith that the woman consented. Of course, all of this furor ignores the serious problem of actually convincing twelve men and women that the actor actually believed the victim consented. If it is true, as the House of Lords maintains, that the jury would not have believed the defendants in *Morgan,* there are not many cases in which they would be duped by a meretricious defendant.

* * *

. . . Focussing on the mistake as a problem of excuse leads invariably to the requirement that the mistake should excuse only if it is free from fault. . . .

Yet the majority of the judges were disinclined to view rape in this way. They were led instead to resolve the problem by construing the intent required for rape as the intent to have intercourse against the woman's will.

* * *

... [T]he required intent must extend to all elements of the prohibited act.... The methodology we propose[] ... [is to] determine which elements adhere to the definition of the offense and require intent as to all those elements.... The consent of the female undoubtedly bears on liability. The question is whether the requirement of intent extends to ... the factor of consent.

If we attempt now to apply our thesis to the problem in *Morgan,* how should we proceed? If we can determine the elements of the definition, then the claim is that the required intent encompasses these and only these elements. But how do we determine whether non-consent is part of the definition of rape? The definition ... is the minimal set of elements necessary to incriminate the actor. Consider the following scale of elements arranged in order of ascending incrimination:

1. touching
2. sexual contact
3. forcible sexual contact
4. non-consensual, forcible sexual contact

It is difficult to argue that touching *per se* is incriminating. In some societies, all forms of human contact must be regarded as trespassing on the domain of another, but we regularly accept a gentle hand on the shoulder as both the price and the benefit of group living. Sexual contact is obviously different. Intimate touching of the genitals is hardly routine; the touching requires a good reason. The reason, or the justification, might be the consent of the person touched or it might be the necessity of performing an operation in an emergency situation. This seems to me to be sufficient to regard the definition of rape as sexual penetration, with consent functioning as a ground for regarding the sexual act as a shared expression of love rather than as an invasion of bodily integrity.

The case in *Morgan* is even clearer, for the penetration was forcible. It is conceivable that a woman would enjoy being taken by force and that her consent would justify the forcible penetration. But it would be implausible to treat non-consent as well as force as necessary conditions for rendering the sexual act suspect. There seems to be little doubt that under the circumstances of *Morgan,* the consent of the woman should have functioned as a justification. And if that is the case, it is wrong to regard the intent required for rape as encompassing a belief in non-consent. If the perpetrators were mistaken about the supposed justification for forcible intercourse, their wrongful act might well be excused. But if the focus is on excusing their conduct, it is appropriate to require ... that their mistake be free from fault. If they were personally culpable in believing Morgan's lies about his wife, they could hardly claim their acts were blameless and therefore properly excused.

NOTES AND QUESTIONS

1. If consent is a defense (excuse or justification) in the context of the crime of rape, do you agree with Professor Fletcher that it is appropriate to require that mistakes as to consent be "free from fault"? Are unreasonable but honest mistakes free from fault? If not, has negligence become a ground for criminal liability for a serious felony? Is there any reason why a man should not be guilty of rape if he negligently believes the woman is consenting to his act of sexual intercourse with her? See the materials on defenses, § § 9.02 and 9.03, *infra*.

2. Consider again the *Reynolds* case, supra. If nonconsent is an element of the crime, should legislators specify that negligence (as opposed to recklessness) is sufficient *mens rea* as to the nonconsent element?

3. Suppose that in *Morgan* the jury had been properly instructed as to the role of mistaken beliefs of consent. Suppose further that the jury returned an acquittal based on its conclusion that the defendants in fact mistakenly believed that Ms. Morgan consented to the acts of sexual intercourse. The implications of the *Morgan* doctrine would appear to be that because an element of the crime had not been proved, no rape had occurred. Indeed, despite her overwhelming feelings of personal violation, Ms. Morgan would not be a rape victim.

On the other hand, different implications follow if the *Morgan* facts generate an acquittal in a jurisdiction treating consent as a defense. Even though the jury acquits due to mistake of fact, the defendants are nevertheless rapists, albeit ones with excuses, and Ms. Morgan has been raped. See the materials on defense theory, § § 9.02 and 9.03, *infra*.

Would women subjected to nonconsensual sexual intercourse take some solace in being treated as victims of excused rapes rather than as nonvictims, even though their male aggressors go free in either case? If so, should policymakers take this consideration into account in deciding whether to require nonconsent as an offense element rather than permitting consent to operate as a defense?

4. If, as in *Smith* and *Mayberry*, only "reasonable" mistakes will exculpate, how is reasonableness to be determined? As *Smith* illustrates, courts and juries look to the woman's conduct in determining whether the alleged rapist's mistake was objectively reasonable. If the woman's actions are in any way equivocal (if she offers little resistance, for example), claims of mistaken consent are often deemed reasonable. Note, *Rethinking the Reasonable Mistake Defense to Rape,* 100 Yale L.J. 2687, 2698—703 (1991). Thus the resistance requirement, abandoned in proving the actus reus of the crime, may be indirectly reinstated at the *mens rea* level. *Id.*

Is this problem solved by defining reasonable mistakes as ones in which "(1) the defendant did not use force and (2) the mistake was not negligent" together with a "rebuttable presumption that a mistake is not reasonable if the victim cried or offered verbal resistance during the encounter"? *Id.* at 2704.

Can you imagine a case of reasonable mistake as to consent where the defendant did use force?

5. For an assessment of the reasonable mistake problem in light of an alleged social convention that "women commonly use nonverbal methods to give consent to sexual intercourse," see Husak and Thomas, *Date Rape, Social Convention, and Reasonable Mistake,* 11 Law and Phil. 95, 116 (1992). Among other things, these authors maintain that women routinely consent to unwanted sex to maintain otherwise desirable relationships with particular men who will terminate the relationship unless sexual activity occurs. *Id.* at 121. Moreover, the authors claim that certain social conventions make it plausible for a male to make a reasonable mistake about a female's consent even when she says "no" or actively resists:

. . . The empirical evidence offers some support for [this view]. In a 1988 study, 39% of Texas female college undergraduates reported they had said "no" when they wanted to have sex. And 60.8% of the sexually experienced women in this study stated that they had said "no" when they intended to have sex. From these data, Abbey concluded: "It is easy to see how a man who has previously turned a 'no' into a 'yes' might force sexual intercourse on a date who says 'no' and means it."

Why would so many women say no when they wanted to have sex? Ninety percent of the women in the Texas study who fit this category said that the fear of appearing promiscuous was at least somewhat important in explaining their behavior. Indeed, compared to other factors such as fear of sexually transmitted diseases and pregnancy, fear of appearing promiscuous explained far more of the variance between women who had used this strategy and those who had not.

* * *

. . . Until we more fully understand the social convention about consent to have sex, any judgment about the reasonableness of a mistake is fragile.

* * *

Social conventions are always changing. The emerging social convention might be shifting more of the risk of error on the consent issue to men imposing an affirmative duty to be more certain that the woman is truly consenting. There are good reasons to hope for such a change. As E.M. Curley argues: "We are dealing here with people who are in a situation in which acting on a false belief involves immediate, serious, and irremediable harm to someone else, while refraining from acting on a true belief would involve only a small loss to anyone." Is the convention really changing in this way? Only careful empirical research, not wishful thinking, can substantiate this hope.

* * *

Some might welcome [the conviction of some men for rape even though they had reason to believe that consent had been given] . . . [O]ne might believe that it is more important to seek to change the social convention or to send a symbolic message than to do justice in an individual case. But if one believes that the criminal law should seek to apply the just result in particular cases, men whose belief in consent is consistent with the social convention seem unlikely candidates for convictions of a serious felony. For this reason, legislatures should proceed slowly when removing some of the common law barriers to rape convictions.

Id. at 122–26 (footnotes omitted).

Should the criminal law reflect social conventions or seek to change them by attributing criminal liability if a given convention is viewed as sexist or otherwise undesirable?

[C] Strict Liability

PEOPLE v. WILLIAMS

Court of Appeals of New York

81 N.Y.2d 303, 598 N.Y.S.2d 167, 614 N.E.2d 730 (1993)

SIMONS, Judge

Defendants have been convicted of multiple counts of rape and sodomy in the first degree. The charges arose after a New Jersey woman alleged defendants forced her into a car outside a Manhattan dance club, took her to a Brooklyn apartment and there raped and sodomized her. . . . They . . . assign error to the trial court's refusal to instruct the jury expressly that acquittal was required if defendants held a mistaken belief that the complainant had consented to sexual relations. The Appellate Division affirmed the judgments . . . , and we now affirm its order in each case.

The complainant, 17 years old, first encountered the three teenage defendants on a street in Manhattan shortly after midnight on August 17, 1989. She and defendant Williams testified at trial and gave dramatically different accounts of what happened thereafter.

Complainant testified that she had come to New York City with a group of friends to go to a dance club and that around midnight, after she began to feel sick, she decided to wait for her companions in the car. A short time later, defendants struck up a conversation with her as she ran an errand to a nearby store and then asked her to accompany them to another club. She refused, but defendants continued to walk alongside her until they passed near defendant Richardson's car. There, defendants surrounded her and, according to her trial testimony, she felt she had no choice but to go with them. She testified that Williams told her, "If you listen, you won't get hurt." Later, in the car, Williams intimated that his two companions were armed.

With Richardson driving and Williams seated next to the complainant in the back seat, defendant took her on a ride through Manhattan and Brooklyn, ultimately arriving at William's Brooklyn apartment in the basement of his family's home. The complainant concedes that the conversation in the car was friendly—an attempt, she testified, to "get on their good side." The complainant testified that during the drive she repeatedly asked to be let out, but defendants refused. Once inside William's apartment, she attempted to flee but found the door locked. She was then forced to engage in acts of sexual intercourse and sodomy by Williams and the others. Afterwards, they all left together, and in the car Williams forced her to perform oral sex on him. She was finally allowed to leave the vehicle near a mass transit station, where she immediately reported the incident to a police officer.

Williams was the only defendant to take the stand. He testified that all the incidents of sexual contact were consensual. According to his testimony, the complainant voluntarily accompanied them to Brooklyn, was affectionate toward him in the car, was never held against her will and had several opportunities to leave the car. He stated that she freely consented to sex with him in a bedroom at the apartment and then agreed to have sex with each of his friends. Later, when defendants let her out of the car near the transit station, he believed she intended to catch a train back to Manhattan to meet her friends. There was testimony from other witnesses which was not conclusive of the ultimate facts but tended to support some of the details in William's account.

The jury credited the testimony of the complainant and convicted defendants of multiple counts of rape in the first degree. . . .

As [a] basis for reversal, defendants contend the trial court erred in refusing to instruct the jury specifically on the mistake of fact defense and on intent as an element of first degree rape and sodomy. They assert that the jury could reasonably have found from the evidence adduced at trial that although the complainant had not consented to sexual relations, defendants mistakenly believed that she had.[3] Under those circumstances, they say, their mistaken belief negated the intent necessary for a finding of guilt on the various counts.

The Penal Law provides that a defendant is guilty of rape, first degree, or sodomy, first degree, when he or she engages in sexual intercourse or deviate sexual intercourse by forcible compulsion. . . . The People must also establish the victim's lack of consent . . . , but lack of consent results from forcible compulsion. . . . Though the statutes are silent on the subject, intent is implicitly an element of these crimes. . . . The intent required is the intent to perform the prohibited act—*i.e.*, the intent to forcibly compel another to engage in intercourse or sodomy.

The question is whether the court's charge, when viewed in its entirety, adequately conveyed to the jury that the defendants acted with the necessary culpable *mens rea*.[4] The court's instructions on forcible compulsion were as follows:

---

[3] The Penal Law recognizes three situations in which a person may be relieved of criminal liability when acting under a mistaken belief of fact: (1)when the factual mistake negates a culpable mental state required as part of the offense, (2)when the statutes defining the offense expressly allow the defense or (3)when the mistake supports a defense of justification. Penal Law § 15.20[1][a], [b], [c]. The statute authorizing a mistake of fact defense to sexual offenses does not apply under the facts of this case, see, Penal Law § 130.10 nor does the defense of justification. Defendants rely on section 15.20(1)(a), a factual mistake negates a culpable mental state, contending that their mistaken belief that complainant consented to intercourse negated the requirement of intent implicit in the element of forcible compulsion.

[4] As a court of law examining the instructions, we must evaluate what the court stated to the jury during the charge, not its misstatements to counsel during colloquy, see, *dissenting opn.*, at 318, at 174 of 598 N.Y.S.2d, at 737 of 614 N.E.2d.

The third and final element [the People must prove] is that the lack of [complainant's] consent resulted from the use of forcible compulsion. . . . Forcible compulsion means to compel by either use of physical force, or a threat, express or implied, which places a person in fear of immediate death or physical injury to herself.

Manifestly, it is unnecessary to forcibly compel another to engage in sexual acts unless that person is an unwilling participant. Thus, the jury, by finding that defendants used forcible compulsion to coerce the victim to engage in sodomy and intercourse, necessarily found that defendants believed the victim did not consent to the sexual activity. The instructions given covered the defense theory and the court did not commit reversible error in declining to give additional instructions on *mens rea* or mistake of fact.

The order of the Appellate Division should be affirmed.

BELLACOSA, J., *dissenting.*

In each case, I respectfully dissent and vote to reverse and order a new trial.

The sole basis upon which I would grant a new trial is that the trial court erred by refusing to instruct the jury on the essential culpable mental state element of criminal intent.

This Court is unanimous that general intent is the culpable mental state of the crimes for which the three defendants were charged and convicted. . . . That being so, we appear to be also unanimous that the trial court's articulation and understanding of this principle was erroneous. In the preinstruction conference and colloquy, the trial court stated:

> "There is no element of intent. . . . [T]he elements of rape and sodomy do not require any intent to do anything. It's a crime of action as opposed to a crime of intent. *It's not a mens rea crime.* . . . You don't have to get into the intent of anybody here. *Intent is not an element of the crime of rape.* . . . [Intent is] not an element of the crime of forcible compulsion. . . . [I]t's a crime of conduct, not a *mens rea,* state of mind. (emphasis added)

Based on that erroneous statement of the concededly applicable principle of law on the pertinent culpable mental state, which the majority characterizes merely as "misstatements to counsel," the trial court rejected the defendants' request to instruct on intent. Thus, my legitimate concern relates not to elaboration of what the trial court stated to the jury, but to what the trial court failed to tell the jury and its reasons for that ruling. . . .

* * *

The Court's analysis, I respectfully submit, also loses its way among crucial words and concepts which have historically governed the imposition of criminal responsibility. To compel by "forcible coercion" is essentially a facet of the traditional *actus reus*—the criminal act; intent is the quintessential *mens rea*—the culpable mental state. . . .

* * *

This case, based on a reading of the whole record, is threaded with an elusive yet worrisome potential risk of miscarriages of justice. That risk is heightened beyond acceptable limits of appellate review by rationalizing away a reversible instructional error.

Notes and Questions

1. Does the *Williams* court fail to instruct the jury on mistake regarding consent because it finds insufficient evidence of mistake to raise the issue? Should the defendant's claims of mistake be sufficient to raise the issue?

On the other hand, is the holding in *Williams* that mistakes about consent, even honest and reasonable ones, are simply irrelevant if the defendant (intentionally?) engages in conduct that results in coercing the victim, whether or not the defendant realizes the coercion? Does it follow, as the court states, that one who coerces another to act against her will necessarily knows (or believes) that the latter is not freely consenting?

Put another way, does *Williams* stand for the view that if, in fact, the victim does not consent, the defendant is strictly liable for mistaken beliefs of consent, even reasonable ones? Is such a view defensible if, as the court suggests in *Williams,* absence of consent is an offense element of rape? Would the strict liability position be more tenable if consent is a "defense" to rape rather than an offense element?

2. Regardless of whether the consent factor functions as an offense element or as a defense, *Williams* represents a commonly held position that rape defendants are held strictly liable for mistaken beliefs of consent. Estrich, *Teaching Rape Law,* 102 Yale L.J. 509, 512 n. 11 (1992). Consider, for example, *People v. Schmidt,* 885 P.2d 312 (Colo. App. 1994), which upheld the trial court's denial of an instruction on "mistake of fact" as to consent. The appellate court refused to recognize a mistake defense, finding simply that "lack of consent is an element of the offense." The facts of *Schmidt* arguably raise a plausible mistake situation.

> The evidence before the court was in conflict. The complainant testified that the defendant threw her on the floor, removed her underclothing and his own, while at all times holding her as she struggled to escape. The defendant testified that the complainant came into his bedroom while he was asleep, awakened him, and wanted to talk to him about a failed love relationship. After putting on his trousers, he joined her in the living room where she sat on his lap and they "messed around." Then, at his request, she preceded him into the bedroom and on to the bed. Although she had said "no" to his requests for intercourse, that response was based on her fear of being discovered by defendant's wife. He further testified that at no time did he apply force, restraint, or threats and that she offered no resistance while he stood to remove his trousers, when he removed her underpants, or when he penetrated her. Defendant testified that he perceived the act of sexual intercourse to have been with her tacit consent. Further, the record is apparently devoid of any evidence of struggle or the application of physical force.

885 P.2d at 317 (Tursi, J., dissenting).

See also *Commonwealth v. Williams,* 439 A.2d 765, 769 (Pa. Super, 1982): "If the element of the defendant's belief as to the victim's state of mind is to be established as a defense to the crime of rape then it should be done by our legislature which has the power to define crimes and offenses. We refuse to create such a defense."

§ 6.04 EVIDENTIARY CONSIDERATIONS

As the Blackstone excerpt at the beginning of this chapter suggests, proving the crime of rape raises controversial evidentiary issues. Historically, the process of proving that a rape was committed was thought to present an implicit risk of convicting the accused on the basis of false testimony by the complainant, whom it was feared would be especially motivated to falsely claim to have been assaulted due to the stigma of participating in fornication. At common law, such concerns were addressed by the creation of several specialized evidentiary rules designed to limit the possibility of conviction based on such false testimony. Moreover, the complainant's sexual history was considered to be relevant and admissible in most cases and, when prior sexual activity could be established, provided a defense to charges of rape in some circumstances.

Such controversial restrictions continue today in some jurisdictions with requirements that complaints be made within a certain time after the alleged event ("prompt complaint" rules) and provisions requiring corroboration of the victim's testimony. While many jurisdictions have reformed traditional rules that permitted evidence of the victim's sexual history as well as her physical dress and appearance to be admitted on the consent issue, debate surrounds the effectiveness and constitutionality of these "rape shield" laws.

Detailed examination of such issues is beyond the scope of these materials and is undertaken in most evidence courses. What follows, therefore, is a brief overview of the past and present status of some of the evidentiary rules unique to rape prosecutions.

DRESSLER

531–35

A common perception is that it is more difficult to obtain convictions for rape and other sex offenses than for other crimes. Two rules of evidence applied solely or primarily in trials involving the prosecution of sex offenses have been blamed by some for making convictions more difficult. . . .

It should be observed at the outset that in an effort to increase the rate of rape convictions, lawmakers in most states have repealed in whole or in part the rules discussed here. Their relevance, therefore, is largely historical. Nonetheless, the reader should consider whether the rules served a legitimate purpose to protect innocent persons from unjust conviction or whether, instead, they represented unsupportable hindrances in the prosecution of rape cases.

CORROBORATION RULE

Until recently most states provided that no person could be convicted of rape upon the uncorroborated testimony of the alleged victim. The corroboration requirement was largely limited to use in prosecution of sex offenses.

As one judge has observed, the corroboration requirement was the result of "legitimate concerns, out-dated beliefs, and deep-seated prejudices." The arguments for the rule focus on the belief that there is a higher risk of conviction of innocent persons in the prosecution of sex offenses than in the prosecution of other crimes. . . .

Why have lawmakers believed that the conviction of an innocent person is more likely in a rape case than, for example, in a robbery? Some of the reasons given are based on entrenched notions regarding sexuality that suggest that the testimony of women in rape prosecutions is particulary suspect. Many people, including some psychiatrists, believe that women fantasize being raped and, therefore, they believe that many women who have consensual intercourse genuinely come to believe that they were raped.

Other persons who favor the corroboration rule believe that women have a strong motive to "cry rape" falsely. Females are expected to avoid sexual relations until marriage; in the past, those who violated this moral code were subject to embarrassment, stigmatization, and even ostracism. An unmarried female who had sexual intercourse or, more significantly, became pregnant had a strong incentive to claim that she was raped rather than to admit that she had consented to the sexual intimacy.

Another aspect of the concern for the accused may be the result of racism. Historically, society disapproved of interracial sexual relations. Racist stereotypes have also suggested that black men are prone to rape white women. A white woman who was known or suspected to have had sexual relations with a black man was under substantial social pressures to claim that she was raped. The corroboration requirement reduces somewhat the risk of unjust racially motivated convictions.

Those who oppose the rule believe that some of the concerns described above—*e.g.,* that the women fantasize rape—are unfounded. The other concerns, they believe, are overstated or outdated. Minority group members previously excluded from jury service now serve regularly on juries, diminishing thereby the risk of false racially based rape convictions. People are also more tolerant of premarital sexual activity so that women have less incentive to claim rape when it is not true.

* * *

In view of the very high penalties set for rape in most states, special concern for the rights of the accused (at least in trials in which consent is a critical issue) may justify a corroboration rule. Nonetheless, opponents of the rule have won the day. The corroboration rule in rape cases has been abolished in virtually all states, although the Model Penal Code . . . retains it.

PRIOR SEXUAL CONDUCT BY THE FEMALE

Ordinarily in a criminal trial two basic principles determine the admissibility of proffered evidence: (1)no evidence is admissible unless it is relevant;

and (2)subject to limited exceptions, relevant evidence is admissible. Evidence is *relevant* if it has the tendency to prove or disprove any disputed fact at issue, including the credibility of a witness. A judge ordinarily has the discretion to exclude relevant evidence if its probative value is outweighed by the danger that it will cause undue prejudice to an opposing party.

In rape trials defense attorneys often wish to introduce evidence of the moral character and prior sexual activities of V, the complaining witness. Specifically, three classes of evidence may be relevant in a rape trial: (1)prior consensual sexual acts of V and D; (2)prior consensual sexual acts of V with persons other than D; and (3)V's reputation for lack of chastity.

The first type of evidence has always been admissible at trial if D contends that V consented to sexual intercourse with him. If V claims that she was raped by D on January 15, it is relevant to the issue of guilt that she consented to sexual relations with D on January 14. Of course, the fact that she consented on one day does not necessarily mean that she consented on another day; nonetheless, the proffered evidence has the tendency to disprove V's claim of lack of consent. Therefore, the jury is entitled to consider such facts and to give them as much weight as it believes they merit. This remains true today.

The introduction of evidence of V's prior sexual conduct with men other than D or of her reputation in the community for lack of chastity has always been more problematical than the introduction of evidence regarding V's sexual history with D. In the past, however, many states permitted the introduction of such testimony as substantive evidence relevant to the issue of V's consent to sexual intercourse with D. Why should V's consensual relations with X or her general lack of chastity be relevant to whether she consented to sexual intercourse with D? The traditional explanation was that

> [no] court can overrule the law of human nature, which declares that one who has already started on the road of [sexual unchastity], would be less reluctant to pursue her way, than another who yet remains at her home of innocence and looks upon such a [pursuit] . . . with horror.

Evidence of V's sexual activities with third parties and of her reputation for lack of chastity were also admissible in the past to impeach her credibility, apparently on the view that there is a logical connection between sexual immorality and lack of veracity.

The effect of these rules of evidence on complaining witnesses was to put their character and prior sexual life on trial at the same time that D's behavior at the time of the alleged rape was litigated. This may be one reason why rape has been a greatly under-reported offense.

Every state has amended its rules of evidence to limit in varying degrees the ability of a defendant to present to the jury evidence of the complaining witness's sexual history and reputation for lack of chastity. In general, so-called "rape-shield" laws treat evidence of the complaining witness's lack of chastity and of her prior sexual conduct with persons other than the defendant as inadmissible unless the defendant can show good cause (as defined in the statute) for its introduction.

Although rape-shield laws reduce the risk that juries will hear information prejudicial to the rape victim, the laws also increase the risk of denying the defendant a fair trial by excluding evidence relevant to his innocence. Specifically, the Sixth Amendment to the Constitution provides that a defendant is entitled to confront and cross-examine his accusers and to compel persons to testify. Consequently, evidentiary rules that restrict the defendant's opportunity to cross-examine the complaining witness about her sexual history and to introduce evidence of her reputation for lack of chastity must be tested against the non-absolute Sixth Amendment rights.

Currently, the legal pendulum has swung dramatically to the side of protecting the interests of the alleged victim. As a result, state courts have consistently upheld rape-shield laws against constitutional attack. Nonetheless, in any particular case a judge's refusal to use his discretion to permit the introduction of highly probative evidence of the alleged victim's prior sexual acts or reputation may violate the defendant's Sixth Amendment rights.

Notes and Questions

1. The traditional "prompt complaint" requirement has been adopted by the Model Penal Code, which requires that complaints be brought to the attention of public authorities within three months of the alleged offense. MPC § 216.6(5). Failure to make a timely complaint precludes prosecution.

While some states follow the Code, others permit the failure of a timely complaint to operate as a rebuttable presumption against the complainant. S. Estrich, Real Rape 53—54 (1987). Some jurisdictions take a less severe view by permitting the staleness of the complaint to be used as a basis to impeach the complainant. Torrey, *When Will We Be Believed? Rape Myths and the Idea of a Fair Trial in Rape Prosecutions,* 24 U.C. Davis L. Rev. 1013, 1046 (1991).

What explains the requirement of a "fresh complaint" of rape? Do these explanations justify the requirement? Why is there no similar requirement for other crimes?

2. Historically, judges in rape trials gave cautionary instructions to the jury. These instructions included the following elements: (1)rape is a charge that is easily made by the victim; (2)rape is a charge that is difficult for the defendant to disprove; and (3)the testimony of the victim requires more careful scrutiny by the jury than the testimony of the other witnesses in the trial. Note, *The Empirical, Historical and Legal Case against the Cautionary Instruction: A Call for Legislative Reform,* 1988, Duke L.J. 154–55. While some states have prohibited such instructions, many continue to permit their use. *Id.* at 156.

Is there any justifiable basis for such instructions in rape trials?

3. In addition to the evidentiary matters discussed, special problems have arisen in connection with admitting evidence of rape trauma syndrome as alluded to in the *Iniguez* case, *supra*. For a discussion of these issues, see Comment, *Rape Trauma Syndrome: Interest of the Victim and Neutral Experts,* 1989 U. Ch. Legal F. 399 (1989). Legal recognition of a rape trauma syndrome is controversial, even among feminists. See, for example, Stefan,

The Protection Racket: Rape Trauma Syndrome, Psychiatric Labeling and Law, 88 Nw.U. L. Rev. 1271, 1273 (1994):

> . . . The creation of these syndromes depoliticized the issue of rape by shifting attention from the prevalence of violence against women to women's reaction to violence. Contrary to popular image, far from validating women's pain, these syndromes delegitimized women's reactions to rape, isolated women as individual subjects of treatment and turned their coping mechanisms into symptoms of disorder. Women who installed locks and purchased security devices, took self-defense classes, carried mace, changed residence, expressed anger at the criminal justice system, and "view[ed] the implications of being raped as extending far beyond the immediate physical and emotional trauma" were characterized as exhibiting pathological symptoms and "adjustment difficulties." By characterizing the reactions of women who had been raped as aberrational, these theories relegated each woman's experience to the realm of aberration.

§ 6.05 GRADING

As mentioned at the beginning of this chapter, rape has historically been punished as a serious felony, one frequently invoking the death penalty. For an argument that on just deserts grounds the crime of rape should not carry a separate penalty but rather should be punished as "ordinary battery," see Davis, *Setting Penalties: What Does Rape Deserve?*, 3 Law and Phil. 61 (1984). For a response to Professor Davis, see Henderson, *Rape and Responsibility*, 11 Law and Phil. 127, 174–77 (1992). See also Dripps, *Beyond Rape: An Essay on the Difference between the Presence of Force and the Absence of Consent*, 92 Colum. L. Rev. 1780 (1992) (arguing for abolition of crime of rape and adoption of new offenses of "sexually motivated assault," punished with same sentence as aggravated assault, and "sexual expropriation," punished by a maximum prison sentence of one year and one day).

As the Blackstone excerpt at the beginning of this chapter indicates, the common law historically distinguished between rapes of adults and the so-called statutory rapes of minors. Apart from the irrelevance of consent in the latter category, jurisdictions sometimes punished the two categories of crime differently. See Perkins and Boyce at 198—99. Several jurisdictions draw further distinctions within the statutory rape category itself, punishing sexual relations with very young minors more severely than those with older ones. MPC § 216.1, Comment at 278. Moreover, some states take the relative ages of the minor victim and the male offender in account by imposing more severe punishment where the age disparity is substantial. See, for example, 2C N.J. Stat. Ann., § 14-2(b) (Supp. 1994) (actor commits aggravated sexual assault if he "commits an act of sexual contact with a victim who is less than 13 years old and the actor is at least 4 years older than the victim").

Recently, some jurisdictions have drawn grading distinctions between categories of adult rape victims. The first move in this direction occurred in 1942 with the passage of a Louisiana statute that punished "aggravated rape" with the death penalty and "simple rape" with a maximum of 20 years in prison. MPC § 216.1, Comment at 278. Aggravated rape was defined to include situations where the "female resists the act to the utmost, but her resistance is overcome by force," and where she is prevented from resisting "by threats of great and immediate bodily harm, accompanied by apparent power of execution." Simple rape was defined to include cases "where the victim is prevented from resisting by drugs, intoxicants, or mental capacity, where she is deceived into believing that the actor is her husband, or where she is mentally incapable of understanding the nature of the act." *Id.*

The Louisiana model was adopted in some other jurisdictions. Moreover, some jurisdictions have enacted more elaborate attempts to differentiate degrees of sexual assault. Michigan, for example, divides "criminal sexual contact" into four degrees, with punishment ranging from life imprisonment for the first degree offense down to two years of imprisonment for the fourth. See Mich. Comp. Laws 750.520 (b–e) (1991).

The Model Penal Code distinguishes § 213.1(1) "rape" (punished as a felony of either the first, second, or third degree), § 213.1(2) "gross sexual imposition" (punished as a felony of the third degree), and § 213.2 "deviate sexual intercourse by force or imposition" (punished as a felony of either the second or third degree). See Appendix, *infra,* for the text of these provisions. The Code Commentary explains the grading rationale of Section 213.1:

> . . . Section 213.1 distributes the offenses with which it deals over the entire range of felony sanctions. This represents a departure from the common law and from a number of statutes that existed at the time the Model Code was drafted. . . .
>
> To begin with lesser felonies, Subsection (2) specifies that gross sexual imposition is a felony of the third degree. This classification includes intercourse with a mentally incompetent female, deception as to the nature of the sexual act or the marital status of the participants, and coercion by threat of harm other than imminent death, serious bodily injury, extreme pain, or kidnapping. Statutory rape of a girl between the ages of 10 and 16 is an offense of the same grade under Section 213.3. These several versions of proscribed conduct share one characteristic relevant to grading: None involves physical injury. At the other extreme, Subsection (1) provides that any of the four versions of rape constitutes a felony of the first degree if "in the course thereof the actor inflicts serious bodily injury upon anyone." Thus, the first and principal grading criterion under Section 213.1 is the use or prospect of violence. The paradigm case of rape as brutal sexual assault continues to command sanctions of the highest degree of severity, while several instances of non-violent sexual imposition are classed as lesser felonies.
>
> It is clear, however, that the presence or absence of violence is not the sole determinant of grading under Section 213.1. At least two of the four instances of rape under Subsection (1)—intercourse with an unconscious female or with a girl under the age of 10—need not involve violence. Additionally, preventing resistance by drugs or intoxicants amounts to use of force only in some highly constructive sense. Yet these three kinds of conduct are proscribed under Subsection (1) and treated more severely than the other sorts of nonviolent behavior covered under Subsection (2). Moreover, Subsection (1) provides for escalation of rape to a felony of the first

degree on grounds other than causing personal injury. Rape is also an offense of the highest grade if "the victim was not a voluntary social companion of the actor upon the occasion of the crime and had not previously permitted him sexual liberties." This basis for aggravation of penalty does not relate to the use or prospect of violence but rather to the absence of any prior relationship between actor and victim.

To the extent that the grading decisions reflected in this section do not relate to violence, they depend in part on varying perceptions of the magnitude of harm caused by the actor's conduct. Thus, for example, statutory rape of a child less than 10 years old is easily understood as a greater wrong than sexual relations with a girl of 15. At the least, the former conduct represents a more dramatic deviation from socially acceptable behavior. Subsection (1)(d) of the rape provision is therefore classed as a felony of higher grade than is corruption of minors under Section 213.3. Similarly, preventing resistance by using agents of incapacitation involves conduct more invasive of individual dignity and more threatening to the general sense of security than does deception as to one's marital status. Consequently, these offenses are differentiated for grading purposes in Subsections (1)(b) and (2)(c). The "no prior relationship" provision for escalating the penalty for rape is also responsive to a concern with the magnitude of harm involved. The law of rape protects against unwanted sexual intimacy, and it is reasonable to believe that such conduct is especially shocking and injurious when the actor is a stranger. In other words, the affront to individual dignity accomplished, for example, by intercourse with an unconscious woman, is thought to be greater when the victim is not a voluntary social companion of the actor and has not previously permitted him sexual liberties.

MPC § 213.1, Commentary at 354–55.

Notes and Questions

1. The above excerpt explains the Code's grading scheme in terms of the gravity of harm caused. Further discussion in the Code Commentary provides additional justification for its provisions as an attempt to reflect "an inevitable unease" about the substantive standards of liability employed in the law of rape. Because the law of rape involves imposing sanctions on "proscribed conduct that, in some circumstances, closely parallels socially accepted behavior," the drafters urge "a healthy sense of caution in assigning sanctions." *Id.* at 355–56. Do you agree with the Code approach?

2. For criticism of aspects of the MPC grading scheme, particularly its downgrading of prior relationship cases, see Estrich, *Rape,* 95 Yale 1087, 1133–47 (1986).

Chapter 7
Inchoate Crimes

§ 7.01 INTRODUCTION

As Chapter 5 shows, criminal liability often entails proof that the defendant's conduct resulted in certain undesirable consequences. In contrast, the criminal law also incorporates an extensive body of law that imposes punishment for activity that anticipates criminal objectives but does not itself result in clearly identifiable harm. This chapter deals primarily with two such "inchoate" offenses—attempt and conspiracy—but also touches briefly on a third—solicitation.

As you read these materials, consider the circumstances, if any, in which punishment for inchoate crimes can be justified. Along these lines, the drafters of the Model Penal Code offer the following:

> [A]ttempt, solicitation, and conspiracy . . . have in common the fact that they deal with conduct that is designed to culminate in the commission of a substantive offense, but has failed in the discrete case to do so or has not yet achieved its culmination because there is something that the actor or another still must do. The offenses are inchoate in this sense.
>
> These, to be sure, are not the only crimes so defined that their commission does not rest on proof of the occurrence of the evil that it is the object of the law to prevent; many specific, substantive offenses also have a large inchoate aspect. This is true not only with respect to crimes of risk creation, such as reckless driving, or specific crimes of preparation, such as possession with unlawful purpose. It is also true, at least in part, of crimes like larceny, forgery, kidnaping and even arson, not to speak of burglary, where a purpose to cause greater harm than that which is implicit in the actor's conduct is an element of the offense. This reservation notwithstanding, attempt, solicitation and conspiracy have such generality of definition and of application as inchoate crimes that it is useful to bring them together in the Code and to confront the common problems they present.
>
> Since these offenses always presuppose a purpose to commit another crime, it is doubtful that the threat of punishment for their commission can significantly add to the deterrent efficacy of the sanction—which the actor by hypothesis ignores—that is threatened for the crime that is his objective. There may be a case where this does occur, as when the actor thinks the chance of apprehension low if he should succeed but high if he should fail in his attempt, or when reflection is promoted at an early stage that otherwise would be postponed until too late, which may be true in some conspiracies. These are, however, special situations. General deterrence is at most a minor function to be served in fashioning provisions of the penal law addressed to these inchoate crimes; that burden is discharged upon the whole by the law dealing with the substantive offenses.

Other and major functions of the penal law remain, however, to be served. They may be summarized as follows:

First: When a person is seriously dedicated to commission of a crime, a firm legal basis is needed for the intervention of the agencies of law enforcement to prevent its consummation. In determining that basis, there must be attention to the danger of abuse; equivocal behavior may be misconstrued by an unfriendly eye as preparation to commit a crime. It is no less important, on the other side, that lines should not be drawn so rigidly that the police confront insoluble dilemmas in deciding when to intervene, facing the risk that if they wait the crime may be committed while if they act they may not yet have any valid charge.

Second: Conduct designed to cause or culminate in the commission of a crime obviously yields an indication that the actor is disposed towards such activity, not alone on this occasion but on others. There is a need, therefore, subject again to proper safeguards, for a legal basis upon which the special danger that such individuals present may be assessed and dealt with. They must be made amenable to the corrective process that the law provides.

Third: Finally, and quite apart from these considerations of prevention, when the actor's failure to commit the substantive offense is due to a fortuity, as when the bullet misses in attempted murder or when the expected response to solicitations is withheld, his exculpation on that ground would involve inequality of treatment that would shock the common sense of justice. Such a situation is unthinkable in any mature system designed to serve the proper goals of penal law.

MPC, Introduction to Art. 5, 293–94

§ 7.02 ATTEMPT

[A] Background

Throughout its history, the common law has embraced a number of offenses, including felonies that are at least partially inchoate crimes. Thus, for example, larceny is defined as a taking with only an *intent* to deprive the owner permanently of property, while burglary is defined as an entry with merely an *intent* to commit a felony. Moreover, to deal with feared incipient crime, the common law employed a variety of methods such as the system of "frank pledge," "surety for the peace," and laws prohibiting vagrancy and nightwalking. Similarly inchoate in nature, the crimes of treason and "encompassing the death of the King" for a time required no overt act at all. Hall at 562–65.

Rex v. Scofield, a 1784 decision of the Court of King's Bench, is generally considered to be the first case upholding a conviction for attempt. See, for example, Sayre, *Criminal Attempts,* 41 Harv. L. Rev. 821, 834–35 (1928). But see Hall at 563–73. The law of attempt is thus a relatively late arrival on the common law scene.

The notion of attempted crimes was similarly absent from the continent in the middle ages. See Grasson, *France in the Later Middle Ages,* in C. von Bar,

A History of Continental Criminal Law, 157 (1916). See also J. Andenaes, The General Part of the Criminal Law of Norway 285 (1965) (general penal provisions proscribing attempt are a 20th century phenomenon). Consider this in light of the arguments, *infra,* for a law of attempt. Was life in the Middle Ages less dangerous than the present? Why would a society's "progress" be accompanied by, *inter alia,* a movement toward punishing attempt? On the other hand, Roman law did proscribe some "attempts." For example, such things as carrying weapons with the intention of killing someone or with the intention to accomplish a theft, and purchasing poison to kill someone, were included under a statute that forbade intentional murder. See von Bar, *supra,* at 20, n. 12.

[B] The *Actus Reus*

REGINA v. EAGLETON

Court of Criminal Appeal

6 Cox C. C. 559, 169 Eng. Rep. 766 (1855)

[Defendant, a baker, contracted with public authorities to supply the poor with loaves of bread weighing three-and-one-half pounds each. Each poor person who presented Defendant with a ticket was to receive such a loaf. Defendant would then redeem the tickets, together with a statement of the number of loaves supplied. The participating townships would credit Defendant for the amount owed him, to be paid at a future date. After the Defendant had submitted the tickets but before such payment was made, the authorities discovered that Defendant had intentionally furnished loaves deficient in weight. Defendant, convicted of attempting to obtain money by false pretenses, appealed.]

PARKE B. . . .

[Defendant contended first] that the attempt to obtain credit in account for a sum of money by delivering up the tickets as vouchers was not in itself an attempt to obtain money within the meaning of the statute, for that credit in account was not equivalent to money;and no doubt the credit in the relieving officer's book was not equivalent to money, and the defendant could not have been convicted of the offense of actually obtaining money by false pretenses.

Secondly, he contended that the credit in account would not necessarily lead to an ultimate payment, for there might be deductions for breaches of contract, which would prevent any payments in cash by the guardians.

We have had great doubt on this part of the case, but do not think that this objection should prevail. We think that the contingency of the whole sum due to him, being subject to deductions in a future event, does not the less make the obtaining credit an attempt to obtain money, if it would be so without that contingency; but our doubt has been whether the obtaining that credit, though undoubtedly a necessary step towards obtaining the money, can be deemed an attempt to do so. Acts remotely leading towards the commission of the offense are not to be considered as attempts to commit it, but acts immediately connected with it are; and if, in this case, after the credit with the relieving officer for the fraudulent overcharge, any further step on the part of the defendant had been necessary to obtain payment, as the making out a further account or producing the vouchers to the Board, we should have thought that the obtaining credit in account with the relieving officer would not have been sufficiently proximate to the obtaining the money. But, on the statement in this case, no other act on the part of the defendant would have been required. It was the last act, depending on himself, towards the payment of the money, and therefore it ought to be considered as an attempt. The receipt of the money appears to have been prevented by a discovery of the fraud by the relieving officer; and it is very much the same case, as if, supposing rendering an account to the guardians at their office, with the vouchers annexed, were a preliminary necessary step to receiving the money, the defendant had gone to the office, rendered the account and vouchers, and then been discovered, and the money consequently refused.

Conviction . . . affirmed.

NOTES AND QUESTIONS

1. *Eagleton* is the earliest case to endeavor to distinguish between innocent preparation and culpable attempt, "the most difficult problem in defining attempt liability." MPC § 5.01, Commentary at 39 (Tent. Draft No. 10, 1958). The case is generally understood to have embraced a "last proximate act" doctrine requiring that the actor do all that he intends to do to accomplish the crime. Thus a would-be murderer who has loaded his gun and taken aim at his intended victim but who is apprehended an instant before he pulls the trigger is not guilty of attempted murder under the *Eagleton* test. Does such a result suggest that the last proximate act standard is too demanding?

2. While commission of the last proximate act is everywhere regarded as sufficient *actus reus* for attempt, the presence of a variety of other tests indicates that the "last act" is generally not necessary for attempt liability. The following case describes several such tests.

UNITED STATES V. JACKSON

United States Court of Appeals, Second Circuit

560 F. 2d 112, cert. denied, 434 U.S. 941 (1977)

Before LUMBARD and OAKES, Circuit Judges, and BRYAN, Senior District Judge. FREDERICK VAN PELT BRYAN, Senior District Judge:

[Appellants Jackson, Scott, and Allen were convicted of conspiracy to rob the Manufacturers Hanover Trust branch bank and attempting to rob the bank on June 14 and 21, 1976. On appeal, appellants do not contest the sufficiency of the evidence on the conspiracy count but they] assert that, as a matter of law, their conduct never crossed the elusive line which separates "mere preparation" from "attempt." This troublesome question was recently examined by this court in *United States v. Stallworth,* 543 F.2d 1038 (2d Cir. 1976), which set forth the applicable legal principles. For the reasons which follow, we affirm the convictions of all three appellants on all four counts.

I.

The Government's evidence at trial consisted largely of the testimony of Vanessa Hodges, an unindicted co-conspirator, and of various FBI agents who surveilled the Manufacturers Hanover branch on June 21, 1976. Since the facts are of critical importance in any attempt case, . . . we shall review the Government's proof in considerable detail.

On June 11, 1976, Vanessa Hodges was introduced to appellant Martin Allen by Pia Longhorne, another unindicted co-conspirator. Hodges wanted to meet someone who would help her carry out a plan to rob the Manufacturers Hanover branch located at 210 Flushing Avenue in Brooklyn, and she invited Allen to join her. Hodges proposed that the bank be robbed the next Monday, June 14th, at about 7:30 AM. She hoped that they could enter with the bank manager at that time, grab the weekend deposits, and leave. Allen agreed to rob the bank with Hodges, and told her he had access to a car, two sawed-off shotguns, and a .38 caliber revolver.

The following Monday, June 14, Allen arrived at Longhorne's house about 7:30 AM in a car driven by appellant Robert Jackson. A suitcase in the back seat of the car contained a sawed-off shotgun, shells, materials intended as masks, and handcuffs to bind the bank manager. While Allen picked up Hodges at Longhorne's, Jackson filled the car with gas. The trio then left for the bank.

When they arrived, it was almost 8:00 AM. It was thus too late to effect the first step of the plan, *viz,* entering the bank as the manager opened the door. They rode around for a while longer, and then went to a restaurant to get something to eat and discuss their next move. After eating, the trio drove back to the bank. Allen and Hodges left the car and walked over to the bank. They peered in and saw the bulky weekend deposits, but decided it was too risky to rob the bank without an extra man.

Consequently, Jackson, Hodges, and Allen drove to Coney Island in search of another accomplice. In front of a housing project on 33rd Street they found appellant William Scott, who promptly joined the team. Allen added to the arsenal another sawed-off shotgun obtained from one of the buildings in the project, and the group drove back to the bank.

When they arrived again, Allen entered the bank to check the location of any surveillance cameras, while Jackson placed a piece of cardboard with a false license number over the authentic license plate of the car. Allen reported back that a single surveillance camera was over the entrance door. After further discussion, Scott left the car and entered the bank. He came back and informed the group that the tellers were separating the weekend deposits and that a number of patrons were now in the bank.

Hodges then suggested that they drop the plans for the robbery that day, and reschedule it for the following Monday, June 21. Accordingly, they left the vicinity of the bank and returned to Coney Island where, before splitting up, they purchased a pair of stockings for Hodges to wear over her head as a disguise and pairs of gloves for Hodges, Scott, and Allen to don before entering the bank. Hodges was arrested on Friday, June 18, 1976, on an unrelated bank robbery charge, and immediately began cooperating with the Government. After relating the events on June 14, she told FBI agents that a robbery of the Manufacturers branch at 210 Flushing Avenue was now scheduled for the following Monday, June 21. The three . . . male robbers, according to Hodges, would be heavily armed with hand and shoulder weapons and expected to use a brown four-door sedan equipped with a cardboard license plate as the getaway car. She told the agents that Jackson, who would drive the car, was light-skinned with a moustache and a cut on his lip, and she described Allen as short, dark-skinned with facial hair, and Scott as 5' 9", slim build, with. . . . some sort of defect in his right eye.

At the request of the agents, Hodges called Allen on Saturday, June 19, and asked if he were still planning to do the job. He said that he was ready. On Sunday she called him again. This time Allen said that he was not going to rob the bank that Monday because he had learned that Hodges had been arrested and he feared that federal agents might be watching. Hodges nevertheless advised the agents that she thought the robbery might still take place as planned with the three men proceeding without her.

At about 7:00 AM on Monday, June 21, 1976, some ten FBI agents took various surveilling positions in the area of the bank. At about 7:39 AM the agents observed a brown four-door Lincoln, with a New York license plate on the front and a cardboard facsimile of a license plate on the rear, moving in an easterly direction on Flushing Avenue past the bank, which was located on the southeast corner of Flushing and Washington Avenues. The front seat of the Lincoln was occupied by a . . . male driver and a . . . male passenger with mutton-chop sideburns. The Lincoln circled the block and came to a stop at a fire hydrant situated at the side of the bank facing Washington Avenue, a short distance south of the corner of Flushing and Washington.

A third . . . male, who appeared to have an eye deformity, got out of the passenger side rear door of the Lincoln, walked to the corner of Flushing and Washington, and stood on the sidewalk in the vicinity of the bank's entrance. He then walked south on Washington Avenue, only to return a short time later with a container of coffee in his hand. He stood again on the corner of Washington and Flushing in front of the bank, drinking the coffee and looking around, before returning to the parked Lincoln.

The Lincoln pulled out, made a left turn onto Flushing, and proceeded in a westerly direction for one block to Waverly Avenue. It stopped, made a U-turn, and parked on the south side of Flushing between Waverly and Washington—a spot on the same side of the street as the bank entrance but separated from it by Washington Avenue. After remaining parked in this position for approximately five minutes, it pulled out and cruised east on Flushing past the bank again. The Lincoln then made a right onto Grand Avenue, the third street east of the bank, and headed south. It stopped halfway down the block, midway between Flushing and Park Avenues, and remained there for several minutes. During this time Jackson was seen working in the front of the car, which had its hood up.

The Lincoln was next sighted several minutes later in the same position it had previously occupied on the south side of Flushing Avenue between Waverly and Washington. The front license plate was now missing. The vehicle remained parked there for close to thirty minutes. Finally, it began moving east on Flushing Avenue once more, in the direction of the bank.

At some point near the bank as they passed down Flushing Avenue, the appellants detected the presence of the surveillance agents. The Lincoln accelerated down Flushing Avenue and turned south on Grand Avenue again. It was overtaken by FBI agents who ordered the appellants out of the car and arrested them. The agents then observed a black and red plaid suitcase in the rear of the car. The zipper of the suitcase was partially open and exposed two loaded sawed-off shotguns, a toy nickel-plated revolver, a pair of handcuffs, and masks. A New York license plate was seen lying on the front floor of the car. All of these items were seized.

In his memorandum of decision, Chief Judge Mishler . . . characterized the question of whether the defendants had attempted a bank robbery as charged . . . or were merely engaged in preparations as "a close one." After canvassing the authorities on what this court one month later called a "perplexing problem," *United States v. Stallworth, supra,* at 1039, Chief Judge Mishler applied the following two-tiered inquiry formulated in *United States v. Mandujano,* 499 F.2d 370, 376 (5th Cir. 1974), *cert. denied,* 419 U.S. 1114 (1975):

> First, the defendant must have been acting with the kind of culpability otherwise required for the commission of the crime which he is charged with attempting. . . .
>
> Second, the defendant must have engaged in conduct which constitutes a substantial step toward commission of the crime. A substantial step must be conduct strongly corroborative of the firmness of the defendant's criminal intent.

He concluded that on June 14 and again on June 21, the defendants took substantial steps, strongly corroborative of the firmness of their criminal intent, toward commission of the crime of bank robbery and found the defendants guilty on each of the two attempt counts. These appeals followed.

II.

"[T]here is no comprehensive statutory definition of attempt in federal law." *United States v. Heng Awkak Roman,* 356 F. Supp. 434, 437 (S.D.N.Y.), *aff'd,* 484 F.2d 1271 (2d Cir. 1973), *cert. denied,* 415 U.S. 978 (1974). Fed. R. Crim. P. 31(c), however, provides in pertinent part that a defendant may be found guilty of an attempt to commit either the offense charged or an offense necessarily included therein if the attempt is an offense." 18 U.S.C. § 2113(a) specifically makes attempted bank robbery an offense.

* * *

In *Stallworth,* the Government provided Rodney Campbell, an informant who had participated in numerous bank robberies, with an undercover vehicle outfitted with a tape recorder and monitoring equipment on the understanding that he would aid in apprehending his former accomplices. Campbell rejoined his companions, and he transported the group in his undercover vehicle as they cased several banks in Queens.

On Wednesday, January 21, they began actual preparations for a robbery by stealing ski masks from a department store, surgical gloves from a hospital, and purchasing a hacksaw and roofing nails to "fix" a shotgun. On Thursday, January 22, the gang selected a target bank in Whitestone, had one member enter it and report on its physical layout, and scheduled the robbery for Friday morning.

On Friday morning, January 23, Campbell and company assembled with a revolver, sawed-off shotgun, and other paraphernalia for a hold-up. On their way to the bank in the undercover vehicle they covered their fingers with bandaids, their hands with the surgical gloves, and put on the ski masks. Gasoline-soaked newspapers were placed under the seats of the car in preparation for its destruction after the getaway.

The car entered the parking lot of the shopping center in which the bank was located and one Sellers got out. He strolled past the bank several times, peeking in at each opportunity, while the car circled the shopping center. Finally, the vehicle pulled up directly in front of the bank and Sellers, armed with the sawed-off shotgun and positioned at an adjacent liquor store, started to approach the bank. Campbell said "let's go," and the occupants of the car reached for the doors. Immediately, FBI agents and New York City policemen who had staked out the parking lot and were monitoring the gang's conversations moved in and arrested the men.

Chief Judge Kaufman, writing for the court, selected the two-tiered inquiry of *United States v. Mandujano, supra,* "properly derived from the writings of many distinguished jurists," 543 F.2d at 1040, as stating the proper test for determining whether the foregoing conduct constituted an attempt. He observed that this analysis "conforms closely to the sensible definition of an attempt proffered by the American Law Institute's Model Penal Code." . . .

The draftsmen of the Model Penal Code recognized the difficulty of arriving at a general standard for distinguishing acts of preparation from acts constituting an attempt. They found general agreement that when an actor committed the "last proximate act," *i.e.,* when he had done all that he believed necessary to effect a particular result which is an element of the offense, he committed an attempt. They also concluded, however, that while the last proximate act is sufficient to constitute an attempt, it is not necessary to such a finding. The problem then was to devise a standard more inclusive than one requiring the last proximate act before attempt liability would attach, but less inclusive than one which would make every act done with the intent to commit a crime criminal. See Model Penal Code § 5.01, Comment at 38–39 (Tent. Draft No. 10, 1960).

The draftsmen considered and rejected the following approaches to distinguishing preparation from attempt, later summarized in *Mandujano:*

(a) The physical proximity doctrine—the overt act required for an attempt must be proximate to the completed crime, or directly tending toward the completion of the crime, or must amount to the commencement of the consummation.

(b) The dangerous proximity doctrine—a test given impetus by Mr. Justice Holmes whereby the greater the gravity and probability of the offense, and the nearer the act to the crime, the stronger is the case for calling the act an attempt.

(c) The indispensable element test—a variation of the proximity tests which emphasizes any indispensable aspect of the criminal endeavor over which the actor has not yet acquired control.

(d) The probable desistance test—the conduct constitutes an attempt if, in the ordinary and natural course of events, without interruption from an outside source, it will result in the crime intended.

(e) The abnormal step approach—an attempt is a step toward crime which goes beyond the point where the normal citizen would think better of his conduct and desist.

(f) The *res ipsa loquitur* or unequivocality test—an attempt is committed when the actor's conduct manifests an intent to commit a crime.

499 F.2d at 373, n. 5.

The formulation upon which the draftsmen ultimately agreed required, in addition to criminal purpose, that an act be a substantial step in a course of conduct designed to accomplish a criminal result, and that it be strongly corroborative of criminal purpose in order for it to constitute such a substantial step. The following differences between this test and previous approaches to the preparation—attempt problem were noted:

First, this formulation shifts the emphasis from what remains to be done—the chief concern of the proximity tests—to what the actor *has already done*. The fact that further major steps must be taken before the crime can be completed does not preclude a finding that the steps already undertaken are substantial. It is expected, in the normal case, that this approach will broaden the scope of attempt liability.

Second, although it is intended that the requirement of a substantial step will result in the imposition of attempt liability only in those instances in which some firmness of criminal purpose is shown, no finding is required as to whether the actor would probably have desisted prior to completing the crime. Potentially the probable desistance test could reach very early steps toward crime—depending upon how one assesses the probabilities of desistance—but since in practice this test follows closely the proximity approaches, rejection of probable desistance will not narrow the scope of attempt liability.

Finally, the requirement of proving a substantial step generally will prove less of a hurdle for the prosecution than the *res ipsa loquitur* approach, which requires that the actor's conduct must itself manifest the criminal purpose. The difference will be illustrated in connection with the present section's requirement of corroboration. Here it should be noted that, in the present formulation, the two purposes to be served by the *res ipsa loquitur* test are, to a large extent, treated separately. Firmness of criminal purpose is intended to be shown by requiring a substantial step, while problems of proof are dealt with by the requirement of corroboration (although, under the reasoning previously expressed, the latter will also tend to establish firmness of purpose).

Model Penal Code § 5.01, Comment at 47 (Tent. Draft No. 10, 1960).

The draftsmen concluded that, in addition to assuring firmness of criminal design, the requirement of a substantial step would preclude attempt liability, with its accompanying harsh penalties, for relatively remote preparatory acts. At the same time, however, by not requiring a "last proximate act" or one of its various analogues it would permit the apprehension of dangerous persons at an earlier stage than the other approaches without immunizing them from attempt liability. *Id.* at 47–48.

Applying the *Mandujano* test, which in turn was derived in large part from the Model Penal Code's standard, Chief Judge Kaufman concluded that since the *Stallworth* appellants had intended to execute a successful bank robbery and took substantial steps in furtherance of their plan that strongly corroborated their criminal intent, their attempted bank robbery convictions were proper.

In the case at bar, Chief Judge Mishler anticipated the precise analysis which this Court adopted in the strikingly similar *Stallworth* case. . . . He concluded that on both occasions these men were seriously dedicated to the commission of a crime, had passed beyond the stage of preparation, and would have assaulted the bank had they not been dissuaded by certain external factors, *viz.,* the breaking up of the weekend deposits and crowd of patrons in the bank on June 14 and the detection of the FBI surveillance on June 21.

We cannot say that these conclusions which Chief Judge Mishler reached as the trier of fact as to what the evidence before him established were erroneous. As in *Stallworth,* the riminal intent of the appellants was beyond dispute. The question remaining then is the substantiality of the steps taken on the dates in question, and how strongly this corroborates the firmness of their obvious criminal intent. This is a matter of degree. See Model Penal Code § 5.01, Comments at 47 (Tent. Draft No. 10, 1960).

On two separate occasions, appellants reconnoitered the place contemplated for the commission of the crime and possessed the paraphernalia to be employed in the commission of the crime—loaded sawed-off shotguns, extra shells, a toy revolver, handcuffs, and masks—which was specially designed for such unlawful use and which could serve no lawful purpose under the circumstances. Under the Model Penal Code formulation, . . . approved by the Stallworth court, either type of conduct, standing alone, was sufficient as a matter of law to constitute a "substantial step" if it strongly corroborated their criminal purpose. Here both types of conduct coincided on both June 14 and June 21, along with numerous other elements strongly corroborative of the firmness of appellants' criminal intent.[8] The steps taken toward a

---

[8] After securing the extra man they needed on June 14, the gang returned to the bank with their weapons ready and the car's license plate disguised for the getaway. Hodges' testimony was that they were ready to rob the bank at that time, but eventually postponed the robbery because conditions did not seem favorable. The fact that they then made further preparations by buying

successful bank robbery thus were not "insubstantial" as a matter of law, and Chief Judge Mishler found them "substantial" as a matter of fact. We are unwilling to substitute our assessment of the evidence for his, and thus affirm the convictions for attempted bank robbery.

The judgments of conviction are affirmed.

NOTES AND QUESTIONS

1. Would the defendants in *Jackson* be guilty of attempt under any of the older tests (last act, probable desistence, *res ipsa loquitur,* etc.) described by the court? If not, does the test in *Jackson* (and that embodied in the Model Penal Code) extend attempt liability too far into the purely subjective area of the defendant's mind without sufficient observable objective conduct? In thinking about this problem, are some concerns alleviated by the following provisions from MPC § 5.01 elaborating on the Code's requirement that defendant engage in conduct "constituting a substantial step in a course of conduct planned to culminate in his commission of the crime"?

Model Penal Code § 5.01

(2) *Conduct That May Be Held Substantial Step under Subsection (1)(c).*

Conduct shall not be held to constitute a substantial step under Subsection (1)(c) of this Section unless it is strongly corroborative of the actor's criminal purpose. Without negating the sufficiency of other conduct, the following, if strongly corroborative of the actor's criminal purpose, shall not be held insufficient as a matter of law:

(a) lying in wait, searching for or following the contemplated victim of the crime;

(b) enticing or seeking to entice the contemplated victim of the crime to go to the place contemplated for its commission;

(c) reconnoitering the place contemplated for the commission of the crime;

(d) unlawful entry of a structure, vehicle or enclosure in which it is contemplated that the crime will be committed;

(e) possession of materials to be employed in the commission of the crime, that are specially designed for such unlawful use or that can serve no lawful purpose of the actor under the circumstances;

---

the stockings and gloves, an afterthought according to Hodges, does not undercut the firmness of their criminal intent when they were at the bank on June 14. By only postponing execution of the plan, appellants did not renounce their criminal purpose, but reaffirmed it. They reflected further upon the plan and embellished it by acquiring the stockings and gloves.

The actions of the appellants on June 21 might not support a finding, as in *Stallworth,* that "a bank robbery was in progress." 543 F.2d at 1041. Such a finding, however, is not essential to attempt liability, . . . which is designed to "encourag[e] early police intervention where a suspect is clearly bent on the commission of crime." *United States v. Stallworth*. On June 21, the firmness of appellants' criminal intent was again evident. The very fact that they showed up at the bank that day after discovering that the agents had arrested Hodges suggests that they were determined to execute their plan. Moreover, they once again had the necessary weapons, the car prepared for escape, and gave every indication that they were ready to strike.

(f) possession, collection or fabrication of materials to be employed in the commission of the crime, at or near the place contemplated for its commission, if such possession, collection or fabrication serves no lawful purpose of the actor under the circumstances;

(g) soliciting an innocent agent to engage in conduct constituting an element of the crime.

(3) *Conduct Designed to Aid Another in Commission of a Crime.* A person who engages in conduct designed to aid another to commit a crime that would establish his complicity under Section 2.06 if the crime were committed by such other person, is guilty of an attempt to commit the crime, although the crime is not committed or attempted by such other person.

2. The requirement that "substantial steps" "strongly corroborate" the actor's criminal "purpose" provides a standard that appears to work well in cases like *Jackson* where strong evidence supports the conclusion that the actor possesses the *mens rea* for attempt. (*Mens rea* issues are taken up in the next section.) Suppose, however, that the presence of *mens rea* is in question. Does the Code's "substantial step" approach preclude inferring "criminal purpose" from the actor's suspicious conduct? If so, is the MPC approach defective in this regard? On the other hand, if finders of fact are permitted to infer *mens rea* from suspicious conduct, is there a danger of "bootstrapping" both the *mens rea* and *actus reus* issues?

3. Several recent cases have involved persons with AIDS biting, spitting, or throwing their blood upon victims. Are these persons guilty of attempted murder? See *State v. Haines,* 545 N.E.2d 834, 839 (Ind. App. 1989) (trial judge erred in ruling that evidence was insufficient to support jury verdict of attempted murder by AIDS patient). Even though the state did not prove that AIDS could be transmitted by an infected person biting, spitting, or throwing blood upon another, the *Haines* court found "[i]t was only necessary for the State to show that [the infected person] did all he believed was necessary to bring about an intended result [infecting others with AIDS] *regardless* of what was *actually* possible." *Accord: New York Times,* Sat., May 19, 1990, p. 25 (AIDS-infected inmate sentenced to 25 years for attempting to murder a prison guard by biting him). On the other hand, where the state fails to show that AIDS can be transmitted by biting, the inmate cannot be convicted of using a "dangerous instrument" causing "serious physical injury." See *Brock v. State,* 555 So. 2d 285 (Ala. App. 1989), later vacated as moot when the state decided not to reprosecute on that charge. 580 So. 2d 1390 (1991). In this regard, consider the material on attempting the impossible, *infra* at 553.

McQuirter v. State

Court of Appeals of Alabama

36 Ala. App. 707, 63 So. 2d 388 (1953)

PRICE, Judge.

Appellant, a Negro man, was found guilty of an attempt to commit an assault with intent to rape, under an indictment charging an assault with intent to rape. The jury assessed a fine of $500.

About 8:00 o'clock on the night of June 29, 1951, Mrs. Ted Allen, a white woman, with her two children and a neighbor's little girl, were drinking Coca-Cola at the "Tiny Diner" in Atmore. When they started in the direction of Mrs. Allen's home she noticed appellant sitting in the cab of a parked truck. As she passed the truck appellant said something unintelligible, opened the truck door and placed his foot on the running board.

Mrs. Allen testified appellant followed her down the street and when she reached Swell Lufkin's house she stopped. As she turned into the Lufkin house appellant was within two or three feet of her. She waited ten minutes for appellant to pass. When she proceeded on her way, appellant came toward her from behind a telephone pole. She told the children to run to Mr. Simmons' house and tell him to come and meet her. When appellant saw Mr. Simmons he turned and went back down the street to the intersection and leaned on a stop sign just across the street from Mrs. Allen's home. Mrs. Allen watched him at the sign from Mr. Simmons' porch for about thirty minutes, after which time he came back down the street and appellant went on home.

* * *

Mr. Clarence Bryars, a policeman in Atmore, testified that appellant stated after his arrest that he came to Atmore with the intention of getting him a white woman that night.

Mr. W. E. Strickland, Chief of Police of Atmore, testified that appellant stated in the Atmore jail he didn't know what was the matter with him; that he was drinking a little; that he and his partner had been to Pensacola; that his partner went to the "Front" to see a colored woman; that he didn't have any money and he sat in the truck and made up his mind he was going to get the first woman that came by and that this was the first woman that came by. He said he got out of the truck, came around the gas tank and watched the lady and when she started off he started off behind her; that he was going to carry her in the cotton patch and if she hollered he was going to kill her. He testified appellant made the same statement in the Brewton jail.

Mr. Norvelle Seals, Chief Deputy Sheriff, corroborated Mr. Strickland's testimony as to the statement by appellant at the Brewton jail.

Appellant, as a witness in his own behalf, testified he and Bill Page, another Negro, carried a load of junk-iron from Monroeville to Pensacola; on their way back to Monroeville they stopped in Atmore. They parked the truck near the

"Tiny Diner" and rode to the "Front," the colored section, in a cab. Appellant came back to the truck around 8:00 o'clock and sat in the truck cab for about thirty minutes. He decided to go back to the "Front" to look for Bill Page. As he started up the street he saw prosecutrix and her children. He turned around and waited until he decided they had gone, then he walked up the street toward the "Front." When he reached the intersection at the telegraph pole he decided he didn't want to go to the "Front" and sat around there a few minutes, then went on to the "Front" and stayed about 25 or 30 minutes, and came back to the truck.

He denied that he followed Mrs. Allen or made any gesture toward molesting her or the children. He denied making the statements testified to by the officers.

He testified he had never been arrested before and introduced testimony by two residents of Monroeville as to his good reputation for peace and quiet and for truth and veracity.

Appellant insists the trial court erred in refusing the general affirmative charge and in denying the motion for a new trial on the ground the verdict was contrary to the evidence.

" 'An attempt to commit an assault with intent to rape,' . . . means an attempt to rape which has not proceeded far enough to amount to an assault." *Burton v. State,* 8 Ala. App. 295, 62 So. 394, 396.

Under the authorities in this state, to justify a conviction for an attempt to commit an assault with intent to rape the jury must be satisfied beyond a reasonable doubt that defendant intended to have sexual intercourse with prosecutrix against her will, by force or by putting her in fear. . . .

Intent is a question to be determined by the jury from the facts and circumstances adduced on the trial, and if there is evidence from which it may be inferred that at the time of the attempt defendant intended to gratify his lustful desires against the resistance of the female a jury question is presented. *McCluskey v. State,* 35 Ala. App. 456, 48 So. 2d 68.

In determining the question of intention the jury may consider social conditions and customs founded upon racial differences, such as that the prosecutrix was a white woman and defendant was a Negro man. . . .

After considering the evidence in this case we are of the opinion it was sufficient to warrant the submission of the question of defendant's guilt to the jury, and was ample to sustain the judgment of conviction.

* * *

Affirmed.

NOTES AND QUESTIONS

1. The racial factors in *McQuirter* raise disturbing questions. Would McQuirter have even been prosecuted had he been the same race as his "victim"? How reliable is the evidence of his intent?

Racial considerations aside, *McQuirter* is still troubling. At the time of McQuirter's arrest and prior to his alleged declarations of intent, what basis supported a belief that he had attempted a crime? Under any of the tests designed to distinguish preparations and attempts, did McQuirter's conduct meet the requirements of the *actus reus* principle? Are those requirements more plausibly met if it is conceded that McQuirter indeed intended to "get the first woman that came by"? If so, did the unique nature of the law of attempt, with its "primacy of the mental element, [create a temptation for] the police to exert pressure in order to obtain a confession"? Ashworth, *Belief, Intent, and Criminal Liability,* Oxford Essays in Jurisprudence, Third Series 1, 2 (J. Eckelaar and J. Bell eds. 1987).

2. In *People v. Berger,* 131 Cal. App. 2d 127, 130, 280 P.2d 136, 138 (Cal. Dist. Ct. App. 1955), the court stated, "where the intent to commit the substantive offense is . . . clearly established . . . acts done towards the commission of the crime may constitute an attempt, where the same acts would be held insufficient to constitute an attempt if the intent with which they were done is equivocal and not clearly proved." The court in *People v. Anderson,* 1 Cal. 2d 687, 690, 37 P.2d 67, 68 (1934), expressed a similar standard: "Whenever the design of a person to commit crime is clearly shown, slight acts in furtherance of the design will constitute an attempt." How, if at all, do such tests differ from the Model Penal Code's requirement of a "substantial step, strongly corroborative of the actor's criminal purpose"?

3. Suppose McQuirter had systematically stalked Mrs. Allen. If so, rather than resorting to the law of attempt, modern prosecutors might choose to charge him under now ubiquitous statutes aimed at preventing such conduct. For a discussion of antistalking legislation, see Note, *Stalking the Stalker: Developing New Laws to Thwart Those Who Terrorize Others,* 27 Ga. L. Rev. 285 (1992).

State v. Otto

Supreme Court of Idaho

102 Idaho 250, 629 P.2d 646 (1981)

McFADDEN, Justice.

The appellant appeals his conviction of attempted first degree murder based on his hiring of an undercover police officer to kill Captain Ailor of the Lewiston Police Department. Appellant had been under investigation by Captain Ailor concerning the disappearance of the appellant's wife in August, 1976.

On October 24, 1976, appellant was in the Long Branch Saloon owned by Stan Kuykendall. Mr. Kuykendall testified that during a conversation appellant expressed a desire to find a "hit-man" to kill Captain Ailor because Ailor had been harassing him over Mrs. Otto's disappearance. Mr. Kuykendall reported this to the Lewiston Police Department. Following this report an officer telephoned appellant and said he was a "hit-man." This officer later testified that appellant stated he was willing to spend $500 to have the killing done, but after dickering a price of $1,000 was agreed upon.

The Lewiston police called in members of the Idaho State Police to assist them in investigating the matter. It was decided that Officer Watts of the Idaho State Police would wear a "bug" and attempt to record his conversations with appellant. On the afternoon of October 26, 1976, Officer Watts, wearing the transmitter, met with appellant at the Long Branch as prearranged earlier in the day. During this conversation, Watts agreed to kill Captain Ailor for $250 "up front" if he were to receive an additional $750 after the killing. It was agreed that appellant would place the $250 in a cup in Watts' pickup, which appellant was seen to do later in the day. Appellant was arrested on October 27 and charged with attempted murder in the first degree. . . .

The essential question before this court is whether the appellant's conduct amounted to more than solicitation of another to murder and reached the extent or degree of an attempt under accepted principles of criminal law. We hold it did not and thus the conviction must be reversed.

The concern of the criminal law is to determine at which points along a continuum of activity criminal liability of differing degrees will attach. There can be no doubt that what the appellant did in this case was criminal as well as reprehensible. But the task facing this court is not merely to pass judgment; we must strive to correctly determine under the accepted precepts of the law whether the appellant's conviction can stand. The sincere desire to protect society from acts such as the appellant's here cannot lead us to slight this duty.

It is recognized, of course, that a close relationship exists between solicitation and attempt. In the early stages of criminal activity, the two offenses may run parallel courses. However, there exists an accepted and distinct difference between them in law, the strength of which cannot be muted by a few courts erroneously treating the terms and concepts as interchangeable.

It is supported beyond contradiction that, regardless how heinous, no man can be convicted for having criminal intent alone. An *actus reus* is essential. And in the sphere of inchoate criminal offenses, it is clear that not every act will, when combined with criminal intent, suffice to establish the basis for an attempt. . . .

While the distinction between acts of preparation and those of commission (or as is more commonly phrased "perpetration") may be difficult to make in many situations, courts have widely adopted the differentiation. . . .

The general rule in regard to solicitations within the context of the preparatory—perpetratory acts sufficient for an attempt[4] is well stated by the Tennessee Supreme Court in *Gervin v. State,* 212 Tenn. 653, 371 S.W.2d 449 (1963): "The weight of American authority holds, as a general proposition, that mere criminal solicitation of another to commit a crime does not constitute an attempt. . . . "

---

[4] The prerequisite to an understanding of the general rule is the recognition that solicitation is in the nature of the incitement or encouragement of another to commit a crime in the future. Thus it is essentially preparatory to the commission of the targeted offense. . . .

. . . A few courts, however, have held that solicitation can be sufficient predicate for an attempt to commit the crime solicited. . . . Since the state relies primarily on the minority view expressed in these last cited cases to support appellant's conviction, a brief discussion of this line of authority is called for.

These decisions rely heavily upon the proposition that when the intent that a crime be committed is clearly shown, "slight acts" on the part of the solicitor will make him liable for an attempt to commit that target crime. . . .

We disagree with the reasoning in the case of *State v. Gay,* 4 Wash. App. 834, 486 P.2d 341 (1971). While that court noted that a "mere" solicitation is not an attempt, the court there held that the transfer of "consideration," *i.e.,* the partial payment for the contracted killing, was a "slight" yet sufficient act upon which an attempt could be found. . . .

Facially there would appear to be no persuasive reason why a request to kill, however phrased or whatever enticement offered, should be treated differently under the law merely because part of the agreed upon fee has passed hands. There is no greater proximity, no significantly greater likelihood of consummation, and no act of a nature other than the incitement or preparation inherent in the solicitation itself. . . .

In *State v. Braham,* . . . 571 P.2d 631 (1977), the most recent adoption of the minority position, the Alaska court . . . recognized that there must be an overt act beyond mere preparation. . . . In the factual context of the *Braham* case, the court found the requisite overt act in the solicitee's visit to the intended victim at the urging of the solicitor for the purpose of gaining the victim's confidence. At that time, the solicitee was still committed to the planned murder; it was only upon later realizing that the police were well informed of the circumstances of the planned murder that the solicitee became an informer. There thus appears to be a valid basis for the Alaska decision holding the solicitor guilty of an attempt. While on the face of the case the citation to the *Gay* . . . precedent would indicate that the solicitor's consummation of the contract to kill or the finding of other "slight acts" on his part supported his conviction of an attempt, the act actually relied upon by the court as satisfying the overt act element was the solicitee's visit with the intended victim pursuant to the plan. It is well accepted that when the parties are acting in furtherance of a plan, the solicitor shares any attempt liability that accrues due to the actions of his agent. Citation to *Gay*. . . is unnecessary.

While the concept of "slight acts" is doubtlessly appealing in some respects, especially to those seeking to punish reprehensible acts when criminal intent is clear, use of this phrase in the manner of the *Gay* . . . decision is improper. The solicitor of another, assuming neither solicitor nor solicitee proximately acts toward the crime's commission, cannot be held for an attempt. He does not by his incitement of another to criminal activity commit a dangerously proximate act of perpetration. . . .

It is foreseeable that jurisdictions faced with a general attempt statute and no means of severely punishing a solicitation to commit a felony might resort to the device of transforming the solicitor's urgings into a proximate attempted commission of the crime urged but doing so violates the very essence of the requirement that a sufficient *actus reus* be proven before criminal liability will attach.

In light of the foregoing discussion, the facts in appellant's situation take on additional clarity. Here appellant desired to have Captain Ailor murdered. In structuring his plan, he solicited an agent to commit the actual act, and in this regard he paid $250 and promised him a larger sum after the crime had been committed. Neither appellant nor the agent ever took any steps of perpetration in dangerous proximity to the commission of the offense planned. The conversation in the Long Branch at which appellant solicited the undercover policeman, and the payment of part of the agreed upon fee, are not acts of perpetration at all but are clearly the preparatory acts of incitement of another to commit a crime, *i.e.,* of mere solicitation. These acts are not sufficient under the law above discussed to support a conviction on the charge of attempted murder. . . .

* * *

Appellant's conviction on the charge of attempted first degree murder is reversed.

DONALDSON and SHEPARD, JJ., *concur*

BAKES, Chief Justice, *dissenting:*

I

The error in the majority opinion begins with the majority's inadequate framing of the issue before us. It presents the essential question as being "whether the appellant's conduct amounted to more than solicitation. . . ." However, we are not involved here with how the appellant's actions relate to the crime of solicitation (if, indeed, there is such a crime in Idaho), but rather the question to be asked is whether the appellant's conduct amounted to an attempt. . . .

Implicit in the majority's rationale is the supposition that the crime of attempt cannot overlap the crime of solicitation. The majority approaches its analysis as though solicitation and attempt were statutory crimes with equal footing, each controlling a specific and exclusive area of conduct. However, there is no statutory crime of solicitation in Idaho, and even if there is a common law crime of solicitation, it is preempted by the Idaho attempt statute, . . . to the extent that the two prohibitions pertain to the same conduct. I.C. § 73–116 provides that "the common law of England . . . *in all cases not provided for in these compiled laws,* is the rule of decision in all the courts of this state." (Emphasis added.) The legislature has, however, provided an attempt statute in I.C. § 18–306, and therefore the common law rule of solicitation is not the rule of decision in the courts of this state when it conflicts with the intended application of the attempt statute.

* * *

. . . In the instant case, the defendant's intent to commit the target crime of first degree murder is more than evident. After first inquiring of a bartender where he could find a "hit man," the defendant was referred to an undercover officer with whom he met for over an hour discussing the details of the killing. While not supplying the murder weapon, the defendant made sure that the murder was to be done in a manner acceptable to him by discussing and approving the type of gun to be used. In the course of the meeting, the defendant stated emphatically, "I don't want that ——— wounded, I want him dead." Even after he was arrested, the defendant was overheard inquiring of a relative whether or not the "hit" had been made. The defendant's intent to murder Captain Ailor was clear and, under the circumstances, the acts of the defendant were more than sufficient to support a conviction for attempted murder under our statute. The defendant had in fact done everything necessary on his part to kill Captain Ailor. All that he had to do was wait for the result. Such a state of events clearly establishes an attempt. . . .

Under I.C. § 18–306, it does not matter that at common law the same conduct may only have been the crime of solicitation. What does matter is whether the conduct is or is not included within the ambit of I.C. § 18.306*

II

The majority also attempts to distinguish between acts of preparation and acts of perpetration. Although this type of analysis has been accepted by some courts, the distinction is in fact highly artificial, since all acts leading up to the ultimate consummation of a crime are by their very nature preparatory. The real question is whether acts of preparation when coupled with intent have reached a point at which they pose a danger to the public so as to be worthy of law's notice. . . .

Although it is not necessarily contended that every solicitation will constitute an attempt, the broad sweep of I.C. § 18–306 indicates that an attempt often may include solicitation within its bounds. This is certainly the case where, as here, the solicitor has done all that he needs to do in accomplishing the target crime. It may even be, under particular fact situations, that intent and danger to the public are so evident that mere solicitation itself might constitute a sufficient overt act to support an attempt conviction. . . .

* * *

Had the defendant been arrested and charged based only on an offer to employ a "hit man," the common law crime of solicitation might be applicable, as the majority urges. However, the acts here went far beyond an offer of "employment." As discussed previously, the type of weapon to be utilized and the manner in which the hit was to be made were discussed, an agreement was reached, payment was made, and the defendant completed all the necessary steps preliminary to the "hit" being made. In view of these facts, it appears that the majority would not find an attempt under our statute until the bullet was sailing through the air. That our legislature intended such a result is inconceivable. For the reasons stated above, I would affirm the conviction.

---

* [Section 18–306 provides, "Every person who attempts to commit any crime, but fails, or is prevented or intercepted in the perpetration thereof, is punishable. . . ."—Eds.]

[The dissenting opinion of Justice Bistine is omitted.]

NOTES AND QUESTIONS

1. As the *Otto* case points out, inciting or soliciting another to commit a crime was itself a crime at common law. Chief Justice Bakes' dissenting opinion notes that the Idaho legislature had failed to codify the crime of solicitation. Until recently, such a situation was common nationwide. With the advent of the Model Penal Code, however, many states have now enacted solicitation provisions, often explicitly reflecting the influence of § 5.02 of the Code, which provides:

(1) *Definition of Solicitation.* A person is guilty of solicitation to commit a crime if with the purpose of promoting or facilitating its commission he commands, encourages or requests another person to engage in specific conduct which would constitute such crime or an attempt to commit such crime or which would establish his complicity in its commission or attempted commission.

(2) *Uncommunicated Solicitation.* It is immaterial under Subsection (1) of this Section that the actor fails to communicate with the person he solicits to commit a crime if his conduct was designed to effect such communication.

(3) *Renunciation of Criminal Purpose.* It is an affirmative defense that the actor, after soliciting another person to commit a crime, persuaded him not to do so or otherwise prevented the commission of the crime, under circumstances manifesting a complete and voluntary renunciation of his criminal purpose.

The Commentary to § 5.02 at 365–66, 370–73 discusses the Code's approach:

. . . There has been difference of opinion as to whether a genuine social danger is presented by solicitation to commit a crime. It has been argued, on the one hand, that such conduct is not dangerous because the resisting will of an independent moral agent is interposed between the solicitor and the commission of the crime that is his object. By the same token it is urged that the solicitor, manifesting his reluctance to commit the crime himself, is not a significant menace. The opposing view is that a solicitation is, if anything, more dangerous than a direct attempt, because it may give rise to the special hazard of cooperation among criminals. Solicitation may, indeed, be thought of as an attempt to conspire. Moreover, the solicitor, working his will through one or more agents, manifests an approach to crime more intelligent and masterful than the efforts of his hireling. . . .

* * *

If behavior is serious enough to be classed as criminal its solicitation should be punishable, and this section so provides. There is no requirement that the solicitation result in action by the person solicited or even that such action seem likely at the time of solicitation. The judgment is that ordinarily a person who tries an unreceptive hearer on one occasion may be more astute in choosing his audience on another occasion. As with attempts,

Section 5.05(2) does permit reduction of the offense or even dismissal if a solicitation is "so inherently unlikely to result or culminate in the commission of a crime that neither such conduct nor the actor presents a public danger warranting" the ordinary grading. . . .

Like Section 5.01 on attempts, 5.02 preserves the traditional requirement of "specific intent." To be liable for solicitation, an actor must have "the purpose of promoting or facilitating" the commission of a crime. It is not enough for a person to be aware that his words may lead to a criminal act or even to be quite sure they will do so; it must be the actor's purpose that the crime be committed. . . .

* * *

. . . While attempts and solicitations have much in common and are closely related in their historical development, this section provides for separate definition of criminal solicitation on the ground that each of the two inchoate offenses presents problems not pertinent to the other. Even so, it is still possible for an act that is a criminal solicitation also to constitute an attempt, as, for example, when an actor's solicitation of another to engage in sodomy is both an invitation to another to commit a crime and an act done for the purpose of enabling the actor to commit a crime.

2. How would the Otto case be resolved under the Model Penal Code? Note that the practical consequences to the defendant may be the same whether his crime is conceptualized as "attempting" or "soliciting" murder. MPC § 5.05 provides in part,

(1) *Grading.* Except as otherwise provided in this Section, attempt [and], solicitation . . . are crimes of the same grade and degree as the most serious offense which is attempted or solicited . . . An attempt [or] solicitation . . . to commit a [capital crime or a] felony of the first degree is a felony of the second degree.

(2) *Mitigation.* If the particular conduct charged to constitute a criminal attempt [or] solicitation . . . is so inherently unlikely to result or culminate in the commission of a crime that neither such conduct nor the actor presents a public danger warranting the grading of such offense under this Section, the Court shall exercise its power under Section 6.12 to enter judgment and impose sentence for a crime of lower grade or degree or, in extreme cases, may dismiss the prosecution.

(3) *Multiple Convictions.* A person may not be convicted of more than one offense defined by this Article for conduct designed to commit or to culminate in the commission of the same crime.

3. Could Otto have been convicted of "conspiring" with the undercover officer to kill Ailor? See § 7.03[2], *infra.*

[C] The *Mens Rea*

THACKER V. COMMONWEALTH

Supreme Court of Appeals of Virginia

134 Va. 767, 114 S.E. 504 (1922)

WEST, J.

This writ of error is to a judgment upon the verdict of a jury finding John Thacker, the accused, guilty of attempting to murder Mrs. J. A. Ratrie, and fixing his punishment at two years in the penitentiary.

* * *

The accused, in company with two other young men, Doc Campbell and Paul Kelly, was attending a church festival in Alleghany county, at which all three became intoxicated. They left the church between 10 and 11 o'clock at night, and walked down the county road about 1½ miles, when they came to a sharp curve. Located in this curve was a tent in which the said Mrs. J. A. Ratrie, her husband, four children, and a servant were camping for the summer. The husband, though absent, was expected home that night, and Mrs. Ratrie, upon retiring, had placed a lighted lamp on a trunk by the head of her bed. After 11 o'clock she was awakened by the shots of a pistol and loud talking in the road near by, and heard a man say, "I am going to shoot that God-damned light out"; and another voice said, "Don't shoot the light out." The accused and his friends then appeared at the back of the tent, where the flaps of the tent were open, and said they were from Bath county and had lost their way, and asked Mrs. Ratrie if she could take care of them all night. She informed them she was camping for the summer, and had no room for them. One of the three thanked her, and they turned away, but after passing around the tent the accused used some vulgar language and did some cursing and singing. When they got back in the road, the accused said again he was going to shoot the light out, and fired three shots, two of which went through the head of the bed in which Mrs. Ratrie was lying, just missing her head and the head of her baby, who was sleeping with her. The accused did not know Mrs. Ratrie, and had never seen her before. He testified he did not know any of the parties in the tent, and had no ill will against either of them; that he simply shot at the light, without any intent to harm Mrs. Ratrie or any one else; that he would not have shot had he been sober, and regretted his action.

* * *

An attempt to commit a crime is composed of two elements: (1) The intent to commit it; and (2) a direct, ineffectual act done towards its commission. The act must reach far enough towards the accomplishment of the desired result to amount to the commencement of the consummation. . . .

The law can presume the intention so far as realized in the act, but not an intention beyond what was so realized. The law does not presume, because an assault was made with a weapon likely to produce death, that it was an assault with the intent to murder. And where it takes a particular intent to constitute a crime, that particular intent must be proved either by direct or circumstantial evidence, which would warrant the inference of the intent with which the act was done.

When a statute makes an offense to consist of an act combined with a particular intent, that intent is just as necessary to be proved as the act itself, and must be found as a matter of fact before a conviction can be had; and no intent in law or mere legal presumption, differing from the intent in fact, can be allowed to supply the place of the latter. . . .

* * *

Mr. Bishop, in his Criminal Law, vol. 1 (8th Ed.), at section 729, says:

When the law makes an act, whether more or less evil in itself, punishable, though done simply from general malevolence, if one takes what, were all accomplished, would be a step towards it, yet if he does not mean to do the whole, no court can justly hold him answerable for more than he does. And when the thing done does not constitute a substantive crime, there is no ground for treating it as an attempt. So that necessarily an act prompted by general malevolence, or by a specific design to do something else, is not an attempt to commit a crime not intended. . . . When we say that a man attempted to do a given wrong, we mean that he intended to do specifically it, and proceeded a certain way in the doing. The intent in the mind covers the thing in full; the act covers it only in part. Thus. . . to commit murder, one need not intend to take life, but to be guilty of an attempt to murder, he must so intend. It is not sufficient that his act, had it proved fatal, would have been murder . . . We have seen that the unintended taking of life may be murder without the specific intent to commit it. . . . For example, if one from a housetop recklessly throws down a billet of wood upon the sidewalk where persons are constantly passing, and it falls upon a person passing by and kills him, this would be the common-law murder, but if, instead of killing, it inflicts only a slight injury, the party could not be convicted of an assault with attempt to commit murder, since, in fact, the murder was not intended.

The application of the foregoing principles to the facts of the instant case shows clearly, as we think, that the judgment complained of is erroneous. While it might possibly be said that the firing of the shot into the head of Mrs. Ratrie's bed was an act done towards the commission of the offense charged, the evidence falls far short of proving that it was fired with the intent to murder her.

However averse we may be to disturb the verdict of the jury, our obligation to the law compels us to do so.

The judgment complained of will be reversed, the verdict of the jury set aside, and the case remanded for a new trial therein, if the commonwealth shall be so advised.

Reversed

NOTES AND QUESTIONS

1. *Thacker* represents the traditional view requiring specific intent to commit the attempted crime. See also *People v. Trinkle,* 369 N.E. 888 (Ill. 1977). This means that the actor must not only "intend to engage in the substantive offense but that the actor intend the prohibited result and the required circumstances of the substantive offense." Robinson, *A Functional Analysis of Criminal Law,* 88 Nw.U.L. Rev. 857, 891 n. 80 (1994). This in turn means, in Modern Penal Code terms, "that the common law rule . . . requires purpose as to the elements of the object offense." Id. Is the common law position sound? Is Thacker not the kind of person at whom the law of attempts is directed? See Williams, *The Problem of Reckless Attempts,* 1983 Crim. L. Rev. 365.

If Thacker is not guilty of attempted murder, is he guilty of any other crime? What about attempted manslaughter? See *Taylor v. State,* 444 So. 2d 931 (Fla. 1983). Could Thacker be convicted of aggravated assault? Assuming no other basis of criminal liability exists, does *Thacker* illustrate the need for a general crime of "reckless endangerment"? See MPC § 211.2, Appendix.

2. X places a bomb on an airplane. She knows that 10 people will be flying on board. The bomb is set to go off while the plane is in flight. Miraculously, the bomb does not detonate. Assuming that X does not desire to kill anyone, is X guilty of attempted murder under *Thacker?* Should X be liable for that crime?

3. A, who plans eventually to threaten to blow up a subway train unless he is paid ransom, carries a small model bomb with him on the subway. It accidently explodes, injuring A severely and several other people as well. He is prosecuted for attempted murder and attempted extortion. What is the likely result of these two charges?

PEPPLE v. KROVARZ

Supreme Court of Colorado, en Banc

697 P. 2d 378 (1985)

DUBOFSKY, Justice.

The Denver District Court acquitted the defendant, Victor Krovarz, of attempted aggravated robbery. . . . The court, relying upon *People v. Frysig,* 628 P.2d 1004 (Colo. 1981), ruled that liability for criminal attempt is predicated upon the specific intent to commit the underlying crime and found that the defendant did not possess the requisite intent. The People appeal the district court's ruling as a question of law under section 16-12-102, 8 C.R.S. (1978). We disapprove the ruling of the district court.

At approximately 11 AM on April 9, 1982, Sandra Tafoya was working as a cashier at a Target store on Sheridan Boulevard in Denver. The defendant came up behind Tafoya, put a putty knife to her throat, and demanded that she hand over the money in her cash register. Gary Hoskins, a customer waiting in the checkout line, circled behind the defendant and wrested the putty knife from his grasp. Hoskins pinned the defendant against a wall until store security guards assumed custody of the defendant. Shortly afterwards, Denver police officers arrived and arrested the defendant. The defendant was charged with attempted aggravated robbery . . . which requires that the prosecution prove, in addition to the usual elements of robbery,[2] that the defendant "by the use of force, threats, or intimidation with a deadly weapon knowingly put[] the person robbed or any other person in reasonable fear of death or bodily injury. . . . "

At trial, the defendant's evidence focused on his mental state. A psychologist testified that the defendant had been a patient at the Bethesda Mental Health Center before his transfer to a halfway house in Denver, from which he was released the morning of the robbery. From his examination of the defendant, the psychologist concluded that the defendant was depressed and suicidal that morning, and, rather than intending to take money, the defendant had committed the robbery in the hope of being returned to a mental hospital where he could receive help. On cross-examination, however, the psychologist stated that the defendant did intend to engage in the conduct constituting the attempted robbery, was aware that he thereby placed the victim in reasonable fear of injury, and was aware that he was practically certain to obtain money as a result of his acts. The defendant confirmed the psychologist's testimony.

After hearing the evidence, the district court ruled that *Frysig* required a specific intent to commit the underlying crime before a defendant may be convicted of criminal attempt. The court found that the prosecution had failed to prove specific intent beyond a reasonable doubt and acquitted the defendant.[3] The court added that "if attempt were a knowing offense, my ruling would be different. . . . " The People on appeal contend that the culpable mental state for attempt is identical to the culpable mental state required for the underlying crime, and that the district court erred in requiring proof of specific intent to commit the underlying offense of aggravated robbery.

Criminal attempt is defined in section 18-2-101(1), 8 C.R.S. (1978):

> A person commits criminal attempt if, acting with the kind of culpability otherwise required for commission of an offense, he engages in conduct constituting a substantial step toward the commission of the offense. A substantial step is any conduct, whether act, omission, or possession, which is strongly corroborative of the firmness of the actor's purpose to complete the commission of the offense. . . .

---

[2] Under section 184-301(1), 8 C.R.S. (1978), "[a] person who knowingly takes anything of value from the person or presence of another by the use of force, threats, or intimidation commits robbery."

[3] Although the defendant's evidence focused on his lack of intent to take a thing of value (money), the district court did not isolate this or any other element in ruling that the defendant lacked specific intent to commit the charged crime. We therefore analyze the required mental state for attempt as it relates to all elements of aggravated robbery.

In *People v. Frysig*, . . . we analyzed the history and language of the criminal attempt statute and concluded that the General Assembly intended to incorporate the traditional rule that an actor may be found guilty of attempt only if he intends to commit the underlying crime, *i.e.*, if he intends to perform the acts and bring about the results proscribed by statute. . . . In reaching this conclusion, we distinguished between the intent necessary to establish a criminal attempt and the culpable mental state of the underlying crime:

> [I]n order to be guilty of criminal attempt, the actor must act with the kind of culpability otherwise required for commission of the underlying offense, and must engage in the conduct which constitutes the substantial step with the further intent to perform acts which, if completed, would constitute the underlying offense.

People v. Frysig, 628 P.2d at 1010.

In the present case, the district court implicitly found that the defendant possessed a culpable mental state of knowledge, which would be sufficient to sustain a conviction for the underlying charge of aggravated robbery. . . . We must determine whether the mental state of knowledge also fulfills the culpable mental state for attempt identified in *Frysig*.

One may be guilty of attempt without having engaged in the harmful conduct or having achieved the harmful result that ordinarily forms the basis for criminal liability; rather, culpability for criminal attempt rests primarily upon the actor's purpose to cause harmful consequences. . . . Punishment is justified where the actor intends harm because there exists a high likelihood that his "unspent" intent will flower into harmful conduct at any moment. . . . The probability of future dangerousness, however, is not confined to actors whose conscious purpose is to perform the proscribed acts or achieve the proscribed results, *i.e.*, those possessing the culpable mental state of specific intent.[7] We believe that this danger is equally present when one acts knowingly.

In analyzing the danger posed by a knowing attempt, we first recognize that the statutory definition of aggravated robbery includes elements of conduct, result and circumstance,[8] and that the definition of the culpable mental state of knowledge differs in relation to each type of element. We therefore examine the mental state of knowledge in relation to each type of element in order to see whether each contains the potential danger that justifies legislative imposition of attempt liability.

---

[7] Section 18-1-501(5), 8 C.R.S. (1978), provides:

All offenses defined in this code in which the mental culpability requirement is expressed as "intentionally" or "with intent" are declared to be specific intent offenses. A person acts "intentionally" or "with intent" when his conscious objective is to cause the specific result proscribed by the statute defining the offense. It is immaterial to the issue of specific intent whether or not the result actually occurred.

[8] Robbery requires a knowing mental state in relation to conduct (use of force, threats or intimidation), result (taking) and circumstance (thing of value from the person or presence of another). *People v. Derrera*, 667 P.2d 1363, 1368 (Colo. 1983). Aggravated robbery under section 18-4-302(1)(b), as charged here, expands the conduct requirement by specifying that the actor must have used a deadly weapon, and expands the result requirement by specifying that the defendant's actions must place the victim in reasonable fear of death or injury.

With respect to a result, one acts knowingly "when he is aware that his conduct is practically certain to cause the result." When one engages in conduct that is practically certain to cause a prohibited result, with awareness of the likely consequence, one in effect chooses to create that result even though he may not actively desire that it occur.[9] In [*People v.*] *Derrera,* [667 P.2d 1363, 1368 (Colo. 1983)], we noted that the culpable mental state of knowledge relative to result "approaches the formulation of a specific intent requirement." For this reason, a number of jurisdictions by statute have extended attempt liability to situations where the actor knowingly obtains the forbidden result. . . . The drafters of the Model Penal Code explained that this extension of liability is warranted because

> the manifestation of dangerousness is as great—or very nearly as great—as in the case of purposive conduct. In both instances a deliberate choice is made to bring about the consequence forbidden by the criminal laws, and the actor has done all within his power to cause this result to occur. The absence in one instance of any desire for the forbidden result is not, under these circumstances, a sufficient basis for differentiating between the two types of conduct involved.
>
> *Id.* § 5.01 comment at 29–30.

We agree with this reasoning; a knowing attempt to attain a proscribed result is a sufficient culpable mental state to justify imposition by the legislature of attempt liability.

We next turn to the question of whether a culpable mental state of knowledge relative to the other two types of elements, conduct and circumstances, is a sufficient index of dangerousness to warrant the punishment established by the legislature for criminal attempt. One acts knowingly with respect to statutorily defined conduct and circumstances "when he is aware that his conduct is of such nature or that such circumstance exists." § 18-1-501(6). Acts undertaken with such awareness are the product of deliberate choice. Indeed, the correlation here between knowledge and intention is even closer than it is with regard to result: knowledge with regard to

---

[9] . . . [T]his line of reasoning does not necessarily extend to crimes predicated upon a culpable mental state of recklessness. One who acts recklessly "consciously disregards a substantial and unjustifiable risk . . . ," § 18-1-501(8); such conscious disregard does not imply that one chooses the result in the same way that one chooses a result he knows to be a practical certainty. Thus, the Model Penal Code, while permitting attempt liability for results obtained knowingly, explicitly excludes results obtained recklessly. Model Penal Code § 5.01 comment at 30 (Tent. Draft No. 10, 1960). In addition, every state court that has considered this question has declined to extend attempt liability to reckless crimes, on the ground that one cannot intend to commit a crime defined as having an unintended result. . .

> Although some . . . cases . . . speak of "specific intent" as a necessary predicate for attempt liability, . . . heir analysis is concerned solely with distinguishing intent from recklessness; the cases do not consider whether attempt liability may be based on knowledge, and therefore they are not contrary to the position we adopt today. This is illustrated by the approach of the Indiana Supreme Court. In *Smith v. State,* 422 N.E.2d 1179, 1185 (Ind. 1981), the court held that there can be no attempt liability for voluntary manslaughter predicated upon recklessness, declaring that the Indiana attempt statute, identical to that of Colorado, applies exclusively to specific intent crimes. One year later, however, the same court acknowledged the existence of attempted voluntary manslaughter based upon "a knowing or intentional state of mind." *Goodwin v. State,* 439 N.E.2d 595, 599 (Ind. 1982).

result requires that the actor be "practically certain" of the consequences, while knowledge with regard to conduct and circumstances requires an "awareness" of the nature of the conduct and the presence of the circumstances. . . . Given this awareness, there is no practical difference between knowledge and intention relative to conduct or circumstances. . . .

The structure of the Colorado Criminal Code supports our conclusion, so far as criminal attempt is concerned, that there is no practical difference between knowledge and intention relative to conduct or circumstances. The mental state of intention is defined relative to result but not relative to conduct or circumstances; knowledge is the most culpable state attached to either of these latter two types of elements. . . . This scheme indicates a legislative judgment that any definition of intent attaching to either conduct or circumstances is superfluous. At least with regard to conduct, this determination was deliberate. When the culpable mental state requirements of the Code were first adopted, the mental state of intention was defined to include the actor's conscious object of engaging in the proscribed conduct. . . . On July 1, 1977, this provision was deleted. Based upon the structure and history of the statutory culpable mental state requirements, we conclude that knowledge as to conduct and circumstances is a sufficient index of potential harm to permit the imposition by the legislature of punishment for criminal attempt.

In addition, the attempt statute indicates a legislative intent to permit imposition of attempt liability based upon a culpable mental state of knowledge relative to circumstances. Section 18-2-101(1), 8 C.R.S. (1978) provides in part: "Factual or legal impossibility of committing the offense is not a defense if the offense could have been committed had the attendant circumstances been as the actor believed them to be. . . ." This provision permits belief in external circumstances, a mental state of lesser culpability than actual awareness, to establish attempt liability as to circumstances.

We hold that a culpable mental state of knowledge suffices to support criminal attempt liability. We recognize that our conclusion that attempt liability may be based on knowing conduct or knowingly attained results conflicts with a plausible reading of *People v. Frysig* . . . that knowledge cannot substitute for intent as a predicate for attempt liability. The precise issue in *Frysig* was whether, in a prosecution for attempted first-degree sexual assault, the trial court erred in failing to instruct the jury that the defendant could be found guilty of attempt only if he intended to commit the underlying crime. The culpable mental state relative to the conduct and result comprised within first-degree sexual assault was, and still is, knowledge. . . . We did not find, however, that the instruction regarding this mental state was an adequate substitute for an instruction on the intent required for attempt; rather, we held that the instruction regarding the "substantial step" necessary for attempt cured the error by referring to "purpose." *Frysig* therefore can be read to imply that knowledge could not substitute for intent as the culpable mental state of attempt. In holding as we do today, we reject such a reading of *Frysig*. The district court erred in requiring a showing of specific intent to commit the underlying crime.

Ruling disapproved.

NOTES AND QUESTIONS

1. Suppose the *Krovarz* facts had arisen in a jurisdiction applying the common law approach reflected in *Thacker.* What result?

2. The Colorado statute interpreted in *Krovarz* adopts some features of the Model Penal Code's *mens rea* approach. In examining the following Code provision and Commentary, consider how the *Thacker* and *Krovarz* cases would be resolved under the MPC.

Section 5.01. Criminal Attempt.

(1) *Definition of Attempt.* A person is guilty of an attempt to commit a crime if, acting with the kind of culpability otherwise required for commission of the crime, he:

   (a) purposely engages in conduct that would constitute the crime if the attendant circumstances were as he believes them to be; or

   (b) when causing a particular result is an element of the crime, does or omits to do anything with the purpose of causing or with the belief that it will cause such result without further conduct on his part; or

   (c) purposely does or omits to do anything that, under the circumstances as he believes them to be, is an act or omission constituting a substantial step in a course of conduct planned to culminate in his commission of the crime.

Comment

Requirement of Purpose. A[n] analysis of Subsection (1) must begin with a discussion of the *mens rea* of attempt. As will be seen, all three of the subdivisions of Subsection (1), with two exceptions to be noted, are designed to follow the conventional pattern of limiting the crime of attempt to purposive conduct. The general principle is thus that the actor must affirmatively desire to engage in the conduct or to cause the result that will constitute the principal offense.

The first exception relates to the circumstances under which the offense must be committed. The requirement of purpose extends to the conduct of the actor and to the results that his conduct causes, but his purpose need not encompass all of the circumstances included in the formal definition of the substantive offense. As to them, it is sufficient that he acts with the culpability that is required for commission of the completed crime.

Several illustrations may serve to clarify the point. Assume, for example, a statute that provides that sexual intercourse with a female under a prescribed age is an offense, and that a mistake as to age will not afford a defense no matter how reasonable its foundation. The policy of the substantive offense as to age, therefore, is one of strict liability, and if the actor has sexual intercourse with a female, he is guilty or not, depending upon her age and irrespective of his views as to her age. Suppose, however, that he is arrested before he engages in the proscribed conduct, and that the charge is an attempt to commit the offense. Should he then be entitled to rely on a mistake as to age as a defense? Or should the policy of the substantive crime on this issue carry over to the attempt as well? Or, assume a statute that makes it a federal offense to murder an FBI agent and treats the agent's status as a member of the FBI as a jurisdictional ingredient, with no culpability required in respect to that element. The question again is whether the policy of the substantive crime should control the same issue when it arises on a charge of attempt, or whether there is a special policy that the law of attempt should embrace to change the result on this point.

Under the formulation in Subsection (1)(c), the proffered defense would not succeed in either case. In the statutory rape example, the actor must have a purpose to engage in sexual intercourse with a female in order to be charged with the attempt, and must engage in a substantial step in a course of conduct planned to culminate in his commission of that act. With respect to the age of the victim, however, it is sufficient if he acts "with the kind of culpability otherwise required for the commission of the crime," which in the case supposed is none at all. Since, therefore, mistake as to age is irrelevant with respect to the substantive offense, it is likewise irrelevant with respect to the attempt. The same result would obtain in the murder illustration. The actor must, in the case supposed, engage in a substantial step in a course of conduct planned to culminate in the death of his victim. But with respect to his awareness of the status of his victim as an FBI agent, a mistake would not be relevant since the policy of the substantive offense controls on such matters and that policy is one of strict liability.

The judgment is thus that if the defendant manifests a purpose to engage in the type of conduct or to cause the type of result that is forbidden by the criminal law, he has sufficiently exhibited his dangerousness to justify the imposition of criminal sanctions, so long as he otherwise acts with the kind of culpability that is sufficient for the completed offense. The objective is to select out those elements of the completed crime that, if the defendant desires to bring them about, indicate with clarity that he poses the type of danger to society that the substantive offense is designed to prevent. . . .

The question might be asked, however, whether the policy of the substantive offense should be allowed to control other culpability questions that might arise. For example, reckless and negligent homicide are offenses under this Code, as they are generally. Cases will arise where the defendant engaged in conduct that recklessly or negligently created a risk of death, but where the death did not result. Should the law of attempts encompass such cases?

The approach of the Model Code is not to treat such behavior as an attempt. Instead the Code creates a separate crime, a misdemeanor, for recklessly placing another person in danger of death or serious bodily injury. The Institute's judgment was that the scope of the criminal law would be unduly extended if one could be liable for an attempt whenever he recklessly or negligently created a risk of any result whose actual occurrence would lead to criminal responsibility. While it was believed that the reckless creation of risk of death or serious bodily harm was grave enough for general coverage, even for this behavior misdemeanor penalties seemed more apt than the severer sanctions attached to felony attempts.

When, on the other hand, a person actually believes that his behavior will produce the proscribed result, it is appropriate to treat him as attempting to cause the result, whether or not that is his purpose.

Subsection (1)(b) provides that when causing a particular result is an element of the crime, as in homicide offenses or criminally obtaining property, an actor commits an attempt when he does or omits to do anything with the purpose of causing "or with the belief that it will cause" such result without further conduct on his part. Thus, a belief that death will ensue from the actor's conduct, or that property will be obtained, will suffice, as well as would a purpose to bring about those results. . . .

. . . [T]he inclusion of such conduct as the basis for liability under Subsection (1)(b) is based on the conclusion that the manifestation of the actor's dangerousness is just as great—or very nearly as great as in the case of purposive conduct. In both instances a deliberate choice is made to bring about the consequence forbidden by the criminal laws, and the actor has done all within his power to cause this result to occur. The absence of any desire that the result occur is not, under these circumstances, a sufficient basis for differentiating between the two types of conduct involved.

3. For a rare case that seems to hold that recklessly creating a risk of death constitutes sufficient *mens rea* for the crime of attempted murder, see *Gentry v. State,* 437 So. 2d 1097–99 (Fla. 1983):

We now hold that there are offenses that may be successfully prosecuted as an attempt without proof of a specific intent to commit the relevant completed offense. The key to recognizing these crimes is to first determine whether the completed offense is a crime requiring specific intent or general intent. If the state is not required to show specific intent to successfully prosecute the completed crime, it will not be required to show specific intent to prosecute an attempt to commit that crime. We believe there is logic in this approach and that it comports with legislative intent. Second-degree and third-degree murder under our statutes are crimes requiring only general intent.

In the instant case, the appellant, while allegedly in a drunken state, swore at his father, choked him, snapped a pistol several times to his head and when the weapon failed to fire, struck the father in the head with the gun. Had a homicide occurred, there can be no doubt that the appellant could have been successfully prosecuted for second-degree murder without the state adducing proof of a specific intent to kill. The fact that the father survived was not the result of any design on the part of the appellant not to effect death but was simply fortuitous. We can think of no good reason to reward the appellant for such fortuity by imposing upon the state the added burden of showing a specific intent to kill in order to successfully prosecute the attempted offense.

Does *Gentry* reach the right result? Does the logic of the Florida court lead to the conclusion that *negligence* might also be a sufficient *mens rea* ground for attempt liability?

Are there problems, semantic and otherwise, with the crime of negligently attempting to commit an offense? For example, suppose X negligently creates a risk of death that fortunately does not cause anyone to die. Would X be guilty of "attempted involuntary manslaughter" under *Gentry?* Should X be guilty of that offense or any other offense?

4. Not surprisingly, the generally held notion that intent is required for an attempt dictates that strict liability offenses can be attempted only if the accused acted with an intent to bring about the result proscribed by the crime attempted. See *Gardner v. Akeroyd,* 2 Q.B. 743 (1952).

[D] Renunciation

PEPOLE v. STAPLES

California Court of Appeals, Second Dist., Div. 5

6 Cal App. 3d 61, 85 Cal Rptr. 589 (1970)

REPPY, Associate Justice.

Defendant was charged in an information with attempted burglary . . . [and] found guilty. . . .

In October 1967, while his wife was away on a trip, defendant, a mathematician, under an assumed name, rented an office on the second floor of a building in Hollywood which was over the mezzanine of a bank. Directly below the mezzanine was the vault of the bank. Defendant was aware of the layout of the building, specifically of the relation of the office he rented to the bank vault. Defendant paid rent for the period from October 23 to November 23. The landlord had 10 days before commencement of the rental period within which to finish some interior repairs and painting. During this prerental period defendant brought into the office certain equipment. This included drilling tools, two acetylene gas tanks, a blow torch, a blanket, and a linoleum rug. The landlord observed these items when he came in from time to time to see how the repair work was progressing. Defendant learned from a custodian that no one was in the building on Saturdays. On Saturday, October 14, defendant drilled two groups of holes into the floor of the office above the mezzanine room. He stopped drilling before the holes went through the floor. He came back to the office several times thinking he might slowly drill down, covering the holes with the linoleum rug. At some point in time he installed a hasp lock on a closet, and planned to, or did, place his tools in it. However, he left the closet keys on the premises. Around the end of November, apparently after November 23, the landlord notified the police and turned the tools and equipment over to them. Defendant did not pay any more rent. It is not clear when he last entered the office, but it could have been after November 23, and even after the landlord had removed the equipment. On February 22, 1968, the police arrested defendant. After receiving advice as to his constitutional rights, defendant voluntarily made an oral statement which he reduced to writing.

Among other things which defendant wrote down were these:

Saturday, the 14th . . . I drilled some small holes in the floor of the room. Because of tiredness, fear, and the implications of what I was doing, I stopped and went to sleep.

At this point I think my motives began to change. The actual commencement of my plan made me begin to realize that even if I were to succeed a fugitive life of living off of stolen money would not give the enjoyment of the life of a mathematician however humble a job I might have.

I still had not given up my plan however. I felt I had made a certain investment of time, money, effort and a certain psychological commitment to the concept.

I came back several times thinking I might store the tools in the closet and slowly drill down. . . . My wife came back and my life as bank robber seemed more and more absurd.

[The court then concluded that sufficient evidence supported defendant's attempt conviction.]

. . . Here, there was no direct proof of any actual interception. But it was clearly inferable by the trial judge that defendant became aware that the landlord had resumed control over the office and had turned defendant's equipment and tools over to the police. This was the equivalent of interception.

The inference of this nonvoluntary character of defendant's abandonment was a proper one for the trial judge to draw. . . . However, it would seem that the character of the abandonment in situations of this type, whether it be voluntary (prompted by pangs of conscience or a change of heart) or nonvoluntary (established by inference in the instant case), is not controlling. The relevant factor is the determination of whether the acts of the perpetrator have reached such a stage of advancement that they can be classified as an attempt. Once that attempt is found there can be no exculpatory abandonment. . . . "One of the purposes of the criminal law is to protect society from those who intend to injure it. When it is established that the defendant intended to commit a specific crime and that in carrying out this intention he committed an act that caused harm or sufficient danger of harm,[5] it is immaterial that for some collateral reason he could not complete the intended crime." (*People v. Comodeca*, 52 Cal. 2d 142, 147, 338 P.2d 903, 906).

The order is affirmed.

NOTES AND QUESTIONS

1. Assuming that Staples was otherwise willing to pay for the physical damage done to the apartment, what "harm" had he done (1) to the landlord and (2) to the bank?

2. *Staples* reflects the majority view that once an attempt has been made, the defendant cannot avoid guilt by abandoning his plan to commit the

---

[5] In the instant case defendant's drilling was done without permission and did cause property damage.

underlying offense. What purposes of punishment are served by this rule? See, for example, *State v. Workman,* 90 Wash. 2d 443, 584 P.2d 38 (1978).

3. As with the crime of solicitation discussed earlier, the Model Penal Code allows a defense of "renunciation" of attempts in certain circumstances. Section 5.01(4) provides:

> (4) *Renunciation of Criminal Purpose.* When the actor's conduct would otherwise constitute an attempt under Subsection (1)(b) or (1)(c) of this Section, it is an affirmative defense that he abandoned his effort to commit the crime or otherwise prevented its commission, under circumstances manifesting a complete and voluntary renunciation of his criminal purpose. The establishment of such defense does not, however, affect the liability of an accomplice who did not join in such abandonment or prevention.
>
> Within the meaning of this Article, renunciation of criminal purpose is not voluntary if it is motivated, in whole or in part, by circumstances, not present or apparent at the inception of the actor's course of conduct, which increase the probability of detection or apprehension or which make more difficult the accomplishment of the criminal purpose. Renunciation is not complete if it is motivated by a decision to postpone the criminal conduct until a more advantageous time or to transfer the criminal effort to another but similar objective or victim.

Would the defendant in *Staples* have a renunciation defense under the MPC? What policy considerations (if any) are promoted by recognizing a defense of renunciation in attempt situations?

4. Defendant stabs victim, then calls an ambulance, and stays with her until she is treated. He seeks to claim abandonment as a defense to a charge of attempted second degree murder. What result? See *Ramirez v. State,* 739 P.2d 1214 (Wyo. 1987), noted 24 Land &Water L. Rev. 219 (1989). See generally Hoeber, *The Abandonment Defense to Criminal Attempt and Other Problems of Temporal Individuation,* 74 Cal. L. Rev. 377 (1986); Comment, 26 Am. Crim. L. Rev. 441 (1988). ("A person who was able to complete a crime, but instead abandoned her attempt, cannot be assumed to need deterrence, rehabilitation, or punishment any more than someone who contemplates a crime but does not have the means available to execute it.")

[E] Attempting Inchoate Crimes

The defendant in *Staples* was convicted of attempted burglary. Burglary, at least under its common law definition of breaking and entering a dwelling of another at night with the intent to commit a felony inside, is itself generally understood to be an inchoate crime dealing with preparatory behavior. Burglary initially developed as a specific variety of attempt, aimed at filling perceived defects in the common law of attempt which required that actors come very close to achieving their criminal goals before being liable for attempt. Thus under doctrines like the "last act" test, a person apprehended while breaking into a dwelling with intent to commit a felony therein would not have committed an attempt because his actions would not be sufficiently proximate to the intended felony. See MPC, Comments to § 221.1 at 62–63. On this view, the crime of attempted burglary constitutes a form of "attempt to attempt," a logical absurdity in the eyes of many. See A. Loewy, Criminal Law 223 (2d ed. 1987).

Nevertheless, the *Staples* court joins a host of other courts in permitting convictions for attempted burglary. See, for example, *DeGidio v. State,* N.W.2d 135 (Minn. 1980); *Taylor v. State,* .W.2d 306 (Tex. Crim. App. 1950). See also *People ex rel. Blumke v. Foster,* .Y. 431, 91 N.E.2d 875 (1950) (attempt to possess burglary tools).

Assault, defined as an attempt to batter, is another substantive crime that possesses characteristics of an inchoate offense. The courts have split on the question of whether attempted assault constitutes a crime. In holding against such a crime, the court in *Wilson v. State,* 53 Ga. 205, 206 (1874), noted,

As an assault is itself an attempt to commit a crime, an attempt to make an assault can only be an attempt to attempt to do it, or to state the matter still more definitely, it is to do any act towards doing an act towards the commission of the offense. This is simply absurd. As soon as any act is done towards committing a violent injury on the person of another, the party doing the act is guilty of an assault, and he is not guilty until he has done the act. Yet it is claimed that [defendant] may be guilty of an attempt to make an assault, when, under the law, he must do an act before the attempt is complete. The refinement and metaphysical acumen that can see a tangible idea in the words *an attempt to attempt to act* is too great for practical use. It is like conceiving of the beginning of eternity or the starting place of infinity.

A variety of other courts have upheld convictions for attempted assault. See, for example, *State v. Wilson,* 218 Or. 575, 346 P.2d 115 (1959); *Miller v. State,* 37 Ala. App. 470, 70 So. 2d 811 (1954). With these considerations in mind, reconsider the *McQuirter* case, *supra,* p. 534, which upheld defendant's conviction for "attempt to commit an assault with intent to rape."

[F] Impossibility

PEOPLE V. JAFFE

New York Court of Appeals

185 N.Y. 497, 78 N.E. 169 (1906)

WILLARD BARTLETT, J.

The indictment charged that the defendant on the 6th day of October, 1902, in the county of New York, feloniously received 20 yards of cloth, of the value of 25 cents a yard, belonging to the copartnership of J. W. Goddard &Son, knowing that the said property had been feloniously stolen, taken, and carried away from the owners. It was found under section 550 of the Penal Code, which provides that a person who buys or receives any stolen property knowing the same to have been stolen is guilty of criminally receiving such property. The defendant was convicted of an attempt to commit the crime charged in the indictment. The proof clearly showed, and the district attorney conceded upon the trial, that the goods which the defendant attempted to purchase on October 6, 1901, had lost their character as stolen goods at the time when they were offered to the defendant and when he sought to buy them. In fact the property had been restored to the owners and was wholly within their control and was offered to the defendant by their authority and through their agency. The question presented by this appeal, therefore, is whether upon an indictment for receiving goods, knowing them to have been stolen, the defendant may be convicted of an attempt to commit the crime where it appears without dispute that the property which he sought to receive was not in fact stolen property.

The conviction was sustained by the Appellate Division chiefly upon the authority of the numerous cases in which it has been held that one may be convicted of an attempt to commit a crime notwithstanding the existence of facts unknown to him which would have rendered the complete perpetration of the crime itself impossible. Notably among these are what may be called the pickpocket cases, where, in prosecutions for attempts to commit larceny from the person by pocket picking, it is held not to be necessary to allege or prove that there was anything in the pocket which could be the subject of larceny. . . .

In passing upon the question here presented for our determination, it is important to bear in mind precisely what it was that the defendant attempted to do. He simply made an effort to purchase certain specific pieces of cloth. He believed the cloth to be stolen property, but it was not such in fact. The purchase, therefore, if it had been completely effected, could not constitute the crime of receiving stolen property, knowing it to be stolen, since there could be no such thing as knowledge on the part of the defendant of a nonexistent fact, although there might be a belief on his part that the fact existed. . . . [I]t is a mere truism that there can be no receiving of stolen goods which have not been stolen. . . . It is equally difficult to perceive how there can be an attempt to receive stolen goods, knowing them to have been stolen, when they have not been stolen in fact.

The crucial distinction between the case before us and the pickpocket cases, and others involving the same principle, lies not in the possibility or impossibility of the commission of the crime, but in the fact that, in the present case, the act, which it was doubtless the intent of the defendant to commit, would not have been a crime if it had been consummated. If he had actually paid for the goods which he desired to buy and received them into his possession, he would have committed no offense under section 550 of the Penal Code, because the very definition in that section of the offense of criminally receiving property makes it an essential element of the crime that the accused shall have known the property to have been stolen or wrongfully appropriated in such a manner as to constitute larceny. This knowledge being a material ingredient of the offense it is manifest that it cannot exist unless the property has in fact been stolen or larcenously appropriated. No man can know that to be so which is not so in truth and in fact. He may believe it to be so but belief is not enough under this statute. In the present case it appeared, not only by proof, but by the express concession of the prosecuting officer, that the goods which the defendant intended to purchase had lost their character as stolen goods at the time of the proposed transaction. Hence, no matter what was the motive of the defendant, and no matter what he supposed, he could do no act which was intrinsically adapted to the then present successful perpetration of the crime denounced by this section of the Penal Code, because neither he nor any one in the world could know that the property was stolen property inasmuch as it was not, in fact, stolen property.

In the pickpocket cases the immediate act which the defendant had in contemplation was an act which, if it could have been carried out, would have been criminal, whereas in the present case the immediate act which the defendant had in contemplation (*to wit,* the purchase of the goods which were brought to his place for sale) could not have been criminal under the statute even if the purchase had been completed, because the goods had not, in fact, been stolen, but were, at the time when they were offered to him, in the custody and under the control of the true owners.

If all which an accused person intends to do would, if done, constitute no crime, it cannot be a crime to attempt to do with the same purpose a part of the thing intended. (1 Bishop's Crim. Law [7th Ed.], Sec. 747.) The crime of which the defendant was convicted necessarily consists of three elements: first, the act; second, the intent; and, third, the knowledge of an existing condition. There was proof tending to establish two of these elements, the first and the second, but none to establish the existence of the third. This was knowledge of the stolen character of the property sought to be acquired. There could be no such knowledge. The defendant could not know that the property possessed the character of stolen property when it had not in fact been acquired by theft.

The language used by Ruger, Ch. J. . . . to the effect that "the question whether an attempt to commit a crime has been made is determinable solely by the condition of the actor's mind and his conduct in the attempted consummation of his design," although accurate in those cases, has no application to a case like this, where, if the accused had completed the act which he attempted to do, he would not be guilty of a criminal offense. A particular belief cannot make that a crime which is not so in the absence of such belief. Take, for example, the case of a young man who attempts to vote, and succeeds in casting his vote under the belief that he is but twenty years of age, when he is in fact over twenty-one and a qualified voter. His intent to commit a crime, and his belief that he was committing a crime, would not make him guilty of any offense under these circumstances, although the moral turpitude of the transaction, on his part, would be just as great as it would if he were in fact under age. So, also, in the case of a prosecution under the statute of this state, which makes it rape in the second degree for a man to perpetrate an act of sexual intercourse with a female not his wife under the age of eighteen years. There could be no conviction if it was established upon the trial that the female was in fact over the age of eighteen years, although the defendant believed her to be younger and intended to commit the crime. No matter how reprehensible would be his act in morals, it would not be the act forbidden by this particular statute. "If what a man contemplates doing would not be in law a crime, he could not be said, in point of law, to intend to commit the crime. If he thinks his act will be a crime, this is a mere mistake of his understanding where the law holds it not to be such, his real intent being to do a particular thing. If the thing is not a crime, he does not intend to commit one whatever he may erroneously suppose." (1 Bishop's Crim. Law [7th Ed.] Sec. 742.)

The judgment of the Appellate Division and of the Court of General Sessions must be reversed, and the defendant discharged upon this indictment, as it is manifest that no conviction can be had thereunder. This discharge, however, in no wise affects the right to prosecute the defendant for other offenses of a like character concerning which there is some proof in the record, but which were not charged in the present indictment.

[Chase, J. dissenting opinion omitted.]

PEOPLE v. DLUGASH

Court of Appeals of New York

41 N.Y.2d 725, 363 N.E.2d 1155, 395 N.Y.S.2d 419 (1977)

JASEN, Judge.

The criminal law is of ancient origin, but criminal liability for attempt to commit a crime is comparatively recent. At the root of the concept of attempt liability are the very aims and purposes of penal law. The ultimate issue is whether an individual's intentions and actions, though failing to achieve a manifest and malevolent criminal purpose, constitute a danger to organized society of sufficient magnitude to warrant the imposition of criminal sanctions. Difficulties in theoretical analysis and concomitant debate over very pragmatic questions of blameworthiness appear dramatically in reference to situations where the criminal attempt failed to achieve its purpose solely because the factual or legal context in which the individual acted was not as the actor supposed them to be. Phrased somewhat differently, the concern centers on whether an individual should be liable for an attempt to commit a crime when, unknown to him, it was impossible to successfully complete the crime attempted. For years, serious studies have been made on the subject in an effort to resolve the continuing controversy when, if at all, the impossibility of successfully completing the criminal act should preclude liability for even making the futile attempt. The 1967 revision of the Penal Law approached the impossibility defense to the inchoate crime of attempt in a novel fashion. The statute provides that, if a person engages in conduct which would otherwise constitute an attempt to commit a crime, "it is no defense to a prosecution for such attempt that the crime charged to have been attempted was, under the attendant circumstances, factually or legally impossible of commission, if such crime could have been committed had the attendant circumstances been as such person believed them to be." (Penal Law, § 110.10.) This appeal presents to us, for the first time, a case involving the application of the modern statute. We hold that, under the proof presented by the People at trial, defendant Melvin Dlugash may be held for attempted murder, though the target of the attempt may have already been slain, by the hand of another, when Dlugash made his felonious attempt.

On December 22, 1973, Michael Geller, 25 years old, was found shot to death in the bedroom of his Brooklyn apartment. The body, which had literally been riddled by bullets, was found lying face up on the floor. An autopsy revealed that the victim had been shot in the face and head no less than seven times. Powder burns on the face indicated that the shots had been fired from within one foot of the victim. Four small caliber bullets were recovered from the victim's skull. The victim had also been critically wounded in the chest. . . .

. . . Defendant stated [to police officers] that, on the night of December 21, 1973, he, [Joe] Bush and Geller had been out drinking. Bush had been staying at Geller's apartment and, during the course of the evening, Geller several times demanded that Bush pay $100 towards the rent on the apartment. According to defendant, Bush rejected these demands, telling Geller that "you better shut up or you're going to get a bullet." All three returned to Geller's apartment at approximately midnight, took seats in the bedroom, and continued to drink until sometime between 3:00 and 3:30 in the morning. When Geller again pressed his demand for rent money, Bush drew his .38 caliber pistol, aimed it at Geller and fired three times. Geller fell to the floor. After the passage of a few minutes, perhaps two, perhaps as much as five, defendant walked over to the fallen Geller, drew his .25 caliber pistol, and fired approximately five shots in the victim's head and face. Defendant contended that, by the time he fired the shots, "it looked like Mike Geller was already dead." . . .

After [Detective] Carrasquillo had taken the bulk of the statement, he asked the defendant why he would do such a thing. According to Carrasquillo, the defendant said, "gee, I really don't know." Carrasquillo repeated the question 10 minutes later, but received the same response. After a while, Carrasquillo asked the question for a third time and defendant replied, "Well, gee, I guess it must have been because I was afraid of Joe Bush.". . .

. . . At the trial, . . . the prosecution sought to establish that Geller was still alive at the time defendant shot him. [Two] physicians testified that each of the two chest wounds, for which defendant alleged Bush to be responsible, would have caused death without prompt medical attention. Moreover, the victim would have remained alive until such time as his chest cavity became fully filled with blood. Depending on the circumstances, it might take 5 to 10 minutes for the chest cavity to fill. Neither prosecution witness could state, with medical certainty, that the victim was still alive when, perhaps five minutes after the initial chest wounds were inflicted, the defendant fired at the victim's head.

The defense produced but a single witness, the former Chief Medical Examiner of New York City. This expert stated that, in his view, Geller might have died of the chest wounds "very rapidly" since, in addition to the bleeding, a large bullet going through a lung and the heart would have other adverse medical effects. . . .

The trial court declined to charge the jury, as requested by the prosecution, that defendant could be guilty of murder on the theory that he had aided and abetted the killing of Geller by Bush. Instead, the court submitted only two theories to the jury: that defendant had either intentionally murdered Geller or had attempted to murder Geller.

The jury found the defendant guilty of murder. . . .

On appeal, the Appellate Division reversed the judgment of conviction on the law and dismissed the indictment. The court ruled that "the People failed to prove beyond a reasonable doubt that Geller had been alive at the time he was shot by defendant; defendant's conviction of murder thus cannot stand." Further, the court held that the judgment could not be modified to reflect a conviction for attempted murder because "the uncontradicted evidence is that the defendant, at the time that he fired the five shots into the body of the decedent, believed him to be dead, and . . . there is not a scintilla of evidence to contradict his assertion in that regard." . . .

Preliminarily, we state our agreement with the Appellate Division that the evidence did not establish, beyond a reasonable doubt, that Geller was alive at the time defendant fired into his body. To sustain a homicide conviction, it must be established, beyond a reasonable doubt, that the defendant caused the death of another person. . . . While the defendant admitted firing five shots at the victim approximately two to five minutes after Bush had fired three times, all three medical expert witnesses testified that they could not, with any degree of medical certainty, state whether the victim had been alive at the time the latter shots were fired by the defendant. Thus, the People failed to prove beyond a reasonable doubt that the victim had been alive at the time he was shot by the defendant. . . .

* * *

[W]e must now decide whether, under the evidence presented, the defendant may be held for attempted murder, though someone else perhaps succeeded in killing the victim.

* * *

The most intriguing attempt cases are those where the attempt to commit a crime was unsuccessful due to mistakes of fact or law on the part of the would-be criminal. A general rule developed in most American jurisdictions that legal impossibility is a good defense but factual impossibility is not. . . . Thus, for example, it was held that defendants who shot at a stuffed deer did not attempt to take a deer out of season, even though they believed the dummy to be a live animal. The court stated that there was no criminal attempt because it was no crime to "take" a stuffed deer, and it is no crime to attempt to do that which is legal. *(State v. Guffey,* 262 S.W.2d 152 [Mo. App.]; see, also, *State v. Taylor,* 345 Mo. 325, 133 S.W.2d 336 [no liability for attempt to bribe a juror where person bribed was not, in fact, a juror].) These cases are illustrative of legal impossibility. . . .

On the other hand, factual impossibility was no defense. For example, a man was held liable for attempted murder when he shot into the room in which his target usually slept and, fortuitously, the target was sleeping elsewhere in the house that night. (*State v. Mitchell,* 170 Mo. 633, 71 S.W. 175.) Although one bullet struck the target's customary pillow, attainment of the criminal objective was factually impossible. . . . On the same view, it was held that men who had sexual intercourse with a woman, with the belief that she was alive and did not consent to the intercourse, could be charged for attempted rape when the woman had, in fact, died from an unrelated ailment prior to the acts of intercourse. (*United States v. Thomas,* 13 U.S.C.M.A. 278.)

* * *

As can be seen from even this abbreviated discussion, the distinction between "factual" and "legal" impossibility was a nice one indeed and the courts tended to place a greater value on legal form than on any substantive danger the defendant's actions posed for society. The approach of the draftsmen of the Model Penal Code [Section 5.01(1)] was to eliminate the defense of impossibility in virtually all situations. Under the code provision, to constitute an attempt, it is still necessary that the result intended or desired by the actor constitute a crime. However, the code suggested a fundamental change to shift the locus of analysis to the actor's mental frame of reference and away from undue dependence upon external considerations. The basic premise of the code provision is that what was in the actor's own mind should be the standard for determining his dangerousness to society and, hence, his liability for attempted criminal conduct. . . .

In the belief that neither of the two branches of the traditional impossibility arguments detracts from the offender's moral culpability . . . , the Legislature substantially carried the [MPC] treatment of impossibility into the 1967 revision of the Penal Law. . . . Thus, a person is guilty of an attempt when, with intent to commit a crime, he engages in conduct which tends to effect the commission of such crime. (Penal Law, § 110.00.) It is no defense that, under the attendant circumstances, the crime was factually or legally impossible of commission, "if such crime could have been committed had the attendant circumstances been as such person believed them to be." (Penal Law, § 110.10.) Thus, if defendant believed the victim to be alive at the time of the shooting, it is no defense to the charge of attempted murder that the victim may have been dead.

Turning to the facts of the case before us, we believe that there is sufficient evidence in the record from which the jury could conclude that the defendant believed Geller to be alive at the time defendant fired shots into Geller's head. Defendant admitted firing five shots at a most vital part of the victim's anatomy from virtually point blank range. Although defendant contended that the victim had already been grievously wounded by another, from the defendant's admitted actions, the jury could conclude that the defendant's purpose and intention was to administer the coup de grace. . . .

* * *

The jury convicted the defendant of murder. Necessarily, they found that defendant intended to kill a live human being. Subsumed within this finding is the conclusion that defendant acted in the belief that Geller was alive. Thus, there is no need for additional fact findings by a jury. Although it was not established beyond a reasonable doubt that Geller was, in fact, alive, such is no defense to attempted murder since a murder would have been committed "had the attendant circumstances been as [defendant] believed them to be."

(Penal Law, § 110.10.) The jury necessarily found that defendant believed Geller to be alive when defendant shot at him.

The Appellate Division erred in not modifying the judgment to reflect a conviction for the lesser included offense of attempted murder. . . .

NOTES AND QUESTIONS

1. Is *Jaffe* soundly decided? How is that case different from the cases that approve convictions for attempting to pick empty pockets? For a case strikingly similar to *Jaffe* that nevertheless sustains a conviction for attempting to receive stolen property that is not really stolen but is only believed to be so by the defendant, see *People v. Rojas,* 55 Cal. 2d 252, 358 P.2d 921 (1961).

2. If the New York statutes had not been amended to reflect the MPC approach, how would *Dlugash* be resolved under *Jaffe* and its common law progeny noted by the Dlugash court? Would *Dlugash* be a "legal" impossibility case a`la the *Guffey* case (no criminal attempt to shoot a stuffed deer out of season) or a "factual" impossibility case a`la the *Thomas* case (defendant commits attempted rape when having sexual relations with a dead woman whom he believes is alive but unconscious and thus unable to consent)? What is the supposed distinction between *Guffey* and *Thomas?* Does it make sense to determine outcomes in terms of the distinction?

Is the "impossibility" problem simply a matter of semantics? Consider the following remark: "All attempts involve impossibility: that is why they are attempts." Alexander, *Inculpatory and Exculpatory Mistakes and the Fact/Law Distinction: An Essay in Memory of Michael Bayles,* 12 Law &Phil. 33, 45 (1993).

3. Suppose that on April 1, X endeavors to pick an empty pocket. On the previous day, March 31, the legislature, unbeknownst to X, repeals the long-standing pickpocketing statute rendering such conduct legally permissible as of March 31. Does X attempt a crime under the common law impossibility cases? Under § 5.01 of the Model Penal Code? As a policy matter, should X be guilty of attempted pickpocketing?

4. Suppose a person attempts to kill by invoking a divine curse upon the intended victim. Assuming that the invoker fully believes and desires that the curse will result in the death of the cursed victim, is he or she guilty of attempted murder? Consider § 5.05(2) of the Model Penal Code in this book's Appendix.

UNITED STATES v. OVIEDO

United States Court of Appeals, Fifth Circuit

525 F.2d 881 (1976)

DYER, Circuit Judge.

Oviedo appeals from a judgment of conviction for the attempted distribution of heroin . . . Oviedo contends that under the facts of this case, he is not guilty of any criminal offense. We agree and reverse.

Oviedo was contacted by an undercover agent, who desired to purchase narcotics. Arrangements were made for the sale of one pound of heroin. The agent met Oviedo at the appointed time and place. Oviedo transferred the substance to the agent, and asked for his money in return. However, the agent informed Oviedo that he would first have to test the substance. A field test was performed with a positive result. Oviedo was placed under arrest.

Subsequent to the arrest, a search warrant was issued for Oviedo's residence. When the search was executed, two pounds of a similar substance was found hidden in a television set. Up to this point, the case appeared unexceptional.

A chemical analysis was performed upon the substances seized, revealing that the substances were not in fact heroin, but rather procaine hydrochloride, an uncontrolled substance.[2] Since any attempt to prosecute for distribution of heroin would have been futile, the defendant was charged with an attempt to distribute heroin.

At trial, Oviedo took the stand and stated that he knew the substance was not heroin, and that he, upon suggestion of his cohorts, was merely attempting to "rip off" the agent. It was, in his view, an easy way to pocket a few thousand dollars.

The court instructed the jury that they could find Oviedo guilty of attempted distribution if he delivered the substance thinking it to be heroin. The jury rejected Oviedo's claimed knowledge of the true nature of the substance, and returned a verdict of guilty. Although Oviedo argues on appeal that there was insufficient evidence to establish that he thought the substance was heroin, this contention is without merit.[3] We thus take as fact Oviedo's belief that the substance was heroin.

The facts before us are therefore simple—Oviedo sold a substance he thought to be heroin, which in reality was an uncontrolled substance. The legal question before us is likewise simple—are these combined acts and intent cognizable as a criminal attempt. . . . The answer, however, is not so simple.

---

[2] Although not an opium derivative, procaine hydrochloride will give a positive reaction to the Marquis Reagent Field Test.

[3] The fact that the procaine was secreted inside a television set, together with the discussions between Oviedo and the undercover agent, lead to the reasonable inference that Oviedo thought the substance to be heroin, and support the jury's conclusion.

Oviedo and the government both agree the resolution of this case rests in an analysis of the doctrines of legal and factual impossibility as defenses to a criminal attempt. . . .

These definitions are not particularly helpful here, for they do nothing more than provide a different focus for the analysis. In one sense, the impossibility involved here might be deemed legal, for those acts which Oviedo set in motion, the transfer of the substance in his possession, were not a crime. In another sense, the impossibility is factual, for the *objective* of Oviedo, the sale of heroin, was proscribed by law, and failed only because of a circumstance unknown to Oviedo.

* * *

When the defendant sells a substance which is actually heroin, it is reasonable to infer that he knew the physical nature of the substance, and to place on him the burden of dispelling that inference. However, if we convict the defendant of attempting to sell heroin for the sale of a non-narcotic substance, we eliminate an objective element that has major evidentiary significance and we increase the risk of mistaken conclusions that the defendant believed the goods were narcotics.[11]

Thus, we demand that in order for a defendant to be guilty of a criminal attempt, the objective acts performed, without any reliance on the accompanying *mens rea*, mark the defendant's conduct as criminal in nature. The acts should be unique rather than so commonplace that they are engaged in by persons not in violation of the law.

Here we have only two objective facts. First, Oviedo told the agent that the substance he was selling was heroin, and second, portions of the substance were concealed in a television set. If another objective fact were present, if the substance were heroin, we would have a strong objective basis for the determination of criminal intent and conduct consistent and supportive of that intent. The test set out above would be met, and, absent a delivery, the criminal attempt would be established. But when this objective basis for the determination of intent is removed, when the substance is not heroin, the conduct becomes ambivalent, and we are left with a sufficiency-of-the-evidence determination of intent rejected in the preparation—attempt dichotomy. We cannot conclude that the objective acts of Oviedo apart from any indirect evidence of intent mark his conduct as criminal in nature. Rather, those acts are consistent with a noncriminal enterprise. Therefore, we will not allow the

---

[11] Enker, *Impossibility in Criminal Attempts—Legality and the Legal Process,* 53 Minn. L.R. 665, 680 (1969).

> *Mens rea* is within one's control but, as already seen, it is not subject to direct proof. More importantly, perhaps, it is not subject to direct refutation either. It is the subject of inference and speculation. The act requirement with its relative fixedness, its greater visibility and difficulty of fabrication, serves to provide additional security and predictability by limiting the scope of the criminal law to those who have engaged in conduct that is itself objectively forbidden and objectively verifiable. Security from officially imposed harm comes not only from the knowledge that one's thoughts are pure but that one's acts are similarly pure. So long as a citizen does not engage in forbidden conduct, he has little need to worry about possible erroneous official conclusions about his guilty mind.

Id. at 688.

jury's determination of Oviedo's intent to form the sole basis of a criminal offense.

* * *

Reversed

NOTES AND QUESTIONS

1. Would any objective facts short of the presence of actual heroin have satisfied the *Oviedo* court that an attempted heroin transaction had occurred? Suppose, for example, it could be shown that Oviedo had paid for his pound of "heroin" at a market price more common for heroin than for procaine hydrochloride. Suppose Oviedo's personal diary indicated that he believed the substance to be heroin.

2. How would *Oviedo* be resolved under Section 5.01 of the Model Penal Code?

3. As a policy matter, how does *Oviedo* affect undercover police operations that sometimes supply contraband to suspects in hopes of apprehending them for their subsequent distribution? See, for example, *Hampton v. United States,* 425 U.S. 484 (1976), where a police informant supplied a suspect with heroin that he, in turn, sold to government agents posing as narcotics buyers. If such transactions are to occur, should the law encourage the police to supply substances like procaine hydrochloride rather than actual heroin? Does *Oviedo* encourage the opposite?

4. For a detailed discussion, see Simon, *Mistake and Impossibility, Law and Fact, and Culpability: A Speculative Essay,* 81 J. Crim. L. &Criminology 447 (1990).

[G] Grading

In many jurisdictions, the crime of attempt is punished less severely than the completed crime. Modern statutory systems commonly punish attempts as crimes "one degree below the object crime." LaFave and Scott at 524. Consider whether differentiation of punishment for attempts and completed crimes makes sense.

The Model Penal Code provides an innovative approach. Section 5.05(1) provides,

> *Grading.* Except as otherwise provided in this Section, attempt . . . is a crime] of the same grade and degree as the most serious offense that is attempted. . . . An attempt . . . to commit a [capital crime or a] felony of the first degree is a felony of the second degree.

The Code Comments explain,

> [Section 5.05(1)] departs from the law that preceded promulgation of the Model Code by treating attempt . . . on a parity for purposes of sentence and by determining the grade or degree of the inchoate crime by the gravity of the most serious offense that is its object. . . .

The theory of this grading system may be stated simply. To the extent that sentencing depends upon the antisocial disposition of the actor and the demonstrated need for a corrective sanction, there is likely to be little difference in the gravity of the required measures depending on the consummation or the failure of the plan. It is only when and insofar as the severity of sentence is designed for general deterrent purposes that a distinction on this ground is likely to have reasonable force. It is doubtful, however, that the threat of punishment for the inchoate crime can add significantly to the net deterrent efficacy of the sanction threatened for the substantive offense that is the actor's object, which he, by hypothesis, ignores. Hence, there is a basis for economizing in use of the heaviest and most afflictive sanctions by removing them from the inchoate crimes. The sentencing provisions for second degree felonies, including the provision for extended terms, should certainly suffice to meet whatever danger is presented by the actor.

On the other side of the equation, it is clear that the inchoate crime should not be graded higher than the substantive offense; it is the danger that the actor's conduct may culminate in its commission that justifies creating the inchoate crime.

MPC, Comment to § 5.05 at 489–90.

The same problem arises when judges have the ability to sentence below the statutory maximum for a specific offense, and may consider the actual "harm" inflicted, or sought to be inflicted, by the defendant. For example, in *United States v. Davern,* 920 F.2d 1490 (6th Cir. 1992), the defendant arranged to purchase 500 grams of cocaine, but actually purchased only 85 grams. The trial court sentenced the defendant on the basis of the 500 grams he attempted to purchase. Assuming that the statutory sentencing guidelines either allowed or required this, is this desirable? (The Sixth Circuit, en banc, said yes.)

[H] The Relevance of Resulting Harm

ASWORTH, *BELIEF, INTENT, AND CRIMINAL LIABILITY*

Oxford Essays in Jurisprudence, 3d Series 7, 29–31

(J. Eckelaar and I. Bell eds. 1989)

[O]ne of [the basic principles of criminal liability] is that a person should be liable to criminal conviction only when, and only to the extent that, he or she chose to do a prohibited act or to bring about a prohibited state of affairs or consequence. Thus, respect for individuals as rational choosing beings suggests that in general it is fair to hold them liable for their conduct on the basis of what they believed they were doing, not on the basis of actual facts and circumstances which were not known to them at the time. This will be termed "the belief principle." The same approach . . . suggests that it is fair to hold individuals liable for what they intended to do or to bring about, and not according to whether the intended state of affairs or consequences did occur. This will be termed "the intent principle." Both principles tend to reduce the effect of chance on the incidence and degree of criminal liability, and to heighten the relationship between criminal liability and the defendant's choices. . . .

* * *

. . . The criminal law calls for a certain amount of self-restraint, specifically requiring individuals to restrain themselves from infringing particular protected interests of other citizens and of the state. The general justification for this is to reduce the frequency of violations of those interests. Respect for the rights of each individual as a rational and choosing member of society requires that criminal liability be restricted (most straightforwardly) to cases where D knows what he is doing and intends to produce the prohibited consequence. The corollary is that individuals who lack the required belief or intent should be exculpated. . . . [I]t is also logical and proper to inculpate those who believe they are doing an act which is in fact prohibited and those who intend and try to produce a prohibited consequence, since their moral culpability is no different from that of individuals whose beliefs are correct and whose efforts come to fruition. In legal terms they should be liable to conviction, probably for an attempted crime. In moral terms the justifications for inculpation are the same, in that both the successful and the unsuccessful have done their best to implement their intentions to commit the crime, and it would be wrong to allow the irrationality of chance to interpose itself in a way which rendered the one liable to conviction and the other not. "Anything which is the product of happy or unhappy contingency is no proper object of moral assessment, and no proper determinant of it, either." Individuals have imperfect knowledge and imperfect control over events, and it is therefore fairer to assess their responsibility on the basis of their beliefs and on what they try to do.

If the belief and intent principles are accepted as *prima facie* necessary elements in criminal liability, what role is left to the requirement of harm? It would still be for the legislators to decide what conduct and what consequences are so harmful as to justify the criminal sanction. The extension proposed here is to hold that the harm requirement is fulfilled not merely where the prohibited harm actually occurs, but also where the individual believes he is causing it or tries to cause it. This approach does not necessarily lead to a widening of the ambit of the criminal law. That remains a question for the legislators, and there may be good reason for redirecting the law towards inchoate offences of violence and away from minor property offences. The approach might, on the other hand, have wider implications for the form of the criminal law. The whole classification of offences might be changed, so that there might be no murders, only attempted murders; no rapes, only attempted rapes; no thefts, only attempted thefts; and so on. Such a change would ensure that the labels of offences reflected the moral equivalence between substantive offences and "complete" attempts to commit them. It would, however, be alien to ordinary linguistic usage, would sometimes misrepresent the external events which took place, and would in turn blur the distinction between incomplete and complete attempts. This last consideration suggests that on balance it is preferable to retain the labeling distinction between attempts and substantive offences and to classify complete attempts as attempts, even though in terms of moral culpability they are equivalent to substantive offences.

DUFF, *CRIMINAL ATTEMPTS*

Intention, Agency, and Criminal Liability 184, 186–92 (1990)

Pat and Jill each fire a shot at an intended victim, intending to kill him: Jill succeeds in killing her victim, but Pat does not (her victim moves and the shot misses). Is there any difference between their two cases which can justify the distinction which the law draws between them, such that Jill is sentenced to life imprisonment for murder, whereas Pat receives a lighter sentence for attempted murder?

* * *

What distinguishes Pat's action from Jill's? Not their subjective character: each intends to kill her victim, and does what she thinks will kill him. If we describe their two actions from the agent's own subjective viewpoint, our description will be the same in each case, since such descriptions are independent of what objectively happens. Whether the gun fires or is jammed; whether the shot hits or misses; whether the victim dies or is saved by prompt medical treatment: both Pat and Jill "try to kill," since both intend to cause death by their actions. The "one vital distinction" between them is that in one case "the killing has not been brought off." . . . This distinction makes Jill guilty of murder and Pat guilty only of attempted murder: but it depends on the objective rather than on the subjective aspects of their conduct. Whether an action counts as an attempt to kill depends essentially on its subjective character: but whether that attempt succeeds or fails depends on the objective matter of what actually happens.

* * *

To justify the legal distinction between attempted and completed crimes, we need to show that the objective aspects of the defendant's conduct can make a relevant difference to the moral character of her action, and to her own moral and legal standing as the agent of that action: but how could this be shown?

* * *

. . . I want to look now, however, at some of the . . . moral implications of success or failure in a wrongful action, in particular at those which may be reflected in the agent's first-person response to what he has done or failed to do, to see if these can have any proper relevance to his criminal liability. . . . Suppose that I have, as I believe, succeeded in killing my enemy, and that I am at once overtaken by remorse: I am horrified by what I have done—by the fact that he is now dead, and that I have murdered him. Quite apart from the legal implications of my crime, I must try to face its moral implications: is there any way in which I can atone or make up for my crime;

how can I face other people (his family, his or my friends) as a murderer; how can I live with what I have done? But then, as I approach what I take to be his corpse, I realize that he is not dead—that my shot missed him, but he fainted from shock. "Thank God," I may cry, "I didn't kill him." What does this signify?

In part, of course, it expresses my relief that he is not dead; a relief which I feel for *him*, that he is still alive: it expresses my renewed concern for him and for his good (a concern that was notably lacking when I tried to kill him). But there is more to it than that, since what I feel is not just the relief I might feel on seeing that the victim of an accident has survived: my relief has also, and essentially, to do with the fact that I have not killed him, although I tried to. It is in part, that is to say, a relief I feel for myself, that I did not succeed in becoming a murderer; and though the fact that I shall not now be sentenced to life imprisonment for murder might play a part in this relief, it can also involve a *moral* relief that I do not have his death (my murder of him) on my conscience. I must, of course, still be horrified by my attempt to kill him, although it failed: I still have that on my conscience, and must repent it and accept punishment for it; I must try to find some way of expiating or making up for it. But what my relief expresses is the thought that to have a failed attempt at murder on my conscience is quite different from having an actual murder on my conscience; and it is that thought which concerns me here.

Such a response to my failure is, I think, entirely natural. Now a subjectivist might insist that, however natural, it is irrational, in so far as it goes beyond the relief for my intended victim that he is not dead, and implies that the fact of failure makes a difference to the character or extent of my own guilt. It embodies, she might argue, the same irrational concentration on what actually happens as is embodied in our existing criminal law: but the mere fact of failure *should* make no difference to my understanding of, or to my response to, the moral character of my action. I think, however, that we can find a morally appropriate meaning in this response, and that this meaning is also relevant to the criminal law's response to my action: it can show why the law should distinguish attempted from completed crimes.

The relief which I feel that I have not murdered my victim has to do, in part, with the *finality* of successful actions. If I succeed in murdering my victim, that harm is done—and cannot be undone: I have brought the evil of his death (his murder) into the world, and cannot remove it. The same is true of less serious wrongs. If I have wounded someone, or damaged her property, there is a sense in which that harm may, unlike the harm of murder, be remediable: wounds can be healed, compensation paid, property repaired or replaced, apologies offered. But the damage has still been done and cannot strictly be undone: the history of my involvement as an agent in the world irrevocably includes the fact that I did this harm. If I have failed to cause the harm which I tried to cause, however, I am as it were given a second chance: I can either try again to cause that harm (to kill my victim, for example); or I can repent, and avoid bringing that evil into the world. Of course, even a failed attempt which does no material damage brings about some harm or evil—the evil involved in a deliberate attack on another person's interests. But a failed attack is still crucially incomplete, since there is one kind of harm or evil which it does not bring about, and its failure gives the agent the chance to make sure that it remains incomplete: whereas if the attempt had succeeded, it is too late for the agent to prevent the occurrence of that evil, however much he repents.

On a strictly subjectivist view the moral character of my actions, and my moral standing as their agent, is determined purely by what I intend and try to do; I am as much a murderer, morally speaking, if I try and fail to kill someone as I am if I succeed in killing her. But the response to a failed attempt which I have sketched here suggests that the objective aspects of an action are also crucial to its moral character and to its agent's moral standing; that I define myself as a moral agent by what I actually do or bring about, and not simply by what I try to do. I define myself as a murderer not just by trying to kill someone, but by actually killing him; if my attempt fails, my action has not acquired the fixed and complete character of an act of murder. For actions aim at success: the paradigm of agency is action that achieves its intended result; and our understanding of the moral significance of an action depends on its relationship to that paradigm. A failed attempt falls short of the paradigm of success, and must be seen as an essentially incomplete action: it will not figure in our or the agent's response to it, or in our understanding of what she has become in doing it, in the same way as a successful action does. A failed killer has not become an actual murderer; and though she must be condemned for her attempt, the character of that condemnation is qualified by the fact of her failure.

But why should that condemnation be qualified by the fact of her failure, since she did all that she could to make herself a murderer and can take no moral credit from her failure? Even if our response to a failed attempt properly includes a relief that it failed, why should that make any difference to the moral condemnation, or to the criminal conviction and punishment, to which she should be subjected? The answer must be that the fact of her failure should qualify these responses to her because it matters: it matters to us, and should matter to her, whether her criminal attempt succeeded or failed, just because it matters to us (and should matter to her) whether or not her victim actually suffered the material harm she tried to cause him. For if the fact of her failure is in this way significant, our responses to her should surely aim to reflect its significance; and they can do that only if they distinguish, as the criminal law does distinguish, between success and failure.

One way to explicate this suggestion is through an account of the purposes of criminal convictions and punishments, according to which one of their essential purposes is to express or communicate, both to the criminal and to the whole community, a proper condemnation of his crime which brings out the character and the seriousness of the wrong he has done. . . . Now to follow the subjectivist's advice, and draw no distinction in the criminal law between attempted and completed offences (to convict both the actual and the failed murderer of the same offense, and subject them to the same punishment), would be to say, in effect, that it does not matter to the law whether the attempt to commit a criminal wrong succeeds or not: the same message, the same condemnation, would be communicated to both the successful and the failed murderer. But it does matter to us, and should matter to the agent, whether his attempt succeeded or not; we are, and he should be, relieved if it failed. Surely, then, the law's response to him should itself reflect this; which is what now happens. A conviction and sentence for murder communicates the message "You have wrongfully killed someone, which is the worst crime that you could have committed." A conviction and lighter sentence for attempted murder, however, expresses the different message "You have wrongfully tried to kill someone; but (thank God) you failed"; that message embodies the relief which we feel (and which we hope that the criminal will feel) at her failure.

This is, I think, the best way to justify the distinction which the law actually draws between attempted and completed crimes, though it clearly needs further explanation and argument than I can provide here. It remains true, however, that the distinction makes criminal liability depend, in part, on the objective aspects of a defendant's conduct, thus making it partly a matter of chance or luck; and this conflicts with the deep-rooted principle which underpins subjectivism—that justice requires us to found criminal liability, like moral culpability, on choice rather than on chance. Now that principle is controversial even in moral contexts. But the account I have outlined here still gives it a central place in the criminal law: for the liability of both the successful and the failed murderer still depends on their deliberate choice and attempt to kill someone. The principle is now qualified, however, by the recognition that we cannot entirely separate the objective from the subjective aspects of an agent's action: that the action's objective character, its success or failure, does help to determine its moral character, and should help to structure both the agent's response to what she has done and the responses of others. The would-be killer whose attempt fails has not in fact made herself a murderer; and that fact should matter to her, to us, and to the criminal law.

SCHULHOFER, *HARM AND PUNISHMENT: A CRITIQUE OF EMPHASIS ON THE RESULTS OF CONDUCT IN THE CRIMINAL LAW*

122 U. Pa. L. Rev. 1497, 1514–17 (1974)

A number of commentators have sought to justify the law's emphasis on the occurrence of harm by arguing that moral fault, the touchstone in the retributive grading of offenses, cannot be measured exclusively by an actor's conduct and state of mind. Resort is had to the "largely intuitive judgment" that "[t]he successful criminal and the person who engaged in an unsuccessful attempt are in some sense not of equal culpability."

The argument is troublesome on several levels. Not the least is its basic anti-rationality. A policy so pervasive and important as the law's emphasis upon results might reasonably be expected to stand upon some fairly weighty reasons capable of coherent explanation. Still, conceding that it might be a mistake to insist on a full articulation of the reasons for every social policy, and conceding that intuitive notions, if widely felt, could sometimes be taken as valid answers to a human problem, there nevertheless remains a major difficulty. The "intuitive judgment" as to culpability cannot claim anything approaching widespread appeal. As we attempt to fill out the fact situations upon which the judgment is made, the notion of a difference in culpability seems more and more implausible. For example, suppose that A and B both shoot their wives, intending to kill. The bullets lodge in precisely the same area of the brain in both cases, but while A's wife dies, B's wife is saved by a miraculous feat of surgery. Is A more culpable than B? More to the point, can we say with any confidence that there would be uniform and fairly widespread agreement with the intuitive proposition that A is more culpable than B? Surely not.

The example, moreover, is far too kind to existing law; we might well have supposed quite different conduct by A and B after the shooting. Suppose that A, who intended to kill the time he shot, suddenly decides he has done a terrible thing, immediately calls a hospital for help, has the country's best neurosurgeon flown in from a great distance to perform the operation, and does all else in his power to save his wife. In spite of everything, she dies. B meanwhile does everything possible to prevent his wounded wife from being discovered or treated. But neighbors have heard the shot, the police get her to the hospital in time, and she recovers. Is A still more culpable than B? Insistence that there simply is a difference in culpability will not convince those who neither "feel" this difference nor comprehend the basis of this feeling in others, and this group is altogether too large to be ignored.

Doubts about the soundness of the "intuitive judgment" are in any event only half of the story. The proposition that if A is more culpable than B, he should be punished more severely than B (other things being equal), can be valid only if retribution (in the sense of condemnation of moral fault) is accepted as a legitimate function of the criminal law. And even for those who believe that moral culpability should affect the severity of punishment, it seems far from evident that this particular moral judgment, the judgment that A is more culpable than B, is one deserving of propagation and reinforcement through the office of the criminal law.

Where we are dealing with the notion that it is wrong to steal, or the notion that it is even more wrong to steal by the use of force, it may make sense to use the criminal law for "sharpening . . . the community's sense of right and wrong." Perhaps there is a value in teaching that it is wrong to cause harm, and that those who do are blameworthy. But the proposition that A is more culpable than B says much more than this. It says that of those who commit the same acts, with the same intentions and the same perceptions as to the risks and consequences of their conduct, the one who actually causes harm is more culpable than the one who, for whatever reason, does not. It says, in effect, that the moral quality of an act is determined not only by factors within an actor's knowledge and control, but also by unseen and unseeable circumstances, by the invisible hand of Fate. To stress the role of an uncontrollable Fate in determining our moral accountability for the harms we cause seems an unlikely way to serve the utilitarian objective of preventing harm and the conduct that causes it. But even in strictly retributive terms, it would seem a perversion of a theory conceived out of concern for moral judgments of some moment, to use the criminal law for "teaching" the soundness of a concept of this sort.

One effort to give content to notions of a difference in culpability has been made with respect to crimes based on reckless or negligent conduct. The argument is that an actor who creates a risk "ought to pay if the gamble with the lives of others does not come off," but if his gamble proves successful, he cannot fairly be subjected to the same penalty. In one sense this suggestion may be taken to state simply that the governing test of fair punishment is proportionality to the harm done; in this sense the argument adds nothing to the retaliation theories already considered. But viewed as an independent guide to fairness, the argument seems misconceived. The creation of crimes based on recklessness or negligence must involve a judgment that the advantages of leaving people free to create certain risks are outweighed by the inevitable social costs. Whether varying policy reasons prompt us to subject the underlying conduct, in the absence of a harmful result, to substantial penalties, to only light penalties, or to no penalty at all, the decision is the same—that these risks ought not to be taken. Accordingly, the actor cannot be regarded as morally free to determine for himself whether the danger is worth risking. When viewed in this light, the culpability of the actor must stem from his having taken the forbidden risk, and he cannot claim that fairness requires imposition of a milder penalty simply because the ultimate harm did not materialize.

NOTES AND QUESTIONS

1. As illustrated by the above excerpts, it is controversial whether punishment should be reduced (or denied altogether) for persons who intend or risk harm but by chance avoid causing it. For more discussion of this debate, see Symposium, *Harm versus Culpability: Which Should Be the Organizing Principle of the Criminal Law?* 5 J. Contemp. L. Issues 1–398 (1994); Kadish, *The Criminal Law and the Luck of the Draw,* 84 J. Crim. L. &Crim. 679 (1994); Comment, *The Role of Luck in the Criminal Law,* 142 U. Pa. L. Rev. 2183 (1994).

2. The excerpt from Professor Schulhofer responds to views such as those held by Judge James Fitzjames Stephen, who wrote,

> If two persons are guilty of the very same act of negligence, and if one of them causes thereby a railway accident, involving the death and mutilation of many persons, whereas the other does no injury to anyone, it seems to me that it would be rather pedantic than rational to say that each had committed the same offense, and should be subjected to the same punishment. In one sense each has committed an offense, but the one has had the bad luck to cause a terrible misfortune, and to attract public attention to it, and the other the good fortune to do no harm. Both certainly deserve punishment but it gratifies a natural public feeling to choose out for punishment the one who actually has caused great harm, and the effect in the way of preventing a repetition of the offense is much the same as if both were punished.

Stephen, 3.11.

Is Schulhofer's critique of such a viewpoint convincing? Are there principled reasons for not imposing attempt liability on people who engage in negligent or reckless conduct but who "luck out" and cause no harm?

Consider the following:

NOTE, *CHANCE, FREEDOM AND CRIMINAL LIABILITY*

87 Colum. L. Rev. 125, 137–40 (1987)

The paradigmatic crime involves an intentional act causing harm for a certain defined class of harms. Legal justice requires that, for this class of harms, the intending perpetrator of the harm be held liable. Certain crimes, however, depart from the paradigm—some by reason of the absence of harm, some by the absence of intent.

Inchoate crimes are nonparadigmatic because an intended harm has fortuitously failed to occur. Nevertheless, one element of the paradigmatic crime is present—intent—and therefore, some liability is appropriate. Attempt liability results from the chance absence of one of the two elements of a paradigmatic crime. Conversely, crimes of negligence are nonparadigmatic because, though unintended, a chance harm has occurred. Liability for criminal negligence, then, results from the chance presence of the harm element of the paradigmatic crime.

* * *

Without providing any role for chance in the criminal law, distinctions between paradigmatic and nonparadigmatic crimes are difficult to draw and justify. Once this role is acknowledged, however, a complete topography of criminal liability becomes apparent—a topography that includes and reconciles the insights of both objectivism [theories linking liability to the consequences of criminal acts rather than the criminality of actors] and subjectivism [theories of criminal liability that place preeminent importance on the mental states of actors]. This topography, moreover, suggests an account of the difference in liability that exists between paradigmatic and nonparadigmatic crimes.

The distinction between paradigmatic and nonparadigmatic crimes depends on the realization that chance intrudes into assessments of criminal liability. This distinction itself, however, is not sufficient to explain the corresponding differences in liability between inchoate and consummated crimes and between eventful and uneventful acts of negligence. A sound explanation of these differences in liability must connect the concepts of chance and freedom within a liberal theory of criminal law.

Since both the elements of an intentional act and resulting harm are present in a paradigmatic crime, both subjectivists and objectivists agree that the imposition of criminal liability is appropriate. Imposing liability vindicates the legal interests that the intentional act offended. Moreover, an infringement on the actor's freedom is justified because the act, in causing harm, infringed another's freedom. In nonparadigmatic crimes, however, the value of freedom and other social values do not align. The chance absence of harm in inchoate crimes appears to prevent the justified infringement on the actor's freedom, even though other social values require vindication. The chance presence of harm in criminal negligence appears to justify an infringement on the freedom of the actor by the state, even though the actor has not intentionally offended any social values that would support imposing criminal liability. This conflict not only explains the basis for the conflicting intuitions between subjectivists and objectivists, but also provides the key to understanding and justifying why a lesser degree of liability attaches to nonparadigmatic crimes than paradigmatic ones.

The tension between the values of freedom and other competing social values when harm is absent is highlighted by victimless crimes. The recurring debates over the criminalization or decriminalization of prostitution, drug use, the sale of pornography, abortion, and consensual sexual conduct are always, at bottom, debates over whether one ought to be free to act provided no harm results. Even assuming the wrongfulness of these acts, the fact that no one is harmed militates against criminalization. Preserving other competing social values, however, militates in favor of criminalization. In different parts of the law, this conflict of values is resolved differently.

In the context of harm without intent, the uncontroversial absence of tort liability for uneventful acts of negligence demonstrates the complete dominance of the value of freedom of action over competing social values. Although consequential luck is present in tort liability, the traditional rule of tort law, that a plaintiff cannot win a case without showing that he has suffered some harm or loss, easily adjusts possible chance differences in consequences to differences in liability. The requirement of harm is so pervasive in tort law that the identical conceptual difficulty that plagues the criminal law does not even ripple the placid surface of tort doctrines. The concept of an inchoate tort is contradictory. Two individuals who act equally negligently towards a plaintiff are viewed as utterly different legal creatures when, by chance, harm ensues from the act of one but not from the other—one is not even a possible tort defendant. Because such a high value is placed on freedom of action, without the presence of a harmful act, an otherwise potential defendant is protected from tort liability.

Like tort law, in cases of criminal negligence, the criminal law generally preserves the supremacy of freedom over other social values—only the existence of isolated reckless endangerments statutes disturbs the congruence. In the case of intentional acts that do not cause harm but are accompanied by an intent to cause harm, however, the value of freedom of action yields to an array of competing values that militate in favor of liability and punishment. While a liberal criminal theory can never disregard the value of freedom of action, the criminal law must provide a means of signaling the importance of other competing social values by criminalizing these acts intended to cause harm. Although precluding liability entirely would displace those social values that rationally militate in favor of liability and punishment, to impose a degree of liability equal to the liability attaching to paradigmatic crimes—as objectivism and subjectivism do—would displace the value of freedom from the criminal law. To avoid both extremes and still to resolve this conflict of values, the criminal law attaches a lesser degree of liability to these acts. This difference in liability serves to signal the preservation of the value of freedom in a liberal theory of criminal law on one hand,

and the importance of other competing social values, on the other. Criminal law resolves this conflict by balancing these social values against one another. Such balancing determines the appropriate degree of liability and thereby accounts for the difference in liability between paradigmatic and nonparadigmatic crimes. The habitual appearance of luck in human affairs and the legal effects that luck's appearance entails provide an occasion to consider the weight and importance law accords to the value of freedom.

§ 7.03 CONSPIRACY

[A] Background

Scholars generally agree that the crime of conspiracy initially emerged from a series of statutes enacted during the reign of Edward I in the late 13th and early 14th centuries aimed at those who "conspired" to hinder justice by bringing false claims, tampering with juries, or engaging in other such acts. Until the early 17th century, the writ of conspiracy would lie only where persons acting in concert initiated legal proceedings against an innocent person who was actually indicted and subsequently acquitted. See Burke and Kadish, *Conspiracy* in 1 Encyclopedia of Crime and Justice 232 (1983). However, in 1611 the Court of Star Chamber, in *Poulterers' Case,* 77 Eng. Rep. 813 (K.B. 1611), expanded the reach of conspiracy by upholding a conviction against defendants who falsely accused a "victim" who was never indicted. *Poulterers' Case* thus gave birth to the notion that the gist of conspiracy lies in the agreement to effectuate undesirable consequences rather than in actually effectuating them. Thus understood, conspiracy was no longer logically limited to cases involving the administration of justice. Indeed, later in the 17th century the courts broadened conspiracy to cover agreements to commit any unlawful act. See Sayre, *Criminal Conspiracy,* 35 Harv. L. Rev. 393, 404 (1922).

[1] Rationale of Conspiracy Law

The commentaries to the Model Penal Code explain the rationale of conspiracy in this way:

> It is worthwhile to note preliminarily that conspiracy as an offense has two different aspects, reflecting the different functions it serves in the legal system. In the first place, conspiracy is an inchoate crime, complementing the provisions dealing with attempt and solicitation in reaching preparatory conduct before it has matured into commission of a substantive offense. Second, it is a means of striking against the special danger incident to group activity, facilitating prosecution of the group, and yielding a basis for imposing added penalties when combination is involved.

> As an inchoate crime, conspiracy fixes the point of legal intervention at agreement to commit a crime, or at agreement coupled with an overt act which may, however, be of very small significance. Conspiracy thus reaches further back into preparatory conduct than attempt.

MPC, Commentary to § 5.03 at 387.

The inchoate aspect of the crime of conspiracy is illustrated by *State v. Burleson,* 50 Ill. App. 3d 629, 365 N.E.2d 1162 (1977), in which the court considered the relationship between conspiracy and attempt:

Section 8-2(a) of the Criminal Code of 1961 provides in pertinent part,

A person commits conspiracy when, with intent that an offense be committed, he *agrees* with another to the commission of that offense. No person may be convicted of conspiracy to commit an offense unless an *act in furtherance* of such agreement is alleged and proved to have been committed by him or by a co-conspirator. (Emphasis added)

Ill. Rev. Stat. 1973, ch. 38, par. 8-2(a).

Section 8-4(a) of the Code provides,

A person commits an attempt when, with intent to commit a specific offense, he does any act which constitutes a substantial step toward the commission of that offense.

Ill. Rev. Stat. 1973, ch. 38, par. 8-4(a).

Both of the quoted sections are contained in that part of the Code concerning inchoate or anticipatory offenses. Another of those sections, section 8-5 of the Code, provides that "[n]o person shall be convicted of both the inchoate and the principal offense" (Ill. Rev. Stat. 1973, ch. 38, par 8-5).

In Illinois, in order for a defendant to be convicted for the offense of conspiracy, the State must establish three elements beyond a reasonable doubt: (1) that the defendant intended to commit an offense; (2) that the defendant and another person entered into an agreement to commit the offense; and (3) that one of the co-conspirators committed an act in furtherance of the agreement. [Ill. Rev. Stat. 1973, ch. 38, par. 8-2(a).] In order for a defendant to be convicted for the offense of attempt, the State must only establish two elements beyond a reasonable doubt: (1) that the defendant intended to commit an offense; and (2) that the defendant took a "substantial step" toward committing that offense. [Ill. Rev. Stat. 1973, ch. 38, par. 8-4(a).] In comparing these two sections of our Criminal Code, we note that the conspiracy provision requires a lesser step to fulfill the act requirement, while the attempt provision requires "a substantial step" toward the commission of the offense. In each situation, as in situations involving other inchoate offenses, the law makes possible some preventive action by the police and courts before a defendant has come dangerously close to committing the intended crime. . . .

The Illinois conspiracy statute construed in *Burleson* requires the State to prove "an act in furtherance of the conspiracy" in addition to a showing that the defendant intentionally agreed with another to commit a crime. Similar "overt act" requirements are common in modern statutory revisions at both the state and federal levels. Section 5.03(5) of the Model Penal Code adopts this approach: "No person may be convicted of conspiracy to commit a crime, other than a felony of the first or second degree, unless an overt act in pursuance of such conspiracy is alleged and proved to have been done by him or by a person with whom he conspired." At common law, however, no requirement of an overt act existed; conspiracy was indictable merely upon the formation of the agreement to commit an unlawful act. Some jurisdictions continue to follow the common law approach. See, for example, *Davis v. State,* 485 So. 2d 1055 (Miss. 1986); *State v. Brown,* 486 A.2d 595 (R.I. 1985); *United States v. Shabani,* 115 S. Ct. 382 (1994) (proof of overt act not required to establish violation of federal drug conspiracy statute).

While conspiracy and attempt share similarities as inchoate crimes, the group activity inherent in conspiracy is sometimes thought to create a special danger not present in attempt and other inchoate crime cases that might even transcend the harm entailed in the unlawful object of the conspiracy. Justice Frankfurter expressed the point this way:

> . . . [C]ollective criminal agreement—partnership in crime—presents a greater potential threat to the public than individual delicts. Concerted action both increases the likelihood that the criminal object will be successfully attained and decreases the probability that the individuals involved will depart from their path of criminality. Group association for criminal purpose often, if not normally, makes possible the attainment of ends more complex than those which one criminal could accomplish. Nor is the danger of a conspiratorial group limited to the particular end toward which it embarked. Combination in crime makes more likely the commission of crimes unrelated to the original purpose for which the group was formed. In sum, the danger which a conspiracy generates is not confined to the substantive offense which is the immediate aim of the enterprise.

Callahan v. United States, 364 U.S. 587, 593 (1961).

Such a view led the *Callahan* Court to conclude that conspiracy constitutes a crime separate and distinct from the substantive object crime of the conspiracy. Therefore, the Court permitted cumulative punishment for conspiracy and the completed substantive offense even though such punishment exceeded the maximum penalty allowed for the substantive offense alone.

Similar to the Illinois statute discussed in *Burleson, supra,* Model Penal Code § 1.07(1) generally rejects the Callahan position:

> (1) *Prosecution for Multiple Offenses* . . . When the same conduct of a defendant may establish the commission of more than one offense, the defendant may be prosecuted for each offense. He may not, however, be convicted of more than one offense if:

> * * *

> (b) one offense consists only of a conspiracy or other form of preparation to commit the other. . . .

But see the Commentary to § 5.03 at 390, which permits cumulative sentences for conspiracy and substantive offenses where "the combination [has] criminal objectives that transcend any particular offenses that have been committed in pursuance of its goals."

The notion of conspiracy "transcending" its object offense(s) provided support for the common law doctrine, embraced during the 18th and 19th centuries, which characterized conspiracy as a felony even where the object offense constituted a mere misdemeanor. Even today, defendants in some jurisdictions may be sentenced to a more severe punishment for conspiring than for the actual object offense itself.

On the other hand, as will be discussed *infra* at § 8.02, some varieties of conspiracy doctrine hold that a conspirator is guilty of *all* substantive offenses committed by any co-conspirator so long as the offense(s) is committed in furtherance of the aims of the conspiracy. Complicity for the substantive offense(s) exists by virtue of being a part of the conspiracy and not necessarily because of any actual aid or encouragement rendered.

[2] Procedural Aspects

In addition to its unique substantive dimensions, a variety of procedural doctrines have grown up around conspiracy. One of these is the so-called "co-conspirator exception" to the hearsay rule. In normal evidence law, A could not testify at C's trial that B told A, outside the courtroom, that B saw C commit a crime. Such evidence is hearsay and is inadmissible against C (unless falling within one of the numerous exceptions to the hearsay rule) because he cannot effectively rebut the validity of the testimony since he was not present when the statement was made and thus cannot contest the validity of the remembered version. If B is C's co-conspirator, however, the co-conspirator exception to the hearsay rule allows the testimony to be introduced against C if B's statement was made during and in furtherance of the conspiracy. The hearsay evidence is admissible only if a preponderance of independent evidence establishes that a conspiracy existed between the defendant and the co-conspirator. However, the courts have not required that initial proof of the conspiracy be established in a hearing free of hearsay. Instead they have permitted the prosecution to present all its evidence, including co-conspirator hearsay, subject to an instruction to the jury that such evidence is not to be considered unless independent proof establishes that the statement was made in the course and in furtherance of a conspiracy between the defendant and the co-conspirator declarant. See *United States v. Vinson,* 606 F.2d 149 (6th Cir. 1979). For discussions and critiques of the co-conspirator exception, see Levie, *Hearsay and Conspiracy,* 52 Mich. L. Rev. 1159 (1954); Note, 25 U. Chi. L. Rev. 530 (1958). See also Morgan, *The Rationale of Vicarious Admissions,* 42 Harv. L Rev. 461 (1929).

Further procedural implications are generated by the "overt act" requirement. As mentioned above, some courts and a number of state statutes require an overt act as an indication that a conspiracy is indeed underway. Although such a requirement appears to protect the defendant, it is an even greater boon for the prosecutor. First, the courts have held that a conspiracy could be prosecuted in any jurisdiction in which an overt act, however minor, had occurred. Thus, *in Smith v. United States,* 92 F.2d 460 (9th Cir. 1937), defendant telephoned a co-conspirator in Los Angeles from Hawaii. Because the phone call constituted an "overt act" in furtherance of the conspiracy, the court held that venue properly existed in the United States District for Southern California, although the majority of the activity had occurred elsewhere, and although defendant had never been in that part of the United States.

A second use of the overt act is to prolong the conspiracy for purposes of the statute of limitations. Thus, if A and B agree, in 1978, to commit a certain crime, and no overt act is required for conspiracy, then a five-year statute of limitations would begin to run from the time of the agreement and would expire in 1983. If, however, an overt act is required and B, in 1980, commits such an act in furtherance of the conspiracy, the statute will not expire until 1985. Because the overt act requirement can be met by virtually any act (certainly by a far less substantial step toward the criminal objective than is required for the crime of attempt, see § 7.02[B], *supra*), the overt act doctrine provides prosecutors broad control over the direction and timing of conspiracy prosecutions.

A final procedural advantage to the prosecution lies in the tradition of joining all the several co-conspirators in a single trial. Among other disadvantages, an individual defendant may face greatly enhanced risks of conviction through joinder, particularly if some of his co-defendants are clearly guilty and perceived by the jury to be dangerous. In any event, in complicated trials with many defendants, juries may have trouble keeping separate evidence and instructions pertaining to the individual liability of each defendant.

These and other facets of conspiracy have rendered its continued status as a criminal offense controversial. Justice Jackson's famous critique, in his concurring opinion in *Krulewitch v. United States,* 336 U.S. 440, 445–54 (1949), voiced these concerns:

> This case illustrates a present drift in the federal law of conspiracy which warrants some further comment because it is characteristic of the long evolution of that elastic, sprawling and pervasive offense. Its history exemplifies the "tendency of a principle to expand itself to the limit of its logic." The unavailing protests of courts against the growing habit to indict for conspiracy in lieu of prosecuting for the substantive offense itself, or in addition thereto, suggests that loose practice as to this offense constitutes a serious threat to fairness in our administration of justice.
>
> The modern crime of conspiracy is so vague that it almost defies definition. Despite certain elementary and essential elements, it also, chameleon-like, takes on a special coloration from each of the many independent offenses on which it may be overlaid. It is always "predominantly mental in composition" because it consists primarily of a meeting of minds and an intent.

* * *

> . . . It is not intended to question that the basic conspiracy principle has some place in modern criminal law, because to unite, back of a criminal purpose, the strength, opportunities and resources of many is obviously more dangerous and more difficult to police than the efforts of a lone wrongdoer. It also may be trivialized, as here, where the conspiracy consists of the concert of a loathsome panderer and a prostitute to go from New York to Florida to ply their trade and it would appear that a simple Mann Act prosecution would vindicate the majesty of federal law. However, even when appropriately invoked, the looseness and pliability of the doctrine present

inherent dangers which should be in the background of judicial thought wherever it is sought to extend the doctrine to meet the exigencies of a particular case.

Conspiracy in federal law aggravates the degree of crime over that of unconcerted offending. The act of confederating to commit a misdemeanor, followed by even an innocent overt act in its execution, is a felony and is such even if the misdemeanor is never consummated. The more radical proposition also is well-established that at common law and under some statutes a combination may be a criminal conspiracy even if it contemplates only acts which are not crimes at all when perpetrated by an individual or by many acting severally.

Thus the conspiracy doctrine will incriminate persons on the fringe of offending who would not be guilty of aiding and abetting or of becoming an accessory, for those charges only lie when an act which is a crime has actually been committed.

Attribution of criminality to a confederation which contemplates no act that would be criminal if carried out by any one of the conspirators is a practice peculiar to Anglo-American law. "There can be little doubt that this wide definition of the crime of conspiracy originates in the criminal equity administered in the Star Chamber." In fact, we are advised that "The modern crime of conspiracy is almost entirely the result of the manner in which conspiracy was treated by the court of Star Chamber." The doctrine does not commend itself to jurists of civil-law countries, despite universal recognition than an organized society must have legal weapons for combating organized criminality. Most other countries have devised what they consider more discriminating principles upon which to prosecute criminal gangs, secret associations and subversive syndicates.

Of course, it is for prosecutors rather than courts to determine when to use a scatter-gun to bring down the defendant, but there are procedural advantages from using it which add to the danger of unguarded extension of the concept.

An accused, under the Sixth Amendment, has the right to trial "by an impartial jury of the State and district wherein the crime shall have been committed." The leverage of a conspiracy charge lifts this limitation from the prosecution and reduces its protection to a phantom, for the crime is considered so vagrant as to have been committed in any district where any one of the conspirators did any one of the acts, however innocent, intended to accomplish its object. The Government may, and often does, compel one to defend at a great distance from any place he ever did any act because some accused confederate did some trivial and by itself innocent act in the chosen district. Circumstances may even enable the prosecution to fix the place of trial in Washington, D.C., where a defendant may lawfully be put to trial before a jury partly or even wholly made up of employees of the Government that accuses him. . . .

When the trial starts, the accused feels the full impact of the conspiracy strategy. Strictly, the prosecution should first establish *prima facie* the conspiracy and identify the conspirators, after which evidence of acts and declarations of each in the course of its execution are admissible against all. But the order of proof of so sprawling a charge is difficult for a judge to control. As a practical matter, the accused often is confronted with a hodgepodge of acts and statements by others which he may never have authorized or intended or even known about, but which help to persuade the jury of existence of the conspiracy itself. In other words, a conspiracy often is proved by evidence that is admissible only upon assumption that conspiracy existed. The naive assumption that prejudicial effects can be overcome by instructions to the jury, . . . all practicing lawyers know to be unmitigated fiction. . . .

A co-defendant in a conspiracy trial occupies an uneasy seat. There generally will be evidence of wrongdoing by somebody. It is difficult for the individual to make his own case stand on its own merits in the minds of jurors who are ready to believe that birds of a feather are flocked together. If he is silent, he is taken to admit it and if, as often happens, co-defendants can be prodded into accusing or contradicting each other, they convict each other. There are many practical difficulties in defending against a charge of conspiracy which I will not enumerate.

On the other hand, many strenuously argue that conspiracy charges, particularly in the federal system, are essential in fighting the intricate networks of organized crime and that charges based on the substantive counts are infinitely harder to prove because they require evidence relating to a specific event rather than of a general agreement or acquiescence. See Blakey, *Aspects of the Evidence Gathering Process in Organized Crime Cases: A Preliminary Analysis* in Task Force Report: Organized Crime 80 (1967). Cf. Wessel, *The Conspiracy Charge as a Weapon Against Organized Crime,* 38 Notre Dame Lawyer 689 (1963). Indeed, in 1970 Congress expanded the power of the federal government to regulate criminal enterprises by enacting the Racketeer Influenced and Corrupt Organizations Act, popularly known as RICO, 18 U.S.C. § § 1961 *et seq.,* aspects of which are considered *infra* at § 7.03[H].

These criticisms and defenses of conspiracy law should be kept in mind as we move through the elements of the crime. In particular, note whether the defendants could have been charged with any other crime, either completed or attempted, since one major explanation of conspiracy is the need to reach defendants who otherwise could not be prosecuted at all. Note also whether in a particular instance conspiracy is utilized as an inchoate offense or as means of addressing the enhanced danger of group criminality.

[B] Conspiratorial Objectives

As alluded to by Justice Jackson in his *Krulewitch* opinion, at common law persons could be guilty of conspiracy even though their contemplated acts were not themselves crimes. During the Star Chamber era, the courts broadened the crime of conspiracy to cover any combination intended to do injury to others. The principle that it could be a crime for several persons to agree to do that which, if done separately, would not be a crime, appears to have originated in *Starling's Case,* 82 Eng. Rep. 1039 (1664). While applied in a variety of contexts, the rule was used in both England (during the 18th century) and in America (during the 19th and early 20th centuries) to restrain the organization of workers. See Bryan, The Development of the English Law of Conspiracy 115–58 (1909); Gilles, The Law of Criminal Conspiracy 146–51 (1981). See, for example, *Rex v. Eccles,* 1 Leach 275, 168 E.R. 240 (1783), in which Lord Mansfield explained that "every man may work at what price he pleases, but a combination not to work under certain prices is an indictable offense." Other manifestations of this rule are reflected in cases such as *Shaw v. Director of Public Prosecutions, supra,* p. 149. See also *Commonwealth v. Donoghue,* 250 Ky. 343, 63 S.W.2d 3 (1933), where the court upheld an indictment for conspiracy to commit the noncriminal offense of charging usurious interest. The *Donoghue* doctrine subsequently has been legislatively rejected. See Ky. Rev. Stat. Ann. § 506.040 (Baldwin 1994) (agreement to commit a "crime" essential for conspiracy).

The Model Penal Code reflects the clear modern trend in rejecting the broad common law standard by requiring that the object of a conspiracy must itself be a crime.

Section 5.03. Criminal Conspiracy.

(1) *Definition of Conspiracy.* A person is guilty of conspiracy with another person or persons to commit a crime if with the purpose of promoting or facilitating its commission he:

(a) agrees with such other person or persons that they or one or more of them will engage in conduct which constitutes such crime or an attempt or solicitation to commit such crime; or

(b) agrees to aid such other person or persons in the planning or commission of such crime or of an attempt or solicitation to commit such a crime.

Many states have adopted definitions similar to the MPC. See, for example, Neb. Rev. Stat. § 28–202 (Reissue 1985); Wash. Rev. Code § 9A.28.040 (1988).

[C] The *Actus Reus*

[1] The Agreement

WENIGER V. UNITED STATES

United States Court of Appeals, Ninth Circuit

47 F.2d 692 (1931)

Before RUDKIN and WILBUR, Circuit Judges, and JAMES, District Judge.

JAMES, District Judge.

Appellants were charged by the indictment in the District Court with having engaged in a conspiracy to violate the National Prohibition Act. Conviction of the offense was followed by judgments of imprisonment. During all of the time that the alleged conspiracy continued, appellant Weniger was the sheriff of the county of Shoshone, in the state of Idaho, and appellant Bloom was a deputy sheriff in the same county. The alleged conspiracy had to do with the selling and dealing in intoxicating liquor in the village of Mullan, which village contained a population of about 3,000 inhabitants and is located seven miles from Wallace, the county seat of Shoshone county, where the sheriff had his office. The deputy Bloom lived in the village of Mullan.

A number of other persons were included as defendants and convicted of the offense charged. Among the latter were persons who had served as members of the board of trustees and police officers of the village. None of the latter appealed from the judgments.

It was the contention of the prosecution, and the evidence shown in the record seems to establish the truth of the charge in that respect, that the city officials of the village of Mullan purposely encouraged and connived at the unlawful sale of liquor within the town by collecting monthly license charges and contributions of money from persons dealing in liquor, in order that the revenue for village upkeep and improvements might be augmented. It was shown, without question, that the city officials did agree that in consideration of the payment of license fees and contributions from liquor sellers, the business of the latter would not be interfered with. It matters not that the ordinances imposing a license tax, as adopted by the board of trustees, might have been within the power of the board to enact. Where the underlying purpose was to use the same in promoting the business of liquor selling in violation of the National Prohibition Act, such purpose, and the conduct of the officers pursuant thereto, would establish the truth of the charge made by the indictment as against the persons so involved.

. . . It is not claimed, nor was it shown, that either of appellants connived with the board of trustees or other village officers in arranging for the collection of the license charges and the money contributions which were collected. This being true, it was necessary that the government show by some substantial evidence the participation by appellants in other ways in the unlawful scheme.

The crime of conspiracy . . . consists in the combining or confederating of two or more persons with the purpose of committing a public offense. It is distinct from the offense intended to be accomplished as a result of the conspiracy and is complete upon the forming of the criminal agreement and the performing of at least one overt act in furtherance of the unlawful design.

The failure of a person to prevent the carrying out of a conspiracy, even though he has the power so to do, will not make him guilty of the offense without further proof that he has in some affirmative way consented to be a party thereto. Neither will the commission of an overt act, though unlawful in itself, be enough to show that the actor was a party to the conspiracy. The law requires proof of the common and unlawful design and the knowing participation therein of the persons charged as conspirators before a conviction is justified.

The United States attorney relies largely upon a showing of inaction on the part of the sheriff of the county and his deputy in enforcing the liquor laws as establishing connection of these appellants with the conspiracy charged.

There existed at the time a law in the state of Idaho prohibiting the sale of intoxicating liquor, and no doubt it was the duty of the sheriff to enforce that law. Apparently he was not disposed to do this and apparently, too, this action on his part applied to all parts of his county, and not in particular to the village of Mullan.

* * *

It was shown that appellant Bloom drank whisky at a place kept by one of the witnesses at Mullan on several occasions; that Bloom did not interfere with the selling of liquor; that in 1928 at Christmas time, the federal officers were reported to be making raids in the village and appellant Bloom said to the witness referred to, "You got your car here, get your stuff in the car and get it out of here, get it out of the way." That on or prior to the day of election when county officers were to be voted for, Bloom solicited the aid of the same witness, and the latter donated the use of his car for election purposes. Appellant Weniger was a candidate for reelection at that time. During the political campaign, appellant Weniger, with other persons, had visited the bar kept by the witness. The witness stated that he had served drinks to the companions of Weniger, but he was not certain whether Weniger had partaken of any intoxicating drinks. On another occasion, after the witness had given an affidavit to federal officers respecting the sale of liquor in Mullan, he was asked to visit the office of the sheriff, who there charged him with making beer. The witness in that connection testified as follows:

> And he (Weniger) made several accusations to try and rile me up, and I told him they were false, and we got to talking things over, and he says I was up in that country stooling, that I was helping the Government men out, that I was stooling on these joints around town, and that the companies—well, through the conversation he told me that the heads of the companies made him run these places, leave them run wide open, and finally then finished up, he told me to keep out of them joints. He accused me of just getting out of jail in Montana, and different things like that and he accused me of not being married.

Another witness named Barron, a miner, testified that he gave information to two federal prohibition agents respecting the liquor traffic in Mullan; that on a certain day thereafter he was in Wallace, the county seat, and saw appellant Weniger; that he (the witness) had an altercation with a woman on the street and that Weniger and Bloom arrested him and put him in jail (he later pleaded guilty to a criminal charge); that Johnson and Webb, federal agents, came to the jail and Weniger said to the agents: "I have got your federal stoolpigeon here. What do you mean by it?" The witness stated further that Weniger wanted to know of the federal agents whether the witness was a federal man or not, and that heated words passed between the men, after which Weniger said: "I wish you would stay out of my county, I can look after my county better without your help." At the time he was arrested by Weniger, the witness stated that a notebook was found on his person and that Weniger remarked to him: "You should not do anything like that, go ahead and stool on these people. I will deport you into Canada if you come up here from Canada and try to get smart."

One of the federal agent's testimony in substance corroborated the statements of the witness Barron. The same agent testified that when he was first assigned to that location, he talked with the sheriff Weniger, and told him that he was going to be stationed there and asked him if there would be a chance to get "a little help if a fellow needed it," to which the sheriff had replied, saying "that he had all he could handle without doing anything with prohibition, and that his men," referring to his deputies, were under bond, "that if they did go out with us fellows, we might shoot somebody and he would get in trouble over it." He testified further that he had never received assistance from the sheriff in his enforcement work.

* * *

The case as made here by the evidence of the prosecution can be said to go no further than to establish that the sheriff of Shoshone county felt no interest in, but was opposed to, the enforcement of the National Prohibition Act. The evidence, in our opinion, falls short of showing that the particular conspiracy which was organized by the city officials of the village of Mullan was joined in by these appellants.

The judgments are reversed.

NOTES AND QUESTIONS

1. If the evidence in *Weniger* fell short of establishing a conspiracy between the police (Weniger and Bloom) and the city officials, what about a conspiracy between Weniger and Bloom themselves? Furthermore, could Weniger and Bloom be liable for aiding and abetting the conspiracy among the city officials? Consider the materials on accomplice liability, *infra* at § 8.01.

2. *Weniger* emphasizes the importance of an agreement in the crime of conspiracy. In *United States v. Alvarez,* 610 F.2d 1250, 1255 (5th Cir. 1980), the court further explained:

> A defendant does not join a conspiracy merely by participating in a substantive offense . . . or by associating with persons who are members of a conspiracy. It is hornbook law that the criminalization of conspiracy does not proscribe purely a mental state; the agreement itself is the criminal act, an act in advancement of the intention which each of [the conspirators] has conceived in his mind.... These elements of the conspiratorial offense may of course be shown by circumstantial evidence.

While essential to a conspiracy, an agreement need not be express or formal. A tacit understanding will suffice and various parties may be co-conspirators even though they never deal directly with one another, *United States v. Fincher,* 723 F.2d 862 (11th Cir. 1984), or know each other's identity, *Blumenthal v. United States,* 332 U.S. 539 (1947), so long as they know there is someone acting in the capacity of co-conspirator. Moreover, because conspirators seldom leave direct evidence establishing a "meeting of the minds," the courts have permitted inferences from circumstantial evidence to prove the agreement. Thus, a famous 19th century English jury instruction provides:

> If you find that these two persons pursued by their acts the same object, often by the same means, one performing one part of an act and the other

another part of the same act, so as to complete it, with a view to the attainment of the object which they were pursuing, you will be at liberty to draw the conclusion that they have been engaged in a conspiracy to effect that object.

Regina v. Murphy, 172 Eng. Rep. 502 (1837).

Does such an instruction threaten to negate the requirement that the government prove an agreement? Is it possible for two persons not to be conspirators if they act in concert to achieve the same criminal object? Consider these cases:

   a. A, B, and C, friends, are walking down the street when C collides with D. An argument ensues, and C and D are soon fighting. If A and B assist C, have they conspired to batter D? If C (or, more difficult, A or B) suddenly knocks D down and grabs D's wallet, is there a conspiracy to rob?

   b. A, B, and C are strangers sitting in a bar watching the local football team being beaten by the Outcity Bandits, when D, a resident of Outcity, comes in and begins to deride the local team. A fight ensues in which all four partake. Are A, B, and C conspirators? If D's wallet is taken by one, have all conspired to rob?

   c. A ship originally intended for shrimp fishing is diverted by its captain to pick up marijuana. Several crewmen learn of the diversion but say nothing directly in opposition to the trip. They watch the ship being loaded and continue their duties for the next few days, after which they are arrested and charged with conspiracy to import marijuana. Has the government proved enough to send the case to the jury? See *United States v. DeWeese,* 632 F.2d 1267 (5th Cir. 1980); *United States v. Freeman,* 660 F.2d 1030 (5th Cir. 1981).

One commentator has observed:

   The basic principle that a conspiracy is not established without proof of an agreement has been weakened, or at least obscured, [by] the courts' unfortunate tendency to overemphasize a rule of evidence at the expense of a rule of law. Conspiracy is by nature a clandestine offense. It is improbable that the parties will enter into their illegal agreement openly; it is not necessary, in fact, that all the parties ever have direct contact with one another, or know one another's identity, or even communicate verbally their intention to agree. It is therefore unlikely that the prosecution will be able to prove the formation of the agreement by direct evidence, and the jury must usually infer its existence from the clear co-operation among the parties. But in their zeal to emphasize that the agreement need not be proved directly, the courts sometimes neglect to say that it need be proved at all.

Note, *Developments in the Law—Criminal Conspiracy,* 72 Harv. L. Rev. 920, 933 (1959).

For further discussion of the relationship between the agreement requirement as a rule of law and the evidentiary rule permitting proof of agreement through circumstantial evidence, see Marcus, *Conspiracy: The Criminal in Theory and in Practice,* 65 Geo. L.J. 925, 952–57 (1977); Cousens, *Agreement as an Element in Conspiracy,* 23 Va. L. Rev. 898 (1937).

[2] Parties to the Agreement

STATE v. ST. CHRISTOPHER

Supreme Court of Minnesota

305 Minn. 226, 232 N.W.2d 798 (1975)

ROGOSHESKE, Justice.

Defendant was found guilty by the court, sitting without a jury, of conspiracy to commit murder, and sentenced under the conspiracy conviction to a maximum indeterminate term of 20 years' imprisonment. He contends upon this appeal from the judgment that he was improperly convicted of conspiracy because the evidence shows that the only party with whom he conspired never intended to aid defendant but merely feigned agreement while cooperating with police. . . We affirm the conviction of conspiracy. . . .

The facts in this case are relatively simple. On March 16, 1974, defendant (who formerly was named Marlin Peter Olson but legally changed his name to Daniel St. Christopher) stated to his cousin, Roger Zobel, that he wanted to kill his mother, Mrs. Marlin Olson, and that he wanted Zobel's help. He would pay him $125,000 over the years, money defendant would get from his father after his mother was dead. Zobel, the key witness against defendant at his trial on the charge of conspiracy, testified that at no time did he ever intend to participate in the murder but that he discussed the matter with defendant on that and subsequent occasions and acted as if he intended to participate in the plan. On March 18, Zobel contacted the police and told them of defendant's plan and they later told him to continue to cooperate with defendant. The plan, which became definite in some detail as early as March 20, was for Zobel to go to the Olson farmhouse on Saturday, March 23, when defendant's father was at the weekly livestock auction. Since defendant's mother was Zobel's aunt, Zobel could gain entrance readily. The idea was for Zobel to break her neck, hide her body in his automobile trunk, and then attach bricks to it and throw it in a nearby river after dark. Later it developed that defendant's father might not go to the sale on Saturday, so a plan was developed whereby defendant would feign car trouble, call his father for help, then signal Zobel when the father was on his way. Police followed defendant on Saturday when he left his apartment and observed him make a number of telephone calls. In one of these he called his father and told him he was having car trouble and asked him to come and help him pay the bill. In a call to Zobel, which was taped, defendant told Zobel that his father was coming and that Zobel should proceed with the plan. Shortly thereafter, police arrested defendant.

During the trial defense counsel, in a motion to dismiss, made it clear to the trial court that he felt defendant could not be convicted of conspiracy. He argued that since Zobel never intended to participate in a murder, he did not really conspire with defendant. . . .

There is extensive authority from other jurisdictions which supports defendant's contention. The reasoning employed in these cases was summarized in Fridman, *Mens Rea in Conspiracy,* 19 Modern L. Rev. 276, as follows:

. . . Conspiracy is the agreement of two or more to effect an unlawful purpose. Two people cannot agree unless they both intend to carry out the purpose which is stated to be the object of their combination. Therefore there is no agreement, and consequently no conspiracy, where one of the two never intends to carry out the unlawful purpose.

* * *

We are persuaded not to accept this rule and base our decision on (a) our belief that the rule is unsound, and (b) our belief that the present conspiracy statute, § 609.175, subd. 2, authorizes a conviction in this situation.

(a) One criticism by a number of commentators of the rule followed in the cited cases is that the courts have reached their conclusion by using as a starting point the definition of conspiracy as an agreement between two or more persons, a definition which was framed in cases not involving the issue. As one commentator put it, "if a conspiracy is arbitrarily defined as 'an agreement of intentions and not merely of language (the intentions being unlawful)' the answer to the problem is undoubtedly that where there is no such agreement of intentions then there is no conspiracy." Fridman, *Mens Rea in Conspiracy,* 19 Modern L. Rev. 276, 278. In other words, the basis for the rule is a strict doctrinal approach toward the conception of conspiracy as an agreement in which two or more parties not only objectively indicate their agreement but actually have a meeting of the minds.

Addressing the rule to be applied as a policy issue, a number of commentators have come to the conclusion that there should be no requirement of a meeting of the minds. Thus, Fridman points to cases holding that factual impossibility is no defense to a charge of attempt to commit a crime and argues that, because of close connections between the origins and purposes of the law of conspiracy and of attempt, a similar rule should obtain in conspiracy. Specifically, he argues that "[t]he fact that, unknown to a man who wishes to enter a conspiracy to commit some criminal purpose, the other person has no intention of fulfilling that purpose ought to be irrelevant as long as the first man does intend to fulfill it if he can" because "a man who believes he is conspiring to commit a crime and wishes to conspire to commit a crime has a guilty mind and has done all in his power to plot the commission of an unlawful purpose."

Professor Glanville Williams makes a somewhat similar argument, basing his opinion on the fact that conspiracy, like attempt, is an inchoate crime and that it is the act of conspiring by a defendant which is the decisive element of criminality, for it makes no difference in logic or public policy that the person with whom the defendant conspires is not himself subject to prosecution. Williams, Criminal Law—The General Part, § 157(a).

The draftsmen of the Model Penal Code take a slightly different approach. They recognize that conspiracy is not just an inchoate crime complementing the law of attempt and solicitation but that it is also a means of striking at the special dangers incident to group activity. A.L.I., Model Penal Code (Tent. Draft No. 10, 1960) § 5.03, Comment. In view of that recognition, it is probably not quite as easy to reject the approach taken by the cases cited, yet this is what the draftsmen have done. The provision which accomplishes this, § 5.03(1), reads as follows:

> A person is guilty of conspiracy with another person or persons to commit a crime if with the purpose of promoting or facilitating its commission he:
>
> (a) agrees with such other person or persons that they or one or more of them will engage in conduct which constitutes such crime or an attempt or solicitation to commit such crime; or
>
> (b) agrees to aid such other person or persons in the planning or commission of such crime or of an attempt or solicitation to commit such crime.

In comments explaining this provision, the reporters state as follows:

2. The Conspiratorial Relationship.

Unilateral Approach of the Draft. The definition of the Draft departs from the traditional view of conspiracy as an entirely bilateral or multilateral relationship, the view inherent in the standard formulation cast in terms of "two or more persons" agreeing or combining to commit a crime. Attention is directed instead to each individual's culpability by framing the definition in terms of the conduct which suffices to establish the liability of any given actor, rather than the conduct of a group of which he is charged to be a part—an approach which in this comment we have designated "unilateral."

One consequence of this approach is to make it immaterial to the guilt of a conspirator whose culpability has been established that the person or all of the persons with whom he conspired have not been or cannot be convicted. Present law frequently holds otherwise, reasoning from the definition of conspiracy as an agreement between two or more persons that there must be at least two guilty conspirators or none. The problem arises in a number of contexts.

* * *

Second: Where the person with whom the defendant conspired secretly intends not to go through with the plan. In these cases it is generally held that neither party can be convicted because there was no "agreement" between two persons. Under the unilateral approach of the Draft, the culpable party's guilt would not be affected by the fact that the other party's agreement was feigned. He has conspired, within the meaning of the definition, in the belief that the other party was with him; apart from the issue of entrapment often presented in such cases, his culpability is not decreased by the other's secret intention. True enough, the project's chances of success have not been increased by the agreement; indeed, its doom may have been sealed by this turn of events. But the major basis of conspiratorial liability—the unequivocal evidence of a firm purpose to commit a crime—remains the same. The result would be the same under the Draft if the only co-conspirator established a defense of renunciation under Section 5.03(6).

While both the Advisory Committee and the Council support the Draft upon this point, it should be noted that the Council vote was 14–11, the dissenting members deeming mutual agreement on the part of two or more essential to the concept of conspiracy.

(b) We find the scholarly literature persuasive on this subject.[7] The question is whether this court can take the recommended approach. We think the answer lies in the wording of our statute. The Minnesota statute formerly dealing with the crime of conspiracy read as follows:

When two or more persons shall conspire:

(1) To commit a crime;

* * *

Every such person shall be guilty of a misdemeanor.

This is the most common type of conspiracy statute, and it is understandable that this type of statute lends itself easily to the result reached by the cases because the statute starts with the phrase, "When two or more persons shall conspire."

However, the Minnesota statute as it presently reads omits this phrase and is now phrased in unilateral terms similar to those used in the Model Penal Code. The provision, Minn. St. 609.175, subd. 2, reads in part:

Whoever conspires with another to commit a crime and in furtherance of the conspiracy one or more of the parties does some overt act in furtherance of such conspiracy may be sentenced as follows: . . .

Because of this wording, we hold that the trial court was free to convict defendant of conspiracy under the facts of this case.

* * *

Affirmed.

NOTES AND QUESTIONS

1. In the *St. Christopher* case, why isn't Zobel guilty of conspiracy? In terms of the "extra danger" approach to the crime, hasn't he made St. Christopher more dangerous by his agreement, however feigned? If we were to take this approach, Zobel would have to justify his agreement (see § 9.05[A][3], *infra*), in which case the degree of recklessness or negligence in which he might have acted would become relevant. Consider, in this regard, the liability, either tort

---

[7] An alternative approach would be to say that in cases of this sort the factfinder may find the defendant guilty of attempted conspiracy. This is the approach recommended in Note, 72 Harv. L. Rev. 920, 926 n. 35. The approach is undesirable because it would result in disparate sentences for defendants whose conduct was the same, the length of sentence turning on a fortuity. Thus, if A agreed with B (a policeman who merely feigns agreement) to commit murder, A would be guilty of attempted conspiracy and could receive a maximum of 10 years' imprisonment, whereas if A agreed with C (who does not feign agreement), A could be guilty of conspiracy and could receive a maximum of 20 years' imprisonment. See Minn. St. 609.17, subd. 4(2), and 609.175, subd. 2(2).

or criminal, of government agents who conduct sting operations, during which, to capture the "big fish," they encourage others to engage in unlawful activity. Suppose, for example, the FBI sets up a front operation purchasing stolen cars. To make the front credible, it gives car thieves orders for specific cars. One of the thieves, in the process of stealing a car pursuant to an order, is surprised by the owner and shoots him to death. Should the FBI be liable?

2. The "unilateral" approach to the agreement of conspiracy adopted by the Model Penal Code and embodied in Minnesota statutory law as interpreted by the court in *St. Christopher* represents the modern trend. Some jurisdictions, however, continue to follow the bilateral approach of the common law. *Regle v. State,* 9 Md. App. 346, 351, 264 A.2d 119, 122 (1970), requires that "at least two persons [have] a meeting of the minds—a unity and purpose," thus maintaining the bilateral approach in a unique factual setting. The defendant invited three other persons to participate in an armed robbery. Unbeknownst to the defendant, one of the three was an undercover police officer and another a police informer, both of whom feigned agreement to engage in the robbery. After planning the robbery, obtaining a gun, and driving to the scene of the intended crime, the undercover officer arrested the defendant and the third person, Fields. Neither the undercover officer nor the informer could be charged with conspiracy, leaving defendant and Fields as the only possible conspirators. At trial, defendant established that Fields was insane at the time of the agreement. The court applied the bilateral doctrine and held that the defendant could not have conspired to rob.

> [C]onspiracy is a joint or group offense requiring a concert of free wills, and the union of the minds of at least two persons is a prerequisite to the commission of the offense. The essence of conspiracy is, therefore, a mental confederation involving at least two persons. . . . [W]e hold that where only two persons are implicated in a conspiracy, and one is shown to have been insane at the time the agreement was concluded, and hence totally incapable of committing any crime, there is no punishable criminal conspiracy, the requisite joint criminal intent being absent.

Id. 9 Md. App. at 355, 264 A.2d at 124

3. Which approach, the bilateral or unilateral, is preferable in a case like *Regle?* Do the underlying policies supporting conspiracy as an inchoate crime dictate an answer one way or the other? What about policy considerations related to the special danger of group activity created by the crime of conspiracy?

4. If the defendant in *Regle* is not guilty of conspiracy, of what crime(s) is he guilty? Attempt to rob? What about an attempt to conspire to rob? See *Developments in the Law—Criminal Conspiracy,* 72 Harv. L. Rev. 920, 927 n. 35 (1959); *Hutchinson v. State,* 315 So. 2d 546 (Fla. App. 1975). Would such a crime be analogous to "conspiring to conspire to rob"? In light of the materials on attempting the impossible, § 7.02[F] *supra,* would the defendant have an impossibility defense if he were charged with attempting to conspire? Would the defendant in *Regle* be guilty of the crime of solicitation if such a crime exists in Maryland?

If *Regle* represents an example of solicitation, does it follow that unilateral conspiracy must be rejected? Note that the Model Penal Code embraces both the crime of solicitation and the doctrine of unilateral conspiracy. Compare §§ 5.02 and 5.03.

5. Analogous to the bilateral agreement doctrine, the common law tradition precludes convicting one conspirator if his sole co-conspirator is acquitted of the conspiracy charge. See, for example, *State v. Valladares,* 99 Wash. 2d 663, 664 P.2d 508 (1983). Not surprisingly, the Model Penal Code rejects the common law rule but takes no position regarding the validity of inconsistent verdicts in a joint trial. See Model Penal Code § 5.03, Comment at 402 (1985).

Gebardi v. United States

Supreme Court of the United States

287 U.S. 112 (1932)

Mr. Justice STONE Delivered the Opinion of the Court.

This case is here . . . to review a judgment of conviction for conspiracy to violate the Mann Act. . . . Petitioners, a man and a woman, not then husband and wife, were indicted in the District Court for Northern Illinois, for conspiring together, and with others not named, to transport the woman from one state to another for the purpose of engaging in sexual intercourse with the man. At the trial without a jury there was evidence from which the court could have found that the petitioners had engaged in illicit sexual relations in the course of each of the journeys alleged; that the man purchased the railway tickets for both petitioners for at least one journey; and that in each instance the woman, in advance of the purchase of the tickets, consented to go on the journey and did go on it voluntarily for the specified immoral purpose. There was no evidence supporting the allegation that any other person had conspired. . . .

* * *

Section 2 of the Mann Act . . . , violation of which is charged by the indictment here as the object of the conspiracy, imposes the penalty upon

> Any person who shall knowingly transport or cause to be transported, or aid or assist in obtaining transportation for, or in transporting, in interstate or foreign commerce . . . any woman or girl for the purpose of prostitution or debauchery, or for any other immoral purpose. . . .

Transportation of a woman or girl whether with or without her consent, or causing or aiding it, or furthering it in any of the specified ways, are the acts punished, when done with a purpose which is immoral within the meaning of the law. . . .

The act does not punish the woman for transporting herself; it contemplates two persons—one to transport and the woman or girl to be transported. For the woman to fall within the ban of the statute she must, at the least, "aid or assist" some one else in transporting or in procuring transportation for herself. But such aid and assistance must . . . be more active than mere agreement on her part to the transportation and its immoral purpose. For the statute is drawn to include those cases in which the woman consents to her own transportation. Yet it does not specifically impose any penalty upon her, although it deals in detail with the person by whom she is transported. In applying this criminal statute we cannot infer that the mere acquiescence of the woman transported was intended to be condemned by the general language punishing those who aid and assist the transporter, any more than it has been inferred that the purchase of liquor was to be regarded as an abettor of the illegal sale. . . . The penalties of the statute are too clearly directed against the acts of the transporter as distinguished from the consent of the subject of the transportation.

We come thus to the main question in the case, whether, admitting that the woman by consenting, has not violated the Mann Act, she may be convicted of a conspiracy with the man to violate it. Section 37 of the Criminal Code (18 U.S.C. § 88), punishes a conspiracy by two or more persons "to commit any offense against the United States." The offense which she is charged with conspiring to commit is that perpetrated by the man, for it is not questioned that in transporting her he contravened § 2 of the Mann Act. . . . Hence we must decide whether her concurrence, which was not criminal before the Mann Act, nor punished by it, may, without more, support a conviction under the conspiracy section, enacted many years before.

. . . [A]n agreement to commit an offense may be criminal, though its purpose is to do what some of the conspirators may be free to do alone. Incapacity of one to commit the substantive offense does not necessarily imply that he may with impunity conspire with others who are able to commit it.[5]

. . .

But in this case we are concerned with something more than an agreement between two persons for one of them to commit an offense which the other cannot commit. There is the added element that the offense planned, the criminal object of the conspiracy, involves the agreement of the woman to her transportation by the man, which is the very conspiracy charged.

Congress set out in the Mann Act to deal with cases which frequently, if not normally, involve consent and agreement on the part of the woman to the forbidden transportation. In every case in which she is not intimidated or forced into the transportation, the statute necessarily contemplates her acquiescence. Yet this acquiescence, though an incident of a type of transportation specifically dealt with by the statute, was not made a crime under the Mann Act itself. Of this class of cases we say that the substantive offense contemplated by the statute itself involves the same combination or community of purpose of two persons only which is prosecuted here as conspiracy. If this were the only case covered by the act, it would be within those decisions which hold, consistently with the theory upon which conspiracies are punished, that where it is impossible under any circumstances to commit the

---

[5] So it has been held repeatedly that one not a bankrupt may be held guilty under § 37 of conspiring that a bankrupt shall conceal property from his trustee. . . .

In like manner *Chadwick v. United States,* 141 Fed. 225, sustained the conviction of one not an officer of a national bank for conspiring with an officer to commit a crime which only he could commit.

substantive offense without co-operative action, the preliminary agreement between the same parties to commit the offense is not an indictable conspiracy either at common law . . . or under the federal statute. . . . But criminal transportation under the Mann Act may be effected without the woman's consent as in cases of intimidation or force (with which we are not now concerned). . . . We place . . . [our decision] upon the ground that we perceive in the failure of the Mann Act to condemn the woman's participation in those transportations which are effected with her mere consent, evidence of an affirmative legislative policy to leave her acquiescence unpunished. We think it a necessary implication of that policy that when the Mann Act and the conspiracy statute came to be construed together, as they necessarily would be, the same participation which the former contemplates an inseparable incident of all cases in which the woman is a voluntary agent at all, but does not punish, was not automatically to be made punishable under the latter. It would contravene that policy to hold that the very passage of the Mann Act effected a withdrawal by the conspiracy statute of that immunity which the Mann Act itself confers.

It is not to be supposed that the consent of an unmarried person to adultery with a married person, where the latter alone is guilty of the substantive offense, would render the former an abettor or a conspirator . . . or that the acquiescence of a woman under the age of consent would make her a co-conspirator with the man to commit statutory rape upon herself. . . . The principle, determinative of this case, is the same.

On the evidence before us the woman petitioner has not violated the Mann Act and, we hold, is not guilty of a conspiracy to do so. As there is no proof that the man conspired with anyone else to bring about the transportation, the convictions of both petitioners must be

Reversed.

Mr. Justice CARDOZO Concurs in the Result.

IANNELLI V. UNITED STATES

Supreme Court of the United States

420 U.S. 770 (1975)

Mr. Justice POWELL Delivered the Opinion of the Court.

This case requires the Court to consider Wharton's Rule, a doctrine of criminal law enunciating an exception to the general principle that a conspiracy and the substantive offense that is its immediate end are discrete crimes for which separate sanctions may be imposed.

I

Petitioners were tried under a six-count indictment alleging a variety of federal gambling offenses. Each of the eight petitioners, along with seven unindicted coconspirators and six codefendants, was charged, *inter alia,* with conspiring to violate and violating 18 U.S.C. § 1955, a federal gambling statute making it a crime for five or more persons to conduct, finance, manage, supervise, direct, or own a gambling business prohibited by state law. Each petitioner was convicted of both offenses, and each was sentenced under both the substantive and conspiracy counts. The Court of Appeals for the Third Circuit affirmed, finding that a recognized exception to Wharton's Rule permitted prosecution and punishment for both offenses. . . .

II

Wharton's Rule owes its name to Francis Wharton, whose treatise on criminal law identified the doctrine and its fundamental rationale:

> When to the idea of an offense plurality of agents is logically necessary, conspiracy, which assumes the voluntary accession of a person to a crime of such a character that is aggravated by a plurality of agents, cannot be maintained. . . . In other words, when the law says, "combination between two persons to effect a particular end shall be called, if the end be effected, by a certain name," it is not lawful for the prosecution to call it by some other name; and when the law says, such an offense, *e.g.*, adultery—shall have a certain punishment, it is not lawful for the prosecution to evade this limitation by indicting the offense as conspiracy.

2F. Wharton, Criminal Law § 1604, p. 1862 (12th ed. 1932).[5]

The Rule has been applied by numerous courts, state and federal alike. It also has been recognized by this Court, although we have had no previous occasion carefully to analyze its justification and proper role in federal law.

* * *

Federal courts . . . likewise have disagreed as to the proper application of the recognized "third-party exception," which renders Wharton's Rule inapplicable when the conspiracy involves the cooperation of a greater number of persons than is required for commission of the substantive offense. . . . In the present case, the Third Circuit concluded that the third-party exception permitted prosecution because the conspiracy involved more than the five persons required to commit the substantive offense. . . . The Seventh Circuit reached the opposite result, however, reasoning that since § 1955 also covers gambling activities involving more than five persons, the third-party exception is inapplicable. . . .

---

[5] The current edition of Wharton's treatise states the Rule more simply:

> An agreement by two persons to commit a particular crime cannot be prosecuted as a conspiracy when the crime is of such a nature as to necessarily require the participation of two persons for its commission.

1 R. Anderson, Wharton's Criminal Law and Procedure § 89, p. 191 (1957).

* * *

III

A

Traditionally the law has considered conspiracy and the completed substantive offense to be separate crimes. Conspiracy is an inchoate offense, the essence of which is an agreement to commit an unlawful act. . . .

* * *

B

The historical difference between the conspiracy and its end has led this Court consistently to attribute to Congress "a tacit purpose—in the absence of any inconsistent expression—to maintain a long-established distinction between offenses essentially different, a distinction whose practical importance in the criminal law is not easily overestimated." . . . Wharton's Rule announces an exception to this general principle.

The Rule traces its origin to the decision of the Pennsylvania Supreme Court in *Shannon v. Commonwealth,* 14 Pa. 226 (1850), a case in which the court ordered dismissal of an indictment alleging conspiracy to commit adultery that was brought after the State had failed to obtain conviction for the substantive offense. Prominent among the concerns voiced in the *Shannon* opinion is the possibility that the State could force the defendant to undergo subsequent prosecution for a lesser offense after failing to prove the greater. The *Shannon* court's holding reflects this concern, stating that "where concert is a constituent part of the act to be done, as it is in fornication and adultery, *a party acquitted of the major cannot be indicted of the minor.*" . . . .

* * *

C

. . . [T]he broadly formulated Wharton's Rule does not rest on principles of double jeopardy. . . . Instead, it has current vitality only as a judicial presumption, to be applied in the absence of legislative intent to the contrary. The classic Wharton's Rule offenses—adultery, incest, bigamy, dueling—are crimes that are characterized by the general congruence of the agreement and the completed substantive offense. The parties to the agreement are the only persons who participate in commission of the substantive offense,[15] and the

---

[15] An exception to the Rule generally is thought to apply in the case in which the conspiracy involves more persons than are required for commission of the substantive offense. For example, while the two persons who commit adultery cannot normally be prosecuted both for that offense and for conspiracy to commit it, the third-party exception would permit the conspiracy charge where a "matchmaker"—the third party—had conspired with the principals to encourage commission of the substantive offense.... The rationale supporting this exception appears to be that the addition of a third party enhances the dangers presented by the crime. Thus, it is thought that the legislature would not have intended to preclude punishment for a combination of greater dimension than that required to commit the substantive offense.

immediate consequences of the crime rest on the parties themselves rather than on society at large. . . . Finally, the agreement that attends the substantive offense does not appear likely to pose the distinct kinds of threats to society that the law of conspiracy seeks to avert. It cannot, for example, readily be assumed that an agreement to commit an offense of this nature will produce agreements to engage in a more general pattern of criminal conduct. . . .

The conduct proscribed by § 1955 is significantly different from the offenses to which the Rule traditionally has been applied. Unlike the consequences of the classic Wharton's Rule offenses, the harm attendant upon the commission of the substantive offense is not restricted to the parties to the agreement. Large-scale gambling activities seek to elicit the participation of additional persons—the bettors—who are parties neither to the conspiracy nor to the substantive offense that results from it. Moreover, the parties prosecuted for the conspiracy need not be the same persons who are prosecuted for commission of the substantive offense. An endeavor as complex as a large-scale gambling enterprise might involve persons who have played appreciably different roles, and whose level of culpability varies significantly. It might, therefore, be appropriate to prosecute the owners and organizers of large-scale gambling operations both for the conspiracy and for the substantive offense but to prosecute the lesser participants only for the substantive offense. Nor can it fairly be maintained that agreements to enter into large-scale gambling activities are not likely to generate additional agreements to engage in other criminal endeavors. . . .

Wharton's Rule applies only to offenses that *require* concerted criminal activity, a plurality of criminal agents. In such cases, a closer relationship exists between the conspiracy and the substantive offense because *both* require collective criminal activity. The substantive offense therefore presents some of the same threats that the law of conspiracy normally is thought to guard against, and it cannot automatically be assumed that the Legislature intended the conspiracy and the substantive offense to remain as discrete crimes upon consummation of the latter. Thus, absent legislative intent to the contrary, the Rule supports a presumption that the two merge when the substantive offense is proved.

But a legal principle commands less respect when extended beyond the logic that supports it. In this case, the significant differences in characteristics and consequences of the kinds of offenses that gave rise to Wharton's Rule and the activities proscribed by § 1955 counsel against attributing significant weight to the presumption the Rule erects. . . .

* * *

Affirmed.

NOTES AND QUESTIONS

1. Suppose A and B agree to commit adultery but do not commit that act. Should Wharton's Rule (or anyone else's) preclude convicting A and B of

conspiracy? See Model Penal Code § 5.03, Comment at 483, which argues against immunizing criminal preparation for offenses entailing concert because in such cases law should allow "a basis for preventive intervention by the agencies of law enforcement and for the corrective treatment of persons who reveal that they are disposed to criminality." The Code therefore rejects Wharton's Rule but achieves at least some of its effects through the provisions of § § 5.04(2) and 1.07(1)(b).

2. Suppose A sells a small amount of a controlled substance to B for the latter's personal use where B's possession renders him guilty merely of a misdemeanor. What result if the state charges A with conspiracy to deliver a controlled substance, a felony? *State v. Smith,* 525 N.W.2d 264 (Wisc. 1995), holds on these facts that A cannot be convicted of conspiracy because that would also make B guilty of a felony (conspiracy), a situation which would improperly permit the state to make a felon of a mere misdemeanant by adding a conspiracy charge to a possession charge. Do you agree with the conclusion and reasoning of the *Smith* court? Is the result in *Smith* supported by either the rationale of *Gebardi* or by application of Wharton's Rule?

[D] The *Mens Rea*

PEOPLE V. LAURIA

Court of Appeals, Second District

59 Cal. Rptr. 628, 251 Cal. App. 2d 471 (1967)

FLEMING, Associate Justice.

In an investigation of call-girl activity the police focused their attention on three prostitutes actively plying their trade on call, each of whom was using Lauria's telephone answering service, presumably for business purposes.

On January 8, 1965, Stella Weeks, a policewoman, signed up for telephone service with Lauria's answering service. Mrs. Weeks, in the course of her conversation with Lauria's office manager, hinted broadly that she was a prostitute concerned with the secrecy of her activities and their concealment from the police. She was assured that the operation of the service was discreet and "about as safe as you can get." It was arranged that Mrs. Weeks need not leave her address with the answering service, but could pick up her calls and pay her bills in person.

On February 11, Mrs. Weeks talked to Lauria on the telephone and told him her business was modeling and she had been referred to the answering service by Terry, one of the three prostitutes under investigation. She complained that because of the operation of the service she had lost two valuable customers, referred to as tricks. Lauria defended his service and said that her friends had probably lied to her about having left calls for her. But he did not respond to Mrs. Weeks' hints that she needed customers in order to make money, other than to invite her to his house for a personal visit in order to get better acquainted. In the course of his talk he said "his business was taking messages."

On February 15, Mrs. Weeks talked on the telephone to Lauria's office manager and again complained of two lost calls, which she described as a $50 and a $100 trick. On investigation the office manager could find nothing wrong, but she said she would alert the switchboard operators about slip-ups on calls.

On April 1, Lauria and the three prostitutes were arrested. Lauria complained to the police that this attention was undeserved, stating that Hollywood Call Board had 60 to 70 prostitutes on its board while his own service had only 9 or 10, that he kept separate records for known or suspected prostitutes for the convenience of himself and the police. When asked if his records were available to police who might come to the office to investigate call girls, Lauria replied that they were whenever the police had a specific name. However, his service didn't "arbitrarily tell the police about prostitutes on our board. As long as they pay their bills we tolerate them." In a subsequent voluntary appearance before the Grand Jury Lauria testified he had always cooperated with the police. But he admitted he knew some of his customers were prostitutes, and he knew Terry was a prostitute because he had personally used her services, and he knew she was paying for 500 calls a month.

Lauria and the three prostitutes were indicted for conspiracy to commit prostitution, and nine overt acts were specified. Subsequently the trial court set aside the indictment as having been brought without reasonable or probable cause. . . . The People have appealed, claiming that a sufficient showing of an unlawful agreement to further prostitution was made.

To establish agreement, the People need show no more than a tacit, mutual understanding between coconspirators to accomplish an unlawful act. . . . Here the People attempted to establish a conspiracy by showing that Lauria, well aware that his codefendants were prostitutes who received business calls from customers through his telephone answering service, continued to furnish them with such service. This approach attempts to equate knowledge of another's criminal activity with conspiracy to further such criminal activity, and poses the question of the criminal responsibility of a furnisher of goods or services who knows his product is being used to assist the operation of an illegal business. Under what circumstances does a supplier become a part of a conspiracy to further an illegal enterprise by furnishing goods or services which he knows are to be used by the buyer for criminal purposes?

The two leading cases on this point face in opposite directions. In *United States v. Falcone,* 311 U.S. 205, the sellers of large quantities of sugar, yeast, and cans were absolved from participation in a moonshining conspiracy among distillers who bought from them, while in *Direct Sales Co. v. United States,* 319 U.S. 703, a wholesaler of drugs was convicted of conspiracy to violate the federal narcotic laws by selling drugs in quantity to a codefendant physician who was supplying them to addicts. The distinction between these two cases appears primarily based on the proposition that distributors of such dangerous products as drugs are required to exercise greater discrimination in the conduct of their business than are distributors of innocuous substances like sugar and yeast.

In the earlier case, *Falcone,* the sellers' knowledge of the illegal use of the goods was insufficient by itself to make the sellers participants in a conspiracy with the distillers who bought from them. Such knowledge fell short of proof of a conspiracy, and evidence on the volume of sales was too vague to support a jury finding that respondents knew of the conspiracy from the size of the sales alone.

In the later case of *Direct Sales,* the conviction of a drug wholesaler for conspiracy to violate federal narcotic laws was affirmed on a showing that it had actively promoted the sale of morphine sulphate in quantity and had sold codefendant physician, who practiced in a small town in South Carolina, more than 300 times his normal requirements of the drug, even though it had been repeatedly warned of the dangers of unrestricted sales of the drug. The court contrasted the restricted goods involved in *Direct Sales* with the articles of free commerce involved in *Falcone:* "All articles of commerce may be put to illegal ends," said the court. "But all do not have inherently the same susceptibility to harmful and illegal use. . . . This difference is important for two purposes. One is for making certain that the seller knows the buyer's intended illegal use. The other is to show that by the sale he intends to further, promote and cooperate in it. This intent, when given effect by overt act, is the gist of conspiracy. While it is not identical with mere knowledge that another purposes unlawful action, it is not unrelated to such knowledge. . . . The step from knowledge to intent and agreement may be taken. There is more than suspicion, more than knowledge, acquiescence, carelessness, indifference, lack of concern. There is informed and interested cooperation, stimulation, instigation. And there is also a —stake in the venture' which, even if it may not be essential, is not irrelevant to the question of conspiracy.". . .

While *Falcone* and *Direct Sales* may not be entirely consistent with each other in their full implications, they do provide us with a framework for the criminal liability of a supplier of lawful goods or services put to unlawful use. Both the element of *knowledge* of the illegal use of the goods or services and the element of *intent* to further that use must be present in order to make the supplier a participant in a criminal conspiracy.

Proof of *knowledge* is ordinarily a question of fact and requires no extended discussion in the present case. The knowledge of the supplier was sufficiently established when Lauria admitted he knew some of his customers were prostitutes and admitted he knew that Terry, an active subscriber to his service, was a prostitute. In the face of these admissions he could scarcely claim to have relied on the normal assumption an operator of a business or service is entitled to make, that his customers are behaving themselves in the eyes of the law. Because Lauria knew in fact that some of his customers were prostitutes, it is a legitimate inference he knew they were subscribing to his answering service for illegal business purposes and were using his service to make assignations for prostitution. On this record we think the prosecution is entitled to claim positive knowledge by Lauria of the use of his service to facilitate the business of prostitution.

The more perplexing issue in the case is the sufficiency of proof of *intent* to further the criminal enterprise. The element of intent may be proved either by direct evidence, or by evidence of circumstances from which an intent to further a criminal enterprise by supplying lawful goods or services may be inferred. Direct evidence of participation, such as advice from the supplier of legal goods or services to the user of those goods or services on their use for illegal purposes, . . . provides the simplest case. When the intent to further and promote the criminal enterprise comes from the lips of the supplier himself, ambiguities of inference from circumstance need not trouble us. But in cases where direct proof of complicity is lacking, intent to further the conspiracy must be derived from the sale itself and its surrounding circumstances in order to establish the supplier's express or tacit agreement to join the conspiracy.

In the case at bench the prosecution argues that since Lauria knew his customers were using his service for illegal purposes but nevertheless continued to furnish it to them, he must have intended to assist them in carrying out their illegal activities. Thus through a union of knowledge and intent he became a participant in a criminal conspiracy. Essentially, the People argue that knowledge alone of the continuing use of his telephone facilities for criminal purposes provided a sufficient basis from which his intent to participate in those criminal activities could be inferred.

In examining precedents in this field we find that sometimes, but not always, the criminal intent of the supplier may be inferred from his knowledge of the unlawful use made of the product he supplies. Some consideration of characteristic patterns may be helpful.

1. Intent may be inferred from knowledge, when the purveyor of legal goods for illegal use has acquired a stake in the venture. (*United States v. Falcone,* 2 Cir., 109 F.2d 579, 581.) For example, in *Regina v. Thomas* (1957), 2 All E.R. 181, 342, a prosecution for living off the earnings of prostitution, the evidence showed that the accused, knowing the woman to be a convicted prostitute, agreed to let her have the use of his room between the hours of 9 PM and 2 AM for a charge of £3 a night. The Court of Criminal Appeal refused an appeal from the conviction, holding that when the accused rented a room at a grossly inflated rent to a prostitute for the purpose of carrying on her trade, a jury could find he was living on the earnings of prostitution.

In the present case, no proof was offered of inflated charges for the telephone answering services furnished the codefendants.

2. Intent may be inferred from knowledge, when no legitimate use for the goods or services exists. The leading California case is *People v. McLaughlin,* 111 Cal, App. 2d 781, 245 P.2d 1076, in which the court upheld a conviction of the suppliers of horse-racing information by wire for conspiracy to promote bookmaking, when it had been established that wire service information had no other use than to supply information needed by bookmakers to conduct illegal gambling operations.

* * *

. . . In such cases the supplier must necessarily have an intent to further the illegal enterprise since there is no known honest use for his goods.

However, there is nothing in the furnishing of telephone answering service which would necessarily imply assistance in the performance of illegal activities. Nor is any inference to be derived from the use of an answering service by women, either in any particular volume of calls, or outside normal working hours. Night-club entertainers, registered nurses, faith healers, public stenographers, photographic models, and free lance substitute employees provide examples of women in legitimate occupations whose employment might cause them to receive a volume of telephone calls at irregular hours.

3. Intent may be inferred from knowledge, when the volume of business with the buyer is grossly disproportionate to any legitimate demand, or when sales for illegal use amount to a high proportion of the seller's total business. In such cases an intent to participate in the illegal enterprise may be inferred from the quantity of the business done. For example, in *Direct Sales, supra,* the sale of narcotics to a rural physician in quantities 300 times greater than he would have normal use for provided potent evidence of an intent to further the illegal activity. In the same case the court also found significant the fact that the wholesaler had attracted as customers a disproportionately large group of physicians who had been convicted of violating the Harrison Act. In *Shaw v. Director of Public Prosecutions,* [1962] A.C. 220, almost the entire business of the directory came from prostitutes.

No evidence of any unusual volume of business with prostitutes was presented by the prosecution against Lauria.

Inflated charges, the sale of goods with no legitimate use, sales in inflated amounts, each may provide a fact of sufficient moment from which the intent of the seller to participate in the criminal enterprise may be inferred. In such instances participation by the supplier of legal goods to the illegal enterprise may be inferred because in one way or another the supplier has acquired a special interest in the operation of the illegal enterprise. His intent to participate in the crime of which he has knowledge may be inferred from the existence of his special interest.

Yet there are cases in which it cannot reasonably be said that the supplier has a stake in the venture or has acquired a special interest in the enterprise, but in which he has been held liable as a participant on the basis of knowledge alone. Some suggestion of this appears in *Direct Sales, supra,* where both the knowledge of the illegal use of the drugs and the intent of the supplier to aid that use were inferred. . . . In *Sykes v. Director of Public Prosecutions,* [1962] A.C. 528, one having knowledge of the theft of 100 pistols, 4 submachine guns, and 1960 rounds of ammunition was convicted of misprision of felony for failure to disclose the theft to the public authorities. It seems apparent from these cases that a supplier who furnishes equipment which he *knows* will be used to commit a serious crime may be deemed from that knowledge alone to have intended to produce the result. Such proof may justify an inference that the furnisher intended to aid the execution of the crime and that he thereby became a participant. For instance, we think the operator of a telephone answering service with positive knowledge that this service was being used to facilitate the extortion of ransom, the distribution of heroin, or the passing of counterfeit money who continued to furnish the service with knowledge of its use, might be chargeable on knowledge alone with participation in a scheme to extort money, to distribute narcotics, or to pass counterfeit money. The same result would follow the seller of gasoline who knew the buyer was using his product to make Molotov cocktails for terroristic use.

Logically, the same reasoning could be extended to crimes of every description. Yet we do not believe an inference of intent drawn from knowledge of criminal use properly applies to the less serious crimes classified as misdemeanors. The duty to take positive action to dissociate oneself from activities helpful to violations of the criminal law is far stronger and more compelling for felonies than it is for misdemeanors or petty offenses. In this respect, as in others, the distinction between felonies and misdemeanors, between more serious and less serious crime, retains continuing vitality. In historically the most serious felony, treason, an individual with knowledge of the treason can be prosecuted for concealing and failing to disclose it. . . .

With respect to misdemeanors, we conclude that positive knowledge of the supplier that his products or services are being used for criminal purposes does not, without more, establish an intent of the supplier to participate in the misdemeanors. With respect to felonies, we do not decide the converse, *viz.*, that in all cases of felony knowledge of criminal use alone may justify an inference of supplier's intent to participate in the crime. The implications of *Falcone* make the matter uncertain with respect to those felonies which are merely prohibited wrongs. . . . But decision on this point is not compelled, and we leave the matter open.

From this analysis of precedent we deduce the following rule: the intent of a supplier who knows of the criminal use to which his supplies are put to participate in the criminal activity connected with the use of his supplies may be established by (1) direct evidence that he intends to participate, or (2) through an inference that he intends to participate based on, (a) his special interest in the activity, or (b) the aggravated nature of the crime itself.

When we review Lauria's activities in the light of this analysis, we find no proof that Lauria took any direct action to further, encourage, or direct the call girl activities of his codefendants and we find an absence of circumstances from which his special interest in their activities could be inferred. Neither excessive charges for standardized services, nor the furnishing of services without a legitimate use, nor an unusual quantity of business with call girls, are present. The offense which he is charged with furthering is a misdemeanor, a category of crime which has never been made a required subject of positive disclosure to public authority. Under these circumstances, although proof of Lauria's knowledge of the criminal activities of his patrons was sufficient to charge him with that fact, there was insufficient evidence that he intended to further their criminal activities, and hence insufficient proof of his participation in a criminal conspiracy with his codefendants to further prostitution. Since the conspiracy centered around the activities of Lauria's telephone answering service, the charges against his codefendants likewise fail for want of proof.

* * *

The order is affirmed.

HERNDON, J., *concurs*

ROTH, P.J., *concurs in the judgment.*

NOTES AND QUESTIONS

1. Apart from *mens rea* considerations, did Lauria's actions constitute the *actus reus* for conspiracy? Was there an agreement for purposes of conspiracy law?

Along these lines, consider the following observation:

The two elements of mental state required by conspiracy are the intent to agree and the intent to promote the unlawful objective of the conspiracy. The first of these elements is almost indistinguishable from the act of agreement. Agreement is in any case morally neutral; its moral character depends upon the nature of the objective of agreement. It is the intention to promote a crime that lends conspiracy its criminal cast.

Burke and Kadish, *Conspiracy* in 1 Encyclopedia of Crime and Justice 235 (1983).

2. What is the required *mens rea* for conspiracy? While Lauria clearly knew of some of his customers' criminal activity and had agreed to assist them in their crimes by means of his answering service, the court holds that he was not conspiring with them. Why not? What more needed to be established to prove the conspiracy? Is the problem simply that the State's proof was deficient in establishing that Lauria merely knew of the criminal activity instead of showing that he intended to promote it? If so, what does the court mean by *intent?* Does it have in mind one of the alternatives to knowledge defined in Model Penal Code § 2.02(2)? See § 5.03 for the Code's approach to the *mens rea* issue.

Suppose the facts of *Lauria* except that Lauria personally put one prostitute subscriber to his service in touch with another so the former could obtain clients from the latter. Assuming that Lauria received no financial reward for arranging the meeting between the two known prostitutes and that he knew that one customer would share her "business" with the other, would Lauria be guilty of conspiracy? See *People v. Roy,* 59 Cal. Rptr. 636, 251 Cal. App. 2d 459 (1967).

3. To what extent is the *mens rea* issue in *Lauria* a subjective issue? Could the government have proved the *mens rea* requirement by simply establishing certain additional objective facts and circumstances (*e.g.,* greater volume of illegal business through the answering service, higher prices charged to prostitute customers then to law-abiding customers)?

4. Why does the *Lauria* court suggest a more rigorous *mens rea* requirement for conspiracies to commit misdemeanors than for felonies? Does such a distinction make sense on either theoretical or policy grounds?

UNITED STATES v. BLANKENSHIP

Seventh Circuit Court of Appeals

970 F.2d 283 (1992)

EASTERBROOK, Circuit Judge.

. . . Nancy Nietupski, a grandmother in her early 60s, ran a methamphetamine ring through her extended family. She started on the west coast, working with her nephew William Zahm. Later she moved to her sister's farm in Illinois. While sister Violet Blankenship supplied a base of operations, nephew Robert Blankenship helped distribute the drug and collect debts.

Nietupski initially bought methamphetamine from outside sources. When these proved unreliable, Zahm helped her enter the manufacturing end of the business. "Cooking" methamphetamine is messy, and there is a risk of explosion when volatile chemicals such as acetone reach high temperatures. Nietupski and Zahm moved their laboratory frequently, to reduce the risk of detection. In February 1989 Zahm leased from Thomas Lawrence a house trailer in which to set up shop for a day. Nietupski told Lawrence what Zahm planned to make and offered $1,000 or one ounce of methamphetamine; Lawrence preferred the cash and took $100 as a down payment. He covered the floor of the trailer with plastic for protection. Zahm postponed the operation when he could not find a heating control. A few days later Lawrence got cold feet, telling Marvin Bland (one of Nietupski's assistants) that he wanted the chemicals and equipment removed. Bland complied.

Zahm soon joined William Worker to set up a new methamphetamine ring. Agents of the DEA infiltrated the Zahm—Worker clique. Zahm cut his losses by turning against his aunt, whose operations collapsed. Eighteen persons from the Nietupski ring were indicted. Robert Blankenship, Thomas Lawrence, and six others were in one group, all charged in a single count with conspiring to manufacture and distribute methamphetamine. 21 U.S.C. § 846. Of the six, three pleaded guilty and three were acquitted. Blankenship and Lawrence, convicted by the jury, received identical sentences of 120 months' imprisonment plus five years' supervised release.

* * *

Lawrence has filed two appeals, one from his sentence and the second from an order denying his motion under Fed. R. Crim. P. 33 for a new trial. . . .

Conspiracy is agreement to violate the law. Unless Lawrence willingly joined the Nietupski venture, he did not commit the crime of conspiracy. What evidence was there that Lawrence knew, let alone joined? Nietupski and Zahm told Lawrence what they planned to do in his trailer; Zahm and Lawrence sampled some of the product scraped off the apparatus; for $1,000 he furnished the space, covered the floor with plastic, supplied refreshments, and let Zahm take a shower to wash some acid off his legs. If providing assistance to a criminal organization were the same thing as conspiracy, then Lawrence would be guilty. Yet there is a difference between supplying goods to a syndicate and joining it, just as there is a difference between selling goods and being an employee of the buyer. Cargill sells malt and barley to Anheuser Busch, knowing that they will be made into beer, without being part of Busch; by parallel reasoning, someone who sells sugar to a bootlegger knowing the use that will be made of that staple is not thereby a conspirator, *United States v. Falcone,* 311 U.S. 205 (1940), and someone who buys one load of marijuana has not conspired with the sellers[.]

Falcone illustrates the doctrine that "mere" sellers and buyers are not automatically conspirators. If it were otherwise, companies that sold cellular phones to teenage punks who have no use for them other than to set up drug deals would be in trouble, and many legitimate businesses would be required to monitor their customers' activities. Cf. *People v. Lauria,* 251 Cal. App. 2d 471, 59 Cal. Rptr. 628 (1967) (answering service furnished to prostitute). Yet this does not get us very far, for no rule says that a supplier cannot join a conspiracy through which the product is put to an unlawful end. *Direct Sales Co. v. United States,* 319 U.S. 703 (1943), makes that point in holding that the jury may infer that a pharmaceutical house selling huge quantities of morphine to a physician over a seven-year span conspired with the physician to distribute the drug illegally.

Where does the "mere" sale end, the conspiracy begin? One may draw a line, as *Falcone* and *Direct Sales* did, between knowledge of other persons' crimes and intent to join them, but this restates the elements of the offense without telling us when an inference of intent to join is permissible. Selling a camera to a spy does not make one a traitor—but selling camera and film, developing the prints, enlarging the detail in the critical areas, and collecting half of the payment for the secret information would assuredly land one in prison. Stating polar cases is easy, but locating the line of demarcation is hard. . . .

When writing for the court of appeals in *Falcone,* Learned Hand concluded that a supplier joins a venture only if his fortunes rise or fall with the venture's, so that he gains by its success. On this view the sale of a staple commodity such as sugar or telephone service does not enlist the seller in the criminal venture; in a competitive market the vendor could sell to someone else at the market price, and the buyer could turn to other sources. Anonymous transactions are the norm in markets and do not create criminal liability; when the seller has knowledge but the terms remain the same, there is no reason to infer participation in the enterprise any more than in the Cargill—Busch case we have given. . . . See . . . Model Penal Code § 2.06(3)(a) and commentary at 315–16 (1985) (supplier culpable only if he has "the purpose of promoting or facilitating" the crime). . . .

Trailers do not rent for $1,000 per week—not in legitimate markets, anyway. By charging a premium price, Lawrence seemingly threw in his lot with the Nietupski operation and may be convicted under Judge Hand's approach. Yet the price cannot be the end of things. What does the $1,000 represent: a piece of the action, or only a premium for the risks? Lawrence bore two. One was that the chemicals would damage his trailer. Although he took precautions by spreading plastic on the floor, an explosion would have spattered chemicals on the walls and ceiling. Lawrence would have charged for taking this risk even if the manufacture of methamphetamine were entirely legal. The other risk was the hazard of criminal liability, a cost of doing business. One who covers his own costs and no more does not share in the venture's success. Using a price calculated by reference to the risk of criminal conviction as support for that conviction would be circular. Reduce the risk of conviction, and you reduce the price. Either way, the price responds to the legal system rather than to the potential profits of the Nietupski gang and does not establish a desire to promote its success. Repeat business, as in *Direct Sales,* might show such a desire, but Lawrence did not carry through with the initial transaction and never realized even the $1,000.

[C]ases from this court speak reverentially of Judge Hand but actually ask a different, and more functional, question. It is whether the imposition of liability on transactions of the class depicted by the case would deter crime without adding unduly to the costs of legitimate transactions. So," [a] stationer who sells an address book to a woman whom he knows to be a prostitute is not an aider and abettor. He can hardly be said to be seeking by his action to make her venture succeed, since the transaction has very little to do with that success and his livelihood will not be affected appreciably by whether her venture succeeds or fails. And, what may well be the same point seen from another angle, punishing him would not reduce the amount of prostitution—the prostitute, at an infinitesimal cost in added inconvenience, would simply shop for address books among stationers who did not know her trade." Treating the stationer as an accomplice would, however, raise the costs of legitimate business, for it would either turn sellers into snoops (lest they sell to the wrong customers) or lead them to hire blind clerks (lest they learn too much about their customers); either way, the costs of business would rise, and honest customers would pay more.

If the product is itself contraband—for example, the methamphetamine Nietupski bought in California early on—the analysis differs but the result is the same: an isolated sale is not the same thing as enlisting in the venture. A sale of methamphetamine is a substantive crime. Because the substance is illegal, the seller knows that the buyer will put the drug to an illegal use, yet this does not make the sale a second, inchoate offense. To treat it as a second crime of aiding and abetting (or conspiring with) the buyer is to multiply the criminal punishment and so distort the penalty system the legislature adopted—for what is the point of setting at five years the maximum penalty for selling a given quantity of methamphetamine if every sale violates a second law and doubles the penalty? [A] long course of sales may permit a finding of conspiracy or aiding and abetting, for such conduct is both more dangerous (it is harder to ferret out crime when the criminals have a closed circle of suppliers) and more likely that the vendor's welfare is bound up with that of the organization to which he sells. So too with "fronting" of drugs, a credit arrangement in which the parties to the sale share the profits.

Sometimes a single transaction extends over a substantial period and is the equivalent of enduring supply. . . .

. . . Lawrence negotiated for one payment, not a stream of rentals. Some states have statutes forbidding "criminal facilitation," an apt description of

Lawrence's acts. *E.g.,* N.Y. Penal Code § 115.05.[1] Lawrence agreed to facilitate the manufacture of methamphetamine, but the United States Code lacks a facilitation statute. It does forbid aiding and abetting substantive offenses. Although Zahm did not complete the "cook," 21 U.S.C. § 846 forbids attempted violations of other drug laws. Yet the prosecutor did not charge Lawrence with assisting this offense—or with assisting a conspiracy to make methamphetamine on his premises. Instead the prosecutor not only selected the conspiracy component of § 846 but also lumped Lawrence with a single, overarching conspiracy, the entire Nietupski venture. Neither joining nor abetting this whole conspiracy is an appropriate description of Lawrence's fling.

In charging Lawrence with joining the Nietupski conspiracy, the prosecutor sought to hold him responsible for that organization's entire activities. . . . Members of conspiracies may be punished for all of the crimes within the scope of the venture. *Pinkerton v. United States,* 328 U.S. 640 (1946)[.] The Sentencing Guidelines, when coupled with the sky-high punishments authorized for drug crimes, produce the same vicarious liability without the bother of obtaining convictions. In a drug case the court must impose a sentence computed by reference to all "acts and omissions that were part of the same course of conduct or common scheme or plan as the offense of conviction."When the "offense of conviction" is a conspiracy, this means counting the full sales of the criminal enterprise throughout its duration. Thus Robert Blankenship, who was a cog of the Nietupski organization from the time his aunt moved to Illinois, and Thomas Lawrence, who obtained $100 by opening his trailer to a single failed "cook," received identical sentences—ten years in prison without possibility of parole.

Neither *Direct Sales* nor any of this court's cases permits a supplier to a criminal organization to be sentenced for all of that organization's sins when he facilitated only one. If the United States Code contained a facilitation statute along the lines of New York's, Lawrence would receive a sentence proportioned to his own iniquity rather than that of Nietupski and her henchmen. So too if the Code penalized abetting criminal attempts. But it does not, and if the only options are conspiracy, with full responsibility for all of the venture's other crimes, and no crime, then no crime comes much closer to describing Lawrence's responsibility. . . .

Let us be clear: we do not hold that in reforming criminal sentences Congress altered the definition of conspiracy. We come to the same conclusion as the Supreme Court did in *Falcone*. Lawrence knew what Zahm wanted to do in the trailer, but there is a gulf between knowledge and conspiracy. There is no evidence that Lawrence recognized, let alone that he joined and promoted, the full scope of the Nietupski organization's activities. He may have joined, or abetted, a more limited agreement to manufacture a quantity of methamphetamine, but he was not charged with that offense. Lawrence

---

[1] "A person is guilty of criminal facilitation in the second degree when, believing it probable that he is rendering aid to a person who intends to commit a class A felony, he engages in conduct which provides such person with means or opportunity for the commission thereof and which in fact aids such person to commit such class A felony. Criminal facilitation in the second degree is a class C felony." Note the difference in degree between the principal and the facilitator, appropriate to the different roles but not achievable when conspiracy or aiding and abetting supplies the theory of responsibility.

facilitated an attempted crime, and probably conspired to do this, but he did not subscribe to the broader agreement on which his conviction depends.

On Lawrence's appeal the judgment is reversed. On Blankenship's appeal, the judgment is affirmed.

NOTES AND QUESTIONS

1. Judge Easterbrook concludes that Lawrence did not "willingly join the Nietupski venture." Do you agree? To what extent is the court's conclusion driven by its concerns about the ramifications of including Lawrence within the Nietupski venture under the *Pinkerton* case (see § 8.02, *infra*) and under the Federal Sentencing Guidelines? How is it, as Judge Easterbrook suggests, that Lawrence would likely have been guilty of "willingly" conspiring to "manufacture a quantity of methamphetamine" had that been the charge? Is there a difference, for *mens rea* purposes, between his "stake in the venture" relative to manufacturing methamphetamine in his trailer and his stake in the entire Nietupski criminal enterprise?

2. Note that *Blankenship* raises two kinds of questions: (1) Did Lawrence possess the *mens rea* for conspiracy? (2) If Lawrence did, what was the extent or scope of the conspiracy he joined? The scope problem is addressed in § 7.03[E], *infra*.

NOTE ON THE CORRUPT MOTIVE DOCTRINE

Suppose in the *Lauria* case that Lauria had entered into an agreement with his customers for the purpose of (*i.e.*, with the intention of) promoting their activities which were criminal but which he mistakenly assumed were lawfully permitted. Would Lauria be guilty of conspiracy under the general rule that ignorance of the law is no excuse, or should an exception be made in conspiracy cases, at least in situations where the substantive crime is perceived to be of the *mala prohibita* variety? Some cases have recognized defenses in the latter class of cases.

In *People v. Powell,* 63 N.Y. 88 (1875), the court held that defendants, city officials, who collectively made city purchases without advertising for bids as required by statute were not guilty of conspiracy because they acted in ignorance of the statutory bid requirement and were thus in good faith. The court found that "implied in the meaning of conspiracy" is a requirement that the agreement "must have been entered into with an evil purpose, as distinguished from a purpose to do the act prohibited in ignorance of the prohibition." *Id,* at 92.

Powell's "corrupt motive" doctrine has met a mixed fate. Some other cases follow it, see, for example, *Commonwealth v. Gormley,* 77 Pa. Super. 298 (1921). But others, perhaps a majority, reject the doctrine, often for reasons similar to those expressed in *United States v. Mack,* 112 F.2d 290, 292 (2d Cir. 1940):

Starting with *People v. Powell* . . . the anomalous doctrine has indeed gained some footing in the circuit courts of appeals that for conspiracy there must be a very "corrupt motive." . . . Yet it is hard to see any reason for this, or why more proof should be necessary than that the parties had in contemplation all the elements of the crime they are charged with conspiracy to commit.

The Model Penal Code follows the trend in rejecting the corrupt motive doctrine:

> The *Powell* rule, and many of the decisions that rely on it, may be viewed as a judicial endeavor to import fair *mens rea* requirements into statutes creating regulatory offenses that do not rest on traditional concepts of personal fault and culpability. This should, however, be the function of the statutes defining such offenses. . . . There is no good reason why the fortuity of concert should be used as a device for limiting criminality in this area, just as there is no good reason for using it as a device to expand liability through imprecise formulations of objectives that include activity not otherwise criminal. The melodramatic and sinister view of conspiracy on which the *Powell* decision seems to rest is largely discredited today. As an uncertain "corrupt motive" requirement, it has little resolving power in particular cases and serves mainly to divert attention from clear analysis of the *mens rea* requirements of conspiracy.

MPC § 5.03 Comment at 417–18 (1985).

On the other hand, if defendants in *Powell*-like situations truly have no intent or desire to break the law, are the objectives of conspiracy law attained by punishing them?

UNITED STATES V. FEOLA

Supreme Court of the United States

420 U.S. 671 (1974)

Mr. Justice BLACKMUN Delivered the Opinion of the Court.

This case presents the issue whether knowledge that the intended victim is a federal officer is a requisite for the crime of conspiracy, under 18 U.S.C. § 371, to commit an offense violative of 18 U.S.C. § 111,[1] that is, an assault upon a federal officer while engaged in the performance of his official duties.

---

[1] "§ 111. Assaulting, resisting, or impeding certain officers or employees.

"Whoever forcibly assaults, resists, opposes, impedes, intimidates, or interferes with any person designated in section 1114 of this title while engaged in or on account of the performance of his official duties shall be fined not more than $5,000 or imprisoned not more than three years, or both.

"Whoever, in the commission of any such acts uses a deadly or dangerous weapon, shall be fined not more than $10,000 or imprisoned not more than ten years, or both."

Among the persons "designated in section 1114" of 18 U.S.C. is "any officer or employee of the Bureau of Narcotics and Dangerous Drugs."

Respondent Feola and three others (Alsondo, Rosa, and Farr) were indicted for violations of § § 371 and 111. A jury found all four defendants guilty of both charges. Feola received a sentence of four years for the conspiracy and one to three years, plus a $3,000 fine, for the assault. . . . The . . . United States Court of Appeals for the Second Circuit . . . affirmed the judgment of conviction on the substantive charges, but reversed the conspiracy convictions. . . . Because of a conflict among the federal Circuits on the scienter issue with respect to a conspiracy charge, we granted the Government's petition for a writ of *certiorari* in Feola's case. . . .

I

The facts reveal a classic narcotics "rip-off." The details are not particularly important for our present purposes. We need note only that the evidence shows that Feola and his confederates arranged for a sale of heroin to buyers who turned out to be undercover agents for the Bureau of Narcotics and Dangerous Drugs. The group planned to palm off on the purchasers, for a substantial sum, a form of sugar in place of heroin and, should that ruse fail, simply to surprise their unwitting buyers and relieve them of the cash they had brought along for payment. The plan failed when one agent, his suspicions being aroused, drew his revolver in time to counter an assault upon another agent from the rear. Instead of enjoying the rich benefits of a successful swindle, Feola and his associates found themselves charged, to their undoubted surprise, with conspiring to assault, and with assaulting, federal officers.

At the trial, the District Court, without objection from the defense, charged the jurors that, in order to find any of the defendants guilty on either the conspiracy count or the substantive one, they were not required to conclude that the defendants were aware that their quarry were federal officers.

The Court of Appeals reversed the conspiracy convictions on a ground not advanced by any of the defendants. Although it approved the trial court's instructions to the jury on the substantive charge of assaulting a federal officer, it nonetheless concluded that the failure to charge that knowledge of the victim's official identity must be proved in order to convict on the conspiracy charge amounted to plain error. . . . The court perceived itself bound by a line of cases, commencing with Judge Learned Hand's opinion in *United States v. Crimmins,* 123 F.2d 271 (CA2 1941), all holding that scienter of a factual element that confers federal jurisdiction, while unnecessary for conviction of the substantive offense, is required in order to sustain a conviction for conspiracy to commit the substantive offense. . . .

II

The Government's plea is for symmetry. It urges that since criminal liability for the offense described in 18 U.S.C. § 111 does not depend on whether the assailant harbored the specific intent to assault a federal officer, no greater scienter requirement can be engrafted upon the conspiracy offense, which is merely an agreement to commit the act proscribed by § 111. Consideration of the Government's contention requires us preliminarily to pass upon its premise, the proposition that responsibility for assault upon a federal officer does not depend upon whether the assailant was aware of the official identity of his victim at the time he acted.

That the "federal officer" requirement is anything other than jurisdictional[9] is not seriously urged upon us; indeed, both Feola and the Court of Appeals . . . concede that scienter is not a necessary element of the substantive offense under § 111. Although some early cases were to the contrary, the concession recognizes what is now the practical unanimity of the Courts of Appeals. Nevertheless, we are not always guided by concessions of the parties, and the very considerations of symmetry urged by the Government suggest that we first turn our attention to the substantive offense.

* * *

In the present case, we see again the possible consequences of an interpretation of § 111 that focuses on only one of the statute's apparent aims. If the primary purpose is to protect federal law enforcement personnel, that purpose could well be frustrated by the imposition of a strict scienter requirement. On the other hand, if § 111 is seen primarily as an anti-obstruction statute, it is likely that Congress intended criminal liability to be imposed only when a person acted with the specific intent to impede enforcement activities. Otherwise, it has been said: "Were knowledge not required in obstruction of justice offenses described by these terms, wholly innocent (or even socially desirable) behavior could be transformed into a felony by the wholly fortuitous circumstance of the concealed identity of the person resisted." Although we adhere to the conclusion . . . that either view of legislative intent is "plausible," we think it plain that Congress intended to protect both federal officers and federal functions, and that, indeed, furtherance of the one policy advances the other. The rejection of a strict scienter requirement is consistent with both purposes.

[The Court then examined the legislative history of § 111.]

We conclude, from all this, that in order to effectuate the congressional purpose of according maximum protection to federal officers by making prosecution for assaults upon them cognizable in the federal courts, § 111 cannot be construed as embodying an unexpressed requirement that an assailant be aware that his victim is a federal officer. All the statute requires is an intent to assault, not an intent to assault a federal officer. A contrary

---

[9] We are content to state the issue this way despite its potential to mislead. Labeling a requirement "jurisdictional" does not necessarily mean, of course, that the requirement is not an element of the offense Congress intended to describe and to punish. Indeed, a requirement is sufficient to confer jurisdiction on the federal courts for what otherwise are state crimes precisely because it implicates factors that are an appropriate subject for federal concern. With respect to the present case, for example, a mere general policy of deterring assaults would probably prove to be an undesirable or insufficient basis for federal jurisdiction; but where Congress seeks to protect the integrity of federal functions and the safety of federal officers, the interest is sufficient to warrant federal involvement. The significance of labeling a statutory requirement as "jurisdictional" is not that the requirement is viewed as outside the scope of the evil Congress intended to forestall, but merely that the existence of the fact that confers federal jurisdiction need not be one in the mind of the actor at the time he perpetrates the act made criminal by the federal statute. The question, then, is not whether the requirement is jurisdictional, but whether it is jurisdictional only.

conclusion would give insufficient protection to the agent enforcing an unpopular law, and none to the agent acting under cover.

This interpretation poses no risk of unfairness to defendants. It is no snare for the unsuspecting. Although the perpetrator of a narcotics "rip-off," such as the one involved here, may be surprised to find that his intended victim is a federal officer in civilian apparel, he nonetheless knows from the very outset that his planned course of conduct is wrongful. The situation is not one where legitimate conduct becomes unlawful solely because of the identity of the individual or agency affected. In a case of this kind the offender takes his victim as he finds him. The concept of criminal intent does not extend so far as to require that the actor understand not only the nature of his act but also its consequence for the choice of a judicial forum.

We are not to be understood as implying that the defendant's state of knowledge is never a relevant consideration under § 111. The statute does require a criminal intent, and there may well be circumstances in which ignorance of the official status of the person assaulted or resisted negates the very existence of *mens rea*. For example, where an officer fails to identify himself or his purpose, his conduct in certain circumstances might reasonably be interpreted as the unlawful use of force directed either at the defendant or his property. In a situation of that kind, one might be justified in exerting an element of resistance, and an honest mistake of fact would not be consistent with criminal intent.

We hold, therefore, that in order to incur criminal liability under § 111 an actor must entertain merely the criminal intent to do the acts therein specified. We now consider whether the rule should be different where persons conspire to commit those acts.

III

Our decisions establish that in order to sustain a judgment of conviction on a charge of conspiracy to violate a federal statute, the Government must prove at least the degree of criminal intent necessary for the substantive offense itself. . . . Respondent Feola urges upon us the proposition that the Government must show a degree of criminal intent in the conspiracy count greater than is necessary to convict for the substantive offense; he urges that even though it is not necessary to show that he was aware of the official identity of his assaulted victims in order to find him guilty of assaulting federal officers, in violation of 18 U.S.C. § 111, the Government nonetheless must show that he was aware that his intended victims were undercover agents, if it is successfully to prosecute him for conspiring to assault federal agents. . . .

The general conspiracy statute, 18 U.S.C. 371, offers no textual support for the proposition that to be guilty of conspiracy a defendant in effect must have known that his conduct violated federal law. The statute makes it unlawful simply to "conspire . . . to commit any offense against the United States." A natural reading of these words would be that since one can violate a criminal statute simply by engaging in the forbidden conduct, a conspiracy to commit that offense is nothing more than an agreement to engage in the prohibited conduct. Then where, as here, the substantive statute does not require that an assailant know the official status of his victim, there is nothing on the face of the conspiracy statute that would seem to require that those agreeing to the assault have a greater degree of knowledge.

* * *

With no support on the face of the general conspiracy statute or in this Court's decisions, respondent relies solely on the line of cases commencing with *United States v. Crimmins,* 123 F.2d 271 (CA2 1941), for the principle that the Government must prove "antifederal" intent in order to establish liability under § 371. In *Crimmins,* the defendant had been found guilty of conspiring to receive stolen bonds that had been transported in interstate commerce. Upon review, the Court of Appeals pointed out that the evidence failed to establish that Crimmins actually knew the stolen bonds had moved into the State. Accepting for the sake of argument the assumption that such knowledge was not necessary to sustain a conviction on the substantive offense, Judge Learned Hand nevertheless concluded that to permit conspiratorial liability where the conspirators were ignorant of the federal implications of their acts would be to enlarge their agreement beyond its terms as they understood them. He capsulized the distinction in what has become well known as his "traffic light" analogy:

> While one may, for instance, be guilty of running past a traffic light of whose existence one is ignorant, one cannot be guilty of conspiring to run past such a light, for one cannot agree to run past a light unless one supposes that there is a light to run past.

Id., at 273.

Judge Hand's attractive, but perhaps seductive, analogy has received a mixed reception in the Courts of Appeals. . . . We conclude that the analogy, though effective prose, is, as applied to the facts before us, bad law.[24]

The question posed by the traffic light analogy is not before us, just as it was not before the Second Circuit in *Crimmins.* Criminal liability, of course, may be imposed on one who runs a traffic light regardless of whether he harbored the "evil intent" of disobeying the light's command; whether he drove so recklessly as to be unable to perceive the light; whether, thinking he was observing all traffic rules, he simply failed to notice the light; or whether, having been reared elsewhere, he thought that the light was only an ornament. Traffic violations generally fall into that category of offenses that dispense with a *mens rea* requirement. . . . These laws embody the social judgment that it is fair to punish one who intentionally engages in conduct that creates a risk to others, even though no risk is intended or the actor, through no fault of his own, is completely unaware of the existence of any risk. The traffic light analogy poses the question whether it is fair to punish parties to an agreement to engage intentionally in apparently innocent

---

[24] The Government rather effectively exposes the fallacy of the *Crimmins* traffic light analogy by recasting it in terms of a jurisdictional element. The suggested example is a traffic light on an Indian reservation. Surely, one may conspire with others to disobey the light but be ignorant of the fact that it is on the reservation. As applied to a jurisdictional element of this kind the formulation makes little sense.

conduct where the unintended result of engaging in that conduct is the violation of a criminal statute.

But this case does not call upon us to answer this question, and we decline to do so. . . . We note in passing, however, that the analogy comes close to stating what has been known as the *"Powell* doctrine," . . . to the effect that a conspiracy, to be criminal, must be animated by a corrupt motive or a motive to do wrong. Under this principle, such a motive could be easily demonstrated if the underlying offense involved an act clearly wrongful in itself; but it had to be independently demonstrated if the acts agreed to were wrongful solely because of statutory proscription. . . .

. . . Fatal to the [*Crimmins* doctrine] is the fact that it was announced in a case to which it could not have been meant to apply. In *Crimmins,* the substantive offense, namely, the receipt of stolen securities that had been in interstate commerce, proscribed clearly wrongful conduct. Such conduct could not be engaged in without an intent to accomplish the forbidden result. So, too, it is with assault, the conduct forbidden by the substantive statute, § 111, presently before us. One may run a traffic light "of whose existence one is ignorant," but assaulting another "of whose existence one is ignorant," probably would require unearthly intervention. Thus, the traffic light analogy, even if it were a correct statement of the law, is inapt, for the conduct proscribed by the substantive offense, here assault, is not of the type outlawed without regard to the intent of the actor to accomplish the result that is made criminal. If the analogy has any vitality at all, it is to conduct of the latter variety; that, however, is a question we save for another day. We hold here only that where a substantive offense embodies only a requirement of *mens rea* as to each of its elements, the general federal conspiracy statute requires no more.

The *Crimmins* rule rests upon another foundation: that it is improper to find conspiratorial liability where the parties to the illicit agreement were not aware of the fact giving rise to federal jurisdiction, because the essence of conspiracy is agreement and persons cannot be punished for acts beyond the scope of their agreement. . . . This "reason" states little more than a conclusion, for it is clear that one may be guilty as a conspirator for acts the precise details of which one does not know at the time of the agreement. . . . The question is not merely whether the official status of an assaulted victim was known to the parties at the time of their agreement, but whether the acts contemplated by the conspirators are to be deemed legally different from those actually performed solely because of the official identity of the victim. Put another way, does the identity of the proposed victim alter the legal character of the acts agreed to, or is it no more germane to the nature of those acts than the color of the victim's hair?

Our analysis of the substantive offense . . . is sufficient to convince us that for the purpose of individual guilt or innocence, awareness of the official identity of the assault victim is irrelevant. We would expect the same to obtain with respect to the conspiracy offense unless one of the policies behind the imposition of conspiratorial liability is not served where the parties to the agreement are unaware that the intended target is a federal law enforcement official.

It is well settled that the law of conspiracy serves ends different from, and complementary to, those served by criminal prohibitions of the substantive offense. Because of this, consecutive sentences may be imposed for the conspiracy and for the underlying crime. . . . Our decisions have identified two independent values served by the law of conspiracy. The first is protection of society from the dangers of concerted criminal activity, . . . That individuals know that their planned joint venture violates federal as well as state law seems totally irrelevant to that purpose of conspiracy law which seeks to protect society from the dangers of concerted criminal activity. . . .

The second aspect is that conspiracy is an inchoate crime. This is to say, that, although the law generally makes criminal only antisocial conduct, at some point in the continuum between preparation and consummation, the likelihood of a commission of an act is sufficiently great and the criminal intent sufficiently well formed to justify the intervention of the criminal law. . . .

Again, we do not see how imposition of a strict "anti-federal" scienter requirement would relate to this purpose of conspiracy law. Given the level of intent needed to carry out the substantive offense, we fail to see how the agreement is any less blameworthy or constitutes less of a danger to society solely because the participants are unaware which body of law they intend to violate. Therefore, we again conclude that imposition of a requirement of knowledge of those facts that serve only to establish federal jurisdiction would render it more difficult to serve the policy behind the law of conspiracy without serving any other apparent social policy.

* * *

Again we point out, however, that the state of knowledge of the parties to an agreement is not always irrelevant in a proceeding charging a violation of conspiracy law. First, the knowledge of the parties is relevant to the same issues and to the same extent as it may be for conviction of the substantive offense. Second, whether conspirators knew the official identity of their quarry may be important, in some cases, in establishing the existence of federal jurisdiction. The jurisdictional requirement is satisfied by the existence of facts tying the proscribed conduct to the area of federal concern delineated by the statute. Federal jurisdiction always exists where the substantive offense is committed in the manner therein described, that is, when a federal officer is attacked. Where, however, there is an unfulfilled agreement to assault, it must be established whether the agreement, standing alone, constituted a sufficient threat to the safety of a federal officer so as to give rise to federal jurisdiction. If the agreement calls for an attack on an individual specifically identified, either by name or by some unique characteristic, as the putative buyers in the present case, and that specifically identified individual is in fact a federal officer, the agreement may be fairly characterized as one calling for an assault upon a federal officer, even though the parties were unaware of the victim's actual identity and even though they would not have agreed to the assault had they known that identity. Where the object of the intended attack is not identified with sufficient specificity so as to give rise to the conclusion that had the attack been carried out the victim would have been a federal officer, it is impossible to assert that the mere act of agreement to assault poses a sufficient threat to federal personnel and functions so as to give rise to federal jurisdiction.

To summarize, with the exception of the infrequent situation in which reference to the knowledge of the parties to an illegal agreement is necessary to establish the existence of federal jurisdiction, we hold that where knowledge of the facts giving rise to federal jurisdiction is not necessary for conviction of a substantive offense embodying a *mens rea* requirement, such knowledge is equally irrelevant to questions of responsibility for conspiracy to commit that offense.

The judgment of the Court of Appeals with respect to the respondent's conspiracy conviction is reversed.

It is so ordered.

Mr. Justice STEWART, with whom Mr. Justice DOUGLAS joins, *dissenting.*

Does an assault on a federal officer violate 18 U.S.C. § 111 even when the assailant is unaware, and has no reason to know, that the victim is other than a private citizen or, indeed, a confederate in crime? . . . .

* * *

The Court recognizes that "[t]he question . . . is not whether the [—federal officer'] requirement is jurisdictional, but whether it is jurisdictional only." . . . Put otherwise, the question is whether Congress intended to write an aggravated assault statute, analogous to the many state statutes which protect the persons and functions of state officers against assault, or whether Congress intended merely to federalize every assault which happens to have a federal officer as its victim. The Court chooses the latter interpretation, reading the federal-officer requirement to bejurisdictional only. This conclusion is inconsistent with the pertinent legislative history, the verbal structure of § 111, accepted canons of statutory construction, and the dictates of common sense.

Many States provide an aggravated penalty for assaults upon state law enforcement officers; typically the victim-status element transforms the assault from a misdemeanor to a felony. These statutes have a twofold purpose: to reflect the societal gravity associated with assaulting a public officer and, by providing an enhanced deterrent against such assault, to accord to public officers and their functions a protection greater than that which the law of assault otherwise provides to private citizens and their private activities. Consonant with these purposes, the accused's knowledge that his victim had an official status or function is invariably recognized by the States as an essential element of the aggravated offense. Where an assailant had no such knowledge, he could not of course be deterred by the statutory threat of enhanced punishment, and it makes no sense to regard the unknowing assault as being any more reprehensible, in a moral or retributive sense, than if the victim had been, as the assailant supposed, a private citizen.

The state statutes protect only state officers. I would read § 111 as filling the gap and supplying analogous protection for federal officers and their functions. An aggravated penalty should apply only where an assailant knew, or had reason to know, that his victim had some official status or function. It is immaterial whether the assailant knew the victim was employed by the federal, as opposed to a state or local, government. That is a matter of "jurisdiction only," for it does not affect the moral gravity of the act. If the victim was a federal officer, § 111 applies; if he was a state or local officer, an analogous state statute or local ordinance will generally apply. But where the assailant reasonably thought his victim a common citizen or, indeed, a confederate in crime, aggravation is simply out of place, and the case should be tried in the appropriate forum under the general law of assault, as are unknowing assaults on state officers.

[The dissent then reviewed the legislative history of § 111.]

* * *

Turning from the history of the statute to its structure, the propriety of implying a scienter requirement becomes manifest. The statute proscribes not only assault but also a whole series of related acts. It applies to any person who "forcibly assaults, *resists, opposes, impedes, intimidates,* or *interferes* with [a federal officer] . . . while engaged in or on account of the performance of his official duties." (Emphasis added.) It can hardly be denied that the emphasized words imply a scienter requirement. Generally speaking, these acts are legal and moral wrongs only if the actor knows that his "victim" enjoys a moral or legal privilege to detain him or order him about. These are terms of art, arising out of the common and statutory law proscribing obstruction of justice. . . .

If the words grouped in the statute with "assaults" require scienter, it follows that scienter is also required for an assault conviction. One need hardly rely on such Latin phrases as *ejusdem generis* and *noscitur a sociis* to reach this obvious conclusion. The Court suggests that assault may be treated differently, "with no risk of unfairness," because an assailant—unlike one who merely "opposes" or "resists"—"knows from the very outset that his planned course of conduct is wrongful" even though he "may be surprised to find that his intended victim is a federal officer in civilian apparel." This argument will not do, either as a matter of statutory construction or as a matter of elementary justice.

The Court is saying that because all assaults are wrong, it is "fair" to regard them all as *equally* wrong. This is a strange theory of justice. As the States recognize, an unknowing assault on an officer is less reprehensible than a knowing assault; to provide that the former may be punished as harshly as the latter is to create a very real "risk of unfairness." It is not unprecedented for Congress to enact stringent legislation, but today it is the Court that rewrites a statute so as to create an inequity which Congress itself had no intention of inflicting.

* * *

For the reasons stated, I believe that before there can be a violation of 18 U.S.C. § 111, an assailant must know or have reason to know that the person he assaults is an officer. It follows *a fortiori* that there can be no criminal conspiracy to violate the statute in the absence of at least equivalent knowledge. Accordingly, I respectfully dissent from the opinion and judgment of the Court.

NOTES AND QUESTIONS

1. In discussing Judge Hand's traffic light analogy, the *Feola* Court states that it "comes close to stating the *Powell* doctrine." To what extent is the traffic light analogy issue different from that encountered by the courts in the corrupt motive cases discussed in the note preceding *Feola?* Are the issues distinct enough to justify different *mens rea* requirements in the traffic light case and the *Powell* case?

2. Suppose the federal assault statute (§ 111) existed within the Model Penal Code system. Under the *Feola* facts, would the parties staging the rip-off be guilty of conspiracy to violate § 111 under MPC § 5.03 and other relevant Code sections? Under the Code, to commit conspiracy, what state of mind is required for the "circumstance" elements of the substantive crime? Consider MPC § 5.03, Explanatory Note at 384, which provides:

> The purpose requirement is meant to extend to result and conduct elements of the offense that is the object of the conspiracy, but whether or how far it also extends to circumstance elements of that offense is meant to be left open to interpretation by the courts.

Compare this approach to that taken by the Code for the state of mind pertaining to circumstance elements in attempt cases, see § 7.02[C] *supra.* Why would the Code permit different *mens rea* approaches for the related crimes of attempt and conspiracy?

In any event, is the federal status circumstance a "material element" of § 111? See MPC § 1.13(9)(10). Why might this question be relevant under the Code's approach to *mens rea* issues?

3. Smith and Jones conspire to steal an item valued at $505, which they (reasonably?) believe has a retail value of $450. The dividing line between grand and petty larceny is $500. Assuming that strict liability is applied to the value of the property for purposes of grading under the law of theft, are Smith and Jones guilty of conspiracy to commit grand larceny under the cases studied?

Would Smith and Jones be guilty of conspiracy under the Model Penal Code? Consider MPC § 223.1 and accompanying Comment (C) at 144–47.

4. Smith and Jones conspire to commit arson, realizing that if the targeted building burns, its janitor inside will surely die. Are Smith and Jones guilty of conspiracy to commit murder? See *State v. Caliguri,* 99 Wash. 2d 501, 664 P.2d 466 (1983).

Are they guilty of conspiracy to commit murder under the Model Penal Code?

5. Suppose conspirators plan to commit a crime that, unbeknownst to them, is actually impossible to commit. What if, as a variation of the *Jaffe* case, p.

553 supra, A and B agree to receive property they believe to be stolen but which actually is not? Unlike cases like *Jaffe* that appeal to the distinction between "legal" and "factual" impossibility in the context of attempt, the courts have tended to reject impossibility in any form as a defense to conspiracy. See, for example, *United States v. Waldron*, 590 F.2d 33 (1st Cir. 1979) (impossibility no defense where A and B conspire to import a painting they believed to be stolen although it actually was not stolen but was instead a forgery). The reasons for the different treatment of impossibility in attempt and impossibility in conspiracy are not obvious. One court offers this explanation:

> The case has been argued as though, for purposes of the defense of impossibility, a conspiracy charge is the same as a charge of attempting to commit a crime. It seems that such an equation could not be sustained, however, because . . . a conspiracy charge focuses primarily on the *intent* of the defendants, while in an attempt case the primary inquiry centers on the defendants' *conduct* tending toward the commission of the substantive crime. The crime of conspiracy is complete once the conspirators, having formed the intent to commit a crime, take any step in preparation; mere preparation, however, is an inadequate basis for an attempt conviction regardless of the intent. . . . Thus, the impossibility that the defendants' conduct will result in the consummation of the contemplated crime is not as pertinent in a conspiracy case as it might be in an attempt prosecution.

State v. Moretti, 244 A.2d 499, 502 (N.J. 1968).

Do you find this explanation convincing? Is impossibility a defense under the conspiracy provisions of the Model Penal Code?

[E] Single or Multiple Conspiracies

Model Penal Code § 5.03, Comment at 422-24 (1985)

Much of the most perplexing litigation in conspiracy has been concerned less with the essential elements of the offense than with the scope to be accorded to a combination, *i.e.*, the singleness or multiplicity of the conspiratorial relationships in a large, complex, and sprawling network of crime. The question here differs from [the question of defining offense elements] in that in most of these cases it is clear that each defendant has committed or conspired to commit one or more crimes; the question now is, to what extent is he a conspirator with each of the persons involved in the larger criminal network to commit the crimes that are their objects.

A narcotics operation may involve smugglers, distributors, and many retail sellers and may result in numerous instances of the commission of different types of crimes, as, for example, importing, possessing, and selling the narcotics. A vice ring may involve an overlord, lesser officers, and numerous runners and prostitutes; it may comprehend countless instances of the commission of such crimes as prostitution, placing a female in a house of prostitution, and receiving money from her earnings. Has a retailer conspired with the smugglers to import the narcotics? Has a prostitute conspired with the leaders of the vice ring to commit the acts of prostitution of each other prostitute who is controlled by the ring?

The inquiry may be crucial for a number of purposes. These include not only defining each defendant's liability, but also the propriety of joint prosecution, admissibility against a defendant of the hearsay acts and declarations of others, questions of multiple prosecution or conviction and double jeopardy, satisfaction of the overt act requirement or statutes of limitation, or rules of jurisdiction and venue, and possibly liability for substantive crimes executed pursuant to the conspiracy. The scope problem is thus central to the concern of courts and commentators about the use of conspiracy, a concern based on the conflict between the need for effective means of prosecuting large criminal organizations, and the dangers of prejudice to individual defendants.

KOTTEAKOS V. UNITED STATES

Supreme Court of the United States

328 U.S. 750 (1946)

Mr. Justice RUTLEDGE Delivered the Opinion of the Court.

The only question is whether petitioners have suffered substantial prejudice from being convicted of a single general conspiracy by evidence which the Government admits proved not one conspiracy but some eight or more different ones of the same sort executed through a common key figure, Simon Brown. Petitioners were convicted under the general conspiracy section of the Criminal Code . . . of conspiring to violate the provisions of the National Housing Act. . . . The judgments were affirmed by the Circuit Court of Appeals. . . .

The indictment named thirty-two defendants, including the petitioners. The gist of the conspiracy, as alleged, was that the defendants had sought to induce various financial institutions to grant credit, with the intent that the loans or advances would then be offered to the Federal Housing Administration for insurance upon applications containing false and fraudulent information.

Simon Brown, who pleaded guilty, was the common and key figure in all of the transactions proven. He was president of the Brownie Lumber Company. Having had experience in obtaining loans under the National Housing Act, he undertook to act as broker in placing for others loans for modernization and renovation, charging a five per cent commission for his services. Brown knew, when he obtained the loans, that the proceeds were not to be used for the purposes stated in the applications.

* * *

The evidence against the other defendants whose cases were submitted to the jury was similar in character. They . . . had transacted business with Brown relating to National Housing Act loans. But no connection was shown between them and petitioners, other than that Brown had been the instrument in each instance for obtaining the loans. In many cases the other defendants did not have any relationship with one another, other than Brown's connection with each transaction. As the Circuit Court of Appeals said, there were "at least eight, and perhaps more, separate and independent groups, none of which had any connection with any other, though all dealt independently with Brown as their agent." . . . As the Government puts it, the pattern was "that of separate spokes meeting at a common center," though we may add without the rim of the wheel to enclose the spokes.

The proof therefore admittedly made out a case, not of a single conspiracy, but of several, notwithstanding only one was charged in the indictment. . . . The Court of Appeals aptly drew analogy in the comment, "Thieves who dispose of their loot to a single receiver—a single —fence'—do not by that face alone become confederates: they may, but it takes more than knowledge that he is a —fence' to make them such." . . . It stated that the trial judge "was plainly wrong in supposing that upon the evidence there could be a single conspiracy; and in the view he took of the law, he should have dismissed the indictment." Nevertheless the appellate court held the error not prejudicial, saying among other things that "especially since guilt was so manifest, it was —proper' to join the conspiracies," and "to reverse the conviction would be a miscarriage of justice." . . .

* * *

. . . [T]he trial court itself was confused in the charge which it gave to guide the jury in deliberation. The court instructed: "The indictment charges but one conspiracy, and to convict each of the defendants of a conspiracy, the Government would have to prove, and you would have to find, that each of the defendants was a member of that conspiracy. You cannot divide it up. It is one conspiracy, and the question is whether or not each of the defendants or which of the defendants, are members of that conspiracy."

On its face, as the Court of Appeals said, this portion of the charge was plainly wrong in application to the proof made; and the error pervaded the entire charge, not merely the portion quoted. The jury could not possibly have found, upon the evidence, that there was only one conspiracy. The trial court was of the view that one conspiracy was made out by showing that each defendant was linked to Brown in one or more transactions, and that it was possible on the evidence for the jury to conclude that all were in a common adventure because of this fact and the similarity of purpose presented in the various applications for loans.

This view, specifically embodied throughout the instructions, obviously confuses the common purpose of a single enterprise with the several, though similar, purposes of numerous separate adventures of like character. It may be that, notwithstanding the misdirection, the jury actually understood correctly the purport of the evidence, as the Government now concedes it to have been; and came to the conclusion that the petitioners were guilty only of the separate conspiracies in which the proof shows they respectively participated. But, in the face of the misdirection and in the circumstances of this case, we cannot assume that the lay triers of fact were so well informed upon the law or that they disregarded the permission expressly given to ignore that vital difference. . . .

As we have said, the error permeated the entire charge, indeed the entire trial. Not only did it permit the jury to find each defendant guilty of conspiring with thirty-five other potential coconspirators, or any less number as the proof might turn out for acquittal of some, when none of the evidence would support such a conviction, as the proof did turn out in fact. It had other effects. One was to prevent the court from giving a precautionary instruction such as would be appropriate, perhaps, required, in cases where related but separate conspiracies are tried together under § 557 of the Code, namely, that the jury should take care to consider the evidence relating to each conspiracy separately from that relating to each other conspiracy charged. The court here was careful to caution the jury to consider each defendant's case separately, in determining his participation in "the scheme" charged. But this obviously does not, and could not, go to keeping distinct conspiracies distinct, in view of the court's conception of the case.

Moreover, the effect of the court's misconception extended also to the proof of overt acts. Carrying forward his premise that the jury could find one conspiracy on the evidence, the trial judge further charged that, if the jury found a conspiracy, "then the acts or the statements of any of those whom you so find to be conspirators between the two dates that I have mentioned, may be considered by you in evidence as against *all* of the defendants whom you so find to be members of the conspiracy." (Emphasis added.) The instructions in this phase also declared:

> It is not necessary, as a matter of law, that an overt act be charged against each defendant. It is sufficient if the conspiracy be established and the defendant be found to be a member of the conspiracy—it is sufficient to allege overt acts on the part of any others who may have been members of the conspiracy, if those acts were done in furtherance of, and for the purpose of accomplishing the conspiracy.

On those instructions it was competent not only for the jury to find that all of the defendants were parties to a single common plan, design and scheme, where none was shown by the proof, but also for them to impute to each defendant the acts and statements of the others without reference to whether they related to one of the schemes proven or another, and to find an overt act affecting all in conduct which admittedly could only have affected some. . . .

* * *

It may be, as the Court of Appeals found, that the evidence concerning each petitioner was so clear that conviction would have been dictated and reversal forbidden, if it had been presented in separate trials for each offense. . . . But whether so or not is neither our problem nor that of the Court of Appeals for this case. . . .We think it highly probable that the error had substantial and injurious effect or influence in determining the jury's verdict.

We have not rested our decision particularly on the fact that the offense charged, and those proved, were conspiracies. That offense is perhaps not greatly different from others when the scheme charged is tight and the number involved small. But as it is broadened to include more and more, in varying degrees of attachment to the confederation, the possibilities for miscarriage of justice to particular individuals become greater and greater. . . . At the outskirts they are perhaps higher than in any other form of criminal trial our system affords. The greater looseness generally allowed for specifying the offense and its details, for receiving proof, and generally in the conduct of the trial, becomes magnified as the numbers involved increase. Here, if anywhere, . . . extraordinary precaution is required, not only that instructions shall not mislead, but that they shall scrupulously safeguard each defendant individually, as far as possible, from loss of identity in the mass. Indeed, the instructions often become, in such cases, his principal protection against unwarranted imputation of guilt from others' conduct. Here also it is of special importance that plain error be not too readily taken to be harmless.

Accordingly the judgments are reversed and the causes are remanded for further proceedings in conformity with this opinion.

Reversed.

Notes and Questions

1. In cases like *Kotteakos,* where a number of people conspire with the same individual or group, the conspiratorial relationship is often analogized to a wheel, with the central figure (Brown in *Kotteakos*) as the hub and the other parties as the spokes. Does *Kotteakos* establish that wheel conspiracies will invariably be viewed as a series of separate conspiracies rather than one, all-encompassing criminal enterprise? In other words, are there cases where the various spokes might be sufficiently connected (rimmed together around the hub) so as to justify the conclusion that a single, large conspiracy exists? If so, does *Kotteakos* provide a standard by which to make such a determination?

In a later case, the Court suggested that the *Kotteakos* wheel might have been viewed differently if certain facts had been otherwise:

> [In *Kotteakos*] [e]ach loan was an end in itself; separate from all others, although all were alike in having similar illegal objects. Except for Brown, the common figure, no conspirator was interested in whether any loan except his own went through. And none aided in any way, by agreement or otherwise, in procuring another's loan. The conspiracies therefore were distinct and disconnected, not parts of a larger general scheme, both in the phase of agreement with Brown and also in the absence of any aid given to others as well as in specific object and result. There was no drawing of all together in a single, over-all, comprehensive plan.

Blumenthal v. United States, 332 U.S. 539, 558 (1947).

2. In *Anderson v. Superior Court,* 78 Cal. App. 2d, 177 P.2d 315 (1947), the court sustained an indictment charging defendant and 16 other persons with conspiring with one Stern to perform illegal abortions. The evidence established that defendant and the others had, for a fee, referred women desiring abortions to Stern. The court concluded that because defendant knew Stern regularly performed abortions and that hers were not his only referrals, she was engaged in a single conspiracy with Stern and the others making referrals even though she did not know their identities. Is *Anderson* consistent with *Kotteakos?* If not, what kinds of additional evidence could "supply proof that

the spokes are bound by a —rim' [so as] to lead to an inference that some form of overall agreement exists"? *United States v. Kenny,* 645 F.2d 1323, 1335 (9th Cir. 1981).

For examples of other wheel arrangements that the courts have found to be single conspiracies, see *United States v. McMurray,* 680 F.2d 695 (10th Cir. 1981); *People v. Quintana,* 189 Colo. 330, 540 P.2d 1097 (1975).

3. In contrast to the wheel relationship in *Kotteakos,* many conspiracies are analogized to chains, usually in contraband distribution schemes involving distributors, middlemen, and ultimate purchasers. *Blumenthal v. United States,* 332 U.S. 539 (1947), provides an example. Whiskey distributors received two carloads of whiskey from an unknown owner of their company which they in turn transferred to their salesmen, who sold the whiskey at prices in excess of the ceiling set by the Office of Price Administration. The distributors and salesmen were convicted of a single conspiracy among themselves and with the unidentified owner. On appeal, the salesmen argued that two conspiracies existed: one between them and the distributors, the other between the distributors and the unknown owner. In holding that the situation constituted one conspiracy, the Court stated,

> We think that in the special circumstances of this case the two agreements were merely steps in the formation of the larger and ultimately more general conspiracy. In that view it would be a perversion of justice to regard the salesmen's ignorance of the unknown owner's participation as furnishing adequate ground for reversal of their convictions. . . . The scheme was in fact the same scheme; the salesmen knew or must have known that others unknown to them were sharing in so large a project; and it hardly can be sufficient to relieve them that they did not know, when they joined the scheme, who those people were or exactly the parts they were playing in carrying out the common design and object of all. By their separate agreements, if such they were, they became parties to the larger common plan, joined together by their knowledge of its essential features and broad scope, though not of its exact limits, and by their common single goal.

* * *

> Here . . . [a]ll knew of and joined in the overriding scheme. All intended to aid the owner . . . to sell whiskey unlawfully, though the two groups of defendants differed on the proof in knowledge and belief concerning the owner's identity. All by reason of their knowledge of the plan's general scope, if not its exact limits, sought a common end, to aid in disposing of the whiskey. True, each salesman aided in selling only his part. But he knew the lot to be sold was larger and thus that he was aiding in a larger plan. He thus became a party to it and not merely to the integrating agreement with [the distributors.]

Blumenthal at 557–59.

4. If *Kotteakos* and *Blumenthal* suggest, respectively, that wheel arrangements are more apt to be viewed as several separate conspiracies, while chain situations likely involve one large conspiracy, how analytically helpful are appeals to the configuration of the conspiratorial pattern in reaching results? Consider the following:

As applied to the long-term operation of an illegal business, the common pictorial distinction between "chain" and "spoke" conspiracies can obscure as much as it clarifies. The chain metaphor is indeed apt in that the links of a narcotics conspiracy are inextricably related to one another, from grower, through exporter and importer, to wholesaler, middleman, and retailer, each depending for his own success on the performance of all the others. But this simple picture tends to obscure that the links at either end are likely to consist of a number of persons who may have no reason to know that others are performing a role similar to theirs—in other words the extreme links of a chain conspiracy may have elements of the spoke conspiracy. Moreover, whatever the value of the chain concept where the problem is to trace a single operation from the start through its various phases to its successful conclusion, it becomes confusing when, over a long period of time, certain links continue to play the same role but with new counterparts, as where importers who regard their partnership as a single continuing one, having successfully distributed one cargo through X distributing organization, turn, years later, to moving another cargo obtained from a different source through Y. Thus, however reasonable the so-called presumption of continuity may be as to all the participants of a conspiracy which intends a single act, such as the robbing of a bank, or even as to the core of a conspiracy to import and resell narcotics, its force is diminished as to the outer links—buyers indifferent to their sources of supply andturning from one source to another, and suppliers equally indifferent to the identity oftheir customers.

United States v. Borelli, 336 F.2d 376, 383–84 (2d Cir. 1964).

The Model Penal Code Comments provide the following discussion of the wheel and chain analogies:

> . . . The relationships in [complex criminal networks] are sometimes analogized to a wheel (or circle) and a chain. . . .

> *United States v. Bruno* [105 F.2d 921 (2d Cir. 1939)] involved both types of relationships. In that case, eighty-eight defendants were indicted for a conspiracy to import, sell, and possess narcotics. The proof showed a vast operation extending over a long period of time, which included smugglers who brought narcotics into New York City, middlemen who paid the smugglers and distributed to retailers, and two groups of retailers selling to addicts, one in New York and the other in Texas and Louisiana. There was no evidence of cooperation or communication between the smugglers and either group of retailers or between the two widely separated groups of retailers. The relationship between the smugglers, the middlemen, and each group of retailers consequently was a typical chain, with communication as well as narcotics passing from smuggler to middleman to retailer. The two groups of retailers, on the other hand, may be considered separate spokes of a wheel whose hub was the middlemen, since they communicated and cooperated only with the middleman and not with one another.

> The appellants argued that the evidence may have established several separate conspiracies, but not the single one alleged. The court held that the jury could have found a single large conspiracy "whose object was to smuggle narcotics into the Port of New York and distribute them to addicts

both in [New York] and in Texas and Louisiana." This required, the court reasoned, the cooperation of all the various groups—smugglers, middlemen, and the two groups of retailers.

> [T]he smugglers knew that the middlemen must sell to retailers, and the retailers knew that the middlemen must buy of importers of one sort or another. Thus the conspirators at one end of the chain knew that the unlawful business would not, and could not, stop with their buyers; and those at the other end knew that it had not begun with their sellers. That being true, a jury might have found that all the accused were embarked upon a venture, in all parts of which each was a participant, and an abettor in the sense that the success of that part with which he was immediately concerned, was dependent upon the success of the whole.

The only possible basis mentioned in the opinion for a finding of separate conspiracies was the fact that there was apparently "no privity" between the two separate groups of retailers. To the argument that there were consequently two conspiracies, one including the smugglers, the middlemen, and the New York retailers, and the other the smugglers, the middlemen, and the Texas and Louisiana retailers, the court replied:

> Clearly, quoad the smugglers, there was but one conspiracy, for it was of no moment to them, whether the middlemen sold to one or more groups of retailers, provided they had a market somewhere. So too of any retailer; he knew that he was a necessary link in a scheme of distribution, and the others, whom he knew to be convenient to its execution, were as much parts of a single undertaking or enterprise as two salesmen in the same shop.

Model Penal Code § 5.03, Comment at 425–27.

5. The Model Penal Code's provision defining the scope of conspiracies is § 5.03(2):

> *Scope of Conspiratorial Relationship.* If a person guilty of conspiracy, as defined by Subsection (1) of this Section, knows that a person with whom he conspires to commit a crime has conspired with another person or persons to commit the same crime, he is guilty of conspiring with such other person or persons, whether or not he knows their identity, to commit such crime.

Under the Code's provision, how would *Kotteakos* be resolved? As to the problem posed by the *Bruno* case, the Code Comments provide,

> The Model Code provision would require a different approach to a case such as *Bruno* and might produce different results. Since the overall operation involved the separate crimes of importing by the smugglers and possession and sale by each group—smugglers, distributors, and retailers—the question as to each defendant would be whether and with whom he conspired to commit each of these crimes, under the criteria set forth in [§ 5.03] Subsections (1) and (2). The conspiratorial objective for the purpose of this inquiry could not be characterized in the manner of the *Bruno* court, as "to smuggle narcotics into the Port of New York and distribute them to addicts both in [New York] and in Texas and Louisiana." This is indeed the overall objective of the entire operation. It also may be true that *some* of

the participants conspired to commit all of the crimes involved in the operation.

With the conspiratorial objectives characterized as the particular crimes and culpability of each participant tested separately, it would be possible to find in a case such as *Bruno,* considering for the moment only each separate chain of distribution, that the smugglers conspired to commit the illegal sales of the retailers, but that the retailers did not conspire to commit the importing of the smugglers. . . .

It also would be possible to find, with the inquiry focused on each individual's culpability as to each criminal objective, that some of the parties in a chain conspired to commit the entire series of crimes while others conspired to commit only some of these crimes. Thus the smugglers and the middlemen in Bruno may have conspired to commit, promote, or facilitate the importing and the possession and sales of all of the parties down to the final retail sale; the retailers might have conspired with them as to their own possession and sales, but might be indifferent to all the steps prior to their receipt of the narcotics. In this situation, a smuggler or a middleman might have conspired with all three groups to commit the entire series of crimes, while a retailer might have conspired with the same parties but to achieve fewer criminal objectives. Such results are conceptually difficult to reach under existing doctrine not only because of the frequent failure to focus separately on the different criminal objectives, but also because of the traditional view of the agreement as a bilateral relationship between each of the parties, congruent in scope both as to its party and its objective dimensions.

MPC § 5.03, Comments at 427–28 (1985).

6. Suppose A, B, and C decide on a single occasion to rob seven different banks on seven different days. Have they committed seven conspiracies or one? In finding one conspiracy in such a case, the Supreme Court stated,

[W]hen to commit one or more substantive crimes is evidenced by an overt act, as the statute requires, the precise nature and extent of the conspiracy must be determined by reference to the agreement which embraces and defines its objects. Whether the object of a single agreement is to commit one or many crimes, it is in either case that agreement which constitutes the conspiracy. . . . The one agreement cannot be taken to be several agreements and hence several conspiracies. . . .

Braverman v. United States, 317 U.S. 49, 53 (1942).

Model Penal Code § 5.03(3) adopts the *Braverman* position:

Conspiracy with Multiple Criminal Objectives. If a person conspires to commit a number of crimes, he is guilty of only one conspiracy so long as such multiple crimes are the object of the same agreement or continuous conspiratorial relationship.

[F] Renunciation and Withdrawal

Although the crime of conspiracy is complete with the making of an agreement with requisite intent and the performance of an overt act if such is required, renunciation of the conspiracy is sometimes recognized as a defense. While the common law traditionally, as with attempt, afforded no affirmative defense, Model Penal Code § § 5.03(6) and 5.03(7)(c) allow a defense if the actor "thwarts the success of the conspiracy, under circumstances manifesting a complete and voluntary renunciation of his criminal purpose." Many jurisdictions now afford a similar defense. Some courts and legislatures, however, consider the requirement that defendant's action actually result in thwarting as too demanding, recognizing that failure to stop the crime might be the fault of the police or others over whom the defendant had no control. They therefore have provided that if the defendant attempts to thwart the object crime, he has "renounced." See, for example, Neb. Rev. Stat. § 28–203 (1995) (renunciation if defendant gives "timely warning to law enforcement authorities or otherwise ma[kes] a reasonable effort to prevent" the object crime). Is a renunciation defense sound on policy grounds?

In contrast to the affirmative defense of renunciation, withdrawal from the conspiracy has always had important consequences. If a conspirator decides not to participate further, the common law recognized a claim of "withdrawal" so long as the conspirator clearly and unequivocally informed each of his cohorts that he was withdrawing prior to the commission of the substantive crime(s), *Loser v. Superior Court,* 78 Cal. App. 2d 30, 177 P.2d 320 (1947). The requirement of notifying each cohort is premised on the assumption that unless they are aware that the withdrawing conspirator has withdrawn, *they* will be encouraged by what *they* believe is his continuing support of their enterprise. An effective withdrawal operates to begin the running of the statute of limitations as to the withdrawing conspirator, *Hyde v. United States,* 225 U.S. 347, 369 (1912). Moreover, effective withdrawal precludes liability for substantive offenses committed in furtherance of the conspiracy, subsequent to the withdrawal. Absent an effective withdrawal, conspirators are held responsible under the *Pinkerton* doctrine for all crimes committed in furtherance of the conspiracy, *State v. Peterson,* 213 Minn. 56, 4 N.W.2d 826 (1942). See *Pinkerton v. United States, infra* at § 8.02.

Model Penal Code § 5.03(7)(c) provides that withdrawal occurs "only if and when [the conspirator] advises those with whom he conspired of his abandonment or he informs the law enforcement authorities of the existence of the conspiracy and of his participation therein." Should informing law enforcement authorities be an absolute prerequisite for any effective withdrawal? The Model Penal Code does not adopt the *Pinkerton* doctrine and treats potential liability for crimes committed by other conspirators, even where the defendant has not clearly withdrawn, under accomplice liability principles. See § 8.02, *infra*. As at common law, withdrawal under the MPC triggers the running of the statute of limitations for conspiracy.

[G] Grading of Punishment

NOTE, CONSPIRACY: STATUTORY REFORM SINCE THE MODEL PENAL CODE

75 Colum. L. Rev. 1122, 1183–87 (1975)

The job of grading the conspiracy offense demands an evaluation of the proper relationship between an inchoate and a substantive crime. The MPC

[§ 5.05(1)] has enjoyed considerable success in pressing the view that the degree of a criminal agreement should depend on the gravity of the substantive offense which is its object. Several pre-reform statutes classify all conspiracies as misdemeanors, regardless of their purpose. . . . But, these statutes are anachronistic. Since the promulgation of the MPC, nearly all jurisdictions concerned with criminal law revision have endorsed conspiracy penalties more closely resembling those assigned to the particular substantive crime intended.

For sentencing purposes, the MPC would treat conspiracy and its object offense identically, unless the latter were a first-degree felony. In that case, conspiracy would be labeled a felony of the second degree. Thirteen states and the Senate version of the proposed Federal Criminal Code have essentially adopted this scheme. The justification for such a grading procedure rests on a conception of conspiracy as inchoate crime, and an accompanying conviction regarding the punishment appropriate for that sort of offense. Apart from retribution, the legitimate ends of punishment as commonly enumerated, are deterrence, reformation, and protection of society through incapacitation of the offender. By definition, a conspirator is one who agrees to commit a crime with the purpose of promoting or facilitating the commission of that crime. Theoretically, then, his criminal intent is established. He is as much in need of correction or reformation as a person successful in committing the crime. On the other hand, sanctions attached to the object offense have not dissuaded the conspirator from aligning himself with others in a plan to violate the law. From this perspective, the potential deterrent efficacy of any conspiracy penalty seems slight. The MPC framers believed that, given this lack of significant deterrent function, the harshest of the law's sanctions could safely be removed from inchoate crimes. Hence, the treatment of conspiracy to commit a first-degree felony. . . . Admittedly, the MPC grading outline, as applied to most conspiracies, provides no marginal inducement to desist between formation of the criminal agreement and commission of the object crime. The renunciation defense is designed to at least partially fill this gap.

* * *

A . . . prevalent alternative to the MPC pattern is the automatic downgrading of the inchoate offense, without regard to indications of the state which the criminal project reached. Sixteen states have chosen to reduce conspiracy one degree from its object crime, and five other jurisdictions have favored even further reductions. . . .

* * *

To complete the grading picture, brief mention must be made of the MPC mitigation provision, which has been embraced in its entirety by just five states. MPC § 5.05(2) grants the court power to "enter judgment and impose sentence for a crime of lower grade or degree or, in extreme cases, [to] dismiss the prosecution" whenever the particular conduct charged to constitute a conspiracy "is so inherently unlikely to result or culminate in the commission of a crime that neither such conduct nor the actor present a public danger warranting" the ordinary grading of such offense. This safety valve is extremely desirable in the inchoate crime area, which, by definition, involves threats of infinitely varying intensity.

[H] RICO

BLAKEY AND GETTINGS, *RACKETEER INFLUENCED AND CORRUPT ORGANIZATIONS (RICO): BASIC CONCEPTS—CRIMINAL AND CIVIL REMEDIES*

53 Temple L.Q. 1009, 1011–14, 1021–25, 1029–31, 1033–35 (1980)

. . . If the law of conspiracy is in good repute among any segment of the bar, it is among the prosecutors. The conspiracy charge has been aptly called by Judge Learned Hand, "the darling of the modern prosecutor's nursery." Were Judge Hand alive today, he might be moved to comment, however, that the fickle fancy of the prosecutor has turned to RICO, the Racketeer Influenced and Corrupt Organizations title (title IX) of the Organized Crime Control Act of 1970. Largely ignored at first, today RICO is widely employed by federal prosecutors, not just by organized crime strike force attorneys, but by prosecutors in United States Attorney's offices; RICO is used not just in organized crime prosecutions, but in white-collar prosecutions (most prominently political corruption cases) as well as in a large variety of violent offenses. . . .

RICO was the end product of a long process of legislative effort to develop new legal remedies to deal with an old problem: "organized crime." As finally enacted, RICO authorized the imposition of enhanced criminal penalties and new civil sanctions to provide new legal remedies for all types of organized criminal behavior, that is, enterprise criminality—from simple political corruption to sophisticated white-collar crime schemes to traditional Mafia-type endeavors. . . .

* * *

A. STANDARDS

RICO makes unlawful, that is, contrary to law, four activities by any person:

(1) using income derived from a pattern of racketeering activity to acquire an interest in an enterprise;

(2) acquiring or maintaining an interest in an enterprise through a pattern of racketeering activity;

(3) conducting the affairs of an enterprise through a pattern of racketeering activity; and

(4) conspiring to commit any of these offenses.

An understanding of these legal standards requires a look at the basic concepts used in their drafting.

B. Concepts

1. Person

Section 1961(3) indicates that "person" "includes . . . any individual or entity capable of holding a legal or beneficial interest in property." . . . Those "persons" who can violate RICO include white-collar criminals as well as members of organized crime.

2. Enterprise

To violate RICO, a person must acquire or maintain an interest in or control of an enterprise, or must conduct or participate in the conduct of an enterprise's affairs. Section 1961(4) provides that "enterprise" "includes any individual, partnership, corporation, association, or other legal entity, and any union or group of individuals associated in fact though not a legal entity."

. . . Private businesses as well as labor organizations are enterprises under RICO, The enterprise need not be legitimate. Government agencies may also be enterprises. In addition, the definition of enterprise encompasses associations in fact. This type of enterprise need not be a legal entity; RICO is directed at groups of individuals informally organized for a common purpose. Associations in fact are often formed for the purpose of engaging in criminal activities, but their purposes may be legitimate as well. The group associated in fact may also change its membership in the course of its activity. . . .

3. Pattern of Racketeering Activity

To violate RICO, the takeover or operation of an enterprise must be accomplished through a "pattern" of "racketeering activity." Section 1961(5) limits "pattern" by requiring that it include "at least two acts . . . , one of which occurred after the effective date of this chapter and the last of which occurred within ten years . . . after the commission of a prior act." Beyond this statutory limitation, the legislative history of RICO as well as its judicial interpretation indicate that the racketeering acts must be "related" to each other. Sporadic activity cannot constitute a pattern of racketeering activity. "The racketeering acts must have been connected with each other by some common scheme, plan, or motive so as to constitute a pattern and not simply a series of disconnected acts." The acts may be unrelated to each other, but held together by a relationship to an enterprise. Patterns have been found where the separate acts have had similar purposes, results, participants, victims, or methods of commission. Under section 1961(1), "racketeering activity" is defined by incorporating state and federal offenses. . . . The state offenses are generically defined. Arson, bribery, and extortion are among the incorporated state crimes.[102] Many federal statutes are incorporated under RICO as well. Mail fraud is the most inclusive of the federal statutes, since it covers a broad range of criminal activity rooted in fraud.

* * *

Section 1963 provides criminal remedies for a violation of RICO's standards. In the event of a criminal conviction, the violator may "be fined not more than

---

[102] 18 U.S.C. § 1961(1)(A) (1976). Other state crimes are murder, kidnaping, gambling, robbery, and dealing in narcotics. *Id.*

$25,000 or imprisoned not more than twenty years, or both." These penalties sometimes, but not always, will exceed those which could be imposed for two violations of the incorporated offenses. In addition to a fine and imprisonment, the violator must forfeit to the United States any interest he has acquired (all his ill-gotten gains) as well as any interest in an enterprise (his economic base) which affords him a source of power over the enterprise involved in the violation of RICO.

UNITED STATES V. SUTHERLAND

United States Court of Appeals, Fifth Circuit

656 F.2d 1181 (1981)

RANDALL, Circuit Judge:

In this case three defendants appeal their convictions for conspiracy to violate the Racketeer Influenced and Corrupt Organizations Act (RICO) in violation of 18 U.S.C. § 1962(d) (1976). The defendants raise . . . an important RICO question: whether and when conspiracies that involve the same enterprise but are otherwise unrelated may be tried together under a single RICO conspiracy count. We consider the defendants' points on appeal . . . and affirm their convictions.

I. THE FACTS

Glen Sutherland, Grace Walker and Edward Maynard were indicted in January 1980 for conspiracy to violate 18 U.S.C. § 1962(c)[1] in violation of 18 U.S.C. § 1962(d)[2]. The indictment charged, in brief, that the three defendants "did knowingly, wilfully, and unlawfully combine, conspire, confederate, and agree together and with each other," from November 1975 until the date of the indictment, to violate section 1962(c). The conspiracy alleged by the

---

[1] 18 U.S.C. § 1962(c) (1976) is as follows:

> It shall be unlawful for any person employed by or associated with any enterprise engaged in, or the activities of which affect, interstate or foreign commerce, to conduct or participate, directly or indirectly, in the conduct of such enterprise's affairs through a pattern of racketeering activity or collection of unlawful debt.

"Enterprise" is defined as follows, 18 U.S.C. § 1961(4):

> [E]nterprise includes any individual, partnership, corporation, association, or other legal entity, and any union or group of individuals associated in fact although not a legal entity.

"Racketeering activity" is defined in pertinent part as follows, 18 U.S.C. § 1961(1):

> Racketeering activity means (A) any act or threat involving murder, kidnaping, gambling, arson, robbery, bribery, extortion, or dealing in narcotic or other dangerous drugs, which is chargeable under State law and punishable by imprisonment for more than one year. . . .

A "pattern of racketeering activity" is defined as follows, 18 U.S.C. § 1961(5):

> [P]attern of racketeering activity requires at least two acts of racketeering activity, one of which occurred after the effective date of this chapter and the last of which occurred within ten years (excluding any period of imprisonment) after the commission of a prior act of racketeering activity.

[2] 18 U.S.C. § 1962(d) is as follows:

> It shall be unlawful for any person to conspire to violate any of the provisions of subsections (a), (b), or (c) of this Section.

government consisted of an agreement to associate with and to participate in the conduct of an enterprise that affects interstate commerce (the Municipal Court of the City of El Paso) through a pattern of racketeering activity (bribery of a state official in violation of state law).

The alleged conspiracy centers around Sutherland, who at the time of these events was a judge of the Municipal Court. According to the government, the defendants agreed that Maynard and Walker would each collect traffic tickets from his or her friends and associates, along with the amount of the statutory fine plus a small premium ($10); that Maynard and Walker would deliver the tickets to Sutherland, who would have the cases transferred to his docket and would then favorably dispose of them; and that the money collected would in each case be split between Sutherland and whichever other defendant collected and delivered the ticket.

Although the indictment frames the conspiracy as a single agreement among all three defendants, the government did not attempt at trial to prove any agreement between Walker and Maynard. . . .

. . . [W]e find the evidence sufficient to support each of two separate conspiracies, one between Walker and Sutherland and the other between Maynard and Sutherland. In each case the evidence is more than sufficient to establish an agreement to participate in the conduct of the Municipal Court through a pattern of racketeering activity. However, the government has pointed to no evidence in the record (and we have found none) that suggests that either Walker or Maynard knew or should have known of the other's similar agreement with Sutherland. The government's evidence as to these two defendants is entirely unrelated and, in fact, places the two conspiracies at different periods of time: the specific instances of bribery alleged between Walker and Sutherland all took place between 1975 and 1977, while those between Maynard and Sutherland all took place in 1979.

II. THE SUFFICIENCY OF THE EVIDENCE

All three defendants challenge the sufficiency of the evidence to support their convictions under 18 U.S.C. § 1962(d). First, each argues that the government failed to establish a "pattern of racketeering activity" since the evidence does not specifically demonstrate "at least two acts of racketeering activity," as required by 18 U.S.C. § 1961(5), *supra* at n. 1.[4] Second, Walker

---

[4] All parties, as well as the district court, refer to the requisite "two acts of racketeering activity." Strictly speaking, the government need not have proven that two such acts were in fact committed. This case was not brought under the substantive RICO provisions, but is instead based on the defendants' *conspiracy* to violate such provisions. The government need not prove in a conspiracy case that a substantive crime was actually committed, but instead need demonstrate that some "overt act" was taken in furtherance of a conspiracy to commit a substantive crime. In particular, the government need show only that "at least one conspirator committed at least one overt act in furtherance of the conspiracy." . . . The overt act need not itself constitute a substantive crime; any act, even if seemingly innocent in itself, is sufficient to support a conspiracy conviction if taken in furtherance of the conspiracy. . . . In this case the government's reliance on specific acts of racketeering activity is understandable, for such evidence constitutes convincing circumstantial evidence of an agreement to violate the substantive RICO provision at issue. Still, however, we find the government's exclusive reliance on these acts for the necessary "overt act" somewhat perplexing in light of the decision (whether made by the government or by the grand jury) not to indict the defendants for a substantive RICO offense.

argues that the evidence does not sufficiently establish any agreement between herself and Sutherland. In considering these arguments we must read the evidence in the light most favorable to the government, and must reverse the convictions if we find that any reasonable jury thus reading the evidence must necessarily have entertained a reasonable doubt as to the defendants' guilt. . . .

The Requisite "Two Acts of Racketeering Activity"

The government proved that a number of specific traffic tickets were (1) given by traffic violators to either Walker or Maynard, and (2) favorably disposed of by Sutherland in his capacity as municipal judge. Through the testimony of Sally Kalastro (a co-worker with Walker at the time of the events in question), the government identified twenty-five individual tickets that had been accepted by Walker. Through the testimony of several persons who submitted tickets to Maynard (including several bogus tickets prepared for the purpose of the investigation), the government identified fifteen individual tickets that had been accepted by Maynard. In the case of each ticket, the government introduced evidence (primarily from Municipal Court records) to establish its favorable disposition (typically a finding of not guilty) by Sutherland.

[The court found that this and other circumstantial evidence sufficiently established an agreement to violate RICO.]

* * *

III. THE MULTIPLE CONSPIRACY DOCTRINE AND RICO

The Trial of Multiple Conspiracies under a Single RICO "Enterprise Conspiracy" Count

It is now well settled that a material variance between the indictment and the government's evidence is created by the government's proof of multiple conspiracies under an indictment alleging a single conspiracy.[5] This "multiple conspiracy doctrine" is commonly illustrated by the Supreme Court's decision in *Kotteakos v. United States,* 328 U.S. 750 (1946). . . .

In this case the government has by its own admission, as in *Kotteakos,* introduced no evidence of a single conspiracy but has instead rested its case on two distinct multiple conspiracies. The government did not attempt at trial to prove an agreement among all three defendants, but instead sought to establish separate conspiracies comprised of (1) Walker and Sutherland, and (2) Maynard and Sutherland. Like the multiple conspiracies in *Kotteakos,* these agreements share a common conspirator and similar objectives, but are otherwise unrelated. The government does not suggest that either bribery scheme was dependent on or benefited from the other, and does not dispute

---

[5] In this case the government introduced no evidence from which a jury could conclude that a single conspiracy existed among the defendants. This case should be distinguished, therefore, from cases in which the record contains, in addition to evidence of multiple conspiracies, sufficient evidence to support a finding of a single conspiracy. If the government sufficiently supports its charge of single conspiracy, evidence at trial of multiple conspiracies does not of itself create a material variance with the indictment; at most, such evidence creates a fact question and entitles the defendants to a jury instruction on the possibility of multiple conspiracies. . . .

the defendants' contentions that neither Walker nor Maynard knew or should have known of the other. "If there is not some interaction between those conspirators who form the spokes of the wheel as to at least one common illegal object, the —wheel' is incomplete, and two conspiracies rather than one are charged." *United States v. Levine,* 546 F.2d 658 663 (5th Cir. 1977).

Of course, the government need not always demonstrate an actual agreement among the various conspirators, or even actual knowledge of each other, in order to establish a single conspiracy. In *Blumenthal v. United States,* 332 U.S. 539 (1947), the Supreme Court recognized that in some cases the interdependent nature of the criminal enterprise is such that each conspirator had to have realized that it extended beyond his individual role. This form of conspiracy is often described as a "chain" rather than a "wheel." . . . The government does not contend that the case at bar is a "chain" conspiracy, and the evidence does not suggest one. Indeed, a chain conspiracy would be difficult to imagine on the facts of this case: while two people may in fact conspire together to bribe a single judge, there is no reason why one who has individually so acted must necessarily have assumed that others have also bribed the same judge.

The government does not defend its joint trial in this case on the basis of traditional conspiracy law, *i.e.,* by arguing either that the evidence connected the spokes of a wheel conspiracy by common knowledge or agreement, or that the evidence demonstrates a chain conspiracy. Instead, the government argues that despite the apparent relevance to this case of the traditional multiple conspiracy doctrine, the defendants were properly tried together for a single "enterprise conspiracy" under RICO. The government contends, in brief, that a single conspiracy to violate a substantive RICO provision may be comprised of a pattern of agreements that absent RICO would constitute multiple conspiracies. The government contends that this is so even where, as here, there is no agreement of any kind between the members of the two separate conspiracies. According to the government, these otherwise multiple conspiracies are tried together by the RICO "enterprise": so long as the object of each conspiracy is participation in the same enterprise in violation of RICO, it matters not that the different conspiracies are otherwise unrelated. Thus, the government argues that it need not demonstrate any connection between Walker and Maynard because the two conspiracies at issue each involved the same RICO enterprise—the Municipal Court of the City of El Paso.

For this proposition the government relies on *United States v. Elliott,* 571 F.2d 880 (5th Cir.), *cert. denied,* 439 U.S. 953 (1978). We held in *Elliott* that a group of defendants who could not have been tried for a single conspiracy to violate any particular predicate crime could nevertheless be tried for a single conspiracy to violate RICO. *Elliott* involved six defendants who had committed a variety of unrelated offenses with no common purpose or agreement as to any of the various crimes. We explained:

> Applying pre-RICO concepts to the facts of this case, we doubt that a single conspiracy could be demonstrated. Foster had no contact with Delph and Taylor during the life of the alleged conspiracy. Delph and Taylor, so far as the evidence revealed, had no contact with Recea Hawkins. The activities allegedly embraced by the illegal agreement in this case are simply too

diverse—(unrelated acts involving arson, murder, theft, drugs, and obstruction of justice) to be tied together on the theory that participation in one activity necessarily implied awareness of others.

571 F.2d at 902.

Despite these facts, we upheld the government's joint trial of the *Elliott* defendants on a single conspiracy count. We defined the RICO enterprise in *Elliott* to consist of at least five persons who joined together to commit crime for profit "a myriopod criminal network, loosely connected but connected nonetheless." . . . Since the defendants had conspired together to participate in that enterprise through a pattern of racketeering activity, we upheld their joint trial despite the absence of an agreement as to any particular predicate crime. We held, in short, that "[RICO's] effect in this case is to free the government from the strictures of the multiple conspiracy doctrine and to allow the joint trial of many persons accused of diversified crimes.". . .

Read out of context, without attention to the facts of the case or to the court's rationale, *Elliott* does seem to support the government's position, *i.e.,* that the defendants' participation in the same RICO enterprise is enough to tie otherwise multiple conspiracies together even where, as here, there is no agreement of any kind between the members of the two separate conspiracies.[7] Indeed, *Elliott* has been thus read by some courts and commentators (and, as so read, has been uniformly criticized). . . .

To put the *Elliott* holding in its proper perspective, we quote our explanation of that holding at length:

> Under the general federal conspiracy statute, "the precise nature and extent of the conspiracy must be determined by reference to the agreement which embraces and defines its objects. Whether the object of a single agreement is to commit one or many crimes, it is in either case that agreement which constitutes the conspiracy which the statute punishes." *Braverman v. United States,* 317 U.S. 49, 53 (1942). In the context of organized crime, this principle inhibited mass prosecutions because a single agreement or "common objective" cannot be inferred from the commission of highly diverse crimes by apparently unrelated individuals. *RICO helps to eliminate this problem by creating a substantive offense which ties together these diverse parties and crimes.* Thus, the object of RICO conspiracy is to violate a substantive RICO provision—here, to conduct or participate in the affairs

---

[7] The government's interpretation rests on some admittedly broad language in *Elliott* that suggests that RICO was intended to alter traditional conspiracy concepts. For example, we stated in *Elliott* that

> through RICO, Congress intended to authorize the single prosecution of a multifaceted, diversified conspiracy by replacing the inadequate "wheel" and "chain" rationales with a new statutory concept: the enterprise.

571 F.2d at 902.

> This and similar statements must, however, be read in the context of the balance of the opinion. In context, as discussed below, this language suggests not that the Congress sought in RICO to change traditional conspiracy concepts, but that the Congress sought instead to expand the reach of traditional conspiracy charges by establishing a new substantive crime around which a conspiracy might center.

of an enterprise through a pattern of racketeering activity—and not merely to commit each of the predicate crimes necessary to demonstrate a pattern of racketeering activity. The gravamen of the conspiracy charge in this case is not that each defendant agreed to commit arson, to steal goods from interstate commerce, to obstruct justice, and to sell narcotics; rather, it is that each agreed to participate, directly and indirectly, in the affairs of the enterprise by committing two or more predicate crimes. Under the statute, it is irrelevant that each defendant participated in the enterprise's affairs through different, even unrelated crimes, so long as we may reasonably infer that each crime was intended to further the enterprise's affairs. *To find a single conspiracy, we still must look for agreement on an overall objective. What Congress did was to define that objective through the substantive provisions of the Act.*

571 F.2d at 902–03 (emphasis added; footnote omitted).

Elliott does indeed hold that on the facts of that case a series of agreements that under pre-RICO law would constitute multiple conspiracies could under RICO be tried as a single "enterprise" conspiracy. But the language of *Elliott* explains that what ties these conspiracies together is not the mere fact that they involve the same enterprise, but is instead as in any other conspiracy an "agreement on an overall objective." What RICO does is to provide a new criminal objective by defining a new substantive crime. In *Elliott,* as here, that crime consists of participation in an enterprise through a pattern of racketeering activity.The defendants in *Elliott* could not have been tried on a single conspiracy count under pre-RICO law because the defendants had not agreed to commit any particular crime. They were properly tried together under RICO only because the evidence established an agreement to commit a substantive RICO offense, *i.e.,* an agreement to participate in an enterprise through a pattern of racketeering activity.

To be sure, the government did not prove in *Elliott* that each of the conspirators had explicitly agreed with all of the others to violate the substantive RICO provision at issue. However, the government did prove that, as in a traditional "chain" conspiracy, the nature of the scheme was such that each defendant must necessarily have known that others were also conspiring to participate in the same enterprise through a pattern of racketeering activity. We found the facts sufficient to demonstrate that the defendants knew they were "directly involved in an enterprise whose purpose was to profit from crime," and that each knew "that the enterprise was bigger than his role in it, and that others unknown to him were participating in its affairs." . . . The agreement among all of the defendants in *Elliott* was an implicit one, but it was an agreement nonetheless.

* * *

. . . Taken to its logical extreme, a rule allowing the joint trial of otherwise unrelated conspiracies solely on the basis of their relationship to a common enterprise—the rule which the government advocates in the case—leads to ridiculous results:

> For example, assuming that our own court the United States Court of Appeals for the Fifth Circuit was alleged to be the enterprise (as we assume

would be proper under our analysis), we question whether an agreement to bribe a court official in El Paso, Texas could be part of the same conspiracy as an unrelated agreement to use a judicial office for illicit profit-making purposes in Fort Lauderdale, Florida, when neither the El Paso nor the Fort Lauderdale conspirators knew of the existence of the other group.

. . . This extreme hypothetical problem is not fundamentally different from the case now before us. Although both conspiracies in the case at bar involved the same judge, it is not that fact which the government argues ties the two conspiracies together. Rather, it is each conspiracy's relationship to the same enterprise (the Municipal Court of the City of El Paso) that is said to provide the necessary link. Thus, the theory urged by the government would bring together individual conspiracies to bribe different judges on the same court.

Our review of *Elliott* . . . convinces us that the government has read this authority too broadly. *Elliott* does not stand for the proposition that multiple conspiracies may be tried on a single "enterprise conspiracy" count under RICO merely because the various conspiracies involve the same enterprise. What *Elliott* does state is two-fold: (1) a pattern of agreements that absent RICO would constitute multiple conspiracies may be joined under a single RICO conspiracy count if the defendants have agreed to commit a substantive RICO offense; and(2) such an agreement to violate RICO may, as in the case of a traditional "chain" or "wheel" conspiracy, be established on circumstantial evidence, *i.e.,* evidence that the nature of the conspiracy is such that each defendant must necessarily have known that others were also conspiring to violate RICO.

In this case the government has not attempted to prove that Walker and Maynard agreed with each other to participate in a bribery scheme with Sutherland, nor has it contended that the nature of each defendant's agreement with Sutherland was such that he or she must necessarily have known that others were also conspiring to commit racketeering offenses in the conduct of the Municipal Court. We must conclude, therefore, that the multiple conspiracy doctrine precluded the joint trial of the two multiple conspiracies involved in this case on a single RICO conspiracy count. In accordance with *Kotteakos* and its progeny, we must reverse the defendants' convictions if this error affected their substantial rights.

[The court went on to decide that the joint trial of the defendants did not violate theirsubstantial rights.]

* * *

Affirmed.

United States v. Licavoli

United States Court of Appeals, Sixth Circuit

725 F.2d 1040 (1984)

CORNELIA G. KENNEDY, Circuit Judge.

The six defendant-appellants were convicted of conspiring to participate in the affairs of an enterprise through a pattern of racketeering activities in violation of the Racketeer Influenced and Corrupt Organizations (RICO) statute, 18 U.S.C. § 1962(c) and (d) following a jury trial, and now appeal those convictions. . . .

I. Facts

Defendant Licavoli is a leader of organized crime in Cleveland. Liberatore is his second-in-command, and Calandra also holds a position of confidence and responsibility within the organization. Carabbia and Cisternino act for the organization, carrying out the orders of the top men. Ciarcia manages a car dealership and supplies vehicles for the organization's criminal activities and also acts on behalf of the organization in other ways.

In the spring of 1976 Licavoli decided that he needed to have one Danny Greene killed. Greene was the leader of a rival criminal organization which had developed a monopoly on criminal activity in West Cleveland. Licavoli had others in his organization contact Raymond Ferritto regarding his wish to have Greene killed.[2] . . .

. . . Liberatore arranged with two other men, Aratari[3] and Guiles, to kill others in Greene's criminal organization, and ultimately to help kill Greene as well. Aratari and Guiles were at times assisted in their efforts by defendants Carabbia, Calandra, Cisternino and Ciarcia. Ciarcia and another man provided Aratari and Guiles with a car and weapons.

Licavoli had Greene's phone tapped in an effort to obtain reliable information regarding Greene's daily activities. Carabbia and Cisternino gave Ferritto the resulting tapes. One tape revealed that Greene was to go to a dentist's appointment at 2:30 PM on Thursday, October 6, 1977. Defendants Licavoli, Cisternino and Carabbia played this tape for Ferritto on Monday, October 3.

On Thursday, the day of Greene's dentist appointment, Cisternino and Ferritto built a bomb in an apartment maintained by Cisternino. Ferritto drove to the vicinity of the dentist's office with the bomb in his car, a Plymouth. Carabbia drove a second car to the office, a Nova. This car had a special box mounted on the side in which the bomb was to be placed. Cisternino remained behind at the apartment to listen to a police scanner for calls. A few minutes after Ferritto and Carabbia arrived at the dentist's, Aratari and Guiles arrived in another car, supplied by Ciarcia as the car to be used in "the Danny Greene case." Guiles was armed with a high powered rifle. The plan was for Guiles

---

[2] Ferritto later testified against all six defendants in their state trials for Greene's murder.

[3] Aratari testified at the trial in this case.

to shoot Greene if he had the opportunity. The bomb was to be used as a backup method.

Greene arrived for his appointment, parked his car and entered the office. Guiles apparently had no opportunity to shoot. A few minutes later a parking space opened next to Greene's car. Ferritto placed the bomb in the box on the side of the Nova, parked the Nova next to Greene's car, and activated the bomb. Then he got into the driver's seat of the Plymouth, which was parked down the block. When Greene emerged from the office Ferritto began to drive away, with Carabbia in the back seat. Carabbia then detonated the bomb with a remote control device and Danny Greene was killed.

All six defendants in the present case were tried for Danny Greene's murder in state court. Cisternino, Carabbia and Ciarcia were convicted of Greene's murder.

The RICO prosecution now on appeal also relied on a separate set of events to establish a predicate criminal act. Ms. Geraldine Rabinowitz[4] worked as a file clerk in the Cleveland office of the FBI, while her then-fiance Jeffrey Rabinowitz worked at the car dealership that Ciarcia managed. In the spring of 1977 Ciarcia asked Ms. Rabinowitz to obtain confidential information from the FBI regarding investigations of himself, Liberatore, and Licavoli. Ms. Rabinowitz complied, after some hesitation, and continued to steal confidential information for Ciarcia from time to time throughout the summer of 1977. Ciarcia assured Ms. Rabinowitz that she would in return be "covered" for a down payment on a new home that she and her fiance planned to buy. On October 12, 1977 the Rabinowitzes met with Liberatore and Ciarcia, and the Rabinowitzes asked for $15,000 for a down payment on the home. Although Liberatore was at first unwilling to comply with this request, the next day he delivered a paper bag to Ms. Rabinowitz containing $15,000 in cash. Counsel for Liberatore characterized this payment as a "loan," but no interest was set, no repayment schedule made, and no collateral specified. The stolen FBI documents were later found at Ciarcia's car dealership. All six defendants were charged with two counts of bribery and one count of conspiracy to commit bribery and were tried in federal court. Ciarcia pleaded guilty to all three counts, and Liberatore was convicted of the conspiracy count and one substantive count.

All six defendants were tried together in federal court for the RICO violation. The jury found all six guilty of having violated RICO. Defendants now raise a large number of issues on appeal.

II. CONSPIRACY TO MURDER MAY BE A PREDICATE ACT FOR A RICO CONVICTION

The District Court instructed the jury that there were three possible acts which the jury could find to serve as predicate acts of racketeering for the RICO charge. These were: 1) conspiracy to murder Danny Greene; 2) the murder of Danny Greene; and 3) bribery. The court instructed that the bribery act applied only to defendants Liberatore and Ciarcia. The jury therefore had to find that the other four defendants both conspired to murder, and murdered Danny Greene in order to convict them of the RICO violation. These four

---

[4] Ms. Rabinowitz testified at the federal bribery trial and the trial in this case.

defendants (Licavoli, Calandra, Carabbia, Cisternino) now argue that conspiracy to commit murder cannot serve as a predicate act for a RICO conviction, and that their RICO convictions therefore cannot stand.

Under 18 U.S.C. § 1961(1)(A) racketeering activity includes "any act or threat involving murder. . . ." Conspiracy to murder on its face fits within this definition of racketeering activity. Conspiracy is "an act . . . involving murder." . . .

* * *

III. MURDER AND CONSPIRACY TO MURDER ARE SEPARATE OFFENSES UNDER OHIO LAW AND MAY BOTH BE PREDICATE ACTS UNDER RICO

For a defendant to be convicted under RICO he must have committed more than one act of racketeering activity. In order for a state crime, such as murder or conspiracy to murder to serve as a predicate act, it must be "chargeable under state law and punishable by imprisonment for more than one year" under 18 U.S.C. § 1961(1)(A). Federal law holds that conspiracy to commit a substantive offense and the substantive offense itself are two separate crimes. See, *e.g., Iannelli v. United States,* 420 U.S. 770, 777 (1975). Under Ohio law, conspiracy to murder and murder are also two separate crimes. However, a person convicted of the substantive crime "shall not be convicted of conspiracy involving the same offense." Ohio Rev. Code § 2923.01(G). Thus under Ohio law a person cannot be convicted of or sentenced for both conspiracy to commit murder and the murder crime itself. Defendants argue that the two acts consequently are not both "chargeable under state law and punishable for more than one year."

We disagree, for two reasons. First Ohio law, in both the Ohio Revised Code and the earlier case law, provides that conspiracy to commit a substantive act and the substantive act are separate offenses, both separately chargeable under state law. . . .

* * *

. . . Murder is a crime, chargeable under Ohio law, . . . and punishable by imprisonment for more than one year. . . . Conspiracy is also a crime in Ohio, . . . and is punishable by imprisonment for more than one year. . . . RICO nowhere indicates that two criminal acts otherwise qualifying as predicate acts may not both constitute predicate acts because under state law a defendant could not be convicted of or sentenced for both crimes.

Secondly, contrary to defendants' contention, it is irrelevant whether these particular defendants could have been charged under Ohio law and imprisoned for more than one year for both conspiracy to murder and murder. This argument has been raised and rejected several times in the context of state statutes of limitations, when the state statute has run on a state crime which is offered as a predicate act for a RICO violation. Courts have held that regardless of the running of the state statute the defendant is still "chargeable" with the state offense within the meaning of [RICO]. . . .

IV. Acquittal in State Court of Criminal Acts Does Not Bar Their Use as Predicate Acts for a RICO Conviction

Defendants Licavoli and Calandra were acquitted in state court proceedings of murdering Greene and conspiring to murder Greene. Consequently, they argue, they were not "chargeable" with the murder or conspiracy to commit murder, as required under 18 U.S.C. § 1961(1)(A), and murder and conspiracy to commit murder could not therefore serve as predicate acts for their RICO convictions.

We disagree. [*United States v.*] *Frumento* [523 F.2d 1083 (3d Cir. 1977)] is directly on point. Defendants in that case were acquitted in state court on charges of bribery, extortion and conspiracy to accept bribes. They were then convicted in federal court of violating 18 U.S.C. § 1962(c) and (d), with the above crimes as predicate acts. On appeal defendants argued that the conviction was barred by the Double Jeopardy Clause of the Fifth Amendment. The Third Circuit disagreed. The court said:

> [RICO] forbids "racketeering," not state offenses *per se*. The state offenses referred to in the federal act are definitional only; racketeering, the federal crime, is defined as a matter of legislative draftsmanship by a reference to state law crimes. This is not to say . . . that the federal statute punishes the same conduct as that reached by state law. The gravamen of section 1962 is a violation of federal law and "reference to state law is necessary only to identify the type of unlawful activity in which the defendant intended to engage." *United States v. Cerone,* 452 F.2d 274, 286 (7th Cir. 1971). (Footnote omitted.)

563 F.2d at 1087 . . .

* * *

VII. Principles of Double Jeopardy Did Not Bar the Government from Using Bribery as a Predicate Offense for the RICO Convictions

Defendants Liberatore and Ciarcia were convicted in federal court of bribing Ms. Rabinowitz. This bribery offense was also used as a predicate act for the RICO convictions of these two defendants. Liberatore and Ciarcia now claim that use of the bribery offense in the RICO prosecution violated the Double Jeopardy Clause of the Fifth Amendment.

* * *

This Court has ruled on a closely related question in *United States v. Morelli,* 643 F.2d 402 (6th Cir.), *cert. denied,* 453 U.S. 912 (1981). Morelli was convicted of two counts of wire fraud, and these acts were used as predicate offenses for a RICO conviction. Morelli complained that he was subject to cruel and unusual punishment in violation of the Eighth Amendment because he was sentenced to fifteen years for the RICO violation, in addition to ten years for the wire fraud crimes. We held that Congress "may constitutionally make the commission of crimes within a specified period of time and within the course of a particular type of enterprise an independent criminal offense. . . . " We now hold that there was no violation of double jeopardy in trying defendants Liberatore and Ciarcia for both the federal bribery charge and the RICO charge.

. . . We affirm defendants' RICO convictions. . . .

MERRITT, Circuit Judge, *concurring.*

I concur in the clear and well reasoned opinion prepared by Judge Kennedy.

It may seem strange for a federal court to uphold convictions under a federal statute based on two underlying predicate state offenses for which a defendant has either been acquitted at state trials (the murder of Danny Greene) or for which he could not be separately convicted or punished under state law (conspiracy to murder Danny Greene). But RICO is now unique. The normal rules of construction do not apply to RICO. Although I had earlier believed that normal canons of construction applicable to other criminal statutes should be applied to RICO, . . . the Supreme Court has now made it clear that RICO is to be given the broadest and most expansive possible interpretation in order to carry out Congressional intent aimed at eliminating organized crime. See *United States v. Turkette,* 452 U.S. 576 (1981), *Russello v. United States,* 464 U.S. 16 (1983). In *Russello,* a unanimous Supreme Court has pointed to RICO as the only federal criminal statute which should receive this kind of broad and expansive interpretation:

> The legislative history clearly demonstrates that the RICO statute was intended to provide new weapons of unprecedented scope for an assault upon organized crime and its economic roots. . . . "The provisions of this title shall be liberally construed to effectuate its remedial purposes." *So far as we have been made aware, this is the only substantive federal criminal statute that contains such a directive.* . . .

Thus, RICO, liberally construed as required by the Supreme Court, can reasonably be interpreted, and therefore should be interpreted, so that a defendant can be convicted even though he has already been acquitted or convicted of the two underlying offenses in state court and even though he could not be convicted or punished for both offenses together under state law.

NOTES AND QUESTIONS

1. The above cases merely touch the surface of the interpretive problems raised by RICO. For a detailed examination of RICO caselaw, see 1 K. Brickey, Corporate Criminal Liability, 229–97 (1984). See also Lynch, *RICO: The Crime of Being a Criminal,* 87 Colum. L. Rev. 661–764, 920–84 (1987); *Symposium, RICO: Something for Everyone,* 35 Vill. L. Rev. 853–947 (1990).

2. As a policy matter, the statute has proven to be controversial. Some critics see RICO's broad language and its liberal construction by the courts as inviting perceived abuses of prosecutorial discretion through charging defendants who fail to fit the classic image of "organized crime" figures. See generally Tarlow, *RICO: The New Darling of the Prosecutor's Nursery,* 49

Fordham L. Rev. 165 (1980). Is such a criticism relevant in the context of a case like *Sutherland,* for example?

Others argue that RICO constitutes unnecessary overkill because existing conspiracy and substantive crime doctrines are adequate to deal with the problem of organized crime. Does *Licavoli* support this objection to RICO?

3. Is the *Sutherland* Court's attempt to distinguish the *Elliot* case convincing? After *Sutherland,* when, if ever, will courts find single RICO conspiracies under facts that would constitute multiple conspiracies under traditional doctrine?

4. In attempts to arm state prosecutors with weapons similar to their federal counterparts, at least 20 states have passed statutes modeled after federal RICO. Note, *"A RICO You Can't Refuse": New York's Organized Crime Control Act,* 53 Brooklyn L. Rev. 979, 981–82 (1988).

Chapter 8
Complicity

§ 8.01 ACCOMPLICE LIABILITY

BLACKSTONE

27–31

. . . [W]e are next to make a few remarks on the different degrees of guilt among persons that are capable of offending; viz., as *principal,* and as *accessory.*

I. A man may be *principal* in an offence in two degrees. A principal in the first degree is he that is the actor, or absolute perpetrator of the crime; and, in the second degree, he who is present, aiding and abetting the fact to be done. Which *presence* need not always be an actual immediate standing by, within sight or hearing of the fact; but there may be also a constructive presence, as when one commits a robbery or murder, and another keeps watch or guard at some convenient distance. . . .

II. An *accessory* is he who is not the chief actor in the offence, nor present at its performance, but is some way concerned therein, either *before or after* the fact committed. . . .

* * *

As to . . . who may be an accessory *before* the fact, Sir Matthew Hale defines him to be one, who being absent at the time of the crime committed, doth yet procure, counsel, or command another to commit a crime. . . . If A. then advises B. to kill another, and B. does it in the absence of A., now B. is principal, and A. is accessory in the murder . . . And it is also settled, that whoever procures a felony to be committed, though it be by the intervention of a third person, is an accessory before the fact. It is likewise a rule, that he who in any wise commands or counsels another to commit an unlawful act, is accessory to all that ensues upon unlawful act, but is not accessory to any act distinct from the other. As if A. commands B. to beat C., and B. beats him so that he dies, B. is guilty of murder as principal, and A. as accessory. But if A. commands B. to burn C.'s house, and he, in so doing, commits a robbery; now A., though accessory to the burning, is not accessory to the robbery, for that is a thing of a distinct and unconsequential nature. But if the felony committed be the same in substance with that which is commanded, and only varying in some circumstantial matters; as if, upon a command to poison Titius, he is stabbed or shot, and dies; the command is still accessory to the murder, for the substance of the thing commanded was the death of Titius, and the manner of its execution is a mere collateral circumstance.

An accessory *after* the fact may be where a person, knowing a felony to have been committed, receives, relieves, comforts, or assists the felon. . . .

* * *

The last point of inquiry is, how accessories are to be treated, considered distinct from principals. And the general rule of the ancient law . . . is this, that accessories shall suffer the same punishment as their principals: if one be liable to death, the other is also liable; as, by the laws of Athens, delinquents and their abettors were to receive the same punishment. Why then, it may be asked, are such elaborate distinctions made between accessories and principals; if both are to suffer the same punishment? For these reasons: 1. To distinguish the nature and denomination of crimes, that the accused may know how to defend himself when indicted; the commission of an actual robbery being quite a different accusation from that of harbouring the robber. 2. Because, though by the ancient common law the rule is as before laid down, that both shall be punished alike, yet "subsequently" a distinction was made between them: accessories *after* the fact being allowed the benefit of clergy in all cases, except horse-stealing and stealing of linen from bleaching grounds, while it was denied to the principals and accessories *before* the fact, in many cases; and especially in murder, robbery, and wilful burning. And, perhaps, if a distinction were constantly to be made between the punishment of principals and accessories, even *before* the fact, the latter to be treated with a little less severity than the former; it might prevent the perpetration of many crimes, by increasing the difficulty of finding a person to execute the deed itself, as his danger would be greater than that of his accomplices, by reason of the difference of his punishment. 3. Because "formerly" no man could be tried as accessory till after the principal was convicted, or at least he must have been tried at the same time with him; though the law "in this respect" is now altered. . . .

NOTES

1. The common law distinctions described by Blackstone between principals in the first and second degrees and between accessories before and after the fact applied only to felonies. At common law, all participants in misdemeanors "before the fact" were equally guilty as "principals," while "after the fact" assistance of a misdemeanant did not constitute criminal liability at all. Dressler at 433, n.36.

While the common law distinctions retained some significance in Blackstone's time, they have subsequently been largely abandoned. Today statutes virtually everywhere have abolished the distinctions between degrees of principals and accessories before the fact, although the common law concepts still appear in a rare statute or an occasional case. Modern statutes generally distinguish only between principal actors and those who aid and abet the principal, providing equal punishment for both classes. The old category of "accessory after the fact" is now generally separated from liability for the offense itself and made a distinct offense. See, for example, Model Penal Code § 242.3:

A person commits an offense if, with purpose to hinder the apprehension, prosecution, conviction or punishment of another for crime, he:

(1) harbors or conceals the other; or

(2) provides or aids in providing a weapon, transportation, disguise or other means of avoiding apprehension or effection escape; or

(3) conceals or destroys evidence of the crime, or tampers with a witness, informant, document or other source of information, regardless of it admissibility in evidence; or

(4) warns the other of impending discovery or apprehension, except that this paragraph does not apply to a warning given in connection with an effort to bring another into compliance with law; or

(5) volunteers false information to a law enforcement officer.

The offense is a felony of the third degree if the conduct which the actor knows has been charged or is liable to be charged against the person aided would be a felony of the first or second degree. Otherwise it is a misdemeanor.

2. The common law crime of "misprison of felony," which consisted of a failure to report or prosecute a known felon, provided a basis of liability analogous to that imposed upon accessories after the fact. While largely rejected in the modern era of organized police forces, some remnants of the crime persist. For example, Title 18 of the United States Code provides:

§ 4. Misprison of felony

Whoever, having knowledge of the actual commission of a felony cognizable by a court of the United States, conceals and does not as soon as possible make known the same to some judge or other person in civil or military authority under the United States, shall be fined not more than $500 or imprisoned not more than three years, or both.

3. As Blackstone points out, "former law," abandoned by his time, required conviction of the principal as a prerequisite to finding liability in an accessory. It is now generally accepted that an accomplice may be convicted even though the "principal in the first degree" has not been prosecuted or has even been acquitted in a separate trial so long as the guilt of the principal is established, beyond a reasonable doubt, at the trial of the accomplice. LaFave and Scott at 591–92.

[A] *Actus Reus*

THE QUEEN V. CONEY

Queen's Bench

[1882] 8 Q.B.D. 534

CAVE, J.

In this case I am of opinion that the direction to the jury was wrong, and consequently that the conviction ought not to stand.

* * *

The prisoners were charged in one count with a common assault on one Burke, and in another count with a like assault on one Mitchell.

The evidence was that on the 16th of June last, at the close of Ascot races, Burke and Mitchell had engaged in a fight near the road from Ascot to Maidenhead; that a ring was formed with posts and ropes; that a large number of persons were present looking on, some of whom were undoubtedly encouraging the fight; that the men fought for some time; and that the three prisoners were seen in the crowd, but were not seen to do anything, and there was no evidence how they got there or how long they stayed there.

The chairman of quarter sessions directed the jury:

> There is no doubt that prize-fights are illegal. . . and all persons who go to a prize fight to see the combatants strike each other, and who are present when they do so are, in point of law, guilty of an assault.

And the chairman added, in the words of Littledale, J., in *Rex v. Murphy* (1): "If they were not casually passing by, but stayed at the place, they encouraged it by their presence, although they did not say or do anything."

By this direction I gather that the chairman laid down as matter of law, first, that the actual fighters in a prize-fight are guilty of an assault; and, secondly, that if any person is shown to have been present in the crowd looking on at the fight, that is not merely evidence, but, if unexplained, conclusive proof that he was aiding and abetting the assault. That seems to be the natural meaning of the language used, and that, from the finding of the jury, appears to me to be the sense in which they understood it. They found . . . as to the three prisoners in question . . . that they were guilty of an assault, and yet that they were not aiding and abetting, which is to my mind an inconsistent finding. Indeed on no other supposition can I understand the verdict, for the evidence against the three prisoners, and especially against Gilliam, is quite consistent with their being labourers working near or persons going quietly home from the races, who, observing a crowd, went up to see what the matter was, and finding it was a fight stayed some short time looking on.

* * *

It was next contended that the chairman was wrong in directing the jury in the words of Littledale, J., in *Rex v. Murphy* (2), that if the prisoners were not merely casually passing by, but stayed at the place, they encouraged it by their presence, although they did not say or do anything.

Now it is a general rule in the case of principals in the second degree that there must be participation in the act, and that, although a man is present whilst a felony is being committed, if he takes no part in it, and does not act in concert with those who commit it he will not be principal in the second degree merely because he does not endeavour to prevent the felony, or apprehend the felon.

* * *

. . . Where presence may be entirely accidental, it is not even evidence of aiding and abetting. Where presence is *prima facie* not accidental it is evidence, but no more than evidence, for the jury.

* * *

[Justice Littledale's] summing up unfortunately appears to be capable of being understood in two different ways. It may mean either that mere presence unexplained is evidence of encouragement, and so of guilt, or that mere presence unexplained is conclusive proof of encouragement, and so of guilt. If the former is the correct meaning, I concur in the law so laid down; if the latter, I am unable to do so. It appears to me that the passage tending to convey the latter view is that which was read by the chairman in this case to the jury, and I cannot help thinking that the chairman believed himself, and meant to direct the jury, and at any rate I feel satisfied that the jury understood him to mean, that mere presence unexplained was conclusive proof of encouragement, and so of guilt; and it is on this ground I hold that this conviction ought not to stand.

MATHEW, J.

. . . It was contended that the presence of persons shown to have assembled for the purpose of witnessing prize-fights did not prove that they were aiding and abetting, and only afforded evidence from which a jury might draw that inference, . . . and that if it were not shown that anything had been said or done by a particular spectator, the jury would be justified in acquitting him.

If this contention were correct some subtle distinctions would have to be made in dealing with the question of the criminality of persons present at prize fights. For instance, it would be clear that those persons who helped to keep the ring, and so to provide sufficient space for the combatants, were aiding and abetting; but those who, in conformity with the arrangements made by the ring-keepers, remained outside the ring with the same object, would not be aiding and abetting unless the jury thought fit to say so. I cannot see the grounds for this distinction.

* * *

It was said by counsel for the defendants that the legislature had not declared that it was criminal to go and see a prize-fight, and that it was not for judges to create a new offense; but the decisions upon which the chairman's direction proceeded do not appear to me to be open to this attack. The learned judges determined, as it seems to me in accordance with reason and principle, what is sufficient in law to establish a charge of countenancing and encouraging a prize-fight. Their reasoning may be stated thus: a prize-fight, which is an assault, and therefore contrary to the law, takes place in public, in order that it may be witnessed by spectators. The spectators by their presence lend themselves to the purpose of the combatants, and countenance and encourage them in a violation of the law. They therefore aid and abet.

I have no doubt in this case that the defendants were spectators, and that the jury meant to find and properly found that they were so; and I am of opinion that they are rightly convicted.

* * *

Conviction quashed.

NOTES AND QUESTIONS

1. In an opinion editorially deleted from the above case, Justice Manisty raises the following hypothetical: "Suppose that the fight in question had resulted in the death of one of the combatants, then if the direction given to the jury was right, every person who was in the crowd was in point of law guilty of manslaughter, though he neither spoke nor did anything." Is this true? Under what theory would the principal be guilty of manslaughter? See *Regina v. Creamer,* [1965] 3 All E.R. 257.

In the context of Justice Manisty's hypothetical, suppose the spectators "did something"—cheered—as the principal battered the soon-to-be-deceased fellow boxer. Would the spectators then (correctly) be guilty of aiding and abetting manslaughter when the fellow boxer died?

Suppose that during a particularly intense baseball game, an umpire's questionable call goes against the home team. An intense argument ensues between the home team's manager and the maker of the controversial call. Thousands of fans scream the familiar slogan "Kill the umpire!" In a fit of rage, the manager does. (He fractures the umpire's skull by hitting him over the head with a bat.) Are the screaming fans accomplices to a homicide? Does it matter (1)what the fans intended by their screams or (2)whether the manager in fact heard their screams? For some preliminary answers to such questions, see *Hicks v. United States,* 150 U.S. 442 (1893).

2. *Coney* stands for the oft-cited doctrine that passive presence at the scene of a crime (even one like illegal prize-fighting which entails spectator participation) is not itself enough to generate accomplice liability even where the passive spectator could have easily and safely prevented the principal from committing the crime. However, the situation is quite different if a passively present spectator has encouraged the principal to commit his crime prior to the time of its commission.

> While it is true that mere presence or negative acquiescence is not enough to constitute a person a principal, one may aid and abet without actively participating in the overt act and if the proof shows that a person was present at the commission of the crime without disapproving or opposing it, it is competent for the trier of fact to consider this conduct in connection with other circumstances and thereby reach a conclusion that such person assented to the commission of the crime, lent to it his countenance and approval and was thereby aiding and abetting the crime. . . . Stated differently, circumstances may show there is common design to do an unlawful act to which all assent, and whatever is done in furtherance of the design is the act of all, making each person guilty of the crime.

People v. Cole, 30 Ill. 2d 375, 379, 196 N.E.2d 691, 693–94 (1964)

3. Suppose that the passive spectator owes a duty of care toward the victim of the principal's violent crime. For a case holding that a mother may be guilty

of aiding and abetting an assault solely on the basis that she was present when her child was assaulted and failed to take reasonable steps to prevent the assault, see *State v. Walden,* 306 N.C. 466, 293 S.E.2d 780 (1982). In such a case, how does the mother "aid" the principal? Suppose the principal is unaware of the mother's presence at the scene of the assault. *But see Knox v. Commonwealth,* 735 S.W.2d 711 (Ky. 1987) (wife held not guilty of complicity to commit rape when she failed to intervene when her husband raped their daughter).

4. While some form of active assistance is generally required, an accomplice may provide such in a variety of ways: acting as a lookout, manning a getaway car, and so on. Sometimes the actual aid rendered the principal actor is minimal. Consider the following case.

WILCOX V. JEFFERY

King's Bench

[1951] 1 All E.R. 464

Lord GODDARD, C.J.:

This is a Case stated by the metropolitan magistrate at Bow Street Magistrate's Court before whom the appellant, Herbert William Wilcox, the proprietor of a periodical called *Jazz Illustrated,* was charged on an information that "on Dec. 11, 1949, he did unlawfully aid and abet one Coleman Hawkins in contravening art. 1(4) of the Aliens Order, 1920, by failing to comply with a condition attached to a grant of leave to land, to wit, that the said Coleman Hawkins should take no employment paid or unpaid while in the United Kingdom, contrary to art. 18(2) of the Aliens Order, 1920." . . .

The case is concerned with the visit of a celebrated professor of the saxophone, a gentleman by the name of Hawkins who was a citizen of the United States. He came here at the invitation of two gentlemen of the name of Curtis and Hughes, connected with a jazz club which enlivens the neighbourhood of Willesden. They, apparently, had applied for permission for Mr. Hawkins to land and it was refused, but, nevertheless, this professor of the saxophone arrived with four French musicians. When they came to the airport, among the people who were there to greet them was the appellant. He had not arranged their visit, but he knew they were coming and he was there to report the arrival of these important musicians for his magazine. So, evidently, he was regarding the visit of Mr. Hawkins as a matter which would be of interest to himself and the magazine which he was editing and selling for profit. Messrs. Curtis and Hughes arranged a concert at the Princes Theatre, London. The appellant attended that concert as a spectator. He paid for his ticket. Mr. Hawkins went on the stage and delighted the audience by playing the saxophone. The appellant did not get up and protest in the name of the musicians of England that Mr. Hawkins ought not to be here competing with them and taking the bread out of their mouths or the wind out of their instruments. It is not found that he actually applauded, but he was there having paid to go in, and, no doubt, enjoying the performance, and then, lo and behold, out comes his magazine with a most laudatory description, fully illustrated, of this concert. On those facts the magistrate has found that he aided and abetted.

Reliance is placed by the prosecution on *R. v. Coney* (1) which dealt with a prize fight. This case relates to a jazz band concert, but the particular nature of the entertainment provided, whether by fighting with bare fists or playing on saxophones, does not seem to me to make any difference to the question which we have to decide. The fact is that a man is charged with aiding and abetting an illegal act, and I can find no authority for saying that it matters what that illegal act is, provided that the aider and abettor knows the facts sufficiently well to know that they would constitute an offense in the principal. . . .

There was not accidental presence in this case. The appellant paid to go to the concert and he went there because he wanted to report it. He must therefore be held to have been present, taking part, concurring, or encouraging, whichever word you like to use for expressing this conception. It was an illegal act on the part of Hawkins to play the saxophone or any other instrument at this concert. The appellant clearly knew that it was an unlawful act for him to play. He had gone there to hear him, and his presence and his payment to go there was an encouragement. He went there to make use of the performance, because he went there, as the magistrate finds and was justified in finding, to get "copy" for his newspaper. It might have been entirely different, as I say, if he had gone there and protested, saying: "The musicians' union do not like you foreigners coming here and playing and you ought to get off the stage." If he had booed, it might have been some evidence that he was not aiding and abetting. If he had gone as a member of a *claque* to try to drown the noise of the saxophone, he might very likely be found not guilty of aiding and abetting. In this case it seems clear that he was there, not only to approve and encourage what was done, but to take advantage of it by getting "copy" for his paper. In those circumstances there was evidence on which the magistrate could find that the appellant aided and abetted, and for these reasons I am of opinion that the appeal fails.

QUESTIONS

1. If Wilcox aids and abets Coleman Hawkins, is similar aid not provided by everyone else in the audience? The court emphasizes that Wilcox knew Hawkins was violating the law, while others in the audience presumably did not. But would the audience's "ignorance of the law" absolve them of liability if they bought tickets and cheered Hawkins on? Of what relevance is the fact that Wilcox financially benefited from the illegal concert by publishing a review after the fact?

2. What causal effect did Wilcox's actions have on Hawkins?

State *ex rel.* Attorney General v. Tally

Supreme Court of Alabama

102 Ala. 25, 15 So. 722 (1894)

McCLELLAN, J.

. . . [In an impeachment proceeding against John B. Tally, a Scottsboro, Alabama, circuit court judge, the evidence revealed the following: Judge Tally learned that his sister-in-law had been seduced by Ross, who had subsequently fled Scottsboro. Tally also knew that her brothers, the Skeltons, were pursuing Ross, seeking his life as revenge for the perceived offense.

A relative of Ross in Scottsboro sent him a telegram through the telegraph operator at Stevenson, Alabama, where Ross intended to catch a train. The telegraph message warned Ross that the Skeltons were pursuing him. Judge Tally was in the Scottsboro telegraph office when the relative of Ross sent the warning telegram. Judge Tally then sent his own telegram to the Stevenson telegraph operator, Huddleston, a friend of Tally's, instructing Huddleston not to deliver the warning telegram to Ross. Huddleston received both telegrams and failed to deliver the warning message to Ross, who was eventually apprehended and killed by the Skeltons. Tally was charged, *inter alia,* as an accomplice to the murder of Ross.]

. . . [W]e . . . consider and determine . . . [w]hether it is essential to the guilt of Judge Tally as charged [in the complicity charge] that the said acts, thus adapted, intended and committed by him, should in fact have aided the said Skeltons to take the life of the said Ross, should have in fact contributed to his death at their hands.

As the life of Ross was not taken by the hands of Tally, the criminal consequences of the homicide could only have been visited upon him at the common law, if at all, as a principal in the second degree or as an accessory before the fact. He could not have been charged, . . . directly with the crime of murder as a principal in the first degree. Our statute has abolished the common law distinctions between accessories before the fact and principals, and between principals in the first and second degrees in cases of felony, and provided that "all persons concerned in the commission of a felony, whether they directly commit the act constituting the offense, or aid or abet in its commission, though not present, must hereafter be indicted, tried, and punished as principals, as in the case of misdemeanors. . . . " We have already stated our conclusion, and the considerations which led us to it, that Judge Tally did not command, direct, incite, counsel, or encourage the Skeltons to the murder of Ross. We have failed to find, and have so stated, that he knew of their felonious purpose before their departure from Scottsboro in pursuit of Ross. Up to that time there was no instigation or incitement by him to the commission of the crime by them, and after that he did not see or communicate with any of them until after the death of Ross, and hence, pending the pursuit, he would not have encouraged or instigated them to kill Ross. Judge Tally was therefore not, on the view we take of the evidence, an accessory before the fact to the killing of Ross. To be guilty of murder, therefore, not being a common-law principal, and not being an accessory before the fact—to be *concerned* in the commission of the offense within the meaning of our statute—he must be found to have aided or abetted the Skeltons in the commission of the offense. . . .

It is enough . . . for the [aider or abettor] to be in position to aid the commission of the crime by others. It is enough if he stands guard while the act is being perpetrated by others to prevent interference with them, or to warn them of the approach of danger; and it is immaterial how distant from the scene of the crime his vigil is maintained, provided it gives some promise of protection to those engaged in its active commission. At whatever distance he may be, he is present in legal contemplation if he is at the time performing any act in furtherance of the crime, or is in a position to give information to the principal which would be helpful to the end in view, or to prevent others from doing any act, by way of warning the intended victim or otherwise, which would be but an obstacle in the way of the consummation of the crime, or render its accomplishment more difficult. . . .

So far, therefore, as presence goes, Judge Tally, on guard at Scottsboro to prevent warnings being sent to Ross, or intercepting, or attempting to intercept, messages of warning which had started on their flight, was in legal contemplation present at Stevenson—the scene of the homicide—standing over Huddleston, to stay him the performance of his duty of delivering warnings to Ross. He was constructively there, and hence, for all practical legal purposes, actually there. Being thus present, did he aid or abet the killing of Ross? . . .

* * *

We are . . . clear to the conclusion that before Judge Tally can be found guilty of aiding and abetting the Skeltons to kill Ross, it must appear that his vigil at Scottsboro to prevent Ross from being warned of his danger was preconcert with them, or at least known to them, whereby they would naturally be incited, encouraged, and emboldened—"given confidence"—to the deed, or that he aided them to kill Ross, contributed to Ross' death in point of physical fact by means of the telegram he sent to Huddleston.

The assistance given, however, need not contribute to the criminal result in the sense that but for it the result would not have ensued. It is quite sufficient if it facilitated a result that would have transpired without it. It is quite enough if the aid merely rendered it easier for the principal actor to accomplish the end intended by him and the aider and abettor, though in all human probability the end would have been attained without it. If the aid in homicide can be shown to have put the deceased at a disadvantage, to have deprived him of a single chance of life, which but for it he would have had, he who furnishes such aid is guilty though it cannot be known or shown that the dead man, in the absence thereof, would have availed himself of that chance. . . .

We have already said enough to indicate the grounds of the conclusion which we now announce, that Tally's standing guard at the telegraph office in

Scottsboro to prevent Ross's being warned of the pursuit of the Skeltons was not by preconcert with them, and was not known to them. It is even clear and more certain that they knew neither of the occasion nor the fact of the sending of the message by him to Huddleston; and hence they were not, and could not have been, aided in the execution of their purpose to kill by the keeping of this vigil, or by the mere fact of the forwarding of the message to Stevenson, since these facts in and of themselves could not have given them any actual, substantial help, as distinguished from incitement and encouragement, and they could not have aided them by way of incitement and encouragement because they were ignorant of them. And so we . . . come to a consideration of the effect, if any, produced upon the situation at Stevenson by the message of Judge Tally to Huddleston. . . .

. . . It is inconceivable to us that after the maturest consideration, reflection, and discussion, but that Ross' predicament was rendered infinitely more desperate, his escape more difficult, and his death of much more easy and certain of accomplishment by the withholding from him of the message of Ed Ross. This withholding was the work of Judge Tally. An intent to aid the Skeltons to take the life of Ross actuated him to it. The intent was effectuated. They thereby were enabled to take him unawares, and to send him to his death without, we doubt not, his ever actually knowing who sought his life or being able to raise a hand in defense, or to take an advised step in retreat. As we are impelled to find that John B. Tally aided and abetted the murder of Robert C. Ross. . . .

No consideration or conclusion of fact in this opinion must be allowed to exert any influence upon the trials of the Skeltons and Judge Tally on the indictments for murder now pending against them.

Notes and Questions

1. If Judge Tally "aided and abetted" the Skeltons, what about Huddleston, the Stevenson telegraph operator? What about the Scottsboro operator who sent Tally's message to Huddleston?

2. Suppose that Huddleston had disregarded Tally's telegram and delivered the warning telegram to Ross, who nevertheless was still murdered by the Skeltons. Of what crime would Tally be guilty? Attempted murder? Murder? What difference would it make at common law? Consider MPC § 2.06(3)(a)(ii):

A person is an accomplice of another person in the commission of an offense if:

(a) with the purpose of promoting or facilitating the commission of the offense, he . . .

(ii) aids or agrees or attempts to aid such other person in planning or committing it.

Suppose that Huddleston had disregarded Tally's telegram and warned Ross, and that Ross had escaped to safety after the Skeltons fired shots at him. Would Tally have attempted murder? Attempted to aid an attempted murder?

Finally, suppose that the Skeltons had known prior to leaving for Stevenson that Tally would instruct Huddleston to disregard any warning telegrams that might be sent to Ross. Would Tally have aided and abetted the Skeltons if Huddleston had disregarded Tally's telegram not to warn and instead had delivered the warning telegram to Ross, who was nevertheless killed by the Skeltons?

3. As in the *Gebardi* case in the context of conspiracy, p. 583 *supra,* persons for whom protective statutes are passed are immune from liability as accomplices to the crime. See *Queen v. Tyrell,* [1893] L.Q.B. 710.

[B] *Mens Rea*

STATE V. GLADSTONE

Washington Supreme Court

78 Wash. 2d 306, 474 P.2d 274 (1970)

HALE, Justice.

A jury found defendant Bruce Gladstone guilty of aiding and abetting one Robert Kent in the unlawful sale of marijuana. . . .

* * *

Gladstone's guilt as an aider and abettor in this case rests solely on evidence of a conversation between him and one Douglas MacArthur Thompson concerning the possible purchase of marijuana from one Robert Kent. There is no other evidence to connect the accused with Kent who ultimately sold some marijuana to Thompson.

When asked by Thompson—an agent of the police—where marijuana could be bought, the defendant did no more than name Kent as an individual who might be willing to sell some and draw a sketch of his location. There was no evidence whatever that the defendant had any association, understanding, agreement or arrangement, direct or indirect, tacit or express with Kent to aid or persuade him in any way in the sale of marijuana.

* * *

. . . [T]wo officers then took Thompson to Kent's residence where marijuana was purchased. The actual purchase was made by Thompson directly from Kent while Officer Gallwas and Lieutenant Seymour stayed in the police car. Kent was subsequently arrested and convicted of selling Thompson approximately 8 ounces of marijuana—the very sale which defendant here was convicted of aiding and abetting.

* * *

If all reasonable inferences favorable to the state are accorded the evidence, it does not, in our opinion, establish the commission of the crime charged. That vital element—a nexus between the accused and the party whom he is charged with aiding and abetting in the commission of crime—is missing. The record contains no evidence whatever that Gladstone had any communication by word, gesture or sign, before or after he drew the map, from which it could be inferred that he counseled, encouraged, hired, commanded, induced or procured Kent to sell marijuana to Douglas Thompson as charged, or took any steps to further the commission of the crime charged. He was not charged with aiding and abetting Thompson in the purchase of marijuana, but with Kent's sale of it.

* * *

... [E]ven without prior agreement, arrangement or understanding, a bystander to a robbery could be guilty of aiding and abetting its commission if he came to the aid of a robber and knowingly assisted him in perpetrating the crime. But regardless of the *modus operandi* and with or without a conspiracy or agreement to commit the crime and whether present or away from the scene of it, there is no aiding and abetting unless one "in some sort associate himself with the venture, that he participate in it as in something that he wishes to bring about, that he seek by his action to make it succeed." *Nye & Nissen v. United States,* 336 U.S. 613, 169 (1949).

* * *

Gladstone's culpability, if at all, must be brought within RCW 9.01.030, which makes a principal of one who aids and abets another in the commission of the crime. Although an aider and abettor need not be physically present at the commission of the crime to be held guilty as a principal, his conviction depends on proof that he did something in association or connection with the principal to accomplish the crime. Learned Hand, J., we think, hit the nail squarely when, in *United States v. Peoni,* 100 F.2d 401, 402 (2d Cir. 1938), he wrote that, in order to aid and abet another to commit a crime, it is necessary that a defendant "in some sort associate himself with the venture, that he participate in it as in something that he wishes to bring about, that he seek by his action to make it succeed. All the words used—even the most colorless, *abet*—carry an implication of purposive attitude towards it." ...

It would be a dangerous precedent indeed to hold that mere communications to the effect that another might or probably would commit a criminal offense amount to an aiding and abetting of the offense should it ultimately be committed.

There being no evidence whatever that the defendant ever communicated to Kent the idea that he would in any way aid him in the sale of any marijuana, or said anything to Kent to encourage or induce him or direct him to do so, or counseled Kent in the sale of marijuana, or did anything more than describe Kent to another person as an individual who might sell some marijuana, or would derive any benefit, consideration or reward from such a sale, there was no proof of an aiding and abetting, and the conviction should, therefore, be reversed as a matter of law. Remanded with directions to dismiss.

HUNTER, C.J., FINLEY, ROSELLINI and NEILL, JJ., and DONWORTH, J. PRO TEM., *concur.*

HAMILTON, Justice *(dissenting).*

. . . I am satisfied that the jury was fully warranted in concluding that appellant, when he affirmatively recommended Kent as a source and purveyor of marijuana, entertained the requisite conscious design and intent that his action would instigate, induce, procure or encourage perpetration of Kent's subsequent crime of selling marijuana to Thompson. . . .

McGOVERN, J., *concurs.*

STATE v. ELLRICH

Supreme Court of New Jersey

10 N.J. 146, 89 A.2d 685 (1952)

WACHENFELD, J.

The appellant, having been convicted by a jury on an indictment for abortion, appeals, claiming he did not instigate the chief actor to perform the unlawful operation and accordingly is not criminally responsible. . . .

A young, single woman residing in Somerville, accompanied by her aunt, visited the defendant, a practicing physician, at his office, 7900 Hudson Boulevard, North Bergen. The young lady told him she was pregnant and asked his help. He refused but "gave me the name of a person who perhaps could help me. He wrote a name and telephone number on a slip of paper and told me to go across the street to the drugstore, I believe it was, and to call this number and say that I was calling from 7900 Hudson Boulevard." The name and number were those of Jean Ellrich.

The woman followed the instructions and as a result of her telephone call she and her aunt went to the Ellrich home in Fairview and made arrangements with him and his wife to have the operation performed about two weeks later. They paid a fee of $800. She testified "he performed the abortion or attempted to" but the proceedings were interrupted by the arrival of the police, who presumably took all present into custody. At their request, a physician made an examination of the patient and testified there had been an attempted abortion which had not been successfully completed.

* * *

The appellant insists the mere giving of the name and address of the one who would perform the unlawful operation does not constitute him an accomplice under the law. As he expresses it, "to incur criminal responsibility under the abortion statute as it is worded, something more than a conversation with the woman is required."

We do not feel called upon to answer so narrow an inquiry, as in our conception of the case the facts so admitted are embellished with a myriad of circumstances the reasonable and logical inferences of which spell out quite clearly and convincingly a criminal concert of action.

Guilty knowledge and a desire for concealment are permissible inferences from the prohibition against the using of the defendant's telephone and the specific instructions to use the pay telephone "across the street." The precaution of using a street address instead of a name to introduce the person making the call implies a knowledge of criminal nature of the transaction and evinces a pre-arranged code between the defendant and Ellrich by which the latter could identify the forwarding agent; while the long journey from Somerville to North Bergen by the victim intimates knowledge that the quest, apparently difficult of accomplishment elsewhere, would be successful here. By referring the patient to a layman, the defendant signified a consciousness that the help sought was not medical treatment or prenatal care but was instead what actually happened.

If the defendant personally arranged with the abortionist for the performance of the illegal operation, he would admittedly be guilty. Likewise, one who directs a woman, under the circumstances here proven, to a third party for the purpose of having such an operation performed, aids and abets in the offense and may be found by the jury to have acted in concert with the chief offender and so be guilty as a principal.

* * *

Here the victim's testimony that she had no prior acquaintance with the Ellriches and met them only as a result of their name and phone number being supplied by the defendant is nowhere challenged or denied. It is not even suggested that she was referred to them for any purpose other than the illegal operation that was subsequently attempted. The defendant was an essential link and, apparently, a conscious one in the chain of events leading up to the commission of the offense. There is sufficient evidence of concerted action in the record to sustain the verdict reached by the jury.

The judgment is affirmed.

NOTES AND QUESTIONS

1. Are Gladstone and *Ellrich* distinguishable? Are they not both cases where the defendant "knowingly facilitates" the criminal offense committed by another?

Are *Gladstone* and *Tally* distinguishable?

A secretary is ordered to type a letter arranging an illegal abortion. Is he guilty of aiding and abetting the abortion? See *R. v. Salford Health Authority ex p. Janaway,* [1988] 2 W.L.R. 442, C.A., affirmed on other grounds, [1988] 3 W.L.R. 1350, H.L.

2. The *Gladstone* court cites Judge Learned Hand's opinion in *United States v. Peoni* as "hitting the [mens rea] nail squarely" by requiring that a defendant charged as an accomplice "associate himself with the venture, that he

participate in it as in something that he wishes to bring about, that he seeks by his action that he make it succeed, [that he manifest a] purposive attitude towards it."

Does *Ellrich* suggest a different approach? consider the words of Judge Parker in *Backun v. United States,* 112 F.2d 635, 637 (4th Cir. 1940):

> Guilt as an accessory depends, not on "having a stake" in the outcome of the crime . . . but on aiding and assisting the perpetrators. . . . The seller may not ignore the purpose for which the purchase is made if he is advised of that purpose, or wash his hands of the aid that he has given the perpetrator of a felony by the plea that he has merely made a sale of merchandise. One who sells a gun to another knowing that he is buying it to commit a murder, would hardly escape conviction as an accessory to the murder by showing that he received full price for the gun.

The problem is similar to that raised earlier in the context of conspiracy. See § 7.03[D], *supra*. As in that area, Judge Friendly's view in *Peoni* is the majority position. Dressler at 411. The Model Penal Code § 2.06(3)(a), with its requirement that the accomplice have "the purpose of promoting or facilitating" the commission of the crime, clearly embraces the approach taken in *Peoni*.

3. The *Gladstone* court notes that the defendant "was not charged with aiding and abetting Thompson in the purchase of marijuana, but with Kent's sale of it." Would the result bedifferent if the government had charged Gladstone with the former rather than the latter offense?

UNITED STATES v. GIOVANETTI

United States Court of Appeals, Seventh Circuit

919 F.2d 1223 (1990)

POSNER, Circuit Judge

The government indicted fifteen men for offenses arising from their participation in an illegal gambling enterprise. . . . Nicholas Janis was convicted of conducting an illegal gambling business or aiding and abetting its conducting, and was sentenced to 60 days.

The head of the gambling enterprise was Thomas Orlando. . . . T]he enterprise operated a succession of "wirerooms," where bets on various sporting events were accepted over the telephone, and it also sponsored "smokers," or casino gambling nights, held at restaurants and bars, where guests played blackjack, craps, and poker. . . . Janis, had [a] minor role in the enterprise. . . . H]e owned a house that the enterprise for a time used as its wireroom.

. . . Janis was a gambler and knew members of the Orlando organization, including Orlando himself and Richard Merino, a bookmaker for the organization. Together with a real estate agent who has not been charged with any wrongdoing, Janis owned, as an investment, a lot in Bridgeview with two houses on it, one behind the other. In the fall of 1982, Merino, who unbeknownst to Janis was a government informant, went to Janis and said he wanted to rent the smaller of the houses, the one in the rear, for his friend Pluta, who was recently divorced. This was done. Pluta did not move in until the spring of the next year (1983), but from November 1982 until July 1983 the house was in continuous use as a wireroom, operated first (it appears) by Merino and then, after Pluta moved in, by Pluta. The house was not used in the gambling enterprise after that, but early the following year the government tape-recorded a telephone conversation between Janis and Orlando in which Janis offered Orlando a key to the house and asked him whether everything was all right. Orlando responded: "Yeah, yeah, they just wanted to get out of there. They spotted some guys out there I guess." Janis replied: "I know." Although Merino and then Pluta were the nominal tenants, often the rent was paid not by either of them but instead by Michael Gioringo, whom Janis knew to be an aide to Thomas Orlando.

The only other evidence of Janis's participation in the gambling enterprise was the testimony of a former friend and fellow gambler, Edward Arnold. Arnold testified that Janis had told him late in 1982 or early in 1983 that he had rented a house in Bridgeview to an acquaintance of Tommy Orlando or Richard Merino. Arnold further testified that shortly after this conversation the phone number that the Orlando enterprise had given him to use in calling in bets was changed to a number that he recognized as a "southwest side" number, an area that, as he knew, included Bridgeview. On the basis of the conversation and the phone number Arnold testified that "in my opinion it was possible that bets were being taken out of that house . . . that Nick was renting."

* * *

Reference to Janis's knowledge brings us to the central issue in the case, the propriety of the judge's having given the "ostrich" instruction, on which see the thorough discussion in *United States v. Jewell,* 532 F.2d 697 (9th Cir. 1976) (en banc). The instruction told the jury, "You may infer knowledge from a combination of suspicion and indifference to the truth. If you find that a person had a strong suspicion that things were not what they seemed or that someone had withheld some important facts, yet shut his eyes for fear that he would learn, you may conclude that he acted knowingly." There is no quarrel with the wording of the instruction, which is verbatim the instruction that we recommended to the district judges of this circuit . . . the question is whether it should have been given.

The ultimate question that the jury had to decide was whether Janis either had participated in conducting the Orlando gambling enterprise or, more plausibly, had aided and abetted the enterprise, by renting the house to Merino knowing it would be used as a wireroom. Now it is not the law that every time a seller sells something that he knows will be used for an illegal purpose he is guilty of aiding and abetting, let alone of actual participation in the illegal conduct. Aiding and abetting requires more, *United States v. Pino-Perez,* 870 F.2d 1230, 1235 (7th Cir. 1989) (en banc); in Learned Hand's words, requires that the alleged aider and abettor "in some sort associate himself with the venture, that he participate in it as in something that he wishes to bring about, that he seek by his action to make it succeed." *United States v. Peoni,* 100 F.2d 401, 402 (2d Cir. 1938). . . .

* * *

It is not the purpose of the ostrich instruction to tell the jury that it does not need direct evidence of guilty knowledge in order to find such knowledge beyond a reasonable doubt. Still less is it to enable conviction of one who merely suspects that he may be involved with wrongdoers. At times during the oral argument of this appeal the government's able lawyer came close to suggesting that the proper office of the ostrich instruction is to enable conviction upon the basis of constructive notice—if a reasonable man who knew what Janis knew would have inquired further and discovered the illegal activity, Janis is an aider and abettor. Not so. Aider and abettor liability is not negligence liability. The abettor and aider must know that he is assisting an illegal activity. We add that if it were the purpose of the ostrich instruction to enable conviction for mere negligence, the instruction would be worded differently.

The most powerful criticism of the ostrich instruction is, precisely, that its tendency is to allow juries to convict upon a finding of negligence for crimes that require intent. The criticism can be deflected by thinking carefully about just what it is that real ostriches do (or at least are popularly supposed to do). They do not just fail to follow through on their suspicions of bad things. They are not merely careless birds. They bury their heads in the sand so that they will not see or hear bad things. They *deliberately* avoid acquiring unpleasant knowledge. The ostrich instruction is designed for cases in which there is evidence that the defendant, knowing or strongly suspecting that he is involved in shady dealings, takes steps to make sure that he does not acquire full or exact knowledge of the nature and extent of those dealings. A deliberate effort to avoid guilty knowledge is all the guilty knowledge the law requires. . . .

The government points out that the rented house in Bridgeview was a short way down a side street from the thoroughfare on which Janis commuted to work daily. It would have been easy for him to drive by the house from time to time to see what was doing, and if he had done so he might have discovered its use as a wireroom. He did not do so. But this is not the active avoidance with which the ostrich doctrine is concerned. It would be if the house had been on the thoroughfare, and Janis, fearful of what he would see if he drove past it, altered his commuting route to avoid it. Janis failed to display curiosity, but he did nothing to prevent the truth from being communicated to him. He did not act to avoid learning the truth.

The critical question so far as Janis's guilt or innocence was concerned is simple (to pose, not necessarily to answer): what did Janis know? Did he know that he was renting his house for use as a wireroom, or did he believe that he was renting his house to the Orlando crew for some private purpose of theirs unconnected with gambling? (Even criminals have private lives.) The ostrich instruction did not advance this inquiry; it confused it, by pointing the jury to circumstances of deliberate avoidance of knowledge that did not exist.

The true intermediate case between a clearly proper giving of the ostrich instruction because the defendant did physical acts to insulate himself from knowledge, and the clearly improper giving of the instruction because the only issue is the defendant's actual knowledge or complete ignorance, is the case of purely psychological avoidance.... In other words, the deliberate effort to avoid guilty knowledge that we said is all the guilty knowledge the law requires can be a mental, as well as a physical, effort—a cutting off of one's normal curiosity by an effort of will. There is no evidence of either sort of effort here.

* * *

Although we think it was an error to give the ostrich instruction in this case, we do not agree with the further suggestion that such an instruction has no possible place in an aider and abettor case. It is true that to be guilty the alleged aider and abettor must want to make the principal's venture succeed, which may seem to imply that he must know what that venture is. But we think not.... We have already given an example, based on the facts of this case, of how an aider and abettor can be an ostrich. If Janis strongly suspected that his house was being used as a wireroom, and to avoid confirming his suspicions he expended resources on avoiding a confrontation with the facts (as by taking a circuitous route to work), then his actions, far from showing that he was not an aider and abettor under Judge Hand's formulation, would show that he was—would show that he wanted the gambling enterprise to succeed so badly that he expended time and effort to avoid acquiring proof of the enterprise's character and with it indisputably guilty knowledge that might compel him to withdraw for fear of being prosecuted with no chance of avoiding conviction by pleading ignorance of what the enterprise was up to.

* * *

Janis's conviction is reversed and the case is remanded for a new trial for him in conformity with the principles set forth in this opinion.

Reversed and remanded.

NOTES AND QUESTIONS

1. Does Judge Posner clearly specify the required state of mind necessary for accomplice liability? To put the question in Model Penal Code terms, must an accomplice "purposely" aid the principal or is he also guilty if he (merely) "knowingly" provides assistance? See MPC, § 2.02(2)(a) and (b). If purpose is the required mental state, is Judge Posner correct in concluding that

> [i]f Janis strongly suspected that his house was being used as a wireroom, and to avoid confirming his suspicions he expended resources on avoiding

a confrontation with the facts . . . then his actions . . . would show that he wanted the gambling enterprise to succeed so badly that he expended time and effort to avoid acquiring proof of the enterprise's character?

If, indeed, Janis went out of his way not to "know" what was going on in the house, does it follow that he necessarily "wanted the gambling enterprise to succeed"?

2. Rather than treating "knowing facilitation" of crime as a basis for accomplice liability for the facilitated crime, a few jurisdictions have created a separate "criminal facilitation" offense which is punished less severely than the facilitated crime. New York, for example, provides for four degrees of criminal facilitation, distinguished on the basis of seriousness of the facilitated crime and whether the person aided is a minor. N.Y. Penal Code § 115.08 (McKinney 1987) defines first degree criminal facilitation as follows:

> A person is guilty of criminal facilitation in the first degree when, believing it probable that he is rendering aid to a person under sixteen years of age who intends to engage in conduct that would constitute a class A felony, he, being over eighteen years of age, engages in conduct which provides such person with means or opportunity for the commission thereof and which in fact aids such person to commit such a class A felony.

Criminal facilitation in the first degree is a class B felony.

STATE v. ETZWEILER

Supreme Court of New Hampshire

125 N.H. 57, 480 A.2d 870 (1984)

BATCHELDER, Justice, with whom BROCK, Justice, *concurs.*

The issues raised in these consolidated cases involve the applicability of New Hampshire's motor vehicle laws and Criminal Code to a simple fact situation. The State and Mark A. Etzweiler, one of the defendants, have stipulated to the following facts. On July 30, 1982, the defendants, Mark Etzweiler and Ralph Bailey, arrived in Etzweiler's automobile at the plant where both were employed. Bailey had been drinking alcoholic beverages and was, allegedly, intoxicated. Etzweiler, allegedly knowing that Bailey was intoxicated, loaned his car to Bailey and proceeded into the plant to begin work. Bailey drove Etzweiler's car away. Approximately ten minutes later, Bailey, driving recklessly, collided with a car driven by Susan Beaulieu. As a result of the accident, two passengers in the Beaulieu car, Kathryn and Nathan Beaulieu, were killed.

On August 26, 1982, the grand jury handed down two indictments charging Etzweiler with negligent homicide . . . and two indictments charging Bailey with manslaughter. . . . Subsequently, on April 6, 1983, the grand jury issued two additional indictments charging Etzweiler with negligent homicide as an accomplice. . . .

Etzweiler filed motions to quash all indictments against him, and the Superior Court transferred to this court the questions of law raised by the motions. . . .

The cases were consolidated on appeal. We dismiss all indictments against Etzweiler and affirm the denial of Bailey's motion to dismiss.

The superior court transferred five questions of law. We need address only the first question: whether the legislature . . . intended to impose criminal liability upon a person who lends his automobile to an intoxicated driver but does not accompany the driver, when the driver's operation of the borrowed automobile causes death.

The first indictments charge Etzweiler with negligent homicide. . . . :

[He] negligently entrusted his motor vehicle to one, Ralph Bailey, knowing that Mr. Bailey was drunk and was going to operate said motor vehicle, that Mr. Bailey while so operating said motor vehicle while drunk did cross into the opposite lane and collide with a motor vehicle in which [decedents were passengers] thereby causing decedent[s'] death[s].

The requisites of the negligent homicide statute are met if a defendant negligently causes death. . . . The State must establish that the defendant failed to become aware of a substantial and unjustifiable risk that his or her conduct may cause the death of another human being. . . .

In this case, however, death resulted not from the conduct of Etzweiler but from the conduct of Bailey, and the accountability of Etzweiler therefore must rest on the complicity of Etzweiler in Bailey's conduct.

At common law, an individual, who did not actually engage in the felonious conduct, could be held criminally liable as a principal if he or she were present during the commission of the crime, aiding and abetting the perpetrator. . . . Thus, the owner of an automobile who lent his or her car to an intoxicated individual, sat by that individual and permitted him to operate the vehicle, may be convicted as a principal to manslaughter if death results from the operation of the vehicle. . . .

At common law, Etzweiler could not have been guilty as a principal. He was not actually or constructively present during the commission of the offense, a necessary prerequisite. . . . If he aided and abetted Bailey, although not present at the commission of the crime, Etzweiler, at common law, may have been guilty as an accessory before the fact to involuntary manslaughter. . . . However, at common law, the crimes of principals and accessories before the fact were distinct and separate. . . .

In 1973, the legislature enacted the Criminal Code and created RSA 626:8, the accomplice liability statute. That statute abrogated the common-law distinction between principals and accessories and narrowly defined those situations in which an individual could be held criminally liable for the conduct of another. . . . Etzweiler's conduct, in lending his automobile to Bailey, must be measured against the standards set forth in the statute.

Etzweiler's conduct *may* fall within the statutory language defining negligent homicide. However, whether to impose criminal liability on Etzweiler involves an important policy decision of broad social consequences. The awesome deliberative task of making such a judgment should not, in the first instance be thrust upon the juries in our trial courts but should be resolved through the legislative process to determine in what manner society seeks to deal with the criminal liability of those who permit unqualified operators to wreak havoc upon our public ways. This is a matter for legislative concern and is not a matter for judicial innovation. . . .

The second indictments charge Etzweiler with the offense of negligent homicide as an accomplice. . . .

RSA 626:8 delineates all situations in which an individual may be held criminally liable for the conduct of another. One situation is when an individual "is an accomplice of [another] in the commission of the offense." RSA 626:8, II(c). Accomplice liability under RSA 626:8, II(c) is defined in two parts, RSA 626:8, III and IV. Section III sets forth the elements which must be present above, beyond, and regardless of the substantive offense. Section IV sets forth the elements of the substantive offense that must be present in order to charge the accomplice.

RSA 626:8, III provides:

A person is an accomplice of another person in the commission of an offense if: (a)with the purpose of promoting or facilitating the commission of the offense, he aids . . . such other person in planning or committing it. . . .

This section sets forth the *conduct element* of accomplice liability, . . . and the necessary accompanying mental state. . . .

Under section III, the State has the burden of establishing that the accomplice acted with the purpose of promoting or facilitating the commission of the substantive offense. . . . This encompasses the requirement that the accomplice's acts were designed to aid the primary actor in committing the offense, . . . and that the accomplice had the purpose to "make the crime succeed.". . . In other words, the accomplice must have the "purpose to advance the criminal end." Model Penal Code § 5.03, comment at 107 (Tent. Draft No. 10, 1960) (RSA 626:8 is based upon the Model Penal Code . . .).

Section IV sets forth the elements of the substantive offense that the State has the burden of establishing against the accomplice. "When causing a particular result is an element of an offense," the accomplice must act "with the kind of culpability, if any, with respect to that result that is sufficient for the commission of the offense.". . .

Our interpretation of the accomplice liability statute effectuates the policy that an accomplice's liability ought not to extend beyond the criminal purposes that he or she shares. Because accomplice liability holds an individual criminally liable for actions done by another, it is important that the prosecution fall squarely within the statute.

Applying these statutory prerequisites, we turn to the indictments charging Etzweiler as an accomplice to negligent homicide.

Mark Etzweiler acted as an accomplice in the conduct which caused the death[s] of Kathryn [and Nathan] Beaulieu when, with a purpose to promote and facilitate the offense of driving under the influence of alcohol, he aided Ralph Bailey in the commission of that offense by lending Ralph Bailey his 1980 AMC automobile, knowing Ralph Bailey was under the influence of alcohol, and encouraging him to drive it on a public way in such condition, and Mark Etzweiler thereby acted negligently with respect to the death[s] of Kathryn [and Nathan] Beaulieu. . . .

The State has alleged that, with the purpose of promoting or facilitating the offense of driving under the influence of alcohol, Etzweiler aided Bailey in the commission of that offense. However, under our statute, the accomplice must aid the primary actor in the substantive offense with the purpose of facilitating the substantive offense—in this case, negligent homicide. Therefore, the indictments against Etzweiler must be quashed. . . .

Even if the indictments tracked the statutory language of RSA 626:8, III and IV, Etzweiler, as a matter of law, could not be an accomplice to negligent homicide. To satisfy the requirements of RSA 626:8, III, the State must establish that Etzeiler's acts were designed to aid Bailey in committing negligent homicide. Yet under the negligent homicide statute, Bailey must be unaware of the risk of death that his conduct created. . . . We cannot see how Etzweiler could intentionally aid Bailey in a crime that Bailey was unaware that he was committing. Thus, we hold, as a matter of law, that, in the present context of the Criminal Code, an individual may not be an accomplice to negligent homicide. We need not reach the question of whether the statute provides for accomplices to manslaughter or murder.

Therefore, we answer the first question posed by the superior court in the negative. . . .

SOUTER, Justice, *concurring specially:*

I concur with the results reached by Justice Batchelder, and I join in his opinion, save in two respects. I do not read RSA 626:8, IV as my brother does. That section provides that

> [w]hen causing a particular result is an element of an offense, an accomplice in the conduct causing such result is an accomplice in the commission of that offense, if he acts with the kind of culpability, if any, with respect to that result that is sufficient for the commission of the offense.

I read this language as an attempt to provide that a person may be criminally liable as an accomplice even if he does not act "with the purpose of promoting or facilitating the commission of an offense." RSA 626:8, III(a).

The attempt fails because the meaning of "accomplice" in section IV is unclear. Section III provides what is necessary to be an "accomplice . . . in the commission of an offense." Among other things, such an accomplice must have a "purpose" to promote or facilitate the commission of the offense. Section IV purports to determine when an accomplice in "conduct" causing a particular result is also an accomplice in the commission of the offense defined by reference to that result. Section IV does not, however, define this new sense of "accomplice" in conduct. One can guess that it means "accomplice" as used in section III minus the "purpose." This is no more than a guess, however. . . . [S]ection IV fails to give any comprehensible, let alone fair, notice of its intended effect and is thus unenforceable. . . .

KING, Chief Justice, Dissenting in *Etzweiler*, with whom DOUGLAS, Justice, *joins.*

For the reasons that follow, I would affirm both sets of indictments against Etzweiler, as . . . an accessory to negligent homicide. . . .

* * *

In construing RSA 626:8—which imputes criminal liability to a person for the conduct of another—to determine whether the indictments in question properly state an offense under that statute, one must define the pertinent statutory language by reference to the definitions provided in the statute itself. . . .

RSA 626:8, I and II(c) assign criminal liability to someone who is "an accomplice of another person in the commission of an offense." This phrase is defined by other provisions in the statute which designate three sets of circumstances under which a person may become "an accomplice of another person in the commission of an offense." They are:

(1) if, "with the purpose of promoting or facilitating the commission of that offense, he solicits such other person in committing it, or aids or agrees or attempts to aid such other person in planning or committing it," RSA 626:8, III(a); or

(2) if "his conduct is expressly declared by law to establish his complicity," RSA 626:8, III(b); or

(3) if, "[w]hen causing a particular result is an element of an offense," the person is "an accomplice in the conduct causing such result" and "he acts with the kind of culpability, if any, with respect to that result that is sufficient for the commission of the offense."

RSA 626:8, IV.

While the statutory phrase "accomplice in the conduct causing [a particular] result" provided by RSA 626:8, IV is not explicitly defined in the statute, when viewed as part of a totality it is implicitly defined by RSA 626:8, III(a). Under section III(a), a person is an accomplice in the principal's criminal conduct causing a particular result if, with the purpose of promoting or facilitating the principal's criminal conduct, the person solicits that conduct, or aids or agrees or attempts to aid that conduct. Section III also assigns liability in those situations in which the accomplice actively seeks the criminal *result* by aiding and abetting the principal without caring precisely how the principal achieves that result.

Therefore, for a person to be criminally liable under RSA 626:8, IV for the crime of a principal, that person must act *purposefully* with respect to the principal's criminal *conduct*. However, with respect to the *result* of the principal's criminal conduct, section IV requires a showing that the person acted with the same state of mind required of the principal. . . . A showing that a person merely acquiesced in or consented to a principal's conduct is not enough to prove purposefulness under section III. . . . Rather, it must be demonstrated that the person participated actively in the principal's conduct. . . .

The second indictments properly allege that Etzweiler acted purposefully to "promote and facilitate" Bailey's criminal conduct—Bailey's alleged intoxicated driving—causing the deaths and "aided" Bailey by "encouraging" him in that conduct. The indictments also allege, as they must, that Etzweiler "thereby acted negligently with respect to" the resulting deaths. Of course, to obtain a conviction of Etzweiler, the State must prove each alleged act and mental state as well as the causal link between *Bailey's* driving and the resulting deaths. Finally, it should be noted that to find Etzweiler guilty, the jury must conclude that he was criminally negligent under RSA 626:2, II(d), a showing of culpability substantially higher than ordinary civil negligence.

While other proffered interpretations of RSA 626:8 may be plausible, they effectively give principal meaning to either section III or section IV of the statute at the expense of the other section. The majority opinion, for example, essentially reads section IV of RSA 626:8 out of the statute, notwithstanding the court's failed attempt to infuse that section with meaning. The statutory analysis herein satisfies the rule of statutory construction that all parts of a statute be read as meaningful and consistent parts of a whole. This analysis also fulfills the court's duty to interpret a statute so as to effectuate its legislative intent: here, to inculpate persons who purposely further the criminal conduct of other while grossly unaware of the substantial and unjustifiable risksattending that criminal conduct.

The court's holding that as a matter of law "a person may not have a purpose of having another commit negligent homicide" is problematic. First, this holding is not supported by the language of RSA 626:8. Second, the court's holding requiring purposeful conduct with respect to the result of the principal's offense, effectively precludes criminal liability of aiding any homicide other than intentional homicide. The justification, theoretical or otherwise, for such an approach to accomplice liability is imperceptible. . . .

NOTES AND QUESTIONS

1. Does the *Etzweiler* majority correctly apply and interpret the provisions of the accomplice statute? Is the dissenting opinion more persuasive?

See *People v. Wheeler,* 772 P.2d 101 (Colo. 1989), which affirms the conviction of a woman for criminal negligent homicide for assisting her boyfriend to engage in conduct "that was a gross deviation from the standard of care that a reasonable person would exercise." The boyfriend's conduct resulted in death, but the court, in applying a statutory provision defining accomplice liability in terms of aiding "with the intent to promote or facilitate the commission of the offense," held that the woman need not have intended or foreseen the death result so long as she "knowingly" aided the conduct.

2. In considering Etzweiler's possible liability as a principal for the crime of negligent homicide, the court concludes that under common law doctrine the deaths "resulted not from the conduct of Etzweiler but from the conduct of Bailey, and the accountability of Etzweiler therefore must rest on the complicity of Etzweiler in Bailey's conduct." Should this approach be followed? Consider the following:

> [I]t is important to reconsider why and when accomplice liability is needed. It is required to establish liability as to one who did not himself engage in the conduct required for commission of the crime, and this becomes most critical when the relevant statute speaks of a specific kind of conduct. For example, the crime of burglary requires (among other things)

a breaking and entering, and thus if A breaks and enters by using a ladder supplied by B and held by C while D keeps a lookout, B, C and D are accountable for the crimes of burglary only if they are accomplices of A for only A has done the requisite breaking and entering. But certain crimes are defined quite differently, in that specific acts are not enumerated; rather, it is only required that the unspecified conduct cause a certain specified result. Such is the case as to criminal negligence involuntary manslaughter. And this is why, if A gives his car to intoxicated B and B runs down and kills C, it is not necessary to find that A is an accomplice to B's crime; if A's own conduct in turning over the car to one known to be intoxicated is itself criminally negligent and if that conduct is found to be the legal cause of the death, then A is guilty of manslaughter on that basis. Indeed, this approach is to be much preferred over the accomplice liability theory, for the latter is not limited by the legal cause requirement and thus could easily be extended to all forms of assistance or encouragement to negligent or reckless conduct.

LaFave and Scott at 85–86.

Should Etzweiler's liability as a principal hinge, as the common law would have it, on whether he was "present" during the commission of the crime? Why is he possibly liable as a principal if he sits by Bailey's side and permits him to drive but escapes liability under that theory when he lends his keys to Bailey and does not ride with him?

3. Suppose Etzweiler had been charged with aiding and abetting Bailey in the crime of manslaughter, under the Model Penal Code, a crime requiring that the defendant act recklessly with respect to both the conduct and resulting death elements. Under the interpretation of the New Hampshire statutes by the *Etzweiler* majority, could Etzweiler be an accomplice to that crime?

Is *Etzweiler* soundly decided on policy grounds? Apart from accomplice liability, could (should?) Etzweiler be guilty as a principal for negligent homicide? See *People v. Kemp,* 150 Cal. App. 2d 654, 310 P.2d 680 (1957); *State v. Hopkins,* 147 Wash. 198, 265 P. 481 (1928).

4. *Etzweiler* arises under an accomplice liability statute patterned after MPC § 2.06(4), which provides:

> When causing a particular result is an element of an offense, an accomplice in the conduct causing such result is an accomplice in the commission of that offense, if he acts with the kind of culpability, if any, with respect to that result that is sufficient for the commission of the offense.

Historically, however, courts and legislatures generally failed to draw distinctions between *mens rea* issues as they relate to conduct versus result elements. Most of the cases focused only on conduct and even there, as reflected by the *Peoni/Backun* differences noted above, were not always in agreement. It is, therefore, not surprising to find that when courts are not guided by explicit provisions such as § 2.06(4), they often reach divergent results when faced with cases like *Etzweiler*. See, *e.g., Stacy v. State,* 228 Ark. 260, 306 S.W.2d 852 (1957) (accomplice liability exists), and *People v. Marshall,* 362 Mich. 170, 106 N.W.2d 842 (1961) (no accomplice liability).

Consider again MPC § 2.06(3)(a)(ii) excerpted in note (2) following the *Tally* case *supra.* The Code restricts accomplice liability to situations where one "purposely" aids another in the "commission of the offense." The language clearly suggests that an accomplice must act purposely with respect to the conduct proscribed by the contemplated offense. But must the accomplice also act purposely regarding the circumstance elements of the offense?

Suppose A encourages B to steal a ring valued at $1,000. Suppose theft of property valued at $1,000 or more constitutes grand theft (a felony), while theft of items valued at less than $1,000 constitutes petty theft (a misdemeanor). Further suppose the crime of grand theft requires no *mens rea* as to the value element. Must A act "purposely" (*i.e.,* be aware or hope that the ring is valued in excess of $1,000) as to the value element in order to "aid" B under § 2.06(3)(a) when B steals the ring? The Code Commentary suggests no clear answer:

> There is deliberate ambiguity as to whether the purpose requirements extends to circumstance elements of the contemplated offense or whether, as in the case of attempts, the policy of the substantive offense on this point should control. . . . The result, therefore, is that the actor must have a purpose with respect to the proscribed conduct . . . with his attitude towards the circumstances to be left to resolution by the courts.

Model Penal Code § 2.06, Comment at 311 n.37 (1985).

5. Returning to the facts of *Etzweiler,* suppose Bailey had been charged with "unlawful-act manslaughter" with reckless driving as the underlying "unlawful act." If Etzweiler aids the crime of reckless driving, he is an accomplice to manslaughter on a "constructive *mens rea*" theory in jurisdictions embracing the unlawful-act—manslaughter doctrine. See, for example, *Wade v. State,* 174 Tenn. 248, 124 S.W.2d 710 (1939); *Black v. State,* 103 Ohio St. 434, 133 N.E. 795 (1921). By the same token, persons who aid others in committing dangerous felonies that result in death are guilty of felony murder even though they neither intentionally, recklessly, nor negligently bring about the homicide. See, for example, *State v. Carothers,* 84 Wash. 2d 256, 525 P.2d 731 (1974); *People v. Cabaltero,* 31 Cal. App. 2d 52, 87 P.2d 364 (1939).

6. Suppose Etzweiler had given Bailey the car keys in hopes that Bailey would end up killing someone while driving in his drunken stupor. If Bailey is guilty of no more than manslaughter, is Etzweiler's liability also limited to manslaughter even if it is assumed that he acted purposely with respect to both the conduct and result elements of the homicides? At least in the area of homicide, the cases hold that accomplices and principals need not be guilty of the same crime. See, for example, *State v. McAllister,* 366 So. 2d 1340 (La. 1978). Therefore, Etzweiler could theoretically be guilty of murder even though the person he aids commits only manslaughter. Similarly, if Bailey, even though drunk, had purposely killed the victims by striking them with Etzweiler's car, he would be guilty of murder, while his accomplice, Etzweiler, could be guilty of a lesser degree of homicide if he was merely reckless or negligent in turning over the car keys to Bailey. See, for example, *Leavine v. State,* 109 Fla. 447, 147 So. 897 (1933). See also *People v. Wheeler,* 772 P.2d 101 (Colo. 1989) (principal guilty of second degree murder; accomplice guilty of aiding criminal negligent homicide).

Outside the homicide context, however, the cases sometimes require that a principal and an accomplice be convicted of exactly the same offense, even though they intended technically different crimes. See, for example, *Regina v. Richards,* [1974] Q.B. 776, where the court quashed a conviction of a wife for the crime of "intentionally causing grievous bodily harm" (a felony) after she had hired two men to beat up her husband. According to her directions, the men beat the husband but were themselves convicted of the lesser crime of "inflicting grievous bodily harm" (a misdemeanor). In finding that only one offense, misdemeanor wounding, had been established, the court stated, "If there is only one offense committed . . . then the person who has requested that offense to be committed, or advised that that offense be committed, cannot be guilty of a graver offense than that in fact which was committed."

7. As a final variation on *Etzweiler,* suppose that instead of killing the victims with Etzweiler's car, Bailey uses a gun to shoot them as he drives down the highway. Assuming that Etzweiler has no reason to believe that Bailey possesses a weapon, does Etzweiler aid and abet the homicides when he loans the drunken Bailey his car?

The general rule is that accomplice liability extend to acts of the principal that are the "natural and probable consequence" of the criminal scheme the accomplice encouraged or aided. See Sayre, *Criminal Responsibility for the Act of Another,* 43 Harv. L. Rev. 689, 702–6 (1930):

Apart from exceptional groups of cases . . . the law may be summarized as follows:

(1) If the defendant can be shown himself to have counseled, procured, commanded, incited, authorized, or encouraged the commission of the particular act which forms the subject of the prosecution, all courts agree in holding him criminally liable, even though the agent committed the act through a different instrumentality, or at a different time, or in a different place from that ordered or authorized.

(2) Where the defendant has neither authorized nor consented to the particular criminal act, even though he has authorized the general business in the course of which the act was committed, the defendant may be civilly, but is not, except as under (3), criminally liable.

(3) On the other hand, even if the particular criminal act has not been authorized or consented to, if it grows out of and is the proximate consequence of one that has been authorized or procured, the defendant is criminally liable, whether or not the agent is acting in the course of the defendant's business.

Whether or not the crime committed is a "proximate consequence" of the crime ordered or procured is often an exceedingly nice question. Such a problem is closely analogous to that arising in the case where one of several accomplices acting in pursuance of a joint plan commits some crime not specifically planned but growing out of the joint enterprise. In such a case, the other accomplices will be liable for the crime thus committed only if it grew out of and was the proximate consequence of the one planned. For instance, where A and B join in a robbery, if A in the commission of the robbery kills the victim, B will be separately liable not only for the robbery, but also for the murder. The same is true where A and B join in concerted burglary. For death is not an improbable consequence of robbery or burglary, and proximate causation can in most such cases be established. On the other hand, if A and B set out to commit larceny, and A while in the commission of the larceny robs a night watchman, B is not guilty of the robbery. So, confederates who combine to commit an assault merely, are not liable for a robbery of the victim by one of their number; nor are confederates who plan to kill A ordinarily liable if one of their number intentionally kills B.

As for Etzweiler's liability in the gun hypothetical, death is surely not an unforeseeable consequence when one loans a car for use by a drunk driver. On the other hand, death caused by gunshots from the drunk driver within the car is another matter, unless of course Etzweiler has prior knowledge of Bailey's gun and his propensity to use it. Thus, while Etzweiler may aid Bailey in reckless driving, accomplice liability would not likely exist for homicides committed by means of the gun. See *Regina v. Anderson and Morris,* 2 W.L.R. 1195 (1966).

[C] Primary and Secondary Liability

STATE V. HAYES

Supreme Court of Missouri

105 Mo. 74, 16 S.W. 514 (1891)

THOMAS, J.

The defendant appeals from a sentence of five years' imprisonment in the penitentiary for burglary and larceny. . . . [Defendant, Hayes, approached an acquaintance, Hill, about a proposed burglary of a general store. Hill feigned agreement in order to arrange for the capture of Hayes when the crime was committed. Hill notified the store owners of the time and place of the proposed crime. Law enforcement personnel stationed themselves near the store to apprehend Hayes. At the time for the proposed burglary, Hill and Hayes arrived at the store together. Hayes raised the store window and boosted Hill inside. Hill handed out a side of bacon. The law enforcement forces then arrested Hayes.] It will be seen the trial court [instructed] the jury . . . that defendant was guilty of burglary if he, with a felonious intent, assisted and aided Hill to enter the building, notwithstanding Hill himself may have had no such intent. In this we think the court erred. One cannot read this record without being convinced beyond a reasonable doubt that Hill did not enter the warehouse with intent to steal. . . . We may assume, then, for the sake of the argument, that Hill committed no crime in entering the wareroom. The act of Hill, however, was by the instruction of the court imputed to defendant. This act, according to the theory of the instructions, so far as Hill was concerned, was not a criminal act but when it was imputed to defendant it became criminal because of the latter's felonious intent. This would probably be true if Hill had acted under the control and compulsion of defendant, and as his passive and submissive agent. But he was not a passive agent in this transaction. He was an active one. He acted of his own volition. He did not raise the window and enter the building with intent to commit crime, but simply to entrap defendant in the commission of crime, and have him captured.

Judge Brewer sets this idea in a very clear light in *State v. Jansen,* 22 Kan. 498. He says "The act of a detective may perhaps be not imputable to the defendant, as there is a want of community of motive. The one has a criminal intent, while the other is seeking the discovery and punishment of crime." Where the owner learns that his property is to be stolen, he may employ detectives and decoys to catch the thief. And we can do no better than to quote again from Judge Brewer, in the case above cited, as to the relation of the acts of detectives and the thief when a crime is alleged to have been committed by the two. He says:

> Where each of the overt acts going to make up the crime charged is personally done by the defendant, and with criminal intent, his guilt is complete, no matter what motives may prompt or what acts be done by the party who is with him, and apparently assisting him. Counsel have cited and commented upon several cases in which detectives figured, and in which defendants were adjudged guiltless of the crimes charged. But this feature distinguishes them: that some act essential to the crime charged was in fact done by the detective, and not by the defendant, and, this act not being imputable to the defendant, the latter's guilt was not made out. The intent and act must combine and all the elements of the act must exist and be imputable to the defendant.

Applying the principle here announced to the case at bar, we find that defendant did not commit every overt act that went to make up the crime. He did not enter the warehouse, either actually or constructively, and hence he did not commit the crime of burglary, no matter what his intent was, it clearly appearing that Hill was guilty of no crime. To make defendant responsible for the acts of Hill, they must have had a common motive and common design. The design and the motives of the two men were not only distinct, but dissimilar, even antagonistic.

. . . Our ruling is that defendant cannot be convicted of burglary and larceny, unless he committed the crimes himself, or was present aiding and abetting another in their commission, that other acting with a felonious intent. The court should instruct the jury that if Hill broke into and entered the wareroom with a felonious intent, and defendant was present, aiding him with the same intent, then he is guilty; but if Hill entered the room with no design to steal, but simply to entrap defendant, and capture him in the commission of crime, and defendant did not enter the room himself, then he is not guilty of burglary and larceny as charged. He may be found guilty, however, of petit larceny, in taking and removing the bacon after it was handed to him. This overt act he did in fact commit. . . . The judgment is reversed and the cause remanded for new trial. All concur.

Regina v. Cogan and Leak

Court of Appeals, Criminal Division

[1975] 2 All E.R. 1059

LAWTON L.J. . . .

[Appellants, Cogan and Leak, appeal their convictions for rape. The indictment charged Cogan with raping Leak's wife and Leak with aiding and abetting that offense. Leak and his wife had been married for five years and the couple had a history of sometimes violent quarrels.]

[On the night of the alleged assault] Leak came home at about 6 PM with Cogan. Both had been drinking. Leak told his wife that Cogan wanted to have sexual intercourse with her and that he, Leak, was going to see she did. She was frightened of him and what he might do, as well she might have been. He made her go upstairs where he took her clothes off and lowered her onto a bed. Cogan then came into the room. Leak asked him twice whether he wanted sexual intercourse with her. On both occasions he said that he did not. Leak then had sexual intercourse with her in the presence of Cogan. When he had finished, Leak again asked Cogan if he wanted sexual intercourse with his wife. This time Cogan said he did. He asked Leak to leave the room but he refused to do so. Cogan then had sexual intercourse with Mrs. Leak. Her husband watched. Whilst all this was going on for most of the time, if not at all, Mrs. Leak was sobbing. She did not struggle when Cogan was on top of her but she did try to turn away from him. When he had finished, he left the room. Leak then had intercourse with her again and behaved in a revolting fashion to her. When he had finished he joined Cogan and the pair of them left the house to renew their drinking. Mrs. Leak dressed. She went to a neighbour's house and then to the police. The two appellants were arrested about three-quarters of an hour later. Both made oral and written statements.

Leak's statement amounted to a confession that he had procured Cogan to have sexual intercourse with his wife. He admitted that whilst Cogan was having intercourse with her she was sobbing "on and off not all the time." There was ample evidence from the terms of his statement that she had not consented to Cogan having intercourse with her. The whole tenor of this statement was that he had procured Cogan to do what he did in order to punish her for past misconduct. He intended that she should be raped and that Cogan's body should provide the physical means to that end.

Cogan, in his written statement, admitted that he had sexual intercourse with Mrs. Leak at Leak's suggestion and that whilst he was on top of her she had been upset and cried. At the trial Cogan gave evidence that he thought Mrs. Leak had consented. The basis for his belief was what he had heard from her husband about her. The drink he had seems to have been a reason, if not the only one, for mistaking her sobs and distress for consent.

The trial started on 23rd October 1974. A few days before, namely on 14th October, press publicity had been given to the fact that this court in *R. v. Morgan* [[1975] 1 All E.R. 8] had certified a point of law of general public importance whether in rape the defendant can properly be convicted notwithstanding that he in fact believed that the woman consented if such belief was not based on reasonable grounds and had given leave to appeal to the House of Lords. In the course of his summing-up the trial judge stressed the need for the jury to be sure before convicting either of the defendants that the wife had not consented to sexual intercourse. He then went on to direct them in relation to Cogan's case in accordance with the decision of this court in *R. v. Morgan.* He prudently decided to ask the jury to make a finding whether any belief in consent which Cogan may have had was based on reasonable grounds. The jury returned a verdict of guilty against Cogan thereby showing that they were sure the wife had not consented. They went on to say that Cogan had believed she was consenting but that he had had no reasonable grounds for such belief.

As to Leak he directed the jury that even if Cogan believed that the wife was consenting and had reasonable grounds for such a belief they would still be entitled to find Leak guilty as charged.

Cogan's appeal against conviction was based on the ground that the decision of the House of Lords in *Director of Public Prosecutions v. Morgan* [[1975] 2 E.R. 347] applied. It did. There is nothing more to be said. It was for this reason that we allowed the appeal and quashed his conviction.

Leak's appeal against conviction was based on the proposition that he could not be found guilty of aiding and abetting Cogan to rape his wife if Cogan was acquitted of that offense as he was deemed in law to have been when his conviction was quashed. . . .

The only case which counsel for Leak submitted that had a direct bearing on the problem of Leak's guilt was *Walters v. Lunt* [[1951] 2 All E.R. 645]. In that case the respondents had been charged under the Larceny Act 1916, § 33(I), with receiving from a child aged seven years, certain articles knowing them to have been stolen. In 1951 a child under eight years was deemed in law to be incapable of committing a crime; it followed that at the time of receipt by the respondents the articles had not been stolen and that the charge had not been proved. That case is very different from this because here one fact is clear—the wife had been raped. Cogan had had sexual intercourse with her without consent. The fact that Cogan was innocent of rape because he believed that she was consenting does not affect the position that she was raped.

Her ravishment had come about because Leak had wanted it to happen and had taken action to see that it did by persuading Cogan to use his body as the instrument for the necessary physical act. In the language of the law the act of sexual intercourse without the wife's consent was the *actus reus;* it had been procured by Leak who had the appropriate *mens rea,* namely his intention that Cogan should have sexual intercourse with her without her consent. Leak was using him as a means to procure a criminal purpose. . . .

. . . The modern law allowed Leak to be tried and punished as a principal offender. In our judgment he could have been indicted as a principal offender. It would have been no defense for him to submit that if Cogan was an "innocent" agent, he was necessarily in the old terminology of the law a principal in the first degree, which was a legal impossibility as a man cannot rape his own wife during cohabitation. The law no longer concerns itself with niceties of degrees in participation in crime; but even if it did, Leak would still be guilty. The reason a man cannot by his own physical act rape his wife during cohabitation is because the law presumes consent from the marriage ceremony. . . . There is no such presumption when a man procures a drunken friend to the physical act for him. . . .

Had Leak been indicted as a principal offender, the case against him would have been clear beyond argument. Should he be allowed to go free because he was charged with "being aider and abettor to the same offense"? If we are right in our opinion that the wife had been raped (and no one outside a court of law would say that she had not been), then the particulars of offense accurately stated what Leak had done, namely he had procured Cogan to commit the offense. This would suffice to uphold the conviction. . . . By his written statement Leak virtually admitted what he had done. As Judge Chapman said in *R. v. Humphreys and Turner* [[1965] 3 All E.R. 689 at 692]:

> It would be anomalous if a person who admitted to a substantial part in the perpetration of a misdemeanor as aider and abettor could not be convicted on his own admission merely because the person alleged to have been aided and abetted was not or could not be convicted.

In the circumstances of this case it would be more than anomalous: it would be an affront to justice and to the common sense of ordinary folk. It was for these reasons that we dismissed the appeal against conviction.

* * *

Appeal of Leak against conviction dismissed.

NOTES AND QUESTIONS

1. Are *Hayes* and *Cogan and Leak* consistent? If *Hayes* stands for the proposition that "It is hornbook law that a defendant charged with aiding and abetting the commission of a crime by another cannot be convicted in the absence of proof that the crime was actually committed," *United States v. Ruffin,* 613 F.2d 408, 412 (2d Cir. 1979), is *Cogan and Leak* at odds with that view? If Cogan lacked the *mens rea* for rape, could he commit that crime? If Leak was liable for "procuring a drunken friend to do the physical act for him," then why not Hayes when he procured an "innocent" person immune from conviction to do the "physical act" for him?

2. Is the English court correct in its view that a rape occurred in *Cogan and Leak* but no theft occurred in *Walters v. Lunt* when the seven-year-old appropriated another's property? Does this mean that if the defendant in *Walters v. Lunt* had encouraged the child to take the property in the first place, the defendant would be immune from theft liability? If not, on what theory would defendant be liable? See *Bailey v. Commonwealth,* 229 Va. 258, 329 S.E.2d 37 (1985); *State v. McCarthy,* 179 Conn. 1, 425 A.2d 924 (1979); *State v. Dowell,* 106 N.C. 168, 11 S.E. 525 (1890).

Model Penal Code § 2.06(1)–(2)(a) provides,

(1) A person is guilty of an offense if it is committed by his own conduct or by the conduct of another person for which he is legally accountable, or both.

(2) A person is legally accountable for the conduct of another person when:

(a) acting with the kind of culpability that is sufficient for the commission of the offense, he causes an innocent or irresponsible person to engage in such conduct.

An analogous Code provision, § 2.06(7), states:

An accomplice may be convicted on proof of the commission of the offense and of his complicity therein, though the person claimed to have committed the offense has not been prosecuted or convicted or has been convicted of a different offense or degree of offense or has an immunity to prosecution or conviction or has been acquitted.

§ 8.02 The Conspiracy—Complicity Doctrine

Pinkerton v. United States

Supreme Court of the United States

328 U.S. 640 (1946)

Mr. Justice DOUGLAS *delivered the opinion of the Court.*

Walter and Daniel Pinkerton are brothers who live a short distance from each other on Daniel's farm. They were indicted for violations of the Internal Revenue Code. The indictment contained ten substantive counts and one conspiracy count. The jury found Walter guilty on nine of the substantive counts and on the conspiracy count. It found Daniel guilty on six of the substantive counts and on the conspiracy count. Walter was fined $500 and sentenced generally on the substantive counts to imprisonment for thirty months. On the conspiracy count he was given a two year sentence to run concurrently with the other sentence. Daniel was fined $1,000 and sentenced generally on the substantive counts to imprisonment for thirty months. On the conspiracy count he was fined $500 and given a two year sentence to run concurrently with the other sentence. . . .

A single conspiracy was charged and proved. . . .

* * *

It is contended that there was insufficient evidence to implicate Daniel in the conspiracy. But we think there was enough evidence for submission of the issue to the jury

There is, however, no evidence to show that Daniel participated directly in the commission of the substantive offenses on which his conviction has been sustained, although there was evidence to show that these substantive offenses were in fact committed by Walter in furtherance of the unlawful agreement of conspiracy existing between the brothers. The question was submitted to the jury on the theory that each petitioner could be found guilty of the substantive offenses, if it was found at the time those offenses were committed petitioners were parties to an unlawful conspiracy and the substantive offenses charged were in fact committed in furtherance of it.

Daniel relies on *United States v. Sall* [116 F.2d 745 (3d Cir. 1940)]. That case held that participation in the conspiracy was not itself enough to sustain a conviction for the substantive offense even though it was committed in furtherance of the conspiracy. The court held that, in addition to evidence that the offense was in fact committed in furtherance of the conspiracy, evidence of direct participation in the commission of the substantive offense or other evidence from which participation might fairly be inferred was necessary.

We take a different view. We have here a continuous conspiracy. There is here no evidence of the affirmative action on the part of Daniel which is necessary to establish his withdrawal from it. *Hyde v. United States,* 225 U.S. 347, 369. As stated in that case,

> Having joined in an unlawful scheme, having constituted agents for its performance, scheme and agency to be continuous until full fruition be secured, until he does some act to disavow or defeat the purpose he is in no situation to claim the delay of the law. As the offense has not been terminated or accomplished, he is still offending. And we think, consciously offending—offending as certainly, as we have said, as at the first moment of his confederation, and consciously through every moment of its existence. . . .

And so long as the partnership in crime continues, the partners act for each other in carrying it forward. It is settled that "an overt act of one partner may be the act of all without any new agree ment specifically directed to that act." . . . Motive or intent may be proved by the acts or declarations of some of the conspirators in furtherance of the common objective. . . . A scheme to use the mails to defraud, which is joined in by more than one person, is a conspiracy. . . . Yet all members are responsible, though only one did the mailing. . . . The governing principle is the same when the substantive offense is committed by one of the conspirators in furtherance of the unlawful project. . . . The criminal intent to do the act is established by the formation of the conspiracy. Each conspirator instigated the commission of the crime. The unlawful agreement contemplated precisely what was done. It was formed for the purpose. The act done was in execution of the enterprise. The rule which holds responsible one who counsels, procures, or commands another to commit a crime is founded on the same principle. That principle is recognized in the law of conspiracy when the overt act of one partner in crime is attributable to all. An overt act is an essential ingredient of the crime of conspiracy. . . . If that can be supplied by the act of one conspirator, we fail to see why the same or other acts in furtherance of the conspiracy are likewise not attributable to the others for the purpose of holding them responsible for the substantive offense.

A different case would arise if the substantive offense committed by one of the conspirators was not in fact done in furtherance of the conspiracy, did not fall within the scope of the unlawful project, or was merely a part of the ramifications of the plan which could not be reasonably foreseen as a necessary or natural consequence of the unlawful agreement. But as we read this record, that is not this case.

Affirmed.

Mr. Justice JACKSON *took no part in the consideration or decision of this case.*

Mr. Justice RUTLEDGE, *dissenting in part.*

The judgment concerning Daniel Pinkerton should be reversed. In my opinion it is without precedent here and is a dangerous precedent to establish.

Daniel and Walter, who were brothers living near each other, were charged in several counts with substantive offenses, and then a conspiracy count was added naming those offenses as overt acts. The proof showed that Walter alone committed the substantive crimes. There was none to establish that Daniel participated in them, aided and abetted Walter in committing them, or knew that he had done so. Daniel in fact was in the penitentiary, under sentence for other crimes, when some of Walter's crimes were done.

There was evidence, however, to show that over several years Daniel and Walter had confederated to commit similar crimes concerned with unlawful possession, transportation, and dealing in whiskey, in fraud of the federal revenues. On this evidence both were convicted of conspiracy. Walter also was convicted on the substantive counts on the proof of his committing the crimes charged. Then, on that evidence without more than the proof of Daniel's criminal agreement with Walter and the latter's overt acts, which were also the substantive offenses charged, the court told the jury they could find Daniel guilty of those substantive offenses. They did so.

I think this ruling violates both the letter and the spirit of what Congress did when it separately defined the three classes of crime, namely, (1) completed substantive offenses; (2) aiding, abetting or counseling another to commit them; and (3) conspiracy to commit them. Not only does this ignore the distinctions Congress has prescribed shall be observed. It either convicts one man for another's crime or punishes the man convicted twice for the same offense.

* * *

. . . Daniel has been held guilty of the substantive crimes committed only by Walter on proof that he did no more than conspire with him to commit offenses of the same general character. There was no evidence that he counseled, advised or had knowledge of those particular acts or offenses. There was, therefore, none that he aided, abetted or took part in them. There was only evidence sufficient to show that he had agreed with Walter at some past time to engage in such transactions generally. As to Daniel this was only evidence of conspiracy, not of substantive crime

The Court's theory seems to be that Daniel and Walter became general partners in crime by virtue of their agreement and because of that agreement without more on his part Daniel became criminally responsible as a principal for everything Walter did thereafter in the nature of a criminal offense of the general sort the agreement contemplated, so long as there was not clear evidence that Daniel had withdrawn from or revoked the agreement. Whether or not his commitment to the penitentiary had that effect, the result is a vicarious criminal responsibility as broad as, or broader than, the vicarious civil liability of a partner for acts done by a co-partner in the course of the firm's business.

* * *

NOTES AND QUESTIONS

1. The *Pinkerton* rule has proven to be controversial. Some jurisdictions embrace it. For example, the Supreme Court of Rhode Island, in *State v. Barton,* 424 A.2d 1033, 1036–38 (R.I. 1981), defended the rule as "sound and viable" and summarized the reasons for its existence:

> The *Pinkerton* rule has found favor with many states under a variety of theories. Under one view, vicarious liability is supported on the premise that criminal acts, apart from the object of the conspiracy, are dependent upon the encouragement and material support of the group as a whole and therefore justify treating each member of the conspiracy as an agent for the others. . . . Under another view, the *Pinkerton* rule is supported on the theory that group activity presents a greater potential threat to the public than individual action. . . . In a similar vein, others have suggested that conspiracy provides a vehicle whereby criminals will engage in more elaborate and complex schemes than they would attempt if working alone, and therefore such activity should be discouraged via the *Pinkerton* rule.

A number of courts, on the other hand, have rejected the *Pinkerton* doctrine. See, for example, *State v. Small,* 301 N.C. 407, 272 S.E.2d 128 (1980); *Commonwealth v. Stasium,* 349 Mass. 38, 206 N.E.2d 672 (1965). In *People v. McGee,* 49 N.Y.2d 48, 424 N.Y.S.2d 157, 399 N.E.2d 1175 (1979), *cert. denied,* 446 U.S. 942 (1980), the New York Court of Appeals rejected *Pinkerton* but recognized that parties to a conspiracy may be held accountable for the "overt acts" of co-conspirators:

> The crime of conspiracy is an offense separate from the crime that is the object of the conspiracy. Once an illicit agreement is shown, the overt act of any conspirator may be attributed to other conspirators to establish the offense of conspiracy and that act may itself be the object crime. But the overt act itself is not the crime in a conspiracy situation; it is merely an element of the crime that has as its basis the agreement. It is not offensive to permit a conviction of conspiracy to stand on the overt act committed by another, for the act merely provides corroboration of existence of the agreement and indicates that the agreement has reached a point where it poses a sufficient threat to society to impose sanctions. But it is repugnant to our system of jurisprudence, where guilt is generally personal to the defendant, to impose punishment, not for the socially harmful agreement

to which the defendant is a party, but for substantive offenses in which he did not participate.

49 N.Y.2d at 57–58, 424 N.Y.S.2d at 162, 399 N.E.2d at 1181–82.

The Model Penal Code also rejects the *Pinkerton* doctrine for reasons detailed in the Commentary to § 2.06 at 307–9:

> The most important point at which the Model Code formulation diverges from the language of many courts is that it does not make "conspiracy" as such a basis of complicity in substantive offenses committed in furtherance of its aims. It asks, instead, more specific questions about the behavior charged to constitute complicity, such as whether the defendant solicited commission of the particular offense or whether he aided, or agreed or attempted to aid, in its commission.
>
> The reason for this treatment is that there appears to be no better way to confine within reasonable limits the scope of liability to which conspiracy may theoretically give rise. In *People v. Luciano,* for example, Luciano and others were convicted of sixty-two counts of compulsory prostitution, receiving money for so doing or receiving money from the earnings of a prostitute—acts proved to have been committed pursuant to a combination to control commercialized vice in New York City.
>
> Liability was properly imposed with respect to these defendants, who directed and controlled the combination. They solicited and aided the commission of numberless specific crimes, including the ones for which they were held. But would so extensive a liability be just for each of the prostitutes or runners involved in the plan? They have, of course, committed their own crimes; they may actually have assisted in others but they exerted no substantial influence on the behavior of a hundred other prostitutes or runners, each pursuing his own ends within the shelter of the combination. A court would and should hold that they are parties to a conspiracy; this is itself a crime, under this Code as well as most others. And they should also be held for those crimes they actually committed, or within the principle of this section for those to which they were accomplices. However, law would lose all sense of just proportion if simply because of the conspiracy itself each were held accountable for thousands of additional offenses of which he was completely unaware and which he did not influence at all.

* * *

> No decision has been found in which the liability of co-conspirators for acts of one another has been pressed to limits such as these, though the limits have been approached. The cases that declare the doctrine normally involve defendants who have had a hand in planning, directing, or executing the crimes charged. When that is so, the other principles of accessorial liability establish guilt, and under this section the defendant has "solicited," "aided," "agreed to aid," or "attempted to aid" in planning or committing the crime. Indeed, when that is not so, courts may be expected to seek ways to avoid the conclusion of complicity, though traditional doctrine hardly points the way. The right way, it is submitted, is to measure liability by the criteria of this section. Conspiracy may prove solicitation, aid or

agreement to aid, etc; it is evidentially important and may be sufficient for that purpose. But whether it suffices ought to be decided by the jurors; they should not be told that it establishes complicity as a matter of law. However proper it may be to draw the necessary inference from proof of the conspiracy, the jury ought to face in concrete cases whether or not, on the evidence, the inference is one that should be drawn.

2. In the following hypothetical, consider the liability of each of the parties for the crimes committed by the others and (a)the normal doctrines of complicity and (b)the *Pinkerton* doctrine:

> A is the organizer and ringleader of a conspiracy to rob banks. He hires B and C to rob banks 1 and 2 respectively. Although B and C do not meet face-to-face, both know that they are members of a large conspiracy and each knows of the other's assignment. At A's instigation, D, knowing of the conspiracy, steals a car for use in the robberies. B and C perform their robberies, the former using D's car.

Developments in the Law—Criminal Conspiracy, 72 Harv. L. Rev. 920, 996 (1959).

3. In *United States v. Molina,* 581 F.2d 56, 61 (2d Cir. 1978), the court stated:

> There are, of course, cases which fall within the exceptions in *Pinkerton* where (1)the substantive offense committed by one of the conspirators was not in fact done in furtherance of the conspiracy, (2)did not fall within the scope of the unlawful project, or (3)was merely a part of the ramifications of the plan which could not reasonably have been foreseen as a necessary or natural consequence of the unlawful agreement.

"It is a question of fact whether there is a conspiracy, . . . and whether the act charged is a natural and probable consequence of the conspiracy." *Martinez v. State,* 413 So. 2d 429, 430 (Fla. Dist. Ct. App. 1982).

4. The Federal Sentencing Guidelines seemingly reduce the impact of the *Pinkerton* Doctrine in federal cases. The Second Circuit has held that "the scope of conduct for which a defendant can be held accountable under the sentencing guidelines is significantly narrower than the conduct embraced by the law of conspiracy." *United States v. Perrone,* 936 F.2d 1403, 1416 (2d Cir. 1991). In determining the base offense level for the purpose of sentencing a defendant under the Federal Sentencing Guidelines, the court will consider as relevant conduct "all reasonably foreseeable acts and omissions of others *in furtherance of the jointly undertaken criminal activity."* United States Sentencing Commission, *Guidelines Manual,* § 1B1.3(a) (Nov. 1994) (emphasis added).

> A "jointly undertaken criminal activity" is a criminal plan, scheme, endeavor, or enterprise undertaken by the defendant in concert with others, whether or not charged as a conspiracy. . . .
>
> Because a count may be worded broadly and include the conduct of many participants over a period of time, the scope of the criminal activity jointly undertaken by the defendant (the "jointly undertaken criminal activity") is not necessarily the same as the scope of the entire conspiracy, and hence relevant conduct is not necessarily the same for every participant. In order

to determine the defendant's accountability for the conduct of others under subsection (a)(1)(B), the court must first determine the scope of the criminal activity the particular defendant agreed to jointly undertake (*i.e.,* the scope of the specific conduct and objectives embraced by the defendant's agreement). The conduct of others that was both in furtherance of, and reasonably foreseeable in connection with, the criminal activity jointly undertaken by the defendant is relevant conduct under this provision. The conduct of others that was not in furtherance of the criminal activity jointly undertaken by the defendant, or was not reasonably foreseeable in connection with that criminal activity, is not relevant conduct under this provision.

U.S.S.G. § 1B1.3, comment (n.2).

Consider the following example:

A, one of the largest drug dealers in the area, hires B to transport 10 grams of cocaine. B knows A's activities and is aware that A has many other employees, including C. Under conspiracy doctrine, B could be found to be a co-conspirator with both A and C to "transport" drugs. If C kills an undercover narcotics agent who is trying to bust the operation, B might be liable under *Pinkerton* for C's homicide if it was committed in furtherance of the conspiracy. Under the Guidelines, however, B appears not responsible for the homicide because his criminal activity is limited to the cocaine he transported, even if he is part of the larger conspiracy and even if C's act is carried out in furtherance thereof and is reasonably foreseeable.

5. For discussion of the *Pinkerton* doctrine, see Perkins, *The Act of One Conspirator,* 26 Hastings L.J. 337 (1974); Marcus, *The Proposed Federal Criminal Code: Conspiracy Provisions,* 1978 Ill. L.F. 379, 381–83; Note, 56 Yale L.J. 371 (1947).

§ 8.03 VICARIOUS LIABILITY

[A] Liability of Natural Persons

ALLEN V. WHITEHEAD

King's Bench Division

[1929] All E.R. 13, [1930] K.B. 211

Lord HEWART, C.J.

This case . . . raises a question under § 44 of the Metropolitan Police Act, 1839. The respondent was summoned to answer an information, laid by the appellant, which charged that the respondent on a day in February, 1929, being the keeper of certain premises where refreshments were sold or consumed, did knowingly suffer prostitutes to meet together and remain therein contrary to § 44 of the statute.* [His Lordship having read the material words

---

* Metropolitan Police Act, 1839, § 44: "And whereas it is expedient that the provisions made by law for preventing disorderly conduct in the houses of licensed victuallers be extended to other houses of public resort. Be it enacted, that every person who shall have or keep any house, shop, room, or place of public resort within the metropolitan police district, wherein provisions, liquors,

of the section, continued:] The magistrate, having heard the evidence, came to the conclusion that the charge was not proved, and the question for this Court is whether he came to a correct determination in point of law in dismissing the case.

The facts of the case are simple enough. It is found as a fact that the respondent, who was the occupier and licensee of a refreshment house, which was open day and night, did not himself manage the premises. He received the profits of the business, but for the purpose of the conduct of the business he chose to employ a manager. In these circumstances it was approved that on a certain day in February, and on each of the seven days following, a number of women, known to the respondent's manager to be prostitutes, resorted to the refreshment house, meeting there together with a number of men and remaining therein between the hours of 8 PM and 4 AM, and using obscene language. There are other findings of fact of a similar character. Before the happening of those events—namely, on September 1, 1928—the respondent had been warned by the police about harbouring prostitutes at his refreshment house. Having received that warning, he gave instructions to the manager that no prostitutes should be allowed to congregate in the premises, and, more than that, a notice was displayed forbidding them to enter the refreshment house after midnight. So far as the respondent's own acts are concerned, the case finds that he visited the premises about once or twice a week.

Now what is the fair meaning of those facts, if it be not this, that the respondent was to all intents and purposes an absentee who had told his manager to use the discretion which, if he had been upon the premises, he must have used himself? . . . The question here was whether it was true to say that the position of the respondent was analogous to that of a licensee under the Licensing Acts, in the sense that he was responsible for the acts of his manager within the scope of his employment. Now here, upon the facts of the case, it is abundantly plain that there was knowledge on the part of the manager. The question is whether upon the proper construction of § 44 of the Metropolitan Police Act, 1839, that knowledge in the servant is to be imputed to the employer so as to make the employer liable. In my opinion, the answer to that question is in the affirmative. The principle seems to me to be that. . . .

> while *prima facie* a principal is not to be made criminally responsible for the acts of his servants, yet the Legislature may prohibit an act or enforce a duty in such words as to make the prohibition or the duty absolute; in which case the principal is liable if the act is in fact done by his servants. To ascertain whether a particular Act of Parliament has that effect or not regard must be had to the object of the statute, the words used, the nature of the duty laid down, the person upon whom it is imposed, the person by whom it would in ordinary circumstances be performed, and the person upon whom the penalty is imposed.

---

or refreshments of any kind shall be sold or consumed, (whether the same shall be kept or retailed therein or procured elsewhere,) and who shall wilfully or knowingly permit drunkenness or other disorderly conduct in such house, shop, room or place . . . or knowingly permit or suffer prostitutes or persons of notoriously bad character to meet together and remain therein, shall for every such offense be liable to a penalty of not more than five pounds. . . . "

Applying that canon to the present case, I think that this provision in this statute would be rendered nugatory if the contention raised on behalf of this respondent were held to prevail. That contention was this, that as the respondent did not himself manage the refreshment house and had no personal knowledge that prostitutes met together and remained therein, and had not been negligent in failing to notice these facts, and had not wilfully closed his eyes to them, he could not in law be held responsible. . . . This seems to me to be a case where the proprietor, the keeper of the house, had delegated his duty to a manager, so far as the conduct of the house was concerned. He had transferred to the manager the exercise of discretion in the conduct of the business, and it seems to me that the only reasonable conclusion is, regard being had to the purposes of this Act, that the knowledge of the manager was the knowledge of the keeper of the house. I think, therefore, that this case ought to go back to the learned magistrate with a direction to convict.

AVORY, J.

I am of the same opinion. I think the manager in this case, although acting contrary to his instructions in doing what he did, was acting in the course of his employment, and that being so, the employer is responsible for his acts.

* * *

BRAND, J.

I agree. The essence of the respondent's case was that he had no personal knowledge of the fact that prostitutes were meeting and remaining upon these premises. It is found that his manager knew, and Lord Coleridge C.J. said . . . "that a man may put another in his position so as to represent him for the purpose of knowledge." I think that is what the respondent has done here and that, consequently, the contention set up by the respondent fails.

I agree that the appeal should be allowed and that the case should go back to the learned magistrate with a direction to convict.

Appeal allowed.

Case remitted for conviction.

NOTES AND QUESTIONS

1. Could the respondent in *Allen* be liable for "aiding and abetting" the crime of the manager? If not, on what basis is liability imposed in *Allen*? Does the court correctly interpret § 44 of the Metropolitan Police Act?

Allen takes place within the common law tradition which imposed criminal liability upon faultless employers for the unauthorized criminal acts of their employees in two isolated instances: nuisance and libel. La Fave and Scott at 251. Does the conduct involved in *Allen* fit within the nuisance category?

2. As *Allen* illustrates, vicarious liability is almost always grounded entirely on the basis of certain status relationships existing between the accused and

the primary actor. The employment relationship provides the most common basis for such liability. A variety of modern statutes have been interpreted to extend vicarious liability outside the traditional nuisance and libel areas to faultless employers whose employees violate the law. See, for example, *People v. Travers,* 52 Cal. App. 3d 111, 124 Cal. Rptr. 728 (1975), where defendant, owner of a gasoline station, was held criminally liable for misrepresentations made by one of his employees as to the viscosity of oil.

Family relationships have also generated statutory attempts to impose vicarious liability, although the constitutionality of such measures is sometimes questionable. See, for example, *State v. Akers,* 119 N.H. 161, 400 A.2d 38 (1979), which strikes down a statute imposing vicarious liability on parents for offenses of minor children in their use of snowmobiles in part because "the status of parenthood cannot be made a crime" under the due process clause of the New Hampshire Constitution.

Sometimes vicarious liability is imposed against defendants who occupy no status relationship with the primary offender. In *Iowa City v. Nolan,* 239 N.W.2d 102 (Iowa 1976), for example, a city ordinance provided if any vehicle is found stopping, standing or parking in any manner violating parking regulations and the identity of the operator cannot be determined, "the owner . . . shall be held *prima facie* responsible for said violation." The Iowa court upheld the statute to maintain proper control of the public highways and found that "not only may public welfare legislation dispense with a *mens rea* or scienter requirement, it may, and frequently does, impose a vicarious —criminal' liability for the acts of another." See also *Commonwealth v. Pauley,* 368 Mass. 286, 331 N.E.2d 901 (1975).

3. As the *Nolan* case in the preceding note points out, vicarious punishment of one person for the crimes of another generally occurs in the context of strict liability, "public welfare" statutes. When such statutes (generally carrying minor penalties) expressly provide for vicarious liability, the courts face few interpretive problems. Thus, for example, where a statute provides that "Every person who by himself or his employee or agent . . . sells any commodity at . . . any weight . . . greater than the true net weight . . . is guilty of a misdemeanor," the courts will impose both strict and vicarious liability on an employer absent at the time his employee sells at short weight, *Ex parte Marley,* 29 Cal. 2d 525, 175 P.2d 832 (1946), even in cases where the employer has specifically instructed the employee not to violate the statute, *State v. Beaudry,* 123 Wis. 2d 40, 365 N.W.2d 593 (1985).

Where strict liability statutes do not expressly provide for vicarious liability, however, difficult interpretive problems are raised. Sometimes courts simply assume that strict liability statutes of necessity also impose vicarious liability. Thus in *United States v. Dotterweich,* 320 U.S. 277 (1943), the United States Supreme Court upheld the conviction of the president of a company that shipped misbranded products in interstate commerce even though he had no contact with the employee who actually shipped the goods. The Court interpreted the statute as dispensing with any *mens rea* requirement and simply assumed from that that the president could also be held liable even though he never performed the *actus reus* of the crime. See also *United States v. Park, supra* at p. 316.

The assumption that vicarious liability necessarily follows from strict liability has been roundly criticized. See, for example, Packer, *Mens Rea and the Supreme Court,* 1962 Sup. Ct. Rev. 107, 116–19. What might be the basis for such criticism?

4. Outside the context of strict liability crimes, the courts have been reluctant to vicariously punish persons for the acts of others.

> [T]he general rule is that where the crime charged involves guilty knowledge or criminal intent, it is essential to the criminal liability of an officer of a corporation that he actually and personally did the acts which constitute the offense, or that they were done under his direction or with his permission.

Bourgeois v. Commonwealth, 217 Va. 268, 274, 227 S.E.2d 714 (1976).

Why should the fact that the crime charged contains a mens rea requirement automatically preclude vicarious liability?

5. Consider the following defense of vicarious liability found in Sayre, *Criminal Responsibility for the Acts of Another,* 43 Harv. L. Rev. 689, 722 (1930):

> What, then, shall be said of the problem of vicarious criminal liability in the case of petty misdemeanors involving merely regulatory offenses? In such cases, there is no question of moral wrongdoing. The objective of the law is not to cure or change the mental processes of the defendant. There is no thought of social treatment or rehabilitation. The law's aim is not reformatory, but almost exclusively deterrent, to prevent future repetitions of similar offenses. To hold the master liable if he fails to prevent his servant from committing the prohibited conduct will have a powerful deterrent effect. On the other hand, to require from the state actual and positive proof of specific authorization or actual knowledge and acquiescence in a matter lying peculiarly within the secret knowledge of the two concerned in the offense, will effectually block most convictions and open the way for successful evasion through secret instructions and covert understandings. The protection of important social interests may thus be sacrificed to a too-zealous concern for individual interests of only trifling importance. Since in such cases deterrence is the essential objective, the present tendency of the law to hold the master criminally liable even for the unauthorized and unknown acts of his servant seems justified, and indicates a direction of sound growth. As long as courts are careful not to permit *respondeat superior* to creep into the true crime cases, masters and principals should be held criminally liable for the petty misdemeanors of their servants and agents which involve no moral delinquency or severe punishment and which are committed in the course of the master's business.

Are you convinced that *criminal,* as opposed to *civil,* vicarious responsibility is justified and desirable?

Commonwealth v. Koczwara

Supreme Court of Pennsylvania

155 A.2d 825 (1959)

COHEN, Justice

This is an appeal from the judgment of the Court of Quarter Sessions of Lackawanna County sentencing the defendant to three months in the Lackawanna County Jail, a fine of five hundred dollars and the costs of prosecution, in a case involving violations of the Pennsylvania Liquor Code.

[Defendant was licensed to operate a tavern. A jury convicted him of permitting the sale of beer to minors and of permitting minors to frequent the premises without parental supervision.]

Defendant raises two contentions, both of which, in effect, question whether the undisputed facts of this case support the judgment and sentence imposed by the Quarter Sessions Court. Judge Hoban found as fact that "in every instance the purchase [by minors] was made from a bartender, not identified by name, and service to the boys was made by the bartender. There was *no* evidence that the defendant was present on any one of the occasions testified to by these witnesses, nor that he had any personal knowledge of the sales to them or to other persons on the premises." We, therefore, must determine the criminal responsibility of a licensee of the Liquor Control Board for acts committed by his employees upon his premises, without his personal knowledge, participation, or presence, which acts violate a valid regulatory statute passed under the Commonwealth's police power.

While an employer in almost all cases is not criminally responsible for the unlawful acts of his employees, unless he consents to, approves, or participates in such acts, courts all over the nation have struggled for years in applying this rule within the framework of "controlling the sale of intoxicating liquor. . . ." At common law, any attempt to invoke the doctrine of *respondeat superior* in a criminal case would have run afoul of our deeply ingrained notions of criminal jurisprudence that guilt must be personal and individual.[1] In recent decades, however, many states have enacted detailed regulatory provisions in fields which are essentially noncriminal, *e.g.,* pure food and drug acts, speeding ordinances, building regulations, and child labor, minimum wage and maximum hour legislation. Such statutes are generally enforceable by light penalties, and although violations are labeled crimes, the considerations applicable to them are totally different from those applicable to true crimes, which involve moral delinquency and which are punishable by imprisonment or another serious penalty. Such so-called statutory crimes are in

---

[1] The distinction between *respondeat superior* in tort law and its application to the criminal law is obvious. In tort law, the doctrine is employed for the purpose of settling the incidence of loss upon the party who can best bear such loss. But the criminal law is supported by totally different concepts. We impose penal treatment upon those who injure or menace social interests, partly in order to reform, partly to prevent the continuation of the anti-social activity and partly to deter others. If a defendant has personally lived up to the social standards of the criminal law and has not menaced or injured anyone, why impose penal treatment?

reality an attempt to utilize the machinery of criminal administration as an enforcing arm for social regulations of a purely civil nature, with the punishment totally unrelated to questions of moral wrongdoing or guilt. It is here that the social interest in the general well-being and security of the populace has been held to outweigh the individual interest of the particular defendant. The penalty is imposed despite the defendant's lack of a criminal intent or *mens rea*.

* * *

In the instant case, the defendant has sought to surround himself with all the safeguards provided to those within the pale of criminal sanctions. He has argued that a statute imposing criminal responsibility should be construed strictly, with all doubts resolved in his favor. While the defendant's position is entirely correct, we must remember that we are dealing with a statutory crime within the state's plenary police power. In the field of liquor regulation, the legislature has enacted a comprehensive Code aimed at regulating and controlling the use and sale of alcoholic beverages. The question here raised is whether the legislature *intended* to impose vicarious criminal liability on the licensee-principal for acts committed on his premises without his presence, participation or knowledge.

* * *

As the defendant has pointed out, there is a distinction between the requirement of a *mens rea* and the imposition of vicarious absolute liability for the acts of another. . . . [W]e fully recognize it. Moreover, we find that the intent of the legislature in enacting this Code was not only to eliminate the common law requirement of a *mens rea,* but also to place a very high degree of responsibility upon the holder of a liquor license to make certain that neither he nor anyone in his employ commit any of the prohibited acts upon the licensed premises. Such a burden of care is imposed upon the licensee in order to protect the public from the potentially noxious effects of an inherently dangerous business. We, of course, express no opinion as to the *wisdom* of the legislature's imposing vicarious responsibility under certain sections of the Liquor Code. There may or may not be an economic-sociological justification for such liability on a theory of deterrence. Such determination is for the legislature to make, so long as the constitutional requirements are met.

Can the legislature, consistent with the requirements of due process, thus establish absolute criminal liability? Were this the defendant's first violation of the Code, and the penalty solely a minor fine of from $100–$300, we would have no hesitation in upholding such a judgment. Defendant, by accepting a liquor license, must bear this financial risk. Because of a prior conviction for violations of the Code, however, the trial judge felt compelled under the mandatory language of the statute to impose not only an increased fine of five hundred dollars, but also a three month sentence of imprisonment. Such sentence of imprisonment in a case where liability is imposed vicariously cannot be sanctioned by this Court consistently with the law of the land clause of Section 9, Article I of the Constitution of the Commonwealth of Pennsylvania.[7]

The Courts of the Commonwealth have already strained to permit the legislature to carry over the civil doctrine of *respondeat superior* and to apply it as a means of enforcing the regulatory scheme that covers the liquor trade. We have done so on the theory that the Code established petty misdemeanors involving only light monetary fines. It would be unthinkable to impose vicarious criminal responsibility in cases involving true crimes. Although to hold a principal criminally liable might possibly be an effective means of enforcing law and order, it would do violence to our more sophisticated modern-day concepts of justice. Liability for all true crimes, wherein an offense carries with it a jail sentence, must be based exclusively upon personal causation. It can be readily imagined that even a licensee who is meticulously careful in the choice of his employees cannot supervise every single act of the subordinates. A man's liberty cannot rest on so frail a reed as whether his employee will commit a mistake in judgment. See Sayre, *Criminal Responsibility for Acts of Another,* 43 Harv. L. Rev. 689 (1930).

This Court is ever mindful of its duty to maintain and establish the proper safeguards in a criminal trial. To sanction the imposition of imprisonment here would make a serious change in the substantive criminal law of the Commonwealth, one for which we find no justification. We have found *no* case in any jurisdiction which has permitted a *prison term* for a vicarious offense. . . .

In holding that the punishment of imprisonment deprives the defendant of due process of law under these facts, we are not declaring that Koczwara must be treated as a first offender under the Code. He has clearly violated the law for a second time and must be punished accordingly. Therefore, we are only holding that so much of the judgment as calls for imprisonment is invalid, and we are leaving intact the five hundred dollar fine imposed by Judge Hoban under the subsequent offense section.

* * *

Judgment, as modified, is affirmed.

MUSSMANO, Justice *(dissenting).*

* * *

The Majority of this Court is doing something which can find no justification in all the law books which ornament the libraries and enlighten the judges and lawyers in this Commonwealth. It sustains the conviction of a person for acts admittedly not committed by him, not performed in his presence, not accomplished at his direction, and not even done within his knowledge. It is stigmatizing him with a conviction for an act which, in point of personal responsibility, is as far removed from him as if it took place across the seas. The Majority's decision is so novel, so unique, and so bizarre that one must put on his spectacles, remove them to wipe the lenses, and then put them on

---

[7] Sec. 9 ". . . nor can he be deprived of his life, liberty or property, unless by the judgment of his peers or the law of the land."

again in order to assure himself that what he reads is a judicial decision proclaimed in Philadelphia, the home of the Liberty Bell, the locale of Independence Hall, and the place where the fathers of our country met to draft the Constitution of the United States, the Magna Charta of the liberties of Americans and the beacon of hope of mankind seeking justice everywhere.

The decision handed down in this case throws a shadow over that Constitution, applies an eraser to the Bill of Rights, and muffles the Liberty Bell which many decades ago sang its song of liberation from monarchial domination over man's inalienable right to life, liberty, and the pursuit of happiness. Our legal system is based on precedent. The decision of today will become a precedent on which future Dracos may feed to their absolutist and tyrannical content.

* * *

The Majority introduces into its discussion a proposition which is shocking to contemplate. It speaks of "vicarious criminal liability." Such a concept is as alien to American soil as the upas tree. There was a time in China when a convicted felon sentenced to death could offer his brother or other close relative in his stead for decapitation. The Chinese law allowed such "vicarious criminal liability." I never thought that Pennsylvania would look with favor on anything approaching so revolting a barbarity.

* * *

. . . The Majority Opinion finds the imprisonment part of the sentence contrary to law. . . . But if the Majority cannot sanction the incarceration of a person for acts of which he had no knowledge, how can it sanction the imposition of a fine? How can it sanction a conviction at all? . . . If it is wrong to send a person to jail for acts committed by another, is it not wrong to convict him at all? There are those who value their good names to the extent that they see as much harm in a degrading criminal conviction as in a jail sentence. The laceration of a man's reputation, the blemishing of his good name, the wrecking of his prestige by a criminal court conviction may blast a person's chances for honorable success in life to such an extent that a jail sentence can hardly add much to the ruin already wrought to him by the conviction alone.

* * *

Notes and Questions

1. The *Koczwara* court says, "it would be unthinkable to impose vicarious liability in cases involving true crimes." Is it? How do you respond to the suggestion that a corporate official might face individual criminal liability "whenever [he or she] knew or should have known of a substantial risk that an illegal act was occurring or would occur within [his or her] realm of authority, and failed to take reasonable steps to prevent the offense"? *Developments—Corporate Crime,* 92 Harv. L. Rev. 1270–71 (1979).

Would it be any less unthinkable to impose strict liability upon defendants who "personally cause" criminal results? Does it matter whether the crime is a "true crime"?

Does the court pay undue attention to the sanction of imprisonment? Should the court have also forbade the imposition of the fine and reversed the conviction? Reconsider the materials in Chapter 2, *supra.*

2. For cases sustaining the constitutionality of statutes imposing imprisonment in vicarious liability situations, see *Ex parte Marley,* 29 Cal. 2d 525, 175 P.2d 832 (1946); *Herschorn v. People,* 108 Colo. 43, 113 P.2d 680 (1941).

3. For vigorous debate on the scope of vicarious strict liability, see Fisse, *The Elimination of Vicarious Liability in Regulatory Offenses,* 44 Aust. L.J. 199 (1968); Rose, *Vicarious Liability in Regulatory Offenses,* 44 Aust. L.J. 147 (1970) (responding to Fisse); Fisse, *Vicarious Responsibility in Regulatory Offenses,* 44 Aust. L.J. 601 (1970) (responding to Rose); Rose, *Vicarious Liability in Statutory Offenses,* 45 Aust. L.J. 252 (1971) (responding to Fisse).

[B] Corporate Criminality

K. BRICKEY, 1 *CORPORATE CRIMINAL LIABILITY*

20–22, 41, 46–47, 49–51 (1984)

From an early age it was established that corporations possessed many of the same capacities attributed to natural persons. A corporation could own property, enter into contracts, sue and be sued. Development of a coherent theory of corporate liabilities, on the other hand, proved to be more problematical. The corporation as a distinct entity was an abstraction. It had no mind. It could not, therefore, form criminal intent. Until the development of a theory of vicarious liability, moreover, it lacked corporeal members and could not act physically. . . .

As early as 1635, however, it was held that a corporation was liable on a presentment for nonfeasance. There, as in a variety of cases arising during the eighteenth and nineteenth centuries, the inhabitants of a governmental unit were charged in a criminal proceeding with failure to repair a public convenience. In decisions imposing liability on such public entities, the courts ordinarily observed that the public convenience in question (usually a bridge or road) had been erected before the present inhabitants took on the responsibilities of the town, parish, or county; that it had been maintained by former inhabitants; and that present inhabitants were bound to do the same. The corporation was responsible for making the needed repairs before the present mayor, aldermen, and burgesses became its directors, and the duty to repair followed the corporation rather than its former members. By mid-nineteenth century it was fairly well established that a corporation was indictable for a breach of duty consisting of inaction, though not for felonies or for crimes involving personal violence.

A theory of corporate acting also was developing over this period. In 1682 it was held that a corporation *qua* corporation could be held liable for the misdeeds of its agents. In that case the mayor of London and several other officials were charged with usurping the powers entrusted to them as directors of a body politic and corporate when they taxed the citizens and then pocketed the money. The officials were found liable and the court ordered forfeiture of the city charter, declaring the acts of the agents to be the acts of the corporation.

Later borrowing the theory of vicarious liability from tort law, courts imposed corporate criminal liability for misconduct of employees acting within the scope of their employment. . . .

* * *

A corporation may be held vicariously liable for criminal acts committed by its agents. It is clear that if any agent possesses the capacity to act on behalf of the corporation—either properly or improperly—it is an executive whose responsibilities include directing corporate affairs. The greater the degree of control an executive exercises over corporate matters, the clearer the rationale for holding the corporation itself bound by his acts. . . .

* * *

The issue of how far—if at all—corporate liability for crime should be extended to include accountability for criminal misconduct of agents outside the highest echelons of the corporate bureaucracy has generated two disparate schools of thought. On the one hand is the relatively conservative position adopted by the drafters of the Model Penal Code. On the other is the relatively expansive view of corporate criminal liability adopted by the federal courts.

The Model Penal Code provision [§ 2.07(1)] governing corporate liability would hold a corporation accountable for the misconduct of its agents only under the following circumstances: (1) the offense is a minor infraction; (2) the offense is defined by a statute that expresses a clear legislative intent to hold corporations liable for the acts of their agents generally; (3) the offense consists of nonfeasance; or (4) the offense is performed, authorized or recklessly tolerated by the board of directors or a high managerial agent acting on behalf of the corporation and within the scope of his employment. The term "high managerial agent" is defined to include only officers of the corporation and other corporate agents whose position in the corporate hierarchy would support a reasonable inference that their conduct reflects corporate policy.

* * *

. . . A substantial body of federal authority recogniz[es] the propriety of holding a corporation liable for the criminal misconduct of its non-executive employees. Most courts that had considered the point had refused to hold that the title or position of a corporate employee was the key to determining whether the employee possessed the power to make the corporation a participant in a criminal transaction.

The rationale underlying judicial extension of corporate liability to include accountability for acts of agents outside the top management of the company is perhaps most easily illustrated when the business entity is a small, closely held corporation. . . .

... [A] small group of individuals cannot carry on a business and at the same time shield themselves from wrongs committed [by their managerial agent] in the conduct of that business in their name and on their behalf simply by interposing between themselves and their managerial agent a document called a corporate charter. To the question whether that proposition should also be deemed to apply to large publicly held corporations, the overwhelming judicial response has been affirmative. Managerial and supervisory personnel who act within the scope of their authority and with the purpose of benefitting the corporation have the capacity to involve the corporation in criminal conduct, regardless of their relatively low status in the corporate hierarchy.

STATE v. CHRISTY PONTIAC—GMC, INC.

Supreme Court of Minnesota

354 N.W.2d 17 (1984)

SIMONETT, Justice.

We hold that a corporation may be convicted of theft and forgery, which are crimes requiring specific intent, and that the evidence sustains defendant corporation's guilt.

In a bench trial, defendant-appellant Christy Pontiac—GMC, Inc., was found guilty of two counts of theft by swindle and two counts of aggravated forgery, and was sentenced to a $1,000 fine on each of the two forgery convictions. Defendant argues that as a corporation it cannot, under our state statutes, be prosecuted or convicted for theft or forgery and that, in any event, the evidence fails to establish that the acts complained of were the acts of the defendant corporation.

Christy Pontiac is a Minnesota corporation, doing business as a car dealership. It is owned by James Christy, a sole stockholder, who serves also as president and as director. In the spring of 1981, General Motors offered a cash rebate program for its dealers. A customer who purchased a new car delivered during the rebate period was entitled to a cash rebate, part paid by GM and part paid by the dealership. GM would pay the entire rebate initially and later charge back, against the dealer, the dealer's portion of the rebate. Apparently it was not uncommon for the dealer to give the customer the dealer's portion of the rebate in the form of a discount on the purchase price.

At this time Phil Hesli was employed by Christy Pontiac as a salesman and fleet manager. On March 27, 1981, James Linden took delivery of a new Grand Prix for his employer, Snyder Brothers. Although the rebate period on this car had expired on March 19, the salesman told Linden that he would still try to get the $700 rebate for Linden. Later, Linden was told by a Christy Pontiac employee that GM had denied the rebate. Subsequently, it was discovered that Hesli had forged Linden's signature twice on the rebate application form submitted by Christy Pontiac to GM, and that the transaction date had been altered and backdated to March 19 on the buyer's order form. Hesli signed the order form as "Sales Manager or Officer of the Company."

On April 6, 1981, Ronald Gores purchased a new Le Mans, taking delivery the next day. The rebate period for this model car had expired on April 4, and apparently Gores was told he would not be eligible for a rebate. Subsequently, it was discovered that Christy Pontiac had submitted a $500 cash rebate application to GM and that Gores' signature had been forged twice by Hesli on the application. It was also discovered that the purchase order form had been backdated to April 3. This order form was signed by Gary Swandy, an officer of Christy Pontiac.

Both purchasers learned of the forged rebate applications when they received a copy of the application in the mail from Christy Pontiac. Both purchasers complained to James Christy, and in both instances conversations ended in angry mutual recriminations. Christy did tell Gores that the rebate on his car was "a mistake" and offered half the rebate to "call it even." After the Attorney General's office made an inquiry, Christy Pontiac contacted GM and arranged for cancellation of the Gores rebate that had been allowed to Christy Pontiac. Subsequent investigation disclosed that of 50 rebate transactions, only the Linden and Gores sales involved irregularities.

In a separate trial, Phil Hesli was acquitted of three felony charges but found guilty on the count of theft for the Gores transaction and was given a misdemeanor disposition. An indictment against James Christy for theft by swindle was dismissed, as was a subsequent complaint for the same charge, for lack of probable cause. Christy Pontiac, the corporation, was also indicted, and the appeal here is from the four convictions on those indictments. Before trial, Mr. Christy was granted immunity and was then called as a prosecution witness. Phil Hesli did not testify at the corporation's trial.

I.

Christy Pontiac argues on several grounds that a corporation cannot be held criminally liable for a specific intent crime. Minn. Stat. § 609.52, subd. 2 (1982), says "whoever" swindles by artifice, trick or other means commits theft. Minn. Stat. § 609.625, subd. 1 (1982), says "whoever" falsely makes or alters a writing with intent to defraud, commits aggravated forgery. Christy Pontiac agrees that the term "whoever" refers to persons, and it agrees that the term "persons" *may* include corporations, see Minn. Stat. § 645.44, subd. 7 (1982), but it argues that when the word "persons" is used here, it should be construed to mean only natural persons. This should be so, argues defendant, because the legislature has defined a crime as "conduct which is prohibited by statute and for which the actor may be sentenced to imprisonment, with or without a fine," Minn. Stat. § 609.02, subd. 1 (1982), and a corporation cannot be imprisoned. Neither, argues defendant, can an artificial person entertain a mental state, let alone have the specific intent required for theft or forgery.

We are not persuaded by these arguments. The Criminal Code is to "be construed according to the fair import of its terms, to promote justice, and to effect its purposes." Minn. Stat. § 609.01, subd. 1 (1982). The legislature has not expressly excluded corporations from criminal liability and, therefore, we take its intent to be that corporations are to be considered persons within the meaning of the Code in the absence of any clear indication to the contrary.

See *e.g.,* Minn. State. § 609.055 (1982) (legislative declaration that children under the age of 14 years are incapable of committing a crime). We do not think the statutory definition of a crime was meant to exclude corporate criminal liability; rather, we construe that definition to mean conduct which is prohibited and, if committed, *may* result in imprisonment. Interestingly, the specific statutes under which the defendant corporation was convicted, sections 609.52 (theft) and 609.625 (aggravated forgery), expressly state that the sentence may be either imprisonment or a fine.

Nor are we troubled by any anthropomorphic implications in assigning specific intent to a corporation for theft or forgery. There was a time when the law, in its logic, declared that a legal fiction could not be a person for purposes of criminal liability, at least with respect to offenses involving specific intent, but that time is gone. If a corporation can be liable in civil tort for both actual and punitive damages for libel, assault and battery, or fraud, it would seem it may also be criminally liable for conduct requiring specific intent. Most courts today recognize that corporations may be guilty of specific intent crimes. . . . Particularly apt candidates for corporate criminality are types of crime, like theft by swindle and forgery, which often occur in a business setting.

We hold, therefore, that a corporation may be prosecuted and convicted for the crimes of theft and forgery.

II.

There remains, however, the evidentiary basis on which criminal responsibility of a corporation is to be determined. Criminal liability, especially for more serious crimes, is thought of as a matter of personal, not vicarious, guilt. One should not be convicted for something one does not do. In that sense, then, does a corporation "do" something for which it can be convicted of a crime? The case law, as illustrated by the authority above cited, takes differing approaches. If a corporation is to be criminally liable, it is clear that the crime must not be a personal aberration of an employee acting on his own; the criminal activity must, in some sense, reflect corporate policy so that it is fair to say that the activity was the activity of the corporation. There must be, as Judge Learned Hand put it, a "kinship of the act to the powers of the officials, who commit it." *United States v. Nearing,* 252 F. 223, 231 (S.D.N.Y. 1918).

We believe, first of all, the jury should be told that it must be satisfied beyond a reasonable doubt that the acts of the individual agent constitute the acts of the corporation. Secondly, as to the kind of proof required, we hold that a corporation may be guilty of a specific intent crime committed by its agent if: (1) the agent was acting within the course and scope of his or her employment, having the authority to act for the corporation with respect to the particular corporate business which was conducted criminally; (2) the agent was acting, at least in part, in furtherance of the corporation's business interests; and (3) the criminal acts were authorized, tolerated, or ratified by corporate management.

This test is not quite the same as the test for corporate vicarious liability for a civil tort of an agent. The burden of proof is different, and, unlike civil liability, criminal guilt requires that the agent be acting at least in part in furtherance of the corporation's business interests. . . . Moreover, it must be shown that corporate management authorized, tolerated, or ratified the criminal activity. Ordinarily, this will be shown by circumstantial evidence, for it is not to be expected that management authorization of illegality would be expressly or openly stated. Indeed, there may be instances where the corporation is criminally liable even though the criminal activity has been expressly forbidden. What must be shown is that from all the facts and circumstances, those in positions of managerial authority or responsibility acted or failed to act in such a manner that the criminal activity reflects corporate policy, and it can be said, therefore, that the criminal act was authorized or tolerated or ratified by the corporation.

* * *

III.

This brings us, then, to the third issue, namely, whether under the proof requirements mentioned above, the evidence is sufficient to sustain the convictions. We hold that it is.

The evidence shows that Hesli, the forger, had authority and responsibility to handle new car sales and to process and sign cash rebate applications. Christy Pontiac, not Hesli, got the GM rebate money, so that Hesli was acting in furtherance of the corporation's business interests. Moreover, there was sufficient evidence of management authorization, toleration, and ratification. Hesli himself, though not an officer, had middle management responsibilities for cash rebate applications. When the customer Gores asked Mr. Benedict, a salesman, about the then discontinued rebate, Benedict referred Gores to Phil Hesli. Gary Swandy, a corporate officer, signed the backdated retail buyer's order form for the Linden sale. James Christy, the president, attempted to negotiate a settlement with Gores after Gores complained. Not until after the Attorney General's inquiry did Christy contact divisional GM headquarters. As the trial judge noted, the rebate money "was so obtained and accepted by Christy Pontiac and kept by Christy Pontiac until somebody blew the whistle." We conclude the evidence establishes that the theft by swindle and the forgeries constituted the acts of the corporation.

We wish to comment further on two aspects of the proof. First, it seems that the state attempted to prosecute both Christy Pontiac and James Christy, but its prosecution of Mr. Christy failed for lack of evidence. We can imagine a different situation where the corporation is the alter ego of its owner and it is the owner who alone commits the crime, where a double prosecution might be deemed fundamentally unfair. Secondly, it may seem incongruous that Hesli, the forger, was acquitted of three of the four criminal counts for which the corporation was convicted. Still, this is not the first time different trials have had different results. See, *e.g., State v. Cegon,* 309 N.W.2d 313 (Minn. 1981). We are reviewing this record, and it sustains the convictions.

Affirmed.

Notes and Questions

1. *Christy* adopts a narrow test defining corporate criminal activity. See also Model Penal Code § 2.07, which provides in part:

(1) A corporation may be convicted of the commission of an offense if:

(a) the offense is a violation or the offense is defined by a statute other than the Code in which a legislative purpose to impose liability on corporations plainly appears and the conduct is performed by an agent of the corporation acting in behalf of the corporation within the scope of his office or employment, except that if the law defining the offense designates the agents for whose conduct the corporation is accountable or the circumstances under which it is accountable, such provisions shall apply; or

(b) the offense consists of an omission to discharge a specific duty or affirmative performance imposed on corporations by law; or

(c) the commission of the offense was authorized, requested, commanded, performed or recklessly tolerated by the board of directors or by a high managerial agent acting in behalf of the corporation within the scope of his office or employment.

* * *

(4) As used in this Section:

(a) "corporation" does not include an entity organized as or by a governmental agency for the execution of a governmental program;

(b) "agent" means any director, officer, servant, employee or other person authorized to act in behalf of the corporation or association and, in the case of an unincorporated association, a member of such association;

(c) "high managerial agent" means an officer of a corporation or an unincorporated association, or, in the case of a partnership, a partner, or any other agent of a corporation or association having duties of such responsibility that his conduct may fairly be assumed to represent the policy of the corporation or association.

(5) In any prosecution of a corporation or an unincorporated association for the commission of an offense included within the terms of Subsection (1)(a) . . . of this Section, other than an offense for which absolute liability has been imposed, it shall be a defense if the defendant proves by a preponderance of evidence that the high managerial agent having supervisory responsibility over the

subject matter of the offense employed due diligence to prevent its commission. This paragraph shall not apply if it is plainly inconsistent with the legislative purpose in defining the particular offense.

2. As Professor Brickey's excerpt, *supra* p. 666, points out, an expanding body of case law rejects the Code's limited approach. For example, and in contrast to *Christy,* consider the following case.

UNITED STATES v. HILTON HOTELS CORPORATION

United States Court of Appeals, Ninth Circuit

467 F.2d 1000 (1972)

BROWNING, Circuit Judge:

This is an appeal from a conviction under an indictment charging a violation of section 1 of the Sherman Act, 15 U.S.C. § 1.

Operators of hotels, restaurants, hotel and restaurant supply companies, and other businesses in Portland, Oregon, organized an association to attract conventions to their city. To finance the association, members were asked to make contributions in predetermined amounts. Companies selling supplies to hotels were asked to contribute an amount equal to one per cent of their sales to hotel members. To aid collections, hotel members, including appellant, agreed to give preferential treatment to suppliers who paid their assessments, and to curtail purchases from those who did not.

The jury was instructed that such an agreement by the hotel members, if proven, would be a per se violation of the Sherman Act. Appellant argues that this was error.

We need not explore the outer limits of the doctrine that joint refusals to deal constitute per se violations of the Act, for the conduct involved here was of the kind long held to be forbidden without more. . . .

* * *

Appellant's president testified that it would be contrary to the policy of the corporation for the manager of one of its hotels to condition purchases upon payment of a contribution to a local association by the supplier. The manager of appellant's Portland hotel and his assistant testified that it was the hotel's policy to purchase supplies solely on the basis of price, quality, and service. They also testified that on two occasions they told the hotel's purchasing agent that he was to take no part in the boycott. The purchasing agent confirmed the receipt of these instructions, but admitted that, despite them, he had threatened a supplier with loss of the hotel's business unless the supplier paid the association assessment. He testified that he violated his instructions because of anger and personal pique toward the individual representing the supplier. . . .

Based upon this testimony, appellant requested certain instructions bearing upon the criminal liability of a corporation for the unauthorized acts of its agents. These requests were rejected by the trial court. The court instructed the jury that a corporation is liable for the acts and statements of its agents "within the scope of their employment," defined to mean "in the corporation's behalf in performance of the agent's general line of work," including "not only that which has been authorized by the corporation, but also that which outsiders could reasonably assume the agent would have authority to do." The court added: "A corporation is responsible for acts and statements of its agents, done or made within the scope of their employment, even though their conduct may be contrary to their actual instructions or contrary to the corporation's stated policies." Appellant objects only to the court's concluding statement.

Congress may constitutionally impose criminal liability upon a business entity for acts or omissions of its agents within the scope of their employment.... Such liability may attach without proof that the conduct was within the agent's actual authority, and even though it may have been contrary to express instructions....

The intention to impose such liability is sometimes express, ... but it may also be implied. The text of the Sherman Act does not expressly resolve the issue. For the reasons that follow, however, we think the construction of the Act that best achieves its purpose is that a corporation is liable for acts of its agents within the scope of their authority even when done against company orders.

* * *

With ... important public interests at stake, it is reasonable to assume that Congress intended to impose liability upon business entities for the acts of those to whom they choose to delegate the conduct of their affairs, thus stimulating a maximum effort by owners and mangers to assure adherence by such agents to the requirements of the Act. ...

Legal commentators have argued forcefully that it is inappropriate and ineffective to impose criminal liability upon a corporation, as distinguished from the human agents who actually perform the unlawful acts. ... But it is the legislative judgment that controls, and "the great mass of legislation calling for corporate criminal liability suggests a widespread belief on the part of legislators that such liability is necessary to effectuate regulatory policy." ALI Model Penal Code, Comment on § 2.07, Tentative Draft No. 4, p.149 (1956). Moreover, the strenuous efforts of corporate defendants to avoid conviction, particularly under the Sherman Act, strongly suggests that Congress is justified in its judgment that exposure of the corporate entity to potential conviction may provide a substantial spur to corporate action to prevent violations by employees. ...

Because of the nature of Sherman Act offenses and the context in which they normally occur, the factors that militate against allowing a corporation to disown the criminal acts of its agents apply with special force to Sherman Act violations.

Sherman Act violations are commercial offenses. They are usually motivated by a desire to enhance profits.[4] They commonly involve large, complex, and

---

[4] A purpose to benefit the corporation is necessary to bring the agent's acts within the scope of his employment. *Standard Oil Co. v. United States,* 307 F.2d 120, 128–129 (5th Cir. 1962).

highly decentralized corporate business enterprises, and intricate business processes, practices, and arrangements. More often than not they also involve basic policy decisions, and must be implemented over an extended period of time.

Complex business structures, characterized by decentralization and delegation of authority, commonly adopted by corporations for business purposes, make it difficult to identify the particular corporate agents responsible for Sherman Act violations. At the same time, it is generally true that high management officials, for whose conduct the corporate directors and stockholders are the most clearly responsible, are likely to have participated in the policy decisions underlying Sherman Act violations, or at least to have become aware of them.

Violations of the Sherman Act are a likely consequence of the pressure to maximize profits that is commonly imposed by corporate owners upon managing agents and, in turn, upon lesser employees. In the face of that pressure, generalized direction to obey the Sherman Act, with the probable effect of forgoing profits, are the least likely to be taken seriously. And if a violation of the Sherman Act occurs, the corporation, and not the individual agents, will have realized the profits from the illegal activity.

In sum, identification of the particular agents responsible for a Sherman Act violation is especially difficult, and their conviction and punishment is peculiarly ineffective as a deterrent. At the same time, conviction and punishment of the business entity itself is likely to be both appropriate and effective.

For these reasons we conclude that as a general rule a corporation is liable under the Sherman Act for the acts of its agents in the scope of their employment, even though contrary to general corporate policy and express instructions to the agent.

Thus the general policy statements of appellant's president were no defense. Nor was it enough that appellant's manager told the purchasing agent that he was not to participate in the boycott. The purchasing agent was authorized to buy all of appellant's supplies. Purchases were made on the basis of specifications, but the purchasing agent exercised complete authority as to source. He was in a unique position to add the corporation's buying power to the force of the boycott. Appellant could not gain exculpation by issuing general instructions without undertaking to enforce those instructions by means commensurate with the obvious risks.

* * *

Affirmed.

Notes and Questions

1. Why were there radically different approaches in *Christy* and *Hilton Hotels*? Does the nature of the crimes in the cases (theft and forgery in *Christy*, antitrust violation in *Hilton Hotels*) and the size of the two corporate entities

(small, intimate organization in *Christy,* corporate giant in *Hilton Hotels*) help explain the different approaches of the respective courts?

2. Consider the following excerpt from the commentary to 3 A.B.A., Standards for Criminal Justice 18.164–69 (2d ed. 1980):

[In recent years] the problem of corporate misconduct has come to the forefront of public attention. Watergate, illegal political contributions, foreign bribes, and alleged violations of penal laws protecting the environment, the consumer, and the worker all of these highly publicized incidents underscore the public interest in achieving a sentencing system capable of deterring the organizational offender. . . .

A number of unique factors, however, both distinguish and complicate the context of organizational crime and in balance make it essential that specially tailored remedies be available to the sentencing court in such cases.

1. Most obviously, the corporation cannot be incarcerated. Thus, normal fine schedules established primarily as a supplementary penalty for individual offenders are likely to be inadequate. . . .

2. Recurrently, costs of compliance with many statutes applicable to organizations exceed the maximum penalties authorized by law. This pattern is most prevalent in the area of safety and environmental regulation, where compliance may entail substantial expenditures. In such instances, not only does crime pay, but management may also misperceive a modest penalty as amounting to only a nuisance tax on the activity in question rather than a "true" criminal prohibition. Unsubstantial fines also remove the incentive for shareholders to hold management accountable for the corporation's loss through the medium of the derivative suit.

3. Although the need for special fine schedules in the case of organizations is thus clear, complete reliance cannot be placed on such a remedy alone. Where exemplary fines are used, the incidence of such penalties falls ultimately on persons who generally may be described as innocent: stockholders, creditors, consumers, and employees of the corporation. Thus, the Model Penal Code counsels restraint in the use of punitive fines to deter corporate misbehavior, because such a policy can amount to imposition of "vicarious criminal liability" on a "group ordinarily innocent of criminal conduct." The dilemma, then, is that for adequate deterrence to be achieved through fines, it may be necessary to increase penalties in a manner that is inversely proportional to the culpability of those who bear them.

4. An alternative policy focusing on the individual decision maker within the organization also encounters unique problems. First, it is a common pattern in many forms of organization crime that the actual decision maker cannot be reliably identified. This may be because no conscious decision to violate the law was ever made. Information often flows poorly within hierarchical organizations, and adverse information in particular may fail to be transmitted upward to those capable of acting on it. As a result, toxic chemicals may be released into a river, workers exposed illegally to harmful substances, or consumers sold a product that test reports suggested had dangerous design defects—all without any senior official being aware of the total pattern of the corporation's activities. . . .

5. A pattern of "corporate recidivism" has characterized a number of corporations. Although this phrase may seem overly dramatic and the evidence cited by some commentators points more to venial sins than to serious crimes, examples can nonetheless be given of corporations that have recurrently run afoul of the antitrust laws, others that have regularly been found guilty of fraudulent activities, and still others whose products or methods of production have repeatedly brought prosecution to health and safety charges. In such cases, to "rehabilitate" the organization, it becomes essential that an effective internal monitoring system be established by which both the court and the corporation's senior management can be apprised of impending developments. Deterrence is only one means to the law's primary goal of crime prevention, and in cases where illegal behavior was either tolerated or ignored as a result of organizational dysfunction, the court is justified in imposing incapacitative restraints.

These complexities have been stressed to demonstrate both the absence of a single optimal sanction for organizational crime and the general inadequacy of the remedies currently available to the sentencing court. There is an unfortunate irony to the contrast existing today between civil and criminal remedies. For example, if a corporation were civilly held liable for creating an actionable nuisance, the court would have available to it a panoply of equitable remedies, including both injunctions and receivership. Yet, if the same corporation were tried and convicted on a criminal charge growing out of the same conduct, then, notwithstanding the higher burden of proof that would have been satisfied, the court would basically lose its ability to impose an equitable remedy and could only order a fine up to the limit authorized by the legislature. . . .

Consider as a response to these and other policy concerns the following from John C. Coffee, Jr.

COFFEE, *CORPORATE CRIMINAL RESPONSIBILITY*

1 Encyclopedia of Crime and Justice

253, 256–61 (S. Kadish ed. 1983)

In the majority of American jurisdictions the corporation is criminally responsible for illegal acts of its agents that are (1) committed within the scope of their employment and (2) intended to benefit the corporation. . . . This simple black-letter rule represents, however, an uneasy marriage of civil and criminal concepts of responsibility that has long proved troubling to legal scholars. . . . Indeed, although the use of criminal sanction against the corporate entity is now relatively common in American courts, the concept of corporate criminal responsibility is accepted to a far more modest extent in Great Britain, and not at all in civil law jurisdictions. . . .

The debate over corporate criminal liability has had two distinct levels, conceptual and pragmatic. On the first level, the American common-law rule of corporate liability for an agent's crimes has been criticized both on the ground that it entails an acceptance of vicarious responsibility (that is, the acts of the agent are imputed to a corporate principal—here, the employer) and because it arguably downgrades the significance of intent and blameworthiness in the criminal law. On the pragmatic level, much skepticism has been expressed about the efficacy of corporate criminal responsibility: Is the corporation an apt or appropriate target for criminal sanctions? Would civil remedies be more effective? Does corporate liability tend to deflect attention from the responsibility of the individual actors? Indeed, can the corporation be deterred at all, if the financial penalties imposed on it can be passed on to others as a business cost?

A Policy Appraisal: Is Corporate Criminal Liability Useful?

"Corporations don't commit crimes; people do." This theme (borrowed, of course, from the opponents of gun control) has been implicit in a substantial body of legal commentary that has criticized the idea of corporate criminal liability. The criticism has had two quite different focal points: (1)the asserted injustice of vicarious criminal liability; and (2)the alleged inefficiency of corporate liability. The following critiques have been repeatedly made. First, with respect to the rationale underlying corporate liability, it has been claimed that:

1. Vicarious liability is appropriate only as a principle of tort law since its justification lies in its allocation of the loss to the party more able to bear it (or at least more deserving of the burden), but it is unrelated to the purposes of retribution, deterrence, prevention, and rehabilitation that underlie the criminal law. . . .

2. Vicarious liability is unjust because its burden falls on the innocent rather than the guilty—that is, the penalty is borne by stockholders and others having an interest in the corporation, rather than by the guilty individual. . . .

3. Vicarious liability results in a disparity between businesses conducted in the corporate form and those run as a proprietorship, since the individual proprietor will not be criminally liable for the independent acts of his employees. . . .

4. Vicarious liability for the corporation may in the future open the door to expanded vicarious criminal liability for individuals as well.

Second, a number of arguments have been advanced to claim that corporate punishment is inefficient or even counterproductive:

1. Corporations are largely undeterrable; fines are ineffective, and only the imprisonment of guilty individuals achieves real deterrence. . . .

2. Prosecution of the corporation may lead courts, juries, and prosecutors to acquit or dismiss charges against individual defendants, and thus corporate liability serves as a shield behind which the truly guilty can hide. . . .

3. Civil remedies are more flexible and potentially as severe, and they also avoid the constitutional restrictions associated with a criminal prosecution. . . .

Although none of these arguments is frivolous, each on closer examination seems seriously overbroad or at least unconfirmed by the relatively slim empirical evidence available. Each will be assessed below, as will the equally debatable arguments for corporate liability.

The Debate over Rationale

Should vicarious liability be limited to the context of tort law as a device for equitable allocation of losses? This argument has a surface plausibility to the extent that tort and criminal law are thought to have substantially different concerns: the former with compensation, the latter with deterrence. Still, vicarious liability may be more closely related to the goal of deterrence than its critics concede. Economists have asserted that the most efficient way to deter organizational crime is to focus on the organization, not the individual. . . . Although others have objected to aspects in this analysis . . . , it does seem likely that the organization has a greater capacity than do public authorities to monitor and police its own internal processes. Thus, if it could be deterred, it would in turn more effectively supervise its agents. Indeed, the corporation could undertake preventive measures in advance of any crime's commission, whereas the state is essentially forced to restrain its own hand until afterward because its right to act (at least insofar as the criminal law is concerned) is initiated only by the commission of the crime.

Conversely, in the absence of corporate penalties, the corporation may, consciously or otherwise, encourage noncompliance by its agents and even pressure for it. . . . Thus, a two-fold answer seems possible to those who object to corporate vicarious criminal liability for criminal acts of an agent: (1)such vicarious liability may well be closely related to the criminal law's chief aim of prevention, both by deterring individual offenders and by encouraging the corporation to install incapacitative monitoring controls; and (2)victim compensation might also be a legitimate goal of the criminal law, both through sentences such as restitution (which the corporation almost uniquely is able to afford) and through the potential collateral estoppel impact of a criminal conviction on civil litigation brought by the victims of the crime.

Still, the argument that the penalty falls on the innocent remains troubling. The traditional answer to this criticism of corporate liability has been that a penalty imposed on the corporation simply eliminates unjust enrichment: since the stockholders indirectly benefited from the crime, they should indirectly bear the penalty. . . . This defense of corporate liability seems oversimple, however, because frequently the penalty will greatly exceed the gain (if any) from the crime. Indeed, many economists believe that adequate deterrence can only result if the expected penalty exceeds the expected gain by a margin sufficient to adjust for limited risk of apprehension and conviction. For example, if the expected gain were $1 million and the risk of apprehension were as low as 10 percent, only a penalty of $10 million would in theory remove the incentive to commit the crime.

This observation heightens the dilemma stemming from the fact that innocent parties suffer when the corporation is punished. But ultimately, the claim that corporate criminal liability is unjust because of the injury caused by the overspill of corporate penalties onto nonculpable shareholders proves too much. First, society does not face this issue exclusively in the context of the criminal law. If avoidance of punitive burdens on shareholders is taken as a first principle, it should also require the elimination of punitive damages in tort cases, treble-damage awards in civil antitrust cases, civil penalties, and possibly the very concept of *respondeat superior* as well. Equally important, the loss imposed on shareholders is generally mitigated through "cost spreading." That is, if a penalty of $10 million were imposed on a company having 100,000 shareholders holding its securities on a pro rata basis, the penalty per shareholder would be only $100 apiece—a loss that is considerably less significant than if the corporation had only a few shareholders. In reality, shareholders protect themselves from such risks through diversification of their investment portfolios, so that their exposure to such penalties is minimal. In short, the problem is not that the impact of a corporate penalty is unjustly severe, but rather that it is so negligible (on a per shareholder basis) that it gives shareholders little incentive to seek to hold management accountable.

The argument that corporate vicarious liability creates an unfair disparity between proprietorships and corporations also seems less than compelling. To be sure, the individual proprietor is not normally criminally liable on a vicarious basis for the criminal acts of his agents, but he is subject to incarcerative penalties if the prosecutor can convince a jury that he conspired with such agents. This risk is real, even if he is innocent, since conspiracy may be proved on circumstantial evidence. One suspects that if a disparity exists here, it favors the corporate shareholder, who seldom will be exposed to a threat of incarceration.

Finally, there remains the "open floodgates" argument: will vicarious liability for the corporation lead to similar liability for individuals? This ominous possibility might well have chilled commentators in 1909, immediately after the *New York Central* case [which upheld as constitutional the imposition of vicarious liability on corporations for a crime that required specific intent], but in the years since that decision, no rush by the legislature to adopt statutes imputing criminal liability from one individual to another has been evident.

In any event, one answer to the "open floodgates" argument may be to redefine corporate criminal responsibility so that it is not truly a species of vicarious criminal liability. At bottom, vicarious liability rests on the imputation of evil intent from one juristic person to another. But such an imputation is not necessary to justify the application of a sanction. Alternatively, one can focus on the negligence or recklessness of the entity in suffering or permitting the act of its agent, and thereby omit the conceptually troublesome fiction of transferring the agent's intent to the entity.

Although this theory—which for the sake of convenience might be called a suretyship rationale—has received little attention from courts, it has been advanced by commentators. One writer has made the interesting suggestion that the corporation should be viewed not as a legal personality but as a "committable common fund" whose "members incur [a] diminished or derivative liability that penalizes them only through their common fund." . . . Conceptually, such a rationale avoids personifying the corporation, instead focusing on the granting of the corporate franchise by the state and construing it as having been conditioned upon an obligation to act as surety for defined criminal acts of its agents.

Under this implied-consent theory, the suretyship is a voluntarily accepted responsibility, to which the stockholder consents in return for the grant of the charter. In contrast, the English law's emphasis on culpability involving an "alter ego" of the corporation sees the corporation not as simply an insurer but as itself morally blameworthy. In essence, then, the English law on corporate responsibility is closely tied to a retributive rationale for punishment. Yet only a few commentators . . . see the corporation as a suitable vehicle for retributively motivated punishment, and there is some risk that in imposing retributive punishment on the corporation the law will appear to many to have been blinded by its own fiction. If so, the special moral and educative force that the criminal law possesses may be compromised.

A surety rationale is also potentially broader than the concept of vicarious liability. Under such a theory, the entity could be held liable for suffering an act by another, even though the individual actor would not necessarily be criminally liable. Thus, if the corporation's agent acts without the requisite level of intent—recklessly but willfully, for example—the corporation cannot today be held liable under a vicarious theory of liability since under such a theory the corporation simply stands in the shoes of its agent, who is not here guilty. Yet it is far from self-evident that the legislature should be denied the power in all cases to so hold the corporation criminally liable; for example, the legislature might wish to hold the corporation more strictly accountable than its agent for tolerating a life-threatening safety hazard to exist, or for suffering an inadequately trained employee to operate a nuclear power plant. These cases can be reached today by making the offense one of strict liability and by enforcing the statute, as a practical matter, only against the corporate principal and not the agent. But a suretyship rationale permits a more formalized distinction between the liability of the individual and that of the entity by creating different standards of culpability for the individual and the entity, thus enabling the legislature to enact substantial deterrent penalties for the entity without permitting incarceration of individuals for behavior that was only negligent.

Similarly, the reach of a vicarious theory of liability may fall short of the surety theory in those cases where the actual actor cannot be identified or where the actor pursues his own ends rather than those of the corporation. For example, sexual harassment of female employees by their male superiors could be criminalized but corporate liability would not normally follow under current law since the agent did not act to benefit the entity. Of course, it is possible to legislate the crime of suffering an act by another, either negligently or as a matter of strict liability, but initially it seems anomalous to create a lower threshold of criminal liability for the party who suffers the act by its agent than for the agent who actually commits it. Yet under a surety rationale it is at least comprehensible that society might, in some limited class of cases, wish to impose a higher standard of intent for the accused individual actor than for the entity employing him, in part because the entity is only being held liable as a guarantor but not "punished" in any retributive sense. This argument raises in turn a more basic question: to the extent that a suretyship rationale is legislatively adopted, should its use be confined to civil rather than criminal sanctions?

As a legal theory, a surety rationale would expand to its logical limits the idea, already inherent in the current federal law of vicarious corporate liability, that a person can be blameworthy for suffering an act by his agent. In practice, such a rationale would modify American law by eliminating the need for the act to be in the interests of the corporation or within the agent's real or apparent authority, and it would permit different levels of intent to govern the liability of the agent and the entity. Yet, although such an expansion of criminal liability is probably constitutional (since strict liability statutes have been upheld), it would leave little remaining distinction between civil and criminal concepts of legal responsibility. From either a civil libertarian perspective or from one that seeks to conserve and protect the special educative force of the criminal law as a legal sanction, it can be questioned whether the gains in deterrence generated by such an expansion justify the potential costs that are risked through overuse of society's most powerful (and theatrical) sanction. The corporation is an anomaly in the criminal process, and the requirement that the agent act to benefit the corporation may well help to rationalize that anomaly and help society conceive of the corporation as a "true" offender.

The Utility of Corporate Punishment

Some critics of corporate liability have doubted whether the corporation itself can be deterred. Such an evaluation seems premature, however, given another conclusion which virtually every commentator on the subject has reached: that corporations tend to receive very small fines in relation to their size, their earnings, or even their expected gain from the criminal transaction. . . . Thus, it is logically difficult to assert simultaneously that corporations are not punished and that they are not deterrable.

But here a problem noted earlier resurfaces: corporate punishment tends to fall on the innocent—not only on stockholders but also on employees (who may be laid off), creditors, the surrounding community, and, of course, the consumer, who may in effect indemnify the corporation if the fine can be passed on as a cost of doing business. Thus, an apparent paradox is reached: the economist's model asserts that only the imposition of severe fines in an amount well in excess of the expected gain will generate adequate deterrence, since it is necessary to compensate for a risk-of-apprehension factor that invariably falls well below 100 percent. But if corporate penalties are escalated in this fashion, the remedy may be worse than the disease, because layoffs, plant closings, and the threatened insolvency of major corporate institutions may be a more adverse result than the financial loss suffered by consumers or the government as a result of price-fixing or tax fraud. . . .

This problem suggests the desirability of corporate penalties that minimize "overspill." . . .

An argument frequently made against corporate liability is that it may interfere with the assignment of individual liability. Here, anecdotal evidence does suggest that juries have sometimes compromised, acquitting all individual defendants while convicting the corporation. . . . The pervasiveness of this pattern cannot be estimated. Still, public-opinion surveys suggest that many white-collar crimes are no longer viewed as mere "regulatory" or technical violations but are ranked relatively high on a scale of seriousness, and consequently this pattern of jury reluctance to convict individual defendants for white-collar crimes may be a declining phenomenon. In any event, the prosecution always has the option of not prosecuting the corporation—or, at least, of not doing so in the same proceeding.

* * *

Still another perspective on the potential utility of corporate criminal liability begins from the much repeated observation that it is frequently difficult to identify the "true" culprit within a firm. Although the point is undoubtedly correct, its truth may lie less in the ability of the "true" culprit to hide his identity than in the absence of any such "true" offender in a broad range of cases. From a social-science perspective, it is virtually a truism that knowledge may exist collectively within an organization, even though it is not localized within any one individual. . . . [I]t is likely that information will exist at one level of an organization that would alter decisions at another, but no mechanism will necessarily force the transmission of this information to where it is needed. Some federal decisions appear to have responded already to such considerations by recognizing a "collective knowledge" doctrine, under which the corporation may be held liable even though no single individual had the requisite information. . . .

These problems indicate one inadequacy of an exclusive focus on the individual decision maker: recurrently, it is unlikely that any single individual within the corporate hierarchy will have the requisite intent, and yet the firm as an entity may have knowledge of an unsafe design, a carcinogenic risk, or a dangerous side effect that its products can cause. In this light, the argument for corporate liability rests not only on the evidentiary problems of identifying the "true" culprit but on the organizational reality that there may be no actual individual culprit at all, because of the diffusion of responsibility within the corporate hierarchy. Moreover, an insistence on finding a responsible individual decision maker might produce a scapegoat system of criminal justice, in which lower-echelon operating officials would probably bear the primary responsibility and risk of exposure.

The forgoing arguments focus on the problem of cognitive failures within the corporation's internal information processing as a justification for corporate liability. An alternative justification proceeds from the motivational failures that also accompany the corporate form. Almost inevitably, there is an incongruence between the interests of the manager and those of the firm as an entity: criminal behavior may be attractive to the pressured or ambitious manager, even if it is not to the corporation. Compounding this problem is the tendency for conflicting signals to issue from the senior levels of the corporate hierarchy to the middle echelons, which tend to be the locus of criminal behavior. Such signals may formally require obedience to law, but they alsodemand and reward short-term profit maximization. The implicit signal may thus be read by middle-level managers as meaning only "don't get caught." Of course, individual criminal liability may partially countervail this pressure on the middle manager. But even if the severity of the criminal sanction vastly exceeds that of the counterthreats the corporation can make, such as dismissal, demotion, or forgone promotion, the absolute severity of the sanction must be discounted by its probability of imposition. . . . This means that the discounted threat of apprehension and conviction by the state for a criminal offense may be less than that of the strong likelihood of internal discipline or dismissal by the corporation for failure to maximize profits. Thus, the manager faces both public and private sanction, and the latter, although lesser in gravity, tend[s] to be higher in probability, making the outcome uncertain and possibly dependent on the level of risk-aversion of the individual manager.

The Alternative of Civil Remedies

Corporate sanctions may be necessary, but it is far from clear that such sanctions must be criminal in nature. Civil penalties are now utilized by many, if not most, administrative agencies. Moreover, a system of civil penalties offers some obvious advantages to the prosecutor. First, the corporation could not claim the protection of constitutional rights, such as the "reasonable doubt" standard or double jeopardy, that are applicable only to criminal proceedings. Second, the possibility of judicial or jury nullification is reduced because of the lesser stigma. Third, courts of equity traditionally have been more able than criminal courts to fashion flexible and novel forms of relief. Thus, from the standpoint of specific deterrence and incapacitation, some have concluded that civil penalties offer significant advantages over criminal law enforcement in the case of the corporation. . . .

In this light, what arguments remain for the use of the criminal law as a preferred legislative strategy? Little agreement exists here, but the following arguments deserve consideration. First, the criminal law has long been thought uniquely capable of performing an educative role in defining and reinforcing the boundaries of acceptable conduct. The civil law's quieter, less theatrical character limits its ability to perform this socializing function. Closely allied to this point is the criminal law's ability to stigmatize and employ publicity as a sanction. The highly publicized prosecution of the Ford Motor Company in 1979 for the allegedly unsafe design of the Pinto illustrates this capacity of the criminal process. Second, the criminal law characteristically moves at a faster pace than the civil law. Thus, to the extent that restitution is an authorized sentence, the criminal law can serve as the engine by which to obtain victim compensation more quickly. In addition, because the double jeopardy clause does not preclude a successive civil prosecution after an acquittal in a criminal trial, the prosecutor can in effect obtain a second chance by proceeding first criminally and then civilly.

Third, courts of equity have traditionally been barred from imposing penalties, and although this does not amount to a constitutional barrier, there may linger a reluctance on the part of courts when operating in a civil mode to pursue deterrent objectives. The basic format of the civil enforcement proceeding also has yet to be resolved, and the fairness and reliability of administratively determined civil penalties is a matter of serious dispute.

Finally, joint prosecutions of the corporation and its agents require a criminal forum if the threat of incarceration is to be used to deter individuals.

From a law enforcement perspective, such joint trials are desirable both because they are less costly than separate prosections and because they permit one prosecutor to pursue the case in an integrated fashion; a separate prosecution, particularly if pursued in a different forum, might require a different prosecutor.

At most, these arguments suggest that corporate prosecutions for truly significant violations might best remain in a criminal courtroom, but they do not deny that corporate prosecutions for many regulatory and strict liability offenses, which today fit awkwardly at best within the criminal process, could be safely transferred to the civil process.

Note

For a discussion of the problem of fashioning punitive sanctions for corporations, see Arlen, *The Potentially Perverse Effects of Corporate Criminal Liability,* 23 J. Leg. Stud. 833 (1994); Coffee, *"No Soul to Damn: No Body to Kick": An Unscandalized Inquiry into the Problem of Corporate Punishment,* 79 Mich. L. Rev. 386 (1980); Laufer, *Corporate Bodies and Guilty Minds,* 43 Emory L.J. 647 (1994). In 1991, the United States Sentencing Commission promulgated guidelines for the sentencing of organizations, which automatically became law due to Congressional inaction in November 1991. See Gruner, *Towards an Organizational Jurisprudence: Transforming Corporate Criminal Law through Federal Sentencing Reform,* 36 Ariz. L. Rev. 407 (1994); Nagel and Swenson, *The Federal Sentencing Guidelines for Corporations: Their Development, Theoretical Underpinnings, and Some Thoughts about Their Future,* 71 Wash. U. L.Q. 205 (1993).

Chapter 9

Defenses

§ 9.01 The Postulate of Free Will

Lynch v. Director of Public Prosecutions

House of Lords

[1975] 1 All E.R. 913

Lord SIMON, . . .

The law accepts generally two concepts as axiomatic even though acknowledging that metaphysicians and psychologists have amongst themselves divergent views on the subject. The first concept which the law accepts generally as a datum is that of the conscious mind. Of course, the law recognizes that exceptionally the mind may be absent, as with a person of very severely subnormal mentality. And, of course, the law does not deny the existence of subconscious psychic activity—indeed, its use of punishment as a deterrent is directed as much to halting action on the verge of consciousness as to instituting a utilitarian debate in the conscious and reasoning mind whereby the pleasures and pains consequent on prohibited action are weighed against each other. But it remains generally true that it is of conscious and provable mental processes that the law takes cognizance. . . .

Largely concomitant with this first datum, the law also accepts generally as an axiom the concept of the free human will—that is a potentiality in the conscious mind to direct conscious action—specifically, the power of choice in regard to action. Even the most devout predestinarian puts off his theology when he put on legal robe.

The general basis of criminal responsibility is the power of choice involved in the axiomatic freedom of the human will.

State v. Sikora

Supreme Court of New Jersey

44 N.J. 453, 210 A.2d 193 (1965)

FRANCIS, J.

Defendant Walter J. Sikora shot and killed Douglas Hooey in the early morning of January 15, 1962. Thereafter, on May 15, 1962, a jury found him guilty of murder in the first degree for the killing, and recommended life imprisonment. . . .

On this appeal defendant contends the trial court committed reversible error . . . in refusing to admit certain psychiatric testimony relative to defendant's capacity to premeditate the killing he committed.

[Defendant, 36 years old at the time of trial, had an unfortunate childhood, moving from one foster home to another and experiencing a variety of physical abuse. As an adult, he fluctuated from one job to another and had infrequent companionships with members of either sex. At the time of the shooting, he had recently broken up with a woman with whom he had been living and upon whom he had become emotionally dependent. Defendant sought to reunite with the woman but she rejected his attempts. After making a phone call to the woman's house that was answered by a male voice, defendant went to a tavern and began to drink. Hooey, the deceased, was present at the bar and made some disparaging remarks about defendant's former girlfriend. According to defendant's testimony Hooey and two or three of his friends attacked defendant, beat him severely, and threw him out of the tavern onto the sidewalk. He reported the incident to the police by phone but declined their request to come to the station and file a complaint. He then went to his home, obtained his merchant marine handgun, and test fired it in preparation for killing Hooey and then his former girlfriend. Defendant returned to the tavern and met and killed Hooey. He then went to the woman's house but found it empty. Police arrested him later that day.]

No defense of insanity was interposed. All the psychiatrists agreed Sikora was legally sane before and at the time of the shooting. Thus it was conceded that he knew the difference between right and wrong; he knew the nature and quality of his act, and he knew that it was wrong to kill.

The error asserted in this Court as requiring reversal of the conviction had its origin in one hypothetical question put by defense counsel to Dr. Noel C. Galen, a psychiatrist produced on behalf of the defendant.

In appearing as a witness, Dr. Galen indicated his function was to help the court understand "the dynamics of what happened to this man with this particular history at this particular time in his life. . . ." Basically Dr. Galen's thesis is that man is a helpless victim of his genes and his life-long environment; that unconscious forces from within dictate the individual's behavior without his being able to alter it.

By way of illustrating the area of psychodynamics under discussion, Dr. Galen referred to a physician friend who, while driving on a public highway, was cut off by another motorist.

[T]his man who is a professional man knows clearly, in a general way, right from wrong, good from evil, if we want to get into that old controversy, but this man chased the car who cut him off and finally cut the car off that cut him off. Now, at this particular time, when he was behaving in this way, which was really endangering the lives of other people, although he was sane at the time, he was acting in an irrational manner with a disturbance of his consciousness; and consciousness is a very difficult thing to define and understand unless one sees it as a dynamic.

The idea seems to be that every deed, no matter how quickly executed, is never fully the result of the apparent immediate cause, and must be judged according to the probable unconscious motivations of an individual with the actor's lifelong history. Therefore, if in the opinion of the psychodynamically oriented psychiatrist, the deed, when evaluated against a background of the individual's life history, was probably produced by unconscious rather than conscious motivations, there was no *mens rea,* no criminal intent, and therefore no criminal guilt. In his view the conduct must be considered as having been conditioned by internal and external forces quite beyond the actor's control.

[In Dr. Galen's opinion] Sikora was suffering from a personality disorder of a passive-dependent type, with aggressive features. This kind of disorder is a function of his personality "which is his way of dealing with himself and with life and with people and with stress. . . ."

Defense counsel addressed a long hypothetical question to Dr. Galen which covered the examination of defendant, his life history, and particularly the events of the several hours preceding the shooting. It concluded with an inquiry as to whether in the doctor's opinion, in view of all those facts and circumstances, Sikora was capable of "premeditating a murder" at the time he killed Hooey. The objection of the State was sustained. No ground was given for the objection. Defense counsel's twice-repeated request to be heard on the law was summarily rejected. On asking the reason for the objection, the court said: "The record is complete. The doctor has testified that the defendant was sane."

When the cause reached this Court, we felt the need for enlightenment as to the nature of the evidence sought to be elicited from Dr. Galen by the hypothetical question. Consequently a remand was ordered for the purpose of further testimonial examination of the doctor. . .

Pursuant to the remand Dr. Galen was recalled and reexamined. . . .

In applying his expertise to this case he reiterated Sikora understood and could differentiate between right and wrong. Also, ordinarily Sikora was able to conceive a design to kill and to deliberate upon it. In fact he was able to do so until a few hours before the homicide occurred. But, because of his individual type of personality disorder, under the stress of certain circumstances which he feels inadequate to cope with, tensions build up within him and his psychological mechanism moves into action which on the surface may seem planned and deliberate but is really in response to unconscious influences and therefore automatic.

According to Dr. Galen, tensions had been building up in Sikora, particularly since his female friend rejected him. When he was humiliated in the tavern by the remarks about her availability for other men because she had broken with him, and then physically beaten by Hooey and his companions, the tensions mounted to the point where they represented a situation in life with which he felt unable to cope. So he began to act in an automatic way; the manner in which a person with his personality inadequacy would characteristically act. He responded to the stress in the way which inevitably would be his way of dealing with that kind of stress. He reacted automatically in the fashion of Dr. Galen's physician friend when he was cut off by another motorist. His successive actions, walking home from the tavern, reporting the assault upon him to the police, deciding against a criminal complaint, obtaining his gun from its place of concealment in the apartment, . . . test firing the gun . . . and putting four bullets into Hooey . . . all showed strong elements of automatism. The beating administered to Hooey in the tavern precipitated the disorganization of his personality to the extent that from then on he probably "acted in at least a semi-automatic way, and probably an automatic way."

The doctor went on to say that . . . [h]e was not "fully conscious of his activities" and not "completely aware" of what he was doing. The stress to which he had been subjected had distorted his personality mechanism. His personality disorder, the kind of man life had made him, when subjected to that stress prevented him from "seeing reality, or premeditating or forming a rational opinion of what is going on in his life." He had been confronted with a situation and reacted with conduct which was his characteristic way of dealing with the particular kind of stress. . . .

In short the doctor opined that the circumstances to which Sikora had been subjected imposed on his personality disorder a stress that impaired or removed his ability consciously to premeditate or weigh a design to kill. The tension was so great that he could handle it only by an automatic reaction motivated by the predetermined influence of his unconscious. Plainly the doctor meant that Sikora's response was not a voluntary exercise of his free will. The stress was such as to distort his mechanisms. During the various actions Sikora took leading up to the killing, which so clearly indicate conception, deliberation and execution of a plan to kill, he was thinking but the thinking was automatic; it was simply subconscious thinking or reaction; it was not conscious thinking. The doctor said Sikora's anxieties at the time were of such a nature that conceivably, his reaction in that automatic way and the commission of the homicide, actually prevented a further disorganization of his personality. The killing, said the doctor, was "a rational murder" but "everything this man did was irrational," and engaged in when he could not conceive the design to kill. . . .

The question now presented is whether psychiatric evidence of the nature described is admissible in first degree murder cases on the issue of premeditation. . . .

[E]vidence of "any defect, deficiency, trait, condition, or illness which rationally bears upon the question" whether the accused did in fact premeditate is admissible in a first degree murder trial. But . . . if such evidence [is] unreliable or too speculative or incompetent when tested by concepts established in law for the determination of criminal responsibility, it should not be received on the issue of guilt or innocence or the degree thereof. That is the situation here. . . . For protection of society the law accepts the thesis that all men are invested with free will and capable of choosing between right and wrong. In the present state of scientific knowledge that thesis cannot be put aside in the administration of the criminal law. Criminal blameworthiness cannot be judged on a basis that negates free will and excuses the offense, wholly or partially, on opinion evidence that the offender's psychological processes or mechanisms were such that even though he knew right from wrong he was predetermined to act the way he did at that time because of unconscious influences set in motion by the emotional stresses then confronting him. In a world of reality such persons must be held responsible for their behavior.

Trite as it may sound to some, the law must distinguish between mental disease and character deformity. . . .

Criminal responsibility must be judged at the level of the conscious. If a person thinks, plans and executes the plan at that level, the criminality of his act cannot be denied, wholly or partially, because, although he did not realize it, his conscious [sic] was influenced to think, to plan and to execute the plan by unconscious influences which were the product of his genes and his lifelong environment. So in the present case, criminal guilt cannot be denied or confined to second degree murder (when the killing was a "rational murder" and the product of thought and action), because Sikora was unaware that his decisions and conduct were mechanistically directed by unconscious influences bound to result from the tensions to which he was subjected at the time. If the law were to accept such a medical doctrine as a basis for a finding of second rather than first degree murder, the legal doctrine of *mens rea* would all but disappear from the law. . . .

In first degree murder cases psychiatric testimony of the type adduced here should be admitted but its probative function limited to the area of sentence or punishment. . . .

In the prosecution of accused for non-capital crimes similar use should be made of the type of medical opinion relied upon here. Under our present system, such psychiatric testimony properly serves a post-conviction purpose. It may be included in the pre-sentence probation report or submitted to the sentencing judge in any other suitable fashion. If in his judgment and discretion it reveals limited criminal blameworthiness, such fact may be reflected in the sentence.

Affirmed.

WEINTRAUB, C.J. *(concurring).*

[T]he question put to Dr. Galen was proper on the surface of things, but the answer we now have reveals his testimony would be incompetent as to guilt for the reason that it does not bear upon the issues as the law conceives them. Rather it simply challenges the law's entire concept of criminal responsibility.

To put the subject in perspective, we must start with the common law's conception of crime. The common law required (1)an evil deed and (2)*mens rea*—a guilty mind. This conception emerged from man's then understanding of himself. It was felt to be unjust to stigmatize a man as a criminal unless his evil deed was accompanied by an evil-meaning mind. Insanity was relevant only insofar as it denied the existence of an evil intent and thus disputed that critical element of the State's charge. It was assumed that all men were able to adhere to the right if they saw the right, and hence insanity was conceived to be such disease of the mind as prevented the accused from understanding the nature of his act and that it was wrong. The law thus separated the sick from the bad upon the basis of a man's capacity to know what was right. Any other imperfection or defect was deemed to be merely a bad trait of character or personality.

The law's conception, resting as it does upon an undemonstrable view of man, is of course vulnerable. But those who attack it cannot offer a view which is demonstrably more authentic. They can tear down the edifice but have nothing better to replace it.

The psychiatric view advanced by Dr. Galen seems quite scientific. It rests upon the elementary concept of cause and effect. The individual is deemed the product of many causes. As a matter of historical fact, he was not the author of any of the formative forces, nor of his capacity or lack of capacity to deal with them. In short, so far as we know, no man is his own maker. I say so far as we know, for man has yet to catch a glimpse of the ultimate truth. The concept of cause-and-effect, satisfying though it may be for most matters, is a dead-end approach to the mystery of our being. . .

Abstractly, the cause-and-effect thesis could suggest a stultifying determinism whereunder every stroke of a man's pen was ordained when time first stirred. But the psychiatrist, awed by it all, wisely leaves that subject to the philosopher. Besides it is not easy for an inquiring mind to believe it is on a string stretching from infinity. Nonetheless the cause-and-effect thesis dominates the psychiatrist's view of his patient. He traces a man's every deed to some cause truly beyond the actor's own making, and says that although the man was aware of his action, he was unaware of assembled forces in his unconscious which decided his course. Thus the conscious is a puppet, and the unconscious the puppeteer.

And so, Dr. Galen, in expounding the psychodynamics of Sikora's murderous exploit, started with the premise that Sikora appreciated the nature of his act and knew it was wrong; that Sikora was aware of the events which indeed he recalled with great detail, but was unaware that his unconscious was so constituted that its reaction to his conscious experience had to be homicidal. The doctor added, as I understand him, that the unconscious probably decided on murder in order to avoid a complete disintegration of the personality.

Now this is interesting, and I will not quarrel with any of it. But the question is whether it has anything to do with the crime of murder. I think it does not.

The witness described Sikora's actions as wholly "automatic." While at times he spoke in other terms, such as that Sikora was really not "fully" conscious of what he was doing despite his "long and rather clear history of what occurred," and although on cross-examination the doctor found himself differentiating between rational and irrational ways of committing murder (a most unscientific discourse, it seems to me), his professional theme remained that the conscious was the unwitting and unsuspecting puppet of the unconscious.

Further, "disease" has nothing to do with this automatic behavior. Although the witness said his "diagnosis" of a "personality disorder of a passive dependent type with aggressive features" describes "a mental disorder" listed in the Manual of the American Psychiatric Association, he denied the reality of such classifications. Rather he said mental disturbances or disorders are merely gradients in the range from "essentially normal" to "marked disturbance of the thinking mechanism." The point I stress is that the automatic thesis in no way depends upon the existence of some "disorder" of the mind. Rather it accounts for all human behavior, whether it be a murder or the retaliatory action of the witness's doctor friend who cut off a motorist who had cut him off, or the raising of one's index finger rather than his pinky, to refer to still another example Dr. Galen gave of the dictatorial control of the unconscious.

Under this psychiatric concept no man could be convicted of anything if the law were to accept the impulses of the unconscious as an excuse for conscious misbehavior. Although the specific question put to Dr. Galen was whether the defendant was capable of premeditating the murder, his answer would have to be the same if he were asked whether defendant was able to form an intent to do grievous bodily harm at all. His answer would have to be that the unconscious directed the killing in response to the stimulus of the events preceding the killing. The same explanation would account for the misbehavior of Dr. Galen's motoring friend if he were charged with a violation of the motor vehicle act.

What then shall we do with our fellow automation whose unconscious directs such antisocial deeds? We could say that in punishing an evil deed accompanied by an evil-meaning mind, the law is concerned only with the existence of a will to do the evil act and it does not matter precisely where within the mind the evil drive resides.

Or we could modify the law's concept of *mens rea* to require an evil-meaning unconscious. The possibilities here are rich. It would be quite a thing to identify the unconscious drive and then decide whether it is evil for the purpose of criminal liability. For example, if we somehow were satisfied that a man murdered another as an alternative to an unconscious demand for suicide or because the unconscious believed it had to kill to avoid a full-blown psychosis, shall we say there was or was not a good defense? Shall we indict for murder a motorist who kills another because, although objectively he was negligent at the worst, the psychoanalyst assures us that the conscious man acted automatically to fulfill an unconscious desire for self-destruction? All of this is fascinating but too frothy to support a structure of criminal law.

Finally, we could amend our concept of criminal responsibility by eliminating the requirement of an evil-meaning mind. That is the true thrust of this psychiatric view of human behavior, for while our criminal law seeks to punish only those who act with a sense of wrongdoing and hence excuses those who because of sickness were bereft of that awareness, the psychiatrist rejects a distinction between the sick and the bad. To him no one is personally blameworthy for his make-up or for his acts. To him the law's distinction between a defect of the mind and a defect of criminal blameworthiness is so obscure that there is an understandable disposition to let anything in for whatever use the jury may wish to make of it. But it will not do merely to receive testimony upon the automaton thesis, for the jury must be told what its legal effect may be. Specifically, the jury must be told whether a man is chargeable with his unconscious drives.

It seems clear to me that the psychiatric view expounded by Dr. Galen is simply irreconcilable with the basic thesis of our criminal law, for while the law requires proof of an evil-meaning mind, this psychiatric thesis denies there is any such thing. To grant a role in our existing structure to the theme that the conscious is just the innocent puppet of a nonculpable unconscious is to make a mishmash of the criminal law, permitting—indeed requiring— each trier of the facts to choose between the automaton thesis and the law's existing concept of criminal accountability. It would be absurd to decide criminal blameworthiness upon a psychiatric thesis which can find no basis for personal blame. So long as we adhere to criminal blameworthiness, *mens rea* must be sought and decided at the level of conscious behavior.

NOTES

1. For further discussion, see Wechsler, *The Criteria of Criminal Responsibility,* 22 U. Chi. L. Rev. 367 (1955); Eser, *Justification and Excuse,* 24 Amer. J. Comp. L. 621 (1976); Shafer, *The Problem of Free Will in Criminology,* 67 J. Crim. L. & Criminology 481 (1977).

2. *Sikora* spells out the law's limits as to the acceptance of determinism. This problem is encountered most directly in the defense of insanity, considered in § 9.05[B][3], *infra.* The remaining materials in this chapter deal with defenses (e.g., self-defense, duress, necessity) involving factors influencing, if not causing, actions by "normal" persons under conditions that render their particular conduct nonpunishable.

§ 9.02 CLASSIFYING DEFENSES

BLACKSTONE

21, 26–27

Now there are three cases, in which the will does not join with the act: 1. Where there is a defect of understanding. For where there is no discernment, there is no choice; and where there is no choice, there can be no act of the will, which is nothing else but a determination of one's choice, to do or to abstain from a particular action: he therefore, that has no understanding, can have no will to guide his conduct. 2. Where there is understanding and will sufficient, residing in the party; but not called forth and exerted at the time of the action done: which is the case of all offenses committed by chance or ignorance. Here the will sits neuter; and neither concurs with the act, nor disagrees to it. 3. Where the action is constrained by some outward force and violence. Here the will counteracts the deed; and is so far from concurring with, that it loathes and disagrees to, what the man is obliged to perform. And, as a vicious will without a vicious act is no civil crime, so, on the other hand, an unwarrantable act without a vicious will is no crime at all. So that to constitute a crime against human laws, there must be, first, a vicious will; and, secondly, an unlawful act consequent upon such vicious will.

Hart

39–40, 45–48

One necessary condition of the just application of a punishment is normally expressed by saying that the agent "could have helped" doing what he did, and hence the need to inquire into the "inner facts" is dictated not by the moral principle that only the doing of an immoral act may be legally punished, but by the moral principle that no one should be punished who could not help doing what he did. This is a necessary condition (unless strict liability is admitted) for the moral propriety of legal punishment and no doubt also for moral censure; in this respect law and morals are similar.

Civil transactions such as wills, contracts, marriages, and the like provide individuals with two inestimable advantages in relation to those areas of conduct they cover. These are (1) the advantage to the individual of determining by his choice what the future shall be and (2) the advantage of being able to predict what the future will be. For these institutions enable the individual (1) to bring into operation the coercive forces of the law so that those legal arrangements he has chosen shall be carried into effect and (2) to plan the rest of his life with certainty or at least the confidence (in a legal system that is working normally) that the arrangements he has made will in fact be carried out. By these devices the individual's choice is brought into the legal system and allowed to determine its future operations in various areas thereby giving him a type of indirect coercive control over, and a power to foresee the development of, official life. This he would not have "naturally;" that is, apart from these legal institutions.

In brief, the function of these institutions of private law is to render effective the individual's preferences in certain areas. It is therefore clear why in this sphere the law treats the mental factors of, say, mistake, ignorance of the nature of the transaction, coercion, undue influence, or insanity as invalidating such civil transactions. For a transaction entered into under such conditions will not represent a real choice: the individual might have chosen one course of events and by the transaction procured another (cases of mistake, ignorance, etc.), or he might have chosen to enter the transaction without coolly and calmly thinking out what he wanted (undue influence), or he might have been subjected to the threats of another who had imposed his choices (coercion).

To see the value of such institutions in rendering effective the individual's considered and informed choices as to what on the whole shall happen, we have but to conduct the experiment of imagining their absence: a system where no mental conditions would be recognized as invalidating such transactions and the consequent loss of control over the future that the individual would suffer. That such institutions do render individual choices effective and increase the powers of individuals to predict the course of events is simply a matter of empirical fact, and no form of determinism, of course, can show this to be false or illusory.

With this in mind we turn back to criminal law and its excusing conditions. We can regard their function as a mechanism for similarly maximizing within the framework of coercive criminal law the efficacy of the individual's informed and considered choice in determining the future and also his power to predict that future. By attaching excusing conditions to criminal responsibility, we provide each individual with benefits he would not have if we made the system of criminal law operate on a basis of total "strict liability." First, we maximize the individual's power at any time to predict the likelihood that the sanctions of the criminal law will be applied to him. Secondly, we introduce the individual's choice as one of the operative factors determining whether or not these sanctions shall be applied to him. He can weigh the cost to him of obeying the law and of sacrificing some satisfaction in order to obey—against obtaining that satisfaction at the cost of paying "the penalty." Thirdly, by adopting this system of attaching excusing conditions we provide that, if the sanctions of the criminal law are applied, the pains of punishment will for each individual represent the price of some satisfaction obtained from breach of law.

Again, the value of these three factors can be realized if we conduct the *Gedanken experiment* of imagining criminal law operating without excusing conditions. First, our power of predicting what will happen to us will be immeasurably diminished; the likelihood that I shall choose to do the forbidden act (*e.g.*, strike someone) and so incur the sanctions of the criminal law may not be very easy to calculate even under our system: as a basis for this prediction we have indeed only the knowledge of our own character and some estimate of the temptations life is likely to offer us. But if we are also to be liable if we strike someone by accident, by mistake, under coercion, etc., the chances that we shall incur the sanctions are immeasurably increased. Secondly, our choice would condition what befalls us to a lesser extent. Thirdly, we should suffer sanctions without having obtained any satisfaction.

ROBINSON, CRIMINAL LAW DEFENSES: A SYSTEMATIC ANALYSIS

82 Colum. L. Rev. 190, 203–04 (1982)

The term "defense" is commonly used, at least in a casual sense, to mean any set of identifiable conditions or circumstances which may prevent a conviction for an offense. Upon examining the functions of and the rationales supporting these rules and doctrines, five general categories become apparent. They may be termed: failure of proof defenses, offense modification defenses, justifications, excuses, and nonexculpatory public policy defenses.*

---

* [In these materials, we are interested only in failure of proof, excuses and justifications. The remaining two categories will not be discussed at length. For the sake of completeness, however, a short description of what Professor Robinson labels "offense modifications" and "public policy" defenses may be helpful. The first of these classifications encompasses cases where "the actor has apparently satisfied all elements of the offense charged (but) has not in fact caused the harm or evil sought to be prevented by the statute defining the offense." Professor Robinson gives, as an example, the exemption for a faculty member to disseminate obscene material. He also notes that it is difficult to distinguish between failure of proof defenses and offense modification, observing that the issue may resolve on the precise drafting of a criminal statute. As for the last category—nonexculpatory public policy defenses—Professor Robinson points to statutes of limitations, double jeopardy protection, diplomatic immunity, and other policies. One of these issues—entrapment—is dealt with in more detail, infra, since it at least arguably deals with the defendant's *mens rea,* and is not unrelated to his culpability.—Eds.]

Failure of proof defenses are nothing more than instances where, because of the "defense," the prosecution is unable to prove all the required elements of the offense, the objective conduct, circumstance, and result elements and their corresponding culpability requirements. Offense modifications are similar in that they essentially modify or refine the criminalization decision embodied in the definition of the particular offense. The remaining three groups of defenses—justifications, excuses, and nonexculpatory public policy defenses—are general defenses; they theoretically apply to all offenses, even when the required elements of an offense are satisfied. They represent principles of exculpation or defense which operate independently of the criminalization decision reflected in the particular offense. A justified actor engages in conduct that is not culpable because its benefits outweigh the harm or evil of the offense; an excused actor admits the harm or evil but nonetheless claims an absence of personal culpability. . . .

A. Failure of Proof Defenses

Failure of proof defenses consist of instances in which, because of the conditions that are the basis for the "defense," all elements of the offense charged cannot be proven. They are in essence no more than the negation of an element required by the definition of the offense. . . . The defendant, as a practical matter, may have to act affirmatively to present evidence on the issue of a given element of the offense; he may have to carry certain evidentiary burdens. But this can be as true with respect to negating any other element of the offense as it is with those situations in which one speaks of the defendant having a failure of proof "defense." The characterization of a given failure of proof as a defense rather than as a defect in proving the offense depends, for the most part, upon common usage of language; whether the defendant will be obliged to present evidence on the issue will depend not on this characterization but rather on whether the prosecutor is able to persuade the jury, on the evidence presented in its case-in-chief, that the required element is satisfied.

Failure of proof defenses often appear to overlap with offense modifications and general defenses. Whether a defense is a failure of proof defense or an offense modification may depend on the form in which it is drafted. General defenses differ conceptually from failure of proof defenses in that the former bar conviction even if all elements of the offense are satisfied, whereas the latter prevent conviction by negating a required element of the offense. But as will be seen, a defense identified by a single name, like mistake or mental illness, may operate in both ways. . . .

* * *

C. Justifications

Justification defenses are not alterations of the statutory definition of the harm sought to be prevented or punished by an offense. The harm caused by the justified behavior remains a legally recognized harm which is to be avoided whenever possible. Under the special justifying circumstances, however, that harm is outweighed by the need to avoid an even greater harm or to further a greater societal interest.

A forest fire rages toward a town of 10,000 unsuspecting inhabitants. The actor burns a field of corn located between the fire and the town; the burned field then serves as a firebreak, saving 10,000 lives. The actor has satisfied all elements of the offense of arson by setting fire to the field with the purpose of destroying it. The immediate harm he has caused—the destruction of the field—is precisely the harm which the statute serves to prevent and punish. Yet the actor is likely to have a complete defense, because his conduct and its harmful consequences were justified. The conduct in this instance is tolerated, even encouraged, by society.

The forest fire case provides an example of the "lesser evils" or "choice of evils" justification (often called "necessity" when the threat of greater harm stems from natural forces). This type of justification defense, though the least common in American criminal codes, most clearly reflects the general principle of justification defenses. In such lesser evils cases, however, the competing harms are more apparent and hence more easily compared than in other types of justification defenses. The interests involved in what might be called "defensive force" and "public authority" justifications are more subtle and abstract, and their relative value more obscure.

D. EXCUSES

Excuses, like justifications, are usually general defenses applicable to all offenses even though the elements of the offense are satisfied. Excuses admit that the deed may be wrong, but excuse the actor because conditions suggest that the actor is not responsible for his deed. For instance, suppose that the actor knocks the mailman over the head with a baseball bat because she believes he is coming to surgically implant a radio receiver which will take control of her body. The defendant has satisfied all elements of the offense of aggravated assault—she struck the mailman with a deadly weapon with the purpose of causing him bodily injury. This is precisely the harm sought to be prevented by the statute, and it is not outweighed by any greater societal harm avoided or greater societal interest furthered. It is conduct that society would in fact condemn and seek to prevent. The defendant is exculpated only because her condition at the time of the offense—her paranoid delusion—suggests that she has not acted through a meaningful exercise of free will and therefore is not an appropriate subject for criminal liability.

Each of the excuse defenses has the following internal structure: a *disability causing an excusing condition*. The *disability* is the abnormal condition of the actor at the time of the offense. We say, for example, that the actor is suffering from insanity, intoxication, subnormality, or immaturity. The disability is a real condition with a variety of observable manifestations apart from the conduct constituting the offense. It may be a long term or even permanent condition, such as subnormality, or it may be a temporary state like intoxication, somnambulism, automatism, or hypnotism. Its cause may be internal, as in insanity, or external, as in duress.

Having a recognized disability at the time of the offense will not alone qualify an actor for an excuse, for it is not the disability that is central to our reason for exculpating the defendant. An actor is not excused because he or she is intoxicated, but because the *effect* of the intoxication in this instance is to create a condition which renders the actor blameless for his conduct constituting the offense. The requirement of an excusing condition, then, is not an element independent of the actor's disability, but rather a requirement that the actor's disability cause a particular result, a particular exculpating mental condition in relation to the conduct constituting the offense.

Society is generally willing to excuse an actor under four types of conditions:

(1) when the conduct constituting the offense is simply not the product of the actor's voluntary effort or determination (*e.g.,* the actor is having a seizure);

(2) when the conduct is the product of the actor's voluntary effort or determination, but he does not accurately perceive the physical nature or consequences of the conduct (*e.g.,* the actor thinks the gun is a paint brush, or accurately sees the physical characteristics of the gun but does not know that the gun shoots bullets that injure people);

(3) when the actor accurately perceives and understands the physical nature of the conduct, its physical results, and physical surroundings, but does not know that the conduct or its results are wrong or criminal (*e.g.,* the actor thinks God has ordered him to sacrifice a neighbor for the good of mankind, or believes, because of paranoid delusions, that the man waiting for a bus is about to assault him); or

(4) when the actor perceives the conduct accurately and fully, understands its physical consequences, and knows its wrongfulness or criminality, but the actor lacks the ability to control his conduct (*e.g.,* because of an insane compulsion or duress) to such an extent that it is no longer proper to hold him accountable for it.

Each of these excusing conditions will give the actor a defense, so long as the condition has been caused by the actor's disability. It is also required that the disability cause an excusing condition for the conduct constituting the offense charged. If A, while killing B, hallucinates that a neighbor's dog has turned into a tiger, he may be considered to be insane at the time of killing B, but he will not be given an insanity excuse if his hallucination plays no part in the murder of B. If he kills the dog/tiger in self-defense, of course, he would be excused. In both cases, A is disabled by insanity. Only if his victim is the dog, however, can the disability be said to have created an excusing condition (type three) that affects his responsibility for the offense.

These, then, are five categories of defenses—failure of proof defenses, offense modifications, justifications, excuses, and nonexculpatory public policy defenses—that provide a conceptual structure useful in the analysis of criminal law defense issues. The scheme is comprehensive; it appears to account for all types of defenses. The bases for the categorizations—those characteristics of each defense which bring it within one or another group—can be articulated. Further, the categories of the scheme have a logical, serial relation. Each successive type of defense need only be considered if those preceding it are unavailable. If there is a failure of proof defense, then there is no offense to be defended against; if there is an offense modification, there is no legally recognized harm that need be justified; if the harm is justified, then nothing remains to be excused; and unless no other defense exists, public policy need not be invoked, for there is no danger of conviction.

A scheme such as this need be neither symmetrical nor unambiguous to be analytically useful, however. The systematic presentation of any significant distinctions, especially where no such structure has been previously proposed, may at least serve to stimulate criticism leading to a better conceptual structure. In the end, the ultimate utility of any scheme will depend on whether the distinctions it draws are in fact the most significant for the goals that area of the law seeks to achieve.

The scheme proposed here does not clearly classify all defenses into one category or another. There are some undeniably problematic defenses. Is provocation a failure of proof defense or an offense modification? Is necessity a justification or an excuse? Is entrapment an excuse or a nonexculpatory public policy defense?

But consider the nature of these problematic classifications. They appear to be precisely those defenses whose proper formulation has been a matter of confusion and debate. If this is true, the fact that these defenses do not fit cleanly into one or another category only reinforces the usefulness of the scheme. If ambiguity in classification coincides with independently generated disputes over proper formulation, it would seem to confirm that the distinctions made by the scheme are central to the ongoing criminal law theory debates, although perhaps not recognized as such.

NOTE

Is there a fundamental disagreement between Hart and Robinson? See Sendor, *Mistakes of Fact: A Study in the Structure of Criminal Conduct,* 25 Wake Forest L. Rev. 707, 737 (1990), arguing that excuse defenses "negate either the capacity or the fair opportunity condition." Sendor also argues that mistake of fact sometimes functions as an excuse, and sometimes as an element negation. Refer back to Chapter 4 and to the *Morgan* case in Chapter 6. How did mistake of fact "function" in those instances?

WILLIAMS, OFFENCES AND DEFENCES

2 Legal Stud. 233, 233–56 (1982)

What, if any, is the distinction between offences and exculpatory defences, between definitional elements and defence elements, between rules and exceptions? In recent years the courts have shown a tendency to attach legal importance to this distinction, even as a matter of substantive law. But ought it to have this importance, and anyway is it usable?

On their face, exculpatory defences often relate to the same kind of question as the inculpation provisions of the criminal law. The offence-creating provision states what must or must not, in general, be done; the exculpatory provision states the limits of the prohibition in particular circumstances. As

Professor Paul Robinson expresses it, defences "refine the wording of the offence;" they provide a more sophisticated account, when needed, of the harm or evil sought to be prohibited. But the refinements may be expressed in the provision itself, as well as in the defences. For what reasons, if any, should the law distinguish between offences and defences?

An example will illustrate the problem. Consider two draft statutes, each of which is intended to turn assault into a statutory offence. The first draft defines an assault as an intentional or reckless attack upon a person without his consent. Non-consent is then, presumably, a definitional element of the offence. The second draft defines assault as an intentional or reckless attack upon a person, but adds the proviso or qualification that the offence is not committed where the person attacked has consented. Consent now appears to be a matter of defence. The distinction has the effect that, according to the present law, under the second draft a mistaken belief in the victim's consent on the part of the attacker would have to be reasonable if it is to be a defence, whereas under the first draft the belief would be an unqualified defence. Yet the difference between the two drafts is purely verbal, a matter of convenience in expression. Is there any reason why rules of substantive law should hinge upon a draftsman's convenience?. . .

A distinction between definitional and defence elements is drawn in relation to the prosecution's pleading, since the prosecution are not required to negative defence elements.

A similar rule applies as a matter of common law to common law defences. It is obviously a rule of convenience. For an indictment or information to have to negative all possible exceptions or defences would be a waste of time. Once the defendant knows the essence of the charge, he can decide for himself which exception, if any, he wishes to urge. It is no hardship for him to be required to do so, even if the question what is an exception has a somewhat arbitrary answer depending on accidents of drafting.

The distinction also has some bearing on the evidential burden. The defendant must adduce evidence to raise some matters in order to negative liability, and these are naturally thought of as defences. He need not, generally, adduce evidence to negative what are regarded as definitional elements if he is content to have the question left to the jury without such evidence. The line between evidential burdens resting on the prosecution and those resting on the defence is not clearly drawn. Some elements thought of as definitional carry an evidential burden for the defence. The law proceeds partly on the basis of convenience, but partly also on the desirability of excluding fanciful defences. The prosecution are not required to negative in advance all the defences that may possibly be raised, and the defendant is not permitted to argue defences before the jury on which he has offered no, or no reasonable, evidence. . . .

So the final question for discussion is whether the attempt to make a strict distinction between offences and defences is theoretically possible. We have seen that, whatever the theoretical difficulties, it has to be used (or rather several different distinctions have to be used) in the law of evidence and procedure. But theoretical difficulties may be regarded as a convincing argument for not importing a generalized distinction between offences and defences into substantive law.

Some definitions of offences seem to look forward to defences by including a comprehensive word or phrase. If the definitional elements of an offence depend upon formal arrangement, the effect of such phrases should be to introduce the negative of defences into definitions.

In any case, distinctions depending upon the arrangement of words can apply only to statutory offences. The distinction between offences and defences applies also to common law offenses of which there is no authoritative expression. We imagine common law offences to have definitions and to carry defences, but there is generally no formal statement of either to give us guidance on which is which.

The foregoing argument suggests that the definition of an offence in a statute is not a comprehensive and safe guide to the "definitional elements of an offence" as contrasted with defences. If this is so, and if we are nevertheless convinced that the phrase "the definitional elements of an offence" expresses a reality, it follows that the definitional elements are those that we choose to pick out from all the elements expressed in the rules relating to the offence, according to some preconceived idea of what the definitional elements should be.

There is no reason why labelling an issue a "defence" by virtue of the definition should affect other legal rules. It may be reasonable to expect the defendant to introduce evidence on a particular issue, but it does not follow that the ordinary principles of *mens rea,* for example, should be modified in respect of it. . . .

A defence by way of excuse can be fairly satisfactorily defined. But an excuse is not necessarily contrasted with the definition of the offence, since absence of *mens rea* or negligence can be an excuse although they are thought of as part of the definition of the offence. It may be important to decide whether a particular defence is an excuse or a justification, but not whether it forms part of the definitional facts.

The conclusion is that we have no satisfactory test of what if anything is meant by the "definition of an offence" as opposed to defences. It is not necessarily the definition in a statute, or the positive elements in a statutory definition, or the minimum definition that looks satisfactory to the eye of common sense. Defences based on the location of the persuasive or evidential burden tend to beg the question. So what we think of as the definition of an offence and what we call a defence can only be regarded as depending largely upon the accidents of language, the convenience of legal drafting, or the unreasoning force of tradition.

§ 9.03 Justification versus Excuse

[A] The Distinction

Hall, Comments on Justification and Excuse

24 Am. J. of Comp. L. 638, 639–40 (1976)

"Justification" and "excuse" are very old concepts. Indeed these words have long been parts of everyday speech; Anglo-American law has used them for centuries and with some sophistication since Bacon's 1630 treatise on the common law. What is common to both concepts is that an injury or damage has been caused by a human being. The difference is that in the former, the actor did the right thing in the circumstances, *e.g.*, he defended himself against an assailant or destroyed property to save life; while in "excuse" the rectitude of the actor or his action is simply irrelevant. What is relevant in excuse, *i.e.*, relevant to penal law, is that for reasons either of incapacity or of extreme pressure, such as the threat of immediate death, the actor should not be held criminally liable; instead he is excused.

These terms, like most words of ordinary speech, are ambiguous. For example, "excuse" in a wide meaning includes all cases where there is no blame and no penal accountability. But in a narrower usage, one excuses only normal adults who were subjected to extreme pressure, *i.e.*, "excuse" is applied to persons who, except for extreme pressure, would be held fully responsible. Second, excusing facts are sometimes accompanied by justifying facts. When an action that caused an injury or damage is justified as the lesser of the threatened evils, it may also be said that the actor is excused since he cannot be blamed for what he did, *e.g.*, a starving man takes food from a shop. Or suppose a bank robber points a gun at the cashier, who hands over a large sum of money. Shall we say that the cashier is excused because he acted under great pressure or shall we say (and indeed would not most people say) that he was justified in what he did?

The interaction of these concepts in actual cases does not negate that justification often has a logical priority since excuses implies that we must first decide, "excuse the actor for doing what?" and that may involve a decision regarding justification.

Eser, Justification and Excuse

24 Am. J. of Comp. L. 621, 635–36 (1976)

Rationale and Grounds of Excuse

Unlike justification, excuse does not affect the unlawfulness of the act; it merely removes the personal blameworthiness of the actor: he is (only) excused. Excuse is granted only to those participants who are acting under excusing conditions; all other participants remain punishable for the illegal act. Contrary to the common law tradition, which seems to limit excuse to insanity, duress and to some extent mistake of law, German law has recognized for quite some time that excessive self-defense by reason of distress, fear or fright. . . necessity . . . and conflict of duties are also grounds of excuse. German criminal theory even makes a distinction between *Schuldausschliessungsgrunde* (such as insanity and unavoidable mistake of law) by which the perpetrator is both excused and, lacking *mens rea,* even deemed to act without guilt, and *Entschuldigungsgrunde* which excuse an act that is unlawful and "guilty" since committed with *mens rea.* Only in this second group (duress, necessity, conflict of duties or excessive self-defense by reason of fear) can we speak of an excuse for an otherwise "culpable" act. And only these grounds of "excuse" are of major concern in our present context.

Although the grounds for exclusion of guilt (*Schuldausschliessungsgrunde*) are characterized by a lack of cognitive (mistake of law) and/or willed (insanity) elements of guilt, grounds of excuse (*Entschuldigungsgrunde*) are rooted in extraordinary psychological pressure on the perpetrator. This at least was Goldschmidt's explanation, which is still accepted by many scholars. The question has been raised however whether all grounds of excuse can indeed be explained simply by this subjective motivation. Thus in the case of excessive self-defense, blameworthiness can be diminished by reason of fear . . . but beyond that we also notice a diminishing of the objective wrong since the perpetrator was reacting—albeit excessively—to an illegal assault. The same applies to excusing necessity. . . where exculpation is based both on acting out of necessity and on preventing damage to a certain legal interest. Therefore, without denying the subjective basis of excuse in some psychological states of necessity or pressure, most German criminal scholars of today treat diminished objective wrongfulness as one of the grounds for excusing the perpetrator.

NOTE

In at least one instance the common law did distinguish between justifiable and excusable acts, even though no "punishment" was visited upon the "excused" actor. In a killing in self-defense the law simply acquitted a "justifiable" actor, but if the act was merely excused, the defendant forfeited his property. (See *infra,* § 9.05[A][4].) This distinction has not, as the following materials will show, remained in the common law. Indeed, Andenaes says that the distinction "involves no legal consequences," and Hall has said the distinction is "fallacious and misleading." As the materials on burden of proof show, see § 9.04, *infra,* however, this is not—or need not be—entirely accurate. Indeed, continental law recognizes the distinction quite graphically. Professor Fletcher has sought to reintroduce the notions to this country. G. Fletcher, Rethinking Criminal Law (1978); Fletcher, *The Individualization of Excusing Conditions,* 47 S. Cal. L. Rev. 1269 (1974). As you read the cases in § 9.05, consider whether the defendant is claiming excuse or justification, as Hall and the continental law define them.

[B] The Distinction Challenged

Dressler, New Thoughts about the Concept of Justification in the Criminal Law: A Critique of Fletcher's Thinking and Rethinking

32 UCLA L. Rev. 61, 84–85 (1984)

Police officer A lawfully enters a house and is suddenly confronted by a six-year old child wielding a real gun, pointing it at A, saying, "Bang, bang." Assuming A has no way to save her life but to fire her gun at the youth, do we feel—do our moral intuitions tell us—that such conduct is good, or is it, perhaps, "not bad" or "tolerable"? Or, suppose that while A is asleep child B puts the gun to A's head, and C shoots B to save A's life. Do we all accept that C did the right thing? Or, if an actor kills an innocent person in order to save ten innocent people, is such a killing morally right, wrong, or "not wrong"? Is the prisoner who flees confinement because he is subject to sexual abuse doing a good act? A bad one? Or is it tolerable?

The purpose of asking these questions is not to answer them, but to suggest that reasonable people, morally sensitive people, even deontologically morally sensitive people, could find any or all of the actions "not right," without considering them "wrong." They could believe that punishment is inappropriate without believing that the actors are in need of excusing circumstances (frequently not present, anyway), in order to avoid criminal punishment.

Yet surely there is conduct for which those moral judgments seem too harsh, or too generous, and for which some other phrase is needed. We want to be provided with a language and a mode of analysis which permits such expression. More significantly, we do not want to be forced to reject a justification theory merely because our language constrains us. After all, the language of the law is a means to an end, not an end in itself. The world too frequently creates situations in which morally sensitive people perceive more gray than they do black and white. The law must provide a way to express such moral ambiguity.

Greenawalt, The Perplexing Borders of Justification and Excuse

84 Colum. L. Rev.1897, 1900–02, 1904, 1910, 1927 (1984)

Systematic distinctions between justifications and excuses might be recommended to further two objectives: (1)producing authoritative determinations of whether persons escaping liability have presented justifications or only excuses and (2)achieving theoretical clarity in the criminal law. The first, more ambitious, goal cannot be fully realized in any system that relies upon a general verdict by lay jurors for tried cases. When only a single ground of acquittal is presented, a not guilty verdict will reveal the ground of the jury's judgment, but if jurors who return a verdict have been presented with claims amounting to justifications and excuses, the legal system will have produced no authoritative determination why liability is not imposed. . . .

* * *

The general verdict is hardly a complete answer to the call for greater rigor in the classification of criminal law defenses, however, for precision can serve other objectives. The educative force of a criminal code may be furthered by a labelling of justifications and excuses that promotes in citizens proper views about how to make difficult choices and how to regard the behavior of others. Clarity in distinctions can enhance understanding of the criminal law and its purposes among those who think about that subject, and can help lay the groundwork for intelligent reform. Although the boundaries of grounds of defenses should be determined in light of all relevant considerations, not dictated by abstract legal definitions of justification and excuse, exploration of the nature of justification and excuse still may affect perceptions about what the overall scope of defenses should be. Finally, conceptual clarity and comprehensiveness may be worth striving after for their own sake. . . .

An act may be thought to be morally permissible even though it is not the best possible among the available alternatives. A person may act in a manner that reflects what most people would do or that in some sense is "within his rights," although a different response would be morally preferable. . . What we have, in fact, is a claim in defense of action that may not fit smoothly into either of the two categories.

* * *

[T]he crucial point for our purposes is that were the law to attempt precise categorization, some actions grounded in factual mistake should be viewed as justified, others as only excused. . . . The critical question is whether for cases in which the criminal law is to relieve actors of liability in either event, it should try to distinguish justifications from excuses. . . .

* * *

Neither the rights of others nor any difference between general and individual claims provides an adequate basis for distinguishing between justifications and excuses. Rather, the central distinction between justification and excuse is between warranted action and unwarranted action for which the actor is not to blame. Although the law's failure to be as precise as it might in reflecting this distinction is partially due to correctable inattention or indifference, much of the imprecision is a consequence of the troubling borderlines of the two concepts, of legal rules that compromise disagreements about substantive morality, and of canons of convenience that support placing similar factual situations under the same rubric in order to focus the jury's efforts on the questions crucial to liability and nonliability.

NOTES

1. Even among those who accept the distinction between justified and excused actions, there is significant disagreement about whether an actor who

is objectively justified will be exculpated if he did not know of the facts that justified his actions. The issue is often called the *Dadson* issue, after the case that is used as a focus. See *Regina v. Dadson,* 4 Cox Crim. Cas. 358 (Ct. Crim. App. 1850). Dadson saw X, who was stealing wood, running away and shot him. This would have violated the common law prohibiting the use of deadly force to prevent a misdemeanor (see *infra,* § 9.05[A][6]) but, unknown to Dadson, the victim had previously been convicted, so the theft was a felony. Use of deadly force to prevent a felony was justified. Should Dadson be exculpated? Compare Robinson, Criminal Law Defenses 12–29 (1984) with Fletcher, Rethinking Criminal Law 555–57 (1978). See also Hogan, *The Dadson Principle,* 1989 Crim. L. Rev. 679; Sullivan, *Bad Thoughts and Bad Acts,* [1990] Crim L. Rev. 559. Who would have more difficulty exculpating *Dadson:* a retributivist or a utilitarian?

2. For further discussion, see J. Smith, Justification and Excuse in the Criminal Law (1989); Husak, *The Serial View of Criminal Law Defenses,* 3 Crim. L. Forum 369 (1992); Quigly, *The Common Law's Theory of Criminal Liability: A Challenge from across the Atlantic,* 11 Whittier L. Rev. 479, 494 (1989) (attempting to differentiate among "defenses" "creates insuperable difficulties of line-drawing . . . serves no practical purpose, and . . . inappropriately separates defenses from the element of the offenses against which they are asserted").

Among the scores of articles on the entire topic of excuse, justification, and the distinction between these concepts, if any, are Bayles, *Character, Purpose, and Criminal Responsibility,* 1 Law & Phil. 5 (1982); Brandt, *The Insanity Defense and the Theory of Motivation,* 7 Law & Phil. 123 (1988); Brandt, *A Motivational Theory of Excuses in the Criminal Law,* 27 Nomos, Criminal Justice 165 (Pennock and Chapman ed. 1985); Corrado, *Notes on the Structure of a Theory of Excuses,* 82 J. Crim. L. & Criminology 465 (1992); Dressler, *Justifications and Excuses: A Brief Review of the Concepts and the Literature,* 33 Wayne L. Rev. 1155 (1987); Fletcher, *The Right Deed for the Wrong Reason: A Reply to Mr. Robinson,* 23 U.C.L.A. L. Rev. 293 (1975); Fletcher, *Should Intolerable Prison Conditions Generate a Justification or an Excuse for Escape?,* 26 U.C.L.A. L. Rev. 1355 (1979); Fletcher, *The Unmet Challenge of Criminal Theory,* 33 Wayne L. Rev. 1439 (1987); Greenawalt, *Conflicts of Law and Morality—Institutions of Amelioration,* 67 Va. L. Rev. 177 (1981); Greenawalt, *Distinguishing Justifications from Excuses,* 49 Law & Contemp. Probs. 89 (1986); Hart, Legal Responsibility and Excuses, in Determinism and Freedom in the Age of Modern Science (Sidney Hook ed. 1961); Kadish, *Excusing Crime,* 75 Cal. L. Rev. 275 (1987); Moore, *Choice, Character and Excuse,* 7 Soc. Phil. & Pol'y 29 (1990); Robinson, *A Theory of Justification: Societal Harm as a Prerequisite for Criminal Liability,* 23 U.C.L.A. L. Rev. 275 (1975); Wasserstrom, *H.L.A. Hart and the Doctrine of Mens Rea and Criminal Responsibility* 35 U. Chi. L. Rev. 92 (1967).

§ 9.04 THE PROCEDURAL IMPLICATIONS OF CLASSIFYING DEFENSES

As the excerpt from *Williams, supra,* p. 694 suggests, the impact of labeling a "fact" as a "defense" rather than as a "failure of proof" may be very significant for procedural purposes as well as for theoretical purity. This requires a close analysis of what is, and is not, an "element" in a crime. Similarly, Dressler and others have suggested that since justification denies the illegality of the act, whereas excuse admits the illegality but proffers some extraneous reason for nonpunishment, that distinction too may have procedural implications.

We have already discussed the critical role played by "element analysis" in the Model Penal Code taxonomy, *supra,* § 4.05. But to understand the current furor that surrounds the questions relating to justifications and excuses, particularly in its constitutional framework, it is important to parse the issue of defining "elements" in the absence of a code that does define them. In Winship, *supra* § 1.02[A], the United States Supreme Court declared that the prosecutor bore the burden of proving, beyond a reasonable doubt, *"every fact necessary to constitute the crime with which [the defendant] is charged."* But that apparently clear statement actually conceals enormously difficult questions: What facts are "necessary" to constitute a crime? And what does "necessary" mean? Are there facts that, as a matter of constitutional law, are "necessary" to constitute guilt? Implicit in *Winship* is the view that the state *may* properly throw upon the defendant the burden of proving those facts that are not elements of the offense, but that the legislature, for whatever reason, has seen fit to include in the statute. Yet, as both the majorities in *Mullaney* and *Patterson, infra,* recognize, there are surely some facts that the state could not, consistent with any fair or constitutional system, require the defendant to prove.

Some cases *seem* easy. Mr. Justice Powell's example in *Patterson* seems the epitome of such a fact; it seems intuitive that the state could not define as a capital crime "being in the presence of a recently killed person" and require the defendant to prove that he did not do the killing in order to avoid capital punishment. We articulate this intuition by saying that *actus reus* is an element of the crime; then, by virtue of *Winship,* the state must prove that the defendant did the act. Yet there are cases that have allowed the state to place upon the defendant the burden of proving "unconsciousness," even though the defendant has argued that because he was "unconscious" or "acting like an automaton," he cannot be said to have committed the "act." See, *e.g., State v. Caddell,* 287 N.C. 266, 215 S.E.2d 348 (1975). *Contra: People v. Newton,* 8 Cal. App. 3d 359, 87 Cal. Rptr. 394 (1970); *People v. Grant* 46 Ill. App. 3d 125, 360 N.E.2d 809 (1977), rev'd, 71 Ill. 2d 551, 377 N.E.2d 4 (1978). Of course, in one sense the cases are not apposite since the defendant in these cases is conceding that his *body* pulled the trigger, but is arguing that he did not have any control over his body, and therefore the pulling of the trigger cannot be reasonably attributed to *him.* But in a more direct sense, these cases raise the core question: What *facts* are essential to the element of actus reus, and which go to "negate" but not "disprove" *actus reus*? And what does the law mean when it says that a fact negates *actus reus* or *mens rea*?

If it is difficult to determine which facts negate the *actus reus,* as is suggested by the conflicting decisions in *Caddell* and *Newton,* then the problem of defining *mens rea* and, more specifically, of defining what negates *mens rea* is even more difficult, perhaps impossible. Yet *Winship* appears to require, as a constitutional matter, that the elements of *mens rea* and the facts that would constitute *mens rea* (and their negations) be defined so that the state be prohibited from either (1) placing the burden of proof on the defendant or (2) "abolishing" those facts as relevant.

The centrality of free will and autonomy to the criminal law, initially seen as academic, may then be critical to a resolution of these constitutional issues. If, for example, only a defendant who has free will is the proper object of blame, and therefore of punishment not only as a matter of principle but as a matter of constitutional law, it is necessary to determine what negates free will. If the defendant does not have free will, then she cannot properly (and hence constitutionally) be punished. And if that is true, then the implication of *Winship* is that any "fact," whether labeled as a defense or not, that goes to the issue of whether defendant had free will (or that amount of free will without which there is no responsibility) must as a constitutional matter be *disproven* by the prosecution before punishment can be properly inflicted.

One further point should be made here. The metaphor that a defense negates a *mens rea* isitself misleading and may well be responsible for the ease with which the law calls these "defenses." The metaphor suggests that the defendant's mind was filled with *mens rea,* but that suddenly it disappeared because it was replaced or erased by a defense. Obviously, this is wrong. If the defendant was acting, *e.g.,* under a mistake, he never had the requisite *mens rea*—or at least no "criminal intent" (see *MacDonald, supra,* p. 264). Instead, the defendant was always innocent in the sense that he had no *mens rea.* If we replace the term *mens rea* with "morally culpable state of mind," the fallacy in the negation metaphor becomes clearer. Of what importance might this be in the practical, real world of criminal law?

There is no easy answer to the question of what facts constitute or negate *mens rea.* Perhaps there is no answer. It is clear, however, that the common law courts did not concern themselves with, much less attempt to resolve, this question generically, although in some instances the argument that a certain datum (*e.g.*, mistake of fact) negated an undisputed element of an offense (*e.g., mens rea* of knowingly) emerged from the decisions. Beyond this, however, there is little assistance from precedent that will help resolve the question.

The excerpt from *Blackstone, supra* p. 689 strives to explicate the relationship between *mens rea* and some "incapacities." But to say that where a defendant has acted under the influence of mistake his free will is "not called forth and exerted at the time," and that the "will sits neuter," as *Blackstone*does, is only a conclusion; it is a metaphor that may help explain why, intuitively, we will not punish such an actor, but has no explanatory power beyond that. More critical is his requirement not merely that the defendant "will" the act, but that the will be "vicious."

Thus the categories of defenses that Professor Robinson lays out, *supra* § 9.02, may hide immense difficulties. First, of course, one must define the "elements" of a crime, no easy task itself, as Professor Williams attempts to demonstrate. But beyond that is the question of the relationship of "defenses," whether denominated "excuses" or "justifications" to those "elements"— constituting the *actus reus* and *mens rea*—on which *Winship* clearly requires the state to carry the burden of proof. The *Segovia* case below deals with the first problem. The ensuing materials demonstrate the conundrum of *mens rea:*

Are the defenses and excusing conditions merely graces of the law, so that they are not relevant to the elements or *mens rea,* or do they negate elements, most importantly *mens rea,* so that the burden of proof of negation falls upon the state? The various murky answers to these questions thus far, culminating in *McMillan, infra,* illustrate both the need for understanding the concepts of *mens rea,* excuses, and justifications as well as the need for a thorough re-examination of criminal liability generally.

[A] Elements Generally

STATE v. SEGOVIA

Supreme Court of Idaho

93 Idaho 208, 457 P.2d 905 (1969)

McFADDEN, Chief Justice.

Appellants Florentino Segovia and Ramiro Hernandez Garcia were by a jury found guilty of illegal possession of a narcotic drug, following which they were sentenced to a term in the state penitentiary not to exceed thirty months. They have appealed from their respective judgments of conviction.

During the course of trial, two police officers testified that on October 14, 1967 they were in their patrol car parked adjacent to a bar on Main Street in Boise, when they saw the defendants walk through the parking lot toward Main Street. The defendants were both smoking a cigarette, passing it back and forth between them. As they approached Main Street, one of the defendants dropped the cigarette, and both defendants turned the corner and went into the bar.

The officers testified they walked to where the cigarette was discarded, searched the area and found only one cigarette in the area, it being still lit and the other end still moist. The officers observed it was a home-made cigarette, broke it open and identified the contents to be marihuana. The officers entered the bar and placed the defendants under arrest. A search of the defendants' persons produced another cigarette from Garcia's pocket which was also determined to contain marihuana. At the police station a more thorough search of their clothing produced loose marihuana and its residue.

On the basis of this testimony the jury found the defendants guilty as charged.

The statute under which the defendants were charged is I.C. § 37-3202 (enacted S.L., 1967, Ch. 435, § 93, 1494), which provides:

> Except as otherwise provided in this act, every person who possesses any narcotic except upon the written prescription of a physician, dentist, podiatrist, osteopath or veterinarian licensed to practice in this state, may be punished by imprisonment in the state prison for a term not to exceed ten (10) years.

No evidence was presented by the state to negate possession by the defendants of a prescription for the marihuana found in their possession, and the defendants contend that absent such proof by the state the facts as proven are insufficient to establish commission of the crime charged. In other words, the defendants assert that the burden is upon the state to negative the exception in I.C. § 37-3202. The state, on the other hand, contends that the burden is upon the defendants to prove that they are within the exception—that it was incumbent upon the defendants to produce a prescription authorizing their possession of the narcotic.

Prior to the enactment of the present narcotic law (S.L. 1967, Ch. 435), Idaho's statutory provisions on narcotics (Title 37, Ch. 23) contained the following provision:

> In any complaint, information, or indictment, and in any action or proceedings brought for the enforcement of any provision of this act, it shall not be necessary to negative any exception, excuse, proviso, or exemption, contained in this act, and the burden of proof of any such exception, excuse, proviso, or exemption, shall be upon the defendant. L.C. § 37–2318.

In 1967, however, the legislature repealed this and all other sections of Chapter 23, Title 37. S.L. 1967, Ch. 435, § 119, p.1469.

In the absence of a statute, the general rule is that the burden is upon the state in a criminal case to negative any exception or proviso appearing in that part of the statute which defines the crime if the exception is "so incorporated with the language describing and defining the offense that the ingredients of the offense cannot be accurately and clearly described if the exception is omitted . . . ," 41 Am. Jur. 2d, *Indictments and Informations,* § 98, pp.940–941. Under such circumstances, the state must prove that the defendant is not within the exception to the statute.

It is our opinion that the exception contained in I.C. § 37-3202 is an integral part of the offense proscribed and is so incorporated with the description of the offense as to be a material element of it. The exception defines the scope of the general prohibition of I.C. § 37-3202 since it is not a crime to possess a narcotic drug pursuant to a valid prescription. The crime is defined as possession without a valid prescription, and thus the absence of such a prescription is of necessity a material element of the offense.

The state strenuously argues that the existence of a prescription is a matter peculiarly within the defendant's own knowledge and that to force the state to prove the non-existence of a prescription imposes an impossible burden upon the state. We do not agree. Whatever may be the situation in other jurisdictions, in Idaho the state has ready access to all prescriptions filled in the state. See I.C. § 37-3017, whereby copies of all narcotic prescriptions filled by pharmacists must be filed monthly with the Idaho State Board of Pharmacy. It is far from impossible for the state to establish a *prima facie* showing of the absence of a prescription. The fact that the legislature repealed the statute relieving the state of this burden and did not see fit to replace it with a comparable provision in the new statute regulating narcotic drugs (S.L. 1967, Ch. 435) is a strong indication that the legislature intended for the state to assume this burden.

However, in regard to marihuana (defined by I.C. § 37-2704), the legislature classified this as a Class A narcotic drug, as follows:

IV MARIHUANA (*Cannabis sativa*), its derivatives or compounds. (Marihuana is not presently used for medicinal purposes in the United States.)L.C. § 37–2702 (S.L. 1967, Ch. 435, § 2, p.1443).

By this classification, with the parenthetical statement that marihuana is not presently used for medicinal purposes, the legislature must have recognized that no prescription for such drug could be obtained, and intended that in a prosecution under the provisions of I.C. § 37-3202 for possession of the narcotic marihuana, it would be a useless act to require the state to prove absence of any prescription for the drug, when the law itself recognizes that no prescription is obtainable. Insofar as the instant case is concerned, the law itself by classification of marihuana as a drug not used for medicinal purposes, negates the burden on the state to prove absence of a prescription.

There being no burden on the state to prove absence of a prescription for marihuana and there being substantial evidence to sustain the judgments, the judgments of conviction are affirmed.

NOTES AND QUESTIONS

1. The general question involved in *Segovia* is often called the "exception" issue. Many states attempt to resolve the issue by a statute precisely like Idaho Code, Title 37, Ch. 23, discussed in *Segovia,* which provided prior to its repeal that "In any complaint, information or indictment, and in any action or proceeding brought for the enforcement of [a specific statute or all criminal statutes] it shall not be necessary to negative any exception, excuse, proviso or exemption contained in such section, and the burden of proof of any such exception, excuse, proviso or exemption shall be upon the defendant." Some state courts view this as putting the burden of persuasion of an exception on the defendant, *e.g., Burgin v. State,* 431 N.E.2d 864 (Ind. App. 1982), while others interpret such statutes to put only the burden of production on the defendant, *e.g., State v. Kahler,* 232 So. 2d 166 (Fla. 1970). As to the specific issue addressed in *Segovia*—whether defendant carries the burden of persuasion on the issue of prescription for a drug—the courts are also split. Compare *State v. Buchman,* 361 So. 2d 692 (Fla. 1978) (yes) with *State v. Carter,* 214 Kan. 533, 521 P.2d. 294 (1974) (defendant carries only burden of production). The Uniform Narcotics Act provides that a person who is not drug-dependent and who sells drugs is guilty of a crime. Is "non—drug-dependence" an element? The decisions are divided. See, *e.g., People v. Hudson,* 130 Ill. App. 2d 1033, 266 N.E.2d 481 (1970); *State v. Gibbs* 239 N.W.2d 866 (Iowa 1976); *Elkins v. State,* 543 S.W.2d 648 (Tex. Crim. 1976) (all holding that the phrase states an element). Recently Connecticut reversed 20 years of decisions so holding, and determined that "non—drug dependence" is not an element. See *State v. Hart,* 221 Conn. 595, 605 A.2d 1366 (1992). The *Hart* court pointed to two factors: (1)"a defendant's drug dependency at the specific point of time . . . is certainly a matter . . . within his own knowledge" and (2)"the state's preparation of its case is hindered because it has no method by which to discover whether drug dependency will be an issue at trial." Are these objections persuasive? As with many other jurisprudential questions, the exception problem has received more attention from English writers than from

American. See, *e.g.,* Bennion, *Statutory Exceptions: A Third Knot in the Golden Thread?,* 1988 Crim. L. Rev. 31; Birch, *Hunting the Snark: The Elusive Statutory Exception,* 1988 Crim. L. Rev. 221; Mayfield, *The Legacy of Hunt,* 1988 Crim. L. Rev. 19. As might be expected in light of his earlier-stated views (see p. 694, *supra*), Professor Williams, *The Logic of "Exceptions",* 47 Cambridge L. J. 261, 280, 278 (1988), thinks the whole discussion is meaningless:

> [L]ooking for the line between a rule and an exception is, to use the proverbial simile, like looking in a dark room for a black cat that isn't here. There are no characteristic features for an exception: "exceptions" are merely linguistic constructs . . . The negative of an element of an offence can be regarded as an exception, and the negative of an exception can be regarded as an element of the offence.

2. Professor Williams targets for particular vehemence the "convenience" argument put forth in *Segovia* by noting that the argument is truest with regard to the defendant's *mens rea.* Do you find the argument persuasive?

3. Suppose a legislature provided that all intentional killings were punishable by death, except those committed on holidays, which would be punished by X years in prison. Assuming the statute to be otherwise constitutional, is "nonholidayness" an element of the offense—or may the burden of proof be placed upon the defendant?

Is the matter simply one of the wording of the legislation? Compare:

    a. "All killings are capitally punishable, except those committed on holidays."

    b. "All killings not committed on holidays are capitally punishable."

    c. "All killings are capitally punishable. If the defendant establishes that the killing was committed on a holiday, the punishment will be X years in prison."

    d. "All killings except those on holidays are capitally punishable. It is presumed, in the absence of evidence from the defendant, that a killing did not occur on a holiday."

4. In the holiday example, it may be suggested that the legislature is giving a "bonus" to those who kill on holidays, since it appears to have nothing to do with the culpability of a killing. But is that clear? And who is to decide? Should not the legislature's statement that there is some relation, even if that statement is tacit, be given substantial, perhaps even conclusive, weight? Why, in the statutes in (3) above, would holidayness but not intent be a bonus?

[B] Elements and Affirmative Defenses

MULLANEY v. WILBUR

Supreme Court of the United States

421 U.S. 684 (1975)

Mr. Justice POWELL *delivered the opinion of the Court.*

The State of Maine requires a defendant charged with murder to prove that he acted "in the heat of passion on sudden provocation" in order to reduce the homicide to manslaughter. We must decide whether this rule comports with the due process requirement, as defined in In re *Winship* [397 U.S. 358 (1970)], that the prosecution prove beyond a reasonable doubt every fact necessary to constitute the crime charged.

In June 1966 a jury found respondent Stillman E. Wilbur, Jr., guilty of murder. The case against him rested on his own pretrial statement and on circumstantial evidence showing that he fatally assaulted Claude Hebert in the latter's hotel room. Respondent's statement, introduced by the prosection, claimed that he had attacked Hebert in a frenzy provoked by Hebert's homosexual advance. The defense offered no evidence, but argued that the homicide was not unlawful since respondent lacked criminal intent. Alternatively, Wilbur's counsel asserted that at most the homicide was manslaughter rather than murder, since it occurred in the heat of passion provoked by the homosexual assault.

The trial court instructed the jury that Maine law recognizes only two kinds of homicide, murder and manslaughter, and that these offenses are not subdivided into different degrees. The common elements of both are that the homicide be unlawful—*i.e.*, neither justifiable nor excusable—and that it be intentional. The prosecution is required to prove these elements by proof beyond a reasonable doubt, and only if they are so proved is the jury to consider the distinction between murder and manslaughter.

In view of the evidence the trial court drew particular attention to the difference between murder and manslaughter. After reading the statutory definitions of both offenses[3] the court charged that "malice aforethought is an essential and indispensable element of the crime of murder," without which the homicide would be manslaughter. The jury was further instructed, however, that if the prosecution established that the homicide was both intentional and unlawful, malice aforethought was to be conclusively implied unless the defendant proved by a fair preponderance of the evidence that he acted in the heat of passion on sudden provocation. The court emphasized that

---

[3] The Maine murder statute, Me. Rev. Stat. Ann., Tit. 17, § 2651 (1964), provides:

Whoever unlawfully kills a human being with malice aforethought, either express or implied, is guilty of murder and shall be punished by imprisonment for life.

The manslaughter statute, Me. Rev. Stat. Ann., Tit. 17, § 2551 (1964), in relevant part provides:

Whoever unlawfully kills a human being in the heat of passion, on sudden provocation, without express or implied malice aforethought . . . shall be punished by a fine of not more than $1,000 or by imprisonment for not more than 20 years.

"malice aforethought and heat of passion on sudden provocation are inconsistent things," thus, by proving the latter the defendant would negate the former and reduce the homicide from murder to manslaughter. The court then concluded its charge with elaborate definitions of "heat of passion"[5] and "sudden provocation."[6]

After retiring to consider its verdict, the jury twice returned to request further instruction. It first sought reinstruction on the doctrine of implied malice aforethought, and later on the definition of "heat of passion." Shortly after the second reinstruction, the jury found respondent guilty of murder.

Respondent appealed to the Maine Supreme Judicial Court, arguing that he had been denied due process because he was required to negate the element of malice aforethought by proving that he had acted in the heat of passion on sudden provocation. He claimed that under Maine law malice aforethought was an essential element of the crime of murder—indeed that it was the sole element distinguishing murder from manslaughter. Respondent contended, therefore, that this Court's decision in *Winship* requires the prosecution to prove the existence of that element beyond a reasonable doubt.

The Maine Supreme Judicial Court rejected this contention, holding that in Maine murder and manslaughter are not distinct crimes but rather different degrees of the single generic offense of felonious homicide. *State v. Wilbur,* 278 A.2d 139 (1971). The court further stated that for more than a century it repeatedly had held that the prosecution could rest on a presumption of implied malice aforethought and require the defendant to prove that he had acted in the heat of passion on sudden provocation in order to reduce murder to manslaughter. With respect to *Winship* which was decided after respondent's trial, the court noted that it did not anticipate the application of the *Winship* principle to a "reductive factor" such as the heat of passion on sudden provocation.

Respondent next successfully petitioned for a writ of habeas corpus in federal district court. . . . The District Court ruled that under the Maine statutes murder and manslaughter are distinct offenses, not different degrees of a single offense. The court further held that "[m]alice aforethought is made the distinguishing element of the offense of murder, and it is explicitly excluded as an element of the offense of manslaughter." Thus, the District Court concluded, *Winship* requires the prosecution to prove malice aforethought beyond a reasonable doubt; it cannot rely on a presumption of implied malice which requires the defendant to prove that he acted in the heat of passion on sudden provocation.

The Court of Appeals for the First Circuit affirmed. Although recognizing that "within broad limits a state court must be the one to interpret its own

---

[5] "Heat of passion . . . means that at the time of the act the reason is disturbed or obscured by passion to an extent which might [make] ordinary men of fair, average disposition liable to act irrationally without due deliberation or reflection, and from passion rather than judgment."

[6] "[H]eat of passion will not avail unless upon sudden provocation. Sudden means happening without previous notice or with very brief notice; coming unexpectedly, precipitated, or unlooked for. . . . It is not every provocation, it is not every rage of passion that will reduce a killing from murder to manslaughter. The provocation must be of such a character and so close upon the act of killing, that for a moment a person could be—that for a moment the defendant could be considered as not being the master of his own understanding."

laws," the court nevertheless ruled that "a totally unsupportable construction which leads to an invasion of constitutional due process is a federal matter." The Court of Appeals equated malice aforethought with "premeditation," and concluded that *Winship* requires the prosecution to prove this fact beyond a reasonable doubt.

Following this decision, the Maine Supreme Judicial Court decided the case of *State v. Lafferty,* 309 A.2d 647 (1973), in which it sharply disputed the First Circuit's view that it was entitled to make an independent determination of Maine law. The Maine court also reaffirmed its earlier opinion that murder and manslaughter are punishment categories of the single offense of felonious homicide. Accordingly, if the prosecution proves a felonious homicide the burden shifts to the defendant to prove that he acted in the heat of passion on sudden provocation in order to receive the lesser penalty prescribed for manslaughter.

In view of the *Lafferty* decision we granted certiorari in this case and remanded to the Court of Appeals for reconsideration. On remand, that court again applied *Winship,* this time to the Maine law as construed by the Maine Supreme Judicial Court. . . . Looking to the "substance" of that law, the court found that the presence or absence of the heat of passion on sudden provocation results in significant differences in the penalties and stigma attaching to conviction. For these reasons the Court of Appeals held that the principles enunciated in *Winship* control, and that to establish murder the prosecution must prove beyond a reasonable doubt that the defendant did not act in the heat of passion on sudden provocation.

Because of the importance of the issues presented, we again granted *certiorari.* . . . We now affirm. . . .

. . . [W]e accept as binding the Maine Supreme Judicial Court's construction of state homicide law.

The Maine law of homicide, as it bears on this case, can be stated succinctly: Absent justification or excuse, all intentional or criminally reckless killings are felonious homicides. Felonious homicide is punished as murder—*i.e.,* by life imprisonment—unless the defendant proves by a fair preponderance of the evidence that it was committed in the heat of passion on sudden provocation, in which case it is punished as manslaughter—*i.e.,* by a fine not to exceed $1,000 or by imprisonment not to exceed 20 years. The issue is whether the Maine rule requiring the defendant to prove that he acted in the heat of passion on sudden provocation accords with due process.

Our analysis may be illuminated if this issue is placed in historical context. At early common law only those homicides committed in the enforcement of justice were considered justifiable; all others were deemed unlawful and were punished by death. Gradually, however, the severity of the common-law punishment for homicide abated. Between the 13th and 16th centuries the class of justifiable homicides expanded to include, for example, accidental homicides and those committed in self-defense. Concurrently, the widespread use of capital punishment was ameliorated further by extension of the ecclesiastic jurisdiction. Almost any person able to read was eligible for "benefit of clergy," a procedural device that effected a transfer from the secular to the ecclesiastic jurisdiction. And under ecclesiastic law a person who committed an unlawful homicide was not executed; instead he received a one-year sentence, had his thumb branded and was required to forfeit his goods. At the turn of the 16th century, English rulers, concerned with the accretion of ecclesiastic jurisdiction at the expense of the secular, enacted a series of statutes eliminating the benefit of clergy in all cases of "murder of malice prepensed." Unlawful homicides that were committed without such malice were designated "manslaughter" and their perpetrators remained eligible for the benefit of clergy.

Even after ecclesiastic jurisdiction was eliminated for all secular offenses the distinction between murder and manslaughter persisted. It was said that "manslaughter arises from the sudden heat of passions, murder from the wickedness of the heart." 4 Blackstone's Commentaries 190. Malice afore-thought was designated as the element that distinguished the two crimes, but it was recognized that such malice could be implied by law as well as proved by evidence. Absent proof that an unlawful homicide resulted from "sudden and sufficiently violent provocation," the homicide was "presumed to be malicious."[15] *Id.*, at 201. In view of this presumption, the early English authorities, relying on the case of *The King v. Oneby*, 92 Eng. Rep. 465 (K.B. 1727), held that once the prosecution proved that the accused had committed the homicide, it was "incumbent on the prisoner to make out . . . all . . . circumstances of justification, excuse or alleviation . . . to the satisfaction of the court and jury." 4 Blackstone's Commentaries 201. See M. Foster, Crown Law 255 (1762). Thus, at common law the burden of proving heat of passion on sudden provocation appears to have rested on the defendant.[16]

In this country the concept of malice aforethought took on two distinct meanings: in some jurisdictions it came to signify a substantive element of intent, requiring the prosecution to prove that the defendant intended to kill or to inflict great bodily harm; in other jurisdictions it remained a policy presumption, indicating only that absent proof to the contrary a homicide was presumed not to have occurred in the heat of passion. . . . [I]n the past half century, the large majority of States now require the prosecution to prove the absence of the heat of passion on sudden provocation beyond a reasonable doubt. . . .

This historical review establishes two important points. First, the fact at issue here—the presence or absence of the heat of passion on sudden provocation—has been, almost from the inception of the common law of homicide, the single most important factor in determining the degree of culpability attaching to an unlawful homicide. And, second, the clear trend has been toward requiring the prosecution to bear the ultimate burden of proving this fact. . . .

---

[15] Thus it appears that the concept of express malice aforethought was surplusage since if the homicide resulted from sudden provocation it was manslaughter; otherwise it was murder. In this respect, Maine law appears to follow the old common law. See generally Note, *The Constitutionality of the Common Law Presumption of Malice in Maine,* 54 B.U.L. Rev. 973, 986–999 (1974).

[16] Fletcher, *Two Kinds of Legal Rules: A Comparative Study of Burden of Persuasion Practices in Criminal Cases,* 77 Yale L.J. 880, 904–07 (1968), disputes this conclusion, arguing that the reliance on *Oneby's Case* was misplaced.

... [Petitioners] note that as a formal matter the absence of the heat of passion on sudden provocation is not a "fact necessary to constitute the crime" of felonious homicide in Maine. *In re Winship,* 397 U.S. at 364. . . . This distinction is relevant according to petitioners, because in *Winship* the facts at issue were essential to establish criminality in the first instance whereas the fact in question here does not come into play until the jury already has determined that the defendant is guilty and may be punished at least for manslaughter. In this situation, petitioners maintain, the defendant's critical interests in liberty and reputation are no longer of paramount concern since, irrespective of the presence or absence of the heat of passion on sudden provocation, he is likely to lose his liberty and certain to be stigmatized.[23] In short, petitioners would limit *Winship* to those facts which, if not proved, would wholly exonerate the defendant.

This analysis fails to recognize that the criminal law of Maine, like that of other jurisdictions, is concerned not only with guilt or innocence in the abstract but also with the degree of criminal culpability. Maine has chosen to distinguish those who kill in the heat of passion from those who kill in the absence of this factor. Because the former are less "blameworth[y]," *State v. Lafferty,* 309 A.2d, at 671, 673 (concurring opinion), they are subject to substantially less severe penalties. By drawing this distinction, while refusing to require the prosecution to establish beyond a reasonable doubt the fact upon which it turns, Maine denigrates the interests found critical in *Winship*.

The safeguards of due process are not rendered unavailing simply because a determination may already have been reached that would stigmatize the defendant and that might lead to a significant impairment of personal liberty. The fact remains that the consequences resulting from a verdict of murder, as compared with a verdict of manslaughter, differ significantly. Indeed, when viewed in terms of the potential difference in restrictions of personal liberty attendant to each conviction, the distinction established by Maine between murder and manslaughter may be of greater importance than the difference between guilt or innocence for many lesser crimes.

Moreover, if *Winship* were limited to those facts that constitute a crime as defined by state law, a State could undermine many of the interests that decision sought to protect without effecting any substantive change in its law. It would only be necessary to redefine the elements that comprise different crimes, characterizing them as factors that bear solely on the extent of punishment. An extreme example of this approach can be fashioned from the law challenged in this case. Maine divides the single generic offense of felonious homicide into three distinct punishment categories—murder, voluntary

---

[23] [P]etitioners seek to buttress this contention by arguing that since the presence or absence of the heat of passion on sudden provocation affects only the extent of punishment it should be considered a matter within the traditional discretion of the sentencing body and therefore not subject to rigorous due process demands. But cf. *United States v. Tucker,* 404 U.S. 443, (1972). There is no incompatibility between our decision today and the traditional discretion afforded sentencing bodies. Under Maine law the jury is given no discretion as to the sentence to be imposed on one found guilty of felonious homicide. If the defendant is found to be a murderer, a mandatory life sentence results. On the other hand, if the jury finds him guilty only of manslaughter it remains for the trial court in the exercise of its discretion to impose a sentence within the statutorily defined limits.

manslaughter, and involuntary manslaughter. Only the first two of these categories require that the homicidal act either be intentional or the result of criminally reckless conduct. . . . But under Maine law these facts of intent are not general elements of the crime of felonious homicide. . . . Instead, they bear only on the appropriate punishment category. Thus, if petitioners' argument were accepted, Maine could impose a life sentence for any felonious homicide—even those that traditionally might be considered involuntary manslaughter—unless the defendant was able to prove that his act was neither intentional nor criminally reckless.[24]

* * *

. . . These interests are implicated to a greater degree in this case than they were in *Winship* itself. Petitioner there faced an 18-month sentence, with a maximum possible extension of an additional four and one-half years, whereas respondent here faces a differential in sentencing ranging from a nominal fine to a mandatory life sentence. Both the stigma to the defendant and the community's confidence in the administration of the criminal law are also of greater consequence in this case,[27] since the adjudication of delinquency involved in *Winship* was "benevolent" in intention, seeking to provide "a generously conceived program of compassionate treatment." *In re Winship*, 397 U.S. at 376. (Burger, J. dissenting).

Not only are the interests underlying *Winship* implicated to a greater degree in this case, but in one respect the protection afforded those interests is less here. In *Winship* the ultimate burden of persuasion remained with the prosecution, although the standard had been reduced to proof by a fair preponderance of the evidence. In this case, by contrast, the State has affirmatively shifted the burden of proof to the defendant. The result, in a case such as this one where the defendant is required to prove the critical fact in dispute, is to increase further the likelihood of an erroneous murder conviction. . . .

It has been suggested that because of the difficulties in negating an argument that the homicide was committed in the heat of passion the burden of proving this fact should rest on the defendant. No doubt this is often a heavy burden for the prosecution to satisfy. The same may be said of the requirement of proof beyond a reasonable doubt of many controverted facts in a criminal trial. But this is the traditional burden which our system of criminal justice deems essential.

. . . [T]he Maine Supreme Judicial Court itself acknowledged that most States require the prosecution to prove the absence of passion beyond a reasonable doubt. *State v. Wilbur,* 278 A.2d, at 146.[28] In this respect, proving

---

[24] Many states impose different statutory sentences on different degrees of assault. If *Winship* were limited to a State's definition of the elements of a crime, these states could define all assaults as a single offense and then require the defendant to disprove the elements of aggravation—*e.g.,* intent to kill or intent to rob. But see *State v. Ferris,* 249 A.2d 523 (Me. 1969) (prosecution must prove elements of aggravation in a criminal assault case by proof beyond a reasonable doubt)

[27] "The penalty authorized by the law of the locality may be taken" as a gauge of its social and ethical judgments.

[28] See Note, 38 Mo. L. Rev. 105 (1973). Many states do require the defendant to show that

that the defendant did not act in the heat of passion on sudden provocation is similar to proving any other element of intent; it may be established by adducing evidence of the factual circumstances surrounding the commission of the homicide. And although intent is typically considered a fact peculiarly within the knowledge of the defendant, this does not, as the Court has long recognized, justify shifting the burden to him. . . .

Nor is the requirement of proving a negative unique in our system of criminal jurisprudence. Maine itself requires the prosecution to prove the absence of self-defense beyond a reasonable doubt. Satisfying this burden imposes an obligation that, in all practical effect, is identical to the burden involved in negating the heat of passion on sudden provocation. Thus, we discern no unique hardship on the prosecution that would justify requiring the defendant to carry the burden of proving a fact so critical to criminal culpability.[31]

Maine law requires a defendant to establish by a preponderance of the evidence that he acted in the heat of passion on sudden provocation in order to reduce murder to manslaughter. Under this burden of proof a defendant can be given a life sentence when the evidence indicates that it is as likely as not that he deserves a significantly lesser sentence. This is an intolerable result in a society where, to paraphrase Mr. Justice Harlan, it is far worse to sentence one guilty only of manslaughter as a murderer than to sentence a murderer for the lesser crime of manslaughter . . . We therefore hold that the Due Process Clause requires the prosecution to prove beyond a reasonable doubt the absence of the heat of passion on sudden provocation when the issue is properly presented in a homicide case. Accordingly, the judgment below is *affirmed.*

---

there is "some evidence" indicating that he acted in the heat of passion before requiring the prosecution to negate this element by proving the absence of passion beyond a reasonable doubt. . . . Nothing in this opinion is intended to affect that requirement.

[31] This conclusion is supported by consideration of a related line of cases. Generally in a criminal case the prosecution bears both the production burden and the persuasion burden. In some instances, however, it is aided by a presumption, see *Davis v. United States,* 160 U.S. 469 (1895) (presumption of sanity), or a permissible inference, see *United States v. Gainey,* 380 U.S. 63 (1965) (inference of knowledge from presence at an illegal still). These procedural devices require (in the case of a presumption) or permit (in the case of an inference) the trier of fact to conclude that the prosecution has met its burden of proof with respect to the presumed or inferred fact by having satisfactorily established other facts. Thus, in effect they require the defendant to present some evidence contesting the otherwise presumed or inferred fact. . . . Since they shift the production burden to the defendant, these devices must satisfy certain due process requirements. . .

  In each of these cases, however, the ultimate burden of persuasion by proof beyond a reasonable doubt remained on the prosecution. . . . Shifting the burden of persuasion to the defendant obviously places an even greater strain upon him since he no longer need only present some evidence with respect to the fact at issue; he must affirmatively establish that fact. Accordingly, the Due Process Clause demands more exacting standards before the State may require a defendant to bear this ultimate burden of persuasion. . .

Mr. Justice REHNQUIST, with whom THE CHIEF JUSTICE joins, *concurring.*

* * *

I agree with the Court that *In re Winship* does require that the prosecution prove beyond a reasonable doubt every element which constitutes the crime charged against a defendant. I see no inconsistency between that holding and the holding of *Leland v. Oregon,* 343 U.S. 790 (1952). In the latter case this Court held that there was no constitutional requirement that the State shoulder the burden of proving the sanity of the defendant.

The Court noted in *Leland* that the issue of insanity as a defense to a criminal charge was considered by the jury only after it had found that all elements of the offense, including the *mens rea* if any required by state law, had been proven beyond a reasonable doubt. *Id.* at 792, 795. Although as the state court's instructions in *Leland* recognized, *Id.* at 794–97, evidence relevant to insanity as defined by state law may also be relevant to whether the required *mens rea* was present, the existence or nonexistence of legal insanity bears no necessary relationship to the existence or nonexistence of the required mental elements of the crime. For this reason, Oregon's placement of the burden of proof of insanity on *Leland,* unlike Maine's redefinition of homicide in the instant case, did not effect an unconstitutional shift in the State's traditional burden of proof beyond a reasonable doubt of all necessary elements of the offense. . . . Both the Court's opinion and the concurring opinion of Mr. Justice Harlan in *In re Winship, supra,* stress the importance of proof beyond a reasonable doubt in a criminal case as "bottomed on a fundamental value determination of our society that it is far worse to convict any innocent man than to let a guilty man go free." 397 U.S. 358, 372 (Harlan, J., concurring). Having once met that rigorous burden of proof that, for example, in a case such as this, the defendant not only killed a fellow human being, but did it with malice aforethought, the State could quite consistently with such a constitutional principle conclude that a defendant who sought to establish the defense of insanity, and thereby escape any punishment whatever for a heinous crime, should bear the laboring oar on such an issue.

NOTES AND QUESTIONS

1. Could a state, after *Mullaney,* simply eliminate "heat of passion" as relevant in homicide? After the *Mullaney* decision, the Maine legislature temporarily rewrote its homicide statutes, defining six degrees of "criminal homicide." Rubin, *Homicide,* 28 Maine L. Rev. 57 (1976). No reference to murder or malice aforethought was retained. The legislature did, however, adopt the "extreme mental or emotional disturbance" language involved in *Patterson,* below. The burden was clearly placed on the defendant to prove such disturbance.

2. Note that in footnote 28 of *Mullaney* the Court leaves open the question of whether the state may put the burden of *production* on the defendant. What criteria might be used in determining under what conditions this would be

permissible? Many states require the defendant to notify the pro-secution if he intends to rely on either an alibi defense or an insanity defense. This is not the sameas requiring defendant to meet the burden of production. What factors would be relevant here?

PATTERSON v. NEW YORK

Supreme Court of the United States

432 U.S. 197 (1977)

Mr. Justice WHITE *delivered the opinion of the Court.*

The question here is the constitutionality under the Fourteenth Amendment's Due Process Clause of burdening the defendant in a New York State murder trial with proving the affirmative defense of extreme emotional disturbance as defined by New York law.

I

After a brief and unstable marriage, the appellant, Gordon Patterson, Jr., became estranged from his wife, Roberta. Roberta resumed an association with John Northrup, a neighbor to whom she had been engaged prior to her marriage to appellant. On December 27, 1970, Patterson borrowed a rifle from an acquaintance and went to the residence of his father-in-law. There, he observed his wife through a window in a state of semiundress in the presence of John Northrup. He entered the house and killed Northrup by shooting him twice in the head.

Patterson was charged with second-degree murder. In New York there are two elements of this crime: (1) "intent to cause the death of another person;" and (2) "caus[ing] the death of such person or of a third person." N.Y. Penal Law § 125.25 (McKinney 1975). Malice aforethought is not an element of the crime. In addition, the State permits a person accused of murder to raise an affirmative defense that he "acted under the influence of extreme emotional disturbance for which there was a reasonable explanation or excuse."[2]

New York also recognizes the crime of manslaughter. A person is guilty of manslaughter if he intentionally kills another person "under circumstances which do not constitute murder because he acts under the influence of extreme

---

[2] Section 125.25 provides in relevant part:

A person is guilty of murder in the second degree when:

1. With intent to cause the death of another person, he causes the death of such person or of a third person; except that in any prosecution under his subdivision, it is an affirmative defense that: (a)The defendant acted under the influence of extreme emotional disturbance for which there was a reasonable explanation or excuse, the reasonableness of which is to be determined from the viewpoint of a person in the defendant's situation under the circumstances as the defendant believed them to be. Nothing contained in this paragraph shall constitute a defense to a prosecution for, or preclude a conviction of, manslaughter in the first degree or any other crime.

emotional disturbance."³ Appellant confessed before trial to killing Northrup, but at trial he raised the defense of extreme emotional disturbance.⁴

The jury was instructed as to the elements of the crime of murder. Focusing on the element of intent, the trial court charged:

> Before you, considering all of the evidence, can convict this defendant or anyone of murder, you must believe and decide that the People have established beyond reasonable doubt that he intended, in firing the gun, to kill either the victim himself or some other human being. . . .
>
> Always remember that you must not expect or require the defendant to prove to your satisfaction that his acts were done without the intent to kill. Whatever proof he may have attempted, however far he may have gone in an effort to convince you of his innocence or guiltlessness, he is not obliged, he is not obligated to prove anything. It is always the People's burden to prove his guilt, and to prove that he intended to kill in this instance beyond a reasonable doubt.⁵

The jury was further instructed, consistently with New York law, that the defendant had the burden of proving his affirmative defense by a preponderance of the evidence. The jury was told that if it found beyond a reasonable doubt that appellant had intentionally killed Northrup but that appellant had demonstrated by a preponderance of the evidence that he had acted under the influence of extreme emotional disturbance, it had to find appellant guilty of manslaughter instead of murder.

The jury found appellant guilty of murder. Judgment was entered on the verdict, and the Appellate Division affirmed. While appeal to the New York Court of Appeals was pending, this Court decided *Mullaney v. Wilbur,* 421 U.S. 684 (1975), in which the Court declared Maine's murder statute unconstitutional. Under the Maine statute, a person accused of murder could rebut the statutory presumption that he committed the offense with "malice aforethought" by proving that he acted in the heat of passion on sudden provocation. The Court held that this scheme improperly shifted the burden of

---

³ Section 125.20(2), N.Y. Penal Law § 125.20(2) (McKinney 1975), provides:

A person is guilty of manslaughter in the first degree when:

. . . With intent to cause the death of another person, he causes the death of such person or of a third person under circumstances which do not constitute murder because he acts under the influence of extreme emotional disturbance, as defined in paragraph (a) of subdivision one of section 125.25. The fact that homicide was committed under the influence of extreme emotional disturbance constitutes a mitigating circumstance reducing murder to manslaughter in the first degree and need not be proved in any prosecution initiated under this subdivision.

⁴ Appellant also contended at trial that the shooting was accidental and that therefore he had no intent to kill Northrup. It is here undisputed, however, that the prosecution proved beyond a reasonable doubt that the killing was intentional

⁵ The trial court's instructions to the jury focused emphatically and repeatedly on the prosecution's burden of proving guilt beyond a reasonable doubt.

> The burden of proving the guilt of a defendant beyond a reasonable doubt rests at all times upon the prosecution. A defendant is never obliged to prove his innocence.
>
> Before you can find a defendant guilty, you must be convinced that each and every element of the crime charged and his guilt has been established to your satisfction by reliable and credible evidence beyond a reasonable doubt

persuasion from the prosecutor to the defendant and was therefore a violation of due process. In the Court of Appeals appellant urged that New York's murder statute is functionally equivalent to the one struck down in *Mullaney* and that therefore his conviction should be reversed.

The Court of Appeals rejected appellant's argument, holding that the New York murder statute is consistent with due process. . . . The Court distinguished *Mullaney* on the ground that the New York statute involved no shifting of the burden to the defendant to disprove any fact essential to the offense charged since the New York affirmative defense of extreme emotional disturbance bears no direct relationship to any element of murder. This appeal ensued, and we noted probable jurisdiction. . . . We affirm.

II

It goes without saying that preventing and dealing with crime is much more the business of the States than it is of the Federal Government . . . and that we should not lightly construe the Constitution so as to intrude upon the administration of justice by the individual States. Among other things, it is normally "within the power of the State to regulate procedures under which its laws are carried out, including the burden of producing evidence and the burden of persuasion," and its decision in this regard is not subject to proscription under the Due Process Clause unless "it offends some principle of justice so rooted in the traditions and conscience of our people as to be ranked as fundamental.". . . *Leland v. Oregon,* 343 U.S. 790, 798 (1952). . .

In determining whether New York's allocation to the defendant of proving the mitigating circumstances of severe emotional disturbance is consistent with due process, it is therefore relevant to note that this defense is a considerably expanded version of the common-law defense of heat of passion on sudden provocation and that at common law the burden of proving the latter, as well as other affirmative defenses—indeed, "all . . . circumstances of justification, excuse or alleviation"—rested on the defendant. 4 W. Blackstone, Commentaries *201; M. Foster, Crown Law 255 (1762); *Mullaney v. Wilbur, supra,* at 693–694. This was the rule when the Fifth Amendment was adopted, and it was the American rule when the Fourteenth Amendment was ratified. *Commonwealth v. York,* 50 Mass. 93 (1845).[8]

III

We cannot conclude that Patterson's conviction under the New York law deprived him of due process of law. The crime of murder is defined by statute, which represents a recent revision of the state criminal code, as causing the death of another person with intent to do so. The death, the intent to kill, and causation are the facts that the State is required to prove beyond a reasonable doubt if a person is to be convicted of murder. No further facts are either presumed or inferred in order to constitute the crime. The statute does provide an affirmative defense—that the defendant acted under the

---

[8] *York,* which relied on American authorities dating back to the early 1800's, confirmed that the common-law and prevailing American view was that the burden was on the defendant to prove provocation. *York* is said to have governed a half century of American burden-of-proof decisions in provocation and self-defense cases.

influence of extreme emotional disturbance for which there was a reasonable explanation—which, if proved by a preponderance of the evidence, would reduce the crime to manslaughter, an offense defined in a separate section of the statute. It is plain enough that if the intentional killing is shown, the State intends to deal with the defendant as a murderer unless he demonstrates the mitigating circumstances.

Here, the jury was instructed in accordance with the statute, and the guilty verdict confirms that the State successfully carried its burden of proving the facts of the crime beyond a reasonable doubt. Nothing in the evidence, including any evidence that might have been offered with respect to Patterson's mental state at the time of the crime, raised a reasonable doubt about his guilt as a murderer; and clearly the evidence failed to convince the jury that Patterson's affirmative defense had been made out. It seems to us that the State satisfied the mandate of *Winship* that it prove beyond a reasonable doubt "every fact necessary to constitute the crime with which [Patterson was] charged.". . . .

In revising its criminal code, New York provided the affirmative defense of extreme emotional disturbance, a substantially expanded version of the older heat-of-passion concept; but it was willing to do so only if the facts making out the defense were established by the defendant with sufficient certainty. The State was itself unwilling to undertake to establish the absence of those facts beyond a reasonable doubt, perhaps fearing that proof would be too difficult and that too many persons deserving treatment as murderers would escape that punishment if the evidence need merely raise a reasonable doubt about the defendant's emotional state. It has been said that the new criminal code of New York contains some 25 affirmative defenses which exculpate or mitigate but which must be established by the defendant to be operative. The Due Process Clause, as we see it, does not put New York to the choice of abandoning those defenses or undertaking to disprove their existence in order to convict of a crime which otherwise is within its constitutional powers to sanction by substantial punishment.

The requirement of proof beyond a reasonable doubt in a criminal case is "bottomed on a fundamental value determination of our society that it is far worse to convict an innocent man than to let a guilty man go free."*Winship*, 397 U.S., at 372 (Harlan, J., concurring). The social cost of placing the burden on the prosecution to prove guilt beyond a reasonable doubt is thus an increased risk that the guilty will go free. While it is clear that our society has willingly chosen to bear a substantial burden in order to protect the innocent, it is equally clear that the risk it must bear is not without limits; and Mr. Justice Harlan's aphorism provides little guidance for determining what those limits are. Due process does not require that every conceivable step be taken, at whatever cost, to eliminate the possibility of convicting an innocent person. Punishment of those found guilty by a jury, for example, is not forbidden merely because there is a remote possibility in some instances that an innocent person might go to jail.

It is said that the common-law rule permits a State to punish one as a murderer when it is as likely as not that he acted in the heat of passion or under severe emotional distress and when, if he did, he is guilty only of manslaughter. But this has always been the case in those jurisdictions adhering to the traditional rule. It is also very likely true that fewer convictions of murder would occur if New York were required to negative the affirmative defense at issue here. But in each instance of a murder conviction under the present law, New York will have proved beyond a reasonable doubt that the defendant has intentionally killed another person, an act which it is not disputed the State may constitutionally criminalize and punish. If the State nevertheless chooses to recognize a factor that mitigates the degree of criminality or punishment, we think the State may assure itself that the fact has been established with reasonable certainty. To recognize at all a mitigating circumstance does not require the State to prove its nonexistence in each case in which the fact is put in issue, if in its judgment this would be too cumbersome, too expensive, and too inaccurate.

We thus decline to adopt as a constitutional imperative, operative countrywide, that a State must disprove beyond a reasonable doubt every fact constituting any and all affirmative defenses related to the culpability of an accused. Traditionally, due process has required that only the most basic procedural safeguards be observed; more subtle balancing of society's interests against those of the accused have been left to the legislative branch. We therefore will not disturb the balance struck in previous cases holding that the Due Process Clause requires the prosecution to prove beyond a reasonable doubt all of the elements included in the definition of the offense of which the defendant is charged. Proof of the non-existence of all affirmative defenses has never been constitutionally required; and we perceive no reason to fashion such a rule in this case and apply it to the statutory defense at issue here.

This view may seem to permit state legislatures to reallocate burdens of proof by labeling as affirmative defenses at least some elements of the crimes now defined in their statutes. But there are obviously constitutional limits beyond which the States may not go in this regard. "[I]t is not within the province of a legislature to declare an individual guilty or presumptively guilty of a crime." *McFarland v. American Sugar Rfg. Co.* 241 U.S. 79, 86 (1916). The legislature cannot "validly command that the finding of an indictment, or mere proof of the identity of the accused, should create a presumption of the existence of all the facts essential to guilt."*Tot v. United States,* 319 U.S. 463, 469 (1943). *Morrison v. California,* 291 U.S. 82 (1934), also makes the point with sufficient clarity.

Long before *Winship,* the universal rule in this country was that the prosecution must prove guilt beyond a reasonable doubt. At the same time, the long-accepted rule was that it was constitutionally permissible to provide that various affirmative defenses were to be proved by the defendant. This did not lead to such abuses or to such widespread redefinition of crime and reduction of the prosecution's burden that a new constitutional rule was required. This was not the problem to which *Winship* was addressed. Nor does the fact that a majority of the States have now assumed the burden of disproving affirmative defenses—for whatever reasons—mean that those States that strike a different balance are in violation of the Constitution.[13]

---

[13] As Chief Judge Breitel cogently stated in concurring in the judgment and opinion below:

A preliminary caveat is indicated. It would be an abuse of affirmative defenses, as it would

IV

It is urged that *Mullaney v. Wilbur* necessarily invalidates Patterson's conviction. In Mullaney the charge was murder, which, the Maine statute defined as the unlawful killing of a human being "with malice aforethought, either express or implied." The trial court instructed the jury that the words "malice aforethought" were most important because "malice aforethought is an essential and indispensable element of the crime of murder." Malice, as the statute indicated and as the court instructed, could be implied and was to be implied from "any deliberate, cruel act committed by one person against another suddenly... or without a considerable provocation," in which event an intentional killing was murder unless by a preponderance of the evidence it was shown that the act was committed "in the heat of passion, on sudden provocation." The instructions emphasized that " 'malice aforethought and heat of passion on sudden provocation are two inconsistent things; thus, by proving the latter the defendant would negate the former." . . .

Mullaney's holding, it is argued, is that the State may not permit the blameworthiness of an act or the severity of punishment authorized for its commission to depend on the presence or absence of an identified fact without assuming the burden of proving the presence of absence of that fact, as the

---

be of presumptions in the criminal law, if the purpose or effect were to unhinge the procedural presumption of innocence which historically and constitutionally shields one charged with crime. Indeed, a by-product of such abuse might well be also to undermine the privilege against self-incrimination by in effect forcing a defendant in a criminal action to testify in his own behalf. Nevertheless, although one should guard against such abuses, it may be misguided, out of excess caution, to forestall or discourage the use of affirmative defenses, where defendant may have the burden of proof but no greater than by a preponderance of the evidence. In the absence of affirmative defenses the impulse to legislators, especially in periods of concern about the rise of crime, would be to define particular crimes in unqualifiedly general terms, and leave only to sentence the adjustment between offenses of lesser and greater degree. In times when there is also a retrogressive impulse in legislation to restrain courts by mandatory sentences, the evil would be compounded.

The affirmative defense, intelligently used, permits the gradation of offenses at the earlier states of prosecution and certainly at the trial, and thus offers the opportunity to a defendant to allege or prove, if he can, the distinction between the offense charged and the mitigating circumstances which should ameliorate the degree or kind of offense. The instant homicide case is a good example. Absent the affirmative defense, the crime of murder or manslaughter could legislatively be defined simply to require an intent to kill, unaffected by the spontaneity with which that intent is formed or the provocative or mitigating circumstances which should legally or morally lower the grade of crime. The placing of the burden of proof on the defense, with a lower threshold, however, is fair because of defendant's knowledge or access to the evidence other than his own on the issue. To require the prosecution to negative the "element" of mitigating circumstances is generally unfair, especially since the conclusion that the negative of the circumstances is necessarily a product of definitional and therefore circular reasoning, and is easily avoided by the likely legislative practice mentioned earlier.

* * *

In sum, the appropriate use of affirmative defenses enlarges the ameliorative aspects of a statutory scheme for the punishment of crime, rather than the other way around—a shift from primitive mechanical classifications based on the bare antisocial act and its consequences, rather than on the nature of the offender and the conditions which produce some degree of excuse for his conduct, is the mark of an advanced criminology.

39 N.Y.2d 288, 305–307, 347 N.E.2d 898, 909–10 (1976).

case may be, beyond a reasonable doubt.[15] In our view, the *Mullaney* holding should not be so broadly read. The concurrence of two Justices in *Mullaney* was necessarily contrary to such a reading. . . .

Mullaney surely held that a State must prove every ingredient of an offense beyond a reasonable doubt, and that it may not shift the burden of proof to the defendant by presuming that ingredient upon proof of the other elements of the offense. This is true even though the State's practice, as in Maine, had been traditionally to the contrary. Such shifting of the burden of persuasion with respect to a fact which the State deems so important that it must be either proved or presumed is impermissible under the Due Process Clause.

It was unnecessary to go further in *Mullaney*. The Maine Supreme Judicial Court made it clear that malice aforethought, which was mentioned in the statutory definition of the crime, was not equivalent to premeditation and that the presumption of malice traditionally arising in intentional homicide cases carried no factual meaning insofar as premeditation was concerned. Even so, a killing became murder in Maine when it resulted from a deliberate, cruel act committed by one person against another, "suddenly without any, or without a considerable provocation." *State v. Lafferty* [309 A.2d 647, 665 (1973)]. Premeditation was not within the definition of murder; but malice, in the sense of absence of provocation, was part of the definition of that crime. Yet malice, *i.e.,* lack of provocation, was presumed be rebutted by the defendant only by proving by a preponderance of the evidence that he acted with heat of passion upon sudden provocation. In *Mullaney* we held that however traditional this mode of proceeding might have been, it is contrary to the Due Process Clause as construed in *Winship*.

As we have explained, nothing was presumed or implied against Patterson; and his conviction is not invalid under any of our prior cases. The judgment of the New York Court of Appeals is

Affirmed.

Mr. Justice Rehnquist took no part in the consideration or decision of this case.

Mr. Justice POWELL, with whom Mr. Justice BRENNAN and Mr. Justice MARSALL join, *dissenting.* . . .

---

[15] There is some language in *Mullaney* that has been understood as perhaps construing the Due Process Clause to require the prosecution to prove beyond a reasonable doubt any fact affecting "the degree of criminal culpability." See, *e.g,* Note, *Affirmative Defenses after Mullaney v. Wilbur: New York's Extreme Emotional Disturbance,* 43 Brooklyn L Rev. 171 (1976); Note, *Affirmative Defenses in Ohio After Mullaney v. Wilbur,* 36 Ohio St. L.J. 828 (1975); Comment, *Unburdening the Criminal Defendant: Mullaney v. Wilbur and the Reasonable Doubt Standard,* 11 Harv. Civ. Rights—Civ. Lib. L. Rev. 390 (1976). It is said that such a rule would deprive legislatures of any discretion whatsoever in allocating the burden of proof, the practical effect of which might be to undermine legislative reform of our criminal justice system. See Part II, *supra.* Carried to its logical extreme, such a reading of *Mullaney* might also, for example, discourage Congress from enacting pending legislation to change the felony-murder rule by permitting the accused to prove by a preponderance of the evidence the affirmative defense that the homicide committed was neither a necessary nor a reasonably foreseeable consequence of the underlying felony. See Senate Bill § 1, 94th Cong., 1st Sess., 118 (1975). The Court did not intend *Mullaney* to have such far-reaching effect

Mullaney held invalid Maine's requirement that the defendant prove heat of passion. The Court today, without disavowing the unanimous holding of *Mullaney,* approves New York's requirement that the defendant prove extreme emotional disturbance. The Court manages to run a constitutional boundary line through the barely visible space that separates Maine's law from New York's. It does so on the basis of distinctions in language that are formalistic rather than substantive.

This result is achieved by a narrowly literal parsing of the holding in *Winship:* "[T]he Due Process Clause protects the accused against conviction except upon proof beyond a reasonable doubt of every fact necessary to constitute the crime with which he is charged." 397 U.S., at 364. . . . The only "facts" necessary to constitute a crime are said to be those that appear on the face of the statute as a part of the definition of the crime. Maine's statute was invalid, the Court reasons, because it "defined [murder] as the unlawful killing of a human being with malice aforethought, either express or implied.". . . "[M]alice," the Court reiterates, "in the sense of the absence of provocation, was part of the definition of that crime.". . . *Winship* was violated only because this "fact"—malice—was "presumed" unless the defendant persuaded the jury otherwise by showing that he acted in the heat of passion. New York, in form presuming no affirmative "fact" against Patterson, and blessed with a statute drafted in the leaner language of the 20th century, escapes constitutional scrutiny unscathed even though the effect on the defendant of New York's placement of the burden of persuasion is exactly the same as Maine's. . . .

This explanation of the *Mullaney* holding bears little resemblance to the basic rationale of that decision. But this is not the cause of greatest concern. The test the Court today establishes allows a legislature to shift, virtually at will, the burden of persuasion with respect to any factor in a criminal case, so long as it is careful not to mention the nonexistence of that factor in the statutory language that defines the crime. The sole requirement is that any references to the factor be confined to those sections that provide for an affirmative defense. . . .

With all respect, this type of constitutional adjudication is indefensibly formalistic. A limited but significant check on possible abuses in the criminal law now becomes an exercise in arid formalities. What *Winship* and *Mullaney* had sought to teach about the limits a free society places on its procedures to safeguard the liberty of its citizens becomes a rather simplistic lesson in statutory draftsmanship. Nothing in the Court's opinion prevents a legislature from applying this new learning to many of the classical elements of the crimes it punishes.[8] It would be preferable, if the Court has found reason to reject

---

[8] For example, a state statute could pass muster under the only solid standard that appears in the Court's opinion if it defined murder as mere physical contact between the defendant and the victim leading to the victim's death, but then set up an affirmative defense leaving it to the defendant to prove that he acted without culpable *mens rea.* The State, in other words, could be relieved altogether of responsibility for proving anything regarding the defendant's state of mind, provided only that the face of the statute meets the Court's drafting formulas.

To be sure, it is unlikely that legislatures will rewrite their criminal laws in this extreme form. The Court seems to think this likelihood of restraint is an added reason for limiting review largely to formalistic examination. . . . But it is completely foreign to this Court's responsibility for constitutional adjudication to limit the scope of judicial review because of the expectation—however reasonable—that legislative bodies will exercise appropriate restraint.

the rationale of *Winship* and *Mullaney,* simply and straightforwardly to overrule those precedents.

The Court understandably manifests some uneasiness that its formalistic approach will give legislatures too much latitude in shifting the burden of persuasion. And so it issues a warning that "there are obviously constitutional limits beyond which the States may not go in this regard." . . . The Court thereby concedes that legislative abuses may occur and that they must be curbed by the judicial branch. But if the State is careful to conform to the drafting formulas articulated today, the constitutional limits are anything but "obvious." This decision simply leaves us without a conceptual framework for distinguishing abuses from legitimate legislative adjustments of the burden of persuasion in criminal cases.

II

It is unnecessary for the Court to retreat to a formalistic test for applying *Winship.* Careful attention to the *Mullaney* decision reveals the principles that should control in this and like cases. *Winship* held that the prosecution must bear the burden of proving beyond a reasonable doubt "the existence of every fact necessary to constitute the crime charged.". . . In *Mullaney* we concluded that heat of passion was one of the "facts" described in *Winship*—that is, a factor as to which the prosecution must bear the burden of persuasion beyond a reasonable doubt. . . . We reached that result only after making two careful inquiries. First, we noted that the presence or absence of heat of passion made a substantial difference in punishment of the offender and in the stigma associated with the conviction. . . . Second, we reviewed the history, in England and this country, of the factor at issue. . . . Central to the holding in *Mullaney* was our conclusion that heat of passion "has been, almost from the inception of the common law of homicide, the single most important factor in determining the degree of culpability attaching to an unlawful homicide."

Implicit in these two inquiries are the principles that should govern this case. The Due Process Clause requires that the prosecutor bear the burden of persuasion beyond a reasonable doubt only if the factor at issue makes a substantial difference in punishment and stigma. The requirement of course applies *a fortiori* if the factor makes the difference between guilt and innocence. But a substantial difference in punishment alone is not enough. It also must be shown that in the Anglo-American legal tradition the factor in question historically has held that level of importance. If either branch of the test is not met, then the legislature retains its traditional authority over matters of proof. But to permit a shift in the burden of persuasion when both branches of this test are satisfied would invite the undermining of the presumption of innocence, "that bedrock —axiomatic and elementary' principle whose —enforcement lies at the foundation of the administration of our criminal law. . . . ' "

III

The Court beats its retreat from *Winship* apparently because of a concern that otherwise the federal judiciary will intrude too far into substantive choices concerning the content of a State's criminal law. The concern is legitimate . . . but misplaced. *Winship* and *Mullaney* are no more than what they purport to be: decisions addressing the procedural requirements that States must meet to comply with due process. They are not outposts for policing the substantive boundaries of the criminal law.

The *Winship/Mullaney* test identifies those factors of such importance, historically, in determining punishment and stigma that the Constitution forbids shifting to the defendant the burden of persuasion when such a factor is at issue. *Winship* and *Mullaney* specify only the procedure that is required when a State elects to use such a factor as part of its substantive criminal law. They do not say that the State must elect to use it. For example, where a State has chosen to retain the traditional distinction between murder and manslaughter, as have New York and Maine, the burden of persuasion must remain on the prosecution with respect to the distinguishing factor, in view of its decisive historical importance. But nothing in *Mullaney* or *Winship* precludes a State from abolishing the distinction between murder and manslaughter and treating all unjustifiable homicide as murder. In this significant respect, neither *Winship* nor *Mullaney* eliminates the substantive flexibility that should remain in legislative hands.

Moreover, it is unlikely that more than a few factors—although important ones—for which a shift in the burden of persuasion seriously would be considered will come within the *Mullaney* holding. With some exceptions, then, the State has the authority "to recognize a factor that mitigates the degree of criminality or punishment" without having "to prove its nonexistence in each case in which the fact is put in issue." . . . New ameliorative affirmative defenses, about which the Court expresses concern, generally remain undisturbed by the holdings in *Winship* and *Mullaney*—and need not be disturbed by a sound holding reversing Patterson's conviction.[15]

Furthermore, as we indicated in *Mullaney* . . . even as to those factors upon which the prosecution must bear the burden of persuasion, the State retains an important procedural device to avoid jury confusion and prevent the prosecution from being unduly hampered. The State normally may shift to the defendant the burden of production,[16] that is, the burden of going forward

---

[15] Numerous examples of such defenses are available: New York subjects an armed robber to lesser punishment than he would otherwise receive if he proves by a preponderance of the evidence that the gun he used was unloaded or inoperative. N.Y. Penal Law § 160.15 (McKinney 1975). A number of States have ameliorated the usual operation of statutes punishing statutory rape, recognizing a defense if the defendant shows that he reasonably believed his partner was of age. *E.g.,* Ky. Rev. Stat. Ann. § § 500.070, 510.030 (1975); Wash. Rev. Code Ann. § 9.79.160(2) (Supp. 1975). Formerly the age of the minor was a strict-liability element of the crime. The Model Penal Code also employs such a shift in the burden of persuasion for a limited number of defenses. For example, a corporation can escape conviction of an offense if it proves by preponderance of the evidence that the responsible supervising officer exercised due diligence to prevent the commission of the offense. § 2.07(5) (Proposed Official Draft 1962).

[16] There are outer limits on shifting the burden of production to a defendant, limits articulated in a long line of cases in this Court passing on the validity of presumption. Most important are the "rational connection" requirement of *Mobile, J. & K. C.R. v. Turnipseed,* 219 U.S. 35, 43 (1910) . . . and also the "comparative convenience" criterion of *Morrison v. California,* 291 U.S. 82 (1934). Caution is appropriate, however, in generalizing about the application of any of these cases to a given procedural device, since the term "presumption" covers a broad range of procedural mechanisms having significant different consequences for the defendant.

with sufficient evidence "to justify [a reasonable] doubt upon the issue." ALI, Model Penal Code § 1.13, Comment, p.110 (Tent. Draft No. 4, 1955). If the defendant's evidence does not cross this threshold, the issue—be it malice, extreme emotional disturbance, self-defense, or whatever—will not be submitted to the jury. . . .

To be sure, there will be many instances when the *Winship/Mullaney* test as I perceive it will be more difficult to apply than the Court's formula. Where I see the need for a careful and discriminating review of history, the Court finds a bright-line standard that can be applied with a quick glance at the face of the statute. But this facile test invites tinkering with the procedural safeguards of the presumption of innocence, and invitation to disregard the principles of *Winship* that I would not extend.

NOTES AND QUESTIONS

1. Suppose a New York defendant, after *Patterson*, wishes to raise, as a defense, that his killing, while within the extreme mental or emotional disturbance language of the New York statute, was also committed under the narrower concept of "heat of passion." Does *Patterson* or *Mullaney* apply? If *Patterson* applies, does this mean that can the state simply shift the burden of proof by redefining or even simply renaming the defense?

2. Robinson, *Criminal Law Defenses: A Systematic Analysis,* 82 Colum. L Rev. 199, 234 (1982):

> Recently, the failure of proof/offense modification distinction has taken on constitutional significance with far-reaching practical implications. In *Patterson v. New York,* the Supreme Court adopted this distinction as the most significant characteristic of the dividing line between those issues for which the state may shift the burden of persuasion to the defendant and those for which it may not. In *Mullaney v. Wilbur* the Court had required that the state of Maine carry the burden of persuasion for the provocation defense. But in *Patterson* it held that New York was permitted to shift this burden to defendants asserting extreme emotional disturbance even though, like provocation, this defense operated to reduce murder to manslaughter under similar, albeit broader, conditions. The Court considered it critical that in *Mullaney* the provocation instructions "emphasized that 'malice aforethought and heat of passion on sudden provocation are two inconsistent things' . . . ; thus, by proving the latter the defendant would negate the former." In other words, provocation was a failure of proof defense that simply negated a required element.

3. Iowa, among other states, makes sale of narcotics a serious offense, but allows a defendant to show that his sale was not for profit, but merely an "accommodation" of a friend, and so on, drastically reducing the seriousness of the offense. In *State v. Monroe,* 236 N.W.2d 24 (Iowa 1975), the court held that *Mullaney* required the state to carry the burden of proof. Would a different result now be required or at least allowable under *Patterson?*

4. As might be expected, there is a rich literature on *Mullaney, Patterson,* and the problems they pose. See, *e.g.,* Allen, *The Restoration of In re Winship:*

A Comment on Burdens of Persuasion in Criminal Cases after Patterson v. New York, 76 Mich. L. Rev. 30 (1977); Tushnet, *Constitutional Limitations of Substantive Criminal Law: An Examination of the Meaning of Mullaney v. Wilbur,* 55 B.U. L. Rev. 775 (1975); Underwood, *The Thumb on the Scales of Justice: Burdens of Persuasion in Criminal Cases,* 86 Yale L.J. 1299 (1977).

McMillan v. Pennsylvania

Supreme Court of the United States

477 U.S. 79 (1986)

Justice REHNQUIST *delivered the opinion of the Court.*

We granted certiorari to consider the constitutionality, under the Due Process Clause of the Fourteenth Amendment and the jury trial guarantee of the Sixth Amendment, of Pennsylvania's Mandatory Minimum Sentencing Act, 42 Pa. Const. Stat. sec. 9712 (1982) (the Act).

The Act was adopted in 1982. It provides that anyone convicted of certain enumerated felonies is subject to a mandatory minimum sentence of five years' imprisonment if the sentencing judge finds, by a preponderance of the evidence, that the person "visibly possessed a firearm" during the commission of the offense. At the sentencing hearing, the judge is directed to consider the evidence introduced at trial and any additional evidence offered by either the defendant or the Commonwealth. . . .

In each case the Commonwealth gave notice that at sentencing it would seek to proceed under the Act. No sec. 9712 hearing was held, however, because each of the sentencing judges before whom petitioners appeared found the Act unconstitutional; each imposed a lesser sentence than that required by the Act.

The Commonwealth appealed all four cases to the Supreme Court of Pennsylvania. That Court consolidated the appeals and unanimously concluded that the Act is consistent with due process. . . . Petitioners' principal argument was that visible possession of a firearm is an element of the crimes for which they were being sentenced and thus must be proved beyond a reasonable doubt under *In re Winship* and *Mullaney v. Wilbur*. . . . After observing that the legislature had expressly provided that visible possession "shall not be an element of the crime," sec. 9712(b), and that the reasonable doubt standard " 'has always been dependent on how a state defines the offense' " in question, . . . the Court rejected the claim that the Act effectively creates a new set of upgraded felonies of which visible possession is an "element." Section 9712, which comes into play only after the defendant has been convicted of an enumerated felony, neither provides for an increase in the maximum sentence for such felony nor authorizes a separate sentence; it merely requires a minimum sentence of five years, which may be more or less than the minimum sentence that might otherwise have been imposed. And consistent with *Winship, Mullaney,* and *Patterson,* the Act "creates no presumption as to any essential fact and places no burden on the defendant;" it "in no way relieve[s] the prosecution of its burden of proving guilt." . . .

Petitioners argue that under the Due Process Clause as interpreted in *Winship* and *Mullaney,* if a State wants to punish visible possession of a firearm it must undertake the burden of proving that fact beyond a reasonable doubt. We disagree. *Winship* held that "the Due Process Clause protects the accused against conviction except upon proof beyond a reasonable doubt of every fact necessary to constitute the crime with which he is charged.". . . In *Mullaney* we held that the Due Process Clause requires the prosecution to prove beyond a reasonable doubt the absence of the heat of passion on sudden provocation when the issue is properly presented in a homicide case.". . . But in *Patterson* . . . we rejected the claim that whenever a State links the "severity of punishment" to "the presence or absence of an identified fact" the State must prove that fact beyond a reasonable doubt.

Patterson stressed that in determining what facts must be proved beyond a reasonable doubt the state legislature's definition of the elements of the offense is usually dispositive: "[T]he Due Process Clause requires the prosecution to prove beyond a reasonable doubt all of the elements *included in the definition of the offence* of which the defendant is charged." . . .

We believe that the present case is controlled by *Patterson,* our most recent pronouncement on this subject, rather than by *Mullaney.* As the Supreme Court of Pennsylvania observed, the Pennsylvania legislature has expressly provided that visible possession of a firearm is not an element of the crimes enumerated in the mandatory sentencing statute, sec. 9712(b), but instead is a sentencing factor that comes into play only after the defendant has been found guilty of one of those crimes beyond a reasonable doubt. Indeed, the elements of the enumerated offenses, like the maximum permissible penalties for those offenses, were established long before the Mandatory Minimum Sentencing Act was passed. While visible possession might well have been included as an element of the enumerated offenses, Pennsylvania chose not to redefine those offenses in order to so include it, and Patterson teaches that we should hesitate to conclude that due process bars the State from pursuing its chosen course in the area of defining crimes and prescribing penalties.

As *Patterson* recognized, of course, there are constitutional limits to the State's power in this regard; in certain limited circumstances *Winship's* reasonable doubt requirement applies to facts not formally identified as elements of the offense charged. Petitioners argue that Pennsylvania has gone beyond those limits and that its formal provision that visible possession is not an element of the crime is therefore of no effect. We do not think so. While we have never attempted to define precisely the constitutional limits noted in Patterson, the extent to which due process forbids the reallocation or reduction of burdens of proof in criminal cases, and do not do so today, we are persuaded by several factors that Pennsylvania's Mandatory Minimum Sentencing Act does not exceed those limits.

We note first that the Act plainly does not transgress the limits expressly set out in *Patterson.* Responding to the concern that its rule would permit States unbridled power to redefine crimes to the detriment of criminal defendants, the *Patterson* Court advanced the unremarkable proposition that the Due Process Clause precludes States from discarding the presumption of innocence:

[I]t is not within the province of a legislature to declare an individual guilty or presumptively guilty of a crime. . . .

Here, of course, the Act creates no presumptions of the sort condemned in *McFarland v. American Sugar Rfg. Co.,* 241 U.S. 79 (1916), . . . or *Tot v. United States,* 319 U.S. 463. . . . Nor does it relieve the prosecution of its burden of proving guilt; Sec. 9712 only becomes applicable after a defendant has been duly convicted of the crime for which he is to be punished.

The Court in *Mullaney* observed, with respect to the main criminal statute invalidated in that case, that once the State proved the elements which Maine required it to prove beyond a reasonable doubt the defendant faced "a differential in sentencing ranging from a nominal fine to a mandatory life sentence." . . . In the present case the situation is quite different. Of the offenses enumerated in the Act, third-degree murder, robbery as defined in 18 Pa. Cons. Stat. sec. 3701(a)(1) (1981), kidnapping, rape, and involuntary deviate sexual intercourse are first-degree felonies subjecting the defendant to a maximum of 20 years' imprisonment. Sec. 1103(1). Voluntary manslaughter and aggravated assault as defined in sec. 2702(a)(1) are felonies of the second degree carrying a maximum sentence of 10 years. Sec. 1103(2). Section 9712 neither alters the maximum penalty for the crime committed nor creates a separate offense calling for a separate penalty; it operates solely to limit the sentencing court's discretion in selecting a penalty within the range already available to it without the special finding of visible possession of a firearm. Section 9712 "ups the ante" for the defendant only by raising to five years the minimum sentence which may be imposed within the statutory plan. The statute gives no impression of having been tailored to permit the visible possession finding to be a tail which wags the dog of the substantive offense. Petitioner's claim that visible possession under the Pennsylvania statute is "really" an element of the offenses for which they are being punished—that Pennsylvania has in effect defined a new set of upgraded felonies—would have at least more superficial appeal if a finding of visible possession exposed them to greater or additional punishment. Cf. 18 U.S.C. Sec. 2113(d) (providing separate and greater punishment for bank robberies accomplished through "use of a dangerous weapon ordevice"), but it does not.

[T]he specter raised by petitioners of States restructuring existing crimes in order to "evade" the commands of *Winship* just does not appear in this case. As noted above, sec. 9712's enumerated felonies retain the same elements they had before the Mandatory Minimum Sentencing Act was passed. The Pennsylvania legislature did not change the definition of any existing offense. It simply took one factor that has always been considered by sentencing courts to bear on punishment—the instrumentality used in committing a violent felony—and dictated the precise weight to be given that factor if the instrumentality is a firearm. Pennsylvania's decision to do so has not transformed against its will a sentencing factor into an "element" of some hypothetical "offense."

Petitioners [observe] . . . that many legislatures have made possession of a weapon an element of various aggravated offenses. But the fact that the States have formulated different statutory schemes to punish armed felons is merely a reflection of our federal system, which demands "[t]olerance for a spectrum of state procedures dealing with a common problem of law enforcement." . . . That Pennsylvania's particular approach has been adopted in few other States does not render Pennsylvania's choice unconstitutional. . . . Nor does the historical test advanced by the *Patterson* dissent, on which petitioners apparently also rely, materially advance their cause. While it is surely true that "[f]or hundreds of years some offenses have been considered more serious and the punishment made more severe if the offense was committed with a weapon or while armed," petitioners do not contend that the particular factor made relevant here—visible possession of a firearm—has historically been treated "in the Anglo-American legal tradition" as requiring proof beyond a reasonable doubt.

* * *

[W]e now turn to petitioners' subsidiary claim that due process nonetheless requires that visible possession be proved by at least clear and convincing evidence. Like the court below, we have little difficulty concluding that in this case the preponderance standard satisfies due process. Indeed, it would be extraordinary if the Due Process Clause as understood in *Patterson* plainly sanctioned Pennsylvania's scheme, while the same clause explained in some other line of less clearly relevant cases imposed more stringent requirements. There is, after all, only one Due Process Clause in the Fourteenth Amendment. Furthermore, petitioners do not and could not claim that a sentencing court may never rely on a particular fact in passing sentence without finding that fact by "clear and convincing evidence." Sentencing courts have traditionally heard evidence and found facts without any prescribed burden of proof at all.[8]

Petitioners apparently concede that Pennsylvania's scheme would pass constitutional muster if only it did not remove the sentencing court's discretion, *i.e.,* if the legislature had simply directed the court to consider visible possession in passing sentence. . . . We have some difficulty fathoming why the due process calculus would change simply because the legislature has seen fit to provide sentencing courts with additional guidance. Nor is there merit to the claim that a heightened burden of proof is required because visible possession is a fact "concerning the crime committed" rather than the background or character of the defendant. . . . Sentencing courts necessarily consider the circumstances of an offense in selecting the appropriate punishment, and we have consistently approved sentencing schemes that mandate consideration of facts related to the crime . . . without suggesting that those facts must be proved beyond a reasonable doubt. The Courts of Appeals have

---

[8] *Addington v. Texas,* 441 U.S. 418, and *Santosky v. Kramer,* 455 U.S. 745 (1982), which respectively applied the "clear and convincing evidence" standard where the State sought involuntary commitment to a mental institution and involuntary termination of parental rights, are not to the contrary. Quite unlike the situation in those cases, criminal sentencing takes place only after a defendant has been adjudged guilty beyond a reasonable doubt. Once the reasonable doubt standard has been applied to obtain a valid conviction, "the criminal defendant has been constitutionally deprived of his liberty to the extent that the State may confine him." *Meachum v. Fano,* 427 U.S. 215, 224 (1976). As noted in the text, sentencing courts have always operated without constitutonally imposed burdens of proof; embracing petitioners' suggestion that we apply the clear and convincing standard here would significantly alter criminal sentencing, for we see no way to distinguish the visible possession finding at issue here from a host of other express or implied findings sentencing judges typically make on the way to passing sentence.

uniformly rejected due process challenges to the preponderance standard under the federal "dangerous special offender" statute, 18 U.S.C. sec. 3575, which provides for an enhanced sentence if the court concludes that the defendant is both "dangerous" and a "special offender." . . .

In light of the foregoing, petitioners' final claim—that the Act denies them their Sixth Amendment right to a trial by jury—merits little discussion. Petitioners again argue that the jury must determine all ultimate facts concerning the offense committed. Having concluded that Pennsylvania may properly treat visible possession as a sentencing consideration and not an element of any offense, we need only note that there is no Sixth Amendment right to jury sentencing, even where the sentence turns on specific findings of fact. . . .

For the foregoing reasons, the judgment of the Supreme Court of Pennsylvania is *affirmed.*

Justice MARSHALL, with whom Justice BRENNAN and Justice BLACKMUM join, *dissenting.*

Whether a particular fact is an element of a criminal offense that, under *In re Winship,* must be proved by the prosecution beyond a reasonable doubt is a question that must be decided by this Court and cannot be abdicated to the States. "[If] *Winship* were limited to those facts that constitute a crime as defined by state law, a State could undermine many of the interests that decision sought to protect without effecting any substantive change in its law." *Mullaney v. Wilbur,* 421 U.S. 684, 698 (1975). The deference that the majority gives to the Pennsylvania legislature's statement that the visible possession of a firearm should not be considered an element of the crime defined by 42 Pa. Cons. Stat. Sec. 9712 (1982) is thus wholly inappropriate.

I would not, however, rely in this case on the formalistic distinction between aggravating and mitigating facts. The "continued functioning of the democratic process," . . . might provide us with some assurance that States will not circumvent the guarantee of *Winship* by criminalizing seemingly innocuous conduct and then placing the burden on the defendant to establish an affirmative defense. . . . But this Court nonetheless must remain ready to enforce that guarantee should the State, by placing upon the defendant the burden of proving certain mitigating facts, effectively lighten the constitutional burden of the prosecution with respect to the elements of the crime. . . . [I]t is enough to agree with Justice Stevens that "if a state provides that a specific component of a prohibited transaction shall give rise both to a special stigma and to a special punishment, that component must be treated as a 'fact necessary to constitute the crime' within the meaning of our holding in *In re Winship."* Pennsylvania has attached just such consequences to a finding that a defendant "visibly possessed a firearm" during the commission of any aggravated assault, and, under *Winship,* the prosecution should not be relieved of proving that fact beyond a reasonable doubt. I dissent.

Justice STEVENS, *dissenting.*

The judge presiding over Dennison's trial, as well as the judges in the other three petitioners' trials and the superior court judges hearing the appeals, all concluded that visible possession of a firearm was an element of the offense. " 'Visibly possessed a firearm' is inarguably language which refers to behavior which the legislature intended to prohibit." . . . As a consequence, the prohibited conduct had to be established by proof beyond a reasonable doubt. The Pennsylvania Supreme Court agreed that visible possession of a firearm is conduct that the Pennsylvania General Assembly intended to prohibit . . . and it recognized that evidence of such conduct would mandate a *minimum* sentence of imprisonment more than twice as severe as the *maximum* the trial judge would otherwise have imposed on petitioner Dennison. . . . But it nonetheless held that visible possession of a firearm was not an element of the offense because the Pennsylvania General Assembly had the foresight to declare in Sec. 9712(b) that "Provisions of this section shall not be an element of the crime."

Today the Court holds that state legislatures may not only define the offense with which a criminal defendant is charged, but may authoritatively determine that the conduct so described—*i.e.,* the prohibited activity which subjects the defendant to criminal sanctions—is *not* an element of the crime which the Due Process Clause requires to be proved by the prosecution beyond a reasonable doubt. In my view, a state legislature may not dispense with the requirement of proof beyond a reasonable doubt for conduct that it targets for severe criminal penalties. Because the Pennsylvania statute challenged in this case describes conduct that the Pennsylvania legislature obviously intended to prohibit, and because it mandates lengthy incarceration for the same, I believe that the conduct so described is an element of the criminal offense to which the proof beyond a reasonable doubt requirement applies.

Once a State defines a criminal offense, the Due Process Clause requires it to prove any component of the prohibited transaction that gives rise to both a special stigma and a special punishment beyond a reasonable doubt.

A State's freedom in this regard, however, has always been understood to reflect the uncontroversial proposition that a State has power, subject of course to constitutional limits, to attach criminal penalties to a wide variety of objectionable transactions; when it does so, the prosecution need establish beyond a reasonable doubt only the constituent elements of the specified criminal transaction. Nothing in *Patterson* or any of its predecessors authorizes a State to decide for itself which of the ingredients of the prohibited transaction are "elements" that it must prove beyond a reasonable doubt at trial.

Indeed, contrary to the supposition of the majority, *Patterson v. New York* is entirely in keeping with the limit on state definitional power implied in *Winship.*

Patterson clarified that the Due Process Clause requires proof beyond a reasonable doubt of conduct which exposes a criminal defendant to greater stigma or punishment, but does not likewise constrain state reductions of criminal penalties—even if such reductions are conditioned on a prosecutor's failure to prove a fact by a preponderance of the evidence or on proof supplied by the criminal defendant.[3]

---

[3] The *Patterson* Court also recognized other "constitutional limits beyond which the States may not go in this regard," . . . *Tot v. United States.* . . . It was on the basis of these cases that

The distinction between aggravating and mitigating facts has been criticized as formalistic. But its ability to identify genuine constitutional threats depends on nothing more than the continued functioning of the democratic process. To appreciate the difference between aggravating and mitigating circumstances, it is important to remember that although states may reach the same destination either by criminalizing conduct and allowing an affirmative defense, or by prohibiting lesser conduct and enhancing the penalty, legislation proceeding along these two paths is very different even if it might theoretically achieve the same result. Consider, for example, a statute making presence "in any private or public place" a "felony punishable by up to five years imprisonment" and yet allowing "an affirmative defense for the defendant to prove, to a preponderance of the evidence, that he was not robbing a bank." Dutile, *The Burden of Proof in Criminal Cases: A Comment on the Mullane—Patterson Doctrine,* 55 Notre Dame L. Rev. 380, 383 (1980). No democratically-elected legislature would enact such a law, and if it did, a broad-based coalition of bankers and bank customers would soon see the legislation repealed. Nor is there a serious danger that a State will soon define murder to be the "mere physical contact between the defendant and the victim leading to the victim's death, but then set up an affirmative defense leaving it to the defendant to prove that he acted without culpable *mens rea.*" . . . No legislator would be willing to expose himself to the severe opprobrium and punishment meted out to murderers for an accidental stumble on the subway. For similar reasons, it can safely be assumed that a State will not "define all assaults as a single offense and then require the defendant to disprove the elements of aggravation." . . . The very inconceivability of the hypothesized legislation—all of which has been sincerely offered to illustrate the dangers of permitting legislative mitigation of punishment in derogation of the requirement of proof beyond a reasonable doubt—is reason enough to feel secure that it will not command a majority of the electorate.

It is not at all inconceivable, however, to fear that a State might subject those individuals convicted of engaging in antisocial conduct to further punishment for aggravating conduct not proved beyond a reasonable doubt. As this case demonstrates, a State may seek to enhance the deterrent effect of its law forbidding the use of firearms in the course of felonies by mandating a minimum sentence of imprisonment upon proof by a preponderance against those already convicted of specified crimes. But *In re Winship* and *Patterson*

Patterson distinguished the Maine statute struck down in *Mullaney v. Wilbur.* . . . *Patterson* clarified that *Mullaney,* like *Tot,* stood for the proposition that "shifting of the burden of persuasion with respect to a fact which the State deems so important that it must be either proved or *presumed* is impermissible under the Due Process Clause." . . . Thus, although Maine could have punished all unlawful, intentional killings with life imprisonment, just as Congress in *Tot* could have punished possession of a firearm by one convicted of a crime of violence, in neither case did the legislature do so. This explanation, although not entirely satisfactory . . . is consistent with the Maine Supreme Court's explanation on direct appeal that State law presumed malice. . . . The state court downplayed this presumption because "no burden is imposed upon defendant until the State has first convinced the jury beyond a reasonable doubt that defendant is guilty of a voluntary and intentional homicide," at which point the issue "is no longer guilt or innocence of felonious homicide but rather the degree of the homicide." . . . As we held in *Mullaney,* "[t]he safeguards of due process are not rendered unavailable simply because a determination may already have been reached that would stigmatize the defendant and that might lead to a significant impairment of personal liberty."

teach that a State may not advance the objectives of its criminal laws at the expense of the accurate fact-finding owed to the criminally accused who suffer the risk of nonpersuasion.

It would demean the importance of the reasonable doubt standard—indeed, it would demean the Constitution itself—if the substance of the standard could be avoided by nothing more than a legislative declaration that prohibited conduct is not an "element" of a crime. A legislative definition of an offense named "assault" could be broad enough to encompass every intentional infliction of harm by one person upon another, but surely the legislature could not provide that only that fact must be proved beyond a reasonable doubt and then specify a range of increased punishments if the prosecution could show by a preponderance of the evidence that the defendant robbed, raped, or killed his victim "during the commission of the offense."

Appropriate respect for the rule of *In re Winship* requires that there be some constitutional limits on the power of a State to define the elements of criminal offenses. The high standard of proof is required because of the immense importance of the individual interest in avoiding both the loss of liberty and the stigma that results from a criminal conviction. It follows, I submit, that if a state provides that a specific component of a prohibited transaction shall give rise both to a special stigma and to a special punishment, that component must be treated as a "fact necessary to constitute the crime" within the meaning of our holding in *In re Winship*.

Pennsylvania's Mandatory Minimum Sentencing Act reflects a legislative determination that a defendant who "visibly possessed a firearm" during the commission of an aggravated assault is more blameworthy than a defendant who did not. A judicial finding that the defendant used a firearm in an aggravated assault places a greater stigma on the defendant's name than a simple finding that he committed an aggravated assault. And not to be overlooked, such a finding with respect to petitioner Dennison automatically mandates a punishment that is more than twice as severe as the *maximum* punishment that the trial judge considered appropriate for his conduct.

It is true, as the Court points out, that the enhanced punishment is within the range that was authorized for any aggravated assault. The fact does not, however, minimize the significance of a finding of visible possession of a firearm whether attention is focused on the stigmatizing or punitive consequences of that finding. . . . The finding identifies conduct that the legislature specifically intended to prohibit and to punish by a special sanction. In my opinion the constitutional significance of the special sanction cannot be avoided by the cavalier observation that it merely "ups the ante" for the defendant. . . . No matter how culpable petitioner Dennison may be, the difference between 11½ months and five years of incarceration merits a more principled justification than the luck of the draw.

I respectfully dissent.

NOTE

In subsequent cases the Court has expanded on the meaning of *McMillan*. In construing a federal statute, the Court, in *Jones v. United States*, 526 U.S.

227, 243 (1999), held that under the Due Process Clause of the Fifth Amendment and the notice and jury trial guarantees of the Sixth Amendment, any fact (other than prior conviction) that increases the maximum penalty for a crime must be charged in an indictment, submitted to a jury, and proven beyond a reasonable doubt."

In *Apprendi v. New Jersey*, 530 U.S. 466 (2000), the Court applied the *Jones* principle, this time under the Fourteenth Amendment, to an interpretation of a state "hate crime" provision. Defendant, Apprendi, fired several bullets into the home of an African-American family. After being arrested, Apprendi made a statement which he later retracted that he had fired the shots because the inhabitants of the house were black in color and that he did not want them in the neighborhood. He was charged under New Jersey law with numerous counts of possession of a firearm for an unlawful purpose. As part of the plea agreement worked out subsequent to Apprendi's indictment, the prosecutors reserved the right to request the court to impose a higher "enhanced" sentence based on a New Jersey "hate crime" statute if Apprendi was found to have committed two counts of second-degree possession of a firearm with a biased purpose. Apprendi plead guilty to the possession charges, and the sentencing judge, having found by a "preponderance of the evidence" that Apprendi's actions were taken "with a purpose to intimidate," held that the hate crime enhancement applied. Thus, although the statutory maximum for the two possession charges was 20 years imprisonment, as a result of the enhancement the maximum on the first count alone was 20 years and the maximum on the two counts in aggregate was 30 years. Apprendi appealed the decision on the grounds that the Due Process Clause of the Fourteenth Amendment requires that the finding of bias upon which his hate crime sentence was based must be proved to a jury beyond a reasonable doubt. The Court agreed, finding that the Constitution requires that any fact that increases the penalty for a crime beyond the prescribed statutory maximum, other than the fact of a prior conviction, must be submitted to a jury and proved beyond a reasonable doubt.

[C] Elements and Presumptions

ULSTER COUNTY COURT v. ALLEN

Supreme Court of the United States

442 U.S. 140 (1979)

Mr. Justice STEVENS *delivered the opinion of the Court.*

A New York statute provides that, with certain exceptions, the presence of a firearm in an automobile is presumptive evidence of its illegal possession by all persons then occupying the vehicle.[1] The United States Court of Appeals

---

[1] New York Penal Law § 265.15(3):

The presence in an automobile, other than a stolen one or a public omnibus, of any firearm, defaced firearm, firearm silencer, bomb, bombshell, gravity knife, switchblade knife, dagger, dirk, stiletto, billy, blackjack, metal knuckles, sandbag, sandclub or slingshot is presumptive evidence of its possession by all persons occupying such automobile at the time such . . . instrument or appliance is found, except under the following circumstances:

(a) . . . if such weapon, instrument or appliance is found upon the person of one of the occupants therein:

for the Second Circuit held that respondents may challenge the constitutionality of this statute in a federal habeas corpus proceeding and that the statute is "unconstitutional on its face." . . .

Four persons, three adult males (respondents) and a 16 year-old girl (Jane Doe, who is not a respondent here), were jointly tried on charges that they possessed two loaded handguns, a loaded machine gun, and over a pound of heroin found in a Chevrolet in which they were riding when it was stopped for speeding on the New York Thruway shortly after noon on March 28, 1973. The two large-caliber handguns, which together with their ammunition weighed approximately six pounds, were seen through the window of the car by the investigating police officer. They were positioned crosswise in an open handbag on either the front floor or the front seat of the car on the passenger side where Jane Doe was sitting. Jane Doe admitted that the handbag was hers. The machine gun and the heroin was discovered in the trunk after the police pried it open. The car had been borrowed from the driver's brother earlier that day; the key to the trunk could not be found in the car or on the person of any of its occupants although there was testimony that two of the occupants had placed something in the trunk before embarking in the borrowed car.[3] The jury convicted all four of possession of the handguns and acquitted them of possession of the contents of the trunk.

Counsel for all four defendants objected to the introduction into evidence of the two handguns, the machine gun, and the drugs, arguing that the State had not adequately demonstrated a connection between their clients and the contraband. The trial court overruled the objection, relying on the presumption of possession created by the New York statute.

Because that presumption does not apply if a weapon is found "upon the person" of one of the occupants of the car, the three male defendants also moved to dismiss the charges relating to the handguns on the ground that the guns were found on the person of Jane Doe. Respondents made this motion both at the close of the prosecution's case and at the close of all evidence. The trial judge twice denied it, concluding that the applicability to the "on the person" exception was a question of fact for the jury. The judge instructed the jurors that they were entitled to infer possession from the defendants' presence in the car. He did not make any reference to the "upon the person" exception in his explanation of the statutory presumption, nor did any of the defendants object to this omission or request alternative or additional instructions on the subject. Respondents filed a petition for a writ of habeas corpus

---

(b) if such weapon, instrument or appliance is found in an automobile which is being operated for hire by a duly licensed driver in the due, lawful and proper pursuit of his trade, then such presumption shall not apply to the driver; or

(c) if the weapon so found is a pistol or revolver and one of the occupants not present under duress, has in his possession a valid license to have and carry concealed the same.

[3] Early that morning, the four defendants had arrived at the Rochester, New York home of the driver's sister in a Cadillac. Using her telephone, the driver called their brother, advising him that "his car ran hot" on the way there from Detroit and asked to borrow the Chevrolet so that the four could continue on to New York City. The brother brought the Chevrolet to the sister's home. He testified that he had recently cleaned out the trunk and had seen no weapons or drugs. The sister also testified stating that she saw two of the defendants transfer some unidentified item or items from the trunk of one vehicle to the trunk of the other while both cars were parked in her driveway.

in the United States District Court for the Southern District of New York contending that they were denied due process of law by the application of the statutory presumption of possession. The District Court issued the writ. The Court of Appeals for the Second Circuit affirmed, but for different reasons. The majority of the court, without deciding whether the presumption was constitutional as applied in this case, concluded that the statute is unconstitutional on its face because the "presumption obviously sweeps within its compass (1) many occupants who may not know they are riding with a gun which may be out of their sight and (2) many who may be aware of the presence of the gun but not permitted access to it."

* * *

Inferences and presumptions are a staple of our adversarial system of fact finding. It is often necessary for the trier of fact to determine the existence of an element of the crime—that is an "ultimate" or "elemental" fact—from the existence of one or more "evidentiary" or "basic" facts.

The value of these evidentiary devices, and their validity under the Due Process Clause, vary from case to case, however, depending on the strength of the connection between the particular basic and elemental facts involved and on the degree to which the device curtails the fact finder's freedom to assess the evidence independently. Nonetheless, in criminal cases, the ultimate test of any device's constitutional validity in a given case remains constant: the device must not undermine the fact finder's responsibility at trial, based on evidence adduced by the State to find the *ultimate* facts *beyond* a reasonable doubt.

The most common evidentiary device is the entirely permissive inferences or presumption, which allows—but does not require—the trier of fact to infer the elemental fact from proof by the prosecutor of the basic one and that places no burden of any kind on the defendant. In that situation the basic fact may constitute *prima facie* evidence of the elemental fact. When reviewing this type of device, the Court has required the party challenging it to demonstrate its invalidity as applied to him.

Because this permissive presumption leaves the trier of fact free to credit or reject the inference and does not shift the burden of proof, it affects the application of the "beyond a reasonable doubt" standard only if under the facts of the case, there is no rational way the trier could make the connection permitted by the inference. For only in that situation is there any risk that an explanation of the permissible inference to a jury, or its use by a jury has caused the presumptively rational fact finder to make an erroneous factual determination.

A mandatory presumption is a far more troublesome evidentiary device. For it may effect not only the strength of the "no reasonable doubt" burden but also the placement of the burden: it tells the trier that he or they must find the elemental fact upon proof of the basic fact at least unless the defendant has come forward with some evidence to rebut the presumed connection between the two facts. *E.g., Turner v. United States,* . . . [396 U.S.,] at 401–402, and n. 1; *Leary v. United States,* 395 U.S. 6, 30; *United States v. Romano,*

382 U.S. 136, 137, and n. 4, 138, 143; *Tot v. United States, supra,* 319 U.S. 469.[16] In this situation, the Court has generally examined the presumption on its face to determine the extent to which the basic and elemental facts coincide.

To the extent that the trier of fact is forced to abide by the presumption, and may not reject it based on an independent evaluation of the particular facts presented by the State, the analysis of the presumption's constitutional validity is logically divorced from those facts and based on the presumption's accuracy in the run of cases.[17] It is for this reason that the Court has held

---

[16] This class of more or less mandatory presumptions can be subdivided into two parts: presumptions that merely shift the burden of production to the defendant, following the satisfaction of which the ultimate burden of persuasion returns to the prosecution; and presumptions that entirely shift the burden of proof to the defendant. The mandatory presumptions examined by our cases have almost uniformly fit into the former subclass in that they never totally removed the ultimate burden of proof beyond a reasonable doubt from the prosecution. *E.g., Tot v. United States, supra,* at 469. See *Roviaro v. United States,* 353 U.S. 53, 63 (describing the operation of the presumption involved).

In deciding what type of inference or presumption is involved in a case, the jury instructions will generally be controlling, although their interpretation may require recourse to the statute involved and the cases decided under it. *Turner v. United States* provides a useful illustration of the different types of presumptions. It analyzes the constitutionality of different presumption statutes (one mandatory and one permissive) as they apply to the basic fact of possession of both heroin and cocaine, and the presumed facts of importation and distribution of narcotic drugs. The jury was charged essentially in the terms of the two statutes.

The importance of focusing attention on the precise presentation of the presumption to the jury and the scope of that presumption is illustrated by a comparison of *United States v. Gainey,* 380 U.S. 63, with *United States v. Romano.* Both cases involved statutory presumptions based on proof that the defendant was present at the site of an illegal still. In *Gainey* the Court sustained a conviction "for carrying on" the business of the distillery in violation of 26 U.S.C. § 5601(a)(4), whereas in *Romano* the Court set aside a conviction for being in "possession, or custody, or . . . control" of such a distillery in violation of § 5601(a)(1). The difference in outcome was attributable to two important differences between the cases. Because the statute involved in *Gainey* was a sweeping prohibition of almost any activity associated with the still, whereas the *Romano* statute involved only one narrow aspect of the total undertaking, there was a much higher probability that mere presence could support an inference of guilt in the former case than in the latter.

Of perhaps greater importance, however, was the difference between the trial judge's instructions to the jury in the two cases. In *Gainey,* the judge had explained that the presumption was permissive; it did not require the jury to convict the defendant even if it was convinced that he was present at the site. On the contrary, the instructions make it clear that presence was only "a circumstance to be considered along with all the other circumstances in the case." As we emphasized, the "jury was thus specifically told that the statutory inference was not conclusive." 380 U.S., at 69–70. In *Romano,* the trial judge told the jury that the defendant's presence at the still "shall be deemed sufficient evidence to authorize conviction." 382 U.S., at 138. Although there was other evidence of guilt, that instruction authorized conviction even if the jury disbelieved all of the testimony except the proof of presence at the site. This Court's holding that the statutory presumption could not support the *Romano* conviction was thus dependent, in part, on the specific instructions given by the trial judge. Under those instructions it was necessary to decide whether, regardless of the specific circumstances of the particular case, the statutory presumption adequately supported the guilty verdict

[17] In addition to the discussion of *Romano* in n. 16, *supra,* this point is illustrated by *Leary v. United States, supra.* In that case, Dr. Timothy Leary, a professor at Harvard University, was stopped by customs inspectors in Laredo, Texas as he was returning from the Mexican side of the international border. Marihuana seed and a silver snuff box filled with semi-refined

it irrelevant in analyzing a mandatory presumption but not in analyzing a purely permissive one that there is ample evidence in the record other than the presumption to support a conviction. *E.g., Turner v. United States, supra,* at 407; *Leary v. United States, supra,* at 31–32.

Without determining whether the presumption in this case was mandatory, the Court of Appeals analyzed it on its face as if it were. In fact, it was not, as the New York Court of Appeals had earlier pointed out.

The trial judge's instructions make it clear that the presumption was merely a part of the prosecution's case,[19] that it gave rise to a permissive inference available only in certain circumstances, rather than a mandatory conclusion of possession, and that it could be ignored by the jury even if there was no affirmative proof offered by defendants in rebuttal. The judge explained that possession could be actual or constructive but that constructive possession could not exist without the intent and ability to exercise control or dominion over the weapons. He also carefully instructed the jury that there is a mandatory presumption of innocence in favor of the defendants that controls unless it, as the exclusive trier of fact, is satisfied beyond a reasonable doubt that the defendants possessed the handguns in the manner described by the judge. In short, the instructions plainly directed the jury to consider all the circumstances tending to support or contradict the inference that all four occupants of the car had possession of the two loaded handguns and to decide the matter for itself without regard to how much evidence the defendants introduced.

Our cases considering the validity of permissive statutory presumptions such as the one involved here have rested on an evaluation of the presumption

---

marihuana and three partially smoked marihuana cigarettes were discovered in his car. He was convicted of having knowingly transported marihuana which he knew had been illegally imported into this country in violation of 21 U.S.C. § 176a. The statute includes a mandatory presumption: "possession shall be deemed sufficient evidence to authorize conviction [for importation] unless the defendant explains his possession to the satisfaction of the jury." Leary admitted possession of the marihuana and claimed that he had carried it from New York to Mexico and then back.

Justice Harlan for the Court found it necessary to test the presumption against the Due Process Clause. Its analysis was facial. Despite the fact that the defendant was well educated and had recently traveled to a country that is a major exporter of marihuana to this country, the Court found the presumption of knowledge of importation from possession irrational. It did so not because Dr. Leary was unlikely to know the source of the marihuana but instead because a "majority of possessors" were unlikely to have such knowledge . . . Because the jury had been instructed to rely on the presumption even if it did not believe the Government's direct evidence of knowledge of importation (unless of course, the defendant met his burden of "satisfying" the jury to the contrary), the Court reversed the conviction.

[19] "It is your duty to consider all the testimony in this case, to weigh it carefully and access the credit to be given to a witness by his apparent intention to speak the truth and by the accuracy of his memory to reconcile, if possible, conflicting statements as to material facts and in such ways to try and get at the truth and to reach a verdict upon the evidence." Tr. 739–740.

"To establish the unlawful possession of the weapons, again the People relied upon the presumption and in addition thereto, the testimony of Anderson and Lemmon who testified in their case in chief." *Id.* at 744. "Accordingly, you would be warranted in returning a verdict of guilt against the defendants or defendant if you find the defendants or defendant was in possession of a machine gun and the other weapons and that the fact of possession was proven to you by the People beyond a reasonable doubt, and an element of such proof is the reasonable presumption of illegal possession of a machine gun or the presumption of illegal possession of firearms, as I have just before explained to you." *Id.* at 746.

as applied to the record before the Court. None suggests that a court should pass on the constitutionality of this kind of statute "on its face." It was error for the Court of Appeals to make such a determination in this case.

III

As applied to the facts of this case, the presumption of possession is entirely rational. 'Notwithstanding the Court of Appeals' analysis, respondents were not "hitch-hikers or other casual passengers," and the guns were neither "a few inches in length" nor "out of [respondents] sight." The argument against possession by any of the respondents was predicted solely on the fact that the guns were in Jane Doe's pocketbook. But several circumstances—which not surprisingly her counsel repeatedly emphasized in his questions and his argument—made it highly improbable that she was the sole custodian of these weapons.

Even if it was reasonable to conclude that she had placed the guns in her purse before the car was stopped by police, the facts strongly suggest that Jane Doe was not the only person able to exercise dominion over them. The two guns were too large to be concealed in her handbag. The bag was consequently open, and part of one of the guns was in plain view, within easy access of the driver of the car and even, perhaps of the other two respondents who were riding in the rear seat.

Moreover, it is highly improbable that the loaded guns belonged to Jane Doe or that she was solely responsible for their being in her purse. As a 16-year-old girl in the company of three adult men she was the least likely of the four to be carrying one let alone two heavy handguns. It is far more probable that she relied on the pocketknife found in her brassiere for any necessary self-protection. Under these circumstances it was not unreasonable for her counsel to argue and for the jury to infer that when the car was halted for speeding the other passengers in the car anticipated the risk of a search and attempted to conceal their weapons in a pocketbook in the front seat. The inference is surely more likely than the notion that these weapons were the sole property of the 16-year-old girl.

Under these circumstances the jury would have been entirely reasonable in rejecting the suggestion—which, incidentally defense counsel did not even advance in their closing arguments to the jury—that the handguns were in the sole possession of Jane Doe. Assuming that the jury did reject it the case is tantamount to one in which the guns were lying on the floor or the seat of the car in the plain view of the three other occupants of the automobile. In such a case it is surely rational to infer that each of the respondents was fully aware of the presence of the guns and had both the ability and the intent to exercise dominion and control over the weapons. The application of the statutory presumption in this case therefore comforts with the standard laid down in *Tot v. United States,* 319 U.S. 463, 467, and restated in *Leary v. United States, supra,* 395 U.S. at 36. For there is a "rational connection" between the basic facts that the prosecution proved and the ultimate fact presumed and the latter is "more likely than not to flow from the former."

Respondents argue, however, that the validity of the New York presumption must be judged by a "reasonable doubt" test rather than the "more likely than not" standard employed in *Leary*. Under the more stringent test, it is argued that a statutory presumption must be rejected unless the evidence necessary to invoke the inference is sufficient for a rational jury to find the inferred fact beyond a reasonable doubt.

Respondents' argument again overlooks the distinction between a permissive presumption on which the prosecution is entitled to rely as one not necessarily sufficient part of its proof and a mandatory presumption which the jury must accept even if it is the sole evidence of an element of the offense.

In the latter situation, since the prosecution bears the burden of establishing guilt, it may not rest its case entirely on a presumption unless the fact proved is sufficent to support the inference of guilt beyond a reasonable doubt. But in the former situation the prosecution may rely on all of the evidence in the record to meet a reasonable doubt standard. There is no more reason to require a permissive statutory presumption to meet a reasonable-doubt standard before it may be permitted to play any part in a trial than there is to require that degree of probative force for other relevant evidence before it may be admitted. As long as it is clear that the presumption is not the sole and sufficient basis for a finding of guilt, it need only satisfy the test described in *Leary*.

The permissive presumption as used in this case satisfied the *Leary* test. And as already noted the New York Court of Appeals has concluded that the record as a whole was sufficient to establish guilt beyond a reasonable doubt.

The judgment is reversed.

Mr. Justice POWELL with whom Mr. Justice BRENNAN, and Mr. Justice STEWART, and Mr. Justice MARSHALL *join, dissenting:*

Legitimate guidance of a jury's deliberations is an indispensable part of our criminal justice system. Nonetheless, the use of presumptions in criminal cases poses at least two distinct perils for defendants' constitutional rights. The Court accurately identifies the first of these as being the danger of interference with "the fact finder's responsibility at trial based on evidence adduced by the State to find the ultimate facts beyond a reasonable doubt." If the jury is instructed that it must infer some ultimate fact (that is, some element of the offense) from proof of other facts unless the defendant disproves the ultimate fact by a preponderance of the evidence then the presumption shifts the burden of proof to the defendant concerning the element thus inferred.

But I do not agree with the Court's conclusion that the only constitutional difficulty with presumptions lies in the danger of lessening the burden of proof the prosecution must bear. As the Court notes the presumptions thus far reviewed by the Court have not shifted the burden of persuasion . . . instead they either have required only that the defendant produce some evidence to rebut the inference suggested by the prosecution's evidence, see *Tot v. United States* . . . or merely have been suggestions to the jury that it would be sensible to draw certain conclusions on the basis of the evidence presented.

Evolving from our decisions, therefore, is a second standard for judging the constitutionality of criminal presumptions which is based—not on the constitutional requirements that the State be put to its proof—but rather on the due process rule that when the jury is encouraged to make factual inferences, those inferences must reflect some valid general observation about the natural connection between events as they occur in our society.

Our decisions uniformly have recognized that due process requires more than merely that the prosecution be put to its proof. In addition the Constitution restricts the court in its charge to the jury by requiring that when particular factual inferences are recommended to the jury those factual inferences be accurate reflections of what history, common sense, and experience tell us about the relations between events in our society. Generally this due process rule has been articulated as requiring that the truth of the inferred fact be more likely than not whenever the premise for the inference is true. Thus, to be constitutional a presumption must be at least more likely than not true.

Undeniably the presumption charged in this case encouraged the jury to draw a particular factual inference regardless of any other evidence presented: to infer that respondents possessed the weapons found in the automobile "upon proof of the presence of the machine gun and the hand weapon" and proof that respondents "occupied the automobile at the time such instruments were found." I believe that the presumption thus charged was unconstitutional because it did not fairly reflect what common sense and experience tell us about passengers in automobiles and the possession of handguns. People present in automobiles where there are weapons simply are not "more likely than not" the possessor of those weapons.

As the Court of Appeals noted, there are countless situations in which individuals are invited as guests into vehicles the contents of which they know nothing about much less have control over. Similarly, those who invite others into their automobile do not generally search them to determine what they may have on their person; nor do they insist that any handguns be identified and placed within reach of the occupants of the automobile. Indeed, handguns are particularly susceptible to concealment and therefore are less likely than are other objects to be observed by those in an automobile.

Because the specific factual inference recommended to the jury in this case is not one that is supported by the general experience of our society, I cannot say that the presumption charge is "more likely than not" to be true. Accordingly respondents' due process rights were violated by the presumption's use.

As I understand it the Court today does not contend that in general those who are present in automobiles are more likely than not to possess any gun contained within their vehicles. It argues, however, that the nature of the presumption here involved requires that we look not only to the immediate facts upon which the jury was encouraged to base its inference but to the other facts "proved" by the prosecution as well. The Court suggests that this is the proper approach when reviewing what it calls "permissive" presumptions because the jury was urged "to consider all the circumstances tending to support or contradict the inference."

It seems to me that the Court mischaracterizes the function of the presumption charged in this case. As it acknowledges was the case in *Romano* . . . the "instruction authorized conviction even if the jury disbelieved all of the testimony except the proof of presence" in the automobile. . . . The Court nevertheless relies on all of the evidence introduced by the prosecution and argues that the "permissive" presumption could not have prejudiced defendants. The possibility that the jury disbelieved all of this evidence, and relied on the presumption is simply ignored.

I agree that the circumstances relied upon by the Court in determining the plausibility of the presumption charged in this case would have made it reasonable for the jury to "infer that each of the respondents was fully aware of the presence of the guns and had both the ability and the intent to exercise dominion and control over the weapons." But the jury was told that it could conclude that respondents possessed the weapons found therein from proof of the mere fact of respondents' presence in the automobile. For all we know the jury rejected all of the prosecution's evidence concerning the location and origin of the guns, and based its conclusion that respondents possessed the weapons solely upon its belief that respondents had been present in the automobile. For purposes of reviewing the constitutionality of the presumption at issues here we must assume that this was the case.

The Court's novel approach in this case appears to contradict prior decisions of this Court reviewing such presumptions. Under the Court's analysis whenever it is determined that an inference is "permissive," the only question is whether in light of all of the evidence adduced at trial the inference recommended to the jury is a reasonable one. The Court has never suggested that the inquiry into the rational basis of a permissible inference may be circumvented in this manner. Quite the contrary, the Court has required that the "evidence necessary to invoke the inference [be] sufficient for a rational juror to find the inferred fact." . . .

Under the presumption charged in this case, the only evidence necessary to invoke the inference was the presence of the weapons in the automobile with respondents—an inference that is plainly irrational.

In sum, it seems to me that the Court today ignores the teaching of our prior decisions. By speculating about what the jury must have done with the factual inference thrust upon it the Court in effect assumes away the inference altogether, constructing a rule that permits the use of any inference—no matter how irrational in itself—provided that otherwise there is sufficient evidence in the record to support a finding of guilt. Applying this novel analysis to the present case the Court upholds the use of a presumption that it makes no effort to defend in isolation. In substance the Court—applying an unarticulated harmless error standard—simply finds that the respondents were guilty as charged. They may well have been but rather than acknowledging this rationale, the Court seems to have made new law with respect to presumptions that could seriously jeopardize a defendant's right to a fair trial. Accordingly, I dissent.

NOTES AND QUESTIONS

1. Does *Ulster County* make it impossible to determine the validity of a statutory presumption before examining the instructions in a given case?

2. In *Iowa City v. Nolan,* 239 N.W.2d 102 (1976), an ordinance provided that if a vehicle was illegally parked, the owner of the vehicle should be presumed liable for the tickets. Is this ordinance consistent with *Ulster County?*

3. A state statute establishing a presumption that the person in charge and possession of a place where utility lines have been tampered with is the person responsible for the tampering was held unconstitutional in *MacMillian v. State,* 358 So. 2d 547 (Fla. 1978). The court applied the *Leary* test of "more likely than not" and said that the inference is "irrational and arbitrary. . . . Common experience tells us that the device or apparatus tampered or altered is generally on the outside of a building and accessible to anyone; that the direct benefits . . . are commonly derived by any occupant of the premises, including family members, business partners, associates, employees, and others."

4. Consider the following statutes:

   a. "In any prosecution under this section, the making, drawing, uttering or delivering of a check, payment of which is refused by the drawee because of lack of funds of credit, shall be *prima facie* evidence of intent to defraud and of knowledge of insufficient funds in, or credit with, such bank unless such maker or drawer shall have paid the drawee thereof the amount due thereon within 10 days after receiving notice." 18 Pa. C.S.A. App. § 4854.

   b. "It shall be *prima facie* evidence upon proof of the fact that the drawer or maker did not have an account with the drawee, at the time of issuance, that the drawer or maker intended to defraud." 96-42 Wyo. Stat.

5. What of a presumption that one who possesses recently stolen articles knows they are stolen? See *Barnes v. United States,* 412 U.S. 837 (1973). But see *West v. Wright,* 931 F.2d 262 (4th Cir. 1991).

6. A number of states allow a presumption that the possessor of a specified amount of drugs (varying in each state) intends to sell or distribute them. Is this constitutional under *Ulster County?* See *Annot.,* A.L.R. 3d 1128.

7. A state statute provides that a person who carries an unlicensed gun and is charged with a crime of violence may be presumed to *intend* such a crime of violence. The defendant is charged with intentional homicide by using an unlicensed gun. The state prosecutor proves that in the past three years 85 percent, 100 percent, and 50 percent of all homicides by gun in the state were committed with unlicensed guns. What is the result? See *State v. Odom,* 83 Wash. 2d 541, 520 P.2d 152 (1974).

8. Schmolesky, *County Court of Ulster County v. Allen and Sandstrom v. Montana: The Supreme Court Lends an Ear But Turns Its Face,* 33 Rutgers L. Rev. 261, 266, 295 (1981):

   [After *Ulster County*] [p]ermissive inferences are twice blessed; the inferential link is not subjected to facial review, that is, it is not tested for accuracy in the abstract but only as applied to the facts of a given case; and there need be only a rational connection between basic and presumed facts. Mandatory presumptions, on the other hand, are doubly burdened by the prospect of appellate review because they will be facially examined by a beyond-a-reasonable-doubt standard. . . . Few drafters of deductive devices will leave the tranquil shallows of a permissible inference to enter the comparatively treacherous waters of a mandatory presumption shifting the burden of production. If this prediction is correct the result will be that the Court will gradually withdraw from the business of reviewing the facial rationality of deductive devices because all such devices will be drafted as permissive inferences.

SANDSTROM V. MONTANA

Supreme Court of the United States

442 U.S. 510 (1979)

Mr. Justice Brennan *delivered the opinion of the Court:*

The question presented is whether, in a case in which intent is an element of the crime charged, the jury instruction, "the law presumes that a person intends the ordinary consequences of his voluntary acts," violates the Fourteenth Amendment's requirement that the State prove every element of a criminal offense beyond a reasonable doubt.

I

On November 22, 1976, 18-year-old David Standstrom confessed to the slaying of Annie Jessen. Based upon the confession and corroborating evidence, petitioner was charged with "deliberate homicide," Mont. Code Ann. § 45-5-102 (1978), in that he "purposely or knowingly caused the death of Annie Jessen." . . . At trial, Sandstrom's attorney informed the jury that, although his client admitted killing Jessen, he did not do so "purposely or knowingly," and was therefore not guilty of "deliberate homicide" but of a lesser crime.

The prosecution requested the trial judge to instruct the jury that "[t]he law presumes that a person intends the ordinary consequences of his voluntary acts." Petitioner's counsel objected, arguing that "the instruction has the effect of shifting the burden of proof on the issue of" purpose or knowledge to the defense, and that "that is impermissible under the Federal Constitution, due process of law."

He offered to provide a number of federal decisions in support of the objection, including this Court's holding in *Mullaney v. Wilbur,* 421 U.S. 684 (1975), but was told by the judge: "You can give those to the Supreme Court. The objection is overruled." The instruction [No. 5] was delivered, the jury found petitioner guilty of deliberate homicide, . . . and petitioner was sentenced to 100 years in prison.

Sandstrom appealed to the Supreme Court of Montana, again contending that the instruction shifted to the defendant the burden of disproving an element of the crime charged in violation of *Mullaney v. Wilbur,* . . . *In re Winship,* and *Patterson v. New York.*

The Montana Court conceded that these cases did prohibit shifting the burden of proof to the defendant by means of a presumption but held that the cases "do not prohibit allocation of some burden of proof to a defendant under certain circumstances." . . . Since in the court's view,

> [d]efendant's sole burden under instruction No. 5 was to produce some evidence that he did not intend the ordinary consequences of his voluntary acts, not to disprove that he acted "purposely" or "knowingly," . . . the instruction does not violate due process standards as defined by the United States or Montana Constitution. . . .

Both federal and state courts have held under a variety of rationales, that the giving of an instruction similar to that challenged here is fatal to the validity of a criminal conviction. We granted *certiorari,* to decide the important question of the instruction's constitutionality. We reverse.

II

The threshold inquiry in ascertaining the constitutional analysis applicable to this kind of jury instruction is to determine the nature of the presumption it describes. See *Ulster County Court v. Allen,* [*supra,* p. 727]. That determination requires careful attention to the words actually spoken to the jury . . . for whether a defendant has been accorded his constitutional rights depends upon the way in which a reasonable juror could have interpreted the instruction.

Respondent argues, first, that the instruction merely described a permissive inference—that is, it allowed but did not require the jury to draw conclusions about defendant's intent from his actions—and that such inferences are constitutional.

These arguments need not detain us long for even respondent admits that "it's possible" that the jury believed they were required to apply the presumptions. Sandstrom's jurors were told that "the law presumes that a person intends the ordinary consequences of his voluntary acts." They were not told that they had a choice or that they might infer that conclusion: they were told only that the law presumed it. It is clear that a reasonable juror could easily have viewed such an instruction as mandatory. See . . . Montana Rules of Evidence 301(a).[4]

In the alternative, respondent urges that even if viewed as a mandatory presumption rather than as a permissive inference, the presumption did not conclusively establish intent but rather could be rebutted. On this view, the instruction required the jury, if satisfied as to the facts which trigger the presumption, to find intent unless the defendant offered evidence to the contrary. Moreover, according to the state, all the defendant had to do to rebut the presumption was produce "some" contrary evidence; he did not have to "prove" that he lacked the required mental state. Thus, "[a]t most, it placed a burden of production on the petitioner," but "did not shift to the petitioner the burden of persuasion with respect to any element of the offense. . . ."

---

[4] "Rule 301(a) Presumption defined. A presumption is an assumption of fact that the law requires to be made from another fact or group of facts found or otherwise established in the action or proceeding."

Again, respondent contends that presumptions with this limited effect pass constitutional muster. We need not view respondent's constitutional argument on this point either, however, for we reject this characterization of the presumption as well. Respondent concedes there is a "risk" that the jury, once having found petitioner's act voluntary, would interpret the instruction as automatically directing a finding of intent. Moreover, the State also concedes that numerous courts "have differed as to the effect of the presumption when given as a jury instruction without further explanation as to its use by the jury," and that some have found it to shift more than the burden of production, and even to have conclusive effect.

Nonetheless, the State contends that the only authoritative reading of the effect of the presumption resided in the Supreme Court of Montana. And the State argued that by holding that "[d]efendant's sole burden under instruction No. 5 was to produce some evidence that he did not intend the ordinary consequences of his voluntary acts, not to disprove that he acted 'purposely' or 'knowingly.' ". . . [T]he Montana Supreme Court decisively established that the presumption at most affected only the burden of going forward with evidence of intent—that is, the burden of production.[5]

The Supreme Court of Montana is, of course, the final authority on the legal weight to be given a presumption under Montana law, but it is not the final authority on the interpretation which a jury could have given the instruction. If Montana intended its presumption to have only the effect described by its Supreme Court, then we are convinced that a reasonable juror could well have been misled by the instruction given, and could have believed that the presumption was not limited to requiring the defendant to satisfy only a burden of production. Petitioner's jury was told that "the law presumes that a person intends the ordinary consequences of his voluntary acts." They were not told that the presumption could be rebutted, as the Montana Supreme Court held, by the defendant's simple presentation of "some" evidence; not even that it could be rebutted at all. Given the common definition of "presume" as "to suppose to be true without proof," Webster's New Collegiate Dictionary 911 (1974), and given the lack of qualifying instructions as to the legal effect of the presumption we cannot discount the possibility that the jury may have interpreted the instruction in either of two more stringent ways.

First, a reasonable jury could well have interpreted the presumption as "conclusive," that is, not technically as a presumption at all, but rather as an irrebuttable direction by the court to find intent once convinced of the facts triggering the presumption. Alternatively the jury may have interpreted the instruction as a direction to find intent upon proof of the defendant's voluntary actions (and their "ordinary" consequences) unless the defendant proved the contrary by some quantum of proof which may well have been considerably

---

[5] For purpose of argument, we accept respondent's definition of the production burden when applied to a defendant in a criminal case. We note, however, that the burden is often described quite differently when it rests upon the prosecution. We also note that the effect of a failure to meet the production burden is significantly different for the defendant and prosecution. When the prosecution fails to meet it, a directed verdict in favor of the defense results. Such a consequence is not possible upon a defendants' failure, however, as verdicts may not be directed against defendants in criminal cases. [Citations omitted.—Eds.]

greater than "some evidence"—thus effectively shifting the burden of persuasion on the element of intent. Numerous federal and state courts have warned that instructions of the type given here can be interpreted in just these ways.

And although the Montana Supreme Court held to the contrary in this case, Montana's own Rules of Evidence expressly state that the presumption at issue here may be overcome only "by a preponderance of evidence contrary to the presumption." Montana Rules of Evidence 301(b)(2). Such a requirement shifts not only the burden of production, but also the ultimate burden of persuasion on the issue of intent.[7]

We do not reject the possibility that some jurors may have interpreted the challenged instruction as permissive, or, if mandatory, as requiring only that the defendant come forward with "some" evidence in rebuttal. However, the fact that a reasonable juror could have given the presumption conclusive or persuasion-shifting effect means that we cannot discount the possibility that Sandstrom's jurors actually did proceed upon one or the other of these latter interpretations. And that means that unless these kinds of presumptions are constitutional the instruction cannot be adjudged valid.[8]

It is the line of cases urged by petitioner, and exemplified by *In re Winship*, 397 U.S. 358 (1970), that provides the appropriate mode of constitutional analysis for these kinds of presumptions.[9]

III

In *Winship*, this Court stated:

> Lest there remain any doubt about the constitutional stature of the reasonable-double standard, we explicitly hold that the Due Process Clause protects the accused against conviction except upon proof beyond a reasonable doubt of *every fact* necessary to constitute the crime with which he is charged.

397 U.S., at 364 (emphasis added).

---

[7] The potential for these interpretations of the presumption was not removed by the other instructions given at the trial. It is true that the jury was instructed generally that the accused was presumed innocent until proven guilty, and that the State had the burden of proving beyond a reasonable doubt that the defendant caused the death of the deceased purposely or knowingly. . . . But this is not rhetorically inconsistent with a conclusive or burden-shifting presumption. The jury could have interpreted the two sets of instructions as indicating that the presumption was a means by which proof beyond a reasonable doubt as to intent could be satisfied. For example, if the presumption were viewed as conclusive, the jury could have believed that, although intent must be proven beyond a reasonable doubt proof of the voluntary slaying and its ordinary consequences constituted proof of intent beyond a reasonable doubt. Cf. *Mullaney v. Wilbur*, 421 U.S. 684, 703 n. 31(1975) ("These procedural devices require (in the case of a presumption) . . . the trier of fact to conclude that the prosecution has met its burden of proof with respect to the presumed . . . fact by having satisfactorily established other facts.")

[8] Given our ultimate result in this case, we do not need to consider what kind of constitutional analysis would be appropriate for other kinds of presumptions.

[9] Another line of our cases also deals with the validity of certain kinds of presumptions. See *Ulster County v. Allen*, 442 U.S. 140 (1979); . . . *Tot v. United States*, 319 U.S. 469 (1943). These cases did not, however, involve presumptions of the conclusive or persuasion-shifting variety. See *Ulster County Court v. Allen*, 442 U.S. 140, 157 and n. 16; and at 169 (Powell, J., dissenting); *Mullaney v. Wilbur*, 421 U.S., at 703 n. 31 (1975).

The petitioner here was charged with and convicted of deliberate homicide, committed purposely or knowingly, under 1947 Mont. Rev. Codes § 94-5-102(a) (Crim. Code of 1973). . . . It is clear that under Montana law, whether the crime was committed purposely or knowingly is a fact necessary to constitute the crime of deliberate homicide. Indeed, it was the lone element of the offense at issue in Sandstrom's trial, as he confessed to causing the death of the victim, told the jury that knowledge and purpose were the only questions he was controverting, and introduced evidence solely on those points. . . . Moreover, it is conceded that proof of defendant's "intent" would be sufficient to establish this element. Thus, the question before this Court is whether the challenged jury instruction had the effect of relieving the State of the burden of proof enunciated in *Winship* on the critical question of petitioner's state of mind. We conclude that under either of the two possible interpretations of the instruction set out above, precisely that effect would result and that the instruction therefore represents constitutional error.

We consider first the validity of a conclusive presumption. This Court has considered such a presumption on at least two prior occasions. In *Morissette v. United States,* 342 U.S. 246 (1952), the defendant was charged with wilful and knowing theft of government property. Although his attorney argued that for his client to be found guilty, "the taking must have been with felonious intent," the trial judge ruled that "[t]hat is presumed by his own act." . . . After first concluding that intent was in fact an element of the crime charged, and after declaring that "[w]here intent of the accused is an ingredient of the crime charged, its existence is a . . . jury issue," *Morissette* held:

> *It follows that the trial court may not withdraw or prejudge the issue by instruction that the law raises a presumption of intent from an act.* It often is tempting to cast in terms of a "presumption" a conclusion which a court thinks probable from given facts. . . . [But] [w]e think presumptive intent had no place in this case. *A conclusive presumption which testimony could not overthrow would effectively eliminate intent as an ingredient of the offense.* A presumption which would permit but not require the jury to assume intent from an isolated fact would prejudge a conclusion which the jury should reach of its own volition. A presumption which would permit the jury to make an assumption which all the evidence considered together does not logically establish would give to a proven fact an artificial and fictional effect. In either case, *this presumption would conflict with the overriding presumption of innocence with which the law endows the accused and which extends to every element of the crime.*

342 U.S., at 274–275. (Emphasis added.)

Just last Term in *United States v. United States Gypsum,* 438 U.S. 422 (1978), we reaffirmed the holding of *Morissette.* In that case defendants, who were charged with criminal violations of the Sherman Act, challenged the following jury instruction:

> The law presumes that a person intends the necessary and natural consequences of his acts. Therefore, if the effect of the exchanges of pricing information was to raise, fix, maintain, and stabilize prices, then the parties to them are presumed, as a matter of law, to have intended that result.

Id., 430.

After again determining that the offense included the element of intent, we held:

> [A] defendant's state of mind or *intent is an element of a criminal antitrust offense which* . . . *cannot be taken from the trier of fact through reliance on a legal presumption of* wrongful intent from proof of effect on prices. Cf. *Morissette v. United States.* . . .
>
> Although an effect on prices may well support an inference that the defendant had knowledge of the probability of such a consequence at the time he acted, the jury must remain free to consider additional evidence before accepting or rejecting the inference. . . . [U]ltimately, the decision on the issue of intent must be left to the trier of fact alone. The instruction given invaded this fact finding function.

438 U.S., at 435, 446 (emphasis added).

As in *Morissette* and *United States Gypsum,* a conclusive presumption in this case would "conflict with the overriding presumption of innocence with which the law endows the accused and which extends to every element of the crime," and would "invade [the] fact finding function" which in a criminal case the law assigns solely to the jury. The instruction announced to David Sandstrom's jury may well have had exactly these consequences. Upon finding proof of one element of the crime (causing death), and of facts insufficient to establish the second (the voluntariness and "ordinary consequences" of defendant's action), Sandstrom's jurors could reasonably have concluded that they were directed to find against defendant on the element of intent.

A presumption which, although not conclusive, had the effect of shifting the burden of persuasion to the defendant, would have suffered from similar infirmities. If Sandstrom's jury interpreted the presumption in that manner, it could have concluded that upon proof by the State of the slaying, and of additional facts not themselves establishing the element of intent, the burden was shifted to the defendant to prove that he lacked the requisite mental state. Such a presumption was found constitutionally deficient in *Mullaney v. Wilbur.* . . .

Because David Sandstrom's jury may have interpreted the judge's instruction as constituting either a burden-shifting presumption like that in *Mullaney,* or a conclusive presumption like those in *Morissette* and *United States Gypsum,* and because either interpretation would have deprived defendant of his right to the due process of law, we hold the instruction given in this case unconstitutional.

Accordingly, the judgment of the Supreme Court of Montana is Reversed, and the case is remanded for proceedings not inconsistent with this opinion.

It is so ordered.

Notes and Questions

1. Chief Judge Ruger, in *People v. Conway,* 97 N.Y. 62, 77 (1884):

Whenever the intent is made an element in determining the character of an act, it is in accordance with our general observation and experience to infer its existence, by reference to the laws which have been usually and generally found to control human conduct. Indeed, this is the only method by which the intent can be made to appear. The intent formed is the secret and silent operation of the mind, and its only visible physical manifestation is in the accomplishment of the thing determined upon. The individual whose intent is sought to be ascertained may remain silent, or if he speaks may, and probably will if he has a crime to conceal, speak untruly, and thus *the mind is compelled from necessity to revert to the actual physical manifestations of the intent, exhibited by the result produced, as the safest if not the only proof of the fact to be ascertained.* This rule is always applied, unless from the circumstances of the case it affirmatively appears that the will of the actor was subordinated to some controlling and irresistible cause precluding the existence of any voluntary mental action. (Emphasis added.—Eds.)

2. Griew, *States of Mind, Presumptions and Inferences,* in Criminal Law: Essays in Honor of J.C. Smith 68 (1987), argues that if the presumption ever really existed, it was only because, until the later 19th century, defendants in both England and America were prohibited from testifying on their own behalf; and without a device to "presume" *mens rea,* prosecutors would have been unable to demonstrate a *prima facie* case. Now that defendants can testify, there is no need for the presumption or even an inference.

The "presumption" has not worn well with many writers. Glanville Williams, for example, declared

> the maxim is tantamount to saying that a consequence is intended though it is not desired, or even foreseen as possible or probable, provided that it was probable in fact, *i.e.,* a reasonable man would have foreseen it as probable. Now the test of reasonable foresight is the very test that is used to establish negligence. . . . Consequently, if it were admitted . . . the result would be to destroy the subjective definition of intention and to efface the line between intention and negligence. Such a mangling of the concept of intention cannot be admitted.

Williams, at 90.

Levitt, *Extent and Function of the Doctrine of* Mens Rea, 17 Ill. L. Rev. 578, 580–81 (1923), supported this view:

> If we solemnly infer the existence of an intent when the facts upon which the inference is based expressly declare that the intent is non-existent, we are going through motions that have no meaning. It is legal catatonia. The courts sententiously declare that "there can be no crime unless there is a joining of a criminal act with a criminal intent" and then they sedulously ignore the intent and examine the act. If they find the act is criminal, they *assume* that the intent exists and proceed to deal with the criminal.

For this reason, perhaps as well as others, the maxim has been under attack. In a series of decisions, federal courts have either invalidated convictions or thrown serious doubt upon the following instruction:

It is reasonable to infer that a person ordinarily intends the natural and probable consequences of acts knowingly done or knowingly omitted. So unless the contrary appears from the evidence, the jury may draw the inference that an accused intended all the consequences which one standing in like circumstances and possessing like knowledge *should reasonably have expected* to result from any act knowingly omitted by an accused.

Mann v. United States, 319 F.2d 404, 407, (5th Cir. 1963) *cert. denied,* 375 U.S. 986 (1964) (emphasis added); see also *United States v. Driscoll,* 454 F.2d 792 (5th Cir. 1972). Still, the Court held in *Rose v. Clark,* 478 U.S. 570 (1986), that a *Sandstrom* instruction *could* be harmless error.

3. The "deadly weapon" doctrine allowed a jury to presume that a person who used a deadly weapon intended to do so with malice aforethought. See, *e.g., The Queen v. Eagle,* 2 F. & F. 827 (1962); *Commonwealth v. Quinby,* 4 Mass. 391 (1808). See generally Oberer, *The Deadly Weapon Doctrine—Common Law Origins,* 75 Harv. L. Rev. 1565 (1962). See, *e.g.,* Belton v. United States, 383 F.2d 150 (D.C. Cir. 1967); *Howard v. United States,* 389 F.2d 287 (D.C. Cir. 1977). Does *Sandstrom* invalidate this presumption? See *Patterson v. State;* 239 Ga. 409, 238 S.E.2d 2 (1977). Does *Ulster County* invalidate the presumption? Is death a "natural and probable" consequence of the use of a deadly weapon? Could expert testimony on this point be relevant?

4. The *Sandstrom* Court struck down the presumption on the basis that it shifted (or could be seen by the jury as shifting) the burden of proof. But is the presumption or even the inference that one intends the natural and probable consequences of one's acts constitutional under *Ulster County?* What are the "natural and probable" consequences of becoming drunk? Of driving while drunk? Of shooting recklessly into a house? See Orchard, *Drunkenness, Drugs and Manslaughter,* 1970 Crim. L. Rev. 132, 138–39.

5. Is the "only" problem with the instruction in *Sandstrom* that it used the word *presume* rather than *infer?* Can other instructions nullify the effect of an otherwise invalid "presumed intent" instruction? In two cases considering this question decided during the same week, two panels of the United States Court of Appeals for the Second Circuit, deciding two appeals from the same trial judge and using essentially identical language, reached opposite results, one finding that there was no error, the other finding error that required reversal. *Rivera v. Combe,* F.2d 697 (2d Cir. 1982); *Ramirez v. Jones,* 683 F.2d 712 (2d Cir. 1982). Is it desirable that (federal) courts pass their time sifting the possible impacts of semantic differences? Would a rule forbidding any mention of any inference (or presumption) be better? More defensible?

6. Is Sandstrom consistent with *Ulster County?* See Allen, *The Constitutional Requirement of Proof beyond a Reasonable Doubt in Criminal Cases: A Comment upon Incipient Chaos in the Lower Courts,* 20 Amer. Crim. L Rev. 1 (1982); *Compare* Schmolesky, *supra;* see Note, *Presumptive Intent Jury Instructions After Sandstrom,* 1980 Wis. L. Rev. 366; Note, *Dietz v. Solem: An Affirmance of the Sandstrom Mandate,* 27 S.D.L. Rev. 65 (1982); Comment, *The Evolving Use of Presumptions in the Criminal Law: Sandstrom v. Montana,* 41 Ohio St. L.J. 1145 (1980).

7. There has been a spate of writing on presumptions. See Abrams, *Statutory Presumptions and the Federal Criminal Law: A Suggested Analysis,* 22 Vand.

§ 9.05 Specific Defenses

[A] Acts "In Extremis"

[1] Duress

[a] Generally

BLACKSTONE

27

Another species of compulsion or necessity is what our law calls *duress per minas;* or threats and menaces, which induce a fear of death or other bodily harm, and which take away for reason the guilt of many crimes and misdemeanors; at least before the human tribunal. But then that fear, which compels a man to do an unwarrantable action, ought to be just and well grounded. . . . Therefore, in time of war or rebellion, a man may be justified in doing many treasonable acts by compulsion of the enemy or rebels, which would admit of no excuse in the time of peace. This however seems only, or at least principally, to hold as to positive crimes, so created by the laws of society; and which therefore society may excuse; but not as to natural offences, so declared by the law of God, wherein human magistrates are only the executioners of divine punishment. And therefore though a man be violently assaulted, and hath no other possible means of escaping death, but by killing an innocent person; this fear and force shall not acquit him of murder; for he ought rather to die himself, than escape by the murder of an innocent. But in such a case he is permitted to kill the assailant; for there the law of nature, and self-defense is its primary canon, have made him his own protector.

STEPHEN

107–08

Criminal law is itself a system of compulsion on the widest scale. It is a collection of threats of injury to life, liberty, and property if people do commit crimes. Are such threats to be withdrawn as soon as they are encountered by opposing threats? The law says to a man intending to commit murder, if you do it I will hang you. Is the law to withdraw its threat if someone else says, if you do not do it I will shoot you? Surely it is at the moment when temptation to crime is strongest that the law should speak most clearly and emphatically to the contrary. It is, of course, a misfortune for a man that he should be placed between two fires, but it would be a much greater misfortune for society at large if criminals could confer impunity upon their agents by threatening them with death or violence if they refused to execute their commands. No doubt the moral guilt of a person who commits crime under compulsion is less than that of a person who commits it freely, but any effect which is thought proper may be given to this circumstance by a proportional mitigation of the offender's punishment. These reasons lead me to think that compulsion by threats ought in no case whatever to be admitted as an excuse for crime, though it may and ought to operate in mitigation of punishment in most though not in all cases.

A. Wertheimer, Coercion

148–49 (1987)

. . . Blackstone's emphasis on the defendant's freedom of will exemplifies the deontological approach. The idea is that it is unjust to punish those who do not will the acts they are "compelled" to perform. Hobbes, on the other hand, offers a distinctly utilitarian explanation of duress. . . . Because punishment would not have a deterrent effect on [a duressed person], and because deterrence is the only legitimate aim of punishment, there should be no punishment.

. . . Bentham developed a similar argument. . . . t is not that it is *unjust* to punish those acting under necessity or duress. On Bentham's view, there is no independent concept of justice. Rather, it is *pointless* to punish those who act under duress, for it will and can have no effect on their actions.

It is a philosophical commonplace that utilitarian footings are extremely unstable: the consequences may go the other way. As Hart points out, even if Bentham is right in claiming that threats of legal punishment have no effect on those actually under duress (and that is by no means self-evident), "the actual *infliction* of punishment on those persons, may secure a higher measure of conformity to law on the part of *other* persons than is secured by the admission of excusing conditions."

Newman and Weitzer, Duress, Free Will, and the Criminal Law

30 Calif. L. Rev. 313, 314–16 (1957)

If "duress" was to excuse, it had to be shown that the compulsion was in its nature such as would induce a well grounded apprehension of death or serious bodily harm. The compulsion had to arise without the negligence or fault of the person claiming aid from the doctrine, and the compulsion had to be instant, present, imminent and impending. The force complained of by the victim must have lasted during the whole time required for the performance of the criminal act. The "duressed" had to show resistance to the point of death (or at least to the instant of serious and grievous bodily harm) before he capitulated and acted. The force had to be exerted, if not on the victim, then on someone close to the victim, such as a wife or child. The "duressed" had to avail himself of any opportunity to avoid or escape from the force.

Depending on the seriousness of the act done, and the nature and imagination of the judicial mind at work, as the court emphasized one, several, or all these standards, so went the defense of duress.

There was good reason for the profusion of standards. The doctrine held within it the germs of potential disorder. The business of excusing individuals from crimes which, in the last analysis, they had committed bodily, was a difficult and dangerous affair. Who could see or wisely guess at the presence of a will which freely motivated the body in that dreadful moment of criminal action? Inference, not observation, was the species of proof; and inferences, it was thought, required the aid of standards. If the doctrine was not to be the plaything of the shrewd and unscrupulous (and were not those suspected of crimes already questionable in that respect?) it had to be well hedged and strict of proof.

It was in this manner that worry about the guilty diverted attention from the innocent (guilt or innocence determined, that is, in terms of the presence or absence of free will). The judicial eye blinked at the question "Was A in fact deprived of his 'free will,'" while turning an open though jaundiced stare toward the problem of determining how much force must be required of the "duressor" (given a particular act) and how much responsibility must be demanded from the "duressed" before he could be excused. By insisting that the compulsion complained of could not be the result of the actor's own fault, the courts were not making a statement about the presence or absence of free will of such a negligent actor. The standard reflected a desire to limit the duress doctrine to the non-negligent, rather than an attempt to establish an impossible relation between fault and free-will. To require resistance up to the point of almost no return (and in some cases up to the point of no return), is to imply that men can act freely up to that instant in time when the threatened danger is to descend on them, or to require that, in spite of the lack of free-will, men will be held responsible for their acts. The requirement that a man avail himself of any opportunity to avoid or escape the force also can hardly be said to be a criterion useful in determining whether the force exerted did or did not deprive the actor of his free will. At best, the standard also reflected the fear which the courts had of the doctrine and their desire to limit its use. The standards devised were, therefore, not so much calculated to show that the actor (within a particular set of circumstances and given the peculiarities of his nature) was actually deprived of his free will as claimed, as much as they were intended to set limits upon the circumstances in which the doctrine could be applied.

On the other hand, the standards were indirectly making judgments about the nature and function of free will. To say that the force exerted on the "duressed" had to be a threat of death or serious bodily harm was to say that man's will was so structured as to make any lesser force incapable of affecting its free operation. To say that the force had to be in continuous operation during the commission of the act was to imply that such a force was only effective in subverting the victim's free will at the time of its application and no longer, and was to overlook the truth that effects follow causes and by their nature exist beyond that which brings them about. To demand a well-grounded apprehension of harm was to claim that, where reason operated properly, the will was subject to the divestment of its freedom, but where passion, ignorance, or individual peculiarity dominated, will was free and a person responsible. Paying little heed to the inconsistency in time of the nature of threats with the harm, and adding their own requirement that the force be instant and present, the courts were also implying that a present threat of harm which would occur too far in the future was not effective in destroying the free-willed quality of an action.

Thus the law of criminal duress opens two avenues of study. The first goes to the core of the problem of freedom since it inquires into those principles of free will which are the justification for the existence of the doctrine of duress. The second line of investigation leads to an examination of the standards which have grown around the doctrine. Standards will not always be the logical outcome of principles. The belief in free will and the desire to excuse compelled action will not always serve to explain or to justify the use of a particular standard—indeed, conflict between principle and standard will often appear the rule rather than the exception.

It may well be that to point out inconsistences and confusions of purposes between principle and standards in no way destroys the need for such standards or principle. But as unnatural as the tendency in the law towards clarity, consistency and systematization may be, it is man's merit that he attempt to clear away the inevitable entanglement to which law in life gives rise.

REGINA v. HUDSON AND TAYLOR

Court of Appeal, Criminal Division

[1971] 2 QB 202, [1971] 2 All ER 244, [1971] 2 WLR 1047

WIDGERY, L.J. delivered the judgment of the court which was read by Lord PARKER, C.J.

The appellants were convicted of perjury at the Manchester Crown Court on 18th May 1970 and each was granted a conditional discharge. They now appeal against their convictions by leave of the single judge. On 6th April 1969 a fight took place in a Salford public house between one Wright and one Mulligan with the result that Wright was charged with wounding Mulligan. Each of the appellants gave statements to the police and they were the principal prosecution witnesses at Wright's trial. The appellant Taylor is 19 and the appellant Hudson is 17. Wright's trial took place on 4th August 1969 but when called to give evidence the appellants failed to identify Wright as Mulligan's assailant.

The appellant Taylor said that she knew no one called Jimmy Wright, and the appellant Hudson said that the only Wright she knew was not the man in the dock.

Wright was accordingly acquitted and, in due course, the appellants were charged with perjury. At their trial they admitted that the evidence which they had given was false but set up the defense of duress. The basis of the defense was that, shortly after the fight between Wright and Mulligan, the appellant Hudson had been approached by a group of men including one Farrell who had a reputation for violence and was warned that if she "told on Wright in court" they would get her and cut her up. The appellant Hudson passed this warning to the appellant Taylor who said that she had also been warned by other girls to be careful or she would be hurt. The appellants said in evidence that in consequence of these threats they were frightened and decided to tell lies in court in order to avoid the consequences which might follow if they testified against Wright. This resolve was strengthened when they arrived at court for Wright's trial and saw that Farrell was in the gallery.

The recorder directed the jury as a matter of law that the defense of duress was not open to the appellants in these circumstances. He said:

> In my direction to you which you have to obey I tell you that duress can only arise when there is a threat made of death or serious personal injury and that threat must be a present immediate threat. . . . [Later he continued:] Assuming everything in favour of [the appellants] . . . assuming that Farrell did make this threat to [the appellant Hudson] . . . assuming that information was passed on by [the appellant Hudson] to [the appellant Taylor] and assuming that [the appellants] believed it; assuming in favour of [the appellant Taylor] and [the appellant Hudson] that [the appellant Taylor] was approached on various occasions by young women who said to her "Be careful and watch it" . . . assuming all that to be 100 per cent in their favour I direct you as a matter of law that does not amount to duress. [The appellants] may very well have thought that if they did not tell lies something very unpleasant might happen to them in the future, but that is not a present immediate threat capable of being then and there carried out because when they told lies they were in a court of law with the recorder of Salford there for protection and with the police there in court and, members of the jury, I direct you that does not amount to duress.

It is now submitted that this was a misdirection in law and that the case should have been left to the jury to determine, as a fact, whether the appellants had acted under duress.

We have been referred to a large number of authorities and to the views of writers of text books. Despite the concern expressed in 2 Stephen's History of the Criminal Law in England that it would be—

> . . . a much greater misfortune for society at large if criminals could confer impunity upon their agents by threatening them with death or violence if they refused to execute their commands . . .

it is clearly established that duress provides a defense in all offences including perjury (except possibly treason or murder as a principal) if the will of the accused has been overborne by threats of death of serious personal injury so that the commission of the alleged offence was no longer the voluntary act of the accused. This appeal raises two main questions; first, as to the nature of the necessary threat and, in particular, whether it must be 'present and immediate'; secondly, as to the extent to which a right to plead duress may be lost if the accused has failed to take steps to remove the threat as, for example, by seeking police protection.

It is essential to the defense of duress that the threat shall be effective at the moment when the crime is committed. The threat must be a 'present' threat in the sense that it is effective to neutralize the will of the accused at that time. Hence an accused who joins a rebellion under the compulsion of threats cannot plead duress if he remains with the rebels after the threats have lost their effect and his own will has had a chance to re-assert itself. . . . Similarly a threat of future violence may be so remote as to be insufficient to overpower the will at the moment when the offence was committed, or the accused may have elected to commit the offence in order to rid himself of a threat hanging over him and not because he was driven to act by immediate and unavoidable pressure. In none of these cases is the defense of duress available because a person cannot justify the commission of a crime merely to secure his own peace of mind.

When, however, there is no opportunity for delaying tactics, and the person threatened must make up his mind whether he is to commit the criminal act or not, the existence at that moment of threats sufficient to destroy his will ought to provide him with a defense even though the threatened injury may not follow instantly, but after an interval.

In the present case the threats of Farrell were likely to be no less compelling, because their execution could not be effected in the court room, if they could be carried out in the streets of Salford the same night. Insofar, therefore, as the recorder ruled as a matter of law that the threats were not sufficiently present and immediate to support the defense of duress we think that he was in error. He should have left the jury to decide whether the threats had overborne the will of the appellants at the time when they gave the false evidence.

Counsel for the Crown, however, contends that the recorder's ruling can be supported on another ground, namely, that the appellants should have taken steps to neutralize the threats by seeking police protection either when they came to court to give evidence, or beforehand. He submits on grounds of public policy that an accused should not be able to plead duress if he had the opportunity to ask for protection from the police before committing the offence and failed to do so. The argument does not distinguish cases in which the police would be able to provide effective protection, from those when they would not, and it would, in effect, restrict the defense of duress to cases where the person threatened had been kept in custody by the maker of the threats, or where the time interval between the making of the threats and the commission of the offence had made recourse to the police impossible. We recognize the need to keep the defense of duress within reasonable bounds but cannot accept so severe a restriction on it.

In the opinion of this court it is always open to the Crown to prove that the accused failed to avail himself of some opportunity which was reasonably open to him to render the threat ineffective, and that on this being established the threat in question can no longer be relied on by the defense. In deciding whether such an opportunity was reasonably open to the accused the jury should have regard to his age and circumstances, and to any risks to him which may be involved in the course of action relied on.

In our judgment the defense of duress should have been left to the jury in the present case, as should any issue raised by the Crown and arising out of the appellants' failure to seek policy protection. The appeals will, therefore, be allowed and the convictions quashed.

MODEL PENAL CODE § 2.09

(1) It is an affirmative defense that the actor engaged in the conduct charged to constitute an offense because he was coerced to do so by the use of, or a threat to use, unlawful force against his person or the person of another, which a person of reasonable firmness in his situation would have been unable to resist.

(2) The defense provided by this Section is unavailable if the actor recklessly placed himself in a situation in which it was probable that he would be subjected to duress. The defense is also unavailable if he was negligent in placing himself in such a situation, whenever negligence suffices to establish culpability for the offense charged.

[b] Rationale of Duress

Mens Rea or Actus Reus? Is the basis of duress a lack of *mens rea* or a lack of *actus reus?* Could it be argued that the act of a duressed person is not "his," and therefore there is no *actus reus?* See Edwards, *Duress and Aiding and Abetting,* 69 L.Q. Rev. 226 (1953). The working party of the English Law Revision Commission has argued that duress negates the *actus reus* rather than *mens rea*. See *Law Commission, Working Paper No. 55, Defences of General Application* 8 (1975). Cf. Aristotle, Ethics, bk. III, 1110a: "it may be debated whether [actions done from fear of greater evils] are involuntary or voluntary." Does this make sense? Does it comport with Blackstone's view? What are the implications of this view? See Williams, 755. Or is it that there is an act, but no *mens rea?* Compare Morawetz, *Reconstructing the Criminal Defenses: The Significance of Justification,* 77 J. Crim. L. & Criminology 277, 297 (1986): "The actor under duress is choosing as deliberately as the person who acts under the pressures of self-defense and necessity. All are exigent situations. Yet in the case of such justifications as self-defense and necessity we do not claim to find an overborne will. These are situations of choice and control." *Accord* 2 Stephen at 102, discussing the question of whether a condemned prisoner "voluntarily" walks to his death: "his motions are just as much voluntary actions as if he (were) going to leave his place of confinement and regain his liberty. He walks to his death because he prefers it to being carried." And see Dressler at 277:

> [I]t is not precisely correct to say that a person is excused for violating the law because she "lacked free will." The coerced actor has the capacity to choose, i.e., she is not an automaton controlled by the coercing party. More to the point, the coerced actor *in fact* chooses to violate the law; she chooses

to commit an offense rather than to accept the threatened consequences. In a sense she "self-consciously subordinates [the law] to the primacy of the person who is the subject of desire," *i.e.,* she chooses to make the coercing party's desires her own for present purposes.

"Failure of Proof" or "Affirmative Defense"? If lack of free will is not the explanation for duress as relevant to criminal liability, what is? Is the change in the meaning of *mens rea* from a notion of general moral blameworthiness to specific *mens rea,* see *supra* § 4.02, relevant here? Fingarette, *Victimization: A Legalist Analysis of Coercion, Deception, Undue Influence, and Excusable Prison Escape,* 42 Wash. and Lee L. Rev. 65 (1985). Consider the following analysis from Rosenthal, *Duress in the Criminal Law,* 32 Crim. L. Q. 199, 203–4 (1989–90):

> Suppose that A, working as a waiter, is handed a glass of wine by B, with instructions to serve it to C. Suppose also that A knows that the wine contains a dose of poison that is probably lethal, that A serves the wine, and that C dies. . . . A would undoubtedly be found guilty of murder: A meant to cause C's death or meant to cause him bodily harm that he knew was likely to cause C's death and was reckless as to whether death ensued.

> Suppose, however, that there are the following additional facts. A's child was visiting at work that day, and B seized the child, put a gun to her head, and ordered A to serve the poisoned wine to C. Suppose, moreover, that A served C a sandwich along with the wine, in the hope that the sandwich would help to dilute the effect of the poison so that C would not die. Would it then still be held that A meant to cause C's death? Or to cause C bodily harm? It is submitted that to say that A meant to cause death or bodily harm in these circumstance would be distorting the meaning of "meant." The evidence of duress should negative A's *mens rea* in such a case.

> On the other hand, if A followed B's instructions to place a gun to C's head and pull the trigger then it could be said that A meant to cause bodily harm to C, although A did so under coercion. In the latter scenario A would need to rely on the *defense* of duress.

Consider also:

> It must be obvious to the deliberate judgment of every reflecting mind that much less freedom of will is required to render a person responsible for crime than to bind him by a sale or other contract. To overcome the will, so far as to render it incapable of contracting a civil obligation, is a mere trifle compared with reducing it to that degree of slavery and submission which will exempt from punishment.

McCoy v. State, 78 Ga. 490, 3 S.E. 768 (1887).

Justification or Excuse? The same lack of certainty surrounds the question of whether duress is an excuse or a justification. The two leading "hornbooks" divide on this issue: Dressler 278 considers the claim as one of excuse, while La Fave and Scott 374–78, consider it a justification. Aside from once again demonstrating the tenuous nature of this distinction, does the conflict help explain the division of the courts on the burden of proof issue, below? See *Williams v. State,* 101 Md. App. 408, 646 A.2d 1101 (1994).

Burden of Proof. The question of whether duress goes to either *actus reus* or *mens rea,* or is an excuse or justification can be cast as a question of the burden of proof—if the claim negates an element of the crime, it would seem that the burden must lie on the prosecutor to defeat the claim, once properly raised. The courts appear to be split on this issue. Compare *United States v. Dominguez-Mestas,* 687 F.2d 1429 (9th Cir. 1988) and *Walker v. Endell,* 850 F.2d 470 (9th Cir. 1987) (recognizing split of courts) (burden can be placed on defendant) with *United States v. Hearst,* 563 F.2d 1331, 1336 n.2 (9th Cir. 1977) (burden is on government).

[c] Definitional Controversies

Immediacy. One of the traditional requirements of a successful plea of duress is that the aggressor must threaten to harm the defendant immediately unless he complies. Recently, however, as in *Hudson and Taylor,* this standard appears to be broadly construed. Thus in *State v. Toscano,* 74 N.J. 421, 378 A.2d 755 (1977), the defendant was convicted of conspiring to obtain money by false pretenses. Defendant claimed that he filled out fraudulent insurance forms only because another conspirator reminded him "[Y]ou just moved into a place that has a very dark entrance and you leave there with your wife. . . You and your wife are going to jump at shadows when you leave that dark entrance." There was no threat that the violence would be "immediate," but the New Jersey Supreme Court, applying the Model Penal Code provision, reversed the conviction.

On the other hand, courts have split on the question posed in *Hudson and Taylor* itself, where the defendant has been threatened with harm unless he either commits perjury or refuses to testify, primarily on whether the threat is "imminent" given that the duressed person could appear before the court and seek assistance. See, *e.g., United States v. Patrick,* 542 F.2d 381 (7th Cir. 1976), and *United States v. Atencio,* 586 F.2d 744 (9th Cir. 1978) (duress not available to charge of contempt where defendant refused to testify). *Contra, United States v. Banks,* 942 F.2d 1576 (11th Cir. 1991). See also *United States v. Jennell,* 749 F.2d 1302 (9th Cir. l984) and *United States v. Contento-Pachon,* 723 F.2d 691 (9th Cir. l984) (whether a defendant who was threatened with death for himself or family if he did not act as a drug courier should have reported threats to authorities when arrested is a question for the jury).

Objective v. Subjective Standard. *Hudson and Taylor* clearly adopts a subjective approach to the doctrine of duress: was *this* defendant's will actually overborne. But the majority view uses an objective standard. Thus, for example Blackstone requires that the defendant suffer from a "well-grounded fear"; the MPC also adopts an objective standard. Why? Consider the following:

> a) It may be said that the whole test as to whether the requirements of duress exist should be subjective, but we feel that this would create too wide a defense. Serious personal injury can cover a wide range of threatened harm, and if the defense is to be available even in respect of the most serious offences, it would be unsatisfactory in the final event to dispense with some objective assessment of whether the defendant could reasonably have been expected to resist the threat. . . . We think that there should be an

objective element in the requirements of the defense so that in the final event it will be for the jury to determine whether the threat was one which the defendant in question could not reasonably have been expected to resist. This will allow the jury to take into account the nature of the offence committed, its relationship to the threats which the defendant believed to exist, the threats themselves and the circumstances in which they were made, and the personal characteristics of the defendant. The last consideration is, we feel, a most important one. Threats directed against a weak, immature or disabled person may well be much more compelling than the same threats directed against a normal healthy person. Indeed, there is some uncertainty whether Hudson and Taylor is still good law even in England. Thus, the Court of Appeals, without overruling the decision, appeared later to embrace an objective standard:

The Law Commission, Defences of General Application, Para. 2.28 (1977, Law Rev. Comm. no. 83).

b) Consistency of approach in defences to criminal liability is obviously desirable. Provocation and duress are analogous. In provocation the words or actions of one person break the self-control of another. In duress the words or actions of one person break the will of another. The law requires a defendant to have the self-control reasonably to be expected of the ordinary citizen in his situation. It should likewise require him to have the steadfastness reasonably to be expected of the ordinary citizen in his situation. So too with self-defense, in which the law permits the use of no more force than is reasonable in the circumstances. And, in general, if a mistake is to excuse what would otherwise be criminal, the mistake must be a reasonable one.

Regina v. Graham, [1982] 1 All E.R. 801, 806–7.

c) The argument . . . is that the maintenance of an objective standard would develop fortitude and stop people from giving way to their fears. However, the possibility of deterrence working upon one who is under immediate threat of death or serious bodily harm is negligible . . . the possibility of frivolous claims of duress is ruled out by the requirement that the perceived threat be one of death or serious bodily harm.

Alldridge, *Duress and the Reasonable Person,* 34 No. Ire. L.Q. 125, 138 (1983).

[d] Homicide and Duress

It is generally believed that the common law did not allow duress as a defense to a homicide charge. See, *e.g., Commonwealth v. Morning wake,* 595 A.2d 158 (Pa. Super. 1991). Why not? In two famous decisions in the 1970s, the House of Lords first decided that duress could be a defense to a charge of homicide against an accomplice, *DPP for No. Ire. v. Lynch,* [1975] A.C. 653, but soon afterward held that it was unavailable if the duressed person actually committed the homicide. *Regina v. Howe,* [1986] 1 All E.R. 771. Some states broaden this ban to all crimes involving offenses involving physical violence. See, *e.g.,* Ind. Code 35-41-3-8(2), applied in *Parker v. State,* 567 N.E. 2d 105 (Ind. App. 1991). Consider the following critique by Professor Smith in *Comment: R. v. Howe,* 1987 Crim. L. Rev. 480, 481–82:

(Assume D has been told) "Kneecap P (*i.e.,* cause him grievous bodily harm) or you will be shot." If D does so and P dies, D may [under the homicide limitation—ed.] properly be charged with murder. Dreadful though the injury caused by "kneecapping" is, might not a reasonable man think it a lesser evil than the loss of his own life—and is it not a threat to which the ordinary man of reasonable fortitude might succumb? If he refuses and dies he may well merit the posthumous award of the George Cross, but it should not be a crime to fail to come up to that exacting and exceptional standard of courage.

Is Smith's critique persuasive? See also Alldridge, *Duress, Murder and the House of Lords,* 52 J. Crim. L. 186 (1988).

J. Andenaes, The General Part of the Criminal Law of Norway 170 (1965), summarizes an opinion of the Norwegian Supreme Court:

During the evacuation of the northernmost districts of the country in the last months of World War II, three Norwegian policemen were forced to participate in the execution of a compatriot who was sentenced to death by a Nazi special court. After the war they were prosecuted under Penal Code § 86 (treason) and § 233 (murder), but argued in their defense that they had acted in a necessity situation; had they refused to follow the order, they, as well as the sentenced person, would have been shot. The court found that this was most probable, but nevertheless did not find it proper to call their act lawful: "And when this is so, the Penal Code will not allow punishment to be dispensed with merely because the accused acted under duress, even where it was such a serious nature as in the case at bar, since according to the decision of the Court of Assize it must be deemed clear that the force did not preclude intentional conduct on the part of the accused."

According to Note, 9 Seton Hall L. Rev. 556, 557 (1978), 11 states that have codified the duress defense define it as a defense to any crime; 6 exclude any capital crime, 8 prohibit it in homicides, and 3, including New Jersey, reduce murder to manslaughter.

[e] Other Considerations

1. *Creating one's own duress.* What is the point of subsection (2) of MPC § 2.09, *supra?* See *Williams v. State,* 646, A.2d 1101 (Md. 1994), where defendant had become involved with a drug gang and was then abducted by former gang members, who sought to have him reveal the location of the gang's stash. Instead, defendant led the abductors to an innocent person's home, where they broke in. When defendant tried to claim duress as a defense to the break-in, the court cited the MPC and rejected the claim. See also *Regina v. Fitzpatrick,* (1977) No. Ire. 20, where a defendant who joined the IRA but later sought to leave was "duressed" to remain and participate in armed robbery. The court held that the defense was not available to him. Granting that the defendant is guilty of being stupid, isn't it nevertheless true that at the time of his act, he was acting with an "overborne will"? Is the proper answer to make joining a gang an offense, rather than have the penalty for that act depend on what the gang member is forced to do? See generally Robinson, *Causing the Conditions of One's Own Defense: A Study in the Limits of Theory in Criminal Law Doctrine,* 71 Va. L. Rev. 1 (1985).

2. *Cumulative threats.* Must the threat to life be the sole motivating factor? In *Regina v. Valderrama Vega,* 1985 Crim. L. Rev. 221, defendant, charged with drug smuggling, argued that cocaine smugglers in Colombia had threatened him and his family with death and with the disclosure of his homosexuality. The trial judge instructed the jury that the threat of death must be the sole cause of defendant's act. The Court of Appeal questioned whether this was accurate, but said that in the case, the instructions as a whole were clear, and therefore the error, if it was error, was harmless. Does the Model Penal Code approach solve this issue?

3. *Duress as a "defense" at all.* For an argument that duress should not be a defense, but should be considered only during sentencing, see Wasik, *Duress and Criminal Responsibility,* 1977 Crim. L. Rev. 453. Accord Kilbrandon, *Duress per Minas as a Defense to Crime I;* Kenny, *Duress per Minas as a Defense to Crime: II;* and Anton, *Duress per Minas as a Defense to Crime: III,* in 1 Law & Phil. 185, 197, and 207 (1982), respectively.

For general discussions, see Dressler, *Exegesis on the Law of Duress: Justifying the Excuse and Searching for Its Proper Limits,* 62 So. Cal. L. Rev. 1331 (1989); Hitchler, *Duress as a Defense in Criminal Cases,* 4 Va. L. Rev. 519 (1917); Perkins, *Impelled Perpetration Restated,* 33 Hastings L.J. 403 (1981).

[2] Superior Orders

Similar to the defense of duress is that of "superior orders" in the military. In a well known decision, the Court of Military Appeals held that a lieutenant in Vietnam who (*arguendo,* for purposes of the appeal) had been ordered to kill helpless women and children had no defense unless a reasonable person would believe the order to be legal (which it clearly was not). This, of course, may well be the effect of the Nuremberg trials and the Holocaust. According to Brewer, *Their's Not to Reason Why—Some Aspects of the Defense of Superior Orders in New Zealand Military Law,* 10 V.U.W. L. Rev. 45 (1979), it is at least arguable that, prior to the Nuremberg Trials, the defense of superior orders was absolute under international law—so long as the defendant obeyed the order, he was not held culpable.

Brewer asserts that the rule applied in the Nuremberg trials was that obedience to superior orders was never a defense, whatever the beliefs of the defendant: "The fact that the defendant acted pursuant to orders of a superior shall not free him from responsibility but may be considered in mitigation of punishment if the tribunal determines that justice so requires." London Agreement, Charter of the International Military Tribunal (1945), art. 8.

Since that time, most nations have ameliorated the new rule substantially, providing that the defendant loses a defense only if the order is "manifestly" criminal, or illegal. The Turkish position went even further:

> [T]he manifest unlawful character of an order, the existence of circumstances from which such a character would obviously be inferred, even a serious doubt, are not sufficient for a subordinate to be held liable; his knowledge of the criminal purpose of the order must be shown.

For a comparative study, see L. Green, *Superior Orders in National and International Law* (1976). See also Creighton, *Superior Orders and Command Responsibility in Canadian Criminal Law,* 38 U. Toronto Fac. L. Rev. 1 (1980).

[3] Necessity

> ROMEO: Come hither, man, I see that thou are poor:
> Hold, for there is forty ducats; let me have
> A dram of poison. . . .
> APOTHECARY: Such mortal drugs I have; but Mantua's law
> Is death to any he that utters them.
> ROMEO: Art thou so base and full of wretchedness
> And fear'st to die? . . .
> The world is not thy friend nor the world's law;
> The world affords no law to make thee rich;
> Then be not poor, but break it, and take this.
> APOTHECARY: My poverty, but not my will, consents.
> ROMEO: I pay thy poverty, and not thy will.

Shakespeare, *Romeo and Juliet, Act V, Scene 1*

BLACKSTONE

27

A SIXTH species of defect of will is that arising from *compulsion* and inevitable *necessity*. These are a constraint upon the will, whereby a man is urged to do that which his judgment disapproves; and which, it is to be presumed, his will (if left to itself) would reject. As punishments are therefore only inflicted for the abuse of that free-will, which God has given to man, it is highly just and equitable that a man should be excused for those acts, which are done through unavoidable force and compulsion.

There is a third species of necessity, which may be distinguished from the actual compulsion of external force or fear; being the result of reason and reflection, which act upon and constrain a man's will, and oblige him to do an action, which without such obligation would be criminal. And that is, when a man has his choice of two evils set before him, and, being under a necessity of choosing one, he chooses the least pernicious of the two. Here the will cannot be said freely to exert itself, being rather passive than active; or, if active, it is rather in rejecting the greater evil than in choosing the less. Of this sort is that necessity where a man by the commandment of the law is bound to arrest another for any capital offense, or to disperse a riot, and resistance is made to his authority: it is here justifiable, and even necessary, to beat, to wound, or perhaps to kill the offenders, rather than permit the murderer to escape or the riot to continue. . . .

Regina v. Dudley and Stephens

The Queen's Bench

14 Q.B.D. 273 (1884)

INDICTMENT for the murder of Richard Parker on the high seas within the jurisdiction of the Admiralty.

At the trial before Huddleston, B., the jury, at the suggestion of the learned judge, found the facts of the case in a special verdict which stated

that on July 5, 1884, the prisoners, Thomas Dudley and Edward Stephens, with one Brooks, all able-bodied English seamen, and the deceased also an English boy, between seventeen and eighteen years of age, the crew of an English yacht, a registered English vessel, were cast away in a storm on the high seas 1600 miles from the Cape of Good Hope, and were compelled to put into an open boat belonging to the said yacht. That in this boat they had no supply of water and no supply of food, except two 1 lb. tins of turnips, and for three days they had nothing else to subsist upon. That on the fourth day they caught a small turtle, upon which they subsisted for a few days, and this was the only food they had up to the twentieth day when the act now in question was committed. That on the twelfth day the remains of the turtle were entirely consumed, and for the next eight days they had nothing to eat. That they had no fresh water, except such rain as they from time to time caught in their oilskin capes. That the boat was drifting on the ocean, and was probably more than 1000 miles away from land. That on the eighteenth day, when they had been seven days without food and five without water, the prisoners spoke to Brooks as to what should be done if no succor came, and suggested that someone should be sacrificed to save the rest, but Brooks dissented, and the boy, to whom they were understood to refer, was not consulted. That on the 24th of July, the day before the act now in question, the prisoner Dudley proposed to Stephens and Brooks that lots should be cast who should be put to death to save the rest, but Brooks refused to consent, and it was not put to the boy, and in point of fact there was no drawing of lots. That on that day the prisoners spoke of their having families, and suggested it would be better to kill the boy that their lives should be saved, and Dudley proposed that if there was no vessel in sight by the morrow morning the boy should be killed. The next day, the 25th of July, no vessel appearing, Dudley told Brooks that he had better go and have a sleep, and made signs to Stephens and Brooks that the boy had better be killed. The prisoner Stephens agreed to the act, but Brooks dissented from it. That the boy was then lying at the bottom of the boat quite helpless, and extremely weakened by famine and by drinking sea water, and unable to make any resistance, nor did he ever assent to his being killed. The prisoner Dudley offered a prayer asking forgiveness for them all if either of them should be tempted to commit a rash act, and that their souls might be saved. That Dudley, with the assent of Stephens, went to the boy, and telling him that his time was come, put a knife into his throat and killed him then and there; that the three men fed upon the body and blood of the boy for four days; that on the fourth day after the act had been committed the boat was picked up by a passing vessel, and the prisoners were rescued, still alive, but in the lowest state of prostration.

That if the men had not fed upon the body of the boy they would probably not have survived to be so picked up and rescued, but would within the four days have died of famine. That the boy, being in a much weaker condition, was likely to have died before them. That at the time of the act in question there was no sail in sight, nor any reasonable prospect of relief. That under these circumstances there appeared to the prisoners every probability that unless they then fed or very soon fed upon the boy or one of themselves they would die of starvation. That there was no appreciable chance of saving life except by killing someone for the others to eat. That assuming any necessity to kill anybody, there was no greater necessity for killing the boy than any of the other three men. But whether upon the whole matter by the jurors found the killing of Richard Parker by Dudley and Stephens be felony and murder the jurors are ignorant, and pray the advice of the Court thereupon, and if upon the whole matter the Court shall be of opinion that the killing of Richard Parker be felony and murder, then the jurors say that Dudley and Stephens were guilty of felony and murder as alleged in the indictment.

The learned judge then adjourned the assizes until the 25th of November at the Royal Courts of Justice. On the application of the Crown they were again adjourned to the 4th of December, and the case ordered to be argued before a Court consisting of five judges.

Lord COLERIDGE, C.J.

From these facts, stated with the cold precision of a special verdict, it appears sufficiently that the prisoners were subject to terrible temptation, to sufferings which might break down the bodily power of the strongest man, and try the conscience of the best. Other details yet more harrowing, facts still more loathsome and appalling, were presented to the jury, and are to be found recorded in my learned Brother's notes. But nevertheless this is clear, that the prisoners put to death a weak and unoffending boy upon the chance of preserving their own lives by feeding upon his flesh and blood after he was killed, and with the certainty of depriving *him* of any possible chance of survival. The verdict finds in terms that "if the men had not fed upon the body of the boy they would *probably* not have survived," and that "the boy being in a much weaker condition was *likely* to have died before them." They might possibly have been picked up next day by a passing ship; they might possibly not have been picked up at all; in either case it is obvious that the killing of the boy would have been an unnecessary and profitless act. It is found by the verdict that the boy was incapable of resistance, and, in fact, made none; and it is not even suggested that his death was due to any violence on his part attempted against, or even so much as feared by, those who killed him. Under these circumstances the jury say that they are ignorant whether those who killed him were guilty of murder, and have referred it to this Court to determine what is the legal consequence which follows from the facts which they have found.

There remains to be considered the real question in the case—whether killing under the circumstances set forth in the verdict be or be not murder. The contention that it could be anything else was, to the minds of us all, both new and strange, and we stopped the Attorney General in his negative argument in order that we might hear what could be said in support of a proposition which appeared to us to be at once dangerous, immoral, and opposed to all legal principle and analogy. All, no doubt, that can be said has been urged before us, and we are now to consider and determine what it amounts to. First it is said that it follows from various definitions of murder in books of authority, which definitions imply, if they do not state, the doctrine, that in order to save your own life you may lawfully take away the life of another, when that other is neither attempting nor threatening yours, nor is guilty of any illegal act whatever towards you or any one else. But if these definitions be looked at they will not be found to sustain this contention. . . .

But, further still, Lord Hale . . . deals with the position asserted by the casuists, and sanctioned, as he says, by Grotius and Puffendorf, that in a case of extreme necessity, either of hunger or clothing, "theft is no theft, or at least not punishable as theft, as some even of our own lawyers have asserted the same." "But," says Lord Hale, "I take it that here in England, that rule, at least by the laws of England, is false; and therefore, if a person, being under necessity for want of victuals or clothes, shall upon that account clandestinely and *animo furandi* steal another man's goods, it is felony, and a crime by the laws of England punishable with death." (Hale, Pleas of the Crown, i. 54.) If, therefore, Lord Hale is clear—as he is—that extreme necessity of hunger does not justify larceny, what would he have said to the doctrine that it justified murder?

Is there, then, any authority for the proposition which has been presented to us? Decided cases there are none. The American case cited by my Brother Stephen in his Digest, from Wharton on Homicide, in which it was decided, correctly indeed, that sailors had no right to throw passengers overboard to save themselves, but on the somewhat strange ground that the proper mode of determining who was to be sacrificed was to vote upon the subject by ballot, can hardly, as my Brother Stephen says, be an authority satisfactory to a court in this country.

. . . We exclude from our consideration all the incidents of war. We are dealing with a case of private homicide, not one imposed upon men in the service of their Sovereign and in the defense of their country. Now it is admitted that the deliberate killing of this unoffending and unresisting boy was clearly murder, unless the killing can be justified by some well-recognized excuse admitted by the law. It is further admitted that there was in this case no such excuse, unless the killing was justified by what has been called "necessity." But the temptation to the act which existed here was not what the law has ever called necessity. . . . Though law and morality are not the same, and many things may be immoral which are not necessarily illegal, yet the absolute divorce of law from morality would be of fatal consequence; and such divorce would follow if the temptation to murder in this case were to be held by law an absolute defense of it. It is not so. To preserve one's life is generally speaking a duty, but it may be the plainest and the highest duty to sacrifice it. War is full of instances in which it is a man's duty not to live, but to die. The duty, in case of shipwreck, of a captain to his crew, of the crew to the passengers, of soldiers to women and children; these duties impose on men the moral necessity, not of the preservation, but of the sacrifice of their lives for others, from which in no country, least of all, it is to be hoped, in England, will men ever shrink, as indeed, they have not shrunk. It is not correct, therefore, to say that there is any absolute or unqualified necessity to preserve one's life.

It is not needful to point out the awful danger of admitting the principle which has been contended for. Who is to be the judge of his sort of necessity? By what measure is the comparative value of lives to be measured? Is it to be strength, or intellect, or what? It is plain that the principle leaves to him who is to profit by it to determine the necessity which will justify him in deliberately taking another's life to save his own. In this case the weakest, the youngest, the most unresisting, was chosen. Was it more necessary to kill him than one of the grown men? The answer must be "No"—

So spake the Fiend, and with necessity,

The tyrant's plea, excused his devilish deeds.

[I]t is quite plain that such a principle once admitted might be made the legal cloak for unbridled passion and atrocious crime. There is no safe path for judges to tread but to ascertain the law to the best of their ability and to declare it according to their judgment; and if in any case the law appears to be too severe on individuals, to leave it to the Sovereign to exercise that prerogative of mercy which the Constitution has intrusted to the hands fittest to dispense it.

It must not be supposed that in refusing to admit temptation to be an excuse for crime it is forgotten how terrible the temptation was; how awful the suffering; how hard in such trials to keep the judgment straight and the conduct pure. We are often compelled to set up standards we cannot reach ourselves, and to lay down rules which we could not ourselves satisfy. But a man has no right to declare temptation to be an excuse, though he might himself have yielded to it, nor allow compassion for the criminal to change or weaken in any manner the legal definition of the crime. It is therefore our duty to declare that the prisoners' act in this case was wilful murder, that the facts as stated in the verdict are no legal justification of the homicide; and to say that in our unanimous opinion the prisoners are upon this special verdict guilty of murder.[1]

THE COURT then proceeded to pass sentence of death upon the prisoners. [This sentence was afterwards commuted by the Crown to six months' imprisonment.—Eds.]

---

[1] My brother Grove has furnished me with the following suggestion, too late to be embodied in the judgment but well worth preserving: "If the two accused men were justified in killing Parker, then if not rescued in time, two of the three survivors would be justified in killing the third, and of the two who remained, the stronger would be justified in killing the weaker, so that three men might be justifiably killed to give the fourth a chance of surviving."—C.

Perka v. The Queen

Supreme Court of Canada

13 D.L.R. (4th) 1 (1984)

DICKSON J:...

I Facts

The appellants are drug smugglers. At trial, they led evidence that in early 1979 three of the appellants were employed, with 16 crew members, to deliver, by ship (the *Samarkanda*) a load of *cannabis* (marijuana) worth $6,000 or $7,000 from a point in international waters off the coast of Columbia, South America to a drop-point in international waters 200 miles off the coast of Alaska. The ship left Tumaco, Colombia, empty with a port-clearance document stating the destination to be Juneau, Alaska. For three weeks the ship remained in international waters off the coast of Colombia. While there, a DC-6 aircraft made four trips, dropping into the water shrimp-nets with a total of 634 bales of *cannabis* which were retrieved by the ship's long-boats.

A "communications" package was also dropped from a light aircraft, giving instructions for a rendezvous with another vessel, the *Julia B,* which was to pick up the cargo of *cannabis* from the *Samarkanda* in international waters off the coast of Alaska. En route, according to the defense evidence, the vessel began to encounter a series of problems: engine breakdowns, overheating generators and malfunctioning navigation devices, aggravated by deteriorating weather. In the meantime, the fourth appellant, Nelson, part-owner of the illicit cargo, and three other persons left Seattle in a small boat, the *Whitecap,* intending to rendezvous with the *Samarkanda* at the drop-point in Alaska. The problems of the *Samarkanda* intensified as fuel was consumed. The vessel became lighter, the intakes in the hull for sea-water, used as a coolant, lost suction and took in air instead, causing the generators to overheat. At this point the vessel was 180 miles from the Canadian coastline. The weather worsened. There were eight-to-ten-foot swells and a rising wind. It was finally decided for the safety of ship and crew to seek refuge on the Canadian shoreline for the purpose of making temporary repairs. The *Whitecap* found a sheltered cove on the west coast of Vancouver Island, "No Name Bay." The *Samarkanda* followed the *Whitecap* into the bay but later grounded amidships on a rock because the depth sounder was not working. The tide ran out. The vessel listed severely to starboard, to the extent that the captain, fearing the vessel was going to capsize, ordered the men to off-load the cargo. That is a brief summary of the defense evidence.

Early on the morning of May 22, 1979, police officers entered No Name Bay in a marked police boat with siren sounding. The *Samarkanda* and the *Whitecap* were arrested, as were all the appellants except Perka and Nelson, the same morning. The vessels and 33.49 tons of *cannabis* marijuana were seized by the police officers.

Charged with importing *cannabis* into Canada and with possession for the purpose of trafficking, the appellants claimed they did not plan to import into

Canada or to leave their cargo of *cannabis* in Canada. They had planned to make repairs and leave. Expert witnesses on marine matters called by the defense testified that the decision to come ashore was, in the opinion of one witness, expedient and prudent and in the opinion of another, essential. At trial, counsel for the Crown alleged that the evidence of the ship's distress was a recent fabrication. Crown counsel relied on the circumstances under which the appellants were arrested to belie the "necessity" defense; when the police arrived on the scene most of the marijuana was already onshore, along with plastic ground sheets, battery-operated lights, liquor, food, clothing, camp stoves and sleeping-bags. Nevertheless, the jury believed the appellants and acquitted them. The acquittal was reversed on appeal.

The appellants have now appealed to this Court. The Crown has raised [the question]: whether the trial judge erred in charging the jury with respect to the necessity defense.

* * *

II THE NECESSITY DEFENSE

(a) History and Background

From earliest times it has been maintained that in some situations the force of circumstances makes it unrealistic and unjust to attach criminal liability to actions which, on their face, violate the law. Aristotle, Ethics (Book III, 1110a), discusses the jettisoning of cargo from a ship in distress and remarks that "any sensible man does so" to secure the safety of himself and his crew. . . .

* * *

In those jurisdictions in which such a general principle has been recognized or codified it is most often referred to by the term "necessity." Classic and harrowing instances which have been cited to illustrate the arguments both for and against the principle include the mother who steals food for her starving child, the shipwrecked mariners who resort to cannibalism (*R. v. Dudley and Stephens* (1884), 14 Q.B.D. 273), or throw passengers overboard to lighten a sinking lifeboat (*United States v. Holmes* (1842), 26 Fed. Cas. 360), and the more mundane case of the motorist who exceeds the speed-limit taking an injured person to the hospital. . . .

* * *

(b) The Conceptual Foundation of the Defense

In *Morgentaler [v. The Queen]* [1976] 1 S.C.R. 616], I characterized necessity as an "ill-defined and elusive concept." Despite the apparently growing consensus as to the existence of a defense of necessity that statement is equally true today.

This is no doubt in part because, though apparently laying down a single rule as to criminal liability, the "defense" of necessity in fact is capable of embracing two different and distinct notions. As Mr. Justice Macdonald observed succinctly but accurately: "Generally speaking, the defense of necessity covers all cases where non-compliance with law is excused by an emergency or justified by the pursuit of some greater good."

Working Paper 29 of the Law Reform Commission of Canada, *Criminal Law: The General Part: Liability and Defences* (1982), p.93, makes this same point in somewhat more detail:

> The rationale of necessity, however, is clear. Essentially it involves two factors. One is the avoidance of greater harm or the pursuit of some greater good, the other is the difficulty of compliance with law in emergencies. From these two factors emerge two different but related principles. The first is a utilitarian principle to the effect that, within certain limits, it is justifiable in an emergency to break the letter of the law if breaking the law will avoid a greater harm than obeying it. The second is a humanitarian principle to the effect that, again within limits, it is excusable in an emergency to break the law if compliance would impose an intolerable burden on the accused.

Despite any superficial similarities, these two principles are in fact quite distinct and many of the confusions and the difficulties in the cases (and, with respect, in academic discussions) arise from a failure to distinguish between them.

[T]he two different approaches to the "defense" of necessity from Blackstone forward correspond, the one to a justification, the other to an excuse. The criminal law recognizes and our *Criminal Code* codifies a number of specific categories of justification and of excuse. The remainder, those instances that conform to the general principle but do not fall within any specific category such as self-defense on the one hand or insanity on the other, purportedly fall within the "residual defense" of necessity.

As a "justification" this residual defense can be related to Blackstone's concept of a "choice of evils." It would exculpate actors whose conduct could reasonably have been viewed as "necessary" in order to prevent a greater evil than that resulting from the violation of the law. As articulated, especially in some of the American cases, it involves a utilitarian balancing of the benefits of obeying the law as opposed to disobeying it and when the balance is clearly in favour of disobeying, exculpates an actor who contravenes a criminal statute. This is the "greater good" formulation of the necessity defense: in some circumstances, it is alleged, the values of society, indeed of the criminal law itself, are better promoted by disobeying a given statute than by observing it. . . .

Conceptualized as an "excuse," however, the residual defense of necessity is, in my view, much less open to criticism. It rests on a realistic assessment of human weakness, recognizing that a liberal and humane criminal law cannot hold people to the strict obedience of laws in emergency situations where normal human instinct, whether of self-preservation or of altruism, overwhelmingly impels disobedience. The objectivity of the criminal law is preserved; such acts are still wrongful, but in the circumstances they are excusable. Praise is indeed not bestowed, but pardon is, when one does a wrongful act under pressure which, in the words of Aristotle in The Nicomachean Ethics, "overstrains human nature and which no one could withstand." . . .

The excuse of necessity does not go to voluntariness in this sense. The lost Alpinist who, on the point of freezing to death, breaks open an isolated mountain cabin is not literally behaving in an involuntary fashion. He has control over his actions to the extent of being physically capable of abstaining from the act.

Realistically, however, his act is not a "voluntary" one. His "choice" to break the law is no true choice at all; it is remorselessly compelled by normal human instincts. This sort of involuntariness is often described as "moral or normative involuntariness." Its place in criminal theory is described by Fletcher at pp.804–5 as follows:

> The notion of voluntariness adds a valuable dimension to the theory of excuses. That conduct is involuntary—even in the normative sense—explains why it cannot fairly be punished. Indeed, H.L.A. Hart builds his theory of excuses on the principle that the distribution of punishment should be reserved for those who voluntarily break the law. Of the arguments he advances for this principle of justice, the most explicit is that it is preferable to live in a society where we have the maximum opportunity to choose whether we shall become the subject of criminal liability. In addition Hart intimates that it is ideologically desirable for the government to treat its citizens as self-actuating, choosing agents. This principle of respect for individual autonomy is implicitly confirmed whenever those who lack an adequate choice are excused for their offenses.

I agree with this formulation of the *rationale* for excuses in the criminal law. In my view, this *rationale* extends beyond specific codified excuses and embraces the residual excuse known as the defense of necessity. At the heart of this defense is the perceived injustice of punishing violations of the law in circumstances in which the person had no other viable or reasonable choice available; the act was wrong but it is excused because it was realistically unavoidable. . . .

(c) Limitations on the Defense

If the defense of necessity is to form a valid and consistent part of our criminal law it must, as has been universally recognized, be strictly controlled and scrupulously limited to situations that correspond to its underlying rationale. That rationale as I have indicated is the recognition that it is inappropriate to punish actions which are normatively "involuntary."

In *Morgentaler, supra,* I was of the view that any defense of necessity was restricted to instances of noncompliance "in urgent situations of clear and imminent peril when compliance with the law is demonstrably impossible." In my opinion, this restriction focuses directly on the "involuntariness" of the purportedly necessitous behaviour by providing a number of tests for determining whether the wrongful act was truly the only realistic reaction open to the actor or whether he was in fact making what in fairness could be called a choice. If he was making a choice, then the wrongful act cannot have been involuntary in the relevant sense.

The requirement that the situation be urgent and the peril be imminent, tests whether it was indeed unavoidable for the actor to act at all. . . .

The requirement that compliance with the law be "demonstrably impossible" takes this assessment one step further. Given that the accused had to act, could he nevertheless realistically have acted to avoid the peril or prevent the harm, without breaking the law? Was there a legal way out? I think this is what Bracton means when he lists "necessity" as a defense, providing the wrongful act was not "avoidable." The question to be asked is whether the agent had any real choice: could he have done otherwise? If there is a reasonable legal alternative to disobeying the law, then the decision to disobey becomes a voluntary one, impelled by some consideration beyond the dictates of "necessity" and human instincts.

The importance of this requirement that there be no reasonable legal alternative cannot be overstressed.

Even if the requirements for urgency and "no legal way out" are met, there is clearly a further consideration. There must be some way of assuring proportionality. No rational criminal justice system, no matter how humane or liberal, could excuse the infliction of a greater harm to allow the actor to avert a lesser evil. In such circumstances we expect the individual to bear the harm and refrain from acting illegally. If he cannot control himself we will not excuse him. According to Fletcher, this requirement is also related to the notion of voluntariness [at p.804]:

> . . . if the gap between the harm done and the benefit accrued becomes too great, the act is more likely to appear voluntary and therefore inexcusable. For example, if the actor has to blow up a whole city in order to avoid the breaking of his finger, we might appropriately expect him to endure the harm to himself. His surrendering to the threat in this case violates our expectations of appropriate and normal resistance to pressure. Yet as we lower the degree of harm to others and increase the threatened harm to the person under duress we will reach a threshold at which, in the language of the Model Penal Code, "a person of reasonable firmness" would be "unable to resist." Determining this threshold is patently a matter of moral judgment about what we expect people to be able to resist in trying situations. A valuable aid in making that judgment is comparing the competing interests at stake and assessing the degree to which the actor inflicts harm beyond the benefit that accrues from his action.

* * *

In my view, the accused's fault in bringing about the situation later invoked to excuse his conduct can be relevant to the availability of the defense of necessity, but not in the sweeping way suggested by some of the commentators and in some of the statutory formulations. In so far as the accused's "fault" reflects on the moral quality of the action taken to meet the emergency, it is irrelevant to the issue of the availability of the defense on the same basis as the illegality or immorality of the actions preceding the emergency are irrelevant. If this fault is capable of attracting criminal or civil liability in its own right, the culprit should be appropriately sanctioned. I see no basis, however, for "transferring" such liability to the actions taken in response to the emergency, especially where to do so would result in attaching criminal consequences on the basis of negligence to actions which would otherwise be excused.

In my view, the better approach to the relationship of fault to the availability of necessity as a defense is based once again on the question of whether the actions sought to be excused were truly "involuntary." If the necessitous situation was clearly foreseeable to a reasonable observer, if the actor contemplated or ought to have contemplated that his actions would likely give rise to an emergency requiring the breaking of the law, then I doubt whether what confronted the accused was in the relevant sense an emergency. His response was in that sense not "involuntary." "Contributory fault" of this nature, but only of this nature, is a relevant consideration to the availability of the defense. . . .

* * *

(e) Onus of Proof

Although necessity is spoken of as a defense, in the sense that it is raised by the accused, the Crown always bears the burden of proving a voluntary act. The prosecution must prove every element of the crime charged. One such element is the voluntariness of the act. Normally, voluntariness can be presumed, but if the accused places before the court, through his own witnesses or through cross-examination of Crown witnesses, evidence sufficient to raise an issue that the situation created by external forces was so emergent that failure to act could endanger life or health and upon any reasonable view of the facts, compliance with the law was impossible, then the Crown must beprepared to meet that issue. There is no onus of proof on the accused.

* * *

(f) Preliminary Conclusions as to the Defense of Necessity

It is now possible to summarize a number of conclusions as to the defense of necessity in terms of its nature, basis and limitations:

(1) the defense of necessity could be conceptualized as either a justification or an excuse;

(2) it should be recognized in Canada as an excuse, operating by virtue of § 7(3) of the Criminal Code;

(3) necessity as an excuse implies no vindication of the deeds of the actor;

(4) the criterion is the moral involuntariness of the wrongful action;

(5) this involuntariness is measured on the basis of society's expectation of appropriate and normal resistance to pressure;

(6) negligence or involvement in criminal or immoral activity does not disentitle the actor to the excuse of necessity;

(7) actions or circumstances which indicate that the wrongful deed was not truly involuntary do disentitle;

(8) the existence of a reasonable legal alternative similarly disentitles; to be involuntary the act must be inevitable, unavoidable and afford no reasonable opportunity for an alternative course of action that does not involve a breach of the law;

(9) the defense only applies in circumstances of imminent risk where the action was taken to avoid a direct and immediate peril;

(10) where the accused places before the court sufficient evidence to raise the issue, the onus is on the Crown to meet it beyond a reasonable doubt.

. . . The summary of conclusions with regard to necessity in the foregoing section indicated that for the defense to succeed, an accused's actions must be, in the relevant sense, an "involuntary" response to an imminent and overwhelming peril. The defense cannot succeed if the response was disproportional to the peril or if it was not "involuntary" in the sense that the emergency was not "real" or not imminent or that there was a reasonble alternative response that was not illegal.

In the course of his charge on the issue of necessity the trial judge instructed the jury . . . to the effect that they must find facts which amount to "an urgent situation of clear and imminent peril when compliance with the law is demonstrably impossible" in order for the appellants' non-compliance with the law against importation and possession of *cannabis* to be excused. That is the correct test. It is, with respect, however, my view that in explaining the meaning and application of this test, the trial judge fell into error.

The trial judge was obliged, in my opinion, to direct the jury's attention to a number of issues pertinent to the test for necessity. Was the emergency a real one? Did it constitute an immediate threat of the harm purportedly feared? Was the response proportionate? In comparing this response to the danger that motivated it, was the danger one that society would reasonably expect the average person to withstand? Was there any reasonable legal alternative to the illegal response open to the accused? Although the trial judge did not explicitly pose each and every one of these questions in my view his charge was adequate to bring the consideration underlying them to the jury's attention on every issue except the last one, the question of a reasonable alternative.

* * *

In his charge, the trial judge . . . [told] the jury that they must find facts capable of showing that "compliance with the law was demonstrably impossible. . . " but on his recharge he put before the jury a significantly different test. The test, he said, is:

. . . can you find facts from this evidence, and that means all the evidence, of course, that the situation of the *Samarkanda* at sea was so appallingly dire and dangerous to life that a reasonable doubt arises as to whether or not their decision was justified?

And again, at the conclusion of the recharge:

There is no need for the evidence to show that a certainty of death would result unless the action complained of by the Crown was taken. It doesn't go so far as that. You have to look at it as reasonable people and decide on any reasonable view of the matter, would these people have been justified in doing what they did? That is all that necessity means.

Both of these passages imply that the crucial consideration was whether the accused acted reasonably in coming into shore with their load of *cannabis* rather than facing death at sea. That is not sufficient as a test. Even if it does deal with the reality of the peril, its imminence and the proportionality of putting into shore, it does not deal at all with the question of whether there existed any other reasonable responses to the peril that were not illegal. Indeed, aside from the initial repetition of the *Morgentaler* formula, the trial judge did not advert to this consideration at all, nor did he direct the jury's attention to the relevance of evidence indicating the possibility of such alternative courses of action. In these respects I believe he erred in law. He did not properly put the question of a "legal way out" before the jury.

In my view, this was a serious error and omission going to the heart of the defense of necessity. The error justifies a new trial.

* * *

WILSON J. . . .

[I]nasmuch as the Chief Justice's conclusion as to the defense of necessity seems clearly correct on the facts of this case and his disposition of the appeal manifestly just in the circumstances, I am dealing in these reasons only with the proposition very forcefully advanced by the Chief Justice in his reasons that the appropriate jurisprudential basis on which to premise the defense of necessity is exclusively that of excuse. My concern is that the learned Chief Justice appears to be closing the door on justification as an appropriate jurisprudential basis in some cases and I am firmly of the view that this is a door which should be left open by the court.

* * *

Turning first to the category of excuse, the concept of "normative involuntariness" stressed in the reasons of the Chief Justice may, on one reading, be said to fit squarely within the framework of an individualized plea which Professor Fletcher indicates characterizes all claims of excusability. The notional involuntariness of the action is assessed in the context of the accused's particular situation. The court must ask not only whether the offensive act accompanied by the requisite culpable mental state (*i.e.,* intention, recklessness, etc.) has been established by the prosecution, but whether or not the accused acted so as to attract society's moral outrage. . . . In evaluating a claim of "normative involuntariness" we seem to be told that the individual's criminally wrongful act was nevertheless blameless in the circumstances.

The position in English law, by contrast, was most accurately stated in the well-known case of *R. v. Dudley and Stephens* in which Lord Coleridge C.J. warned against allowing "compassion for the criminal to change or weaken in any manner the legal definition of the crime." The underlying principle here is the universality of rights, that all individuals whose actions are subjected to legal evaluation must be considered equal in standing. Indeed, it may be said that this concept of equal assessment of every actor, regardless of his particular motives or the particular pressures operating upon his will, is so fundamental to the criminal law as rarely to receive explicit articulation. However, the entire premise expressed by such thinkers as Kant and Hegal that man is by nature a rational being, and that this rationality finds expression both in the human capacity to overcome the impulses of one's own will and in the universal right to be free from the imposition of the impulses and will of others (see Hegel's, Philosophy of Right (Knox, translator, 1952), at pp.226–7) supports the view that an individualized assessment of offensive conduct is simply not possible. If the obligation to refrain from criminal behaviour is perceived as a reflection of the fundamental duty to be rationally cognizant of the equal freedom of all individuals, then the focus of an analysis of culpability must be on the act itself (including its physical and mental elements) and not on the actor. The universality of such obligations precludes the relevance of what Fletcher refers to as "an individualized excusing condition."

On the other hand, the necessity of an act may be said to exempt an actor from punishment, since the person who acts in a state of what the Chief Justice calls "normative involuntariness" may be viewed as having been moved to act by the instinct for self-preservation. If so, the defense does not invoke the court's compassion but rather embodies an implicit statement that the sanction threatened by law (*i.e.*, future punishment in one form or another) could never overcome the fear of immediate death which the accused faced. Accordingly, in such a case the law is incapable of controlling the accused's conduct and responding to it with any punishment at all. Although such an act dictated by the necessity of self-preservation is a voluntary one (in the normal sense of the word), its "normative involuntariness" (in the sense that the actor faced no realistic choice) may form the basis of a defense if this is conceived as based on the pointlessness of punishment rather than on a view of the act itself as one the accused was entitled to commit. . . .

[A]n analytic focus on excusing conditions is often premised on the fact that punishment in such situations will not serve the further goals of deterrence, rehabilitation, etc. Such considerations, however, cannot form the basis of an acceptable defense since they seem to view criminal culpability merely as a phenomenon in a chain of cause and effect. From an instrumentalist point of view the question is not whether liability is demanded in and of itself (as Lord Coleridge C.J. insisted must be the case in *Dudley and Stephens, supra*), but rather whether the infliction of punishment will have some positive consequential effect: see, *e.g.*, J. Bentham, An Introduction to the Principles of Morals and Legislation, 2nd ed. (1823), vol. II, p.1.

The view of criminal liability as purposive only when it serves as a means to a further end is inherently problematic since the further goals of punishment are by their very nature one step removed from the determination of guilt or innocence. Just as we do not inquire into the socio-economic effects of a particular remedy for determining parties' respective rights in civil litigation . . . it does not seem possible to evaluate criminality with regard to the end results which punishment will or will not achieve. Accordingly, if the basis for the accused's defense is reducible to compassion for his individual attributes or predicament, or the ineffectiveness of punishment in rehabilitating him or deterring future acts, the question raised is the type of remedy and the fashioning of an appropriate sentence. The concerns embodied in such a defense are legitimately addressed to the sentencing process but cannot, in my view, be the basis of a successful defense leading to an acquittal.

This, however, is distinguishable from the situation in which punishment cannot on any grounds be justified, such as the situation where a person has acted in order to save his own life. As Kant indicates, although the law must refrain from asserting that conduct which otherwise constitutes an offence is rightful if done for the sake of self-preservation, there is no punishment which could conceivably be appropriate to the accused's act. As such, the actor falling within the Chief Justice's category of "normative involuntariness" is excused not because there is no instrumental ground on which to justify his punishment, but because no purpose inherent to criminal liability and punishment—*i.e.*, the setting right of a wrongful act—can be accomplished for an act which no rational person would avoid.

Returning to the defense of necessity as a justification, it may generally be said that an act is justified on grounds of necessity if the court can say that not only was the act a necessary one but it was rightful rather than wrongful. When grounded on the fundamental principle that a successful defense must characterize an act as one which the accused was within his rights to commit, it becomes immediately apparent that the defense does not depend on the immediacy or "normative involuntariness" of the accused's act unless, of course, the involuntariness is such as to be pertinent to the ordinary analysis of *mens rea*. The fact that one act is done out of a sense of immediacy or urgency and another after some contemplation cannot, in my view, serve to distinguish the quality of the act in terms of right or wrong. Rather, the justification must be premised on the need to fulfil a duty conflicting with the one which the accused is charged with having breached. . . .

[T]he Chief Justice in his reasons for judgment in the present case correctly underlines the fact that a utilitarian balancing of the benefits of obeying the law as opposed to disobeying it cannot possibly represent a legitimate principle against which to measure the legality of an action since any violation of right permitted to be justified on such a utilitarian calculus does not, in the Chief Justice's words, "fit[s] well with the judicial function." The maximization of social utility may well be a goal of legislative policy but it is not part of the judicial task of delineating right and wrong. . . .

Not only can the system of positive law not tolerate an individual opting to act in accordance with the dictates of his conscience in the event of a conflict with legal duties, but it cannot permit acts in violation of legal obligations to be justified on the grounds that social utility is thereby increased. In both situations the conflicting "duty" to which the defense arguments point is one which the court cannot take into account as it invokes considerations external to a judicial analysis of the rightness or wrongness of the impugned act.

Notes and Questions

1. Consider the rationale of necessity. Were the defendants in *Dudley and Stephens* trying to justify their act or excuse it? See Fletcher, *The Individualization of Excusing Conditions,* 47 S. Cal. L. Rev. 1269, 1274–75 (1974). Some have argued that if conduct is justified, the case so finding will set a precedent (because all similar acts must be similarly justified, and therefore legal),

whereas if conduct is excused, the decision will be unique to the individual. Is that observation, assuming it is doctrinally accurate, relevant in considering whether a particular defense, such as necessity, is a justification or an excuse? Consider its cogency when wrestling with the issue of insanity, *infra* § 9.05[B][3], which all concede is an excuse.

What purpose(s) of punishment would be served by convicting and punishing the defendants in either *Dudley or Perka* (a) according to Lord Coleridge, (b) according to utilitarian theory, (c) according to retributivist theory?

The court in *Perka* suggests that defendants in necessity situations are not "acting" "voluntarily." How does that square with the doctrine of duress? Note also that the court holds—possibly on the basis of this analysis—that the state carries the burden of persuasion on the claim. Are there other conceptualizations of necessity that would permit placing the burden of persuasion on the defendant?

Depending on the answer to the questions raised here, does necessity (or duress) apply to strict liability crimes? Consider A, who lives in a remote area and has had her driving license suspended. A's spouse, B, is seriously injured. A is the only person within miles who can drive B to the hospital. A speeds while attempting to get there and, upon arrival, parks in a no-parking zone. Evidence is clear that had A not so acted, B would have died. A is charged with

1. Driving with a suspended license.
2. Speeding.
3. Parking in a no-parking zone in a hospital.

Assuming that all three are strict liability crimes, to which charges, if any, can A successfully plead necessity? See *State v. Cole,* 403 S.E. 2d 117 (S.C. 1991); *Regina v. Conway* [1988] 3 W.L.R. 1238; *Regina v. Martin* [1989] 1 All E.R. 652. See Gardner, *Necessity's Newest Invention* 11 Ox. J. Leg. Stud. 125 (1991). Note that some states expressly provide by statute for a necessity claim in strict liability situations. *E.g.,* Ore. Rev. Stat. 811.180(1)(a), applied in *State v. Brown,* 306 Ore. 599, 761 P.2d 1300 (1988). Does this imply that the claim would not be allowed in the absence of such a provision?

Is your answer different to any or all three of these questions if B, rather than being injured, is a person who broke into A's house, and, at gunpoint, demanded that A drive him to the hospital, at breakneck speed, and park where he did? Would you need to know B's reason for the event?

2. *Dudley and Stephens* is one of the classic cases of criminal law. For a fascinating glimpse into the facts of the case and the public furor it created, see A.W.B. Simpson, Cannibalism and the Common Law (1984). See also Note, *In Warm Blood: Some Historical and Procedural Aspects of Regina v. Dudley and Stephens,* 34 U. Chi. L. Rev. 387 (1967).

3. The facts of *Dudley and Stephens* may have allowed the court to avoid at least some of the more difficult problems posed by the issue of necessity. One of these is posed by Justice Cardozo's comment on the case: "Who shall know when the masts and sails of rescue may emerge out of the fog?" B. Cardozo, Law and Literature 113 (1931). A brilliant effort to preclude the

factual "escape hatches" that Cardozo erects and therefore to pose the moral issues in their largest form is Fuller, *The Case of the Speluncean Explorers,* 62 Harv. L. Rev. 616 (1949).

4. Assuming that *Dudley and Stephens* is still good law, does *Perka* suggest that it is limited to homicide cases? See, *e.g., Nelson v. State,* 597 P.2d 977 (Alaska 1979); *United States v. Ashton,* 24 F. Cas. 873 No. 14,470 (C.C.D. Mass. 1834).

5. Although the necessity claim was essentially moribund over the past century or so, defendants in a variety of cases have recently raised the issue. Persons frustrated with the pace or conclusions reached by normal governmental processes have sought, in a number of instances, to claim necessity. Thus, persons who have used prohibited drugs, such as marijuana or laetrile, because they believe it will reduce pain from serious diseases, such as cancer, have sought to claim necessity. See, *e.g., State v. Diana,* 24 Wash. App. 908, 604 P.2d 1312 (1979); *Commonwealth v. Hutchins,* 410 Mass. 776, 575 N.E. 2d 741 (1991); *State v. Tate,* 102 N.J. 64, 505 A.2d 941 (1986). Similarly, a number of cases have arisen where persons on the grounds that the prevention of AIDS necessitates such acts have distributed clean needles to heroin addicts, thereby violating laws prohibiting the distribution of drug paraphernalia. See *Commonwealth v. Lino,* 415 Mass. 835, 616 N.E. 2d 453 (1993). Is the claim valid? See Editorial, *New York Times,* p.18 (Aug. 3, 1991). Is the necessity claim helped or hurt by the fact that a number of cities, including Seattle, New York, Tacoma, and Vancouver, have adopted plans to distribute clean needles?

Defendants who sit in or demonstrate to prevent what they consider to be immoral or illegal acts occurring on the premises often claim necessity as a defense to a charge of trespass. See *State v. Dorsey,* 118 N.H. 844, 395 A.2d 885 (1978); *State v. Warshow,* 138 Vt. 22, 410 A.2d 1000 (1979) (both protesting nuclear power facilities); *United States v. Montgomery,* 772 F.2d 734 (11th Cir. 1985) (protest against nuclear war and weapons); *United States v. Dorrell,* 758 F.2d 427 (9th Cir. 1985) (attempting to destroy a nuclear missile). See also *State v. Sahr,* 470 N.W. 2d 185 (N.D. 1991); *State v. Cozzens,* 241 Neb. 565, 490 N.W. 2d 184 (1992); *Sigma Reproductive Health Center v. State,* 297 Md. 660, 467 A.2d 483 (1983) (demonstrators from Operation Rescue protesting abortions). See Apel, *Operation Rescue and the Necessity Defense: Beginning a Feminist Deconstruction,* 48 Wash. and Lee L. Rev. 41 (1991); Russell, *Status of the Texas Necessity Defense in Abortion Clinic Trespass Cases Assuming the Demise of Roe v. Wade,* 17 Am. J. Crim. L. 1 (1989). See also Lippmann, *The Necessity Defense and Political Protest,* 26 Crim. L. Bull. 317 (1920). Some commentators suggest a distinction between "indirect" civil disobedience, such as that involved in the paragraph immediately above, and "direct" disobedience, where the disobedience itself prevents the protested governmental action. Is the distinction viable? Is it useful in deciding the legal parameters of the cases?

In 1994, Paul Hill, who killed both a doctor associated with an abortion clinic and his bodyguard, sought to claim necessity. The trial judge precluded the claim, Hill was convicted, and sentenced to die. See *Time,* August 15, 1994, p.39. The issue also created a substantial public furor when a proposed law review article exploring the question of whether such killings could be justified was suddenly withdrawn by its author. See 80 A.B.A.J. 26 (Dec. 1994). The issue of how the law should deal with political offenders is considered *infra*, § 9.05[E][2][a][ii]. In this connection, see *Apel, supra,* distinguishing between persons who protest in order to prevent acts from immediately occurring and those who protest to garner public support against a policy or current position of law.

According to Note, 30 Emory L.J. 958 (1981), religious deprogrammers charged with kidnapping or assault, have successfully argued necessity as a defense. In particular, see *United States v. Patrick,* 532 F.2d 142 (9th Cir. 1976). See also Note, 80 Mich. L. Rev. 271 (1981).

Finally, as discussed, *infra*, § 9.05[E][1], prisoners who escape from prison in response to threats of homosexual attack sometimes seek to claim necessity. These claims initially were rejected solely because there was no "teleological force" involved, as was required under the "black letter law" of necessity. Recent decisions have taken a more ameliorative approach. See especially *United States v. Lopez,* 662 F. Supp. 1083 (N.D. Cal. 1987) (recognizing that prison escape cases do not fit either duress nor necessity paradigms, but allowing defense anyway). See generally Gardner, *The Right to Escape from Prison—A Step Towards Incarceration Free from Sexual Assault,* 49 S. Cal. L. Rev. 110 (1975).

6. D, a bartender, is assaulted and stabbed by V. D tries to grab a club beneath the bar and his hand happens upon a gun that does not belong to him. He shoots V. "Possession" of a gun by D is a felony because he is an exfelon. Is he guilty of that crime, assuming that he "controlled" the gun long enough for possession? Or did D act out of necessity? Is this a viable jury issue? See *United States v. Panter,* 688 F.2d 268 (5th Cir. 1982). For other variations on this theme, see *Commonwealth v. Lindsey,* 396 Mass. 840, 489 N.E. 2d 666 (1986); *People v. King,* 22 Cal. 3d 12 (1987).

7. For general discussion of the law of necessity, see Arnolds and Garland, *The Defense of Necessity in Criminal Law: The Right to Choose the Lesser Evil,* 65 J. Crim. L. & Criminology 289 (1974); Glazebrook, *The Necessity Plea in English Criminal Law,* 30 Cambridge L.J. 87 (1972); Huxley, *Proposals and Counter Proposals on the Defense of Necessity,* 1978 Crim. L. Rev. 141; Williams, *The Defense of Necessity,* 6 Current Leg. Prob. 216 (1953); Williams, Necessity, 1978 Crim. L. Rev. 128.

[a] Codifying Necessity

English antipathy to the defense of necessity was so great that in 1977, the Law Revision Commission, rejecting the recommendation of its "Working Party" that the defense be codified, instead endorsed legislation totally abolishing the defense in England. Law Revision Commission, Report No. 83—Defenses of General Application 19-32 (1977):

> An immediate blood transfusion must be made in order to save an injured person: the only one who has the same blood type as the injured [person] refuses to give blood. Can he be overpowered, and the blood taken from him? The necessity defense advocated by the working party would by its terms

almost certainly answer this in the affirmative. But one of those commenting on the working paper expressed doubts as to whether this would be regarded as a generally acceptable solution. We share these doubts. It is however, almost, if not entirely, impossible to devise any generalized exception which would exclude the availability of a general defense in this situation. It may, of course, be objected that such examples are mere academic puzzles, and are so unlikely to arise in practice that they may safely be ignored. . . .

It is probable that situations where necessity may be in issue are so diverse as not to be readily classifiable; and in this respect the difference between, on the one hand, necessity and, on the other, duress and other defenses applicable in more narrowly defined circumstances, such as self-defense, is perhaps more fundamental than the working party appreciated. Significantly, in our view, even some of those who, on the whole, were inclined to favor the creation of a general defense were in doubt as to how it would operate in relation to many offenses. We are very doubtful whether a defense operating with such a degree of uncertainty ought to find a place in a code. . . .

Nevertheless, the Model Penal Code has a necessity provision, adopted in many states. Other states, as well as many other countries have enacted other statutory versions of necessity. See Sullivan, *The Defense of Necessity in Texas: Legislative Invention Comes of Age,* 16 Hous. L. Rev. 333 (1979); Tiffany and Anderson, *Legislating the Necessity Defense in Criminal Law,* 52 Den. L.J. 839 (1975).

MODEL PENAL CODE § 3.02

(1) Conduct which the actor believes to be necessary to avoid a harm or evil to himself or to another is justifiable, provided that:

> (a) the harm or evil sought to be avoided by such conduct is greater than that sought to be prevented by the law defining the offense charged; and
>
> (b) neither the Code nor other law defining the offense provides exceptions or defenses dealing with specific situation involved; and
>
> (c) a legislative purpose to exclude the justification claimed does not otherwise plainly appear.

NEW YORK PENAL LAW § 35.05

(Amended 1968)

§ 35.05; GENERALLY

Unless otherwise limited by the ensuing provisions of this article defining justifiable use of physical force, or with some other provision of law, conduct which would otherwise constitute an offense is justifiable and not criminal when:

Such conduct is necessary as an emergency measure to avoid an imminent public or private injury which is about to occur by reason of a situation occasioned or developed through no fault of the actor, and which is of such gravity that, according to ordinary standards of intelligence and morality, the desirability and urgency of avoiding such injury clearly outweigh the desirability of avoiding the injury sought to be prevented by the statute defining the offense in issue. The necessity and justifiability of such conduct may not rest upon considerations pertaining only to the morality and advisability of the statute, either in its general application or with respect to its application to a particular class of cases arising thereunder. Whenever evidence relating to the defense of justification under this subdivision is offered by the defendant, the court shall rule as a matter of law whether the claimed facts and circumstances would, if established, constitute a defense.

GERMAN PENAL CODE 1969 § § 34 AND 35

Effective Jan. 1, 1975

§ 34 NECESSITY WHICH JUSTIFIES

One who commits an act in order to save himself or another from an imminent and otherwise unavoidable danger to life, person, freedom, honor, property or other legally protected interest, does not act unlawfully if, in weighing the conflicting interests, particularly the legally protected interest which is threatened and the degree of the threat, the interest he protects significantly outweighs the interest he harms. However, the foregoing applies only insofar as the act committed is an appropriate measure for avoiding the danger.

§ 35 NECESSITY WHICH EXCUSES

Whoever commits an unlawful act in order to prevent a present danger to the life, limb or liberty of himself, a relative or a close person, acts without guilt. However, this does not apply if . . . the perpetrator should be expected to cope with the danger.

SWEDISH PENAL CODE

Ch. 24 § § 4 and 5 1963)

§ 4. A person, who acts out of necessity in order to avert danger to life or health, save valuable property or for other reasons, shall also be free from punishment if the act must be considered justifiable in view of the nature of the danger, the harm caused another and the circumstances in general.

§ 5. If, in a case referred to in Sections 1–4, some one has used greater force or caused more serious harm than is permissible in each case, he shall nevertheless not be punished, so long as the circumstances were such that he could hardly have stopped to think.

NOTES AND QUESTIONS

1. Why does the Model Penal Code deal with necessity only in terms of justification rather than in terms of excuse as well? Would Dudley and Stephens have a defense under § 3.02? Under the New York Code? Under the German or Swedish codes?

2. Kadish and Paulsen, Criminal Law and Its Processes (1961), have given the following hypothetical: A is driving down a mountain road when he discovers, around a curve, two persons lying in the road. He has two choices: (1) hit the two persons, almost surely killing them, (2) swerve and plunge off the cliff to a certain death. Does § 3.02 apply? Suppose the driver does not "choose" an option, but acts instinctively? Suppose, in a variation of the hypothetical, his instinctive act is to swerve, but in so doing he actually hits three other persons, unseen by him, killing all three?

3. In supporting its position on necessity, the commentary to the Model Penal Code poses a hypothetical where a person makes a breach in a dike, knowing that this will inundate a farm, but adopting the only course available to save a whole town. The Code indicates that the "net saving of innocent lives" would justify the act. The result is not necessarily applauded by all, however, as the following excerpt shows:

> The MPC analysis can be faulted for several reasons. The superiority of the value of saving a town's populace may seem "obvious" when compared to that of saving a family, because the disparity of numbers is so great, but as the numerical difference becomes smaller, the distinction pales. The outcome becomes foolish when the town's numbers are so pared that, for example, five are being sacrificed to save six.
>
> An approach that affirmatively condones the killing of innocent persons and places the stamp of public affirmation on acts leading to that end is wrong. Excuse is the more appropriate means of defending homicidal conduct and acts necessary to self-preservation.

Note, *Justification: The Impact of the Model Penal Code on Statutory Reform,* 75 Colum. L. Rev. 914, 922–23 (1975).

4. The MPC § 3.02(2) also provides that

> When the actor was reckless or negligent in bringing about the situation requiring a choice of harms or evils or in appraising the necessity for his conduct, the justification afforded by this Section is unavailable in a prosecution for any offense for which recklessness or negligence, as the case may be, suffices to establish culpability.

Are the two cases below different? How would they fare under the MPC?

    a. D negligently runs over A and then breaks the speed limit in order to take A to a hospital.

    b. D negligently runs out of gas. To avoid obstructing traffic, she pulls onto the median, which is prohibited.

5. What are the differences between § 2.09 (duress) and § 3.02 of the Model Penal Code? What situations are covered by § 3.02 that are not covered by § 2.09 and vice versa? Are there cases that might not literally be covered by either, but which seem to fall within the spirit of one or the other?

6. Under which of the previous statutes would the actors below be guilty:

   a. A, B, C, and D are, respectively, mountain climbers hanging over a cliff from a rope. There is a belief that unless C cuts the rope between C and D, all four will fall. If C, under the direction of B and A, cuts the rope, is C guilty? Suppose C acts without consulting B and A? Suppose that A, believing that he must cut the rope just below him, does so? A recent book, Touching the Void, describes how a mountaineer, Joe Simpson, while climbing in the Andes, slipped off a 19,000-foot cliff edge and was left dangling on a rope. For an hour, his only companion, Simon Yates, held him, becoming more and more exhausted and numb with cold. If he clung on much longer, he too would go over the edge. He cut the rope and Simpson hurtled into space. Yates writes, "I might as well have put a gun to his head and shot him." But in fact it was not so, because, almost miraculously, Simpson landed on a snowy ice bridge 100 feet below the cliff edge and survived. When they met again, Simpson said to Yates, "You did right." [Did he do right in law?] J. Smith, Justification and Excuse in the Criminal Law 79 (1988).

   b. In 1987, a boat capsized with nearly 1,500 people on board. Several, according to testimony given at the inquest, swam to a rope ladder up which they might climb to safety. On the ladder, "petrified with cold or fear, or both, was a young man, Z, unable to move up or down. No one could get past him. X shouted at him for 10 minutes with no effect. Eventually X instructed someone else who was nearer to the young man Z to push him off the ladder. The young man then was pushed off and he fell into the water . . . X and others were then able to climb up the ladder to safety." J. Smith, Justification and Excuse in the Criminal Law 73 (1988). Assuming Z drowned, is X criminally liable? Is the person who actually pushed him back into the water liable?

[4] Self-Defense

Until approximately the middle of the 14th century, the common law did not recognize any defense to a charge of homicide. The defendant who killed in self-defense, by accident, or while insane was nevertheless subject to capital punishment; only the king's pardon, which was totally discretionary, could save him from the gallows. However, the king generally would grant such a pardon if the jury found, and relayed to the king, that the killing had been committed in one of these circumstances. By 1400, these circumstances became recognized as bases for acquittal and pardons issued as a matter of course (*de curso*). Nevertheless, as with all other grounds for the king's pardon, the defendant was required to forfeit all his land and chattels to the Crown.

During the time of Henry VIII, Parliament provided by statute that persons killing to prevent felonies, or who were the victims of unprovoked murderous assaults on the highway or in their homes, should not be required to forfeit their goods. 24 Henry VIII c. 5 (1532). Thus these killings were "justifiable," while other killings, which continued to require forfeiture, were "excusable." By Blackstone's time the law was fairly clear.

BLACKSTONE

177–87

I. Justifiable homicide is of diverse kinds . . . as, for instance, by virtue of such an office as obliges one, in the execution of public justice, to put a malefactor to death, who had forfeited his life by the laws and verdict of his country. This is an act of necessity, and even of civil duty; and therefore not only justifiable, but commendable, where the law requires it. . . .

Such homicide as is committed for the prevention of any forcible and atrocious crime, is justifiable by the laws of nature; and also by the law of England, as it stood so early as the time of Bracton. . . .

In these instances of justifiable homicide, it may be observed that the slayer is in no kind of fault whatsoever, not even in the minutest degree; and is therefore to be totally acquitted and discharged with commendation rather than blame. But that is not quite the case in excusable homicide, the very name whereof imports some fault, some error, or omission; so trivial, however, that the law excuses it from the guilt of felony, though in strictness it judges it deserving of some little degree of punishment. . . .

Homicide in self-defense or *se defendendo,* upon a sudden affray, is also excusable, rather than justifiable, by the English law. This species of self-defense must be distinguished from that just now mentioned, as calculated to hinder the perpetration of a capital crime; which is not only a matter of excuse, but of justification. But the self-defense which we are now speaking of, is that whereby a man may protect himself from an assault or the like, in the course of a sudden brawl or quarrel, by killing him who assaults him. And this is what the law expresses by the word *chance-medley* or *chaud-medley,* the former of which in its etymology signifies a casual affray, the latter an affray in the heat of blood or passion; . . . to excuse homicide by the plea of self-defense, it must appear that the slayer had no other possible (or, at least, probable) means of escaping from his assailant. . . .

The law requires that the person, who kills another in his own defense, should have retreated as far as he conveniently or safely can, to avoid the violence of the assault, before he turns upon his assailant. . . . The party assaulted must therefore flee as far as he conveniently can, either by reason of some wall, ditch, or other impediment; or as far as the fierceness of the assault will permit him; for it may be so fierce as not to allow him to yield a step, without manifest danger of his life, or enormous bodily harm; and then in his defense he may kill his assailant instantly. . . .

And as to the necessity which excuses a man who kills another *se defendendo,* Lord Bacon entitles it *necessitas culpabilis,* and thereby distinguishes it from the forced necessity of killing a thief or a malefactor. For the law intends that the quarrel or assault arose from some unknown wrong, or some provocation, either in word or deed; and since in quarrels both parties may be, and usually are, in some fault; and it scarce can be tried who was originally in the wrong; the law will not hold the survivor entirely guiltless. But it is clear, in the other case, that where I kill a thief that breaks into my house, the original default can never be upon my side.

The doctrine of self-defense can be relatively quickly stated. For example, *People v. Williams,* 56 Ill. App. 2d 159, 165–66, 205 N.E. 2d 749, 752 (1965), provides the following definition:

> [We] now turn to the elements, which if present, justify the use of force in the defense of a person. These elements are: (1) that force is threatened against a person; (2) that the person threatened is not the aggressor; (3) that the danger of harm is imminent; (4) that the force threatened is unlawful; (5) that the person threatened must actually believe: (a) that a danger exists, (b) that the use of force is necessary to avert the danger, (c) that the kind and amount of force which he uses is necessary; and (6) that the above beliefs are reasonable. There is a further principle involved, when . . . the defendant uses deadly force. This principle limits the use of deadly force to those situations in which, (a) the threatened force will cause death or great bodily harm or (b) the force threatened is a forcible felony.

The Model Penal Code defines the claim as follows:

MODEL PENAL CODE §§ 3.04 AND 3.09

§ 3.04. USE OF FORCE IN SELF-PROTECTION

(1) Use of Force Justifiable for Protection of the Person. Subject to the provisions of this Section and of Section 3.09, the use of force upon or toward another person is justifiable when the actor believes that such force is immediately necessary for the purpose of protecting himself against the use of unlawful force by such other person on the present occasion.

* * *

(b) The use of deadly force is not justifiable under this Section unless the actor believes that such force is necessary to protect himself against death, serious bodily harm, kidnapping or sexual intercourse compelled by force or threat; nor is it justifiable if:

> (i) the actor, with the purpose of causing death or serious bodily harm, provoked the use of force against himself in the same encounter; or

> (ii) the actor knows that he can avoid the necessity of using such force with complete safety by retreating or by surrendering possession of a thing to a person asserting a claim of right thereto or by complying with a demand that he abstain from any action which he has no duty to take, except that:

>> (1) the actor is not obligated to retreat from his dwelling or place of work, unless he was the initial aggressor or is assailed in his place of

work by another person whose place of work the actor knows it to be; . . .

* * *

(c) Except as required by paragraph [] . . . (b) of this Subsection, a person employing protective force may estimate the necessity thereof under the circumstances as he believes them to be when the force is used, without retreating, surrendering possession, doing any other act which he has no legal duty to do or abstaining from any lawful action.

3.09. MISTAKE OF LAW AS TO UNLAWFULNESS OF FORCE. . . .

* * *

(2) When the actor believes that the use of force upon or toward the person of another is necessary for any of the purposes for which such belief would establish a justification under Sections 3.03 to 3.08 but the actor is reckless or negligent in having such belief or in acquiring or failing to acquire any knowledge or belief which is material to the justifiability of his use of force, the justification afforded by those Sections is unavailable in a prosecution for an offense for which recklessness or negligence, as the case may be, suffices to establish culpability.

[a] The Rationale of Self-Defense and Doctrinal Confusion

What is the rationale for allowing self-defense as a relevant claim? Philosophers as well as the common law courts offer several explanations. First, it can be argued that a person who has chosen to take an innocent person's life has forfeited his right to protection against force. See, e.g., Kadish, *Respect for Life and Regard for Rights in the Criminal Law,* 64 Calif. L. Rev. 871 (1976). Second, it can be argued that the victim of the aggression has a "natural right" to life and to resist aggression. Fletcher, *Proportionality and the Psychotic Aggressor: A Vignette in Comparative Criminal Theory,* 8 Israel L. Rev. 367 (1973); Uniacke, *Self Defense and Natural Law,* 36 Am. J. Juris. 73 (1991). See, however, *Rowe v. Debruyn,* 17 F.3d 1047 (7th Cir. 1994) (no constitutional right to plead self-defense in a prison disciplinary setting since self-defense is not a natural right). Related to this notion is the argument that if the victim has given up this "natural right" in exchange for governmental protection from such assaults, the right is reactivated when the government is unable to provide such protection. Utilitarians also endorse legal recognition of the right to self-defense, either because they think it will deter aggressors, see Williams, *Offences and Defences,* 2 Legal Studies 233, 250 (1982), or because victims of aggression are simply not deterred by the law's threat that, if they act in self-defense, they will be punished at a later time. As Justice Holmes put it, "Detached reflection cannot be expected in the presence of an uplifted knife." *Brown v. United States,* 256 U.S. 335, 343 (1921). See also

McCord and Lyons, *Moral Reasoning and the Criminal Law: The Example of Self-Defense,* 30 Amer. Cr. L. Rev. 97 (1992).

On a different line, one could ask whether the defendant who kills in self-defense has the requisite *mens rea* for the crime of homicide. Consider the following explanation (often characterized as the "Double Effect Doctrine") of self-defense: "[S]elf-defense is not wrong, because our object is not to take another man's life, but simply to preserve our own, and the moral worth of an action is determined by that which is, not by which is not, its object." F. Spirago, The Catechism Explained 388 (1961). See also S. Uniacke, Permissible Killing 92–155 (1994). Put in a slightly differ ent way, it could be argued that the slayer in a self-defense setting does not act "purposely" or even "knowingly" (in Model Penal Code terms) with regard to the death of his aggressor—his object is to escape, and he would be just as happy (in most instances at least) if his aggressor were merely wounded, or incapacitated, in order to permit the escape. While there would be a stronger argument that he has acted "recklessly," (whether or not under circumstances mainfesting extreme indifference for the value of human life) this too might fail in a number of situations. But see the ambiguous remarks of the United States Supreme Court in *Matthews v. United States,* 485 U.S. 58 (1988): "The affirmative defense of self-defense is, of course, inconsistent with the claim that the defendant killed in the heat of passion."

Still another variation on this theme would stem from the perception—captured in the slogan that self-defense "sounds" in necessity or "*in extremis*"—that self-defenders (like those who act under duress and in necessitous circumstances) are caught up in the "maelstrom of circumstance" and both do not have, and can not be expected to have, "a full mens." In this light, consider the words of Bracton, written nearly 700 years ago: "If . . . he slew a man without any meditation of hatred, in fear and grief of mind in delivering himself and his property, when he could not otherwise escape, he is not liable to the punishment of homicide." Bracton, De Legibus Anglae 276–7 (c. 1250). This thought is also reflected by Section 33 of the Strafgesetzbuch (German Criminal Code), which declares that "If the actor exceeds the limits of self-defense because of confusion, fear, or fright, he is not to be punished." In the celebrated Bernhard Goetz trial discussed in Note (1) following the *Wanrow* case *infra,* the jury was told that Goetz fired five shots on "automatic pilot" as part of a normal "adrenaline response" to such a situation. Should the defense (indeed each of the claims reviewed thus far in this chapter) be renamed "the law of apparent necessity under emotional stress"?

These issues may also be seen in the debate over whether self-defense is a "justification" or an "excuse." Most writers agree that *actual* self-defense is justified because the defendant did the "right" thing. But how do we know that the defendant did the right thing? By hypothesis, the defendant has killed what appeared to be the original aggressor before the aggressor killed the slayer—in many instances before the aggressor even attempted to injure the slayer. Consider the following typical case: Jack, saying he is going to kill Sally, puts his hand around the trigger of a gun, and points it at Sally's temple; Sally kills him first. Can we be sure that Jack would have (tried to) kill Sally? Professor Sendor has declared

The problem of retrospective determination of the accuracy of a defendant's perception of justificatory circumstances can apply to apparent threats from *natural* forces because of the difficulty of reconstructing the relevant causal chain. The problem is even greater in cases of apparent *human* threats to rights. . . . How . . . should we categorize such allegedly justified conduct when we cannot in retrospect know with certainty whether the defendant correctly or mistakenly assessed the presence of justificatory circumstances at the time of his act? I suggest that . . . criminal law should give the defendant the normative benefit of the doubt and classify his conduct as justified.

Sendor, *Mistake of Fact: A Study in the Structure of Criminal Conduct,* 25 Wake For. L. Rev. 707, 776 (1990).

[b] Mistake and "Imperfect Self Defense"

But if the criminal law is only giving the "benefit of the doubt" in cases where it appears that the aggressor would carry out the threat, what if, *ex post,* it is clear that the aggressor would not or could not have carried out the threat (*e.g.,* had blanks in the gun or was reaching for a handkerchief)? The question as to the effect of mistake upon justification is not unique to self-defense; it arises in every case when the actor (1)is mistaken as to the need to use force at all or (2)uses excessive force. *Dudley and Stephens supra,* p. 751, may well have been arguing mistake—reasonable or not—as to the necessity of killing Parker given the uncertainty about when (if ever) they would be rescued and when Parker might die of natural causes. Thus, if Dudley and Stephens were seeking to excuse their act rather than justify it, they might concede that they should have waited until Parker (or one of the other passengers) died or to see whether a ship would in fact "appear out of the mist." But they could claim mistake in the sense that they were mistaken about the unlikelihood of rescue, and about the need to kill Parker before they all were so emaciated as to make killing Parker a futile gesture. Reconsider now the opinion in that case, in particular the statement that the law never allows the killing of an innocent person.

Originally, the common law of self-defense exonerated any honestly mistaken or excessive actor, see Singer, *The Resurgence of Mens Rea: II—Honest but Unreasonable Mistake of Fact in Self-Defense,* 28 B.C. L. Rev. 459 (1987), but during the 19th century American courts altered this view to require that the mistake be "reasonable." Which is the preferred position? The impact in the 19th century of the newly coined requirement of reasonableness upon the claim of self-defense was enormous. A defendant who, in the exigency of the moment, made an "unreasonable" judgment was deprived totally of the defense of self-defense and so stood convicted of intentional murder—first degree in many situations. In the past several decades, however, many states have ameliorated the doctrine by establishing a notion of "imperfect self-defense" by which the unreasonable but honest defender is convicted of manslaughter rather than murder. Although this falls short of calling self-defense, or even imperfect self-defense, an "excuse," it certainly suggests a willingness to recognize the extraordinary circumstances under which the defendant was required to make split-second judgments. Is this like a "chance medley" where the defendant has been provoked? Is it an analog to killing in "heat of passion"? Or is it merely another instance of the courts seeking to avoid the possible imposition of the death penalty?

The Model Penal Code has adopted the imperfect self-defense rule, though with some changes. See MPC § 3.09(2) cited *supra* and in the Appendix. The New Jersey Supreme Court has held that the legislature's explicit repeal of (the equivalent of) Model Penal Code § 3.09 and the injection of the word *reasonable* in the self-defense section require the conclusion that New Jersey does not recognize "imperfect self-defense." Said the court, "Were we to create an unspecified form of manslaughter to accommodate this uncertainty in the Code, we would be doing just that" (*i.e.*, "creating" a new form). However, having just rejected "imperfectness," the New Jersey Supreme Court, per Justice Hern, went on to hold that "in many, if not most, circumstances . . . the proffered evidence may certainly bear directly on the question of wheher the homicide was knowing or purposeful, and would be admissible to counter these essential elements of the offense of murder." In so holding, the court distinguished between "the existence of a fact that negates an essential element of the crime as defined, and the narrower concept of an affirmative defense that excuses conduct that is otherwise unlawful." The court then concluded that "(e)vidence of imperfect self-defense does not justify the conduct, it mitigates the offense." *State v. Bowen,* 108 N.J. 622, 633, 532 A.2d 215, 221 (1987).

Is it rational to treat a defendant who honestly but unreasonably believes he must use deadly force in the same manner as a cold-blooded assassin for hire or even a defendant who heedlessly throws a bomb into a crowded room? A penetrating analysis is found in *People v. Flannel,* 25 Cal. 3d 668, 160 Cal. Rptr. 84, 603 P.2d 1 (1979). See Note, 1982 N. Ill. U. L.F. 217. Cf. N. Morris and C. Howard, Studies in Criminal Law 114 (1964) (In Australia, such a killing is manslaughter). See also Kuvacs, *Excessive Self-Defense in Homicide Cases: Some Fundamental Problems in Australia Law,* 4 Monash U. L. Rev. 50 (1977).

Until the Model Penal Code (at least), the courts drew no distinction for defense purposes between "tort" negligence, or unreasonableness, and "criminal negligence." A defendant charged with "negligent" homicide or "involuntary manslaughter" would be entitled to a charge that informed the jury that only "criminal" unreasonableness would suffice for conviction. See *e.g., Fitzgerald v. State,* p. 436, *supra.* Where a defendant sought to raise the issue of self-defense, how ever, the jury would receive no such instruction, simply being told that the defendant had to be "reasonable" under the circumstances. Unless juries instinctively knew the difference between criminal and tort unreasonableness it is possible that defendants who raised self-defense were being convicted of murder (because their mistake was "tortiously unreasonable") although, had they been charged with negligent homicide, they might have been acquitted (because their actions were not "grossly negligent"). The Code, at least, tries to remedy this situation. See MPC § 3.09.

[c] The "Retreat" Rule

As Blackstone indicates, the common law distinguished between justifiable and excusable self-defense. In the latter, retreat was required, whereas in the former the fully innocent target of an unprovoked attack could stand his ground and kill. Moreover, in justifiable homicide any mistake as to the necessity of the slaying exonerated, whereas in excusable homicide, since the defendant was already somewhat at fault, courts were more apt to require that a mistake be reasonable. When the practice of forfeiture, which operationally distinguished the two categories of self-defense, ended in the early 19th century, courts and writers merged justifiable prevention of a felony into *se defendendo* killings and began to require both retreat and reasonable mistake even in instances that would have been previously labeled justifiable. See Singer, *The Resurgence of Mens Rea II: Honest But Unreasonable Mistake of Fact in Self-Defense,* 28 B.C. L. Rev. 459 (1987); Fletcher, *The Individualization of Excusing Conditions,* 47 S. Cal. L. Rev. 1269 (1974). For a synopsis of the early writers, see Snelling, *Killing in Self-Defence,* 34 Aust. L.J. 130 (1960).

In addition to any other faults, this blurring has resulted in conflict over the theory of self-defense. Thus, for example, it is easier to argue that self-defense is a justification if it is limited to "felony prevention" events. Moreover, the argument that the victim has forfeited his life because of his aggression is more palatable where he was the only aggressor, rather than where both victim and slayer have begun a mutual battle. This explanation also faces problems where the victim, although undoubtedly the initial aggressor, is not acting immorally or unlawfully. Thus, for example, if a small child or a clearly mentally incompetent person aims a gun at D, and the only way D can escape death is to shoot the child or insane person, it is difficult to argue that the aggressor forfeited his right to life because of that aggression. See *e.g.,* Fletcher, 8 Israel L. Rev. 367, *supra;* McMahan, *Self-Defense and the Problem of the Innocent Attacker,* 104 Ethics 252 (1994); Otsuka, *Killing the Innocent in Self-Defense,* 23 Phil. and Pub. Affairs 74 (1994). Is a killer of an innocent aggressor excused or justified? See Alexander, *Justification and Innocent Aggressors,* 33 Wayne L. Rev. 1177 (1987), and Quigley, *The Common Law's Theory of Criminal Liability: A Challenge from Across the Atlantic,* 11 Whittier L. Rev. 479 (1989) (arguing that the debate shows the frail line between excuse and justification).

The confusion between excused and justified self defense is nowhere more obvious than in the doctrines with regard to the duty to retreat. According to Perkins, *Self-Defense Re-Examined,* 1 U.C.L.A. L. Rev. 133, 140 (1953), the phrase *retreat to the wall* alluded to by Blackstone, *supra,* came from an early English case where "the defendant . . . had been driven to a certain wall situated between two houses beyond which he was not able in any way to pass. Only there did the defendant stand and kill the other in his own defense." Quoting Anonymous, Fitzherbert, Grand Abridgment, C. and P.C. No. 284 (1328). Another more romantic notion is that *wall* refers to the wall of the city—that the defendant would be required to go (at least figuratively and almost literally) to the ends of civilization before being excused (or justified) for taking life.

Whatever its origins, the retreat requirement was not applied to "prevention of felony" killings until the middle of the 19th century. But with the collapse of the two different kinds of self-defense into one label plus the invention of the portable revolver, courts began requiring retreat either in all cases or in none. While at least a sizable minority (and perhaps a majority) of states never require retreat, LaFave and Scott at 460–61, many jurisdictions follow the lead of the Model Penal Code and include a retreat requirement. See MPC and Commentaries, Comment at 55 (1985). Even in those jurisdictions requiring retreat, however, the defendant need not retreat if (1) he would not lessen the danger to himself by doing so and (2) he is in a "nonretreat" place.

The first exception is captured by the Model Penal Code, § 3.04(2)(b)(ii), which declares that the defendant is required to retreat only if he "knows" that he can avoid the necessity of using deadly force "with complete safety." In an era of the firearm, how often is that likely to be the case? Has the Code paid homage to the retreat requirement, while allowing virtually every defendant to stand her ground?

The law on the second exception is extremely arcane. Thus the vast majority of states that otherwise require retreat do not so require if the defendant is on his own property. *E.g., People v. Tomlins,* 213 N.Y. 240, 197 N.E. 496 (1914). See also Harlow, *Self-Defence: Public Right or Private Privilege,* 1974 Crim. L. Rev. 528. Some courts, however, narrowly define "property" to be limited only to the defendant's house, *e.g., State v. Page,* 418 So. 2d 254 (Fla. 1982) (common walkway to apartment is not part of "house"); *Commonwealth v. Marcocelli,* 271 Pa. Super. 411, 413 A.2d 732 (1979) (lawn is not part of "home"). What about a porch around the house? *State v. Bonano,* 59 N.J. 515, 284 A.2d 345 (1971). Some courts continue to rely on the archaic definitions of "house" and "home" in determining whether a self-defense retreat instruction is required. See, *e.g., State v. Martinez,* 229 N.J. Super. 593, 552 A.2d 232 (App. Div. 1989), where defendant was held entitled to a "no retreat" instruction because the victim's first punch hit the door of the defendant's home. The court ignored the fact that the defendant had gone inside his home, closed the door, and then returned with a screwdriver, which he concealed, and with which eventually he killed the victim.

The situation is even more complicated when both the defendant and the victim (such as husband and wife) have a right to be in the house, *People v. Lenkevick,* 394 Mich. 117, 229 N.W.2d 298 (1975); a codweller, *State v. Shaw,* 185 Conn. 372, 441 A.2d 561 (1981); or a host and an invitee, *Oney v. Commonwealth,* 225 Ky. 590, 9 S.W.2d 723 (1928). Cf. *Ripple v. State,* 404 So. 2d 160 (Fla. Dist. Ct. App. 1981) (co-occupant need not leave house, but may be required to leave room). See 52 A.L.R.2d 1458 (1957); 100 A.L.R.3d 532 (1980). Why should the law allow a defendant to take the life of an aggressor rather than require the defendant simply to leave his house, assuming the defendant knows that he can do so with complete safety both for himself and others? Is the principle merely a reflex extension of the maxim that one's home is one's castle? Or is there something more to it?

The law as to retreat from the house is a paragon of clarity when compared to other areas. The Model Penal Code, for example, does not require retreat (even if it can be done in complete safety) from a "dwelling" or "place of work" unless the defender was "the initial aggressor or is assailed in his place of work by another person whose place of work the actor knows it to be." Sec. 3.04(2)(b)(ii)(1). Why the exemption for a place of work? And why the exception to the exemption with regard to a place of work, but not for the home? Some states, moreover, have expanded the exception to other locales. *State v. Marlowe,* 120 S.C. 205, 112 S.E. 921 (1921) (defendant's private club); *State v. Borwich,* 193 Iowa 639, 197 N.W. 460 (1922) (defendant's car). Does the purpose of the rule not requiring retreat in the home apply to these places? Why should the purpose of the rule be dominant, rather than the issue of the defendant's actual state of mind?

A number of jurisdictions have taken what might be called a middle position—that there is no hard rule on whether the defendant must retreat, but that the failure to retreat is only one of several factors to be considered in determining whether the use of force was reasonable and proportionate. See, *e.g., Brown v. United States,* 256 U.S. 335, 343 (1921) (per Justice Holmes); *Commonwealth v. Shaffer,* 367 Mass. 508, 326 N.E.2d 880 (1975). Norse law takes this approach. J. Andenaes, The General Part of the Criminal Law of Norway 160 (1965). The German code requires retreat if the attacked person can evade the assault "without losing face." Eser, *Justification and Excuse,* 24 Amer. J. Comp. L. 621, 632 (1976).

One reason for not requiring retreat is the notion that the victim of the aggression has a "natural law" right to remain where he is:

> Three reasons for the [no-retreat] approach might be advanced: a show of strength may often discourage a pending attack (*si vis pacem para bellum*); it is wrong that a criminal should be able to oblige a law-abiding citizen to make a timid and dishonorable withdrawal; and moreover a law which purports to curb the basic instinct toward self-preservation will prove unenforceable. A person attacked should therefore be entitled to stand fast and to repel force by force until that is no longer necessary for self-protection.

Ashworth, *Self-Defense and the Right to Life,* 34 Cambridge L.J. 282, 289–90 (1975).

Accord Beale, *Retreat from a Murderous Assault,* 16 Harv. L. Rev. 567 (1903), urging that one might establish a duty not to retreat to avoid allowing an unlawful aggressor to continue his illegal acts.

[d] The "Rules" of Self-Defense

Withdrawal and Self-Defense. The usual rule is that self-defense is not available to a defendant who was the original aggressor. But that is true only as to the aggressor who uses deadly force. If A begins a fist fight with B, who then pulls out a switchblade knife and attempts to kill A, A has the right to use deadly force in return. Similarly, if A starts with deadly force, but withdraws from the initial fray, and B then pursues A, the doctrinal explanation for allowing A to use deadly force in self-defense is that this is a "new encounter," having nothing to do with the first, in which A is the "victim" of "new" aggression. See Dressler at 201–02. Even if this were "obvious" when A kills B three years after the initial melee, it is still true (by hypothesis) that but for A's assault, B would not have assaulted A. Why, then, is A allowed to regain the right of self-defense vis-à-vis B?

A corollary of the withdrawal requirement is that A, the initial aggressor, must fully communicate his withdrawal, lest B believe (reasonably?) that A's withdrawal is merely a ploy. See *People v. Button,* 106 Cal. 628, 39 P. 1073 (1895); *Stoffer v. State,* 45 Ohio St. 47 (1864). But assuming that A's withdrawal is genuine, why should he be deprived of the right of self-defense simply because of B's (unreasonable?) perception that the fight continues?

Defense of Others. Suppose that Carl, walking along the street, suddenly sees Alan striking Bill. Carl intervenes to prevent what he perceives to be a beating. If Alan was illegally striking Bill, Carl has justifiably assisted Bill. But suppose that Alan is justified in striking Bill (either because Bill was an initial aggressor or because Alan is a police officer using reasonable force making an arrest). Should Carl still have a defense to his (now not factually justified) beating of Alan? Should it matter whether Carl's judgment was reasonable? The majority rule—referred to as the *alter ego rule*—is that Carl is exonerated only if Alan could have used such force. The rule is at least as old as *Stanley's Case,* J. Kel 86 (circa 1700). The court there said that

> A man must take heed how he joineth in any unlawful act, as fight is; for, if he doth, he is guilty of all that follows . . . his ignorance will not excuse him where the fact is made murder by the law, without any malice precedent. . . .

This view continues today in many jurisdictions. See, *e.g., People v. Young,* 11 N.Y.2d 274, 183 N.E.2d 319 (1962). Thus even if Carl's mistake is reasonable, he is still guilty. What explains such a rule? The *Young* court said that allowing (reasonable but mistaken) intervention and use of force as a defense "would not be conducive to an orderly society." *Contra State v. Chiarello,* 69 N.J. Super. 470, 174 A.2d 506 (App. Div. 1961); *State v. Fair,* 45 N.J. 77, 211 A.2d 359 (1965). The New York legislature eventually overruled *Young* by statutorily providing a defense in such a situation. See, *e.g.,* New York Penal Law § 35.15 (1968).* Even where the defendant acted on behalf of the initial victim, early common law restricted such intervention to family members. (Thus, in the example above, if Carl was unrelated to Bill, Carl would have no defense even if Bill was the initial victim.) Most jurisdictions that have abolished the alter ego rule have also abolished this restriction. See generally Note, *Criminal Culpability for Defense of Third Persons,* 20 Wash. & Lee L. Rev. 98 (1963); Note, 9 Capital U.L. Rev. 827 (1980). See MPC, § 3.05, Appendix.

---

* N.Y. Penal Code § 35.15:

A person may . . . use physical force upon another person when and to the extent he reasonably believes such to be necessary to defend himself or a third person from what he reasonably believes to be the use or imminent use of unlawful physical force be such other person unless:

(a) The latter's conduct was provoked by the actor himself with intent to cause physical injury to another person; or

(b) The actor was the initial aggressor; except that in such case his use of physical force is nevertheless justifiable if he has withdrawn from the encounter and effectively communicated such withdrawal to such other person but the latter persists in continuing the incident by the use or threatened imminent use of unlawful physical force; or

(c) The physical force involved is the product of a combat by agreement not specifically authorized by law.

Are the utilitarian reasons for supporting a self-defense doctrine also present and as strong in a defense of third-party case? Are the retributivist reasons?

STATE v. WANROW

Supreme Court of Washington

88 Wash. 2d 221, 559 P.2d 548 (1977)

UTTER, Associate Justice.

Yvonne Wanrow was convicted by a jury of second-degree murder and first-degree assault. She appealed her conviction to the Court of Appeals.

On the afternoon of August 11, 1972, defendant's (respondent's) two children were staying at the home of Ms. Hooper, a friend of defendant. Defendant's son was playing in the neighborhood and came back to Ms. Hooper's house and told her that a man tried to pull him off his bicycle and drag him into a house. Some months earlier, Ms. Hooper's 7-year-old daughter had developed a rash on her body which was diagnosed as venereal disease. Ms. Hooper had been unable to persuade her daughter to tell her who had molested her. It was not until the night of the shooting that Ms. Hooper discovered it was Willaim Wesler (decedent) who allegedly had violated her daughter. A few minutes after the defendant's son related his story to Ms. Hooper about the man who tried to detain him, Mr. Wesler appeared on the porch of the Hooper house and stated through the door, "I didn't touch the kid, I didn't touch the kid." At that moment, the Hooper girl, seeing Wesler at the door, indicated to her mother that Wesler was the man who had molested her. Joseph Fah, Ms. Hooper's landlord, saw Wesler as he was leaving and informed Shirley Hooper that Wesler had tried to molest a young boy who had earlier lived in the same house, and that Wesler had previously been committed to the Eastern State Hospital for the mentally ill. Immediately after this revelation from Mr. Fah, Ms. Hooper called the police who, upon their arrival at the Hooper residence, were informed of all the events which had transpired that day. Ms. Hooper requested that Wesler be arrested then and there, but the police stated, "We can't, until Monday morning." Ms. Hooper was urged by the police officer to go to the police station Monday morning and "swear out a warrant." Ms. Hooper's landlord, who was present during the conversation, suggested that Ms. Hooper get a baseball bat located at the corner of the house and "conk him over the head" should Wesler try to enter the house uninvited during the weekend. To this suggestion, the policeman replied, "Yes, but wait until he gets in the house." (A week before this incident Shirley Hooper had noticed someone prowling around her house at night. Two days before the shooting someone had attempted to get into Ms. Hooper's bedroom and had slashed the window screen. She suspected that such person was Wesler.)

That evening, Ms. Hooper called the defendant and asked her to spend the night with her in the Hooper house. At that time she related to Ms. Wanrow the facts we have previously set forth. The defendant arrived sometime after 6 P.M. with a pistol in her handbag. The two women ultimately determined that they were too afraid to stay alone and decided to ask some friends to come over for added protection. The two women then called the defendant's sister and brother-in-law, Angie and Chuck Michel. The four adults did not go to bed that evening, but remained awake talking and watching for any possible prowlers. There were eight young children in the house with them. At around 5 A.M., Chuck Michel, without the knowledge of the women in the house, went to Wesler's house, carrying a baseball bat. Upon arriving at the Wesler residence, Mr. Michel accused Wesler of molesting little children. Mr. Wesler then suggested that they go over to the Hooper residence and get the whole thing straightened out. Another man, one David Kelly, was also present, and together the three men went over to the Hooper house. Mr. Michel and Mr. Kelly remained outside while Wesler entered the residence.

The testimony as to what next took place is considerably less precise. It appears that Wesler, a large man who was visibly intoxicated, entered the home and when told to leave declined to do so. A good deal of shouting and confusion then arose, and a young child, asleep on the couch, awoke crying. The testimony indicates that Wesler then approached this child, stating, "My what a cute little boy," or words to that effect, and that the child's mother, Ms. Michel, stepped between Wesler and the child. By this time Hooper was screaming for Wesler to get out. Ms. Wanrow, a 5'4" woman who at the time had a broken leg and was using a crutch, testified that she then went to the front door to enlist the aid of Chuck Michel. She stated that she shouted for him and, upon turning around to reenter the living room, found Wesler standing directly behind her. She testified to being gravely startled by this situation and to having then shot Wesler in what amounted to a reflex action.

Instruction No. 10, setting forth the law of self-defense, incorrectly limited the jury's consideration of acts and circumstances pertinent to respondent's perception of the alleged threat to her person. An examination of the record of the testimony and of the colloquies which took place with regard to the instructions on self-defense indicate the critical importance of these instructions to the respondent's theory of the case. Based upon the evidence we have already set out, it is obviously crucial that the jury be precisely instructed as to the defense of justification.

In the opening paragraph of instruction No. 10, the jury, in evaluating the gravity of the danger to the respondent, was directed to consider only those acts and circumstances occurring "at or immediately before the killing. . . ."[7] This is not now, and never has been, the law of self-defense in Washington. On the contrary, the justification of self-defense is to be evaluated in light of all the facts and circumstances known to the defendant, including those known substantially before the killing.

State v. Tribett, 74 Wash. 125, 132 P. 875 (1913), is in accord. There this court approved an instruction which twice directed the jury to evaluate the

---

[7] Instruction No. 10 reads:

To justify killing in self-defense, there need be no actual or real danger to the life or person of the party killing, but there must be, or reasonably appear to be, at or immediately before the killing, some overt act, or some circumstances which would reasonably indicate to the party killing that the person slain, is, at the time, endeavoring to kill him or inflict upon him great bodily harm.

reasonableness of the defendant's actions in defense of himself "in the light of all the circumstances." *Tribett,* at 130, 132 P. at 877. Such circumstances included those existing and known long before the killing, such as the reputation of the place of the killing for lawlessness. This court stated with reference to the self-defense instruction:

> All of these facts and circumstances should have been placed before the jury, to the end that they could put themselves in the place of the appellant, get the point of view which he had at the time of the tragedy, and view the conduct of the [deceased] with all its pertinent sidelights as the appellant was warranted in viewing it. In no other way could the jury safely say what a reasonably prudent man similarly situated would have done.

The second paragraph of instruction No. 10 contains an equally erroneous and prejudicial statement of the law. That portion of the instruction reads:

> However, when there is no reasonable ground for the person attacked to believe that *his* person is in imminent danger of death or great bodily harm, and it appears to *him* that only an ordinary battery is all that is intended, and all that *he* has reasonable grounds to fear from *his* assailant, *he* has a right to stand *his* ground and repel such threatened assault, yet *he* has no right to repel a threatened assault with naked hands, by the use of a deadly weapon in a deadly manner, unless *he* believes, *and has reasonable grounds* to believe, that *he* is in imminent danger of death or great bodily harm. [Emphasis added.]

In our society women suffer from a conspicuous lack of access to training in and the means of developing those skills necessary to effectively repel a male assailant without resorting to the use of deadly weapons.[8] Instruction No. 12 does indicate that the "relative size and strength of the persons involved" may be considered; however, it does not make clear that the defendant's actions are to be judged against her own subjective impressions and not those which a detached jury might determine to be objectively reasonable.

The second paragraph of instruction No. 10 not only establishes an objective standard, but through the persistent use of the masculine gender leaves the jury with the impression the objective standard to be applied is that applicable to an altercation between two men. The impression created—that a 5'4" woman with a cast on her leg and using a crutch must, under the law, somehow repel an assault by a 6'2" intoxicated man without employing weapons in her defense, unless the jury finds her determination of the degree of danger to be objectively reasonable—constitutes a separate and distinct misstatement of the law and, in the context of this case, violates the respondent's right to equal protection of the law. The respondent was entitled to have the jury consider her actions in the light of her own perceptions of the situation, including those perceptions which were the product of our nation's "long and unfortunate history of sex discrimination." Until such time as the effects of that history are eradicated, care must be taken to assure that our self-defense instructions afford women the right to have their conduct judged

---

[8] See B. Babock, A. Freedman, E. Norton, and S. Ross, Sex Discrimination and the Law: Causes and Remedies 943–1070 (1975);S. Brownmiller, Against Our Will;Men, Women and Rape (1975).

in light of the individual physical handicaps which are the product of sex discrimination. To fail to do so is to deny the right of the individual woman involved to trial by the same rules which are applicable to male defendants. The portion of the instruction above quoted misstates our law in creating an objective standard of "reasonableness." It then compounds that error by utilizing language suggesting that the respondent's conduct must be measured against that of a reasonable male individual finding himself in the same circumstances.

We conclude that the instruction here in question contains an improper statement of the law on a vital issue in the case, is inconsistent, misleading and prejudicial when read in conjunction with other instructions pertaining to the same issue, and therefore is a proper basis for a finding of reversible error.

Finally, we agree with the conclusion of the Court of Appeals that the trial court cannot be said to have abused its discretion in this case in declining to allow defendant's counsel to call an expert witness to present opinion evidence on the effects of defendant's Indian culture upon her perception and actions. . . . The conviction is reversed, and the case remanded for a new trial.

NOTES AND QUESTIONS

1. *Reasonableness and Subjectivity.* *Wanrow* raises again the question of whether to use a subjective or objective standard in assessing the actor's liability. The court clearly accepts the view that "social acculturation" is relevant in determining the proper instruction. See Schneider, *Equal Rights to Trial for Women: Sex Bias in the Law of Self-Defense,* 15 Harv. C.R.C.L. L. Rev. 623 (1980). See also Sagawa, *A Hard Case for Feminists: People v. Goetz,* 10 Harv. Women's L. J. 253 (1987). For an illuminating article, arguing that the principle of *Wanrow* should be expanded to allow nervous self-defenders full exoneration if they deem the use of force necessary, even if the force is "objectively" excessive, see LaFond, *The Case for Liberalizing the Use of Deadly Force in Self-Defense,* 6 U. Puget. Sound. L. Rev. 237 (1983).

The English courts seem now to have adopted a fully subjective view on self-defense. See *Gladstone Williams,* (1984) 78 Cr. App. R. 276, and *Beckford v. Regina,* (1987) 85 Cr. App. R. 378. Alldridge, *Mistake in Criminal Law—Subjectivism Reasserted in the Court of Appeal,* 35 No. Ire. L. Q. 263 (1984). But see Giles, *Self-Defence and Mistake: A Way Forward,* 53 Mod. L. Rev. 187 (1990). American jurisdictions initially applied the full subjective test. See, *e.g.,* the statement of the court in *Batten v. State,* 80 Ind. 394 (1881):

> An ideal man is thus (by the lower court's instruction) made the standard by which the guilt or innocence of the accused is to be determined. Is this correct? Should not the standard be the man himself? Ought regard to be had to real things, the man, the situation, the surroundings, or should some imaginary person be taken as the guide? There is some conflict in the cases. Our conclusion is that the question must be decided upon the appearances present to the eyes and mind of the accused himself, and upon the belief

actually and in good faith entertained by him. . . . The court is not to set up, as the standard by which the appearances are to be measured or the belief tested, an ideal man. In cases involving life, actual, real things rather than ideal should be taken as standards and tests. It is much safer and better to take the real man, the actual situation, and the real surroundings.

For a variety of reasons, however, the majority of courts (including Indiana) has now endorsed the use of the reasonable person test. Singer, *The Resurgence of Mens Rea: II—Honest but Unreasonable Mistake of Fact in Self-Defense,* 28 B.C. L. Rev. 459, 482–86 (1987).

If the fully subjective test (did the defendant honestly believe) is not to be used as the standard, three other possibilities may be suggested: (1)Would a reasonable person have so acted (believed)? (2)Would a reasonable person with (some, all) of the defendant's traits have so acted (believed)? (3)Did the defendant, given (some, all) of his traits, act (believe) reasonably? Which of these is preferable?

What factors should be considered as part of the reasonable person's circumstances? The defendant's infirmity of vision? See *Yates v. People,* 32 N.Y. 509 (1865). The defendant's size and weight relative to that of the victim? *People v. Collins,* 189 Cal. App. 2d 575, 11 Cal. Rptr. 504 (1961). What if the deceased has threatened to kill the defendant and the defendant has heard about the threats—does the reasonable person have such knowledge? See *Marts v. State,* 26 Ohio St. Rep. 162 (1875). Should the defendant be required to show that he actually knew of the threats? Suppose the deceased has a reputation for violence, but has never threatened the defendant? See Comment, 13 Suffolk U.L. Rev. 1136 (1979); Annot., 1 A.L.R.3d 571. What of the holding in *Tribett,* cited in *Wanrow,* that the reasonable person knows that the area in which he is walking has a reputation as a high crime area?

What about prior events in the defendant's personal background? Consider the case of infamous subway-shooter Bernhard Goetz. Goetz was on a New York subway late at night when he was approached by four black teenagers, one of whom asked him for five dollars. According to Goetz, he "knew" that the teenagers were intent on robbing him. Goetz then pulled out a gun (which he illegally possessed on the subway) and shot them each once, then returned, and shot one of the boys again. Among other claims, Goetz argued that his belief that he was about to be robbed and beaten was "reasonable" for him, and he sought to introduce evidence that (1) he personally had been mugged several times and beaten once and (2) his doorman had recently been beaten and nearly killed by black youths. Should this evidence be admitted? Is it the kind of information that the reasonable person has, or only Bernhard Goetz? In holding that New York follows an "objective" standard, the New York Court of Appeals nevertheless expressly stated that these experiences and others were admissible. See *People v. Goetz,* 68 N.Y.2d 96, 497 N.E.2d 41 (1986). See G. Fletcher, A Crime of Self-Defense: Bernhard Goetz & the Law on Trial (1988). According to the account of one juror in Goetz, this information was seriously considered by the jury. M. Lesly, Subway Gunman: A Juror's Account of the Bernhard Goetz Trial 287–92 (1988). Suppose the defendant has never known anyone who has been mugged, but reads about such events in the daily papers? Or has a fixation on crime and reads the *Police Gazette?* At what point does the subjectivization of the reasonable person turn into a completely subjective standard? See Dressler 213–14: "Increasingly, courts and statutes are 'subjectivizing' the 'reasonable man' *i.e.,* infusing characteristics of the defendant in the objective standard. . . . There comes a point at which D's characteristics are so deeply infused in the 'reasonable person' that the test of reasonableness loses its value as basis for moral judgment of D's conduct."

Should the defendant's low mental state, edginess, or even his cowardice be construed as part of the reasonable person if a quasi-objective test is to be used? Should a coward be held to the standard of the reasonably brave person? Are these questions the same as asking whether such characteristics should be considered in assessing the effect of a provocative act? See *supra* § 5.03[B][1].

2. *Imminence.* It is generally required that the threat of danger be imminent. But what does that mean? How imminent was the threat to the defendant or her children in *Wanrow?*

Suppose the victim has previously threatened the defendant and walks toward him menacingly? Breaks down his door? See *Commonwealth v. Colandro,* 231 Pa. 343, 80 A. 571 (1911). Suppose the defendant, fearful of the threat, arms himself and (a)goes looking for the victim, meets him, and shoots him? (b)inadvertently meets the victim and then purposely shoots him? *State v. Bristol,* 53 Wyo. 304, 84 P.2d 757 (1938); *Bohannon v. Commonwealth,* 8 Bush. 481 (1781).

In *State v. Schroder,* 199 Neb. 822, 261 N.W. 2d 759 (1978), the defendant, a 19-year-old prisoner, was told by his cell mate Riggs, to whom he owed approximately $3,000, that Riggs "might walk in his sleep that night and —collect some of this money I got owed to me tonight.' "Defendant, construing this as a threat of homosexual rape, waited until Riggs was asleep and then stabbed him once and hit him with a metal ashtray several times. Defendant's conviction for assault with intent to inflict great bodily injury was upheld on appeal, the court refusing to allow a claim of self-defense, on the ground that "There is a very real danger in a rule which would legalize preventive assaults involving the use of deadly force where there has been nothing more than threats." Nevertheless, because "this is a difficult case . . . [where] there are extenuating circumstances . . . ," the court reduced the sentence imposed by the trial court. How much longer should defendant have waited before acting? How much longer would a reasonable person have waited? Consider, the words of the court in *Carico v. Commonwealth.,* 70 Ky. 124 (1870):

> Why should he be required still to wait an assault and to endure longer haunting and hazard when he might at any moment become the victim of his own forbearance, and when self-defense might be impossible or unavailing? Why let the sword still hang over him? Why not remove it out of sight when he may, and not passively linger until it unexpectedly falls and strikes his heart unresisted? The recognition of the perfect right to do so in such a crisis appears to us consistent with both principle and policy. It seems to us conservative. It might afford more security and prevent more assassinations than the lame law of punishment ever could, and the manly and opportune assertion of this universal birthright may teach the reckless who thus maliciously beset the pathway of the peaceable that they will be likely

to bring destruction on their own heads. This preventive principle will go hand in hand with civilization and philosophical jurisprudence as a palladium of personal security and social order and peace. Properly guarded, it may do more good than harm.

Rosen, *On Self-Defense, Imminence, and Women Who Kill Their Batterers,* 71 N.Car. L. Rev. 371, 380–81 (1993) offers this insight:

> In self-defense, the concept of imminence has no significance independent of the notion of necessity. It is, in other words, a "translator" of the underlying principle of necessity, not the principle itself. . . . Because imminence serves only to further the necessity principle, if there is a conflict between imminence and necessity, necessity must prevail. If action is *really* necessary, to avert a threatened harm, society should allow the action, or at least not punish it, even if the harm is not imminent. . . . In cases where the principle, *i.e.,* necessity is present, and the translator, *i.e.,* imminence, is not, this choice mandates ignoring the principle because of the absence of the translator.

Schopp, Sturgis, and Sullivan, *Battered Woman Syndrome, Expert Testimony, and the Distinction between Justification and Excuse,* 1994 U. Ill. L. Rev. 45, 68–69, add the following:

> [S]ome writers interpret necessity as the core of self-defense doctrine. Imminence of harm remains consistent with this theoretical foundation when it serves as a factor regarding judgments of necessity because in most circumstances the judgment that no nonviolent alternative will suffice is more likely to be accurate regarding an imminent harm than a remote one. Imminence of harm can undermine these justificatory theories, however, if it is accepted as an independent requirement of the defense.

Does Model Penal Code § 3.04 (1), *supra,* abolish the requirements of imminence with its language of "on the present occasion"? See C. Gillespie, Justifiable Homicide 186 (1989), arguing that the Code's language would "open up the time frame enough so that persons who have good reason to believe that an assailant is about to launch an attack . . . can act before it is too late. It appears to work quite well in the states that have adopted this provision of the Code."

These questions are sometimes dealt with under the rubric of whether the law of self-defense allows a preemptive strike, a question answered in the affirmative in international law. See P. Ramsy, The Just War, Force and Political Responsibility 61–69 (1968); Note, *Preemptive Strikes against Nuclear Terrorists and Their Sponsors: A Reasonable Solution,* 14 N.Y. L. Sch. J. Int'l & Comp. L. 375 (1993).

3. *Battered Spouses.* In the past two decades incontrovertible data have established the epidemic of spouse battering, almost all by men, in this country. See *Developments in the Law—Legal Responses to Domestic Violence,* 106 Harv. L. Rev. 1499 (1993). Although statistics vary somewhat, it has been estimated that at least 2,000,000 women are beaten every year by their significant others. Straus, *Wife Beating: How Common and Why?* 2 Victimology 443 (1977–78). See also J. Jones, *Battered Spouses' State Law Damage Actions Against the Unresponsive Police,* 23 Rutgers L. J. 1 (1991); M. Straus,

R. Gelles, and S. Steimetz, Behind Closed Doors: Violence in the American Family (1980). Over two-thirds of violent victimizations against women were committed by someone known to them; only 31 percent of female victims reported that the offender was a stranger. U.S. Dept. of Justice, Bureau of Justice Statistics, *Preventing Domestic Violence Against Women* (1986). Six percent of all pregnant women report being beaten. See *N.Y. Times,* March 4, 1994, p.23, col. 1.

Various steps have been taken or suggested to attempt to stem this spate of violence. Shelters for abused women have been established throughout the country. In response to a perception that police were unresponsive to calls involving domestic violence, some states have adopted policies mandating arrest of the abuser even if the victim does not seek to press charges. (The efficacy of this remedy, however, has recently been challenged. See Note, 43 DePaul L. Rev. 1133 (1994), arguing that recent data suggest that arresting unemployed batterers actually results in an increase in battering.) Similarly, some courts have allowed civil law suits against the police. Restraining orders and other such remedies have also proved sporadically successful as has counseling of the battering partner.

As put by two commentators:

> If she seeks criminal remedy, the police may or may not respond. Even if her call is answered, she will probably receive no protection. If she requests a warrant, she would have to survive the scrutiny of the prosecuting attorney and prove she is a worthy victim, primarily through her decision to go through with the divorce. Having completed that stage, she may then enter a reconciliation court . . . In a criminal court she is told wife assault is not a crime but a family matter; in civil court she is told it is a crime which must be enforced by public officials. And, society tells her it is her fault; she provokes it, she tolerates it, she may even like it.

Eisenberg and Micklow, *The Assaultive Wife: "Catch 22" Revisited,* 3 Women's Rts L. Rep. 138, 159 (1977). Even assuming some hyperbole, could the "reasonable battered woman" believe the use of deadly force is required?

Not infrequently, these batterings result in the death of the female partner, in which case the male is prosecuted, usually for murder.* But sometimes, as in *Norman, infra,* the female responds and kills the batterer. In most of those cases, the killing occurs during the battering, and the usual doctrines of self-defense are applied by the courts. See Maguigan, *Battered Women and Self-Defense: Myths and Misconceptions in Current Reform Proposals,* 140 U. Pa. L. Rev. 379 (1991). In a small percentage of these instances, however, such as the *Norman* case, the killing occurs while the batterer is asleep or otherwise not engaged in beating the wife/lover. These cases have forced the law to confront a number of doctrinal questions that had rarely, if ever, been examined minutely in previous cases.

---

* But see Spatz, *A "Lesser" Crime: A Comparative Study of Legal Defenses for Men Who Kill Their Wives,* 24 Colum. J. of Law and Soc. Probs. 597 (1991) (studying three systems, including the United States, in which, according to the author, wife-killing is either totally exonerated, mitigated by virtue of specific events (such as adultery), or punished less seriously)

State v. Norman

Supreme Court of North Carolina

324 N.C. 253, 378 S.E.2d 8 (1989)

MITCHELL, Justice.

The defendant was tried at the 16 February 1987 Criminal Session of Superior Court for Rutherford County upon a proper indictment charging her with the first degree murder of her husband. The jury found the defendant guilty of voluntary manslaughter. The defendant appealed from the trial court's judgment sentencing her to six years imprisonment.

The Court of Appeals granted a new trial, citing as error the trial court's refusal to submit a possible verdict of acquittal by reason of perfect self-defense. Notwithstanding the uncontroverted evidence that the defendant shot her husband three times in the back of the head as he lay sleeping in his bed, the Court of Appeals held that the defendant's evidence that she exhibited what has come to be called "the battered wife syndrome" entitled her to have the jury consider whether the homicide was an act of perfect self-defense and, thus, not a legal wrong.

We conclude that the evidence introduced in this case would not support a finding that the defendant killed her husband due to a reasonable fear of imminent death or great bodily harm, as is required before a defendant is entitled to jury instructions concerning either perfect or imperfect self-defense. Therefore, the trial court properly declined to instruct the jury on the law relating to self-defense. Accordingly, we reverse the Court of Appeals.

At trial, the State presented the testimony of Deputy Sheriff R.H. Epley of the Rutherford County Sheriff's Department, who was called to the Norman residence on the night of 12 June 1985. Inside the home, Epley found the defendant's husband, John Thomas Norman, lying on a bed in a rear bedroom with his face toward the wall and his back toward the middle of the room. He was dead, but blood was still coming from wounds to the back of his head. A later autopsy revealed three gunshot wounds to the head, two of which caused fatal brain injury. The autopsy also revealed a .12 percent blood alcohol level in the victim's body.

Later that night, the defendant related an account of the events leading to the killing, after Epley had advised her of her constitutional rights and she had waived her right to remain silent. The defendant told Epley that her husband had been beating her all day and had made her lie down on the floor while he slept on the bed. After her husband fell asleep, the defendant carried her grandchild to the defendant's mother's house. The defendant took a pistol from her mother's purse and walked the short distance back to her home. She pointed the pistol at the back of her sleeping husband's head, but it jammed the first time she tried to shoot him. She fixed the gun and then shot her husband in the back of the head as he lay sleeping. After one shot, she felt her husband's chest and determined that he was still breathing and making sounds. She then shot him twice more in the back of the head. The defendant told Epley that she killed her husband because "she took all she was going to take from him so she shot him."

The defendant presented evidence tending to show a long history of physical and mental abuse by her husband due to his alcoholism. At the time of the killing, the 39 year old defendant and her husband had been married almost 25 years and had several children. The defendant testified that her husband had started drinking and abusing her about five years after they were married. His physical abuse of her consisted of frequent assaults that included slapping, punching and kicking her, striking her with various objects, and throwing glasses, beer bottles and other objects at her. The defendant described other specific incidents of abuse, such as her husband putting her cigarettes out on her, throwing hot coffee on her, breaking glass against her face and crushing food on her face. Although the defendant did not present evidence of ever having received medical treatment for any physical injuries inflicted by her husband, she displayed several scars about her face which she attributed to her husband's assaults.

The defendant's evidence also tended to show other indignities inflicted upon her by her husband. Her evidence tended to show that her husband did not work and forced her to make money by prostitution, and that he made humor of the fact to family and friends. He would beat her if she resisted going out to prostitute herself or if he was unsatisfied with the amounts of money she made. He routinely called the defendant "dog," "bitch" and "whore," and on a few occasions made her eat pet food out of the pet's bowls and bark like a dog. He often made her sleep on the floor. At times, he deprived her of food and refused to let her get food for the family. During those years of abuse, the defendant's husband threatened numerous times to kill her and to maim her in various ways.

The defendant said her husband's abuse occurred only when he was intoxicated, but that he would not give up drinking. She said she and her husband "got along very well when he was sober," and that he was "a good guy" when he was not drunk. She had accompanied her husband to the local mental health center for sporadic counseling sessions for his problem, but he continued to drink.

In the early morning hours on the day before his death, the defendant's husband, who was intoxicated, went to a rest area off I-85 near Kings Mountain where the defendant was engaging in prostitution and assaulted her. While driving home, he was stopped by a patrolman and jailed on a charge of driving while impaired. After the defendant's mother got him out of jail at the defendant's request later that morning, he resumed his drinking and abuse of the defendant.

The defendant's evidence also tended to show that her husband seemed angrier than ever after he was released from jail and that his abuse of the defendant was more frequent. That evening, sheriff's deputies were called to the Norman residence, and the defendant complained that her husband had been beating her all day and she could not take it anymore. The defendant was advised to file a complaint, but she said she was afraid her husband would kill her if she had him arrested. The deputies told her they needed a warrant before they could arrest her husband, and they left the scene.

The deputies were called back less than an hour later after the defendant had taken a bottle of pills. The defendant's husband cursed her and called her names as she was attended by paramedics, and he told them to let her die. A sheriff's deputy finally chased him back into his house as the defendant was put into an ambulance. The defendant's stomach was pumped at the local hospital, and she was sent home with her mother.

While in the hospital, the defendant was visited by a therapist with whom she discussed filing charges against her husband and having him committed for treatment. Before the therapist left, the defendant agreed to go to the mental health center the next day to discuss those possibilities. The therapist testified at trial that the defendant seemed depressed in the hospital, and that she expressed considerable anger toward her husband. He testified that the defendant threatened a number of times that night to kill her husband and that she said she should kill him "because of the things he had done to her."

The next day, the day she shot her husband, the defendant went to the mental health center to talk about charges and possible commitment, and she confronted her husband with that possibility. She testified that she told her husband later that day: "J.T., straighten up. Quit drinking. I'm going to have you committed to help you." She said her husband then told her he would "see them coming" and would cut her throat before they got to him.

The defendant also went to the social services office that day to seek welfare benefits, but her husband followed her there, interrupted her interview and made her go home with him. He continued his abuse of her, threatening to kill and to maim her, slapping her, kicking her, and throwing objects at her. At one point he took her cigarette and put it out on her, causing a small burn on her upper torso. He would not let her eat or bring food into the house for their children.

That evening, the defendant and her husband went into their bedroom to lie down, and he called her a "dog" and made her lie on the floor when he lay down on the bed. Their daughter brought in her baby to leave with the defendant, and the defendant's husband agreed to let her baby-sit. After the defendant's husband fell asleep, the baby started crying and the defendant took it to her mother's house so it would not wake up her husband. She returned shortly with the pistol and killed her husband.

The defendant testified at trial that she was too afraid of her husband to press charges against him or to leave him. She said that she had temporarily left their home on several previous occasions, but he had always found her, brought her home and beaten her. Asked why she killed her husband, the defendant replied: "Because I was scared of him and I knowed when he woke up, it was going to be the same thing, and I was scared when he took me to the truck stop that night it was going to be worse than he had ever been. I just couldn't take it no more. There ain't no way, even if it means going to prison. It's better than living in that. That's worse hell than anything."

The defendant and other witnesses testified that for years her husband had frequently threatened to kill her and to maim her. When asked if she believed those threats, the defendant replied: "Yes. I believed him; he would, he would kill me if he got a chance. If he thought he wouldn't a had to went to jail, he would a done it."

Two expert witnesses in forensic psychology and psychiatry who examined the defendant after the shooting, Dr. William Tyson and Dr. Robert Rollins, testified that the defendant fit the profile of battered wife syndrome. This condition, they testified, is characterized by such abuse and degradation that the battered wife comes to believe she is unable to help herself and cannot expect help from anyone else. She believes that she cannot excape the complete control of her husband and that he is invulnerable to law enforcement and other sources of help.

Dr. Tyson, a psychologist, was asked his opinion as to whether, on 12 June 1985, "it appeared reasonably necessary for Judy Norman to shoot J.T. Norman?" He replied: "I believe that . . . Mrs. Norman believed herself to be doomed . . . to a life of the worst kind of torture and abuse, degradation that she had experienced over the years in a progressive way; that it would only get worse, and that death was inevitable. . . . " Dr. Tyson later added "I think Judy Norman felt that she had no choice, both in the protection of herself and her family, but to engage, exhibit deadly force against Mr. Norman, and that in so doing, she was sacrificing herself, both for herself and for her family."

Dr. Rollins, who was the defendant's attending physician at Dorothea Dix Hospital when she was sent there for evaluation, testified that in his opinion the defendant was a typical abused spouse and that "[s]he saw herself as powerless to deal with the situation, that there was no alternative, no way she could escape it." Dr. Rollins was asked his opinion as to whether "on June 12th, 1985, it appeared reasonably necessary that Judy Norman would take the life of J.T. Norman?" Dr. Rollins replied that in his opinion, "that course of action did appear necessary to Mrs. Norman."

Based on the evidence that the defendant exhibited battered wife syndrome, that she believed she could not escape her husband nor expect help from others, that her husband had threatened her, and that her husband's abuse of her had worsened in the two days preceding his death, the Court of Appeals concluded that a jury reasonably could have found that her killing of her husband was justified as an act of perfect self-defense. The Court of Appeals reasoned that the nature of battered wife syndrome is such that a jury could not be precluded from finding the defendant killed her husband lawfully in perfect self-defense, even though he was asleep when she killed him. We disagree.

* * *

In North Carolina, a defendant is entitled to have the jury consider acquittal by reason of perfect self-defense when the evidence, viewed in the light most favorable to the defendant, tends to show that at the time of the killing it appeared to the defendant and she believed it to be necessary to kill the decedent to save herself from imminent death or great bodily harm. That belief must be reasonable, however, in that the circumstances as they appeared to the defendant would create such a belief in the mind of a person of ordinary firmness. Further, the defendant must not have been the initial aggressor provoking the fatal confrontation. A killing in the proper exercise of the right of perfect self-defense is always completely justified in law and constitutes no legal wrong.

Our law also recognizes an imperfect right of self-defense in certain circumstances, including, for example, when the defendant is the initial aggressor, but without intent to kill or to seriously injure the decedent, and the decedent escalates the confrontation to a point where it reasonably appears to the defendant to be necessary to kill the decedent to save herself from imminent death or great bodily harm. Although the culpability of a defendant who kills in the exercise of imperfect self-defense is reduced, such a defendant is not justified in the killing so as to be entitled to acquittal, but is guilty at least of voluntary manslaughter.

The defendant in the present case was not entitled to a jury instruction on either perfect or imperfect self-defense. The trial court was not required to instruct on either form of self-defense unless evidence was introduced tending to show that at the time of the killing the defendant reasonably believed herself to be confronted by circumstances which necessitated her killing her husband to save herself from imminent death or great bodily harm. No such evidence was introduced in this case, and it would have been error for the trial court to instruct the jury on either perfect or imperfect self-defense.

The jury found the defendant guilty only of voluntary manslaughter in the present case. As we have indicated, an instruction on imperfect self-defense would have entitled the defendant to nothing more, since one who kills in the exercise of imperfect self-defense is guilty at least of voluntary manslaughter. Therefore, even if it is assumed *arguendo* that the defendant was entitled to an instruction of imperfect self-defense—a notion we have specifically rejected—the failure to give such an instruction was harmless in this case. Accordingly, although we recognize that the imminence requirement applies to both types of self-defense or almost identical reasons, we limit our consideration in the remainder of this opinion to the issue of whether the trial court erred in failing to instruct the jury to consider acquittal on the ground that the killing was justified and, thus, lawful as an act of perfect self-defense.

The killing of another human being is the most extreme recourse to our inherent right of self-preservation and can be justified in law only by the utmost real or apparent necessity brought about by the decedent. For that reason, our law of self-defense has required that a defendant claiming that a homicide was justified and, as a result, inherently lawful by reason of perfect self-defense must establish that she reasonably believed at the time of the killing she otherwise would have immediately suffered death or great bodily harm. Only if defendants are required to show that they killed due to a reasonable belief that death or great bodily harm was imminent can the justification for homicide remain clearly and firmly rooted in necessity. The imminence requirement ensures that deadly force will be used only where it is necessary as a last resort in the exercise of the inherent right of self-preservation. It also ensures that before a homicide is justified and, as a result, not a legal wrong, it will be reliably determined that the defendant reasonably believed that absent the use of deadly force, not only would an unlawful attack have occurred, but also that the attack would have caused death or great bodily harm. The law does not sanction the use of deadly force to repel simple assaults.

The term "imminent," as used to describe such perceived threats of death or great bodily harm as will justify a homicide by reason of perfect self-defense, has been defined as "immediate danger, such as must be instantly met, such as cannot be guarded against by calling for the assistance of others or the protection of the law.". . .

The evidence in this case did not tend to show that the defendant reasonably believed that she was confronted by a threat of imminent death or great bodily harm. The evidence tended to show that no harm was "imminent" or about to happen to the defendant when she shot her husband. The uncontroverted evidence was that her husband had been asleep for some time when she walked to her mother's house, returned with the pistol, fixed the pistol after it jammed and then shot her husband three times in the back of the head. The defendant was not faced with an instantaneous choice between killing her husband or being killed or seriously injured. Instead, all of the evidence tended to show that the defendant had ample time and opportunity to resort to other means of preventing further abuse by her husband. There was no action underway by the decedent from which the jury could have found that the defendant had reasonable grounds to believe either that a felonious assault was imminent or that it might result in her death or great bodily injury. Additionally, no such action by the decedent had been underway immediately prior to his falling asleep.

Faced with somewhat similar facts, we have previously held that a defendant who believed himself to be threatened by the decedent was not entitled to a jury instruction on either perfect or imperfect self-defense when it was the defendant who went to the decedent and initiated the final fatal confrontation. *State v. Mize,* 316 N.C. 48, 340 S.E. 2d 439 (1986). In *Mize,* the decedent Joe McDonald was reported to be looking for the defendant George Mize to get revenge for Mize's alleged rape of McDonald's girlfriend, which had exacerbated existing animosity between Mize and McDonald. After hiding from McDonald for most of the day, Mize finally went to McDonald's residence, woke him up and then shot and killed him. Mize claimed that he feared McDonald was going to kill him and that his killing of McDonald was in self-defense. Rejecting Mize's argument that his jury should have been instructed on self-defense, we stated:

> Here, although the victim had pursued defendant during the day approximately eight hours before the killing, defendant Mize was in no imminent danger while McDonald was at home asleep. When Mize went to McDonald's trailer with his shotgun, it was a new confrontation. Therefore, even if Mize believed it was necessary to kill McDonald to avoid his own imminent death, that belief was unreasonable. 316 N.C. at 53, 340 S.E. 2d at 442 (citations omitted).

The same reasoning applies in the present case.

Additionally, the lack of any belief by the defendant—reasonable or otherwise—that she faced a threat of imminent death or great bodily harm from the drunk and sleeping victim in the present case was illustrated by the defendant and her own expert witnesses when testifying about her subjective assessment of her situation at the time of the killing. The psychologist and psychiatrist replied affirmatively when asked their opinions of whether killing her husband "appeared reasonably necessary" to the defendant at the time of the homicide. That testimony spoke of no imminent threat nor of any fear by the defendant of death or great bodily harm, imminent or otherwise. Testimony in the form of a conclusion that a killing "appeared reasonably necessary" to a defendant does not tend to show all that must be shown to establish self-defense. More specifically, for a killing to be in self-defense, the perceived necessity must arise from a reasonable fear of imminent death or great bodily harm.

Dr. Tyson additionally testified that the defendant "believed herself to be doomed . . . to a life of the worst kind of torture and abuse, degradation that she had experienced over the years in a progressive way; that it would only get worse and that death was inevitable." Such evidence of the defendant's speculative beliefs concerning her remote and indefinite future, while indicating she had felt generally threatened, did not tend to show that she killed in the belief—reasonable or otherwise—that her husband presented a threat of imminent death or great bodily harm. Under our law of self-defense, a defendant's subjective belief of what might be "inevitable" at some indefinite point in the future does not equate to what she believes to be "imminent." Dr. Tyson's opinion that the defendant believed it was necessary to kill her husband for "the protection of herself and her family" was similarly indefinite and devoid of time frame and did not tend to show a threat or fear of imminent harm.

The defendant testified that, "I knowed when he woke up, it was going to be the same thing, and I was scared when he took me to the truck stop that night it was going to be worse than he had ever been." She also testified, when asked if she believed her husband's threats: "Yes . . . [H]e would kill me if he got a chance. If he thought he wouldn't a had to went to jail, he would a done it." Testimony about such indefinite fears concerning what her sleeping husband might do at some time in the future did not tend to establish a fear—reasonable or otherwise—of imminent death or great bodily harm at the time of the killing.

We are not persuaded by the reasoning of our Court of Appeals in this case that when there is evidence of battered wife syndrome, neither an actual attack nor threat of attack by the husband at the moment the wife uses deadly force is required to justify the wife's killing of him in perfect self-defense. The Court of Appeals concluded that to impose such requirements would ignore the "learned helplessness," meekness and other realities of battered wife syndrome and would effectively preclude such women from exercising their right of self-defense. 89 N.C. App. 384, 392–93, 366 S.E. 2d 586, 591–92 (1988). See Mather, *The Skeleton in the Closet: The Battered Woman Syndrome, Self-Defense, and Expert Testimony,* 39 Mercer L. Rev. 545 (1988); Eber, *The Battered Wife's Dilemma: To Kill or to Be Killed,* 32 Hastings L.J. 895 (1981). Other jurisdictions that have addressed this question under similar facts are divided in their views, and we can discern no clear majority position on facts closely similar to those of this case. Compare, *e.g., Commonwealth v. Grove,* 363 Pa. Super. 328, 526 A.2d 369, appeal denied 517 Pa. 630, 539 A.2d 810 (1987) (abused wife who killed her sleeping husband not entitled to self-defense instructions—no immediate threat was posed by the decedent), with

State v. Gallegos, 104 N.M. 247, 719 P.2d 1268 (1986) (abused wife could claim self-defense where she walked into bedroom with gun and killed husband who was awake but lying on the bed).

The reasoning of our Court of Appeals in this case proposes to change the established law of self-defense by giving the term "imminent" a meaning substantially more indefinite and all-encompassing than its present meaning. This would result in substantial relaxation of the requirement of real or apparent necessity to justify homicide. Such reasoning proposes justifying the taking of human life not upon the reasonable belief it is necessary to prevent death or great bodily harm—which the imminence requirement ensures—but upon purely subjective speculation that the decedent probably would present a threat to life at a future time and that the defendant would not be able to avoid the predicted threat.

The Court of Appeals suggests that such speculation would have been particularly reliable in the present case because the jury, based on the evidence of the decedent's intensified abuse during the thirty-six hours preceding his death, could have found that the decedent's passive state at the time of his death was "but a momentary hiatus in a continuous reign of terror by the decedent [and] the defendant merely took advantage of her first opportunity to protect herself." Requiring jury instructions on perfect self-defense in such situations, however, would still tend to make opportune homicide lawful as a result of mere subjective predictions of indefinite future assaults and circumstances. Such predictions of future assaults to justify the defendant's use of deadly force in this case would be entirely speculative, because there was no evidence that her husband had ever inflicted any harm upon her that approached life-threatening injury, even during the "reign of terror." It is far from clear in the defendant's poignant evidence that any abuse by the decedent had ever involved the degree of physical threat required to justify the defendant in using deadly force, even when those threats were imminent. The use of deadly force in self-defense to prevent harm other than death or great bodily harm is excessive as a matter of law. *State v. Hunter,* 315 N.C. 371, 338 S.E. 2d 99 (1986).

As we have stated, stretching the law of self-defense to fit the facts of this case would require changing the "imminent death or great bodily harm" requirement to something substantially more indefinite than previously required and would weaken our assurances that justification for the taking of human life remains firmly rooted in real or apparent necessity. That result in principle could not be limited to a few cases decided on evidence as poignant as this. The relaxed requirements for perfect self-defense proposed by our Court of Appeals would tend to categorically legalize the opportune killing of abusive husbands by their wives solely on the basis of the wives' testimony concerning their subjective speculation as to the probability of future felonious assaults by their husbands. Homicidal self-help would then become a lawful solution, and perhaps the easiest and most effective solution to this problem. See generally Rosen, *The Excuse of Self-Defense: Correcting a Historical Accident on Behalf of Battered Women Who Kill,* 36 Am. U. L. Rev. 11 (1986) (advocating changing the basis of self-defense acquittals to excuse rather than justification, so that excusing battered women's killing of their husband under circumstances not fitting within the traditional requirements of self-defense would not be seen as justifying and therefore encouraging such self-help killing); Mitchell, *Does Wife Abuse Justify Homicide?*, 24 Wayne L. Rev. 1705 (1978) (advocating institutional rather than self-help solutions to wife abuse and citing case studies at the trial level where traditional defenses to homicide appeared stretched to accommodate poignant facts, resulting in justifications of some killings which appeared to be motivated by revenge rather than protection from death or great bodily harm). It has even been suggested that the relaxed requirements of self-defense found in what is often called the "battered woman's defense" could be extended in principle to *any type of case* in which a defendant testified that he or she subjectively believed that killing was necessary and proportionate to any perceived threat.

In conclusion, we decline to expand our law of self-defense beyond the limits of immediacy and necessity which have heretofore provided an appropriately narrow but firm basis upon which homicide may be justified and, thus, lawful by reason of perfect self-defense or upon which a defendant's culpability may be reduced by reason of imperfect self-defense. As we have shown, the evidence in this case did not entitle the defendant to jury instructions on either perfect or imperfect self-defense.

For the foregoing reasons, we conclude that the defendant's conviction for voluntary manslaughter and the trial court's judgment sentencing her to a six-year term of imprisonment were without error. Therefore, we must reverse the decision of the Court of Appeals which awarded the defendant a new trial.

Reversed.

MARTIN, Justice, *dissenting.*

At the outset it is to be noted that the peril of fabricated evidence is not unique to the trials of battered wives who kill. The possibility of invented evidence arises in all cases in which a party is seeking the benefit of self-defense. Moreover, in this case there were a number of witnesses other than defendant who testified as to the actual presence of circumstances supporting a claim of self-defense. This record contains no reasonable basis to attack the credibility of evidence for the defendant.

Likewise, the difficulty of rebutting defendant's evidence because the only other witness to many of the events is deceased is not unique to this type of case. This situation is also commonplace in cases in which self-defense is raised, although, again, in the case *sub judice* there was more than one surviving witness to such events. In considering the argument that the State is faced with a difficult burden in attempting to rebut evidence of which defendant is the only surviving witness, one must not overlook the law: the burden is always on the state to prove that the killing was intentional beyond a reasonable doubt. . . .

At the heart of the majority's reasoning is its unsubstantiated concern that to find that the evidence presented by defendant would support an instruction on self-defense would "expand our law of self-defense beyond the limits of immediacy and necessity." Defendant does not seek to expand or relax the requirements of self-defense and thereby "legalize the opportune killing of allegedly abusive husbands by their wives," as the majority overstates. Rather, defendant contends that the evidence as gauged by the existing laws of self-defense is sufficient to require the submission of a self-defense instruction to the jury. The proper issue for this Court is to determine whether the evidence, viewed in the light most favorable to the defendant, was sufficient to require the trial court to instruct on the law of self-defense. I conclude that it was.

In every jury trial, it is the duty of the court to charge the jury on all substantial features of the case arising on the evidence, whether or not such instructions have been requested. All defenses presented by the defendant's evidence are substantial features of the case, even if that evidence contains discrepancies or is contradicted by evidence from the state. This rule reflects the principle in our jurisprudence that it is the jury, not the judge, that weighs the evidence.

A defendant is entitled to an instruction on self-defense when there is evidence, viewed in the light most favorable to the defendant, that these four elements existed at the time of the killing: (1) it appeared to defendant and he believed it to be necessary to kill the deceased in order to save himself from death or great bodily harm; and (2) defendant's belief was reasonable in that the circumstances as they appeared to him at the time were sufficient to create such a belief in the mind of a person of ordinary firmness; and (3) defendant was not the aggressor in bringing on the affray, *i.e.,* he did not aggressively and willingly enter into the fight without legal excuse or provocation; and (4) defendant did not use excessive force, *i.e.,* did not use more force than was necessary or reasonably appeared to him to be necessary under the circumstances to protect himself from death or great bodily harm. The first element requires that there be evidence that the defendant believed it was necessary to kill in order to protect herself from serious bodily harm or death; the second requires that the circumstances as defendant perceived them were sufficient to create such a belief in the mind of a person of ordinary firmness. Both elements were supported by evidence at defendant's trial.

Evidence presented by defendant described a twenty-year history of beatings and other dehumanizing and degrading treatment by her husband. In his expert testimony a clinical psychologist concluded that defendant fit "and exceed[ed]" the profile of an abused or battered spouse, analogizing this treatment to the dehumanization process suffered by prisoners of war under the Nazis during the Second World War and the brainwashing techniques of the Korean War. The psychologist described the defendant as a woman incarcerated by abuse, by fear, and by her conviction that her husband was invincible and inescapable: Mrs. Norman didn't leave because she believed, fully believed that escape was totally impossible. There was no place to go. She had left before; he had come and gotten her. She had gone to the Department of Social Services. He had come and gotten her. The law, she believed the law could not protect her; no one could protect her, and I must admit, looking over the records, that there was nothing done that would contradict that belief. She fully believed that he was invulnerable to the law and to all social agencies that were available; that nobody could withstand his power. As a result, there was no such thing as escape.

When asked if he had an opinion whether it appeared reasonably necessary for Judy Norman to shoot her husband, this witness responded: "Yes . . . I believe that in examining the facts of this case and examining the psychological data, that Mrs. Norman believed herself to be doomed . . . to a life of the worst kind of torture and abuse, degradation that she had experienced over the years in a progressive way; that it would only get worse, and that death was inevitable; death of herself, which was not such, I don't think was such an issue for her, as she had attempted to commit suicide, and in her continuing conviction of J.T. Norman's power over her, and even failed at that form of escape. I believe she also came to the point of beginning to fear for family members and her children, that were she to commit suicide that the abuse and the treatment that was heaped on her would be transferred onto them." This testimony describes defendant's perception of circumstances in which she was held hostage to her husband's abuse for two decades and which ultimately compelled her to kill him. This testimony alone is evidence amply indicating the first two elements required for entitlement to an instruction on self-defense.

In addition to the testimony of the clinical psychologist, defendant presented the testimony of witnesses who had actually seen defendant's husband abuse her. These witnesses described circumstances that caused not only defendant to believe escape was impossible, but that also convinced them of its impossibility. Defendant's isolation and helplessness were evident in testimony that her family was intimidated by her husband into acquiescing in his torture of her. Witnesses also described defendant's experience with social service agencies and the law, which had contributed to her sense of futility and abandonment through the inefficacy of their protection and the strength of her husband's wrath when they failed. Where torture appears interminable and escape impossible, the belief that only the death of the oppressor can provide relief is reasonable in the mind of a person of ordinary firmness, let alone in the mind of the defendant, who, like a prisoner of war of some years, had been deprived of her humanity and is held hostage by fear.

In *State v. Mize,* this Court noted that if the defendant was in "no imminent danger" at the time of the killing, then his belief that it was necessary to kill the man who had pursued him eight hours before was unreasonable. The second element of self-defense was therefore not satisfied. In the context of the doctrine of self-defense, the definition of "imminent" must be informed by the defendant's perceptions. It is not bounded merely by measurable time, but by all of the facts and circumstances. Its meaning depends upon the assessment of the facts by one of "ordinary firmness" with regard to whether the defendant's perception of impending death or injury was so pressing as to render reasonable her belief that it was necessary to kill.

Evidence presented in the case *sub judice* revealed no letup of tension or fear, no moment in which the defendant felt released from impending serious harm, even while the decedent slept. This, in fact, is a state of mind common to the battered spouse, and one that dramatically distinguishes Judy Norman's belief in the imminence of serious harm from that asserted by the defendant in *Mize.* Psychologists have observed and commentators have described a "constant state of fear" brought on by the cyclical nature of battering as well as the battered spouse's perception that her abuser is both "omnipotent and unstoppable." See Comment, *The Admissibility of Expert Testimony on the Battered Woman Syndrome in Support of a Claim of Self-Defense,* 15 Conn.

L. Rev. 121, 131 (1982). Constant fear means a perpetual anticipation of the next blow, a perpetual expectation that the next blow will kill. "[T]he battered wife is constantly in a heightened state of terror because she is certain that one day her husband will kill her during the course of a beating. . . . Thus from the perspective of the battered wife, the danger is constantly 'immediate.'" "Eber, *The Battered Wife's Dilemma: To Kill or to Be Killed,* 32 Hastings L. J. 895, 928–29 (1981). For the battered wife, if there is no escape, if there is no window of relief or momentary sense of safety, then the next attack, which could be the fatal one, is imminent. In the context of the doctrine of self-defense, "imminent" is a term the meaning of which must be grasped from the defendant's point of view. Properly stated, the second prong of the question is not whether the threat was *in fact* imminent, but whether defendant's belief in the impending nature of the threat, given the circumstances as she saw them, was reasonable in the mind of a person of ordinary firmness.

Defendant's intense fear, based on her belief that her husband intended not only to maim or deface her, as he had in the past, but to kill her, was evident in the testimony of witnesses who recounted events of the last three days of the decedent's life. This testimony could have led a juror to conclude that defendant reasonably perceived a threat to her life as "imminent," even while her husband slept. Over these three days, her husband's anger was exhibited in an unprecedented crescendo of violence. The evidence showed defendant's fear and sense of hopelessness similarly intensifying, leading to an unsuccessful attempt to escape through suicide and culminating in her belief that escape would be possible only through her husband's death.

Defendant testified that on 10 June, two days before her husband's death, he had again forced her to go to a reststop near Kings Mountain to make money by prostitution. Her daughter Phyllis and Phyllis's boyfriend Mark Navarra accompanied her on this occasion because, defendant said, whenever her husband took her there, he would beat her. Phyllis corroborated this account. She testified that her father had arrived some time later and had begun beating her mother, asking how much money she had. Defendant said they all then drove off. Shortly afterwards an officer arrested defendant's husband for driving under the influence. He spent the night in jail and was released the next morning on bond paid by defendant's mother.

Defendant testified that her husband was argumentative and abusive all through the next day, 11 June. Mark Navarra testified that at one point defendant's husband threw a sandwich that defendant had made for him on the floor. She made another; he threw it on the floor as well, then insisted she prepare one without touching it. Defendant's husband had then taken the third sandwich, which defendant had wrapped in paper towels, and smeared it on her face. Both Navarra and Phyllis testified that they had later watched defendant's husband seize defendant's cigarette and put it out on her neck, the scars from which defendant displayed to the jury.

A police officer testified that he arrived at defendant's home at 8:00 that evening in response to a call reporting a domestic quarrel. Defendant, whose face was bruised, was crying, and she told the officer that her husband had beaten her all day long and that she could not take it any longer. The officer told her that he could do nothing for her unless she took out a warrant on her husband. She responded that if she did, her husband would kill her. The officer left but was soon radioed to return because defendant had taken an overdose of pills. The officer testified that defendant's husband was interfering with ambulance attendants, saying "Let the bitch die." When he refused to respond to the officer's warning that if he continued to hinder the attendants, he would be arrested, the officer was compelled to chase him into the house.

Defendant's mother testified that her son-in-law had reacted to the discovery that her daughter had taken the pills with cursing and obscenities and threats such as, "Now, you're going to pay for taking those pills," and "I'll kill you, your mother and your grandmother." His rage was such that defendant's mother feared he might kill the whole family, and knowing defendant's sister had a gun in her purse, she took the gun and placed it in her own.

Defendant was taken to the hospital, treated, and released at 2:30 A.M. She spent the remainder of the night at her grandmother's house. Defendant testified that the next day, 12 June, she felt dazed all day long. She went in the morning to the county mental health center for guidance on domestic abuse. When she returned home, she tried to talk to her husband, telling him to "straighten up. Quit drinking . . . I'm going to have you committed to help you." Her husband responded, "If you do, I'll see them coming and before they get here, I'll cut your throat."

Later, her husband made her drive him and his friend to Spartanburg to pick up the friend's paycheck. On the way, the friend testified, defendant's husband "started slapping on her" when she was following a truck too closely, and he periodically poured his beer into a glass, then reached over and poured it on defendant's head. At one point defendant's husband lay down on the front seat with his head on the arm rest, "like he was going to go to sleep," and kicked defendant, who was still driving, in the side of the head.

Mark Navarra testified that in the year and a half he had lived with the Normans, he had never seen defendant's husband madder than he was on 12 June, opining that it was the DUI arrest two days before that had ignited J.T's fury. Phyllis testified that her father had beaten her mother "all day long." She testified that this was the third day defendant's husband had forbidden her to eat any food. Phyllis said defendant's family tried to get her to eat, but defendant, fearing a beating, would not. Although Phyllis's grandmother had sent over a bag of groceries that day, defendant's husband had made defendant put them back in the bag and would not let anyone eat them.

Early in the evening of 12 June, defendant's husband told defendant, "Let's go to bed." Phyllis testified that although there were two beds in the room, her father had forbidden defendant from sleeping on either. Instead, he had made her lie down on the concrete floor between the two beds, saying, "Dogs don't lay in the bed. They lay in the floor." Shortly afterward defendant testified, Phyllis came in and asked her father if defendant could take care of her baby while she went to the store. He assented and eventually went to sleep. Defendant was still on the floor, the baby on the small bed. The baby started to cry and defendant "snuck up and took him out there to [her] mother's [house]." She asked her mother to watch the baby, then asked if her mother had anything for headache, as her head was "busting." Her mother responded that she had some pain pills in her purse. Defendant went in to get the pills, "and the gun was in there, and I don't know, I just seen the gun, and I took it out, and I went back there and shot him."

From this evidence of the exacerbated nature of the last three days of twenty years of provocation, a juror could conclude that defendant believed that her husband's threats to her life were viable, that serious bodily harm was imminent, and that it was necessary to kill her husband to escape that harm. And from this evidence a juror could find defendant's belief in the necessity to kill her husband not merely reasonable but compelling.

The third element for entitlement to an instruction on self-defense requires that there be evidence that the defendant was not the aggressor in bringing on the affray. If the defendant was the aggressor and killed with murderous intent, that is, that intent to kill or inflict serious bodily harm, then she is not entitled to an instruction on self-defense. A hiatus between provocation by the decedent and the killing can mark the initiation of a new confrontation between the defendant and the decedent, such that the defendant's earlier perception of imminent danger no longer appears reasonable and the defendant becomes the aggressor. For example, in *Mize,* the defendant, who had been told the day before that the decedent was "out to get" him, went to the decedent's trailer with a shotgun, knocked on the front door, and hid under the steps when the decedent opened the door and asked who was there. Defendant then went to the back door, knocked again, and shot the decedent. When the defendant went with his shotgun to the decedent's trailer, this court said, it was a new confrontation, and if the defendant still believed that it was necessary to kill the decedent to avoid his own imminent death, that belief was unreasonable.

Where the defendant is a battered wife, there is no analogue to the victim-turned-aggressor, who, as in *Mize,* turns the table on the decedent in a fresh confrontation. Where the defendant is a battered wife, the affray out of which the killing arises can be a continuing assault. There was evidence before the jury that it had not been defendant but her husband who had initiated "the affray," which the jury could have regarded as lasting twenty years, three days, or any number of hours preceding his death. And there was evidence from which the jury could infer that in defendant's mind the affray reached beyond the moment at which her husband fell asleep. Like the ongoing threats of death or great bodily harm, which she might reasonably have perceived as imminent, her husband continued to be the aggressor and she the victim.

Finally, the fourth element of self-defense poses the question of whether there was any evidence tending to show that the force used by defendant to repel her husband was not excessive, that is, more than reasonably appeared to be necessary under the circumstances. This question is answered in part by abundant testimony describing defendant's immobilization by fear caused by abuse by her husband. Three witnesses, including the decedent's best friend, all recounted incidents in which defendant passively accepted beating, kicks, commands, or humiliating affronts without striking back. From such evidence that she was paralyzed by her husband's presence, a jury could infer that it reasonably appeared to defendant to be necessary to kill her husband in order ultimately to protect herself from the death he had threatened and from severe bodily injury, a foretaste of which she had already experienced.

* * *

By his barbaric conduct over the course of twenty years, J.T. Norman reduced the quality of the defendant's life to such an abysmal state that, given the opportunity to do so, the jury might well have found that she was justified in acting in self-defense for the preservation of her tragic life.

It is to be remembered that defendant does not have the burden of persuasion as to self-defense; the burden remains with the state to prove beyond a reasonable doubt that defendant intentionally killed decedent without excuse or justification. . . . If the evidence in support of self-defense is sufficient to create a reasonable doubt in the mind of a rational juror whether the state has proved an intentional killing without justification or excuse, self-defense must be submitted to the jury. This is such a case.

Notes and Questions

1. The *Norman* case, while typical of the "nonconfrontational" killings by battered wives, is well known because of the opinion of the Court of Appeals, 89 N.C. 384, 366 S.E. 2d 586 (1988), which reversed Ms. Norman's conviction. In that opinion, the court made the following observations of fact and law:

   a. "When defendant was pregnant with her youngest child, Norman beat her and kicked her down a flight of steps, causing the baby to be born prematurely the next day."

   b. "Norman beat defendant 'most every day,' especially when he was drunk and when other people were around, to 'show off.' He would beat defendant with whatever was handy—his fist, a fly swatter, a baseball bat, his shoe, or a bottle; he put out cigarettes on defendant's skin; he threw food and drink in her face and refused to let her eat for days at a time; and he threw glasses, ashtrays, and beer bottles at her and once smashed a glass in her face. Defendant exhibited to the jury scars on her face from these incidents. Norman would often make defendant bark like a dog, and if she refused, he would beat her. He often forced defendant to sleep on the concrete floor of their home and on several occasions forced her to eat dog or cat food out of the dog or cat bowl."

   c. "On the day of the killing one of the Normans' daughters, Loretta, reported to defendant's mother that her father was beating her mother again. Defendant's mother called the sheriff's department, but no help arrived at that time."

   d. "A jury, in our view, could find that decedent's sleep was but a momentary hiatus in a continuous reign of terror by the decedent, that defendant merely took advantage of her first opportunity to protect herself, and that defendant's act was not without the provocation required for perfect self-defense."

Do any of these findings clarify the issues in the case? In other nonconfrontational cases, the states have varied. In *State v. Leidholm,* 334 N.W.2d 811

(N.D. 1983), the defendant-wife stabbed her husband repeatedly after he was asleep; the court allowed the possibility of a defense. But in *State v. Stewart,* 243 Kan. 639, 763 P.2d 577 (1989), the court took the same approach taken in *Norman*—that the "event" of aggression ceased when the husband went to sleep, and the wife thereafter became the "aggressor." In another widely known but not officially reported case, Francine Hughes poured kerosene over her sleeping husband and the house, and lit the kerosene. See F. McNulty, The Burning Bed (1980).

2. *Norman* assumes the admissibility of expert testimony on the battered wife syndrome, which attempts to explain why such wives often not only do not leave, but continue to take the husband back, aware of the risk that beatings will be renewed. Initially the courts were divided on whether such evidence is admissible, but the vast majority now allow such evidence, and at least eight state legislatures have so provided by statute. See Development Note, 106 Harv. L. Rev. *supra,* at 1582–86. Indeed, Maryland admits evidence of the battered woman syndrome "notwithstanding evidence that the defendant was the first aggressor, used excessive force, or failed to retreat at the time of the alleged offense". Md. Code Ann., Cts. and Jud. Proc. sec. 10-91(b) (Supp. 1992). Just as it is being accepted by courts, however, the methodology used by those who "discovered" the syndrome is coming under attack. See Schopp, Sturgis, and Sullivan, *Battered Woman Syndrome, Expert Testimony and the Distinction Between Justification and Excuse,* 1994 U.Ill. L. Rev. 45, 53–64. In *Ibn-Tamas v. United States,* 407 A.2d 626 (D.C. 1979), the testimony was held admissible, but on remand the trial court in *Ibn-Tamas* found that the proffered expert there (and in other cases) did not show that her methodology was sound. The District of Columbia Court of Appeals affirmed in a one-paragraph opinion. *Ibn-Tamas v. United States,* 455 A.2d 893 (D.C. Ct. App. 1983). Are battered wife cases like insanity cases *infra,* § 9.05[B][3], an area where fear that experts will dominate the trial may be relevant or is there another explanation? Or do these cases, and the battered child cases, note 4 below, raise greater concerns of the so-called abuse excuse?

Schopp *et. al., supra,* previous paragraph, at 86–87, argue not only that the evidence for battered spouse syndrome is weak or misleading, but that it can sometimes divert attention from the real facts of the case. They argue, essentially, that these spouses have a valid case of excused self-defense *without* the syndrome evidence and that the syndrome is, at best, neutral, and at worst distracting to the trial:

> [I]f defendants have basis in experience for anticipating a future attack, no duty to retreat, no access to legal alternatives, and good reason to believe that they will be unable to effectively protect themselves at the time of the attack, then they might reasonably believe that immediate defensive force is necessary to protect themselves from the unlawful use of force by their batterers. . . . Expert testimony regarding depression, decreased self-esteem, learned helplessness, or other psychological characteristics of the defendant does not show the defendant's "reasonableness." Such testimony may assist the jury in understanding the defendant, but it does not inform them regarding the events and information that would lead the jurors to the inference of necessity. . . . The evidence required to establish the

defendant's reasonable belief in the necessity of deadly force must demonstrate the pattern of battering and the lack of available legal alternatives to defensive force, rather than the presence of the battered woman syndrome.

Do you agree?

3. Prior to the 19th century, wives who killed their husbands were convicted not merely of murder, but of "petit treason," having killed the "king of the household." For this they could, like other traitors, be drawn and quartered or burned at the stake, a far more serious death penalty than that imposed for "mere murderers." Moreover, husbands were permitted to "discipline" their wives by beating them, provided that the implement was no thicker than a thumb (hence the "rule of thumb"). Islamic law has a similar provision. See Note, *History of Abuse: Society, Judicial, and Legislative Responses to the Problem of Wife Beating,* 23 Suffolk L. Rev. 983 (1989). While this sexist history does not itself explain the doctrinal narrowness of the "self-defense" doctrine, it may help explain why women have more difficulty obtaining even mitigation in their killings. See generally, Marcus, *Conjugal Violence: The Law of Force and the Force of Law,* 69 Calif. L. Rev. 1657 (1981); Note, *The Battered Wife's Dilemma: To Kill or Be Killed,* 32 Hastings L.J. 895 (1981); Note, *The Battered Wife Syndrome: A Potential Defense to a Homicide Charge,* 6 Pepperdine L. Rev. 213 (1978). Littleton, *Women's Experience and the Problem of Transition: Perspectives on Male Battering of Women,* 1989 U. Chi. Legal F. 23, argues that treating the battered wife who kills as acting "unreasonably" or even "reasonably given her emotional state" is sexist. Given that many battered wives are in fact murdered by their husbands during a (frequently drunken) beating, she argues that the killing is reasonable as an empirical matter as well as a subjective matter.

English courts have analyzed the few battered spouse cases they have confronted as raising issues of provocation, rather than of self defense, perfect or imperfect. See, *e.g., R. v. Ahluwalia* (1993) 96 Cr. App. R. 133 (Ct. App.). What are the tactical, as well as doctrinal, strengths and weaknesses of such an approach?

4. *Battered Child Syndrome.* Every year, about 400 parents are killed by their children. Many of these defendants are now raising a self-defense plea similar to that of the battered spouse. See Moreno, *Killing Daddy: Developing a Self-Defense Strategy for the Abused Child,* 137 U. Pa. L. Rev. 1281 (1989); Sambeek, *Parricide as Self-Defense,* 7 Law and Inequality 87 (1988); Note, 40 Wayne L. Rev. 237 (1993). The cases are divided as to the admissibility of expert testimony relevant to a battered child syndrome defense. See *State v. Janes,* 64 Wash. App. 134, 822 P.2d 1238 (1992) (allowing testimony); *Jahnke v. State,* 682 P.2d 991 (Wyo. 1984) (disallowing testimony). Are the questions of necessity the same in these instances as in the battered spouse cases?

5. Are battered children and spouses attempting to justify their actions or to excuse them? What differences might this make as to (a) the admissibility of evidence of past beatings and (b) the burden of proof as to both the credibility of such evidence and its causal relation to the slaying?

· Suppose a battered spouse or child elicits the aid of a third party in killing the abuser to prevent further abuse. Does it matter for purposes of assessing the possible liability of the third party whether the killing by the spouse or child is justified rather than excused?

[5] Defense of Property/Habitation

LAW v. MARYLAND

Maryland Court of Special Appeals

21 Md. App. 13, 318 A.2d 859 (1974)

LOWE, Judge.

When James Cecil Law, Jr. purchased a thirty-nine dollar shotgun for "house protection," he could not possibly have conceived of the ordeal it would cause him to undergo.

Mr. Law, a 32 year old black man, had recently married and moved to a predominantly white middle-class neighborhood. Within two weeks his home was broken into and a substantial amount of clothing and personal property was taken. The investigating officer testified that Mr. Law was highly agitated following the burglary and indicated that he would take the matter in his own hands. The officer quoted Mr. Law as saying: "I will take care of the job. I know who it is." The officer went on to say that Law told him ". . . he knew somebody he could get a gun from in D.C. and he was going to kill the man and he was going take care of it." Two days later he purchased a 12 gauge shotgun and several "double ought" shells.

The intruder entered the Law's home between 6:30 and 9:00 in the evening by breaking a windowpane in the kitchen door which opened onto a screened back porch. The intruder then apparently reached in and unlocked the door. Law later installed "double locks" which required the use of a key both inside and outside. He replaced the glass in the door window in a temporary manner by holding it in place with a few pieces of molding, without using the customary glazing compound to seal it in.

One week after the break-in a well meaning neighbor saw a flickering light in the Law's otherwise darkened house and became suspicious. Aware of the previous burglary, he reported to the police that some one was breaking into the Laws' home. Although the hour was 8:00 P.M., Mr. Law and his bride had retired for the evening. When the police arrived, a fuse of circumstances ignited by fear exploded into a tragedy of errors.

The police did not report to or question the calling neighbor. Instead they went about routinely checking the house seeking the possible illegal point of entry. They raised storm windows where they could reach them and shook the inside windows to see if they were locked. They shined flashlights upon the windows out of reach, still seeking evidence of unlawful entry. Finding none, two officers entered the back screened porch to check the back door, whereupon they saw the windowpane which appeared to have been temporarily put in place with a few pieces of molding. These officers apparently had not known of the repair or the cause of damage.

Upstairs Mr. and Mrs. Law heard what sounded like attempts to enter their home. Keenly aware of the recent occurrence, Mr. Law went downstairs, obtained and loaded his newly acquired shotgun and, apparently facing the rear door of the house, listened for more sounds.

In the meantime, the uniformed officers found what they thought to be the point of entry of a burglar, and were examining the recently replaced glass. While Officer Adams held the flashlight on the recently replaced pane of glass, Officer Garrison removed the molding and the glass, laid them down and stated that he was going to reach in and unlock the door from the inside to see if entry could be gained. Officer Adams testified that they "were talking in a tone a little lower than normal at this point." Officer Adams stated that Officer Garrison then tested the inside lock, discovered it was a deadlock and decided no one could have gotten in the door without a key. A law enforcement student, riding with Officer Garrison that evening, testified that he then heard a rattling noise and someone saying "if there was somebody here, he's still in there." As Officer Garrison removed his hand from the window he was hit by a shotgun blast which Law fired through the door. Officer Garrison was dead on arrival at the hospital.

Officer Potts, the officer next to arrive at the scene, saw Officer Adams running to his car to call for reinforcements. He heard another shot and Officer Adams yell "they just shot at me."

The tragedy of errors had only begun. The officers, having obtained reinforcements and apparently believing they had cornered a burglar, subjected the house to a fusillade of gun fire evinced by over forty bullet holes in the bottom of the kitchen door and the police department transcription of a telephone conversation during the ensuing period of incomprehensible terror.

Mr. Law testified that while he stood listening to the sounds and voices at the door, fearful that someone was about to come in ". . . the gun went off, like that, and when it went off like that it scared me and I was so scared because I had never shot a shotgun before and then I heard a voice on the outside say that someone had been shot." Mr. Law was not able to hear who had been shot but he then ". . . hollered up to my wife, call a police officer, I think I shot a burglar." His wife called the police and most of her conversation was recorded. . . .

* * *

The appellant, James Cecil Law, Jr. was found guilty of murder in the second degree and of assault with intent to murder. He was convicted by a jury in the Circuit Court for Charles County following removal from Prince George's County. Judge James C. Mitchell sentenced him to concurrent ten year terms.

* * *

I.

The appellant's first question assigning error for failure to grant his motion for judgment of acquittal is a request for our review of the trial court's constitutional responsibility to pass upon the sufficiency of the evidence. In doing so we are not permitted to substitute our judgment of whether there was reasonable doubt of the defendant's guilt for that exercised by the jury. The limit of our review is to determine whether there was relevant and legally sufficient evidence, properly before the jury, to sustain a conviction. . . .

The necessity of responding to this question is diminished by the result we reach here;* however, appellant's assertion of the defense of habitation requires that we do more than summarily declare the question moot.

There is a dearth of Maryland authority upon the question of what constitutes justifiable homicide in the defense of one's home. We hasten to note, however, that the single case directly meeting the question does so concisely and clearly. In 1962, the Court of Appeals in *Crawford v. State,* 231 Md. 354, 190 A.2d 538, reversed a conviction of manslaughter against a 42 year old man, suffering from a nervous condition and ulcers, whose home was being broken into by a 23 year old man and a partner. The decedent had knocked out a piece of masonite replacing one of four glass panes in the door. Crawford fired a shotgun through the door killing the attacker before he was able to enter.

Certain of the circumstances of that case coincide remarkably with the case at bar. It is as remarkably distinguished, however, by the character and purpose of the decedent, who had previously beaten Crawford and was returning to rob and beat him again after threatening to do so. Without digression on tangential issues, Chief Judge Brune noted with little discussion, as we do here, the appropriateness of the [view] . . . that one not seeking a fight may arm himself in anticipation of a violent attack.

The defense of habitation is explained by text writers and treated in *Crawford* as an extension of the right of self-defense. The distinction between the defense of home and the defense of person is primarily that in the former there is no duty to retreat. . . .

The regal aphorism that a man's home is his castle has obscured the limitations on the right to preserve one's home as a sanctuary from fear of force or violence.

Crawford articulates the rule well, distilling it from a review of cases in many jurisdictions:

> Most American jurisdictions in which the question has been decided have taken the view that if an assault on a dwelling and an attempted forcible entry are made under circumstances which would create *a reasonable apprehension* that it is the design of the assailant to *commit a felony* or to inflict on the inhabitants injury which may result in loss of life or great bodily harm, and that the danger that the design will be carried into effect is imminent, a lawful occupant of the dwelling may prevent the entry even by the taking of the intruder's life. [Emphasis added.]

The felonies the prevention of which justifies the taking of a life "are such and only such as are committed by forcible means, violence, and surprise such

---

* [In a portion of the opinion omitted here, the court reersed the convictions and remanded for a new trial because unconstitutionally obtained statements by law were received in evidence at trial.—Eds.]

as murder, robbery, burglary, rape or arson." . . . [I]t is "essential that killing is *necessary* to prevent the commission of the felony in question. If other methods would prevent its commission, a homicide is not justified; all other means of preventing the crime must first be exhausted." . . .

The right thus rests upon real or apparent necessity. It is this need for caution in exercising the right that has been relegated to obscurity. The position espoused by appellant typifies the misunderstanding of the extent of the right to defend one's home against intrusion. He says:

> The defendant is not required to act as a reasonable, prudent and cautious individual, nor was he required to limit his force to only that that was required under the circumstances—not when the defendant was in his own home, and believed he was being set upon, or about to be set upon by would be robbers or burglars who were in the act of breaking into his home at the time.

The judgment which must usually be made precipitously under frightening conditions nevertheless demands a certain presence of mind and reasonableness of judgment. Although one is "not obliged to retreat . . . but . . . may even pursue the assailant until he finds himself or his property out of danger. . . , this will not justify a person['s] firing upon everyone who forcibly enters his house, even at night." . . .

* * *

II.

Appellant points to a portion of the court's instructions which he feels indicates an erroneous shifting of the burden of proof. He contends this is tantamount to removing the presumptive cloak of innocence constitutionally enveloping a defendant. The judge issued a variant of the stock instruction that once an illegal homicide is established the law presumes it to be murder in the second degree. He then went on to say that:

> *the burden rests upon the accused as part of his defense to prove by a fair preponderance of the evidence* circumstances of a deviation or mitigation, which would lower, reduce the crime to manslaughter or he may show, by way of defense, that the killing was justifiable or excusable and that therefore he should not be held criminally accountable for any crime and the State has the burden of proving not by merely a preponderance of the greater weight of the evidence, but proving beyond a reasonable doubt the element which will raise the crime from second degree murder to first degree. [Emphasis supplied by appellant.]

We are unable to see how the "trial judge illegally shifted the burden of proof to the defendant." Appellant points to cases that draw semantic distinctions between the shifting of the burden of proof and the burden of going forward with the evidence. Undoubtedly the judge chose to avoid confusing the jury with the fine academic distinctions of shifting burdens. His choice of words was not such as appear misleading or prejudicial. . . .

Any possibility of a misunderstanding was averted by emphatically placing upon the State the burden of proving guilt beyond a reasonable doubt. The judge elaborated upon that instruction as well as the presumption of innocence favoring the accused. . . .

* * *

III.

The same authorities answer appellant's third assignment of error that answered his first. Appellant argues that in defense of his home he "is not subject to the standards of a reasonable, prudent and cautious person, nor is his degree of force limited only to that required under the circumstances to repel the intruder." Quite the contrary, we do not find the right to defend one's habitation to be so absolute as to sanction promiscuous shooting upon a baseless apprehension by an unreasonable person. The permissible degree of force used to repel an intruder must not be excessive. . . . The question of excessive force to resist the intrusion, in most instances, as in *Crawford, supra,* is the most difficult problem the jury has to cope with when death of the intruder was the result. Apropos of the appellant's question is the statement in *State v. Sorrentino,* 31 Wyo. 129, 224 P. 420, 423, that a defendant is not justified in taking a life "[i]f a cautious and prudent man, under the same circumstances, would not believe the danger to have been real. . . ."[4]

* * *

[Based upon violations of Miranda rights, discussion of which is omitted here] [j]udgments reversed; case remanded for a new trial.

NOTES AND QUESTIONS

1. In light of *Mullaney v. Wilbur,* and *Patterson v. New York, supra,* § 9.04[B], did the court in *Law* properly instruct the jury on the burden of proof issue?

2. *Law* recognizes a limited defense of habitation by means of deadly force. Is the defense too limited? What should Mr. Law have done under the circumstances of his case?

Apart from the exemption of the requirement to retreat (if it applies in the jurisdiction), is the defense of habitation in *Law* any different than self-defense? Some cases suggest an additional distinction. Defense of habitation may permit use of deadly force before the perceived danger becomes as

---

[4] Equally apropos are the circumstances in *sorrentino* which created the reasonable belief of danger.

> The effect upon the human mind of darkness n the stillness of the night is a factor well known. . . . A sudden appearance from out the darkness is apt to give at least a temporary nervous shock to the stoutest heart. Much more is that apt to bt true when, roused from rest or slumber, footsteps and other sounds are heard which are calculated, of giving the impression of boding no good. . . .

immediate as required by self-defense. Thus a householder fearing an unlawful entry by one intent on doing violence to the householder need not wait until the assailant is upon him in the house, but may open the door and shoot while the assailant is still outside. *People v. Givens,* 26 Ill. 2d 371, 375, 186 N.E. 2d 225, 227 (1962); *People v. Gray,* 162 N.C. 608, 614, 77 S.E. 833, 834 (1913). Other cases extend the habitation defense even further by permitting the use of deadly force to repel unlawful entries into the home by persons intending assaults upon those therein which are neither intended nor likely to kill or inflict great bodily injury. *People v. Eatman,* 405 Ill. 491, 498, 91 N.E. 2d 387, 390 (1950). See Jacobs, *Privileges for the Use of Deadly Force Against a Residence-Intruder: A Comparison of the Jewish Law and the United States Common Law,* 63 Temp. L. Q. 31 (1990).

Some jurisdictions have enacted statutory provisions affording citizens broad rights of self-defense within their homes. For example, see *People v. Young,* 825 P.2d 1004 (Colo. App. 1991) discussing Colorado's "make my day" statute which provides:

> [A]ny occupant of a dwelling is justified in using any degree of physical force, including deadly physical force, against another person when that other person has made an unlawful entry into the dwelling, and when the occupant has a reasonable belief that such other person has committed a crime in the dwelling in addition to the uninvited entry, or is committing or intends to commit a crime against a person or property in addition to the uninvited entry, and when the occupant reasonably believes that such other person might use any physical force, no matter how slight, against any occupant.

Colo. Rev. Stat. § 18-1-704.5(2)(1986).

3. Courts have generally condemned the use of deadly mechanical devices to protect habitations from trespassing wrongdoers. Thus most cases hold that homeowners are not permitted to use spring guns where they could cause the death of one attempting to burglarize the house, even if there are no other reasonable ways to protect the property. *People v. Ceballos,* 12 Cal. 3d 470, 116 Cal. Rptr. 233, 526 P.2d 241 (1974).

4. Many jurisdictions have codified the rules governing defense of property. The following Model Penal Code provisions have been influential:

§ 3.06 Use of Force for the Protection of Property.

(1) *Use of Force Justifiable for Protection of Property.* Subject to the provisions of this Section and of Section 3.09, the use of force upon or toward the person of another is justifiable when the actor believes that such force is immediately necessary:

(a) to prevent or terminate an unlawful entry or other trespass upon land or a trespass against or the unlawful carrying away of tangible, movable property, provided that such land or movable property is, or is believed by the actor to be, in his possession or in the possession of another person for whose protection he acts; or

(b) to effect an entry or re-entry upon land or to retake tangible movable property, provided that the actor believes that he or the person by whose authority he acts or a person from whom he or such other person derives title was unlawfully dispossessed of such land or movable property and is entitled to possession, and provided, further, that:

(i) the force is used immediately or on fresh pursuit after such dispossession; or

(ii) the actor believes that the person against whom he uses force has no claim of right to the possession of the property and, in the case of land, the circumstances, as the actor believes them to be, are of such urgency that it would be an exceptional hardship to postpone the entry or re-entry until a court order is obtained.

* * *

(3) *Limitations on Justifiable Use of Force.*

(a) *Request to Desist.* The use of force is justifiable under this Section only if the actor first requests the person against whom such force is used to desist from his interference with the property, unless the actor believes that:

(i) such request would be useless; or

(ii) it would be dangerous to himself or another person to make the request; or

(iii) substantial harm will be done to the physical condition of the property that is sought to be protected before the request can effectively be made.

(b) *Exclusion of Trespasser.* The use of force to prevent or terminate a trespass is not justifiable under this Section if the actor knows that the exclusion of the trespasser will expose him to substantial danger of serious bodily harm.

(c) *Resistance of Lawful Re-entry or Recaption.* The use of force to prevent an entry or re-entry upon land or the recaption of movable property is not justifiable under this Section, although the actor believes that such re-entry or recaption is unlawful, if:

(i) the re-entry or recaption is made by or on behalf of a person who was actually dispossessed of the property; and

(ii) it is otherwise justifiable under Subsection (1)(b) of this Section.

(d) *Use of Deadly Force.* The use of deadly force is not justifiable under this Section unless the actor believes that:

(i) the person against whom the force is used is attempting to dispossess him of his dwelling otherwise than under a claim of right to its possession; or

(ii) the person against whom the force is used is attempting to commit or consummate arson, burglary, robbery or other felonious theft or property destruction and either:

(1) has employed or threatened deadly force against or in the presence of the actor; or

(2) the use of force other than deadly force to prevent the commission or the consummation of the crime would expose the actor or another in his presence to substantial danger of serious bodily harm.

4. *Use of Confinement as Protective Force.* The justification afforded by this Section extends to the use of confinement as protective force only if the actor takes all reasonable measures to terminate the confinement as soon as he knows that he can do so with safety to the property, unless the person confined has been arrested on a charge of crime.

5. *Use of Device to Protect Property.* The justification afforded by this Section extends to the use of a device for the purpose of protecting property only if:

(a) the device is not designed to cause or known to create a substantial risk of causing death or serious bodily harm; and

(b) the use of the particular device to protect the property from entry or trespass is reasonable under the circumstances, as the actor believes them to be; and

(c) the device is one customarily used for such a purpose or reasonable care is taken to make known to probable intruders the fact that it is used.

* * *

[6] Law Enforcement Defenses

TENNESSEE V. GARNER

Supreme Court of the United States

471 U.S. 1 (1985)

Justice WHITE *delivered the opinion of the Court.*

This case requires us to determine the constitutionality of the use of deadly force to prevent the escape of an apparently unarmed suspected felon. We conclude that such force may not be used unless it is necessary to prevent the escape and the officer has probable cause to believe that the suspect poses a significant threat of death or serious physical injury to the officer or others.

I

At about 10:45 P.M. on October 3, 1974, Memphis Police Officers Elton Hymon and Leslie Wright were dispatched to answer a "prowler inside call." Upon arriving at the scene they saw a woman standing on her porch and gesturing toward the adjacent house. She told them she had heard glass breaking and that "they" or "someone" was breaking in next door. While Wright radioed the dispatcher to say that they were on the scene, Hymon went behind the house. He heard a door slam and saw someone run across the back yard. The fleeing suspect, who was appellee—respondent's decedent, Edward

Garner, stopped at a 6 feet-high chain link fence at the edge of the yard. With the aid of a flashlight, Hymon was able to see Garner's face and hands. He saw no sign of a weapon, and, though not certain, was "reasonably sure" and "figured" that Garner was unarmed. . . . He thought Garner was 17 or 18 years old and about 5'5" or 5'7" tall.[2] While Garner was crouched at the base of the fence, Hymon called out "police, halt" and took a few steps toward him. Garner then began to climb over the fence. Convinced that if Garner made it over the fence he would elude capture, Hymon shot him. The bullet hit Garner in the back of the head. Garner was taken by ambulance to a hospital, where he died on the operating table. Ten dollars and a purse taken from the house were found on his body. . . .

In using deadly force to prevent the escape, Hymon was acting under the authority of a Tennessee statute and pursuant to Police Department policy. The statute provides that "[i]f, after notice of the intention to arrest the defendant, he either flee or forcibly resist, the officer may use all the necessary means to effect the arrest.". . . [5]

Garner's father . . . brought this action in the Federal District Court for the Western District of Tennessee, seeking damages under 42 U.S.C. § 1983 for asserted violations of Garner's constitutional rights. The complaint alleged that the shooting violated the Fourth, Fifth, Sixth, Eighth, and Fourteenth Amendments of the United States Constitution. It named as defendants Officer Hymon, the Police Department, its Director, and the Mayor and city of Memphis. . . . [T]he District Court entered judgment for all defendants. . . . It . . . concluded that Hymon's actions were authorized by the Tennessee statute, which in turn was constitutional. Hymon had employed the only reasonable and practicable means of preventing Garner's escape. Garner had "recklessly and heedlessly attempted to vault over the fence to escape, thereby assuming the risk of being fired upon." . . .

* * *

The Court of Appeals reversed and remanded. . . . It reasoned that the killing of a fleeing suspect is a "seizure" under the Fourth Amendment,[6] and is therefore constitutional only if "reasonable." The Tennessee statute failed as applied to this case because it did not adequately limit the use of deadly force by distinguishing between felonies of different magnitudes. . . . [7]

The State of Tennessee, which had intervened to defend the statute, . . . appealed to this Court. . . .

---

[2] In fact, Garner, an eighth-grader, was 15. He was 5'4" tall and weighed somewhere around 100 or 110 pounds. . . .

[5] Although the statute does not say so explicitly, Tennessee law forbids the use of deadly force in the arrest of a misdemeanant. See *Johnson v. State,* 173 Tenn. 134, 114S.W.3d 819 (1938).

[6] "The right of the people to be secure in their persons. . . against unreasonable searches and seizures, shall not be violated. . . . " U.S. Const, Amdt. 4.

[7] The Court of Appeals concluded that the rule set out in the Model Penal Code [§ 3.07(2)(b)] "accurately states Fourth Amendment limitations on the use of deadly force against fleeing felons.". . .

II

Whenever an officer restrains the freedom of a person to walk away, he has seized that person. . . . While it is not always clear just when minimal police interference becomes a seizure, . . . there can be no question that apprehension by the use of deadly force is a seizure subject to the reasonableness requirement of the Fourth Amendment.

A police officer may arrest a person if he has probable cause to believe that person committed a crime. . . . Petitioners and appellant argue that if this requirement is satisfied the Fourth Amendment has nothing to say about how that seizure is made. This submission ignores the many cases in which this Court, by balancing the extent of the intrusion against the need for it, has examined the reasonableness of the manner in which a search or seizure is conducted. . . .

* * *

. . . [N]ot withstanding probable cause to seize a suspect, an officer may not always do so by killing him. The intrusiveness of a seizure by means of deadly force is unmatched. The suspect's fundamental interest in his own life need not be elaborated upon. The use of deadly force also frustrates the interest of the individual, and of society, in judicial determination of guilt and punishment. Against these interests are ranged governmental interests in effective law enforcement.[8] It is argued that overall violence will be reduced by encouraging the peaceful submission of suspects who know that they may be shot if they flee. Effectiveness in making arrests requires the resort to deadly force, or at least the meaningful threat thereof. "Being able to arrest such individuals is a condition precedent to the state's entire system of law enforcement." . . .

Without in any way disparaging the importance of these goals, we are not convinced that the use of deadly force is a sufficiently productive means of accomplishing them to justify the killing of nonviolent suspects. . . . The use of deadly force is a self-defeating way of apprehending a suspect and so setting the criminal justice mechanism in motion. If successful, it guarantees that mechanism will not be set in motion. And while the meaningful threat of deadly force might be thought to lead to the arrest of more live suspects by discouraging escape attempts,[9] the presently available evidence does not

---

[8] The dissent emphasizes that subsequent investigation cannot replace immediate apprehension. We recognize that this is so. . . . ;indeed, that is the reason why there is any dispute. If subsequent arrest were assured, no one would argue that use of deadly force was justified. Thus, we proceed on the assumption that subsequent arrest is not likely. Nonetheless, it should be remembered that failure to apprehend at the scene does not necessarily mena that the suspect will never be caught. . . .

[9] We note that the usual manner of deterring illegal conduct—through punishment—has been largely ignored in connection with flight from arrest. Arkansas, for example, specifically excepts flight from arrest from the offense of "obstruction of governmental operations." The comentary notes that this "reflects the basic policy judgment that, absent the use of force or violence, a mere attempt to avoid apprehension by a law enforcement officer does not give rise to an independent offense.". . . In the few States that do outlaw flight from an arresting officer, the crime is only a misdemeanor. . . . Even forceful resistance, though generally a separate offense, is classified as a misdemeanor. . . .

support this thesis. The fact is that a majority of police departments in this country have forbidden the use of deadly force against nonviolent suspects. . . . If those charged with the enforcement of the criminal law have abjured the use of deadly force in arresting nondangerous felons, there is a substantial basis for doubting that the use of such force is an essential attribute of the arrest power in all felony cases. . . . Petitioners and appellant have not persuaded us that shooting nondangerous fleeing suspects is so vital as to outweigh the suspect's interest in his own life.

The use of deadly force to prevent the escape of all felony suspects, whatever the circumstances, is constitutionally unreasonable. It is not better that all felony suspects die than that they escape. Where the suspect poses no immediate threat to the officer and no threat to others, the harm resulting from failing to apprehend him does not justify the use of deadly force to do so. It is no doubt unfortunate when a suspect who is in sight escapes, but the fact that the police arrive a little late or are a little slower afoot does not always justify killing the suspect. A police officer may not seize an unarmed, nondangerous suspect by shooting him dead. The Tennessee statute is unconstitutional insofar as it authorizes the use of deadly force against such fleeing suspects.

It is not however, unconstitutional on its face. Where the officer has probable cause to believe that the suspect poses a threat of serious physical harm, either to the officer or to others, it is not constitutionally unreasonable to prevent escape by using deadly force. Thus, if the suspect threatens the officer with a weapon or there is probable cause to believe that he has committed a crime involving the infliction or threatened infliction of serious physical harm, deadly force may be used if necessary to prevent escape, and if, where feasible, some warning has been given. As applied in such circumstances, the Tennessee statute would pass constitutional muster.

III

It is insisted that the Fourth Amendment must be construed in light of the common-law rule, which allowed the use of whatever force was necessary to effect the arrest of a fleeing felon, though not a misdemeanant. . . . Most American jurisdictions also imposed a flat prohibition against the use of deadly force to stop a fleeing misdemeanant, coupled with a general privilege to use such force to stop a fleeing felon. . . .

The State and city argue that because this was the prevailing rule at the time of the adoption of the Fourth Amendment and for some time thereafter, and is still in force in some States, use of deadly force against a fleeing felon must be "reasonable." It is true that this Court has often looked to the common law in evaluating the reasonableness, for Fourth Amendment purposes, of

---

This lenient approach does avoid the anomaly of automatically transforming every fleeing misdemenant into a fleeing felon—subject, under the common-law rule, to apprehension by deadly force—solely by virtue of his flight. However, it is in real tension with the harsh consequences of flight in cases where deadly foce is employed. For example, Tennessee does not outlaw fleeing from arrest. The Memphis City Code does, . . . subjecting the offender to a maximum fine of $50. . . . Thus, Garner's attempted escape subjected him to (a) a $50 fine and (b) being shot.

police activity. . . . On the other hand, it "has not simply frozen into constitutional law those law enforcement practices that existed at the time of the Fourth Amendment's passage." . . . Because of sweeping change in the legal and technological context, reliance on the common-law rule in this case would be a mistaken literalism that ignores the purposes of a historical inquiry.

It has been pointed out many times that the common-law rule is best understood in light of the fact that it arose at a time when virtually all felonies were punishable by death. "Though effected without the protections and formalities of an orderly trial and conviction, the killing of a resisting or fleeing felon resulted in no greater consequences than those authorized for punishment of the felony of which the individual was charged or suspected." . . . Courts have also justified the common-law rule by emphasizing the relative dangerousness of felons. . . .

Neither of these justifications makes sense today. Almost all crimes formerly punishable by death no longer are or can be. . . . And while in earlier times "the gulf between the felonies and the minor offenses was broad and deep," . . . today the distinction is minor and often arbitrary. Many crimes classified as misdemeanors, or nonexistent, at common law are now felonies. . . . These changes have undermined the concept, which was questionable to begin with, that use of deadly force against a fleeing felon is merely a speedier execution of someone who has already forfeited his life. They have also made the assumption that a "felon" is more dangerous than a misdemeanant untenable. Indeed, numerous misdemeanors involve conduct more dangerous than many felonies.[12]

There is an additional reason why the common-law rule cannot be directly translated to the present day. The common-law rule developed at a time when weapons were rudimentary. Deadly force could be inflicted almost solely in a hand-to-hand struggle during which, necessarily, the safety of the arresting officer was at risk. Handguns were not carried by police officers until the latter half of the last century. . . . Only then did it become possible to use deadly force from a distance as a means of apprehension. As a practical matter, the use of deadly force under the standard articulation of the common-law rule has an altogether different meaning—and harsher consequences—now than in past centuries. . . .

One other aspect of the common-law rule bears emphasis. It forbids the use of deadly force to apprehend a misdemeanant, condemning such action as disproportionately severe. See *Holloway v. Moser,* 193 N.C., at 187, 136 S.E., at 376; *State v. Smith,* 127 Iowa, at 535, 103 N.W., at 945. See generally Annot., 83 A.L.R.3d 238 (1978).

In short, though the common law pedigree of Tennessee's rule is pure on its face, changes in the legal and technological context mean the rule is distorted almost beyond recognition when literally applied.

In evaluating the reasonableness of police procedures under the Fourth Amendment, we have also looked to prevailing rules in individual jurisdictions. . . . Some 19 States have codified the common-law rule. . . . Four

---

[12] White collar crime, for example, poses a less significant physical threat than, say, drunken driving. . . .

States, though without a relevant statute, apparently retain the common-law rule. Two States have adopted the Model Penal Code's provision verbatim. Eighteen others allow, in slightly varying language, the use of deadly force only if the suspect has committed a felony involving the use or threat of physical or deadly force, or is escaping with a deadly weapon, or is likely to endanger life or inflict serious physical injury if not arrested. . . .

It cannot be said that there is a constant or overwhelming trend away from the common-law rule. . . . Nonetheless, the long-term movement has been away from the rule that deadly force may be used against any fleeing felon, and that remains the rule in less than half the States.

This trend is more evident and impressive when viewed in light of the policies adopted by the police departments themselves. Overwhelmingly, these are more restrictive than the common-law rule. . . . The Federal Bureau of Investigation and the New York City Police Department, for example, both forbid the use of firearms except when necessary to prevent death or grievous bodily harm. Overall, only 7.5% of departmental and municipal policies explicitly permit the use of deadly force against any felon; 86.8% explicitly do not. . . . In light of the rules adopted by those who must actually administer them, the older and fading common-law view is a dubious indicium of the constitutionality of the Tennessee statute now before us.

Actual departmental policies are important for an additional reason. We would hesitate to declare a police practice of long standing "unreasonable" if doing so would severely hamper effective law enforcement. But the indications are to the contrary. There has been no suggestion that crime has worsened in any way in jurisdictions that have adopted, by legislation or departmental policy, rules similar to that announced today. . . . The submission is that the obvious state interests in apprehension are not sufficiently served to warrant the use of lethal weapons against all fleeing felons. . . .

* * *

IV

In reversing, the Court of Appeals accepted the District Court's factual conclusions and held that "the facts, as found, did not justify the use of deadly force." . . . We agree. Officer Hymon could not reasonably have believed that Garner—young, slight, and unarmed—posed any threat. Indeed, Hymon never attempted to justify his actions on any basis other than the need to prevent an escape. . . .

The dissent argues that the shooting was justified by the fact that Officer Hymon had probable cause to believe that Garner had committed a nighttime burglary. . . . While we agree that burglary is a serious crime, we cannot agree that it is so dangerous as automatically to justify the use of deadly force. . . . Although the armed burglar would present a different situation, the fact that an unarmed suspect has broken into a dwelling at night does not automatically mean he is physically dangerous. . . . In fact, the available statistics demonstrate the burglaries only rarely involve physical violence.

During the 10-year period from 1973–1982, only 3.8% of all burglaries involved violent crime. . . . [23]

* * *

The judgment of the Court of Appeals is affirmed, and the case is remanded for further proceedings consistent with this opinion.

So ordered.

Justice O'CONNOR, with whom THE CHIEF JUSTICE and Justice REHNQUIST join, *dissenting.*

The Court today holds that the Fourth Amendment prohibits a police officer from using deadly force as a last resort to apprehend a criminal suspect who refuses to halt when fleeing the scene of a nighttime burglary. This conclusion rests on the majority's balancing of the interests of the suspect and the public interest in effective law enforcement. . . . Notwithstanding the venerable common-law rule authorizing the use of deadly force if necessary to apprehend a fleeing felon, and continued acceptance of this rule by nearly half the States, . . . the majority concludes that Tennessee's statute is unconstitutional inasmuch as it allows the use of such force to apprehend a burglary suspect who is not obviously armed or otherwise dangerous. Although the circumstances of this case are unquestionably tragic and unfortunate, our constitutional holdings must be sensitive both to the history of the Fourth Amendment and to the general implications of the Court's reasoning. By disregarding the serious and dangerous nature of residential burglaries and the longstanding practice of many States, the Court effectively creates a Fourth Amendment right allowing a burglary suspect to flee unimpeded from a police officer who has probable cause to arrest, who has ordered the suspect to halt, and who has no means short of firing his weapon to prevent escape. I do not believe that the Fourth Amendment supports such a right, and I accordingly dissent.

* * *

. . . [I]t is crucial to acknowledge that police use of deadly force to apprehend a fleeing criminal suspect falls within the "rubric of police conduct . . . necessarily [involving] swift action predicated upon the on-the-spot observations of the officer on the beat." . . . The clarity of hindsight cannot provide the standard for judging the reasonableness of police decisions made in uncertain and often dangerous circumstances. Moreover, I am far more

---

[23] The dissent points out that three-fifths of all rapes in the home, three-fifths of all home robberies, and about a third of home assaults are committed by burglars. . . . These figures mean only that if one knows that a suspect committed a rape in the home, there is a good chance that the suspect is also a burglar. That has nothing to do with the question here, which is whether the fact that someone has committed a burglary indicates that he has committed, or might commit, a violent crime.

The dissent also points out that this 3.8% adds up to 2.8 million violent crimes over a 10-year period, as if to imply that today's holding will let loose 2.8 million violent burglars. The relevant universe is, of course, far smaller. At issue is only that tiny fraction of cases where violence has taken place and an officer who has no other means of apprehending the suspect is unaware of its occurrence.

reluctant than is the Court to conclude that the Fourth Amendment proscribes a police practice that was accepted at the time of the adoption of the Bill of Rights and has continued to receive the support of many state legislatures. Although the Court has recognized that the requirements of the Fourth Amendment must respond to the reality of social and technological change, fidelity to the notion of constitutional—as opposed to purely judicial—limits on governmental action requires us to impose a heavy burden on those who claim that practices accepted when the Fourth Amendment was adopted are now constitutionally impermissible. . . .

The public interest involved in the use of deadly force as a last resort to apprehend a fleeing burglary suspect relates primarily to the serious nature of the crime. Household burglaries represent not only the illegal entry into a person's home, but also "pos[e] real risk of serious harm to others." . . . According to recent Department of Justice statistics,"[t]hree-fifths of all rapes in the home, three-fifths of all home robberies, and about a third of home aggravated and simple assaults are committed by burglars." . . . During the period 1973–1982, 2.8 million such violent crimes were committed in the course of burglaries. . . . Victims of a forcible intrusion into their home by a nighttime prowler will find little consolation in the majority's confident assertion that "burglaries only rarely involve physical violence." . . . Moreover, even if a particular burglary, when viewed in retrospect, does not involve physical harm to others, the "harsh potentialities for violence" inherent in the forced entry into a home preclude characterization of the crime as "innocuous, inconsequential, minor, or nonviolent." . . .

Because burglary is a serious and dangerous felony, the public interest in the prevention and detection of the crime is of compelling importance. Where a police officer has probable cause to arrest a suspected burglar, the use of deadly force as a last resort might well be the only means of apprehending the suspect. With respect to a particular burglary, subsequent investigation simply cannot represent a substitute for immediate apprehension of the criminal suspect at the scene. . . . Although some law enforcement agencies may choose to assume the risk that a criminal will remain at large, the Tennessee statute reflects a legislative determination that the use of deadly force in prescribed circumstances will serve generally to protect the public. Such statutes assist the police in apprehending suspected perpetrators of serious crimes and provide notice that a lawful police order to stop and submit to arrest may not be ignored with impunity. . . .

The Court unconvincingly dismisses the general deterrence effects by stating that "the presently available evidence does not support [the] thesis" that the threat of force discourages escape and that "there is a substantial basis for doubting that the use of such force is an essential attribute to the arrest power in all felon cases." . . . There is no question that the effectiveness of police use of deadly force is arguable and that many States or individual police departments have decided not to authorize it in circumstances similar to those presented here. But it should go without saying that the effectiveness or popularity of a particular police practice does not determine its constitutionality. . . . Moreover, the fact that police conduct pursuant to a state statute is challenged on constitutional grounds does not impose a burden on the State to produce social science statistics or to dispel any possible doubts about the necessity of the conduct. This observation, I believe, has particular force where the challenged practice both predates enactment of the Bill of Rights and continues to be accepted by a substantial number of the States.

Against the strong public interests justifying the conduct at issue here must be weighed the individual interests implicated in the use of deadly force by police officers. The majority declares that "[t]he suspect's fundamental interest in his own life need not be elaborated upon." . . . This blithe assertion hardly provides an adequate substitute for the majority's failure to acknowledge the distinctive manner in which the suspect's interest in his life is even exposed to risk. For purposes of this case, we must recall that the police officer, in the course of investigating a nighttime burglary, had reasonable cause to arrest the suspect and ordered him to halt. The officer's use of force resulted because the suspected burglar refused to heed this command and the officer reasonably believed that there was no means short of firing his weapon to apprehend the suspect. Without questioning the importance of a person's interest in his life, I do not think this interest encompasses a right to flee unimpeded from the scene of a burglary. . . . The legitimate interests of the suspect in these circumstances are adequately accommodated by the Tennessee statute: to avoid the use of deadly force and the consequent risk to his life, the suspect need merely obey the valid order to halt.

A proper balancing of the interests involved suggests that use of deadly force as a last resort to apprehend a criminal suspect fleeing from the scene of a nighttime burglary is not unreasonable within the meaning of the Fourth Amendment. Admittedly, the events giving rise to this case are in retrospect deeply regrettable. No one can view the death of an unarmed and apparently nonviolent 15-year old without sorrow, much less disapproval. Nonetheless, the reasonableness of Officer Hymon's conduct for purposes of the Fourth Amendment cannot be evaluated by what later appears to have been a preferable course of police action. The officer pursued a suspect in the darkened backyard of a house that from all indications had just been burglarized. The police officer was not certain whether the suspect was alone or unarmed; nor did he know what had transpired inside the house. He ordered the suspect to halt, and when the suspect refused to obey and attempted to flee into the night, the officer fired his weapon to prevent escape. The reasonableness of this action for purposes of the Fourth Amendment is not determined by the unfortunate nature of this particular case; instead, the question is whether it is constitutionally impermissible for police officers, as a last resort, to shoot a burglary suspect fleeing the scene of the crime.

* * *

The Court's silence on critical factors in the decision to use deadly force simply invites second-guessing of difficult police decisions that must be made quickly in the most trying of circumstances. . . . Police are given no guidance for determining which objects, among an array of potentially lethal weapons ranging from guns to knives to baseball bats to rope, will justify the use of deadly force. The Court also declines to outline the additional factors necessary to provide "probable cause" for believing that a suspect "poses a significant threat of death or serious physical injury," . . . when the officer has probable cause to arrest and the suspect refuses to obey an order to halt. But even if it were appropriate in this case to limit the use of deadly force to that ambiguous class of suspects, I believe the class should include nighttime residential burglars who resist arrest by attempting to flee the scene of the crime. We can expect an escalating volume of litigation as the lower courts struggle to determine if a police officer's split-second decision to shoot was justified by the danger posed by a particular object and other facts related to the crime. Thus, the majority opinion portends a burgeoning area of Fourth Amendment doctrine concerning the circumstances in which police officers can reasonably employ deadly force.

. . . I cannot accept the majority's creation of a constitutional right to flight for burglary suspects seeking to avoid capture at the scene of the crime. Whatever the constitutional limits on police use of deadly force in order to apprehend a fleeing felon, I do not believe they are exceeded in a case in which a police officer has probable cause to arrest a suspect at the scene of a residential burglary, orders the suspect to halt, and then fires his weapon as a last resort to prevent the suspect's escape into the night. I respectfully dissent.

NOTES AND QUESTIONS

1. As *Garner* points out, the common law granted broad authority to persons enforcing the law to employ force against those suspected of committing crimes. At the time these rules emerged, no organized police forces as we now know them existed. The rules thus applied to any person, private citizen or police officer, who acted in a law enforcement capacity. The law permitted the use of force to prevent the commission of, or to apprehend for, a felony or breach of the peace. Boyce, Encyclopedia of Crime and Justice 953 (1983).

With the emergence of organized police departments, the common law eventually began to reduce citizen law enforcement authority. At common law, private persons, as well as police officers, are entitled to use reasonable force to arrest, without warrants, persons committing crimes in the presence of the arrestor. For crimes not committed in the presence of the arrestor, police officers can arrest without warrants if they possess reasonable grounds to believe that a felony has been committed by the person to be arrested. Private persons, however, can arrest under similar circumstances only if a felony has in fact been committed. Arrests by either police or private citizens for misdemeanors committed outside the presence of the arrestor required arrest warrants at common law. LaFave and Scott at 470.

As for the degree of permissible force, the courts also distinguished between private citizens and police officers. While the common law rule rejected in *Garner* allowed persons enforcing the law to employ deadly force when necessary to effectuate arrest of any suspected felon, some courts permitted private citizens to employ deadly force only when arresting for certain felonies which had in fact been committed by the person to be arrested. See, *e.g.,*

Commonwealth v. Chermansky, 430 Pa. 170, 173–74, 242 A.2d 237, 239–40 (1968).

Garner apparently leaves unaffected the common law rule which permits arresting officers, and perhaps private citizens as well, to use any force necessary to subdue arrestees who resist arrest and place the arrestor in reasonable fear of immediate bodily harm or death. See *Durham v. State,* 199 Ind. 567, 159 N.E. 147 (1927). The permissible use of force against persons resisting arrest applies in either the felony or misdemeanor context and is essentially a self-defense principle except that it exempts the arrestor from any retreat requirements should such exist.

2. If Officer Hymon was not "entitled" to use deadly force in the *Garner* situation, does it follow that he is guilty of some level of homicide? If so, which? Apart from a defense of justifiable force, would Hymon have any other valid defense claims should he be charged with homicide?

3. Most jurisdictions have now codified the rules governing the use of force in law enforcement for both police officers and private citizens. Many statutes reflect the influence of the following provisions of the Model Penal Code:

§ 3.07 Use of Force in Law Enforcement.

(1) *Use of Force Justifiable to Effect an Arrest.* Subject to the provisions of this Section and of Section 3.09, the use of force upon or toward the person of another is justifiable when the actor is making or assisting in making an arrest and the actor believes that such force is immediately necessary to effect a lawful arrest.

(2) *Limitations on the Use of Force.*

   (a) The use of force is not justifiable under this Section unless:

   (i) the actor makes known the purpose of the arrest or believes that it is otherwise known by or cannot reasonably be made known to the person to be arrested; and

   (ii) when the arrest is made under a warrant, the warrant is valid or believed by the actor to be valid.

   (b) The use of deadly force is not justifiable under this Section unless:

   (i) the arrest is for a felony; and

   (ii) the person effecting the arrest is authorized to act as a peace officer or is assisting a person whom he believes to be authorized to act as a peace officer;

   (iii) the actor believes that the force employed creates no substantial risk of injury to innocent persons; and

   (iv) the actor believes that:

   (1) the crime for which the arrest is made involved conduct including the use or threatened use of deadly force; or

   (2) there is a substantial risk that the person to be arrested will cause death or serious bodily harm if his apprehension is delayed.

* * *

(4) *Use of Force by Private Person Assisting an Unlawful Arrest.*

(a) A private person who is summoned by a peace officer to assist in effecting an unlawful arrest, is justified in using any force which he would be justified in using if the arrest were lawful, provided that he does not believe the arrest is unlawful.

(b) A private person who assists another private person in effecting an unlawful arrest, or who, not being summoned, assists a peace officer in effecting an unlawful arrest, is justified in using any force which he would be justified in using if the arrest were lawful, provided that (i) he believes the arrest is lawful, and (ii) the arrest would be lawful if the facts were as he believes them to be.

4. A different variety of defense within the law enforcement context arises when the arrested, rather than the arresting, person claims a right to use force. As noted above in the section on self-defense, at common law persons could resist unlawful arrests by reasonable, nondeadly force. The modern trend, however, requires unlawfully arrested persons to submit to the arrest when it is clear or should be clear that the person making the arrest is a police officer acting in the performance of his duties. See, *e.g., People v. Curtis,* 70 Cal. 2d 347, 74 Cal. Rptr. 713, 450 P.2d 33 (1969). The Model Penal Code at § 3.04(2)(i) rejects the common law rule: "The use of force is not justifiable . . . to resist an arrest which the actor knows is being made by a police officer, although the arrest is unlawful."

For arguments that resistance to unlawful arrests should be allowable, at least in certain circumstances, see *Wainwright v. New Orleans,* 392 U.S. 598, 610–613 (1968) (Douglas, J. dissenting from dismissal of *certiorari*), and Chevigny, *The Right to Resist an Unlawful Arrest,* 78 Yale L.J. 1128 (1969).

On the other hand, an arrestee may use reasonable force to protect his person where police officers use excessive force that threatens serious injury regardless of the legality of the arrest. *State v. Mulvihill,* 57 N.J. 151, 270 A.2d 277 (1970); *State v. Westlund,* 13 Wash. App. 460, 536 P.2d 20 (1975).

[B] Mental Abnormality

The problem of the mentally abnormal offender arises in a variety of contexts within the criminal justice system. While this section attends primarily to the problems of the insanity defense and mental abnormality as negation of the *mens rea* element of the crime charged (sometimes called the doctrine of diminished capacity or diminished responsibility), the issues of incompetency to stand trial and insanity of those sentenced to death deserve brief mention.

[1] Incompetency to Stand Trial

Defendants who are mentally incompetent at the time of trial cannot be prosecuted as a matter of due process, *Pate v. Robinson,* 383 U.S. 375 (1966).

The test for incompetency is sometimes statutorily defined, often along the lines of Model Penal Code § 4.04: "No person who as a result of mental disease or defect lacks capacity to understand the proceedings against him or to assist in his own defense shall be tried, convicted or sentenced for the commission of an offense so long as such incapacity endures." Other jurisdictions are less specific in simply providing that defendants "insane" at the time of trial cannot be proceeded against. Such imprecise formulations risk confusion of the issues of responsibility at the time of the offense (the traditional insanity inquiry) with mental ability to comprehend the nature of the proceedings at the time of trial (the traditional incompetency inquiry).

This is not to suggest that the insanity and incompetency issues are unrelated. Many incompetent defendants are also insane. Indeed, in practice the incompetency determination often operates as a substitute for the insanity defense by removing the need for an inquiry into the insanity issue. Consider these observations from A. Matthews, Mental Disability and the Criminal Law 90–92 (1970):

> . . . The initiation of competency proceedings is the major access route in the criminal process to psychiatric intervention, a necessary prerequisite if some informal psychiatric disposition is to occur. Since competency proceedings provide that access, both sides have reasons for invoking them. When the prosecution and the defense are agreed on allowing the accused to be treated on an outpatient basis or to be civilly committed, and thus on disposing of the criminal charges, both want to know if such treatment is psychiatrically indicated and feasible. Since the prosecutor has no funds in his budget for this purpose, and the defendant typically is indigent, both sides may agree to raise the competency issue to get a medical consultation. The judge may also want some help in disposing of the offender, initially or subsequently, in a perhaps more humane and effective way than sentencing him to the county jail. . . . In many cases this is a conscious use of competency proceedings in which the judge, the prosecutor, and defense counsel concur. Whether by plan or by accident, the psychiatric report, irrespective of its impact on the competency issue, is a highly influential factor in determining the final disposition.

> Another shared reason for initiating competency proceedings is to develop evidence on the issue of criminal responsibility. Many lawyers think the standard for incompetency is broader than that for criminal responsibility. . . . Lawyers sometimes told us they thought an incompetency disposition by a judge was more likely in certain cases than an irresponsibility disposition by a jury. The judge, in the view of his brothers in the legal profession, is less likely than a jury to be prejudiced by the fact, for example, that the offense is particularly violent or atrocious. At times the competency hearing itself (when there is one) approaches a proceeding in which the court reaches a "summary judgment" of insanity. The prosecutor can avoid a public trial which may carry with it public pressure, usually in the direction of severity; if the accused can be found incompetent, the case can later be disposed of quietly. The result in some cases is a conscious substitution of a finding of incompetency for a trial by jury on the responsibility issue—a result tacitly agreed to by both sides. This practice tends to occur in the

more serious cases, especially those involving capital crimes, and helps explain why findings of incompetency outnumber findings of not guilty by reason of insanity.

A finding of incompetence does not mean that the defendant is simply released until competency is regained. As the excerpt from Matthews intimates, indeterminate confinement in a mental institution has been the plight of the incompetent, particularly those charged with serious offenses. The Supreme Court, in *Jackson v. Indiana,* 406 U.S. 715, 738 (1971), recognized certain procedural protections required in hospitalizing those incompetent to stand trial:

> [A] person charged by a State with a criminal offense who is committed solely on account of his incapacity to proceed to trial cannot be held more than the reasonable period of time necessary to determine whether there is a substantial probability that he will attain that capacity in the foreseeable future. If it is determined that this is not the case, then the State must either institute the customary civil commitment proceeding that would be required to commit indefinitely any other citizen, or release the defendant. Furthermore, even if it is determined that the defendant probably soon will be able to stand trial, his continued commitment must be justified by progress toward that goal.

For an argument espousing the abolition of the special plea of incompetency to stand trial in favor of a system granting "trial continuance by reason of disability," see N. Morris, Madness and the Criminal Law 33–53 (1982). Morris would eventually try the "untriable" defendant, on the grounds that he might be exonerated.

[2] Insanity and Execution

The common law for centuries has prohibited the execution of the insane. The test for postconviction incompetence was generally whether the defendant was incapable of comprehending that he has been convicted and sentenced to death. *Commonwealth v. Moon,* 383 Pa. 18, 117 A.2d 96 (1955). This common law tradition finds support in the Eighth Amendment's bar against cruel and unusual punishment. In *Ford v. Wainright,* 477 U.S. 399, 406–10 (1986), the Supreme Court appealed to the rationale of the common law rule in holding that the procedures for determining a prisoner's sanity for purposes of execution must comport with due process standards because execution of the insane is constitutionally prohibited by the Eighth Amendment:

> The bar against executing a prisoner who has lost his sanity bears impressive historical credentials; the practice consistently has been branded "savage and inhuman." 4 W. Blackstone, Commentaries* 24–25 (1769). Blackstone explained:
>
>> [I]diots and lunatics are not chargeable for their own acts, if committed when under these incapacities: no, not even for treason itself. . . . If, after

---

* At one point, Henry VIII enacted a law requiring that if a man convicted of treason fell mad, he should nevertheless be executed. 33 Hen. VIII, c. 20. This law was uniformly condemned. See Blackstone *25; 1 Hale 35; 1 Hawkins 2. The "cruel and inhumane" Law lived not long, but was repealed, for in that point also it was against the Common Law. . . . Coke 6.

he be tried and found guilty, he becomes of nonsane memory, execution shall be stayed:for per adventure, says the humanity of the English law, had the prisoner been of sound memory, he might have alleged something in stay of judgment or execution.

Sir Edward Coke had earlier expressed the same view of the common law of England: "[B]y intendment of Law the execution of the offender is for example, . . . but so it is not when a mad man is executed, but should be a miserable spectacle, both against Law, and of extreme inhumanity and cruelty, and can be no example to others." E. Coke, Third Institute 6 (6th ed. 1680) (hereinafter Coke). . . . As is often true of common-law principles, . . . the reasons for the rule are less sure and less uniform than the rule itself. One explanation is that the execution of an insane person simply offends humanity, . . . another, that it provides no example to others and thus contributes nothing to whatever deterrence value is intended to be served by capital punishment. Other commentators postulate religious underpinnings: that it is uncharitable to dispatch an offender "into another world, when his is not of a capacity to fit himself for it," Hawles, [Remarks on the Trial of Mr. Charles Bateman 477 (1685)]. It is also said that execution serves no purpose in these cases because madness is its own punishment: *furious solo furor punitur.* Blackstone, *supra,* at 395. More recent commentators opine that the community's quest for "retribution"—th e need to offset a criminal act by a punishment of equivalent "moral quality"—is not served by execution of an insane person, which has a "lesser value" than that of the crime for which he is to be punished. Hazard & Louisell, *Death, the State, and the Insane: Stay of Execution,* 9 U.C.L.A. L. Rev. 381, 387 (1962). Unanimity of rationale, therefore, we do not find. "But whatever the reason of the law is, it is plain the law is so." Hawles, *supra.* We know of virtually no authority condoning the execution of the insane at English common law.*

This ancestral legacy has not outlived its time. Today, no State in the Union permits the execution of the insane. It is clear that the ancient and humane limitation upon the State's ability to execute its sentences has as firm a hold upon the jurisprudence of today as it had centuries ago in England. The various reasons put forth in support of the common-law restriction have no less logical, moral, and practical force than they did when first voiced. For today, no less than before, we may seriously question the retributive value of executing a person who has no comprehension of why he has been singled out and stripped of his fundamental right to life. See Note, *The Eighth Amendment and the Execution of the Presently Incompetent,* 32 Stan. L. Rev. 765, 777, n. 58 (1980). Similarly, the natural abhorrence civilized societies feel at killing one who has no capacity to come to grips with his own conscience or deity is still vivid today. And the intuition that such an execution simply offends humanity is evidently shared across this Nation. Faced with such widespread evidence of a restriction upon sovereign power, this Court is compelled to conclude that the Eighth Amendment prohibits a State from carrying out a sentence of death upon a prisoner who is insane. Whether its aim be to protect the condemned from fear and pain without comfort of understanding, or to protect the dignity of society itself from the barbarity of exacting mindless vengeance, the restriction finds enforcement in the Eighth Amendment.

[The Court discussed and rejected the argument that Ford could not be executed if he were found insane because an insane person is incapable of assisting counsel in the fight to keep the death penalty from being imposed.]

NOTES AND QUESTIONS

1. How convincing are the *Ford* Court's reasons for its holding? In light of the materials on punishment, § 2.02, *supra,* is it meaningful for Blackstone and others to maintain that insanity is itself a form of "punishment"? Why is it supposedly more "inhumane" to execute insane offenders than sane ones? Does the Court's appeal to deterrence theory focus too heavily on special deterrence without attending to considerations of general deterrence? In what sense does retributive theory preclude executing the insane? If the offender was culpable when he committed his offense, what difference should it make on retributive grounds that he later became insane? Is the Court's recognition of religious considerations appropriate? For consideration of the question of the death penalty *per se,* see § 5.04, *supra.*

2. Does the inherent stress of life on death row itself cause insanity in many condemned prisoners? See Lewis, *Psychiatric, Neurological, and Psychoeducational Characteristics of Fifteen Death Row Inmates in the United States,* 143 Am. J. Psych. 838 (July 1986) (study conducted by psychiatrists who found extremely high incidence of psychoses in death row inmates); H. Bedau, The Death Penalty in America 379 (1982). Does the rule against executing the insane encourage feigned insanity claims to avoid execution? If so, can the malingerers be distinguished from the truly insane? See Ennis and Litwack, *Psychiatry and the Presumption of Expertise: Flipping Coins in the Courtroom,* 62 Calif. L. Rev. 693 (1974).

3. The decision to stay execution due to insanity is temporary in all states imposing the death penalty. When the prisoner is cured, he is executed. Does this create a conflict of interest for mental health professionals treating the insane individual? See Adler, *The Cure That Kills,* The American Lawyer 1, 29 (Sept. 1986).

Is it perhaps less humanitarian to execute a sane man while staying the execution of the insane until the prisoner understands the nature and reason for his punishment? If the prisoner was sane enough to stand trial and be convicted, has he already sufficiently understood the nature and reason for his punishment even though he subsequently became insane? Consider the remarks of Justice Roger Traynor: "Is it not an inverted humanitarianism that deplores as barbarous the capital punishment of those who have become insane after trial and conviction, but accepts the capital punishment of sane men, a curious reasoning that would free a man from capital punishment only if he is not in full possession of his senses?" *Phyle v. Duffy,* 34 Cal. 2d 144, 158, 208 P.2d 668, 676–77 (1949).

4. For discussion of the rule against executing the insane, see, in addition to the sources cited in Ford, Note, *Insanity and Condemned,* 88 Yale L.J. 533 (1979); Note, *Eighth Amendment—The Constitutional Rights of the Insane on Death Row,* 77 J. Crim. L. & Criminology 844(1986); Note, *The Eighth*

Amendment, Due Process and Insanity on Death Row, 89 N. Ill. U. L.Rev. 89 (1986).

[3] The Defense of Insanity

[a] Development of Tests for Insanity

AMERICAN BAR ASSOCIATION STANDING COMMITTEE ON
ASSOCIATION STANDARDS FOR CRIMINAL JUSTICE,
PROPOSED CRIMINAL JUSTICE MENTAL HEALTH STANDARDS

316-17, 323 (1984)

Almost 150 years ago, Daniel M'Naghten was acquitted "by reason of insanity" on charges of murdering the private secretary of Prime Minister Robert Peel. The verdict caused an uproar in England and moved the House of Lords to scrutinize carefully the grounds upon which a mentally disordered person should be excused from crime. Since that time, probably no other area of the criminal law has attracted as much professional or public attention as the doctrine these standards refer to as the defense of mental nonresponsibility. The amount of scholarly, judicial and legislative energy expended on this subject on both sides of the Atlantic has been prodigious and, some would say, excessive. The best evidence suggests that the mental nonresponsibility defense is raised in less than one percent of all felony cases in the United States and is successful in about a fourth of these. In 1978, there were approximately 1,600 defendants acquitted by reason of mental nonresponsibility nationwide, an average of 32 per state. In terms of its incidence, the defense occupies a very small nook of the criminal justice system.

Yet it continues to command a large portion of our attention. In 1982, John W. Hinckley, Jr.'s attempted assassination of President Reagan resulted in a new round of controversy over the defense, rivaling the *M'Naghten* experience. Hinckley's subsequent acquittal "by reason of insanity" prompted the introduction of over two score bills to abolish or reform the insanity defense during the 97th Congress and legislatures in many states also began considering the different alternatives. The hostile public mood which sparked this flurry of legislative activity echoed the reaction of Queen Victoria (herself once the target of a gunman later acquitted on "insanity" grounds) upon hearing the outcome of the *M'Naghten* case: "The law may be perfect, but how is it that whenever a case for its application arises, it proves to be of no avail?"

* * *

[The] jurisprudential underpinnings [of the defense of mental nonresponsibility] reach back to the origins of Western ethical and legal thought. As early as the sixth century b.c., commentary on the Hebrew scriptures distinguished between the harmful act traceable to fault and that which occurs without fault. To these ancient scholars, the paradigm of the latter type of act was one committed by a child, who was seen as incapable of weighing the moral implications of his or her behavior, even when willful; likened to the child were the retarded and the insane. The Greek moral philosophers, at least as far back as the fifth century b.c., considered the distinction between a culpable and nonculpable act to be among the "unwritten laws of nature supported by the universal moral sense of mankind." The same view pervaded Roman law and appears in the teaching of the early Christian Church Fathers. It emerges in Anglo-Saxon law no later than the twelfth century, the result of the "mutual influences and interaction of Christian theology and Anglo-Saxon law." The idea was reinforced in England when the Norman invasion brought continental legal thought, itself strongly influenced by Christian ethics and canon law, which had already absorbed Jewish ethical teachings, classical philosophy, and Roman law.

Thus, at least as early as 1300, records show that English kings were pardoning murderers because their crimes were committed "while suffering from madness." The first recorded jury acquittal by reason of insanity was in 1505. Sir Matthew Hale, a 17th century jurist, summarized centuries of thought when he stated: "The consent of the will is that which renders human actions either commendable or culpable. . . . And because the liberty or choice of the will presupposeth an act of understanding to know the thing or action chosen by the will, it follows that where there is a total defect of the understanding there is no free act of the will." . . .

[I]f one focuses solely on Anglo-American jurisprudence in relatively recent times, several different formulations of the mental nonresponsibility defense emerge. Writing in the early seventeenth century, Sir Edward Coke held that both "idiots" and "madmen" who "wholly loseth their memory and understanding" should be found nonresponsible. Later in the same century, Sir Matthew Hale concluded that the "best measure" for determining "insanity" was whether the accused had "as great understanding as ordinarily a child of fourteen hath." In 1723, Justice Tracey instructed a jury that in order to be found nonresponsible "a man must be totally deprived of his understanding and memory so as not to know what he is doing, no more than an infant, brute or a wild beast." At about the same time, other English courts were excusing those who lacked the capacity to distinguish "good from evil" or "right from wrong."

It was this latter approach which, in slightly modified form, became the "*M'Naghten* test of insanity." . . . Although this was the first time an appellate court in either England or the United States had declared a rule for determining mental nonresponsibility, the *M'Naghten* test became the accepted standard in both countries within a short period of time.

DANIEL M'NAGHTEN'S CASE

10 Cl. & F. 200, 8 Eng. Rep. 718 (1843)

[In 1843, a Scotsman by the name of Daniel M'Naghten shot and killed Edmund Drummond, the secretary to Prime Minister of England Robert Peel. At his trial, M'Naghten introduced evidence of his belief that Peel headed a conspiracy to kill him and that he mistakenly shot Drummond believing him to be Peel. M'Naghten claimed that his delusional state constituted insanity and that he was therefore not responsible for Drummond's death. The jury agreed and returned a verdict of not guilty by reason of insanity.

The verdict was controversial. In its wake, the House of Lords, at the behest of Queen Victoria, invited 15 members of the English judiciary to meet with the Lords to determine what rules should be applied in future insanity cases. The *M'Naghten Rule* is found in the answers of Lord Chief Justice Tindal (who had earlier presided at the trial of Daniel M'Naghten), speaking for the assembled judges in response to certain questions posed by the Lords.]

Your Lordships are pleased to inquire of us, "What are the proper questions to be submitted to the jury, where a person alleged to be afflicted with insane delusion respecting one or more particular subjects or persons, is charged with the commission of a crime (murder, for example), and insanity is set up as a defense?" And, . . . "In what terms ought the question to be left to the jury as to the prisoner's state of mind at the time when the act was committed?" And as these two questions appear to us to be more conveniently answered together, we have to submit our opinion to be, that the jurors ought to be told in all cases that every man is to be presumed to be sane, and to possess a sufficient degree of reason to be responsible for his crimes, until the contrary be proved to their satisfaction; and that to establish a defense on the ground of insanity, it must be clearly proved that, at the time of the committing of the act, the party accused was labouring under such a defect of reason, from disease of the mind, as not to know the nature and quality of the act he was doing; or, if he did know it, that he did not know he was doing what was wrong. The mode of putting the latter part of the question to the jury on these occasions has generally been, whether the accused at the time of doing the act knew the difference between right and wrong: which mode, though rarely, if ever, leading to any mistake with the jury, is not, as we conceive, so accurate when put generally and in the abstract, as when put with reference to the party's knowledge of right and wrong in respect to the very act with which he is charged. If the question were to be put as to the knowledge of the accused solely and exclusively with reference to the law of the land, it might tend to confound the jury, by inducing them to believe that an actual knowledge of the law of the land was essential in order to lead to a conviction; whereas the law is administered upon the principle that every one must be taken conclusively to know it, without proof that he does know it. If the accused was conscious that the act was one which he ought not to do, and if the act was at the same time contrary to the law of the land, he is punishable; and the usual course therefore has been to leave the question to the jury, whether the party accused had a sufficient degree of reason to know that he was doing an act that was wrong: and this course we think is correct, accompanied with such observations and explanations as the circumstances of each particular case may require.

Notes and Questions

1. *The "Nature and Quality" of the Act. M'Naghten* defines insanity, under one formulation, in terms of the defendant's failure to know the "nature and

quality" of his act. What does this mean? Commentators suggest that the nature and quality test carries little independent significance.

The phrase "nature and quality of the act" is sometimes omitted completely from the charge to the jury. More often, it is either stated to the jury without explanation or treated as adding nothing to the requirement that the accused know his act was wrong. The underlying theory is that if the accused did not know the nature and quality of his act, he would have been incapable of knowing it was wrong. There have been a few efforts to treat the phrase as if it added something to the rule. In England, for example, it was suggested that "nature" meant the act's physical nature, while "quality" referred to its moral aspect. The court rejected the suggestion, holding that "nature and quality" refers solely to the physical character of the act. In the United States, the rule seems to be similar, though the Wisconsin court has held that "nature and quality" gives "important emphasis" to the realization of the wrongfulness of an act. It marks the distinction between "vaguely . . . [realizing] that particular conduct is forbidden" and "real insight into the conduct." This construction illustrates the close connection between the definition of "know" and that of "nature and quality." The broader reading of "nature and quality" carries with it the broader construction of "know" and vice versa. To know the quality of an act, with all its social and emotional implications, requires more than an abstract, purely intellectual knowledge. Likewise, to talk of appreciating the full significance of an act means that "nature and quality" must be understood as including more than the physical nature of the act.

A. Goldstein, The Insanity Defense 50–51 (1967).

Could many of the criticisms of *M'Naghten* as unduly limiting the focus to cognitive impairment (see pp. 820–32 *infra*) be rebutted by a broad reading of the "nature and quality" language?

2. *Knowledge That the Act Was Wrong.* Even if the defendant knew the nature and quality of his acts, he might nevertheless be insane under *M'Naghten* if "he did not know he was doing what was wrong." As Dean Goldstein suggests in the quoted excerpt, this prong of the test has assumed major significance.

M'Naghten did not invent the "right/wrong" test. Some earlier cases had applied a standard couched in terms of whether the defendant had the capacity to distinguish right from wrong. See Platt and Diamond, *The Origins of the "Right and Wrong" Test of Criminal Responsibility and Its Subsequent Development in the United States: A Historical Survey,* 54 Calif. L. Rev. 1227 (1966). See also S. Glueck, Mental Disorder and the Criminal Law 123–60 (1925); Crotty, *The History of Insanity as a Defense to Crime in English Criminal Law,* 12 Calif. L. Rev. 105 (1924). Are there significant differences in tests asking "whether the defendant had the capacity to distinguish right from wrong" and those asking whether the defendant in the particular case "knew his act to be wrong"?

The question of whether "wrong" in the test means "morally wrong" or "legally wrong" has perplexed many. English law has adopted the view that "legal wrong" is meant, *R. v. Windle* (1952), 2 Q.B. 826. Other commonwealth countries have taken the "moral wrong" view. Australia: *R. v. Poter* (1933), 55 C.L.R. 182; *Stapleton v. R.* (1952), 86 C.L.R. 358; New Zealand:by legislation—Crimes Act 1961, § 23(2)(b). The American decisions are split. For example, some cases find insanity under *M'Naghten* if the defendant knew his actions were legally wrong but believed them morally permissible, while others deny insanity if the defendant knew his actions to be contrary to law regardless of his perceptions of morality. The issue frequently arises in cases where the defendant knowingly violates the law because of a perceived religious obligation arising from an insane delusion.

In *People v. Schmidt,* 216 N.Y. 324, 110 N.E. 945 (1915), Justice Cardozo, then a member of the New York Court of Appeals, interpreted *M'Naghten* to permit an acquittal by reason of insanity for a defendant who claimed to hear the voice of God calling upon him to kill the victim as a sacrifice and atonement even though the defendant realized that his act was illegal. Alleging to be in the visible presence of God at the time of his crime, defendant took the life of the victim. The evidence supported a finding that defendant suffered insane delusions that did not necessarily affect his awareness of the illegality of his actions. The trial court, erroneously in Cardozo's opinion for the Court of Appeals, instructed the jury to find defendant guilty if he knew his act was legally wrong even if he entertained a "good faith" belief that God had commanded his actions. For a more recent case following the *Schmidt* approach, see *State v. Cameron,* 100 Wash. 2d 520, 674 P.2d 650 (*en blanc* 1983).

A contrary approach is reflected in *McElroy v. State,* 242 S.W. 883 (Tenn. 1922), which holds that an offender who believes his act is commanded by God is nevertheless sane if he knew the act was legally prohibited. See also *State v. Andrews,* 357 P.2d 739, 747–48 (Kan. 1961), which holds that a defendant who believed his act was morally permissible is nevertheless criminally responsible if he knew his act was against the law.

Which line of case law is preferable: *Schmidt/Cameron* or *McElroy/Andrews?* What tensions concerning the insanity defense—and indeed of the purposes of the criminal law generally—are reflected by the different interpretations? If legal insanity exists because of an absence of knowledge of the illegality of one's actions, to what extent is the *M'Naghten* test in conflict with the general rule that ignorance of the law is no excuse, *supra,* § 4.06[B][1]?

3. *"Disease of the Mind."* In *State v. Crenshaw,* 98 Wash. 2d 789, 659 P.2d 488 (1983), the court held that defendant's claim that he killed his adulteress wife out of religious duty under his "Moscovite" faith was irrelevant for purposes of the insanity defense because Moscovite beliefs are not "insane delusions." *Crenshaw* thus illustrates that failure to know right from wrong is not a defense unless linked to mental illness or, in the language of *M'Naghten* to "a defect of reason from a disease of the mind." Indeed, all tests for insanity embrace the "medical model" of insanity by requiring mental illness as a necessary (but not a sufficient) condition of legal insanity, see pp. 820–32 *infra.* Why require mental illness? Why not, for example, excuse defendants if depraved cultural or economic backgrounds render them unable to know "the nature and quality of their acts" or to know "right from wrong"? For an account of Chief Judge David Bazelon's views advocating rejection of the medical model of insanity, see Wales, *The Rise, The Fall and the Resur*

rection of the Medical Model, 63 Geo. L.J. 87 (1974). For arguments that the requirement of mental illness or "craziness" is an analytically necessary condition for tests of legal insanity, see Morse, *Excusing the Crazy: The Insanity Defense Reconsidered,* 58 S. Cal. L. Rev. 777, 780–90, 820 (1985).

The "disease of the mind" requirement creates a variety of problems. At the conceptual level, courts have struggled with the problem of defining mental diseases and defects, relying heavily on the inexact science of psychiatry to provide expertise. A notorious example of the kind of difficulty that can arise is illustrated by *Blocker v. United States,* 274 F.2d 573 (D.C. Cir. 1959), which describes a series of events in which the staff at St. Elizabeth's Hospital, which provides the District of Columbia courts with most of their experts on the insanity issue, suddenly decided for the first time to incorporate the personality disorders, including the so-called sociopathic personality, within the definition of mental disease for purposes of the insanity defense. Thus, in the space of a few days, sociopaths previously unable to plead insanity (because they were not suffering from a mental disease or defect) had their status totally reversed by psychiatric fiat.

The problem in *Blocker* arose in a jurisdiction that at that time applied a liberal test for insanity, see note 4 p. 820 *infra.* Courts have generally denied the status of mental illness to the personality disorders in insanity defense contexts. The kinds of mental abnormalities qualifying for insanity are summarized by G. Melton, J. Petrila, N. Poythress, and C. Slobogin, Psychological Evaluations for the Courts 118–19 (1987):

> The term "mental disease" has usually been equated with "mental illness," while the term "mental defect" is usually thought to be synonymous with "mental retardation," although some courts have indicated that "defect" refers to any condition that is incapable of improving.
>
> It has been suggested that this threshold adds nothing to the test for insanity beyond the . . . preference for endogenous causes. . . . In other words, any mental disability that causes significant cognitive or volitional impairment will meet the threshold.
>
> This statement is probably true to the extent that it implies that courts and juries pay more attention to the degree of impairment than to the specific mental disability suffered by the defendant. But it can also be misleading. In historical fact, most successful insanity defenses are based on the presence of one of two mental conditions: psychosis or mental retardation. . . [V]irtually all studies of the subject indicate that the majority (60–90%) of defendants acquitted by reason of insanity are diagnosed as psychotic. To judges, lawyers, and juries, these individuals are more sick than evil, and do not deserve criminal punishment. Moreover, some offenders who may be able to meet the second "functional" part of the tests are clearly not the types of individuals the law wishes to excuse. For example, sociopaths (or, using modern nomenclature, "antisocial personalities") are individuals who may very well be unable to "appreciate" the quality or wrongfulness of a criminal act because of their lack of moral inhibition; yet they are not generally considered legally insane. . . . Similarly, most courts would probably not consider any condition listed in the third edition of the Diagnostic and Statistical Manual of Mental Disorders (DSM-III) a "mental disease or defect"

for purposes of the insanity test* merely because defendants can show that such a condition substantially impaired their capacity to appreciate the criminality of or to control their acts.

The actual number of written opinions attempting to grapple with the definition of "mental disease or defect" for purposes of the insanity defense is extremely small. But those decisions that do exist define the concept narrowly. Some courts have emphasized that mild symptomatology will not support a defense, presumably even if the individual is psychotic. A few have expressed some distaste for "temporary insanity"—pleas based on nonpsychotic disorders such as "dissociative states," which appear to take hold of the defendant at the time of the offense, but at no other time. Finally, alcohol-or-drug-in duced "insanity" is rarely a successful claim, especially when the dysfunction is caused by short-term or one-time use of the psychoactive substance. Usually, only in cases involving "settled insanity" from prolonged alcohol or drug abuse (resulting in significant organic damage) are the courts willing to recognize an insanity defense.

The courts have encountered additional problems in determining whether certain diseases of the brain such as psychomotor epilepsy or hypoglycemia should be treated as "diseases of the mind" and thus as matters of insanity rather than as relevant excusing conditions under other defense theories. These issues are explored in greater depth at § 9.05[B][3][d], *infra*.

Finally, the medical model of insanity has created a constant tension between mental health professionals and lawyers. The law has always sought out the expertise of the mental health community which, in being expected to provide its input within the context of the legal test of insanity, has often felt captured by considerations irrelevant to medical science. While input on the "mental illness" issue may be problematic for mental health experts if courts place limitations on the kinds of abnormalities which qualify for insanity consideration, the experts often encounter even greater difficulties when testifying on the issue of the relation of the illness to the defendant's capacity to distinguish right and wrong at the time of the crime. Guttmacher, *Principal Difficulties with the Present Criteria of Responsibility and Possible Alternatives,* in Commentary to Model Penal Code 170–71 (Tent. Draft No. 4, 1955). Many mental health professionals feel incapable of offering opinions about the moral issue of the defendant's capacity for responsible conduct; when such opinions are offered there is always a danger that the trier of fact will place undue importance on the expert testimony to the extent that it becomes outcome determinative. These problems are explored in H. Fingarette, The Meaning of Criminal Insanity 1–120 (1972); see also A. Goldstein, The Insanity Defense 98–105 (1967).

4. *The "Product Test" as an Alternative to M'Naghten.* From its inception, the M'Naghten test was subjected to criticism for being too restrictive. Many complained that *M'Naghten's* requirement of total cognitive incapacity limited the flow of psychiatric expertise to the jury by failing to permit consideration

---

* [For example, DSM-III-R includes such things as caffeine intoxication and nicotine withdrawal as mental disorders. See American Psychiatric Association, Diagnostic and Statistical Manual of Mental Disorders 138–39, 150–51 (3d ed. rev. 1987).—Eds.]

of subtle forms of mental illness that influence behavior. See, e.g., H. Weihofen, Insanity as a Defense in the Criminal Law 29–31 (1933). But see A. Goldstein, The Insanity Defense 49–51 (1967).

The New Hampshire Supreme Court found such criticisms telling. In *State v. Pike,* 49 N.H. 399 (1870), the court severely criticized *M'Naghten,* rejecting that test altogether in *State v. Jones,* 50 N.H. 369 (1871), which articulated a new standard, commonly known as the *product test:* "No man shall be held accountable, criminally, for an act which was the offspring and product of mental disease."

With the celebrated exception of the decision of the Court of Appeals for the District of Columbia in *Durham v. United States,* 214 F.2d 862 (D.C. Cir. 1954), the product test failed to win judicial or legislative support. The *Durham* product test was subsequently abandoned by the D.C. Circuit in *United States v. Brawner,* 471 F.2d 969 (D.C. Cir. 1972) in favor of the Model Penal Code test, discussed at p. 827, *infra.*

Is the product test a significant departure from *M'Naghten?* Consider the following hypothetical posed by Model Penal Code § 4.01, Comment at 173, n. 24: X believes, as a result of mental disease, that he will inherit a large sum of money upon the death of a wealthy relative. Acting upon this belief, X kills the relative. X's capacities of understanding and control are not impaired. Is X insane under *M'Naghten?* Under the product test? Should the law grant an insanity excuse in X's case?

5. *"Emotional" Impairment.* Probably the single most controversial legacy of *M'Naghten* is its requirement of cognitive impairment which, as a consequence, denies a defense of insanity to defendants who "knew" what they were doing when they committed their crimes even though they might have suffered from substantial emotional or volitional abnormalities. In assessing this criticism of *M'Naghten,* examine the following case and consider whether the defendant has a viable insanity defense under *M'Naghten* and, if not, whether she, nevertheless, ought to be assessed legally insane.

COMMONWEALTH V. TEMPEST

Supreme Court of Pennsylvania

436 Pa. 436, 437 A.2d 952 (1981)

LARSON, Justice. . . .

[Appellant, Mrs Patricia Tempest, was convicted of murdering her six-year-old son and sentenced to life imprisonment. Among other things, appellant claimed on appeal that the trial evidence was insufficient to find her sane under Pennsylvania law, which placed the burden of proving sanity on the State. (For a discussion of the burden of proof issue in insanity cases, see § 9.05[B][3][e], *infra.*) The Pennsylvania Supreme Court sustained Tempest's conviction, finding insufficient evidence of insanity under *M'Naghten.*]

The record discloses that appellant has been emotionally disturbed since adolescence. Evidently, appellant suffers from depression and low self-esteem, and perceives herself as unattractive and a loner. Prior to the homicide, appellant had been hospitalized for mental illness seven or eight times, the first time at age fifteen and twice following suicide attempts. But despite her problems, appellant married Ronald Tempest and had one son, Gregory, the victim. A psychiatrist who counseled the Tempest family described them as an intact and affectionate family.

On June 18, 1976, tragedy struck this family. Appellant's confession relates in part the facts:

> I got up quarter to eleven or something like that. My husband had already left to go to work. I gave Gregory his breakfast. He was already up watching T.V. It was the last day for kindergarten. I was packing him a lunch for his picnic. I gave him juice with vitamin E. I told him he had to get a bath. He didn't want to go right away. He wanted to finish watching his program so I told him to come up after he did. I went upstairs and filled the tub. I filled it more than normal. When he came upstairs he noticed and said it was kind of deep. He got in the tub himself. I washed the front of his body, then I told him to turn around on his stomach. He told me I didn't wash his face yet. So, I washed his face. I told him to turn on his stomach. When he did I pushed his face down. He struggled and cried, "Mommy you're drowning me." He kept fighting for a couple of minutes—it could have been longer. He still tried to move a little but I kept his head under until he stopped. He didn't move any more so I got out of the tub, I had gotten into the tub to hold him down. I didn't know how long it would take to drown, so I left him there in the tub. He was on his back. I sat there and told him "I had to kill you. I'm sorry." I went into the bedroom, put the television on and watched the movie. I went downstairs and got a banana and ate it, and also took my medicine. I came back upstairs and watched another program, $20,000 *Pyramid*. My husband came home at 25 of 4. I told him I killed Greg. I'd drowned him. He went upstairs and came back and looked very sad.

Appellant's husband summoned the police. Appellant was taken into custody at 3:40 P.M., was given *Miranda* warnings, and signed the aforementioned lucid confession at 5:40 P.M. Additionally in this confession, appellant describes her motive for the killing in these disturbing terms:

Q: Why did you drown Greg?

A: My husband made friends down the street. Greg played with Joey, the little boy down the street. I didn't have any friends. I'm afraid of everybody. I don't really know why I did it. I just did—I didn't want Ronnie and Greg in my life anymore.

Q: Why didn't you want them in your life any more?

A: Greg was too demanding. He got on my nerves. Just having to do things for him. I didn't want the responsibility. I didn't want him to go into 1st grade because I would have to talk to other people. I didn't want to be a housekeeper and have people come to my house. My husband did most of the work.

Appellant repeated essentially the same statement of motive to the arresting officer, her husband, and a psychiatrist.

A psychiatrist who examined appellant after the homicide diagnosed her as suffering from chronic schizophrenia, acute type. . . .

. . . This Court has adopted the test for legal sanity announced in *The Queen v. M'Naghten*. . . . Appellant introduced psychiatric testimony that she did not know right from wrong, hence appellant's insanity claim rests on the second part of the *M'Naghten* test. We find, however, that the evidence (read in the light most favorable to the Commonwealth as verdict winner), proved beyond a reasonable doubt that appellant did know the killing was wrong.

Appellant's acts and statements near the time of the killing clearly support the inference that she knew the killing was wrong. . . . Appellant confessed that she told her dead child, "I had to kill you, I'm sorry." Moreover, when asked by the interrogating detective, "Do you know the difference between right and wrong?" Appellant responded, "Yes, I know killing Greg was wrong." All other portions of appellant's confession are coherent and evince appellant's lucidity. Furthermore, the testimony of lay witnesses can establish appellant's sanity. . . . The interrogating detective testified that appellant was lucid and responsive throughout the interview. Appellant's husband, the first person on the scene, testified that his wife was calm. Finally, the medical testimony in this case belies appellant's insanity claim. Dr. Burt and Dr. Glass, both called for the defense, testified that appellant could tell right from wrong. Dr. Glass so stated unequivocally. Dr. Burt, while admitting that appellant could tell right from wrong "on the surface", claimed that she really could not, due to her psychosis. The trial court expressly rejected Dr. Burt's testimony as vacillating and imprecise. The trier can repudiate even expert psychiatric testimony of insanity. . . . Accordingly, the evidence is sufficient to sustain a finding that appellant was sane.

Undoubtedly, appellant's terrible deed is not the product of a sound mind. But mental illness alone cannot absolve appellant from criminal responsibility. . . . The *M'Naghten* test can embrace those mentally disturbed in the category of those criminally responsible. . . .

Judgment of conviction affirmed.

NOTE ON VOLITIONAL IMPAIRMENT

Even though Ms. Tempest knew killing Gregory was wrong, should her emotional abnormalities be recognized as sufficiently substantial to disqualify her from criminal punishments? Suppose at the time she killed Gregory she was under the illusion that he was Satan incarnate. See *State v. Cameron*, 100 Wash. 2d 520, 674 P.2d 650 (*en banc* 1983). Why might she be insane under those conditions but not under the actual facts? Could she indeed be insane under *M'Naghten* if the court broadly interpreted the test's nature and quality language? See the Wisconsin interpretation referred to by Dean Goldstein in note 1, section 3, *supra*.

Tempest raises the problem of whether emotional impairment should supplement cognitive impairment as a basis for legal insanity. A similar problem is posed by defendants whose cognitive abilities are apparently intact but who claim inability to control their behavior because of mental disease. Mental abnormalities such as pyromania and kleptomania provide paradigmatic examples of mental disorders that leave their respective victims with the knowledge of right and wrong but with impaired ability to resist the compulsions to set fires or to steal.

Often, however, allegations of loss of self-control through mental abnormality are more subtle. Consider the following case.

UNITED STATES v. POLLARD

United States District Court, Eastern District Michigan, Southern Division

171 F. Supp. 474 (1959)

LEVIN, District Judge.

[The defendant was charged with three counts of robbery. Defendant pleaded not guilty by reason of insanity, waived his right to a jury trial, and was convicted. The court explained its reasons for rejecting the plea of insanity:]

The defendant [Pollard] is an intelligent, twenty-nine year old man. In 1949, he married and, during the next four years, three sons and a daughter were born of this marriage. He was apparently a well adjusted, happy, family man. In 1952, he became a member of the Police Department of the City of Detroit and continued to work as a policeman until he was apprehended for the acts for which he is now being prosecuted. In April, 1956, his wife and infant daughter were brutally killed in an unprovoked attack by a drunken neighbor.

On May 21, 1958, one day before he remarried, at about 11:00 A.M., defendant entered the 24th Michigan Branch of the Detroit Bank & Trust Company. He paused for a few moments to look over the bank and then proceeded to an enclosure in which a bank official was at work. He told the official, whom he believed to be the manager, that he wanted to open a savings account. He then walked through a swinging gate into the enclosure, sat down at the desk, pulled out a gun and pointed it at the official. He ordered the official to call a teller. When the teller arrived, the defendant handed a brown paper grocery bag to him and told him to fill it with money. While it was being filled, defendant kept the bank official covered. The teller filled the bag with money as ordered and turned it over to the defendant. Thereupon, defendant ordered the bank official to accompany him to the exit. As both the defendant and bank official approached the exit, the official suddenly wrapped his arms around the defendant, who then dropped the bag and fled from the bank and escaped.

About 4:00 P.M., on the same day, he entered the Chene-Medbury Branch of the Bank of the Commonwealth and walked to a railing behind which a bank employee was sitting. He pointed his gun at the man and told him to sit quietly. The employee, however, did not obey this order but instead raised an alarm, whereupon the defendant ran from the bank and again escaped.

After the defendant was apprehended by the Detroit Police under circumstances which I shall later relate, he admitted to agents of the Federal Bureau of Investigation that after his abortive attempts to rob the two banks, he decided to rob a third bank and actually proceeded on the same day to an unnamed bank he had selected but decided not to make the attempt when he discovered that the bank was "too wide open"—had too much window area so that the possibility of apprehension was enhanced.

On June 3, at about 3:00 P.M., the defendant entered the Woodrow Wilson-Davison Branch of the Bank of Commonwealth and went directly to an enclosure behind which a male and female employee were sitting at desks facing each other. Defendant held his gun under a jacket which he carried over his right arm. He ordered the woman employee to come out from behind the railing. In doing so, she grasped the edge of her desk. Defendant, in the belief that she may have pushed an alarm button, decided to leave but ordered the woman to accompany him out of the bank. When they reached the street, he told her to walk ahead of him, but not to attract attention. Defendant noticed a police car approaching the bank and waited until it passed him, then ran across an empty lot to his car and again escaped.

On June 11, 1958, he attempted to hold up a grocery market. He was thwarted in the attempt when the proprietor screamed and, becoming frightened, the defendant fled. In doing so, he abandoned his automobile in back of the market where he had parked it during the holdup attempt. Routinely, this car was placed under surveillance and later when the defendant, dressed in his Detroit Police Officer's uniform, attempted to get in it, he was arrested by detectives of the Detroit Police Force.

After his apprehension, the defendant confessed to eleven other robberies, or attempted robberies.

The three psychiatrists who submitted the written report, all qualified and respected members of their profession, testified that in their opinion the defendant, at the time he committed the criminal acts, knew the difference between right and wrong and knew that the acts he committed were wrong but was suffering from a "traumatic neurosis" or "dissociative reaction," characterized by moods of depression and severe feelings of guilt, induced by the traumatic effect of the death of his wife and child and his belief that he was responsible for their deaths because by his absence from home he left them exposed to the actions of the crazed, drunken neighbor. They further stated that he had a unconscious desire to be punished by society to expiate these guilt feelings and that the governing power of his mind was so destroyed or impaired that he was unable to resist the commission of the criminal acts. In their opinion, however, the defendant was not then, nor is he now, psychotic or committable to a mental institution.

Three of defendant's fellow police officers, called as defense witnesses, testified that during the period in which the defendant committed the criminal acts he had a tendency to be late for work; that at times he was despondent; and that he occasionally seemed to be lost in thought and did not promptly respond to questions directed to him. One of the officers testified that on one occasion, he repeatedly beat the steering wheel of the police car in which they were riding, while at the same time reiterating the name of his murdered wife.

However, none of them found his conduct or moods to be of such consequence that they believed it necessary to report the defendant to a superior officer.

Defendant's present wife . . . testified that on two occasions defendant suddenly, and for no reason apparent to her, lapsed into crying spells and that he talked to her once or twice about committing suicide. She also testified that during one such period of depression he pointed a gun at himself; that she became frightened and called the police; that the police came, relieved him of his gun, and took him to the precinct police station; and that after his release he appeared jovial and acted as if nothing had happened. Defendant's brother-in-law stated that the defendant had always been a very happy person but that he became noticeably despondent after the death of his wife and child and expressed a desire to commit suicide because he now no longer had a reason for living.

A police lieutenant of the Detroit Police Department testified that the defendant's police work, during the period with which we are now concerned, as evidenced by his efficiency rating and his written duty reports, was, if anything, more effective than his service prior to the death of his wife.

Counsel for defendant contends that since all the medical testimony was to the effect that the defendant was suffering from an irresistible impulse at the time of the commission of the offenses, this Court must accept this uncontroverted expert testimony and find him not guilty by reason of insanity.

[The court then evaluated the expert testimony, noted that it was premised on a "deterministic position with regard to behavior," and found it unpersuasive because defendant's "conscious desire not to be apprehended and punished was demonstrably greater than his unconscious desire to the contrary." The court concluded that the defendant's robbery attempts "were made as the result of impulses the defendant did not choose voluntarily to resist because, to him, the possibility of success outweighed the likelihood of detection which is in essence a motivation for all criminal conduct." Therefore, the "impulse being resistible, the defendant is accountable for his criminal conduct."]

NOTE

Should Pollard be granted a defense of insanity even though he clearly "knew" what he was doing? Are there problems in excusing a defendant because, in the view of the psychiatric experts, his mental illness manifests itself through "unconscious desire(s)" that "impair the governing power of the mind" to such an extent that the defendant was "unable to resist the commission of the criminal acts"? Is it ever clear whether offenders were "unable to resist" desires to commit crime as opposed to simply failing to resist such desires? For discussion of the problem of unconscious motivation as a possible defense, see *State v. Sikora, supra* § 9.02.

In any event, several jurisdictions, prior to the advent of the Model Penal Code, perceived a weakness in *M'Naghten* and supplemented it with a "volitional impairment" test as an independent ground of exculpation. The court in *Parsons v. State,* 81 Ala. 577, 596, 2 So. 854, 866–67 (1886), offered an early recognition of volitional impairment:

[D]id he know right from wrong, as applied to the particular act in question? . . . If he did have such knowledge, he may nevertheless not be legally responsible if the two following conditions concur: (1)If, by reason of the duress of such mental disease, he had so far lost the *power to choose* between the right and wrong, and to avoid doing the act in question, as that his free agency was at the time destroyed; (2) and if, at the same time, the alleged crime was so connected with such mental disease, in the relation of cause and effect, as to have been the product of it *solely.*

A few other jurisdictions followed. See, *e.g., State v. Reidell,* 14 Del. 470, 472, 14 A. 550, 551 (Oyer and Terminer 1888) (test is whether defendant was "capable of controlling himself"); *Commonwealth v. Chester,* 337 Mass. 702, 712, 150 N.E.2d 914, 919 (1958) (test is whether defendant acted from an "irresistible and uncontrollable impulse").

Morse, *Culpability and Control*

142 U. Pa. L. Rev. 1587, 1637-40 (1994)

Adherents of psychodynamic psychological theories claim that much of human behavior is caused by psychological motives that are dynamically unconscious, that is, prevented from reaching awareness because recognition of them would provoke dreadful anxiety and other unpleasant feelings. An example of such motivation might be the bank robber who robs to pay gambling debts, but who executes his crimes in a manner that virtually insures that he will be caught. A psychodynamic formulation of the causes of his action might include the hypothesis that the robber unconsciously feels unworthy and guilty and desires, without being aware of it, of course, to be punished. As a result, and again without being aware of it, he commits his robberies in an unnecessarily incompetent manner, guaranteeing capture, conviction, and punishment. According to the dynamicist, such unconscious motivation is ubiquitous; there is, so to speak, a "shadow" system of practical reasoning of varying rationality that accompanies and influences our conscious motivation.

Assuming the validity of such hypotheses, what is their bearing on control excuses? First note that dynamically unconscious motivation does not negate intention or choice. The hapless bank robber may not have been aware of the "real" reason he robbed the bank, but he surely chose to rob it and did so intentionally. Moreover, he was fully conscious in the legal sense because he did not rob during a dissociative state. If psychodynamic motivation produces a lack of intention in some hard to fathom manner or, more plausibly but rarely, it causes a dissociative state, then the absence of *mens rea* or dissociation is doing the work.

Should dynamically unconscious motivation have excusing force? Here are two theories that might support such an excuse. The first is that an agent who is unaware of the "real" reason for conduct is not rational; the second is that dynamic unconscious motivation somehow compels the agent to perform the conduct so motivated. Consider our sad bank robber again. He was quite consciously rational: he knew the relevant facts about the world and his conscious reason for robbing the bank—to obtain needed money—was certainly rational, if not laudable. Moreover, his will translated his desires into action. Is knowing the entire set of causes for one's behavior necessary for responsibility? All of us almost always lack full awareness of the *present* variables causally influencing us, whether they are of the dynamic type or not. If the presence of dynamically unconscious causes or other unperceived causes negated responsibility, no one would ever be responsible because such causes are always operative. Only if dynamically unconscious motives were distinguishable for these purposes would this theory have plausibility. But because dynamic motivation is ubiquitous, we would then need a further theory and method for distinguishing unconscious motives that render the consciously rational agent actually irrational from unconscious motives that did not have this effect. For example, we might try to distinguish rational and irrational *unconscious* motivation. Even if this were possible, which is entirely a tooth fairy hypothesis, the excuse would be irrationality, not lack of control, except in the extended sense that irrationality makes flying straight harder. [Throughout his article, Professor Morse discusses "flying straight" as the ability of humans to manage to behave ourselves in the face of ubiquitous antisocial desires.]

* * *

Let us turn to the alternatives, compulsion theory. How might dynamically unconscious causes "compel" conduct? Why are dynamically unconscious causes any more compelling than the other, myriad causes of behavior of which we are unaware? Causes, even if they are unconscious, are not excuses. Of course, it is arguable that self-awareness about one's "true" motives, in addition to self-awareness about what one is consciously doing, makes it easier to control conduct. But empirical research suggests that becoming aware of dynamically unconscious motives, that is, achieving "insight" into repressed psychological contents, does not help people to change, producing doubt about this argument. And, the argument is not about hard choice, but about another attribute, self-awareness, that may be self-protective. Should lack of such awareness excuse in general or in the case of (some? which?) dynamic motives? If so, it would excuse because we believe that the self-protective variable is so important that lacking it makes it too difficult to fly straight. But there is no reason to believe this in general or in the case of dynamic motivation in particular. The "compulsion theory," if supportable at all, reduces to a standard "hard to fly straight" theory, much akin to irrationality claims. I conclude that as long as the agent is consciously rational and not constrained by a perceived, blameless hard choice, justification for an excuse is lacking.

NOTE ON THE MODEL PENAL CODE APPROACH

Does Morse show convincingly that Pollard should not be excused for his botched bank robberies? If "subconscious motives" should not excuse, are they relevant as sentencing considerations? Is Pollard as culpable as one who robs merely to satisfy motives for pecuniary gain?

Model Penal Code § 4.01 offers its own volitional impairment supplement to the traditional cognitive impairment standard:

(1) A person is not responsible for criminal conduct if at the time of such conduct as a result of mental disease or defect he lacks substantial capacity either to appreciate the criminality [wrongfulness] of his conduct or to conform his conduct to the requirements of law.

(2) As used in this Article, the terms "mental disease or defect" do not include an abnormality manifested only by repeated criminal or otherwise anti-social conduct.

Until the verdict in the *Hinckley* case precipitated a movement away from volitional impairment tests (see note 2, p. 831 immediately following the *Johnson* case, *infra*), the MPC test was emerging as the dominant standard in the United States. The reasons for the test's attractiveness are summarized by the court in the following case.

STATE v. JOHNSON

Supreme Court of Rhode Island

121 R.I. 254, 399 A.2d 469 (1979)

DORIS, Justice.

The sole issue presented by this appeal is whether this court should abandon the *M'Naghten* test in favor of a new standard for determining the criminal responsibility of those who claim they are blameless by reason of mental illness. . . . For the reasons stated herein, we have concluded that the time has arrived to modernize our rule governing this subject.

Before punishing one who has invaded a protected interest, the criminal law generally requires some showing of culpability in the offender. The requirement of a *mens rea,* or guilty mind, is the most notable example of the concept that before punishment may be exacted, blameworthiness must be demonstrated. That some deterrent, restraint, or rehabilitative purpose may be served is alone insufficient. It has been stated that the criminal law reflects the moral sense of the community. "The fact that the law has, for centuries, regarded certain wrongdoers as improper subjects for punishment is a testament to the extent to which that moral sense has developed. Thus, society has recognized over the years that none of the three asserted purposes of the criminal law—rehabilitation, deterrence and retribution—is satisfied when the truly irresponsible, those who lack substantial capacity to control their actions, are punished." *United States v. Freeman,* 357 F.2d 606, 615 (2d Cir. 1966). The law appreciates that those who are substantially unable to restrain their conduct are, by definition, incapable of being deterred and their punishment in a correctional institution provides no example for others.

The law of criminal responsibility has its roots in the concept of free will. As Mr. Justice Jackson stated:

How far one by an exercise of free will may determine his general destiny or his course in a particular matter and how far he is the toy of circumstance has been debated through the ages by theologians, philosophers, and scientists. Whatever doubts they have entertained as to the matter, the practical business of government and administration of the law is obliged to proceed on more or less rough and ready judgments based on the assumption that mature and rational persons are in control of their own conduct.

Gregg Cartage & Storage Co. v. United States, 316 U.S. 74, 79–80 (1942).

Our law proceeds from this postulate and seeks to fashion a standard by which criminal offenders whose free will has been sufficiently impaired can be identified and treated in a manner that is both humane and beneficial to society at large. The problem has been aptly described as distinguishing between those cases for which a correctional-puniti ve disposition is appropriate and those in which a medical-custodial disposition is the only kind that is legally permissible. . . .

Because language is inherently imprecise and there is a wide divergence of opinion within the medical profession, no exact definition of "insanity" is possible . . . Every legal definition comprehends elements of abstraction and approximation that are particularly difficult to apply in marginal cases. Our inability to guarantee that a new rule will always be infallible, however, cannot justify unyielding adherence to an outmoded standard, solely at variance with contemporary medical and legal knowledge. Any legal standard designed to assess criminal responsibility must satisfy several objectives. It must accurately reflect the underlying principles of substantive law and community values while comporting with the realities of scientific understanding. The standard must be phrased in order to make fully available to the jury such psychiatric information as medical science has to offer regarding the individual defendant, yet be comprehensible to the experts, lawyers, and jury alike. Finally, the definition must preserve to the trier of facts, be it judge or jury, its full authority to render a final decision. . . . These considerations are paramount in our consideration of the rule to be applied in this jurisdiction in cases in which the defense of lack of criminal responsibility due to a mental illness is raised.

* * *

This jurisdiction has long adhered to the *M'Naghten* standard for determining criminal responsibility. . . . The *M'Naghten* rule has been the subject of considerable criticism and controversy for over a century. . . . The test's emphasis upon knowledge of right or wrong abstracts a single element of personality as the sole symptom or manifestation of mental illness. *M'Naghten* refuses to recognize volitional or emotional impairments, viewing the cognitive element as the singular cause of conduct. . . . *M'Naghten* has been further criticized for being predicated upon an outmoded psychological concept because modern science recognizes that "insanity" affects the whole personality of the defendant, including the will and emotions. . . . One of the most frequent criticisms of *M'Naghten* has been directed at its all-or-nothing approach, requiring total incapacity of cognition. . . . We agree that:

> Nothing makes the inquiry into responsibility more unreal for the psychiatrist than limitation of the issue to some ultimate extreme of total

incapacity, when clinical experience reveals only a graded scale with marks along the way. . . .

The law must recognize that when there is no black and white it must content itself with different shades of gray. Model Penal Code, § 4.01, Comment at 158 (Tent. Draft No. 4, 1955).

By focusing upon total cognitive incapacity, the *M'Naghten* rule compels the psychiatrist to testify in terms of unrealistic concepts having no medical meaning. Instead of scientific opinions, the rule calls for moral or ethical judgment from the expert which judgment contributes to usurpation of the jury's function as decision maker. . . . That these criticisms have had a pronounced effect is evidenced by the large and growing number of jurisdictions that have abandoned their former allegiance to *M'Naghten* in favor of the Model Penal Code formulation; . . . We also find these criticisms persuasive and agree that *M'Naghten's* serious deficiencies necessitate a new approach.

Responding to the criticism of the *M'Naghten* and irresistible impulse rules, the American Law Institute incorporated a new test of criminal responsibility into its Model Penal Code. The Model Penal Code test has received widespread and evergrowing acceptance. It has been adopted with varying degrees of modification in 26 states and by every federal court of appeals that has addressed the issue. Although no definition can be accurately described as the perfect or ultimate pronouncement, we believe that the Model Penal Code standard represents a significant, positive improvement over our existing rule. Most importantly, it acknowledges that volitional as well as cognitive impairments must be considered by the jury in its resolution of the responsibility issue. The test replaces *M'Naghten's* unrealistic all or nothing approach with the concept of "substantial" capacity. Additionally, the test employs vocabulary sufficiently in the common ken that its use at trial will permit a reasonable three-way dialogue between the law-trained judges and lawyers, the medical-trained experts, and the jury. . . .

Without question the essential dilemma in formulating any standard of criminal responsibility is encouraging a maximum informational input from the expert witnesses while preserving to the jury its role as trier of fact and ultimate decision maker. As one court has aptly observed:

> At bottom, the determination whether a man is or is not held responsible for his conduct is not a medical but a legal, social, or moral judgment. Ideally, psychiatrists—much like experts in other fields—should provide grist for the legal mill, should furnish the raw data upon which the legal judgment is based. It is the psychiatrist who informs as to the mental state of the accused—his characteristics, his potentialities, his capabilities. But once this information is disclosed, it is society as a whole, represented by judge or jury, which decides whether a man with the characteristics described should or should not be held accountable for his acts.

United States v. Freeman, 357 F.2d at 619–620.

Because of our overriding concern that the jury's function remain inviolate, we today adopt the following formulation of the Model Penal Code test:

A person is not responsible for criminal conduct if at the time of such conduct, as a result of mental disease or defect, his capacity either to appreciate the wrongfulness of his conduct or to conform his conduct to the requirements of law is so substantially impaired that he cannot justly be held responsible.

The terms "mental disease or defect" do not include an abnormality manifested only by repeated criminal or otherwise antisocial conduct.

There are several important reasons why we prefer this formulation. The greatest strength of our test is that it clearly delegates the issue of criminal responsibility to the jury, thus precluding possible usurpation of the ultimate decision by the expert witnesses. Under the test we have adopted, the jury's attention is appropriately focused upon the legal and moral aspects of responsibility because it must evaluate the defendant's blameworthiness in light of prevailing community standards. Far from setting the jury at large, as in the majority Model Penal Code test, the defendant must demonstrate a certain form of incapacity. That is, the jury must find that a mental disease or defect caused a substantial impairment of the defendant's capacity to appreciate the wrongfulness of his act or to conform his conduct to legal requirements. Our new test emphasizes that the degree of "substantial" impairment required is essentially a legal rather than a medical question. Where formerly under *M'Naghten* total incapacity was necessary for exculpation, the new standard allows the jury to find that incapacity less than total is sufficient. Because impairment is a matter of degree, the precise degree demanded is necessarily governed by the community sense of justice as represented by the trier of fact.

Several other components of our new test require elucidation. Our test consciously employs the more expansive term "appreciate" rather than "know." Implicit in this choice is the recognition that mere theoretical awareness that a certain course of conduct is wrong, when divorced from appreciation or understanding of the moral or legal impact of behavior, is of little import. . . . A significant difference from our former rule is inclusion in the new test of the concept that a defendant is not criminally responsible if he lacked substantial capacity to conform his conduct to the requirements of law. As we noted at the outset, our law assumes that a normal individual has the capacity to control his behavior; should an individual manifest free will in the commission of a criminal act, he must be held responsible for that conduct. Mental illness, however, can effectively destroy an individual's capacity for choice and impair behavioral controls.

The drafters of the Model Penal Code left to each jurisdiction a choice between the terms "wrongfulness" and "criminality." We prefer the word "wrongfulness" because we believe that a person who, knowing an act to be criminal, committed it because of a delusion that the act was morally justified, should not be automatically foreclosed from raising the defense of lack of criminal responsibility.

The second paragraph of our test is designed to exclude from the concept of "mental disease or defect" the so-called psychopathic or sociopathic personality . . . We have included this language in our test to make clear that mere recidivism alone does not justify acquittal. . . .

As we have emphasized previously, preserving the respective provinces of the jury and experts is an important concern. Consonant with modern medical understanding, our test is intended to allow the psychiatrist to place before the jury all of the relevant information that it must consider in reaching its decision. We adhere to Dean Wigmore's statement that when criminal responsibility is in issue, "any and all conduct of the person is admissible in evidence." 2 Wigmore, Evidence section 228 (1940). Nevertheless, the charge to the jury must include unambiguous instructions stressing that regardless of the nature and extent of the experts' testimony, the issue of exculpation remains at all times a legal and not a medical question. In determining the issue of responsibility the jury has two important tasks. First, it must measure the extent to which the defendant's mental and emotional processes were impaired at the time of the unlawful conduct. The answer to that inquiry is a difficult and elusive one, but no more so than numerous other facts that a jury must find in a criminal trial. Second, the jury must assess that impairment in light of community standards of blameworthiness. The jury's unique qualifications for making that determination justify our unusual deference to the jury's resolution of the issue of responsibility. . . . For it has been stated that the essential feature of a jury "lies in the interposition between the accused and his accuser of the commonsense judgment of a group of laymen, and in the community participation and shared responsibility that results from that group's determination of guilt or innocence. . . ." Therefore, the charge should leave no doubt that it is for the jury to determine: 1) the existence of a cognizable mental disease or defect, 2) whether such a disability resulted in a substantial impairment at the time of the unlawful conduct of the accused's capacity either to appreciate the wrongfulness of his conduct or to conform his conduct to the requirements of the law, and consequently, 3) whether there existed a sufficient relationship between the mental abnormality and the condemned behavior to warrant the conclusion that the defendant cannot justly be held responsible for his acts.

So there will be no misunderstanding of the thrust of this opinion, mention should be made of the treatment to be afforded individuals found lacking criminal responsibility due to a mental illness under the test we have adopted. Unquestionably the security of the community must be the paramount interest. Society withholds criminal sanctions out of a sense of compassion and understanding when the defendant is found to lack capacity. It would be an intolerable situation if those suffering from a mental disease or defect of such a nature as to relieve them from criminal responsibility were to be released to continue to pose a threat to life and property. The General Laws provide that a person found not guilty because he was "insane" at the time of the commission of a crime shall be committed to the Director of the State Department of Mental Health for observation. At a subsequent judicial hearing if he is found to be dangerous, the person must be committed to a public institution for care and treatment. . . . This procedure insures society's protection and affords the incompetent criminal offender necessary medical attention.

NOTES AND QUESTIONS

1. Note that by means of the *Johnson* decision, Rhode Island is the only jurisdiction to embrace the MPC variation couched in terms of whether the defendant can "justly be held responsible" for his actions. That formulation of the test was considered but rejected by the Council of the American Law Institute. Model Penal Code § 4.01, Comment at 172, n. 19 (1985). Is an explicit "justice" standard desirable?

2. The emerging recognition of the MPC test came to an abrupt halt in 1982 with the trial of John W. Hinckley for the attempted assassination of President Ronald Reagan. Hinckley was acquitted by reason of insanity under the MPC standard after a lengthy trial, observed closely by the public through extensive media coverage. The acquittal precipitated considerable public outrage and focused antipathy toward the insanity defense and its administration.

Powerful organizations called for the elimination of the volitional impairment test. The American Psychiatric Association advocated a return to *M'Naghten* principles by excusing the defendant only if, as a result of mental disease or retardation, he is "unable to appreciate the wrongfulness of his conduct at the time of the offense." The American Psychiatric Association, *Statement on the Insanity Defense,* December 1982, declared:

> [M]any psychiatrists . . . believe that psychiatric information relevant to determining whether a defendant understood the nature of his act . . . is more reliable and has a stronger scientific basis than, for example, does psychiatric information relevant to whether a defendant was able to control his behavior. The line between an irresistible impulse and an impulse not resisted is probably no sharper than that between twilight and dusk. . . . The concept of volition is the subject of some disagreement among psychiatrists. Many . . . believe that psychiatric testimony . . . about volition is more likely to produce confusion for jurors than is psychiatric testimony relevant to a defendant's appreciation or understanding.

Similarly, the American Bar Association adopted a position against the use of any volitional test:

> [O]ur proposed test eliminates the "volitional" part of the ALI test. This is a noteworthy aspect of our proposal for it would do away with that portion of expert testimony regarding the impairment of "normal" behavioral controls. And, we submit, it is just this volitional or behavioral part of the ALI test that has brought the insanity defense under increasing attack. During the 1950's a wave of clinical optimism suggested that scientific knowledge concerning psychopathology had expanded to the extent that informed judgments could be made regarding impairment of behavioral control. That optimism was reflected in the volitional portion of the ALI test. Yet, experience confirms that there is still no accurate scientific basis for measuring one's capacity for self-control or for calibrating the impairment of such capacity. There is, in short, no objective basis for distinguishing between offenders who were undeterrable and those who were merely undeterred, between the impulse that was irresistible and the impulse not

resisted, or between substantial impairment of the capacity and some lesser impairment. Whatever the precise terms of the volitional test, the question is unanswerable or, at best, can be answered only by "moral (*and not medical*) guesses." In our opinion, to even ask the volitional question invites fabricated expert claims, undermines the equal administration of the penal law and compromises the law's deterrent effect.

Report of the Standing Committee on Association Standards for Criminal Justice and Commission on the Mentally Disabled, 108 Rep. of the A.B.A. 715, 717 (1983) (Recommendation approved by the House of Delegates, February 9, 1983, 108 Rep. of the ABA at 380.)

In 1983 the American Medical Association approved a more radical measure, recommending abolition of the insanity defense altogether with evidence of mental abnormality being admissible only on the issue of whether the defendant possessed the *mens rea* required as an element of the crime charged. *Insanity Defense in Criminal Trials and Limitations of Psychiatric Testimony,* Report of Board of Trustees, Committee on Medicolegal Problems, American Medical Association, 251 J.A.M.A. 2967 (1984).

The states of Montana, Idaho, and Utah have statutorily enacted provisions similar to the AMA proposal. The abolitionist movement is more fully discussed at § 9.05[B][5][b], *infra.*

Congressional reaction to the *Hinckley* verdict was swift. At the time of his acquittal, the MPC test or variations thereof had been adopted in each of the federal circuits. In 1984 Congress for the first time passed a statute governing the federal insanity defense. 18 U.S.C. § 17 (1984). The new legislation eliminated the volitional prong of the defense and placed the burden of proving insanity on the defendant:

> (a) Affirmative Defense.—It is an affirmative defense to a prosecution under any federal statute that, at the time of the commission of the acts constituting the offense, the defendant as a result of a severe mental disease or defect, was unable to appreciate the nature and quality or the wrongfulness of his acts. Mental disease or defect does not otherwise constitute a defense.
>
> (b) Burden of Proof.—The defendant has the burden of proving the defense of insanity by clear and convincing evidence.

See the discussion of burdens of proof in insanity cases, § 9.05 [B][3][e], *infra.*

3. Is all the discussion about the phraseology of the test a tempest in an academic teapot? Can juries—do juries—rigorously apply the tests, or do they decide the moral, commonsense issue without much regard for linguistic niceties? For a detailed attempt to document whether the form of the insanity test makes a difference in jury deliberations, see R. Simon, The Jury and the Defense of Insanity (1967). Professor Simon's results are equivocal. For example, for some crimes but not for others, the rate of juror acquittals significantly varies depending upon whether the instruction is in terms of the *M'Naghten* rather than the *Durham* test for insanity. *Id.* at 215–16.

[b] Disposition of Offenders Not Guilty by Reason of Insanity

While the *Hinckley* verdict precipitated wholesale doctrinal re-evaluation, other forces also contributed to the growing disenchantment with the insanity defense and its administration. Among the most important of such forces was the reform movement toward deinstitutionalization tion of the mentally ill. See Stone, *The Insanity Defense on Trial,* 33 Harv. L. Sch. Bull., 15, 19–20 (Fall 1982).

Available evidence suggests that prior to 1800 a defendant acquitted by reason of insanity was treated, at least as a matter of law, like any other acquittee who simply walked out of the courtroom a free person. In 1800, however, England's Parliament provided for the automatic confinement of such persons to mental institutions, where they were to remain "at the pleasure of the king," a euphemism for an indefinite commitment, often for the remainder of the acquittee's life. For 150 years, this was the virtually uniform practice in this country as well, whether specifically authorized by statute or not.

In the 1960s and 70s, however, serious criticisms were made of this practice in light of its underlying presumptions that insanity acquittees, having committed criminal acts, are dangerous and that their insanity, proven at trial to have existed at the time of their acts, continues. Neither of these presumptions is necessarily true. The acquittee may not pose an ongoing danger. His offense may have been minor in the first place, or, even if it was serious (for example, murdering one's spouse), the acquittee may pose little risk of recidivism. Moreover, either naturally or by treatment, the acquittee may have recovered his sanity between the time of the criminal act and the acquittal. Some courts found such criticisms convincing and so have invalidated automatic commitment practices. See, *e.g., Bolton v. Harris,* 395 F.2d 642 (D.C. Cir. 1968).

The Supreme Court first addressed dispositional issues in the following case.

JONES V. UNITED STATES

Supreme Court of the United States

463 U.S. 354 (1968)

Justice POWELL *delivered the opinion of the Court.*

[The case raised the question whether automatic commitment of insanity acquittees was constitutional under the Due Process Clause even though the government was not required to prove that the acquittee was mentally ill or dangerous at the time of commitment. The statutory scheme at issue required the defendant at the guilt stage to prove insanity at the time of the crime by a preponderance of the evidence. (The burden of proof issue in insanity defense cases is discussed in this casebook at § 9.05[B][3][e], *infra.*) Acquittees meeting this burden were then subjected to automatic commitment for diagnosis for up to 50 days after which the acquittee could move for a judicial release hearing at which he bore the burden of proving, again by a preponderance of the evidence, that he was no longer mentally ill or dangerous. Failing to obtain release at the 50-day hearing, the acquittee was entitled to a judicial release hearing every six months, at which he again carried the burden of proving by a preponderance of the evidence that the release was appropriate because of the absence of mental illness or dangerousness. A third release mechanism was available if the court approved a certification of recovery by the hospital chief of staff.

The acquittee petitioner raised three issues: 1)whether automatic commitment, even if only for 50 days for diagnosis, is constitutional without a showing of mental illness and dangerousness at the time of commitment; 2)whether the Constitution permits hospitalizing insanity acquittees without the government meeting the standards required in ordinary civil commitment proceedings, specifically proof by clear and convincing evidence that the person to be committed is mentally ill and dangerous; and 3)whether an insanity acquittee could constitutionally be confined for a longer period of time than he could have been confined had he been convicted of the crime. The Court found against the acquittee petitioner on all three issues.]

It is clear that "commitment for any purpose constitutes a significant deprivation of liberty that requires due process protection." *Addington v. Texas,* 441 U.S. 418 (1979). Therefore, a State must have "a constitutionally adequate purpose for the confinement." . . . Congress has determined that a criminal defendant found not guilty by reason of insanity in the District of Columbia should be committed indefinitely to a mental institution for treatment and the protection of society. . . .

Petitioner's argument rests principally on *Addington v. Texas, supra,* in which the Court held that the Due Process Clause requires the Government in a civil commitment proceeding to demonstrate by clear and convincing evidence that the individual is mentally ill and dangerous. Petitioner contends that these due process standards were not met in his case because the judgment of not guilty by reason of insanity did not constitute a finding of present mental illness and dangerousness and because it was established only by a preponderance of the evidence. Petitioner then concludes that the Government's only conceivably legitimate justification for automatic commitment is to ensure that insanity acquittees do not escape confinement entirely, and that this interest can justify commitment at most for a period equal to the maximum prison sentence the acquittee could have received if convicted. Because petitioner has been hospitalized for longer than the one year he might have served in prison, he asserts that he should be released unconditionally or recommitted under the District's civil-commitment procedures.

We turn first to the question whether the finding of insanity at the criminal trial is sufficiently probative of mental illness and dangerousness to justify commitment. A verdict of not guilty by reason of insanity establishes two facts: (i) the defendant committed an act that constitutes a criminal offense, and (ii) he committed the act because of mental illness. Congress has determined that these findings constitute an adequate basis for hospitalizing the acquittee as a dangerous and mentally ill person. See H.R. Rep. No. 91-907, at 74 (expressing fear that "dangerous criminals, particularly psychopaths, [may] win acquittals of serious criminal charges on grounds of insanity" and yet "escape hospital commitment"); S. Rep. No. 1170, 84th Cong., 1st Sess. 13 (1955) ("Where [the] accused has pleaded insanity as a defense to a crime, and the jury has found that the defendant was, in fact, insane at the time the crime was committed, it is just and reasonable in the Committee's opinion that the insanity, once established, should be presumed to continue and that the accused should automatically be confined for treatment until it can be shown that he has recovered"). We cannot say that it was unreasonable and therefore unconstitutional for Congress to make this determination.

The fact that a person has been found, beyond a reasonable doubt, to have committed a criminal act certainly indicates dangerousness. Indeed, this concrete evidence generally may be at least as persuasive as any predictions about dangerousness that might be made in a civil-commitment proceeding. We do not agree with petitioner's suggestion that the requisite dangerousness is not established by proof that a person committed a non-violent crime against property. This Court never has held that "violence," however that term might be defined, is a prerequisite for a constitutional commitment.

Nor can we say that it was unreasonable for Congress to determine that the insanity acquittal supports an inference of continuing mental illness. It comports with common sense to conclude that someone whose mental illness was sufficient to lead him to commit a criminal act is likely to remain ill and in need of treatment. The precise evidentiary force of the acquittal, of course, may vary from case to case, but the Due Process Clause does not require Congress to make classifications that fit every individual with the same degree of relevance. Because a hearing is provided within 50 days of the commitment, there is assurance that every acquittee has prompt opportunity to obtain release if he has recovered.

* * *

. . . We therefore conclude that a finding of not guilty by reason of insanity is a sufficient foundation for commitment of an insanity acquittee for the purposes of treatment and the protection of society.

Petitioner next contends that his indefinite commitment is unconstitutional because the proof of his insanity was based only on a preponderance of the evidence, as compared to *Addington's* civil-commitment requirement of proof by clear and convincing evidence. In equating these situations, petitioner ignores important differences between the class of potential civil-commitment candidates and the class of insanity acquittees that justify differing standards of proof. The *Addington* Court expressed particular concern that members of the public could be confined on the basis of "some abnormal behavior which might be perceived by some as symptomatic of a mental or emotional disorder, but which is in fact within a range of conduct that is generally acceptable." . . . In view of this concern, the Court deemed it inappropriate to ask the individual "to share equally with society the risk of error." . . . But since automatic commitment under Section 24-301(d)(1) follows only if the *acquittee himself* advances insanity as a defense and proves that his criminal act was a product of his mental illness, there is good reason for diminished concern as to the risk of error. More important, the proof that he committed a criminal act as a result of mental illness eliminates the risk that he is being committed for mere "idiosyncratic behavior." . . . A criminal act by definition is not "within a range of conduct that is generally acceptable." . . .

We therefore conclude that concerns critical to our decision in *Addington* are diminished or absent in the case of insanity acquittees. Accordingly, there is no reason for adopting the same standard of proof in both cases. . . . The preponderance of the evidence standard comports with due process for commitment of insanity acquittees.

The remaining question is whether petitioner nonetheless is entitled to his release because he has been hospitalized for a period longer than he could have been incarcerated if convicted. The Due Process Clause "requires that the nature and duration of commitment bear some reasonable relation to the purpose for which the individual is committed." *Jackson v. Indiana,* 406 U.S. 715, 738 (1972). The purpose of commitment following an insanity acquittal, like that of civil commitment, is to treat the individual's mental illness and protect him and society from his potential dangerousness. The committed acquittee is entitled to release when he has recovered his sanity or is no longer dangerous. . . . And because it is impossible to predict how long it will take for any given individual to recover—or indeed whether he ever will recover—Congress has chosen, as it has with respect to civil commitment, to leave the length of commitment indeterminate, subject to periodic review of the patient's suitability for release.

* * *

. . . There simply is no necessary correlation between severity of the offense and length of time necessary for recovery. The length of the acquittee's hypothetical criminal sentence therefore is irrelevant to the purposes of his commitment.

We hold that when a criminal defendant establishes by a preponderance of the evidence that he is not guilty of a crime by reason of insanity, the Constitution permits the Government, on the basis of the insanity judgment, to confine him to a mental institution until such time as he has regained his sanity or is no longer a danger to himself or society. This holding accords with the widely and reasonably held view that insanity acquittees constitute a special class that should be treated differently from other candidates for commitment. . . .

NOTES AND QUESTIONS

1. Would the result in *Jones* be different if the burden of proof on the insanity defense issue had been on the government? Suppose, for example, that the government was assessed the burden of showing beyond a reasonable doubt that the defendant was not insane. If so, would the automatic commitment procedure in *Jones* be constitutional? The release mechanisms?

2. Does Jones leave intact the following practices described in J. German and A. Singer, *Punishing the Not Guilty: Hospitalization of Persons Acquitted*

by Reason of Insanity, 29 Rutgers L. Rev. 1011, 1037–38, 1053–54, 1064–66 (1976):

The conditions under which most NGI's [persons acquitted by reason of insanity] are housed stand in stark contrast to those under which most other civil mental patients are confined. Non-NGI civil patients are usually afforded gradually progressive pass privileges as they are able to demonstrate greater responsibility. Home passes and visits are usually permitted. Telephone calls and correspondence are not likely to be limited. The patients are generally hospitalized near their homes, facilitating visits by friends and relatives. Chains, handcuffs, and barred cells are not in general use. In other words, although locked wards are present in most mental hospitals, security is not given the primary emphasis.

It is not surprising that statistics demonstrate that NGI's are hospitalized for far longer periods than other civil patients, the duration more likely to be related to the seriousness of the criminal acts than to the patient's improvement within the hospital. An especially egregious example of this practice is the unwritten "ten-year rule" whereby patients at California's Atascadero State Hospital who have been acquitted of murder by reason of insanity are not considered for release or transfer for ten years. Similarly, patients charged with serious assaults are not released for three years after their symptoms abate.

* * *

Of all the circumstances affecting an acquitted patient's existence, none is more unfair or diverges farther from the norms applicable to other committed patients than the procedures and standards controlling his release. . . .

. . . . While statutes in nearly every state permit an administrative discharge by the hospital director when he believes a patient no longer requires hospitalization, about half of the states require court orders for discharge of NGI's. The burden of proof may be heavier and the standards for release more stringent for NGI's. The procedure for release is often more cumbersome, involving the prosecutor or attorney general and the same judge who signed the commitment order. And NGI's may be denied discharge through periodic review and conditional discharge, avenues open to other patients.

* * *

Another source of discrimination against NGI's is the tremendous burden they must bear to attain their release, once they do get into court. Some courts, continuing to regard NGI's as an "exceptional class," have held that they must prove beyond a reasonable doubt that they are fit to be released into society. This burden seems practically impossible to meet, since it involves proving the negative—that an NGI will not be dangerous. It is especially onerous when the NGI is kept in strict custody and allowed no opportunity to demonstrate what his behavior would be if he were given his liberty, increasing the likelihood that judges will continue confinement even in the face of unanimous psychiatric testimony that the patient should be released.

* * *

There is great variety in the standards of release for NGI's. Many states, including New York, require an end to dangerousness. Some courts have held that dangerousness must relate to mental illness, since any other construction could not be a valid basis for indeterminate confinement where treatment would be of no use. Some courts have adopted civil hospitalization standards, discharging those patients who fail to meet the criteria. However, still other courts have held that mental illness need not be a component of the release formula if the patient is otherwise still "dangerous." Such construction is unheard of in the regular civil commitment context.

Do such practices as those described in the above article make a plausible case for its authors' conclusion, expressed in the article's title, that insanity acquittees are often "punished"? Reconsider § 2.02, *supra*. What are the legal implications of "punishing" the not guilty?

3. The deinstitutionalization movement has waned in recent years insofar as insanity acquittees are concerned. As *Jones* represents, concern over premature release has led some jurisdictions that might otherwise be swayed by the logic of not distinguishing between NGIs and other involuntarily hospitalized persons, to adopt provisions that facilitate the confinement and retention of NGIs as a special class. See, *e.g.*, Neb. Rev. Stats. § § 29-2203, 29-3705 (Reissue 1989) (assigning burden of proving insanity on defendant and placing hospital release decision within the sole jurisdiction of the court that initially committed the NGI to the hospital). However, as the following case suggests, some state attempts to enhance the confinement of NGIs meet with disapproval from the Supreme Court.

FOUCHA v. LOUISIANA

Supreme Court of the United States

504 U.S. 71 (1992)

Justice WHITE *delivered the opinion of the Court, except as to Part III.*

When a defendant in a criminal case pending in Louisiana is found not guilty by reason of insanity, he is committed to a psychiatric hospital unless he proves that he is not dangerous. This is so whether or not he is then insane. After commitment, if the acquittee or the superintendent begins release proceedings, a review panel at the hospital makes a written report on the patient's mental condition and whether he can be released without danger to himself or others. If release is recommended, the court must hold a hearing to determine dangerousness; the acquittee has the burden of proving that he is not dangerous. If found to be dangerous, the acquittee may be returned to the mental institution whether or not he is then mentally ill. Petitioner contends that this scheme denies him due process and equal protection because it allows a person acquitted by reason of insanity to be committed to a mental institution until he is able to demonstrate that he is not dangerous to himself and others, even though he does not suffer from any mental illness.

I

Petitioner Terry Foucha was charged by Louisiana authorities with aggravated burglary and illegal discharge of a firearm . . . [On October 12, 1984 the trial court ruled that Foucha was not guilty by reason of insanity. In addition, the court found that Foucha was "presently insane and a menace to himself and others" and committed him to a mental institution until such time as the medical authorities and the court recommend release.] In March, 1988, a panel of medical authorities recommended conditional discharge, noting "that there had been no evidence of mental illness since admission."[2] The trial judge appointed a two-member sanity commission made up of the same two doctors who had conducted the pretrial examination. Their written report stated that Foucha "is presently in remission from mental illness [but] [w]e cannot certify that he would not constitute a menace to himself or others if released." One of the doctors testified at a hearing that upon commitment Foucha probably suffered from a drug induced psychosis but that he had recovered from that temporary condition; that he evidenced no signs of psychosis or neurosis and was in "good shape" mentally; that he has, however, an antisocial personality, a condition that is not a mental disease and that is untreatable. The doctor also testified that Foucha had been involved in several altercations [while in the institution] and that he, the doctor, would not "feel comfortable in certifying that [Foucha] would not be a danger to himself or to other people."

After it was stipulated that the other doctor, if he were present, would give essentially the same testimony, the court ruled that Foucha was dangerous to himself and others and ordered him returned to the mental institution. The Court of Appeals refused supervisory writs, and the State Supreme Court affirmed, holding that Foucha had not carried the burden placed upon him by statute to prove that he was not dangerous, that our decision in *Jones v. United States,* 463 U.S. 354 (1983), did not require Foucha's release, and that neither the Due Process Clause nor the Equal Protection Clause was violated by the statutory provision permitting confinement of an insanity acquittee based on dangerousness alone.

Because the case presents an important issue and was decided by the court below in a manner arguably at odds with prior decisions of this Court, we granted certiorari.

II

Addington v. Texas, 441 U.S. 418 (1979), held that to commit an individual to a mental institution in a civil proceeding, the State is required by the Due

---

[2] The panel unanimously recommended that petitioner be conditionally discharged with recommendations that he (1)be placed on probation; (2)remain free from intoxicating and mind-altering substances; (3)attend a substance abuse clinic on a regular basis; (4)submit to regular and random urine drug screening; and (5)be actively employed or seeking employment. (App. 10-11) Although the panel recited that it was charged with determining dangerousness, its report did not expressly make a finding in that regard.

Process Clause to prove by clear and convincing evidence the two statutory preconditions to commitment: that the person sought to be committed is mentally ill and that he requires hospitalization for his own welfare and protection of others. Proof beyond reasonable doubt was not required, but proof by preponderance of the evidence fell short of satisfying due process.

When a person charged with having committed a crime is found not guilty by reason of insanity, however, a State may commit that person without satisfying the *Addington* burden with respect to mental illness and dangerousness. Such a verdict, we observed in *Jones,* "establishes two facts: (i)the defendant committed an act that constitutes a criminal offense, and (ii)he committed the act because of mental illness," an illness that the defendant adequately proved in this context by a preponderance of the evidence. From these two facts, it could be properly inferred that at the time of the verdict, the defendant was still mentally ill and dangerous and hence could be committed.

We held, however, that "[t]he committed acquittee is entitled to release when he has recovered his sanity or is no longer dangerous"; *i.e.* the acquittee may be held as long as he is both mentally ill and dangerous, but no longer. We relied on *O'Connor v. Donaldson,* 422 U.S. 563 (1975), which held as a matter of due process that it was unconstitutional for a State to continue to confine a harmless, mentally ill person. Even if the initial commitment was permissible, "it could not constitutionally continue after that basis no longer existed." In the summary of our holdings in our opinion we stated that "the Constitution permits the Government, on the basis of the insanity judgment, to confine him to a mental institution until such time as he has regained his sanity or is no longer a danger to himself or society." The court below was in error in characterizing the above language from *Jones* as merely an interpretation of the pertinent statutory law in the District of Columbia and as having no constitutional significance. In this case, Louisiana does not contend that Foucha was mentally ill at the time of the trial court's hearing. Thus, the basis for holding Foucha in a psychiatric facility as an insanity acquittee has disappeared, and the State is no longer entitled to hold him on that basis.

The State, however, seeks to perpetuate Foucha's confinement . . . on the basis of his antisocial personality which, as evidenced by his conduct at the facility, the court found rendered him a danger to himself or others. There are at least three difficulties with this position. First, even if his continued confinement were constitutionally permissible, keeping Foucha against his will in a mental institution is improper absent a determination in civil commitment proceedings of current mental illness and dangerousness. In *Vitek v. Jones,* 445 U.S. 480 (1980), we held that a convicted felon serving his sentence has a liberty interest, not extinguished by his confinement as a criminal, in not being transferred to a mental institution and hence classified as mentally ill without appropriate procedures to prove that he was mentally ill. "The loss of liberty produced by an involuntary commitment is more than a loss of freedom from confinement." Due process requires that the nature of commitment bear some reasonable relation to the purpose for which the individual is committed. Here, according to the testimony given at the hearing in the trial court, Foucha is not suffering from a mental disease or illness. If he is to be held, he should not be held as a mentally ill person.

Second, if Foucha can no longer be held as an insanity acquittee in a mental hospital, he is entitled to constitutionally adequate procedures to establish the grounds for his confinement. [The Court discusses *Jackson v. Indiana,* noted at § 9.05[B][1] *supra.*]

Third, "the Due Process Clause contains a substantive component that bars certain arbitrary, wrongful government actions 'regardless of the fairness of the procedures used to implement them.'" Freedom from bodily restraint has always been at the core of the liberty protected by the Due Process Clause from arbitrary governmental action.

A State, pursuant to its police power, may of course imprison convicted criminals for the purposes of deterrence and retribution. But there are constitutional limitations on the conduct that a State may criminalize. Here, the State has no such punitive interest. As Foucha was not convicted, he may not be punished. Here, Louisiana has by reason of his acquittal exempted Foucha from criminal responsibility[.]

The State may also confine a mentally ill person if it shows "by clear and convincing evidence that the individual is mentally ill and dangerous[.]" Here, the State has not carried that burden; indeed, the State does not claim that Foucha is now mentally ill.

We have also held that in certain narrow circumstances persons who pose a danger to others or to the community may be subject to limited confinement and it is on these cases, particularly *United States v. Salerno,* [481 U.S. 739 (1987)], that the State relies in this case.

Salerno, unlike this case, involved pretrial detention. We observed in *Salerno* that the "government's interest in preventing crime by arrestees is both legitimate and compelling," and that the statute involved there was a constitutional implementation of that interest. The statute carefully limited the circumstances under which detention could be sought to those involving the most serious of crimes (crimes of violence, offenses punishable by life imprisonment or death, serious drug offenses, or certain repeat offenders), and was narrowly focused on a particularly acute problem in which the government interests are overwhelming. In addition to first demonstrating probable cause, the government was required, in a "full-blown adversary hearing," to convince a neutral decisionmaker by clear and convincing evidence that no conditions of release can reasonably assure the safety of the community or any person, *i.e.,* that the "arrestee presents an identified and articulable threat to an individual or the community." Furthermore, the duration of confinement under the Act was strictly limited. The arrestee was entitled to a prompt detention hearing and the maximum length of pretrial detention was limited by the "stringent time limitations of the Speedy Trial Act." If the arrestee were convicted, he would be confined as a criminal proved guilty; if he were acquitted, he would go free. Moreover, the Act required that detainees be housed, to the extent practicable, in a facility separate from persons awaiting or serving sentences or awaiting appeal.

Salerno does not save Louisiana's detention of insanity acquittees who are no longer mentally ill. Unlike the sharply focused scheme at issue in *Salerno,* the Louisiana scheme of confinement is not carefully limited. Under the state statute, Foucha is not now entitled to an adversary hearing at which the State must prove by clear and convincing evidence that he is demonstrably dangerous to the community. Indeed, the State need prove nothing to justify continued detention, for the statute places the burden on the detainee to prove that he is not dangerous. At the hearing which ended with Foucha's recommittal, no doctor or any other person testified positively that in his opinion Foucha would be a danger to the community, let alone gave the basis for such an opinion. There was only a description of Foucha's behavior [in the institution] and his antisocial personality, along with a refusal to certify that he would not be dangerous. When directly asked whether Foucha would be dangerous, Dr. Ritter said only "I don't think I would feel comfortable in certifying that he would not be a danger to himself or to other people." This, under the Louisiana statute, was enough to defeat Foucha's interest in physical liberty. It is not enough to defeat Foucha's liberty interest under the Constitution in being freed from indefinite confinement in a mental facility.

Furthermore, if Foucha committed criminal acts while [in the institution], such as assault, the State does not explain why its interest would not be vindicated by the ordinary criminal processes involving charge and conviction, the use of enhanced sentences for recidivists, and other permissible ways of dealing with patterns of criminal conduct. These are the normal means of dealing with persistent criminal conduct. Had they been employed against Foucha when he assaulted other inmates, there is little doubt that if then sane he could have been convicted and incarcerated in the usual way.

It was emphasized in *Salerno* that the detention we found constitutionally permissible was strictly limited in duration. Here, in contrast, the State asserts that because Foucha once committed a criminal act and now has an antisocial personality that sometimes leads to aggressive conduct, a disorder for which there is no effective treatment, he may be held indefinitely. This rationale would permit the State to hold indefinitely any other insanity acquittee not mentally ill who could be shown to have a personality disorder that may lead to criminal conduct. The same would be true of any convicted criminal, even though he has completed his prison term. It would also be only a step away from substituting confinements for dangerousness for our present system which, with only narrow exceptions and aside from permissible confinements for mental illness, incarcerates only those who are proved beyond reasonable doubt to have violated a criminal law.

III

It should be apparent from what has been said earlier in this opinion that the Louisiana statute also discriminates against Foucha in violation of the Equal Protection Clause of the Fourteenth Amendment. *Jones* established that insanity acquittees may be treated differently in some respects from those persons subject to civil commitment, but Foucha, who is not now thought to be insane, can no longer be so classified. The State nonetheless insists on holding him indefinitely because he at one time committed a criminal act and does not now prove he is not dangerous. Louisiana law, however, does not provide for similar confinement for other classes of persons who have committed criminal acts and who cannot later prove they would not be dangerous.

Criminals who have completed their prison terms, or are about to do so, are an obvious and large category of such persons. Many of them will likely suffer from the same sort of personality disorder that Foucha exhibits. However, state law does not allow for their continuing confinement based merely on dangerousness. Instead, the State controls the behavior of these similarly situated citizens by relying on other means, such as punishment, deterrence, and supervised release. Freedom from physical restraint being a fundamental right, the State must have a particularly convincing reason, which it has not put forward, for such discrimination against insanity acquittees who are no longer mentally ill.

Furthermore, in civil commitment proceedings the State must establish the grounds of insanity and dangerousness permitting confinement by clear and convincing evidence. Similarly, the State must establish insanity and dangerousness by clear and convincing evidence in order to confine an insane convict beyond his criminal sentence, when the basis for his original confinement no longer exists. However, the State now claims that it may continue to confine Foucha, who is not now considered to be mentally ill, solely because he is deemed dangerous, but without assuming the burden of proving even this ground for confinement by clear and convincing evidence. The court below gave no convincing reason why the procedural safeguards against unwarranted confinement which are guaranteed to insane persons and those who have been convicted may be denied to a sane acquittee, and the State has done no better in this Court.

For the foregoing reasons the judgment of the Louisiana Supreme Court is reversed.

So ordered.

[The concurring opinion of Justice O'Connor and the dissenting opinions of Justice Kennedy, joined by Chief Justice Rehnquist, and of Justice Thomas, joined by Chief Justice Rehnquist and Justice Scalia, are omitted.]

Notes and Questions

1. In an omitted opinion, Justice Kennedy questioned the implications of the *Foucha* Court's opinion regarding the continued use of dangerousness as a (the?) consideration in parole release decisions. Does *Foucha* call into constitutional question decisions to continue incarceration in penal institutions based on the perceived dangerousness of an individual offender? What about initial decisions to incarcerate based on perceived dangerousness? Is *Foucha* limited in any principled sense to insanity aquittees?

2. Consider the material on incapacitation at § 2.03, *supra.*

3. The conclusion that NGIs require special dispositional treatment may be based on faulty empirical perceptions about the insanity defense, the consequences of its successful invocation, and the nature of insanity acquittees. Studies indicate that the public generally assumes that the insanity defense is widely raised, usually successfully, and that NGIs are released upon

acquittal or shortly thereafter even though they are extremely dangerous. G. Melton, J. Petrila, N. Poythress, and C. Slobogin, Psychological Evaluations for the Courts 112 (1987). In fact, the defense is rarely raised. In many jurisdictions it is employed in substantially less than 1 percent of felony cases, and is successful nationally only about 25 percent of the time when raised. *Id.* at 112–13. Insanity acquittees do not, of course, enjoy quick and easy freedom. As for the perception that insanity acquittees are especially dangerous as a class, Melton *et al.* observe:

> There are no studies examining the "dangerousness" of persons found NGRI at the time of acquittal, since . . . these individuals are almost always automatically institutionalized and subjected to treatment. However, there are three studies comparing the recidivism rates of NGRI individuals who have been released after hospitalization with released felons charged with similar offenses. Two of the studies indicated that NGRI individuals as a group were slightly less likely to have recidivating members than felons as a group (although of those who did recidivate, those found NGRI repeated more often than the felons), and the third study showed the recidivism rates between the two groups to be about even. As with research comparing the recidivism rates of those who are civilly committed to those of the general population, these studies tentatively suggest that the most accurate predictor of violence is the number and nature of prior offenses, not mental illness. They also suggest that the treatment provided to those found NGRI is not particularly effective at removing criminal tendencies. What they do not support is the contention that typical released insanity acquittees are "abnormally" dangerous or that such persons should be confined longer than felons because they are more likely to recidivate than their convicted counterparts.

Id. at 114–15.

4. Because the NGI verdict results in a special disposition for the acquittee, many argue that the jury should be informed of the significance of the verdict lest they assume that the NGI acquittee (often perceived to be dangerous) will receive an outright release. Without knowledge of its consequences, the jury might improperly reject the NGI verdict out of a misplaced fear of releasing dangerous offenders back into society. For these reasons a minority of state courts require that the jury be instructed on the consequences of an NGI verdict if the defendant so requests. See, *e.g., Roberts v. State,* 335 So. 2d 285 (Fla. 1976); LaFave and Scott at 358–59. On the other hand, others argue that the jury should not be informed of the dispositional implications of successful NGI defenses because such information might distract them from the insanity issue and invite compromise verdicts. *Id.* The United States Supreme Court has held that in federal cases the jury need not be instructed as to the consequences of a finding of NGI. *Shannon v. United States,* 114 S. Ct. 2419 (1994).

5. A variety of commentators have examined the practice of treating insanity acquittees as a special class for commitment purposes. In addition to the German and Singer article excerpted at p. 836 above, see, *e.g.,* S. Brakel, J. Parry, and B. Weiner, The Mentally Disabled and the Law 725–34 (3d ed. 1985); Note, *Commitment Following an Insanity Acquittal,* 94 Harv. L. Rev. 605 (1981).

6. Given the usual consequences of a successful insanity defense, might the defense be unattractive to some defendants even though they possess valid insanity claims? Suppose the court or prosecutor seeks to pursue the "defense" over the objections of the defendant? Do the judicial and executive branches have an obligation to ensure that a "nonguilty" person is not convicted? Or should the defendant have a right to refuse a defense of insanity? See A. Singer, *The Imposition of the Insanity Defense on an Unwilling Defendant*, 41 Ohio St. L.J. 637 (1980). If the defendant does have a right to refuse the defense, could the right meaningfully be grounded on his right to be punished? See § 2.03[C][3] *supra*. Consider in this regard *United States v. Wright*, 627 F.2d 1300, 1302, 1305 (D.C. Cir. 1980):

> Between 11:30 and 11:45 A.M. on the day of the offense, appellant [Beachey Wright] entered the United States Capitol building, and began "walking around observing the tourists, taking in the building and the artworks and exhibits that were on display." Wright then was "inspired" by the Holy Spirit to commit a symbolic act, intended to warn people of God's impending judgment that the nation "has deviated from his original designs." Wright saw a metal stanchion, used with a cordon to rope off displays. He also noticed a replica of the Capitol building behind a glass display case. He "tossed" the stanchion at the model and the glass case, causing both to break. A police officer on duty heard the crash and arrested Wright.

* * *

> The appellant, Beachey Wright testified that he had been educated in a private Seventh Day Adventists grammar school. He described religious experiences starting while he was stationed with the army in Vietnam. After an honorable discharge, he attended college but left in 1971 because "God had told me to go and prophesy" about God's plan to destroy the government. He traveled to Washington, D.C. where he burned American flags in public places. He returned to college, and then traveled again to Washington to perform his prophetic mission. His activities at that time led to an indictment, and ultimately commitment to St. Elizabeth's Hospital. Wright said that after visiting religious colleges in the South, he arrived in California, where he worked as a construction worker. Then he left for Washington once more to fulfill his mission—and performed the acts giving rise to the instant indictment.

> Wright told the court that he declined to raise the insanity defense not for fear of stigma: "I have a stigma of being an ex-mental patient, as it is." . . . Instead, Wright said he rejected the defense because

>> The whole idea of the notion that I am suffering from some kind of mental illness is absurd to me. I know I express a great amount of religious conviction, more so than the ordinary person, but that is not in itself, as far as I am concerned, an indication of mental illness. I cannot accept a mental insanity plea because it would be a compromise of my faith and the principles that have motivated me up to this point. It would discredit everything that I represent in coming here.

[c] The Rationale of the Defense of Insanity

II Bentham, *Theory of Legislation*

122-23 (1914)

When Punishment Ought Not to Be Inflicted

The cases in which punishment should not be inflicted may be reduced to four heads: (I.) When such punishment would be groundless; (II.) when it would be inefficacious; (III.) when it would be superfluous; and (IV.) when it would be too expensive.

* * *

II. INEFFICACIOUS PUNISHMENTS.—I describe as inefficacious such punishments as cannot produce any effect on the will, and, consequently, cannot serve to prevent the commission of like acts.

Punishments are inefficacious when directed against persons who had no power or opportunity of acquainting themselves with the particular law; or who have acted unintentionally; or who have done the mischief innocently under a mistaken supposition or some irresistible compulsion. Children, idiots, and madmen, although they may, up to a certain point, be controlled by rewards and threats, have not a sufficiently clear conception of the future to be restrained by punishments to be inflicted at some distant date: so far as they are concerned, penal laws will, therefore, be inefficacious.

Brandt, *A Utilitarian Theory of Excuses*

78 Phil.Rev. 337 (1969).

[T]he rule-utilitarian theory of right and wrong leads naturally to a theory of excuses. . . . [T]he rule-utilitarian holds that the right action is the one that would not be prohibited by the moral code the currency of which in the agent's society would (roughly) maximize utility. But which moral code will maximize utility is partly a function of the system of excuses it contains—just as the utility of a legal system is partly a function of its system of legal excuses. For when we are seeking to determine the utility of a certain moral system, we are not merely inquiring what would be the advantage in a certain kind of *prohibited behavior not occurring;* we are trying to answer a much more complex question about the gains and losses partly from the decrease of the prohibited behavior, but also from the very existence of the moral system—the costs of teaching it, the psychological burden and risks of living with it, and so on. Therefore, different sets of excuses will be features defining different moral systems, some of which will have more utility than others just on this account. So if a rule-utilitarian affirms that an act is objectively right if it would be permitted by the moral code which will have the best consequences, then, since the best moral system will also contain a system of excuses, the utilitarian will presumably say that behavior in some way out of line *should be excused* if its excuse would be provided for in the total moral system which would have the best consequences. Of course, there are two types of excuse which the rule-utilitarian presumably can and should recognize. First, total excuses, exculpations: an action is totally excused if the moral system with best consequences would not condemn it at all. Second, mitigating excuses: an action has a mitigating excuse if, in view of some feature, the moral system with best consequences would condemn it *less severely* than where this feature is not present.

To see the reasoning more clearly, let us pursue a bit further the analogy with the law. Let us suppose a utilitarian is considering what should be the penalties affixed to the act of homicide. He will follow Bentham in deciding such matters by applying the principle of marginal utility to punishment, or what might be called the principle of "least necessary punishment." For, since punishment is an evil, the utilitarian will want to inflict it only in order to avoid a greater cost. In the case of homicide the utilitarian will insist on having some penalty for the offense; otherwise, everyone is invited to indulge in homicide when it suits his ends. The utilitarian will consider successively more severe penalties, and each time he will count the loss of the punishment against the predicted gain, primarily in crime prevention because of the threat of punishment. When he arrives at a degree of severity such that the utility of the crime prevention just equals the disutility to society of the punishment itself, he will decide that the punishment is just severe enough. In making the calculations, the utilitarian will take into account how the utility of the system is affected if certain defenses (such as insanity) are allowed and if certain circumstances are regarded as mitigating (different degrees of homicide recognized). Whether such defenses or mitigations are allowed will make a great deal of difference to the utility of the system as a whole. Obviously, if every homicide were a capital offense, and no defenses of mistake or accident or insanity were admitted, the total effect would be intolerable; anyone who drove a motorcar would be continuously under the shadow of a threat to life which no voluntary act of his could remove. Of course, there are also disadvantages in having such defenses, since their existence is something of an invitation to crime, in that a person may hope that skillful maneuvering and a clever lawyer may prevent a deliberate crime from being punished. Nevertheless, it seems clear that the utilitarian will conclude that the best system of criminal law will combine a fairly heavy penalty for homicide with a system of exculpations and mitigations for certain circumstances. This system will yield a high degree of deterrence combined with lower social costs, as compared with any system which had no provision for excuses.

GOLDSTEIN AND KATZ, ABOLISH THE "INSANITY DEFENSE"—WHY NOT?

72 Yale L.J. 853, 854, 864-66, 868 (1963)

Criminal responsibility results when each element of crime charged against an accused has been established beyond a reasonable doubt. Only then is the state authorized to exercise its power to impose certain specified sanctions against the offender. "Insanity at the time of the offense," we are told, relieves the offending actor of criminal responsibility. This may mean either that "insanity" is to serve as *evidence* which precludes establishing a crime by leaving in doubt some material element of an offense, or that "insanity" is to serve as a *defense* to a crime, even though each of its elements can be established beyond doubt, in order to protect a preferred value threatened by the imposition of an authorized sanction.

* * *

In our efforts to understand the suggested relationship between "insanity" and *"mens rea"* there emerges a purpose for the "insanity defense" which, though there to be seen, has remained of extremely low visibility. That purpose seems to be obscured because thinking about such a relationship has generally been blocked by unquestioning and disarming references to our collective conscience and our religious and moral traditions. Assuming the existence of the suggested relationship between "insanity" and *"mens rea,"* the defense is not to absolve of criminal responsibility "sick" persons who would otherwise be subject to criminal sanction. Rather, its real function is to authorize the state to hold those "who must be found not to possess the guilty mind *mens rea,*" even though the criminal law demands that no person be held criminally responsible if doubt is cast on any material element of the offense charged. . . . .

[T]he insanity defense is not designed, as is the defense of self-defense, to define an exception to criminal liability, but rather to define for sanction an exception from among those who would be free of liability. It is as if the insanity defense were prompted by an affirmative answer to the silently posed question: "Does *mens rea* or any essential element of an offense exclude from liability a group of persons whom the community wishes to restrain?" If the suggested relationship between *mens rea* and "insanity" means that "insanity" precludes proof beyond doubt of *mens rea* then the "defense" is designed to authorize the holding of persons who have committed no crime. So conceived, the problem really facing the criminal process has been how to obtain authority to sanction the "insane" who would be excluded from liability by an overall application of the general principles of the criminal law.

Furthermore, even if the relationship between insanity and *"mens rea"* is rejected, this same purpose re-emerges when we try to understand why the consequence of this defense, unlike other defenses, is restraint, not release. Even though each of the elements of an offense may be established, release will follow acquittal or dismissal if, for example, entrapment, self-defense, or the statute of limitations are successfully pleaded. Assuming, then, that all elements of an offense are to be established before the insanity defense becomes operative, the question remains: "Why restrain rather than release?" Restraint cannot be attributed to potential "dangerousness" associated with the crime charged, no matter how serious, for that kind of "dangerousness" is characteristic of defendants whose defenses prevail. The crucial variable leading to restraint seems to be the "insanity at the time of the offense," *i.e.,* a fear of danger seen in the combination of "mental sickness" and "crime." . . . Thus the insanity defense is not a defense, it is a device for triggering indeterminate restraint.

Kadish, Decline of Innocence

26 Cambridge L.J. 273-75 (1968)

The criminal law constitutes a description of harms which a society seeks to discourage with the threat of criminal punishment for those who commit those harms. At the same time the criminal law comprises an elaborate body of qualifications to these prohibitions and threats. It used to be common, and it still is not unknown, to express all of these qualifications to liability in terms of the requirement of *mens rea*. This is the thought behind the classic maxim, "*Actus non facit reum, nisi mens sit rea.*" Or in Blackstone's translation, "An unwarrantable act without a vicious will is no crime at all." The vicious will was the *mens rea*. Reduced to its essence it referred to the choice to do a blameworthy act. The requirement of *mens rea* was rationalized on the common sense view of justice that blame and punishment were inappropriate and unjust in the absence of that choice.

It is more helpful (and also more usual today) to speak more discriminatingly of the various classes of circumstances in which criminal liability is qualified by the requirement of blameworthiness. Putting aside the circumstances of justification and excuse (they are relevant but not central to the controversy) there are two principal categories of *mens rea* which should be distinguished.

The *first* category we can call *mens rea* in its special sense. In this special sense *mens rea* refers only to the mental state which is required by the definition of the offense to accompany the act which produces or threatens the harm. An attempt to commit a crime consists of an act which comes close to its commission done *with the purpose that the crime be committed*. Unlawful assembly is joining with a group in a public place *with intent to commit unlawful acts*. Larceny consists of the appropriation of another's property *knowing* it is not your own with intent to deprive the owner or possessor of it permanently. Receiving stolen goods is a crime when one receives those goods *knowing they are stolen*. Manslaughter is the killing of another by an act done with *awareness* of a substantial and unjustifiable risk of doing so.

That the absence of the *mens rea* in this special sense of the required mental state precludes liability in all of these cases is of course the merest tautology. This is the way these crimes are defined. But it is important to see that they are so defined because the special *mens rea* element is crucial to the description of the conduct we want to make criminal. And description is crucial in so far as it is regarded as important to exclude from the definition of criminality what we do not want to punish as criminal. To revert to the examples just given, it would not be regarded as appropriate to make criminal the taking of another's property where the taker believed honestly that he was taking his own property. Neither would it make sense to make a person guilty of receiving stolen goods where he neither knew nor had occasion to know that the goods were stolen. And surely we should see nothing criminal in joining a group in a public place, apart from the intent to commit unlawful acts.

The *second* category of *mens rea* qualifications to liability is that of legal responsibility, which includes the familiar defenses of legal insanity and infancy. These qualifications differ in several particulars from the *mens rea* qualifications of the first category. In requiring *mens rea* in the first, special, sense the law is saying that it does not hold a person where he has shown himself by his conduct, judged in terms of its totality, including his mental state, to be no different than the rest of us, or not different enough to justify the criminal sanction. In requiring *mens rea* in the sense of legal responsibility, the law absolves a person precisely because his deficiencies of temperament, personality or maturity distinguish him so utterly from the rest of us to whom the law's threats are addressed that we do not expect him to comply.

Morse, Excusing the Crazy: The Insanity Defense Reconsidered

58 S. Cal. L. Rev. 777, 782-83, 788 (1985)

The insanity defense is rooted in moral principles of excuse that are accepted in both ordinary human interaction and criminal law. Our intuition is that minimal rationality (a cognitive capacity) and minimal self-control or lack of compulsion (a volitional capacity) are the essential preconditions for responsibility. Young children are not considered responsible for the harms they cause precisely because they lack these capacities. Similarly, adults who cause harm while terrifically distraught because of a personal tragedy, for instance, will typically be thought less responsible and culpable for the harm than if they had been normally rational and in control. Aristotle recognized these fundamental requirements for responsibility by noting that persons may be less blameworthy for actions committed under the influence of mistake (a cognitive problem) or compulsion (a so-called volitional problem).

Criminal law defenses that focus on the moral attributes of the defendant are based on these same intuitions and principles. Even if the defendant's conduct fulfills the usual requirements for *prima facie* guilt—that is, act, mental state, causation, result—the defendant will be found not guilty, not culpable, if the acts committed were the products of cognitive (*e.g.,* infancy) or volitional (*e.g.,* duress) circumstances that were not under the defendant's control. These defenses are considered relevant at the time of guilt determination as well as at the time of sentencing. It would be indeed illogical in a criminal justice system based partly on desert to hold that a defendant with a valid claim of duress is culpable (because he or she intended to do the compelled act), but then to decide to release the defendant because he or she does not deserve punishment. To convict a person with a meritorious defense would offend our conception of the relationship between legal guilt and blameworthiness. A person acting under duress is not culpable, although it is unfortunate that a prohibited act has been committed.

In sum, the moral basis of the insanity defense is that there is no just punishment without desert and no desert without responsibility. Responsibility is, in turn, based on minimal cognitive and volitional competence. Thus, an actor who lacks such competence is not responsible, does not deserve punishment, and cannot justly be punished.

* * *

The insanity defense issue is whether in some cases extreme craziness (involved in the defendant's offensive conduct) so compromises the defendant's rationality or creates such compulsion that it would be unjust to hold the defendant responsible.

KADISH, *EXCUSING CRIME*

75 Cal. L. Rev. 257, 278-81 (1987)

The modern tests of legal insanity are varied and controversial, but they all rest on the view that the claim of incapacity to comply with the law because of defects of understanding or self-control is an excuse only if it is the result of a mental disease. Here, then, it is precisely the individual's personal incapacities that serve as the basis of the excuse, whereas, in other cases, saving cases of physical and physiological compulsion, the law declines to permit individualized inquiries into the capacities of the defendant. Why should the presence of mental disease make all this difference?

One answer is a wholly practical one. We cannot allow personal incapacity as an excuse generally without unduly compromising the deterrent effectiveness of the law. Proof would be too speculative and uncertain, acquittals would be invited based on the jury's subjective attitudes toward the defendant, there would be too great a chance of erroneous acquittals, and less incentive would be given potential violators to make every effort to comply. Narrowing the excuse to those who can be identified, through medical testimony, as having a mental disease helps to meet these practical concerns. There is support for this explanation in the efforts from time to time (and certainly in these times) to limit or abolish the defense, precisely on the ground that the requirement of a mental disease is inadequate to meet these concerns.

Without denying that this practical explanation plays a part, I suggest it is not the heart of the matter. The explanation seems to accept that the reason for disallowing an unqualified defense that the defendant could not understand or control his conduct is wholly a matter of expediency. But neither in moral judgments nor in legal ones do we ask of a person who wrongs another whether he could have helped choosing to do so. Being responsible for our characters means that we are responsible for our choices, even if in some sense they have their causes, like any other events, in the world.

What, then, is different about a person whose disabilities result from mental disease? The answer, I believe, is that the concept of mental disease serves to identify so complete a breakdown of the normal human capacities of judgment and practical reason that the afflicted person cannot fairly be held liable. That concept, it should be emphasized, is not synonymous with the varieties of mental illness identified for therapeutic purposes. Categories developed with regard to whether and how a person can be helped by psychiatry are not designed to determine whether a person may be justly punished. They have some evidentiary relevance to the questions of judgment and moral responsibility which are the law's concern, but that is all.

Though the prevailing tests of legal insanity speak in one way or another of inability of the defendant, because of mental disease, to know the nature of wrongfulness of his action or (sometimes) to choose to comply with the law, it is apparent that "know" and "choose" in these tests mean more than what those terms signify in casual discourse. Many defendants acquitted on grounds of legal insanity, particularly those with psychoses, "knew" what they were doing and "meant" to do it in a literal sense.

Consider the facts of a famous California case, *People v. Wolff* [61 Cal. 2d 795, 394 P.2d 959, 40 Cal. Rptr. 271 (1964)]: A schizophrenic teenager, after previous failed attempts, killed his mother with an axe because he saw her as an obstacle to fulfilling his bizarre sexual fantasies. He kept a list of seven girls he had not met whom he planned to chloroform and kidnap and bring back to his home, where he would rape them and photograph them nude. In such a case, surely the defendant knows well enough what he is doing and acts with deliberate choice. But he may nonetheless be excused if his disease of the mind has so far impaired his rationality that he has ceased to be a moral agent. . . .

Seen in this way, it is apparent why the excuse of legal insanity is fundamental. No blaming system would be coherent if it imposed blame without regard to moral agency. We may become angry with an object or an animal that thwarts us, but we can't blame it.

Of course, being beyond the reach of moral responsibility, not being a moral agent, is not the same as being nonhuman. The acts of insane people are usually ambiguous between deliberate actions and pointless, unreasoned behavior; they are not mere events, like rocks falling. Insane people are *just* beyond responsibility, and that is why they are so disturbing. Nevertheless, blaming them commits an anomaly (we would say an "injustice" as applied to people) similar to that entailed in blaming a rock for falling or a dog for barking.

This, then, explains the distinctive and fundamental character of the defense of legal insanity. . . .

MOORE, CAUSATION AND THE EXCUSES

73 Cal. L. Rev. 1091, 1137-39 (1985)

It is not because crazy people are caused to do what they do that they are excused; rather, crazy people are excused because they are crazy. Mental illness is directly relevant to responsibility in a way that other illnesses that may also cause crime, such as blindness, deafness, stomach cramps, and heart conditions, are not. Insanity betokens a difference so fundamental that we deny moral agency to those afflicted with it. The insane, like young infants, lack one of the essential attributes of personhood—rationality. For this reason, human beings who are insane are no more the proper subjects of moral evaluation than are young infants, animals, or even stones. Only beings who, like most of us, are fairly good practical reasoners can be the subjects of moral norms.

. . . It is not because their mental disease causes the insane to commit crimes that we excuse them, no more than it is because an infant's lack of rationality causes him to do bad that we excuse him. Rather, in both cases, we excuse because the actors lack the status of moral agents. Although we may colloquially attribute particular actions to their insanity, we do not mean that they are to be excused because of some supposed causal relation. We mean that they cannot fairly be blamed because *in general* they lack our rational capacities.

Doctrinal support for this view of legal insanity is admittedly scarcer than one might hope. The pre-*M'Naghten* test, for one, was consistent with this view. According to that test, . . . the accused was not legally insane if he could tell the difference between right and wrong. This capacity was chosen as the mark of sufficient mental maturity that an offender could be held responsible. The test had been adopted from the test for responsibility for children, which as early as the fourteenth century drew the line of accountability at the ability to know of good and evil. That language was drawn from the passage in the Book of Genesis in which God likens humans to God once they have come to know of good and evil. Insofar as the law asked whether a person knew right from wrong, it was asking whether he was sufficiently like us to be a moral agent and thus responsible for his acts.

When the *M'Naghten* test was adopted in 1843, however, this ancient wisdom was forgotten. The test measuring moral agency was supplanted by the language of mistake: only if the accused did not know the nature and quality of the particular act he did, or he did not know that it was wrong, was he to be excused. *M'Naghten* transformed the insanity defense into a version of the mistake excuses.

All the other tests for insanity repeated this tendency. Rather than trying to determine when a being is enough like us to be considered a moral agent, courts have officially treated insanity as a true excuse rather than a status excuse.* The status conception of the excuse, however, refuses to die. Jurors refuse to convict seriously deranged people even if these people are sane by the *M'Naghten* test or any other test, and jurors convict less seriously deranged individuals even if these people quite literally satisfy the terms of the applicable test. As the Royal Commission on Capital Punishment observed about English juries: "However much you charge a jury as to the *M'Naghten* Rules or any other test, the question they would put to themselves when they retire is—"Is this man mad or not?" Psychiatrists serving as expert witnesses often do the same thing. In New Hampshire, for example, where an accused is excused only if his act was the "product" of "mental illness," psychiatrists at the state hospital have given their own meaning to the phrase "mental illness" when they testify. This meaning is not the expansive one they use

---

* [Earlier in his paper, Professor Moore distinguished "true excuses" (defenses like the mistake and compulsion excuses that explain the defendant's particular actions in light of the events or states at the time of the action) from "status excuses" (defenses that make a claim about the accused's general status, not his state of mind at the time he acted).—Eds.]

in clinical practice, but rather the more restrictive meaning captured by the popular labels "mad" or "crazy." More generally, psychiatrists testifying under any test typically assume that "mental illness," "disease of the mind," "abnormality of mind," and like phrases appearing in the various insanity tests should be taken to mean, roughly, the extreme psychoses.

Thus, the "unofficial" version of the insanity test—the test as actually applied by psychiatrists and jurors—restricts the excuse of legal insanity to those who are so lacking in rationality that they are popularly considered crazy. This is because those psychiatrists and jurors have glimpsed a moral truth: the very status of being crazy precludes responsibility. Seeking some hidden cause of the accused's criminal behavior is, accordingly, simply beside the point.

NOTES AND QUESTIONS

1. The Bentham, Brandt, and Goldstein/Katz selections offer utilitarian explanations for the existence of the insanity defense. Can the defense be accounted for solely in utilitarian terms?

2. How convincing is the Goldstein/Katz conclusion that insanity is not a defense at all? Do these authors forget Kadish's distinction between *"mens rea* in its special sense" and *"mens rea* in the sense of legal responsibility"? Are Goldstein and Katz correct in concluding that criminally insane people routinely lack the specific *mens rea* element(s) of the crime? Consider the following observations from Morse, *Undiminished Confusion in Diminished Capacity,* 75 J. Crim. L. & Criminology 1, 40–42 (1984):

> *[M]ens rea,* properly understood, is rarely negated by mental abnormality, no matter how severe the disorder or defect. This is not a point I can prove empirically with rigor, but experience with cases at the trial level, readings of hundreds of appellate . . . cases, and my years of experience as a practicing mental health clinician have convinced me of its truth. From all that experience, I can find only one case in which *mens rea* was truly negated, and even that case gives me substantial pause because I fear the defendant was a clever malingerer. . . . Craziness seems to affect impulses, controls, and motivations for actions, but it does not stop persons from intending to do what they do or from narrowly knowing factually what they are doing. For instance, a person who kills because he feels totally controlled by an influencing machine operated by hostile forces may ultimately be legally insane, but surely he intends to kill his victims. It is no accident that he kills them; it is what he means to do. Absurd claims about mental disorder negating *mens rea* can only be maintained by blinking both the general truth that this rarely occurs and the specific truth presented by the utterly contradictory facts of almost all individual cases.

* * *

Much as mental disorder virtually never negates *mens rea* in fact, it also seldom negates the capacity to form it. A *mens rea* is a relatively simple mental state; it requires little cognitive capacity to intend to do something or to know legally relevant facts, such as that the car one is driving across the border contains contraband in a hidden compartment. A mentally abnormal person may not form a requisite intent or have the required knowledge, but it will rarely be because he lacked the capacity to form the *mens rea*. . . .

3. How do the Morse, Kadish, and Moore theories differ from the Bentham, Brandt, and Goldstein/Katz views?

4. Applying Moore's distinction between true excuses and status excuses, how would you characterize Morse's position? Does his Aristotelian account of responsibility in terms of concepts of mistake and compulsion commit him to the true excuse theory? Does Kadish give a true excuse or status excuse explanation? Is Moore's conceptualization of insanity as a status excuse conceptually sound? What about the case of an insane person who murders for irrational reasons one day and robs for rational reasons the next? Would Moore's theory require excusing the robbery as well as the murder? Conversely, what of the otherwise normal person whose ability to reason practically is seriously deficient for a short period of time during which he commits a crime? Is such person not a candidate for an insanity defense on Moore's view because he lacks the general status of a deficient practical reasoner? See Slobogin, *A Rational Approach to Responsibility,* 83 Mich. L. Rev. 820, 832–33 (1985).

What practical difference does it make whether insanity is a true excuse or status excuse? Fletcher, 836:

> There is a fundamental conceptual and functional difference between treating the insane as a class exempt from criminal punishment and treating insanity as an excuse for a particular act. The first trades on the analogy between insanity and infancy; the second, on the analogy between insanity and duress. The distinction between these two conceptions of insanity has profound implications. If insanity is an excuse, then it comes to bear on liability only if it is first established that the act of the accused is wrongful. If the allegedly insane defendant killed another in a barroom brawl, a good defense or even a reasonable doubt of self-defense should preclude consideration of insanity. If, in contrast, insanity is a condition akin to infancy, it would be appropriate to raise the issue at the very outset of the case. The claim of insanity would function as a challenge to the criminal jurisdiction of the court. A determination of insanity would justify the court's assuming an administrative role and ordering civil commitment. Most observers would probably agree that insanity is a subsidiary issue, appropriately considered only as excuse to a wrongful act. But those who draw the analogy between insanity and infancy may have a different view.

For further discussion of the true excuse versus status excuse views of insanity, compare H. Fingarette and A. Hesse, Mental Disability and Criminal Responsibility 1–43 (1979), with R. Gerber, The Insanity Defense 71–75 (1984).

5. The scholarly literature on the rationale of the insanity defense is vast. See, *e.g.,* M. Moore, Law and Psychiatry (1984); M. Perlin, The Jurisprudence of the Insanity Defense (1994); R. Schopp, Automatism, Insanity and the

Psychology of Criminal Responsibility (1991). For an extensive bibliography of the literature, see M. Perlin, Law and Mental Disability 781–838 (1994).

[d] Insanity and Automatism

FULCHER v. STATE

Supreme Court of Wyoming

633 P.2d 142 (1981)

Before ROSE, C. J., and RAPER, THOMAS, ROONEY and BROWN, JJ.

BROWN, Justice. Appellant-defendant was found guilty of aggravated assault without dangerous weapon in violation of Section 6-4-506(a), W.S. 1977, by the district court sitting without a jury. While appellant characterizes the issues on appeal differently, we believe the issues to be:

(1) Is it necessary for a defendant to plead "not guilty by reason of mental illness or deficiency" before evidence of unconsciousness can be presented?

(2) Was there sufficient evidence to sustain appellant's conviction?

We will affirm.

On November 17, 1979, the appellant consumed seven or eight shots of whiskey over a period of four hours in a Torrington bar, and had previously had a drink at home.

Appellant claims he got in a fight in the bar restroom, then left the bar to find a friend. According to his testimony, the last thing he remembers until awakening in jail, is going out of the door at the bar.

Appellant and his friend were found lying in the alley behind the bar by a police officer who noted abrasions on their fists and faces. Appellant and his friend swore, were uncooperative, and combative. They were subsequently booked for public intoxication and disturbing the peace. During booking appellant continued to swear, and said he and his friend were jumped by a "bunch of Mexicans." Although his speech was slurred, he was able to verbally count his money, roughly $500 to $600 in increments of $20, and was able to walk to his cell without assistance.

Appellant was placed in a cell with one Martin Hernandez who was lying unconscious on the floor of the cell. After the jailer left the cell, he heard something that sounded like someone being kicked. He ran back to the cell and saw appellant standing by Hernandez. When the jailer started to leave again, the kicking sound resumed, and he observed appellant kicking and stomping on Hernandez's head. Appellant told the officer Hernandez had fallen out of bed. Hernandez was bleeding profusely and was taken to the hospital for some 52 stitches in his head and mouth. He had lost two or three teeth as a result of the kicking. . . .

At his first arraignment in district court, appellant first entered a plea of "not guilty by reason of temporary mental illness." Upon being advised by the trial judge that he would have to be committed for examination pursuant to [state statute] he withdrew that plea and entered a plea of not guilty.

In preparation for trial, appellant was examined by Dr. Breck LeBegue, a forensic psychiatrist. The doctor reviewed the police report and conducted a number of tests.

At the trial Dr. LeBegue testified that in his expert medical opinion appellant suffered brain injury and was in a state of traumatic automatism at the time of his attack on Hernandez. Dr. LeBegue defined traumatic automatism as the state of mind in which a person does not have conscious and willful control over his actions, and lacks the ability to be aware of and to perceive his external environment. Dr. LeBegue further testified that another possible symptom is an inability to remember what occurred while in a state of traumatic automatism. . . .

We hold that the trial court properly received and considered evidence of unconsciousness absent a plea of "not guilty by reason of mental illness or deficiency."

The defense of unconsciousness perhaps should be more precisely denominated as the defense of automatism. Automatism is the state of a person who, though capable of action, is not conscious of what he is doing. While in an automatistic state, an individual performs complex actions without an exercise of will. Because these actions are performed in a state of unconsciousness, they are involuntary. Automatistic behavior may be followed by complete or partial inability to recall the actions performed while unconscious. Thus, a person who acts automatically does so without intent, exercise of free will, or knowledge of the act.

Automatism may be caused by an abnormal condition of the mind—capable of being designated a mental illness or deficiency. Automatism may also be manifest in a person with a perfectly healthy mind. In this opinion we are only concerned with the defense of automatism occurring in a person with a healthy mind. To further narrow the issue to be decided in this case, we are concerned with alleged automatism caused by concussion.

The defense of automatism, while not an entirely new development in the criminal law, has been discussed in relatively few decisions by American appellate courts, most of these being in California where the defense is statutory. Some courts have held that insanity and automatism are separate and distinct defenses, and that evidence of automatism may be presented under a plea of not guilty. Some states have made this distinction by statute. In other states the distinction is made by case law. . . .

> The defenses of insanity and unconsciousness are not the same in nature, for unconsciousness at the time of the allege criminal act need not be the result of a disease or defect of the mind. As a consequence, the two defenses are not the same in effect, for a defendant found not guilty by reason of unconsciousness, as distinct from insanity, is not subject to commitment to a hospital for the mentally ill.

State v. Caddell, 287 N.C. 266, 215 S.E.2d 348, 360 (1975).

The principal reason for making a distinction between the defense of unconsciousness and insanity is that the consequences which follow an acquittal will differ. The defense of unconsciousness is usually a complete defense.... That is, there are no follow-up consequences after an acquittal; all action against a defendant is concluded.

However, in the case of a finding of not guilty by reason of insanity, the defendant is ordinarily committed to a mental institution.

* * *

In some states the commitment is automatic after a finding of not guilty by reason of insanity. In Wyoming the trial judge may commit a defendant based on evidence produced at trial or the commitment may be by separate proceedings.

The mental illness or deficiency plea does not adequately cover automatic behavior. Unless the plea of automatism, separate and apart from the plea of mental illness or deficiency is allowed, certain anomalies will result. For example, if the court determines that the automatistic defendant is sane, but refuses to recognize automatism, the defendant has no defense to the crime with which he is charged. If found guilty, he faces a prison term. The rehabilitative value of imprisonment for the automatistic offender who has committed the offense unconsciously is nonexistent. The cause of the act was an uncontrollable physical disorder that may never recur and is not a moral deficiency.

If, however, the court treats automatism as insanity and then determines that the defendant is insane, he will be found not guilty. He then will be committed to a mental institution for an indefinite period. The commitment of an automatistic individual to a mental institution for rehabilitation has absolutely no value. Mental hospitals generally treat people with psychiatric or psychological problems. This form of treatment is not suited to unconscious behavior resulting from a bump on the head.

It may be argued that evidence of unconsciousness cannot be received unless a plea of not guilty by reason of mental illness or deficiency is made.... We believe this approach to be illogical.

... Insanity is incapacity from disease of the mind, to know the nature and quality of one's act or to distinguish between right and wrong in relation thereto. In contrast, a person who is completely unconscious when he commits an act otherwise punishable as a crime cannot know the nature and quality thereof or whether it is right or wrong....

It does not seem that the definition of "mental deficiency" in § 7-11-301(a)(iii),[7] W.S. 1977, which includes "brain damage," encompasses simple brain trauma with no permanent after effects. It is our view that the "brain damage" contemplated in the statute is some serious and irreversible condition having an impact upon the ability of the person to function. It is undoubtedly something far more significant than a temporary and transitory condition. The two defenses are merged, in effect, if a plea of "not guilty by reason of mental illness or deficiency" is a prerequisite for using the defense of unconsciousness....

---

[7] Section 7-11-301(a)(iii): "—Mental deficiency' means a defect attributable to mental retardation, brain damage and learning disabilities." [The statute defines mental deficiency for insanity defense purposes as well as for the issues of competency to stand trial and to be punished.—Eds.]

Although courts hold that unconsciousness and insanity are separate and distinct defenses, there has been some uncertainty concerning the burden of proof. We believe the better rule to be that stated in *State v. Caddell, supra,* 215 S.E.2d at 363:

> We now hold that, under the law of this state, unconsciousness, or automatism, is a complete defense to the criminal charge, separate and apart from the defense of insanity; that *it is an affirmative defense: and that the burden rests upon the defendant to establish this defense, unless it arises out of the State's own evidence,* to the satisfaction of the jury. (Emphasis added.)

The rationale for this rule is that the defendant is the only person who knows his actual state of consciousness. *Hill v. Baxter,* 1 All E.R. 193 (1958), 1 Q.B. 277.

Our ruling on the facts of this case is that the defense of unconsciousness resulting from a concussion with no permanent brain damage is an affirmative defense and is a defense separate from the defense of not guilty by reason of mental illness or deficiency.

The appellant's conviction must, nevertheless, be affirmed. Dr. LeBegue was unable to state positively whether or not appellant had the requisite mental state for aggravated assault. He could not state that the character of the act was devoid of criminal intent because of the mind alteration. The presumption of mental competency was never overcome by appellant and the evidence presented formed a reasonable basis on which the trial judge could find and did find that the State had met the required burden of proof. . . .

Affirmed.

[In a concurring opinion, Justice Raper, joined by Justice Rooney, argued that because appellant's defense was based on evidence of "brain damage," a form of "mental deficiency" under § 7-11-301(a)(iii), the legislature intended the insanity defense to be the sole guilt stage theory under which the evidence could be admitted.]

NOTES AND QUESTIONS

1. Is the *Fulcher* court's assessment of the burden of proof issue unconstitutional in light of the Supreme Court case law discussed at § 9.04 [B], *supra?*

2. The relationship between insanity and automatism has been explored in a series of English decisions. In *Regina v. Charlson* [1955], 1 All E.R. 859, the defendant was acquitted of assaulting his son after the trial court instructed the jury on the automatism theory, permitting them to consider defendant's evidence that he suffered from a cerebral tumor which caused outbursts of impulsive violence over which he had no control. The defendant in *Charlson* did not plead insanity and evidence was offered that he was not suffering from mental disease. On the other hand, in *Regina v. Kemp* [1957], 1 Q.B. 399, the trial court refused to instruct on automatism and limited defendant to an insanity instruction after he had introduced evidence establishing that he had not known what he was doing at the time he assaulted

his wife with a hammer because he suffered from arteriosclerosis. The trial court's ruling that hardening of the arteries is a "disease of the mind" under *M'Naghten* was based largely on the policy concern that people who commit crimes of violence, even though not responsible for their actions because of a lingering health problem, ought not be allowed an outright acquittal because they pose an ongoing danger. The problem was addressed by the House of Lords in *Bratty v. Attorney General for Northern Ireland* [1961], 3 All E.R. 523, which held that psychomotor epilepsy was a "disease of the mind" and that only a defense of insanity (and not of automatism) would be available. Lord Denning defined "disease of the mind" as "any mental disorder which has manifested itself in violence and is prone to recur." *Bratty* suggested, therefore, that *some* automatism might be seen as non-insane, such as that caused by an external factor like a blow to the head. Finally, in *Regina v. Quick* [1973], Q.B. 910, the Court of Appeal held that a transitory malfunctioning of the mind "externally" caused by hypoglycemia was not a "disease of the mind" and thus might trigger an outright acquittal under the automatism defense. The *Quick* court noted, however, that the defense would be unavailing to defendants who themselves are responsible for episodes of hypoglycemia by culpably failing to take an "antidote" such as a lump of sugar.

[e] Burden of Proof and the Insanity Defense

Because the defendant is presumed to be sane, the initial burden of coming forward with evidence of insanity is invariably placed upon the defendant. Many jurisdictions also require the defendant to notify the prosecution in advance of the trial of an intended defense of insanity and to submit to psychiatric examination by court-appointed experts. Failure to comply with such pretrial conditions generally results in denial of a defense of insanity at trial.

Assuming the defendant has satisfied any pretrial requirements, he must then satisfy the requirement of coming forward with evidence. The standards for meeting this burden vary, ranging from a minimal "some evidence" test in some jurisdictions to a more stringent "reasonable doubt of sanity" test in others. For a full discussion, see Eule, *The Presumption of Sanity: Bursting the Bubble,* 25 U.C.L.A. L. Rev. 637 (1978).

Once the initial burden is met, it must be determined which party has the burden of persuasion. In about half the states, the prosecution must then proceed to prove responsibility beyond a reasonable doubt. The remainder of the jurisdictions place the burden of persuasion on the defendant, generally requiring proof of insanity by a preponderance of the evidence. Recent legislation has placed upon defendants in the federal system the burden of proving insanity by "clear and convincing evidence." See 18 U.S.C. § 20, note 8 following *Johnson,* § 9.05[B][3][a], *supra.*

As for the constitutionality of placing the burden of persuasion on the defendant, the Supreme Court has apparently given its blessing. In Leland v. Oregon, 343 U.S. 790 (1942), the Court upheld a since-repealed Oregon statute that required defendants to prove their insanity beyond a reasonable doubt. The issue again arose subsequent to the Court's decisions in *In re Winship,* 397 U.S. 358 (1970), and *Mullaney v. Wilber,* 421 U.S. 684 (1975), which held that due process requires the government to prove beyond a reasonable doubt every fact necessary to constitute the crime charged. See § 1.02[A] and § 9.04[B], *supra. In Rivera v. Delaware,* 429 U.S. 877 (1976), the Court dismissed as not presenting a substantial federal question an appeal claiming that a state statute placing the burden of persuasion in insanity cases on the defendant was unconstitutional under *Winship* and *Mullaney.* Finally, in *Patterson v. New York,* 432 U.S. 197, 206–07 (1977), the Court expressly reaffirmed the *Rivera* holding.

[4] Diminished Capacity

UNITED STATES V. BRAWNER

Circuit Court of Appeals, District of Columbia

471 F.2d 969 (1972)

LEVENTHAL, J. . . . .

[Following a day of wine-drinking, defendant Brawner was involved in a brawl at a party with several acquaintances. After sustaining several injuries in the fight, Brawner became angry and left the party to obtain a gun. He returned to the site of the party and fired five shots through the closed metal door of the apartment in which the party was proceeding. Two shots struck and killed the victim.

Brawner was charged with murder. After considering the government's evidence, the trial court found insufficient evidence of "deliberation" to support first degree murder and therefore directed a verdict of acquittal on that charge.

The trial proceeded with both sides calling expert witnesses to testify regarding Brawner's mental condition at the time of the killing. The experts agreed that Brawner suffered from a mental abnormality, described variously by such labels as "epileptic personality disorder," "personality disorder associated with epilepsy," and "explosive personality." After considering the expert testimony, the jury returned a verdict of second degree murder.

On appeal, the Court of Appeals, *en banc,* used the occasion to, *inter alia,* prospectively rule on the admissibility of evidence of mental abnormality not constituting legal insanity.]

Mental condition, though insufficient to exonerate, may be relevant to specific mental elements of certain crimes or degrees of crime.

Our decision accompanies the redefinition of when a mental condition exonerates a defendant from criminal responsibility with the doctrine that expert testimony as to a defendant's abnormal mental condition may be received and considered, as tending to show, in a responsible way, that defendant did not have the specific mental state required for a particular crime or degree of crime—even though he was aware that his act was wrongful and was able to control it, and hence was not entitled to complete exoneration.

Some of the cases following this doctrine use the term "diminished responsibility," but we prefer the example of the cases that avoid this term, for its convenience is outweighed by its confusion: Our doctrine has nothing to do with "diminishing" responsibility of a defendant because of his impaired mental condition, but rather with determining whether the defendant had the mental state that must be proved as to all defendants.

Procedurally, the issue of abnormal mental condition negativing a person's intent may arise in different ways: For example, the defendant may offer evidence of mental condition not qualifying as mental disease under *McDonald [v. United States,* 312 F.2d 847 (D.C. Cir. 1962)].* Or, he may tender evidence that qualifies under *McDonald,* yet the jury may conclude from all the evidence that defendant has knowledge and control capacity sufficient for responsibility under the ALI rule.

The issue often arises with respect to mental condition tendered as negativing the element of premeditation in a charge of first degree premeditated murder. . . .

An offense like deliberated and premeditated murder requires a specific intent that cannot be satisfied merely by showing that defendant failed to conform to an objective standard.

This is plainly established by the defense of voluntary intoxication. . .

In *Bishop v. United States,* 71 App. D.C. 132, 136, 107 F.2d 297, 301 (1939), Justice Vinson noted that while voluntary intoxication *per se* is no defense to guilt, "the stated condition of a defendant's mind at the time of the killing . . . is now a proper subject for consideration, inquiry, and determinationby the jury." Thus "voluntary intoxication will not excuse murder, but it may negative the ability of the defendant" as to premeditation, and hence effect "a reduction to second degree murder. . . ."

Neither logic nor justice can tolerate a jurisprudence that defines the elements of an offense as requiring a mental state such that one defendant can properly argue that his voluntary drunkenness removed his capacity to form the specific intent but another defendant is inhibited from a submission of his contention that an abnormal mental condition, for which he was in no way responsible, negated his capacity to form a particular specific intent, even though the condition did not exonerate him from all criminal responsibilities. . . .

[The court then discussed and rejected its earlier precedents which had denied the introduction of mental abnormality on the premeditation issue.]

Our rule permits the introduction of expert testimony, as to abnormal condition if it is relevant to negative, or establish, the specific mental condition that is an element of the crime. The receipt of this expert testimony to negative the mental condition of specific intent requires careful administration by the trial judge. Where the proof is not offered in the first instance as evidence of exonerating mental disease or defect within the ALI rule the judge may, and ordinarily would, require counsel first to make a proffer of the proof to be adduced outside the presence of the jury. The judge will then determine whether the testimony is grounded in sufficient scientific support to warrant

---

* [In *McDonald,* the court defined "mental disease or defect" as "any abnormal condition of the mind which substantially affects mental or emotional processes and substantially impairs behavior controls."—Eds.]

use in the courtroom, and whether it would aid the jury in reaching a decision on the ultimate issues.

NOTES

1. The Model Penal Code at § 4.02 offers the following version of the doctrine espoused in *Brawner*: "Evidence that the defendant suffered from a mental disease or defect is admissible whenever it is relevant to prove that the defendant did or did not have a state of mind which is an element of the offense."

2. Some jurisdictions permit evidence of mental abnormality to negate *mens rea* in only certain circumstances. See, *e.g., Commonwealth v. Walzack,* 468 Pa. 210, 360 A.2d 914 (1976) (evidence of mental abnormality admissible only on issue of premeditation); *McCarthy v. State,* 372 A.2d 180, 183 (Del. 1977) (evidence of mental abnormality admissible only for crimes embodying "lesser included offenses" that lack the requisite "specific intent" of the greater offense). Some courts reject the doctrine altogether. *Bethea v. United States,* 365 A.2d 64, 83–92 (D.C. App. 1976), *cert. denied,* 433 U.S. 911 (1977).

MORSE, UNDIMINISHED CONFUSION IN DIMINISHED CAPACITY

75 J. Crim. L. & Criminology 1, 5-9 (1984)

The diminished capacity doctrine allows a criminal defendant to introduce evidence of mental abnormality at trial either to negate a mental element of the crime charged, thereby exonerating the defendant of that charge, or to reduce the degree of crime for which the defendant may be convicted, even if the defendant's conduct satisfied all the formal elements of a higher offense. The first variant of diminished capacity, which I shall refer to as the *"mens rea"* variant, is the dominant approach in the United States. The second, which I shall refer to as the "partial responsibility" variant, is the rule in Great Britain and in indirect form has been adopted in a substantial number of American jurisdictions.

* * *

The prosecution always bears the burden of proving beyond a reasonable doubt its *prima facie* case, the definitional elements necessary to find the defendant guilty of the crime charged or lesser included offenses. Cases of strict liability aside, all crimes include a mental element, a *mens rea,* that the prosecution must prove. If the prosecution fails to carry its persuasion burden on a requisite mental element, the defendant must be acquitted of any crime that includes such an element in its definition. As a matter of constitutional law, the defendant is entitled to introduce competent and relevant evidence to disprove any element of any crime charged subject to few and limited exceptions.

In light of these elementary principles of criminal law, it is clear that the *mens rea* variant of diminished capacity is not a separate defense that deserves to be called "diminished capacity" or any other name connoting that it is some sort of special, affirmative defense. The defendant is simply introducing evidence, in this case evidence of mental abnormality, to make the following claim: "I did not commit the crime charged because I did not possess the requisite *mens rea.*" This is not an affirmative defense whereby the defendant admits or has proved against him the elements of the crime charged, but then raises a claim of justification or excuse. Further, a defendant claiming no *mens rea* because of mental disorder is not asserting some lesser form of legal insanity, that is, he is not claiming that he is partially or less responsible for the crime charged. Rather, the defendant is straightforwardly denying the prosecution's claim that a requisite mental element was present at the time of the offense. He is claiming that he is not guilty of that crime at all, although he may be guilty of a lesser crime if all the elements of the latter are proven. It is as if, for example, a defendant charged with murder on an intent-to-kill theory pleads not guilty on the ground that he thought he was shooting at a tree and therefore lacked the requisite intent to kill.

* * *

Many courts and legislatures have been convinced of the fundamental fairness and consequent necessity of allowing defendants to attempt to cast doubt on the prosecution's case using evidence of mental abnormality, but they have usually placed illogical limitations on the defendant's ability to do so. A smaller number of courts and legislatures have refused to permit the admission of any evidence of mental abnormality, except on the issue of legal insanity. I believe that most, if not all, limitations on the *mens rea* variant are unconstitutional. In an adversary system of criminal justice, where liberty and stigma are at stake, it is a violation of the defendant's sixth and fourteenth amendment rights to prevent him from introducing competent and relevant evidence to defeat the state's case unless there are powerful justifications for the prohibition. . . .

* * *

Courts commonly reject the *mens rea* variant because they mistakenly believe that it is a form of partial insanity or partial responsibility. They argue that so momentous a change in substantive criminal law as adopting a defense of partial insanity is a task appropriately left to the legislature. I completely agree with this argument, but it does not respond to the argument for acceptance of the *mens rea* variant. As I just demonstrated, the defendant claiming no *mens rea* is not attempting to prove that he is less criminally responsible in general. . . . Courts and commentators consistently fall prey to confusing "special" *mens rea,* the specific mental state element that is part of the definition of the crime and thus part of the prosecution's *prima facie case,* and "general" *mens rea,* a generic term for lack of responsibility that might be produced in whole or in part by factors such as legal insanity, duress, or partial responsibility. The confusion is compounded by use of the term "criminal intent." Sometimes, this term is a shorthand designation for all the special *mens rea,* such as intent, knowledge, recklessness, and negligence. When so used, it tends to obscure understanding of which specific *mens rea* is required by the definition of the crime. At other times, unfortunately, it is used as a synonym for general *mens rea*.

Whether or not one accepts the special/general *mens rea* terminology or any other set of terms, there is no doubt that the phenomena being described by those terms are conceptually distinct. A defendant who lacks special *mens rea* is acquitted because his conduct fails to satisfy the state's definition of the offense, not because he lacks responsibility. The conduct of a defendant who lacks general *mens rea* almost always satisfies the elements of the *prima facie* case including the special *mens rea,* but he is acquitted because he is not considered responsible for his conduct. The claim that the state's *prima facie* case cannot be proven is entirely different from the claim of partial insanity or partial responsibility. A court faced with an attempt to admit evidence of mental abnormality to negate *mens rea* can completely exclude such evidence only by demonstrating that the evidence is not relevant to the evaluation of *mens rea* or, even if it is relevant, that it should be excluded for other, powerful policy reasons. Thus, the *mens rea* variant is mandated by current law and does not represent any substantive change.

* * *

The argument in favor of the constitutional and logical necessity of adopting the *mens rea* variant is predicated on the position that intent, purpose, knowledge, and recklessness are subjective *mens rea;* that is, the defendant must subjectively intend, know, or be aware of a risk in order for criminal liability to be imposed. If criminal liability is based on subjective mental states, then it is, of course, possible that the defendant did not actually have the requisite mental state at the time of the offense. By contrast, if these *mens rea* are objective, the arguments for limiting the introduction of evidence of mental abnormality to negate *mens rea* gain coherence; the issue, then, is what the *reasonable* person's state of mind would have been, rather than what the defendant's actual state of mind actually was. Evidence concerning the defendant's actual state of mind is less relevant if subjective *mens rea* is not the issue.

There is resistance in the criminal law to the idea that liability should purely or primarily be based on subjective mental states. If *mens rea* is subjective, a highly unreasonable and dangerous defendant may be freed entirely if he can prove that *mens rea* was actually absent. This is an uncongenial result to many and leads to tensions and ambiguities in the definitions of intent, knowledge, and recklessness. The better solution would be to confront openly our willingness to impose liability on objective grounds.

NOTES AND QUESTIONS

1. The "partial responsibility" variant of diminished capacity described by Professor Morse has enjoyed some popularity in Anglo-American law. For example, Section 2 of the English Homicide Act of 1957, 5 & 6 El. z. II, ch. II, Section 2(1) provides

Where a person kills or is a party to the killing of another, he shall not be convicted of murder if he was suffering from such abnormality of mind (whether arising from a condition of arrested or retarded development of mind or any inherent causes or induced by disease or injury) as substantially impaired the mental responsibility for acts and omissions in doing or being a party to the killing. . . . A person who but for this section would be liable . . . to be convicted of murder shall be liable instead to be convicted of manslaughter.

The Model Penal Code's doctrine of "extreme emotional disturbance," which reduces a homicide from murder to manslaughter, is also a form of partial responsibility. The Code defines manslaughter at § 210.3(1)(b) as.

. . . homicide which would otherwise be murder [but] is committed under the influence of extreme mental or emotional disturbance for which there is reasonable explanation or excuse. The reasonableness of such explanation or excuse shall be determined from the viewpoint of a person in the actor's situation under the circumstances as he believes them to be.

2. Some courts have interpreted the *mens rea* elements of certain crimes in such a way as to recognize the doctrine of partial responsibility. The most vivid example is the California experience in interpreting the concepts of "premeditation" and "malice aforethought" in murder cases.

In *People v. Wolff,* 61 Cal. 2d, 795, 821, 394 P.2d 959, 975, 40 Cal. Rptr. 271, 287 (1964), the California Supreme Court defined "premeditation" as the ability to "maturely and meaningfully reflect upon the gravity of one's acts." The court, in *People v. Conley,* 64 Cal. 2d 310, 322, 411 P.2d 911, 918, 49 Cal. Rptr. 815, 822 (1966), and *People v. Poddar,* 10 Cal. 3d 750, 758, 518 P.2d 342, 348, 11 Cal. Rptr. 910, 916 (1974), defined "malice aforethought" as the ability to "comprehend and act according to one's duty to obey the law." As a result of such cases, defendants possessing the *mens rea* for first degree murder ("premeditation") under common definitions of that term, could introduce evidence of mental abnormality to reduce the crime to a lesser degree of murder or even to manslaughter if the mental abnormality suggested an absence of "malice aforethought."

For a critical review of the partial responsibility doctrine in California, see Arenella, *The Diminished Capacity and Diminished Responsibility Defense: Two Children of a Doomed Marriage,* 77 Colum. L. Rev. 827, 836–49 (1977); Morse, article excerpted immediately *supra* at 25–28.

The California legislature eventually abolished the partial responsibility doctrine in homicide cases but embraced the *mens rea* variant of diminished capacity, although only in the context of "specific intent" crimes. Section 189 of the California Penal Code now reads in part: "To prove the killing was deliberate and premeditated, it shall not be necessary to prove the defendant maturely and meaningfully reflected upon the gravity of his or her act." Cal. Penal Code § 189 (West 1987). Section 188 now reads in part

When it is shown that the killing resulted from the intentional doing of an act with express or implied malice . . . , no other mental state need be shown to establish the mental state of malice aforethought. Neither an awareness of the obligation to act within the general body of laws regulating society nor acting despite such awareness is included within the definition of malice.

Its section 28(a) now reads

(a) Evidence of mental disease, mental defect, or mental disorder shall not be admitted to show or negate the capacity to form any mental state, including, but not limited to, purpose, intent, knowledge, premeditation, deliberation, or malice aforethought, with which the accused committed the act. Evidence of mental disease, mental defect, or mental disorder is admissible solely on the issue of whether or not the accused actually formed a required specific intent, premeditated, deliberated, or harbored malice aforethought, when a specific intent crime is charged.

Why might the California legislature have found the partial responsibility doctrine objectionable?

3. While analytically distinct, the *mens rea* and partial responsibility variants of diminished capacity are sometimes confused. Consider the following case.

JOHNSON V. STATE

Court of Appeals of Maryland

292 Md. 405, 439 A.2d 542 (1982)

DIGGES, Judge

Lawrence Johnson was convicted . . . by a jury in the Circuit Court for Calvert County of first degree murder (both premeditated and in the commission of a felony), first degree rape, kidnapping, and use of handgun during the commission of a felony or a crime of violence. The same jury subsequently sentenced Johnson to death for murder. . . .

The sordid chronicle of this crime spree was related by the appellant, Lawrence Johnson, at trial. It began in the early morning of February 23, 1980, when he was suddenly awakened by a friend, Amos Batts, while perched on the couch at the home of his cousin, Dwayne Mayers. At the urging of Batts, Johnson followed his friend outside to a car being operated by the cousin. It soon became apparent to Johnson that Mayers and Batts had stolen the vehicle during the night and had abducted its owner, Betty Toulson, in the process. Although Johnson had earlier declined to participate when the other two decided to obtain some money through crime, the defendant this time joined them in the car with the victim. After a brief discussion, Mayers started the vehicle and drove around while the three men smoked "parsley flakes sprayed with some kind of embalming fluid." The victim remained silent throughout this journey "with her head down." Later, after driving to a remote area of Baltimore County, Mayers stopped the car and asked whether his companions "wanted to have sex" with their prisoner. Mayers and the appellant eventually raped the woman on the back seat of her car. The trio then drove the victim to another location nearby where Mayers stripped Ms. Toulson of her coat and pocketbook. After discussing the problem presented by the victim's knowledge of their identities, Mayers returned to the automobile, removed a pistol from under the seat, and presented it to the appellant with instructions to kill the woman. Johnson led her into the woods and complied with the directive. Ms. Toulson's snow-covered body was recovered five days later; she had received fatal shots in the head and chest.

* * *

Johnson . . . asserts that the trial court erred in not admitting certain psychological evidence at trial where he sought to use this information, not to establish his legal insanity, but rather, to demonstrate that he lacked a sufficient mental capacity to form the requisite intent to commit murder in the first degree. As an aid to an understanding of this issue we set out its factual predicate.

At trial, the defense called Dr. Ernest Kamm, a clinical psychologist at the Clifton T. Perkins Hospital Center. Dr. Kamm had conducted a psychological examination of Johnson as part of the court ordered evaluation performed by the Perkins staff and had prepared a report of his findings. Counsel for Johnson proffered that he wished to use Dr. Kamm's entire report and testimony "to go to the mitigation of First Degree Murder and any specific [intent] crimes," rather than to raise the issue of defendant's sanity. The court allowed the psychologist to read to the jury only parts of his report relating to intelligence tests he had administered to Johnson and his conclusion, based on those tests, that the defendant "functions at the borderline intellectual level (I.Q. 72)." Appellant urges that the entire report is relevant to his defense of "diminished capacity"—that is, he did not have sufficient mental capacity to form the requisite specific intent to commit some of the crimes with which he is charged. Consequently, the argument goes, it was error to keep that information from the jury when it determines the guilt issue. In order to decide whether this ruling on the evidence was erroneous, however, we must first examine whether the criminal defense known as "diminished capacity," or as it is sometimes called, "diminished responsibility," is recognized in this State. Only if such a doctrine exists in our jurisprudence is defendant arguably entitled to produce evidence in support of it. Because we here determine, however, that this State does not recognize diminished capacity as a legal doctrine operating to negate specific criminal intent, it was not error to exclude evidence in support of it.

Before expounding on why the principle of diminished capacity has been rejected in Maryland as a criminal defense relevant to the issue of guilt, and why we adhere to that position now, it may prove helpful to explore briefly our understanding of the doctrine and its background. The basic outline of diminished capacity has been summarized as follows:

> [S]ince certain crimes, by definition, require the existence of specific intent, any evidence relevant to the existence of that intent, including evidence of an abnormal mental condition not constituting legal insanity, is competent for the purpose of [negating] that intent. . . .
>
> [T]he actual purpose of such evidence is to establish, by negating the requisite intent for a higher degree of offense, that in fact a lesser degree of the offense was committed. . . .

Thus, only after a defendant has been determined to be criminally accountable for his actions (legally sane) has the doctrine been applied to admit expert testimony as to a defendant's mental condition in order to determine the degree of criminality for which the accused will be held responsible.

The states are less than unanimous in their resolution of the question whether application of diminished capacity to criminal trials on the issue of guilt represents a legally sound resolution of the pressing problem of how the criminal law should treat evidence of mental abnormality that does not establish the actor's legal insanity. . . . It is generally recognized, however, that adoption of the concept of diminished capacity as a separate defense involves "a fundamental change in the common law theory of [criminal] responsibility," *Fisher v. United States,* 328 U.S. 463, 476 (1946). This is true because the introduction of expert psychiatric testimony concerning the defendant's mental aberrations when the basic sanity of the accused is not at issue conflicts with the governing principle of the criminal law that all legally sane individuals are equally capable of forming and possessing the same types and degrees of intent. Consequently, an individual determined to be "sane" within the traditional constructs of the criminal law is held accountable for his action, regardless of his particular disabilities, weaknesses, poverty, religious beliefs, social deprivation or educational background. The most that is proper to do with such information is to weigh it during sentencing. This view of the relation of diminished capacity to criminal responsibility is exemplified by . . . Judge Leventhal concurring in *United States v. Moore,* 486 F.2d 1139, 1179–80 (D.C. Cir. 1973) *(en banc), cert. denied,* 414 U.S. 980 (1973):

> [t]he legal conception of criminal capacity cannot be limited to those of unusual endowment or even average powers. A few may be recognized as so far from normal as to be entirely beyond the reach of criminal justice, but in general the criminal law is a means of social control that must be potentially capable of reaching the vast bulk of the population. Criminal responsibility is a concept that not only extends to the bulk of those below the median line of responsibility, but specifically extends to those who have a realistic problem of substantial impairment and lack of capacity. . . . The criminal law cannot "vary legal norms with the individual's capacity to meet the standards they prescribe, absent a disability that is both gross and verifiable, such as the mental disease or defect that may establish irresponsibility. The most that is feasible to do with lesser disabilities is to accord them proper weight in sentencing."

A review of our prior decisions in this area as they interact with legislative enactments on the subject demonstrates that this State has consistently adhered to the just articulated view that the criminal law as an instrument of social control cannot allow a legally sane defendant's lesser disabilities to be a part of the guilt determining calculus. For the purpose of guilt determination, an offender is either wholly sane or wholly insane. In 1888, this Court, following the lead of the celebrated English *McNaughten* case, first enunciated the test for criminal responsibility. . . .

Upon this common law doctrinal base, the General Assembly passed in 1967 a massive remodeling of the limits of criminal culpability [by adopting] a broader rule patterned after that expressed in the American Law Institute Model Penal Code (section 4.01). . . . By thus defining . . . the limits of criminal culpability as expressed in the definition of legal insanity, the General Assembly has exercised its unique prerogative to balance the interests of the community and the individual accused in this regard. We here reaffirm our position that "the concepts of both diminished capacity and insanity involve a moral choice by the community to withhold a finding of responsibility and its consequence of punishment," . . . and on this basis are indistinguishable.[10] Accordingly, because the legislature, reflecting community morals, has, by its definition of criminal insanity already determined which states of mental disorder ought to relieve one from criminal responsibility, this court is without authority to impose our views in this regard even if they differed.

In light of criticism of the *McNaughten* insanity test, diminished capacity has been viewed as a solution to some of the inadequacies of the traditional approach to criminal responsibility, and many decisions allowing evidence of a sane defendant's mental abnormalities arise in jurisdictions which define criminal insanity in terms of the *McNaughten* principle. In fact, some assert that the judicial development of the diminished capacity defense assuaged dissatisfaction with the *McNaughten* and actually inhibited reform of it. Arenella, *The Diminished Capacity and Diminished Responsibility Defenses: Two Children of a Doomed Marriage,* 77 Colum. L. Rev. 827, 854–55 (1977). With the broadening of the concept of criminal insanity however, the arguable need for a doctrine such as diminished capacity to ameliorate the law governing criminal responsibility prescribed by the *McNaughten* rule has been eliminated to the extent the legislature has deemed it advisable to do so.

---

[10] Given the primary assumption in the criminal law concerning a defendant's criminal culpability regardless of his lesser abilities, whatever they may be, and "recognizing the unique position of the concept of insanity in the framework of criminal responsibility," *Bethea v. United States,* 365 A.2d 64, 86 (D.C. App. 1976), we cannot agree with those courts which easily declare that evidence of a legally sane defendant's mental impairment is always probative on the factual question of whether a particular accused entertained requisite mental state. See, *e.g., State v. DiPaolo,* 34 N.J. 279, 168 A.2d 401 (1961), cert. denied, 368 U.S. 880 (1961). There is a fundamental difference between evidence demonstrating that the defendant did not as a fact possess the requisite mental state, here premeditation and deliberation, as opposed to evidence establishing that the defendant was generally less capable than a normal person of forming a requisite *mens rea.* Certainly, we recognize the basic proposition that the state must prove every element of a crime beyond a reasonable doubt including specific intent if necessary, and that an accused is entitled to rebut the state's case. . . . The doctrine of diminished capacity, in our view, however, does not operate to demonstrate that, as a fact, a defendant did not entertain a requisite mental state; rather the principle is used to establish a legally sane but mentally impaired defendant's diminished culpability for a particular criminal act.

Moreover, facile comparison of the doctrine of diminished capacity with the rule allowing certain evidence of a defendant's intoxication on the issue of *mens rea* does not withstand scrutiny. The degree of intoxication necessary to negate *mens rea* is great and is comparable with that degree of mental incapacity that will render a defendant legally insane. As noted in *state v. GGover,* 267 Md. 602, 298 A.2d 378, 382 (1973):

> if the trier of fact determines that at the time the alleged criminal act occurred, the accused had become so inebriated that he possessed no reason or understanding, then he has reached that stage of intoxication that renders him incapable of forming the requisite *mens rea* which is a necessary element of all specific intent crimes.
>
> Lesser degrees of incapacity, whether produced by intoxication or organic mental impairment will not relieve a defendant of full responsibility of his acts. . .

* * *

What has just been iterated does not mean, however, that evidence of a defendant's mental abnormality which does not establish his insanity has been totally precluded from the consideration of those operating the machinery of our criminal justice system. Such evidence typically constitutes part of the range of data upon which the trial judge, following establishment of guilt, focuses attention when sentencing the individual accused. Such use of this information squares with the practice prevailing in our jurisprudence of permitting the judge wide latitude in making individualized sentencing decisions after consideration of information both in aggravation and mitigation of penalty. . .

[The death sentence was held invalid on other grounds, and the case was remanded to the trial court for a new sentencing proceeding.]

ELDRIDGE, Judge *dissenting:*

* * *

. . . On appeal to this Court . . . appellant contended that the trial judge erred in not allowing all of the psychologist's report to be presented to the jury. The State without disputing the admissibility of the expert testimony, argued that the trial court correctly excluded a portion of the report because it "was simply not germane to the issue of diminished capacity." . . .

The majority opinion, instead of deciding the issue which was presented . . . now holds that the entire expert testimony and the entire report was inadmissible. On this basis, the majority finds no reversible error in the exclusion of a portion of the psychologist's report. . . .

Turning to the merits of the majority's position, in my view the trial court correctly held that evidence of Johnson's mental condition was admissible for the purpose of showing the absence of certain elements of first degree murder and of the other specific intent crimes with which Johnson was charged. The majority's contrary holding represents an abrupt departure from prior Maryland law as well as from the prevailing view throughout the country. Moreover, it constitutes an unwarranted limitation upon a criminal defendant's constitutional right to present relevant evidence in his own defense.

The majority arrives at its holding by confusing two entirely distinct matters: (1)the existence of criminal conduct when a particular mental state is an element of the crime charged; and (2)responsibility for criminal conduct. The confusion is enhanced by the majority's use of the terms "capacity" and "capability" interchangeably with "responsibility" and "culpability."

The defendant Johnson, *inter alia,* was charged with murder in the first degree. In order to constitute first degree murder the homicide must be a "wilful, deliberate and premeditated killing." Consequently, the State had the burden of proving the existence of these three elements. The mental condition of the defendant is obviously relevant to willfulness, deliberation and premeditation. . . . Evidence designed to show that a particular defendant was incapable of having the requisite mental state is nothing more or less than evidence designed to show that he did not commit the crime with which he was charged.

On the other hand, under Maryland law criminal responsibility due to mental condition is a wholly different matter. Unlike the common law concept of "not guilty by reason of insanity," the Maryland statutory scheme concerning criminal responsibility contemplates an initial determination that the defendant did commit the crime charged before there is an inquiry into his responsibility therefore. . . .

The majority purports to recognize that the State must prove every element of a crime, including mental elements such as specific intent, premeditation, and deliberation. Nevertheless the majority asserts, without any reasoning, that "[t]here is a fundamental difference between evidence demonstrating that the defendant did not *as a fact* possess the requisite mental state, here premeditation and deliberation, as opposed to evidence establishing that the defendant *was generally less capable* than a normal person of forming a requisite *mens rea*." However, I fail to perceive this "fundamental difference" referred to by the majority. A particular individual's abnormal mental capability is a fact. It is part of his mental state or condition. . . .

As Justice Powell stated for the Supreme Court in *Chambers v. Mississippi*, 410 U.S. 284, 302 (1973), "[f]ew rights are more fundamental than that of an accused to present witnesses in his own defense." By holding that one accused of first degree murder is no longer entitled to present relevant testimony of his mental condition for the purpose of negating the elements of first degree murder, the majority today imposes an unjustified limitation upon the right of a criminal defendant to present evidence in his own behalf.

Notes and Questions

1. What is the issue in the *Johnson case?* Does the *Johnson* majority, particularly in its discussion at footnote 10, confuse the *mens rea* and partial responsibility variants of diminished capacity? Is this the same objection raised by Judge Eldridge in his *Johnson* dissent in which he criticizes the majority for failing to distinguish responsibility and culpability issues?

2. Are there valid objections to the *mens rea* variant of diminished capacity? The court in *Wahrlich v. Arizona,* 479 F.2d 1137, 1138 (9th Cir. 1973), expressed a common argument against the doctrine:

> While there may be superficial appeal to the idea that the standards of criminal responsibility should be applied as subjectively as possible, the overriding danger of the disputed doctrine is that it would discard the traditional presumptions concerning *mens rea* without providing for a corresponding adjustment in the means whereby society is enabled to protect itself from those who cannot or will not conform their conduct to the requirements of the law.
>
> Under the present statutory scheme, a successful plea of insanity avoids a conviction, but confronts the accused with the very real possibility of prolonged therapeutic confine ment. If, however, psychiatric testimony were

generally admissible to cast a reasonable doubt upon whatever degree of *mens rea* was necessary for the charged offense, thus resulting in outright acquittal, there would be scant reason indeed for a defendant to risk such confinement by arguing the greater form of mental deficiency. Thus, quite apart from the argument that the diminished capacity doctrine would result in a considerably greater likelihood of acquittal for those who by traditional standards would be held responsible, the future safety of the offender as well as the community would be jeopardized by the possibility that one who is genuinely dangerous might obtain his complete freedom merely by applying his psychiatric evidence to the threshold of intent.

Are such concerns justified? Do they support recognizing the mens rea variant only in cases where outright acquittal is not possible? For example, should the doctrine be applicable only on the premeditation issue in first degree murder cases, thereby assuring a conviction for second degree murder should diminished capacity be shown? On the other hand, does the logic of the mens rea variant require its across-the-board application even if acquittal might result?

People v. Wetmore

Supreme Court of California

22 Cal. 3d 318, 583 P.2d 1308 (1978)

TOBRINER, Justice.

Charged with burglary, defendant argued that psychiatric reports showed that as a result of mental illness he lacked the specific intent required for conviction of that crime. Relying on a dictum in *People v. Wells* (1949), 33 Cal. 2d 330, 202 P.2d 53, the trial court reasoned that because the reports described defendant's insanity as well as his diminished capacity, such description of defendant's condition in those reports should not be admitted to prove lack of specific intent. The court found defendant guilty of second degree burglary; subsequently, relying on the psychiatric reports, it found him insane [and ordered him hospitalized for treatment pursuant to statutory provisions for the confinement of persons acquitted by reason of insanity].

We hold that the dictum from *Wells* on which the trial court relied must be rejected. The state bears the burden of proving every element of the offense charged; defendant cannot logically or constitutionally be denied the right to present probative evidence rebutting an element of the crime merely because such evidence also suggests insanity. Defendant's evidence established that he entered an apartment under a delusion that he owned that apartment and thus did not enter with the intent of committing a theft or felony. That evidence demonstrated that defendant lacked the specific intent required for a conviction of burglary; the trial court's refusal to consider the evidence at the guilt phase of the trial therefore constituted prejudicial error.

We reject the suggestion . . . that we sustain the trial court by holding that a defense of diminished capacity cannot be raised whenever, owing to the lack of a lesser included offense, it might result in the defendant's acquittal. A defendant who, because of diminished capacity, does not entertain the specific intent required for a particular crime is entitled to be acquitted of that crime. If he cannot be convicted of a lesser offense and cannot safely be released, the state's remedy is to institute civil commitment proceedings, not to convict him of a specific intent crime which he did not commit.

The only evidence submitted to the trial court in this case was the testimony of Joseph Cacciatore, the victim of the burglary, at the preliminary hearing, and three psychiatric reports. Cacciatore testified that he left his apartment on March 7, 1975. When he returned three days later, he discovered defendant in his apartment. Defendant was wearing Cacciatore's clothes and cooking his food. The lock on the front door had been broken; the apartment lay in a shambles. Cacciatore called the police who arrested defendant for burglary. Later Cacciatore discovered that a ring, a watch, a credit card, and items of clothing were missing.

The psychiatric reports submitted to the court explain defendant's long history of psychotic illness, including at least 10 occasions of hospital confinement for treatment. According to the reports, defendant, shortly after his last release from Brentwood Veteran's Hospital, found himself with no place to go. He began to believe that he "owned" property, and was "directed" to Cacciatore's apartment. When he found the door unlocked he was sure he owned the apartment, destroyed some advertising he felt was inappropriate, and put on Cacciatore's clothes. When the police arrived, defendant was shocked and embarrassed, and only then understood that he did not own the apartment.

* * *

In holding that defendant's psychiatric evidence could not be utilized to prove that he lacked the specific intent required for the offense of burglary, the trial court followed a dictum laid down in our decision in *Wells*. . . . *Wells*, the seminal decision which established the doctrine of diminished capacity in California law, held that "evidence of diminished mental capacity, whether caused by intoxication, trauma, or disease, can be used to show that a defendant did not have a specific mental state essential to an offense." In dictum, however, *Wells* stated that since sanity is conclusively presumed at the guilt trial, "evidence tending to show lack of mental capacity to commit the crime because of legal insanity is barred at that stage." The *Wells* opinion later restated that conclusion in different terms: "if the proffered evidence tends to show not merely that he [defendant] did or did not, but rather that because of legal insanity he could not, entertain the specific intent or other essential mental state, then that evidence is inadmissible under the not guilty plea. . .

As we shall explain, the *Wells* dictum imposes an illogical and unworkable rule which has not been followed in subsequent cases. *Wells* spoke of excluding evidence which tended to prove "lack of mental capacity . . . because of legal insanity." Mental incapacity does not occur "because of legal insanity;" instead both insanity and diminished capacity are legal conclusions derived from evidence of defendant's mental condition. Consequently, if the evidence of a defendant's mental illness indicates that the defendant lacked the specific intent to commit the charged crime such evidence cannot reasonably be ignored at the guilt trial merely because it might (but might not) also persuade the trier of fact that the defendant is insane.

Wells' distinction between evidence that defendant did not entertain the requisite intent, which is admissible, and evidence that he could not entertain that intent, which is inadmissible, cannot be supported. "[A]s a matter of logic, any proof tending to show that a certain mental condition could not exist is relevant and should be admissible to show that it did not exist. And, of course, proof that something could not exist is the best possible evidence that it did not exist." (Louisell and Hazard, Insanity as a Defense: The Bifurcated Trial (1961), 49 Calif. L. Rev. 805, 819.) Moreover, . . . evidence which tends to prove that a defendant could not entertain a certain intent may, when subject to cross-examination, convince the trier of fact that defendant was able to entertain the intent but did not do so on the occasion of the crime. Thus,. . . . the trial court cannot refuse to admit such evidence when offered to prove diminished capacity.

* * *

We therefore hold that evidence of diminished capacity is admissible at the guilt phase whether or not that evidence may also be probative of insanity. The trial court erred when, relying on the *Wells* dictum, it refused to consider evidence of diminished capacity in determining defendant's guilt.

Amicus Los Angeles City Attorney urges that we sustain the trial court's ruling on a different ground. He contends that a defendant should be permitted to assert the defense of diminished capacity caused by mental disease or defect only to reduce a specific crime to a lesser included offense. Claiming that there is no lesser included offense in burglary, *Amicus* argues that the trial court correctly refused to consider evidence of defendant Wetmore's diminished mental capacity.

* * *

[It is] our conclusion that a defense of diminished capacity arising from mental disease or defense of diminished capacity arising from mental disease or defect extends to all specific intent crimes, whether or not they encompass lesser included offenses. Clearly, if a crime requires specific intent, a defendant who because of mental disease or defect lacks that intent, cannot commit that crime. The presence or absence of a lesser included offense within the charged crime cannot affect the result. The prosecution must prove all elements of the crime beyond a reasonable doubt; we do not perceive how a defendant who has in his possession evidence which rebuts an element of the crime can logically be denied the right to present that evidence merely because it will result in his acquittal.

Amicus' argument, although legally flawed, addresses a matter of real concern. A defendant whose criminal activity arises from mental disease or defect usually requires confinement and special treatment. Penal Code sections 1026 and 1026a provide such confinement and treatment for persons found not guilty by reason of insanity. A defendant acquitted because, as a result of diminished capacity, he lacked the specific intent required for the crime cannot be confined pursuant to sections 1026 and 1026a, yet often he cannot be released without endangering the public safety.

The same danger may arise, however, when a diminished capacity defense does not result in the defendant's acquittal but in his conviction for a lesser included offense. A defendant convicted of a lesser included misdemeanor, for example, will be confined for a relatively short period in a facility which probably lacks a suitable treatment program, and may later, having served his term, be released to become a public danger. The solution to this problem thus does not lie in barring the defense of diminished capacity when the charged crime lacks a lesser included offense, but in providing for the confinement and treatment of defendants with diminished capacity arising from mental disease or defect.

The Lanterman—Petris—Short Act provides for the civil commitment of any person who, "as a result of mental disorder, is a danger to others, or to himself, or gravely disabled." Recognizing that evidence of such mental disorder may arise at trial, the Legislature provided that a judge of the county where a prisoner is confined may institute evaluation and treatment procedures under the Lanterman—Petris—S hort Act. Thus if evidence adduced in support of a successful diminished capacity defense indicates to the trial judge that the defendant is dangerous, the court is not compelled to foist the defendant upon the public; it may, instead, initiate procedures for civil commitment.

The Attorney General points out that a person who commits a crime against property, such as defendant Wetmore, might not be committable under the Lanterman-Petris-Short Act unless he were "gravely disabled." A more serious omission lies in the act's failure to provide for long term commitment of persons dangerous to others; unless found "gravely disabled," a "person who, as a result of mental disorder, presents an imminent threat of substantial physical harm to others" cannot be confined beyond the initial 90-day postcertification treatment. If the Lanterman—Petris—S hort Act does not adequately protect the public against crimes committed by persons with diminished mental capacity, the answer lies either in amendment to that act or in the enactment of legislation that would provide for commitment of persons acquitted by virtue of a successful diminished capacity defense in the same manner as persons acquitted by reason of insanity are presently committed. It does not lie in judicial creation of an illogical—and possibly unconstitutional—r ule denying the defense of diminished capacity to persons charged with crimes lacking a lesser included offense.

* * *

In conclusion, the trial court in the present case erroneously refused to consider at the guilt phase evidence which clearly indicated that defendant believed that he owned the apartment and its contents, and thus entered the apartment without specific intent to commit a theft or felony. If the court had considered that evidence, it is reasonably probable that it would not have found defendant guilty of burglary; thus the error was prejudicial. Although defendant might have been subject to civil commitment proceedings even if acquitted of burglary, he would not have been subject to commitment [under the special provisions reserved for those acquitted by reason of insanity].

The judgment (order of commitment) is reversed and the cause remanded for further proceedings consistent with this opinion.

NOTES AND QUESTIONS

1. The *Wetmore* case occurs within a "bifurcated" procedure in which the issues of "guilt or innocence" and "insanity" are tried in successive stages with separate verdicts. California is one of only a few states which require bifurcation although many other jurisdictions permit it in the discretion of the trial judge. Only a few jurisdictions forbid bifurcation altogether.

Bifurcation offers several supposed advantages. By deferring psychiatric testimony to the second stage, juries are not tempted to reach a compromise insanity verdict in lieu of either an outright acquittal or a finding of guilt. Moreover, the defendant's ability to exercise his privilege against self-incrimination is arguably protected. The insanity defense almost always requires the defendant to make statements about the crime, often resulting in admissions of the offense. Bifurcation permits the defendant to remain silent at the guilt stage while the state proves the elements of the crime while retaining the right to raise the insanity issue at the insanity phase of the proceedings.

Does the *Wetmore* holding defeat the purposes of bifurcation?

2. On the other hand, would Wetmore's constitutional rights have been violated had the court denied the admissibility of his evidence of mental abnormality at the guilt phase? The courts have reached contrary conclusions. See, *e.g., Hendershott v. People,* 653 P.2d 385 (Colo. 1985) (exclusion of psychiatric evidence on issue of whether defendant in fact possessed the requisite mental state violates defendant's constitutional right to present evidence in his behalf); *Wahrlich v. Arizona,* 479 F.2d 1137 (9th Cir. 1973) (nonrecognition of *mens rea* variant of diminished capacity is constitutionally permissible).

An interesting constitutional development has occurred in the Seventh Circuit Court of Appeals in cases arising from the State of Wisconsin. In *Hughes v. Matthews,* 576 F.2d 1250 (7th Cir. 1978), the court concluded that Hughes, convicted of first degree murder by a Wisconsin jury, had been denied due process when the trial court prevented him from introducing psychiatric testimony to show that he lacked the *mens rea* for the charged crime and was thus guilty of only second degree murder. A panel of the Seventh Circuit upheld a grant of habeas corpus issued by the federal district court. Citing the principle that a defendant's due process right to present evidence is violated where the state has recognized as "relevant and competent" the testimony of [a given] type of witness but has arbitrarily barred its use by the defendant, the court assumed that psychiatric evidence was "relevant" and "competent" on the *mens rea* issue because Wisconsin permitted psychiatric expertise on a variety of other legal issues. The court then found the state's justifications for excluding the evidence, a fear that legally sane defendants will escape punishment if the evidence is admitted and a concern that such admission would result in a duplication of evidence at both stages of the state's bifurcated system, to be arbitrary. Permitting the defendant to admit the evidence could not result in his "escaping punishment" because a successful negation of *mens rea* for first degree murder would still leave him liable for second degree murder. As for duplication of evidence, no such possibility existed given the fact that the defendant did not raise a defense of insanity and thus no second proceeding was at issue.

Subsequent to *Hughes,* the Wisconsin Supreme Court held, in *Steele v. State,* 97 Wis. 2d 72, 294 N.W.2d 2, 13 (1980), that while psychiatric testimony was relevant and competent to make the "gross evaluation" of whether a defendant is criminally responsible under the insanity defense, such testimony was not relevant or competent for the "fine tuning" necessary to determine capacity to form the various states of mind required in the criminal law.

In light of *Steele,* in *Muench v. Israel,* 715 F.2d 1125 (7th Cir. 1983), a separate panel of the Seventh Circuit from that deciding Hughes reached a contrary constitutional conclusion to *Hughes* by upholding a Wisconsin court denial of the admissibility of psychiatric evidence on the *mens rea* issue.

See Huckabee, *Evidence of Mental Disorder on Mens Rea: Constitutionality of Drawing the Line of the Insanity Defense,* 16 Pepp. L. Rev. 573 (1989), arguing that states both do and can constitutionally forbid all evidence "below the insanity line," thus precluding diminished capacity or partial responsibility theories.

3. Is the *Steele* court's conclusion that psychiatric expertise is more relevant and competent on the insanity issue than on the diminished capacity issue defensible? Is the nature of psychiatric testimony different on the two issues?

[5] New Alternatives

[a] The Guilty But Mentally Ill Verdict

MICKENBERG, *A PLEASANT SURPRISE: THE GUILTY BUT MENTALLY ILL VERDICT HAS BOTH SUCCEEDED IN ITS OWN RIGHT AND SUCCESSFULLY PRESERVED THE TRADITIONAL ROLE OF THE INSANITY DEFENSE*

55 U. Cin. L. Rev. 943, 987-91 (1987)

The GBMI [guilty but mentally ill] verdict was first adopted by Michigan in 1975 as part of the legislative response to *People v. McQuillan.** Since then GBMI proposals based on the Michigan plan have been adopted by statute in ten other states and by judicial decision in one. Since all of the extent

---

* [392 Mich. 511, 221 N.W.2d 569 (1974). Earlier in his article, Professor Mickenberg discussed the controversy surrounding the case. McQuillan held that insanity acquittees [NGRIs] must be granted the same procedural protections for commitment to and release from mental institutions as those granted to civilly committed persons. *McQuillan* was given retroactive application and played a role in the release of sixty-four previously hospitalized NGRIs. Within a year of their release, two of the NGRIs committed new violent crimes. The crimes were widely publicized and triggered intense public opposition to the insanity defense.—Eds.]

(GBMI) laws are virtually identical to that of Michigan, the following discussion of Michigan's rules are applicable to any jurisdiction that has adopted GBMI.

The GBMI verdict in Michigan does not abolish the insanity defense, but supplements it by providing juries with an alternative to the stark choice between "Guilty" and NGRI. When a defendant raises the insanity defense at trial, the court must instruct the jury as to four possible verdicts: guilty, not guilty, not guilty by reason of insanity, and guilty but mentally ill. The first three of these options are defined just as they were prior to the adoption of GBMI. A defendant must be found GBMI, however, if the jury finds beyond a reasonable doubt that the following conditions have been met:

1) the defendant has fulfilled every element of the crime charged; 2) the defendant was mentally ill at the time he committed the criminal act; and 3) although mentally ill, the defendant cannot be found NGRI because he was not legally insane at the time he committed the crime.

Thus, a finding of GBMI may be made only after the jury decides to reject the insanity defense, thereby establishing that the defendant, although mentally ill, was sufficiently in possession of his faculties to be morally blameworthy for his acts. A GBMI holding is therefore considered a criminal conviction equivalent to a verdict of guilty. A defendant can also enter a plea of GBMI, which the court may accept after holding an evidentiary hearing on the issue of the defendant's mental condition at the time of the criminal offense. If the plea is accepted, the defendant is treated just as if the GBMI verdict had been returned by a jury.

When a defendant is found GBMI, either by verdict or by plea, the court may impose any sentence permitted by law for the offense of which he was convicted. This may involve prison, probation, a fine, or any authorized alternative. If a jail term is imposed, the defendant must be evaluated by the Department of Mental Health and receive "such [medical] treatment as is psychiatrically indicated." If inpatient treatment is considered necessary, the defendant may be committed to a state mental hospital instead of prison. If hospitalization is not indicated, or when after completing such treatment he is deemed clinically ready for discharge, the defendant is returned to prison to serve the balance of his sentence. Credit is granted toward completion of prison term for any time spent confined in the mental institution.

The most obvious and important function of the GBMI verdict is to permit juries to make an unambiguous statement about the factual guilt, mental condition, and moral responsibility of a defendant. Theoretically, this should allow jurors to feel more comfortable in returning NGRI verdicts in cases where the defendant committed a criminal act but fit the statutory definition of insanity. Conversely, juries should also feel more confident in convicting a mentally ill defendant when appropriate, because they are able to recommend treatment and make a mitigating statement concerning mental illness. In both situations, members of the jury and the public should be satisfied that the issue of moral blameworthiness was resolved by a knowing decision about the relationship between a defendant's misdeeds and illness.

* * *

The insanity defense is usually available only to the defendants who because of mental illness are unable to understand the nature of their acts or to conform their behavior to the requirements of the law. This does not exonerate mentally ill defendants whose cognitive and volitional abilities are unimpaired. Such defendants are considered morally blameworthy because they still have the capacity to choose between right and wrong. Society recognizes, however, the benefits of mitigating the punishment of such people by affording them treatment for their mental illness in the hope of avoiding recidivism after their release. One function of the GBMI verdict is to permit such treatment. Consequently, . . . GBMI provide[s] necessary and acceptable mitigation in the form of psychiatric assistance for the convicts while they serve their sentences.

Considering the advantages offered by the GBMI verdict in restoring public confidence in the criminal law and affording treatment for mentally ill convicts, GBMI proposals should be welcomed by representatives of all factions of the criminal justice system. Surprisingly, however, the verdict has been almost universally attacked by prosecutors, defense attorneys, and academics.

The most fervent objections to GBMI proposals come from proponents of the insanity defense who claim that GBMI is nothing more than a disguised attempt to abolish the NGRI verdict. The argument continues that the real purpose of GBMI is to encourage jurors hostile to the concept of an insanity defense to reach impermissible compromises by returning verdicts of GBMI for defendants who should be found NGRI. Further, the use of the word "but" in "guilty but mentally ill" gives jurors the impression that the GBMI verdict mitigates blame, when it really only suggests treatment for a blameworthy defendant. Consequently, juries uncomfortable with the idea of pronouncing a nonresponsible defendant "not guilty" may compromise and return a verdict of GBMI in the mistaken belief that it does not entail criminal punishment.

Other opponents of the GBMI verdict contend that even if juries do not intentionally use it as a vehicle for impermissible compromise, the difference between mental illness and legal insanity will prove too confusing for jurors to understand. Thus, GBMI verdicts will be returned every time a jury believes that a "crazy" defendant committed a criminal act.

The fears of insanity defense proponents that GBMI would *de facto* eliminate the NGRI plea are in large part derived from statements made by advocates of the GBMI verdict. In virtually every state that has debated a GBMI statute, proponents have claimed that its main function would be to reduce the number of insanity acquittals and insure that persons who committed a criminal act would be imprisoned regardless of their mental condition. In Michigan, for example, legislators openly argued that GBMI would "circumvent the *McQuillan* decision" and reduce, if not eliminate NGRI verdicts.

* * *

At the present time there is a widespread public belief that the insanity defense fosters recidivism, encourages the feigning of mental illness, and results in overly lenient treatment of criminals. Although each of these charges is false, the fact that the public believes them to be true has caused a serious loss of confidence in the ability of the law to protect the public. Numerous proposed solutions have been advanced to deal with these perceived problems, including the so-called *mens rea* alternatives and the GBMI verdict. These proposals should not be discarded simply because they would work some change on the traditional structure of the insanity plea. Instead, they should only be rejected if they would alter the defense in a way that would abandon those notions of moral responsibility that are the very reason the insanity verdict exists.

* * *

NOTE

In addition to Professor Mickenberg's article, see Slobogin, *The Guilty but Mentally Ill Verdict: An Idea Whose Time Should Not Have Come,* 53 Geo. Wash. L. Rev. 494 (1985), for an evaluation of the GBMI verdict.

[b] Abolition of the Defense of Insanity

Perhaps the most dramatic consequence of the disenchantment with the insanity defense has been its outright abolition in at least three states: Montana, Idaho, and Utah. In all three jurisdictions, evidence of mental abnormality is now inadmissible except on the issue of whether the defendant formulated the specific *mens rea* of the charged offense. For a discussion of the Idaho statute, see Elkins, *Idaho's Repeal of the Insanity Defense: What Are We Trying to Prove?* 31 Idaho L. Rev. 151 (1994). The Montana statute provides in Section 46-14-201, Mont. Rev. Codes Ann.:

> (1) Evidence of mental disease or defect is not admissible in a trial on the merits unless the defendant . . . files a written notice of his purpose to rely on a mental disease or defect to prove he did not have a particular state of mind which is an essential element of the offense charged. . . .
>
> (2) When the defendant is found not guilty of the charged offense or offenses or any lesser included offense for the reason that due to a mental disease or defect, he could not have a particular state of mind that is an essential element of the offense charged, the verdict and judgment shall so state.

Unlike the Idaho and Utah analogues, which rely on ordinary civil commitment procedures to confine *mens rea* acquittees, Montana has enacted special dispositional provisions to facilitate confinement of Section 46-14-201 acquittees. Mont. Rev. Codes Ann. Sections 46-14-301 *et seq.,* provide a mechanism, not unlike that applicable to insanity acquittees in many jurisdictions, by which *mens rea* acquittees may be hospitalized for "custody, care, and treatment." The acquittee is entitled to a hearing to determine "present mental condition" and "dangerousness." Once hospitalized, the acquittee is entitled to periodic judicial hearings at which he must carry the burden of proving that he may be released "without danger to others."

The Montana Supreme Court rejected arguments that the insanity defense was so firmly entrenched in the common law that its availability constituted a fundamental right therefore rendering abolition of the defense a violation of due process. *State v. Korell,* 690 P.2d 992 (Mont. 1984). In upholding the Montana scheme, the *Korell* court distinguished several early decisions *(e.g., State v. Strasburg,* 60 Wash. 106, 110 P. 1010 (1910); *Sinclair v. State,* 161 Miss. 142, 132 So. 581 (1931)) that held abolition of the insanity defense unconstitutional under statutes that denied trial consideration of mental abnormality on both the insanity and diminished capacity issues. In *Cowan v. Montana,* 114 S. Ct. 1371 (1994), the Supreme Court denied certiorari in a case upholding the Montana abolition statute. For a discussion of *Cowan,* see Note, *State v. Cowan: The Consequences of Montana's Abolition of the Insanity Defense,* 55 Mont. L. Rev. 503 (1994).

The literature for and against abolition of the insanity defense is voluminous. The following excerpts provide many of the traditional arguments.

Morris, *Madness and the Criminal Law*

53-54, 57-64, 72-74 (1982)

Abolition of the defense of insanity has received exhaustive attention in the literature; the informed reader is entitled, therefore, to be notified of where the argument leads so that he may avoid the sharper irritations of redundancy. In accordance with the thesis of separation of the mental health law and the criminal-law powers to incarcerate, I propose the abolition of the special defense of insanity. A fall-back alternative position, in no way conflicting with the separation thesis, is for the abolition of the special defense and for legislative substitution of a qualified defense of diminished responsibility to a charge of murder having the effect, if successful, of a conviction of manslaughter with the usual sentencing discretion attached to that crime.

* * *

Why, then, go beyond the simple rule, to give mental illness the same exculpatory effect as, say, blindness or deafness? Evidence of the latter afflictions may be admitted as indicative of lack of both the *actus reus* (prohibited act) and the *mens rea* of a crime. Why go further? The answer lies in the pervasive moral sense that when choice to do ill is lacking, it is improper to impute guilt. And hence there is pressure for special defense of insanity, just as there is pressure for a special defense of infancy or duress. Let us consider what has been offered by way of larger statements of the ends to be served by a special defense of insanity.

* * *

In *Durham* [214 F.2d 862, 876 (D.C. Cir. 1954)], Judge Bazelon put the matter curtly and clearly: "Our collective conscience does not allow punishment where it cannot impose blame." Such a rationale claims too much, assumes our possession of finely calibrated moral scales, and flies in the face of observation of the gross daily work of our criminal courts. It is hortatory rather than descriptive but it does state a justification that a generous mind may accept as an aim though doubt as a reality.

Historically, of course, the special defense made good sense in relation to one punishment. Capital punishment infused it with meaning. But even perfervid advocates of capital punishment do not favor the execution of the mentally ill, and this justification for the special defense is now sufficiently covered by the rules and practices of sentencing.

One is left, therefore, with the feeling that the special defense is a genuflection to a deep-seated moral sense that the mentally ill lack freedom of choice to guide and govern their conduct and that therefore blame should not be imputed them for their otherwise criminal acts nor should punishment to be imposed. . . . [I]t is important not to assume that those who advocate the abolition of the special defense of insanity are recommending the wholesale punishment of the sick. They are urging rather that mental illness be given the same exculpatory effect as other adversities that bear upon criminal guilt. And they add the not unfair criticism of the conventional position that they observe the widespread conviction and punishment of the mentally ill, the special defense being an ornate rarity, a tribute to our capacity to pretend to a moral position while pursuing profoundly different practices.

* * *

It is unthinkable that mental illness should be given a lesser reach than drunkenness. If a given mental condition (intent, recklessness) is required for the conviction of a criminal offense then, as a proposition requiring no discussion, in the absence of that mental condition there can be no conviction. This holds true whether the absence of that condition is attributable to blindness, deafness, drunkenness, mental illness or retardation, linguistic difficulties, or, if it could be established, hypnotic control. But this states basic principles of criminal law, not a special defense. The main reasons for defining a "special defense" beyond the traditional common-law relationship between mental illness and the *actus reus* and *mens rea* of crime are, I think, twofold: expediency in crime control and fairness.

The expediency rationale can be quickly advanced and disposed of; the fairness rationale is more difficult.

. . . . J. Goldstein and J. Katz accurately perceived that "the insanity defense is not a defense, it is a device for triggering indeterminate restraint" of those who were mentally ill at the time of the crime but are not civilly committable now. In considerable part, that has been its role since 1800 when the emergence of the special defense in England led to the Criminal Lunatics Act of 1800, which provided indeterminate custody for those not found guilty by reason of insanity, with similar legislation spreading in the states and federal systems in this country.

Few are prepared any longer to justify the special defense on this crime control basis, as a means of confining the dangerous though not civilly committable. It would be a strange "defense," an unusual benevolence, whose purpose is confinement of those who cold not otherwise be confined.

Hence we are brought to the central issue—the question of fairness, the sense that it is unjust and unfair to stigmatize the mentally ill as criminals and to punish them for their crimes. The criminal law exists to deter and to punish those who would or who do choose to do wrong. If they cannot exercise choice, they cannot be deterred and it is a moral outrage to punish them. The argument sounds powerful but its premise is weak.

Choice is neither present nor absent in the typical case where the insanity defense is currently pleaded; what is at issue is the degree of freedom of choice on a continuum from the hypothetically entirely rational to the hypothetically pathologically determined—in states of consciousness neither polar condition exists.

The moral issue sinks into the sands of reality. Certainly it is true that in a situation of total absence of choice it is outrageous to inflict punishment; but the frequency of such situations to the problems of criminal responsibility becomes an issue of fact in which tradition and clinical knowledge and practice are in conflict. The traditions of being possessed of evil spirits, of being bewitched, confront the practices of a mental health system which increasingly fashions therapeutic practices to hold patients responsible for their conduct. And suppose we took the moral argument seriously and eliminated responsibility in those situations where we thought there had been a substantial impairment of the capacity to choose between crime and no crime (I set aside problems of strict liability and of negligence for the time being). Would we not have to, as a matter of moral fairness, fashion a special defense of gross social adversity? The matter might be tested by asking which is the more criminogenic, psychosis or serious social deprivation? In an article in 1968 on this topic I raised the question of whether there should be a special defense of dwelling in a black ghetto. Some literal-minded commentators castigated me severely for such a recommendation, mistaking a form of argument, the *reductio ad absurdum,* for a recommendation. But let me again press the point. If one were asked how to test the criminogenic effect of any factor in man or in the environment, the answer would surely follow empirical lines. One would measure and try to isolate the impact of that factor on behavior, with particular reference to criminal behavior. To isolate genetic pressure toward crime one might pursue twin studies or cohort studies, one might look at patterns of adoption and the criminal behavior of natural fathers and adoptive fathers and see whether they were related to the criminal behavior of their children. Somewhat similar measuring techniques would be followed if one were trying to search out the relationship between unemployment and criminality, or a Bowlby-like study of the effects of maternal separation or maternal deprivation on later criminal behavior. Our answers to the question of the determining effects of such conditions would be found empirically and not in a priori arguing about their relationships to crime, though there may be ample room for argument involved in the empirical studies.

Hence, at first blush, it seems a perfectly legitimate correlation and, I submit, causal inquiry, whether psychosis, or any particular type of psychosis, is more closely related to criminal behavior than, say, being born to a one-parent family living on welfare in a black inner-city area. And there is no doubt of the empirical answer. Social adversity is grossly more potent in its pressure toward criminality, certainly toward all forms of violence and street crime as distinct from white-collar crime, than is any psychotic condition. As a factual matter, the exogenous pressures are very much stronger than the endogenous.

But the argument feels wrong. Surely there is more to it than the simple calculation of criminogenic impact. Is this unease rationally based? I think not, though the question certainly merits further consideration. As a rational matter it is hard to see why one should be more responsible for what is done to one than for what one is. Yet major contributors to jurisprudence and criminal law theory insist that it is necessary to maintain the denial of responsibility on grounds of mental illness to preserve the moral infrastructure of the criminal law. For many years I have struggled with this opinion by those whose work I deeply respect, yet I remain unpersuaded. Indeed, they really don't try to persuade, but rather affirm and reaffirm with vehemence and almost mystical sincerity the necessity of retaining the special defense of insanity as a moral prop to the entire criminal law.

And indeed I think that much of the discussion of the defense of insanity is the discussion of a myth rather than of a reality. It is no minor debating point that in fact we lack a defense of insanity as an operating tool of the criminal law other than in relation to a very few particularly heinous and heavily punished offenses. There is not an operating defense of insanity in relation to burglary or theft, or the broad sweep of index crimes generally; the plea of not guilty on the ground of insanity is rarely to be heard in city courts of first instance which handle the grist of the mill of the criminal law—though a great deal of pathology is to be seen in the parade of accused and convicted persons before these courts. As a practical matter we reserve this defense for a few sensational cases where it may be in the interest of the accused either to escape the possibility of capital punishment (though in cases where serious mental illness is present, the risk of execution is slight) or where the likely punishment is of a sufficient severity to make the indeterminate commitment of the accused a preferable alternative to a criminal conviction. Operationally the defense of insanity is a tribute, it seems to me, to our hypocrisy rather than to our morality.

To be less aggressive about the matter and to put aside anthropomorphic allegations of hypocrisy, the special defense of insanity may properly be indicated as producing a morally unsatisfactory classification on the continuum between guilt and innocence. It applies in practice to only a few mentally ill criminals, thus omitting many others with guilt-reducing relationships between their mental illness and their crime; it excludes other powerful pressures on human behavior, thus giving excessive weight to the psychological over the social. It is a false classification in the sense that if a team of the world's most sensitive and trained psychiatrists and moralists were to select from all those found guilty of felonies and those found not guilty by reason of insanity any given number who should not be stigmatized as criminals, very few of those found not guilty by reason of insanity would be selected. How to offer proof of this? The only proof, I regret, is to be found by personal contact with a flow of felony cases through the courts and into the prisons. No one of serious perception will fail to recognize both the extent of mental illness and retardation among the prison population and the overwhelming weight of adverse social circumstances on criminal behavior. This is, of course, not an argument that social adversities should lead to acquittals; they should be taken into account in sentencing. And the same is true of the guilt and sentencing of those pressed by psychological adversities. The special defense is thus a morally false classification. And it is a false classification also in the sense that it does not select from the prison population those most in need of psychiatric treatment.

* * *

The whole argument for abolition of the insanity defense is misconceived, it might be argued. These trials have little to do with the accused; he is highly likely to be protractedly incarcerated whatever the outcome and it doesn't matter much where. The thesis is disingenuous, the criticism would continue; it fails to appreciate the larger function of the sensational trials of mad murderers and insane assassins. They are the modern "Everyman;" they are public morality plays, spectacles, moral circuses for the masses to educate them in virtue and in moral sensitivity. For mass consumption they distinguish the mad from the bad, even though on close analysis that is a philosophically impossible trick to perform.

It is not easy to respond to such high-flying rhetoric except to reject it as a prescription. As a description it has truth but I doubt strongly that community moral values are in any way strengthened by the more publicized insanity defenses. At the time of writing, John Hinckley, who shot President Reagan and most seriously injured James Brady, is about to go on trial, the announced defense being that of insanity. One wonders what social purposes are to be served by what will indeed be a massively publicized performance. The reputations of several psychiatrists and lawyers will be made, their fee scales enhanced. Passionate and ill-informed discussion will engulf dinner tables throughout the country. Hinckley will not be at large for many years. He clearly planned and intended to shoot the President. His need for psychiatric assistance may or may not be real and lasting; if it is, we should see that he gets it. But the interstitial orgy of psychiatric moralizing seems of no social utility.

Lurking within this rhetorically overblown argument may be a more subtle and difficult point. It may be argued that, in addition to deterrent purposes, criminal trials and convictions have another important purpose, that of dramatically and formally affirming minimum standards of moral conduct, of stigmatizing the wicked and only the wicked. Seen thus, the criminal justice system is a name-calling, stigmatizing, community superego reinforcing system—a system which should not be used against the mentally ill. They are mad, not bad, sick not wicked; it is important that we should not misclassify them.

Again, in my view, practice casts down theory. We fail in this classificatory effort and are doomed to failure no matter how we try since the distinction surpasses our moral and intellectual capacities. And, in any event, we do not stigmatize the insane killer (who is at the heart of the argument about the special defense) or other psychologically disturbed persons who commit serious criminal acts as either bad or mad; in practice, we stigmatize them as *both* bad and mad.

This double stigmatization of the subjects of our inquiry can be seen by anyone who visits a prison containing mentally ill prisoners or a mental hospital holding the unfit to plead or those found not guilty by reason of insanity. Prison authorities regard their inmates in the facilities for the psychologically disturbed, no matter how they got there, as both criminal and insane, as bad and mad. And it is a regrettable fact that conditions in both types of institutions are often adjusted adversely to the inmate to accommodate the larger political risks that would flow from his escape because of that double stigmatization.

And as a final sad point on this question: it is not only the public and those working in prisons and mental hospitals who doubly rather than alternatively stigmatize in these cases, the patient-inmates in my experience also see themselves as both bad and mad, though it is a tribute to divine mercy and the human spirit that processes of repentance and cognitive dissonance help them to fashion some sort of a life despite that miserable, doubly blemished self-image.

NOTE

For an assessment of Dean Morris's arguments, see Singer, *Abolition of the Insanity Defense: Madness and the Criminal Law,* 4 Cardozo L. Rev. 683 (1983).

WALES *AN ANALYSIS OF THE PROPOSAL TO "ABOLISH" THE INSANITY DEFENSE IN S.1.: SQUEEZING A LEMON*

124 U. Pa. L. Rev. 687, 710 (1976)

In urging the abolition of a separate insanity defense, Dean Morris observed, "It too often is overlooked that one group's exculpation from criminal responsibility confirms the inculpation of other groups." That simple perception provides as well the principal justification for retention of the defense. For it is through the ongoing, case-by-case process of exculpating the non-responsible that society evolves its concepts of individual autonomy and accountability. As long as we retain our commitment to the political ideal that an individual is able in some degree to control his own destiny, we shall resist efforts to eliminate our principal mechanism for testing that capacity in our criminal law. If we abolish in large measure the defense of blamelessness, we detract from our ability to impose blame. The numbers of offenders so exculpated is likely to remain small; they are the exception we use to prove the rule of personal accountability. Symbolically, their significance outstrips the social gains to be realized by submitting them to our largely ineffective correctional process.

STONE, *THE INSANITY DEFENSE ON TRIAL*

33 Harv. L. Sch. Bull. 15, 21 (Fall 1982)

So finally, why not abolish the insanity defense? Who is standing in the way? My answer is the law itself. By the law, I mean those people—lawyers, judges, legislatures, and citizens—who have a profound concern for the morality of the law itself and who believe that the law should reflect our most basic human intuitions of morality. I maintain that every moral philosopher in every culture has realized that morality requires that man has free will. Our legal system and the law are inspired by that moral intuition. At the same time, I maintain that every moral philosopher who has thought about human nature has also concluded that at sometime in a man's life, he feels he has no choice. The contradiction between this experience of being without choice and the moral intuition of free will is one of the inescapable contradictions of human existence. That contradiction is expressed and denied by the insanity defense. The insanity defense is the exception that "proves" the rule of the law. I bowdlerize the maxim because today the insanity defense does more than test the law, it demonstrates that all other criminals had free will—the ability to choose between good and evil—but that they chose evil and therefore deserve to be punished.

It is not psychiatrists, it is not criminals, it is not the insane who need the insanity defense. The insanity defense is the exception that "proves" the rule of free will. It is required by the law itself, and it is this vision of law which has throughout history required resistance to abolition of the insanity defense.

BONNIE, *THE MORAL BASIS OF THE INSANITY DEFENSE*

69 A.B.A. J. 194-96 (1983)

Two fundamentally distinct questions are intertwined in discussions of the insanity defense. One concerns the moral issue of responsibility, a question looking backward to the offender's mental condition at the time of offense. The other is essentially dispositional and looks forward in time: what should be done with mentally disordered offenders, including those who are acquitted by reason of insanity, to minimize the risk of future recidivism?

This article addresses the issue of responsibility. Sweeping proposals to abolish the insanity defense should be rejected in favor of proposals to narrow it and shift the burden of proof to the defendant. The moral core of the defense must be retained, in my opinion, because some defendants afflicted by severe mental disorder who are out of touch with reality and are unable to appreciate the wrongfulness of their acts cannot justly be blamed and do not therefore deserve to be punished. The insanity defense, in short, is essential to the moral integrity of the criminal law.

But there are several observations to be made about the dispositional issues now receiving legislative attention.

First, the present dissatisfaction with the insanity defense is largely rooted in public concern about the premature release of dangerous persons acquitted by reason of insanity. Increased danger to the public, however, is not a necessary consequence of the insanity defense. The public can be better protected than is now the case in many states by a properly designed dispositional statute that assures that violent offenders acquitted by reason of insanity are committed for long-term treatment, including a period of post-discharge supervision or "hospital parole."

[Professor Bonnie then discusses the "guilty but mentally ill" verdict and the problem of mental health professionals' participation at the guilt stage.]

The historical evolution of the insanity defense has been influenced by the ebb and flow of informed opinion concerning scientific understanding of mental illness and its relation to criminal behavior. But it is well to remember that, at bottom, the debate about the insanity defense and the idea of criminal responsibility raises fundamentally moral questions, not scientific ones. As Lord Hale observed three centuries ago, in *History of Pleas of the Crown,* the ethical foundations of the criminal law are rooted in beliefs about human rationality, deterrability, and free will. But these are articles of moral faith rather than scientific fact.

Some critics of the insanity defense believe that mentally ill persons are not substantially less able to control their behavior than normal persons and that, in any case, a decent respect for the dignity of those persons requires that they be held accountable for their wrong-doing on the same terms as everyone else. On the other hand, proponents of the defense, among whom I count myself, believe that it is fundamentally wrong to condemn and punish a person whose rational control over his or her behavior was impaired by the incapacitating effects of severe mental illness.

* * *

If the insanity defense were abolished, the law would not take adequate account of the incapacitating effects of severe mental illness. Some mentally ill defendants who were psychotic and grossly out of touch with reality may be said to have "intended" to do what they did but nonetheless may have been so severely disturbed that they were unable to understand or appreciate the significance of their actions. These cases do not arise frequently, but when they do a criminal conviction, which signifies the societal judgment that the defendant deserves to be punished, would offend the basic moral intuitions of the community. Judges and juries would be forced either to return a verdict of conviction, which they would regard as morally obtuse, or to acquit the defendant in defiance of the law. They should be spared that moral embarrassment.

The moral difficulty with the *mens rea* approach is illustrated by a case involving Joy Baker, a 31-year-old woman who shot and killed her aunt. According to her account—which no one has ever doubted—she became increasingly agitated and fearful during the days before the shooting; she was worried that her dogs, her children (ages 8 and 11), and her neighbors were becoming possessed by the devil and that she was going to be "annihilated."

On the morning of the shooting, after a sleepless night, she ran frantically around the house clutching a gun to her breast. Worried about what the children might do to her if they became demonically "possessed" and about what she might do to them to defend herself, she made them read and reread the 23rd Psalm. Suddenly her aunt arrived unexpectedly. Unable to open the locked front door, and ignoring Mrs. Baker's frantic pleas to go away, the aunt came to the back door. When she reached through the broken screening to unlock the door, Mrs. Baker shot her.

The aunt then fell backward into the mud behind the porch, bleeding profusely. "Why, Joy?" she asked. "Because you're the devil, and you came to hurt me," Joy answered. Her aunt said, "Honey, no, I came to help you." At this point, Mrs. Baker said she became very confused and "I took the gun and shot her again just to relieve the pain she was having because she said she was hurt."

All the psychiatrists who examined Mrs. Baker concluded that she was acutely psychotic at the time she killed her aunt. The police who arrested her and others in the small rural community agreed that she must have been crazy because there was no rational explanation for her conduct. She was acquitted. Yet, had there been no insanity defense, she could have been acquitted only in defiance of the law. Although she was clearly out of touch with reality and unable to understand the wrongfulness of her conduct, she had the "criminal intent" or *mens rea* required for some form of criminal homicide. It we look only at her conscious motivation for the second shot and do not take into account her high regressed and disorganized emotional condition, she was technically guilty of murder (euthanasia being no justification, of course). Moreover, even if the first shot had been fatal, she probably would have been guilty of manslaughter because her delusional belief that she was in imminent danger of demonic annihilation was, by definition, unreasonable.

These technical points, of course, may make little practical difference in the courtroom. If the expert testimony in Joy Baker's case were admitted to disprove *mens rea,* juries might ignore the law and decide, very bluntly, whether the defendant was "too crazy" to be convicted. The cause of rational criminal law reform, however, is not well served by designing rules of law in the expectation that they will be ignored or nullified when they appear unjust in individual cases.

[C] Intoxication

The relationship between alcohol and drug consumption and crime appears significant. Available data suggest that often the perpetrators of crime and/or their victims are intoxicated at the time the crime occurs.

In a study of 588 criminal homicides committed in Philadelphia during a five-year period, alcohol was present in both victim and offender in 44 percent of the cases. The authors of this study concluded that those victims who drank were twice as likely to have initiated the violence as victim who were not drinking prior to being killed.[1] Another study of 882 persons arrested during

---

[1] Wolfgang and Strohm, *The Relationship between Alcohol and Criminal Homicide,* 41 Q.J. of Stud. in Alcohol 411 (1956).

or immediately after committing a felony concluded alcoholic involvement was significant in 64 percent of the sample.[2] A third report found 56 percent of 5,622 patients admitted to a hospital emergency room with injuries resulting from fights or assaults to have positive alcohol levels measured by breath analysis.[3]

In an investigation of homicides in St. Louis during 1973, 85 of the 168 victims examined had been drinking at the time of death.[4] One researcher concludes that two-thirds of recorded homicides result from "drunken brawls" at home or in a tavern.[5] Finally, a Law Enforcement Assistance Administration study claimed that at least 24 percent of violent index crimes involve alcohol.[6]

A report published in 1980 studied 57 Alaskan homicide defendants (30 Alaska natives and 27 non-natives) referred for psychiatric evaluation after being indicted. Alcoholism was the most frequent psychiatric diagnosis made of the offenders. Eighty-three percent of the native offenders consumed alcohol, in most cases quite heavily, at the time of the homicide. Fifty-six percent of the non-native subjects used alcohol at the time of the homicides. Ninety percent of the natives and 59 percent of the non-natives had a prior history of alcoholism or episodic abuse. Forty percent of the natives and 11 percent of the non-natives had a past history of alcoholism treatment.[7]

A 1979 survey of state prisoners found that half of them self-reported drinking heavily on the day of the crime, and 20 percent reported drinking heavily every day for the year preceding their crime.[8]

Drug consumption is also a highly relevant factor in criminal activity. In a study by the Drug Use Forecasting System, a program founded in 1987 by the National Institute of Justice, 53 to 79 percent of men arrested in 12 major cities tested positive for illegal drug use. Even excluding tests for marijuana, 25 to 74 percent showed positive results for illegal drug use. The findings were based on voluntary urine tests of more than 2,000 men arrested by local police departments in June and November 1987.[9]

Justice Kennedy expressed the following regarding the relationship between drug use and crime in his concurring opinion in *Harmelin v. Michigan,* p. 139, supra:

> Quite apart from the pernicious effects on the individual who consumes illegal drugs, such drugs relate to crime in at least three ways: (1)A drug user may commit crime because of drug-induced changes in physiological

---

[2] Shupe, *Alcohol and Crime,* 44 J. Crim. L., Criminology, & Police Sd. 661 (1954).

[3] Thum, Wechsler, and Demone, *Alcohol Levels of Emergency Service Patients Injured in Fights and Assaults,* 10 Criminology 487 (1973).

[4] Herjanic and Meyer, *Notes on Epidemiology of Homicide in an Urban Area,* 8 Forensic Sci. 235 (1976).

[5] Davis, *Alcohol as a Precursor to Violent Death,* 5 J. Drug Issues 270 (1975).

[6] Erskine, H., *Alcohol and the Criminal Justice System: Challenge and Response* (1972).

[7] Bloom, J. D., *Forensic Psychiatric Evaluation of Alaska Native Homicide Offenders,* 3 Int. J.L. Psych. 163–71 (1980).

[8] *Prisoners and Alcohol,* Bureau of Just. Statistics Bull. (1983).

[9] *New York Times,* Jan. 22, 1988, § 1, at 1, col. 6.

functions, cognitive ability, and mood; (2)A drug user may commit crime in order to obtain money to buy drugs; and (3)A violent crime may occur as part of the drug business or culture. . . . Studies bear out these possibilities, and demonstrate a direct nexus between illegal drugs and crimes of violence. To mention but a few examples, 57 percent of a national sample of males arrested in 1989 for homicide tested positive for illegal drugs. . . . The comparable statistics for assault, robbery, and weapons arrests were 55, 73 and 63 percent, respectively. In Detroit, Michigan in 1988, 68 percent of a sample of male arrestees and 81 percent of a sample of female arrestees tested positive for illegal drugs. . . . Fifty-one percent of males and seventy-one percent of females tested positive for cocaine. And last year an estimated 60 percent of the homicides in Detroit were drug-related, primarily cocaine-related.

501 U.S. at 1002–03 (cites to empirical studies omitted).

The studies, of course, do not demonstrate that drinking or drug use are the "cause" of crime; indeed, that victims and/or defendants were "drinking" may not indicate substantial levels of intoxication. Nevertheless, the figures are striking, and would seem to urge a careful examination by the criminal law of the effect of intoxication, or drinking, upon criminal liability.

PEOPLE V. LOW

Supreme Court of Colorado, En Banc

732 P.2d 622 (1987)

ERICKSON, Justice.

This is an appeal by the prosecution on a point of law following the acquittal of defendant Robert Eugene Low in a trial to the court on a charge of assault in the first degree and all lesser included offenses. The trial court found the defendant not guilty because the prosecution did not establish that the defendant had the required specific or general intent necessary to commit assault in the first, second, and third degree.[1] The trial court acquitted the defendant because he had consumed an excessive amount of "HOLD" cough drops which caused him to become "temporarily insane" and incapable of formulating either a specific or general criminal intent.

The prosecution asserts that the trial court erred as a matter of law in considering evidence of the defendant's chemically induced insanity because the defendant did not specially plead at arraignment the defense of insanity as required by section 16-8-103(1), 8A C.R.S. (1986), or the defense of impaired mental condition as required by section 16-8-103.5(1), 8A C.R.S. (1986). It is

---

[1] In Colorado, "all offenses . . . in which the mental culpability requirement is expressed as 'intentionally' or 'with intent' are declared to be specific intent offenses." § 18-1-501(5), 8B C.R.S. (1986). The crimes of first degree assault, as defined in section 18-3-202(1)(a), (b), and (g), are specific intent crimes. Only those offenses that contain the mental culpability element of "knowingly" or "willfully" are general intent crimes. § 18-1-501(6), 8B C.R.S. (1986). We use the term "general intent" to signify any crime which does not require proof of a specific intent and is not a crime of strict liability

undisputed that the defendant did not follow the statutory procedure for pleading insanity or the defense of impaired mental condition. We disapprove of the trial court's entry of a judgment of acquittal for the reasons set forth in this opinion.

Defendant Robert Eugene Low was president and general manager of Prime, Inc., a trucking company in Springfield, Missouri. Low and his fourteen-year old stepson Shane Low (Shane), together with several friends from Springfield, Missouri, arranged a hunting trip to Creede, Colorado.

The hunters planned to meet in Creede on Friday, October 14, 1983. On October 13, 1983, Low worked at his trucking company all day, and then he and Shane attended a hunter's safety class that evening so that they could obtain Colorado hunting licenses. After the hunter's safety class, Low drove all night to be in Creede at the agreed time. Low and Shane arrived in Creede at approximately 3:00 P.M. on October 14, and after some delay, located Kim McCowan (Kim), the brother of the victim in this case, and Jerry Roller (Roller), both of whom were friends from Missouri. Kim and Roller led the way up the canyon to the campsite in a four-wheel-drive vehicle, followed by Low and Shane in Low's pickup truck.

On the trip up the mountain road, the defendant became increasingly anxious and apprehensive, and had feelings of unreality. He began to notice that the trees surrounding the road had a particular type of bark that was "soft and unnatural." He was paranoid and questioned his stepson about what was occurring and why he was being "tricked." At approximately the halfway point to the camp, the defendant stopped his pickup truck. When Kim and Roller stopped their truck to make sure everything was all right, Low demanded that all of the individuals kneel in prayer with him. Kim testified that he had never known Low to be "a religious person," but imagined that the beauty of the wilderness inspired Low to demand the prayer session. Upon concluding the prayer, Low insisted that Roller drive Shane to the campsite in Kim's truck, and that Kim drive Low's truck with Low as a passenger. Kim complied because Low appeared to be tired from his trip from Missouri. During the remainder of the ride to the campsite, the defendant speculated on whether he was alive or dead.

When the parties arrived at the campsite, the defendant, according to the testimony, was convinced that he was dead and had gone to hell. Kim, still believing that the defendant was exhausted, suggested that Low rest in the small cabin at the campsite while the others unload his truck and erect his tent. Low went to the cabin and rested for five or ten minutes. While in the cabin, the defendant concluded that he was a corpse in a mausoleum and that it was necessary to redeem himself in order to get to heaven. He then walked out of the cabin and up a small knoll and, referring to his tent, said, "we're going to bring it up here. We're going to raise the temple here." The other members of the hunting party took Low's tent up the knoll and began to set it up. Low approached A. D. McCowan (Duane or A. D.), who was helping with the tent, and said, "You're the devil, Duane." A. D. made a response relating to Low's ingratitude and Low said, "If you're not the devil, stand up and look me in the eye." A. D. did so, and the confrontation seemingly ended.

Low went down the knoll to his truck while Kim and A. D. continued to set up the tent. He asked for his rifle and told his stepson to get him some shells for the gun. The other hunters realized by this time that Low was disturbed in some way and took the rifle from him. The defendant then unbuckled his hunting knife, went to his tent, and stabbed A. D. in the upper back. Low was immediately subdued. His friends testified that Low repeatedly called his tent a temple, and that he was acting in an irrational and crazy manner. McCowan suffered serious injuries and was taken to Creede, and from there he was transferred by ambulance to a hospital in Del Norte.

Kim and Shane remained at the campsite to look after Low while the others took A. D. to the hospital. Low tried to stab himself when Kim attempted to take the hunting knife away from him, but Kim obtained the knife after a brief struggle. Low then returned to his truck, removed a can of kerosene from the truck bed, and went into the partially erected tent. He poured kerosene on the floor, sat in a folding chair, and ignited the tent while he was still inside of it. Kim unsuccessfully attempted to get Low out of the burning tent. Convinced that Low was "crazy," Kim grabbed a gun and ammunition and took Shane into the woods to avoid a further confrontation until help arrived. Low left the tent shortly before it was burned completely and fell asleep on the ground. After a short nap, he began questioning what had happened, and then returned to the cabin and lay down. He dozed and awakened from time to time and began feeling sensations of being cold and again questioned whether or not he was in fact dead. When the police arrived and arrested the defendant the next day, he told them that the unreal nightmare was finally over.

The uncontradicted testimony was that the defendant, for several months prior to the attack on A. D. McCowan, had ingested forty to fifty "HOLD" cough drops a day. The defendant's use of the cough drops had developed over the course of five to six months. He initially took the cough drops after developing a lingering cough and cold but continued to take them as a partial substitute for chewing tobacco and in an effort to quit smoking. On his trip to Colorado, the defendant did not sleep and consumed approximately one hundred twenty cough drops within a twenty-four-hour period. Prior to his attack on McCowan, the defendant had never felt any adverse or intoxicating effects from the cough drops.

Dr. Frederick A. Lewis, a psychiatrist, examined the defendant in June 1984, and concluded that Low was not mentally ill at the time of the examination. "HOLD" cough drops contain the drug dextromethorphan hydrobromide. Dr. Lewis stated that Low ingested approximately one gram of dextromethorphan when he consumed twelve packages of the cough drops in the twenty-four hours preceding the attack on McCowan. In Dr. Lewis's opinion, there was very little doubt that the dextromethorphan caused a psychotic disorder known as "organic delusional syndrome" or "toxic psychosis." Symptoms of toxic psychosis include a distorted perception of reality, paranoia, auditory hallucinations, and delusions. From his medical research, the accounts of the incident by the other witnesses, and his examination of the defendant, Dr. Lewis concluded that Low was psychotic and delusional at the time he attacked McCowan. Dr. Lewis testified that Low was incapable of distinguishing right from wrong at the time of the alleged assault, and that Low did not have the ability to formulate the specific intent to commit a criminal act. . . .

The defendant entered a plea of not guilty and waived his right to a jury trial. Both the prosecution and the court were advised that the defendant was not entering a plea of not guilty by reason of insanity, and elected not to plead the affirmative defense of impaired mental condition. . . .

Prior to trial, defense counsel gave a notice of defenses to the court and to the prosecutor. The affirmative defense of involuntary intoxication was raised in the notice. The defense claimed that the warning on the cough drop box did not alert the defendant to the danger of intoxication.[5] The notice also stated that the defense would rely upon the absence of the requisite specific intent to commit the crime of assault in the first degree.

The trial judge, at the close of the case, found that the prosecution proved beyond a reasonable doubt that Low caused serious bodily injury to A. D. McCowan by means of a deadly weapon. In considering whether Low acted with the specific intent required by the first-degree-assault statute, the affirmative defense of involuntary intoxication was reviewed by the court. However, the trial judge did not make an explicit finding of involuntary intoxication, impaired mental condition or insanity, but acquitted the defendant because the prosecution "failed to prove an element of the offense or any lesser included offense; namely, the culpability element of *mens rea.*"

The question before us is whether the failure of the defendant to plead the defense of insanity or impaired mental condition precludes the introduction of evidence of insanity or impaired mental condition to establish the absence of *mens rea*.

The power to define criminal conduct and to establish the legal components of criminal liability is vested with the General Assembly. . . . The legislature is also empowered to formulate principles of criminal responsibility and justification and, within constitutional limitations, to restrict defenses to particular crimes. . . . The General Assembly can require certain matters to be raised by a special plea without offending the constitutional rights of the accused. . . .

The only disputed factual issue in this case was whether the defendant had the requisite mental culpability to commit first-degree assault or any lesser included offense. It was stipulated that the defendant, with or by means of a hunting knife, a deadly weapon, stabbed A. D. McCowan in the back and inflicted serious bodily injury.

---

[5] The cough drops were sold over the counter without a prescription. "HOLD" cough drops had the following warning on the box:

> WARNING: If cough persists or is accompanied by high fever, consult a physician promptly. Do not administer to children under six. Keep out of reach of children.
>
> CAUTION: If you are pregnant or nursing a baby, seek the advice of a health professional before using this product.
>
> NOT HABIT FORMING: Contains 7.5 milligrams of dextromethorphan HBr per lozenge.

THE AFFIRMATIVE DEFENSE OF INTOXICATION

Intoxication, voluntary or involuntary, is a "disturbance of mental or physical capacities resulting from the introduction of any substance into the body...." Voluntary or self-induced intoxication is "caused by substances which the defendant knows or ought to know have the tendency to cause intoxication and which he knowingly introduced or allowed to be introduced into his body...." Involuntary intoxication is intoxication that is not self-induced, and by definition occurs when the defendant does not knowingly ingest an intoxicating substance, or ingests a substance not known to be an intoxicant....

While the characterization of intoxication as self-induced or involuntary depends on the facts of each case, the legal consequences of voluntary or involuntary intoxication are clear. An involuntarily intoxicated person is not criminally responsible for his conduct if at the time of the alleged offense the defendant "lacks the capacity to conform his conduct to the requirements of law...." Involuntary intoxication is in this respect similar to "temporary insanity" because there is no immoral or blameworthy stigma attached to the condition. See generally, R. Perkins & R. Boyce, Criminal Law 1005 (3d ed. 1982) (involuntary intoxication establishes that the accused's "derangement is without culpability and hence is to be dealt with the same as if it were the result of mental disease or defect....") The General Assembly... has made involuntary intoxication a complete defense to all crimes....

Voluntary intoxication "may be offered by the defendant when it is relevant to negate the existence of a specific intent if such intent is an element of the crime charged." Consequently, evidence of voluntary intoxication constitutes a defense to specific intent crimes, but is incompetent as a defense to general intent crimes...

* * *

Low claimed that the manufacturer's warning did not indicate that intoxication was a possible side effect of ingesting large quantities of the medication, and Low's previous experience with "HOLD" did not alert him to the possibility of intoxication. Expert testimony established that Low's consumption of excessive quantities of dextromethorphan hydrobromide resulted in delusional and psychotic behavior, precluding Low from conforming his conduct to the requirements of the law. Had the trial court found as a factual matter that Low was involuntarily intoxicated, assuming the finding was supported by sufficient competent evidence, its judgment of acquittal would have been proper. There are no special pleading requirements for the affirmative defense of involuntary intoxication, and an involuntarily intoxicated defendant is absolved of responsibility for all criminal acts.

[The court went on to "disapprove" of the trial court's judgment of acquittal. The basis of the acquittal, the state's failure to prove the *mens rea* elements of the charged offenses, was improper because the defendant had not met the special pleading requirements for raising the defenses of insanity or of "impaired mental condition," Colorado's version of "diminished capacity." Those issues were, therefore, not before the trial court. Moreover, even if the defendant had properly raised the "impaired mental condition" issue, the defense could only negate the *mens rea* for "specific intent" crimes thus leaving unaffected the state's proof of "the lesser included offenses" of assault in the second and third degrees.]

Model Penal Code § 2.08

(4) Intoxication which (a)is not self-induced or (b)is pathological is an affirmative defense if by reason of such intoxication the actor at the time of his conduct lacks substantial capacity either to appreciate its criminality [wrongfulness] or to conform his conduct to the requirements of law.

(5) *Definitions.* In this Section unless a different meaning plainly is required:

(a) "intoxication" means a disturbance of mental or physical capacities resulting from the introduction of substances into the body;

(b) "self-induced intoxication" means intoxication caused by substances which the actor knowingly introduces into his body, the tendency of which to cause intoxication he knows or ought to know, unless he introduces them pursuant to medical advice or under such circumstances as would afford a defense to a charge of crime;

(c) "pathological intoxication" means intoxication grossly excessive in degree, given the amount of the intoxicant, to which the actor does not know he is susceptible.

People v. Kelley

Court of Appeals of Michigan

21 Mich. App. 612, 176 N.W.2d 435 (1970)

LEVIN, Judge.

The defendant appeals his conviction of armed robbery. We reverse because of instructional error concerning the intoxication defense.

The people's evidence showed that the defendant and George Moore entered a drug store at 8:30 P.M. and held it up using revolvers.

At the trial the defendant testified that for several days before the robbery he had been drinking heavily. He claimed that after drinking 20 to 25 bottles of beer during the morning of the day the crime was committed he drove his car to Moore's house to buy some insulation from him. After purchasing the insulation the defendant and Moore made 2 automobile trips to the defendant's house transporting the insulation. The defendant further testified that he continued to drink throughout the morning; he said that he and Moore consumed some 24 bottles of beer transporting the first load of insulation, and that additional beer was consumed delivering the second load. The defendant said he then took a couple of benzedrine capsules to "appease" Moore. The defendant claimed that he had no recollection of anything that occurred that day after taking the benzedrine owing to an alcoholic blackout.[2] Thus, he said, he could not recall his participation in the robbery.

The defendant also provided an extensive history of alcoholism beginning at the age of 15, reflected in military service and civilian criminal records. In 1956 he was convicted of armed robbery; he was intoxicated when that offense was committed. He said, however, that he had an awareness of his actions at that time which he did not have at the time the currently charged robbery was committed.

He stated he could recall only one previous incident of overtly antisocial behavior after blacking out due to intoxication, when, as a soldier and while grossly intoxicated, he was removed from a machine gun behind the lines and struck the company commander in a fight. The defendant said he had experienced many blackouts of an uneventual nature. He had previously committed at least one crime while sober.

The defense in this case was that by reason of intoxication the defendant was not aware of, and, therefore, was not criminally responsible for, his actions at the time the crime was committed.

At common law, a trespass was not criminal unless the actor entertained that culpable state of mind termed *mens rea*. This element of every common law crime is sometimes referred to as general intent. The universally accepted rule in this country is that general intent cannot be negatived by evidence that the actor was intoxicated at the time the crime was committed. This doctrine is expressed in the oft-repeated maxim that "voluntary intoxication is no excuse for crime."

The rigor of this doctrine has been relaxed where the People must prove that the actor entertained a specific intent in addition to general intent. Thus, although intoxication is not a defense where only general intent needs to be shown, *e.g.,* where the crime charged is involuntary manslaughter or statutory rape, the Michigan Supreme Court has held that it can be shown to negative the requisite specific intent where the crime charged is assault with intent to murder, assault with intent to rape and assault with intent to do great bodily harm less than the crime of murder. And since larceny "does not consist in the wrongful taking of the property, for that might be a mere trespass; but it consists in the wrongful taking with felonious intent," intoxication can be shown to negative that felonious intent. . . .

In this case the prosecutor concedes, the trial judge charged the jury and we agree that armed robbery is a specific intent crime. Robbery is larceny committed by assault or putting in fear and, as we have already seen, larceny is a specific intent crime.

---

[2] "After numerous overindulgences some drinkers may begin to experience mental blackouts. After a certain point in a drinking bout they are unable to remember what happened. They do not pass out or become unconscious, but their intelligence is as clouded as that of a psychotic, and their control is equally impaired." Deddens, *Volitional Fault and the Intoxicated Criminal Offender,* 36 U. Cin. L. Rev. 258 (1967), citing a study of the Public Health Service, U.S. Department of Health, Education and Welfare.

The intoxication defense was first discussed by the Michigan Supreme Court in *People v. Garbutt* (1868), 17 Mich. 9. Garbutt was convicted of murder. The Court held that the trial judge had correctly refused to charge the jury that they must acquit the defendant if they believed that he was intoxicated to such an extent that he was not conscious of what he was doing at the time the offense was committed. The Court stated that to recognize intoxication as a defense:

> would be a most alarming [doctrine] to admit in the criminal jurisprudence of the country, and we think the recorder was right in rejecting it. *A man who voluntarily puts himself in condition to have no control of his actions, must be held to intend the consequences.* The safety of the community requires this rule. Intoxication is so easily counterfeited, and when real it is so often resorted to as a means of nerving the person up to the commission of some desperate act, and is withal so inexcusable in itself, that the law has never recognized it as an excuse for crime. [Emphasis supplied.]

Two years later, in *Roberts v. People* (1870), 19 Mich. 401, the Michigan Supreme Court for the first time drew the distinction between general and specific intent. Roberts was convicted of assault with intent to murder. The Court referred to *Garbutt* and stated that the consequences which a man who voluntarily becomes intoxicated is held, as a matter of law, to intend is "the crime actually committed; and not in this case the intent charged, if the defendant was at the time incapable of entertaining it, and did not in fact entertain it."

* * *

> . . . A person who voluntarily puts himself in a state of intoxication is deemed to intend the consequences which actually ensue, the crime actually committed, in this case armed robbery. Or, to state it differently, as a matter of law, voluntary intoxication may not be shown for the purpose of establishing that the defendant did not entertain the general intent (*mens rea* or culpability) necessary to commit the crime.

> Since armed robbery is, as we have previously stated, a crime of specific intent, the trial judge properly went on to charge that if the defendant's mental faculties were so far overcome by intoxication that he was not conscious of what he was doing, or he did not know what he was doing, then he could not entertain that specific intent and, therefore . . . there being "no such intent, the crime cannot have been committed."

> The last sentence of this portion of the instruction, *viz:*

>> However, I also instruct you that if the respondent had knowledge that when he drinks he may lose his faculties, and without control over his actions commit a crime, then such prior knowledge of criminal propensity would be a basis for your finding that he intended to do what he did

> was, however, erroneous. This portion of the charge seems to be modeled on *Roberts,* butmistakenly.

> In the situation hypothesized in Roberts, a defendant "had formed the intent" to commit the crime before he became intoxicated. It is not claimed,

however, that the defendant Kelley while he was sober formed the specific intent requisite to the commission of the crime of which he was convicted. . . .

It was, therefore, incorrect to charge that intoxication would not be a defense if Kelley knew before he began to drink that if he became drunk he might commit "a crime"—any crime. Under *Roberts,* to entirely eliminate intoxication as a defense, a defendant must, while sober, have formed the specific intent requisite to the commission of the particular crime he is charged with committing.

The defendant in *Roberts* also claimed insanity but introduced no evidence tending to show insanity distinct from and independent of the effects of intoxication. The Supreme Court ruled that if the jury found that Roberts knew that intoxication would trigger a dormant tendency to insanity, then insanity would be a defense only if the defendant was insane without regard to his intoxication. That cannot be read, as the trial judge appears to have read it in this case, as meaning that if the defendant Kelley had knowledge that when he drinks he may lose his faculties and without control over his actions commit "a crime," such prior knowledge of criminal propensity would be a basis for a finding that he entertained the intent required to commit the particular crime he was convicted of committing. The *Roberts* opinion states only that intoxication may not be relied upon to establish a defense *other* than intoxication when the actor knows before he begins to drink that drinking may cause a condition which would create a factual basis for that defense. This did not create an exception to the intoxication defense itself.

The instruction given in this case eliminates the very distinction drawn in *Roberts,* the distinction between general intent and specific intent. The judge's charge that the intoxication defense is unavailable if the jury finds that the defendant knew while sober that when he drinks he may commit a crime, any crime, means that a defendant's knowledge of a propensity to commit when drunk, say, the crime of blasphemy, or gambling, or gross indecency or murder, would eliminate the defense even if the crime actually charged is, say, armed robbery or some other crime of specific intent. That is not the law. Prior knowledge of a propensity to commit some crime cannot be made the basis of a finding by a jury that a defendant while sober entertained the requisite specific intent to commit a particular crime.

* * *

During the discussion of his proposed jury charge with counsel for the parties the trial judge expressed the view that a man with the defendant's history of intoxication should be deemed fully accountable for the crimes he commits while intoxicated. We agree with the judge that one who has a history of committing serious crimes when he drinks is a threat to the safety of the community and that in the spectrum of moral responsibility one who has such a history and commits a crime in that condition is generally more heinous than one who commits a crime while intoxicated but who has no such history.

The question before us, however, is one of criminal responsibility, not moral responsibility. Present law simply does not differentiate between wrongdoers based on their propensity for crime, holding one with a prior history of committing crimes while intoxicated to a higher standard of criminal responsibility than one who has no such history.

It has been suggested that the law needs revision. One commentator would eliminate the intoxication defense where a normal drinker knows of his propensity to commit crime while intoxicated; but that innovation would not be of much value when the drinker, like the defendant Kelley, is an alcoholic.

It has also been suggested that a person who has a prior history of commission of crime while drunk and nevertheless drinks and commits a crime should not be held responsible for the commission of that crime, but rather for the crime of drinking knowing of that propensity; that he should be charged with the commission of a newly created offense of reckless or negligent intoxication in lieu of the offense which he committed while drunk.

* * *

It has also been maintained that the availability of the intoxication defense should not depend on whether a court chooses to characterize an element of the crime charged as separate from the element of general intent. It has been observed that neither common experience nor psychology knows of any such phenomenon as "general intent" distinguishable from "specific intent." It does seem incongruous to make the admissibility of mitigating evidence depend on whether the statutory definition of a crime includes a separately stated intent, and other methods of defining specific intent are highly manipulable.

The clumsiness of the exculpatory device has been criticized. A defendant who is charged with a specific intent crime may go free if he can prove he was intoxicated; this result contrasts sharply with the absolute denial of relief to the intoxicated offender charged with a crime of general intent.

If the function of the general/specific intent distinction is to eliminate the defense as to lesser included offenses, *e.g.,* assault and battery, but to retain it for the more serious offenses, *e.g.,* armed robbery, and in that manner mitigate the general rule that intoxication is not a defense, then manifestly this should be done on a consistent basis. The right to interpose this defense should depend on something more substantial than a technical distinction that was seized upon by a judge 130 years ago and adopted by other judges to reach results thought sound in the cases then before them.

* * *

As long as the general/specific intent distinction is conceptually the controlling one, proof of the actor's general recklessness cannot be made to substitute for proof of his specific intent to commit a particular crime. Under existing precedent if the crime charged cannot be committed unless the actor entertained a specific intent at the time the crime was committed, he is not guilty if he did not entertain that intent by reason of intoxication.

* * *

Reversed and remanded for a new trial.

NOTES

1. *Kelley* represents the traditional common law rule: Voluntary intoxication is admissible when relevant to disprove a "specific intent" that is an element of the crime charged, but not to disprove a "general intent" when that is the required element. The "specific" versus "general" intent distinction has proven notoriously obscure. Sometimes "specific intent" is defined as "some intent in addition to the intent to do the physical act which the crime requires," LaFave and Scott, p.389. Thus, as *Kelley* suggests, "assault with intent to murder" is a specific intent crime while "assault with a deadly weapon" is considered a crime of general intent. See *People v. Rocha*, 3 Cal. 3d 893, 479 P.2d 372 (1971). Yet, if assault in the latter context is given its usual meaning of attempting a violent injury or acting with the *intent* to commit a violent injury, then it appears that "assault with a deadly weapon" would also be a specific intent crime. See the analysis of Chief Justice Traynor in *People v. Hood*, 1 Cal. 3d 444, 462 P.2d 370 (1969).

The Comments to Model Penal Code § 2.08 offer a different explication of the specific-general intent distinction:.

> . . . To the extent . . . that the actual decisions have given a concrete content to these vague conceptions, the net effect of this rule seems to have come to this: when purpose or knowledge, as those culpability factors are defined in Section 2.02 of the Model Code, must be proved as an element of the offense, intoxication may generally be adduced in disproof if it is logically relevant. When, on the other hand, recklessness or negligence, as those culpability factors are defined in Section 2.02, suffices to establish the offense, an exculpation based on intoxication is precluded by the law. Moreover, since recklessness is sufficient to establish *mens rea* for most offenses, intoxication is ordinarily not permitted to establish a defense, whatever its effect on the awareness or knowledge of the actor.

MPC § 2.08, Comment at 354.

2. Although most writers and courts now acknowledge that the "specific versus general" intent approach is nothing more than a legal fiction (designed, according to Hall, *Intoxication and Criminal Responsibility,* 57 Harv. L. Rev. 1045 (1944), to allow drunken offenders to avoid liability for capital homicide), most courts continue to follow the doctrine in an effort to accommodate the interest of reducing culpability of drunken offenders while still promoting interests in deterrence and incapacitation. Thus, in *D.P.P. v. Majewski,* 2 W.L.R. 623 (1976), the House of Lords reaffirmed the "specific—general" intent doctrine. Each of the opinions recognized that limiting the effect of intoxication to "specific intent" crimes was not logical, but rejected logic as the only relevant guide. In one of the more notable passages, Lord Salmon said,

I accept that there is a degree of illogicality in the rule that intoxication may excuse or expunge one type of intention and not another. This illogicality is, however, acceptable to me because the benevolent part of the rule removes undue harshness without imperiling safety and the stricter part of the rule works without imperiling justice. It would be just as ridiculous to remove the benevolent part of the rule (which no one suggests) as it would be to adopt the alternative of removing the stricter part of the rule for the sake of preserving absolute logic. Absolute logic in human affairs is an uncertain guide and a very dangerous matter.

See Dashwood, *Logic and the Lords in Majewski,* 1977 Crim. L. Rev. 532.

A straightforward embrace of social protection occurred in *People v. Hood,* 1 Cal. 3d 444, 462 P.2d 370 (1969). There the California Supreme Court abandoned the distinction between specific and general intents, finding it opaque and confusing.

The court then went on, however, to hold that intoxication could be no defense to a charge of assault, whether it was a specific or general intent crime:

> . . . The problem is to reconcile two competing theories of what is just in the treatment of those who commit crimes while intoxicated. On the one hand, the moral culpability of a drunken criminal is frequently less than that of a sober person effecting a like injury. On the other hand, it is commonly felt that a person who voluntarily gets drunk and while in that state commits a crime should not escape the consequences. (See Hall, General Principles of Criminal Law 537 (2d ed. 1960).)
>
> Before the nineteenth century, the common law refused to give any effect to the fact that an accused committed a crime while intoxicated. The judges were apparently troubled by this rigid traditional rule, however, for there were a number of attempts during the early part of the nineteenth century to arrive at a more humane, yet workable doctrine. The theory that these judges explored was that evidence of intoxication could be considered to negate intent, whenever intent was an element of the crime charged. As Professor Hall notes, however, such an exculpatory doctrine could eventually have undermined the traditional rule entirely, since some form of *mens rea* is a requisite of all but strict liability offenses. (Hall, Intoxication and Criminal Responsibility, 57 Harv. L. Rev. 1045, 1049.) To limit the operation of the doctrine and achieve a compromise between the conflicting feelings of sympathy and reprobation for the intoxicated offender, later courts both in England and this country drew a distinction between so-called specific intent and general intent crimes.

* * *

> A compelling consideration is the effect of alcohol on human behavior. A significant effect of alcohol is to distort judgment and relax the controls on aggressive and anti-social impulses. (Beck and Parker, The Intoxicated Offender—A Problem of Responsibility (1966), 44 Can. B. Rev. 563, 570–573; Muelberger, *Medico-Legal Aspects of Alcohol Intoxication,* 35 Mich. St. B.J. 36, 40–41 (1956).) Alcohol apparently has less effect on the ability to engage

in simple goal-directed behavior, although it may impair the efficiency of that behavior. In other words, a drunk man is capable of forming an intent to do something simple, such as strike another, unless he is so drunk that he has reached the stage of unconsciousness. What he is not as capable as a sober man of doing is exercising judgment about the social consequences of his acts or controlling his impulses toward antisocial acts. He is more likely to act rashly and impulsively and to be susceptible to passion and anger. It would therefore be anomalous to allow evidence of intoxication to relieve a man of responsibility for the crimes of assault with a deadly weapon or simple assault, which are so frequently committed in just such a manner. As the court said in *Parker v. United States,* 23 U.S. App. D.C. 343, 359 F.2d 1009, 1012–1013 (1966), "Whatever ambiguities there may be in distinguishing between specific and general intent to determine whether drunkenness constitutes a defense, an offense of this nature is not one which requires an intent that is susceptible to negation through a showing of voluntary intoxication."

People v. Hood, at 455–58, 462 P.2d at 377–79.

But see People v. Rocha, 3 Cal. 3d 893, 479 P.2d 372 (1971), which appears to reintroduce the specific—general intent distinction to California law by holding that assault with a deadly weapon is a "general intent" crime for which the defense of intoxication is irrelevant.

3. The most important effect of the intoxication "defense" in the United States is that it allows a drunken killer to negate the "specific intent" or "premeditation" necessary for firstdegree murder, thus reducing the crime to second degree (noncapital) murder. Even injurisdictions where intoxication is otherwise deemed irrelevant to guilt, *e.g., Chittum v. Commonwealth,* 211 Va. 12, 174 S.E.2d 1129 (1979), the courts have recognized the doctrine in first degree murder cases.

4. The suggestion, noted in *Kelley,* that the current law be radically changed and that legislatures create a new crime, such as "reckless drinking" or "drinking while knowing of a propensity to commit a crime (or become violent, etc.)" has been made by a number of writers. See, *e.g.,* Williams at 566 *et seq:* Frankel, *Narcotic Addiction, Criminal Responsibility, and Civil Commitment,* 1966 Utah L. Rev. 581; Ashworth, *Intoxication and General Defences,* 1980 Cr. L. Rev. 556; Comment, *Volitional Fault and the Intoxicated Criminal Offender,* 36 U. Cin. L. Rev. 258 (1967). *Contra:* Bryden, *Mens Rea and the Intoxicated Offenders,* 1968 Jud. Rev. 48.

5. The Model Penal Code § 2.08 and Comments at 358–59 offers its own version of the defense of intoxication:

> (1) Except as provided in Subsection (4) [see p. 884 immediately following the Low case, *supra]* of this Section, intoxication of the actor is not a defense unless it negatives an element of the offense.

> (2) When recklessness establishes an element of the offense, if the actor, due to self-induced intoxication, is unaware of a risk of which he would have been aware had he been sober, such unawareness is immaterial.

> (3) Intoxication does not, in itself, constitute mental disease within the meaning of Section 4.01.

* * *

Comments:

Those who oppose a special rule for drunkenness in relation to awareness of the risk in recklessness draw strength initially from the presumptive disfavor of any special rules of liability. . . . The protagonists of this position draw further strength from the proposition that it is precisely the awareness of the risk in recklessness that is the essence of its moral culpability—a culpability dependent upon the magnitude of the specific risk knowingly created. When that risk is greater in degree than that which the actor perceives at the time of getting drunk, as is frequently the case, the result of a special rule is bound to be a liability disproportionate to culpability. Hence the solution urged is to dispense with any special rule, relying rather on the possibility of proving foresight at the time of drinking and, when this cannot be proved, upon a generalized prohibition of being drunk and dangerous, with sanctions appropriate for such behavior. This approach would also permit prosecution for negligence if negligent commission of the act in question was sufficient to establish criminal liability. With respect to negligence, the essence of the culpability is the failure to perceive a risk that the actor should have perceived. The actor's culpability in failing to perceive a risk would be judged against the standard of a man in normal possession of his faculties. Thus, the fact that the defendant was drunk will not exculpate him from a charge of negligence. Indeed, often drunkenness would be substantial evidence that he had acted negligently.

The case thus made is worthy of respect, but there are strong considerations on the other side. There is first the weight of the antecedent law which here, more clearly than in England, has tended toward a special rule for drunkenness in this context. Beyond this, there is the fundamental point that awareness of the potential consequences of excessive drinking on the capacity of human beings to gauge the risks incident to their conduct is by now so dispersed in our culture that it is not unfair to postulate a general equivalence between the risks created by the conduct of the drunken actor and the risks created by his conduct in becoming drunk. Becoming so drunk as to destroy temporarily the actor's powers of perception and judgment is conduct that plainly has no affirmative social value to counterbalance the potential danger. The actor's moral culpability lies in engaging in such conduct. Added to this are the impressive difficulties posed in litigating the foresight of any particular actor at the time when he imbibes and the relative rarity of cases where intoxication really does engender unawareness as distinguished from imprudence. These considerations led to the conclusion, on balance, that the Model Code should declare that unawareness of a risk, of which the actor would have been aware had he been sober, is immaterial.

Montana v. Egelhoff

Supreme Court of the United States

518 U.S. 37 (1996)

Justice SCALIA announced the judgment of the Court and delivered an opinion, in which THE CHIEF JUSTICE, Justice KENNEDY, and Justice THOMAS *join.*

We consider in this case whether the Due Process Clause is violated by Montana Code Annotated § 45-2-203, which provides, in relevant part, that voluntary intoxication "may not be taken into consideration in determining the existence of a mental state which is an element of [a criminal] offense."

I

In July 1992, while camping out in the Yaak region of northwestern Montana to pick mushrooms, respondent made friends with Roberta Pavola and John Christenson, who were doing the same. On Sunday, July 12, the three sold the mushrooms they had collected and spent the rest of the day and evening drinking, in bars and at a private party in Troy, Montana. Some time after 9 p.m., they left the party in Christenson's 1974 Ford Galaxy station wagon. The drinking binge apparently continued, as respondent was seen buying beer at 9:20 p.m. and recalled "sitting on a hill or a bank passing a bottle of Black Velvet back and forth" with Christenson.

At about midnight that night, officers of the Lincoln County, Montana, sheriff's department, responding to reports of a possible drunk driver, discovered Christenson's station wagon stuck in a ditch along U.S. Highway 2. In the front seat were Pavola and Christenson, each dead from a single gunshot to the head. In the rear of the car lay respondent, alive and yelling obscenities. His blood-alcohol content measured .36 percent over one hour later. On the floor of the car, near the brake pedal, lay respondent's .38 caliber handgun, with four loaded rounds and two empty casings; respondent had gunshot residue on his hands.

Respondent was charged with two counts of deliberate homicide, a crime defined by Montana law as "purposely" or "knowingly" causing the death of another human being. A portion of the jury charge, uncontested here, instructed that "[a] person acts purposely when it is his conscious object to engage in conduct of that nature or to cause such a result," and that "[a] person acts knowingly when he is aware of his conduct or when he is aware under the circumstances his conduct constitutes a crime; or, when he is aware there exists the high probability that his conduct will cause a specific result." Respondent's defense at trial was that an unidentified fourth person must have committed the murders; his own extreme intoxication, he claimed, had rendered him physically incapable of committing the murders, and accounted for his inability to recall the events of the night of July 12. Although respondent was allowed to make this use of the evidence that he was intoxicated, the jury was instructed, pursuant to Mont.Code Ann. § 45-2-203

(1995), that it could not consider respondent's "intoxicated condition. . . in determining the existence of a mental state which is an element of the offense." The jury found respondent guilty on both counts, and the court sentenced him to 84 years' imprisonment.

The Supreme Court of Montana reversed. It reasoned (1) that respondent "had a due process right to present and have considered by the jury all relevant evidence to rebut the State's evidence on all elements of the offense charged," and (2) that evidence of respondent's voluntary intoxication was "clear[ly] . . . relevant to the issue of whether [respondent] acted knowingly and purposely." Because § 45-2-203 prevented the jury from considering that evidence with regard to that issue, the court concluded that the State had been "relieved of part of its burden to prove beyond a reasonable doubt every fact necessary to constitute the crime charged," and that respondent had therefore been denied due process. We granted certiorari.

II

The cornerstone of the Montana Supreme Court's judgment was the proposition that the Due Process Clause guarantees a defendant the right to present and have considered by the jury "all relevant evidence to rebut the State's evidence on all elements of the offense charged." Respondent does not defend this categorical rule; he acknowledges that the right to present relevant evidence "has not been viewed as absolute." That is a wise concession, since the proposition that the Due Process Clause guarantees the right to introduce all relevant evidence is simply indefensible. As we have said: "The accused does not have an unfettered right to offer [evidence] that is incompetent, privileged, or otherwise inadmissible under standard rules of evidence." Relevant evidence may, for example, be excluded on account of a defendant's failure to comply with procedural requirements. And any number of familiar and unquestionably constitutional evidentiary rules also authorize the exclusion of relevant evidence. For example, Federal (and Montana) Rule of Evidence 403 provides: "Although relevant, evidence may be excluded if its probative value is substantially outweighed by the danger of unfair prejudice, confusion of the issues, or misleading the jury, or by considerations of undue delay, waste of time, or needless presentation of cumulative evidence." Hearsay rules similarly prohibit the introduction of testimony which, though unquestionably relevant, is deemed insufficiently reliable.[1] Of course, to say that the right to introduce relevant evidence is not absolute is not to say that the Due Process Clause places no limits upon restriction of that right. But

---

[1] Justice O'CONNOR agrees that "a defendant does not enjoy an absolute right to present evidence relevant to his defense," and does not dispute the validity of the evidentiary rules mentioned above. She contends, however, that Montana's rule is not like these because it "places a blanket exclusion on a category of evidence that would allow the accused to negate the offense's mental-state element." Of course hearsay is a "category" of evidence as well; what Justice O'CONNOR apparently has in mind is that this particular category relates to evidence tending to prove a particular fact. That is indeed a distinction, but it is hard to understand why it should make a difference. So long as the category of excluded evidence is selected on a basis that has good and traditional policy support, it ought to be valid. We do not entirely understand Justice O'CONNOR's argument that the vice of § 45-2-203 is that it excludes evidence "essential to the accused's defense." Evidence of intoxication is not always "essential," any more than hearsay evidence is always "nonessential."

it is to say that the defendant asserting such a limit must sustain the usual heavy burden that a due process claim entails:

> [P]reventing and dealing with crime is much more the business of the States than it is of the Federal Government, and . . . we should not lightly construe the Constitution so as to intrude upon the administration of justice by the individual States. Among other things, it is normally 'within the power of the State to regulate procedures under which its laws are carried out' . . . and its decision in this regard is not subject to proscription under the Due Process Clause unless "it offends some principle of justice so rooted in the traditions and conscience of our people as to be ranked as fundamental."

Our primary guide in determining whether the principle in question is fundamental is, of course, historical practice. Here that gives respondent little support. By the laws of England, wrote Hale, the intoxicated defendant "shall have no privilege by this voluntarily contracted madness, but shall have the same judgment as if he were in his right senses." 1 M. Hale, Pleas of the Crown *32-33. According to Blackstone and Coke, the law's condemnation of those suffering from dementia affectata was harsher still: Blackstone, citing Coke, explained that the law viewed intoxication "as an aggravation of the offence, rather than an excuse for any criminal misbehaviour." 4 W. Blackstone, Commentaries *25-26. This stern rejection of inebriation as a defense became a fixture of early American law as well. The American editors of the 1847 edition of Hale wrote:

> Drunkenness, it was said in an early case, can never be received as a ground to excuse or palliate an offence: this is not merely the opinion of a speculative philosopher, the argument of counsel, or the obiter dictum of a single judge, but it is a sound and long established maxim of judicial policy, from which perhaps a single dissenting voice cannot be found. But if no other authority could be adduced, the uniform decisions of our own Courts from the first establishment of the government, would constitute it now a part of the common law of the land.

In an opinion citing the foregoing passages from Blackstone and Hale, Justice Story rejected an objection to the exclusion of evidence of intoxication as follows:

> This is the first time, that I ever remember it to have been contended, that the commission of one crime was an excuse for another. Drunkenness is a gross vice, and in the contemplation of some of our laws is a crime; and I learned in my earlier studies, that so far from its being in law an excuse for murder, it is rather an aggravation of its malignity. *United States v. Cornell*, 25 F. Cas. 650, 657-658 (No. 14,868) (CC R.I. 1820).

The historical record does not leave room for the view that the common law's rejection of intoxication as an "excuse" or "justification" for crime would nonetheless permit the defendant to show that intoxication prevented the requisite *mens rea*. Hale, Coke and Blackstone were familiar, to say the least, with the concept of *mens rea*, and acknowledged that drunkenness "deprive[s] men of the use of reason," Hale; see also *Blackstone*. It is inconceivable that they did not realize that an offender's drunkenness might impair his ability to form the requisite intent; and inconceivable that their failure to note this massive exception from the general rule of disregard of intoxication was an oversight. Hale's statement that a drunken offender shall have the same judgment "as if he were in his right senses" must be understood as precluding a defendant from arguing that, because of his intoxication, he could not have possessed the *mens rea* required to commit the crime. And the same must be said of the exemplar of the common-law rule cited by both Hale and Blackstone, which is Serjeant Pollard's argument to the King's Bench in *Reniger v. Fogossa*, 1 Plowd. 1, 19, 75 Eng. Rep. 1, 31 (K.B.1550): "[I]f a person that is drunk kills another, this shall be Felony, and he shall be hanged for it, and yet he did it through Ignorance, for when he was drunk he had no Understanding nor Memory; but inasmuch as that Ignorance was occasioned by his own Act and Folly, and he might have avoided it, he shall not be privileged thereby." See also *Beverley's Case*, 4 Co. Rep. 123b, 125a, 76 Eng. Rep. 1118, 1123 (K.B.1603) ("although he who is drunk, is for the time *non compos mentis*, yet his drunkenness does not extenuate his act or offence, nor turn to his avail.")

Against this extensive evidence of a lengthy common-law tradition decidedly against him, the best argument available to respondent is the one made by his amicus and conceded by the State: Over the course of the 19th century, courts carved out an exception to the common law's traditional across-the-board condemnation of the drunken offender, allowing a jury to consider a defendant's intoxication when assessing whether he possessed the mental state needed to commit the crime charged, where the crime was one requiring a "specific intent." The emergence of this new rule is often traced to an 1819 English case, in which Justice Holroyd is reported to have held that "though voluntary drunkenness cannot excuse from the commission of crime, yet where, as on a charge of murder, the material question is, whether an act was premeditated or done only with sudden heat and impulse, the fact of the party being intoxicated [is] a circumstance proper to be taken into consideration." 1 W. Russell, Crimes and Misdemeanors *8 (citing *King v. Grindley*, Worcester Sum. Assizes 1819, MS). This exception was "slow to take root," however, Hall, *Intoxication and Criminal Responsibility*, 57 Harv. L.Rev. 1045, 1049 (1944), even in England. Indeed, in the 1835 case of *King v. Carroll*, Justice Park claimed that Holroyd had "retracted his opinion" in *Grindley*, and said "there is no doubt that that case is not law." In this country, as late as 1858 the Missouri Supreme Court could speak as categorically as this:

> To look for deliberation and forethought in a man maddened by intoxication is vain, for drunkenness has deprived him of the deliberating faculties to a greater or less extent; and if this deprivation is to relieve him of all responsibility or to diminish it, the great majority of crimes committed will go unpunished. This however is not the doctrine of the common law; and to its maxims, based as they obviously are upon true wisdom and sound policy, we must adhere.

And as late as 1878, the Vermont Supreme Court upheld the giving of the following instruction at a murder trial:

> 'The voluntary intoxication of one who without provocation commits a homicide, although amounting to a frenzy, that is, although the intoxication amounts to a frenzy, does not excuse him from the same construction

of his conduct, and the same legal inferences upon the question of premeditation and intent, as affecting the grade of his crime, which are applicable to a person entirely sober.'

Eventually, however, the new view won out, and by the end of the 19th century, in most American jurisdictions, intoxication could be considered in determining whether a defendant was capable of forming the specific intent necessary to commit the crime charged.

On the basis of this historical record, respondent's *amicus* argues that "[t]he old common-law rule . . . was no longer deeply rooted at the time the Fourteenth Amendment was ratified." That conclusion is questionable, but we need not pursue the point, since the argument of amicus mistakes the nature of our inquiry. It is not the State which bears the burden of demonstrating that its rule is "deeply rooted," but rather respondent who must show that the principle of procedure violated by the rule (and allegedly required by due process) is " 'so rooted in the traditions and conscience of our people as to be ranked as fundamental.' " Thus, even assuming that when the Fourteenth Amendment was adopted the rule Montana now defends was no longer generally applied, this only cuts off what might be called an *a fortiori* argument in favor of the State. The burden remains upon respondent to show that the "new common law" rule that intoxication may be considered on the question of intent was so deeply rooted at the time of the Fourteenth Amendment (or perhaps has become so deeply rooted since) as to be a fundamental principle which that Amendment ensh

That showing has not been made. Instead of the uniform and continuing acceptance we would expect for a rule that enjoys "fundamental principle" status, we find that fully one-fifth of the States either never adopted the "new common-law" rule at issue here or have recently abandoned it.[2]

It is not surprising that many States have held fast to or resurrected the common-law rule prohibiting consideration of voluntary intoxication in the determination of *mens rea*, because that rule has considerable justification which alone casts doubt upon the proposition that the opposite rule is a "fundamental principle." A large number of crimes, especially violent crimes, are committed by intoxicated offenders; modern studies put the numbers as high as half of all homicides, for example. Disallowing consideration of voluntary intoxication has the effect of increasing the punishment for all unlawful acts

---

[2] Besides Montana, those States are Arizona, see State v. Ramos, 133 Ariz. 4, 6, 648 P.2d 119, 121 (1982) (upholding statute precluding jury consideration of intoxication for purposes of determining whether defendant acted "knowingly"); Ariz.Rev.Stat. Ann. § 13-503 (Supp.1995-1996) (voluntary intoxication "is not a defense for any criminal act or requisite state of mind"); Arkansas, see White v. State, 290 Ark. 130, 134-137, 717 S.W.2d 784, 786-788 (1986) (interpreting Ark.Code Ann. § 5-2-207 (1993)); Delaware, see Wyant v. State, 519 A.2d 649, 651 (1986) (interpreting Del.Code Ann., Tit. 11, § 421 (1995)); Georgia, see Foster v. State, 258 Ga. 736, 742-745, 374 S.E.2d 188, 194-196 (1988) (interpreting Ga.Code Ann. § 16-3-4 (1992)), cert. denied, 490 U.S. 1085 (1989); Hawaii, see Haw.Rev.Stat. § 702-230(2) (1993), State v. Souza, 72 Haw. 246, 248, 813 P.2d 1384, 1386 (1991) (§ 702-230(2) is constitutional); Mississippi, see Lanier v. State, 533 So.2d 473, 478-479 (1988); Missouri, see Mo.Rev.Stat. § 562.076 (1994), State v. Erwin, 848 S.W.2d 476, 482 (§ 562.076 is constitutional), cert. denied, 510 U.S. 826 (1993); South Carolina, see State v. Vaughn, 268 S.C. 119, 124-126, 232 S.E.2d 328, 330-331 (1977); and Texas, see Hawkins v. State, 605 S.W.2d 586, 589 (Tex.Crim.App.1980) (interpreting Tex. Penal Code Ann. § 8.04).

committed in that state, and thereby deters drunkenness or irresponsible behavior while drunk. The rule also serves as a specific deterrent, ensuring that those who prove incapable of controlling violent impulses while voluntarily intoxicated go to prison. And finally, the rule comports with and implements society's moral perception that one who has voluntarily impaired his own faculties should be responsible for the consequences.

There is, in modern times, even more justification for laws such as § 45-2-203 than there used to be. Some recent studies suggest that the connection between drunkenness and crime is as much cultural as pharmacological that is, that drunks are violent not simply because alcohol makes them that way, but because they are behaving in accord with their learned belief that drunks are violent. This not only adds additional support to the traditional view that an intoxicated criminal is not deserving of exoneration, but it suggests that juries who possess the same learned belief as the intoxicated offender will be too quick to accept the claim that the defendant was biologically incapable of forming the requisite *mens rea*. Treating the matter as one of excluding misleading evidence therefore makes some sense.[5]

In sum, not every widespread experiment with a procedural rule favorable to criminal defendants establishes a fundamental principle of justice. Although the rule allowing a jury to consider evidence of a defendant's voluntary intoxication where relevant to *mens rea* has gained considerable acceptance, it is of too recent vintage, and has not received sufficiently uniform and permanent allegiance to qualify as fundamental, especially since it displaces a lengthy common-law tradition which remains supported by valid justifications today.[6]

III

The Supreme Court of Montana's conclusion that Mont.Code Ann. § 45-2-203 violates the Due Process Clause purported to rest on two lines of our jurisprudence. First, it derived its view that the Due Process Clause requires the admission of all relevant evidence from the statement in *Chambers v. Mississippi*, 410 U.S. 284 (1973), that "[t]he right of an accused in a criminal trial to due process is, in essence, the right to a fair opportunity to defend against the State's accusations." Respondent relies heavily on this statement, which he terms "the *Chambers* principle."

---

[5] These many valid policy reasons for excluding evidence of voluntary intoxication refute Justice O'CONNOR's claim that § 45-2-203 has no purpose other than to improve the State's likelihood of winning a conviction. Such a claim is no more accurate as applied to this provision than it would have been as applied to the New York law in Patterson v. New York, which placed upon the defendant the burden of proving the affirmative defense of extreme emotional disturbance. We upheld that New York law, even though we found it "very likely true that fewer convictions of murder would occur if New York were required to negative the affirmative defense at issue here." Here, as in Patterson, any increase in the chance of obtaining a conviction is merely a consequence of pursuing legitimate penological goals.

[6] Justice O'CONNOR maintains that "to determine whether a fundamental principle of justice has been violated here, we cannot consider only the historical disallowance of intoxication evidence, but must also consider the 'fundamental principle' that a defendant has a right to a fair opportunity to put forward his defense." What Justice O'CONNOR overlooks, however, is that the historical disallowance of intoxication evidence sheds light upon what our society has understood by a "fair opportunity to put forward [a] defense." That "fundamental principle" has demonstrably not included the right to introduce intoxication evidence.

We held in *Chambers* that "the exclusion of [certain] critical evidence, coupled with the State's refusal to permit [petitioner] to cross-examine McDonald, denied him a trial in accord with traditional and fundamental standards of due process." We continued, however:

> In reaching this judgment, we establish no new principles of constitutional law. Nor does our holding signal any diminution in the respect traditionally accorded to the States in the establishment and implementation of their own criminal trial rules and procedures. Rather, we hold quite simply that under the facts and circumstances of this case the rulings of the trial court deprived Chambers of a fair trial.

In other words, *Chambers* was an exercise in highly case-specific error correction. At issue were two rulings by the state trial court at Chambers' murder trial: denial of Chambers' motion to treat as an adverse witness one McDonald, who had confessed to the murder for which Chambers was on trial, but later retracted the confession; and exclusion, on hearsay grounds, of testimony of three witnesses who would testify that McDonald had confessed to them. We held that both of these rulings were erroneous, the former because McDonald's testimony simply was adverse, and the second because the statements "were originally made and subsequently offered at trial under circumstances that provided considerable assurance of their reliability," and were "well within the basic rationale of the exception for declarations against interest." Thus, the holding of *Chambers* if one can be discerned from such a fact-intensive case is certainly not that a defendant is denied "a fair opportunity to defend against the State's accusations" whenever "critical evidence" favorable to him is excluded, but rather that erroneous evidentiary rulings can, in combination, rise to the level of a due process violation.

* * *

The second line of our cases invoked by the Montana Supreme Court's opinion requires even less discussion. *In re Winship* announced the proposition that the Due Process Clause requires proof beyond a reasonable doubt of every fact necessary to constitute the charged crime, and *Sandstrom v. Montana* established a corollary, that a jury instruction which shifts to the defendant the burden of proof on a requisite element of mental state violates due process. These decisions simply are not implicated here because, as the Montana court itself recognized, "[t]he burden is not shifted" under § 45-2-203. The trial judge instructed the jury that "[t]he State of Montana has the burden of proving the guilt of the Defendant beyond a reasonable doubt," and that "[a] person commits the offense of deliberate homicide if he purposely or knowingly causes the death of another human being." Thus, failure by the State to produce evidence of respondent's mental state would have resulted in an acquittal. That acquittal did not occur was presumably attributable to the fact, noted by the Supreme Court of Montana, that the State introduced considerable evidence from which the jury might have concluded that respondent acted "purposely" or "knowingly." For example, respondent himself testified that, several hours before the murders, he had given his handgun to Pavola and asked her to put it in the glove compartment of Christenson's car. That he had to retrieve the gun from the glove compartment before he used it was strong evidence that it was his "conscious object" to commit the charged crimes; as was the execution-style manner in which a single shot was fired into the head of each victim.

Recognizing that *Sandstrom* is not directly on point, the Supreme Court of Montana described § 45-2-203 as a burden-reducing, rather than burden-shifting, statute. This obviously was not meant to suggest that the statute formally reduced the burden of proof to clear-and-convincing, or to a mere preponderance; there is utterly no basis for that, neither in the text of the law nor in the jury instruction that was given. What the court evidently meant is that, by excluding a significant line of evidence that might refute *mens rea*, the statute made it easier for the State to meet the requirement of proving *mens rea* beyond a reasonable doubt reduced the burden in the sense of making the burden easier to bear. But any evidentiary rule can have that effect. "Reducing" the State's burden in this manner is not unconstitutional, unless the rule of evidence itself violates a fundamental principle of fairness (which, as discussed, this one does not). We have "reject[ed] the view that anything in the Due Process Clause bars States from making changes in their criminal law that have the effect of making it easier for the prosecution to obtain convictions."

Finally, we may comment upon the Montana Supreme Court's citation of the following passage in *Martin v. Ohio*, 480 U.S. 228 (1987), a case upholding a state law that placed on the defendant the burden of proving self-defense by a preponderance of the evidence:

> It would be quite different if the jury had been instructed that self-defense evidence could not be considered in determining whether there was a reasonable doubt about the State's case, i.e., that self-defense evidence must be put aside for all purposes unless it satisfied the preponderance standard. Such instruction would relieve the State of its burden and plainly run afoul of [*In re*] *Winship*'s mandate. The instructions in this case . . . are adequate to convey to the jury that all of the evidence, including the evidence going to self-defense, must be considered in deciding whether there was a reasonable doubt about the sufficiency of the State's proof of the elements of the crime.

This passage can be explained in various ways e.g., as an assertion that the right to have a jury consider self-defense evidence (unlike the right to have a jury consider evidence of voluntary intoxication), is fundamental, a proposition that the historical record may support. But the only explanation needed for present purposes is: "It is to the holdings of our cases, rather than their *dicta*, that we must attend." If the *Martin* dictum means that the Due Process Clause requires all relevant evidence bearing on the elements of a crime to be admissible, the decisions we have discussed show it to be incorrect.

* * *

"The doctrines of *actus reus, mens rea*, insanity, mistake, justification, and duress have historically provided the tools for a constantly shifting adjustment of the tension between the evolving aims of the criminal law and changing religious, moral, philosophical, and medical views of the nature of man. This process of adjustment has always been thought to be the province of the States." *Powell v. Texas*, 392 U.S. 514 (1968) (plurality opinion). The people of Montana have decided to resurrect the rule of an earlier era, disallowing consideration of voluntary intoxication when a defendant's state of mind is at issue. Nothing in the Due Process Clause prevents them from doing so, and the judgment of the Supreme Court of Montana to the contrary must be reversed.

It is so ordered.

Justice GINSBURG, *concurring in the judgment.*

The Court divides in this case on a question of characterization. The State's law, Mont.Code Ann. § 45-2-203 (1995), prescribes that voluntary intoxication "may not be taken into consideration in determining the existence of a mental state which is an element of [a criminal] offense." For measurement against federal restraints on state action, how should we type that prescription? If § 45-2-203 is simply a rule designed to keep out "relevant, exculpatory evidence," Justice O'Connor maintains, Montana's law offends due process. If it is, instead, a redefinition of the mental-state element of the offense, on the other hand, Justice O'Connor's due process concern "would not be at issue," for "[a] state legislature certainly has the authority to identify the elements of the offenses it wishes to punish," and to exclude evidence irrelevant to the crime it has defined.

Beneath the labels (rule excluding evidence or redefinition of the offense) lies the essential question: Can a State, without offense to the Federal Constitution, make the judgment that two people are equally culpable where one commits an act stone sober, and the other engages in the same conduct after his voluntary intoxication has reduced his capacity for self-control? For the reasons that follow, I resist categorizing § 45-2-203 as merely an evidentiary prescription, but join the Court's judgment refusing to condemn the Montana statute as an unconstitutional enactment.

Section 45-2-203 does not appear in the portion of Montana's Code containing evidentiary rules, the expected placement of a provision regulating solely the admissibility of evidence at trial. Instead, Montana's intoxication statute appears in Title 45 ("Crimes"), as part of a chapter entitled "General Principles of Liability." No less than adjacent provisions governing duress and entrapment, § 45-2-203 embodies a legislative judgment regarding the circumstances under which individuals may be held criminally responsible for their actions.

As urged by Montana and its *amici*, § 45-2-203 "extract[s] the entire subject of voluntary intoxication from the *mens rea* inquiry," thereby rendering evidence of voluntary intoxication logically irrelevant to proof of the requisite mental state. Thus, in a prosecution for deliberate homicide, the State need not prove that the defendant "purposely or knowingly cause[d] the death of another," Mont.Code Ann. § 45-5-102(a) (1995), in a purely subjective sense. To obtain a conviction, the prosecution must prove only that (1) the defendant caused the death of another with actual knowledge or purpose, or (2) that the defendant killed "under circumstances that would otherwise establish knowledge or purpose'but for '[the defendant's] voluntary intoxication." Accordingly,

§ 45-2-203 does not "lighte[n] the prosecution's burden to prove [the] mental-state element beyond a reasonable doubt," as Justice O'Connor suggests for "[t]he applicability of the reasonable-doubt standard . . . has always been dependent on how a State defines the offense that is charged."

Comprehended as a measure redefining *mens rea*, § 45-2-203 encounters no constitutional shoal. States enjoy wide latitude in defining the elements of criminal offenses, particularly when determining "the extent to which moral culpability should be a prerequisite to conviction of a crime." When a State's power to define criminal conduct is challenged under the Due Process Clause, we inquire only whether the law "offends some principle of justice so rooted in the traditions and conscience of our people as to be ranked as fundamental." Defining *mens rea* to eliminate the exculpatory value of voluntary intoxication does not offend a "fundamental principle of justice," given the lengthy common-law tradition, and the adherence of a significant minority of the States to that position today.

* * *

The Montana Supreme Court's judgment, in sum, strikes down a statute whose text displays no constitutional infirmity. If the Montana court considered its analysis forced by this Court's precedent, it is proper for this Court to say what prescriptions federal law leaves to the States,[3] and thereby dispel confusion to which we may have contributed, and attendant state-court misperception.

Justice O'CONNOR, with whom Justice STEVENS, Justice SOUTER, and Justice BREYER join, *dissenting*.

The Montana Supreme Court unanimously held that Mont.Code Ann. § 45-2-203 (1995) violates due process. I agree. Our cases establish that due process sets an outer limit on the restrictions that may be placed on a defendant's ability to raise an effective defense to the State's accusations. Here, to impede the defendant's ability to throw doubt on the State's case, Montana has removed from the jury's consideration a category of evidence relevant to determination of mental state where that mental state is an essential element of the offense that must be proved beyond a reasonable doubt. Because this disallowance eliminates evidence with which the defense might negate an essential element, the State's burden to prove its case is made correspondingly easier. The justification for this disallowance is the State's desire to increase the likelihood of conviction of a certain class of defendants who might otherwise be able to prove that they did not satisfy a requisite element of the offense. In my view, the statute's effect on the criminal proceeding violates due process.

I

This Court's cases establish that limitations placed on the accused's ability to present a fair and complete defense can, in some circumstances, be severe enough to violate due process. "The right of an accused in a criminal trial to

---

[3] As the United States observed, it is generally within the States' domain "to determine what are the elements of criminal responsibility."

due process is, in essence, the right to a fair opportunity to defend against the State's accusations." *Chambers v. Mississippi*. Applying our precedent, the Montana Supreme Court held that keeping intoxication evidence away from the jury, where such evidence was relevant to establishment of the requisite mental state, violated the due process right to present a defense and that the instruction pursuant to § 45-2-203 was not harmless error. In rejecting the Montana Supreme Court's conclusion, the Court emphasizes that "any number of familiar and unquestionably constitutional evidentiary rules" permit exclusion of relevant evidence. It is true that a defendant does not enjoy an absolute right to present evidence relevant to his defense. But none of the "familiar" evidentiary rules operates as Montana's does. The Montana statute places a blanket exclusion on a category of evidence that would allow the accused to negate the offense's mental-state element. In so doing, it frees the prosecution, in the face of such evidence, from having to prove beyond a reasonable doubt that the defendant nevertheless possessed the required mental state. In my view, this combination of effects violates due process.

The proposition that due process requires a fair opportunity to present a defense in a criminal prosecution is not new. In *Chambers*, the defendant had been prevented from cross-examining a witness and from presenting witnesses on his own behalf by operation of Mississippi's "voucher" and hearsay rules. The Court held that the application of these evidentiary rules deprived the defendant of a fair trial. "[W]here constitutional rights directly affecting the ascertainment of guilt are implicated, the hearsay rule may not be applied mechanistically to defeat the ends of justice." The plurality's characterization of *Chambers* as "case-specific error correction," cannot diminish its force as a prohibition on enforcement of state evidentiary rules that lead, without sufficient justification, to the establishment of guilt by suppression of evidence supporting the defendant's case.

* * *

In *Washington v. Texas*, 388 U.S. 14 (1967), the trial court refused to permit a defense witness to testify on the basis of Texas statutes providing that persons charged or convicted as co-participants in the same crime could not testify for one another, although they could testify for the State. The Court held that the Constitution prohibited a State from establishing rules to prevent whole categories of defense witnesses from testifying out of a belief that such witnesses were untrustworthy. Such action by the State detracted too severely and arbitrarily from the defendant's right to call witnesses in his favor.

These cases, taken together, illuminate a simple principle: Due process demands that a criminal defendant be afforded a fair opportunity to defend against the State's accusations. Meaningful adversarial testing of the State's case requires that the defendant not be prevented from raising an effective defense, which must include the right to present relevant, probative evidence. To be sure, the right to present evidence is not limitless; for example, it does not permit the defendant to introduce any and all evidence he believes might work in his favor, nor does it generally invalidate the operation of testimonial privileges. Nevertheless, "an essential component of procedural fairness is an opportunity to be heard. That opportunity would be an empty one if the State were permitted to exclude competent, reliable evidence" that is essential to the accused's defense. Section 45-2-203 forestalls the defendant's ability to raise an effective defense by placing a blanket exclusion on the presentation of a type of evidence that directly negates an element of the crime, and by doing so, it lightens the prosecution's burden to prove that mental-state element beyond a reasonable doubt.

This latter effect is as important to the due process analysis as the former. A state legislature certainly has the authority to identify the elements of the offenses it wishes to punish, but once its laws are written, a defendant has the right to insist that the State prove beyond a reasonable doubt every element of an offense charged. See *McMillan v. Pennsylvania; Patterson v. New York*, ("The applicability of the reasonable-doubt standard, however, has always been dependent on how a State defines the offense that is charged"). "[T]he Due Process Clause protects the accused against conviction except upon proof beyond a reasonable doubt of every fact necessary to constitute the crime with which he is charged." Because the Montana Legislature has specified that a person commits "deliberate homicide" only if he "purposely or knowingly causes the death of another human being," Mont.Code Ann. § 45-5-102(1)(a) (1995), the prosecution must prove the existence of such mental state in order to convict. That is, unless the defendant is shown to have acted purposely or knowingly, he is not guilty of the offense of deliberate homicide. The Montana Supreme Court found that it was inconsistent with the legislature's requirement of the mental state of "purposely" or "knowingly" to prevent the jury from considering evidence of voluntary intoxication, where that category of evidence was relevant to establishment of that mental-state element.

Where the defendant may introduce evidence to negate a subjective mental-state element, the prosecution must work to overcome whatever doubts the defense has raised about the existence of the required mental state. On the other hand, if the defendant may not introduce evidence that might create doubt in the factfinder's mind as to whether that element was met, the prosecution will find its job so much the easier. A subjective mental state is generally proved only circumstantially. If a jury may not consider the defendant's evidence of his mental state, the jury may impute to the defendant the culpability of a mental state he did not possess.

In *Martin v. Ohio*, 480 U.S. 228 (1987), the Court considered an Ohio statute providing that a defendant bore the burden of proving, by a preponderance of the evidence, an affirmative defense such as self-defense. We held that placing that burden on the defendant did not violate due process. The Court noted in explanation that it would nevertheless have been error to instruct the jury "that self-defense evidence could not be considered in determining whether there was a reasonable doubt about the State's case" where Ohio's definition of the intent element made self-defense evidence relevant to the State's burden. "Such an instruction would relieve the State of its burden and plainly run afoul of *Winship*'s mandate." In other words, the State's right to shift the burden of proving an affirmative defense did not include the power to prevent the defendant from attempting to prove self-defense in an effort to cast doubt on the State's case. *Dictum* or not, this observation explained our reasoning and is similarly applicable here, where the State has benefitted from the defendant's inability to make an argument which, if accepted, could throw reasonable doubt on the State's proof. The placement of the burden of proof for affirmative defenses should not be confused with the use of evidence to negate elements of the offense charged.

* * *

The Court ignores [the] caution that the prosecution must be put to a full test. Rather, it. . . emphasize[s] that "introduction of relevant evidence can be limited by the State for a 'valid' reason, as it has been by Montana." The State's brief to this Court enunciates a single reason: due to the well-known risks related to voluntary intoxication, it seeks to prevent a defendant's use of his own voluntary intoxication as basis for exculpation. That is, its interest is to ensure that even a defendant who lacked the required mental-state element and is therefore not guilty is nevertheless convicted of the offense. The Court elaborates on reasons why Montana might wish to preclude exculpation on the basis of voluntary intoxication, but these reasons increased punishment and concomitant deterrence for those who commit unlawful acts while drunk, and implementation of society's moral perception that those who become drunk should bear the consequences merely explain the State's purpose in trying to improve its likelihood of winning convictions. The final justification proffered by the Court on Montana's behalf is that Montana's rule perhaps prevents juries, who might be otherwise be misled, from being "too quick to accept the claim that the [drunk] defendant was biologically incapable of forming the requisite *mens rea*." But this proffered justification is inconsistent with § 45-2-203's exception for persons who are involuntarily intoxicated. That exception makes plain that Montana does not consider intoxication evidence misleading but rather considers it relevant for the determination of a person's capacity to form the requisite mental state.

A State's placement of a significant limitation on the right to defend against the State's accusations "requires that the competing interest be closely examined." Montana has specified that to prove guilt, the State must establish that the defendant acted purposely or knowingly, but has prohibited a category of defendants from effectively disputing guilt through presentation of evidence relevant to that essential element. And the evidence is indisputably relevant: The Montana Supreme Court held that evidence of intoxication is relevant to proof of mental state, and furthermore, § 45-2-203's exception for involuntary intoxication shows that the legislature does consider intoxication relevant to mental state. Montana has barred the defendant's use of a category of relevant, exculpatory evidence for the express purpose of improving the State's likelihood of winning a conviction against a certain type of defendant. The plurality's observation that all evidentiary rules that exclude exculpatory evidence reduce the State's burden to prove its case is beside the point. The purpose of the familiar evidentiary rules is not to alleviate the State's burden, but rather, to vindicate some other goal or value e.g., to ensure the reliability and competency of evidence or to encourage effective communications within certain relationships. Such rules may or may not help the prosecution, and when they do help, do so only incidentally. While due process does not "ba[r] States from making changes. . . that have the effect of making it easier for the prosecution to obtain convictions," an evidentiary rule whose sole purpose is to boost the State's likelihood of conviction distorts the adversary process. Unlike *Chambers* and *Washington,* where the State at least claimed that the evidence at issue was unreliable, Montana does not justify its rule on grounds such as that intoxication evidence is unreliable, cumulative, privileged, or irrelevant. The sole purpose for this disallowance is to keep from the jury's consideration a category of evidence that helps the defendant's case and weakens the government's case.

The plurality brushes aside this Court's precedents as variously fact-bound, irrelevant, and dicta. I would afford more weight to principles enunciated in our case law than is accorded in the Court's opinion today. It seems to me that a State may not first determine the elements of the crime it wishes to punish, and then thwart the accused's defense by categorically disallowing the very evidence that would prove him innocent.

II

The Court does, however, raise an important argument for the statute's validity: the disallowance, at common law, of consideration of voluntary intoxication where a defendant's state of mind is at issue. Because this disallowance was permitted at common law, the plurality argues, its disallowance by Montana cannot amount to a violation of a "fundamental principle of justice."

From 1551 until its shift in the 19th century, the common-law rule prevailed that a defendant could not use intoxication as an excuse or justification for an offense, or, it must be assumed, to rebut establishment of a requisite mental state. "Early law was indifferent to the defence of drunkenness because the theory of criminal liability was then too crude and too undeveloped to admit of exceptions. . . . But with the refinement in the theory of criminal liability . . . a modification of the rigid old rule on the defence of drunkenness was to be expected." Singh, History of the Defense of Drunkenness in English Criminal Law, 49 L.Q. Rev. 528, 537 (1933) (footnote omitted). As the plurality concedes, that significant modification took place in the 19th century. Courts acknowledged the fundamental incompatibility of a particular mental-state requirement on the one hand, and the disallowance of consideration of evidence that might defeat establishment of that mental state on the other. In the slow progress typical of the common law, courts began to recognize that evidence of intoxication was properly admissible for the purpose of ascertaining whether a defendant had met the required mental-state element of the offense charged.

This recognition, courts believed, was consistent with the common-law rule that voluntary intoxication did not excuse commission of a crime; rather, an element of the crime, the requisite mental state, was not satisfied and therefore the crime had not been committed. As one influential mid-19th century case explained, "Drunkenness is no excuse for crime; yet, in that class of crimes and offences which depend upon guilty knowledge, or the coolness and deliberation with which they shall have been perpetrated, to constitute their commission . . . [drunkenness] should be submitted to the consideration of the Jury"; for, where the crime required a particular mental state, "it is proper to show any state or condition of the person that is adverse to the proper exercise of the mind" in order "[t]o rebut" the mental state or "to enable the Jury to judge rightly of the matter." ("The rule is well settled that intoxication is not a justification or an excuse for crime. . . . But in many cases evidence of intoxication is admissible with a view to the question whether a crime has been committed; . . . As [mental state], in such case, is of the essence of the offense, it is possible that in proving intoxication you go far to prove that no offense was committed").

Courts across the country agreed that where a subjective mental state was an element of the crime to be proved, the defense must be permitted to show, by reference to intoxication, the absence of that element. One court commented that it seemed "incontrovertible and to be universally applicable" that "where the nature and essence of the crime are made by law to depend upon the peculiar state and condition of the criminal's mind at the time with reference to the act done, drunkenness may be a proper subject for the consideration of the jury, not to excuse or mitigate the offence but to show that it was not committed."

With similar reasoning, the Montana Supreme Court recognized the incompatibility of a jury instruction pursuant to § 45-2-203 in conjunction with the legislature's decision to require a mental state of "purposely" or "knowingly" for deliberate homicide. It held that intoxication is relevant to formation of the requisite mental state. Unless a defendant is proved beyond a reasonable doubt to have possessed the requisite mental state, he did not commit the offense. Elimination of a critical category of defense evidence precludes a defendant from effectively rebutting the mental-state element, while simultaneously shielding the State from the effort of proving the requisite mental state in the face of negating evidence. It was this effect on the adversarial process that persuaded the Montana Supreme Court that the disallowance was unconstitutional.

The Due Process Clause protects those "'principle[s] of justice so rooted in the traditions and conscience of our people as to be ranked as fundamental.'" "At the time the Fourteenth Amendment was ratified, the common-law rule on consideration of intoxication evidence was in flux. The Court argues that rejection of the historical rule in the 19th century simply does not establish that the "new common law" rule is a principle of procedure so "deeply rooted" as to be ranked "fundamental." But to determine whether a fundamental principle of justice has been violated here, we cannot consider only the historical disallowance of intoxication evidence, but must also consider the "fundamental principle" that a defendant has a right to a fair opportunity to put forward his defense, in adversarial testing where the State must prove the elements of the offense beyond a reasonable doubt. As concepts of *mens rea* and burden of proof developed, these principles came into conflict, as the shift in the common law in the 19th century reflects.

III

Justice Ginsburg concurs in the Court's judgment based on her determination that § 45-2-203 amounts to a redefinition of the offense that renders evidence of voluntary intoxication irrelevant to proof of the requisite mental state. The concurrence emphasizes that States enjoy wide latitude in defining the elements of crimes and concludes that, "[c]omprehended as a measure redefining *mens rea*, § 45-2-203 encounters no constitutional shoal."

A state legislature certainly possesses the authority to define the offenses it wishes to punish. If the Montana legislature chose to redefine this offense so as to alter the requisite mental-state element, the due process problem presented in this case would not be at issue.

There is, however, no indication that such a "redefinition" occurred. Justice Ginsburg's reading of Montana law is plainly inconsistent with that given by the Montana Supreme Court, and therefore cannot provide a valid basis to uphold § 45-2-203's operation. "We are, of course, bound to accept the interpretation of [state] law by the highest court of the State." The Montana Supreme Court held that evidence of voluntary intoxication was relevant to the requisite mental state. And in summing up the court's holding, Justice Nelson's concurrence explains that while the legislature may enact the statutes it chooses, § 45-2-203 "effectively and impermissibly . . . lessens the burden of the State to prove beyond a reasonable doubt an essential element of the offense charged the mental state element by statutorily precluding the jury from considering the very evidence that might convince them that the State had not proven that element." The Montana Supreme Court's decision cannot be read consistently with a "redefinition" of the offense.

Because the management of criminal justice is within the province of the States, this Court is properly reluctant to interfere in the States' authority in these matters. Nevertheless, the Court must invalidate those rules that violate the requirements of due process. The Court acknowledges that a reduction of the State's burden through disallowance of exculpatory evidence is unconstitutional if it violates a principle of fairness. I believe that such a violation is present here. Montana's disallowance of consideration of voluntary-intoxication evidence removes too critical a category of relevant, exculpatory evidence from the adversarial process by prohibiting the defendant from making an essential argument and permitting the prosecution to benefit from its suppression. Montana's purpose is to increase the likelihood of conviction of a certain class of defendants, who might otherwise be able to prove that they did not satisfy a requisite element of the offense. The historical fact that this disallowance once existed at common law is not sufficient to save the statute today. I would affirm the judgment of the Montana Supreme Court.

Justice SOUTER, *dissenting*.

I have no doubt that a State may so define the mental element of an offense that evidence of a defendant's voluntary intoxication at the time of commission does not have exculpatory relevance and, to that extent, may be excluded without raising any issue of due process. I would have thought the statute at issue here (Mont.Code Ann. § 45-2-203 (1995)) had implicitly accomplished such a redefinition, but I read the opinion of the Supreme Court of Montana as indicating that it had no such effect, and I am bound by the state court's statement of its domestic law.

Even on the assumption that Montana's definitions of the purposeful and knowing culpable mental states were untouched by § 45-2-203, so that voluntary intoxication remains relevant to each, it is not a foregone conclusion that our cases preclude the State from declaring such intoxication evidence inadmissible. A State may typically exclude even relevant and exculpatory evidence if it presents a valid justification for doing so. There may (or may not) be a valid justification to support a State's decision to exclude, rather than render irrelevant, evidence of a defendant's voluntary intoxication. Montana has not endeavored, however, to advance an argument to that effect. Rather, the State has effectively restricted itself to advancing undoubtedly sound reasons for defining the mental state element so as to make voluntary intoxication generally irrelevant (though its own Supreme Court has apparently said the legislature failed to do that) and to demonstrating that evidence of voluntary intoxication was irrelevant at common law (a fact that goes part way, but not all the way, to answering the due process objection). In short, I read the State Supreme Court opinion as barring one interpretation that would leave the statutory scheme constitutional, while the State's failure to offer a justification for excluding relevant evidence leaves us unable to discern whether there may be a valid reason to support the statute as the State Supreme Court appears to view it. I therefore respectfully dissent from the Court's judgment.

I

The plurality opinion convincingly demonstrates that when the Fourteenth Amendment's Due Process Clause was added to the Constitution in 1868, the common law as it then stood either rejected the notion that voluntary intoxication might be exculpatory, or was at best in a state of flux on that issue. That is enough to show that Montana's rule that evidence of voluntary intoxication is inadmissible on the issue of culpable mental state contravenes no principle " 'so rooted in the traditions and conscience of our people,' " as they stood in 1868, " 'as to be ranked as fundamental.' " But this is not the end of the due process enquiry. Justice Harlan's dissenting opinion in *Poe v. Ullman*, 367 U.S. 497 (1961), teaches that the "tradition" to which we are tethered "is a living thing." What the historical practice does not rule out as inconsistent with "the concept of ordered liberty," must still pass muster as rational in today's world. (Although "historical pedigree can give a procedural practice a presumption of constitutionality . . . the presumption must surely be

In this case, the second step of the due process enquiry leads to a line of precedent discussed in Justice O'Connor's dissent, involving the right to present a defense. Collectively, these cases stand for the proposition . . . that while the right to present relevant evidence may be limited, the Constitution "requires that the competing interest [said to justify the limitation] be closely examined."

II

Given the foregoing line of authority, Montana had at least one way to give effect to its judgment that defendants should not be permitted to use evidence of their voluntary intoxication to defeat proof of culpable mental state, and perhaps a second. First, it could have defined culpable mental state so as to give voluntary intoxication no exculpatory relevance. While the Due Process Clause requires the government to prove the existence of every element of the offense beyond a reasonable doubt, within fairly broad limits the definition of those elements is up to the State. . . .

While I therefore find no apparent constitutional reason why Montana could not render evidence of voluntary intoxication excludable as irrelevant by redefining "knowledge" and "purpose," as they apply to the mental state element of its substantive offenses, or by making some other provision for mental state, I do not believe that I am free to conclude that Montana has done so here. Our view of state law is limited by its interpretation in the State's highest court, and I am not able to square the State Supreme Court's opinion in this case with the position advanced by the State here (and supported by the United States, as amicus curiae), that Montana's legislature changed the definition of culpable mental states when it enacted § 45-2-203.

A second possible (although by no means certain) option may also be open. Even under a definition of the mental state element that would treat evidence of voluntary intoxication as relevant and exculpatory, the exclusion of such evidence is typically permissible so long as a State presents a " 'valid' reason" to justify keeping it out. . . .

Hence, I do not rule out the possibility of justifying exclusion of relevant intoxication evidence in a case like this. At the least, there may be reasons beyond those actually advanced by Montana that might have induced a state to reject its prior law freely admitting intoxication evidence going to mental state.

A State (though not necessarily Montana) might, for example, argue that admitting intoxication evidence on the issue of culpable mental state but not on a defense of incapacity (as to which it is widely assumed to be excludable as generally irrelevant)[3] would be irrational since both capacity to obey the law and purpose to accomplish a criminal result presuppose volitional ability. See Model Penal Code § 4.01 ("A person is not responsible for criminal conduct if at the time of such conduct as a result of mental disease or defect he lacks substantial capacity . . . to conform his conduct to the requirements of law") and Model Penal Code §.02(2)(a)(i) ("A person acts purposely with respect to a material element of an offense when . . . it is his conscious object to engage in conduct of that nature or to cause such a result"). And quite apart from any technical irrationality, a State might think that admitting the evidence in question on culpable mental state but not capacity (when each was a jury issue in a given case) would raise too high a risk of juror confusion. "[U]se of [intoxication] evidence runs an unacceptable risk of potential manipulation by defendants and [will lead to] confusion of juries, who may not adequately appreciate that intoxication evidence is to be used for the question of mental state, not for purposes of showing an excuse"). While Thomas Reed Powell

---

[3] See American Law Institute, Model Penal Code § 2.08(4) (1985), which deems intoxication relevant for this purpose only where by reason of "pathological intoxication" an "actor at the time of his conduct lacks substantial capacity. . . to conform his conduct to the requirements of law." The Model Penal Code further defines "pathological intoxication" as "intoxication grossly excessive in degree, given the amount of the intoxicant, to which the actor does not know he is susceptible." Id., § 2.08(5)(c).

reportedly suggested that "learning to think like a lawyer is when you learn to think about one thing that is connected to another without thinking about the other thing it is connected to," a State might argue that its law should be structured on the assumption that its jurors typically will not suffer from this facility.

Quite apart from the fact that Montana has made no such arguments for justification here, however, I am not at all sure why such arguments would go any further than justifying redefinition of mental states (the first option above). I do not understand why they would justify the state in cutting the conceptual corner by leaving the definitions of culpable mental states untouched but excluding evidence relevant to this proof. Absent a convincing argument for cutting that corner, *Chambers* and the like constrain us to hold the current Montana statute unconstitutional. I therefore respectfully dissent.

Justice BREYER, with whom Justice STEVENS joins, *dissenting.*

I join Justice O'Connor's dissent. As the dissent says, and as Justice Souter agrees, the Montana Supreme Court did not understand Montana's statute to have redefined the mental element of deliberate homicide. In my view, however, this circumstance is not simply happenstance or a technical matter that deprives us of the power to uphold that statute. To have read the statute differently to treat it as if it had redefined the mental element would produce anomalous results. A statute that makes voluntary intoxication the legal equivalent of purpose or knowledge but only where external circumstances would establish purpose or knowledge in the absence of intoxication is a statute that turns guilt or innocence not upon state of mind, but upon irrelevant external circumstances. An intoxicated driver stopped at an intersection who unknowingly accelerated into a pedestrian would likely be found guilty, for a jury unaware of intoxication would likely infer knowledge or purpose. An identically intoxicated driver racing along a highway who unknowingly sideswiped another car would likely be found innocent, for a jury unaware of intoxication would likely infer negligence. Why would a legislature want to write a statute that draws such a distinction, upon which a sentence of life imprisonment, or death, may turn? If the legislature wanted to equate voluntary intoxication, knowledge, and purpose, why would it not write a statute that plainly says so, instead of doing so in a roundabout manner that would affect, in dramatically different ways, those whose minds, deeds, and consequences seem identical? I would reserve the question of whether or not such a hypothetical statute might exceed constitutional limits.

NOTES AND QUESTIONS

1. In examining the issue whether a "fundamental principle" of justice is violated by denying intoxication evidence, is it helpful to remember that for much of its history, the common law conceptualized *mens rea* in terms of the generalized notion of an "evil mind" or a "wicked disposition?" See generally, Gardner, *The* Mens Rea *Enigma: Observations on the Role of Motive in the Criminal Law Past and Present*, 1993 Utah L. Rev. 635. Does intoxication evidence become more relevant as the common law moved towards treating

mens rea (or *mentes reae*) as specific states of mind ("purposely" or "knowingly" in the homicide statute in *Egelhoff*) for specific offenses? See *id;* see also the *Faulkner* and *Cunningham* cases, *supra* pages 230-34.

What does Justice Ginsburg mean in her *Egelhoff* concurrence when she says that by denying evidence of voluntary intoxication in prosecutions for deliberate homicide, "the State need not prove that the defendant 'purposely or knowingly cause[d] the death of another' *in a purely subjective sense*" (emphasis added)? Justice Ginsburg concludes that the prosecution may legitimately convict if it proves either that the defendant "caused the death of another with actual knowledge or purpose" or that he "killed under circumstances that would otherwise establish knowledge or purpose 'but for 'the defendant's voluntary intoxication." Does this latter basis for liability suggest that the act of becoming intoxicated is sufficiently "evil" so as to satisfy the *mens rea* requirement thus hearkening back to original notice of *mens rea* as a generalized "evil mind"?

2. Would the defendant in *Egelhoff* have fared better if he had argued that his intoxication precluded him from performing the *actus reus* for the crime rather than from formulating the required *mens rea*? Is the state equally free to define (or define away) *actus reus* elements as it is *mens rea* elements? Compare *Patterson v. New York, supra* page 711, with *Robinson v. California, supra* page 201. See also, *People v. Decina, supra* page 188.

3. For early critical review of *Egelhoff, see, e.g.*, Husak and Singer, *Innocence and Innocents*, Mens Rea *in the Supreme Court Since Herbert Packer,* 2 Buff. Crim. L. Rev. 859 (1999); Note, *Montana v. Egelhoff: Voluntary Intoxication, Mortality, and the Constitution,* 46 Am. U. L. Rev. 1245 (1997); Note, *Montana v. Egelhoff: Abandoning a Defendant's Fundamental Right to a Defense,* 46 Cath. U. L. Rev. 1349 (1997).

NOTE ON ALCOHOL AND DRUG ADDICTION

The doctrines thus far examined have dealt essentially with "normal" persons who, while intoxicated, committed an act that, if done while sober, would undoubtedly bring criminal liability. But what if the defendant claims that he is an alcoholic and therefore has no control over his drinking? After *Robinson v. California, supra,* § 3.01[B], some courts held that an alcoholic would have a defense to criminal liability, at least for some crimes, since holding the alcoholic criminally liable would constitute punishment for a disease, contrary to the Eighth Amendment as interpreted by *Robinson. Easter v. District of Columbia,* 362 F.2d 50 (D.C. Cir. 1966). The issue reached the Supreme Court in *Powell v. Texas,* 392 U.S. 514 (1968). Four Justices of the Court, led by Justice Marshall, rejected the defense entirely, fearing that it would require a "constitutionalization ation" of all criminal defenses. The plurality construed *Robinson* only to prohibit the punishment of status offenses where there was no act at all by the defendant. Four Justices dissented, saying that at least as to the crime of public drunkenness, a showing of alcoholism should be a defense if there were also a showing that "going into public" was a "part and pattern" of the disease. This notion was obviously aimed at precluding alcoholism as a defense to crimes such as robbery and homicide. Mr. Justice White appeared to accept the dissent's test, but found that "going into public" was not part of the disease of alcoholism, and he therefore concurred in the judgment of the Marshall plurality.

The issue raised in *Powell* seems to have died in the reported cases. However, judicial attention has been directed to the analogous problem of criminal activity by drug addicts. See, *e.g., United States v. Moore,* 486 F.2d 1139 (D.C. Cir. 1973), where the court rejected a heroin addict's argument that he could not be held criminally responsible for the crime of heroin possession.

[D] Entrapment

SHERMAN V. UNITED STATES

Supreme Court of the United States

356 U.S. 369 (1958)

Mr. Chief Justice WARREN *delivered the opinion of the Court.*

The issue before us is whether petitioner's conviction should be set aside on the ground that as a matter of law the defense of entrapment was established. Petitioner was convicted under an indictment charging three sales of narcotics. . . . In late August 1951, Kalchinian, a government informer, first met petitioner at a doctor's office where apparently both were being treated to be cured of narcotics addiction. Several accidental meetings followed, either at the doctor's office or at the pharmacy where both filled their prescriptions from the doctor. From mere greetings, conversation progressed to a discussion of mutual experiences and problems, including their attempts to overcome addiction to narcotics. Finally Kalchinian asked petitioner if he knew of a good source of narcotics. He asked petitioner to supply him with a source because he was not responding to treatment. From the first, petitioner tried to avoid the issue. Not until after a number of repetitions of the request, predicated on Kalchinian's presumed suffering, did petitioner finally acquiesce. Several times thereafter he obtained a quantity of narcotics which he shared with Kalchinian. Each time petitioner told Kalchinian that the total cost of narcotics he obtained was twenty-five dollars and that Kalchinian owed him fifteen dollars. The informer thus bore the cost of his share of the narcotics plus the taxi and other expenses necessary to obtain the drug. After several such sales Kalchinian informed agents of the Bureau of Narcotics that he had another seller for them. On three occasions during November 1951, government agents observed petitioner give narcotics to Kalchinian in return for money supplied by the Government.

At the trial the factual issue was whether the informer had convinced an otherwise unwilling person to commit a criminal act or whether petitioner was already predisposed to commit the act and exhibited only the natural hesitancy of one acquainted with the narcotics trade. The issue of entrapment went to the jury, and a conviction resulted. Petitioner was sentenced to imprisonment for ten years. The Court of Appeals for the Second Circuit affirmed. We granted certiorari.

In *Sorrells v. United States,* 287 U.S. 435 [1932], this Court firmly recognized the defense of entrapment in the federal courts. The intervening years have in no way detracted from the principles underlying that decision. The function of law enforcement is the prevention of crime and the apprehension of criminals. Manifestly, that function does not include the manufacturing of crime. Criminal activity is such that stealth and strategy are necessary weapons in the arsenal of the police officer. However, "A different question is presented when the criminal design originates with the officials of the government, and they implant in the mind of an innocent person the disposition to commit the alleged offense and induce its commission in order that they may prosecute." The stealth and strategy become as objectionable police methods as the coerced confession and the unlawful search. Congress could not have intended that its statutes were to be enforced by tempting innocent persons into violations.

However, the fact that government agents "merely afford opportunities or facilities for the commission of the offense does not" constitute entrapment. Entrapment occurs only when the criminal conduct was "the product of the creative activity" of law-enforcement officials. To determine whether entrapment has been established, a line must be drawn between the trap for the unwary innocent and the trap for the unwary criminal. The principles by which the courts are to make this determination were outlined in *Sorrells*. On the one hand, at trial the accused may examine the conduct of the government agent; and on the other hand, the accused will be subjected to an "appropriate and searching inquiry into his own conduct and predisposition" as bearing on his claim of innocence.

We conclude from the evidence that entrapment was established as a matter of law. . . . It is patently clear that petitioner was induced by Kalchinian. The informer himself testified that, believing petitioner to be undergoing a cure for narcotics addiction, he nonetheless sought to persuade petitioner to obtain for him a source of narcotics. In Kalchinian's own words we are told of the accidental, yet recurring, meetings, the ensuing conversations concerning mutual experiences in regard to narcotics addiction, and then of Kalchinian's resort to sympathy. One request was not enough, for Kalchinian tells us that additional ones were necessary to overcome, first, petitioner's refusal, then his evasiveness, and then his hesitancy in order to achieve capitulation. Kalchinian not only procured a source of narcotics but apparently also induced petitioner to return to the habit. Finally, assured of a catch, Kalchinian informed the authorities so that they could close the net. The Government cannot disown Kalchinian and insist it is not responsible for his actions. Although he was not being paid, Kalchinian was an active government informer who had but recently been the instigator of at least two other prosecutions. Undoubtedly the impetus for such achievements was the fact that in 1951 Kalchinian was himself under criminal charges for illegally selling narcotics and had not yet been sentenced. It makes no difference that the sales for which petitioner was convicted occurred after a series of sales. They were not independent acts subsequent to the inducement but part of a course of conduct which was the product of the inducement. In his testimony the federal agent in charge of the case admitted that he never bothered to question Kalchinian about the way he had made contact with petitioner. The

Government cannot make such use of an informer and then claim disassociation through ignorance.

The Government sought to overcome the defense of entrapment by claiming that petitioner evinced a "ready complaisance" to accede to Kalchinian's request. Aside from a record of past convictions, which we discuss in the following paragraph, the Government's case is unsupported. There is no evidence that petitioner himself was in the trade. When his apartment was searched after arrest, no narcotics were found. There is no significant evidence that petitioner even made a profit on any sale to Kalchinian. The Government's characterization of petitioner's hesitancy to Kalchinian's request as the natural wariness of the criminal cannot fill the evidentiary void.

The Government's additional evidence in the second trial to show that petitioner was ready and willing to sell narcotics should the opportunity present itself was petitioner's record of two past narcotics convictions. In 1942 petitioner was convicted of illegally selling narcotics; in 1946 he was convicted of illegally possessing them. However, a nine-year-old sales conviction and a five-year-old possession conviction are insufficient to prove petitioner had a readiness to sell narcotics at the time Kalchinian approached him, particularly when we must assume from the record he was trying to overcome the narcotics habit at the time.

The case at bar illustrates an evil which the defense of entrapment is designed to overcome. The government informer entices someone attempting to avoid narcotics not only into carrying out an illegal sale but also into returning to the habit of use. Selecting the proper time, the informer then tells the government agent. The set-up is accepted by the agent without even a question as to the manner in which the informer encountered the seller. Thus the Government plays on the weaknesses of an innocent party and beguiles him into committing crimes which he otherwise would not have attempted. Law enforcement does not require methods such as this.

It has been suggested that in overturning this conviction we should reassess the doctrine of entrapment according to principles announced in the separate opinion of Mr. Justice Roberts in *Sorrells*. To do so would be to decide the case on grounds rejected by the majority in *Sorrells* and, so far as the record shows, not raised here or below by the parties before us. We do not ordinarily decide issues not presented by the parties and there is good reason not to vary that practice in this case.

At least two important issues of law enforcement and trial procedure would have to be decided without the benefit of argument by the parties, one party being the Government. Mr. Justice Roberts asserted that although the defendant could claim that the Government had induced him to commit the crime, the Government could not reply by showing that the defendant's criminal conduct was due to his own readiness and not to the persuasion of government agents. The handicap thus placed on the prosecution is obvious. Furthermore, it was the position of Mr. Justice Roberts that the factual issue of entrapment—now limited to the question of what the government agents did—should be decided by the judge, not the jury. Not only was this rejected by the Court in *Sorrells,* but where the issue has been presented to them, the Courts of Appeals have since *Sorrells* unanimously concluded that unless it can be decided as a matter of law, the issue of whether a defendant has been entrapped is for the jury as part of its function of determining the guilt or innocence of the accused.

To dispose of this case on the ground suggested would entail both overruling a leading decision of this Court and brushing aside the possibility that we would be creating more problems than we would supposedly be solving.

The judgment of the Court of Appeals is reversed and the case is remanded to the District Court with instructions to dismiss the indictment.

Reversed and remanded.

Mr. Justice FRANKFURTER, whom Mr. Justice DOUGLAS, Mr. Justice HARLAN, and Mr. Justice BRENNAN join, *concurring in the result.*

Although agreeing with the Court that the undisputed facts show entrapment as a matter of law, I reach this result by a route different from the Court's.

* * *

Today's opinion . . . accepts without re-examination the theory espoused in *Sorrels* over strong protest by Mr. Justice Roberts, speaking for Brandeis and Stone, JJ., as well as himself. . . . In a matter of this kind the Court should not rest on the first attempt at an explanation for what sound instinct counsels. It should not forgo re-examination to achieve clarity of thought, because confused and inadequate analysis is too apt gradually to lead to a course of decisions that diverges from the true ends to be pursued.

It is surely sheer fiction to suggest that a conviction cannot be had when a defendant has been entrapped by government officers or informers because "Congress could not have intended that its statutes were to be enforced by tempting innocent persons into violations." In these cases raising claims of entrapment, the only legislative intention that can with any show of reason be extracted from the statute is the intention to make criminal precisely the conduct in which the defendant has engaged. That conduct includes all the elements necessary to constitute criminality. Without compulsion and "knowingly," where that is requisite, the defendant has violated the statutory command. If he is to be relieved from the usual punitive consequences, it is on no account because he is innocent of the offense described. In these circumstances, conduct is not less criminal because the result of temptation, whether the tempter is a private person or government agent or informer.

The courts refuse to convict an entrapped defendant, not because his conduct falls outside the proscription of the statute, but because, even if his guilt be admitted, the methods employed on behalf of the Government to bring about conviction cannot be countenanced. . . . The federal courts have an obligation to set their face against enforcement of the law by lawless means or means that violate rationally vindicated standards of justice, and to refuse to sustain such methods by effectuating them. They do this in the exercise of a recognized jurisdiction to formulate and apply "proper standards for the enforcement of the federal criminal law in the federal courts," an obligation that goes beyond the conviction of the particular defendant before the court.

Public confidence in the fair and honorable administration of justice, upon which ultimately depends the rule of law, is the transcending value at stake.

The formulation of these standards does not in any way conflict with the statute the defendant has violated, or involve the initiation of a judicial policy disregarding or qualifying that framed by Congress. A false choice is put when it is said that either the defendant's conduct does not fall within the statute or he must be convicted. The statute is wholly directed to defining and prohibiting the substantive offense concerned and expresses no purpose, either permissive or prohibitory, regarding the police conduct that will be tolerated in the detection of crime. A statute prohibiting the sale of narcotics is as silent on the question of entrapment as it is on the admissibility of illegally obtained evidence. It is enacted, however, on the basis of certain presuppositions concerning the established legal order and the role of the courts within that system in formulating standards for the administration of criminal justice when Congress itself has not specifically legislated to that end. Specific statutes are to be fitted into an antecedent legal system.

* * *

The crucial question, not easy of answer, to which the court must direct itself is whether the police conduct revealed in the particular case falls below standards, to which common feelings respond, for the proper use of governmental power. For answer it is wholly irrelevant to ask if the "intention" to commit the crime originated with the defendant or government officers, or if the criminal conduct was the product of "the creative activity" of law enforcement officials. Yet in the present case the Court repeats and purports to apply these unrevealing tests. Of course in every case of this kind the intention that the particular crime be committed originates with the police, and without their inducement the crime would not have occurred. But it is perfectly clear, where the police simply [furnish] the opportunity for the commission of the crime, that this is not enough to enable the defendant to escape conviction.

The intention referred to, therefore, must be a general intention or predisposition to commit, whenever the opportunity should arise, crimes of the kind solicited, and in proof of such a predisposition evidence has often been admitted to show the defendant's reputation, criminal activities, and prior disposition. The danger of prejudice in such a situation, particularly if the issue of entrapment must be submitted to the jury and disposed of by a general verdict of guilty or innocent, is evident. The defendant must either forgo the claim of entrapment or run the substantial risk that, in spite of instructions, the jury will allow a criminal record or bad reputation to weigh in its determination of guilt of the specific offense of which he stands charged. Furthermore, a test that looks to the character and predisposition of the defendant rather than the conduct of the police loses sight of the underlying reason for the defense of entrapment. No matter what the defendant's past record and present inclinations to criminality, or the depths to which he has sunk in the estimation of society, certain police conduct to ensnare him into further crime is not to be tolerated by an advanced society. And in the present case it is clear that the Court in fact reverses the conviction because of the conduct of the informer Kalchinian, and not because the Government has failed to draw a convincing picture of petitioner's past criminal conduct. Permissible police activity does not vary according to the particular defendant concerned; surely if two suspects have been solicited at the same time in the same manner, one should not go to jail simply because he has been convicted before and is said to have a criminal disposition. No more does it very according to the suspicions, reasonable or unreasonable, of the police concerning the defendant's activities. Appeals to sympathy, friendship, the possibility of exorbitant gain, and so forth, can no more be tolerated when directed against a past offender than against an ordinary law-abiding citizen. A contrary view runs afoul of fundamental principles of equality under law, and would espouse the notion that when dealing with the criminal classes anything goes. The possibility that no matter what his past crimes and general disposition the defendant might not have committed the particular crime unless confronted with inordinate inducements, must not be ignored. Past crimes do not forever outlaw the criminal and open him to police practices, aimed at securing his repeated conviction, from which the ordinary citizen is protected. The whole ameliorative hopes of modern penology and prison administration strongly counsel against such a view.

This does not mean that the police may not act so as to detect those engaged in criminal conduct and ready and willing to commit further crimes should the occasion arise. Such indeed is their obligation. It does mean that in holding out inducements they should act in such a manner as is likely to induce to the commission of crime only these persons and not others who would normally avoid crime and through self-struggle resist ordinary temptations. This test shifts attention from the record and predisposition of the particular defendant to the conduct of the police and the likelihood, objectively considered, that it would entrap only those ready and willing to commit crime. It is as objective a test as the subject matter permits, and will give guidance in regulating police conduct that is lacking when the reasonableness of police suspicions must be judged or the criminal disposition of the defendant retrospectively appraised. It draws directly on the fundamental intuition that led in the first instance to the outlawing of "entrapment" as a prosecutorial instrument. The power of government is abused and directed to an end for which it was not constituted when employed to promote rather than detect crime and to bring about the downfall of those who, left to themselves, might well have obeyed the law. Human nature is weak enough and sufficiently beset by temptations without government adding to them and generating crime.

As Mr. Justice Roberts convincingly urged in the *Sorrells* case, such a judgment, aimed at blocking off areas of impermissible police conduct, is appropriate for the court and not the jury. "The protection of its own functions and the preservation of the purity of its own temple belongs only to the court. It is the province of the court and of the court alone to protect itself and the government from such prostitution of the criminal law. The violation of the principles of justice by the entrapment of the unwary into crime should be dealt with by the court no matter by whom or at what stage of the proceedings the facts are brought to its attention." Equally important is the consideration that a jury verdict, although it may settle the issue of entrapment in the particular case, cannot give significant guidance for official conduct for the future. Only the court, through the gradual evolution of explicit standards in accumulated precedents, can do this with the degree of certainty that the wise administration of criminal justice demands.

NOTES AND QUESTIONS

1. In Professor Robinson's conceptual scheme, see § 9.02, *supra,* into which defense category does the *Sherman* majority's theory of entrapment fit? Does the defense fit within a different category under the theory espoused by Justice Frankfurter in his concurring opinion in *Sherman?* Under either theory, could the defendant constitutionally be required to carry the burden of persuasion on the entrapment issue? Under both theories? See § 9.04, *supra.*

Which theory of entrapment (the majority or concurring view) more accurately captures the nature of the defense? In thinking about this question, consider the following variation on *Sherman:*

Suppose the facts of the case except assume that Kalchinian is not a governmental informer and that the police "innocently" happen to observe Sherman transferring the drugs to Kalchinian. Assuming that Sherman obtains the drugs for Kalchinian under exactly the same conditions and for the same reasons as detailed in *Sherman,* would Sherman have a defense? If not, does that suggest that perhaps Justice Frankfurter more accurately captured the gist of the entrapment defense than the *Sherman* majority?

2. The Supreme Court has subsequently refined the *Sherman* majority's "predisposition" test. In *Jacobson v. United States,* 503 U.S. 540 (1992), the Court held that when a defendant argues entrapment, the government must show that he was "predisposed" to commit crime prior to the time the government encouraged the crime in question. The Court noted that "[l]aw enforcement officials go too far when they —implant in the mind of an innocent person the disposition to commit [an] offense and induce its commission in order that they may prosecute.' "503 U.S. at 553, quoting *Sorrells v. United States,* 287 U.S. 435, 442 (1932).

3. The *Sherman* majority's test, with *Jacobson's* gloss, is the rule in the federal system and probably also in a majority of the states. See P. Robinson, 2 Criminal Law Defenses 509–12 (1984). That test, with its focus on criminal predisposition and subjective guilt, is often characterized as the "subjective approach." See, *e.g.,* LaFave and Scott at 422. Frankfurter's concurrence in *Sherman,* on the other hand, is contrasted as an "objective approach" to defining entrapment in terms of police misconduct rather than the culpability of the particular defendant. *Id.,* at 423–25.

The Model Penal Code embraces a version of the objective approach. Section 2.13 provides

(1) A public law enforcement official or a person acting in cooperation with such an official perpetrates an entrapment if for the purpose of obtaining evidence of the commission of an offense, he induces or encourages another person to engage in conduct constituting such offense by either:

(a) making knowingly false representations designed to induce the belief that such conduct is not prohibited; or

(b) employing methods of persuasion or inducement which create a substan-tial risk that such an offense will be committed by persons other than those who are ready to commit it.

(2) Except as provided in Subsection (3) of this Section, a person prosecuted for an offense shall be acquitted if he proves by a preponderance of evidence that his conduct occurred in response to an entrapment. The issue of entrapment shall be tried by the Court in the absence of the jury.

(3) The defense afforded by this Section is unavailable when causing or threatening bodily injury is an element of the offense charged and the prosecution is based on conduct causing or threatening such injury to a person other than the person perpetrating the entrapment.

A dozen or so states have adopted one variety or another of the objective approach. See Piccaretta and Keenan, *Entrapment Targets and Tactics: Jacobson v. United States,* 29 Crim. L. Bull. 241, 252 (1993).

4. For discussion of the relative merits of the subjective and the objective approaches, see LaFave and Scott at 425–27; DeFeo, *Entrapment as a Defense to Criminal Responsibility,* 1 U.S.F. L. Rev. 243 (1967); Park, *The Entrapment Controversy,* 60 Minn. L. Rev. 163 (1976); Seidman, *The Supreme Court, Entrapment, and Our Criminal Justice Dilemma,* 1981 Sup. Ct. Rev. 111.

[E] Expanding Excuses

[1] In General

WILLIAMS, *THE THEORY OF EXCUSES*

1982 Crim. L. Rev. 732, 741-42

Once it is recognized that excuses are based on notions of justice, and show the law's consideration for the defendant's predicament in particular circumstances, it becomes obvious that the list of excuses need not be regarded as closed. Our judges are so costive in their attitude to defenses that there is perhaps no immediate hope of a change of attitude on their part; but if the call for new defenses is made insistently enough it may be heeded eventually.

ARISTOTLE, *NICOMACHEAN ETHICS*

1114a 3-11

People who appear unaware that what they are doing is wrong are actually people who are responsible for becoming men of that kind, and . . . make themselves responsible for being unjust or self-indulgent, in the one case by cheating and in the other by spending their time in drunken bouts and the like, for it is activities exercised on particular objects that make the corresponding character. . . . Now *not to know* that it is from the exercise of activities on particular objects that states of character are produced is the mark of a thoroughly senseless person.

UNITED STATES V. BAILEY

United States Circuit Court of Appeals, District of Columbia

585 F.2d 1087 (1978)

[A series of cases in the early 1970s involved defendants charged with escape from a prison. In many of these cases, defendants argued that they escaped because they had been threatened with homosexual rape and had been told by the prison officials that they were helpless to prevent the assault. In the early cases, the courts rejected such claims because they were not cognizable under typical defenses. In the eyes of these courts, the escape was not under duress (see *supra*, § 9.05[A][1]) because the threateners had not ordered them to escape "or else." (Indeed, the threateners did not want them to escape.) And the escape was not a matter of necessity (see *supra*, § 9.05[A][3]) because the common law generally required that the "choice of evils" be triggered by a natural, nonhuman source. However, in *People v. Lovercamp,* 43 Cal. App. 3d 832, 118 Cal. Rptr. 110 (1974), the court enunciated a five-prong test that "blended" duress and necessity elements. In holding that the defense was available to the defendants, the court set forth five conditions that must be established before the defense could be submitted to the jury:

> [W]e hold that the proper rule is that a limited defense of necessity is available if the following conditions exist:
>
> (1) The prisoner is faced with a specific threat of death, forcible sexual attack or substantial bodily injury in the immediate future;
>
> (2) There is no time for a complaint to the authorities or there exists a history of futile complaints which make any result from such complaints illusory;
>
> (3) There is no time or opportunity to resort to the courts;
>
> (4) There is no evidence of force or violence used towards prison personnel or other "innocent" persons in the escape; and
>
> (5) The prisoner immediately reports to the proper authorities when he has attained a position of safety from the immediate threat.

In *Bailey,* defendants did not claim homosexual rape as the impetus of their escape from jail; their claim was, among other things, that they lacked the *mens rea* for escape due to deplorable jail conditions. The defendants alleged that the jail had inadequate medical care, had brutal guards, and was a fire trap. The trial court, using *Lovercamp,* refused to instruct the jury on the claim since the defendants had not turned themselves in immediately after escaping. The opinion below by Judge Wright should not be read as restricted to prison escape cases; it raises much more general and theoretical problems than that.—Eds.]

WRIGHT, Chief Judge:

* * *

The District Court's attachment to a definition of "escape" that would effectively prevent the jury from considering the evidence of conditions in the jail, assault, and threats in relation to appellants' intent reflects a line of cases in which courts, moved by fears of undermining prison discipline or encouraging mass escapes, have hesitated to allow juries even to consider such allegedly exculpatory evidence in escape cases unless various rigorous conditions have been satisfied. We find no adequate justification for this special broad proscription against admission of such probative defense evidence relating to intent. Juries are accustomed to determining the intent of alleged criminals, and we see nothing in the context of prosecutions for escape that requires the court to risk denying the defendant a fair trial by denying the jury its normal function. The escape cases in which juries have been allowed to consider exculpatory evidence offer no support for fears that jurors are unable reasonably to consider all the aspects of escape cases or that juries will render decisions that will "encourage" escapes. . . . [T]he pernicious consequences of the restrictive rules are all too clear from the reported cases . . . the proper approach is to inform the jury of those considerations that are relevant to its deliberations. Not to take the issue out of its hands . . . allowing the jury to perform its accustomed role in escape cases may make those responsible for prison conditions more conscious of their responsibilities and may well lead to fewer, rather than more, escapes.

The defenses usually raised under the duress/necessity labels reflect two different general principles of exculpation. One of these principles, exemplified by the notion of duress as compulsion, dictates that a person will not be held responsible for an offense he commits under threats or conditions that a person of ordinary firmness would have been unable to resist. . . .

The other general principle reflected in the discussions of duress/necessity defenses is one of justification by choice of the lesser evil. . . Courts and legislatures that have recognized this type of defense have often reflected the theoretical confusion surrounding the duress/necessity labels more than the fundamental choice of evils principle by creating "fixed rules which depart somewhat from the rationale underlying the [general] rule." The tendency of courts to structure duress/necessity defenses in terms of such fixed rules has been particularly pronounced in escape cases. . . .

In regard to the choice-of-evils-type defense, this particular case in its present posture at most presents the relatively narrow question whether a jury should be allowed to consider an otherwise sufficiently supported choice of evils defense in the absence of one of the special prerequisites some courts have imposed upon such defenses in escape cases—the requirement that an escapee turn himself in to the authorities immediately after escaping. . . .

Under the circumstances of this case it is unnecessary for us to consider exhaustively the proper prerequisites to a choice of evils defense in escape cases. The trial court apparently gave this question considerable attention, and we do not know the nature of its prepared instruction except that were it not for the return requirement, which must be modified in accordance with our opinion, it was willing to have the jury consider the defense. . . .

Reversed and remanded

WILKEY, Circuit Judge, *dissenting.*

Traditionally, claims of compulsion have been governed by strict standards; defendants have been required to raise such issues within the framework of the affirmative defenses of duress and necessity, and these defenses have been precisely defined, carefully hedged, and subject to strict proof. In a radical departure from this approach, the majority holds that even if evidence is insufficient as a matter of law to make out a duress or necessity defense, it must nevertheless be presented to the jury as bearing, in some nebulous and undefined way, on a defendant's "voluntariness" and "intent." Although my colleagues do not seem to realize it, this bouleversement effectively abolishes the defenses of duress and necessity and the salutary standards embodied in them. In their stead it places vague, expanded, and essentially deterministic concepts of "intent" and "voluntariness," whose just application, no matter how well-intentioned, is obviously fraught with difficulties. . .

[Judge Wilkey then argued that the claims here met neither traditional duress nor necessity standards.]

IV. THE MAJORITY'S "VOLUNTARINESS" THEORY

The majority suggests that, regardless of whether the evidence presented by defendants was sufficient as a matter of law to make out an affirmative defense of duress, it should have been submitted to the jury as relevant to the "voluntariness" of defendants' actions. Finding that "voluntariness" is a necessary "element" of the crime of escape, the majority concludes that the trial court erred in precluding jury consideration of defendants' evidence of medical inattention, assaults, and fires. . . .

The second way in which the term "voluntary" is used refers to exercise of the *free will*. In this context, an act is said to be "involuntary" where the will of an actor is subject to such coercive pressure *(vis compulsiva)* that it is overborne and the actor—"against his own will"—chooses to violate the law rather than obey it. Thus, for example, if a prisoner is forced at gunpoint to walk out of prison "against his own will," then he has not acted "voluntarily." It is in this "free will" sense that the majority uses the term "voluntary," and it is in this sense that the term will be used in this section.

The majority is unquestionably correct when it says that "voluntariness"—free will—is a necessary element in the crime of escape, for it is a necessary element in *all* true crimes. It is a basic precept in Anglo-American law that the exercise of "free" will is essential to criminal responsibility. A person who has been compelled to act against his will should not be held responsible and punished for his actions.

With respect to the present case, the majority's position is simply this: the defendants' evidence regarding fires, assaults, and medical care have some bearing on whether the defendants were exercising "free will" when they departed from prison; therefore, the evidence should have been submitted to the jury on the issue of "voluntariness," even though it did not make out a defense of duress.

This position is utterly untenable. It is black-letter law that, in cases such as this, issues of "voluntariness" are to be raised through the affirmative defense of duress. When a defendant asserts that he was deprived of free will and did not act "voluntarily" because he was compelled to violate the law either by force of circumstances or by the threats of other persons, then he must raise these matters within the framework of the duress defense. This is why I stated at the outset that my colleagues did not seem to realize the radical revolution they were writing into the law, such a bouleversement that it in reality abolishes the salutary standards that heretofore have governed the defenses of duress and necessity.

The doctrine of duress has been fashioned precisely for dealing with the issue of free will. As Professor Burdick writes in his treatise on criminal law:

> Since every crime requires a willing or voluntary mind, it may be a defense to a criminal charge that the criminal act was not committed voluntarily but was the result of coercion, compulsion, or necessity. As said by Lord Mansfield: "Whenever necessity forces a man to do an illegal act, [whatever] *forces* him to do it, justifies him, because no man can be guilty of a crime without the will and intention of the mind." Blackstone has also said: "A species of defect of will is that arising from compulsion and inevitable necessity. These are a constraint upon the will whereby a man is urged to do that which his judgment disapproves, and which it is to be presumed, his will (if left to itself) would reject. As punishments are therefore only inflicted for the abuse of that free will which God has given to man, it is highly just and equitable that a man should be excused for those acts which are done through unavoidable force and compulsion.". . . .

Thus, the positive law that defines where free will ends and exculpating compulsion begins is embodied in the duress doctrine and no where else. The rule of law embodied in the doctrine is this: A defendant's actions are deemed voluntary, even though he has been subject to compulsion, unless the compulsion is such as to induce a well-grounded apprehension of immediate and avoidable death or serious bodily harm. If a defendant fails to adduce evidence of such duress, then as a matter of law he has acted voluntarily. Only when he has adduced such evidence can there be a reasonable doubt as to his voluntariness. In short, the issue of duress by definition determines the issue of voluntariness: if legally sufficient duress exists, then the defendant may be acting involuntarily; if legally sufficient duress does not exist, then the defendant is deemed to be acting voluntarily as a matter of law. . . .

The practical effect of the majority's decision is to abolish the strict standards governing claims of "involuntariness" that were formerly embodied in the affirmative defense of duress and to replace them with a nebulous and essentially deterministic view of "voluntariness," or free will. What really takes shape is a "totality of the circumstances" test. Defendant would be able to adduce any and all evidence that may have some kind of bearing on his motivation. Evidence as to every conceivable unpleasantry that may exist in the prison may be thrown into the hodge-podge. Moreover, presumably evidence concerning motivation stemming from conditions external to the prison could be adduced by the defendant, *i.e.,* that he was driven by a desire to see his dying mother. Confronted with this unstructured evidence the jury would then be expected to find whether from all the circumstances there is any reasonable doubt as to whether the defendant acted voluntarily. This deterministic approach is a prescription for chaos and has wisely been rejected in the criminal law for hundreds of years.

Notes and Questions

1. On appeal, the United States Supreme Court reversed *Bailey,* holding that the federal escape statute established two separate offenses: (1)escape and (2)remaining absent after escape. Since there was no dispute that the defendants in *Bailey* had in fact remained absent after escaping, the Court found no defense. *United States v. Bailey,* 444 U.S. 394 (1980). The Court thereby avoided the nettlesome issue of whether the defendants' plea sounded in necessity, duress, or, as the D.C. Circuit had held, *mens rea,* without regard to a specific label.

Indeed, the Court, per Mr. Justice Rehnquist, explicitly refused to grapple with the issue:

While the suggested element-by-element analysis is a useful tool for making sense of an otherwise opaque concept, it is not the only principle to be considered. The administration of the federal system of criminal justice is confined to ordinary mortals, whether they be lawyers, judges or jurors. This system could easily fall of its own weight if courts or scholars become obsessed with hair-splitting distinctions, either traditional or novel, that Congress neither stated nor implied when it made the conduct criminal.

44 U.S. at 406–07.

2. The prison escape cases resurrected the issues of duress and necessity in American law. Not surprisingly, therefore, the law reviews also blossomed with materials. See, *e.g.,* Gardner, *The Defense of Necessity and the Right to Escape from Prison—A Step Towards Incarceration Free from Sexual Assault,* 49 S. Cal. L. Rev. 110 (1975). The cases and the commentary continue even after the Supreme Court decision in *Bailey.* See also *People v. Unger,* 362 N.E. 2d 319 (Ill. 1977). For example, Missouri, interpreting its statute differently from the Supreme Court's reading of the federal statute, has now held that an escapee may have a defense, and that the presence of that defense does not depend on meeting specific criteria. *State v. Baker,* 598 S.W.2d, 540 (Mo. Ct. App. 1980). For a fascinating debate over whether these cases should be considered ones of duress or necessity, see Comment, *Intolerable Conditions as a Defense to Prison Escapes,* 26 U.C.L.A. L. Rev. 1126 (1979); Fletcher, *Should Intolerable Prison Conditions Generate a Justification or an Excuse for Escape?,* 26 U.C.L.A. L. Rev. 1355 (1979) (responding to the Comment). See also Comment, 67 Calif. L. Rev. 1183 (1979).

3. Judge Wilkey says that defenses such as necessity and duress are carefully defined "affirmative defenses" and do not go to the *mens rea* issue raised in *Bailey.* What does that mean? Why should a question of defendant's liability be required to fit neatly into one or another category?

[2] General Issues of Free Will and Science

The question of free will versus determinism, predestination, karma, and so on far transcends the criminal law. But to the extent that the criminal law is based on blameworthiness (and possibly even deterrence), the assumption of free will may be one that, true or not, the criminal law must make. (See, *supra,* § 9.01.) It is possible to see in the response to claims of diminished capacity, irresistible impulse, and other such potential excuses as well as the rigid requirements for self-defense, duress, necessity, and even provocation, the persistent reluctance of the common law even to consider doctrines that substantially undermine the idea that virtually all choices of most persons are "free."

Yet scientists, moralists, and others have consistently sought to demonstrate that immorality or criminality is indeed "caused" or at least substantially influenced by factors beyond the control of the actor. Thus, for example, Cesare Lombroso introduced the idea of phrenology, arguing that by carefully analyzing the facial and cranial physiology of a person, one could determine whether he would become a criminal. C. Lombroso, Criminal Man (1911). In the early 20th century, there was much support, in this country and others, for the view that criminality was hereditary. Many states provided for the sterilization of criminals. See M. Haller, Eugenics (1963); K. Ludmerer, Genetics and American Society (1972). See also Sixty-Third Report of the Board of Inspectors the Eastern State Penitentiary of Philadelphia 104 (1893). In the one Supreme Court decision concerning these statutes, the Court held that the Oklahoma statute in question was unconstitutional not because it provided for sterilization of some thieves, but because it did not also impose the penalty upon other thieves, thereby depriving the defendant of equal protection. *Skinner v. Oklahoma,* 316 U.S. 535 (1942). Exploration for physical or other determinants of criminality as well as other conduct has continued; numerous writings, for example, discuss the connection between certain physical disorders and crime. See, *e.g.,* Shah and Roth, *Biological and Psychophysiologica l Factors in Criminality,* in Handbook of Criminology 101 (D. Glasser ed. 1974).

Within the past century, the emergence of psychiatry has added yet another force that seeks to explain criminality. The dominance of that approach to insanity has been noted as has the reluctance of some courts to adopt any but the most rigid test for insanity since they fear that acceptance of the determinism promoted by psychiatrists might lead to the downfall of the criminal system—*tout comprendre, c'est tout pardonner.*

Still a third explanatory engine is sociology—the view that people become what they are not from nature, but from nurture, and that a criminal (or noncriminal) is "determined" by the forces she encounters in her life. To some extent we have seen this view adopted in *Wanrow, supra* p. 776, where the court accepted the argument that women as a class are "socially acculturated" either to submit to male force or to kill rather than use less than nondeadly force. Other sociological explanations of crime and criminogenic conditions are now being suggested as excuses for criminals.

The materials below sketch briefly some attempts to introduce into the criminal law new excuses based upon one or more of these schools of thought. The data given are incomplete, as is sometimes the case in even the most thorough research on the particular symptom. The interested reader will necessarily have to read the literature much more deeply to ascertain even preliminarily the strength of the argument concerning each of these proffered defenses.

Beyond the question of the data's power, however, is the critical issue, which is one of faith and philosophy: Assuming that the evidence sustained the argument that a particular defendant's criminal acts were "caused" or "heavily influenced" by the forces delineated, should the criminal law recognize these forces as an excuse, either full or partial? Or should the law refuse to undercut potentially the entire premise of free will and moral culpability? If the law recognized all of these defenses (and those to come) would the criminal law retain its unique character? Could we continue to talk about "morally blameworthy acts"? Would even deterrence be a feasible goal? These questions and the questions they raise in turn may suggest why the law has typically been loathe to expand excuses.

GROSS, *SOME UNACCEPTABLE EXCUSES*

19 Wayne L. Rev. 997, 1001-2 (1973)

There is a false exculpatory move which is commonplace in legal and other determinations of responsibility. It is said that certain things caused a person to behave badly and since they were not his making—indeed their existence was beyond his control—he ought not to be held responsible for their effects. Causes under this view are things but for which the criminal behavior would have been unlikely. . . . Those offering the excuse assume that conduct cannot be blameworthy unless the existence of those conditions that were necessary for its occurrence were within the actor's control. This, however, is not so. We are all of us all the time subject to such alien influences, but so long as we have control over how these influences affect our conduct we are responsible agents. All that is required for responsibility is that we be able to modify such influences by inhibitory processes. Even though certain background conditions may have been necessary for behavior constituting criminal conduct—but for those conditions the conduct almost certainly would not have been engaged in—we do not excuse the conduct unless the outcome of those conditions is beyond the inhibitory powers of the actor. In short, responsibility for conduct does not require that the actor be responsible for those elements but for whose influence he would not have acted as he did. It requires only that he be able to frustrate their effect.

[a] Physiologically Based Excuses for Criminality

Clearly the closest to the "nature" philosophy of the causes of behavior are those claims that rely upon the idea that "criminals are born, not made" and that their criminality is in their body, in one way or another, far beyond their ability to control or alter.

XYY. Of all the theories thus far proffered by serious scientists, the XYY chromosomal abnormality theory is in many ways the broadest for it literally suggests that criminality is genetic in nature. In the early 1960s a series of medical journal articles suggested that a chromosomal variance might be responsible for at least some criminal action. Researchers in British prisons discovered that a substantial percentage of the inmates—much higher than in the general population—had an extra Y chromosome. (A female has two X and no Y chromosomes. A male generally has one X and one Y chromosome. The subjects had two Y chromosomes.) This led to speculation that the extra Y chromosome might cause some persons to be more "masculine" (which was then read to mean aggressive) and therefore to commit crime. Later investigation, however, threw doubt both upon the raw findings and upon the alleged link between the extra chromosome and criminal propensity. The defense was rejected in *Millard v. State,* 8 Md. App. 419, 261 A.2d 227 (1970), where the defendant had sought to establish XYY as a form of insanity. There is today virtually total agreement that there is no relationship between XYY and criminal behavior. See generally Burke, *The "XYY Syndrome": Genetics, Behavior and the Law,* 46 Den. L.J. 261 (1969); Fox, *The XYY Offender: A Modern Myth?,* 62 J. Crim. L. Criminology & Pol. Sci. 59 (1971); Taylor, *Genetically Influenced Anti-Social Conduct and the Criminal Justice System,* 330 No. Ire. L.Q. 214 (1982). Still, the moral and philosophical issue is posed: Suppose the data were more conclusive. Should the criminal law nevertheless ignore the scientific findings? Can these issues be avoided by requiring *absolute* certainty since that is impossible?

Genetic Causation

NOTE, THE GENETIC DEFENSE: EXCUSE OR EXPLANATION?

35 Wm. & Mary L. Rev. 353, 390-96 (1993)

The causal nexus hurdle may prove more difficult to surmount. Although studies have shown consistent correlation between certain conditions and criminal behavior, they have not produced definitive evidence regarding the nature and extent of causation. Indeed, many experts warn that in seeking to identify the root causes of physical or behavioral symptoms and to predict future conditions in the absence of manifest symptoms, correlation can easily be misperceived as causation, especially by nonscientists using the tests for policy purposes. In other words, the presence of a genetic or biological condition may be confused with inevitable expression of the actual disease.

Moreover, most genetic disorders are polygenic, or the product of the interaction of several genes with a person's environment. Thus, even if a test can detect with complete reliability a gene, a cluster of genes, or an extra chromosome, it will not necessarily provide information about the timing or severity of a disability or how it might affect the normal functioning of the afflicted individual. "Tests that identify genetic traits are intrinsically incapable of accounting for other variables—diet, lifestyle, the effect of environmental or social interactions—that may influence their manifestation in disease."
. . . Not only have experts been unable to identify definitive and predictable causal relations between certain conditions and subsequent behavioral manifestations, but they also remain unsure as to how many forms of genetic aberration actually exist. . . .

A system which denies excuse to those who suffer biological disorders not satisfying the criteria of legal insanity implicitly demands that these persons be held criminally responsible for their behavior. Whereas society may not find this abstract concept too disturbing when weighed against the countervailing objectives of safety and order, the determination of suitable punishment poses a more troublesome dilemma.

. . . Penalties for the "normal" offender may be justified by the goals of retribution, deterrence, isolation, and rehabilitation. Incarcerating the biologically impaired individual, however, serves these objectives imperfectly, if at all. If a definite link is established between the presence of a biological condition and antisocial behavior, society will be faced with an individual who may not be able to control his behavior or be rehabilitated by imprisonment, and whose biological propensity for antisocial behavior is not "curable."

Theoretically, society would gain little satisfaction in seeking retribution against one who is neither responsible for, nor capable of changing, his physical constitution. Under such circumstances, retribution would be, in effect, exacting vengeance for a birth defect. As for deterrence, effectiveness assumes that a criminal reflects rationally on the potential consequences of his acts. If the offender's behavior is to some extent driven by factors beyond his understanding or control, however, to what extent would threat of punishment be effective?

Given the disparate functions of law and science, models of human behavior based exclusively on either free will or determinism prove problematic. On the one hand, an assumption that all individuals possess similar control over their actions directly conflicts with evidence demonstrating different genetic susceptibilities. On the other hand, an assumption that all actions are caused by factors beyond our control effectively eliminates personal accountability in a system that predicates punishment upon moral blame. Some theories attempt to reconcile determinism and free will. "Degree determinism," for instance, denies that all human actions are fully caused; instead, a continuum exists in which different actions can be more or less determined and thus are more or less free. Certain factors predispose individuals to specific behavior, but do not operate as either a necessary or a sufficient condition for that behavior. Degree determinism, or a "conditional free will" theory, is based on probabilities. "Numerous causes or alternatives are presented to explain an effect, with each cause having a certain probability of resulting in that outcome." When certain factors make the probabilities of deviant behavior strong enough, responsibility is excused.

A model integrating the influences of free will and determinism would not necessarily overturn or undermine existing foundations of the legal system. Although a revised paradigm would recognize empirical data demonstrating that genetic conditions may predispose the development and manifestations of antisocial behavior, it would not foreclose automatically the possibility of an appreciable degree of free will, or preclude the imposition of social regulation based upon that residual self-control.

In sum, to deny that biological aberrations and dysfunctions exert some influence on an individual's decisions and actions in certain environments would be to dispute scientific reality. With the trend of modern genetic research, science will now, or in the near future, be able to satisfy courts' demands for sufficiently substantiated and accepted proof of actual genetic disorders.

This recognition of biological determinism need not require the adoption of a constitutional or special "genetic defense." Because an individual may be more vulnerable to developing a chemical addiction or an antisocial personality disorder does not mean that that individual in fact will develop those conditions, or that the individual has absolutely no control over such development. The existence of a genetic condition merely provides more insight into whether a person possessed enough free will or rational ability to control and understand her behavior. The difficulty with a model of degree determinism, then, is twofold: separating the causal factors to assess their relative contributions and identifying the "baseline" of criminal responsibility—the point in the continuum of free will and causation in which responsibility ends and excuse begins. Science cannot now, and may not in the near future, assign exact probabilities or make definitive causal connections between genetic abnormalities and human behavior. To summarily dismiss the probative value of an individual diagnosis because of this lack of certainty, however, is unwarranted. Instead, courts should admit evidence of a medically diagnosable disorder as a relevant factor in determining whether an individual possessed the requisite amount of control or understanding of his behavior to be held legally responsible.

Again, although the putative "free will" basis of criminal responsibility must be reassessed and reformulated to acknowledge a greater degree of determinism, that acknowledgment need not result in an abandonment of the fundamental standards by which an individual is held accountable for his actions. Adherence to intellectual honesty may require simply an admission that the criminal justice system is not based solely on attribution of moral blame. Society may decide that, in some instances, the need for civil order and protection may override subjective culpability as a justification for criminal sanctions.

Unquestionably, a minimal level of conformity is a prerequisite for orderly human interaction; underconformity, or lawlessness, threatens the core of civilized society. Consequently, the State attaches a broad responsibility to the condition of citizenship: persons within the jurisdiction must obey the law. Ordinarily, both the intention and the ability to do otherwise are necessary for full moral responsibility. But the two elements are not always required for the ascription of legal responsibility. A particular responsibility rule may require both elements, either one, or neither.

Accordingly, responsibility may be defined in consideration of social welfare: offenders should be deemed "responsible" for their crimes at the point at which social utility is maximized. Utilitarian theories of punishment do not require that an actor be responsible in a morally significant sense. An individual's metaphysical or psychological condition at the time of the act is not the appropriate focus. Rather, the inquiry is whether punishment will serve any societal interest. If society finds punishing an individual for crimes for which he is not responsible in the traditional sense to be morally offensive, then the punishment cannot be justified unless it is outweighed by a greater good. In short, the rightness or wrongness of action can be measured by its consequences. While incarceration of a genetically afflicted offender would not serve the traditional objectives of retribution and deterrence, society nonetheless may determine that the isolation function outweighs these factors pursuant to a utilitarian concept of responsibility. Although an individual, through no fault of her own, may be born with an immutable predisposition to behavior that society has deemed unacceptable, in some cases the normative ends—for example, removing a potentially dangerous offender from the street—may justify the morally debatable means.

On the other hand, consider the following from the *New York Times,* Jan. 21, 1994(sect. 4), p.1.

NATALIE ANGIER, *ELEMENTARY, DR. WATSON.* THE *NEUROTRANSMITTERS DID IT*

[A] growing number of researchers are seeking to train the might of molecular science on the greatest sickness of all—violent crime. They believe there is much to be gained by exploring the neurobiological basis of aggression, the biochemical gunpowder in the brain that prompts a person to explode in mortal fury. Already scientists have identified several important signaling molecules, or neurotransmitters, that seem to play a role in aggressive and potentially dangerous behavior, some of which are described in three articles appearing in the current issue of the *Archives of General Psychiatry.* And recently researchers from the Netherlands announced the link between a gene and a rare hereditary disease in which afflicted men impulsively commit violent acts.

Given these and other successes, the study of the biology of violence has lately gained new credibility and cachet. Less than two years ago, the Federal Government pulled its financial support from a conference to be held at the University of Maryland on the genetics of criminal behavior, when the political heat grew too scorching. Now the money is being reinstated, and the university hopes to hold the conference in 1995.

Yet even as some scientists vigorously promote the new work, they . . . say there is not likely to be a single gene for violence, or even a tidy handful of genes. And they emphasize that, while they have implicated some neurotransmitters in impulsive and aggressive behavior, their work is in an embryonic stage, far from producing any miracle cures."

Although I think the genetic and biological research angles should be pursued," said Dr. Gregory Carey, a behavioral geneticist at the University of Colorado in Boulder, "the possibility that there will be any immediate, short-term payoff is relatively remote."

And some critics of the new line of research doubt that any of the recent biological revelations will be of use in tackling urban crime, bound up as it is with poverty, miserable living conditions, drugs, low educational achievement, availability of guns and other old-fashioned sociocultural afflictions. They see current efforts to explain crime in genetic or physiological terms as yet another swing in the unending nature-versus-nurture debate. They say that people are lulled by the undeniable accomplishments of the biomedical revolution into believing that all problems can be solved, or at least soothed, by the proper application of science. . . .

"People want simple explanations for hard-core problems," said Dr. Anne Fausto-Sterling, a geneticist at Brown University. "If there was an anti-testosterone drug that we could inject to make young boys nice, that would be a lot easier and cheaper than transforming schools or society or whatever is at the heart of the problem." Dr. Fausto-Sterling warned against the sort of zealous faith in science that led in the 19th century to eugenics and the infamous "science" of phrenology, measuring the skull as a way of identifying personality types (the telltale features of a potential criminal, by this analysis: a low forehead and protuberant brow). Even as recently as the 1970's, she said, "people were talking about finding the parts of the brain that trigger violence, with the idea that hardened criminals could be treated by selectively ablating those regions of the brain."

Yet with all the fears and caveats, those who focus on biology of aggression say violence cannot be explained by environmental circumstances alone.

Based on studies that compare fraternal twins, who share only half their genes with one another, and identical twins who are genetically identical, Dr. Emil F. Coccaro, director of clinical neuroscience research at the Medical College of Pennsylvania in Philadelphia, estimated that the heritability of impulsive-aggressi ve behavior is between 25 and 40 percent.

Several experts have settled on the neurotransmitter serotonin as a major player in aggressive and impulsive behaviors. This chemical messenger, a molecular celebrity for its role as the target of the popular antidepressant drug Prozac, has long been implicated in animal studies as a mediator of sexual and social behaviors. Now scientists have reason to suspect that low serotonin in the brain can lead to all sorts of problems. Studying impulsively violent offenders, who have killed or attempted to kill in a burst of unpremeditated fury they have found comparatively low levels of serotonin.

COMPLICATING FACTORS

Some of the discrepancy may be hereditary. In a related study, for example, the scientists found that a group of people prone to suicidal behavior while drunk had inherited a genetic variant that resulted in low serotonin release in the brain, particularly in the frontal lobes. However, low serotonin in the brain may result from habits as well as genes: liquor, some drugs and stress are all thought to depress serotonin.

Scientists also warn that serotonin is only one of many chemical actors in anti-social behavior. Perhaps not surprisingly, [one researcher] also found that violent offenders had abnormally high levels of testosterone, the male hormone long known as a mediator of aggression.

Dr. Craig Ferris, of the University of Massachusetts Medical Center in Worcester, has found that vasopressin, another hormone, is one signal that turns an animal aggressive. Unfortunately for those who might consider a vasopressin-blocki ng drug as a means of controlling aggression, vasopressin has also been shown to allow male animals to bond with their mates and protect their young. Indeed, skeptics point out that all compounds in the brain have multiple effects on personality and behavior, and one signaling system invariably interacts with many others. Serotonin, dopamine, adrenaline, noradrenaline: all these neurotransmitters and hormones talk to one another and sorting out the many chattering conversations will likely take years, if not decades.

Even if low serotonin does prove to be an important predisposing factor for violence-prone personalities, nobody is ready to propose that children in urban areas take Prozac, a drug known to raise serotonin levels. . .

Critics said that, for all the scientific insights that may or may not come out of understanding the biology of violence, any solutions to the problem on a broad scale are likely to be environmental. . . .

"I would say, don't hold your breath if you think looking for genes is going to help you understand violence," said Dr. Balaban. "I would put my money on clever environmental manipulations, because in the end you're going to go there anyway."

For just part of the huge literature that is accruing in this area, see Mednick, Pollock, Volavka, and Garbrielli, *Biology and Violence* in Criminal Violence (M. Wolfgang and N. Weiner eds. 1982); *The Causes of Crime: New Biological Approaches* (S. Mednick, T. Moffit, and S. Stacks eds. 1987); Taylor, Born to Crime: The Genetic Causes of Criminal Behavior (1984); Norrie, *Freewill, Determinism and Criminal Justice,* 3 Legal Stud. (1983); Biosocial Bases of Criminal Behavior (S. Mednick and K. Christiansen eds. 1977); Biology, Crime and Ethics: A Study of Biological Explanations for Criminal Behavior (F. Marsh and J. Katz eds. 1985); Colloquium on the Correlates of Crime and the Determinants of Criminal Behavior (L. Otten ed. 1978); *Plasma Levels in the Rapist,* 38 Psychosomatic Med. 257 (1976); Bain et al., *Sex Hormones in Murderers and Assaulters,* 5 Behavior Sci. & L. 95 (1987); Ecologic-Biochemic al Approaches to Treatment of Delinquents and Criminals (L. Hippchen ed. 1978); *EEG Studies:* Hill, 98 J. Mental Sci. 23 (1952); D. Denno, Biology and Violence: From Birth to Adulthood (1989); D. Hamparian et al., The Violent Few: A Study of Dangerous Juvenile Offenders (1978).

Premenstrual Syndrome (PMS). For many decades, it has been obvious that most women suffer some discomfort before and during menstruation, and that some become severely irritable, depressed, somewhat unable to control their behavior, and sometimes suicidal. In the past two decades, several writers have suggested that in a small percentage of women (3 to 5 percent) these symptoms become so severe as to alter significantly the woman's behavior controls, thus hinting at a link between PMS and criminality. The first major legal work was Wallach and Rubin, *The Premenstrual Syndrome and Criminal Responsibility,* 19 U.C.L.A. L. Rev. 210 (1971). Among other studies, Wallach and Rubin cited one reporting that of all women committing violent crime in a given year in Paris, a disproportionately large* percentage was in the menstrual period. *Id.* at 228. Similarly, Ellis and Austin, *Menstruation and Aggressive Behavior in a Correctional Center for Women,* 62 J. Crim. L., Criminology & Police Sci. 388 (1971), found that 41 percent of all "aggressive" acts by inmates occurred during the premenstrual and menstrual cycles. This data, and the inferences drawn, have been subjected to scathing skepticism by Horney, *Menstrual Cycles and Criminal Responsibility,* 2 Law & Hum. Behav. 25 (1978).

The literature is vast. See, *e.g.,* Dalton, Menstruation and Crime (1961), Brit. Med. J. 1752; d'Orban and Dalton, *Violent Crime and the Menstrual Cycle,* 10 Psychol. Med. 353 (1980); Pallis, *The Menstrual Cycle and Suicidal Attempt,* 8 J. Biosoc. Soc. 27 (1976); Brahams, *Medicine and the Law,* Lancet (November 28, 1981), p.1238.

The cases are unreported as of now, but are discussed in Note, *Criminal Law: Premenstrual Syndrome in the Courts,* 24 Washburn L.J. 54 (1984). In one case, a 36-year-old English woman ended a love affair by deliberately running down her lover with her car and killing him. She pled guilty to manslaughter because of diminished responsibility due to PMS and was discharged from custody, having her driver's license revoked for one year. In another case, a woman who had already been on probation for stabbing a colleague to death was convicted of carrying a knife and threatening to kill a policeman, and again put on probation. In both instances the woman argued that she was suffering from PMS, which the court recognized as a mitigating factor in sentencing.

Under what currently existing doctrine, if any, could this claim be recognized? Is the woman suffering from diminished capacity as it is recognized in this country? Could a killing committed in such a situation be deemed provoked? Would she be acting "under extreme mental or emotional disturbance" in a Model Penal Code jurisdiction? See Note, 1983 Duke L.J. 176. There is some indication that PMS was relied on 140 years ago to obtain an acquittal on insanity grounds. R. Smith, Trial by Medicine 118–19 (1981). Note, 6 Cooley L. Rev. 323 at 331 (1989) cites Norris and Sullivan, PMS: Premenstrual Syndrome 270 (1983), for the proposition that "in the past, the law has recognized menstrual disorders as defense for various criminal acts." What doctrinal difficulties are there with this analysis?

In 1994, the American Psychiatric Association added premenstrual dysphoric disorder (PMDD), a severe form of premenstrual syndrome, to the list of depressive disorders in its Diagnostic and Statistical Manual (DSM-IV). The definition is such that it applies to a small percentage (2–6%) of women. The

---

* The argument here is that, assuming a 7-day menstruation cycle and a 28-day month, if mere randomness were at work and there were no connection between PMS and criminality, one would expect that only 25 percent of crimes committed by women would occur during this seven-day period. If the percentage of crimes actually committed by women is higher than 25 percent, the argument continues, this suggests a causal link between PMS and criminality. It is suggested that the discrepancy between the 25 percent random distribution to be expected and the 41 percent in this study (other percentages appear in other studies) supports, the view that PMS makes a woman more susceptible to loss of normal controls and moral inhibitors, and thus "causes" her crimes.

DSM expressly states that its classifications are not to be used in non-psychiatric settings (e.g., in court), but lawyers have consistently relied upon its authority in the past. This might mean that (1) other women will be excluded from claiming PMS; (2) women who claim PMDD will be treated as suffering from a mental illness, with possible commitment after a successful defense. Is this a sound approach? See Solomon, *Premenstrual Syndrome: The Debate Surrounding Criminal Defense,* 54 Md. L. Rev. 571 (1995).

PMS apparently can be prevented by progesterone treatment. Can this disease then be handled by the criminal law by analogy to epilepsy? See *Decina, supra,* § 3.01[A]. See also Note, 15 N.C. Cent. L.J. 246, 272 (1981), urging that PMS be considered a factor only in mitigation of the charged offense at sentence so as to reduce possibility of abuse while "protecting a PMS defendant from the stigma of institutionalizati on," but then later stating that "[I]f a defendant could show that she could respond to PMS treatment, the best solution, in light of all purposes for punishment, would be a limited confinement to a medical facility for treatment and observation."

Hypoglycemia. As we have already seen in § 3.01[A], *supra,* the law recognizes that bodily movements that occur during an epileptic seizure are not "voluntary" and hence cannot be the basis for criminal liability, although the failure to take medication can itself become the basis. A number of other physical disabilities arguably have similar impact on the individual. In *Regina v. Quick* [1973], 3 W.L.R. 26 (Ct. of Crim. App.), the court was confronted with a defendant who claimed that his acts were performed while he was in a state of hypoglycemia brought about by his taking more insulin (for his diabetes) than his body sugar could adequately handle. According to expert testimony, this could make the patient "more than aggressive, for a while he may start being physically violent and then he will be in a semi-conscious state . . . then he may have a fit, then he may stay deeply unconscious for quite a while." The *Quick* court held that such a defendant could argue lack of a voluntary act and was not limited to an insanity defense, even though if the defendant were found not guilty by reason of insanity he could be confined, whereas if the defense were allowed under the voluntary act rubric, the defendant would be eligible for complete freedom. Should the law recognize a defense at all in a case like *Quick?* How would one apply this to women with premenstrual syndrome?

Senility and Alzheimer's Disease Professor Cohen has predicted that the criminal law will soon be faced with elderly criminals claiming an excuse due to their age and the effects of physical deterioration on the mental processes. Cohen, *Old Age as a Criminal Defense,* 21 Crim. L. Bull. 5 (1985). How should a utilitarian react to such a suggestion? Both tort law and criminal law treat juvenile actors differently—the former by establishing an exception to the reasonably prudent person standard for children, the latter by establishing an entirely different administrative process (not even labeled criminal). Yet tort law does not establish such an exception for either the insane or the elderly. The criminal law does, as we have seen, distinguish the insane. Should it similarly give an exception for the (non-insane) senile? Are the tort law's reasons for not establishing an exception for the senile actor nevertheless to be followed by the criminal law? Why?

Sleep Disorders In *People v. Cegers,* 7 Cal. App. 4th 988, 2 Cal. Rptr. 2d 297 (1992), defendant, upon being awakened from a deep sleep, aggravated by severe intoxication, rose suddenly, put on his trousers, and flailed with knives at family members in his house. In a prosecution for assault, he was allowed to introduce evidence that he suffered from sleep apnea, a defect in breathing patterns that causes diminished oxygen level, which results in confusion and abnormal behavior upon being suddenly awakened. The trial court, however, precluded psychological evidence from an expert in sleep disorders that the defendant suffered from "confusional arousal syndrome." What result on appeal?

Brain Scan Evidence. The positron emission tomograph (PET) scan is the most recent and apparently most accurate brain imaging technique. It shows organic damage in the brain and is often used to support insanity pleas. Two other types of imaging—CAT scans and magnetic resonance imaging (MRI)—each give detailed anatomical pictures of the brain, while the PETs can show brain metabolic activity. Are these physiological or psychological evidence of insanity? Are they more acceptable forms of evidence than psychiatric testimony because of their hard science shape?

SUGGESTED READING

For a broader discussion of all these issues, see Fox, *Physical Disorder, Consequences, and Criminal Liability,* 63 Colum. L. Rev. 645 (1963).

---

[b] Psychologically Based Excuses for Criminality

To some degree, this category may be fictitious since some would now argue that most behavior disorders that we now attribute to mental illness are probably physiologically based, even if we are presently ignorant about the physiological causes. The dramatic success that psychotropic drugs have shown in curbing mental illness, or at least the behavior disorders affiliated with some mental illness, gives credence to this view.* Yet there are still many disorders that we call mental rather than physical. Whether this simply reflects the current lack of understanding or a deeper intuition (or fear) about the relationship of body and mind is not clear and probably not relevant to the criminal law. In any event, there are some "excuses" that seem to be more psychologically related than others. We explore these below.

Brainwashing. The notion that (1)one would be brainwashed into committing a crime and (2)the actual actor should not be punished for that crime obtained national headlines with the prosecution of Patricia Hearst for bank robbery. Hearst, daughter of a wealthy newspaper publisher, was kidnapped by a revolutionary group, the Symbionese Liberation Army (SLA), and held for several months. She suddenly appeared with members of the SLA during a bank robbery, holding a machine gun, and dressed, as they were, in military attire. She then disappeared. She was found several months later by the FBI,

---

* There is some recent suggestion that schizophrenia and perhaps other mental illnesses are genetic in origin. The overlap with this category of excuses and those in the first section becomes apparent.

living independently in San Francisco. When arrested, she gave her occupation as "revolutionary" and declared that during her capture she had become convinced that the SLA's perspective on politics and crime was the right perspective. At her trial, however, she argued that she had been brainwashed into believing this and that she never would have voluntarily participated in the bank robbery or thought of herself as a revolutionary but for the extreme physical and mental torment she had experienced during her early days of captivity. The jury convicted her of bank robbery.

The case raised the question of whether, assuming Hearst's story was believed, she should be excused. Professor Richard Delgado argued in favor of the excuse:

> Consideration of theories traditionally believed to justify punishment also suggests that coercive persuasion should be taken into account in assessing a defendant's criminal guilt. . . . Punitive treatment of coercively persuaded defendants is difficult to reconcile with [societal safety, rehabilitation, deterrence, or retribution]. . . [M]ost such victims, once removed from the coercive environment, soon lose their inculcated responses and return to their former modes of thinking and acting. . . . Punishment of such individuals does little to promote the rationales of the criminal justice system. . . .
>
> [D]efendants who have undergone coercive persuasion apparently are neither insane, coerced, or acting under diminished capacity, and yet they seem less than fully responsible for their acts. This is so because the coercively persuaded defendant's choice to act criminally was not freely made and, indeed, appears to be not his choice at all.
>
> The victim of thought reform typically commits criminal acts fully aware of their wrongfulness. He acts consciously, even enthusiastically, and without overt coercion. Yet, in an important sense, the guilty mind with which he acts is not his own. Rather, his mental state is more appropriately ascribed to the captors who instilled it in him for their own purposes. Explication of the concept of transferred or superimposed *mens rea* . . . is thus the principal [issue].
>
> Since traditional *actus reus* and *mens rea* defenses have been declared inapplicable and courts have been reluctant to extend existing defenses to thought reform victims, development of a new defense along lines suggested here may well constitute the minimal departure from existing theory that Occam's principle demands.
>
> It is proposed that the following elements must be shown to exist:
>
> (1) that coercive persuasion actually occurred;
>
> (2) that the defendant's unlawful action was the proximate result of that coercive persuasion; and
>
> (3) that exculpation for the act committed is morally justified.
>
> Refusal to recognize a defense for fear of difficult line drawing problems is . . . needless and potentially inhumane. . . . [T]he coercive persuasion defense is no different from the insanity defense, or, indeed, criminal responsibility itself. Fear of such problems need not prevent us from

addressing those compelling polar cases that call for compassionate, informed treatment. It is hardly a noble doctrine that sacrifices individuals for the sake of preserving an artificial conceptual simplicity in the law of criminal excuses.

Delgado, *Ascription of Criminal States of Mind: Toward a Defense Theory for the Coercively Persuaded ("Brainwashed") Defendant,* 63 Minn. L. Rev. 1, 8–11, 19, 27 (1978).

To this Professor Dressler responded:

> Delgado's doctrinal argument is predicated on the unique theory of a superimposed *mens rea*. Because the mental state of the coercively persuaded victim is inculcated by another person, Delgado would create a new legal fiction by treating the actor's *mens rea* as legally noncognizable. Legal blame would attach solely to the indoctrinator.
>
> Such a proposal is doctrinally untenable. All ideas and intents originate outside the individual, in the sense that they are shaped by experiences and environment. . . .
>
> The difficulty with Delgado's *mens rea* analysis is that the actor does possess the requisite mental state. . . . [T]he decision on how to release the anger is personal, as is the decision on how to alleviate fears. The defendant could have vented his anger in many noncriminal ways. . . .
>
> If the law creates such a fiction in some cases by ignoring the intent of the actorbecause of dismay over the way he came to have it, there is no logical reason to limitsuch inquiry. Delgado's *mens rea* thesis, therefore, violates his own goal of logically but minimally extending the law. His concept would constitute an abrupt, unprecedented, and potentially unlimitable change in legal doctrine.
>
> [Delgado's] defense would still be open to challenge on the ground that it does not impose clear and just limitations on the excuse's applicability. This failure forces society to choose between two alternatives, both of which are antithetical to current concepts of criminal responsibility. It must either allow some morally blameworthy actors to be excused, while not excusing some morally blameless actors, or accept a theory of criminal responsibility that embraces a determinist view of society.
>
> Delgado's defense . . . advocates the drawing of a new, morally doubtful line between criminal responsibility and blamelessness. There are only two ways to avoid such an unfair result: either reaffirm current law, which is strict but clear, or enlarge the coercive persuasion defense to include within its possible reach the full panoply of environmental influences. . . . With the adoption of this test, however, determinists virtually win their case. Abundant scientific evidence demonstrates that the ordinary person will reject his preexisting moral values to obey antisocial orders even under comparatively noncoercive circumstances. [A] defense based on reduced choice . . . must permit persons to present their entire life histories as part of a "blamelessness" defense to crime.

Dressler, *Professor Delgado's "Brainwashing" Defense: Courting a Determinist Legal System,* 63 Minn. L. Rev. 335, 342–43, 346–49, 354, 359–60 (1979).

See also Lunde and Wilson, *Brainwashing as a Defense to Criminal Liability: Patty Hearst Revisited,* 13 Crim. L. Bull. 341 (1977); Note, *Brainwashing: Fact, Fiction and Criminal Defense,* 44 U.M.K.C. L. Rev. 438 (1976).

Pathological Behavior. The Revised Third Edition of the American Psychiatric Association's Diagnostic and Statistical Manual of Mental Disorders 324 (1987) (DSM-III-R) greatly increased the number of professionally recognized behavior or mental disorders as mental illness of one sort or another. Among them is pathological gambling.

> The essential features of this disorder are a chronic and progressive failure to resist impulses to gamble, and gambling behavior that compromises, disrupts, or damages personal, family, or vocational pursuits. The gambling preoccupation, urge, and activity increase during periods of stress. Problems that arise as a result of the gambling lead to an intensification of gambling behavior. Characteristic problems include extensive indebtedness and consequent default on debts and other financial responsibilities, disruptive family relationships, inattention to work, and financially motivated illegal activities to pay for gambling.

Should a pathological gambler be acquitted of a charge of illegal gambling on the basis of DSM-III-R? What if he embezzles money with which to gamble? See *State v. Lafferty,* No. 44359 (Conn. Super. Ct., June 5, 1981), noted 14 Conn. L. Rev. 341 (1982); *United States v. Lewellyn,* 723 F.2d 615 (8th Cir. 1983). What of other pathological disorders?

Other Concerns. For notes on post partum psychosis as a defense for mothers who kill their newborn children, see Note, *Postpartum Psychosis: The Birth of a New Defense?,* 6 Cooley L. Rec. 323 (1989); Note, 15 N.C. Cent. L.J. 246 (1985); Note, *Postpartum Psychosis as a Defense to Infant Murder,* 5 Touro L. Rev. 287 (1989). See also *Commonwealth v. Comitz,* 530 A.2d 473 (Pa. Super. 1987).

As the materials on insanity demonstrated, the common law severely restricted the mental disorders that could be considered as a predicate for that claim. Recently, however, psychiatry has broadened the definitions of mental illness and mental disability to cover very broad areas of everyday life. Thus, for example, DSM-III-R lists as "organic mental disorders" both tobacco withdrawal and caffeine intoxication. Among the "substance use disorders" is tobacco dependence. Despite a clear statement in DSM-III-R that it is not intended to establish categories for legal use, the spectacle of a defendant claiming an excuse for a crime because he was addicted to cigarettes is surely at the base of much opposition to the use of psychiatry generally in legal (especially criminal) proceedings. How should the criminal law resolve these tensions?

[c] Sociologically Based Excuses for Criminality"

"Rotten Social Background" (RSB): "I'm Depraved on Accounta I'm Deprived." The decision in *Wanrow,* § 9.05[A][4], *supra,* may be a narrow one, yet it could be seen as the opening wedge in an attempt to make the criminal law more responsive to general attitudes of classes or subclasses of persons in our society. Prime among these is the argument that poverty, discrimination (racial or otherwise), and other such social factors create criminals. It is, of course, no answer to this to say that not all ghetto dwellers or victims of racial discrimination and so on commit crime. Not all schizophrenics kill, but when one does, we are willing to recognize the possibility that his mental disorder should be considered in assessing his guilt.

The argument must be taken seriously. One reason given by Professor Norval Morris, for example, in urging that we abolish the insanity defense, see, *supra* § 9.05[B][5][b], is that it is unjust to recognize insanity as a defense when statistics can show that "rotten social background" is more criminogenic, thereby suggesting (he says) that persons with RSB have less control and choice over their acts than do insane persons. Morris's solution, however, is not to endorse RSB as an excuse but to eliminate insanity as one.

Professor Richard Delgado, on the other hand, takes the step Morris is unwilling to take and urges RSB as a defense. See Delgado, *"Rotten Social Background": Should the Criminal Law Recognize a Defense of Severe Environmental Deprivation?*, 3 Law & Inequality 9, 54–56, 75–77 (1985):

> An environment of extreme poverty and deprivation creates in individuals a propensity to commit crimes. In some cases, a defendant's impoverished background so greatly determines his or her criminal behavior that we feel it unfair to punish the individual. This sense of unfairness arises from the morality of the criminal law itself. . . .
>
> Where extreme social and economic disadvantage demonstrably creates a defendant's criminal propensity, punishment may be inappropriate from two perspectives; first, because the RSB criminal's behavior can be defended on theories of justification and excuses; and second, because society's rationales for inflicting punishment are undermined. . . .
>
> Evidence of a rotten social background could be introduced in criminal trials in various ways. It could be relevant . . . to a public policy defense relating to society's responsibility for the rotten social background. . . .
>
> a. *Involuntary Rage.* Under this model, the RSB defendant would argue that a precipitating event evoked rage so powerful as to block his or her consciousness, rendering subsequent actions involuntary. Studies of repressed anger . . . indicate that long-term exposure to environmental insult can make an individual a virtual "time bomb." Such a person may react to a seemingly minor provocation with a violent response of which he or she is scarcely aware. . . .
>
> When extreme environmental deprivation causes the type of physical disorder required by the conventional defense, then the RSB person should be exculpated. The defense, however, should not be limited to cases of physical disorder. . . . The kind of pent-up rage and despair that can result from living in a crowded, violent neighborhood can cause an explosion of violence just as disordered brain circuits can. When this occurs, a defense should be available. The defense would require provng: (i)that the defendant was acting automatically; and (ii)that the automatic state was caused by the extreme deprivation. . . .

b. *Isolation from Dominant Culture.* The theory underlying this model of the defense is that some urban ghettos are social and cultural islands unto themselves, with their own rules, norms and values. A person who has lived since birth in such an environment may be so strongly socialized by it that he or she has little sense of the values of the large society or opportunity to acquire the norms necessary to function responsibly in that society. This defense would be particularly appropriate for a young defendant who has had little or no exposure to life outside the ghetto, and for whom acquiescence to ghetto norms was required to survive. It would require a psychological and sociological analysis of the defendant's development, and proof that the defendant did not adequately internalize the values of the larger society, while in fact living by ghetto norms endorsing violence and other criminal behavior.

c. *Inability to Control Conduct.* This model assumes that a rotten social background can cause inability to control conduct as insanity does. This defense would require a broad definition of disability, for instance. . . . that at the time of the defendant's unlawfu l conduct his or her mental or emotional processes or behavioral controls were impaired to such an extent that he or she cannot justly be held responsible for his or her act.

KADISH, *EXCUSING CRIME*

75 Cal. L. Rev. 257, 284-5 (1987)

Social deprivation may well establish a credible explanation of how the defendant has come to have the character he has. But it does not establish a moral excuse any more than a legal one, for there is a difference between explaining a person's wrongful behavior and explaining it away. Explanations are not excuses if they merely explain how the defendant came to have the character of someone who could do such a thing. Otherwise, there would be no basis for moral responsibility in any case where we knew enough about the person to understand him. And that would mean every case, because ignorance about a person could hardly stand as a justification for blaming him.

The reason the argument fails to make out a moral excuse, as insanity does, is that it fails to establish the breakdown of rationality and judgment that is incompatible with moral agency. It may be conceded that cultural deprivation contributed to making the defendant what he is (though, of course, only some people so brought up end up committing crimes). But what is he? He is a person with wrong values and inclinations, not a human being whose powers of judgment and rational action have been so destroyed that he must be dealt with like an infant, a machine, or an animal. Those who propose this defense are plainly moved by compassion for the downtrodden, to whom, however, it is nonetheless an insult.

NOTES

These defenses, and others likely to be raised in the future, continue the debate between those who fear that all (dangerous) acts will become "excused" or "understood," and those who see the need to grant excuse or mitigation where there is no true culpability, without regard to the dangerousness issue being addressed by the criminal law. See generally, Allen, *Criminal Law and the Modern Consciousness: Some Observations on Blameworthiness,* 44 Tenn. L. Rev. 735 (1977); Bazelon, *The Morality of the Criminal Law,* 49 S. Cal. L. Rev. 385 (1976); Diamond, *Social and Cultural Factors as a Diminished Capacity Defense in Criminal Law,* 6 Bull. Am. Acad. Psychiat. & L. 195 (1978); Floud, *Sociology and the Theory of Responsibility: Social Background as an Excuse for Crime,* in The Science of Society and the Unity of Mankind (R. Fletcher, ed., 1974); Morris, *The Twilight of Welfare Criminology: A Reply to Judge Bazelon,* 49 S. Cal. L. Rev. 1247 (1976); Morse, *Culpability and Control,* 142 U. Pa. L. Rev. 1587 (1994).

Many are worried about the explosion of new excuses seen throughout the 1980s and 90s. Some are concerned that they are illegitimate. See, for example, the comment of Dr. John McKinlay, an epidemiologist at Boston University. After first arguing that there is no such thing as male midlife crisis, Dr. McKinlay went on to say, "I think by the year 2000 the syndrome will exist. There's very strong interest in treating aging men for a profit, just as there is for menopausal women." *New York Times,* May 20, 1992, p.C14, col. 2.

Still others have greater concerns. Professor Alan Dershowitz, for example, lists the following syndromes (in addition to ones we have discussed) that have been raised (not necessarily successfully) in at least one case. Among these are:

Adopted child syndrome

American dream syndrome

Black rage syndrome

Distant father syndrome

Elderly abuse syndrome

False memory syndrome

Fetal alcohol syndrome

Gangster syndrome

Holocaust survivor syndrome

Parental alienation syndrome

Patient—therapist sex syndrome

Repressed (or recovered) memory syndrome

Ritual abuse (satanic cults) syndrome

Roid rage (violence caused by steroids)

Situational stress syndrome

Super Bowl Sunday syndrome

"Television made me do it" syndrome

Urban survival syndrome

In his book The Abuse Excuse (1994), Dershowitz explores at least some of these in great detail, arguing vehemently that acceptance of these or other such claims is weakening not only the criminal law but also our general sense of responsibility, both individually and as a nation. See also Morse, The *"New Syndrome Excuse Syndrome,"* 14 Crim. Just. Ethics 3 (1995).

To what extent is a reluctance to accept new defenses a function of distrust of the jury? See J. Smith, Justification and Excuse in the Criminal Law 97–98 (1989), discussing his own experience on criminal law committees, where judges have openly expressed the concern that juries may be fooled. And consider the proposition, put forth by Lord Chief Justice Lane in the Court of Appeal in *Howe and Bannister,* [1986] 1 Q.B. 76 [1986] 1 All E.R. 833, that judges might more readily accept a defense or a more broadly based defense, if the burden of proof were on the defendant. Is this a possible "solution"? Is it a principled one? Consider again the *Mullaney* and *Patterson* cases, *supra* § 9.04[B].

[3] The Role of Motive

[a] The General Doctrine

REGINA V. HICKLIN

Court of the Queen's Bench

11 Cox C.C. 19 (1868)

[Defendant, a vitriolic anti-Catholic, sold copies of a book that purported to demonstrate that Catholicism was ungodly and obscene, selecting pieces from the works of various theologians. He sold the pamphlets at cost. The court declared that "About one-half of the pamphlet relates to casuistical and controversial questions which are not obscene, but the remainder of the pamphlet is obscene in fact as relating to impure and filthy acts, words, and ideas." The books were seized and ordered to be destroyed. The defendant contended that his sole purpose in publishing the book was "to [show] the depravity of the Romish priesthood, the iniquity of the confessional and the questions put to females in confession." The defendant lost in the lower court, but on appeal to a Recorder, the order was quashed, the Recorder determining that the sale and distribution of the pamphlets would not be a misdemeanor. The Crown appealed.]

COCKBURN, C.J.:

[The Recorder] reversed [the lower court] decision upon the ground that although this work was an obscene publication . . . yet the immediate intention of the appellant was not so to affect the public mind, but to expose the practices and errors of the confessional system in the Roman Catholic churches. Now we must take it upon this finding. . . . That such was the motive of this publication. . . . If there be an infraction of the law, and an intention to break the law, the criminal character of such publication is not affected or qualified by there being some ulterior object, which is the immediate and primary objects of the parties in view, of a different and of an honest character. . . .

We have it, therefore, that the publication itself is a breach of the law. But then it is said, "Yes, but the purpose was not to deprave the public mind; the purpose was to expose the errors ofthe Roman Catholic religion, especially in the matter of the confessional." Be it so. But then the question presents itself in this simple form—May you commit an offense against the law in order that thereby you may effect some ulterior object which you have in view, which may be an honest and even a laudable one? My answer is emphatically "No."

[T]he effect of the work is mischievous, and against the law; and is not to be justified because the immediate object of the party is not to deprave the public mind, but it may be to destroy and extirpate Roman Catholicism. I think the old, sound, and honest maxim that "you shall not do evil that good may come" is applicable in law as well as in morals; and here we have a certain and positive evil produced for the purpose of effecting an uncertain, remote, and very doubtful good. I think, therefore, the case for the order is made out, and although I quite concur in thinking that the motive of the parties who published this work, however mistaken, was an honest one, yet I cannot suppose but what they had that intention which constitutes the criminality of the act. . . . [I]t does not lie in the mouth of the man who does it to say, "Well, I was breaking the law, but I was breaking it for some wholesome and salutary purpose." The law does not allow that. You must abide by the law, and if you accomplish your object, you must do it in a legal manner or let it alone. You must not do it in a manner which is illegal.

Notes and Questions

1. Was defendant seeking to justify or excuse his conduct?

2. Suppose defendant had been charged with "distributing obscene pamphlets with the intent to deprave morals"? Is his motive then relevant? Is the motive relevant in a charge of "assault with intent to kill"?

3. Defendant, a member of the city council, went to a gambling parlor and placed a bet. It was stipulated that he went there and placed the bet solely to obtain evidence to "disarm suspicion and enable him to secure evidence to convict these habitual violators of the law." Dissenting from a judgment overturning his conviction, Ellison, J., stated:

It will not do to say that he had no intention to gamble, for he did gamble, but said he did so with the view of detecting others. That was merely his motive, as distinguished from his intention. His intention was to do the prohibited and his motive was to catch others. But one's motive, however sincere, will not excuse his violation of the penal statute.

State v. Torphy, 78 Mo. App. 206, 209 (1899) (Ellison, J., dissenting).

4. Stevens, Circuit Judge (later Justice), in *United States v. Cullen,* 454 F.2d 386, 390–92 (7th Cir. 1971):

[T]he term "intent" may be used in at least three different senses: First, that the prohibited act was performed deliberately; second, that defendant knew it was wrong; and third, that it was designed to further some ultimate goal. In the narrowest sense, every crime must be the product of defendant's free will; it must reflect his choice to perform the criminal act. . . . In a second sense, the term "intent" encompasses a "consciousness of wrongdoing." . . . A third sense in which the term "intent" is sometimes used is that of ultimate purpose or "motive" as that term was used in the district court's instructions. In some situations the defendant's ultimate objective may be an element of the particular offense charged. . . . But improper motive is not an element of either of the offenses committed by appellant; accordingly, evidence which merely relates to his good motive does not tend to disprove his admitted consciousness of wrongdoing. . . . If defendant's theory of defense were valid, the character of his conduct would be judged not by the rule of law but by the end which his means were designed to serve. His theory is merely another variety of an age-old argument. If a religious, moral, or political purpose may exculpate illegal behavior, one might commit bigamy to avoid eternal damnation; steal from the rich to give alms to the poor; burn and destroy, not merely public records or perhaps buildings but even public servants as well, to implement a Utopian design. One who elects to serve mankind by taking the law into his own hands thereby demonstrates his conviction that his own ability to determine policy is superior to democratic decision making. Appellant's professed unselfish motivation, rather than a justification, actually identifies a form of arrogance which organized society cannot tolerate. A simple rule, reiterated by a peace-loving scholar, amply refutes appellant's arrogant theory of defense: "No man or group is above the law."

5. Would a defendant pleading self-defense be wrong if he said: "Of course I intended to kill him, but my motive was to escape from his aggressive, murderous attack on me"? What of the defendant who says: "I did steal the money, but my motive was to prevent him from killing my entire family"? Does this suggest that the law does sometimes consider motive? Or is it merely that these defendants do not understand why self-defense or duress is sometimes allowed as a relevant factor? For a discussion of the role of motive in the criminal law, see Gardner, *The Mens Rea Enigma: Observations on the Role of Motive in the Criminal Law Past and Present,* 1993 Utah L. Rev. 635.

6. Hitchler, *Motive as an Essential Element of Crime,* 35 Dick. L. Rev. 105, 105, 110–11 (1931):

Motive is a desire prompting conduct. It is a desire transformed into a practical incentive or excitant to action. A motive is thus a desire viewed in its relation to a particular action, to the carrying out of which it urges or prompts.

A rule which made the existence of a bad motive the test of the criminality of an act would be popular because it would tend to bring the law into accord with the popular feeling that the ethical quality of one's act should be the measure of criminal liability.

[An] objection to making motive the test of the criminality of an act is the difficulty of ascertaining with precision the motive for any given act. This objection is of ancient origin. "The thought of man shall not be tried," said Chief Justice Brian, one of the best of medieval lawyers, "for the devil himself knoweth not the thought of man." An equally eminent English judge has declared that "secret things belong to God" and the Pennsylvania court has said that "motives be left to Him who searches the heart" or to the "Unseen Eye from whom the secrets of no heart can be hidden."

7. Husak, *Motive and Criminal Liability,* Criminal Justice Ethics 3 (Winter/ Spring 1989):

Modern penal codes typically identify only four culpable states (purpose, knowledge, recklessness, and negligence) that are relevant to the defendant's liability. All other "mentalistic" factors that bear on his blameworthiness are consigned to the sentencing stage. Foremost (but not alone) among these is his motive. But there is no good reason why the *mens rea* component of liability should be construed so narrowly as to include only these four "mental states." No satisfactory explanation supports the decision to relegate a factor to one stage or the other. Why are such issues as whether the defendant succeeds in killing his victim, as opposed to failing in his attempt, material to his liability but not to his punishment? Why are such issues as his stress, economic background, ignorance of law, inherited character, education, amount of temptation, or degree of complicity in the offense, material to his punishment but not to his liability? The writings of orthodox criminal theorists provide no principled answers to these questions.

Lately, however, this traditional (but largely unprincipled) consensus to relegate a consideration of motives to the sentencing stage of the criminal justice system has been eroding. Impetus for change has come not from theoreticians of liability, but from advocates of sentencing reform. The traditional treatment of motives is at odds with recent (and welcome) trends in sentencing theory. Perhaps the most noteworthy aspect of the revival of retributivism (or "just deserts") is the reduction of discretion among sentencing authorities. If the severity of the defendant's punishment is to be proportionate to his desert and not responsive to the need to deter or to rehabilitate him, there is almost no reason to allow sentencing authorities the wide discretion they have generally exercised in the last several decades. But any effective strategy to lessen discretion in sentencing will prove draconian in implementation without revising the substantive criminal law.

Several advantages would follow if motives were sometimes considered to be relevant to liability. The incorporation of motives into the substantive criminal law would publicize whatever significance motives are thought to have. For example, if an assault motivated by racial hatred is believed to be more reprehensible than an assault motivated by sexual jealousy, this judgment should be explicitly included in a criminal code. A properly drafted criminal code should provide effective notice. Statutes not only should identify objectionable conduct, but also should draw whatever distinctions are necessary to indicate the extent to which conduct is blameworthy. The public is less likely to be informed of the relevance of such judgments as long as the evaluation of motives is reserved to the less visible decision of sentencing authorities.

On the other hand, there are obvious limits to the number of variables that a criminal code can effectively include. Offenses would become horribly complex if all (or even most) factors relevant to blameworthiness were incorporated into statutes. It is unclear exactly when this limit is exceeded. Perhaps draftsmen of criminal codes should proceed cautiously by explicitly identifying only a few especially benevolent or malevolent motives, leaving finer distinctions to sentencing authorities.

The exceptional significance Anglo-American criminal law attaches to intention stands in stark contrast to its (alleged) complete disregard of motive. This disparate treatment demands attention. Perhaps an explanation is to be found in whatever distinguishes intention from motive. Alleged differences and similarities between these concepts provide a useful means to introduce the two most familiar attempts of criminal theorists to analyze motives. According to the first school of thought, motives are one species of the genus intention. According to the second, motives and intentions are logically separate types.

Neither account is altogether satisfactory. The correct view, I believe, is that some but not all motives are intentions; motives and intentions are not separate types, but not all motives can be subsumed under the broader category of intentions. But I am less interested to defend the philosophically correct account of motives than to argue that motives are relevant to criminal liability according to any plausible conception.

Those who construe motives as conceptually distinct from intentions, typically regard motives as "springs" or "originators" of actions. Differences between theorists of this school derive largely from disagreements about the nature of practical reasoning. Some accept the Humean account according to which reason is inert in producing action, and thereby liken motives to urges or desires. Others reject the Humean account, and allow that motives can function as reasons for action. But whatever the nature of reason in influencing behavior, the contrast between motive and intention is expressed by the principle that motives explain why a person acted, while intentions describe what action was performed. The principle that motives explain while intentions describe is affirmed by all theorists who regard motives and intentions as logically distinct. Gross writes: "A motive can be distinguished from an intention as an explanation of an act and not a description of it." This view is appealing because it lends itself to a theory about why intention but not motive is material to liability. According to this theory, criminal statutes simply describe unlawful conduct.

This theory could be challenged at its foundation. Why should the criminal law merely describe illegal conduct? It must be conceded that many factors that are relevant to a defendant's blameworthiness are excluded from a description of his conduct (when the scope of a description is confined to his *actus reus* and his intention). Why should these factors be pertinent only to sentencing, and not to liability? A deeper justification is required to support treating variables that describe conduct as relevant only to liability, while treating variables that explain conduct as material only to punishment. Surely it is insufficient to simply reply without supporting argument that liability is "action-directed," while punishment is "person-directed." Theories of liability and theories of sentencing each seem to contain assessments of actions as well as of persons, insofar as evaluations of actions and of persons can be clearly distinguished in the first place. Until this "deeper justification" is produced in detail, judgment about this sketch of a theory should be withheld.

Moreover, the claim that intentions describe while motives explain cannot be assessed without sophisticated theories of descriptions and explanations, and no criminal theorist has yet produced them. In the absence of a theory, there is no obvious fact of the matter that settles whether a proposition qualifies as a description or as an explanation of conduct.

8. The question of the role of motive is, of course, only one of several issues raised by those exploring the interrelations of the role of motive, character, mercy, justice, forgiveness, and moral philosophy generally. For broader discussions, see P. Arenella, in Praise of Blaming: The Centrality of Character (1989); M. Brand, Intending and Acting (1984); R. Brandt, Ethical Theory (1959); N. Lacey, State Punishment (1988); R. Nozick, Philosophical Explanations (1981). For a marvelous symposium of essays, see 7 Social Philosophy and Policy (Issue 2, 1990).

[b] Specific Cases

[i] Euthanasia

STATE v. FORREST

Supreme Court of North Carolina

321 N.C. 186, 362 S.E.2d 252 (1987)

MEYER, Justice.

Defendant was convicted of the first-degree murder of his father, Clyde Forrest . . . [and] was sentenced accordingly to life imprisonment.

On 22 December 1985, defendant John Forrest admitted his critically ill father, Clyde Forrest, Sr., to Moore Memorial Hospital. Defendant's father, who had previously been hospitalized, was suffering from numerous serious ailments, including severe heart disease, hypertension, a thoracic aneurysm, numerous pulmonary emboli, and a peptic ulcer. By the morning of 23 December 1985, his medical condition was determined to be untreatable and terminal. Accordingly, he was classified as "No Code," meaning that no extraordinary measures would be used to save his life, and he was moved to a more comfortable room.

On 24 December 1985, defendant went to the hospital to visit his ailing father. No other family members were present in his father's room when he arrived. While one of the nurse's assistants was tending to his father, defendant told her, "There is no need in doing that. He's dying." She responded, "Well, I think he's better." The nurse's assistant noticed that defendant was sniffing as though crying and that he kept his hand in his pocket during their conversation. She subsequently went to get the nurse.

When the nurse's assistant returned with the nurse, defendant once again stated his belief that his father was dying. The nurse tried to comfort defendant, telling him, "I don't think your father is as sick as you think he is." Defendant, very upset, responded, "Go to hell. I've been taking care of him for years. I'll take care of him." Defendant was then left alone in the room with his father.

Alone at his father's bedside, defendant began to cry and to tell his father how much he loved him. His father began to cough, emitting a gurgling and rattling noise. Extremely upset, defendant pulled a small pistol from his pants pocket, put it to his father's temple, and fired. He subsequently fired three more times and walked out into the hospital corridor, dropping the gun to the floor just outside his father's room.

Following the shooting, defendant, who was crying and upset, neither ran nor threatened anyone. Moreover, he never denied shooting his father and talked openly with law enforcement officials. Specifically, defendant made the following oral statements: "You can't do anything to him now. He's out of his suffering." "I killed my daddy." "He won't have to suffer anymore." "I know they can burn me for it, but my dad will not have to suffer anymore." "I know the doctors couldn't do it, but I could." "I promised my dad I wouldn't let him suffer."

[D]efendant asserts that the trial court committed reversible error in its instruction to the jury concerning the issue of malice. Defendant makes three specific arguments in support of his position on this assignment of error. First, states defendant, the instruction permitting an inference of malice from the use of a deadly weapon on these particular facts constituted an impermissible shift of the burden of persuasion on the issue of malice to defendant. Second, continues defendant, the trial court erred in giving incomplete instructions on the element of malice and in thereby improperly suggesting that the mitigating evidence presented at trial neither negated malice nor showed heat of passion. Third, concludes defendant, the trial court erred more generally in giving instructions on malice which were simply erroneous and misleading. . . .

On the issue of malice, the trial court consistently instructed the jury as follows:

> Malice means not only hatred, ill-will or spite, as it is ordinarily understood; to be sure that's malice. But it also means that condition of the mind that prompts a person to take the life of another intentionally, or to intentionally inflict serious bodily harm which proximately results in his death without just cause, excuse or justification.
>
> If the State proves beyond a reasonable doubt that the defendant killed the victim with a deadly weapon, or intentionally inflicted a wound upon the victim with a deadly weapon that proximately [sic] caused the victim's death you may infer, first, that the killing was unlawful. Second, that it was done with malice. But you are not compelled to do so. You may consider this, along with all other facts and circumstances in determining whether the killing was unlawful and whether it was done with malice.
>
> I charge that it is not a legal defense to the offense of murder if the defendant, John Forrest, at the time of the shooting believed his father, Clyde Forrest, to be terminally ill or in danger of immediate death. But you may consider such belief in determining whether the killing was done with malice. . . .

Defendant first argues that, on the particular facts of this case, the trial court's instruction permitting an inference of malice from the use of a deadly weapon improperly shifted the burden of persuasion on the issue of malice to defendant. Here, claims defendant, where the facts presented tended to show a distraught son who wanted merely to end his father's suffering, the evidence in fact negated the element of malice. According to defendant, there was no rational connection here between the fact proved [intentional use of a dangerous weapon] and the fact inferred [malice]. Therefore, concludes defendant, use of an inference under these circumstances was tantamount to shifting the burden of persuasion to defendant, because first, the jury was encouraged to draw the inference regardless of any other evidence presented, and second, it was told, in effect, that the inference could not be overcome—that the direct evidence was not a "legal defense." We cannot agree.

Significantly, the trial court did not instruct the jury that malice should be presumed. On the contrary, the trial court instructed the jury that it "may infer" that the killing was unlawful and committed with malice, but that it was not compelled to do so. The trial court properly instructed the jury that it should consider this permissive inference along with all the other facts and circumstances, including defendant's belief that his father was terminally ill or in danger of immediate death, in deciding whether the State had proven malice beyond a reasonable doubt. . . .

Defendant argues second that the trial court erred in giving incomplete instructions on the issue of malice, thereby improperly suggesting that any mitigating evidence presented did not negate malice or show heat of passion. While conceding that the instruction here was technically correct, defendant claims that it was nevertheless inadequate and misleading in that it failed to define what was meant by the phrase "just cause, excuse or justification." According to defendant, there is abundant evidence in the record that, upon seeing his father at the hospital, he was overwhelmed by the futile, horrible suffering before him and that, in a highly emotional state, he killed to bring relief to the man he deeply loved. The jury instruction employed by the trial court, concludes defendant, because it did not instruct on heat of passion, for all intents and purposes precluded the jury from considering these critical facts in mitigation of the offense. We do not agree with defendant, and we hold that a heat of passion jury instruction on facts such as those of the case at bar is improper.

In essence, defendant asks the Court to hold that his extreme distress over his father's suffering was adequate provocation, as in the "heat of passion" doctrine, to negate the malice element required for a murder conviction. Our Court has held on numerous occasions that, under certain circumstances, one who kills another human being in the "heat of passion" produced by adequate provocation sufficient to negate malice, is guilty of manslaughter rather than murder. . . . A killing in the "heat of passion" on sudden and adequate provocation means a killing without premeditation under the influence of a sudden passion which renders the mind incapable of cool reflection. . . .

We are unwilling to hold that, as in the case at bar, where defendant kills a loved one in order to end the deceased's suffering, adequate provocation to negate malice is necessarily present. The "heat of passion" doctrine is meant to reduce murder to manslaughter when defendant kills without premeditation and deliberation and without malice, but rather under the influence of the heat of passion suddenly aroused which renders the mind temporarily incapable of cool reflection. Here, irrefutable proof of premeditation and deliberation is clearly present. This defendant, though clearly upset by his father's condition, indicated by his actions and his statements that his crime was premeditated and deliberate. . . .

Defendant argues third that the trial court committed reversible error in giving instructions on the issue of malice which were erroneous and generally misleading. Defendant's objection here is essentially a grammatical one and is directed at that portion of the jury instruction which reads as follows:

> [Malice] also means that condition of the mind that prompts a person to take the life of another intentionally. . . . without just cause, excuse or justification.

The trial court, argues defendant, failed to explicitly and specifically qualify the particular definition of malice as "that condition of the mind that prompts a person to take the life of another intentionally" with the important phrase "without just cause, excuse or justification." This, claims defendant, almost certainly led the jury to conclude that the intentional shooting alone required them to find malice, despite any evidence to the contrary. The trial court, adds defendant, should have defined malice in its instruction as follows:

> That condition of the mind which prompts a person, without just cause, excuse or justification to take the life of another intentionally. . . .

We do not agree, and we therefore decline defendant's invitation to adopt a new jury instruction concerning the issue of malice. The instruction employed by the trial court is consistent with the *North Carolina Pattern Jury Instructions* and is the very instruction we have previously expressly approved on numerous occasions. . . . Moreover, the instruction used at trial is, on its face, in essence the same as that for which defendant argues. Defendant's third argument in support of this assignment of error is without merit, and the assignment as a whole is hereby overruled.

In his second assignment of error, defendant asserts that the trial court committed reversible error in denying his motion for directed verdict as to the first-degree murder charge. Specifically, defendant argues that the trial court's submission of the first-degree murder charge was improper because there was insufficient evidence of premeditation and deliberation presented at trial. . . .

We recently addressed this very issue in the case of *State v. Jackson*, 317 N.C. 1, 343 S.E.2d 814 (1986). Our analysis of the relevant law in that case is instructive in the case at bar:

> Before the issue of a defendant's guilt may be submitted to the jury, the trial court must be satisfied that substantial evidence has been introduced tending to prove each essential element of the offense charged and that the defendant was the perpetrator. . . . Substantial evidence must be existing and real, but need not exclude every reasonable hypothesis of innocence. . . . In considering a motion to dismiss, the trial court must examine the evidence in the light most favorable to the State, and the State is entitled to every reasonable intendment and inference to be drawn

therefrom. . . . Contradictions and discrepancies in the evidence are for the jury to resolve and do not warrant dismissal. . . .

First-degree murder is the intentional and unlawful killing of a human being with malice and with premeditation and deliberation. . . . N.C.G.S. § 14-17 (1981 and Cum. Supp. 1985). Premeditation means that the act was thought out beforehand for some length of time, however short, but no particular amount of time is necessary for the mental process of premeditation. . . . Deliberation means an intent to kill, carried out in a cool state of blood, in furtherance of a fixed design for revenge or to accomplish an unlawful purpose and not under the influence of a violent passion, suddenly aroused by lawful or just cause or legal provocation . . . The phrase "cool state of blood" means that the defendant's anger or emotion must not have been such as to overcome his reason. . . .

[I]n the present case there was substantial evidence that the killing was premeditated and deliberate and the trial court did not err in submitting to the jury the question of defendant's guilt of first-degree murder based upon premeditation and deliberation. Here, many of the circumstances that we have held to establish a factual basis for a finding of premeditation and deliberation are present. It is clear, for example, that the seriously ill deceased did nothing to provoke defendant's action. Moreover, the deceased was lying helpless in a hospital bed when defendant shot him four separate times. In addition, defendant's revolver was a five-shot single-action gun which had to be cocked each time before it could be fired. Interestingly, although defendant testified that he always carried the gun in his job as a truck driver, he was not working on the day in question but carried the gun to the hospital nonetheless.

Most persuasive of all on the issue of premeditation and deliberation, however, are defendant's own statements following the incident. Among other things, defendant stated that he had thought about putting his father out of his misery because he knew he was suffering. He stated further that he had promised his father that he would not let him suffer and that, though he did not think he could do it, he just could not stand to see his father suffer any more. These statements, together with the other circumstances mentioned above, make it clear that the trial court did not err in submitting to the jury the issue of first-degree murder based upon premeditation and deliberation. . . .

Affirmed.

EXUM, Chief Justice, *dissenting.*

Almost all would agree that someone who kills because of a desire to end a loved one's physical suffering caused by an illness which is both terminal and incurable should not be deemed in law as culpable and deserving of the same punishment as one who kills because of unmitigated spite, hatred or ill-will. Yet the Court's decision in this case essentially says there is no legal distinction between the two kinds of killing.

Our law of homicide should not be so roughly hewn as to be incapable of recognizing the difference. I believe there are legal principles which, when properly applied, draw the desirable distinction and that both the trial court and this Court have failed to recognize and apply them.

The difference, legally, between the two kinds of killings hinges on the element of malice, the former being without, and the latter with, malice. The absence of malice, however, does not mean the killing is justified or excused so as not to be unlawful; it means simply that the killing is mitigated so as not to be murder but manslaughter. Our cases have traditionally recognized the distinction between mitigation and excuse in the law of homicide. . . .

The error in the trial court's instructions stems from the failure to recognize this difference between mitigation and excuse. The trial court instructed that malice was "that condition of mind that prompts a person to take the life of another intentionally. . . . without just cause, excuse or justification." This instruction, correct insofar as it goes, is incomplete. The trial court should have added "and without mitigation."

Failure to include circumstances in mitigation as capable of rebutting malice, in effect, precluded the jury from considering at all defendant's reasons for killing his father or the issue of whether he acted with malice. The instructions were that only matters which excused the killing altogether were sufficient to rebut the element of malice. The trial court then told the jury that defendant's reasons for killing his father would not excuse the killing, saying,

> I charge that it is not a legal defense to the offense of murder if the defendant, John Forrest, at the time of the shooting believed his father, Clyde Forrest, to be terminally ill or in danger of immediate death.

Although the trial court followed this immediately with, "But you may consider such belief in determining whether the killing was done with malice," he gave the jury no theory by which the circumstances might in law rebut the inference of malice which arose from the intentional killing with a deadly weapon. In essence this instruction was superfluous because the jury had already been told that only legal defenses, as opposed to circumstances in mitigation, could be considered on the issue of malice. At best the instructions were conflicting on the crucial element in the case. Ordinarily this kind of error calls for a new trial. . . .

The jury's confusion concerning the malice instructions is revealed by their three requests that the trial court repeat them and the trial court's finally submitting them to the jury in writing.

For this error in the trial court's instructions, I vote to give defendant a new trial.

DAUGHTER FREED AFTER MERCY KILLING OF FATHER

By Joseph D. Whitaker

Washington Post Staff Writer

Washington Post, May 24, 1979, p.1

Patricia Stephens carried a pair of scissors in her purse last Friday night when she went to visit her critically ill father at Howard University Hospital.

When the attending nurse left the room, Stephens snipped the tubes that fed oxygen and liquid food to her father, who lay in a coma suffering from cancer, pneumonia and heart disease.

Then, Patricia Stephens, 39, unplugged the machine that kept her father breathing and sat quietly by his bedside and awaited his final heartbeats. After his final breath, she stood and made the sign of the cross over his body.

Stephens later told D.C. police detectives that she decided to take her father's life because she could not bear to see him suffer any longer.

D.C. Medical Examiner Dr. James L. Luke said that the death of Jeremiah Stephens, 65, was a case of euthanasia and that, to his knowledge, it was the first such case in the District of Columbia.

Details of Stephens' death have been recounted by various sources familiar with the case, which was classified by Luke as a homicide. Three days after the death, the U.S. Attorney's office presented evidence to a D.C. Superior Court grand jury. But the grand jury declined to bring any charges against Patricia Stephens.

It was learned that the grand jury's decision not to return an indictment in the case reflected the panel's sympathetic view toward Stephens' action.

Yesterday, Patricia Stephens, a British citizen who is a sociologist in London, attended her father's funeral with her family in their home town of Mt. Lambert, Trinidad, and could not be reached for comment.

Luke said his autopsy of Stephens showed that Stephens suffered cancer of the esophagus, which almost completely blocked his throat. Because Stephens could receive no solid foods, his 5-foot, 10-inch frame became extremely emaciated, Luke said.

According to Luke, Stephens also had suffered numerous heart attacks since he was admitted to Howard University Hospital on April 11. Stephens had gone into a coma following the first heart attack about 10 days before his death, Luke said.

"There is no question that the man was terminally ill," Luke said. "He would have died within hours or days of when this incident happened."

Shortly after his arrival here, Stephens was hospitalized at the Washington Adventist Hospital in Tacoma Park for radiation treatment of extensive cancer of the throat, sources said.

Patricia Stephens arrived in Washington earlier this year, when her father's health grew worse. In a diary that police confiscated from Patricia Stephens as evidence, she expressed her desire to end her father's suffering according to the sources.

LaRue Cook, the assistant hospital administrator on duty at the time, said yesterday that shortly after her father was pronounced dead, Patricia Stephens agreed to write a statement at the hospital's request, in which she described what she did and why she did it.

"Without hesitating or showing any great concern," Cook said, "she sat down and made out a statement in longhand describing what happened."

Another source said Stephens wrote two pages of longhand in which she expressed her strong desire to see her father "die in peace." The hospital had asked Stephens to write the statement to relieve the hospital of liability for Stephens' death, Cook said.

Shortly after hospital officials learned of Stephens' death, they contacted 3d District Police, who immediately turned the case over to homicide detectives for investigation.

According to a police spokesman, the U.S. Attorney's office agreed to present evidence to the grand jury on Monday and told police there was no need to arrest Patricia Stephens.

The U.S. Attorney's office would not comment on the case yesterday.

Notes and Questions

1. Many cases that grapple with the problem of mercy killings are not criminal cases at all. One of the best known is *Repouille v. United States,* 165 F.2d 152 (2d Cir. 1947). Repouille filed for naturalization, one requirement of which was a showing that he was of "good moral character" for the five years preceding the filing. Four years and 10 months before the filing, however, he had deliberately put to death his 13-year-old son, who was blind, mute, and deformed, and whose care had been a burden to the care of the four other children in the family. Although there was no doubt that he was guilty of first degree murder, the jury convicted him of involuntary manslaughter, and the judge imposed a 10-year sentence, suspended. In the naturalization proceedings, the trial judge had granted the petition for naturalization, finding that Repouille was of good character. On appeal, held, per Judge Learned Hand, Judge Jerome Frank dissenting: reversed. Although the moral question of euthanasia is a difficult one, "we feel reasonably secure in holding that only a minority of virtuous persons would deem the practice morally justifiable . . . even when the provocation is as overwhelming as it was in this instance." The court took great pains, however, to note that if Repouille refiled for naturalization now, the crime would have been more than five years old, and there was no question but that he would obtain relief.

For comments on the issue, see G. Williams, The Sanctity of Life and the Criminal Law (1957); Kamisar, *Some Non-Religious Views against Proposed "Mercy-Killing" Legislation,* 42 Minn. L. Rev. 969 (1958); Sanders, *Euthanasia: None Dare Call It Murder,* 60 J. Crim. L., Criminology & Police Sci. 351 (1969); Silving, *Euthanasia: A Study in Comparative Criminal Law,* 103 U. Pa. L. Rev. 350 (1954); Williams, *Mercy-Killing Legislation—A Rejoinder,* 43 Minn. L. Rev. 1 (1958); Note, 39 Notre Dame Law. 461 (1959).

2. In *Griffith v. State,* 546 So. 2d 244 (Fla. App. 1989), defendant shot his three-year-old daughter after she had been in a vegetative state for eight months, requiring continuous intensive hospital care, but not artificial maintenance of her respiratory and circulatory functions, after a "bizarre and tragic accident in which her head became caught in the footrest of a living room chair." The jury convicted him of first degree murder, and he was sentenced to life imprisonment without the possibility of parole for 25 years.

The court reversed his conviction, on other grounds, but was very clear that this was a first degree murder case, although acknowledging that "the defendant's state of mind concerning the victim's condition may. . . . be pertinent to the vital issue of premeditation, on which the jury was fully instructed here." Similarly, the court in *Gilbert v. State,* 487 So. 2d 1185 (Fla. App. 1986), upheld a first degree murder conviction (which is punished by 25 years without parole) of a 75-year-old husband who shot his wife of 51 years because she had Alzheimer's disease and was in pain, and said "Somebody help me." The appellate court hinted that there was some reason to doubt that the sole or even primary motivation was concern for the victim: "The manifestation of Emily's illness which appeared to bother appellant the most was her increased dependence on him." The court upheld the refusal of the trial court to give an instruction to the effect that first degree murder requires that the killing be done "feloniously," *i.e.,* "proceeding from an evil heart or purpose . . . malignantly; maliciously. . . .

In August 1988, 15-month-old Sammy Linares choked on a balloon. For several months, the child remained in a persistent vegetative state. Then, in April 1989, Rudy Linares removed his son from a respirator while holding the hospital staff at bay with a.357 Magnum. The grand jury refused to indict for this act, although he pleaded guilty to a weapons charge. As a result of the grand jury action, the State's Attorney of Cook County convened a large public Task Force on the Forgoing of Life-Sustaining Treatment. After a year's work, the Task Force emerged with some consensus positions about the general desirability of withholding such treatment in terminal cases, concluding that "public policy should continue to endorse the prevailing view that active euthanasia is morally unacceptable and ethically impermissible." *Report of the Cook County State's Attorney's Task Force on the Forgoing of Life-Sustaining Treatment* (March 1990). This, of course, is not necessarily responsive to the question of whether the active euthanasiast should be criminally punished, even assuming that society does not with to publicly endorse euthanasia.

3. Today the issue of euthanasia often becomes largely one of medical ethics and law. Most mercy killings now are performed by physicians who fail to use extraordinary means to keep alive a person whom the physician (frequently with at least tacit approval of the patient, the family, or both) has decided will live a meaningless existence. Obviously, the sophisticated technology by which life may be prolonged has moved this dilemma from house to hospital.

The moral issues of ending life and of the value of life have therefore come resoundingly to the fore, and the question of emotionally motivated conduct is less frequent. What implications might this have for the criminal law? See Fletcher, *Prolonging Life: Some Legal Considerations,* in A. Downey, Euthanasia and the Right to Die 71 (1969); O. Russell, Freedom to Die (1975). Many states have enacted laws allowing living wills by which a person may authorize a physician to forgo extraordinary life-prolonging efforts. In the landmark case of *In re Quinlan,* 70 N.J. 10, 355 A.2d 647 (1976), the New Jersey Supreme Court held that, under some circumstances, a person may obtain a court order allowing the termination of extraordinary care to a comatose patient. More recently, the court has added a new dimension to the already existing cases on this subject. In *In re Farrell,* 108 N.J. 335, 529 A.2d 404 (1987), the court first established procedures by which a competent patient could refuse life-sustaining medical treatment. The court then declared, "No civil or criminal liability will be incurred by any person who, in good faith reliance on the procedures established in this opinion, withdraws life-sustaining treatment." In two companion cases, the court established procedures for patients who have lapsed into a persistent vegetative state before making the choice to refuse treatment. *In re Peter,* 108 N.J. 365, 529 A.2d 419 (1987), and *In re Jobes,* 108 N.J. 394, 529 A.2d 434 (1987). For a cogent analysis of New Jersey law in this area, see Moore, *"Two Steps Forward, One Step Back:"An Analysis of New Jersey's Latest "Right to Die" Decisions,* 19 Rutgers L.J. 955 (1988).

4. Curtin, *Euthanasia, A Clarification,* in The Human Side of Homicide 98 (Danto et al. eds. 1983) divides euthanasia into the following categories:

1. Voluntary mercy killing—assisted suicide.

2. Death authorized by the individual—prior authorization—livi ng will.

3. Death not authorized by the individual.

4. Death for merciful reasons.

5. Withholding of life support systems.

6. Eugenic killings.

7. Medical triage.

8. Therapeutic euthanasia.

Clearly the best-known person assisting suicide is Dr. Jack Kevorkian, a pathologist. In June 1990, Dr. Kevorkian, using a crude device that allowed her to inject herself slowly with poison,assisted Janet Adkins, a woman suffering from Alzheimer's disease, in committing suicide in the state of Michigan. *New York Times,* June 6, 1990, p.A1. That state, unlike many others, did not at that time have a statute prohibiting the assistance of suicide. When Kevorkian was charged by the state with Adkins' murder, the charges were dismissed by the state trial judge, see N.Y.L.J., Dec. 17, 1990, p.3, but Kevorkian was later enjoined from using the machine. Michigan Lawyers Weekly, Feb. 11, 1991, p.3. Thereafter, Michigan passed a statute prohibiting assisting suicide, and Kevorkian was indicted for helping two other persons in committing suicide. In 1994, the Michigan Supreme Court upheld indictments against Kevorkian under this new statute, rejecting his argument that punishing assisting suicide unconstitutionally restricted the patient's rights of self-determination *People v. Kevorkian,* 447 Mich. 436, 527 N.W.2d 714 (1994). *Accord Quill v. Koppel,* 870 F. Supp. 78 (S.D.N.Y. 1994).

Are doctors such as Kevorkian in the same situation as a relative of the patient? A defendant such as Forrest, however else characterized, has personal involvement in the matter—not only has he (or the family) suffered psychologically during what may have been years of physical deterioration of the victim, but the defendant also has emotional ties with the "victim." The physician, on the other hand, while sensitive to and aware of those wrenching situations, has no direct personal involvement. Might one of these classes of actors be arguing that euthanasia is justified while the other is arguing that it is excused? What difference might it make which way the defense is conceptualized? See Gardner, *The Mens Rea Enigma: Observations on the Role of Motive in Criminal Law Past and Present,* 1993 Utah L. Rev. 635, 743–46.

5. The Criminal Law Reform Commission of Canada has expressly dealt with the topic in its new proposals, declaring that the definition of murder does not apply "to the administration of palliative care appropriate in the circumstances for the control or elimination of a person's pain and suffering even if such care shortens his life expectancy, unless the patient refuses such care." Recodifying Criminal Law 6(6) (1987).

Most continental countries have explicit methods of dealing with euthanasia and other problems of motive. Several provide that a killing done with good motive is to be punished less severely or not at all. Many have provisions that provide that "homicide upon request" (of the victim) is either no crime or a minor crime. Finally, some provide for a separate crime such as "manslaughter with extenuation." See generally Note, 6 B.C. Intl. & Comp. L. Rev. 533 (1983). Typical of these statutes is that of § 235 of the Penal Code of Norway:

If somebody is killed or seriously injured in body or health with his own consent or if anybody kills a hopelessly sick person out of mercy, or is accessory thereto, the punishment may be reduced below the minimum provided, and to a milder form of punishment.

[i] Political Offenders: Civil Disobedients and Terrorists

UNITED STATES v. MERKT

United States Court of Appeals for the Fifth Circuit

794 F.2d 950 (1986)

JONES, Circuit Judge:

In August 1984, Jose Andres Mendez-Valle and Maria Calletano Rosales-Cruz, El Salvadoran citizens, along with three El Salvadoran juveniles (hereinafter collectively referred to as "illegal aliens" or "aliens") left El Salvador. Having reached Saltillo, Mexico, by bus, Mendez-Valle contacted relatives in Washington, D.C., who instructed him to remain in Mexico until further notice. Several weeks later, two American women came and took the aliens to a church in Matamoros, Mexico, near the Rio Grande River. The aliens spent the night at the church and, the following morning, a man escorted them to the river and directed them to cross at a point where the appellant, John B. Elder, was waiting on the other side.

Once in the United States, Elder drove the illegal aliens to the self-styled sanctuary, Casa Oscar Romero, in San Benito, Texas, where they remained for approximately fifteen days. While at Casa Oscar Romero, Mendez-Valle occasionally saw Elder, who directed the house, and also became acquainted with the appellant, Stacey Lynn Merkt, a volunteer there, when Mendez-Valle gave her money to buy the aliens bus tickets to Houston.

In the early morning hours of November 21, Mendez-Valle was given five bus tickets. Merkt drove the aliens to the bus station in McAllen, Texas, where they were directed to the proper bus. En route to Houston, the bus stopped in Weslaco. There, U.S. Border Patrol agents boarded the bus to check for illegal aliens. Mendez-Valle, Rosales-Cruz, and the three juveniles were arrested, given *Miranda* warnings, and taken to the Border Patrol station in Mercedes, Texas. There, the agents learned that the aliens might have been smuggled into the United States. Accordingly, after initial processing, the aliens were sent to the Anti-Smuggling Unit in McAllen.

At the Border Patrol station in McAllen, Mendez-Valle generally described and later identified both Elder and Merkt. Rosales-Cruz was not able to identify either defendant from a photographic line-up.

Elder was indicted, charged, and convicted of two counts of conspiracy, two counts of bringing in and landing illegal aliens, in violation of 8 U.S.C. § 1324(a)(1), and two counts of transporting illegal aliens, in violation of 8 U.S.C. § 1324(a)(2). Merkt, indicted on one conspiracy count and two substantive transportation counts, was found guilty only of the conspiracy counts.

Appellants contend that their convictions are barred by their religiously motivated "sanctuary" activities for El Salvadorans, which give rise to First Amendment immunity from punishment for violating 8 U.S.C. § 1324.

American society extols its tradition as a haven for those to whom obligations of piety and conscience rank higher than the goods of this world. The tradition, at one level, was embodied in the "Free Exercise" Clause of the Bill of Rights. While respecting the rights of citizens to adhere to different religions, however, it has never been doubted that the government's duty to all may, in some circumstances, encroach upon the practices of a few. Appellants Merkt and Elder seek sanctuary in the "Free Exercise" Clause against their violation of national border control laws. This court, whose sanctuary power is rigidly controlled by precedent, cannot grant their request.

Enforcement of 8 U.S.C. § 1324 cannot brook exceptions for those who claim to obey a higher authority. The prohibition on the landing and transport of illegal aliens represents but one facet of the comprehensive legal framework governing entry into the United States and admission to its citizenship. The importance of the prohibition is reflected in the criminalization of conduct, as opposed to milder enforcement sanctions. Control of one's borders and of the identity of one's citizens is an essential feature of national sovereignty. Relinquish this control and it may fairly be said that there remains no territorial or social body which can be called a sovereign nation. The peace, order, and very existence of society are bound up in its border control laws as much as in its criminal and conscription laws. Although their scope and application may be justly criticized, there can be no doubt that, until Congress changes the border control laws, they must be uniformly obeyed. On this basis alone, the First Amendment challenge of Merkt and Elder to their convictions fails.

It is not clear to us how enforcement of 8 U.S.C. § 1324 unduly burdens appellants' free exercise of religion. The statute relates only to conduct that aids or shelters illegal aliens and contains no explicit prohibition on religious practices or beliefs. The sincerity of appellants' religious motivation to aid El Salvadorans was not doubted by the trial court. Whether such motivation, in turn, required defiance of the nation's border control laws, hence, whether enforcement of those laws so as to inhibit and punish appellants burdened their religious practice, is another matter. Representatives of Catholic and Methodist clergy testified at the pretrial hearing and at trial. None suggested that devout Christian belief mandates participation in the "sanctuary movement." Obviously, appellants could have assisted beleaguered El Salvadorans in many ways which did not affront the border control laws: they could have collected and distributed monetary and other donations, aided in preparing petitions for legal entry and assisted El Salvadorans legally in this country, or, in the Christian missionary tradition, they could have performed their ministry in El Salvador or neighboring countries where El Salvadorans are refugees. They chose confrontational, illegal means to practice their religious views—the "burden" was voluntarily assumed and not imposed on them by the government.

Second, contrary to appellants' assertions, there is a compelling state interest in the government's uniform enforcement of border control laws. The statute under which appellants were convicted is part of a comprehensive, essential sovereign policy. We cannot engraft judicial exceptions to the illegality of transporting undocumented El Salvadorans without thereby *de facto* revising, for the unique benefit of El Salvadorans, the legal conditions under which they may abide in this country. This result would create a preference utterly at odds with the fine balancing of national origin quotas, visa preference tables, and alien residency requirements promulgated and enforced pursuant to the Immigration and Nationality Act of 1952, as amended, 8 U.S.C.§ § 110 1–1524, *passim*.

An even more basic objection to requiring the government to adopt a less restrictive alternative that would protect the appellants' choice of religious practices is the open-endess of their demand. Judge Head eloquently captured the ramifications of appellants' position in the following analysis:

> If the Government attempted to accommodate into its immigration policy [appellants'] religious beliefs, the Government's efforts would result in no immigration policy at all. As testimony from [appellants'] witnesses indicated, the moral obligation to assist others crosses religious and denominational lines. These widely-held beliefs allow adherents to exercise considerable discretion and would permit religious individuals to form personal immigration policies. . . .

[Appellants wish] to limit this Court's view solely to the violence in El Salvador; however, the human condition remains miserable in many parts of the globe. Man's inhumanity to man, as well as nature's, has been unrelenting throughout history. Many people live on this planet who logically are no less worthy of [appellants'] Christian charity than the Salvadorans. The consciences of others religiously motivated may conclude that the starving and impoverished of North Africa, Asia, or Mexico are equally entitled to enter this country without review by the INS.

Appellants' "do it yourself" immigration policy, even if grounded in sincerely held religious conviction, is irreconcilably, voluntarily, and knowingly at war with the duly legislated border control policy. In this case, the claims of conscience must yield to the twin imperatives of evenhanded enforcement of criminal laws and preservation of our national identity as defined by the immigration laws.

NOTES

1. *Mahatma Ghandi, A Plea for the Severest Penalty upon Sedition*, reprinted in The Law as Literature 459–60 (E. London ed. 1960):

> I consider it to be a sin to have affection for the system. . . . In my humble opinion, non-cooperation with evil is as much a duty as is cooperation with good. . . . Non-violence implies voluntary submission to the penalty for non-cooperation with evil. I am here, therefore, to invite and submit cheerfully to the highest penalty that can be inflicted upon me for what in law is a deliberate crime and what appears to me to be the highest duty of a citizen.

2. The true political offender poses in crystalline form the problem of how, if at all, the jury should consider motive since there is no doubt that such an offender (1) recognizes that the law forbids the act he performs as a matter of political protest and (2) believes his act serves and perhaps is compelled by a higher morality. The phenomenon of civil disobedience, manifested by politically motivated defendants, is beyond the scope of this work. But the law has consistently forbidden such defendants to even argue such motives as a mitigating force. See Note, 24 Am. U.L. Rev. 797 (1975). As already noted, *supra*, § 1.03[C], the issue of jury nullification is frequently raised in such instances, and juries on occasion exculpate despite the obvious legal violation that has occurred.

3. For another case rejecting necessity in a sanctuary setting, see *United States v. Aguilar*, 871 F.2d 1436 (9th Cir. 1989). Citing the "four requirements of necessity" (choice of the lesser evil; imminent harm; reasonable causal link between act and avoidance of harm; no legal alternatives), the court declared that the defendants failed to show that there were no legal alternatives. For example, said the court, the defendants did not seek judicial help in reversing what the defendants believed to be INS's niggardly application of asylum principles; since some cases have given relief and have effected changes in INS detention and asylum procedures, said the court, there is no reason to believe that other courts would have been less receptive. As in *Merkt* and other cases, the court also rejected a First Amendment argument, holding that the defendants' mistaken belief that persons they harbored were, as a matter of national and international law, entitled to be classified as political refugees was not a defense to charges of smuggling, transporting, and harboring them. The court essentially argued that this would allow every case to "degenerate" into the facts of each refugee. For a detailed examination of the sanctuary movement, see A. Crittendon, Sanctuary: A Story of American Conscience and the Law in Collision (1988).

F. Allen, The Crimes of Politics

29, 57 (1974)

Because the political offender is significantly different from, and morally superior to, those who commit common crimes, it follows that the penalties imposed on him should reflect these differences being less rigorous and debasing, and by manifesting the state's perception of the dignity of the conscientious law violator. Moreover, the nature of the political offender's motives causes him to be less amenable to the deterrent threat of criminal punishment. To impose harsh penalties on the nondeterrable is both futile and cruel. The doctrine is one of mitigation, not of excuse or justification. The political offense is not to be overlooked, but the necessary restraints on the offender should interfere with the normal pattern of his life as little as possible. After the Munich putsch of 1923, for example, Adolph Hitler, as a political offender, was awarded the special form of confinement known as *festungshaft* at Landsberg Prison, and under this mild regime he found the conditions favorable for writing Mein Kampf.

Whatever may be the ultimate judgment about the realism and feasibility of this application of the political offense concept, it has an unquestioned ethical appeal. Moreover, for reasons that perhaps are not wholly selfish, this version of the political offense doctrine coincides with the expectations of the political offender, and when those expectations are disappointed (as very often occurs), a sense of injustice is produced in the offender and his supporters.

* * *

An argument familiar to criminologists is that society "needs its criminals." The punishment of deviancy, it is suggested, represents a ritualistic reaffirmation of the community's values and strengthens the sense of personal worth of the noncriminal majority by identifying its members as parts of a group possessing distinctive convictions and aspirations. This view might be thought to apply with particular force to the prosecution of political crimes. Thus, the punishment of the traitor both dramatizes the reality of the community and reinforces the sense of dentity of its constituent members. One need not deny all validity to these concepts to recognize that in a society in which consensus is suffering substantial erosion, the social effects of imposing punishment on political deviants may be quite different from that suggested by the theory. If the deviant is part of an infinitesimal minority, or a member of a large but powerless group, then his symbolic sacrifice to the values of the dominant group may conceivably enhance the vigor and cohesion of the majority. But if the deviant groups are substantial in size, assertive in demand, and vigorous in defense of their values, if they are recruited in significant measure from persons born close to the centers of power as well as from the dispossessed; attempts at criminal repression may produce a clamor that assaults the confidence of the majority group and which weakens rather than fortifies its sense of identity. To obtain the satisfying feeling of truth vindicated may then require a quantum of force not available to the majority or, if available and employed, which threatens or destroys the libertarian assumptions of the society.

NOTE

See also McEwen, *The Defense of Justification and Its Use by the Protestor: A Focus on Pennsylvania,* 91 Dick. L. Rev. 1 (1986).

APPENDIX

MODEL PENAL CODE

AMERICAN LAW INSTITUTE MODEL PENAL CODE
OFFICIAL DRAFT–1962*

TABLE OF CONTENTS
MODEL PENAL CODE

PART I. GENERAL PROVISIONS

ARTICLE 1. PRELIMINARY

1.01. Title and Effective Date	App.–11
1.02. Purposes; Principles of Construction	App.–11
1.03. Territorial Applicability	App.–12
1.04. Classes of Crimes; Violations	App.–12
1.05. All Offenses Defined by Statute; Application of General Provisions of the Code	App.–13
1.06. Time Limitations	App.–13
1.07. Method of Prosecution When Conduct Constitutes More Than One Offense	App.–14
1.08. When Prosecution Barred by Former Prosecution for the Same Offense	App.–15
1.09. When Prosecution Barred by Former Prosecution for Different Offense	App.–15
1.10. Former Prosecution in Another Jurisdiction: When a Bar	App.–16
1.11. Former Prosecution Before Court Lacking Jurisdiction or When Fraudulently Procured by the Defendant	App.–16
1.12. Proof Beyond a Reasonable Doubt; Affirmative Defenses; Burden of Proving Fact When Not an Element of an Offense; Presumptions	App.–17
1.13. General Definitions	App.–18

ARTICLE 2. GENERAL PRINCIPLES OF LIABILITY

2.01. Requirement of Voluntary Act; Omission as Basis of Liability; Possession as an Act	App.–19
2.02. General Requirements of Culpability	App.–19
2.03. Causal Relationship Between Conduct and Result; Divergence Between Result Designed or Contemplated and Actual Result or Between Probable and Actual Result	App.–21
2.04. Ignorance or Mistake	App.–21
2.05. When Culpability Requirements Are Inapplicable to Violations and to Offenses Defined by Other Statutes; Effect of Absolute Liability in Reducing Grade of Offense to Violation	App.–22
2.06. Liability for Conduct of Another; Complicity	App.–23
2.07. Liability of Corporations, Unincorporated Associations and Persons Acting, or Under a Duty to Act, in Their Behalf	App.–24
2.08. Intoxication	App.–25

---

* Copyright 1962 by The American Law Institute. Reprinted with permission of The American Law Institute.

2.09. Duress App.–26
2.10. Military Orders App.–26
2.11. Consent App.–26
2.12. De Minimis Infractions App.–27
2.13. Entrapment App.–27

ARTICLE 3. GENERAL PRINCIPLES OF JUSTIFICATION

3.01. Justification an Affirmative Defense; Civil Remedies Unaffected App.–27
3.02. Justification Generally: Choice of Evils App.–28
3.03. Execution of Public Duty App.–28
3.04. Use of Force in Self–Protection App.–30
3.05. Use of Force for the Protection of Other Persons App.–30
3.06. Use of Force for the Protection of Property App.-30
3.07. Use of Force in Law Enforcement App.–32
3.08. Use of Force by Persons With Special Responsibility or Care, Discipline or Safety of Others App.–34
3.09. Mistake of Law as to Unlawfulness of Force or Legality of Arrest; Reckless or Negligent Use of Otherwise Justifiable Force; Reckless or Negligent Injury or Risk of Injury to Innocent Persons App.–35
3.10. Justification in Property Crimes App.–36
3.11. Definitions App.–36

ARTICLE 4. RESPONSIBILITY

4.01. Mental Disease or Defect Excluding Responsibility ... App.–37
4.02. Evidence of Mental Disease or Defect Admissible When Relevant to Element of the Offense; Mental Disease or Defect Impairing Capacity as Ground for Mitigation of Punishment in Capital Cases App.–37
4.03. Mental Disease or Defect Excluding Responsibility is Affirmative Defense; Requirement of Notice; Form of Verdict and Judgement When Finding of Irresponsibility is Made App.–37
4.04. Mental Disease or Defect Excluding Fitness to Proceed App.–37
4.05. Psychiatric Examination of Defendant With Respect to Mental Disease or Defect App.–37
4.06. Determination of Fitness to Proceed; Effect of Finding of Unfitness; Proceedings if Fitness is Regained [; Post-Commitment Hearing] App.-38
4.07. Determination of Irresponsibility on Basis of Report; Access to Defendant by Psychiatrist of His Own Choice; Form of Expert Testimony When Issue of Responsibility is Tried App.–39
4.08. Legal Effect of Acquittal on the Ground of Mental Disease or Defect Excluding Responsibility; Commitment; Release or Discharge App.–40
4.09. Statements for Purposes of Examination or Treatment Inadmissible Except on Issue of Mental Condition App.–41
4.10. Immaturity Excluding Criminal Conviction; Transfer of Proceedings to Juvenile Court App.–42

ARTICLE 5. INCHOATE CRIMES

5.01. Criminal Attempt App.–42
5.02. Criminal Solicitation App.–43
5.03. Criminal Conspiracy App.–44
5.04. Incapacity, Irresponsibility or Immunity of Party to Solicitation or Conspiracy App.–45
5.05. Grading of Criminal Attempt, Solicitation and Conspiracy; Mitigation in Cases of Lesser Danger; Multiple Convictions Barred App.–45
5.06. Possessing Instruments of Crime; Weapons App.–46
5.07. Prohibited Offensive Weapons App.-47

ARTICLE 6. AUTHORIZED DISPOSITION OF OFFENDERS

6.01. Degrees of Felonies App.–47
6.02. Sentence in Accordance With Code; Authorized Dispositions ... App.–47
6.03. Fines App.–48
6.04. Penalties Against Corporations and Unincorporated Associations; Forfeiture of Corporate Charter or Revocation of Certificate Authorizing Foreign Corporation to Do Business in The State App.–48
6.05. Young Adult Offenders App.–49
6.06. Sentence of Imprisonment for Felony; Ordinary Terms App.–50
6.07. Sentence of Imprisonment for Felony; Extended Terms App.–50
6.08. Sentence of Imprisonment for Misdemeanors and Petty Misdemeanors; Ordinary Terms App.–51
6.09. Sentence of Imprisonment for Misdemeanors and Petty Misdemeanors; Extended Terms App.–51
6.10. First Release of All Offenders on Parole; Sentence of Imprisonment Includes Separate Parole Term; Length of Parole Term; Length of Recommitment and Reparole After Revocation of Parole; Final Unconditional Release App.–51
6.11. Place of Imprisonment App.-52
6.12. Reduction of Conviction by Court to Lesser Degree of Felony or to Misdemeanor App.–52
6.13. Civil Commitment in Lieu of Prosecution or of Sentence App.-52

ARTICLE 7. AUTHORITY OF COURT IN SENTENCING

7.01. Criteria for Withholding Sentence of Imprisonment and for Placing Defendant on Probation App.–52
7.02. Criteria for Imposing Fines App.–53
7.03. Criteria for Sentence of Extended Term of Imprisonment; Felonies App.–54
7.04. Criteria for Sentence of Extended Term of Imprisonment; Misdemeanors and Petty Misdemeanors App.–55
7.05. Former Conviction in Another Jurisdiction; Definition and Proof of Conviction; Sentence Taking into Account Admitted Crimes Bars Subsequent Conviction for Such Crimes App.–56

7.06. Multiple Sentences; Concurrent and Consecutive Terms App.–56
7.07. Procedure on Sentence; Pre-sentence Investigation and Report; Remand for Psychiatric Examination; Transmission of Records to Department of Correction App.–58
7.08. Commitment for Observation; Sentence of Imprisonment for Felony Deemed Tentative for Period of One Year; Resentence on Petition of Commissioner of Correction App.-59
7.09. Credit for Time of Detention Prior to Sentence; Credit for Imprisonment Under Earlier Sentence for the Same Crime App.–60

PART II. DEFINITION OF SPECIFIC CRIMES OFFENSES AGAINST EXISTENCE OR STABILITY OF THE STATE OFFENSES INVOLVING DANGER TO THE PERSON

ARTICLE 210. CRIMINAL HOMICIDE

210.0. Definitions App.–61
210.1. Criminal Homicide App.–61
210.2. Murder App.–61
210.3. Manslaughter App.–62
210.4. Negligent Homicide App.–62
210.5. Causing or Aiding Suicide App.–62
210.6. Sentence of Death for Murder; Further Proceedings to Determine Sentence App.–62

ARTICLE 211. ASSAULT; RECKLESS ENDANGERING; THREATS

211.0. Definitions App.–65
211.1. Assault App.–65
211.2. Recklessly Endangering Another Person App.–65
211.3. Terroristic Threats App.–65

ARTICLE 212. KIDNAPPING AND RELATED OFFENSES; COERCION

212.0. Definitions App.–65
212.1. Kidnapping App.–65
212.2. Felonious Restraint App.–66
212.3. False Imprisonment App.–66
212.4. Interference With Custody App.–66
212.5. Criminal Coercion App.–67

ARTICLE 213. SEXUAL OFFENSES

213.0. Definitions App.–67
213.1. Rape and Related Offenses App.–67
213.2. Deviate Sexual Intercourse by Force or Imposition App.–68
213.3. Corruption of Minors and Seduction App.–68
213.4. Sexual Assault App.–69

213.5. Indecent Exposure	App.–69
213.6. Provisions Generally Applicable to Article 213	App.–69

OFFENSES AGAINST PROPERTY

Article 220. ARSON, CRIMINAL MISCHIEF, AND OTHER PROPERTY DESTRUCTION

220.1. Arson and Related Offenses	App.–70
220.2. Causing or Risking Catastrophe	App.–71
220.3. Criminal Mischief	App.–71

Article 221. BURGLARY AND OTHER CRIMINAL INTRUSION

221.0. Definitions	App.–71
221.1. Burglary	App.–72
221.2. Criminal Trespass	App.–72

ARTICLE 222. ROBBERY

222.1. Robbery	App.–73

ARTICLE 223. THEFT AND RELATED OFFENSES

223.0. Definitions	App.–73
223.1. Consolidation of Then Offenses; Grading; Provisions Applicable to Theft Generally	App.–74
223.2. Theft by Unlawful Taking or Disposition	App.–75
223.3. Theft by Deception	App.–75
223.4. Theft by Extortion	App.–75
223.5. Theft of Property Lost, Mislaid or Delivered by Mistake	App.–76
223.6. Receiving Stolen Property	App.–76
223.7. Theft of Services	App.–76
223.8. Theft by Failure to Make Required Disposition of Funds Received	App.–76
223.9. Unauthorized Use of Automobiles and Other Vehicles	App.–77

ARTICLE 224. FORGERY AND FRAUDULENT PRACTICES

224.0. Definitions	App.–77
224.1. Forgery	App.–77
224.2. Simulating Objects of Antiquity, Rarity, Etc.	App.–77
224.3. Fraudulent Destruction, Removal or Concealment of Recordable Instruments	App.–78
224.4. Tampering With Records	App.–78
224.5. Bad Checks	App.–78
224.6. Credit Cards	App.–78
224.7. Deceptive Business Practices	App.–78
224.8. Commercial Bribery and Breach of Duty to Act Disinterestedly	App.–79

224.9. Rigging Publicly Exhibited Contest App.–79
224.10. Defrauding Secured Creditors App.–80
224.11. Fraud in Insolvency App.–80
224.12. Receiving Deposits in a Failing Financial Institution App.–80
224.13. Misapplication of Entrusted Property and Property of Government or Financial Institution App.–80
224.14. Securing Execution of Documents by Deception App.–81

OFFENSES AGAINST THE FAMILY

Article 230. OFFENSES AGAINST THE FAMILY

230.1. Bigamy and Polygamy App.–81
230.2. Incest App.–81
230.3. Abortion App.–81
230.4. Endangering Welfare of Children App.–83
230.5. Persistent Non-support App.–83

OFFENSES AGAINST PUBLIC ADMINISTRATION

Article 240. BRIBERY AND CORRUPT INFLUENCE

240.0. Definitions App.–83
240.1. Bribery in Official and Political Matters App.–84
240.2. Threats and Other Improper Influence in Official and Political Matters App.–84
240.3. Compensation for Past Official Behavior App.–84
240.4. Retaliation for Past Official Action App.–85
240.5. Gifts to Public Servants by Persons Subject to Their Jurisdiction App.–85
240.6. Compensating Public Servant for Assisting Private Interests in Relation to Matters Before Him App.–86
240.7. Selling Political Endorsement; Special Influence App.–86

ARTICLE 241. PERJURY AND OTHER FALSIFICATION IN OFFICIAL MATTERS

241.0. Definitions App.–86
241.1. Perjury App.–86
241.2. False Swearing App.–87
241.3. Unsworn Falsification to Authorities App.–87
241.4. False Alarms to Agencies of Public Safety App.–88
241.5. False Reports to Law Enforcement Authorities App.–88
241.6. Tampering With Witnesses and Informants; Retaliation vAgainst Them App.–88
241.7. Tampering With or Fabricating Physical Evidence App.–89
241.8. Tampering With Public Records or Information App.–89
241.9. Impersonating a Public Servant App.–89

ARTICLE 242. OBSTRUCTING GOVERNMENTAL, OPERATIONS; ESCAPES

242.0. Definitions App.-89
242.1. Obstructing Administration of Law or Other Governmental Function App.-89
242.2. Resisting Arrest or Other Law Enforcement App.-89
242.3. Hindering Apprehension or Prosecution App.-90
242.4. Aiding Consummation of Crime App.-90
242.5. Compounding App.-90
242.6. Escape App.-90
242.7. Implements for Escape; Other Contraband App.-91
242.8. Bail Jumping; Default in Required Appearance App.-91

Article 243. ABUSE OF OFFICE

243.0. Definitions App.-91
243.1. Official Oppression App.-91
243.2. Speculating or Wagering on Official Action or Information ... App.-92

OFFENSES AGAINST PUBLIC ORDER AND DECENCY

ARTICLE 250. RIOT, DISORDERLY CONDUCT, AND RELATED OFFENSES

250.1. Riot; Failure to Disperse App.-92
250.2. Disorderly Conduct App.-92
250.3. False Public Alarms App.-93
250.4. Harassment App.-93
250.5. Public Drunkenness; Drug Incapacitation App.-93
250.6. Loitering or Prowling App.-93
250.7. Obstructing Highways and Other Public Passages App.-94
250.8. Disrupting Meetings and Processions App.-94
250.9. Desecration of Venerated Objects App.-94
250.10. Abuse of Corpse App.-94
250.11. Cruelty to Animals App.-94
250.12. Violation of Privacy App.-95

ARTICLE 251. PUBLIC INDECENCY

251.1. Open Lewdness App.-95
251.2. Prostitution and Related Offenses App.-95
251.3. Loitering to Solicit Deviate Sexual Relations App.-97
251.4. Obscenity App.-97

ADDITIONAL ARTICLES

PART III. TREATMENT AND CORRECTION [OMITTED]

PART IV. ORGANIZATION OF CORRECTION [OMITTED]

PART I.

GENERAL PROVISIONS

ARTICLE 1. PRELIMINARY

Section 1.01 Title and Effective Date.

(1) This Act is called the Penal and Correctional Code and may be cited as P.C.C. It shall become effective on —.

(2) Except as provided in Subsections (3) and (4) of this Section, the Code does not apply to offenses committed prior to its effective date and prosecutions for such offenses shall be governed by the prior law, which is continued in effect for that purpose, as if this Code were not in force. For the purposes of this Section, an offense was committed prior to the effective date of the Code if any of the elements of the offense occurred prior thereto.

(3) In any case pending on or after the effective date of the Code, involving an offense committed prior to such date:

(a) procedural provisions of the Code shall govern, insofar as they are justly applicable and their application does not introduce confusion or delay;

(b) provisions of the Code according a defense or mitigation shall apply, with the consent of the defendant;

(c) the Court, with the consent of the defendant, may impose sentence under the provisions of the Code applicable to the offense and the offender.

(4) Provisions of the Code governing the treatment and the release or discharge of prisoners, probationers and parolees shall apply to persons under sentence for offenses committed prior to the effective date of the Code, except that the minimum or maximum period of their detention or supervision shall in no case be increased.

Section 1.02 Purposes; Principles of Construction.

(1) The general purposes of the provisions governing the definition of offenses are:

(a) to forbid and prevent conduct that unjustifiably and inexcusably inflicts or threatens substantial harm to individual or public interests;

(b) to subject to public control persons whose conduct indicates that they are disposed to commit crimes;

(c) to safeguard conduct that is without fault from condemnation as criminal;

(d) to give fair warning of the nature of the conduct declared to constitute an offense;

(e) to differentiate on reasonable grounds between serious and minor offenses.

(2) The general purposes of the provisions governing the sentencing and treatment of offenders are:

(a) to prevent the commission of offenses;

(b) to promote the correction and rehabilitation of offenders;

(c) to safeguard offenders against excessive, disproportionate or arbitrary punishment;

(d) to give fair warning of the nature of the sentences that may be imposed on conviction of an offense;

(e) to differentiate among offenders with a view to a just individualization in their treatment;

(f) to define, coordinate and harmonize the powers, duties and functions of the courts and of administrative officers and agencies responsible for dealing with offenders;

(g) to advance the use of generally accepted scientific methods and knowledge in the sentencing and treatment of offenders;

(h) to integrate responsibility for the administration of the correctional system in a State Department of Correction [or other single department or agency].

(3) The provisions of the Code shall be construed according to the fair import of their terms but when the language is susceptible of differing constructions it shall be interpreted to further the general purposes stated in this Section and the special purposes of the particular provision involved. The discretionary powers conferred by the Code shall be exercised in accordance with the criteria stated in the Code and, insofar as such criteria are not decisive, to further the general purposes stated in this Section.

Section 1.03 Territorial Applicability.

(1) Except as otherwise provided in this Section, a person may be convicted under the law of this State of an offense committed by his own conduct or the conduct of another for which he is legally accountable if:

(a) either the conduct which is an element of the offense or the result which is such an element occurs within this State; or

(b) conduct occurring outside the State is sufficient under the law of this State to constitute an attempt to commit an offense within the State; or

(c) conduct occurring outside the State is sufficient under the law of this State to constitute a conspiracy to commit an offense within the State and an overt act in furtherance of such conspiracy occurs within the State; or

(d) conduct occurring within the State establishes complicity in the commission of, or an attempt, solicitation or conspiracy to commit, an offense in another jurisdiction which also is an offense under the law of this State; or

(e) the offense consists of the omission to perform a legal duty imposed by the law of this State with respect to domicile, residence or a relationship to a person, thing or transaction in the State; or

(f) the offense is based on a statute of this State which expressly prohibits conduct outside the State, when the conduct bears a reasonable relation to a legitimate interest of this State and the actor knows or should know that his conduct is likely to affect that interest.

(2) Subsection (1)(a) does not apply when either causing a specified

result or a purpose to cause or danger of causing such a result is an element of an offense and the result occurs or is designed or likely to occur only in another jurisdiction where the conduct charged would not constitute an offense, unless a legislative purpose plainly appears to declare the conduct criminal regardless of the place of the result.

(3) Subsection (1)(a) does not apply when causing a particular result is an element of an offense and the result is caused by conduct occurring outside the State which would not constitute an offense if the result had occurred there, unless the actor purposely or knowingly caused the result within the State.

(4) When the offense is homicide, either the death of the victim or the bodily impact causing death constitutes a "result," within the meaning of Subsection (1)(a) and if the body of a homicide victim is found within the State, it is presumed that such result occurred within the State.

(5) This State includes the land and water and the air space above such land and water with respect to which the State has legislative jurisdiction.

Section 1.04 Classes of Crimes; Violations.

(1) An offense defined by this Code or by any other statute of this State, for which a sentence of [death or of] imprisonment is authorized, constitutes a crime. Crimes are classified as felonies, misdemeanors or petty misdemeanors.

(2) A crime is a felony if it is so designated in this Code or if persons convicted thereof may be sentenced [to death or] to imprisonment for a term which, apart from an extended term, is in excess of one year.

(3) A crime is a misdemeanor if it is so designated in this Code or in a statute other than this Code enacted subsequent thereto.

(4) A crime is a petty misdemeanor if it is so designated in this Code or in a statute other than this Code enacted subsequent thereto or if it is defined by a statute other than this Code which now provides that persons convicted thereof may be sentenced to imprisonment for a term of which the maximum is less than one year.

(5) An offense defined by this Code or by any other statute of this State constitutes a violation if it is so designated in this Code or in the law defining the offense or if no other sentence than a fine, or fine and forfeiture or other civil penalty is authorized upon conviction or if it is defined by a statute other than this Code which now provides that the offense shall not constitute a crime. A violation does not constitute a crime and conviction of a violation shall not give rise to any disability or legal disadvantage based on conviction of a criminal offense.

(6) Any offense declared by law to constitute a crime, without specification of the grade thereof or of the sentence authorized upon conviction, is a misdemeanor.

(7) An offense defined by any statute of this State other than this Code shall be classified as provided in this Section and the sentence that may be imposed upon conviction thereof shall hereafter be governed by this Code.

Section 1.05 All Offenses Defined by Statute; Application of General Provisions of the Code.

(1) No conduct constitutes an offense unless it is a crime or violation under this Code or another statute of this State.

(2) The provisions of Part I of the Code are applicable to offenses defined by other statutes, unless the Code otherwise provides.

(3) This Section does not affect the power of a court to punish for contempt or to employ any sanction authorized by law for the enforcement of an order or a civil judgment or decree.

Section 1.06 Time Limitations.

(1) A prosecution for murder may be commenced at anytime.

(2) Except as otherwise provided in this Section, prosecutions for other offenses are subject to the following periods of limitation:

(a) a prosecution for a felony of the first degree must be commenced within six years after it is committed;

(b) a prosecution for any other felony must be commenced within three years after it is committed;

(c) a prosecution for a misdemeanor must be commenced within two years after it is committed;

(d) a prosecution for a petty misdemeanor or a violation must be commenced within six months after it is committed.

(3) If the period prescribed in Subsection (2) has expired, a prosecution may nevertheless be commenced for:

(a) any offense a material element of which is either fraud or a breach of fiduciary obligation within one year after discovery of the offense by an aggrieved party or by a person who has legal duty to represent an aggrieved party and who is himself not a party to the offense, but in no case shall this provision extend the period of limitation otherwise applicable by more than three years; and

(b) any offense based upon misconduct in office by a public officer or employee at any time when the defendant is in public office or employment or within two years thereafter, but in no case shall this provision extend the period of limitation otherwise applicable by more than three years.

(4) An offense is committed either when every element occurs, or, if a legislative purpose to prohibit a continuing course of conduct plainly appears, at the time when the course of conduct or the defendant's complicity therein is terminated. Time starts to run on the day after the offense is committed.

(5) A prosecution is commenced either when an indictment is found [or an information filed] or when a warrant or other process is issued, provided that such warrant or process is executed without unreasonable delay.

(6) The period of limitation does not run:

(a) during any time when the accused is continuously absent from the State or has no reasonably ascertainable place of abode or work within the State, but in no case shall this provision extend the period of limitation otherwise applicable by more than three years; or

(b) during any time when a prosecution against the accused for the same conduct is pending in this State.

Section 1.07 Method of Prosecution When Conduct Constitutes More Than One Offense.

(1) Prosecution for Multiple Offenses; Limitation on Convictions. When the same conduct of a defendant may establish the commission of more than one offense, the defendant may be prosecuted for each such offense. He may not, however, be convicted of more than one offense if:

(a) one offense is included in the other, as defined in Subsection (4) of this Section; or

(b) one offense consists only of a conspiracy or other form of preparation to commit the other; or

(c) inconsistent findings of fact are required to establish the commission of the offenses; or

(d) the offenses differ only in that one is defined to prohibit a designated kind of conduct generally and the other to prohibit a specific instance of such conduct; or

(e) the offense is defined as a continuing course of conduct and the defendant's course of conduct was uninterrupted, unless the law provides that specific periods of such conduct constitute separate offenses.

(2) Limitation on Separate Trials for Multiple Offenses. Except as provided in Subsection (3) of this Section, a defendant shall not be subject to separate trials for multiple offenses based on the same conduct or arising from the same criminal episode, if such offenses are known to the appropriate prosecuting officer at the time of the commencement of the first trial and are within the jurisdiction of a single court.

(3) Authority of Court to Order Separate Trials. When a defendant is charged with two or more offenses based on the same conduct or arising from the same criminal episode, the Court, on application of the prosecuting attorney or of the defendant, may order any such charge to be tried separately, if it is satisfied that justice so requires.

(4) Conviction of Included Offense Permitted. A defendant may be convicted of an offense included in an offense charged in the indictment [or the information]. An offense is so included when:

(a) it is established by proof of the same or less than all the facts required to establish the commission of the offense charged; or

(b) it consists of an attempt or solicitation to commit the offense charged or to commit an offense otherwise included therein; or

(c) it differs from the offense charged only in the respect that a less serious injury or risk of injury to the same person, property or public interest or a lesser kind of culpability suffices to establish its commission.

(5) Submission of Included Offense to Jury. The Court shall not be obligated to charge the jury with respect to an included offense unless there is a rational basis for a verdict acquitting the defendant of the offense charged and convicting him of the included offense.

Section 1.08 When Prosecution Barred by Former Prosecution for the Same Offense.

When a prosecution is for a violation of the same provision of the statutes and is based upon the same facts as a former prosecution, it is barred by such former prosecution under the following circumstances:

(1) The former prosecution resulted in an acquittal. There is an acquittal if the prosecution resulted in a finding of not guilty by the trier of fact or in a determination that there was insufficient evidence to warrant a conviction. A finding of guilty of a lesser included offense is an acquittal of the greater inclusive offense, although the conviction is subsequently set aside.

(2) The former prosecution was terminated, after the information had been filed or the indictment found, by a final order or judgment for the defendant, which has not been set aside, reversed, or vacated and which necessarily required a determination inconsistent with a fact or a legal proposition that must be established for conviction of the offense.

(3) The former prosecution resulted in a conviction. There is a conviction if the prosecution resulted in a judgment of conviction which has not been reversed or vacated, a verdict of guilty which has not been set aside and which is capable of supporting a judgment, or a plea of guilty accepted by the Court. In the latter two cases failure to enter judgment must be for a reason other than a motion of the defendant.

(4) The former prosecution was improperly terminated. Except as provided in this Subsection, there is an improper termination of a prosecution if the termination is for reasons not amounting to an acquittal, and it takes place after the first witness is sworn but before verdict. Termination under any of the following circumstances is not improper:

(a) The defendant consents to the termination or waives, by motion to dismiss or otherwise, his right to object to the termination.

(b) The trial court finds that the termination is necessary because:

(i) it is physically impossible to proceed with the trial in conformity with law; or

(ii) there is a legal defect in the proceedings which would make any judgment entered upon a verdict reversible as a matter of law; or

(iii) prejudicial conduct, in or outside the courtroom, makes it impossible to proceed with the trial without injustice to either the defendant or the State; or

(iv) the jury is unable to agree upon a verdict; or

(v) false statements of a juror on voir dire prevent a fair trial.

Section 1.09 When Prosecution Barred by Former Prosecution for Different Offense.

Although a prosecution is for a violation of a different provision of the statutes than a former prosecution or is based on different facts, it is barred by such former prosecution under the following circumstances:

(1) The former prosecution resulted in an acquittal or in a conviction as defined in Section 1.08 and the subsequent prosecution is for:

(a) any offense of which the

defendant could have been convicted on the first prosecution; or

(b) any offense for which the defendant should have been tried on the first prosecution under Section 1.07, unless the Court ordered a separate trial of the charge of such offense; or

(c) the same conduct, unless (i) the offense of which the defendant was formerly convicted or acquitted and the offense for which he is subsequently prosecuted each requires proof of a fact not required by the other and the law defining each of such offenses is intended to prevent a substantially different harm or evil, or (ii) the second offense was not consummated when the former trial began.

(2) The former prosecution was terminated, after the information was filed or the indictment found, by an acquittal or by a final order or judgment for the defendant which has not been set aside, reversed or vacated and which acquittal, final order or judgment necessarily required a determination inconsistent with a fact which must be established for conviction of the second offense.

(3) The former prosecution was improperly terminated, as improper termination is defined in Section 1.08, and the subsequent prosecution is for an offense of which the defendant could have been convicted had the former prosecution not been improperly terminated.

Section 1.10 Former Prosecution in Another Jurisdiction: When a Bar.

When conduct constitutes an offense within the concurrent jurisdiction of this State and of the United States or another State, a prosecution in any such other jurisdiction is a bar to a subsequent prosecution in this State under the following circumstances:

(1) The first prosecution resulted in an acquittal or in a conviction as defined in Section 1.08 and the subsequent prosecution is based on the same conduct, unless (a) the offense of which the defendant was formerly convicted or acquitted and the offense for which he is subsequently prosecuted each requires proof of a fact not required by the other and the law defining each of such offenses is intended to prevent a substantially different harm or evil or (b) the second offense was not consummated when the former trial began; or

(2) The former prosecution was terminated, after the information was filed or the indictment found, by an acquittal or by a final order or judgment for the defendant which has not been set aside, reversed or vacated and which acquittal, final order or judgment necessarily required a determination inconsistent with a fact which must be established for conviction of the offense of which the defendant is subsequently prosecuted.

Section 1.11 Former Prosecution Before Court Lacking Jurisdiction or When Fraudulently Procured by the Defendant.

A prosecution is not a bar within the meaning of Sections 1.08, 1.09 and 1.10 under any of the following circumstances:

(1) The former prosecution was before a court which lacked

jurisdiction over the defendant or the offense; or

(2) The former prosecution was procured by the defendant without the knowledge of the appropriate prosecuting officer and with the purpose of avoiding the sentence which might otherwise be imposed; or

(3) The former prosecution resulted in a judgment of conviction which was held invalid in a subsequent proceeding on a writ of habeas corpus, coram nobis or similar process.

Section 1.12 Proof Beyond a Reasonable Doubt; Affirmative Defenses; Burden of Proving Fact When Not an Element of an Offense; Presumptions.

(1) No person may be convicted of an offense unless each element of such offense is proved beyond a reasonable doubt. In the absence of such proof, the innocence of the defendant is assumed.

(2) Subsection (1) of this Section does not:

(a) require the disproof of an affirmative defense unless and until there is evidence supporting such defense; or

(b) apply to any defense which the Code or another statute plainly requires the defendant to prove by a preponderance of evidence.

(3) A ground of defense is affirmative, within the meaning of Subsection (2)(a) of this Section, when:

(a) it arises under a section of the Code which so provides; or

(b) it relates to an offense defined by a statute other than the Code and such statute so provides; or

(c) it involves a matter of excuse or justification peculiarly within the knowledge of the defendant on which he can fairly be required to adduce supporting evidence.

(4) When the application of the Code depends upon the finding of a fact which is not an element of an offense, unless the Code otherwise provides:

(a) the burden of proving the fact is on the prosecution or defendant, depending on whose interest or contention will be furthered if the finding should be made; and

(b) the fact must be proved to the satisfaction of the Court or jury, as the case may be.

(5) When the Code establishes a presumption with respect to any fact which is an element of an offense, it has the following consequences:

(a) when there is evidence of the facts which give rise to the presumption, the issue of the existence of the presumed fact must be submitted to the jury, unless the Court is satisfied that the evidence as a whole clearly negatives the presumed fact; and

(b) when the issue of the existence of the presumed fact is submitted to the jury, the Court shall charge that while the presumed fact must, on all the evidence, be proved beyond a reasonable doubt, the law declares that the jury may regard the facts giving rise to the presumption as sufficient evidence of the presumed fact.

(6) A presumption not established by the Code or inconsistent with it has

the consequences otherwise accorded it by law.

Section 1.13 General Definitions.

In this Code, unless a different meaning plainly is required:

(1) "statute" includes the Constitution and a local law or ordinance of a political subdivision of the State;

(2) "act" or "action" means a bodily movement whether voluntary or involuntary;

(3) "voluntary" has the meaning specified in Section 2.01;

(4) "omission" means a failure to act;

(5) "conduct" means an action or omission and its accompanying state of mind, or, where relevant, a series of acts and omissions;

(6) "actor" includes, where relevant, a person guilty of an omission;

(7) "acted" includes, where relevant, "omitted to act";

(8) "person," "he" and "actor" include any natural person and, where relevant, a corporation or an unincorporated association;

(9) "element of an offense" means (i) such conduct or (ii) such attendant circumstances or (iii) such a result of conduct as

(a) is included in the description of the forbidden conduct in the definition of the offense; or

(b) establishes the required kind of culpability; or

(c) negatives an excuse or justification for such conduct; or

(d) negatives a defense under the statute of limitations; or

(e) establishes jurisdiction or venue;

(10) "material element of an offense" means an element that does not relate exclusively to the statute of limitations, jurisdiction, venue or to any other matter similarly unconnected with (i) the harm or evil, incident to conduct, sought to be prevented by the law defining the offense, or (ii) the existence of a justification or excuse for such conduct;

(11) "purposely" has the meaning specified in Section 2.02 and equivalent terms such as "with purpose," "designed" or "with design" have the same meaning;

(12) "intentionally" or "with intent" means purposely;

(13) "knowingly" has the meaning specified in Section 2.02 and equivalent terms such as "knowing" or "with knowledge" have the same meaning;

(14) "recklessly" has the meaning specified in Section 2.02 and equivalent terms such as "recklessness" or "with recklessness" have the same meaning;

(15) "negligently" has the meaning specified in Section 2.02 and equivalent terms such as "negligence" or "with negligence" have the same meaning;

(16) "reasonably believes" or "reasonable belief" designates a belief which the actor is not reckless or negligent in holding.

ARTICLE 2. GENERAL PRINCIPLES OF LIABILITY

Section 2.01 Requirement of Voluntary Act; Omission as Basis of Liability; Possession as an Act.

(1) A person is not guilty of an offense unless his liability is based on conduct which includes a voluntary act or the omission to perform an act of which he is physically capable.

(2) The following are not voluntary acts within the meaning of this Section:

(a) a reflex or convulsion;

(b) a bodily movement during unconsciousness or sleep;

(c) conduct during hypnosis or resulting from hypnotic suggestion;

(d) a bodily movement that otherwise is not a product of the effort or determination of the actor, either conscious or habitual.

(3) Liability for the commission of an offense may not be based on an omission unaccompanied by action unless:

(a) the omission is expressly made sufficient by the law defining the offense; or

(b) a duty to perform the omitted act is otherwise imposed by law.

(4) Possession is an act, within the meaning of this Section, if the possessor knowingly procured or received the thing possessed or was aware of his control thereof for a sufficient period to have been able to terminate his possession.

Section 2.02 General Requirements of Culpability.

(1) Minimum Requirements of Culpability. Except as provided in Section 2.05, a person is not guilty of an offense unless he acted purposely, knowingly, recklessly or negligently, as the law may require, with respect to each material element of the offense.

(2) Kinds of Culpability Defined.

(a) *Purposely*.

A person acts purposely with respect to a material element of an offense when:

(i) if the element involves the nature of his conduct or a result thereof, it is his conscious object to engage in conduct of that nature or to cause such a result; and

(ii) if the element involves the attendant circumstances, he is aware of the existence of such circumstances or he believes or hopes that they exist.

(b) *Knowingly*.

A person acts knowingly with respect to a material element of an offense when:

(i) if the element involves the nature of his conduct or the attendant circumstances, he is aware that his conduct is of that nature or that such circumstances exist; and

(ii) if the element involves a result of his conduct, he is aware that it is practically certain that his conduct will cause such a result.

(c) *Recklessly*.

A person acts recklessly with respect to a material element of an offense when he consciously disregards a substantial and unjustifiable risk that the material element exists or will result from his conduct. The risk must be of such a nature and degree that, considering the nature and purpose of the actor's conduct and the circumstances known to him, its disregard involves a gross deviation from the standard of conduct that a law-abiding person would observe in the actor's situation.

(d) *Negligently.*

A person acts negligently with respect to a material element of an offense when he should be aware of a substantial and unjustifiable risk that the material element exists or will result from his conduct. The risk must be of such a nature and degree that the actor's failure to perceive it, considering the nature and purpose of his conduct and the circumstances known to him, involves a gross deviation from the standard of care that a reasonable person would observe in the actor's situation.

(3) Culpability Required Unless Otherwise Provided. When the culpability sufficient to establish a material element of an offense is not prescribed by law, such element is established if a person acts purposely, knowingly or recklessly with respect thereto.

(4) Prescribed Culpability Requirement Applies to All Material Elements. When the law defining an offense prescribes the kind of culpability that is sufficient for the commission of an offense, without distinguishing among the material elements thereof, such provision shall apply to all the material elements of the offense, unless a contrary purpose plainly appears.

(5) Substitutes for Negligence, Recklessness and Knowledge. When the law provides that negligence suffices to establish an element of an offense, such element also is established if a person acts purposely, knowingly or recklessly. When recklessness suffices to establish an element, such element also is established if a person acts purposely or knowingly. When acting knowingly suffices to establish an element, such element also is established if a person acts purposely.

(6) Requirement of Purpose Satisfied if Purpose Is Conditional. When a particular purpose is an element of an offense, the element is established although such purpose is conditional, unless the condition negatives the harm or evil sought to be prevented by the law defining the offense.

(7) Requirement of Knowledge Satisfied by Knowledge of High Probability. When knowledge of the existence of a particular fact is an element of an offense, such knowledge is established if a person is aware of a high probability of its existence, unless he actually believes that it does not exist.

(8) Requirement of Willfulness Satisfied by Acting Knowingly. A requirement that an offense be committed wilfully is satisfied if a person acts knowingly with respect to the material elements of the offense, unless a purpose to impose further requirements appears.

(9) Culpability as to Illegality of Conduct. Neither knowledge nor recklessness or negligence as to whether conduct constitutes an offense or as to the existence, meaning or application of the law determining the elements of an offense is an element of such offense, unless the definition

of the offense or the Code so provides.

(10) Culpability as Determinant of Grade of Offense. When the grade or degree of an offense depends on whether the offense is committed purposely, knowingly, recklessly or negligently, its grade or degree shall be the lowest for which the determinative kind of culpability is established with respect to any material element of the offense.

Section 2.03 Causal Relationship Between Conduct and Result; Divergence Between Result Designed or Contemplated and Actual Result or Between Probable and Actual Result.

(1) Conduct is the cause of a result when:

(a) it is an antecedent but for which the result in question would not have occurred; and

(b) the relationship between the conduct and result satisfies any additional causal requirements imposed by the Code or by the law defining the offense.

(2) When purposely or knowingly causing a particular result is an element of an offense, the element is not established if the actual result is not within the purpose or the contemplation of the actor unless:

(a) the actual result differs from that designed or contemplated, as the case may be, only in the respect that a different person or different property is injured or affected or that the injury or harm designed or contemplated would have been more serious or more extensive than that caused; or

(b) the actual result involves the same kind of injury or harm as that designed or contemplated and is not too remote or accidental in its occurrence to have a [just] bearing on the actor's liability or on the gravity of his offense.

(3) When recklessly or negligently causing a particular result is an element of an offense, the element is not established if the actual result is not within the risk of which the actor is aware or, in the case of negligence, of which he should be aware unless:

(a) the actual result differs from the probable result only in the respect that a different person or different property is injured or affected or that the probable injury or harm would have been more serious or more extensive than that caused; or

(b) the actual result involves the same kind of injury or harm as the probable result and is not too remote or accidental in its occurrence to have a [just] bearing on the actor's liability or on the gravity of his offense.

(4) When causing a particular result is a material element of an offense for which absolute liability is imposed by law, the element is not established unless the actual result is a probable consequence of the actor's conduct.

Section 2.04 Ignorance or Mistake.

(1) Ignorance or mistake as to a matter of fact or law is a defense if:

(a) the ignorance or mistake negatives the purpose, knowledge, belief, recklessness or negligence required to establish a material element of the offense; or

(b) the law provides that the state of mind established by such ignorance or mistake constitutes a defense.

(2) Although ignorance or mistake would otherwise afford a defense to the offense charged, the defense is not available if the defendant would be guilty of another offense had the situation been as he supposed. In such case, however, the ignorance or mistake of the defendant shall reduce the grade and degree of the offense of which he may be convicted to those of the offense of which he would be guilty had the situation been as he supposed.

(3) A belief that conduct does not legally constitute an offense is a defense to a prosecution for that offense based upon such conduct when:

(a) the statute or other enactment defining the offense is not known to the actor and has not been published or otherwise reasonably made available prior to the conduct alleged; or

(b) he acts in reasonable reliance upon an official statement of the law, afterward determined to be invalid or erroneous, contained in (i) a statute or other enactment; (ii) a judicial decision, opinion or judgment; (iii) an administrative order or grant of permission; or (iv) an official interpretation of the public officer or body charged by law with responsibility for the interpretation, administration or enforcement of the law defining the offense.

(4) The defendant must prove a defense arising under Subsection (3) of this Section by a preponderance of evidence.

Section 2.05 When Culpability Requirements Are Inapplicable to Violations and to Offenses Defined by Other Statutes; Effect of Absolute Liability in Reducing Grade of Offense to Violation.

(1) The requirements of culpability prescribed by Sections 2.01 and 2.02 do not apply to:

(a) offenses which constitute violations, unless the requirement involved is included in the definition of the offense or the Court determines that its application is consistent with effective enforcement of the law defining the offense; or

(b) offenses defined by statutes other than the Code, insofar as a legislative purpose to impose absolute liability for such offenses or with respect to any material element thereof plainly appears.

(2) Notwithstanding any other provision of existing law and unless a subsequent statute otherwise provides:

(a) when absolute liability is imposed with respect to any material element of an offense defined by a statute other than the Code and a conviction is based upon such liability, the offense constitutes a violation; and

(b) although absolute liability is imposed by law with respect to one or more of the material elements of an offense defined by a statute other than the Code, the culpable commission of the offense may be charged and proved, in which event negligence with respect to such elements constitutes sufficient culpability and the classification of the offense and the sentence that may be imposed therefor upon conviction are determined by Section 1.04 and Article 6 of the Code.

Section 2.06 Liability for Conduct of Another; Complicity.

(1) A person is guilty of an offense if it is committed by his own conduct or by the conduct of another person for which he is legally accountable, or both.

(2) A person is legally accountable for the conduct of another person when:

(a) acting with the kind of culpability that is sufficient for the commission of the offense, he causes an innocent or irresponsible person to engage in such conduct; or

(b) he is made accountable for the conduct of such other person by the Code or by the law defining the offense; or

(c) he is an accomplice of such other person in the commission of the offense.

(3) A person is an accomplice of another person in the commission of an offense if:

(a) with the purpose of promoting or facilitating the commission of the offense, he

(i) solicits such other person to commit it; or

(ii) aids or agrees or attempts to aid such other person in planning or committing it; or

(iii) having a legal duty to prevent the commission of the offense, fails to make proper effort so to do; or

(b) his conduct is expressly declared by law to establish his complicity.

(4) When causing a particular result is an element of an offense, an accomplice in the conduct causing such result is an accomplice in the commission of that offense, if he acts with the kind of culpability, if any, with respect to that result that is sufficient for the commission of the offense.

(5) A person who is legally incapable of committing a particular offense himself may be guilty thereof if it is committed by the conduct of another person for which he is legally accountable, unless such liability is inconsistent with the purpose of the provision establishing his incapacity.

(6) Unless otherwise provided by the Code or by the law defining the offense, a person is not an accomplice in an offense committed by another person if:

(a) he is a victim of that offense; or

(b) the offense is so defined that his conduct is inevitably incident to its commission; or

(c) he terminates his complicity prior to the commission of the offense and

(i) wholly deprives it of effectiveness in the commission of the offense; or

(ii) gives timely warning to the law enforcement authorities or otherwise makes proper effort to prevent the commission of the offense.

(7) An accomplice may be convicted on proof of the commission of the offense and of his complicity

therein, though the person claimed to have committed the offense has not been prosecuted or convicted or has been convicted of a different offense or degree of offense or has an immunity to prosecution or conviction or has been acquitted.

Section 2.07 Liability of Corporations, Unincorporated Associations and Persons Acting, or Under a Duty to Act, in Their Behalf.

(1) A corporation may be convicted of the commission of an offense if:

(a) the offense is a violation or the offense is defined by a statute other than the Code in which a legislative purpose to impose liability on corporations plainly appears and the conduct is performed by an agent of the corporation acting in behalf of the corporation within the scope of his office or employment, except that if the law defining the offense designates the agents for whose conduct the corporation is accountable or the circumstances under which it is accountable, such provisions shall apply; or

(b) the offense consists of an omission to discharge a specific duty of affirmative performance imposed on corporations by law; or

(c) the commission of the offense was authorized, requested, commanded, performed or recklessly tolerated by the board of directors or by a high managerial agent acting in behalf of the corporation within the scope of his office or employment.

(2) When absolute liability is imposed for the commission of an offense, a legislative purpose to impose liability on a corporation shall be assumed, unless the contrary plainly appears.

(3) An unincorporated association may be convicted of the commission of an offense if:

(a) the offense is defined by a statute other than the Code which expressly provides for the liability of such an association and the conduct is performed by an agent of the association acting in behalf of the association within the scope of his office or employment, except that if the law defining the offense designates the agents for whose conduct the association is accountable or the circumstances under which it is accountable, such provisions shall apply; or

(b) the offense consists of an omission to discharge a specific duty of affirmative performance imposed on associations by law.

(4) As used in this Section:

(a) "corporation" does not include an entity organized as or by a governmental agency for the execution of a governmental program;

(b) "agent" means any director, officer, servant, employee or other person authorized to act in behalf of the corporation or association and, in the case of an unincorporated association, a member of such association;

(c) "high managerial agent" means an officer of a corporation or an unincorporated association, or, in the case of a partnership, a partner, or any other agent of a corporation or association having duties of such responsibility that his conduct may fairly be assumed to represent the policy of the corporation or association.

(5) In any prosecution of a corporation or an unincorporated association for the commission of an offense included within the terms of Subsection (1)(a) or Subsection (3)(a) of this Section, other than an offense for which absolute liability has been imposed, it shall be a defense if the defendant proves by a preponderance of evidence that the high managerial agent having supervisory responsibility over the subject matter of the offense employed due diligence to prevent its commission. This paragraph shall not apply if it is plainly inconsistent with the legislative purpose in defining the particular offense.

(6)(a) A person is legally accountable for any conduct he performs or causes to be performed in the name of the corporation or an unincorporated association or in its behalf to the same extent as if it were performed in his own name or behalf.

(b) Whenever a duty to act is imposed by law upon a corporation or an unincorporated association, any agent of the corporation or association having primary responsibility for the discharge of the duty is legally accountable for a reckless omission to perform the required act to the same extent as if the duty were imposed by law directly upon himself.

(c) When a person is convicted of an offense by reason of his legal accountability for the conduct of a corporation or an unincorporated association, he is subject to the sentence authorized by law when a natural person is convicted of an offense of the grade and the degree involved.

Section 2.08 Intoxication.

(1) Except as provided in Subsection (4) of this Section, intoxication of the actor is not a defense unless it negatives an element of the offense.

(2) When recklessness establishes an element of the offense, if the actor, due to self-induced intoxication, is unaware of a risk of which he would have been aware had he been sober, such unawareness is immaterial.

(3) Intoxication does not, in itself, constitute mental disease within the meaning of Section 4.01.

(4) Intoxication which (a) is not self-induced or (b) is pathological is an affirmative defense if by reason of such intoxication the actor at the time of his conduct lacks substantial capacity either to appreciate its criminality [wrongfulness] or to conform his conduct to the requirements of law.

(5) Definitions. In this Section unless a different meaning plainly is required:

(a) "intoxication" means a disturbance of mental or physical capacities resulting from the introduction of substances into the body;

(b) "self-induced intoxication" means intoxication caused by substances which the actor knowingly introduces into his body, the tendency of which to cause intoxication he knows or ought to know, unless he introduces them pursuant to medical advice or under such circumstances as would afford a defense to a charge of crime;

(c) "pathological intoxication" means intoxication grossly excessive in degree, given the amount of the intoxicant, to which the actor does not know he is susceptible.

Section 2.09   Duress.

(1) It is an affirmative defense that the actor engaged in the conduct charged to constitute an offense because he was coerced to do so by the use of, or a threat to use, unlawful force against his person or the person of another, which a person of reasonable firmness in his situation would have been unable to resist.

(2) The defense provided by this Section is unavailable if the actor recklessly placed himself in a situation in which it was probable that he would be subjected to duress. The defense is also unavailable if he was negligent in placing himself in such a situation, whenever negligence suffices to establish culpability for the offense charged.

(3) It is not a defense that a woman acted on the command of her husband, unless she acted under such coercion as would establish a defense under this Section. [The presumption that a woman, acting in the presence of her husband, is coerced is abolished.]

(4) When the conduct of the actor would otherwise be justifiable under Section 3.02, this Section does not preclude such defense.

Section 2.10   Military Orders.

It is an affirmative defense that the actor, in engaging in the conduct charged to constitute an offense, does no more than execute an order of his superior in the armed services which he does not know to be unlawful.

Section 2.11   Consent.

(1) In General. The consent of the victim to conduct charged to constitute an offense or to the result thereof is a defense if such consent negatives an element of the offense or precludes the infliction of the harm or evil sought to be prevented by the law defining the offense.

(2) Consent to Bodily Injury. When conduct is charged to constitute an offense because it causes or threatens bodily injury, consent to such conduct or to the infliction of such injury is a defense if:

(a) the bodily injury consented to or threatened by the conduct consented to is not serious; or

(b) the conduct and the injury are reasonably foreseeable hazards of joint participation in a lawful athletic contest or competitive sport or other concerted activity not forbidden by law; or

(c) the consent establishes a justification for the conduct under Article 3 of the Code.

(3) Ineffective Consent. Unless otherwise provided by the Code or by the law defining the offense, assent does not constitute consent if:

(a) it is given by a person who is legally incompetent to authorize the conduct charged to constitute the offense; or

(b) it is given by a person who by reason of youth, mental disease or defect or intoxication is manifestly unable or known by the actor to be unable to make a reasonable judgment as to the nature or harmfulness of the conduct charged to constitute the offense; or

(c) it is given by a person whose improvident consent is sought to be prevented by the law defining the offense; or

(d) it is induced by force, duress or deception of a kind sought to be prevented by the law defining the offense.

Section 2.12 De Minimis Infractions.

The Court shall dismiss a prosecution if, having regard to the nature of the conduct charged to constitute an offense and the nature of the attendant circumstances, it finds that the defendant's conduct:

(1) was within a customary license or tolerance, neither expressly negatived by the person whose interest was infringed nor inconsistent with the purpose of the law defining the offense; or

(2) did not actually cause or threaten the harm or evil sought to be prevented by the law defining the offense or did so only to an extent too trivial to warrant the condemnation of conviction; or

(3) presents such other extenuations that it cannot reasonably be regarded as envisaged by the legislature in forbidding the offense.

The Court shall not dismiss a prosecution under Subsection (3) of this Section without filing a written statement of its reasons.

Section 2.13 Entrapment.

(1) A public law enforcement official or a person acting in cooperation with such an official perpetrates an entrapment if for the purpose of obtaining evidence of the commission of an offense, he induces or encourages another person to engage in conduct constituting such offense by either:

(a) making knowingly false representations designed to induce the belief that such conduct is not prohibited; or

(b) employing methods of persuasion or inducement which create a substantial risk that such an offense will be committed by persons other than those who are ready to commit it.

(2) Except as provided in Subsection (3) of this Section, a person prosecuted for an offense shall be acquitted if he proves by a preponderance of evidence that his conduct occurred in response to an entrapment. The issue of entrapment shall be tried by the Court in the absence of the jury.

(3) The defense afforded by this Section is unavailable when causing or threatening bodily injury is an element of the offense charged and the prosecution is based on conduct causing or threatening such injury to a person other than the person perpetrating the entrapment.

ARTICLE 3. GENERAL PRINCIPLES OF JUSTIFICATION

Section 3.01 Justification an Affirmative Defense; Civil Remedies Unaffected.

(1) In any prosecution based on conduct which is justifiable under this Article, justification is an affirmative defense.

(2) The fact that conduct is justifiable under this Article does not abolish or impair any remedy for such conduct which is available in any civil action.

Section 3.02 Justification Generally: Choice of Evils.

(1) Conduct which the actor believes to be necessary to avoid a harm or evil to himself or to another is justifiable, provided that:

(a) the harm or evil sought to be avoided by such conduct is greater than that sought to be prevented by the law defining the offense charged; and

(b) neither the Code nor other law defining the offense provides exceptions or defenses dealing with the specific situation involved; and

(c) a legislative purpose to exclude the justification claimed does not otherwise plainly appear.

(2) When the actor was reckless or negligent in bringing about the situation requiring a choice of harms or evils or in appraising the necessity for his conduct, the justification afforded by this Section is unavailable in a prosecution for any offense for which recklessness or negligence, as the case may be, suffices to establish culpability.

Section 3.03 Execution of Public Duty.

(1) Except as provided in Subsection (2) of this Section, conduct is justifiable when it is required or authorized by:

(a) the law defining the duties or functions of a public officer or the assistance to be rendered to such officer in the performance of his duties; or

(b) the law governing the execution of legal process; or

(c) the judgment or order of a competent court or tribunal; or

(d) the law governing the armed services or the lawful conduct of war; or

(e) any other provision of law imposing a public duty.

(2) The other sections of this Article apply to:

(a) the use of force upon or toward the person of another for any of the purposes dealt with in such sections; and

(b) the use of deadly force for any purpose, unless the use of such force is otherwise expressly authorized by law or occurs in the lawful conduct of war.

(3) The justification afforded by Subsection (1) of this Section applies:

(a) when the actor believes his conduct to be required or authorized by the judgment or direction of a competent court or tribunal or in the lawful execution of legal process, notwithstanding lack of jurisdiction of the court or defect in the legal process; and

(b) when the actor believes his conduct to be required or authorized to assist a public officer in the performance of his duties, notwithstanding that the officer exceeded his legal authority.

Section 3.04 Use of Force in Self-Protection.

(1) Use of Force Justifiable for Protection of the Person. Subject to the provisions of this Section and of Section 3.09, the use of force upon or toward another person is justifiable when the actor believes that such force is immediately necessary for the purpose of protecting himself against the use of unlawful force by such other person on the present occasion.

(2) Limitations on Justifying Necessity for Use of Force.

(a) The use of force is not justifiable under this Section:

(i) to resist an arrest which the actor knows is being made by a peace officer, although the arrest is unlawful; or

(ii) to resist force used by the occupier or possessor of property or by another person on his behalf, where the actor knows that the person using the force is doing so under a claim of right to protect the property, except that this limitation shall not apply if:

(1) the actor is a public officer acting in the performance of his duties or a person lawfully assisting him therein or a person making or assisting in a lawful arrest; or

(2) the actor has been unlawfully dispossessed of the property and is making a re-entry or recaption justified by Section 3.06; or

(3) the actor believes that such force is necessary to protect himself against death or serious bodily harm.

(b) The use of deadly force is not justifiable under this Section unless the actor believes that such force is necessary to protect himself against death, serious bodily harm, kidnapping or sexual intercourse compelled by force or threat; nor is it justifiable if:

(i) the actor, with the purpose of causing death or serious bodily harm, provoked the use of force against himself in the same encounter; or

(ii) the actor knows that he can avoid the necessity of using such force with complete safety by retreating or by surrendering possession of a thing to a person asserting a claim of right thereto or by complying with a demand that he abstain from any action which he has no duty to take, except that:

(1) the actor is not obliged to retreat from his dwelling or place of work, unless he was the initial aggressor or is assailed in his place of work by another person whose place of work the actor knows it to be; and

(2) a public officer justified in using force in the performance of his duties or a person justified in using force in his assistance or a person justified in using force in making an arrest or preventing an escape is not obliged to desist from efforts to perform such duty, effect such arrest or prevent such escape because of resistance or threatened resistance by or on behalf of the person against whom such action is directed.

(c) Except as required by paragraphs (a) and (b) of this Subsection, a person employing protective force may estimate the necessity thereof under the circumstances as he believes them to be when the force is used, without retreating, surrendering possession, doing any other act which he has no legal duty to do or abstaining from any lawful action.

(3) Use of Confinement as Protective Force. The justification afforded by this Section extends to the use of confinement as protective force only if the actor takes all reasonable measures to terminate the confinement as soon as he knows that he safely can,

unless the person confined has been arrested on a charge of crime.

Section 3.05 Use of Force for the Protection of Other Persons.

(1) Subject to the provisions of this Section and of Section 3.09, the use of force upon or toward the person of another is justifiable to protect a third person when:

(a) the actor would be justified under Section 3.04 in using such force to protect himself against the injury he believes to be threatened to the person whom he seeks to protect; and

(b) under the circumstances as the actor believes them to be, the person whom he seeks to protect would be justified in using such protective force; and

(c) the actor believes that his intervention is necessary for the protection of such other person.

(2) Notwithstanding Subsection (1) of this Section:

(a) when the actor would be obliged under Section 3.04 to retreat, to surrender the possession of a thing or to comply with a demand before using force in self-protection, he is not obliged to do so before using force for the protection of another person, unless he knows that he can thereby secure the complete safety of such other person; and

(b) when the person whom the actor seeks to protect would be obliged under Section 3.04 to retreat, to surrender the possession of a thing or to comply with a demand if he knew that he could obtain complete safety by so doing, the actor is obliged to try to cause him to do so before using force in his protection if the actor knows that he can obtain complete safety in that way; and

(c) neither the actor nor the person whom he seeks to protect is obliged to retreat when in the other's dwelling or place of work to any greater extent than in his own.

Section 3.06 Use of Force for the Protection of Property.

(1) Use of Force Justifiable for Protection of Property. Subject to the provisions of this Section and of Section 3.09, the use of force upon or toward the person of another is justifiable when the actor believes that such force is immediately necessary:

(a) to prevent or terminate an unlawful entry or other trespass upon land or a trespass against or the unlawful carrying away of tangible, movable property, provided that such land or movable property is, or is believed by the actor to be, in his possession or in the possession of another person for whose protection he acts; or

(b) to effect an entry or re-entry upon land or to retake tangible movable property, provided that the actor believes that he or the person by whose authority he acts or a person from whom he or such other person derives title was unlawfully dispossessed of such land or movable property and is entitled to possession, and provided, further, that:

(i) the force is used immediately or on fresh pursuit after such dispossession; or

(ii) the actor believes that the person against whom he uses force has no claim of right to the possession of the property and, in the case of land, the circumstances, as the actor believes them to be, are of such urgency that it would be an exceptional hardship to postpone the entry or re-entry until a court order is obtained.

(2) *Meaning of Possession.* For the purposes of Subsection (1) of this Section:

(a) a person who has parted with the custody of property to another who refuses to restore it to him is no longer in possession, unless the property is movable and was and still is located on land in his possession;

(b) a person who has been dispossessed of land does not regain possession thereof merely by setting foot thereon;

(c) a person who has a license to use or occupy real property is deemed to be in possession thereof except against the licensor acting under claim of right.

(3) *Limitations on Justifiable Use of Force.*

(a) *Request to Desist.* The use of force is justifiable under this Section only if the actor first requests the person against whom such force is used to desist from his interference with the property, unless the actor believes that:

(i) such request would be useless; or

(ii) it would be dangerous to himself or another person to make the request; or

(iii) substantial harm will be done to the physical condition of the property which is sought to be protected before the request can effectively be made.

(b) *Exclusion of Trespasser.* The use of force to prevent or terminate a trespass is not justifiable under this Section if the actor knows that the exclusion of the trespasser will expose him to substantial danger of serious bodily harm.

(c) *Resistance of Lawful Re-entry or Re-caption.* The use of force to prevent an entry or re-entry upon land or the recaption of movable property is not justifiable under this Section, although the actor believes that such re-entry or recaption is unlawful, if:

(i) the re-entry or recaption is made by or on behalf of a person who was actually dispossessed of the property; and

(ii) it is otherwise justifiable under paragraph (1)(b) of this Section.

(d) *Use of Deadly Force.* The use of deadly force is not justifiable under this Section unless the actor believes that:

(i) the person against whom the force is used is attempting to dispossess him of his dwelling otherwise than under a claim of right to its possession; or

(ii) the person against whom the force is used is attempting to commit or consummate arson, burglary, robbery or other felonious theft or property destruction and either:

(1) has employed or threatened deadly force against or in the presence of the actor; or

(2) the use of force other than deadly force to prevent the commission or the consummation of the crime would expose the actor or another in his presence to substantial danger of serious bodily harm.

(4) Use of Confinement as Protective Force. The justification afforded by this Section extends to the use of confinement as protective force only if the actor takes all reasonable measures to terminate the confinement as soon as he knows that he can do so with safety to the property, unless the person confined has been arrested on a charge of crime.

(5) Use of Device to Protect Property. The justification afforded by this Section extends to the use of a device for the purpose of protecting property only if:

(a) the device is not designed to cause or known to create a substantial risk of causing death or serious bodily harm; and

(b) the use of the particular device to protect the property from entry or trespass is reasonable under the circumstances, as the actor believes them to be; and

(c) the device is one customarily used for such a purpose or reasonable care is taken to make known to probable intruders the fact that it is used.

(6) Use of Force to Pass Wrongful Obstructor. The use of force to pass a person whom the actor believes to be purposely or knowingly and unjustifiably obstructing the actor from going to a place to which he may lawfully go is justifiable, provided that:

(a) the actor believes that the person against whom he uses force has no claim of right to obstruct the actor; and

(b) the actor is not being obstructed from entry or movement on land which he knows to be in the possession or custody of the person obstructing him, or in the possession or custody of another person by whose authority the obstructor acts, unless the circumstances, as the actor believes them to be, are of such urgency that it would not be reasonable to postpone the entry or movement on such land until a court order is obtained; and

(c) the force used is not greater than would be justifiable if the person obstructing the actor were using force against him to prevent his passage.

Section 3.07 Use of Force in Law Enforcement.

(1) Use of Force Justifiable to Effect an Arrest. Subject to the provisions of this Section and of Section 3.09, the use of force upon or toward the person of another is justifiable when the actor is making or assisting in making an arrest and the actor believes that such force is immediately necessary to effect a lawful arrest.

(2) Limitations on the Use of Force.

(a) The use of force is not justifiable under this Section unless:

(i) the actor makes known the purpose of the arrest or believes that it is otherwise known by or cannot reasonably be made known to the person to be arrested; and

(ii) when the arrest is made

under a warrant, the warrant is valid or believed by the actor to be valid.

(b) The use of deadly force is not justifiable under this Section unless:

(i) the arrest is for a felony; and

(ii) the person effecting the arrest is authorized to act as a peace officer or is assisting a person whom he believes to be authorized to act as a peace officer; and

(iii) the actor believes that the force employed creates no substantial risk of injury to innocent persons; and

(iv) the actor believes that:

(1) the crime for which the arrest is made involved conduct including the use or threatened use of deadly force; or

(2) there is a substantial risk that the person to be arrested will cause death or serious bodily harm if his apprehension is delayed.

(3) Use of Force to Prevent Escape from Custody. The use of force to prevent the escape of an arrested person from custody is justifiable when the force could justifiably have been employed to effect the arrest under which the person is in custody, except that a guard or other person authorized to act as a peace officer is justified in using any force, including deadly force, which he believes to be immediately necessary to prevent the escape of a person from a jail, prison, or other institution for the detention of persons charged with or convicted of a crime.

(4) Use of Force by Private Person Assisting an Unlawful Arrest.

(a) A private person who is summoned by a peace officer to assist in effecting an unlawful arrest, is justified in using any force which he would be justified in using if the arrest were lawful provided that he does not believe the arrest is unlawful.

(b) A private person who assists another private person in effecting an unlawful arrest, or who, not being summoned, assists a peace officer in effecting an unlawful arrest, is justified in using any force which he would be justified in using if the arrest were lawful, provided that (i) he believes the arrest is lawful, and (ii) the arrest would be lawful if the facts were as he believes them to be.

(5) Use of Force to Prevent Suicide or the Commission of a Crime.

(a) The use of force upon or toward the person of another is justifiable when the actor believes that such force is immediately necessary to prevent such other person from committing suicide, inflicting serious bodily harm upon himself, committing or consummating the commission of a crime involving or threatening bodily harm, damage to or loss of property or a breach of the peace, except that:

(i) any limitations imposed by the other provisions of this Article on the justifiable use of force in self-protection, for the protection of others, the protection of property, the effectuation of an arrest or the prevention of an escape from custody shall apply notwithstanding the criminality of the conduct against which such force is used; and

(ii) the use of deadly force is not in any event justifiable under this Subsection unless:

(1) the actor believes that there is a substantial risk that the person whom he seeks to prevent from committing a crime will cause death or serious bodily harm to another unless the commission or the consummation of the crime is prevented and that the use of such force presents no substantial risk of injury to innocent persons; or

(2) the actor believes that the use of such force is necessary to suppress a riot or mutiny after the rioters or mutineers have been ordered to disperse and warned, in any particular manner that the law may require, that such force will be used if they do not obey.

(b) The justification afforded by this Subsection extends to the use of confinement as preventive force only if the actor takes all reasonable measures to terminate the confinement as soon as he knows that he safely can, unless the person confined has been arrested on a charge of crime.

Section 3.08 Use of Force by Persons With Special Responsibility for Care, Discipline or Safety of Others.

The use of force upon or toward the person of another is justifiable if:

(1) the actor is the parent or guardian or other person similarly responsible for the general care and supervision of a minor or a person acting at the request of such parent, guardian or other responsible person and:

(a) the force is used for the purpose of safeguarding or promoting the welfare of the minor, including the prevention or punishment of his misconduct; and

(b) the force used is not designed to cause or known to create a substantial risk of causing death, serious bodily harm, disfigurement, extreme pain or mental distress or gross degradation; or

(2) the actor is a teacher or a person otherwise entrusted with the care or supervision for a special purpose of a minor and:

(a) the actor believes that the force used is necessary to further such special purpose, including the maintenance of reasonable discipline in a school, class or other group, and that the use of such force is consistent with the welfare of the minor; and

(b) the degree of force, if it had been used by the parent or guardian of the minor, would not be unjustifiable under Subsection (1)(b) of this Section; or

(3) the actor is the guardian or other person similarly responsible for the general care and supervision of an incompetent person; and:

(a) the force is used for the purpose of safeguarding or promoting the welfare of the incompetent person, including the prevention of his misconduct, or, when such incompetent person is in a hospital or other institution for his care and custody, for the maintenance of reasonable discipline in such institution; and

(b) the force used is not designed to cause or known to create a substantial risk of causing death, serious bodily harm, disfigurement, extreme or unnecessary pain, mental distress, or humiliation; or

(4) the actor is a doctor or other therapist or a person assisting him at his direction, and:

(a) the force is used for the purpose of administering a recognized form of treatment which the actor believes to be adapted to promoting the physical or mental health of the patient; and

(b) the treatment is administered with the consent of the patient or, if the patient is a minor or an incompetent person, with the consent of his parent or guardian or other person legally competent to consent in his behalf, or the treatment is administered in an emergency when the actor believes that no one competent to consent can be consulted and that a reasonable person, wishing to safeguard the welfare of the patient, would consent; or

(5) the actor is a warden or other authorized official of a correctional institution, and:

(a) he believes that the force used is necessary for the purpose of enforcing the lawful rules or procedures of the institution, unless his belief in the lawfulness of the rule or procedure sought to be enforced is erroneous and his error is due to ignorance or mistake as to the provisions of the Code, any other provision of the criminal law or the law governing the administration of the institution; and

(b) the nature or degree of force used is not forbidden by Article 303 or 304 of the Code; and

(c) if deadly force is used, its use is otherwise justifiable under this Article; or

(6) the actor is a person responsible for the safety of a vessel or an aircraft or a person acting at his direction, and

(a) he believes that the force used is necessary to prevent interference with the operation of the vessel or aircraft or obstruction of the execution of a lawful order, unless his belief in the lawfulness of the order is erroneous and his error is due to ignorance or mistake as to the law defining his authority; and

(b) if deadly force is used, its use is otherwise justifiable under this Article; or

(7) the actor is a person who is authorized or required by law to maintain order or decorum in a vehicle, train or other carrier or in a place where others are assembled, and:

(a) he believes that the force used is necessary for such purpose; and

(b) the force used is not designed to cause or known to create a substantial risk of causing death, bodily harm, or extreme mental distress.

Section 3.09 Mistake of Law as to Unlawfulness of Force or Legality of Arrest; Reckless or Negligent Use of Otherwise Justifiable Force; Reckless or Negligent Injury or Risk of Injury to Innocent Persons.

(1) The justification afforded by

Sections 3.04 to 3.07, inclusive, is unavailable when:

(a) the actor's belief in the unlawfulness of the force or conduct against which he employs protective force or his belief in the lawfulness of an arrest which he endeavors to effect by force is erroneous; and

(b) his error is due to ignorance or mistake as to the provisions of the Code, any other provision of the criminal law or the law governing the legality of an arrest or search.

(2) When the actor believes that the use of force upon or toward the person of another is necessary for any of the purposes for which such belief would establish a justification under Sections 3.03 to 3.08 but the actor is reckless or negligent in having such belief or in acquiring or failing to acquire any knowledge or belief which is material to the justifiability of his use of force, the justification afforded by those Sections is unavailable in a prosecution for an offense for which recklessness or negligence, as the case may be, suffices to establish culpability.

(3) When the actor is justified under Sections 3.03 to 3.08 in using force upon or toward the person of another but he recklessly or negligently injures or creates a risk of injury to innocent persons, the justification afforded by those Sections is unavailable in a prosecution for such recklessness or negligence towards innocent persons.

Section 3.10 Justification in Property Crimes.

Conduct involving the appropriation, seizure or destruction of, damage to, intrusion on or interference with property is justifiable under circumstances which would establish a defense of privilege in a civil action based thereon, unless:

(1) the Code or the law defining the offense deals with the specific situation involved; or

(2) a legislative purpose to exclude the justification claimed otherwise plainly appears.

Section 3.11 Definitions.

In this Article, unless a different meaning plainly is required:

(1) "unlawful force" means force, including confinement, which is employed without the consent of the person against whom it is directed and the employment of which constitutes an offense or actionable tort or would constitute such offense or tort except for a defense (such as the absence of intent, negligence, or mental capacity; duress; youth; or diplomatic status) not amounting to a privilege to use the force. Assent constitutes consent, within the meaning of this Section, whether or not it otherwise is legally effective, except assent to the infliction of death or serious bodily harm.

(2) "deadly force" means force which the actor uses with the purpose of causing or which he knows to create a substantial risk of causing death or serious bodily harm. Purposely firing a firearm in the direction of another person or at a vehicle in which another person is believed to be constitutes deadly force. A threat to cause death or serious bodily harm, by the production of a weapon or otherwise, so long as the actor's purpose is limited to creating an apprehension that he will use deadly force if necessary, does not constitute deadly force;

(3) "dwelling" means any building or structure, though movable or temporary, or a portion thereof, which is for the time being the actor's home or place of lodging.

ARTICLE 4. RESPONSIBILITY

Section 4.01 Mental Disease or Defect Excluding Responsibility.

(1) A person is not responsible for criminal conduct if at the time of such conduct as a result of mental disease or defect he lacks substantial capacity either to appreciate the criminality [wrongfulness] of his conduct or to conform his conduct to the requirements of law.

(2) As used in this Article, the terms "mental disease or defect" do not include an abnormality manifested only by repeated criminal or otherwise anti-social conduct.

Section 4.02 Evidence of Mental Disease or Defect Admissible When Relevant to Element of the Offense; [Mental Disease or Defect Impairing Capacity as Ground for Mitigation of Punishment in Capital Cases].

(1) Evidence that the defendant suffered from a mental disease or defect is admissible whenever it is relevant to prove that the defendant did or did not have a state of mind which is an element of the offense.

[(2) Whenever the jury or the Court is authorized to determine or to recommend whether or not the defendant shall be sentenced to death or imprisonment upon conviction, evidence that the capacity of the defendant to appreciate the criminality [wrongfulness] of his conduct or to conform his conduct to the requirements of law was impaired as a result of mental disease or defect is admissible in favor of sentence of imprisonment.]

Section 4.03 Mental Disease or Defect Excluding Responsibility is Affirmative Defense; Requirement of Notice; Form of Verdict and Judgment When Finding of Irresponsibility is Made.

(1) Mental disease or defect excluding responsibility is an affirmative defense.

(2) Evidence of mental disease or defect excluding responsibility is not admissible unless the defendant, at the time of entering his plea of not guilty or within ten days thereafter or at such later time as the Court may for good cause permit, files a written notice of his purpose to rely on such defense.

(3) When the defendant is acquitted on the ground of mental disease or defect excluding responsibility, the verdict and the judgment shall so state.

Section 4.04 Mental Disease or Defect Excluding Fitness to Proceed.

No person who as a result of mental disease or defect lacks capacity to understand the proceedings against him or to assist in his own defense shall be tried, convicted or sentenced for the commission of an offense so long as such incapacity endures.

Section 4.05 Psychiatric Examination of Defendant With Respect to Mental Disease or Defect.

(1) Whenever the defendant has filed a notice of intention to rely on

the defense of mental disease or defect excluding responsibility, or there is reason to doubt his fitness to proceed, or reason to believe that mental disease or defect of the defendant will otherwise become an issue in the cause, the Court shall appoint at least one qualified psychiatrist or shall request the Superintendent of the Hospital to designate at least one qualified psychiatrist, which designation may be or include himself, to examine and report upon the mental condition of the defendant. The Court may order the defendant to be committed to a hospital or other suitable facility for the purpose of the examination for a period of not exceeding sixty days or such longer period as the Court determines to be necessary for the purpose and may direct that a qualified psychiatrist retained by the defendant be permitted to witness and participate in the examination.

(2) In such examination any method may be employed which is accepted by the medical profession for the examination of those alleged to be suffering from mental disease or defect.

(3) The report of the examination shall include the following: (a) a description of the nature of the examination; (b) a diagnosis of the mental condition of the defendant; (c) if the defendant suffers from a mental disease or defect, an opinion as to his capacity to understand the proceedings against him and to assist in his own defense; (d) when a notice of intention to rely on the defense of irresponsibility has been filed, an opinion as to the extent, if any, to which the capacity of the defendant to appreciate the criminality [wrongfulness] of his conduct or to conform his conduct to the requirements of law was impaired at the time of the criminal conduct charged; and (e) when directed by the Court, an opinion as to the capacity of the defendant to have a particular state of mind which is an element of the offense charged.

If the examination can not be conducted by reason of the unwillingness of the defendant to participate therein, the report shall so state and shall include, if possible, an opinion as to whether such unwillingness of the defendant was the result of mental disease or defect.

The report of the examination shall be filed [in triplicate] with the clerk of the Court, who shall cause copies to be delivered to the district attorney and to counsel for the defendant.

Section 4.06 Determination of Fitness to Proceed; Effect of Finding of Unfitness; Proceedings if Fitness is Regained [; Post-Commitment Hearing].

(1) When the defendant's fitness to proceed is drawn in question, the issue shall be determined by the Court. If neither the prosecuting attorney nor counsel for the defendant contests the finding of the report filed pursuant to Section 4.05, the Court may make the determination on the basis of such report. If the finding is contested, the Court shall hold a hearing on the issue. If the report is received in evidence upon such hearing, the party who contests the finding thereof shall have the right to summon and to cross-examine the psychiatrists who joined in the report and to offer evidence upon the issue.

(2) If the Court determines that the defendant lacks fitness to proceed, the proceeding against him shall be suspended, except as provided in Subsection (3) [Subsections (3) and (4)] of this Section, and the Court shall commit him to the custody of the

Commissioner of Mental Hygiene [Public Health or Correction] to be placed in an appropriate institution of the Department of Mental Hygiene [Public Health or Correction] for so long as such unfitness shall endure. When the Court, on its own motion or upon the application of the Commissioner of Mental Hygiene [Public Health or Correction] or the prosecuting attorney, determines, after a hearing if a hearing is requested, that the defendant has regained fitness to proceed, the proceeding shall be resumed. If, however, the Court is of the view that so much time has elapsed since the commitment of the defendant that it would be unjust to resume the criminal proceeding, the Court may dismiss the charge and may order the defendant to be discharged or, subject to the law governing the civil commitment of persons suffering from mental disease or defect, order the defendant to be committed to an appropriate institution of the Department of Mental Hygiene [Public Health].

(3) The fact that the defendant is unfit to proceed does not preclude any legal objection to the prosecution which is susceptible of fair determination prior to trial and without the personal participation of the defendant.

[Alternative: (3) At any time within ninety days after commitment as provided in Subsection (2) of this Section, or at any later time with permission of the Court granted for good cause, the defendant or his counsel or the Commissioner of Mental Hygiene [Public Health or Correction] may apply for a special post-commitment hearing. If the application is made by or on behalf of a defendant not represented by counsel, he shall be afforded a reasonable opportunity to obtain counsel, and if he lacks funds to do so, counsel shall be assigned by the Court. The application shall be granted only if the counsel for the defendant satisfies the Court by affidavit or otherwise that as an attorney he has reasonable grounds for a good faith belief that his client has, on the facts and the law, a defense to the charge other than mental disease or defect excluding responsibility.

[(4) If the motion for a special post-commitment hearing is granted, the hearing shall be by the Court without a jury. No evidence shall be offered at the hearing by either party on the issue of mental disease or defect as a defense to, or in mitigation of, the crime charged. After hearing, the Court may in an appropriate case quash the indictment or other charge, or find it to be defective or insufficient, or determine that it is not proved beyond a reasonable doubt by the evidence, or otherwise terminate the proceedings on the evidence or the law. In any such case, unless all defects in the proceedings are promptly cured, the Court shall terminate the commitment ordered under Subsection (2) of this Section and order the defendant to be discharged or, subject to the law governing the civil commitment of persons suffering from mental disease or defect, order the defendant to be committed to an appropriate institution of the Department of Mental Hygiene [Public Health].]

Section 4.07 Determination of Irresponsibility on Basis of Report; Access to Defendant by Psychiatrist of His Own Choice; Form of Expert Testimony When Issue of Responsibility is Tried.

(1) If the report filed pursuant to Section 4.05 finds that the defendant

at the time of the criminal conduct charged suffered from a mental disease or defect which substantially impaired his capacity to appreciate the criminality [wrongfulness] of his conduct or to conform his conduct to the requirements of law, and the Court, after a hearing if a hearing is requested by the prosecuting attorney or the defendant, is satisfied that such impairment was sufficient to exclude responsibility, the Court on motion of the defendant shall enter judgment of acquittal on the ground of mental disease or defect excluding responsibility.

(2) When, notwithstanding the report filed pursuant to Section 4.05, the defendant wishes to be examined by a qualified psychiatrist or other expert of his own choice, such examiner shall be permitted to have reasonable access to the defendant for the purposes of such examination.

(3) Upon the trial, the psychiatrists who reported pursuant to Section 4.05 may be called as witnesses by the prosecution, the defendant or the Court. If the issue is being tried before a jury, the jury may be informed that the psychiatrists were designated by the Court or by the Superintendent of the Hospital at the request of the Court as the case may be. If called by the Court, the witness shall be subject to cross-examination by the prosecution and by the defendant. Both the prosecution and the defendant may summon any other qualified psychiatrist or other expert to testify, but no one who has not examined the defendant shall be competent to testify to an expert opinion with respect to the mental condition or responsibility of the defendant, as distinguished from the validity of the procedure followed by, or the general scientific propositions stated by, another witness.

(4) When a psychiatrist or other expert who has examined the defendant testifies concerning his mental condition, he shall be permitted to make a statement as to the nature of his examination, his diagnosis of the mental condition of the defendant at the time of the commission of the offense charged and his opinion as to the extent, if any, to which the capacity of the defendant to appreciate the criminality [wrongfulness] of his conduct or to conform his conduct to the requirements of law or to have a particular state of mind which is an element of the offense charged was impaired as a result of mental disease or defect at that time. He shall be permitted to make any explanation reasonably serving to clarify his diagnosis and opinion and may be cross-examined as to any matter bearing on his competency or credibility or the validity of his diagnosis or opinion.

Section 4.08 Legal Effect of Acquittal on the Ground of Mental Disease or Defect Excluding Responsibility; Commitment; Release or Discharge.

(1) When a defendant is acquitted on the ground of mental disease or defect excluding responsibility, the Court shall order him to be committed to the custody of the Commissioner of Mental Hygiene [Public Health] to be placed in an appropriate institution for custody, care and treatment.

(2) If the Commissioner of Mental Hygiene [Public Health] is of the view that a person committed to his custody, pursuant to paragraph (1) of this Section, may be discharged or released on condition without danger to himself or to others, he shall make application for the discharge or release of such person in a report to the

Court by which such person was committed and shall transmit a copy of such application and report to the prosecuting attorney of the county [parish] from which the defendant was committed. The Court shall thereupon appoint at least two qualified psychiatrists to examine such person and to report within sixty days, or such longer period as the Court determines to be necessary for the purpose, their opinion as to his mental condition. To facilitate such examination and the proceedings thereon, the Court may cause such person to be confined in any institution located near the place where the Court sits, which may hereafter be designated by the Commissioner of Mental Hygiene [Public Health] as suitable for the temporary detention of irresponsible persons.

(3) If the Court is satisfied by the report filed pursuant to paragraph (2) of this Section and such testimony of the reporting psychiatrists as the Court deems necessary that the committed person may be discharged or released on condition without danger to himself or others, the Court shall order his discharge or his release on such conditions as the Court determines to be necessary. If the Court is not so satisfied, it shall promptly order a hearing to determine whether such person may safely be discharged or released. Any such hearing shall be deemed a civil proceeding and the burden shall be upon the committed person to prove that he may safely be discharged or released. According to the determination of the Court upon the hearing, the committed person shall thereupon be discharged or released on such conditions as the Court determines to be necessary, or shall be recommitted to the custody of the Commissioner of Mental Hygiene [Public Health], subject to discharge or release only in accordance with the procedure prescribed above for a first hearing.

(4) If, within [five] years after the conditional release of a committed person, the Court shall determine, after hearing evidence, that the conditions of release have not been fulfilled and that for the safety of such person or for the safety of others his conditional release should be revoked, the Court shall forthwith order him to be recommitted to the Commissioner of Mental Hygiene [Public Health], subject to discharge or release only in accordance with the procedure prescribed above for a first hearing.

(5) A committed person may make application for his discharge or release to the Court by which he was committed, and the procedure to be followed upon such application shall be the same as that prescribed above in the case of an application by the Commissioner of Mental Hygiene [Public Health]. However, no such application by a committed person need be considered until he has been confined for a period of not less than [six months] from the date of the order of commitment, and if the determination of the Court be adverse to the application, such person shall not be permitted to file a further application until [one year] has elapsed from the date of any preceding hearing on an application for his release or discharge.

Section 4.09 Statements for Purposes of Examination or Treatment Inadmissible Except on Issue of Mental Condition.

A statement made by a person subjected to psychiatric examination or treatment pursuant to Sections 4.05, 4.06 or 4.08 for the purposes of such examination or treatment shall not be admissible in evidence against him in any criminal proceeding on any issue other than that of his mental condition but it shall be admissible upon that issue, whether or not it would otherwise be deemed a privileged communication [, unless such statement constitutes an admission of guilt of the crime charged].

Section 4.10 Immaturity Excluding Criminal Conviction; Transfer of Proceedings to Juvenile Court.

(1) A person shall not be tried for or convicted of an offense if:

(a) at the time of the conduct charged to constitute the offense he was less than sixteen years of age [, in which case the Juvenile Court shall have exclusive jurisdiction*]; or

(b) at the time of the conduct charged to constitute the offense he was sixteen or seventeen years of age unless:

(i) the Juvenile Court has no jurisdiction over him, or,

(ii) the Juvenile Court has entered an order waiving jurisdiction and consenting to the institution of criminal proceedings against him.

(2) No court shall have jurisdiction to try or convict a person of an offense if criminal proceedings against him are barred by Subsection (1) of this Section. When it appears that a person charged with the commission of an offense may be of such an age that criminal proceedings may be barred under Subsection (1) of this Section, the Court shall hold a hearing thereon, and the burden shall be on the prosecution to establish to the satisfaction of the Court that the criminal proceeding is not barred upon such grounds. If the Court determines that the proceeding is barred, custody of the person charged shall be surrendered to the Juvenile Court, and the case, including all papers and processes relating thereto, shall be transferred.

ARTICLE 5. INCHOATE CRIMES

Section 5.01 Criminal Attempt.

(1) Definition of Attempt. A person is guilty of an attempt to commit a crime if, acting with the kind of culpability otherwise required for commission of the crime, he:

(a) purposely engages in conduct which would constitute the crime if the attendant circumstances were as he believes them to be; or

(b) when causing a particular result is an element of the crime, does or omits to do anything with the purpose of causing or with the belief that it will cause such result without further conduct on his part; or

(c) purposely does or omits to do anything which, under the circumstances as he believes them to be, is an act or omission constituting a substantial step in a course of conduct planned to culminate in his commission of the crime.

(2) Conduct Which May Be Held Substantial Step Under Subsection (1) (c). Conduct shall not be held to constitute a substantial step under Subsection (1) (c) of this Section unless it is strongly corroborative of the actor's criminal purpose. Without

---

* The bracketed words are unnecessary if the Juvenile Court Act so provides or is amended accordingly.

negativing the sufficiency of other conduct, the following, if strongly corroborative of the actor's criminal purpose, shall not be held insufficient as a matter of law:

(a) lying in wait, searching for or following the contemplated victim of the crime;

(b) enticing or seeking to entice the contemplated victim of the crime to go to the place contemplated for its commission;

(c) reconnoitering the place contemplated for the commission of the crime;

(d) unlawful entry of a structure, vehicle or enclosure in which it is contemplated that the crime will be committed;

(e) possession of materials to be employed in the commission of the crime, which are specially designed for such unlawful use or which can serve no lawful purpose of the actor under the circumstances;

(f) possession, collection or fabrication of materials to be employed in the commission of the crime, at or near the place contemplated for its commission, where such possession, collection or fabrication serves no lawful purpose of the actor under the circumstances;

(g) soliciting an innocent agent to engage in conduct constituting an element of the crime.

(3) Conduct Designed to Aid Another in Commission of a Crime. A person who engages in conduct designed to aid another to commit a crime which would establish his complicity under Section 2.06 if the crime were committed by such other person, is guilty of an attempt to commit the crime, although the crime is not committed or attempted by such other person.

(4) Renunciation of Criminal Purpose. When the actor's conduct would otherwise constitute an attempt under Subsection (1)(b) or (1)(c) of this Section, it is an affirmative defense that he abandoned his effort to commit the crime or otherwise prevented its commission, under circumstances manifesting a complete and voluntary renunciation of his criminal purpose. The establishment of such defense does not, however, affect the liability of an accomplice who did not join in such abandonment or prevention.

Within the meaning of this Article, renunciation of criminal purpose is not voluntary if it is motivated, in whole or in part, by circumstances, not present or apparent at the inception of the actor's course of conduct, which increase the probability of detection or apprehension or which make more difficult the accomplishment of the criminal purpose. Renunciation is not complete if it is motivated by a decision to postpone the criminal conduct until a more advantageous time or to transfer the criminal effort to another but similar objective or victim.

Section 5.02 Criminal Solicitation.

(1) Definition of Solicitation. A person is guilty of solicitation to commit a crime if with the purpose of promoting or facilitating its commission he commands, encourages or requests another person to engage in specific conduct which would constitute such crime or an attempt to commit such crime or which would

establish his complicity in its commission or attempted commission.

(2) Uncommunicated Solicitation. It is immaterial under Subsection (1) of this Section that the actor fails to communicate with the person he solicits to commit a crime if his conduct was designed to effect such communication.

(3) Renunciation of Criminal Purpose. It is an affirmative defense that the actor, after soliciting another person to commit a crime, persuaded him not to do so or otherwise prevented the commission of the crime, under circumstances manifesting a complete and voluntary renunciation of his criminal purpose.

Section 5.03 Criminal Conspiracy.

(1) Definition of Conspiracy. A person is guilty of conspiracy with another person or persons to commit a crime if with the purpose of promoting or facilitating its commission he:

(a) agrees with such other person or persons that they or one or more of them will engage in conduct which constitutes such crime or an attempt or solicitation to commit such crime; or

(b) agrees to aid such other person or persons in the planning or commission of such crime or of an attempt or solicitation to commit such crime.

(2) Scope of Conspiratorial Relationship. If a person guilty of conspiracy, as defined by Subsection (1) of this Section, knows that a person with whom he conspires to commit a crime has conspired with another person or persons to commit the same crime, he is guilty of conspiring with such other person or persons, whether or not he knows their identity, to commit such crime.

(3) Conspiracy With Multiple Criminal Objectives. If a person conspires to commit a number of crimes, he is guilty of only one conspiracy so long as such multiple crimes are the object of the same agreement or continuous conspiratorial relationship.

(4) Joinder and Venue in Conspiracy Prosecutions.

(a) Subject to the provisions of paragraph (b) of this Subsection, two or more persons charged with criminal conspiracy may be prosecuted jointly if:

(i) they are charged with conspiring with one another; or

(ii) the conspiracies alleged, whether they have the same or different parties, are so related that they constitute different aspects of a scheme of organized criminal conduct.

(b) In any joint prosecution under paragraph (a) of this Subsection:

(i) no defendant shall be charged with a conspiracy in any county [parish or district] other than one in which he entered into such conspiracy or in which an overt act pursuant to such conspiracy was done by him or by a person with whom he conspired; and

(ii) neither the liability of any defendant nor the admissibility against him of evidence of acts or declarations of another shall be enlarged by such joinder; and

(iii) the Court shall order a severance or take a special verdict as to any defendant who so requests, if it deems it necessary or appropriate to promote the fair determination of his guilt or innocence, and shall take any other proper measures to protect the fairness of the trial.

(5) Overt Act. No person may be convicted of conspiracy to commit a crime, other than a felony of the first or second degree, unless an overt act in pursuance of such conspiracy is alleged and proved to have been done by him or by a person with whom he conspired.

(6) Renunciation of Criminal Purpose. It is an affirmative defense that the actor, after conspiring to commit a crime, thwarted the success of the conspiracy, under circumstances manifesting a complete and voluntary renunciation of his criminal purpose.

(7) Duration of Conspiracy. For purposes of Section 1.06(4):

(a) conspiracy is a continuing course of conduct which terminates when the crime or crimes which are its object are committed or the agreement that they be committed is abandoned by the defendant and by those with whom he conspired; and

(b) such abandonment is presumed if neither the defendant nor anyone with whom he conspired does any overt act in pursuance of the conspiracy during the applicable period of limitation; and

(c) if an individual abandons the agreement, the conspiracy is terminated as to him only if and when he advises those with whom he conspired of his abandonment or he informs the law enforcement authorities of the existence of the conspiracy and of his participation therein.

Section 5.04 Incapacity, Irresponsibility or Immunity of Party to Solicitation or Conspiracy.

(1) Except as provided in Subsection (2) of this Section, it is immaterial to the liability of a person who solicits or conspires with another to commit a crime that:

(a) he or the person whom he solicits or with whom he conspires does not occupy a particular position or have a particular characteristic which is an element of such crime, if he believes that one of them does; or

(b) the person whom he solicits or with whom he conspires is irresponsible or has an immunity to prosecution or conviction for the commission of the crime.

(2) It is a defense to a charge of solicitation or conspiracy to commit a crime that if the criminal object were achieved, the actor would not be guilty of a crime under the law defining the offense or as an accomplice under Section 2.06(5) or 2.06(6) (a) or (b).

Section 5.05 Grading of Criminal Attempt, Solicitation and Conspiracy; Mitigation in Cases of Lesser Danger; Multiple Convictions Barred.

(1) Grading. Except as otherwise provided in this Section, attempt, solicitation and conspiracy are crimes of the same grade and degree as the most serious offense which is attempted or solicited or is an object of the conspiracy. An attempt, solicitation or conspiracy to commit a [capital crime or a] felony of the first degree is a felony of the second degree.

(2) Mitigation. If the particular conduct charged to constitute a criminal attempt, solicitation or conspiracy is so inherently unlikely to result or culminate in the commission of a crime that neither such conduct nor the actor presets a public danger warranting the grading of such offense under this Section, the Court shall exercise its power under Section 6.12 to enter judgment and impose sentence for a crime of lower grade or degree or, in extreme cases, may dismiss the prosecution.

(3) Multiple Convictions. A person may not be convicted of more than one offense defined by this Article for conduct designed to commit or to culminate in the commission of the same crime.

Section 5.06 Possessing Instruments of Crime; Weapons.

(1) Criminal Instruments Generally. A person commits a misdemeanor if he possesses any instrument of crime with purpose to employ it criminally. "Instrument of crime" means:

(a) anything specially made or specially adapted for criminal use; or

(b) anything commonly used for criminal purposes and possessed by the actor under circumstances which do not negative unlawful purpose.

(2) Presumption of Criminal Purpose from Possession of Weapon. If a person possesses a firearm or other weapon on or about his person, in a vehicle occupied by him, or otherwise readily available for use, it is presumed that he had the purpose to employ it criminally, unless:

(a) the weapon is possessed in the actor's home or place of business;

(b) the actor is licensed or otherwise authorized by law to possess such weapon; or

(c) the weapon is of a type commonly used in lawful sport.

"Weapon" means anything readily capable of lethal use and possessed under circumstances not manifestly appropriate for lawful uses which it may have; the term includes a firearm which is not loaded or lacks a clip or other component to render it immediately operable, and components which can readily be assembled into a weapon.

(3) Presumptions as to Possession of Criminal Instruments in Automobiles. Where a weapon or other instrument of crime is found in an automobile, it shall be presumed to be in the possession of the occupant if there is but one. If there is more than one occupant, it shall be presumed to be in the possession of all, except under the following circumstances:

(a) where it is found upon the person of one of the occupants;

(b) where the automobile is not a stolen one and the weapon or instrument is found out of view in a glove compartment, car trunk, or other enclosed customary depository, in which case it shall be presumed to be in the possession of the occupant or occupants who own or have authority to operate the automobile;

(c) in the case of a taxicab, a weapon or instrument found in the passengers' portion of the vehicle shall be presumed to be in the possession of all the passengers, if there are any, and, if not, in the possession of the driver.

Section 5.07 Prohibited Offensive Weapons.

A person commits a misdemeanor if, except as authorized by law, he makes, repairs, sells, or otherwise deals in, uses, or possesses any offensive weapon. "Offensive weapon" means any bomb, machine gun, sawed-off shotgun, firearm specially made or specially adapted for concealment or silent discharge, any blackjack, sandbag, metal knuckles, dagger, or other implement for the infliction of serious bodily injury which serves no common lawful purpose. It is a defense under this Section for the defendant to prove by a preponderance of evidence that he possessed or dealt with the weapon solely as a curio or in a dramatic performance, or that he possessed it briefly in consequence of having found it or taken it from an aggressor, or under circumstances similarly negativing any purpose or likelihood that the weapon would be used unlawfully. The presumptions provided in Section 5.06(3) are applicable to prosecutions under this Section.

ARTICLE 6. AUTHORIZED DISPOSITION OF OFFENDERS

Section 6.01 Degrees of Felonies.

(1) Felonies defined by this Code are classified, for the purpose of sentence, into three degrees, as follows:

(a) felonies of the first degree;

(b) felonies of the second degree;

(c) felonies of the third degree.

A felony is of the first or second degree when it is so designated by the Code. A crime declared to be a felony, without specification of degree, is of the third degree.

(2) Notwithstanding any other provision of law, a felony defined by any statute of this State other than this Code shall constitute for the purpose of sentence a felony of the third degree.

Section 6.02 Sentence in Accordance With Code; Authorized Dispositions.

(1) No person convicted of an offense shall be sentenced otherwise than in accordance with this Article.

[(2) The Court shall sentence a person who has been convicted of murder to death or imprisonment, in accordance with Section 210.6.]

(3) Except as provided in Subsection (2) of this Section and subject to the applicable provisions of the Code, the Court may suspend the imposition of sentence on a person who has been convicted of a crime, may order him to be committed in lieu of sentence, in accordance with Section 6.13, or may sentence him as follows:

(a) to pay a fine authorized by Section 6.03; or

(b) to be placed on probation [, and, in the case of a person convicted of a felony or misdemeanor to imprisonment for a term fixed by the Court not exceeding thirty days to be served as a condition of probation]; or

(c) to imprisonment for a term authorized by Sections 6.05, 6.06, 6.07, 6.08, 6.09, or 7.06; or

(d) to fine and probation or fine and imprisonment, but not to probation and imprisonment [, except as authorized in paragraph (b) of this Subsection].

(4) The Court may suspend the imposition of sentence on a person who has been convicted of a violation or may sentence him to pay a fine authorized by Section 6.03.

(5) This Article does not deprive the Court of any authority conferred by law to decree a forfeiture of property, suspend or cancel a license, remove a person from office, or impose any other civil penalty. Such a judgment or order may be included in the sentence.

Section 6.03 Fines.

A person who has been convicted of an offense may be sentenced to pay a fine not exceeding:

(1) $10,000, when the conviction is of a felony of the first or second degree;

(2) $5,000, when the conviction is of a felony of the third degree;

(3) $1,000, when the conviction is of a misdemeanor;

(4) $500, when the conviction is of a petty misdemeanor or a violation;

(5) any higher amount equal to double the pecuniary gain derived from the offense by the offender;

(6) any higher amount specifically authorized by statute.

Section 6.04 Penalties Against Corporations and Unincorporated Associations; Forfeiture of Corporate Charter or Revocation of Certificate Authorizing Foreign Corporation to Do Business in the State.

(1) The Court may suspend the sentence of a corporation or an unincorporated association which has been convicted of an offense or may sentence it to pay a fine authorized by Section 6.03.

(2)(a) The [prosecuting attorney] is authorized to institute civil proceedings in the appropriate court of general jurisdiction to forfeit the charter of a corporation organized under the laws of this State or to revoke the certificate authorizing a foreign corporation to conduct business in this State. The Court may order the charter forfeited or the certificate revoked upon finding (i) that the board of directors or a high managerial agent acting in behalf of the corporation has, in conducting the corporation's affairs, purposely engaged in a persistent course of criminal conduct and (ii) that for the prevention of future criminal conduct of the same character, the public interest requires the charter of the corporation to be forfeited and the corporation to be dissolved or the certificate to be revoked.

(b) When a corporation is convicted of a crime or a high managerial agent of a corporation, as defined in Section 2.07, is convicted of a crime committed in the conduct of the affairs of the corporation, the Court, in sentencing the corporation or the agent, may direct the [prosecuting attorney] to institute proceedings authorized by paragraph (a) of this Subsection.

(c) The proceedings authorized by paragraph (a) of this Subsection shall be conducted in accordance with the procedures authorized by law for the involuntary dissolution of a corporation or the revocation of the certificate authorizing a foreign corporation to conduct business in this State. Such proceedings shall be deemed additional to any other proceedings authorized by law for the purpose of forfeiting the charter of a corporation or revoking the certificate of a foreign corporation.

Section 6.05 Young Adult Offenders.

(1) Specialized Correctional Treatment. A young adult offender is a person convicted of a crime who, at the time of sentencing, is sixteen but less than twenty-two years of age. A young adult offender who is sentenced to a term of imprisonment which may exceed thirty days [alternatives: (1) ninety days; (2) one year] shall be committed to the custody of the Division of Young Adult Correction of the Department of Correction, and shall receive, as far as practicable, such special and individualized correctional and rehabilitative treatment as may be appropriate to his needs.

(2) Special Term. A young adult offender convicted of a felony may, in lieu of any other sentence of imprisonment authorized by this Article, be sentenced to a special term of imprisonment without a minimum and with a maximum of four years, regardless of the degree of the felony involved, if the Court is of the opinion that such special term is adequate for his correction and rehabilitation and will not jeopardize the protection of the public.

[(3) Removal of Disabilities; Vacation of Conviction.

(a) In sentencing a young adult offender to the special term provided by this Section or to any sentence other than one of imprisonment, the Court may order that so long as he is not convicted of another felony, the judgment shall not constitute a conviction for the purposes of any disqualification or disability imposed by law upon conviction of a crime.

(b) When any young adult offender is unconditionally discharged from probation or parole before the expiration of the maximum term thereof, the Court may enter an order vacating the judgment of conviction.]

[(4) Commitment for Observation. If, after pre-sentence investigation, the Court desires additional information concerning a young adult offender before imposing sentence, it may order that he be committed, for a period not exceeding ninety days, to the custody of the Division of Young Adult Correction of the Department of Correction for observation and study at an appropriate reception or classification center. Such Division of the Department of Correction and the [Young Adult Division of the] Board of Parole shall advise the Court of their findings and recommendations on or before the expiration of such ninety-day period.]

Subsection (3) should be eliminated if Section 306.6, dealing with removal of disabilities generally, is adopted.

Subsection (4) should be eliminated if Subsection (1) of Section

7.08, dealing with commitments for observation generally, is adopted.

Section 6.06 Sentence of Imprisonment for Felony; Ordinary Terms.

A person who has been convicted of a felony may be sentenced to imprisonment, as follows:

(1) in the case of a felony of the first degree, for a term the minimum of which shall be fixed by the Court at not less than one year nor more than ten years, and the maximum of which shall be life imprisonment;

(2) in the case of a felony of the second degree, for a term the minimum of which shall be fixed by the Court at not less than one year nor more than three years, and the maximum of which shall be ten years;

(3) in the case of a felony of the third degree, for a term the minimum of which shall be fixed by the Court at not less than one year nor more than two years, and the maximum of which shall be five years.

Alternate Section 6.06. Sentence of Imprisonment for Felony; Ordinary Terms.

A person who has been convicted of a felony may be sentenced to imprisonment, as follows:

(1) in the case of a felony of the first degree, for a term the minimum of which shall be fixed by the Court at not less than one year nor more than ten years, and the maximum at not more than twenty years or at life imprisonment;

(2) in the case of a felony of the second degree, for a term the minimum of which shall be fixed by the Court at not less than one year nor more than three years, and the maximum at not more than ten years;

(3) in the case of a felony of the third degree, for a term the minimum of which shall be fixed by the Court at not less than one year nor more than two years, and the maximum at not more than five years.

No sentence shall be imposed under this Section of which the minimum is longer than one-half the maximum, or, when the maximum is life imprisonment, longer than ten years.

Section 6.07 Sentence of Imprisonment for Felony; Extended Terms.

In the cases designated in Section 7.03, a person who has been convicted of a felony may be sentenced to an extended term of imprisonment, as follows:

(1) in the case of a felony of the first degree, for a term the minimum of which shall be fixed by the Court at not less than five years nor more than ten years, and the maximum of which shall be life imprisonment;

(2) in the case of a felony of the second degree, for a term the minimum of which shall be fixed by the Court at not less than one year nor more than five years, and the maximum of which shall be fixed by the Court at not less than ten nor more than twenty years;

(3) in the case of a felony of the third degree, for a term the minimum of which shall be fixed by the Court at not less than one year nor more than three years, and the maximum of which shall be fixed

by the Court at not less than five nor more than ten years.

Section 6.08 Sentence of Imprisonment for Misdemeanors and Petty Misdemeanors; Ordinary Terms.

A person who has been convicted of a misdemeanor or a petty misdemeanor may be sentenced to imprisonment for a definite term which shall be fixed by the Court and shall not exceed one year in the case of a misdemeanor or thirty days in the case of a petty misdemeanor.

Section 6.09 Sentence of Imprisonment for Misdemeanors and Petty Misdemeanors; Extended Terms.

(1) In the cases designated in Section 7.04, a person who has been convicted of a misdemeanor or a petty misdemeanor may be sentenced to an extended term of imprisonment, as follows:

(a) in the case of a misdemeanor, for a term the minimum of which shall be fixed by the Court at not more than one year and the maximum of which shall be three years;

(b) in the case of a petty misdemeanor, for a term the minimum of which shall be fixed by the Court at not more than six months and the maximum of which shall be two years.

(2) No such sentence for an extended term shall be imposed unless:

(a) the Director of Correction has certified that there is an institution in the Department of Correction, or in a county, city [or other appropriate political subdivision of the State] which is appropriate for the detention and correctional treatment of such misdemeanants or petty misdemeanants, and that such institution is available to receive such commitments; and

(b) the [Board of Parole] [Parole Administrator] has certified that the Board of Parole is able to visit such institution and to assume responsibility for the release of such prisoners on parole and for their parole supervision.

Section 6.10 First Release of All Offenders on Parole; Sentence of Imprisonment Includes Separate Parole Term; Length of Parole Term; Length of Recommitment and Reparole After Revocation of Parole; Final Unconditional Release.

(1) First Release of All Offenders on Parole. An offender sentenced to an indefinite term of imprisonment in excess of one year under Section 6.05, 6.06, 6.07, 6.09 or 7.06 shall be released conditionally on parole at or before the expiration of the maximum of such term, in accordance with Article 305.

(2) Sentence of Imprisonment Includes Separate Parole Term; Length of Parole Term. A sentence to an indefinite term of imprisonment in excess of one year under Section 6.05, 6.06, 6.07, 6.09 or 7.06 includes as a separate portion of the sentence a term of parole or of recommitment for violation of the conditions of parole which governs the duration of parole or recommitment after the offender's first conditional release on parole. The minimum of such term is one year and the maximum is five years, unless the sentence was imposed under Section 6.05(2) or

Section 6.09, in which case the maximum is two years.

(3) Length of Recommitment and Reparole After Revocation of Parole. If an offender is recommitted upon revocation of his parole, the term of further imprisonment upon such recommitment and of any subsequent reparole or recommitment under the same sentence shall be fixed by the Board of Parole but shall not exceed in aggregate length the unserved balance of the maximum parole term provided by Subsection (2) of this Section.

(4) Final Unconditional Release. When the maximum of his parole term has expired or he has been sooner discharged from parole under Section 305.12, an offender shall be deemed to have served his sentence and shall be released unconditionally.

Section 6.11 Place of Imprisonment.

(1) When a person is sentenced to imprisonment for an indefinite term with a maximum in excess of one year, the Court shall commit him to the custody of the Department of Correction [or other single department or agency] for the term of his sentence and until released in accordance with law.

(2) When a person is sentenced to imprisonment for a definite term, the Court shall designate the institution or agency to which he is committed for the term of his sentence and until released in accordance with law.

Section 6.12 Reduction of Conviction by Court to Lesser Degree of Felony or to Misdemeanor.

If, when a person has been convicted of a felony, the Court, having regard to the nature and circumstances of the crime and to the history and character of the defendant, is of the view that it would be unduly harsh to sentence the offender in accordance with the Code, the Court may enter judgment of conviction for a lesser degree of felony or for a misdemeanor and impose sentence accordingly.

Section 6.13 Civil Commitment in Lieu of Prosecution or of Sentence.

(1) When a person prosecuted for a [felony of the third degree,] misdemeanor or petty misdemeanor is a chronic alcoholic, narcotic addict [or prostitute] or person suffering from mental abnormality and the Court is authorized by law to order the civil commitment of such person to a hospital or other institution for medical, psychiatric or other rehabilitative treatment, the Court may order such commitment and dismiss the prosecution. The order of commitment may be made after conviction, in which event the Court may set aside the verdict or judgment of conviction and dismiss the prosecution.

(2) The Court shall not make an order under Subsection (1) of this Section unless it is of the view that it will substantially further the rehabilitation of the defendant and will not jeopardize the protection of the public.

ARTICLE 7. AUTHORITY OF COURT IN SENTENCING

Section 7.01 Criteria for Withholding Sentence of Imprisonment and for Placing Defendant on Probation.

(1) The Court shall deal with a person who has been convicted of a

crime without imposing sentence of imprisonment unless, having regard to the nature and circumstances of the crime and the history, character and condition of the defendant, it is of the opinion that his imprisonment is necessary for protection of the public because:

(a) there is undue risk that during the period of a suspended sentence or probation the defendant will commit another crime; or

(b) the defendant is in need of correctional treatment that can be provided most effectively by his commitment to an institution; or

(c) a lesser sentence will depreciate the seriousness of the defendant's crime.

(2) The following grounds, while not controlling the discretion of the Court, shall be accorded weight in favor of withholding sentence of imprisonment:

(a) the defendant's criminal conduct neither caused nor threatened serious harm;

(b) the defendant did not contemplate that his criminal conduct would cause or threaten serious harm;

(c) the defendant acted under a strong provocation;

(d) there were substantial grounds tending to excuse or justify the defendant's criminal conduct, though failing to establish a defense;

(e) the victim of the defendant's criminal conduct induced or facilitated its commission;

(f) the defendant has compensated or will compensate the victim of his criminal conduct for the damage or injury that he sustained;

(g) the defendant has no history of prior delinquency or criminal activity or has led a law-abiding life for a substantial period of time before the commission of the present crime;

(h) the defendant's criminal conduct was the result of circumstances unlikely to recur;

(i) the character and attitudes of the defendant indicate that he is unlikely to commit another crime;

(j) the defendant is particularly likely to respond affirmatively to probationary treatment;

(k) the imprisonment of the defendant would entail excessive hardship to himself or his dependents.

(3) When a person who has been convicted of a crime is not sentenced to imprisonment, the Court shall place him on probation if he is in need of the supervision, guidance, assistance or direction that the probation service can provide.

Section 7.02 Criteria for Imposing Fines.

(1) The Court shall not sentence a defendant only to pay a fine, when any other disposition is authorized by law, unless having regard to the nature and circumstances of the crime and to the history and character of the defendant, it is of the opinion that the fine alone suffices for protection of the public.

(2) The Court shall not sentence a defendant to pay a fine in addition to a sentence of imprisonment or probation unless:

(a) the defendant has derived a pecuniary gain from the crime; or

(b) the Court is of opinion that a fine is specially adapted to deterrence of the crime involved or to the correction of the offender.

(3) The Court shall not sentence a defendant to pay a fine unless:

(a) the defendant is or will be able to pay the fine; and

(b) the fine will not prevent the defendant from making restitution or reparation to the victim of the crime.

(4) In determining the amount and method of payment of a fine, the Court shall take into account the financial resources of the defendant and the nature of the burden that its payment will impose.

Section 7.03 Criteria for Sentence of Extended Term of Imprisonment; Felonies.

The Court may sentence a person who has been convicted of a felony to an extended term of imprisonment if it finds one or more of the grounds specified in this Section. The finding of the Court shall be incorporated in the record.

(1) The defendant is a persistent offender whose commitment for an extended term is necessary for protection of the public.

The Court shall not make such a finding unless the defendant is over twenty-one years of age and has previously been convicted of two felonies or of one felony and two misdemeanors, committed at different times when he was over [insert Juvenile Court age] years of age.

(2) The defendant is a professional criminal whose commitment for an extended term is necessary for protection of the public.

The Court shall not make such a finding unless the defendant is over twenty-one years of age and:

(a) the circumstances of the crime show that the defendant has knowingly devoted himself to criminal activity as a major source of livelihood; or

(b) the defendant has substantial income or resources not explained to be derived from a source other than criminal activity.

(3) The defendant is a dangerous, mentally abnormal person whose commitment for an extended term is necessary for protection of the public.

The Court shall not make such a finding unless the defendant has been subjected to a psychiatric examination resulting in the conclusions that his mental condition is gravely abnormal; that his criminal conduct has been characterized by a pattern of repetitive or compulsive behavior or by persistent aggressive behavior with heedless indifference to consequences; and that such condition makes him a serious danger to others.

(4) The defendant is a multiple offender whose criminality was so extensive that a sentence of imprisonment for an extended term is warranted.

The Court shall not make such a finding unless:

(a) the defendant is being sentenced for two or more felonies, or is already under sentence of imprisonment for felony, and the sentences of imprisonment involved will run concurrently under Section 7.06; or

(b) the defendant admits in open court the commission of one or more other felonies and asks that they be taken into account when he is sentenced; and

(c) the longest sentences of imprisonment authorized for each of the defendant's crimes, including admitted crimes taken into account, if made to run consecutively would exceed in length the minimum and maximum of the extended term imposed.

Section 7.04 Criteria for Sentence of Extended Term of Imprisonment; Misdemeanors and Petty Misdemeanors.

The Court may sentence a person who has been convicted of a misdemeanor or petty misdemeanor to an extended term of imprisonment if it finds one or more of the grounds specified in this Section. The finding of the Court shall be incorporated in the record.

(1) The defendant is a persistent offender whose commitment for an extended term is necessary for protection of the public.

The Court shall not make such a finding unless the defendant has previously been convicted of two crimes, committed at different times when he was over [insert Juvenile Court age] years of age.

(2) The defendant is a professional criminal whose commitment for an extended term is necessary for protection of the public.

The Court shall not make such a finding unless:

(a) the circumstances of the crime show that the defendant has knowingly devoted himself to criminal activity as a major source of livelihood; or

(b) the defendant has substantial income or resources not explained to be derived from a source other than criminal activity.

(3) The defendant is a chronic alcoholic, narcotic addict, prostitute or person of abnormal mental condition who requires rehabilitative treatment for a substantial period of time.

The Court shall not make such a finding unless, with respect to the particular category to which the defendant belongs, the Director of Correction has certified that there is a specialized institution or facility which is satisfactory for the rehabilitative treatment of such persons and which otherwise meets the requirements of Section 6.09, Subsection (2).

(4) The defendant is a multiple offender whose criminality was so extensive that a sentence of imprisonment for an extended term is warranted.

The Court shall not make such a finding unless:

(a) the defendant is being sentenced for a number of misdemeanors or petty misdemeanors or is already under sentence of imprisonment for crime of such grades, or admits in open court the commission of one or more such crimes and asks that they be taken into account when he is sentenced; and

(b) maximum fixed sentences of imprisonment for each of the defendant's crimes, including admitted crimes taken into account, if made to run consecutively, would exceed in length the maximum period of the extended term imposed.

Section 7.05 Former Conviction in Another Jurisdiction; Definition and Proof of Conviction; Sentence Taking into Account Admitted Crimes Bars Subsequent Conviction for Such Crimes.

(1) For purposes of paragraph (1) of Section 7.03 or 7.04, a conviction of the commission of a crime in another jurisdiction shall constitute a previous conviction. Such conviction shall be deemed to have been of a felony if sentence of death or of imprisonment in excess of one year was authorized under the law of such other jurisdiction, of a misdemeanor if sentence of imprisonment in excess of thirty days but not in excess of a year was authorized and of a petty misdemeanor if sentence of imprisonment for not more than thirty days was authorized.

(2) An adjudication by a court of competent jurisdiction that the defendant committed a crime constitutes a conviction for purposes of Sections 7.03 to 7.05 inclusive, although sentence or the execution thereof was suspended, provided that the time to appeal has expired and that the defendant was not pardoned on the ground of innocence.

(3) Prior conviction may be proved by any evidence, including fingerprint records made in connection with arrest, conviction or imprisonment, that reasonably satisfies the Court that the defendant was convicted.

(4) When the defendant has asked that other crimes admitted in open court be taken into account when he is sentenced and the Court has not rejected such request, the sentence shall bar the prosecution or conviction of the defendant in this State for any such admitted crime.

Section 7.06 Multiple Sentences; Concurrent and Consecutive Terms.

(1) Sentences of Imprisonment for More Than One Crime. When multiple sentences of imprisonment are imposed on a defendant for more than one crime, including a crime for which a previous suspended sentence or sentence of probation has been revoked, such multiple sentences shall run concurrently or consecutively as the Court determines at the time of sentence, except that:

(a) a definite and an indefinite term shall run concurrently and both sentences shall be satisfied by service of the indefinite term; and

(b) the aggregate of consecutive definite terms shall not exceed one year; and

(c) the aggregate of consecutive indefinite terms shall not exceed in minimum or maximum length the longest extended term authorized for the highest grade and degree of crime for which any of the sentences was imposed; and

(d) not more than one sentence for an extended term shall be imposed.

(2) Sentences of Imprisonment

Imposed at Different Times. When a defendant who has previously been sentenced to imprisonment is subsequently sentenced to another term for a crime committed prior to the former sentence, other than a crime committed while in custody:

(a) the multiple sentences imposed shall so far as possible conform to Subsection (1) of this Section; and

(b) whether the Court determines that the terms shall run concurrently or consecutively, the defendant shall be credited with time served in imprisonment on the prior sentence in determining the permissible aggregate length of the term or terms remaining to be served; and

(c) when a new sentence is imposed on a prisoner who is on parole, the balance of the parole term on the former sentence shall be deemed to run during the period of the new imprisonment.

(3) Sentence of Imprisonment for Crime Committed While on Parole. When a defendant is sentenced to imprisonment for a crime committed while on parole in this State, such term of imprisonment and any period of reimprisonment that the Board of Parole may require the defendant to serve upon the revocation of his parole shall run concurrently, unless the Court orders them to run consecutively.

(4) Multiple Sentences of Imprisonment in Other Cases. Except as otherwise provided in this Section, multiple terms of imprisonment shall run concurrently or consecutively as the Court determines when the second or subsequent sentence is imposed.

(5) Calculation of Concurrent and Consecutive Terms of Imprisonment.

(a) When indefinite terms run concurrently, the shorter minimum terms merge in and are satisfied by serving the longest minimum term and the shorter maximum terms merge in and are satisfied by discharge of the longest maximum term.

(b) When indefinite terms run consecutively, the minimum terms are added to arrive at an aggregate minimum to be served equal to the sum of all minimum terms and the maximum terms are added to arrive at an aggregate maximum equal to the sum of all maximum terms.

(c) When a definite and an indefinite term run consecutively, the period of the definite term is added to both the minimum and maximum of the indefinite term and both sentences are satisfied by serving the indefinite term.

(6) Suspension of Sentence or Probation and Imprisonment; Multiple Terms of Suspension and Probation. When a defendant is sentenced for more than one offense or a defendant already under sentence is sentenced for another offense committed prior to the former sentence:

(a) the Court shall not sentence to probation a defendant who is under sentence of imprisonment [with more than thirty days to run] or impose a sentence of probation and a sentence of imprisonment [, except as authorized by Section 6.02(3)(b)]; and

(b) multiple periods of suspension or probation shall run concurrently from the date of the first such disposition; and

(c) when a sentence of imprisonment is imposed for an indefinite term, the service of such sentence shall satisfy a suspended sentence on another count or a prior suspended sentence or sentence to probation; and

(d) when a sentence of imprisonment is imposed for a definite term, the period of a suspended sentence on another count or a prior suspended sentence or sentence to probation shall run during the period of such imprisonment.

(7) Offense Committed While Under Suspension of Sentence or Probation. When a defendant is convicted of an offense committed while under suspension of sentence or on probation and such suspension or probation is not revoked:

(a) if the defendant is sentenced to imprisonment for an indefinite term, the service of such sentence shall satisfy the prior suspended sentence or sentence to probation; and

(b) if the defendant is sentenced to imprisonment for a definite term, the period of the suspension or probation shall not run during the period of such imprisonment; and

(c) if sentence is suspended or the defendant is sentenced to probation, the period of such suspension or probation shall run concurrently with or consecutively to the remainder of the prior periods, as the Court determines at the time of sentence.

Section 7.07 Procedure on Sentence; Presentence Investigation and Report; Remand for Psychiatric Examination; Transmission of Records to Department of Correction.

(1) The Court shall not impose sentence without first ordering a presentence investigation of the defendant and according due consideration to a written report of such investigation where:

(a) the defendant has been convicted of a felony; or

(b) the defendant is less than twenty-two years of age and has been convicted of a crime; or

(c) the defendant will be [placed on probation or] sentenced to imprisonment for an extended term.

(2) The Court may order a presentence investigation in any other case.

(3) The pre-sentence investigation shall include an analysis of the circumstances attending the commission of the crime, the defendant's history of delinquency or criminality, physical and mental condition, family situation and background, economic status, education, occupation and personal habits and any other matters that the probation officer deems relevant or the Court directs to be included.

(4) Before imposing sentence, the Court may order the defendant to submit to psychiatric observation and examination for a period of not exceeding sixty days or such longer period as the Court determines to be necessary for the purpose. The defendant may be remanded for this purpose to any available clinic or mental

hospital or the Court may appoint a qualified psychiatrist to make the examination. The report of the examination shall be submitted to the Court.

(5) Before imposing sentence, the Court shall advise the defendant or his counsel of the factual contents and the conclusions of any pre-sentence investigation or psychiatric examination and afford fair opportunity, if the defendant so requests, to controvert them. The sources of confidential information need not, however, be disclosed.

(6) The Court shall not impose a sentence of imprisonment for an extended term unless the ground therefor has been established at a hearing after the conviction of the defendant and on written notice to him of the ground proposed. Subject to the limitation of Subsection (5) of this Section, the defendant shall have the right to hear and controvert the evidence against him and to offer evidence upon the issue.

(7) If the defendant is sentenced to imprisonment, a copy of the report of any pre-sentence investigation or psychiatric examination shall be transmitted forthwith to the Department of Correction [or other state department or agency] or, when the defendant is committed to the custody of a specific institution, to such institution.

Section 7.08 Commitment for Observation; Sentence of Imprisonment for Felony Deemed Tentative for Period of One Year; Re-sentence on Petition of Commissioner of Correction.

(1) If, after pre-sentence investigation, the Court desires additional information concerning an offender convicted of a felony or misdemeanor before imposing sentence, it may order that he be committed, for a period not exceeding ninety days, to the custody of the Department of Correction, or, in the case of a young adult offender, to the custody of the Division of Young Adult Correction, for observation and study at an appropriate reception or classification center. The Department and the Board of Parole, or the Young Adult Divisions thereof, shall advise the Court of their findings and recommendations on or before the expiration of such ninety-day period. If the offender is thereafter sentenced to imprisonment, the period of such commitment for observation shall be deducted from the maximum term and from the minimum, if any, of such sentence.

(2) When a person has been sentenced to imprisonment upon conviction of a felony, whether for an ordinary or extended term, the sentence shall be deemed tentative, to the extent provided in this Section, for the period of one year following the date when the offender is received in custody by the Department of Correction [or other state department or agency].

(3) If, as a result of the examination and classification by the Department of Correction [or other state department or agency] of a person under sentence of imprisonment upon conviction of a felony, the Commissioner of Correction [or other department head] is satisfied that the sentence of the Court may have been based upon a misapprehension as to the history, character or physical or mental condition of the offender, the Commissioner, during the period when the offender's sentence is deemed tentative under Subsection (2) of this Section shall file in the sentencing Court a petition to resentence the offender. The petition shall set forth the information as to the offender that is

deemed to warrant his re-sentence and may include a recommendation as to the sentence to be imposed.

(4) The Court may dismiss a petition filed under Subsection (3) of this Section without a hearing if it deems the information set forth insufficient to warrant reconsideration of the sentence. If the Court is of the view that the petition warrants such reconsideration, a copy of the petition shall be served on the offender, who shall have the right to be heard on the issue and to be represented by counsel.

(5) When the Court grants a petition filed under Subsection (3) of this Section, it shall resentence the offender and may impose any sentence that might have been imposed originally for the felony of which the defendant was convicted. The period of his imprisonment prior to resentence and any reduction for good behavior to which he is entitled shall be applied in satisfaction of the final sentence.

(6) For all purposes other than this Section, a sentence of imprisonment has the same finality when it is imposed that it would have if this Section were not in force.

(7) Nothing in this Section shall alter the remedies provided by law for vacating or correcting an illegal sentence.

Section 7.09 Credit for Time of Detention Prior to Sentence; Credit for Imprisonment Under Earlier Sentence for the Same Crime.

(1) When a defendant who is sentenced to imprisonment has previously been detained in any state or local correctional or other institution following his [conviction of] [arrest for] the crime for which such sentence is imposed, such period of detention following his [conviction] [arrest] shall be deducted from the maximum term, and from the minimum, if any, of such sentence. The officer having custody of the defendant shall furnish a certificate to the Court at the time of sentence, showing the length of such detention of the defendant prior to sentence in any state or local correctional or other institution, and the certificate shall be annexed to the official records of the defendant's commitment.

(2) When a judgment of conviction is vacated and a new sentence is thereafter imposed upon the defendant for the same crime, the period of detention and imprisonment theretofore served shall be deducted from the maximum term, and from the minimum, if any, of the new sentence. The officer having custody of the defendant shall furnish a certificate to the Court at the time of sentence, showing the period of imprisonment served under the original sentence, and the certificate shall be annexed to the official records of the defendant's new commitment.

PART II.

DEFINITION OF SPECIFIC CRIMES

OFFENSES AGAINST EXISTENCE OR STABILITY OF THE STATE

[This category of offenses, including treason, sedition, espionage and like crimes, was excluded from the scope of the Model Penal Code. These offenses are peculiarly the concern of the federal government. The Constitution itself defines treason: "Treason against the United States shall consist only in levying War against them, or in adhering to their Enemies, giving them Aid and Comfort. * * *" Article III, Section 3; cf. Pennsylvania v. Nelson, 350 U.S. 497 (supersession of state sedition legislation by federal law). Also, the definition of offenses against the stability of the state is inevitably affected by special political considerations. These factors militated against the use of the Institute's limited resources to attempt to draft "model" provisions in this area. However we provide at this point in the Plan of the Model Penal Code for an Article 200, where definitions of offenses against the existence or stability of the state may be incorporated.]

ARTICLE 210. CRIMINAL HOMICIDE

Section 210.0 Definitions.

In Articles 210–213, unless a different meaning plainly is required:

(1) "human being" means a person who has been born and is alive;

(2) "bodily injury" means physical pain, illness or any impairment of physical condition;

(3) "serious bodily injury" means bodily injury which creates a substantial risk of death or which causes serious, permanent disfigurement, or protracted loss or impairment of the function of any bodily member or organ;

(4) "deadly weapon" means any firearm, or other weapon, device, instrument, material or substance, whether animate or inanimate, which in the manner it is used or is intended to be used is known to be capable of producing death or serious bodily injury.

Section 210.1 Criminal Homicide.

(1) A person is guilty of criminal homicide if he purposely, knowingly, recklessly or negligently causes the death of another human being.

(2) Criminal homicide is murder, manslaughter or negligent homicide.

Section 210.2 Murder.

(1) Except as provided in Section 210.3(1)(b), criminal homicide constitutes murder when:

(a) it is committed purposely or knowingly; or

(b) it is committed recklessly under circumstances manifesting extreme indifference to the value of human life. Such recklessness and indifference are presumed if the actor is engaged or is an accomplice in the commission of, or an attempt to commit, or flight after committing or attempting to commit robbery, rape or deviate sexual intercourse by force or threat of force, arson, burglary, kidnapping or felonious escape.

(2) Murder is a felony of the first degree [but a person convicted of murder may be sentenced to death, as provided in Section 210.6].

Section 210.3   Manslaughter.

(1) Criminal homicide constitutes manslaughter when:

(a) it is committed recklessly; or

(b) a homicide which would otherwise be murder is committed under the influence of extreme mental or emotional disturbance for which there is reasonable explanation or excuse. The reasonableness of such explanation or excuse shall be determined from the viewpoint of a person in the actor's situation under the circumstances as he believes them to be.

(2) Manslaughter is a felony of the second degree.

Section 210.4   Negligent Homicide.

(1) Criminal homicide constitutes negligent homicide when it is committed negligently.

(2) Negligent homicide is a felony of the third degree.

Section 210.5   Causing or Aiding Suicide.

(1) Causing Suicide as Criminal Homicide. A person may be convicted of criminal homicide for causing another to commit suicide only if he purposely causes such suicide by force, duress or deception.

(2) Aiding or Soliciting Suicide as an Independent Offense. A person who purposely aids or solicits another to commit suicide is guilty of a felony of the second degree if his conduct causes such suicide or an attempted suicide, and otherwise of a misdemeanor.

Section 210.6   Sentence of Death for Murder; Further Proceedings to Determine Sentence.

(1) Death Sentence Excluded. When a defendant is found guilty of murder, the Court shall impose sentence for a felony of the first degree if it is satisfied that:

(a) none of the aggravating circumstances enumerated in Subsection (3) of this Section was established by the evidence at the trial or will be established if further proceedings are initiated under Subsection (2) of this Section; or

(b) substantial mitigating circumstances, established by the evidence at the trial, call for leniency; or

(c) the defendant, with the consent of the prosecuting attorney and the approval of the Court, pleaded guilty to murder as a felony of the first degree; or

(d) the defendant was under 18 years of age at the time of the commission of the crime; or

(e) the defendant's physical or mental condition calls for leniency; or

(f) although the evidence suffices to sustain the verdict, it does not foreclose all doubt respecting the defendant's guilt.

(2) Determination by Court or by

Court and Jury. Unless the Court imposes sentence under Subsection (1) of this Section, it shall conduct a separate proceeding to determine whether the defendant should be sentenced for a felony of the first degree or sentenced to death. The proceeding shall be conducted before the Court alone if the defendant was convicted by a Court sitting without a jury or upon his plea of guilty or if the prosecuting attorney and the defendant waive a jury with respect to sentence. In other cases it shall be conducted before the Court sitting with the jury which determined the defendant's guilt or, if the Court for good cause shown discharges that jury, with a new jury empanelled for the purpose.

In the proceeding, evidence may be presented as to any matter that the Court deems relevant to sentence, including but not limited to the nature and circumstances of the crime, the defendant's character, background, history, mental and physical condition and any of the aggravating or mitigating circumstances enumerated in Subsections (3) and (4) of this Section. Any such evidence, not legally privileged, which the Court deems to have probative force may be received, regardless of its admissibility under the exclusionary rules of evidence, provided that the defendant's counsel is accorded a fair opportunity to rebut such evidence. The prosecuting attorney and the defendant or his counsel shall be permitted to present argument for or against sentence of death.

The determination whether sentence of death shall be imposed shall be in the discretion of the Court, except that when the proceeding is conducted before the Court sitting with a jury, the Court shall not impose sentence of death unless it submits to the jury the issue whether the defendant should be sentenced to death or to imprisonment and the jury returns a verdict that the sentence should be death. If the jury is unable to reach a unanimous verdict, the Court shall dismiss the jury and impose sentence for a felony of the first degree.

The Court, in exercising its discretion as to sentence, and the jury, in determining upon its verdict, shall take into account the aggravating and mitigating circumstances enumerated in Subsections (3) and (4) and any other facts that it deems relevant, but it shall not impose or recommend sentence of death unless it finds one of the aggravating circumstances enumerated in Subsection (3) and further finds that there are no mitigating circumstances sufficiently substantial to call for leniency. When the issue is submitted to the jury, the Court shall so instruct and also shall inform the jury of the nature of the sentence of imprisonment that may be imposed, including its implication with respect to possible release upon parole, if the jury verdict is against sentence of death.

Alternative formulation of Subsection (2):

(2) Determination by Court. Unless the Court imposes sentence under Subsection (1) of this Section, it shall conduct a separate proceeding to determine whether the defendant should be sentenced for a felony of the first degree or sentenced to death. In the proceeding, the Court, in accordance with Section 7.07, shall consider the report of the pre-sentence investigation and, if a psychiatric examination has been ordered, the report of such examination. In addition, evidence may be presented as to any matter that the Court deems relevant to sentence, including but not limited to the nature and circumstances of the crime, the

defendant's character, background, history, mental and physical condition and any of the aggravating or mitigating circumstances enumerated in Subsections (3) and (4) of this Section. Any such evidence, not legally privileged, which the Court deems to have probative force may be received, regardless of its admissibility under the exclusionary rules of evidence, provided that the defendant's counsel is accorded a fair opportunity to rebut such evidence. The prosecuting attorney and the defendant or his counsel shall be permitted to present argument for or against sentence of death.

The determination whether sentence of death shall be imposed shall be in the discretion of the Court. In exercising such discretion, the Court shall take into account the aggravating and mitigating circumstances enumerated in Subsections (3) and (4) and any other facts that it deems relevant but shall not impose sentence of death unless it finds one of the aggravating circumstances enumerated in Subsection (3) and further finds that there are no mitigating circumstances sufficiently substantial to call for leniency.

(3) Aggravating Circumstances.

(a) The murder was committed by a convict under sentence of imprisonment.

(b) The defendant was previously convicted of another murder or of a felony involving the use or threat of violence to the person.

(c) At the time the murder was committed the defendant also committed another murder.

(d) The defendant knowingly created a great risk of death to many persons.

(e) The murder was committed while the defendant was engaged or was an accomplice in the commission of, or an attempt to commit, or flight after committing or attempting to commit robbery, rape or deviate sexual intercourse by force or threat of force, arson, burglary or kidnapping.

(f) The murder was committed for the purpose of avoiding or preventing a lawful arrest or effecting an escape from lawful custody.

(g) The murder was committed for pecuniary gain.

(h) The murder was especially heinous, atrocious or cruel, manifesting exceptional depravity.

(4) Mitigating Circumstances.

(a) The defendant has no significant history of prior criminal activity.

(b) The murder was committed while the defendant was under the influence of extreme mental or emotional disturbance.

(c) The victim was a participant in the defendant's homicidal conduct or consented to the homicidal act.

(d) The murder was committed under circumstances which the defendant believed to provide a moral justification or extenuation for his conduct.

(e) The defendant was an accomplice in a murder committed by another person and his participation in the homicidal act was relatively minor.

(f) The defendant acted under duress or under the domination of another person.

(g) At the time of the murder, the capacity of the defendant to appreciate the criminality [wrongfulness] of his conduct or to conform his conduct to the requirements of law was impaired as a result of mental disease or defect or intoxication.

(h) The youth of the defendant at the time of the crime.]

ARTICLE 211. ASSAULT; RECKLESS ENDANGERING; THREATS

Section 211.0 Definitions.

In this Article, the definitions given in Section 210.0 apply unless a different meaning plainly is required.

Section 211.1 Assault.

(1) Simple Assault. A person is guilty of assault if he:

(a) attempts to cause or purposely, knowingly or recklessly causes bodily injury to another; or

(b) negligently causes bodily injury to another with a deadly weapon; or

(c) attempts by physical menace to put another in fear of imminent serious bodily injury.

Simple assault is a misdemeanor unless committed in a fight or scuffle entered into by mutual consent, in which case it is a petty misdemeanor.

(2) Aggravated Assault. A person is guilty of aggravated assault if he:

(a) attempts to cause serious bodily injury to another, or causes such injury purposely, knowingly or recklessly under circumstances manifesting extreme indifference to the value of human life; or

(b) attempts to cause or purposely or knowingly causes bodily injury to another with a deadly weapon.

Aggravated assault under paragraph (a) is a felony of the second degree; aggravated assault under paragraph (b) is a felony of the third degree.

Section 211.2 Recklessly Endangering Another Person.

A person commits a misdemeanor if he recklessly engages in conduct which places or may place another person in danger of death or serious bodily injury. Recklessness and danger shall be presumed where a person knowingly points a firearm at or in the direction of another, whether or not the actor believed the firearm to be loaded.

Section 211.3 Terroristic Threats.

A person is guilty of a felony of the third degree if he threatens to commit any crime of violence with purpose to terrorize another or to cause evacuation of a building, place of assembly, or facility of public transportation, or otherwise to cause serious public inconvenience, or in reckless disregard of the risk of causing such terror or inconvenience.

ARTICLE 212. KIDNAPPING AND RELATED OFFENSES; COERCION

Section 212.0 Definitions.

In this Article, the definitions given in Section 210.0 apply unless a different meaning plainly is required.

Section 212.1 Kidnapping.

A person is guilty of kidnapping if he unlawfully removes another from his place of residence or business, or a substantial distance from the vicinity where he is found, or if he unlawfully confines another for a substantial period in a place of isolation, with any of the following purposes:

(a) to hold for ransom or reward, or as a shield or hostage; or

(b) to facilitate commission of any felony or flight thereafter; or

(c) to inflict bodily injury on or to terrorize the victim or another; or

(d) to interfere with the performance of any governmental or political function.

Kidnapping is a felony of the first degree unless the actor voluntarily releases the victim alive and in a safe place prior to trial, in which case it is a felony of the second degree. A removal or confinement is unlawful within the meaning of this Section if it is accomplished by force, threat or deception, or, in the case of a person who is under the age of 14 or incompetent, if it is accomplished without the consent of a parent, guardian or other person responsible for general supervision of his welfare.

Section 212.2 Felonious Restraint.

A person commits a felony of the third degree if he knowingly:

(a) restrains another unlawfully in circumstances exposing him to risk of serious bodily injury; or

(b) holds another in a condition of involuntary servitude.

Section 212.3 False Imprisonment.

A person commits a misdemeanor if he knowingly restrains another unlawfully so as to interfere substantially with his liberty.

Section 212.4 Interference With Custody.

(1) Custody of Children. A person commits an offense if he knowingly or recklessly takes or entices any child under the age of 18 from the custody of its parent, guardian or other lawful custodian, when he has no privilege to do so. It is an affirmative defense that:

(a) the actor believed that his action was necessary to preserve the child from danger to its welfare; or

(b) the child, being at the time not less than 14 years old, was taken away at its own instigation without enticement and without purpose to commit a criminal offense with or against the child.

Proof that the child was below the critical age gives rise to a presumption that the actor knew the child's age or acted in reckless disregard thereof. The offense is a misdemeanor unless the actor, not being a parent or person in equivalent relation to the child, acted with knowledge that his conduct would cause serious alarm for the child's safety, or in reckless disregard of a likelihood of causing such alarm, in which case the offense is a felony of the third degree.

(2) Custody of Committed Persons. A person is guilty of a misdemeanor if he knowingly or recklessly takes or entices any committed person away from lawful custody when he is not privileged to do so. "Committed person" means, in addition to anyone committed under judicial warrant, any orphan, neglected or delinquent child,

mentally defective or insane person, or other dependent or incompetent person entrusted to another's custody by or through a recognized social agency or otherwise by authority of law.

Section 212.5 Criminal Coercion.

(1) Offense Defined. A person is guilty of criminal coercion if, with purpose unlawfully to restrict another's freedom of action to his detriment, he threatens to:

    (a) commit any criminal offense; or

    (b) accuse anyone of a criminal offense; or

    (c) expose any secret tending to subject any person to hatred, contempt or ridicule, or to impair his credit or business repute; or

    (d) take or withhold action as an official, or cause an official to take or withhold action.

It is an affirmative defense to prosecution based on paragraphs (b), (c) or (d) that the actor believed the accusation or secret to be true or the proposed official action justified and that his purpose was limited to compelling the other to behave in a way reasonably related to the circumstances which were the subject of the accusation, exposure or proposed official action, as by desisting from further misbehavior, making good a wrong done, refraining from taking any action or responsibility for which the actor believes the other disqualified.

(2) Grading. Criminal coercion is a misdemeanor unless the threat is to commit a felony or the actor's purpose is felonious, in which cases the offense is a felony of the third degree.

ARTICLE 213. SEXUAL OFFENSES

Section 213.0 Definitions.

In this Article, the definitions given in Section 210.0 apply unless a different meaning plainly is required. Sexual intercourse includes intercourse per os or per anum, with some penetration however slight; emission is not required.

Deviate sexual intercourse means sexual intercourse per os or per anum between human beings who are not husband and wife, and any form of sexual intercourse with an animal.

Section 213.1 Rape and Related Offenses.

(1) Rape. A male who has sexual intercourse with a female not his wife is guilty of rape if:

    (a) he compels her to submit by force or by threat of imminent death, serious bodily injury, extreme pain or kidnapping, to be inflicted on anyone; or

    (b) he has substantially impaired her power to appraise or control her conduct by administering or employing without her knowledge drugs, intoxicants or other means for the purpose of preventing resistance; or

    (c) the female is unconscious; or

    (d) the female is less than 10 years old.

Rape is a felony of the second degree unless (i) in the course thereof the actor inflicts serious bodily injury upon anyone, or (ii) the victim was not a voluntary social companion of the actor upon the occasion of the crime and had not previously permitted him sexual liberties, in which cases the offense is a felony of the first degree.

(2) Gross Sexual Imposition. A male who has sexual intercourse with a female not his wife commits a felony of the third degree if:

(a) he compels her to submit by any threat that would prevent resistance by a woman of ordinary resolution; or

(b) he knows that she suffers from a mental disease or defect which renders her incapable of appraising the nature of her conduct; or

(c) he knows that she is unaware that a sexual act is being committed upon her or that she submits because she mistakenly supposes that he is her husband.

Section 213.2 Deviate Sexual Intercourse by Force or Imposition.

(1) By Force or Its Equivalent. A person who engages in deviate sexual intercourse with another person, or who causes another to engage in deviate sexual intercourse, commits a felony of the second degree if:

(a) he compels the other person to participate by force or by threat of imminent death, serious bodily injury, extreme pain or kidnapping, to be inflicted on anyone; or

(b) he has substantially impaired the other person's power to appraise or control his conduct, by administering or employing without the knowledge of the other person drugs, intoxicants or other means for the purpose of preventing resistance; or

(c) the other person is unconscious; or

(d) the other person is less than 10 years old.

(2) By Other Imposition. A person who engages in deviate sexual intercourse with another person, or who causes another to engage in deviate sexual intercourse, commits a felony of the third degree if:

(a) he compels the other person to participate by any threat that would prevent resistance by a person of ordinary resolution; or

(b) he knows that the other person suffers from a mental disease or defect which renders him incapable of appraising the nature of his conduct; or

(c) he knows that the other person submits because he is unaware that a sexual act is being committed upon him.

Section 213.3 Corruption of Minors and Seduction.

(1) Offense Defined. A male who has sexual intercourse with a female not his wife, or any person who engages in deviate sexual intercourse or causes another to engage in deviate sexual intercourse, is guilty of an offense if:

(a) the other person is less than [16] years old and the actor is at least [4] years older than the other person, or

(b) the other person is less than 21 years old and the actor is his guardian or otherwise responsible for general supervision of his welfare; or

(c) the other person is in custody of law or detained in a hospital or other institution and the actor has supervisory or disciplinary authority over him; or

(d) the other person is a female who is induced to participate by a promise of marriage which the actor does not mean to perform.

(2) Grading. An offense under paragraph (a) of Subsection (1) is a felony of the third degree. Otherwise an offense under this section is a misdemeanor.

Section 213.4 Sexual Assault.

A person who has sexual contact with another not his spouse, or causes such other to have sexual intercourse with him, is guilty of sexual assault, a misdemeanor, if:

(1) he knows that the contact is offensive to the other person; or

(2) he knows that the other person suffers from a mental disease or defect which renders him or her incapable of appraising the nature of his or her conduct; or

(3) he knows that the other person is unaware that a sexual act is being committed; or

(4) the other person is less than 10 years old; or

(5) he has substantially impaired the other person's power to appraise or control his or her conduct, by administering or employing without the other's knowledge drugs, intoxicants or other means for the purpose of preventing resistance; or

(6) the other person is less than [16] years old and the actor is at least [4] years older than the other person; or

(7) the other person is less than 21 years old and the actor is his guardian or otherwise responsible for general supervision of his welfare; or

(8) the other person is in custody of law or detained in a hospital or other institution and the actor has supervisory or disciplinary authority over him.

Sexual contact is any touching of the sexual or other intimate parts of the person for the purpose of arousing or gratifying sexual desire.

Section 213.5 Indecent Exposure.

A person commits a misdemeanor if, for the purpose of arousing or gratifying sexual desire of himself or of any person other than his spouse, he exposes his genitals under circumstances in which he knows his conduct is likely to cause affront or alarm.

Section 213.6 Provisions Generally Applicable to Article 213.

(1) Mistake as to Age. Whenever in this Article the criminality of conduct depends on a child's being below the age of 10, it is no defense that the actor did not know the child's age, or reasonably believed the child to be older than 10. When criminality depends on the child's being below a critical age other than 10, it is a defense for the actor to prove by a preponderance of the evidence that he reasonably believed the child to be above the critical age.

(2) Spouse Relationships. Whenever in this Article the definition of an offense excludes conduct with a spouse, the exclusion shall be deemed to extend to persons living as man and wife, regardless of the legal status of their relationship. The exclusion shall be inoperative as respects spouses

living apart under a decree of judicial separation. Where the definition of an offense excludes conduct with a spouse or conduct by a woman, this shall not preclude conviction of a spouse or woman as accomplice in a sexual act which he or she causes another person, not within the exclusion, to perform.

(3) Sexually Promiscuous Complainants. It is a defense to prosecution under Section 213.3 and paragraphs (6), (7) and (8) of Section 213.4 for the actor to prove by a preponderance of the evidence that the alleged victim had, prior to the time of the offense charged, engaged promiscuously in sexual relations with others.

(4) Prompt Complaint. No prosecution may be instituted or maintained under this Article unless the alleged offense was brought to the notice of public authority within [3] months of its occurrence or, where the alleged victim was less than [16] years old or otherwise incompetent to make complaint, within [3] months after a parent, guardian or other competent person specially interested in the victim learns of the offense.

(5) Testimony of Complainants. No person shall be convicted of any felony under this Article upon the uncorroborated testimony of the alleged victim. Corroboration may be circumstantial. In any prosecution before a jury for an offense under this Article, the jury shall be instructed to evaluate the testimony of a victim or complaining witness with special care in view of the emotional involvement of the witness and the difficulty of determining the truth with respect to alleged sexual activities carried out in private.

ARTICLE 220. ARSON, CRIMINAL MISCHIEF, AND OTHER PROPERTY DESTRUCTION

Section 220.1 Arson and Related Offenses.

(1) Arson. A person is guilty of arson, a felony of the second degree, if he starts a fire or causes an explosion with the purpose of:

(a) destroying a building or occupied structure of another; or

(b) destroying or damaging any property, whether his own or another's, to collect insurance for such loss. It shall be an affirmative defense to prosecution under this paragraph that the actor's conduct did not recklessly endanger any building or occupied structure of another or place any other person in danger of death or bodily injury.

(2) Reckless Burning or Exploding. A person commits a felony of the third degree if he purposely starts a fire or causes an explosion, whether on his own property or another's, and thereby recklessly:

(a) places another person in danger of death or bodily injury; or

(b) places a building or occupied structure of another in danger of damage or destruction.

(3) Failure to Control or Report Dangerous Fire. A person who knows that a fire is endangering life or a substantial amount of property of another and fails to take reasonable measures to put out or control the fire, when he can do so without substantial risk to himself, or to give a prompt fire alarm, commits a misdemeanor if:

(a) he knows that he is under an official, contractual, or other legal duty to prevent or combat the fire; or

(b) the fire was started, albeit lawfully, by him or with his assent, or on property in his custody or control.

(4) Definitions. "Occupied structure" includes a ship, trailer, sleeping car, airplane, or other vehicle, structure or place adapted for overnight accommodation of persons or for carrying on business therein, whether or not a person is actually present. Property is that of another, for the purposes of this section, if anyone other than the actor has a possessory or proprietary interest therein. If a building or structure is divided into separately occupied units, any unit not occupied by the actor is an occupied structure of another.

Section 220.2 Causing or Risking Catastrophe.

(1) Causing Catastrophe. A person who causes a catastrophe by explosion, fire, flood, avalanche, collapse of building, release of poison gas, radioactive material or other harmful or destructive force or substance, or by any other means of causing potentially widespread injury or damage, commits a felony of the second degree if he does so purposely or knowingly, or a felony of the third degree if he does so recklessly.

(2) Risking Catastrophe. A person is guilty of a misdemeanor if he recklessly creates a risk of catastrophe in the employment of fire, explosives or other dangerous means listed in Subsection (1).

(3) Failure to Prevent Catastrophe. A person who knowingly or recklessly fails to take reasonable measures to prevent or mitigate a catastrophe commits a misdemeanor if:

(a) he knows that he is under an official, contractual or other legal duty to take such measures; or

(b) he did or assented to the act causing or threatening the catastrophe.

Section 220.3 Criminal Mischief.

(1) Offense Defined. A person is guilty of criminal mischief if he:

(a) damages tangible property of another purposely, recklessly, or by negligence in the employment of fire, explosives, or other dangerous means listed in Section 220.2(1); or

(b) purposely or recklessly tampers with tangible property of another so as to endanger person or property; or

(c) purposely or recklessly causes another to suffer pecuniary loss by deception or threat.

(2) Grading. Criminal mischief is a felony of the third degree if the actor purposely causes pecuniary loss in excess of $5,000, or a substantial interruption or impairment of public communication, transportation, supply of water, gas or power, or other public service. It is a misdemeanor if the actor purposely causes pecuniary loss in excess of $100, or a petty misdemeanor if he purposely or recklessly causes pecuniary loss in excess of $25. Otherwise criminal mischief is a violation.

ARTICLE 221. BURGLARY AND OTHER CRIMINAL INTRUSION

Section 221.0 Definitions.

In this Article, unless a different meaning plainly is required:

(1) "occupied structure" means

any structure, vehicle or place adapted for overnight accommodation of persons, or for carrying on business therein, whether or not a person is actually present.

(2) "night" means the period between thirty minutes past sunset and thirty minutes before sunrise.

Section 221.1 Burglary.

(1) Burglary Defined. A person is guilty of burglary if he enters a building or occupied structure, or separately secured or occupied portion thereof, with purpose to commit a crime therein, unless the premises are at the time open to the public or the actor is licensed or privileged to enter. It is an affirmative defense to prosecution for burglary that the building or structure was abandoned.

(2) Grading. Burglary is a felony of the second degree if it is perpetrated in the dwelling of another at night, or if, in the course of committing the offense, the actor:

(a) purposely, knowingly or recklessly inflicts or attempts to inflict bodily injury on anyone; or

(b) is armed with explosives or a deadly weapon.

Otherwise, burglary is a felony of the third degree. An act shall be deemed "in the course of committing" an offense if it occurs in an attempt to commit the offense or in flight after the attempt or commission.

(3) Multiple Convictions. A person may not be convicted both for burglary and for the offense which it was his purpose to commit after the burglarious entry or for an attempt to commit that offense, unless the additional offense constitutes a felony of the first or second degree.

Section 221.2 Criminal Trespass.

(1) Buildings and Occupied Structures. A person commits an offense if, knowing that he is not licensed or privileged to do so, he enters or surreptitiously remains in any building or occupied structure, or separately secured or occupied portion thereof. An offense under this Subsection is a misdemeanor if it is committed in a dwelling at night. Otherwise it is a petty misdemeanor.

(2) Defiant Trespasser. A person commits an offense if, knowing that he is not licensed or privileged to do so, he enters or remains in any place as to which notice against trespass is given by:

(a) actual communication to the actor; or

(b) posting in a manner prescribed by law or reasonably likely to come to the attention of intruders; or

(c) fencing or other enclosure manifestly designed to exclude intruders.

An offense under this Subsection constitutes a petty misdemeanor if the offender defies an order to leave personally communicated to him by the owner of the premises or other authorized person. Otherwise it is a violation.

(3) Defenses. It is an affirmative defense to prosecution under this Section that:

(a) a building or occupied structure involved in an offense under Subsection (1) was abandoned; or

(b) the premises were at the time open to members of the public and the actor complied with all lawful conditions imposed on access to or remaining in the premises; or

(c) the actor reasonably believed that the owner of the premises, or other person empowered to license access thereto, would have licensed him to enter or remain.

ARTICLE 222. ROBBERY

Section 222.1 Robbery.

(1) Robbery Defined. A person is guilty of robbery if, in the course of committing a theft, he:

(a) inflicts serious bodily injury upon another; or

(b) threatens another with or purposely puts him in fear of immediate serious bodily injury; or

(c) commits or threatens immediately to commit any felony of the first or second degree.

An act shall be deemed "in the course of committing a theft" if it occurs in an attempt to commit theft or in flight after the attempt or commission.

(2) Grading. Robbery is a felony of the second degree, except that it is a felony of the first degree if in the course of committing the theft the actor attempts to kill anyone, or purposely inflicts or attempts to inflict serious bodily injury.

ARTICLE 223. THEFT AND RELATED OFFENSES

Section 223.0 Definitions.

In this Article, unless a different meaning plainly is required:

(1) "deprive" means: (a) to withhold property of another permanently or for so extended a period as to appropriate a major portion of its economic value, or with intent to restore only upon payment of reward or other compensation; or (b) to dispose of the property so as to make it unlikely that the owner will recover it.

(2) "financial institution" means a bank, insurance company, credit union, building and loan association, investment trust or other organization held out to the public as a place of deposit of funds or medium of savings or collective investment.

(3) "government" means the United States, any State, county, municipality, or other political unit, or any department, agency or subdivision of any of the foregoing, or any corporation or other association carrying out the functions of government.

(4) "movable property" means property the location of which can be changed, including things growing on, affixed to, or found in land, and documents although the rights represented thereby have no physical location. "Immovable property" is all other property.

(5) "obtain" means: (a) in relation to property, to bring about a transfer or purported transfer of a legal interest in the property, whether to the obtainer or another; or (b) in relation to labor or service, to secure performance thereof.

(6) "property" means anything of value, including real estate, tangible and intangible personal property, contract rights, choses-in-action and other interests in or claims to wealth, admission or transportation tickets, captured or domestic animals, food and drink, electric or other power.

(7) "property of another" includes property in which any person other than the actor has an interest which the actor is not privileged to infringe, regardless of the fact that the actor also has an interest in the property and regardless of the fact that the other person might be precluded from civil recovery because the property was used in an unlawful transaction or was subject to forfeiture as contraband. Property in possession of the actor shall not be deemed property of another who has only a security interest therein, even if legal title is in the creditor pursuant to a conditional sales contract or other security agreement.

Section 223.1 Consolidation of Theft Offenses; Grading; Provisions Applicable to Theft Generally.

(1) Consolidation of Theft Offenses. Conduct denominated theft in this Article constitutes a single offense. An accusation of theft may be supported by evidence that it was committed in any manner that would be theft under this Article, notwithstanding the specification of a different manner in the indictment or information, subject only to the power of the Court to ensure fair trial by granting a continuance or other appropriate relief where the conduct of the defense would be prejudiced by lack of fair notice or by surprise.

(2) Grading of Theft Offenses.

(a) Theft constitutes a felony of the third degree if the amount involved exceeds $500, or if the property stolen is a fire-arm, automobile, airplane, motorcycle, motorboat or other motor-propelled vehicle, or in the case of theft by receiving stolen property, if the receiver is in the business of buying or selling stolen property.

(b) Theft not within the preceding paragraph constitutes a misdemeanor, except that if the property was not taken from the person or by threat, or in breach of a fiduciary obligation, and the actor proves by a preponderance of the evidence that the amount involved was less than $50, the offense constitutes a petty misdemeanor.

(c) The amount involved in a theft shall be deemed to be the highest value, by any reasonable standard, of the property or services which the actor stole or attempted to steal. Amounts involved in thefts committed pursuant to one scheme or course of conduct, whether from the same person or several persons, may be aggregated in determining the grade of the offense.

(3) Claim of Right. It is an affirmative defense to prosecution for theft that the actor:

(a) was unaware that the property or service was that of another; or

(b) acted under an honest claim of right to the property or service involved or that he had a right to acquire or dispose of it as he did; or

(c) took property exposed for sale, intending to purchase and pay for it promptly, or reasonably believing that the owner, if present, would have consented.

(4) Theft from Spouse. It is no defense that theft was from the actor's spouse, except that misappropriation of household and personal effects, or other property normally accessible to

both spouses, is theft only if it occurs after the parties have ceased living together.

Section 223.2 Theft by Unlawful Taking or Disposition.

(1) Movable Property. A person is guilty of theft if he unlawfully takes, or exercises unlawful control over, movable property of another with purpose to deprive him thereof.

(2) Immovable Property. A person is guilty of theft if he unlawfully transfers immovable property of another or any interest therein with purpose to benefit himself or another not entitled thereto.

Section 223.3 Theft by Deception.

A person is guilty of theft if he purposely obtains property of another by deception. A person deceives if he purposely:

(1) creates or reinforces a false impression, including false impressions as to law, value, intention or other state of mind; but deception as to a person's intention to perform a promise shall not be inferred from the fact alone that he did not subsequently perform the promise; or

(2) prevents another from acquiring information which would affect his judgment of a transaction; or

(3) fails to correct a false impression which the deceiver previously created or reinforced, or which the deceiver knows to be influencing another to whom he stands in a fiduciary or confidential relationship; or

(4) fails to disclose a known lien, adverse claim or other legal impediment to the enjoyment of property which he transfers or encumbers in consideration for the property obtained, whether such impediment is or is not valid, or is or is not a matter of official record.

The term "deceive" does not, however, include falsity as to matters having no pecuniary significance, or puffing by statements unlikely to deceive ordinary persons in the group addressed.

Section 223.4 Theft by Extortion.

A person is guilty of theft if he purposely obtains property of another by threatening to:

(1) inflict bodily injury on anyone or commit any other criminal offense; or

(2) accuse anyone of a criminal offense; or

(3) expose any secret tending to subject any person to hatred, contempt or ridicule, or to impair his credit or business repute; or

(4) take or withhold action as an official, or cause an official to take or withhold action; or

(5) bring about or continue a strike, boycott or other collective unofficial action, if the property is not demanded or received for the benefit of the group in whose interest the actor purports to act; or

(6) testify or provide information or withhold testimony or information with respect to another's legal claim or defense; or

(7) inflict any other harm which would not benefit the actor.

It is an affirmative defense to prosecution based on paragraphs (2), (3) or (4) that the property obtained by threat of accusation, exposure, lawsuit or other invocation of official action was honestly claimed as restitution or indemnification for harm done in the circumstances to which such accusation, exposure, lawsuit or other official action relates, or as compensation for property or lawful services.

Section 223.5   Theft of Property Lost, Mislaid, or Delivered by Mistake.

A person who comes into control of property of another that he knows to have been lost, mislaid, or delivered under a mistake as to the nature or amount of the property or the identity of the recipient is guilty of theft if, with purpose to deprive the owner thereof, he fails to take reasonable measures to restore the property to a person entitled to have it.

Section 223.6   Receiving Stolen Property.

(1) Receiving. A person is guilty of theft if he purposely receives, retains, or disposes of movable property of another knowing that it has been stolen, or believing that it has probably been stolen, unless the property is received, retained, or disposed with purpose to restore it to the owner. "Receiving" means acquiring possession, control or title, or lending on the security of the property.

(2) Presumption of Knowledge. The requisite knowledge or belief is presumed in the case of a dealer who:

(a) is found in possession or control of property stolen from two or more persons on separate occasions; or

(b) has received stolen property in another transaction within the year preceding the transaction charged; or

(c) being a dealer in property of the sort received, acquires it for a consideration which he knows is far below its reasonable value.

"Dealer" means a person in the business of buying or selling goods, including a pawnbroker.

Section 223.7   Theft of Services.

(1) A person is guilty of theft if he purposely obtains services which he knows are available only for compensation, by deception or threat, or by false token or other means to avoid payment for the service. "Services" includes labor, professional service, transportation, telephone or other public service, accommodation in hotels, restaurants or elsewhere, admission to exhibitions, use of vehicles or other movable property. Where compensation for service is ordinarily paid immediately upon the rendering of such service, as in the case of hotels and restaurants, refusal to pay or absconding without payment or offer to pay gives rise to a presumption that the service was obtained by deception as to intention to pay.

(2) A person commits theft if, having control over the disposition of services of others, to which he is not entitled, he knowingly diverts such services to his own benefit or to the benefit of another not entitled thereto.

Section 223.8   Theft by Failure to Make Required Disposition of Funds Received.

A person who purposely obtains property upon agreement, or subject to a known legal obligation, to make specified payment or other disposition, whether from such property or its proceeds or from his own property to be reserved in equivalent amount, is guilty of theft if he deals with the property obtained as his own and fails to make the required payment or disposition. The foregoing applies notwithstanding that it may be impossible to identify particular property as belonging to the victim at the time of the actor's failure to make the required payment or disposition. An officer or employee of the government or of a financial institution is presumed: (i) to know any legal obligation relevant to his criminal liability under this Section, and (ii) to have dealt with the property as his own if he fails to pay or account upon lawful demand, or if an audit reveals a shortage or falsification of accounts.

Section 223.9 Unauthorized Use of Automobiles and Other Vehicles.

A person commits a misdemeanor if he operates another's automobile, airplane, motorcycle, motorboat, or other motorpropelled vehicle without consent of the owner. It is an affirmative defense to prosecution under this Section that the actor reasonably believed that the owner would have consented to the operation had he known of it.

ARTICLE 224. FORGERY AND FRAUDULENT PRACTICES

Section 224.0 Definitions.

In this Article, the definitions given in Section 223.0 apply unless a different meaning plainly is required.

Section 224.1 Forgery.

(1) Definition. A person is guilty of forgery if, with purpose to defraud or injure anyone, or with knowledge that he is facilitating a fraud or injury to be perpetrated by anyone, the actor:

(a) alters any writing of another without his authority; or

(b) makes, completes, executes, authenticates, issues or transfers any writing so that it purports to be the act of another who did not authorize that act, or to have been executed at a time or place or in a numbered sequence other than was in fact the case, or to be a copy of an original when no such original existed; or

(c) utters any writing which he knows to be forged in a manner specified in paragraphs (a) or (b).

"Writing" includes printing or any other method of recording information, money, coins, tokens, stamps, seals, credit cards, badges, trademarks, and other symbols of value, right, privilege, or identification.

(2) Grading. Forgery is a felony of the second degree if the writing is or purports to be part of an issue of money, securities, postage or revenue stamps, or other instruments issued by the government, or part of an issue of stock, bonds or other instruments representing interests in or claims against any property or enterprise. Forgery is a felony of the third degree if the writing is or purports to be a will, deed, contract, release, commercial instrument, or other document evidencing, creating, transferring, altering, terminating, or otherwise affecting legal relations. Otherwise forgery is a misdemeanor.

Section 224.2 Simulating Objects of Antiquity, Rarity, Etc.

A person commits a misdemeanor if, with purpose to defraud anyone or with knowledge that he is facilitating a fraud to be perpetrated by anyone, he makes, alters or utters any object so that it appears to have value because of antiquity, rarity, source, or authorship which it does not possess.

Section 224.3 Fraudulent Destruction, Removal or Concealment of Recordable Instruments.

A person commits a felony of the third degree if, with purpose to deceive or injure anyone, he destroys, removes or conceals any will, deed, mortgage, security instrument or other writing for which the law provides public recording.

Section 224.4 Tampering With Records.

A person commits a misdemeanor if, knowing that he has no privilege to do so, he falsifies, destroys, removes or conceals any writing or record, with purpose to deceive or injure anyone or to conceal any wrongdoing.

Section 224.5 Bad Checks.

A person who issues or passes a check or similar sight order for the payment of money, knowing that it will not be honored by the drawee, commits a misdemeanor. For the purposes of this Section as well as in any prosecution for theft committed by means of a bad check, an issuer is presumed to know that the check or order (other than a post-dated check or order) would not be paid, if:

(1) the issuer had no account with the drawee at the time the check or order was issued; or

(2) payment was refused by the drawee for lack of funds, upon presentation within 30 days after issue, and the issuer failed to make good within 10 days after receiving notice of that refusal.

Section 224.6 Credit Cards.

A person commits an offense if he uses a credit card for the purpose of obtaining property or services with knowledge that:

(1) the card is stolen or forged; or

(2) the card has been revoked or cancelled; or

(3) for any other reason his use of the card is unauthorized.

It is an affirmative defense to prosecution under paragraph (3) if the actor proves by a preponderance of the evidence that he had the purpose and ability to meet all obligations to the issuer arising out of his use of the card. "Credit card" means a writing or other evidence of an undertaking to pay for property or services delivered or rendered to or upon the order of a designated person or bearer. An offense under this Section is a felony of the third degree if the value of the property or services secured or sought to be secured by means of the credit card exceeds $500; otherwise it is a misdemeanor.

Section 224.7 Deceptive Business Practices.

A person commits a misdemeanor if in the course of business he:

(1) uses or possesses for use a false weight or measure, or any other device for falsely determining or recording any quality or quantity; or

(2) sells, offers or exposes for sale, or delivers less than the

represented quantity of any commodity or service; or

(3) takes or attempts to take more than the represented quantity of any commodity or service when as buyer he furnishes the weight or measure; or

(4) sells, offers or exposes for sale adulterated or mislabeled commodities. "Adulterated" means varying from the standard of composition or quality prescribed by or pursuant to any statute providing criminal penalties for such variance, or set by established commercial usage. "Mislabeled" means varying from the standard of truth or disclosure in labeling prescribed by or pursuant to any statute providing criminal penalties for such variance, or set by established commercial usage; or

(5) makes a false or misleading statement in any advertisement addressed to the public or to a substantial segment thereof for the purpose of promoting the purchase or sale of property or services; or

(6) makes a false or misleading written statement for the purpose of obtaining property or credit; or

(7) makes a false or misleading written statement for the purpose of promoting the sale of securities, or omits information required by law to be disclosed in written documents relating to securities.

It is an affirmative defense to prosecution under this Section if the defendant proves by a preponderance of the evidence that his conduct was not knowingly or recklessly deceptive.

Section 224.8 Commercial Bribery and Breach of Duty to Act Disinterestedly.

(1) A person commits a misdemeanor if he solicits, accepts or agrees to accept any benefit as consideration for knowingly violating or agreeing to violate a duty of fidelity to which he is subject as:

(a) agent or employee of another;

(b) trustee, guardian, or other fiduciary;

(c) Lawyer, physician, accountant, appraiser, or other professional adviser or informant;

(d) officer, director, manager or other participant in the direction of the affairs of an incorporated or unincorporated association; or

(e) arbitrator or other purportedly disinterested adjudicator or referee.

(2) A person who holds himself out to the public as being engaged in the business of making disinterested selection, appraisal, or criticism of commodities or services commits a misdemeanor if he solicits, accepts or agrees to accept any benefit to influence his selection, appraisal or criticism.

(3) A person commits a misdemeanor if he confers, or offers or agrees to confer, any benefit the acceptance of which would be criminal under this Section.

Section 224.9 Rigging Publicly Exhibited Contest.

(1) A person commits a misdemeanor if, with purpose to prevent a publicly exhibited contest from being conducted in accordance with the

rules and usages purporting to govern it, he:

(a) confers or offers or agrees to confer any benefit upon, or threatens any injury to a participant, official or other person associated with the contest or exhibition; or

(b) tampers with any person, animal or thing.

(2) Soliciting or Accepting Benefit for Rigging. A person commits a misdemeanor if he knowingly solicits, accepts or agrees to accept any benefit the giving of which would be criminal under Subsection (1).

(3) Participation in Rigged Contest. A person commits a misdemeanor if he knowingly engages in, sponsors, produces, judges, or otherwise participates in a publicly exhibited contest knowing that the contest is not being conducted in compliance with the rules and usages purporting, to govern it, by reason of conduct which would be criminal under this Section.

Section 224.10 Defrauding Secured Creditors.

A person commits a misdemeanor if he destroys, removes, conceals, encumbers, transfers or otherwise deals with property subject to a security interest with purpose to hinder enforcement of that interest.

Section 224.11 Fraud in Insolvency.

A person commits a misdemeanor if, knowing that proceedings have been or are about to be instituted for the appointment of a receiver or other person entitled to administer property for the benefit of creditors, or that any other composition or liquidation for the benefit of creditors has been or is about to be made, he:

(a) destroys, removes, conceals, encumbers, transfers, or otherwise deals with any property with purpose to defeat or obstruct the claim of any creditor, or otherwise to obstruct the operation of any law relating to administration of property for the benefit of creditors; or

(b) knowingly falsifies any writing or record relating to the property; or

(c) knowingly misrepresents or refuses to disclose to a receiver or other person entitled to administer property for the benefit of creditors, the existence, amount or location of the property, or any other information which the actor could be legally required to furnish in relation to such administration.

Section 224.12 Receiving Deposits in a Failing Financial Institution.

An officer, manager or other person directing or participating in the direction of a financial institution commits a misdemeanor if he receives or permits the receipt of a deposit, premium payment or other investment in the institution knowing that:

(1) due to financial difficulties the institution is about to suspend operations or go into receivership or reorganization; and

(2) the person making the deposit or other payment is unaware of the precarious situation of the institution.

Section 224.13 Misapplication of Entrusted Property and Property of Government or Financial Institution.

A person commits an offense if he applies or disposes of property that has been entrusted to him as a fiduciary, or property of the government or of a financial institution, in a manner which he knows is unlawful and involves substantial risk of loss or detriment to the owner of the property or to a person for whose benefit the property was entrusted. The offense is a misdemeanor if the amount involved exceeds $50; otherwise it is a petty misdemeanor. "Fiduciary" includes trustee, guardian, executor, administrator, receiver and any person carrying on fiduciary functions on behalf of a corporation or other organization which is a fiduciary.

Section 224.14 Securing Execution of Documents by Deception.

A person commits a misdemeanor if by deception he causes another to execute any instrument affecting or purporting to affect or likely to affect the pecuniary interest of any person.

ARTICLE 230. OFFENSES AGAINST THE FAMILY

Section 230.1 Bigamy and Polygamy.

(1) Bigamy. A married person is guilty of bigamy, a misdemeanor, if he contracts or purports to contract another marriage, unless at the time of the subsequent marriage:

(a) the actor believes that the prior spouse is dead; or

(b) the actor and the prior spouse have been living apart for five consecutive years throughout which the prior spouse was not known by the actor to be alive; or

(c) a Court has entered a judgment purporting to terminate or annul any prior disqualifying marriage, and the actor does not know that judgment to be invalid; or

(d) the actor reasonably believes that he is legally eligible to remarry.

(2) Polygamy. A person is guilty of polygamy, a felony of the third degree, if he marries or cohabits with more than one spouse at a time in purported exercise of the right of plural marriage. The offense is a continuing one until all cohabitation and claim of marriage with more than one spouse terminates. This Section does not apply to parties to a polygamous marriage, lawful in the country of which they are residents or nationals, while they are in transit through or temporarily visiting this State.

(3) Other Party to Bigamous or Polygamous Marriage. A person is guilty of bigamy or polygamy, as the case may be, if he contracts or purports to contract marriage with another knowing that the other is thereby committing bigamy or polygamy.

Section 230.2 Incest.

A person is guilty of incest, a felony of the third degree, if he knowingly marries or cohabits or has sexual intercourse with an ancestor or descendant, a brother or sister of the whole or half blood [or an uncle, aunt, nephew or niece of the whole blood]. "Cohabit" means to live together under the representation or appearance of being married. The relationships referred to herein include blood relationships without regard to legitimacy, and relationship of parent and child by adoption.

Section 230.3 Abortion.

(1) Unjustified Abortion. A person

who purposely and unjustifiably terminates the pregnancy of another otherwise than by a live birth commits a felony of the third degree or, where the pregnancy has continued beyond the twenty-sixth week, a felony of the second degree.

(2) Justifiable Abortion. A licensed physician is justified in terminating a pregnancy if he believes there is substantial risk that continuance of the pregnancy would gravely impair the physical or mental health of the mother or that the child would be born with grave physical or mental defect, or that the pregnancy resulted from rape, incest, or other felonious intercourse. All illicit intercourse with a girl below the age of 16 shall be deemed felonious for purposes of this subsection. Justifiable abortions shall be performed only in a licensed hospital except in case of emergency when hospital facilities are unavailable. [Additional exceptions from the requirement of hospitalization may be incorporated here to take account of situations in sparsely settled areas where hospitals are not generally accessible.]

(3) Physicians' Certificates; Presumption from Non-Compliance. No abortion shall be performed unless two physicians, one of whom may be the person performing the abortion, shall have certified in writing the circumstances which they believe to justify the abortion. Such certificate shall be submitted before the abortion to the hospital where it is to be performed and, in the case of abortion following felonious intercourse, to the prosecuting attorney or the police. Failure to comply with any of the requirements of this Subsection gives rise to a presumption that the abortion was unjustified.

(4) Self-Abortion. A woman whose pregnancy has continued beyond the twenty-sixth week commits a felony of the third degree if she purposely terminates her own pregnancy otherwise than by a live birth, or if she uses instruments, drugs or violence upon herself for that purpose. Except as justified under Subsection (2), a person who induces or knowingly aids a woman to use instruments, drugs or violence upon herself for the purpose of terminating her pregnancy otherwise than by a live birth commits a felony of the third degree whether or not the pregnancy has continued beyond the twenty-sixth week.

(5) Pretended Abortion. A person commits a felony of the third degree if, representing that it is his purpose to perform an abortion, he does an act adapted to cause abortion in a pregnant woman although the woman is in fact not pregnant, or the actor does not believe she is. A person charged with unjustified abortion under Subsection (1) or an attempt to commit that offense may be convicted thereof upon proof of conduct prohibited by this Subsection.

(6) Distribution of Abortifacients. A person who sells, offers to sell, possesses with intent to sell, advertises, or displays for sale anything specially designed to terminate a pregnancy, or held out by the actor as useful for that purpose, commits a misdemeanor, unless:

(a) the sale, offer or display is to a physician or druggist or to an intermediary in a chain of distribution to physicians or druggists; or

(b) the sale is made upon prescription or order of a physician; or

(c) the possession is with intent to sell as authorized in paragraphs (a) and (b); or

(d) the advertising is addressed to persons named in paragraph (a) and confined to trade or professional channels not likely to reach the general public.

(7) Section Inapplicable to Prevention of Pregnancy. Nothing in this Section shall be deemed applicable to the prescription, administration or distribution of drugs or other substances for avoiding pregnancy, whether by preventing implantation of a fertilized ovum or by any other method that operates before, at or immediately after fertilization.

Section 230.4 Endangering Welfare of Children.

A parent, guardian, or other person supervising the welfare of a child under 18 commits a misdemeanor if he knowingly endangers the child's welfare by violating a duty of care, protection or support.

Section 230.5 Persistent Nonsupport.

A person commits a misdemeanor if he persistently fails to provide support which he can provide and which he knows he is legally obliged to provide to a spouse, child or other defendant.

ARTICLE 240. BRIBERY AND CORRUPT INFLUENCE

Section 240.0 Definitions.

In Articles 240–243, unless a different meaning plainly is required:

(1) "benefit" means gain or advantage, or anything regarded by the beneficiary as gain or advantage, including benefit to any other person or entity in whose welfare he is interested, but not an advantage promised generally to a group or class of voters as a consequence of public measures which a candidate engages to support or oppose;

(2) "government" includes any branch, subdivision or agency of the government of the State or any locality within it;

(3) "harm" means loss, disadvantage or injury, or anything so regarded by the person affected, including loss, disadvantage or injury to any other person or entity in whose welfare he is interested;

(4) "official proceeding" means a proceeding heard or which may be heard before any legislative, judicial, administrative or other governmental agency or official authorized to take evidence under oath, including any referee, hearing examiner, commissioner, notary or other person taking testimony or deposition in connection with any such proceeding;

(5) "party official" means a person who holds an elective or appointive post in a political party in the United States by virtue of which he directs or conducts, or participates in directing or conducting party affairs at any level of responsibility;

(6) "pecuniary benefit" is benefit in the form of money, property, commercial interests or anything else the primary significance of which is economic gain;

(7) "public servant" means any officer or employee of government, including legislators and judges, and any person participating as juror, advisor, consultant or otherwise, in performing a govern-

mental function; but the term does not include witnesses;

(8) "administrative proceeding" means any proceeding other than a judicial proceeding the outcome of which is required to be based on a record or documentation prescribed by law, or in which law or regulation is particularized in application to individuals.

Section 240.1 Bribery in Official and Political Matters.

A person is guilty of bribery, a felony of the third degree, if he offers, confers or agrees to confer upon another, or solicits, accepts or agrees to accept from another:

(1) any pecuniary benefit as consideration for the recipient's decision, opinion, recommendation, vote or other exercise of discretion as a public servant, party official or voter; or

(2) any benefit as consideration for the recipient's decision, vote, recommendation or other exercise of official discretion in a judicial or administrative proceeding; or

(3) any benefit as consideration for a violation of a known legal duty as public servant or party official.

It is no defense to prosecution under this section that a person whom the actor sought to influence was not qualified to act in the desired way whether because he had not yet assumed office, or lacked jurisdiction, or for any other reason.

Section 240.2 Threats and Other Improper Influence in Official and Political Matters.

(1) Offenses Defined. A person commits an offense if he:

(a) threatens unlawful harm to any person with purpose to influence his decision, opinion, recommendation, vote or other exercise of discretion as a public servant, party official or voter; or

(b) threatens harm to any public servant with purpose to influence his decision, opinion, recommendation, vote or other exercise of discretion in a judicial or administrative proceeding; or

(c) threatens harm to any public servant or party official with purpose to influence him to violate his known legal duty; or

(d) privately addresses to any public servant who has or will have an official discretion in a judicial or administrative proceeding any representation, entreaty, argument or other communication with purpose to influence the outcome on the basis of considerations other than those authorized by law.

It is no defense to prosecution under this Section that a person whom the actor sought to influence was not qualified to act in the desired way, whether because he had not yet assumed office, or lacked jurisdiction, or for any other reason.

(2) Grading. An offense under this Section is a misdemeanor unless the actor threatened to commit a crime or made a threat with purpose to influence a judicial or administrative proceeding, in which cases the offense is a felony of the third degree.

Section 240.3 Compensation for Past Official Behavior.

A person commits a misdemeanor if he solicits, accepts or agrees to accept any pecuniary benefit as compensation for hav ing, as public servant, given a decision, opinion, recommendation or vote favorable to another, or for having otherwise exercised a discretion in his favor, or for having violated his duty. A person commits a misdemeanor if he offers, confers or agrees to confer compensation acceptance of which is prohibited by this Section.

Section 240.4 Retaliation for Past Official Action.

A person commits a misdemeanor if he harms another by any unlawful act in retaliation for anything lawfully done by the latter in the capacity of public servant.

Section 240.5 Gifts to Public Servants by Persons Subject to Their Jurisdiction.

(1) Regulatory and Law Enforcement Officials. No public servant in any department or agency exercising regulatory functions, or conducting inspections or investigations, or carrying on civil or criminal litigation on behalf of the government, or having custody of prisoners, shall solicit, accept or agree to accept any pecuniary benefit from a person known to be subject to such regulation, inspection, investigation or custody, or against whom such litigation is known to be pending or contemplated.

(2) Officials Concerned with Government Contracts and Pecuniary Transactions. No public servant having any discretionary function to perform in connection with contracts, purchases, payments, claims or other pecuniary transactions of the government shall solicit, accept or agree to accept any pecuniary benefit from any person known to be interested in or likely to become interested in any such contract, purchase, payment, claim or transaction.

(3) Judicial and Administrative Officials. No public servant having judicial or administrative authority and no public servant employed by or in a court or other tribunal having such authority, or participating in the enforcement of its decisions, shall solicit, accept or agree to accept any pecuniary benefit from a person known to be interested in or likely to become interested in any matter before such public servant or a tribunal with which he is associated.

(4) Legislative Officials. No legislator or public servant employed by the legislature or by any committee or agency thereof shall solicit, accept or agree to accept any pecuniary benefit from any person known to be interested in a bill, transaction or proceeding, pending or contemplated, before the legislature or any committee or agency thereof.

(5) Exceptions. This Section shall not apply to:

    (a) fees prescribed by law to be received by a public servant, or any other benefit for which the recipient gives legitimate consideration or to which he is otherwise legally entitled; or

    (b) gifts or other benefits conferred on account of kinship or other personal, professional or business relationship independent of the official status of the receiver; or

    (c) trivial benefits incidental to personal, professional or business contacts and involving no substantial risk of undermining official impartiality.

(6) Offering Benefits Prohibited.

No person shall knowingly confer, or offer or agree to confer, any benefit prohibited by the foregoing Subsections.

(7) Grade of Offense. An offense under this Section is a misdemeanor.

Section 240.6 Compensating Public Servant for Assisting Private Interests in Relation to Matters Before Him.

(1) Receiving Compensation. A public servant commits a misdemeanor if he solicits, accepts or agrees to accept compensation for advice or other assistance in preparing or promoting a bill, contract, claim, or other transaction or proposal as to which he knows that he has or is likely to have an official discretion to exercise.

(2) Paying Compensation. A person commits a misdemeanor if he pays or offers or agrees to pay compensation to a public servant with knowledge that acceptance by the public servant is unlawful.

Section 240.7 Selling Political Endorsement; Special Influence.

(1) Selling Political Endorsement. A person commits a misdemeanor if he solicits, receives, agrees to receive, or agrees that any political party or other person shall receive, any pecuniary benefit as consideration for approval or disapproval of an appointment or advancement in public service, or for approval or disapproval of any person or transaction for any benefit conferred by an official or agency of government. "Approval" includes recommendation, failure to disapprove, or any other manifestation of favor or acquiescence. "Disapproval" includes failure to approve, or any other manifestation of disfavor or nonacquiescence.

(2) Other Trading in Special Influence. A person commits a misdemeanor if he solicits, receives or agrees to receive any pecuniary benefit as consideration for exerting special influence upon a public servant or procuring another to do so. "Special influence" means power to influence through kinship, friendship or other relationship, apart from the merits of the transaction.

(3) Paying for Endorsement or Special Influence. A person commits a misdemeanor if he offers, confers or agrees to confer any pecuniary benefit receipt of which is prohibited by this Section.

ARTICLE 241. PERJURY AND OTHER FALSIFICATION IN OFFICIAL MATTERS

Section 241.0 Definitions.

In this Article, unless a different meaning plainly is required:

(1) the definitions given in Section 240.0 apply; and

(2) "statement" means any representation, but includes a representation of opinion, belief or other state of mind only if the representation clearly relates to state of mind apart from or in addition to any facts which are the subject of the representation.

Section 241.1 Perjury.

(1) Offense Defined. A person is guilty of perjury, a felony of the third degree, if in any official proceeding he makes a false statement under oath or equivalent affirmation, or swears or affirms the truth of a statement previously made, when the statement is material and he does not believe it to be true.

(2) Materiality. Falsification is material, regardless of the admissibility of the statement under rules of evidence, if it could have affected the course or outcome of the proceeding. It is no defense that the declarant mistakenly believed the falsification to be immaterial. Whether a falsification is material in a given factual situation is a question of law.

(3) Irregularities No Defense. It is not a defense to prosecution under this Section that the oath or affirmation was administered or taken in an irregular manner or that the declarant was not competent to make the statement. A document purporting to be made upon oath or affirmation at any time when the actor presents it as being so verified shall be deemed to have been duly sworn or affirmed.

(4) Retraction. No person shall be guilty of an offense under this Section if he retracted the falsification in the course of the proceeding in which it was made before it became manifest that the falsification was or would be exposed and before the falsification substantially affected the proceeding.

(5) Inconsistent Statements. Where the defendant made inconsistent statements under oath or equivalent affirmation, both having been made within the period of the statute of limitations, the prosecution may proceed by setting forth the inconsistent statements in a single count alleging in the alternative that one or the other was false and not believed by the defendant. In such case it shall not be necessary for the prosecution to prove which statement was false but only that one or the other was false and not believed by the defendant to be true.

(6) Corroboration. No person shall be convicted of an offense under this Section where proof of falsity rests solely upon contradiction by testimony of a single person other than the defendant.

Section 241.2 False Swearing.

(1) False Swearing in Official Matters. A person who makes a false statement under oath or equivalent affirmation, or swears or affirms the truth of such a statement previously made, when he does not believe the statement to be true, is guilty of a misdemeanor if:

    (a) the falsification occurs in an official proceeding; or

    (b) the falsification is intended to mislead a public servant in performing his official function.

(2) Other False Swearing. A person who makes a false statement under oath or equivalent affirmation, or swears or affirms the truth of such a statement previously made, when he does not believe the statement to be true, is guilty of a petty misdemeanor, if the statement is one which is required by law to be sworn or affirmed before a notary or other person authorized to administer oaths.

(3) Perjury Provisions Applicable. Subsections (3) to (6) of Section 241.1 apply to the present Section.

Section 241.3 Unsworn Falsification to Authorities.

(1) In General. A person commits a misdemeanor if, with purpose to mislead a public servant in performing his official function, he:

    (a) makes any written false statement which he does not believe to be true; or

    (b) purposely creates a false impression in a written application for any pecuniary or other benefit, by omitting information necessary to prevent statements therein from being misleading; or

(c) submits or invites reliance on any writing which he knows to be forged, altered or otherwise lacking in authenticity; or

(d) submits or invites reliance on any sample, specimen, map, boundary-mark, or other object which he knows to be false.

(2) Statements "Under Penalty." A person commits a petty misdemeanor if he makes a written false statement which he does not believe to be true, on or pursuant to a form bearing notice, authorized by law, to the effect that false statements made therein are punishable.

(3) Perjury Provisions Applicable. Subsections (3) to (6) of Section 241.1 apply to the present Section.

Section 241.4 False Alarms to Agencies of Public Safety.

A person who knowingly causes a false alarm of fire or other emergency to be transmitted to or within any organization, official or volunteer, for dealing with emergencies involving danger to life or property commits a misdemeanor.

Section 241.5 False Reports to Law Enforcement Authorities.

(1) Falsely Incriminating Another. A person who knowingly gives false information to any law enforcement officer with purpose to implicate another commits a misdemeanor.

(2) Fictitious Reports. A person commits a petty misdemeanor if he:

(a) reports to law enforcement authorities an offense or other incident within their concern knowing that it did not occur; or

(b) pretends to furnish such authorities with information relating to an offense or incident when he knows he has no information relating to such offense or incident.

Section 241.6 Tampering With Witnesses and Informants; Retaliation Against Them.

(1) Tampering. A person commits an offense if, believing that an official proceeding or investigation is pending or about to be instituted, he attempts to induce or otherwise cause a witness or informant to:

(a) testify or inform falsely; or

(b) withhold any testimony, information, document or thing; or

(c) elude legal process summoning him to testify or supply evidence; or

(d) absent himself from any proceeding or investigation to which he has been legally summoned.

The offense is a felony of the third degree if the actor employs force, deception, threat or offer of pecuniary benefit. Otherwise it is a misdemeanor.

(2) Retaliation Against Witness or Informant. A person commits a misdemeanor if he harms another by any unlawful act in retaliation for anything lawfully done in the capacity of witness or informant.

(3) Witness or Informant Taking Bribe. A person commits a felony of the third degree if he solicits, accepts or agrees to accept any benefit in consideration of his doing any of the

things specified in clauses (a) to (d) of Subsection (1).

Section 241.7 Tampering With or Fabricating Physical Evidence.

A person commits a misdemeanor if, believing that an official proceeding or investigation is pending or about to be instituted, he:

(1) alters, destroys, conceals or removes any record, document or thing with purpose to impair its verity or availability in such proceeding or investigation; or

(2) makes, presents or uses any record, document or thing knowing it to be false and with purpose to mislead a public servant who is or may be engaged in such proceeding or investigation.

Section 241.8 Tampering With Public Records or Information.

(1) Offense Defined. A person commits an offense if he:

(a) knowingly makes a false entry in, or false alteration of, any record, document or thing belonging to, or received or kept by, the government for information or record, or required by law to be kept by others for information of the government; or

(b) makes, presents or uses any record, document or thing knowing it to be false, and with purpose that it be taken as a genuine part of information or records referred to in paragraph (a); or

(c) purposely and unlawfully destroys, conceals, removes or otherwise impairs the verity or availability of any such record, document or thing.

(2) Grading. An offense under this Section is a misdemeanor unless the actor's purpose is to defraud or injury anyone, in which case the offense is a felony of the third degree.

Section 241.9 Impersonating a Public Servant.

A person commits a misdemeanor if he falsely pretends to hold a position in the public service with purpose to induce another to submit to such pretended official authority or otherwise to act in reliance upon that pretense to his prejudice.

ARTICLE 242. OBSTRUCTING GOVERNMENTAL OPERATIONS; ESCAPES

Section 242.0 Definitions.

In this Article, unless another meaning plainly is required, the definitions given in Section 240.0 apply.

Section 242.1 Obstructing Administration of Law or Other Governmental Function.

A person commits a misdemeanor if he purposely obstructs, impairs or perverts the administration of law or other governmental function by force, violence, physical interference or obstacle, breach of official duty, or any other unlawful act, except that this Section does not apply to flight by a person charged with crime, refusal to submit to arrest, failure to perform a legal duty other than an official duty, or any other means of avoiding compliance with law without affirmative interference with governmental functions.

Section 242.2 Resisting Arrest or Other Law Enforcement.

A person commits a misdemeanor if, for the purpose of preventing a public servant from effecting a lawful arrest or discharging any other duty, the person creates a substantial risk of bodily injury to the public servant or anyone else, or employs means justifying or requiring substantial force to overcome the resistance.

Section 242.3 Hindering Apprehension or Prosecution.

A person commits an offense if, with purpose to hinder the apprehension, prosecution, conviction or punishment of another for crime, he:

(1) harbors or conceals the other; or

(2) provides or aids in providing a weapon, transportation, disguise or other means of avoiding apprehension or affecting escape; or

(3) conceals or destroys evidence of the crime, or tampers with a witness, informant, document or other source of information, regardless of its admissibility in evidence; or

(4) warns the other of impending discovery or apprehension, except that this paragraph does not apply to a warning given in connection with an effort to bring another into compliance with law; or

(5) volunteers false information to a law enforcement officer.

The offense is a felony of the third degree if the conduct which the actor knows has been charged or is liable to be charged against the person aided would constitute a felony of the first or second degree. Otherwise it is a misdemeanor.

Section 242.4 Aiding Consummation of Crime.

A person commits an offense if he purposely aids another to accomplish an unlawful object of a crime, as by safeguarding the proceeds thereof or converting the proceeds into negotiable funds. The offense is a felony of the third degree if the principal offense was a felony of the first or second degree. Otherwise it is a misdemeanor.

Section 242.5 Compounding.

A person commits a misdemeanor if he accepts or agrees to accept any pecuniary benefit in consideration of refraining from reporting to law enforcement authorities the commission or suspected commission of any offense or information relating to an offense. It is an affirmative defense to prosecution under this Section that the pecuniary benefit did not exceed an amount which the actor believed to be due as restitution or indemnification for harm caused by the offense.

Section 242.6 Escape.

(1) Escape. A person commits an offense if he unlawfully removes himself from official detention or fails to return to official detention following temporary leave granted for a specific purpose or limited period. "Official detention" means arrest, detention in any facility for custody of persons under charge or conviction of crime or alleged or found to be delinquent, detention for extradition or deportation, or any other detention for law enforcement purposes; but "official detention" does not include supervision of probation or parole, or constraint incidental to release on bail.

(2) Permitting or Facilitating Escape. A public servant concerned in detention commits an offense if he knowingly or recklessly permits an escape. Any person who knowingly

causes or facilitates an escape commits an offense.

(3) Effect of Legal Irregularity in Detention. Irregularity in bringing about or maintaining detention, or lack of jurisdiction of the committing or detaining authority, shall not be a defense to prosecution under this Section if the escape is from a prison or other custodial facility or from detention pursuant to commitment by official proceedings. In the case of other detentions, irregularity or lack of jurisdiction shall be a defense only if:

(a) the escape involved no substantial risk of harm to the person or property of anyone other than the detainee; or

(b) the detaining authority did not act in good faith under color of law.

(4) Grading of Offenses. An offense under this Section is a felony of the third degree where:

(a) the actor was under arrest for or detained on a charge of felony or following conviction of crime; or

(b) the actor employs force, threat, deadly weapon or other dangerous instrumentality to effect the escape; or

(c) a public servant concerned in detention of persons convicted of crime purposely facilitates or permits an escape from a detention facility.

Otherwise an offense under this section is a misdemeanor.

Section 242.7 Implements for Escape; Other Contraband.

(1) Escape Implements. A person commits a misdemeanor if he unlawfully introduces within a detention facility, or unlawfully provides an inmate with, any weapon, tool or other thing which may be useful for escape. An inmate commits a misdemeanor if he unlawfully procures, makes, or otherwise provides himself with, or has in his possession, any such implement of escape. "Unlawfully" means sur repetitiously or contrary to law, regulation or order of the detaining authority.

(2) Other Contraband. A person commits a petty misdemeanor if he provides an inmate with anything which the actor knows it is unlawful for the inmate to possess.

Section 242.8 Bail Jumping; Default in Required Appearance.

A person set at liberty by court order, with or without bail, upon condition that he will subsequently appear at a specified time and place, commits a misdemeanor if, without lawful excuse, he fails to appear at that time and place. The offense constitutes a felony of the third degree where the required appearance was to answer to a charge of felony, or for disposition of any such charge, and the actor took flight or went into hiding to avoid apprehension, trial or punishment. This Section does not apply to obligations to appear incident to release under suspended sentence or on probation or parole.

ARTICLE 243. ABUSE OF OFFICE

Section 243.0 Definitions.

In this Article, unless a different meaning plainly is required, the definitions given in Section 240.0 apply.

Section 243.1 Official Oppression.

A person acting or purporting to act

in an official capacity or taking advantage of such actual or purported capacity commits a misdemeanor if, knowing that his conduct is illegal, he:

(a) subjects another to arrest, detention, search, seizure, mistreatment, dispossession, assessment, lien or other infringement of personal or property rights; or

(b) denies or impedes another in the exercise or enjoyment of any right, privilege, power or immunity.

Section 243.2 Speculating or Wagering on Official Action or Information.

A public servant commits a misdemeanor if, in contemplation of official action by himself or by a governmental unit with which he is associated, or in reliance on information to which he has access in his official capacity and which has not been made public, he:

(1) acquires a pecuniary interest in any property, transaction or enterprise which may be affected by such information or official action; or

(2) speculates or wagers on the basis of such information or official action; or

(3) aids another to do any of the foregoing.

ARTICLE 250. RIOT, DISORDERLY CONDUCT, AND RELATED OFFENSES

Section 250.1 Riot; Failure to Disperse.

(1) Riot. A person is guilty of riot, a felony of the third degree, if he participates with [two] or more others in a course of disorderly conduct:

(a) with purpose to commit or facilitate the commission of a felony or misdemeanor;

(b) with purpose to prevent or coerce official action; or

(c) when the actor or any other participant to the knowledge of the actor uses or plans to use a firearm or other deadly weapon.

(2) Failure of Disorderly Persons to Disperse Upon Official Order. Where [three] or more persons are participating in a course of disorderly conduct likely to cause substantial harm or serious inconvenience, annoyance or alarm, a peace officer or other public servant engaged in executing or enforcing the law may order the participants and others in the immediate vicinity to disperse. A person who refuses or knowingly fails to obey such an order commits a misdemeanor.

Section 250.2 Disorderly Conduct.

(1) Offense Defined. A person is guilty of disorderly conduct if, with purpose to cause public inconvenience, annoyance or alarm, or recklessly creating a risk thereof, he:

(a) engages in fighting or threatening, or in violent or tumultuous behavior; or

(b) makes unreasonable noise or offensively coarse utterance, gesture or display, or addresses abusive language to any person present; or

(c) creates a hazardous or physically offensive condition by any act which serves no legitimate purpose of the actor.

"Public" means affecting or likely to affect persons in a place to which the public or a substantial group has access; among the places included are highways, transport facilities, schools, prisons, apartment houses, places of business or amusement, or any neighborhood.

(2) Grading. An offense under this section is a petty misdemeanor if the actor's purpose is to cause substantial harm or serious inconvenience, or if he persists in disorderly conduct after reasonable warning or request to desist. Otherwise disorderly conduct is a violation.

Section 250.3 False Public Alarms.

A person is guilty of a misdemeanor if he initiates or circulates a report or warning of an impending bombing or other crime or catastrophe, knowing that the report or warning is false or baseless and that it is likely to cause evacuation of a building, place of assembly, or facility of public transport, or to cause public inconvenience or alarm.

Section 250.4 Harassment.

A person commits a petty misdemeanor if, with purpose to harass another, he:

(1) makes a telephone call without purpose of legitimate communication; or

(2) insults, taunts or challenges another in a manner likely to provoke violent or disorderly response; or

(3) makes repeated communications anonymously or at extremely inconvenient hours, or in offensively coarse language; or

(4) subjects another to an offensive touching; or

(5) engages in any other course of alarming conduct serving no legitimate purpose of the actor.

Section 250.5 Public Drunkenness; Drug Incapacitation.

A person is guilty of an offense if he appears in any public place manifestly under the influence of alcohol, narcotics or other drug, not therapeutically administered, to the degree that he may endanger himself or other persons or property, or annoy persons in his vicinity. An offense under this Section constitutes a petty misdemeanor if the actor has been convicted hereunder twice before within a period of one year. Otherwise the offense constitutes a violation.

Section 250.6 Loitering or Prowling.

A person commits a violation if he loiters or prowls in a place, at a time, or in a manner not usual for law-abiding individuals under circumstances that warrant alarm for the safety of persons or property in the vicinity. Among the circumstances which may be considered in determining whether such alarm is warranted is the fact that the actor takes flight upon appearance of a peace officer, refuses to identify himself, or manifestly endeavors to conceal himself or any object. Unless flight by the actor or other circumstance makes it impracticable, a peace officer shall prior to any arrest for an offense under this section afford the actor an opportunity to dispel any alarm which would otherwise be warranted, by requesting him to identify himself and explain his presence and conduct. No person shall be convicted of an offense under this Section if the peace officer did not comply with the preceding sentence, or if it appears at trial that the explanation given by the actor was true and, if believed by the peace officer at the time, would have dispelled the alarm.

Section 250.7 Obstructing Highways and Other Public Passages.

(1) A person, who, having no legal privilege to do so, purposely or recklessly obstructs any highway or other public passage, whether alone or with others, commits a violation, or, in case he persists after warning by a law officer, a petty misdemeanor. "Obstructs" means renders impassable without unreasonable inconvenience or hazard. No person shall be deemed guilty of recklessly obstructing in violation of this Subsection solely because of a gathering of persons to hear him speak or otherwise communicate, or solely because of being a member of such a gathering.

(2) A person in a gathering commits a violation if he refuses to obey a reasonable official request or order to move:

(a) to prevent obstruction of a highway or other public passage; or

(b) to maintain public safety by dispersing those gathered in dangerous proximity to a fire or other hazard.

An order to move, addressed to a person whose speech or other lawful behavior attracts an obstructing audience, shall not be deemed reasonable if the obstruction can be readily remedied by police control of the size or location of the gathering.

Section 250.8 Disrupting Meetings and Processions.

A person commits a misdemeanor if, with purpose to prevent or disrupt a lawful meeting, procession or gathering, he does any act tending to obstruct or interfere with it physically, or makes any utterance, gesture or display designed to outrage the sensibilities of the group.

Section 250.9 Desecration of Venerated Objects.

A person commits a misdemeanor if he purposely desecrates any public monument or structure, or place of worship or burial, or if he purposely desecrates the national flag or any other object of veneration by the public or a substantial segment thereof in any public place. "Desecrate" means defacing, damaging, polluting or otherwise physically mistreating in a way that the actor knows will outrage the sensibilities of persons likely to observe or discover his action.

Section 250.10 Abuse of Corpse.

Except as authorized by law, a person who treats a corpse in a way that he knows would outrage ordinary family sensibilities commits a misdemeanor.

Section 250.11 Cruelty to Animals.

A person commits a misdemeanor if he purposely or recklessly:

(1) subjects any animal to cruel mistreatment; or

(2) subjects any animal in his custody to cruel neglect; or

(3) kills or injures any animal

belonging to another without legal privilege or consent of the owner.

Subsections (1) and (2) shall not be deemed applicable to accepted veterinary practices and activities carried on for scientific research.

Section 250.12 Violation of Privacy.

(1) Unlawful Eavesdropping or Surveillance. A person commits a misdemeanor if, except as authorized by law, he:

(a) trespasses on property with purpose to subject anyone to eavesdropping or other surveillance in a private place; or

(b) installs in any private place, without the consent of the person or persons entitled to privacy there, any device for observing, photographing, recording, amplifying or broadcasting sounds or events in such place, or uses any such unauthorized installation; or

(c) installs or uses outside a private place any device for hearing, recording, amplifying or broadcasting sounds originating in such place which would not ordinarily be audible or comprehensible outside, without the consent of the person or persons entitled to privacy there.

"Private place" means a place where one may reasonably expect to be safe from casual or hostile intrusion or surveillance, but does not include a place to which the public or a substantial group thereof has access.

(2) Other Breach of Privacy of Messages. A person commits a misdemeanor if, except as authorized by law, he:

(a) intercepts without the consent of the sender or receiver a message by telephone, telegraph, letter or other means of communicating privately; but this paragraph does not extend to (i) overhearing of messages through a regularly installed instrument on a telephone party line or on an extension, or (ii) interception by the telephone company or subscriber incident to enforcement of regulations limiting use of the facilities or incident to other normal operation and use; or

(b) divulges without the consent of the sender or receiver the existence or contents of any such message if the actor knows that the message was illegally intercepted, or if he learned of the message in the course of employment with an agency engaged in transmitting it.

ARTICLE 251. PUBLIC INDECENCY

Section 251.1 Open Lewdness.

A person commits a petty misdemeanor if he does any lewd act which he knows is likely to be observed by others who would be affronted or alarmed.

Section 251.2 Prostitution and Related Offenses.

(1) Prostitution. A person is guilty of prostitution, a petty misdemeanor, if he or she:

(a) is an inmate of a house of prostitution or otherwise engages in sexual activity as a business; or

(b) loiters in or within view of any public place for the purpose of being hired to engage in sexual activity.

"Sexual activity" includes homosexual and other deviate sexual relations.

A "house of prostitution" is any place where prostitution or promotion of prostitution is regularly carried on by one person under the control, management or supervision of another. An "inmate" is a person who engages in prostitution in or through the agency of a house of prostitution. "Public place" means any place to which the public or any substantial group thereof has access.

(2) Promoting Prostitution. A person who knowingly promotes prostitution of another commits a misdemeanor or felony as provided in Subsection (3). The following acts shall, without limitation of the foregoing, constitute promoting prostitution:

(a) owning, controlling, managing, supervising or otherwise keeping, alone or in association with others, a house of prostitution or a prostitution business; or

(b) procuring an inmate for a house of prostitution or a place in a house of prostitution for one who would be an inmate; or

(c) encouraging, inducing, or otherwise purposely causing another to become or remain a prostitute; or

(d) soliciting a person to patronize a prostitute; or

(e) procuring a prostitute for a patron; or

(f) transporting a person into or within this state with purpose to promote that person's engaging in prostitution, or procuring or paying for transportation with that purpose; or

(g) leasing or otherwise permitting a place controlled by the actor, alone or in association with others, to be regularly used for prostitution or the promotion of prostitution, or failure to make reasonable effort to abate such use by ejecting the tenant, notifying law enforcement authorities, or other legally available means; or

(h) soliciting, receiving, or agreeing to receive any benefit for doing or agreeing to do anything forbidden by this Subsection.

(3) Grading of Offenses Under Subsection (2). An offense under Subsection (2) constitutes a felony of the third degree if:

(a) the offense falls within paragraph (a), (b) or (c) of Subsection (2); or

(b) the actor compels another to engage in or promote prostitution; or

(c) the actor promotes prostitution of a child under 16, whether or not he is aware of the child's age; or

(d) the actor promotes prostitution of his wife, child, ward or any person for whose care, protection or support he is responsible.

Otherwise the offense is a misdemeanor.

(4) Presumption from Living off Prostitutes. A person, other than the prostitute or the prostitute's minor child or other legal dependent incapable of self-support, who is supported in whole or substantial part by the proceeds of prostitution is presumed to be knowingly promoting prostitution in violation of Subsection (2).

(5) Patronizing Prostitutes. A person commits a violation if he hires a prostitute to engage in sexual activity

with him, or if he enters or remains in a house of prostitution for the purpose of engaging in sexual activity.

(6) Evidence. On the issue whether a place is a house of prostitution the following shall be admissible evidence: its general repute; the repute of the persons who reside in or frequent the place; the frequency, timing and duration of visits by non-residents. Testimony of a person against his spouse shall be admissible to prove offenses under this Section.

Section 251.3 Loitering to Solicit Deviate Sexual Relations.

A person is guilty of a petty misdemeanor if he loiters in or near any public place for the purpose of soliciting or being solicited to engage in deviate sexual relations.

Section 251.4 Obscenity.

(1) Obscene Defined. Material is obscene if, considered as a whole, its predominant appeal is to prurient interest, that is, a shameful or morbid interest, in nudity, sex or excretion, and if in addition it goes substantially beyond customary limits of candor in describing or representing such matters. Predominant appeal shall be judged with reference to ordinary adults unless it appears from the character of the material or the circumstances of its dissemination to be designed for children or other specially susceptible audience. Undeveloped photographs, molds, printing plates, and the like, shall be deemed obscene notwithstanding that processing or other acts may be required to make the obscenity patent or to disseminate it.

(2) Offenses. Subject to the affirmative defense provided in Subsection (3), a person commits a misdemeanor if he knowingly or recklessly:

(a) sells, delivers or provides, or offers or agrees to sell, deliver or provide, any obscene writing, picture, record or other representation or embodiment of the obscene; or

(b) presents or directs an obscene play, dance or performance, or participates in that portion thereof which makes it obscene; or

(c) publishes, exhibits or otherwise makes available any obscene material; or

(d) possesses any obscene material for purposes of sale or other commercial dissemination; or

(e) sells, advertises or otherwise commercially disseminates material, whether or not obscene, by representing or suggesting that it is obscene.

A person who disseminates or possesses obscene material in the course of his business is presumed to do so knowingly or recklessly.

(3) Justifiable and Non-Commercial Private Dissemination. It is an affirmative defense to prosecution under this Section that dissemination was restricted to:

(a) institutions or persons having scientific, educational, governmental or other similar justification for possessing obscene material; or

(b) non-commercial dissemination to personal associates of the actor.

(4) Evidence; Adjudication of Obscenity. In any prosecution under this Section evidence shall be admissible to show:

(a) the character of the audience for which the material was designed or to which it was directed;

(b) what the predominant appeal of the material would be for ordinary adults or any special audience to which it was directed, and what effect, if any, it would probably have on conduct of such people;

(c) artistic, literary, scientific, educational or other merits of the material;

(d) the degree of public acceptance of the material in the United States;

(e) appeal to prurient interest, or absence thereof, in advertising or other promotion of the material; and

(f) the good repute of the author, creator, publisher or other person from whom the material originated.

Expert testimony and testimony of the author, creator, publisher or other person from whom the material originated, relating to factors entering into the determination of the issue of obscenity, shall be admissible. The Court shall dismiss a prosecution for obscenity if it is satisfied that the material is not obscene.

ADDITIONAL ARTICLES

[At this point, a State enacting a new Penal Code may insert additional Articles dealing with special topics such as narcotics, alcoholic beverages, gambling and offenses against tax and trade laws. The Model Penal Code project did not extend to these, partly because a higher priority on limited time and resources was accorded to branches of the penal law which have not received close legislative scrutiny. Also, in legislation dealing with narcotics, liquor, tax evasion, and the like, penal provisions have been so intermingled with regulatory and procedural provisions that the task of segregating one group from the other presents special difficulty for model legislation.]

TABLE OF CASES

[References are to sections.]

A

Aaron; People v. . . . . 5.03[A][4][a]
A. Magnano Co. v. Hamilton . . . 2.02[B][5]
Addington v. Texas . . . . 1.02[A]; 2.01; 9.04[B]n8; 9.05[B][3][b]
Afroyim v. Rusk . . . . 2.02[A]
Aguilar; United States v. . . 9.05[E][3][b][i]
Akers; State v. . . . . 8.03[A]
Alexander v. United States . . . . 2.02[B][6]
Alleged Contempt of (see name of party)
Allen v. Illinois . . . . 2.02[B][1]
Allen v. Whitehead . . . . *8.03[A]*
Altschul v. State . . . . 4.07[A]
Alvarez; United States v. . . . . . 7.03[C][1]
Anderson; People v. . . . 5.03[A][1]; 7.02[B]
Anderson v. State . . . . 4.07[A]
Anderson v. Superior Court . . . . . 7.03[E]
Andrews; State v. . . . . 9.05[B][3][a]
Angelo; People v. 3.01
Antick; People v. . . . . 5.03[A][4][e]
Appeal of (see name of party)
Appeal of Estate of (see name of party)
Application of (see name of applicant)
Apprendi v. New Jersey . . . . 9.04[B]
Arata; State v. . . . . 5.03[A][1]
Argersinger v. Hamlin . . . . 1.02[C]
As in Bennis v. Michigan . . . . . 2.02[B][6]
Ashland; People v. . . . . 5.03[B][1]
Ashton; United States v. . . . . . 9.05[A][3]
Atencio; United States v. . . . . 9.05[A][1][c]
Austin v. United States . . . . . . 2.02[B][6]; 2.04[B]; 5.03[A]

B

B. v. Director of Public Prosecutions, H.L. . . 4.07[A]
Bailey v. Commonwealth . . . . 8.01[C]
Bailey; United States v. . . . . *9.05[E][1]*
Bajakajian; United States v. . . . 2.02[B][6]
Baker; State v. . . . . 5.03[A][4][e]
Baldwin v. New York . . . . 2.02[B][2]
Balint; United States v. . . . . 4.07[B]
Ballard v. United States . . . . . . 1.02[D][2]
Ballew v. Georgia . . . . 1.02[D][2]
Banks; United States v . . . . *5.03[A][2]*; 9.05[A][1][c]
Barber v. Superior Court . . . . 3.03; 5.02[B]
Barker; United States v. . . . . . . 4.06[B][1]
Barnes v. Comm. . . . . 4.07[A]
Barnes; People v. . . . . 6.02[A]
Barnes v. United States . . . . 9.04[C]
barnett; State v., 5.03[B][1][a]
Barrows v. Jackson . . . . 1.02[D][2]

Bartram v. State . . . . 5.03[B][1]
Bateman; State v. . . . . 2.06[A]
Batson v. Kentucky . . . . 1.02[D][2]
Batten v. State . . . . 9.05[A][4][d]
B.C. Motor Vehicle Act, *In re* . . . . 4.07[A]
Beardsley; People v. 3.03
Beaudry; State v. . . . . 8.03[A]
Beaver v. Queen . . . . 4.06[A]
Bell v. Wolfish . . . . 2.02[B][1]
Belton v. United States . . . . 9.04[C]
Bennett; People v. . . . . 5.03[B][2][a]
Bennis v. Michigan . . . . 2.02[B][6]
Bentley v. State . . . . 5.03[A][2]
Berger; People v. . . . . 7.02[B]
Bergman; United States v. . . . . . *2.03[D]*
Berkowitz; Commonwealth v. . . . . *6.02[A]*
Bernstein; State v. . . . . 4.06[B][2][a]
Berrois; United States v. . . . . . . 1.02[B]
Berry; People v. . . . . *5.03[B][1]*
Bertucci; People v. . . . . 2.02[B][4]
Bethea v. United States . . . 9.05[B][4], n10
Bingham; State v. . . . . *5.03[A][1]*
Birch v. Louisiana . . . . 1.02[D][2]
Birney v. State . . . . 4.07[A]
Bishop v. United States . . . . 9.05[B][4]
Bishop; United States v. . . . . 4.06[B][2][d]
Black v. State . . . . 8.01[B]
Blankenship; United States v. . . . . *7.03[D]*
Blansett v. State . . . . 5.03[A][4][e]
Blanton v. Nevada . . . . 1.02[D][2]
Blocker v. United States . . . . 9.05[B][3][a]
Blodgett, *In re* . . . . 2.02[B][1]
Boro v. Superior Court . . . . *6.02[B]*
Blumenthal v. United States . . . 7.03[C][1], [E], [H]
Blumke v. Foster . . . . 7.02[E]
Bohannon v. Commonwealth . . 9.05[A][4][d]
Bolton v. Harris . . . . 9.05[B][3][b]
Bonano; State v. . . . . 9.05[A][4][c]
Bonds; People v. . . . . 5.03[A][4][a]
Bonilla; People v. . . . . 5.02[B]
Borches; People v. . . . . 5.03[B][1]
Bordenkircher v. Hayes . . . . 1.02[B]
Borelli; United States v. . . . . 7.03[E]
Borwich; State v. . . . . 9.05[A][4][c]
Bouie v. Columbia, City of . . . . . . 2.05[C]
Bourgeois v. Commonwealth . . . . . 8.03[A]
Bouse; People v. . . . . 5.02[D]
Bowen; State v. . . . . 9.05[A][4][b]
Bowers v. Hardwick . . . . 2.06[A]
Boyce v. California . . . . 1.02[A]
Boynton; Commonwealth v. . . . . . 4.07[A]
Bradford; United States v. . . . 5.03[B][2][b]
Bradley v. State 3.01

TC-1

[References are to sections.]

Braham; State v.	7.02[B]
Braithwaite; People v.	5.03[A][4][e]
Brandon; United States v.	4.06[A]
Bratty v. Attorney General for Northern Ireland	9.05[B][3][d]
Braverman v. United States	7.03[E], [H]
Brawner; United States v.	9.05[B][3][a]
Brent v. State	4.06[B][2][a]
Bright; United States v.	4.06[A]
Brinegar v. United States	1.02[A]
Bristol; State v.	9.05[A][4][d]
Brock v. State	5.02[A]; 7.02[B]
Broome v. Cassell	4.03[A][ii]
Brown v. Multnomah County District Court	*2.02[B][3]*; 2.02[B][4]
Brown v. State	4.06[B][2][d]
Brown; State v.	5.03[A][1]; 7.03[A][1]; 9.05[A][3]
Brown v. United States	9.05[A][4][a], [c]
Brown; United States v.	4.06[B][1]
Browning-Ferris Industries v. Kelco Disposal, Inc.	2.02[B][6]
Bruno; United States v.	7.03[E]
Buchman; State v.	9.04[A]
Bullock; People v.	2.04[B]
Burden; People v.	5.03[A][2]
Burgin v. State	9.04[A]
Burleson; State v.	7.03[A][1]
Burns v. State	4.06[B][2][d]
Burton; People v.	5.03[A][4][d]
Burton v. State	7.02[B]
Bushell's Case	1.02[D][2]
Bussard v. State	5.03[B][2][a]
Button; People v.	9.05[A][4][d]

C

Cabaltero; People v.	8.01[B]
Caddell; State v.	9.04; 9.05[B][3][d]
Cage v. Louisiana	1.02[A]
Calder v. Bull	2.05[C]
Calero-Toledo v. Pearson Yacht Leasing Co.	2.02[B][6]
Calhoun; State v.	2.02[B][3]
Cali; Commonwealth v.	3.02[A]
Caliguri; State v.	7.03[D]
Callahan v. United States	7.03[A][1]
Cameron; State v.	4.07[A]; 9.05[B][3][a]
Canola; State v.	3.04[D]; *5.03[A][4][e]*
Cardwell; People v.	5.03[A][1]
Carico v. Commonwealth.	9.05[A][4][d]
Carothers; State v.	8.01[B]
Carroll; Commonwealth v.	5.03[A][1]
Carter v. Jury Commission	1.02[D][2]
Carter v. Jury Commission of Greene County	1.02[D][2]
Carter; People v.	3.04[C][1]
Carter; State v.	9.04[A]
Cass; Commonwealth v.	2.05[C]; 5.02[C]
Castaneda v. Partida	1.02[D][2]
Ceballos; People v.	9.05[A][5]
Cegers; People v.	9.05[E][2][a]
Cegon; State v.	8.03[B]
Cerone; United States v.	7.03[H]
Chadwick v. United States	7.03[C][2]n5
Chambers v. Mississippi	9.05[B][4], [C]
Chambers; State v.	5.03[A][4][b]
Chapman v. United States	2.04[A]
Chase v. United States	1.02[D][2]
Chavez; People v.	2.05[C]
Check v. United States	*4.06[B][2][d]*; 4.07[B]n3
Cheek; United States v.	4.06[B][2][d]
Chermansky; Commonwealth v.	9.05[A][6]
Chester; Commonwealth v.	9.05[B][3][a]
Chevalier; People v.	5.03[B][1]
Chiarello; State v.	9.05[A][4][d]
Chicago, City of v. Morales	2.05[B]
Chittum v. Commonwealth	9.05[C]
Chopra; People v.	5.03[A][2]
Christy Pontiac-GMC, Inc,	*8.03[B]*
Cifizzari; Commonwealth v.	5.03[A][4][d]
City v. (see name of defendant)	
City and County of (see name of city and county)	
Clary; United States v.	2.04[A]
Coe; State v.	4.03[B]
Coffin v. United States	1.02[A]
Cohen; United States v.	1.02[D][2]
Coker v. Georgia	5.04[B]; 6.01
Colandro; Commonwealth v.	9.05[A][4][d]
Cole; People v.	8.01[A]
Cole; State v.	9.05[A][3]
Colero-Toledo v. Pearson Yacht Leasing Co.	2.02[B][6]
Collins; People v.	9.05[A][4][d]
Comitz; Commonwealth v.	9.05[E][2][b]
Comm. v. Barboza	1.02[D][2]
Comm v. N.Y. Cent. & H. Co.	4.07[B]
Commission v. (see name of opposing party)	
Commissioner v. (see name of opposing party)	
Commissioner of Internal Revenue (see name of defendant)	
Commonwealth v. (see name of defendant)	
Commonwealth ex rel. (see name of relator)	
Comodeca; People v.	7.02[D]
Conley; People v.	9.05[B][4]
Connally v. General Constr. Co.	2.05[B]n17, [C]
Conservatorship of (see name of party)	
Consider R. v. Ross	4.06[B][1]
Cornell; United States v.	9.05[C]
Cotterill v. Penn	*4.04[B]*; 4.05[D];4.05[E]
The Cotton Planter	4.06[B][1]
Couch v. State	3.04[A]

TABLE OF CASES

[References are to sections.]

County v. (see name of defendant)
County of (see name of county)
Cowan v. Montana . . . . 9.05[B][5][b]
Cowan; State v. . . . . 9.05[B][5][b]
Cox v. Louisiana . . . . 4.06[B][2][c]
Cox; United States v. . . . . 1.02[B]
Cozzens; State v. . . . . 9.05[A][3]
Crabfree v. State . . . . 4.07[A]
Craig v. State 3.03n3
Crenshaw; State v. . . . . 9.05[B][3][a]
Crimmins; United States v. . . . . . 7.03[D]
Curtis; People v. . . . . 9.05[A][6]
Custody of (see name of party)
Cutter v. State . . . . 4.06[B][2][b]

D

Daly; State v. . . . . 3.02[A]
Daniel M'Naghten's Case . . . *9.05[B][3][a]*
Davern; United States v. . . . . 7.02[G]
Davis; People v. . . . . 5.02[C]
Davis v. State . . . . 7.03[A][1]
Davis v. United States . . . . 1.02[A];
 9.04[B]n31
Davis, In re . . . . 2.05[C]
DeGidio v. State . . . . 7.02[E]
De La O, In re . . . . *2.02[B][2];*
 3.01[B];4.03[A][ii]
De Veau v. Braisted . . . . 2.02[A]
Dear Wing Jung v. United States . . 1.02[B]
Decina; People v. . . *3.01[A];* 3.02[A];9.05[C]
Delahoussaye; United States v. . . . 4.03[B]
Delamater v. South Dakota . . 4.06[B][2][a]
Department of Revenue of Mont. v. Kurth Ranch
 . . . . . . 2.02[B][4];*2.02[B][5]*
Derrera; People v. . . . . 7.02[C]n8
DeWeese; United States v. . . . . 7.03[C][1]
D.G.W., State in Interest of . . . . 2.02[B][4]
Diana; State v. . . . . 9.05[A][3]
Dietz v. Solem . . . . 9.04[C]
Dillon; People v. . . . . 5.03[A][4][a]
Dillon; State v. . . . . 2.02[B][4]
DiPaolo; State v. . . . . 9.05[B][4]n10
Director of Public Prosecutions v. Camplin
 . . . . *5.03[B][1]*
Director of Public Prosecutions v. Morgan .
 6.03[A]; 6.03[B]
Direct Sales Co. v. United States . . 7.03[D]
Dobbins's Distillery v. United States . . . . .
 2.02[B][6]
Dominguez-Mestas; United States v. . . . . . .
 9.05[A][1][b]
Donoghue; Commonwealth v. . . . . 7.03[B]
Donovan; United States v. . . . 4.06[B][2][d]
Dorazio; Commonwealth v. . . . *5.03[A][3]*
Dorrell; United States v. . . . . . . 9.05[A][3]
Dorsey; State v. . . . . 9.05[A][3]

Dotterweich; United States v. . . . . 4.07[A],
 [B]; 8.03[A]
Dougherty; United States v. . . . 1.02[D][2]
Dowell; State v. . . . . 8.01[C]
Downey v. Perini . . . . 2.04[B]
D.P.P. v. Majewski . . . . 9.05[C]
DPP for No. Ire. v. Lynch . . . 9.05[A][1][d]
Driscoll; United States v. . . . . 9.04[C]
Duncan v. Louisiana . . . . . 1.02[A], [D][2]
Duren v. Missouri . . . . 1.02[D][2]
Durham v. State . . . . 9.05[A][6]
Durham v. United States . . . . 9.05[B][3][a]

E

Easter v. District of Columbia . . . . 9.05[C]
Eatman; People v. . . . . 9.05[A][5]
Edmondson v. Leesville Concrete Co. . . . . .
 1.02[D][2]
Eisenstadt v. Baird . . . . 2.06[A]
Ekwunoh; United States v. . . . . . . 4.06[A]
Elder; People v. . . . . 3.04[C][1]
Elkins v. State . . . . 9.04[A]
Elliott; United States v. . . . . 7.03[H]
Ellis; State v. . . . . 4.06[B][2][a]
Elrich; State v. . . . . *8.01[B]*
Employment Division, Oregon Department of
 Human Resources v. Smith . . 4.06[B][1]
Enmund v. Florida . . . . 5.04[B]
Erickson; State v. . . . . 2.06[A]
Erie R.R. v. Stewart 3.03
Erwin; State v. . . . . 9.05[C]n2
Est. of (see name of party)
Estate of (see name of party)
Etiene Barronnet and Edmond Allain, In The
 Matter of . . . . 4.06[B][1]
Etzweiler; State v. . . . . *8.01[B]*
Ex parte (see name of applicant)
Ex rel. (see name of relator)

F

Fagan v. Metropolitan Police Commissioner
 . . . . 3.02[A]
Fain v. Commonwealth 3.01
Fair; State v. . . . . 9.05[A][4][d]
Falcone; United States v. . . . . 7.03[D]
Falcone, United States v. . . . . 7.03[D]
Falk; United States v. . . . . 1.02[B]
Farrell v. State . . . . 4.06[A]
Farrell, In re . . . . 9.05[E][3][b][i]
Fatico; United States v. . . . . 1.02[A]
Fay v. New York . . . . 1.02[D][2]
the Federal Sentencing Guidelines." United
 States v. Ocasio-Rivera . . . . . . 2.04[A]
Feinberg; Commonwealth v. . . . . . 3.04[B]
Felder, In re . . . . *2.02[B][2]*
Feola v. United States . . . . *4.06[A];7.03[D]*

TABLE OF CASES

[References are to sections.]

Ferris; State v. . . . . 9.04[B]n24
Fierro; State v. . . . . *5.02[B]*
Fincher; United States v. . . . . . 7.03[C][1]
Fioretti; People v. . . . . 2.02[B][3]
Fisher v. United States . . . . . . 9.05[B][4]
Fisse, Probability and the Proudman v. Dayman Defence of Reasonable Mistaken Belief . . . . 4.07[A]
Fitzgerald v. State . . . . *5.03[B][1][a]*
 9.05[A][4][b]
Flannel; People v. . . . . 9.05[A][4][b]
Flemming v. Nestor . . . . *2.02[A];*
 2.02[B][4];2.05
Ford; People v. . . . . 5.03[A][4][b]
Ford v. Wainright . . . . 9.05[B][2]
Forrest; State v. . . . . *9.05[E][3][b]*
Foster v. State . . . . 9.05[C]n2
Foster; State v. . . . . 4.06[B][2][c]
Foucha v. Louisiana . . . .
 2.02[B][6];*9.05[B][3][b]*
Frazier; State v. . . . . 3.04[A]
Freddo v. State . . . . 5.03[B][1]
Freed; United States v. . . . . . . 4.06[B][1];
 4.07[B]
Freeman; People v. . . . . 1.02[A]
Freeman; United States v. . . . . 4.06[B][1];
 7.03[C][1]; 9.05[B][3][a]
Frysig; People v. . . . . 7.02[C]
Fulcher v. State . . . . *9.05[B][3][d]*
Fuller; People v. . . . . 5.03[A][4][b]
Furman v. Georgia . . . . 5.04[B]

G

Gainey; United States v. . . . . . 9.04[B]n31,
 [C]n16
Gallegos; State v. . . . . 9.05[A][4][d]
Garbutt; People v. . . . . 9.05[C]
Gardner v. Akeroyd . . . . 7.02[C]
Garrett; United States v. . . . . . *4.03[B]*
Gault, In re . . . . 2.02[B][2]
Gay; State v. . . . . 7.02[B]
Gebardi v. United States . . . . . *7.03[C][2]*
Gentry v. State . . . . 7.02[C]
Georgia v. McCollum . . . . 1.02[D][2]
Gervin v. State . . . . 7.02[B]
Gibbs; State v. . . . . 9.04[A]
Gideon v. Wainwright . . . . 1.02[C]
Gilbert; People v. . . . . 5.03[A][4][e]
Gilbert v. State . . . . 9.05[E][3][b][i]
Giovanetti; United States v. . . . . . *8.01[B]*
Givens; People v. . . . . 9.05[A][5]
Gladman; People v. . . . . 5.03[A][4][c]
Gladstone; State v. . . . . *8.01[B]*
Goetz; People v. . . . . 9.05[A][4][d]
Goetz v. State . . . . 4.06[A]
Goldberg v. State . . . . 6.02[A]
Good; People v. . . . . 2.02[B][4]

Goodenow; State v. . . . . 4.06[B][2][b]
Goodrow v. Perrin . . . . 4.07[A]
Goodwin v. State . . . . 7.02[C]n9
Gooze; State v. 3.01
Gormley; Commonwealth v. . . . . . 7.03[D]
Gounagias; State v. . . . . 5.03[B][1]
Granda; United States v. . . . . . 4.06[B][1]
Grant; People v. 9.04
Gray; People v. . . . . 9.05[A][5]
Greer; People v. . . . . 5.02[C]
Gregg v. Georgia . . . . 5.04[A][2], [B]
Gregg Cartage & Storage Co. v. United States
 . . . . 9.05[B][3][a]
Griffith v. State . . . . 9.05[E][3][b][i]
Griswold v. Connecticut . . . . *2.06[A]*
Grove; Commonwealth v. . . . . 9.05[A][4][d]
Guardianship of (see name of party)
Guirlando; State v. . . . . 1.02[D][2]

H

Haack; People v. . . . . *5.03[A][1]*
Haines; State v. . . . . 5.02[A]; 7.02[B]
Haley v. Ohio . . . . 4.06[B][2][c]
Halper; United States v. . . . *2.02[B][4]* , [5],
 [6], n6
Halper and Austin; United States v. . . . . .
 2.02[B][6]
Halper and Department of Revenue of Mont. v.
 Kurth Ranch . . . . 2.02[B][4]
Halper, Austin, and Department of Revenue of
 Mont. v. Kurth Ranch . . . . . 2.02[B][6]
Hamling v. United States . . . . . 1.02[D][2]
Hampton v. United States . . . . . . 7.02[F]
Ham, qui tam v. McClaws . . . . . 4.06[B][1]
Hamilton v. People . . . . 4.06[B][2][c]
Hanaphy; State v. . . . . 4.06[B][2][a]
Hansen v. Harris . . . . 4.06[B][2][c]
Hansen v. United States . . . . . 1.02[D][2]
Harding v. Price . . . . 4.07[A]
Harmelin v. Michigan . . . . 2.04[B]; 9.05[C]
Harmony v. United States . . . . . 2.02[B][6]
Harris; State v. . . . . 5.03[A][1]
Hart; State v. . . . . 9.04[A]
Hatch; State v. . . . . 4.06[B][1]
Hawkins v. State . . . . 9.05[C]n2
Hayes; State v. . . . . *8.01[C]*
Haynes v. State . . . . 4.07[A]
Heacock v. Commonwealth . . . 5.03[A][4][b]
Healy v. Edwards and Taylor . . . 1.02[D][2]
Hearst; United States v. . . . . . 9.05[A][1][b]
Heigho, *In re* . . . . 3.04[A]
Heil; People v. . . . . 2.02[B][4]n2
Helverling v. Michell . . . . 2.02[B][5]
Hendershott v. People . . . . 9.05[B][4]
Heng Awkak Roman; United States v. . . . .
 7.02[B]
Henzey; People v. . . . . 1.02[B]

[References are to sections.]

Hermelin v. Michigan	*2.04[B]*
Herschorn v. People	8.03[A]
Hickman; People v.	5.03[A][4][e]
Hicks v. United States	8.01[A]
Hill v. Baxter	9.05[B][3][d]
Hilton Hotels Corporation; United States v.	*8.03[B]*
Hinkle; State v.	5.03[A][4][d]
HM Advocate v. Fraser	3.01
Hobbins v. Attorney General	5.02[D]
Hoflin; United States v.	4.04[B]
Holland v. Illinois	1.02[D][2]
Hollis v. Commonwealth	5.02[C]
Holloway v. Moser	9.05[A][6]
Holmes; United States v.	9.05[A][3]
Home; State v.	2.05[C]
Hood; People v.	4.03[A][2]; 9.05[C]
Hopkins v. State	4.06[B][2][c]
Hopkins; State v.	8.01[B]
Hornbeck v. State	5.03[A][4][e]
Horne; State v.	5.02[C]
Horton v. Gwynne	4.04[B]
Hough; People v.	6.02[B]
Howard v. United States	9.04[C]
Hoyt v. Florida	1.02[D][2]
Hudson; People v.	9.04[A]
Hudson v. United States	2.02[B][6]n6
Huff; State v.	*4.06[B][2][c]*
Hughes v. Matthews	9.05[B][4]
Hunter v. State	4.06[B][2][b]
Hunter; State v.	9.05[A][4][d]
Hupf; State v.	5.03[B][2][b]
Hutchins; Commonwealth v.	9.05[A][3]
Hutchinson v. Bank of Wheeling	1.02[B]
Hutchinson v. State	7.03[C][2]
Hyde v. United States	7.03[F]; 8.02

I

Iannelli v. United States	7.03[H]
Ibn-Tamas v. United States	9.05[A][4][d]
Imbler v. Pachtman	1.02[B]
In re (see name of party)	
Iniguez; People v.	*6.02[A]*
United States v. Cullen	9.05[E][3][a]
International Longshoremen Warehouseman's Union v. Ackerman	1.02[D][2]
International Minerals and Chemical Corp.; United States v.	4.06[B][1];4.07[B]n3
International Union, United Mine Workers of America v. Bagwell	2.02[B][1]
Iowa City v. Nolan	8.03[A]; 9.04[C]
Ireland; People v.	5.03[A][4][d]

J

Jackson v. Indiana	9.05[B][3][b]
Jackson v. State	3.04[D]
Jackson; State v.	9.05[E][3][b][i]
Jackson; United States v.	*2.04[A]*
Jackson v. Virginia	5.03[A][1]
Jacobson v. Massachusetts	3.01
Jacobson v. United States	9.05[D]
Jaffe; People v.	*7.02[F]*
Jahnke v. State	9.05[A][4][d]
Janes; State v.	9.05[A][4][d]
Jansen; State v.	8.01[C]
J.E.B. v. Alabama Ex rel T.B.	1.02[D][2]
Jefferson; People v.	5.03[A][3]
Jellico Coal Min. Co. v. Comm.	4.06[B][1]
Jennell; United States v.	9.05[A][1][c]
Jensen; State v.	5.03[A][1]
Jenson v. Fletcher	3.01
Jewell; United States v.	4.06[A]; 8.01[B]
Jobes, In re	9.05[E][3][b][i]
Johnson v. Glick	2.02[B][1]
Johnson v. Louisiana	1.02[D][2]
Johnson v. Sargant and Sons	4.06[B][1]
Johnson v. State	5.03[A][4][e]; 9.05[A][6]n5;*9.05[B][3][a]*
Johnson; State v. 5.03[A][1]	*Johnson v. State of Florida* 2.05[C]
Johnson v. Williford	4.06[B][2][c]
Johnson and Towers; United States v.	4.04[B]
Jones; State v.	9.05[B][3][a]
Jones v. United States	*3.03[C]* 9.05[B][3][b]
Joseph G., In re	*5.02[D]*
Jung Yul Yu; United States v.	4.06[B][1]
Jurek v. Texas	5.04[B]
J.W. Goldsmith, Jr.-Grant Co. v. United States	2.02[B][6]

K

Kahler; State v.	9.04[A]
Kansas v. Hendricks	2.02[B][3]
Keaton v. State	5.03[A][4][e]
Keihn; State v.	4.07[A]
Keller v. Superior Court	*2.05[C]*
Kelley; People v.	*9.05[C]*
Kelly v. Gwinnell	3.03
Kelly; State v.	4.07[A]
Kelso; People v.	5.03[A][4][d]
Kemp; People v.	8.01[B]
Kendall v. State	4.07[A]
Kennedy v. Mendoza-Martinez	2.02[A], [B][1], [3], [4], [6]n6
Kenny; United States v.	7.03[E]
Kervorkian; People v.	5.02[D]
Kevorkian; People v.	9.05[E][3][b][i]
King v. Carroll, Justice Park	9.05[C]
The King v. Cogdon	3.01
King v. Grindley	9.05[C]
The King v. Oneby	9.04[B]

[References are to sections.]

King; People v. . . . . 9.05[A][3]
Kistenmacher; State v. . . . . 4.03[A][2]
Kitson, *In re* . . . . 3.02[A]
Knowles; United States v. 3.03n4
Knox v. Comm. 3.03
Knox v. Commonwealth . . . . 8.01[A]
Koczwara; Commonwealth v. . . . . 8.03[A]
Koilender v. Lawson . . . . 2.05[B]
Kominis; State v. . . . . 4.07[A]
Konz; Commonwealth v. 3.03
Korell; State v. . . . . 9.05[B][5][b]
Kotteakos v. United States . . . . . . 7.03[E];
7.03[H]
Kress; State v. . . . . 3.04[D]
Krovarz; People v. . . . . 7.02[C]
Krulewitch v. United States . . . 7.03[A][2]
Kryske; United States v. . . . . . 1.02[D][2]

L

Ladd; Commonwealth v. . . . . 5.02[A]
Lafferty; State v. . . . . 9.04[B];9.05[E][2][b]
Lambert v. California . . . . 4.06[B][1]
Lanier v. State . . . . 9.05[C]n2
Lanzetta v. New Jersey . . . . 2.05[B];
4.06[B][2][a]
Lashley; State v. . . . . 5.03[A][4][b]
Later, in Stanford v. Kentucky . . . 5.04[B]
Lauria; People v . . . . 7.03[D]
Law v. Maryland . . . . 9.05[A][5]
Lazy FC Ranch; United States v. . . . . . .
4.06[B][2][c]
Leary v. United States . . . . . 9.04[C], n17
Leavine v. State . . . . 8.01[B]
Leidholm; State v. . . . . 9.05[A][4][d]
Leland v. Oregon . . . 9.04[B]; 9.05[B][3][e]
Lenkevick; People v. . . . . 9.05[A][4][c]
Levine; United States v. . . . . 7.03[H]
Lewellyn; United States v. . . . 9.05[E][2][b]
Lewis v. State 3.01
Libretti v. United States . . . . . . 2.02[B][6]
Licavoli; United States v. . . . . . . 7.03[H]
License of (see name of party)
Lindsey; Commonwealth v. . . . . 9.05[A][3]
Lino; Commonwealth v. . . . . . . 9.05[A][3]
Liparota v. United States . . . . . . 4.04[B];
4.06[B][1]; 4.07[B]
Littledale, J., in Rex v. Murphy (1) . . . . . .
8.01[A]
Littledale, J., in Rex v. Murphy (2) . . . . . .
8.01[A]
Lockett v. Ohio . . . . 5.04[B]
Lockyer v. Gibb . . . . 4.06[A]
Logan; People v. . . . . 5.03[B][1]
Long v. State . . . . 4.06[B][2][b]
Lopez; United States v. . . . . . . 9.05[A][3]
Loser v. Superior Court . . . . 7.03[F]
Lovercamp; People v. . . . . 9.05[E][1]

Low; People v. . . . . 9.05[C]
Luciano; People v. 8.02
Lynch, *In re* . . . . 2.04[B]
Lynch v. Director of Public Prosecutions . .
9.01

M

Mack; People v. . . . . 3.02[B]
Mack; United States v. . . . . . 5.03[A][4][c];
7.03[D]
MacMillian v. State . . . . 9.04[C]
Maher v. People . . . . 5.03[B][1]
Maldonado; State v. . . 3.04[D]; 5.03[A][4][b]
Malloy; Commonwealth v. . . . . . . 1.02[B]
Malone; Commonwealth v. . . . . 5.03[A][2];
5.03[B][2][a]
Mandujano; United States v. . . . . . 7.02[B]
Mann v. United States . . . . 9.04[C]
Marcocelli; Commonwealth v. . . . .
9.05[A][4][c]
Markowitz; People v. . . . . . . 4.06[B][2][c]
Marley, Ex parte . . . . 8.03[A]
Marlowe; State v. . . . . 9.05[A][4][c]
Marrero; People v. . . . . 4.06[B][2][a]
Marriage of (see name of party)
Marshall; People v. . . . . 8.01[B]
Marshall; United States v. . . . . . . 2.04[A]
Martin v. Ohio . . . . 9.05[C]
Martin v. State . . . . 3.01[B]
Martinez v. State 8.02
Martinez; State v. . . . . 9.05[A][4][c]
Marts v. State . . . . 9.05[A][4][d]
Massie v. State . . . . 5.03[A][4][d]
Matlock; People v. . . . . 5.02[D]
Matter of (see name of party)
Matthews v. United States . . . 9.05[A][4][a]
Mauldin; State v. . . . . 5.03[A][4][c]
Mayberry; People v. . . . . 6.03[B]
Mays; People v. . . . . 5.03[A][2]
McAllister; State v. . . . . . 5.03[B][1]; 8.01[B]
McCall; State v. . . . . 5.03[B][2][a]
McCarthy v. State . . . . 9.05[B][4]
McCarthy; State v. . . . . 8.01[C]
McCleskey v. Kemp . . . . 5.04[B]
McCluskey v. State . . . . 7.02[B]
McCollum v. McConaughy . . . 4.06[B][2][a]
McCoy v. State . . . . 9.05[A][1][b]
McCullough v. State . . . . 1.02[A]
McDougle v. Maxwell . . . . 2.04[B]
McDonald;State v. . . . . 4.06[A]
McElroy v. State . . . . 9.05[B][3][a]
McFarland v. American Sugar Rfg. Co. . . .
9.04[B]
McGee; People v. 8.02
McKeiver v. Pennsylvania . . . . 1.02[D][2];
2.02[B][2]
McKiever; State v. . . . . 5.03[A][4][a]

TABLE OF CASES

[References are to sections.]

McLaughlin, 111 Cal, App. 2d 781; People v.
.... 7.03[D]
McMillan v. Pennsylvania ...... 9.04[B];
9.05[C]
McMurray; United States v. ..... 7.03[E]
McQuillan.; People v. ..... 9.05[B][5][a]n*
McQuirter v. State ..... 7.02[B]; 7.02[E]
Meachum v. Fano .... 9.04[B]n8
Merkt; United State v. .... 9.05[E][3][b]
Merrill v. Fed. Crop. Ins. Corp. ....
4.06[B][2][c]
Merrill; State v. .... 5.02[C]
Midgett v. State .... 5.03[A][3]
Miers v. State .... 5.03[A][4][e]
Millard v. State .... 9.05[E][2][a]
Miller v. California .... 4.04[B]
Miller; People v. .... 5.03[A][4][d]
Miller v. State .... 7.02[E]
Minkowski; People v. .... 6.02[B]
Minster; State v. .... 5.02[A]
Mistretta; United States v. ...... 2.04[A]
Mitchell; State v. .... 7.02[F]
Mixer; Commonwealth .... 4.07[A]
Mize; State v. .... 9.05[A][4][d]
Mlinarich; Commonwealth v. .... 6.02[A]
Mobile, J. & K. C.R. v. Turnipseed .....
9.04[B]n16
Molina; United States v. 8.02
Moncini; United States v. .... 4.06[B][1]
Monroe; State v. .... 9.04[B]
Montana v. Egelhoff .... 9.05[C]
Montgomery; State v. ..... 5.03[A][4][c]
Montgomery; United States v. .. 9.05[A][3]
Moon; Commonwealth v. ..... 9.05[B][2]
Moore v. Dempsey .... 5.04[B]
Moore; United States v. .... 5.02[A];
9.05[B][4], [C]
Moran; People v. .... 5.03[A][4][d]
Moran; United States v. .... 4.06[B][2][d]
Morelli; United States v. .... 7.03[H]
Moretti; State v. .... 7.03[D]
Morissette v. United States .. 4.01; 4.07[A];
4.07[B]; 9.04[C]
Morning; Commonwealth v. .. 9.05[A][1][d]
Morris; People v. .... 5.03[A][4][e]
Morris; United States v. .... 4.04[B]
Morrison v. California ...... 9.04[B], n16
Morse; State v. .... 2.02[B][4]
Moylan; United States v. ..... 1.02[D][2]
Mullaney v. Wilber .... 9.05[B][3]e]
Mullaney v. Wilbur .. 9.04[B], n3, n15, [C],
n7;9.04[C]n9;9.04[B]n3
Mulvihill; State v. .... 9.05[A][6]
Murdock; United States v. ... 4.06[B][2][d]
Murry v. State .... 5.03[A][1]
Myers v. Conn. .... 4.06[A]
Myers; State v. .... 2.02[B][3]

N

Natal Rivera; United States v. . . . 4.06[B][1]
Nearing; United States v. .... 8.03[B]
Neitzel v. State .... 5.03[A][2]
Nelson v. Heyne .... 2.02[B][2]
Nelson v. State .... 9.05[A][3]
New Hampshire v. Elbert ..... 1.02[D][2]
New York v. Ferber .... 4.04[B]
Newman v. United States ...... 1.02[B]
Newton; People v. 9.04
NGI. Shannon v. United States ....
9.05[B][3][b]
Nofziger; United States v. .... 4.04[B]
Norman; State v. ....
5.03[B][2][a];9.05[A][4][c]
Northington v. State .... 5.03[A][2]
Nye & Nissen v. United States . . . 8.01[B]

O

Obiechie; United States v. . . . 4.06[B][2][d]
O'Blasney; State v. .... 5.03[A][4][d]
O'Brien; People v. .... 4.06[B][2][c]
O'Connor v. Donaldson ..... 9.05[B][3][b]
Odom; State v. .... 9.04[C]
ark; United States v. O'Neill; State v. ....
4.06[B][2][a]
Oney v. Commonwealth ..... 9.05[A][4][c]
Ott; State v. .... 5.03[B][1]
Otto; State v. .... 7.02[B]
Oviedo; United States v. .... 7.02[F]

P

Pagach v. Klein .... 1.02[B]
Page; State v. .... 9.05[A][4][c]
Palmer v. State .... 5.03[B][2][a]
Panter; United States v. .... 9.05[A][3]
Papachristou v. Jacksonville, City of .....
2.05[B], n21
Park; United States v. .... 4.07[B]; 8.03[A]
Parker v. State .... 9.05[A][1][d]
Parker v. United States .... 9.05[C]
Parsons v. State .... 9.05[B][3][a]
Pate v. Robinson .... 9.05[B][1]
Patrick; United States v. .. 9.05[A][1][c], [3]
Patterson; People v. .... 5.03[A][4][b]
Patterson v. New York .... 9.04[B];
9.05[B][3][e];9.05[C], n5
Patterson v. State .... 9.04[C]
Pauley; Commonwealth v. .... 8.03[A]
Payne; People v. .... 5.03[A][4][e]
Pears v. State .... 5.03[A][2]
Peisch v. Ware .... 2.02[B][6]
Pennsylvania Supreme Court,
Commonwealth v. Almeida ....
5.03[A][4][e]

TABLE OF CASES

[References are to sections.]

Peoni; United States v.	8.01[B]
People v. (see name of defendant)	
People ex (see name of defendant)	
People ex rel. (see name of defendant)	
Perez v. Brownell	2.02[A]
Perka v. The Queen	*9.05[A][3]*
Perrone; United States v.	8.02
Peter, *In re*	9.05[E][3][b][i]
Peters v. Kiff	1.02[D][2]
Peterson; State v.	7.03[F]
Petition of (see name of party)	
Pettit; People v.	*2.02[B][4]*
Phillimore, L.J., in Broome v. Cassell	4.03[A][2]
Phillips; People v.	5.03[A][4][b]
Phyle v. Duffy	9.05[B][2]
Pierce; Commonwealth v.	*4.03[A][ii]*
Pike; State v.	9.05[B][3][a]
Pinkerton v. United States	7.03[D], [F], 8.02
Pino-Perez; United States v.	8.01[B]
Pizano v. Superior Court	3.04[D]
Planned Parenthood v. Casey	2.06[A]
Plenty Horse; State v.	1.02[D][2]
Poddar; People v.	9.05[B][4]
Poe v. Ullman	9.05[C]
Pollard; United States v.	*9.05[B][3][a]*
Pollock v. Farmers' Loan & T. Co.	3.03
Pomponio; United States v.	4.06[B][2][d]
Post v. State	2.06[A]
Powell; People v.	7.03[D]
Powell v. Texas	3.01; 9.05[C]
Preslar; State v.	3.04[B]
Price, People ex rel. v. Sheffield Farms	4.07[A]
Proffitt v. Florida	5.04[B]
Proudman v. Dayman	4.07[A]

Q

The Queen v. Coney	*8.01[A]*
The Queen v. Eagle	*9.04[C]*
The Queen v. M'Naghten	9.05[B][3][a]
Queen v. Senior	3.03
Queen v. Tyrell	8.01[A]
Quill v. Koppel	9.05[E][3][b][i]
Quinby; Commonwealth v.	9.04[C]
Quinlan, In re	9.05[E][3][b][i]
Quintana; People v.	7.03[E]

R

R. v. Church	3.04[D]
R. v. Coney (1)	8.01[A]
R. v. Dudley and Stephens	9.05[A]3
R. v. Forbes and Webb	4.07[A]
R. v. Howe	9.05[A][1][d]
R. v. Humphreys and Turner	8.01[C]
R. v. Kennedy	4.07[B]
R. v. MacLean	4.06[B][2][c]
R. v. Morgan	8.01[C]
R. v. Morgan. He	8.01[C]
R. v. Paul	4.07[B]
R. v. Poter	9.05[B][3][a]
R. v. Salford Health Authority	8.01[B]
R. v. Smith	3.03
R. v. Tolson	4.07[A]
R. v. Windle	9.05[B][3][a]
R. v. Woodrow, 15 M & W 404	4.07[A]
Ragen; United States v.	2.05[B]
Ramirez v. Jones	9.04[C]
Ramirez v. State	7.02[D]
Ramos; State v.	9.05[C]n2
Ratzlaf v. United States	4.06[B][2][d]
Ravin v. State	2.06[A]
Rawlins v. Georgia	1.02[D][2]
Redline; Commonwealth v.	5.03[A][4][e]
Reed., *In re*	2.02[B][3]
Regina v. Ali	5.03[B][1]
Regina v. Anderson and Morris	8.01[B]
Regina v. Benge and Another	*3.04[C][2]*
Regina v. Charlson	9.05[B][3][d]
Regina v. Cogan and Leak	*8.01[C]*
Regina v. Conway	9.05[A]3
Regina v. Creamer	8.01[A]
Regina v. Cunningham	*4.03[A][iii]*
Regina v. Dadson	9.03[B]
Regina v. Eagleton	*7.02[B]*
Regina v. Faulkner	*4.03[A][ii];* 4.03[B];4.05[D];4.05[F]
Regina v. Graham	9.05[A][1][c]
Regina v. Hicklin	*9.05[E][3][a]*
Regina v. Horsey, 3 F & F 287	5.03[A][4][a]
Regina v. Howe	9.05[A][1][d]
Regina v. Hudson and Taylor	*9.05[A][1][a];* 9.05[A][1][c]
Regina v. Kemp	9.05[B][3][d]
Regina v. Martin	9.05[A]3
Regina v. Morgan, the Lords	6.03[B]
Regina v. Murphy	7.03[C][1]
Regina v. Pembltion	*4.03[A][ii]*
Regina v. Prince	4.07[A]
Regina v. Quick	9.05[E][2][a]
Regina v. Richards	8.01[B]
Regina v. Sargeant	2.03[B][4]
Regina v. Serne	5.03[A][4][b]
Regina v. Stone	3.03
Regina v. Thomas	7.03[D]
Regina v. Tolson	6.03[A]
Regina v. Valderrama Vega	9.05[A][1][e]
Regle v. State	7.03[C][2]
Reidell; State v.	9.05[B][3][a]
Reisman; People v.	4.06[A]
Reitze; State v.	3.03n4
Repouille v. United States	9.05[E][3][b][i]

TABLE OF CASES

[References are to sections.]

Rex v. Bailey	4.06[B][1]
Rex v. Eccles	7.03[B]
Rex v. Heath	3.02[B]
Rex v. Scofield	7.02[A]
Rex. v. Sinnisiak	4.06[A]
Reynolds v. State	*6.03[A]*; 6.03[B]
Rhodes; Commonwealth v.	6.02[A]
Riley; Commonwealth v.	4.07[A]
Ripple v. State	9.05[A][4][c]
Rivera v. Combe	9.04[C]
Rivera v. Delaware	9.05[B][3][e]
Robbins v. People	5.03[A][4][e]
Robbins v. State	5.03[A][1]
Roberts v. Louisiana	5.04[B]
Roberts v. People	9.05[C]
Roberts v. State	9.05[B][3][b]
Robinson v. California	2.02[B][2];2.04[B];3.01[B];9.05[C]
Robinson. Easter v. District of Columbia	9.05[C]
Rocha; People v.	4.03[A][2]; 9.05[C]
Roe v. Wade	2.06[A]
Rojas; People v.	7.02[F]
Romano; United States v.	9.04[C]
Rose v. Clark	9.04[C]
Roth; State v.	5.03[A][2]
Rothenberg; State v.	6.03[B]
Roviaro v. United States	9.04[C]n16
Rowe v. Burton	2.02[B][3]
Rowe v. Debruyn	9.05[A][4][a]
Roy; People v.	7.03[D]
Ruffin; United States v.	8.01[C]
Rummel v. Estelle	2.04[B]
Russell, Status of the Texas Necessity Defense in Abortion C v. Wade	9.05[A][3]
Russello v. United States	7.03[H]
Russo; State v.	5.03[B][1]
Ryan; People v.	*4.06[A]*

S

Sahr; State v.	9.05[A][3]
Salerno; United States v.	*2.02[B][1]*; 2.03[B][2]; 9.05[B][3][b]
Sall; United States v.	8.02
Sanchez; United States v.	2.02[B][5]
Sandoval v. California	1.02[A]
Sandstrom v. Montana	*9.04[C]* ; 9.05[C]
Santillanes v. State	*4.03[B]*
Santobello v. New York	1.02[B]
Santosky v. Kramer	9.04[B]n8
Saunders; State v.	2.06[A]
Schall v. Martin	2.02[B][1]
Schmidt; People v.	6.03[C]; 9.05[B][3][a]
Schochet v. Maryland	2.06[A]
Schroder; State v.	9.05[A][4][d]
Scott v. Illinois	1.02[C]
Scott; People v.	3.04[C][1]
Sears; People v.	*5.03[A][4][d]*
Segovia; State v.	*9.04[A]*
Seluk; United States v.	2.04[A]
Serafin v. Serafin	5.02[A]
Shabani; United States v.	7.03[A][1]
Shaffer; Commonwealth v.	9.05[A][4][c]
Shannon v. Commonwealth	7.03[C][2]
Shaughnessy; People v.	*3.02[A]*
Shaw v. Director of Public Prosecutions	*2.05[A]*; 7.03[B], [D]
Shaw; State v.	9.05[A][4][c]
Shelledy; State v.	3.04[B]
Shepard; People v.	2.06[A]
Sheriff, Clark County v. Morris	5.03[A][4][b]
Shockley; People v.	5.03[A][4][d]
Siggelkow v. State	5.03[A][2]
Sigma Reproductive Health Center v. State	9.05[A][3]
Sikora; State v.	*9.01*; 9.05[B][3][a]
Sinclair v. State	9.05[B][5][b]
Siruckmeyer v. C. J., and Hays, Holohan and Gordon, JJ.	5.02[B]
Skinner v. Oklahoma	9.05[E][2]
Small; State v.	8.02
Smith v. California	4.04[B]; 4.07[B]
Smith; People v.	5.03[A][4][d]
Smith v. State	7.02[C]n9
Smith; State v.	3.03;*6.03[B]*; 7.03[C][2]
Solem v. Helm	2.04[A], [B]
Sorrells v. United States	9.05[D]
Sorrentino; State v.	9.05[A][5]
Souza; State v.	9.05[C]n2
Spallone; Commonwealth v.	5.03[A][4][c]
Sparf v. United States	1.02[D][2]
Sparf and Hansen v. United States	1.02[D][2]
Speach; United States v.	4.04[B]
St. Christopher; State v.	7.03[C][2]
Stacy v. State	8.01[B]
Staley; State v.	*4.06[B][2][b]*
Stallworth; United States v.	7.02[B]
Stamp; People v.	5.03[A][4][a]
Standard Oil Co. v. United States	8.03[B]n4
Staples; People v.	*7.02[D]*
Staples v. United States	4.04[B];*4.07[B]*
Stapleton v. R.	9.05[B][3][a]
Stasium; Commonwealth v.	8.02
State v. (see name of defendant)	
State ex (see name of state)	
State ex rel. (see name of state)	
State of (see name of state)	
Steele v. State	9.05[B][4]
Steele, in Muench v. Israel	9.05[B][4]
Steger; People v.	5.03[A][1]
Stephenson v. state	*3.04[B]*
Stern v. The State	*4.06[A]*

[References are to sections.]

Stevenson; People v.	5.02[A], n1
Stoffer v. State	9.05[A][4][d]
Stokes v. McRae	5.03[A][4][d]
Strasburg; State v.	9.05[B][5][b]
Strauder v. West Virginia	1.02[D][2]
Striggles; Stae v.	*4.06[B][2][a]*
Strong; Peopl v.	*5.03[B][1][a]*
Superior Court; State v.	4.07[A]
Surrey County Council v. Battersby	4.06[B][2][c]
Sutherland; United States v.	*7.03[H]*
Swanson; United States v.	1.02[B]
Sweeny v. State	3.02[A]
Swincher v. Commonwealth	4.06[B][2][a]
Sykes v. Director of Public Prosecutions	7.03[D]

T

Tally;State ex. Rel Attorney General v.	*8.01[A]*
Tate; State v.	9.05[A][3]
Taylor; People v.	5.03[A][4][d]
Taylor v. Louisiana	*1.02[D][2]*
Taylor v. State	5.03[A][4][e]; 7.02[C], [E]
Taylor; State v.	7.02[F]
Taylor v. Superior Court	5.03[A][4][e]
Tempest; Commonwealth v.	*9.05[B][3][a]*
Tenement House Department of City of New York v. McDevitt, 1915	4.07[A]
Tennessee v. Garner	*9.05[A][6]*
Territory of Montana v. Manton	3.03
Texas v. Johnson	2.06
Thabo Meli v. Regina	3.04[D]
Thacker v. Commonwealth	*7.02[C]*
Thiede v. State	5.03[B][2][b]
Thiel v. Southern Pacific Co.	1.02[D][2]
Thomas; People v.	5.03[A][1]
Thomas; United States v.	4.04[B]; 7.02[F]
Thomas C., In re	5.02[D]
Thomas, In re	5.03[A][1]
Thomerson v. Lockhart	5.03[A][1]
Thompson v. Oklahoma	5.04[B]
Thompson; State v.	5.03[A][4][d]
Tilley; People v.	5.03[A][1]
Tison v. Arizona	*5.04[B]*
Tomlins; People v.	9.05[A][4][c]
Tomlinson; Commonwealth v.	5.03[A][4][c]
Torphy; State v.	9.05[E][3][a]
Toscano; State v.	9.05[A][1][c]
Tot v. United States	9.04[B], [C], n9, n16
Trambitas, In re	2.02[B][1]
Travers; People v.	8.03[A]
Tribett; State v.	9.05[A][4][d]
Trinkle; People v.	7.02[C]
Tripp v. State	*5.03[B][1]*
Trop v. Dulles	2.02[A], [B][2]
Trust Estate of (see name of party)	
Tucker; United States v.	9.04[B]n23
Turkette; United States v.	7.03[H]
Turner v. United States	9.04[C], n16

U

Ulster County v. Allen	*9.04[C]*, n9
Unger; People v.	9.05[E][1]
United States v. (see name of defendant)	
United States District Court for Central District of Califor; United States v.	4.04[B]n26
United States Gypsum Co.; United States v.	4.03[B]; 4.07[B]
Ursery; United States v.	2.02[B][3], [4], [6]

V

Vacco v. Quill	5.02[D]
Valentine; People v.	5.03[B][1]
Valladares; State v.	7.03[C][2]
Van Oster v. Kansas	2.02[B][6]
Vaughn; State v.	9.05[C]n2
Victor v. Nebraska	1.02[A]
Vinson; United States v.	7.03[A][2]
Vitek v. Jones	9.05[B][3][b]
Voytko v. Ramada Inn of Atlantic City	1.02[B]

W

Wade v. State	8.01[B]
Wagner; People v.	5.03[A][4][d]
Wahrlich v. Arizona	9.05[B][4]
Wainwright v. New Orleans	9.05[A][6]
Wake; United States v.	4.07[A]
Walden; State v.	8.01[A]
Waldron; United States v.	7.03[D]
Walker; Commonwealth v.	1.02[B]
Walker; United States v.	*5.03[B][1][b]*
Walker v. Endell	9.05[A][1][b]
Wallace v. State	5.03[B][2][b]
Walters v. Lunt	8.01[C]
Walters; United States v.	4.06[B][2][b], [d]
Walzack; Commonwealth v.	9.05[B][4]
Wanrow; State v.	9.05[A][4][a];*9.05[A][4][c]*; 9.05[E][2]
Ward; United States v.	2.02[B][4]
Ward and Kennedy; United States v.	2.02[B][4]
Warren v. State	*6.02[C]*
Warshow; State v.	9.05[A][3]
Washington; People v.	5.03[A][4][e], [B][1]

TABLE OF CASES

[References are to sections.]

Washington v. Texas . . . . 9.05[C]
Waters; People v. . . . . *5.03[A][1]*
Watson v. United States . . . . . . 5.03[A][1]
Webb; State v. . . . . 3.02[A]
Weems v. United States . . . . 5.04[B]
Weisberg; State v. . . . . 4.07[A]
Welansky; Commonwealth v. . . . . 5.03[B][2][a]
Wellar v. People . . . . 5.03[A][3]
Wells; People v. . . . . 9.05[B][4]
Weniger v. United Staes . . . . . *7.03[C][1]*
West v. Wright . . . . 9.04[C]
Western Union Tel. Co.; State v. . . . . 4.06[B][2][b]
Westlund; State v. . . . . 9.05[A][6]
Wheeler; People v. . . . . 8.01[B]
While Heacock v. Commonwealth . . . . 5.03[A][4][b]
White v. State . . . . . . 4.07[A]; 9.05[C]n2
Whitehead v. State . . . . 5.03[B][1]
Whitman v. People . . . . 5.03[A][4][c]
Whitner v. State . . . . 2.05[C]
Wiesenfeld Warehouse Co.; United States v. . . . . 4.07[B]
Wilbur; State v. . . . . 9.04[B]
Wilbur, 278 A.2d, at 146.; State v. . . . . . . 9.04[B]n28
Wilcox v. Jeffery . . . . *8.01[A]*
Willard v. State . . . . 2.05[A]
William M., *In re* . . . . 2.02[B][2]
Williams; Commonwealth v. . . . . . 6.03[C]
Williams v. Florida . . . . 1.02[D][2]
Will*iams; People v.* . . . . 5.03[A][4][b];*6.03[C]*;9.05[A][4]
Williams v. State . . . . 9.05[A][1][b]
Williams; State v. . . . *4.07[A]*; 5.03[A][4][e]
Wilson; People v. . . . . 5.03[A][4][d]
Wilson v. State . . . . 7.02[E]
Wilson; State v. . . . . 7.02[E]
Winne; State v. . . . . 1.02[B]
Winship and Patterson, In re . . . . 9.04[B]
Winship, and Patterson, In re v. New York. . . . . 9.04[C]
Winship, In re . . *1.02[A];* 2.01; 9.04[B], [C]; 9.05[B][3][e], [C]
Winston; People v. . . . . 2.02[B][4]
Winters v. New York . . . . 2.05[B]n18
Wisconsin v. Yoder 2.06
Wolff; People v. . . . . 9.05[B][3][c], [4]
Woodson v. North Carolina . . . . . . 5.04[B]
Workman; State v. . . . . 7.02[D]
Wright; People v. . . . . 5.03[A][4][a]
Wright; State v. . . . . 2.02[B][4]
Wright; United States v. . . . . 9.05[B][3][b]
Wu; People v. . . . . *3.01[A];* 4.06[B][1]; 5.03[B][1]
Wyant v. State . . . . 9.05[C]n2
Wyley v. Warden . . . . 1.02[D][2]

X

X-Citement Video; United States v. . . . . 4.07[B]

Y

Yaselli v. Goff . . . . 1.02[B]
Yates v. People . . . . 9.05[A][4][d]
York; Commonwealth v. . . . . 9.04[B]
Young; People v. . . 2.02[B][2]; 9.05[A][4][d], [5]
Young; State v. . . . . 5.02[A]
Yu; United States v. . . . . 4.06[B][1]

Z

Zakrasek v. State . . . . 4.06[B][1]

TABLE OF STATUTES

[References are to sections.]

State

Alabama code
13A-6-2(a)(2) .... 5.03[A][2]

Arizona Revised Statutes
13-804(a) .... 2.02[B][4]

Arkansas Statutes Annotated
41-1504(91)(d) .... 3.04[D]

California Health and Safety Code
11721 .... 3.01[B]

California Penal Code
28(a) .... 9.05[B][4]
187 .... 5.03[A]
188 .... 5.03[A]; 9.05[B][4]
189 .... 5.03[A]; 9.05[B][4]
266c .... 6.02[B]
1170 .... 2.03[A]

Colorado Revised Statutes
18-1-704.5(2) .... 9.05[A][5]
18-3-102(1)(d) .... 5.03[A][2]
18-3-103(1)(a) .... 5.03[A][2]

Colorado Statutes Annotated
18-3-102(1)(d) .... 5.03[A][2]

District of Columbia Code
22-902 .... 3.03

Florida Statutes Annotated
782.09 .... 5.02[C]

Illinois Revised Statutes
Chapter 38
8-2(a) .... 7.03[A][1]
8-4(a) .... 7.03[A][1]
8-5 .... 7.03[A][1]

Indiana Code
35-41-3-8(2) .... 9.05[A][1][d]

Iowa Code Annotated
707.7 .... 5.02[C]

Kansas Statutes
21-3404 .... 5.03[B][2][b]

Kentucky Revised Statutes Annoted
500.070 .... 9.04[B]
500.030 .... 9.04[B]

Maine Revised Statutes Annotated
Title 17
2551 .... 9.04[B]
2651 .... 9.04[B]

Michigan Compiled Laws
750.520b 6.02
750.520(b-e) 6.05

Minnesota Statutes Annotated
609.2661 .... 5.02[C]
609.2662 .... 5.02[C]

Montana Revised Codes Annotated
46-14-201 .... 9.05[B][5][b]

Nebraska Revised Statutes
28-202 .... 7.03[B]
28-302 .... 5.03[A]
28-303 .... 5.03[A]
28-304 .... 5.03[A]
38-305 .... 5.03[A][2]; 5.03[B][1]
28-711 .... 3.03
29-1606 .... 1.02[B]

New Jersey Statutes Annotated
2C:2-4d .... 4.06[B][2][d]

New York Penal Law
35.05 .... 9.05[A][3][a]
35.15 .... 9.05[A][4][c]
115.08 .... 8.01[B]
125.00 .... 5.03[A][1]
125.20(2) .... 9.04[B]
125.25 .... 5.03[A][1]; 9.04[B]
125.25(2) .... 5.03[A][2]
125.27 .... 5.03[A][1]
160.15 .... 9.04[B]
265.15(3) .... 9.04[C]

North Carolina General Statutes
14-17 .... 5.03[A][1]

Pennsylvania Consolidated Statutes
Title 18
126 .... 6.02[A]
2501 .... 5.03[A]
2502 .... 5.03[A]
2503 .... 5.03[B][1]
3107 .... 6.02[A]
4854 .... 9.04[C]

South District of Carolina Annotated
16-3-60 .... 5.03[B][2][a]

[References are to sections.]

Utah Code Annotated
76-5-402 .... 6.02

Vermont Statutes Annotated
Title 12
519 .... 3.03

Virginia Code Annotated
18.2-61 .... 6.02

Washington Revised Code
9.79.160(2) .... 9.04[B]
9A.28.040 .... 7.03[B]
9A.32.070 .... 5.03[B][2][a]

Wyoming Statutes
96-42 .... 9.04[C]

Federal

Comprehensive Crime Control Act of 1984
general .... 2.03[A]

Federal Rules of Criminal Procedure
7(case) .... 1.02[B]

Sentencing Reform Act of 1984
general .... 2.04[A]

United States Code
Title 18
20 .... 9.05[B][3][e]
207(c) .... 4.04[B]
1080(a)(5)(a) .... 4.04[B]
1961(1) .... 7.03[G]
1961(1)(A) .... 7.03[G]
1961(4) .... 7.03[G]
1961(5) .... 7.03[G]
1962(c) .... 7.03[G]
1962(d) .... 7.03[G]
3553 .... 2.03[A]
Title 21
331(k) .... 4.07[B]
335 .... 4.07[B]
342 .... 4.07[B]
3333(a) .... 4.07[B]
3333(b) .... 4.07[B]
Title 26
5845(a)(8) .... 4.07[B]
5845(f)(1)(B) .... 4.07[B]
Title 42
6928(d) .... 4.04[B]

United States Constitution
Amendment V .... 2.02[B][5]
Amendment VI .... 2.02[A]
Article I, Sec. 9 .... 2.02[A]
Article III, Sec. 2 .... 2.02[A]

Miscellaneous

Restatement of Torts
402A .... 4.07[A]

Uniform Commercial Code
2-314-316 .... 4.07[A]

International

Chinese Criminal Code
Art. 16 .... 4.06[B][2][d]

German Penal Code 1969
34 .... 9.05[A][3][a]
35 .... 9.05[A][3][a]

Japanese Criminal Code
Art 21 II .... 4.06[B]2][d]

Korean Code of 1953
Art. 16 .... 4.06[B]2][d]

Norwegian Penal Code
57 .... 4.06[B]2][d]

Swedish Penal Code
Chapter 24
4 .... 9.05[A][3][a]
5 .... 9.05[A][3][a]

West German Penal Code
17 .... 4.06[B]2][d]

TABLE OF THE MODEL PENAL CODE

[References are to pages.]

Art. 1	App. 11
Art. 2	App. 20
Art. 3	App. 28
Art. 4	App. 38
Art. 5	7.01; App. 43
Art. 6	App. 48
Art. 7	App. 53
Art. 210	App. 62
Art. 211	App. 66
Art. 212	App. 66
Art. 213	App. 68
Art. 220	App. 71
Art. 221	App. 72
Art. 222	App. 74
Art. 223	App. 74
Art. 224	App. 78
Art. 230	App. 82
Art. 240	App. 84
Art. 241	App. 87
Art. 242	App. 90
Art. 243	App. 92
Art. 250	App. 93
Art. 251	App. 96
1.01	App. 11
1.01(1)	App. 11
1.01(2)	App. 11
1.01(3)	App. 11
1.01(3)(a)	App. 11
1.01(3)(b)	App. 11
1.01(3)(c)	App. 11
1.01(4)	App. 11
1.02	2.03[A]; App. 11
1.02(1)	App. 11
1.02(1)(a)	App. 11
1.02(1)(b)	App. 11
1.02(1)(c)	App. 11
1.02(1)(d)	App. 11
1.02(1)(e)	App. 11
1.02(2)	App. 11
1.02(2)(a)	App. 11
1.02(2)(b)	App. 11
1.02(2)(c)	App. 11
1.02(2)(d)	App. 11
1.02(2)(e)	App. 11
1.02(2)(f)	App. 11
1.02(2)(g)	App. 11
1.02(2)(h)	App. 12
1.02(3)	App. 12
1.03	App. 12
1.03(1)	App. 12
1.03(1)(a)	App. 12
1.03(1)(b)	App. 12
1.03(1)(c)	App. 12
1.03(1)(d)	App. 12
1.03(1)(e)	App. 12
1.03(1)(f)	App. 12
1.03(2)	App. 12
1.03(3)	App. 13
1.03(4)	App. 13
1.03(5)	App. 13
1.04	2.02[B][3]; App. 13; App. 24
1.04(1)	App. 13
1.04(2)	App. 13
1.04(3)	App. 13
1.04(4)	App. 13
1.04(5)	4.07[A]; App. 13
1.04(6)	App. 13
1.04(7)	App. 13
1.05	App. 14
1.05(1)	App. 14
1.05(2)	App. 14
1.05(3)	App. 14
1.06	App. 14
1.06(1)	App. 14
1.06(2)	App. 14
1.06(2)(a)	App. 14
1.06(2)(b)	App. 14
1.06(2)(c)	App. 14
1.06(2)(d)	App. 14
1.06(3)	App. 14
1.06(3)(a)	App. 14
1.06(3)(b)	App. 14
1.06(4)	App. 14; App. 46
1.06(5)	App. 14
1.06(6)	App. 14
1.06(6)(a)	App. 14
1.06(6)(b)	App. 15
1.07	App. 15
1.07(1)	7.03[A][1]; App. 15
1.07(1)(a)	App. 15
1.07(1)(b)	App. 15
1.07(1)(c)	App. 15
1.07(1)(d)	App. 15
1.07(1)(e)	App. 15
1.07(2)	App. 15
1.07(3)	App. 15
1.07(4)	App. 15
1.07(4)(a)	App. 15
1.07(4)(b)	App. 15
1.07(4)(c)	App. 15
1.07(5)	App. 15
1.08	App. 16; App. 17
1.08(1)	App. 16
1.08(2)	App. 16
1.08(3)	App. 16
1.08(4)	App. 16
1.08(4)(a)	App. 16
1.08(4)(b)	App. 16
1.08(4)(b)(i)	App. 16
1.08(4)(b)(ii)	App. 16

[References are to pages.]

1.08(4)(b)(iii)	App. 16
1.08(4)(b)(iv)	App. 16
1.08(4)(b)(v)	App. 16
1.09	App. 16
1.09(1)	App. 16
1.09(1)(a)	App. 17
1.09(1)(b)	App. 17
1.09(1)(c)	App. 17
1.09(2)	App. 17
1.09(3)	App. 17
1.10	App. 17
1.10(1)	App. 17
1.10(2)	App. 17
1.11	App. 17
1.11(1)	App. 18
1.11(2)	App. 18
1.11(3)	App. 18
1.12	App. 18
1.12(1)	App. 18
1.12(2)	App. 18
1.12(2)(a)	App. 18
1.12(2)(b)	App. 18
1.12(3)	App. 18
1.12(3)(a)	App. 18
1.12(3)(b)	App. 18
1.12(3)(c)	App. 18
1.12(4)	App. 18
1.12(4)(a)	App. 18
1.12(4)(b)	App. 18
1.12(5)	5.03[A][4][a]; App. 18
1.12(5)(a)	App. 18
1.12(5)(b)	App. 18
1.12(6)	App. 18
1.13	4.05[B]; App. 19
1.13(1)	App. 19
1.13(2)	App. 19
1.13(3)	App. 19
1.13(4)	App. 19
1.13(5)	App. 19
1.13(6)	App. 19
1.13(7)	App. 19
1.13(8)	App. 19
1.13(9)	App. 19
1.13(9)(a)	App. 19
1.13(9)(b)	App. 19
1.13(9)(c)	App. 19
1.13(9)(d)	App. 19
1.13(9)(e)	App. 19
1.13(10)	4.05[B]; App. 19
1.13(11)	App. 19
1.13(12)	App. 19
1.13(13)	App. 19
1.13(14)	App. 19
1.13(15)	App. 19
1.13(16)	App. 19
2.01	3.01[B]; App. 20
2.01(1)	App. 20
2.01(2)	App. 20
2.01(2)(a)	App. 20
2.01(2)(b)	App. 20
2.01(2)(c)	App. 20
2.01(2)(d)	App. 20
2.01(3)	App. 20
2.01(3)(a)	App. 20
2.01(3)(b)	App. 20
2.01(4)	3.02[B]; App. 20
2.02	4.05[A]; App. 20
2.02(a)	4.06[B][2][d]
2.02(d)	4.05[C]
2.02(1)	4.05[B]; App. 20
2.02(2)	App. 20
2.02(2)(a)	App. 20
2.02(2)(a)(i)	App. 20
2.02(2)(a)(ii)	App. 20
2.02(2)(b)	App. 20
2.02(2)(b)(i)	App. 20
2.02(2)(b)(ii)	App. 20
2.02(2)(c)	App. 20
2.02(2)(d)	App. 21
2.02(3)	4.05[D]; App. 21
2.02(4)	4.05[C]; 4.05[D]; App. 21
2.02(5)	App. 21
2.02(6)	App. 21
2.02(7)	App. 21
2.02(8)	App. 21
2.02(9)	App. 21
2.02(10)	App. 22
2.03	3.04[D]; App. 22
2.03(1)	App. 22
2.03(1)(a)	App. 22
2.03(1)(b)	App. 22
2.03(2)	App. 22
2.03(2)(a)	App. 22
2.03(2)(b)	App. 22
2.03(3)	App. 22
2.03(3)(a)	App. 22
2.03(3)(b)	App. 22
2.04	4.06[A]; 4.06[B][2][d]; App. 22
2.04(1)	App. 22
2.04(1)(a)	App. 22
2.04(1)(b)	App. 23
2.04(2)	4.07[A]; App. 23
2.04(3)	4.06[B][2][d]; App. 23
2.04(3)(a)	App. 23
2.04(3)(b)	App. 23
2.04(4)	App. 23
2.05	4.07[A; App. 23
2.05(1)	App. 23
2.05(1)(a)	App. 23
2.05(1)(b)	App. 23
2.05(2)	App. 23
2.05(2)(a)	App. 23
2.05(2)(b)	App. 23
2.06	8.01[B]; 8.02; App. 24
2.06(1)	8.01[C]; App. 24
2.06(2)	App. 24

TABLE OF THE MODEL PENAL CODE

[References are to pages.]

2.06(2)(a)	8.01[C]; App. 24
2.06(2)(b)	App. 24
2.06(2)(c)	App. 24
2.06(3)	App. 24
2.06(3)(a)	8.01[B]; App. 24
2.06(3)(a)(i)	App. 24
2.06(3)(a)(ii)	8.01[A]; App. 24
2.06(3)(a)(iii)	App. 24
2.06(3)(b)	App. 24
2.06(4)	8.01[B]; App. 24
2.06(5)	App. 24
2.06(6)	App. 24
2.06(6)(a)	App. 24
2.06(6)(b)	App. 24
2.06(6)(c)	App. 24
2.06(6)(c)(i)	App. 24
2.06(6)(c)(ii)	App. 24
2.06(7)	8.01[C]; App. 24
2.07	8.03[B]; App. 25
2.07(1)	App. 25
2.07(1)(a)	App. 25
2.07(1)(b)	App. 25
2.07(2)	App. 25
2.07(2)(c)	App. 25
2.07(3)	App. 25
2.07(3)(a)	App. 25
2.07(3)(b)	App. 25
2.07(4)	App. 25
2.07(4)(a)	App. 25
2.07(4)(b)	App. 25
2.07(4)(c)	App. 25
2.07(5)	9.04[B]; App. 26
2.07(6)(a)	App. 26
2.07(6)(b)	App. 26
2.07(6)(c)	App. 26
2.08	4.03[A][ii]; 9.05[C]; App. 26
2.08(1)	App. 26
2.08(2)	App. 26
2.08(3)	App. 26
2.08(4)	App. 26
2.08(5)	App. 26
2.08(5)(a)	App. 26
2.08(5)(b)	App. 26
2.08(5)(c)	App. 26
2.09	9.05[A][1][a]; App. 27
2.09(1)	App. 27
2.09(2)	App. 27
2.09(3)	App. 27
2.09(4)	App. 27
2.10	App. 27
2.11	6.03[A]; App. 27
2.11(1)	App. 27
2.11(2)	App. 27
2.11(2)(a)	App. 27
2.11(2)(b)	App. 27
2.11(2)(c)	App. 27
2.11(3)	App. 27
2.11(3)(a)	App 27
2.11(3)(b)	App. 27
2.11(3)(c)	App. 27
2.12	App. 28
2.12(1)	App. 28
2.12(2)	App. 28
2.12(3)	App. 28
2.13	9.05[D]; App. 28
2.13(1)	App. 28
2.13(1)(a)	App. 28
2.13(1)(b)	App. 28
2.13(2)	App. 28
2.13(3)	App. 28
3.01	App. 28
3.01(1)	App. 28
3.01(2)	App. 28
3.02	9.05[A][3][a]; App. 28
3.02(1)	App. 28
3.02(1)(a)	App. 29
3.02(1)(b)	App. 29
3.02(1)(c)	App. 29
3.02(2)	App. 29
3.03	App. 29
3.03(1)	App. 29
3.03(1)(a)	App. 29
3.03(1)(b)	App. 29
3.03(1)(c)	App. 29
3.03(1)(d)	App. 29
3.03(1)(e)	App. 29
3.03(2)	App. 29
3.03(2)(a)	App. 29
3.03(2)(b)	App. 29
3.03(3)	App. 29
3.03(3)(a)	App. 29
3.03(3)(b)	App. 29
3.04	9.05[A][4]; App. 29; App. 37
3.04(b)(ii)	9.05[A][4][b]
3.04(1)	App. 29
3.04(2)	App. 29
3.04(2)(a)	App. 29
3.04(2)(a)(i)	App. 30
3.04(2)(a)(ii)	App. 30
3.04(2)(a)(ii)(1)	App. 30
3.04(2)(a)(ii)(2)	App. 30
3.04(2)(a)(ii)(3)	App. 30
3.04(2)(b)	App. 30
3.04(2)(b)(i)	App. 30
3.04(2)(b)(ii)	App. 30
3.04(2)(b)(ii)(1)	App. 30
3.04(2)(b)(ii)(2)	App. 30
3.04(2)(c)	App. 30
3.04(3)	App. 30
3.05	App. 31
3.05(1)	App. 31
3.05(1)(a)	App. 31
3.05(1)(b)	App. 13
3.05(1)(c)	App. 31
3.05(2)	App. 31
3.05(2)(a)	App. 31

MPC–3

[References are to pages.]

3.05(2)(b)	App. 31
3.05(2)(c)	App. 31
3.06	9.05[A][5]; App. 31
3.06(1)	App. 31
3.06(1)(a)	App. 31
3.06(1)(b)	App. 13
3.06(1)(b)(i)	App. 31
3.06(1)(b)(ii)	App. 31
3.06(2)	App. 32
3.06(2)(a)	App. 32
3.06(2)(b)	App. 32
3.06(2)(c)	App. 32
3.06(3)	App. 32
3.06(3)(a)	App. 32
3.06(3)(a)(i)	App. 32
3.06(3)(a)(ii)	App. 32
3.06(3)(a)(iii)	App. 32
3.06(3)(b)	App. 32
3.06(3)(c)	App. 32
3.06(3)(c)(i)	App. 32
3.06(3)(c)(ii)	App. 32
3.06(3)(d)	App. 32
3.06(3)(d)(i)	App. 32
3.06(3)(d)(ii)	App. 32
3.06(3)(d)(ii)(1)	App. 32
3.06(3)(d)(ii)(2)	App. 33
3.06(4)	App. 33
3.06(5)	App. 33
3.06(5)(a)	App. 33
3.06(5)(b)	App. 33
3.06(5)(c)	App. 33
3.06(6)	App. 33
3.06(6)(a)	App. 33
3.06(6)(b)	App. 33
3.06(6)(c)	App. 33
3.07	9.05[A][6]; App. 33; App. 37
3.07(1)	App. 33
3.07(2)	App. 33
3.07(2)(a)	App. 33
3.07(2)(a)(i)	App. 33
3.07(2)(a)(ii)	App. 33
3.07(2)(b)	9.05[A][6]; App. 34
3.07(2)(b)(i)	App. 34
3.07(2)(b)(ii)	App. 34
3.07(2)(b)(iii)	App. 34
3.07(2)(b)(iv)	App. 34
3.07(2)(b)(iv)(1)	App. 34
3.07(2)(b)(iv)(2)	App. 34
3.07(3)	App. 34
3.07(4)	App. 34
3.07(4)(a)	App. 34
3.07(4)(b)	App. 34
3.07(5)(a)	App. 34
3.07(5)(a)(i)	App. 34
3.07(5)(a)(ii)	App. 35
3.07(5)(a)(ii)(1)	App. 35
3.07(5)(a)(ii)(2)	App. 35
3.07(5)(b)	App. 35
3.08	App. 35
3.08(1)	App. 35
3.08(1)(a)	App. 35
3.08(1)(b)	App. 35
3.08(2)	App. 35
3.08(2)(a)	App. 35
3.08(2)(b)	App. 35
3.08(3)	App. 35
3.08(3)(a)	App. 35
3.08(3)(b)	App. 36
3.08(4)	App. 36
3.08(4)(a)	App. 36
3.08(4)(b)	App. 36
3.08(5)	App. 36
3.08(5)(a)	App. 36
3.08(5)(b)	App. 36
3.08(5)(c)	App. 36
3.08(6)	App. 36
3.08(6)(a)	App. 36
3.08(6)(b)	App. 36
3.08(7)	App. 36
3.08(7)(a)	App. 36
3.08(7)(b)	App. 36
3.09	9.05[A][4]; App. 36
3.09(1)	App. 36
3.09(1)(a)	App. 37
3.09(1)(b)	App. 37
3.09(3)	App. 37
3.10	App. 37
3.10(1)	App. 37
3.10(2)	App. 37
3.11	App. 37
3.11(1)	App. 37
3.11(2)	App. 37
3.11(3)	App. 38
4.01	App. 38
4.01(1)	App. 38
4.01(2)	App. 38
4.02	9.05[B][4]; App. 38
4.02(1)	App. 38
4.02(2)	App. 38
4.03	App. 38
4.03(1)	App. 38
4.03(2)	App. 38
4.03(3)	App. 38
4.04	App. 38
4.05	App. 35; App. 38; App. 42
4.05(1)	App. 38
4.05(2)	App. 39
4.05(3)	App. 39
4.06	App. 39; App. 42
4.06(1)	App. 39
4.06(2)	App. 39
4.06(3)	App. 40
4.06(4)	App. 40
4.07	App. 40
4.07(1)	App. 40
4.07(2)	App. 41

TABLE OF THE MODEL PENAL CODE

[References are to pages.]

4.07(3)	App. 41
4.07(4)	App. 41
4.08	App. 41; App. 42
4.08(1)	App. 41
4.08(2)	App. 41
4.08(3)	App. 42
4.08(4)	App. 42
4.08(5)	App. 42
4.09	App. 42
4.10	App. 43
4.10(1)	App. 43
4.10(1)(a)	App. 43
4.10(1)(b)	App. 43
4.10(1)(b)(i)	App. 43
4.10(1)(b)(ii)	App. 43
4.10(2)	App. 43
5.01	7.02[B]; 7.02[C]; App. 43
5.01(1)	App. 43
5.01(1)(a)	App. 43
5.01(1)(b)	App. 43
5.01(1)(c)	App. 43
5.01(2)	App. 43
5.01(2)(a)	App. 44
5.01(2)(b)	App. 44
5.01(2)(c)	App. 44
5.01(2)(d)	App. 44
5.01(2)(e)	App. 44
5.01(2)(f)	App. 44
5.01(2)(g)	App. 44
5.01(3)	App. 44
5.01(4)	7.02[D]; App. 44
5.02	7.02[B]; App. 44
5.02(1)	App. 44
5.02(2)	App. 45
5.02(3)	App. 45
5.03	7.03[A][1]; 7.03[B]; 7.03[C][2]; 7.03[D]; 7.03[E]; App. 45
5.03(1)	App. 45
5.03(1)(a)	App. 45
5.03(1)(b)	App. 45
5.03(2)	7.03[E]; App. 45
5.03(3)	7.03[E]; App. 45
5.03(4)	App. 45
5.03(4)(a)	App. 45
5.03(4)(a)(i)	App. 45
5.03(4)(a)(ii)	App. 45
5.03(4)(b)	App. 45
5.03(4)(b)(i)	App. 45
5.03(4)(b)(ii)	App. 45
5.03(4)(b)(iii)	App. 45
5.03(5)	App. 46
5.03(6)	7.03[F]; App. 46
5.03(7)	App. 46
5.03(7)(a)	App. 46
5.03(7)(b)	App. 46
5.03(7)(c)	7.03[F]; App. 46
5.04	App. 46
5.04(1)	App. 46
5.04(1)(a)	App. 46
5.04(1)(b)	App. 46
5.04(2)	App. 46
5.05	2.06[B][1]; 7.02[B]; App. 46
5.05(1)	App. 46
5.05(2)	App. 47
5.05(3)	App. 47
5.06	App. 47
5.06(1)	App. 47
5.06(1)(a)	App. 47
5.06(1)(b)	App. 47
5.06(2)	App. 47
5.06(2)(a)	App. 47
5.06(2)(b)	App. 47
5.06(2)(c)	App. 47
5.06(3)	App. 47
5.06(3)(a)	App. 47
5.06(3)(b)	App. 47
5.06(3)(c)	App. 47
5.07	App. 48
5.50(1)	7.02[G]
6.01	App. 48
6.01(1)	App. 48
6.01(1)(a)	App. 48
6.01(1)(b)	App. 48
6.01(1)(c)	App. 48
6.01(2)	App. 48
6.02	App. 48
6.02(1)	App. 48
6.02(2)	App. 48
6.02(3)	App. 48
6.02(3)(a)	App. 48
6.02(3)(b)	App. 48; App. 58
6.02(3)(c)	App. 48
6.02(3)(d)	App. 48
6.02(4)	App. 49
6.02(5)	App. 49
6.03	App. 49
6.03(1)	App. 49
6.03(2)	App. 49
6.03(3)	App. 49
6.03(4)	App. 49
6.03(5)	App. 49
6.03(6)	App. 49
6.04	App. 49
6.04(2)(a)	App. 49
6.04(2)(b)	App. 49
6.04(2)(c)	App. 50
6.05	App. 48; App. 50; App. 52
6.05(1)	App. 50
6.05(2)	App. 45; App. 50
6.05(3)	App. 50
6.05(3)(a)	App. 50
6.05(3)(b)	App. 50
6.05(4)	App. 50
6.06	5.03[B][2][a]; App. 48; App. 51; App. 52
6.06(1)	App. 51

Section	Page	Section	Page
6.06(2)	App. 51	7.03(3)	App. 55
6.06(3)	App. 51	7.03(4)	App. 55
6.07	App. 51; App. 52	7.03(4)(a)	App. 55
6.07(1)	App. 51	7.03(4)(b)	App. 56
6.07(2)	App. 51	7.03(4)(c)	App. 56
6.07(3)	App. 51	7.04	App. 56
6.08	App. 52	7.04(1)	App. 56
6.09	App. 56	7.04(2)	App. 56
6.09(1)	App. 52	7.04(2)(a)	App. 56
6.09(1)(a)	App. 52	7.04(2)(b)	App. 56
6.09(1)(b)	App. 52	7.04(3)	App. 56
6.09(2)	App. 52	7.04(4)	App. 56
6.09(2)(a)	App. 52	7.04(4)(a)	App. 56
6.09(2)(b)	App. 52	7.04(4)(b)	App. 57
6.10	App. 52	7.05	App. 57
6.10(1)	App. 52	7.05(1)	App. 57
6.10(2)	App. 52	7.05(2)	App. 57
6.10(3)	App. 53	7.05(3)	App. 57
6.10(4)	App. 53	7.05(4)	App. 57
6.11	App. 53	7.06	App. 48; App. 52; App. 57
6.11(1)	App. 53	7.06(1)	App. 57
6.11(2)	App. 53	7.06(1)(a)	App. 57
6.12	App. 53	7.06(1)(b)	App. 57
6.13	App. 53	7.06(1)(c)	App. 57
6.13(1)	App. 53	7.06(1)(d)	App. 57
6.13(2)	App. 53	7.06(2)	App. 57
7.01	App. 53	7.06(2)(a)	App. 58
7.01(1)	App. 53	7.06(2)(b)	App. 58
7.01(1)(a)	App. 54	7.06(2)(c)	App. 58
7.01(1)(b)	App. 54	7.06(3)	App. 58
7.01(1)(c)	App. 54	7.06(4)	App. 58
7.01(2)	App. 54	7.06(5)	App. 58
7.01(2)(a)	App. 54	7.06(5)(a)	App. 58
7.01(2)(b)	App. 54	7.06(5)(b)	App. 58
7.01(2)(c)	App. 54	7.06(5)(c)	App. 58
7.01(2)(d)	App. 44	7.06(6)	App. 58
7.01(2)(e)	App. 54	7.06(6)(a)	App. 58
7.01(2)(f)	App. 54	7.06(6)(b)	App. 58
7.01(2)(g)	App. 54	7.06(6)(c)	App. 59
7.01(2)(h)	App. 54	7.06(6)(d)	App. 59
7.01(2)(i)	App. 54	7.06(7)	App. 59
7.01(2)(j)	App. 54	7.06(7)(a)	App. 59
7.01(2)(k)	App. 54	7.06(7)(b)	App. 59
7.01(3)	App. 54	7.06(7)(c)	App. 59
7.02	App. 54	7.07	App. 59
7.02(1)	App. 54	7.07(1)	App. 59
7.02(2)	App. 54	7.07(1)(a)	App. 59
7.02(2)(a)	App. 55	7.07(1)(b)	App. 59
7.02(2)(b)	App. 55	7.07(1)(c)	App. 59
7.02(3)	App. 55	7.07(2)	App. 59
7.02(3)(a)	App. 55	7.07(3)	App. 59
7.02(3)(b)	App. 55	7.07(4)	App. 59
7.02(4)	App. 55	7.07(5)	App. 60
7.03	App. 57	7.07(6)	App. 60
7.03(1)	App. 55	7.07(7)	App. 60
7.03(2)	App. 55	7.08	App. 51; App. 60
7.03(2)(a)	App. 55	7.08(1)	App. 60
7.03(2)(b)	App. 55	7.08(2)	App. 60

[References are to pages.]

7.08(3)	App. 60	210.6(4)(g)	App. 66
7.08(4)	App. 61	210.6(4)(h)	App. 66
7.08(5)	App. 61	211.0	App. 66
7.08(6)	App. 61	211.1	App. 66
7.08(7)	App. 61	211.1(1)	App. 66
7.09	App. 61	211.1(1)(a)	App. 66
7.09(1)	App. 61	211.1(1)(b)	App. 66
7.09(2)	App. 61	211.1(1)(c)	App. 66
210.0	App. 61	211.1(2)	App. 66
210.0(1)	App. 62	211.1(2)(a)	App. 66
210.0(2)	App. 62	211.1(2)(b)	App. 66
210.0(3)	App. 62	211.2	App. 66
210.0(4)	App. 62	211.3	App. 66
210.1	5.02[A]; App. 62	212.0	App. 66
210.1(1)	App. 62	212.1	App. 66
210.1(2)	App. 62	212.1(a)	App. 67
210.2	5.03[A]; 5.03[A][2]; 5.03[A][3]; 5.03[A][4][a]; 5.03[A][4][b]; App. 62	212.1(b)	App. 67
		212.1(c)	App. 67
210.2(1)	App. 62	212.1(d)	App. 67
210.2(1)(a)	App. 62	212.2	App. 67
210.2(1)(b)	App. 62	212.2(a)	App. 67
210.2(2)	App. 63	212.2(b)	App. 67
210.3	5.03[B][1]; 5.03[B][2][b]; App. 63	212.3	App. 67
210.3(a)	5.03[B][2][a]	212.4	App. 67
210.3(1)(a)	App. 63	212.4(1)	App. 67
210.3(1)(b)	App. 63	212.4(1)(a)	App. 67
210.3(2)	App. 63	212.4(1)(b)	App. 67
210.4	App. 63	212.4(2)	App. 67
210.4(1)	App. 63	212.5	App. 68
210.4(2)	App. 63	212.5(1)	App. 68
210.5	5.02[D]; App. 63	212.5(1)(a)	App. 68
210.5(1)	App. 63	212.5(1)(b)	App. 68
210.5(2)	App. 63	212.5(1)(c)	App. 68
210.6	5.04[A][2]; App. 48; App. 63	212.5(1)(d)	App. 68
210.6(1)	App. 63	212.5(2)	App. 68
210.6(1)(a)	App. 63	213.0	App. 68
210.6(1)(b)	App. 63	213.1	6.02; 6.02[A]; 6.02[C]; 6.03[A]; 6.05; App. 68
210.6(1)(c)	App. 63		
210.6(1)(d)	App. 63	213.1(1)	6.05; App. 68
210.6(1)(e)	App. 63	213.1(1)(a)	App. 68
210.6(1)(f)	App. 63	213.1(1)(b)	App. 68
210.6(2)	App. 63	213.1(1)(c)	App. 68
210.6(3)	App. 65	213.1(1)(d)	App. 68
210.6(3)(a)	App. 65	213.1(2)	6.05; App. 69
210.6(3)(b)	App. 65	213.1(2)(a)	App. 69
210.6(3)(c)	App. 65	213.1(2)(b)	App. 69
210.6(3)(d)	App. 65	213.1(2)(c)	App. 69
210.6(3)(e)	App. 65	213.2	App. 69
210.6(3)(f)	App. 65	213.2(1)	App. 69
210.6(3)(g)	App. 65	213.2(1)(a)	App. 69
210.6(3)(h)	App. 65	213.2(1)(b)	App. 69
210.6(4)	App. 65	213.2(1)(c)	App. 69
210.6(4)(a)	App. 65	213.2(1)(d)	App. 69
210.6(4)(b)	App. 65	213.2(2)	App. 69
210.6(4)(c)	App. 65	213.2(2)(a)	App. 69
210.6(4)(d)	App. 65	213.2(2)(b)	App. 69
210.6(4)(e)	App. 65	213.2(2)(c)	App. 69
210.6(4)(f)	App. 65	213.3	App. 69

[References are to pages.]

213.3(1)	App. 69	221.2(2)(a)	App. 73
213.3(1)(a)	App. 69	221.2(2)(b)	App. 73
213.3(1)(b)	App. 69	221.2(2)(c)	App. 73
213.3(1)(c)	App. 69	221.2(3)	App. 73
213.3(1)(d)	App. 70	221.2(3)(a)	App. 73
213.3(2)	App. 70	221.2(3)(b)	App. 73
213.4	6.02[A]; App. 70; App. 71	221.2(3)(c)	App. 74
213.4(1)	App. 70	222.1	App. 74
213.4(2)	App. 70	222.1(1)	App. 74
213.4(3)	App. 70	222.1(1)(a)	App. 74
213.4(4)	App. 70	222.1(1)(b)	App. 74
213.4(5)	App. 70	222.1(1)(c)	App. 74
213.4(6)	App. 70	222.1(2)	App. 74
213.4(7)	App. 70	223.0	App. 74; App. 78
213.4(8)	App. 70	223.0(1)	App. 74
213.5	App. 70	223.0(2)	App. 74
213.6	App. 70	223.0(3)	App. 74
213.6(1)	4.07[A]; App. 70	223.0(4)	App. 74
213.6(2)	App. 70	223.0(5)	App. 74
213.6(3)	App. 71	223.0(6)	App. 74
213.6(4)	App. 71	223.0(7)	App. 75
213.6(5)	App. 71	223.1	App. 75
216.6(5)	6.04	223.1(1)	App. 75
220.1	App. 71	223.1(2)	App. 75
220.1(1)	App. 71	223.1(2)(a)	App. 75
220.1(1)(a)	App. 71	223.1(2)(b)	App. 75
220.1(1)(b)	App. 71	223.1(2)(c)	App. 75
220.1(2)	App. 71	223.1(3)	App. 75
220.1(2)(a)	App. 71	223.1(3)(a)	App. 75
220.1(2)(b)	App. 71	223.1(3)(b)	App. 75
220.1(3)	App. 71	223.1(3)(c)	App. 75
220.1(3)(a)	App. 71	223.1(4)	App. 75
220.1(3)(b)	App. 72	223.2	App. 76
220.1(4)	App. 72	223.2(1)	App. 76
220.2	App. 72	223.2(2)	App. 76
220.2(1)	App. 72	223.3	App. 76
220.2(2)	App. 72	223.3(1)	App. 76
220.2(3)	App. 72	223.3(2)	App. 76
220.2(3)(a)	App. 72	223.3(3)	App. 76
220.2(3)(b)	App. 72	223.3(4)	App. 76
220.3	App. 72	223.4	App. 76
220.3(1)	App. 72	223.4(1)	App. 76
220.3(1)(a)	App. 72	223.4(2)	App. 76
220.3(1)(b)	App. 72	223.4(3)	App. 76
220.3(1)(c)	App. 72	223.4(4)	App. 76
220.3(2)	App. 72	223.4(5)	App. 76
221.0	App. 72	223.4(6)	App. 76
221.0(1)	App. 72	223.4(7)	App. 76
221.0(2)	App. 73	223.5	App. 77
221.1	7.02[E]; App. 73	223.6	App. 77
221.1(1)	App. 73	223.6(1)	App. 77
221.1(2)	App. 73	223.6(2)	App. 77
221.1(2)(a)	App. 73	223.6(2)(a)	App. 77
221.1(2)(b)	App. 73	223.6(2)(b)	App. 77
221.1(3)	App. 73	223.6(2)(c)	App. 77
221.2	App. 73	223.7	App. 77
221.2(1)	App. 73	223.7(1)	App. 77
221.2(2)	App. 73	223.7(2)	App. 77

TABLE OF THE MODEL PENAL CODE

[References are to pages.]

223.8	App. 77
223.9	App. 78
224.0	App. 78
224.1	App. 78
224.1(1)(a)	App. 78
224.1(1)(b)	App. 78
224.1(1)(c)	App. 78
224.1(2)	App. 78
224.2	App. 78
224.3	App. 79
224.4	App. 79
224.5	App. 79
224.5(1)	App. 79
224.5(2)	App. 79
224.6	App. 79
224.6(1)	App. 79
224.6(2)	App. 79
224.6(3)	App. 79
224.7	App. 79
224.7(1)	App. 79
224.7(2)	App. 79
224.7(3)	App. 80
224.7(4)	App. 80
224.7(5)	App. 80
224.7(6)	App. 80
224.7(7)	App. 80
224.8	App. 80
224.8(1)	App. 80
224.8(1)(a)	App. 80
224.8(1)(b)	App. 80
224.8(1)(c)	App. 80
224.8(1)(d)	App. 80
224.8(1)(e)	App. 80
224.8(2)	App. 80
224.8(3)	App. 80
224.9	App. 80
224.9(1)	App. 80
224.9(1)(a)	App. 81
224.9(1)(b)	App. 81
224.9(2)	App. 81
224.9(3)	App. 81
224.10	App. 81
224.11	App. 81
224.11(a)	App. 81
224.11(b)	App. 81
224.11(c)	App. 81
224.12	App. 81
224.12(1)	App. 81
224.12(2)	App. 81
224.13	App. 81
224.14	App. 82
230.1	App. 82
230.1(1)	App. 82
230.1(1)(a)	App. 82
230.1(1)(b)	App. 82
230.1(1)(c)	App. 82
230.1(1)(d)	App. 82
230.1(2)	App. 82
230.1(3)	App. 82
230.2	App. 82
230.3	App. 82
230.3(1)	App. 82
230.3(2)	App. 83
230.3(3)	App. 83
230.3(4)	App. 83
230.3(5)	App. 83
230.3(6)	App. 83
230.3(6)(a)	App. 83
230.3(6)(b)	App. 83
230.3(6)(c)	App. 83
230.3(6)(d)	App. 84
230.3(7)	App. 84
230.4	App. 84
230.5	App. 84
240.0	App. 84; App. 87; App. 90
240.0(1)	App. 84
240.0(2)	App. 84
240.0(3)	App. 84
240.0(4)	App. 84
240.0(5)	App. 84
240.0(6)	App. 84
240.0(7)	App. 84
240.0(8)	App. 85
240.1	App. 85
240.1(1)	App. 85
240.2	App. 85
240.2(1)	App. 85
240.2(1)(a)	App. 85
240.2(1)(b)	App. 85
240.2(1)(c)	App. 85
240.2(1)(d)	App. 85
240.2(2)	App. 85
240.2(3)	App. 85
240.3	App. 85
240.4	App. 86
240.5	App. 86
240.5(1)	App. 86
240.5(2)	App. 86
240.5(3)	App. 86
240.5(4)	App. 86
240.5(5)	App. 86
240.5(5)(a)	App. 86
240.5(5)(b)	App. 86
240.5(5)(c)	App. 86
240.5(6)	App. 86
240.5(7)	App. 87
240.6	App. 87
240.6(1)	App. 87
240.6(2)	App. 87
240.7	App. 87
240.7(1)	App. 87
240.7(2)	App. 87
240.7(3)	App. 87
241.0	App. 87
241.0(1)	App. 87
241.0(2)	App. 87

[References are to pages.]

241.1	App. 87; App. 88
241.1(1)	App. 87
241.1(2)	App. 88
241.1(3)	App. 88
241.1(4)	App. 88
241.1(5)	App. 88
241.1(6)	App. 88
241.2	App. 88
241.2(1)	App. 88
241.2(1)(a)	App. 88
241.2(1)(b)	App. 88
241.2(2)	App. 88
241.2(3)	App. 88
241.3	App. 88
241.3(1)	App. 88
241.3(1)(a)	App. 88
241.3(1)(b)	App. 88
241.3(1)(c)	App. 89
241.3(1)(d)	App. 89
241.3(2)	App. 89
241.3(3)	App. 89
241.4	App. 89
241.5	App. 89
241.5(1)	App. 89
241.5(2)	App. 89
241.5(2)(a)	App. 89
241.5(2)(b)	App. 89
241.6	App. 89
241.6(1)	App. 89
241.6(1)(a)	App. 89
241.6(1)(b)	App. 89
241.6(1)(c)	App. 89
241.6(1)(d)	App. 89
241.6(2)	App. 89
241.6(3)	App. 89
241.7	App. 90
241.7(1)	App. 90
241.7(2)	App. 90
241.8	App. 90
241.8(1)	App. 90
241.8(1)(a)	App. 90
241.8(1)(b)	App. 90
241.8(1)(c)	App. 90
241.8(2)	App. 90
241.9	App. 90
242.0	App. 90
242.1	App. 90
242.2	App. 90
242.3	8.01; App. 91
242.3(1)	App. 91
242.3(2)	App. 91
242.3(3)	App. 91
242.3(4)	App. 91
242.3(5)	App. 91
242.4	App. 91
242.5	App. 91
242.6	App. 91
242.6(1)	App. 91
242.6(2)	App. 91
242.6(3)	App. 92
242.6(3)(a)	App. 92
242.6(3)(b)	App. 92
242.6(4)	App. 92
242.6(4)(a)	App. 92
242.6(4)(b)	App. 92
242.6(4)(c)	App. 92
242.7	4.05[F]; App. 92
242.7(1)	App. 92
242.7(2)	App. 92
242.8	App. 92
243.0	App. 92
243.1	App. 92
243.1(a)	App. 93
243.1(b)	App. 93
243.2	App. 93
243.2(1)	App. 93
243.2(2)	App. 93
243.2(3)	App. 93
250.1	App. 93
250.1(1)	App. 93
250.1(1)(a)	App. 93
250.1(1)(b)	App. 93
250.1(1)(c)	App. 93
250.1(2)	App. 93
250.2	App. 93
250.2(1)	App. 93
250.2(1)(a)	App. 93
250.2(1)(b)	App. 93
250.2(1)(c)	App. 93
250.2(2)	App. 94
250.3	App. 94
250.4	App. 94
250.4(1)	App. 94
250.4(2)	App. 94
250.4(3)	App. 94
250.4(4)	App. 94
250.4(5)	App. 94
250.5	App. 94
250.6	2.05[B]; App. 94
250.7	App. 95
250.7(1)	App. 95
250.7(2)	App. 95
250.7(2)(a)	App. 95
250.7(2)(b)	App. 95
250.8	App. 95
250.9	App. 95
250.10	App. 95
250.11	App. 95
250.11(1)	App. 95
250.11(2)	App. 95
250.11(3)	App. 95
250.12	App. 96
250.12(1)	App. 96
250.12(1)(a)	App. 96
250.12(1)(b)	App. 96
250.12(1)(c)	App. 96

TABLE OF THE MODEL PENAL CODE

[References are to pages.]

Section	Page	Section	Page
250.12(2)	App. 96	251.2(4)	App. 97
250.12(2)(a)	App. 96	251.2(5)	App. 97
250.12(2)(b)	App. 96	251.2(6)	App. 98
251.1	App. 96	251.3	App. 98
251.2	App. 96	251.4	App. 98
251.2(1)	App. 96	251.4(1)	App. 98
251.2(1)(a)	App. 96	251.4(2)	App. 98
251.2(1)(b)	App. 96	251.4(2)(a)	App. 98
251.2(2)	App. 97	251.4(2)(b)	App. 98
251.2(2)(a)	App. 97	251.4(2)(c)	App. 98
251.2(2)(b)	App. 97	251.4(2)(d)	App. 98
251.2(2)(c)	App. 97	251.4(2)(e)	App. 98
251.2(2)(d)	App. 97	251.4(3)	App. 98
251.2(2)(e)	App. 97	251.4(3)(a)	App. 98
251.2(2)(f)	App. 97	251.4(3)(b)	App. 98
251.2(2)(g)	App. 97	251.4(4)	App. 98
251.2(2)(h)	App. 97	251.4(4)(a)	App. 98
251.2(3)	App. 97	251.4(4)(b)	App. 99
251.2(3)(a)	App. 97	251.4(4)(c)	App. 99
251.2(3)(b)	App. 97	251.4(4)(d)	App. 99
251.2(3)(c)	App. 97	251.4(4)(e)	App. 99
251.2(3)(d)	App. 97	251.4(4)(f)	App. 99

INDEX

[References are to pages.]

A

"ABANDONED AND MALIGNANT HEART" MURDER
Generally . . . 534–545

ABORTIONS UNLAWFULLY PERFORMED
Accomplice liability . . . 864–865

ABSOLUTE LIABILITY (See "STRICT" LIABILITY)

ACCESSORIES (See ACCOMPLICE LIABILITY)

ACCOMPLICE LIABILITY
Generally . . . 845–847
Accessories at common law . . . 845–847
Actus reus . . . 853–862
Mens rea . . . 862–879
Primary and secondary liability . . 879–880
Principals . . . 851; 859

ACTUS REUS
Accomplice liability . . . 853–862
Attempt . . . 727–745
Causation . . . 335–346
Conspiracy . . . 787–803
Drug possession . . . 327–329
Duress . . . 997–999
Epileptic attack, acts during . . . 316–319
Homicide . . . 486–508
Knowing failure to act . . . 325–329
Omissions . . . 329–335
Punishable acts (See CONDUCT PUNISHABLE)
Rape . . . 669–693
Requirement of "act" . . . 303–304
Sleep, acts during . . . 312–316
Status crimes . . . 320–324
"Unconsciousness," acts during state of . . . 304–320

ADMINISTRATIVE REGULATIONS
Ignorance of law . . . 415–416

ADOPTED CHILD SYNDROME
Defense . . . 1227

ADULTERY
Mistake of law . . . 422

ADVICE OF COUNSEL
Mistake of law defense . . . 420–423

AFFIRMATIVE DEFENSES
(See also DEFENSES)
Burden of proof . . . 946–973
Duress . . . 998–999

AGE OF MAJORITY
Mistake of fact . . . 398–399; 453–454

AGREEMENT
Conspiracy . . . 787–790

AIDS-INDUCED HOMICIDES
Causation, timing of . . . 489–490

ALCOHOL ADDICTION
Defense of intoxication . . . 1197–1198
Fetal alcohol syndrome . . . 1227

ALZHEIMER'S DISEASE DEFENSE
Generally . . . 1220

AMERICAN DREAM SYNDROME
Defense . . . 1227

ANTITRUST VIOLATIONS
Corporate criminality . . . 906–908

APPEALS
Victim's standing . . . 12–14

ARMED ROBBERY
Intoxication defense . . . 1169–1174

ARSON-RELATED DEATHS
Felony murder . . . 552

ASSAULT AND BATTERY
Accomplice liability . . . 853–856
Attempt to batter as "assault" . . . 758–759
Conspiracy to assault federal officer 815–824
Intent-to-cause-serious-bodily-injury murder . . . 546–550
Intoxication defense . . . 1164–1169
Mistake of fact . . . 397–398; 407

ASSISTED SUICIDE
Euthanasia . . . 1233–1243
Homicide . . . 500–508

ATTEMPT
Generally . . . 726–727
Actus reus . . . 727–745
Grading . . . 769–770
Harm resulting, relevance of . . . 770–780
Impossibility . . . 759–769
Inchoate crimes, attempting . . . 758–759
Mens rea . . . 746–756
Preparation versus . . . 727–744
Renunciation . . . 756–758
"Substantial steps" test . . . 728–736

AUTOMATISM AND INSANITY
Generally . . . 1128–1131

I–1

INDEX

[References are to pages.]

B

BAD CHECKS
Presumption to defraud . . . 982

BANK ROBBERY
Attempt . . . 728–735

BATTERED CHILD
Self-defense by . . . 1059–1060

BATTERED SPOUSES
Self-defense . . . 1041–1060

BIFURCATED PROCEDURE
Insanity determinations . . . 1149

BIGAMY
Mistake of law . . . 420–421
"Strict" liability . . . 454

BIRTH CONTROL LAWS
Constitutionally protected conduct 281–283

BLACK RAGE SYNDROME
Defense . . . 1227

BLUNT OBJECT KILLINGS
Premeditation . . . 520; 529–532

BRAIN DAMAGE
Defenses . . . 1221

BRAIN DEAD VICTIMS
What constitutes "death" . . . 490–493

BRAINWASHING DEFENSE
Generally . . . 1221–1224

BURDEN OF PROOF
Affirmative defenses . . . 946–973
Due process
    Elements of offenses and defenses . . . 946–973
    Juvenile proceedings . . . 5–8
Duress . . . 999
Elements of offense
    "Exception" issue . . . 942–945
    Lesser offense . . . 946–954
"Exception" issue . . . 942–945
"Hate crime" enhanced penalties . . . 973
Insanity defense . . . 1132–1133
Mandatory minimum sentences . . 965–973
Presumptions, effect of . . . 973–991
Reasonable doubt standard . . . 5–10
Voluntary manslaughter . . . 946–954

BURGLARY
Accomplice liability . . . 879–880
Attempt, renunciation of . . . 756–758
Diminished capacity defense . . . 1145–1149

C

CAPITAL PUNISHMENT (See DEATH PENALTY)

CARDIAC ARREST
Felony murder . . . 551–552

CAUSATION
Generally . . . 335
Conduct and result, relationship between . . . 344–345
Eggshell victims . . . 336
Felony murder limitations . . . 581–591
Joint causation . . . 345–346
Natural forces . . . 343–344
Superseding causes . . . 341
Third parties' acts . . . 341–343
Victims' acts . . . 337–340

"CHAIN" CONSPIRACIES
Generally . . . 830–833

CHILD ABUSE
Negligence . . . 370–374
Omission, acts of . . . 329–335
Self-defense by battered child . . 1059–1060

CHILD, FAILURE TO PROVIDE MEDICAL ATTENTION FOR
Criminal negligence manslaughter 625–628

CHILD PORNOGRAPHY
Ignorance of law . . . 408–411

CHILD, STARVATION OF
Depraved heart murder . . . 543–545

CHURCH LIQUOR SALES
Mistake of law . . . 421–422

CIVIL COMMITMENT
Sexually violent predators . . . 58–68

CIVIL DISOBEDIENCE
Excuse defense . . . 1243–1248

CIVIL PUNITIVE SANCTIONS
Criminal punishment versus . . . 152–155

"CLAIMS OF RIGHT"
Mistake of law . . . 435

COCAINE POSSESSION
Life imprisonment without possibility of parole . . . 230–241

CO-CONSPIRATOR HEARSAY EXCEPTION
Generally . . . 783

COERCION (See DURESS)

COERCIVE THERAPY VERSUS PUNISHMENT
Generally . . . 68–78

COMPENSATION VERSUS PUNISHMENT
Generally . . . 96–109

COMPLICITY
Accomplice liability (See ACCOMPLICE LIABILITY)
Conspiracy . . . 884–890
Vicarious liability (See VICARIOUS LIABILITY)

CONCEALED WEAPONS, CARRYING OF
Mistake of law . . . 419

CONDUCT PUNISHABLE
Generally . . . 280–281
Constitutionally protected conduct 281–286
Harm . . . 286–289; 296–298
Immorality . . . 290–301
Policy issues . . . 286–301

CONSPIRACY
Generally . . . 780
Actus reus . . . 787–803
Agreement . . . 787–790
"Chains" . . . 830–833
Co-conspirator hearsay exception . . . 783
Complicity doctrine . . . 884–890
Corrupt motive doctrine . . . 810–815
Criticism of crime . . . 784–786
Grading . . . 834–836
Mens rea . . . 803–825
Objectives of . . . 786–787
"Overt act" . . . 783–784
Parties to agreement . . . 792–803
Procedural aspects . . . 783–786
Rationale behind law . . . 780–783
Renunciation and withdrawal . . . 833–834
RICO . . . 836–849
Single or multiple
    Generally . . . 825–833
    RICO actions . . . 838–844
Wharton's rule . . . 797–803
"Wheel" arrangements . . 826–827; 830–831

CONSTRUCTION OF STATUTES
Generally . . . 262–280
Mens rea words . . . 378–389

CORPORATE CRIMINALITY
Generally . . . 899–918

CORROBORATION RULE
Rape . . . 719

CORRUPT MOTIVE DOCTRINE
Conspiracy . . . 810–815

COURT, RELIANCE ON
Mistake of law . . . 416–419

CRIMES, FAIR NOTICE OF
Generally . . . 252–280

CRIMES, JUDICIAL CREATION OF
Generally . . . 252–257

CRIMINAL JUSTICE SYSTEM
Overview . . . 1–4

CRUEL AND UNUSUAL PUNISHMENT
Disproportionality . . . 230–252
Forfeitures . . . 242–252
Life imprisonment without possibility of parole . . . 230–241
Rape, death penalty for . . . 663

CULPABILITY (See MENS REA)

CULTURAL DEFENSE
Ignorance of law . . . 409–413

CULTURAL STEREOTYPES
Rape . . . 667–668

D

DAMAGES
Punishment versus compensation . . 96–109

DANGEROUS DRUG TAXES
Punishment versus taxation . . . 109–115

"DANGEROUS" FELONIES
Felony murder . . . 561–573

DEADLY FORCE
Defense of property/habitation 1060–1067
Law enforcement officers . . . 1067–1078
Self-defense (See SELF-DEFENSE)

DEATH PENALTY
Deterrence . . . 640–644
Insane persons . . . 1080–1082
Legal issues . . . 644–662
Rape . . . 663
Retribution . . . 635–640
Supreme Court cases in brief . . . 658–662

DECEPTION
Rape . . . 684–688

DEFENSE COUNSEL
Generally . . . 20–21
Mistaken reliance on counsel . . . 420–423

DEFENSE OF OTHERS
Generally . . . 1034–1035

[References are to pages.]

DEFENSE OF PROPERTY/HABITATION
Generally . . . 1060–1067

DEFENSES
Adopted child syndrome . . . 1227
Alzheimer's disease . . . 1220
American dream syndrome . . . 1227
Attempt, renunciation of . . . 756–758
Black rage syndrome . . . 1227
Brain damage . . . 1221
Brainwashing . . . 1221–1224
Classifying
    Generally . . . 926–934
    Procedural implications . . . 939–991
Conspiracy, renunciation of . . . 833–834
Conspiracy, withdrawal from . . . 833–834
Cultural defense . . . 409–413
Defense of others . . . 1034–1035
Defense of property/habitation 1060–1067
Diminished capacity . . . 1133–1150
Distant father syndrome . . . 1227
Duress (See DURESS)
Elderly abuse syndrome . . . 1227
Elements, proof of
    Generally . . . 942–945
    Affirmative defenses . . . 946–973
    Insanity defense . . . 1132–1133
Entrapment . . . 1198–1205
Excuse (See EXCUSE)
"Failure of proof" classification . . . 929
False memory syndrome . . . 1227
Fetal alcohol syndrome . . . 1227
Free will . . . 913–920
Gangster syndrome . . . 1227
Genetic defense . . . 1212–1216
Guilty but mentally ill . . . 1150–1153
Holocaust survivor syndrome . . . 1227
Hypoglycemia . . . 1220
Ignorance of fact . . . 396–408
Ignorance of law . . . 408–417
Impossibility defense to attempt . . 759–769
Incompetency to stand trial . . . 1078–1080
Insane persons
    Defense of insanity (See INSANITY DEFENSE)
    Execution of . . . 1080–1082
Intoxication . . . 1162–1198
Justification . . . 929–930; 935–939
Law enforcement defenses . . . 1067–1078
Mental abnormality (See MENTAL ABNORMALITY)
Military orders of superior officers 1002–1003
Mistake of fact (See MISTAKE OF FACT)
Mistake of law (See MISTAKE OF LAW)
Necessity defense
    Generally . . . 1003–1020
    Codification of . . . 1020–1024

DEFENSES—Cont.
Parental alienation syndrome . . . 1227
Pathological behavior . . . 1224
Patient-therapist sex syndrome . . . 1227
Post partum psychosis . . . 1224
Premenstrual syndrome . . . 1218–1220
Repressed (or recovered) memory syndrome . . . 1227
Ritual abuse syndrome . . . 1227
Road rage . . . 1227
"Rotten social background" (RSB) 1224–1228
Satanic cult syndrome . . . 1227
Self-defense (See SELF-DEFENSE)
Senility . . . 1220
Situational stress syndrome . . . 1227
Sleep disorders . . . 1221
Super Bowl Sunday syndrome . . . 1227
"Television made me do it" syndrome 1227
Urban survival syndrome . . . 1227

DELIBERATION
Intent-to-kill murder . . . 526–527

DENUNCIATION
Justification for punishment . . . 178–188

DEPRAVED HEART MURDER
Generally . . . 534–545

DETENTION
Punishment versus preventive detention . . 51–68

DETERMINATE VERSUS INDETERMINATE SENTENCES
Generally . . . 211–230

DETERRENCE
Justification for punishment . . . 159–167
"Strict" liability laws . . . 457–459

DIMINISHED CAPACITY
Defense of . . . 1133–1149

"DISEASE OF THE MIND"
Insanity defense . . . 1087–1089

DISTANT FATHER SYNDROME
Defense . . . 1227

DISTRICT ATTORNEYS (See PROSECUTORS)

DOMESTIC DISPUTES RESULTING IN DEATH
Felony murder doctrine . . . 574–581
Self-defense by battered spouse 1043–1057
Voluntary manslaughter 598–601; 603–606

DOUBLE JEOPARDY
Compensation and punishment . . 100–108
Forfeiture and punishment . . . 138–152
Megan's Laws . . . 87–88
Taxation and punishment . . . 109–115

DRAMSHOP LIABILITY
Omission, acts of . . . 334

DRIVING UNDER THE INFLUENCE
Accomplice liability . . . 870–875
Depraved heart murder . . . 537–540
Regulatory penalties versus punishment . . 78–82

DRUG ADDICTION
Actus reus . . . 320–324
Coercive therapy versus punishment 68–73
Defense of intoxication . . . 1197–1198

DRUG DELIVERY TO FETUS OR NEWBORN
Statutory interpretation . . . 274–280

DRUG FORFEITURE STATUTES
Punishment versus actions in rem 116–124; 138–152

DRUG POSSESSION
Actus reus . . . 327–329
Life imprisonment without possibility of parole . . . 230–241
Mistake of fact . . . 402–407
Necessity defense . . . 1008–1009

DRUG-RELATED DEATHS
Felony murder . . . 562–573

DRUG "RINGS"
Mens rea . . . 810–814

DRUG SALES/DISTRIBUTION
Accomplice liability . . . 862–864
Attempt, impossibility of . . . 767–769
"Chain" conspiracies . . . 830–833
Entrapment defense . . . 1198–1204
Necessity defense . . . 1008–1009

DRUG TAXES
Punishment versus taxation . . . 109–115

DRUNKENNESS
Defense of intoxication . . . 1162–1198
Driving under the influence (See DRIVING UNDER THE INFLUENCE)

DUE PROCESS
Anti-assisted suicide laws . . . 500–508
Burden of proof
    Elements of offenses and defenses . . . 946–973
    Juvenile proceedings . . . 5–8

DUE PROCESS—Cont.
Civil forfeitures . . . 125–138
Insanity acquittees, disposition of 1105–1107
Intoxication defense, disallowance of 1178–1196
Mandatory minimum sentencing . . 965–973
Presumptions . . . 983–988
Pretrial detention . . . 52–57
Restitution as condition of probation 97–99
Sexually violent predator detention 58–68
"Void for vagueness" doctrine . . . 257–262

DUII
Accomplice liability . . . 870–875
Depraved heart murder . . . 537–540
Regulatory penalties versus punishment . . 78–82

DURESS
Generally . . . 991–997
Burden of proof . . . 999
Creating one's own duress . . . 1001
Cumulative threats . . . 1002
"Defense," questionableness as . . . 1002
Definitional controversies . . . 999–1000
"Failure of proof" or "affirmative" defense . . . 998–999
Homicide and . . . 1000–1001
Immediacy . . . 999
Justification or excuse . . . 998
Mens rea or actus reus . . . 997–999
Military orders of superior officers 1002–1003
Objective versus subjective standard 999–1000
Rape . . . 671–684; 693–714
Rationale of . . . 997–999

E

EGGSHELL VICTIMS
Causation . . . 336

ELDERLY ABUSE SYNDROME
Defense . . . 1227

ELEMENTS OF OFFENSE
Burden of proof
    Generally . . . 946–954
    "Exception" issue . . . 942–945
    Lesser offense . . . 946–954
Presumptions . . . 973–991

EMERGENCY MEDICAL CARE
Omission, acts of . . . 333–334

EMINENT DOMAIN
Civil forfeitures . . . 125–138

[References are to pages.]

"EMOTIONAL" IMPAIRMENT
Insanity defense . . . 1090–1092

ENTRAPMENT DEFENSE
Generally . . . 1198–1205

EPILEPTICS
Vehicular homicide . . . 316–319

EQUAL PROTECTION
Jury selection . . . 24–30

EUTHANASIA
Motive and . . . 1233–1243

"EXCEPTION" ISSUE
Burden of proof . . . 942–945

EXCESSIVE FINES
Civil forfeitures . . . 116–124

EXCUSE
Generally . . . 930–932; 1205–1210
Duress (See DURESS)
Euthanasia, motive and . . . 1233–1243
Free will and . . . 1210–1212
Justification versus . . . 935–939
Motive, role of . . . 1228–1248
Physiologically based excuses . . 1212–1221
Political offenders . . . 1243–1248
Psychologically based excuses . . 1221–1224
Sociologically based excuses . . . 1224–1228

EXECUTION (See DEATH PENALTY)

EXPATRIATION STATUTES
What constitutes punishment . . . 47–48

EX POST FACTO LAWS
Megan's Laws . . . 87–88
Sexually violent predator detentions 58–68
What constitutes punishment . . . 42–47

EXPRESSIVE FUNCTION
Punishment . . . 48–51; 182–188

EXTREME EMOTIONAL DISTURBANCE
Murder case, proof of defense in . . 954–964

F

FACILITATION
Generally . . . 866–869

FAIR-CROSS-SECTION
Jury selection . . . 24–30

FAIR NOTICE OF CRIMES
Generally . . . 252–280

FALSE MEMORY SYNDROME
Defense . . . 1227

FALSE PRETENSES, OBTAINING MONEY BY
Attempt . . . 727–728

FAMILY RELATIONSHIPS
Vicarious liability . . . 893

FDA VIOLATIONS
"Strict" liability . . . 461–467

FEAR AND DURESS
Rape . . . 675–684

FEDERAL PROPERTY
"Strict" liability statutes . . . 446–447

FELONY MURDER
Generally . . . 551–561
Abolition of doctrine . . . 591–595
Causation limitations . . . 581–591
"Dangerous" felonies . . . 561–573
Death penalty . . . 644–658
Duration of felony . . . 573–574
Merger doctrine . . . 574–581

FETAL ALCOHOL SYNDROME
Defense . . . 1227

FETUSES
Criminal statutes, interpretation of 263–280
HIV transmissions . . . 278; 286
Homicide . . . 263–273; 493–495

FIREARMS
Machinegun possession, "strict" liability for . . . 468–480
Negligent possession . . . 374–378
Presumption of illegal possession 973–981
Unlawful act manslaughter . . . 631–633

FISHING VIOLATIONS
Mistake of law . . . 423
"Strict" liability statutes . . . 442–445

FIST-FIGHTING
Accomplice liability for prizefighting 853–856
Intent-to-cause-serious-bodily-injury murder . . . 546–547; 550

FORCE
Deadly force (See DEADLY FORCE)
Duress (See DURESS)
Rape, nonconsent and force in . . . 671–684; 693–714

FOREIGNERS
Ignorance of law . . . 409–413

FORFEITURES
Cruel and unusual punishment . . 242–252
What constitutes punishment . . . 116–152

[References are to pages.]

FORGERY
Corporate criminality . . . 901–904

FORMER JEOPARDY (See DOUBLE JEOPARDY)

FRAUD
Rape . . . 684–688

FREE WILL
Generally . . . 913–920
Excuses and . . . 1210–1212

"FRESH COMPLAINT" RULES
Rape . . . 666; 718; 721

G

GAMBLING ACTIVITIES OR DEVICES
Accomplice liability . . . 866–869
Mistake of law . . . 416–418
Pathological behavior defense . . . 1224

GANGSTER SYNDROME
Defense . . . 1227

GENETIC DEFENSE
Generally . . . 1212–1216

GUILTY BUT MENTALLY ILL
Generally . . . 1150–1153

GUILTY PLEAS
"On the nose" . . . 16–17

GUNS (See FIREARMS)

H

HARM
Attempt, relevance of resulting harm to . . . 770–780
Conduct punishable . . . 286–289; 296–298

"HATE CRIME" ENHANCED PENALTIES
Burden of proof . . . 973

HEART ATTACK-RELATED DEATHS
Felony murder . . . 551–552

HEAT OF PASSION KILLINGS
Voluntary manslaughter . . . 595–617

HIV
AIDS-induced homicides . . . 489–490
Fetuses, transmission to . . . 279; 286

HOLOCAUST SURVIVOR SYNDROME
Defense . . . 1227

HOMICIDE
Generally . . . 485–486
Actus reus . . . 486–508

HOMICIDE—Cont.
Assisted suicide . . . 500–508
Battered children . . . 1059–1060
Battered spouses . . . 1043–1057
Brain dead victims . . . 490–493
Causation, timing of . . . 486–490
Death penalty (See DEATH PENALTY)
Duress and . . . 1000–1001
Euthanasia . . . 1233–1243
Felony murder (See FELONY MURDER)
Fetuses . . . 263–273; 493–495
Manslaughter (See MANSLAUGHTER)
Mens rea . . . 510–635
Murder (See MURDER)
Necessity defense . . . 1004–1007
Negligent third party acts . . . 341–343
Omission, acts of . . . 329–335
Self-defense (See SELF-DEFENSE)
Somnambulistic homicide . . . 312–316
Suicide pacts . . . 495–499
"Unconsciousness" defense . . . 304–320
Vehicular homicide (See VEHICULAR HOMICIDE)
Victims' acts, effect of . . . 337–340

HONEST VERSUS REASONABLE MISTAKES
Generally . . . 400–402

HUSBAND AND WIFE
Bigamy
    Mistake of law . . . 420–421
    "Strict" liability . . . 454
Omission, acts of . . . 334
Self-defense by battered spouse 1043–1057

HUSBAND'S RAPE OF WIFE
Generally . . . 689–693
Accomplice liability . . . 881–883

HYPOGLYCEMIA DEFENSE
Generally . . . 1220

I

IGNORANCE OF FACT
Generally . . . 396–408
Conspiracy to assault federal officer 815–824
"Willful blindness" rule . . . 408

IGNORANCE OF LAW
Generally . . . 408–417

ILLEGAL ALIENS, BRINGING IN
Religious motivation . . . 1243–1246

IMMORALITY
Conduct punishable . . . 290–301

[References are to pages.]

IMPOSSIBILITY
Attempt . . . 759–769

INCAPACITATION
Justification for punishment . . . 167–173

INCHOATE CRIMES
Generally . . . 725–726
Attempt (See ATTEMPT)
Conspiracy (See CONSPIRACY)

INDETERMINATE VERSUS DETERMINATE SENTENCES
Generally . . . 211–230

INFANTS, DRUG DELIVERY TO
Statutory interpretation . . . 274–280

IN REM ACTIONS VERSUS PUNISHMENT
Generally . . . 116–152

INSANE PERSONS
Death penalty . . . 1080–1082
Defense of insanity (See INSANITY DEFENSE)
Guilty but mentally ill . . . 1150–1153

INSANITY DEFENSE
Abolition of . . . 1153–1162
Automatism and insanity . . . 1128–1131
Burden of proof . . . 1132–1133
"Disease of the mind" . . . 1087–1089
Disposition of offenders not guilty by reason of insanity . . . 1105–1117
"Emotional" impairment . . . 1090–1092
Knowledge that act was wrong 1086–1087
M'Naghten test . . . 1083–1085
MPC approach . . . 1097–1098
"Nature and quality" of act . . . 1085–1086
"Product test" . . . 1089–1090
Rationale . . . 1118–1128
Tests for, development of . . . 1083–1104
"Unconscious" motivation . . . 1095–1097
"Volitional" impairment . . . 1092–1095

INTENT
(See also MENS REA)
Criminal liability and . . . 770–771
Oblique intent . . . 352–353
Presumptions . . . 983–988
Rape . . . 693–700
"Specific" and "general" intents . . 353–365

INTENT-TO-CAUSE-SERIOUS-BODILY-INJURY MURDER
Generally . . . 546–551

INTENT-TO-KILL MURDER
Generally . . . 514–534

INTERPRETATION OF STATUTES
Generally . . . 262–280
Mens rea words . . . 378–390

INTERVENING CAUSE
Generally . . . 345–346

INTOXICATION
Defense . . . 1162–1198
Driving under the influence (See DRIVING UNDER THE INFLUENCE)

INVOLUNTARY MANSLAUGHTER
Criminal negligence manslaughter 617–631
Unlawful act manslaughter . . . 631–635

J

JOINT CAUSATION
Generally . . . 345–346

JUDICIAL CREATION OF CRIMES
Generally . . . 252–257

JURY
Historical sketch . . . 21–24
Selection (See JURY SELECTION)
Size and unanimity . . . 32–33

JURY NULLIFICATION
Generally . . . 33–36

JURY SELECTION
Challenges . . . 30–31
Fair-cross-section requirement . . . 24–30
Process . . . 30–31

JUSTIFICATION DEFENSE
Generally . . . 929–930
Excuse versus . . . 935–939

JUSTIFICATIONS FOR PUNISHMENT
Generally . . . 155–159
Death penalty . . . 635–644
Deterrence
    Generally . . . 159–167
    "Strict" liability laws . . . 457–459
Incapacitation . . . 167–173
Inchoate crimes . . . 725–726
Retributivism . . . 188–204
Theory into practice . . . 204–211
Utilitarianism . . . 159–188

JUVENILE DELINQUENTS
Burden of proof . . . 5–8
Coercive therapy versus punishment 74–78

[References are to pages.]

K

KNOWING FAILURE TO ACT
Generally . . . 325–329

"KNOWINGLY"
Ignorance of fact . . . 396–408
Ignorance of law . . . 408–417
Interpretation of term . . . 381–390
Model Penal Code . . . 390–391

L

LARCENY (See THEFT)

LAW ENFORCEMENT
Defenses . . . 1067–1078
Entrapment . . . 1198–1205
Police role . . . 2–3

LEGALITY PRINCIPLE
Punishment . . . 252–280

LIFE IMPRISONMENT WITHOUT POSSIBILITY OF PAROLE
Cruel and unusual punishment . . 230–241

LIFE-SUSTAINING TREATMENT, WITHDRAWAL OF
Homicide . . . 500–508

LIQUOR, ILLEGAL TRANSPORTATION OF
"Strict" liability statutes . . . 438–440

LIQUOR SALES
Mistake of law . . . 421–422
Vicarious liability for sales to minors 895–898

LOITERING STATUTES
"Void for vagueness" doctrine . . . 260–262

LOTTERIES
Mistake of law . . . 419

M

MACHINEGUN POSSESSION
"Strict" liability . . . 468–480

MAGISTRATES
Generally . . . 3

MALICE AFORETHOUGHT
Murder . . . 510–512; 526–527

"MALICIOUSLY"
Interpretation of term . . . 378

MANDATORY MINIMUM SENTENCES
Burden of proof . . . 965–973

MANN ACT
Conspiracy to violate . . . 797–799

MANSLAUGHTER
Involuntary manslaughter
    Criminal negligence manslaughter . . . 617–631; 870–879
    Unlawful act manslaughter . . 631–635
Negligent third party acts . . . 341–343
Omission, acts of . . . 329–335
Recklessness . . . 362–365
Voluntary manslaughter . . . 595–617

MARITAL RAPE
Generally . . . 689–693
Accomplice liability . . . 881–883

MEGAN'S LAWS
Regulatory penalties versus punishment . . 83–96

MENS REA
Generally . . . 347–348
Accomplice liability . . . 862–879
Applying to elements of offense
    Generally . . . 379–390
    Model Penal Code approach 392–394
Attempt . . . 746–756
Common law development . . . 349–352
Conspiracy . . . 803–825
Diminished capacity . . . 1133–1149
Duress . . . 997–999
Future of . . . 481–484
Homicide . . . 510–635
Ignorance of fact . . . 396–408
Ignorance of law . . . 408–417
Insanity defense (See INSANITY DEFENSE)
Intent and recklessness . . . 352–365
Malice aforethought . . . 510–512
Mental abnormality (See MENTAL ABNORMALITY)
Mistake of fact (See MISTAKE OF FACT)
Mistake of law (See MISTAKE OF LAW)
Model Penal Code . . . 390–396
Motive
    Corrupt motive doctrine . . . 810–815
    Excuses . . . 1228–1248
Negligence (See NEGLIGENCE)
Premeditation to kill . . . 517–534
Presumptions . . . 983–988
Rape (See RAPE)
Recklessness (See RECKLESSNESS)
Statutory interpretation . . . 378–390
"Strict" liability (See "STRICT" LIABILITY)

MENTAL ABNORMALITY
Diminished capacity . . . 1133–1149
Free will and . . . 913–920
Guilty but mentally ill . . . 1150–1153

[References are to pages.]

MENTAL ABNORMALITY—Cont.
Incompetency to stand trial . . . 1078–1080
Insane persons
    Defense of insanity (See INSANITY DEFENSE)
    Execution of . . . 1080–1082

MENTAL STATE (See MENS REA)

MERCY KILLINGS
Generally . . . 1233–1243

MERGER DOCTRINE
Felony murder . . . 574–581

MILITARY ORDERS OF SUPERIOR OFFICERS
Defense of . . . 1002–1003

MISPRISON OF FELONY
Accomplice liability . . . 853

MISTAKE OF FACT
Generally . . . 396–408
Honest versus reasonable mistakes 400–402
"Imperfect self-defense" . . . 1029–1030
Intent-to-kill murder . . . 514–517
Legal mistake, disparate treatment of 436–437
Sexual intercourse, consent to . . . 693–700; 714–718
"Willful blindness" rule . . . 408

MISTAKE OF LAW
Generally . . . 416–417
Common law, relaxing of . . . 425–437
Factual mistake, disparate treatment of . . 436–437
Force, unlawful use of . . . 1027
Reliance on counsel . . . 420–423
Reliance on court . . . 417–420
Reliance on official . . . 423–425

M'NAGHTEN TEST
Insanity . . . 1083–1085

MODEL PENAL CODE
Accomplice liability . . 852–853; 861; 883–884
Actus reus . . . 323
Attempt . . . 735–736; 752–756; 758; 769
Causation . . . 344–345
Conspiracy 787; 825–826; 832–833; 834–836
Conspiracy-complicity doctrine . . . 888
Corporate criminality . . . 905–906
Defense of property/habitation 1065–1067
Duress . . . 997
Entrapment defense . . . 1204–1205
Insanity defense . . . 1097–1098

MODEL PENAL CODE—Cont.
Intoxication defense . . . 1169; 1176
Law enforcement, use of force in 1077–1078
Mens rea . . . 390–396
Mistake of law or fact . . . 426–427
Murder, degrees of . . . 514
Necessity defense . . . 1021
Punishment, justification for . . . 156–157
Rape . . . 670; 692
Renunciation of criminal purpose . . . 758
Self-defense . . . 1026–1027
Solicitation . . . 744–745
Suicide, causing or aiding of . . . 499

MOTIVE
Corrupt motive doctrine . . . 810–815
Excuses . . . 1228–1248

MURDER
Accomplice liability . . . 859–861
Attempt . . . 746–748
Attempt, impossibility of . . . 762–766
Battered spouse, self-defense by 1043–1057
Conspiracy to commit . . . 792–797
Defense of property/habitation 1060–1067
Degrees of . . . 511–514
Depraved heart murder . . . 534–545
Diminished capacity defense . . . 1133–1144
Euthanasia . . . 1233–1243
Extreme emotional disturbance, proof of . . 954–964
Felony murder (See FELONY MURDER)
Fetal death . . . 263–273
Intent-to-cause-serious-bodily-injury murder . . . 546–551
Intent-to-kill murder . . . 514–534
Malice aforethought . . . 510–512; 526–527
RICO convictions . . . 845–849
Solicitation . . . 739–744
"Unconsciousness" defense . . . 304–316
Victims' acts, effect of . . . 337–340

MUSICAL CONCERT UNLAWFULLY PERFORMED
Spectator's accomplice liability . . . 857–858

N

NATURAL FORCES
Causation . . . 343–344

NECESSITY DEFENSE
Generally . . . 1003–1020
Codification of . . . 1020–1024

NEGLIGENCE
(See also MENS REA)

[References are to pages.]

NEGLIGENCE—Cont.
Manslaughter . . . 617–631; 870–879
Model Penal Code . . . 391
Predicate for criminal liability . . . 365–378
Third parties' acts . . . 341–342

NEUROBIOLOGY OF VIOLENT BEHAVIOR
Generally . . . 1216–1218

NEWBORNS, DRUG DELIVERY TO
Statutory interpretation . . . 274–280

NO PUNISHMENT WITHOUT LAW
Generally . . . 252–280

NOT GUILTY BY REASON OF INSANITY
(See also INSANITY DEFENSE)
Disposition of offenders . . . 1105–1117

NULLA POENA SINE LEGE
Generally . . . 252–280

O

OBLIQUE INTENT
Generally . . . 352–353

OFFICIAL, RELIANCE ON
Mistake of law . . . 423–425

OMISSIONS
Generally . . . 329–335

"ON THE NOSE" GUILTY PLEAS
Generally . . . 16–17

ORDEALS
Burden of proof . . . 9–10

"OVERT ACT"
Conspiracy . . . 783–784

P

PARENTAL ALIENATION SYNDROME
Defense . . . 1227

PARENT AND CHILD
Distant father syndrome . . . 1227
Medical attention for child, failure to provide
. . . 625–628
Omission, acts of . . . 334
Parental alienation syndrome . . . 1227
Starvation of child . . . 543–545

PASSENGERS
Knowing failure to act . . . 325–327

PATHOLOGICAL BEHAVIOR
Defense . . . 1224

PATIENT-THERAPIST SEX SYNDROME
Defense . . . 1227

PHYSICIAN-ASSISTED SUICIDE
Homicide . . . 500–508

PHYSICIAN RAPE
Deception . . . 684–688

PINKERTON RULE
Generally . . . 884–890

PLEA BARGAINING
Generally . . . 4; 16–17
Prosecutorial discretion . . . 19–20

PMS DEFENSE
Generally . . . 1218–1220

POISONING
Premeditation . . . 522–523

POLICE (See LAW ENFORCEMENT)

POLITICAL OFFENDERS
Excuse defense . . . 1243–1248

PORNOGRAPHY
Ignorance of law . . . 408–411

POST PARTUM PSYCHOSIS
Defense . . . 1224

PREDATORY SEXUAL OFFENDERS
Detention as punishment . . . 58–68

PREMEDITATION
Intent-to-kill murder . . . 517–534
Malice aforethought . . . 510–512; 526–527

PREMENSTRUAL SYNDROME
Defense . . . 1218–1220

PREPARATION VERSUS ATTEMPT
Generally . . . 727–744

PRESUMPTIONS
Elements of offense . . . 973–991
Intent . . . 983–988

PRETRIAL DETENTION
Punishment, preventative detention versus
. . . 51–58

PRIZEFIGHTING
Accomplice liability . . . 853–856

PROFITS FROM CRIMES
Forfeitures versus punishment . . . 116–152

PROHIBITION LAW
Conspiracy to violate . . . 787–790

"PROMPT COMPLAINT" RULES
Rape . . . 666; 718; 721

PROPORTIONALITY
Punishment . . . 230–252

[References are to pages.]

PROSECUTORS
Generally . . . 4
Discretion to prosecute . . . 14–20
German prosecutors . . . 17–19
Public versus private prosecution . . 11–16

PROSTITUTION
Conspiracy to commit . . . 803–809
Conspiracy to violate Mann Act . . 797–799
Rape of prostitute . . . 664
Vicarious liability . . . 890–892

PROVOCATION
Voluntary manslaughter . . . 595–617

PUBLIC DEFENDERS
State office . . . 20–21

PUBLIC WELFARE OFFENSES
"Strict" liability 447–448; 456–457; 480; 893

PUNISHMENT
(See also SENTENCING)
Generally . . . 37–39
Attempt . . . 769–770
Civil punitive sanctions . . . 152–155
Coercive therapy versus . . . 68–78
Compensation versus . . . 96–109
Conduct punishable . . . 280–301
Conspiracy . . . 780; 834–836
Corporate punishment, utility of . . 915–917
Cruel and unusual (See CRUEL AND UNUSUAL PUNISHMENT)
Death penalty (See DEATH PENALTY)
Defined . . . 40–50
Denunciation justification . . . 178–188
Deterrence justification . . . 159–167
Expressive function . . . 48–51; 182–188
Incapacitation justification . . . 167–173
In rem actions versus . . . 116–152
Justifications for (See JUSTIFICATIONS FOR PUNISHMENT)
Legality principle . . . 252–280
Nonpunitive sanctions . . . 51–152
Preventive detention versus . . . 51–68
Proportionality . . . 230–252
Rape . . . 722–724
Regulatory penalties versus . . . 78–96
Rehabilitation justification . . . 173–178
Taxation versus . . . 109–115
Utilitarianism . . . 159–188
Vicarious liability . . . 893

"PURPOSELY"
Model Penal Code . . . 391

R

RACKETEER INFLUENCED AND CORRUPT ORGANIZATIONS (RICO)
Generally . . . 836–849

RAPE
Generally . . . 663–668
Accomplice liability . . . 881–883
Actus reus . . . 669–693
Attempt . . . 736–739
Corroboration rule . . . 719
Cultural stereotypes . . . 667–668
Deception . . . 684–688
Evidentiary considerations . . . 718–721
Fear and duress . . . 675–684
Force and nonconsent . . . 671–684; 693–714
Grading . . . 722–724
Marital exemption . . . 689–693
Mens rea
    Objective liability . . . 705–714
    Strict liability . . . 714–718
    Subjective fault . . . 693–704
"Prompt complaint" rules . . . 666; 718; 721
Resistance . . 672; 673; 676; 679–680; 700–701; 705; 706; 709; 715
Seduction . . . 687–688
Victim's conduct
    Generally . . . 666–667
    Prior sexual conduct . . . 719–721
Victim's testimony . . . 664

RAPE SHIELD LAW
Generally . . . 719–721

RAPE TRAUMA SYNDROME
Generally . . . 721–722

REASONABLE DOUBT STANDARD
Burden of proof . . . 5–10

RECEIVING STOLEN PROPERTY
Attempt, impossibility of . . . 759–762

RECKLESSNESS
(See also MENS REA)
Generally . . . 358–365
Depraved heart murder . . . 534–545
Mistake of law . . . 425–426
Model Penal Code . . . 391; 393–394

REGULATORY PENALTIES VERSUS PUNISHMENT
Generally . . . 78–96

REHABILITATION
Justification for punishment . . . 173–178

RELIANCE ON COUNSEL
Mistake of law . . . 420–423

RELIANCE ON COURT
Mistake of law . . . 417–420

RELIANCE ON OFFICIAL
Mistake of law . . . 423–425

RENUNCIATION
Attempt . . . 756–758
Conspiracy . . . 833–834

REPRESSED (OR RECOVERED) MEMORY SYNDROME
Defense . . . 1227

REPROBATIVE FUNCTION
Punishment . . . 48–51

RESISTANCE
Rape . . . 672; 673; 676; 679–680; 700–701; 705; 706; 709; 715

RESTITUTION
Punishment versus compensation . . 96–109

"RETREAT" RULE
Self-defense . . . 1030–1033

RETRIBUTIVISM
Death penalty . . . 635–640
Just deserts and the obligation to punish . . . 188–198
Just deserts and the right to be punished . . . 202–204
Just deserts as a limiting principle 196–201

RICO
Generally . . . 836–849

RIGHT TO JURY TRIAL
Jury selection . . . 24–30

RITUAL ABUSE SYNDROME
Defense . . . 1227

ROAD RAGE
Defense . . . 1227

ROBBERY
Attempt . . . 728–735; 748–752
Intoxication defense . . . 1169–1174

"ROTTEN SOCIAL BACKGROUND" (RSB) DEFENSE
Generally . . . 1224–1228

RSB DEFENSE
Generally . . . 1224–1228

RUSSIAN ROULETTE
Depraved heart murder . . . 542–543

S

SANCTIONS
Civil punitive sanctions . . . 152–155
Corporate civil punishment . . . 917–918
Criminal (See PUNISHMENT)
Nonpunitive sanctions . . . 51–152

SATANIC CULT SYNDROME
Defense . . . 1227

SEDUCTION
Rape . . . 687–688

SELF-DEFENSE
Generally . . . 1024–1027
Battered spouses . . . 1043–1057
Imminent threat of danger . . . 1040–1042
Mistake and "imperfect self-defense" 1029–1030
Rationale and doctrinal confusion 1027–1029
Reasonableness and subjectivity 1038–1039
"Retreat" rule . . . 1030–1033
"Rules" of . . . 1026–1053
Withdrawal and . . . 1026–1027

SENILITY DEFENSE
Generally . . . 1220

SENTENCING
Commissions . . . 212–214
Grids . . . 219–221
Indeterminate versus determinate sentences . . . 211–230
Mandatory minimum sentencing . . 965–973
Proportionality . . . 230–252

SENTENCING GUIDELINES
Generally . . . 214–225
Federal . . . 227–230

SEXISM IN THE LAW
Rape, crime of . . . 665–666; 667

SEX OFFENDER REGISTRATION AND NOTIFICATION STATUTES
Regulatory penalties versus punishment . . 83–96

"SEXUAL ACTIVITY" CASES
"Strict" liability laws . . . 450–456

SEXUAL ASSAULT (See RAPE)

SEXUAL INTIMACY
Punishable conduct . . . 283–285; 298–300

SEXUALLY VIOLENT PREDATORS
Detention as punishment . . . 58–68

[References are to pages.]

SHERMAN ACT VIOLATIONS
Corporate criminality . . . 906–908

SITUATIONAL STRESS SYNDROME
Defense . . . 1227

SLEEP DISORDERS
Defenses . . . 1221
Somnambulistic homicide . . . 312–316

SOCIAL DEPRIVATION DEFENSE
Generally . . . 1224–1228

SOCIAL SECURITY BENEFITS
Termination as punishment . . . 42–47

SODOMY
Conduct deemed punishable . . . 284–285
Provocation for voluntary manslaughter . . . 607
Rape (See RAPE)

SOLICITATION
Generally . . . 739–744

SOMNAMBULISTIC HOMICIDE
Generally . . . 312–316

"SPOKE" CONSPIRACIES
Generally . . . 826–827; 830–831

SPOUSAL ABUSE
Self-defense by battered spouse 1043–1057

SPOUSAL RAPE
Generally . . . 689–693
Accomplice liability . . . 883–883

SPOUSES (See HUSBAND AND WIFE)

SPRING GUNS
Defense of property/habitation . . . 1065

STABBING TO DEATH
Premeditation . . . 532–533

STALKING STATUTES
"Void for vagueness" doctrine . . . 262

STANDING
Appeal by victim . . . 12–14

STARVATION OF CHILD
Reckless homicide . . . 543–545

STATE OF MIND (See MENS REA)

STATUS CRIMES
Actus reus . . . 320–324

STATUTORY INTERPRETATION
Generally . . . 262–280
Mens rea words . . . 378–390

STEROID RAGE
Defense . . . 1227

STRANGULATION
Premeditation . . . 517–519
Voluntary manslaughter . . . 603–606

"STRICT" LIABILITY
Generally . . . 437–460
Federal view . . . 460–481
Public welfare offenses . . 447–448; 456–457; 480; 893
Rape . . . 714–718
Vicarious liability, distinguished . . . 449

SUICIDE, ASSISTED
Euthanasia . . . 1233–1243
Homicide . . . 500–508

SUICIDE PACTS
Homicide . . . 495–499

SUPER BOWL SUNDAY SYNDROME
Defense . . . 1227

SUPERIOR ORDERS
Duress . . . 1002–1003

SUPERSEDING CAUSES
Generally . . . 341

T

"TAKINGS" ISSUES
Civil forfeitures . . . 125–138

TAXATION VERSUS PUNISHMENT
Generally . . . 109–115

TAX EVASION
Mistake of law . . . 427–434

"TELEVISION MADE ME DO IT" SYNDROME
Defense . . . 1227

TENEMENT HOUSE REGULATIONS
"Strict" liability laws . . . 448–449

TERRORISTS
Excuse defense . . . 1243–1248

THEFT
Armed robbery . . . 1169–1174
Attempted robbery . . . 728–735; 748–752
Corporate liability . . . 901–904
Receiving stolen property, impossibility of . . . 759–762

THERAPY
Coercive therapy versus punishment 68–78
Patient-therapist sex syndrome . . . 1227

[References are to pages.]

THIRD PARTIES' ACTS
Criminal acts . . . 341
Negligent acts . . . 341–342

TRAFFIC INFRACTIONS
Regulatory penalties versus punishment . . 78–82

TRAINS, SHOOTING AT
Depraved heart murder . . . 534–535

U

"UNCONSCIOUS" MOTIVATION
Insanity defense . . . 1095–1097

"UNCONSCIOUSNESS" DEFENSE
Insanity and automatism . . . 1128–1131
Murder . . . 304–316

UNUSUAL PUNISHMENT (See CRUEL AND UNUSUAL PUNISHMENT)

URBAN SURVIVAL SYNDROME
Defense . . . 1227

UTILITARIANISM
Justification for punishment . . . 159–187

UTILITY LINE TAMPERING
Presumption of responsibility . . . 982

UTTERING
Presumption to defraud . . . 982

V

VAGRANCY STATUTES
"Void for vagueness" doctrine . . . 260–262

VAGUENESS AND OVERBREADTH
Generally . . . 257–262

VEHICLE PASSENGERS
Knowing failure to act . . . 325–327

VEHICULAR ASSAULT
Intent-to-cause-serious-bodily-injury murder . . . 548–550

VEHICULAR HOMICIDE
Generally . . . 541
Accomplice liability . . . 870–879
Criminal negligence manslaughter 620–622; 870–879
Epileptic attack, commission during 316–319

VICARIOUS LIABILITY
Corporate criminality . . . 899–918
Natural persons . . . 890–899
"Strict" liability, distinguished . . . 449

VICTIMS
Acts, effect of . . . 337–340
Appeal, standing to . . . 12–14
Brain dead victims . . . 490–493
Eggshell victims . . . 336
Rape victim's conduct
   Generally . . . 666–667
   Prior sexual conduct . . . 719–721
Rape victim's testimony . . . 664

"VOID FOR VAGUENESS" DOCTRINE
Generally . . . 257–262

"VOLITIONAL" IMPAIRMENT
Insanity defense . . . 1092–1095

VOLUNTARY MANSLAUGHTER
Generally . . . 595–617

W

"WANTONLY"
Interpretation of term . . . 378

WEAPONS
Concealed weapon, mistake of law in carrying . . . 419
Firearms (See FIREARMS)

WHARTON'S RULE
Conspiracy . . . 797–803

"WHEEL" ARRANGEMENTS
Conspiracy . . . 826–827; 830–831

"WILFULLY"
Free will . . . 913–920; 1210–1212
Interpretation of term . . . 378; 379

"WILLFUL BLINDNESS" RULE"
Generally . . . 408

WITHDRAWAL
Conspiracy . . . 833–834
Self-defense and . . . 1026–1027

WOMEN
Jury selection . . . 24–30

Y

"YEAR AND A DAY RULE"
Homicide . . . 486–488